INGENIX®

2009 Product Alert

Ingenix Has You Covered!

ICD-9-CM INGENIX EDGE

With semi-annual ICD-9-CM changes effective April 1 and October 1, it is more important than ever to have up-to-date ICD-9-CM coding information in order to stay in compliance with HIPAA regulations. Ingenix is committed to providing you and your staff with the ICD-9-CM code update information you need to code accurately and efficiently. We are offering several ways to make sure you are always up-to-date.

- **Updateable Expert ICD-9-CM code books.** The February update will have any new codes effective April 1.
- **Annual Expert and Professional ICD-9-CM editions.** Just visit www.shopIngenix.com/productalerts and select the View ICD-9-CM official alerts link.

No extra charge to view and download the code changes. No additional cost for updated books. No hassle for you or your staff.

Revised Coding Guidelines

The official coding guidelines included in this edition became effective on October 1, 2007. Signifi cant revisions were made to chapter-specific guidelines, the V code table and the Present on Admission Reporting Guidelines.

Only this set of guidelines, approved by the Cooperating Parties, is official. Adherence to these guidelines when assigning ICD-9-CM diagnosis and procedure codes is required under the Health Insurance Portability and Accountability Act (HIPAA).

The Cooperating Parties for ICD-9-CM continue to review and revise the coding guidelines. Should an updated version of the offi cial ICD-9-CM coding guidelines be released, Ingenix will post the revised guidelines on our Web site. Please visit www.shopingenix.com/productalerts and select View ICD-9-CM official alerts link to view and download the revised guidleines.

Medicare Code Edits Notice

Not all Medicare edits for the new 2009 ICD-9-CM codes were released in time to be published in this edition. Once these edits are released we will post them on our Web site. Please visit www.shopingenix.com/productalerts and click on the View ICD-9-CM offi cial alerts link to view these edits.

Get in the loop and join the Ingenix Coding Circle today!

Ever feel like you're the last to know about code updates, Medicare changes and ICD-10 developments? Ever wish you could connect with others in your industry to share ideas, ask questions and voice frustrations? Well quit daydreaming and get in the loop! Join the Coding Circle – the new ShopIngenix. com eCommunity that allows health care professionals just like you to access the latest industry news and ICD-10 developments, share ideas, test coding skills and connect with colleagues!

As a member you will have access to these great features:

- **ICD-10 Corner.** View the latest developments in ICD-10 for a smooth transition to this new coding system. Coding scenarios are posted for real case coding practice.
- **Coding Circle Profile.** Submit or update your personal profile information, browse other member profiles.
- **Member Directory.** Network with other Coding Circle members by searching our database.
- **Coding Circle eLink.** Access timely industry news along with coding, billing and reimbursement case studies and analyses.
- **Code This!** Check out a variety of coding scenarios to help you test, develop and improve your coding skills.
- **Submit your ideas for new products.**
- **Earn special discounts and rewards.**

Visit www.
shopingenix.com/
codingcircle
to sign up today–
membership is FREE!

Ingenix | Intelligence for Health Care | Call toll-free 1.800.INGENIX (464.3649), option 1.

100% Money Back Guarantee If our merchandise ever fails to meet your expectations, please contact our Customer Service Department toll-free at 1.800.INGENIX (464.3649), option 1, for an immediate response. Software: Credit will be granted for unopened packages only.

Also available from your medical bookstore or distributor.

FOBA09

www.shopingenix.com

INGENIX®

2009 HCPCS Level II Expert

ISBN: 978-1-60151-157-7
Item Number: HC09
Available: December 2008
Price: $86.95

ISBN: 978-1-60151-155-3
Item Number: HS09
Available: December 2008
Price: $99.95

Item Number: 4524
Available: Now
Price: $149.95

Timely and Accurate Coding Made Easy.

Meticulous coders know that staying on top of code changes is the key to timely and accurate reimbursement. This reliable HCPCS Level II book features the most current HCPCS codes and regulations for the most meticulous, HIPAA-compliant coders and provides authoritative answers to your coding questions.

← **Keep up-to-date with revenue using accurate coding**

← **Understand and adopt changes faster**

← **Benefit from a comprehensive collection of HCPCS sources**

Key Features and Benefits

The ***HCPCS Level II Expert*** compiles codes from every source that generates HCPCS codes, including CMS, OPPS addendum B and the physician fee schedule, to provide one of the most complete code sets available.

- **PQRI Ready! Icons denoting which HCPCS codes and their denominators are part of the Physician Quality Reporting Initiative help you get your bonus.**
- **IngenixEdge®—Expert Exclusive—National Medicare and commercial fees.** Organized and easy-to-follow information helps identify reimbursement based on Medicare and private payer fee data.
- **IngenixEdge®—Email alerts.** Keep current with late-breaking news through quarterly special reports to ensure the most up-to-date codes and regulations.
- **IngenixEdge®—Comprehensive code updates.** Includes all HCPCS, MPFS and OPPS files for HCPCS Level II as well as deleted codes for 2009.
- **IngenixEdge®—Color-coded icons.** Flags signal Pub. 100 references, DMEPOS, age and sex edits, new, deleted or revised code changes and government coverage and rules.
- **Plus all these features for effective HCPCS coding.** Table of Drugs, APC status indicators, ASC group symbols, in-depth illustrations, AHA *Coding Clinic for HCPCS* references and a user-friendly appendix.

SAVE 20%

when you order at www.shopingenix.com and enter source code FOBAW9 in the lower right-hand corner of the home page.

Ingenix | Intelligence for Health Care | Call toll-free 1.800.INGENIX (464.3649), option 1.

100% Money Back Guarantee If our merchandise ever fails to meet your expectations, please contact our Customer Service Department toll-free at 1.800.INGENIX (464.3649), option 1, for an immediate response. Software: Credit will be granted for unopened packages only.

Also available from your medical bookstore or distributor.

FOBA09

INGENIX®

Four simple ways to place an order.

Call

1.800.ingenix (464.3649), option 1. Mention source code FOBA09 when ordering.

Mail

PO Box 27116
Salt Lake City, UT 84127-0116
With payment and/or purchase order.

Fax

801.982.4033
With credit card information and/or purchase order.

Click

www.shopingenix.com
Save 20% when you order online today—use source code FOBAW9.

ingenix esmart
ShopIngenix.com frequent buyer program

GET REWARDS FOR SHOPPING ONLINE!
To find out more, visit www.shopingenix.com

eSmart program available only to Ingenix customers who are not part of Medallion, Gold Medallion or Partner Accounts programs. You must be registered at ShopIngenix.com to have your online purchases tracked for rewards purposes. Shipping charges and taxes still apply and cannot be used for rewards. Offer valid online only.

100% Money Back Guarantee

If our merchandise* ever fails to meet your expectations, please contact our Customer Service Department toll-free at 1.800.ingenix (464.3649), option 1 for an immediate response.

*Software: Credit will be granted for unopened packages only.

Customer Service Hours

7:00 am - 5:00 pm Mountain Time
9:00 am - 7:00 pm Eastern Time

Shipping and Handling

no. of items	fee
1	$10.95
2-4	$12.95
5-7	$14.95
8-10	$19.95
11+	Call

Order Form

Information

Customer No. ____________ Contact No. ____________

Source Code ____________

Contact Name ____________

Title ____________ Specialty ____________

Company ____________

Street Address ____________
NO PO BOXES, PLEASE

City ____________ State ______ Zip ______

Telephone (   ) ____________ Fax (   ) ____________
IN CASE WE HAVE QUESTIONS ABOUT YOUR ORDER

E-mail ____________ @ ____________
REQUIRED FOR ORDER CONFIRMATION AND SELECT PRODUCT DELIVERY.

Ingenix respects your right to privacy. We will not sell or rent your e-mail address or fax number to anyone outside Ingenix and its business partners. If you would like to remove your name from Ingenix promotion, please call 1.800.ingenix (464.3649), option 1.

Product

Item No.	Qty	Description	Price	Total

Subtotal ______

UT, VA, TN, OH, CT, IA, MD, MN, NC & NJ residents, please add applicable Sales tax ______

(See chart on the left) Shipping & handling charges ______
All foreign orders, please call for shipping costs

Total ______

Payment

○ Please bill my credit card ○ MasterCard ○ VISA ○ Amex ○ Discover

Card No. ____________ Expires ______
MONTH YEAR

Signature ____________

○ Check enclosed, made payable to: Ingenix, Inc. ○ Please bill my office

Purchase Order No. ____________
ATTACH COPY OF PURCHASE ORDER

2009

INGENIX®

ICD-9-CM Professional

for Physicians
Volumes 1 & 2

International Classification of Diseases
9th Revision
Clinical Modification

Sixth Edition

Edited by:
Anita C. Hart, RHIA, CCS, CCS-P
Melinda S. Stegman, MBA, CCS
Beth Ford, RHIT, CCS

Ingenix is committed to providing you with the ICD-9-CM code update information you need to code accurately and to be in compliance with HIPAA regulations. In case of adoption of additional ICD-9-CM code changes effective April 1, 2009, Ingenix will provide these code changes to you at no additional cost! Just check back at www.shopingenix.com/productalerts to review the latest information concerning any new code changes.

Codes Valid October 1, 2008, through September 30, 2009

First Printing — August 2008
Made in the USA

Additional copies may be ordered from:
Your local bookstore
or
1-800-INGENIX (464-3649)

IPP ISBN 978-1-60151-122-5

PUBLISHER'S NOTICE

All codes, indexes, and other material in the ICD-9-CM are compiled from official ICD-9-CM codes and instructions as well as the Medicare regulations and manuals issued or authorized by the Centers for Medicare and Medicaid Services. The code book is designed to provide accurate and authoritative information in regard to the subject covered, and every reasonable effort has been made to ensure the accuracy of the information within these pages. However, the ultimate responsibility for correct coding lies with the provider of services.

Ingenix, its employees, agents and staff make no representation, warranty or guarantee that this compilation of codes and narratives is error-free or that the use of this code book will prevent differences of opinion or disputes with Medicare or other third-party payers as to the codes that are accepted or the amounts that will be paid to providers for services, and will bear no responsibility or liability for the results or consequences of the use of this code book.

OUR COMMITMENT TO ACCURACY

Ingenix is committed to producing accurate and reliable materials. To report corrections, please visit www.ingenixonline.com/accuracy or email accuracy@ingenix.com. You can also reach customer service by calling 1.800.INGENIX (464.3649), option 1.

Preface

ICD-9-CM for Physicians has been designed with the physician office coder in mind. The most recent official government versions of volumes 1 and 2 have been combined to provide physicians and their office staff with an ICD-9-CM book that is easy to use.

In addition, our technical experts have drawn upon their extensive hands-on experience to enhance the government's official version with valuable features essential to correct coding and reimbursement. With these enhancements, physician office health information professionals will increase the efficiency and timeliness of claim submission for both Medicare and other third-party payers.

As you review the content, you'll find the following:

- All the official ICD-9-CM codes, indexes, notes, footnotes and symbols
- Complete official coding guidelines
- Our exclusive color coding, symbols, and footnotes that alert coders to coding and reimbursement issues. Medicare outpatient code edits, such as invalid fourth or fifth digit for diagnosis codes are identified.
- Illustrations and clinically oriented definitions to aid in correct code assignment
- Symbols identifying new codes and text revisions; pages are dated to indicate when the changes were made
- Exclusive QuickFlip Color Tabs for quick, easy location of terms and codes in the Alphabetic Index and Tabular List

Use of Official Sources

This *ICD-9-CM for Physicians* contains the official U.S. Department of Health and Human Services, ICD-9-CM codes, effective for the current year.

The color coding, footnotes and symbols, which identify coding and reimbursement issues, are derived from official federal government sources, including the Medicare Outpatient Code Editor as well as the knowledge of our technical experts.

The American Hospital Association's (AHA) *Coding Clinic for ICD-9-CM* references are used with permission of the AHA.

Important Information About Your Subscription Service

If you have purchased the updateable *ICD-9-CM for Physicians*, your subscription includes an updating service throughout the year to keep the code book current and accurate. Whenever CMS issues changes or corrections to the ICD-9-CM codes, We will issue an update to the book. In July you will receive a list of all new, revised, and invalid codes for the upcoming year.

Technical Editors

Anita C. Hart, RHIA, CCS, CCS-P, *Product Manager, Ingenix*
Ms. Hart's experience includes 15 years conducting and publishing research in clinical medicine and human genetics for Yale University, Massachusetts General Hospital, and Massachusetts Institute of Technology. In addition, Ms. Hart has supervised medical records management, health information management, coding and reimbursement, and worker's compensation issues as the office manager for a physical therapy rehabilitation clinic. Ms. Hart is an expert in physician and facility coding, reimbursement systems, and compliance issues. Ms. Hart has developed and has served as technical consultant for numerous other publications for hospital and physician practices. Currrently, Ms. Hart is the Product Manager and Technical Editor for the ICD-9-CM and ICD-10-CM/PCS product lines.

Melinda S. Stegman, MBA, CCS,*Clinical/Technical Editor, Ingenix*
Ms. Stegman has 27 years of experience in the HIM profession and has been responsible for managing the clinical aspects of the HSS/Ingenix HIM Consulting practice in the Washington, DC area office. Her areas of specialization include training on inpatient and DRG coding, outpatient coding, and Ambulatory Payment Classifications (APCs) for HIM professionals, software developers, and other clients; developing an outpatient billing/coding compliance tool for a major accounting firm; and managing HIM consulting practices. Ms. Stegman is a regular contributing author for *Advance for Health Information Management Professionals* and for the *Journal of Health Care Compliance*. She has performed coding assessments and educational sessions throughout the country.

Beth Ford, RHIT, CCS, *Clinical/Technical Editor, Ingenix*
Ms. Ford is a clinical/technical editor for Ingenix. She has extensive background in both physician and facility ICD-9-CM and CPT/HCPCS coding. Ms. Ford has served as a coding specialist, coding manager, coding trainer/educator and coding consultant, as well as a health information management director. She is an active member of the American Heath Information Management Association (AHIMA).

In addition to the editors, the following people have contributed to this book:

Stacy Perry, *Manager, Desktop Publishing*
Tracy Betzler, *Desktop Publishing Specialist*
Hope Dunn, *Desktop Publishing Specialist*
Toni Stewart, *Desktop Publishing Specialist*
Kate Holden, *Editor*

What to Do If You Have Questions

If you have any questions call our customer service department toll-free at 800-INGENIX (464-3649), option 1.

If you have comments on the content of this book, please e-mail them to customerservice@ingenix.com or fax to 801-982-4033.

Introduction

History and Future of ICD-9

The International Classification of Diseases, Ninth Revision, Clinical Modification (ICD-9-CM) is based on the official version of the World Health Organization's Ninth Revision, International Classification of Diseases (ICD-9). ICD-9-CM classifies morbidity and mortality information for statistical purposes, indexing of hospital records by disease and operations, data storage, and retrieval.

This modification of ICD-9 supplants the Eighth Revision International Classification of Diseases, Adapted for Use in the United States (ICDA-8) and the Hospital Adaptation of ICDA (H-ICDA).

The concept of extending the International Classification of Diseases for use in hospital indexing was originally developed in response to a need for a more efficient basis for storage and retrieval of diagnostic data. In 1950, the U.S. Public Health Service and the Veterans Administration began independent tests of the International Classification of Diseases for hospital indexing purposes. The following year, the Columbia Presbyterian Medical Center in New York City adopted the International Classification of Diseases, Sixth Revision, with some modifications for use in its medical record department. A few years later, the Commission on Professional and Hospital Activities (CPHA) in Ann Arbor, Mich., adopted the International Classification of Diseases with similar modifications for use in hospitals participating in the Professional Activity Study.

The problem of adapting ICD for indexing hospital records was addressed by the U.S. National Committee on Vital and Health Statistics through its subcommittee on hospital statistics. The subcommittee reviewed the modifications made by the various users of ICD and proposed that uniform changes be made. This was done by a small working party.

In view of the growing interest in the use of the International Classification of Diseases for hospital indexing, a study was undertaken in 1956 by the American Hospital Association and the American Medical Record Association (then the American Association of Medical Record Librarians) of the relative efficiencies of coding systems for diagnostic indexing. This study indicated the International Classification of Diseases provided a suitable and efficient framework for indexing hospital records. The major users of the International Classification of Diseases for hospital indexing purposes then consolidated their experiences, and an adaptation was first published in December 1959. A revision was issued in 1962 and the first "Classification of Operations and Treatments" was included.

In 1966, the international conference for revising the International Classification of Diseases noted the eighth revision of ICD had been constructed with hospital indexing in mind and considered the revised classification suitable, in itself, for hospital use in some countries. However, it was recognized that the basic classification might provide inadequate detail for diagnostic indexing in other countries. A group of consultants was asked to study the eighth revision of ICD (ICD-8) for applicability to various users in the United States. This group recommended that further detail be provided for coding of hospital and morbidity data. The American Hospital Association was requested to develop the needed adaptation proposals. This was done by an advisory committee (the Advisory Committee to the Central Office on ICDA). In 1968 the United States Public Health Service published the product, Eighth Revision International Classification of Diseases, Adapted for Use in the United States. This became commonly known as ICDA-8, and beginning in 1968 it served as the basis for coding diagnostic data for both official morbidity and mortality statistics in the United States.

In 1968, the CPHA published the Hospital Adaptation of ICDA (H-ICDA) based on both the original ICD-8 and ICDA-8. In 1973, CPHA published a revision of H-ICDA, referred to as H-ICDA-2. Hospitals throughout the United States were divided in their use of these classifications until January 1979, when ICD-9-CM was made the single classification intended primarily for use in the United States, replacing these earlier related, but somewhat dissimilar, classifications.

Physicians have been required by law to submit diagnosis codes for Medicare reimbursement since the passage of the Medicare Catastrophic Coverage Act of 1988. This act requires physician offices to include the appropriate diagnosis codes when billing for services provided to Medicare beneficiaries on or after April 1, 1989. The Centers for Medicare and Medicaid Services (CMS) designated ICD-9-CM as the coding system physicians must use.

In 1993 the World Health Organization published the newest version of International Classification of Diseases, Tenth Revision, ICD-10. This version contains the greatest number of changes in the history of ICD. There are more codes (5,500 more than ICD-9) to allow more specific reporting of diseases and newly recognized conditions. ICD-10 consists of three volumes; Tabular List (volume I), instructions (volume 2) and the Alphabetic Index (volume 3). It contains 21 chapters including two supplementary ones. The codes are alphanumeric (A00–T98, V01–Y98 and Z00–Z99). Currently ICD-10 is being used in some European countries with implementation expected after the year 2011 in the United States.

ICD-9-CM Background

In February 1977, a steering committee was convened by the National Center for Health Statistics to provide advice and counsel in developing a clinical modification of ICD-9. The organizations represented on the steering committee included the following:

- American Association of Health Data Systems
- American Hospital Association
- American Medical Record Association
- Association for Health Records
- Council on Clinical Classifications
- Centers for Medicare and Medicaid Services, Department of Health and Human Services
- WHO Center for Classification of Diseases for North America, sponsored by the National Center for Health Statistics, Department of Health and Human Services

The Council on Clinical Classifications was sponsored by the following:

- American Academy of Pediatrics
- American College of Obstetricians and Gynecologists
- American College of Physicians
- American College of Surgeons
- American Psychiatric Association
- Commission on Professional and Hospital Activities

The steering committee met periodically in 1977. Clinical guidance and technical input were provided by task forces on classification from the Council on Clinical Classification's sponsoring organizations.

ICD-9-CM is a clinical modification of the World Health Organization's ICD-9. The term "clinical" is used to emphasize the modification's intent: to serve as a useful tool to classify morbidity data for indexing medical records, medical care review, and ambulatory and other medical care programs, as well as for basic health statistics. To describe the clinical picture of the patient, the codes must be more precise than those needed only for statistical groupings and trend analysis.

Characteristics of ICD-9-CM

ICD-9-CM far exceeds its predecessors in the number of codes provided. The disease classification has been expanded to include health-related conditions and to provide greater specificity at the fifth-digit level of detail. These fifth digits are not optional; they are intended for use in recording the information substantiated in the clinical record.

Volume I (Tabular List) of ICD-9-CM contains four appendices:

Appendix A:	Morphology of Neoplasms
Appendix B:	Deleted effective October 1, 2004
Appendix C:	Classification of Drugs by American Hospital Formulary Service List Number and Their ICD-9-CM Equivalents
Appendix D:	Classification of Industrial Accidents According to Agency
Appendix E:	List of Three-Digit Categories

These appendices are included as a reference to provide further information about the patient's clinical picture, to further define a diagnostic statement, to aid in classifying new drugs or to reference three-digit categories.

Volume 2 (Alphabetic Index) of ICD-9-CM contains many diagnostic terms that do not appear in volume I since the index includes most diagnostic terms currently in use.

The Disease Classification

ICD-9-CM is totally compatible with its parent system, ICD-9, thus meeting the need for comparability of morbidity and mortality statistics at the international level. A few fourth-digit codes were created in existing three-digit rubrics only when the necessary detail could not be accommodated by the use of a fifth-digit subclassification. To ensure that each rubric of ICD-9-CM collapses back to its ICD-9 counterpart the following specifications governed the ICD-9-CM disease classification:

Specifications for the Tabular List:

1. Three-digit rubrics and their contents are unchanged from ICD-9.
2. The sequence of three-digit rubrics is unchanged from ICD-9.
3. Three-digit rubrics are not added to the main body of the classification.
4. Unsubdivided three-digit rubrics are subdivided where necessary to
   - add clinical detail
   - solate terms for clinical accuracy
5. The modification in ICD-9-CM is accomplished by adding a fifth digit to existing ICD-9 rubrics, except as noted under #7 below.
6. The optional dual classification in ICD-9 is modified.
   - Duplicate rubrics are deleted:
     - four-digit manifestation categories duplicating etiology entries
     - manifestation inclusion terms duplicating etiology entries[2]
   - Manifestations of disease are identified, to the extent possible, by creating five-digit codes in the etiology rubrics.
   - When the manifestation of a disease cannot be included in the etiology rubrics, provision for its identification is made by retaining the ICD-9 rubrics used for classifying manifestations of disease.
7. The format of ICD-9-CM is revised from that used in ICD-9.
   - American spelling of medical terms is used.
   - Inclusion terms are indented beneath the titles of codes.
   - Codes not to be used for primary tabulation of disease are printed in italics with the notation, "code first underlying disease."

Specifications for the Alphabetic Index:

1. The format of the Alphabetic Index follows that of ICD-9.
2. When two codes are required to indicate etiology and manifestation, the manifestation code appears in brackets (e.g., diabetic cataract 250.5 [*366.41*]).

The ICD-9-CM Coordination and Maintenance Committee

The four cooperating parties involved in maintaining the ICD-9-CM classification system include representatives of the American Hospital Association (AHA), the Centers for Medicare and Medicaid Services (CMS), the National Center for Health Statistics (NCHS), and the American Health Information Management Association (AHIMA).

Proposals for changes to the ICD-9-CM classification system are submitted and discussed in two open forum meetings held in March and September of each year at the Headquarters of the Centers for Medicare and Medicaid Services, Baltimore, Maryland. Comments received during and after the meetings are then discussed by the Committee. A notice of the new codes and code revisions approved by the Committee are published in the *Federal Register* as part of the proposed and final rule for the changes to the inpatient prospective payment system. The complete official document of changes to the classification system is released as the Addenda for the *International Classification of Diseases, Ninth Revision, Clinical Modification, Sixth Edition, Volumes 1, 2 and 3.*

How to Use the ICD-9-CM for Physicians (Volume 1 & 2)

ICD-9-CM for Physicians is based on the official version of the International Classification of Diseases, Ninth Revision, Clinical Modification, Sixth Edition, issued by the U.S. Department of Health and Human Services. Annual code changes are implemented by the government and are effective Oct. 1 and valid through Sept. 30 of the following year.

To accommodate the coder's approach to coding, the Alphabetic Index (Volume 2) has been placed before the Tabular List (Volume 1). This allows the user to locate the term in the index, then confirm the accuracy of the code in the Tabular List.

10 Steps to Correct Coding

To code accurately, it is necessary to have a working knowledge of medical terminology and to understand the characteristics, terminology and conventions of ICD-9-CM. Transforming descriptions of diseases, injuries, conditions and procedures into numerical designations (coding) is a complex activity and should not be undertaken without proper training.

Originally, coding allowed retrieval of medical information by diagnoses and operations for medical research, education and administration. Coding today is used to describe the medical necessity of a procedure and facilitate payment of health services, to evaluate utilization patterns and to study the appropriateness of health care costs. Coding provides the basis for epidemiological studies and research into the quality of health care. Incorrect or inaccurate coding can lead to investigations of fraud and abuse. Therefore, coding must be performed correctly and consistently to produce meaningful statistics to aid in planning for the health needs of the nation.

Follow the steps below to code correctly:

Step 1: Identify the reason for the visit (e.g., sign, symptom, diagnosis, condition to be coded).

Physicians describe the patient's condition using terminology that includes specific diagnoses as well as symptoms, problems or reasons for the encounter. If symptoms are present but a definitive diagnosis has not yet been determined, code the symptoms. Do not code conditions that are referred to as "rule out," "suspected," "probable" or "questionable."

Step 2: Always consult the Alphabetic Index, Volume 2, before turning to the Tabular List.

The most critical rule is to begin a code search in the index. Never turn first to the Tabular List (Volume 1), as this will lead to coding errors and less specificity in code assignments. To prevent coding errors, use both the Alphabetic Index and the Tabular List when locating and assigning a code.

Step 3: Locate the main entry term.

The Alphabetic Index is arranged by condition. Conditions may be expressed as nouns, adjectives and eponyms. Some conditions have multiple entries under their synonyms. Main terms are identified using boldface type.

Step 4: Read and interpret any notes listed with the main term

Notes are identified using italicized type.

Step 5: Review entries for modifiers

Nonessential modifiers are in parentheses. These parenthetical terms are supplementary words or explanatory information that may either be present or absent in the diagnostic statement and do not affect code assignment.

Step 6: Interpret abbreviations, cross-references, symbols and brackets

Cross-references used are "*see*," "*see* category" or "*see* also." The abbreviation NEC may follow main terms or subterms. NEC (not elsewhere classified) indicates that there is no specific code for the condition even though the medical documentation may be very specific. The ☑ box indicates the code requires an additional digit. If the appropriate digits are not found in the index, in a box beneath the main term, you MUST refer to the Tabular List. Italicized brackets [ ], are used to enclose a second code number that must be used with the code immediately preceding it and in that sequence.

Step 7: Choose a tentative code and locate it in the Tabular List.

Be guided by any inclusion or exclusion terms, notes or other instructions, such as "*code first*" and "use additional code," that would direct the use of a different or additional code from that selected in the index for a particular diagnosis, condition or disease.

Step 8: Determine whether the code is at the highest level of specificity.

Assign three-digit codes (category codes) if there are no four-digit codes within the code category. Assign four-digit codes (subcategory codes) if there are no five-digit codes for that category. Assign five-digit codes (fifth-digit subclassification codes) for those categories where they are available.

Step 9: Consult the color coding and reimbursement prompts, including the age, sex and Medicare as secondary payer edits.

Consult the official ICD-9-CM guidelines for coding and reporting, and refer to the AHA's *Coding Clinic for ICD-9-CM* for coding guidelines governing the use of specific codes.

Step 10: Assign the code.

Organization

Introduction

The introductory material in this book includes the history and future of ICD-9-CM as well as an overview of the classification system

Official ICD-9-CM Conventions

This section provides a full explanation of all the official footnotes, symbols, instructional notes, and conventions found in the official government version

Additional Conventions

Exclusive color-coding, symbols, and notations have been included in the *ICD-9-CM for Physicians, Volumes 1 and 2* to alert coders to important coding and reimbursement issues. This section provides a full explanation of the additional conventions used throughout this book.

Summary of Code Changes

This section includes a complete listing of all code changes for the current year.

Summary of AHA's Coding Clinic for ICD-9-CM Topics

This is a brief summary of the official advice concerning coding topics covered in the latest issues of AHA's *Coding Clinic for ICD-9-CM* and is found ONLY in the *ICD-9-CM Expert for Physicians* updateable edition.

Coding Guidelines

Included in this book are the official ICD-9-CM coding guidelines as approved by the four cooperating parties of the ICD-9-CM Coordination and Maintenance Committee. Failure to comply with these official coding guidelines may result in denied or delayed claims.

Disease Classification: Alphabetic Index to Diseases

The Alphabetic Index to Diseases is separated by tabs labeled with the letters of the alphabet, contains diagnostic terms for illnesses, injuries and reasons for encounters with health care professionals. Both the Table of Drugs and Chemicals and the Alphabetic Index to External Causes of Injury and Poisoning are easily located with the tabs in this section.

The warning statement at the bottom of every page of the index, Subterms under main terms may continue to next column or page, is a reminder to always check for additional subterms before making final selection.

Disease Classification: Tabular List of Diseases

The Tabular List of Diseases arranges the ICD-9-CM codes and descriptors numerically. Tabs divide this section into chapters, identified by the code range on the tab.

The Tabular List includes two supplementary classifications:

- V Codes–Supplementary Classification of Factors Influencing Health Status and Contact with Health Services (V01–V89)
- E Codes–Supplementary Classification of External Causes of Injury and Poisoning (E800–E999)

ICD-9-CM includes four official appendixes.

- Appendix A Morphology of Neoplasms
- Appendix B Deleted effective October 1, 2004
- Appendix C Classification of Drugs by AHFS List
- Appendix D Classification of Industrial Accidents According to Agency
- Appendix E List of Three-digit Categories

These appendices are included as a reference to provide further information about the patient's circumstances, help further define a diagnostic statement, maintain a tumor registry and aid in classifying new drugs.

Resources

Listed below are the exclusive resources found ONLY in the *ICD-9-CM Expert for Physicians, Volumes 1 & 2.*

10 Steps to Correct Coding

This is a valuable resource that takes the coder step by step through the coding process with detailed explanations accompanied by coding examples that demonstrate the practical application of ICD-9-CM conventions and coding guidelines in 10 steps.

Valid Three-digit Code Table

ICD-9-CM is composed of codes with either 3, 4, or 5 digits. A code is invalid if it has not been coded to the full number of digits required for that code. There are a certain number codes that are valid for reporting as three digit codes. A list of these valid three-digit code is included as a convenient reference when auditing claims.

Code Tables

Exclusive coding tables covering abortion, burns, complications, diabetes, hernia, pregnancy, and others are provided to simplify those complex coding issues.

ICD-9-CM Official Conventions

ICD-9-CM Footnotes, Symbols, Instructional Notes and Conventions

This *ICD-9-CM for Physicians* preserves all the footnotes, symbols, instructional notes and conventions found in the government's official version. Accurate coding depends upon understanding the meaning of these elements.

The following appear in the disease Tabular List, unless otherwise noted.

Official Government Symbols

§ The section mark preceding a code denotes a footnote on the page. This symbol is used in the Tabular List of Diseases.

ICD-9-CM Conventions Used in the Tabular List

In addition to the symbols and footnotes above, the ICD-9-CM disease tabular has certain abbreviations, punctuation, symbols and other conventions. Our *ICD-9-CM for Physicians* preserves these conventions. Proper use of the conventions will lead to efficient and accurate coding.

Abbreviations

NEC Not elsewhere classifiable
This abbreviation is used when the ICD-9-CM system does not provide a code specific for the patient's condition.

NOS Not otherwise specified
This abbreviation is the equivalent of "unspecified" and is used only when the coder lacks the information necessary to code to a more specific four-digit subcategory.

[ ] Brackets enclose synonyms, alternative terminology or explanatory phrases:

482.2 Pneumonia due to Hemophilus influenzae [H. influenzae]

Brackets that appear beneath a code indicate the fifth digits that are considered valid fifth digits for the code. This convention is applied for those instances in ICD-9-CM where not all common fifth digits are considered valid for each subcategory within a category.

715.0 Osteoarthrosis, generalized
[0,4,9]

Generalized arthrosis can only be assigned in cases for which the degenerative joint disease involves multiple joints. Therefore, this code is considered for arthrosis in the sites described as unspecified, hand (which consists of multiple joints), or multiple sites. Therefore, only fifth digits 0, 4, and 9 are valid with subcategory 715.0.

[ ] Slanted brackets that appear in the Alphabetic Index indicate mandatory multiple coding. Both codes must be assigned to fully describe the condition and are sequenced in the order listed.

Tachycardia
ventricular (paroxysmal)
psychogenic 316 *[427.1]*

Psychogenic paroxysmal tachycardia is reported using both 316, Psychogenic factors associated with diseases classified elsewhere, and 427.1, Paroxysmal ventricular tachydcardia.

( ) Parentheses enclose supplementary words, called nonessential modifiers, that may be present in the narrative description of a disease without affecting the code assignment:

198.4 Other parts of nervous system
Meninges (cerebral) (spinal)

: Colons are used in the Tabular List after an incomplete term that needs one or more of the modifiers that follow in order to make it assignable to a given category:

021.1 Enteric tularemia
Tularemia:
cryptogenic
intestinal
typhoidal

} Braces enclose a series of terms, each of which is modified by the statement appearing to the right of the brace:

560.2 Volvulus
Knotting
Strangulation
Torsion
Twist
} if intestine, bowel, or colon

Other Conventions

Boldface Boldface type is used for all codes and titles in the Tabular List.

Italicized Italicized type is used for all exclusion notes and to identify codes that should not be used for describing the primary diagnosis.

Instructional Notes Used in the Tabular List

These notes appear only in the Tabular List of Diseases:

Includes An includes note further defines or clarifies the content of the chapter, subchapter, category, subcategory or subclassification. The includes note in the example below applies only to category 461.

Excludes following the word "Excludes" are not classified to the chapter, subchapter, category, subcategory or specific subclassification code under which it is found. The note also may provide the location of the excluded diagnosis. Excludes notes are italicized.

461 Acute sinusitis
INCLUDES abscess
empyema
infection
inflammation
suppuration
} acute, of sinus (accessory) (nasal)

EXCLUDES *chronic or unspecified sinusitis (473.0-473.9)*

Use additional code:
This instruction signals the coder that an additional code should be used if the information is available to provide a more complete picture of that diagnosis.

362.13 Changes in vascular appearance
Vascular sheathing of retina
Use additional code for any associated atherosclerosis (440.8)

There are coding circumstances outside of the etiology/manifestation convention when multiple coding for a single condition is required. The "Use additional code" note will be found under the associated condition code in the tabular. In the index, the multiple coding requirement is indicated by the use of the slanted bracket. The two codes are to be sequenced as listed in the index. For example, retinal arteriosclerosis must be coded using two codes sequenced as listed in the index.

Arteriosclerosis, arteriosclerotic
retinal (vascular) 440.8 *[362.13]*

Code first underlying disease:

The *"Code first underlying"* instructional note found under certain codes is a sequencing rule. Most often this sequencing rule applies to the etiology/manifestation convention and is found under the manifestation code. The manifestation code may never be used alone or as a primary diagnosis (i.e., sequenced first). The instructional note, the code and its descriptor appear in italics in the Tabular List.

590.81 Pyelitis or pyelonephritis in diseases classified elsewhere
Code first underlying disease as:
tuberculosis (016.0)

Not all codes with a "Code first underlying disease" instructional note are part of the etiology/manifestation convention. The `Code first' note will appear, but the title of the code and the instructional note are not in italics. These codes may be reported alone or as the secondary diagnosis. For example, disseminated chorioretinitis may be reported as a principal diagnosis. However, if the underlying condition that caused disseminated chorioretinitis is known, such as tuberculous disseminated chorioretinitis, two codes are required and sequenced as listed in the index.

363.13 Disseminated choroiditis and chorioretinitis, generalized
Code first underlying disease as:
tuberculosis (017.3)

Code, if applicable, any causal condition first:

A code with this note indicates that this code may be assigned as a principal diagnosis when the causal condition is unknown or not applicable. If a causal condition is known, then the code for that condition should be sequenced as the principal or first-listed diagnosis.

590.0 Chronic pyelonephritis
Chronic pyelitis
Chronic pyonephrosis
Code, if applicable, any causal condition first

Instructional Notes Used in the Index

Omit code:

"*Omit code*" is used to instruct the coder that no code is to be assigned. When this instruction is found in the Alphabetic Index to Diseases the medical term should not be coded as a diagnosis.

Metaplasia
cervix — *omit code*

See Condition:

The "see condition" note found in the Alphabetic Index to Disease instructs the coder to refer to a main term for the condition. This note will follow index terms that are nouns for anatomical sites or adjectival forms of disease term. In the example below, the index terms "Cervix" and "Diffuse" are followed by the — see condition. Coders should search the index using a condition term such as atrophy or prolapse.

Cervix — *see* condition

Diffuse — *see* condition

Morphology Codes:

For each neoplastic disease listed in the index, a morphology code is provided that identifies histological type and behavior.

Example:

Myelolipoma (M8870/0) — *see* Neoplasm, by site, benign

The histology is identified by the first four digits and the behavior is identified by the digit following the slash. Appendix A of Volume 1 contains a listing of morphology codes. This appendix is helpful when the pathology report identifies the neoplasm by using an M code. The coder may refer to Appendix A to determine the nomenclature of the neoplasm that will be the main term to search in the Index. The behavior classification is as follows:

0 Benign

1 Uncertain behavior

2 Carcinoma in situ

3 Malignant, primary site

6 Malignant, secondary site.

Additional Conventions

Symbols and Notations

New and Revised Text Symbols

● A bullet at a code or line of text indicates that the entry is new.

▲ A triangle in the Tabular List indicates that the code title is revised. In the Alphabetic Index the triangle indicates that a code has changed.

►◄ These symbols appear at the beginning and at the end of a section of new or revised text.

When these symbols appear on a page there will be a date on the lower outside corner of the page indicating the date of the change, (e.g., October 2008).

Additional Digits Required

✓4th This symbol indicates that the code requires a fourth digit.

✓5th This symbol indicates that a code requires a fifth digit.

☑ This symbol found only in the Alphabetic Index sections and the Table of Drugs and Chemicals indicates that an additional digit is required. Referring to the tabular section is essential to locate the appropriate additional digit.

AHA's Coding Clinic for ICD-9-CM References

The four cooperating parties have designated the AHA's *Coding Clinic for ICD-9-CM* as the official publication for coding guidelines. The references are identified by the notation **AHA:** followed by the issue, year and page number.

In the example below, AHA's *Coding Clinic for ICD-9-CM*, third quarter 1991, page 15, contains a discussion on code assignment for vitreous hemorrhage:

379.23 Vitreous hemorrhage

AHA: 3Q, '91, 15

The table below explains the abbreviations in the *Coding Clinic* references:

J-F	January/February
M-A	March/April
M-J	May/June
J-A	July/August
S-O	September/October
N-D	November/December
1Q	First quarter
2Q	Second quarter
3Q	Third quarter
4Q	Fourth quarter

Age and Sex Edit Symbols

The age edits below address OCE edits and are used to detect inconsistencies between the patient's age and diagnosis. They appear in the Tabular List of Diseases to the right of the code description.

Newborn Age: 0
These diagnoses are intended for newborns and neonates and the patient's age must be 0 years.

Pediatric Age: 0-17
These diagnoses are intended for children and the patient's age must between 0 and 17 years.

Maternity Age: 12-55
These diagnoses are intended for the patients between the age of 12 and 55 years.

Adult Age: 15-124
These diagnoses are intended for the patients between the age of 15 and 124 years.

The sex symbols below address OCE edits and are used to detect inconsistencies between the patient's sex and diagnosis. They appear in the Tabular List of Diseases to the right of the code description:

♂ **Male diagnosis only**
This symbol appears to the right of the code description. This reference appears in the disease Tabular List.

♀ **Female diagnosis only**
This symbol appears to the right of the code description. This reference appears in the disease Tabular List.

Color Coding

To alert the coder to Medicare outpatient code edits and other important reimbursement issues, color bars have been added over the code descriptors in the Tabular List. Some codes carry more than one color.

Carriers use the Medicare Outpatient Code Editor (OCE) to examine claims for coding and billing accuracy and completeness. Color codes in this book signify Medicare code edits for manifestation codes not to be reported as a primary diagnosis, and when a more specific diagnosis code should be used.

Manifestation Code
These codes will appear in italic type as well as with a blue color bar over the code title. A manifestation code is not allowed to be reported as a primary diagnosis because each describes a manifestation of some other underlying disease, not the disease itself. This is referred to as mandatory multiple coding of etiology and manifestation. Code the underlying disease first. A *Code first underlying disease* instructional note will appear with underlying disease codes identified. In the Alphabetic Index these codes are listed as the secondary code in slanted brackets with the code for the underlying disease listed first.

Other Specified Code
These codes will appear with a gray color bar over the code title. Use these codes when the documentation indicates a specified diagnosis, but the ICD-9-CM system does not have a specific code that describes the diagnosis. These codes are may be stated as "Other" or "Not elsewhere classified (NEC)."

Unspecified Code
These codes will have a yellow color bar over the code title. Use these codes when the neither the diagnostic statement nor the documentation provides enough information to assign a more specified diagnosis code. These codes may be stated as "Unspecified" or "Not otherwise specified (NOS)." Note: Do not assign these codes when a more specific diagnosis has been determined.

Other Notations

DEF: This symbol indicates a definition of disease term. The definition will appear in blue type in the Disease Tabular Lists.

PDx This symbol identifies a V code that generally is for use as a first listed diagnosis only but may be used as an additional diagnosis if the patient has more than one encounter on one day or there is more than one reason for the encounter.

SDx This symbol identifies a V code that can only be used as a secondary diagnosis.

Note: A V code without a symbol may be used as either a primary or secondary diagnosis.

Note: Please note that the symbols indicating the V code "primary only" and "secondary only" designation and the V Code Table included in the official coding guidelines

[Section 1.C.18.e] are consistent with reporting guidelines for healthcare encounters *excluding acute care inpatient admissions*. These V code edits are often in conflict with the inpatient prospective payment system (IPPS) edits. For example, V22.0, Encounter for supervision of a normal first pregnancy, may be an appropriate primary reason for an outpatient encounter. However, supervision for a normal pregnancy is not an acceptable principal diagnosis for an inpatient admission and will have an unacceptable prinicpal diagnosis edit under IPPS.

Medicare as Secondary Payer (MSP)

Note: This edit is no longer included in the official Medicare Code Editor (MCE).The Medicare as Secondary Payer (MSP) alert identified trauma diagnoses that may be covered under automobile insurance, no-fault insurance, workmen's compensation or other types of liability insurance for which Medicare should be a secondary payer. Providers must verify MSP information prior to submitting the claim to Medicare.

Alphabetic Indexes

Subterms under main terms may continue to next column or page.

This warning statement is a reminder to always check for additional subterms and information that may continue on to the next page or column before making a final selection.

Summary of Code Changes

DIAGNOSIS TABULAR (VOLUME 1)

006.8 Exclusion term revised

▲ 045-049 POLIOMYELITIS AND OTHER NON-ARTHROPOD-BORNE VIRAL DISEASES ▶AND PRION DISEASES◀ OF CENTRAL NERVOUS SYSTEM (045-049)

▲ 038.11 ▶Methicillin susceptible◀ Staphylococcus aureus septicemia
Inclusion terms added

● 038.12 Methicillin resistant Staphylococcus aureus septicemia

▲ 041.11 ▶Methicillin susceptible◀ Staphylococcus aureus
Inclusion terms added

● 041.12 Methicillin resistant Staphylococcus aureus
Inclusion term added

▲ 046 Slow virus infections ▶and prion diseases◀ of central nervous system

046.1 Inclusion term deleted

● 046.11 Variant Creutzfeldt-Jakob disease
Inclusion term added

● 046.19 Other and unspecified Creutzfeldt-Jakob disease
Inclusion terms added
Exclusion term added

● 046.7 Other specified prion diseases of central nervous system
Exclusion terms added

● 046.71 Gerstmann-Sträussler-Scheinker syndrome
Inclusion term added

● 046.72 Fatal familial insomnia
Inclusion term added

● 046.79 Other and unspecified prion disease of central nervous system

▲ 050-059 VIRAL DISEASES ACCOMPANIED BY EXANTHEM ▶(050-059)◀

▲ 051.0 Cowpox ▶and vaccinia not from vaccination◀
Inclusion term deleted
Exclusion term deleted

● 051.01 Cowpox

● 051.02 Vaccinia not from vaccination
Exclusion term added

058 ~~OTHER HUMAN HERPESVIRUSES (058)~~

● 059 Other poxvirus infections
Exclusion terms added

● 059.0 Other orthopoxvirus infections

● 059.00 Orthopoxvirus infection, unspecified

● 059.01 Monkeypox

● 059.09 Other orthopoxvirus infections

● 059.1 Other parapoxvirus infections

● 059.10 Parapoxvirus infection, unspecified

● 059.11 Bovine stomatitis

● 059.12 Sealpox

● 059.19 Other parapoxvirus infections

● 059.2 Yatapoxvirus infections

● 059.20 Yatapoxvirus infection, unspecified

● 059.21 Tanapox

● 059.22 Yaba monkey tumor virus

● 059.8 Other poxvirus infections

● 059.9 Poxvirus infections, unspecified

078.10 Inclusion term deleted
Inclusion term revised

078.11 Inclusion terms added

● 078.12 Plantar wart
Inclusion term added

078.19 Inclusion terms added
Inclusion terms deleted
Inclusion term revised

118 Use additional code note added

136.2 Inclusion term deleted

● 136.21 Specific infection due to acanthamoeba
Use additional code note added

● 136.29 Other specific infections by free-living amebae
Inclusion term added

Chapter 2 note added:

151 Exclusion terms added
Exclusion term deleted

152 Exclusion terms added
Exclusion term deleted

153 Exclusion terms added

154 Exclusion terms added

162 Exclusion terms added

164.0 Exclusion terms added

171 Includes term deleted
Exclusion term revised

172 Includes term added

189 Exclusion terms added

194 Use additional code note deleted
Exclusion term added

199 Exclusion terms added

● 199.2 Malignant neoplasm associated with transplant organ
Code first note added
Use additional code note added

▲ 203.00 Multiple myeloma, without mention of ▶having achieved◀ remission
Inclusion term added

● 203.02 Multiple myeloma, in relapse

▲ 203.10 Plasma cell leukemia, without mention of ▶having achieved◀ remission
Inclusion term added

● 203.12 Plasma cell leukemia, in relapse

▲ 203.80 Other immunoproliferative neoplasms, without mention of ▶having achieved◀ remission
Inclusion term added

● 203.82 Other immunoproliferative neoplasms, in relapse

▲ 204.00 Acute lymphoid leukemia, without mention of ▶having achieved◀ remission
Inclusion term added

● 204.02 Acute lymphoid leukemia, in relapse

▲ 204.10 Chronic lymphoid leukemia, without mention of ▶having achieved◀ remission
Inclusion term added

● 204.12 Chronic lymphoid leukemia, in relapse

▲ 204.20 Subacute lymphoid leukemia, without mention of ▶having achieved◀ remission
Inclusion term added

● 204.22 Subacute lymphoid leukemia, in relapse

▲ 204.80 Other lymphoid leukemia, without mention of ▶having achieved◀ remission
Inclusion term added

● 204.82 Other lymphoid leukemia, in relapse

▲ 204.90 Unspecified lymphoid leukemia, without mention of ▶having achieved◀ remission
Inclusion term added

● 204.92 Unspecified lymphoid leukemia, in relapse

▲ 205.00 Acute myeloid leukemia, without mention of ▶having achieved◀ remission
Inclusion term added

● 205.02 Acute myeloid leukemia, in relapse

▲ 205.10 Chronic myeloid leukemia, without mention of ▶having achieved◀ remission
Inclusion term added

● 205.12 Chronic myeloid leukemia, in relapse

▲ 205.20 Subacute myeloid leukemia, without mention of ▶having achieved◀ remission
Inclusion term added

● 205.22 Subacute myeloid leukemia, in relapse

▲ 205.30 Myeloid sarcoma, without mention of ▶having achieved◀ remission
Inclusion term added

● 205.32 Myeloid sarcoma, in relapse

▲ 205.80 Other myeloid leukemia, without mention of ▶having achieved◀ remission
Inclusion term added

● 205.82 Other myeloid leukemia, in relapse

▲ 205.90 Unspecified myeloid leukemia, without mention of ▶having achieved◀ remission
Inclusion term added

● 205.92 Unspecified myeloid leukemia, in relapse

▲ 206.00 Acute monocytic leukemia, without mention of ▶having achieved◀ remission
Inclusion term added

● 206.02 Acute monocytic leukemia, in relapse

▲ 206.10 Chronic monocytic leukemia, without mention of ▶having achieved◀ remission
Inclusion term added
● 206.12 Chronic monocytic leukemia, in relapse
▲ 206.20 Subacute monocytic leukemia, without mention of ▶having achieved◀ remission
Inclusion term added
● 206.22 Subacute monocytic leukemia, in relapse
▲ 206.80 Other monocytic leukemia, without mention of ▶having achieved◀ remission
Inclusion term added
● 206.82 Other monocytic leukemia, in relapse
▲ 206.90 Unspecified monocytic leukemia, without mention of ▶having achieved◀ remission
Inclusion term added
● 206.92 Unspecified monocytic leukemia, in relapse
▲ 207.00 Acute erythremia and erythroleukemia, without mention of ▶having achieved◀ remission
Inclusion term added
● 207.02 Acute erythremia and erythroleukemia, in relapse
▲ 207.10 Chronic erythremia, without mention of ▶having achieved◀ remission
Inclusion term added
● 207.12 Chronic erythremia, in relapse
▲ 207.20 Megakaryocytic leukemia, without mention of ▶having achieved◀ remission
Inclusion term added
● 207.22 Megakaryocytic leukemia, in relapse
▲ 207.80 Other specified leukemia, without mention of ▶having achieved◀ remission
Inclusion term added
● 207.82 Other specified leukemia, in relapse
▲ 208.00 Acute leukemia of unspecified cell type, without mention of ▶having achieved◀ remission
Inclusion term added
● 208.02 Acute leukemia of unspecified cell type, in relapse
▲ 208.10 Chronic leukemia of unspecified cell type, without mention of ▶having achieved◀ remission
Inclusion term added
● 208.12 Chronic leukemia of unspecified cell type, in relapse
▲ 208.20 Subacute leukemia of unspecified cell type, without mention of ▶having achieved◀ remission
Inclusion term added
● 208.22 Subacute leukemia of unspecified cell type, in relapse
▲ 208.80 Other leukemia of unspecified cell type, without mention of ▶having achieved◀ remission
Inclusion term added
● 208.82 Other leukemia of unspecified cell type, in relapse
▲ 208.90 Unspecified leukemia, without mention of ▶having achieved◀ remission
Inclusion term added
● 208.92 Unspecified leukemia, in relapse
● 209 Neuroendocrine tumors
Code first note added
Use additional code note added
Exclusion term added
● 209.0 Malignant carcinoid tumors of the small intestine
● 209.00 Malignant carcinoid tumor of the small intestine, unspecified portion
● 209.01 Malignant carcinoid tumor of the duodenum
● 209.02 Malignant carcinoid tumor of the jejunum
● 209.03 Malignant carcinoid tumor of the ileum
New subcategory 209.1 Malignant carcinoid tumors of the appendix, large intestine, and rectum
● 209.10 Malignant carcinoid tumor of the large intestine, unspecified portion
Inclusion term added
● 209.11 Malignant carcinoid tumor of the appendix
● 209.12 Malignant carcinoid tumor of the cecum
● 209.13 Malignant carcinoid tumor of the ascending colon
● 209.14 Malignant carcinoid tumor of the transverse colon
● 209.15 Malignant carcinoid tumor of the descending colon
● 209.16 Malignant carcinoid tumor of the sigmoid colon
● 209.17 Malignant carcinoid tumor of the rectum
● 209.2 Malignant carcinoid tumors of other and unspecified sites
● 209.20 Malignant carcinoid tumor of unknown primary site
● 209.21 Malignant carcinoid tumor of the bronchus and lung
● 209.22 Malignant carcinoid tumor of the thymus
● 209.23 Malignant carcinoid tumor of the stomach
● 209.24 Malignant carcinoid tumor of the kidney
● 209.25 Malignant carcinoid tumor of foregut, not otherwise specified
● 209.26 Malignant carcinoid tumor of midgut, not otherwise specified
● 209.27 Malignant carcinoid tumor of hindgut, not otherwise specified
● 209.29 Malignant carcinoid tumor of other sites
● 209.3 Malignant poorly differentiated neuroendocrine tumors
● 209.30 Malignant poorly differentiated neuroendocrine carcinoma, any site
Inclusion terms added
● 209.4 Benign carcinoid tumors of the small intestine
● 209.40 Benign carcinoid tumor of the small intestine, unspecified portion
● 209.41 Benign carcinoid tumor of the duodenum
● 209.42 Benign carcinoid tumor of the jejunum
● 209.43 Benign carcinoid tumor of the ileum
● 209.5 Benign carcinoid tumors of the appendix, large intestine, and rectum
● 209.50 Benign carcinoid tumor of the large intestine, unspecified portion
Inclusion term added
● 209.51 Benign carcinoid tumor of the appendix
● 209.52 Benign carcinoid tumor of the cecum
● 209.53 Benign carcinoid tumor of the ascending colon
● 209.54 Benign carcinoid tumor of the transverse colon
● 209.55 Benign carcinoid tumor of the descending colon
● 209.56 Benign carcinoid tumor of the sigmoid colon
● 209.57 Benign carcinoid tumor of the rectum
● 209.6 Benign carcinoid tumors of other and unspecified sites
● 209.60 Benign carcinoid tumor of unknown primary site
Inclusion terms added
● 209.61 Benign carcinoid tumor of the bronchus and lung
● 209.62 Benign carcinoid tumor of the thymus
● 209.63 Benign carcinoid tumor of the stomach
● 209.64 Benign carcinoid tumor of the kidney
● 209.65 Benign carcinoid tumor of foregut, not otherwise specified
● 209.66 Benign carcinoid tumor of midgut, not otherwise specified
● 209.67 Benign carcinoid tumor of hindgut, not otherwise specified
● 209.69 Benign carcinoid tumor of other sites
211.1 Exclusion term added
211.2 Exclusion term added
211.3 Exclusion term added
211.4 Exclusion term added
212.3 Exclusion term added
212.6 Exclusion term added
223.0 Exclusion term added
232 Exclusion term added
233.1 Inclusion term revised
238.7 Exclusion term deleted
● 238.77 Post-transplant lymphoproliferative disorder [PTLD]
Code first note added
▲ 249-259 DISEASES OF OTHER ENDOCRINE GLANDS ▶(249-259)◀
● 249 Secondary diabetes mellitus
Fifth digit definitions added
Inclusion terms added
Exclusion terms added

Code	Change
	Use additional code note added
● 249.00	Secondary diabetes mellitus without mention of complication, not stated as uncontrolled, or unspecified
	Inclusion term added
● 249.01	Secondary diabetes mellitus without mention of complication, uncontrolled
	Inclusion term added
● 249.10	Secondary diabetes mellitus with ketoacidosis, not stated as uncontrolled, or unspecified
	Inclusion terms added
● 249.11	Secondary diabetes mellitus with ketoacidosis, uncontrolled
	Inclusion terms added
● 249.20	Secondary diabetes mellitus with hyperosmolarity, not stated as uncontrolled, or unspecified
	Inclusion term added
● 249.21	Secondary diabetes mellitus with hyperosmolarity, uncontrolled
	Inclusion term added
● 249.30	Secondary diabetes mellitus with other coma, not stated as uncontrolled, or unspecified
	Inclusion terms added
	Exclusion term added
● 249.31	Secondary diabetes mellitus with other coma, uncontrolled
	Inclusion terms added
	Exclusion term added
● 249.40	Secondary diabetes mellitus with renal manifestations, not stated as uncontrolled, or unspecified
	Use additional code note added
● 249.41	Secondary diabetes mellitus with renal manifestations, uncontrolled
	Use additional code note added
● 249.50	Secondary diabetes mellitus with ophthalmic manifestations, not stated as uncontrolled, or unspecified
	Use additional code note added
● 249.51	Secondary diabetes mellitus with ophthalmic manifestations, uncontrolled
	Use additional code note added
● 249.60	Secondary diabetes mellitus with neurological manifestations, not stated as uncontrolled, or unspecified
	Use additional code note added
● 249.61	Secondary diabetes mellitus with neurological manifestations, uncontrolled
	Use additional code note added
● 249.70	Secondary diabetes mellitus with peripheral circulatory disorders, not stated as uncontrolled, or unspecified
	Use additional code note added
● 249.71	Secondary diabetes mellitus with peripheral circulatory disorders, uncontrolled
	Use additional code note added
● 249.80	Secondary diabetes mellitus with other specified manifestations, not stated as uncontrolled, or unspecified
	Inclusion terms added
	Use additional code note added
● 249.81	Secondary diabetes mellitus with other specified manifestations, uncontrolled
	Inclusion terms added
	Use additional code note added
● 249.90	Secondary diabetes mellitus with unspecified complication, not stated as uncontrolled, or unspecified
● 249.91	Secondary diabetes mellitus with unspecified complication, uncontrolled
250	Exclusion term added
250.6	Use additional code note revised
250.8	Inclusion terms revised
	Use additional code note deleted
251.0	Exclusion term revised
251.1	Exclusion term revised
251.2	Exclusion term revised
252	Exclusion term added
257.8	Exclusion term revised
259.5	Inclusion terms deleted
● 259.50	Androgen insensitivity, unspecified
● 259.51	Androgen insensitivity syndrome
	Inclusion terms added
● 259.52	Partial androgen insensitivity
	Inclusion terms added
271	Exclusion term revised
275.4	Exclusion term added
● 275.5	Hungry bone syndrome
276.2	Exclusion term revised
● 279.5	Graft-versus-host disease
	Code first note added
	Use additional code note added
● 279.50	Graft-versus-host disease, unspecified
● 279.51	Acute graft-versus-host disease
● 279.52	Chronic graft-versus-host disease
● 279.53	Acute on chronic graft-versus-host disease
287.4	Exclusion term added
288.0	Use additional code note revised
289.82	Exclusion term added
289.83	Use additional code notes added
● 289.84	Heparin-induced thrombocytopenia [HIT]
306.4	Exclusion term added
307.5	Exclusion term revised
	Exclusion term added
307.81	Exclusion terms added
310.2	Use additional code note added
315.34	Use additional code note deleted
323.41	Exclusion term revised
331	Use additional code note revised
337.0	Inclusion terms deleted
● 337.00	Idiopathic peripheral autonomic neuropathy, unspecified
● 337.01	Carotid sinus syndrome
	Inclusion term added
● 337.09	Other idiopathic peripheral autonomic neuropathy
	Inclusion term added
337.1	Code first note revised
337.20	Inclusion term added
337.21	Inclusion term added
337.22	Inclusion term added
337.29	Inclusion term added
337.3	Use additional code note revised
338	Exclusion terms added
● OTHER HEADACHE SYNDROMES (349)	
● 339	Other headache syndromes
	Exclusion terms added
● 339.0	Cluster headaches and other trigeminal autonomic cephalgias
	Inclusion term added
● 339.00	Cluster headache syndrome, unspecified.
	Inclusion terms added
● 339.01	Episodic cluster headache
● 339.02	Chronic cluster headache
● 339.03	Episodic paroxysmal hemicrania
	Inclusion term added
● 339.04	Chronic paroxysmal hemicrania
● 339.05	Short lasting unilateral neuralgiform headache with conjunctival injection and tearing
	Inclusion term added
● 339.09	Other trigeminal autonomic cephalgias
● 339.1	Tension type headache
	Exclusion terms added
● 339.10	Tension type headache, unspecified
● 339.11	Episodic tension type headache
● 339.12	Chronic tension type headache
● 339.2	Post-traumatic headache
● 339.20	Post-traumatic headache, unspecified
● 339.21	Acute post-traumatic headache
● 339.22	Chronic post-traumatic headache
● 339.3	Drug induced headache, not elsewhere classified
	Inclusion terms added
● 339.4	Complicated headache syndromes
● 339.41	Hemicrania continua
● 339.42	New daily persistent headache
	Inclusion term added
● 339.43	Primary thunderclap headache
● 339.44	Other complicated headache syndrome
● 339.8	Other specified headache syndromes
● 339.81	Hypnic headache
● 339.82	Headache associated with sexual activity
● 339.83	Primary cough headache
● 339.84	Primary exertional headache
● 339.85	Primary stabbing headache
● 339.89	Other headache syndromes
346	Exclusion terms added
	Fifth-digit definitions revised
	Fifth-digit definitions added
346.0	Inclusion term deleted
	Inclusion term added
	Exclusion term added
▲ 346.00	~~Classical~~ Migraine ▶with aura,◀ without mention of intractable migraine ▶without mention of status migrainosus◀
▲ 346.01	~~Classical~~ Migraine ▶with aura,◀ with intractable migraine, so stated, ▶without mention of status migrainosus◀

▶◀ **Revised Text** ● **New Code** ▲ **Revised Code Title**

● 346.02 Migraine with aura, without mention of intractable migraine with status migrainosus

● 346.03 Migraine with aura, with intractable migraine, so stated, with status migrainosus

346.1 Inclusion terms deleted
Inclusion term added

▲ 346.10 ~~Common~~ Migraine ▶without aura,◀ without mention of intractable migraine ▶without mention of status migrainosus◀

▲ 346.11 ~~Common~~ Migraine ▶without aura,◀ with intractable migraine, so stated, ▶without mention of status migrainosus◀

● 346.12 Migraine without aura, without mention of intractable migraine with status migrainosus

● 346.13 Migraine without aura, with intractable migraine, so stated, with status migrainosus

346.2 Inclusion terms deleted
Inclusion terms added
Exclusion terms added

▲ 346.20 Variants of migraine, ▶not elsewhere classified,◀ without mention of intractable migraine ▶without mention of status migrainosus◀

▲ 346.21 Variants of migraine, ▶not elsewhere classified,◀ with intractable migraine, so stated, ▶without mention of status migrainosus◀

● 346.22 Variants of migraine, not elsewhere classified, without mention of intractable migraine with status migrainosus

● 346.23 Variants of migraine, not elsewhere classified, with intractable migraine, so stated, with status migrainosus

346.3 Inclusion terms added

● 346.30 Hemiplegic migraine, without mention of intractable migraine without mention of status migrainosus

● 346.31 Hemiplegic migraine, with intractable migraine, so stated, without mention of status migrainosus

● 346.32 Hemiplegic migraine, without mention of intractable migraine with status migrainosus

● 346.33 Hemiplegic migraine, with intractable migraine, so stated, with status migrainosus

346.4 Inclusion terms added

● 346.40 Menstrual migraine, without mention of intractable migraine without mention of status migrainosus

● 346.41 Menstrual migraine, with intractable migraine, so stated, without mention of status migrainosus

● 346.42 Menstrual migraine, without mention of intractable migraine with status migrainosus

● 346.43 Menstrual migraine, with intractable migraine, so stated, with status migrainosus

346.5 Inclusion term added

● 346.50 Persistent migraine aura without cerebral infarction, without mention of intractable migraine without mention of status migrainosus

● 346.51 Persistent migraine aura without cerebral infarction, with intractable migraine, so stated, without mention of status migrainosus

● 346.52 Persistent migraine aura without cerebral infarction, without mention of intractable migraine with status migrainosus

● 346.53 Persistent migraine aura without cerebral infarction, with intractable migraine, so stated, with status migrainosus

● 346.60 Persistent migraine aura with cerebral infarction, without mention of intractable migraine without mention of status migrainosus

● 346.61 Persistent migraine aura with cerebral infarction, with intractable migraine, so stated, without mention of status migrainosus

● 346.62 Persistent migraine aura with cerebral infarction, without mention of intractable migraine with status migrainosus

● 346.63 Persistent migraine aura with cerebral infarction, with intractable migraine, so stated, with status migrainosus

346.7 Inclusion term added

● 346.70 Chronic migraine without aura, without mention of intractable migraine without mention of status migrainosus

● 346.71 Chronic migraine without aura, with intractable migraine, so stated, without mention of status migrainosus

● 346.72 Chronic migraine without aura, without mention of intractable migraine with status migrainosus

● 346.73 Chronic migraine without aura, with intractable migraine, so stated, with status migrainosus

346.8 Inclusion terms deleted

▲ 346.80 Other forms of migraine, without mention of intractable migraine ▶without mention of status migrainosus◀

▲ 346.81 Other forms of migraine, with intractable migraine, so stated, ▶without mention of status migrainosus◀

● 346.82 Other forms of migraine, without mention of intractable migraine with status migrainosus

● 346.83 Other forms of migraine, with intractable migraine, so stated, with status migrainosus

▲ 346.90 Migraine, unspecified, without mention of intractable migraine ▶without mention of status migrainosus◀

▲ 346.91 Migraine, unspecified, with intractable migraine, so stated, ▶without mention of status migrainosus◀

● 346.92 Migraine, unspecified, without mention of intractable migraine with status migrainosus

● 346.93 Migraine, unspecified, with intractable migraine, so stated, with status migrainosus

● 349.3 Dural tear

● 349.31 Accidental puncture or laceration of dura during a procedure
Inclusion term added

● 349.39 Other dural tear

353.1 Code first note deleted

353.5 Code first note added

354.4 Inclusion term added
Exclusion term added

355.71 Exclusion term added

355.9 Exclusion terms added

357.2 Code first note revised

358.1 Code first note revised

360-379 Use additional code note added

362.0 Code first note revised

● 362.20 Retinopathy of prematurity, unspecified
Inclusion term added

362.21 Inclusion term added

● 362.22 Retinopathy of prematurity, stage 0

● 362.23 Retinopathy of prematurity, stage 1

● 362.24 Retinopathy of prematurity, stage 2

● 362.25 Retinopathy of prematurity, stage 3

● 362.26 Retinopathy of prematurity, stage 4

● 362.27 Retinopathy of prematurity, stage 5

● 364.82 Plateau iris syndrome

365.41 Code first note deleted

365.42 Code first note deleted

365.43 Code first note deleted

365.51 Use additional code note deleted

365.52 Use additional code note deleted

365.59 Use additional code note deleted

365.61 Use additional code note deleted

365.62 Use additional code note deleted

365.63 Use additional code note deleted

365.64 Use additional code note deleted

365.65 Use additional code note deleted

366.41 Code first note revised

366.43 Code first note revised

368.16 Inclusion terms added

370.8 Code first note added

372.33 Code first note revised

● 372.34 Pingueculitis

380-389 Use additional code note added

▲ 386.0 ▶Ménière's◀ disease
Inclusion term revised

▲ 386.00 ▶Ménière's◀ disease, unspecified
Inclusion term revised

▲ 386.01 Active ▶Ménière's◀ disease, cochleovestibular

▲ 386.02 Active ▶Ménière's◀ disease, cochlear
▲ 386.03 Active ▶Ménière's◀ disease, vestibular
▲ 386.04 Inactive ▶Ménière's◀ disease
Inclusion term revised
391 Exclusion term revised
403 Includes note revised
411.1 Exclusion term deleted
Exclusion term added
● 414.3 Coronary atherosclerosis due to lipid rich plaque
Code first note added
415.11 Use additional code note added
433 Use additional code note added
434 Use additional code note added
443.81 Code first note revised
447.0 Exclusion term revised
459.0 Exclusion term added
480-488 Exclusion term added
▲ 482.41 ▶Methicillin susceptible◀ pneumonia due to Staphylococcus aureus
Inclusion terms added
● 482.42 Methicillin resistant pneumonia due to Staphylococcus aureus
511 Exclusion term deleted
511.8 Exclusion terms deleted
● 511.81 Malignant pleural effusion
Code first note added
● 511.89 Other specified forms of effusion, except tuberculous
Inclusion terms added
525.71 Inclusion terms added
525.72 Inclusion terms added
525.73 Inclusion terms added
528.0 Exclusion term added
Exclusion term deleted
530.1 Inclusion terms deleted
530.10 Inclusion term added
● 530.13 Eosinophilic esophagitis
530.19 Inclusion term added
535.4 Exclusion term added
● 535.70 Eosinophilic gastritis, without mention of hemorrhage
● 535.71 Eosinophilic gastritis, with hemorrhage
536.2 Inclusion term added
Exclusion term revised
Exclusion term added
536.3 Code first note revised
557 Exclusion term revised
● 558.4 Eosinophilic gastroenteritis and colitis
● 558.41 Eosinophilic gastroenteritis
Inclusion term added
● 558.42 Eosinophilic colitis
● 569.44 Dysplasia of anus
Inclusion terms added
Exclusion terms added
● 571.42 Autoimmune hepatitis
571.5 Code first note added
581.81 Code first note revised
583.81 Code first note revised
584.9 Inclusion term added
Exclusion term added
586 Exclusion term deleted
587 Exclusion terms deleted
● 599.70 Hematuria, unspecified
● 599.71 Gross hematuria
● 599.72 Microscopic hematuria

▲ DISORDERS OF THE BREAST ▶(610-612)◀
611.1 Exclusion terms added
611.3 Code first note added
611.8 Inclusion terms deleted
● 611.81 Ptosis of breast
Exclusion term added
● 611.82 Hypoplasia of breast
Inclusion term added
Exclusion term added
● 611.83 Capsular contracture of breast implant
● 611.89 Other specified disorders of breast
Inclusion terms added
New category 612 Deformity and disproportion of reconstructed breast
● 612.0 Deformity of reconstructed breast
Inclusion terms added
● 612.1 Disproportion of reconstructed breast
Inclusion terms added
616.1 Exclusion term added
622.1 Exclusion term added
623.0 Inclusion term added
Exclusion terms added
625.4 Inclusion terms deleted
Inclusion term added
Exclusion term added
New subcategory 625.7 Vulvodynia
● 625.70 Vulvodynia, unspecified
Inclusion term added
● 625.71 Vulvar vestibulitis
● 625.79 Other vulvodynia
▲ 630-679 COMPLICATIONS OF PREGNANCY, CHILDBRITH, AND THE PUERPERIUM ▶(630-679)◀
640 Instructional note revised
641 Instructional note revised
642 Instructional note revised
643 Instructional note revised
644 Instructional note revised
645 Instructional note revised
646 Instructional note revised
647 Instructional noterevised
647.6 Conditions classifiable to note revised
648 Instructional note revised
Exclusion term added
648.0 Inclusion term revised648.9
Inclusion term revised
649 Instructional note added
649.6 Exclusion term added
649.7 Exclusion term added
● 649.70 Cervical shortening, unspecified as to episode of care or not applicable
● 649.71 Cervical shortening, delivered, with or without mention of antepartum condition
● 649.73 Cervical shortening, antepartum condition or complication
651.0 Exclusion term added
653.7 Inclusion term deleted
Exclusion term added

▲ 656 Other ▶known or suspected◀ fetal and placental problems affecting management of mother
Exclusion terms added
656.8 Inclusion term added
657 Exclusion term added
658 Exclusion term added
● 678-679 OTHER MATERNAL AND FETAL COMPLICATIONS (678-679)
Fifth-digit definitions with instructional note added
● 678 Other fetal conditions
● 678.0 Fetal hematologic conditions
Inclusion terms added
Exclusion terms added
● 678.00 Fetal hematologic conditions, unspecified as to episode of care or not applicable
● 678.01 Fetal hematologic conditions, delivered, with or without mention of antepartum condition
● 678.03 Fetal hematologic conditions, antepartum condition or complication
● 678.1 Fetal conjoined twins
● 678.10 Fetal conjoined twins, unspecified as to episode of care or not applicable
● 678.11 Fetal conjoined twins, delivered, with or without mention of antepartum condition
● 678.13 Fetal conjoined twins, antepartum condition or complication
● 679 Complications of in utero procedures
● 679.0 Maternal complications from in utero procedure
Exclusion term added
● 679.00 Maternal complications from in utero procedure, unspecified as to episode of care or not applicable
● 679.01 Maternal complications from in utero procedure, delivered, with or without mention of antepartum condition
● 679.02 Maternal complications from in utero procedure, delivered, with mention of postpartum complication
● 679.03 Maternal complications from in utero procedure, antepartum condition or complication
● 679.04 Maternal complications from in utero procedure, postpartum condition or complication
● 679.1 Fetal complications from in utero procedure
Exclusion term added
● 679.10 Fetal complications from in utero procedure, unspecified as to episode of care or not applicable
● 679.11 Fetal complications from in utero procedure, delivered, with or without mention of antepartum condition
● 679.12 Fetal complications from in utero procedure, delivered, with mention of postpartum complication

▶◀ Revised Text ● New Code ▲ Revised Code Title

Code	Change
● 679.13	Fetal complications from in utero procedure, antepartum condition or complication
● 679.14	Fetal complications from in utero procedure, postpartum condition or complication
● 695	Erythematous conditions
● 695.1	Erythema multiforme Inclusion terms deleted Use additional code notes added Exclusion term added
● 695.10	Erythema multiforme, unspecified Inclusion terms added
● 695.11	Erythema multiforme minor
● 695.12	Erythema multiforme major
● 695.13	Stevens-Johnson syndrome
● 695.14	Stevens-Johnson syndrome-toxic epidermal necrolysis overlap syndrome Inclusion term added
● 695.15	Toxic epidermal necrolysis Inclusion terms added
● 695.19	Other erythema multiforme
● 695.5	Exfoliation due to erythematous conditions according to extent of body surface involved Code first note added
● 695.50	Exfoliation due to erythematous condition involving less than 10 percent of body surface Inclusion term added
● 695.51	Exfoliation due to erythematous condition involving 10-19 percent of body surface
● 695.52	Exfoliation due to erythematous condition involving 20-29 percent of body surface
● 695.53	Exfoliation due to erythematous condition involving 30-39 percent of body surface
● 695.54	Exfoliation due to erythematous condition involving 40-49 percent of body surface
● 695.55	Exfoliation due to erythematous condition involving 50-59 percent of body surface
● 695.56	Exfoliation due to erythematous condition involving 60-69 percent of body surface
● 695.57	Exfoliation due to erythematous condition involving 70-79 percent of body surface
● 695.58	Exfoliation due to erythematous condition involving 80-89 percent of body surface
● 695.59	Exfoliation due to erythematous condition involving 90 percent or more of body surface
695.81	Inclusion term added Use additional note added
707	Exclusion term deleted
▲ 707.0	~~Decubitus~~ ▶Pressure◀ ulcer Inclusion term revised Inclusion term deleted Use additional note added
▲ 707.00	~~Decubitus~~ ▶Pressure◀ ulcer, unspecified site
▲ 707.01	~~Decubitus~~ ▶Pressure◀ ulcer, elbow
▲ 707.02	~~Decubitus~~ ▶Pressure◀ ulcer, upper back

Code	Change
▲ 707.03	~~Decubitus~~ ▶Pressure◀ ulcer, lower back
▲ 707.04	~~Decubitus~~ ▶Pressure◀ ulcer, hip
▲ 707.05	~~Decubitus~~ ▶Pressure◀ ulcer, buttock
▲ 707.06	~~Decubitus~~ ▶Pressure◀ ulcer, ankle
▲ 707.07	~~Decubitus~~ ▶Pressure◀ ulcer, heel
▲ 707.09	~~Decubitus~~ ▶Pressure◀ ulcer, other site
▲ 707.1	Ulcer of lower limbs, except ~~decubitus~~ ▶pressure ulcer◀ Code first note added
▲ 707.10	Ulcer of lower limbs, except ~~decubitus~~ ▶pressure ulcer◀, ulcer of unspecified site
▲ 707.11	Ulcer of lower limbs, except ~~decubitus~~ ▶pressure ulcer◀, ulcer of thigh
▲ 707.12	Ulcer of lower limbs, except ~~decubitus~~ ▶pressure ulcer◀, ulcer of calf
▲ 707.13	Ulcer of lower limbs, except ~~decubitus~~ ▶pressure ulcer◀, ulcer of ankle
▲ 707.14	Ulcer of lower limbs, except ~~decubitus~~ ▶pressure ulcer◀, heel and midfoot
▲ 707.15	Ulcer of lower limbs, except ~~decubitus~~ ▶pressure ulcer◀, other part of foot
▲ 707.19	Ulcer of lower limbs, except ~~decubitus~~ ▶pressure ulcer◀, other part of lower limb
● 707.2	Pressure ulcer stages Code first note added
● 707.20	Pressure ulcer, unspecified stage Inclusion terms added
● 707.21	Pressure ulcer stage I Inclusion terms added
● 707.22	Pressure ulcer stage II Inclusion terms added
● 707.23	Pressure ulcer stage III Inclusion terms added
● 707.24	Pressure ulcer stage IV Inclusion terms added
● 707.25	Pressure ulcer, unstageable
710-739	Use additional code note added
713.3	Code first note revised
713.5	Code first note revised
728	Exclusion term added
729.7	Code first note added
729.9	Inclusion term deleted
● 729.90	Disorders of soft tissue, unspecified
● 729.91	Post-traumatic seroma Exclusion term added
● 729.92	Nontraumatic hematoma of soft tissue Inclusion term added
● 729.99	Other disorders of soft tissue Inclusion term added
731.8	Code first note revised
733.0	Use additional note added
733.93	Use additional note added
733.49	Use additional note added
733.95	Use additional note added Exclusion terms added
● 733.96	Stress fracture of femoral neck Inclusion term added Use additional note added

Code	Change
● 733.97	Stress fracture of shaft of femur Inclusion term added Use additional note added
● 733.98	Stress fracture of pelvis Inclusion term added Use additional note added
746.84	Inclusion term added Use additional note added
751.7	Exclusion term revised Exclusion terms deleted
752	Exclusion terms deleted
752.7	Exclusion terms added Exclusion terms deleted
756	Exclusion term added
757.6	Inclusion term deleted Exclusion term added
▲ 760.6	Surgical operation on mother ▶and fetus◀ Exclusion term deleted
● 760.61	Newborn affected by amniocentesis Exclusion term added
● 760.62	Newborn affected by other in utero procedure Exclusion term added
● 760.63	Newborn affected by other surgical operations on mother during pregnancy Exclusion term added
● 760.64	Newborn affected by previous surgical procedure on mother not associated with pregnancy
763	Exclusion term added
763.89	Inclusion term deleted
771.81	Use additional code note added
▲ 776	Hematological disorders of ~~fetus and~~ newborn Inclusion term revised Exclusion term added
▲ 777.5	Necrotizing enterocolitis in ~~fetus or~~ newborn
● 777.50	Necrotizing enterocolitis in newborn, unspecified Inclusion term added
● 777.51	Stage I necrotizing enterocolitis in newborn
● 777.52	Stage II necrotizing enterocolitis in newborn Inclusion term added
● 777.53	Stage III necrotizing enterocolitis in newborn Inclusion term added
780.0	Exclusion term revised
▲ 780.6	Fever ▶and other physiologic disturbances of temperature regulation◀ Inclusion terms deleted Code first note deleted Exclusion terms deleted Exclusion terms added
● 780.60	Fever, unspecified Inclusion terms added Exclusion terms added
● 780.61	Fever presenting with conditions classified elsewhere Code first note added
● 780.62	Postprocedural fever Exclusion term added
● 780.63	Postvaccination fever Inclusion term added

▶◀ **Revised Text** ● **New Code** ▲ **Revised Code Title**

● 780.64 Chills (without fever)
Inclusion term added
Exclusion terms added
● 780.65 Hypothermia not associated with low environmental temperature
Exclusion term added
● 780.72 Functional quadriplegia
Inclusion term added
Exclusion terms added
780.9 Exclusion terms deleted
Exclusion terms added
780.99 Inclusion terms deleted
782.3 Exclusion term revised
787.0 Exclusion terms added
788 Exclusion term revised
788.3 Exclusion terms added
788.9 Inclusion terms deleted
● 788.91 Functional urinary incontinence
Inclusion term added
Exclusion terms added
● 788.99 Other symptoms involving urinary system
Inclusion term added
790.2 Exclusion term revised
791 Exclusion term revised
795 Exclusion terms added
795.0 Exclusion terms added
Exclusion term revised
795.00 Inclusion term revised
● 795.07 Satisfactory cervical smear but lacking transformation zone
▲ 795.08 Unsatisfactory ▶cervical cytology◀smear
Inclusion term revised
▲ 795.1 ~~Nonspecific abnormal Papanicolaou smear of other site~~ ▶Abnormal Papanicolaou smear of vagina and vaginal HPV◀
Inclusion term added
Use additional code note added
Exclusion terms added
● 795.10 Abnormal glandular Papanicolaou smear of vagina
Inclusion term added
● 795.11 Papanicolaou smear of vagina with atypical squamous cells of undetermined significance (ASC-US)
● 795.12 Papanicolaou smear of vagina with atypical squamous cells cannot exclude high grade squamous intraepithelial lesion (ASC-H)
● 795.13 Papanicolaou smear of vagina with low grade squamous intraepithelial lesion (LGSIL)
● 795.14 Papanicolaou smear of vagina with high grade squamous intraepithelial lesion (HGSIL)
● 795.15 Vaginal high risk human papillomavirus (HPV) DNA test positive
Exclusion terms added
● 795.16 Papanicolaou smear of vagina with cytologic evidence of malignancy
● 795.18 Unsatisfactory vaginal cytology smear
Inclusion term added
● 795.19 Other abnormal Papanicolaou smear of vagina and vaginal HPV
Inclusion term added
Use additional code note added
● 796.7 Abnormal cytologic smear of anus and anal HPV
Exclusion terms added
● 796.70 Abnormal glandular Papanicolaou smear of anus
Inclusion term added
● 796.71 Papanicolaou smear of anus with atypical squamous cells of undetermined significance (ASC-US)
● 796.72 Papanicolaou smear of anus with atypical squamous cells cannot exclude high grade squamous intraepithelial lesion (ASC-H)
● 796.73 Papanicolaou smear of anus with low grade squamous intraepithelial lesion (LGSIL)
● 796.74 Papanicolaou smear of anus with high grade squamous intraepithelial lesion (HGSIL)
● 796.75 Anal high risk human papillomavirus (HPV) DNA test positive
● 796.76 Papanicolaou smear of anus with cytologic evidence of malignancy
● 796.77 Satisfactory anal smear but lacking transformation zone
● 796.78 Unsatisfactory anal cytology smear
Inclusion term added
● 796.79 Other abnormal Papanicolaou smear of anus and anal HPV
Inclusion term added
Use additional code note added
797 Inclusion term added
▲ 850.4 Concussion, with prolonged loss of ▶consciousness,◀ without return to pre-existing conscious level
866 Exclusion term added
958 Exclusion term added
991.6 Exclusion term revised
994.5 Exclusion term revised
994.8 Inclusion term added
995.6 Inclusion term added
996 Exclusion term added
996.49 Inclusion terms added
996.62 Exclusion terms added
996.7 Exclusion term added
996.8 Use additional code note added
996.85 Inclusion term deleted
997.3 Inclusion terms deleted
● 997.31 Ventilator associated pneumonia
Use additional code note added
● 997.39 Other respiratory complications
Inclusion terms added
998.2 Exclusion terms added
▲ 998.3 Disruption of ~~operation~~ wound
Inclusion term added
● 998.30 Disruption of wound, unspecified
Inclusion term added
▲ 998.31 Disruption of internal operation ▶(surgical)◀ wound
Inclusion terms added
Exclusion terms added
▲ 998.32 Disruption of external operation ▶(surgical)◀ wound
Inclusion terms added
● 998.33 Disruption of traumatic injury wound repair
Inclusion terms added
999.0 Exclusion term added
999.2 Exclusion term added
999.31 Inclusion term revised
Inclusion terms added
999.4 Inclusion term added
▲ 999.8 Other ▶infusion and◀ transfusion reaction
Inclusion terms deleted
● 999.81 Extravasation of vesicant chemotherapy
Inclusion term added
● 999.82 Extravasation of other vesicant agent
Inclusion term added
● 999.88 Other infusion reaction
● 999.89 Other transfusion reaction
Inclusion term added
Use additional code note added
999.9 Exclusion term added
V02 Inclusion term added
● V02.53 Methicillin susceptible Staphylococcus aureus
Inclusion term added
● V02.54 Methicillin resistant Staphylococcus aureus
Inclusion term added
● V07.5 Prophylactic use of agents affecting estrogen receptors and estrogen levels
Code first note added
Use additional note added
Exclusion term added
● V07.51 Prophylactic use of selective estrogen receptor modulators (SERMs)
Inclusion terms added
● V07.52 Prophylactic use of aromatase inhibitors
Inclusion terms added
● V07.59 Prophylactic use of other agents affecting estrogen receptors and estrogen levels
Inclusion terms added
V09.0 Inclusion term deleted
V10 Code first note added
● V12.04 Methicillin resistant Staphylococcus aureus MRSA
Inclusion term added
● V13.51 Pathologic fracture
Inclusion term added
Exclusion term added
● V13.52 Stress fracture
Inclusion term added
Exclusion term added
● V13.59 Other musculoskeletal disorders
V15 Exclusion term added
▲ V15.2 Surgery to other ~~major~~ organs
● V15.21 Personal history of undergoing in utero procedure during pregnancy
● V15.22 Personal history of undergoing in utero procedure while a fetus
● V15.29 Surgery to other organs

▶◀ Revised Text ● New Code ▲ Revised Code Title

● V15.51 Traumatic fracture
Inclusion term added
Exclusion term added
● V15.59 Other injury
V15.8 Exclusion term added
V15.81 Exclusion term added
V15.89 Exclusion terms added
● V23.85 Pregnancy resulting from assisted reproductive technology
Inclusion term added
● V23.86 Pregnancy with history of in utero procedure during previous pregnancy
Exclusion term added
V28 Exclusion term added
▲ V28.3 ►Encounter for routine◄ screening for malformation using ultrasonics
Inclusion term added
Exclusion terms added
● V28.81 Encounter for fetal anatomic survey
● V28.82 Encounter for screening for risk of pre-term labor
● V28.89 Other specified antenatal screening
Inclusion terms added
V29 Exclusion term added
V43 Exclusion terms added
V45.1 Inclusion terms deleted
● V45.11 Renal dialysis status
Inclusion terms added
● V45.12 Noncompliance with renal dialysis
▲ V45.71 Acquired absence of breast ►and nipple◄
V45.77 Exclusion term added
● V45.87 Transplanted organ removal status
Inclusion term added
Exclusion term added
● V45.88 Status post administration of tPA (rtPA) in a different facility within the last 24 hours prior to admission to current facility
Code first note added
▲ V46 Other dependence on machines ►and devices◄
● V46.3 Wheelchair dependence
Inclusion terms added
Code first note added
V46.8 Exclusion term revised
V50.1 Exclusion term added
Exclusion term revised
V51 Exclusion term revised
● V51.0 Encounter for breast reconstruction following mastectomy
Exclusion term added
● V51.8 Other aftercare involving the use of plastic surgery
V52.4 Inclusion terms added
Exclusion terms added
Exclusion term revised
V56.0 Exclusion term revised
V58.1 Exclusion term deleted
V58.41 Exclusion term revised
V58.6 Exclusion terms added
V58.69 Inclusion terms added

V61.0 Inclusion terms deleted
● V61.01 Family disruption due to family member on military deployment
Inclusion terms added
● V61.02 Family disruption due to return of family member from military deployment
Inclusion terms added
● V61.03 Family disruption due to divorce or legal separation
● V61.04 Family disruption due to parent-child estrangement
Exclusion term added
● V61.05 Family disruption due to child in welfare custody
● V61.06 Family disruption due to child in foster care or in care of non-parental family member
● V61.09 Other family disruption
Inclusion terms added
V62.2 Inclusion terms deleted
● V62.21 Personal current military deployment status
Inclusion term added
● V62.22 Personal history of return from military deployment
Inclusion term added
● V62.29 Other occupational circumstances or maladjustment
Inclusion term added
V64.05 Exclusion term added
V67.01 Use additional code note revised
V71 Exclusion term added
V71.8 Exclusion term added
V76.47 Use additional code note revised
● OTHER SPECIFIED PERSONAL EXPOSURES AND HISTORY PRESENTING HAZARDS TO HEALTH (V87)
● V87 Other specified personal exposures and history presenting hazards to health
● V87.0 Contact with and (suspected) exposure to hazardous metals
Exclusion term added
● V87.01 Arsenic
● V87.09 Other hazardous metals
Inclusion terms added
● V87.1 Contact with and (suspected) exposure to hazardous aromatic compounds
Exclusion term added
● V87.11 Aromatic amines
● V87.12 Benzene
● V87.19 Other hazardous aromatic compounds
Inclusion terms added
● V87.2 Contact with and (suspected) exposure to other potentially hazardous chemicals
Inclusion terms added
Exclusion terms added
● V87.3 Contact with and (suspected) exposure to other potentially hazardous substances
Exclusion terms added
● V87.31 Exposure to mold
● V87.39 Contact with and (suspected) exposure to other potentially hazardous substances

● V87.4 Personal history of drug therapy
Exclusion term added
● V87.41 Personal history of antineoplastic chemotherapy
● V87.42 Personal history of monoclonal drug therapy
● V87.49 Personal history of other drug therapy
● ACQUIRED ABSENCE OF OTHER ORGANS AND TISSUE (V88)
● V88 Acquired absence of other organs and tissue
● V88.0 Acquired absence of cervix and uterus
● V88.01 Acquired absence of both cervix and uterus
Inclusion terms added
● V88.02 Acquired absence of uterus with remaining cervical stump
Inclusion terms added
● V88.03 Acquired absence of cervix with remaining uterus
● OTHER SUSPECTED CONDITIONS NOT FOUND (V89)
● V89 Other suspected conditions not found
● V89.0 Suspected maternal and fetal conditions not found
Exclusion terms added
● V89.01 Suspected problem with amniotic cavity and membrane not found
Inclusion terms added
● V89.02 Suspected placental problem not found
● V89.03 Suspected fetal anomaly not found
● V89.04 Suspected problem with fetal growth not found
● V89.05 Suspected cervical shortening not found
● V89.09 Other suspected maternal and fetal condition not found
E800-E999 Inclusion term added
E885.1 Inclusion terms added
▲ E927 Overexertion and strenuous ►and repetitive◄ movements ►or loads◄
Inclusion terms deleted
● E927.0 Overexertion from sudden strenuous movement
Inclusion term added
● E927.1 Overexertion from prolonged static position
Inclusion terms added
● E927.2 Excessive physical exertion from prolonged activity
● E927.3 Cumulative trauma from repetitive motion
Inclusion terms added
● E927.4 Cumulative trauma from repetitive impact
● E927.8 Other overexertion and strenuous and repetitive movements or load
● E927.9 Unspecified overexertion and strenuous and repetitive movements or loads
E928.6 Inclusion term revised

Coding Guidelines

Effective October 1, 2007
Narrative changes appear in bold text. Items underlined have been moved within the guidelines since November 15, 2006. The guidelines include the updated V Code Table

The Centers for Medicare and Medicaid Services (CMS) and the National Center for Health Statistics (NCHS), two departments within the U.S. Federal Government's Department of Health and Human Services (DHHS) provide the following guidelines for coding and reporting using the International Classification of Diseases, 9th Revision, Clinical Modification (ICD-9-CM). These guidelines should be used as a companion document to the official version of the ICD-9CM as published on CD-ROM by the U.S. Government Printing Office (GPO).

These guidelines have been approved by the four organizations that make up the Cooperating Parties for the ICD-9-CM: the American Hospital Association (AHA), the American Health Information Management Association (AHIMA), CMS, and NCHS. These guidelines are included on the official government version of the ICD-9-CM, and also appear in "*Coding Clinic for ICD-9-CM*" published by the AHA.

These guidelines are a set of rules that have been developed to accompany and complement the official conventions and instructions provided within the ICD-9-CM itself. These guidelines are based on the coding and sequencing instructions in Volumes I, II and III of ICD-9-CM, but provide additional instruction. Adherence to these guidelines when assigning ICD-9-CM diagnosis and procedure codes is required under the Health Insurance Portability and Accountability Act (HIPAA). The diagnosis codes (Volumes 1-2) have been adopted under HIPAA for all healthcare settings. Volume 3 procedure codes have been adopted for inpatient procedures reported by hospitals. A joint effort between the healthcare provider and the coder is essential to achieve complete and accurate documentation, code assignment, and reporting of diagnoses and procedures. These guidelines have been developed to assist both the healthcare provider and the coder in identifying those diagnoses and procedures that are to be reported. The importance of consistent, complete documentation in the medical record cannot be overemphasized. Without such documentation accurate coding cannot be achieved. The entire record should be reviewed to determine the specific reason for the encounter and the conditions treated.

The term encounter is used for all settings, including hospital admissions. In the context of these guidelines, the term provider is used throughout the guidelines to mean physician or any qualified health care practitioner who is legally accountable for establishing the patient's diagnosis. Only this set of guidelines, approved by the Cooperating Parties, is official.

The guidelines are organized into sections. Section I includes the structure and conventions of the classification and general guidelines that apply to the entire classification, and chapter-specific guidelines that correspond to the chapters as they are arranged in the classification. Section II includes guidelines for selection of principal diagnosis for non-outpatient settings. Section III includes guidelines for reporting additional diagnoses in non-outpatient settings. Section IV is for outpatient coding and reporting.

Section I. Conventions, general coding guidelines and chapter specific guidelines

A. Conventions for the ICD-9-CM
   1. Format:
   2. Abbreviations
      a. Index abbreviations
      b. Tabular abbreviations
   3. Punctuation
   4. Includes and Excludes Notes and Inclusion terms
   5. Other and Unspecified codes
      a. "Other" codes
      b. "Unspecified" codes
   6. Etiology/manifestation convention ("code first", "use additional code" and "in diseases classified elsewhere" notes)
   7. "And"
   8. "With"
   9. "See" and "See Also"
B. General Coding Guidelines
   1. Use of Both Alphabetic Index and Tabular List
   2. Locate each term in the Alphabetic Index
   3. Level of Detail in Coding
   4. Code or codes from 001.0 through V89.09
   5. Selection of codes 001.0 through 999.9
   6. Signs and symptoms
   7. Conditions that are an integral part of a disease process
   8. Conditions that are not an integral part of a disease process
   9. Multiple coding for a single condition
   10. Acute and Chronic Conditions
   11. Combination Code
   12. Late Effects
   13. Impending or Threatened Condition
C. Chapter-Specific Coding Guidelines
   1. Chapter 1: Infectious and Parasitic Diseases (001-139)
      a. Human Immunodeficiency Virus (HIV) Infections
      b. Septicemia, Systemic Inflammatory Response Syndrome (SIRS), Sepsis, Severe Sepsis and Septic Shock
   2. Chapter 2: Neoplasms (140-239)
      a. Treatment directed at the malignancy
      b. Treatment of secondary site
      c. Coding and sequencing of complications
      d. Primary malignancy previously excised
      e. Admissions/Encounters involving chemotherapy, immunotherapy and radiation therapy
      f. Admission/encounter to determine extent of malignancy
      g. Symptoms, signs, and ill-defined conditions listed in Chapter 16 **associated with neoplasms**
      h. Admission/encounter for pain control/management
   3. Chapter 3: Endocrine, Nutritional, and Metabolic Diseases and Immunity Disorders (240-279)
      a. Diabetes mellitus
   4. Chapter 4: Diseases of Blood and Blood Forming Organs (280-289)
      a. Anemia of chronic disease
   5. Chapter 5: Mental Disorders (290-319)
      Reserved for future guideline expansion
   6. Chapter 6: Diseases of Nervous System and Sense Organs (320-389)
      a. Pain - Category 338
   7. Chapter 7: Diseases of Circulatory System (390-459)
      a. Hypertension
      b. Cerebral infarction/stroke/cerebrovascular accident (CVA)
      c. Postoperative cerebrovascular accident
      d. Late Effects of Cerebrovascular Disease
      e. Acute myocardial infarction (AMI)
   8. Chapter 8: Diseases of Respiratory System (460-519)
      a. Chronic Obstructive Pulmonary Disease [COPD] and Asthma
      b. Chronic Obstructive Pulmonary Disease [COPD] and Bronchitis
      c. Acute Respiratory Failure
      d. Influenza due to identified avian influenza virus (avian influenza)
   9. Chapter 9: Diseases of Digestive System (520-579)
      Reserved for future guideline expansion
   10. Chapter 10: Diseases of Genitourinary System (580-629)
      a. Chronic kidney disease
   11. Chapter 11: Complications of Pregnancy, Childbirth, and the Puerperium (630-677)
      a. General Rules for Obstetric Cases
      b. Selection of OB Principal or First-listed Diagnosis
      c. Fetal Conditions Affecting the Management of the Mother
      d. HIV Infection in Pregnancy, Childbirth and the Puerperium
      e. Current Conditions Complicating Pregnancy
      f. Diabetes mellitus in pregnancy
      g. Gestational diabetes
      h. Normal Delivery, Code 650
      i. The Postpartum and Peripartum Periods
      j. Code 677, Late effect of complication of pregnancy
      k. Abortions
   12. Chapter 12: Diseases Skin and Subcutaneous Tissue (680-709)
      Reserved for future guideline expansion
   13. Chapter 13: Diseases of Musculoskeletal and Connective Tissue (710-739)
      a. Coding of Pathologic Fractures
   14. Chapter 14: Congenital Anomalies (740-759)
      a. Codes in categories 740-759, Congenital Anomalies
   15. Chapter 15: Newborn (Perinatal) Guidelines (760-779)
      a. General Perinatal Rules

  - b. Use of codes V30-V39
  - c. Newborn transfers
  - d. Use of category V29
  - e. Use of other V codes on perinatal records
  - f. Maternal Causes of Perinatal Morbidity
  - g. Congenital Anomalies in Newborns
  - h. Coding Additional Perinatal Diagnoses
  - i. Prematurity and Fetal Growth Retardation
  - j. Newborn sepsis

16. Chapter 16: Signs, Symptoms and Ill-Defined Conditions (780-799)
    Reserved for future guideline expansion
17. Chapter 17: Injury and Poisoning (800-999)
    - a. Coding of Injuries
    - b. Coding of Traumatic Fractures
    - c. Coding of Burns
    - d. Coding of Debridement of Wound, Infection, or Burn
    - e. Adverse Effects, Poisoning and Toxic Effects
    - f. Complications of care
    - g. SIRS due to Non-infectious Process
18. Classification of Factors Influencing Health Status and Contact with Health Service (Supplemental V01-V89)
    - a. Introduction
    - b. V codes use in any healthcare setting
    - c. V Codes indicate a reason for an encounter
    - d. Categories of V Codes
    - e. V Code Table
19. Supplemental Classification of External Causes of Injury and Poisoning (E-codes, E800-E999)
    - a. General E Code Coding Guidelines
    - b. Place of Occurrence Guideline
    - c. Adverse Effects of Drugs, Medicinal and Biological Substances Guidelines
    - d. Multiple Cause E Code Coding Guidelines
    - e. Child and Adult Abuse Guideline
    - f. Unknown or Suspected Intent Guideline
    - g. Undetermined Cause
    - h. Late Effects of External Cause Guidelines
    - i. Misadventures and Complications of Care Guidelines
    - j. Terrorism Guidelines

Section II. Selection of Principal Diagnosis

A. Codes for symptoms, signs, and ill-defined conditions
B. Two or more interrelated conditions, each potentially meeting the definition for principal diagnosis
C. Two or more diagnoses that equally meet the definition for principal diagnosis
D. Two or more comparative or contrasting conditions
E. A symptom(s) followed by contrasting/comparative diagnoses
F. Original treatment plan not carried out
G. Complications of surgery and other medical care
H. Uncertain Diagnosis
I. Admission from Observation Unit
   1. Admission Following Medical Observation
   2. Admission Following Post-Operative Observation
J. Admission from Outpatient Surgery

Section III. Reporting Additional Diagnoses

A. Previous conditions
B. Abnormal findings
C. Uncertain Diagnosis

Section IV. Diagnostic Coding and Reporting Guidelines for Outpatient Services

A. Selection of first-listed condition
   1. Outpatient Surgery
   2. Observation Stay
B. Codes from 001.0 through V84.8
C. Accurate reporting of ICD-9-CM diagnosis codes
D. Selection of codes 001.0 through 999.9
E. Codes that describe symptoms and signs
F. Encounters for circumstances other than a disease or injury
G. Level of Detail in Coding
   1. ICD-9-CM codes with 3, 4, or 5 digits
   2. Use of full number of digits required for a code
H. ICD-9-CM code for the diagnosis, condition, problem, or other reason for encounter/visit
I. Uncertain diagnosis
J. Chronic diseases
K. Code all documented conditions that coexist
L. Patients receiving diagnostic services only
M. Patients receiving therapeutic services only
N. Patients receiving preoperative evaluations only
O. Ambulatory surgery
P. Routine outpatient prenatal visits

Appendix I: Present on Admission Reporting Guidelines

Section I. Conventions, General Coding Guidelines and Chapter Specific Guidelines

The conventions, general guidelines and chapter-specific guidelines are applicable to all health care settings unless otherwise indicated.

A. Conventions for the ICD-9-CM

The conventions for the ICD-9-CM are the general rules for use of the classification independent of the guidelines. These conventions are incorporated within the index and tabular of the ICD-9-CM as instructional notes. The conventions are as follows:

1. Format:

The ICD-9-CM uses an indented format for ease in reference

2. Abbreviations

a. Index abbreviations

NEC "Not elsewhere classifiable"
This abbreviation in the index represents "other specified" when a specific code is not available for a condition the index directs the coder to the "other specified" code in the tabular.

b. Tabular abbreviations

NEC "Not elsewhere classifiable"
This abbreviation in the tabular represents "other specified". When a specific code is not available for a condition the tabular includes an NEC entry under a code to identify the code as the "other specified" code. *(See Section I.A.5.a. "Other" codes").*

NOS "Not otherwise specified"
This abbreviation is the equivalent of unspecified. *(See Section I.A.5.b., "Unspecified" codes)*

3. Punctuation

[ ] Brackets are used in the tabular list to enclose synonyms, alternative wording or explanatory phrases. Brackets are used in the index to identify manifestation codes. *(See Section I.A.6. "Etiology/manifestations")*

( ) Parentheses are used in both the index and tabular to enclose supplementary words that may be present or absent in the statement of a disease or procedure without affecting the code number to which it is assigned. The terms within the parentheses are referred to as nonessential modifiers.

: Colons are used in the Tabular list after an incomplete term which needs one or more of the modifiers following the colon to make it assignable to a given category.

4. Includes and Excludes Notes and Inclusion terms

Includes: This note appears immediately under a three-digit code title to further define, or give examples of, the content of the category.

Excludes: An excludes note under a code indicates that the terms excluded from the code are to be coded elsewhere. In some cases the codes for the excluded terms should not be used in conjunction with the code from which it is excluded. An example of this is a congenital condition excluded from an acquired form of the same condition. The congenital and acquired codes should not be used together. In other cases, the excluded terms may be used together with an excluded code. An example of this is when fractures of different bones are coded to different codes. Both codes may be used together if both types of fractures are present.

 Revised text in bold font.

Inclusion terms: List of terms is included under certain four and five digit codes. These terms are the conditions for which that code number is to be used. The terms may be synonyms of the code title, or, in the case of "other specified" codes, the terms are a list of the various conditions assigned to that code. The inclusion terms are not necessarily exhaustive. Additional terms found only in the index may also be assigned to a code.

5. **Other and Unspecified codes**
   a. **"Other" codes**
      Codes titled "other" or "other specified" (usually a code with a 4th digit 8 or fifth-digit 9 for diagnosis codes) are for use when the information in the medical record provides detail for which a specific code does not exist. Index entries with NEC in the line designate "other" codes in the tabular. These index entries represent specific disease entities for which no specific code exists so the term is included within an "other" code.
   b. **"Unspecified" codes**
      Codes (usually a code with a 4th digit 9 or 5th digit 0 for diagnosis codes) titled "unspecified" are for use when the information in the medical record is insufficient to assign a more specific code.
6. **Etiology/manifestation convention ("Code first," "Use additional code" and "In diseases classified elsewhere" notes)**
   Certain conditions have both an underlying etiology and multiple body system manifestations due to the underlying etiology. For such conditions, the ICD-9-CM has a coding convention that requires the underlying condition be sequenced first followed by the manifestation. Wherever such a combination exists, there is a "Use additional code" note at the etiology code, and a "Code first" note at the manifestation code. These instructional notes indicate the proper sequencing order of the codes, etiology followed by manifestation.
   In most cases the manifestation codes will have in the code title, "In diseases classified elsewhere." Codes with this title are a component of the etiology/ manifestation convention. The code title indicates that it is a manifestation code. "In diseases classified elsewhere" codes are never permitted to be used as first listed or principal diagnosis codes. They must be used in conjunction with an underlying condition code and they must be listed following the underlying condition.
   There are manifestation codes that do not have "In diseases classified elsewhere" in the title. For such codes a "Use additional code" note will still be present and the rules for sequencing apply.
   In addition to the notes in the tabular, these conditions also have a specific index entry structure. In the index both conditions are listed together with the etiology code first followed by the manifestation codes in brackets. The code in brackets is always to be sequenced second.
   The most commonly used etiology/manifestation combinations are the codes for Diabetes mellitus, category 250. For each code under category 250 there is a use additional code note for the manifestation that is specific for that particular diabetic manifestation. Should a patient have more than one manifestation of diabetes, more than one code from category 250 may be used with as many manifestation codes as are needed to fully describe the patient's complete diabetic condition. The category 250 diabetes codes should be sequenced first, followed by the manifestation codes.
   "Code first" and "Use additional code" notes are also used as sequencing rules in the classification for certain codes that are not part of an etiology/ manifestation combination.
   See - Section I.B.9. "Multiple coding for a single condition."
7. **"And"**
   The word "and" should be interpreted to mean either "and" or "or" when it appears in a title.
8. **"With"**
   The word "with" in the alphabetic index is sequenced immediately following the main term, not in alphabetical order.
9. **"See" and "See Also"**
   The "see" instruction following a main term in the index indicates that another term should be referenced. It is necessary to go to the main term referenced with the "see" note to locate the correct code.
   A "see also" instruction following a main term in the index instructs that there is another main term that may also be referenced that may provide additional index entries that may be useful. It is not necessary to follow the "see also" note when the original main term provides the necessary code.

B. **General Coding Guidelines**
1. **Use of Both Alphabetic Index and Tabular List** Use both the Alphabetic Index and the Tabular List when locating and assigning a code. Reliance on only the Alphabetic Index or the Tabular List leads to errors in code assignments and less specificity in code selection.
2. **Locate each term in the Alphabetic Index**
   Locate each term in the Alphabetic Index and verify the code selected in the Tabular List. Read and be guided by instructional notations that appear in both the Alphabetic Index and the Tabular List.
3. **Level of Detail in Coding**
   Diagnosis and procedure codes are to be used at their highest number of digits available.
   ICD-9-CM diagnosis codes are composed of codes with 3, 4, or 5 digits. Codes with three digits are included in ICD-9-CM as the heading of a category of codes that may be further subdivided by the use of fourth and/or fifth digits, which provide greater detail.
   A three-digit code is to be used only if it is not further subdivided. Where fourth-digit subcategories and/or fifth-digit subclassifications are provided, they must be assigned. A code is invalid if it has not been coded to the full number of digits required for that code. For example, Acute myocardial infarction, code 410, has fourth digits that describe the location of the infarction (e.g., 410.2, Of inferolateral wall), and fifth digits that identify the episode of care. It would be incorrect to report a code in category 410 without a fourth and fifth digit.
   ICD-9-CM Volume 3 procedure codes are composed of codes with either 3 or 4 digits. Codes with two digits are included in ICD-9-CM as the heading of a category of codes that may be further subdivided by the use of third and/or fourth digits, which provide greater detail.
4. **Code or codes from 001.0 through V89.09**
   The appropriate code or codes from 001.0 through V89.09 must be used to identify diagnoses, symptoms, conditions, problems, complaints or other reason(s) for the encounter/visit.
5. **Selection of codes 001.0 through 999.9**
   The selection of codes 001.0 through 999.9 will frequently be used to describe the reason for the admission/encounter. These codes are from the section of ICD-9-CM for the classification of diseases and injuries (e.g., infectious and parasitic diseases; neoplasms; symptoms, signs, and ill-defined conditions, etc.).
6. **Signs and symptoms**
   Codes that describe symptoms and signs, as opposed to diagnoses, are acceptable for reporting purposes when a related definitive diagnosis has not been established (confirmed) by the provider. Chapter 16 of ICD-9-CM, Symptoms, Signs, and Ill-defined conditions (codes 780.0 - 799.9) contain many, but not all codes for symptoms.
7. **Conditions that are an integral part of a disease process**
   Signs and symptoms that are **associated routinely with a** disease process should not be assigned as additional codes, unless otherwise instructed by the classification.
8. **Conditions that are not an integral part of a disease process**
   Additional signs and symptoms that may not be associated routinely with a disease process should be coded when present.
9. **Multiple coding for a single condition**
   In addition to the etiology/manifestation convention that requires two codes to fully describe a single condition that affects multiple body systems, there are other single conditions that also require more than one code. "Use additional code" notes are found in the tabular at codes that are not part of an etiology/manifestation pair where a secondary code is useful to fully describe a condition. The sequencing rule is the same as the etiology/manifestation pair - , "Use additional code" indicates that a secondary code should be added.
   For example, for infections that are not included in chapter 1, a secondary code from category 041, Bacterial infection in conditions classified elsewhere and of unspecified site, may be required to identify the bacterial organism causing the infection. A "Use additional code" note will normally be found at the infectious disease code, indicating a need for the organism code to be added as a secondary code.
   "Code first" notes are also under certain codes that are not specifically manifestation codes but may be due to an underlying cause. When a "Code first" note is present and an underlying condition is present the underlying condition should be sequenced first.
   "Code, if applicable, any causal condition first", notes indicate that this code may be assigned as a principal diagnosis when the

Revised text in bold font.

causal condition is unknown or not applicable. If a causal condition is known, then the code for that condition should be sequenced as the principal or first-listed diagnosis.

Multiple codes may be needed for late effects, complication codes and obstetric codes to more fully describe a condition. See the specific guidelines for these conditions for further instruction.

10. **Acute and Chronic Conditions**

If the same condition is described as both acute (subacute) and chronic, and separate subentries exist in the Alphabetic Index at the same indentation level, code both and sequence the acute (subacute) code first.

11. **Combination Code**

A combination code is a single code used to classify:

- Two diagnoses, or
- A diagnosis with an associated secondary process (manifestation)
- A diagnosis with an associated complication

Combination codes are identified by referring to subterm entries in the Alphabetic Index and by reading the inclusion and exclusion notes in the Tabular List.

Assign only the combination code when that code fully identifies the diagnostic conditions involved or when the Alphabetic Index so directs. Multiple coding should not be used when the classification provides a combination code that clearly identifies all of the elements documented in the diagnosis. When the combination code lacks necessary specificity in describing the manifestation or complication, an additional code should be used as a secondary code.

12. **Late Effects**

A late effect is the residual effect (condition produced) after the acute phase of an illness or injury has terminated. There is no time limit on when a late effect code can be used. The residual may be apparent early, such as in cerebrovascular accident cases, or it may occur months or years later, such as that due to a previous injury. Coding of late effects generally requires two codes sequenced in the following order: The condition or nature of the late effect is sequenced first. The late effect code is sequenced second.

An exception to the above guidelines are those instances where the code for late effect is followed by a manifestation code identified in the Tabular List and title, or the late effect code has been expanded (at the fourth and fifth-digit levels) to include the manifestation(s). The code for the acute phase of an illness or injury that led to the late effect is never used with a code for the late effect.

13. **Impending or Threatened Condition**

Code any condition described at the time of discharge as "impending" or "threatened" as follows:

If it did occur, code as confirmed diagnosis. If it did not occur, reference the Alphabetic Index to determine if the condition has a subentry term for "impending" or "threatened" and also reference main term entries for "Impending" and for "Threatened." If the subterms are listed, assign the given code. If the subterms are not listed, code the existing underlying condition(s) and not the condition described as impending or threatened.

C. **Chapter-Specific Coding Guidelines**

In addition to general coding guidelines, there are guidelines for specific diagnoses and/or conditions in the classification. Unless otherwise indicated, these guidelines apply to all health care settings. Please refer to Section II for guidelines on the selection of principal diagnosis.

1. **Chapter 1: Infectious and Parasitic Diseases (001-139)**

a. **Human Immunodeficiency Virus (HIV) Infections**

1) **Code only confirmed cases**

Code only confirmed cases of HIV infection/illness. This is an exception to the hospital inpatient guideline Section II, H.

In this context, "confirmation" does not require documentation of positive serology or culture for HIV; the provider's diagnostic statement that the patient is HIV positive, or has an HIV-related illness is sufficient.

2) **Selection and sequencing of HIV codes**

(a) Patient admitted for HIV-related condition

If a patient is admitted for an HIV-related condition, the principal diagnosis should be 042, followed by additional diagnosis codes for all reported HIV-related conditions.

(b) Patient with HIV disease admitted for unrelated condition

If a patient with HIV disease is admitted for an unrelated condition (such as a traumatic injury), the code for the unrelated condition (e.g., the nature of injury code) should be the principal diagnosis. Other diagnoses would be 042 followed by additional diagnosis codes for all reported HIV-related conditions.

(c) Whether the patient is newly diagnosed

Whether the patient is newly diagnosed or has had previous admissions/encounters for HIV conditions is irrelevant to the sequencing decision.

(d) Asymptomatic human immunodeficiency virus

V08 Asymptomatic human immunodeficiency virus [HIV] infection, is to be applied when the patient without any documentation of symptoms is listed as being "HIV positive," "known HIV," "HIV test positive," or similar terminology. Do not use this code if the term "AIDS" is used or if the patient is treated for any HIV-related illness or is described as having any condition(s) resulting from his/her HIV positive status; use 042 in these cases.

(e) Patients with inconclusive HIV serology

Patients with inconclusive HIV serology, but no definitive diagnosis or manifestations of the illness, may be assigned code 795.71, Inconclusive serologic test for Human Immunodeficiency Virus [HIV].

(f) Previously diagnosed HIV-related illness

Patients with any known prior diagnosis of an HIV-related illness should be coded to 042. Once a patient has developed an HIV-related illness, the patient should always be assigned code 042 on every subsequent admission/encounter. Patients previously diagnosed with any HIV illness (042) should never be assigned to 795.71 or V08.

(g) HIV Infection in Pregnancy, Childbirth and the Puerperium

During pregnancy, childbirth or the puerperium, a patient admitted (or presenting for a health care encounter) because of an HIV-related illness should receive a principal diagnosis code of 647.6X, Other specified infectious and parasitic diseases in the mother classifiable elsewhere, but complicating the pregnancy, childbirth or the puerperium, followed by 042 and the code(s) for the HIV-related illness(es). Codes from Chapter 15 always take sequencing priority.

Patients with asymptomatic HIV infection status admitted (or presenting for a health care encounter) during pregnancy, childbirth, or the puerperium should receive codes of 647.6X and V08.

(h) Encounters for testing for HIV

If a patient is being seen to determine his/her HIV status, use code V73.89, Screening for other specified viral disease. Use code V69.8, Other problems related to lifestyle, as a secondary code if an asymptomatic patient is in a known high risk group for HIV. Should a patient with signs or symptoms or illness, or a confirmed HIV related diagnosis be tested for HIV, code the signs and symptoms or the diagnosis. An additional counseling code V65.44 may be used if counseling is provided during the encounter for the test.

When a patient returns to be informed of his/her HIV test results use code V65.44, HIV counseling, if the results of the test are negative.

If the results are positive but the patient is asymptomatic use code V08, Asymptomatic HIV infection. If the results are positive and the patient is symptomatic use code 042, HIV infection, with codes for the HIV related symptoms or diagnosis. The HIV counseling code may also be used if counseling is provided for patients with positive test results.

b. Septicemia, Systemic Inflammatory Response Syndrome (SIRS), Sepsis, Severe Sepsis, and Septic Shock

1) SIRS, Septicemia, and Sepsis

(a) The terms *septicemia* and *sepsis* are often used interchangeably by providers, however they are not considered synonymous terms. The following descriptions are provided for reference but do not preclude querying the provider for clarification about terms used in the documentation:

(i) Septicemia generally refers to a systemic disease associated with the presence of pathological microorganisms or toxins in the blood, which can include bacteria, viruses, fungi or other organisms.

(ii) Systemic inflammatory response syndrome (SIRS) generally refers to the systemic response to infection, trauma/burns, or other insult (such as cancer) with symptoms including fever, tachycardia, tachypnea, and leukocytosis.

(iii) Sepsis generally refers to SIRS due to infection.

(iv) Severe sepsis generally refers to sepsis with associated acute organ dysfunction.

(b) The coding of SIRS, sepsis and severe sepsis

The coding of SIRS, sepsis and severe sepsis requires a minimum of 2 codes: a code for the underlying cause (such as infection or trauma) and a code from subcategory 995.9 Systemic inflammatory response syndrome (SIRS).

(i) The code for the underlying cause (such as infection or trauma) must be sequenced before the code from subcategory 995.9 Systemic inflammatory response syndrome (SIRS).

(ii) Sepsis and severe sepsis require a code for the systemic infection (038.xx, 112.5, etc.) and either code 995.91, Sepsis, or 995.92, Severe sepsis. If the causal organism is not documented, assign code 038.9, Unspecified septicemia.

(iii) Severe sepsis requires additional code(s) for the associated acute organ dysfunction(s).

(iv) If a patient has sepsis with multiple organ dysfunctions, follow the instructions for coding severe sepsis.

(v) Either the term sepsis or SIRS must be documented to assign a code from subcategory 995.9.

(vi) See Section I.C.17.g), Injury and poisoning, for information regarding systemic inflammatory response syndrome (SIRS) due to trauma/burns and other non-infectious processes.

(c) Due to the complex nature of sepsis and severe sepsis, some cases may require querying the provider prior to assignment of the codes.

2) Sequencing sepsis and severe sepsis

(a) Sepsis and severe sepsis as principal diagnosis

If sepsis or severe sepsis is present on admission, and meets the definition of principal diagnosis, the systemic infection code (e.g., 038.xx, 112.5, etc) should be assigned as the principal diagnosis, followed by code 995.91, Sepsis, or 995.92, Severe sepsis, as required by the sequencing rules in the Tabular List. Codes from subcategory 995.9 can never be assigned as a principal diagnosis. A code should also be assigned for any localized infection, if present.

If the sepsis or severe sepsis is due to a postprocedural infection, see Section I.C.10 for guidelines related to sepsis due to postprocedural infection.

(b) Sepsis and severe sepsis as secondary diagnoses

When sepsis or severe sepsis develops during the encounter (it was not present on admission), the systemic infection code and code 995.91 or 995.92 should be assigned as secondary diagnoses.

(c) Documentation unclear as to whether sepsis or severe sepsis is present on admission

Sepsis or severe sepsis may be present on admission but the diagnosis may not be confirmed until sometime after admission**.** If the documentation is not clear whether the sepsis **or severe sepsis** was present on admission, the provider should be queried.

3) Sepsis/SIRS with Localized Infection

If the reason for admission is both sepsis, severe sepsis, or SIRS and a localized infection, such as pneumonia or cellulitis, a code for the systemic infection (038.xx, 112.5, etc) should be assigned first, then code 995.91 or 995.92, followed by the code for the localized infection. If the patient is admitted with a localized infection, such as pneumonia, and sepsis/SIRS doesn't develop until after admission, see guideline **I.C.1.b.**2.b).

If the localized infection is postprocedural, ***see Section I.C.10 for guidelines related to sepsis due to postprocedural infection.***

Note: The term urosepsis is a nonspecific term. If that is the only term documented then only code 599.0 should be assigned based on the default for the term in the ICD-9-CM index, in addition to the code for the causal organism if known.

4) Bacterial Sepsis and Septicemia

In most cases, it will be a code from category 038, Septicemia, that will be used in conjunction with a code from subcategory 995.9 such as the following:

(a) Streptococcal sepsis

If the documentation in the record states streptococcal sepsis, codes 038.0, Streptococcal septicemia, and code 995.91 should be used, in that sequence.

(b) Streptococcal septicemia

If the documentation states streptococcal septicemia, only code 038.0 should be assigned, however, the provider should be queried whether the patient has sepsis, an infection with SIRS.

5) Acute organ dysfunction that is not clearly associated with the sepsis

If a patient has sepsis and an acute organ dysfunction, but the medical record documentation indicates that the acute organ dysfunction is related to a medical condition other than the sepsis, do not assign code 995.92, Severe sepsis. An acute organ dysfunction must be associated with the sepsis in order to assign the severe sepsis code. If the documentation is not clear as to whether an acute organ dysfunction is related to the sepsis or another medical condition, query the provider.

6) Septic shock

(a) Sequencing of septic shock

Septic shock generally refers to circulatory failure associated with severe sepsis, and, therefore, it represents a type of acute organ dysfunction.

For all cases of septic shock, the code for the systemic infection should be sequenced first, followed by codes 995.92 and 785.52. Any additional codes for other acute organ dysfunctions should also be assigned. As noted in the sequencing instructions in the Tabular List, the code for septic shock cannot be assigned as a principal diagnosis.

(b) Septic Shock without documentation of severe sepsis

Septic shock indicates the presence of severe sepsis.

Code 995.92, Severe sepsis, must be assigned with code 785.52, Septic shock, even if the term severe sepsis is not documented in the record. The "Use additional code" note and the "Code first" note in the tabular support this guideline.

7) Sepsis and septic shock complicating abortion and pregnancy

Sepsis and septic shock complicating abortion, ectopic pregnancy, and molar pregnancy are classified to category codes in Chapter 11 (630-639).

See section I.C.11.

8) Negative or inconclusive blood cultures

Negative or inconclusive blood cultures do not preclude a diagnosis of septicemia or sepsis in patients with clinical evidence of the condition, however, the provider should be queried.

9) **Newborn sepsis**
See Section I.C.15.j for information on the coding of newborn sepsis.

10) **Sepsis due to a postprocedural infection**

(a) **Documentation of causal relationship**
As with all postprocedural complications, code assignment is based on the provider's documentation of the relationship between the infection and the procedure.

(b) **Sepsis due to postprocedural infection**
In cases of postprocedural sepsis, the complication code, such as code 998.59, Other postoperative infection, or 674.3x, Other complications of obstetrical surgical wounds should be coded first followed by the appropriate sepsis codes (systemic infection code and either code 995.91or 995.92). An additional code(s) for any acute organ dysfunction should also be assigned for cases of severe sepsis.

11) **External cause of injury codes with SIRS**
Refer to Section I.C.19.a.7 for instruction on the use of external cause of injury codes with codes for SIRS resulting from trauma.

12) **Sepsis and severe sepsis associated with noninfectious process**

(a) **Sequencing of sepsis/severe sepsis associated with non-infectious process**
In some cases, a non-infectious process, such as trauma, may lead to an infection which can result in sepsis or severe sepsis. If sepsis or severe sepsis is documented as associated with a non-infectious condition, such as a burn or serious injury, and this condition meets the definition for principal diagnosis, the code for the noninfectious condition should be sequenced first, followed by the code for the systemic infection and either code 995.91, Sepsis, or 995.92, Severe sepsis. Additional codes for any associated acute organ dysfunction(s) should also be assigned for cases of severe sepsis. If the sepsis or severe sepsis meets the definition of principal diagnosis, the systemic infection and sepsis codes should be sequenced before the non-infectious condition. When both the associated non-infectious condition and the sepsis or severe sepsis meet the definition of principal diagnosis, either may be assigned as principal diagnosis.

See Section I.C.1.b.2) (a) for guidelines pertaining to sepsis or severe sepsis as the principal diagnosis.

(b) **Only one SIRS (subcategory 995.9) code should be assigned**
Only one code from subcategory 995.9 should be assigned for SIRS associated with trauma or other non-infectious condition. Assign the SIRS code (subcategory 995.9) that corresponds to the principal diagnosis. That is, if trauma or a noninfectious condition is the underlying cause, assign code 995.93 or 995.94. If an infection is the underlying cause, assign code 995.91 or 995.92.

See Section I.C.17.g for information on the coding of SIRS due to trauma/burns or other non-infectious disease processes.

2. **Chapter 2: Neoplasms (140-239)**

General guidelines

Chapter 2 of the ICD-9-CM contains the codes for most benign and all malignant neoplasms. Certain benign neoplasms, such as prostatic adenomas, may be found in the specific body system chapters. To properly code a neoplasm it is necessary to determine from the record if the neoplasm is benign, in-situ, malignant, or of uncertain histologic behavior. If malignant, any secondary (metastatic) sites should also be determined.

The neoplasm table in the Alphabetic Index should be referenced first. However, if the histological term is documented, that term should be referenced first, rather than going immediately to the Neoplasm Table, in order to determine which column in the Neoplasm Table is appropriate. For example, if the documentation indicates "adenoma," refer to the term in the Alphabetic Index to review the entries under this term and the instructional note to "see also neoplasm, by site, benign." The table provides the proper code based on the type of neoplasm and the site. It is important to select the proper column in the table that corresponds to the type of neoplasm. The tabular should then be referenced to verify that the correct code has been selected from the table and that a more specific site code does not exist.

See Section I. C. 18.d.4. for information regarding V codes for genetic susceptibility to cancer.

a. **Treatment directed at the malignancy**
If the treatment is directed at the malignancy, designate the malignancy as the principal diagnosis.

b. **Treatment of secondary site**
When a patient is admitted because of a primary neoplasm with metastasis and treatment is directed toward the secondary site only, the secondary neoplasm is designated as the principal diagnosis even though the primary malignancy is still present.

c. **Coding and sequencing of complications**
Coding and sequencing of complications associated with the malignancies or with the therapy thereof are subject to the following guidelines:

1) **Anemia associated with malignancy**
When admission/encounter is for management of an anemia associated with the malignancy, and the treatment is only for anemia, the appropriate anemia code (such as code 285.22, Anemia in neoplastic disease) is designated as the principal diagnosis and is followed by the appropriate code(s) for the malignancy.
Code 285.22 may also be used as a secondary code if the patient suffers from anemia and is being treated for the malignancy.

2) **Anemia associated with chemotherapy, immunotherapy and radiation therapy**
When the admission/encounter is for management of an anemia associated with chemotherapy, immunotherapy or radiotherapy and the only treatment is for the anemia, the anemia is sequenced first followed by code E933.1. The appropriate neoplasm code should be assigned as an additional code.

3) **Management of dehydration due to the malignancy**
When the admission/encounter is for management of dehydration due to the malignancy or the therapy, or a combination of both, and only the dehydration is being treated (intravenous rehydration), the dehydration is sequenced first, followed by the code(s) for the malignancy.

4) **Treatment of a complication resulting from a surgical procedure**
When the admission/encounter is for treatment of a complication resulting from a surgical procedure, designate the complication as the principal or first-listed diagnosis if treatment is directed at resolving the complication.

d. **Primary malignancy previously excised**
When a primary malignancy has been previously excised or eradicated from its site and there is no further treatment directed to that site and there is no evidence of any existing primary malignancy, a code from category V10, Personal history of malignant neoplasm, should be used to indicate the former site of the malignancy. Any mention of extension, invasion, or metastasis to another site is coded as a secondary malignant neoplasm to that site. The secondary site may be the principal or first-listed with the V10 code used as a secondary code.

e. **Admissions/Encounters involving chemotherapy, immunotherapy and radiation therapy**

1) **Episode of care involves surgical removal of neoplasm**
When an episode of care involves the surgical removal of a neoplasm, primary or secondary site, followed by adjunct chemotherapy or radiation treatment during the same episode of care, the neoplasm code should be assigned as principal or first-listed diagnosis, using codes in the 140-198 series or where appropriate in the 200-203 series.

2) **Patient admission/encounter solely for administration of chemotherapy, immunotherapy and radiation therapy**
If a patient admission/encounter is solely for the administration of chemotherapy, immunotherapy or

radiation therapy assign code V58.0, Encounter for radiation therapy, or V58.11, Encounter for antineoplastic chemotherapy, or V58.12, Encounter for antineoplastic immunotherapy as the first-listed or principal diagnosis. If a patient receives more than one of these therapies during the same admission more than one of these codes may be assigned, in any sequence.

3) **Patient admitted for radiotherapy/chemotherapy and immunotherapy and develops complications**
When a patient is admitted for the purpose of radiotherapy, immunotherapy or chemotherapy and develops complications such as uncontrolled nausea and vomiting or dehydration, the principal or first-listed diagnosis is V58.0, Encounter for radiotherapy, or V58.11, Encounter for antineoplastic chemotherapy, or V58.12, Encounter for antineoplastic immunotherapy followed by any codes for the complications.

f. **Admission/encounter to determine extent of malignancy**
When the reason for admission/encounter is to determine the extent of the malignancy, or for a procedure such as paracentesis or thoracentesis, the primary malignancy or appropriate metastatic site is designated as the principal or first-listed diagnosis, even though chemotherapy or radiotherapy is administered.

g. **Symptoms, signs, and ill-defined conditions listed in Chapter 16 associated with neoplasms**
Symptoms, signs, and ill-defined conditions listed in Chapter 16 characteristic of, or associated with, an existing primary or secondary site malignancy cannot be used to replace the malignancy as principal or first-listed diagnosis, regardless of the number of admissions or encounters for treatment and care of the neoplasm.
See section I.C.18.d.14, Encounter for prophylactic organ removal.

h. **Admission/encounter for pain control/management**
See Section I.C.6.a.5 for information on coding admission/encounter for pain control/management.

3. **Chapter 3: Endocrine, Nutritional, and Metabolic Diseases and Immunity Disorders (240-279)**

a. **Diabetes mellitus**
Codes under category 250, Diabetes mellitus, identify complications/manifestations associated with diabetes mellitus. A fifth-digit is required for all category 250 codes to identify the type of diabetes mellitus and whether the diabetes is controlled or uncontrolled.

1) **Fifth digits for category 250:**
The following are the fifth digits for the codes under category 250:
0 type II or unspecified type, not stated as uncontrolled
1 type I, [juvenile type], not stated as uncontrolled
2 type II or unspecified type, uncontrolled
3 type I, [juvenile type], uncontrolled
The age of a patient is not the sole determining factor, though most type I diabetics develop the condition before reaching puberty. For this reason type I diabetes mellitus is also referred to as juvenile diabetes.

2) **Type of diabetes mellitus not documented**
If the type of diabetes mellitus is not documented in the medical record the default is type II.

3) **Diabetes mellitus and the use of insulin**
All type I diabetics must use insulin to replace what their bodies do not produce. However, the use of insulin does not mean that a patient is a type I diabetic. Some patients with type II diabetes mellitus are unable to control their blood sugar through diet and oral medication alone and do require insulin.
If the documentation in a medical record does not indicate the type of diabetes but does indicate that the patient uses insulin, the appropriate fifth-digit for type II must be used. For type II patients who routinely use insulin, code V58.67, Long-term (current) use of insulin, should also be assigned to indicate that the patient uses insulin. Code V58.67 should not be assigned if insulin is given temporarily to bring a type II patient's blood sugar under control during an encounter.

4) **Assigning and sequencing diabetes codes and associated conditions**
When assigning codes for diabetes and its associated conditions, the code(s) from category 250 must be sequenced before the codes for the associated conditions. The diabetes codes and the secondary codes that correspond to them are paired codes that follow the etiology/manifestation convention of the classification *(See Section I.A.6., Etiology/manifestation convention)*. Assign as many codes from category 250 as needed to identify all of the associated conditions that the patient has. The corresponding secondary codes are listed under each of the diabetes codes.

(a) **Diabetic retinopathy/diabetic macular edema**
Diabetic macular edema, code 362.07, is only present with diabetic retinopathy. Another code from subcategory 362.0, Diabetic retinopathy, must be used with code 362.07. Codes under subcategory 362.0 are diabetes manifestation codes, so they must be used following the appropriate diabetes code.

5) **Diabetes mellitus in pregnancy and gestational diabetes**
(a) For diabetes mellitus complicating pregnancy, *see Section I.C.11.f., Diabetes mellitus in pregnancy.*
(b) For gestational diabetes, *see Section I.C.11, g., Gestational diabetes.*

6) **Insulin pump malfunction**
(a) **Underdose of insulin due insulin pump failure**
An underdose of insulin due to an insulin pump failure should be assigned 996.57, Mechanical complication due to insulin pump, as the principal or first listed code, followed by the appropriate diabetes mellitus code based on documentation.
(b) **Overdose of insulin due to insulin pump failure**
The principal or first listed code for an encounter due to an insulin pump malfunction resulting in an overdose of insulin, should also be 996.57, Mechanical complication due to insulin pump, followed by code 962.3, Poisoning by insulins and antidiabetic agents, and the appropriate diabetes mellitus code based on documentation.

4. **Chapter 4: Diseases of Blood and Blood Forming Organs (280-289)**

a. **Anemia of chronic disease**
Subcategory 285.2, Anemia in chronic illness, has codes for anemia in chronic kidney disease, code 285.21; anemia in neoplastic disease, code 285.22; and anemia in other chronic illness, code 285.29. These codes can be used as the principal/first listed code if the reason for the encounter is to treat the anemia. They may also be used as secondary codes if treatment of the anemia is a component of an encounter, but not the primary reason for the encounter. When using a code from subcategory 285 it is also necessary to use the code for the chronic condition causing the anemia.

1) **Anemia in chronic kidney disease**
When assigning code 285.21, Anemia in chronic kidney disease, it is also necessary to assign a code from category 585, Chronic kidney disease, to indicate the stage of chronic kidney disease.
See I.C.10.a. Chronic kidney disease (CKD).

2) **Anemia in neoplastic disease**
When assigning code 285.22, Anemia in neoplastic disease, it is also necessary to assign the neoplasm code that is responsible for the anemia. Code 285.22 is for use for anemia that is due to the malignancy, not for anemia due to antineoplastic chemotherapy drugs, which is an adverse effect.
See I.C.2.c.1 Anemia associated with malignancy. See I.C.2.c.2 Anemia associated with chemotherapy, immunotherapy and radiation therapy. See I.C.17.e.1. Adverse effects.

5. **Chapter 5: Mental Disorders (290-319)**
Reserved for future guideline expansion

6. **Chapter 6: Diseases of Nervous System and Sense Organs (320-389)**

a. **Pain - Category 338**

1) **General coding information**
Codes in category 338 may be used in conjunction with codes from other categories and chapters to provide more detail about acute or chronic pain and neoplasm-related pain, **unless otherwise indicated below.**

If the pain is not specified as acute or chronic, do not assign codes from category 338, except for post-thoracotomy pain, postoperative pain, neoplasm related pain, **or central pain syndrome.**

A code from subcategories 338.1 and 338.2 should not be assigned if the underlying (definitive) diagnosis is known, unless the reason for the encounter is pain control/management and not management of the underlying condition.

(a) Category 338 codes as principal or first-listed diagnosis

Category 338 codes are acceptable as principal diagnosis or the first-listed code:

- When pain control or pain management is the reason for the admission/encounter (e.g., a patient with displaced intervertebral disc, nerve impingement and severe back pain presents for injection of steroid into the spinal canal). The underlying cause of the pain should be reported as an additional diagnosis, if known.
- **When an admission or encounter is for a procedure aimed at treating the underlying condition (e.g., spinal fusion, kyphoplasty), a code for the underlying condition (e.g., vertebral fracture, spinal stenosis) should be assigned as the principal diagnosis. No code from category 338 should be assigned.**
- **When a patient is admitted for the insertion of a neurostimulator for pain control, assign the appropriate pain code as the principal or first listed diagnosis. When an admission or encounter is for a procedure aimed at treating the underlying condition and a neurostimulator is inserted for pain control during the same admission/encounter, a code for the underlying condition should be assigned as the principal diagnosis and the appropriate pain code should be assigned as a secondary diagnosis.**

(b) Use of category 338 codes in conjunction with site specific pain codes

(i) Assigning category 338 codes and site-specific pain codes

Codes from category 338 may be used in conjunction with codes that identify the site of pain (including codes from chapter 16) if the category 338 code provides additional information. For example, if the code describes the site of the pain, but does not fully describe whether the pain is acute or chronic, then both codes should be assigned.

(ii) Sequencing of category 338 codes with site-specific pain codes

The sequencing of category 338 codes with site-specific pain codes (including chapter 16 codes), is dependent on the circumstances of the encounter/admission as follows:

- If the encounter is for pain control or pain management, assign the code from category 338 followed by the code identifying the specific site of pain (e.g., encounter for pain management for acute neck pain from trauma is assigned code 338.11, Acute pain due to trauma, followed by code 723.1, Cervicalgia, to identify the site of pain).
- If the encounter is for any other reason except pain control or pain management, and a related definitive diagnosis has not been established (confirmed) by the provider, assign the code for the specific site of pain first, followed by the appropriate code from category 338.

2) Pain due to devices, <u>implants and grafts</u> Pain associated with devices, **implants or grafts** left in a surgical site (**for example painful hip prosthesis**) is assigned to the appropriate code(s) found in Chapter 17, Injury and Poisoning. **Use additional code(s) from category 338 to identify acute or chronic pain due to presence of the device, implant or graft (338.18-338.19 or 338.28-338.29).**

3) Postoperative pain

Post-thoracotomy pain and other postoperative pain are classified to subcategories 338.1 and 338.2, depending on whether the pain is acute or chronic. The default for post-thoracotomy and other postoperative pain not specified as acute or chronic is the code for the acute form.

<u>Routine or expected postoperative pain immediately after surgery should not be coded.</u>

(a) Postoperative pain not associated with specific postoperative complication

Postoperative pain not associated with a specific postoperative complication is assigned to the appropriate postoperative pain code in category 338.

(b) Postoperative pain associated with specific postoperative complication

Postoperative pain associated with a specific postoperative complication (such as **painful wire sutures**) is assigned to the appropriate code(s) found in Chapter 17, Injury and Poisoning. **If appropriate, use additional code(s) from category 338 to identify acute or chronic pain (338.18 or 338.28).** If pain control/management is the reason for the encounter, a code from category 338 should be assigned as the principal or first-listed diagnosis in accordance with *Section I.C.6.a.1.a above.*

(c) Postoperative pain as principal or first-listed diagnosis

Postoperative pain may be reported as the principal or first-listed diagnosis when the stated reason for the admission/encounter is documented as postoperative pain control/management.

(d) Postoperative pain as secondary diagnosis

Postoperative pain may be reported as a secondary diagnosis code when a patient presents for outpatient surgery and develops an unusual or inordinate amount of postoperative pain.

The provider's documentation should be used to guide the coding of postoperative pain, as well as *Section III. Reporting Additional Diagnoses* and *Section IV. Diagnostic Coding and Reporting in the Outpatient Setting.*

See Section II.I.2 for information on sequencing of diagnoses for patients admitted to hospital inpatient care following post-operative observation.

See Section II.J for information on sequencing of diagnoses for patients admitted to hospital inpatient care from outpatient surgery.

See Section IV.A.2 for information on sequencing of diagnoses for patients admitted for observation.

4) Chronic pain

Chronic pain is classified to subcategory 338.2. There is no time frame defining when pain becomes chronic pain. The provider's documentation should be used to guide use of these codes.

5) Neoplasm related pain

Code 338.3 is assigned to pain documented as being related, associated or due to cancer, primary or secondary malignancy, or tumor. This code is assigned regardless of whether the pain is acute or chronic.

This code may be assigned as the principal or first-listed code when the stated reason for the admission/encounter is documented as pain control/pain management. The underlying neoplasm should be reported as an additional diagnosis.

When the reason for the admission/encounter is management of the neoplasm and the pain associated with the neoplasm is also documented, code 338.3 may be assigned as an additional diagnosis.

See Section I.C.2 for instructions on the sequencing of neoplasms for all other stated reasons for the admission/encounter (except for pain control/pain management).

6) **Chronic pain syndrome**
This condition is different than the term "chronic pain," and therefore this code should only be used when the provider has specifically documented this condition.

7. **Chapter 7: Diseases of Circulatory System (390-459)**

a. **Hypertension**
Hypertension Table
The Hypertension Table, found under the main term, "Hypertension," in the Alphabetic Index, contains a complete listing of all conditions due to or associated with hypertension and classifies them according to malignant, benign, and unspecified.

1) **Hypertension, essential, or NOS**
Assign hypertension (arterial) (essential) (primary) (systemic) (NOS) to category code 401 with the appropriate fourth digit to indicate malignant (.0), benign (.1), or unspecified (.9). Do not use either .0 malignant or .1 benign unless medical record documentation supports such a designation.

2) **Hypertension with heart disease**
Heart conditions (425.8, 429.0-429.3, 429.8, 429.9) are assigned to a code from category 402 when a causal relationship is stated (due to hypertension) or implied (hypertensive). Use an additional code from category 428 to identify the type of heart failure in those patients with heart failure. More than one code from category 428 may be assigned if the patient has systolic or diastolic failure and congestive heart failure.
The same heart conditions (425.8, 429.0-429.3, 429.8, 429.9) with hypertension, but without a stated causal relationship, are coded separately. Sequence according to the circumstances of the admission/encounter.

3) **Hypertensive chronic kidney disease**
Assign codes from category 403, Hypertensive chronic kidney disease, when conditions classified to categories 585-587 are present. Unlike hypertension with heart disease, ICD-9-CM presumes a cause-and-effect relationship and classifies chronic kidney disease (CKD) with hypertension as hypertensive chronic kidney disease.
Fifth digits for category 403 should be assigned as follows:
- 0 with CKD stage I through stage IV, or unspecified.
- 1 with CKD stage V or end stage renal disease.

The appropriate code from category 585, Chronic kidney disease, should be used as a secondary code with a code from category 403 to identify the stage of chronic kidney disease.
See Section I.C.10.a for information on the coding of chronic kidney disease.

4) **Hypertensive heart and chronic kidney disease**
Assign codes from combination category 404, Hypertensive heart and chronic kidney disease, when both hypertensive kidney disease and hypertensive heart disease are stated in the diagnosis. Assume a relationship between the hypertension and the chronic kidney disease, whether or not the condition is so designated. Assign an additional code from category 428, to identify the type of heart failure. More than one code from category 428 may be assigned if the patient has systolic or diastolic failure and congestive heart failure.
Fifth digits for category 404 should be assigned as follows:
- 0 without heart failure and with chronic kidney disease (CKD) stage I through stage IV, or unspecified
- 1 with heart failure and with CKD stage I through stage IV, or unspecified
- 2 without heart failure and with CKD stage V or end stage renal disease
- 3 with heart failure and with CKD stage V or end stage renal disease

The appropriate code from category 585, Chronic kidney disease, should be used as a secondary code with a code from category 404 to identify the stage of kidney disease.
See Section I.C.10.a for information on the coding of chronic kidney disease.

5) **Hypertensive cerebrovascular disease**
First assign codes from 430-438, Cerebrovascular disease, then the appropriate hypertension code from categories 401-405.

6) **Hypertensive retinopathy**
Two codes are necessary to identify the condition. First assign the code from subcategory 362.11, Hypertensive retinopathy, then the appropriate code from categories 401-405 to indicate the type of hypertension.

7) **Hypertension, secondary**
Two codes are required: one to identify the underlying etiology and one from category 405 to identify the hypertension. Sequencing of codes is determined by the reason for admission/encounter.

8) **Hypertension, transient**
Assign code 796.2, Elevated blood pressure reading without diagnosis of hypertension, unless patient has an established diagnosis of hypertension. Assign code 642.3x for transient hypertension of pregnancy.

9) **Hypertension, controlled**
Assign appropriate code from categories 401-405. This diagnostic statement usually refers to an existing state of hypertension under control by therapy.

10) **Hypertension, uncontrolled**
Uncontrolled hypertension may refer to untreated hypertension or hypertension not responding to current therapeutic regimen. In either case, assign the appropriate code from categories 401-405 to designate the stage and type of hypertension. Code to the type of hypertension.

11) **Elevated blood pressure**
For a statement of elevated blood pressure without further specificity, assign code 796.2, Elevated blood pressure reading without diagnosis of hypertension, rather than a code from category 401.

b. **Cerebral infarction/stroke/cerebrovascular accident (CVA)**
The terms stroke and CVA are often used interchangeably to refer to a cerebral infarction. The terms stroke, CVA, and cerebral infarction NOS are all indexed to the default code 434.91, Cerebral artery occlusion, unspecified, with infarction. Code 436, Acute, but ill-defined, cerebrovascular disease, should not be used when the documentation states stroke or CVA.

c. **Postoperative cerebrovascular accident**
A cerebrovascular hemorrhage or infarction that occurs as a result of medical intervention is coded to 997.02, Iatrogenic cerebrovascular infarction or hemorrhage. Medical record documentation should clearly specify the cause- and-effect relationship between the medical intervention and the cerebrovascular accident in order to assign this code. A secondary code from the code range 430-432 or from a code from subcategories 433 or 434 with a fifth digit of "1" should also be used to identify the type of hemorrhage or infarct.
This guideline conforms to the use additional code note instruction at category 997. Code 436, Acute, but ill-defined, cerebrovascular disease, should not be used as a secondary code with code 997.02.

d. **Late Effects of cerebrovascular disease**

1) **Category 438, late effects of cerebrovascular disease**
Category 438 is used to indicate conditions classifiable to categories 430-437 as the causes of late effects (neurologic deficits), themselves classified elsewhere. These "late effects" include neurologic deficits that persist after initial onset of conditions classifiable to 430-437. The neurologic deficits caused by cerebrovascular disease may be present from the onset or may arise at any time after the onset of the condition classifiable to 430-437.

2) **Codes from category 438 with codes from 430-437**
Codes from category 438 may be assigned on a health care record with codes from 430-437, if the patient has a current cerebrovascular accident (CVA) and deficits from an old CVA.

3) **Code V12.54**
Assign code V12.**54, Transient ischemic attack (TIA), and cerebral infarction without residual deficits** (and not a code from category 438) as an additional code for history of cerebrovascular disease when no neurologic deficits are present.

e. **Acute myocardial infarction (AMI)**

1) **ST elevation myocardial infarction (STEMI) and non ST elevation myocardial infarction (NSTEMI)**
The ICD-9-CM codes for acute myocardial infarction (AMI) identify the site, such as anterolateral wall or true posterior wall. Subcategories 410.0-410.6 and 410.8 are used for ST elevation myocardial infarction (STEMI). Subcategory 410.7, Subendocardial infarction, is used for non ST elevation myocardial infarction (NSTEMI) and nontransmural MIs.

2) **Acute myocardial infarction, unspecified**
Subcategory 410.9 is the default for the unspecified term acute myocardial infarction. If only STEMI or transmural MI without the site is documented, query the provider as to the site, or assign a code from subcategory 410.9.

3) **AMI documented as nontransmural or subendocardial but site provided**
If an AMI is documented as nontransmural or subendocardial, but the site is provided, it is still coded as a subendocardial AMI. If NSTEMI evolves to STEMI, assign the STEMI code. If STEMI converts to NSTEMI due to thrombolytic therapy, it is still coded as STEMI.

8. **Chapter 8: Diseases of Respiratory System (460-519)**

a. **Chronic obstructive pulmonary disease [COPD] and asthma**

1) **Conditions that comprise COPD and asthma**
The conditions that comprise COPD are obstructive chronic bronchitis, subcategory 491.2, and emphysema, category 492. All asthma codes are under category 493, Asthma. Code 496, Chronic airway obstruction, not elsewhere classified, is a nonspecific code that should only be used when the documentation in a medical record does not specify the type of COPD being treated.

2) **Acute exacerbation of chronic obstructive bronchitis and asthma**
The codes for chronic obstructive bronchitis and asthma distinguish between uncomplicated cases and those in acute exacerbation. An acute exacerbation is a worsening or a decompensation of a chronic condition. An acute exacerbation is not equivalent to an infection superimposed on a chronic condition, though an exacerbation may be triggered by an infection.

3) **Overlapping nature of the conditions that comprise COPD and asthma**
Due to the overlapping nature of the conditions that make up COPD and asthma, there are many variations in the way these conditions are documented. Code selection must be based on the terms as documented. When selecting the correct code for the documented type of COPD and asthma, it is essential to first review the index, and then verify the code in the tabular list. There are many instructional notes under the different COPD subcategories and codes. It is important that all such notes be reviewed to assure correct code assignment.

4) **Acute exacerbation of asthma and status asthmaticus**
An acute exacerbation of asthma is an increased severity of the asthma symptoms, such as wheezing and shortness of breath. Status asthmaticus refers to a patient's failure to respond to therapy administered during an asthmatic episode and is a life threatening complication that requires emergency care. If status asthmaticus is documented by the provider with any type of COPD or with acute bronchitis, the status asthmaticus should be sequenced first. It supersedes any type of COPD including that with acute exacerbation or acute bronchitis. It is inappropriate to assign an asthma code with 5th digit 2, with acute exacerbation, together with an asthma code with 5th digit 1, with status asthmatics. Only the 5th digit 1 should be assigned.

b. **Chronic obstructive pulmonary disease [COPD] and bronchitis**

1) **Acute bronchitis with COPD**
Acute bronchitis, code 466.0, is due to an infectious organism. When acute bronchitis is documented with COPD, code 491.22, Obstructive chronic bronchitis with acute bronchitis, should be assigned. It is not necessary to also assign code 466.0. If a medical record documents acute bronchitis with COPD with acute exacerbation, only code 491.22 should be assigned. The acute bronchitis included in code 491.22 supersedes the acute exacerbation. If a medical record documents COPD with acute exacerbation without mention of acute bronchitis, only code 491.21 should be assigned.

c. **Acute Respiratory Failure**

1) **Acute respiratory failure as principal diagnosis**
Code 518.81, Acute respiratory failure, may be assigned as a principal diagnosis when it is the condition established after study to be chiefly responsible for occasioning the admission to the hospital, and the selection is supported by the Alphabetic Index and Tabular List. However, chapter-specific coding guidelines (such as obstetrics, poisoning, HIV, newborn) that provide sequencing direction take precedence.

2) **Acute respiratory failure as secondary diagnosis**
Respiratory failure may be listed as a secondary diagnosis if it occurs after admission, or if it is present on admission, but does not meet the definition of principal diagnosis.

3) **Sequencing of acute respiratory failure and another acute condition**
When a patient is admitted with respiratory failure and another acute condition, (e.g., myocardial infarction, cerebrovascular accident), the principal diagnosis will not be the same in every situation. Selection of the principal diagnosis will be dependent on the circumstances of admission. If both the respiratory failure and the other acute condition are equally responsible for occasioning the admission to the hospital, and there are no chapter-specific sequencing rules, the guideline regarding two or more diagnoses that equally meet the definition for principal diagnosis *(Section II, C.)* may be applied in these situations.

If the documentation is not clear as to whether acute respiratory failure and another condition are equally responsible for occasioning the admission, query the provider for clarification.

d. **Influenza due to identified avian influenza virus (avian influenza)**

Code only confirmed cases of avian influenza. This is an exception to the hospital inpatient guideline Section II, H. (Uncertain Diagnosis).

In this context, "confirmation" does not require documentation of positive laboratory testing specific for avian influenza. However, coding should be based on the provider's diagnostic statement that the patient has avian influenza.

If the provider records "suspected or possible or probable avian influenza," the appropriate influenza code from category 487 should be assigned. Code 488, Influenza due to identified avian influenza virus, should not be assigned.

9. **Chapter 9: Diseases of Digestive System (520-579)**
Reserved for future guideline expansion

10. **Chapter 10: Diseases of Genitourinary System (580-629)**

a. **Chronic kidney disease**

1) **Stages of chronic kidney disease (CKD)**
The ICD-9-CM classifies CKD based on severity. The severity of CKD is designated by stages I-V. Stage II, code 585.2, equates to mild CKD; stage III, code 585.3, equates to moderate CKD; and stage IV, code 585.4, equates to severe CKD. Code 585.6, End stage renal disease (ESRD), is assigned when the provider has documented end-stage-renal disease (ESRD).

If both a stage of CKD and ESRD are documented, assign code 585.6 only.

2) **Chronic kidney disease and kidney transplant status**
Patients who have undergone kidney transplant may still have some form of CKD, because the kidney transplant may not fully restore kidney function. Therefore, the presence of CKD alone does not constitute a transplant complication. Assign the appropriate 585 code for the patient's stage of CKD and code V42.0. If a transplant complication such as failure or rejection is documented, see section I.C.17.f.1.b for information on coding complications of a kidney transplant. If the documentation is unclear as to whether the patient has a complication of the transplant, query the provider.

3) Chronic kidney disease with other conditions
Patients with CKD may also suffer from other serious conditions, most commonly diabetes mellitus and hypertension. The sequencing of the CKD code in relationship to codes for other contributing conditions is based on the conventions in the tabular list.

See I.C.3.a.4 for sequencing instructions for diabetes.
See I.C.4.a.1 for anemia in CKD.
See I.C.7.a.3 for hypertensive chronic kidney disease.
See I.C.17.f.1.b, Kidney transplant complications, for instructions on coding of documented rejection or failure.

11. Chapter 11: Complications of Pregnancy, Childbirth, and the Puerperium (630-679)

a. General Rules for Obstetric Cases

1) Codes from chapter 11 and sequencing priority
Obstetric cases require codes from chapter 11, codes in the range 630-679, Complications of Pregnancy, Childbirth, and the Puerperium. Chapter 11 codes have sequencing priority over codes from other chapters. Additional codes from other chapters may be used in conjunction with chapter 11 codes to further specify conditions. Should the provider document that the pregnancy is incidental to the encounter, then code V22.2 should be used in place of any chapter 11 codes. It is the provider's responsibility to state that the condition being treated is not affecting the pregnancy.

2) Chapter 11 codes used only on the maternal record
Chapter 11 codes are to be used only on the maternal record, never on the record of the newborn.

3) Chapter 11 fifth digits
Categories 640-648, 651-676 have required fifth-digits, which indicate whether the encounter is antepartum, postpartum and whether a delivery has also occurred.

4) Fifth digits, appropriate for each code
The fifth digits, which are appropriate for each code number, are listed in brackets under each code. The fifth digits on each code should all be consistent with each other. That is, should a delivery occur all of the fifth-digits should indicate the delivery.

b. Selection of OB Principal or First-listed Diagnosis

1) Routine outpatient prenatal visits
For routine outpatient prenatal visits when no complications are present codes V22.0, Supervision of normal first pregnancy, and V22.1, Supervision of other normal pregnancy, should be used as the first-listed diagnoses. These codes should not be used in conjunction with chapter 11 codes.

2) Prenatal outpatient visits for high-risk patients
For prenatal outpatient visits for patients with high-risk pregnancies, a code from category V23, Supervision of high-risk pregnancy, should be used as the first-listed diagnosis. Secondary chapter 11 codes may be used in conjunction with these codes if appropriate.

3) Episodes when no delivery occurs
In episodes when no delivery occurs, the principal diagnosis should correspond to the principal complication of the pregnancy, which necessitated the encounter. Should more than one complication exist, all of which are treated or monitored, any of the complications codes may be sequenced first.

4) When a delivery occurs
When a delivery occurs, the principal diagnosis should correspond to the main circumstances or complication of the delivery. In cases of cesarean delivery, the selection of the principal diagnosis should correspond to the reason the cesarean delivery was performed unless the reason for admission/encounter was unrelated to the condition resulting in the cesarean delivery.

5) Outcome of delivery
An outcome of delivery code, V27.0-V27.9, should be included on every maternal record when a delivery has occurred. These codes are not to be used on subsequent records or on the newborn record.

c. Fetal conditions affecting the management of the mother

1) Codes from category 655
Known or suspected fetal abnormality affecting management of the mother, and category 656, Other fetal and placental problems affecting the management of the mother, are assigned only when the fetal condition is actually responsible for modifying the management of the mother, i.e., by requiring diagnostic studies, additional observation, special care, or termination of pregnancy. The fact that the fetal condition exists does not justify assigning a code from this series to the mother's record.

2) In utero surgery
In cases when surgery is performed on the fetus, a diagnosis code from category 655, Known or suspected fetal abnormalities affecting management of the mother, should be assigned identifying the fetal condition. Procedure code 75.36, Correction of fetal defect, should be assigned on the hospital inpatient record.

No code from Chapter 15, the perinatal codes, should be used on the mother's record to identify fetal conditions. Surgery performed in utero on a fetus is still to be coded as an obstetric encounter.

d. HIV infection in pregnancy, childbirth and the puerperium
During pregnancy, childbirth or the puerperium, a patient admitted because of an HIV-related illness should receive a principal diagnosis of 647.6X, Other specified infectious and parasitic diseases in the mother classifiable elsewhere, but complicating the pregnancy, childbirth or the puerperium, followed by 042 and the code(s) for the HIV-related illness(es).

Patients with asymptomatic HIV infection status admitted during pregnancy, childbirth, or the puerperium should receive codes of 647.6X and V08.

e. Current conditions complicating pregnancy
Assign a code from subcategory 648.x for patients that have current conditions when the condition affects the management of the pregnancy, childbirth, or the puerperium. Use additional secondary codes from other chapters to identify the conditions, as appropriate.

f. Diabetes mellitus in pregnancy
Diabetes mellitus is a significant complicating factor in pregnancy. Pregnant women who are diabetic should be assigned code 648.0x, Diabetes mellitus complicating pregnancy, and a secondary code from category 250, Diabetes mellitus, to identify the type of diabetes.

Code V58.67, Long-term (current) use of insulin, should also be assigned if the diabetes mellitus is being treated with insulin.

g. Gestational diabetes
Gestational diabetes can occur during the second and third trimester of pregnancy in women who were not diabetic prior to pregnancy. Gestational diabetes can cause complications in the pregnancy similar to those of pre-existing diabetes mellitus. It also puts the woman at greater risk of developing diabetes after the pregnancy. Gestational diabetes is coded to 648.8x, Abnormal glucose tolerance. Codes 648.0x and 648.8x should never be used together on the same record.

Code V58.67, Long-term (current) use of insulin, should also be assigned if the gestational diabetes is being treated with insulin.

h. Normal delivery, Code 650

1) Normal delivery
Code 650 is for use in cases when a woman is admitted for a full-term normal delivery and delivers a single, healthy infant without any complications antepartum, during the delivery, or postpartum during the delivery episode. Code 650 is always a principal diagnosis. It is not to be used if any other code from chapter 11 is needed to describe a current complication of the antenatal, delivery, or perinatal period. Additional codes from other chapters may be used with code 650 if they are not related to or are in any way complicating the pregnancy.

2) Normal delivery with resolved antepartum complication
Code 650 may be used if the patient had a complication at some point during her pregnancy, but the complication is not present at the time of the admission for delivery.

3) V27.0, Single liveborn, outcome of delivery
V27.0, Single liveborn, is the only outcome of delivery code appropriate for use with 650.

i. The postpartum and peripartum periods

1) Postpartum and peripartum periods
The postpartum period begins immediately after delivery and continues for six weeks following delivery. The peripartum period is defined as the last month of pregnancy to five months postpartum.

2) **Postpartum complication**
A postpartum complication is any complication occurring within the six-week period.

3) **Pregnancy-related complications after 6 week period**
Chapter 11 codes may also be used to describe pregnancy-related complications after the six-week period should the provider document that a condition is pregnancy related.

4) **Postpartum complications occurring during the same admission as delivery**
Postpartum complications that occur during the same admission as the delivery are identified with a fifth digit of "2." Subsequent admissions/encounters for postpartum complications should be identified with a fifth digit of "4."

5) **Admission for routine postpartum care following delivery outside hospital**
When the mother delivers outside the hospital prior to admission and is admitted for routine postpartum care and no complications are noted, code V24.0, Postpartum care and examination immediately after delivery, should be assigned as the principal diagnosis.

6) **Admission following delivery outside hospital with postpartum conditions**
A delivery diagnosis code should not be used for a woman who has delivered prior to admission to the hospital. Any postpartum conditions and/or postpartum procedures should be coded.

j. **Code 677, Late effect of complication of pregnancy**

1) **Code 677**
Code 677, Late effect of complication of pregnancy, childbirth, and the puerperium is for use in those cases when an initial complication of a pregnancy develops a sequelae requiring care or treatment at a future date.

2) **After the initial postpartum period**
This code may be used at any time after the initial postpartum period.

3) **Sequencing of Code 677**
This code, like all late effect codes, is to be sequenced following the code describing the sequelae of the complication.

k. **Abortions**

1) **Fifth digits required for abortion categories**
Fifth digits are required for abortion categories 634-637. Fifth digit 1, incomplete, indicates that all of the products of conception have not been expelled from the uterus. Fifth digit 2, complete, indicates that all products of conception have been expelled from the uterus prior to the episode of care.

2) **Code from categories 640-648 and 651-659**
A code from categories 640-648 and 651-659 may be used as additional codes with an abortion code to indicate the complication leading to the abortion.
Fifth digit 3 is assigned with codes from these categories when used with an abortion code because the other fifth digits will not apply. Codes from the 660-669 series are not to be used for complications of abortion.

3) **Code 639 for complications**
Code 639 is to be used for all complications following abortion. Code 639 cannot be assigned with codes from categories 634-638.

4) **Abortion with liveborn fetus**
When an attempted termination of pregnancy results in a liveborn fetus assign code 644.21, Early onset of delivery, with an appropriate code from category V27, Outcome of Delivery. The procedure code for the attempted termination of pregnancy should also be assigned.

5) **Retained products of conception following an abortion**
Subsequent admissions for retained products of conception following a spontaneous or legally induced abortion are assigned the appropriate code from category 634, Spontaneous abortion, or 635 Legally induced abortion, with a fifth digit of "1" (incomplete). This advice is appropriate even when the patient was discharged previously with a discharge diagnosis of complete abortion.

12. **Chapter 12: Diseases of Skin and Subcutaneous Tissue (680-709)**
Reserved for future guideline expansion

13. **Chapter 13: Diseases of Musculoskeletal and Connective Tissue (710-739)**

a. **Coding of pathologic fractures**

1) **Acute fractures vs. aftercare**
Pathologic fractures are reported using subcategory 733.1, when the fracture is newly diagnosed. Subcategory 733.1 may be used while the patient is receiving active treatment for the fracture. Examples of active treatment are: surgical treatment, emergency department encounter, evaluation and treatment by a new physician.
Fractures are coded using the aftercare codes (subcategories V54.0, V54.2, V54.8 or V54.9) for encounters after the patient has completed active treatment of the fracture and is receiving routine care for the fracture during the healing or recovery phase. Examples of fracture aftercare are: cast change or removal, removal of external or internal fixation device, medication adjustment, and follow up visits following fracture treatment.
Care for complications of surgical treatment for fracture repairs during the healing or recovery phase should be coded with the appropriate complication codes.
Care of complications of fractures, such as malunion and nonunion, should be reported with the appropriate codes.
See Section I. C. 17.b for information on the coding of traumatic fractures.

14. **Chapter 14: Congenital Anomalies (740-759)**

a. **Codes in categories 740-759, congenital anomalies**
Assign an appropriate code(s) from categories 740-759, Congenital Anomalies, when an anomaly is documented. A congenital anomaly may be the principal/first listed diagnosis on a record or a secondary diagnosis.
When a congenital anomaly does not have a unique code assignment, assign additional code(s) for any manifestations that may be present.
When the code assignment specifically identifies the congenital anomaly, manifestations that are an inherent component of the anomaly should not be coded separately. Additional codes should be assigned for manifestations that are not an inherent component.
Codes from Chapter 14 may be used throughout the life of the patient. If a congenital anomaly has been corrected, a personal history code should be used to identify the history of the anomaly. Although present at birth, a congenital anomaly may not be identified until later in life. Whenever the condition is diagnosed by the physician, it is appropriate to assign a code from codes 740-759.
For the birth admission, the appropriate code from category V30, Liveborn infants, according to type of birth should be sequenced as the principal diagnosis, followed by any congenital anomaly codes, 740-759.

15. **Chapter 15: Newborn (Perinatal) Guidelines (760-779)**
For coding and reporting purposes the perinatal period is defined as before birth through the 28th day following birth. The following guidelines are provided for reporting purposes. Hospitals may record other diagnoses as needed for internal data use.

a. **General perinatal rules**

1) **Chapter 15 Codes**
They are never for use on the maternal record. Codes from Chapter 11, the obstetric chapter, are never permitted on the newborn record. Chapter 15 code may be used throughout the life of the patient if the condition is still present.

2) **Sequencing of perinatal codes**
Generally, codes from Chapter 15 should be sequenced as the principal/first-listed diagnosis on the newborn record, with the exception of the appropriate V30 code for the birth episode, followed by codes from any other chapter that provide additional detail. The "use additional code" note at the beginning of the chapter supports this guideline. If the index does not provide a specific code for a perinatal condition, assign code 779.89, Other specified conditions originating in the perinatal period, followed by the code from another chapter that specifies the condition. Codes for signs and symptoms may be assigned when a definitive diagnosis has not been established.

3) **Birth process or community acquired conditions**
If a newborn has a condition that may be either due to the birth process or community acquired and the documentation does not indicate which it is, the default is due to the birth process and the code from Chapter 15 should be used. If the condition is community-acquired, a code from Chapter 15 should not be assigned.

4) **Code all clinically significant conditions**
All clinically significant conditions noted on routine newborn examination should be coded. A condition is clinically significant if it requires:

- clinical evaluation; or
- therapeutic treatment; or
- diagnostic procedures; or
- extended length of hospital stay; or
- increased nursing care and/or monitoring; or
- has implications for future health care needs

Note: The perinatal guidelines listed above are the same as the general coding guidelines for "additional diagnoses", except for the final point regarding implications for future health care needs. Codes should be assigned for conditions that have been specified by the provider as having implications for future health care needs. Codes from the perinatal chapter should not be assigned unless the provider has established a definitive diagnosis.

b. **Use of codes V30-V39**
When coding the birth of an infant, assign a code from categories V30-V39, according to the type of birth. A code from this series is assigned as a principal diagnosis, and assigned only once to a newborn at the time of birth.

c. **Newborn transfers**
If the newborn is transferred to another institution, the V30 series is not used at the receiving hospital.

d. **Use of category V29**

1) **Assigning a code from category V29**
Assign a code from category V29, Observation and evaluation of newborns and infants for suspected conditions not found, to identify those instances when a healthy newborn is evaluated for a suspected condition that is determined after study not to be present. Do not use a code from category V29 when the patient has identified signs or symptoms of a suspected problem; in such cases, code the sign or symptom.

A code from category V29 may also be assigned as a principal code for readmissions or encounters when the V30 code no longer applies. Codes from category V29 are for use only for healthy newborns and infants for which no condition after study is found to be present.

2) **V29 code on a birth record**
A V29 code is to be used as a secondary code after the V30, Outcome of delivery, code.

e. **Use of other V codes on perinatal records**
V codes other than V30 and V29 may be assigned on a perinatal or newborn record code. The codes may be used as a principal or first-listed diagnosis for specific types of encounters or for readmissions or encounters when the V30 code no longer applies.

See Section I.C.18 for information regarding the assignment of V codes.

f. **Maternal causes of perinatal morbidity**
Codes from categories 760-763, Maternal causes of perinatal morbidity and mortality, are assigned only when the maternal condition has actually affected the fetus or newborn. The fact that the mother has an associated medical condition or experiences some complication of pregnancy, labor or delivery does not justify the routine assignment of codes from these categories to the newborn record.

g. **Congenital anomalies in newborns**
For the birth admission, the appropriate code from category V30, Liveborn infants according to type of birth, should be used, followed by any congenital anomaly codes, categories 740-759. Use additional secondary codes from other chapters to specify conditions associated with the anomaly, if applicable.

Also, see Section I.C.14 for information on the coding of congenital anomalies.

h. **Coding additional perinatal diagnoses**

1) **Assigning codes for conditions that require treatment**
Assign codes for conditions that require treatment or further investigation, prolong the length of stay, or require resource utilization.

2) **Codes for conditions specified as having implications for future health care needs**
Assign codes for conditions that have been specified by the provider as having implications for future health care needs.

Note: This guideline should not be used for adult patients.

3) **Codes for newborn conditions originating in the perinatal period**
Assign a code for newborn conditions originating in the perinatal period (categories 760-779), as well as complications arising during the current episode of care classified in other chapters, only if the diagnoses have been documented by the responsible provider at the time of transfer or discharge as having affected the fetus or newborn.

i. **Prematurity and fetal growth retardation**
Providers utilize different criteria in determining prematurity. A code for prematurity should not be assigned unless it is documented. The 5th digit assignment for codes from category 764 and subcategories 765.0 and 765.1 should be based on the recorded birth weight and estimated gestational age.

A code from subcategory 765.2, Weeks of gestation, should be assigned as an additional code with category 764 and codes from 765.0 and 765.1 to specify weeks of gestation as documented by the provider in the record.

j. **Newborn sepsis**
Code 771.81, Septicemia [sepsis] of newborn, should be assigned with a secondary code from category 041, Bacterial infections in conditions classified elsewhere and of unspecified site, to identify the organism. It is not necessary to use a code from subcategory 995.9, Systemic inflammatory response syndrome (SIRS), on a newborn record. A code from category 038, Septicemia, should not be used on a newborn record. Code 771.81 describes the sepsis.

16. **Chapter 16: Signs, Symptoms and Ill-Defined Conditions (780-799)**
Reserved for future guideline expansion

17. **Chapter 17: Injury and Poisoning (800-999)**

a. **Coding of injuries**
When coding injuries, assign separate codes for each injury unless a combination code is provided, in which case the combination code is assigned. Multiple injury codes are provided in ICD-9-CM, but should not be assigned unless information for a more specific code is not available. These codes are not to be used for normal, healing surgical wounds or to identify complications of surgical wounds.

The code for the most serious injury, as determined by the provider and the focus of treatment, is sequenced first.

1) **Superficial injuries**
Superficial injuries such as abrasions or contusions are not coded when associated with more severe injuries of the same site.

2) **Primary injury with damage to nerves/blood vessels**
When a primary injury results in minor damage to peripheral nerves or blood vessels, the primary injury is sequenced first with additional code(s) from categories 950-957, Injury to nerves and spinal cord, and/or 900-904, Injury to blood vessels. When the primary injury is to the blood vessels or nerves, that injury should be sequenced first.

b. **Coding of traumatic fractures**
The principles of multiple coding of injuries should be followed in coding fractures. Fractures of specified sites are coded individually by site in accordance with both the provisions within categories 800-829 and the level of detail furnished by medical record content. Combination categories for multiple fractures are provided for use when there is insufficient detail in the medical record (such as trauma cases transferred to another hospital), when the reporting form limits the number of codes that can be used in reporting pertinent clinical data, or when there is insufficient specificity at the fourth-digit or fifth-digit level. More specific guidelines are as follows:

1) **Acute fractures vs. aftercare**
Traumatic fractures are coded using the acute fracture codes (800-829) while the patient is receiving active treatment for the fracture. Examples of active treatment are: surgical treatment, emergency department encounter, and evaluation and treatment by a new physician.
Fractures are coded using the aftercare codes (subcategories V54.0, V54.1, V54.8, or V54.9) for encounters after the patient has completed active treatment of the fracture and is receiving routine care for the fracture during the healing or recovery phase. Examples of fracture aftercare are: cast change or removal, removal of external or internal fixation device, medication adjustment, and follow up visits following fracture treatment.
Care for complications of surgical treatment for fracture repairs during the healing or recovery phase should be coded with the appropriate complication codes.
Care of complications of fractures, such as malunion and nonunion, should be reported with the appropriate codes.
Pathologic fractures are not coded in the 800-829 range, but instead are assigned to subcategory 733.1. *See Section I.C.13.a for additional information.*

2) **Multiple fractures of same limb**
Multiple fractures of same limb classifiable to the same three-digit or four-digit category are coded to that category.

3) **Multiple unilateral or bilateral fractures of same bone**
Multiple unilateral or bilateral fractures of same bone(s) but classified to different fourth-digit subdivisions (bone part) within the same three-digit category are coded individually by site.

4) **Multiple fracture categories 819 and 828**
Multiple fracture categories 819 and 828 classify bilateral fractures of both upper limbs (819) and both lower limbs (828), but without any detail at the fourth-digit level other than open and closed type of fractures.

5) **Multiple fractures sequencing**
Multiple fractures are sequenced in accordance with the severity of the fracture. The provider should be asked to list the fracture diagnoses in the order of severity.

c. **Coding of burns**
Current burns (940-948) are classified by depth, extent and by agent (E code). Burns are classified by depth as first degree (erythema), second degree (blistering), and third degree (full-thickness involvement).

1) **Sequencing of burn and related condition codes**
Sequence first the code that reflects the highest degree of burn when more than one burn is present.

a. When the reason for the admission or encounter is for treatment of external multiple burns, sequence first the code that reflects the burn of the highest degree.
b. When a patient has both internal and external burns, the circumstances of admission govern the selection of the principal diagnosis or first-listed diagnosis.
c. When a patient is admitted for burn injuries and other related conditions such as smoke inhalation and/or respiratory failure, the circumstances of admission govern the selection of the principal or first-listed diagnosis.

2) **Burns of the same local site**
Classify burns of the same local site (three-digit category level, 940-947) but of different degrees to the subcategory identifying the highest degree recorded in the diagnosis.

3) **Non-healing burns**
Non-healing burns are coded as acute burns.
Necrosis of burned skin should be coded as a non-healed burn.

4) **Code 958.3, posttraumatic wound infection**
Assign code 958.3, Posttraumatic wound infection, not elsewhere classified, as an additional code for any documented infected burn site.

5) **Assign separate codes for each burn site**
When coding burns, assign separate codes for each burn site. Category 946 Burns of Multiple specified sites, should only be used if the location of the burns are not documented.
Category 949, Burn, unspecified, is extremely vague and should rarely be used.

6) **Assign codes from category 948, burns**
Burns classified according to extent of body surface involved, when the site of the burn is not specified or when there is a need for additional data. It is advisable to use category 948 as additional coding when needed to provide data for evaluating burn mortality, such as that needed by burn units. It is also advisable to use category 948 as an additional code for reporting purposes when there is mention of a third-degree burn involving 20 percent or more of the body surface.
In assigning a code from category 948:

Fourth-digit codes are used to identify the percentage of total body surface involved in a burn (all degree).

Fifth-digits are assigned to identify the percentage of body surface involved in third-degree burn.

Fifth-digit zero (0) is assigned when less than 10 percent or when no body surface is involved in a third-degree burn.

Category 948 is based on the classic "rule of nines" in estimating body surface involved: head and neck are assigned nine percent, each arm nine percent, each leg 18 percent, the anterior trunk 18 percent, posterior trunk 18 percent, and genitalia one percent. Providers may change these percentage assignments where necessary to accommodate infants and children who have proportionately larger heads than adults and patients who have large buttocks, thighs, or abdomen that involve burns.

7) **Encounters for treatment of late effects of burns**
Encounters for the treatment of the late effects of burns (i.e., scars or joint contractures) should be coded to the residual condition (sequelae) followed by the appropriate late effect code (906.5-906.9). A late effect E code may also be used, if desired.

8) **Sequelae with a late effect code and current burn**
When appropriate, both a sequelae with a late effect code, and a current burn code may be assigned on the same record (when both a current burn and sequelae of an old burn exist).

d. **Coding of debridement of wound, infection, or burn**
Excisional debridement involves surgical removal or cutting away, as opposed to a mechanical (brushing, scrubbing, washing) debridement.
For coding purposes, excisional debridement is assigned to code 86.22.
Nonexcisional debridement is assigned to code 86.28.

e. **Adverse effects, poisoning and toxic effects**
The properties of certain drugs, medicinal and biological substances or combinations of such substances, may cause toxic reactions. The occurrence of drug toxicity is classified in ICD-9-CM as follows:

1) **Adverse effect**
When the drug was correctly prescribed and properly administered, code the reaction plus the appropriate code from the E930-E949 series. Codes from the E930-E949 series must be used to identify the causative substance for an adverse effect of drug, medicinal and biological substances, correctly prescribed and properly administered. The effect, such as tachycardia, delirium, gastrointestinal hemorrhaging, vomiting, hypokalemia, hepatitis, renal failure, or respiratory failure, is coded and followed by the appropriate code from the E930-E949 series.
Adverse effects of therapeutic substances correctly prescribed and properly administered (toxicity, synergistic reaction, side effect, and idiosyncratic reaction) may be due to (1) differences among patients, such as age, sex, disease, and genetic factors, and (2) drug-related factors, such as type of drug, route of administration, duration of therapy, dosage, and bioavailability.

2) **Poisoning**

(a) **Error was made in drug prescription**
Errors made in drug prescription or in the administration of the drug by provider, nurse, patient, or other person, use the appropriate poisoning code from the 960-979 series.

(b) **Overdose of a drug intentionally taken**
If an overdose of a drug was intentionally taken or administered and resulted in drug toxicity, it would be coded as a poisoning (960-979 series).

(c) **Nonprescribed drug taken with correctly prescribed and properly administered drug**
If a nonprescribed drug or medicinal agent was taken in combination with a correctly prescribed and properly administered drug, any drug toxicity or other reaction resulting from the interaction of the two drugs would be classified as a poisoning.

(d) **Sequencing of poisoning**
When coding a poisoning or reaction to the improper use of a medication (e.g., wrong dose, wrong substance, wrong route of administration) the poisoning code is sequenced first, followed by a code for the manifestation. If there is also a diagnosis of drug abuse or dependence to the substance, the abuse or dependence is coded as an additional code.

See Section I.C.3.a.6.b. if poisoning is the result of insulin pump malfunctions and Section I.C.19 for general use of E-codes.

3) **Toxic effects**

(a) **Toxic effect codes**
When a harmful substance is ingested or comes in contact with a person, this is classified as a toxic effect. The toxic effect codes are in categories 980-989.

(b) **Sequencing toxic effect codes**
A toxic effect code should be sequenced first, followed by the code(s) that identify the result of the toxic effect.

(c) **External cause codes for toxic effects**
An external cause code from categories E860-E869 for accidental exposure, codes E950.6 or E950.7 for intentional self-harm, category E962 for assault, or categories E980-E982, for undetermined, should also be assigned to indicate intent.

f. **Complications of care**

1) **Transplant complications**

(a) **Transplant complications other than kidney**
Codes under subcategory 996.8, Complications of transplanted organ, are for use for both complications and rejection of transplanted organs. A transplant complication code is only assigned if the complication affects the function of the transplanted organ. Two codes are required to fully describe a transplant complication, the appropriate code from subcategory 996.8 and a secondary code that identifies the complication.

Pre-existing conditions or conditions that develop after the transplant are not coded as complications unless they affect the function of the transplanted organs.

(b) **Kidney transplant complications**
Code 996.81 should be assigned for documented complications of a kidney transplant, such as transplant failure or rejection. Code 996.81 should not be assigned for post kidney transplant patients who have chronic kidney (CKD) unless a transplant complication such as transplant failure or rejection is documented. If the documentation is unclear as to whether the patient has a complication of the transplant, query the provider.

For patients with CKD following a kidney transplant, but who do not have a complication such as failure or rejection, *see section I.C.10.a.2, Chronic kidney disease and kidney transplant status.*

g. **SIRS due to non-infectious process**
The systemic inflammatory response syndrome (SIRS) can develop as a result of certain non-infectious disease processes, such as trauma, malignant neoplasm, or pancreatitis. When SIRS is documented with a noninfectious condition, and no subsequent infection is documented, the code for the underlying condition, such as an injury, should be assigned, followed by code 995.93, Systemic inflammatory response syndrome due to noninfectious process without acute organ dysfunction, or 995.94, Systemic inflammatory response syndrome due to non-infectious process with acute organ dysfunction. If an acute organ dysfunction is documented, the appropriate code(s) for the associated acute organ dysfunction(s) should be assigned in addition to code 995.94. If acute organ dysfunction is documented, but it cannot be determined if the acute organ dysfunction is associated with SIRS or due to another condition (e.g., directly due to the trauma), the provider should be queried.

When the non-infectious condition has led to an infection that results in SIRS, *see Section I.C.1.b.11 for the guideline for sepsis and severe sepsis associated with a non-infectious process.*

18. **Classification of Factors Influencing Health Status and Contact with Health Service (Supplemental V01-V89)**
Note: The chapter specific guidelines provide additional information about the use of V codes for specified encounters.

a. **Introduction**
ICD-9-CM provides codes to deal with encounters for circumstances other than a disease or injury. The Supplementary Classification of Factors Influencing Health Status and Contact with Health Services (V01.0 - V89.09) is provided to deal with occasions when circumstances other than a disease or injury (codes 001-999) are recorded as a diagnosis or problem.

There are four primary circumstances for the use of V codes:

1) A person who is not currently sick encounters the health services for some specific reason, such as to act as an organ donor, to receive prophylactic care, such as inoculations or health screenings, or to receive counseling on health related issues.
2) A person with a resolving disease or injury, or a chronic, long-term condition requiring continuous care, encounters the health care system for specific aftercare of that disease or injury (e.g., dialysis for renal disease; chemotherapy for malignancy; cast change). A diagnosis/symptom code should be used whenever a current, acute, diagnosis is being treated or a sign or symptom is being studied.
3) Circumstances or problems influence a person's health status but are not in themselves a current illness or injury.
4) Newborns, to indicate birth status

b. **V codes use in any healthcare setting**
V codes are for use in any healthcare setting. V codes may be used as either a first listed (principal diagnosis code in the inpatient setting) or secondary code, depending on the circumstances of the encounter. Certain V codes may only be used as first listed, others only as secondary codes.
See Section I.C.18.e, V Code Table.

c. **V Codes indicate a reason for an encounter**
They are not procedure codes. A corresponding procedure code must accompany a V code to describe the procedure performed.

d. **Categories of V codes**

1) **Contact/exposure**
Category V01 indicates contact with or exposure to communicable diseases. These codes are for patients who do not show any sign or symptom of a disease but have been exposed to it by close personal contact with an infected individual or are in an area where a disease is epidemic. These codes may be used as a first listed code to explain an encounter for testing, or, more commonly, as a secondary code to identify a potential risk.

2) **Inoculations and vaccinations**
Categories V03-V06 are for encounters for inoculations and vaccinations. They indicate that a patient is being seen to receive a prophylactic inoculation against a disease. The injection itself must be represented by the appropriate procedure code. A code from V03-V06 may be used as a secondary code if the inoculation is given as a routine part of preventive health care, such as a well-baby visit.

3) **Status**
Status codes indicate that a patient is either a carrier of a disease or has the sequelae or residual of a past disease or condition. This includes such things as the presence of prosthetic or mechanical devices resulting from past treatment. A status code is informative, because the

status may affect the course of treatment and its outcome. A status code is distinct from a history code. The history code indicates that the patient no longer has the condition.

A status code should not be used with a diagnosis code from one of the body system chapters, if the diagnosis code includes the information provided by the status code. For example, code V42.1, Heart transplant status, should not be used with code 996.83, Complications of transplanted heart. The status code does not provide additional information. The complication code indicates that the patient is a heart transplant patient.

The status V codes/categories are:

V02 Carrier or suspected carrier of infectious diseases
Carrier status indicates that a person harbors the specific organisms of a disease without manifest symptoms and is capable of transmitting the infection.

V08 Asymptomatic HIV infection status
This code indicates that a patient has tested positive for HIV but has manifested no signs or symptoms of the disease.

V09 Infection with drug-resistant microorganisms
This category indicates that a patient has an infection that is resistant to drug treatment. Sequence the infection code first.

V21 Constitutional states in development

V22.2 Pregnant state, incidental
This code is a secondary code only for use when the pregnancy is in no way complicating the reason for visit. Otherwise, a code from the obstetric chapter is required.

V26.5x Sterilization status

V42 Organ or tissue replaced by transplant

V43 Organ or tissue replaced by other means

V44 Artificial opening status

V45 Other postsurgical states

V46 Other dependence on machines

V49.6 Upper limb amputation status

V49.7 Lower limb amputation status
Note: Categories V42-V46, and subcategories V49.6, V49.7 are for use only if there are no complications or malfunctions of the organ or tissue replaced, the amputation site or the equipment on which the patient is dependent.

V49.81 Postmenopausal status

V49.82 Dental sealant status

V49.83 Awaiting organ transplant status

V58.6**x** Long-term (current) drug use
Codes from this subcategory indicate a patient's continuous use of a prescribed drug (including such things as aspirin therapy) for the long-term treatment of a condition or for prophylactic use. It is not for use for patients who have addictions to drugs.
Assign a code from subcategory V58.6, Long-term (current) drug use, if the patient is receiving a medication for an extended period as a prophylactic measure (such as for the prevention of deep vein thrombosis) or as treatment of a chronic condition (such as arthritis) or a disease requiring a lengthy course of treatment (such as cancer). Do not assign a code from subcategory V58.6 for medication being administered for a brief period of time to treat an acute illness or injury (such as a course of antibiotics to treat acute bronchitis).

V83 Genetic carrier status
Genetic carrier status indicates that a person carries a gene, associated with a particular disease, which may be passed to offspring who may develop that disease. The person does not have the disease and is not at risk of developing the disease.

V84 Genetic susceptibility status
Genetic susceptibility indicates that a person has a gene that increases the risk of that person developing the disease.
Codes from category V84, Genetic susceptibility to disease, should not be used as principal or first-listed codes. If the patient has the condition to which he/she is susceptible, and that condition is the reason for the encounter, the code for the current condition should be sequenced first. If the patient is being seen for follow-up after completed treatment for this condition, and the condition no longer exists, a follow-up code should be sequenced first, followed by the appropriate personal history and genetic susceptibility codes. If the purpose of the encounter is genetic counseling associated with procreative management, a code from subcategory V26.3, Genetic counseling and testing, should be assigned as the first-listed code, followed by a code from category V84. Additional codes should be assigned for any applicable family or personal history.
See Section I.C. 18.d.14 for information on prophylactic organ removal due to a genetic susceptibility.

V86 Estrogen receptor status

4) **History (of)**

There are two types of history V codes, personal and family. Personal history codes explain a patient's past medical condition that no longer exists and is not receiving any treatment, but that has the potential for recurrence, and therefore may require continued monitoring. The exceptions to this general rule are category V14, Personal history of allergy to medicinal agents, and subcategory V15.0, Allergy, other than to medicinal agents. A person who has had an allergic episode to a substance or food in the past should always be considered allergic to the substance.

Family history codes are for use when a patient has a family member(s) who has had a particular disease that causes the patient to be at higher risk of also contracting the disease.

Personal history codes may be used in conjunction with follow-up codes and family history codes may be used in conjunction with screening codes to explain the need for a test or procedure. History codes are also acceptable on any medical record regardless of the reason for visit. A history of an illness, even if no longer present, is important information that may alter the type of treatment ordered.

The history V code categories are:

V10 Personal history of malignant neoplasm

V12 Personal history of certain other diseases

V13 Personal history of other diseases
Except: V13.4, Personal history of arthritis, and V13.6, Personal history of congenital malformations. These conditions are life-long so are not true history codes.

V14 Personal history of allergy to medicinal agents

V15 Other personal history presenting hazards to health
Except: V15.7, Personal history of contraception.

V16 Family history of malignant neoplasm

V17 Family history of certain chronic disabling diseases

V18 Family history of certain other specific diseases

V19 Family history of other conditions

5) **Screening**

Screening is the testing for disease or disease precursors in seemingly well individuals so that early detection and treatment can be provided for those who test positive for the disease. Screenings that are recommended for many subgroups in a population include: routine mammograms for women over 40, a fecal occult blood test for everyone over 50, an amniocentesis to rule out a fetal anomaly for pregnant women over 35, because the incidence of breast cancer and colon cancer in these subgroups is higher than in the general population, as is the incidence of Down's syndrome in older mothers.

The testing of a person to rule out or confirm a suspected diagnosis because the patient has some sign or symptom is a diagnostic examination, not a screening. In these cases, the sign or symptom is used to explain the reason for the test.

A screening code may be a first listed code if the reason for the visit is specifically the screening exam. It may also be used as an additional code if the screening is done during an office visit for other health problems. A screening code is not necessary if the screening is inherent to a routine examination, such as a pap smear done during a routine pelvic examination.

Should a condition be discovered during the screening then the code for the condition may be assigned as an additional diagnosis.

The V code indicates that a screening exam is planned. A procedure code is required to confirm that the screening was performed.

The screening V code categories:

V28	Antenatal screening
V73-V82	Special screening examinations

6) **Observation**

There are two observation V code categories. They are for use in very limited circumstances when a person is being observed for a suspected condition that is ruled out. The observation codes are not for use if an injury or illness or any signs or symptoms related to the suspected condition are present. In such cases the diagnosis/symptom code is used with the corresponding E code to identify any external cause.

The observation codes are to be used as principal diagnosis only. The only exception to this is when the principal diagnosis is required to be a code from the V30, Live born infant, category. Then the V29 observation code is sequenced after the V30 code. Additional codes may be used in addition to the observation code but only if they are unrelated to the suspected condition being observed.

The observation V code categories:

V29	Observation and evaluation of newborns for suspected condition not found For the birth encounter, a code from category V30 should be sequenced before the V29 code.
V71	Observation and evaluation for suspected condition not found

7) **Aftercare**

Aftercare visit codes cover situations when the initial treatment of a disease or injury has been performed and the patient requires continued care during the healing or recovery phase, or for the long-term consequences of the disease. The aftercare V code should not be used if treatment is directed at a current, acute disease or injury. The diagnosis code is to be used in these cases. Exceptions to this rule are codes V58.0, Radiotherapy, and codes from subcategory V58.1, Encounter for chemotherapy and immunotherapy for neoplastic conditions. These codes are to be first listed, followed by the diagnosis code when a patient's encounter is solely to receive radiation therapy or chemotherapy for the treatment of a neoplasm. Should a patient receive both chemotherapy and radiation therapy during the same encounter code V58.0 and V58.1 may be used together on a record with either one being sequenced first.

The aftercare codes are generally first listed to explain the specific reason for the encounter. An aftercare code may be used as an additional code when some type of aftercare is provided in addition to the reason for admission and no diagnosis code is applicable. An example of this would be the closure of a colostomy during an encounter for treatment of another condition.

Certain aftercare V code categories need a secondary diagnosis code to describe the resolving condition or sequelae, for others, the condition is inherent in the code title.

Additional V code aftercare category terms include, fitting and adjustment, and attention to artificial openings.

Status V codes may be used with aftercare V codes to indicate the nature of the aftercare. For example code V45.81, Aortocoronary bypass status, may be used with code V58.73, Aftercare following surgery of the circulatory system, NEC, to indicate the surgery for which the aftercare is being performed. Also, a transplant status code may be used following code V58.44, Aftercare following organ transplant, to identify the organ transplanted. A status code should not be used when the aftercare code indicates the type of status, such as using V55.0, Attention to tracheostomy with V44.0, Tracheostomy status.

The aftercare V category/codes:

V52	Fitting and adjustment of prosthetic device and implant
V53	Fitting and adjustment of other device
V54	Other orthopedic aftercare
V55	Attention to artificial openings
V56	Encounter for dialysis and dialysis catheter care
V57	Care involving the use of rehabilitation procedures
V58.0	Radiotherapy
V58.11	Encounter for antineoplastic chemotherapy
V58.12	Encounter for antineoplastic immunotherapy
V58.3x	Attention to dressings and sutures
V58.41	Encounter for planned post-operative wound closure
V58.42	Aftercare, surgery, neoplasm
V58.43	Aftercare, surgery, trauma
V58.44	Aftercare involving organ transplant
V58.49	Other specified aftercare following surgery
V58.7x	Aftercare following surgery
V58.81	Fitting and adjustment of vascular catheter
V58.82	Fitting and adjustment of non-vascular catheter
V58.83	Monitoring therapeutic drug
V58.89	Other specified aftercare

8) **Follow-up**

The follow-up codes are used to explain continuing surveillance following completed treatment of a disease, condition, or injury. They imply that the condition has been fully treated and no longer exists. They should not be confused with aftercare codes that explain current treatment for a healing condition or its sequelae. Follow-up codes may be used in conjunction with history codes to provide the full picture of the healed condition and its treatment. The follow-up code is sequenced first, followed by the history code.

A follow-up code may be used to explain repeated visits. Should a condition be found to have recurred on the follow-up visit, then the diagnosis code should be used in place of the follow-up code.

The follow-up V code categories:

V24	Postpartum care and evaluation
V67	Follow-up examination

9) **Donor**

Category V59 is the donor codes. They are used for living individuals who are donating blood or other body tissue. These codes are only for individuals donating for others, not for self donations. They are not for use to identify cadaveric donations.

10) **Counseling**

Counseling V codes are used when a patient or family member receives assistance in the aftermath of an illness or injury, or when support is required in coping with family or social problems. They are not necessary for use in conjunction with a diagnosis code when the counseling component of care is
considered integral to standard treatment.

The counseling V categories/codes:

V25.0	General counseling and advice for contraceptive management
V26.3	Genetic counseling
V26.4	General counseling and advice for procreative management
V61	Other family circumstances
V65.1	Person consulted on behalf of another person

V65.3 Dietary surveillance and counseling
V65.4 Other counseling, not elsewhere classified

11) Obstetrics and related conditions

See Section I.C.11., the Obstetrics guidelines for further instruction on the use of these codes.

V codes for pregnancy are for use in those circumstances when none of the problems or complications included in the codes from the Obstetrics chapter exist (a routine prenatal visit or postpartum care). Codes V22.0, Supervision of normal first pregnancy, and V22.1, Supervision of other normal pregnancy, are always first listed and are not to be used with any other code from the OB chapter.

The outcome of delivery, category V27, should be included on all maternal delivery records. It is always a secondary code.

V codes for family planning (contraceptive) or procreative management and counseling should be included on an obstetric record either during the pregnancy or the postpartum stage, if applicable.

Obstetrics and related conditions V code categories:

V22 Normal pregnancy
V23 Supervision of high-risk pregnancy
Except: V23.2, Pregnancy with history of abortion. Code 646.3, Habitual aborter, from the OB chapter is required to indicate a history of abortion during a pregnancy.
V24 Postpartum care and evaluation
V25 Encounter for contraceptive management
Except V25.0x
(See Section I.C.18.d.11, Counseling)
V26 Procreative management
Except V26.5x, Sterilization status, V26.3 and V26.4
(See Section I.C.18.d.11., Counseling)
V27 Outcome of delivery
V28 Antenatal screening
(See Section I.C.18.d.6., Screening)

12) Newborn, infant and child

See Section I.C.15, the Newborn guidelines for further instruction on the use of these codes.

Newborn V code categories:

V20 Health supervision of infant or child
V29 Observation and evaluation of newborns for suspected condition not found
(See Section I.C.18.d.7, Observation)
V30-V39 Liveborn infant according to type of birth

13) Routine and administrative examinations

The V codes allow for the description of encounters for routine examinations, such as, a general check-up, or, examinations for administrative purposes, such as, a pre-employment physical. The codes are not to be used if the examination is for diagnosis of a suspected condition or for treatment purposes. In such cases the diagnosis code is used. During a routine exam, should a diagnosis or condition be discovered, it should be coded as an additional code. Pre-existing and chronic conditions and history codes may also be included as additional codes as long as the examination is for administrative purposes and not focused on any particular condition.

Pre-operative examination V codes are for use only in those situations when a patient is being cleared for surgery and no treatment is given.

The V codes categories/code for routine and administrative examinations:

V20.2 Routine infant or child health check
Any injections given should have a corresponding procedure code.
V70 General medical examination
V72 Special investigations and examinations
Codes V72.5 and V72.6 may be used if the reason for the patient encounter is for routine laboratory/radiology testing in the absence of any signs, symptoms, or associated diagnosis. If routine testing is performed during the same encounter as a test to evaluate a sign, symptom, or diagnosis, it is appropriate to assign both the V code and the code describing the reason for the non-routine test.

14) Miscellaneous V codes

The miscellaneous V codes capture a number of other health care encounters that do not fall into one of the other categories. Certain of these codes identify the reason for the encounter, others are for use as additional codes that provide useful information on circumstances that may affect a patient's care and treatment.

Prophylactic organ removal

For encounters specifically for prophylactic removal of breasts, ovaries, or another organ due to a genetic susceptibility to cancer or a family history of cancer, the principal or first listed code should be a code from subcategory V50.4, Prophylactic organ removal, followed by the appropriate genetic susceptibility code and the appropriate family history code.

If the patient has a malignancy of one site and is having prophylactic removal at another site to prevent either a new primary malignancy or metastatic disease, a code for the malignancy should also be assigned in addition to a code from subcategory V50.4. A V50.4 code should not be assigned if the patient is having organ removal for treatment of a malignancy, such as the removal of the testes for the treatment of prostate cancer.

Miscellaneous V code categories/codes:

V07 Need for isolation and other prophylactic measures
V50 Elective surgery for purposes other than remedying health states
V58.5 Orthodontics
V60 Housing, household, and economic circumstances
V62 Other psychosocial circumstances
V63 Unavailability of other medical facilities for care
V64 Persons encountering health services for specific procedures, not carried out
V66 Convalescence and palliative care
V68 Encounters for administrative purposes
V69 Problems related to lifestyle
V85 Body Mass Index

15) Nonspecific V codes

Certain V codes are so non-specific, or potentially redundant with other codes in the classification, that there can be little justification for their use in the inpatient setting. Their use in the outpatient setting should be limited to those instances when there is no further documentation to permit more precise coding. Otherwise, any sign or symptom or any other reason for visit that is captured in another code should be used.

Nonspecific V code categories/codes:

V11 Personal history of mental disorder A code from the mental disorders chapter, with an in remission fifth-digit, should be used.
V13.4 Personal history of arthritis
V13.6 Personal history of congenital malformations
V15.7 Personal history of contraception
V23.2 Pregnancy with history of abortion
V40 Mental and behavioral problems
V41 Problems with special senses and other special functions
V47 Other problems with internal organs
V48 Problems with head, neck, and trunk
V49 Problems with limbs and other problems
Exception:
V49.6 Upper limb amputation status
V49.7 Lower limb amputation status
V49.81 Postmenopausal status
V49.82 Dental sealant status
V49.83 Awaiting organ transplant status
V51 Aftercare involving the use of plastic surgery
V58.2 Blood transfusion, without reported diagnosis
V58.9 Unspecified aftercare
See Section IV.K. and Section IV.L. of the Outpatient guidelines.

V CODE TABLE

October 1, 2007 (FY2008)

Items in bold indicate a new entry or change from the November 2006 table

The following V code table contains columns for 1st listed, 1st or additional, additional only, and non-specific. Each code or category is listed on the left hand column and the allowable sequencing of the code or codes within the category is noted under the appropriate column.

Code(s)	Description	1st Dx Only[1]	1st or Add'l Dx[2]	Add'l Dx Only[3]	Non-Specific Diagnosis[4]
V01.X	Contact with or exposure to communicable diseases		X		
V02.X	Carrier or suspected carrier of infectious diseases		X		
V03.X	Need for prophylactic vaccination and inoculation against bacterial diseases		X		
V04.X	Need for prophylactic vaccination and inoculation against certain diseases		X		
V05.X	Need for prophylactic vaccination and inoculation against single diseases		X		
V06.X	Need for prophylactic vaccination and inoculation against combinations of diseases		X		
V07.X	Need for isolation and other prophylactic measures		X		
V08	Asymptomatic HIV infection status		X		
V09.X	Infection with drug resistant organisms			X	
V10.X	Personal history of malignant neoplasm		X		
V11.X	Personal history of mental disorder				X
V12.X	Personal history of certain other diseases		X		
V13.0X	Personal history of other disorders of urinary system		X		
V13.1	Personal history of trophoblastic disease		X		
V13.2X	Personal history of other genital system and obstetric disorders		X		
V13.3	Personal history of diseases of skin and subcutaneous tissue		X		
V13.4	Personal history of arthritis				X
V13.5	Personal history of other musculoskeletal disorders		X		
V13.61	Personal history of hypospadias			X	
V13.69	Personal history of congenital malformations				X
V13.7	Personal history of perinatal problems		X		
V13.8	Personal history of other specified diseases		X		
V13.9	Personal history of unspecified disease				X
V14.X	Personal history of allergy to medicinal agents			X	
V15.0X	Personal history of allergy, other than to medicinal agents			X	
V15.1	Personal history of surgery to heart and great vessels			X	
V15.2	Personal history of surgery to other major organs			X	
V15.3	Personal history of irradiation			X	
V15.4X	Personal history of psychological trauma			X	
V15.5	Personal history of injury			X	
V15.6	Personal history of poisoning			X	
V15.7	Personal history of contraception				X
V15.81	Personal history of noncompliance with medical treatment			X	
V15.82	Personal history of tobacco use			X	
V15.84	Personal history of exposure to asbestos			X	
V15.85	Personal history of exposure to potentially hazardous body fluids			X	
V15.86	Personal history of exposure to lead			X	
V15.87	Personal history of extracorporeal membrane oxygenation [ECMO]			X	
V15.88	History of fall		X		
V15.89	Other specified personal history presenting hazards to health			X	
V16.X	Family history of malignant neoplasm		X		
V17.X	Family history of certain chronic disabling diseases		X		
V18.X	Family history of certain other specific conditions		X		
V19.X	Family history of other conditions		X		
V20.X	Health supervision of infant or child	X			
V21.X	Constitutional states in development			X	
V22.0	Supervision of normal first pregnancy	X			
V22.1	Supervision of other normal pregnancy	X			
V22.2	Pregnancy state, incidental			X	
V23.X	Supervision of high-risk pregnancy		X		
V24.X	Postpartum care and examination	X			
V25.X	Encounter for contraceptive management		X		
V26.0	Tuboplasty or vasoplasty after previous sterilization		X		
V26.1	Artificial insemination		X		
V26.2X	Procreative management investigation and testing		X		
V26.3X	Procreative management, genetic counseling and testing		X		
V26.4X	Procreative management, genetic counseling and advice		X		
V26.5X	Procreative management, sterilization status			X	
V26.81	**Encounter for assisted reproductive fertility procedure cycle**	**X**			
V26.89	Other specified procreative management		X		
V26.9	Unspecified procreative management		X		

1. Generally for use as first listed only but may be used as additional if patient has more than one encounter on one day **or there is more than one reason for the encounter**
2. These codes may be used as first listed or additional codes
3. These codes are only for use as additional codes
4. These codes are primarily for use in the nonacute setting and should be limited to encounters for which no sign or symptom or reason for visit is documented in the record. Their use may be as either a first listed or additional code.

Code(s)	Description	1st Dx Only[1]	1st or Add'l Dx[2]	Add'l Dx Only[3]	Non-Specific Diagnosis[4]
V27.X	Outcome of delivery			X	
V28.X	Encounter for antenatal screening of mother		X		
V29.X	Observation and evaluation of newborns for suspected condition not found		X		
V30.X	Single liveborn	X			
V31.X	Twin, mate liveborn	X			
V32.X	Twin, mate stillborn	X			
V33.X	Twin, unspecified	X			
V34.X	Other multiple, mates all liveborn	X			
V35.X	Other multiple, mates all stillborn	X			
V36.X	Other multiple, mates live- and stillborn	X			
V37.X	Other multiple, unspecified	X			
V39.X	Unspecified	X			
V40.X	Mental and behavioral problems				X
V41.X	Problems with special senses and other special functions				X
V42.X	Organ or tissue replaced by transplant			X	
V43.0	Organ or tissue replaced by other means, eye globe			X	
V43.1	Organ or tissue replaced by other means, lens			X	
V43.21	Organ or tissue replaced by other means, heart assist device			X	
V43.22	Fully implantable artificial heart status		X		
V43.3	Organ or tissue replaced by other means, heart valve			X	
V43.4	Organ or tissue replaced by other means, blood vessel			X	
V43.5	Organ or tissue replaced by other means, bladder			X	
V43.6X	Organ or tissue replaced by other means, joint			X	
V43.7	Organ or tissue replaced by other means, limb			X	
V43.8X	Other organ or tissue replaced by other means			X	
V44.X	Artificial opening status			X	
V45.0X	Cardiac device in situ			X	
V45.1	Renal dialysis status			X	
V45.2	Presence of cerebrospinal fluid drainage device			X	
V45.3	Intestinal bypass or anastomosis status			X	
V45.4	Arthrodesis status			X	
V45.5X	Presence of contraceptive device			X	
V45.6X	States following surgery of eye and adnexa			X	
V45.7X	Acquired absence of organ		X		
V45.8X	Other postprocedural status			X	
V46.0	Other dependence on machines, aspirator			X	
V46.11	Dependence on respiratory, status			X	
V46.12	Encounter for respirator dependence during power failure	X			
V46.13	Encounter for weaning from respirator [ventilator]	X			
V46.14	Mechanical complication of respirator [ventilator]		X		
V46.2	Other dependence on machines, supplemental oxygen			X	
V46.8	Other dependence on other enabling machines			X	
V46.9	Unspecified machine dependence				X
V47.X	Other problems with internal organs				X
V48.X	Problems with head, neck and trunk				X
V49.0	Deficiencies of limbs				X
V49.1	Mechanical problems with limbs				X
V49.2	Motor problems with limbs				X
V49.3	Sensory problems with limbs				X
V49.4	Disfigurements of limbs				X
V49.5	Other problems with limbs				X
V49.6X	Upper limb amputation status		X		
V49.7X	Lower limb amputation status		X		
V49.81	Asymptomatic postmenopausal status (age-related) (natural)		X		
V49.82	Dental sealant status			X	
V49.83	Awaiting organ transplant status			X	
V49.84	Bed confinement status		X		
V49.85	**Dual sensory impairment**			**X**	
V49.89	Other specified conditions influencing health status		X		
V49.9	Unspecified condition influencing health status				X
V50.X	Elective surgery for purposes other than remedying health states		X		
V51	Aftercare involving the use of plastic surgery				X
V52.X	Fitting and adjustment of prosthetic device and implant		X		
V53.X	Fitting and adjustment of other device		X		
V54.X	Other orthopedic aftercare		X		
V55.X	Attention to artificial openings		X		
V56.0	Extracorporeal dialysis	X			
V56.1	Encounter for fitting and adjustment of extracorporeal dialysis catheter		X		

1. Generally for use as first listed only but may be used as additional if patient has more than one encounter on one day **or there is more than one reason for the encounter**
2. These codes may be used as first listed or additional codes
3. These codes are only for use as additional codes
4. These codes are primarily for use in the nonacute setting and should be limited to encounters for which no sign or symptom or reason for visit is documented in the record. Their use may be as either a first listed or additional code.

Code(s)	Description	1st Dx Only[1]	1st or Add'l Dx[2]	Add'l Dx Only[3]	Non-Specific Diagnosis[4]
V56.2	Encounter for fitting and adjustment of peritoneal dialysis catheter		X		
V56.3X	Encounter for adequacy testing for dialysis		X		
V56.8	Encounter for other dialysis and dialysis catheter care		X		
V57.X	Care involving use of rehabilitation procedures	X			
V58.0	Radiotherapy	X			
V58.11	Encounter for antineoplastic chemotherapy	X			
V58.12	Encounter for antineoplastic immunotherapy	X			
V58.2	Blood transfusion without reported diagnosis				X
V58.3X	Attention to dressings and sutures		X		
V58.4X	Other aftercare following surgery		X		
V58.5	Encounter for orthodontics				X
V58.6X	Long term (current) drug use			X	
V58.7X	Aftercare following surgery to specified body systems, not elsewhere classified		X		
V58.8X	Other specified procedures and aftercare		X		
V58.9	Unspecified aftercare				X
V59.X	Donors	X			
V60.X	Housing, household, and economic circumstances			X	
V61.X	Other family circumstances		X		
V62.X	Other psychosocial circumstances			X	
V63.X	Unavailability of other medical facilities for care		X		
V64.X	Persons encountering health services for specified procedure, not carried out			X	
V65.X	Other persons seeking consultation without complaint or sickness		X		
V66.0	Convalescence and palliative care following surgery	X			
V66.1	Convalescence and palliative care following radiotherapy	X			
V66.2	Convalescence and palliative care following chemotherapy	X			
V66.3	Convalescence and palliative care following psychotherapy and other treatment for mental disorder	X			
V66.4	Convalescence and palliative care following treatment of fracture	X			
V66.5	Convalescence and palliative care following other treatment	X			
V66.6	Convalescence and palliative care following combined treatment	X			
V66.7	Encounter for palliative care			X	
V66.9	Unspecified convalescence	X			
V67.X	Follow-up examination		X		
V68.X	Encounters for administrative purposes	X			
V69.X	Problems related to lifestyle		X		
V70.0	Routine general medical examination at a health care facility	X			
V70.1	General psychiatric examination, requested by the authority	X			
V70.2	General psychiatric examination, other and unspecified	X			
V70.3	Other medical examination for administrative purposes	X			
V70.4	Examination for medicolegal reasons	X			
V70.5	Health examination of defined subpopulations	X			
V70.6	Health examination in population surveys	X			
V70.7	Examination of participant in clinical trial		X		
V70.8	Other specified general medical examinations	X			
V70.9	Unspecified general medical examination	X			
V71.X	Observation and evaluation for suspected conditions not found	X			
V72.0	Examination of eyes and vision		X		
V72.1X	Examination of ears and hearing		X		
V72.2	Dental examination		X		
V72.3X	Gynecological examination		X		
V72.4X	Pregnancy examination or test		X		
V72.5	Radiological examination, NEC		X		
V72.6	Laboratory examination		X		
V72.7	Diagnostic skin and sensitization tests		X		
V72.81	Preoperative cardiovascular examination		X		
V72.82	Preoperative respiratory examination		X		
V72.83	Other specified preoperative examination		X		
V72.84	Preoperative examination, unspecified		X		
V72.85	Other specified examination		X		
V72.86	Encounter for blood typing		X		
V72.9	Unspecified examination				X
V73.X	Special screening examination for viral and chlamydial diseases		X		
V74.X	Special screening examination for bacterial and spirochetal diseases		X		
V75.X	Special screening examination for other infectious diseases		X		
V76.X	Special screening examination for malignant neoplasms		X		
V77.X	Special screening examination for endocrine, nutritional, metabolic and immunity disorders		X		
V78.X	Special screening examination for disorders of blood and blood-forming organs		X		
V79.X	Special screening examination for mental disorders and developmental handicaps		X		

1. Generally for use as first listed only but may be used as additional if patient has more than one encounter on one day **or there is more than one reason for the encounter**
2. These codes may be used as first listed or additional codes
3. These codes are only for use as additional codes
4. These codes are primarily for use in the nonacute setting and should be limited to encounters for which no sign or symptom or reason for visit is documented in the record. Their use may be as either a first listed or additional code.

Code(s)	Description	1st Dx Only[1]	1st or Add'l Dx[2]	Add'l Dx Only[3]	Non-Specific Diagnosis[4]
V80.X	Special screening examination for neurological, eye, and ear diseases		X		
V81.X	Special screening examination for cardiovascular, respiratory, and genitourinary diseases		X		
V82.X	Special screening examination for other conditions		X		
V83.X	Genetic carrier status		X		
V84.X	Genetic susceptibility to disease			X	
V85	Body mass index			X	
V86	Estrogen receptor status			X	

1. Generally for use as first listed only but may be used as additional if patient has more than one encounter on one day **or there is more than one reason for the encounter**
2. These codes may be used as first listed or additional codes
3. These codes are only for use as additional codes
4. These codes are primarily for use in the nonacute setting and should be limited to encounters for which no sign or symptom or reason for visit is documented in the record. Their use may be as either a first listed or additional code.

19. Supplemental Classification of External Causes of Injury and Poisoning (E codes, E800-E999)

Introduction: These guidelines are provided for those who are currently collecting E codes in order that there will be standardization in the process. If your institution plans to begin collecting E codes, these guidelines are to be applied. The use of E codes is supplemental to the application of ICD-9-CM diagnosis codes. E codes are never to be recorded as principal diagnoses (first-listed in non-inpatient setting) and are not required for reporting to CMS.

External causes of injury and poisoning codes (E codes) are intended to provide data for injury research and evaluation of injury prevention strategies. E codes capture how the injury or poisoning happened (cause), the intent (unintentional or accidental; or intentional, such as suicide or assault), and the place where the event occurred.

Some major categories of E codes include:

- transport accidents
- poisoning and adverse effects of drugs, medicinal substances and biologicals
- accidental falls
- accidents caused by fire and flames
- accidents due to natural and environmental factors
- late effects of accidents, assaults or self injury
- assaults or purposely inflicted injury
- suicide or self inflicted injury

These guidelines apply for the coding and collection of E codes from records in hospitals, outpatient clinics, emergency departments, other ambulatory care settings and provider offices, and nonacute care settings, except when other specific guidelines apply.

a. General E code coding guidelines

1) Used with any code in the range of 001-V89.09

An E code may be used with any code in the range of 001-V89.09, which indicates an injury, poisoning, or adverse effect due to an external cause.

2) Assign the appropriate E code for all initial treatments

Assign the appropriate E code for the initial encounter of an injury, poisoning, or adverse effect of drugs, not for subsequent treatment.

External cause of injury codes (E-codes) may be assigned while the acute fracture codes are still applicable.

See Section I.C.17.b.1 for coding of acute fractures.

3) Use the full range of E codes

Use the full range of E codes to completely describe the cause, the intent and the place of occurrence, if applicable, for all injuries, poisonings, and adverse effects of drugs.

4) Assign as many E codes as necessary

Assign as many E codes as necessary to fully explain each cause. If only one E code can be recorded, assign the E code most related to the principal diagnosis.

5) The selection of the appropriate E code

The selection of the appropriate E code is guided by the Index to External Causes, which is located after the alphabetical index to diseases and by Inclusion and Exclusion notes in the Tabular List.

6) E code can never be a principal diagnosis

An E code can never be a principal (first listed) diagnosis.

7) External cause code(s) with systemic inflammatory response syndrome (SIRS)

An external cause code is not appropriate with a code from subcategory 995.9, unless the patient also has an injury, poisoning, or adverse effect of drugs.

b. Place of occurrence guideline

Use an additional code from category E849 to indicate the Place of Occurrence for injuries and poisonings. The Place of Occurrence describes the place where the event occurred and not the patient's activity at the time of the event.

Do not use E849.9 if the place of occurrence is not stated.

c. Adverse effects of drugs, medicinal and biological substances guidelines

1) Do not code directly from the Table of Drugs

Do not code directly from the Table of Drugs and Chemicals. Always refer back to the Tabular List.

2) Use as many codes as necessary to describe

Use as many codes as necessary to describe completely all drugs, medicinal or biological substances.

3) If the same E code would describe the causative agent

If the same E code would describe the causative agent for more than one adverse reaction, assign the code only once.

4) If two or more drugs, medicinal or biological substances

If two or more drugs, medicinal or biological substances are reported, code each individually unless the combination code is listed in the Table of Drugs and Chemicals. In that case, assign the E code for the combination.

5) When a reaction results from the interaction of a drug(s)

When a reaction results from the interaction of a drug(s) and alcohol, use poisoning codes and E codes for both.

6) If the reporting format limits the number of E codes

If the reporting format limits the number of E codes that can be used in reporting clinical data, code the one most related to the principal diagnosis. Include at least one from each category (cause, intent, place) if possible.

If there are different fourth digit codes in the same three digit category, use the code for "Other specified" of that category. If there is no "Other specified" code in that category, use the appropriate "Unspecified" code in that category.

If the codes are in different three digit categories, assign the appropriate E code for other multiple drugs and medicinal substances.

7) Codes from the E930-E949 series

Codes from the E930-E949 series must be used to identify the causative substance for an adverse effect of drug, medicinal and biological substances, correctly prescribed and properly administered. The effect, such as tachycardia, delirium, gastrointestinal hemorrhaging, vomiting, hypokalemia, hepatitis, renal failure, or respiratory failure, is coded and followed by the appropriate code from the E930-E949 series.

d. Multiple cause E code coding guidelines

If two or more events cause separate injuries, an E code should be assigned for each cause. The first listed E code will be selected in the following order:

E codes for child and adult abuse take priority over all other E codes.

See Section I.C.19.e., Child and Adult abuse guidelines.

E codes for terrorism events take priority over all other E codes except child and adult abuse.

E codes for cataclysmic events take priority over all other E codes except child and adult abuse and terrorism.

E codes for transport accidents take priority over all other E codes except cataclysmic events and child and adult abuse and terrorism.

The first-listed E code should correspond to the cause of the most serious diagnosis due to an assault, accident, or self-harm, following the order of hierarchy listed above.

e. Child and adult abuse guideline

1) Intentional injury

When the cause of an injury or neglect is intentional child or adult abuse, the first listed E code should be assigned from categories E960-E968, Homicide and injury purposely inflicted by other persons, (except category E967). An E code from category E967, Child and adult battering and other maltreatment, should be added as an additional code to identify the perpetrator, if known.

2) Accidental intent

In cases of neglect when the intent is determined to be accidental E code E904.0, Abandonment or neglect of infant and helpless person, should be the first listed E code.

f. Unknown or suspected intent guideline

1) If the intent (accident, self-harm, assault) of the cause of an injury or poisoning is unknown

If the intent (accident, self-harm, assault) of the cause of an injury or poisoning is unknown or unspecified, code the intent as undetermined E980-E989.

2) If the intent (accident, self-harm, assault) of the cause of an injury or poisoning is questionable

If the intent (accident, self-harm, assault) of the cause of an injury or poisoning is questionable, probable or suspected, code the intent as undetermined E980-E989.

g. Undetermined cause

When the intent of an injury or poisoning is known, but the cause is unknown, use codes: E928.9, Unspecified accident, E958.9, Suicide and self-inflicted injury by unspecified means, and E968.9, Assault by unspecified means.

These E codes should rarely be used, as the documentation in the medical record, in both the inpatient outpatient and other settings, should normally provide sufficient detail to determine the cause of the injury.

h. Late effects of external cause guidelines

1) Late effect E codes

Late effect E codes exist for injuries and poisonings but not for adverse effects of drugs, misadventures and surgical complications.

2) Late effect E codes (E929, E959, E969, E977, E989, or E999.1)

A late effect E code (E929, E959, E969, E977, E989, or E999.1) should be used with any report of a late effect or sequela resulting from a previous injury or poisoning (905 909).

3) Late effect E code with a related current injury

A late effect E code should never be used with a related current nature of injury code.

4) Use of late effect E codes for subsequent visits

Use a late effect E code for subsequent visits when a late effect of the initial injury or poisoning is being treated. There is no late effect E code for adverse effects of drugs. Do not use a late effect E code for subsequent visits for follow-up care (e.g., to assess healing, to receive rehabilitative therapy) of the injury or poisoning when no late effect of the injury has been documented.

i. Misadventures and complications of care guidelines

1) Code range E870-E876

Assign a code in the range of E870-E876 if misadventures are stated by the provider.

2) Code range E878-E879

Assign a code in the range of E878-E879 if the provider attributes an abnormal reaction or later complication to a surgical or medical procedure, but does not mention misadventure at the time of the procedure as the cause of the reaction.

j. Terrorism guidelines

1) Cause of injury identified by the Federal Government (FBI) as terrorism

When the cause of an injury is identified by the Federal Government (FBI) as terrorism, the first-listed E-code should be a code from category E979, Terrorism. The definition of terrorism employed by the FBI is found at the inclusion note at E979. The terrorism E-code is the only E-code that should be assigned. Additional E codes from the assault categories should not be assigned.

2) Cause of an injury is suspected to be the result of terrorism

When the cause of an injury is suspected to be the result of terrorism a code from category E979 should not be assigned. Assign a code in the range of E codes based circumstances on the documentation of intent and mechanism.

3) Code E979.9, Terrorism, secondary effects

Assign code E979.9, Terrorism, secondary effects, for conditions occurring subsequent to the terrorist event. This code should not be assigned for conditions that are due to the initial terrorist act.

4) Statistical tabulation of terrorism codes

For statistical purposes these codes will be tabulated within the category for assault, expanding the current category from E960-E969 to include E979 and E999.1.

Section II. Selection of Principal Diagnosis

The circumstances of inpatient admission always govern the selection of principal diagnosis. The principal diagnosis is defined in the Uniform Hospital Discharge Data Set (UHDDS) as "that condition established after study to be chiefly responsible for occasioning the admission of the patient to the hospital for care."

The UHDDS definitions are used by hospitals to report inpatient data elements in a standardized manner. These data elements and their definitions can be found in the July 31, 1985, Federal Register (Vol. 50, No. 147), pp. 31038-40.

Since that time the application of the UHDDS definitions has been expanded to include all non-outpatient settings (acute care, short term, long term care and psychiatric hospitals; home health agencies; rehab facilities; nursing homes, etc).

In determining principal diagnosis the coding conventions in the ICD-9-CM, Volumes I and II take precedence over these official coding guidelines.

(See Section I.A., Conventions for the ICD-9-CM)

The importance of consistent, complete documentation in the medical record cannot be overemphasized. Without such documentation the application of all coding guidelines is a difficult, if not impossible, task.

A. Codes for symptoms, signs, and ill-defined conditions

Codes for symptoms, signs, and ill-defined conditions from Chapter 16 are not to be used as principal diagnosis when a related definitive diagnosis has been established.

B. Two or more interrelated conditions, each potentially meeting the definition for principal diagnosis

When there are two or more interrelated conditions (such as diseases in the same ICD-9-CM chapter or manifestations characteristically associated with a certain disease) potentially meeting the definition of principal diagnosis, either condition may be sequenced first, unless the circumstances of the admission, the therapy provided, the Tabular List, or the Alphabetic Index indicate otherwise.

C. Two or more diagnoses that equally meet the definition for principal diagnosis

In the unusual instance when two or more diagnoses equally meet the criteria for principal diagnosis as determined by the circumstances of admission, diagnostic workup and/or therapy provided, and the Alphabetic Index, Tabular List, or another coding guidelines does not provide sequencing direction, any one of the diagnoses may be sequenced first.

D. Two or more comparative or contrasting conditions

In those rare instances when two or more contrasting or comparative diagnoses are documented as "either/or" (or similar terminology), they are coded as if the diagnoses were confirmed and the diagnoses are sequenced according to the circumstances of the admission. If no further determination can be made as to which diagnosis should be principal, either diagnosis may be sequenced first.

E. A symptom(s) followed by contrasting/comparative diagnoses

When a symptom(s) is followed by contrasting/comparative diagnoses, the symptom code is sequenced first. All the contrasting/comparative diagnoses should be coded as additional diagnoses.

F. Original treatment plan not carried out

Sequence as the principal diagnosis the condition, which after study occasioned the admission to the hospital, even though treatment may not have been carried out due to unforeseen circumstances.

G. Complications of surgery and other medical care

When the admission is for treatment of a complication resulting from surgery or other medical care, the complication code is sequenced as the principal diagnosis. If the complication is classified to the 996-999 series and the code lacks the necessary specificity in describing the complication, an additional code for the specific complication should be assigned.

H. Uncertain diagnosis

If the diagnosis documented at the time of discharge is qualified as "probable", "suspected", "likely", "questionable", "possible", or "still to be ruled out", or other similar terms indicating uncertainty, code the condition as if it existed or was established. The bases for these guidelines are the diagnostic workup, arrangements for further workup or observation, and initial therapeutic approach that correspond most closely with the established diagnosis.

Note: This guideline is applicable only to inpatient admissions to short-term, acute, long-term care and psychiatric hospitals.

I. Admission from observation unit

1. Admission following medical observation

When a patient is admitted to an observation unit for a medical condition, which either worsens or does not improve, and is subsequently admitted as an inpatient of the same hospital for this same medical condition, the principal diagnosis would be the medical condition which led to the hospital admission.

2. Admission following post-operative observation

When a patient is admitted to an observation unit to monitor a condition (or complication) that develops following outpatient surgery, and then is subsequently admitted as an inpatient of the same hospital, hospitals should apply the Uniform Hospital Discharge Data Set (UHDDS) definition of principal diagnosis as "that condition established after study to be chiefly responsible for occasioning the admission of the patient to the hospital for care."

J. Admission from outpatient surgery

When a patient receives surgery in the hospital's outpatient surgery department and is subsequently admitted for continuing inpatient care at the same hospital, the following guidelines should be followed in selecting the principal diagnosis for the inpatient admission:

- If the reason for the inpatient admission is a complication, assign the complication as the principal diagnosis.
- If no complication, or other condition, is documented as the reason for the inpatient admission, assign the reason for the outpatient surgery as the principal diagnosis.
- If the reason for the inpatient admission is another condition unrelated to the surgery, assign the unrelated condition as the principal diagnosis.

Section III. Reporting Additional Diagnoses

GENERAL RULES FOR OTHER (ADDITIONAL) DIAGNOSES

For reporting purposes the definition for "other diagnoses" is interpreted as additional conditions that affect patient care in terms of requiring:

clinical evaluation; or
therapeutic treatment; or
diagnostic procedures; or
extended length of hospital stay; or
increased nursing care and/or monitoring.

The UHDDS item #11-b defines Other Diagnoses as "all conditions that coexist at the time of admission, that develop subsequently, or that affect the treatment received and/or the length of stay. Diagnoses that relate to an earlier episode which have no bearing on the current hospital stay are to be excluded." UHDDS definitions apply to inpatients in acute care, short-term, long term care and psychiatric hospital setting. The UHDDS definitions are used by acute care short-term hospitals to report inpatient data elements in a standardized manner. These data elements and their definitions can be found in the July 31, 1985, Federal Register (Vol. 50, No, 147), pp. 31038-40.

Since that time the application of the UHDDS definitions has been expanded to include all non-outpatient settings (acute care, short term, long term care and psychiatric hospitals; home health agencies; rehab facilities; nursing homes, etc).

The following guidelines are to be applied in designating "other diagnoses" when neither the Alphabetic Index nor the Tabular List in ICD-9-CM provide direction. The listing of the diagnoses in the patient record is the responsibility of the attending provider.

A. Previous conditions

If the provider has included a diagnosis in the final diagnostic statement, such as the discharge summary or the face sheet, it should ordinarily be coded. Some providers include in the diagnostic statement resolved conditions or diagnoses and status-post procedures from previous admission that have no bearing on the current stay. Such conditions are not to be reported and are coded only if required by hospital policy.

However, history codes (V10-V19) may be used as secondary codes if the historical condition or family history has an impact on current care or influences treatment.

B. Abnormal findings

Abnormal findings (laboratory, x-ray, pathologic, and other diagnostic results) are not coded and reported unless the provider indicates their clinical significance. If the findings are outside the normal range and the attending provider has ordered other tests to evaluate the condition or prescribed treatment, it is appropriate to ask the provider whether the abnormal finding should be added.

Please note: This differs from the coding practices in the outpatient setting for coding encounters for diagnostic tests that have been interpreted by a provider.

C. Uncertain diagnosis

If the diagnosis documented at the time of discharge is qualified as "probable", "suspected", "likely", "questionable", "possible", or "still to be ruled out" or other similar terms indicating uncertainty, code the condition as if it existed or was established. The bases for these guidelines are the diagnostic workup, arrangements for further workup or observation, and initial therapeutic approach that correspond most closely with the established diagnosis.

Note: This guideline is applicable only to inpatient admissions to short-term, acute, long-term care and psychiatric hospitals.

Section IV. Diagnostic Coding and Reporting Guidelines for Outpatient Services

These coding guidelines for outpatient diagnoses have been approved for use by hospitals/ providers in coding and reporting hospital-based outpatient services and provider-based office visits.

Information about the use of certain abbreviations, punctuation, symbols, and other conventions used in the ICD-9-CM Tabular List (code numbers and titles), can be found in Section IA of these guidelines, under "Conventions Used in the Tabular List." Information about the correct sequence to use in finding a code is also described in Section I.

The terms encounter and visit are often used interchangeably in describing outpatient service contacts and, therefore, appear together in these guidelines without distinguishing one from the other.

Though the conventions and general guidelines apply to all settings, coding guidelines for outpatient and provider reporting of diagnoses will vary in a number of instances from those for inpatient diagnoses, recognizing that:

The Uniform Hospital Discharge Data Set (UHDDS) definition of principal diagnosis applies only to inpatients in acute, short-term, long-term care and psychiatric hospitals.

Coding guidelines for inconclusive diagnoses (probable, suspected, rule out, etc.) were developed for inpatient reporting and do not apply to outpatients.

A. Selection of first-listed condition

In the outpatient setting, the term first-listed diagnosis is used in lieu of principal diagnosis.

In determining the first-listed diagnosis the coding conventions of ICD-9-CM, as well as the general and disease specific guidelines take precedence over the outpatient guidelines.

Diagnoses often are not established at the time of the initial encounter/visit. It may take two or more visits before the diagnosis is confirmed.

The most critical rule involves beginning the search for the correct code assignment through the Alphabetic Index. Never begin searching initially in the Tabular List as this will lead to coding errors.

1. Outpatient surgery

When a patient presents for outpatient surgery, code the reason for the surgery as the first-listed diagnosis (reason for the encounter), even if the surgery is not performed due to a contraindication.

2. Observation stay

When a patient is admitted for observation for a medical condition, assign a code for the medical condition as the first-listed diagnosis.

When a patient presents for outpatient surgery and develops complications requiring admission to observation, code the reason for the surgery as the first reported diagnosis (reason for the encounter), followed by codes for the complications as secondary diagnoses.

B. Codes from 001.0 through V89.09

The appropriate code or codes from 001.0 through V89.09 must be used to identify diagnoses, symptoms, conditions, problems, complaints, or other reason(s) for the encounter/visit.

C. Accurate reporting of ICD-9-CM diagnosis codes

For accurate reporting of ICD-9-CM diagnosis codes, the documentation should describe the patient's condition, using terminology which includes specific diagnoses as well as symptoms, problems, or reasons for the encounter. There are ICD-9-CM codes to describe all of these.

D. Selection of codes 001.0 through 999.9

The selection of codes 001.0 through 999.9 will frequently be used to describe the reason for the encounter. These codes are from the section of ICD-9-CM for the classification of diseases and injuries (e.g. infectious and parasitic diseases; neoplasms; symptoms, signs, and ill-defined conditions, etc.).

E. Codes that describe symptoms and signs

Codes that describe symptoms and signs, as opposed to diagnoses, are acceptable for reporting purposes when a diagnosis has not been established (confirmed) by the provider. Chapter 16 of ICD-9-CM, Symptoms, Signs, and Ill-defined conditions (codes 780.0 - 799.9) contain many, but not all codes for symptoms.

F. Encounters for circumstances other than a disease or injury

ICD-9-CM provides codes to deal with encounters for circumstances other than a disease or injury. The Supplementary Classification of factors Influencing Health Status and Contact with Health Services (V01.0- V84.8) is provided to deal with occasions when circumstances other than a disease or injury are recorded as diagnosis or problems.

See Section I.C. 18 for information on V-codes

G. Level of detail in coding

1. ICD-9-CM codes with 3, 4, or 5 digits

ICD-9-CM is composed of codes with either 3, 4, or 5 digits. Codes with three digits are included in ICD-9-CM as the heading of a category of codes that may be further subdivided by the use of fourth and/or fifth digits, which provide greater specificity.

2. Use of full number of digits required for a code

A three-digit code is to be used only if it is not further subdivided. Where fourth-digit subcategories and/or fifth-digit subclassifications are provided, they must be assigned. A code is invalid if it has not been coded to the full number of digits required for that code.

See also discussion under Section I.b.3., General Coding Guidelines, Level of Detail in Coding.

H. ICD-9-CM code for the diagnosis, condition, problem, or other reason for encounter/visit

List first the ICD-9-CM code for the diagnosis, condition, problem, or other reason for encounter/visit shown in the medical record to be chiefly responsible for the services provided. List additional codes that describe any coexisting conditions. In some cases the first-listed diagnosis may be a symptom when a diagnosis has not been established (confirmed) by the physician.

I. Uncertain diagnosis

Do not code diagnoses documented as "probable", "suspected," "questionable," "rule out," or "working diagnosis" or other similar terms indicating uncertainty. Rather, code the condition(s) to the highest degree of certainty for that encounter/visit, such as symptoms, signs, abnormal test results, or other reason for the visit.

Please note: This differs from the coding practices used by short-term, acute care, long-term care and psychiatric hospitals.

J. Chronic diseases

Chronic diseases treated on an ongoing basis may be coded and reported as many times as the patient receives treatment and care for the condition(s)

K. Code all documented conditions that coexist

Code all documented conditions that coexist at the time of the encounter/visit, and require or affect patient care treatment or management. Do not code conditions that were previously treated and no longer exist. However, history codes (V10-V19) may be used as secondary codes if the historical condition or family history has an impact on current care or influences treatment.

L. Patients receiving diagnostic services only

For patients receiving diagnostic services only during an encounter/visit, sequence first the diagnosis, condition, problem, or other reason for encounter/visit shown in the medical record to be chiefly responsible for the outpatient services provided during the encounter/visit. Codes for other diagnoses (e.g., chronic conditions) may be sequenced as additional diagnoses.

For encounters for routine laboratory/radiology testing in the absence of any signs, symptoms, or associated diagnosis, assign V72.5 and V72.6. If routine testing is performed during the same encounter as a test to evaluate a sign, symptom, or diagnosis, it is appropriate to assign both the V code and the code describing the reason for the non-routine test.

For outpatient encounters for diagnostic tests that have been interpreted by a physician, and the final report is available at the time of coding, code any confirmed or definitive diagnosis(es) documented in the interpretation. Do not code related signs and symptoms as additional diagnoses.

Please note: This differs from the coding practice in the hospital inpatient setting regarding abnormal findings on test results.

M. Patients receiving therapeutic services only

For patients receiving therapeutic services only during an encounter/visit, sequence first the diagnosis, condition, problem, or other reason for encounter/visit shown in the medical record to be chiefly responsible for the outpatient services provided during the encounter/visit. Codes for other diagnoses (e.g., chronic conditions) may be sequenced as additional diagnoses.

The only exception to this rule is that when the primary reason for the admission/encounter is chemotherapy, radiation therapy, or rehabilitation, the appropriate V code for the service is listed first, and the diagnosis or problem for which the service is being performed listed second.

N. Patients receiving preoperative evaluations only

For patients receiving preoperative evaluations only, sequence first a code from category V72.8, Other specified examinations, to describe the pre-op consultations. Assign a code for the condition to describe the reason for the surgery as an additional diagnosis. Code also any findings related to the pre-op evaluation.

O. Ambulatory surgery

For ambulatory surgery, code the diagnosis for which the surgery was performed. If the postoperative diagnosis is known to be different from the preoperative diagnosis at the time the diagnosis is confirmed, select the postoperative diagnosis for coding, since it is the most definitive.

P. Routine outpatient prenatal visits

For routine outpatient prenatal visits when no complications are present, codes V22.0, Supervision of normal first pregnancy, or V22.1, Supervision of other normal pregnancy, should be used as the principal diagnosis. These codes should not be used in conjunction with chapter 11 codes.

Appendix I. Present on Admission Reporting Guidelines

Introduction

These guidelines are to be used as a supplement to the *ICD-9-CM Official Guidelines for Coding and Reporting* to facilitate the assignment of the Present on Admission (POA) indicator for each diagnosis and external cause of injury code reported on claim forms (UB-04 and 837 Institutional).

These guidelines are not intended to replace any guidelines in the main body of the *ICD-9-CM Official Guidelines for Coding and Reporting.* The POA guidelines are not intended to provide guidance on when a condition should be coded, but rather, how to apply the POA indicator to the final set of diagnosis codes that have been assigned in accordance with Sections I, II, and III of the official coding guidelines. Subsequent to the assignment of the ICD-9-CM codes, the POA indicator should then be assigned to those conditions that have been coded.

As stated in the Introduction to the ICD-9-CM Official Guidelines for Coding and Reporting, a joint effort between the healthcare provider and the coder is essential to achieve complete and accurate documentation, code assignment, and reporting of diagnoses and procedures. The importance of consistent, complete documentation in the medical record cannot be overemphasized. Medical record documentation from any provider involved in the care and treatment of the patient may be used to support the determination of whether a condition was present on admission or not. In the context of the official coding guidelines, the term "provider" means a physician or any qualified healthcare practitioner who is legally accountable for establishing the patient's diagnosis.

General Reporting Requirements

All claims involving inpatient admissions to general acute care hospitals or other facilities that are subject to a law or regulation mandating collection of present on admission information.

Present on admission is defined as present at the time the order for inpatient admission occurs -- conditions that develop during an outpatient encounter, including emergency department, observation, or outpatient surgery, are considered as present on admission.

POA indicator is assigned to principal and secondary diagnoses (as defined in Section II of the Official Guidelines for Coding and Reporting) and the external cause of injury codes.

Issues related to inconsistent, missing, conflicting or unclear documentation must still be resolved by the provider.

If a condition would not be coded and reported based on UHDDS definitions and current official coding guidelines, then the POA indicator would not be reported.

Reporting Options

Y - Yes

N - No

U - Unknown

W – Clinically undetermined

Unreported/Not used – (Exempt from POA reporting)

Reporting Definitions

Y = present at the time of inpatient admission

N = not present at the time of inpatient admission

U = documentation is insufficient to determine if condition is present on admission

W = provider is unable to clinically determine whether condition was present on admission or not

Assigning the POA Indicator

Condition is on the "Exempt from Reporting" list Leave the "present on admission" field blank if the condition is on the list of ICD-9-CM codes for which this field is not applicable. This is the only circumstance in which the field may be left blank.

POA explicitly documented

Assign Y for any condition the provider explicitly documents as being present on admission.

Assign N for any condition the provider explicitly documents as not present at the time of admission.

Conditions diagnosed prior to inpatient admission

Assign "Y" for conditions that were diagnosed prior to admission (example: hypertension, diabetes mellitus, asthma)

Conditions diagnosed during the admission but clearly present before admission

Assign "Y" for conditions diagnosed during the admission that were clearly present but not diagnosed until after admission occurred.

Diagnoses subsequently confirmed after admission are considered present on admission if at the time of admission they are documented as suspected, possible, rule out, differential diagnosis, or constitute an underlying cause of a symptom that is present at the time of admission.

Condition develops during outpatient encounter prior to inpatient admission

Assign Y for any condition that develops during an outpatient encounter prior to a written order for inpatient admission.

Documentation does not indicate whether condition was present on admission

Assign "U" when the medical record documentation is unclear as to whether the condition was present on admission. "U" should not be routinely assigned and used only in very limited circumstances. Coders are encouraged to query the providers when the documentation is unclear.

Documentation states that it cannot be determined whether the condition was or was not present on admission

Assign "W" when the medical record documentation indicates that it cannot be clinically determined whether or not the condition was present on admission.

Chronic condition with acute exacerbation during the admission

If the code is a combination code that identifies both the chronic condition and the acute exacerbation, see POA guidelines pertaining to combination codes.

If the combination code only identifies the chronic condition and not the acute exacerbation (e.g., acute exacerbation of CHF), assign "Y."

Conditions documented as possible, probable, suspected, or rule out at the time of discharge

If the final diagnosis contains a possible, probable, suspected, or rule out diagnosis, and this diagnosis was suspected at the time of inpatient admission, assign "Y."

If the final diagnosis contains a possible, probable, suspected, or rule out diagnosis, and this diagnosis was based on symptoms or clinical findings that were not present on admission, assign "N".

Conditions documented as impending or threatened at the time of discharge

If the final diagnosis contains an impending or threatened diagnosis, and this diagnosis is based on symptoms or clinical findings that were present on admission, assign "Y".

If the final diagnosis contains an impending or threatened diagnosis, and this diagnosis is based on symptoms or clinical findings that were **not** present on admission, assign "N".

Acute and chronic conditions

Assign "Y" for acute conditions that are present at time of admission and N for acute conditions that are not present at time of admission.

Assign "Y" for chronic conditions, even though the condition may not be diagnosed until after admission.

If a single code identifies both an acute and chronic condition, see the POA guidelines for combination codes.

Combination codes

Assign "N" if any part of the combination code was not present on admission (e.g., obstructive chronic bronchitis with acute exacerbation and the exacerbation was not present on admission; gastric ulcer that does not start bleeding until after admission; asthma patient develops status asthmaticus after admission)

Assign "Y" if all parts of the combination code were present on admission (e.g., patient with diabetic nephropathy is admitted with uncontrolled diabetes)

If the final diagnosis includes comparative or contrasting diagnoses, and both were present, or suspected, at the time of admission, assign "Y".

For infection codes that include the causal organism, assign "Y" if the infection (or signs of the infection) was present on admission, even though the culture results may not be known until after admission (e.g., patient is admitted with pneumonia and the provider documents pseudomonas as the causal organism a few days later).

Obstetrical conditions

Whether or not the patient delivers during the current hospitalization does not affect assignment of the POA indicator. The determining factor for POA assignment is whether the pregnancy complication or obstetrical condition described by the code was present at the time of admission or not.

If the pregnancy complication or obstetrical condition was present on admission (e.g., patient admitted in preterm labor), assign "Y".

If the pregnancy complication or obstetrical condition was not present on admission (e.g., 2nd degree laceration during delivery, postpartum hemorrhage that occurred during current hospitalization, fetal distress develops after admission), assign "N".

If the obstetrical code includes more than one diagnosis and any of the diagnoses identified by the code were not present on admission (e.g., Code 642.7, Pre-eclampsia or eclampsia superimposed on preexisting hypertension) assign "N".

If the obstetrical code includes information that is not a diagnosis, do not consider that information in the POA determination. Example, code 652.1x, Breech or other malpresentation successfully converted to cephalic presentation, should be reported as present on admission if the fetus was breech on admission but was converted to cephalic presentation after admission. Since the conversion to cephalic presentation does not represent a diagnosis, the fact that the conversion occurred after admission has no bearing on the POA determination.

Perinatal conditions

Newborns are not considered to be admitted until after birth. Therefore, any condition present at birth or that developed in utero is considered present at admission and should be assigned "Y". This includes conditions that occur during delivery (e.g., injury during delivery, meconium aspiration, exposure to streptococcus B in the vaginal canal).

Congenital conditions and anomalies

Assign "Y" for congenital conditions and anomalies. Congenital conditions are always considered present on admission.

External cause of injury codes

Assign "Y" for any E code representing an external cause of injury or poisoning that occurred prior to inpatient admission (e.g., patient fell out of bed at home, patient fell out of bed in emergency room prior to admission)

Assign "N" for any E code representing an external cause of injury or poisoning that occurred during inpatient hospitalization (e.g., patient fell out of hospital bed during hospital stay, patient experienced an adverse reaction to a medication administered after inpatient admission)

Categories and Codes Exempt from Diagnosis Present on Admission Requirement

Note: "Diagnosis present on admission" for these code categories are exempt because they represent circumstances regarding the healthcare encounter or factors influencing health status that do not represent a current disease or injury or are always present on admission

137-139 Late effects of infectious and parasitic diseases
268.1 Rickets, late effect
326 Late effects of intracranial abscess or pyogenic infection
412 Old myocardial infarction
438 Late effects of cerebrovascular disease
650 Normal delivery
660.7 Failed forceps or vacuum extractor, unspecified
677 Late effect of complication of pregnancy, childbirth, and the puerperium
905-909 Late effects of injuries, poisonings, toxic effects, and other external causes
V02 Carrier or suspected carrier of infectious diseases
V03 Need for prophylactic vaccination and inoculation against bacterial diseases
V04 Need for prophylactic vaccination and inoculation against certain viral diseases
V05 Need for other prophylactic vaccination and inoculation against single diseases
V06 Need for prophylactic vaccination and inoculation against combinations of diseases
V07 Need for isolation and other prophylactic measures
V10 Personal history of malignant neoplasm
V11 Personal history of mental disorder
V12 Personal history of certain other diseases
V13 Personal history of other diseases
V14 Personal history of allergy to medicinal agents
V15 Other personal history presenting hazards to health
V16 Family history of malignant neoplasm
V17 Family history of certain chronic disabling diseases
V18 Family history of certain other specific conditions
V19 Family history of other conditions
V20 Health supervision of infant or child
V21 Constitutional states in development
V22 Normal pregnancy
V23 Supervision of high-risk pregnancy
V24 Postpartum care and examination
V25 Encounter for contraceptive management
V26 Procreative management
V27 Outcome of delivery
V28 Antenatal screening
V29 Observation and evaluation of newborns for suspected condition not found
V30-V39 Liveborn infants according to type of birth
V42 Organ or tissue replaced by transplant
V43 Organ or tissue replaced by other means
V44 Artificial opening status
V45 Other postprocedural states
V46 Other dependence on machines
V49.60-V49.77 Upper and lower limb amputation status
V49.81-V49.84 Other specified conditions influencing health status
V50 Elective surgery for purposes other than remedying health states
V51 Aftercare involving the use of plastic surgery
V52 Fitting and adjustment of prosthetic device and implant
V53 Fitting and adjustment of other device
V54 Other orthopedic aftercare
V55 Attention to artificial openings
V56 Encounter for dialysis and dialysis catheter care
V57 Care involving use of rehabilitation procedures
V58 Encounter for other and unspecified procedures and aftercare
V59 Donors
V60 Housing, household, and economic circumstances
V61 Other family circumstances
V62 Other psychosocial circumstances
V64 Persons encountering health services for specific procedures, not carried out
V65 Other persons seeking consultation
V66 Convalescence and palliative care
V67 Follow-up examination
V68 Encounters for administrative purposes
V69 Problems related to lifestyle
V70 General medical examination
V71 Observation and evaluation for suspected condition not found
V72 Special investigations and examinations
V73 Special screening examination for viral and chlamydial diseases
V74 Special screening examination for bacterial and spirochetal diseases
V75 Special screening examination for other infectious diseases
V76 Special screening for malignant neoplasms
V77 Special screening for endocrine, nutritional, metabolic, and immunity disorders
V78 Special screening for disorders of blood and blood-forming organs
V79 Special screening for mental disorders and developmental handicaps
V80 Special screening for neurological, eye, and ear diseases
V81 Special screening for cardiovascular, respiratory, and genitourinary diseases
V82 Special screening for other conditions
V83 Genetic carrier status
V84 Genetic susceptibility to disease
V85 Body Mass Index
V86 Estrogen receptor status
E800-E807 Railway accidents
E810-E819 Motor vehicle traffic accidents
E820-E825 Motor vehicle nontraffic accidents E826-E829, Other road vehicle accidents
E830-E838 Water transport accidents
E840-E845 Air and space transport accidents
E846-E848 Vehicle accidents not elsewhere classifiable
E849.0-E849.6 Place of occurrence
E849.8-E849.9 Place of occurrence
E883.1 Accidental fall into well
E883.2 Accidental fall into storm drain or manhole
E884.0 Fall from playground equipment
E884.1 Fall from cliff
E885.0 Fall from (nonmotorized) scooter
E885.1 Fall from roller skates
E885.2 Fall from skateboard
E885.3 Fall from skis
E885.4 Fall from snowboard
E886.0 Fall on same level from collision, pushing, or shoving, by or with other person, In sports
E890.0-E890.9 Conflagration in private dwelling
E893.0 Accident caused by ignition of clothing, from controlled fire in private dwelling
E893.2 Accident caused by ignition of clothing, from controlled fire not in building or structure
E894 Ignition of highly inflammable material
E895 Accident caused by controlled fire in private dwelling
E897 Accident caused by controlled fire not in building or structure
E898.0-E898.1 Accident caused by other specified fire and flames
E917.0 Striking against or struck accidentally by objects or persons, in sports without subsequent fall
E917.1 Striking against or struck accidentally by objects or persons, caused by a crowd, by collective fear or panic without subsequent fall
E917.2 Striking against or struck accidentally by objects or persons, in running water without subsequent fall
E917.5 Striking against or struck accidentally by objects or persons, object in sports with subsequent fall
E917.6 Striking against or struck accidentally by objects or persons, caused by a crowd, by collective fear or panic with subsequent fall
E919.0-E919.1 Accidents caused by machinery
E919.3-E919.9 Accidents caused by machinery
E921.0-E921.9 Accident caused by explosion of pressure vessel
E922.0-E922.9 Accident caused by firearm and air gun missile
E924.1 Caustic and corrosive substances
E926.2 Visible and ultraviolet light sources

E928.0-E928.8	Other and unspecified environmental and accidental causes
E929.0-E929.9	Late effects of accidental injury
E959	Late effects of self-inflicted injury
E970-E978	Legal intervention
E979	Terrorism
E981.0-E981.8	**Poisoning by gases in domestic use, undetermined whether accidentally or purposely inflicted**
E982.0-E982.9	Poisoning by other gases, undetermined whether accidentally or purposely inflicted
E985.0-E985.7	Injury by firearms, air guns and explosives, undetermined whether accidentally or purposely inflicted
E987.0	Falling from high place, undetermined whether accidentally or purposely inflicted, residential premises
E987.2	Falling from high place, undetermined whether accidentally or purposely inflicted, natural sites
E989	Late effects of injury, undetermined whether accidentally or purposely inflicted
E990-E999	Injury resulting from operations of war

POA Examples

General Medical Surgical

1. Patient is admitted for diagnostic work-up for cachexia. The final diagnosis is malignant neoplasm of lung with metastasis.
   Assign "Y" on the POA field for the malignant neoplasm. The malignant neoplasm was clearly present on admission, although it was not diagnosed until after the admission occurred.
2. A patient undergoes outpatient surgery. During the recovery period, the patient develops atrial fibrillation and the patient is subsequently admitted to the hospital as an inpatient.
   Assign "Y" on the POA field for the atrial fibrillation since it developed prior to a written order for inpatient admission.
3. A patient is treated in observation and while in Observation, the patient falls out of bed and breaks a hip. The patient is subsequently admitted as an inpatient to treat the hip fracture.
   Assign "Y" on the POA field for the hip fracture since it developed prior to a written order for inpatient admission.
4. A patient with known congestive heart failure is admitted to the hospital after he develops decompensated congestive heart failure.
   Assign "Y" on the POA field for the congestive heart failure. The ICD-9-CM code identifies the chronic condition and does not specify the acute exacerbation.
5. A patient undergoes inpatient surgery. After surgery, the patient develops fever and is treated aggressively. The physician's final diagnosis documents "possible postoperative infection following surgery."
   Assign "N" on the POA field for the postoperative infection since final diagnoses that contain the terms "possible", "probable", "suspected" or "rule out" and that are based on symptoms or clinical findings that were not present on admission should be reported as "N".
6. A patient with severe cough and difficulty breathing was diagnosed during his hospitalization to have lung cancer.
   Assign "Y" on the POA field for the lung cancer. Even though the cancer was not diagnosed until after admission, it is a chronic condition that was clearly present before the patient's admission.
7. A patient is admitted to the hospital for a coronary artery bypass surgery. Postoperatively he developed a pulmonary embolism.
   Assign "N" on the POA field for the pulmonary embolism. This is an acute condition that was not present on admission.
8. A patient is admitted with a known history of coronary atherosclerosis, status post myocardial infarction five years ago is now admitted for treatment of impending myocardial infarction. The final diagnosis is documented as "impending myocardial infarction."
   Assign "Y" to the impending myocardial infarction because the condition is present on admission.
9. A patient with diabetes mellitus developed uncontrolled diabetes on day 3 of the hospitalization.
   Assign "N" to the diabetes code because the "uncontrolled" component of the code was not present on admission.
10. A patient is admitted with high fever and pneumonia. The patient rapidly deteriorates and becomes septic. The discharge diagnosis lists sepsis and pneumonia. The documentation is unclear as to whether the sepsis was present on admission or developed shortly after admission.
    Query the physician as to whether the sepsis was present on admission, developed shortly after admission, or it cannot be clinically determined as to whether it was present on admission or not.
11. A patient is admitted for repair of an abdominal aneurysm. However, the aneurysm ruptures after hospital admission.
    Assign "N" for the ruptured abdominal aneurysm. Although the aneurysm was present on admission, the "ruptured" component of the code description did not occur until after admission.
12. A patient with viral hepatitis B progresses to hepatic coma after admission.
    Assign "N" for the viral hepatitis B with hepatic coma because part of the code description did not develop until after admission.
13. A patient with a history of varicose veins and ulceration of the left lower extremity strikes the area against the side of his hospital bed during an inpatient hospitalization. It bleeds profusely. The final diagnosis lists varicose veins with ulcer and hemorrhage.
    Assign "Y" for the varicose veins with ulcer. Although the hemorrhage occurred after admission, the code description for varicose veins with ulcer does not mention hemorrhage.
14. **The nursing initial assessment upon admission documents the presence of a decubitus ulcer. There is no mention of the decubitus ulcer in the physician documentation until several days after admission.**
    Query the physician as to whether the decubitus ulcer was present on admission, or developed after admission. Both diagnosis code assignment and determination of whether a condition was present on admission must be based on provider documentation in the medical record (per the definition of "provider" found at the beginning of these POA guidelines and in the introductory section of the ICD-9-CM Official Guidelines for Coding and Reporting). If it cannot be determined from the provider documentation whether or not a condition was present on admission, the provider should be queried.

Obstetrics

1. A female patient was admitted to the hospital and underwent a normal delivery.
   Leave the "present on admission" (POA) field blank. Code 650, Normal delivery, is on the "exempt from reporting" list.
2. Patient admitted in late pregnancy due to excessive vomiting and dehydration. During admission patient goes into premature labor
   Assign "Y" for the excessive vomiting and the dehydration.
   Assign "N" for the premature labor
3. Patient admitted in active labor. During the stay, a breast abscess is noted when mother attempted to breast feed. Provider is unable to determine whether the abscess was present on admission
   Assign "W" for the breast abscess.
4. Patient admitted in active labor. After 12 hours of labor it is noted that the infant is in fetal distress and a Cesarean section is performed
   Assign "N" for the fetal distress.

Newborn

1. A single liveborn infant was delivered in the hospital via Cesarean section. The physician documented fetal bradycardia during labor in the final diagnosis in the newborn record.
   Assign " Y" because the bradycardia developed prior to the newborn admission (birth).
2. A newborn developed diarrhea which was believed to be due to the hospital baby formula.
   Assign " N" because the diarrhea developed after admission.

A

- **AAT** (alpha-1 antitrypsin) deficiency 273.4
- **AAV (disease) (illness) (infection)** — *see* Human immunodeficiency virus (disease) (illness) (infection)
- **Abactio** — *see* Abortion, induced
- **Abactus venter** — *see* Abortion, induced
- **Abarognosis** 781.99
- **Abasia** (-astasia) 307.9
  - atactica 781.3
  - choreic 781.3
  - hysterical 300.11
  - paroxysmal trepidant 781.3
  - spastic 781.3
  - trembling 781.3
  - trepidans 781.3
- **Abderhalden-Kaufmann-Lignac syndrome** (cystinosis) 270.0
- **Abdomen, abdominal** — *see also* condition
  - accordion 306.4
  - acute 789.0 ☑
  - angina 557.1
  - burst 868.00
  - convulsive equivalent (*see also* Epilepsy) 345.5 ☑
  - heart 746.87
  - muscle deficiency syndrome 756.79
  - obstipum 756.79
- **Abdominalgia** 789.0 ☑
  - periodic 277.31
- **Abduction contracture, hip or other joint** — *see* Contraction, joint
- **Abercrombie's syndrome** (amyloid degeneration) 277.39
- **Aberrant** (congenital) — *see also* Malposition, congenital
  - adrenal gland 759.1
  - blood vessel NEC 747.60
    - arteriovenous NEC 747.60
    - cerebrovascular 747.81
    - gastrointestinal 747.61
    - lower limb 747.64
    - renal 747.62
    - spinal 747.82
    - upper limb 747.63
  - breast 757.6
  - endocrine gland NEC 759.2
  - gastrointestinal vessel (peripheral) 747.61
  - hepatic duct 751.69
  - lower limb vessel (peripheral) 747.64
  - pancreas 751.7
  - parathyroid gland 759.2
  - peripheral vascular vessel NEC 747.60
  - pituitary gland (pharyngeal) 759.2
  - renal blood vessel 747.62
  - sebaceous glands, mucous membrane, mouth 750.26
  - spinal vessel 747.82
  - spleen 759.0
  - testis (descent) 752.51
  - thymus gland 759.2
  - thyroid gland 759.2
  - upper limb vessel (peripheral) 747.63
- **Aberratio**
  - lactis 757.6
  - testis 752.51
- **Aberration** — *see also* Anomaly
  - chromosome — *see* Anomaly, chromosome(s)
  - distantial 368.9
  - mental (*see also* Disorder, mental, nonpsychotic) 300.9
- **Abetalipoproteinemia** 272.5
- **Abionarce** 780.79
- **Abiotrophy** 799.89
- **Ablatio**
  - placentae — *see* Placenta, ablatio
  - retinae (*see also* Detachment, retina) 361.9
- **Ablation**
  - pituitary (gland) (with hypofunction) 253.7
  - placenta — *see* Placenta, ablatio

- **Ablation** — *continued*
  - uterus 621.8
- **Ablepharia, ablepharon, ablephary** 743.62
- **Ablepsia** — *see* Blindness
- **Ablepsy** — *see* Blindness
- **Ablutomania** 300.3
- **Abnormal, abnormality, abnormalities** — *see also* Anomaly
  - acid-base balance 276.4
    - fetus or newborn — *see* Distress, fetal
  - adaptation curve, dark 368.63
  - alveolar ridge 525.9
  - amnion 658.9 ☑
    - affecting fetus or newborn 762.9
  - anatomical relationship NEC 759.9
  - apertures, congenital, diaphragm 756.6
  - auditory perception NEC 388.40
  - autosomes NEC 758.5
    - 13 758.1
    - 18 758.2
    - 21 or 22 758.0
    - D_1 758.1
    - E_3 758.2
    - G 758.0
  - ballistocardiogram 794.39
  - basal metabolic rate (BMR) 794.7
  - biosynthesis, testicular androgen 257.2
  - blood level (of)
    - cobalt 790.6
    - copper 790.6
    - iron 790.6
    - lead 790.6
    - lithium 790.6
    - magnesium 790.6
    - mineral 790.6
    - zinc 790.6
  - blood pressure
    - elevated (without diagnosis of hypertension) 796.2
    - low (*see also* Hypotension) 458.9
      - reading (incidental) (isolated) (nonspecific) 796.3
  - blood sugar 790.29
  - bowel sounds 787.5
  - breathing behavior — *see* Respiration
  - caloric test 794.19
  - cervix (acquired) NEC 622.9
    - congenital 752.40
    - in pregnancy or childbirth 654.6 ☑
      - causing obstructed labor 660.2 ☑
        - affecting fetus or newborn 763.1
  - chemistry, blood NEC 790.6
  - chest sounds 786.7
  - chorion 658.9 ☑
    - affecting fetus or newborn 762.9
  - chromosomal NEC 758.89
    - analysis, nonspecific result 795.2
    - autosomes (*see also* Abnormal, autosomes NEC) 758.5
    - fetal, (suspected) affecting management of pregnancy 655.1 ☑
    - sex 758.81
  - clinical findings NEC 796.4
  - communication — *see* Fistula
  - configuration of pupils 379.49
  - coronary
    - artery 746.85
    - vein 746.9
  - cortisol-binding globulin 255.8
  - course, Eustachian tube 744.24
  - creatinine clearance 794.4 ●
  - dentofacial NEC 524.9
    - functional 524.50
    - specified type NEC 524.89
  - development, developmental NEC 759.9
    - bone 756.9
    - central nervous system 742.9
  - direction, teeth 524.30

- **Abnormal, abnormality, abnormalities** — *see also* Anomaly — *continued*
  - Dynia (*see also* Defect, coagulation) 286.9
  - Ebstein 746.2
  - echocardiogram 793.2
  - echoencephalogram 794.01
  - echogram NEC — *see* Findings, abnormal, structure
  - electrocardiogram (ECG) (EKG) 794.31
  - electroencephalogram (EEG) 794.02
  - electromyogram (EMG) 794.17
    - ocular 794.14
  - electro-oculogram (EOG) 794.12
  - electroretinogram (ERG) 794.11
  - erythrocytes 289.9
    - congenital, with perinatal jaundice 282.9 *[774.0]*
  - Eustachian valve 746.9
  - excitability under minor stress 301.9
  - fat distribution 782.9
  - feces 787.7
  - fetal heart rate — *see* Distress, fetal
  - fetus NEC
    - affecting management of pregnancy — *see* Pregnancy, management affected by, fetal
    - causing disproportion 653.7 ☑
      - affecting fetus or newborn 763.1
      - causing obstructed labor 660.1 ☑
        - affecting fetus or newborn 763.1
  - findings without manifest disease — *see* Findings, abnormal
  - fluid
    - amniotic 792.3
    - cerebrospinal 792.0
    - peritoneal 792.9
    - pleural 792.9
    - synovial 792.9
    - vaginal 792.9
  - forces of labor NEC 661.9 ☑
    - affecting fetus or newborn 763.7
  - form, teeth 520.2
  - function studies
    - auditory 794.15
    - bladder 794.9
    - brain 794.00
    - cardiovascular 794.30
    - endocrine NEC 794.6
    - kidney 794.4
    - liver 794.8
    - nervous system
      - central 794.00
      - peripheral 794.19
    - oculomotor 794.14
    - pancreas 794.9
    - placenta 794.9
    - pulmonary 794.2
    - retina 794.11
    - special senses 794.19
    - spleen 794.9
    - thyroid 794.5
    - vestibular 794.16
  - gait 781.2
    - hysterical 300.11
  - gastrin secretion 251.5
  - globulin
    - cortisol-binding 255.8
    - thyroid-binding 246.8
  - glucagon secretion 251.4
  - glucose 790.29
    - in pregnancy, childbirth, or puerperium 648.8 ☑
      - fetus or newborn 775.0
    - non-fasting 790.29
  - gravitational (G) forces or states 994.9
  - hair NEC 704.2
  - hard tissue formation in pulp 522.3
  - head movement 781.0

- **Abnormal, abnormality, abnormalities** — *see also* Anomaly — *continued*
  - heart
    - rate
      - fetus, affecting liveborn infant
        - before the onset of labor 763.81
        - during labor 763.82
        - unspecified as to time of onset 763.83
      - intrauterine
        - before the onset of labor 763.81
        - during labor 763.82
        - unspecified as to time of onset 763.83
      - newborn
        - before the onset of labor 763.81
        - during labor 763.82
        - unspecified as to time of onset 763.83
    - shadow 793.2
    - sounds NEC 785.3
  - hemoglobin (*see also* Disease, hemoglobin) 282.7
    - trait — *see* Trait, hemoglobin, abnormal
  - hemorrhage, uterus — *see* Hemorrhage, uterus
  - histology NEC 795.4
  - increase
    - in
      - appetite 783.6
      - development 783.9
  - involuntary movement 781.0
  - jaw closure 524.51
  - karyotype 795.2
  - knee jerk 796.1
  - labor NEC 661.9 ☑
    - affecting fetus or newborn 763.7
  - laboratory findings — *see* Findings, abnormal
  - length, organ or site, congenital — *see* Distortion
  - liver function test 790.6 ●
  - loss of height 781.91
  - loss of weight 783.21
  - lung shadow 793.1
  - mammogram 793.80
    - calcification 793.89
    - calculus 793.89
    - microcalcification 793.81
  - Mantoux test 795.5
  - membranes (fetal)
    - affecting fetus or newborn 762.9
    - complicating pregnancy 658.8 ☑
  - menstruation — *see* Menstruation
  - metabolism (*see also* condition) 783.9
  - movement 781.0
    - disorder NEC 333.90
      - sleep related, unspecified 780.58
      - specified NEC 333.99
    - head 781.0
    - involuntary 781.0
    - specified type NEC 333.99
  - muscle contraction, localized 728.85
  - myoglobin (Aberdeen) (Annapolis) 289.9
  - narrowness, eyelid 743.62
  - optokinetic response 379.57
  - organs or tissues of pelvis NEC
    - in pregnancy or childbirth 654.9 ☑
      - affecting fetus or newborn 763.89
      - causing obstructed labor 660.2 ☑
        - affecting fetus or newborn 763.1
  - origin — *see* Malposition, congenital
  - palmar creases 757.2
  - Papanicolaou (smear)
    - anus 796.70 ●

Abnormal, abnormality, abnormalities — *see also* Anomaly — *continued*
- Papanicolaou — *continued*
  - anus — *continued*
    - with ●
      - atypical squamous cells ●
        - cannot exclude high grade squamous intraepithelial lesion (ASC-H) 796.72 ●
        - of undetermined significance (ASC-US) 796.71 ●
      - cytologic evidence of malignancy 796.76 ●
      - high grade squamous intraepithelial lesion (HGSIL) 796.74 ●
      - low grade squamous intraepithelial lesion (LGSIL) 796.73 ●
    - glandular 796.70 ●
    - specified finding NEC 796.79 ●
  - cervix 795.00
    - with
      - atypical squamous cells
        - cannot exclude high grade squamous intraepithelial lesion (ASC-H) 795.02
        - of undetermined significance (ASC-US) 795.01
      - cytologic evidence of malignancy 795.06
      - high grade squamous intraepithelial lesion (HGSIL) 795.04
      - low grade squamous intraepithelial lesion (LGSIL) 795.03
    - nonspecific finding NEC 795.09
  - other site 796.9 ▲
  - vagina 795.10 ●
    - with ●
      - atypical squamous cells ●
        - cannot exclude high grade squamous intraepithelial lesion (ASC-H) 795.12 ●
        - of undetermined significance (ASC-US) 795.11 ●
      - cytologic evidence of malignancy 795.16 ●
      - high grade squamous intraepithelial lesion (HGSIL) 795.14 ●
      - low grade squamous intraepithelial lesion (LGSIL) 795.13 ●
    - glandular 795.10 ●
    - specified finding NEC 795.19 ●
- parturition
  - affecting fetus or newborn 763.9
  - mother — *see* Delivery, complicated
- pelvis (bony) — *see* Deformity, pelvis
- percussion, chest 786.7
- periods (grossly) (*see also* Menstruation) 626.9
- phonocardiogram 794.39
- placenta — *see* Placenta, abnormal
- plantar reflex 796.1
- plasma protein — *see* Deficiency, plasma, protein
- pleural folds 748.8
- position (*see also* Malposition)
  - gravid uterus 654.4 ☑
    - causing obstructed labor 660.2 ☑
      - affecting fetus or newborn 763.1
- posture NEC 781.92
- presentation (fetus) — *see* Presentation, fetus, abnormal
- product of conception NEC 631
- puberty — *see* Puberty
- pulmonary
  - artery 747.3
  - function, newborn 770.89
  - test results 794.2
  - ventilation, newborn 770.89
    - hyperventilation 786.01
- pulsations in neck 785.1
- pupil reflexes 379.40
- quality of milk 676.8 ☑
- radiological examination 793.99
  - abdomen NEC 793.6
  - biliary tract 793.3
  - breast 793.89
    - mammogram NOS 793.80
    - mammographic
      - calcification 793.89
      - calculus 793.89
      - microcalcification 793.81
  - gastrointestinal tract 793.4
  - genitourinary organs 793.5
  - head 793.0
  - image test inconclusive due to excess body fat 793.91
  - intrathoracic organ NEC 793.2
  - lung (field) 793.1
  - musculoskeletal system 793.7
  - retroperitoneum 793.6
  - skin and subcutaneous tissue 793.99
  - skull 793.0
- red blood cells 790.09
  - morphology 790.09
  - volume 790.09
- reflex NEC 796.1
- renal function test 794.4
- respiration signs — *see* Respiration
- response to nerve stimulation 794.10
- retinal correspondence 368.34
- rhythm, heart (*see also* Arrhythmia)
  - fetus — *see* Distress, fetal
- saliva 792.4
- scan
  - brain 794.09
  - kidney 794.4
  - liver 794.8
  - lung 794.2
  - thyroid 794.5
- secretion
  - gastrin 251.5
  - glucagon 251.4
- semen 792.2
- serum level (of)
  - acid phosphatase 790.5
  - alkaline phosphatase 790.5
  - amylase 790.5
  - enzymes NEC 790.5
  - lipase 790.5
- shape
  - cornea 743.41
  - gallbladder 751.69
  - gravid uterus 654.4 ☑
    - affecting fetus or newborn 763.89
    - causing obstructed labor 660.2 ☑
      - affecting fetus or newborn 763.1
  - head (*see also* Anomaly, skull) 756.0
  - organ or site, congenital NEC — *see* Distortion
- sinus venosus 747.40
- size
  - fetus, complicating delivery 653.5 ☑
    - causing obstructed labor 660.1 ☑
  - gallbladder 751.69
  - head (*see also* Anomaly, skull) 756.0
  - organ or site, congenital NEC — *see* Distortion
  - teeth 520.2
- skin and appendages, congenital NEC 757.9
- soft parts of pelvis — *see* Abnormal, organs or tissues of pelvis
- spermatozoa 792.2
- sputum (amount) (color) (excessive) (odor) (purulent) 786.4
- stool NEC 787.7
  - bloody 578.1
    - occult 792.1
  - bulky 787.7
  - color (dark) (light) 792.1
  - content (fat) (mucus) (pus) 792.1
  - occult blood 792.1
- synchondrosis 756.9
- test results without manifest disease — *see* Findings, abnormal
- thebesian valve 746.9
- thermography — *see* Findings, abnormal, structure
- threshold, cones or rods (eye) 368.63
- thyroid-binding globulin 246.8
- thyroid product 246.8
- toxicology (findings) NEC 796.0
- tracheal cartilage (congenital) 748.3
- transport protein 273.8
- ultrasound results — *see* Findings, abnormal, structure
- umbilical cord
  - affecting fetus or newborn 762.6
  - complicating delivery 663.9 ☑
  - specified NEC 663.8 ☑
- union
  - cricoid cartilage and thyroid cartilage 748.3
  - larynx and trachea 748.3
  - thyroid cartilage and hyoid bone 748.3
- urination NEC 788.69
  - psychogenic 306.53
  - stream
    - intermittent 788.61
    - slowing 788.62
    - splitting 788.61
    - weak 788.62
  - urgency 788.63
- urine (constituents) NEC 791.9
- uterine hemorrhage (*see also* Hemorrhage, uterus) 626.9
  - climacteric 627.0
  - postmenopausal 627.1
- vagina (acquired) (congenital)
  - in pregnancy or childbirth 654.7 ☑
    - affecting fetus or newborn 763.89
    - causing obstructed labor 660.2 ☑
      - affecting fetus or newborn 763.1
- vascular sounds 785.9
- vectorcardiogram 794.39
- visually evoked potential (VEP) 794.13
- vulva (acquired) (congenital)
  - in pregnancy or childbirth 654.8 ☑
    - affecting fetus or newborn 763.89
    - causing obstructed labor 660.2 ☑
      - affecting fetus or newborn 763.1
- weight
  - gain 783.1
    - of pregnancy 646.1 ☑
      - with hypertension — *see* Toxemia, of pregnancy
  - loss 783.21
- x-ray examination — *see* Abnormal, radiological examination

Abnormally formed uterus — *see* Anomaly, uterus

Abnormity (any organ or part) — *see* Anomaly

ABO
- hemolytic disease 773.1
- incompatibility reaction 999.6

Abocclusion 524.20

Abolition, language 784.69

Aborter, habitual or recurrent NEC
- without current pregnancy 629.81
- current abortion (*see also* Abortion, spontaneous) 634.9 ☑
  - affecting fetus or newborn 761.8
- observation in current pregnancy 646.3 ☑

Abortion (complete) (incomplete) (inevitable) (with retained products of conception) 637.9 ☑

> *Note — Use the following fifth-digit subclassification with categories 634–637:*
>
> 0 *unspecified*
>
> 1 *incomplete*
>
> 2 *complete*

- with
  - complication(s) (any) following previous abortion — *see* category 639 ☑
  - damage to pelvic organ (laceration) (rupture) (tear) 637.2 ☑
  - embolism (air) (amniotic fluid) (blood clot) (pulmonary) (pyemic) (septic) (soap) 637.6 ☑
  - genital tract and pelvic infection 637.0 ☑
  - hemorrhage, delayed or excessive 637.1 ☑
  - metabolic disorder 637.4 ☑
  - renal failure (acute) 637.3 ☑
  - sepsis (genital tract) (pelvic organ) 637.0 ☑
    - urinary tract 637.7 ☑
  - shock (postoperative) (septic) 637.5 ☑
  - specified complication NEC 637.7 ☑
  - toxemia 637.3 ☑
  - unspecified complication(s) 637.8 ☑
  - urinary tract infection 637.7 ☑
- accidental — *see* Abortion, spontaneous
- artificial — *see* Abortion, induced
- attempted (failed) — *see* Abortion, failed
- criminal — *see* Abortion, illegal
- early — *see* Abortion, spontaneous
- elective — *see* Abortion, legal
- failed (legal) 638.9
  - with
    - damage to pelvic organ (laceration) (rupture) (tear) 638.2
    - embolism (air) (amniotic fluid) (blood clot) (pulmonary) (pyemic) (septic) (soap) 638.6
    - genital tract and pelvic infection 638.0
    - hemorrhage, delayed or excessive 638.1
    - metabolic disorder 638.4
    - renal failure (acute) 638.3
    - sepsis (genital tract) (pelvic organ) 638.0
      - urinary tract 638.7
    - shock (postoperative) (septic) 638.5

- **Abortion** — *continued*
  - failed — *continued*
    - with — *continued*
      - specified complication NEC 638.7
      - toxemia 638.3
      - unspecified complication(s) 638.8
      - urinary tract infection 638.7
  - fetal indication — *see* Abortion, legal
  - fetus 779.6
  - following threatened abortion — *see* Abortion, by type
  - habitual or recurrent (care during pregnancy) 646.3 ☑
    - with current abortion (*see also* Abortion, spontaneous) 634.9 ☑
      - affecting fetus or newborn 761.8
    - without current pregnancy 629.81
  - homicidal — *see* Abortion, illegal
  - illegal 636.9 ☑
    - with
      - damage to pelvic organ (laceration) (rupture) (tear) 636.2 ☑
      - embolism (air) (amniotic fluid) (blood clot) (pulmonary) (pyemic) (septic) (soap) 636.6 ☑
      - genital tract and pelvic infection 636.0 ☑
      - hemorrhage, delayed or excessive 636.1 ☑
      - metabolic disorder 636.4 ☑
      - renal failure 636.3 ☑
      - sepsis (genital tract) (pelvic organ) 636.0 ☑
        - urinary tract 636.7 ☑
      - shock (postoperative) (septic) 636.5 ☑
      - specified complication NEC 636.7 ☑
      - toxemia 636.3 ☑
      - unspecified complication(s) 636.8 ☑
      - urinary tract infection 636.7 ☑
    - fetus 779.6
  - induced 637.9 ☑
    - illegal — *see* Abortion, illegal
    - legal indications — *see* Abortion, legal
    - medical indications — *see* Abortion, legal
    - therapeutic — *see* Abortion, legal
  - late — *see* Abortion, spontaneous
  - legal (legal indication) (medical indication) (under medical supervision) 635.9 ☑
    - with
      - damage to pelvic organ (laceration) (rupture) (tear) 635.2 ☑
      - embolism (air) (amniotic fluid) (blood clot) (pulmonary) (pyemic) (septic) (soap) 635.6 ☑
      - genital tract and pelvic infection 635.0 ☑
      - hemorrhage, delayed or excessive 635.1 ☑
      - metabolic disorder 635.4 ☑
      - renal failure (acute) 635.3 ☑
      - sepsis (genital tract) (pelvic organ) 635.0 ☑
        - urinary tract 635.7 ☑
      - shock (postoperative) (septic) 635.5 ☑
      - specified complication NEC 635.7 ☑
      - toxemia 635.3 ☑
      - unspecified complication(s) 635.8 ☑
      - urinary tract infection 635.7 ☑
    - fetus 779.6

- **Abortion** — *continued*
  - medical indication — *see* Abortion, legal
  - mental hygiene problem — *see* Abortion, legal
  - missed 632
  - operative — *see* Abortion, legal
  - psychiatric indication — *see* Abortion, legal
  - recurrent — *see* Abortion, spontaneous
  - self-induced — *see* Abortion, illegal
  - septic — *see* Abortion, by type, with sepsis
  - spontaneous 634.9 ☑
    - with
      - damage to pelvic organ (laceration) (rupture) (tear) 634.2 ☑
      - embolism (air) (amniotic fluid) (blood clot) (pulmonary) (pyemic) (septic) (soap) 634.6 ☑
      - genital tract and pelvic infection 634.0 ☑
      - hemorrhage, delayed or excessive 634.1 ☑
      - metabolic disorder 634.4 ☑
      - renal failure 634.3 ☑
      - sepsis (genital tract) (pelvic organ) 634.0 ☑
        - urinary tract 634.7 ☑
      - shock (postoperative) (septic) 634.5 ☑
      - specified complication NEC 634.7 ☑
      - toxemia 634.3 ☑
      - unspecified complication(s) 634.8 ☑
      - urinary tract infection 634.7 ☑
    - fetus 761.8
    - threatened 640.0 ☑
      - affecting fetus or newborn 762.1
  - surgical — *see* Abortion, legal
  - therapeutic — *see* Abortion, legal
  - threatened 640.0 ☑
    - affecting fetus or newborn 762.1
  - tubal — *see* Pregnancy, tubal
  - voluntary — *see* Abortion, legal
- **Abortus fever** 023.9
- **Aboulomania** 301.6
- **Abrachia** 755.20
- **Abrachiatism** 755.20
- **Abrachiocephalia** 759.89
- **Abrachiocephalus** 759.89
- **Abrami's disease** (acquired hemolytic jaundice) 283.9
- **Abramov-Fiedler myocarditis** (acute isolated myocarditis) 422.91
- **Abrasion** — *see also* Injury, superficial, by site
  - cornea 918.1
  - dental 521.20
    - extending into
      - dentine 521.22
      - pulp 521.23
    - generalized 521.25
    - limited to enamel 521.21
    - localized 521.24
  - teeth, tooth (dentifrice) (habitual) (hard tissues) (occupational) (ritual) (traditional) (wedge defect) (*see also* Abrasion, dental) 521.20
- **Abrikossov's tumor** (M9580/0) — *see also* Neoplasm, connective tissue, benign
  - malignant (M9580/3) — *see* Neoplasm, connective tissue, malignant
- **Abrism** 988.8
- **Abruption, placenta** — *see* Placenta, abruptio
- **Abruptio placentae** — *see* Placenta, abruptio

- **Abscess** (acute) (chronic) (infectional) (lymphangitic) (metastatic) (multiple) (pyogenic) (septic) (with lymphangitis) — *see also* Cellulitis 682.9
  - abdomen, abdominal
    - cavity 567.22
    - wall 682.2
  - abdominopelvic 567.22
  - accessory sinus (chronic) (*see also* Sinusitis) 473.9
  - adrenal (capsule) (gland) 255.8
  - alveolar 522.5
    - with sinus 522.7
  - amebic 006.3
    - bladder 006.8
    - brain (with liver or lung abscess) 006.5
    - liver (without mention of brain or lung abscess) 006.3
      - with
        - brain abscess (and lung abscess) 006.5
        - lung abscess 006.4
    - lung (with liver abscess) 006.4
      - with brain abscess 006.5
    - seminal vesicle 006.8
    - specified site NEC 006.8
    - spleen 006.8
  - anaerobic 040.0
  - ankle 682.6
  - anorectal 566
  - antecubital space 682.3
  - antrum (chronic) (Highmore) (*see also* Sinusitis, maxillary) 473.0
  - anus 566
  - apical (tooth) 522.5
    - with sinus (alveolar) 522.7
  - appendix 540.1
  - areola (acute) (chronic) (nonpuerperal) 611.0
    - puerperal, postpartum 675.1 ☑
  - arm (any part, above wrist) 682.3
  - artery (wall) 447.2
  - atheromatous 447.2
  - auditory canal (external) 380.10
  - auricle (ear) (staphylococcal) (streptococcal) 380.10
  - axilla, axillary (region) 682.3
    - lymph gland or node 683
  - back (any part) 682.2
  - Bartholin's gland 616.3
    - with
      - abortion — *see* Abortion, by type, with sepsis
      - ectopic pregnancy (*see also* categories 633.0–633.9) 639.0
      - molar pregnancy (*see also* categories 630–632) 639.0
    - complicating pregnancy or puerperium 646.6 ☑
    - following
      - abortion 639.0
      - ectopic or molar pregnancy 639.0
  - bartholinian 616.3
  - Bezold's 383.01
  - bile, biliary, duct or tract (*see also* Cholecystitis) 576.8
  - bilharziasis 120.1
  - bladder (wall) 595.89
    - amebic 006.8
  - bone (subperiosteal) (*see also* Osteomyelitis) 730.0 ☑
    - accessory sinus (chronic) (*see also* Sinusitis) 473.9
    - acute 730.0 ☑
    - chronic or old 730.1 ☑
    - jaw (lower) (upper) 526.4
    - mastoid — *see* Mastoiditis, acute
    - petrous (*see also* Petrositis) 383.20
    - spinal (tuberculous) (*see also* Tuberculosis) 015.0 ☑ *[730.88]*
      - nontuberculous 730.08
  - bowel 569.5

- **Abscess** — *see also* Cellulitis — *continued*
  - brain (any part) 324.0
    - amebic (with liver or lung abscess) 006.5
    - cystic 324.0
    - late effect — *see* category 326
    - otogenic 324.0
    - tuberculous (*see also* Tuberculosis) 013.3 ☑
  - breast (acute) (chronic) (nonpuerperal) 611.0
    - newborn 771.5
    - puerperal, postpartum 675.1 ☑
    - tuberculous (*see also* Tuberculosis) 017.9 ☑
  - broad ligament (chronic) (*see also* Disease, pelvis, inflammatory) 614.4
    - acute 614.3
  - Brodie's (chronic) (localized) (*see also* Osteomyelitis) 730.1 ☑
  - bronchus 519.19
  - buccal cavity 528.3
  - bulbourethral gland 597.0
  - bursa 727.89
    - pharyngeal 478.29
  - buttock 682.5
  - canaliculus, breast 611.0
  - canthus 372.20
  - cartilage 733.99
  - cecum 569.5
    - with appendicitis 540.1
  - cerebellum, cerebellar 324.0
    - late effect — *see* category 326
  - cerebral (embolic) 324.0
    - late effect — *see* category 326
  - cervical (neck region) 682.1
    - lymph gland or node 683
    - stump (*see also* Cervicitis) 616.0
  - cervix (stump) (uteri) (*see also* Cervicitis) 616.0
  - cheek, external 682.0
    - inner 528.3
  - chest 510.9
    - with fistula 510.0
    - wall 682.2
  - chin 682.0
  - choroid 363.00
  - ciliary body 364.3
  - circumtonsillar 475
  - cold (tuberculous) (*see also* Tuberculosis, abscess)
    - articular — *see* Tuberculosis, joint
  - colon (wall) 569.5
  - colostomy or enterostomy 569.61
  - conjunctiva 372.00
  - connective tissue NEC 682.9
  - cornea 370.55
    - with ulcer 370.00
  - corpus
    - cavernosum 607.2
    - luteum (*see also* Salpingo-oophoritis) 614.2
  - Cowper's gland 597.0
  - cranium 324.0
  - cul-de-sac (Douglas') (posterior) (*see also* Disease, pelvis, inflammatory) 614.4
    - acute 614.3
  - dental 522.5
    - with sinus (alveolar) 522.7
  - dentoalveolar 522.5
    - with sinus (alveolar) 522.7
  - diaphragm, diaphragmatic 567.22
  - digit NEC 681.9
  - Douglas' cul-de-sac or pouch (*see also* Disease, pelvis, inflammatory) 614.4
    - acute 614.3
  - Dubois' 090.5
  - ductless gland 259.8
  - ear
    - acute 382.00
    - external 380.10
    - inner 386.30

Abscess — *see also* Cellulitis — *continued*
- ear — *continued*
  - middle — *see* Otitis media
- elbow 682.3
- endamebic — *see* Abscess, amebic
- entamebic — *see* Abscess, amebic
- enterostomy 569.61
- epididymis 604.0
- epidural 324.9
  - brain 324.0
  - late effect — *see* category 326
  - spinal cord 324.1
- epiglottis 478.79
- epiploon, epiploic 567.22
- erysipelatous (*see also* Erysipelas) 035
- esophagostomy 530.86
- esophagus 530.19
- ethmoid (bone) (chronic) (sinus) (*see also* Sinusitis, ethmoidal) 473.2
- external auditory canal 380.10
- extradural 324.9
  - brain 324.0
  - late effect — *see* category 326
  - spinal cord 324.1
- extraperitoneal — *see* Abscess, peritoneum
- eye 360.00
- eyelid 373.13
- face (any part, except eye) 682.0
- fallopian tube (*see also* Salpingo-oophoritis) 614.2
- fascia 728.89
- fauces 478.29
- fecal 569.5
- femoral (region) 682.6
- filaria, filarial (*see also* Infestation, filarial) 125.9
- finger (any) (intrathecal) (periosteal) (subcutaneous) (subcuticular) 681.00
- fistulous NEC 682.9
- flank 682.2
- foot (except toe) 682.7
- forearm 682.3
- forehead 682.0
- frontal (sinus) (chronic) (*see also* Sinusitis, frontal) 473.1
- gallbladder (*see also* Cholecystitis, acute) 575.0
- gastric 535.0 ☑
- genital organ or tract NEC
  - female 616.9
    - with
      - abortion — *see* Abortion, by type, with sepsis
      - ectopic pregnancy (*see also* categories 633.0–633.9) 639.0
      - molar pregnancy (*see also* categories 630–632) 639.0
    - following
      - abortion 639.0
      - ectopic or molar pregnancy 639.0
    - puerperal, postpartum, childbirth 670.0 ☑
  - male 608.4
- genitourinary system, tuberculous (*see also* Tuberculosis) 016.9 ☑
- gingival 523.30
- gland, glandular (lymph) (acute) NEC 683
- glottis 478.79
- gluteal (region) 682.5
- gonorrheal NEC (*see also* Gonococcus) 098.0
- groin 682.2
- gum 523.30
- hand (except finger or thumb) 682.4
- head (except face) 682.8
- heart 429.89
- heel 682.7
- helminthic (*see also* Infestation, by specific parasite) 128.9
- hepatic 572.0
  - amebic (*see also* Abscess, liver, amebic) 006.3
  - duct 576.8
- hip 682.6
  - tuberculous (active) (*see also* Tuberculosis) 015.1 ☑
- ileocecal 540.1
- ileostomy (bud) 569.61
- iliac (region) 682.2
  - fossa 540.1
- iliopsoas 567.31
  - nontuberculous 728.89
  - tuberculous (*see also* Tuberculosis) 015.0 ☑ *[730.88]*
- infraclavicular (fossa) 682.3
- inguinal (region) 682.2
  - lymph gland or node 683
- intersphincteric (anus) 566
- intestine, intestinal 569.5
  - rectal 566
- intra-abdominal (*see also* Abscess, peritoneum) 567.22
  - postoperative 998.59
- intracranial 324.0
  - late effect — *see* category 326
- intramammary — *see* Abscess, breast
- intramastoid (*see also* Mastoiditis, acute) 383.00
- intraorbital 376.01
- intraperitoneal 567.22
- intraspinal 324.1
  - late effect — *see* category 326
- intratonsillar 475
- iris 364.3
- ischiorectal 566
- jaw (bone) (lower) (upper) 526.4
  - skin 682.0
- joint (*see also* Arthritis, pyogenic) 711.0 ☑
  - vertebral (tuberculous) (*see also* Tuberculosis) 015.0 ☑ *[730.88]*
    - nontuberculous 724.8
- kidney 590.2
  - with
    - abortion — *see* Abortion, by type, with urinary tract infection
    - calculus 592.0
    - ectopic pregnancy (*see also* categories 633.0–633.9) 639.8
    - molar pregnancy (*see also* categories 630–632) 639.8
  - complicating pregnancy or puerperium 646.6 ☑
    - affecting fetus or newborn 760.1
  - following
    - abortion 639.8
    - ectopic or molar pregnancy 639.8
- knee 682.6
  - joint 711.06
  - tuberculous (active) (*see also* Tuberculosis) 015.2 ☑
- labium (majus) (minus) 616.4
  - complicating pregnancy, childbirth, or puerperium 646.6 ☑
- lacrimal (passages) (sac) (*see also* Dacryocystitis) 375.30
  - caruncle 375.30
  - gland (*see also* Dacryoadenitis) 375.00
- lacunar 597.0
- larynx 478.79
- lateral (alveolar) 522.5
  - with sinus 522.7
- leg, except foot 682.6
- lens 360.00
- lid 373.13
- lingual 529.0
  - tonsil 475
- lip 528.5
- Littre's gland 597.0
- liver 572.0
  - amebic 006.3
    - with
      - brain abscess (and lung abscess) 006.5
      - lung abscess 006.4
  - due to Entamoeba histolytica 006.3
  - dysenteric (*see also* Abscess, liver, amebic) 006.3
  - pyogenic 572.0
  - tropical (*see also* Abscess, liver, amebic) 006.3
- loin (region) 682.2
- lumbar (tuberculous) (*see also* Tuberculosis) 015.0 ☑ *[730.88]*
  - nontuberculous 682.2
- lung (miliary) (putrid) 513.0
  - amebic (with liver abscess) 006.4
    - with brain abscess 006.5
- lymphangitic, acute — *see* Cellulitis
- lymph, lymphatic, gland or node (acute) 683
  - any site, except mesenteric 683
  - mesentery 289.2
- malar 526.4
- mammary gland — *see* Abscess, breast
- marginal (anus) 566
- mastoid (process) (*see also* Mastoiditis, acute) 383.00
  - subperiosteal 383.01
- maxilla, maxillary 526.4
  - molar (tooth) 522.5
    - with sinus 522.7
  - premolar 522.5
  - sinus (chronic) (*see also* Sinusitis, maxillary) 473.0
- mediastinum 513.1
- meibomian gland 373.12
- meninges (*see also* Meningitis) 320.9
- mesentery, mesenteric 567.22
- mesosalpinx (*see also* Salpingo-oophoritis) 614.2
- milk 675.1 ☑
- Monro's (psoriasis) 696.1
- mons pubis 682.2
- mouth (floor) 528.3
- multiple sites NEC 682.9
- mural 682.2
- muscle 728.89
  - psoas 567.31
- myocardium 422.92
- nabothian (follicle) (*see also* Cervicitis) 616.0
- nail (chronic) (with lymphangitis) 681.9
  - finger 681.02
  - toe 681.11
- nasal (fossa) (septum) 478.19
  - sinus (chronic) (*see also* Sinusitis) 473.9
- nasopharyngeal 478.29
- nates 682.5
- navel 682.2
  - newborn NEC 771.4
- neck (region) 682.1
  - lymph gland or node 683
- nephritic (*see also* Abscess, kidney) 590.2
- nipple 611.0
  - puerperal, postpartum 675.0 ☑
- nose (septum) 478.19
  - external 682.0
- omentum 567.22
- operative wound 998.59
- orbit, orbital 376.01
- ossifluent — *see* Abscess, bone
- ovary, ovarian (corpus luteum) (*see also* Salpingo-oophoritis) 614.2
- oviduct (*see also* Salpingo-oophoritis) 614.2
- palate (soft) 528.3
  - hard 526.4
- palmar (space) 682.4
- pancreas (duct) 577.0
- paradontal 523.30
- parafrenal 607.2
- parametric, parametrium (chronic) (*see also* Disease, pelvis, inflammatory) 614.4
  - acute 614.3
- paranephric 590.2
- parapancreatic 577.0
- parapharyngeal 478.22
- pararectal 566
- parasinus (*see also* Sinusitis) 473.9
- parauterine (*see also* Disease, pelvis, inflammatory) 614.4
  - acute 614.3
- paravaginal (*see also* Vaginitis) 616.10
- parietal region 682.8
- parodontal 523.30
- parotid (duct) (gland) 527.3
  - region 528.3
- parumbilical 682.2
  - newborn 771.4
- pectoral (region) 682.2
- pelvirectal 567.22
- pelvis, pelvic
  - female (chronic) (*see also* Disease, pelvis, inflammatory) 614.4
    - acute 614.3
  - male, peritoneal (cellular tissue) — *see* Abscess, peritoneum
  - tuberculous (*see also* Tuberculosis) 016.9 ☑
- penis 607.2
  - gonococcal (acute) 098.0
    - chronic or duration of 2 months or over 098.2
- perianal 566
- periapical 522.5
  - with sinus (alveolar) 522.7
- periappendiceal 540.1
- pericardial 420.99
- pericecal 540.1
- pericemental 523.30
- pericholecystic (*see also* Cholecystitis, acute) 575.0
- pericoronal 523.30
- peridental 523.30
- perigastric 535.0 ☑
- perimetric (*see also* Disease, pelvis, inflammatory) 614.4
  - acute 614.3
- perinephric, perinephritic (*see also* Abscess, kidney) 590.2
- perineum, perineal (superficial) 682.2
  - deep (with urethral involvement) 597.0
  - urethra 597.0
- periodontal (parietal) 523.31
  - apical 522.5
- periosteum, periosteal (*see also* Periostitis) 730.3 ☑
  - with osteomyelitis (*see also* Osteomyelitis) 730.2 ☑
    - acute or subacute 730.0 ☑
    - chronic or old 730.1 ☑
- peripleuritic 510.9
  - with fistula 510.0
- periproctic 566
- periprostatic 601.2
- perirectal (staphylococcal) 566
- perirenal (tissue) (*see also* Abscess, kidney) 590.2
- perisinuous (nose) (*see also* Sinusitis) 473.9
- peritoneum, peritoneal (perforated) (ruptured) 567.22
  - with
    - abortion — *see* Abortion, by type, with sepsis
    - appendicitis 540.1
    - ectopic pregnancy (*see also* categories 633.0–633.9) 639.0

- **Abscess** — *see also* Cellulitis — *continued*
  - peritoneum, peritoneal — *continued*
    - with — *continued*
      - molar pregnancy (*see also* categories 630–632) 639.0
    - following
      - abortion 639.0
      - ectopic or molar pregnancy 639.0
    - pelvic, female (*see also* Disease, pelvis, inflammatory) 614.4
      - acute 614.3
    - postoperative 998.59
    - puerperal, postpartum, childbirth 670.0 ☑
    - tuberculous (*see also* Tuberculosis) 014.0 ☑
  - peritonsillar 475
  - perityphlic 540.1
  - periureteral 593.89
  - periurethral 597.0
    - gonococcal (acute) 098.0
      - chronic or duration of 2 months or over 098.2
  - periuterine (*see also* Disease, pelvis, inflammatory) 614.4
    - acute 614.3
  - perivesical 595.89
  - pernicious NEC 682.9
  - petrous bone — *see* Petrositis
  - phagedenic NEC 682.9
    - chancroid 099.0
  - pharynx, pharyngeal (lateral) 478.29
  - phlegmonous NEC 682.9
  - pilonidal 685.0
  - pituitary (gland) 253.8
  - pleura 510.9
    - with fistula 510.0
  - popliteal 682.6
  - postanal 566
  - postcecal 540.1
  - postlaryngeal 478.79
  - postnasal 478.19
  - postpharyngeal 478.24
  - posttonsillar 475
  - posttyphoid 002.0
  - Pott's (*see also* Tuberculosis) 015.0 ☑ *[730.88]*
  - pouch of Douglas (chronic) (*see also* Disease, pelvis, inflammatory) 614.4
  - premammary — *see* Abscess, breast
  - prepatellar 682.6
  - prostate (*see also* Prostatitis) 601.2
    - gonococcal (acute) 098.12
      - chronic or duration of 2 months or over 098.32
  - psoas 567.31
    - nontuberculous 728.89
    - tuberculous (*see also* Tuberculosis) 015.0 ☑ *[730.88]*
  - pterygopalatine fossa 682.8
  - pubis 682.2
  - puerperal — *see* Puerperal, abscess, by site
  - pulmonary — *see* Abscess, lung
  - pulp, pulpal (dental) 522.0
    - finger 681.01
    - toe 681.10
  - pyemic — *see* Septicemia
  - pyloric valve 535.0 ☑
  - rectovaginal septum 569.5
  - rectovesical 595.89
  - rectum 566
  - regional NEC 682.9
  - renal (*see also* Abscess, kidney) 590.2
  - retina 363.00
  - retrobulbar 376.01
  - retrocecal 567.22
  - retrolaryngeal 478.79
  - retromammary — *see* Abscess, breast
  - retroperineal 682.2
  - retroperitoneal 567.38
    - postprocedural 998.59

- **Abscess** — *see also* Cellulitis — *continued*
  - retropharyngeal 478.24
    - tuberculous (*see also* Tuberculosis) 012.8 ☑
  - retrorectal 566
  - retrouterine (*see also* Disease, pelvis, inflammatory) 614.4
    - acute 614.3
  - retrovesical 595.89
  - root, tooth 522.5
    - with sinus (alveolar) 522.7
  - round ligament (*see also* Disease, pelvis, inflammatory) 614.4
    - acute 614.3
  - rupture (spontaneous) NEC 682.9
  - sacrum (tuberculous) (*see also* Tuberculosis) 015.0 ☑ *[730.88]*
    - nontuberculous 730.08
  - salivary duct or gland 527.3
  - scalp (any part) 682.8
  - scapular 730.01
  - sclera 379.09
  - scrofulous (*see also* Tuberculosis) 017.2 ☑
  - scrotum 608.4
  - seminal vesicle 608.0
    - amebic 006.8
  - septal, dental 522.5
    - with sinus (alveolar) 522.7
  - septum (nasal) 478.19
  - serous (*see also* Periostitis) 730.3 ☑
  - shoulder 682.3
  - side 682.2
  - sigmoid 569.5
  - sinus (accessory) (chronic) (nasal) (*see also* Sinusitis) 473.9
    - intracranial venous (any) 324.0
      - late effect — *see* category 326
  - Skene's duct or gland 597.0
  - skin NEC 682.9
    - tuberculous (primary) (*see also* Tuberculosis) 017.0 ☑
  - sloughing NEC 682.9
  - specified site NEC 682.8
    - amebic 006.8
  - spermatic cord 608.4
  - sphenoidal (sinus) (*see also* Sinusitis, sphenoidal) 473.3
  - spinal
    - cord (any part) (staphylococcal) 324.1
      - tuberculous (*see also* Tuberculosis) 013.5 ☑
    - epidural 324.1
  - spine (column) (tuberculous) (*see also* Tuberculosis) 015.0 ☑ *[730.88]*
    - nontuberculous 730.08
  - spleen 289.59
    - amebic 006.8
  - staphylococcal NEC 682.9
  - stitch 998.59
  - stomach (wall) 535.0 ☑
  - strumous (tuberculous) (*see also* Tuberculosis) 017.2 ☑
  - subarachnoid 324.9
    - brain 324.0
    - cerebral 324.0
    - late effect — *see* category 326
    - spinal cord 324.1
  - subareolar (*see also* Abscess, breast)
    - puerperal, postpartum 675.1 ☑
  - subcecal 540.1
  - subcutaneous NEC 682.9
  - subdiaphragmatic 567.22
  - subdorsal 682.2
  - subdural 324.9
    - brain 324.0
    - late effect — *see* category 326
    - spinal cord 324.1
  - subgaleal 682.8
  - subhepatic 567.22
  - sublingual 528.3
    - gland 527.3
  - submammary — *see* Abscess, breast

- **Abscess** — *see also* Cellulitis — *continued*
  - submandibular (region) (space) (triangle) 682.0
    - gland 527.3
  - submaxillary (region) 682.0
    - gland 527.3
  - submental (pyogenic) 682.0
    - gland 527.3
  - subpectoral 682.2
  - subperiosteal — *see* Abscess, bone
  - subperitoneal 567.22
  - subphrenic (*see also* Abscess, peritoneum) 567.22
    - postoperative 998.59
  - subscapular 682.2
  - subungual 681.9
  - suburethral 597.0
  - sudoriparous 705.89
  - suppurative NEC 682.9
  - supraclavicular (fossa) 682.3
  - suprahepatic 567.22
  - suprapelvic (*see also* Disease, pelvis, inflammatory) 614.4
    - acute 614.3
  - suprapubic 682.2
  - suprarenal (capsule) (gland) 255.8
  - sweat gland 705.89
  - syphilitic 095.8
  - teeth, tooth (root) 522.5
    - with sinus (alveolar) 522.7
    - supporting structures NEC 523.30
  - temple 682.0
  - temporal region 682.0
  - temporosphenoidal 324.0
    - late effect — *see* category 326
  - tendon (sheath) 727.89
  - testicle — *see* Orchitis
  - thecal 728.89
  - thigh (acquired) 682.6
  - thorax 510.9
    - with fistula 510.0
  - throat 478.29
  - thumb (intrathecal) (periosteal) (subcutaneous) (subcuticular) 681.00
  - thymus (gland) 254.1
  - thyroid (gland) 245.0
  - toe (any) (intrathecal) (periosteal) (subcutaneous) (subcuticular) 681.10
  - tongue (staphylococcal) 529.0
  - tonsil(s) (lingual) 475
  - tonsillopharyngeal 475
  - tooth, teeth (root) 522.5
    - with sinus (alveolar) 522.7
    - supporting structure NEC 523.30
  - trachea 478.9
  - trunk 682.2
  - tubal (*see also* Salpingo-oophoritis) 614.2
  - tuberculous — *see* Tuberculosis, abscess
  - tubo-ovarian (*see also* Salpingo-oophoritis) 614.2
  - tunica vaginalis 608.4
  - umbilicus NEC 682.2
    - newborn 771.4
  - upper arm 682.3
  - upper respiratory 478.9
  - urachus 682.2
  - urethra (gland) 597.0
  - urinary 597.0
  - uterus, uterine (wall) (*see also* Endometritis) 615.9
    - ligament (*see also* Disease, pelvis, inflammatory) 614.4
      - acute 614.3
    - neck (*see also* Cervicitis) 616.0
  - uvula 528.3
  - vagina (wall) (*see also* Vaginitis) 616.10
  - vaginorectal (*see also* Vaginitis) 616.10
  - vas deferens 608.4
  - vermiform appendix 540.1

- **Abscess** — *see also* Cellulitis — *continued*
  - vertebra (column) (tuberculous) (*see also* Tuberculosis) 015.0 ☑ *[730.88]*
    - nontuberculous 730.0 ☑
  - vesical 595.89
  - vesicouterine pouch (*see also* Disease, pelvis, inflammatory) 614.4
  - vitreous (humor) (pneumococcal) 360.04
  - vocal cord 478.5
  - von Bezold's 383.01
  - vulva 616.4
    - complicating pregnancy, childbirth, or puerperium 646.6 ☑
  - vulvovaginal gland (*see also* Vaginitis) 616.3
  - web-space 682.4
  - wrist 682.4
- **Absence** (organ or part) (complete or partial)
  - acoustic nerve 742.8
  - adrenal (gland) (congenital) 759.1
    - acquired V45.79
  - albumin (blood) 273.8
  - alimentary tract (complete) (congenital) (partial) 751.8
    - lower 751.5
    - upper 750.8
  - alpha-fucosidase 271.8
  - alveolar process (acquired) 525.8
    - congenital 750.26
  - anus, anal (canal) (congenital) 751.2
  - aorta (congenital) 747.22
  - aortic valve (congenital) 746.89
  - appendix, congenital 751.2
  - arm (acquired) V49.60
    - above elbow V49.66
    - below elbow V49.65
    - congenital (*see also* Deformity, reduction, upper limb) 755.20
      - lower — *see* Absence, forearm, congenital
      - upper (complete) (partial) (with absence of distal elements, incomplete) 755.24
        - with
          - complete absence of distal elements 755.21
          - forearm (incomplete) 755.23
  - artery (congenital) (peripheral) NEC (*see also* Anomaly, peripheral vascular system) 747.60
    - brain 747.81
    - cerebral 747.81
    - coronary 746.85
    - pulmonary 747.3
    - umbilical 747.5
  - atrial septum 745.69
  - auditory canal (congenital) (external) 744.01
  - auricle (ear) (with stenosis or atresia of auditory canal), congenital 744.01
  - bile, biliary duct (common) or passage (congenital) 751.61
  - bladder (acquired) V45.74
    - congenital 753.8
  - bone (congenital) NEC 756.9
    - marrow 284.9
      - acquired (secondary) 284.89
      - congenital 284.09
      - hereditary 284.09
      - idiopathic 284.9
    - skull 756.0
  - bowel sounds 787.5
  - brain 740.0
    - specified part 742.2
  - breast(s) (acquired) V45.71
    - congenital 757.6
  - broad ligament (congenital) 752.19
  - bronchus (congenital) 748.3
  - calvarium, calvaria (skull) 756.0

Absence — *continued*
- canaliculus lacrimalis, congenital 743.65
- carpal(s) (congenital) (complete) (partial) (with absence of distal elements, incomplete) (*see also* Deformity, reduction, upper limb) 755.28
  - with complete absence of distal elements 755.21
- cartilage 756.9
- caudal spine 756.13
- cecum (acquired) (postoperative) (posttraumatic) V45.72
  - congenital 751.2
- cementum 520.4
- cerebellum (congenital) (vermis) 742.2
- cervix (acquired) (uteri) V88.01 ▲
  - with remaining uterus V88.03 ●
  - and uterus V88.01 ●
  - congenital 752.49
- chin, congenital 744.89
- cilia (congenital) 743.63
  - acquired 374.89
- circulatory system, part NEC 747.89
- clavicle 755.51
- clitoris (congenital) 752.49
- coccyx, congenital 756.13
- cold sense (*see also* Disturbance, sensation) 782.0
- colon (acquired) (postoperative) V45.72
  - congenital 751.2
- congenital
  - lumen — *see* Atresia
  - organ or site NEC — *see* Agenesis
  - septum — *see* Imperfect, closure
- corpus callosum (congenital) 742.2
- cricoid cartilage 748.3
- diaphragm (congenital) (with hernia) 756.6
  - with obstruction 756.6
- digestive organ(s) or tract, congenital (complete) (partial) 751.8
  - acquired V45.79
  - lower 751.5
  - upper 750.8
- ductus arteriosus 747.89
- duodenum (acquired) (postoperative) V45.72
  - congenital 751.1
- ear, congenital 744.09
  - acquired V45.79
  - auricle 744.01
  - external 744.01
  - inner 744.05
  - lobe, lobule 744.21
  - middle, except ossicles 744.03
    - ossicles 744.04
  - ossicles 744.04
- ejaculatory duct (congenital) 752.89
- endocrine gland NEC (congenital) 759.2
- epididymis (congenital) 752.89
  - acquired V45.77
- epiglottis, congenital 748.3
- epileptic (atonic) (typical) (*see also* Epilepsy) 345.0 ☑
- erythrocyte 284.9
- erythropoiesis 284.9
  - congenital 284.01
- esophagus (congenital) 750.3
- Eustachian tube (congenital) 744.24
- extremity (acquired)
  - congenital (*see also* Deformity, reduction) 755.4
  - lower V49.70
  - upper V49.60
- extrinsic muscle, eye 743.69
- eye (acquired) V45.78
  - adnexa (congenital) 743.69
  - congenital 743.00
  - muscle (congenital) 743.69
- eyelid (fold), congenital 743.62
  - acquired 374.89

Absence — *continued*
- face
  - bones NEC 756.0
  - specified part NEC 744.89
- fallopian tube(s) (acquired) V45.77
  - congenital 752.19
- femur, congenital (complete) (partial) (with absence of distal elements, incomplete) (*see also* Deformity, reduction, lower limb) 755.34
  - with
    - complete absence of distal elements 755.31
    - tibia and fibula (incomplete) 755.33
- fibrin 790.92
- fibrinogen (congenital) 286.3
  - acquired 286.6
- fibula, congenital (complete) (partial) (with absence of distal elements, incomplete) (*see also* Deformity, reduction, lower limb) 755.37
  - with
    - complete absence of distal elements 755.31
    - tibia 755.35
      - with
        - complete absence of distal elements 755.31
        - femur (incomplete) 755.33
          - with complete absence of distal elements 755.31
- finger (acquired) V49.62
  - congenital (complete) (partial) (*see also* Deformity, reduction, upper limb) 755.29
    - meaning all fingers (complete) (partial) 755.21
    - transverse 755.21
- fissures of lungs (congenital) 748.5
- foot (acquired) V49.73
  - congenital (complete) 755.31
- forearm (acquired) V49.65
  - congenital (complete) (partial) (with absence of distal elements, incomplete) (*see also* Deformity, reduction, upper limb) 755.25
    - with
      - complete absence of distal elements (hand and fingers) 755.21
      - humerus (incomplete) 755.23
- fovea centralis 743.55
- fucosidase 271.8
- gallbladder (acquired) V45.79
  - congenital 751.69
- gamma globulin (blood) 279.00
- genital organs
  - acquired V45.77
  - congenital
    - female 752.89
      - external 752.49
      - internal NEC 752.89
    - male 752.89
      - penis 752.69
- genitourinary organs, congenital NEC 752.89
- glottis 748.3
- gonadal, congenital NEC 758.6
- hair (congenital) 757.4
  - acquired — *see* Alopecia
- hand (acquired) V49.63
  - congenital (complete) (*see also* Deformity, reduction, upper limb) 755.21
- heart (congenital) 759.89
  - acquired — *see* Status, organ replacement
- heat sense (*see also* Disturbance, sensation) 782.0

Absence — *continued*
- humerus, congenital (complete) (partial) (with absence of distal elements, incomplete) (*see also* Deformity, reduction, upper limb) 755.24
  - with
    - complete absence of distal elements 755.21
    - radius and ulna (incomplete) 755.23
- hymen (congenital) 752.49
- ileum (acquired) (postoperative) (posttraumatic) V45.72
  - congenital 751.1
- immunoglobulin, isolated NEC 279.03
  - IgA 279.01
  - IgG 279.03
  - IgM 279.02
- incus (acquired) 385.24
  - congenital 744.04
- internal ear (congenital) 744.05
- intestine (acquired) (small) V45.72
  - congenital 751.1
    - large 751.2
  - large V45.72
    - congenital 751.2
- iris (congenital) 743.45
- jaw — *see* Absence, mandible
- jejunum (acquired) V45.72
  - congenital 751.1
- joint, congenital NEC 755.8
- kidney(s) (acquired) V45.73
  - congenital 753.0
- labium (congenital) (majus) (minus) 752.49
- labyrinth, membranous 744.05
- lacrimal apparatus (congenital) 743.65
- larynx (congenital) 748.3
- leg (acquired) V49.70
  - above knee V49.76
  - below knee V49.75
  - congenital (partial) (unilateral) (*see also* Deformity, reduction, lower limb) 755.31
    - lower (complete) (partial) (with absence of distal elements, incomplete) 755.35
      - with
        - complete absence of distal elements (foot and toes) 755.31
        - thigh (incomplete) 755.33
          - with complete absence of distal elements 755.31
    - upper — *see* Absence, femur
- lens (congenital) 743.35
  - acquired 379.31
- ligament, broad (congenital) 752.19
- limb (acquired)
  - congenital (complete) (partial) (*see also* Deformity, reduction) 755.4
    - lower 755.30
      - complete 755.31
      - incomplete 755.32
      - longitudinal — *see* Deficiency, lower limb, longitudinal
      - transverse 755.31
    - upper 755.20
      - complete 755.21
      - incomplete 755.22
      - longitudinal — *see* Deficiency, upper limb, longitudinal
      - transverse 755.21
  - lower NEC V49.70
  - upper NEC V49.60
- lip 750.26
- liver (congenital) (lobe) 751.69
- lumbar (congenital) (vertebra) 756.13
  - isthmus 756.11
  - pars articularis 756.11

Absence — *continued*
- lumen — *see* Atresia
- lung (bilateral) (congenital) (fissure) (lobe) (unilateral) 748.5
  - acquired (any part) V45.76
- mandible (congenital) 524.09
- maxilla (congenital) 524.09
- menstruation 626.0
- metacarpal(s), congenital (complete) (partial) (with absence of distal elements, incomplete) (*see also* Deformity, reduction, upper limb) 755.28
  - with all fingers, complete 755.21
- metatarsal(s), congenital (complete) (partial) (with absence of distal elements, incomplete) (*see also* Deformity, reduction, lower limb) 755.38
  - with complete absence of distal elements 755.31
- muscle (congenital) (pectoral) 756.81
  - ocular 743.69
- musculoskeletal system (congenital) NEC 756.9
- nail(s) (congenital) 757.5
- neck, part 744.89
- nerve 742.8
- nervous system, part NEC 742.8
- neutrophil 288.00
- nipple (congenital) 757.6
  - acquired V45.71 ●
- nose (congenital) 748.1
  - acquired 738.0
- nuclear 742.8
- ocular muscle (congenital) 743.69
- organ
  - of Corti (congenital) 744.05
  - or site
    - acquired V45.79
    - congenital NEC 759.89
- osseous meatus (ear) 744.03
- ovary (acquired) V45.77
  - congenital 752.0
- oviduct (acquired) V45.77
  - congenital 752.19
- pancreas (congenital) 751.7
  - acquired (postoperative) (posttraumatic) V45.79
- parathyroid gland (congenital) 759.2
- parotid gland(s) (congenital) 750.21
- patella, congenital 755.64
- pelvic girdle (congenital) 755.69
- penis (congenital) 752.69
  - acquired V45.77
- pericardium (congenital) 746.89
- perineal body (congenital) 756.81
- phalange(s), congenital 755.4
  - lower limb (complete) (intercalary) (partial) (terminal) (*see also* Deformity, reduction, lower limb) 755.39
    - meaning all toes (complete) (partial) 755.31
    - transverse 755.31
  - upper limb (complete) (intercalary) (partial) (terminal) (*see also* Deformity, reduction, upper limb) 755.29
    - meaning all digits (complete) (partial) 755.21
    - transverse 755.21
- pituitary gland (congenital) 759.2
- postoperative — *see* Absence, by site, acquired
- prostate (congenital) 752.89
  - acquired V45.77
- pulmonary
  - artery 747.3
  - trunk 747.3
  - valve (congenital) 746.01
  - vein 747.49
- punctum lacrimale (congenital) 743.65
- radius, congenital (complete) (partial) (with absence of distal elements, incomplete) 755.26

Absence — *continued*
- radius, congenital — *continued*
  - with
    - complete absence of distal elements 755.21
    - ulna 755.25
      - with
        - complete absence of distal elements 755.21
        - humerus (incomplete) 755.23
- ray, congenital 755.4
  - lower limb (complete) (partial) (*see also* Deformity, reduction, lower limb) 755.38
    - meaning all rays 755.31
    - transverse 755.31
  - upper limb (complete) (partial) (*see also* Deformity, reduction, upper limb) 755.28
    - meaning all rays 755.21
    - transverse 755.21
- rectum (congenital) 751.2
  - acquired V45.79
- red cell 284.9
  - acquired (secondary) 284.81
  - congenital 284.01
  - hereditary 284.01
  - idiopathic 284.9
- respiratory organ (congenital) NEC 748.9
- rib (acquired) 738.3
  - congenital 756.3
- roof of orbit (congenital) 742.0
- round ligament (congenital) 752.89
- sacrum, congenital 756.13
- salivary gland(s) (congenital) 750.21
- scapula 755.59
- scrotum, congenital 752.89
- seminal tract or duct (congenital) 752.89
  - acquired V45.77
- septum (congenital) (*see also* Imperfect, closure, septum)
  - atrial 745.69
    - and ventricular 745.7
  - between aorta and pulmonary artery 745.0
  - ventricular 745.3
    - and atrial 745.7
- sex chromosomes 758.81
- shoulder girdle, congenital (complete) (partial) 755.59
- skin (congenital) 757.39
- skull bone 756.0
  - with
    - anencephalus 740.0
    - encephalocele 742.0
    - hydrocephalus 742.3
      - with spina bifida (*see also* Spina bifida) 741.0 ☑
    - microcephalus 742.1
- spermatic cord (congenital) 752.89
- spinal cord 742.59
- spine, congenital 756.13
- spleen (congenital) 759.0
  - acquired V45.79
- sternum, congenital 756.3
- stomach (acquired) (partial) (postoperative) V45.75
  - with postgastric surgery syndrome 564.2
  - congenital 750.7
- submaxillary gland(s) (congenital) 750.21
- superior vena cava (congenital) 747.49
- tarsal(s), congenital (complete) (partial) (with absence of distal elements, incomplete) (*see also* Deformity, reduction, lower limb) 755.38
- teeth, tooth (congenital) 520.0
  - with abnormal spacing 524.30
  - acquired 525.10
    - with malocclusion 524.30
    - due to
      - caries 525.13

Absence — *continued*
- teeth, tooth — *continued*
  - acquired — *continued*
    - due to — *continued*
      - extraction 525.10
      - periodontal disease 525.12
      - trauma 525.11
- tendon (congenital) 756.81
- testis (congenital) 752.89
  - acquired V45.77
- thigh (acquired) 736.89
- thumb (acquired) V49.61
  - congenital 755.29
- thymus gland (congenital) 759.2
- thyroid (gland) (surgical) 246.8
  - with hypothyroidism 244.0
  - cartilage, congenital 748.3
  - congenital 243
- tibia, congenital (complete) (partial) (with absence of distal elements, incomplete) (*see also* Deformity, reduction, lower limb) 755.36
  - with
    - complete absence of distal elements 755.31
    - fibula 755.35
      - with
        - complete absence of distal elements 755.31
        - femur (incomplete) 755.33
          - with complete absence of distal elements 755.31
- toe (acquired) V49.72
  - congenital (complete) (partial) 755.39
    - meaning all toes 755.31
    - transverse 755.31
  - great V49.71
- tongue (congenital) 750.11
- tooth, teeth (congenital) 520.0
  - with abnormal spacing 524.30
  - acquired 525.10
    - with malocclusion 524.30
    - due to
      - caries 525.13
      - extraction 525.10
      - periodontal disease 525.12
      - trauma 525.11
- trachea (cartilage) (congenital) (rings) 748.3
- transverse aortic arch (congenital) 747.21
- tricuspid valve 746.1
- ulna, congenital (complete) (partial) (with absence of distal elements, incomplete) (*see also* Deformity, reduction, upper limb) 755.27
  - with
    - complete absence of distal elements 755.21
    - radius 755.25
      - with
        - complete absence of distal elements 755.21
        - humerus (incomplete) 755.23
- umbilical artery (congenital) 747.5
- ureter (congenital) 753.4
  - acquired V45.74
- urethra, congenital 753.8
  - acquired V45.74
- urinary system, part NEC, congenital 753.8
  - acquired V45.74
- uterus (acquired) V88.01 ▲
  - with remaining cervical stump V88.02 ●
  - and cervix V88.01 ●
  - congenital 752.3
- uvula (congenital) 750.26
- vagina, congenital 752.49
  - acquired V45.77
- vas deferens (congenital) 752.89
  - acquired V45.77

Absence — *continued*
- vein (congenital) (peripheral) NEC (*see also* Anomaly, peripheral vascular system) 747.60
  - brain 747.81
  - great 747.49
  - portal 747.49
  - pulmonary 747.49
- vena cava (congenital) (inferior) (superior) 747.49
- ventral horn cell 742.59
- ventricular septum 745.3
- vermis of cerebellum 742.2
- vertebra, congenital 756.13
- vulva, congenital 752.49

Absentia epileptica — *see also* Epilepsy 345.0 ☑

Absinthemia — *see also* Dependence 304.6 ☑

Absinthism — *see also* Dependence 304.6 ☑

Absorbent system disease 459.89

Absorption
- alcohol, through placenta or breast milk 760.71
- antibiotics, through placenta or breast milk 760.74
- anticonvulsants, through placenta or breast milk 760.77
- antifungals, through placenta or breast milk 760.74
- anti-infective, through placenta or breast milk 760.74
- antimetabolics, through placenta or breast milk 760.78
- chemical NEC 989.9
  - specified chemical or substance — *see* Table of Drugs and Chemicals
  - through placenta or breast milk (fetus or newborn) 760.70
    - alcohol 760.71
    - anticonvulsants 760.77
    - antifungals 760.74
    - anti-infective agents 760.74
    - antimetabolics 760.78
    - cocaine 760.75
    - "crack" 760.75
    - diethylstilbestrol [DES] 760.76
    - hallucinogenic agents 760.73
    - medicinal agents NEC 760.79
    - narcotics 760.72
    - obstetric anesthetic or analgesic drug 763.5
    - specified agent NEC 760.79
    - suspected, affecting management of pregnancy 655.5 ☑
- cocaine, through placenta or breast milk 760.75
- drug NEC (*see also* Reaction, drug)
  - through placenta or breast milk (fetus or newborn) 760.70
    - alcohol 760.71
    - anticonvulsants 760.77
    - antifungals 760.74
    - anti-infective agents 760.74
    - antimetabolics 760.78
    - cocaine 760.75
    - "crack" 760.75
    - diethylstilbestrol [DES] 760.76
    - hallucinogenic agents 760.73
    - medicinal agents NEC 760.79
    - narcotics 760.72
    - obstetric anesthetic or analgesic drug 763.5
    - specified agent NEC 760.79
    - suspected, affecting management of pregnancy 655.5 ☑
- fat, disturbance 579.8
- hallucinogenic agents, through placenta or breast milk 760.73
- immune sera, through placenta or breast milk 760.79
- lactose defect 271.3

Absorption — *continued*
- medicinal agents NEC, through placenta or breast milk 760.79
- narcotics, through placenta or breast milk 760.72
- noxious substance — *see* Absorption, chemical
- protein, disturbance 579.8
- pus or septic, general — *see* Septicemia
- quinine, through placenta or breast milk 760.74
- toxic substance — *see* Absorption, chemical
- uremic — *see* Uremia

Abstinence symptoms or syndrome
- alcohol 291.81
- drug 292.0

Abt-Letterer-Siwe syndrome (acute histiocytosis X) (M9722/3) 202.5 ☑

Abulia 799.89

Abulomania 301.6

Abuse
- adult 995.80
  - emotional 995.82
  - multiple forms 995.85
  - neglect (nutritional) 995.84
  - physical 995.81
  - psychological 995.82
  - sexual 995.83
- alcohol — *see* also Alcoholism 305.0 ☑
  - dependent 303.9 ☑
  - non-dependent 305.0 ☑
- child 995.50
  - counseling
    - perpetrator
      - non-parent V62.83
      - parent V61.22
    - victim V61.21
  - emotional 995.51
  - multiple forms 995.59
  - neglect (nutritional) 995.52
  - physical 995.54
    - shaken infant syndrome 995.55
  - psychological 995.51
  - sexual 995.53
- drugs, nondependent 305.9 ☑

> *Note — Use the following fifth-digit subclassification with the following codes: 305.0, 305.2–305.9:*
>
> | | |
> |---|---|
> | *0* | *unspecified* |
> | *1* | *continuous* |
> | *2* | *episodic* |
> | *3* | *in remission* |

  - amphetamine type 305.7 ☑
  - antidepressants 305.8 ☑
  - anxiolytic 305.4 ☑
  - barbiturates 305.4 ☑
  - caffeine 305.9 ☑
  - cannabis 305.2 ☑
  - cocaine type 305.6 ☑
  - hallucinogens 305.3 ☑
  - hashish 305.2 ☑
  - hypnotic 305.4 ☑
  - inhalant 305.9 ☑
  - LSD 305.3 ☑
  - marijuana 305.2 ☑
  - mixed 305.9 ☑
  - morphine type 305.5 ☑
  - opioid type 305.5 ☑
  - phencyclidine (PCP) 305.9 ☑
  - sedative 305.4 ☑
  - specified NEC 305.9 ☑
  - tranquilizers 305.4 ☑
- spouse 995.80
- tobacco 305.1

Acalcerosis 275.40

Acalcicosis 275.40

Acalculia 784.69
- developmental 315.1

Acanthocheilonemiasis 125.4

Acanthocytosis 272.5

Acanthokeratodermia 701.1
Acantholysis 701.8
- bullosa 757.39

Acanthoma (benign) (M8070/0) — *see also* Neoplasm, by site, benign
- malignant (M8070/3) — *see* Neoplasm, by site, malignant

Acanthosis (acquired) (nigricans) 701.2
- adult 701.2
- benign (congenital) 757.39
- congenital 757.39
- glycogenic
  - esophagus 530.89
- juvenile 701.2
- tongue 529.8

Acanthrocytosis 272.5
Acapnia 276.3
Acarbia 276.2
Acardia 759.89
Acardiacus amorphus 759.89
Acardiotrophia 429.1
Acardius 759.89
Acariasis 133.9
- sarcoptic 133.0

Acaridiasis 133.9
Acarinosis 133.9
Acariosis 133.9
Acarodermatitis 133.9
- urticarioides 133.9

Acarophobia 300.29
Acatalasemia 277.89
Acatalasia 277.89
Acatamathesia 784.69
Acataphasia 784.5
Acathisia 781.0
- due to drugs 333.99

Acceleration, accelerated
- atrioventricular conduction 426.7
- idioventricular rhythm 427.89

Accessory (congenital)
- adrenal gland 759.1
- anus 751.5
- appendix 751.5
- atrioventricular conduction 426.7
- auditory ossicles 744.04
- auricle (ear) 744.1
- autosome(s) NEC 758.5
  - 21 or 22 758.0
- biliary duct or passage 751.69
- bladder 753.8
- blood vessels (peripheral) (congenital) NEC (*see also* Anomaly, peripheral vascular system) 747.60
  - cerebral 747.81
  - coronary 746.85
- bone NEC 756.9
  - foot 755.67
- breast tissue, axilla 757.6
- carpal bones 755.56
- cecum 751.5
- cervix 752.49
- chromosome(s) NEC 758.5
  - 13-15 758.1
  - 16-18 758.2
  - 21 or 22 758.0
  - autosome(s) NEC 758.5
  - D_1 758.1
  - E_3 758.2
  - G 758.0
  - sex 758.81
- coronary artery 746.85
- cusp(s), heart valve NEC 746.89
  - pulmonary 746.09
- cystic duct 751.69
- digits 755.00
- ear (auricle) (lobe) 744.1
- endocrine gland NEC 759.2
- external os 752.49
- eyelid 743.62
- eye muscle 743.69
- face bone(s) 756.0
- fallopian tube (fimbria) (ostium) 752.19
- fingers 755.01
- foreskin 605
- frontonasal process 756.0

Accessory — *continued*
- gallbladder 751.69
- genital organ(s)
  - female 752.89
    - external 752.49
    - internal NEC 752.89
  - male NEC 752.89
    - penis 752.69
- genitourinary organs NEC 752.89
- heart 746.89
  - valve NEC 746.89
    - pulmonary 746.09
- hepatic ducts 751.69
- hymen 752.49
- intestine (large) (small) 751.5
- kidney 753.3
- lacrimal canal 743.65
- leaflet, heart valve NEC 746.89
  - pulmonary 746.09
- ligament, broad 752.19
- liver (duct) 751.69
- lobule (ear) 744.1
- lung (lobe) 748.69
- muscle 756.82
- navicular of carpus 755.56
- nervous system, part NEC 742.8
- nipple 757.6
- nose 748.1
- organ or site NEC — *see* Anomaly, specified type NEC
- ovary 752.0
- oviduct 752.19
- pancreas 751.7
- parathyroid gland 759.2
- parotid gland (and duct) 750.22
- pituitary gland 759.2
- placental lobe — *see* Placenta, abnormal
- preauricular appendage 744.1
- prepuce 605
- renal arteries (multiple) 747.62
- rib 756.3
  - cervical 756.2
- roots (teeth) 520.2
- salivary gland 750.22
- sesamoids 755.8
- sinus — *see* condition
- skin tags 757.39
- spleen 759.0
- sternum 756.3
- submaxillary gland 750.22
- tarsal bones 755.67
- teeth, tooth 520.1
  - causing crowding 524.31
- tendon 756.89
- thumb 755.01
- thymus gland 759.2
- thyroid gland 759.2
- toes 755.02
- tongue 750.13
- tragus 744.1
- ureter 753.4
- urethra 753.8
- urinary organ or tract NEC 753.8
- uterus 752.2
- vagina 752.49
- valve, heart NEC 746.89
  - pulmonary 746.09
- vertebra 756.19
- vocal cords 748.3
- vulva 752.49

Accident, accidental — *see also* condition
- birth NEC 767.9
- cardiovascular (*see also* Disease, cardiovascular) 429.2
- cerebral (*see also* Disease, cerebrovascular, acute) 434.91
- cerebrovascular (current) (CVA) (*see also* Disease, cerebrovascular, acute) 434.91
  - aborted 434.91
  - embolic 434.11
  - healed or old V12.54
  - hemorrhagic — *see* Hemorrhage, brain

Accident, accidental — *see also* condition — *continued*
- cerebrovascular (*see also* Disease, cerebrovascular, acute) — *continued*
  - impending 435.9
  - ischemic 434.91
  - late effect — *see* Late effect(s) (of) cerebrovascular disease
  - postoperative 997.02
  - thrombotic 434.01
- coronary (*see also* Infarct, myocardium) 410.9 ☑
- craniovascular (*see also* Disease, cerebrovascular, acute) 436
- during pregnancy, to mother, affecting fetus or newborn 760.5
- heart, cardiac (*see also* Infarct, myocardium) 410.9 ☑
- intrauterine 779.89
- vascular — *see* Disease, cerebrovascular, acute

Accommodation
- disorder of 367.51
  - drug-induced 367.89
  - toxic 367.89
- insufficiency of 367.4
- paralysis of 367.51
  - hysterical 300.11
- spasm of 367.53

Accouchement — *see* Delivery
Accreta placenta (without hemorrhage) 667.0 ☑
- with hemorrhage 666.0 ☑

Accretio cordis (nonrheumatic) 423.1
Accretions on teeth 523.6
Accumulation secretion, prostate 602.8
Acephalia, acephalism, acephaly 740.0
Acephalic 740.0
Acephalobrachia 759.89
Acephalocardia 759.89
Acephalocardius 759.89
Acephalochiria 759.89
Acephalochirus 759.89
Acephalogaster 759.89
Acephalostomus 759.89
Acephalothorax 759.89
Acephalus 740.0
Acetonemia 790.6
- diabetic 250.1 ☑
  - due to secondary diabetes 249.1 ☑ ●

Acetonglycosuria 982.8
Acetonuria 791.6
Achalasia 530.0
- cardia 530.0
- digestive organs congenital NEC 751.8
- esophagus 530.0
- pelvirectal 751.3
- psychogenic 306.4
- pylorus 750.5
- sphincteral NEC 564.89

Achard-Thiers syndrome (adrenogenital) 255.2
Ache(s) — *see* Pain
Acheilia 750.26
Acheiria 755.21
Achillobursitis 726.71
Achillodynia 726.71
Achlorhydria, achlorhydric 536.0
- anemia 280.9
- diarrhea 536.0
- neurogenic 536.0
- postvagotomy 564.2
- psychogenic 306.4
- secondary to vagotomy 564.2

Achloroblepsia 368.52
Achloropsia 368.52
Acholia 575.8
Acholuric jaundice (familial) (splenomegalic) — *see also* Spherocytosis 282.0
- acquired 283.9

Achondroplasia 756.4
Achrestic anemia 281.8
Achroacytosis, lacrimal gland 375.00

Achroacytosis, lacrimal gland — *continued*
- tuberculous (*see also* Tuberculosis) 017.3 ☑

Achroma, cutis 709.00
Achromate (congenital) 368.54
Achromatopia 368.54
Achromatopsia (congenital) 368.54
Achromia
- congenital 270.2
- parasitica 111.0
- unguium 703.8

Achylia
- gastrica 536.8
  - neurogenic 536.3
  - psychogenic 306.4
- pancreatica 577.1

Achylosis 536.8
Acid
- burn (*see also* Burn, by site)
  - from swallowing acid — *see* Burn, internal organs
- deficiency
  - amide nicotinic 265.2
  - amino 270.9
  - ascorbic 267
  - folic 266.2
  - nicotinic (amide) 265.2
  - pantothenic 266.2
- intoxication 276.2
- peptic disease 536.8
- stomach 536.8
  - psychogenic 306.4

Acidemia 276.2
- arginosuccinic 270.6
- fetal
  - affecting management of pregnancy 656.3 ☑
  - before onset of labor, in liveborn infant 768.2
  - during labor and delivery in liveborn infant 768.3
  - intrauterine 656.3 ☑
  - unspecified as to time of onset, in liveborn infant 768.4
- newborn 775.81
- pipecolic 270.7

Acidity, gastric (high) (low) 536.8
- psychogenic 306.4

Acidocytopenia 288.59
Acidocytosis 288.3
Acidopenia 288.59
Acidosis 276.2
- diabetic 250.1 ☑
  - due to secondary diabetes 249.1 ☑ ●
- fetal, affecting management of pregnancy 756.8 ☑
- fetal, affecting newborn 775.81
- kidney tubular 588.89
  - newborn 775.81
- lactic 276.2
- metabolic NEC 276.2
  - with respiratory acidosis 276.4
    - of newborn 775.81
  - late, of newborn 775.7
- newborn 775.81
- renal
  - hyperchloremic 588.89
  - tubular (distal) (proximal) 588.89
- respiratory 276.2
  - complicated by
    - metabolic acidosis 276.4
      - of newborn 775.81
    - metabolic alkalosis 276.4

Aciduria 791.9
- arginosuccinic 270.6
- beta-aminoisobutyric (BAIB) 277.2
- glutaric
  - type I 270.7
  - type II (type IIA, IIB, IIC) 277.85
  - type III 277.86
- glycolic 271.8
- methylmalonic 270.3
  - with glycinemia 270.7
- organic 270.9

- **Aciduria** — *continued*
  - orotic (congenital) (hereditary) (pyrimidine deficiency) 281.4
- **Acladiosis** 111.8
  - skin 111.8
- **Aclasis**
  - diaphyseal 756.4
  - tarsoepiphyseal 756.59
- **Acleistocardia** 745.5
- **Aclusion** 524.4
- **Acmesthesia** 782.0
- **Acne** (pustular) (vulgaris) 706.1
  - agminata (*see also* Tuberculosis) 017.0 ☑
  - artificialis 706.1
  - atrophica 706.0
  - cachecticorum (Hebra) 706.1
  - conglobata 706.1
  - conjunctiva 706.1
  - cystic 706.1
  - decalvans 704.09
  - erythematosa 695.3
  - eyelid 706.1
  - frontalis 706.0
  - indurata 706.1
  - keloid 706.1
  - lupoid 706.0
  - necrotic, necrotica 706.0
    - miliaris 704.8
  - neonatal 706.1
  - nodular 706.1
  - occupational 706.1
  - papulosa 706.1
  - rodens 706.0
  - rosacea 695.3
  - scorbutica 267
  - scrofulosorum (Bazin) (*see also* Tuberculosis) 017.0 ☑
  - summer 692.72
  - tropical 706.1
  - varioliformis 706.0
- **Acneiform drug eruptions** 692.3
- **Acnitis** (primary) — *see also* Tuberculosis 017.0 ☑
- **Acomia** 704.00
- **Acontractile bladder** 344.61
- **Aconuresis** — *see also* Incontinence 788.30
- **Acosta's disease** 993.2
- **Acousma** 780.1
- **Acoustic** — *see* condition
- **Acousticophobia** 300.29
- **Acquired** — *see* condition
- **Acquired immune deficiency syndrome** — *see* Human immunodeficiency virus (disease) (illness) (infection)
- **Acquired immunodeficiency syndrome** — *see* Human immunodeficiency virus (disease) (illness) (infection)
- **Acragnosis** 781.99
- **Acrania** 740.0
- **Acroagnosis** 781.99
- **Acroasphyxia, chronic** 443.89
- **Acrobrachycephaly** 756.0
- **Acrobystiolith** 608.89
- **Acrobystitis** 607.2
- **Acrocephalopolysyndactyly** 755.55
- **Acrocephalosyndactyly** 755.55
- **Acrocephaly** 756.0
- **Acrochondrohyperplasia** 759.82
- **Acrocyanosis** 443.89
  - newborn 770.83
    - meaning transient blue hands and feet — *omit code*
- **Acrodermatitis** 686.8
  - atrophicans (chronica) 701.8
  - continua (Hallopeau) 696.1
  - enteropathica 686.8
  - Hallopeau's 696.1
  - perstans 696.1
  - pustulosa continua 696.1
  - recalcitrant pustular 696.1
- **Acrodynia** 985.0
- **Acrodysplasia** 755.55
- **Acrohyperhidrosis** — *see also* Hyperhidrosis 780.8
- **Acrokeratosis verruciformis** 757.39
- **Acromastitis** 611.0
- **Acromegaly, acromegalia** (skin) 253.0
- **Acromelalgia** 443.82
- **Acromicria, acromikria** 756.59
- **Acronyx** 703.0
- **Acropachyderma** 757.39
- **Acropachy, thyroid** — *see also* Thyrotoxicosis 242.9 ☑
- **Acroparesthesia** 443.89
  - simple (Schultz's type) 443.89
  - vasomotor (Nothnagel's type) 443.89
- **Acropathy thyroid** — *see also* Thyrotoxicosis 242.9 ☑
- **Acrophobia** 300.29
- **Acroposthitis** 607.2
- **Acroscleriasis** — *see also* Scleroderma 710.1
- **Acroscleroderma** — *see also* Scleroderma 710.1
- **Acrosclerosis** — *see also* Scleroderma 710.1
- **Acrosphacelus** 785.4
- **Acrosphenosyndactylia** 755.55
- **Acrospiroma, eccrine** (M8402/0) — *see* Neoplasm, skin, benign
- **Acrostealgia** 732.9
- **Acrosyndactyly** — *see also* Syndactylism 755.10
- **Acrotrophodynia** 991.4
- **Actinic** — *see also* condition
  - cheilitis (due to sun) 692.72
    - chronic NEC 692.74
    - due to radiation, except from sun 692.82
  - conjunctivitis 370.24
  - dermatitis (due to sun) (*see also* Dermatitis, actinic) 692.70
    - due to
      - roentgen rays or radioactive substance 692.82
      - ultraviolet radiation, except from sun 692.82
    - sun NEC 692.70
  - elastosis solare 692.74
  - granuloma 692.73
  - keratitis 370.24
  - ophthalmia 370.24
  - reticuloid 692.73
- **Actinobacillosis, general** 027.8
- **Actinobacillus**
  - lignieresii 027.8
  - mallei 024
  - muris 026.1
- **Actinocutitis** NEC — *see also* Dermatitis, actinic 692.70
- **Actinodermatitis** NEC — *see also* Dermatitis, actinic 692.70
- **Actinomyces**
  - israelii (infection) — *see* Actinomycosis
  - muris-ratti (infection) 026.1
- **Actinomycosis, actinomycotic** 039.9
  - with
    - pneumonia 039.1
  - abdominal 039.2
  - cervicofacial 039.3
  - cutaneous 039.0
  - pulmonary 039.1
  - specified site NEC 039.8
  - thoracic 039.1
- **Actinoneuritis** 357.89
- **Action, heart**
  - disorder 427.9
    - postoperative 997.1
  - irregular 427.9
    - postoperative 997.1
    - psychogenic 306.2
- **Active** — *see* condition
- **Activity decrease, functional** 780.99
- **Acute** — *see also* condition
  - abdomen NEC 789.0 ☑
  - gallbladder (*see also* Cholecystitis, acute) 575.0
- **Acyanoblepsia** 368.53
- **Acyanopsia** 368.53
- **Acystia** 753.8
- **Acystinervia** — *see* Neurogenic, bladder
- **Acystineuria** — *see* Neurogenic, bladder
- **Adactylia, adactyly** (congenital) 755.4
  - lower limb (complete) (intercalary) (partial) (terminal) (*see also* Deformity, reduction, lower limb) 755.39
    - meaning all digits (complete) (partial) 755.31
    - transverse (complete) (partial) 755.31
  - upper limb (complete) (intercalary) (partial) (terminal) (*see also* Deformity, reduction, upper limb) 755.29
    - meaning all digits (complete) (partial) 755.21
    - transverse (complete) (partial) 755.21
- **Adair-Dighton syndrome** (brittle bones and blue sclera, deafness) 756.51
- **Adamantinoblastoma** (M9310/0) — *see* Ameloblastoma
- **Adamantinoma** (M9310/0) — *see* Ameloblastoma
- **Adamantoblastoma** (M9310/0) — *see* Ameloblastoma
- **Adams-Stokes (-Morgagni) disease or syndrome** (syncope with heart block) 426.9
- **Adaptation reaction** — *see also* Reaction, adjustment 309.9
- **Addiction** — *see also* Dependence
  - absinthe 304.6 ☑
  - alcoholic (ethyl) (methyl) (wood) 303.9 ☑
    - complicating pregnancy, childbirth, or puerperium 648.4 ☑
      - affecting fetus or newborn 760.71
    - suspected damage to fetus affecting management of pregnancy 655.4 ☑
  - drug (*see also* Dependence) 304.9 ☑
  - ethyl alcohol 303.9 ☑
  - heroin 304.0 ☑
  - hospital 301.51
  - methyl alcohol 303.9 ☑
  - methylated spirit 303.9 ☑
  - morphine (-like substances) 304.0 ☑
  - nicotine 305.1
  - opium 304.0 ☑
  - tobacco 305.1
  - wine 303.9 ☑
- **Addison's**
  - anemia (pernicious) 281.0
  - disease (bronze) (primary adrenal insufficiency) 255.41
    - tuberculous (*see also* Tuberculosis) 017.6 ☑
  - keloid (morphea) 701.0
  - melanoderma (adrenal cortical hypofunction) 255.41
- **Addison-Biermer anemia** (pernicious) 281.0
- **Addison-Gull disease** — *see* Xanthoma
- **Addisonian crisis or melanosis** (acute adrenocortical insufficiency) 255.41
- **Additional** — *see also* Accessory
  - chromosome(s) 758.5
    - 13-15 758.1
    - 16-18 758.2
    - 21 758.0
    - autosome(s) NEC 758.5
    - sex 758.81
- **Adduction contracture, hip or other joint** — *see* Contraction, joint
- **ADEM** (acute disseminated encephalomyelitis) (postinfectious) 136.9 *[323.61]*
  - infectious 136.9 *[323.61]*
  - noninfectious 323.81
- **Adenasthenia gastrica** 536.0
- **Aden fever** 061
- **Adenitis** — *see also* Lymphadenitis 289.3
- **Adenitis** — *see also* Lymphadenitis — *continued*
  - acute, unspecified site 683
    - epidemic infectious 075
  - axillary 289.3
    - acute 683
    - chronic or subacute 289.1
  - Bartholin's gland 616.89
  - bulbourethral gland (*see also* Urethritis) 597.89
  - cervical 289.3
    - acute 683
    - chronic or subacute 289.1
  - chancroid (Ducrey's bacillus) 099.0
  - chronic (any lymph node, except mesenteric) 289.1
    - mesenteric 289.2
  - Cowper's gland (*see also* Urethritis) 597.89
  - epidemic, acute 075
  - gangrenous 683
  - gonorrheal NEC 098.89
  - groin 289.3
    - acute 683
    - chronic or subacute 289.1
  - infectious 075
  - inguinal (region) 289.3
    - acute 683
    - chronic or subacute 289.1
  - lymph gland or node, except mesenteric 289.3
    - acute 683
    - chronic or subacute 289.1
    - mesenteric (acute) (chronic) (nonspecific) (subacute) 289.2
  - mesenteric (acute) (chronic) (nonspecific) (subacute) 289.2
    - due to Pasteurella multocida (P. septica) 027.2
  - parotid gland (suppurative) 527.2
  - phlegmonous 683
  - salivary duct or gland (any) (recurring) (suppurative) 527.2
  - scrofulous (*see also* Tuberculosis) 017.2 ☑
  - septic 289.3
  - Skene's duct or gland (*see also* Urethritis) 597.89
  - strumous, tuberculous (*see also* Tuberculosis) 017.2 ☑
  - subacute, unspecified site 289.1
  - sublingual gland (suppurative) 527.2
  - submandibular gland (suppurative) 527.2
  - submaxillary gland (suppurative) 527.2
  - suppurative 683
  - tuberculous — *see* Tuberculosis, lymph gland
  - urethral gland (*see also* Urethritis) 597.89
  - venereal NEC 099.8
  - Wharton's duct (suppurative) 527.2
- **Adenoacanthoma** (M8570/3) — *see* Neoplasm, by site, malignant
- **Adenoameloblastoma** (M9300/0) 213.1
  - upper jaw (bone) 213.0

Adenocarcinoma (M8140/3) — *see also* Neoplasm, by site, malignant

> *Note — The list of adjectival modifiers below is not exhaustive. A description of adenocarcinoma that does not appear in this list should be coded in the same manner as carcinoma with that description. Thus, "mixed acidophil-basophil adenocarcinoma," should be coded in the same manner as "mixed acidophil-basophil carcinoma," which appears in the list under "Carcinoma."*
>
> *Except where otherwise indicated, the morphological varieties of adenocarcinoma in the list below should be coded by site as for "Neoplasm, malignant."*

- with
  - apocrine metaplasia (M8573/3)
  - cartilaginous (and osseous) metaplasia (M8571/3)
  - osseous (and cartilaginous) metaplasia (M8571/3)
  - spindle cell metaplasia (M8572/3)
  - squamous metaplasia (M8570/3)
- acidophil (M8280/3)
  - specified site — *see* Neoplasm, by site, malignant
  - unspecified site 194.3
- acinar (M8550/3)
- acinic cell (M8550/3)
- adrenal cortical (M8370/3) 194.0
- alveolar (M8251/3)
  - and
    - epidermoid carcinoma, mixed (M8560/3)
    - squamous cell carcinoma, mixed (M8560/3)
- apocrine (M8401/3)
  - breast — *see* Neoplasm, breast, malignant
  - specified site NEC — *see* Neoplasm, skin, malignant
  - unspecified site 173.9
- basophil (M8300/3)
  - specified site — *see* Neoplasm, by site, malignant
  - unspecified site 194.3
- bile duct type (M8160/3)
  - liver 155.1
  - specified site NEC — *see* Neoplasm, by site, malignant
  - unspecified site 155.1
- bronchiolar (M8250/3) — *see* Neoplasm, lung, malignant
- ceruminous (M8420/3) 173.2
- chromophobe (M8270/3)
  - specified site — *see* Neoplasm, by site, malignant
  - unspecified site 194.3
- clear cell (mesonephroid type) (M8310/3)
- colloid (M8480/3)
- cylindroid type (M8200/3)
- diffuse type (M8145/3)
  - specified site — *see* Neoplasm, by site, malignant
  - unspecified site 151.9
- duct (infiltrating) (M8500/3)
  - with Paget's disease (M8541/3) — *see* Neoplasm, breast, malignant
  - specified site — *see* Neoplasm, by site, malignant
  - unspecified site 174.9
- embryonal (M9070/3)
- endometrioid (M8380/3) — *see* Neoplasm, by site, malignant
- eosinophil (M8280/3)
  - specified site — *see* Neoplasm, by site, malignant
  - unspecified site 194.3
- follicular (M8330/3)
  - and papillary (M8340/3) 193
  - moderately differentiated type (M8332/3) 193

Adenocarcinoma — *see also* Neoplasm, by site, malignant — *continued*
- follicular — *continued*
  - pure follicle type (M8331/3) 193
  - specified site — *see* Neoplasm, by site, malignant
  - trabecular type (M8332/3) 193
  - unspecified type 193
  - well differentiated type (M8331/3) 193
- gelatinous (M8480/3)
- granular cell (M8320/3)
- Hürthle cell (M8290/3) 193
- in
  - adenomatous
    - polyp (M8210/3)
    - polyposis coli (M8220/3) 153.9
  - polypoid adenoma (M8210/3)
  - tubular adenoma (M8210/3)
  - villous adenoma (M8261/3)
- infiltrating duct (M8500/3)
  - with Paget's disease (M8541/3) — *see* Neoplasm, breast, malignant
  - specified site — *see* Neoplasm, by site, malignant
  - unspecified site 174.9
- inflammatory (M8530/3)
  - specified site — *see* Neoplasm, by site, malignant
  - unspecified site 174.9
- in situ (M8140/2) — *see* Neoplasm, by site, in situ
- intestinal type (M8144/3)
  - specified site — *see* Neoplasm, by site, malignant
  - unspecified site 151.9
- intraductal (noninfiltrating) (M8500/2)
  - papillary (M8503/2)
    - specified site — *see* Neoplasm, by site, in situ
    - unspecified site 233.0
  - specified site — *see* Neoplasm, by site, in situ
  - unspecified site 233.0
- islet cell (M8150/3)
  - and exocrine, mixed (M8154/3)
    - specified site — *see* Neoplasm, by site, malignant
    - unspecified site 157.9
  - pancreas 157.4
  - specified site NEC — *see* Neoplasm, by site, malignant
  - unspecified site 157.4
- lobular (M8520/3)
  - specified site — *see* Neoplasm, by site, malignant
  - unspecified site 174.9
- medullary (M8510/3)
- mesonephric (M9110/3)
- mixed cell (M8323/3)
- mucinous (M8480/3)
- mucin-producing (M8481/3)
- mucoid (M8480/3) (*see also* Neoplasm, by site, malignant)
  - cell (M8300/3)
    - specified site — *see* Neoplasm, by site, malignant
    - unspecified site 194.3
- nonencapsulated sclerosing (M8350/3) 193
- oncocytic (M8290/3)
- oxyphilic (M8290/3)
- papillary (M8260/3)
  - and follicular (M8340/3) 193
  - intraductal (noninfiltrating) (M8503/2)
    - specified site — *see* Neoplasm, by site, in situ
    - unspecified site 233.0
  - serous (M8460/3)
    - specified site — *see* Neoplasm, by site, malignant
    - unspecified site 183.0

Adenocarcinoma — *see also* Neoplasm, by site, malignant — *continued*
- papillocystic (M8450/3)
  - specified site — *see* Neoplasm, by site, malignant
  - unspecified site 183.0
- pseudomucinous (M8470/3)
  - specified site — *see* Neoplasm, by site, malignant
  - unspecified site 183.0
- renal cell (M8312/3) 189.0
- sebaceous (M8410/3)
- serous (M8441/3) (*see also* Neoplasm, by site, malignant)
  - papillary
    - specified site — *see* Neoplasm, by site, malignant
    - unspecified site 183.0
- signet ring cell (M8490/3)
- superficial spreading (M8143/3)
- sweat gland (M8400/3) — *see* Neoplasm, skin, malignant
- trabecular (M8190/3)
- tubular (M8211/3)
- villous (M8262/3)
- water-clear cell (M8322/3) 194.1

Adenofibroma (M9013/0)
- clear cell (M8313/0) — *see* Neoplasm, by site, benign
- endometrioid (M8381/0) 220
  - borderline malignancy (M8381/1) 236.2
  - malignant (M8381/3) 183.0
- mucinous (M9015/0)
  - specified site — *see* Neoplasm, by site, benign
  - unspecified site 220
- prostate 600.20
  - with
    - other lower urinary tract symptoms (LUTS) 600.21
    - urinary
      - obstruction 600.21
      - retention 600.21
- serous (M9014/0)
  - specified site — *see* Neoplasm, by site, benign
  - unspecified site 220
- specified site — *see* Neoplasm, by site, benign
- unspecified site 220

Adenofibrosis
- breast 610.2
- endometrioid 617.0

Adenoiditis 474.01
- acute 463
- chronic 474.01
  - with chronic tonsillitis 474.02

Adenoids (congenital) (of nasal fossa) 474.9
- hypertrophy 474.12
- vegetations 474.2

Adenolipomatosis (symmetrical) 272.8

Adenolymphoma (M8561/0)
- specified site — *see* Neoplasm, by site, benign
- unspecified 210.2

Adenomatosis (M8220/0)
- endocrine (multiple) (M8360/1)
  - single specified site — *see* Neoplasm, by site, uncertain behavior
  - two or more specified sites 237.4
  - unspecified site 237.4
- erosive of nipple (M8506/0) 217
- pluriendocrine — *see* Adenomatosis, endocrine
- pulmonary (M8250/1) 235.7
  - malignant (M8250/3) — *see* Neoplasm, lung, malignant
- specified site — *see* Neoplasm, by site, benign
- unspecified site 211.3

Adenomatous
- cyst, thyroid (gland) — *see* Goiter, nodular

Adenomatous — *continued*
- goiter (nontoxic) (*see also* Goiter, nodular) 241.9
  - toxic or with hyperthyroidism 242.3 ☑

Adenoma (sessile) (M8140/0) — *see also* Neoplasm, by site, benign

> *Note — Except where otherwise indicated, the morphological varieties of adenoma in the list below should be coded by site as for "Neoplasm, benign."*

- acidophil (M8280/0)
  - specified site — *see* Neoplasm, by site, benign
  - unspecified site 227.3
- acinar (cell) (M8550/0)
- acinic cell (M8550/0)
- adrenal (cortex) (cortical) (functioning) (M8370/0) 227.0
  - clear cell type (M8373/0) 227.0
  - compact cell type (M8371/0) 227.0
  - glomerulosa cell type (M8374/0) 227.0
  - heavily pigmented variant (M8372/0) 227.0
  - mixed cell type (M8375/0) 227.0
- alpha cell (M8152/0)
  - pancreas 211.7
  - specified site NEC — *see* Neoplasm, by site, benign
  - unspecified site 211.7
- alveolar (M8251/0)
- apocrine (M8401/0)
  - breast 217
  - specified site NEC — *see* Neoplasm, skin, benign
  - unspecified site 216.9
- basal cell (M8147/0)
- basophil (M8300/0)
  - specified site — *see* Neoplasm, by site, benign
  - unspecified site 227.3
- beta cell (M8151/0)
  - pancreas 211.7
  - specified site NEC — *see* Neoplasm, by site, benign
  - unspecified site 211.7
- bile duct (M8160/0) 211.5
- black (M8372/0) 227.0
- bronchial (M8140/1) 235.7
  - carcinoid type (M8240/3) — *see* Neoplasm, lung, malignant
  - cylindroid type (M8200/3) — *see* Neoplasm, lung, malignant
- ceruminous (M8420/0) 216.2
- chief cell (M8321/0) 227.1
- chromophobe (M8270/0)
  - specified site — *see* Neoplasm, by site, benign
  - unspecified site 227.3
- clear cell (M8310/0)
- colloid (M8334/0)
  - specified site — *see* Neoplasm, by site, benign
  - unspecified site 226
- cylindroid type, bronchus (M8200/3) — *see* Neoplasm, lung, malignant
- duct (M8503/0)
- embryonal (M8191/0)
- endocrine, multiple (M8360/1)
  - single specified site — *see* Neoplasm, by site, uncertain behavior
  - two or more specified sites 237.4
  - unspecified site 237.4
- endometrioid (M8380/0) (*see also* Neoplasm, by site, benign)
  - borderline malignancy (M8380/1) — *see* Neoplasm, by site, uncertain behavior
- eosinophil (M8280/0)
  - specified site — *see* Neoplasm, by site, benign
  - unspecified site 227.3

- **Adenoma** — *see* also Neoplasm, by site, benign — *continued*
  - fetal (M8333/0)
    - specified site — *see* Neoplasm, by site, benign
    - unspecified site 226
  - follicular (M8330/0)
    - specified site — *see* Neoplasm, by site, benign
    - unspecified site 226
  - hepatocellular (M8170/0) 211.5
  - Hürthle cell (M8290/0) 226
  - intracystic papillary (M8504/0)
  - islet cell (functioning) (M8150/0)
    - pancreas 211.7
    - specified site NEC — *see* Neoplasm, by site, benign
    - unspecified site 211.7
  - liver cell (M8170/0) 211.5
  - macrofollicular (M8334/0)
    - specified site NEC — *see* Neoplasm, by site, benign
    - unspecified site 226
  - malignant, malignum (M8140/3) — *see* Neoplasm, by site, malignant
  - mesonephric (M9110/0)
  - microfollicular (M8333/0)
    - specified site — *see* Neoplasm, by site, benign
    - unspecified site 226
  - mixed cell (M8323/0)
  - monomorphic (M8146/0)
  - mucinous (M8480/0)
  - mucoid cell (M8300/0)
    - specified site — *see* Neoplasm, by site, benign
    - unspecified site 227.3
  - multiple endocrine (M8360/1)
    - single specified site — *see* Neoplasm, by site, uncertain behavior
    - two or more specified sites 237.4
    - unspecified site 237.4
  - nipple (M8506/0) 217
  - oncocytic (M8290/0)
  - oxyphilic (M8290/0)
  - papillary (M8260/0) (*see also* Neoplasm, by site, benign)
    - intracystic (M8504/0)
  - papillotubular (M8263/0)
  - Pick's tubular (M8640/0)
    - specified site — *see* Neoplasm, by site, benign
    - unspecified site
      - female 220
      - male 222.0
  - pleomorphic (M8940/0)
  - polypoid (M8210/0)
  - prostate (benign) 600.20
    - with
      - other lower urinary tract symptoms (LUTS) 600.21
      - urinary
        - obstruction 600.21
        - retention 600.21
  - rete cell 222.0
  - sebaceous, sebaceum (gland) (senile) (M8410/0) (*see also* Neoplasm, skin, benign)
    - disseminata 759.5
  - Sertoli cell (M8640/0)
    - specified site — *see* Neoplasm, by site, benign
    - unspecified site
      - female 220
      - male 222.0
  - skin appendage (M8390/0) — *see* Neoplasm, skin, benign
  - sudoriferous gland (M8400/0) — *see* Neoplasm, skin, benign
  - sweat gland or duct (M8400/0) — *see* Neoplasm, skin, benign
  - testicular (M8640/0)
    - specified site — *see* Neoplasm, by site, benign
- **Adenoma** — *see* also Neoplasm, by site, benign — *continued*
  - testicular — *continued*
    - unspecified site
      - female 220
      - male 222.0
  - thyroid 226
  - trabecular (M8190/0)
  - tubular (M8211/0) (*see also* Neoplasm, by site, benign)
    - papillary (M8460/3)
    - Pick's (M8640/0)
      - specified site — *see* Neoplasm, by site, benign
      - unspecified site
        - female 220
        - male 222.0
  - tubulovillous (M8263/0)
  - villoglandular (M8263/0)
  - villous (M8261/1) — *see* Neoplasm, by site, uncertain behavior
  - water-clear cell (M8322/0) 227.1
  - wolffian duct (M9110/0)
- **Adenomyoma** (M8932/0) — *see also* Neoplasm, by site, benign
  - prostate 600.20
    - with
      - other lower urinary tract symptoms (LUTS) 600.21
      - urinary
        - obstruction 600.21
        - retention 600.21
- **Adenomyometritis** 617.0
- **Adenomyosis** (uterus) (internal) 617.0
- **Adenopathy** (lymph gland) 785.6
  - inguinal 785.6
  - mediastinal 785.6
  - mesentery 785.6
  - syphilitic (secondary) 091.4
  - tracheobronchial 785.6
    - tuberculous (*see also* Tuberculosis) 012.1 ☑
      - primary, progressive 010.8 ☑
  - tuberculous (*see also* Tuberculosis, lymph gland) 017.2 ☑
    - tracheobronchial 012.1 ☑
      - primary, progressive 010.8 ☑
- **Adenopharyngitis** 462
- **Adenophlegmon** 683
- **Adenosalpingitis** 614.1
- **Adenosarcoma** (M8960/3) 189.0
- **Adenosclerosis** 289.3
- **Adenosis**
  - breast (sclerosing) 610.2
  - vagina, congenital 752.49
- **Adentia** (complete) (partial) — *see also* Absence, teeth 520.0
- **Adherent**
  - labium (minus) 624.4
  - pericardium (nonrheumatic) 423.1
    - rheumatic 393
  - placenta 667.0 ☑
    - with hemorrhage 666.0 ☑
  - prepuce 605
  - scar (skin) NEC 709.2
  - tendon in scar 709.2
- **Adhesion(s), adhesive** (postinfectional) (postoperative)
  - abdominal (wall) (*see also* Adhesions, peritoneum) 568.0
  - amnion to fetus 658.8 ☑
    - affecting fetus or newborn 762.8
  - appendix 543.9
  - arachnoiditis — *see* Meningitis
  - auditory tube (Eustachian) 381.89
  - bands (*see also* Adhesions, peritoneum)
    - cervix 622.3
    - uterus 621.5
  - bile duct (any) 576.8
  - bladder (sphincter) 596.8
  - bowel (*see also* Adhesions, peritoneum) 568.0
  - cardiac 423.1
    - rheumatic 398.99
- **Adhesion(s), adhesive** — *continued*
  - cecum (*see also* Adhesions, peritoneum) 568.0
  - cervicovaginal 622.3
    - congenital 752.49
    - postpartal 674.8 ☑
      - old 622.3
  - cervix 622.3
  - clitoris 624.4
  - colon (*see also* Adhesions, peritoneum) 568.0
  - common duct 576.8
  - congenital (*see also* Anomaly, specified type NEC)
    - fingers (*see also* Syndactylism, fingers) 755.11
    - labium (majus) (minus) 752.49
    - omental, anomalous 751.4
    - ovary 752.0
    - peritoneal 751.4
    - toes (*see also* Syndactylism, toes) 755.13
    - tongue (to gum or roof of mouth) 750.12
  - conjunctiva (acquired) (localized) 372.62
    - congenital 743.63
    - extensive 372.63
  - cornea — *see* Opacity, cornea
  - cystic duct 575.8
  - diaphragm (*see also* Adhesions, peritoneum) 568.0
  - due to foreign body — *see* Foreign body
  - duodenum (*see also* Adhesions, peritoneum) 568.0
    - with obstruction 537.3
  - ear, middle — *see* Adhesions, middle ear
  - epididymis 608.89
  - epidural — *see* Adhesions, meninges
  - epiglottis 478.79
  - Eustachian tube 381.89
  - eyelid 374.46
    - postoperative 997.99
      - surgically created V45.69
  - gallbladder (*see also* Disease, gallbladder) 575.8
  - globe 360.89
  - heart 423.1
    - rheumatic 398.99
  - ileocecal (coil) (*see also* Adhesions, peritoneum) 568.0
  - ileum (*see also* Adhesions, peritoneum) 568.0
  - intestine (postoperative) (*see also* Adhesions, peritoneum) 568.0
    - with obstruction 560.81
      - with hernia (*see also* Hernia, by site, with obstruction)
        - gangrenous — *see* Hernia, by site, with gangrene
  - intra-abdominal (*see also* Adhesions, peritoneum) 568.0
  - iris 364.70
    - to corneal graft 996.79
  - joint (*see also* Ankylosis) 718.5 ☑
  - kidney 593.89
  - labium (majus) (minus), congenital 752.49
  - liver 572.8
  - lung 511.0
  - mediastinum 519.3
  - meninges 349.2
    - cerebral (any) 349.2
      - congenital 742.4
    - congenital 742.8
    - spinal (any) 349.2
      - congenital 742.59
    - tuberculous (cerebral) (spinal) (*see also* Tuberculosis, meninges) 013.0 ☑
  - mesenteric (*see also* Adhesions, peritoneum) 568.0
  - middle ear (fibrous) 385.10
    - drum head 385.19
- **Adhesion(s), adhesive** — *continued*
  - middle ear — *continued*
    - drum head — *continued*
      - to
        - incus 385.11
        - promontorium 385.13
        - stapes 385.12
    - specified NEC 385.19
  - nasal (septum) (to turbinates) 478.19
  - nerve NEC 355.9
    - spinal 355.9
      - root 724.9
        - cervical NEC 723.4
        - lumbar NEC 724.4
        - lumbosacral 724.4
        - thoracic 724.4
  - ocular muscle 378.60
  - omentum (*see also* Adhesions, peritoneum) 568.0
  - organ or site, congenital NEC — *see* Anomaly, specified type NEC
  - ovary 614.6
    - congenital (to cecum, kidney, or omentum) 752.0
  - parauterine 614.6
  - parovarian 614.6
  - pelvic (peritoneal)
    - female (postoperative) (postinfection) 614.6
    - male (postoperative) (postinfection) (*see also* Adhesions, peritoneum) 568.0
    - postpartal (old) 614.6
    - tuberculous (*see also* Tuberculosis) 016.9 ☑
  - penis to scrotum (congenital) 752.69
  - periappendiceal (*see also* Adhesions, peritoneum) 568.0
  - pericardium (nonrheumatic) 423.1
    - rheumatic 393
    - tuberculous (*see also* Tuberculosis) 017.9 ☑ *[420.0]*
  - pericholecystic 575.8
  - perigastric (*see also* Adhesions, peritoneum) 568.0
  - periovarian 614.6
  - periprostatic 602.8
  - perirectal (*see also* Adhesions, peritoneum) 568.0
  - perirenal 593.89
  - peritoneum, peritoneal (fibrous) (postoperative) 568.0
    - with obstruction (intestinal) 560.81
      - with hernia (*see also* Hernia, by site, with obstruction)
        - gangrenous — *see* Hernia, by site, with gangrene
      - duodenum 537.3
    - congenital 751.4
    - female (postoperative) (postinfective) 614.6
    - pelvic, female 614.6
    - pelvic, male 568.0
    - postpartal, pelvic 614.6
    - to uterus 614.6
  - peritubal 614.6
  - periureteral 593.89
  - periuterine 621.5
  - perivesical 596.8
  - perivesicular (seminal vesicle) 608.89
  - pleura, pleuritic 511.0
    - tuberculous (*see also* Tuberculosis, pleura) 012.0 ☑
  - pleuropericardial 511.0
  - postoperative (gastrointestinal tract) (*see also* Adhesions, peritoneum) 568.0
    - eyelid 997.99
      - surgically created V45.69
    - pelvic female 614.9
    - pelvic male 568.0
    - urethra 598.2
  - postpartal, old 624.4
  - preputial, prepuce 605
  - pulmonary 511.0

Adhesion(s), adhesive — *continued*
- pylorus (*see also* Adhesions, peritoneum) 568.0
- Rosenmüller's fossa 478.29
- sciatic nerve 355.0
- seminal vesicle 608.89
- shoulder (joint) 726.0
- sigmoid flexure (*see also* Adhesions, peritoneum) 568.0
- spermatic cord (acquired) 608.89
  - congenital 752.89
- spinal canal 349.2
  - nerve 355.9
    - root 724.9
      - cervical NEC 723.4
      - lumbar NEC 724.4
      - lumbosacral 724.4
      - thoracic 724.4
- stomach (*see also* Adhesions, peritoneum) 568.0
- subscapular 726.2
- tendonitis 726.90
  - shoulder 726.0
- testicle 608.89
- tongue (congenital) (to gum or roof of mouth) 750.12
  - acquired 529.8
- trachea 519.19
- tubo-ovarian 614.6
- tunica vaginalis 608.89
- ureter 593.89
- uterus 621.5
  - to abdominal wall 614.6
    - in pregnancy or childbirth 654.4 ☑
      - affecting fetus or newborn 763.89
- vagina (chronic) (postoperative) (postradiation) 623.2
- vaginitis (congenital) 752.49
- vesical 596.8
- vitreous 379.29

Adie (-Holmes) syndrome (tonic pupillary reaction) 379.46

Adiponecrosis neonatorum 778.1

Adiposa dolorosa 272.8

Adiposalgia 272.8

Adiposis
- cerebralis 253.8
- dolorosa 272.8
- tuberosa simplex 272.8

Adiposity 278.02
- heart (*see also* Degeneration, myocardial) 429.1
- localized 278.1

Adiposogenital dystrophy 253.8

Adjustment
- prosthesis or other device — *see* Fitting of
- reaction — *see* Reaction, adjustment

Administration, prophylactic
- antibiotics V07.39
- antitoxin, any V07.2
- antivenin V07.2
- chemotherapeutic agent NEC V07.39
- chemotherapy NEC V07.39
- diphtheria antitoxin V07.2
- fluoride V07.31
- gamma globulin V07.2
- immune sera (gamma globulin) V07.2
- passive immunization agent V07.2
- RhoGAM V07.2

Admission (encounter)
- as organ donor — *see* Donor
- by mistake V68.9
- for
  - adequacy testing (for)
    - hemodialysis V56.31
    - peritoneal dialysis V56.32
  - adjustment (of)
    - artificial
      - arm (complete) (partial) V52.0
      - eye V52.2
      - leg (complete) (partial) V52.1
    - brain neuropacemaker V53.02

Admission — *continued*
- for — *continued*
  - adjustment — *continued*
    - breast
      - implant V52.4
        - exchange (different material) (different size) V52.4 ●
      - prosthesis V52.4
    - cardiac device V53.39
      - defibrillator, automatic implantable V53.32
      - pacemaker V53.31
        - carotid sinus V53.39
    - catheter
      - non-vascular V58.82
      - vascular V58.81
    - cerebral ventricle (communicating) shunt V53.01
    - colostomy belt V55.3
    - contact lenses V53.1
    - cystostomy device V53.6
    - dental prosthesis V52.3
    - device, unspecified type V53.90
      - abdominal V53.5
      - cardiac V53.39
        - defibrillator, automatic implantable V53.32
        - pacemaker V53.31
      - carotid sinus V53.39
      - cerebral ventricle (communicating) shunt V53.01
      - insulin pump V53.91
      - intrauterine contraceptive V25.1
      - nervous system V53.09
      - orthodontic V53.4
      - other device V53.99
      - prosthetic V52.9
        - breast V52.4
        - dental V52.3
        - eye V52.2
        - specified type NEC V52.8
      - special senses V53.09
      - substitution
        - auditory V53.09
        - nervous system V53.09
        - visual V53.09
      - urinary V53.6
    - dialysis catheter
      - extracorporeal V56.1
      - peritoneal V56.2
    - diaphragm (contraceptive) V25.02
    - growth rod V54.02
    - hearing aid V53.2
    - ileostomy device V55.2
    - intestinal appliance or device NEC V53.5
    - intrauterine contraceptive device V25.1
    - neuropacemaker (brain) (peripheral nerve) (spinal cord) V53.02
    - orthodontic device V53.4
    - orthopedic (device) V53.7
      - brace V53.7
      - cast V53.7
      - shoes V53.7
    - pacemaker
      - brain V53.02
      - cardiac V53.31
      - carotid sinus V53.39
      - peripheral nerve V53.02
      - spinal cord V53.02
    - prosthesis V52.9
      - arm (complete) (partial) V52.0
      - breast V52.4
      - dental V52.3
      - eye V52.2
      - leg (complete) (partial) V52.1
      - specified type NEC V52.8
    - spectacles V53.1
    - wheelchair V53.8

Admission — *continued*
- for — *continued*
  - adoption referral or proceedings V68.89
  - aftercare (*see also* Aftercare) V58.9
    - cardiac pacemaker V53.31
    - chemotherapy V58.11
    - dialysis
      - extracorporeal (renal) V56.0
      - peritoneal V56.8
      - renal V56.0
    - fracture (*see also* Aftercare, fracture) V54.9
    - medical NEC V58.89
    - organ transplant V58.44
    - orthopedic V54.9
      - specified care NEC V54.89
    - pacemaker device
      - brain V53.02
      - cardiac V53.31
      - carotid sinus V53.39
      - nervous system V53.02
      - spinal cord V53.02
    - postoperative NEC V58.49
      - wound closure, planned V58.41
    - postpartum
      - immediately after delivery V24.0
      - routine follow-up V24.2
    - postradiation V58.0
    - radiation therapy V58.0
    - removal of
      - non-vascular catheter V58.82
      - vascular catheter V58.81
    - specified NEC V58.89
    - surgical NEC V58.49
      - wound closure, planned V58.41
  - antineoplastic
    - chemotherapy V58.11
    - immunotherapy V58.12
  - artificial insemination V26.1
  - assisted reproductive fertility procedure cycle V26.81
  - attention to artificial opening (of) V55.9
    - artificial vagina V55.7
    - colostomy V55.3
    - cystostomy V55.5
    - enterostomy V55.4
    - gastrostomy V55.1
    - ileostomy V55.2
    - jejunostomy V55.4
    - nephrostomy V55.6
    - specified site NEC V55.8
      - intestinal tract V55.4
      - urinary tract V55.6
    - tracheostomy V55.0
    - ureterostomy V55.6
    - urethrostomy V55.6
  - battery replacement
    - cardiac pacemaker V53.31
  - blood typing V72.86
    - Rh typing V72.86
  - boarding V65.0
  - breast
    - augmentation or reduction V50.1
    - implant exchange (different material) (different size) V52.4 ●
    - reconstruction following mastectomy V51.0 ●
    - removal
      - prophylactic V50.41 ●
      - tissue expander without synchronous insertion of permanent implant V52.4 ●
  - change of
    - cardiac pacemaker (battery) V53.31
    - carotid sinus pacemaker V53.39

Admission — *continued*
- for — *continued*
  - change of — *continued*
    - catheter in artificial opening — *see* Attention to, artificial, opening
    - drains V58.49
    - dressing
      - wound V58.30
        - nonsurgical V58.30
        - surgical V58.31
    - fixation device
      - external V54.89
      - internal V54.01
    - Kirschner wire V54.89
    - neuropacemaker device (brain) (peripheral nerve) (spinal cord) V53.02
    - nonsurgical wound dressing V58.30
    - pacemaker device
      - brain V53.02
      - cardiac V53.31
      - carotid sinus V53.39
      - nervous system V53.02
    - plaster cast V54.89
    - splint, external V54.89
    - Steinmann pin V54.89
    - surgical wound dressing V58.31
    - traction device V54.89
    - wound packing V58.30
      - nonsurgical V58.30
      - surgical V58.31
  - checkup only V70.0
  - chemotherapy, antineoplastic V58.11
  - circumcision, ritual or routine (in absence of medical indication) V50.2
  - clinical research investigation (control) (normal comparison) (participant) V70.7
  - closure of artificial opening — *see* Attention to, artificial, opening
  - contraceptive
    - counseling V25.09
      - emergency V25.03
      - postcoital V25.03
    - management V25.9
      - specified type NEC V25.8
  - convalescence following V66.9
    - chemotherapy V66.2
    - psychotherapy V66.3
    - radiotherapy V66.1
    - surgery V66.0
    - treatment (for) V66.5
      - combined V66.6
      - fracture V66.4
      - mental disorder NEC V66.3
      - specified condition NEC V66.5
  - cosmetic surgery NEC V50.1
    - breast reconstruction following mastectomy V51.0 ●
    - following healed injury or operation V51.8 ▲
  - counseling (*see also* Counseling) V65.40
    - without complaint or sickness V65.49
    - contraceptive management V25.09
      - emergency V25.03
      - postcoital V25.03
    - dietary V65.3
    - exercise V65.41
    - for
      - nonattending third party V65.19
      - pediatric pre-birth visit for expectant mother V65.11
      - victim of abuse
        - child V61.21
        - partner or spouse V61.11

☑ Additional Digit Required — Refer to the Tabular List for Digit Selection

Subterms under main terms may continue to next column or page

▶◀ Revised Text ● New Line ▲ Revised Code

Admission — *continued*
for — *continued*
counseling (*see also* Counseling) — *continued*
genetic V26.33
gonorrhea V65.45
HIV V65.44
human immunodeficiency virus V65.44
injury prevention V65.43
insulin pump training V65.46
natural family planning
procreative V26.41
to avoid pregnancy V25.04
procreative management V26.49
using natural family planning V26.41
sexually transmitted disease NEC V65.45
HIV V65.44
specified reason NEC V65.49
substance use and abuse V65.42
syphilis V65.45
victim of abuse
child V61.21
partner or spouse V61.11
desensitization to allergens V07.1
dialysis V56.0
catheter
fitting and adjustment
extracorporeal V56.1
peritoneal V56.2
removal or replacement
extracorporeal V56.1
peritoneal V56.2
extracorporeal (renal) V56.0
peritoneal V56.8
renal V56.0
dietary surveillance and counseling V65.3
drug monitoring, therapeutic V58.83
ear piercing V50.3
elective surgery V50.9
breast
augmentation or reduction V50.1
reconstruction following mastectomy V51.0 ●
removal, prophylactic V50.41
circumcision, ritual or routine (in absence of medical indication) V50.2
cosmetic NEC V50.1
breast reconstruction following mastectomy V51.0 ●
following healed injury or operation V51.8 ▲
ear piercing V50.3
face-lift V50.1
hair transplant V50.0
plastic
breast reconstruction following mastectomy V51.0 ●
cosmetic NEC V50.1
following healed injury or operation V51.8 ▲
prophylactic organ removal V50.49
breast V50.41
ovary V50.42
repair of scarred tissue (following healed injury or operation) V51.8 ▲
specified type NEC V50.8
end-of-life care V66.7
examination (*see also* Examination) V70.9
administrative purpose NEC V70.3
adoption V70.3
allergy V72.7
at health care facility V70.0

Admission — *continued*
for — *continued*
examination (*see also* Examination) — *continued*
athletic team V70.3
camp V70.3
cardiovascular, preoperative V72.81
clinical research investigation (control) (participant) V70.7
dental V72.2
developmental testing (child) (infant) V20.2
donor (potential) V70.8
driver's license V70.3
ear V72.19
employment V70.5
eye V72.0
follow-up (routine) — *see* Examination, follow-up
for admission to
old age home V70.3
school V70.3
general V70.9
specified reason NEC V70.8
gynecological V72.31
health supervision (child) (infant) V20.2
hearing V72.19
following failed hearing screening V72.11
immigration V70.3
infant, routine V20.2
insurance certification V70.3
laboratory V72.6
marriage license V70.3
medical (general) (*see also* Examination, medical) V70.9
medicolegal reasons V70.4
naturalization V70.3
pelvic (annual) (periodic) V72.31
postpartum checkup V24.2
pregnancy (possible) (unconfirmed) V72.40
negative result V72.41
positive result V72.42
preoperative V72.84
cardiovascular V72.81
respiratory V72.82
specified NEC V72.83
preprocedural V72.84
cardiovascular V72.81
general physical V72.83
respiratory V72.82
specified NEC V72.83
prison V70.3
psychiatric (general) V70.2
requested by authority V70.1
radiological NEC V72.5
respiratory, preoperative V72.82
school V70.3
screening — *see* Screening
skin hypersensitivity V72.7
specified type NEC V72.85
sport competition V70.3
vision V72.0
well baby and child care V20.2
exercise therapy V57.1
face-lift, cosmetic reason V50.1
fitting (of)
artificial
arm (complete) (partial) V52.0
eye V52.2
leg (complete) (partial) V52.1
biliary drainage tube V58.82
brain neuropacemaker V53.02
breast V52.4
implant V52.4
prosthesis V52.4
cardiac pacemaker V53.31
catheter
non-vascular V58.82
vascular V58.81

Admission — *continued*
for — *continued*
fitting — *continued*
cerebral ventricle (communicating) shunt V53.01
chest tube V58.82
colostomy belt V55.2
contact lenses V53.1
cystostomy device V53.6
dental prosthesis V52.3
device, unspecified type V53.90
abdominal V53.5
cerebral ventricle (communicating) shunt V53.01
insulin pump V53.91
intrauterine contraceptive V25.1
nervous system V53.09
orthodontic V53.4
other device V53.99
prosthetic V52.9
breast V52.4
dental V52.3
eye V52.2
special senses V53.09
substitution
auditory V53.09
nervous system V53.09
visual V53.09
diaphragm (contraceptive) V25.02
fistula (sinus tract) drainage tube V58.82
growth rod V54.02
hearing aid V53.2
ileostomy device V55.2
intestinal appliance or device NEC V53.5
intrauterine contraceptive device V25.1
neuropacemaker (brain) (peripheral nerve) (spinal cord) V53.02
orthodontic device V53.4
orthopedic (device) V53.7
brace V53.7
cast V53.7
shoes V53.7
pacemaker
brain V53.02
cardiac V53.31
carotid sinus V53.39
spinal cord V53.02
pleural drainage tube V58.82
portacath V58.81 ●
prosthesis V52.9
arm (complete) (partial) V52.0
breast V52.4
dental V52.3
eye V52.2
leg (complete) (partial) V52.1
specified type NEC V52.8
spectacles V53.1
wheelchair V53.8
follow-up examination (routine) (following) V67.9
cancer chemotherapy V67.2
chemotherapy V67.2
high-risk medication NEC V67.51
injury NEC V67.59
psychiatric V67.3
psychotherapy V67.3
radiotherapy V67.1
specified surgery NEC V67.09
surgery V67.00
vaginal pap smear V67.01
treatment (for) V67.9
combined V67.6
fracture V67.4
involving high-risk medication NEC V67.51
mental disorder V67.3
specified NEC V67.59

Admission — *continued*
for — *continued*
hair transplant, for cosmetic reason V50.0
health advice, education, or instruction V65.4 ☑
hearing conservation and treatment V72.12
hormone replacement therapy (postmenopausal) V07.4
hospice care V66.7
immunotherapy, antineoplastic V58.12
insertion (of)
subdermal implantable contraceptive V25.5
insulin pump titration V53.91
insulin pump training V65.46
intrauterine device
insertion V25.1
management V25.42
investigation to determine further disposition V63.8
in vitro fertilization cycle V26.81
isolation V07.0
issue of
disability examination certificate V68.01
medical certificate NEC V68.09
repeat prescription NEC V68.1
contraceptive device NEC V25.49
kidney dialysis V56.0
lengthening of growth rod V54.02
mental health evaluation V70.2
requested by authority V70.1
natural family planning counseling and advice
procreative V26.41
to avoid pregnancy V25.04
nonmedical reason NEC V68.89
nursing care evaluation V63.8
observation (without need for further medical care) (*see also* Observation) V71.9
accident V71.4
alleged rape or seduction V71.5
criminal assault V71.6
following accident V71.4
at work V71.3
foreign body ingestion V71.89
growth and development variations, childhood V21.0
inflicted injury NEC V71.6
ingestion of deleterious agent or foreign body V71.89
injury V71.6
malignant neoplasm V71.1
mental disorder V71.09
newborn — *see* Observation, suspected, condition, newborn
rape V71.5
specified NEC V71.89
suspected
abuse V71.81
accident V71.4
at work V71.3
benign neoplasm V71.89
cardiovascular V71.7
disorder V71.9 ●
exposure
anthrax V71.82
biological agent NEC V71.83
SARS V71.83
heart V71.7
inflicted injury NEC V71.6
malignant neoplasm V71.1
maternal and fetal problem ●
not found ●
amniotic cavity and membrane V89.01 ●
cervical shortening V89.05 ●
fetal anomaly V89.03 ●

- **Admission** — *continued*
  - for — *continued*
    - observation (*see also* Observation) — *continued*
      - suspected — *continued*
        - maternal and fetal problem not found — *continued*
          - fetal growth V89.04 ●
          - oligohydramnios V89.01 ●
          - other specified NEC V89.09 ●
          - placenta V89.02 ●
          - polyhydramnios V89.01 ●
        - mental NEC V71.09
        - neglect V71.81
        - specified condition NEC V71.89
        - tuberculosis V71.2
      - tuberculosis V71.2
    - occupational therapy V57.21
    - organ transplant, donor — *see* Donor
    - ovary, ovarian removal, prophylactic V50.42
    - palliative care V66.7
    - Papanicolaou smear
      - cervix V76.2
        - for suspected malignant neoplasm V76.2
          - no disease found V71.1
        - routine, as part of gynecological examination V72.31
        - to confirm findings of recent normal smear following initial abnormal smear V72.32
      - vaginal V76.47
        - following hysterectomy for malignant condition V67.01
    - passage of sounds or bougie in artificial opening — *see* Attention to, artificial, opening
    - paternity testing V70.4
    - peritoneal dialysis V56.32
    - physical therapy NEC V57.1
    - plastic surgery
      - breast reconstruction following mastectomy V51.0 ●
      - cosmetic NEC V50.1
      - following healed injury or operation V51.8 ▲
    - postmenopausal hormone replacement therapy V07.4
    - postpartum observation
      - immediately after delivery V24.0
      - routine follow-up V24.2
    - poststerilization (for restoration) V26.0
    - procreative management V26.9
      - assisted reproductive fertility procedure cycle V26.81
      - in vitro fertilization cycle V26.81
      - specified type NEC V26.89
    - prophylactic
      - administration of
        - antibiotics V07.39
        - antitoxin, any V07.2
        - antivenin V07.2
        - chemotherapeutic agent NEC V07.39
        - chemotherapy NEC V07.39
        - diphtheria antitoxin V07.2
        - fluoride V07.31
        - gamma globulin V07.2
        - immune sera (gamma globulin) V07.2
        - RhoGAM V07.2
        - tetanus antitoxin V07.2
      - breathing exercises V57.0
      - chemotherapy NEC V07.39
        - fluoride V07.31
      - measure V07.9
        - specified type NEC V07.8

- **Admission** — *continued*
  - for — *continued*
    - prophylactic — *continued*
      - organ removal V50.49
        - breast V50.41
        - ovary V50.42
    - psychiatric examination (general) V70.2
      - requested by authority V70.1
    - radiation management V58.0
    - radiotherapy V58.0
    - reconstruction following mastectomy V51.0 ●
    - reforming of artificial opening — *see* Attention to, artificial, opening
    - rehabilitation V57.9
      - multiple types V57.89
      - occupational V57.21
      - orthoptic V57.4
      - orthotic V57.81
      - physical NEC V57.1
      - specified type NEC V57.89
      - speech V57.3
      - vocational V57.22
    - removal of
      - breast tissue expander without synchronous insertion of permanent implant V52.4 ●
      - cardiac pacemaker V53.31
      - cast (plaster) V54.89
      - catheter from artificial opening — *see* Attention to, artificial, opening
      - cerebral ventricle (communicating) shunt V53.01
      - cystostomy catheter V55.5
      - device
        - cerebral ventricle (communicating) shunt V53.01
        - fixation
          - external V54.89
          - internal V54.01
        - intrauterine contraceptive V25.42
        - traction, external V54.89
      - drains V58.49
      - dressing
        - wound V58.30
          - nonsurgical V58.30
          - surgical V58.31
      - fixation device
        - external V54.89
        - internal V54.01
      - intrauterine contraceptive device V25.42
      - Kirschner wire V54.89
      - neuropacemaker (brain) (peripheral nerve) (spinal cord) V53.02
      - nonsurgical wound dressing V58.30
      - orthopedic fixation device
        - external V54.89
        - internal V54.01
      - pacemaker device
        - brain V53.02
        - cardiac V53.31
        - carotid sinus V53.39
        - nervous system V53.02
      - plaster cast V54.89
      - plate (fracture) V54.01
      - rod V54.01
      - screw (fracture) V54.01
      - splint, traction V54.89
      - staples V58.32
      - Steinmann pin V54.89
      - subdermal implantable contraceptive V25.43
      - surgical wound dressing V58.31
      - sutures V58.32
      - traction device, external V54.89
      - ureteral stent V53.6
      - wound packing V58.30
        - nonsurgical V58.30

- **Admission** — *continued*
  - for — *continued*
    - removal of — *continued*
      - wound packing — *continued*
        - surgical V58.31
    - repair of scarred tissue (following healed injury or operation) V51.8 ▲
    - reprogramming of cardiac pacemaker V53.31
    - respirator [ventilator] dependence during
      - mechanical failure V46.14
      - power failure V46.12
      - for weaning V46.13
    - restoration of organ continuity (poststerilization) (tuboplasty) (vasoplasty) V26.0
    - Rh typing V72.86
    - sensitivity test (*see also* Test, skin)
      - allergy NEC V72.7
      - bacterial disease NEC V74.9
      - Dick V74.8
      - Kveim V82.89
      - Mantoux V74.1
      - mycotic infection NEC V75.4
      - parasitic disease NEC V75.8
      - Schick V74.3
      - Schultz-Charlton V74.8
    - social service (agency) referral or evaluation V63.8
    - speech therapy V57.3
    - sterilization V25.2
    - suspected disorder (ruled out) (without need for further care) — *see* Observation
    - terminal care V66.7
    - tests only — *see* Test
    - therapeutic drug monitoring V58.83
    - therapy
      - blood transfusion, without reported diagnosis V58.2
      - breathing exercises V57.0
      - chemotherapy, antineoplastic V58.11
        - prophylactic NEC V07.39
          - fluoride V07.31
      - dialysis (intermittent) (treatment)
        - extracorporeal V56.0
        - peritoneal V56.8
        - renal V56.0
        - specified type NEC V56.8
      - exercise (remedial) NEC V57.1
        - breathing V57.0
      - immunotherapy, antineoplastic V58.12
      - long-term (current) drug use NEC V58.69
        - antibiotics V58.62
        - anticoagulants V58.61
        - anti-inflammatories, non-steroidal (NSAID) V58.64
        - antiplatelets V58.63
        - antithrombotics V58.63
        - aspirin V58.66
        - high-risk medications NEC V58.69
        - insulin V58.67
        - methadone V58.69 ●
        - opiate analgesic V58.69 ●
        - steroids V58.65
      - occupational V57.21
      - orthoptic V57.4
      - physical NEC V57.1
      - radiation V58.0
      - speech V57.3
      - vocational V57.22
    - toilet or cleaning
      - of artificial opening — *see* Attention to, artificial, opening
      - of non-vascular catheter V58.82
      - of vascular catheter V58.81
    - tubal ligation V25.2

- **Admission** — *continued*
  - for — *continued*
    - tuboplasty for previous sterilization V26.0
    - ultrasound, routine fetal V28.3 ●
    - vaccination, prophylactic (against)
      - arthropod-borne virus, viral NEC V05.1
        - disease NEC V05.1
        - encephalitis V05.0
      - Bacille Calmette Guérin (BCG) V03.2
      - BCG V03.2
      - chickenpox V05.4
      - cholera alone V03.0
        - with typhoid-paratyphoid (cholera + TAB) V06.0
      - common cold V04.7
      - dengue V05.1
      - diphtheria alone V03.5
      - diphtheria-tetanus-pertussis (DTP) (DTaP) V06.1
        - with
          - poliomyelitis (DTP + polio) V06.3
          - typhoid-paratyphoid (DTP + TAB) V06.2
      - diphtheria-tetanus [Td] [DT] without pertussis V06.5
      - disease (single) NEC V05.9
        - bacterial NEC V03.9
          - specified type NEC V03.89
        - combinations NEC V06.9
          - specified type NEC V06.8
        - specified type NEC V05.8
        - viral NEC V04.89
      - encephalitis, viral, arthropod-borne V05.0
      - Hemophilus influenzae, type B [Hib] V03.81
      - hepatitis, viral V05.3
      - human papillomavirus (HPV) V04.89
      - immune sera (gamma globulin) V07.2
      - influenza V04.81
        - with
          - Streptococcus pneumoniae [pneumococcus] V06.6
      - Leishmaniasis V05.2
      - measles alone V04.2
      - measles-mumps-rubella (MMR) V06.4
      - mumps alone V04.6
        - with measles and rubella (MMR) V06.4
      - not done because of contraindication V64.09
      - pertussis alone V03.6
      - plague V03.3
      - pneumonia V03.82
      - poliomyelitis V04.0
        - with diphtheria-tetanus-pertussis (DTP+ polio) V06.3
      - rabies V04.5
      - respiratory syncytial virus (RSV) V04.82
      - rubella alone V04.3
        - with measles and mumps (MMR) V06.4
      - smallpox V04.1
      - specified type NEC V05.8
      - Streptococcus pneumoniae [pneumococcus] V03.82
        - with
          - influenza V06.6
      - tetanus toxoid alone V03.7
        - with diphtheria [Td] [DT] V06.5
          - and pertussis (DTP) (DTaP) V06.1
      - tuberculosis (BCG) V03.2
      - tularemia V03.4
      - typhoid alone V03.1

- **Admission** — *continued*
  - for — *continued*
    - vaccination, prophylactic — *continued*
      - typhoid alone — *continued*
        - with diphtheria-tetanus-pertussis (TAB + DTP) V06.2
      - typhoid-paratyphoid alone (TAB) V03.1
      - typhus V05.8
      - varicella (chicken pox) V05.4
      - viral encephalitis, arthropod-borne V05.0
      - viral hepatitis V05.3
      - yellow fever V04.4
    - vasectomy V25.2
    - vasoplasty for previous sterilization V26.0
    - vision examination V72.0
    - vocational therapy V57.22
    - waiting period for admission to other facility V63.2
      - undergoing social agency investigation V63.8
    - well baby and child care V20.2
    - x-ray of chest
      - for suspected tuberculosis V71.2
      - routine V72.5
- **Adnexitis** (suppurative) — *see also* Salpingo-oophoritis 614.2
- **Adolescence** NEC V21.2
- **Adoption**
  - agency referral V68.89
  - examination V70.3
  - held for V68.89
- **Adrenal gland** — *see* condition
- **Adrenalism** 255.9
  - tuberculous (*see also* Tuberculosis) 017.6 ☑
- **Adrenalitis, adrenitis** 255.8
  - meningococcal hemorrhagic 036.3
- **Adrenarche, precocious** 259.1
- **Adrenocortical syndrome** 255.2
- **Adrenogenital syndrome** (acquired) (congenital) 255.2
  - iatrogenic, fetus or newborn 760.79
- **Adrenoleukodystrophy** 277.86
  - neonatal 277.86
  - x-linked 277.86
- **Adrenomyeloneuropathy** 277.86
- **Adventitious bursa** — *see* Bursitis
- **Adynamia** (episodica) (hereditary) (periodic) 359.3
- **Adynamic**
  - ileus or intestine (*see also* Ileus) 560.1
  - ureter 753.22
- **Aeration lung, imperfect, newborn** 770.5
- **Aerobullosis** 993.3
- **Aerocele** — *see* Embolism, air
- **Aerodermectasia**
  - subcutaneous (traumatic) 958.7
    - surgical 998.81
  - surgical 998.81
- **Aerodontalgia** 993.2
- **Aeroembolism** 993.3
- **Aerogenes capsulatus infection** — *see also* Gangrene, gas 040.0
- **Aero-otitis media** 993.0
- **Aerophagy, aerophagia** 306.4
  - psychogenic 306.4
- **Aerosinusitis** 993.1
- **Aerotitis** 993.0
- **Affection, affections** — *see also* Disease
  - sacroiliac (joint), old 724.6
  - shoulder region NEC 726.2
- **Afibrinogenemia** 286.3
  - acquired 286.6
  - congenital 286.3
  - postpartum 666.3 ☑
- **African**
  - sleeping sickness 086.5
  - tick fever 087.1
  - trypanosomiasis 086.5
- **African** — *continued*
  - trypanosomiasis — *continued*
    - Gambian 086.3
    - Rhodesian 086.4
- **Aftercare** V58.9
  - amputation stump V54.89
  - artificial openings — *see* Attention to, artificial, opening
  - blood transfusion without reported diagnosis V58.2
  - breathing exercise V57.0
  - cardiac device V53.39
    - defibrillator, automatic implantable V53.32
    - pacemaker V53.31
      - carotid sinus V53.39
  - carotid sinus pacemaker V53.39
  - cerebral ventricle (communicating) shunt V53.01
  - chemotherapy session (adjunctive) (maintenance) V58.11
  - defibrillator, automatic implantable cardiac V53.32
  - exercise (remedial) (therapeutic) V57.1
    - breathing V57.0
  - extracorporeal dialysis (intermittent) (treatment) V56.0
  - following surgery NEC V58.49
    - for
      - injury V58.43
      - neoplasm V58.42
      - organ transplant V58.44
      - trauma V58.43
    - joint replacement V54.81
    - of
      - circulatory system V58.73
      - digestive system V58.75
      - genital organs V58.76
      - genitourinary system V58.76
      - musculoskeletal system V58.78
      - nervous system V58.72
      - oral cavity V58.75
      - respiratory system V58.74
      - sense organs V58.71
      - skin V58.77
      - subcutaneous tissue V58.77
      - teeth V58.75
      - urinary system V58.76
    - spinal — *see* Aftercare, following surgery, of, specified body system
    - wound closure, planned V58.41
  - fracture V54.9
    - healing V54.89
      - pathologic
        - ankle V54.29
        - arm V54.20
          - lower V54.22
          - upper V54.21
        - finger V54.29
        - foot V54.29
        - hand V54.29
        - hip V54.23
        - leg V54.24
          - lower V54.26
          - upper V54.25
        - pelvis V54.29
        - specified site NEC V54.29
        - toe(s) V54.29
        - vertebrae V54.27
        - wrist V54.29
      - traumatic
        - ankle V54.19
        - arm V54.10
          - lower V54.12
          - upper V54.11
        - finger V54.19
        - foot V54.19
        - hand V54.19
        - hip V54.13
        - leg V54.14
          - lower V54.16
          - upper V54.15
        - pelvis V54.19
        - specified site NEC V54.19
        - toe(s) V54.19
- **Aftercare** — *continued*
  - fracture — *continued*
    - healing — *continued*
      - traumatic — *continued*
        - vertebrae V54.17
        - wrist V54.19
    - removal of
      - external fixation device V54.89
      - internal fixation device V54.01
    - specified care NEC V54.89
  - gait training V57.1
    - for use of artificial limb(s) V57.81
  - internal fixation device V54.09
  - involving
    - dialysis (intermittent) (treatment)
      - extracorporeal V56.0
      - peritoneal V56.8
      - renal V56.0
    - gait training V57.1
      - for use of artificial limb(s) V57.81
    - growth rod
      - adjustment V54.02
      - lengthening V54.02
    - internal fixation device V54.09
    - orthoptic training V57.4
    - orthotic training V57.81
    - radiotherapy session V58.0
    - removal of
      - drains V58.49
      - dressings
        - wound V58.30
          - nonsurgical V58.30
          - surgical V58.31
      - fixation device
        - external V54.89
        - internal V54.01
      - fracture plate V54.01
      - nonsurgical wound dressing V58.30
      - pins V54.01
      - plaster cast V54.89
      - rods V54.01
      - screws V58.32
      - staples V58.32
      - surgical wound dressings V58.31
      - sutures V58.32
      - traction device, external V54.89
      - wound packing V58.30
        - nonsurgical V58.30
        - surgical V58.31
    - neuropacemaker (brain) (peripheral nerve) (spinal cord) V53.02
    - occupational therapy V57.21
    - orthodontic V58.5
    - orthopedic V54.9
      - change of external fixation or traction device V54.89
      - following joint replacement V54.81
      - internal fixation device V54.09
      - removal of fixation device
        - external V54.89
        - internal V54.01
      - specified care NEC V54.89
    - orthoptic training V57.4
    - orthotic training V57.81
    - pacemaker
      - brain V53.02
      - cardiac V53.31
      - carotid sinus V53.39
      - peripheral nerve V53.02
      - spinal cord V53.02
    - peritoneal dialysis (intermittent) (treatment) V56.8
    - physical therapy NEC V57.1
      - breathing exercises V57.0
    - radiotherapy session V58.0
    - rehabilitation procedure V57.9
      - breathing exercises V57.0
      - multiple types V57.89
      - occupational V57.21
      - orthoptic V57.4
      - orthotic V57.81
      - physical therapy NEC V57.1
      - remedial exercises V57.1
- **Aftercare** — *continued*
  - rehabilitation procedure — *continued*
    - specified type NEC V57.89
    - speech V57.3
    - therapeutic exercises V57.1
    - vocational V57.22
  - renal dialysis (intermittent) (treatment) V56.0
  - specified type NEC V58.89
    - removal of non-vascular catheter V58.82
    - removal of vascular catheter V58.81
  - speech therapy V57.3
  - stump, amputation V54.89
  - vocational rehabilitation V57.22
- **After-cataract** 366.50
  - obscuring vision 366.53
  - specified type, not obscuring vision 366.52
- **Agalactia** 676.4 ☑
- **Agammaglobulinemia** 279.00
  - with lymphopenia 279.2
  - acquired (primary) (secondary) 279.06
  - Bruton's X-linked 279.04
  - infantile sex-linked (Bruton's) (congenital) 279.04
  - Swiss-type 279.2
- **Aganglionosis** (bowel) (colon) 751.3
- **Age** (old) — *see also* Senile 797
- **Agenesis** — *see also* Absence, by site, congenital
  - acoustic nerve 742.8
  - adrenal (gland) 759.1
  - alimentary tract (complete) (partial) NEC 751.8
    - lower 751.2
    - upper 750.8
  - anus, anal (canal) 751.2
  - aorta 747.22
  - appendix 751.2
  - arm (complete) (partial) (*see also* Deformity, reduction, upper limb) 755.20
  - artery (peripheral) NEC (*see also* Anomaly, peripheral vascular system) 747.60
    - brain 747.81
    - coronary 746.85
    - pulmonary 747.3
    - umbilical 747.5
  - auditory (canal) (external) 744.01
  - auricle (ear) 744.01
  - bile, biliary duct or passage 751.61
  - bone NEC 756.9
  - brain 740.0
    - specified part 742.2
  - breast 757.6
  - bronchus 748.3
  - canaliculus lacrimalis 743.65
  - carpus NEC (*see also* Deformity, reduction, upper limb) 755.28
  - cartilage 756.9
  - cecum 751.2
  - cerebellum 742.2
  - cervix 752.49
  - chin 744.89
  - cilia 743.63
  - circulatory system, part NEC 747.89
  - clavicle 755.51
  - clitoris 752.49
  - coccyx 756.13
  - colon 751.2
  - corpus callosum 742.2
  - cricoid cartilage 748.3
  - diaphragm (with hernia) 756.6
  - digestive organ(s) or tract (complete) (partial) NEC 751.8
    - lower 751.2
    - upper 750.8
  - ductus arteriosus 747.89
  - duodenum 751.1
  - ear NEC 744.09
    - auricle 744.01
    - lobe 744.21

Agenesis — *see also* Absence, by site, congenital — *continued*
ejaculatory duct 752.89
endocrine (gland) NEC 759.2
epiglottis 748.3
esophagus 750.3
Eustachian tube 744.24
extrinsic muscle, eye 743.69
eye 743.00
adnexa 743.69
eyelid (fold) 743.62
face
bones NEC 756.0
specified part NEC 744.89
fallopian tube 752.19
femur NEC (*see also* Absence, femur, congenital) 755.34
fibula NEC (*see also* Absence, fibula, congenital) 755.37
finger NEC (*see also* Absence, finger, congenital) 755.29
foot (complete) (*see also* Deformity, reduction, lower limb) 755.31
gallbladder 751.69
gastric 750.8
genitalia, genital (organ)
female 752.89
external 752.49
internal NEC 752.89
male 752.89
penis 752.69
glottis 748.3
gonadal 758.6
hair 757.4
hand (complete) (*see also* Deformity, reduction, upper limb) 755.21
heart 746.89
valve NEC 746.89
aortic 746.89
mitral 746.89
pulmonary 746.01
hepatic 751.69
humerus NEC (*see also* Absence, humerus, congenital) 755.24
hymen 752.49
ileum 751.1
incus 744.04
intestine (small) 751.1
large 751.2
iris (dilator fibers) 743.45
jaw 524.09
jejunum 751.1
kidney(s) (partial) (unilateral) 753.0
labium (majus) (minus) 752.49
labyrinth, membranous 744.05
lacrimal apparatus (congenital) 743.65
larynx 748.3
leg NEC (*see also* Deformity, reduction, lower limb) 755.30
lens 743.35
limb (complete) (partial) (*see also* Deformity, reduction) 755.4
lower NEC 755.30
upper 755.20
lip 750.26
liver 751.69
lung (bilateral) (fissures) (lobe) (unilateral) 748.5
mandible 524.09
maxilla 524.09
metacarpus NEC 755.28
metatarsus NEC 755.38
muscle (any) 756.81
musculoskeletal system NEC 756.9
nail(s) 757.5
neck, part 744.89
nerve 742.8
nervous system, part NEC 742.8
nipple 757.6
nose 748.1
nuclear 742.8
organ
of Corti 744.05
or site not listed — *see* Anomaly, specified type NEC
osseous meatus (ear) 744.03

Agenesis — *see also* Absence, by site, congenital — *continued*
ovary 752.0
oviduct 752.19
pancreas 751.7
parathyroid (gland) 759.2
patella 755.64
pelvic girdle (complete) (partial) 755.69
penis 752.69
pericardium 746.89
perineal body 756.81
pituitary (gland) 759.2
prostate 752.89
pulmonary
artery 747.3
trunk 747.3
vein 747.49
punctum lacrimale 743.65
radioulnar NEC (*see also* Absence, forearm, congenital) 755.25
radius NEC (*see also* Absence, radius, congenital) 755.26
rectum 751.2
renal 753.0
respiratory organ NEC 748.9
rib 756.3
roof of orbit 742.0
round ligament 752.89
sacrum 756.13
salivary gland 750.21
scapula 755.59
scrotum 752.89
seminal duct or tract 752.89
septum
atrial 745.69
between aorta and pulmonary artery 745.0
ventricular 745.3
shoulder girdle (complete) (partial) 755.59
skull (bone) 756.0
with
anencephalus 740.0
encephalocele 742.0
hydrocephalus 742.3
with spina bifida (*see also* Spina bifida) 741.0 ☑
microcephalus 742.1
spermatic cord 752.89
spinal cord 742.59
spine 756.13
lumbar 756.13
isthmus 756.11
pars articularis 756.11
spleen 759.0
sternum 756.3
stomach 750.7
tarsus NEC 755.38
tendon 756.81
testicular 752.89
testis 752.89
thymus (gland) 759.2
thyroid (gland) 243
cartilage 748.3
tibia NEC (*see also* Absence, tibia, congenital) 755.36
tibiofibular NEC 755.35
toe (complete) (partial) (*see also* Absence, toe, congenital) 755.39
tongue 750.11
trachea (cartilage) 748.3
ulna NEC (*see also* Absence, ulna, congenital) 755.27
ureter 753.4
urethra 753.8
urinary tract NEC 753.8
uterus 752.3
uvula 750.26
vagina 752.49
vas deferens 752.89
vein(s) (peripheral) NEC (*see also* Anomaly, peripheral vascular system) 747.60
brain 747.81
great 747.49
portal 747.49

Agenesis — *see also* Absence, by site, congenital — *continued*
vein(s) (*see also* Anomaly, peripheral vascular system) — *continued*
pulmonary 747.49
vena cava (inferior) (superior) 747.49
vermis of cerebellum 742.2
vertebra 756.13
lumbar 756.13
isthmus 756.11
pars articularis 756.11
vulva 752.49
Ageusia — *see also* Disturbance, sensation 781.1
Aggressiveness 301.3
Aggressive outburst — *see also* Disturbance, conduct 312.0 ☑
in children or adolescents 313.9
Aging skin 701.8
Agitated — *see* condition
Agitation 307.9
catatonic (*see also* Schizophrenia) 295.2 ☑
Aglossia (congenital) 750.11
Aglycogenosis 271.0
Agnail (finger) (with lymphangitis) 681.02
Agnosia (body image) (tactile) 784.69
verbal 784.69
auditory 784.69
secondary to organic lesion 784.69
developmental 315.8
secondary to organic lesion 784.69
visual 368.16
object 368.16 ●
Agoraphobia 300.22
with panic disorder 300.21
Agrammatism 784.69
Agranulocytopenia — *see also* Agranulocytosis 288.09
Agranulocytosis (angina) 288.09
chronic 288.09
cyclical 288.02
genetic 288.01
infantile 288.01
periodic 288.02
pernicious 288.09
Agraphia (absolute) 784.69
with alexia 784.61
developmental 315.39
Agrypnia — *see also* Insomnia 780.52
Ague — *see also* Malaria 084.6
brass-founders' 985.8
dumb 084.6
tertian 084.1
Agyria 742.2
Ahumada-del Castillo syndrome (nonpuerperal galactorrhea and amenorrhea) 253.1
AIDS 042
AIDS-associated retrovirus (disease) (illness) 042
infection — *see* Human immunodeficiency virus, infection
AIDS-associated virus (disease) (illness) 042
infection — *see* Human immunodeficiency virus, infection
AIDS-like disease (illness) (syndrome) 042
AIDS-related complex 042
AIDS-related conditions 042
AIDS-related virus (disease) (illness) 042
infection — *see* Human immunodeficiency virus, infection
AIDS virus (disease) (illness) 042
infection — *see* Human immunodeficiency virus, infection
Ailment, heart — *see* Disease, heart
Ailurophobia 300.29
Ainhum (disease) 136.0
AIN I [anal intraepithelial neoplasia I] (histologically confirmed) 569.44 ● ●
AIN II [anal intraepithelial neoplasia II] (histologically confirmed) 569.44 ● ●

AIN III [anal intraepithelial neoplasia III] 230.6 ● ●
anal canal 230.5 ●
Air
anterior mediastinum 518.1
compressed, disease 993.3
embolism (any site) (artery) (cerebral) 958.0
with
abortion — *see* Abortion, by type, with embolism
ectopic pregnancy (*see also* categories 633.0–633.9) 639.6
molar pregnancy (*see also* categories 630–632) 639.6
due to implanted device — *see* Complications, due to (presence of) any device, implant, or graft classified to 996.0–996.5 NEC
following
abortion 639.6
ectopic or molar pregnancy 639.6
infusion, perfusion, or transfusion 999.1
in pregnancy, childbirth, or puerperium 673.0 ☑
traumatic 958.0
hunger 786.09
psychogenic 306.1
leak (lung) (pulmonary) (thorax) 512.8
iatrogenic 512.1
postoperative 512.1
rarefied, effects of — *see* Effect, adverse, high altitude
sickness 994.6
Airplane sickness 994.6
Akathisia, acathisia 781.0
due to drugs 333.99
neuroleptic-induced acute 333.99
Akinesia algeria 352.6
Akiyami 100.89
Akureyri disease (epidemic neuromyasthenia) 049.8
Alacrima (congenital) 743.65
Alactasia (hereditary) 271.3
Alagille syndrome 759.89
Alalia 784.3
developmental 315.31
receptive-expressive 315.32
secondary to organic lesion 784.3
Alaninemia 270.8
Alastrim 050.1
Albarrán's disease (colibacilluria) 791.9
Albers-Schönberg's disease (marble bones) 756.52
Albert's disease 726.71
Albinism, albino (choroid) (cutaneous) (eye) (generalized) (isolated) (ocular) (oculocutaneous) (partial) 270.2
Albinismus 270.2
Albright (-Martin) (-Bantam) disease (pseudohypoparathyroidism) 275.49
Albright (-McCune) (-Sternberg) syndrome (osteitis fibrosa disseminata) 756.59
Albuminous — *see* condition
Albuminuria, albuminuric (acute) (chronic) (subacute) 791.0
Bence-Jones 791.0
cardiac 785.9
complicating pregnancy, childbirth, or puerperium 646.2 ☑
with hypertension — *see* Toxemia, of pregnancy
affecting fetus or newborn 760.1
cyclic 593.6
gestational 646.2 ☑
gravidarum 646.2 ☑
with hypertension — *see* Toxemia, of pregnancy
affecting fetus or newborn 760.1
heart 785.9

☑ Additional Digit Required — Refer to the Tabular List for Digit Selection
Subterms under main terms may continue to next column or page

- **Albuminuria, albuminuric** — *continued*
  - idiopathic 593.6
  - orthostatic 593.6
  - postural 593.6
  - pre-eclamptic (mild) 642.4 ☑
    - affecting fetus or newborn 760.0
    - severe 642.5 ☑
      - affecting fetus or newborn 760.0
  - recurrent physiologic 593.6
  - scarlatinal 034.1
- **Albumosuria** 791.0
  - Bence-Jones 791.0
  - myelopathic (M9730/3) 203.0 ☑
- **Alcaptonuria** 270.2
- **Alcohol, alcoholic**
  - abstinence 291.81
  - acute intoxication 305.0 ☑
    - with dependence 303.0 ☑
  - addiction (*see also* Alcoholism) 303.9 ☑
    - maternal
      - with suspected fetal damage affecting management of pregnancy 655.4 ☑
      - affecting fetus or newborn 760.71
  - amnestic disorder, persisting 291.1
  - anxiety 291.89
  - brain syndrome, chronic 291.2
  - cardiopathy 425.5
  - chronic (*see also* Alcoholism) 303.9 ☑
  - cirrhosis (liver) 571.2
  - delirium 291.0
    - acute 291.0
    - chronic 291.1
    - tremens 291.0
    - withdrawal 291.0
  - dementia NEC 291.2
  - deterioration 291.2
  - drunkenness (simple) 305.0 ☑
  - hallucinosis (acute) 291.3
  - induced
    - circadian rhythm sleep disorder 291.82
    - hypersomnia 291.82
    - insomnia 291.82
    - mental disorder 291.9
      - anxiety 291.89
      - mood 291.89
      - sexual 291.89
      - sleep 291.82
      - specified type 291.89
    - parasomnia 291.82
    - persisting
      - amnestic disorder 291.1
      - dementia 291.2
    - psychotic disorder
      - with
        - delusions 291.5
        - hallucinations 291.3
    - sleep disorder 291.82
  - insanity 291.9
  - intoxication (acute) 305.0 ☑
    - with dependence 303.0 ☑
    - pathological 291.4
  - jealousy 291.5
  - Korsakoff's, Korsakov's, Korsakow's 291.1
  - liver NEC 571.3
    - acute 571.1
    - chronic 571.2
  - mania (acute) (chronic) 291.9
  - mood 291.89
  - paranoia 291.5
  - paranoid (type) psychosis 291.5
  - pellagra 265.2
  - poisoning, accidental (acute) NEC 980.9
    - specified type of alcohol — *see* Table of Drugs and Chemicals
  - psychosis (*see also* Psychosis, alcoholic) 291.9
    - Korsakoff's, Korsakov's, Korsakow's 291.1
    - polyneuritic 291.1
- **Alcohol, alcoholic** — *continued*
  - psychosis (*see also* Psychosis, alcoholic) — *continued*
    - polyneuritic — *continued*
      - with
        - delusions 291.5
        - hallucinations 291.3
  - related disorder 291.9
  - withdrawal symptoms, syndrome NEC 291.81
    - delirium 291.0
    - hallucinosis 291.3
- **Alcoholism** 303.9 ☑

> *Note — Use the following fifth-digit subclassification with category 303:*
>
> 0 *unspecified*
>
> 1 *continuous*
>
> 2 *episodic*
>
> 3 *in remission*

-
  - with psychosis (*see also* Psychosis, alcoholic) 291.9
  - acute 303.0 ☑
  - chronic 303.9 ☑
    - with psychosis 291.9
  - complicating pregnancy, childbirth, or puerperium 648.4 ☑
    - affecting fetus or newborn 760.71
  - history V11.3
  - Korsakoff's, Korsakov's, Korsakow's 291.1
  - suspected damage to fetus affecting management of pregnancy 655.4 ☑
- **Alder's anomaly or syndrome** (leukocyte granulation anomaly) 288.2
- **Alder-Reilly anomaly** (leukocyte granulation) 288.2
- **Aldosteronism** (primary) 255.10
  - congenital 255.10
  - familial type I 255.11
  - glucocorticoid-remediable 255.11
  - secondary 255.14
- **Aldosteronoma** (M8370/1) 237.2
- **Aldrich (-Wiskott) syndrome** (eczema thrombocytopenia) 279.12
- **Aleppo boil** 085.1
- **Aleukemic** — *see* condition
- **Aleukia**
  - congenital 288.09
  - hemorrhagica 284.9
    - acquired (secondary) 284.89
    - congenital 284.09
    - idiopathic 284.9
  - splenica 289.4
- **Alexia** (congenital) (developmental) 315.01
  - secondary to organic lesion 784.61
- **Algoneurodystrophy** 733.7
- **Algophobia** 300.29
- **Alibert-Bazin disease** (M9700/3) 202.1 ☑
- **Alibert's disease** (mycosis fungoides) (M9700/3) 202.1 ☑
- **Alice in Wonderland syndrome** 293.89
- **Alienation, mental** — *see also* Psychosis 298.9
- **Alkalemia** 276.3
- **Alkalosis** 276.3
  - metabolic 276.3
    - with respiratory acidosis 276.4
  - respiratory 276.3
- **Alkaptonuria** 270.2
- **Allen-Masters syndrome** 620.6
- **Allergic bronchopulmonary aspergillosis** 518.6
- **Allergy, allergic** (reaction) 995.3
  - air-borne substance — *see also* Fever, hay 477.9
    - specified allergen NEC 477.8
  - alveolitis (extrinsic) 495.9
    - due to
      - Aspergillus clavatus 495.4
      - cryptostroma corticale 495.6
- **Allergy, allergic** — *continued*
  - alveolitis — *continued*
    - due to — *continued*
      - organisms (fungal, thermophilic actinomycete, other) growing in ventilation (air conditioning systems) 495.7
    - specified type NEC 495.8
  - anaphylactic shock 999.4
    - due to food — *see* Anaphylactic shock, due to, food
  - angioneurotic edema 995.1
  - animal (cat) (dog) (epidermal) 477.8
    - dander 477.2
    - hair 477.2
  - arthritis (*see also* Arthritis, allergic) 716.2 ☑
  - asthma — *see* Asthma
  - bee sting (anaphylactic shock) 989.5
  - biological — *see* Allergy, drug
  - bronchial asthma — *see* Asthma
  - conjunctivitis (eczematous) 372.14
  - dander, animal (cat) (dog) 477.2
  - dandruff 477.8
  - dermatitis (venenata) — *see* Dermatitis
  - diathesis V15.09
  - drug, medicinal substance, and biological (any) (correct medicinal substance properly administered) (external) (internal) 995.27
    - wrong substance given or taken NEC 977.9
      - specified drug or substance — *see* Table of Drugs and Chemicals
  - dust (house) (stock) 477.8
  - eczema — *see* Eczema
  - endophthalmitis 360.19
  - epidermal (animal) 477.8
  - existing dental restorative material 525.66
  - feathers 477.8
  - food (any) (ingested) 693.1
    - atopic 691.8
    - in contact with skin 692.5
  - gastritis 535.4 ☑
  - gastroenteritis 558.3
  - gastrointestinal 558.3
  - grain 477.0
  - grass (pollen) 477.0
    - asthma (*see also* Asthma) 493.0 ☑
    - hay fever 477.0
  - hair, animal (cat) (dog) 477.2
  - hay fever (grass) (pollen) (ragweed) (tree) (*see also* Fever, hay) 477.9
  - history (of) V15.09
    - to
      - eggs V15.03
      - food additives V15.05
      - insect bite V15.06
      - latex V15.07
      - milk products V15.02
      - nuts V15.05
        - peanuts V15.01
      - radiographic dye V15.08
      - seafood V15.04
      - specified food NEC V15.05
      - spider bite V15.06
  - horse serum — see Allergy, serum
  - inhalant 477.9
    - dust 477.8
    - pollen 477.0
    - specified allergen other than pollen 477.8
  - kapok 477.8
  - medicine — *see* Allergy, drug
  - migraine 339.00 ▲
  - milk protein 558.3
  - pannus 370.62
  - pneumonia 518.3
  - pollen (any) (hay fever) 477.0
    - asthma (*see also* Asthma) 493.0 ☑
  - primrose 477.0
- **Allergy, allergic** — *continued*
  - primula 477.0
  - purpura 287.0
  - ragweed (pollen) (Senecio jacobae) 477.0
    - asthma (*see also* Asthma) 493.0 ☑
    - hay fever 477.0
  - respiratory (*see also* Allergy, inhalant) 477.9
    - due to
      - drug — *see* Allergy, drug
      - food — *see* Allergy, food
  - rhinitis (*see also* Fever, hay) 477.9
    - due to food 477.1
  - rose 477.0
  - Senecio jacobae 477.0
  - serum (prophylactic) (therapeutic) 999.5
    - anaphylactic shock 999.4
  - shock (anaphylactic) (due to adverse effect of correct medicinal substance properly administered) 995.0
    - food — *see* Anaphylactic shock, due to, food
    - from serum or immunization 999.5
      - anaphylactic 999.4
  - sinusitis (*see also* Fever, hay) 477.9
  - skin reaction 692.9
    - specified substance — *see* Dermatitis, due to
  - tree (any) (hay fever) (pollen) 477.0
    - asthma (*see also* Asthma) 493.0 ☑
  - upper respiratory (*see also* Fever, hay) 477.9
  - urethritis 597.89
  - urticaria 708.0
  - vaccine — *see* Allergy, serum
- **Allescheriosis** 117.6
- **Alligator skin disease** (ichthyosis congenita) 757.1
  - acquired 701.1
- **Allocheiria, allochiria** — *see also* Disturbance, sensation 782.0
- **Almeida's disease** (Brazilian blastomycosis) 116.1
- **Alopecia** (atrophicans) (pregnancy) (premature) (senile) 704.00
  - adnata 757.4
  - areata 704.01
  - celsi 704.01
  - cicatrisata 704.09
  - circumscripta 704.01
  - congenital, congenitalis 757.4
  - disseminata 704.01
  - effluvium (telogen) 704.02
  - febrile 704.09
  - generalisata 704.09
  - hereditaria 704.09
  - marginalis 704.01
  - mucinosa 704.09
  - postinfectional 704.09
  - seborrheica 704.09
  - specific 091.82
  - syphilitic (secondary) 091.82
  - telogen effluvium 704.02
  - totalis 704.09
  - toxica 704.09
  - universalis 704.09
  - x-ray 704.09
- **Alpers' disease** 330.8
- **Alpha-lipoproteinemia** 272.4
- **Alpha thalassemia** 282.49
- **Alphos** 696.1
- **Alpine sickness** 993.2
- **Alport's syndrome** (hereditary hematurianephropathy-deafness) 759.89
- **Alteration** (of), altered
  - awareness 780.09
    - transient 780.02
  - consciousness 780.09
    - persistent vegetative state 780.03
    - transient 780.02
  - mental status 780.97
    - amnesia (retrograde) 780.93
    - memory loss 780.93

- **Alternaria** (infection) 118
- **Alternating** — *see* condition
- **Altitude, high** (effects) — *see* Effect, adverse, high altitude
- **Aluminosis** (of lung) 503
- **Alvarez syndrome** (transient cerebral ischemia) 435.9
- **Alveolar capillary block syndrome** 516.3
- **Alveolitis**
  - allergic (extrinsic) 495.9
    - due to organisms (fungal, thermophilic actinomycete, other) growing in ventilation (air conditioning systems) 495.7
    - specified type NEC 495.8
  - due to
    - Aspergillus clavatus 495.4
    - Cryptostroma corticale 495.6
  - fibrosing (chronic) (cryptogenic) (lung) 516.3
    - idiopathic 516.3
    - rheumatoid 714.81
  - jaw 526.5
  - sicca dolorosa 526.5
- **Alveolus, alveolar** — *see* condition
- **Alymphocytosis** (pure) 279.2
- **Alymphoplasia, thymic** 279.2
- **Alzheimer's**
  - dementia (senile)
    - with behavioral disturbance 331.0 *[294.11]*
    - without behavioral disturbance 331.0 *[294.10]*
  - disease or sclerosis 331.0
    - with dementia — *see* Alzheimer's, dementia
- **Amastia** — *see also* Absence, breast 611.89 ▲
- **Amaurosis** (acquired) (congenital) — *see also* Blindness 369.00
  - fugax 362.34
  - hysterical 300.11
  - Leber's (congenital) 362.76
  - tobacco 377.34
  - uremic — *see* Uremia
- **Amaurotic familial idiocy** (infantile) (juvenile) (late) 330.1
- **Ambisexual** 752.7
- **Amblyopia** (acquired) (congenital) (partial) 368.00
  - color 368.59
    - acquired 368.55
  - deprivation 368.02
  - ex anopsia 368.00
  - hysterical 300.11
  - nocturnal 368.60
    - vitamin A deficiency 264.5
  - refractive 368.03
  - strabismic 368.01
  - suppression 368.01
  - tobacco 377.34
  - toxic NEC 377.34
  - uremic — *see* Uremia
- **Ameba, amebic** (histolytica) — *see also* Amebiasis
  - abscess 006.3
    - bladder 006.8
    - brain (with liver and lung abscess) 006.5
    - liver 006.3
      - with
        - brain abscess (and lung abscess) 006.5
        - lung abscess 006.4
    - lung (with liver abscess) 006.4
      - with brain abscess 006.5
    - seminal vesicle 006.8
    - spleen 006.8
  - carrier (suspected of) V02.2
  - meningoencephalitis
    - due to Naegleria (gruberi) 136.29 ▲
    - primary 136.29 ▲
- **Amebiasis** NEC 006.9
- **Amebiasis** — *continued*
  - with
    - brain abscess (with liver or lung abscess) 006.5
    - liver abscess (without mention of brain or lung abscess) 006.3
    - lung abscess (with liver abscess) 006.4
      - with brain abscess 006.5
  - acute 006.0
  - bladder 006.8
  - chronic 006.1
  - cutaneous 006.6
  - cutis 006.6
  - due to organism other than Entamoeba histolytica 007.8
  - hepatic (*see also* Abscess, liver, amebic) 006.3
  - nondysenteric 006.2
  - seminal vesicle 006.8
  - specified
    - organism NEC 007.8
    - site NEC 006.8
- **Ameboma** 006.8
- **Amelia** 755.4
  - lower limb 755.31
  - upper limb 755.21
- **Ameloblastoma** (M9310/0) 213.1
  - jaw (bone) (lower) 213.1
    - upper 213.0
  - long bones (M9261/3) — *see* Neoplasm, bone, malignant
  - malignant (M9310/3) 170.1
    - jaw (bone) (lower) 170.1
      - upper 170.0
  - mandible 213.1
  - tibial (M9261/3) 170.7
- **Amelogenesis imperfecta** 520.5
  - nonhereditaria (segmentalis) 520.4
- **Amenorrhea** (primary) (secondary) 626.0
  - due to ovarian dysfunction 256.8
  - hyperhormonal 256.8
- **Amentia** — *see also* Retardation, mental 319
  - Meynert's (nonalcoholic) 294.0
    - alcoholic 291.1
  - nevoid 759.6
- **American**
  - leishmaniasis 085.5
  - mountain tick fever 066.1
  - trypanosomiasis — *see* Trypanosomiasis, American
- **Ametropia** — *see also* Disorder, accommodation 367.9
- **Amianthosis** 501
- **Amimia** 784.69
- **Amino acid**
  - deficiency 270.9
    - anemia 281.4
  - metabolic disorder (*see also* Disorder, amino acid) 270.9
- **Aminoaciduria** 270.9
  - imidazole 270.5
- **Amnesia** (retrograde) 780.93
  - auditory 784.69
    - developmental 315.31
    - secondary to organic lesion 784.69
  - dissociative 300.12
  - hysterical or dissociative type 300.12
  - psychogenic 300.12
  - transient global 437.7
- **Amnestic** (confabulatory) **syndrome** 294.0
  - alcohol-induced persisting 291.1
  - drug-induced persisting 292.83
  - posttraumatic 294.0
- **Amniocentesis screening** (for) V28.2
  - alphafetoprotein level, raised V28.1
  - chromosomal anomalies V28.0
- **Amnion, amniotic** — *see also* condition
  - nodosum 658.8 ☑
- **Amnionitis** (complicating pregnancy) 658.4 ☑
  - affecting fetus or newborn 762.7
- **Amoral trends** 301.7
- **Amotio retinae** — *see also* Detachment, retina 361.9
- **Ampulla**
  - lower esophagus 530.89
  - phrenic 530.89
- **Amputation**
  - any part of fetus, to facilitate delivery 763.89
  - cervix (supravaginal) (uteri) 622.8
    - in pregnancy or childbirth 654.6 ☑
      - affecting fetus or newborn 763.89
  - clitoris — *see* Wound, open, clitoris
  - congenital
    - lower limb 755.31
    - upper limb 755.21
  - neuroma (traumatic) (*see also* Injury, nerve, by site)
    - surgical complication (late) 997.61
  - penis — *see* Amputation, traumatic, penis
  - status (without complication) — *see* Absence, by site, acquired
  - stump (surgical) (posttraumatic)
    - abnormal, painful, or with complication (late) 997.60
    - healed or old NEC (*see also* Absence, by site, acquired)
      - lower V49.70
      - upper V49.60
  - traumatic (complete) (partial)

> *Note — "Complicated" includes traumatic amputation with delayed healing, delayed treatment, foreign body, or infection.*

  - arm 887.4
    - at or above elbow 887.2
      - complicated 887.3
    - below elbow 887.0
      - complicated 887.1
    - both (bilateral) (any level(s)) 887.6
      - complicated 887.7
    - complicated 887.5
  - finger(s) (one or both hands) 886.0
    - with thumb(s) 885.0
      - complicated 885.1
    - complicated 886.1
  - foot (except toe(s) only) 896.0
    - and other leg 897.6
      - complicated 897.7
    - both (bilateral) 896.2
      - complicated 896.3
    - complicated 896.1
    - toe(s) only (one or both feet) 895.0
      - complicated 895.1
  - genital organ(s) (external) NEC 878.8
    - complicated 878.9
  - hand (except finger(s) only) 887.0
    - and other arm 887.6
      - complicated 887.7
    - both (bilateral) 887.6
      - complicated 887.7
    - complicated 887.1
    - finger(s) (one or both hands) 886.0
      - with thumb(s) 885.0
        - complicated 885.1
      - complicated 886.1
    - thumb(s) (with fingers of either hand) 885.0
      - complicated 885.1
  - head 874.9
  - late effect — *see* Late, effects (of), amputation
  - leg 897.4
    - and other foot 897.6
      - complicated 897.7
    - at or above knee 897.2
      - complicated 897.3
    - below knee 897.0
      - complicated 897.1
    - both (bilateral) 897.6
      - complicated 897.7
- **Amputation** — *continued*
  - traumatic — *continued*
    - leg — *continued*
      - complicated 897.5
    - lower limb(s) except toe(s) — *see* Amputation, traumatic, leg
    - nose — *see* Wound, open, nose
    - penis 878.0
      - complicated 878.1
    - sites other than limbs — *see* Wound, open, by site
    - thumb(s) (with finger(s) of either hand) 885.0
      - complicated 885.1
    - toe(s) (one or both feet) 895.0
      - complicated 895.1
    - upper limb(s) — *see* Amputation, traumatic, arm
- **Amputee** (bilateral) (old) — *see also* Absence, by site, acquired V49.70
- **Amusia** 784.69
  - developmental 315.39
  - secondary to organic lesion 784.69
- **Amyelencephalus** 740.0
- **Amyelia** 742.59
- **Amygdalitis** — *see* Tonsillitis
- **Amygdalolith** 474.8
- **Amyloid disease or degeneration** 277.30
  - heart 277.39 *[425.7]*
- **Amyloidosis** (familial) (general) (generalized) (genetic) (primary) 277.30 ▲
  - with lung involvement 277.39 *[517.8]*
  - cardiac, hereditary 277.39
  - heart 277.39 *[425.7]*
  - nephropathic 277.39 *[583.81]*
  - neuropathic (Portuguese) (Swiss) 277.39 *[357.4]*
  - pulmonary 277.39 *[517.8]*
  - secondary 277.39
  - systemic, inherited 277.39
- **Amylopectinosis** (brancher enzyme deficiency) 271.0
- **Amylophagia** 307.52
- **Amyoplasia, congenita** 756.89
- **Amyotonia** 728.2
  - congenita 358.8
- **Amyotrophia, amyotrophy, amyotrophic** 728.2
  - congenita 756.89
  - diabetic 250.6 ☑ *[353.5]* ▲
    - due to secondary diabetes ● 249.6 ☑ *[353.5]* ●
  - lateral sclerosis (syndrome) 335.20
  - neuralgic 353.5
  - sclerosis (lateral) 335.20
  - spinal progressive 335.21
- **Anacidity, gastric** 536.0
  - psychogenic 306.4
- **Anaerosis of newborn** 770.88
- **Analbuminemia** 273.8
- **Analgesia** — *see also* Anesthesia 782.0
- **Analphalipoproteinemia** 272.5
- **Anaphylactic shock or reaction** (correct substance properly administered) 995.0
  - due to
    - food 995.60
      - additives 995.66
      - crustaceans 995.62
      - eggs 995.68
      - fish 995.65
      - fruits 995.63
      - milk products 995.67
      - nuts (tree) 995.64
      - peanuts 995.61
      - seeds 995.64
      - specified NEC 995.69
      - tree nuts 995.64
      - vegetables 995.63
    - immunization 999.4
    - overdose or wrong substance given or taken 977.9
      - specified drug — *see* Table of Drugs and Chemicals

Anaphylactic shock or reaction — *continued*
due to — *continued*
serum 999.4
following sting(s) 989.5
purpura 287.0
serum 999.4
Anaphylactoid shock or reaction — *see* Anaphylactic shock
Anaphylaxis — *see* Anaphylactic shock
Anaplasia, cervix 622.10
Anarthria 784.5
Anarthritic rheumatoid disease 446.5
Anasarca 782.3
cardiac (*see also* Failure, heart) 428.0
fetus or newborn 778.0
lung 514
nutritional 262
pulmonary 514
renal (*see also* Nephrosis) 581.9
Anaspadias 752.62
Anastomosis
aneurysmal — *see* Aneurysm
arteriovenous, congenital NEC (*see also* Anomaly, arteriovenous) 747.60
ruptured, of brain (*see also* Hemorrhage, subarachnoid) 430
intestinal 569.89
complicated NEC 997.4
involving urinary tract 997.5
retinal and choroidal vessels 743.58
acquired 362.17
Anatomical narrow angle (glaucoma) 365.02
Ancylostoma (infection) (infestation) 126.9
americanus 126.1
braziliense 126.2
caninum 126.8
ceylanicum 126.3
duodenale 126.0
Necator americanus 126.1
Ancylostomiasis (intestinal) 126.9
ancylostoma
americanus 126.1
caninum 126.8
ceylanicum 126.3
duodenale 126.0
braziliense 126.2
Necator americanus 126.1
Anders' disease or syndrome (adiposis tuberosa simplex) 272.8
Andersen's glycogen storage disease 271.0
Anderson's disease 272.7
Andes disease 993.2
Andrews' disease (bacterid) 686.8
Androblastoma (M8630/1)
benign (M8630/0)
specified site — *see* Neoplasm, by site, benign
unspecified site
female 220
male 222.0
malignant (M8630/3)
specified site — *see* Neoplasm, by site, malignant
unspecified site
female 183.0
male 186.9
specified site — *see* Neoplasm, by site, uncertain behavior
tubular (M8640/0)
with lipid storage (M8641/0)
specified site — *see* Neoplasm, by site, benign
unspecified site
female 220
male 222.0
specified site — *see* Neoplasm, by site, benign
unspecified site
female 220
male 222.0
Androblastoma — *continued*
unspecified site
female 236.2
male 236.4
Android pelvis 755.69
with disproportion (fetopelvic) 653.3 ☑
affecting fetus or newborn 763.1
causing obstructed labor 660.1 ☑
affecting fetus or newborn 763.1
Anectasis, pulmonary (newborn or fetus) 770.5
Anemia 285.9
with
disorder of
anaerobic glycolysis 282.3
pentose phosphate pathway 282.2
koilonychia 280.9
6-phosphogluconic dehydrogenase deficiency 282.2
achlorhydric 280.9
achrestic 281.8
Addison's (pernicious) 281.0
Addison-Biermer (pernicious) 281.0
agranulocytic 288.09
amino acid deficiency 281.4
aplastic 284.9
acquired (secondary) 284.89 ▲
congenital 284.01
constitutional 284.01
due to
antineoplastic chemotherapy 284.89 ●
chronic systemic disease 284.89
drugs 284.89
infection 284.89
radiation 284.89
idiopathic 284.9
myxedema 244.9
of or complicating pregnancy 648.2 ☑
red cell (acquired) (adult) (with thymoma) 284.81
congenital 284.01
pure 284.01
specified type NEC 284.89
toxic (paralytic) 284.89
aregenerative 284.9
congenital 284.01
asiderotic 280.9
atypical (primary) 285.9
autohemolysis of Selwyn and Dacie (type I) 282.2
autoimmune hemolytic 283.0
Baghdad Spring 282.2
Balantidium coli 007.0
Biermer's (pernicious) 281.0
blood loss (chronic) 280.0
acute 285.1
bothriocephalus 123.4
brickmakers' (*see also* Ancylostomiasis) 126.9
cerebral 437.8
childhood 282.9
chlorotic 280.9
chronica congenita aregenerativa 284.01
chronic simple 281.9
combined system disease NEC 281.0 *[336.2]*
due to dietary deficiency 281.1 *[336.2]*
complicating pregnancy or childbirth 648.2 ☑
congenital (following fetal blood loss) 776.5
aplastic 284.01
due to isoimmunization NEC 773.2
Heinz-body 282.7
hereditary hemolytic NEC 282.9
nonspherocytic
Type I 282.2
Type II 282.3
pernicious 281.0
spherocytic (*see also* Spherocytosis) 282.0
Anemia — *continued*
Cooley's (erythroblastic) 282.49
crescent — *see* Disease, sickle-cell
cytogenic 281.0
Dacie's (nonspherocytic)
type I 282.2
type II 282.3
Davidson's (refractory) 284.9
deficiency 281.9
2, 3 diphosphoglycurate mutase 282.3
2, 3 PG 282.3
6-PGD 282.2
6-phosphogluronic dehydrogenase 282.2
amino acid 281.4
combined B_{12} and folate 281.3
enzyme, drug-induced (hemolytic) 282.2
erythrocytic glutathione 282.2
folate 281.2
dietary 281.2
drug-induced 281.2
folic acid 281.2
dietary 281.2
drug-induced 281.2
G-6-PD 282.2
GGS-R 282.2
glucose-6-phosphate dehydrogenase (G-6-PD) 282.2
glucose-phosphate isomerase 282.3
glutathione peroxidase 282.2
glutathione reductase 282.2
glyceraldehyde phosphate dehydrogenase 282.3
GPI 282.3
G SH 282.2
hexokinase 282.3
iron (Fe) 280.9
specified NEC 280.8
nutritional 281.9
with
poor iron absorption 280.9
specified deficiency NEC 281.8
due to inadequate dietary iron intake 280.1
specified type NEC 281.8
of or complicating pregnancy 648.2 ☑
pentose phosphate pathway 282.2
PFK 282.3
phosphofructo-aldolase 282.3
phosphofructokinase 282.3
phosphoglycerate kinase 282.3
PK 282.3
protein 281.4
pyruvate kinase (PK) 282.3
TPI 282.3
triosephosphate isomerase 282.3
vitamin B_{12} NEC 281.1
dietary 281.1
pernicious 281.0
Diamond-Blackfan (congenital hypoplastic) 284.01
dibothriocephalus 123.4
dimorphic 281.9
diphasic 281.8
diphtheritic 032.89
Diphyllobothrium 123.4
drepanocytic (*see also* Disease, sickle-cell) 282.60
due to
blood loss (chronic) 280.0
acute 285.1
defect of Embden-Meyerhof pathway glycolysis 282.3
disorder of glutathione metabolism 282.2
drug — *see* Anemia, by type (*see also* Table of Drugs and Chemicals) ●
fetal blood loss 776.5
fish tapeworm (D. latum) infestation 123.4
Anemia — *continued*
due to — *continued*
glutathione metabolism disorder 282.2
hemorrhage (chronic) 280.0
acute 285.1
hexose monophosphate (HMP) shunt deficiency 282.2
impaired absorption 280.9
loss of blood (chronic) 280.0
acute 285.1
myxedema 244.9
Necator americanus 126.1
prematurity 776.6
selective vitamin B_{12} malabsorption with proteinuria 281.1
Dyke-Young type (secondary) (symptomatic) 283.9
dyserythropoietic (congenital) (types I, II, III) 285.8
dyshemopoietic (congenital) 285.8
Egypt (*see also* Ancylostomiasis) 126.9
elliptocytosis (*see also* Elliptocytosis) 282.1
enzyme deficiency, drug-induced 282.2
epidemic (*see also* Ancylostomiasis) 126.9
EPO resistant 285.21
erythroblastic
familial 282.49
fetus or newborn (*see also* Disease, hemolytic) 773.2
late 773.5
erythrocytic glutathione deficiency 282.2
erythropoietin-resistant (EPO resistant anemia) 285.21
essential 285.9
Faber's (achlorhydric anemia) 280.9
factitious (self-induced blood letting) 280.0
familial erythroblastic (microcytic) 282.49
Fanconi's (congenital pancytopenia) 284.09
favism 282.2
fetal 678.0 ☑ ▲
following blood loss, affecting newborn 776.5 ●
fetus or newborn
due to
ABO
antibodies 773.1
incompatibility, maternal/fetal 773.1
isoimmunization 773.1
Rh
antibodies 773.0
incompatibility, maternal/fetal 773.0
isoimmunization 773.0
following fetal blood loss 776.5
fish tapeworm (D. latum) infestation 123.4
folate (folic acid) deficiency 281.2
dietary 281.2
drug-induced 281.2
folate malabsorption, congenital 281.2
folic acid deficiency 281.2
dietary 281.2
drug-induced 281.2
G-6-PD 282.2
general 285.9
glucose-6-phosphate dehydrogenase deficiency 282.2
glutathione-reductase deficiency 282.2
goat's milk 281.2
granulocytic 288.09
Heinz-body, congenital 282.7
hemoglobin deficiency 285.9
hemolytic 283.9
acquired 283.9
with hemoglobinuria NEC 283.2

☑ Additional Digit Required — Refer to the Tabular List for Digit Selection
▽ Subterms under main terms may continue to next column or page

- **Anemia** — *continued*
  - hemolytic — *continued*
    - acquired — *continued*
      - autoimmune (cold type) (idiopathic) (primary) (secondary) (symptomatic) (warm type) 283.0
      - due to
        - cold reactive antibodies 283.0
        - drug exposure 283.0
        - warm reactive antibodies 283.0
      - fragmentation 283.19
      - idiopathic (chronic) 283.9
      - infectious 283.19
        - autoimmune 283.0
      - non-autoimmune 283.10
      - toxic 283.19
      - traumatic cardiac 283.19
    - acute 283.9
      - due to enzyme deficiency NEC 282.3
      - fetus or newborn (*see also* Disease, hemolytic) 773.2
        - late 773.5
      - Lederer's (acquired infectious hemolytic anemia) 283.19
    - autoimmune (acquired) 283.0
    - chronic 282.9
      - idiopathic 283.9
    - cold type (secondary) (symptomatic) 283.0
    - congenital (spherocytic) (*see also* Spherocytosis) 282.0
      - nonspherocytic — *see* Anemia, hemolytic, nonspherocytic, congenital
    - drug-induced 283.0
      - enzyme deficiency 282.2
    - due to
      - cardiac conditions 283.19
      - drugs 283.0
      - enzyme deficiency NEC 282.3
        - drug-induced 282.2
      - presence of shunt or other internal prosthetic device 283.19
      - thrombotic thrombocytopenic purpura 446.6
    - elliptocytotic (*see also* Elliptocytosis) 282.1
    - familial 282.9
    - hereditary 282.9
      - due to enzyme deficiency NEC 282.3
      - specified NEC 282.8
    - idiopathic (chronic) 283.9
    - infectious (acquired) 283.19
    - mechanical 283.19
    - microangiopathic 283.19
    - non-autoimmune NEC 283.10
    - nonspherocytic
      - congenital or hereditary NEC 282.3
        - glucose-6-phosphate dehydrogenase deficiency 282.2
        - pyruvate kinase (PK) deficiency 282.3
        - type I 282.2
        - type II 282.3
      - type I 282.2
      - type II 282.3
    - of or complicating pregnancy 648.2 ☑
    - resulting from presence of shunt or other internal prosthetic device 283.19
    - secondary 283.19
      - autoimmune 283.0
    - sickle-cell — *see* Disease, sickle-cell
    - Stransky-Regala type (Hb-E) (*see also* Disease, hemoglobin) 282.7

- **Anemia** — *continued*
  - hemolytic — *continued*
    - symptomatic 283.19
      - autoimmune 283.0
    - toxic (acquired) 283.19
    - uremic (adult) (child) 283.11
    - warm type (secondary) (symptomatic) 283.0
  - hemorrhagic (chronic) 280.0
    - acute 285.1
  - HEMPAS 285.8
  - hereditary erythroblast multinuclearity-positive acidified serum test 285.8
  - Herrick's (hemoglobin S disease) 282.61
  - hexokinase deficiency 282.3
  - high A_2 282.49
  - hookworm (*see also* Ancylostomiasis) 126.9
  - hypochromic (idiopathic) (microcytic) (normoblastic) 280.9
    - with iron loading 285.0
    - due to blood loss (chronic) 280.0
      - acute 285.1
    - familial sex linked 285.0
    - pyridoxine-responsive 285.0
  - hypoplasia, red blood cells 284.81
    - congenital or familial 284.01
  - hypoplastic (idiopathic) 284.9
    - congenital 284.01
    - familial 284.01
    - of childhood 284.09
  - idiopathic 285.9
    - hemolytic, chronic 283.9
  - in
    - chronic illness NEC 285.29
    - chronic kidney disease 285.21
    - end-stage renal disease 285.21
    - neoplastic disease 285.22
  - infantile 285.9
  - infective, infectional 285.9
  - intertropical (*see also* Ancylostomiasis) 126.9
  - iron (Fe) deficiency 280.9
    - due to blood loss (chronic) 280.0
      - acute 285.1
    - of or complicating pregnancy 648.2 ☑
    - specified NEC 280.8
  - Jaksch's (pseudoleukemia infantum) 285.8
  - Joseph-Diamond-Blackfan (congenital hypoplastic) 284.01
  - labyrinth 386.50
  - Lederer's (acquired infectious hemolytic anemia) 283.19
  - leptocytosis (hereditary) 282.49
  - leukoerythroblastic 284.2
  - macrocytic 281.9
    - nutritional 281.2
    - of or complicating pregnancy 648.2 ☑
    - tropical 281.2
  - malabsorption (familial), selective B_{12} with proteinuria 281.1
  - malarial (*see also* Malaria) 084.6
  - malignant (progressive) 281.0
  - malnutrition 281.9
  - marsh (*see also* Malaria) 084.6
  - Mediterranean (with hemoglobinopathy) 282.49
  - megaloblastic 281.9
    - combined B_{12} and folate deficiency 281.3
    - nutritional (of infancy) 281.2
    - of infancy 281.2
    - of or complicating pregnancy 648.2 ☑
    - refractory 281.3
    - specified NEC 281.3
  - megalocytic 281.9
  - microangiopathic hemolytic 283.19
  - microcytic (hypochromic) 280.9
    - due to blood loss (chronic) 280.0
      - acute 285.1

- **Anemia** — *continued*
  - microcytic — *continued*
    - familial 282.49
    - hypochromic 280.9
  - microdrepanocytosis 282.49
  - miners' (*see also* Ancylostomiasis) 126.9
  - myelopathic 285.8
  - myelophthisic (normocytic) 284.2
  - newborn (*see also* Disease, hemolytic) 773.2
    - due to isoimmunization (*see also* Disease, hemolytic) 773.2
    - late, due to isoimmunization 773.5
    - posthemorrhagic 776.5
  - nonregenerative 284.9
  - nonspherocytic hemolytic — *see* Anemia, hemolytic, nonspherocytic
  - normocytic (infectional) (not due to blood loss) 285.9
    - due to blood loss (chronic) 280.0
      - acute 285.1
    - myelophthisic 284.2
  - nutritional (deficiency) 281.9
    - with
      - poor iron absorption 280.9
      - specified deficiency NEC 281.8
    - due to inadequate dietary iron intake 280.1
    - megaloblastic (of infancy) 281.2
  - of childhood 282.9
  - of chronic
    - disease NEC 285.29
    - illness NEC 285.29
  - of or complicating pregnancy 648.2 ☑
    - affecting fetus or newborn 760.8
  - of prematurity 776.6
  - orotic aciduric (congenital) (hereditary) 281.4
  - osteosclerotic 289.89
  - ovalocytosis (hereditary) (*see also* Elliptocytosis) 282.1
  - paludal (*see also* Malaria) 084.6
  - pentose phosphate pathway deficiency 282.2
  - pernicious (combined system disease) (congenital) (dorsolateral spinal degeneration) (juvenile) (myelopathy) (neuropathy) (posterior sclerosis) (primary) (progressive) (spleen) 281.0
    - of or complicating pregnancy 648.2 ☑
  - pleochromic 285.9
    - of sprue 281.8
  - portal 285.8
  - posthemorrhagic (chronic) 280.0
    - acute 285.1
    - newborn 776.5
  - postoperative
    - due to (acute) blood loss 285.1
      - chronic blood loss 280.0
    - other 285.9
  - postpartum 648.2 ☑
  - pressure 285.9
  - primary 285.9
  - profound 285.9
  - progressive 285.9
    - malignant 281.0
    - pernicious 281.0
  - protein-deficiency 281.4
  - pseudoleukemica infantum 285.8
  - puerperal 648.2 ☑
  - pure red cell 284.81
    - congenital 284.01
  - pyridoxine-responsive (hypochromic) 285.0
  - pyruvate kinase (PK) deficiency 282.3
  - refractoria sideroblastica 238.72
  - refractory (primary) 238.72
    - with
      - excess
        - blasts-1 (RAEB-1) 238.73
        - blasts-2 (RAEB-2) 238.73
      - hemochromatosis 238.72

- **Anemia** — *continued*
  - refractory — *continued*
    - with — *continued*
      - ringed sideroblasts (RARS) 238.72
    - due to ●
      - drug 285.0 ●
      - myelodysplastic syndrome 238.72 ●
      - toxin 285.0 ●
    - hereditary 285.0 ●
    - idiopathic 238.72 ●
    - megaloblastic 281.3
    - sideroblastic 238.72
      - hereditary 285.0 ●
    - sideropenic 280.9
  - Rietti-Greppi-Micheli (thalassemia minor) 282.49
  - scorbutic 281.8
  - secondary (to) 285.9
    - blood loss (chronic) 280.0
      - acute 285.1
    - hemorrhage 280.0
      - acute 285.1
    - inadequate dietary iron intake 280.1
  - semiplastic 284.9
  - septic 285.9
  - sickle-cell (*see also* Disease, sickle-cell) 282.60
  - sideroachrestic 285.0
  - sideroblastic (acquired) (any type) (congenital) (drug-induced) (due to disease) (hereditary) (primary) (secondary) (sex-linked hypochromic) (vitamin B_6 responsive) 285.0
    - refractory 238.72
      - congenital 285.0 ●
      - drug-induced 285.0 ●
      - hereditary 285.0 ●
      - sex-linked hypochromic 285.0 ●
      - vitamin B_6-responsive 285.0 ●
  - sideropenic (refractory) 280.9
    - due to blood loss (chronic) 280.0
      - acute 285.1
  - simple chronic 281.9
  - specified type NEC 285.8
  - spherocytic (hereditary) (*see also* Spherocytosis) 282.0
  - splenic 285.8
    - familial (Gaucher's) 272.7
  - splenomegalic 285.8
  - stomatocytosis 282.8
  - syphilitic 095.8
  - target cell (oval) 282.49
  - thalassemia 282.49
  - thrombocytopenic (*see also* Thrombocytopenia) 287.5
  - toxic 284.89
  - triosephosphate isomerase deficiency 282.3
  - tropical, macrocytic 281.2
  - tuberculous (*see also* Tuberculosis) 017.9 ☑
  - vegan's 281.1
  - vitamin
    - B_6-responsive 285.0
    - B_{12} deficiency (dietary) 281.1
      - pernicious 281.0
  - von Jaksch's (pseudoleukemia infantum) 285.8
  - Witts' (achlorhydric anemia) 280.9
  - Zuelzer (-Ogden) (nutritional megaloblastic anemia) 281.2
- **Anencephalus, anencephaly** 740.0
  - fetal, affecting management of pregnancy 655.0 ☑
- **Anergasia** — *see also* Psychosis, organic 294.9
  - senile 290.0
- **Anesthesia, anesthetic** 782.0
  - complication or reaction NEC 995.22

Anesthesia, anesthetic — *continued*
- complication or reaction — *continued*
  - due to
    - correct substance properly administered 995.22
    - overdose or wrong substance given 968.4
      - specified anesthetic — *see* Table of Drugs and Chemicals
- cornea 371.81
- death from
  - correct substance properly administered 995.4
  - during delivery 668.9 ☑
  - overdose or wrong substance given 968.4
  - specified anesthetic — *see* Table of Drugs and Chemicals
- eye 371.81
- functional 300.11
- hyperesthetic, thalamic 338.0
- hysterical 300.11
- local skin lesion 782.0
- olfactory 781.1
- sexual (psychogenic) 302.72
- shock
  - due to
    - correct substance properly administered 995.4
    - overdose or wrong substance given 968.4
    - specified anesthetic — *see* Table of Drugs and Chemicals
- skin 782.0
- tactile 782.0
- testicular 608.9
- thermal 782.0

Anetoderma (maculosum) 701.3

Aneuploidy NEC 758.5

Aneurin deficiency 265.1

Aneurysm (anastomotic) (artery) (cirsoid) (diffuse) (false) (fusiform) (multiple) (ruptured) (saccular) (varicose) 442.9
- abdominal (aorta) 441.4
  - ruptured 441.3
  - syphilitic 093.0
- aorta, aortic (nonsyphilitic) 441.9
  - abdominal 441.4
    - dissecting 441.02
    - ruptured 441.3
    - syphilitic 093.0
  - arch 441.2
    - ruptured 441.1
  - arteriosclerotic NEC 441.9
    - ruptured 441.5
  - ascending 441.2
    - ruptured 441.1
  - congenital 747.29
  - descending 441.9
    - abdominal 441.4
      - ruptured 441.3
    - ruptured 441.5
    - thoracic 441.2
      - ruptured 441.1
  - dissecting 441.00
    - abdominal 441.02
    - thoracic 441.01
    - thoracoabdominal 441.03
  - due to coarctation (aorta) 747.10
  - ruptured 441.5
  - sinus, right 747.29
  - syphilitic 093.0
  - thoracoabdominal 441.7
    - ruptured 441.6
  - thorax, thoracic (arch) (nonsyphilitic) 441.2
    - dissecting 441.01
    - ruptured 441.1
    - syphilitic 093.0
  - transverse 441.2
    - ruptured 441.1
  - valve (heart) (*see also* Endocarditis, aortic) 424.1

Aneurysm — *continued*
- arteriosclerotic NEC 442.9
  - cerebral 437.3
    - ruptured (*see also* Hemorrhage, subarachnoid) 430
- arteriovenous (congenital) (peripheral) NEC (*see also* Anomaly, arteriovenous) 747.60
  - acquired NEC 447.0
    - brain 437.3
      - ruptured (*see also* Hemorrhage, subarachnoid) 430
    - coronary 414.11
    - pulmonary 417.0
  - brain (cerebral) 747.81
    - ruptured (*see also* Hemorrhage, subarachnoid) 430
  - coronary 746.85
  - pulmonary 747.3
  - retina 743.58
  - specified site NEC 747.89
    - acquired 447.0
  - traumatic (*see also* Injury, blood vessel, by site) 904.9
- basal — *see* Aneurysm, brain
- berry (congenital) (ruptured) (*see also* Hemorrhage, subarachnoid) 430
- brain 437.3
  - arteriosclerotic 437.3
    - ruptured (*see also* Hemorrhage, subarachnoid) 430
  - arteriovenous 747.81
    - acquired 437.3
      - ruptured (*see also* Hemorrhage, subarachnoid) 430
    - ruptured (*see also* Hemorrhage, subarachnoid) 430
  - berry (congenital) (ruptured) (*see also* Hemorrhage, subarachnoid) 430
  - congenital 747.81
    - ruptured (*see also* Hemorrhage, subarachnoid) 430
  - meninges 437.3
    - ruptured (*see also* Hemorrhage, subarachnoid) 430
  - miliary (congenital) (ruptured) (*see also* Hemorrhage, subarachnoid) 430
  - mycotic 421.0
    - ruptured (*see also* Hemorrhage, subarachnoid) 430
  - nonruptured 437.3
  - ruptured (*see also* Hemorrhage, subarachnoid) 430
    - syphilitic 094.87
  - syphilitic (hemorrhage) 094.87
  - traumatic — *see* Injury, intracranial
- cardiac (false) (*see also* Aneurysm, heart) 414.10
- carotid artery (common) (external) 442.81
  - internal (intracranial portion) 437.3
    - extracranial portion 442.81
    - ruptured into brain (*see also* Hemorrhage, subarachnoid) 430
  - syphilitic 093.89
    - intracranial 094.87
- cavernous sinus (*see also* Aneurysm, brain) 437.3
  - arteriovenous 747.81
    - ruptured (*see also* Hemorrhage, subarachnoid) 430
  - congenital 747.81
    - ruptured (*see also* Hemorrhage, subarachnoid) 430
- celiac 442.84
- central nervous system, syphilitic 094.89
- cerebral — *see* Aneurysm, brain
- chest — *see* Aneurysm, thorax

Aneurysm — *continued*
- circle of Willis (*see also* Aneurysm, brain) 437.3
  - congenital 747.81
    - ruptured (*see also* Hemorrhage, subarachnoid) 430
  - ruptured (*see also* Hemorrhage, subarachnoid) 430
- common iliac artery 442.2
- congenital (peripheral) NEC 747.60
  - brain 747.81
    - ruptured (*see also* Hemorrhage, subarachnoid) 430
  - cerebral — *see* Aneurysm, brain, congenital
  - coronary 746.85
  - gastrointestinal 747.61
  - lower limb 747.64
  - pulmonary 747.3
  - renal 747.62
  - retina 743.58
  - specified site NEC 747.89
  - spinal 747.82
  - upper limb 747.63
- conjunctiva 372.74
- conus arteriosus (*see also* Aneurysm, heart) 414.10
- coronary (arteriosclerotic) (artery) (vein) (*see also* Aneurysm, heart) 414.11
  - arteriovenous 746.85
  - congenital 746.85
  - syphilitic 093.89
- cylindrical 441.9
  - ruptured 441.5
  - syphilitic 093.9
- dissecting 442.9
  - aorta 441.00
    - abdominal 441.02
    - thoracic 441.01
    - thoracoabdominal 441.03
  - syphilitic 093.9
- ductus arteriosus 747.0
- embolic — *see* Embolism, artery
- endocardial, infective (any valve) 421.0
- femoral 442.3
- gastroduodenal 442.84
- gastroepiploic 442.84
- heart (chronic or with a stated duration of over 8 weeks) (infectional) (wall) 414.10
  - acute or with a stated duration of 8 weeks or less (*see also* Infarct, myocardium) 410.9 ☑
  - congenital 746.89
  - valve — *see* Endocarditis
- hepatic 442.84
- iliac (common) 442.2
- infective (any valve) 421.0
- innominate (nonsyphilitic) 442.89
  - syphilitic 093.89
- interauricular septum (*see also* Aneurysm, heart) 414.10
- interventricular septum (*see also* Aneurysm, heart) 414.10
- intracranial — *see* Aneurysm, brain
- intrathoracic (nonsyphilitic) 441.2
  - ruptured 441.1
  - syphilitic 093.0
- jugular vein 453.8
- lower extremity 442.3
- lung (pulmonary artery) 417.1
- malignant 093.9
- mediastinal (nonsyphilitic) 442.89
  - syphilitic 093.89
- miliary (congenital) (ruptured) (*see also* Hemorrhage, subarachnoid) 430
- mitral (heart) (valve) 424.0
- mural (arteriovenous) (heart) (*see also* Aneurysm, heart) 414.10
- mycotic, any site 421.0
  - without endocarditis — *see* Aneurysm by site
  - ruptured, brain (*see also* Hemorrhage, subarachnoid) 430

Aneurysm — *continued*
- myocardium (*see also* Aneurysm, heart) 414.10
- neck 442.81
- pancreaticoduodenal 442.84
- patent ductus arteriosus 747.0
- peripheral NEC 442.89
  - congenital NEC (*see also* Aneurysm, congenital) 747.60
- popliteal 442.3
- pulmonary 417.1
  - arteriovenous 747.3
    - acquired 417.0
  - syphilitic 093.89
  - valve (heart) (*see also* Endocarditis, pulmonary) 424.3
- racemose 442.9
  - congenital (peripheral) NEC 747.60
- radial 442.0
- Rasmussen's (*see also* Tuberculosis) 011.2 ☑
- renal 442.1
- retinal (acquired) 362.17
  - congenital 743.58
  - diabetic 250.5 ☑ *[362.01]*
    - due to secondary diabetes 249.5 ☑ *[362.01]* ●
- sinus, aortic (of Valsalva) 747.29
- specified site NEC 442.89
- spinal (cord) 442.89
  - congenital 747.82
  - syphilitic (hemorrhage) 094.89
- spleen, splenic 442.83
- subclavian 442.82
  - syphilitic 093.89
- superior mesenteric 442.84
- syphilitic 093.9
  - aorta 093.0
  - central nervous system 094.89
  - congenital 090.5
  - spine, spinal 094.89
- thoracoabdominal 441.7
  - ruptured 441.6
- thorax, thoracic (arch) (nonsyphilitic) 441.2
  - dissecting 441.01
  - ruptured 441.1
  - syphilitic 093.0
- traumatic (complication) (early) — *see* Injury, blood vessel, by site
- tricuspid (heart) (valve) — *see* Endocarditis, tricuspid
- ulnar 442.0
- upper extremity 442.0
- valve, valvular — *see* Endocarditis
- venous 456.8
  - congenital NEC (*see also* Aneurysm, congenital) 747.60
- ventricle (arteriovenous) (*see also* Aneurysm, heart) 414.10
- visceral artery NEC 442.84

Angiectasis 459.89

Angiectopia 459.9

Angiitis 447.6
- allergic granulomatous 446.4
- hypersensitivity 446.20
  - Goodpasture's syndrome 446.21
  - specified NEC 446.29
- necrotizing 446.0
- Wegener's (necrotizing respiratory granulomatosis) 446.4

Angina (attack) (cardiac) (chest) (effort) (heart) (pectoris) (syndrome) (vasomotor) 413.9
- abdominal 557.1
- accelerated 411.1
- agranulocytic 288.03
- aphthous 074.0
- catarrhal 462
- crescendo 411.1
- croupous 464.4
- cruris 443.9

- **Angina** — *continued*
  - cruris — *continued*
    - due to atherosclerosis NEC (*see also* Arteriosclerosis, extremities) 440.20
  - decubitus 413.0
  - diphtheritic (membranous) 032.0
  - erysipelatous 034.0
  - erythematous 462
  - exudative, chronic 476.0
  - faucium 478.29
  - gangrenous 462
    - diphtheritic 032.0
  - infectious 462
  - initial 411.1
  - intestinal 557.1
  - ludovici 528.3
  - Ludwig's 528.3
  - malignant 462
    - diphtheritic 032.0
  - membranous 464.4
    - diphtheritic 032.0
  - mesenteric 557.1
  - monocytic 075
  - nocturnal 413.0
  - phlegmonous 475
    - diphtheritic 032.0
  - preinfarctional 411.1
  - Prinzmetal's 413.1
  - progressive 411.1
  - pseudomembranous 101
  - psychogenic 306.2
  - pultaceous, diphtheritic 032.0
  - scarlatinal 034.1
  - septic 034.0
  - simple 462
  - stable NEC 413.9
  - staphylococcal 462
  - streptococcal 034.0
  - stridulous, diphtheritic 032.3
  - syphilitic 093.9
    - congenital 090.5
  - tonsil 475
  - trachealis 464.4
  - unstable 411.1
  - variant 413.1
  - Vincent's 101
- **Angioblastoma** (M9161/1) — *see* Neoplasm, connective tissue, uncertain behavior
- **Angiocholecystitis** — *see also* Cholecystitis, acute 575.0
- **Angiocholitis** — *see also* Cholecystitis, acute 576.1
- **Angiodysgensis spinalis** 336.1
- **Angiodysplasia** (intestinalis) (intestine) 569.84
  - with hemorrhage 569.85
  - duodenum 537.82
    - with hemorrhage 537.83
  - stomach 537.82
    - with hemorrhage 537.83
- **Angioedema** (allergic) (any site) (with urticaria) 995.1
  - hereditary 277.6
- **Angioendothelioma** (M9130/1) — *see also* Neoplasm, by site, uncertain behavior
  - benign (M9130/0) (*see also* Hemangioma, by site) 228.00
  - bone (M9260/3) — *see* Neoplasm, bone, malignant
  - Ewing's (M9260/3) — *see* Neoplasm, bone, malignant
  - nervous system (M9130/0) 228.09
- **Angiofibroma** (M9160/0) — *see also* Neoplasm, by site, benign
  - juvenile (M9160/0) 210.7
    - specified site — *see* Neoplasm, by site, benign
    - unspecified site 210.7
- **Angiohemophilia** (A) (B) 286.4
- **Angioid streaks** (choroid) (retina) 363.43
- **Angiokeratoma** (M9141/0) — *see also* Neoplasm, skin, benign
  - corporis diffusum 272.7
- **Angiokeratosis**
  - diffuse 272.7
- **Angioleiomyoma** (M8894/0) — *see* Neoplasm, connective tissue, benign
- **Angioleucitis** 683
- **Angiolipoma** (M8861/0) — *see also* Lipoma, by site 214.9
  - infiltrating (M8861/1) — *see* Neoplasm, connective tissue, uncertain behavior
- **Angioma** (M9120/0) — *see also* Hemangioma, by site 228.00
  - capillary 448.1
  - hemorrhagicum hereditaria 448.0
  - malignant (M9120/3) — *see* Neoplasm, connective tissue, malignant
  - pigmentosum et atrophicum 757.33
  - placenta — *see* Placenta, abnormal
  - plexiform (M9131/0) — *see* Hemangioma, by site
  - senile 448.1
  - serpiginosum 709.1
  - spider 448.1
  - stellate 448.1
- **Angiomatosis** 757.32
  - bacillary 083.8
  - corporis diffusum universale 272.7
  - cutaneocerebral 759.6
  - encephalocutaneous 759.6
  - encephalofacial 759.6
  - encephalotrigeminal 759.6
  - hemorrhagic familial 448.0
  - hereditary familial 448.0
  - heredofamilial 448.0
  - meningo-oculofacial 759.6
  - multiple sites 228.09
  - neuro-oculocutaneous 759.6
  - retina (Hippel's disease) 759.6
  - retinocerebellosa 759.6
  - retinocerebral 759.6
  - systemic 228.09
- **Angiomyolipoma** (M8860/0)
  - specified site — *see* Neoplasm, connective tissue, benign
  - unspecified site 223.0
- **Angiomyoliposarcoma** (M8860/3) — *see* Neoplasm, connective tissue, malignant
- **Angiomyoma** (M8894/0) — *see* Neoplasm, connective tissue, benign
- **Angiomyosarcoma** (M8894/3) — *see* Neoplasm, connective tissue, malignant
- **Angioneurosis** 306.2
- **Angioneurotic edema** (allergic) (any site) (with urticaria) 995.1
  - hereditary 277.6
- **Angiopathia, angiopathy** 459.9
  - diabetic (peripheral) 250.7 ☑ *[443.81]*
    - due to secondary diabetes 249.7 ☑ *[443.81]* ●
  - peripheral 443.9
    - diabetic 250.7 ☑ *[443.81]*
      - due to secondary diabetes 249.7 ☑ *[443.81]* ●
    - specified type NEC 443.89
  - retinae syphilitica 093.89
  - retinalis (juvenilis) 362.18
    - background 362.10
    - diabetic 250.5 ☑ *[362.01]*
      - due to secondary diabetes 249.5 ☑ *[362.01]* ●
    - proliferative 362.29
    - tuberculous (*see also* Tuberculosis) 017.3 ☑ *[362.18]*
- **Angiosarcoma** (M9120/3) — *see* Neoplasm, connective tissue, malignant
- **Angiosclerosis** — *see* Arteriosclerosis
- **Angioscotoma, enlarged** 368.42
- **Angiospasm** 443.9
  - brachial plexus 353.0
  - cerebral 435.9
  - cervical plexus 353.2
- **Angiospasm** — *continued*
  - nerve
    - arm 354.9
      - axillary 353.0
      - median 354.1
      - ulnar 354.2
    - autonomic (*see also* Neuropathy, peripheral, autonomic) 337.9
    - axillary 353.0
    - leg 355.8
      - plantar 355.6
    - lower extremity — *see* Angiospasm, nerve, leg
    - median 354.1
    - peripheral NEC 355.9
    - spinal NEC 355.9
    - sympathetic (*see also* Neuropathy, peripheral, autonomic) 337.9
    - ulnar 354.2
    - upper extremity — *see* Angiospasm, nerve, arm
  - peripheral NEC 443.9
  - traumatic 443.9
    - foot 443.9
    - leg 443.9
  - vessel 443.9
- **Angiospastic disease or edema** 443.9
- **Angle's**
  - class I 524.21
  - class II 524.22
  - class III 524.23
- **Anguillulosis** 127.2
- **Angulation**
  - cecum (*see also* Obstruction, intestine) 560.9
  - coccyx (acquired) 738.6
    - congenital 756.19
  - femur (acquired) 736.39
    - congenital 755.69
  - intestine (large) (small) (*see also* Obstruction, intestine) 560.9
  - sacrum (acquired) 738.5
    - congenital 756.19
  - sigmoid (flexure) (*see also* Obstruction, intestine) 560.9
  - spine (*see also* Curvature, spine) 737.9
  - tibia (acquired) 736.89
    - congenital 755.69
  - ureter 593.3
  - wrist (acquired) 736.09
    - congenital 755.59
- **Angulus infectiosus** 686.8
- **Anhedonia** 780.99
- **Anhidrosis** (lid) (neurogenic) (thermogenic) 705.0
- **Anhydration** 276.51
  - with
    - hypernatremia 276.0
    - hyponatremia 276.1
- **Anhydremia** 276.52
  - with
    - hypernatremia 276.0
    - hyponatremia 276.1
- **Anidrosis** 705.0
- **Aniridia** (congenital) 743.45
- **Anisakiasis** (infection) (infestation) 127.1
- **Anisakis larva infestation** 127.1
- **Aniseikonia** 367.32
- **Anisocoria** (pupil) 379.41
  - congenital 743.46
- **Anisocytosis** 790.09
- **Anisometropia** (congenital) 367.31
- **Ankle** — *see* condition
- **Ankyloblepharon** (acquired) (eyelid) 374.46
  - filiforme (adnatum) (congenital) 743.62
  - total 743.62
- **Ankylodactly** — *see also* Syndactylism 755.10
- **Ankyloglossia** 750.0
- **Ankylosis** (fibrous) (osseous) 718.50
  - ankle 718.57
  - any joint, produced by surgical fusion V45.4
- **Ankylosis** — *continued*
  - cricoarytenoid (cartilage) (joint) (larynx) 478.79
  - dental 521.6
  - ear ossicle NEC 385.22
    - malleus 385.21
  - elbow 718.52
  - finger 718.54
  - hip 718.55
  - incostapedial joint (infectional) 385.22
  - joint, produced by surgical fusion NEC V45.4
  - knee 718.56
  - lumbosacral (joint) 724.6
  - malleus 385.21
  - multiple sites 718.59
  - postoperative (status) V45.4
  - sacroiliac (joint) 724.6
  - shoulder 718.51
  - specified site NEC 718.58
  - spine NEC 724.9
  - surgical V45.4
  - teeth, tooth (hard tissues) 521.6
  - temporomandibular joint 524.61
  - wrist 718.53
- **Ankylostoma** — *see* Ancylostoma
- **Ankylostomiasis** (intestinal) — *see* Ancylostomiasis
- **Ankylurethria** — *see also* Stricture, urethra 598.9
- **Annular** — *see also* condition
  - detachment, cervix 622.8
  - organ or site, congenital NEC — *see* Distortion
  - pancreas (congenital) 751.7
- **Anodontia** (complete) (partial) (vera) 520.0
  - with abnormal spacing 524.30
  - acquired 525.10
    - causing malocclusion 524.30
    - due to
      - caries 525.13
      - extraction 525.10
      - periodontal disease 525.12
      - trauma 525.11
- **Anomaly, anomalous** (congenital) (unspecified type) 759.9
  - abdomen 759.9
  - abdominal wall 756.70
  - acoustic nerve 742.9
  - adrenal (gland) 759.1
  - Alder (-Reilly) (leukocyte granulation) 288.2
  - alimentary tract 751.9
    - lower 751.5
    - specified type NEC 751.8
    - upper (any part, except tongue) 750.9
      - tongue 750.10
        - specified type NEC 750.19
  - alveolar 524.70
    - ridge (process) 525.8
    - specified NEC 524.79
  - ankle (joint) 755.69
  - anus, anal (canal) 751.5
  - aorta, aortic 747.20
    - arch 747.21
    - coarctation (postductal) (preductal) 747.10
    - cusp or valve NEC 746.9
    - septum 745.0
    - specified type NEC 747.29
  - aorticopulmonary septum 745.0
  - apertures, diaphragm 756.6
  - appendix 751.5
  - aqueduct of Sylvius 742.3
    - with spina bifida (*see also* Spina bifida) 741.0 ☑
  - arm 755.50
    - reduction (*see also* Deformity, reduction, upper limb) 755.20
  - arteriovenous (congenital) (peripheral) NEC 747.60
    - brain 747.81
    - cerebral 747.81
    - coronary 746.85

- **Anomaly, anomalous** — *continued*
  - arteriovenous — *continued*
    - gastrointestinal 747.61
      - acquired — *see* Angiodysplasia
    - lower limb 747.64
    - renal 747.62
    - specified site NEC 747.69
    - spinal 747.82
    - upper limb 747.63
  - artery (*see also* Anomaly, peripheral vascular system) NEC 747.60
    - brain 747.81
    - cerebral 747.81
    - coronary 746.85
    - eye 743.9
    - pulmonary 747.3
    - renal 747.62
    - retina 743.9
    - umbilical 747.5
  - arytenoepiglottic folds 748.3
  - atrial
    - bands 746.9
    - folds 746.9
    - septa 745.5
  - atrioventricular
    - canal 745.69
    - common 745.69
    - conduction 426.7
    - excitation 426.7
    - septum 745.4
  - atrium — *see* Anomaly, atrial
  - auditory canal 744.3
    - specified type NEC 744.29
      - with hearing impairment 744.02
  - auricle
    - ear 744.3
      - causing impairment of hearing 744.02
    - heart 746.9
      - septum 745.5
  - autosomes, autosomal NEC 758.5
  - Axenfeld's 743.44
  - back 759.9
  - band
    - atrial 746.9
    - heart 746.9
    - ventricular 746.9
  - Bartholin's duct 750.9
  - biliary duct or passage 751.60
    - atresia 751.61
  - bladder (neck) (sphincter) (trigone) 753.9
    - specified type NEC 753.8
  - blood vessel 747.9
    - artery — *see* Anomaly, artery
    - peripheral vascular — *see* Anomaly, peripheral vascular system
    - vein — *see* Anomaly, vein
  - bone NEC 756.9
    - ankle 755.69
    - arm 755.50
    - chest 756.3
    - cranium 756.0
    - face 756.0
    - finger 755.50
    - foot 755.67
    - forearm 755.50
    - frontal 756.0
    - head 756.0
    - hip 755.63
    - leg 755.60
    - lumbosacral 756.10
    - nose 748.1
    - pelvic girdle 755.60
    - rachitic 756.4
    - rib 756.3
    - shoulder girdle 755.50
    - skull 756.0
      - with
        - anencephalus 740.0
        - encephalocele 742.0
        - hydrocephalus 742.3
          - with spina bifida (*see also* Spina bifida) 741.0 ☑
        - microcephalus 742.1
    - toe 755.66
  - brain 742.9
    - multiple 742.4
    - reduction 742.2
    - specified type NEC 742.4
    - vessel 747.81
  - branchial cleft NEC 744.49
    - cyst 744.42
    - fistula 744.41
    - persistent 744.41
    - sinus (external) (internal) 744.41
  - breast 757.9
  - broad ligament 752.10
    - specified type NEC 752.19
  - bronchus 748.3
  - bulbar septum 745.0
  - bulbus cordis 745.9
    - persistent (in left ventricle) 745.8
  - bursa 756.9
  - canal of Nuck 752.9
  - canthus 743.9
  - capillary NEC (*see also* Anomaly, peripheral vascular system) 747.60
  - cardiac 746.9
    - septal closure 745.9
      - acquired 429.71
    - valve NEC 746.9
      - pulmonary 746.00
      - specified type NEC 746.89
  - cardiovascular system 746.9
    - complicating pregnancy, childbirth, or puerperium 648.5 ☑
  - carpus 755.50
  - cartilage, trachea 748.3
  - cartilaginous 756.9
  - caruncle, lacrimal, lachrymal 743.9
  - cascade stomach 750.7
  - cauda equina 742.59
  - cecum 751.5
  - cerebral (*see also* Anomaly, brain vessels) 747.81
  - cerebrovascular system 747.81
  - cervix (uterus) 752.40
    - with doubling of vagina and uterus 752.2
    - in pregnancy or childbirth 654.6 ☑
      - affecting fetus or newborn 763.89
      - causing obstructed labor 660.2 ☑
        - affecting fetus or newborn 763.1
  - Chédiak-Higashi (-Steinbrinck) (congenital gigantism of peroxidase granules) 288.2
  - cheek 744.9
  - chest (wall) 756.3
  - chin 744.9
    - specified type NEC 744.89
  - chordae tendineae 746.9
  - choroid 743.9
    - plexus 742.9
  - chromosomes, chromosomal 758.9
    - 13 (13-15) 758.1
    - 18 (16-18) 758.2
    - 21 or 22 758.0
    - autosomes NEC (*see also* Abnormal, autosomes) 758.5
      - deletion 758.39
    - Christchurch 758.39
    - D_1 758.1
    - E_3 758.2
    - G 758.0
    - mitochondrial 758.9
    - mosaics 758.89
    - sex 758.81
      - complement, XO 758.6
      - complement, XXX 758.81
      - complement, XXY 758.7
      - complement, XYY 758.81
      - gonadal dysgenesis 758.6
      - Klinefelter's 758.7
      - Turner's 758.6
    - trisomy 21 758.0
  - cilia 743.9
  - circulatory system 747.9
    - specified type NEC 747.89
  - clavicle 755.51
  - clitoris 752.40
  - coccyx 756.10
  - colon 751.5
  - common duct 751.60
  - communication
    - coronary artery 746.85
    - left ventricle with right atrium 745.4
  - concha (ear) 744.3
  - connection
    - renal vessels with kidney 747.62
    - total pulmonary venous 747.41
  - connective tissue 756.9
    - specified type NEC 756.89
  - cornea 743.9
    - shape 743.41
    - size 743.41
    - specified type NEC 743.49
  - coronary
    - artery 746.85
    - vein 746.89
  - cranium — *see* Anomaly, skull
  - cricoid cartilage 748.3
  - cushion, endocardial 745.60
    - specified type NEC 745.69
  - cystic duct 751.60
  - dental arch 524.20
    - specified NEC 524.29
  - dental arch relationship 524.20
    - angle's class I 524.21
    - angle's class II 524.22
    - angle's class III 524.23
    - articulation
      - anterior 524.27
      - posterior 524.27
      - reverse 524.27
    - disto-occlusion 524.22
      - division I 524.22
      - division II 524.22
    - excessive horizontal overlap 524.26
    - interarch distance (excessive) (inadequate) 524.28
    - mesio-occlusion 524.23
    - neutro-occlusion 524.21
    - open
      - anterior occlusal relationship 524.24
      - posterior occlusal relationship 524.25
    - specified NEC 524.29
  - dentition 520.6
  - dentofacial NEC 524.9
    - functional 524.50
    - specified type NEC 524.89
  - dermatoglyphic 757.2
  - Descemet's membrane 743.9
    - specified type NEC 743.49
  - development
    - cervix 752.40
    - vagina 752.40
    - vulva 752.40
  - diaphragm, diaphragmatic (apertures) NEC 756.6
  - digestive organ(s) or system 751.9
    - lower 751.5
    - specified type NEC 751.8
    - upper 750.9
  - distribution, coronary artery 746.85
  - ductus
    - arteriosus 747.0
    - Botalli 747.0
  - duodenum 751.5
  - dura 742.9
    - brain 742.4
    - spinal cord 742.59
  - ear 744.3
    - causing impairment of hearing 744.00
      - specified type NEC 744.09
    - external 744.3
      - causing impairment of hearing 744.02
      - specified type NEC 744.29
    - inner (causing impairment of hearing) 744.05
    - middle, except ossicles (causing impairment of hearing) 744.03
      - ossicles 744.04
    - ossicles 744.04
    - prominent auricle 744.29
    - specified type NEC 744.29
      - with hearing impairment 744.09
  - Ebstein's (heart) 746.2
    - tricuspid valve 746.2
  - ectodermal 757.9
  - Eisenmenger's (ventricular septal defect) 745.4
  - ejaculatory duct 752.9
    - specified type NEC 752.89
  - elbow (joint) 755.50
  - endocardial cushion 745.60
    - specified type NEC 745.69
  - endocrine gland NEC 759.2
  - epididymis 752.9
  - epiglottis 748.3
  - esophagus 750.9
    - specified type NEC 750.4
  - Eustachian tube 744.3
    - specified type NEC 744.24
  - eye (any part) 743.9
    - adnexa 743.9
      - specified type NEC 743.69
    - anophthalmos 743.00
    - anterior
      - chamber and related structures 743.9
        - angle 743.9
          - specified type NEC 743.44
        - specified type NEC 743.44
      - segment 743.9
        - combined 743.48
        - multiple 743.48
        - specified type NEC 743.49
    - cataract (*see also* Cataract) 743.30
    - glaucoma (*see also* Buphthalmia) 743.20
    - lid 743.9
      - specified type NEC 743.63
    - microphthalmos (*see also* Microphthalmos) 743.10
    - posterior segment 743.9
      - specified type NEC 743.59
      - vascular 743.58
      - vitreous 743.9
        - specified type NEC 743.51
    - ptosis (eyelid) 743.61
    - retina 743.9
      - specified type NEC 743.59
    - sclera 743.9
      - specified type NEC 743.47
    - specified type NEC 743.8
  - eyebrow 744.89
  - eyelid 743.9
    - specified type NEC 743.63
  - face (any part) 744.9
    - bone(s) 756.0
    - specified type NEC 744.89
  - fallopian tube 752.10
    - specified type NEC 752.19
  - fascia 756.9
    - specified type NEC 756.89
  - femur 755.60
  - fibula 755.60
  - finger 755.50
    - supernumerary 755.01
    - webbed (*see also* Syndactylism, fingers) 755.11

Anomaly, anomalous — *continued*
fixation, intestine 751.4
flexion (joint) 755.9
hip or thigh (*see also* Dislocation, hip, congenital) 754.30
folds, heart 746.9
foot 755.67
foramen
Botalli 745.5
ovale 745.5
forearm 755.50
forehead (*see also* Anomaly, skull) 756.0
form, teeth 520.2
fovea centralis 743.9
frontal bone (*see also* Anomaly, skull) 756.0
gallbladder 751.60
Gartner's duct 752.41
gastrointestinal tract 751.9
specified type NEC 751.8
vessel 747.61
genitalia, genital organ(s) or system
female 752.9
external 752.40
specified type NEC 752.49
internal NEC 752.9
male (external and internal) 752.9
epispadias 752.62
hidden penis 752.65
hydrocele, congenital 778.6
hypospadias 752.61
micropenis 752.64
testis, undescended 752.51
retractile 752.52
specified type NEC 752.89
genitourinary NEC 752.9
Gerbode 745.4
globe (eye) 743.9
glottis 748.3
granulation or granulocyte, genetic 288.2
constitutional 288.2
leukocyte 288.2
gum 750.9
gyri 742.9
hair 757.9
specified type NEC 757.4
hand 755.50
hard tissue formation in pulp 522.3
head (*see also* Anomaly, skull) 756.0
heart 746.9
auricle 746.9
bands 746.9
fibroelastosis cordis 425.3
folds 746.9
malposition 746.87
maternal, affecting fetus or newborn 760.3
obstructive NEC 746.84
patent ductus arteriosus (Botalli) 747.0
septum 745.9
acquired 429.71
aortic 745.0
aorticopulmonary 745.0
atrial 745.5
auricular 745.5
between aorta and pulmonary artery 745.0
endocardial cushion type 745.60
specified type NEC 745.69
interatrial 745.5
interventricular 745.4
with pulmonary stenosis or atresia, dextraposition of aorta, and hypertrophy of right ventricle 745.2
acquired 429.71
specified type NEC 745.8
ventricular 745.4

Anomaly, anomalous — *continued*
heart — *continued*
septum — *continued*
ventricular — *continued*
with pulmonary stenosis or atresia, dextraposition of aorta, and hypertrophy of right ventricle 745.2
acquired 429.71
specified type NEC 746.89
tetralogy of Fallot 745.2
valve NEC 746.9
aortic 746.9
atresia 746.89
bicuspid valve 746.4
insufficiency 746.4
specified type NEC 746.89
stenosis 746.3
subaortic 746.81
supravalvular 747.22
mitral 746.9
atresia 746.89
insufficiency 746.6
specified type NEC 746.89
stenosis 746.5
pulmonary 746.00
atresia 746.01
insufficiency 746.09
stenosis 746.02
infundibular 746.83
subvalvular 746.83
tricuspid 746.9
atresia 746.1
stenosis 746.1
ventricle 746.9
heel 755.67
Hegglin's 288.2
hemianencephaly 740.0
hemicephaly 740.0
hemicrania 740.0
hepatic duct 751.60
hip (joint) 755.63
hourglass
bladder 753.8
gallbladder 751.69
stomach 750.7
humerus 755.50
hymen 752.40
hypersegmentation of neutrophils, hereditary 288.2
hypophyseal 759.2
ileocecal (coil) (valve) 751.5
ileum (intestine) 751.5
ilium 755.60
integument 757.9
specified type NEC 757.8
interarch distance (excessive) (inadequate) 524.28
intervertebral cartilage or disc 756.10
intestine (large) (small) 751.5
fixational type 751.4
iris 743.9
specified type NEC 743.46
ischium 755.60
jaw NEC 524.9
closure 524.51
size (major) NEC 524.00
specified type NEC 524.89
jaw-cranial base relationship 524.10
specified NEC 524.19
jejunum 751.5
joint 755.9
hip
dislocation (*see also* Dislocation, hip, congenital) 754.30
predislocation (*see also* Subluxation, congenital, hip) 754.32
preluxation (*see also* Subluxation, congenital, hip) 754.32
subluxation (*see also* Subluxation, congenital, hip) 754.32
lumbosacral 756.10

Anomaly, anomalous — *continued*
joint — *continued*
lumbosacral — *continued*
spondylolisthesis 756.12
spondylosis 756.11
multiple arthrogryposis 754.89
sacroiliac 755.69
Jordan's 288.2
kidney(s) (calyx) (pelvis) 753.9
vessel 747.62
Klippel-Feil (brevicollis) 756.16
knee (joint) 755.64
labium (majus) (minus) 752.40
labyrinth, membranous (causing impairment of hearing) 744.05
lacrimal
apparatus, duct or passage 743.9
specified type NEC 743.65
gland 743.9
specified type NEC 743.64
Langdon Down (mongolism) 758.0
larynx, laryngeal (muscle) 748.3
web, webbed 748.2
leg (lower) (upper) 755.60
reduction NEC (*see also* Deformity, reduction, lower limb) 755.30
lens 743.9
shape 743.36
specified type NEC 743.39
leukocytes, genetic 288.2
granulation (constitutional) 288.2
lid (fold) 743.9
ligament 756.9
broad 752.10
round 752.9
limb, except reduction deformity 755.9
lower 755.60
reduction deformity (*see also* Deformity, reduction, lower limb) 755.30
specified type NEC 755.69
upper 755.50
reduction deformity (*see also* Deformity, reduction, upper limb) 755.20
specified type NEC 755.59
lip 750.9
harelip (*see also* Cleft, lip) 749.10
specified type NEC 750.26
liver (duct) 751.60
atresia 751.69
lower extremity 755.60
vessel 747.64
lumbosacral (joint) (region) 756.10
lung (fissure) (lobe) NEC 748.60
agenesis 748.5
specified type NEC 748.69
lymphatic system 759.9
Madelung's (radius) 755.54
mandible 524.9
size NEC 524.00
maxilla 524.9
size NEC 524.00
May (-Hegglin) 288.2
meatus urinarius 753.9
specified type NEC 753.8
meningeal bands or folds, constriction of 742.8
meninges 742.9
brain 742.4
spinal 742.59
meningocele (*see also* Spina bifida) 741.9 ☑
acquired 349.2
mesentery 751.9
metacarpus 755.50
metatarsus 755.67
middle ear, except ossicles (causing impairment of hearing) 744.03
ossicles 744.04
mitral (leaflets) (valve) 746.9
atresia 746.89
insufficiency 746.6
specified type NEC 746.89
stenosis 746.5
mouth 750.9

Anomaly, anomalous — *continued*
mouth — *continued*
specified type NEC 750.26
multiple NEC 759.7
specified type NEC 759.89
muscle 756.9
eye 743.9
specified type NEC 743.69
specified type NEC 756.89
musculoskeletal system, except limbs 756.9
specified type NEC 756.9
nail 757.9
specified type NEC 757.5
narrowness, eyelid 743.62
nasal sinus or septum 748.1
neck (any part) 744.9
specified type NEC 744.89
nerve 742.9
acoustic 742.9
specified type NEC 742.8
optic 742.9
specified type NEC 742.8
specified type NEC 742.8
nervous system NEC 742.9
brain 742.9
specified type NEC 742.4
specified type NEC 742.8
neurological 742.9
nipple 757.6
nonteratogenic NEC 754.89
nose, nasal (bone) (cartilage) (septum) (sinus) 748.1
ocular muscle 743.9
omphalomesenteric duct 751.0
opening, pulmonary veins 747.49
optic
disc 743.9
specified type NEC 743.57
nerve 742.9
opticociliary vessels 743.9
orbit (eye) 743.9
specified type NEC 743.66
organ
of Corti (causing impairment of hearing) 744.05
or site 759.9
specified type NEC 759.89
origin
both great arteries from same ventricle 745.11
coronary artery 746.85
innominate artery 747.69
left coronary artery from pulmonary artery 746.85
pulmonary artery 747.3
renal vessels 747.62
subclavian artery (left) (right) 747.21
osseous meatus (ear) 744.03
ovary 752.0
oviduct 752.10
palate (hard) (soft) 750.9
cleft (*see also* Cleft, palate) 749.00
pancreas (duct) 751.7
papillary muscles 746.9
parathyroid gland 759.2
paraurethral ducts 753.9
parotid (gland) 750.9
patella 755.64
Pelger-Huët (hereditary hyposegmentation) 288.2
pelvic girdle 755.60
specified type NEC 755.69
pelvis (bony) 755.60
complicating delivery 653.0 ☑
rachitic 268.1
fetal 756.4
penis (glans) 752.69
pericardium 746.89
peripheral vascular system NEC 747.60
gastrointestinal 747.61
lower limb 747.64
renal 747.62
specified site NEC 747.69

Anomaly, anomalous — *continued*
peripheral vascular system — *continued*
spinal 747.82
upper limb 747.63
Peter's 743.44
pharynx 750.9
branchial cleft 744.41
specified type NEC 750.29
Pierre Robin 756.0
pigmentation 709.00
congenital 757.33
specified NEC 709.09
pituitary (gland) 759.2
pleural folds 748.8
portal vein 747.40
position tooth, teeth 524.30
crowding 524.31
displacement 524.30
horizontal 524.33
vertical 524.34
distance
interocclusal
excessive 524.37
insufficient 524.36
excessive spacing 524.32
rotation 524.35
specified NEC 524.39
preauricular sinus 744.46
prepuce 752.9
prostate 752.9
pulmonary 748.60
artery 747.3
circulation 747.3
specified type NEC 748.69
valve 746.00
atresia 746.01
insufficiency 746.09
specified type NEC 746.09
stenosis 746.02
infundibular 746.83
subvalvular 746.83
vein 747.40
venous
connection 747.49
partial 747.42
total 747.41
return 747.49
partial 747.42
total (TAPVR) (complete) (subdiaphragmatic) (supradiaphragmatic) 747.41
pupil 743.9
pylorus 750.9
hypertrophy 750.5
stenosis 750.5
rachitic, fetal 756.4
radius 755.50
rectovaginal (septum) 752.40
rectum 751.5
refraction 367.9
renal 753.9
vessel 747.62
respiratory system 748.9
specified type NEC 748.8
rib 756.3
cervical 756.2
Rieger's 743.44
rings, trachea 748.3
rotation (*see also* Malrotation)
hip or thigh (*see also* Subluxation, congenital, hip) 754.32
round ligament 752.9
sacroiliac (joint) 755.69
sacrum 756.10
saddle
back 754.2
nose 754.0
syphilitic 090.5
salivary gland or duct 750.9
specified type NEC 750.26
scapula 755.50
sclera 743.9
specified type NEC 743.47
scrotum 752.9

Anomaly, anomalous — *continued*
sebaceous gland 757.9
seminal duct or tract 752.9
sense organs 742.9
specified type NEC 742.8
septum
heart — *see* Anomaly, heart, septum
nasal 748.1
sex chromosomes NEC (*see also* Anomaly, chromosomes) 758.81
shoulder (girdle) (joint) 755.50
specified type NEC 755.59
sigmoid (flexure) 751.5
sinus of Valsalva 747.29
site NEC 759.9
skeleton generalized NEC 756.50
skin (appendage) 757.9
specified type NEC 757.39
skull (bone) 756.0
with
anencephalus 740.0
encephalocele 742.0
hydrocephalus 742.3
with spina bifida (*see also* Spina bifida) 741.0 ☑
microcephalus 742.1
specified type NEC
adrenal (gland) 759.1
alimentary tract (complete) (partial) 751.8
lower 751.5
upper 750.8
ankle 755.69
anus, anal (canal) 751.5
aorta, aortic 747.29
arch 747.21
appendix 751.5
arm 755.59
artery (peripheral) NEC (*see also* Anomaly, peripheral vascular system) 747.60
brain 747.81
coronary 746.85
eye 743.58
pulmonary 747.3
retinal 743.58
umbilical 747.5
auditory canal 744.29
causing impairment of hearing 744.02
bile duct or passage 751.69
bladder 753.8
neck 753.8
bone(s) 756.9
arm 755.59
face 756.0
leg 755.69
pelvic girdle 755.69
shoulder girdle 755.59
skull 756.0
with
anencephalus 740.0
encephalocele 742.0
hydrocephalus 742.3
with spina bifida (*see also* Spina bifida) 741.0 ☑
microcephalus 742.1
brain 742.4
breast 757.6
broad ligament 752.19
bronchus 748.3
canal of Nuck 752.89
cardiac septal closure 745.8
carpus 755.59
cartilaginous 756.9
cecum 751.5
cervix 752.49
chest (wall) 756.3
chin 744.89
ciliary body 743.46
circulatory system 747.89
clavicle 755.51
clitoris 752.49
coccyx 756.19

Anomaly, anomalous — *continued*
specified type — *continued*
colon 751.5
common duct 751.69
connective tissue 756.89
cricoid cartilage 748.3
cystic duct 751.69
diaphragm 756.6
digestive organ(s) or tract 751.8
lower 751.5
upper 750.8
duodenum 751.5
ear 744.29
auricle 744.29
causing impairment of hearing 744.02
causing impairment of hearing 744.09
inner (causing impairment of hearing) 744.05
middle, except ossicles 744.03
ossicles 744.04
ejaculatory duct 752.89
endocrine 759.2
epiglottis 748.3
esophagus 750.4
Eustachian tube 744.24
eye 743.8
lid 743.63
muscle 743.69
face 744.89
bone(s) 756.0
fallopian tube 752.19
fascia 756.89
femur 755.69
fibula 755.69
finger 755.59
foot 755.67
fovea centralis 743.55
gallbladder 751.69
Gartner's duct 752.89
gastrointestinal tract 751.8
genitalia, genital organ(s)
female 752.89
external 752.49
internal NEC 752.89
male 752.89
penis 752.69
scrotal transposition 752.81
genitourinary tract NEC 752.89
glottis 748.3
hair 757.4
hand 755.59
heart 746.89
valve NEC 746.89
pulmonary 746.09
hepatic duct 751.69
hydatid of Morgagni 752.89
hymen 752.49
integument 757.8
intestine (large) (small) 751.5
fixational type 751.4
iris 743.46
jejunum 751.5
joint 755.8
kidney 753.3
knee 755.64
labium (majus) (minus) 752.49
labyrinth, membranous 744.05
larynx 748.3
leg 755.69
lens 743.39
limb, except reduction deformity 755.8
lower 755.69
reduction deformity (*see also* Deformity, reduction, lower limb) 755.30
upper 755.59
reduction deformity (*see also* Deformity, reduction, upper limb) 755.20
lip 750.26
liver 751.69
lung (fissure) (lobe) 748.69
meatus urinarius 753.8

Anomaly, anomalous — *continued*
specified type — *continued*
metacarpus 755.59
mouth 750.26
muscle 756.89
eye 743.69
musculoskeletal system, except limbs 756.9
nail 757.5
neck 744.89
nerve 742.8
acoustic 742.8
optic 742.8
nervous system 742.8
nipple 757.6
nose 748.1
organ NEC 759.89
of Corti 744.05
osseous meatus (ear) 744.03
ovary 752.0
oviduct 752.19
pancreas 751.7
parathyroid 759.2
patella 755.64
pelvic girdle 755.69
penis 752.69
pericardium 746.89
peripheral vascular system NEC (*see also* Anomaly, peripheral vascular system) 747.60
pharynx 750.29
pituitary 759.2
prostate 752.89
radius 755.59
rectum 751.5
respiratory system 748.8
rib 756.3
round ligament 752.89
sacrum 756.19
salivary duct or gland 750.26
scapula 755.59
sclera 743.47
scrotum 752.89
transposition 752.81
seminal duct or tract 752.89
shoulder girdle 755.59
site NEC 759.89
skin 757.39
skull (bone(s)) 756.0
with
anencephalus 740.0
encephalocele 742.0
hydrocephalus 742.3
with spina bifida (*see also* Spina bifida) 741.0 ☑
microcephalus 742.1
specified organ or site NEC 759.89
spermatic cord 752.89
spinal cord 742.59
spine 756.19
spleen 759.0
sternum 756.3
stomach 750.7
tarsus 755.67
tendon 756.89
testis 752.89
thorax (wall) 756.3
thymus 759.2
thyroid (gland) 759.2
cartilage 748.3
tibia 755.69
toe 755.66
tongue 750.19
trachea (cartilage) 748.3
ulna 755.59
urachus 753.7
ureter 753.4
obstructive 753.29
urethra 753.8
obstructive 753.6
urinary tract 753.8
uterus 752.3
uvula 750.26
vagina 752.49

Anomaly, anomalous — *continued*
specified type — *continued*
vascular NEC (*see also* Anomaly, peripheral vascular system) 747.60
brain 747.81
vas deferens 752.89
vein(s) (peripheral) NEC (*see also* Anomaly, peripheral vascular system) 747.60
brain 747.81
great 747.49
portal 747.49
pulmonary 747.49
vena cava (inferior) (superior) 747.49
vertebra 756.19
vulva 752.49
spermatic cord 752.9
spine, spinal 756.10
column 756.10
cord 742.9
meningocele (*see also* Spina bifida) 741.9 ☑
specified type NEC 742.59
spina bifida (*see also* Spina bifida) 741.9 ☑
vessel 747.82
meninges 742.59
nerve root 742.9
spleen 759.0
Sprengel's 755.52
sternum 756.3
stomach 750.9
specified type NEC 750.7
submaxillary gland 750.9
superior vena cava 747.40
talipes — *see* Talipes
tarsus 755.67
with complete absence of distal elements 755.31
teeth, tooth NEC 520.9
position 524.30
crowding 524.31
displacement 524.30
horizontal 524.33
vertical 524.34
distance
interocclusal
excessive 524.37
insufficient 524.36
excessive spacing 524.32
rotation 524.35
specified NEC 524.39
spacing 524.30
tendon 756.9
specified type NEC 756.89
termination
coronary artery 746.85
testis 752.9
thebesian valve 746.9
thigh 755.60
flexion (*see also* Subluxation, congenital, hip) 754.32
thorax (wall) 756.3
throat 750.9
thumb 755.50
supernumerary 755.01
thymus gland 759.2
thyroid (gland) 759.2
cartilage 748.3
tibia 755.60
saber 090.5
toe 755.66
supernumerary 755.02
webbed (*see also* Syndactylism, toes) 755.13
tongue 750.10
specified type NEC 750.19
trachea, tracheal 748.3
cartilage 748.3
rings 748.3
tragus 744.3
transverse aortic arch 747.21
trichromata 368.59
trichromatopsia 368.59

Anomaly, anomalous — *continued*
tricuspid (leaflet) (valve) 746.9
atresia 746.1
Ebstein's 746.2
specified type NEC 746.89
stenosis 746.1
trunk 759.9
Uhl's (hypoplasia of myocardium, right ventricle) 746.84
ulna 755.50
umbilicus 759.9
artery 747.5
union, trachea with larynx 748.3
unspecified site 759.9
upper extremity 755.50
vessel 747.63
urachus 753.7
specified type NEC 753.7
ureter 753.9
obstructive 753.20
specified type NEC 753.4
obstructive 753.29
urethra (valve) 753.9
obstructive 753.6
specified type NEC 753.8
urinary tract or system (any part, except urachus) 753.9
specified type NEC 753.8
urachus 753.7
uterus 752.3
with only one functioning horn 752.3
in pregnancy or childbirth 654.0 ☑
affecting fetus or newborn 763.89
causing obstructed labor 660.2 ☑
affecting fetus or newborn 763.1
uvula 750.9
vagina 752.40
valleculae 748.3
valve (heart) NEC 746.9
formation, ureter 753.29
pulmonary 746.00
specified type NEC 746.89
vascular NEC (*see also* Anomaly, peripheral vascular system) 747.60
ring 747.21
vas deferens 752.9
vein(s) (peripheral) NEC (*see also* Anomaly, peripheral vascular system) 747.60
brain 747.81
cerebral 747.81
coronary 746.89
great 747.40
specified type NEC 747.49
portal 747.40
pulmonary 747.40
retina 743.9
vena cava (inferior) (superior) 747.40
venous — *see* Anomaly, vein ●
venous return (pulmonary) 747.49
partial 747.42
total 747.41
ventricle, ventricular (heart) 746.9
bands 746.9
folds 746.9
septa 745.4
vertebra 756.10
vesicourethral orifice 753.9
vessels NEC (*see also* Anomaly, peripheral vascular system) 747.60
optic papilla 743.9
vitelline duct 751.0
vitreous humor 743.9
specified type NEC 743.51
vulva 752.40
wrist (joint) 755.50
Anomia 784.69
Anonychia 757.5
acquired 703.8
Anophthalmos, anophthalmus (clinical) (congenital) (globe) 743.00

Anophthalmos, anophthalmus — *continued*
acquired V45.78
Anopsia (altitudinal) (quadrant) 368.46
Anorchia 752.89
Anorchism, anorchidism 752.89
Anorexia 783.0
hysterical 300.11
nervosa 307.1
Anosmia — *see also* Disturbance, sensation 781.1
hysterical 300.11
postinfectional 478.9
psychogenic 306.7
traumatic 951.8
Anosognosia 780.99
Anosphrasia 781.1
Anosteoplasia 756.50
Anotia 744.09
Anovulatory cycle 628.0
Anoxemia 799.02
newborn 770.88
Anoxia 799.02
altitude 993.2
cerebral 348.1
with
abortion — *see* Abortion, by type, with specified complication NEC
ectopic pregnancy (*see also* categories 633.0–633.9) 639.8
molar pregnancy (*see also* categories 630–632) 639.8
complicating
delivery (cesarean) (instrumental) 669.4 ☑
ectopic or molar pregnancy 639.8
obstetric anesthesia or sedation 668.2 ☑
during or resulting from a procedure 997.01
following
abortion 639.8
ectopic or molar pregnancy 639.8
newborn (*see also* Distress, fetal, liveborn infant) 770.88
due to drowning 994.1
fetal, affecting newborn 770.88
heart — *see* Insufficiency, coronary
high altitude 993.2
intrauterine
fetal death (before onset of labor) 768.0
during labor 768.1
liveborn infant — *see* Distress, fetal, liveborn infant
myocardial — *see* Insufficiency, coronary
newborn 768.9
mild or moderate 768.6
severe 768.5
pathological 799.02
Anteflexion — *see* Anteversion
Antenatal
care, normal pregnancy V22.1
first V22.0
sampling ●
chorionic villus V28.89 ●
screening of mother (for) V28.9
based on amniocentesis NEC V28.2
chromosomal anomalies V28.0
raised alphafetoprotein levels V28.1
chromosomal anomalies V28.0
fetal growth retardation using ulatrasonics V28.4
genomic V28.89 ●
isoimmunization V28.5
malformations using ulatrasonics V28.3
proteomic V28.89 ●
raised alphafetoprotein levels in amniotic fluid V28.1

Antenatal — *continued*
screening of mother — *continued*
risk ●
pre-term labor V28.82 ●
specified condition NEC V28.89 ▲
Streptococcus B V28.6
survey ●
fetal anatomic V28.81 ●
testing ●
nuchal translucency V28.89 ●
Antepartum — *see* condition
Anterior — *see also* condition
spinal artery compression syndrome 721.1
Antero-occlusion 524.24
Anteversion
cervix — *see* Anteversion, uterus
femur (neck), congenital 755.63
uterus, uterine (cervix) (postinfectional) (postpartal, old) 621.6
congenital 752.3
in pregnancy or childbirth 654.4 ☑
affecting fetus or newborn 763.89
causing obstructed labor 660.2 ☑
affecting fetus or newborn 763.1
Anthracosilicosis (occupational) 500
Anthracosis (lung) (occupational) 500
lingua 529.3
Anthrax 022.9
with pneumonia 022.1 *[484.5]*
colitis 022.2
cutaneous 022.0
gastrointestinal 022.2
intestinal 022.2
pulmonary 022.1
respiratory 022.1
septicemia 022.3
specified manifestation NEC 022.8
Anthropoid pelvis 755.69
with disproportion (fetopelvic) 653.2 ☑
affecting fetus or newborn 763.1
causing obstructed labor 660.1 ☑
affecting fetus or newborn 763.1
Anthropophobia 300.29
Antibioma, breast 611.0
Antibodies
maternal (blood group) (*see also* Incompatibility) 656.2 ☑
anti-D, cord blood 656.1 ☑
fetus or newborn 773.0
Antibody deficiency syndrome
agammaglobulinemic 279.00
congenital 279.04
hypogammaglobulinemic 279.00
Anticoagulant, circulating — *see also* Circulating anticoagulants 286.5
Antimongolism syndrome 758.39
Antimonial cholera 985.4
Antisocial personality 301.7
Antithrombinemia — *see also* Circulating anticoagulants 286.5
Antithromboplastinemia — *see also* Circulating anticoagulants 286.5
Antithromboplastinogenemia — *see also* Circulating anticoagulants 286.5
Antitoxin complication or reaction — *see* Complications, vaccination
Anton (-Babinski) syndrome (hemiasomatognosia) 307.9
Antritis (chronic) 473.0
maxilla 473.0
acute 461.0
stomach 535.4 ☑
Antrum, antral — *see* condition
Anuria 788.5
with
abortion — *see* Abortion, by type, with renal failure
ectopic pregnancy (*see also* categories 633.0–633.9) 639.3

☑ Additional Digit Required — Refer to the Tabular List for Digit Selection
Subterms under main terms may continue to next column or page
▸◂ Revised Text ● New Line ▲ Revised Code

- **Anuria** — *continued*
  - with — *continued*
    - molar pregnancy (*see also* categories 630–632) 639.3
  - calculus (impacted) (recurrent) 592.9
    - kidney 592.0
    - ureter 592.1
  - congenital 753.3
  - due to a procedure 997.5
  - following
    - abortion 639.3
    - ectopic or molar pregnancy 639.3
  - newborn 753.3
  - postrenal 593.4
  - puerperal, postpartum, childbirth 669.3 ☑
  - specified as due to a procedure 997.5
  - sulfonamide
    - correct substance properly administered 788.5
    - overdose or wrong substance given or taken 961.0
  - traumatic (following crushing) 958.5
- **Anus, anal** — *see* ▶*also*◀ condition
  - high risk human papillomavirus (HPV) DNA test positive 796.75 ●
  - low risk human papillomavirus (HPV) DNA test positive 796.79 ●
- **Anusitis** 569.49
- **Anxiety** (neurosis) (reaction) (state) 300.00
  - alcohol-induced 291.89
  - depression 300.4
  - drug-induced 292.89
  - due to or associated with physical condition 293.84
  - generalized 300.02
  - hysteria 300.20
  - in
    - acute stress reaction 308.0
    - transient adjustment reaction 309.24
  - panic type 300.01
  - separation, abnormal 309.21
  - syndrome (organic) (transient) 293.84
- **Aorta, aortic** — *see* condition
- **Aortectasia** 441.9
- **Aortitis** (nonsyphilitic) 447.6
  - arteriosclerotic 440.0
  - calcific 447.6
  - Döhle-Heller 093.1
  - luetic 093.1
  - rheumatic (*see also* Endocarditis, acute, rheumatic) 391.1
  - rheumatoid — *see* Arthritis, rheumatoid
  - specific 093.1
  - syphilitic 093.1
    - congenital 090.5
- **Apathetic thyroid storm** — *see also* Thyrotoxicosis 242.9 ☑
- **Apepsia** 536.8
  - achlorhydric 536.0
  - psychogenic 306.4
- **Aperistalsis, esophagus** 530.0
- **Apert-Gallais syndrome** (adrenogenital) 255.2
- **Apertognathia** 524.20
- **Apert's syndrome** (acrocephalosyndactyly) 755.55
- **Aphagia** 787.20
  - psychogenic 307.1
- **Aphakia** (acquired) (bilateral) (postoperative) (unilateral) 379.31
  - congenital 743.35
- **Aphalangia** (congenital) 755.4
  - lower limb (complete) (intercalary) (partial) (terminal) 755.39
    - meaning all digits (complete) (partial) 755.31
    - transverse 755.31
  - upper limb (complete) (intercalary) (partial) (terminal) 755.29
    - meaning all digits (complete) (partial) 755.21
    - transverse 755.21
- **Aphasia** (amnestic) (ataxic) (auditory) (Broca's) (choreatic) (classic) (expressive) (global) (ideational) (ideokinetic) (ideomotor) (jargon) (motor) (nominal) (receptive) (semantic) (sensory) (syntactic) (verbal) (visual) (Wernicke's) 784.3
  - developmental 315.31
  - syphilis, tertiary 094.89
  - uremic — *see* Uremia
- **Aphemia** 784.3
  - uremic — *see* Uremia
- **Aphonia** 784.41
  - clericorum 784.49
  - hysterical 300.11
  - organic 784.41
  - psychogenic 306.1
- **Aphthae, aphthous** — *see also* condition
  - Bednar's 528.2
  - cachectic 529.0
  - epizootic 078.4
  - fever 078.4
  - oral 528.2
  - stomatitis 528.2
  - thrush 112.0
  - ulcer (oral) (recurrent) 528.2
    - genital organ(s) NEC
      - female 616.50
      - male 608.89
    - larynx 478.79
- **Apical** — *see* condition
- **Apical ballooning syndrome** 429.83
- **Aplasia** — *see also* Agenesis
  - alveolar process (acquired) 525.8
    - congenital 750.26
  - aorta (congenital) 747.22
  - aortic valve (congenital) 746.89
  - axialis extracorticalis (congenital) 330.0
  - bone marrow (myeloid) 284.9
    - acquired (secondary) 284.89
    - congenital 284.01
    - idiopathic 284.9
  - brain 740.0
    - specified part 742.2
  - breast 757.6
  - bronchus 748.3
  - cementum 520.4
  - cerebellar 742.2
  - congenital (pure) red cell 284.01
  - corpus callosum 742.2
  - erythrocyte 284.81
    - congenital 284.01
  - extracortical axial 330.0
  - eye (congenital) 743.00
  - fovea centralis (congenital) 743.55
  - germinal (cell) 606.0
  - iris 743.45
  - labyrinth, membranous 744.05
  - limb (congenital) 755.4
    - lower NEC 755.30
    - upper NEC 755.20
  - lung (bilateral) (congenital) (unilateral) 748.5
  - nervous system NEC 742.8
  - nuclear 742.8
  - ovary 752.0
  - Pelizaeus-Merzbacher 330.0
  - prostate (congenital) 752.89
  - red cell (with thymoma) (adult) 284.81
    - acquired (secondary) 284.81
    - congenital 284.01
    - hereditary 284.01
    - of infants 284.01
    - primary 284.01
    - pure 284.01
  - round ligament (congenital) 752.89
  - salivary gland 750.21
  - skin (congenital) 757.39
  - spinal cord 742.59
  - spleen 759.0
  - testis (congenital) 752.89
  - thymic, with immunodeficiency 279.2
  - thyroid 243
  - uterus 752.3
  - ventral horn cell 742.59
- **Apleuria** 756.3
- **Apnea, apneic** (spells) 786.03
  - newborn, neonatorum 770.81
    - essential 770.81
    - obstructive 770.82
    - primary 770.81
    - sleep 770.81
    - specified NEC 770.82
  - psychogenic 306.1
  - sleep, unspecified 780.57
    - with
      - hypersomnia, unspecified 780.53
      - hyposomnia, unspecified 780.51
      - insomnia, unspecified 780.51
      - sleep disturbance 780.57
    - central, in conditions classified elsewhere 327.27
    - obstructive (adult) (pediatric) 327.23
    - organic 327.20
      - other 327.29
    - primary central 327.21
- **Apneumatosis newborn** 770.4
- **Apodia** 755.31
- **Aponeurosis** 726.90
- **Apophysitis** (bone) — *see also* Osteochondrosis 732.9
  - calcaneus 732.5
  - juvenile 732.6
- **Apoplectiform convulsions** — *see also* Disease, cerebrovascular, acute 436
- **Apoplexia, apoplexy, apoplectic** — *see also* Disease, cerebrovascular, acute 436
  - abdominal 569.89
  - adrenal 036.3
  - attack 436
  - basilar (*see also* Disease, cerebrovascular, acute) 436
  - brain (*see also* Disease, cerebrovascular, acute) 436
  - bulbar (*see also* Disease, cerebrovascular, acute) 436
  - capillary (*see also* Disease, cerebrovascular, acute) 436
  - cardiac (*see also* Infarct, myocardium) 410.9 ☑
  - cerebral (*see also* Disease, cerebrovascular, acute) 436
  - chorea (*see also* Disease, cerebrovascular, acute) 436
  - congestive (*see also* Disease, cerebrovascular, acute) 436
    - newborn 767.4
  - embolic (*see also* Embolism, brain) 434.1 ☑
  - fetus 767.0
  - fit (*see also* Disease, cerebrovascular, acute) 436
  - healed or old V12.54
  - heart (auricle) (ventricle) (*see also* Infarct, myocardium) 410.9 ☑
  - heat 992.0
  - hemiplegia (*see also* Disease, cerebrovascular, acute) 436
  - hemorrhagic (stroke) (*see also* Hemorrhage, brain) 432.9
  - ingravescent (*see also* Disease, cerebrovascular, acute) 436
  - late effect — *see* Late effect(s) (of) cerebrovascular disease
  - lung — *see* Embolism, pulmonary
  - meninges, hemorrhagic (*see also* Hemorrhage, subarachnoid) 430
  - neonatorum 767.0
  - newborn 767.0
  - pancreatitis 577.0
  - placenta 641.2 ☑
  - progressive (*see also* Disease, cerebrovascular, acute) 436
  - pulmonary (artery) (vein) — *see* Embolism, pulmonary
  - sanguineous (*see also* Disease, cerebrovascular, acute) 436
- **Apoplexia, apoplexy, apoplectic** — *see also* Disease, cerebrovascular, acute — *continued*
  - seizure (*see also* Disease, cerebrovascular, acute) 436
  - serous (*see also* Disease, cerebrovascular, acute) 436
  - spleen 289.59
  - stroke (*see also* Disease, cerebrovascular, acute) 436
  - thrombotic (*see also* Thrombosis, brain) 434.0 ☑
  - uremic — *see* Uremia
  - uteroplacental 641.2 ☑
- **Appendage**
  - fallopian tube (cyst of Morgagni) 752.11
  - intestine (epiploic) 751.5
  - preauricular 744.1
  - testicular (organ of Morgagni) 752.89
- **Appendicitis** 541
  - with
    - perforation, peritonitis (generalized), or rupture 540.0
      - with peritoneal abscess 540.1
    - peritoneal abscess 540.1
  - acute (catarrhal) (fulminating) (gangrenous) (inflammatory) (obstructive) (retrocecal) (suppurative) 540.9
    - with
      - perforation, peritonitis, or rupture 540.0
        - with peritoneal abscess 540.1
      - peritoneal abscess 540.1
  - amebic 006.8
  - chronic (recurrent) 542
  - exacerbation — *see* Appendicitis, acute
  - fulminating — *see* Appendicitis, acute
  - gangrenous — *see* Appendicitis, acute
  - healed (obliterative) 542
  - interval 542
  - neurogenic 542
  - obstructive 542
  - pneumococcal 541
  - recurrent 542
  - relapsing 542
  - retrocecal 541
  - subacute (adhesive) 542
  - subsiding 542
  - suppurative — *see* Appendicitis, acute
  - tuberculous (*see also* Tuberculosis) 014.8 ☑
- **Appendiclausis** 543.9
- **Appendicolithiasis** 543.9
- **Appendicopathia oxyurica** 127.4
- **Appendix, appendicular** — *see also* condition
  - Morgagni (male) 752.89
    - fallopian tube 752.11
- **Appetite**
  - depraved 307.52
  - excessive 783.6
    - psychogenic 307.51
  - lack or loss (*see also* Anorexia) 783.0
    - nonorganic origin 307.59
  - perverted 307.52
    - hysterical 300.11
- **Apprehension, apprehensiveness** (abnormal) (state) 300.00
  - specified type NEC 300.09
- **Approximal wear** 521.10
- **Apraxia** (classic) (ideational) (ideokinetic) (ideomotor) (motor) 784.69
  - oculomotor, congenital 379.51
  - verbal 784.69
- **Aptyalism** 527.7
- **Aqueous misdirection** 365.83
- **Arabicum elephantiasis** — *see also* Infestation, filarial 125.9
- **Arachnidism** 989.5
- **Arachnitis** — *see* Meningitis
- **Arachnodactyly** 759.82
- **Arachnoidism** 989.5

- **Arachnoiditis** (acute) (adhesive) (basic) (brain) (cerebrospinal) (chiasmal) (chronic) (spinal) — *see also* Meningitis 322.9
  - meningococcal (chronic) 036.0
  - syphilitic 094.2
  - tuberculous (*see also* Tuberculosis, meninges) 013.0 ☑
- **Araneism** 989.5
- **Arboencephalitis, Australian** 062.4
- **Arborization block** (heart) 426.6
- **Arbor virus, arbovirus** (infection) NEC 066.9
- **ARC** 042
- **Arches** — *see* condition
- **Arcuatus uterus** 752.3
- **Arcus** (cornea)
  - juvenilis 743.43
    - interfering with vision 743.42
  - senilis 371.41
- **Arc-welders' lung** 503
- **Arc-welders' syndrome** (photokeratitis) 370.24
- **Areflexia** 796.1
- **Areola** — *see* condition
- **Argentaffinoma** (M8241/1) — *see also* Neoplasm, by site, uncertain behavior
  - benign (M8241/0) — *see* Neoplasm, by site, benign
  - malignant (M8241/3) — *see* Neoplasm, by site, malignant
  - syndrome 259.2
- **Argentinian hemorrhagic fever** 078.7
- **Arginosuccinicaciduria** 270.6
- **Argonz-Del Castillo syndrome** (nonpuerperal galactorrhea and amenorrhea) 253.1
- **Argyll-Robertson phenomenon, pupil, or syndrome** (syphilitic) 094.89
  - atypical 379.45
  - nonluetic 379.45
  - nonsyphilitic 379.45
  - reversed 379.45
- **Argyria, argyriasis** NEC 985.8
  - conjunctiva 372.55
  - cornea 371.16
  - from drug or medicinal agent
    - correct substance properly administered 709.09
    - overdose or wrong substance given or taken 961.2
- **Arhinencephaly** 742.2
- **Arias-Stella phenomenon** 621.30
- **Ariboflavinosis** 266.0
- **Arizona enteritis** 008.1
- **Arm** — *see* condition
- **Armenian disease** 277.31
- **Arnold-Chiari obstruction or syndrome** — *see also* Spina bifida 741.0 ☑
  - type I 348.4
  - type II (*see also* Spina bifida) 741.0 ☑
  - type III 742.0
  - type IV 742.2
- **Arousals**
  - confusional 327.41
- **Arrest, arrested**
  - active phase of labor 661.1 ☑
    - affecting fetus or newborn 763.7
  - any plane in pelvis
    - complicating delivery 660.1 ☑
      - affecting fetus or newborn 763.1
  - bone marrow (*see also* Anemia, aplastic) 284.9
  - cardiac 427.5
    - with
      - abortion — *see* Abortion, by type, with specified complication NEC
      - ectopic pregnancy (*see also* categories 633.0–633.9) 639.8
      - molar pregnancy (*see also* categories 630–632) 639.8
- **Arrest, arrested** — *continued*
  - cardiac — *continued*
    - complicating
      - anesthesia
        - correct substance properly administered 427.5
        - obstetric 668.1 ☑
        - overdose or wrong substance given 968.4
        - specified anesthetic — *see* Table of Drugs and Chemicals
      - delivery (cesarean) (instrumental) 669.4 ☑
      - ectopic or molar pregnancy 639.8
      - surgery (nontherapeutic) (therapeutic) 997.1
    - fetus or newborn 779.85
    - following
      - abortion 639.8
      - ectopic or molar pregnancy 639.8
    - personal history, successfully resuscitated V12.53
    - postoperative (immediate) 997.1
      - long-term effect of cardiac surgery 429.4
  - cardiorespiratory (*see also* Arrest, cardiac) 427.5
  - deep transverse 660.3 ☑
    - affecting fetus or newborn 763.1
  - development or growth
    - bone 733.91
    - child 783.40
    - fetus 764.9 ☑
      - affecting management of pregnancy 656.5 ☑
    - tracheal rings 748.3
  - epiphyseal 733.91
  - granulopoiesis 288.09
  - heart — *see* Arrest, cardiac
  - respiratory 799.1
    - newborn 770.87
  - sinus 426.6
  - transverse (deep) 660.3 ☑
    - affecting fetus or newborn 763.1
- **Arrhenoblastoma** (M8630/1)
  - benign (M8630/0)
    - specified site — *see* Neoplasm, by site, benign
    - unspecified site
      - female 220
      - male 222.0
  - malignant (M8630/3)
    - specified site — *see* Neoplasm, by site, malignant
    - unspecified site
      - female 183.0
      - male 186.9
  - specified site — *see* Neoplasm, by site, uncertain behavior
  - unspecified site
    - female 236.2
    - male 236.4
- **Arrhinencephaly** 742.2
  - due to
    - trisomy 13 (13-15) 758.1
    - trisomy 18 (16-18) 758.2
- **Arrhythmia** (auricle) (cardiac) (cordis) (gallop rhythm) (juvenile) (nodal) (reflex) (sinus) (supraventricular) (transitory) (ventricle) 427.9
  - bigeminal rhythm 427.89
  - block 426.9
  - bradycardia 427.89
  - contractions, premature 427.60
  - coronary sinus 427.89
  - ectopic 427.89
  - extrasystolic 427.60
  - postoperative 997.1
  - psychogenic 306.2
  - vagal 780.2
- **Arrillaga-Ayerza syndrome** (pulmonary artery sclerosis with pulmonary hypertension) 416.0
- **Arsenical**
  - dermatitis 692.4
  - keratosis 692.4
  - pigmentation 985.1
    - from drug or medicinal agent
      - correct substance properly administered 709.09
      - overdose or wrong substance given or taken 961.1
- **Arsenism** 985.1
  - from drug or medicinal agent
    - correct substance properly administered 692.4
    - overdose or wrong substance given or taken 961.1
- **Arterial** — *see* condition
- **Arteriectasis** 447.8
- **Arteriofibrosis** — *see* Arteriosclerosis
- **Arteriolar sclerosis** — *see* Arteriosclerosis
- **Arteriolith** — *see* Arteriosclerosis
- **Arteriolitis** 447.6
  - necrotizing, kidney 447.5
  - renal — *see* Hypertension, kidney
- **Arteriolosclerosis** — *see* Arteriosclerosis
- **Arterionephrosclerosis** — *see also* Hypertension, kidney 403.90
- **Arteriopathy** 447.9
- **Arteriosclerosis, arteriosclerotic** (artery) (deformans) (diffuse) (disease) (endarteritis) (general) (obliterans) (obliterative) (occlusive) (senile) (with calcification) 440.9
  - with
    - gangrene 440.24
    - psychosis (*see also* Psychosis, arteriosclerotic) 290.40
    - ulceration 440.23
  - aorta 440.0
  - arteries of extremities — *see* Arteriosclerosis, extremities
  - basilar (artery) (*see also* Occlusion, artery, basilar) 433.0 ☑
  - brain 437.0
  - bypass graft
    - coronary artery 414.05
      - autologous artery (gastroepiploic) (internal mammary) 414.04
      - autologous vein 414.02
      - nonautologous biological 414.03
      - of transplanted heart 414.07
    - extremity 440.30
      - autologous vein 440.31
      - nonautologous biological 440.32
  - cardiac — *see* Arteriosclerosis, coronary
  - cardiopathy — *see* Arteriosclerosis, coronary
  - cardiorenal (*see also* Hypertension, cardiorenal) 404.90
  - cardiovascular (*see also* Disease, cardiovascular) 429.2
  - carotid (artery) (common) (internal) (*see also* Occlusion, artery, carotid) 433.1 ☑
  - central nervous system 437.0
  - cerebral 437.0
    - late effect — *see* Late effect(s) (of) cerebrovascular disease
  - cerebrospinal 437.0
  - cerebrovascular 437.0
  - coronary (artery) 414.00
    - due to lipid rich plaque 414.3 ●
    - graft — *see* Arteriosclerosis, bypass graft
    - native artery 414.01
      - of transplanted heart 414.06
  - extremities (native artery) NEC 440.20
    - bypass graft 440.30
      - autologous vein 440.31
      - nonautologous biological 440.32
    - claudication (intermittent) 440.21
      - and
        - gangrene 440.24
        - rest pain 440.22
- **Arteriosclerosis, arteriosclerotic** — *continued*
  - extremities — *continued*
    - claudication — *continued*
      - and — *continued*
        - rest pain — *continued*
          - and
            - gangrene 440.24
            - ulceration 440.23
              - and gangrene 440.24
        - ulceration 440.23
          - and gangrene 440.24
    - gangrene 440.24
    - rest pain 440.22
      - and
        - gangrene 440.24
        - ulceration 440.23
          - and gangrene 440.24
    - specified site NEC 440.29
    - ulceration 440.23
      - and gangrene 440.24
  - heart (disease) (*see also* Arteriosclerosis, coronary)
    - valve 424.99
      - aortic 424.1
      - mitral 424.0
      - pulmonary 424.3
      - tricuspid 424.2
  - kidney (*see also* Hypertension, kidney) 403.90
  - labyrinth, labyrinthine 388.00
  - medial NEC (*see also* Arteriosclerosis, extremities) 440.20
  - mesentery (artery) 557.1
  - Mönckeberg's (*see also* Arteriosclerosis, extremities) 440.20
  - myocarditis 429.0
  - nephrosclerosis (*see also* Hypertension, kidney) 403.90
  - peripheral (of extremities) — *see* Arteriosclerosis, extremities
  - precerebral 433.9 ☑
    - specified artery NEC 433.8 ☑
  - pulmonary (idiopathic) 416.0
  - renal (*see also* Hypertension, kidney) 403.90
    - arterioles (*see also* Hypertension, kidney) 403.90
    - artery 440.1
  - retinal (vascular) 440.8 *[362.13]*
  - specified artery NEC 440.8
    - with gangrene 440.8 *[785.4]*
  - spinal (cord) 437.0
  - vertebral (artery) (*see also* Occlusion, artery, vertebral) 433.2 ☑
- **Arteriospasm** 443.9
- **Arteriovenous** — *see* condition
- **Arteritis** 447.6
  - allergic (*see also* Angiitis, hypersensitivity) 446.20
  - aorta (nonsyphilitic) 447.6
    - syphilitic 093.1
  - aortic arch 446.7
  - brachiocephalica 446.7
  - brain 437.4
    - syphilitic 094.89
  - branchial 446.7
  - cerebral 437.4
    - late effect — *see* Late effect(s) (of) cerebrovascular disease
    - syphilitic 094.89
  - coronary (artery) (*see also* Arteriosclerosis, coronary)
    - rheumatic 391.9
      - chronic 398.99
    - syphilitic 093.89
  - cranial (left) (right) 446.5
  - deformans — *see* Arteriosclerosis
  - giant cell 446.5
  - necrosing or necrotizing 446.0
  - nodosa 446.0
  - obliterans (*see also* Arteriosclerosis)
    - subclaviocarotica 446.7
  - pulmonary 417.8
  - retina 362.18

Arteritis — *continued*
- rheumatic — *see* Fever, rheumatic
- senile — *see* Arteriosclerosis
- suppurative 447.2
- syphilitic (general) 093.89
  - brain 094.89
  - coronary 093.89
  - spinal 094.89
- temporal 446.5
- young female, syndrome 446.7

Artery, arterial — *see* condition

Arthralgia — *see also* Pain, joint 719.4 ☑
- allergic (*see also* Pain, joint) 719.4 ☑
- in caisson disease 993.3
- psychogenic 307.89
- rubella 056.71
- Salmonella 003.23
- temporomandibular joint 524.62

Arthritis, arthritic (acute) (chronic) (subacute) 716.9 ☑
- meaning Osteoarthritis — *see* Osteoarthrosis

> *Note — Use the following fifth-digit subclassification with categories 711–712, 715–716:*
>
> 0 *site unspecified*
> 1 *shoulder region*
> 2 *upper arm*
> 3 *forearm*
> 4 *hand*
> 5 *pelvic region and thigh*
> 6 *lower leg*
> 7 *ankle and foot*
> 8 *other specified sites*
> 9 *multiple sites*

- allergic 716.2 ☑
- ankylosing (crippling) (spine) 720.0
  - sites other than spine 716.9 ☑
- atrophic 714.0
  - spine 720.9
- back (*see also* Arthritis, spine) 721.90
- Bechterew's (ankylosing spondylitis) 720.0
- blennorrhagic 098.50
- cervical, cervicodorsal (*see also* Spondylosis, cervical) 721.0
- Charcôt's 094.0 [713.5]
  - diabetic 250.6 ☑ [713.5]
    - due to secondary diabetes ● 249.6 ☑ [713.5] ●
  - syringomyelic 336.0 [713.5]
  - tabetic 094.0 [713.5]
- chylous (*see also* Filariasis) 125.9 [711.7] ☑
- climacteric NEC 716.3 ☑
- coccyx 721.8
- cricoarytenoid 478.79
- crystal (-induced) — *see* Arthritis, due to crystals
- deformans (*see also* Osteoarthrosis) 715.9 ☑
  - spine 721.90
    - with myelopathy 721.91
- degenerative (*see also* Osteoarthrosis) 715.9 ☑
  - idiopathic 715.09
  - polyarticular 715.09
  - spine 721.90
    - with myelopathy 721.91
- dermatoarthritis, lipoid 272.8 [713.0]
- due to or associated with
  - acromegaly 253.0 [713.0]
  - actinomycosis 039.8 [711.4] ☑
  - amyloidosis 277.39 [713.7]
  - bacterial disease NEC 040.89 [711.4] ☑
  - Behçet's syndrome 136.1 [711.2] ☑
  - blastomycosis 116.0 [711.6] ☑
  - brucellosis (*see also* Brucellosis) 023.9 [711.4] ☑

Arthritis, arthritic — *continued*
- due to or associated with — *continued*
  - caisson disease 993.3
  - coccidioidomycosis 114.3 [711.6] ☑
  - coliform (Escherichia coli) 711.0 ☑
  - colitis, ulcerative (*see also* Colitis, ulcerative) 556.9 [713.1]
  - cowpox 051.01 [711.5] ☑ ▲
  - crystals (*see also* Gout)
    - dicalcium phosphate 275.49 [712.1] ☑
    - pyrophosphate 275.49 [712.2] ☑
    - specified NEC 275.49 [712.8] ☑
  - dermatoarthritis, lipoid 272.8 [713.0]
  - dermatological disorder NEC 709.9 [713.3]
  - diabetes 250.6 ☑ [713.5]
    - due to secondary diabetes ● 249.6 ☑ [713.5] ●
  - diphtheria 032.89 [711.4] ☑
  - dracontiasis 125.7 [711.7] ☑
  - dysentery 009.0 [711.3] ☑
  - endocrine disorder NEC 259.9 [713.0]
  - enteritis NEC 009.1 [711.3] ☑
    - infectious (*see also* Enteritis, infectious) 009.0 [711.3] ☑
      - specified organism NEC 008.8 [711.3] ☑
    - regional (*see also* Enteritis, regional) 555.9 [713.1]
    - specified organism NEC 008.8 [711.3] ☑
  - epiphyseal slip, nontraumatic (old) 716.8 ☑
  - erysipelas 035 [711.4] ☑
  - erythema
    - epidemic 026.1
    - multiforme 695.10 [713.3] ▲
    - nodosum 695.2 [713.3]
  - Escherichia coli 711.0 ☑
  - filariasis NEC 125.9 [711.7] ☑
  - gastrointestinal condition NEC 569.9 [713.1]
  - glanders 024 [711.4] ☑
  - Gonococcus 098.50
  - gout 274.0
  - helminthiasis NEC 128.9 [711.7] ☑
  - hematological disorder NEC 289.9 [713.2]
  - hemochromatosis 275.0 [713.0]
  - hemoglobinopathy NEC (*see also* Disease, hemoglobin) 282.7 [713.2]
  - hemophilia (*see also* Hemophilia) 286.0 [713.2]
  - Hemophilus influenzae (H. influenzae) 711.0 ☑
  - Henoch (-Schönlein) purpura 287.0 [713.6]
  - H. influenzae 711.0 ☑
  - histoplasmosis NEC (*see also* Histoplasmosis) 115.99 [711.6] ☑
  - human parvovirus 079.83 [711.5] ☑
  - hyperparathyroidism 252.00 [713.0]
  - hypersensitivity reaction NEC 995.3 [713.6]
  - hypogammaglobulinemia (*see also* Hypogamma-globulinemia) 279.00 [713.0]
  - hypothyroidism NEC 244.9 [713.0]
  - infection (*see also* Arthritis, infectious) 711.9 ☑
  - infectious disease NEC 136.9 [711.8] ☑
  - leprosy (*see also* Leprosy) 030.9 [711.4] ☑
  - leukemia NEC (M9800/3) 208.9 [713.2]

Arthritis, arthritic — *continued*
- due to or associated with — *continued*
  - lipoid dermatoarthritis 272.8 [713.0]
  - Lyme disease 088.81 [711.8] ☑
  - Mediterranean fever, familial 277.31 [713.7]
  - meningococcal infection 036.82
  - metabolic disorder NEC 277.9 [713.0]
  - multiple myelomatosis (M9730/3) 203.0 [713.2]
  - mumps 072.79 [711.5] ☑
  - mycobacteria 031.8 [711.4] ☑
  - mycosis NEC 117.9 [711.6] ☑
  - neurological disorder NEC 349.9 [713.5]
  - ochronosis 270.2 [713.0]
  - O'Nyong Nyong 066.3 [711.5] ☑
  - parasitic disease NEC 136.9 [711.8] ☑
  - paratyphoid fever (*see also* Fever, paratyphoid) 002.9 [711.3] ☑
  - parvovirus B19 079.83 [711.5] ☑
  - Pneumococcus 711.0 ☑
  - poliomyelitis (*see also* Poliomyelitis) 045.9 ☑ [711.5] ☑
  - Pseudomonas 711.0 ☑
  - psoriasis 696.0
  - pyogenic organism (E. coli) (H. influenzae) (Pseudomonas) (Streptococcus) 711.0 ☑
  - rat-bite fever 026.1 [711.4] ☑
  - regional enteritis (*see also* Enteritis, regional) 555.9 [713.1]
  - Reiter's disease 099.3 [711.1] ☑
  - respiratory disorder NEC 519.9 [713.4]
  - reticulosis, malignant (M9720/3) 202.3 [713.2]
  - rubella 056.71
  - salmonellosis 003.23
  - sarcoidosis 135 [713.7]
  - serum sickness 999.5 [713.6]
  - Staphylococcus 711.0 ☑
  - Streptococcus 711.0 ☑
  - syphilis (*see also* Syphilis) 094.0 [711.4] ☑
  - syringomyelia 336.0 [713.5]
  - thalassemia 282.49 [713.2]
  - tuberculosis (*see also* Tuberculosis, arthritis) 015.9 ☑ [711.4] ☑
  - typhoid fever 002.0 [711.3] ☑
  - ulcerative colitis (*see also* Colitis, ulcerative) 556.9 [713.1]
  - urethritis
    - nongonococcal (*see also* Urethritis, nongonococcal) 099.40 [711.1] ☑
    - nonspecific (*see also* Urethritis, nongonococcal) 099.40 [711.1] ☑
    - Reiter's 099.3
  - viral disease NEC 079.99 [711.5] ☑
- erythema epidemic 026.1
- gonococcal 098.50
- gouty (acute) 274.0
- hypertrophic (*see also* Osteoarthrosis) 715.9 ☑
  - spine 721.90
    - with myelopathy 721.91
- idiopathic, blennorrheal 099.3
- in caisson disease 993.3 [713.8]
- infectious or infective (acute) (chronic) (subacute) NEC 711.9 ☑
  - nonpyogenic 711.9 ☑
  - spine 720.9
- inflammatory NEC 714.9
- juvenile rheumatoid (chronic) (polyarticular) 714.30
  - acute 714.31
  - monoarticular 714.33
  - pauciarticular 714.32
- lumbar (*see also* Spondylosis, lumbar) 721.3

Arthritis, arthritic — *continued*
- meningococcal 036.82
- menopausal NEC 716.3 ☑
- migratory — *see* Fever, rheumatic
- neuropathic (Charcôt's) 094.0 [713.5]
  - diabetic 250.6 ☑ [713.5]
    - due to secondary diabetes ● 249.6 ☑ [713.5] ●
  - nonsyphilitic NEC 349.9 [713.5]
  - syringomyelic 336.0 [713.5]
  - tabetic 094.0 [713.5]
- nodosa (*see also* Osteoarthrosis) 715.9 ☑
  - spine 721.90
    - with myelopathy 721.91
- nonpyogenic NEC 716.9 ☑
  - spine 721.90
    - with myelopathy 721.91
- ochronotic 270.2 [713.0]
- palindromic (*see also* Rheumatism, palindromic) 719.3 ☑
- pneumococcal 711.0 ☑
- postdysenteric 009.0 [711.3] ☑
- postrheumatic, chronic (Jaccoud's) 714.4
- primary progressive 714.0
  - spine 720.9
- proliferative 714.0
  - spine 720.0
- psoriatic 696.0
- purulent 711.0 ☑
- pyogenic or pyemic 711.0 ☑
- rheumatic 714.0
  - acute or subacute — *see* Fever, rheumatic
  - chronic 714.0
  - spine 720.9
- rheumatoid (nodular) 714.0
  - with
    - splenoadenomegaly and leukopenia 714.1
    - visceral or systemic involvement 714.2
  - aortitis 714.89
  - carditis 714.2
  - heart disease 714.2
  - juvenile (chronic) (polyarticular) 714.30
    - acute 714.31
    - monoarticular 714.33
    - pauciarticular 714.32
  - spine 720.0
- rubella 056.71
- sacral, sacroiliac, sacrococcygeal (*see also* Spondylosis, sacral) 721.3
- scorbutic 267
- senile or senescent (*see also* Osteoarthrosis) 715.9 ☑
  - spine 721.90
    - with myelopathy 721.91
- septic 711.0 ☑
- serum (nontherapeutic) (therapeutic) 999.5 [713.6]
- specified form NEC 716.8 ☑
- spine 721.90
  - with myelopathy 721.91
  - atrophic 720.9
  - degenerative 721.90
    - with myelopathy 721.91
  - hypertrophic (with deformity) 721.90
    - with myelopathy 721.91
  - infectious or infective NEC 720.9
  - Marie-Strümpell 720.0
  - nonpyogenic 721.90
    - with myelopathy 721.91
  - pyogenic 720.9
  - rheumatoid 720.0
  - traumatic (old) 721.7
  - tuberculous (*see also* Tuberculosis) 015.0 ☑ [720.81]
- staphylococcal 711.0 ☑
- streptococcal 711.0 ☑
- suppurative 711.0 ☑
- syphilitic 094.0 [713.5]
  - congenital 090.49 [713.5]

- **Arthritis, arthritic** — *continued*
  - syphilitica deformans (Charcôt) 094.0 *[713.5]*
  - temporomandibular joint 524.69
  - thoracic (*see also* Spondylosis, thoracic) 721.2
  - toxic of menopause 716.3 ☑
  - transient 716.4 ☑
  - traumatic (chronic) (old) (post) 716.1 ☑
    - current injury — *see* nature of injury
  - tuberculous (*see also* Tuberculosis, arthritis) 015.9 ☑ *[711.4]* ☑
  - urethritica 099.3 *[711.1]* ☑
  - urica, uratic 274.0
  - venereal 099.3 *[711.1]* ☑
  - vertebral (*see also* Arthritis, spine) 721.90
  - villous 716.8 ☑
  - von Bechterew's 720.0
- **Arthrocele** — *see also* Effusion, joint 719.0 ☑
- **Arthrochondritis** — *see* Arthritis
- **Arthrodesis status** V45.4
- **Arthrodynia** — *see also* Pain, joint 719.4 ☑
  - psychogenic 307.89
- **Arthrodysplasia** 755.9
- **Arthrofibrosis joint** — *see also* Ankylosis 718.5 ☑
- **Arthrogryposis** 728.3
  - multiplex, congenita 754.89
- **Arthrokatadysis** 715.35
- **Arthrolithiasis** 274.0
- **Arthro-onychodysplasia** 756.89
- **Arthro-osteo-onychodysplasia** 756.89
- **Arthropathy** — *see also* Arthritis 716.9 ☑

Note — Use the following fifth-digit subclassification with categories 711–712, 716:

0	*site unspecified*
1	*shoulder region*
2	*upper arm*
3	*forearm*
4	*hand*
5	*pelvic region and thigh*
6	*lower leg*
7	*ankle and foot*
8	*other specified sites*
9	*multiple sites*

  - Behçet's 136.1 *[711.2]* ☑
  - Charcôt's 094.0 *[713.5]*
    - diabetic 250.6 ☑ *[713.5]*
      - due to secondary diabetes 249.6 ☑ *[713.5]* ●
    - syringomyelic 336.0 *[713.5]*
    - tabetic 094.0 *[713.5]*
  - crystal (-induced) — *see* Arthritis, due to crystals
  - gouty 274.0
  - neurogenic, neuropathic (Charcôt's) (tabetic) 094.0 *[713.5]*
    - diabetic 250.6 ☑ *[713.5]*
      - due to secondary diabetes 249.6 ☑ *[713.5]* ●
    - nonsyphilitic NEC 349.9 *[713.5]*
    - syringomyelic 336.0 *[713.5]*
  - postdysenteric NEC 009.0 *[711.3]* ☑
  - postrheumatic, chronic (Jaccoud's) 714.4
  - psoriatic 696.0
  - pulmonary 731.2
  - specified NEC 716.8 ☑
  - syringomyelia 336.0 *[713.5]*
  - tabes dorsalis 094.0 *[713.5]*
  - tabetic 094.0 *[713.5]*
  - transient 716.4 ☑
  - traumatic 716.1 ☑
- **Arthropathy** — *see also* Arthritis — *continued*
  - uric acid 274.0
- **Arthrophyte** — *see also* Loose, body, joint 718.1 ☑
- **Arthrophytis** 719.80
  - ankle 719.87
  - elbow 719.82
  - foot 719.87
  - hand 719.84
  - hip 719.85
  - knee 719.86
  - multiple sites 719.89
  - pelvic region 719.85
  - shoulder (region) 719.81
  - specified site NEC 719.88
  - wrist 719.83
- **Arthropyosis** — *see also* Arthritis, pyogenic 711.0 ☑
- **Arthroscopic surgical procedure converted to open procedure** V64.43
- **Arthrosis** (deformans) (degenerative) — *see also* Osteoarthrosis 715.9 ☑
  - Charcôt's 094.0 *[713.5]*
  - polyarticular 715.09
  - spine (*see also* Spondylosis) 721.90
- **Arthus phenomenon** 995.21
  - due to
    - correct substance properly administered 995.21
    - overdose or wrong substance given or taken 977.9
      - specified drug — *see* Table of Drugs and Chemicals
    - serum 999.5
- **Articular** — *see also* condition
  - disc disorder (reducing or non-reducing) 524.63
  - spondylolisthesis 756.12
- **Articulation**
  - anterior 524.27
  - posterior 524.27
  - reverse 524.27
- **Artificial**
  - device (prosthetic) — *see* Fitting, device
  - insemination V26.1
  - menopause (states) (symptoms) (syndrome) 627.4
  - opening status (functioning) (without complication) V44.9
    - anus (colostomy) V44.3
    - colostomy V44.3
    - cystostomy V44.50
      - appendico-vesicostomy V44.52
      - cutaneous-vesicostomy V44.51
      - specified type NEC V44.59
    - enterostomy V44.4
    - gastrostomy V44.1
    - ileostomy V44.2
    - intestinal tract NEC V44.4
    - jejunostomy V44.4
    - nephrostomy V44.6
    - specified site NEC V44.8
    - tracheostomy V44.0
    - ureterostomy V44.6
    - urethrostomy V44.6
    - urinary tract NEC V44.6
    - vagina V44.7
  - vagina status V44.7
- **ARV** (disease) (illness) (infection) — *see* Human immunodeficiency virus (disease) (illness) (infection)
- **Arytenoid** — *see* condition
- **Asbestosis** (occupational) 501
- **Asboe-Hansen's disease** (incontinentia pigmenti) 757.33
- **Ascariasis** (intestinal) (lung) 127.0
- **Ascaridiasis** 127.0
- **Ascaridosis** 127.0
- **Ascaris** 127.0
  - lumbricoides (infestation) 127.0
  - pneumonia 127.0
- **Ascending** — *see* condition
- **ASC-H** (atypical squamous cells cannot exclude high grade squamous intraepithelial lesion)
  - anus 796.72 ●
  - cervix 795.02 ●
  - vagina 795.12 ●
- **Aschoff's bodies** — *see also* Myocarditis, rheumatic 398.0
- **Ascites** 789.59
  - abdominal NEC 789.59
  - cancerous (M8000/6) 789.51
  - cardiac 428.0
  - chylous (nonfilarial) 457.8
    - filarial (*see also* Infestation, filarial) 125.9
  - congenital 778.0
  - due to S. japonicum 120.2
  - fetal, causing fetopelvic disproportion 653.7 ☑
  - heart 428.0
  - joint (*see also* Effusion, joint) 719.0 ☑
  - malignant (M8000/6) 789.51
  - pseudochylous 789.59
  - syphilitic 095.2
  - tuberculous (*see also* Tuberculosis) 014.0 ☑
- **Ascorbic acid** (vitamin C) **deficiency** (scurvy) 267
- **ASC-US** (atypical squamous cells of undetermined significance)
  - anus 796.71 ●
  - cervix 795.01 ●
  - vagina 795.11 ●
- **ASCVD** (arteriosclerotic cardiovascular disease) 429.2
- **Aseptic** — *see* condition
- **Asherman's syndrome** 621.5
- **Asialia** 527.7
- **Asiatic cholera** — *see also* Cholera 001.9
- **Asocial personality or trends** 301.7
- **Asomatognosia** 781.8
- **Aspergillosis** 117.3
  - with pneumonia 117.3 *[484.6]*
  - allergic bronchopulmonary 518.6
  - nonsyphilitic NEC 117.3
- **Aspergillus** (flavus) (fumigatus) (infection) (terreus) 117.3
- **Aspermatogenesis** 606.0
- **Aspermia** (testis) 606.0
- **Asphyxia, asphyxiation** (by) 799.01
  - antenatal — *see* Distress, fetal
  - bedclothes 994.7
  - birth (*see also* Asphyxia, newborn) 768.9
  - bunny bag 994.7
  - carbon monoxide 986
  - caul (*see also* Asphyxia, newborn) 768.9
  - cave-in 994.7
    - crushing — *see* Injury, internal, intrathoracic organs
  - constriction 994.7
  - crushing — *see* Injury, internal, intrathoracic organs
  - drowning 994.1
  - fetal, affecting newborn 768.9
  - food or foreign body (in larynx) 933.1
    - bronchioles 934.8
    - bronchus (main) 934.1
    - lung 934.8
    - nasopharynx 933.0
    - nose, nasal passages 932
    - pharynx 933.0
    - respiratory tract 934.9
      - specified part NEC 934.8
    - throat 933.0
    - trachea 934.0
  - gas, fumes, or vapor NEC 987.9
    - specified — *see* Table of Drugs and Chemicals
  - gravitational changes 994.7
  - hanging 994.7
  - inhalation — *see* Inhalation
  - intrauterine
    - fetal death (before onset of labor) 768.0
- **Asphyxia, asphyxiation** — *continued*
  - intrauterine — *continued*
    - fetal death — *continued*
      - during labor 768.1
    - liveborn infant — *see* Distress, fetal, liveborn infant
  - local 443.0
  - mechanical 994.7
    - during birth (*see also* Distress, fetal) 768.9
  - mucus 933.1
    - bronchus (main) 934.1
    - larynx 933.1
    - lung 934.8
    - nasal passages 932
    - newborn 770.18
    - pharynx 933.0
    - respiratory tract 934.9
      - specified part NEC 934.8
    - throat 933.0
    - trachea 934.0
    - vaginal (fetus or newborn) 770.18
  - newborn 768.9
    - with neurologic involvement 768.5
    - blue 768.6
    - livida 768.6
    - mild or moderate 768.6
    - pallida 768.5
    - severe 768.5
    - white 768.5
  - pathological 799.01
  - plastic bag 994.7
  - postnatal (*see also* Asphyxia, newborn) 768.9
    - mechanical 994.7
  - pressure 994.7
  - reticularis 782.61
  - strangulation 994.7
  - submersion 994.1
  - traumatic NEC — *see* Injury, internal, intrathoracic organs
  - vomiting, vomitus — *see* Asphyxia, food or foreign body
- **Aspiration**
  - acid pulmonary (syndrome) 997.39 ▲
    - obstetric 668.0 ☑
  - amniotic fluid 770.13
    - with respiratory symptoms 770.14
  - bronchitis 507.0
  - clear amniotic fluid 770.13
    - with
      - pneumonia 770.14
      - pneumonitis 770.14
      - respiratory symptoms 770.14
  - contents of birth canal 770.17
    - with respiratory symptoms 770.18
  - fetal 770.10
    - blood 770.15
      - with
        - pneumonia 770.16
        - pneumonitis 770.16
    - pneumonitis 770.18
  - food, foreign body, or gasoline (with asphyxiation) — *see* Asphyxia, food or foreign body
  - meconium 770.11
    - with
      - pneumonia 770.12
      - pneumonitis 770.12
      - respiratory symptoms 770.12
    - below vocal cords 770.11
      - with respiratory symptoms 770.12
  - mucus 933.1
    - into
      - bronchus (main) 934.1
      - lung 934.8
      - respiratory tract 934.9
        - specified part NEC 934.8
      - trachea 934.0
    - newborn 770.17
    - vaginal (fetus or newborn) 770.17
  - newborn 770.10
    - with respiratory symptoms 770.18
    - blood 770.15

- **Aspiration** — *continued*
  - newborn — *continued*
    - blood — *continued*
      - with
        - pneumonia 770.16
        - pneumonitis 770.16
        - respiratory symptoms 770.16
  - pneumonia 507.0
    - fetus or newborn 770.18
      - meconium 770.12
  - pneumonitis 507.0
    - fetus or newborn 770.18
      - meconium 770.12
    - obstetric 668.0 ☑
  - postnatal stomach contents 770.85
    - with
      - pneumonia 770.86
      - pneumonitis 770.86
      - respiratory symptoms 770.86
  - syndrome of newborn (massive) 770.18
    - meconium 770.12
  - vernix caseosa 770.12
- **Asplenia** 759.0
  - with mesocardia 746.87
- **Assam fever** 085.0
- **Assimilation, pelvis**
  - with disproportion 653.2 ☑
    - affecting fetus or newborn 763.1
    - causing obstructed labor 660.1 ☑
      - affecting fetus or newborn 763.1
- **Assmann's focus** — *see also* Tuberculosis 011.0 ☑
- **Astasia** (-abasia) 307.9
  - hysterical 300.11
- **Asteatosis** 706.8
  - cutis 706.8
- **Astereognosis** 780.99
- **Asterixis** 781.3
  - in liver disease 572.8
- **Asteroid hyalitis** 379.22
- **Asthenia, asthenic** 780.79
  - cardiac (*see also* Failure, heart) 428.9
    - psychogenic 306.2
  - cardiovascular (*see also* Failure, heart) 428.9
    - psychogenic 306.2
  - heart (*see also* Failure, heart) 428.9
    - psychogenic 306.2
  - hysterical 300.11
  - myocardial (*see also* Failure, heart) 428.9
    - psychogenic 306.2
  - nervous 300.5
  - neurocirculatory 306.2
  - neurotic 300.5
  - psychogenic 300.5
  - psychoneurotic 300.5
  - psychophysiologic 300.5
  - reaction, psychoneurotic 300.5
  - senile 797
  - Stiller's 780.79
  - tropical anhidrotic 705.1
- **Asthenopia** 368.13
  - accommodative 367.4
  - hysterical (muscular) 300.11
  - psychogenic 306.7
- **Asthenospermia** 792.2
- **Asthma, asthmatic** (bronchial) (catarrh) (spasmodic) 493.9 ☑

> *Note — Use the following fifth-digit subclassification with category 493:*
>
> 0 *without mention of status asthmaticus or acute exacerbation or unspecified*
>
> 1 *with status asthmaticus*
>
> 2 *with acute exacerbation*

  - with
    - chronic obstructive pulmonary disease (COPD) 493.2 ☑
    - hay fever 493.0 ☑
    - rhinitis, allergic 493.0 ☑
  - allergic 493.9 ☑

- **Asthma, asthmatic** — *continued*
  - allergic — *continued*
    - stated cause (external allergen) 493.0 ☑
  - atopic 493.0 ☑
  - cardiac (*see also* Failure, ventricular, left) 428.1
  - cardiobronchial (*see also* Failure, ventricular, left) 428.1
  - cardiorenal (*see also* Hypertension, cardiorenal) 404.90
  - childhood 493.0 ☑
  - Colliers' 500
  - cough variant 493.82
  - croup 493.9 ☑
  - detergent 507.8
  - due to
    - detergent 507.8
    - inhalation of fumes 506.3
    - internal immunological process 493.0 ☑
  - endogenous (intrinsic) 493.1 ☑
  - eosinophilic 518.3
  - exercise induced bronchospasm 493.81
  - exogenous (cosmetics) (dander or dust) (drugs) (dust) (feathers) (food) (hay) (platinum) (pollen) 493.0 ☑
  - extrinsic 493.0 ☑
  - grinders' 502
  - hay 493.0 ☑
  - heart (*see also* Failure, ventricular, left) 428.1
  - IgE 493.0 ☑
  - infective 493.1 ☑
  - intrinsic 493.1 ☑
  - Kopp's 254.8
  - late-onset 493.1 ☑
  - meat-wrappers' 506.9
  - Millar's (laryngismus stridulus) 478.75
  - millstone makers' 502
  - miners' 500
  - Monday morning 504
  - New Orleans (epidemic) 493.0 ☑
  - platinum 493.0 ☑
  - pneumoconiotic (occupational) NEC 505
  - potters' 502
  - psychogenic 316 *[493.9]* ☑
  - pulmonary eosinophilic 518.3
  - red cedar 495.8
  - Rostan's (*see also* Failure, ventricular, left) 428.1
  - sandblasters' 502
  - sequoiosis 495.8
  - stonemasons' 502
  - thymic 254.8
  - tuberculous (*see also* Tuberculosis, pulmonary) 011.9 ☑
  - Wichmann's (laryngismus stridulus) 478.75
  - wood 495.8
- **Astigmatism** (compound) (congenital) 367.20
  - irregular 367.22
  - regular 367.21
- **Astroblastoma** (M9430/3)
  - nose 748.1
  - specified site — *see* Neoplasm, by site, malignant
  - unspecified site 191.9
- **Astrocytoma** (cystic) (M9400/3)
  - anaplastic type (M9401/3)
    - specified site — *see* Neoplasm, by site, malignant
    - unspecified site 191.9
  - fibrillary (M9420/3)
    - specified site — *see* Neoplasm, by site, malignant
    - unspecified site 191.9
  - fibrous (M9420/3)
    - specified site — *see* Neoplasm, by site, malignant
    - unspecified site 191.9

- **Astrocytoma** — *continued*
  - gemistocytic (M9411/3)
    - specified site — *see* Neoplasm, by site, malignant
    - unspecified site 191.9
  - juvenile (M9421/3)
    - specified site — *see* Neoplasm, by site, malignant
    - unspecified site 191.9
  - nose 748.1
  - pilocytic (M9421/3)
    - specified site — *see* Neoplasm, by site, malignant
    - unspecified site 191.9
  - piloid (M9421/3)
    - specified site — *see* Neoplasm, by site, malignant
    - unspecified site 191.9
  - protoplasmic (M9410/3)
    - specified site — *see* Neoplasm, by site, malignant
    - unspecified site 191.9
  - specified site — *see* Neoplasm, by site, malignant
  - subependymal (M9383/1) 237.5
    - giant cell (M9384/1) 237.5
  - unspecified site 191.9
- **Astroglioma** (M9400/3)
  - nose 748.1
  - specified site — *see* Neoplasm, by site, malignant
  - unspecified site 191.9
- **Asymbolia** 784.60
- **Asymmetrical breathing** 786.09
- **Asymmetry** — *see also* Distortion
  - breast, between native and reconstructed 612.1 ●
  - chest 786.9
  - face 754.0
  - jaw NEC 524.12
    - maxillary 524.11
  - pelvis with disproportion 653.0 ☑
    - affecting fetus or newborn 763.1
    - causing obstructed labor 660.1 ☑
      - affecting fetus or newborn 763.1
- **Asynergia** 781.3
- **Asynergy** 781.3
  - ventricular 429.89
- **Asystole** (heart) — *see also* Arrest, cardiac 427.5
- **Ataxia, ataxy, ataxic** 781.3
  - acute 781.3
  - brain 331.89
  - cerebellar 334.3
    - hereditary (Marie's) 334.2
    - in
      - alcoholism 303.9 ☑ *[334.4]*
      - myxedema (*see also* Myxedema) 244.9 *[334.4]*
      - neoplastic disease NEC 239.9 *[334.4]*
  - cerebral 331.89
  - family, familial 334.2
    - cerebral (Marie's) 334.2
    - spinal (Friedreich's) 334.0
  - Friedreich's (heredofamilial) (spinal) 334.0
  - frontal lobe 781.3
  - gait 781.2
    - hysterical 300.11
  - general 781.3
  - hereditary NEC 334.2
    - cerebellar 334.2
    - spastic 334.1
    - spinal 334.0
  - heredofamilial (Marie's) 334.2
  - hysterical 300.11
  - locomotor (progressive) 094.0
    - diabetic 250.6 ☑ *[337.1]*
      - due to secondary diabetes 249.6 ☑ *[337.1]* ●
  - Marie's (cerebellar) (heredofamilial) 334.2
  - nonorganic origin 307.9
  - partial 094.0
  - postchickenpox 052.7

- **Ataxia, ataxy, ataxic** — *continued*
  - progressive locomotor 094.0
  - psychogenic 307.9
  - Sanger-Brown's 334.2
  - spastic 094.0
    - hereditary 334.1
    - syphilitic 094.0
  - spinal
    - hereditary 334.0
    - progressive locomotor 094.0
  - telangiectasia 334.8
- **Ataxia-telangiectasia** 334.8
- **Atelectasis** (absorption collapse) (complete) (compression) (massive) (partial) (postinfective) (pressure collapse) (pulmonary) (relaxation) 518.0
  - newborn (congenital) (partial) 770.5
    - primary 770.4
  - primary 770.4
  - tuberculous (*see also* Tuberculosis, pulmonary) 011.9 ☑
- **Ateleiosis, ateliosis** 253.3
- **Atelia** — *see* Distortion
- **Ateliosis** 253.3
- **Atelocardia** 746.9
- **Atelomyelia** 742.59
- **Athelia** 757.6
- **Atheroembolism**
  - extremity
    - lower 445.02
    - upper 445.01
  - kidney 445.81
  - specified site NEC 445.89
- **Atheroma, atheromatous** — *see also* Arteriosclerosis 440.9
  - aorta, aortic 440.0
    - valve (*see also* Endocarditis, aortic) 424.1
  - artery — *see* Arteriosclerosis
  - basilar (artery) (*see also* Occlusion, artery, basilar) 433.0 ☑
  - carotid (artery) (common) (internal) (*see also* Occlusion, artery, carotid) 433.1 ☑
  - cerebral (arteries) 437.0
  - coronary (artery) — *see* Arteriosclerosis, coronary
  - degeneration — *see* Arteriosclerosis
  - heart, cardiac — *see* Arteriosclerosis, coronary
  - mitral (valve) 424.0
  - myocardium, myocardial — *see* Arteriosclerosis, coronary
  - pulmonary valve (heart) (*see also* Endocarditis, pulmonary) 424.3
  - skin 706.2
  - tricuspid (heart) (valve) 424.2
  - valve, valvular — *see* Endocarditis
  - vertebral (artery) (*see also* Occlusion, artery, vertebral) 433.2 ☑
- **Atheromatosis** — *see also* Arteriosclerosis
  - arterial, congenital 272.8
- **Atherosclerosis** — *see* Arteriosclerosis
- **Athetosis** (acquired) 781.0
  - bilateral 333.79
  - congenital (bilateral) 333.6
  - double 333.71
  - unilateral 781.0
- **Athlete's**
  - foot 110.4
  - heart 429.3
- **Athletic team examination** V70.3
- **Athrepsia** 261
- **Athyrea** (acquired) — *see also* Hypothyroidism 244.9
  - congenital 243
- **Athyreosis** (congenital) 243
  - acquired — *see* Hypothyroidism
- **Athyroidism** (acquired) — *see also* Hypothyroidism 244.9
  - congenital 243
- **Atmospheric pyrexia** 992.0
- **Atonia, atony, atonic**
  - abdominal wall 728.2

Atonia, atony, atonic — *continued*
- bladder (sphincter) 596.4
  - neurogenic NEC 596.54
    - with cauda equina syndrome 344.61
- capillary 448.9
- cecum 564.89
  - psychogenic 306.4
- colon 564.89
  - psychogenic 306.4
- congenital 779.89
- dyspepsia 536.3
  - psychogenic 306.4
- intestine 564.89
  - psychogenic 306.4
- stomach 536.3
  - neurotic or psychogenic 306.4
  - psychogenic 306.4
- uterus 661.2 ☑
  - with hemorrhage (postpartum) 666.1 ☑
  - without hemorrhage
    - intrapartum 661.2 ☑
    - postpartum 669.8 ☑
- vesical 596.4

Atopy NEC V15.09

Atransferrinemia, congenital 273.8

Atresia, atretic (congenital) 759.89
- alimentary organ or tract NEC 751.8
  - lower 751.2
  - upper 750.8
- ani, anus, anal (canal) 751.2
- aorta 747.22
  - with hypoplasia of ascending aorta and defective development of left ventricle (with mitral valve atresia) 746.7
  - arch 747.11
  - ring 747.21
- aortic (orifice) (valve) 746.89
  - arch 747.11
- aqueduct of Sylvius 742.3
  - with spina bifida (*see also* Spina bifida) 741.0 ☑
- artery NEC (*see also* Atresia, blood vessel) 747.60
  - cerebral 747.81
  - coronary 746.85
  - eye 743.58
  - pulmonary 747.3
  - umbilical 747.5
- auditory canal (external) 744.02
- bile, biliary duct (common) or passage 751.61
  - acquired (*see also* Obstruction, biliary) 576.2
- bladder (neck) 753.6
- blood vessel (peripheral) NEC 747.60
  - cerebral 747.81
  - gastrointestinal 747.61
  - lower limb 747.64
  - pulmonary artery 747.3
  - renal 747.62
  - spinal 747.82
  - upper limb 747.63
- bronchus 748.3
- canal, ear 744.02
- cardiac
  - valve 746.89
    - aortic 746.89
    - mitral 746.89
    - pulmonary 746.01
    - tricuspid 746.1
- cecum 751.2
- cervix (acquired) 622.4
  - congenital 752.49
  - in pregnancy or childbirth 654.6 ☑
    - affecting fetus or newborn 763.89
    - causing obstructed labor 660.2 ☑
      - affecting fetus or newborn 763.1
- choana 748.0
- colon 751.2
- cystic duct 751.61

Atresia, atretic — *continued*
- cystic duct — *continued*
  - acquired 575.8
    - with obstruction (*see also* Obstruction, gallbladder) 575.2
- digestive organs NEC 751.8
- duodenum 751.1
- ear canal 744.02
- ejaculatory duct 752.89
- epiglottis 748.3
- esophagus 750.3
- Eustachian tube 744.24
- fallopian tube (acquired) 628.2
  - congenital 752.19
- follicular cyst 620.0
- foramen of
  - Luschka 742.3
    - with spina bifida (*see also* Spina bifida) 741.0 ☑
  - Magendie 742.3
    - with spina bifida (*see also* Spina bifida) 741.0 ☑
- gallbladder 751.69
- genital organ
  - external
    - female 752.49
    - male NEC 752.89
      - penis 752.69
  - internal
    - female 752.89
    - male 752.89
- glottis 748.3
- gullet 750.3
- heart
  - valve NEC 746.89
    - aortic 746.89
    - mitral 746.89
    - pulmonary 746.01
    - tricuspid 746.1
- hymen 752.42
  - acquired 623.3
  - postinfective 623.3
- ileum 751.1
- intestine (small) 751.1
  - large 751.2
- iris, filtration angle (*see also* Buphthalmia) 743.20
- jejunum 751.1
- kidney 753.3
- lacrimal, apparatus 743.65
  - acquired — *see* Stenosis, lacrimal
- larynx 748.3
- ligament, broad 752.19
- lung 748.5
- meatus urinarius 753.6
- mitral valve 746.89
  - with atresia or hypoplasia of aortic orifice or valve, with hypoplasia of ascending aorta and defective development of left ventricle 746.7
- nares (anterior) (posterior) 748.0
- nasolacrimal duct 743.65
- nasopharynx 748.8
- nose, nostril 748.0
  - acquired 738.0
- organ or site NEC — *see* Anomaly, specified type NEC
- osseous meatus (ear) 744.03
- oviduct (acquired) 628.2
  - congenital 752.19
- parotid duct 750.23
  - acquired 527.8
- pulmonary (artery) 747.3
  - valve 746.01
  - vein 747.49
- pulmonic 746.01
- pupil 743.46
- rectum 751.2
- salivary duct or gland 750.23
  - acquired 527.8
- sublingual duct 750.23
  - acquired 527.8
- submaxillary duct or gland 750.23
  - acquired 527.8

Atresia, atretic — *continued*
- trachea 748.3
- tricuspid valve 746.1
- ureter 753.29
- ureteropelvic junction 753.21
- ureterovesical orifice 753.22
- urethra (valvular) 753.6
- urinary tract NEC 753.29
- uterus 752.3
  - acquired 621.8
- vagina (acquired) 623.2
  - congenital 752.49
  - postgonococcal (old) 098.2
  - postinfectional 623.2
  - senile 623.2
- vascular NEC (*see also* Atresia, blood vessel) 747.60
  - cerebral 747.81
- vas deferens 752.89
- vein NEC (*see also* Atresia, blood vessel) 747.60
  - cardiac 746.89
  - great 747.49
  - portal 747.49
  - pulmonary 747.49
- vena cava (inferior) (superior) 747.49
- vesicourethral orifice 753.6
- vulva 752.49
  - acquired 624.8

Atrichia, atrichosis 704.00
- congenital (universal) 757.4

Atrioventricularis commune 745.69

At risk for falling V15.88

Atrophia — *see also* Atrophy
- alba 709.09
- cutis 701.8
  - idiopathica progressiva 701.8
  - senilis 701.8
- dermatological, diffuse (idiopathic) 701.8
- flava hepatis (acuta) (subacuta) (*see also* Necrosis, liver) 570
- gyrata of choroid and retina (central) 363.54
  - generalized 363.57
- senilis 797
  - dermatological 701.8
- unguium 703.8
  - congenita 757.5

Atrophoderma, atrophodermia 701.9
- diffusum (idiopathic) 701.8
- maculatum 701.3
  - et striatum 701.3
    - due to syphilis 095.8
  - syphilitic 091.3
- neuriticum 701.8
- pigmentosum 757.33
- reticulatum symmetricum faciei 701.8
- senile 701.8
- symmetrical 701.8
- vermiculata 701.8

Atrophy, atrophic
- adrenal (autoimmune) (capsule) (cortex) (gland) 255.41
  - with hypofunction 255.41
- alveolar process or ridge (edentulous) 525.20
  - mandible 525.20
    - minimal 525.21
    - moderate 525.22
    - severe 525.23
  - maxilla 525.20
    - minimal 525.24
    - moderate 525.25
    - severe 525.26
- appendix 543.9
- Aran-Duchenne muscular 335.21
- arm 728.2
- arteriosclerotic — *see* Arteriosclerosis
- arthritis 714.0
  - spine 720.9
- bile duct (any) 576.8
- bladder 596.8
- blanche (of Milian) 701.3
- bone (senile) 733.99

Atrophy, atrophic — *continued*
- bone — *continued*
  - due to
    - disuse 733.7
    - infection 733.99
    - tabes dorsalis (neurogenic) 094.0
  - posttraumatic 733.99
- brain (cortex) (progressive) 331.9
  - with dementia 290.10
  - Alzheimer's 331.0
    - with dementia — *see* Alzheimer's, dementia
  - circumscribed (Pick's) 331.11
    - with dementia
      - with behavioral disturbance 331.11 *[294.11]*
      - without behavioral disturbance 331.11 *[294.10]*
  - congenital 742.4
  - hereditary 331.9
  - senile 331.2
- breast 611.4
  - puerperal, postpartum 676.3 ☑
- buccal cavity 528.9
- cardiac (brown) (senile) (*see also* Degeneration, myocardial) 429.1
- cartilage (infectional) (joint) 733.99
- cast, plaster of Paris 728.2
- cerebellar — *see* Atrophy, brain
- cerebral — *see* Atrophy, brain
- cervix (endometrium) (mucosa) (myometrium) (senile) (uteri) 622.8
  - menopausal 627.8
- Charcôt-Marie-Tooth 356.1
- choroid 363.40
  - diffuse secondary 363.42
  - hereditary (*see also* Dystrophy, choroid) 363.50
    - gyrate
      - central 363.54
      - diffuse 363.57
      - generalized 363.57
  - senile 363.41
- ciliary body 364.57
- colloid, degenerative 701.3
- conjunctiva (senile) 372.89
- corpus cavernosum 607.89
- cortical (*see also* Atrophy, brain) 331.9
- Cruveilhier's 335.21
- cystic duct 576.8
- dacryosialadenopathy 710.2
- degenerative
  - colloid 701.3
  - senile 701.3
- Déjérine-Thomas 333.0
- diffuse idiopathic, dermatological 701.8
- disuse
  - bone 733.7
  - muscle 728.2
  - pelvic muscles and anal sphincter 618.83
- Duchenne-Aran 335.21
- ear 388.9
- edentulous alveolar ridge 525.20
  - mandible 525.20
    - minimal 525.21
    - moderate 525.22
    - severe 525.23
  - maxilla 525.20
    - minimal 525.24
    - moderate 525.25
    - severe 525.26
- emphysema, lung 492.8
- endometrium (senile) 621.8
  - cervix 622.8
- enteric 569.89
- epididymis 608.3
- eyeball, cause unknown 360.41
- eyelid (senile) 374.50
- facial (skin) 701.9
- facioscapulohumeral (Landouzy-Déjérine) 359.1
- fallopian tube (senile), acquired 620.3
- fatty, thymus (gland) 254.8

- **Atrophy, atrophic** — *continued*
  - gallbladder 575.8
  - gastric 537.89
  - gastritis (chronic) 535.1 ☑
  - gastrointestinal 569.89
  - genital organ, male 608.89
  - glandular 289.3
  - globe (phthisis bulbi) 360.41
  - gum (*see also* Recession, gingival) 523.20
  - hair 704.2
  - heart (brown) (senile) (*see also* Degeneration, myocardial) 429.1
  - hemifacial 754.0
    - Romberg 349.89
  - hydronephrosis 591
  - infantile 261
    - paralysis, acute (*see also* Poliomyelitis, with paralysis) 045.1 ☑
  - intestine 569.89
  - iris (generalized) (postinfectional) (sector shaped) 364.59
    - essential 364.51
    - progressive 364.51
    - sphincter 364.54
  - kidney (senile) (*see also* Sclerosis, renal) 587
    - with hypertension (*see also* Hypertension, kidney) 403.90
    - congenital 753.0
    - hydronephrotic 591
    - infantile 753.0
  - lacrimal apparatus (primary) 375.13
    - secondary 375.14
  - Landouzy-Déjérine 359.1
  - laryngitis, infection 476.0
  - larynx 478.79
  - Leber's optic 377.16
  - lip 528.5
  - liver (acute) (subacute) (*see also* Necrosis, liver) 570
    - chronic (yellow) 571.8
    - yellow (congenital) 570
      - with
        - abortion — *see* Abortion, by type, with specified complication NEC
        - ectopic pregnancy (*see also* categories 633.0–633.9) 639.8
        - molar pregnancy (*see also* categories 630–632) 639.8
      - chronic 571.8
      - complicating pregnancy 646.7 ☑
      - following
        - abortion 639.8
        - ectopic or molar pregnancy 639.8
      - from injection, inoculation or transfusion (onset within 8 months after administration) — *see* Hepatitis, viral
      - healed 571.5
      - obstetric 646.7 ☑
      - postabortal 639.8
      - postimmunization — *see* Hepatitis, viral
      - posttransfusion — *see* Hepatitis, viral
      - puerperal, postpartum 674.8 ☑
  - lung (senile) 518.89
    - congenital 748.69
  - macular (dermatological) 701.3
    - syphilitic, skin 091.3
      - striated 095.8
  - muscle, muscular 728.2
    - disuse 728.2
    - Duchenne-Aran 335.21
    - extremity (lower) (upper) 728.2
    - familial spinal 335.11
    - general 728.2
    - idiopathic 728.2
    - infantile spinal 335.0
    - myelopathic (progressive) 335.10

- **Atrophy, atrophic** — *continued*
  - muscle, muscular — *continued*
    - myotonic 359.21
    - neuritic 356.1
    - neuropathic (peroneal) (progressive) 356.1
    - peroneal 356.1
    - primary (idiopathic) 728.2
    - progressive (familial) (hereditary) (pure) 335.21
      - adult (spinal) 335.19
      - infantile (spinal) 335.0
      - juvenile (spinal) 335.11
      - spinal 335.10
        - adult 335.19
        - hereditary or familial 335.11
        - infantile 335.0
    - pseudohypertrophic 359.1
    - spinal (progressive) 335.10
      - adult 335.19
      - Aran-Duchenne 335.21
      - familial 335.11
      - hereditary 335.11
      - infantile 335.0
      - juvenile 335.11
    - syphilitic 095.6
  - myocardium (*see also* Degeneration, myocardial) 429.1
  - myometrium (senile) 621.8
    - cervix 622.8
  - myotatic 728.2
  - myotonia 359.21
  - nail 703.8
    - congenital 757.5
  - nasopharynx 472.2
  - nerve (*see also* Disorder, nerve)
    - abducens 378.54
    - accessory 352.4
    - acoustic or auditory 388.5
    - cranial 352.9
      - first (olfactory) 352.0
      - second (optic) (*see also* Atrophy, optic nerve) 377.10
      - third (oculomotor) (partial) 378.51
        - total 378.52
      - fourth (trochlear) 378.53
      - fifth (trigeminal) 350.8
      - sixth (abducens) 378.54
      - seventh (facial) 351.8
      - eighth (auditory) 388.5
      - ninth (glossopharyngeal) 352.2
      - tenth (pneumogastric) (vagus) 352.3
      - eleventh (accessory) 352.4
      - twelfth (hypoglossal) 352.5
    - facial 351.8
    - glossopharyngeal 352.2
    - hypoglossal 352.5
    - oculomotor (partial) 378.51
      - total 378.52
    - olfactory 352.0
    - peripheral 355.9
    - pneumogastric 352.3
    - trigeminal 350.8
    - trochlear 378.53
    - vagus (pneumogastric) 352.3
  - nervous system, congenital 742.8
  - neuritic (*see also* Disorder, nerve) 355.9
  - neurogenic NEC 355.9
    - bone
      - tabetic 094.0
  - nutritional 261
  - old age 797
  - olivopontocerebellar 333.0
  - optic nerve (ascending) (descending) (infectional) (nonfamilial) (papillomacular bundle) (postretinal) (secondary NEC) (simple) 377.10
    - associated with retinal dystrophy 377.13
    - dominant hereditary 377.16
    - glaucomatous 377.14
    - hereditary (dominant) (Leber's) 377.16

- **Atrophy, atrophic** — *continued*
  - optic nerve — *continued*
    - Leber's (hereditary) 377.16
    - partial 377.15
    - postinflammatory 377.12
    - primary 377.11
    - syphilitic 094.84
      - congenital 090.49
      - tabes dorsalis 094.0
  - orbit 376.45
  - ovary (senile), acquired 620.3
  - oviduct (senile), acquired 620.3
  - palsy, diffuse 335.20
  - pancreas (duct) (senile) 577.8
  - papillary muscle 429.81
  - paralysis 355.9
  - parotid gland 527.0
  - patches skin 701.3
    - senile 701.8
  - penis 607.89
  - pharyngitis 472.1
  - pharynx 478.29
  - pluriglandular 258.8
  - polyarthritis 714.0
  - prostate 602.2
  - pseudohypertrophic 359.1
  - renal (*see also* Sclerosis, renal) 587
  - reticulata 701.8
  - retina (*see also* Degeneration, retina) 362.60
    - hereditary (*see also* Dystrophy, retina) 362.70
  - rhinitis 472.0
  - salivary duct or gland 527.0
  - scar NEC 709.2
  - sclerosis, lobar (of brain) 331.0
    - with dementia
      - with behavioral disturbance 331.0 *[294.11]*
      - without behavioral disturbance 331.0 *[294.10]*
  - scrotum 608.89
  - seminal vesicle 608.89
  - senile 797
    - degenerative, of skin 701.3
  - skin (patches) (senile) 701.8
  - spermatic cord 608.89
  - spinal (cord) 336.8
    - acute 336.8
    - muscular (chronic) 335.10
      - adult 335.19
      - familial 335.11
      - juvenile 335.10
    - paralysis 335.10
      - acute (*see also* Poliomyelitis, with paralysis) 045.1 ☑
  - spine (column) 733.99
  - spleen (senile) 289.59
  - spots (skin) 701.3
    - senile 701.8
  - stomach 537.89
  - striate and macular 701.3
    - syphilitic 095.8
  - subcutaneous 701.9
    - due to injection 999.9
  - sublingual gland 527.0
  - submaxillary gland 527.0
  - Sudeck's 733.7
  - suprarenal (autoimmune) (capsule) (gland) 255.41
    - with hypofunction 255.41
  - tarso-orbital fascia, congenital 743.66
  - testis 608.3
  - thenar, partial 354.0
  - throat 478.29
  - thymus (fat) 254.8
  - thyroid (gland) 246.8
    - with
      - cretinism 243
      - myxedema 244.9
    - congenital 243
  - tongue (senile) 529.8
    - papillae 529.4
    - smooth 529.4
  - trachea 519.19
  - tunica vaginalis 608.89

- **Atrophy, atrophic** — *continued*
  - turbinate 733.99
  - tympanic membrane (nonflaccid) 384.82
    - flaccid 384.81
  - ulcer (*see also* Ulcer, skin) 707.9
  - upper respiratory tract 478.9
  - uterus, uterine (acquired) (senile) 621.8
    - cervix 622.8
    - due to radiation (intended effect) 621.8
  - vagina (senile) 627.3
  - vascular 459.89
  - vas deferens 608.89
  - vertebra (senile) 733.99
  - vulva (primary) (senile) 624.1
  - Werdnig-Hoffmann 335.0
  - yellow (acute) (congenital) (liver) (subacute) (*see also* Necrosis, liver) 570
    - chronic 571.8
    - resulting from administration of blood, plasma, serum, or other biological substance (within 8 months of administration) — *see* Hepatitis, viral

- **Attack**
  - akinetic (*see also* Epilepsy) 345.0 ☑
  - angina — *see* Angina
  - apoplectic (*see also* Disease, cerebrovascular, acute) 436
  - benign shuddering 333.93
  - bilious — *see* Vomiting
  - cataleptic 300.11
  - cerebral (*see also* Disease, cerebrovascular, acute) 436
  - coronary (*see also* Infarct, myocardium) 410.9 ☑
  - cyanotic, newborn 770.83
  - epileptic (*see also* Epilepsy) 345.9 ☑
  - epileptiform 780.39
  - heart (*see also* Infarct, myocardium) 410.9 ☑
  - hemiplegia (*see also* Disease, cerebrovascular, acute) 436
  - hysterical 300.11
  - jacksonian (*see also* Epilepsy) 345.5 ☑
  - myocardium, myocardial (*see also* Infarct, myocardium) 410.9 ☑
  - myoclonic (*see also* Epilepsy) 345.1 ☑
  - panic 300.01
  - paralysis (*see also* Disease, cerebrovascular, acute) 436
  - paroxysmal 780.39
  - psychomotor (*see also* Epilepsy) 345.4 ☑
  - salaam (*see also* Epilepsy) 345.6 ☑
  - schizophreniform (*see also* Schizophrenia) 295.4 ☑
  - sensory and motor 780.39
  - syncope 780.2
  - toxic, cerebral 780.39
  - transient ischemic (TIA) 435.9
  - unconsciousness 780.2
    - hysterical 300.11
  - vasomotor 780.2
  - vasovagal (idiopathic) (paroxysmal) 780.2

- **Attention to**
  - artificial opening (of) V55.9
    - digestive tract NEC V55.4
    - specified site NEC V55.8
    - urinary tract NEC V55.6
    - vagina V55.7
  - colostomy V55.3
  - cystostomy V55.5
  - dressing
    - wound V58.30
      - nonsurgical V58.30
      - surgical V58.31
  - gastrostomy V55.1
  - ileostomy V55.2
  - jejunostomy V55.4
  - nephrostomy V55.6
  - surgical dressings V58.31

Attention to — *continued*
  sutures V58.32
  tracheostomy V55.0
  ureterostomy V55.6
  urethrostomy V55.6
Attrition
  gum (*see also* Recession, gingival) 523.20
  teeth (hard tissues) 521.10
    excessive 521.10
      extending into
        dentine 521.12
        pulp 521.13
      generalized 521.15
      limited to enamel 521.11
      localized 521.14
Atypical — *see also* condition
  cells
    endocervical 795.00
    endometrial 795.00
    glandular
      anus 796.70 ●
      cervical 795.00 ●
      vaginal 795.10 ●
  distribution, vessel (congenital) (peripheral) NEC 747.60
  endometrium 621.9
  kidney 593.89
Atypism, cervix 622.10
Audible tinnitus — *see also* Tinnitus 388.30
Auditory — *see* condition
Audry's syndrome (acropachyderma) 757.39
Aujeszky's disease 078.89
Aura
  jacksonian (*see also* Epilepsy) 345.5 ☑ ●
  persistent migraine 346.5 ☑ ●
    with cerebral infarction 346.6 ☑ ●
    without cerebral infarction 346.5 ☑ ●
Aurantiasis, cutis 278.3
Auricle, auricular — *see* condition
Auriculotemporal syndrome 350.8
Australian
  Q fever 083.0
  X disease 062.4
Autism, autistic (child) (infantile) 299.0 ☑
Autodigestion 799.89
Autoerythrocyte sensitization 287.2
Autographism 708.3
Autoimmune
  cold sensitivity 283.0
  disease NEC 279.4
  hemolytic anemia 283.0
  thyroiditis 245.2
Autoinfection, septic — *see* Septicemia
Autointoxication 799.89
Automatism 348.8
  epileptic (*see also* Epilepsy) 345.4 ☑
  paroxysmal, idiopathic (*see also* Epilepsy) 345.4 ☑
Autonomic, autonomous
  bladder 596.54
    neurogenic 596.54
      with cauda equina 344.61
  dysreflexia 337.3
  faciocephalalgia (*see also* Neuropathy, peripheral, autonomic) 337.9
  hysterical seizure 300.11
  imbalance (*see also* Neuropathy, peripheral, autonomic) 337.9
Autophony 388.40
Autosensitivity, erythrocyte 287.2
Autotopagnosia 780.99
Autotoxemia 799.89
Autumn — *see* condition
Avellis' syndrome 344.89
Aviators
  disease or sickness (*see also* Effect, adverse, high altitude) 993.2
  ear 993.0
  effort syndrome 306.2
Avitaminosis (multiple NEC) — *see also* Deficiency, vitamin 269.2
  A 264.9
  B 266.9
    with
      beriberi 265.0
      pellagra 265.2
  B_1 265.1
  B_2 266.0
  B_6 266.1
  B_{12} 266.2
  C (with scurvy) 267
  D 268.9
    with
      osteomalacia 268.2
      rickets 268.0
  E 269.1
  G 266.0
  H 269.1
  K 269.0
  multiple 269.2
  nicotinic acid 265.2
  P 269.1
Avulsion (traumatic) 879.8
  blood vessel — *see* Injury, blood vessel, by site
  cartilage (*see also* Dislocation, by site)
    knee, current (*see also* Tear, meniscus) 836.2
    symphyseal (inner), complicating delivery 665.6 ☑
  complicated 879.9
  diaphragm — *see* Injury, internal, diaphragm
  ear — *see* Wound, open, ear
  epiphysis of bone — *see* Fracture, by site
  external site other than limb — *see* Wound, open, by site
  eye 871.3
  fingernail — *see* Wound, open, finger
  fracture — *see* Fracture, by site
  genital organs, external — *see* Wound, open, genital organs
  head (intracranial) NEC (*see also* Injury, intracranial, with open intracranial wound)
    complete 874.9
    external site NEC 873.8
      complicated 873.9
  internal organ or site — *see* Injury, internal, by site
  joint (*see also* Dislocation, by site)
    capsule — *see* Sprain, by site
  ligament — *see* Sprain, by site
  limb (*see also* Amputation, traumatic, by site)
    skin and subcutaneous tissue — *see* Wound, open, by site
  muscle — *see* Sprain, by site
  nerve (root) — *see* Injury, nerve, by site
  scalp — *see* Wound, open, scalp
  skin and subcutaneous tissue — *see* Wound, open, by site
  symphyseal cartilage (inner), complicating delivery 665.6 ☑
  tendon (*see also* Sprain, by site)
    with open wound — *see* Wound, open, by site
  toenail — *see* Wound, open, toe(s)
  tooth 873.63
    complicated 873.73
Awaiting organ transplant status V49.83
Awareness of heart beat 785.1
Axe grinders' disease 502
Axenfeld's anomaly or syndrome 743.44
Axilla, axillary — *see also* condition
  breast 757.6
Axonotmesis — *see* Injury, nerve, by site
Ayala's disease 756.89
Ayerza's disease or syndrome (pulmonary artery sclerosis with pulmonary hypertension) 416.0
Azoospermia 606.0
Azorean disease (of the nervous system) 334.8
Azotemia 790.6
  meaning uremia (*see also* Uremia) 586
Aztec ear 744.29
Azygos lobe, lung (fissure) 748.69

B

Baader's syndrome (erythema multiforme exudativum) 695.19 ▲
Baastrup's syndrome 721.5
Babesiasis 088.82
Babesiosis 088.82
Babington's disease (familial hemorrhagic telangiectasia) 448.0
Babinski-Fröhlich syndrome (adiposogenital dystrophy) 253.8
Babinski-Nageotte syndrome 344.89
Babinski's syndrome (cardiovascular syphilis) 093.89
Bacillary — *see* condition
Bacilluria 791.9
  asymptomatic, in pregnancy or puerperium 646.5 ☑
  tuberculous (*see also* Tuberculosis) 016.9 ☑
Bacillus — *see also* Infection, bacillus
  abortus infection 023.1
  anthracis infection 022.9
  coli
    infection 041.4
      generalized 038.42
      intestinal 008.00
    pyemia 038.42
    septicemia 038.42
  Flexner's 004.1
  fusiformis infestation 101
  mallei infection 024
  Shiga's 004.0
  suipestifer infection (*see also* Infection, Salmonella) 003.9
Back — *see* condition
Backache (postural) 724.5
  psychogenic 307.89
  sacroiliac 724.6
Backflow (pyelovenous) — *see also* Disease, renal 593.9
Backknee — *see also* Genu, recurvatum 736.5
Bacteremia 790.7
  newborn 771.83
Bacteria
  in blood (*see also* Bacteremia) 790.7
  in urine (*see also* Bacteriuria) 599.0
Bacterial — *see* condition
Bactericholia — *see also* Cholecystitis, acute 575.0
Bacterid, bacteride (Andrews' pustular) 686.8
Bacteriuria, bacteruria 791.9
  with
    urinary tract infection 599.0
  asymptomatic 791.9
    in pregnancy or puerperium 646.5 ☑
      affecting fetus or newborn 760.1
Bad
  breath 784.99
  heart — *see* Disease, heart
  trip (*see also* Abuse, drugs, nondependent) 305.3 ☑
Baehr-Schiffrin disease (thrombotic thrombocytopenic purpura) 446.6
Baelz's disease (cheilitis glandularis apostematosa) 528.5
Baerensprung's disease (eczema marginatum) 110.3
Bagassosis (occupational) 495.1
Baghdad boil 085.1
Bagratuni's syndrome (temporal arteritis) 446.5
Baker's
  cyst (knee) 727.51
    tuberculous (*see also* Tuberculosis) 015.2 ☑
  itch 692.89
Bakwin-Krida syndrome (craniometaphyseal dysplasia) 756.89
Balanitis (circinata) (gangraenosa) (infectious) (vulgaris) 607.1
  amebic 006.8
  candidal 112.2
  chlamydial 099.53
  due to Ducrey's bacillus 099.0
  erosiva circinata et gangraenosa 607.1
  gangrenous 607.1
  gonococcal (acute) 098.0
    chronic or duration of 2 months or over 098.2
  nongonococcal 607.1
  phagedenic 607.1
  venereal NEC 099.8
  xerotica obliterans 607.81
Balanoposthitis 607.1
  chlamydial 099.53
  gonococcal (acute) 098.0
    chronic or duration of 2 months or over 098.2
  ulcerative NEC 099.8
Balanorrhagia — *see* Balanitis
Balantidiasis 007.0
Balantidiosis 007.0
Balbuties, balbutio 307.0
Bald
  patches on scalp 704.00
  tongue 529.4
Baldness — *see also* Alopecia 704.00
Balfour's disease (chloroma) 205.3 ☑
Balint's syndrome (psychic paralysis of visual fixation) 368.16
Balkan grippe 083.0
Ball
  food 938
  hair 938
Ballantyne (-Runge) syndrome (postmaturity) 766.22
Balloon disease — *see also* Effect, adverse, high altitude 993.2
Ballooning posterior leaflet syndrome 424.0
Baló's disease or concentric sclerosis 341.1
Bamberger's disease (hypertrophic pulmonary osteoarthropathy) 731.2
Bamberger-Marie disease (hypertrophic pulmonary osteoarthropathy) 731.2
Bamboo spine 720.0
Bancroft's filariasis 125.0
Band(s)
  adhesive (*see also* Adhesions, peritoneum) 568.0
  amniotic 658.8 ☑
    affecting fetus or newborn 762.8
  anomalous or congenital (*see also* Anomaly, specified type NEC)
    atrial 746.9
    heart 746.9
    intestine 751.4
    omentum 751.4
    ventricular 746.9
  cervix 622.3
  gallbladder (congenital) 751.69
  intestinal (adhesive) (*see also* Adhesions, peritoneum) 568.0
    congenital 751.4
  obstructive (*see also* Obstruction, intestine) 560.81
  periappendiceal (congenital) 751.4
  peritoneal (adhesive) (*see also* Adhesions, peritoneum) 568.0
    with intestinal obstruction 560.81
    congenital 751.4
  uterus 621.5
  vagina 623.2
Bandemia (without diagnosis of specific infection) 288.66

Bandl's ring (contraction)
- complicating delivery 661.4 ☑
  - affecting fetus or newborn 763.7

Bang's disease (Brucella abortus) 023.1
Bangkok hemorrhagic fever 065.4
Bannister's disease 995.1
Bantam-Albright-Martin disease (pseudohypoparathyroidism) 275.49
Banti's disease or syndrome (with cirrhosis) (with portal hypertension) — *see* Cirrhosis, liver
Bar
- calcaneocuboid 755.67
- calcaneonavicular 755.67
- cubonavicular 755.67
- prostate 600.90
  - with
    - other lower urinary tract symptoms (LUTS) 600.91
    - urinary
      - obstruction 600.91
      - retention 600.91
- talocalcaneal 755.67

Baragnosis 780.99
Barasheh, barashek 266.2
Barcoo disease or rot — *see also* Ulcer, skin 707.9
Bard-Pic syndrome (carcinoma, head of pancreas) 157.0
Bärensprung's disease (eczema marginatum) 110.3
Baritosis 503
Barium lung disease 503
Barlow (-Möller) disease or syndrome (meaning infantile scurvy) 267
Barlow's syndrome (meaning mitral valve prolapse) 424.0
Barodontalgia 993.2
Baron Münchausen syndrome 301.51
Barosinusitis 993.1
Barotitis 993.0
Barotrauma 993.2
- odontalgia 993.2
- otitic 993.0
- sinus 993.1

Barraquer's disease or syndrome (progressive lipodystrophy) 272.6
Barré-Guillain syndrome 357.0
Barrel chest 738.3
Barré-Liéou syndrome (posterior cervical sympathetic) 723.2
Barrett's esophagus 530.85
Barrett's syndrome or ulcer (chronic peptic ulcer of esophagus) 530.85
Bársony-Polgár syndrome (corkscrew esophagus) 530.5
Bársony-Teschendorf syndrome (corkscrew esophagus) 530.5
Bartholin's
- adenitis (*see also* Bartholinitis) 616.89
- gland — *see* condition

Bartholinitis (suppurating) 616.89
- gonococcal (acute) 098.0
  - chronic or duration of 2 months or over 098.2

Barth syndrome 759.89
Bartonellosis 088.0
Bartter's syndrome (secondary hyperaldosteronism with juxtaglomerular hyperplasia) 255.13
Basal — *see* condition
Basan's (hidrotic) **ectodermal dysplasia** 757.31
Baseball finger 842.13
Basedow's disease or syndrome (exophthalmic goiter) 242.0 ☑
Basic — *see* condition
Basilar — *see* condition
Bason's (hidrotic) **ectodermal dysplasia** 757.31
Basopenia 288.59
Basophilia 288.65
Basophilism (corticoadrenal) (Cushing's) (pituitary) (thymic) 255.0
Bassen-Kornzweig syndrome (abetalipoproteinemia) 272.5
Bat ear 744.29
Bateman's
- disease 078.0
- purpura (senile) 287.2

Bathing cramp 994.1
Bathophobia 300.23
Batten's disease, retina 330.1 *[362.71]*
Batten-Mayou disease 330.1 *[362.71]*
Batten-Steinert syndrome 359.21
Battered
- adult (syndrome) 995.81
- baby or child (syndrome) 995.54
- spouse (syndrome) 995.81

Battey mycobacterium infection 031.0
Battledore placenta — *see* Placenta, abnormal
Battle exhaustion — *see also* Reaction, stress, acute 308.9
Baumgarten-Cruveilhier (cirrhosis) **disease, or syndrome** 571.5
Bauxite
- fibrosis (of lung) 503
- workers' disease 503

Bayle's disease (dementia paralytica) 094.1
Bazin's disease (primary) — *see also* Tuberculosis 017.1 ☑
Beach ear 380.12
Beaded hair (congenital) 757.4
Beals syndrome 759.82
Beard's disease (neurasthenia) 300.5
Bearn-Kunkel (-Slater) syndrome (lupoid hepatitis) 571.49
Beat
- elbow 727.2
- hand 727.2
- knee 727.2

Beats
- ectopic 427.60
- escaped, heart 427.60
  - postoperative 997.1
- premature (nodal) 427.60
  - atrial 427.61
  - auricular 427.61
  - postoperative 997.1
  - specified type NEC 427.69
  - supraventricular 427.61
  - ventricular 427.69

Beau's
- disease or syndrome (*see also* Degeneration, myocardial) 429.1
- lines (transverse furrows on fingernails) 703.8

Bechterew's disease (ankylosing spondylitis) 720.0
Bechterew-Strümpell-Marie syndrome (ankylosing spondylitis) 720.0
Becker's
- disease
  - idiopathic mural endomyocardial disease 425.2
  - myotonia congenita, recessive form 359.22
- dystrophy 359.22

Beck's syndrome (anterior spinal artery occlusion) 433.8 ☑
Beckwith (-Wiedemann) syndrome 759.89
Bedbugs bite(s) — *see* Injury, superficial, by site ●
Bedclothes, asphyxiation or suffocation by 994.7
Bed confinement status V49.84
Bednar's aphthae 528.2
Bedsore ▶(*see also* Ulcer, pressure)◀ 707.00
- with gangrene 707.00 *[785.4]*

Bedwetting — *see also* Enuresis 788.36
Beer-drinkers' heart (disease) 425.5
Bee sting (with allergic or anaphylactic shock) 989.5
Begbie's disease (exophthalmic goiter) 242.0 ☑
Behavior disorder, disturbance — *see also* Disturbance, conduct
Behavior disorder, disturbance — *see also* Disturbance, conduct — *continued*
- antisocial, without manifest psychiatric disorder
  - adolescent V71.02
  - adult V71.01
  - child V71.02
- dyssocial, without manifest psychiatric disorder
  - adolescent V71.02
  - adult V71.01
  - child V71.02
- high risk — *see* Problem

Behçet's syndrome 136.1
Behr's disease 362.50
Beigel's disease or morbus (white piedra) 111.2
Bejel 104.0
Bekhterev's disease (ankylosing spondylitis) 720.0
Bekhterev-Strümpell-Marie syndrome (ankylosing spondylitis) 720.0
Belching — *see also* Eructation 787.3
Bell's
- disease (*see also* Psychosis, affective) 296.0 ☑
- mania (*see also* Psychosis, affective) 296.0 ☑
- palsy, paralysis 351.0
  - infant 767.5
  - newborn 767.5
  - syphilitic 094.89
- spasm 351.0

Bence-Jones albuminuria, albuminosuria, or proteinuria 791.0
Bends 993.3
Benedikt's syndrome (paralysis) 344.89
Benign — *see also* condition
- cellular changes, cervix 795.09
- prostate
  - with
    - other lower urinary tract symptoms (LUTS) 600.21
    - urinary
      - obstruction 600.21
      - retention 600.21
  - hyperplasia 600.20
  - neoplasm 222.2

Bennett's
- disease (leukemia) 208.9 ☑
- fracture (closed) 815.01
  - open 815.11

Benson's disease 379.22
Bent
- back (hysterical) 300.11
- nose 738.0
  - congenital 754.0

Bereavement V62.82
- as adjustment reaction 309.0

Bergeron's disease (hysteroepilepsy) 300.11
Berger's paresthesia (lower limb) 782.0
Beriberi (acute) (atrophic) (chronic) (dry) (subacute) (wet) 265.0
- with polyneuropathy 265.0 *[357.4]*
- heart (disease) 265.0 *[425.7]*
- leprosy 030.1
- neuritis 265.0 *[357.4]*

Berlin's disease or edema (traumatic) 921.3
Berloque dermatitis 692.72
Bernard-Horner syndrome — *see also* Neuropathy, peripheral, autonomic 337.9
Bernard-Sergent syndrome (acute adrenocortical insufficiency) 255.41
Bernard-Soulier disease or thrombopathy 287.1
Bernhardt's disease or paresthesia 355.1
Bernhardt-Roth disease or syndrome (paresthesia) 355.1
Bernheim's syndrome — *see also* Failure, heart 428.0
Bertielliasis 123.8
Bertolotti's syndrome (sacralization of fifth lumbar vertebra) 756.15
Berylliosis (acute) (chronic) (lung) (occupational) 503
Besnier's
- lupus pernio 135
- prurigo (atopic dermatitis) (infantile eczema) 691.8

Besnier-Boeck disease or sarcoid 135
Besnier-Boeck-Schaumann disease (sarcoidosis) 135
Best's disease 362.76
Bestiality 302.1
Beta-adrenergic hyperdynamic circulatory state 429.82
Beta-aminoisobutyric aciduria 277.2
Beta-mercaptolactate-cysteine disulfiduria 270.0
Beta thalassemia (major) (minor) (mixed) 282.49
Beurmann's disease (sporotrichosis) 117.1
Bezoar 938
- intestine 936
- stomach 935.2

Bezold's abscess — *see also* Mastoiditis 383.01
Bianchi's syndrome (aphasia-apraxia-alexia) 784.69
Bicornuate or bicornis uterus 752.3
- in pregnancy or childbirth 654.0 ☑
  - with obstructed labor 660.2 ☑
    - affecting fetus or newborn 763.1
  - affecting fetus or newborn 763.89

Bicuspid aortic valve 746.4
Biedl-Bardet syndrome 759.89
Bielschowsky's disease 330.1
Bielschowsky-Jansky
- amaurotic familial idiocy 330.1
- disease 330.1

Biemond's syndrome (obesity, polydactyly, and mental retardation) 759.89
Biermer's anemia or disease (pernicious anemia) 281.0
Biett's disease 695.4
Bifid (congenital) — *see also* Imperfect, closure
- apex, heart 746.89
- clitoris 752.49
- epiglottis 748.3
- kidney 753.3
- nose 748.1
- patella 755.64
- scrotum 752.89
- toe 755.66
- tongue 750.13
- ureter 753.4
- uterus 752.3
- uvula 749.02
  - with cleft lip (*see also* Cleft, palate, with cleft lip) 749.20

Biforis uterus (suprasimplex) 752.3
Bifurcation (congenital) — *see also* Imperfect, closure
- gallbladder 751.69
- kidney pelvis 753.3
- renal pelvis 753.3
- rib 756.3
- tongue 750.13
- trachea 748.3
- ureter 753.4
- urethra 753.8
- uvula 749.02
  - with cleft lip (*see also* Cleft, palate, with cleft lip) 749.20
- vertebra 756.19

Bigeminal pulse 427.89
Bigeminy 427.89
Big spleen syndrome 289.4
Bilateral — *see* condition
Bile duct — *see* condition
Bile pigments in urine 791.4
Bilharziasis — *see also* Schistosomiasis 120.9
- chyluria 120.0
- cutaneous 120.3

Bilharziasis — *see also* Schistosomiasis — *continued*
galacturia 120.0
hematochyluria 120.0
intestinal 120.1
lipemia 120.9
lipuria 120.0
Oriental 120.2
piarhemia 120.9
pulmonary 120.2
tropical hematuria 120.0
vesical 120.0
Biliary — *see* condition
Bilious (attack) — *see also* Vomiting
fever, hemoglobinuric 084.8
Bilirubinuria 791.4
Biliuria 791.4
Billroth's disease
meningocele (*see also* Spina bifida) 741.9 ☑
Bilobate placenta — *see* Placenta, abnormal
Bilocular
heart 745.7
stomach 536.8
Bing-Horton syndrome (histamine cephalgia) 339.00 ▲
Binswanger's disease or dementia 290.12
Biörck (-Thorson) syndrome (malignant carcinoid) 259.2
Biparta, bipartite — *see also* Imperfect, closure
carpal scaphoid 755.59
patella 755.64
placenta — *see* Placenta, abnormal
vagina 752.49
Bird
face 756.0
fanciers' lung or disease 495.2
Bird's disease (oxaluria) 271.8
Birth
abnormal fetus or newborn 763.9
accident, fetus or newborn — *see* Birth, injury
complications in mother — *see* Delivery, complicated
compression during NEC 767.9
defect — *see* Anomaly
delayed, fetus 763.9
difficult NEC, affecting fetus or newborn 763.9
dry, affecting fetus or newborn 761.1
forced, NEC, affecting fetus or newborn 763.89
forceps, affecting fetus or newborn 763.2
hematoma of sternomastoid 767.8
immature 765.1 ☑
extremely 765.0 ☑
inattention, after or at 995.52
induced, affecting fetus or newborn 763.89
infant — *see* Newborn
injury NEC 767.9
adrenal gland 767.8
basal ganglia 767.0
brachial plexus (paralysis) 767.6
brain (compression) (pressure) 767.0
cerebellum 767.0
cerebral hemorrhage 767.0
conjunctiva 767.8
eye 767.8
fracture
bone, any except clavicle or spine 767.3
clavicle 767.2
femur 767.3
humerus 767.3
long bone 767.3
radius and ulna 767.3
skeleton NEC 767.3
skull 767.3
spine 767.4
tibia and fibula 767.3

Birth — *continued*
injury — *continued*
hematoma 767.8
liver (subcapsular) 767.8
mastoid 767.8
skull 767.19
sternomastoid 767.8
testes 767.8
vulva 767.8
intracranial (edema) 767.0
laceration
brain 767.0
by scalpel 767.8
peripheral nerve 767.7
liver 767.8
meninges
brain 767.0
spinal cord 767.4
nerves (cranial, peripheral) 767.7
brachial plexus 767.6
facial 767.5
paralysis 767.7
brachial plexus 767.6
Erb (-Duchenne) 767.6
facial nerve 767.5
Klumpke (-Déjérine) 767.6
radial nerve 767.6
spinal (cord) (hemorrhage) (laceration) (rupture) 767.4
rupture
intracranial 767.0
liver 767.8
spinal cord 767.4
spleen 767.8
viscera 767.8
scalp 767.19
scalpel wound 767.8
skeleton NEC 767.3
specified NEC 767.8
spinal cord 767.4
spleen 767.8
subdural hemorrhage 767.0
tentorial, tear 767.0
testes 767.8
vulva 767.8
instrumental, NEC, affecting fetus or newborn 763.2
lack of care, after or at 995.52
multiple
affected by maternal complications of pregnancy 761.5
healthy liveborn — *see* Newborn, multiple
neglect, after or at 995.52
newborn — *see* Newborn
palsy or paralysis NEC 767.7
precipitate, fetus or newborn 763.6
premature (infant) 765.1 ☑
prolonged, affecting fetus or newborn 763.9
retarded, fetus or newborn 763.9
shock, newborn 779.89
strangulation or suffocation
due to aspiration of clear amniotic fluid 770.13
with respiratory symptoms 770.14
mechanical 767.8
trauma NEC 767.9
triplet
affected by maternal complications of pregnancy 761.5
healthy liveborn — *see* Newborn, multiple
twin
affected by maternal complications of pregnancy 761.5
healthy liveborn — *see* Newborn, twin
ventouse, affecting fetus or newborn 763.3
Birthmark 757.32
Birt-Hogg-Dube syndrome 759.89 ●
Bisalbuminemia 273.8
Biskra button 085.1

Bite(s)
with intact skin surface — *see* Contusion
animal — *see* Wound, open, by site
intact skin surface — *see* Contusion
bedbug — *see* Injury, superficial, by site ●
centipede 989.5
chigger 133.8
fire ant 989.5
flea — *see* Injury, superficial, by site
human (open wound) (*see also* Wound, open, by site)
intact skin surface — *see* Contusion
insect
nonvenomous — *see* Injury, superficial, by site
venomous 989.5
mad dog (death from) 071
open
anterior 524.24
posterior 524.25
poisonous 989.5
red bug 133.8
reptile 989.5
nonvenomous — *see* Wound, open, by site
snake 989.5
nonvenomous — *see* Wound, open, by site
spider (venomous) 989.5
nonvenomous — *see* Injury, superficial, by site
venomous 989.5
Biting
cheek or lip 528.9
nail 307.9
Black
death 020.9
eye NEC 921.0
hairy tongue 529.3
heel 924.20
lung disease 500
palm 923.20
Blackfan-Diamond anemia or syndrome (congenital hypoplastic anemia) 284.01
Blackhead 706.1
Blackout 780.2
Blackwater fever 084.8
Bladder — *see* condition
Blast
blindness 921.3
concussion — *see* Blast, injury
injury 869.0
with open wound into cavity 869.1
abdomen or thorax — *see* Injury, internal, by site
brain (*see also* Concussion, brain) 850.9
with skull fracture — *see* Fracture, skull
ear (acoustic nerve trauma) 951.5
with perforation, tympanic membrane — *see* Wound, open, ear, drum
lung (*see also* Injury, internal, lung) 861.20
otitic (explosive) 388.11
Blastomycosis, blastomycotic (chronic) (cutaneous) (disseminated) (lung) (pulmonary) (systemic) 116.0
Brazilian 116.1
European 117.5
keloidal 116.2
North American 116.0
primary pulmonary 116.0
South American 116.1
Bleb(s) 709.8
emphysematous (bullous) (diffuse) (lung) (ruptured) (solitary) 492.0
filtering, eye (postglaucoma) (status) V45.69
with complication 997.99

Bleb(s) — *continued*
filtering, eye — *continued*
postcataract extraction (complication) 997.99
lung (ruptured) 492.0
congenital 770.5
subpleural (emphysematous) 492.0
Bleeder (familial) (hereditary) — *see also* Defect, coagulation 286.9
nonfamilial 286.9
Bleeding — *see also* Hemorrhage 459.0
anal 569.3
anovulatory 628.0
atonic, following delivery 666.1 ☑
capillary 448.9
due to subinvolution 621.1
puerperal 666.2 ☑
ear 388.69
excessive, associated with menopausal onset 627.0
familial (*see also* Defect, coagulation) 286.9
following intercourse 626.7
gastrointestinal 578.9
gums 523.8
hemorrhoids — *see* Hemorrhoids, bleeding
intermenstrual
irregular 626.6
regular 626.5
intraoperative 998.11
irregular NEC 626.4
menopausal 627.0
mouth 528.9
nipple 611.79
nose 784.7
ovulation 626.5
postclimacteric 627.1
postcoital 626.7
postmenopausal 627.1
following induced menopause 627.4
postoperative 998.11
preclimacteric 627.0
puberty 626.3
excessive, with onset of menstrual periods 626.3
rectum, rectal 569.3
tendencies (*see also* Defect, coagulation) 286.9
throat 784.8
umbilical stump 772.3
umbilicus 789.9
unrelated to menstrual cycle 626.6
uterus, uterine 626.9
climacteric 627.0
dysfunctional 626.8
functional 626.8
unrelated to menstrual cycle 626.6
vagina, vaginal 623.8
functional 626.8
vicarious 625.8
Blennorrhagia, blennorrhagic — *see* Blennorrhea
Blennorrhea (acute) 098.0
adultorum 098.40
alveolaris 523.40
chronic or duration of 2 months or over 098.2
gonococcal (neonatorum) 098.40
inclusion (neonatal) (newborn) 771.6
neonatorum 098.40
Blepharelosis — *see also* Entropion 374.00
Blepharitis (eyelid) 373.00
angularis 373.01
ciliaris 373.00
with ulcer 373.01
marginal 373.00
with ulcer 373.01
scrofulous (*see also* Tuberculosis) 017.3 ☑ *[373.00]*
squamous 373.02
ulcerative 373.01
Blepharochalasis 374.34
congenital 743.62

☑ Additional Digit Required — Refer to the Tabular List for Digit Selection
▽ Subterms under main terms may continue to next column or page

- **Blepharoclonus** 333.81
- **Blepharoconjunctivitis** — *see also* Conjunctivitis 372.20
  - angular 372.21
  - contact 372.22
- **Blepharophimosis** (eyelid) 374.46
  - congenital 743.62
- **Blepharoplegia** 374.89
- **Blepharoptosis** 374.30
  - congenital 743.61
- **Blepharopyorrhea** 098.49
- **Blepharospasm** 333.81
  - due to drugs 333.85
- **Blessig's cyst** 362.62
- **Blighted ovum** 631
- **Blind**
  - bronchus (congenital) 748.3
  - eye (*see also* Blindness)
    - hypertensive 360.42
    - hypotensive 360.41
  - loop syndrome (postoperative) 579.2
  - sac, fallopian tube (congenital) 752.19
  - spot, enlarged 368.42
  - tract or tube (congenital) NEC — *see* Atresia
- **Blindness** (acquired) (congenital) (both eyes) 369.00
  - with deafness V49.85
  - blast 921.3
    - with nerve injury — *see* Injury, nerve, optic
  - Bright's — *see* Uremia
  - color (congenital) 368.59
    - acquired 368.55
    - blue 368.53
    - green 368.52
    - red 368.51
    - total 368.54
  - concussion 950.9
  - cortical 377.75
  - day 368.10
    - acquired 368.10
    - congenital 368.10
    - hereditary 368.10
    - specified type NEC 368.10
  - due to
    - injury NEC 950.9
    - refractive error — *see* Error, refractive
  - eclipse (total) 363.31
  - emotional 300.11
  - face 368.16 ●
  - hysterical 300.11
  - legal (both eyes) (USA definition) 369.4
    - with impairment of better (less impaired) eye
      - near-total 369.02
        - with
          - lesser eye impairment 369.02
            - near-total 369.04
            - total 369.03
      - profound 369.05
        - with
          - lesser eye impairment 369.05
            - near-total 369.07
            - profound 369.08
            - total 369.06
      - severe 369.21
        - with
          - lesser eye impairment 369.21
            - blind 369.11
            - near-total 369.13
            - profound 369.14
            - severe 369.22
            - total 369.12
      - total
        - with lesser eye impairment
          - total 369.01
  - mind 784.69
  - moderate
    - both eyes 369.25
      - with impairment of lesser eye (specified as)
        - blind, not further specified 369.15
        - low vision, not further specified 369.23
        - near-total 369.17
        - profound 369.18
        - severe 369.24
        - total 369.16
    - one eye 369.74
      - with vision of other eye (specified as)
        - near-normal 369.75
        - normal 369.76
  - near-total
    - both eyes 369.04
      - with impairment of lesser eye (specified as)
        - blind, not further specified 369.02
        - total 369.03
    - one eye 369.64
      - with vision of other eye (specified as)
        - near-normal 369.65
        - normal 369.66
  - night 368.60
    - acquired 368.62
    - congenital (Japanese) 368.61
    - hereditary 368.61
    - specified type NEC 368.69
    - vitamin A deficiency 264.5
  - nocturnal — *see* Blindness, night
  - one eye 369.60
    - with low vision of other eye 369.10
  - profound
    - both eyes 369.08
      - with impairment of lesser eye (specified as)
        - blind, not further specified 369.05
        - near-total 369.07
        - total 369.06
    - one eye 369.67
      - with vision of other eye (specified as)
        - near-normal 369.68
        - normal 369.69
  - psychic 784.69
  - severe
    - both eyes 369.22
      - with impairment of lesser eye (specified as)
        - blind, not further specified 369.11
        - low vision, not further specified 369.21
        - near-total 369.13
        - profound 369.14
        - total 369.12
    - one eye 369.71
      - with vision of other eye (specified as)
        - near-normal 369.72
        - normal 369.73
  - snow 370.24
  - sun 363.31
  - temporary 368.12
  - total
    - both eyes 369.01
    - one eye 369.61
      - with vision of other eye (specified as)
        - near-normal 369.62
        - normal 369.63
  - transient 368.12
  - traumatic NEC 950.9
  - word (developmental) 315.01
    - acquired 784.61
    - secondary to organic lesion 784.61
- **Blister** — *see also* Injury, superficial, by site
  - beetle dermatitis 692.89
  - due to burn — *see* Burn, by site, second degree
  - fever 054.9
  - multiple, skin, nontraumatic 709.8
- **Bloating** 787.3
- **Bloch-Siemens syndrome** (incontinentia pigmenti) 757.33
- **Bloch-Stauffer dyshormonal dermatosis** 757.33
- **Bloch-Sulzberger disease or syndrome** (incontinentia pigmenti) (melanoblastosis) 757.33
- **Block**
  - alveolar capillary 516.3
  - arborization (heart) 426.6
  - arrhythmic 426.9
  - atrioventricular (AV) (incomplete) (partial) 426.10
    - with
      - 2:1 atrioventricular response block 426.13
      - atrioventricular dissociation 426.0
    - first degree (incomplete) 426.11
    - second degree (Mobitz type I) 426.13
      - Mobitz (type) II 426.12
    - third degree 426.0
    - complete 426.0
      - congenital 746.86
    - congenital 746.86
    - Mobitz (incomplete)
      - type I (Wenckebach's) 426.13
      - type II 426.12
    - partial 426.13
  - auriculoventricular (*see also* Block, atrioventricular) 426.10
    - complete 426.0
      - congenital 746.86
    - congenital 746.86
  - bifascicular (cardiac) 426.53
  - bundle branch (complete) (false) (incomplete) 426.50
    - bilateral 426.53
    - left (complete) (main stem) 426.3
      - with right bundle branch block 426.53
      - anterior fascicular 426.2
        - with
          - posterior fascicular block 426.3
          - right bundle branch block 426.52
      - hemiblock 426.2
      - incomplete 426.2
        - with right bundle branch block 426.53
      - posterior fascicular 426.2
        - with
          - anterior fascicular block 426.3
          - right bundle branch block 426.51
    - right 426.4
      - with
        - left bundle branch block (incomplete) (main stem) 426.53
        - left fascicular block 426.53
          - anterior 426.52
          - posterior 426.51
    - Wilson's type 426.4
  - cardiac 426.9
  - conduction 426.9
    - complete 426.0
  - Eustachian tube (*see also* Obstruction, Eustachian tube) 381.60
  - fascicular (left anterior) (left posterior) 426.2
  - foramen Magendie (acquired) 331.3
    - congenital 742.3
      - with spina bifida (*see also* Spina bifida) 741.0 ☑
  - heart 426.9
    - first degree (atrioventricular) 426.11
    - second degree (atrioventricular) 426.13
    - third degree (atrioventricular) 426.0
    - bundle branch (complete) (false) (incomplete) 426.50
      - bilateral 426.53
      - left (*see also* Block, bundle branch, left) 426.3
      - right (*see also* Block, bundle branch, right) 426.4
    - complete (atrioventricular) 426.0
    - congenital 746.86
    - incomplete 426.13
    - intra-atrial 426.6
    - intraventricular NEC 426.6
    - sinoatrial 426.6
    - specified type NEC 426.6
  - hepatic vein 453.0
  - intraventricular (diffuse) (myofibrillar) 426.6
    - bundle branch (complete) (false) (incomplete) 426.50
      - bilateral 426.53
      - left (*see also* Block, bundle branch, left) 426.3
      - right (*see also* Block, bundle branch, right) 426.4
  - kidney (*see also* Disease, renal) 593.9
    - postcystoscopic 997.5
  - myocardial (*see also* Block, heart) 426.9
  - nodal 426.10
  - optic nerve 377.49
  - organ or site (congenital) NEC — *see* Atresia
  - parietal 426.6
  - peri-infarction 426.6
  - portal (vein) 452
  - sinoatrial 426.6
  - sinoauricular 426.6
  - spinal cord 336.9
  - trifascicular 426.54
  - tubal 628.2
  - vein NEC 453.9
- **Blocq's disease or syndrome** (astasia-abasia) 307.9
- **Blood**
  - constituents, abnormal NEC 790.6
  - disease 289.9
    - specified NEC 289.89
  - donor V59.01
    - other blood components V59.09
    - stem cells V59.02
    - whole blood V59.01
  - dyscrasia 289.9
    - with
      - abortion — *see* Abortion, by type, with hemorrhage, delayed or excessive
      - ectopic pregnancy (*see also* categories 633.0–633.9) 639.1
      - molar pregnancy (*see also* categories 630–632) 639.1
    - fetus or newborn NEC 776.9
    - following
      - abortion 639.1
      - ectopic or molar pregnancy 639.1
    - puerperal, postpartum 666.3 ☑
  - flukes NEC (*see also* Infestation, Schistosoma) 120.9
  - in
    - feces (*see also* Melena) 578.1
      - occult 792.1
    - urine (*see also* Hematuria) 599.70 ▲
  - mole 631
  - occult 792.1
  - poisoning (*see also* Septicemia) 038.9

Index
Blepharoclonus — Blood

- **Blood** — *continued*
  - pressure
    - decreased, due to shock following injury 958.4
    - fluctuating 796.4
    - high (*see also* Hypertension) 401.9
      - incidental reading (isolated) (nonspecific), without diagnosis of hypertension 796.2
    - low (*see also* Hypotension) 458.9
      - incidental reading (isolated) (nonspecific), without diagnosis of hypotension 796.3
  - spitting (*see also* Hemoptysis) 786.3
  - staining cornea 371.12
  - transfusion
    - without reported diagnosis V58.2
    - donor V59.01
      - stem cells V59.02
    - reaction or complication — *see* Complications, transfusion
  - tumor — *see* Hematoma
  - vessel rupture — *see* Hemorrhage
  - vomiting (*see also* Hematemesis) 578.0
- **Blood-forming organ disease** 289.9
- **Bloodgood's disease** 610.1
- **Bloodshot eye** 379.93
- **Bloom (-Machacek) (-Torre) syndrome** 757.39
- **Blotch, palpebral** 372.55
- **Blount-Barber syndrome** (tibia vara) 732.4
- **Blount's disease** (tibia vara) 732.4
- **Blue**
  - baby 746.9
  - bloater 491.20
    - with
      - acute bronchitis 491.22
      - exacerbation (acute) 491.21
  - diaper syndrome 270.0
  - disease 746.9
  - dome cyst 610.0
  - drum syndrome 381.02
  - sclera 743.47
    - with fragility of bone and deafness 756.51
  - toe syndrome 445.02
- **Blueness** — *see also* Cyanosis 782.5
- **Blurring, visual** 368.8
- **Blushing** (abnormal) (excessive) 782.62
- **BMI** (body mass index)
  - adult
    - 25.0-25.9 V85.21
    - 26.0-26.9 V85.22
    - 27.0-27.9 V85.23
    - 28.0-28.9 V85.24
    - 29.0-29.9 V85.25
    - 30.0-30.9 V85.30
    - 31.0-31.9 V85.31
    - 32.0-32.9 V85.32
    - 33.0-33.9 V85.33
    - 34.0-34.9 V85.34
    - 35.0-35.9 V85.35
    - 36.0-36.9 V85.36
    - 37.0-37.9 V85.37
    - 38.0-38.9 V85.38
    - 39.0-39.9 V85.39
    - 40 and over V85.4
    - between 19-24 V85.1
    - less than 19 V85.0
  - pediatric
    - 5th percentile to less than 85th percentile for age V85.52
    - 85th percentile to less than 95th percentile for age V85.53
    - greater than or equal to 95th percentile for age V85.54
    - less than 5th percentile for age V85.51
- **Boarder, hospital** V65.0
  - infant V65.0
- **Bockhart's impetigo** (superficial folliculitis) 704.8
- **Bodechtel-Guttmann disease** (subacute sclerosing panencephalitis) 046.2
- **Boder-Sedgwick syndrome** (ataxia-telangiectasia) 334.8
- **Body, bodies**
  - Aschoff (*see also* Myocarditis, rheumatic) 398.0
  - asteroid, vitreous 379.22
  - choroid, colloid (degenerative) 362.57
    - hereditary 362.77
  - cytoid (retina) 362.82
  - drusen (retina) (*see also* Drusen) 362.57
    - optic disc 377.21
  - fibrin, pleura 511.0
  - foreign — *see* Foreign body
  - Hassall-Henle 371.41
  - loose
    - joint (*see also* Loose, body, joint) 718.1 ☑
      - knee 717.6
    - knee 717.6
    - sheath, tendon 727.82
  - Mallory's 034.1
  - mass index (BMI)
    - adult
      - 25.0-25.9 V85.21
      - 26.0-26.9 V85.22
      - 27.0-27.9 V85.23
      - 28.0-28.9 V85.24
      - 29.0-29.9 V85.25
      - 30.0-30.9 V85.30
      - 31.0-31.9 V85.31
      - 32.0-32.9 V85.32
      - 33.0-33.9 V85.33
      - 34.0-34.9 V85.34
      - 36.0-36.9 V85.36
      - 37.0-37.9 V85.37
      - 38.0-38.9 V85.38
      - 39.0-39.9 V85.39
      - 40 and over V85.4
      - between 19-24 V85.1
      - less than 19 V85.0
    - pediatric
      - 5th percentile to less than 85th percentile for age V85.52
      - 85th percentile to less than 95th percentile for age V85.53
      - greater than or equal to 95th percentile for age V85.54
      - less than 5th percentile for age V85.51
  - Mooser 081.0
  - Negri 071
  - rice (joint) (*see also* Loose, body, joint) 718.1 ☑
    - knee 717.6
  - rocking 307.3
- **Boeck's**
  - disease (sarcoidosis) 135
  - lupoid (miliary) 135
  - sarcoid 135
- **Boerhaave's syndrome** (spontaneous esophageal rupture) 530.4
- **Boggy**
  - cervix 622.8
  - uterus 621.8
- **Boil** — *see also* Carbuncle 680.9
  - abdominal wall 680.2
  - Aleppo 085.1
  - ankle 680.6
  - anus 680.5
  - arm (any part, above wrist) 680.3
  - auditory canal, external 680.0
  - axilla 680.3
  - back (any part) 680.2
  - Baghdad 085.1
  - breast 680.2
  - buttock 680.5
  - chest wall 680.2
  - corpus cavernosum 607.2
  - Delhi 085.1
  - ear (any part) 680.0
  - eyelid 373.13
  - face (any part, except eye) 680.0
- **Boil** — *see also* Carbuncle — *continued*
  - finger (any) 680.4
  - flank 680.2
  - foot (any part) 680.7
  - forearm 680.3
  - Gafsa 085.1
  - genital organ, male 608.4
  - gluteal (region) 680.5
  - groin 680.2
  - hand (any part) 680.4
  - head (any part, except face) 680.8
  - heel 680.7
  - hip 680.6
  - knee 680.6
  - labia 616.4
  - lacrimal (*see also* Dacryocystitis) 375.30
    - gland (*see also* Dacryoadenitis) 375.00
    - passages (duct) (sac) (*see also* Dacryocystitis) 375.30
  - leg, any part, except foot 680.6
  - multiple sites 680.9
  - natal 085.1
  - neck 680.1
  - nose (external) (septum) 680.0
  - orbit, orbital 376.01
  - partes posteriores 680.5
  - pectoral region 680.2
  - penis 607.2
  - perineum 680.2
  - pinna 680.0
  - scalp (any part) 680.8
  - scrotum 608.4
  - seminal vesicle 608.0
  - shoulder 680.3
  - skin NEC 680.9
  - specified site NEC 680.8
  - spermatic cord 608.4
  - temple (region) 680.0
  - testis 608.4
  - thigh 680.6
  - thumb 680.4
  - toe (any) 680.7
  - tropical 085.1
  - trunk 680.2
  - tunica vaginalis 608.4
  - umbilicus 680.2
  - upper arm 680.3
  - vas deferens 608.4
  - vulva 616.4
  - wrist 680.4
- **Bold hives** — *see also* Urticaria 708.9
- **Bolivian hemorrhagic fever** 078.7
- **Bombé, iris** 364.74
- **Bomford-Rhoads anemia** (refractory) 238.72
- **Bone** — *see* condition
- **Bonnevie-Ullrich syndrome** 758.6
- **Bonnier's syndrome** 386.19
- **Bonvale Dam fever** 780.79
- **Bony block of joint** 718.80
  - ankle 718.87
  - elbow 718.82
  - foot 718.87
  - hand 718.84
  - hip 718.85
  - knee 718.86
  - multiple sites 718.89
  - pelvic region 718.85
  - shoulder (region) 718.81
  - specified site NEC 718.88
  - wrist 718.83
- ● **BOOP** (bronchiolitis obliterans organized pneumonia) 516.8
- **Borderline**
  - intellectual functioning V62.89
  - ● osteopenia 733.90
  - pelvis 653.1 ☑
    - with obstruction during labor 660.1 ☑
      - affecting fetus or newborn 763.1
  - psychosis (*see also* Schizophrenia) 295.5 ☑
- **Borderline** — *continued*
  - psychosis (*see also* Schizophrenia) — *continued*
    - of childhood (*see also* Psychosis, childhood) 299.8 ☑
  - schizophrenia (*see also* Schizophrenia) 295.5 ☑
- **Borna disease** 062.9
- **Bornholm disease** (epidemic pleurodynia) 074.1
- **Borrelia vincentii** (mouth) (pharynx) (tonsils) 101
- **Bostock's catarrh** — *see also* Fever, hay 477.9
- **Boston exanthem** 048
- **Botalli, ductus** (patent) (persistent) 747.0
- **Bothriocephalus latus infestation** 123.4
- **Botulism** 005.1
  - food poisoning 005.1
  - infant 040.41
  - non-foodborne 040.42
  - wound 040.42
- **Bouba** — *see also* Yaws 102.9
- **Bouffée délirante** 298.3
- **Bouillaud's disease or syndrome** (rheumatic heart disease) 391.9
- **Bourneville's disease** (tuberous sclerosis) 759.5
- **Boutonneuse fever** 082.1
- **Boutonniere**
  - deformity (finger) 736.21
  - hand (intrinsic) 736.21
- **Bouveret (-Hoffmann) disease or syndrome** (paroxysmal tachycardia) 427.2
- **Bovine heart** — *see* Hypertrophy, cardiac
- **Bowel** — *see* condition
- **Bowen's**
  - dermatosis (precancerous) (M8081/2) — *see* Neoplasm, skin, in situ
  - disease (M8081/2) — *see* Neoplasm, skin, in situ
  - epithelioma (M8081/2) — *see* Neoplasm, skin, in situ
  - type
    - epidermoid carcinoma in situ (M8081/2) — *see* Neoplasm, skin, in situ
    - intraepidermal squamous cell carcinoma (M8081/2) — *see* Neoplasm, skin, in situ
- **Bowing**
  - femur 736.89
    - congenital 754.42
  - fibula 736.89
    - congenital 754.43
  - forearm 736.09
    - away from midline (cubitus valgus) 736.01
    - toward midline (cubitus varus) 736.02
  - leg(s), long bones, congenital 754.44
  - radius 736.09
    - away from midline (cubitus valgus) 736.01
    - toward midline (cubitus varus) 736.02
  - tibia 736.89
    - congenital 754.43
- **Bowleg(s)** 736.42
  - congenital 754.44
  - rachitic 268.1
- ● **Boyd's dysentery** 004.2
- **Brachial** — *see* condition
- **Brachman-de Lange syndrome** (Amsterdam dwarf, mental retardation, and brachycephaly) 759.89
- **Brachycardia** 427.89
- **Brachycephaly** 756.0
- **Brachymorphism and ectopia lentis** 759.89
- **Bradley's disease** (epidemic vomiting) 078.82
- **Bradycardia** 427.89

Bradycardia — *continued*
chronic (sinus) 427.81
newborn 779.81
nodal 427.89
postoperative 997.1
reflex 337.09 ▲
sinoatrial 427.89
with paroxysmal tachyarrhythmia or tachycardia 427.81
chronic 427.81
sinus 427.89
with paroxysmal tachyarrhythmia or tachycardia 427.81
chronic 427.81
persistent 427.81
severe 427.81
tachycardia syndrome 427.81
vagal 427.89
Bradypnea 786.09
Brailsford's disease 732.3
radial head 732.3
tarsal scaphoid 732.5
Brailsford-Morquio disease or syndrome (mucopolysaccharidosis IV) 277.5
Brain — *see also* condition
death 348.8
syndrome (acute) (chronic) (nonpsychotic) (organic) (with neurotic reaction) (with behavioral reaction) (*see also* Syndrome, brain) 310.9
with
presenile brain disease 290.10
psychosis, psychotic reaction (*see also* Psychosis, organic) 294.9
congenital (*see also* Retardation, mental) 319
Branched-chain amino-acid disease 270.3
Branchial — *see* condition
Brandt's syndrome (acrodermatitis enteropathica) 686.8
Brash (water) 787.1
Brass-founders' ague 985.8
Bravais-Jacksonian epilepsy — *see also* Epilepsy 345.5 ☑
Braxton Hicks contractions 644.1 ☑
Braziers' disease 985.8
Brazilian
blastomycosis 116.1
leishmaniasis 085.5
BRBPR (bright red blood per rectum) 569.3
Break
cardiorenal — *see* Hypertension, cardiorenal
retina (*see also* Defect, retina) 361.30
Breakbone fever 061
Breakdown
device, implant, or graft — *see* Complications, mechanical
nervous (*see also* Disorder, mental, nonpsychotic) 300.9
perineum 674.2 ☑
Breast — *see also* condition
buds 259.1 ●
in newborn 779.89 ●
dense — *omit code* ●
nodule 793.89 ●
Breast feeding difficulties 676.8 ☑
Breath
foul 784.99
holder, child 312.81
holding spells 786.9
shortness 786.05
Breathing
asymmetrical 786.09
bronchial 786.09
exercises V57.0
labored 786.09
mouth 784.99
causing malocclusion 524.59
periodic 786.09
high altitude 327.22
Breathing — *continued*
tic 307.20
Breathlessness 786.09
Breda's disease — *see also* Yaws 102.9
Breech
delivery, affecting fetus or newborn 763.0
extraction, affecting fetus or newborn 763.0
presentation (buttocks) (complete) (frank) 652.2 ☑
with successful version 652.1 ☑
before labor, affecting fetus or newborn 761.7
during labor, affecting fetus or newborn 763.0
Breisky's disease (kraurosis vulvae) 624.09
Brennemann's syndrome (acute mesenteric lymphadenitis) 289.2
Brenner's
tumor (benign) (M9000/0) 220
borderline malignancy (M9000/1) 236.2
malignant (M9000/3) 183.0
proliferating (M9000/1) 236.2
Bretonneau's disease (diphtheritic malignant angina) 032.0
Breus' mole 631
Brevicollis 756.16
Bricklayers' itch 692.89
Brickmakers' anemia 126.9
Bridge
myocardial 746.85
Bright's
blindness — *see* Uremia
disease (*see also* Nephritis) 583.9
arteriosclerotic (*see also* Hypertension, kidney) 403.90
Bright red blood per rectum (BRBPR) 569.3
Brill's disease (recrudescent typhus) 081.1
flea-borne 081.0
louse-borne 081.1
Brill-Symmers disease (follicular lymphoma) (M9690/3) 202.0 ☑
Brill-Zinsser disease (recrudescent typhus) 081.1
Brinton's disease (linitis plastica) (M8142/3) 151.9
Brion-Kayser disease — *see also* Fever, paratyphoid 002.9
Briquet's disorder or syndrome 300.81
Brissaud's
infantilism (infantile myxedema) 244.9
motor-verbal tic 307.23
Brissaud-Meige syndrome (infantile myxedema) 244.9
Brittle
bones (congenital) 756.51
nails 703.8
congenital 757.5
Broad — *see also* condition
beta disease 272.2
ligament laceration syndrome 620.6
Brock's syndrome (atelectasis due to enlarged lymph nodes) 518.0
Brocq's disease 691.8
atopic (diffuse) neurodermatitis 691.8
lichen simplex chronicus 698.3
parakeratosis psoriasiformis 696.2
parapsoriasis 696.2
Brocq-Duhring disease (dermatitis herpetiformis) 694.0
Brodie's
abscess (localized) (chronic) (*see also* Osteomyelitis) 730.1 ☑
disease (joint) (*see also* Osteomyelitis) 730.1 ☑
Broken
arches 734
congenital 755.67
back — *see* Fracture, vertebra, by site
bone — *see* Fracture, by site
compensation — *see* Disease, heart
Broken — *continued*
heart syndrome 429.83
implant or internal device — *see* listing under Complications, mechanical
neck — *see* Fracture, vertebra, cervical
nose 802.0
open 802.1
tooth, teeth 873.63
complicated 873.73
Bromhidrosis 705.89
Bromidism, bromism
acute 967.3
correct substance properly administered 349.82
overdose or wrong substance given or taken 967.3
chronic (*see also* Dependence) 304.1 ☑
Bromidrosiphobia 300.23
Bromidrosis 705.89
Bronchi, bronchial — *see* condition
Bronchiectasis (cylindrical) (diffuse) (fusiform) (localized) (moniliform) (postinfectious) (recurrent) (saccular) 494.0
with acute exacerbation 494.1
congenital 748.61
tuberculosis (*see also* Tuberculosis) 011.5 ☑
Bronchiolectasis — *see* Bronchiectasis
Bronchiolitis (acute) (infectious) (subacute) 466.19
with
bronchospasm or obstruction 466.19
influenza, flu, or grippe 487.1
catarrhal (acute) (subacute) 466.19
chemical 506.0
chronic 506.4
chronic (obliterative) 491.8
due to external agent — *see* Bronchitis, acute, due to
fibrosa obliterans 491.8
influenzal 487.1
obliterans 491.8
with organizing pneumonia ▶(BOOP)◀ 516.8
status post lung transplant 996.84
obliterative (chronic) (diffuse) (subacute) 491.8
due to fumes or vapors 506.4
respiratory syncytial virus 466.11
vesicular — *see* Pneumonia, broncho-
Bronchitis (diffuse) (hypostatic) (infectious) (inflammatory) (simple) 490
with
emphysema — *see* Emphysema
influenza, flu, or grippe 487.1
obstruction airway, chronic 491.20
with
acute bronchitis 491.22
exacerbation (acute) 491.21
tracheitis 490
acute or subacute 466.0
with bronchospasm or obstruction 466.0
chronic 491.8
acute or subacute 466.0
with
bronchiectasis 494.1 ●
bronchospasm 466.0
obstruction 466.0
tracheitis 466.0
chemical (due to fumes or vapors) 506.0
due to
fumes or vapors 506.0
radiation 508.8
allergic (acute) (*see also* Asthma) 493.9 ☑
arachidic 934.1
aspiration 507.0
due to fumes or vapors 506.0
asthmatic (acute) 493.90
Bronchitis — *continued*
asthmatic — *continued*
with
acute exacerbation 493.92
status asthmaticus 493.91
chronic 493.2 ☑
capillary 466.19
with bronchospasm or obstruction 466.19
chronic 491.8
caseous (*see also* Tuberculosis) 011.3 ☑
Castellani's 104.8
catarrhal 490
acute — *see* Bronchitis, acute
chronic 491.0
chemical (acute) (subacute) 506.0
chronic 506.4
due to fumes or vapors (acute) (subacute) 506.0
chronic 506.4
chronic 491.9
with
tracheitis (chronic) 491.8
asthmatic 493.2 ☑
catarrhal 491.0
chemical (due to fumes and vapors) 506.4
due to
fumes or vapors (chemical) (inhalation) 506.4
radiation 508.8
tobacco smoking 491.0
mucopurulent 491.1
obstructive 491.20
with
acute bronchitis 491.22
exacerbation (acute) 491.21
purulent 491.1
simple 491.0
specified type NEC 491.8
croupous 466.0
with bronchospasm or obstruction 466.0
due to fumes or vapors 506.0
emphysematous 491.20
with
acute bronchitis 491.22
exacerbation (acute) 491.21
exudative 466.0
fetid (chronic) (recurrent) 491.1
fibrinous, acute or subacute 466.0
with bronchospasm or obstruction 466.0
grippal 487.1
influenzal 487.1
membranous, acute or subacute 466.0
with bronchospasm or obstruction 466.0
moulders' 502
mucopurulent (chronic) (recurrent) 491.1
acute or subacute 466.0
obliterans 491.8
obstructive (chronic) 491.20
with
acute bronchitis 491.22
exacerbation (acute) 491.21
pituitous 491.1
plastic (inflammatory) 466.0
pneumococcal, acute or subacute 466.0
with bronchospasm or obstruction 466.0
pseudomembranous 466.0
purulent (chronic) (recurrent) 491.1
acute or subacute 466.0
with bronchospasm or obstruction 466.0
putrid 491.1
scrofulous (*see also* Tuberculosis) 011.3 ☑
senile 491.9
septic, acute or subacute 466.0

Bronchitis — *continued*
septic, acute or subacute — *continued*
with bronchospasm or obstruction 466.0
smokers' 491.0
spirochetal 104.8
suffocative, acute or subacute 466.0
summer (*see also* Asthma) 493.9 ☑
suppurative (chronic) 491.1
acute or subacute 466.0
tuberculous (*see also* Tuberculosis) 011.3 ☑
ulcerative 491.8
Vincent's 101
Vincent's 101
viral, acute or subacute 466.0
Bronchoalveolitis 485
Bronchoaspergillosis 117.3
Bronchocele
meaning
dilatation of bronchus 519.19
goiter 240.9
Bronchogenic carcinoma 162.9
Bronchohemisporosis 117.9
Broncholithiasis 518.89
tuberculous (*see also* Tuberculosis) 011.3 ☑
Bronchomalacia 748.3
Bronchomoniliasis 112.89
Bronchomycosis 112.89
Bronchonocardiosis 039.1
Bronchopleuropneumonia — *see* Pneumonia, broncho-
Bronchopneumonia — *see* Pneumonia, broncho-
Bronchopneumonitis — *see* Pneumonia, broncho-
Bronchopulmonary — *see* condition
Bronchopulmonitis — *see* Pneumonia, broncho-
Bronchorrhagia 786.3
newborn 770.3
tuberculous (*see also* Tuberculosis) 011.3 ☑
Bronchorrhea (chronic) (purulent) 491.0
acute 466.0
Bronchospasm 519.11
with
asthma — *see* Asthma
bronchiolitis, acute 466.19
due to respiratory syncytial virus 466.11
bronchitis — *see* Bronchitis
chronic obstructive pulmonary disease (COPD) 496
emphysema — *see* Emphysema
due to external agent — *see* Condition, respiratory, acute, due to
acute 519.11
exercise induced 493.81
Bronchospirochetosis 104.8
Bronchostenosis 519.19
Bronchus — *see* condition
Bronze, bronzed
diabetes 275.0
disease (Addison's) (skin) 255.41
tuberculous (*see also* Tuberculosis) 017.6 ☑
Brooke's disease or tumor (M8100/0) — *see* Neoplasm, skin, benign
Brown enamel of teeth (hereditary) 520.5
Brown-Séquard's paralysis (syndrome) 344.89
Brown's tendon sheath syndrome 378.61
Brow presentation complicating delivery 652.4 ☑
Brucella, brucellosis (infection) 023.9
abortus 023.1
canis 023.3
dermatitis, skin 023.9
melitensis 023.0
mixed 023.8

Brucella, brucellosis — *continued*
suis 023.2
Bruck-de Lange disease or syndrome (Amsterdam dwarf, mental retardation, and brachycephaly) 759.89
Bruck's disease 733.99
Brugada syndrome 746.89
Brug's filariasis 125.1
Brugsch's syndrome (acropachyderma) 757.39
Bruhl's disease (splenic anemia with fever) 285.8
Bruise (skin surface intact) — *see also* Contusion
with
fracture — *see* Fracture, by site
open wound — *see* Wound, open, by site
internal organ (abdomen, chest, or pelvis) — *see* Injury, internal, by site
umbilical cord 663.6 ☑
affecting fetus or newborn 762.6
Bruit 785.9
arterial (abdominal) (carotid) 785.9
supraclavicular 785.9
Brushburn — *see* Injury, superficial, by site
Bruton's X-linked agammaglobulinemia 279.04
Bruxism 306.8
sleep related 327.53
Bubbly lung syndrome 770.7
Bubo 289.3
blennorrhagic 098.89
chancroidal 099.0
climatic 099.1
due to Hemophilus ducreyi 099.0
gonococcal 098.89
indolent NEC 099.8
inguinal NEC 099.8
chancroidal 099.0
climatic 099.1
due to H. ducreyi 099.0
scrofulous (*see also* Tuberculosis) 017.2 ☑
soft chancre 099.0
suppurating 683
syphilitic 091.0
congenital 090.0
tropical 099.1
venereal NEC 099.8
virulent 099.0
Bubonic plague 020.0
Bubonocele — *see* Hernia, inguinal
Buccal — *see* condition
Buchanan's disease (juvenile osteochondrosis of iliac crest) 732.1
Buchem's syndrome (hyperostosis corticalis) 733.3
Buchman's disease (osteochondrosis, juvenile) 732.1
Bucket handle fracture (semilunar cartilage) — *see also* Tear, meniscus 836.2
Budd-Chiari syndrome (hepatic vein thrombosis) 453.0
Budgerigar-fanciers' disease or lung 495.2
Büdinger-Ludloff-Läwen disease 717.89
Buds ●
breast 259.1 ●
in newborn 779.89 ●
Buerger's disease (thromboangiitis obliterans) 443.1
Bulbar — *see* condition
Bulbus cordis 745.9
persistent (in left ventricle) 745.8
Bulging fontanels (congenital) 756.0
Bulimia 783.6
nervosa 307.51
nonorganic origin 307.51
Bulky uterus 621.2
Bulla(e) 709.8
lung (emphysematous) (solitary) 492.0

Bullet wound — *see also* Wound, open, by site
fracture — *see* Fracture, by site, open
internal organ (abdomen, chest, or pelvis) — *see* Injury, internal, by site, with open wound
intracranial — *see* Laceration, brain, with open wound
Bullis fever 082.8
Bullying — *see also* Disturbance, conduct 312.0 ☑
Bundle
branch block (complete) (false) (incomplete) 426.50
bilateral 426.53
left (*see also* Block, bundle branch, left) 426.3
hemiblock 426.2
right (*see also* Block, bundle branch, right) 426.4
of His — *see* condition
of Kent syndrome (anomalous atrioventricular excitation) 426.7
Bungpagga 040.81
Bunion 727.1
Bunionette 727.1
Bunyamwera fever 066.3
Buphthalmia, buphthalmos (congenital) 743.20
associated with
keratoglobus, congenital 743.22
megalocornea 743.22
ocular anomalies NEC 743.22
isolated 743.21
simple 743.21
Bürger-Grütz disease or syndrome (essential familial hyperlipemia) 272.3
Buried roots 525.3
Burke's syndrome 577.8
Burkitt's
tumor (M9750/3) 200.2 ☑
type malignant, lymphoma, lymphoblastic, or undifferentiated (M9750/3) 200.2 ☑
Burn (acid) (cathode ray) (caustic) (chemical) (electric heating appliance) (electricity) (fire) (flame) (hot liquid or object) (irradiation) (lime) (radiation) (steam) (thermal) (x-ray) 949.0

Note — Use the following fifth-digit subclassification with category 948 to indicate the percent of body surface with third degree burn:

0	*Less than 10% or unspecified*
1	*10–19%*
2	*20–29%*
3	*30–39%*
4	*40–49%*
5	*50–59%*
6	*60–69%*
7	*70–79%*
8	*80–89%*
9	*90% or more of body surface*

with
blisters — *see* Burn, by site, second degree
erythema — *see* Burn, by site, first degree
skin loss (epidermal) (*see also* Burn, by site, second degree)
full thickness (*see also* Burn, by site, third degree)
with necrosis of underlying tissues — *see* Burn, by site, third degree, deep
first degree — *see* Burn, by site, first degree
second degree — *see* Burn, by site, second degree

Burn — *continued*
third degree — *see* Burn, by site, third degree
deep — *see* Burn, by site, third degree, deep
abdomen, abdominal (muscle) (wall) 942.03
with
trunk — *see* Burn, trunk, multiple sites
first degree 942.13
second degree 942.23
third degree 942.33
deep 942.43
with loss of body part 942.53
ankle 945.03
with
lower limb(s) — *see* Burn, leg, multiple sites
first degree 945.13
second degree 945.23
third degree 945.33
deep 945.43
with loss of body part 945.53
anus — *see* Burn, trunk, specified site NEC
arm(s) 943.00
first degree 943.10
second degree 943.20
third degree 943.30
deep 943.40
with loss of body part 943.50
lower — *see* Burn, forearm(s)
multiple sites, except hand(s) or wrist(s) 943.09
first degree 943.19
second degree 943.29
third degree 943.39
deep 943.49
with loss of body part 943.59
upper 943.03
first degree 943.13
second degree 943.23
third degree 943.33
deep 943.43
with loss of body part 943.53
auditory canal (external) — *see* Burn, ear
auricle (ear) — *see* Burn, ear
axilla 943.04
with
upper limb(s), except hand(s) or wrist(s) — *see* Burn, arm(s), multiple sites
first degree 943.14
second degree 943.24
third degree 943.34
deep 943.44
with loss of body part 943.54
back 942.04
with
trunk — *see* Burn, trunk, multiple sites
first degree 942.14
second degree 942.24
third degree 942.34
deep 942.44
with loss of body part 942.54
biceps
brachii — *see* Burn, arm(s), upper
femoris — *see* Burn, thigh
breast(s) 942.01
with
trunk — *see* Burn, trunk, multiple sites
first degree 942.11
second degree 942.21
third degree 942.31
deep 942.41
with loss of body part 942.51
brow — *see* Burn, forehead
buttock(s) — *see* Burn, back
canthus (eye) 940.1
chemical 940.0

Burn — *continued*
  cervix (uteri) 947.4
  cheek (cutaneous) 941.07
    with
      face or head — *see* Burn, head, multiple sites
    first degree 941.17
    second degree 941.27
    third degree 941.37
      deep 941.47
        with loss of body part 941.57
  chest wall (anterior) 942.02
    with
      trunk — *see* Burn, trunk, multiple sites
    first degree 942.12
    second degree 942.22
    third degree 942.32
      deep 942.42
        with loss of body part 942.52
  chin 941.04
    with
      face or head — *see* Burn, head, multiple sites
    first degree 941.14
    second degree 941.24
    third degree 941.34
      deep 941.44
        with loss of body part 941.54
  clitoris — *see* Burn, genitourinary organs, external
  colon 947.3
  conjunctiva (and cornea) 940.4
    chemical
      acid 940.3
      alkaline 940.2
  cornea (and conjunctiva) 940.4
    chemical
      acid 940.3
      alkaline 940.2
  costal region — *see* Burn, chest wall
  due to ingested chemical agent — *see* Burn, internal organs
  ear (auricle) (canal) (drum) (external) 941.01
    with
      face or head — *see* Burn, head, multiple sites
    first degree 941.11
    second degree 941.21
    third degree 941.31
      deep 941.41
        with loss of a body part 941.51
  elbow 943.02
    with
      hand(s) and wrist(s) — *see* Burn, multiple specified sites
      upper limb(s), except hand(s) or wrist(s) (*see also* Burn, arm(s), multiple sites)
    first degree 943.12
    second degree 943.22
    third degree 943.32
      deep 943.42
        with loss of body part 943.52
  electricity, electric current — *see* Burn, by site
  entire body — *see* Burn, multiple, specified sites
  epididymis — *see* Burn, genitourinary organs, external
  epigastric region — *see* Burn, abdomen
  epiglottis 947.1
  esophagus 947.2
  extent (percent of body surface)
    less than 10 percent 948.0 ☑
    10-19 percent 948.1 ☑
    20-29 percent 948.2 ☑
    30-39 percent 948.3 ☑
    40-49 percent 948.4 ☑
    50-59 percent 948.5 ☑
    60-69 percent 948.6 ☑
    70-79 percent 948.7 ☑

Burn — *continued*
  extent — *continued*
    80-89 percent 948.8 ☑
    90 percent or more 948.9 ☑
  extremity
    lower — *see* Burn, leg
    upper — *see* Burn, arm(s)
  eye(s) (and adnexa) (only) 940.9
    with
      face, head, or neck 941.02
        first degree 941.12
        second degree 941.22
        third degree 941.32
          deep 941.42
            with loss of body part 941.52
      other sites (classifiable to more than one category in 940–945) — *see* Burn, multiple, specified sites
      resulting rupture and destruction of eyeball 940.5
    specified part — *see* Burn, by site
  eyeball (*see also* Burn, eye)
    with resulting rupture and destruction of eyeball 940.5
  eyelid(s) 940.1
    chemical 940.0
  face — *see* Burn, head
  finger (nail) (subungual) 944.01
    with
      hand(s) — *see* Burn, hand(s), multiple sites
      other sites — *see* Burn, multiple, specified sites
      thumb 944.04
        first degree 944.14
        second degree 944.24
        third degree 944.34
          deep 944.44
            with loss of body part 944.54
    first degree 944.11
    second degree 944.21
    third degree 944.31
      deep 944.41
        with loss of body part 944.51
    multiple (digits) 944.03
      with thumb — *see* Burn, finger, with thumb
      first degree 944.13
      second degree 944.23
      third degree 944.33
        deep 944.43
          with loss of body part 944.53
  flank — *see* Burn, abdomen
  foot 945.02
    with
      lower limb(s) — *see* Burn, leg, multiple sites
    first degree 945.12
    second degree 945.22
    third degree 945.32
      deep 945.42
        with loss of body part 945.52
  forearm(s) 943.01
    with
      upper limb(s), except hand(s) or wrist(s) — *see* Burn, arm(s), multiple sites
    first degree 943.11
    second degree 943.21
    third degree 943.31
      deep 943.41
        with loss of body part 943.51
  forehead 941.07
    with
      face or head — *see* Burn, head, multiple sites
    first degree 941.17
    second degree 941.27
    third degree 941.37
      deep 941.47
        with loss of body part 941.57

Burn — *continued*
  fourth degree — *see* Burn, by site, third degree, deep
  friction — *see* Injury, superficial, by site
  from swallowing caustic or corrosive substance NEC — *see* Burn, internal organs
  full thickness — *see* Burn, by site, third degree
  gastrointestinal tract 947.3
  genitourinary organs
    external 942.05
      with
        trunk — *see* Burn, trunk, multiple sites
      first degree 942.15
      second degree 942.25
      third degree 942.35
        deep 942.45
          with loss of body part 942.55
    internal 947.8
  globe (eye) — *see* Burn, eyeball
  groin — *see* Burn, abdomen
  gum 947.0
  hand(s) (phalanges) (and wrist) 944.00
    first degree 944.10
    second degree 944.20
    third degree 944.30
      deep 944.40
        with loss of body part 944.50
    back (dorsal surface) 944.06
      first degree 944.16
      second degree 944.26
      third degree 944.36
        deep 944.46
          with loss of body part 944.56
    multiple sites 944.08
      first degree 944.18
      second degree 944.28
      third degree 944.38
        deep 944.48
          with loss of body part 944.58
  head (and face) 941.00
    first degree 941.10
    second degree 941.20
    third degree 941.30
      deep 941.40
        with loss of body part 941.50
    eye(s) only 940.9
      specified part — *see* Burn, by site
    multiple sites 941.09
      with eyes — *see* Burn, eyes, with face, head, or neck
      first degree 941.19
      second degree 941.29
      third degree 941.39
        deep 941.49
          with loss of body part 941.59
  heel — *see* Burn, foot
  hip — *see* Burn, trunk, specified site NEC
  iliac region — *see* Burn, trunk, specified site NEC
  infected 958.3
  inhalation (*see also* Burn, internal organs) 947.9
  internal organs 947.9
    from caustic or corrosive substance (swallowing) NEC 947.9
    specified NEC (*see also* Burn, by site) 947.8
  interscapular region — *see* Burn, back
  intestine (large) (small) 947.3
  iris — *see* Burn, eyeball
  knee 945.05
    with
      lower limb(s) — *see* Burn, leg, multiple sites
    first degree 945.15
    second degree 945.25

Burn — *continued*
  knee — *continued*
    third degree 945.35
      deep 945.45
        with loss of body part 945.55
  labium (majus) (minus) — *see* Burn, genitourinary organs, external
  lacrimal apparatus, duct, gland, or sac 940.1
    chemical 940.0
  larynx 947.1
  late effect — *see* Late, effects (of), burn
  leg 945.00
    first degree 945.10
    second degree 945.20
    third degree 945.30
      deep 945.40
        with loss of body part 945.50
    lower 945.04
      with other part(s) of lower limb(s) — *see* Burn, leg, multiple sites
      first degree 945.14
      second degree 945.24
      third degree 945.34
        deep 945.44
          with loss of body part 945.54
    multiple sites 945.09
      first degree 945.19
      second degree 945.29
      third degree 945.39
        deep 945.49
          with loss of body part 945.59
    upper — *see* Burn, thigh
  lightning — *see* Burn, by site
  limb(s)
    lower (including foot or toe(s)) — *see* Burn, leg
    upper (except wrist and hand) — *see* Burn, arm(s)
  lip(s) 941.03
    with
      face or head — *see* Burn, head, multiple sites
    first degree 941.13
    second degree 941.23
    third degree 941.33
      deep 941.43
        with loss of body part 941.53
  lumbar region — *see* Burn, back
  lung 947.1
  malar region — *see* Burn, cheek
  mastoid region — *see* Burn, scalp
  membrane, tympanic — *see* Burn, ear
  midthoracic region — *see* Burn, chest wall
  mouth 947.0
  multiple (*see also* Burn, unspecified) 949.0
    specified sites classifiable to more than one category in 940-945 ☑, 946.0
      first degree 946.1
      second degree 946.2
      third degree 946.3
        deep 946.4
          with loss of body part 946.5
  muscle, abdominal — *see* Burn, abdomen
  nasal (septum) — *see* Burn, nose
  neck 941.08
    with
      face or head — *see* Burn, head, multiple sites
    first degree 941.18
    second degree 941.28
    third degree 941.38
      deep 941.48
        with loss of body part 941.58
  nose (septum) 941.05
    with
      face or head — *see* Burn, head, multiple sites

Burn — *continued*
- nose — *continued*
  - first degree 941.15
  - second degree 941.25
  - third degree 941.35
    - deep 941.45
      - with loss of body part 941.55
- occipital region — *see* Burn, scalp
- orbit region 940.1
  - chemical 940.0
- oronasopharynx 947.0
- palate 947.0
- palm(s) 944.05
  - with
    - hand(s) and wrist(s) — *see* Burn, hand(s), multiple sites
  - first degree 944.15
  - second degree 944.25
  - third degree 944.35
    - deep 944.45
      - with loss of a body part 944.55
- parietal region — *see* Burn, scalp
- penis — *see* Burn, genitourinary organs, external
- perineum — *see* Burn, genitourinary organs, external
- periocular area 940.1
  - chemical 940.0
- pharynx 947.0
- pleura 947.1
- popliteal space — *see* Burn, knee
- prepuce — *see* Burn, genitourinary organs, external
- pubic region — *see* Burn, genitourinary organs, external
- pudenda — *see* Burn, genitourinary organs, external
- rectum 947.3
- sac, lacrimal 940.1
  - chemical 940.0
- sacral region — *see* Burn, back
- salivary (ducts) (glands) 947.0
- scalp 941.06
  - with
    - face or neck — *see* Burn, head, multiple sites
  - first degree 941.16
  - second degree 941.26
  - third degree 941.36
    - deep 941.46
      - with loss of body part 941.56
- scapular region 943.06
  - with
    - upper limb(s), except hand(s) or wrist(s) — *see* Burn, arm(s), multiple sites
  - first degree 943.16
  - second degree 943.26
  - third degree 943.36
    - deep 943.46
      - with loss of body part 943.56
- sclera — *see* Burn, eyeball
- scrotum — *see* Burn, genitourinary organs, external
- septum, nasal — *see* Burn, nose
- shoulder(s) 943.05
  - with
    - hand(s) and wrist(s) — *see* Burn, multiple, specified sites
    - upper limb(s), except hand(s) or wrist(s) — *see* Burn, arm(s), multiple sites
  - first degree 943.15
  - second degree 943.25
  - third degree 943.35
    - deep 943.45
      - with loss of body part 943.55
- skin NEC (*see also* Burn, unspecified) 949.0
- skull — *see* Burn, head
- small intestine 947.3
- sternal region — *see* Burn, chest wall
- stomach 947.3

Burn — *continued*
- subconjunctival — *see* Burn, conjunctiva
- subcutaneous — *see* Burn, by site, third degree
- submaxillary region — *see* Burn, head
- submental region — *see* Burn, chin
- sun — *see* Sunburn
- supraclavicular fossa — *see* Burn, neck
- supraorbital — *see* Burn, forehead
- temple — *see* Burn, scalp
- temporal region — *see* Burn, scalp
- testicle — *see* Burn, genitourinary organs, external
- testis — *see* Burn, genitourinary organs, external
- thigh 945.06
  - with
    - lower limb(s) — *see* Burn, leg, multiple sites
  - first degree 945.16
  - second degree 945.26
  - third degree 945.36
    - deep 945.46
      - with loss of body part 945.56
- thorax (external) — *see* Burn, chest wall
- throat 947.0
- thumb(s) (nail) (subungual) 944.02
  - with
    - finger(s) — *see* Burn, finger, with other sites, thumb
    - hand(s) and wrist(s) — *see* Burn, hand(s), multiple sites
  - first degree 944.12
  - second degree 944.22
  - third degree 944.32
    - deep 944.42
      - with loss of body part 944.52
- toe (nail) (subungual) 945.01
  - with
    - lower limb(s) — *see* Burn, leg, multiple sites
  - first degree 945.11
  - second degree 945.21
  - third degree 945.31
    - deep 945.41
      - with loss of body part 945.51
- tongue 947.0
- tonsil 947.0
- trachea 947.1
- trunk 942.00
  - first degree 942.10
  - second degree 942.20
  - third degree 942.30
    - deep 942.40
      - with loss of body part 942.50
  - multiple sites 942.09
    - first degree 942.19
    - second degree 942.29
    - third degree 942.39
      - deep 942.49
        - with loss of body part 942.59
  - specified site NEC 942.09
    - first degree 942.19
    - second degree 942.29
    - third degree 942.39
      - deep 942.49
        - with loss of body part 942.59
- tunica vaginalis — *see* Burn, genitourinary organs, external
- tympanic membrane — *see* Burn, ear
- tympanum — *see* Burn, ear
- ultraviolet 692.82
- unspecified site (multiple) 949.0
  - with extent of body surface involved specified
    - less than 10 percent 948.0 ☑
    - 10-19 percent 948.1 ☑
    - 20-29 percent 948.2 ☑
    - 30-39 percent 948.3 ☑
    - 40-49 percent 948.4 ☑

Burn — *continued*
- unspecified site — *continued*
  - with extent of body surface involved specified — *continued*
    - 50-59 percent 948.5 ☑
    - 60-69 percent 948.6 ☑
    - 70-79 percent 948.7 ☑
    - 80-89 percent 948.8 ☑
    - 90 percent or more 948.9 ☑
  - first degree 949.1
  - second degree 949.2
  - third degree 949.3
    - deep 949.4
      - with loss of body part 949.5
- uterus 947.4
- uvula 947.0
- vagina 947.4
- vulva — *see* Burn, genitourinary organs, external
- wrist(s) 944.07
  - with
    - hand(s) — *see* Burn, hand(s), multiple sites
  - first degree 944.17
  - second degree 944.27
  - third degree 944.37
    - deep 944.47
      - with loss of body part 944.57

Burnett's syndrome (milk-alkali) 275.42

Burnier's syndrome (hypophyseal dwarfism) 253.3

Burning
- feet syndrome 266.2
- sensation (*see also* Disturbance, sensation) 782.0
- tongue 529.6

Burns' disease (osteochondrosis, lower ulna) 732.3

Bursa — *see also* condition
- pharynx 478.29

Bursitis NEC 727.3
- Achilles tendon 726.71
- adhesive 726.90
  - shoulder 726.0
- ankle 726.79
- buttock 726.5
- calcaneal 726.79
- collateral ligament
  - fibular 726.63
  - tibial 726.62
- Duplay's 726.2
- elbow 726.33
- finger 726.8
- foot 726.79
- gonococcal 098.52
- hand 726.4
- hip 726.5
- infrapatellar 726.69
- ischiogluteal 726.5
- knee 726.60
- occupational NEC 727.2
- olecranon 726.33
- pes anserinus 726.61
- pharyngeal 478.29
- popliteal 727.51
- prepatellar 726.65
- radiohumeral 727.3
- scapulohumeral 726.19
  - adhesive 726.0
- shoulder 726.10
  - adhesive 726.0
- subacromial 726.19
  - adhesive 726.0
- subcoracoid 726.19
- subdeltoid 726.19
  - adhesive 726.0
- subpatellar 726.69
- syphilitic 095.7
- Thornwaldt's, Tornwaldt's (pharyngeal) 478.29
- toe 726.79
- trochanteric area 726.5
- wrist 726.4

Burst stitches or sutures (complication of surgery) (external) ▶(*see also* Dehiscence)◀ 998.32

Burst stitches or sutures ▶(*see also* Dehiscence)◀ — *continued*
- internal 998.31

Buruli ulcer 031.1

Bury's disease (erythema elevatum diutinum) 695.89

Buschke's disease or scleredema (adultorum) 710.1

Busquet's disease (osteoperiostitis) — *see also* Osteomyelitis 730.1 ☑

Busse-Buschke disease (cryptococcosis) 117.5

Buttock — *see* condition

Button
- Biskra 085.1
- Delhi 085.1
- oriental 085.1

Buttonhole hand (intrinsic) 736.21

Bwamba fever (encephalitis) 066.3

Byssinosis (occupational) 504

Bywaters' syndrome 958.5

C

Cacergasia 300.9

Cachexia 799.4
- cancerous (*see also* Neoplasm, by site, malignant) 799.4
- cardiac — *see* Disease, heart
- dehydration 276.51
  - with
    - hypernatremia 276.0
    - hyponatremia 276.1
- due to malnutrition 799.4
- exophthalmic 242.0 ☑
- heart — *see* Disease, heart
- hypophyseal 253.2
- hypopituitary 253.2
- lead 984.9
  - specified type of lead — *see* Table of Drugs and Chemicals
- malaria 084.9
- malignant (*see also* Neoplasm, by site, malignant) 799.4
- marsh 084.9
- nervous 300.5
- old age 797
- pachydermic — *see* Hypothyroidism
- paludal 084.9
- pituitary (postpartum) 253.2
- renal (*see also* Disease, renal) 593.9
- saturnine 984.9
  - specified type of lead — *see* Table of Drugs and Chemicals
- senile 797
- Simmonds' (pituitary cachexia) 253.2
- splenica 289.59
- strumipriva (*see also* Hypothyroidism) 244.9
- tuberculous NEC (*see also* Tuberculosis) 011.9 ☑

Café au lait spots 709.09

Caffey's disease or syndrome (infantile cortical hyperostosis) 756.59

Caisson disease 993.3

Caked breast (puerperal, postpartum) 676.2 ☑

Cake kidney 753.3

Calabar swelling 125.2

Calcaneal spur 726.73

Calcaneoapophysitis 732.5

Calcaneonavicular bar 755.67

Calcareous — *see* condition

Calcicosis (occupational) 502

Calciferol (vitamin D) **deficiency** 268.9
- with
  - osteomalacia 268.2
  - rickets (*see also* Rickets) 268.0

Calcification
- adrenal (capsule) (gland) 255.41
  - tuberculous (*see also* Tuberculosis) 017.6 ☑
- aorta 440.0
- artery (annular) — *see* Arteriosclerosis
- auricle (ear) 380.89
- bladder 596.8
  - due to S. hematobium 120.0

Calcification — *continued*
brain (cortex) — *see* Calcification, cerebral
bronchus 519.19
bursa 727.82
cardiac (*see also* Degeneration, myocardial) 429.1
cartilage (postinfectional) 733.99
cerebral (cortex) 348.8
artery 437.0
cervix (uteri) 622.8
choroid plexus 349.2
conjunctiva 372.54
corpora cavernosa (penis) 607.89
cortex (brain) — *see* Calcification, cerebral
dental pulp (nodular) 522.2
dentinal papilla 520.4
disc, intervertebral 722.90
cervical, cervicothoracic 722.91
lumbar, lumbosacral 722.93
thoracic, thoracolumbar 722.92
fallopian tube 620.8
falx cerebri — *see* Calcification, cerebral
fascia 728.89
gallbladder 575.8
general 275.40
heart (*see also* Degeneration, myocardial) 429.1
valve — *see* Endocarditis
intervertebral cartilage or disc (postinfectional) 722.90
cervical, cervicothoracic 722.91
lumbar, lumbosacral 722.93
thoracic, thoracolumbar 722.92
intracranial — *see* Calcification, cerebral
intraspinal ligament 728.89
joint 719.80
ankle 719.87
elbow 719.82
foot 719.87
hand 719.84
hip 719.85
knee 719.86
multiple sites 719.89
pelvic region 719.85
shoulder (region) 719.81
specified site NEC 719.88
wrist 719.83
kidney 593.89
tuberculous (*see also* Tuberculosis) 016.0 ☑
larynx (senile) 478.79
lens 366.8
ligament 728.89
intraspinal 728.89
knee (medial collateral) 717.89
lung 518.89
active 518.89
postinfectional 518.89
tuberculous (*see also* Tuberculosis, pulmonary) 011.9 ☑
lymph gland or node (postinfectional) 289.3
tuberculous (*see also* Tuberculosis, lymph gland) 017.2 ☑
mammographic 793.89
massive (paraplegic) 728.10
medial NEC (*see also* Arteriosclerosis, extremities) 440.20
meninges (cerebral) 349.2
metastatic 275.40
Mönckeberg's — *see* Arteriosclerosis
muscle 728.10
heterotopic, postoperative 728.13
myocardium, myocardial (*see also* Degeneration, myocardial) 429.1
ovary 620.8
pancreas 577.8
penis 607.89
periarticular 728.89
pericardium (*see also* Pericarditis) 423.8
pineal gland 259.8

Calcification — *continued*
pleura 511.0
postinfectional 518.89
tuberculous (*see also* Tuberculosis, pleura) 012.0 ☑
pulp (dental) (nodular) 522.2
renal 593.89
Rider's bone 733.99
sclera 379.16
semilunar cartilage 717.89
spleen 289.59
subcutaneous 709.3
suprarenal (capsule) (gland) 255.41
tendon (sheath) 727.82
with bursitis, synovitis or tenosynovitis 727.82
trachea 519.19
ureter 593.89
uterus 621.8
vitreous 379.29
Calcified — *see also* Calcification
hematoma NEC 959.9
Calcinosis (generalized) (interstitial) (tumoral) (universalis) 275.49
circumscripta 709.3
cutis 709.3
intervertebralis 275.49 *[722.90]*
Raynaud's phenomenonsclerodactylytelangiectasis (CRST) 710.1
Calciphylaxis — *see also* Calcification, by site 275.49
Calcium
blood
high (*see also* Hypercalcemia) 275.42
low (*see also* Hypocalcemia) 275.41
deposits (*see also* Calcification, by site)
in bursa 727.82
in tendon (sheath) 727.82
with bursitis, synovitis or tenosynovitis 727.82
salts or soaps in vitreous 379.22
Calciuria 791.9
Calculi — *see* Calculus
Calculosis, intrahepatic — *see* Choledocholithiasis
Calculus, calculi, calculous 592.9
ampulla of Vater — *see* Choledocholithiasis
anuria (impacted) (recurrent) 592.0
appendix 543.9
bile duct (any) — *see* Choledocholithiasis
biliary — *see* Cholelithiasis
bilirubin, multiple — *see* Cholelithiasis
bladder (encysted) (impacted) (urinary) 594.1
diverticulum 594.0
bronchus 518.89
calyx (kidney) (renal) 592.0
congenital 753.3
cholesterol (pure) (solitary) — *see* Cholelithiasis
common duct (bile) — *see* Choledocholithiasis
conjunctiva 372.54
cystic 594.1
duct — *see* Cholelithiasis
dental 523.6
subgingival 523.6
supragingival 523.6
epididymis 608.89
gallbladder (*see also* Cholelithiasis)
congenital 751.69
hepatic (duct) — *see* Choledocholithiasis
intestine (impaction) (obstruction) 560.39
kidney (impacted) (multiple) (pelvis) (recurrent) (staghorn) 592.0
congenital 753.3
lacrimal (passages) 375.57
liver (impacted) — *see* Choledocholithiasis

Calculus, calculi, calculous — *continued*
lung 518.89
mammographic 793.89
nephritic (impacted) (recurrent) 592.0
nose 478.19
pancreas (duct) 577.8
parotid gland 527.5
pelvis, encysted 592.0
prostate 602.0
pulmonary 518.89
renal (impacted) (recurrent) 592.0
congenital 753.3
salivary (duct) (gland) 527.5
seminal vesicle 608.89
staghorn 592.0
Stensen's duct 527.5
sublingual duct or gland 527.5
congenital 750.26
submaxillary duct, gland, or region 527.5
suburethral 594.8
tonsil 474.8
tooth, teeth 523.6
tunica vaginalis 608.89
ureter (impacted) (recurrent) 592.1
urethra (impacted) 594.2
urinary (duct) (impacted) (passage) (tract) 592.9
lower tract NEC 594.9
specified site 594.8
vagina 623.8
vesical (impacted) 594.1
Wharton's duct 527.5
Caliectasis 593.89
California
disease 114.0
encephalitis 062.5
Caligo cornea 371.03
Callositas, callosity (infected) 700
Callus (infected) 700
bone 726.91
excessive, following fracture (*see also* Late, effect (of), fracture)
Calvé (-Perthes) disease (osteochondrosis, femoral capital) 732.1
Calvities — *see also* Alopecia 704.00
Cameroon fever — *see also* Malaria 084.6
Camptocormia 300.11
Camptodactyly (congenital) 755.59
Camurati-Engelmann disease (diaphyseal sclerosis) 756.59
Canal — *see* condition
Canaliculitis (lacrimal) (acute) 375.31
Actinomyces 039.8
chronic 375.41
Canavan's disease 330.0
Cancer (M8000/3) — *see also* Neoplasm, by site, malignant

Note — The term "cancer" when modified by an adjective or adjectival phrase indicating a morphological type should be coded in the same manner as "carcinoma" with that adjective or phrase. Thus, "squamous-cell cancer" should be coded in the same manner as "squamous-cell carcinoma," which appears in the list under "Carcinoma."

bile duct type (M8160/3), liver 155.1
hepatocellular (M8170/3) 155.0
Cancerous (M8000/3) — *see* Neoplasm, by site, malignant
Cancerphobia 300.29
Cancrum oris 528.1
Candidiasis, candidal 112.9
with pneumonia 112.4
balanitis 112.2
congenital 771.7
disseminated 112.5
endocarditis 112.81
esophagus 112.84
intertrigo 112.3
intestine 112.85
lung 112.4
meningitis 112.83

Candidiasis, candidal — *continued*
mouth 112.0
nails 112.3
neonatal 771.7
onychia 112.3
otitis externa 112.82
otomycosis 112.82
paronychia 112.3
perionyxis 112.3
pneumonia 112.4
pneumonitis 112.4
skin 112.3
specified site NEC 112.89
systemic 112.5
urogenital site NEC 112.2
vagina 112.1
vulva 112.1
vulvovaginitis 112.1
Candidiosis — *see* Candidiasis
Candiru infection or infestation 136.8
Canities (premature) 704.3
congenital 757.4
Canker (mouth) (sore) 528.2
rash 034.1
Cannabinosis 504
Canton fever 081.9
Cap
cradle 690.11
Capillariasis 127.5
Capillary — *see* condition
Caplan-Colinet syndrome 714.81
Caplan's syndrome 714.81
Capsule — *see* condition
Capsulitis (joint) 726.90
adhesive (shoulder) 726.0
hip 726.5
knee 726.60
labyrinthine 387.8
thyroid 245.9
wrist 726.4
Caput
crepitus 756.0
medusae 456.8
succedaneum 767.19
Carapata disease 087.1
Carate — *see* Pinta
Carbohydrate-deficient glycoprotein syndrome (CGDS) 271.8
Carboxyhemoglobinemia 986
Carbuncle 680.9
abdominal wall 680.2
ankle 680.6
anus 680.5
arm (any part, above wrist) 680.3
auditory canal, external 680.0
axilla 680.3
back (any part) 680.2
breast 680.2
buttock 680.5
chest wall 680.2
corpus cavernosum 607.2
ear (any part) (external) 680.0
eyelid 373.13
face (any part, except eye) 680.0
finger (any) 680.4
flank 680.2
foot (any part) 680.7
forearm 680.3
genital organ (male) 608.4
gluteal (region) 680.5
groin 680.2
hand (any part) 680.4
head (any part, except face) 680.8
heel 680.7
hip 680.6
kidney (*see also* Abscess, kidney) 590.2
knee 680.6
labia 616.4
lacrimal
gland (*see also* Dacryoadenitis) 375.00
passages (duct) (sac) (*see also* Dacryocystitis) 375.30
leg, any part except foot 680.6

- **Carbuncle** — *continued*
  - lower extremity, any part except foot 680.6
  - malignant 022.0
  - multiple sites 680.9
  - neck 680.1
  - nose (external) (septum) 680.0
  - orbit, orbital 376.01
  - partes posteriores 680.5
  - pectoral region 680.2
  - penis 607.2
  - perineum 680.2
  - pinna 680.0
  - scalp (any part) 680.8
  - scrotum 608.4
  - seminal vesicle 608.0
  - shoulder 680.3
  - skin NEC 680.9
  - specified site NEC 680.8
  - spermatic cord 608.4
  - temple (region) 680.0
  - testis 608.4
  - thigh 680.6
  - thumb 680.4
  - toe (any) 680.7
  - trunk 680.2
  - tunica vaginalis 608.4
  - umbilicus 680.2
  - upper arm 680.3
  - urethra 597.0
  - vas deferens 608.4
  - vulva 616.4
  - wrist 680.4
- **Carbunculus** — *see also* Carbuncle 680.9
- **Carcinoid** (tumor) (M8240/1) — *see* ▶Tumor, carcinoid◀
  - and struma ovarii (M9091/1) 236.2
  - argentaffin (M8241/1) — *see* Neoplasm, by site, uncertain behavior
    - malignant (M8241/3) — *see* Neoplasm, by site, malignant
  - benign (M9091/0) 220
  - composite (M8244/3) — *see* Neoplasm, by site, malignant
  - goblet cell (M8243/3) — *see* Neoplasm, by site, malignant
  - malignant (M8240/3) — *see* Neoplasm, by site, malignant
  - nonargentaffin (M8242/1) (*see also* Neoplasm, by site, uncertain behavior)
    - malignant (M8242/3) — *see* Neoplasm, by site, malignant
  - strumal (M9091/1) 236.2
  - syndrome (intestinal) (metastatic) 259.2
  - type bronchial adenoma (M8240/3) — *see* Neoplasm, lung, malignant
- **Carcinoidosis** 259.2
- **Carcinomaphobia** 300.29
- **Carcinomatosis**
  - peritonei (M8010/6) 197.6
  - specified site NEC (M8010/3) — *see* Neoplasm, by site, malignant
  - unspecified site (M8010/6) 199.0
- **Carcinoma** (M8010/3) — *see also* Neoplasm, by site, malignant

> *Note — Except where otherwise indicated, the morphological varieties of carcinoma in the list below should be coded by site as for "Neoplasm, malignant."*

  - with
    - apocrine metaplasia (M8573/3)
    - cartilaginous (and osseous) metaplasia (M8571/3)
    - osseous (and cartilaginous) metaplasia (M8571/3)
    - productive fibrosis (M8141/3)
    - spindle cell metaplasia (M8572/3)
    - squamous metaplasia (M8570/3)
  - acidophil (M8280/3)
    - specified site — *see* Neoplasm, by site, malignant
    - unspecified site 194.3

- **Carcinoma** — *see also* Neoplasm, by site, malignant — *continued*
  - acidophil-basophil, mixed (M8281/3)
    - specified site — *see* Neoplasm, by site, malignant
    - unspecified site 194.3
  - acinar (cell) (M8550/3)
  - acinic cell (M8550/3)
  - adenocystic (M8200/3)
  - adenoid
    - cystic (M8200/3)
    - squamous cell (M8075/3)
  - adenosquamous (M8560/3)
  - adnexal (skin) (M8390/3) — *see* Neoplasm, skin, malignant
  - adrenal cortical (M8370/3) 194.0
  - alveolar (M8251/3)
    - cell (M8250/3) — *see* Neoplasm, lung, malignant
  - anaplastic type (M8021/3)
  - apocrine (M8401/3)
    - breast — *see* Neoplasm, breast, malignant
    - specified site NEC — *see* Neoplasm, skin, malignant
    - unspecified site 173.9
  - basal cell (pigmented) (M8090/3) (*see also* Neoplasm, skin, malignant)
    - fibro-epithelial type (M8093/3) — *see* Neoplasm, skin, malignant
    - morphea type (M8092/3) — *see* Neoplasm, skin, malignant
    - multicentric (M8091/3) — *see* Neoplasm, skin, malignant
  - basaloid (M8123/3)
  - basal-squamous cell, mixed (M8094/3) — *see* Neoplasm, skin, malignant
  - basophil (M8300/3)
    - specified site — *see* Neoplasm, by site, malignant
    - unspecified site 194.3
  - basophil-acidophil, mixed (M8281/3)
    - specified site — *see* Neoplasm, by site, malignant
    - unspecified site 194.3
  - basosquamous (M8094/3) — *see* Neoplasm, skin, malignant
  - bile duct type (M8160/3)
    - and hepatocellular, mixed (M8180/3) 155.0
    - liver 155.1
    - specified site NEC — *see* Neoplasm, by site, malignant
    - unspecified site 155.1
  - branchial or branchiogenic 146.8
  - bronchial or bronchogenic — *see* Neoplasm, lung, malignant
  - bronchiolar (terminal) (M8250/3) — *see* Neoplasm, lung, malignant
  - bronchiolo-alveolar (M8250/3) — *see* Neoplasm, lung, malignant
  - bronchogenic (epidermoid) 162.9
  - C cell (M8510/3)
    - specified site — *see* Neoplasm, by site, malignant
    - unspecified site 193
  - ceruminous (M8420/3) 173.2
  - chorionic (M9100/3)
    - specified site — *see* Neoplasm, by site, malignant
    - unspecified site
      - female 181
      - male 186.9
  - chromophobe (M8270/3)
    - specified site — *see* Neoplasm, by site, malignant
    - unspecified site 194.3
  - clear cell (mesonephroid type) (M8310/3)
  - cloacogenic (M8124/3)
    - specified site — *see* Neoplasm, by site, malignant
    - unspecified site 154.8

- **Carcinoma** — *see also* Neoplasm, by site, malignant — *continued*
  - colloid (M8480/3)
  - cribriform (M8201/3)
  - cylindroid type (M8200/3)
  - diffuse type (M8145/3)
    - specified site — *see* Neoplasm, by site, malignant
    - unspecified site 151.9
  - duct (cell) (M8500/3)
    - with Paget's disease (M8541/3) — *see* Neoplasm, breast, malignant
    - infiltrating (M8500/3)
      - specified site — *see* Neoplasm, by site, malignant
      - unspecified site 174.9
  - ductal (M8500/3)
  - ductular, infiltrating (M8521/3)
  - embryonal (M9070/3)
    - and teratoma, mixed (M9081/3)
    - combined with choriocarcinoma (M9101/3) — *see* Neoplasm, by site, malignant
    - infantile type (M9071/3)
    - liver 155.0
    - polyembryonal type (M9072/3)
  - endometrioid (M8380/3)
  - eosinophil (M8280/3)
    - specified site — *see* Neoplasm, by site, malignant
    - unspecified site 194.3
  - epidermoid (M8070/3) (*see also* Carcinoma, squamous cell)
    - and adenocarcinoma, mixed (M8560/3)
    - in situ, Bowen's type (M8081/2) — *see* Neoplasm, skin, in situ
    - intradermal — *see* Neoplasm, skin, in situ
  - fibroepithelial type basal cell (M8093/3) — *see* Neoplasm, skin, malignant
  - follicular (M8330/3)
    - and papillary (mixed) (M8340/3) 193
    - moderately differentiated type (M8332/3) 193
    - pure follicle type (M8331/3) 193
    - specified site — *see* Neoplasm, by site, malignant
    - trabecular type (M8332/3) 193
    - unspecified site 193
    - well differentiated type (M8331/3) 193
  - gelatinous (M8480/3)
  - giant cell (M8031/3)
    - and spindle cell (M8030/3)
  - granular cell (M8320/3)
  - granulosa cell (M8620/3) 183.0
  - hepatic cell (M8170/3) 155.0
  - hepatocellular (M8170/3) 155.0
    - and bile duct, mixed (M8180/3) 155.0
  - hepatocholangiolitic (M8180/3) 155.0
  - Hürthle cell (thyroid) 193
  - hypernephroid (M8311/3)
  - in
    - adenomatous
      - polyp (M8210/3)
      - polyposis coli (M8220/3) 153.9
    - pleomorphic adenoma (M8940/3)
    - polypoid adenoma (M8210/3)
    - situ (M8010/3) — *see* Carcinoma, in situ
    - tubular adenoma (M8210/3)
    - villous adenoma (M8261/3)
  - infiltrating duct (M8500/3)
    - with Paget's disease (M8541/3) — *see* Neoplasm, breast, malignant
    - specified site — *see* Neoplasm, by site, malignant
    - unspecified site 174.9

- **Carcinoma** — *see also* Neoplasm, by site, malignant — *continued*
  - inflammatory (M8530/3)
    - specified site — *see* Neoplasm, by site, malignant
    - unspecified site 174.9
  - in situ (M8010/2) (*see also* Neoplasm, by site, in situ)
    - epidermoid (M8070/2) (*see also* Neoplasm, by site, in situ)
      - with questionable stromal invasion (M8076/2)
        - specified site — *see* Neoplasm, by site, in situ
        - unspecified site 233.1
      - Bowen's type (M8081/2) — *see* Neoplasm, skin, in situ
    - intraductal (M8500/2)
      - specified site — *see* Neoplasm, by site, in situ
      - unspecified site 233.0
    - lobular (M8520/2)
      - specified site — *see* Neoplasm, by site, in situ
      - unspecified site 233.0
    - papillary (M8050/2) — *see* Neoplasm, by site, in situ
    - squamous cell (M8070/2) (*see also* Neoplasm, by site, in situ)
      - with questionable stromal invasion (M8076/2)
        - specified site — *see* Neoplasm, by site, in situ
        - unspecified site 233.1
    - transitional cell (M8120/2) — *see* Neoplasm, by site, in situ
  - intestinal type (M8144/3)
    - specified site — *see* Neoplasm, by site, malignant
    - unspecified site 151.9
  - intraductal (noninfiltrating) (M8500/2)
    - papillary (M8503/2)
      - specified site — *see* Neoplasm, by site, in situ
      - unspecified site 233.0
    - specified site — *see* Neoplasm, by site, in situ
    - unspecified site 233.0
  - intraepidermal (M8070/2) (*see also* Neoplasm, skin, in situ)
    - squamous cell, Bowen's type (M8081/2) — *see* Neoplasm, skin, in situ
  - intraepithelial (M8010/2) (*see also* Neoplasm, by site, in situ)
    - squamous cell (M8072/2) — *see* Neoplasm, by site, in situ
  - intraosseous (M9270/3) 170.1
    - upper jaw (bone) 170.0
  - islet cell (M8150/3)
    - and exocrine, mixed (M8154/3)
      - specified site — *see* Neoplasm, by site, malignant
      - unspecified site 157.9
    - pancreas 157.4
    - specified site NEC — *see* Neoplasm, by site, malignant
    - unspecified site 157.4
  - juvenile, breast (M8502/3) — *see* Neoplasm, breast, malignant
  - Kulchitsky's cell (carcinoid tumor of intestine) 259.2
  - large cell (M8012/3)
    - squamous cell, non-keratinizing type (M8072/3)
  - Leydig cell (testis) (M8650/3)
    - specified site — *see* Neoplasm, by site, malignant
    - unspecified site 186.9
      - female 183.0
      - male 186.9
  - liver cell (M8170/3) 155.0
  - lobular (infiltrating) (M8520/3)
    - non-infiltrating (M8520/3)
      - specified site — *see* Neoplasm, by site, in situ

Carcinoma — *see also* Neoplasm, by site, malignant — *continued*
lobular — *continued*
non-infiltrating — *continued*
unspecified site 233.0
specified site — *see* Neoplasm, by site, malignant
unspecified site 174.9
lymphoepithelial (M8082/3)
medullary (M8510/3)
with
amyloid stroma (M8511/3)
specified site — *see* Neoplasm, by site, malignant
unspecified site 193
lymphoid stroma (M8512/3)
specified site — *see* Neoplasm, by site, malignant
unspecified site 174.9
mesometanephric (M9110/3)
mesonephric (M9110/3)
metastatic (M8010/6) — *see* Metastasis, cancer
metatypical (M8095/3) — *see* Neoplasm, skin, malignant
morphea type basal cell (M8092/3) — *see* Neoplasm, skin, malignant
mucinous (M8480/3)
mucin-producing (M8481/3)
mucin-secreting (M8481/3)
mucoepidermoid (M8430/3)
mucoid (M8480/3)
cell (M8300/3)
specified site — *see* Neoplasm, by site, malignant
unspecified site 194.3
mucous (M8480/3)
neuroendocrine ●
high grade (M8240/3) 209.30 ●
malignant poorly differentiated (M8240/3) 209.30 ●
nonencapsulated sclerosing (M8350/3) 193
noninfiltrating
intracystic (M8504/2) — *see* Neoplasm, by site, in situ
intraductal (M8500/2)
papillary (M8503/2)
specified site — *see* Neoplasm, by site, in situ
unspecified site 233.0
specified site — *see* Neoplasm, by site, in situ
unspecified site 233.0
lobular (M8520/2)
specified site — *see* Neoplasm, by site, in situ
unspecified site 233.0
oat cell (M8042/3)
specified site — *see* Neoplasm, by site, malignant
unspecified site 162.9
odontogenic (M9270/3) 170.1
upper jaw (bone) 170.0
onocytic (M8290/3)
oxyphilic (M8290/3)
papillary (M8050/3)
and follicular (mixed) (M8340/3) 193
epidermoid (M8052/3)
intraductal (noninfiltrating) (M8503/2)
specified site — *see* Neoplasm, by site, in situ
unspecified site 233.0
serous (M8460/3)
specified site — *see* Neoplasm, by site, malignant
surface (M8461/3)
specified site — *see* Neoplasm, by site, malignant
unspecified site 183.0
unspecified site 183.0

Carcinoma — *see also* Neoplasm, by site, malignant — *continued*
papillary — *continued*
squamous cell (M8052/3)
transitional cell (M8130/3)
papillocystic (M8450/3)
specified site — *see* Neoplasm, by site, malignant
unspecified site 183.0
parafollicular cell (M8510/3)
specified site — *see* Neoplasm, by site, malignant
unspecified site 193
pleomorphic (M8022/3)
polygonal cell (M8034/3)
prickle cell (M8070/3)
pseudoglandular, squamous cell (M8075/3)
pseudomucinous (M8470/3)
specified site — *see* Neoplasm, by site, malignant
unspecified site 183.0
pseudosarcomatous (M8033/3)
regaud type (M8082/3) — *see* Neoplasm, nasopharynx, malignant
renal cell (M8312/3) 189.0
reserve cell (M8041/3)
round cell (M8041/3)
Schmincke (M8082/3) — *see* Neoplasm, nasopharynx, malignant
Schneiderian (M8121/3)
specified site — *see* Neoplasm, by site, malignant
unspecified site 160.0
scirrhous (M8141/3)
sebaceous (M8410/3) — *see* Neoplasm, skin, malignant
secondary (M8010/6) — *see* Neoplasm, by site, malignant, secondary
secretory, breast (M8502/3) — *see* Neoplasm, breast, malignant
serous (M8441/3)
papillary (M8460/3)
specified site — *see* Neoplasm, by site, malignant
unspecified site 183.0
surface, papillary (M8461/3)
specified site — *see* Neoplasm, by site, malignant
unspecified site 183.0
Sertoli cell (M8640/3)
specified site — *see* Neoplasm, by site, malignant
unspecified site 186.9
signet ring cell (M8490/3)
metastatic (M8490/6) — *see* Neoplasm, by site, secondary
simplex (M8231/3)
skin appendage (M8390/3) — *see* Neoplasm, skin, malignant
small cell (M8041/3)
fusiform cell type (M8043/3)
squamous cell, non-keratinizing type (M8073/3)
solid (M8230/3)
with amyloid stroma (M8511/3)
specified site — *see* Neoplasm, by site, malignant
unspecified site 193
spheroidal cell (M8035/3)
spindle cell (M8032/3)
and giant cell (M8030/3)
spinous cell (M8070/3)
squamous (cell) (M8070/3)
adenoid type (M8075/3)
and adenocarcinoma, mixed (M8560/3)
intraepidermal, Bowen's type — *see* Neoplasm, skin, in situ

Carcinoma — *see also* Neoplasm, by site, malignant — *continued*
squamous — *continued*
keratinizing type (large cell) (M8071/3)
large cell, non-keratinizing type (M8072/3)
microinvasive (M8076/3)
specified site — *see* Neoplasm, by site, malignant
unspecified site 180.9
non-keratinizing type (M8072/3)
papillary (M8052/3)
pseudoglandular (M8075/3)
small cell, non-keratinizing type (M8073/3)
spindle cell type (M8074/3)
verrucous (M8051/3)
superficial spreading (M8143/3)
sweat gland (M8400/3) — *see* Neoplasm, skin, malignant
theca cell (M8600/3) 183.0
thymic (M8580/3) 164.0
trabecular (M8190/3)
transitional (cell) (M8120/3)
papillary (M8130/3)
spindle cell type (M8122/3)
tubular (M8211/3)
undifferentiated type (M8020/3)
urothelial (M8120/3)
ventriculi 151.9
verrucous (epidermoid) (squamous cell) (M8051/3)
villous (M8262/3)
water-clear cell (M8322/3) 194.1
wolffian duct (M9110/3)
Carcinosarcoma (M8980/3) — *see also* Neoplasm, by site, malignant
embryonal type (M8981/3) — *see* Neoplasm, by site, malignant
Cardiac — *see also* condition
death — *see* Disease, heart
device
defibrillator, automatic implantable V45.02
in situ NEC V45.00
pacemaker
cardiac
fitting or adjustment V53.31
in situ V45.01
carotid sinus
fitting or adjustment V53.39
in situ V45.09
pacemaker — *see* Cardiac, device, pacemaker
tamponade 423.3
Cardia, cardial — *see* condition
Cardialgia — *see also* Pain, precordial 786.51
Cardiectasis — *see* Hypertrophy, cardiac
Cardiochalasia 530.81
Cardiomalacia — *see also* Degeneration, myocardial 429.1
Cardiomegalia glycogenica diffusa 271.0
Cardiomegaly — *see also* Hypertrophy, cardiac 429.3
congenital 746.89
glycogen 271.0
hypertensive (*see also* Hypertension, heart) 402.90
idiopathic 429.3
Cardiomyoliposis — *see also* Degeneration, myocardial 429.1
Cardiomyopathy (congestive) (constrictive) (familial) (infiltrative) (obstructive) (restrictive) (sporadic) 425.4
alcoholic 425.5
amyloid 277.39 *[425.7]*
beriberi 265.0 *[425.7]*
cobalt-beer 425.5
congenital 425.3
due to
amyloidosis 277.39 *[425.7]*
beriberi 265.0 *[425.7]*
cardiac glycogenosis 271.0 *[425.7]*

Cardiomyopathy — *continued*
due to — *continued*
Chagas' disease 086.0
Friedreich's ataxia 334.0 *[425.8]*
hypertension — *see* Hypertension, with, heart involvement
mucopolysaccharidosis 277.5 *[425.7]*
myotonia atrophica 359.21 *[425.8]*
progressive muscular dystrophy 359.1 *[425.8]*
sarcoidosis 135 *[425.8]*
glycogen storage 271.0 *[425.7]*
hypertensive — *see* Hypertension, with, heart involvement
hypertrophic
nonobstructive 425.4
obstructive 425.1
congenital 746.84
idiopathic (concentric) 425.4
in
Chagas' disease 086.0
sarcoidosis 135 *[425.8]*
ischemic 414.8
metabolic NEC 277.9 *[425.7]*
amyloid 277.39 *[425.7]*
thyrotoxic (*see also* Thyrotoxicosis) 242.9 ☑ *[425.7]*
thyrotoxicosis (*see also* Thyrotoxicosis) 242.9 ☑ *[425.7]*
newborn 425.4
congenital 425.3
nutritional 269.9 *[425.7]*
beriberi 265.0 *[425.7]*
obscure of Africa 425.2
peripartum 674.5 ☑
postpartum 674.5 ☑
primary 425.4
secondary 425.9
stress inuced 429.83
takotsubo 429.83
thyrotoxic (*see also* Thyrotoxicosis) 242.9 ☑ *[425.7]*
toxic NEC 425.9
tuberculous (*see also* Tuberculosis) 017.9 ☑ *[425.8]*
Cardionephritis — *see* Hypertension, cardiorenal
Cardionephropathy — *see* Hypertension, cardiorenal
Cardionephrosis — *see* Hypertension, cardiorenal
Cardioneurosis 306.2
Cardiopathia nigra 416.0
Cardiopathy — *see also* Disease, heart 429.9
hypertensive (*see also* Hypertension, heart) 402.90
idiopathic 425.4
mucopolysaccharidosis 277.5 *[425.7]*
Cardiopericarditis — *see also* Pericarditis 423.9
Cardiophobia 300.29
Cardioptosis 746.87
Cardiorenal — *see* condition
Cardiorrhexis — *see also* Infarct, myocardium 410.9 ☑
Cardiosclerosis — *see* Arteriosclerosis, coronary
Cardiosis — *see* Disease, heart
Cardiospasm (esophagus) (reflex) (stomach) 530.0
congenital 750.7
Cardiostenosis — *see* Disease, heart
Cardiosymphysis 423.1
Cardiothyrotoxicosis — *see* Hyperthyroidism
Cardiovascular — *see* condition
Carditis (acute) (bacterial) (chronic) (subacute) 429.89
Coxsackie 074.20
hypertensive (*see also* Hypertension, heart) 402.90
meningococcal 036.40
rheumatic — *see* Disease, heart, rheumatic

Carditis — *continued*
- rheumatoid 714.2

Care (of)
- child (routine) V20.1
- convalescent following V66.9
  - chemotherapy V66.2
  - medical NEC V66.5
  - psychotherapy V66.3
  - radiotherapy V66.1
  - surgery V66.0
  - surgical NEC V66.0
  - treatment (for) V66.5
    - combined V66.6
    - fracture V66.4
    - mental disorder NEC V66.3
    - specified type NEC V66.5
- end-of-life V66.7
- family member (handicapped) (sick)
  - creating problem for family V61.49
  - provided away from home for holiday relief V60.5
  - unavailable, due to
    - absence (person rendering care) (sufferer) V60.4
    - inability (any reason) of person rendering care V60.4
- holiday relief V60.5
- hospice V66.7
- lack of (at or after birth) (infant) (child) 995.52
  - adult 995.84
- lactation of mother V24.1
- palliative V66.7
- postpartum
  - immediately after delivery V24.0
  - routine follow-up V24.2
- prenatal V22.1
  - first pregnancy V22.0
  - high-risk pregnancy V23.9
    - specified problem NEC V23.89
- terminal V66.7
- unavailable, due to
  - absence of person rendering care V60.4
  - inability (any reason) of person rendering care V60.4
- well baby V20.1

Caries (bone) — *see also* Tuberculosis, bone 015.9 ☑ *[730.8]* ☑
- arrested 521.04
- cementum 521.03
- cerebrospinal (tuberculous) 015.0 ☑ *[730.88]*
- dental (acute) (chronic) (incipient) (infected) 521.00
  - with pulp exposure 521.03
  - extending to
    - dentine 521.02
    - pulp 521.03
  - other specified NEC 521.09
  - pit and fissure 521.06
  - primary
    - pit and fissure origin 521.06
    - root surface 521.08
    - smooth surface origin 521.07
  - root surface 521.08
  - smooth surface 521.07
- dentin (acute) (chronic) 521.02
- enamel (acute) (chronic) (incipient) 521.01
- external meatus 380.89
- hip (*see also* Tuberculosis) 015.1 ☑ *[730.85]*
- initial 521.01
- knee 015.2 ☑ *[730.86]*
- labyrinth 386.8
- limb NEC 015.7 ☑ *[730.88]*
- mastoid (chronic) (process) 383.1
- middle ear 385.89
- nose 015.7 ☑ *[730.88]*
- orbit 015.7 ☑ *[730.88]*
- ossicle 385.24
- petrous bone 383.20
- sacrum (tuberculous) 015.0 ☑ *[730.88]*

Caries — *see also* Tuberculosis, bone — *continued*
- spine, spinal (column) (tuberculous) 015.0 ☑ *[730.88]*
- syphilitic 095.5
  - congenital 090.0 *[730.8]* ☑
- teeth (internal) 521.00
  - initial 521.01
- vertebra (column) (tuberculous) 015.0 ☑ *[730.88]*

Carini's syndrome (ichthyosis congenita) 757.1

Carious teeth 521.00

Carneous mole 631

Carnosinemia 270.5

Carotid body or sinus syndrome 337.01 ▲

Carotidynia 337.01 ▲

Carotinemia (dietary) 278.3

Carotinosis (cutis) (skin) 278.3

Carpal tunnel syndrome 354.0

Carpenter's syndrome 759.89

Carpopedal spasm — *see also* Tetany 781.7

Carpoptosis 736.05

Carrier (suspected) **of**
- amebiasis V02.2
- bacterial disease (meningococcal, staphylococcal) NEC V02.59
- cholera V02.0
- cystic fibrosis gene V83.81
- defective gene V83.89
- diphtheria V02.4
- dysentery (bacillary) V02.3
  - amebic V02.2
- Endamoeba histolytica V02.2
- gastrointestinal pathogens NEC V02.3
- genetic defect V83.89
- gonorrhea V02.7
- group B streptococcus V02.51
- HAA (hepatitis Australian-antigen) V02.61
- hemophilia A (asymptomatic) V83.01
  - symptomatic V83.02
- hepatitis V02.60
  - Australian-antigen (HAA) V02.61
  - B V02.61
  - C V02.62
  - serum V02.61
  - specified type NEC V02.69
  - viral V02.60
- infective organism NEC V02.9
- malaria V02.9
- paratyphoid V02.3
- Salmonella V02.3
  - typhosa V02.1
- serum hepatitis V02.61
- Shigella V02.3
- Staphylococcus NEC V02.59
  - methicillin ●
    - resistant Staphylococcus aureus V02.54 ●
    - susceptible Staphylococcus aureus V02.53 ●
- Streptococcus NEC V02.52
  - group B V02.51
- typhoid V02.1
- venereal disease NEC V02.8

Carrión's disease (Bartonellosis) 088.0

Car sickness 994.6

Carter's
- relapsing fever (Asiatic) 087.0

Cartilage — *see* condition

Caruncle (inflamed)
- abscess, lacrimal (*see also* Dacryocystitis) 375.30
- conjunctiva 372.00
  - acute 372.00
- eyelid 373.00
- labium (majus) (minus) 616.89
- lacrimal 375.30
- urethra (benign) 599.3
- vagina (wall) 616.89

Cascade stomach 537.6

Caseation lymphatic gland — *see also* Tuberculosis 017.2 ☑

Caseous
- bronchitis — *see* Tuberculosis, pulmonary
- meningitis 013.0 ☑
- pneumonia — *see* Tuberculosis, pulmonary

Cassidy (-Scholte) syndrome (malignant carcinoid) 259.2

Castellani's bronchitis 104.8

Castleman's tumor or lymphoma (mediastinal lymph node hyperplasia) 785.6

Castration, traumatic 878.2
- complicated 878.3

Casts in urine 791.7

Catalepsy 300.11
- catatonic (acute) (*see also* Schizophrenia) 295.2 ☑
- hysterical 300.11
- schizophrenic (*see also* Schizophrenia) 295.2 ☑

Cataphasia 307.0

Cataplexy (idiopathic) — *see* Narcolepsy

Cataract (anterior cortical) (anterior polar) (black) (capsular) (central) (cortical) (hypermature) (immature) (incipient) (mature) 366.9
- anterior
  - and posterior axial embryonal 743.33
  - pyramidal 743.31
  - subcapsular polar
    - infantile, juvenile, or presenile 366.01
    - senile 366.13
- associated with
  - calcinosis 275.40 *[366.42]*
  - craniofacial dysostosis 756.0 *[366.44]*
  - galactosemia 271.1 *[366.44]*
  - hypoparathyroidism 252.1 *[366.42]*
  - myotonic disorders 359.21 *[366.43]*
  - neovascularization 366.33
- blue dot 743.39
- cerulean 743.39
- complicated NEC 366.30
- congenital 743.30
  - capsular or subcapsular 743.31
  - cortical 743.32
  - nuclear 743.33
  - specified type NEC 743.39
  - total or subtotal 743.34
  - zonular 743.32
- coronary (congenital) 743.39
  - acquired 366.12
- cupuliform 366.14
- diabetic 250.5 ☑ *[366.41]*
  - due to secondary diabetes 249.5 ☑ *[366.41]* ●
- drug-induced 366.45
- due to
  - chalcosis 360.24 *[366.34]*
  - chronic choroiditis (*see also* Choroiditis) 363.20 *[366.32]*
  - degenerative myopia 360.21 *[366.34]*
  - glaucoma (*see also* Glaucoma) 365.9 *[366.31]*
  - infection, intraocular NEC 366.32
  - inflammatory ocular disorder NEC 366.32
  - iridocyclitis, chronic 364.10 *[366.33]*
  - pigmentary retinal dystrophy 362.74 *[366.34]*
  - radiation 366.46
- electric 366.46
- glassblowers' 366.46
- heat ray 366.46
- heterochromic 366.33
- in eye disease NEC 366.30
- infantile (*see also* Cataract, juvenile) 366.00
- intumescent 366.12
- irradiational 366.46
- juvenile 366.00

Cataract — *continued*
- juvenile — *continued*
  - anterior subcapsular polar 366.01
  - combined forms 366.09
  - cortical 366.03
  - lamellar 366.03
  - nuclear 366.04
  - posterior subcapsular polar 366.02
  - specified NEC 366.09
  - zonular 366.03
- lamellar 743.32
  - infantile, juvenile, or presenile 366.03
- morgagnian 366.18
- myotonic 359.21 *[366.43]*
- myxedema 244.9 *[366.44]*
- nuclear 366.16
- posterior, polar (capsular) 743.31
  - infantile, juvenile, or presenile 366.02
  - senile 366.14
- presenile (*see also* Cataract, juvenile) 366.00
- punctate
  - acquired 366.12
  - congenital 743.39
- secondary (membrane) 366.50
  - obscuring vision 366.53
  - specified type, not obscuring vision 366.52
- senile 366.10
  - anterior subcapsular polar 366.13
  - combined forms 366.19
  - cortical 366.15
  - hypermature 366.18
  - immature 366.12
  - incipient 366.12
  - mature 366.17
  - nuclear 366.16
  - posterior subcapsular polar 366.14
  - specified NEC 366.19
  - total or subtotal 366.17
- snowflake 250.5 ☑ *[366.41]*
  - due to secondary diabetes 249.5 ☑ *[366.41]* ●
- specified NEC 366.8
- subtotal (senile) 366.17
  - congenital 743.34
- sunflower 360.24 *[366.34]*
- tetanic NEC 252.1 *[366.42]*
- total (mature) (senile) 366.17
  - congenital 743.34
  - localized 366.21
  - traumatic 366.22
- toxic 366.45
- traumatic 366.20
  - partially resolved 366.23
  - total 366.22
- zonular (perinuclear) 743.32
  - infantile, juvenile, or presenile 366.03

Cataracta 366.10
- brunescens 366.16
- cerulea 743.39
- complicata 366.30
- congenita 743.30
- coralliformis 743.39
- coronaria (congenital) 743.39
  - acquired 366.12
- diabetic 250.5 ☑ *[366.41]*
  - due to secondary diabetes 249.5 ☑ *[366.41]* ●
- floriformis 360.24 *[366.34]*
- membranacea
  - accreta 366.50
  - congenita 743.39
- nigra 366.16

Catarrh, catarrhal (inflammation) — *see also* condition 460
- acute 460
- asthma, asthmatic (*see also* Asthma) 493.9 ☑
- Bostock's (*see also* Fever, hay) 477.9
- bowel — *see* Enteritis
- bronchial 490
  - acute 466.0

Catarrh, catarrhal — *see also* condition — *continued*
  bronchial — *continued*
    chronic 491.0
    subacute 466.0
  cervix, cervical (canal) (uteri) — *see* Cervicitis
  chest (*see also* Bronchitis) 490
  chronic 472.0
  congestion 472.0
  conjunctivitis 372.03
  due to syphilis 095.9
    congenital 090.0
  enteric — *see* Enteritis
  epidemic 487.1
  Eustachian 381.50
  eye (acute) (vernal) 372.03
  fauces (*see also* Pharyngitis) 462
  febrile 460
  fibrinous acute 466.0
  gastroenteric — *see* Enteritis
  gastrointestinal — *see* Enteritis
  gingivitis 523.00
  hay (*see also* Fever, hay) 477.9
  infectious 460
  intestinal — *see* Enteritis
  larynx (*see also* Laryngitis, chronic) 476.0
  liver 070.1
    with hepatic coma 070.0
  lung (*see also* Bronchitis) 490
    acute 466.0
    chronic 491.0
  middle ear (chronic) — *see* Otitis media, chronic
  mouth 528.00
  nasal (chronic) (*see also* Rhinitis) 472.0
    acute 460
  nasobronchial 472.2
  nasopharyngeal (chronic) 472.2
    acute 460
  nose — *see* Catarrh, nasal
  ophthalmia 372.03
  pneumococcal, acute 466.0
  pulmonary (*see also* Bronchitis) 490
    acute 466.0
    chronic 491.0
  spring (eye) 372.13
  suffocating (*see also* Asthma) 493.9 ☑
  summer (hay) (*see also* Fever, hay) 477.9
  throat 472.1
  tracheitis 464.10
    with obstruction 464.11
  tubotympanal 381.4
    acute (*see also* Otitis media, acute, nonsuppurative) 381.00
    chronic 381.10
  vasomotor (*see also* Fever, hay) 477.9
  vesical (bladder) — *see* Cystitis
Catarrhus aestivus — *see also* Fever, hay 477.9
Catastrophe, cerebral — *see also* Disease, cerebrovascular, acute 436
Catatonia, catatonic (acute) 781.99
  with
    affective psychosis — *see* Psychosis, affective
  agitation 295.2 ☑
  dementia (praecox) 295.2 ☑
  due to or associated with physical condition 293.89
  excitation 295.2 ☑
  excited type 295.2 ☑
  in conditions classified elsewhere 293.89
  schizophrenia 295.2 ☑
  stupor 295.2 ☑
Cat's ear 744.29
Cat-scratch — *see also* Injury, superficial
  disease or fever 078.3
Cauda equina — *see also* condition
  syndrome 344.60
Cauliflower ear 738.7
Caul over face 768.9
Causalgia 355.9
  lower limb 355.71
  upper limb 354.4
Cause
  external, general effects NEC 994.9
  not stated 799.9
  unknown 799.9
Caustic burn — *see also* Burn, by site
  from swallowing caustic or corrosive substance — *see* Burn, internal organs
Cavare's disease (familial periodic paralysis) 359.3
Cave-in, injury
  crushing (severe) (*see also* Crush, by site) 869.1
  suffocation 994.7
Cavernitis (penis) 607.2
  lymph vessel — *see* Lymphangioma
Cavernositis 607.2
Cavernous — *see* condition
Cavitation of lung — *see also* Tuberculosis 011.2 ☑
  nontuberculous 518.89
  primary, progressive 010.8 ☑
Cavity
  lung — *see* Cavitation of lung
  optic papilla 743.57
  pulmonary — *see* Cavitation of lung
  teeth 521.00
  vitreous (humor) 379.21
Cavovarus foot, congenital 754.59
Cavus foot (congenital) 754.71
  acquired 736.73
Cazenave's
  disease (pemphigus) NEC 694.4
  lupus (erythematosus) 695.4
CDGS (carbohydrate-deficient glycoprotein syndrome) 271.8
Cecitis — *see* Appendicitis
Cecocele — *see* Hernia
Cecum — *see* condition
Celiac
  artery compression syndrome 447.4
  disease 579.0
  infantilism 579.0
Cell, cellular — *see also* condition
  anterior chamber (eye) (positive aqueous ray) 364.04
Cellulitis (diffuse) (with lymphangitis) — *see also* Abscess 682.9
  abdominal wall 682.2
  anaerobic (*see also* Gas gangrene) 040.0
  ankle 682.6
  anus 566
  areola 611.0
  arm (any part, above wrist) 682.3
  auditory canal (external) 380.10
  axilla 682.3
  back (any part) 682.2
  breast 611.0
    postpartum 675.1 ☑
  broad ligament (*see also* Disease, pelvis, inflammatory) 614.4
    acute 614.3
  buttock 682.5
  cervical (neck region) 682.1
  cervix (uteri) (*see also* Cervicitis) 616.0
  cheek, external 682.0
    internal 528.3
  chest wall 682.2
  chronic NEC 682.9
  colostomy 569.61
  corpus cavernosum 607.2
  digit 681.9
  Douglas' cul-de-sac or pouch (chronic) (*see also* Disease, pelvis, inflammatory) 614.4
    acute 614.3
  drainage site (following operation) 998.59
  ear, external 380.10
  enterostomy 569.61
  erysipelar (*see also* Erysipelas) 035
Cellulitis — *see also* Abscess — *continued*
  esophagostomy 530.86
  eyelid 373.13
  face (any part, except eye) 682.0
  finger (intrathecal) (periosteal) (subcutaneous) (subcuticular) 681.00
  flank 682.2
  foot (except toe) 682.7
  forearm 682.3
  gangrenous (*see also* Gangrene) 785.4
  genital organ NEC
    female — *see* Abscess, genital organ, female
    male 608.4
  glottis 478.71
  gluteal (region) 682.5
  gonococcal NEC 098.0
  groin 682.2
  hand (except finger or thumb) 682.4
  head (except face) NEC 682.8
  heel 682.7
  hip 682.6
  jaw (region) 682.0
  knee 682.6
  labium (majus) (minus) (*see also* Vulvitis) 616.10
  larynx 478.71
  leg, except foot 682.6
  lip 528.5
  mammary gland 611.0
  mouth (floor) 528.3
  multiple sites NEC 682.9
  nasopharynx 478.21
  navel 682.2
    newborn NEC 771.4
  neck (region) 682.1
  nipple 611.0
  nose 478.19
    external 682.0
  orbit, orbital 376.01
  palate (soft) 528.3
  pectoral (region) 682.2
  pelvis, pelvic
    with
      abortion — *see* Abortion, by type, with sepsis
      ectopic pregnancy (*see also* categories 633.0–633.9) 639.0
      molar pregnancy (*see also* categories 630–632) 639.0
    female (*see also* Disease, pelvis, inflammatory) 614.4
      acute 614.3
    following
      abortion 639.0
      ectopic or molar pregnancy 639.0
    male 567.21
    puerperal, postpartum, childbirth 670.0 ☑
  penis 607.2
  perineal, perineum 682.2
  perirectal 566
  peritonsillar 475
  periurethral 597.0
  periuterine (*see also* Disease, pelvis, inflammatory) 614.4
    acute 614.3
  pharynx 478.21
  phlegmonous NEC 682.9
  rectum 566
  retromammary 611.0
  retroperitoneal (*see also* Peritonitis) 567.2 ☑, 567.38
  round ligament (*see also* Disease, pelvis, inflammatory) 614.4
    acute 614.3
  scalp (any part) 682.8
    dissecting 704.8
  scrotum 608.4
  seminal vesicle 608.0
  septic NEC 682.9
  shoulder 682.3
  specified sites NEC 682.8
Cellulitis — *see also* Abscess — *continued*
  spermatic cord 608.4
  submandibular (region) (space) (triangle) 682.0
    gland 527.3
  submaxillary 528.3
    gland 527.3
  submental (pyogenic) 682.0
    gland 527.3
  suppurative NEC 682.9
  testis 608.4
  thigh 682.6
  thumb (intrathecal) (periosteal) (subcutaneous) (subcuticular) 681.00
  toe (intrathecal) (periosteal) (subcutaneous) (subcuticular) 681.10
  tonsil 475
  trunk 682.2
  tuberculous (primary) (*see also* Tuberculosis) 017.0 ☑
  tunica vaginalis 608.4
  umbilical 682.2
    newborn NEC 771.4
  vaccinal 999.39
  vagina — *see* Vaginitis
  vas deferens 608.4
  vocal cords 478.5
  vulva (*see also* Vulvitis) 616.10
  wrist 682.4
Cementoblastoma, benign (M9273/0) 213.1
  upper jaw (bone) 213.0
Cementoma (M9273/0) 213.1
  gigantiform (M9276/0) 213.1
    upper jaw (bone) 213.0
  upper jaw (bone) 213.0
Cementoperiostitis 523.40
  acute 523.33 ●
  apical 523.40 ●
Cephalgia, cephalagia — *see also* Headache 784.0
  histamine 339.00 ▲
  nonorganic origin 307.81
  other trigeminal autonomic (TACS) 339.09 ●
  psychogenic 307.81
  tension 307.81
Cephalhematocele, cephalematocele
  due to birth injury 767.19
  fetus or newborn 767.19
  traumatic (*see also* Contusion, head) 920
Cephalhematoma, cephalematoma (calcified)
  due to birth injury 767.19
  fetus or newborn 767.19
  traumatic (*see also* Contusion, head) 920
Cephalic — *see* condition
Cephalitis — *see* Encephalitis
Cephalocele 742.0
Cephaloma — *see* Neoplasm, by site, malignant
Cephalomenia 625.8
Cephalopelvic — *see* condition
Cercomoniasis 007.3
Cerebellitis — *see* Encephalitis
Cerebellum (cerebellar) — *see* condition
Cerebral — *see* condition
Cerebritis — *see* Encephalitis
Cerebrohepatorenal syndrome 759.89
Cerebromacular degeneration 330.1
Cerebromalacia — *see also* Softening, brain 434.9 ☑
Cerebrosidosis 272.7
Cerebrospasticity — *see* Palsy, cerebral
Cerebrospinal — *see* condition
Cerebrum — *see* condition
Ceroid storage disease 272.7
Cerumen (accumulation) (impacted) 380.4
Cervical — *see also* condition
  auricle 744.43

- **Cervical** — *see also* condition — *continued*
  - high risk human papillomavirus (HPV) DNA test positive 795.05
  - intraepithelial glandular neoplasia 233.1
  - low risk human papillomavirus (HPV) DNA test positive 795.09
  - rib 756.2
  - shortening — *see* Short, cervical ●
- **Cervicalgia** 723.1
- **Cervicitis** (acute) (chronic) (nonvenereal) (subacute) (with erosion or ectropion) 616.0
  - with
    - abortion — *see* Abortion, by type, with sepsis
    - ectopic pregnancy (*see also* categories 633.0–633.9) 639.0
    - molar pregnancy (*see also* categories 630–632) 639.0
    - ulceration 616.0
  - chlamydial 099.53
  - complicating pregnancy or puerperium 646.6 ☑
    - affecting fetus or newborn 760.8
  - following
    - abortion 639.0
    - ectopic or molar pregnancy 639.0
  - gonococcal (acute) 098.15
    - chronic or duration of 2 months or more 098.35
  - senile (atrophic) 616.0
  - syphilitic 095.8
  - trichomonal 131.09
  - tuberculous (*see also* Tuberculosis) 016.7 ☑
- **Cervicoaural fistula** 744.49
- **Cervicocolpitis** (emphysematosa) — *see also* Cervicitis 616.0
- **Cervix** — *see* condition
- **Cesarean delivery, operation or section** NEC 669.7 ☑
  - affecting fetus or newborn 763.4
  - post mortem, affecting fetus or newborn 761.6
  - previous, affecting management of pregnancy 654.2 ☑
- **Céstan-Chenais paralysis** 344.89
- **Céstan-Raymond syndrome** 433.8 ☑
- **Céstan's syndrome** 344.89
- **Cestode infestation** NEC 123.9
  - specified type NEC 123.8
- **Cestodiasis** 123.9
- **CGF** (congenital generalized fibromatosis) 759.89
- **Chabert's disease** 022.9
- **Chacaleh** 266.2
- **Chafing** 709.8
- **Chagas' disease** — *see also* Trypanosomiasis, American 086.2
  - with heart involvement 086.0
- **Chagres fever** 084.0
- **Chalasia** (cardiac sphincter) 530.81
- **Chalazion** 373.2
- **Chalazoderma** 757.39
- **Chalcosis** 360.24
  - cornea 371.15
  - crystalline lens 360.24 *[366.34]*
  - retina 360.24
- **Chalicosis** (occupational) (pulmonum) 502
- **Chancre** (any genital site) (hard) (indurated) (infecting) (primary) (recurrent) 091.0
  - congenital 090.0
  - conjunctiva 091.2
  - Ducrey's 099.0
  - extragenital 091.2
  - eyelid 091.2
  - Hunterian 091.0
  - lip (syphilis) 091.2
  - mixed 099.8
  - nipple 091.2
  - Nisbet's 099.0
- **Chancre** — *continued*
  - of
    - carate 103.0
    - pinta 103.0
    - yaws 102.0
  - palate, soft 091.2
  - phagedenic 099.0
  - Ricord's 091.0
  - Rollet's (syphilitic) 091.0
  - seronegative 091.0
  - seropositive 091.0
  - simple 099.0
  - soft 099.0
    - bubo 099.0
  - urethra 091.0
  - yaws 102.0
- **Chancriform syndrome** 114.1
- **Chancroid** 099.0
  - anus 099.0
  - penis (Ducrey's bacillus) 099.0
  - perineum 099.0
  - rectum 099.0
  - scrotum 099.0
  - urethra 099.0
  - vulva 099.0
- **Chandipura fever** 066.8
- **Chandler's disease** (osteochondritis dissecans, hip) 732.7
- **Change(s)** (of) — *see also* Removal of
  - arteriosclerotic — *see* Arteriosclerosis
  - battery
    - cardiac pacemaker V53.31
  - bone 733.90
    - diabetic 250.8 ☑ *[731.8]*
      - due to secondary diabetes 249.8 ☑ *[731.8]* ●
    - in disease, unknown cause 733.90
  - bowel habits 787.99
  - cardiorenal (vascular) (*see also* Hypertension, cardiorenal) 404.90
  - cardiovascular — *see* Disease, cardiovascular
  - circulatory 459.9
  - cognitive or personality change of other type, nonpsychotic 310.1
  - color, teeth, tooth
    - during formation 520.8
    - extrinsic 523.6
    - intrinsic posteruptive 521.7
  - contraceptive device V25.42
  - cornea, corneal
    - degenerative NEC 371.40
    - membrane NEC 371.30
    - senile 371.41
  - coronary (*see also* Ischemia, heart) 414.9
  - degenerative
    - chamber angle (anterior) (iris) 364.56
    - ciliary body 364.57
    - spine or vertebra (*see also* Spondylosis) 721.90
  - dental pulp, regressive 522.2
  - drains V58.49
  - dressing
    - wound V58.30
      - nonsurgical V58.30
      - surgical V58.31
  - fixation device V54.89
    - external V54.89
    - internal V54.01
  - heart (*see also* Disease, heart)
  - hip joint 718.95
  - hyperplastic larynx 478.79
  - hypertrophic
    - nasal sinus (*see also* Sinusitis) 473.9
    - turbinate, nasal 478.0
    - upper respiratory tract 478.9
  - inflammatory — *see* Inflammation
  - joint (*see also* Derangement, joint) 718.90
    - sacroiliac 724.6
  - Kirschner wire V54.89
  - knee 717.9
  - macular, congenital 743.55
- **Change(s)** — *see also* Removal of — *continued*
  - malignant (M — — /3) (*see also* Neoplasm, by site, malignant)

> *Note — for malignant change occurring in a neoplasm, use the appropriate M code with behavior digit /3 e.g., malignant change in uterine fibroid — M8890/3. For malignant change occurring in a nonneoplastic condition (e.g., gastric ulcer) use the M code M8000/3.*

  - mental (status) NEC 780.97
    - due to or associated with physical condition — *see* Syndrome, brain
  - myocardium, myocardial — *see* Degeneration, myocardial
  - of life (*see also* Menopause) 627.2
  - pacemaker battery (cardiac) V53.31
  - peripheral nerve 355.9
  - personality (nonpsychotic) NEC 310.1
  - plaster cast V54.89
  - refractive, transient 367.81
  - regressive, dental pulp 522.2
  - retina 362.9
    - myopic (degenerative) (malignant) 360.21
    - vascular appearance 362.13
  - sacroiliac joint 724.6
  - scleral 379.19
    - degenerative 379.16
  - senile (*see also* Senility) 797
  - sensory (*see also* Disturbance, sensation) 782.0
  - skin texture 782.8
  - spinal cord 336.9
  - splint, external V54.89
  - subdermal implantable contraceptive V25.5
  - suture V58.32
  - traction device V54.89
  - trophic 355.9
    - arm NEC 354.9
    - leg NEC 355.8
    - lower extremity NEC 355.8
    - upper extremity NEC 354.9
  - vascular 459.9
  - vasomotor 443.9
  - voice 784.49
    - psychogenic 306.1
  - wound packing V58.30
    - nonsurgical V58.30
    - surgical V58.31
- **Changing sleep-work schedule, affecting sleep** 327.36
- **Changuinola fever** 066.0
- **Chapping skin** 709.8
- **Character**
  - depressive 301.12
- **Charcôt's**
  - arthropathy 094.0 *[713.5]*
  - cirrhosis — *see* Cirrhosis, biliary
  - disease 094.0
    - spinal cord 094.0
  - fever (biliary) (hepatic) (intermittent) — *see* Choledocholithiasis
  - joint (disease) 094.0 *[713.5]*
    - diabetic 250.6 ☑ *[713.5]*
      - due to secondary diabetes 249.6 ☑ *[713.5]* ●
    - syringomyelic 336.0 *[713.5]*
  - syndrome (intermittent claudication) 443.9
    - due to atherosclerosis 440.21
- **Charcôt-Marie-Tooth disease, paralysis, or syndrome** 356.1
- **CHARGE association** (syndrome) 759.89
- **Charleyhorse** (quadriceps) 843.8
  - muscle, except quadriceps — *see* Sprain, by site
- **Charlouis' disease** — *see also* Yaws 102.9
- **Chauffeur's fracture** — *see* Fracture, ulna, lower end
- **Cheadle (-Möller) (-Barlow) disease or syndrome** (infantile scurvy) 267
- **Checking** (of)
  - contraceptive device (intrauterine) V25.42
  - device
    - fixation V54.89
      - external V54.89
      - internal V54.09
    - traction V54.89
  - Kirschner wire V54.89
  - plaster cast V54.89
  - splint, external V54.89
- **Checkup**
  - following treatment — *see* Examination
  - health V70.0
  - infant (not sick) V20.2
  - newborn, routine
    - initial V20.2
    - subsequent V20.2
  - pregnancy (normal) V22.1
    - first V22.0
    - high-risk pregnancy V23.9
      - specified problem NEC V23.89
- **Chédiak-Higashi (-Steinbrinck) anomaly, disease, or syndrome** (congenital gigantism of peroxidase granules) 288.2
- **Cheek** — *see also* condition
  - biting 528.9
- **Cheese itch** 133.8
- **Cheese washers' lung** 495.8
- **Cheilitis** 528.5
  - actinic (due to sun) 692.72
    - chronic NEC 692.74
      - due to radiation, except from sun 692.82
    - due to radiation, except from sun 692.82
  - acute 528.5
  - angular 528.5
  - catarrhal 528.5
  - chronic 528.5
  - exfoliative 528.5
  - gangrenous 528.5
  - glandularis apostematosa 528.5
  - granulomatosa 351.8
  - infectional 528.5
  - membranous 528.5
  - Miescher's 351.8
  - suppurative 528.5
  - ulcerative 528.5
  - vesicular 528.5
- **Cheilodynia** 528.5
- **Cheilopalatoschisis** — *see also* Cleft, palate, with cleft lip 749.20
- **Cheilophagia** 528.9
- **Cheiloschisis** — *see also* Cleft, lip 749.10
- **Cheilosis** 528.5
  - with pellagra 265.2
  - angular 528.5
  - due to
    - dietary deficiency 266.0
    - vitamin deficiency 266.0
- **Cheiromegaly** 729.89
- **Cheiropompholyx** 705.81
- **Cheloid** — *see also* Keloid 701.4
- **Chemical burn** — *see also* Burn, by site
  - from swallowing chemical — *see* Burn, internal organs
- **Chemodectoma** (M8693/1) — *see* Paraganglioma, nonchromaffin
- **Chemoprophylaxis** NEC V07.39
- **Chemosis, conjunctiva** 372.73
- **Chemotherapy**
  - convalescence V66.2
  - encounter (for) V58.11
  - maintenance V58.11
  - prophylactic NEC V07.39
    - fluoride V07.31
- **Cherubism** 526.89
- **Chest** — *see* condition
- **Cheyne-Stokes respiration** (periodic) 786.04

- **Chiari's**
  - disease or syndrome (hepatic vein thrombosis) 453.0
  - malformation
    - type I 348.4
    - type II (*see also* Spina bifida) 741.0 ☑
    - type III 742.0
    - type IV 742.2
  - network 746.89
- **Chiari-Frommel syndrome** 676.6 ☑
- **Chicago disease** (North American blastomycosis) 116.0
- **Chickenpox** — *see also* Varicella 052.9
  - exposure to V01.71
  - vaccination and inoculation (prophylactic) V05.4
- **Chiclero ulcer** 085.4
- **Chiggers** 133.8
- **Chignon** 111.2
  - fetus or newborn (from vacuum extraction) 767.19
- **Chigoe disease** 134.1
- **Chikungunya fever** 066.3
- **Chilaiditi's syndrome** (subphrenic displacement, colon) 751.4
- **Chilblains** 991.5
  - lupus 991.5
- **Child**
  - behavior causing concern V61.20
- **Childbed fever** 670.0 ☑
- **Childbirth** — *see also* Delivery
  - puerperal complications — *see* Puerperal
- **Childhood, period of rapid growth** V21.0
- **Chill(s)** 780.64 ▲
  - with fever 780.60 ▲
  - without fever 780.64 ●
  - congestive 780.99
    - in malarial regions 084.6
  - septic — *see* Septicemia
  - urethral 599.84
- **Chilomastigiasis** 007.8
- **Chin** — *see* condition
- **Chinese dysentery** 004.9
- **Chiropractic dislocation** — *see also* Lesion, nonallopathic, by site 739.9
- **Chitral fever** 066.0
- **Chlamydia, chlamydial** — *see* condition
- **Chloasma** 709.09
  - cachecticorum 709.09
  - eyelid 374.52
    - congenital 757.33
    - hyperthyroid 242.0 ☑
  - gravidarum 646.8 ☑
  - idiopathic 709.09
  - skin 709.09
  - symptomatic 709.09
- **Chloroma** (M9930/3) 205.3 ☑
- **Chlorosis** 280.9
  - Egyptian (*see also* Ancylostomiasis) 126.9
  - miners' (*see also* Ancylostomiasis) 126.9
- **Chlorotic anemia** 280.9
- **Chocolate cyst** (ovary) 617.1
- **Choked**
  - disc or disc — *see* Papilledema
  - on food, phlegm, or vomitus NEC (*see also* Asphyxia, food) 933.1
  - phlegm 933.1
  - while vomiting NEC (*see also* Asphyxia, food) 933.1
- **Chokes** (resulting from bends) 993.3
- **Choking sensation** 784.99
- **Cholangiectasis** — *see also* Disease, gallbladder 575.8
- **Cholangiocarcinoma** (M8160/3)
  - and hepatocellular carcinoma, combined (M8180/3) 155.0
  - liver 155.1
  - specified site NEC — *see* Neoplasm, by site, malignant
  - unspecified site 155.1
- **Cholangiohepatitis** 575.8
- **Cholangiohepatitis** — *continued*
  - due to fluke infestation 121.1
- **Cholangiohepatoma** (M8180/3) 155.0
- **Cholangiolitis** (acute) (chronic) (extrahepatic) (gangrenous) 576.1
  - intrahepatic 575.8
  - paratyphoidal (*see also* Fever, paratyphoid) 002.9
  - typhoidal 002.0
- **Cholangioma** (M8160/0) 211.5
  - malignant — *see* Cholangiocarcinoma
- **Cholangitis** (acute) (ascending) (catarrhal) (chronic) (infective) (malignant) (primary) (recurrent) (sclerosing) (secondary) (stenosing) (suppurative) 576.1
  - chronic nonsuppurative destructive 571.6
  - nonsuppurative destructive (chronic) 571.6
- **Cholecystdocholithiasis** — *see* Choledocholithiasis
- **Cholecystitis** 575.10
  - with
    - calculus, stones in
      - bile duct (common) (hepatic) — *see* Choledocholithiasis
      - gallbladder — *see* Cholelithiasis
  - acute 575.0
  - acute and chronic 575.12
  - chronic 575.11
  - emphysematous (acute) (*see also* Cholecystitis, acute) 575.0
  - gangrenous (*see also* Cholecystitis, acute) 575.0
  - paratyphoidal, current (*see also* Fever, paratyphoid) 002.9
  - suppurative (*see also* Cholecystitis, acute) 575.0
  - typhoidal 002.0
- **Choledochitis** (suppurative) 576.1
- **Choledocholith** — *see* Choledocholithiasis
- **Choledocholithiasis** 574.5 ☑

Note — Use the following fifth-digit subclassification with category 574:

0	*without mention of obstruction*
1	*with obstruction*

  - with
    - cholecystitis 574.4 ☑
      - acute 574.3 ☑
      - chronic 574.4 ☑
    - cholelithiasis 574.9 ☑
      - with
        - cholecystitis 574.7 ☑
          - acute 574.6 ☑
            - and chronic 574.8 ☑
          - chronic 574.7 ☑
- **Cholelithiasis** (impacted) (multiple) 574.2 ☑

Note — Use the following fifth-digit subclassification with category 574:

0	*without mention of obstruction*
1	*with obstruction*

  - with
    - cholecystitis 574.1 ☑
      - acute 574.0 ☑
      - chronic 574.1 ☑
    - choledocholithiasis 574.9 ☑
      - with
        - cholecystitis 574.7 ☑
          - acute 574.6 ☑
            - and chronic 574.8 ☑
          - chronic cholecystitis 574.7 ☑
- **Cholemia** — *see also* Jaundice 782.4
  - familial 277.4
  - Gilbert's (familial nonhemolytic) 277.4
- **Cholemic gallstone** — *see* Cholelithiasis
- **Choleperitoneum, choleperitonitis** — *see also* Disease, gallbladder 567.81
- **Cholera** (algid) (Asiatic) (asphyctic) (epidemic) (gravis) (Indian) (malignant) (morbus) (pestilential) (spasmodic) 001.9
  - antimonial 985.4
  - carrier (suspected) of V02.0
  - classical 001.0
  - contact V01.0
  - due to
    - Vibrio
      - cholerae (Inaba, Ogawa, Hikojima serotypes) 001.0
        - El Tor 001.1
  - El Tor 001.1
  - exposure to V01.0
  - vaccination, prophylactic (against) V03.0
- **Cholerine** — *see also* Cholera 001.9
- **Cholestasis** 576.8
  - due to total parenteral nutrition (TPN) 573.8
- **Cholesteatoma** (ear) 385.30
  - attic (primary) 385.31
  - diffuse 385.35
  - external ear (canal) 380.21
  - marginal (middle ear) 385.32
    - with involvement of mastoid cavity 385.33
    - secondary (with middle ear involvement) 385.33
  - mastoid cavity 385.30
  - middle ear (secondary) 385.32
    - with involvement of mastoid cavity 385.33
  - postmastoidectomy cavity (recurrent) 383.32
  - primary 385.31
  - recurrent, postmastoidectomy cavity 383.32
  - secondary (middle ear) 385.32
    - with involvement of mastoid cavity 385.33
- **Cholesteatosis** (middle ear) — *see also* Cholesteatoma 385.30
  - diffuse 385.35
- **Cholesteremia** 272.0
- **Cholesterin**
  - granuloma, middle ear 385.82
  - in vitreous 379.22
- **Cholesterol**
  - deposit
    - retina 362.82
    - vitreous 379.22
  - elevated (high) 272.0
    - with elevated (high) triglycerides 272.2
  - imbibition of gallbladder (*see also* Disease, gallbladder) 575.6
- **Cholesterolemia** 272.0
  - essential 272.0
  - familial 272.0
  - hereditary 272.0
- **Cholesterosis, cholesterolosis** (gallbladder) 575.6
  - with
    - cholecystitis — *see* Cholecystitis
    - cholelithiasis — *see* Cholelithiasis
  - middle ear (*see also* Cholesteatoma) 385.30
- **Cholocolic fistula** — *see also* Fistula, gallbladder 575.5
- **Choluria** 791.4
- **Chondritis** (purulent) 733.99
  - auricle 380.03
  - costal 733.6
    - Tietze's 733.6
  - patella, posttraumatic 717.7
  - pinna 380.03
  - posttraumatica patellae 717.7
  - tuberculous (active) (*see also* Tuberculosis) 015.9 ☑
    - intervertebral 015.0 ☑ *[730.88]*
- **Chondroangiopathia calcarea seu punctate** 756.59
- **Chondroblastoma** (M9230/0) — *see also* Neoplasm, bone, benign
- **Chondroblastoma** — *see also* Neoplasm, bone, benign — *continued*
  - malignant (M9230/3) — *see* Neoplasm, bone, malignant
- **Chondrocalcinosis** (articular) (crystal deposition) (dihydrate) — *see also* Arthritis, due to, crystals 275.49 *[712.3]* ☑
  - due to
    - calcium pyrophosphate 275.49 *[712.2]* ☑
    - dicalcium phosphate crystals 275.49 *[712.1]* ☑
    - pyrophosphate crystals 275.49 *[712.2]* ☑
- **Chondrodermatitis nodularis helicis** 380.00
- **Chondrodysplasia** 756.4
  - angiomatose 756.4
  - calcificans congenita 756.59
  - epiphysialis punctata 756.59
  - hereditary deforming 756.4
  - rhizomelic punctata 277.86
- **Chondrodystrophia** (fetalis) 756.4
  - calcarea 756.4
  - calcificans congenita 756.59
  - fetalis hypoplastica 756.59
  - hypoplastica calcinosa 756.59
  - punctata 756.59
  - tarda 277.5
- **Chondrodystrophy** (familial) (hypoplastic) 756.4
  - myotonic (congenital) 359.23
- **Chondroectodermal dysplasia** 756.55
- **Chondrolysis** 733.99
- **Chondroma** (M9220/0) — *see also* Neoplasm cartilage, benign
  - juxtacortical (M9221/0) — *see* Neoplasm, bone, benign
  - periosteal (M9221/0) — *see* Neoplasm, bone, benign
- **Chondromalacia** 733.92
  - epiglottis (congenital) 748.3
  - generalized 733.92
  - knee 717.7
  - larynx (congenital) 748.3
  - localized, except patella 733.92
  - patella, patellae 717.7
  - systemic 733.92
  - tibial plateau 733.92
  - trachea (congenital) 748.3
- **Chondromatosis** (M9220/1) — *see* Neoplasm, cartilage, uncertain behavior
- **Chondromyxosarcoma** (M9220/3) — *see* Neoplasm, cartilage, malignant
- **Chondro-osteodysplasia** (Morquio-Brailsford type) 277.5
- **Chondro-osteodystrophy** 277.5
- **Chondro-osteoma** (M9210/0) — *see* Neoplasm, bone, benign
- **Chondropathia tuberosa** 733.6
- **Chondrosarcoma** (M9220/3) — *see also* Neoplasm, cartilage, malignant
  - juxtacortical (M9221/3) — *see* Neoplasm, bone, malignant
  - mesenchymal (M9240/3) — *see* Neoplasm, connective tissue, malignant
- **Chordae tendineae rupture** (chronic) 429.5
- **Chordee** (nonvenereal) 607.89
  - congenital 752.63
  - gonococcal 098.2
- **Chorditis** (fibrinous) (nodosa) (tuberosa) 478.5
- **Chordoma** (M9370/3) — *see* Neoplasm, by site, malignant
- **Chorea** (gravis) (minor) (spasmodic) 333.5
  - with
    - heart involvement — *see* Chorea with rheumatic heart disease

Chorea — *continued*
with — *continued*
rheumatic heart disease (chronic, inactive, or quiescent) (conditions classifiable to 393–398) (*see* rheumatic heart condition involved)
active or acute (conditions classifiable to 391) 392.0
acute — *see* Chorea, Sydenham's
apoplectic (*see also* Disease, cerebrovascular, acute) 436
chronic 333.4
electric 049.8
gravidarum — *see* Eclampsia, pregnancy
habit 307.22
hereditary 333.4
Huntington's 333.4
posthemiplegic 344.89
pregnancy — *see* Eclampsia, pregnancy
progressive 333.4
chronic 333.4
hereditary 333.4
rheumatic (chronic) 392.9
with heart disease or involvement — *see* Chorea, with rheumatic heart disease
senile 333.5
Sydenham's 392.9
with heart involvement — *see* Chorea, with rheumatic heart disease
nonrheumatic 333.5
variabilis 307.23
Choreoathetosis (paroxysmal) 333.5
Chorioadenoma (destruens) (M9100/1) 236.1
Chorioamnionitis 658.4 ☑
affecting fetus or newborn 762.7
Chorioangioma (M9120/0) 219.8
Choriocarcinoma (M9100/3)
combined with
embryonal carcinoma (M9101/3) — *see* Neoplasm, by site, malignant
teratoma (M9101/3) — *see* Neoplasm, by site, malignant
specified site — *see* Neoplasm, by site, malignant
unspecified site
female 181
male 186.9
Chorioencephalitis, lymphocytic (acute) (serous) 049.0
Chorioepithelioma (M9100/3) — *see* Choriocarcinoma
Choriomeningitis (acute) (benign) (lymphocytic) (serous) 049.0
Chorionepithelioma (M9100/3) — *see* Choriocarcinoma
Chorionitis — *see also* Scleroderma 710.1
Chorioretinitis 363.20
disseminated 363.10
generalized 363.13
in
neurosyphilis 094.83
secondary syphilis 091.51
peripheral 363.12
posterior pole 363.11
tuberculous (*see also* Tuberculosis) 017.3 ☑ *[363.13]*
due to
histoplasmosis (*see also* Histoplasmosis) 115.92
toxoplasmosis (acquired) 130.2
congenital (active) 771.2
focal 363.00
juxtapapillary 363.01
peripheral 363.04
posterior pole NEC 363.03
juxtapapillaris, juxtapapillary 363.01
progressive myopia (degeneration) 360.21

Chorioretinitis — *continued*
syphilitic (secondary) 091.51
congenital (early) 090.0 *[363.13]*
late 090.5 *[363.13]*
late 095.8 *[363.13]*
tuberculous (*see also* Tuberculosis) 017.3 ☑ *[363.13]*
Choristoma — *see* Neoplasm, by site, benign
Choroid — *see* condition
Choroideremia, choroidermia (initial stage) (late stage) (partial or total atrophy) 363.55
Choroiditis — *see also* Chorioretinitis 363.20
leprous 030.9 *[363.13]*
senile guttate 363.41
sympathetic 360.11
syphilitic (secondary) 091.51
congenital (early) 090.0 *[363.13]*
late 090.5 *[363.13]*
late 095.8 *[363.13]*
Tay's 363.41
tuberculous (*see also* Tuberculosis) 017.3 ☑ *[363.13]*
Choroidopathy NEC 363.9
degenerative (*see also* Degeneration, choroid) 363.40
hereditary (*see also* Dystrophy, choroid) 363.50
specified type NEC 363.8
Choroidoretinitis — *see* Chorioretinitis
Choroidosis, central serous 362.41
Choroidretinopathy, serous 362.41
Christian's syndrome (chronic histiocytosis X) 277.89
Christian-Weber disease (nodular nonsuppurative panniculitis) 729.30
Christmas disease 286.1
Chromaffinoma (M8700/0) — *see also* Neoplasm, by site, benign
malignant (M8700/3) — *see* Neoplasm, by site, malignant
Chromatopsia 368.59
Chromhidrosis, chromidrosis 705.89
Chromoblastomycosis 117.2
Chromomycosis 117.2
Chromophytosis 111.0
Chromotrichomycosis 111.8
Chronic — *see* condition
Churg-Strauss syndrome 446.4
Chyle cyst, mesentery 457.8
Chylocele (nonfilarial) 457.8
filarial (*see also* Infestation, filarial) 125.9
tunica vaginalis (nonfilarial) 608.84
filarial (*see also* Infestation, filarial) 125.9
Chylomicronemia (fasting) (with hyperprebetalipoproteinemia) 272.3
Chylopericardium (acute) 420.90
Chylothorax (nonfilarial) 457.8
filarial (*see also* Infestation, filarial) 125.9
Chylous
ascites 457.8
cyst of peritoneum 457.8
hydrocele 603.9
hydrothorax (nonfilarial) 457.8
filarial (*see also* Infestation, filarial) 125.9
Chyluria 791.1
bilharziasis 120.0
due to
Brugia (malayi) 125.1
Wuchereria (bancrofti) 125.0
malayi 125.1
filarial (*see also* Infestation, filarial) 125.9
filariasis (*see also* Infestation, filarial) 125.9
nonfilarial 791.1
Cicatricial (deformity) — *see* Cicatrix
Cicatrix (adherent) (contracted) (painful) (vicious) 709.2
adenoid 474.8

Cicatrix — *continued*
alveolar process 525.8
anus 569.49
auricle 380.89
bile duct (*see also* Disease, biliary) 576.8
bladder 596.8
bone 733.99
brain 348.8
cervix (postoperative) (postpartal) 622.3
in pregnancy or childbirth 654.6 ☑
causing obstructed labor 660.2 ☑
chorioretinal 363.30
disseminated 363.35
macular 363.32
peripheral 363.34
posterior pole NEC 363.33
choroid — *see* Cicatrix, chorioretinal
common duct (*see also* Disease, biliary) 576.8
congenital 757.39
conjunctiva 372.64
cornea 371.00
tuberculous (*see also* Tuberculosis) 017.3 ☑ *[371.05]*
duodenum (bulb) 537.3
esophagus 530.3
eyelid 374.46
with
ectropion — *see* Ectropion
entropion — *see* Entropion
hypopharynx 478.29
knee, semilunar cartilage 717.5
lacrimal
canaliculi 375.53
duct
acquired 375.56
neonatal 375.55
punctum 375.52
sac 375.54
larynx 478.79
limbus (cystoid) 372.64
lung 518.89
macular 363.32
disseminated 363.35
peripheral 363.34
middle ear 385.89
mouth 528.9
muscle 728.89
nasolacrimal duct
acquired 375.56
neonatal 375.55
nasopharynx 478.29
palate (soft) 528.9
penis 607.89
prostate 602.8
rectum 569.49
retina 363.30
disseminated 363.35
macular 363.32
peripheral 363.34
posterior pole NEC 363.33
semilunar cartilage — *see* Derangement, meniscus
seminal vesicle 608.89
skin 709.2
infected 686.8
postinfectional 709.2
tuberculous (*see also* Tuberculosis) 017.0 ☑
specified site NEC 709.2
throat 478.29
tongue 529.8
tonsil (and adenoid) 474.8
trachea 478.9
tuberculous NEC (*see also* Tuberculosis) 011.9 ☑
ureter 593.89
urethra 599.84
uterus 621.8
vagina 623.4
in pregnancy or childbirth 654.7 ☑
causing obstructed labor 660.2 ☑

Cicatrix — *continued*
vocal cord 478.5
wrist, constricting (annular) 709.2
CIDP (chronic inflammatory demyelinating polyneuropathy) 357.81
CIN I [cervical intraepithelial neoplasia I] 622.11
CIN II [cervical intraepithelial neoplasia II] 622.12
CIN III [cervical intraepithelial neoplasia III] 233.1
Cinchonism
correct substance properly administered 386.9
overdose or wrong substance given or taken 961.4
Circine herpes 110.5
Circle of Willis — *see* condition
Circular — *see also* condition
hymen 752.49
Circulating anticoagulants 286.5
following childbirth 666.3 ☑
postpartum 666.3 ☑
Circulation
collateral (venous), any site 459.89
defective 459.9
congenital 747.9
lower extremity 459.89
embryonic 747.9
failure 799.89
fetus or newborn 779.89
peripheral 785.59
fetal, persistent 747.83
heart, incomplete 747.9
Circulatory system — *see* condition
Circulus senilis 371.41
Circumcision
in absence of medical indication V50.2
ritual V50.2
routine V50.2
status (post), female 629.20
Circumscribed — *see* condition
Circumvallata placenta — *see* Placenta, abnormal
Cirrhosis, cirrhotic 571.5
with alcoholism 571.2
alcoholic (liver) 571.2
atrophic (of liver) — *see* Cirrhosis, portal
Baumgarten-Cruveilhier 571.5
biliary (cholangiolitic) (cholangitic) (cholestatic) (extrahepatic) (hypertrophic) (intrahepatic) (nonobstructive) (obstructive) (pericholangiolitic) (posthepatic) (primary) (secondary) (xanthomatous) 571.6
due to
clonorchiasis 121.1
flukes 121.3
brain 331.9
capsular — *see* Cirrhosis, portal
cardiac 571.5
alcoholic 571.2
central (liver) — *see* Cirrhosis, liver
Charcôt's 571.6
cholangiolitic — *see* Cirrhosis, biliary
cholangitic — *see* Cirrhosis, biliary
cholestatic — *see* Cirrhosis, biliary
clitoris (hypertrophic) 624.2
coarsely nodular 571.5
congestive (liver) — *see* Cirrhosis, cardiac
Cruveilhier-Baumgarten 571.5
cryptogenic (of liver) 571.5
alcoholic 571.2
dietary (*see also* Cirrhosis, portal) 571.5
due to
bronzed diabetes 275.0
congestive hepatomegaly — *see* Cirrhosis, cardiac
cystic fibrosis 277.00
hemochromatosis 275.0
hepatolenticular degeneration 275.1

☑ Additional Digit Required — Refer to the Tabular List for Digit Selection

Subterms under main terms may continue to next column or page

▶◀ Revised Text ● New Line ▲ Revised Code

Cirrhosis, cirrhotic — *continued*
due to — *continued*
passive congestion (chronic) — *see* Cirrhosis, cardiac
Wilson's disease 275.1
xanthomatosis 272.2
extrahepatic (obstructive) — *see* Cirrhosis, biliary
fatty 571.8
alcoholic 571.0
florid 571.2
Glisson's — *see* Cirrhosis, portal
Hanot's (hypertrophic) — *see* Cirrhosis, biliary
hepatic — *see* Cirrhosis, liver
hepatolienal — *see* Cirrhosis, liver
hobnail — *see* Cirrhosis, portal
hypertrophic (*see also* Cirrhosis, liver)
biliary — *see* Cirrhosis, biliary
Hanot's — *see* Cirrhosis, biliary
infectious NEC — *see* Cirrhosis, portal
insular — *see* Cirrhosis, portal
intrahepatic (obstructive) (primary) (secondary) — *see* Cirrhosis, biliary
juvenile (*see also* Cirrhosis, portal) 571.5
kidney (*see also* Sclerosis, renal) 587
Laennec's (of liver) 571.2
nonalcoholic 571.5
liver (chronic) (hepatolienal) (hypertrophic) (nodular) (splenomegalic) (unilobar) 571.5
with alcoholism 571.2
alcoholic 571.2
congenital (due to failure of obliteration of umbilical vein) 777.8
cryptogenic 571.5
alcoholic 571.2
fatty 571.8
alcoholic 571.0
macronodular 571.5
alcoholic 571.2
micronodular 571.5
alcoholic 571.2
nodular, diffuse 571.5
alcoholic 571.2
pigmentary 275.0
portal 571.5
alcoholic 571.2
postnecrotic 571.5
alcoholic 571.2
syphilitic 095.3
lung (chronic) (*see also* Fibrosis, lung) 515
macronodular (of liver) 571.5
alcoholic 571.2
malarial 084.9
metabolic NEC 571.5
micronodular (of liver) 571.5
alcoholic 571.2
monolobular — *see* Cirrhosis, portal
multilobular — *see* Cirrhosis, portal
nephritis (*see also* Sclerosis, renal) 587
nodular — *see* Cirrhosis, liver
nutritional (fatty) 571.5
obstructive (biliary) (extrahepatic) (intrahepatic) — *see* Cirrhosis, biliary
ovarian 620.8
paludal 084.9
pancreas (duct) 577.8
pericholangiolitic — *see* Cirrhosis, biliary
periportal — *see* Cirrhosis, portal
pigment, pigmentary (of liver) 275.0
portal (of liver) 571.5
alcoholic 571.2
posthepatitic (*see also* Cirrhosis, postnecrotic) 571.5
postnecrotic (of liver) 571.5
alcoholic 571.2
primary (intrahepatic) — *see* Cirrhosis, biliary

Cirrhosis, cirrhotic — *continued*
pulmonary (*see also* Fibrosis, lung) 515
renal (*see also* Sclerosis, renal) 587
septal (*see also* Cirrhosis, postnecrotic) 571.5
spleen 289.51
splenomegalic (of liver) — *see* Cirrhosis, liver
stasis (liver) — *see* Cirrhosis, liver
stomach 535.4 ☑
Todd's (*see also* Cirrhosis, biliary) 571.6
toxic (nodular) — *see* Cirrhosis, postnecrotic
trabecular — *see* Cirrhosis, postnecrotic
unilobar — *see* Cirrhosis, liver
vascular (of liver) — *see* Cirrhosis, liver
xanthomatous (biliary) (*see also* Cirrhosis, biliary) 571.6
due to xanthomatosis (familial) (metabolic) (primary) 272.2
Cistern, subarachnoid 793.0
Citrullinemia 270.6
Citrullinuria 270.6
Ciuffini-Pancoast tumor (M8010/3) (carcinoma, pulmonary apex) 162.3
Civatte's disease or poikiloderma 709.09
CJD (Creutzfeldt-Jakob disease) 046.19 ●
variant (vCJD) 046.11 ●
Clam diggers' itch 120.3
Clap — *see* Gonorrhea
Clarke-Hadfield syndrome (pancreatic infantilism) 577.8
Clark's paralysis 343.9
Clastothrix 704.2
Claude Bernard-Horner syndrome — *see also* Neuropathy, peripheral, autonomic 337.9
Claude's syndrome 352.6
Claudication, intermittent 443.9
cerebral (artery) (*see also* Ischemia, cerebral, transient) 435.9
due to atherosclerosis 440.21
spinal cord (arteriosclerotic) 435.1
syphilitic 094.89
spinalis 435.1
venous (axillary) 453.8
Claudicatio venosa intermittens 453.8
Claustrophobia 300.29
Clavus (infected) 700
Clawfoot (congenital) 754.71
acquired 736.74
Clawhand (acquired) 736.06
congenital 755.59
Clawtoe (congenital) 754.71
acquired 735.5
Clay eating 307.52
Clay shovelers' fracture — *see* Fracture, vertebra, cervical
Cleansing of artificial opening — *see also* Attention to artificial opening V55.9
Cleft (congenital) — *see also* Imperfect, closure
alveolar process 525.8
branchial (persistent) 744.41
cyst 744.42
clitoris 752.49
cricoid cartilage, posterior 748.3
facial (*see also* Cleft, lip) 749.10
lip 749.10
with cleft palate 749.20
bilateral (lip and palate) 749.24
with unilateral lip or palate 749.25
complete 749.23
incomplete 749.24
unilateral (lip and palate) 749.22
with bilateral lip or palate 749.25
complete 749.21

Cleft — *see also* Imperfect, closure — *continued*
lip — *continued*
with cleft palate — *continued*
unilateral — *continued*
incomplete 749.22
bilateral 749.14
with cleft palate, unilateral 749.25
complete 749.13
incomplete 749.14
unilateral 749.12
with cleft palate, bilateral 749.25
complete 749.11
incomplete 749.12
nose 748.1
palate 749.00
with cleft lip 749.20
bilateral (lip and palate) 749.24
with unilateral lip or palate 749.25
complete 749.23
incomplete 749.24
unilateral (lip and palate) 749.22
with bilateral lip or palate 749.25
complete 749.21
incomplete 749.22
bilateral 749.04
with cleft lip, unilateral 749.25
complete 749.03
incomplete 749.04
unilateral 749.02
with cleft lip, bilateral 749.25
complete 749.01
incomplete 749.02
penis 752.69
posterior, cricoid cartilage 748.3
scrotum 752.89
sternum (congenital) 756.3
thyroid cartilage (congenital) 748.3
tongue 750.13
uvula 749.02
with cleft lip (*see also* Cleft, lip, with cleft palate) 749.20
water 366.12
Cleft hand (congenital) 755.58
Cleidocranial dysostosis 755.59
Cleidotomy, fetal 763.89
Cleptomania 312.32
Clérambault's syndrome 297.8
erotomania 302.89
Clergyman's sore throat 784.49
Click, clicking
systolic syndrome 785.2
Clifford's syndrome (postmaturity) 766.22
Climacteric — *see also* Menopause 627.2
arthritis NEC (*see also* Arthritis, climacteric) 716.3 ☑
depression (*see also* Psychosis, affective) 296.2 ☑
disease 627.2
recurrent episode 296.3 ☑
single episode 296.2 ☑
female (symptoms) 627.2
male (symptoms) (syndrome) 608.89
melancholia (*see also* Psychosis, affective) 296.2 ☑
recurrent episode 296.3 ☑
single episode 296.2 ☑
paranoid state 297.2
paraphrenia 297.2
polyarthritis NEC 716.39
male 608.89
symptoms (female) 627.2
Clinical research investigation (control) (participant) V70.7
Clinodactyly 755.59
Clitoris — *see* condition
Cloaca, persistent 751.5
Clonorchiasis 121.1
Clonorchiosis 121.1

Clonorchis infection, liver 121.1
Clonus 781.0
Closed bite 524.20
Closed surgical procedure converted to open procedure
arthroscopic V64.43
laparoscopic V64.41
thoracoscopic V64.42
Closure
artificial opening (*see also* Attention to artificial opening) V55.9
congenital, nose 748.0
cranial sutures, premature 756.0
defective or imperfect NEC — *see* Imperfect, closure
fistula, delayed — *see* Fistula
fontanelle, delayed 756.0
foramen ovale, imperfect 745.5
hymen 623.3
interauricular septum, defective 745.5
interventricular septum, defective 745.4
lacrimal duct 375.56
congenital 743.65
neonatal 375.55
nose (congenital) 748.0
acquired 738.0
vagina 623.2
valve — *see* Endocarditis
vulva 624.8
Clot (blood)
artery (obstruction) (occlusion) (*see also* Embolism) 444.9
atrial appendage 429.89
bladder 596.7
brain (extradural or intradural) (*see also* Thrombosis, brain) 434.0 ☑
late effect — *see* Late effect(s) (of) cerebrovascular disease
circulation 444.9
heart (*see also* Infarct, myocardium) 410.9 ☑
without myocardial infarction 429.89
vein (*see also* Thrombosis) 453.9
Clotting defect NEC — *see also* Defect, coagulation 286.9
Clouded state 780.09
epileptic (*see also* Epilepsy) 345.9 ☑
paroxysmal (idiopathic) (*see also* Epilepsy) 345.9 ☑
Clouding
corneal graft 996.51
Cloudy
antrum, antra 473.0
dialysis effluent 792.5
Clouston's (hidrotic) ectodermal dysplasia 757.31
Clubbing of fingers 781.5
Clubfinger 736.29
acquired 736.29
congenital 754.89
Clubfoot (congenital) 754.70
acquired 736.71
equinovarus 754.51
paralytic 736.71
Club hand (congenital) 754.89
acquired 736.07
Clubnail (acquired) 703.8
congenital 757.5
Clump kidney 753.3
Clumsiness 781.3
syndrome 315.4
Cluttering 307.0
Clutton's joints 090.5
Coagulation, intravascular (diffuse) (disseminated) — *see also* Fibrinolysis 286.6
newborn 776.2
Coagulopathy — *see also* Defect, coagulation 286.9
consumption 286.6
intravascular (disseminated) NEC 286.6
newborn 776.2

- **Coalition**
  - calcaneoscaphoid 755.67
  - calcaneus 755.67
  - tarsal 755.67
- **Coal miners'**
  - elbow 727.2
  - lung 500
- **Coal workers' lung or pneumoconiosis** 500
- **Coarctation**
  - aorta (postductal) (preductal) 747.10
  - pulmonary artery 747.3
- **Coated tongue** 529.3
- **Coats' disease** 362.12
- **Cocainism** — *see also* Dependence 304.2 ☑
- **Coccidioidal granuloma** 114.3
- **Coccidioidomycosis** 114.9
  - with pneumonia 114.0
  - cutaneous (primary) 114.1
  - disseminated 114.3
  - extrapulmonary (primary) 114.1
  - lung 114.5
    - acute 114.0
    - chronic 114.4
    - primary 114.0
  - meninges 114.2
  - primary (pulmonary) 114.0
    - acute 114.0
  - prostate 114.3
  - pulmonary 114.5
    - acute 114.0
    - chronic 114.4
    - primary 114.0
  - specified site NEC 114.3
- **Coccidioidosis** 114.9
  - lung 114.5
    - acute 114.0
    - chronic 114.4
    - primary 114.0
  - meninges 114.2
- **Coccidiosis** (colitis) (diarrhea) (dysentery) 007.2
- **Cocciuria** 791.9
- **Coccus in urine** 791.9
- **Coccydynia** 724.79
- **Coccygodynia** 724.79
- **Coccyx** — *see* condition
- **Cochin-China**
  - diarrhea 579.1
    - anguilluliasis 127.2
  - ulcer 085.1
- **Cockayne's disease or syndrome** (microcephaly and dwarfism) 759.89
- **Cockayne-Weber syndrome** (epidermolysis bullosa) 757.39
- **Cocked-up toe** 735.2
- **Cock's peculiar tumor** 706.2
- **Codman's tumor** (benign chondroblastoma) (M9230/0) — *see* Neoplasm, bone, benign
- **Coenurosis** 123.8
- **Coffee workers' lung** 495.8
- **Cogan's syndrome** 370.52
  - congenital oculomotor apraxia 379.51
  - nonsyphilitic interstitial keratitis 370.52
- **Coiling, umbilical cord** — *see* Complications, umbilical cord
- **Coitus, painful** (female) 625.0
  - male 608.89
  - psychogenic 302.76
- **Cold** 460
  - with influenza, flu, or grippe 487.1
  - abscess (*see also* Tuberculosis, abscess)
    - articular — *see* Tuberculosis, joint
  - agglutinin
    - disease (chronic) or syndrome 283.0
    - hemoglobinuria 283.0
      - paroxysmal (cold) (nocturnal) 283.2
  - allergic (*see also* Fever, hay) 477.9
  - bronchus or chest — *see* Bronchitis
    - with grippe or influenza 487.1

Cold — *continued*

  - common (head) 460
    - vaccination, prophylactic (against) V04.7
  - deep 464.10
  - effects of 991.9
    - specified effect NEC 991.8
  - excessive 991.9
    - specified effect NEC 991.8
  - exhaustion from 991.8
  - exposure to 991.9
    - specified effect NEC 991.8
  - grippy 487.1
  - head 460
  - injury syndrome (newborn) 778.2
  - intolerance 780.99
  - on lung — *see* Bronchitis
  - rose 477.0
  - sensitivity, autoimmune 283.0
  - virus 460
- **Coldsore** — *see also* Herpes, simplex 054.9
- **Colibacillosis** 041.4
  - generalized 038.42
- **Colibacilluria** 791.9
- **Colic** (recurrent) 789.0 ☑
  - abdomen 789.0 ☑
    - psychogenic 307.89
  - appendicular 543.9
  - appendix 543.9
  - bile duct — *see* Choledocholithiasis
  - biliary — *see* Cholelithiasis
  - bilious — *see* Cholelithiasis
  - common duct — *see* Choledocholithiasis
  - Devonshire NEC 984.9
    - specified type of lead — *see* Table of Drugs and Chemicals
  - flatulent 787.3
  - gallbladder or gallstone — *see* Cholelithiasis
  - gastric 536.8
  - hepatic (duct) — *see* Choledocholithiasis
  - hysterical 300.11
  - infantile 789.0 ☑
  - intestinal 789.0 ☑
  - kidney 788.0
  - lead NEC 984.9
    - specified type of lead — *see* Table of Drugs and Chemicals
  - liver (duct) — *see* Choledocholithiasis
  - mucous 564.9
    - psychogenic 316 *[564.9]*
  - nephritic 788.0
  - painter's NEC 984.9
  - pancreas 577.8
  - psychogenic 306.4
  - renal 788.0
  - saturnine NEC 984.9
    - specified type of lead — *see* Table of Drugs and Chemicals
  - spasmodic 789.0 ☑
  - ureter 788.0
  - urethral 599.84
    - due to calculus 594.2
  - uterus 625.8
    - menstrual 625.3
  - vermicular 543.9
  - virus 460
  - worm NEC 128.9
- **Colicystitis** — *see also* Cystitis 595.9
- **Colitis** (acute) (catarrhal) (croupous) (cystica superficialis) (exudative) (hemorrhagic) (noninfectious) (phlegmonous) (presumed noninfectious) 558.9
  - adaptive 564.9
  - allergic 558.3
  - amebic (*see also* Amebiasis) 006.9
    - nondysenteric 006.2
  - anthrax 022.2
  - bacillary (*see also* Infection, Shigella) 004.9
  - balantidial 007.0
  - chronic 558.9

Colitis — *continued*

  - chronic — *continued*
    - ulcerative (*see also* Colitis, ulcerative) 556.9
  - coccidial 007.2
  - dietetic 558.9
  - due to radiation 558.1
  - eosinophilic 558.41 ●
  - functional 558.9
  - gangrenous 009.0
  - giardial 007.1
  - granulomatous 555.1
  - gravis (*see also* Colitis, ulcerative) 556.9
  - infectious (*see also* Enteritis, due to, specific organism) 009.0
    - presumed 009.1
  - ischemic 557.9
    - acute 557.0
    - chronic 557.1
    - due to mesenteric artery insufficiency 557.1
  - membranous 564.9
    - psychogenic 316 *[564.9]*
  - mucous 564.9
    - psychogenic 316 *[564.9]*
  - necrotic 009.0
  - polyposa (*see also* Colitis, ulcerative) 556.9
  - protozoal NEC 007.9
  - pseudomembranous 008.45
  - pseudomucinous 564.9
  - regional 555.1
  - segmental 555.1
  - septic (*see also* Enteritis, due to, specific organism) 009.0
  - spastic 564.9
    - psychogenic 316 *[564.9]*
  - Staphylococcus 008.41
    - food 005.0
  - thromboulcerative 557.0
  - toxic 558.2
  - transmural 555.1
  - trichomonal 007.3
  - tuberculous (ulcerative) 014.8 ☑
  - ulcerative (chronic) (idiopathic) (nonspecific) 556.9
    - entero- 556.0
    - fulminant 557.0
    - ileo- 556.1
    - left-sided 556.5
    - procto- 556.2
    - proctosigmoid 556.3
    - psychogenic 316 *[556]* ☑
    - specified NEC 556.8
    - universal 556.6
- **Collagen disease** NEC 710.9
  - nonvascular 710.9
  - vascular (allergic) (*see also* Angiitis, hypersensitivity) 446.20
- **Collagenosis** — *see also* Collagen disease 710.9
  - cardiovascular 425.4
  - mediastinal 519.3
- **Collapse** 780.2
  - adrenal 255.8
  - cardiorenal (*see also* Hypertension, cardiorenal) 404.90
  - cardiorespiratory 785.51
    - fetus or newborn 779.85
  - cardiovascular (*see also* Disease, heart) 785.51
    - fetus or newborn 779.85
  - circulatory (peripheral) 785.59
    - with
      - abortion — *see* Abortion, by type, with shock
      - ectopic pregnancy (*see also* categories 633.0–633.9) 639.5
      - molar pregnancy (*see also* categories 630–632) 639.5
    - during or after labor and delivery 669.1 ☑
    - fetus or newborn 779.85

Collapse — *continued*

  - circulatory — *continued*
    - following
      - abortion 639.5
      - ectopic or molar pregnancy 639.5
    - during or after labor and delivery 669.1 ☑
      - fetus or newborn 779.89
  - external ear canal 380.50
    - secondary to
      - inflammation 380.53
      - surgery 380.52
      - trauma 380.51
  - general 780.2
  - heart — *see* Disease, heart
  - heat 992.1
  - hysterical 300.11
  - labyrinth, membranous (congenital) 744.05
  - lung (massive) (*see also* Atelectasis) 518.0
    - pressure, during labor 668.0 ☑
  - myocardial — *see* Disease, heart
  - nervous (*see also* Disorder, mental, nonpsychotic) 300.9
  - neurocirculatory 306.2
  - nose 738.0
  - postoperative (cardiovascular) 998.0
  - pulmonary (see also Atelectasis) 518.0
    - fetus or newborn 770.5
      - partial 770.5
      - primary 770.4
  - thorax 512.8
    - iatrogenic 512.1
    - postoperative 512.1
  - trachea 519.19
  - valvular — *see* Endocarditis
  - vascular (peripheral) 785.59
    - with
      - abortion — *see* Abortion, by type, with shock
      - ectopic pregnancy (*see also* categories 633.0–633.9) 639.5
      - molar pregnancy (*see also* categories 630–632) 639.5
    - cerebral (*see also* Disease, cerebrovascular, acute) 436
    - during or after labor and delivery 669.1 ☑
    - fetus or newborn 779.89
    - following
      - abortion 639.5
      - ectopic or molar pregnancy 639.5
  - vasomotor 785.59
  - vertebra 733.13
- **Collateral** — *see also* condition
  - circulation (venous) 459.89
  - dilation, veins 459.89
- **Colles' fracture** (closed) (reversed) (separation) 813.41
  - open 813.51
- **Collet-Sicard syndrome** 352.6
- **Collet's syndrome** 352.6
- **Colliculitis urethralis** — *see also* Urethritis 597.89
- **Colliers'**
  - asthma 500
  - lung 500
  - phthisis (*see also* Tuberculosis) 011.4 ☑
- **Collodion baby** (ichthyosis congenita) 757.1
- **Colloid milium** 709.3
- **Coloboma** NEC 743.49
  - choroid 743.59
  - fundus 743.52
  - iris 743.46
  - lens 743.36
  - lids 743.62
  - optic disc (congenital) 743.57
    - acquired 377.23
  - retina 743.56
  - sclera 743.47

Coloenteritis — *see* Enteritis
Colon — *see* condition
Colonization ●
MRSA (methicillin resistant Staphylococcus aureus) V02.54 ●
MSSA (methicillin susceptible Staphylococcus aureus) V02.53 ●
Coloptosis 569.89
Color
amblyopia NEC 368.59
acquired 368.55
blindness NEC (congenital) 368.59
acquired 368.55
Colostomy
attention to V55.3
fitting or adjustment V55.3
malfunctioning 569.62
status V44.3
Colpitis — *see also* Vaginitis 616.10
Colpocele 618.6
Colpocystitis — *see also* Vaginitis 616.10
Colporrhexis 665.4 ☑
Colpospasm 625.1
Column, spinal, vertebral — *see* condition
Coma 780.01
apoplectic (*see also* Disease, cerebrovascular, acute) 436
diabetic (with ketoacidosis) 250.3 ☑
due to secondary diabetes 249.3 ☑ ●
hyperosmolar 250.2 ☑
due to secondary diabetes 249.2 ☑ ●
eclamptic (*see also* Eclampsia) 780.39
epileptic 345.3
hepatic 572.2
hyperglycemic 250.2 ☑
due to secondary diabetes 249.2 ☑ ●
hyperosmolar (diabetic) (nonketotic) 250.2 ☑
due to secondary diabetes 249.2 ☑ ●
hypoglycemic 251.0
diabetic 250.3 ☑
due to secondary diabetes 249.3 ☑ ●
insulin 250.3 ☑
due to secondary diabetes 249.3 ☑ ●
hyperosmolar 250.2 ☑
due to secondary diabetes 249.2 ☑ ●
non-diabetic 251.0
organic hyperinsulinism 251.0
Kussmaul's (diabetic) 250.3 ☑
due to secondary diabetes 249.3 ☑ ●
liver 572.2
newborn 779.2
prediabetic 250.2 ☑
due to secondary diabetes 249.2 ☑ ●
uremic — *see* Uremia
Combat fatigue — *see also* Reaction, stress, acute 308.9
Combined — *see* condition
Comedo 706.1
Comedocarcinoma (M8501/3) — *see also* Neoplasm, breast, malignant
noninfiltrating (M8501/2)
specified site — *see* Neoplasm, by site, in situ
unspecified site 233.0
Comedomastitis 610.4
Comedones 706.1
lanugo 757.4
Comma bacillus, carrier (suspected) of V02.3
Comminuted fracture — *see* Fracture, by site
Common
aortopulmonary trunk 745.0

Common — *continued*
atrioventricular canal (defect) 745.69
atrium 745.69
cold (head) 460
vaccination, prophylactic (against) V04.7
truncus (arteriosus) 745.0
ventricle 745.3
Commotio (current)
cerebri (*see also* Concussion, brain) 850.9
with skull fracture — *see* Fracture, skull, by site
retinae 921.3
spinalis — *see* Injury, spinal, by site
Commotion (current)
brain (without skull fracture) (*see also* Concussion, brain) 850.9
with skull fracture — *see* Fracture, skull, by site
spinal cord — *see* Injury, spinal, by site
Communication
abnormal (*see also* Fistula)
between
base of aorta and pulmonary artery 745.0
left ventricle and right atrium 745.4
pericardial sac and pleural sac 748.8
pulmonary artery and pulmonary vein 747.3
congenital, between uterus and anterior abdominal wall 752.3
bladder 752.3
intestine 752.3
rectum 752.3
left ventricular — right atrial 745.4
pulmonary artery — pulmonary vein 747.3
Compartment syndrome — *see* Syndrome, compartment
Compensation
broken — *see* Failure, heart
failure — *see* Failure, heart
neurosis, psychoneurosis 300.11
Complaint — *see also* Disease
bowel, functional 564.9
psychogenic 306.4
intestine, functional 564.9
psychogenic 306.4
kidney (*see also* Disease, renal) 593.9
liver 573.9
miners' 500
Complete — *see* condition
Complex
cardiorenal (*see also* Hypertension, cardiorenal) 404.90
castration 300.9
Costen's 524.60
ego-dystonic homosexuality 302.0
Eisenmenger's (ventricular septal defect) 745.4
homosexual, ego-dystonic 302.0
hypersexual 302.89
inferiority 301.9
jumped process
spine — *see* Dislocation, vertebra
primary, tuberculosis (*see also* Tuberculosis) 010.0 ☑
regional pain syndrome 355.9 ●
type I 337.20 ●
lower limb 337.22 ●
specified site NEC 337.29 ●
upper limb 337.21 ●
type II ●
lower limb 355.71 ●
upper limb 354.4 ●
Taussig-Bing (transposition, aorta and overriding pulmonary artery) 745.11
Complications
abortion NEC — *see* categories 634-639 ☑

Complications — *continued*
accidental puncture or laceration during a procedure 998.2
amniocentesis, fetal 679.1 ☑ ●
amputation stump (late) (surgical) 997.60
traumatic — *see* Amputation, traumatic
anastomosis (and bypass) (*see also* Complications, due to (presence of) any device, implant, or graft classified to 996.0–996.5 NEC)
hemorrhage NEC 998.11
intestinal (internal) NEC 997.4
involving urinary tract 997.5
mechanical — *see* Complications, mechanical, graft
urinary tract (involving intestinal tract) 997.5
anesthesia, anesthetic NEC (*see also* Anesthesia, complication) 995.22
in labor and delivery 668.9 ☑
affecting fetus or newborn 763.5
cardiac 668.1 ☑
central nervous system 668.2 ☑
pulmonary 668.0 ☑
specified type NEC 668.8 ☑
aortocoronary (bypass) graft 996.03
atherosclerosis — *see* Arteriosclerosis, coronary
embolism 996.72
occlusion NEC 996.72
thrombus 996.72
arthroplasty (*see also* Complications, prosthetic joint) 996.49
artificial opening
cecostomy 569.60
colostomy 569.60
cystostomy 997.5
enterostomy 569.60
esophagostomy 530.87
infection 530.86
mechanical 530.87
gastrostomy 536.40
ileostomy 569.60
jejunostomy 569.60
nephrostomy 997.5
tracheostomy 519.00
ureterostomy 997.5
urethrostomy 997.5
bariatric surgery 997.4
bile duct implant (prosthetic) NEC 996.79
infection or inflammation 996.69
mechanical 996.59
bleeding (intraoperative) (postoperative) 998.11
blood vessel graft 996.1
aortocoronary 996.03
atherosclerosis — *see* Arteriosclerosis, coronary
embolism 996.72
occlusion NEC 996.72
thrombus 996.72
atherosclerosis — *see* Arteriosclerosis, extremities
embolism 996.74
occlusion NEC 996.74
thrombus 996.74
bone growth stimulator NEC 996.78
infection or inflammation 996.67
bone marrow transplant 996.85
breast implant (prosthetic) NEC 996.79
infection or inflammation 996.69
mechanical 996.54
bypass (*see also* Complications, anastomosis)
aortocoronary 996.03
atherosclerosis — *see* Arteriosclerosis, coronary
embolism 996.72
occlusion NEC 996.72
thrombus 996.72
carotid artery 996.1

Complications — *continued*
bypass (*see also* Complications, anastomosis) — *continued*
carotid artery — *continued*
atherosclerosis — *see* Arteriosclerosis, extremities
embolism 996.74
occlusion NEC 996.74
thrombus 996.74
cardiac (*see also* Disease, heart) 429.9
device, implant, or graft NEC 996.72
infection or inflammation 996.61
long-term effect 429.4
mechanical (*see also* Complications, mechanical, by type) 996.00
valve prosthesis 996.71
infection or inflammation 996.61
postoperative NEC 997.1
long-term effect 429.4
cardiorenal (*see also* Hypertension, cardiorenal) 404.90
carotid artery bypass graft 996.1
atherosclerosis — *see* Arteriosclerosis, extremities
embolism 996.74
occlusion NEC 996.74
thrombus 996.74
cataract fragments in eye 998.82
catheter device NEC (*see also* Complications, due to (presence of) any device, implant, or graft classified to 996.0–996.5 NEC)
mechanical — *see* Complications, mechanical, catheter
cecostomy 569.60
cesarean section wound 674.3 ☑
chemotherapy (antineoplastic) 995.29
chin implant (prosthetic) NEC 996.79
infection or inflammation 996.69
mechanical 996.59
colostomy (enterostomy) 569.60
specified type NEC 569.69
contraceptive device, intrauterine NEC 996.76
infection 996.65
inflammation 996.65
mechanical 996.32
cord (umbilical) — *see* Complications, umbilical cord
cornea
due to
contact lens 371.82
coronary (artery) bypass (graft) NEC 996.03
atherosclerosis — *see* Arteriosclerosis, coronary
embolism 996.72
infection or inflammation 996.61
mechanical 996.03
occlusion NEC 996.72
specified type NEC 996.72
thrombus 996.72
cystostomy 997.5
delivery 669.9 ☑
procedure (instrumental) (manual) (surgical) 669.4 ☑
specified type NEC 669.8 ☑
dialysis (hemodialysis) (peritoneal) (renal) NEC 999.9
catheter NEC (*see also* Complications, due to (presence of) any device, implant, or graft classified to 996.0–996.5 NEC)
infection or inflammation 996.62
peritoneal 996.68
mechanical 996.1
peritoneal 996.56
drug NEC 995.29

Complications — *continued*
due to (presence of) any device, implant, or graft classified to 996.0–996.5 NEC 996.70
with infection or inflammation — *see* Complications, infection or inflammation, due to (presence of) any device, implant, or graft classified to 996.0–996.5 NEC
arterial NEC 996.74
coronary NEC 996.03
atherosclerosis — *see* Arteriosclerosis, coronary
embolism 996.72
occlusion NEC 996.72
specified type NEC 996.72
thrombus 996.72
renal dialysis 996.73
arteriovenous fistula or shunt NEC 996.74
bone growth stimulator 996.78
breast NEC 996.79
cardiac NEC 996.72
defibrillator 996.72
pacemaker 996.72
valve prosthesis 996.71
catheter NEC 996.79
spinal 996.75
urinary, indwelling 996.76
vascular NEC 996.74
renal dialysis 996.73
ventricular shunt 996.75
coronary (artery) bypass (graft) NEC 996.03
atherosclerosis — *see* Arteriosclerosis, coronary
embolism 996.72
occlusion NEC 996.72
thrombus 996.72
electrodes
brain 996.75
heart 996.72
esophagostomy 530.87
gastrointestinal NEC 996.79
genitourinary NEC 996.76
heart valve prosthesis NEC 996.71
infusion pump 996.74
insulin pump 996.57
internal
joint prosthesis 996.77
orthopedic NEC 996.78
specified type NEC 996.79
intrauterine contraceptive device NEC 996.76
joint prosthesis, internal NEC 996.77
mechanical — *see* Complications, mechanical
nervous system NEC 996.75
ocular lens NEC 996.79
orbital NEC 996.79
orthopedic NEC 996.78
joint, internal 996.77
renal dialysis 996.73
specified type NEC 996.79
urinary catheter, indwelling 996.76
vascular NEC 996.74
ventricular shunt 996.75
during dialysis NEC 999.9
ectopic or molar pregnancy NEC 639.9
electroshock therapy NEC 999.9
enterostomy 569.60
specified type NEC 569.69
esophagostomy 530.87
infection 530.86
mechanical 530.87
external (fixation) device with internal component(s) NEC 996.78
infection or inflammation 996.67
mechanical 996.49
extracorporeal circulation NEC 999.9
eye implant (prosthetic) NEC 996.79
infection or inflammation 996.69
mechanical
ocular lens 996.53

Complications — *continued*
eye implant — *continued*
mechanical — *continued*
orbital globe 996.59
fetal, from amniocentesis 679.1 ☑ ●
gastrointestinal, postoperative NEC (*see also* Complications, surgical procedures) 997.4
gastrostomy 536.40
specified type NEC 536.49
genitourinary device, implant or graft NEC 996.76
infection or inflammation 996.65
urinary catheter, indwelling 996.64
mechanical (*see also* Complications, mechanical, by type) 996.30
specified NEC 996.39
graft (bypass) (patch) (*see also* Complications, due to (presence of) any device, implant, or graft classified to 996.0–996.5 NEC)
bone marrow 996.85
corneal NEC 996.79
infection or inflammation 996.69
rejection or reaction 996.51
mechanical — *see* Complications, mechanical, graft
organ (immune or nonimmune cause) (partial) (total) 996.80
bone marrow 996.85
heart 996.83
intestines 996.87
kidney 996.81
liver 996.82
lung 996.84
pancreas 996.86
specified NEC 996.89
skin NEC 996.79
infection or inflammation 996.69
rejection 996.52
artificial 996.55
decellularized allodermis 996.55
heart (*see also* Disease, heart transplant (immune or nonimmune cause)) 996.83
hematoma (intraoperative) (postoperative) 998.12
hemorrhage (intraoperative) (postoperative) 998.11
hyperalimentation therapy NEC 999.9
immunization (procedure) — *see* Complications, vaccination
implant (*see also* Complications, due to (presence of) any device, implant, or graft classified to 996.0–996.5 NEC)
dental placement, hemorrhagic 525.71
mechanical — *see* Complications, mechanical, implant
infection and inflammation
due to (presence of) any device, implant or graft classified to 996.0–996.5 NEC 996.60
arterial NEC 996.62
coronary 996.61
renal dialysis 996.62
arteriovenous fistula or shunt 996.62
artificial heart 996.61
bone growth stimulator 996.67
breast 996.69
cardiac 996.61
catheter NEC 996.69
central venous 999.31
Hickman 999.31
peripherally inserted central (PICC) 999.31
peritoneal 996.68
portacath (port-a-cath) 999.31 ●

Complications — *continued*
infection and inflammation — *continued*
due to any device, implant or graft classified to 996.0–996.5 — *continued*
catheter — *continued*
spinal 996.63
triple lumen 999.31
umbilical venous 999.31 ●
urinary, indwelling 996.64
vascular (arterial) (dialysis) (peripheral venous) NEC 996.62
ventricular shunt 996.63
central venous catheter 999.31
coronary artery bypass 996.61
electrodes
brain 996.63
heart 996.61
gastrointestinal NEC 996.69
genitourinary NEC 996.65
indwelling urinary catheter 996.64
heart assist device 996.61
heart valve 996.61
Hickman catheter 999.31
infusion pump 996.62
insulin pump 996.69
intrauterine contraceptive device 996.65
joint prosthesis, internal 996.66
ocular lens 996.69
orbital (implant) 996.69
orthopedic NEC 996.67
joint, internal 996.66
peripherally inserted central catheter (PICC) 999.31
portacath (port-a-cath) 999.31 ●
specified type NEC 996.69
triple lumen catheter 999.31
umbilical venous catheter 999.31 ●
urinary catheter, indwelling 996.64
ventricular shunt 996.63
infusion (procedure) 999.88 ▲
blood — *see* Complications, transfusion
infection NEC 999.39
sepsis NEC 999.39
inhalation therapy NEC 999.9
injection (procedure) 999.9
drug reaction (*see also* Reaction, drug) 995.27
infection NEC 999.39
sepsis NEC 999.39
serum (prophylactic) (therapeutic) — *see* Complications, vaccination
vaccine (any) — *see* Complications, vaccination
inoculation (any) — *see* Complications, vaccination
insulin pump 996.57
internal device (catheter) (electronic) (fixation) (prosthetic) (*see also* Complications, due to (presence of) any device, implant, or graft classified to 996.0–996.5 NEC)
mechanical — *see* Complications, mechanical
intestinal transplant (immune or nonimmune cause) 996.87
intraoperative bleeding or hemorrhage 998.11
intrauterine contraceptive device (*see also* Complications, contraceptive device) 996.76
with fetal damage affecting management of pregnancy 655.8 ☑
infection or inflammation 996.65
in utero procedure ●
fetal 679.1 ☑ ●
maternal 679.0 ☑ ●
jejunostomy 569.60

Complications — *continued*
kidney transplant (immune or nonimmune cause) 996.81
labor 669.9 ☑
specified condition NEC 669.8 ☑
liver transplant (immune or nonimmune cause) 996.82
lumbar puncture 349.0
mechanical
anastomosis — *see* Complications, mechanical, graft
artificial heart 996.09
bypass — *see* Complications, mechanical, graft
catheter NEC 996.59
cardiac 996.09
cystostomy 996.39
dialysis (hemodialysis) 996.1
peritoneal 996.56
during a procedure 998.2
urethral, indwelling 996.31
colostomy 569.62
device NEC 996.59
balloon (counterpulsation), intra-aortic 996.1
cardiac 996.00
automatic implantable defibrillator 996.04
long-term effect 429.4
specified NEC 996.09
contraceptive, intrauterine 996.32
counterpulsation, intra-aortic 996.1
fixation, external, with internal components 996.49
fixation, internal (nail, rod, plate) 996.40
genitourinary 996.30
specified NEC 996.39
insulin pump 996.57
nervous system 996.2
orthopedic, internal 996.40
prosthetic joint (*see also* Complications, mechanical, device, orthopedic, prosthetic, joint) 996.47
prosthetic NEC 996.59
joint (*see also* Complications, prosthetic joint) 996.47
articular bearing surface wear 996.46
aseptic loosening 996.41
breakage 996.43
dislocation 996.42
failure 996.43
fracture 996.43
around prosthetic 996.44
peri-prosthetic 996.44
instability 996.42
loosening 996.41
peri-prosthetic osteolysis 996.45
subluxation 996.42
wear 996.46
umbrella, vena cava 996.1
vascular 996.1
dorsal column stimulator 996.2
electrode NEC 996.59
brain 996.2
cardiac 996.01
spinal column 996.2
enterostomy 569.62
esophagostomy 530.87
fistula, arteriovenous, surgically created 996.1
gastrostomy 536.42
graft NEC 996.52
aortic (bifurcation) 996.1
aortocoronary bypass 996.03
blood vessel NEC 996.1
bone 996.49
cardiac 996.00
carotid artery bypass 996.1

☑ Additional Digit Required — Refer to the Tabular List for Digit Selection

Subterms under main terms may continue to next column or page

▶◀ Revised Text ● New Line ▲ Revised Code

Complications — *continued*
mechanical — *continued*
graft — *continued*
cartilage 996.49
corneal 996.51
coronary bypass 996.03
decellularized allodermis 996.55
genitourinary 996.30
specified NEC 996.39
muscle 996.49
nervous system 996.2
organ (immune or nonimmune cause) 996.80
heart 996.83
intestines 996.87
kidney 996.81
liver 996.82
lung 996.84
pancreas 996.86
specified NEC 996.89
orthopedic, internal 996.49
peripheral nerve 996.2
prosthetic NEC 996.59
skin 996.52
artificial 996.55
specified NEC 996.59
tendon 996.49
tissue NEC 996.52
tooth 996.59
ureter, without mention of resection 996.39
vascular 996.1
heart valve prosthesis 996.02
long-term effect 429.4
implant NEC 996.59
cardiac 996.00
automatic implantable defibrillator 996.04
long-term effect 429.4
specified NEC 996.09
electrode NEC 996.59
brain 996.2
cardiac 996.01
spinal column 996.2
genitourinary 996.30
nervous system 996.2
orthopedic, internal 996.49
prosthetic NEC 996.59
in
bile duct 996.59
breast 996.54
chin 996.59
eye
ocular lens 996.53
orbital globe 996.59
vascular 996.1
insulin pump 996.57
nonabsorbable surgical material 996.59
pacemaker NEC 996.59
brain 996.2
cardiac 996.01
nerve (phrenic) 996.2
patch — *see* Complications, mechanical, graft
prosthesis NEC 996.59
bile duct 996.59
breast 996.54
chin 996.59
ocular lens 996.53
reconstruction, vas deferens 996.39
reimplant NEC 996.59
extremity (*see also* Complications, reattached, extremity) 996.90
organ (*see also* Complications, transplant, organ, by site) 996.80
repair — *see* Complications, mechanical, graft
respirator [ventilator] V46.14
shunt NEC 996.59
arteriovenous, surgically created 996.1

Complications — *continued*
mechanical — *continued*
shunt — *continued*
ventricular (communicating) 996.2
stent NEC 996.59
tracheostomy 519.02
vas deferens reconstruction 996.39
ventilator [respirator] V46.14
medical care NEC 999.9
cardiac NEC 997.1
gastrointestinal NEC 997.4
nervous system NEC 997.00
peripheral vascular NEC 997.2
respiratory NEC 997.39 ▲
urinary NEC 997.5
vascular
mesenteric artery 997.71
other vessels 997.79
peripheral vessels 997.2
renal artery 997.72
nephrostomy 997.5
nervous system
device, implant, or graft NEC 349.1
mechanical 996.2
postoperative NEC 997.00
obstetric 669.9 ☑
procedure (instrumental) (manual) (surgical) 669.4 ☑
specified NEC 669.8 ☑
surgical wound 674.3 ☑
ocular lens implant NEC 996.79
infection or inflammation 996.69
mechanical 996.53
organ transplant — *see* Complications, transplant, organ, by site
orthopedic device, implant, or graft
internal (fixation) (nail) (plate) (rod) NEC 996.78
infection or inflammation 996.67
joint prosthesis 996.77
infection or inflammation 996.66
mechanical 996.40
pacemaker (cardiac) 996.72
infection or inflammation 996.61
mechanical 996.01
pancreas transplant (immune or nonimmune cause) 996.86
perfusion NEC 999.9
perineal repair (obstetrical) 674.3 ☑
disruption 674.2 ☑
pessary (uterus) (vagina) — *see* Complications, contraceptive device
phototherapy 990
postcystoscopic 997.5
postmastoidectomy NEC 383.30
postoperative — *see* Complications, surgical procedures
pregnancy NEC 646.9 ☑
affecting fetus or newborn 761.9
prosthetic device, internal (*see also* Complications, due to (presence of) any device, implant or graft classified to 996.0–996.5 NEC)
mechanical NEC (*see also* Complications, mechanical) 996.59
puerperium NEC (*see also* Puerperal) 674.9 ☑
puncture, spinal 349.0
pyelogram 997.5
radiation 990
radiotherapy 990
reattached
body part, except extremity 996.99
extremity (infection) (rejection) 996.90
arm(s) 996.94
digit(s) (hand) 996.93
foot 996.95
finger(s) 996.93
foot 996.95
forearm 996.91
hand 996.92
leg 996.96

Complications — *continued*
reattached — *continued*
extremity — *continued*
lower NEC 996.96
toe(s) 996.95
upper NEC 996.94
reimplant NEC (*see also* Complications, due to (presence of) any device, implant, or graft classified to 996.0–996.5 NEC)
bone marrow 996.85
extremity (*see also* Complications, reattached, extremity) 996.90
due to infection 996.90
mechanical — *see* Complications, mechanical, reimplant
organ (immune or nonimmune cause) (partial) (total) (*see also* Complications, transplant, organ, by site) 996.80
renal allograft 996.81
renal dialysis — *see* Complications, dialysis
respirator [ventilator], mechanical V46.14
respiratory 519.9
device, implant or graft NEC 996.79
infection or inflammation 996.69
mechanical 996.59
distress syndrome, adult, following trauma or surgery 518.5
insufficiency, acute, postoperative 518.5
postoperative NEC 997.39 ▲
therapy NEC 999.9
sedation during labor and delivery 668.9 ☑
affecting fetus or newborn 763.5
cardiac 668.1 ☑
central nervous system 668.2 ☑
pulmonary 668.0 ☑
specified type NEC 668.8 ☑
seroma (intraoperative) (postoperative) (noninfected) 998.13
infected 998.51
shunt (*see also* Complications, due to (presence of) any device, implant, or graft classified to 996.0–996.5 NEC)
mechanical — *see* Complications, mechanical, shunt
specified body system NEC
device, implant, or graft — *see* Complications, due to (presence of) any device, implant, or graft classified to 996.0–996.5 NEC
postoperative NEC 997.99
spinal puncture or tap 349.0
stomach banding 997.4
stomach stapling 997.4
stoma, external
gastrointestinal tract
colostomy 569.60
enterostomy 569.60
esophagostomy 530.87
infection 530.86
mechanical 530.87
gastrostomy 536.40
urinary tract 997.5
surgical procedures 998.9
accidental puncture or laceration 998.2
amputation stump (late) 997.60
anastomosis — *see* Complications, anastomosis
burst stitches or sutures (external) ▶(*see also* Dehiscence)◀ 998.32
internal 998.31
cardiac 997.1
long-term effect following cardiac surgery 429.4
cataract fragments in eye 998.82

Complications — *continued*
surgical procedures — *continued*
catheter device — *see* Complications, catheter device
cecostomy malfunction 569.62
colostomy malfunction 569.62
cystostomy malfunction 997.5
dehiscence (of incision) (external) ▶(*see also* Dehiscence)◀ 998.32
internal 998.31
dialysis NEC (*see also* Complications, dialysis) 999.9
disruption ▶(*see also* Dehiscence)◀
anastomosis (internal) — *see* Complications, mechanical, graft
internal suture (line) 998.31
wound (external) 998.32
internal 998.31
dumping syndrome (postgastrectomy) 564.2
elephantiasis or lymphedema 997.99
postmastectomy 457.0
emphysema (surgical) 998.81
enterostomy malfunction 569.62
esophagostomy malfunction 530.87
evisceration 998.32
fistula (persistent postoperative) 998.6
foreign body inadvertently left in wound (sponge) (suture) (swab) 998.4
from nonabsorbable surgical material (Dacron) (mesh) (permanent suture) (reinforcing) (Teflon) — *see* Complications, due to (presence of) any device, implant, or graft classified to 996.0–996.5 NEC
gastrointestinal NEC 997.4
gastrostomy malfunction 536.42
hematoma 998.12
hemorrhage 998.11
ileostomy malfunction 569.62
internal prosthetic device NEC (*see also* Complications, internal device) 996.70
hemolytic anemia 283.19
infection or inflammation 996.60
malfunction — *see* Complications, mechanical
mechanical complication — *see* Complications, mechanical
thrombus 996.70
jejunostomy malfunction 569.62
nervous system NEC 997.00
obstruction, internal anastomosis — *see* Complications, mechanical, graft
other body system NEC 997.99
peripheral vascular NEC 997.2
postcardiotomy syndrome 429.4
postcholecystectomy syndrome 576.0
postcommissurotomy syndrome 429.4
postgastrectomy dumping syndrome 564.2
postmastectomy lymphedema syndrome 457.0
postmastoidectomy 383.30
cholesteatoma, recurrent 383.32
cyst, mucosal 383.31
granulation 383.33
inflammation, chronic 383.33
postvagotomy syndrome 564.2
postvalvulotomy syndrome 429.4
reattached extremity (infection) (rejection) (*see also* Complications, reattached, extremity) 996.90
respiratory NEC 997.39 ▲

- **Complications** — *continued*
  - surgical procedures — *continued*
    - seroma 998.13
    - shock (endotoxic) (hypovolemic) (septic) 998.0
    - shunt, prosthetic (thrombus) (*see also* Complications, due to (presence of) any device, implant, or graft classified to 996.0–996.5 NEC)
      - hemolytic anemia 283.19
    - specified complication NEC 998.89
    - stitch abscess 998.59
    - transplant — *see* Complications, graft
    - ureterostomy malfunction 997.5
    - urethrostomy malfunction 997.5
    - urinary NEC 997.5
    - vascular
      - mesenteric artery 997.71
      - other vessels 997.79
      - peripheral vessels 997.2
      - renal artery 997.72
    - wound infection 998.59
  - therapeutic misadventure NEC 999.9
    - surgical treatment 998.9
  - tracheostomy 519.00
  - transfusion (blood) (lymphocytes) (plasma) NEC 999.89 ▲
    - acute lung injury (TRALI) 518.7
    - atrophy, liver, yellow, subacute (within 8 months of administration) — *see* Hepatitis, viral
    - bone marrow 996.85
    - embolism
      - air 999.1
      - thrombus 999.2
    - hemolysis NEC 999.89 ▲
      - bone marrow 996.85
    - hepatitis (serum) (type B) (within 8 months after administration) — *see* Hepatitis, viral
    - incompatibility reaction (ABO) (blood group) 999.6
      - Rh (factor) 999.7
    - infection 999.39
    - jaundice (serum) (within 8 months after administration) — *see* Hepatitis, viral
    - sepsis 999.39
    - shock or reaction NEC 999.89 ▲
      - bone marrow 996.85
    - subacute yellow atrophy of liver (within 8 months after administration) — *see* Hepatitis, viral
    - thromboembolism 999.2
  - transplant NEC (*see also* Complications, due to (presence of) any device, implant, or graft classified to 996.0–996.5 NEC)
    - bone marrow 996.85
    - organ (immune or nonimmune cause) (partial) (total) 996.80
      - bone marrow 996.85
      - heart 996.83
      - intestines 996.87
      - kidney 996.81
      - liver 996.82
      - lung 996.84
      - pancreas 996.86
      - specified NEC 996.89
  - trauma NEC (early) 958.8
  - ultrasound therapy NEC 999.9
  - umbilical cord
    - affecting fetus or newborn 762.6
    - complicating delivery 663.9 ☑
      - affecting fetus or newborn 762.6
      - specified type NEC 663.8 ☑
  - urethral catheter NEC 996.76
    - infection or inflammation 996.64
    - mechanical 996.31
  - urinary, postoperative NEC 997.5
  - vaccination 999.9
    - anaphylaxis NEC 999.4
    - cellulitis 999.39

- **Complications** — *continued*
  - vaccination — *continued*
    - encephalitis or encephalomyelitis 323.51
    - hepatitis (serum) (type B) (within 8 months after administration) — *see* Hepatitis, viral
    - infection (general) (local) NEC 999.39
    - jaundice (serum) (within 8 months after administration) — *see* Hepatitis, viral
    - meningitis 997.09 *[321.8]*
    - myelitis 323.52
    - protein sickness 999.5
    - reaction (allergic) 999.5
      - Herxheimer's 995.0
      - serum 999.5
    - sepsis 999.39
    - serum intoxication, sickness, rash, or other serum reaction NEC 999.5
    - shock (allergic) (anaphylactic) 999.4
    - subacute yellow atrophy of liver (within 8 months after administration) — *see* Hepatitis, viral
    - vaccinia (generalized) 999.0
      - localized 999.39
  - vascular
    - device, implant, or graft NEC 996.74
      - infection or inflammation 996.62
      - mechanical NEC 996.1
        - cardiac (*see also* Complications, mechanical, by type) 996.00
    - following infusion, perfusion, or transfusion 999.2
    - postoperative NEC 997.2
      - mesenteric artery 997.71
      - other vessels 997.79
      - peripheral vessels 997.2
      - renal artery 997.72
  - ventilation therapy NEC 999.9
  - ventilator [respirator], mechanical V46.14
- **Compound presentation, complicating delivery** 652.8 ☑
  - causing obstructed labor 660.0 ☑
- **Compressed air disease** 993.3
- **Compression**
  - with injury — *see* specific injury
  - arm NEC 354.9
  - artery 447.1
    - celiac, syndrome 447.4
  - brachial plexus 353.0
  - brain (stem) 348.4
    - due to
      - contusion, brain — *see* Contusion, brain
      - injury NEC (*see also* Hemorrhage, brain, traumatic)
        - birth — *see* Birth, injury, brain
      - laceration, brain — *see* Laceration, brain
    - osteopathic 739.0
  - bronchus 519.19
  - by cicatrix — *see* Cicatrix
  - cardiac 423.9
  - cauda equina 344.60
    - with neurogenic bladder 344.61
  - celiac (artery) (axis) 447.4
  - cerebral — *see* Compression, brain
  - cervical plexus 353.2
  - cord (umbilical) — *see* Compression, umbilical cord
  - cranial nerve 352.9
    - second 377.49
    - third (partial) 378.51
      - total 378.52
    - fourth 378.53
    - fifth 350.8

- **Compression** — *continued*
  - cranial nerve — *continued*
    - sixth 378.54
    - seventh 351.8
  - divers' squeeze 993.3
  - duodenum (external) (*see also* Obstruction, duodenum) 537.3
  - during birth 767.9
  - esophagus 530.3
    - congenital, external 750.3
  - Eustachian tube 381.63
  - facies (congenital) 754.0
  - fracture — *see* Fracture, by site
  - heart — *see* Disease, heart
  - intestine (*see also* Obstruction, intestine) 560.9
    - with hernia — *see* Hernia, by site, with obstruction
  - laryngeal nerve, recurrent 478.79
  - leg NEC 355.8
  - lower extremity NEC 355.8
  - lumbosacral plexus 353.1
  - lung 518.89
  - lymphatic vessel 457.1
  - medulla — *see* Compression, brain
  - nerve NEC (*see also* Disorder, nerve)
    - arm NEC 354.9
    - autonomic nervous system (*see also* Neuropathy, peripheral, autonomic) 337.9
    - axillary 353.0
    - cranial NEC 352.9
    - due to displacement of intervertebral disc 722.2
      - with myelopathy 722.70
      - cervical 722.0
        - with myelopathy 722.71
      - lumbar, lumbosacral 722.10
        - with myelopathy 722.73
      - thoracic, thoracolumbar 722.11
        - with myelopathy 722.72
    - iliohypogastric 355.79
    - ilioinguinal 355.79
    - leg NEC 355.8
    - lower extremity NEC 355.8
    - median (in carpal tunnel) 354.0
    - obturator 355.79
    - optic 377.49
    - plantar 355.6
    - posterior tibial (in tarsal tunnel) 355.5
    - root (by scar tissue) NEC 724.9
      - cervical NEC 723.4
      - lumbar NEC 724.4
      - lumbosacral 724.4
      - thoracic 724.4
    - saphenous 355.79
    - sciatic (acute) 355.0
    - sympathetic 337.9
    - traumatic — *see* Injury, nerve
    - ulnar 354.2
    - upper extremity NEC 354.9
  - peripheral — *see* Compression, nerve
  - spinal (cord) (old or nontraumatic) 336.9
    - by displacement of intervertebral disc — *see* Displacement, intervertebral disc
    - nerve
      - root NEC 724.9
        - postoperative 722.80
          - cervical region 722.81
          - lumbar region 722.83
          - thoracic region 722.82
        - traumatic — *see* Injury, nerve, spinal
      - traumatic — *see* Injury, nerve, spinal
    - spondylogenic 721.91
      - cervical 721.1
      - lumbar, lumbosacral 721.42
      - thoracic 721.41
    - traumatic (*see also* Injury, spinal, by site)

- **Compression** — *continued*
  - spinal — *continued*
    - traumatic (*see also* Injury, spinal, by site) — *continued*
      - with fracture, vertebra — *see* Fracture, vertebra, by site, with spinal cord injury
  - spondylogenic — *see* Compression, spinal cord, spondylogenic
  - subcostal nerve (syndrome) 354.8
  - sympathetic nerve NEC 337.9
  - syndrome 958.5
  - thorax 512.8
    - iatrogenic 512.1
    - postoperative 512.1
  - trachea 519.19
    - congenital 748.3
  - ulnar nerve (by scar tissue) 354.2
  - umbilical cord
    - affecting fetus or newborn 762.5
      - cord prolapsed 762.4
    - complicating delivery 663.2 ☑
      - cord around neck 663.1 ☑
      - cord prolapsed 663.0 ☑
  - upper extremity NEC 354.9
  - ureter 593.3
  - urethra — *see* Stricture, urethra
  - vein 459.2
  - vena cava (inferior) (superior) 459.2
  - vertebral NEC — *see* Compression, spinal (cord)
- **Compulsion, compulsive**
  - eating 307.51
  - neurosis (obsessive) 300.3
  - personality 301.4
  - states (mixed) 300.3
  - swearing 300.3
    - in Gilles de la Tourette's syndrome 307.23
  - tics and spasms 307.22
  - water drinking NEC (syndrome) 307.9
- **Concato's disease** (pericardial polyserositis) 423.2
  - peritoneal 568.82
  - pleural — *see* Pleurisy
- **Concavity, chest wall** 738.3
- **Concealed**
  - hemorrhage NEC 459.0
  - penis 752.65
- **Concentric fading** 368.12
- **Concern** (normal) **about sick person in family** V61.49
- **Concrescence** (teeth) 520.2
- **Concretio cordis** 423.1
  - rheumatic 393
- **Concretion** — *see also* Calculus
  - appendicular 543.9
  - canaliculus 375.57
  - clitoris 624.8
  - conjunctiva 372.54
  - eyelid 374.56
  - intestine (impaction) (obstruction) 560.39
  - lacrimal (passages) 375.57
  - prepuce (male) 605
    - female (clitoris) 624.8
  - salivary gland (any) 527.5
  - seminal vesicle 608.89
  - stomach 537.89
  - tonsil 474.8
- **Concussion** (current) 850.9
  - with
    - loss of consciousness 850.5
      - brief (less than one hour)
        - 30 minutes or less 850.11
        - 31-59 minutes 850.12
      - moderate (1-24 hours) 850.2
      - prolonged (more than 24 hours) (with complete recovery) (with return to pre-existing conscious level) 850.3
        - without return to pre-existing conscious level 850.4

Concussion — *continued*
- with — *continued*
  - mental confusion or disorientation (without loss of consciousness) 850.0
    - with loss of consciousness — *see* Concussion, with, loss of consciousness
- without loss of consciousness 850.0
- blast (air) (hydraulic) (immersion) (underwater) 869.0
  - with open wound into cavity 869.1
  - abdomen or thorax — *see* Injury, internal, by site
  - brain — *see* Concussion, brain
  - ear (acoustic nerve trauma) 951.5
    - with perforation, tympanic membrane — *see* Wound, open, ear drum
  - thorax — *see* Injury, internal, intrathoracic organs NEC
- brain or cerebral (without skull fracture) 850.9
  - with
    - loss of consciousness 850.5
      - brief (less than one hour)
        - 30 minutes or less 850.11
        - 31-59 minutes 850.12
      - moderate (1-24 hours) 850.2
      - prolonged (more than 24 hours) (with complete recovery) (with return to pre-existing conscious level) 850.3
        - without return to pre-existing conscious level 850.4
    - mental confusion or disorientation (without loss of consciousness) 850.0
      - with loss of consciousness — *see* Concussion, brain, with, loss of consciousness
    - skull fracture — *see* Fracture, skull, by site
  - without loss of consciousness 850.0
- cauda equina 952.4
- cerebral — *see* Concussion, brain
- conus medullaris (spine) 952.4
- hydraulic — *see* Concussion, blast
- internal organs — *see* Injury, internal, by site
- labyrinth — *see* Injury, intracranial
- ocular 921.3
- osseous labyrinth — *see* Injury, intracranial
- spinal (cord) (*see also* Injury, spinal, by site)
  - due to
    - broken
      - back — *see* Fracture, vertebra, by site, with spinal cord injury
      - neck — *see* Fracture, vertebra, cervical, with spinal cord injury
    - fracture, fracture dislocation, or compression fracture of spine or vertebra — *see* Fracture, vertebra, by site, with spinal cord injury
- syndrome 310.2
- underwater blast — *see* Concussion, blast

Condition — *see also* Disease
- fetal hematologic 678.0 ☑ ●
- psychiatric 298.9
- respiratory NEC 519.9
  - acute or subacute NEC 519.9
    - due to
      - external agent 508.9
        - specified type NEC 508.8

Condition — *see also* Disease — *continued*
- respiratory — *continued*
  - acute or subacute — *continued*
    - due to — *continued*
      - fumes or vapors (chemical) (inhalation) 506.3
      - radiation 508.0
  - chronic NEC 519.9
    - due to
      - external agent 508.9
        - specified type NEC 508.8
      - fumes or vapors (chemical) (inhalation) 506.4
      - radiation 508.1
  - due to
    - external agent 508.9
      - specified type NEC 508.8
    - fumes or vapors (chemical) (inhalation) 506.9

Conduct disturbance — *see also* Disturbance, conduct 312.9
- adjustment reaction 309.3
- hyperkinetic 314.2

Condyloma NEC 078.11 ▲
- acuminatum 078.11
- gonorrheal 098.0
- latum 091.3
- syphilitic 091.3
  - congenital 090.0
- venereal, syphilitic 091.3

Confinement — *see* Delivery

Conflagration — *see also* Burn, by site
- asphyxia (by inhalation of smoke, gases, fumes, or vapors) 987.9
  - specified agent — *see* Table of Drugs and Chemicals

Conflict
- family V61.9
  - specified circumstance NEC V61.8
- interpersonal NEC V62.81
- marital V61.10
  - involving
    - divorce V61.03 ●
    - estrangement V61.09 ●
- parent-child V61.20
- partner V61.10

Confluent — *see* condition

Confusional arousals 327.41

Confusion, confused (mental) (state) — *see also* State, confusional 298.9
- acute 293.0
- epileptic 293.0
- postoperative 293.9
- psychogenic 298.2
- reactive (from emotional stress, psychological trauma) 298.2
- subacute 293.1

Congelation 991.9

Congenital — *see also* condition
- aortic septum 747.29
- generalized fibromatosis (CGF) 759.89
- intrinsic factor deficiency 281.0
- malformation — *see* Anomaly

Congestion, congestive
- asphyxia, newborn 768.9
- bladder 596.8
- bowel 569.89
- brain (*see also* Disease, cerebrovascular NEC) 437.8
  - malarial 084.9
- breast 611.79
- bronchi 519.19
- bronchial tube 519.19
- catarrhal 472.0
- cerebral — *see* Congestion, brain
- cerebrospinal — *see* Congestion, brain
- chest 786.9
- chill 780.99
  - malarial (*see also* Malaria) 084.6
- circulatory NEC 459.9
- conjunctiva 372.71
- due to disturbance of circulation 459.9
- duodenum 537.3
- enteritis — *see* Enteritis

Congestion, congestive — *continued*
- eye 372.71
- fibrosis syndrome (pelvic) 625.5
- gastroenteritis — *see* Enteritis
- general 799.89
- glottis 476.0
- heart (*see also* Failure, heart) 428.0
- hepatic 573.0
- hypostatic (lung) 514
- intestine 569.89
- intracranial — *see* Congestion, brain
- kidney 593.89
- labyrinth 386.50
- larynx 476.0
- liver 573.0
- lung 786.9
  - active or acute (*see also* Pneumonia) 486
    - congenital 770.0
  - chronic 514
  - hypostatic 514
  - idiopathic, acute 518.5
  - passive 514
- malaria, malarial (brain) (fever) (*see also* Malaria) 084.6
- medulla — *see* Congestion, brain
- nasal 478.19
- nose 478.19
- orbit, orbital 376.33
  - inflammatory (chronic) 376.10
    - acute 376.00
- ovary 620.8
- pancreas 577.8
- pelvic, female 625.5
- pleural 511.0
- prostate (active) 602.1
- pulmonary — *see* Congestion, lung
- renal 593.89
- retina 362.89
- seminal vesicle 608.89
- spinal cord 336.1
- spleen 289.51
  - chronic 289.51
- stomach 537.89
- trachea 464.11
- urethra 599.84
- uterus 625.5
  - with subinvolution 621.1
- viscera 799.89

Congestive — *see* Congestion

Conical
- cervix 622.6
- cornea 371.60
- teeth 520.2

Conjoined twins 759.4
- causing disproportion (fetopelvic) 678.1 ☑ ▲
- fetal 678.1 ☑ ●

Conjugal maladjustment V61.10
- involving
  - divorce V61.03 ●
  - estrangement V61.09 ●

Conjunctiva — *see* condition

Conjunctivitis (exposure) (infectious) (nondiphtheritic) (pneumococcal) (pustular) (staphylococcal) (streptococcal) NEC 372.30
- actinic 370.24
- acute 372.00
  - atopic 372.05
  - contagious 372.03
  - follicular 372.02
  - hemorrhagic (viral) 077.4
- adenoviral (acute) 077.3
- allergic (chronic) 372.14
  - with hay fever 372.05
- anaphylactic 372.05
- angular 372.03
- Apollo (viral) 077.4
- atopic 372.05
- blennorrhagic (neonatorum) 098.40
- catarrhal 372.03
- chemical 372.01
  - allergic 372.05
  - meaning corrosion — *see* Burn, conjunctiva

Conjunctivitis — *continued*
- chlamydial 077.98
  - due to
    - Chlamydia trachomatis — *see* Trachoma
    - paratrachoma 077.0
- chronic 372.10
  - allergic 372.14
  - follicular 372.12
  - simple 372.11
  - specified type NEC 372.14
  - vernal 372.13
- diphtheritic 032.81
- due to
  - dust 372.05
  - enterovirus type 70 077.4
  - erythema multiforme 695.10 *[372.33]* ▲
  - filariasis (*see also* Filariasis) 125.9 *[372.15]*
  - mucocutaneous
    - disease NEC 372.33
    - leishmaniasis 085.5 *[372.15]*
  - Reiter's disease 099.3 *[372.33]*
  - syphilis 095.8 *[372.10]*
  - toxoplasmosis (acquired) 130.1
    - congenital (active) 771.2
  - trachoma — *see* Trachoma
- dust 372.05
- eczematous 370.31
- epidemic 077.1
  - hemorrhagic 077.4
- follicular (acute) 372.02
  - adenoviral (acute) 077.3
  - chronic 372.12
- glare 370.24
- gonococcal (neonatorum) 098.40
- granular (trachomatous) 076.1
  - late effect 139.1
- hemorrhagic (acute) (epidemic) 077.4
- herpetic (simplex) 054.43
  - zoster 053.21
- inclusion 077.0
- infantile 771.6
- influenzal 372.03
- Koch-Weeks 372.03
- light 372.05
- medicamentosa 372.05
- membranous 372.04
- meningococcic 036.89
- Morax-Axenfeld 372.02
- mucopurulent NEC 372.03
- neonatal 771.6
  - gonococcal 098.40
- Newcastle's 077.8
- nodosa 360.14
- of Beal 077.3
- parasitic 372.15
  - filariasis (*see also* Filariasis) 125.9 *[372.15]*
  - mucocutaneous leishmaniasis 085.5 *[372.15]*
- Parinaud's 372.02
- petrificans 372.39
- phlyctenular 370.31
- pseudomembranous 372.04
  - diphtheritic 032.81
- purulent 372.03
- Reiter's 099.3 *[372.33]*
- rosacea 695.3 *[372.31]*
- serous 372.01
  - viral 077.99
- simple chronic 372.11
- specified NEC 372.39
- sunlamp 372.04
- swimming pool 077.0
- trachomatous (follicular) 076.1
  - acute 076.0
  - late effect 139.1
- traumatic NEC 372.39
- tuberculous (*see also* Tuberculosis) 017.3 ☑ *[370.31]*
- tularemic 021.3
- tularensis 021.3
- vernal 372.13
  - limbar 372.13 *[370.32]*

- **Conjunctivitis** — *continued*
  - viral 077.99
    - acute hemorrhagic 077.4
    - specified NEC 077.8
- **Conjunctivochalasis** 372.81
- **Conjunctoblepharitis** — *see* Conjunctivitis
- **Connective tissue** — *see* condition
- **Conn (-Louis) syndrome** (primary aldosteronism) 255.12
- **Conradi (-Hünermann) syndrome or disease** (chondrodysplasia calcificans congenita) 756.59
- **Consanguinity** V19.7
- **Consecutive** — *see* condition
- **Consolidated lung** (base) — *see* Pneumonia, lobar
- **Constipation** 564.00
  - atonic 564.09
  - drug induced
    - correct substance properly administered 564.09
    - overdose or wrong substance given or taken 977.9
      - specified drug — *see* Table of Drugs and Chemicals
  - neurogenic 564.09
  - other specified NEC 564.09
  - outlet dysfunction 564.02
  - psychogenic 306.4
  - simple 564.00
  - slow transit 564.01
  - spastic 564.09
- **Constitutional** — *see also* condition
  - arterial hypotension (*see also* Hypotension) 458.9
  - obesity 278.00
    - morbid 278.01
  - psychopathic state 301.9
  - short stature in childhood 783.43
  - state, developmental V21.9
    - specified development NEC V21.8
  - substandard 301.6
- **Constitutionally substandard** 301.6
- **Constriction**
  - anomalous, meningeal bands or folds 742.8
  - aortic arch (congenital) 747.10
  - asphyxiation or suffocation by 994.7
  - bronchus 519.19
  - canal, ear (*see also* Stricture, ear canal, acquired) 380.50
  - duodenum 537.3
  - gallbladder (*see also* Obstruction, gallbladder) 575.2
    - congenital 751.69
  - intestine (*see also* Obstruction, intestine) 560.9
  - larynx 478.74
    - congenital 748.3
  - meningeal bands or folds, anomalous 742.8
  - organ or site, congenital NEC — *see* Atresia
  - prepuce (congenital) 605
  - pylorus 537.0
    - adult hypertrophic 537.0
    - congenital or infantile 750.5
    - newborn 750.5
  - ring (uterus) 661.4 ☑
    - affecting fetus or newborn 763.7
  - spastic (*see also* Spasm)
    - ureter 593.3
    - urethra — *see* Stricture, urethra
  - stomach 537.89
  - ureter 593.3
  - urethra — *see* Stricture, urethra
  - visual field (functional) (peripheral) 368.45
- **Constrictive** — *see* condition
- **Consultation**
  - without complaint or sickness V65.9
    - feared complaint unfounded V65.5
    - specified reason NEC V65.8
  - medical (*see also* Counseling, medical)
  - specified reason NEC V65.8
- **Consumption** — *see* Tuberculosis
- **Contact**
  - with
    - AIDS virus V01.79
    - anthrax V01.81
    - cholera V01.0
    - communicable disease V01.9
      - specified type NEC V01.89
      - viral NEC V01.79
    - Escherichia coli (E. coli) V01.83
    - German measles V01.4
    - gonorrhea V01.6
    - HIV V01.79
    - human immunodeficiency virus V01.79
    - meningococcus V01.84
    - parasitic disease NEC V01.89
    - poliomyelitis V01.2
    - rabies V01.5
    - rubella V01.4
    - SARS-associated coronavirus V01.82
    - smallpox V01.3
    - syphilis V01.6
    - tuberculosis V01.1
    - varicella V01.71
    - venereal disease V01.6
    - viral disease NEC V01.79
  - dermatitis — *see* Dermatitis
- **Contamination, food** — *see also* Poisoning, food 005.9
- **Contraception, contraceptive**
  - advice NEC V25.09
    - family planning V25.09
    - fitting of diaphragm V25.02
    - prescribing or use of
      - oral contraceptive agent V25.01
      - specified agent NEC V25.02
  - counseling NEC V25.09
    - emergency V25.03
    - family planning V25.09
    - fitting of diaphragm V25.02
    - prescribing or use of
      - oral contraceptive agent V25.01
        - emergency V25.03
        - postcoital V25.03
      - specified agent NEC V25.02
  - device (in situ) V45.59
    - causing menorrhagia 996.76
    - checking V25.42
    - complications 996.32
    - insertion V25.1
    - intrauterine V45.51
    - reinsertion V25.42
    - removal V25.42
    - subdermal V45.52
  - fitting of diaphragm V25.02
  - insertion
    - intrauterine contraceptive device V25.1
    - subdermal implantable V25.5
  - maintenance V25.40
    - examination V25.40
      - oral contraceptive V25.41
      - specified method NEC V25.49
      - subdermal implantable V25.43
        - intrauterine device V25.42
    - intrauterine device V25.42
    - oral contraceptive V25.41
    - specified method NEC V25.49
    - subdermal implantable V25.43
  - management NEC V25.49
  - prescription
    - oral contraceptive agent V25.01
      - emergency V25.03
      - postcoital V25.03
      - repeat V25.41
    - specified agent NEC V25.02
      - repeat V25.49
  - sterilization V25.2
  - surveillance V25.40
    - intrauterine device V25.42
    - oral contraceptive agent V25.41
      - subdermal implantable V25.43
    - specified method NEC V25.49
- **Contraction, contracture, contracted**
  - Achilles tendon (*see also* Short, tendon, Achilles) 727.81
  - anus 564.89
  - axilla 729.90 ▲
  - bile duct (*see also* Disease, biliary) 576.8
  - bladder 596.8
    - neck or sphincter 596.0
  - bowel (*see also* Obstruction, intestine) 560.9
  - Braxton Hicks 644.1 ☑
  - breast implant, capsular 611.83 ●
  - bronchus 519.19
  - burn (old) — *see* Cicatrix
  - capsular, of breast implant 611.83 ●
  - cecum (*see also* Obstruction, intestine) 560.9
  - cervix (*see also* Stricture, cervix) 622.4
    - congenital 752.49
  - cicatricial — *see* Cicatrix
  - colon (*see also* Obstruction, intestine) 560.9
  - conjunctiva trachomatous, active 076.1
    - late effect 139.1
  - Dupuytren's 728.6
  - eyelid 374.41
  - eye socket (after enucleation) 372.64
  - face 729.90 ▲
  - fascia (lata) (postural) 728.89
    - Dupuytren's 728.6
    - palmar 728.6
    - plantar 728.71
  - finger NEC 736.29
    - congenital 755.59
    - joint (*see also* Contraction, joint) 718.44
  - flaccid, paralytic
    - joint (*see also* Contraction, joint) 718.4 ☑
    - muscle 728.85
      - ocular 378.50
  - gallbladder (*see also* Obstruction, gallbladder) 575.2
  - hamstring 728.89
    - tendon 727.81
  - heart valve — *see* Endocarditis
  - Hicks' 644.1 ☑
  - hip (*see also* Contraction, joint) 718.4 ☑
  - hourglass
    - bladder 596.8
      - congenital 753.8
    - gallbladder (*see also* Obstruction, gallbladder) 575.2
      - congenital 751.69
    - stomach 536.8
      - congenital 750.7
      - psychogenic 306.4
    - uterus 661.4 ☑
      - affecting fetus or newborn 763.7
  - hysterical 300.11
  - infantile (*see also* Epilepsy) 345.6 ☑
  - internal os (*see also* Stricture, cervix) 622.4
  - intestine (*see also* Obstruction, intestine) 560.9
  - joint (abduction) (acquired) (adduction) (flexion) (rotation) 718.40
    - ankle 718.47
    - congenital NEC 755.8
      - generalized or multiple 754.89
        - lower limb joints 754.89
      - hip (*see also* Subluxation, congenital, hip) 754.32
      - lower limb (including pelvic girdle) not involving hip 754.89
      - upper limb (including shoulder girdle) 755.59
    - elbow 718.42
    - foot 718.47
    - hand 718.44
    - hip 718.45
    - hysterical 300.11

Contraction, contracture, contracted — *continued*

  - joint — *continued*
    - knee 718.46
    - multiple sites 718.49
    - pelvic region 718.45
    - shoulder (region) 718.41
    - specified site NEC 718.48
    - wrist 718.43
  - kidney (granular) (secondary) (*see also* Sclerosis, renal) 587
    - congenital 753.3
    - hydronephritic 591
    - pyelonephritic (*see also* Pyelitis, chronic) 590.00
    - tuberculous (*see also* Tuberculosis) 016.0 ☑
  - ligament 728.89
    - congenital 756.89
  - liver — *see* Cirrhosis, liver
  - muscle (postinfectional) (postural) NEC 728.85
    - congenital 756.89
      - sternocleidomastoid 754.1
    - extraocular 378.60
    - eye (extrinsic) (*see also* Strabismus) 378.9
      - paralytic (*see also* Strabismus, paralytic) 378.50
    - flaccid 728.85
    - hysterical 300.11
    - ischemic (Volkmann's) 958.6
    - paralytic 728.85
    - posttraumatic 958.6
    - psychogenic 306.0
      - specified as conversion reaction 300.11
  - myotonic 728.85
  - neck (*see also* Torticollis) 723.5
    - congenital 754.1
    - psychogenic 306.0
  - ocular muscle (*see also* Strabismus) 378.9
    - paralytic (*see also* Strabismus, paralytic) 378.50
  - organ or site, congenital NEC — *see* Atresia
  - outlet (pelvis) — *see* Contraction, pelvis
  - palmar fascia 728.6
  - paralytic
    - joint (*see also* Contraction, joint) 718.4 ☑
    - muscle 728.85
      - ocular (*see also* Strabismus, paralytic) 378.50
  - pelvis (acquired) (general) 738.6
    - affecting fetus or newborn 763.1
    - complicating delivery 653.1 ☑
      - causing obstructed labor 660.1 ☑
      - generally contracted 653.1 ☑
        - causing obstructed labor 660.1 ☑
      - inlet 653.2 ☑
        - causing obstructed labor 660.1 ☑
      - midpelvic 653.8 ☑
        - causing obstructed labor 660.1 ☑
      - midplane 653.8 ☑
        - causing obstructed labor 660.1 ☑
      - outlet 653.3 ☑
        - causing obstructed labor 660.1 ☑
  - plantar fascia 728.71
  - premature
    - atrial 427.61
    - auricular 427.61
    - auriculoventricular 427.61
    - heart (junctional) (nodal) 427.60
    - supraventricular 427.61
    - ventricular 427.69
  - prostate 602.8
  - pylorus (*see also* Pylorospasm) 537.81

- **Contraction, contracture, contracted** — *continued*
  - rectosigmoid (*see also* Obstruction, intestine) 560.9
  - rectum, rectal (sphincter) 564.89
    - psychogenic 306.4
  - ring (Bandl's) 661.4 ☑
    - affecting fetus or newborn 763.7
  - scar — *see* Cicatrix
  - sigmoid (*see also* Obstruction, intestine) 560.9
  - socket, eye 372.64
  - spine (*see also* Curvature, spine) 737.9
  - stomach 536.8
    - hourglass 536.8
      - congenital 750.7
    - psychogenic 306.4
  - tendon (sheath) (*see also* Short, tendon) 727.81
  - toe 735.8
  - ureterovesical orifice (postinfectional) 593.3
  - urethra 599.84
  - uterus 621.8
    - abnormal 661.9 ☑
      - affecting fetus or newborn 763.7
    - clonic, hourglass or tetanic 661.4 ☑
      - affecting fetus or newborn 763.7
    - dyscoordinate 661.4 ☑
      - affecting fetus or newborn 763.7
    - hourglass 661.4 ☑
      - affecting fetus or newborn 763.7
    - hypotonic NEC 661.2 ☑
      - affecting fetus or newborn 763.7
    - incoordinate 661.4 ☑
      - affecting fetus or newborn 763.7
    - inefficient or poor 661.2 ☑
      - affecting fetus or newborn 763.7
    - irregular 661.2 ☑
      - affecting fetus or newborn 763.7
    - tetanic 661.4 ☑
      - affecting fetus or newborn 763.7
  - vagina (outlet) 623.2
  - vesical 596.8
    - neck or urethral orifice 596.0
  - visual field, generalized 368.45
  - Volkmann's (ischemic) 958.6
- **Contusion** (skin surface intact) 924.9
  - with
    - crush injury — *see* Crush
    - dislocation — *see* Dislocation, by site
    - fracture — *see* Fracture, by site
    - internal injury (*see also* Injury, internal, by site)
      - heart — *see* Contusion, cardiac
      - kidney — *see* Contusion, kidney
      - liver — *see* Contusion, liver
      - lung — *see* Contusion, lung
      - spleen — *see* Contusion, spleen
    - intracranial injury — *see* Injury, intracranial
    - nerve injury — *see* Injury, nerve
    - open wound — *see* Wound, open, by site
  - abdomen, abdominal (muscle) (wall) 922.2
    - organ(s) NEC 868.00
  - adnexa, eye NEC 921.9
  - ankle 924.21
    - with other parts of foot 924.20
  - arm 923.9
    - lower (with elbow) 923.10
    - upper 923.03
      - with shoulder or axillary region 923.09
  - auditory canal (external) (meatus) (and other part(s) of neck, scalp, or face, except eye) 920
  - auricle, ear (and other part(s) of neck, scalp, or face except eye) 920
  - axilla 923.02
    - with shoulder or upper arm 923.09
  - back 922.31
- **Contusion** — *continued*
  - bone NEC 924.9
  - brain (cerebral) (membrane) (with hemorrhage) 851.8 ☑

> *Note — Use the following fifth-digit subclassification with categories 851–854:*
>
> *0 unspecified state of consciousness*
>
> *1 with no loss of consciousness*
>
> *2 with brief [less than one hour] loss of consciousness*
>
> *3 with moderate [1–24 hours] loss of consciousness*
>
> *4 with prolonged [more than 24 hours] loss of consciousness and return to pre-existing conscious level*
>
> *5 with prolonged [more than 24 hours] loss of consciousness, without return to pre-existing conscious level*
>
> *Use fifth-digit 5 to designate when a patient is unconscious and dies before regaining consciousness, regardless of the duration of the loss of consciousness*
>
> *6 with loss of consciousness of unspecified duration*
>
> *9 with concussion, unspecified*

  - brain — *continued*
    - with
      - open intracranial wound 851.9 ☑
      - skull fracture — *see* Fracture, skull, by site
    - cerebellum 851.4 ☑
      - with open intracranial wound 851.5 ☑
    - cortex 851.0 ☑
      - with open intracranial wound 851.1 ☑
    - occipital lobe 851.4 ☑
      - with open intracranial wound 851.5 ☑
    - stem 851.4 ☑
      - with open intracranial wound 851.5 ☑
  - breast 922.0
  - brow (and other part(s) of neck, scalp, or face, except eye) 920
  - buttock 922.32
  - canthus 921.1
  - cardiac 861.01
    - with open wound into thorax 861.11
  - cauda equina (spine) 952.4
  - cerebellum — *see* Contusion, brain, cerebellum
  - cerebral — *see* Contusion, brain
  - cheek(s) (and other part(s) of neck, scalp, or face, except eye) 920
  - chest (wall) 922.1
  - chin (and other part(s) of neck, scalp, or face, except eye) 920
  - clitoris 922.4
  - conjunctiva 921.1
  - conus medullaris (spine) 952.4
  - cornea 921.3
  - corpus cavernosum 922.4
  - cortex (brain) (cerebral) — *see* Contusion, brain, cortex
  - costal region 922.1
  - ear (and other part(s) of neck, scalp, or face except eye) 920
  - elbow 923.11
    - with forearm 923.10
  - epididymis 922.4
  - epigastric region 922.2
  - eye NEC 921.9
  - eyeball 921.3
  - eyelid(s) (and periocular area) 921.1
  - face (and neck, or scalp, any part, except eye) 920
  - femoral triangle 922.2
  - fetus or newborn 772.6
  - finger(s) (nail) (subungual) 923.3
  - flank 922.2
  - foot (with ankle) (excluding toe(s)) 924.20
  - forearm (and elbow) 923.10
  - forehead (and other part(s) of neck, scalp, or face, except eye) 920
  - genital organs, external 922.4
  - globe (eye) 921.3
  - groin 922.2
  - gum(s) (and other part(s) of neck, scalp, or face, except eye) 920
  - hand(s) (except fingers alone) 923.20
  - head (any part, except eye) (and face) (and neck) 920
  - heart — *see* Contusion, cardiac
  - heel 924.20
  - hip 924.01
    - with thigh 924.00
  - iliac region 922.2
  - inguinal region 922.2
  - internal organs (abdomen, chest, or pelvis) NEC — *see* Injury, internal, by site
  - interscapular region 922.33
  - iris (eye) 921.3
  - kidney 866.01
    - with open wound into cavity 866.11
  - knee 924.11
    - with lower leg 924.10
  - labium (majus) (minus) 922.4
  - lacrimal apparatus, gland, or sac 921.1
  - larynx (and other part(s) of neck, scalp, or face, except eye) 920
  - late effect — *see* Late, effects (of), contusion
  - leg 924.5
    - lower (with knee) 924.10
  - lens 921.3
  - lingual (and other part(s) of neck, scalp, or face, except eye) 920
  - lip(s) (and other part(s) of neck, scalp, or face, except eye) 920
  - liver 864.01
    - with
      - laceration — *see* Laceration, liver
      - open wound into cavity 864.11
  - lower extremity 924.5
    - multiple sites 924.4
  - lumbar region 922.31
  - lung 861.21
    - with open wound into thorax 861.31
  - malar region (and other part(s) of neck, scalp, or face, except eye) 920
  - mandibular joint (and other part(s) of neck, scalp, or face, except eye) 920
  - mastoid region (and other part(s) of neck, scalp, or face, except eye) 920
  - membrane, brain — *see* Contusion, brain
  - midthoracic region 922.1
  - mouth (and other part(s) of neck, scalp, or face, except eye) 920
  - multiple sites (not classifiable to same three-digit category) 924.8
    - lower limb 924.4
    - trunk 922.8
    - upper limb 923.8
  - muscle NEC 924.9
  - myocardium — *see* Contusion, cardiac
  - nasal (septum) (and other part(s) of neck, scalp, or face, except eye) 920
  - neck (and scalp or face, any part, except eye) 920
  - nerve — *see* Injury, nerve, by site
  - nose (and other part(s) of neck, scalp, or face, except eye) 920
  - occipital region (scalp) (and neck or face, except eye) 920
    - lobe — *see* Contusion, brain, occipital lobe
  - orbit (region) (tissues) 921.2
  - palate (soft) (and other part(s) of neck, scalp, or face, except eye) 920
  - parietal region (scalp) (and neck, or face, except eye) 920
    - lobe — *see* Contusion, brain
  - penis 922.4
  - pericardium — *see* Contusion, cardiac
  - perineum 922.4
  - periocular area 921.1
  - pharynx (and other part(s) of neck, scalp, or face, except eye) 920
  - popliteal space (*see also* Contusion, knee) 924.11
  - prepuce 922.4
  - pubic region 922.4
  - pudenda 922.4
  - pulmonary — *see* Contusion, lung
  - quadriceps femoralis 924.00
  - rib cage 922.1
  - sacral region 922.32
  - salivary ducts or glands (and other part(s) of neck, scalp, or face, except eye) 920
  - scalp (and neck, or face any part, except eye) 920
  - scapular region 923.01
    - with shoulder or upper arm 923.09
  - sclera (eye) 921.3
  - scrotum 922.4
  - shoulder 923.00
    - with upper arm or axillar regions 923.09
  - skin NEC 924.9
  - skull 920
  - spermatic cord 922.4
  - spinal cord (*see also* Injury, spinal, by site)
    - cauda equina 952.4
    - conus medullaris 952.4
  - spleen 865.01
    - with open wound into cavity 865.11
  - sternal region 922.1
  - stomach — *see* Injury, internal, stomach
  - subconjunctival 921.1
  - subcutaneous NEC 924.9
  - submaxillary region (and other part(s) of neck, scalp, or face, except eye) 920
  - submental region (and other part(s) of neck, scalp, or face, except eye) 920
  - subperiosteal NEC 924.9
  - supraclavicular fossa (and other part(s) of neck, scalp, or face, except eye) 920
  - supraorbital (and other part(s) of neck, scalp, or face, except eye) 920
  - temple (region) (and other part(s) of neck, scalp, or face, except eye) 920
  - testis 922.4
  - thigh (and hip) 924.00
  - thorax 922.1
    - organ — *see* Injury, internal, intrathoracic
  - throat (and other part(s) of neck, scalp, or face, except eye) 920
  - thumb(s) (nail) (subungual) 923.3
  - toe(s) (nail) (subungual) 924.3
  - tongue (and other part(s) of neck, scalp, or face, except eye) 920
  - trunk 922.9
    - multiple sites 922.8

Contusion — *continued*
  trunk — *continued*
    specified site — *see* Contusion, by site
  tunica vaginalis 922.4
  tympanum (membrane) (and other part(s) of neck, scalp, or face, except eye) 920
  upper extremity 923.9
    multiple sites 923.8
  uvula (and other part(s) of neck, scalp, or face, except eye) 920
  vagina 922.4
  vocal cord(s) (and other part(s) of neck, scalp, or face, except eye) 920
  vulva 922.4
  wrist 923.21
    with hand(s), except finger(s) alone 923.20
Conus (any type) (congenital) 743.57
  acquired 371.60
  medullaris syndrome 336.8
Convalescence (following) V66.9
  chemotherapy V66.2
  medical NEC V66.5
  psychotherapy V66.3
  radiotherapy V66.1
  surgery NEC V66.0
  treatment (for) NEC V66.5
    combined V66.6
    fracture V66.4
    mental disorder NEC V66.3
    specified disorder NEC V66.5
Conversion
  closed surgical procedure to open procedure
    arthroscopic V64.43
    laparoscopic V64.41
    thoracoscopic V64.42
  hysteria, hysterical, any type 300.11
  neurosis, any 300.11
  reaction, any 300.11
Converter, tuberculosis (test reaction) 795.5
Convulsions (idiopathic) 780.39
  apoplectiform (*see also* Disease, cerebrovascular, acute) 436
  brain 780.39
  cerebral 780.39
  cerebrospinal 780.39
  due to trauma NEC — *see* Injury, intracranial
  eclamptic (*see also* Eclampsia) 780.39
  epileptic (*see also* Epilepsy) 345.9 ☑
  epileptiform (*see also* Seizure, epileptiform) 780.39
  epileptoid (*see also* Seizure, epileptiform) 780.39
  ether
    anesthetic
      correct substance properly administered 780.39
      overdose or wrong substance given 968.2
    other specified type — *see* Table of Drugs and Chemicals
  febrile (simple) 780.31
    complex 780.32
  generalized 780.39
  hysterical 300.11
  infantile 780.39
    epilepsy — *see* Epilepsy
  internal 780.39
  jacksonian (*see also* Epilepsy) 345.5 ☑
  myoclonic 333.2
  newborn 779.0
  paretic 094.1
  pregnancy (nephritic) (uremic) — *see* Eclampsia, pregnancy
  psychomotor (*see also* Epilepsy) 345.4 ☑
  puerperal, postpartum — *see* Eclampsia, pregnancy
  recurrent 780.39
    epileptic — *see* Epilepsy

Convulsions — *continued*
  reflex 781.0
  repetitive 780.39
    epileptic — *see* Epilepsy
  salaam (*see also* Epilepsy) 345.6 ☑
  scarlatinal 034.1
  spasmodic 780.39
  tetanus, tetanic (*see also* Tetanus) 037
  thymic 254.8
  uncinate 780.39
  uremic 586
Convulsive — *see also* Convulsions
  disorder or state 780.39
    epileptic — *see* Epilepsy
  equivalent, abdominal (*see also* Epilepsy) 345.5 ☑
Cooke-Apert-Gallais syndrome (adrenogenital) 255.2
Cooley's anemia (erythroblastic) 282.49
Coolie itch 126.9
Cooper's
  disease 610.1
  hernia — *see* Hernia, Cooper's
Coordination disturbance 781.3
Copper wire arteries, retina 362.13
Copra itch 133.8
Coprolith 560.39
Coprophilia 302.89
Coproporphyria, hereditary 277.1
Coprostasis 560.39
  with hernia (*see also* Hernia, by site, with obstruction)
    gangrenous — *see* Hernia, by site, with gangrene
Cor
  biloculare 745.7
  bovinum — *see* Hypertrophy, cardiac
  bovis (*see also* Hypertrophy, cardiac)
  pulmonale (chronic) 416.9
    acute 415.0
  triatriatum, triatrium 746.82
  triloculare 745.8
    biatriatum 745.3
    biventriculare 745.69
Corbus' disease 607.1
Cord — *see also* condition
  around neck (tightly) (with compression)
    affecting fetus or newborn 762.5
    complicating delivery 663.1 ☑
      without compression 663.3 ☑
        affecting fetus or newborn 762.6
  bladder NEC 344.61
    tabetic 094.0
  prolapse
    affecting fetus or newborn 762.4
    complicating delivery 663.0 ☑
Cord's angiopathy — *see also* Tuberculosis 017.3 ☑ *[362.18]*
Cordis ectopia 746.87
Corditis (spermatic) 608.4
Corectopia 743.46
Cori type glycogen storage disease — *see* Disease, glycogen storage
Cork-handlers' disease or lung 495.3
Corkscrew esophagus 530.5
Corlett's pyosis (impetigo) 684
Corn (infected) 700
Cornea — *see also* condition
  donor V59.5
  guttata (dystrophy) 371.57
  plana 743.41
Cornelia de Lange's syndrome (Amsterdam dwarf, mental retardation, and brachycephaly) 759.89
Cornual gestation or pregnancy — *see* Pregnancy, cornual
Cornu cutaneum 702.8
Coronary (artery) — *see also* condition
  arising from aorta or pulmonary trunk 746.85
Corpora — *see also* condition
  amylacea (prostate) 602.8
  cavernosa — *see* condition
Corpulence — *see* Obesity

Corpus — *see* condition
Corrigan's disease — *see* Insufficiency, aortic
Corrosive burn — *see* Burn, by site
Corsican fever — *see also* Malaria 084.6
Cortical — *see also* condition
  blindness 377.75
  necrosis, kidney (bilateral) 583.6
Corticoadrenal — *see* condition
Corticosexual syndrome 255.2
Coryza (acute) 460
  with grippe or influenza 487.1
  syphilitic 095.8
    congenital (chronic) 090.0
Costen's syndrome or complex 524.60
Costiveness — *see also* Constipation 564.00
Costochondritis 733.6
Cotard's syndrome (paranoia) 297.1
Cot death 798.0
Cotia virus 059.8 ●
Cotungo's disease 724.3
Cough 786.2
  with hemorrhage (*see also* Hemoptysis) 786.3
  affected 786.2
  bronchial 786.2
    with grippe or influenza 487.1
  chronic 786.2
  epidemic 786.2
  functional 306.1
  hemorrhagic 786.3
  hysterical 300.11
  laryngeal, spasmodic 786.2
  nervous 786.2
  psychogenic 306.1
  smokers' 491.0
  tea tasters' 112.89
Counseling NEC V65.40
  without complaint or sickness V65.49
  abuse victim NEC V62.89
    child V61.21
    partner V61.11
    spouse V61.11
  child abuse, maltreatment, or neglect V61.21
  contraceptive NEC V25.09
    device (intrauterine) V25.02
    maintenance V25.40
      intrauterine contraceptive device V25.42
      oral contraceptive (pill) V25.41
      specified type NEC V25.49
      subdermal implantable V25.43
    management NEC V25.9
    oral contraceptive (pill) V25.01
      emergency V25.03
      postcoital V25.03
    prescription NEC V25.02
      oral contraceptive (pill) V25.01
        emergency V25.03
        postcoital V25.03
        repeat prescription V25.41
      repeat prescription V25.40
    subdermal implantable V25.43
    surveillance NEC V25.40
  dietary V65.3
  exercise V65.41
  expectant mother, pediatric pre-birth visit V65.11
  explanation of
    investigation finding NEC V65.49
    medication NEC V65.49
  family planning V25.09
    natural
      procreative V26.41
      to avoid pregnancy V25.04
  for nonattending third party V65.19
  genetic V26.33
  gonorrhea V65.45
  health (advice) (education) (instruction) NEC V65.49
  HIV V65.44
  human immunodeficiency virus V65.44
  injury prevention V65.43

Counseling — *continued*
  insulin pump training V65.46
  marital V61.10
  medical (for) V65.9
    boarding school resident V60.6
    condition not demonstrated V65.5
    feared complaint and no disease found V65.5
    institutional resident V60.6
    on behalf of another V65.19
    person living alone V60.3
  natural family planning
    procreative V26.41
    to avoid pregnancy V25.04
  parent-child conflict V61.20
    specified problem NEC V61.29
  partner abuse
    perpetrator V61.12
    victim V61.11
  pediatric pre-birth visit for expectant mother V65.11
  perpetrator of
    child abuse V62.83
      parental V61.22
    partner abuse V61.12
    spouse abuse V61.12
  procreative V65.49
  sex NEC V65.49
    transmitted disease NEC V65.45
      HIV V65.44
  specified reason NEC V65.49
  spousal abuse
    perpetrator V61.12
    victim V61.11
  substance use and abuse V65.42
  syphilis V65.45
  victim (of)
    abuse NEC V62.89
    child abuse V61.21
    partner abuse V61.11
    spousal abuse V61.11
Coupled rhythm 427.89
Couvelaire uterus (complicating delivery) — *see* Placenta, separation
Cowper's gland — *see* condition
Cowperitis — *see also* Urethritis 597.89
  gonorrheal (acute) 098.0
    chronic or duration of 2 months or over 098.2
Cowpox (abortive) 051.01 ▲
  due to vaccination 999.0
  eyelid 051.01 *[373.5]* ▲
    postvaccination 999.0 *[373.5]*
Coxa
  plana 732.1
  valga (acquired) 736.31
    congenital 755.61
    late effect of rickets 268.1
  vara (acquired) 736.32
    congenital 755.62
    late effect of rickets 268.1
Coxae malum senilis 715.25
Coxalgia (nontuberculous) 719.45
  tuberculous (*see also* Tuberculosis) 015.1 ☑ *[730.85]*
Coxalgic pelvis 736.30
Coxitis 716.65
Coxsackie (infection) (virus) 079.2
  central nervous system NEC 048
  endocarditis 074.22
  enteritis 008.67
  meningitis (aseptic) 047.0
  myocarditis 074.23
  pericarditis 074.21
  pharyngitis 074.0
  pleurodynia 074.1
  specific disease NEC 074.8
Crabs, meaning pubic lice 132.2
Crack baby 760.75
Cracked
  nipple 611.2
    puerperal, postpartum 676.1 ☑
  tooth 521.81
Cradle cap 690.11
Craft neurosis 300.89
Craigiasis 007.8

Cramp(s) 729.82
- abdominal 789.0 ☑
- bathing 994.1
- colic 789.0 ☑
  - psychogenic 306.4
- due to immersion 994.1
- extremity (lower) (upper) NEC 729.82
- fireman 992.2
- heat 992.2
- hysterical 300.11
- immersion 994.1
- intestinal 789.0 ☑
  - psychogenic 306.4
- linotypist's 300.89
  - organic 333.84
- muscle (extremity) (general) 729.82
  - due to immersion 994.1
  - hysterical 300.11
- occupational (hand) 300.89
  - organic 333.84
- psychogenic 307.89
- salt depletion 276.1
- sleep related leg 327.52
- stoker 992.2
- stomach 789.0 ☑
- telegraphers' 300.89
  - organic 333.84
- typists' 300.89
  - organic 333.84
- uterus 625.8
  - menstrual 625.3
- writers' 333.84
  - organic 333.84
  - psychogenic 300.89

Cranial — *see* condition
Cranioclasis, fetal 763.89
Craniocleidodysostosis 755.59
Craniofenestria (skull) 756.0
Craniolacunia (skull) 756.0
Craniopagus 759.4
Craniopathy, metabolic 733.3
Craniopharyngeal — *see* condition
Craniopharyngioma (M9350/1) 237.0
Craniorachischisis (totalis) 740.1
Cranioschisis 756.0
Craniostenosis 756.0
Craniosynostosis 756.0
Craniotabes (cause unknown) 733.3
- rachitic 268.1
- syphilitic 090.5

Craniotomy, fetal 763.89
Cranium — *see* condition
Craw-craw 125.3
CRBSI (catheter-related bloodstream infection) 999.31
Creaking joint 719.60
- ankle 719.67
- elbow 719.62
- foot 719.67
- hand 719.64
- hip 719.65
- knee 719.66
- multiple sites 719.69
- pelvic region 719.65
- shoulder (region) 719.61
- specified site NEC 719.68
- wrist 719.63

Creeping
- eruption 126.9
- palsy 335.21
- paralysis 335.21

Crenated tongue 529.8
Creotoxism 005.9
Crepitus
- caput 756.0
- joint 719.60
  - ankle 719.67
  - elbow 719.62
  - foot 719.67
  - hand 719.64
  - hip 719.65
  - knee 719.66
  - multiple sites 719.69
  - pelvic region 719.65
  - shoulder (region) 719.61
  - specified site NEC 719.68

Crepitus — *continued*
- joint — *continued*
  - wrist 719.63

Crescent or conus choroid, congenital 743.57
Cretin, cretinism (athyrotic) (congenital) (endemic) (metabolic) (nongoitrous) (sporadic) 243
- goitrous (sporadic) 246.1
- pelvis (dwarf type) (male type) 243
  - with disproportion (fetopelvic) 653.1 ☑
    - affecting fetus or newborn 763.1
    - causing obstructed labor 660.1 ☑
      - affecting fetus or newborn 763.1
- pituitary 253.3

Cretinoid degeneration 243
Creutzfeldt-Jakob disease ▶(CJD)◀ (syndrome) 046.19 ▲
- with dementia
  - with behavioral disturbance 046.19 *[294.11]* ▲
  - without behavioral disturbance 046.19 *[294.10]* ▲
- familial 046.19 ●
- iatrogenic 046.19 ●
- specified NEC 046.19 ●
- sporadic 046.19 ●
- variant (vCJD) 046.11 ●
  - with dementia ●
    - with behavioral disturbance 046.11 *[294.11]* ●
    - without behavioral disturbance 046.11 *[294.10]* ●

Crib death 798.0
Cribriform hymen 752.49
Cri-du-chat syndrome 758.31
Crigler-Najjar disease or syndrome (congenital hyperbilirubinemia) 277.4
Crimean hemorrhagic fever 065.0
Criminalism 301.7
Crisis
- abdomen 789.0 ☑
- addisonian (acute adrenocortical insufficiency) 255.41
- adrenal (cortical) 255.41
- asthmatic — *see* Asthma
- brain, cerebral (*see also* Disease, cerebrovascular, acute) 436
- celiac 579.0
- Dietl's 593.4
- emotional NEC 309.29
  - acute reaction to stress 308.0
  - adjustment reaction 309.9
  - specific to childhood or adolescence 313.9
- gastric (tabetic) 094.0
- glaucomatocyclitic 364.22
- heart (*see also* Failure, heart) 428.9
- hypertensive — *see* Hypertension
- nitritoid
  - correct substance properly administered 458.29
  - overdose or wrong substance given or taken 961.1
- oculogyric 378.87
  - psychogenic 306.7
- Pel's 094.0
- psychosexual identity 302.6
- rectum 094.0
- renal 593.81
- sickle cell 282.62
- stomach (tabetic) 094.0
- tabetic 094.0
- thyroid (*see also* Thyrotoxicosis) 242.9 ☑
- thyrotoxic (*see also* Thyrotoxicosis) 242.9 ☑
- vascular — *see* Disease, cerebrovascular, acute

Crocq's disease (acrocyanosis) 443.89
Crohn's disease — *see also* Enteritis, regional 555.9
Cronkhite-Canada syndrome 211.3
Crooked septum, nasal 470
Cross
- birth (of fetus) complicating delivery 652.3 ☑
  - with successful version 652.1 ☑
  - causing obstructed labor 660.0 ☑
- bite, anterior or posterior 524.27
- eye (*see also* Esotropia) 378.00

Crossed ectopia of kidney 753.3
Crossfoot 754.50
Croup, croupous (acute) (angina) (catarrhal) (infective) (inflammatory) (laryngeal) (membranous) (nondiphtheritic) (pseudomembranous) 464.4
- asthmatic (*see also* Asthma) 493.9 ☑
- bronchial 466.0
- diphtheritic (membranous) 032.3
- false 478.75
- spasmodic 478.75
  - diphtheritic 032.3
- stridulous 478.75
  - diphtheritic 032.3

Crouzon's disease (craniofacial dysostosis) 756.0
Crowding, teeth 524.31
CRST syndrome (cutaneous systemic sclerosis) 710.1
Cruchet's disease (encephalitis lethargica) 049.8
Cruelty in children — *see also* Disturbance, conduct 312.9
Crural ulcer — *see also* Ulcer, lower extremity 707.10
Crush, crushed, crushing (injury) 929.9
- abdomen 926.19
  - internal — *see* Injury, internal, abdomen
- ankle 928.21
  - with other parts of foot 928.20
- arm 927.9
  - lower (and elbow) 927.10
  - upper 927.03
    - with shoulder or axillary region 927.09
- axilla 927.02
  - with shoulder or upper arm 927.09
- back 926.11
- breast 926.19
- buttock 926.12
- cheek 925.1
- chest — *see* Injury, internal, chest
- ear 925.1
- elbow 927.11
  - with forearm 927.10
- face 925.1
- finger(s) 927.3
  - with hand(s) 927.20
    - and wrist(s) 927.21
- flank 926.19
- foot, excluding toe(s) alone (with ankle) 928.20
- forearm (and elbow) 927.10
- genitalia, external (female) (male) 926.0
  - internal — *see* Injury, internal, genital organ NEC
- hand, except finger(s) alone (and wrist) 927.20
- head — *see* Fracture, skull, by site
- heel 928.20
- hip 928.01
  - with thigh 928.00
- internal organ (abdomen, chest, or pelvis) — *see* Injury, internal, by site
- knee 928.11
  - with leg, lower 928.10
- labium (majus) (minus) 926.0
- larynx 925.2
- late effect — *see* Late, effects (of), crushing
- leg 928.9
  - lower 928.10
    - and knee 928.11

Crush, crushed, crushing — *continued*
- leg — *continued*
  - upper 928.00
- limb
  - lower 928.9
    - multiple sites 928.8
  - upper 927.9
    - multiple sites 927.8
- multiple sites NEC 929.0
- neck 925.2
- nerve — *see* Injury, nerve, by site
- nose 802.0
  - open 802.1
- penis 926.0
- pharynx 925.2
- scalp 925.1
- scapular region 927.01
  - with shoulder or upper arm 927.09
- scrotum 926.0
- shoulder 927.00
  - with upper arm or axillary region 927.09
- skull or cranium — *see* Fracture, skull, by site
- spinal cord — *see* Injury, spinal, by site
- syndrome (complication of trauma) 958.5
- testis 926.0
- thigh (with hip) 928.00
- throat 925.2
- thumb(s) (and fingers) 927.3
- toe(s) 928.3
  - with foot 928.20
    - and ankle 928.21
- tonsil 925.2
- trunk 926.9
  - chest — *see* Injury, internal, intrathoracic organs NEC
  - internal organ — *see* Injury, internal, by site
  - multiple sites 926.8
  - specified site NEC 926.19
- vulva 926.0
- wrist 927.21
  - with hand(s), except fingers alone 927.20

Crusta lactea 690.11
Crusts 782.8
Crutch paralysis 953.4
Cruveilhier-Baumgarten cirrhosis, disease, or syndrome 571.5
Cruveilhier's disease 335.21
Cruz-Chagas disease — *see also* Trypanosomiasis 086.2
Crying
- constant, continuous
  - adolescent 780.95
  - adult 780.95
  - baby 780.92
  - child 780.95
  - infant 780.92
  - newborn 780.92
- excessive
  - adolescent 780.95
  - adult 780.95
  - baby 780.92
  - child 780.95
  - infant 780.92
  - newborn 780.92

Cryofibrinogenemia 273.2 ●
Cryoglobulinemia (mixed) 273.2
Crypt (anal) (rectal) 569.49
Cryptitis (anal) (rectal) 569.49
Cryptococcosis (European) (pulmonary) (systemic) 117.5
Cryptococcus 117.5
- epidermicus 117.5
- neoformans, infection by 117.5

Cryptopapillitis (anus) 569.49
Cryptophthalmos (eyelid) 743.06
Cryptorchid, cryptorchism, cryptorchidism 752.51
Cryptosporidiosis 007.4
Cryptotia 744.29

Crystallopathy
- calcium pyrophosphate (*see also* Arthritis) 275.49 *[712.2]* ☑
- dicalcium phosphate (*see also* Arthritis) 275.49 *[712.1]* ☑
- gouty 274.0
- pyrophosphate NEC (*see also* Arthritis) 275.49 *[712.2]* ☑
- uric acid 274.0

Crystalluria 791.9

Csillag's disease (lichen sclerosis et atrophicus) 701.0

Cuban itch 050.1

Cubitus
- valgus (acquired) 736.01
  - congenital 755.59
  - late effect of rickets 268.1
- varus (acquired) 736.02
  - congenital 755.59
  - late effect of rickets 268.1

Cultural deprivation V62.4

Cupping of optic disc 377.14

Curling esophagus 530.5

Curling's ulcer — *see* Ulcer, duodenum

Curschmann (-Batten) (-Steinert) disease or syndrome 359.21

Curvature
- organ or site, congenital NEC — *see* Distortion
- penis (lateral) 752.69
- Pott's (spinal) (*see also* Tuberculosis) 015.0 ☑ *[737.43]*
- radius, idiopathic, progressive (congenital) 755.54
- spine (acquired) (angular) (idiopathic) (incorrect) (postural) 737.9
  - congenital 754.2
  - due to or associated with
    - Charcôt-Marie-Tooth disease 356.1 *[737.40]*
    - mucopolysaccharidosis 277.5 *[737.40]*
    - neurofibromatosis 237.71 *[737.40]*
    - osteitis
      - deformans 731.0 *[737.40]*
      - fibrosa cystica 252.01 *[737.40]*
    - osteoporosis (*see also* Osteoporosis) 733.00 *[737.40]*
    - poliomyelitis (*see also* Poliomyelitis) 138 *[737.40]*
    - tuberculosis (Pott's curvature) (*see also* Tuberculosis) 015.0 ☑ *[737.43]*
  - kyphoscoliotic (*see also* Kyphoscoliosis) 737.30
  - kyphotic (*see also* Kyphosis) 737.10
  - late effect of rickets 268.1 *[737.40]*
  - Pott's 015.0 ☑ *[737.40]*
  - scoliotic (*see also* Scoliosis) 737.30
  - specified NEC 737.8
  - tuberculous 015.0 ☑ *[737.40]*

Cushing's
- basophilism, disease, or syndrome (iatrogenic) (idiopathic) (pituitary basophilism) (pituitary dependent) 255.0
- ulcer — *see* Ulcer, peptic

Cushingoid due to steroid therapy
- correct substance properly administered 255.0
- overdose or wrong substance given or taken 962.0

Cut (external) — *see* Wound, open, by site

Cutaneous — *see also* condition
- hemorrhage 782.7
- horn (cheek) (eyelid) (mouth) 702.8
- larva migrans 126.9

Cutis — *see also* condition
- hyperelastic 756.83
  - acquired 701.8
- laxa 756.83
  - senilis 701.8

Cutis — *see also* condition — *continued*
- marmorata 782.61
- osteosis 709.3
- pendula 756.83
  - acquired 701.8
- rhomboidalis nuchae 701.8
- verticis gyrata 757.39
  - acquired 701.8

Cyanopathy, newborn 770.83

Cyanosis 782.5
- autotoxic 289.7
- common atrioventricular canal 745.69
- congenital 770.83
- conjunctiva 372.71
- due to
  - endocardial cushion defect 745.60
  - nonclosure, foramen botalli 745.5
  - patent foramen botalli 745.5
  - persistent foramen ovale 745.5
- enterogenous 289.7
- fetus or newborn 770.83
- ostium primum defect 745.61
- paroxysmal digital 443.0
- retina, retinal 362.10

Cycle
- anovulatory 628.0
- menstrual, irregular 626.4

Cyclencephaly 759.89

Cyclical vomiting 536.2
- associated with migraine 346.2 ☑ ●
- psychogenic 306.4

Cyclitic membrane 364.74

Cyclitis — *see also* Iridocyclitis 364.3
- acute 364.00
  - primary 364.01
  - recurrent 364.02
- chronic 364.10
  - in
    - sarcoidosis 135 *[364.11]*
    - tuberculosis (*see also* Tuberculosis) 017.3 ☑ *[364.11]*
- Fuchs' heterochromic 364.21
- granulomatous 364.10
- lens induced 364.23
- nongranulomatous 364.00
- posterior 363.21
- primary 364.01
- recurrent 364.02
- secondary (noninfectious) 364.04
  - infectious 364.03
- subacute 364.00
  - primary 364.01
  - recurrent 364.02

Cyclokeratitis — *see* Keratitis

Cyclophoria 378.44

Cyclopia, cyclops 759.89

Cycloplegia 367.51

Cyclospasm 367.53

Cyclosporiasis 007.5

Cyclothymia 301.13

Cyclothymic personality 301.13

Cyclotropia 378.33

Cyesis — *see* Pregnancy

Cylindroma (M8200/3) — *see also* Neoplasm, by site, malignant
- eccrine dermal (M8200/0) — *see* Neoplasm, skin, benign
- skin (M8200/0) — *see* Neoplasm, skin, benign

Cylindruria 791.7

Cyllosoma 759.89

Cynanche
- diphtheritic 032.3
- tonsillaris 475

Cynorexia 783.6

Cyphosis — *see* Kyphosis

Cyprus fever — *see also* Brucellosis 023.9

Cyriax's syndrome (slipping rib) 733.99

Cyst (mucus) (retention) (serous) (simple)

> *Note — In general, cysts are not neoplastic and are classified to the appropriate category for disease of the specified anatomical site. This generalization does not apply to certain types of cysts which are neoplastic in nature, for example, dermoid, nor does it apply to cysts of certain structures, for example, branchial cleft, which are classified as developmental anomalies.*
>
> *The following listing includes some of the most frequently reported sites of cysts as well as qualifiers which indicate the type of cyst. The latter qualifiers usually are not repeated under the anatomical sites. Since the code assignment for a given site may vary depending upon the type of cyst, the coder should refer to the listings under the specified type of cyst before consideration is given to the site.*

- accessory, fallopian tube 752.11
- adenoid (infected) 474.8
- adrenal gland 255.8
  - congenital 759.1
- air, lung 518.89
- allantoic 753.7
- alveolar process (jaw bone) 526.2
- amnion, amniotic 658.8 ☑
- anterior chamber (eye) 364.60
  - exudative 364.62
  - implantation (surgical) (traumatic) 364.61
  - parasitic 360.13
- anterior nasopalatine 526.1
- antrum 478.19
- anus 569.49
- apical (periodontal) (tooth) 522.8
- appendix 543.9
- arachnoid, brain 348.0
- arytenoid 478.79
- auricle 706.2
- Baker's (knee) 727.51
  - tuberculous (*see also* Tuberculosis) 015.2 ☑
- Bartholin's gland or duct 616.2
- bile duct (*see also* Disease, biliary) 576.8
- bladder (multiple) (trigone) 596.8
- Blessig's 362.62
- blood, endocardial (*see also* Endocarditis) 424.90
- blue dome 610.0
- bone (local) 733.20
  - aneurysmal 733.22
  - jaw 526.2
    - developmental (odontogenic) 526.0
    - fissural 526.1
    - latent 526.89
  - solitary 733.21
  - unicameral 733.21
- brain 348.0
  - congenital 742.4
  - hydatid (*see also* Echinococcus) 122.9
  - third ventricle (colloid) 742.4
- branchial (cleft) 744.42
- branchiogenic 744.42
- breast (benign) (blue dome) (pedunculated) (solitary) (traumatic) 610.0
  - involution 610.4
  - sebaceous 610.8
- broad ligament (benign) 620.8
  - embryonic 752.11
- bronchogenic (mediastinal) (sequestration) 518.89
  - congenital 748.4
- buccal 528.4
- bulbourethral gland (Cowper's) 599.89
- bursa, bursal 727.49
  - pharyngeal 478.26

Cyst — *continued*
- calcifying odontogenic (M9301/0) 213.1
  - upper jaw (bone) 213.0
- canal of Nuck (acquired) (serous) 629.1
  - congenital 752.41
- canthus 372.75
- carcinomatous (M8010/3) — *see* Neoplasm, by site, malignant
- cartilage (joint) — *see* Derangement, joint
- cauda equina 336.8
- cavum septi pellucidi NEC 348.0
- celomic (pericardium) 746.89
- cerebellopontine (angle) — *see* Cyst, brain
- cerebellum — *see* Cyst, brain
- cerebral — *see* Cyst, brain
- cervical lateral 744.42
- cervix 622.8
  - embryonal 752.41
  - nabothian (gland) 616.0
- chamber, anterior (eye) 364.60
  - exudative 364.62
  - implantation (surgical) (traumatic) 364.61
  - parasitic 360.13
- chiasmal, optic NEC (*see also* Lesion, chiasmal) 377.54
- chocolate (ovary) 617.1
- choledochal (congenital) 751.69
  - acquired 576.8
- choledochus 751.69
- chorion 658.8 ☑
- choroid plexus 348.0
- chyle, mesentery 457.8
- ciliary body 364.60
  - exudative 364.64
  - implantation 364.61
  - primary 364.63
- clitoris 624.8
- coccyx (*see also* Cyst, bone) 733.20
- colloid
  - third ventricle (brain) 742.4
  - thyroid gland — *see* Goiter
- colon 569.89
- common (bile) duct (*see also* Disease, biliary) 576.8
- congenital NEC 759.89
  - adrenal glands 759.1
  - epiglottis 748.3
  - esophagus 750.4
  - fallopian tube 752.11
  - kidney 753.10
    - multiple 753.19
    - single 753.11
  - larynx 748.3
  - liver 751.62
  - lung 748.4
  - mediastinum 748.8
  - ovary 752.0
  - oviduct 752.11
  - pancreas 751.7
  - periurethral (tissue) 753.8
  - prepuce NEC 752.69
    - penis 752.69
  - sublingual 750.26
  - submaxillary gland 750.26
  - thymus (gland) 759.2
  - tongue 750.19
  - ureterovesical orifice 753.4
  - vulva 752.41
- conjunctiva 372.75
- cornea 371.23
- corpora quadrigemina 348.0
- corpus
  - albicans (ovary) 620.2
  - luteum (ruptured) 620.1
- Cowper's gland (benign) (infected) 599.89
- cranial meninges 348.0
- craniobuccal pouch 253.8
- craniopharyngeal pouch 253.8
- cystic duct (*see also* Disease, gallbladder) 575.8

Cyst — *continued*
  Cysticercus (any site) 123.1
  Dandy-Walker 742.3
    with spina bifida (*see also* Spina bifida) 741.0 ☑
  dental 522.8
    developmental 526.0
    eruption 526.0
    lateral periodontal 526.0
    primordial (keratocyst) 526.0
    root 522.8
  dentigerous 526.0
    mandible 526.0
    maxilla 526.0
  dermoid (M9084/0) (*see also* Neoplasm, by site, benign)
    with malignant transformation (M9084/3) 183.0
    implantation
      external area or site (skin) NEC 709.8
      iris 364.61
      skin 709.8
      vagina 623.8
      vulva 624.8
    mouth 528.4
    oral soft tissue 528.4
    sacrococcygeal 685.1
      with abscess 685.0
  developmental of ovary, ovarian 752.0
  dura (cerebral) 348.0
    spinal 349.2
  ear (external) 706.2
  echinococcal (*see also* Echinococcus) 122.9
  embryonal
    cervix uteri 752.41
    genitalia, female external 752.41
    uterus 752.3
    vagina 752.41
  endometrial 621.8
    ectopic 617.9
  endometrium (uterus) 621.8
    ectopic — *see* Endometriosis
  enteric 751.5
  enterogenous 751.5
  epidermal (inclusion) (*see also* Cyst, skin) 706.2
  epidermoid (inclusion) (*see also* Cyst, skin) 706.2
    mouth 528.4
    not of skin — *see* Cyst, by site
    oral soft tissue 528.4
  epididymis 608.89
  epiglottis 478.79
  epiphysis cerebri 259.8
  epithelial (inclusion) (*see also* Cyst, skin) 706.2
  epoophoron 752.11
  eruption 526.0
  esophagus 530.89
  ethmoid sinus 478.19
  eye (retention) 379.8
    congenital 743.03
    posterior segment, congenital 743.54
  eyebrow 706.2
  eyelid (sebaceous) 374.84
    infected 373.13
    sweat glands or ducts 374.84
  falciform ligament (inflammatory) 573.8
  fallopian tube 620.8
    congenital 752.11 ●
  female genital organs NEC 629.89
  fimbrial (congenital) 752.11
  fissural (oral region) 526.1
  follicle (atretic) (graafian) (ovarian) 620.0
    nabothian (gland) 616.0
  follicular (atretic) (ovarian) 620.0
    dentigerous 526.0
  frontal sinus 478.19
  gallbladder or duct 575.8
  ganglion 727.43
  Gartner's duct 752.41

Cyst — *continued*
  gas, of mesentery 568.89
  gingiva 523.8
  gland of moll 374.84
  globulomaxillary 526.1
  graafian follicle 620.0
  granulosal lutein 620.2
  hemangiomatous (M9121/0) (*see also* Hemangioma) 228.00
  hydatid (*see also* Echinococcus) 122.9
    fallopian tube (Morgagni) 752.11
    liver NEC 122.8
    lung NEC 122.9
    Morgagni 752.89
      fallopian tube 752.11
    specified site NEC 122.9
  hymen 623.8
    embryonal 752.41
  hypopharynx 478.26
  hypophysis, hypophyseal (duct) (recurrent) 253.8
    cerebri 253.8
  implantation (dermoid)
    anterior chamber (eye) 364.61
    external area or site (skin) NEC 709.8
    iris 364.61
    vagina 623.8
    vulva 624.8
  incisor, incisive canal 526.1
  inclusion (epidermal) (epithelial) (epidermoid) (mucous) (squamous) (*see also* Cyst, skin) 706.2
    not of skin — *see* Neoplasm, by site, benign
  intestine (large) (small) 569.89
  intracranial — *see* Cyst, brain
  intraligamentous 728.89
    knee 717.89
  intrasellar 253.8
  iris (idiopathic) 364.60
    exudative 364.62
    implantation (surgical) (traumatic) 364.61
    miotic pupillary 364.55
    parasitic 360.13
  Iwanoff's 362.62
  jaw (bone) (aneurysmal) (extravasation) (hemorrhagic) (traumatic) 526.2
    developmental (odontogenic) 526.0
    fissural 526.1
  keratin 706.2
  kidney (congenital) 753.10
    acquired 593.2
    calyceal (*see also* Hydronephrosis) 591
    multiple 753.19
    pyelogenic (*see also* Hydronephrosis) 591
    simple 593.2
    single 753.11
    solitary (not congenital) 593.2
  labium (majus) (minus) 624.8
    sebaceous 624.8
  lacrimal
    apparatus 375.43
    gland or sac 375.12
  larynx 478.79
  lens 379.39
    congenital 743.39
  lip (gland) 528.5
  liver 573.8
    congenital 751.62
    hydatid (*see also* Echinococcus) 122.8
      granulosis 122.0
      multilocularis 122.5
  lung 518.89
    congenital 748.4
    giant bullous 492.0
  lutein 620.1
  lymphangiomatous (M9173/0) 228.1
  lymphoepithelial
    mouth 528.4
    oral soft tissue 528.4

Cyst — *continued*
  macula 362.54
  malignant (M8000/3) — *see* Neoplasm, by site, malignant
  mammary gland (sweat gland) (*see also* Cyst, breast) 610.0
  mandible 526.2
    dentigerous 526.0
    radicular 522.8
  maxilla 526.2
    dentigerous 526.0
    radicular 522.8
  median
    anterior maxillary 526.1
    palatal 526.1
  mediastinum (congenital) 748.8
  meibomian (gland) (retention) 373.2
    infected 373.12
  membrane, brain 348.0
  meninges (cerebral) 348.0
    spinal 349.2
  meniscus knee 717.5
  mesentery, mesenteric (gas) 568.89
    chyle 457.8
    gas 568.89
  mesonephric duct 752.89
  mesothelial
    peritoneum 568.89
    pleura (peritoneal) 568.89
  milk 611.5
  miotic pupillary (iris) 364.55
  Morgagni (hydatid) 752.89
    fallopian tube 752.11
  mouth 528.4
  ▶Müllerian◀ duct 752.89
    appendix testis 608.89 ●
    cervix (embryonal) 752.41 ●
    fallopian tube 752.11 ●
    prostatic utricle 599.89 ●
    vagina (embryonal) 752.41 ●
  multilocular (ovary) (M8000/1) 239.5
  myometrium 621.8
  nabothian (follicle) (ruptured) 616.0
  nasal sinus 478.19
  nasoalveolar 528.4
  nasolabial 528.4
  nasopalatine (duct) 526.1
    anterior 526.1
  nasopharynx 478.26
  neoplastic (M8000/1) (*see also* Neoplasm, by site, unspecified nature)
    benign (M8000/0) — *see* Neoplasm, by site, benign
    uterus 621.8
  nervous system — *see* Cyst, brain
  neuroenteric 742.59
  neuroepithelial ventricle 348.0
  nipple 610.0
  nose 478.19
    skin of 706.2
  odontogenic, developmental 526.0
  omentum (lesser) 568.89
    congenital 751.8
  oral soft tissue (dermoid) (epidermoid) (lymphoepithelial) 528.4
  ora serrata 361.19
  orbit 376.81
  ovary, ovarian (twisted) 620.2
    adherent 620.2
    chocolate 617.1
    corpus
      albicans 620.2
      luteum 620.1
    dermoid (M9084/0) 220
    developmental 752.0
    due to failure of involution NEC 620.2
    endometrial 617.1
    follicular (atretic) (graafian) (hemorrhagic) 620.0
    hemorrhagic 620.2
    in pregnancy or childbirth 654.4 ☑
      affecting fetus or newborn 763.89

Cyst — *continued*
  ovary, ovarian — *continued*
    in pregnancy or childbirth — *continued*
      causing obstructed labor 660.2 ☑
        affecting fetus or newborn 763.1
    multilocular (M8000/1) 239.5
    pseudomucinous (M8470/0) 220
    retention 620.2
    serous 620.2
    theca lutein 620.2
    tuberculous (*see also* Tuberculosis) 016.6 ☑
    unspecified 620.2
  oviduct 620.8
  palatal papilla (jaw) 526.1
  palate 526.1
    fissural 526.1
    median (fissural) 526.1
  palatine, of papilla 526.1
  pancreas, pancreatic 577.2
    congenital 751.7
    false 577.2
    hemorrhagic 577.2
    true 577.2
  paralabral ●
    hip 718.85 ●
    shoulder 840.7 ●
  paramesonephric duct — *see* Cyst, Müllerian duct ●
  paranephric 593.2
  para ovarian 752.11
  paraphysis, cerebri 742.4
  parasitic NEC 136.9
  parathyroid (gland) 252.8
  paratubal (fallopian) 620.8
  paraurethral duct 599.89
  paroophoron 752.11
  parotid gland 527.6
    mucous extravasation or retention 527.6
  parovarian 752.11
  pars planus 364.60
    exudative 364.64
    primary 364.63
  pelvis, female
    in pregnancy or childbirth 654.4 ☑
      affecting fetus or newborn 763.89
      causing obstructed labor 660.2 ☑
        affecting fetus or newborn 763.1
  penis (sebaceous) 607.89
  periapical 522.8
  pericardial (congenital) 746.89
    acquired (secondary) 423.8
  pericoronal 526.0
  perineural (Tarlov's) 355.9
  periodontal 522.8
    lateral 526.0
  peripancreatic 577.2
  peripelvic (lymphatic) 593.2
  peritoneum 568.89
    chylous 457.8
  pharynx (wall) 478.26
  pilonidal (infected) (rectum) 685.1
    with abscess 685.0
    malignant (M9084/3) 173.5
  pituitary (duct) (gland) 253.8
  placenta (amniotic) — *see* Placenta, abnormal
  pleura 519.8
  popliteal 727.51
  porencephalic 742.4
    acquired 348.0
  postanal (infected) 685.1
    with abscess 685.0
  posterior segment of eye, congenital 743.54
  postmastoidectomy cavity 383.31
  preauricular 744.47
  prepuce 607.89
    congenital 752.69

Cyst — *continued*
primordial (jaw) 526.0
prostate 600.3
pseudomucinous (ovary) (M8470/0) 220
pudenda (sweat glands) 624.8
pupillary, miotic 364.55
sebaceous 624.8
radicular (residual) 522.8
radiculodental 522.8
ranular 527.6
Rathke's pouch 253.8
rectum (epithelium) (mucous) 569.49
renal — *see* Cyst, kidney
residual (radicular) 522.8
retention (ovary) 620.2
retina 361.19
macular 362.54
parasitic 360.13
primary 361.13
secondary 361.14
retroperitoneal 568.89
sacrococcygeal (dermoid) 685.1
with abscess 685.0
salivary gland or duct 527.6
mucous extravasation or retention 527.6
Sampson's 617.1
sclera 379.19
scrotum (sebaceous) 706.2
sweat glands 706.2
sebaceous (duct) (gland) 706.2
breast 610.8
eyelid 374.84
genital organ NEC
female 629.89
male 608.89
scrotum 706.2
semilunar cartilage (knee) (multiple) 717.5
seminal vesicle 608.89
serous (ovary) 620.2
sinus (antral) (ethmoidal) (frontal) (maxillary) (nasal) (sphenoidal) 478.19
Skene's gland 599.89
skin (epidermal) (epidermoid, inclusion) (epithelial) (inclusion) (retention) (sebaceous) 706.2
breast 610.8
eyelid 374.84
genital organ NEC
female 629.89
male 608.89
neoplastic 216.3
scrotum 706.2
sweat gland or duct 705.89
solitary
bone 733.21
kidney 593.2
spermatic cord 608.89
sphenoid sinus 478.19
spinal meninges 349.2
spine (*see also* Cyst, bone) 733.20
spleen NEC 289.59
congenital 759.0
hydatid (*see also* Echinococcus) 122.9
spring water (pericardium) 746.89
subarachnoid 348.0
intrasellar 793.0
subdural (cerebral) 348.0
spinal cord 349.2
sublingual gland 527.6
mucous extravasation or retention 527.6
submaxillary gland 527.6
mucous extravasation or retention 527.6
suburethral 599.89
suprarenal gland 255.8
suprasellar — *see* Cyst, brain
sweat gland or duct 705.89
sympathetic nervous system 337.9
synovial 727.40
popliteal space 727.51

Cyst — *continued*
Tarlov's 355.9
tarsal 373.2
tendon (sheath) 727.42
testis 608.89
theca-lutein (ovary) 620.2
Thornwaldt's, Tornwaldt's 478.26
thymus (gland) 254.8
thyroglossal (duct) (infected) (persistent) 759.2
thyroid (gland) 246.2
adenomatous — *see* Goiter, nodular
colloid (*see also* Goiter) 240.9
thyrolingual duct (infected) (persistent) 759.2
tongue (mucous) 529.8
tonsil 474.8
tooth (dental root) 522.8
tubo-ovarian 620.8
inflammatory 614.1
tunica vaginalis 608.89
turbinate (nose) (*see also* Cyst, bone) 733.20
Tyson's gland (benign) (infected) 607.89
umbilicus 759.89
urachus 753.7
ureter 593.89
ureterovesical orifice 593.89
congenital 753.4
urethra 599.84
urethral gland (Cowper's) 599.89
uterine
ligament 620.8
embryonic 752.11
tube 620.8
uterus (body) (corpus) (recurrent) 621.8
embryonal 752.3
utricle (ear) 386.8
prostatic 599.89
utriculus masculinus 599.89
vagina, vaginal (squamous cell) (wall) 623.8
embryonal 752.41
implantation 623.8
inclusion 623.8
vallecula, vallecular 478.79
ventricle, neuroepithelial 348.0
verumontanum 599.89
vesical (orifice) 596.8
vitreous humor 379.29
vulva (sweat glands) 624.8
congenital 752.41
implantation 624.8
inclusion 624.8
sebaceous gland 624.8
vulvovaginal gland 624.8
wolffian 752.89
Cystadenocarcinoma (M8440/3) — *see also* Neoplasm, by site, malignant
bile duct type (M8161/3) 155.1
endometrioid (M8380/3) — *see* Neoplasm, by site, malignant
mucinous (M8470/3)
papillary (M8471/3)
specified site — *see* Neoplasm, by site, malignant
unspecified site 183.0
specified site — *see* Neoplasm, by site, malignant
unspecified site 183.0
papillary (M8450/3)
mucinous (M8471/3)
specified site — *see* Neoplasm, by site, malignant
unspecified site 183.0
pseudomucinous (M8471/3)
specified site — *see* Neoplasm, by site, malignant
unspecified site 183.0
serous (M8460/3)
specified site — *see* Neoplasm, by site, malignant
unspecified site 183.0

Cystadenocarcinoma — *see also* Neoplasm, by site, malignant — *continued*
papillary — *continued*
specified site — *see* Neoplasm, by site, malignant
unspecified site 183.0
pseudomucinous (M8470/3)
papillary (M8471/3)
specified site — *see* Neoplasm, by site, malignant
unspecified site 183.0
specified site — *see* Neoplasm, by site, malignant
unspecified site 183.0
serous (M8441/3)
papillary (M8460/3)
specified site — *see* Neoplasm, by site, malignant
unspecified site 183.0
specified site — *see* Neoplasm, by site, malignant
unspecified site 183.0
Cystadenofibroma (M9013/0)
clear cell (M8313/0) — *see* Neoplasm, by site, benign
endometrioid (M8381/0) 220
borderline malignancy (M8381/1) 236.2
malignant (M8381/3) 183.0
mucinous (M9015/0)
specified site — *see* Neoplasm, by site, benign
unspecified site 220
serous (M9014/0)
specified site — *see* Neoplasm, by site, benign
unspecified site 220
specified site — *see* Neoplasm, by site, benign
unspecified site 220
Cystadenoma (M8440/0) — *see also* Neoplasm, by site, benign
bile duct (M8161/0) 211.5
endometrioid (M8380/0) (*see also* Neoplasm, by site, benign)
borderline malignancy (M8380/1) — *see* Neoplasm, by site, uncertain behavior
malignant (M8440/3) — *see* Neoplasm, by site, malignant
mucinous (M8470/0)
borderline malignancy (M8470/1)
specified site — *see* Neoplasm, uncertain behavior
unspecified site 236.2
papillary (M8471/0)
borderline malignancy (M8471/1)
specified site — *see* Neoplasm, by site, uncertain behavior
unspecified site 236.2
specified site — *see* Neoplasm, by site, benign
unspecified site 220
specified site — *see* Neoplasm, by site, benign
unspecified site 220
papillary (M8450/0)
borderline malignancy (M8450/1)
specified site — *see* Neoplasm, by site, uncertain behavior
unspecified site 236.2
lymphomatosum (M8561/0) 210.2
mucinous (M8471/0)
borderline malignancy (M8471/1)
specified site — *see* Neoplasm, by site, uncertain behavior
unspecified site 236.2
specified site — *see* Neoplasm, by site, benign
unspecified site 220

Cystadenoma — *see also* Neoplasm, by site, benign — *continued*
papillary — *continued*
pseudomucinous (M8471/0)
borderline malignancy (M8471/1)
specified site — *see* Neoplasm, by site, uncertain behavior
unspecified site 236.2
specified site — *see* Neoplasm, by site, benign
unspecified site 220
serous (M8460/0)
borderline malignancy (M8460/1)
specified site — *see* Neoplasm, by site, uncertain behavior
unspecified site 236.2
specified site — *see* Neoplasm, by site, benign
unspecified site 220
specified site — *see* Neoplasm, by site, benign
unspecified site 220
pseudomucinous (M8470/0)
borderline malignancy (M8470/1)
specified site — *see* Neoplasm, by site, uncertain behavior
unspecified site 236.2
papillary (M8471/0)
borderline malignancy (M8471/1)
specified site — *see* Neoplasm, by site, uncertain behavior
unspecified site 236.2
specified site — *see* Neoplasm, by site, benign
unspecified site 220
specified site — *see* Neoplasm, by site, benign
unspecified site 220
serous (M8441/0)
borderline malignancy (M8441/1)
specified site — *see* Neoplasm, by site, uncertain behavior
unspecified site 236.2
papillary (M8460/0)
borderline malignancy (M8460/1)
specified site — *see* Neoplasm, by site, uncertain behavior
unspecified site 236.2
specified site — *see* Neoplasm, by site, benign
unspecified site 220
specified site — *see* Neoplasm, by site, benign
unspecified site 220
thyroid 226
Cystathioninemia 270.4
Cystathioninuria 270.4
Cystic — *see also* condition
breast, chronic 610.1
corpora lutea 620.1
degeneration, congenital
brain 742.4
kidney (*see also* Cystic, disease, kidney) 753.10
disease
breast, chronic 610.1
kidney, congenital 753.10
medullary 753.16
multiple 753.19
polycystic — *see* Polycystic, kidney
single 753.11
specified NEC 753.19
liver, congenital 751.62
lung 518.89
congenital 748.4

Additional Digit Required — Refer to the Tabular List for Digit Selection
Subterms under main terms may continue to next column or page

▶◀ Revised Text ● New Line ▲ Revised Code

Cystic — *see also* condition — *continued*
disease — *continued*
pancreas, congenital 751.7
semilunar cartilage 717.5
duct — *see* condition
eyeball, congenital 743.03
fibrosis (pancreas) 277.00
with
manifestations
gastrointestinal 277.03
pulmonary 277.02
specified NEC 277.09
meconium ileus 277.01
pulmonary exacerbation 277.02
hygroma (M9173/0) 228.1
kidney, congenital 753.10
medullary 753.16
multiple 753.19
polycystic — *see* Polycystic, kidney
single 753.11
specified NEC 753.19
liver, congenital 751.62
lung 518.89
congenital 748.4
mass — *see* Cyst
mastitis, chronic 610.1
ovary 620.2
pancreas, congenital 751.7
Cysticerciasis 123.1
Cysticercosis (mammary) (subretinal) 123.1
Cysticercus 123.1
cellulosae infestation 123.1
Cystinosis (malignant) 270.0
Cystinuria 270.0
Cystitis (bacillary) (colli) (diffuse) (exudative) (hemorrhagic) (purulent) (recurrent) (septic) (suppurative) (ulcerative) 595.9
with
abortion — *see* Abortion, by type, with urinary tract infection
ectopic pregnancy (*see also* categories 633.0–633.9) 639.8
fibrosis 595.1
leukoplakia 595.1
malakoplakia 595.1
metaplasia 595.1
molar pregnancy (*see also* categories 630–632) 639.8
actinomycotic 039.8 *[595.4]*
acute 595.0
of trigone 595.3
allergic 595.89
amebic 006.8 *[595.4]*
bilharzial 120.9 *[595.4]*
blennorrhagic (acute) 098.11
chronic or duration of 2 months or more 098.31
bullous 595.89
calculous 594.1
chlamydial 099.53
chronic 595.2
interstitial 595.1
of trigone 595.3
complicating pregnancy, childbirth, or puerperium 646.6 ☑
affecting fetus or newborn 760.1
cystic(a) 595.81
diphtheritic 032.84
echinococcal
granulosus 122.3 *[595.4]*
multilocularis 122.6 *[595.4]*
emphysematous 595.89
encysted 595.81
follicular 595.3
following
abortion 639.8
ectopic or molar pregnancy 639.8
gangrenous 595.89
glandularis 595.89
gonococcal (acute) 098.11
chronic or duration of 2 months or more 098.31
incrusted 595.89
interstitial 595.1
irradiation 595.82
irritation 595.89
malignant 595.89
monilial 112.2
of trigone 595.3
panmural 595.1
polyposa 595.89
prostatic 601.3
radiation 595.82
Reiter's (abacterial) 099.3
specified NEC 595.89
subacute 595.2
submucous 595.1
syphilitic 095.8
trichomoniasis 131.09
tuberculous (*see also* Tuberculosis) 016.1 ☑
ulcerative 595.1
Cystocele
female (without uterine prolapse) 618.01
with uterine prolapse 618.4
complete 618.3
incomplete 618.2
lateral 618.02
midline 618.01
paravaginal 618.02
in pregnancy or childbirth 654.4 ☑
affecting fetus or newborn 763.89
causing obstructed labor 660.2 ☑
affecting fetus or newborn 763.1
male 596.8
Cystoid
cicatrix limbus 372.64
degeneration macula 362.53
Cystolithiasis 594.1
Cystoma (M8440/0) — *see also* Neoplasm, by site, benign
endometrial, ovary 617.1
mucinous (M8470/0)
specified site — *see* Neoplasm, by site, benign
unspecified site 220
serous (M8441/0)
specified site — *see* Neoplasm, by site, benign
unspecified site 220
simple (ovary) 620.2
Cystoplegia 596.53
Cystoptosis 596.8
Cystopyelitis — *see also* Pyelitis 590.80
Cystorrhagia 596.8
Cystosarcoma phyllodes (M9020/1) 238.3
benign (M9020/0) 217
malignant (M9020/3) — *see* Neoplasm, breast, malignant
Cystostomy status V44.50
with complication 997.5
appendico-vesicostomy V44.52
cutaneous-vesicostomy V44.51
specified type NEC V44.59
Cystourethritis — *see also* Urethritis 597.89
Cystourethrocele — *see also* Cystocele
female (without uterine prolapse) 618.09
with uterine prolapse 618.4
complete 618.3
incomplete 618.2
male 596.8
Cytomegalic inclusion disease 078.5
congenital 771.1
Cytomycosis, reticuloendothelial — *see also* Histoplasmosis, American 115.00
Cytopenia 289.9
refractory
with
multilineage dysplasia (RCMD) 238.72
and ringed sideroblasts (RCMD-RS) 238.72

D

- **Daae (-Finsen) disease** (epidemic pleurodynia) 074.1
- **Dabney's grip** 074.1
- **Da Costa's syndrome** (neurocirculatory asthenia) 306.2
- **Dacryoadenitis, dacryadenitis** 375.00
  - acute 375.01
  - chronic 375.02
- **Dacryocystitis** 375.30
  - acute 375.32
  - chronic 375.42
  - neonatal 771.6
  - phlegmonous 375.33
  - syphilitic 095.8
    - congenital 090.0
  - trachomatous, active 076.1
    - late effect 139.1
  - tuberculous (*see also* Tuberculosis) 017.3 ☑
- **Dacryocystoblenorrhea** 375.42
- **Dacryocystocele** 375.43
- **Dacryolith, dacryolithiasis** 375.57
- **Dacryoma** 375.43
- **Dacryopericystitis** (acute) (subacute) 375.32
  - chronic 375.42
- **Dacryops** 375.11
- **Dacryosialadenopathy, atrophic** 710.2
- **Dacryostenosis** 375.56
  - congenital 743.65
- **Dactylitis**
  - bone (*see also* Osteomyelitis) 730.2 ☑
  - sickle-cell 282.62
    - Hb-C 282.64
    - Hb-SS 282.62
    - specified NEC 282.69
  - syphilitic 095.5
  - tuberculous (*see also* Tuberculosis) 015.5 ☑
- **Dactylolysis spontanea** 136.0
- **Dactylosymphysis** — *see also* Syndactylism 755.10
- **Damage**
  - arteriosclerotic — *see* Arteriosclerosis
  - brain 348.9
    - anoxic, hypoxic 348.1
      - during or resulting from a procedure 997.01
      - ischemic, in newborn 768.7
    - child NEC 343.9
    - due to birth injury 767.0
    - minimal (child) (*see also* Hyperkinesia) 314.9
    - newborn 767.0
  - cardiac (*see also* Disease, heart)
  - cardiorenal (vascular) (*see also* Hypertension, cardiorenal) 404.90
  - central nervous system — *see* Damage, brain
  - cerebral NEC — *see* Damage, brain
  - coccyx, complicating delivery 665.6 ☑
  - coronary (*see also* Ischemia, heart) 414.9
  - eye, birth injury 767.8
  - heart (*see also* Disease, heart)
    - valve — *see* Endocarditis
  - hypothalamus NEC 348.9
  - liver 571.9
    - alcoholic 571.3
  - medication 995.20
  - myocardium (*see also* Degeneration, myocardial) 429.1
  - pelvic
    - joint or ligament, during delivery 665.6 ☑
    - organ NEC
      - with
        - abortion — *see* Abortion, by type, with damage to pelvic organs
        - ectopic pregnancy (*see also* categories 633.0–633.9) 639.2

- **Damage** — *continued*
  - pelvic — *continued*
    - organ — *continued*
      - with — *continued*
        - molar pregnancy (*see also* categories 630–632) 639.2
      - during delivery 665.5 ☑
      - following
        - abortion 639.2
        - ectopic or molar pregnancy 639.2
  - renal (*see also* Disease, renal) 593.9
  - skin, solar 692.79
    - acute 692.72
    - chronic 692.74
  - subendocardium, subendocardial (*see also* Degeneration, myocardial) 429.1
  - vascular 459.9
- **Dameshek's syndrome** (erythroblastic anemia) 282.49
- **Dana-Putnam syndrome** (subacute combined sclerosis with pernicious anemia) 281.0 *[336.2]*
- **Danbolt (-Closs) syndrome** (acrodermatitis enteropathica) 686.8
- **Dandruff** 690.18
- **Dandy fever** 061
- **Dandy-Walker deformity or syndrome** (atresia, foramen of Magendie) 742.3
  - with spina bifida (*see also* Spina bifida) 741.0 ☑
- **Dangle foot** 736.79
- **Danielssen's disease** (anesthetic leprosy) 030.1
- **Danlos' syndrome** 756.83
- **Darier's disease** (congenital) (keratosis follicularis) 757.39
  - due to vitamin A deficiency 264.8
  - meaning erythema annulare centrifugum 695.0
- **Darier-Roussy sarcoid** 135
- **Darling's**
  - disease (*see also* Histoplasmosis, American) 115.00
  - histoplasmosis (*see also* Histoplasmosis, American) 115.00
- **Dartre** 054.9
- **Darwin's tubercle** 744.29
- **Davidson's anemia** (refractory) 284.9
- **Davies-Colley syndrome** (slipping rib) 733.99
- **Davies' disease** 425.0
- **Dawson's encephalitis** 046.2
- **Day blindness** — *see also* Blindness, day 368.60
- **Dead**
  - fetus
    - retained (in utero) 656.4 ☑
      - early pregnancy (death before 22 completed weeks gestation) 632
      - late (death after 22 completed weeks gestation) 656.4 ☑
    - syndrome 641.3 ☑
  - labyrinth 386.50
  - ovum, retained 631
- **Deaf and dumb** NEC 389.7
- **Deaf mutism** (acquired) (congenital) NEC 389.7
  - endemic 243
  - hysterical 300.11
  - syphilitic, congenital 090.0
- **Deafness** (acquired) (complete) (congenital) (hereditary) (middle ear) (partial) 389.9
  - with
    - blindness V49.85
    - blue sclera and fragility of bone 756.51
  - auditory fatigue 389.9
  - aviation 993.0
    - nerve injury 951.5
  - boilermakers' 951.5

- **Deafness** — *continued*
  - central 389.14
    - with conductive hearing loss 389.20
      - bilateral 389.22
      - unilateral 389.21
  - conductive (air) 389.00
    - with sensorineural hearing loss 389.20
      - bilateral 389.22
      - unilateral 389.21
    - bilateral 389.06
    - combined types 389.08
    - external ear 389.01
    - inner ear 389.04
    - middle ear 389.03
    - multiple types 389.08
    - tympanic membrane 389.02
    - unilateral 389.05
  - emotional (complete) 300.11
  - functional (complete) 300.11
  - high frequency 389.8
  - hysterical (complete) 300.11
  - injury 951.5
  - low frequency 389.8
  - mental 784.69
  - mixed conductive and sensorineural 389.20
    - bilateral 389.22
    - unilateral 389.21
  - nerve
    - with conductive hearing loss 389.20
      - bilateral 389.22
      - unilateral 389.21
    - bilateral 389.12
    - unilateral 389.13
  - neural
    - with conductive hearing loss 389.20
      - bilateral 389.22
      - unilateral 389.21
    - bilateral 389.12
    - unilateral 389.13
  - noise-induced 388.12
    - nerve injury 951.5
  - nonspeaking 389.7
  - perceptive 389.10
    - with conductive hearing loss 389.20
      - bilateral 389.22
      - unilateral 389.21
    - central 389.14
    - neural
      - bilateral 389.12
      - unilateral 389.13
    - sensorineural 389.10
      - asymmetrical 389.16
      - bilateral 389.18
      - unilateral 389.15
    - sensory
      - bilateral 389.11
      - unilateral 389.17
  - psychogenic (complete) 306.7
  - sensorineural (*see also* Deafness, perceptive) 389.10
    - asymmetrical 389.16
    - bilateral 389.18
    - unilateral 389.15
  - sensory
    - with conductive hearing loss 389.20
      - bilateral 389.22
      - unilateral 389.21
    - bilateral 389.11
    - unilateral 389.17
  - specified type NEC 389.8
  - sudden NEC 388.2
  - syphilitic 094.89
  - transient ischemic 388.02
  - transmission — *see* Deafness, conductive
  - traumatic 951.5
  - word (secondary to organic lesion) 784.69
    - developmental 315.31

- **Death**
  - after delivery (cause not stated) (sudden) 674.9 ☑
  - anesthetic
    - due to
      - correct substance properly administered 995.4
      - overdose or wrong substance given 968.4
        - specified anesthetic — *see* Table of Drugs and Chemicals
    - during delivery 668.9 ☑
  - brain 348.8
  - cardiac (sudden) (SCD) — code to underlying condition
    - family history of V17.41
    - personal history of, successfully resuscitated V12.53
  - cause unknown 798.2
  - cot (infant) 798.0
  - crib (infant) 798.0
  - fetus, fetal (cause not stated) (intrauterine) 779.9
    - early, with retention (before 22 completed weeks gestation) 632
    - from asphyxia or anoxia (before labor) 768.0
      - during labor 768.1
    - late, affecting management of pregnancy (after 22 completed weeks gestation) 656.4 ☑
  - from pregnancy NEC 646.9 ☑
  - instantaneous 798.1
  - intrauterine (*see also* Death, fetus) 779.9
    - complicating pregnancy 656.4 ☑
  - maternal, affecting fetus or newborn 761.6
  - neonatal NEC 779.9
  - sudden (cause unknown) 798.1
    - cardiac (SCD)
      - family history of V17.41
      - personal history of, successfully resuscitated V12.53
    - during delivery 669.9 ☑
      - under anesthesia NEC 668.9 ☑
    - infant, syndrome (SIDS) 798.0
    - puerperal, during puerperium 674.9 ☑
  - unattended (cause unknown) 798.9
  - under anesthesia NEC
    - due to
      - correct substance properly administered 995.4
      - overdose or wrong substance given 968.4
        - specified anesthetic — *see* Table of Drugs and Chemicals
    - during delivery 668.9 ☑
  - violent 798.1
- **de Beurmann-Gougerot disease** (sporotrichosis) 117.1
- **Debility** (general) (infantile) (postinfectional) 799.3
  - with nutritional difficulty 269.9
  - congenital or neonatal NEC 779.9
  - nervous 300.5
  - old age 797
  - senile 797
- **Débove's disease** (splenomegaly) 789.2
- **Decalcification**
  - bone (*see also* Osteoporosis) 733.00
  - teeth 521.89
- **Decapitation** 874.9
  - fetal (to facilitate delivery) 763.89
- **Decapsulation, kidney** 593.89
- **Decay**
  - dental 521.00
  - senile 797
  - tooth, teeth 521.00
- **Decensus, uterus** — *see* Prolapse, uterus

- **Deciduitis** (acute)
  - with
    - abortion — see Abortion, by type, with sepsis
    - ectopic pregnancy (see also categories 633.0–633.9) 639.0
    - molar pregnancy (see also categories 630–632) 639.0
  - affecting fetus or newborn 760.8
  - following
    - abortion 639.0
    - ectopic or molar pregnancy 639.0
  - in pregnancy 646.6 ☑
  - puerperal, postpartum 670.0 ☑
- **Deciduoma malignum** (M9100/3) 181
- **Deciduous tooth** (retained) 520.6
- **Decline** (general) — see also Debility 799.3
- **Decompensation**
  - cardiac (acute) (chronic) (see also Disease, heart) 429.9
    - failure — see Failure, heart
  - cardiorenal (see also Hypertension, cardiorenal) 404.90
  - cardiovascular (see also Disease, cardiovascular) 429.2
  - heart (see also Disease, heart) 429.9
    - failure — see Failure, heart
  - hepatic 572.2
  - myocardial (acute) (chronic) (see also Disease, heart) 429.9
    - failure — see Failure, heart
  - respiratory 519.9
- **Decompression sickness** 993.3
- **Decrease, decreased**
  - blood
    - platelets (see also Thrombocytopenia) 287.5
    - pressure 796.3
      - due to shock following
        - injury 958.4
        - operation 998.0
    - white cell count 288.50
      - specified NEC 288.59
  - cardiac reserve — see Disease, heart
  - estrogen 256.39
    - postablative 256.2
  - fetal movements 655.7 ☑
  - fragility of erythrocytes 289.89
  - function
    - adrenal (cortex) 255.41
      - medulla 255.5
    - ovary in hypopituitarism 253.4
    - parenchyma of pancreas 577.8
    - pituitary (gland) (lobe) (anterior) 253.2
      - posterior (lobe) 253.8
  - functional activity 780.99
  - glucose 790.29
  - haptoglobin (serum) NEC 273.8
  - leukocytes 288.50
  - libido 799.81
  - lymphocytes 288.51
  - platelets (see also Thrombocytopenia) 287.5
  - pulse pressure 785.9
  - respiration due to shock following injury 958.4
  - sexual desire 799.81
  - tear secretion NEC 375.15
  - tolerance
    - fat 579.8
    - salt and water 276.9
  - vision NEC 369.9
  - white blood cell count 288.50
- **Decubital gangrene** — ▶see also Ulcer, pressure◀ 707.00 *[785.4]*
- **Decubiti** — see also ▶Ulcer, pressure◀ 707.00
- **Decubitus** (ulcer) — ▶see also Ulcer, pressure◀ 707.00
  - with gangrene 707.00 *[785.4]*
  - ankle 707.06
  - back
    - lower 707.03
    - upper 707.02
- **Decubitus** — ▶see also Ulcer, pressure◀ — *continued*
  - buttock 707.05
  - elbow 707.01
  - head 707.09
  - heel 707.07
  - hip 707.04
  - other site 707.09
  - sacrum 707.03
  - shoulder blades 707.02
- **Deepening acetabulum** 718.85
- **Defect, defective** 759.9
  - 3-beta-hydroxysteroid dehydrogenase 255.2
  - 11-hydroxylase 255.2
  - 21-hydroxylase 255.2
  - abdominal wall, congenital 756.70
  - aorticopulmonary septum 745.0
  - aortic septal 745.0
  - atrial septal (ostium secundum type) 745.5
    - acquired 429.71
    - ostium primum type 745.61
    - sinus venosus 745.8
  - atrioventricular
    - canal 745.69
    - septum 745.4
      - acquired 429.71
  - atrium secundum 745.5
    - acquired 429.71
  - auricular septal 745.5
    - acquired 429.71
  - bilirubin excretion 277.4
  - biosynthesis, testicular androgen 257.2
  - bridge 525.60
  - bulbar septum 745.0
  - butanol-insoluble iodide 246.1
  - chromosome — see Anomaly, chromosome
  - circulation (acquired) 459.9
    - congenital 747.9
    - newborn 747.9
  - clotting NEC (see also Defect, coagulation) 286.9
  - coagulation (factor) (see also Deficiency, coagulation factor) 286.9
    - with
      - abortion — see Abortion, by type, with hemorrhage
      - ectopic pregnancy (see also categories 634–638) 639.1
      - molar pregnancy (see also categories 630–632) 639.1
    - acquired (any) 286.7
    - antepartum or intrapartum 641.3 ☑
      - affecting fetus or newborn 762.1
    - causing hemorrhage of pregnancy or delivery 641.3 ☑
    - complicating pregnancy, childbirth, or puerperium 649.3 ☑
    - due to
      - liver disease 286.7
      - vitamin K deficiency 286.7
    - newborn, transient 776.3
    - postpartum 666.3 ☑
    - specified type NEC 286.9
  - conduction (heart) 426.9
    - bone (see also Deafness, conductive) 389.00
  - congenital, organ or site NEC (see also Anomaly)
    - circulation 747.9
    - Descemet's membrane 743.9
      - specified type NEC 743.49
    - diaphragm 756.6
    - ectodermal 757.9
    - esophagus 750.9
    - pulmonic cusps — see Anomaly, heart valve
    - respiratory system 748.9
      - specified type NEC 748.8
  - crown 525.60
  - cushion endocardial 745.60
  - dental restoration 525.60
- **Defect, defective** — *continued*
  - dentin (hereditary) 520.5
  - Descemet's membrane (congenital) 743.9
    - acquired 371.30
    - specific type NEC 743.49
  - deutan 368.52
  - developmental (see also Anomaly, by site)
    - cauda equina 742.59
    - left ventricle 746.9
      - with atresia or hypoplasia of aortic orifice or valve, with hypoplasia of ascending aorta 746.7
      - in hypoplastic left heart syndrome 746.7
    - testis 752.9
    - vessel 747.9
  - diaphragm
    - with elevation, eventration, or hernia — see Hernia, diaphragm
    - congenital 756.6
      - with elevation, eventration, or hernia 756.6
      - gross (with elevation, eventration, or hernia) 756.6
  - ectodermal, congenital 757.9
  - Eisenmenger's (ventricular septal defect) 745.4
  - endocardial cushion 745.60
    - specified type NEC 745.69
  - esophagus, congenital 750.9
  - extensor retinaculum 728.9
  - fibrin polymerization (see also Defect, coagulation) 286.3
  - filling
    - biliary tract 793.3
    - bladder 793.5
    - dental 525.60
    - gallbladder 793.3
    - kidney 793.5
    - stomach 793.4
    - ureter 793.5
  - fossa ovalis 745.5
  - gene, carrier (suspected) of V83.89
  - Gerbode 745.4
  - glaucomatous, without elevated tension 365.89
  - Hageman (factor) (see also Defect, coagulation) 286.3
  - hearing (see also Deafness) 389.9
  - high grade 317
  - homogentisic acid 270.2
  - interatrial septal 745.5
    - acquired 429.71
  - interauricular septal 745.5
    - acquired 429.71
  - interventricular septal 745.4
    - with pulmonary stenosis or atresia, dextraposition of aorta, and hypertrophy of right ventricle 745.2
    - acquired 429.71
    - in tetralogy of Fallot 745.2
  - iodide trapping 246.1
  - iodotyrosine dehalogenase 246.1
  - kynureninase 270.2
  - learning, specific 315.2
  - major osseous 731.3
  - mental (see also Retardation, mental) 319
  - osseous, major 731.3
  - osteochondral NEC 738.8
  - ostium
    - primum 745.61
    - secundum 745.5
  - pericardium 746.89
  - peroxidase-binding 246.1
  - placental blood supply — see Placenta, insufficiency
  - platelet (qualitative) 287.1
    - constitutional 286.4
  - postural, spine 737.9
  - protan 368.51
  - pulmonic cusps, congenital 746.00
- **Defect, defective** — *continued*
  - renal pelvis 753.9
    - obstructive 753.29
    - specified type NEC 753.3
  - respiratory system, congenital 748.9
    - specified type NEC 748.8
  - retina, retinal 361.30
    - with detachment (see also Detachment, retina, with retinal defect) 361.00
    - multiple 361.33
      - with detachment 361.02
    - nerve fiber bundle 362.85
    - single 361.30
      - with detachment 361.01
  - septal (closure) (heart) NEC 745.9
    - acquired 429.71
    - atrial 745.5
    - specified type NEC 745.8
  - speech NEC 784.5
    - developmental 315.39
    - secondary to organic lesion 784.5
  - Taussig-Bing (transposition, aorta and overriding pulmonary artery) 745.11
  - teeth, wedge 521.20
  - thyroid hormone synthesis 246.1
  - tritan 368.53
  - ureter 753.9
    - obstructive 753.29
  - vascular (acquired) (local) 459.9
    - congenital (peripheral) NEC 747.60
      - gastrointestinal 747.61
      - lower limb 747.64
      - renal 747.62
      - specified NEC 747.69
      - spinal 747.82
      - upper limb 747.63
  - ventricular septal 745.4
    - with pulmonary stenosis or atresia, dextraposition of aorta, and hypertrophy of right ventricle 745.2
    - acquired 429.71
    - atrioventricular canal type 745.69
    - between infundibulum and anterior portion 745.4
    - in tetralogy of Fallot 745.2
    - isolated anterior 745.4
  - vision NEC 369.9
  - visual field 368.40
    - arcuate 368.43
    - heteronymous, bilateral 368.47
    - homonymous, bilateral 368.46
    - localized NEC 368.44
    - nasal step 368.44
    - peripheral 368.44
    - sector 368.43
  - voice 784.40
  - wedge, teeth (abrasion) 521.20
- **Defeminization syndrome** 255.2
- **Deferentitis** 608.4
  - gonorrheal (acute) 098.14
    - chronic or duration of 2 months or over 098.34
- **Defibrination syndrome** — see also Fibrinolysis 286.6
- **Deficiency, deficient**
  - 3-beta-hydroxysteroid dehydrogenase 255.2
  - 6-phosphogluconic dehydrogenase (anemia) 282.2
  - 11-beta-hydroxylase 255.2
  - 17-alpha-hydroxylase 255.2
  - 18-hydroxysteroid dehydrogenase 255.2
  - 20-alpha-hydroxylase 255.2
  - 21-hydroxylase 255.2
  - AAT (alpha-1 antitrypsin) 273.4
  - abdominal muscle syndrome 756.79
  - accelerator globulin (Ac G) (blood) (see also Defect, coagulation) 286.3
  - AC globulin (congenital) (see also Defect, coagulation) 286.3
    - acquired 286.7

☑ Additional Digit Required — Refer to the Tabular List for Digit Selection

▽ Subterms under main terms may continue to next column or page

Deficiency, deficient — *continued*
activating factor (blood) (*see also* Defect, coagulation) 286.3
adenohypophyseal 253.2
adenosine deaminase 277.2
aldolase (hereditary) 271.2
alpha-1-antitrypsin 273.4
alpha-1-trypsin inhibitor 273.4
alpha-fucosidase 271.8
alpha-lipoprotein 272.5
alpha-mannosidase 271.8
amino acid 270.9
anemia — *see* Anemia, deficiency
aneurin 265.1
with beriberi 265.0
antibody NEC 279.00
antidiuretic hormone 253.5
antihemophilic
factor (A) 286.0
B 286.1
C 286.2
globulin (AHG) NEC 286.0
antithrombin III 289.81
antitrypsin 273.4
argininosuccinate synthetase or lyase 270.6
ascorbic acid (with scurvy) 267
autoprothrombin
I (*see also* Defect, coagulation) 286.3
II 286.1
C (*see also* Defect, coagulation) 286.3
bile salt 579.8
biotin 266.2
biotinidase 277.6
bradykinase-1 277.6
brancher enzyme (amylopectinosis) 271.0
calciferol 268.9
with
osteomalacia 268.2
rickets (*see also* Rickets) 268.0
calcium 275.40
dietary 269.3
calorie, severe 261
carbamyl phosphate synthetase 270.6
cardiac (*see also* Insufficiency, myocardial) 428.0
carnitine 277.81
due to
hemodialysis 277.83
inborn errors of metabolism 277.82
valproic acid therapy 277.83
iatrogenic 277.83
palmitoyltransferase (CPT1, CPT2) 277.85
palmityl transferase (CPT1, CPT2) 277.85
primary 277.81
secondary 277.84
carotene 264.9
Carr factor (*see also* Defect, coagulation) 286.9
central nervous system 349.9
ceruloplasmin 275.1
cevitamic acid (with scurvy) 267
choline 266.2
Christmas factor 286.1
chromium 269.3
citrin 269.1
clotting (blood) (*see also* Defect, coagulation) 286.9
coagulation factor NEC 286.9
with
abortion — *see* Abortion, by type, with hemorrhage
ectopic pregnancy (*see also* categories 634–638) 639.1
molar pregnancy (*see also* categories 630–632) 639.1
acquired (any) 286.7
antepartum or intrapartum 641.3 ☑
affecting fetus or newborn 762.1

Deficiency, deficient — *continued*
coagulation factor — *continued*
complicating pregnancy, childbirth, or puerperium 649.3 ☑
due to
liver disease 286.7
vitamin K deficiency 286.7
newborn, transient 776.3
postpartum 666.3 ☑
specified type NEC 286.3
color vision (congenital) 368.59
acquired 368.55
combined glucocorticoid and mineralocorticoid 255.41
combined, two or more coagulation factors (*see also* Defect, coagulation) 286.9
complement factor NEC 279.8
contact factor (*see also* Defect, coagulation) 286.3
copper NEC 275.1
corticoadrenal 255.41
craniofacial axis 756.0
cyanocobalamin (vitamin B_{12}) 266.2
debrancher enzyme (limit dextrinosis) 271.0
desmolase 255.2
diet 269.9
dihydrofolate reductase 281.2
dihydropteridine reductase 270.1
disaccharidase (intestinal) 271.3
disease NEC 269.9
ear(s) V48.8
edema 262
endocrine 259.9
enzymes, circulating NEC (*see also* Deficiency, by specific enzyme) 277.6
ergosterol 268.9
with
osteomalacia 268.2
rickets (*see also* Rickets) 268.0
erythrocytic glutathione (anemia) 282.2
eyelid(s) V48.8
factor (*see also* Defect, coagulation) 286.9
I (congenital) (fibrinogen) 286.3
antepartum or intrapartum 641.3 ☑
affecting fetus or newborn 762.1
newborn, transient 776.3
postpartum 666.3 ☑
II (congenital) (prothrombin) 286.3
V (congenital) (labile) 286.3
VII (congenital) (stable) 286.3
VIII (congenital) (functional) 286.0
with
functional defect 286.0
vascular defect 286.4
IX (Christmas) (congenital) (functional) 286.1
X (congenital) (Stuart-Prower) 286.3
XI (congenital) (plasma thromboplastin antecedent) 286.2
XII (congenital) (Hageman) 286.3
XIII (congenital) (fibrin stabilizing) 286.3
Hageman 286.3
multiple (congenital) 286.9
acquired 286.7
fibrinase (*see also* Defect, coagulation) 286.3
fibrinogen (congenital) (*see also* Defect, coagulation) 286.3
acquired 286.6
fibrin-stabilizing factor (congenital) (*see also* Defect, coagulation) 286.3
finger — *see* Absence, finger
fletcher factor (*see also* Defect, coagulation) 286.9
fluorine 269.3
folate, anemia 281.2

Deficiency, deficient — *continued*
folic acid (vitamin B_c) 266.2
anemia 281.2
follicle-stimulating hormone (FSH) 253.4
fructokinase 271.2
fructose-1, 6-diphosphate 271.2
fructose-1-phosphate aldolase 271.2
FSH (follicle-stimulating hormone) 253.4
fucosidase 271.8
galactokinase 271.1
galactose-1-phosphate uridyl transferase 271.1
gamma globulin in blood 279.00
glass factor (*see also* Defect, coagulation) 286.3
glucocorticoid 255.41
glucose-6-phosphatase 271.0
glucose-6-phosphate dehydrogenase anemia 282.2
glucuronyl transferase 277.4
glutathione-reductase (anemia) 282.2
glycogen synthetase 271.0
growth hormone 253.3
Hageman factor (congenital) (*see also* Defect, coagulation) 286.3
head V48.0
hemoglobin (*see also* Anemia) 285.9
hepatophosphorylase 271.0
hexose monophosphate (HMP) shunt 282.2
HGH (human growth hormone) 253.3
HG-PRT 277.2
homogentisic acid oxidase 270.2
hormone (*see also* Deficiency, by specific hormone)
anterior pituitary (isolated) (partial) NEC 253.4
growth (human) 253.3
follicle-stimulating 253.4
growth (human) (isolated) 253.3
human growth 253.3
interstitial cell-stimulating 253.4
luteinizing 253.4
melanocyte-stimulating 253.4
testicular 257.2
human growth hormone 253.3
humoral 279.00
with
hyper-IgM 279.05
autosomal recessive 279.05
X-linked 279.05
increased IgM 279.05
congenital hypogammaglobulinemia 279.04
non-sex-linked 279.06
selective immunoglobulin NEC 279.03
IgA 279.01
IgG 279.03
IgM 279.02
increased 279.05
specified NEC 279.09
hydroxylase 255.2
hypoxanthine-guanine phosphoribosyltransferase (HG-PRT) 277.2
ICSH (interstitial cell-stimulating hormone) 253.4
immunity NEC 279.3
cell-mediated 279.10
with
hyperimmunoglobulinemia 279.2
thrombocytopenia and eczema 279.12
specified NEC 279.19
combined (severe) 279.2
syndrome 279.2
common variable 279.06
humoral NEC 279.00
IgA (secretory) 279.01
IgG 279.03
IgM 279.02
immunoglobulin, selective NEC 279.03

Deficiency, deficient — *continued*
immunoglobulin, selective — *continued*
IgA 279.01
IgG 279.03
IgM 279.02
inositol (B complex) 266.2
interferon 279.4
internal organ V47.0
interstitial cell-stimulating hormone (ICSH) 253.4
intrinsic factor (Castle's) (congenital) 281.0
intrinsic (urethral) sphincter (ISD) 599.82
invertase 271.3
iodine 269.3
iron, anemia 280.9
labile factor (congenital) (*see also* Defect, coagulation) 286.3
acquired 286.7
lacrimal fluid (acquired) 375.15
congenital 743.64
lactase 271.3
Laki-Lorand factor (*see also* Defect, coagulation) 286.3
lecithin-cholesterol acyltranferase 272.5
LH (luteinizing hormone) 253.4
limb V49.0
lower V49.0
congenital (*see also* Deficiency, lower limb, congenital) 755.30
upper V49.0
congenital (*see also* Deficiency, upper limb, congenital) 755.20
lipocaic 577.8
lipoid (high-density) 272.5
lipoprotein (familial) (high density) 272.5
liver phosphorylase 271.0
long chain 3-hydroxyacyl CoA dehydrogenase (LCHAD) 277.85
long chain/very long chain acyl CoA dehydrogenase (LCAD, VLCAD) 277.85
lower limb V49.0
congenital 755.30
with complete absence of distal elements 755.31
longitudinal (complete) (partial) (with distal deficiencies, incomplete) 755.32
with complete absence of distal elements 755.31
combined femoral, tibial, fibular (incomplete) 755.33
femoral 755.34
fibular 755.37
metatarsal(s) 755.38
phalange(s) 755.39
meaning all digits 755.31
tarsal(s) 755.38
tibia 755.36
tibiofibular 755.35
transverse 755.31
luteinizing hormone (LH) 253.4
lysosomal alpha-1, 4 glucosidase 271.0
magnesium 275.2
mannosidase 271.8
medium chain acyl CoA dehydrogenase (MCAD) 277.85
melanocyte-stimulating hormone (MSH) 253.4
menadione (vitamin K) 269.0
newborn 776.0
mental (familial) (hereditary) (*see also* Retardation, mental) 319
methylenetetrahydrofolate reductase (MTHFR) 270.4
mineral NEC 269.3
mineralocorticoid 255.42

Deficiency, deficient — *continued*
- molybdenum 269.3
- moral 301.7
- multiple, syndrome 260
- myocardial (*see also* Insufficiency, myocardial) 428.0
- myophosphorylase 271.0
- NADH-diaphorase or reductase (congenital) 289.7
- NADH (DPNH)-methemoglobin-reductase (congenital) 289.7
- neck V48.1
- niacin (amide) (-tryptophan) 265.2
- nicotinamide 265.2
- nicotinic acid (amide) 265.2
- nose V48.8
- number of teeth (*see also* Anodontia) 520.0
- nutrition, nutritional 269.9
  - specified NEC 269.8
- ornithine transcarbamylase 270.6
- ovarian 256.39
- oxygen (*see also* Anoxia) 799.02
- pantothenic acid 266.2
- parathyroid (gland) 252.1
- phenylalanine hydroxylase 270.1
- phosphoenolpyruvate carboxykinase 271.8
- phosphofructokinase 271.2
- phosphoglucomutase 271.0
- phosphohexosisomerase 271.0
- phosphomannomutase 271.8
- phosphomannose isomerase 271.8
- phosphomannosyl mutase 271.8
- phosphorylase kinase, liver 271.0
- pituitary (anterior) 253.2
  - posterior 253.5
- placenta — *see* Placenta, insufficiency
- plasma
  - cell 279.00
  - protein (paraproteinemia) (pyroglobulinemia) 273.8
    - gamma globulin 279.00
  - thromboplastin
    - antecedent (PTA) 286.2
    - component (PTC) 286.1
- platelet NEC 287.1
  - constitutional 286.4
- polyglandular 258.9
- potassium (K) 276.8
- proaccelerin (congenital) (*see also* Defect, congenital) 286.3
  - acquired 286.7
- proconvertin factor (congenital) (*see also* Defect, coagulation) 286.3
  - acquired 286.7
- prolactin 253.4
- protein 260
  - anemia 281.4
  - C 289.81
  - plasma — *see* Deficiency, plasma, protein
  - S 289.81
- prothrombin (congenital) (*see also* Defect, coagulation) 286.3
  - acquired 286.7
- Prower factor (*see also* Defect, coagulation) 286.3
- PRT 277.2
- pseudocholinesterase 289.89
- psychobiological 301.6
- PTA 286.2
- PTC 286.1
- purine nucleoside phosphorylase 277.2
- pyracin (alpha) (beta) 266.1
- pyridoxal 266.1
- pyridoxamine 266.1
- pyridoxine (derivatives) 266.1
- pyruvate carboxylase 271.8
- pyruvate dehydrogenase 271.8
- pyruvate kinase (PK) 282.3
- riboflavin (vitamin B_2) 266.0
- saccadic eye movements 379.57
- salivation 527.7
- salt 276.1

Deficiency, deficient — *continued*
- secretion
  - ovary 256.39
  - salivary gland (any) 527.7
  - urine 788.5
- selenium 269.3
- serum
  - antitrypsin, familial 273.4
  - protein (congenital) 273.8
- short chain acyl CoA dehydrogenase (SCAD) 277.85
- short stature homeobox gene (SHOX)
  - with
    - dyschondrosteosis 756.89
    - short stature (idiopathic) 783.43
    - Turner's syndrome 758.6
- smooth pursuit movements (eye) 379.58
- sodium (Na) 276.1
- SPCA (*see also* Defect, coagulation) 286.3
- specified NEC 269.8
- stable factor (congenital) (*see also* Defect, coagulation) 286.3
  - acquired 286.7
- Stuart (-Prower) factor (*see also* Defect, coagulation) 286.3
- sucrase 271.3
- sucrase-isomaltase 271.3
- sulfite oxidase 270.0
- syndrome, multiple 260
- thiamine, thiaminic (chloride) 265.1
- thrombokinase (*see also* Defect, coagulation) 286.3
  - newborn 776.0
- thrombopoieten 287.39
- thymolymphatic 279.2
- thyroid (gland) 244.9
- tocopherol 269.1
- toe — *see* Absence, toe
- tooth bud (*see also* Anodontia) 520.0
- trunk V48.1
- UDPG-glycogen transferase 271.0
- upper limb V49.0
  - congenital 755.20
    - with complete absence of distal elements 755.21
    - longitudinal (complete) (partial) (with distal deficiencies, incomplete) 755.22
      - carpal(s) 755.28
      - combined humeral, radial, ulnar (incomplete) 755.23
      - humeral 755.24
      - metacarpal(s) 755.28
      - phalange(s) 755.29
        - meaning all digits 755.21
      - radial 755.26
      - radioulnar 755.25
      - ulnar 755.27
    - transverse (complete) (partial) 755.21
- vascular 459.9
- vasopressin 253.5
- viosterol (*see also* Deficiency, calciferol) 268.9
- vitamin (multiple) NEC 269.2
  - A 264.9
    - with
      - Bitôt's spot 264.1
        - corneal 264.2
          - with corneal ulceration 264.3
      - keratomalacia 264.4
      - keratosis, follicular 264.8
      - night blindness 264.5
      - scar of cornea, xerophthalmic 264.6
      - specified manifestation NEC 264.8
        - ocular 264.7
      - xeroderma 264.8
      - xerophthalmia 264.7
      - xerosis
        - conjunctival 264.0

Deficiency, deficient — *continued*
- vitamin — *continued*
  - A — *continued*
    - with — *continued*
      - xerosis — *continued*
        - conjunctival — *continued*
          - with Bitôt's spot 264.1
        - corneal 264.2
          - with corneal ulceration 264.3
  - B (complex) NEC 266.9
    - with
      - beriberi 265.0
      - pellagra 265.2
    - specified type NEC 266.2
  - B_1 NEC 265.1
    - beriberi 265.0
  - B_2 266.0
  - B_6 266.1
  - B_{12} 266.2
  - B_c (folic acid) 266.2
  - C (ascorbic acid) (with scurvy) 267
  - D (calciferol) (ergosterol) 268.9
    - with
      - osteomalacia 268.2
      - rickets (*see also* Rickets) 268.0
  - E 269.1
  - folic acid 266.2
  - G 266.0
  - H 266.2
  - K 269.0
    - of newborn 776.0
  - nicotinic acid 265.2
  - P 269.1
  - PP 265.2
  - specified NEC 269.1
- zinc 269.3

Deficient — *see also* Deficiency
- blink reflex 374.45
- craniofacial axis 756.0
- number of teeth (*see also* Anodontia) 520.0
- secretion of urine 788.5

Deficit
- neurologic NEC 781.99
  - due to
    - cerebrovascular lesion (*see also* Disease, cerebrovascular, acute) 436
      - late effect — *see* Late effect(s) (of) cerebrovascular disease
    - transient ischemic attack 435.9
  - ischemic
    - reversible (RIND) 434.91
      - history of (personal) V12.54
      - prolonged (PRIND) 434.91
        - history of (personal) V12.54
- oxygen 799.02

Deflection
- radius 736.09
- septum (acquired) (nasal) (nose) 470
- spine — *see* Curvature, spine
- turbinate (nose) 470

Defluvium
- capillorum (*see also* Alopecia) 704.00
- ciliorum 374.55
- unguium 703.8

Deformity 738.9
- abdomen, congenital 759.9
- abdominal wall
  - acquired 738.8
  - congenital 756.70
    - muscle deficiency syndrome 756.79
- acquired (unspecified site) 738.9
  - specified site NEC 738.8
- adrenal gland (congenital) 759.1
- alimentary tract, congenital 751.9
  - lower 751.5
  - specified type NEC 751.8
  - upper (any part, except tongue) 750.9

Deformity — *continued*
- alimentary tract, congenital — *continued*
  - upper — *continued*
    - specified type NEC 750.8
    - tongue 750.10
      - specified type NEC 750.19
- ankle (joint) (acquired) 736.70
  - abduction 718.47
  - congenital 755.69
  - contraction 718.47
  - specified NEC 736.79
- anus (congenital) 751.5
  - acquired 569.49
- aorta (congenital) 747.20
  - acquired 447.8
  - arch 747.21
    - acquired 447.8
  - coarctation 747.10
- aortic
  - arch 747.21
    - acquired 447.8
  - cusp or valve (congenital) 746.9
    - acquired (*see also* Endocarditis, aortic) 424.1
  - ring 747.21
- appendix 751.5
- arm (acquired) 736.89
  - congenital 755.50
- arteriovenous (congenital) (peripheral) NEC 747.60
  - gastrointestinal 747.61
  - lower limb 747.64
  - renal 747.62
  - specified NEC 747.69
  - spinal 747.82
  - upper limb 747.63
- artery (congenital) (peripheral) NEC (*see also* Deformity, vascular) 747.60
  - acquired 447.8
  - cerebral 747.81
  - coronary (congenital) 746.85
    - acquired (*see also* Ischemia, heart) 414.9
  - retinal 743.9
  - umbilical 747.5
- atrial septal (congenital) (heart) 745.5
- auditory canal (congenital) (external) (*see also* Deformity, ear) 744.3
  - acquired 380.50
- auricle
  - ear (congenital) (*see also* Deformity, ear) 744.3
    - acquired 380.32
  - heart (congenital) 746.9
- back (acquired) — *see* Deformity, spine
- Bartholin's duct (congenital) 750.9
- bile duct (congenital) 751.60
  - acquired 576.8
    - with calculus, choledocholithiasis, or stones — *see* Choledocholithiasis
- biliary duct or passage (congenital) 751.60
  - acquired 576.8
    - with calculus, choledocholithiasis, or stones — *see* Choledocholithiasis
- bladder (neck) (sphincter) (trigone) (acquired) 596.8
  - congenital 753.9
- bone (acquired) NEC 738.9
  - congenital 756.9
  - turbinate 738.0
- boutonniere (finger) 736.21
- brain (congenital) 742.9
  - acquired 348.8
  - multiple 742.4
  - reduction 742.2
  - vessel (congenital) 747.81
- breast (acquired) 611.89 ▲
  - congenital 757.9
  - reconstructed 612.0 ●
- bronchus (congenital) 748.3

Deformity — *continued*
bronchus — *continued*
acquired 519.19
bursa, congenital 756.9
canal of Nuck 752.9
canthus (congenital) 743.9
acquired 374.89
capillary (acquired) 448.9
congenital NEC (*see also* Deformity, vascular) 747.60
cardiac — *see* Deformity, heart
cardiovascular system (congenital) 746.9
caruncle, lacrimal (congenital) 743.9
acquired 375.69
cascade, stomach 537.6
cecum (congenital) 751.5
acquired 569.89
cerebral (congenital) 742.9
acquired 348.8
cervix (acquired) (uterus) 622.8
congenital 752.40
cheek (acquired) 738.19
congenital 744.9
chest (wall) (acquired) 738.3
congenital 754.89
late effect of rickets 268.1
chin (acquired) 738.19
congenital 744.9
choroid (congenital) 743.9
acquired 363.8
plexus (congenital) 742.9
acquired 349.2
cicatricial — *see* Cicatrix
cilia (congenital) 743.9
acquired 374.89
circulatory system (congenital) 747.9
clavicle (acquired) 738.8
congenital 755.51
clitoris (congenital) 752.40
acquired 624.8
clubfoot — *see* Clubfoot
coccyx (acquired) 738.6
congenital 756.10
colon (congenital) 751.5
acquired 569.89
concha (ear) (congenital) (*see also* Deformity, ear) 744.3
acquired 380.32
congenital, organ or site not listed (*see also* Anomaly) 759.9
cornea (congenital) 743.9
acquired 371.70
coronary artery (congenital) 746.85
acquired (*see also* Ischemia, heart) 414.9
cranium (acquired) 738.19
congenital (*see also* Deformity, skull, congenital) 756.0
cricoid cartilage (congenital) 748.3
acquired 478.79
cystic duct (congenital) 751.60
acquired 575.8
Dandy-Walker 742.3
with spina bifida (*see also* Spina bifida) 741.0 ☑
diaphragm (congenital) 756.6
acquired 738.8
digestive organ(s) or system (congenital) NEC 751.9
specified type NEC 751.8
ductus arteriosus 747.0
duodenal bulb 537.89
duodenum (congenital) 751.5
acquired 537.89
dura (congenital) 742.9
brain 742.4
acquired 349.2
spinal 742.59
acquired 349.2
ear (congenital) 744.3
acquired 380.32
auricle 744.3
causing impairment of hearing 744.02

Deformity — *continued*
ear — *continued*
causing impairment of hearing 744.00
external 744.3
causing impairment of hearing 744.02
internal 744.05
lobule 744.3
middle 744.03
ossicles 744.04
ossicles 744.04
ectodermal (congenital) NEC 757.9
specified type NEC 757.8
ejaculatory duct (congenital) 752.9
acquired 608.89
elbow (joint) (acquired) 736.00
congenital 755.50
contraction 718.42
endocrine gland NEC 759.2
epididymis (congenital) 752.9
acquired 608.89
torsion 608.24
epiglottis (congenital) 748.3
acquired 478.79
esophagus (congenital) 750.9
acquired 530.89
Eustachian tube (congenital) NEC 744.3
specified type NEC 744.24
extremity (acquired) 736.9
congenital, except reduction deformity 755.9
lower 755.60
upper 755.50
reduction — *see* Deformity, reduction
eye (congenital) 743.9
acquired 379.8
muscle 743.9
eyebrow (congenital) 744.89
eyelid (congenital) 743.9
acquired 374.89
specified type NEC 743.62
face (acquired) 738.19
congenital (any part) 744.9
due to intrauterine malposition and pressure 754.0
fallopian tube (congenital) 752.10
acquired 620.8
femur (acquired) 736.89
congenital 755.60
fetal
with fetopelvic disproportion 653.7 ☑
affecting fetus or newborn 763.1
causing obstructed labor 660.1 ☑
affecting fetus or newborn 763.1
known or suspected, affecting management of pregnancy 655.9 ☑
finger (acquired) 736.20
boutonniere type 736.21
congenital 755.50
flexion contracture 718.44
swan neck 736.22
flexion (joint) (acquired) 736.9
congenital NEC 755.9
hip or thigh (acquired) 736.39
congenital (*see also* Subluxation, congenital, hip) 754.32
foot (acquired) 736.70
cavovarus 736.75
congenital 754.59
congenital NEC 754.70
specified type NEC 754.79
valgus (acquired) 736.79
congenital 754.60
specified type NEC 754.69
varus (acquired) 736.79
congenital 754.50
specified type NEC 754.59
forearm (acquired) 736.00
congenital 755.50
forehead (acquired) 738.19

Deformity — *continued*
forehead — *continued*
congenital (*see also* Deformity, skull, congenital) 756.0
frontal bone (acquired) 738.19
congenital (*see also* Deformity, skull, congenital) 756.0
gallbladder (congenital) 751.60
acquired 575.8
gastrointestinal tract (congenital) NEC 751.9
acquired 569.89
specified type NEC 751.8
genitalia, genital organ(s) or system NEC
congenital 752.9
female (congenital) 752.9
acquired 629.89
external 752.40
internal 752.9
male (congenital) 752.9
acquired 608.89
globe (eye) (congenital) 743.9
acquired 360.89
gum (congenital) 750.9
acquired 523.9
gunstock 736.02
hand (acquired) 736.00
claw 736.06
congenital 755.50
minus (and plus) (intrinsic) 736.09
pill roller (intrinsic) 736.09
plus (and minus) (intrinsic) 736.09
swan neck (intrinsic) 736.09
head (acquired) 738.10
congenital (*see also* Deformity, skull congenital) 756.0
specified NEC 738.19
heart (congenital) 746.9
auricle (congenital) 746.9
septum 745.9
auricular 745.5
specified type NEC 745.8
ventricular 745.4
valve (congenital) NEC 746.9
acquired — *see* Endocarditis
pulmonary (congenital) 746.00
specified type NEC 746.89
ventricle (congenital) 746.9
heel (acquired) 736.76
congenital 755.67
hepatic duct (congenital) 751.60
acquired 576.8
with calculus, choledocholithiasis, or stones — *see* Choledocholithiasis
hip (joint) (acquired) 736.30
congenital NEC 755.63
flexion 718.45
congenital (*see also* Subluxation, congenital, hip) 754.32
hourglass — *see* Contraction, hourglass
humerus (acquired) 736.89
congenital 755.50
hymen (congenital) 752.40
hypophyseal (congenital) 759.2
ileocecal (coil) (valve) (congenital) 751.5
acquired 569.89
ileum (intestine) (congenital) 751.5
acquired 569.89
ilium (acquired) 738.6
congenital 755.60
integument (congenital) 757.9
intervertebral cartilage or disc (acquired) (*see also* Displacement, intervertebral disc)
congenital 756.10
intestine (large) (small) (congenital) 751.5
acquired 569.89
iris (acquired) 364.75
congenital 743.9
prolapse 364.89

Deformity — *continued*
ischium (acquired) 738.6
congenital 755.60
jaw (acquired) (congenital) NEC 524.9
due to intrauterine malposition and pressure 754.0
joint (acquired) NEC 738.8
congenital 755.9
contraction (abduction) (adduction) (extension) (flexion) — *see* Contraction, joint
kidney(s) (calyx) (pelvis) (congenital) 753.9
acquired 593.89
vessel 747.62
acquired 459.9
Klippel-Feil (brevicollis) 756.16
knee (acquired) NEC 736.6
congenital 755.64
labium (majus) (minus) (congenital) 752.40
acquired 624.8
lacrimal apparatus or duct (congenital) 743.9
acquired 375.69
larynx (muscle) (congenital) 748.3
acquired 478.79
web (glottic) (subglottic) 748.2
leg (lower) (upper) (acquired) NEC 736.89
congenital 755.60
reduction — *see* Deformity, reduction, lower limb
lens (congenital) 743.9
acquired 379.39
lid (fold) (congenital) 743.9
acquired 374.89
ligament (acquired) 728.9
congenital 756.9
limb (acquired) 736.9
congenital, except reduction deformity 755.9
lower 755.60
reduction (*see also* Deformity, reduction, lower limb) 755.30
upper 755.50
reduction (*see also* Deformity, reduction, upper limb) 755.20
specified NEC 736.89
lip (congenital) NEC 750.9
acquired 528.5
specified type NEC 750.26
liver (congenital) 751.60
acquired 573.8
duct (congenital) 751.60
acquired 576.8
with calculus, choledocholithiasis, or stones — *see* Choledocholithiasis
lower extremity — *see* Deformity, leg
lumbosacral (joint) (region) (congenital) 756.10
acquired 738.5
lung (congenital) 748.60
acquired 518.89
specified type NEC 748.69
lymphatic system, congenital 759.9
Madelung's (radius) 755.54
maxilla (acquired) (congenital) 524.9
meninges or membrane (congenital) 742.9
brain 742.4
acquired 349.2
spinal (cord) 742.59
acquired 349.2
mesentery (congenital) 751.9
acquired 568.89
metacarpus (acquired) 736.00
congenital 755.50
metatarsus (acquired) 736.70
congenital 754.70
middle ear, except ossicles (congenital) 744.03

Deformity — *continued*
middle ear, except ossicles — *continued*
ossicles 744.04
mitral (leaflets) (valve) (congenital) 746.9
acquired — *see* Endocarditis, mitral
Ebstein's 746.89
parachute 746.5
specified type NEC 746.89
stenosis, congenital 746.5
mouth (acquired) 528.9
congenital NEC 750.9
specified type NEC 750.26
multiple, congenital NEC 759.7
specified type NEC 759.89
muscle (acquired) 728.9
congenital 756.9
specified type NEC 756.89
sternocleidomastoid (due to intrauterine malposition and pressure) 754.1
musculoskeletal system, congenital NEC 756.9
specified type NEC 756.9
nail (acquired) 703.9
congenital 757.9
nasal — *see* Deformity, nose
neck (acquired) NEC 738.2
congenital (any part) 744.9
sternocleidomastoid 754.1
nervous system (congenital) 742.9
nipple (congenital) 757.9
acquired 611.89 ▲
nose, nasal (cartilage) (acquired) 738.0
bone (turbinate) 738.0
congenital 748.1
bent 754.0
squashed 754.0
saddle 738.0
syphilitic 090.5
septum 470
congenital 748.1
sinus (wall) (congenital) 748.1
acquired 738.0
syphilitic (congenital) 090.5
late 095.8
ocular muscle (congenital) 743.9
acquired 378.60
opticociliary vessels (congenital) 743.9
orbit (congenital) (eye) 743.9
acquired NEC 376.40
associated with craniofacial deformities 376.44
due to
bone disease 376.43
surgery 376.47
trauma 376.47
organ of Corti (congenital) 744.05
ovary (congenital) 752.0
acquired 620.8
oviduct (congenital) 752.10
acquired 620.8
palate (congenital) 750.9
acquired 526.89
cleft (congenital) (*see also* Cleft, palate) 749.00
hard, acquired 526.89
soft, acquired 528.9
pancreas (congenital) 751.7
acquired 577.8
parachute, mitral valve 746.5
parathyroid (gland) 759.2
parotid (gland) (congenital) 750.9
acquired 527.8
patella (acquired) 736.6
congenital 755.64
pelvis, pelvic (acquired) (bony) 738.6
with disproportion (fetopelvic) 653.0 ☑
affecting fetus or newborn 763.1
causing obstructed labor 660.1 ☑
affecting fetus or newborn 763.1

Deformity — *continued*
pelvis, pelvic — *continued*
congenital 755.60
rachitic (late effect) 268.1
penis (glans) (congenital) 752.9
acquired 607.89
pericardium (congenital) 746.9
acquired — *see* Pericarditis
pharynx (congenital) 750.9
acquired 478.29
Pierre Robin (congenital) 756.0
pinna (acquired) 380.32
congenital 744.3
pituitary (congenital) 759.2
pleural folds (congenital) 748.8
portal vein (congenital) 747.40
posture — *see* Curvature, spine
prepuce (congenital) 752.9
acquired 607.89
prostate (congenital) 752.9
acquired 602.8
pulmonary valve — *see* Endocarditis, pulmonary
pupil (congenital) 743.9
acquired 364.75
pylorus (congenital) 750.9
acquired 537.89
rachitic (acquired), healed or old 268.1
radius (acquired) 736.00
congenital 755.50
reduction — *see* Deformity, reduction, upper limb
rectovaginal septum (congenital) 752.40
acquired 623.8
rectum (congenital) 751.5
acquired 569.49
reduction (extremity) (limb) 755.4
brain 742.2
lower limb 755.30
with complete absence of distal elements 755.31
longitudinal (complete) (partial) (with distal deficiencies, incomplete) 755.32
with complete absence of distal elements 755.31
combined femoral, tibial, fibular (incomplete) 755.33
femoral 755.34
fibular 755.37
metatarsal(s) 755.38
phalange(s) 755.39
meaning all digits 755.31
tarsal(s) 755.38
tibia 755.36
tibiofibular 755.35
transverse 755.31
upper limb 755.20
with complete absence of distal elements 755.21
longitudinal (complete) (partial) (with distal deficiencies, incomplete) 755.22
with complete absence of distal elements 755.21
carpal(s) 755.28
combined humeral, radial, ulnar (incomplete) 755.23
humeral 755.24
metacarpal(s) 755.28
phalange(s) 755.29
meaning all digits 755.21
radial 755.26
radioulnar 755.25
ulnar 755.27
transverse (complete) (partial) 755.21
renal — *see* Deformity, kidney
respiratory system (congenital) 748.9
specified type NEC 748.8
rib (acquired) 738.3
congenital 756.3
cervical 756.2

Deformity — *continued*
rotation (joint) (acquired) 736.9
congenital 755.9
hip or thigh 736.39
congenital (*see also* Subluxation, congenital, hip) 754.32
sacroiliac joint (congenital) 755.69
acquired 738.5
sacrum (acquired) 738.5
congenital 756.10
saddle
back 737.8
nose 738.0
syphilitic 090.5
salivary gland or duct (congenital) 750.9
acquired 527.8
scapula (acquired) 736.89
congenital 755.50
scrotum (congenital) 752.9
acquired 608.89
sebaceous gland, acquired 706.8
seminal tract or duct (congenital) 752.9
acquired 608.89
septum (nasal) (acquired) 470
congenital 748.1
shoulder (joint) (acquired) 736.89
congenital 755.50
specified type NEC 755.59
contraction 718.41
sigmoid (flexure) (congenital) 751.5
acquired 569.89
sinus of Valsalva 747.29
skin (congenital) 757.9
acquired NEC 709.8
skull (acquired) 738.19
congenital 756.0
with
anencephalus 740.0
encephalocele 742.0
hydrocephalus 742.3
with spina bifida (*see also* Spina bifida) 741.0 ☑
microcephalus 742.1
due to intrauterine malposition and pressure 754.0
soft parts, organs or tissues (of pelvis)
in pregnancy or childbirth NEC 654.9 ☑
affecting fetus or newborn 763.89
causing obstructed labor 660.2 ☑
affecting fetus or newborn 763.1
spermatic cord (congenital) 752.9
acquired 608.89
torsion 608.22
extravaginal 608.21
intravaginal 608.22
spinal
column — *see* Deformity, spine
cord (congenital) 742.9
acquired 336.8
vessel (congenital) 747.82
nerve root (congenital) 742.9
acquired 724.9
spine (acquired) NEC 738.5
congenital 756.10
due to intrauterine malposition and pressure 754.2
kyphoscoliotic (*see also* Kyphoscoliosis) 737.30
kyphotic (*see also* Kyphosis) 737.10
lordotic (*see also* Lordosis) 737.20
rachitic 268.1
scoliotic (*see also* Scoliosis) 737.30
spleen
acquired 289.59
congenital 759.0
Sprengel's (congenital) 755.52
sternum (acquired) 738.3

Deformity — *continued*
sternum — *continued*
congenital 756.3
stomach (congenital) 750.9
acquired 537.89
submaxillary gland (congenital) 750.9
acquired 527.8
swan neck (acquired)
finger 736.22
hand 736.09
talipes — *see* Talipes
teeth, tooth NEC 520.9
testis (congenital) 752.9
acquired 608.89
torsion 608.20
thigh (acquired) 736.89
congenital 755.60
thorax (acquired) (wall) 738.3
congenital 754.89
late effect of rickets 268.1
thumb (acquired) 736.20
congenital 755.50
thymus (tissue) (congenital) 759.2
thyroid (gland) (congenital) 759.2
cartilage 748.3
acquired 478.79
tibia (acquired) 736.89
congenital 755.60
saber 090.5
toe (acquired) 735.9
congenital 755.66
specified NEC 735.8
tongue (congenital) 750.10
acquired 529.8
tooth, teeth NEC 520.9
trachea (rings) (congenital) 748.3
acquired 519.19
transverse aortic arch (congenital) 747.21
tricuspid (leaflets) (valve) (congenital) 746.9
acquired — *see* Endocarditis, tricuspid
atresia or stenosis 746.1
specified type NEC 746.89
trunk (acquired) 738.3
congenital 759.9
ulna (acquired) 736.00
congenital 755.50
upper extremity — *see* Deformity, arm
urachus (congenital) 753.7
ureter (opening) (congenital) 753.9
acquired 593.89
urethra (valve) (congenital) 753.9
acquired 599.84
urinary tract or system (congenital) 753.9
urachus 753.7
uterus (congenital) 752.3
acquired 621.8
uvula (congenital) 750.9
acquired 528.9
vagina (congenital) 752.40
acquired 623.8
valve, valvular (heart) (congenital) 746.9
acquired — *see* Endocarditis
pulmonary 746.00
specified type NEC 746.89
vascular (congenital) (peripheral) NEC 747.60
acquired 459.9
gastrointestinal 747.61
lower limb 747.64
renal 747.62
specified site NEC 747.69
spinal 747.82
upper limb 747.63
vas deferens (congenital) 752.9
acquired 608.89
vein (congenital) NEC (*see also* Deformity, vascular) 747.60
brain 747.81
coronary 746.9
great 747.40

Deformity — *continued*
- vena cava (inferior) (superior) (congenital) 747.40
- vertebra — *see* Deformity, spine
- vesicourethral orifice (acquired) 596.8
  - congenital NEC 753.9
    - specified type NEC 753.8
- vessels of optic papilla (congenital) 743.9
- visual field (contraction) 368.45
- vitreous humor (congenital) 743.9
  - acquired 379.29
- vulva (congenital) 752.40
  - acquired 624.8
- wrist (joint) (acquired) 736.00
  - congenital 755.50
  - contraction 718.43
  - valgus 736.03
    - congenital 755.59
  - varus 736.04
    - congenital 755.59

Degeneration, degenerative
- adrenal (capsule) (gland) 255.8
  - with hypofunction 255.41
  - fatty 255.8
  - hyaline 255.8
  - infectional 255.8
  - lardaceous 277.39
- amyloid (any site) (general) 277.39
- anterior cornua, spinal cord 336.8
- anterior labral 840.8 ●
- aorta, aortic 440.0
  - fatty 447.8
  - valve (heart) (*see also* Endocarditis, aortic) 424.1
- arteriovascular — *see* Arteriosclerosis
- artery, arterial (atheromatous) (calcareous) (*see also* Arteriosclerosis)
  - amyloid 277.39
  - lardaceous 277.39
  - medial NEC (*see also* Arteriosclerosis, extremities) 440.20
- articular cartilage NEC (*see also* Disorder, cartilage, articular) 718.0 ☑
  - elbow 718.02
  - knee 717.5
  - patella 717.7
  - shoulder 718.01
  - spine (*see also* Spondylosis) 721.90
- atheromatous — *see* Arteriosclerosis
- bacony (any site) 277.39
- basal nuclei or ganglia NEC 333.0
- bone 733.90
- brachial plexus 353.0
- brain (cortical) (progressive) 331.9
  - arteriosclerotic 437.0
  - childhood 330.9
    - specified type NEC 330.8
  - congenital 742.4
  - cystic 348.0
    - congenital 742.4
  - familial NEC 331.89
  - grey matter 330.8
  - heredofamilial NEC 331.89
  - in
    - alcoholism 303.9 ☑ *[331.7]*
    - beriberi 265.0 *[331.7]*
    - cerebrovascular disease 437.9 *[331.7]*
    - congenital hydrocephalus 742.3 *[331.7]*
      - with spina bifida (*see also* Spina bifida) 741.0 ☑ *[331.7]*
    - Fabry's disease 272.7 *[330.2]*
    - Gaucher's disease 272.7 *[330.2]*
    - Hunter's disease or syndrome 277.5 *[330.3]*
    - lipidosis
      - cerebral 330.1
      - generalized 272.7 *[330.2]*
    - mucopolysaccharidosis 277.5 *[330.3]*
    - myxedema (*see also* Myxedema) 244.9 *[331.7]*

Degeneration, degenerative — *continued*
- brain — *continued*
  - in — *continued*
    - neoplastic disease NEC (M8000/1) 239.9 *[331.7]*
    - Niemann-Pick disease 272.7 *[330.2]*
    - sphingolipidosis 272.7 *[330.2]*
    - vitamin B_{12} deficiency 266.2 *[331.7]*
  - motor centers 331.89
  - senile 331.2
  - specified type NEC 331.89
- breast — *see* Disease, breast
- Bruch's membrane 363.40
- bundle of His 426.50
  - left 426.3
  - right 426.4
- calcareous NEC 275.49
- capillaries 448.9
  - amyloid 277.39
  - fatty 448.9
  - lardaceous 277.39
- cardiac (brown) (calcareous) (fatty) (fibrous) (hyaline) (mural) (muscular) (pigmentary) (senile) (with arteriosclerosis) (*see also* Degeneration, myocardial) 429.1
  - valve, valvular — *see* Endocarditis
- cardiorenal (*see also* Hypertension, cardiorenal) 404.90
- cardiovascular (*see also* Disease, cardiovascular) 429.2
  - renal (*see also* Hypertension, cardiorenal) 404.90
- cartilage (joint) — *see* Derangement, joint
- cerebellar NEC 334.9
  - primary (hereditary) (sporadic) 334.2
- cerebral — *see* Degeneration, brain
- cerebromacular 330.1
- cerebrovascular 437.1
  - due to hypertension 437.2
  - late effect — *see* Late effect(s) (of) cerebrovascular disease
- cervical plexus 353.2
- cervix 622.8
  - due to radiation (intended effect) 622.8
    - adverse effect or misadventure 622.8
- changes, spine or vertebra (*see also* Spondylosis) 721.90
- chitinous 277.39
- chorioretinal 363.40
  - congenital 743.53
  - hereditary 363.50
- choroid (colloid) (drusen) 363.40
  - hereditary 363.50
  - senile 363.41
    - diffuse secondary 363.42
- cochlear 386.8
- collateral ligament (knee) (medial) 717.82
  - lateral 717.81
- combined (spinal cord) (subacute) 266.2 *[336.2]*
  - with anemia (pernicious) 281.0 *[336.2]*
    - due to dietary deficiency 281.1 *[336.2]*
  - due to vitamin B_{12} deficiency anemia (dietary) 281.1 *[336.2]*
- conjunctiva 372.50
  - amyloid 277.39 *[372.50]*
- cornea 371.40
  - calcerous 371.44
  - familial (hereditary) (*see also* Dystrophy, cornea) 371.50
    - macular 371.55
    - reticular 371.54
  - hyaline (of old scars) 371.41
  - marginal (Terrien's) 371.48
  - mosaic (shagreen) 371.41

Degeneration, degenerative — *continued*
- cornea — *continued*
  - nodular 371.46
  - peripheral 371.48
  - senile 371.41
- cortical (cerebellar) (parenchymatous) 334.2
  - alcoholic 303.9 ☑ *[334.4]*
  - diffuse, due to arteriopathy 437.0
- corticostriatal-spinal 334.8
- cretinoid 243
- cruciate ligament (knee) (posterior) 717.84
  - anterior 717.83
- cutis 709.3
  - amyloid 277.39
- dental pulp 522.2
- disc disease — *see* Degeneration, intervertebral disc
- dorsolateral (spinal cord) — *see* Degeneration, combined
- endocardial 424.90
- extrapyramidal NEC 333.90
- eye NEC 360.40
  - macular (*see also* Degeneration, macula) 362.50
    - congenital 362.75
    - hereditary 362.76
- fatty (diffuse) (general) 272.8
  - liver 571.8
    - alcoholic 571.0
  - localized site — *see* Degeneration, by site, fatty
  - placenta — *see* Placenta, abnormal
- globe (eye) NEC 360.40
  - macular — *see* Degeneration, macula
- grey matter 330.8
- heart (brown) (calcareous) (fatty) (fibrous) (hyaline) (mural) (muscular) (pigmentary) (senile) (with arteriosclerosis) (*see also* Degeneration, myocardial) 429.1
  - amyloid 277.39 *[425.7]*
  - atheromatous — *see* Arteriosclerosis, coronary
  - gouty 274.82
  - hypertensive (*see also* Hypertension, heart) 402.90
  - ischemic 414.9
  - valve, valvular — *see* Endocarditis
- hepatolenticular (Wilson's) 275.1
- hepatorenal 572.4
- heredofamilial
  - brain NEC 331.89
  - spinal cord NEC 336.8
- hyaline (diffuse) (generalized) 728.9
  - localized (*see also* Degeneration, by site)
    - cornea 371.41
    - keratitis 371.41
- hypertensive vascular — *see* Hypertension
- infrapatellar fat pad 729.31
- internal semilunar cartilage 717.3
- intervertebral disc 722.6
  - with myelopathy 722.70
  - cervical, cervicothoracic 722.4
    - with myelopathy 722.71
  - lumbar, lumbosacral 722.52
    - with myelopathy 722.73
  - thoracic, thoracolumbar 722.51
    - with myelopathy 722.72
- intestine 569.89
  - amyloid 277.39
  - lardaceous 277.39
- iris (generalized) (*see also* Atrophy, iris) 364.59
  - pigmentary 364.53
  - pupillary margin 364.54
- ischemic — *see* Ischemia
- joint disease (*see also* Osteoarthrosis) 715.9 ☑
  - multiple sites 715.09
  - spine (*see also* Spondylosis) 721.90

Degeneration, degenerative — *continued*
- kidney (*see also* Sclerosis, renal) 587
  - amyloid 277.39 *[583.81]*
  - cyst, cystic (multiple) (solitary) 593.2
    - congenital (*see also* Cystic, disease, kidney) 753.10
  - fatty 593.89
  - fibrocystic (congenital) 753.19
  - lardaceous 277.39 *[583.81]*
  - polycystic (congenital) 753.12
    - adult type (APKD) 753.13
    - autosomal dominant 753.13
    - autosomal recessive 753.14
    - childhood type (CPKD) 753.14
    - infantile type 753.14
  - waxy 277.39 *[583.81]*
- Kuhnt-Junius (retina) 362.52
- labyrinth, osseous 386.8
- lacrimal passages, cystic 375.12
- lardaceous (any site) 277.39
- lateral column (posterior), spinal cord (*see also* Degeneration, combined) 266.2 *[336.2]*
- lattice 362.63
- lens 366.9
  - infantile, juvenile, or presenile 366.00
  - senile 366.10
- lenticular (familial) (progressive) (Wilson's) (with cirrhosis of liver) 275.1
  - striate artery 437.0
- lethal ball, prosthetic heart valve 996.02
- ligament
  - collateral (knee) (medial) 717.82
    - lateral 717.81
  - cruciate (knee) (posterior) 717.84
    - anterior 717.83
- liver (diffuse) 572.8
  - amyloid 277.39
  - congenital (cystic) 751.62
  - cystic 572.8
    - congenital 751.62
  - fatty 571.8
    - alcoholic 571.0
  - hypertrophic 572.8
  - lardaceous 277.39
  - parenchymatous, acute or subacute (*see also* Necrosis, liver) 570
  - pigmentary 572.8
  - toxic (acute) 573.8
  - waxy 277.39
- lung 518.89
- lymph gland 289.3
  - hyaline 289.3
  - lardaceous 277.39
- macula (acquired) (senile) 362.50
  - atrophic 362.51
  - Best's 362.76
  - congenital 362.75
  - cystic 362.54
  - cystoid 362.53
  - disciform 362.52
  - dry 362.51
  - exudative 362.52
  - familial pseudoinflammatory 362.77
  - hereditary 362.76
  - hole 362.54
  - juvenile (Stargardt's) 362.75
  - nonexudative 362.51
  - pseudohole 362.54
  - wet 362.52
- medullary — *see* Degeneration, brain
- membranous labyrinth, congenital (causing impairment of hearing) 744.05
- meniscus — *see* Derangement, joint
- microcystoid 362.62
- mitral — *see* Insufficiency, mitral
- Mönckeberg's (*see also* Arteriosclerosis, extremities) 440.20

Degeneration, degenerative — *continued*
- moral 301.7
- motor centers, senile 331.2
- mural (*see also* Degeneration, myocardial) 429.1
  - heart, cardiac (*see also* Degeneration, myocardial) 429.1
  - myocardium, myocardial (*see also* Degeneration, myocardial) 429.1
- muscle 728.9
  - fatty 728.9
  - fibrous 728.9
  - heart (*see also* Degeneration, myocardial) 429.1
  - hyaline 728.9
- muscular progressive 728.2
- myelin, central nervous system NEC 341.9
- myocardium, myocardial (brown) (calcareous) (fatty) (fibrous) (hyaline) (mural) (muscular) (pigmentary) (senile) (with arteriosclerosis) 429.1
  - with rheumatic fever (conditions classifiable to 390) 398.0
    - active, acute, or subacute 391.2
      - with chorea 392.0
    - inactive or quiescent (with chorea) 398.0
  - amyloid 277.39 *[425.7]*
  - congenital 746.89
  - fetus or newborn 779.89
  - gouty 274.82
  - hypertensive (*see also* Hypertension, heart) 402.90
  - ischemic 414.8
  - rheumatic (*see also* Degeneration, myocardium, with rheumatic fever) 398.0
  - syphilitic 093.82
- nasal sinus (mucosa) (*see also* Sinusitis) 473.9
  - frontal 473.1
  - maxillary 473.0
- nerve — *see* Disorder, nerve
- nervous system 349.89
  - amyloid 277.39 *[357.4]*
  - autonomic (*see also* Neuropathy, peripheral, autonomic) 337.9
  - fatty 349.89
  - peripheral autonomic NEC (*see also* Neuropathy, peripheral, autonomic) 337.9
- nipple 611.9
- nose 478.19
- oculoacousticocerebral, congenital (progressive) 743.8
- olivopontocerebellar (familial) (hereditary) 333.0
- osseous labyrinth 386.8
- ovary 620.8
  - cystic 620.2
  - microcystic 620.2
- pallidal, pigmentary (progressive) 333.0
- pancreas 577.8
  - tuberculous (*see also* Tuberculosis) 017.9 ☑
- papillary muscle 429.81
- paving stone 362.61
- penis 607.89
- peritoneum 568.89
- pigmentary (diffuse) (general)
  - localized — *see* Degeneration, by site
  - pallidal (progressive) 333.0
  - secondary 362.65
- pineal gland 259.8
- pituitary (gland) 253.8
- placenta (fatty) (fibrinoid) (fibroid) — *see* Placenta, abnormal
- popliteal fat pad 729.31

Degeneration, degenerative — *continued*
- posterolateral (spinal cord) (*see also* Degeneration, combined) 266.2 *[336.2]*
- pulmonary valve (heart) (*see also* Endocarditis, pulmonary) 424.3
- pulp (tooth) 522.2
- pupillary margin 364.54
- renal (*see also* Sclerosis, renal) 587
  - fibrocystic 753.19
  - polycystic 753.12
    - adult type (APKD) 753.13
    - autosomal dominant 753.13
    - autosomal recessive 753.14
    - childhood type (CPKD) 753.14
    - infantile type 753.14
- reticuloendothelial system 289.89
- retina (peripheral) 362.60
  - with retinal defect (*see also* Detachment, retina, with retinal defect) 361.00
  - cystic (senile) 362.50
  - cystoid 362.53
  - hereditary (*see also* Dystrophy, retina) 362.70
    - cerebroretinal 362.71
    - congenital 362.75
    - juvenile (Stargardt's) 362.75
    - macula 362.76
  - Kuhnt-Junius 362.52
  - lattice 362.63
  - macular (*see also* Degeneration, macula) 362.50
  - microcystoid 362.62
  - palisade 362.63
  - paving stone 362.61
  - pigmentary (primary) 362.74
    - secondary 362.65
  - posterior pole (*see also* Degeneration, macula) 362.50
  - secondary 362.66
  - senile 362.60
    - cystic 362.53
    - reticular 362.64
- saccule, congenital (causing impairment of hearing) 744.05
- sacculocochlear 386.8
- senile 797
  - brain 331.2
  - cardiac, heart, or myocardium (*see also* Degeneration, myocardial) 429.1
  - motor centers 331.2
  - reticule 362.64
  - retina, cystic 362.50
  - vascular — *see* Arteriosclerosis
- silicone rubber poppet (prosthetic valve) 996.02
- sinus (cystic) (*see also* Sinusitis) 473.9
  - polypoid 471.1
- skin 709.3
  - amyloid 277.39
  - colloid 709.3
- spinal (cord) 336.8
  - amyloid 277.39
  - column 733.90
  - combined (subacute) (*see also* Degeneration, combined) 266.2 *[336.2]*
    - with anemia (pernicious) 281.0 *[336.2]*
  - dorsolateral (*see also* Degeneration, combined) 266.2 *[336.2]*
  - familial NEC 336.8
  - fatty 336.8
  - funicular (*see also* Degeneration, combined) 266.2 *[336.2]*
  - heredofamilial NEC 336.8
  - posterolateral (*see also* Degeneration, combined) 266.2 *[336.2]*
  - subacute combined — *see* Degeneration, combined
  - tuberculous (*see also* Tuberculosis) 013.8 ☑
- spine 733.90

Degeneration, degenerative — *continued*
- spleen 289.59
  - amyloid 277.39
  - lardaceous 277.39
- stomach 537.89
  - lardaceous 277.39
- strionigral 333.0
- sudoriparous (cystic) 705.89
- suprarenal (capsule) (gland) 255.8
  - with hypofunction 255.41
- sweat gland 705.89
- synovial membrane (pulpy) 727.9
- tapetoretinal 362.74
  - adult or presenile form 362.50
- testis (postinfectional) 608.89
- thymus (gland) 254.8
  - fatty 254.8
  - lardaceous 277.39
- thyroid (gland) 246.8
- tricuspid (heart) (valve) — *see* Endocarditis, tricuspid
- tuberculous NEC (*see also* Tuberculosis) 011.9 ☑
- turbinate 733.90
- uterus 621.8
  - cystic 621.8
- vascular (senile) (*see also* Arteriosclerosis)
  - hypertensive — *see* Hypertension
- vitreoretinal (primary) 362.73
  - secondary 362.66
- vitreous humor (with infiltration) 379.21
- wallerian NEC — *see* Disorder, nerve
- waxy (any site) 277.39
- Wilson's hepatolenticular 275.1

Deglutition
- paralysis 784.99
  - hysterical 300.11
- pneumonia 507.0

Degos' disease or syndrome 447.8

Degradation disorder, branched-chain amino acid 270.3

Dehiscence
- anastomosis — *see* Complications, anastomosis
- cesarean wound 674.1 ☑
- closure of ●
  - cornea 998.32 ●
  - fascia, superficial or muscular 998.31 ●
  - internal organ 998.31 ●
  - mucosa 998.32 ●
  - muscle or muscle flap 998.31 ●
  - ribs or rib cage 998.31 ●
  - skin 998.32 ●
  - skull or craniotomy 998.31 ●
  - sternum or sternotomy 998.31 ●
  - subcutaneous tissue 998.32 ●
  - tendon or ligament 998.31 ●
  - traumatic laceration (external) (internal) 998.33 ●
- episiotomy 674.2 ☑
- operation wound 998.32
  - deep 998.31 ●
  - external 998.32 ●
  - internal 998.31
  - superficial 998.32 ●
- perineal wound (postpartum) 674.2 ☑
- postoperative 998.32
  - abdomen 998.32
    - internal 998.31
  - internal 998.31
- traumatic injury wound repair 998.33 ●
- uterine wound 674.1 ☑

Dehydration (cachexia) 276.51
- with
  - hypernatremia 276.0
  - hyponatremia 276.1
- newborn 775.5

Deiters' nucleus syndrome 386.19

Déjérine's disease 356.0

Déjérine-Klumpke paralysis 767.6

Déjérine-Roussy syndrome 338.0

Déjérine-Sottas disease or neuropathy (hypertrophic) 356.0

Déjérine-Thomas atrophy or syndrome 333.0

de Lange's syndrome (Amsterdam dwarf, mental retardation, and brachycephaly) 759.89

Delay, delayed
- adaptation, cones or rods 368.63
- any plane in pelvis
  - affecting fetus or newborn 763.1
  - complicating delivery 660.1 ☑
- birth or delivery NEC 662.1 ☑
  - affecting fetus or newborn 763.89
  - second twin, triplet, or multiple mate 662.3 ☑
- closure (*see also* Fistula)
  - cranial suture 756.0
  - fontanel 756.0
- coagulation NEC 790.92
- conduction (cardiac) (ventricular) 426.9
- delivery NEC 662.1 ☑
  - second twin, triplet, etc. 662.3 ☑
    - affecting fetus or newborn 763.89
- development
  - in childhood 783.40
    - physiological 783.40
  - intellectual NEC 315.9
  - learning NEC 315.2
  - reading 315.00
  - sexual 259.0
  - speech 315.39
    - and language due to hearing loss 315.34
    - associated with hyperkinesis 314.1
  - spelling 315.09
- gastric emptying 536.8
- menarche 256.39
  - due to pituitary hypofunction 253.4
- menstruation (cause unknown) 626.8
- milestone in childhood 783.42
- motility — *see* Hypomotility
- passage of meconium (newborn) 777.1
- primary respiration 768.9
- puberty 259.0
- separation of umbilical cord 779.83
- sexual maturation, female 259.0
- vaccination V64.00 ●

Del Castillo's syndrome (germinal aplasia) 606.0

Déleage's disease 359.89

Deletion syndrome
- 5p 758.31
- 22q11.2 758.32
- autosomal NEC 758.39
- constitutional 5q deletion 758.39

Delhi (boil) (button) (sore) 085.1

Delinquency (juvenile) 312.9
- group (*see also* Disturbance, conduct) 312.2 ☑
- neurotic 312.4

Delirium, delirious 780.09
- acute (psychotic) 293.0
- alcoholic 291.0
  - acute 291.0
  - chronic 291.1
- alcoholicum 291.0
- chronic (*see also* Psychosis) 293.89
  - due to or associated with physical condition — *see* Psychosis, organic
- drug-induced 292.81
- due to conditions classified elsewhere 293.0
- eclamptic (*see also* Eclampsia) 780.39
- exhaustion (*see also* Reaction, stress, acute) 308.9
- hysterical 300.11
- in
  - presenile dementia 290.11
  - senile dementia 290.3
- induced by drug 292.81

Delirium, delirious — *continued*
  manic, maniacal (acute) (*see also* Psychosis, affective) 296.0 ☑
    recurrent episode 296.1 ☑
    single episode 296.0 ☑
  puerperal 293.9
  senile 290.3
  subacute (psychotic) 293.1
  thyroid (*see also* Thyrotoxicosis) 242.9 ☑
  traumatic (*see also* Injury, intracranial)
    with
      lesion, spinal cord — *see* Injury, spinal, by site
      shock, spinal — *see* Injury, spinal, by site
  tremens (impending) 291.0
  uremic — *see* Uremia
  withdrawal
    alcoholic (acute) 291.0
      chronic 291.1
    drug 292.0

Delivery

> *Note — Use the following fifth-digit subclassification with categories 640–▶649◀, 651–676:*
>
> 0 *unspecified as to episode of care*
>
> 1 *delivered, with or without mention of antepartum condition*
>
> 2 *delivered, with mention of postpartum complication*
>
> 3 *antepartum condition or complication*
>
> 4 *postpartum condition or complication*

  breech (assisted) (buttocks) (complete) (frank) (spontaneous) 652.2 ☑
    affecting fetus or newborn 763.0
    extraction NEC 669.6 ☑
  cesarean (for) 669.7 ☑
    abnormal
      cervix 654.6 ☑
      pelvic organs or tissues 654.9 ☑
      pelvis (bony) (major) NEC 653.0 ☑
      presentation or position 652.9 ☑
        in multiple gestation 652.6 ☑
      size, fetus 653.5 ☑
      soft parts (of pelvis) 654.9 ☑
      uterus, congenital 654.0 ☑
      vagina 654.7 ☑
      vulva 654.8 ☑
    abruptio placentae 641.2 ☑
    acromion presentation 652.8 ☑
    affecting fetus or newborn 763.4
    anteversion, cervix or uterus 654.4 ☑
    atony, uterus 661.2 ☑
      with hemorrhage 666.1 ☑
    bicornis or bicornuate uterus 654.0 ☑
    breech presentation (buttocks) (complete) (frank) 652.2 ☑
    brow presentation 652.4 ☑
    cephalopelvic disproportion (normally formed fetus) 653.4 ☑
    chin presentation 652.4 ☑
    cicatrix of cervix 654.6 ☑
    contracted pelvis (general) 653.1 ☑
      inlet 653.2 ☑
      outlet 653.3 ☑
    cord presentation or prolapse 663.0 ☑
    cystocele 654.4 ☑
    deformity (acquired) (congenital)
      pelvic organs or tissues NEC 654.9 ☑
      pelvis (bony) NEC 653.0 ☑
    displacement, uterus NEC 654.4 ☑
    disproportion NEC 653.9 ☑

Delivery — *continued*
  cesarean — *continued*
    distress
      fetal 656.8 ☑
      maternal 669.0 ☑
    eclampsia 642.6 ☑
    face presentation 652.4 ☑
    failed
      forceps 660.7 ☑
      trial of labor NEC 660.6 ☑
      vacuum extraction 660.7 ☑
      ventouse 660.7 ☑
    fetal deformity 653.7 ☑
    fetal-maternal hemorrhage 656.0 ☑
    fetus, fetal
      distress 656.8 ☑
      prematurity 656.8 ☑
    fibroid (tumor) (uterus) 654.1 ☑
    footling 652.8 ☑
      with successful version 652.1 ☑
    hemorrhage (antepartum) (intrapartum) NEC 641.9 ☑
    hydrocephalic fetus 653.6 ☑
    incarceration of uterus 654.3 ☑
    incoordinate uterine action 661.4 ☑
    inertia, uterus 661.2 ☑
      primary 661.0 ☑
      secondary 661.1 ☑
    lateroversion, uterus or cervix 654.4 ☑
    mal lie 652.9 ☑
    malposition
      fetus 652.9 ☑
        in multiple gestation 652.6 ☑
      pelvic organs or tissues NEC 654.9 ☑
      uterus NEC or cervix 654.4 ☑
    malpresentation NEC 652.9 ☑
      in multiple gestation 652.6 ☑
    maternal
      diabetes mellitus ▶(conditions classifiable to 249 and 250)◀ 648.0 ☑
      heart disease NEC 648.6 ☑
    meconium in liquor 656.8 ☑
      staining only 792.3
    oblique presentation 652.3 ☑
    oversize fetus 653.5 ☑
    pelvic tumor NEC 654.9 ☑
    placental insufficiency 656.5 ☑
    placenta previa 641.0 ☑
      with hemorrhage 641.1 ☑
    poor dilation, cervix 661.0 ☑
    pre-eclampsia 642.4 ☑
      severe 642.5 ☑
    previous
      cesarean delivery, section 654.2 ☑
      surgery (to)
        cervix 654.6 ☑
        gynecological NEC 654.9 ☑
        rectum 654.8 ☑
        uterus NEC 654.9 ☑
          previous cesarean delivery, section 654.2 ☑
        vagina 654.7 ☑
    prolapse
      arm or hand 652.7 ☑
      uterus 654.4 ☑
    prolonged labor 662.1 ☑
    rectocele 654.4 ☑
    retroversion, uterus or cervix 654.3 ☑
    rigid
      cervix 654.6 ☑
      pelvic floor 654.4 ☑
      perineum 654.8 ☑
      vagina 654.7 ☑
      vulva 654.8 ☑
    sacculation, pregnant uterus 654.4 ☑

Delivery — *continued*
  cesarean — *continued*
    scar(s)
      cervix 654.6 ☑
      cesarean delivery, section 654.2 ☑
      uterus NEC 654.9 ☑
        due to previous cesarean delivery, section 654.2 ☑
    Shirodkar suture in situ 654.5 ☑
    shoulder presentation 652.8 ☑
    stenosis or stricture, cervix 654.6 ☑
    transverse presentation or lie 652.3 ☑
    tumor, pelvic organs or tissues NEC 654.4 ☑
    umbilical cord presentation or prolapse 663.0 ☑
  completely normal case — *see* category 650
  complicated (by) NEC 669.9 ☑
    abdominal tumor, fetal 653.7 ☑
      causing obstructed labor 660.1 ☑
    abnormal, abnormality of
      cervix 654.6 ☑
        causing obstructed labor 660.2 ☑
      forces of labor 661.9 ☑
      formation of uterus 654.0 ☑
      pelvic organs or tissues 654.9 ☑
        causing obstructed labor 660.2 ☑
      pelvis (bony) (major) NEC 653.0 ☑
        causing obstructed labor 660.1 ☑
      presentation or position NEC 652.9 ☑
        causing obstructed labor 660.0 ☑
      size, fetus 653.5 ☑
        causing obstructed labor 660.1 ☑
      soft parts (of pelvis) 654.9 ☑
        causing obstructed labor 660.2 ☑
      uterine contractions NEC 661.9 ☑
      uterus (formation) 654.0 ☑
        causing obstructed labor 660.2 ☑
      vagina 654.7 ☑
        causing obstructed labor 660.2 ☑
    abnormally formed uterus (any type) (congenital) 654.0 ☑
      causing obstructed labor 660.2 ☑
    acromion presentation 652.8 ☑
      causing obstructed labor 660.0 ☑
    adherent placenta 667.0 ☑
      with hemorrhage 666.0 ☑
    adhesions, uterus (to abdominal wall) 654.4 ☑
    advanced maternal age NEC 659.6 ☑
      multigravida 659.6 ☑
      primigravida 659.5 ☑
    air embolism 673.0 ☑
    amnionitis 658.4 ☑
    amniotic fluid embolism 673.1 ☑
    anesthetic death 668.9 ☑
    annular detachment, cervix 665.3 ☑
    antepartum hemorrhage — *see* Delivery, complicated, hemorrhage
    anteversion, cervix or uterus 654.4 ☑
      causing obstructed labor 660.2 ☑
    apoplexy 674.0 ☑

Delivery — *continued*
  complicated — *continued*
    apoplexy — *continued*
      placenta 641.2 ☑
    arrested active phase 661.1 ☑
    asymmetrical pelvis bone 653.0 ☑
      causing obstructed labor 660.1 ☑
    atony, uterus with hemorrhage (hypotonic) (inertia) 666.1 ☑
      hypertonic 661.4 ☑
    Bandl's ring 661.4 ☑
    battledore placenta — *see* Placenta, abnormal
    bicornis or bicornuate uterus 654.0 ☑
      causing obstructed labor 660.2 ☑
    birth injury to mother NEC 665.9 ☑
    bleeding (*see also* Delivery, complicated, hemorrhage) 641.9 ☑
    breech presentation (assisted) (buttocks) (complete) (frank) (spontaneous) 652.2 ☑
      with successful version 652.1 ☑
    brow presentation 652.4 ☑
    cephalopelvic disproportion (normally formed fetus) 653.4 ☑
      causing obstructed labor 660.1 ☑
    cerebral hemorrhage 674.0 ☑
    cervical dystocia 661.2 ☑
    chin presentation 652.4 ☑
      causing obstructed labor 660.0 ☑
    cicatrix
      cervix 654.6 ☑
        causing obstructed labor 660.2 ☑
      vagina 654.7 ☑
        causing obstructed labor 660.2 ☑
    coagulation defect 649.3 ☑
    colporrhexis 665.4 ☑
      with perineal laceration 664.0 ☑
    compound presentation 652.8 ☑
      causing obstructed labor 660.0 ☑
    compression of cord (umbilical) 663.2 ☑
      around neck 663.1 ☑
      cord prolapsed 663.0 ☑
    contraction, contracted pelvis 653.1 ☑
      causing obstructed labor 660.1 ☑
      general 653.1 ☑
        causing obstructed labor 660.1 ☑
      inlet 653.2 ☑
        causing obstructed labor 660.1 ☑
      midpelvic 653.8 ☑
        causing obstructed labor 660.1 ☑
      midplane 653.8 ☑
        causing obstructed labor 660.1 ☑
      outlet 653.3 ☑
        causing obstructed labor 660.1 ☑
    contraction ring 661.4 ☑
    cord (umbilical) 663.9 ☑
      around neck, tightly or with compression 663.1 ☑
        without compression 663.3 ☑
      bruising 663.6 ☑
      complication NEC 663.9 ☑
        specified type NEC 663.8 ☑
      compression NEC 663.2 ☑
      entanglement NEC 663.3 ☑
        with compression 663.2 ☑
      forelying 663.0 ☑

Delivery — *continued*
complicated — *continued*
cord — *continued*
hematoma 663.6 ☑
marginal attachment 663.8 ☑
presentation 663.0 ☑
prolapse (complete) (occult) (partial) 663.0 ☑
short 663.4 ☑
specified complication NEC 663.8 ☑
thrombosis (vessels) 663.6 ☑
vascular lesion 663.6 ☑
velamentous insertion 663.8 ☑
Couvelaire uterus 641.2 ☑
cretin pelvis (dwarf type) (male type) 653.1 ☑
causing obstructed labor 660.1 ☑
crossbirth 652.3 ☑
with successful version 652.1 ☑
causing obstructed labor 660.0 ☑
cyst (Gartner's duct) 654.7 ☑
cystocele 654.4 ☑
causing obstructed labor 660.2 ☑
death of fetus (near term) 656.4 ☑
early (before 22 completed weeks gestation) 632
deformity (acquired) (congenital)
fetus 653.7 ☑
causing obstructed labor 660.1 ☑
pelvic organs or tissues NEC 654.9 ☑
causing obstructed labor 660.2 ☑
pelvis (bony) NEC 653.0 ☑
causing obstructed labor 660.1 ☑
delay, delayed
delivery in multiple pregnancy 662.3 ☑
due to locked mates 660.5 ☑
following rupture of membranes (spontaneous) 658.2 ☑
artificial 658.3 ☑
depressed fetal heart tones 659.7 ☑
diastasis recti 665.8 ☑
dilatation
bladder 654.4 ☑
causing obstructed labor 660.2 ☑
cervix, incomplete, poor or slow 661.0 ☑
diseased placenta 656.7 ☑
displacement uterus NEC 654.4 ☑
causing obstructed labor 660.2 ☑
disproportion NEC 653.9 ☑
causing obstructed labor 660.1 ☑
disruptio uteri — *see* Delivery, complicated, rupture, uterus
distress
fetal 656.8 ☑
maternal 669.0 ☑
double uterus (congenital) 654.0 ☑
causing obstructed labor 660.2 ☑
dropsy amnion 657.0 ☑
dysfunction, uterus 661.9 ☑
hypertonic 661.4 ☑
hypotonic 661.2 ☑
primary 661.0 ☑
secondary 661.1 ☑
incoordinate 661.4 ☑
dystocia
cervical 661.2 ☑
fetal — *see* Delivery, complicated, abnormal, presentation

Delivery — *continued*
complicated — *continued*
dystocia — *continued*
maternal — *see* Delivery, complicated, prolonged labor
pelvic — *see* Delivery, complicated, contraction pelvis
positional 652.8 ☑
shoulder girdle 660.4 ☑
eclampsia 642.6 ☑
ectopic kidney 654.4 ☑
causing obstructed labor 660.2 ☑
edema, cervix 654.6 ☑
causing obstructed labor 660.2 ☑
effusion, amniotic fluid 658.1 ☑
elderly multigravida 659.6 ☑
elderly primigravida 659.5 ☑
embolism (pulmonary) 673.2 ☑
air 673.0 ☑
amniotic fluid 673.1 ☑
blood clot 673.2 ☑
cerebral 674.0 ☑
fat 673.8 ☑
pyemic 673.3 ☑
septic 673.3 ☑
entanglement, umbilical cord 663.3 ☑
with compression 663.2 ☑
around neck (with compression) 663.1 ☑
eversion, cervix or uterus 665.2 ☑
excessive
fetal growth 653.5 ☑
causing obstructed labor 660.1 ☑
size of fetus 653.5 ☑
causing obstructed labor 660.1 ☑
face presentation 652.4 ☑
causing obstructed labor 660.0 ☑
to pubes 660.3 ☑
failure, fetal head to enter pelvic brim 652.5 ☑
causing obstructed labor 660.0 ☑
female genital mutilation 660.8 ☑
fetal
acid-base balance 656.8 ☑
death (near term) NEC 656.4 ☑
early (before 22 completed weeks gestation) 632
deformity 653.7 ☑
causing obstructed labor 660.1 ☑
distress 656.8 ☑
heart rate or rhythm 659.7 ☑
reduction of multiple fetuses reduced to single fetus 651.7 ☑
fetopelvic disproportion 653.4 ☑
causing obstructed labor 660.1 ☑
fever during labor 659.2 ☑
fibroid (tumor) (uterus) 654.1 ☑
causing obstructed labor 660.2 ☑
fibromyomata 654.1 ☑
causing obstructed labor 660.2 ☑
forelying umbilical cord 663.0 ☑
fracture of coccyx 665.6 ☑
hematoma 664.5 ☑
broad ligament 665.7 ☑
ischial spine 665.7 ☑
pelvic 665.7 ☑
perineum 664.5 ☑
soft tissues 665.7 ☑
subdural 674.0 ☑
umbilical cord 663.6 ☑
vagina 665.7 ☑
vulva or perineum 664.5 ☑

Delivery — *continued*
complicated — *continued*
hemorrhage (uterine) (antepartum) (intrapartum) (pregnancy) 641.9 ☑
accidental 641.2 ☑
associated with
afibrinogenemia 641.3 ☑
coagulation defect 641.3 ☑
hyperfibrinolysis 641.3 ☑
hypofibrinogenemia 641.3 ☑
cerebral 674.0 ☑
due to
low-lying placenta 641.1 ☑
placenta previa 641.1 ☑
premature separation of placenta (normally implanted) 641.2 ☑
retained placenta 666.0 ☑
trauma 641.8 ☑
uterine leiomyoma 641.8 ☑
marginal sinus rupture 641.2 ☑
placenta NEC 641.9 ☑
postpartum (atonic) (immediate) (within 24 hours) 666.1 ☑
with retained or trapped placenta 666.0 ☑
delayed 666.2 ☑
secondary 666.2 ☑
third stage 666.0 ☑
hourglass contraction, uterus 661.4 ☑
hydramnios 657.0 ☑
hydrocephalic fetus 653.6 ☑
causing obstructed labor 660.1 ☑
hydrops fetalis 653.7 ☑
causing obstructed labor 660.1 ☑
hypertension — *see* Hypertension, complicating pregnancy
hypertonic uterine dysfunction 661.4 ☑
hypotonic uterine dysfunction 661.2 ☑
impacted shoulders 660.4 ☑
incarceration, uterus 654.3 ☑
causing obstructed labor 660.2 ☑
incomplete dilation (cervix) 661.0 ☑
incoordinate uterus 661.4 ☑
indication NEC 659.9 ☑
specified type NEC 659.8 ☑
inertia, uterus 661.2 ☑
hypertonic 661.4 ☑
hypotonic 661.2 ☑
primary 661.0 ☑
secondary 661.1 ☑
infantile
genitalia 654.4 ☑
causing obstructed labor 660.2 ☑
uterus (os) 654.4 ☑
causing obstructed labor 660.2 ☑
injury (to mother) NEC 665.9 ☑
intrauterine fetal death (near term) NEC 656.4 ☑
early (before 22 completed weeks gestation) 632
inversion, uterus 665.2 ☑
kidney, ectopic 654.4 ☑
causing obstructed labor 660.2 ☑
knot (true), umbilical cord 663.2 ☑
labor, premature (before 37 completed weeks gestation) 644.2 ☑
laceration 664.9 ☑
anus (sphincter) (healed) (old) 654.8 ☑
with mucosa 664.3 ☑

Delivery — *continued*
complicated — *continued*
laceration — *continued*
anus — *continued*
not associated with third-degree perineal laceration 664.6 ☑
bladder (urinary) 665.5 ☑
bowel 665.5 ☑
central 664.4 ☑
cervix (uteri) 665.3 ☑
fourchette 664.0 ☑
hymen 664.0 ☑
labia (majora) (minora) 664.0 ☑
pelvic
floor 664.1 ☑
organ NEC 665.5 ☑
perineum, perineal 664.4 ☑
first degree 664.0 ☑
second degree 664.1 ☑
third degree 664.2 ☑
fourth degree 664.3 ☑
central 664.4 ☑
extensive NEC 664.4 ☑
muscles 664.1 ☑
skin 664.0 ☑
slight 664.0 ☑
peritoneum 665.5 ☑
periurethral tissue 664.8 ☑
rectovaginal (septum) (without perineal laceration) 665.4 ☑
with perineum 664.2 ☑
with anal or rectal mucosa 664.3 ☑
skin (perineum) 664.0 ☑
specified site or type NEC 664.8 ☑
sphincter ani (healed) (old) 654.8 ☑
with mucosa 664.3 ☑
not associated with third-degree perineal laceration 664.6 ☑
urethra 665.5 ☑
uterus 665.1 ☑
before labor 665.0 ☑
vagina, vaginal (deep) (high) (sulcus) (wall) (without perineal laceration) 665.4 ☑
with perineum 664.0 ☑
muscles, with perineum 664.1 ☑
vulva 664.0 ☑
lateroversion, uterus or cervix 654.4 ☑
causing obstructed labor 660.2 ☑
locked mates 660.5 ☑
low implantation of placenta — *see* Delivery, complicated, placenta, previa
mal lie 652.9 ☑
malposition
fetus NEC 652.9 ☑
causing obstructed labor 660.0 ☑
pelvic organs or tissues NEC 654.9 ☑
causing obstructed labor 660.2 ☑
placenta 641.1 ☑
without hemorrhage 641.0 ☑
uterus NEC or cervix 654.4 ☑
causing obstructed labor 660.2 ☑
malpresentation 652.9 ☑
causing obstructed labor 660.0 ☑
marginal sinus (bleeding) (rupture) 641.2 ☑
maternal hypotension syndrome 669.2 ☑
meconium in liquor 656.8 ☑

Delivery — *continued*
complicated — *continued*
membranes, retained — *see* Delivery, complicated, placenta, retained
mentum presentation 652.4 ☑
causing obstructed labor 660.0 ☑
metrorrhagia (myopathia) — *see* Delivery, complicated, hemorrhage
metrorrhexis — *see* Delivery, complicated, rupture, uterus
multiparity (grand) 659.4 ☑
myelomeningocele, fetus 653.7 ☑
causing obstructed labor 660.1 ☑
Nägele's pelvis 653.0 ☑
causing obstructed labor 660.1 ☑
nonengagement, fetal head 652.5 ☑
causing obstructed labor 660.0 ☑
oblique presentation 652.3 ☑
causing obstructed labor 660.0 ☑
obstetric
shock 669.1 ☑
trauma NEC 665.9 ☑
obstructed labor 660.9 ☑
due to
abnormality of pelvic organs or tissues (conditions classifiable to 654.0–654.9) 660.2 ☑
deep transverse arrest 660.3 ☑
impacted shoulders 660.4 ☑
locked twins 660.5 ☑
malposition and malpresentation of fetus (conditions classifiable to 652.0–652.9) 660.0 ☑
persistent occipitoposterior 660.3 ☑
shoulder dystocia 660.4 ☑
occult prolapse of umbilical cord 663.0 ☑
oversize fetus 653.5 ☑
causing obstructed labor 660.1 ☑
pathological retraction ring, uterus 661.4 ☑
pelvic
arrest (deep) (high) (of fetal head) (transverse) 660.3 ☑
deformity (bone) (*see also* Deformity, pelvis, with disproportion)
soft tissue 654.9 ☑
causing obstructed labor 660.2 ☑
tumor NEC 654.9 ☑
causing obstructed labor 660.2 ☑
penetration, pregnant uterus by instrument 665.1 ☑
perforation — *see* Delivery, complicated, laceration
persistent
hymen 654.8 ☑
causing obstructed labor 660.2 ☑
occipitoposterior 660.3 ☑
placenta, placental
ablatio 641.2 ☑
abnormality 656.7 ☑
with hemorrhage 641.2 ☑
abruptio 641.2 ☑
accreta 667.0 ☑
with hemorrhage 666.0 ☑
adherent (without hemorrhage) 667.0 ☑

Delivery — *continued*
complicated — *continued*
placenta, placental — *continued*
adherent — *continued*
with hemorrhage 666.0 ☑
apoplexy 641.2 ☑
battledore placenta — *see* Placenta, abnormal
detachment (premature) 641.2 ☑
disease 656.7 ☑
hemorrhage NEC 641.9 ☑
increta (without hemorrhage) 667.0 ☑
with hemorrhage 666.0 ☑
low (implantation) 641.1 ☑
without hemorrhage 641.0 ☑
malformation 656.7 ☑
with hemorrhage 641.2 ☑
malposition 641.1 ☑
without hemorrhage 641.0 ☑
marginal sinus rupture 641.2 ☑
percreta 667.0 ☑
with hemorrhage 666.0 ☑
premature separation 641.2 ☑
previa (central) (lateral) (marginal) (partial) 641.1 ☑
without hemorrhage 641.0 ☑
retained (with hemorrhage) 666.0 ☑
without hemorrhage 667.0 ☑
rupture of marginal sinus 641.2 ☑
separation (premature) 641.2 ☑
trapped 666.0 ☑
without hemorrhage 667.0 ☑
vicious insertion 641.1 ☑
polyhydramnios 657.0 ☑
polyp, cervix 654.6 ☑
causing obstructed labor 660.2 ☑
precipitate labor 661.3 ☑
premature
labor (before 37 completed weeks gestation) 644.2 ☑
rupture, membranes 658.1 ☑
delayed delivery following 658.2 ☑
presenting umbilical cord 663.0 ☑
previous
cesarean delivery, section 654.2 ☑
surgery
cervix 654.6 ☑
causing obstructed labor 660.2 ☑
gynecological NEC 654.9 ☑
causing obstructed labor 660.2 ☑
perineum 654.8 ☑
rectum 654.8 ☑
uterus NEC 654.9 ☑
due to previous cesarean delivery, section 654.2 ☑
vagina 654.7 ☑
causing obstructed labor 660.2 ☑
vulva 654.8 ☑
primary uterine inertia 661.0 ☑
primipara, elderly or old 659.5 ☑
prolapse
arm or hand 652.7 ☑
causing obstructed labor 660.0 ☑
cord (umbilical) 663.0 ☑
fetal extremity 652.8 ☑
foot or leg 652.8 ☑
causing obstructed labor 660.0 ☑
umbilical cord (complete) (occult) (partial) 663.0 ☑
uterus 654.4 ☑

Delivery — *continued*
complicated — *continued*
prolapse — *continued*
uterus — *continued*
causing obstructed labor 660.2 ☑
prolonged labor 662.1 ☑
first stage 662.0 ☑
second stage 662.2 ☑
active phase 661.2 ☑
due to
cervical dystocia 661.2 ☑
contraction ring 661.4 ☑
tetanic uterus 661.4 ☑
uterine inertia 661.2 ☑
primary 661.0 ☑
secondary 661.1 ☑
latent phase 661.0 ☑
pyrexia during labor 659.2 ☑
rachitic pelvis 653.2 ☑
causing obstructed labor 660.1 ☑
rectocele 654.4 ☑
causing obstructed labor 660.2 ☑
retained membranes or portions of placenta 666.2 ☑
without hemorrhage 667.1 ☑
retarded (prolonged) birth 662.1 ☑
retention secundines (with hemorrhage) 666.2 ☑
without hemorrhage 667.1 ☑
retroversion, uterus or cervix 654.3 ☑
causing obstructed labor 660.2 ☑
rigid
cervix 654.6 ☑
causing obstructed labor 660.2 ☑
pelvic floor 654.4 ☑
causing obstructed labor 660.2 ☑
perineum or vulva 654.8 ☑
causing obstructed labor 660.2 ☑
vagina 654.7 ☑
causing obstructed labor 660.2 ☑
Robert's pelvis 653.0 ☑
causing obstructed labor 660.1 ☑
rupture (*see also* Delivery, complicated, laceration)
bladder (urinary) 665.5 ☑
cervix 665.3 ☑
marginal sinus 641.2 ☑
membranes, premature 658.1 ☑
pelvic organ NEC 665.5 ☑
perineum (without mention of other laceration) — *see* Delivery, complicated, laceration, perineum
peritoneum 665.5 ☑
urethra 665.5 ☑
uterus (during labor) 665.1 ☑
before labor 665.0 ☑
sacculation, pregnant uterus 654.4 ☑
sacral teratomas, fetal 653.7 ☑
causing obstructed labor 660.1 ☑
scar(s)
cervix 654.6 ☑
causing obstructed labor 660.2 ☑
cesarean delivery, section 654.2 ☑
causing obstructed labor 660.2 ☑
perineum 654.8 ☑
causing obstructed labor 660.2 ☑
uterus NEC 654.9 ☑

Delivery — *continued*
complicated — *continued*
scar(s) — *continued*
uterus — *continued*
causing obstructed labor 660.2 ☑
due to previous cesarean delivery, section 654.2 ☑
vagina 654.7 ☑
causing obstructed labor 660.2 ☑
vulva 654.8 ☑
causing obstructed labor 660.2 ☑
scoliotic pelvis 653.0 ☑
causing obstructed labor 660.1 ☑
secondary uterine inertia 661.1 ☑
secundines, retained — *see* Delivery, complicated, placenta, retained
separation
placenta (premature) 641.2 ☑
pubic bone 665.6 ☑
symphysis pubis 665.6 ☑
septate vagina 654.7 ☑
causing obstructed labor 660.2 ☑
shock (birth) (obstetric) (puerperal) 669.1 ☑
short cord syndrome 663.4 ☑
shoulder
girdle dystocia 660.4 ☑
presentation 652.8 ☑
causing obstructed labor 660.0 ☑
Siamese twins 678.1 ☑ ▲
causing obstructed labor 660.1 ☑
slow slope active phase 661.2 ☑
spasm
cervix 661.4 ☑
uterus 661.4 ☑
spondylolisthesis, pelvis 653.3 ☑
causing obstructed labor 660.1 ☑
spondylolysis (lumbosacral) 653.3 ☑
causing obstructed labor 660.1 ☑
spondylosis 653.0 ☑
causing obstructed labor 660.1 ☑
stenosis or stricture
cervix 654.6 ☑
causing obstructed labor 660.2 ☑
vagina 654.7 ☑
causing obstructed labor 660.2 ☑
sudden death, unknown cause 669.9 ☑
tear (pelvic organ) (*see also* Delivery, complicated, laceration) 664.9 ☑
anal sphincter (healed) (old) 654.8 ☑
not associated with third-degree perineal laceration 664.6 ☑
teratomas, sacral, fetal 653.7 ☑
causing obstructed labor 660.1 ☑
tetanic uterus 661.4 ☑
tipping pelvis 653.0 ☑
causing obstructed labor 660.1 ☑
transverse
arrest (deep) 660.3 ☑
presentation or lie 652.3 ☑
with successful version 652.1 ☑
causing obstructed labor 660.0 ☑
trauma (obstetrical) NEC 665.9 ☑

Delivery — *continued*
complicated — *continued*
tumor
abdominal, fetal 653.7 ☑
causing obstructed labor 660.1 ☑
pelvic organs or tissues NEC 654.9 ☑
causing obstructed labor 660.2 ☑
umbilical cord (*see also* Delivery, complicated, cord) 663.9 ☑
around neck tightly, or with compression 663.1 ☑
entanglement NEC 663.3 ☑
with compression 663.2 ☑
prolapse (complete) (occult) (partial) 663.0 ☑
unstable lie 652.0 ☑
causing obstructed labor 660.0 ☑
uterine
inertia (*see also* Delivery, complicated, inertia, uterus) 661.2 ☑
spasm 661.4 ☑
vasa previa 663.5 ☑
velamentous insertion of cord 663.8 ☑
young maternal age 659.8 ☑
delayed NEC 662.1 ☑
following rupture of membranes (spontaneous) 658.2 ☑
artificial 658.3 ☑
second twin, triplet, etc. 662.3 ☑
difficult NEC 669.9 ☑
previous, affecting management of pregnancy or childbirth V23.49
specified type NEC 669.8 ☑
early onset (spontaneous) 644.2 ☑
footling 652.8 ☑
with successful version 652.1 ☑
forceps NEC 669.5 ☑
affecting fetus or newborn 763.2
missed (at or near term) 656.4 ☑
multiple gestation NEC 651.9 ☑
with fetal loss and retention of one or more fetus(es) 651.6 ☑
following (elective) fetal reduction 651.7 ☑
specified type NEC 651.8 ☑
with fetal loss and retention of one or more fetus(es) 651.6 ☑
following (elective) fetal reduction 651.7 ☑
nonviable infant 656.4 ☑
normal — *see* category 650
precipitate 661.3 ☑
affecting fetus or newborn 763.6
premature NEC (before 37 completed weeks gestation) 644.2 ☑
previous, affecting management of pregnancy V23.41
quadruplet NEC 651.2 ☑
with fetal loss and retention of one or more fetus(es) 651.5 ☑
following (elective) fetal reduction 651.7 ☑
quintuplet NEC 651.8 ☑
with fetal loss and retention of one or more fetus(es) 651.6 ☑
following (elective) fetal reduction 651.7 ☑
sextuplet NEC 651.8 ☑
with fetal loss and retention of one or more fetus(es) 651.6 ☑
following (elective) fetal reduction 651.7 ☑
specified complication NEC 669.8 ☑
stillbirth (near term) NEC 656.4 ☑
early (before 22 completed weeks gestation) 632

Delivery — *continued*
term pregnancy (live birth) NEC — *see* category 650
stillbirth NEC 656.4 ☑
threatened premature 644.2 ☑
triplets NEC 651.1 ☑
with fetal loss and retention of one or more fetus(es) 651.4 ☑
delayed delivery (one or more mates) 662.3 ☑
following (elective) fetal reduction 651.7 ☑
locked mates 660.5 ☑
twins NEC 651.0 ☑
with fetal loss and retention of one fetus 651.3 ☑
delayed delivery (one or more mates) 662.3 ☑
following (elective) fetal reduction 651.7 ☑
locked mates 660.5 ☑
uncomplicated — *see* category 650
vacuum extractor NEC 669.5 ☑
affecting fetus or newborn 763.3
ventouse NEC 669.5 ☑
affecting fetus or newborn 763.3
Dellen, cornea 371.41
Delusions (paranoid) 297.9
grandiose 297.1
parasitosis 300.29
systematized 297.1
Dementia 294.8
alcohol-induced persisting (*see also* Psychosis, alcoholic) 291.2
Alzheimer's — *see* Alzheimer's, dementia
arteriosclerotic (simple type) (uncomplicated) 290.40
with
acute confusional state 290.41
delirium 290.41
delusions 290.42
depressed mood 290.43
depressed type 290.43
paranoid type 290.42
Binswanger's 290.12
catatonic (acute) (*see also* Schizophrenia) 295.2 ☑
congenital (*see also* Retardation, mental) 319
degenerative 290.9
presenile-onset — *see* Dementia, presenile
senile-onset — *see* Dementia, senile
developmental (*see also* Schizophrenia) 295.9 ☑
dialysis 294.8
transient 293.9
drug-induced persisting (*see also* Psychosis, drug) 292.82
due to or associated with condition(s) classified elsewhere
Alzheimer's
with behavioral disturbance 331.0 *[294.11]*
without behavioral disturbance 331.0 *[294.10]*
cerebral lipidoses
with behavioral disturbance 330.1 *[294.11]*
without behavioral disturbance 330.1 *[294.10]*
epilepsy
with behavioral disturbance 345.9 ☑ *[294.11]*
without behavioral disturbance 345.9 ☑ *[294.10]*
hepatolenticular degeneration
with behavioral disturbance 275.1 *[294.11]*
without behavioral disturbance 275.1 *[294.10]*
HIV
with behavioral disturbance 042 *[294.11]*

Dementia — *continued*
due to or associated with condition(s) classified elsewhere — *continued*
HIV — *continued*
without behavioral disturbance 042 *[294.10]*
Huntington's chorea
with behavioral disturbance 333.4 *[294.11]*
without behavioral disturbance 333.4 *[294.10]*
Jakob-Creutzfeldt disease ▶(CJD)◀
with behavioral disturbance 046.19 *[294.11]* ▲
without behavioral disturbance 046.19 *[294.10]* ▲
variant (vCJD) 046.11 ●
with dementia ●
with behavioral disturbance ●
046.11 *[294.11]* ●
without behavioral disburbance ●
046.11 *[294.10]* ●
Lewy bodies
with behavioral disturbance 331.82 *[294.11]*
without behavioral disturbance 331.82 *[294.10]*
multiple sclerosis
with behavioral disturbance 340 *[294.11]*
without behavioral disturbance 340 *[294.10]*
neurosyphilis
with behavioral disturbance 094.9 *[294.11]*
without behavioral disturbance 094.9 *[294.10]*
Parkinsonism
with behavioral disturbance 331.82 *[294.11]*
without behavioral disturbance 331.82 *[294.10]*
Pelizaeus-Merzbacher disease
with behavioral disturbance 333.0 *[294.11]*
without behavioral disturbance 333.0 *[294.10]*
Pick's disease
with behavioral disturbance 331.11 *[294.11]*
without behavioral disturbance 331.11 *[294.10]*
polyarteritis nodosa
with behavioral disturbance 446.0 *[294.11]*
without behavioral disturbance 446.0 *[294.10]*
syphilis
with behavioral disturbance 094.1 *[294.11]*
without behavioral disturbance 094.1 *[294.10]*
Wilson's disease
with behavioral disturbance 275.1 *[294.11]*
without behavioral disturbance 275.1 *[294.10]*
frontal 331.19
with behavioral disturbance 331.19 *[294.11]*
without behavioral disturbance 331.19 *[294.10]*
frontotemporal 331.19
with behavioral disturbance 331.19 *[294.11]*
without behavioral disturbance 331.19 *[294.10]*
hebephrenic (acute) 295.1 ☑
Heller's (infantile psychosis) (*see also* Psychosis, childhood) 299.1 ☑
idiopathic 290.9
presenile-onset — *see* Dementia, presenile

Dementia — *continued*
idiopathic — *continued*
senile-onset — *see* Dementia, senile
in
arteriosclerotic brain disease 290.40
senility 290.0
induced by drug 292.82
infantile, infantilia (*see also* Psychosis, childhood) 299.0 ☑
Lewy body 331.82
with behavioral disturbance 331.82 *[294.11]*
without behavioral disturbance 331.82 *[294.10]*
multi-infarct (cerebrovascular) (*see also* Dementia, arteriosclerotic) 290.40
old age 290.0
paralytica, paralytic 094.1
juvenilis 090.40
syphilitic 094.1
congenital 090.40
tabetic form 094.1
paranoid (*see also* Schizophrenia) 295.3 ☑
paraphrenic (*see also* Schizophrenia) 295.3 ☑
paretic 094.1
praecox (*see also* Schizophrenia) 295.9 ☑
presenile 290.10
with
acute confusional state 290.11
delirium 290.11
delusional features 290.12
depressive features 290.13
depressed type 290.13
paranoid type 290.12
simple type 290.10
uncomplicated 290.10
primary (acute) (*see also* Schizophrenia) 295.0 ☑
progressive, syphilitic 094.1
puerperal — *see* Psychosis, puerperal
schizophrenic (*see also* Schizophrenia) 295.9 ☑
senile 290.0
with
acute confusional state 290.3
delirium 290.3
delusional features 290.20
depressive features 290.21
depressed type 290.21
exhaustion 290.0
paranoid type 290.20
simple type (acute) (*see also* Schizophrenia) 295.0 ☑
simplex (acute) (*see also* Schizophrenia) 295.0 ☑
syphilitic 094.1
uremic — *see* Uremia
vascular 290.40
with
delirium 290.41
delusions 290.42
depressed mood 290.43
Demerol dependence — *see also* Dependence 304.0 ☑
Demineralization, ankle — *see also* Osteoporosis 733.00
Demodex folliculorum (infestation) 133.8
de Morgan's spots (senile angiomas) 448.1
Demyelinating
polyneuritis, chronic inflammatory 357.81
Demyelination, demyelinization
central nervous system 341.9
specified NEC 341.8
corpus callosum (central) 341.8
global 340
Dengue (fever) 061
sandfly 061

Dengue — *continued*
- vaccination, prophylactic (against) V05.1
- virus hemorrhagic fever 065.4

Dens
- evaginatus 520.2
- in dente 520.2
- invaginatus 520.2

Dense ●
- breast(s) — *omit code* ●

Density
- increased, bone (disseminated) (generalized) (spotted) 733.99
- lung (nodular) 518.89

Dental — *see also* condition
- examination only V72.2

Dentia praecox 520.6

Denticles (in pulp) 522.2

Dentigerous cyst 526.0

Dentin
- irregular (in pulp) 522.3
- opalescent 520.5
- secondary (in pulp) 522.3
- sensitive 521.89

Dentinogenesis imperfecta 520.5

Dentinoma (M9271/0) 213.1
- upper jaw (bone) 213.0

Dentition 520.7
- abnormal 520.6
- anomaly 520.6
- delayed 520.6
- difficult 520.7
- disorder of 520.6
- precocious 520.6
- retarded 520.6

Denture sore (mouth) 528.9

Dependence

> *Note — Use the following fifth-digit subclassification with category 304:*
>
> 0 *unspecified*
>
> 1 *continuous*
>
> 2 *episodic*
>
> 3 *in remission*

- with
  - withdrawal symptoms
    - alcohol 291.81
    - drug 292.0
- 14-hydroxy-dihydromorphinone 304.0 ☑
- absinthe 304.6 ☑
- acemorphan 304.0 ☑
- acetanilid(e) 304.6 ☑
- acetophenetidin 304.6 ☑
- acetorphine 304.0 ☑
- acetyldihydrocodeine 304.0 ☑
- acetyldihydrocodeinone 304.0 ☑
- Adalin 304.1 ☑
- Afghanistan black 304.3 ☑
- agrypnal 304.1 ☑
- alcohol, alcoholic (ethyl) (methyl) (wood) 303.9 ☑
  - maternal, with suspected fetal damage affecting management of pregnancy 655.4 ☑
- allobarbitone 304.1 ☑
- allonal 304.1 ☑
- allylisopropylacetylurea 304.1 ☑
- alphaprodine (hydrochloride) 304.0 ☑
- Alurate 304.1 ☑
- Alvodine 304.0 ☑
- amethocaine 304.6 ☑
- amidone 304.0 ☑
- amidopyrine 304.6 ☑
- aminopyrine 304.6 ☑
- amobarbital 304.1 ☑
- amphetamine(s) (type) (drugs classifiable to 969.7) 304.4 ☑
- amylene hydrate 304.6 ☑
- amylobarbitone 304.1 ☑
- amylocaine 304.6 ☑
- Amytal (sodium) 304.1 ☑
- analgesic (drug) NEC 304.6 ☑

Dependence — *continued*
- analgesic — *continued*
  - synthetic with morphine-like effect 304.0 ☑
- anesthetic (agent) (drug) (gas) (general) (local) NEC 304.6 ☑
- Angel dust 304.6 ☑
- anileridine 304.0 ☑
- antipyrine 304.6 ☑
- anxiolytic 304.1 ☑
- aprobarbital 304.1 ☑
- aprobarbitone 304.1 ☑
- atropine 304.6 ☑
- Avertin (bromide) 304.6 ☑
- barbenyl 304.1 ☑
- barbital(s) 304.1 ☑
- barbitone 304.1 ☑
- barbiturate(s) (compounds) (drugs classifiable to 967.0) 304.1 ☑
- barbituric acid (and compounds) 304.1 ☑
- benzedrine 304.4 ☑
- benzylmorphine 304.0 ☑
- Beta-chlor 304.1 ☑
- bhang 304.3 ☑
- blue velvet 304.0 ☑
- Brevital 304.1 ☑
- bromal (hydrate) 304.1 ☑
- bromide(s) NEC 304.1 ☑
- bromine compounds NEC 304.1 ☑
- bromisovalum 304.1 ☑
- bromoform 304.1 ☑
- Bromo-seltzer 304.1 ☑
- bromural 304.1 ☑
- butabarbital (sodium) 304.1 ☑
- butabarpal 304.1 ☑
- butallylonal 304.1 ☑
- butethal 304.1 ☑
- buthalitone (sodium) 304.1 ☑
- Butisol 304.1 ☑
- butobarbitone 304.1 ☑
- butyl chloral (hydrate) 304.1 ☑
- caffeine 304.4 ☑
- cannabis (indica) (sativa) (resin) (derivatives) (type) 304.3 ☑
- carbamazepine 304.6 ☑
- Carbrital 304.1 ☑
- carbromal 304.1 ☑
- carisoprodol 304.6 ☑
- Catha (edulis) 304.4 ☑
- chloral (betaine) (hydrate) 304.1 ☑
- chloralamide 304.1 ☑
- chloralformamide 304.1 ☑
- chloralose 304.1 ☑
- chlordiazepoxide 304.1 ☑
- Chloretone 304.1 ☑
- chlorobutanol 304.1 ☑
- chlorodyne 304.1 ☑
- chloroform 304.6 ☑
- Cliradon 304.0 ☑
- coca (leaf) and derivatives 304.2 ☑
- cocaine 304.2 ☑
  - hydrochloride 304.2 ☑
  - salt (any) 304.2 ☑
- codeine 304.0 ☑
- combination of drugs (excluding morphine or opioid type drug) NEC 304.8 ☑
  - morphine or opioid type drug with any other drug 304.7 ☑
- croton-chloral 304.1 ☑
- cyclobarbital 304.1 ☑
- cyclobarbitone 304.1 ☑
- dagga 304.3 ☑
- Delvinal 304.1 ☑
- Demerol 304.0 ☑
- desocodeine 304.0 ☑
- desomorphine 304.0 ☑
- desoxyephedrine 304.4 ☑
- DET 304.5 ☑
- dexamphetamine 304.4 ☑
- dexedrine 304.4 ☑
- dextromethorphan 304.0 ☑
- dextromoramide 304.0 ☑

Dependence — *continued*
- dextronorpseudoephedrine 304.4 ☑
- dextrorphan 304.0 ☑
- diacetylmorphine 304.0 ☑
- Dial 304.1 ☑
- diallylbarbituric acid 304.1 ☑
- diamorphine 304.0 ☑
- diazepam 304.1 ☑
- dibucaine 304.6 ☑
- dichloroethane 304.6 ☑
- diethyl barbituric acid 304.1 ☑
- diethylsulfone-diethylmethane 304.1 ☑
- difencloxazine 304.0 ☑
- dihydrocodeine 304.0 ☑
- dihydrocodeinone 304.0 ☑
- dihydrohydroxycodeinone 304.0 ☑
- dihydroisocodeine 304.0 ☑
- dihydromorphine 304.0 ☑
- dihydromorphinone 304.0 ☑
- dihydroxcodeinone 304.0 ☑
- Dilaudid 304.0 ☑
- dimenhydrinate 304.6 ☑
- dimethylmeperidine 304.0 ☑
- dimethyltriptamine 304.5 ☑
- Dionin 304.0 ☑
- diphenoxylate 304.6 ☑
- dipipanone 304.0 ☑
- d-lysergic acid diethylamide 304.5 ☑
- DMT 304.5 ☑
- Dolophine 304.0 ☑
- DOM 304.2 ☑
- Doriden 304.1 ☑
- dormiral 304.1 ☑
- Dormison 304.1 ☑
- Dromoran 304.0 ☑
- drug NEC 304.9 ☑
  - analgesic NEC 304.6 ☑
  - combination (excluding morphine or opioid type drug) NEC 304.8 ☑
    - morphine or opioid type drug with any other drug 304.7 ☑
  - complicating pregnancy, childbirth, or puerperium 648.3 ☑
    - affecting fetus or newborn 779.5
  - hallucinogenic 304.5 ☑
  - hypnotic NEC 304.1 ☑
  - narcotic NEC 304.9 ☑
  - psychostimulant NEC 304.4 ☑
  - sedative 304.1 ☑
  - soporific NEC 304.1 ☑
  - specified type NEC 304.6 ☑
  - suspected damage to fetus affecting management of pregnancy 655.5 ☑
  - synthetic, with morphine-like effect 304.0 ☑
  - tranquilizing 304.1 ☑
- duboisine 304.6 ☑
- ectylurea 304.1 ☑
- Endocaine 304.6 ☑
- Equanil 304.1 ☑
- Eskabarb 304.1 ☑
- ethchlorvynol 304.1 ☑
- ether (ethyl) (liquid) (vapor) (vinyl) 304.6 ☑
- ethidene 304.6 ☑
- ethinamate 304.1 ☑
- ethoheptazine 304.6 ☑
- ethyl
  - alcohol 303.9 ☑
  - bromide 304.6 ☑
  - carbamate 304.6 ☑
  - chloride 304.6 ☑
  - morphine 304.0 ☑
- ethylene (gas) 304.6 ☑
  - dichloride 304.6 ☑
- ethylidene chloride 304.6 ☑
- etilfen 304.1 ☑
- etorphine 304.0 ☑
- etoval 304.1 ☑
- eucodal 304.0 ☑

Dependence — *continued*
- euneryl 304.1 ☑
- Evipal 304.1 ☑
- Evipan 304.1 ☑
- fentanyl 304.0 ☑
- ganja 304.3 ☑
- gardenal 304.1 ☑
- gardenpanyl 304.1 ☑
- gelsemine 304.6 ☑
- Gelsemium 304.6 ☑
- Gemonil 304.1 ☑
- glucochloral 304.1 ☑
- glue (airplane) (sniffing) 304.6 ☑
- glutethimide 304.1 ☑
- hallucinogenics 304.5 ☑
- hashish 304.3 ☑
- headache powder NEC 304.6 ☑
- Heavenly Blue 304.5 ☑
- hedonal 304.1 ☑
- hemp 304.3 ☑
- heptabarbital 304.1 ☑
- Heptalgin 304.0 ☑
- heptobarbitone 304.1 ☑
- heroin 304.0 ☑
  - salt (any) 304.0 ☑
- hexethal (sodium) 304.1 ☑
- hexobarbital 304.1 ☑
- Hycodan 304.0 ☑
- hydrocodone 304.0 ☑
- hydromorphinol 304.0 ☑
- hydromorphinone 304.0 ☑
- hydromorphone 304.0 ☑
- hydroxycodeine 304.0 ☑
- hypnotic NEC 304.1 ☑
- Indian hemp 304.3 ☑
- inhalant 304.6 ☑
- intranarcon 304.1 ☑
- Kemithal 304.1 ☑
- ketobemidone 304.0 ☑
- khat 304.4 ☑
- kif 304.3 ☑
- Lactuca (virosa) extract 304.1 ☑
- lactucarium 304.1 ☑
- laudanum 304.0 ☑
- Lebanese red 304.3 ☑
- Leritine 304.0 ☑
- lettuce opium 304.1 ☑
- Levanil 304.1 ☑
- Levo-Dromoran 304.0 ☑
- levo-iso-methadone 304.0 ☑
- levorphanol 304.0 ☑
- Librium 304.1 ☑
- Lomotil 304.6 ☑
- Lotusate 304.1 ☑
- LSD (-25) (and derivatives) 304.5 ☑
- Luminal 304.1 ☑
- lysergic acid 304.5 ☑
  - amide 304.5 ☑
- maconha 304.3 ☑
- magic mushroom 304.5 ☑
- marihuana 304.3 ☑
- MDA (methylene dioxyamphetamine) 304.4 ☑
- Mebaral 304.1 ☑
- Medinal 304.1 ☑
- Medomin 304.1 ☑
- megahallucinogenics 304.5 ☑
- meperidine 304.0 ☑
- mephobarbital 304.1 ☑
- meprobamate 304.1 ☑
- mescaline 304.5 ☑
- methadone 304.0 ☑
- methamphetamine(s) 304.4 ☑
- methaqualone 304.1 ☑
- metharbital 304.1 ☑
- methitural 304.1 ☑
- methobarbitone 304.1 ☑
- methohexital 304.1 ☑
- methopholine 304.6 ☑
- methyl
  - alcohol 303.9 ☑
  - bromide 304.6 ☑
  - morphine 304.0 ☑
  - sulfonal 304.1 ☑

- **Dependence** — *continued*
  - methylaparafynol 304.1 ☑
  - methylated spirit 303.9 ☑
  - methylbutinol 304.6 ☑
  - methyldihydromorphinone 304.0 ☑
  - methylene
    - chloride 304.6 ☑
    - dichloride 304.6 ☑
    - dioxyamphetamine (MDA) 304.4 ☑
  - methylphenidate 304.4 ☑
  - methyprylone 304.1 ☑
  - metopon 304.0 ☑
  - Miltown 304.1 ☑
  - morning glory seeds 304.5 ☑
  - morphinan(s) 304.0 ☑
  - morphine (sulfate) (sulfite) (type) (drugs classifiable to 965.00–965.09) 304.0 ☑
  - morphine or opioid type drug (drugs classifiable to 965.00–965.09) with any other drug 304.7 ☑
  - morphinol(s) 304.0 ☑
  - morphinon 304.0 ☑
  - morpholinylethylmorphine 304.0 ☑
  - mylomide 304.1 ☑
  - myristicin 304.5 ☑
  - narcotic (drug) NEC 304.9 ☑
  - nealbarbital 304.1 ☑
  - nealbarbitone 304.1 ☑
  - Nembutal 304.1 ☑
  - Neonal 304.1 ☑
  - Neraval 304.1 ☑
  - Neravan 304.1 ☑
  - neurobarb 304.1 ☑
  - nicotine 305.1
  - Nisentil 304.0 ☑
  - nitrous oxide 304.6 ☑
  - Noctec 304.1 ☑
  - Noludar 304.1 ☑
  - nonbarbiturate sedatives and tranquilizers with similar effect 304.1 ☑
  - noptil 304.1 ☑
  - normorphine 304.0 ☑
  - noscapine 304.0 ☑
  - Novocaine 304.6 ☑
  - Numorphan 304.0 ☑
  - nunol 304.1 ☑
  - Nupercaine 304.6 ☑
  - Oblivon 304.1 ☑
  - on
    - aspirator V46.0
    - hemodialysis V45.11 ▲
    - hyperbaric chamber V46.8
    - iron lung V46.11
    - machine (enabling) V46.9
      - specified type NEC V46.8
    - peritoneal dialysis V45.11 ▲
    - Possum (Patient-Operated-Selector-Mechanism) V46.8
    - renal dialysis machine V45.11 ▲
    - respirator [ventilator] V46.11
      - encounter
        - during
          - mechanical failure V46.14
          - power failure V46.12
        - for weaning V46.13
    - supplemental oxygen V46.2
    - wheelchair V46.3 ●
  - opiate 304.0 ☑
  - opioids 304.0 ☑
  - opioid type drug 304.0 ☑
    - with any other drug 304.7 ☑
  - opium (alkaloids) (derivatives) (tincture) 304.0 ☑
  - ortal 304.1 ☑
  - Oxazepam 304.1 ☑
  - oxycodone 304.0 ☑
  - oxymorphone 304.0 ☑
  - Palfium 304.0 ☑
  - Panadol 304.6 ☑
  - pantopium 304.0 ☑
  - pantopon 304.0 ☑
  - papaverine 304.0 ☑
  - paracetamol 304.6 ☑
  - paracodin 304.0 ☑
- **Dependence** — *continued*
  - paraldehyde 304.1 ☑
  - paregoric 304.0 ☑
  - Parzone 304.0 ☑
  - PCP (phencyclidine) 304.6 ☑
  - Pearly Gates 304.5 ☑
  - pentazocine 304.0 ☑
  - pentobarbital 304.1 ☑
  - pentobarbitone (sodium) 304.1 ☑
  - Pentothal 304.1 ☑
  - Percaine 304.6 ☑
  - Percodan 304.0 ☑
  - Perichlor 304.1 ☑
  - Pernocton 304.1 ☑
  - Pernoston 304.1 ☑
  - peronine 304.0 ☑
  - pethidine (hydrochloride) 304.0 ☑
  - petrichloral 304.1 ☑
  - peyote 304.5 ☑
  - Phanodron 304.1 ☑
  - phenacetin 304.6 ☑
  - phenadoxone 304.0 ☑
  - phenaglycodol 304.1 ☑
  - phenazocine 304.0 ☑
  - phencyclidine 304.6 ☑
  - phenmetrazine 304.4 ☑
  - phenobal 304.1 ☑
  - phenobarbital 304.1 ☑
  - phenobarbitone 304.1 ☑
  - phenomorphan 304.0 ☑
  - phenonyl 304.1 ☑
  - phenoperidine 304.0 ☑
  - pholcodine 304.0 ☑
  - piminodine 304.0 ☑
  - Pipadone 304.0 ☑
  - Pitkin's solution 304.6 ☑
  - Placidyl 304.1 ☑
  - polysubstance 304.8 ☑
  - Pontocaine 304.6 ☑
  - pot 304.3 ☑
  - potassium bromide 304.1 ☑
  - Preludin 304.4 ☑
  - Prinadol 304.0 ☑
  - probarbital 304.1 ☑
  - procaine 304.6 ☑
  - propanal 304.1 ☑
  - propoxyphene 304.6 ☑
  - psilocibin 304.5 ☑
  - psilocin 304.5 ☑
  - psilocybin 304.5 ☑
  - psilocyline 304.5 ☑
  - psilocyn 304.5 ☑
  - psychedelic agents 304.5 ☑
  - psychostimulant NEC 304.4 ☑
  - psychotomimetic agents 304.5 ☑
  - pyrahexyl 304.3 ☑
  - Pyramidon 304.6 ☑
  - quinalbarbitone 304.1 ☑
  - racemoramide 304.0 ☑
  - racemorphan 304.0 ☑
  - Rela 304.6 ☑
  - scopolamine 304.6 ☑
  - secobarbital 304.1 ☑
  - Seconal 304.1 ☑
  - sedative NEC 304.1 ☑
    - nonbarbiturate with barbiturate effect 304.1 ☑
  - Sedormid 304.1 ☑
  - sernyl 304.1 ☑
  - sodium bromide 304.1 ☑
  - Soma 304.6 ☑
  - Somnal 304.1 ☑
  - Somnos 304.1 ☑
  - Soneryl 304.1 ☑
  - soporific (drug) NEC 304.1 ☑
  - specified drug NEC 304.6 ☑
  - speed 304.4 ☑
  - spinocaine 304.6 ☑
  - Stovaine 304.6 ☑
  - STP 304.5 ☑
  - stramonium 304.6 ☑
  - Sulfonal 304.1 ☑
  - sulfonethylmethane 304.1 ☑
  - sulfonmethane 304.1 ☑
- **Dependence** — *continued*
  - Surital 304.1 ☑
  - synthetic drug with morphine-like effect 304.0 ☑
  - talbutal 304.1 ☑
  - tetracaine 304.6 ☑
  - tetrahydrocannabinol 304.3 ☑
  - tetronal 304.1 ☑
  - THC 304.3 ☑
  - thebacon 304.0 ☑
  - thebaine 304.0 ☑
  - thiamil 304.1 ☑
  - thiamylal 304.1 ☑
  - thiopental 304.1 ☑
  - tobacco 305.1
  - toluene, toluol 304.6 ☑
  - tranquilizer NEC 304.1 ☑
    - nonbarbiturate with barbiturate effect 304.1 ☑
  - tribromacetaldehyde 304.6 ☑
  - tribromethanol 304.6 ☑
  - tribromomethane 304.6 ☑
  - trichloroethanol 304.6 ☑
  - trichoroethyl phosphate 304.1 ☑
  - triclofos 304.1 ☑
  - Trional 304.1 ☑
  - Tuinal 304.1 ☑
  - Turkish Green 304.3 ☑
  - urethan(e) 304.6 ☑
  - Valium 304.1 ☑
  - Valmid 304.1 ☑
  - veganin 304.0 ☑
  - veramon 304.1 ☑
  - Veronal 304.1 ☑
  - versidyne 304.6 ☑
  - vinbarbital 304.1 ☑
  - vinbarbitone 304.1 ☑
  - vinyl bitone 304.1 ☑
  - vitamin B_6 266.1
  - wine 303.9 ☑
  - Zactane 304.6 ☑
- **Dependency**
  - passive 301.6
  - reactions 301.6
- **Depersonalization** (episode, in neurotic state) (neurotic) (syndrome) 300.6
- **Depletion**
  - carbohydrates 271.9
  - complement factor 279.8
  - extracellular fluid 276.52
  - plasma 276.52
  - potassium 276.8
    - nephropathy 588.89
  - salt or sodium 276.1
    - causing heat exhaustion or prostration 992.4
    - nephropathy 593.9
  - volume 276.50
    - extracellular fluid 276.52
    - plasma 276.52
- **Deposit**
  - argentous, cornea 371.16
  - bone, in Boeck's sarcoid 135
  - calcareous, calcium — *see* Calcification
  - cholesterol
    - retina 362.82
    - skin 709.3
    - vitreous (humor) 379.22
  - conjunctival 372.56
  - cornea, corneal NEC 371.10
    - argentous 371.16
    - in
      - cystinosis 270.0 *[371.15]*
      - mucopolysaccharidosis 277.5 *[371.15]*
  - crystalline, vitreous (humor) 379.22
  - hemosiderin, in old scars of cornea 371.11
  - metallic, in lens 366.45
  - skin 709.3
  - teeth, tooth (betel) (black) (green) (materia alba) (orange) (soft) (tobacco) 523.6
- **Deposit** — *continued*
  - urate, in kidney (*see also* Disease, renal) 593.9
- **Depraved appetite** 307.52
- **Depression** 311
  - acute (*see also* Psychosis, affective) 296.2 ☑
    - recurrent episode 296.3 ☑
    - single episode 296.2 ☑
  - agitated (*see also* Psychosis, affective) 296.2 ☑
    - recurrent episode 296.3 ☑
    - single episode 296.2 ☑
  - anaclitic 309.21
  - anxiety 300.4
  - arches 734
    - congenital 754.61
  - autogenous (*see also* Psychosis, affective) 296.2 ☑
    - recurrent episode 296.3 ☑
    - single episode 296.2 ☑
  - basal metabolic rate (BMR) 794.7
  - bone marrow 289.9
  - central nervous system 799.1
    - newborn 779.2
  - cerebral 331.9
    - newborn 779.2
  - cerebrovascular 437.8
    - newborn 779.2
  - chest wall 738.3
  - endogenous (*see also* Psychosis, affective) 296.2 ☑
    - recurrent episode 296.3 ☑
    - single episode 296.2 ☑
  - functional activity 780.99
  - hysterical 300.11
  - involutional, climacteric, or menopausal (*see also* Psychosis, affective) 296.2 ☑
    - recurrent episode 296.3 ☑
    - single episode 296.2 ☑
  - manic (*see also* Psychosis, affective) 296.80
  - medullary 348.8
    - newborn 779.2
  - mental 300.4
  - metatarsal heads — *see* Depression, arches
  - metatarsus — *see* Depression, arches
  - monopolar (*see also* Psychosis, affective) 296.2 ☑
    - recurrent episode 296.3 ☑
    - single episode 296.2 ☑
  - nervous 300.4
  - neurotic 300.4
  - nose 738.0
  - postpartum 648.4 ☑
  - psychogenic 300.4
    - reactive 298.0
  - psychoneurotic 300.4
  - psychotic (*see also* Psychosis, affective) 296.2 ☑
    - reactive 298.0
    - recurrent episode 296.3 ☑
    - single episode 296.2 ☑
  - reactive 300.4
    - neurotic 300.4
    - psychogenic 298.0
    - psychoneurotic 300.4
    - psychotic 298.0
  - recurrent 296.3 ☑
  - respiratory center 348.8
    - newborn 770.89
  - scapula 736.89
  - senile 290.21
  - situational (acute) (brief) 309.0
    - prolonged 309.1
  - skull 754.0
  - sternum 738.3
  - visual field 368.40
- **Depressive reaction** — *see also* Reaction, depressive
  - acute (transient) 309.0
    - with anxiety 309.28
  - prolonged 309.1
  - situational (acute) 309.0

Depressive reaction — *see also* Reaction, depressive — *continued*
- situational — *continued*
  - prolonged 309.1

Deprivation
- cultural V62.4
- emotional V62.89
  - affecting
    - adult 995.82
    - infant or child 995.51
- food 994.2
  - specific substance NEC 269.8
- protein (familial) (kwashiorkor) 260
- sleep V69.4
- social V62.4
  - affecting
    - adult 995.82
    - infant or child 995.51
- symptoms, syndrome
  - alcohol 291.81
  - drug 292.0
- vitamins (*see also* Deficiency, vitamin) 269.2
- water 994.3

de Quervain's
- disease (tendon sheath) 727.04
- syndrome 259.51 ●
- thyroiditis (subacute granulomatous thyroiditis) 245.1

Derangement
- ankle (internal) 718.97
  - current injury (*see also* Dislocation, ankle) 837.0
  - recurrent 718.37
- cartilage (articular) NEC (*see also* Disorder, cartilage, articular) 718.0 ☑
  - knee 717.9
    - recurrent 718.36
  - recurrent 718.3 ☑
- collateral ligament (knee) (medial) (tibial) 717.82
  - current injury 844.1
    - lateral (fibular) 844.0
  - lateral (fibular) 717.81
    - current injury 844.0
- cruciate ligament (knee) (posterior) 717.84
  - anterior 717.83
    - current injury 844.2
  - current injury 844.2
- elbow (internal) 718.92
  - current injury (*see also* Dislocation, elbow) 832.00
  - recurrent 718.32
- gastrointestinal 536.9
- heart — *see* Disease, heart
- hip (joint) (internal) (old) 718.95
  - current injury (*see also* Dislocation, hip) 835.00
  - recurrent 718.35
- intervertebral disc — *see* Displacement, intervertebral disc
- joint (internal) 718.90
  - ankle 718.97
  - current injury (*see also* Dislocation, by site)
    - knee, meniscus or cartilage (*see also* Tear, meniscus) 836.2
  - elbow 718.92
  - foot 718.97
  - hand 718.94
  - hip 718.95
  - knee 717.9
  - multiple sites 718.99
  - pelvic region 718.95
  - recurrent 718.30
    - ankle 718.37
    - elbow 718.32
    - foot 718.37
    - hand 718.34
    - hip 718.35
    - knee 718.36
    - multiple sites 718.39
    - pelvic region 718.35

Derangement — *continued*
- joint — *continued*
  - recurrent — *continued*
    - shoulder (region) 718.31
    - specified site NEC 718.38
    - temporomandibular (old) 524.69
    - wrist 718.33
  - shoulder (region) 718.91
  - specified site NEC 718.98
  - spine NEC 724.9
  - temporomandibular 524.69
  - wrist 718.93
- knee (cartilage) (internal) 717.9
  - current injury (*see also* Tear, meniscus) 836.2
  - ligament 717.89
    - capsular 717.85
    - collateral — *see* Derangement, collateral ligament
    - cruciate — *see* Derangement, cruciate ligament
    - specified NEC 717.85
  - recurrent 718.36
- low back NEC 724.9
- meniscus NEC (knee) 717.5
  - current injury (*see also* Tear, meniscus) 836.2
  - lateral 717.40
    - anterior horn 717.42
    - posterior horn 717.43
    - specified NEC 717.49
  - medial 717.3
    - anterior horn 717.1
    - posterior horn 717.2
  - recurrent 718.3 ☑
  - site other than knee — *see* Disorder, cartilage, articular
- mental (*see also* Psychosis) 298.9
- rotator cuff (recurrent) (tear) 726.10
  - current 840.4
- sacroiliac (old) 724.6
  - current — *see* Dislocation, sacroiliac
- semilunar cartilage (knee) 717.5
  - current injury 836.2
    - lateral 836.1
    - medial 836.0
  - recurrent 718.3 ☑
- shoulder (internal) 718.91
  - current injury (*see also* Dislocation, shoulder) 831.00
  - recurrent 718.31
- spine (recurrent) NEC 724.9
  - current — *see* Dislocation, spine
- temporomandibular (internal) (joint) (old) 524.69
  - current — *see* Dislocation, jaw

Dercum's disease or syndrome (adiposis dolorosa) 272.8

Derealization (neurotic) 300.6

Dermal — *see* condition

Dermaphytid — *see* Dermatophytosis

Dermatergosis — *see* Dermatitis

Dermatitis (allergic) (contact) (occupational) (venenata) 692.9
- ab igne 692.82
- acneiform 692.9
- actinic (due to sun) 692.70
  - acute 692.72
  - chronic NEC 692.74
  - other than from sun NEC 692.82
- ambustionis
  - due to
    - burn or scald — *see* Burn, by site
    - sunburn (*see also* Sunburn) 692.71
- amebic 006.6
- ammonia 691.0
- anaphylactoid NEC 692.9
- arsenical 692.4
- artefacta 698.4
  - psychogenic 316 *[698.4]*
- asthmatic 691.8
- atopic (allergic) (intrinsic) 691.8
  - psychogenic 316 *[691.8]*

Dermatitis — *continued*
- atrophicans 701.8
  - diffusa 701.8
  - maculosa 701.3
- berlock, berloque 692.72
- blastomycetic 116.0
- blister beetle 692.89
- Brucella NEC 023.9
- bullosa 694.9
  - striata pratensis 692.6
- bullous 694.9
  - mucosynechial, atrophic 694.60
    - with ocular involvement 694.61
  - seasonal 694.8
- calorica
  - due to
    - burn or scald — *see* Burn, by site
    - cold 692.89
    - sunburn (*see also* Sunburn) 692.71
- caterpillar 692.89
- cercarial 120.3
- combustionis
  - due to
    - burn or scald — *see* Burn, by site
    - sunburn (*see also* Sunburn) 692.71
- congelationis 991.5
- contusiformis 695.2
- diabetic 250.8 ☑
- diaper 691.0
- diphtheritica 032.85
- due to
  - acetone 692.2
  - acids 692.4
  - adhesive plaster 692.4
  - alcohol (skin contact) (substances classifiable to 980.0–980.9) 692.4
    - taken internally 693.8
  - alkalis 692.4
  - allergy NEC 692.9
  - ammonia (household) (liquid) 692.4
  - animal
    - dander (cat) (dog) 692.84
    - hair (cat) (dog) 692.84
  - arnica 692.3
  - arsenic 692.4
    - taken internally 693.8
  - blister beetle 692.89
  - cantharides 692.3
  - carbon disulphide 692.2
  - caterpillar 692.89
  - caustics 692.4
  - cereal (ingested) 693.1
    - contact with skin 692.5
  - chemical(s) NEC 692.4
    - internal 693.8
    - irritant NEC 692.4
    - taken internally 693.8
  - chlorocompounds 692.2
  - coffee (ingested) 693.1
    - contact with skin 692.5
  - cold weather 692.89
  - cosmetics 692.81
  - cyclohexanes 692.2
  - dander, animal (cat) (dog) 692.84
  - deodorant 692.81
  - detergents 692.0
  - dichromate 692.4
  - drugs and medicinals (correct substance properly administered) (internal use) 693.0
    - external (in contact with skin) 692.3
      - wrong substance given or taken 976.9
        - specified substance — *see* Table of Drugs and Chemicals
    - wrong substance given or taken 977.9

Dermatitis — *continued*
- due to — *continued*
  - drugs and medicinals — *continued*
    - wrong substance given or taken — *continued*
      - specified substance — *see* Table of Drugs and Chemicals
  - dyes 692.89
    - hair 692.89
  - epidermophytosis — *see* Dermatophytosis
  - esters 692.2
  - external irritant NEC 692.9
    - specified agent NEC 692.89
  - eye shadow 692.81
  - fish (ingested) 693.1
    - contact with skin 692.5
  - flour (ingested) 693.1
    - contact with skin 692.5
  - food (ingested) 693.1
    - in contact with skin 692.5
  - fruit (ingested) 693.1
    - contact with skin 692.5
  - fungicides 692.3
  - furs 692.84
  - glycols 692.2
  - greases NEC 692.1
  - hair, animal (cat) (dog) 692.84
  - hair dyes 692.89
  - hot
    - objects and materials — *see* Burn, by site
    - weather or places 692.89
  - hydrocarbons 692.2
  - infrared rays, except from sun 692.82
    - solar NEC (*see also* Dermatitis, due to, sun) 692.70
  - ingested substance 693.9
    - drugs and medicinals (*see also* Dermatitis, due to, drugs and medicinals) 693.0
    - food 693.1
    - specified substance NEC 693.8
  - ingestion or injection of chemical 693.8
    - drug (correct substance properly administered) 693.0
    - wrong substance given or taken 977.9
      - specified substance — *see* Table of Drugs and Chemicals
  - insecticides 692.4
  - internal agent 693.9
    - drugs and medicinals (*see also* Dermatitis, due to, drugs and medicinals) 693.0
    - food (ingested) 693.1
      - in contact with skin 692.5
    - specified agent NEC 693.8
  - iodine 692.3
  - iodoform 692.3
  - irradiation 692.82
  - jewelry 692.83
  - keratolytics 692.3
  - ketones 692.2
  - lacquer tree (Rhus verniciflua) 692.6
  - light (sun) NEC (*see also* Dermatitis, due to, sun) 692.70
    - other 692.82
  - low temperature 692.89
  - mascara 692.81
  - meat (ingested) 693.1
    - contact with skin 692.5
  - mercury, mercurials 692.3
  - metals 692.83
  - milk (ingested) 693.1
    - contact with skin 692.5
  - Neomycin 692.3
  - nylon 692.4
  - oils NEC 692.1
  - paint solvent 692.2

- **Dermatitis** — *continued*
  - due to — *continued*
    - pediculocides 692.3
    - petroleum products (substances classifiable to 981) 692.4
    - phenol 692.3
    - photosensitiveness, photosensitivity (sun) 692.72
      - other light 692.82
    - plants NEC 692.6
    - plasters, medicated (any) 692.3
    - plastic 692.4
    - poison
      - ivy (Rhus toxicodendron) 692.6
      - oak (Rhus diversiloba) 692.6
      - plant or vine 692.6
      - sumac (Rhus venenata) 692.6
      - vine (Rhus radicans) 692.6
    - preservatives 692.89
    - primrose (primula) 692.6
    - primula 692.6
    - radiation 692.82
      - sun NEC (*see also* Dermatitis, due to, sun) 692.70
      - tanning bed 692.82
    - radioactive substance 692.82
    - radium 692.82
    - ragweed (Senecio jacobae) 692.6
    - Rhus (diversiloba) (radicans) (toxicodendron) (venenata) (verniciflua) 692.6
    - rubber 692.4
    - scabicides 692.3
    - Senecio jacobae 692.6
    - solar radiation — *see* Dermatitis, due to, sun
    - solvents (any) (substances classifiable to 982.0–982.8) 692.2
      - chlorocompound group 692.2
      - cyclohexane group 692.2
      - ester group 692.2
      - glycol group 692.2
      - hydrocarbon group 692.2
      - ketone group 692.2
      - paint 692.2
    - specified agent NEC 692.89
    - sun 692.70
      - acute 692.72
      - chronic NEC 692.74
      - specified NEC 692.79
    - sunburn (*see also* Sunburn) 692.71
    - sunshine NEC (*see also* Dermatitis, due to, sun) 692.70
    - tanning bed 692.82
    - tetrachlorethylene 692.2
    - toluene 692.2
    - topical medications 692.3
    - turpentine 692.2
    - ultraviolet rays, except from sun 692.82
      - sun NEC (*see also* Dermatitis, due to, sun) 692.70
    - vaccine or vaccination (correct substance properly administered) 693.0
      - wrong substance given or taken
        - bacterial vaccine 978.8
          - specified — *see* Table of Drugs and Chemicals
        - other vaccines NEC 979.9
          - specified — *see* Table of Drugs and Chemicals
    - varicose veins (*see also* Varicose, vein, inflamed or infected) 454.1
    - x-rays 692.82
  - dyshydrotic 705.81
  - dysmenorrheica 625.8
  - eczematoid NEC 692.9
    - infectious 690.8
  - eczematous NEC 692.9
  - epidemica 695.89
  - erysipelatosa 695.81
  - escharotica — *see* Burn, by site
  - exfoliativa, exfoliative 695.89
    - generalized 695.89
    - infantum 695.81
    - neonatorum 695.81
  - eyelid 373.31
    - allergic 373.32
    - contact 373.32
    - eczematous 373.31
    - herpes (zoster) 053.20
      - simplex 054.41
    - infective 373.5
      - due to
        - actinomycosis 039.3 *[373.5]*
        - herpes
          - simplex 054.41
          - zoster 053.20
        - impetigo 684 *[373.5]*
        - leprosy (*see also* Leprosy) 030.0 *[373.4]*
        - lupus vulgaris (tuberculous) (*see also* Tuberculosis) 017.0 ☑ *[373.4]*
        - mycotic dermatitis (*see also* Dermatomycosis) 111.9 *[373.5]*
        - vaccinia 051.02 *[373.5]* ▲
          - postvaccination 999.0 *[373.5]*
        - yaws (*see also* Yaws) 102.9 *[373.4]*
  - facta, factitia 698.4
    - psychogenic 316 *[698.4]*
  - ficta 698.4
    - psychogenic 316 *[698.4]*
  - flexural 691.8
  - follicularis 704.8
  - friction 709.8
  - fungus 111.9
    - specified type NEC 111.8
  - gangrenosa, gangrenous (infantum) (*see also* Gangrene) 785.4
  - gestationis 646.8 ☑
  - gonococcal 098.89
  - gouty 274.89
  - harvest mite 133.8
  - heat 692.89
  - herpetiformis (bullous) (erythematous) (pustular) (vesicular) 694.0
    - juvenile 694.2
    - senile 694.5
  - hiemalis 692.89
  - hypostatic, hypostatica 454.1
    - with ulcer 454.2
  - impetiginous 684
  - infantile (acute) (chronic) (intertriginous) (intrinsic) (seborrheic) 690.12
  - infectiosa eczematoides 690.8
  - infectious (staphylococcal) (streptococcal) 686.9
    - eczematoid 690.8
  - infective eczematoid 690.8
  - Jacquet's (diaper dermatitis) 691.0
  - leptus 133.8
  - lichenified NEC 692.9
  - lichenoid, chronic 701.0
  - lichenoides purpurica pigmentosa 709.1
  - meadow 692.6
  - medicamentosa (correct substance properly administered) (internal use) (*see also* Dermatitis, due to, drugs or medicinals) 693.0
    - due to contact with skin 692.3
  - mite 133.8
  - multiformis 694.0
    - juvenile 694.2
    - senile 694.5
  - napkin 691.0
  - neuro 698.3
  - neurotica 694.0
  - nummular NEC 692.9
  - osteatosis, osteatotic 706.8
  - papillaris capillitii 706.1
  - pellagrous 265.2
  - perioral 695.3
  - perstans 696.1
  - photosensitivity (sun) 692.72
    - other light 692.82
  - pigmented purpuric lichenoid 709.1
  - polymorpha dolorosa 694.0
  - primary irritant 692.9
  - pruriginosa 694.0
  - pruritic NEC 692.9
  - psoriasiform nodularis 696.2
  - psychogenic 316
  - purulent 686.00
  - pustular contagious 051.2
  - pyococcal 686.00
  - pyocyaneus 686.09
  - pyogenica 686.00
  - radiation 692.82
  - repens 696.1
  - Ritter's (exfoliativa) 695.81
  - Schamberg's (progressive pigmentary dermatosis) 709.09
  - schistosome 120.3
  - seasonal bullous 694.8
  - seborrheic 690.10
    - infantile 690.12
  - sensitization NEC 692.9
  - septic (*see also* Septicemia) 686.00
    - gonococcal 098.89
  - solar, solare NEC (*see also* Dermatitis, due to, sun) 692.70
  - stasis 454.1 ▲
    - due to
      - postphlebitic syndrome 459.12
        - with ulcer 459.13
      - varicose veins — *see* Varicose
    - ulcerated or with ulcer (varicose) 454.2
  - sunburn (*see also* Sunburn) 692.71
  - suppurative 686.00
  - traumatic NEC 709.8
  - trophoneurotica 694.0
  - ultraviolet, except from sun 692.82
    - due to sun NEC (*see also* Dermatitis, due to, sun) 692.82
  - varicose 454.1
    - with ulcer 454.2
  - vegetans 686.8
  - verrucosa 117.2
  - xerotic 706.8
- **Dermatoarthritis, lipoid** 272.8 *[713.0]*
- **Dermatochalasia, dermatochalasis** 374.87
- **Dermatofibroma** (lenticulare) (M8832/0) — *see also* Neoplasm, skin, benign
  - protuberans (M8832/1) — *see* Neoplasm, skin, uncertain behavior
- **Dermatofibrosarcoma** (protuberans) (M8832/3) — *see* Neoplasm, skin, malignant
- **Dermatographia** 708.3
- **Dermatolysis** (congenital) (exfoliativa) 757.39
  - acquired 701.8
  - eyelids 374.34
  - palpebrarum 374.34
  - senile 701.8
- **Dermatomegaly** NEC 701.8
- **Dermatomucomyositis** 710.3
- **Dermatomycosis** 111.9
  - furfuracea 111.0
  - specified type NEC 111.8
- **Dermatomyositis** (acute) (chronic) 710.3
- **Dermatoneuritis of children** 985.0
- **Dermatophiliasis** 134.1
- **Dermatophytide** — *see* Dermatophytosis
- **Dermatophytosis** (Epidermophyton) (infection) (microsporum) (tinea) (Trichophyton) 110.9
  - beard 110.0
  - body 110.5
  - deep seated 110.6
  - fingernails 110.1
  - foot 110.4
  - groin 110.3
  - hand 110.2
  - nail 110.1
  - perianal (area) 110.3
  - scalp 110.0
  - scrotal 110.8
  - specified site NEC 110.8
  - toenails 110.1
  - vulva 110.8
- **Dermatopolyneuritis** 985.0
- **Dermatorrhexis** 756.83
  - acquired 701.8
- **Dermatosclerosis** — *see also* Scleroderma 710.1
  - localized 701.0
- **Dermatosis** 709.9
  - Andrews' 686.8
  - atopic 691.8
  - Bowen's (M8081/2) — *see* Neoplasm, skin, in situ
  - bullous 694.9
    - specified type NEC 694.8
  - erythematosquamous 690.8
  - exfoliativa 695.89
  - factitial 698.4
  - gonococcal 098.89
  - herpetiformis 694.0
    - juvenile 694.2
    - senile 694.5
  - hysterical 300.11
  - linear IgA 694.8
  - menstrual NEC 709.8
  - neutrophilic, acute febrile 695.89
  - occupational (*see also* Dermatitis) 692.9
  - papulosa nigra 709.8
  - pigmentary NEC 709.00
    - progressive 709.09
    - Schamberg's 709.09
    - Siemens-Bloch 757.33
  - progressive pigmentary 709.09
  - psychogenic 316
  - pustular subcorneal 694.1
  - Schamberg's (progressive pigmentary) 709.09
  - senile NEC 709.3
  - specified NEC 702.8
  - Unna's (seborrheic dermatitis) 690.10
- **Dermographia** 708.3
- **Dermographism** 708.3
- **Dermoid** (cyst) (M9084/0) — *see also* Neoplasm, by site, benign
  - with malignant transformation (M9084/3) 183.0
- **Dermopathy**
  - infiltrative, with thyrotoxicosis 242.0 ☑
  - nephrogenic fibrosing 701.8 ●
  - senile NEC 709.3
- **Dermophytosis** — *see* Dermatophytosis
- **Descemet's membrane** — *see* condition
- **Descemetocele** 371.72
- **Descending** — *see* condition
- **Descensus uteri** (complete) (incomplete) (partial) (without vaginal wall prolapse) 618.1
  - with mention of vaginal wall prolapse — *see* Prolapse, uterovaginal
- **Desensitization to allergens** V07.1
- **Desert**
  - rheumatism 114.0
  - sore (*see also* Ulcer, skin) 707.9
- **Desertion** (child) (newborn) 995.52
  - adult 995.84
- **Desmoid** (extra-abdominal) (tumor) (M8821/1) — *see also* Neoplasm, connective tissue, uncertain behavior
  - abdominal (M8822/1) — *see* Neoplasm, connective tissue, uncertain behavior
- **Despondency** 300.4
- **Desquamative dermatitis** NEC 695.89
- **Destruction**
  - articular facet (*see also* Derangement, joint) 718.9 ☑

☑ Additional Digit Required — Refer to the Tabular List for Digit Selection
Subterms under main terms may continue to next column or page

Destruction — *continued*
articular facet (*see also* Derangement, joint) — *continued*
vertebra 724.9
bone 733.90
syphilitic 095.5
joint (*see also* Derangement, joint) 718.9 ☑
sacroiliac 724.6
kidney 593.89
live fetus to facilitate birth NEC 763.89
ossicles (ear) 385.24
rectal sphincter 569.49
septum (nasal) 478.19
tuberculous NEC (*see also* Tuberculosis) 011.9 ☑
tympanic membrane 384.82
tympanum 385.89
vertebral disc — *see* Degeneration, intervertebral disc
Destructiveness — *see also* Disturbance, conduct 312.9
adjustment reaction 309.3
Detachment
cartilage (*see also* Sprain, by site)
knee — *see* Tear, meniscus
cervix, annular 622.8
complicating delivery 665.3 ☑
choroid (old) (postinfectional) (simple) (spontaneous) 363.70
hemorrhagic 363.72
serous 363.71
knee, medial meniscus (old) 717.3
current injury 836.0
ligament — *see* Sprain, by site
placenta (premature) — *see* Placenta, separation
retina (recent) 361.9
with retinal defect (rhegmatogenous) 361.00
giant tear 361.03
multiple 361.02
partial
with
giant tear 361.03
multiple defects 361.02
retinal dialysis (juvenile) 361.04
single defect 361.01
retinal dialysis (juvenile) 361.04
single 361.01
subtotal 361.05
total 361.05
delimited (old) (partial) 361.06
old
delimited 361.06
partial 361.06
total or subtotal 361.07
pigment epithelium (RPE) (serous) 362.42
exudative 362.42
hemorrhagic 362.43
rhegmatogenous (*see also* Detachment, retina, with retinal defect) 361.00
serous (without retinal defect) 361.2
specified type NEC 361.89
traction (with vitreoretinal organization) 361.81
vitreous humor 379.21
Detergent asthma 507.8
Deterioration
epileptic
with behavioral disturbance 345.9 ☑ *[294.11]*
without behavioral disturbance 345.9 ☑ *[294.10]*
heart, cardiac (*see also* Degeneration, myocardial) 429.1
mental (*see also* Psychosis) 298.9
myocardium, myocardial (*see also* Degeneration, myocardial) 429.1
senile (simple) 797

Deterioration — *continued*
transplanted organ — *see* Complications, transplant, organ, by site
de Toni-Fanconi syndrome (cystinosis) 270.0
Deuteranomaly 368.52
Deuteranopia (anomalous trichromat) (complete) (incomplete) 368.52
Deutschländer's disease — *see* Fracture, foot
Development
abnormal, bone 756.9
arrested 783.40
bone 733.91
child 783.40
due to malnutrition (protein-calorie) 263.2
fetus or newborn 764.9 ☑
tracheal rings (congenital) 748.3
defective, congenital (*see also* Anomaly)
cauda equina 742.59
left ventricle 746.9
with atresia or hypoplasia of aortic orifice or valve with hypoplasia of ascending aorta 746.7
in hypoplastic left heart syndrome 746.7
delayed (*see also* Delay, development) 783.40
arithmetical skills 315.1
language (skills) 315.31
and speech due to hearing loss 315.34
expressive 315.31
mixed receptive-expressive 315.32
learning skill, specified NEC 315.2
mixed skills 315.5
motor coordination 315.4
reading 315.00
specified
learning skill NEC 315.2
type NEC, except learning 315.8
speech 315.39
and language due to hearing loss 315.34
associated with hyperkinesia 314.1
phonological 315.39
spelling 315.09
written expression 315.2
imperfect, congenital (*see also* Anomaly)
heart 746.9
lungs 748.60
improper (fetus or newborn) 764.9 ☑
incomplete (fetus or newborn) 764.9 ☑
affecting management of pregnancy 656.5 ☑
bronchial tree 748.3
organ or site not listed — *see* Hypoplasia
respiratory system 748.9
sexual, precocious NEC 259.1
tardy, mental (*see also* Retardation, mental) 319
Developmental — *see* condition
Devergie's disease (pityriasis rubra pilaris) 696.4
Deviation
conjugate (eye) 378.87
palsy 378.81
spasm, spastic 378.82
esophagus 530.89
eye, skew 378.87
mandible, opening and closing 524.53
midline (jaw) (teeth) 524.29
specified site NEC — *see* Malposition
occlusal plane 524.76
organ or site, congenital NEC — *see* Malposition, congenital
septum (acquired) (nasal) 470
congenital 754.0

Deviation — *continued*
sexual 302.9
bestiality 302.1
coprophilia 302.89
ego-dystonic
homosexuality 302.0
lesbianism 302.0
erotomania 302.89
Clérambault's 297.8
exhibitionism (sexual) 302.4
fetishism 302.81
transvestic 302.3
frotteurism 302.89
homosexuality, ego-dystonic 302.0
pedophilic 302.2
lesbianism, ego-dystonic 302.0
masochism 302.83
narcissism 302.89
necrophilia 302.89
nymphomania 302.89
pederosis 302.2
pedophilia 302.2
sadism 302.84
sadomasochism 302.84
satyriasis 302.89
specified type NEC 302.89
transvestic fetishism 302.3
transvestism 302.3
voyeurism 302.82
zoophilia (erotica) 302.1
teeth, midline 524.29
trachea 519.19
ureter (congenital) 753.4
Devic's disease 341.0
Device
cerebral ventricle (communicating) in situ V45.2
contraceptive — *see* Contraceptive, device
drainage, cerebrospinal fluid V45.2
Devil's
grip 074.1
pinches (purpura simplex) 287.2
Devitalized tooth 522.9
Devonshire colic 984.9
specified type of lead — *see* Table of Drugs and Chemicals
Dextraposition, aorta 747.21
with ventricular septal defect, pulmonary stenosis or atresia, and hypertrophy of right ventricle 745.2
in tetralogy of Fallot 745.2
Dextratransposition, aorta 745.11
Dextrinosis, limit (debrancher enzyme deficiency) 271.0
Dextrocardia (corrected) (false) (isolated) (secondary) (true) 746.87
with
complete transposition of viscera 759.3
situs inversus 759.3
Dextroversion, kidney (left) 753.3
Dhobie itch 110.3

Diabetes, diabetic (brittle) (congenital) (familial) (mellitus) (poorly controlled) (severe) (slight) (without complication) 250.0 ☑

Note — Use the following fifth-digit subclassification with category 250:

0 type II or unspecified type, not stated as uncontrolled

Fifth-digit 0 is for use for type II patients, even if the patient requires insulin

1 type I [juvenile type], not stated as uncontrolled

2 type II or unspecified type, uncontrolled

Fifth-digit 2 is for use for type II patients, even if the patient requires insulin

3 type I [juvenile type], uncontrolled

with
coma (with ketoacidosis) 250.3 ☑
due to secondary diabetes 249.3 ☑ ●
hyperosmolar (nonketotic) 250.2 ☑
due to secondary diabetes 249.2 ☑ ●
complication NEC 250.9 ☑
due to secondary diabetes 249.9 ☑ ●
specified NEC 250.8 ☑
due to secondary diabetes 249.8 ☑ ●
gangrene 250.7 ☑ *[785.4]*
due to secondary diabetes 249.7 ☑ *[785.4]* ●
hyperglycemia — code to Diabetes, by type, with 5th digit for not stated as uncontrolled ●
hyperosmolarity 250.2 ☑
due to secondary diabetes 249.2 ☑ ●
ketosis, ketoacidosis 250.1 ☑
due to secondary diabetes 249.1 ☑ ●
osteomyelitis 250.8 ☑ *[731.8]*
due to secondary diabetes 249.8 ☑ *[731.8]* ●
specified manisfestations NEC 250.8 ☑
due to secondary diabetes 249.8 ☑ ●
acetonemia 250.1 ☑
due to secondary diabetes 249.1 ☑ ●
acidosis 250.1 ☑
due to secondary diabetes 249.1 ☑ ●
amyotrophy 250.6 ☑ *[353.5]* ▲
due to secondary diabetes 249.6 ☑ *[353.5]* ●
angiopathy, peripheral 250.7 ☑ *[443.81]*
due to secondary diabetes 249.7 ☑ *[443.81]* ●
asymptomatic 790.29
autonomic neuropathy (peripheral) 250.6 ☑ *[337.1]*
due to secondary diabetes 249.6 ☑ *[337.1]* ●
bone change 250.8 ☑ *[731.8]*
due to secondary diabetes 249.8 ☑ *[731.8]* ●
bronze, bronzed 275.0
cataract 250.5 ☑ *[366.41]*
due to secondary diabetes 249.5 ☑ *[366.41]* ●
chemical ▶induced — *see* Diabetes, secondary◀

Diabetes, diabetic — *continued*
- chemical ▶induced — *see* Diabetes, secondary◀ — *continued*
  - complicating pregnancy, childbirth, or puerperium 648.0 ☑ ▲
- coma (with ketoacidosis) 250.3 ☑
  - due to secondary diabetes 249.3 ☑
  - hyperglycemic 250.3 ☑
    - due to secondary diabetes 249.3 ☑
  - hyperosmolar (nonketotic) 250.2 ☑
    - due to secondary diabetes 249.2 ☑
  - hypoglycemic 250.3 ☑
    - due to secondary diabetes 249.3 ☑
  - insulin 250.3 ☑
    - due to secondary diabetes 249.3 ☑
- complicating pregnancy, childbirth, or puerperium (maternal) ▶(conditions classifiable to 249 and 250)◀ 648.0 ☑
  - affecting fetus or newborn 775.0
- complication NEC 250.9 ☑
  - due to secondary diabetes 249.9 ☑
  - specified NEC 250.8 ☑
    - due to secondary diabetes 249.8 ☑
- dorsal sclerosis 250.6 ☑ *[340]*
  - due to secondary diabetes 249.6 ☑ *[340]*
- drug-induced — *see also* Diabetes, secondary
  - overdose or wrong substance given or taken — *see* Table of Drugs and Chemicals
- due to
  - cystic fibrosis — *see* Diabetes, secondary
  - infection — *see* Diabetes, secondary
- dwarfism-obesity syndrome 258.1
- gangrene 250.7 ☑ *[785.4]*
  - due to secondary diabetes 249.7 ☑ *[785.4]*
- gastroparesis 250.6 ☑ *[536.3]*
  - due to secondary diabetes 249.6 ☑ *[536.3]*
- gestational 648.8 ☑
  - complicating pregnancy, childbirth, or puerperium 648.8 ☑
- glaucoma 250.5 ☑ *[365.44]*
  - due to secondary diabetes 249.5 ☑ *[365.44]*
- glomerulosclerosis (intercapillary) 250.4 ☑ *[581.81]*
  - due to secondary diabetes 249.4 ☑ *[581.81]*
- glycogenosis, secondary 250.8 ☑ *[259.8]*
  - due to secondary diabetes 249.8 ☑ *[259.8]*
- hemochromatosis 275.0
- hyperosmolar coma 250.2 ☑
  - due to secondary diabetes 249.2 ☑
- hyperosmolarity 250.2 ☑
  - due to secondary diabetes 249.2 ☑
- hypertension-nephrosis syndrome 250.4 ☑ *[581.81]*
  - due to secondary diabetes 249.4 ☑ *[581.81]*
- hypoglycemia 250.8 ☑
  - due to secondary diabetes 249.8 ☑
- hypoglycemic shock 250.8 ☑
  - due to secondary diabetes 249.8 ☑

Diabetes, diabetic — *continued*
- inadequately controlled — code to Diabetes, by type, with 5th digit for not stated as uncontrolled
- insipidus 253.5
  - nephrogenic 588.1
  - pituitary 253.5
  - vasopressin-resistant 588.1
- intercapillary glomerulosclerosis 250.4 ☑ *[581.81]*
  - due to secondary diabetes 249.4 ☑ *[581.81]*
- iritis 250.5 ☑ *[364.42]*
  - due to secondary diabetes 249.5 ☑ *[364.42]*
- ketosis, ketoacidosis 250.1 ☑
  - due to secondary diabetes 249.1 ☑
- Kimmelstiel (-Wilson) disease or syndrome (intercapillary glomerulosclerosis) 250.4 ☑ *[581.81]*
  - due to secondary diabetes 249.4 ☑ *[581.81]*
- Lancereaux's (diabetes mellitus with marked emaciation) 250.8 ☑ *[261]*
  - due to secondary diabetes 249.8 ☑ *[261]*
- latent (chemical) ▶— *see* Diabetes, secondary◀
  - complicating pregnancy, childbirth, or puerperium 648.0 ☑ ▲
- lipoidosis 250.8 ☑ *[272.7]*
  - due to secondary diabetes 249.8 ☑ *[272.7]*
- macular edema 250.5 ☑ *[362.07]*
  - due to secondary diabetes 249.5 ☑ *[362.07]*
- maternal
  - with manifest disease in the infant 775.1
  - affecting fetus or newborn 775.0
- microaneurysms, retinal 250.5 ☑ *[362.01]*
  - due to secondary diabetes 249.5 ☑ *[362.01]*
- mononeuropathy 250.6 ☑ *[355.9]*
  - due to secondary diabetes 249.6 ☑ *[355.9]*
- neonatal, transient 775.1
- nephropathy 250.4 ☑ *[583.81]*
  - due to secondary diabetes 249.4 ☑ *[581.81]*
- nephrosis (syndrome) 250.4 ☑ *[581.81]*
  - due to secondary diabetes 249.4 ☑ *[581.81]*
- neuralgia 250.6 ☑ *[357.2]*
  - due to secondary diabetes 249.6 ☑ *[357.2]*
- neuritis 250.6 ☑ *[357.2]*
  - due to secondary diabetes 249.6 ☑ *[357.2]*
- neurogenic arthropathy 250.6 ☑ *[713.5]*
  - due to secondary diabetes 249.6 ☑ *[713.5]*
- neuropathy 250.6 ☑ *[357.2]*
  - due to secondary diabetes 249.6 ☑ *[357.2]*
- nonclinical 790.29
- osteomyelitis 250.8 ☑ *[731.8]*
  - due to secondary diabetes 249.8 ☑ *[731.8]*
- out of control — code to Diabetes, by type, with 5th digit for uncontrolled
- peripheral autonomic neuropathy 250.6 ☑ *[337.1]*
  - due to secondary diabetes 249.6 ☑ *[337.1]*
- phosphate 275.3

Diabetes, diabetic — *continued*
- polyneuropathy 250.6 ☑ *[357.2]*
  - due to secondary diabetes 249.6 ☑ *[357.2]*
- poorly controlled — code to Diabetes, by type, with 5th digit for not stated as uncontrolled
- renal (true) 271.4
- retinal
  - edema 250.5 ☑ *[362.07]*
    - due to secondary diabetes 249.5 ☑ *[362.07]*
  - hemorrhage 250.5 ☑ *[362.01]*
    - due to secondary diabetes 249.5 ☑ *[362.01]*
  - microaneurysms 250.5 ☑ *[362.01]*
    - due to secondary diabetes 249.5 ☑ *[362.01]*
- retinitis 250.5 ☑ *[362.01]*
  - due to secondary diabetes 249.5 ☑ *[362.01]*
- retinopathy 250.5 ☑ *[362.01]*
  - background 250.5 ☑ *[362.01]*
    - due to secondary diabetes 249.5 ☑ *[362.01]*
  - due to secondary diabetes 249.5 ☑ *[362.01]*
  - nonproliferative 250.5 ☑ *[362.03]*
    - due to secondary diabetes 249.5 ☑ *[362.03]*
    - mild 250.5 ☑ *[362.04]*
      - due to secondary diabetes 249.5 ☑ *[362.04]*
    - moderate 250.5 ☑ *[362.05]*
      - due to secondary diabetes 249.5 ☑ *[362.05]*
    - severe 250.5 ☑ *[362.06]*
      - due to secondary diabetes 249.5 ☑ *[362.06]*
  - proliferative 250.5 ☑ *[362.02]*
    - due to secondary diabetes 249.5 ☑ *[362.02]*
- secondary (chemical-induced) (due to chronic condition) (due to infection) (drug-induced) 249.0 ☑
  - with
    - coma (with ketoacidosis) 249.3 ☑
      - hyperosmolar (nonketotic) 249.2 ☑
    - complication NEC 249.9 ☑
      - specified NEC 249.8 ☑
    - gangrene 249.7 ☑ *[785.4]*
    - hyperosmolarity 249.2 ☑
    - ketosis, ketoacidosis 249.1 ☑
    - osteomyelitis 249.8 ☑ *[731.8]*
    - specified manifestations NEC 249.8 ☑
  - acetonemia 249.1 ☑
  - acidosis 249.1 ☑
  - amyotrophy 249.6 ☑ *[353.5]*
  - angiopathy, peripheral 249.7 ☑ *[443.81]*
  - autonomic neuropathy (peripheral) 249.6 ☑ *[337.1]*
  - bone change 249.8 ☑ *[731.8]*
  - cataract 249.5 ☑ *[366.41]*
  - coma (with ketoacidosis) 249.3 ☑
    - hyperglycemic 249.3 ☑
    - hyperosmolar (nonketotic) 249.2 ☑
    - hypoglycemic 249.3 ☑
    - insulin 249.3 ☑
  - complicating pregnancy, childbirth, or puerperium (maternal) 648.0 ☑
    - affecting fetus or newborn 775.0
  - complication NEC 249.9 ☑
    - specified NEC 249.8 ☑
  - dorsal sclerosis 249.6 ☑ *[340]*

Diabetes, diabetic — *continued*
- secondary — *continued*
  - due to overdose or wrong substance given or taken — *see* Table of Drugs and Chemicals
  - gangrene 249.7 ☑ *[785.4]*
  - gastroparesis 249.6 ☑ *[536.3]*
  - glaucoma 249.5 ☑ *[365.44]*
  - glomerulosclerosis (intercapillary) 249.4 ☑ *[581.81]*
  - glycogenosis, secondary 249.8 ☑ *[259.8]*
  - hyperosmolar coma 249.2 ☑
  - hyperosmolarity 249.2 ☑
  - hypertension-nephrosis syndrome 249.4 ☑ *[581.81]*
  - hypoglycemia 249.8 ☑
  - hypoglycemic shock 249.8 ☑
  - intercapillary glomerulosclerosis 249.4 ☑ *[581.81]*
  - iritis 249.5 ☑ *[364.42]*
  - ketosis, ketoacidosis 249.1 ☑
  - Kimmelstiel (-Wilson) disease or syndrome (intercapillary glomerulosclerosis) 249.4 ☑ *[581.81]*
  - Lancereaux's (diabetes mellitus with marked emaciation) 249.8 ☑ *[261]*
  - lipoidosis 249.8 ☑ *[272.7]*
  - macular edema 249.5 ☑ *[362.07]*
  - maternal
    - with manifest disease in the infant 775.1
    - affecting fetus or newborn 775.0
  - microaneurysms, retinal 249.5 ☑ *[362.01]*
  - mononeuropathy 249.6 ☑ *[355.9]*
  - nephropathy 249.4 ☑ *[581.81]*
  - nephrosis (syndrome) 249.4 ☑ *[581.81]*
  - neuralgia 249.6 ☑ *[357.2]*
  - neuritis 249.6 ☑ *[357.2]*
  - neurogenic arthropathy 249.6 ☑ *[713.5]*
  - neuropathy 249.6 ☑ *[357.2]*
  - osteomyelitis 249.8 ☑ *[731.8]*
  - peripheral autonomic neuropathy 249.6 ☑ *[337.1]*
  - polyneuropathy 249.6 ☑ *[357.2]*
  - retinal
    - edema 249.5 ☑ *[362.07]*
    - hemorrhage 249.5 ☑ *[362.01]*
    - microaneurysms 249.5 ☑ *[362.01]*
  - retinitis 249.5 ☑ *[362.01]*
  - retinopathy 249.5 ☑ *[362.01]*
    - background 249.5 ☑ *[362.01]*
    - nonproliferative 249.5 ☑ *[362.03]*
      - mild 249.5 ☑ *[362.04]*
      - moderate 249.5 ☑ *[362.05]*
      - severe 249.5 ☑ *[362.06]*
    - proliferative 249.5 ☑ *[362.02]*
  - ulcer (skin) 249.8 ☑ *[707.9]*
    - lower extemity 249.8 ☑ *[707.10]*
      - ankle 249.8 ☑ *[707.13]*
      - calf 249.8 ☑ *[707.12]*
      - foot 249.8 ☑ *[707.15]*
      - heel 249.8 ☑ *[707.14]*
      - knee 249.8 ☑ *[707.19]*
      - specified site NEC 249.8 ☑ *[707.19]*
      - thigh 249.8 ☑ *[707.11]*
      - toes 249.8 ☑ *[707.15]*
    - specified site NEC 249.8 ☑ *[707.8]*
  - xanthoma 249.8 ☑ *[272.2]*
- steroid induced ▶— *see also* Diabetes, secondary◀
  - overdose or wrong substance given or taken 962.0

☑ Additional Digit Required — Refer to the Tabular List for Digit Selection

Subterms under main terms may continue to next column or page

▶◀ Revised Text ● New Line ▲ Revised Code

Diabetes, diabetic — *continued*
- stress 790.29
- subclinical 790.29
- subliminal 790.29
- sugar 250.0 ☑
- ulcer (skin) 250.8 ☑ *[707.9]*
  - due to secondary diabetes 249.8 ☑ *[707.9]* ●
  - lower extremity 250.8 ☑ *[707.10]*
    - ankle 250.8 ☑ *[707.13]*
      - due to secondary diabetes 249.8 ☑ *[707.13]* ●
    - calf 250.8 ☑ *[707.12]*
      - due to secondary diabetes 249.8 ☑ *[707.12]* ●
    - due to secondary diabetes 249.8 ☑ *[707.10]* ●
    - foot 250.8 ☑ *[707.15]*
      - due to secondary diabetes 249.8 ☑ *[707.15]* ●
    - heel 250.8 ☑ *[707.14]*
      - due to secondary diabetes 249.8 ☑ *[707.14]* ●
    - knee 250.8 ☑ *[707.19]*
      - due to secondary diabetes 249.8 ☑ *[707.19]* ●
    - specified site NEC 250.8 ☑ *[707.19]*
      - due to secondary diabetes 249.8 ☑ *[707.19]* ●
    - thigh 250.8 ☑ *[707.11]*
      - due to secondary diabetes 249.8 ☑ *[707.11]* ●
    - toes 250.8 ☑ *[707.15]*
      - due to secondary diabetes 249.8 ☑ *[707.15]* ●
  - specified site NEC 250.8 ☑ *[707.8]*
    - due to secondary diabetes 249.8 ☑ *[707.8]* ●
- xanthoma 250.8 ☑ *[272.2]*
  - due to secondary diabetes 249.8 ☑ *[272.2]* ●

Diacyclothrombopathia 287.1

Diagnosis deferred 799.9

Dialysis (intermittent) (treatment)
- anterior retinal (juvenile) (with detachment) 361.04
- extracorporeal V56.0
- hemodialysis V56.0
  - status only V45.11 ▲
- peritoneal V56.8
  - status only V45.11 ▲
- renal V56.0
  - status only V45.11 ▲
- specified type NEC V56.8

Diamond-Blackfan anemia or syndrome (congenital hypoplastic anemia) 284.01

Diamond-Gardener syndrome (autoerythrocyte sensitization) 287.2

Diaper rash 691.0

Diaphoresis (excessive) NEC — *see also* Hyperhidrosis) 780.8

Diaphragm — *see* condition

Diaphragmalgia 786.52

Diaphragmitis 519.4

Diaphyseal aclasis 756.4

Diaphysitis 733.99

Diarrhea, diarrheal (acute) (autumn) (bilious) (bloody) (catarrhal) (choleraic) (chronic) (gravis) (green) (infantile) (lienteric) (noninfectious) (presumed noninfectious) (putrefactive) (secondary) (sporadic) (summer) (symptomatic) (thermic) 787.91
- achlorhydric 536.0
- allergic 558.3
- amebic (*see also* Amebiasis) 006.9
  - with abscess — *see* Abscess, amebic
  - acute 006.0
  - chronic 006.1
  - nondysenteric 006.2
- bacillary — *see* Dysentery, bacillary
- bacterial NEC 008.5

Diarrhea, diarrheal — *continued*
- balantidial 007.0
- bile salt-induced 579.8
- cachectic NEC 787.91
- chilomastix 007.8
- choleriformis 001.1
- coccidial 007.2
- Cochin-China 579.1
  - anguilluliasis 127.2
  - psilosis 579.1
- Dientamoeba 007.8
- dietetic 787.91
- due to
  - achylia gastrica 536.8
  - Aerobacter aerogenes 008.2
  - Bacillus coli — *see* Enteritis, E. coli
  - bacteria NEC 008.5
  - bile salts 579.8
  - Capillaria
    - hepatica 128.8
    - philippinensis 127.5
  - Clostridium perfringens (C) (F) 008.46
  - Enterobacter aerogenes 008.2
  - enterococci 008.49
  - Escherichia coli — *see* Enteritis, E. coli
  - Giardia lamblia 007.1
  - Heterophyes heterophyes 121.6
  - irritating foods 787.91
  - Metagonimus yokogawai 121.5
  - Necator americanus 126.1
  - Paracolobactrum arizonae 008.1
  - Paracolon bacillus NEC 008.47
    - Arizona 008.1
  - Proteus (bacillus) (mirabilis) (Morganii) 008.3
  - Pseudomonas aeruginosa 008.42
  - S. japonicum 120.2
  - specified organism NEC 008.8
    - bacterial 008.49
    - viral NEC 008.69
  - Staphylococcus 008.41
  - Streptococcus 008.49
    - anaerobic 008.46
  - Strongyloides stercoralis 127.2
  - Trichuris trichiuria 127.3
  - virus NEC (*see also* Enteritis, viral) 008.69
- dysenteric 009.2
  - due to specified organism NEC 008.8
- dyspeptic 787.91
- endemic 009.3
  - due to specified organism NEC 008.8
- epidemic 009.2
  - due to specified organism NEC 008.8
- fermentative 787.91
- flagellate 007.9
- Flexner's (ulcerative) 004.1
- functional 564.5
  - following gastrointestinal surgery 564.4
  - psychogenic 306.4
- giardial 007.1
- Giardia lamblia 007.1
- hill 579.1
- hyperperistalsis (nervous) 306.4
- infectious 009.2
  - due to specified organism NEC 008.8
  - presumed 009.3
- inflammatory 787.91
  - due to specified organism NEC 008.8
- malarial (*see also* Malaria) 084.6
- mite 133.8
- mycotic 117.9
- nervous 306.4
- neurogenic 564.5
- parenteral NEC 009.2
- postgastrectomy 564.4
- postvagotomy 564.4
- prostaglandin induced 579.8

Diarrhea, diarrheal — *continued*
- protozoal NEC 007.9
- psychogenic 306.4
- septic 009.2
  - due to specified organism NEC 008.8
- specified organism NEC 008.8
  - bacterial 008.49
  - viral NEC 008.69
- Staphylococcus 008.41
- Streptococcus 008.49
  - anaerobic 008.46
- toxic 558.2
- travelers' 009.2
  - due to specified organism NEC 008.8
- trichomonal 007.3
- tropical 579.1
- tuberculous 014.8 ☑
- ulcerative (chronic) (*see also* Colitis, ulcerative) 556.9
- viral (*see also* Enteritis, viral) 008.8
- zymotic NEC 009.2

Diastasis
- cranial bones 733.99
  - congenital 756.0
- joint (traumatic) — *see* Dislocation, by site
- muscle 728.84
  - congenital 756.89
- recti (abdomen) 728.84
  - complicating delivery 665.8 ☑
  - congenital 756.79

Diastema, teeth, tooth 524.30

Diastematomyelia 742.51

Diataxia, cerebral, infantile 343.0

Diathesis
- allergic V15.09
- bleeding (familial) 287.9
- cystine (familial) 270.0
- gouty 274.9
- hemorrhagic (familial) 287.9
  - newborn NEC 776.0
- oxalic 271.8
- scrofulous (*see also* Tuberculosis) 017.2 ☑
- spasmophilic (*see also* Tetany) 781.7
- ulcer 536.9
- uric acid 274.9

Diaz's disease or osteochondrosis 732.5

Dibothriocephaliasis 123.4
- larval 123.5

Dibothriocephalus (infection) (infestation) (latus) 123.4
- larval 123.5

Dicephalus 759.4

Dichotomy, teeth 520.2

Dichromat, dichromata (congenital) 368.59

Dichromatopsia (congenital) 368.59

Dichuchwa 104.0

Dicroceliasis 121.8

Didelphys, didelphic — *see also* Double uterus 752.2

Didymitis — *see also* Epididymitis 604.90

Died — *see also* Death
- without
  - medical attention (cause unknown) 798.9
  - sign of disease 798.2

Dientamoeba diarrhea 007.8

Dietary
- inadequacy or deficiency 269.9
- surveillance and counseling V65.3

Dietl's crisis 593.4

Dieulafoy lesion (hemorrhagic)
- of
  - duodenum 537.84
  - esophagus 530.82
  - intestine 569.86
  - stomach 537.84

Difficult
- birth, affecting fetus or newborn 763.9
- delivery NEC 669.9 ☑

Difficulty
- feeding 783.3
  - adult 783.3
  - breast 676.8 ☑
  - child 783.3
  - elderly 783.3
  - infant 783.3
  - newborn 779.3
  - nonorganic (infant) NEC 307.59
- mechanical, gastroduodenal stoma 537.89
- reading 315.00
- specific, spelling 315.09
- swallowing (*see also* Dysphagia) 787.20
- walking 719.7

Diffuse — *see* condition

Diffused ganglion 727.42

Di George's syndrome (thymic hypoplasia) 279.11

Digestive — *see* condition

Di Guglielmo's disease or syndrome (M9841/3) 207.0 ☑

Diktyoma (M9051/3) — *see* Neoplasm, by site, malignant

Dilaceration, tooth 520.4

Dilatation
- anus 564.89
  - venule — *see* Hemorrhoids
- aorta (focal) (general) (*see also* Aneurysm, aorta) 441.9
  - congenital 747.29
  - infectional 093.0
  - ruptured 441.5
  - syphilitic 093.0
- appendix (cystic) 543.9
- artery 447.8
- bile duct (common) (cystic) (congenital) 751.69
  - acquired 576.8
- bladder (sphincter) 596.8
  - congenital 753.8
  - in pregnancy or childbirth 654.4 ☑
    - causing obstructed labor 660.2 ☑
      - affecting fetus or newborn 763.1
- blood vessel 459.89
- bronchus, bronchi 494.0
  - with acute exacerbation 494.1
- calyx (due to obstruction) 593.89
- capillaries 448.9
- cardiac (acute) (chronic) (*see also* Hypertrophy, cardiac) 429.3
  - congenital 746.89
    - valve NEC 746.89
      - pulmonary 746.09
  - hypertensive (*see also* Hypertension, heart) 402.90
- cavum septi pellucidi 742.4
- cecum 564.89
  - psychogenic 306.4
- cervix (uteri) (*see also* Incompetency, cervix)
  - incomplete, poor, slow
    - affecting fetus or newborn 763.7
    - complicating delivery 661.0 ☑
      - affecting fetus or newborn 763.7
- colon 564.7
  - congenital 751.3
  - due to mechanical obstruction 560.89
  - psychogenic 306.4
- common bile duct (congenital) 751.69
  - acquired 576.8
    - with calculus, choledocholithiasis, or stones — *see* Choledocholithiasis
- cystic duct 751.69
  - acquired (any bile duct) 575.8
- duct, mammary 610.4
- duodenum 564.89
- esophagus 530.89
  - congenital 750.4

☑ Additional Digit Required — Refer to the Tabular List for Digit Selection
Subterms under main terms may continue to next column or page

- **Dilatation** — *continued*
  - esophagus — *continued*
    - due to
      - achalasia 530.0
      - cardiospasm 530.0
  - Eustachian tube, congenital 744.24
  - fontanel 756.0
  - gallbladder 575.8
    - congenital 751.69
  - gastric 536.8
    - acute 536.1
    - psychogenic 306.4
  - heart (acute) (chronic) (*see also* Hypertrophy, cardiac) 429.3
    - congenital 746.89
    - hypertensive (*see also* Hypertension, heart) 402.90
    - valve (*see also* Endocarditis)
      - congenital 746.89
  - ileum 564.89
    - psychogenic 306.4
  - inguinal rings — *see* Hernia, inguinal
  - jejunum 564.89
    - psychogenic 306.4
  - kidney (calyx) (collecting structures) (cystic) (parenchyma) (pelvis) 593.89
  - lacrimal passages 375.69
  - lymphatic vessel 457.1
  - mammary duct 610.4
  - Meckel's diverticulum (congenital) 751.0
  - meningeal vessels, congenital 742.8
  - myocardium (acute) (chronic) (*see also* Hypertrophy, cardiac) 429.3
  - organ or site, congenital NEC — *see* Distortion
  - pancreatic duct 577.8
  - pelvis, kidney 593.89
  - pericardium — *see* Pericarditis
  - pharynx 478.29
  - prostate 602.8
  - pulmonary
    - artery (idiopathic) 417.8
      - congenital 747.3
    - valve, congenital 746.09
  - pupil 379.43
  - rectum 564.89
  - renal 593.89
  - saccule vestibularis, congenital 744.05
  - salivary gland (duct) 527.8
  - sphincter ani 564.89
  - stomach 536.8
    - acute 536.1
    - psychogenic 306.4
  - submaxillary duct 527.8
  - trachea, congenital 748.3
  - ureter (idiopathic) 593.89
    - congenital 753.20
    - due to obstruction 593.5
  - urethra (acquired) 599.84
  - vasomotor 443.9
  - vein 459.89
  - ventricular, ventricle (acute) (chronic) (*see also* Hypertrophy, cardiac) 429.3
    - cerebral, congenital 742.4
    - hypertensive (*see also* Hypertension, heart) 402.90
  - venule 459.89
    - anus — *see* Hemorrhoids
  - vesical orifice 596.8
- **Dilated, dilation** — *see* Dilatation
- **Diminished**
  - hearing (acuity) (*see also* Deafness) 389.9
  - pulse pressure 785.9
  - vision NEC 369.9
  - vital capacity 794.2
- **Diminuta taenia** 123.6
- **Diminution, sense or sensation** (cold) (heat) (tactile) (vibratory) — *see also* Disturbance, sensation 782.0
- **Dimitri-Sturge-Weber disease** (encephalocutaneous angiomatosis) 759.6
- **Dimple**
  - parasacral 685.1
    - with abscess 685.0
  - pilonidal 685.1
    - with abscess 685.0
  - postanal 685.1
    - with abscess 685.0
- **Dioctophyma renale** (infection) (infestation) 128.8
- **Dipetalonemiasis** 125.4
- **Diphallus** 752.69
- **Diphtheria, diphtheritic** (gangrenous) (hemorrhagic) 032.9
  - carrier (suspected) of V02.4
  - cutaneous 032.85
  - cystitis 032.84
  - faucial 032.0
  - infection of wound 032.85
  - inoculation (anti) (not sick) V03.5
  - laryngeal 032.3
  - myocarditis 032.82
  - nasal anterior 032.2
  - nasopharyngeal 032.1
  - neurological complication 032.89
  - peritonitis 032.83
  - specified site NEC 032.89
- **Diphyllobothriasis** (intestine) 123.4
  - larval 123.5
- **Diplacusis** 388.41
- **Diplegia** (upper limbs) 344.2
  - brain or cerebral 437.8
  - congenital 343.0
  - facial 351.0
    - congenital 352.6
  - infantile or congenital (cerebral) (spastic) (spinal) 343.0
  - lower limbs 344.1
  - syphilitic, congenital 090.49
- **Diplococcus, diplococcal** — *see* condition
- **Diplomyelia** 742.59
- **Diplopia** 368.2
  - refractive 368.15
- **Dipsomania** — *see also* Alcoholism 303.9 ☑
  - with psychosis (*see also* Psychosis, alcoholic) 291.9
- **Dipylidiasis** 123.8
  - intestine 123.8
- **Direction, teeth, abnormal** 524.30
- **Dirt-eating child** 307.52
- **Disability**
  - heart — *see* Disease, heart
  - learning NEC 315.2
  - special spelling 315.09
- **Disarticulation** — *see also* Derangement, joint 718.9 ☑
  - meaning
    - amputation
      - status — *see* Absence, by site
      - traumatic — *see* Amputation, traumatic
    - dislocation, traumatic or congenital — *see* Dislocation
- **Disaster, cerebrovascular** — *see also* Disease, cerebrovascular, acute 436
- **Discharge**
  - anal NEC 787.99
  - breast (female) (male) 611.79
  - conjunctiva 372.89
  - continued locomotor idiopathic (*see also* Epilepsy) 345.5 ☑
  - diencephalic autonomic idiopathic (*see also* Epilepsy) 345.5 ☑
  - ear 388.60
    - blood 388.69
    - cerebrospinal fluid 388.61
  - excessive urine 788.42
  - eye 379.93
  - nasal 478.19
  - nipple 611.79
- **Discharge** — *continued*
  - patterned motor idiopathic (*see also* Epilepsy) 345.5 ☑
  - penile 788.7
  - postnasal — *see* Sinusitis
  - sinus, from mediastinum 510.0
  - umbilicus 789.9
  - urethral 788.7
    - bloody 599.84
  - vaginal 623.5
- **Discitis** 722.90
  - cervical, cervicothoracic 722.91
  - lumbar, lumbosacral 722.93
  - thoracic, thoracolumbar 722.92
- **Discogenic syndrome** — *see* Displacement, intervertebral disc
- **Discoid**
  - kidney 753.3
  - meniscus, congenital 717.5
  - semilunar cartilage 717.5
- **Discoloration**
  - mouth 528.9
  - nails 703.8
  - teeth 521.7
    - due to
      - drugs 521.7
      - metals (copper) (silver) 521.7
      - pulpal bleeding 521.7
    - during formation 520.8
    - extrinsic 523.6
    - intrinsic posteruptive 521.7
- **Discomfort**
  - chest 786.59
  - visual 368.13
- **Discomycosis** — *see* Actinomycosis
- **Discontinuity, ossicles, ossicular chain** 385.23
- **Discrepancy**
  - centric occlusion
    - maximum intercuspation 524.55
    - of teeth 524.55
  - leg length (acquired) 736.81
    - congenital 755.30
  - uterine size-date 649.6 ☑
- **Discrimination**
  - political V62.4
  - racial V62.4
  - religious V62.4
  - sex V62.4
- **Disease, diseased** — *see also* Syndrome
  - Abrami's (acquired hemolytic jaundice) 283.9
  - absorbent system 459.89
  - accumulation — *see* Thesaurismosis
  - acid-peptic 536.8
  - Acosta's 993.2
  - Adams-Stokes (-Morgagni) (syncope with heart block) 426.9
  - Addison's (bronze) (primary adrenal insufficiency) 255.41
    - anemia (pernicious) 281.0
    - tuberculous (*see also* Tuberculosis) 017.6 ☑
  - Addison-Gull — *see* Xanthoma
  - adenoids (and tonsils) (chronic) 474.9
  - adrenal (gland) (capsule) (cortex) 255.9
    - hyperfunction 255.3
    - hypofunction 255.41
    - specified type NEC 255.8
  - ainhum (dactylolysis spontanea) 136.0
  - akamushi (scrub typhus) 081.2
  - Akureyri (epidemic neuromyasthenia) 049.8
  - Albarrán's (colibacilluria) 791.9
  - Albers-Schönberg's (marble bones) 756.52
  - Albert's 726.71
  - Albright (-Martin) (-Bantam) 275.49
  - Alibert's (mycosis fungoides) (M9700/3) 202.1 ☑
  - Alibert-Bazin (M9700/3) 202.1 ☑
  - alimentary canal 569.9
  - alligator skin (ichthyosis congenita) 757.1
    - acquired 701.1
- **Disease, diseased** — *see also* Syndrome — *continued*
  - Almeida's (Brazilian blastomycosis) 116.1
  - Alpers' 330.8
  - alpine 993.2
  - altitude 993.2
  - alveoli, teeth 525.9
  - Alzheimer's — *see* Alzheimer's
  - amyloid (any site) 277.30
  - anarthritic rheumatoid 446.5
  - Anders' (adiposis tuberosa simplex) 272.8
  - Andersen's (glycogenosis IV) 271.0
  - Anderson's (angiokeratoma corporis diffusum) 272.7
  - Andes 993.2
  - Andrews' (bacterid) 686.8
  - angiospastic, angiospasmodic 443.9
    - cerebral 435.9
      - with transient neurologic deficit 435.9
    - vein 459.89
  - anterior
    - chamber 364.9
    - horn cell 335.9
      - specified type NEC 335.8
  - antral (chronic) 473.0
    - acute 461.0
  - anus NEC 569.49
  - aorta (nonsyphilitic) 447.9
    - syphilitic NEC 093.89
  - aortic (heart) (valve) (*see also* Endocarditis, aortic) 424.1
  - apollo 077.4
  - aponeurosis 726.90
  - appendix 543.9
  - aqueous (chamber) 364.9
  - arc-welders' lung 503
  - Armenian 277.31
  - Arnold-Chiari (*see also* Spina bifida) 741.0 ☑
  - arterial 447.9
    - occlusive (*see also* Occlusion, by site) 444.22
      - with embolus or thrombus — *see* Occlusion, by site
      - due to stricture or stenosis 447.1
    - specified type NEC 447.8
  - arteriocardiorenal (*see also* Hypertension, cardiorenal) 404.90
  - arteriolar (generalized) (obliterative) 447.9
    - specified type NEC 447.8
  - arteriorenal — *see* Hypertension, kidney
  - arteriosclerotic (*see also* Arteriosclerosis)
    - cardiovascular 429.2
    - coronary — *see* Arteriosclerosis, coronary
    - heart — *see* Arteriosclerosis, coronary
    - vascular — *see* Arteriosclerosis
  - artery 447.9
    - cerebral 437.9
    - coronary — *see* Arteriosclerosis, coronary
    - specified type NEC 447.8
  - arthropod-borne NEC 088.9
    - specified type NEC 088.89
  - Asboe-Hansen's (incontinentia pigmenti) 757.33
  - atticoantral, chronic (with posterior or superior marginal perforation of ear drum) 382.2
  - auditory canal, ear 380.9
  - Aujeszky's 078.89
  - auricle, ear NEC 380.30
  - Australian X 062.4
  - autoimmune NEC 279.4
    - hemolytic (cold type) (warm type) 283.0
    - parathyroid 252.1
    - thyroid 245.2

Disease, diseased — *see also* Syndrome — *continued*
aviators' (*see also* Effect, adverse, high altitude) 993.2
ax(e)-grinders' 502
Ayala's 756.89
Ayerza's (pulmonary artery sclerosis with pulmonary hypertension) 416.0
Azorean (of the nervous system) 334.8
Babington's (familial hemorrhagic telangiectasia) 448.0
back bone NEC 733.90
bacterial NEC 040.89
zoonotic NEC 027.9
specified type NEC 027.8
Baehr-Schiffrin (thrombotic thrombocytopenic purpura) 446.6
Baelz's (cheilitis glandularis apostematosa) 528.5
Baerensprung's (eczema marginatum) 110.3
Balfour's (chloroma) 205.3 ☑
balloon (*see also* Effect, adverse, high altitude 993.2
Baló's 341.1
Bamberger (-Marie) (hypertrophic pulmonary osteoarthropathy) 731.2
Bang's (Brucella abortus) 023.1
Bannister's 995.1
Banti's (with cirrhosis) (with portal hypertension) — *see* Cirrhosis, liver
Barcoo (*see also* Ulcer, skin) 707.9
barium lung 503
Barlow (-Möller) (infantile scurvy) 267
barometer makers' 985.0
Barraquer (-Simons) (progressive lipodystrophy) 272.6
basal ganglia 333.90
degenerative NEC 333.0
specified NEC 333.89
Basedow's (exophthalmic goiter) 242.0 ☑
basement membrane NEC 583.89
with
pulmonary hemorrhage (Goodpasture's syndrome) 446.21 *[583.81]*
Bateman's 078.0
purpura (senile) 287.2
Batten's 330.1 *[362.71]*
Batten-Mayou (retina) 330.1 *[362.71]*
Batten-Steinert 359.21
Battey 031.0
Baumgarten-Cruveilhier (cirrhosis of liver) 571.5
bauxite-workers' 503
Bayle's (dementia paralytica) 094.1
Bazin's (primary) (*see also* Tuberculosis) 017.1 ☑
Beard's (neurasthenia) 300.5
Beau's (*see also* Degeneration, myocardial) 429.1
Bechterew's (ankylosing spondylitis) 720.0
Becker's
idiopathic mural endomyocardial disease 425.2
myotonia congenita, recessive form 359.22
Begbie's (exophthalmic goiter) 242.0 ☑
Behr's 362.50
Beigel's (white piedra) 111.2
Bekhterev's (ankylosing spondylitis) 720.0
Bell's (*see also* Psychosis, affective) 296.0 ☑
Bennett's (leukemia) 208.9 ☑
Benson's 379.22
Bergeron's (hysteroepilepsy) 300.11
Berlin's 921.3
Bernard-Soulier (thrombopathy) 287.1
Bernhardt (-Roth) 355.1
beryllium 503

Disease, diseased — *see also* Syndrome — *continued*
Besnier-Boeck (-Schaumann) (sarcoidosis) 135
Best's 362.76
Beurmann's (sporotrichosis) 117.1
Bielschowsky (-Jansky) 330.1
Biermer's (pernicious anemia) 281.0
Biett's (discoid lupus erythematosus) 695.4
bile duct (*see also* Disease, biliary) 576.9
biliary (duct) (tract) 576.9
with calculus, choledocholithiasis, or stones — *see* Choledocholithiasis
Billroth's (meningocele) (*see also* Spina bifida) 741.9 ☑
Binswanger's 290.12
Bird's (oxaluria) 271.8
bird fanciers' 495.2
black lung 500
bladder 596.9
specified NEC 596.8
bleeder's 286.0
Bloch-Sulzberger (incontinentia pigmenti) 757.33
Blocq's (astasia-abasia) 307.9
blood (-forming organs) 289.9
specified NEC 289.89
vessel 459.9
Bloodgood's 610.1
Blount's (tibia vara) 732.4
blue 746.9
Bodechtel-Guttmann (subacute sclerosing panencephalitis) 046.2
Boeck's (sarcoidosis) 135
bone 733.90
fibrocystic NEC 733.29
jaw 526.2
marrow 289.9
Paget's (osteitis deformans) 731.0
specified type NEC 733.99
von Recklinghausen's (osteitis fibrosa cystica) 252.01
Bonfils' — *see* Disease, Hodgkin's
Borna 062.9
Bornholm (epidemic pleurodynia) 074.1
Bostock's (*see also* Fever, hay) 477.9
Bouchard's (myopathic dilatation of the stomach) 536.1
Bouillaud's (rheumatic heart disease) 391.9
Bourneville (-Brissaud) (tuberous sclerosis) 759.5
Bouveret (-Hoffmann) (paroxysmal tachycardia) 427.2
bowel 569.9
functional 564.9
psychogenic 306.4
Bowen's (M8081/2) — *see* Neoplasm, skin, in situ
Bozzolo's (multiple myeloma) (M9730/3) 203.0 ☑
Bradley's (epidemic vomiting) 078.82
Brailsford's 732.3
radius, head 732.3
tarsal, scaphoid 732.5
Brailsford-Morquio (mucopolysaccharidosis IV) 277.5
brain 348.9
Alzheimer's 331.0
with dementia — *see* Alzheimer's, dementia
arterial, artery 437.9
arteriosclerotic 437.0
congenital 742.9
degenerative — *see* Degeneration, brain
inflammatory (*see also* Encephalitis)
late effect — *see* category 326
organic 348.9
arteriosclerotic 437.0
parasitic NEC 123.9

Disease, diseased — *see also* Syndrome — *continued*
brain — *continued*
Pick's 331.11
with dementia
with behavioral disturbance 331.11 *[294.11]*
without behavioral disturbance 331.11 *[294.10]*
senile 331.2
braziers' 985.8
breast 611.9
cystic (chronic) 610.1
fibrocystic 610.1
inflammatory 611.0
Paget's (M8540/3) 174.0
puerperal, postpartum NEC 676.3 ☑
specified NEC 611.89 ▲
Breda's (*see also* Yaws) 102.9
Breisky's (kraurosis vulvae) 624.09
Bretonneau's (diphtheritic malignant angina) 032.0
Bright's (*see also* Nephritis) 583.9
arteriosclerotic (*see also* Hypertension, kidney) 403.90
Brill's (recrudescent typhus) 081.1
flea-borne 081.0
louse-borne 081.1
Brill-Symmers (follicular lymphoma) (M9690/3) 202.0 ☑
Brill-Zinsser (recrudescent typhus) 081.1
Brinton's (leather bottle stomach) (M8142/3) 151.9
Brion-Kayser (*see also* Fever, paratyphoid) 002.9
broad
beta 272.2
ligament, noninflammatory 620.9
specified NEC 620.8
Brocq's 691.8
meaning
atopic (diffuse) neurodermatitis 691.8
dermatitis herpetiformis 694.0
lichen simplex chronicus 698.3
parapsoriasis 696.2
prurigo 698.2
Brocq-Duhring (dermatitis herpetiformis) 694.0
Brodie's (joint) (*see also* Osteomyelitis) 730.1 ☑
bronchi 519.19
bronchopulmonary 519.19
bronze (Addison's) 255.41
tuberculous (*see also* Tuberculosis) 017.6 ☑
Brown-Séquard 344.89
Bruck's 733.99
Bruck-de Lange (Amsterdam dwarf, mental retardation and brachycephaly) 759.89
Bruhl's (splenic anemia with fever) 285.8
Bruton's (X-linked agammaglobulinemia) 279.04
buccal cavity 528.9
Buchanan's (juvenile osteochondrosis, iliac crest) 732.1
Buchman's (osteochondrosis juvenile) 732.1
Budgerigar-Fanciers' 495.2
Büdinger-Ludloff-Läwen 717.89
Buerger's (thromboangiitis obliterans) 443.1
Bürger-Grütz (essential familial hyperlipemia) 272.3
Burns' (lower ulna) 732.3
bursa 727.9
Bury's (erythema elevatum diutinum) 695.89
Buschke's 710.1
Busquet's (*see also* Osteomyelitis) 730.1 ☑
Busse-Buschke (cryptococcosis) 117.5

Disease, diseased — *see also* Syndrome — *continued*
C_2 (*see also* Alcoholism) 303.9 ☑
Caffey's (infantile cortical hyperostosis) 756.59
caisson 993.3
calculous 592.9
California 114.0
Calvé (-Perthes) (osteochondrosis, femoral capital) 732.1
Camurati-Engelmann (diaphyseal sclerosis) 756.59
Canavan's 330.0
capillaries 448.9
Carapata 087.1
cardiac — *see* Disease, heart
cardiopulmonary, chronic 416.9
cardiorenal (arteriosclerotic) (hepatic) (hypertensive) (vascular) (*see also* Hypertension, cardiorenal) 404.90
cardiovascular (arteriosclerotic) 429.2
congenital 746.9
hypertensive (*see also* Hypertension, heart) 402.90
benign 402.10
malignant 402.00
renal (*see also* Hypertension, cardiorenal) 404.90
syphilitic (asymptomatic) 093.9
carotid gland 259.8
Carrión's (Bartonellosis) 088.0
cartilage NEC 733.90
specified NEC 733.99
Castellani's 104.8
cat-scratch 078.3
Cavare's (familial periodic paralysis) 359.3
Cazenave's (pemphigus) 694.4
cecum 569.9
celiac (adult) 579.0
infantile 579.0
cellular tissue NEC 709.9
central core 359.0
cerebellar, cerebellum — *see* Disease, brain
cerebral (*see also* Disease, brain) 348.9
arterial, artery 437.9
degenerative — *see* Degeneration, brain
cerebrospinal 349.9
cerebrovascular NEC 437.9
acute 436
embolic — *see* Embolism, brain
late effect — *see* Late effect(s) (of) cerebrovascular disease
puerperal, postpartum, childbirth 674.0 ☑
thrombotic — *see* Thrombosis, brain
arteriosclerotic 437.0
embolic — *see* Embolism, brain
ischemic, generalized NEC 437.1
late effect — *see* Late effect(s) (of) cerebrovascular disease
occlusive 437.1
puerperal, postpartum, childbirth 674.0 ☑
specified type NEC 437.8
thrombotic — *see* Thrombosis, brain
ceroid storage 272.7
cervix (uteri)
inflammatory 616.0
noninflammatory 622.9
specified NEC 622.8
Chabert's 022.9
Chagas' (*see also* Trypanosomiasis, American) 086.2
Chandler's (osteochondritis dissecans, hip) 732.7
Charcôt-Marie-Tooth 356.1
Charcôt's (joint) 094.0 *[713.5]*
spinal cord 094.0

- **Disease, diseased** — *see also* Syndrome — *continued*
  - Charlouis' (*see also* Yaws) 102.9
  - Cheadle (-Möller) (-Barlow) (infantile scurvy) 267
  - Chédiak-Steinbrinck (-Higashi) (congenital gigantism of peroxidase granules) 288.2
  - cheek, inner 528.9
  - chest 519.9
  - Chiari's (hepatic vein thrombosis) 453.0
  - Chicago (North American blastomycosis) 116.0
  - chignon (white piedra) 111.2
  - chigoe, chigo (jigger) 134.1
  - childhood granulomatous 288.1
  - Chinese liver fluke 121.1
  - chlamydial NEC 078.88
  - cholecystic (*see also* Disease, gallbladder) 575.9
  - choroid 363.9
    - degenerative (*see also* Degeneration, choroid) 363.40
    - hereditary (*see also* Dystrophy, choroid) 363.50
    - specified type NEC 363.8
  - Christian's (chronic histiocytosis X) 277.89
  - Christian-Weber (nodular nonsuppurative panniculitis) 729.30
  - Christmas 286.1
  - ciliary body 364.9
    - specified NEC 364.89
  - circulatory (system) NEC 459.9
    - chronic, maternal, affecting fetus or newborn 760.3
    - specified NEC 459.89
    - syphilitic 093.9
      - congenital 090.5
  - Civatte's (poikiloderma) 709.09
  - climacteric 627.2
    - male 608.89
  - coagulation factor deficiency (congenital) (*see also* Defect, coagulation) 286.9
  - Coats' 362.12
  - coccidioidal pulmonary 114.5
    - acute 114.0
    - chronic 114.4
    - primary 114.0
    - residual 114.4
  - Cockayne's (microcephaly and dwarfism) 759.89
  - Cogan's 370.52
  - cold
    - agglutinin 283.0
      - or hemoglobinuria 283.0
        - paroxysmal (cold) (nocturnal) 283.2
    - hemagglutinin (chronic) 283.0
  - collagen NEC 710.9
    - nonvascular 710.9
    - specified NEC 710.8
    - vascular (allergic) (*see also* Angiitis, hypersensitivity) 446.20
  - colon 569.9
    - functional 564.9
      - congenital 751.3
    - ischemic 557.0
  - combined system (of spinal cord) 266.2 *[336.2]*
    - with anemia (pernicious) 281.0 *[336.2]*
  - compressed air 993.3
  - Concato's (pericardial polyserositis) 423.2
    - peritoneal 568.82
    - pleural — *see* Pleurisy
  - congenital NEC 799.89
  - conjunctiva 372.9
    - chlamydial 077.98
      - specified NEC 077.8
    - specified type NEC 372.89
    - viral 077.99
      - specified NEC 077.8
  - connective tissue, diffuse (*see also* Disease, collagen) 710.9
  - Conor and Bruch's (boutonneuse fever) 082.1
  - Conradi (-Hünermann) 756.59
  - Cooley's (erythroblastic anemia) 282.49
  - Cooper's 610.1
  - Corbus' 607.1
  - cork-handlers' 495.3
  - cornea (*see also* Keratopathy) 371.9
  - coronary (*see also* Ischemia, heart) 414.9
    - congenital 746.85
    - ostial, syphilitic 093.20
      - aortic 093.22
      - mitral 093.21
      - pulmonary 093.24
      - tricuspid 093.23
  - Corrigan's — *see* Insufficiency, aortic
  - Cotugno's 724.3
  - Coxsackie (virus) NEC 074.8
  - cranial nerve NEC 352.9
  - Creutzfeldt-Jakob ▶(CJD)◀ 046.19 ▲
    - with dementia
      - with behavioral disturbance 046.19 *[294.11]* ▲
      - without behavioral disturbance 046.19 *[294.10]* ▲
    - familial 046.19 ●
    - iatrogenic 046.19 ●
    - specified NEC 046.19 ●
    - sporadic 046.19 ●
    - variant (vCJD) 046.11 ●
      - with dementia ●
        - with behavioral disturbance ● 046.11 *[294.11]* ●
        - without behavioral disturbance ● 046.11 *[294.10]* ●
  - Crigler-Najjar (congenital hyperbilirubinemia) 277.4
  - Crocq's (acrocyanosis) 443.89
  - Crohn's (intestine) (*see also* Enteritis, regional) 555.9
  - Crouzon's (craniofacial dysostosis) 756.0
  - Cruchet's (encephalitis lethargica) 049.8
  - Cruveilhier's 335.21
  - Cruz-Chagas (*see also* Trypanosomiasis, American) 086.2
  - crystal deposition (*see also* Arthritis, due to, crystals) 712.9 ☑
  - Csillag's (lichen sclerosus et atrophicus) 701.0
  - Curschmann's 359.21
  - Cushing's (pituitary basophilism) 255.0
  - cystic
    - breast (chronic) 610.1
    - kidney, congenital (*see also* Cystic, disease, kidney) 753.10
    - liver, congenital 751.62
    - lung 518.89
      - congenital 748.4
    - pancreas 577.2
      - congenital 751.7
    - renal, congenital (*see also* Cystic, disease, kidney) 753.10
    - semilunar cartilage 717.5
  - cysticercus 123.1
  - cystine storage (with renal sclerosis) 270.0
  - cytomegalic inclusion (generalized) 078.5
    - with
      - pneumonia 078.5 *[484.1]*
    - congenital 771.1
  - Daae (-Finsen) (epidemic pleurodynia) 074.1
  - dancing 297.8
  - Danielssen's (anesthetic leprosy) 030.1
  - Darier's (congenital) (keratosis follicularis) 757.39
    - erythema annulare centrifugum 695.0
    - vitamin A deficiency 264.8
  - Darling's (histoplasmosis) (*see also* Histoplasmosis, American) 115.00
  - Davies' 425.0
  - de Beurmann-Gougerot (sporotrichosis) 117.1
  - Débove's (splenomegaly) 789.2
  - deer fly (*see also* Tularemia) 021.9
  - deficiency 269.9
  - degenerative (*see also* Degeneration)
    - disc — *see* Degeneration, intervertebral disc
  - Degos' 447.8
  - Déjérine (-Sottas) 356.0
  - Déleage's 359.89
  - demyelinating, demyelinizating (brain stem) (central nervous system) 341.9
    - multiple sclerosis 340
    - specified NEC 341.8
  - de Quervain's (tendon sheath) 727.04
    - thyroid (subacute granulomatous thyroiditis) 245.1
  - Dercum's (adiposis dolorosa) 272.8
  - Deutschländer's — *see* Fracture, foot
  - Devergie's (pityriasis rubra pilaris) 696.4
  - Devic's 341.0
  - diaphorase deficiency 289.7
  - diaphragm 519.4
  - diarrheal, infectious 009.2
  - diatomaceous earth 502
  - Diaz's (osteochondrosis astragalus) 732.5
  - digestive system 569.9
  - Di Guglielmo's (erythemic myelosis) (M9841/3) 207.0 ☑
  - Dimitri-Sturge-Weber (encephalocutaneous angiomatosis) 759.6
  - disc, degenerative — *see* Degeneration, intervertebral disc
  - discogenic (*see also* Disease, intervertebral disc) 722.90
  - diverticular — *see* Diverticula
  - Down's (mongolism) 758.0
  - Dubini's (electric chorea) 049.8
  - Dubois' (thymus gland) 090.5
  - Duchenne's 094.0
    - locomotor ataxia 094.0
    - muscular dystrophy 359.1
    - paralysis 335.22
    - pseudohypertrophy, muscles 359.1
  - Duchenne-Griesinger 359.1
  - ductless glands 259.9
  - Duhring's (dermatitis herpetiformis) 694.0
  - Dukes (-Filatov) 057.8
  - duodenum NEC 537.9
    - specified NEC 537.89
  - Duplay's 726.2
  - Dupré's (meningism) 781.6
  - Dupuytren's (muscle contracture) 728.6
  - Durand-Nicolas-Favre (climatic bubo) 099.1
  - Duroziez's (congenital mitral stenosis) 746.5
  - Dutton's (trypanosomiasis) 086.9
  - Eales' 362.18
  - ear (chronic) (inner) NEC 388.9
    - middle 385.9
      - adhesive (*see also* Adhesions, middle ear) 385.10
      - specified NEC 385.89
  - Eberth's (typhoid fever) 002.0
  - Ebstein's
    - heart 746.2
    - meaning diabetes 250.4 ☑ *[581.81]*
      - due to secondary diabetes ● 249.4 ☑ *[581.81]* ●
  - Echinococcus (*see also* Echinococcus) 122.9
  - ECHO virus NEC 078.89
  - Economo's (encephalitis lethargica) 049.8
  - Eddowes' (brittle bones and blue sclera) 756.51
  - Edsall's 992.2
  - Eichstedt's (pityriasis versicolor) 111.0
  - Ellis-van Creveld (chondroectodermal dysplasia) 756.55
  - endocardium — *see* Endocarditis
  - endocrine glands or system NEC 259.9
    - specified NEC 259.8
  - endomyocardial, idiopathic mural 425.2
  - Engelmann's (diaphyseal sclerosis) 756.59
  - Engel-von Recklinghausen (osteitis fibrosa cystica) 252.01
  - English (rickets) 268.0
  - Engman's (infectious eczematoid dermatitis) 690.8
  - enteroviral, enterovirus NEC 078.89
    - central nervous system NEC 048
  - epidemic NEC 136.9
  - epididymis 608.9
  - epigastric, functional 536.9
    - psychogenic 306.4
  - Erb (-Landouzy) 359.1
  - Erb-Goldflam 358.00
  - Erichsen's (railway spine) 300.16
  - esophagus 530.9
    - functional 530.5
    - psychogenic 306.4
  - Eulenburg's (congenital paramyotonia) 359.29
  - Eustachian tube 381.9
  - Evans' (thrombocytopenic purpura) 287.32
  - external auditory canal 380.9
  - extrapyramidal NEC 333.90
  - eye 379.90
    - anterior chamber 364.9
    - inflammatory NEC 364.3
    - muscle 378.9
  - eyeball 360.9
  - eyelid 374.9
  - eyeworm of Africa 125.2
  - Fabry's (angiokeratoma corporis diffusum) 272.7
  - facial nerve (seventh) 351.9
    - newborn 767.5
  - Fahr-Volhard (malignant nephrosclerosis) 403.00
  - fallopian tube, noninflammatory 620.9
    - specified NEC 620.8
  - familial periodic 277.31
    - paralysis 359.3
  - Fanconi's (congenital pancytopenia) 284.09
  - Farber's (disseminated lipogranulomatosis) 272.8
  - fascia 728.9
    - inflammatory 728.9
  - Fauchard's (periodontitis) 523.40
  - Favre-Durand-Nicolas (climatic bubo) 099.1
  - Favre-Racouchot (elastoidosis cutanea nodularis) 701.8
  - Fede's 529.0
  - Feer's 985.0
  - Felix's (juvenile osteochondrosis, hip) 732.1
  - Fenwick's (gastric atrophy) 537.89
  - Fernels' (aortic aneurysm) 441.9
  - fibrocaseous, of lung (*see also* Tuberculosis, pulmonary) 011.9 ☑

Disease, diseased — *see also* Syndrome — *continued*
fibrocystic (*see also* Fibrocystic, disease)
newborn 277.01
Fiedler's (leptospiral jaundice) 100.0
fifth 057.0
Filatoff's (infectious mononucleosis) 075
Filatov's (infectious mononucleosis) 075
file-cutters' 984.9
specified type of lead — *see* Table of Drugs and Chemicals
filterable virus NEC 078.89
fish skin 757.1
acquired 701.1
Flajani (-Basedow) (exophthalmic goiter) 242.0 ☑
Flatau-Schilder 341.1
flax-dressers' 504
Fleischner's 732.3
flint 502
fluke — *see* Infestation, fluke
Følling's (phenylketonuria) 270.1
foot and mouth 078.4
foot process 581.3
Forbes' (glycogenosis III) 271.0
Fordyce's (ectopic sebaceous glands) (mouth) 750.26
Fordyce-Fox (apocrine miliaria) 705.82
Fothergill's
meaning scarlatina anginosa 034.1
neuralgia (*see also* Neuralgia, trigeminal) 350.1
Fournier's 608.83
fourth 057.8
Fox (-Fordyce) (apocrine miliaria) 705.82
Francis' (*see also* Tularemia) 021.9
Franklin's (heavy chain) 273.2
Frei's (climatic bubo) 099.1
Freiberg's (flattening metatarsal) 732.5
Friedländer's (endarteritis obliterans) — *see* Arteriosclerosis
Friedreich's
combined systemic or ataxia 334.0
facial hemihypertrophy 756.0
myoclonia 333.2
Fröhlich's (adiposogenital dystrophy) 253.8
Frommel's 676.6 ☑
frontal sinus (chronic) 473.1
acute 461.1
Fuller's earth 502
fungus, fungous NEC 117.9
Gaisböck's (polycythemia hypertonica) 289.0
gallbladder 575.9
congenital 751.60
Gamna's (siderotic splenomegaly) 289.51
Gamstorp's (adynamia episodica hereditaria) 359.3
Gandy-Nanta (siderotic splenomegaly) 289.51
Gannister (occupational) 502
Garré's (*see also* Osteomyelitis) 730.1 ☑
gastric (*see also* Disease, stomach) 537.9
gastroesophageal reflux (GERD) 530.81 ●
gastrointestinal (tract) 569.9
amyloid 277.39
functional 536.9
psychogenic 306.4
Gaucher's (adult) (cerebroside lipidosis) (infantile) 272.7
Gayet's (superior hemorrhagic polioencephalitis) 265.1
Gee (-Herter) (-Heubner) (-Thaysen) (nontropical sprue) 579.0
generalized neoplastic (M8000/6) 199.0
genital organs NEC
female 629.9
specified NEC 629.89
male 608.9
Gerhardt's (erythromelalgia) 443.82
Gerlier's (epidemic vertigo) 078.81
Gibert's (pityriasis rosea) 696.3
Gibney's (perispondylitis) 720.9
Gierke's (glycogenosis I) 271.0
Gilbert's (familial nonhemolytic jaundice) 277.4
Gilchrist's (North American blastomycosis) 116.0
Gilford (-Hutchinson) (progeria) 259.8
Gilles de la Tourette's (motor-verbal tic) 307.23
Giovannini's 117.9
gland (lymph) 289.9
Glanzmann's (hereditary hemorrhagic thrombasthenia) 287.1
glassblowers' 527.1
Glénard's (enteroptosis) 569.89
Glisson's (*see also* Rickets) 268.0
glomerular
membranous, idiopathic 581.1
minimal change 581.3
glycogen storage (Andersen's) (Cori types 1-7) (Forbes') (McArdle-Schmid-Pearson) (Pompe's) (types I-VII) 271.0
cardiac 271.0 *[425.7]*
generalized 271.0
glucose-6-phosphatase deficiency 271.0
heart 271.0 *[425.7]*
hepatorenal 271.0
liver and kidneys 271.0
myocardium 271.0 *[425.7]*
von Gierke's (glycogenosis I) 271.0
Goldflam-Erb 358.00
Goldscheider's (epidermolysis bullosa) 757.39
Goldstein's (familial hemorrhagic telangiectasia) 448.0
gonococcal NEC 098.0
Goodall's (epidemic vomiting) 078.82
Gordon's (exudative enteropathy) 579.8
Gougerot's (trisymptomatic) 709.1
Gougerot-Carteaud (confluent reticulate papillomatosis) 701.8
Gougerot-Hailey-Hailey (benign familial chronic pemphigus) 757.39
graft-versus-host 279.50 ▲
acute 279.51 ●
on chronic 279.53 ●
chronic 279.52 ●
grain-handlers' 495.8
Grancher's (splenopneumonia) — *see* Pneumonia
granulomatous (childhood) (chronic) 288.1
graphite lung 503
Graves' (exophthalmic goiter) 242.0 ☑
Greenfield's 330.0
green monkey 078.89
Griesinger's (*see also* Ancylostomiasis) 126.9
grinders' 502
Grisel's 723.5
Gruby's (tinea tonsurans) 110.0
Guertin's (electric chorea) 049.8
Guillain-Barré 357.0
Guinon's (motor-verbal tic) 307.23
Gull's (thyroid atrophy with myxedema) 244.8
Gull and Sutton's — *see* Hypertension, kidney
gum NEC 523.9
Günther's (congenital erythropoietic porphyria) 277.1
gynecological 629.9
specified NEC 629.89
H 270.0
Haas' 732.3
Habermann's (acute parapsoriasis varioliformis) 696.2
Haff 985.1
Hageman (congenital factor XII deficiency) (*see also* Defect, congenital) 286.3
Haglund's (osteochondrosis os tibiale externum) 732.5
Hagner's (hypertrophic pulmonary osteoarthropathy) 731.2
Hailey-Hailey (benign familial chronic pemphigus) 757.39
hair (follicles) NEC 704.9
specified type NEC 704.8
Hallervorden-Spatz 333.0
Hallopeau's (lichen sclerosus et atrophicus) 701.0
Hamman's (spontaneous mediastinal emphysema) 518.1
hand, foot, and mouth 074.3
Hand-Schüller-Christian (chronic histiocytosis X) 277.89
Hanot's — *see* Cirrhosis, biliary
Hansen's (leprosy) 030.9
benign form 030.1
malignant form 030.0
Harada's 363.22
Harley's (intermittent hemoglobinuria) 283.2
Hartnup (pellagra-cerebellar ataxia-renal aminoaciduria) 270.0
Hart's (pellagra-cerebellar ataxia-renal aminoaciduria) 270.0
Hashimoto's (struma lymphomatosa) 245.2
Hb — *see* Disease, hemoglobin
heart (organic) 429.9
with
acute pulmonary edema (*see also* Failure, ventricular, left) 428.1
hypertensive 402.91
with renal failure 404.93
benign 402.11
with renal failure 404.13
malignant 402.01
with renal failure 404.03
kidney disease — *see* Hypertension, cardiorenal
rheumatic fever (conditions classifiable to 390)
active 391.9
with chorea 392.0
inactive or quiescent (with chorea) 398.90
amyloid 277.39 *[425.7]*
aortic (valve) (*see also* Endocarditis, aortic) 424.1
arteriosclerotic or sclerotic (minimal) (senile) — *see* Arteriosclerosis, coronary
artery, arterial — *see* Arteriosclerosis, coronary
atherosclerotic — *see* Arteriosclerosis, coronary
beer drinkers' 425.5
beriberi 265.0 *[425.7]*
black 416.0
congenital NEC 746.9
cyanotic 746.9
maternal, affecting fetus or newborn 760.3
specified type NEC 746.89
congestive (*see also* Failure, heart) 428.0
coronary 414.9
cryptogenic 429.9
due to
amyloidosis 277.39 *[425.7]*
beriberi 265.0 *[425.7]*

Disease, diseased — *see also* Syndrome — *continued*
heart — *continued*
due to — *continued*
cardiac glycogenosis 271.0 *[425.7]*
Friedreich's ataxia 334.0 *[425.8]*
gout 274.82
mucopolysaccharidosis 277.5 *[425.7]*
myotonia atrophica 359.21 *[425.8]*
progressive muscular dystrophy 359.1 *[425.8]*
sarcoidosis 135 *[425.8]*
fetal 746.9
inflammatory 746.89
fibroid (*see also* Myocarditis) 429.0
functional 427.9
postoperative 997.1
psychogenic 306.2
glycogen storage 271.0 *[425.7]*
gonococcal NEC 098.85
gouty 274.82
hypertensive (*see also* Hypertension, heart) 402.90
benign 402.10
malignant 402.00
hyperthyroid (*see also* Hyperthyroidism) 242.9 ☑ *[425.7]*
incompletely diagnosed — *see* Disease, heart
ischemic (chronic) (*see also* Ischemia, heart) 414.9
acute (*see also* Infarct, myocardium) 410.9 ☑
without myocardial infarction 411.89
with coronary (artery) occlusion 411.81
asymptomatic 412
diagnosed on ECG or other special investigation but currently presenting no symptoms 412
kyphoscoliotic 416.1
mitral (*see also* Endocarditis, mitral) 394.9
muscular (*see also* Degeneration, myocardial) 429.1
postpartum 674.8 ☑
psychogenic (functional) 306.2
pulmonary (chronic) 416.9
acute 415.0
specified NEC 416.8
rheumatic (chronic) (inactive) (old) (quiescent) (with chorea) 398.90
active or acute 391.9
with chorea (active) (rheumatic) (Sydenham's) 392.0
specified type NEC 391.8
maternal, affecting fetus or newborn 760.3
rheumatoid — *see* Arthritis, rheumatoid
sclerotic — *see* Arteriosclerosis, coronary
senile (*see also* Myocarditis) 429.0
specified type NEC 429.89
syphilitic 093.89
aortic 093.1
aneurysm 093.0
asymptomatic 093.89
congenital 090.5
thyroid (gland) (*see also* Hyperthyroidism) 242.9 ☑ *[425.7]*
thyrotoxic (*see also* Thyrotoxicosis) 242.9 ☑ *[425.7]*
tuberculous (*see also* Tuberculosis) 017.9 ☑ *[425.8]*
valve, valvular (obstructive) (regurgitant) (*see also* Endocarditis)

Disease, diseased — *see also* Syndrome — *continued*
- heart — *continued*
  - valve, valvular (*see also* Endocarditis) — *continued*
    - congenital NEC (*see also* Anomaly, heart, valve) 746.9
      - pulmonary 746.00
      - specified type NEC 746.89
  - vascular — *see* Disease, cardiovascular
- heavy-chain (gamma G) 273.2
- Heberden's 715.04
- Hebra's
  - dermatitis exfoliativa 695.89
  - erythema multiforme exudativum 695.19 ▲
  - pityriasis
    - maculata et circinata 696.3
    - rubra 695.89
      - pilaris 696.4
  - prurigo 698.2
- Heerfordt's (uveoparotitis) 135
- Heidenhain's 290.10
  - with dementia 290.10
- Heilmeyer-Schöner (M9842/3) 207.1 ☑
- Heine-Medin (*see also* Poliomyelitis) 045.9 ☑
- Heller's (*see also* Psychosis, childhood) 299.1 ☑
- Heller-Döhle (syphilitic aortitis) 093.1
- hematopoietic organs 289.9
- hemoglobin (Hb) 282.7
  - with thalassemia 282.49
  - abnormal (mixed) NEC 282.7
    - with thalassemia 282.49
  - AS genotype 282.5
  - Bart's 282.49
  - C (Hb-C) 282.7
    - with other abnormal hemoglobin NEC 282.7
    - elliptocytosis 282.7
    - Hb-S (without crisis) 282.63
      - with
        - crisis 282.64
        - vaso-occlusive pain 282.64
    - sickle-cell (without crisis) 282.63
      - with
        - crisis 282.64
        - vaso-occlusive pain 282.64
    - thalassemia 282.49
  - constant spring 282.7
  - D (Hb-D) 282.7
    - with other abnormal hemoglobin NEC 282.7
    - Hb-S (without crisis) 282.68
      - with crisis 282.69
    - sickle-cell (without crisis) 282.68
      - with crisis 282.69
    - thalassemia 282.49
  - E (Hb-E) 282.7
    - with other abnormal hemoglobin NEC 282.7
    - Hb-S (without crisis) 282.68
      - with crisis 282.69
    - sickle-cell (without crisis) 282.68
      - with crisis 282.69
    - thalassemia 282.49
  - elliptocytosis 282.7
  - F (Hb-F) 282.7
  - G (Hb-G) 282.7
  - H (Hb-H) 282.49
  - hereditary persistence, fetal (HPFH) ("Swiss variety") 282.7
  - high fetal gene 282.7
  - I thalassemia 282.49
  - M 289.7
  - S (*see also* Disease, sickle-cell, Hb-S)

Disease, diseased — *see also* Syndrome — *continued*
- hemoglobin — *continued*
  - S (*see also* Disease, sickle-cell, Hb-S) — *continued*
    - thalassemia (without crisis) 282.41
      - with
        - crisis 282.42
        - vaso-occlusive pain 282.42
  - spherocytosis 282.7
  - unstable, hemolytic 282.7
  - Zurich (Hb-Zurich) 282.7
- hemolytic (fetus) (newborn) 773.2
  - autoimmune (cold type) (warm type) 283.0
  - due to or with
    - incompatibility
      - ABO (blood group) 773.1
      - blood (group) (Duffy) (Kell) (Kidd) (Lewis) (M) (S) NEC 773.2
      - Rh (blood group) (factor) 773.0
    - Rh negative mother 773.0
  - unstable hemoglobin 282.7
- hemorrhagic 287.9
  - newborn 776.0
- Henoch (-Schönlein) (purpura nervosa) 287.0
- hepatic — *see* Disease, liver
- hepatolenticular 275.1
- heredodegenerative NEC
  - brain 331.89
  - spinal cord 336.8
- Hers' (glycogenosis VI) 271.0
- Herter (-Gee) (-Heubner) (nontropical sprue) 579.0
- Herxheimer's (diffuse idiopathic cutaneous atrophy) 701.8
- Heubner's 094.89
- Heubner-Herter (nontropical sprue) 579.0
- high fetal gene or hemoglobin thalassemia 282.49
- Hildenbrand's (typhus) 081.9
- hip (joint) NEC 719.95
  - congenital 755.63
  - suppurative 711.05
  - tuberculous (*see also* Tuberculosis) 015.1 ☑ *[730.85]*
- Hippel's (retinocerebral angiomatosis) 759.6
- Hirschfeld's (acute diabetes mellitus) (*see also* Diabetes) 250.0 ☑
  - due to secondary diabetes 249.0 ☑ ●
- Hirschsprung's (congenital megacolon) 751.3
- His (-Werner) (trench fever) 083.1
- HIV 042
- Hodgkin's (M9650/3) 201.9 ☑

Note — Use the following fifth-digit subclassification with category 201:

0	*unspecified site*
1	*lymph nodes of head, face, and neck*
2	*intrathoracic lymph nodes*
3	*intra-abdominal lymph nodes*
4	*lymph nodes of axilla and upper limb*
5	*lymph nodes of inguinal region and lower limb*
6	*intrapelvic lymph nodes*
7	*spleen*
8	*lymph nodes of multiple sites*

  - lymphocytic
    - depletion (M9653/3) 201.7 ☑
      - diffuse fibrosis (M9654/3) 201.7 ☑

Disease, diseased — *see also* Syndrome — *continued*
- Hodgkin's — *continued*
  - lymphocytic — *continued*
    - depletion — *continued*
      - reticular type (M9655/3) 201.7 ☑
    - predominance (M9651/3) 201.4 ☑
  - lymphocytic-histiocytic predominance (M9651/3) 201.4 ☑
  - mixed cellularity (M9652/3) 201.6 ☑
  - nodular sclerosis (M9656/3) 201.5 ☑
    - cellular phase (M9657/3) 201.5 ☑
- Hodgson's 441.9
  - ruptured 441.5
- Hoffa (-Kastert) (liposynovitis prepatellaris) 272.8
- Holla (*see also* Spherocytosis) 282.0
- homozygous-Hb-S 282.61
- hoof and mouth 078.4
- hookworm (*see also* Ancylostomiasis) 126.9
- Horton's (temporal arteritis) 446.5
- host-versus-graft (immune or nonimmune cause) 279.50 ▲
- HPFH (hereditary persistence of fetal hemoglobin) ("Swiss variety") 282.7
- Huchard's disease (continued arterial hypertension) 401.9
- Huguier's (uterine fibroma) 218.9
- human immunodeficiency (virus) 042
- hunger 251.1
- Hunt's
  - dyssynergia cerebellaris myoclonica 334.2
  - herpetic geniculate ganglionitis 053.11
- Huntington's 333.4
- Huppert's (multiple myeloma) (M9730/3) 203.0 ☑
- Hurler's (mucopolysaccharidosis I) 277.5
- Hutchinson-Boeck (sarcoidosis) 135
- Hutchinson-Gilford (progeria) 259.8
- Hutchinson's, meaning
  - angioma serpiginosum 709.1
  - cheiropompholyx 705.81
  - prurigo estivalis 692.72
- hyaline (diffuse) (generalized) 728.9
  - membrane (lung) (newborn) 769
- hydatid (*see also* Echinococcus) 122.9
- Hyde's (prurigo nodularis) 698.3
- hyperkinetic (*see also* Hyperkinesia) 314.9
  - heart 429.82
- hypertensive (*see also* Hypertension) 401.9
- hypophysis 253.9
  - hyperfunction 253.1
  - hypofunction 253.2
- Iceland (epidemic neuromyasthenia) 049.8
- I cell 272.7
- ill-defined 799.89
- immunologic NEC 279.9
- immunoproliferative 203.8 ☑
- inclusion 078.5
  - salivary gland 078.5
- infancy, early NEC 779.9
- infective NEC 136.9
- inguinal gland 289.9
- internal semilunar cartilage, cystic 717.5
- intervertebral disc 722.90
  - with myelopathy 722.70
  - cervical, cervicothoracic 722.91
    - with myelopathy 722.71
  - lumbar, lumbosacral 722.93
    - with myelopathy 722.73
  - thoracic, thoracolumbar 722.92
    - with myelopathy 722.72

Disease, diseased — *see also* Syndrome — *continued*
- intestine 569.9
  - functional 564.9
    - congenital 751.3
    - psychogenic 306.4
  - lardaceous 277.39
  - organic 569.9
  - protozoal NEC 007.9
- iris 364.9
  - specified NEC 364.89
- iron
  - metabolism 275.0
  - storage 275.0
- Isambert's (*see also* Tuberculosis, larynx) 012.3 ☑
- Iselin's (osteochondrosis, fifth metatarsal) 732.5
- island (scrub typhus) 081.2
- itai-itai 985.5
- Jadassohn's (maculopapular erythroderma) 696.2
- Jadassohn-Pellizari's (anetoderma) 701.3
- Jakob-Creutzfeldt ▶(CJD)◀ 046.19 ▲
  - with dementia
    - with behavioral disturbance 046.19 *[294.11]* ▲
    - without behavioral disturbance 046.19 *[294.10]* ▲
  - familial 046.19 ●
  - iatrogenic 046.19 ●
  - specified NEC 046.19 ●
  - sporadic 046.19 ●
  - variant (vCJD) 046.11 ●
    - with dementia ●
      - with behavioral disturbance 046.11 *[294.11]* ●
      - without behavioral disturbance 046.11 *[294.10]* ●
- Jaksch (-Luzet) (pseudoleukemia infantum) 285.8
- Janet's 300.89
- Jansky-Bielschowsky 330.1
- jaw NEC 526.9
  - fibrocystic 526.2
- Jensen's 363.05
- Jeune's (asphyxiating thoracic dystrophy) 756.4
- jigger 134.1
- Johnson-Stevens (erythema multiforme exudativum) 695.13 ▲
- joint NEC 719.9 ☑
  - ankle 719.97
  - Charcôt 094.0 *[713.5]*
  - degenerative (*see also* Osteoarthrosis) 715.9 ☑
    - multiple 715.09
    - spine (*see also* Spondylosis) 721.90
  - elbow 719.92
  - foot 719.97
  - hand 719.94
  - hip 719.95
  - hypertrophic (chronic) (degenerative) (*see also* Osteoarthrosis) 715.9 ☑
    - spine (*see also* Spondylosis) 721.90
  - knee 719.96
  - Luschka 721.90
  - multiple sites 719.99
  - pelvic region 719.95
  - sacroiliac 724.6
  - shoulder (region) 719.91
  - specified site NEC 719.98
  - spine NEC 724.9
    - pseudarthrosis following fusion 733.82
    - sacroiliac 724.6
  - wrist 719.93
- Jourdain's (acute gingivitis) 523.00
- Jüngling's (sarcoidosis) 135

☑ Additional Digit Required — Refer to the Tabular List for Digit Selection

Subterms under main terms may continue to next column or page

▶◀ Revised Text ● New Line ▲ Revised Code

Disease, diseased — *see also* Syndrome — *continued*
Kahler (-Bozzolo) (multiple myeloma) (M9730/3) 203.0 ☑
Kalischer's 759.6
Kaposi's 757.33
lichen ruber 697.8
acuminatus 696.4
moniliformis 697.8
xeroderma pigmentosum 757.33
Kaschin-Beck (endemic polyarthritis) 716.00
ankle 716.07
arm 716.02
lower (and wrist) 716.03
upper (and elbow) 716.02
foot (and ankle) 716.07
forearm (and wrist) 716.03
hand 716.04
leg 716.06
lower 716.06
upper 716.05
multiple sites 716.09
pelvic region (hip) (thigh) 716.05
shoulder region 716.01
specified site NEC 716.08
Katayama 120.2
Kawasaki 446.1
Kedani (scrub typhus) 081.2
kidney (functional) (pelvis) (*see also* Disease, renal) 593.9
chronic 585.9
requiring chronic dialysis 585.6
stage
I 585.1
II (mild) 585.2
III (moderate) 585.3
IV (severe) 585.4
V 585.5
cystic (congenital) 753.10
multiple 753.19
single 753.11
specified NEC 753.19
fibrocystic (congenital) 753.19
in gout 274.10
polycystic (congenital) 753.12
adult type (APKD) 753.13
autosomal dominant 753.13
autosomal recessive 753.14
childhood type (CPKD) 753.14
infantile type 753.14
Kienböck's (carpal lunate) (wrist) 732.3
Kimmelstiel (-Wilson) (intercapillary glomerulosclerosis) 250.4 ☑ *[581.81]*
due to secondary diabetes 249.4 ☑ *[581.81]* ●
Kinnier Wilson's (hepatolenticular degeneration) 275.1
kissing 075
Kleb's (*see also* Nephritis) 583.9
Klinger's 446.4
Klippel's 723.8
Klippel-Feil (brevicollis) 756.16
knight's 911.1
Köbner's (epidermolysis bullosa) 757.39
Koenig-Wichmann (pemphigus) 694.4
Köhler's
first (osteoarthrosis juvenilis) 732.5
second (Freiberg's infraction, metatarsal head) 732.5
patellar 732.4
tarsal navicular (bone) (osteoarthrosis juvenilis) 732.5
Köhler-Freiberg (infraction, metatarsal head) 732.5
Köhler-Mouchet (osteoarthrosis juvenilis) 732.5
Köhler-Pellegrini-Stieda (calcification, knee joint) 726.62
Kok 759.89
König's (osteochondritis dissecans) 732.7
Korsakoff's (nonalcoholic) 294.0

Disease, diseased — *see also* Syndrome — *continued*
Korsakoff's — *continued*
alcoholic 291.1
Kostmann's (infantile genetic agranulocytosis) 288.01
Krabbe's 330.0
Kraepelin-Morel (*see also* Schizophrenia) 295.9 ☑
Kraft-Weber-Dimitri 759.6
Kufs' 330.1
Kugelberg-Welander 335.11
Kuhnt-Junius 362.52
Kümmell's (-Verneuil) (spondylitis) 721.7
Kundrat's (lymphosarcoma) 200.1 ☑
kuru 046.0
Kussmaul (-Meier) (polyarteritis nodosa) 446.0
Kyasanur Forest 065.2
Kyrle's (hyperkeratosis follicularis in cutem penetrans) 701.1
labia
inflammatory 616.10
noninflammatory 624.9
specified NEC 624.8
labyrinth, ear 386.8
lacrimal system (apparatus) (passages) 375.9
gland 375.00
specified NEC 375.89
Lafora's 333.2
Lagleyze-von Hippel (retinocerebral angiomatosis) 759.6
Lancereaux-Mathieu (leptospiral jaundice) 100.0
Landry's 357.0
Lane's 569.89
lardaceous (any site) 277.39
Larrey-Weil (leptospiral jaundice) 100.0
Larsen (-Johansson) (juvenile osteopathia patellae) 732.4
larynx 478.70
Lasègue's (persecution mania) 297.9
Leber's 377.16
Lederer's (acquired infectious hemolytic anemia) 283.19
Legg's (capital femoral osteochondrosis) 732.1
Legg-Calvé-Perthes (capital femoral osteochondrosis) 732.1
Legg-Calvé-Waldenström (femoral capital osteochondrosis) 732.1
Legg-Perthes (femoral capital osteochrondosis) 732.1
Legionnaires' 482.84
Leigh's 330.8
Leiner's (exfoliative dermatitis) 695.89
Leloir's (lupus erythematosus) 695.4
Lenegre's 426.0
lens (eye) 379.39
Leriche's (osteoporosis, posttraumatic) 733.7
Letterer-Siwe (acute histiocytosis X) (M9722/3) 202.5 ☑
Lev's (acquired complete heart block) 426.0
Lewandowski's (*see also* Tuberculosis) 017.0 ☑
Lewandowski-Lutz (epidermodysplasia verruciformis) 078.19
Lewy body 331.82
with dementia
with behavioral disturbance 331.82 *[294.11]*
without behavioral disturbance 331.82 *[294.10]*
Leyden's (periodic vomiting) 536.2
Libman-Sacks (verrucous endocarditis) 710.0 *[424.91]*
Lichtheim's (subacute combined sclerosis with pernicious anemia) 281.0 *[336.2]*
ligament 728.9
light chain 203.0 ☑

Disease, diseased — *see also* Syndrome — *continued*
Lightwood's (renal tubular acidosis) 588.89
Lignac's (cystinosis) 270.0
Lindau's (retinocerebral angiomatosis) 759.6
Lindau-von Hippel (angiomatosis retinocerebellosa) 759.6
lip NEC 528.5
lipidosis 272.7
lipoid storage NEC 272.7
Lipschütz's 616.50
Little's — *see* Palsy, cerebral
liver 573.9
alcoholic 571.3
acute 571.1
chronic 571.3
chronic 571.9
alcoholic 571.3
cystic, congenital 751.62
drug-induced 573.3
due to
chemicals 573.3
fluorinated agents 573.3
hypersensitivity drugs 573.3
isoniazids 573.3
end stage NEC 572.8
due to hepatitis — *see* Hepatitis
fibrocystic (congenital) 751.62
glycogen storage 271.0
organic 573.9
polycystic (congenital) 751.62
Lobo's (keloid blastomycosis) 116.2
Lobstein's (brittle bones and blue sclera) 756.51
locomotor system 334.9
Lorain's (pituitary dwarfism) 253.3
Lou Gehrig's 335.20
Lucas-Championnière (fibrinous bronchitis) 466.0
Ludwig's (submaxillary cellulitis) 528.3
luetic — *see* Syphilis
lumbosacral region 724.6
lung NEC 518.89
black 500
congenital 748.60
cystic 518.89
congenital 748.4
fibroid (chronic) (*see also* Fibrosis, lung) 515
fluke 121.2
oriental 121.2
in
amyloidosis 277.39 *[517.8]*
polymyositis 710.4 *[517.8]*
sarcoidosis 135 *[517.8]*
Sjögren's syndrome 710.2 *[517.8]*
syphilis 095.1
systemic lupus erythematosus 710.0 *[517.8]*
systemic sclerosis 710.1 *[517.2]*
interstitial (chronic) 515
acute 136.3
nonspecific, chronic 496
obstructive (chronic) (COPD) 496
with
acute
bronchitis 491.22
exacerbation NEC 491.21
alveolitis, allergic (*see also* Alveolitis, allergic) 495.9
asthma (chronic) (obstructive) 493.2 ☑
bronchiectasis 494.0
with acute exacerbation 494.1
bronchitis (chronic) 491.20
with
acute bronchitis 491.22
exacerbation (acute) 491.21

Disease, diseased — *see also* Syndrome — *continued*
lung — *continued*
obstructive — *continued*
with — *continued*
decompensated 491.21
with exacerbation 491.21
emphysema NEC 492.8
diffuse (with fibrosis) 496
polycystic 518.89
asthma (chronic) (obstructive) 493.2 ☑
congenital 748.4
purulent (cavitary) 513.0
restrictive 518.89
rheumatoid 714.81
diffuse interstitial 714.81
specified NEC 518.89
Lutembacher's (atrial septal defect with mitral stenosis) 745.5
Lutz-Miescher (elastosis perforans serpiginosa) 701.1
Lutz-Splendore-de Almeida (Brazilian blastomycosis) 116.1
Lyell's (toxic epidermal necrolysis) 695.15 ▲
due to drug
correct substance properly administered 695.15 ▲
overdose or wrong substance given or taken 977.9
specific drug — *see* Table of Drugs and Chemicals
Lyme 088.81
lymphatic (gland) (system) 289.9
channel (noninfective) 457.9
vessel (noninfective) 457.9
specified NEC 457.8
lymphoproliferative (chronic) (M9970/1) 238.79
Machado-Joseph 334.8
Madelung's (lipomatosis) 272.8
Madura (actinomycotic) 039.9
mycotic 117.4
Magitot's 526.4
Majocchi's (purpura annularis telangiectodes) 709.1
malarial (*see also* Malaria) 084.6
Malassez's (cystic) 608.89
Malibu 919.8
infected 919.9
malignant (M8000/3) (*see also* Neoplasm, by site, malignant)
previous, affecting management of pregnancy V23.89
Manson's 120.1
maple bark 495.6
maple syrup (urine) 270.3
Marburg (virus) 078.89
Marchiafava (-Bignami) 341.8
Marfan's 090.49
congenital syphilis 090.49
meaning Marfan's syndrome 759.82
Marie-Bamberger (hypertrophic pulmonary osteoarthropathy) (secondary) 731.2
primary or idiopathic (acropachyderma) 757.39
pulmonary (hypertrophic osteoarthropathy) 731.2
Marie-Strümpell (ankylosing spondylitis) 720.0
Marion's (bladder neck obstruction) 596.0
Marsh's (exophthalmic goiter) 242.0 ☑
Martin's 715.27
mast cell 757.33
systemic (M9741/3) 202.6 ☑
mastoid (*see also* Mastoiditis) 383.9
process 385.9
maternal, unrelated to pregnancy NEC, affecting fetus or newborn 760.9
Mathieu's (leptospiral jaundice) 100.0
Mauclaire's 732.3

Disease, diseased — *see also* Syndrome — *continued*
Mauriac's (erythema nodosum syphiliticum) 091.3
Maxcy's 081.0
McArdle (-Schmid-Pearson) (glycogenosis V) 271.0
mediastinum NEC 519.3
Medin's (*see also* Poliomyelitis) 045.9 ☑
Mediterranean (with hemoglobinopathy) 282.49
medullary center (idiopathic) (respiratory) 348.8
Meige's (chronic hereditary edema) 757.0
Meleda 757.39
Ménétrier's (hypertrophic gastritis) 535.2 ☑
Ménière's (active) 386.00
cochlear 386.02
cochleovestibular 386.01
inactive 386.04
in remission 386.04
vestibular 386.03
meningeal — *see* Meningitis
mental (*see also* Psychosis) 298.9
Merzbacher-Pelizaeus 330.0
mesenchymal 710.9
mesenteric embolic 557.0
metabolic NEC 277.9
metal polishers' 502
metastatic — *see* Metastasis
Mibelli's 757.39
microdrepanocytic 282.49
microvascular — code to condition
Miescher's 709.3
Mikulicz's (dryness of mouth, absent or decreased lacrimation) 527.1
Milkman (-Looser) (osteomalacia with pseudofractures) 268.2
Miller's (osteomalacia) 268.2
Mills' 335.29
Milroy's (chronic hereditary edema) 757.0
Minamata 985.0
Minor's 336.1
Minot's (hemorrhagic disease, newborn) 776.0
Minot-von Willebrand-Jürgens (angiohemophilia) 286.4
Mitchell's (erythromelalgia) 443.82
mitral — *see* Endocarditis, mitral
Mljet (mal de Meleda) 757.39
Möbius', Moebius' 346.2 ☑ ▲
Moeller's 267
Möller (-Barlow) (infantile scurvy) 267
Mönckeberg's (*see also* Arteriosclerosis, extremities) 440.20
Mondor's (thrombophlebitis of breast) 451.89
Monge's 993.2
Morel-Kraepelin (*see also* Schizophrenia) 295.9 ☑
Morgagni's (syndrome) (hyperostosis frontalis interna) 733.3
Morgagni-Adams-Stokes (syncope with heart block) 426.9
Morquio (-Brailsford) (-Ullrich) (mucopolysaccharidosis IV) 277.5
Morton's (with metatarsalgia) 355.6
Morvan's 336.0
motor neuron (bulbar) (mixed type) 335.20
Mouchet's (juvenile osteochondrosis, foot) 732.5
mouth 528.9
Moyamoya 437.5
Mucha's (acute parapsoriasis varioliformis) 696.2
mu-chain 273.2
mucolipidosis (I) (II) (III) 272.7
Münchmeyer's (exostosis luxurians) 728.11
Murri's (intermittent hemoglobinuria) 283.2

Disease, diseased — *see also* Syndrome — *continued*
muscle 359.9
inflammatory 728.9
ocular 378.9
musculoskeletal system 729.90 ▲
mushroom workers' 495.5
Myà's (congenital dilation, colon) 751.3
mycotic 117.9
myeloproliferative (chronic) (M9960/1) 238.79
myocardium, myocardial (*see also* Degeneration, myocardial) 429.1
hypertensive (*see also* Hypertension, heart 402.90
primary (idiopathic) 425.4
myoneural 358.9
Naegeli's 287.1
nail 703.9
specified type NEC 703.8
Nairobi sheep 066.1
nasal 478.19
cavity NEC 478.19
sinus (chronic) — *see* Sinusitis
navel (newborn) NEC 779.89
delayed separation of umbilical cord 779.83
nemaline body 359.0
neoplastic, generalized (M8000/6) 199.0
nerve — *see* Disorder, nerve
nervous system (central) 349.9
autonomic, peripheral (*see also* Neuropathy, peripheral, autonomic) 337.9
congenital 742.9
inflammatory — *see* Encephalitis
parasympathetic (*see also* Neuropathy, peripheral, autonomic) 337.9
peripheral NEC 355.9
prion NEC 046.79 ●
specified NEC 349.89
sympathetic (*see also* Neuropathy, peripheral, autonomic) 337.9
vegetative (*see also* Neuropathy, peripheral, autonomic) 337.9
Nettleship's (urticaria pigmentosa) 757.33
Neumann's (pemphigus vegetans) 694.4
neurologic (central) NEC (*see also* Disease, nervous system) 349.9
peripheral NEC 355.9
neuromuscular system NEC 358.9
Newcastle 077.8
Nicolas (-Durand) — Favre (climatic bubo) 099.1
Niemann-Pick (lipid histiocytosis) 272.7
nipple 611.9
Paget's (M8540/3) 174.0
Nishimoto (-Takeuchi) 437.5
nonarthropod-borne NEC 078.89
central nervous system NEC 049.9
enterovirus NEC 078.89
nonautoimmune hemolytic NEC 283.10
Nonne-Milroy-Meige (chronic hereditary edema) 757.0
Norrie's (congenital progressive oculoacousticocerebral degeneration) 743.8
nose 478.19
nucleus pulposus — *see* Disease, intervertebral disc
nutritional 269.9
maternal, affecting fetus or newborn 760.4
oasthouse, urine 270.2
obliterative vascular 447.1
Odelberg's (juvenile osteochondrosis) 732.1
Oguchi's (retina) 368.61
Ohara's (*see also* Tularemia) 021.9

Disease, diseased — *see also* Syndrome — *continued*
Ollier's (chondrodysplasia) 756.4
Opitz's (congestive splenomegaly) 289.51
Oppenheim's 358.8
Oppenheim-Urbach (necrobiosis lipoidica diabeticorum) 250.8 ☑ *[709.3]*
due to secondary diabetes ●
249.8 ☑ *[709.3]* ●
optic nerve NEC 377.49
orbit 376.9
specified NEC 376.89
Oriental liver fluke 121.1
Oriental lung fluke 121.2
Ormond's 593.4
Osgood-Schlatter 732.4
Osgood's tibia (tubercle) 732.4
Osler (-Vaquez) (polycythemia vera) (M9950/1) 238.4
Osler-Rendu (familial hemorrhagic telangiectasia) 448.0
osteofibrocystic 252.01
Otto's 715.35
outer ear 380.9
ovary (noninflammatory) NEC 620.9
cystic 620.2
polycystic 256.4
specified NEC 620.8
Owren's (congenital) (*see also* Defect, coagulation) 286.3
Paas' 756.59
Paget's (osteitis deformans) 731.0
with infiltrating duct carcinoma of the breast (M8541/3) — *see* Neoplasm, breast, malignant
bone 731.0
osteosarcoma in (M9184/3) — *see* Neoplasm, bone, malignant
breast (M8540/3) 174.0
extramammary (M8542/3) (*see also* Neoplasm, skin, malignant)
anus 154.3
skin 173.5
malignant (M8540/3)
breast 174.0
specified site NEC (M8542/3) — *see* Neoplasm, skin, malignant
unspecified site 174.0
mammary (M8540/3) 174.0
nipple (M8540/3) 174.0
palate (soft) 528.9
Paltauf-Sternberg 201.9 ☑
pancreas 577.9
cystic 577.2
congenital 751.7
fibrocystic 277.00
Panner's 732.3
capitellum humeri 732.3
head of humerus 732.3
tarsal navicular (bone) (osteochondrosis) 732.5
panvalvular — *see* Endocarditis, mitral
parametrium 629.9
parasitic NEC 136.9
cerebral NEC 123.9
intestinal NEC 129
mouth 112.0
skin NEC 134.9
specified type — *see* Infestation
tongue 112.0
parathyroid (gland) 252.9
specified NEC 252.8
Parkinson's 332.0
parodontal 523.9
Parrot's (syphilitic osteochondritis) 090.0
Parry's (exophthalmic goiter) 242.0 ☑
Parson's (exophthalmic goiter) 242.0 ☑
Pavy's 593.6
Paxton's (white piedra) 111.2

Disease, diseased — *see also* Syndrome — *continued*
Payr's (splenic flexure syndrome) 569.89
pearl-workers' (chronic osteomyelitis) (*see also* Osteomyelitis) 730.1 ☑
Pel-Ebstein — *see* Disease, Hodgkin's
Pelizaeus-Merzbacher 330.0
with dementia
with behavioral disturbance 330.0 *[294.11]*
without behavioral disturbance 330.0 *[294.10]*
Pellegrini-Stieda (calcification, knee joint) 726.62
pelvis, pelvic
female NEC 629.9
specified NEC 629.89
gonococcal (acute) 098.19
chronic or duration of 2 months or over 098.39
infection (*see also* Disease, pelvis, inflammatory) 614.9
inflammatory (female) (PID) 614.9
with
abortion — *see* Abortion, by type, with sepsis
ectopic pregnancy (*see also* categories 633.0–633.9) 639.0
molar pregnancy (*see also* categories 630–632) 639.0
acute 614.3
chronic 614.4
complicating pregnancy 646.6 ☑
affecting fetus or newborn 760.8
following
abortion 639.0
ectopic or molar pregnancy 639.0
peritonitis (acute) 614.5
chronic NEC 614.7
puerperal, postpartum, childbirth 670.0 ☑
specified NEC 614.8
organ, female NEC 629.9
specified NEC 629.89
peritoneum, female NEC 629.9
specified NEC 629.89
penis 607.9
inflammatory 607.2
peptic NEC 536.9
acid 536.8
periapical tissues NEC 522.9
pericardium 423.9
specified type NEC 423.8
perineum
female
inflammatory 616.9
specified NEC 616.89
noninflammatory 624.9
specified NEC 624.8
male (inflammatory) 682.2
periodic (familial) (Reimann's) NEC 277.31
paralysis 359.3
periodontal NEC 523.9
specified NEC 523.8
periosteum 733.90
peripheral
arterial 443.9
autonomic nervous system (*see also* Neuropathy, autonomic) 337.9
nerve NEC (*see also* Neuropathy) 356.9
multiple — *see* Polyneuropathy
vascular 443.9
specified type NEC 443.89
peritoneum 568.9
pelvic, female 629.9
specified NEC 629.89
Perrin-Ferraton (snapping hip) 719.65

☑ Additional Digit Required — Refer to the Tabular List for Digit Selection
Subterms under main terms may continue to next column or page

Disease, diseased — *see also* Syndrome — *continued*
persistent mucosal (middle ear) (with posterior or superior marginal perforation of ear drum) 382.2
Perthes' (capital femoral osteochondrosis) 732.1
Petit's (*see also* Hernia, lumbar) 553.8
Peutz-Jeghers 759.6
Peyronie's 607.85
Pfeiffer's (infectious mononucleosis) 075
pharynx 478.20
Phocas' 610.1
photochromogenic (acid-fast bacilli) (pulmonary) 031.0
nonpulmonary 031.9
Pick's
brain 331.11
with dementia
with behavioral disturbance 331.11 *[294.11]*
without behavioral disturbance 331.11 *[294.10]*
cerebral atrophy 331.11
with dementia
with behavioral disturbance 331.11 *[294.11]*
without behavioral disturbance 331.11 *[294.10]*
lipid histiocytosis 272.7
liver (pericardial pseudocirrhosis of liver) 423.2
pericardium (pericardial pseudocirrhosis of liver) 423.2
polyserositis (pericardial pseudocirrhosis of liver) 423.2
Pierson's (osteochondrosis) 732.1
pigeon fanciers' or breeders' 495.2
pineal gland 259.8
pink 985.0
Pinkus' (lichen nitidus) 697.1
pinworm 127.4
pituitary (gland) 253.9
hyperfunction 253.1
hypofunction 253.2
pituitary snuff-takers' 495.8
placenta
affecting fetus or newborn 762.2
complicating pregnancy or childbirth 656.7 ☑
pleura (cavity) (*see also* Pleurisy) 511.0
Plummer's (toxic nodular goiter) 242.3 ☑
pneumatic
drill 994.9
hammer 994.9
policeman's 729.2
Pollitzer's (hidradenitis suppurativa) 705.83
polycystic (congenital) 759.89
congenital 748.4
kidney or renal 753.12
adult type (APKD) 753.13
autosomal dominant 753.13
autosomal recessive 753.14
childhood type (CPKD) 753.14
infantile type 753.14
liver or hepatic 751.62
lung or pulmonary 518.89
ovary, ovaries 256.4
spleen 759.0
Pompe's (glycogenosis II) 271.0
Poncet's (tuberculous rheumatism) (*see also* Tuberculosis) 015.9 ☑
Posada-Wernicke 114.9
Potain's (pulmonary edema) 514
Pott's (*see also* Tuberculosis) 015.0 ☑ *[730.88]*
osteomyelitis 015.0 ☑ *[730.88]*
paraplegia 015.0 ☑ *[730.88]*
spinal curvature 015.0 ☑ *[737.43]*
spondylitis 015.0 ☑ *[720.81]*
Potter's 753.0
Poulet's 714.2

Disease, diseased — *see also* Syndrome — *continued*
pregnancy NEC (*see also* Pregnancy) 646.9 ☑
Preiser's (osteoporosis) 733.09
Pringle's (tuberous sclerosis) 759.5
Profichet's 729.90 ▲
prostate 602.9
specified type NEC 602.8
protozoal NEC 136.8
intestine, intestinal NEC 007.9
pseudo-Hurler's (mucolipidosis III) 272.7
psychiatric (*see also* Psychosis) 298.9
psychotic (*see also* Psychosis) 298.9
Puente's (simple glandular cheilitis) 528.5
puerperal NEC (*see also* Puerperal) 674.9 ☑
pulmonary (*see also* Disease, lung)
amyloid 277.39 *[517.8]*
artery 417.9
circulation, circulatory 417.9
specified NEC 417.8
diffuse obstructive (chronic) 496
with
acute bronchitis 491.22
asthma (chronic) (obstructive) 493.2 ☑
exacerbation NEC (acute) 491.21
heart (chronic) 416.9
specified NEC 416.8
hypertensive (vascular) 416.0
cardiovascular 416.0
obstructive diffuse (chronic) 496
with
acute bronchitis 491.22
asthma (chronic) (obstructive) 493.2 ☑
bronchitis (chronic) 491.20
with
exacerbation (acute) 491.21
acute 491.22
exacerbation NEC (acute) 491.21
decompensated 491.21
with exacerbation 491.21
valve (*see also* Endocarditis, pulmonary) 424.3
pulp (dental) NEC 522.9
pulseless 446.7
Putnam's (subacute combined sclerosis with pernicious anemia) 281.0 *[336.2]*
Pyle (-Cohn) (craniometaphyseal dysplasia) 756.89
pyramidal tract 333.90
Quervain's
tendon sheath 727.04
thyroid (subacute granulomatous thyroiditis) 245.1
Quincke's — *see* Edema, angioneurotic
Quinquaud (acne decalvans) 704.09
rag sorters' 022.1
Raynaud's (paroxysmal digital cyanosis) 443.0
reactive airway — *see* Asthma
Recklinghausen's (M9540/1) 237.71
bone (osteitis fibrosa cystica) 252.01
Recklinghausen-Applebaum (hemochromatosis) 275.0
Reclus' (cystic) 610.1
rectum NEC 569.49
Refsum's (heredopathia atactica polyneuritiformis) 356.3
Reichmann's (gastrosuccorrhea) 536.8
Reimann's (periodic) 277.31
Reiter's 099.3
renal (functional) (pelvis) (*see also* Disease, kidney) 593.9

Disease, diseased — *see also* Syndrome — *continued*
renal (*see also* Disease, kidney) — *continued*
with
edema (*see also* Nephrosis) 581.9
exudative nephritis 583.89
lesion of interstitial nephritis 583.89
stated generalized cause — *see* Nephritis
acute 593.9
basement membrane NEC 583.89
with
pulmonary hemorrhage (Goodpasture's syndrome) 446.21 *[583.81]*
chronic (*see also* Disease, kidney, chronic) 585.9
complicating pregnancy or puerperium NEC 646.2 ☑
with hypertension — *see* Toxemia, of pregnancy
affecting fetus or newborn 760.1
cystic, congenital (*see also* Cystic, disease, kidney) 753.10
diabetic 250.4 ☑ *[583.81]*
due to secondary diabetes ●
249.4 ☑ *[581.81]* ●
due to
amyloidosis 277.39 *[583.81]*
diabetes mellitus 250.4 ☑ *[583.81]*
due to secondary diabetes ●
249.4 ☑ *[581.81]* ●
systemic lupus erythematosis 710.0 *[583.81]*
end-stage 585.6
exudative 583.89
fibrocystic (congenital) 753.19
gonococcal 098.19 *[583.81]*
gouty 274.10
hypertensive (*see also* Hypertension, kidney) 403.90
immune complex NEC 583.89
interstitial (diffuse) (focal) 583.89
lupus 710.0 *[583.81]*
maternal, affecting fetus or newborn 760.1
hypertensive 760.0
phosphate-losing (tubular) 588.0
polycystic (congenital) 753.12
adult type (APKD) 753.13
autosomal dominant 753.13
autosomal recessive 753.14
childhood type (CPKD) 753.14
infantile type 753.14
specified lesion or cause NEC (*see also* Glomerulonephritis) 583.89
subacute 581.9
syphilitic 095.4
tuberculous (*see also* Tuberculosis) 016.0 ☑ *[583.81]*
tubular (*see also* Nephrosis, tubular) 584.5
Rendu-Osler-Weber (familial hemorrhagic telangiectasia) 448.0
renovascular (arteriosclerotic) (*see also* Hypertension, kidney) 403.90
respiratory (tract) 519.9
acute or subacute (upper) NEC 465.9
due to fumes or vapors 506.3
multiple sites NEC 465.8
noninfectious 478.9
streptococcal 034.0
chronic 519.9
arising in the perinatal period 770.7
due to fumes or vapors 506.4
due to
aspiration of liquids or solids 508.9
external agents NEC 508.9

Disease, diseased — *see also* Syndrome — *continued*
respiratory — *continued*
due to — *continued*
external agents — *continued*
specified NEC 508.8
fumes or vapors 506.9
acute or subacute NEC 506.3
chronic 506.4
fetus or newborn NEC 770.9
obstructive 496
specified type NEC 519.8
upper (acute) (infectious) NEC 465.9
multiple sites NEC 465.8
noninfectious NEC 478.9
streptococcal 034.0
retina, retinal NEC 362.9
Batten's or Batten-Mayou 330.1 *[362.71]*
degeneration 362.89
vascular lesion 362.17
rheumatic (*see also* Arthritis) 716.8 ☑
heart — *see* Disease, heart, rheumatic
rheumatoid (heart) — *see* Arthritis, rheumatoid
rickettsial NEC 083.9
specified type NEC 083.8
Riedel's (ligneous thyroiditis) 245.3
Riga (-Fede) (cachectic aphthae) 529.0
Riggs' (compound periodontitis) 523.40
Ritter's 695.81
Rivalta's (cervicofacial actinomycosis) 039.3
Robles' (onchocerciasis) 125.3 *[360.13]*
Roger's (congenital interventricular septal defect) 745.4
Rokitansky's (*see also* Necrosis, liver) 570
Romberg's 349.89
Rosenthal's (factor XI deficiency) 286.2
Rossbach's (hyperchlorhydria) 536.8
psychogenic 306.4
Roth (-Bernhardt) 355.1
Runeberg's (progressive pernicious anemia) 281.0
Rust's (tuberculous spondylitis) (*see also* Tuberculosis) 015.0 ☑ *[720.81]*
Rustitskii's (multiple myeloma) (M9730/3) 203.0 ☑
Ruysch's (Hirschsprung's disease) 751.3
Sachs (-Tay) 330.1
sacroiliac NEC 724.6
salivary gland or duct NEC 527.9
inclusion 078.5
streptococcal 034.0
virus 078.5
Sander's (paranoia) 297.1
Sandhoff's 330.1
sandworm 126.9
Savill's (epidemic exfoliative dermatitis) 695.89
Schamberg's (progressive pigmentary dermatosis) 709.09
Schaumann's (sarcoidosis) 135
Schenck's (sporotrichosis) 117.1
Scheuermann's (osteochondrosis) 732.0
Schilder (-Flatau) 341.1
Schimmelbusch's 610.1
Schlatter-Osgood 732.4
Schlatter's tibia (tubercle) 732.4
Schmorl's 722.30
cervical 722.39
lumbar, lumbosacral 722.32
specified region NEC 722.39
thoracic, thoracolumbar 722.31
Scholz's 330.0
Schönlein (-Henoch) (purpura rheumatica) 287.0
Schottmüller's (*see also* Fever, paratyphoid) 002.9

Disease, diseased — *see also* Syndrome — *continued*
Schüller-Christian (chronic histiocytosis X) 277.89
Schultz's (agranulocytosis) 288.09
Schwalbe-Ziehen-Oppenheimer 333.6
Schwartz-Jampel 359.23
Schweninger-Buzzi (macular atrophy) 701.3
sclera 379.19
scrofulous (*see also* Tuberculosis) 017.2 ☑
scrotum 608.9
sebaceous glands NEC 706.9
Secretan's (posttraumatic edema) 782.3
semilunar cartilage, cystic 717.5
seminal vesicle 608.9
Senear-Usher (pemphigus erythematosus) 694.4
serum NEC 999.5
Sever's (osteochondrosis calcaneum) 732.5
sexually transmitted — *see* Disease, venereal
Sézary's (reticulosis) (M9701/3) 202.2 ☑
Shaver's (bauxite pneumoconiosis) 503
Sheehan's (postpartum pituitary necrosis) 253.2
shimamushi (scrub typhus) 081.2
shipyard 077.1
sickle cell 282.60
with
crisis 282.62
Hb-S disease 282.61
other abnormal hemoglobin (Hb-D) (Hb-E) (Hb-G) (Hb-J) (Hb-K) (Hb-O) (Hb-P) (high fetal gene) (without crisis) 282.68
with crisis 282.69
elliptocytosis 282.60
Hb-C (without crisis) 282.63
with
crisis 282.64
vaso-occlusive pain 282.64
Hb-S 282.61
with
crisis 282.62
Hb-C (without crisis) 282.63
with
crisis 282.64
vaso-occlusive pain 282.64
other abnormal hemoglobin (Hb-D) (Hb-E) (Hb-G) (Hb-J) (Hb-K) (Hb-O) (Hb-P) (high fetal gene) (without crisis) 282.68
with crisis 282.69
spherocytosis 282.60
thalassemia (without crisis) 282.41
with
crisis 282.42
vaso-occlusive pain 282.42
Siegal-Cattan-Mamou (periodic) 277.31
silo fillers' 506.9
Simian B 054.3
Simmonds' (pituitary cachexia) 253.2
Simons' (progressive lipodystrophy) 272.6
Sinding-Larsen (juvenile osteopathia patellae) 732.4
sinus (*see also* Sinusitis)
brain 437.9
specified NEC 478.19
Sirkari's 085.0
sixth (*see also* Exanthem subitum) 058.10
Sjögren (-Gougerot) 710.2
with lung involvement 710.2 *[517.8]*
Skevas-Zerfus 989.5

Disease, diseased — *see also* Syndrome — *continued*
skin NEC 709.9
due to metabolic disorder 277.9
specified type NEC 709.8
sleeping (*see also* Narcolepsy) 347.00
meaning sleeping sickness (*see also* Trypanosomiasis) 086.5
small vessel 443.9
Smith-Strang (oasthouse urine) 270.2
Sneddon-Wilkinson (subcorneal pustular dermatosis) 694.1
South African creeping 133.8
Spencer's (epidemic vomiting) 078.82
Spielmeyer-Stock 330.1
Spielmeyer-Vogt 330.1
spine, spinal 733.90
combined system (*see also* Degeneration, combined) 266.2 *[336.2]*
with pernicious anemia 281.0 *[336.2]*
cord NEC 336.9
congenital 742.9
demyelinating NEC 341.8
joint (*see also* Disease, joint, spine) 724.9
tuberculous 015.0 ☑ *[730.8]* ☑
spinocerebellar 334.9
specified NEC 334.8
spleen (organic) (postinfectional) 289.50
amyloid 277.39
lardaceous 277.39
polycystic 759.0
specified NEC 289.59
sponge divers' 989.5
Stanton's (melioidosis) 025
Stargardt's 362.75
Startle 759.89
Steinert's 359.21
Sternberg's — *see* Disease, Hodgkin's
Stevens-Johnson (erythema multiforme exudativum) 695.13 ▲
Sticker's (erythema infectiosum) 057.0
Stieda's (calcification, knee joint) 726.62
Still's (juvenile rheumatoid arthritis) 714.30
adult onset 714.2 ●
Stiller's (asthenia) 780.79
Stokes' (exophthalmic goiter) 242.0 ☑
Stokes-Adams (syncope with heart block) 426.9
Stokvis (-Talma) (enterogenous cyanosis) 289.7
stomach NEC (organic) 537.9
functional 536.9
psychogenic 306.4
lardaceous 277.39
stonemasons' 502
storage
glycogen (*see also* Disease, glycogen storage) 271.0
lipid 272.7
mucopolysaccharide 277.5
striatopallidal system 333.90
specified NEC 333.89
Strümpell-Marie (ankylosing spondylitis) 720.0
Stuart's (congenital factor X deficiency) (*see also* Defect, coagulation) 286.3
Stuart-Prower (congenital factor X deficiency) (*see also* Defect, coagulation) 286.3
Sturge (-Weber) (-Dimitri) (encephalocutaneous angiomatosis) 759.6
Stuttgart 100.89
Sudeck's 733.7
supporting structures of teeth NEC 525.9
suprarenal (gland) (capsule) 255.9
hyperfunction 255.3
hypofunction 255.41
Sutton's 709.09

Disease, diseased — *see also* Syndrome — *continued*
Sutton and Gull's — *see* Hypertension, kidney
sweat glands NEC 705.9
specified type NEC 705.89
sweating 078.2
Sweeley-Klionsky 272.4
Swift (-Feer) 985.0
swimming pool (bacillus) 031.1
swineherd's 100.89
Sylvest's (epidemic pleurodynia) 074.1
Symmers (follicular lymphoma) (M9690/3) 202.0 ☑
sympathetic nervous system (*see also* Neuropathy, peripheral, autonomic) 337.9
synovium 727.9
syphilitic — *see* Syphilis
systemic tissue mast cell (M9741/3) 202.6 ☑
Taenzer's 757.4
Takayasu's (pulseless) 446.7
Talma's 728.85
Tangier (familial high-density lipoprotein deficiency) 272.5
Tarral-Besnier (pityriasis rubra pilaris) 696.4
Taylor's 701.8
Tay-Sachs 330.1
tear duct 375.69
teeth, tooth 525.9
hard tissues 521.9
specified NEC 521.89
pulp NEC 522.9
tendon 727.9
inflammatory NEC 727.9
terminal vessel 443.9
testis 608.9
Thaysen-Gee (nontropical sprue) 579.0
Thomsen's 359.22
Thomson's (congenital poikiloderma) 757.33
Thornwaldt's, Tornwaldt's (pharyngeal bursitis) 478.29
throat 478.20
septic 034.0
thromboembolic (*see also* Embolism) 444.9
thymus (gland) 254.9
specified NEC 254.8
thyroid (gland) NEC 246.9
heart (*see also* Hyperthyroidism) 242.9 ☑ *[425.7]*
lardaceous 277.39
specified NEC 246.8
Tietze's 733.6
Tommaselli's
correct substance properly administered 599.70 ▲
overdose or wrong substance given or taken 961.4
tongue 529.9
tonsils, tonsillar (and adenoids) (chronic) 474.9
specified NEC 474.8
tooth, teeth 525.9
hard tissues 521.9
specified NEC 521.89
pulp NEC 522.9
Tornwaldt's (pharyngeal bursitis) 478.29
Tourette's 307.23
trachea 519.19
tricuspid — *see* Endocarditis, tricuspid
triglyceride-storage, type I, II, III 272.7
triple vessel (coronary arteries) — *see* Arteriosclerosis, coronary
trisymptomatic, Gourgerot's 709.1
trophoblastic (*see also* Hydatidiform mole) 630
previous, affecting management of pregnancy V23.1
tsutsugamushi (scrub typhus) 081.2

Disease, diseased — *see also* Syndrome — *continued*
tube (fallopian), noninflammatory 620.9
specified NEC 620.8
tuberculous NEC (*see also* Tuberculosis) 011.9 ☑
tubo-ovarian
inflammatory (*see also* Salpingo-oophoritis) 614.2
noninflammatory 620.9
specified NEC 620.8
tubotympanic, chronic (with anterior perforation of ear drum) 382.1
tympanum 385.9
Uhl's 746.84
umbilicus (newborn) NEC 779.89
delayed separation 779.83
Underwood's (sclerema neonatorum) 778.1
undiagnosed 799.9
Unna's (seborrheic dermatitis) 690.18
unstable hemoglobin hemolytic 282.7
Unverricht (-Lundborg) 333.2
Urbach-Oppenheim (necrobiosis lipoidica diabeticorum) 250.8 ☑ *[709.3]*
due to secondary diabetes ●
249.8 ☑ *[709.3]* ●
Urbach-Wiethe (lipoid proteinosis) 272.8
ureter 593.9
urethra 599.9
specified type NEC 599.84
urinary (tract) 599.9
bladder 596.9
specified NEC 596.8
maternal, affecting fetus or newborn 760.1
Usher-Senear (pemphigus erythematosus) 694.4
uterus (organic) 621.9
infective (*see also* Endometritis) 615.9
inflammatory (*see also* Endometritis) 615.9
noninflammatory 621.9
specified type NEC 621.8
uveal tract
anterior 364.9
posterior 363.9
vagabonds' 132.1
vagina, vaginal
inflammatory 616.10
noninflammatory 623.9
specified NEC 623.8
Valsuani's (progressive pernicious anemia, puerperal) 648.2 ☑
complicating pregnancy or puerperium 648.2 ☑
valve, valvular — ▶*see also*◀ Endocarditis
congenital NEC (*see also* Anomaly, heart, valve) 746.9 ●
pulmonary 746.00 ●
specified type NEC 746.89 ●
van Bogaert-Nijssen (-Peiffer) 330.0
van Creveld-von Gierke (glycogenosis I) 271.0
van den Bergh's (enterogenous cyanosis) 289.7
van Neck's (juvenile osteochondrosis) 732.1
Vaquez (-Osler) (polycythemia vera) (M9950/1) 238.4
vascular 459.9
arteriosclerotic — *see* Arteriosclerosis
hypertensive — *see* Hypertension
obliterative 447.1
peripheral 443.9
occlusive 459.9
peripheral (occlusive) 443.9
in diabetes mellitus 250.7 ☑ *[443.81]*

Disease, diseased — *see also* Syndrome — *continued*
vascular — *continued*
peripheral — *continued*
in diabetes mellitus — *continued*
due to secondary diabetes ● 249.7 ☑ *[443.81]* ●
specified type NEC 443.89
vas deferens 608.9
vasomotor 443.9
vasospastic 443.9
vein 459.9
venereal 099.9
chlamydial NEC 099.50
anus 099.52
bladder 099.53
cervix 099.53
epididymis 099.54
genitourinary NEC 099.55
lower 099.53
specified NEC 099.54
pelvic inflammatory disease 099.54
perihepatic 099.56
peritoneum 099.56
pharynx 099.51
rectum 099.52
specified site NEC 099.59
testis 099.54
vagina 099.53
vulva 099.53
complicating pregnancy, childbirth, or puerperium 647.2 ☑
fifth 099.1
sixth 099.1
specified nature or type NEC 099.8
chlamydial — *see* Disease, venereal, chlamydial
Verneuil's (syphilitic bursitis) 095.7
Verse's (calcinosis intervertebralis) 275.49 *[722.90]*
vertebra, vertebral NEC 733.90
disc — *see* Disease, Intervertebral disc
vibration NEC 994.9
Vidal's (lichen simplex chronicus) 698.3
Vincent's (trench mouth) 101
Virchow's 733.99
virus (filterable) NEC 078.89
arbovirus NEC 066.9
arthropod-borne NEC 066.9
central nervous system NEC 049.9
specified type NEC 049.8
complicating pregnancy, childbirth, or puerperium 647.6 ☑
contact (with) V01.79
varicella V01.71
exposure to V01.79
varicella V01.71
Marburg 078.89
maternal
with fetal damage affecting management of pregnancy 655.3 ☑
nonarthropod-borne NEC 078.89
central nervous system NEC 049.9
specified NEC 049.8
vaccination, prophylactic (against) V04.89
vitreous 379.29
vocal cords NEC 478.5
Vogt's (Cecile) 333.71
Vogt-Spielmeyer 330.1
Volhard-Fahr (malignant nephrosclerosis) 403.00
Volkmann's
acquired 958.6
von Bechterew's (ankylosing spondylitis) 720.0
von Economo's (encephalitis lethargica) 049.8
von Eulenburg's (congenital paramyotonia) 359.29

Disease, diseased — *see also* Syndrome — *continued*
von Gierke's (glycogenosis I) 271.0
von Graefe's 378.72
von Hippel's (retinocerebral angiomatosis) 759.6
von Hippel-Lindau (angiomatosis retinocerebellosa) 759.6
von Jaksch's (pseudoleukemia infantum) 285.8
von Recklinghausen's (M9540/1) 237.71
bone (osteitis fibrosa cystica) 252.01
von Recklinghausen-Applebaum (hemochromatosis) 275.0
von Willebrand (-Jürgens) (angiohemophilia) 286.4
von Zambusch's (lichen sclerosus et atrophicus) 701.0
Voorhoeve's (dyschondroplasia) 756.4
Vrolik's (osteogenesis imperfecta) 756.51
vulva
inflammatory 616.10
noninflammatory 624.9
specified NEC 624.8
Wagner's (colloid milium) 709.3
Waldenström's (osteochondrosis capital femoral) 732.1
Wallgren's (obstruction of splenic vein with collateral circulation) 459.89
Wardrop's (with lymphangitis) 681.9
finger 681.02
toe 681.11
Wassilieff's (leptospiral jaundice) 100.0
wasting NEC 799.4
due to malnutrition 261
paralysis 335.21
Waterhouse-Friderichsen 036.3
waxy (any site) 277.39
Weber-Christian (nodular nonsuppurative panniculitis) 729.30
Wegner's (syphilitic osteochondritis) 090.0
Weil's (leptospiral jaundice) 100.0
of lung 100.0
Weir Mitchell's (erythromelalgia) 443.82
Werdnig-Hoffmann 335.0
Werlhof's (*see also* Purpura, thrombocytopenic) 287.39
Wermer's 258.01
Werner's (progeria adultorum) 259.8
Werner-His (trench fever) 083.1
Werner-Schultz (agranulocytosis) 288.09
Wernicke's (superior hemorrhagic polioencephalitis) 265.1
Wernicke-Posadas 114.9
Whipple's (intestinal lipodystrophy) 040.2
whipworm 127.3
White's (congenital) (keratosis follicularis) 757.39
white
blood cell 288.9
specified NEC 288.8
spot 701.0
Whitmore's (melioidosis) 025
Widal-Abrami (acquired hemolytic jaundice) 283.9
Wilkie's 557.1
Wilkinson-Sneddon (subcorneal pustular dermatosis) 694.1
Willis' (diabetes mellitus) (*see also* Diabetes) 250.0 ☑
due to secondary diabetes ● 249.0 ☑ ●
Wilson's (hepatolenticular degeneration) 275.1
Wilson-Brocq (dermatitis exfoliativa) 695.89
winter vomiting 078.82

Disease, diseased — *see also* Syndrome — *continued*
Wise's 696.2
Wohlfart-Kugelberg-Welander 335.11
Woillez's (acute idiopathic pulmonary congestion) 518.5
Wolman's (primary familial xanthomatosis) 272.7
wool-sorters' 022.1
Zagari's (xerostomia) 527.7
Zahorsky's (exanthem subitum) 058.10
Ziehen-Oppenheim 333.6
zoonotic, bacterial NEC 027.9
specified type NEC 027.8
Disfigurement (due to scar) 709.2
head V48.6
limb V49.4
neck V48.7
trunk V48.7
Disgerminoma — *see* Dysgerminoma
Disinsertion, retina 361.04
Disintegration, complete, of the body 799.89
traumatic 869.1
Disk kidney 753.3
Dislocatable hip, congenital — *see also* Dislocation, hip, congenital 754.30
Dislocation (articulation) (closed) (displacement) (simple) (subluxation) 839.8

Note — "Closed" includes simple, complete, partial, uncomplicated, and unspecified dislocation.

"Open" includes dislocation specified as infected or compound and dislocation with foreign body.

"Chronic," "habitual," "old," or "recurrent" dislocations should be coded as indicated under the entry "Dislocation, recurrent," and "pathological" as indicated under the entry "Dislocation, pathological."

For late effect of dislocation see Late, effect, dislocation.

with fracture — *see* Fracture, by site
acromioclavicular (joint) (closed) 831.04
open 831.14
anatomical site (closed)
specified NEC 839.69
open 839.79
unspecified or ill-defined 839.8
open 839.9
ankle (scaphoid bone) (closed) 837.0
open 837.1
arm (closed) 839.8
open 839.9
astragalus (closed) 837.0
open 837.1
atlanto-axial (closed) 839.01
open 839.11
atlas (closed) 839.01
open 839.11
axis (closed) 839.02
open 839.12
back (closed) 839.8
open 839.9
Bell-Daly 723.8
breast bone (closed) 839.61
open 839.71
capsule, joint — *see* Dislocation, by site
carpal (bone) — *see* Dislocation, wrist
carpometacarpal (joint) (closed) 833.04
open 833.14
cartilage (joint) (*see also* Dislocation, by site)
knee — *see* Tear, meniscus
cervical, cervicodorsal, or cervicothoracic (spine) (vertebra) — *see* Dislocation, vertebra, cervical
chiropractic (*see also* Lesion, nonallopathic) 739.9

Dislocation — *continued*
chondrocostal — *see* Dislocation, costochondral
chronic — *see* Dislocation, recurrent
clavicle (closed) 831.04
open 831.14
coccyx (closed) 839.41
open 839.51
collar bone (closed) 831.04
open 831.14
compound (open) NEC 839.9
congenital NEC 755.8
hip (*see also* Dislocation, hip, congenital) 754.30
lens 743.37
rib 756.3
sacroiliac 755.69
spine NEC 756.19
vertebra 756.19
coracoid (closed) 831.09
open 831.19
costal cartilage (closed) 839.69
open 839.79
costochondral (closed) 839.69
open 839.79
cricoarytenoid articulation (closed) 839.69
open 839.79
cricothyroid (cartilage) articulation (closed) 839.69
open 839.79
dorsal vertebrae (closed) 839.21
open 839.31
ear ossicle 385.23
elbow (closed) 832.00
anterior (closed) 832.01
open 832.11
congenital 754.89
divergent (closed) 832.09
open 832.19
lateral (closed) 832.04
open 832.14
medial (closed) 832.03
open 832.13
open 832.10
posterior (closed) 832.02
open 832.12
recurrent 718.32
specified type NEC 832.09
open 832.19
eye 360.81
lateral 376.36
eyeball 360.81
lateral 376.36
femur
distal end (closed) 836.50
anterior 836.52
open 836.62
lateral 836.53
open 836.63
medial 836.54
open 836.64
open 836.60
posterior 836.51
open 836.61
proximal end (closed) 835.00
anterior (pubic) 835.03
open 835.13
obturator 835.02
open 835.12
open 835.10
posterior 835.01
open 835.11
fibula
distal end (closed) 837.0
open 837.1
proximal end (closed) 836.59
open 836.69
finger(s) (phalanx) (thumb) (closed) 834.00
interphalangeal (joint) 834.02
open 834.12
metacarpal (bone), distal end 834.01
open 834.11
metacarpophalangeal (joint) 834.01

Index

Disease, diseased — Dislocation

- **Dislocation** — *continued*
  - finger(s) — *continued*
    - metacarpophalangeal — *continued*
      - open 834.11
    - open 834.10
    - recurrent 718.34
  - foot (closed) 838.00
    - open 838.10
    - recurrent 718.37
  - forearm (closed) 839.8
    - open 839.9
  - fracture — *see* Fracture, by site
  - glenoid (closed) 831.09
    - open 831.19
  - habitual — *see* Dislocation, recurrent
  - hand (closed) 839.8
    - open 839.9
  - hip (closed) 835.00
    - anterior 835.03
      - obturator 835.02
        - open 835.12
      - open 835.13
    - congenital (unilateral) 754.30
      - with subluxation of other hip 754.35
      - bilateral 754.31
    - developmental 718.75
    - open 835.10
    - posterior 835.01
      - open 835.11
    - recurrent 718.35
  - humerus (closed) 831.00
    - distal end (*see also* Dislocation, elbow) 832.00
    - open 831.10
    - proximal end (closed) 831.00
      - anterior (subclavicular) (subcoracoid) (subglenoid) (closed) 831.01
        - open 831.11
      - inferior (closed) 831.03
        - open 831.13
      - open 831.10
      - posterior (closed) 831.02
        - open 831.12
  - implant — *see* Complications, mechanical
  - incus 385.23
  - infracoracoid (closed) 831.01
    - open 831.11
  - innominate (pubic junction) (sacral junction) (closed) 839.69
    - acetabulum (*see also* Dislocation, hip) 835.00
    - open 839.79
  - interphalangeal (joint)
    - finger or hand (closed) 834.02
      - open 834.12
    - foot or toe (closed) 838.06
      - open 838.16
  - jaw (cartilage) (meniscus) (closed) 830.0
    - open 830.1
    - recurrent 524.69
  - joint NEC (closed) 839.8
    - developmental 718.7 ☑
    - open 839.9
    - pathological — *see* Dislocation, pathological
    - recurrent — *see* Dislocation, recurrent
  - knee (closed) 836.50
    - anterior 836.51
      - open 836.61
    - congenital (with genu recurvatum) 754.41
    - habitual 718.36
    - lateral 836.54
      - open 836.64
    - medial 836.53
      - open 836.63
    - old 718.36
    - open 836.60
    - posterior 836.52
      - open 836.62

- **Dislocation** — *continued*
  - knee — *continued*
    - recurrent 718.36
    - rotatory 836.59
      - open 836.69
  - lacrimal gland 375.16
  - leg (closed) 839.8
    - open 839.9
  - lens (crystalline) (complete) (partial) 379.32
    - anterior 379.33
    - congenital 743.37
    - ocular implant 996.53
    - posterior 379.34
    - traumatic 921.3
  - ligament — *see* Dislocation, by site
  - lumbar (vertebrae) (closed) 839.20
    - open 839.30
  - lumbosacral (vertebrae) (closed) 839.20
    - congenital 756.19
    - open 839.30
  - mandible (closed) 830.0
    - open 830.1
  - maxilla (inferior) (closed) 830.0
    - open 830.1
  - meniscus (knee) (*see also* Tear, meniscus)
    - other sites — *see* Dislocation, by site
  - metacarpal (bone)
    - distal end (closed) 834.01
      - open 834.11
    - proximal end (closed) 833.05
      - open 833.15
  - metacarpophalangeal (joint) (closed) 834.01
    - open 834.11
  - metatarsal (bone) (closed) 838.04
    - open 838.14
  - metatarsophalangeal (joint) (closed) 838.05
    - open 838.15
  - midcarpal (joint) (closed) 833.03
    - open 833.13
  - midtarsal (joint) (closed) 838.02
    - open 838.12
  - Monteggia's — *see* Dislocation, hip
  - multiple locations (except fingers only or toes only) (closed) 839.8
    - open 839.9
  - navicular (bone) foot (closed) 837.0
    - open 837.1
  - neck (*see also* Dislocation, vertebra, cervical) 839.00
  - Nélaton's — *see* Dislocation, ankle
  - nontraumatic (joint) — *see* Dislocation, pathological
  - nose (closed) 839.69
    - open 839.79
  - not recurrent, not current injury — *see* Dislocation, pathological
  - occiput from atlas (closed) 839.01
    - open 839.11
  - old — *see* Dislocation, recurrent
  - open (compound) NEC 839.9
  - ossicle, ear 385.23
  - paralytic (flaccid) (spastic) — *see* Dislocation, pathological
  - patella (closed) 836.3
    - congenital 755.64
    - open 836.4
  - pathological NEC 718.20
    - ankle 718.27
    - elbow 718.22
    - foot 718.27
    - hand 718.24
    - hip 718.25
    - knee 718.26
    - lumbosacral joint 724.6
    - multiple sites 718.29
    - pelvic region 718.25
    - sacroiliac 724.6
    - shoulder (region) 718.21
    - specified site NEC 718.28
    - spine 724.8

- **Dislocation** — *continued*
  - pathological — *continued*
    - spine — *continued*
      - sacroiliac 724.6
    - wrist 718.23
  - pelvis (closed) 839.69
    - acetabulum (*see also* Dislocation, hip) 835.00
    - open 839.79
  - phalanx
    - foot or toe (closed) 838.09
      - open 838.19
    - hand or finger (*see also* Dislocation, finger) 834.00
  - postpoliomyelitic — *see* Dislocation, pathological
  - prosthesis, internal — *see* Complications, mechanical
  - radiocarpal (joint) (closed) 833.02
    - open 833.12
  - radioulnar (joint)
    - distal end (closed) 833.01
      - open 833.11
    - proximal end (*see also* Dislocation, elbow) 832.00
  - radius
    - distal end (closed) 833.00
      - open 833.10
    - proximal end (closed) 832.01
      - open 832.11
  - recurrent (*see also* Derangement, joint, recurrent) 718.3 ☑
    - elbow 718.32
    - hip 718.35
    - joint NEC 718.38
    - knee 718.36
    - lumbosacral (joint) 724.6
    - patella 718.36
    - sacroiliac 724.6
    - shoulder 718.31
    - temporomandibular 524.69
  - rib (cartilage) (closed) 839.69
    - congenital 756.3
    - open 839.79
  - sacrococcygeal (closed) 839.42
    - open 839.52
  - sacroiliac (joint) (ligament) (closed) 839.42
    - congenital 755.69
    - open 839.52
    - recurrent 724.6
  - sacrum (closed) 839.42
    - open 839.52
  - scaphoid (bone)
    - ankle or foot (closed) 837.0
      - open 837.1
    - wrist (closed) (*see also* Dislocation, wrist) 833.00
      - open 833.10
  - scapula (closed) 831.09
    - open 831.19
  - semilunar cartilage, knee — *see* Tear, meniscus
  - septal cartilage (nose) (closed) 839.69
    - open 839.79
  - septum (nasal) (old) 470
  - sesamoid bone — *see* Dislocation, by site
  - shoulder (blade) (ligament) (closed) 831.00
    - anterior (subclavicular) (subcoracoid) (subglenoid) (closed) 831.01
      - open 831.11
    - chronic 718.31
    - inferior 831.03
      - open 831.13
    - open 831.10
    - posterior (closed) 831.02
      - open 831.12
    - recurrent 718.31
  - skull — *see* Injury, intracranial
  - Smith's — *see* Dislocation, foot
  - spine (articular process) (*see also* Dislocation, vertebra) (closed) 839.40

- **Dislocation** — *continued*
  - spine (*see also* Dislocation, vertebra) — *continued*
    - atlanto-axial (closed) 839.01
      - open 839.11
      - recurrent 723.8
    - cervical, cervicodorsal, cervicothoracic (closed) (*see also* Dislocation, vertebrae, cervical) 839.00
      - open 839.10
      - recurrent 723.8
    - coccyx 839.41
      - open 839.51
    - congenital 756.19
    - due to birth trauma 767.4
    - open 839.50
    - recurrent 724.9
    - sacroiliac 839.42
      - recurrent 724.6
    - sacrum (sacrococcygeal) (sacroiliac) 839.42
      - open 839.52
  - spontaneous — *see* Dislocation, pathological
  - sternoclavicular (joint) (closed) 839.61
    - open 839.71
  - sternum (closed) 839.61
    - open 839.71
  - subastragalar — *see* Dislocation, foot
  - subglenoid (closed) 831.01
    - open 831.11
  - symphysis
    - jaw (closed) 830.0
      - open 830.1
    - mandibular (closed) 830.0
      - open 830.1
    - pubis (closed) 839.69
      - open 839.79
  - tarsal (bone) (joint) 838.01
    - open 838.11
  - tarsometatarsal (joint) 838.03
    - open 838.13
  - temporomandibular (joint) (closed) 830.0
    - open 830.1
    - recurrent 524.69
  - thigh
    - distal end (*see also* Dislocation, femur, distal end) 836.50
    - proximal end (*see also* Dislocation, hip) 835.00
  - thoracic (vertebrae) (closed) 839.21
    - open 839.31
  - thumb(s) (*see also* Dislocation, finger) 834.00
  - thyroid cartilage (closed) 839.69
    - open 839.79
  - tibia
    - distal end (closed) 837.0
      - open 837.1
    - proximal end (closed) 836.50
      - anterior 836.51
        - open 836.61
      - lateral 836.54
        - open 836.64
      - medial 836.53
        - open 836.63
      - open 836.60
      - posterior 836.52
        - open 836.62
      - rotatory 836.59
        - open 836.69
  - tibiofibular
    - distal (closed) 837.0
      - open 837.1
    - superior (closed) 836.59
      - open 836.69
  - toe(s) (closed) 838.09
    - open 838.19
  - trachea (closed) 839.69
    - open 839.79
  - ulna
    - distal end (closed) 833.09
      - open 833.19

Dislocation — *continued*
- ulna — *continued*
  - proximal end — *see* Dislocation, elbow
- vertebra (articular process) (body) (closed) (traumatic) 839.40
  - cervical, cervicodorsal or cervicothoracic (closed) 839.00
    - first (atlas) 839.01
      - open 839.11
    - second (axis) 839.02
      - open 839.12
    - third 839.03
      - open 839.13
    - fourth 839.04
      - open 839.14
    - fifth 839.05
      - open 839.15
    - sixth 839.06
      - open 839.16
    - seventh 839.07
      - open 839.17
    - congential 756.19
    - multiple sites 839.08
      - open 839.18
    - open 839.10
  - congenital 756.19
  - dorsal 839.21
    - open 839.31
    - recurrent 724.9
  - lumbar, lumbosacral 839.20
    - open 839.30
  - non-traumatic — *see* Displacement, intervertebral disc
  - open NEC 839.50
  - recurrent 724.9
  - specified region NEC 839.49
    - open 839.59
  - thoracic 839.21
    - open 839.31
- wrist (carpal bone) (scaphoid) (semilunar) (closed) 833.00
  - carpometacarpal (joint) 833.04
    - open 833.14
  - metacarpal bone, proximal end 833.05
    - open 833.15
  - midcarpal (joint) 833.03
    - open 833.13
  - open 833.10
  - radiocarpal (joint) 833.02
    - open 833.12
  - radioulnar (joint) 833.01
    - open 833.11
  - recurrent 718.33
  - specified site NEC 833.09
    - open 833.19
- xiphoid cartilage (closed) 839.61
  - open 839.71

Dislodgement
- artificial skin graft 996.55
- decellularized allodermis graft 996.55

Disobedience, hostile (covert) (overt) — *see also* Disturbance, conduct 312.0 ☑

Disorder — *see also* Disease
- academic underachievement, childhood and adolescence 313.83
- accommodation 367.51
  - drug-induced 367.89
  - toxic 367.89
- adjustment (*see also* Reaction, adjustment) 309.9
  - with
    - anxiety 309.24
    - anxiety and depressed mood 309.28
    - depressed mood 309.0
    - disturbance of conduct 309.3
    - disturbance of emotions and conduct 309.4
- adrenal (capsule) (cortex) (gland) 255.9
  - specified type NEC 255.8
- adrenogenital 255.2
- affective (*see also* Psychosis, affective) 296.90

Disorder — *see also* Disease — *continued*
- affective (*see also* Psychosis, affective) — *continued*
  - atypical 296.81
- aggressive, unsocialized (*see also* Disturbance, conduct) 312.0 ☑
- alcohol, alcoholic (*see also* Alcohol) 291.9
- allergic — *see* Allergy
- amino acid (metabolic) (*see also* Disturbance, metabolism, amino acid) 270.9
  - albinism 270.2
  - alkaptonuria 270.2
  - argininosuccinicaciduria 270.6
  - beta-amino-isobutyricaciduria 277.2
  - cystathioninuria 270.4
  - cystinosis 270.0
  - cystinuria 270.0
  - glycinuria 270.0
  - homocystinuria 270.4
  - imidazole 270.5
  - maple syrup (urine) disease 270.3
  - neonatal, transitory 775.89
  - oasthouse urine disease 270.2
  - ochronosis 270.2
  - phenylketonuria 270.1
  - phenylpyruvic oligophrenia 270.1
  - purine NEC 277.2
  - pyrimidine NEC 277.2
  - renal transport NEC 270.0
  - specified type NEC 270.8
  - transport NEC 270.0
    - renal 270.0
  - xanthinuria 277.2
- amnestic (*see also* Amnestic syndrome) 294.8
  - alcohol-induced persisting 291.1
  - drug-induced persisting 292.83
  - in conditions classified elsewhere 294.0
- anaerobic glycolysis with anemia 282.3
- anxiety (*see also* Anxiety) 300.00
  - due to or associated with physical condition 293.84
- arteriole 447.9
  - specified type NEC 447.8
- artery 447.9
  - specified type NEC 447.8
- articulation — *see* Disorder, joint
- Asperger's 299.8 ☑
- attachment of infancy or early childhood 313.89
- attention deficit 314.00
  - with hyperactivity 314.01
  - predominantly
    - combined hyperactive/inattentive 314.01
    - hyperactive/impulsive 314.01
    - inattentive 314.00
  - residual type 314.8
- auditory processing disorder 388.45
  - acquired 388.45
  - developmental 315.32
- autistic 299.0 ☑
- autoimmune NEC 279.4
  - hemolytic (cold type) (warm type) 283.0
  - parathyroid 252.1
  - thyroid 245.2
- avoidant, childhood or adolescence 313.21
- balance
  - acid-base 276.9
    - mixed (with hypercapnia) 276.4
  - electrolyte 276.9
  - fluid 276.9
- behavior NEC (*see also* Disturbance, conduct) 312.9
  - disruptive 312.9
- bilirubin excretion 277.4

Disorder — *see also* Disease — *continued*
- bipolar (affective) (alternating) 296.80

> *Note — Use the following fifth-digit subclassification with categories 296.0–296.6:*
>
> 0 *unspecifed*
>
> 1 *mild*
>
> 2 *moderate*
>
> 3 *severe, without mention of psychotic behavior*
>
> 4 *severe, specified as with psychotic behavior*
>
> 5 *in partial or unspecified remission*
>
> 6 *in full remission*

  - atypical 296.7
  - currently
    - depressed 296.5 ☑
    - hypomanic 296.4 ☑
    - manic 296.4 ☑
  - mixed 296.6 ☑
  - specified type NEC 296.89
  - type I 296.7
    - most recent episode (or current)
      - depressed 296.5 ☑
      - hypomanic 296.4 ☑
      - manic 296.4 ☑
      - mixed 296.6 ☑
      - unspecified 296.7
    - single manic episode 296.0 ☑
  - type II (recurrent major depressive episodes with hypomania) 296.89
- bladder 596.9
  - functional NEC 596.59
  - specified NEC 596.8
- bleeding 286.9
- bone NEC 733.90
  - specified NEC 733.99
- brachial plexus 353.0
- branched-chain amino-acid degradation 270.3
- breast 611.9
  - puerperal, postpartum 676.3 ☑
  - specified NEC 611.89 ▲
- Briquet's 300.81
- bursa 727.9
  - shoulder region 726.10
- carbohydrate metabolism, congenital 271.9
- cardiac, functional 427.9
  - postoperative 997.1
  - psychogenic 306.2
- cardiovascular, psychogenic 306.2
- cartilage NEC 733.90
  - articular 718.00
    - ankle 718.07
    - elbow 718.02
    - foot 718.07
    - hand 718.04
    - hip 718.05
    - knee 717.9
    - multiple sites 718.09
    - pelvic region 718.05
    - shoulder region 718.01
    - specified
      - site NEC 718.08
      - type NEC 733.99
    - wrist 718.03
- catatonic — *see* Catatonia
- central auditory processing 315.32
  - acquired 388.45
  - developmental 315.32
- cervical region NEC 723.9
- cervical root (nerve) NEC 353.2
- character NEC (*see also* Disorder, personality) 301.9
- ciliary body 364.9
  - specified NEC 364.89
- coagulation (factor) (*see also* Defect, coagulation) 286.9

Disorder — *see also* Disease — *continued*
- coagulation (*see also* Defect, coagulation) — *continued*
  - factor VIII (congenital) (functional) 286.0
  - factor IX (congenital) (functional) 286.1
  - neonatal, transitory 776.3
- coccyx 724.70
  - specified NEC 724.79
- cognitive 294.9
- colon 569.9
  - functional 564.9
    - congenital 751.3
- communication 307.9
- conduct (*see also* Disturbance, conduct) 312.9
  - adjustment reaction 309.3
  - adolescent onset type 312.82
  - childhood onset type 312.81
  - compulsive 312.30
    - specified type NEC 312.39
  - hyperkinetic 314.2
  - onset unspecified 312.89
  - socialized (type) 312.20
    - aggressive 312.23
    - unaggressive 312.21
  - specified NEC 312.89
- conduction, heart 426.9
  - specified NEC 426.89
- conflict
  - sexual orientation 302.0
- congenital
  - glycosylation (CDG) 271.8
- convulsive (secondary) (*see also* Convulsions) 780.39
  - due to injury at birth 767.0
  - idiopathic 780.39
- coordination 781.3
- cornea NEC 371.89
  - due to contact lens 371.82
- corticosteroid metabolism NEC 255.2
- cranial nerve — *see* Disorder, nerve, cranial
- cyclothymic 301.13
- degradation, branched-chain amino acid 270.3
- delusional 297.1
- dentition 520.6
- depersonalization 300.6
- depressive NEC 311
  - atypical 296.82
  - major (*see also* Psychosis, affective) 296.2 ☑
    - recurrent episode 296.3 ☑
    - single episode 296.2 ☑
- development, specific 315.9
  - associated with hyperkinesia 314.1
  - coordination 315.4
  - language 315.31
    - and speech due to hearing loss 315.34
  - learning 315.2
    - arithmetical 315.1
    - reading 315.00
  - mixed 315.5
  - motor coordination 315.4
  - specified type NEC 315.8
  - speech 315.39
    - and language due to hearing loss 315.34
- diaphragm 519.4
- digestive 536.9
  - fetus or newborn 777.9
    - specified NEC 777.8
  - psychogenic 306.4
- disintegrative, childhood 299.1 ☑
- dissociative 300.15
  - identity 300.14
  - nocturnal 307.47
- drug-related 292.9
- dysmorphic body 300.7
- dysthymic 300.4
- ear 388.9
  - degenerative NEC 388.00

Disorder — *see also* Disease — *continued*

- ear — *continued*
  - external 380.9
    - specified 380.89
  - pinna 380.30
  - specified type NEC 388.8
  - vascular NEC 388.00
- eating NEC 307.50
- electrolyte NEC 276.9
  - with
    - abortion — *see* Abortion, by type, with metabolic disorder
    - ectopic pregnancy (*see also* categories 633.0–633.9) 639.4
    - molar pregnancy (*see also* categories 630–632) 639.4
  - acidosis 276.2
    - metabolic 276.2
    - respiratory 276.2
  - alkalosis 276.3
    - metabolic 276.3
    - respiratory 276.3
  - following
    - abortion 639.4
    - ectopic or molar pregnancy 639.4
  - neonatal, transitory NEC 775.5
- emancipation as adjustment reaction 309.22
- emotional (*see also* Disorder, mental, nonpsychotic) V40.9
- endocrine 259.9
  - specified type NEC 259.8
- esophagus 530.9
  - functional 530.5
  - psychogenic 306.4
- explosive
  - intermittent 312.34
  - isolated 312.35
- expressive language 315.31
- eye 379.90
  - globe — *see* Disorder, globe
  - ill-defined NEC 379.99
  - limited duction NEC 378.63
  - specified NEC 379.8
- eyelid 374.9
  - degenerative 374.50
  - sensory 374.44
  - specified type NEC 374.89
  - vascular 374.85
- factitious (with combined psychological and physical signs and symptoms) (with predominantly physical signs and symptoms) 300.19
  - with predominantly psychological signs and symptoms 300.16
- factor, coagulation (*see also* Defect, coagulation) 286.9
  - IX (congenital) (funcitonal) 286.1
  - VIII (congenital) (functional) 286.0
- fascia 728.9
- fatty acid oxidation 277.85
- feeding — *see* Feeding
- female sexual arousal 302.72
- fluid NEC 276.9
- gastric (functional) 536.9
  - motility 536.8
  - psychogenic 306.4
  - secretion 536.8
- gastrointestinal (functional) NEC 536.9
  - newborn (neonatal) 777.9
    - specified NEC 777.8
  - psychogenic 306.4
- gender (child) 302.6
  - adult 302.85
- gender identity (childhood) 302.6
  - adolescents 302.85
  - adults (-life) 302.85
- genitourinary system, psychogenic 306.50
- globe 360.9

Disorder — *see also* Disease — *continued*

- globe — *continued*
  - degenerative 360.20
    - specified NEC 360.29
  - specified type NEC 360.89
- hearing (*see also* Deafness)
  - conductive type (air) (*see also* Deafness, conductive) 389.00
  - mixed conductive and sensorineural 389.20
    - bilateral 389.22
    - unilateral 389.21
  - nerve
    - bilateral 389.12
    - unilateral 389.13
  - perceptive (*see also* Deafness, perceptive) 389.10
  - sensorineural type NEC (*see also* Deafness, sensorineural 389.10
- heart action 427.9
  - postoperative 997.1
- hematological, transient neonatal 776.9
  - specified type NEC 776.8
- hematopoietic organs 289.9
- hemorrhagic NEC 287.9
  - due to intrinsic circulating anticoagulants 286.5
  - specified type NEC 287.8
- hemostasis (*see also* Defect, coagulation) 286.9
- homosexual conflict 302.0
- hypomanic (chronic) 301.11
- identity
  - childhood and adolescence 313.82
  - gender 302.6
- immune mechanism (immunity) 279.9
  - single complement (C1-C9) 279.8
  - specified type NEC 279.8
- impulse control (*see also* Disturbance, conduct, compulsive) 312.30
- infant sialic acid storage 271.8
- integument, fetus or newborn 778.9
  - specified type NEC 778.8
- interactional psychotic (childhood) (*see also* Psychosis, childhood) 299.1 ☑
- intermittent explosive 312.34
- intervertebral disc 722.90
  - cervical, cervicothoracic 722.91
  - lumbar, lumbosacral 722.93
  - thoracic, thoracolumbar 722.92
- intestinal 569.9
  - functional NEC 564.9
    - congenital 751.3
    - postoperative 564.4
  - psychogenic 306.4
- introverted, of childhood and adolescence 313.22
- involuntary emotional expression (IEED) 310.8
- iris 364.9
  - specified NEC 364.89
- iron, metabolism 275.0
- isolated explosive 312.35
- joint NEC 719.90
  - ankle 719.97
  - elbow 719.92
  - foot 719.97
  - hand 719.94
  - hip 719.95
  - knee 719.96
  - multiple sites 719.99
  - pelvic region 719.95
  - psychogenic 306.0
  - shoulder (region) 719.91
  - specified site NEC 719.98
  - temporomandibular 524.60
    - sounds on opening or closing 524.64
    - specified NEC 524.69
  - wrist 719.93
- kidney 593.9
  - functional 588.9

Disorder — *see also* Disease — *continued*

- kidney — *continued*
  - functional — *continued*
    - specified NEC 588.89
- labyrinth, labyrinthine 386.9
  - specified type NEC 386.8
- lactation 676.9 ☑
- language (developmental) (expressive) 315.31
  - mixed receptive-expressive 315.32
- learning 315.9
- ligament 728.9
- ligamentous attachments, peripheral (*see also* Enthesopathy)
  - spine 720.1
- limb NEC 729.90 ▲
  - psychogenic 306.0
- lipid
  - metabolism, congenital 272.9
  - storage 272.7
- lipoprotein deficiency (familial) 272.5
- low back NEC 724.9
  - psychogenic 306.0
- lumbosacral
  - plexus 353.1
  - root (nerve) NEC 353.4
- lymphoproliferative (chronic) NEC (M9970/1) 238.79
  - post-transplant (PTLD) 238.77 ●
- major depressive (*see also* Psychosis, affective) 296.2 ☑
  - recurrent episode 296.3 ☑
  - single episode 296.2 ☑
- male erectile 607.84
  - nonorganic origin 302.72
- manic (*see also* Psychosis, affective) 296.0 ☑
  - atypical 296.81
- mathematics 315.1
- meniscus NEC (*see also* Disorder, cartilage, articular) 718.0 ☑
- menopausal 627.9
  - specified NEC 627.8
- menstrual 626.9
  - psychogenic 306.52
  - specified NEC 626.8
- mental (nonpsychotic) 300.9
  - affecting management of pregnancy, childbirth, or puerperium 648.4 ☑
  - drug-induced 292.9
    - hallucinogen persisting perception 292.89
    - specified type NEC 292.89
  - due to or associated with
    - alcoholism 291.9
    - drug consumption NEC 292.9
      - specified type NEC 292.89
    - physical condition NEC 293.9
  - induced by drug 292.9
    - specified type NEC 292.89
  - neurotic (*see also* Neurosis) 300.9
  - of infancy, childhood or adolescence 313.9
  - persistent
    - other
      - due to conditions classified elsewhere 294.8
    - unspecified
      - due to conditions classified elsewhere 294.9
  - presenile 310.1
    - psychotic NEC 290.10
  - previous, affecting management of pregnancy V23.89
  - psychoneurotic (*see also* Neurosis) 300.9
  - psychotic (*see also* Psychosis) 298.9
    - brief 298.8
    - senile 290.20
  - specific, following organic brain damage 310.9
    - cognitive or personality change of other type 310.1

Disorder — *see also* Disease — *continued*

- mental — *continued*
  - specific, following organic brain damage — *continued*
    - frontal lobe syndrome 310.0
    - postconcussional syndrome 310.2
    - specified type NEC 310.8
  - transient
    - in conditions classified elsewhere 293.9
- metabolism NEC 277.9
  - with
    - abortion — *see* Abortion, by type, with metabolic disorder
    - ectopic pregnancy (*see also* categories 633.0–633.9) 639.4
    - molar pregnancy (*see also* categories 630–632) 639.4
  - alkaptonuria 270.2
  - amino acid (*see also* Disorder, amino acid) 270.9
    - specified type NEC 270.8
  - ammonia 270.6
  - arginine 270.6
  - argininosuccinic acid 270.6
  - basal 794.7
  - bilirubin 277.4
  - calcium 275.40
  - carbohydrate 271.9
    - specified type NEC 271.8
  - cholesterol 272.9
  - citrulline 270.6
  - copper 275.1
  - corticosteroid 255.2
  - cystine storage 270.0
  - cystinuria 270.0
  - fat 272.9
  - fatty acid oxidation 277.85
  - following
    - abortion 639.4
    - ectopic or molar pregnancy 639.4
  - fructosemia 271.2
  - fructosuria 271.2
  - fucosidosis 271.8
  - galactose-1-phosphate uridyl transferase 271.1
  - glutamine 270.7
  - glycine 270.7
  - glycogen storage NEC 271.0
    - hepatorenal 271.0
  - hemochromatosis 275.0
  - in labor and delivery 669.0 ☑
  - iron 275.0
  - lactose 271.3
  - lipid 272.9
    - specified type NEC 272.8
    - storage 272.7
  - lipoprotein (*see also* Hyperlipemia deficiency (familial)) 272.5
  - lysine 270.7
  - magnesium 275.2
  - mannosidosis 271.8
  - mineral 275.9
    - specified type NEC 275.8
  - mitochondrial 277.87
  - mucopolysaccharide 277.5
  - nitrogen 270.9
  - ornithine 270.6
  - oxalosis 271.8
  - pentosuria 271.8
  - phenylketonuria 270.1
  - phosphate 275.3
  - phosphorous 275.3
  - plasma protein 273.9
    - specified type NEC 273.8
  - porphyrin 277.1
  - purine 277.2
  - pyrimidine 277.2
  - serine 270.7
  - sodium 276.9
  - specified type NEC 277.89

- **Disorder** — *see also* Disease — *continued*
  - metabolism — *continued*
    - steroid 255.2
    - threonine 270.7
    - urea cycle 270.6
    - xylose 271.8
  - micturition NEC 788.69
    - psychogenic 306.53
  - misery and unhappiness, of childhood and adolescence 313.1
  - mitochondrial metabolism 277.87
  - mitral valve 424.0
  - mood (*see also* Disorder, bipolar) 296.90
    - episodic 296.90
      - specified NEC 296.99
    - in conditions classified elsewhere 293.83
  - motor tic 307.20
    - chronic 307.22
    - transient (childhood) 307.21
  - movement NEC 333.90
    - hysterical 300.11
    - medication-induced 333.90
    - periodic limb 327.51
    - sleep related, unspecified 780.58
      - other organic 327.59
    - specified type NEC 333.99
    - stereotypic 307.3
  - mucopolysaccharide 277.5
  - muscle 728.9
    - psychogenic 306.0
    - specified type NEC 728.3
  - muscular attachments, peripheral (*see also* Enthesopathy)
    - spine 720.1
  - musculoskeletal system NEC 729.90 ▲
    - psychogenic 306.0
  - myeloproliferative (chronic) NEC (M9960/1) 238.79
  - myoneural 358.9
    - due to lead 358.2
    - specified type NEC 358.8
    - toxic 358.2
  - myotonic 359.29
  - neck region NEC 723.9
  - nerve 349.9
    - abducens NEC 378.54
    - accessory 352.4
    - acoustic 388.5
    - auditory 388.5
    - auriculotemporal 350.8
    - axillary 353.0
    - cerebral — *see* Disorder, nerve, cranial
    - cranial 352.9
      - first 352.0
      - second 377.49
      - third
        - partial 378.51
        - total 378.52
      - fourth 378.53
      - fifth 350.9
      - sixth 378.54
      - seventh NEC 351.9
      - eighth 388.5
      - ninth 352.2
      - tenth 352.3
      - eleventh 352.4
      - twelfth 352.5
      - multiple 352.6
    - entrapment — *see* Neuropathy, entrapment
    - facial 351.9
      - specified NEC 351.8
    - femoral 355.2
    - glossopharyngeal NEC 352.2
    - hypoglossal 352.5
    - iliohypogastric 355.79
    - ilioinguinal 355.79
    - intercostal 353.8
    - lateral
      - cutaneous of thigh 355.1
      - popliteal 355.3
    - lower limb NEC 355.8
    - medial, popliteal 355.4
    - median NEC 354.1
    - obturator 355.79
    - oculomotor
      - partial 378.51
      - total 378.52
    - olfactory 352.0
    - optic 377.49
      - hypoplasia 377.43
      - ischemic 377.41
      - nutritional 377.33
      - toxic 377.34
    - peroneal 355.3
    - phrenic 354.8
    - plantar 355.6
    - pneumogastric 352.3
    - posterior tibial 355.5
    - radial 354.3
    - recurrent laryngeal 352.3
    - root 353.9
      - specified NEC 353.8
    - saphenous 355.79
    - sciatic NEC 355.0
    - specified NEC 355.9
      - lower limb 355.79
      - upper limb 354.8
    - spinal 355.9
    - sympathetic NEC 337.9
    - trigeminal 350.9
      - specified NEC 350.8
    - trochlear 378.53
    - ulnar 354.2
    - upper limb NEC 354.9
    - vagus 352.3
  - nervous system NEC 349.9
    - autonomic (peripheral) (*see also* Neuropathy, peripheral, autonomic) 337.9
    - cranial 352.9
    - parasympathetic (*see also* Neuropathy, peripheral, autonomic) 337.9
    - specified type NEC 349.89
    - sympathetic (*see also* Neuropathy, peripheral, autonomic) 337.9
    - vegetative (*see also* Neuropathy, peripheral, autonomic) 337.9
  - neurohypophysis NEC 253.6
  - neurological NEC 781.99
    - peripheral NEC 355.9
  - neuromuscular NEC 358.9
    - hereditary NEC 359.1
    - specified NEC 358.8
    - toxic 358.2
  - neurotic 300.9
    - specified type NEC 300.89
  - neutrophil, polymorphonuclear (functional) 288.1
  - nightmare 307.47
  - night terror 307.46
  - obsessive-compulsive 300.3
  - oppositional defiant, childhood and adolescence 313.81
  - optic
    - chiasm 377.54
      - associated with
        - inflammatory disorders 377.54
        - neoplasm NEC 377.52
          - pituitary 377.51
        - pituitary disorders 377.51
        - vascular disorders 377.53
    - nerve 377.49
    - radiations 377.63
    - tracts 377.63
  - orbit 376.9
    - specified NEC 376.89
  - orgasmic
    - female 302.73
    - male 302.74
  - overanxious, of childhood and adolescence 313.0
  - oxidation, fatty acid 277.85
  - pancreas, internal secretion (other than diabetes mellitus) 251.9
    - specified type NEC 251.8
  - panic 300.01
    - with agoraphobia 300.21
  - papillary muscle NEC 429.81
  - paranoid 297.9
    - induced 297.3
    - shared 297.3
  - parathyroid 252.9
    - specified type NEC 252.8
  - paroxysmal, mixed 780.39
  - pentose phosphate pathway with anemia 282.2
  - periodic limb movement 327.51
  - peroxisomal 277.86
  - personality 301.9
    - affective 301.10
    - aggressive 301.3
    - amoral 301.7
    - anancastic, anankastic 301.4
    - antisocial 301.7
    - asocial 301.7
    - asthenic 301.6
    - avoidant 301.82
    - borderline 301.83
    - compulsive 301.4
    - cyclothymic 301.13
    - dependent-passive 301.6
    - dyssocial 301.7
    - emotional instability 301.59
    - epileptoid 301.3
    - explosive 301.3
    - following organic brain damage 310.1
    - histrionic 301.50
    - hyperthymic 301.11
    - hypomanic (chronic) 301.11
    - hypothymic 301.12
    - hysterical 301.50
    - immature 301.89
    - inadequate 301.6
    - introverted 301.21
    - labile 301.59
    - moral deficiency 301.7
    - narcissistic 301.81
    - obsessional 301.4
    - obsessive-compulsive 301.4
    - overconscientious 301.4
    - paranoid 301.0
    - passive (-dependent) 301.6
    - passive-aggressive 301.84
    - pathological NEC 301.9
    - pseudosocial 301.7
    - psychopathic 301.9
    - schizoid 301.20
      - introverted 301.21
      - schizotypal 301.22
    - schizotypal 301.22
    - seductive 301.59
    - type A 301.4
    - unstable 301.59
  - pervasive developmental 299.9 ☑
    - childhood-onset 299.8 ☑
    - specified NEC 299.8 ☑
  - phonological 315.39
  - pigmentation, choroid (congenital) 743.53
  - pinna 380.30
    - specified type NEC 380.39
  - pituitary, thalamic 253.9
    - anterior NEC 253.4
    - iatrogenic 253.7
    - postablative 253.7
    - specified NEC 253.8
  - pityriasis-like NEC 696.8
  - platelets (blood) 287.1
  - polymorphonuclear neutrophils (functional) 288.1
  - porphyrin metabolism 277.1
  - postmenopausal 627.9
    - specified type NEC 627.8
  - post-transplant lymphoproliferative (PTLD) 238.77 ●
  - posttraumatic stress 309.81
  - post-traumatic stress (PTSD) 309.81
    - acute 309.81
    - brief 309.81
    - chronic 309.81
  - premenstrual dysphoric (PMDD) 625.4
  - psoriatic-like NEC 696.8
  - psychic, with diseases classified elsewhere 316
  - psychogenic NEC (*see also* condition) 300.9
    - allergic NEC
      - respiratory 306.1
    - anxiety 300.00
      - atypical 300.00
      - generalized 300.02
    - appetite 307.59
    - articulation, joint 306.0
    - asthenic 300.5
    - blood 306.8
    - cardiovascular (system) 306.2
    - compulsive 300.3
    - cutaneous 306.3
    - depressive 300.4
    - digestive (system) 306.4
    - dysmenorrheic 306.52
    - dyspneic 306.1
    - eczematous 306.3
    - endocrine (system) 306.6
    - eye 306.7
    - feeding 307.59
    - functional NEC 306.9
    - gastric 306.4
    - gastrointestinal (system) 306.4
    - genitourinary (system) 306.50
    - heart (function) (rhythm) 306.2
    - hemic 306.8
    - hyperventilatory 306.1
    - hypochondriacal 300.7
    - hysterical 300.10
    - intestinal 306.4
    - joint 306.0
    - learning 315.2
    - limb 306.0
    - lymphatic (system) 306.8
    - menstrual 306.52
    - micturition 306.53
    - monoplegic NEC 306.0
    - motor 307.9
    - muscle 306.0
    - musculoskeletal 306.0
    - neurocirculatory 306.2
    - obsessive 300.3
    - occupational 300.89
    - organ or part of body NEC 306.9
    - organs of special sense 306.7
    - paralytic NEC 306.0
    - phobic 300.20
    - physical NEC 306.9
    - pruritic 306.3
    - rectal 306.4
    - respiratory (system) 306.1
    - rheumatic 306.0
    - sexual (function) 302.70
      - specified type NEC 302.79
    - sexual orientation conflict 302.0
    - skin (allergic) (eczematous) (pruritic) 306.3
    - sleep 307.40
      - initiation or maintenance 307.41
        - persistent 307.42
        - transient 307.41
      - movement 780.58
      - sleep terror 307.46
      - specified type NEC 307.49
    - specified part of body NEC 306.8
    - stomach 306.4
  - psychomotor NEC 307.9
    - hysterical 300.11
  - psychoneurotic (*see also* Neurosis) 300.9

☑ Additional Digit Required — Refer to the Tabular List for Digit Selection
Subterms under main terms may continue to next column or page
▶◀ Revised Text ● New Line ▲ Revised Code

- **Disorder** — *see also* Disease — *continued*
  - psychoneurotic (*see also* Neurosis) — *continued*
    - mixed NEC 300.89
  - psychophysiologic (*see also* Disorder, psychosomatic) 306.9
  - psychosexual identity (childhood) 302.6
    - adult-life 302.85
  - psychosomatic NEC 306.9
    - allergic NEC
      - respiratory 306.1
    - articulation, joint 306.0
    - cardiovascular (system) 306.2
    - cutaneous 306.3
    - digestive (system) 306.4
    - dysmenorrheic 306.52
    - dyspneic 306.1
    - endocrine (system) 306.6
    - eye 306.7
    - gastric 306.4
    - gastrointestinal (system) 306.4
    - genitourinary (system) 306.50
    - heart (functional) (rhythm) 306.2
    - hyperventilatory 306.1
    - intestinal 306.4
    - joint 306.0
    - limb 306.0
    - lymphatic (system) 306.8
    - menstrual 306.52
    - micturition 306.53
    - monoplegic NEC 306.0
    - muscle 306.0
    - musculoskeletal 306.0
    - neurocirculatory 306.2
    - organs of special sense 306.7
    - paralytic NEC 306.0
    - pruritic 306.3
    - rectal 306.4
    - respiratory (system) 306.1
    - rheumatic 306.0
    - sexual (function) 302.70
    - skin 306.3
    - specified part of body NEC 306.8
    - specified type NEC 302.79
    - stomach 306.4
  - psychotic (*see also* Psychosis) 298.9
    - brief 298.8
  - purine metabolism NEC 277.2
  - pyrimidine metabolism NEC 277.2
  - reactive attachment of infancy or early childhood 313.89
  - reading, developmental 315.00
  - reflex 796.1
  - REM sleep behavior 327.42
  - renal function, impaired 588.9
    - specified type NEC 588.89
  - renal transport NEC 588.89
  - respiration, respiratory NEC 519.9
    - due to
      - aspiration of liquids or solids 508.9
      - inhalation of fumes or vapors 506.9
    - psychogenic 306.1
  - retina 362.9
    - specified type NEC 362.89
  - rumination 307.53
  - sacroiliac joint NEC 724.6
  - sacrum 724.6
  - schizo-affective (*see also* Schizophrenia) 295.7 ☑
  - schizoid, childhood or adolescence 313.22
  - schizophreniform 295.4 ☑
  - schizotypal personality 301.22
  - secretion, thyrocalcitonin 246.0
  - seizure 345.9 ☑
    - recurrent 345.9 ☑
      - epileptic — *see* Epilepsy
  - semantic pragmatic 315.39 ●
    - with autism 299.0 ☑ ●
  - sense of smell 781.1
    - psychogenic 306.7
  - separation anxiety 309.21
- **Disorder** — *see also* Disease — *continued*
  - sexual (*see also* Deviation, sexual) 302.9
    - aversion 302.79
    - desire, hypoactive 302.71
    - function, psychogenic 302.70
  - shyness, of childhood and adolescence 313.21
  - single complement (C1-C9) 279.8
  - skin NEC 709.9
    - fetus or newborn 778.9
      - specified type 778.8
    - psychogenic (allergic) (eczematous) (pruritic) 306.3
    - specified type NEC 709.8
    - vascular 709.1
  - sleep 780.50
    - with apnea — *see* Apnea, sleep
    - alcohol induced 291.82
    - arousal 307.46
      - confusional 327.41
    - circadian rhythm 327.30
      - advanced sleep phase type 327.32
      - alcohol induced 291.82
      - delayed sleep phase type 327.31
      - drug induced 292.85
      - free running type 327.34
      - in conditions classified elsewhere 327.37
      - irregular sleep-wake type 327.33
      - jet lag type 327.35
      - other 327.39
      - shift work type 327.36
    - drug induced 292.85
    - initiation or maintenance (*see also* Insomnia) 780.52
      - nonorganic origin (transient) 307.41
        - persistent 307.42
    - nonorganic origin 307.40
      - specified type NEC 307.49
    - organic specified type NEC 327.8
    - periodic limb movement 327.51
    - specified NEC 780.59
    - wake
      - cycle — *see* Disorder, sleep, circadian rhythm
      - schedule — *see* Disorer, sleep, circadian rhythm
  - social, of childhood and adolescence 313.22
  - soft tissue 729.90 ▲
    - specified type NEC 729.99 ●
  - somatization 300.81
  - somatoform (atypical) (undifferentiated) 300.82
    - severe 300.81
    - specified type NEC 300.89
  - speech NEC 784.5
    - nonorganic origin 307.9
  - spine NEC 724.9
    - ligamentous or muscular attachments, peripheral 720.1
  - steroid metabolism NEC 255.2
  - stomach (functional) (*see also* Disorder, gastric) 536.9
    - psychogenic 306.4
  - storage, iron 275.0
  - stress (*see also* Reaction, stress, acute) 308.3
    - posttraumatic
      - acute 309.81
      - brief 309.81
      - chronic 309.81
  - substitution 300.11
  - suspected — *see* Observation
  - synovium 727.9
  - temperature regulation, fetus or newborn 778.4
  - temporomandibular joint NEC 524.60
    - sounds on opening or closing 524.64
    - specified NEC 524.69
- **Disorder** — *see also* Disease — *continued*
  - tendon 727.9
    - shoulder region 726.10
  - thoracic root (nerve) NEC 353.3
  - thyrocalcitonin secretion 246.0
  - thyroid (gland) NEC 246.9
    - specified type NEC 246.8
  - tic 307.20
    - chronic (motor or vocal) 307.22
    - motor-verbal 307.23
    - organic origin 333.1
    - transient (of childhood) 307.21
  - tooth NEC 525.9
    - development NEC 520.9
      - specified type NEC 520.8
    - eruption 520.6
    - specified type NEC 525.8
  - Tourette's 307.23
  - transport, carbohydrate 271.9
    - specified type NEC 271.8
  - tubular, phosphate-losing 588.0
  - tympanic membrane 384.9
  - unaggressive, unsocialized (*see also* Disturbance, conduct) 312.1 ☑
  - undersocialized, unsocialized (*see also* Disturbance, conduct)
    - aggressive (type) 312.0 ☑
    - unaggressive (type) 312.1 ☑
  - vision, visual NEC 368.9
    - binocular NEC 368.30
    - cortex 377.73
      - associated with
        - inflammatory disorders 377.73
        - neoplasms 377.71
        - vascular disorders 377.72
    - pathway NEC 377.63
      - associated with
        - inflammatory disorders 377.63
        - neoplasms 377.61
        - vascular disorders 377.62
  - vocal tic
    - chronic 307.22
  - wakefulness (*see also* Hypersomnia) 780.54
    - nonorganic origin (transient) 307.43
      - persistent 307.44
  - written expression 315.2
- **Disorganized globe** 360.29
- **Displacement, displaced**

> *Note — For acquired displacement of bones, cartilage, joints, tendons, due to injury, see also Dislocation.*
>
> *Displacements at ages under one year should be considered congenital, provided there is no indication the condition was acquired after birth.*

  - acquired traumatic of bone, cartilage, joint, tendon NEC (without fracture) (*see also* Dislocation) 839.8
    - with fracture — *see* Fracture, by site
  - adrenal gland (congenital) 759.1
  - alveolus and teeth, vertical 524.75
  - appendix, retrocecal (congenital) 751.5
  - auricle (congenital) 744.29
  - bladder (acquired) 596.8
    - congenital 753.8
  - brachial plexus (congenital) 742.8
  - brain stem, caudal 742.4
  - canaliculus lacrimalis 743.65
  - cardia, through esophageal hiatus 750.6
  - cerebellum, caudal 742.4
  - cervix — *see* Displacement, uterus
  - colon (congenital) 751.4
  - device, implant, or graft — *see* Complications, mechanical
  - epithelium
    - columnar of cervix 622.10
- **Displacement, displaced** — *continued*
  - epithelium — *continued*
    - cuboidal, beyond limits of external os (uterus) 752.49
  - esophageal mucosa into cardia of stomach, congenital 750.4
  - esophagus (acquired) 530.89
    - congenital 750.4
  - eyeball (acquired) (old) 376.36
    - congenital 743.8
    - current injury 871.3
    - lateral 376.36
  - fallopian tube (acquired) 620.4
    - congenital 752.19
    - opening (congenital) 752.19
  - gallbladder (congenital) 751.69
  - gastric mucosa 750.7
    - into
      - duodenum 750.7
      - esophagus 750.7
      - Meckel's diverticulum, congenital 750.7
  - globe (acquired) (lateral) (old) 376.36
    - current injury 871.3
  - graft
    - artificial skin graft 996.55
    - decellularized allodermis graft 996.55
  - heart (congenital) 746.87
    - acquired 429.89
  - hymen (congenital) (upward) 752.49
  - internal prosthesis NEC — *see* Complications, mechanical
  - intervertebral disc (with neuritis, radiculitis, sciatica, or other pain) 722.2
    - with myelopathy 722.70
    - cervical, cervicodorsal, cervicothoracic 722.0
      - with myelopathy 722.71
      - due to major trauma — *see* Dislocation, vertebra, cervical
    - due to trauma — *see* Dislocation, vertebra
    - lumbar, lumbosacral 722.10
      - with myelopathy 722.73
      - due to major trauma — *see* Dislocation, vertebra, lumbar
    - thoracic, thoracolumbar 722.11
      - with myelopathy 722.72
      - due to major trauma — *see* Dislocation, vertebra, thoracic
  - intrauterine device 996.32
  - kidney (acquired) 593.0
    - congenital 753.3
  - lacrimal apparatus or duct (congenital) 743.65
  - macula (congenital) 743.55
  - Meckel's diverticulum (congenital) 751.0
  - nail (congenital) 757.5
    - acquired 703.8
  - opening of Wharton's duct in mouth 750.26
  - organ or site, congenital NEC — *see* Malposition, congenital
  - ovary (acquired) 620.4
    - congenital 752.0
    - free in peritoneal cavity (congenital) 752.0
    - into hernial sac 620.4
  - oviduct (acquired) 620.4
    - congenital 752.19
  - parathyroid (gland) 252.8
  - parotid gland (congenital) 750.26
  - punctum lacrimale (congenital) 743.65
  - sacroiliac (congenital) (joint) 755.69
    - current injury — *see* Dislocation, sacroiliac
    - old 724.6
  - spine (congenital) 756.19
  - spleen, congenital 759.0

Displacement, displaced — *continued*
stomach (congenital) 750.7
acquired 537.89
subglenoid (closed) 831.01
sublingual duct (congenital) 750.26
teeth, tooth 524.30
horizontal 524.33
vertical 524.34
tongue (congenital) (downward) 750.19
trachea (congenital) 748.3
ureter or ureteric opening or orifice (congenital) 753.4
uterine opening of oviducts or fallopian tubes 752.19
uterus, uterine (*see also* Malposition, uterus) 621.6
congenital 752.3
ventricular septum 746.89
with rudimentary ventricle 746.89
xyphoid bone (process) 738.3
Disproportion 653.9 ☑
affecting fetus or newborn 763.1
breast, reconstructed 612.1 ●
between native and reconstructed 612.1 ●
caused by
conjoined twins 678.1 ☑ ▲
contraction, pelvis (general) 653.1 ☑
inlet 653.2 ☑
midpelvic 653.8 ☑
midplane 653.8 ☑
outlet 653.3 ☑
fetal
ascites 653.7 ☑
hydrocephalus 653.6 ☑
hydrops 653.7 ☑
meningomyelocele 653.7 ☑
sacral teratoma 653.7 ☑
tumor 653.7 ☑
hydrocephalic fetus 653.6 ☑
pelvis, pelvic, abnormality (bony) NEC 653.0 ☑
unusually large fetus 653.5 ☑
causing obstructed labor 660.1 ☑
cephalopelvic, normally formed fetus 653.4 ☑
causing obstructed labor 660.1 ☑
fetal NEC 653.5 ☑
causing obstructed labor 660.1 ☑
fetopelvic, normally formed fetus 653.4 ☑
causing obstructed labor 660.1 ☑
mixed maternal and fetal origin, normally formed fetus 653.4 ☑
pelvis, pelvic (bony) NEC 653.1 ☑
causing obstructed labor 660.1 ☑
specified type NEC 653.8 ☑
Disruption
cesarean wound 674.1 ☑
family V61.09 ▲
due to ●
child in ●
care of non-parental family member V61.06 ●
foster care V61.06 ●
welfare custody V61.05 ●
divorce V61.03 ●
estrangement V61.09 ●
parent-child V61.04 ●
family member ●
on military deployment V61.01 ●
return from military deployment V61.02 ●
legal separation V61.03 ●
gastrointestinal anastomosis 997.4
ligament(s) (*see also* Sprain)
knee
current injury — *see* Dislocation, knee
old 717.89
capsular 717.85
collateral (medial) 717.82
lateral 717.81
Disruption — *continued*
ligament(s) (*see also* Sprain) — *continued*
knee — *continued*
old — *continued*
cruciate (posterior) 717.84
anterior 717.83
specified site NEC 717.85
marital V61.10
involving
divorce V61.03 ●
estrangement V61.09 ●
operation wound (external) ▶(*see also* Dehiscence)◀ 998.32
internal 998.31
organ transplant, anastomosis site — *see* Complications, transplant, organ, by site
ossicles, ossicular chain 385.23
traumatic — *see* Fracture, skull, base
parenchyma
liver (hepatic) — *see* Laceration, liver, major
spleen — *see* Laceration, spleen, parenchyma, massive
phase-shift, of 24-hour sleep-wake cycle, unspecified 780.55
nonorganic origin 307.45
sleep-wake cycle (24-hour), unspecified 780.55
circadian rhythm 327.33
nonorganic origin 307.45
suture line (external) ▶(*see also* Dehiscence)◀ 998.32
internal 998.31
wound 998.30 ▲
cesarean operation 674.1 ☑
episiotomy 674.2 ☑
operation ▶(surgical)◀ 998.32
cesarean 674.1 ☑
internal 998.31
perineal (obstetric) 674.2 ☑
uterine 674.1 ☑
Disruptio uteri — *see also* Rupture, uterus
complicating delivery — *see* Delivery, complicated, rupture, uterus
Dissatisfaction with
employment V62.29 ▲
school environment V62.3
Dissecting — *see* condition
Dissection
aorta 441.00
abdominal 441.02
thoracic 441.01
thoracoabdominal 441.03
artery, arterial
carotid 443.21
coronary 414.12
iliac 443.22
renal 443.23
specified NEC 443.29
vertebral 443.24
vascular 459.9
wound — *see* Wound, open, by site
Disseminated — *see* condition
Dissociated personality NEC 300.15
Dissociation
auriculoventricular or atrioventricular (any degree) (AV) 426.89
with heart block 426.0
interference 426.89
isorhythmic 426.89
rhythm
atrioventricular (AV) 426.89
interference 426.89
Dissociative
identity disorder 300.14
reaction NEC 300.15
Dissolution, vertebra — *see also* Osteoporosis 733.00
Distention
abdomen (gaseous) 787.3
bladder 596.8
cecum 569.89
Distention — *continued*
colon 569.89
gallbladder 575.8
gaseous (abdomen) 787.3
intestine 569.89
kidney 593.89
liver 573.9
seminal vesicle 608.89
stomach 536.8
acute 536.1
psychogenic 306.4
ureter 593.5
uterus 621.8
Distichia, distichiasis (eyelid) 743.63
Distoma hepaticum infestation 121.3
Distomiasis 121.9
bile passages 121.3
due to Clonorchis sinensis 121.1
hemic 120.9
hepatic (liver) 121.3
due to Clonorchis sinensis (clonorchiasis) 121.1
intestinal 121.4
liver 121.3
due to Clonorchis sinensis 121.1
lung 121.2
pulmonary 121.2
Distomolar (fourth molar) 520.1
causing crowding 524.31
Disto-occlusion (division I) (division II) 524.22
Distortion (congenital)
adrenal (gland) 759.1
ankle (joint) 755.69
anus 751.5
aorta 747.29
appendix 751.5
arm 755.59
artery (peripheral) NEC (*see also* Distortion, peripheral vascular system) 747.60
cerebral 747.81
coronary 746.85
pulmonary 747.3
retinal 743.58
umbilical 747.5
auditory canal 744.29
causing impairment of hearing 744.02
bile duct or passage 751.69
bladder 753.8
brain 742.4
bronchus 748.3
cecum 751.5
cervix (uteri) 752.49
chest (wall) 756.3
clavicle 755.51
clitoris 752.49
coccyx 756.19
colon 751.5
common duct 751.69
cornea 743.41
cricoid cartilage 748.3
cystic duct 751.69
duodenum 751.5
ear 744.29
auricle 744.29
causing impairment of hearing 744.02
causing impairment of hearing 744.09
external 744.29
causing impairment of hearing 744.02
inner 744.05
middle, except ossicles 744.03
ossicles 744.04
ossicles 744.04
endocrine (gland) NEC 759.2
epiglottis 748.3
Eustachian tube 744.24
eye 743.8
adnexa 743.69
face bone(s) 756.0
fallopian tube 752.19
femur 755.69
Distortion — *continued*
fibula 755.69
finger(s) 755.59
foot 755.67
gallbladder 751.69
genitalia, genital organ(s)
female 752.89
external 752.49
internal NEC 752.89
male 752.89
penis 752.69
glottis 748.3
gyri 742.4
hand bone(s) 755.59
heart (auricle) (ventricle) 746.89
valve (cusp) 746.89
hepatic duct 751.69
humerus 755.59
hymen 752.49
ileum 751.5
intestine (large) (small) 751.5
with anomalous adhesions, fixation or malrotation 751.4
jaw NEC 524.89
jejunum 751.5
kidney 753.3
knee (joint) 755.64
labium (majus) (minus) 752.49
larynx 748.3
leg 755.69
lens 743.36
liver 751.69
lumbar spine 756.19
with disproportion (fetopelvic) 653.0 ☑
affecting fetus or newborn 763.1
causing obstructed labor 660.1 ☑
lumbosacral (joint) (region) 756.19
lung (fissures) (lobe) 748.69
nerve 742.8
nose 748.1
organ
of Corti 744.05
of site not listed — *see* Anomaly, specified type NEC
ossicles, ear 744.04
ovary 752.0
oviduct 752.19
pancreas 751.7
parathyroid (gland) 759.2
patella 755.64
peripheral vascular system NEC 747.60
gastrointestinal 747.61
lower limb 747.64
renal 747.62
spinal 747.82
upper limb 747.63
pituitary (gland) 759.2
radius 755.59
rectum 751.5
rib 756.3
sacroiliac joint 755.69
sacrum 756.19
scapula 755.59
shoulder girdle 755.59
site not listed — *see* Anomaly, specified type NEC
skull bone(s) 756.0
with
anencephalus 740.0
encephalocele 742.0
hydrocephalus 742.3
with spina bifida (*see also* Spina bifida) 741.0 ☑
microcephalus 742.1
spinal cord 742.59
spine 756.19
spleen 759.0
sternum 756.3
thorax (wall) 756.3
thymus (gland) 759.2
thyroid (gland) 759.2
cartilage 748.3
tibia 755.69

Index

Displacement, displaced — Distortion

☑ Additional Digit Required — Refer to the Tabular List for Digit Selection
Subterms under main terms may continue to next column or page

Distortion — *continued*
- toe(s) 755.66
- tongue 750.19
- trachea (cartilage) 748.3
- ulna 755.59
- ureter 753.4
  - causing obstruction 753.20
- urethra 753.8
  - causing obstruction 753.6
- uterus 752.3
- vagina 752.49
- vein (peripheral) NEC (*see also* Distortion, peripheral vascular system) 747.60
  - great 747.49
  - portal 747.49
  - pulmonary 747.49
- vena cava (inferior) (superior) 747.49
- vertebra 756.19
- visual NEC 368.15
  - shape or size 368.14
- vulva 752.49
- wrist (bones) (joint) 755.59

Distress
- abdomen 789.0 ☑
- colon 564.9
- emotional V40.9
- epigastric 789.0 ☑
- fetal (syndrome) 768.4
  - affecting management of pregnancy or childbirth 656.8 ☑
  - liveborn infant 768.4
    - first noted
      - before onset of labor 768.2
      - during labor and delivery 768.3
  - stillborn infant (death before onset of labor) 768.0
    - death during labor 768.1
- gastrointestinal (functional) 536.9
  - psychogenic 306.4
- intestinal (functional) NEC 564.9
  - psychogenic 306.4
- intrauterine — *see* Distress, fetal
- leg 729.5
- maternal 669.0 ☑
- mental V40.9
- respiratory 786.09
  - acute (adult) 518.82
  - adult syndrome (following shock, surgery, or trauma) 518.5
    - specified NEC 518.82
  - fetus or newborn 770.89
  - syndrome (idiopathic) (newborn) 769
- stomach 536.9
  - psychogenic 306.4

Distribution vessel, atypical NEC 747.60
- coronary artery 746.85
- spinal 747.82

Districhiasis 704.2

Disturbance — *see also* Disease
- absorption NEC 579.9
  - calcium 269.3
  - carbohydrate 579.8
  - fat 579.8
  - protein 579.8
  - specified type NEC 579.8
  - vitamin (*see also* Deficiency, vitamin) 269.2
- acid-base equilibrium 276.9
- activity and attention, simple, with hyperkinesis 314.01
- amino acid (metabolic) (*see also* Disorder, amino acid) 270.9
  - imidazole 270.5
  - maple syrup (urine) disease 270.3
  - transport 270.0
- assimilation, food 579.9
- attention, simple 314.00
  - with hyperactivity 314.01
- auditory, nerve, except deafness 388.5
- behavior (*see also* Disturbance, conduct) 312.9

Disturbance — *see also* Disease — *continued*
- blood clotting (hypoproteinemia) (mechanism) (*see also* Defect, coagulation) 286.9
- central nervous system NEC 349.9
- cerebral nerve NEC 352.9
- circulatory 459.9
- conduct 312.9

> *Note — Use the following fifth-digit subclassification with categories 312.0–312.2:*
>
> *0 unspecified*
> *1 mild*
> *2 moderate*
> *3 severe*

  - adjustment reaction 309.3
  - adolescent onset type 312.82
  - childhood onset type 312.81
  - compulsive 312.30
    - intermittent explosive disorder 312.34
    - isolated explosive disorder 312.35
    - kleptomania 312.32
    - pathological gambling 312.31
    - pyromania 312.33
  - hyperkinetic 314.2
  - intermittent explosive 312.34
  - isolated explosive 312.35
  - mixed with emotions 312.4
  - socialized (type) 312.20
    - aggressive 312.23
    - unaggressive 312.21
  - specified type NEC 312.89
  - undersocialized, unsocialized
    - aggressive (type) 312.0 ☑
    - unaggressive (type) 312.1 ☑
- coordination 781.3
- cranial nerve NEC 352.9
- deep sensibility — *see* Disturbance, sensation
- digestive 536.9
  - psychogenic 306.4
- electrolyte — *see* Imbalance, electrolyte
- emotions specific to childhood or adolescence 313.9
  - with
    - academic underachievement 313.83
    - anxiety and fearfulness 313.0
    - elective mutism 313.23
    - identity disorder 313.82
    - jealousy 313.3
    - misery and unhappiness 313.1
    - oppositional defiant disorder 313.81
    - overanxiousness 313.0
    - sensitivity 313.21
    - shyness 313.21
    - social withdrawal 313.22
    - withdrawal reaction 313.22
  - involving relationship problems 313.3
  - mixed 313.89
  - specified type NEC 313.89
- endocrine (gland) 259.9
  - neonatal, transitory 775.9
    - specified NEC 775.89
- equilibrium 780.4
- feeding (elderly) (infant) 783.3
  - newborn 779.3
  - nonorganic origin NEC 307.59
  - psychogenic NEC 307.59
- fructose metabolism 271.2
- gait 781.2
  - hysterical 300.11
- gastric (functional) 536.9
  - motility 536.8
  - psychogenic 306.4
  - secretion 536.8
- gastrointestinal (functional) 536.9
  - psychogenic 306.4

Disturbance — *see also* Disease — *continued*
- habit, child 307.9
- hearing, except deafness 388.40
- heart, functional (conditions classifiable to 426, 427, 428)
  - due to presence of (cardiac) prosthesis 429.4
  - postoperative (immediate) 997.1
    - long-term effect of cardiac surgery 429.4
  - psychogenic 306.2
- hormone 259.9
- innervation uterus, sympathetic, parasympathetic 621.8
- keratinization NEC
  - gingiva 523.10
  - lip 528.5
  - oral (mucosa) (soft tissue) 528.79
    - residual ridge mucosa
      - excessive 528.72
      - minimal 528.71
  - tongue 528.79
- labyrinth, labyrinthine (vestibule) 386.9
- learning, specific NEC 315.2
- memory (*see also* Amnesia) 780.93
  - mild, following organic brain damage 310.8
- mental (*see also* Disorder, mental) 300.9
  - associated with diseases classified elsewhere 316
- metabolism (acquired) (congenital) (*see also* Disorder, metabolism) 277.9
  - with
    - abortion — *see* Abortion, by type, with metabolic disorder
    - ectopic pregnancy (*see also* categories 633.0–633.9) 639.4
    - molar pregnancy (*see also* categories 630–632) 639.4
  - amino acid (*see also* Disorder, amino acid) 270.9
    - aromatic NEC 270.2
    - branched-chain 270.3
    - specified type NEC 270.8
    - straight-chain NEC 270.7
    - sulfur-bearing 270.4
    - transport 270.0
  - ammonia 270.6
  - arginine 270.6
  - argininosuccinic acid 270.6
  - carbohydrate NEC 271.9
  - cholesterol 272.9
  - citrulline 270.6
  - cystathionine 270.4
  - fat 272.9
  - following
    - abortion 639.4
    - ectopic or molar pregnancy 639.4
  - general 277.9
    - carbohydrate 271.9
    - iron 275.0
    - phosphate 275.3
    - sodium 276.9
  - glutamine 270.7
  - glycine 270.7
  - histidine 270.5
  - homocystine 270.4
  - in labor or delivery 669.0 ☑
  - iron 275.0
  - isoleucine 270.3
  - leucine 270.3
  - lipoid 272.9
    - specified type NEC 272.8
  - lysine 270.7
  - methionine 270.4
  - neonatal, transitory 775.9
    - specified type NEC 775.89
  - nitrogen 788.99 ▲
  - ornithine 270.6

Disturbance — *see also* Disease — *continued*
- metabolism (*see also* Disorder, metabolism) — *continued*
  - phosphate 275.3
  - phosphatides 272.7
  - serine 270.7
  - sodium NEC 276.9
  - threonine 270.7
  - tryptophan 270.2
  - tyrosine 270.2
  - urea cycle 270.6
  - valine 270.3
- motor 796.1
- nervous functional 799.2
- neuromuscular mechanism (eye) due to syphilis 094.84
- nutritional 269.9
  - nail 703.8
- ocular motion 378.87
  - psychogenic 306.7
- oculogyric 378.87
  - psychogenic 306.7
- oculomotor NEC 378.87
  - psychogenic 306.7
- olfactory nerve 781.1
- optic nerve NEC 377.49
- oral epithelium, including tongue 528.79
  - residual ridge mucosa
    - excessive 528.72
    - minimal 528.71
- personality (pattern) (trait) (*see also* Disorder, personality) 301.9
  - following organic brain damage 310.1
- polyglandular 258.9
- psychomotor 307.9
- pupillary 379.49
- reflex 796.1
- rhythm, heart 427.9
  - postoperative (immediate) 997.1
    - long-term effect of cardiac surgery 429.4
  - psychogenic 306.2
- salivary secretion 527.7
- sensation (cold) (heat) (localization) (tactile discrimination localization) (texture) (vibratory) NEC 782.0
  - hysterical 300.11
  - skin 782.0
  - smell 781.1
  - taste 781.1
- sensory (*see also* Disturbance, sensation) 782.0
  - innervation 782.0
- situational (transient) (*see also* Reaction, adjustment) 309.9
  - acute 308.3
- sleep 780.50
  - with apnea — *see* Apnea, sleep
  - initiation or maintenance (*see also* Insomnia) 780.52
    - nonorganic origin 307.41
  - nonorganic origin 307.40
    - specified type NEC 307.49
  - specified NEC 780.59
    - nonorganic origin 307.49
  - wakefulness (*see also* Hypersomnia) 780.54
    - nonorganic origin 307.43
- sociopathic 301.7
- speech NEC 784.5
  - developmental 315.39
    - associated with hyperkinesis 314.1
  - secondary to organic lesion 784.5
- stomach (functional) (*see also* Disturbance, gastric) 536.9
- sympathetic (nerve) (*see also* Neuropathy, peripheral, autonomic) 337.9
- temperature sense 782.0
  - hysterical 300.11

Disturbance — *see also* Disease — *continued*
- tooth
  - eruption 520.6
  - formation 520.4
  - structure, hereditary NEC 520.5
- touch (*see also* Disturbance, sensation) 782.0
- vascular 459.9
  - arteriosclerotic — *see* Arteriosclerosis
- vasomotor 443.9
- vasospastic 443.9
- vestibular labyrinth 386.9
- vision, visual NEC 368.9
  - psychophysical 368.16
  - specified NEC 368.8
  - subjective 368.10
- voice 784.40
- wakefulness (initiation or maintenance) (*see also* Hypersomnia) 780.54
  - nonorganic origin 307.43

Disulfiduria, beta-mercaptolactate-cysteine 270.0

Disuse atrophy, bone 733.7

Ditthomska syndrome 307.81

Diuresis 788.42

Divers'
- palsy or paralysis 993.3
- squeeze 993.3

Diverticula, diverticulosis, diverticulum (acute) (multiple) (perforated) (ruptured) 562.10
- with diverticulitis 562.11
- aorta (Kommerell's) 747.21
- appendix (noninflammatory) 543.9
- bladder (acquired) (sphincter) 596.3
  - congenital 753.8
- broad ligament 620.8
- bronchus (congenital) 748.3
  - acquired 494.0
    - with acute exacerbation 494.1
- calyx, calyceal (kidney) 593.89
- cardia (stomach) 537.1
- cecum 562.10
  - with
    - diverticulitis 562.11
      - with hemorrhage 562.13
    - hemorrhage 562.12
  - congenital 751.5
- colon (acquired) 562.10
  - with
    - diverticulitis 562.11
      - with hemorrhage 562.13
    - hemorrhage 562.12
  - congenital 751.5
- duodenum 562.00
  - with
    - diverticulitis 562.01
      - with hemorrhage 562.03
    - hemorrhage 562.02
  - congenital 751.5
- epiphrenic (esophagus) 530.6
- esophagus (congenital) 750.4
  - acquired 530.6
  - epiphrenic 530.6
  - pulsion 530.6
  - traction 530.6
  - Zenker's 530.6
- Eustachian tube 381.89
- fallopian tube 620.8
- gallbladder (congenital) 751.69
- gastric 537.1
- heart (congenital) 746.89
- ileum 562.00
  - with
    - diverticulitis 562.01
      - with hemorrhage 562.03
    - hemorrhage 562.02
- intestine (large) 562.10
  - with
    - diverticulitis 562.11
      - with hemorrhage 562.13
    - hemorrhage 562.12
  - congenital 751.5

Diverticula, diverticulosis, diverticulum — *continued*
- intestine — *continued*
  - small 562.00
    - with
      - diverticulitis 562.01
        - with hemorrhage 562.03
      - hemorrhage 562.02
    - congenital 751.5
- jejunum 562.00
  - with
    - diverticulitis 562.01
      - with hemorrhage 562.03
    - hemorrhage 562.02
- kidney (calyx) (pelvis) 593.89
  - with calculus 592.0
- Kommerell's 747.21
- laryngeal ventricle (congenital) 748.3
- Meckel's (displaced) (hypertrophic) 751.0
- midthoracic 530.6
- organ or site, congenital NEC — *see* Distortion
- pericardium (conginital) (cyst) 746.89
  - acquired (true) 423.8
- pharyngoesophageal (pulsion) 530.6
- pharynx (congenital) 750.27
- pulsion (esophagus) 530.6
- rectosigmoid 562.10
  - with
    - diverticulitis 562.11
      - with hemorrhage 562.13
    - hemorrhage 562.12
  - congenital 751.5
- rectum 562.10
  - with
    - diverticulitis 562.11
      - with hemorrhage 562.13
    - hemorrhage 562.12
- renal (calyces) (pelvis) 593.89
  - with calculus 592.0
- Rokitansky's 530.6
- seminal vesicle 608.0
- sigmoid 562.10
  - with
    - diverticulitis 562.11
      - with hemorrhage 562.13
    - hemorrhage 562.12
  - congenital 751.5
- small intestine 562.00
  - with
    - diverticulitis 562.01
      - with hemorrhage 562.03
    - hemorrhage 562.02
- stomach (cardia) (juxtacardia) (juxtapyloric) (acquired) 537.1
  - congenital 750.7
- subdiaphragmatic 530.6
- trachea (congenital) 748.3
  - acquired 519.19
- traction (esophagus) 530.6
- ureter (acquired) 593.89
  - congenital 753.4
- ureterovesical orifice 593.89
- urethra (acquired) 599.2
  - congenital 753.8
- ventricle, left (congenital) 746.89
- vesical (urinary) 596.3
  - congenital 753.8
- Zenker's (esophagus) 530.6

Diverticulitis (acute) — *see also* Diverticula 562.11
- with hemorrhage 562.13
- bladder (urinary) 596.3
- cecum (perforated) 562.11
  - with hemorrhage 562.13
- colon (perforated) 562.11
  - with hemorrhage 562.13
- duodenum 562.01
  - with hemorrhage 562.03
- esophagus 530.6
- ileum (perforated) 562.01
  - with hemorrhage 562.03
- intestine (large) (perforated) 562.11
  - with hemorrhage 562.13
  - small 562.01

Diverticulitis — *see also* Diverticula — *continued*
- intestine — *continued*
  - small — *continued*
    - with hemorrhage 562.03
- jejunum (perforated) 562.01
  - with hemorrhage 562.03
- Meckel's (perforated) 751.0
- pharyngoesophageal 530.6
- rectosigmoid (perforated) 562.11
  - with hemorrhage 562.13
- rectum 562.11
  - with hemorrhage 562.13
- sigmoid (old) (perforated) 562.11
  - with hemorrhage 562.13
- small intestine (perforated) 562.01
  - with hemorrhage 562.03
- vesical (urinary) 596.3

Diverticulosis — *see* Diverticula

Division
- cervix uteri 622.8
  - external os into two openings by frenum 752.49
- external (cervical) into two openings by frenum 752.49
- glans penis 752.69
- hymen 752.49
- labia minora (congenital) 752.49
- ligament (partial or complete) (current) (*see also* Sprain, by site)
  - with open wound — *see* Wound, open, by site
- muscle (partial or complete) (current) (*see also* Sprain, by site)
  - with open wound — *see* Wound, open, by site
- nerve — *see* Injury, nerve, by site
- penis glans 752.69
- spinal cord — *see* Injury, spinal, by site
- vein 459.9
  - traumatic — *see* Injury, vascular, by site

Divorce V61.03 ▲

Dix-Hallpike neurolabyrinthitis 386.12

Dizziness 780.4
- hysterical 300.11
- psychogenic 306.9

Doan-Wiseman syndrome (primary splenic neutropenia) 289.53

Dog bite — *see* Wound, open, by site

Döhle body-panmyelopathic syndrome 288.2

Döhle-Heller aortitis 093.1

Dolichocephaly, dolichocephalus 754.0

Dolichocolon 751.5

Dolichostenomelia 759.82

Donohue's syndrome (leprechaunism) 259.8

Donor
- blood V59.01
  - other blood components V59.09
  - stem cells V59.02
  - whole blood V59.01
- bone V59.2
  - marrow V59.3
- cornea V59.5
- egg (oocyte) (ovum) V59.70
  - over age 35 V59.73
    - anonymous recipient V59.73
    - designated recipient V59.74
  - under age 35 V59.71
    - anonymous recipient V59.71
    - designated recipient V59.72
- heart V59.8
- kidney V59.4
- liver V59.6
- lung V59.8
- lymphocyte V59.8
- organ V59.9
  - specified NEC V59.8
- potential, examination of V70.8
- skin V59.1
- specified organ or tissue NEC V59.8
- sperm V59.8
- stem cells V59.02

Donor — *continued*
- tissue V59.9
  - specified type NEC V59.8

Donovanosis (granuloma venereum) 099.2

DOPS (diffuse obstructive pulmonary syndrome) 496

Double
- albumin 273.8
- aortic arch 747.21
- auditory canal 744.29
- auricle (heart) 746.82
- bladder 753.8
- external (cervical) os 752.49
- kidney with double pelvis (renal) 753.3
- larynx 748.3
- meatus urinarius 753.8
- organ or site NEC — *see* Accessory orifice
  - heart valve NEC 746.89
    - pulmonary 746.09
- outlet, right ventricle 745.11
- pelvis (renal) with double ureter 753.4
- penis 752.69
- tongue 750.13
- ureter (one or both sides) 753.4
  - with double pelvis (renal) 753.4
- urethra 753.8
- urinary meatus 753.8
- uterus (any degree) 752.2
  - with doubling of cervix and vagina 752.2
  - in pregnancy or childbirth 654.0 ☑
    - affecting fetus or newborn 763.89
- vagina 752.49
  - with doubling of cervix and uterus 752.2
- vision 368.2
- vocal cords 748.3
- vulva 752.49
- whammy (syndrome) 360.81

Douglas' pouch, cul-de-sac — *see* condition

Down's disease or syndrome (mongolism) 758.0

Down-growth, epithelial (anterior chamber) 364.61

Dracontiasis 125.7

Dracunculiasis 125.7

Dracunculosis 125.7

Drainage
- abscess (spontaneous) — *see* Abscess
- anomalous pulmonary veins to hepatic veins or right atrium 747.41
- stump (amputation) (surgical) 997.62
- suprapubic, bladder 596.8

Dream state, hysterical 300.13

Drepanocytic anemia — *see also* Disease, sickle cell 282.60

Dresbach's syndrome (elliptocytosis) 282.1

Dreschlera (infection) 118
- hawaiiensis 117.8

Dressler's syndrome (postmyocardial infarction) 411.0

Dribbling (post-void) 788.35

Drift, ulnar 736.09

Drinking (alcohol) — *see also* Alcoholism
- excessive, to excess NEC (*see also* Abuse, drugs, nondependent) 305.0 ☑
  - bouts, periodic 305.0 ☑
  - continual 303.9 ☑
  - episodic 305.0 ☑
  - habitual 303.9 ☑
  - periodic 305.0 ☑

Drip, postnasal (chronic) 784.91
- due to
  - allergic rhinitis — *see* Rhinitis, allergic
  - common cold 460
  - gastroesophageal reflux — *see* Reflux, gastroesophageal

Drip, postnasal — *continued*
due to — *continued*
nasopharyngitis — *see* Nasopharyngitis
other known condition — code to condition
sinusitis — *see* Sinusitis
Drivers' license examination V70.3
Droop
Cooper's 611.81 ▲
facial 781.94
Drop
finger 736.29
foot 736.79
hematocrit (precipitous) 790.01
toe 735.8
wrist 736.05
Dropped
dead 798.1
heart beats 426.6
Dropsy, dropsical — *see also* Edema 782.3
abdomen 789.59
amnion (*see also* Hydramnios) 657.0 ☑
brain — *see* Hydrocephalus
cardiac (*see also* Failure, heart) 428.0
cardiorenal (*see also* Hypertension, cardiorenal) 404.90
chest 511.9
fetus or newborn 778.0
due to isoimmunization 773.3
gangrenous (*see also* Gangrene) 785.4
heart (*see also* Failure, heart) 428.0
hepatic — *see* Cirrhosis, liver
infantile — *see* Hydrops, fetalis
kidney (*see also* Nephrosis) 581.9
liver — *see* Cirrhosis, liver
lung 514
malarial (*see also* Malaria) 084.9
neonatorum — *see* Hydrops, fetalis
nephritic 581.9
newborn — *see* Hydrops, fetalis
nutritional 269.9
ovary 620.8
pericardium (*see also* Pericarditis) 423.9
renal (*see also* Nephrosis) 581.9
uremic — *see* Uremia
Drowned, drowning ▶(near)◀ 994.1
lung 518.5
Drowsiness 780.09
Drug — *see also* condition
addiction (*see also* listing under Dependence) 304.9 ☑
adverse effect NEC, correct substance properly administered 995.20
allergy 995.27
dependence (*see also* listing under Dependence) 304.9 ☑
habit (*see also* listing under Dependence) 304.9 ☑
hypersensitivity 995.27
induced
circadian rhythm sleep disorder 292.85
hypersomnia 292.85
insomnia 292.85
mental disorder 292.9
anxiety 292.89
mood 292.84
sexual 292.89
sleep 292.85
specified type 292.89
parasomnia 292.85
persisting
amnestic disorder 292.83
dementia 292.82
psychotic disorder
with
delusions 292.11
hallucinations 292.12
sleep disorder 292.85
intoxication 292.89
overdose — *see* Table of Drugs and Chemicals
Drug — *see also* condition — *continued*
poisoning — *see* Table of Drugs and Chemicals
therapy (maintenance) status NEC
chemotherapy, antineoplastic V58.11
immunotherapy, antineoplastic V58.12
long-term (current) use V58.69
antibiotics V58.62
anticoagulants V58.61
anti-inflammatories, non-steroidal (NSAID) V58.64
antiplatelets V58.63
antithrombotics V58.63
aspirin V58.66
high-risk medications NEC V58.69
insulin V58.67
methadone V58.69 ●
opiate analgesic V58.69 ●
steroids V58.65
wrong substance given or taken in error — *see* Table of Drugs and Chemicals
Drunkenness — *see also* Abuse, drugs, nondependent 305.0 ☑
acute in alcoholism (*see also* Alcoholism) 303.0 ☑
chronic (*see also* Alcoholism) 303.9 ☑
pathologic 291.4
simple (acute) 305.0 ☑
in alcoholism 303.0 ☑
sleep 307.47
Drusen
optic disc or papilla 377.21
retina (colloid) (hyaloid degeneration) 362.57
hereditary 362.77
Drusenfieber 075
Dry, dryness — *see also* condition
eye 375.15
syndrome 375.15
larynx 478.79
mouth 527.7
nose 478.19
skin syndrome 701.1
socket (teeth) 526.5
throat 478.29
DSAP (disseminated superficial actinic porokeratosis) 692.75
Duane's retraction syndrome 378.71
Duane-Stilling-Türk syndrome (ocular retraction syndrome) 378.71
Dubini's disease (electric chorea) 049.8
Dubin-Johnson disease or syndrome 277.4
Dubois' abscess or disease 090.5
Duchenne's
disease 094.0
locomotor ataxia 094.0
muscular dystrophy 359.1
pseudohypertrophy, muscles 359.1
paralysis 335.22
syndrome 335.22
Duchenne-Aran myelopathic, muscular atrophy (nonprogressive) (progressive) 335.21
Duchenne-Griesinger disease 359.1
Ducrey's
bacillus 099.0
chancre 099.0
disease (chancroid) 099.0
Duct, ductus — *see* condition
Duengero 061
Duhring's disease (dermatitis herpetiformis) 694.0
Dukes (-Filatov) disease 057.8
Dullness
cardiac (decreased) (increased) 785.3
Dumb ague — *see also* Malaria 084.6
Dumbness — *see also* Aphasia 784.3
Dumdum fever 085.0
Dumping syndrome (postgastrectomy) 564.2
Dumping syndrome — *continued*
nonsurgical 536.8
Duodenitis (nonspecific) (peptic) 535.60
with hemorrhage 535.61
due to
Strongyloides stercoralis 127.2
Duodenocholangitis 575.8
Duodenum, duodenal — *see* condition
Duplay's disease, periarthritis, or syndrome 726.2
Duplex — *see also* Accessory
kidney 753.3
placenta — *see* Placenta, abnormal
uterus 752.2
Duplication — *see also* Accessory
anus 751.5
aortic arch 747.21
appendix 751.5
biliary duct (any) 751.69
bladder 753.8
cecum 751.5
and appendix 751.5
clitoris 752.49
cystic duct 751.69
digestive organs 751.8
duodenum 751.5
esophagus 750.4
fallopian tube 752.19
frontonasal process 756.0
gallbladder 751.69
ileum 751.5
intestine (large) (small) 751.5
jejunum 751.5
kidney 753.3
liver 751.69
nose 748.1
pancreas 751.7
penis 752.69
respiratory organs NEC 748.9
salivary duct 750.22
spinal cord (incomplete) 742.51
stomach 750.7
ureter 753.4
vagina 752.49
vas deferens 752.89
vocal cords 748.3
Dupré's disease or syndrome (meningism) 781.6
Dupuytren's
contraction 728.6
disease (muscle contracture) 728.6
fracture (closed) 824.4
ankle (closed) 824.4
open 824.5
fibula (closed) 824.4
open 824.5
open 824.5
radius (closed) 813.42
open 813.52
muscle contracture 728.6
Durand-Nicolas-Favre disease (climatic bubo) 099.1
Durotomy, incidental (inadvertent) — ●
see also Tear, dural 349.31 ●
Duroziez's disease (congenital mitral stenosis) 746.5
Dust
conjunctivitis 372.05
reticulation (occupational) 504
Dutton's
disease (trypanosomiasis) 086.9
relapsing fever (West African) 087.1
Dwarf, dwarfism 259.4
with infantilism (hypophyseal) 253.3
achondroplastic 756.4
Amsterdam 759.89
bird-headed 759.89
congenital 259.4
constitutional 259.4
hypophyseal 253.3
infantile 259.4
Levi type 253.3
Lorain-Levi (pituitary) 253.3
Lorain type (pituitary) 253.3
metatropic 756.4
Dwarf, dwarfism — *continued*
nephrotic-glycosuric, with hypophosphatemic rickets 270.0
nutritional 263.2
ovarian 758.6
pancreatic 577.8
pituitary 253.3
polydystrophic 277.5
primordial 253.3
psychosocial 259.4
renal 588.0
with hypertension — *see* Hypertension, kidney
Russell's (uterine dwarfism and craniofacial dysostosis) 759.89
Dyke-Young anemia or syndrome (acquired macrocytic hemolytic anemia) (secondary) (symptomatic) 283.9
Dynia abnormality — *see also* Defect, coagulation 286.9
Dysacousis 388.40
Dysadrenocortism 255.9
hyperfunction 255.3
hypofunction 255.41
Dysarthria 784.5
Dysautonomia — *see also* Neuropathy, peripheral, autonomic 337.9
familial 742.8
Dysbarism 993.3
Dysbasia 719.7
angiosclerotica intermittens 443.9
due to atherosclerosis 440.21
hysterical 300.11
lordotica (progressiva) 333.6
nonorganic origin 307.9
psychogenic 307.9
Dysbetalipoproteinemia (familial) 272.2
Dyscalculia 315.1
Dyschezia — *see also* Constipation 564.00
Dyschondroplasia (with hemangiomata) 756.4
Voorhoeve's 756.4
Dyschondrosteosis 756.59
Dyschromia 709.00
Dyscollagenosis 710.9
Dyscoria 743.41
Dyscraniopyophalangy 759.89
Dyscrasia
blood 289.9
with antepartum hemorrhage 641.3 ☑
fetus or newborn NEC 776.9
hemorrhage, subungual 287.8
puerperal, postpartum 666.3 ☑
ovary 256.8
plasma cell 273.9
pluriglandular 258.9
polyglandular 258.9
Dysdiadochokinesia 781.3
Dysectasia, vesical neck 596.8
Dysendocrinism 259.9
Dysentery, dysenteric (bilious) (catarrhal) (diarrhea) (epidemic) (gangrenous) (hemorrhagic) (infectious) (sporadic) (tropical) (ulcerative) 009.0
abscess, liver (*see also* Abscess, amebic) 006.3
amebic (*see also* Amebiasis) 006.9
with abscess — *see* Abscess, amebic
acute 006.0
carrier (suspected) of V02.2
chronic 006.1
arthritis (*see also* Arthritis, due to, dysentery) 009.0 *[711.3]* ☑
bacillary 004.9 *[711.3]* ☑
asylum 004.9
bacillary 004.9
arthritis 004.9 *[711.3]* ☑
Boyd 004.2
Flexner 004.1
Schmitz (-Stutzer) 004.0
Shiga 004.0

Dysentery, dysenteric — *continued*
- bacillary — *continued*
  - Shigella 004.9
    - group A 004.0
    - group B 004.1
    - group C 004.2
    - group D 004.3
    - specified type NEC 004.8
  - Sonne 004.3
  - specified type NEC 004.8
- bacterium 004.9
- balantidial 007.0
- Balantidium coli 007.0
- Boyd's 004.2
- Chilomastix 007.8
- Chinese 004.9
- choleriform 001.1
- coccidial 007.2
- Dientamoeba fragilis 007.8
- due to specified organism NEC — *see* Enteritis, due to, by organism
- Embadomonas 007.8
- Endolimax nana — *see* Dysentery, amebic
- Entamoba, entamebic — *see* Dysentery, amebic
- Flexner's 004.1
- Flexner-Boyd 004.2
- giardial 007.1
- Giardia lamblia 007.1
- Hiss-Russell 004.1
- lamblia 007.1
- leishmanial 085.0
- malarial (*see also* Malaria) 084.6
- metazoal 127.9
- Monilia 112.89
- protozoal NEC 007.9
- Russell's 004.8
- salmonella 003.0
- schistosomal 120.1
- Schmitz (-Stutzer) 004.0
- Shiga 004.0
- Shigella NEC (*see also* Dysentery, bacillary) 004.9
  - boydii 004.2
  - dysenteriae 004.0
    - Schmitz 004.0
    - Shiga 004.0
  - flexneri 004.1
  - group A 004.0
  - group B 004.1
  - group C 004.2
  - group D 004.3
  - Schmitz 004.0
  - Shiga 004.0
  - Sonnei 004.3
- Sonne 004.3
- strongyloidiasis 127.2
- trichomonal 007.3
- tuberculous (*see also* Tuberculosis) 014.8 ☑
- viral (*see also* Enteritis, viral) 008.8

Dysequilibrium 780.4

Dysesthesia 782.0
- hysterical 300.11

Dysfibrinogenemia (congenital) — *see also* Defect, coagulation 286.3

Dysfunction
- adrenal (cortical) 255.9
  - hyperfunction 255.3
  - hypofunction 255.41
- associated with sleep stages or arousal from sleep 780.56
  - nonorganic origin 307.47
- bladder NEC 596.59
- bleeding, uterus 626.8
- brain, minimal (*see also* Hyperkinesia) 314.9
- cerebral 348.30
- colon 564.9
  - psychogenic 306.4
- colostomy or enterostomy 569.62
- cystic duct 575.8
- diastolic 429.9
  - with heart failure — *see* Failure, heart

Dysfunction — *continued*
- diastolic — *continued*
  - due to
    - cardiomyopathy — *see* Cardiomyopathy
    - hypertension — *see* Hypertension, heart
- endocrine NEC 259.9
- endometrium 621.8
- enteric stoma 569.62
- enterostomy 569.62
- erectile 607.84
  - nonorganic origin 302.72
- esophagostomy 530.87
- Eustachian tube 381.81
- gallbladder 575.8
- gastrointestinal 536.9
- gland, glandular NEC 259.9
- heart 427.9
  - postoperative (immediate) 997.1
    - long-term effect of cardiac surgery 429.4
- hemoglobin 289.89
- hepatic 573.9
- hepatocellular NEC 573.9
- hypophysis 253.9
  - hyperfunction 253.1
  - hypofunction 253.2
  - posterior lobe 253.6
    - hypofunction 253.5
- kidney (*see also* Disease, renal) 593.9
- labyrinthine 386.50
  - specified NEC 386.58
- liver 573.9
  - constitutional 277.4
- minimal brain (child) (*see also* Hyperkinesia) 314.9
- ovary, ovarian 256.9
  - hyperfunction 256.1
    - estrogen 256.0
  - hypofunction 256.39
    - postablative 256.2
  - postablative 256.2
  - specified NEC 256.8
- papillary muscle 429.81
  - with myocardial infarction 410.8 ☑
- parathyroid 252.8
  - hyperfunction 252.00
  - hypofunction 252.1
- pineal gland 259.8
- pituitary (gland) 253.9
  - hyperfunction 253.1
  - hypofunction 253.2
  - posterior 253.6
    - hypofunction 253.5
- placental — *see* Placenta, insufficiency
- platelets (blood) 287.1
- polyglandular 258.9
  - specified NEC 258.8
- psychosexual 302.70
  - with
    - dyspareunia (functional) (psychogenic) 302.76
    - frigidity 302.72
    - impotence 302.72
    - inhibition
      - orgasm
        - female 302.73
        - male 302.74
      - sexual
        - desire 302.71
        - excitement 302.72
    - premature ejaculation 302.75
    - sexual aversion 302.79
    - specified disorder NEC 302.79
    - vaginismus 306.51
- pylorus 537.9
- rectum 564.9
  - psychogenic 306.4
- segmental (*see also* Dysfunction, somatic) 739.9
- senile 797
- sexual 302.70
- sinoatrial node 427.81
- somatic 739.9
  - abdomen 739.9

Dysfunction — *continued*
- somatic — *continued*
  - acromioclavicular 739.7
  - cervical 739.1
  - cervicothoracic 739.1
  - costochondral 739.8
  - costovertebral 739.8
  - extremities
    - lower 739.6
    - upper 739.7
  - head 739.0
  - hip 739.5
  - lumbar, lumbosacral 739.3
  - occipitocervical 739.0
  - pelvic 739.5
  - pubic 739.5
  - rib cage 739.8
  - sacral 739.4
  - sacrococcygeal 739.4
  - sacroiliac 739.4
  - specified site NEC 739.9
  - sternochondral 739.8
  - sternoclavicular 739.7
  - temporomandibular 739.0
  - thoracic, thoracolumbar 739.2
- stomach 536.9
  - psychogenic 306.4
- suprarenal 255.9
  - hyperfunction 255.3
  - hypofunction 255.41
- symbolic NEC 784.60
  - specified type NEC 784.69
- systolic 429.9
  - with heart failure — *see* Failure, heart
- temporomandibular (joint) (joint-pain-syndrome) NEC 524.60
  - sounds on opening or closing 524.64
  - specified NEC 524.69
- testicular 257.9
  - hyperfunction 257.0
  - hypofunction 257.2
  - specified type NEC 257.8
- thymus 254.9
- thyroid 246.9
  - complicating pregnancy, childbirth, or puerperium 648.1 ☑
  - hyperfunction — *see* Hyperthyroidism
  - hypofunction — *see* Hypothyroidism
- uterus, complicating delivery 661.9 ☑
  - affecting fetus or newborn 763.7
  - hypertonic 661.4 ☑
  - hypotonic 661.2 ☑
    - primary 661.0 ☑
    - secondary 661.1 ☑
- velopharyngeal (acquired) 528.9
  - congenital 750.29
- ventricular 429.9
  - with congestive heart failure (*see also* Failure, heart) 428.0
  - due to
    - cardiomyopathy — *see* Cardiomyopathy
    - hypertension — *see* Hypertension, heart
  - left, reversible following sudden emotional stress 429.83
- vesicourethral NEC 596.59
- vestibular 386.50
  - specified type NEC 386.58

Dysgammaglobulinemia 279.06

Dysgenesis
- gonadal (due to chromosomal anomaly) 758.6
  - pure 752.7
- kidney(s) 753.0
- ovarian 758.6
- renal 753.0
- reticular 279.2
- seminiferous tubules 758.6
- tidal platelet 287.31

Dysgerminoma (M9060/3)
- specified site — *see* Neoplasm, by site, malignant
- unspecified site
  - female 183.0
  - male 186.9

Dysgeusia 781.1

Dysgraphia 781.3

Dyshidrosis 705.81

Dysidrosis 705.81

Dysinsulinism 251.8

Dyskaryotic cervical smear 795.09

Dyskeratosis — *see also* Keratosis 701.1
- bullosa hereditaria 757.39
- cervix 622.10
- congenital 757.39
- follicularis 757.39
  - vitamin A deficiency 264.8
- gingiva 523.8
- oral soft tissue NEC 528.79
- tongue 528.79
- uterus NEC 621.8

Dyskinesia 781.3
- biliary 575.8
- esophagus 530.5
- hysterical 300.11
- intestinal 564.89
- neuroleptic-induced tardive 333.85
- nonorganic origin 307.9
- orofacial 333.82
  - due to drugs 333.85
- psychogenic 307.9
- subacute, due to drugs 333.85
- tardive (oral) 333.85

Dyslalia 784.5
- developmental 315.39

Dyslexia 784.61
- developmental 315.02
- secondary to organic lesion 784.61

Dyslipidemia 272.4

Dysmaturity — *see also* Immaturity 765.1 ☑
- lung 770.4
- pulmonary 770.4

Dysmenorrhea (essential) (exfoliative) (functional) (intrinsic) (membranous) (primary) (secondary) 625.3
- psychogenic 306.52

Dysmetabolic syndrome X 277.7

Dysmetria 781.3

Dysmorodystrophia mesodermalis congenita 759.82

Dysnomia 784.3

Dysorexia 783.0
- hysterical 300.11

Dysostosis
- cleidocranial, cleidocranialis 755.59
- craniofacial 756.0
- Fairbank's (idiopathic familial generalized osteophytosis) 756.50
- mandibularis 756.0
- mandibulofacial, incomplete 756.0
- multiplex 277.5
- orodigitofacial 759.89

Dyspareunia (female) 625.0
- male 608.89
- psychogenic 302.76

Dyspepsia (allergic) (congenital) (fermentative) (flatulent) (functional) (gastric) (gastrointestinal) (neurogenic) (occupational) (reflex) 536.8
- acid 536.8
- atonic 536.3
  - psychogenic 306.4
- diarrhea 787.91
  - psychogenic 306.4
- intestinal 564.89
  - psychogenic 306.4
- nervous 306.4
- neurotic 306.4
- psychogenic 306.4

Dysphagia 787.20
- cervical 787.29
- functional 300.11
- hysterical 300.11
- nervous 300.11

Dysphagia — *continued*
neurogenic 787.29
oral phase 787.21
oropharyngeal phase 787.22
pharyngeal phase 787.23
pharyngoesophageal phase 787.24
psychogenic 306.4
sideropenic 280.8
spastica 530.5
specified NEC 787.29
Dysphagocytosis, congenital 288.1
Dysphasia 784.5
Dysphonia 784.49
clericorum 784.49
functional 300.11
hysterical 300.11
psychogenic 306.1
spastica 478.79
Dyspigmentation — *see also* Pigmentation
eyelid (acquired) 374.52
Dyspituitarism 253.9
hyperfunction 253.1
hypofunction 253.2
posterior lobe 253.6
Dysplasia — *see also* Anomaly
anus 569.44 ●
intraepithelial neoplasia I [AIN I] (histologically confirmed) 569.44 ●
intraepithelial neoplasia II [AIN II] (histologically confirmed) 569.44 ●
intraepithelial neoplasia III [AIN III] 230.6 ●
anal canal 230.5 ●
mild (histologically confirmed) 569.44 ●
moderate (histologically confirmed) 569.44 ●
severe 230.6 ●
anal canal 230.5 ●
artery
fibromuscular NEC 447.8
carotid 447.8
renal 447.3
bladder 596.8
bone (fibrous) NEC 733.29
diaphyseal, progressive 756.59
jaw 526.89
monostotic 733.29
polyostotic 756.54
solitary 733.29
brain 742.9
bronchopulmonary, fetus or newborn 770.7
cervix (uteri) 622.10
cervical intraepithelial neoplasia I [CIN I] 622.11
cervical intraepithelial neoplasia II [CIN II] 622.12
cervical intraepithelial neoplasia III [CIN III] 233.1
CIN I 622.11
CIN II 622.12
CIN III 233.1
mild 622.11
moderate 622.12
severe 233.1
chondroectodermal 756.55
chondromatose 756.4
colon 211.3
craniocarpotarsal 759.89
craniometaphyseal 756.89
dentinal 520.5
diaphyseal, progressive 756.59
ectodermal (anhidrotic) (Bason) (Clouston's) (congenital) (Feinmesser) (hereditary) (hidrotic) (Marshall) (Robinson's) 757.31
epiphysealis 756.9
multiplex 756.56
punctata 756.59
epiphysis 756.9
multiple 756.56

Dysplasia — *see also* Anomaly — *continued*
epithelial
epiglottis 478.79
uterine cervix 622.10
erythroid NEC 289.89
eye (*see also* Microphthalmos) 743.10
familial metaphyseal 756.89
fibromuscular, artery NEC 447.8
carotid 447.8
renal 447.3
fibrous
bone NEC 733.29
diaphyseal, progressive 756.59
jaw 526.89
monostotic 733.29
polyostotic 756.54
solitary 733.29
high-grade, focal — *see* Neoplasm, by site, benign
hip (congenital) 755.63
with dislocation (*see also* Dislocation, hip, congenital) 754.30
hypohidrotic ectodermal 757.31
joint 755.8
kidney 753.15
leg 755.69
linguofacialis 759.89
lung 748.5
macular 743.55
mammary (benign) (gland) 610.9
cystic 610.1
specified type NEC 610.8
metaphyseal 756.9
familial 756.89
monostotic fibrous 733.29
muscle 756.89
myeloid NEC 289.89
nervous system (general) 742.9
neuroectodermal 759.6
oculoauriculovertebral 756.0
oculodentodigital 759.89
olfactogenital 253.4
osteo-onycho-arthro (hereditary) 756.89
periosteum 733.99
polyostotic fibrous 756.54
progressive diaphyseal 756.59
prostate 602.3
intraepithelial neoplasia I [PIN I] 602.3
intraepithelial neoplasia II [PIN II] 602.3
intraepithelial neoplasia III [PIN III] 233.4
renal 753.15
renofacialis 753.0
retinal NEC 743.56
retrolental ▶(*see also* Retinopathy of prematurity)◀ 362.21
skin 709.8 ●
spinal cord 742.9
thymic, with immunodeficiency 279.2
vagina 623.0
mild 623.0 ●
moderate 623.0 ●
severe 233.31
vocal cord 478.5
vulva 624.8
intraepithelial neoplasia I [VIN I] 624.01
intraepithelial neoplasia II [VIN II] 624.02
intraepithelial neoplasia III [VIN III] 233.32
mild 624.01
moderate 624.02
severe 233.32
VIN I 624.01
VIN II 624.02
VIN III 233.32
Dyspnea (nocturnal) (paroxysmal) 786.09
asthmatic (bronchial) (*see also* Asthma) 493.9 ☑
with bronchitis (*see also* Asthma) 493.9 ☑

Dyspnea — *continued*
asthmatic (*see also* Asthma) — *continued*
with bronchitis (*see also* Asthma) — *continued*
chronic 493.2 ☑
cardiac (*see also* Failure, ventricular, left) 428.1
cardiac (*see also* Failure, ventricular, left) 428.1
functional 300.11
hyperventilation 786.01
hysterical 300.11
Monday morning 504
newborn 770.89
psychogenic 306.1
uremic — *see* Uremia
Dyspraxia 781.3
syndrome 315.4
Dysproteinemia 273.8
transient with copper deficiency 281.4
Dysprothrombinemia (constitutional) — *see also* Defect, coagulation 286.3
Dysreflexia, autonomic 337.3
Dysrhythmia
cardiac 427.9
postoperative (immediate) 997.1
long-term effect of cardiac surgery 429.4
specified type NEC 427.89
cerebral or cortical 348.30
Dyssecretosis, mucoserous 710.2
Dyssocial reaction, without manifest psychiatric disorder
adolescent V71.02
adult V71.01
child V71.02
Dyssomnia NEC 780.56
nonorganic origin 307.47
Dyssplenism 289.4
Dyssynergia
biliary (*see also* Disease, biliary) 576.8
cerebellaris myoclonica 334.2
detrusor sphincter (bladder) 596.55
ventricular 429.89
Dystasia, hereditary areflexic 334.3
Dysthymia 300.4
Dysthymic disorder 300.4
Dysthyroidism 246.9
Dystocia 660.9 ☑
affecting fetus or newborn 763.1
cervical 661.2 ☑
affecting fetus or newborn 763.7
contraction ring 661.4 ☑
affecting fetus or newborn 763.7
fetal 660.9 ☑
abnormal size 653.5 ☑
affecting fetus or newborn 763.1
deformity 653.7 ☑
maternal 660.9 ☑
affecting fetus or newborn 763.1
positional 660.0 ☑
affecting fetus or newborn 763.1
shoulder (girdle) 660.4 ☑
affecting fetus or newborn 763.1
uterine NEC 661.4 ☑
affecting fetus or newborn 763.7
Dystonia
acute
due to drugs 333.72
neuroleptic-induced acute 333.72
deformans progressiva 333.6
lenticularis 333.6
musculorum deformans 333.6
torsion (idiopathic) 333.6
acquired 333.79
fragments (of) 333.89
genetic 333.6
symptomatic 333.79
Dystonic
movements 781.0
Dystopia kidney 753.3
Dystrophia myotonica 359.2 ☑
Dystrophy, dystrophia 783.9
adiposogenital 253.8
asphyxiating thoracic 756.4

Dystrophy, dystrophia — *continued*
Becker's type 359.22
brevicollis 756.16
Bruch's membrane 362.77
cervical (sympathetic) NEC 337.09 ▲
chondro-osseus with punctate epiphyseal dysplasia 756.59
choroid (hereditary) 363.50
central (areolar) (partial) 363.53
total (gyrate) 363.54
circinate 363.53
circumpapillary (partial) 363.51
total 363.52
diffuse
partial 363.56
total 363.57
generalized
partial 363.56
total 363.57
gyrate
central 363.54
generalized 363.57
helicoid 363.52
peripapillary — *see* Dystrophy, choroid, circumpapillary
serpiginous 363.54
cornea (hereditary) 371.50
anterior NEC 371.52
Cogan's 371.52
combined 371.57
crystalline 371.56
endothelial (Fuchs') 371.57
epithelial 371.50
juvenile 371.51
microscopic cystic 371.52
granular 371.53
lattice 371.54
macular 371.55
marginal (Terrien's) 371.48
Meesman's 371.51
microscopic cystic (epithelial) 371.52
nodular, Salzmann's 371.46
polymorphous 371.58
posterior NEC 371.58
ring-like 371.52
Salzmann's nodular 371.46
stromal NEC 371.56
dermatochondrocorneal 371.50
Duchenne's 359.1
due to malnutrition 263.9
Erb's 359.1
familial
hyperplastic periosteal 756.59
osseous 277.5
foveal 362.77
Fuchs', cornea 371.57
Gowers' muscular 359.1
hair 704.2
hereditary, progressive muscular 359.1
hypogenital, with diabetic tendency 759.81
Landouzy-Déjérine 359.1
Leyden-Möbius 359.1
mesodermalis congenita 759.82
muscular 359.1
congenital (hereditary) 359.0
myotonic 359.22
distal 359.1
Duchenne's 359.1
Erb's 359.1
fascioscapulohumeral 359.1
Gowers' 359.1
hereditary (progressive) 359.1
Landouzy-Déjérine 359.1
limb-girdle 359.1
myotonic 359.21
progressive (hereditary) 359.1
Charcôt-Marie-Tooth 356.1
pseudohypertrophic (infantile) 359.1
myocardium, myocardial (*see also* Degeneration, myocardial) 429.1
myotonic 359.21

☑ Additional Digit Required — Refer to the Tabular List for Digit Selection
Subterms under main terms may continue to next column or page

▶◀ Revised Text ● New Line ▲ Revised Code

Dystrophy, dystrophia — *continued*
  myotonica 359.21
  nail 703.8
    congenital 757.5
  neurovascular (traumatic) (*see also* Neuropathy, peripheral, autonomic) 337.9
  nutritional 263.9
  ocular 359.1
  oculocerebrorenal 270.8
  oculopharyngeal 359.1
  ovarian 620.8
  papillary (and pigmentary) 701.1
  pelvicrural atrophic 359.1
  pigmentary (*see also* Acanthosis) 701.2
  pituitary (gland) 253.8
  polyglandular 258.8
  posttraumatic sympathetic — *see* Dystrophy, sympathetic
  progressive ophthalmoplegic 359.1
  reflex neuromuscular — *see* Dystrophy, sympathetic ●
  retina, retinal (hereditary) 362.70
    albipunctate 362.74
    Bruch's membrane 362.77
    cone, progressive 362.75
    hyaline 362.77
    in
      Bassen-Kornzweig syndrome 272.5 *[362.72]*
      cerebroretinal lipidosis 330.1 *[362.71]*
      Refsum's disease 356.3 *[362.72]*
      systemic lipidosis 272.7 *[362.71]*
    juvenile (Stargardt's) 362.75
    pigmentary 362.74
    pigment epithelium 362.76
    progressive cone (-rod) 362.75
    pseudoinflammatory foveal 362.77
    rod, progressive 362.75
    sensory 362.75
    vitelliform 362.76
  Salzmann's nodular 371.46
  scapuloperoneal 359.1
  skin NEC 709.9
  sympathetic (posttraumatic) (reflex) 337.20
    lower limb 337.22
    specified site NEC 337.29
    upper limb 337.21
  tapetoretinal NEC 362.74
  thoracic asphyxiating 756.4
  unguium 703.8
    congenital 757.5
  vitreoretinal (primary) 362.73
    secondary 362.66
  vulva 624.09
Dysuria 788.1
  psychogenic 306.53

E

Eagle-Barrett syndrome 756.71
Eales' disease (syndrome) 362.18
Ear — *see also* condition
  ache 388.70
    otogenic 388.71
    referred 388.72
  lop 744.29
  piercing V50.3
  swimmers' acute 380.12
  tank 380.12
  tropical 111.8 *[380.15]*
  wax 380.4
Earache 388.70
  otogenic 388.71
  referred 388.72
Early satiety 780.94
Eaton-Lambert syndrome — *see also* Neoplasm, by site, malignant 199.1 *[358.1]*
Eberth's disease (typhoid fever) 002.0
Ebstein's
  anomaly or syndrome (downward displacement, tricuspid valve into right ventricle) 746.2
Ebstein's — *continued*
  disease (diabetes) 250.4 ☑ *[581.81]*
    due to secondary diabetes 249.4 ☑ *[581.81]* ●
Eccentro-osteochondrodysplasia 277.5
Ecchondroma (M9210/0) — *see* Neoplasm, bone, benign
Ecchondrosis (M9210/1) 238.0
Ecchordosis physaliphora 756.0
Ecchymosis (multiple) 459.89
  conjunctiva 372.72
  eye (traumatic) 921.0
  eyelids (traumatic) 921.1
  newborn 772.6
  spontaneous 782.7
  traumatic — *see* Contusion
Echinococciasis — *see* Echinococcus
Echinococcosis — *see* Echinococcus
Echinococcus (infection) 122.9
  granulosus 122.4
    liver 122.0
    lung 122.1
    orbit 122.3 *[376.13]*
    specified site NEC 122.3
    thyroid 122.2
  liver NEC 122.8
    granulosus 122.0
    multilocularis 122.5
  lung NEC 122.9
    granulosus 122.1
    multilocularis 122.6
  multilocularis 122.7
    liver 122.5
    specified site NEC 122.6
  orbit 122.9 *[376.13]*
    granulosus 122.3 *[376.13]*
    multilocularis 122.6 *[376.13]*
  specified site NEC 122.9
    granulosus 122.3
    multilocularis 122.6 *[376.13]*
  thyroid NEC 122.9
    granulosus 122.2
    multilocularis 122.6
Echinorhynchiasis 127.7
Echinostomiasis 121.8
Echolalia 784.69
ECHO virus infection NEC 079.1
Eclampsia, eclamptic (coma) (convulsions) (delirium) 780.39
  female, child-bearing age NEC — *see* Eclampsia, pregnancy
  gravidarum — *see* Eclampsia, pregnancy
  male 780.39
  not associated with pregnancy or childbirth 780.39
  pregnancy, childbirth, or puerperium 642.6 ☑
    with pre-existing hypertension 642.7 ☑
    affecting fetus or newborn 760.0
  uremic 586
Eclipse blindness (total) 363.31
Economic circumstance affecting care V60.9
  specified type NEC V60.8
Economo's disease (encephalitis lethargica) 049.8
Ectasia, ectasis
  aorta (*see also* Aneurysm, aorta) 441.9
    ruptured 441.5
  breast 610.4
  capillary 448.9
  cornea (marginal) (postinfectional) 371.71
  duct (mammary) 610.4
  gastric antral vascular (GAVE) 537.82
    with hemorrhage 537.83
    without hemorrhage 537.82
  kidney 593.89
  mammary duct (gland) 610.4
  papillary 448.9
  renal 593.89
  salivary gland (duct) 527.8
  scar, cornea 371.71
  sclera 379.11
Ecthyma 686.8
  contagiosum 051.2
  gangrenosum 686.09
  infectiosum 051.2
Ectocardia 746.87
Ectodermal dysplasia, congenital 757.31
Ectodermosis erosiva pluriorificialis 695.19 ▲
Ectopic, ectopia (congenital) 759.89
  abdominal viscera 751.8
    due to defect in anterior abdominal wall 756.79
  ACTH syndrome 255.0
  adrenal gland 759.1
  anus 751.5
  auricular beats 427.61
  beats 427.60
  bladder 753.5
  bone and cartilage in lung 748.69
  brain 742.4
  breast tissue 757.6
  cardiac 746.87
  cerebral 742.4
  cordis 746.87
  endometrium 617.9
  gallbladder 751.69
  gastric mucosa 750.7
  gestation — *see* Pregnancy, ectopic
  heart 746.87
  hormone secretion NEC 259.3
  hyperparathyroidism 259.3
  kidney (crossed) (intrathoracic) (pelvis) 753.3
    in pregnancy or childbirth 654.4 ☑
      causing obstructed labor 660.2 ☑
  lens 743.37
  lentis 743.37
  mole — *see* Pregnancy, ectopic
  organ or site NEC — *see* Malposition, congenital
  ovary 752.0
  pancreas, pancreatic tissue 751.7
  pregnancy — *see* Pregnancy, ectopic
  pupil 364.75
  renal 753.3
  sebaceous glands of mouth 750.26
  secretion
    ACTH 255.0
    adrenal hormone 259.3
    adrenalin 259.3
    adrenocorticotropin 255.0
    antidiuretic hormone (ADH) 259.3
    epinephrine 259.3
    hormone NEC 259.3
    norepinephrine 259.3
    pituitary (posterior) 259.3
  spleen 759.0
  testis 752.51
  thyroid 759.2
  ureter 753.4
  ventricular beats 427.69
  vesicae 753.5
Ectrodactyly 755.4
  finger (*see also* Absence, finger, congenital) 755.29
  toe (*see also* Absence, toe, congenital) 755.39
Ectromelia 755.4
  lower limb 755.30
  upper limb 755.20
Ectropion 374.10
  anus 569.49
  cervix 622.0
    with mention of cervicitis 616.0
  cicatricial 374.14
  congenital 743.62
  eyelid 374.10
    cicatricial 374.14
    congenital 743.62
    mechanical 374.12
    paralytic 374.12
    senile 374.11
    spastic 374.13
  iris (pigment epithelium) 364.54
Ectropion — *continued*
  lip (congenital) 750.26
    acquired 528.5
  mechanical 374.12
  paralytic 374.12
  rectum 569.49
  senile 374.11
  spastic 374.13
  urethra 599.84
  uvea 364.54
Eczema (acute) (allergic) (chronic) (erythematous) (fissum) (occupational) (rubrum) (squamous) 692.9
  asteatotic 706.8
  atopic 691.8
  contact NEC 692.9
  dermatitis NEC 692.9
  due to specified cause — *see* Dermatitis, due to
  dyshidrotic 705.81
  external ear 380.22
  flexural 691.8
  gouty 274.89
  herpeticum 054.0
  hypertrophicum 701.8
  hypostatic — *see* Varicose, vein
  impetiginous 684
  infantile (acute) (chronic) (due to any substance) (intertriginous) (seborrheic) 690.12
  intertriginous NEC 692.9
    infantile 690.12
  intrinsic 691.8
  lichenified NEC 692.9
  marginatum 110.3
  nummular 692.9
  pustular 686.8
  seborrheic 690.18
    infantile 690.12
  solare 692.72
  stasis (lower extremity) 454.1
    ulcerated 454.2
  vaccination, vaccinatum 999.0
  varicose (lower extremity) — *see* Varicose, vein
  verrucosum callosum 698.3
Eczematoid, exudative 691.8
Eddowes' syndrome (brittle bones and blue sclera) 756.51
Edema, edematous 782.3
  with nephritis (*see also* Nephrosis) 581.9
  allergic 995.1
  angioneurotic (allergic) (any site) (with urticaria) 995.1
    hereditary 277.6
  angiospastic 443.9
  Berlin's (traumatic) 921.3
  brain 348.5
    due to birth injury 767.8
    fetus or newborn 767.8
  cardiac (*see also* Failure, heart) 428.0
  cardiovascular (*see also* Failure, heart) 428.0
  cerebral — *see* Edema, brain
  cerebrospinal vessel — *see* Edema, brain
  cervix (acute) (uteri) 622.8
    puerperal, postpartum 674.8 ☑
  chronic hereditary 757.0
  circumscribed, acute 995.1
    hereditary 277.6
  complicating pregnancy (gestational) 646.1 ☑
    with hypertension — *see* Toxemia, of pregnancy
  conjunctiva 372.73
  connective tissue 782.3
  cornea 371.20
    due to contact lenses 371.24
    idiopathic 371.21
    secondary 371.22
  cystoid macular 362.53
  due to
    lymphatic obstruction — *see* Edema, lymphatic

Edema, edematous — *continued*
due to — *continued*
salt retention 276.0
epiglottis — *see* Edema, glottis
essential, acute 995.1
hereditary 277.6
extremities, lower — *see* Edema, legs
eyelid NEC 374.82
familial, hereditary (legs) 757.0
famine 262
fetus or newborn 778.5
genital organs
female 629.89
male 608.86
gestational 646.1 ☑
with hypertension — *see* Toxemia, of pregnancy
glottis, glottic, glottides (obstructive) (passive) 478.6
allergic 995.1
hereditary 277.6
due to external agent — *see* Condition, respiratory, acute, due to specified agent
heart (*see also* Failure, heart) 428.0
newborn 779.89
heat 992.7
hereditary (legs) 757.0
inanition 262
infectious 782.3
intracranial 348.5
due to injury at birth 767.8
iris 364.89
joint (*see also* Effusion, joint) 719.0 ☑
larynx (*see also* Edema, glottis) 478.6
legs 782.3
due to venous obstruction 459.2
hereditary 757.0
localized 782.3
due to venous obstruction 459.2
lower extremity 459.2
lower extremities — *see* Edema, legs
lung 514
acute 518.4
with heart disease or failure (*see also* Failure, ventricular, left) 428.1
congestive 428.0
chemical (due to fumes or vapors) 506.1
due to
external agent(s) NEC 508.9
specified NEC 508.8
fumes and vapors (chemical) (inhalation) 506.1
radiation 508.0
chemical (acute) 506.1
chronic 506.4
chronic 514
chemical (due to fumes or vapors) 506.4
due to
external agent(s) NEC 508.9
specified NEC 508.8
fumes or vapors (chemical) (inhalation) 506.4
radiation 508.1
due to
external agent 508.9
specified NEC 508.8
high altitude 993.2
near drowning 994.1
postoperative 518.4
terminal 514
lymphatic 457.1
due to mastectomy operation 457.0
macula 362.83
cystoid 362.53
diabetic 250.5 ☑ *[362.07]*
due to secondary diabetes ●
249.5 ☑ *[362.07]* ●
malignant (*see also* Gangrene, gas) 040.0
Milroy's 757.0
nasopharynx 478.25
neonatorum 778.5

Edema, edematous — *continued*
nutritional (newborn) 262
with dyspigmentation, skin and hair 260
optic disc or nerve — *see* Papilledema
orbit 376.33
circulatory 459.89
palate (soft) (hard) 528.9
pancreas 577.8
penis 607.83
periodic 995.1
hereditary 277.6
pharynx 478.25
pitting 782.3
pulmonary — *see* Edema, lung
Quincke's 995.1
hereditary 277.6
renal (*see also* Nephrosis) 581.9
retina (localized) (macular) (peripheral) 362.83
cystoid 362.53
diabetic 250.5 ☑ *[362.07]*
due to secondary diabetes ●
249.5 ☑ *[362.07]* ●
salt 276.0
scrotum 608.86
seminal vesicle 608.86
spermatic cord 608.86
spinal cord 336.1
starvation 262
stasis (*see also* Hypertension, venous) 459.30
subconjunctival 372.73
subglottic (*see also* Edema, glottis) 478.6
supraglottic (*see also* Edema, glottis) 478.6
testis 608.86
toxic NEC 782.3
traumatic NEC 782.3
tunica vaginalis 608.86
vas deferens 608.86
vocal cord — *see* Edema, glottis
vulva (acute) 624.8
Edentia (complete) (partial) — *see also* Absence, tooth 520.0
acquired (*see also* Edentulism) 525.40
due to
caries 525.13
extraction 525.10
periodontal disease 525.12
specified NEC 525.19
trauma 525.11
causing malocclusion 524.30
congenital (deficiency of tooth buds) 520.0
Edentulism 525.40
complete 525.40
class I 525.41
class II 525.42
class III 525.43
class IV 525.44
partial 525.50
class I 525.51
class II 525.52
class III 525.53
class IV 525.54
Edsall's disease 992.2
Educational handicap V62.3
Edwards' syndrome 758.2
Effect, adverse NEC
abnormal gravitational (G) forces or states 994.9
air pressure — *see* Effect, adverse, atmospheric pressure
altitude (high) — *see* Effect, adverse, high altitude
anesthetic
in labor and delivery NEC 668.9 ☑
affecting fetus or newborn 763.5
antitoxin — *see* Complications, vaccination
atmospheric pressure 993.9
due to explosion 993.4
high 993.3

Effect, adverse — *continued*
atmospheric pressure — *continued*
low — *see* Effect, adverse, high altitude
specified effect NEC 993.8
biological, correct substance properly administered (*see also* Effect, adverse, drug) 995.20
blood (derivatives) (serum) (transfusion) — *see* Complications, transfusion
chemical substance NEC 989.9
specified — *see* Table of Drugs and Chemicals
cobalt, radioactive (*see also* Effect, adverse, radioactive substance) 990
cold (temperature) (weather) 991.9
chilblains 991.5
frostbite — *see* Frostbite
specified effect NEC 991.8
drugs and medicinals 995.20
correct substance properly administered 995.20
overdose or wrong substance given or taken 977.9
specified drug — *see* Table of Drugs and Chemicals
electric current (shock) 994.8
burn — *see* Burn, by site
electricity (electrocution) (shock) 994.8
burn — *see* Burn, by site
exertion (excessive) 994.5
exposure 994.9
exhaustion 994.4
external cause NEC 994.9
fallout (radioactive) NEC 990
fluoroscopy NEC 990
foodstuffs
allergic reaction (*see also* Allergy, food) 693.1
anaphylactic shock due to food NEC 995.60
noxious 988.9
specified type NEC (*see also* Poisoning, by name of noxious foodstuff) 988.8
gases, fumes, or vapors — *see* Table of Drugs and Chemicals
glue (airplane) sniffing 304.6 ☑
heat — *see* Heat
high altitude NEC 993.2
anoxia 993.2
on
ears 993.0
sinuses 993.1
polycythemia 289.0
hot weather — *see* Heat
hunger 994.2
immersion, foot 991.4
immunization — *see* Complications, vaccination
immunological agents — *see* Complications, vaccination
implantation (removable) of isotope or radium NEC 990
infrared (radiation) (rays) NEC 990
burn — *see* Burn, by site
dermatitis or eczema 692.82
infusion — *see* Complications, infusion
ingestion or injection of isotope (therapeutic) NEC 990
irradiation NEC (*see also* Effect, adverse, radiation) 990
isotope (radioactive) NEC 990
lack of care (child) (infant) (newborn) 995.52
adult 995.84
lightning 994.0
burn — *see* Burn, by site
Lirugin — *see* Complications, vaccination
medicinal substance, correct, properly administered (*see also* Effect, adverse, drugs) 995.20

Effect, adverse — *continued*
mesothorium NEC 990
motion 994.6
noise, inner ear 388.10
other drug, medicinal and biological substance 995.29
overheated places — *see* Heat
polonium NEC 990
psychosocial, of work environment V62.1
radiation (diagnostic) (fallout) (infrared) (natural source) (therapeutic) (tracer) (ultraviolet) (x-ray) NEC 990
with pulmonary manifestations
acute 508.0
chronic 508.1
dermatitis or eczema 692.82
due to sun NEC (*see also* Dermatitis, due to, sun) 692.70
fibrosis of lungs 508.1
maternal with suspected damage to fetus affecting management of pregnancy 655.6 ☑
pneumonitis 508.0
radioactive substance NEC 990
dermatitis or eczema 692.82
radioactivity NEC 990
radiotherapy NEC 990
dermatitis or eczema 692.82
radium NEC 990
reduced temperature 991.9
frostbite — *see* Frostbite
immersion, foot (hand) 991.4
specified effect NEC 991.8
roentgenography NEC 990
roentgenoscopy NEC 990
roentgen rays NEC 990
serum (prophylactic) (therapeutic) NEC 999.5
specified NEC 995.89
external cause NEC 994.9
strangulation 994.7
submersion 994.1
teletherapy NEC 990
thirst 994.3
transfusion — *see* Complications, transfusion
ultraviolet (radiation) (rays) NEC 990
burn (*see also* Burn, by site)
from sun (*see also* Sunburn) 692.71
dermatitis or eczema 692.82
due to sun NEC (*see also* Dermatitis, due to, sun) 692.70
uranium NEC 990
vaccine (any) — *see* Complications, vaccination
weightlessness 994.9
whole blood (*see also* Complications, transfusion)
overdose or wrong substance given (*see also* Table of Drugs and Chemicals) 964.7
working environment V62.1
x-rays NEC 990
dermatitis or eczema 692.82
Effect, remote
of cancer — *see* condition
Effects, late — *see* Late, effect (of)
Effluvium, telogen 704.02
Effort
intolerance 306.2
syndrome (aviators) (psychogenic) 306.2
Effusion
amniotic fluid (*see also* Rupture, membranes, premature) 658.1 ☑
brain (serous) 348.5
bronchial (*see also* Bronchitis) 490
cerebral 348.5
cerebrospinal (*see also* Meningitis) 322.9

- **Effusion** — *continued*
  - cerebrospinal (*see also* Meningitis) — *continued*
    - vessel 348.5
  - chest — *see* Effusion, pleura
  - intracranial 348.5
  - joint 719.00
    - ankle 719.07
    - elbow 719.02
    - foot 719.07
    - hand 719.04
    - hip 719.05
    - knee 719.06
    - multiple sites 719.09
    - pelvic region 719.05
    - shoulder (region) 719.01
    - specified site NEC 719.08
    - wrist 719.03
  - meninges (*see also* Meningitis) 322.9
  - pericardium, pericardial (*see also* Pericarditis) 423.9
    - acute 420.90
  - peritoneal (chronic) 568.82
  - pleura, pleurisy, pleuritic, pleuropericardial 511.9
    - bacterial, nontuberculous 511.1
    - fetus or newborn 511.9
    - malignant 511.81 ▲
    - nontuberculous 511.9
      - bacterial 511.1
    - pneumococcal 511.1
    - staphylococcal 511.1
    - streptococcal 511.1
    - traumatic 862.29
      - with open wound 862.39
    - tuberculous (*see also* Tuberculosis, pleura) 012.0 ☑
      - primary progressive 010.1 ☑
  - pulmonary — *see* Effusion, pleura
  - spinal (*see also* Meningitis) 322.9
  - thorax, thoracic — *see* Effusion, pleura
- **Egg** (oocyte) (ovum)
  - donor V59.70
    - over age 35 V59.73
      - anonymous recipient V59.73
      - designated recipient V59.74
    - under age 35 V59.71
      - anonymous recipient V59.71
      - designated recipient V59.72
- **Eggshell nails** 703.8
  - congenital 757.5
- **Ego-dystonic**
  - homosexuality 302.0
  - lesbianism 302.0
  - sexual orientation 302.0
- **Egyptian splenomegaly** 120.1
- **Ehlers-Danlos syndrome** 756.83
- **Ehrlichiosis** 082.40
  - chaffeensis 082.41
  - specified type NEC 082.49
- **Eichstedt's disease** (pityriasis versicolor) 111.0
- **Eisenmenger's complex or syndrome** (ventricular septal defect) 745.4
- **Ejaculation, semen**
  - painful 608.89
    - psychogenic 306.59
  - premature 302.75
  - retrograde 608.87
- **Ekbom syndrome** (restless legs) 333.94
- **Ekman's syndrome** (brittle bones and blue sclera) 756.51
- **Elastic skin** 756.83
  - acquired 701.8
- **Elastofibroma** (M8820/0) — *see* Neoplasm, connective tissue, benign
- **Elastoidosis**
  - cutanea nodularis 701.8
  - cutis cystica et comedonica 701.8
- **Elastoma** 757.39
  - juvenile 757.39
  - Miescher's (elastosis perforans serpiginosa) 701.1
- **Elastomyofibrosis** 425.3
- **Elastosis** 701.8
- **Elastosis** — *continued*
  - atrophicans 701.8
  - perforans serpiginosa 701.1
  - reactive perforating 701.1
  - senilis 701.8
  - solar (actinic) 692.74
- **Elbow** — *see* condition
- **Electric**
  - current, electricity, effects (concussion) (fatal) (nonfatal) (shock) 994.8
    - burn — *see* Burn, by site
  - feet (foot) syndrome 266.2
  - ● shock from electroshock gun (taser) 994.8 ●
- **Electrocution** 994.8
- **Electrolyte imbalance** 276.9
  - with
    - abortion — *see* Abortion, by type, with metabolic disorder
    - ectopic pregnancy (*see also* categories 633.0–633.9) 639.4
    - hyperemesis gravidarum (before 22 completed weeks gestation) 643.1 ☑
    - molar pregnancy (*see also* categories 630–632) 639.4
  - following
    - abortion 639.4
    - ectopic or molar pregnancy 639.4
- **Elephantiasis** (nonfilarial) 457.1
  - arabicum (*see also* Infestation, filarial) 125.9
  - congenita hereditaria 757.0
  - congenital (any site) 757.0
  - due to
    - Brugia (malayi) 125.1
    - mastectomy operation 457.0
    - Wuchereria (bancrofti) 125.0
      - malayi 125.1
  - eyelid 374.83
  - filarial (*see also* Infestation, filarial) 125.9
  - filariensis (*see also* Infestation, filarial) 125.9
  - gingival 523.8
  - glandular 457.1
  - graecorum 030.9
  - lymphangiectatic 457.1
  - lymphatic vessel 457.1
    - due to mastectomy operation 457.0
  - neuromatosa 237.71
  - postmastectomy 457.0
  - scrotum 457.1
  - streptococcal 457.1
  - surgical 997.99
    - postmastectomy 457.0
  - telangiectodes 457.1
  - vulva (nonfilarial) 624.8
- **Elephant man syndrome** 237.71
- **Elevated** — *see* Elevation
- **Elevation**
  - 17-ketosteroids 791.9
  - acid phosphatase 790.5
  - alkaline phosphatase 790.5
  - amylase 790.5
  - antibody titers 795.79
  - basal metabolic rate (BMR) 794.7
  - blood pressure (*see also* Hypertension) 401.9
    - reading (incidental) (isolated) (nonspecific), no diagnosis of hypertension 796.2
  - blood sugar 790.29
  - body temperature (of unknown origin) (*see also* Pyrexia) 780.60 ▲
  - cancer antigen 125 [CA 125] 795.82
  - carcinoembryonic antigen [CEA] 795.81
  - cholesterol 272.0
    - with ▶high◀ triglycerides 272.2
  - conjugate, eye 378.81
  - C-reactive protein (CRP) 790.95
  - CRP (C-reactive protein) 790.95
  - diaphragm, congenital 756.6
- **Elevation** — *continued*
  - glucose
    - fasting 790.21
    - tolerance test 790.22
  - immunoglobulin level 795.79
  - indolacetic acid 791.9
  - lactic acid dehydrogenase (LDH) level 790.4
  - leukocytes 288.60
  - lipase 790.5
  - lipoprotein a level 272.8
  - liver function test (LFT) 790.6
    - alkaline phosphatase 790.5
    - aminotransferase 790.4
    - bilirubin 782.4
    - hepatic enzyme NEC 790.5
    - lactate dehydrogenase 790.4
  - lymphocytes 288.61
  - prostate specific antigen (PSA) 790.93
  - renin 790.99
    - in hypertension (*see also* Hypertension, renovascular) 405.91
  - Rh titer 999.7
  - scapula, congenital 755.52
  - sedimentation rate 790.1
  - SGOT 790.4
  - SGPT 790.4
  - transaminase 790.4
  - triglycerides 272.1
    - with ▶high◀ cholesterol 272.2
  - vanillylmandelic acid 791.9
  - venous pressure 459.89
  - VMA 791.9
  - white blood cell count 288.60
    - specified NEC 288.69
- **Elliptocytosis** (congenital) (hereditary) 282.1
  - Hb-C (disease) 282.7
  - hemoglobin disease 282.7
  - sickle-cell (disease) 282.60
    - trait 282.5
- **Ellison-Zollinger syndrome** (gastric hypersecretion with pancreatic islet cell tumor) 251.5
- **Ellis-van Creveld disease or syndrome** (chondroectodermal dysplasia) 756.55
- **Elongation, elongated** (congenital) — *see also* Distortion
  - bone 756.9
  - cervix (uteri) 752.49
    - acquired 622.6
    - hypertrophic 622.6
  - colon 751.5
  - common bile duct 751.69
  - cystic duct 751.69
  - frenulum, penis 752.69
  - labia minora, acquired 624.8
  - ligamentum patellae 756.89
  - petiolus (epiglottidis) 748.3
  - styloid bone (process) 733.99
  - tooth, teeth 520.2
  - uvula 750.26
    - acquired 528.9
- **Elschnig bodies or pearls** 366.51
- **El Tor cholera** 001.1
- **Emaciation** (due to malnutrition) 261
- **Emancipation disorder** 309.22
- **Embadomoniasis** 007.8
- **Embarrassment heart, cardiac** — *see* Disease, heart
- **Embedded tooth, teeth** 520.6
  - root only 525.3
- **Embolic** — *see* condition
- **Embolism** 444.9
  - with
    - abortion — *see* Abortion, by type, with embolism
    - ectopic pregnancy (*see also* categories 633.0–633.9) 639.6
    - molar pregnancy (*see also* categories 630–632) 639.6
  - air (any site) 958.0
    - with
      - abortion — *see* Abortion, by type, with embolism
- **Embolism** — *continued*
  - air — *continued*
    - with — *continued*
      - ectopic pregnancy (*see also* categories 633.0–633.9) 639.6
      - molar pregnancy (*see also* categories 630–632) 639.6
    - due to implanted device — *see* Complications, due to (presence of) any device, implant, or graft classified to 996.0–996.5 NEC
    - following
      - abortion 639.6
      - ectopic or molar pregnancy 639.6
      - infusion, perfusion, or transfusion 999.1
    - in pregnancy, childbirth, or puerperium 673.0 ☑
    - traumatic 958.0
  - amniotic fluid (pulmonary) 673.1 ☑
    - with
      - abortion — *see* Abortion, by type, with embolism
      - ectopic pregnancy (*see also* categories 633.0–633.9) 639.6
      - molar pregnancy (*see also* categories 630–632) 639.6
    - following
      - abortion 639.6
      - ectopic or molar pregnancy 639.6
  - aorta, aortic 444.1
    - abdominal 444.0
    - bifurcation 444.0
    - saddle 444.0
    - thoracic 444.1
  - artery 444.9
    - auditory, internal 433.8 ☑
    - basilar (*see also* Occlusion, artery, basilar) 433.0 ☑
    - bladder 444.89
    - carotid (common) (internal) (*see also* Occlusion, artery, carotid) 433.1 ☑
    - cerebellar (anterior inferior) (posterior inferior) (superior) 433.8 ☑
    - cerebral (*see also* Embolism, brain) 434.1 ☑
    - choroidal (anterior) 433.8 ☑
    - communicating posterior 433.8 ☑
    - coronary (*see also* Infarct, myocardium) 410.9 ☑
      - without myocardial infarction 411.81
    - extremity 444.22
      - lower 444.22
      - upper 444.21
    - hypophyseal 433.8 ☑
    - mesenteric (with gangrene) 557.0
    - ophthalmic (*see also* Occlusion, retina) 362.30
    - peripheral 444.22
    - pontine 433.8 ☑
    - precerebral NEC — *see* Occlusion, artery, precerebral
    - pulmonary — *see* Embolism, pulmonary
    - pyemic 449
      - pulmonary 415.12
    - renal 593.81
    - retinal (*see also* Occlusion, retina) 362.30
    - septic 449
      - pulmonary 415.12
    - specified site NEC 444.89
    - vertebral (*see also* Occlusion, artery, vertebral) 433.2 ☑
  - auditory, internal 433.8 ☑
  - basilar (artery) (*see also* Occlusion, artery, basilar) 433.0 ☑

- **Embolism** — *continued*
  - birth, mother — *see* Embolism, obstetrical
  - blood-clot
    - with
      - abortion — *see* Abortion, by type, with embolism
      - ectopic pregnancy (*see also* categories 633.0–633.9) 639.6
      - molar pregnancy (*see also* categories 630–632) 639.6
    - following
      - abortion 639.6
      - ectopic or molar pregnancy 639.6
    - in pregnancy, childbirth, or puerperium 673.2 ☑
  - brain 434.1 ☑
    - with
      - abortion — *see* Abortion, by type, with embolism
      - ectopic pregnancy (*see also* categories 633.0–633.9) 639.6
      - molar pregnancy (*see also* categories 630–632) 639.6
    - following
      - abortion 639.6
      - ectopic or molar pregnancy 639.6
    - late effect — *see* Late effect(s) (of) cerebrovascular disease
    - puerperal, postpartum, childbirth 674.0 ☑
  - capillary 448.9
  - cardiac (*see also* Infarct, myocardium) 410.9 ☑
  - carotid (artery) (common) (internal) (*see also* Occlusion, artery, carotid) 433.1 ☑
  - cavernous sinus (venous) — *see* Embolism, intracranial venous sinus
  - cerebral (*see also* Embolism, brain) 434.1 ☑
  - cholesterol — *see* Atheroembolism
  - choroidal (anterior) (artery) 433.8 ☑
  - coronary (artery or vein) (systemic) (*see also* Infarct, myocardium) 410.9 ☑
    - without myocardial infarction 411.81
  - due to (presence of) any device, implant, or graft classifiable to 996.0–996.5 — *see* Complications, due to (presence of) any device, implant, or graft classified to 996.0–996.5 NEC
  - encephalomalacia (*see also* Embolism, brain) 434.1 ☑
  - extremities 444.22
    - lower 444.22
    - upper 444.21
  - eye 362.30
  - fat (cerebral) (pulmonary) (systemic) 958.1
    - with
      - abortion — *see* Abortion, by type, with embolism
      - ectopic pregnancy (*see also* categories 633.0–633.9) 639.6
      - molar pregnancy (*see also* categories 630–632) 639.6
    - complicating delivery or puerperium 673.8 ☑
    - following
      - abortion 639.6
      - ectopic or molar pregnancy 639.6
    - in pregnancy, childbirth, or the puerperium 673.8 ☑
  - femoral (artery) 444.22
    - vein 453.8
      - deep 453.41

- **Embolism** — *continued*
  - following
    - abortion 639.6
    - ectopic or molar pregnancy 639.6
    - infusion, perfusion, or transfusion
      - air 999.1
      - thrombus 999.2
  - heart (fatty) (*see also* Infarct, myocardium) 410.9 ☑
  - hepatic (vein) 453.0
  - iliac (artery) 444.81
  - iliofemoral 444.81
  - in pregnancy, childbirth, or puerperium (pulmonary) — *see* Embolism, obstetrical
  - intestine (artery) (vein) (with gangrene) 557.0
  - intracranial (*see also* Embolism, brain) 434.1 ☑
    - venous sinus (any) 325
      - late effect — *see* category 326
      - nonpyogenic 437.6
        - in pregnancy or puerperium 671.5 ☑
  - kidney (artery) 593.81
  - lateral sinus (venous) — *see* Embolism, intracranial venous sinus
  - longitudinal sinus (venous) — *see* Embolism, intracranial venous sinus
  - lower extremity 444.22
  - lung (massive) — *see* Embolism, pulmonary
  - meninges (*see also* Embolism, brain) 434.1 ☑
  - mesenteric (artery) (with gangrene) 557.0
  - multiple NEC 444.9
  - obstetrical (pulmonary) 673.2 ☑
    - air 673.0 ☑
    - amniotic fluid (pulmonary) 673.1 ☑
    - blood-clot 673.2 ☑
    - cardiac 674.8 ☑
    - fat 673.8 ☑
    - heart 674.8 ☑
    - pyemic 673.3 ☑
    - septic 673.3 ☑
    - specified NEC 674.8 ☑
  - ophthalmic (*see also* Occlusion, retina) 362.30
  - paradoxical NEC 444.9
  - penis 607.82
  - peripheral arteries NEC 444.22
    - lower 444.22
    - upper 444.21
  - pituitary 253.8
  - popliteal (artery) 444.22
  - portal (vein) 452
  - postoperative NEC 997.2
    - cerebral 997.02
    - mesenteric artery 997.71
    - other vessels 997.79
    - peripheral vascular 997.2
    - pulmonary 415.11
      - septic 415.11 ▲
    - renal artery 997.72
  - precerebral artery (*see also* Occlusion, artery, precerebral) 433.9 ☑
  - puerperal — *see* Embolism, obstetrical
  - pulmonary (artery) (vein) 415.19
    - with
      - abortion — *see* Abortion, by type, with embolism
      - ectopic pregnancy (*see also* categories 633.0–633.9) 639.6
      - molar pregnancy (*see also* categories 630–632) 639.6
    - following
      - abortion 639.6
      - ectopic or molar pregnancy 639.6
    - iatrogenic 415.11

- **Embolism** — *continued*
  - pulmonary — *continued*
    - in pregnancy, childbirth, or puerperium — *see* Embolism, obstetrical
    - postoperative 415.11
    - septic 415.12
  - pyemic (multiple) (*see also* Septicemia) 415.12
    - with
      - abortion — *see* Abortion, by type, with embolism
      - ectopic pregnancy (*see also* categories 633.0–633.9) 639.6
      - molar pregnancy (*see also* categories 630–632) 639.6
    - Aerobacter aerogenes 415.12
    - enteric gram-negative bacilli 415.12
    - Enterobacter aerogenes 415.12
    - Escherichia coli 415.12
    - following
      - abortion 639.6
      - ectopic or molar pregnancy 639.6
    - Hemophilus influenzae 415.12
    - pneumococcal 415.12
    - Proteus vulgaris 415.12
    - Pseudomonas (aeruginosa) 415.12
    - puerperal, postpartum, childbirth (any organism) 673.3 ☑
    - Serratia 415.12
    - specified organism NEC 415.12
    - staphylococcal 415.12
      - aureus 415.12
      - specified organism NEC 415.12
    - streptococcal 415.12
  - renal (artery) 593.81
    - vein 453.3
  - retina, retinal (*see also* Occlusion, retina) 362.30
  - saddle (aorta) 444.0
  - septic 415.12
    - arterial 449
  - septicemic — *see* Embolism, pyemic
  - sinus — *see* Embolism, intracranial venous sinus
  - soap
    - with
      - abortion — *see* Abortion, by type, with embolism
      - ectopic pregnancy (*see also* categories 633.0–633.9) 639.6
      - molar pregnancy (*see also* categories 630–632) 639.6
    - following
      - abortion 639.6
      - ectopic or molar pregnancy 639.6
  - spinal cord (nonpyogenic) 336.1
    - in pregnancy or puerperium 671.5 ☑
    - pyogenic origin 324.1
      - late effect — *see* category 326
  - spleen, splenic (artery) 444.89
  - thrombus (thromboembolism) following infusion, perfusion, or transfusion 999.2
  - upper extremity 444.21
  - vein 453.9
    - with inflammation or phlebitis — *see* Thrombophlebitis
    - cerebral (*see also* Embolism, brain) 434.1 ☑
    - coronary (*see also* Infarct, myocardium) 410.9 ☑
      - without myocardial infarction 411.81
    - hepatic 453.0
    - lower extremity 453.8
      - deep 453.40
        - calf 453.42
        - distal (lower leg) 453.42
        - femoral 453.41

- **Embolism** — *continued*
  - vein — *continued*
    - lower extremity — *continued*
      - deep — *continued*
        - iliac 453.41
        - lower leg 453.42
        - peroneal 453.42
        - popliteal 453.41
        - proximal (upper leg) 453.41
        - thigh 453.41
        - tibial 453.42
    - mesenteric (with gangrene) 557.0
    - portal 452
    - pulmonary — *see* Embolism, pulmonary
    - renal 453.3
    - specified NEC 453.8
      - with inflammation or phlebitis — *see* Thrombophlebitis
  - vena cava (inferior) (superior) 453.2
  - vessels of brain (*see also* Embolism, brain) 434.1 ☑
- **Embolization** — *see* **Embolism**
- **Embolus** — *see* Embolism
- **Embryoma (M9080/1)** — *see also* Neoplasm, by site, uncertain behavior
  - benign (M9080/0) — *see* Neoplasm, by site, benign
  - kidney (M8960/3) 189.0
  - liver (M8970/3) 155.0
  - malignant (M9080/3) (*see also* Neoplasm, by site, malignant)
    - kidney (M8960/3) 189.0
    - liver (M8970/3) 155.0
    - testis (M9070/3) 186.9
      - undescended 186.0
  - testis (M9070/3) 186.9
    - undescended 186.0
- **Embryonic**
  - circulation 747.9
  - heart 747.9
  - vas deferens 752.89
- **Embryopathia NEC** 759.9
- **Embryotomy, fetal** 763.89
- **Embryotoxon** 743.43
  - interfering with vision 743.42
- **Emesis** — *see also* Vomiting
  - gravidarum — *see* Hyperemesis, gravidarum
- **Emissions, nocturnal** (semen) 608.89
- **Emotional**
  - crisis — *see* Crisis, emotional
  - disorder (*see also* Disorder, mental) 300.9
  - instability (excessive) 301.3
  - overlay — *see* Reaction, adjustment
  - upset 300.9
- **Emotionality, pathological** 301.3
- **Emotogenic disease** — *see also* Disorder, psychogenic 306.9
- **Emphysema** (atrophic) (centriacinar) (centrilobular) (chronic) (diffuse) (essential) (hypertrophic) (interlobular) (lung) (obstructive) (panlobular) (paracicatricial) (paracinar) (postural) (pulmonary) (senile) (subpleural) (traction) (unilateral) (unilobular) (vesicular) 492.8
  - with bronchitis
    - chronic 491.20
      - with
        - acute bronchitis 491.22
        - exacerbation (acute) 491.21
  - bullous (giant) 492.0
  - cellular tissue 958.7
    - surgical 998.81
  - compensatory 518.2
  - congenital 770.2
  - conjunctiva 372.89
  - connective tissue 958.7
    - surgical 998.81
  - due to fumes or vapors 506.4
  - eye 376.89
  - eyelid 374.85
    - surgical 998.81
    - traumatic 958.7

Emphysema — *continued*
- fetus or newborn (interstitial) (mediastinal) (unilobular) 770.2
- heart 416.9
- interstitial 518.1
  - congenital 770.2
  - fetus or newborn 770.2
- laminated tissue 958.7
  - surgical 998.81
- mediastinal 518.1
  - fetus or newborn 770.2
- newborn (interstitial) (mediastinal) (unilobular) 770.2
- obstructive diffuse with fibrosis 492.8
- orbit 376.89
- subcutaneous 958.7
  - due to trauma 958.7
  - nontraumatic 518.1
  - surgical 998.81
- surgical 998.81
- thymus (gland) (congenital) 254.8
- traumatic 958.7
- tuberculous (*see also* Tuberculosis, pulmonary) 011.9 ☑

Employment examination (certification) V70.5

Empty sella (turcica) syndrome 253.8

Empyema (chest) (diaphragmatic) (double) (encapsulated) (general) (interlobar) (lung) (medial) (necessitatis) (perforating chest wall) (pleura) (pneumococcal) (residual) (sacculated) (streptococcal) (supradiaphragmatic) 510.9
- with fistula 510.0
- accessory sinus (chronic) (*see also* Sinusitis) 473.9
- acute 510.9
  - with fistula 510.0
- antrum (chronic) (*see also* Sinusitis, maxillary) 473.0
- brain (any part) (*see also* Abscess, brain) 324.0
- ethmoidal (sinus) (chronic) (*see also* Sinusitis, ethmoidal) 473.2
- extradural (*see also* Abscess, extradural) 324.9
- frontal (sinus) (chronic) (*see also* Sinusitis, frontal) 473.1
- gallbladder (*see also* Cholecystitis, acute) 575.0
- mastoid (process) (acute) (*see also* Mastoiditis, acute) 383.00
- maxilla, maxillary 526.4
  - sinus (chronic) (*see also* Sinusitis, maxillary) 473.0
- nasal sinus (chronic) (*see also* Sinusitis) 473.9
- sinus (accessory) (nasal) (*see also* Sinusitis) 473.9
- sphenoidal (chronic) (sinus) (*see also* Sinusitis, sphenoidal) 473.3
- subarachnoid (*see also* Abscess, extradural) 324.9
- subdural (*see also* Abscess, extradural) 324.9
- tuberculous (*see also* Tuberculosis, pleura) 012.0 ☑
- ureter (*see also* Ureteritis) 593.89
- ventricular (*see also* Abscess, brain) 324.0

Enameloma 520.2

Encephalitis (bacterial) (chronic) (hemorrhagic) (idiopathic) (nonepidemic) (spurious) (subacute) 323.9
- acute (*see also* Encephalitis, viral)
  - disseminated (postinfectious) NEC 136.9 *[323.61]*
    - postimmunization or postvaccination 323.51
  - inclusional 049.8
  - inclusion body 049.8
  - necrotizing 049.8
- arboviral, arbovirus NEC 064
- arthropod-borne (*see also* Encephalitis, viral, arthropod-borne) 064

Encephalitis — *continued*
- Australian X 062.4
- Bwamba fever 066.3
- California (virus) 062.5
- Central European 063.2
- Czechoslovakian 063.2
- Dawson's (inclusion body) 046.2
- diffuse sclerosing 046.2
- due to
  - actinomycosis 039.8 *[323.41]*
  - cat-scratch disease 078.3 *[323.01]*
  - human herpesvirus NEC 058.29
  - human herpesvirus 6 058.21
  - human herpesvirus 7 058.29
  - infection classified elsewhere 136.9 *[323.41]*
  - infectious mononucleosis 075 *[323.01]*
  - malaria (*see also* Malaria) 084.6 *[323.2]*
  - Negishi virus 064
  - ornithosis 073.7 *[323.01]*
  - prophylactic inoculation against smallpox 323.51
  - rickettsiosis (*see also* Rickettsiosis) 083.9 *[323.1]*
  - rubella 056.01
  - toxoplasmosis (acquired) 130.0
    - congenital (active) 771.2 *[323.41]*
  - typhus (fever) (*see also* Typhus) 081.9 *[323.1]*
  - vaccination (smallpox) 323.51
- Eastern equine 062.2
- endemic 049.8
- epidemic 049.8
- equine (acute) (infectious) (viral) 062.9
  - Eastern 062.2
  - Venezuelan 066.2
  - Western 062.1
- Far Eastern 063.0
- following vaccination or other immunization procedure 323.51
- herpes 054.3
- human herpesvirus NEC 058.29
- human herpesvirus 6 058.21
- human herpesvirus 7 058.29
- Ilheus (virus) 062.8
- inclusion body 046.2
- infectious (acute) (virus) NEC 049.8
- influenzal 487.8 *[323.41]*
  - lethargic 049.8
- Japanese (B type) 062.0
- La Crosse 062.5
- Langat 063.8
- late effect — *see* Late, effect, encephalitis
- lead 984.9 *[323.71]*
- lethargic (acute) (infectious) (influenzal) 049.8
- lethargica 049.8
- louping ill 063.1
- lupus 710.0 *[323.81]*
- lymphatica 049.0
- Mengo 049.8
- meningococcal 036.1
- mumps 072.2
- Murray Valley 062.4
- myoclonic 049.8
- Negishi virus 064
- otitic NEC 382.4 *[323.41]*
- parasitic NEC 123.9 *[323.41]*
- periaxialis (concentrica) (diffusa) 341.1
- postchickenpox 052.0
- postexanthematous NEC 057.9 *[323.62]*
- postimmunization 323.51
- postinfectious NEC 136.9 *[323.62]*
- postmeasles 055.0
- posttraumatic 323.81
- postvaccinal (smallpox) 323.51
- postvaricella 052.0
- postviral NEC 079.99 *[323.62]*
  - postexanthematous 057.9 *[323.62]*
    - specified NEC 057.8 *[323.62]*
- Powassan 063.8

Encephalitis — *continued*
- progressive subcortical (Binswanger's) 290.12
- Rasmussen 323.81
- Rio Bravo 049.8
- rubella 056.01
- Russian
  - autumnal 062.0
  - spring-summer type (taiga) 063.0
- saturnine 984.9 *[323.71]*
- Semliki Forest 062.8
- serous 048
- slow-acting virus NEC 046.8
- specified cause NEC 323.81
- St. Louis type 062.3
- subacute sclerosing 046.2
- subcorticalis chronica 290.12
- summer 062.0
- suppurative 324.0
- syphilitic 094.81
  - congenital 090.41
- tick-borne 063.9
- torula, torular 117.5 *[323.41]*
- toxic NEC 989.9 *[323.71]*
- toxoplasmic (acquired) 130.0
  - congenital (active) 771.2 *[323.41]*
- trichinosis 124 *[323.41]*
- Trypanosomiasis (*see also* Trypanosomiasis) 086.9 *[323.2]*
- tuberculous (*see also* Tuberculosis) 013.6 ☑
- type B (Japanese) 062.0
- type C 062.3
- van Bogaert's 046.2
- Venezuelan 066.2
- Vienna type 049.8
- viral, virus 049.9
  - arthropod-borne NEC 064
    - mosquito-borne 062.9
      - Australian X disease 062.4
      - California virus 062.5
      - Eastern equine 062.2
      - Ilheus virus 062.8
      - Japanese (B type) 062.0
      - Murray Valley 062.4
      - specified type NEC 062.8
      - St. Louis 062.3
      - type B 062.0
      - type C 062.3
      - Western equine 062.1
    - tick-borne 063.9
      - biundulant 063.2
      - Central European 063.2
      - Czechoslovakian 063.2
      - diphasic meningoencephalitis 063.2
      - Far Eastern 063.0
      - Langat 063.8
      - louping ill 063.1
      - Powassan 063.8
      - Russian spring-summer (taiga) 063.0
      - specified type NEC 063.8
    - vector unknown 064
    - Western equine 062.1
  - slow acting NEC 046.8
  - specified type NEC 049.8
  - vaccination, prophylactic (against) V05.0
- von Economo's 049.8
- Western equine 062.1
- West Nile type 066.41

Encephalocele 742.0
- orbit 376.81

Encephalocystocele 742.0

Encephalomalacia (brain) (cerebellar) (cerebral) (cerebrospinal) — *see also* Softening, brain 434.9 ☑
- due to
  - hemorrhage (*see also* Hemorrhage, brain) 431
  - recurrent spasm of artery 435.9
- embolic (cerebral) (*see also* Embolism, brain) 434.1 ☑
- subcorticalis chronicus arteriosclerotica 290.12

Encephalomalacia — *see also* Softening, brain — *continued*
- thrombotic (*see also* Thrombosis, brain) 434.0 ☑

Encephalomeningitis — *see* Meningoencephalitis

Encephalomeningocele 742.0

Encephalomeningomyelitis — *see* Meningoencephalitis

Encephalomeningopathy — *see also* Meningoencephalitis 349.9

Encephalomyelitis (chronic) (granulomatous) (myalgic, benign) — *see also* Encephalitis 323.9
- abortive disseminated 049.8
- acute disseminated (ADEM) (postinfectious) 136.9 *[323.61]*
  - infectious 136.9 *[323.61]*
  - noninfectious 323.81
  - postimmunization 323.51
- due to
  - cat-scratch disease 078.3 *[323.01]*
  - infectious mononucleosis 075 *[323.01]*
  - ornithosis 073.7 *[323.01]*
  - vaccination (any) 323.51
- equine (acute) (infectious) 062.9
  - Eastern 062.2
  - Venezuelan 066.2
  - Western 062.1
- funicularis infectiosa 049.8
- late effect — *see* Late, effect, encephalitis
- Munch-Peterson's 049.8
- postchickenpox 052.0
- postimmunization 323.51
- postmeasles 055.0
- postvaccinal (smallpox) 323.51
- rubella 056.01
- specified cause NEC 323.81
- syphilitic 094.81
- West Nile 066.41

Encephalomyelocele 742.0

Encephalomyelomeningitis — *see* Meningoencephalitis

Encephalomyeloneuropathy 349.9

Encephalomyelopathy 349.9
- subacute necrotizing (infantile) 330.8

Encephalomyeloradiculitis (acute) 357.0

Encephalomyeloradiculoneuritis (acute) 357.0

Encephalomyeloradiculopathy 349.9

Encephalomyocarditis 074.23

Encephalopathia hyperbilirubinemica, newborn 774.7
- due to isoimmunization (conditions classifiable to 773.0–773.2) 773.4

Encephalopathy (acute) 348.30
- alcoholic 291.2
- anoxic — *see* Damage, brain, anoxic
- arteriosclerotic 437.0
  - late effect — *see* Late effect(s) (of) cerebrovascular disease
- bilirubin, newborn 774.7
  - due to isoimmunization 773.4
- congenital 742.9
- demyelinating (callosal) 341.8
- due to
  - birth injury (intracranial) 767.8
  - dialysis 294.8
    - transient 293.9
  - drugs — (*see also* Table of Drugs and Chemicals) 348.39 ●
  - hyperinsulinism — *see* Hyperinsulinism
  - influenza (virus) 487.8
  - lack of vitamin (*see also* Deficiency, vitamin) 269.2
  - nicotinic acid deficiency 291.2
  - serum (nontherapeutic) (therapeutic) 999.5
  - syphilis 094.81
  - trauma (postconcussional) 310.2

Index

Emphysema — Encephalopathy

Encephalopathy — *continued*
due to — *continued*
trauma — *continued*
current (*see also* Concussion, brain) 850.9
with skull fracture — *see* Fracture, skull, by site, with intracranial injury
vaccination 323.51
hepatic 572.2
hyperbilirubinemic, newborn 774.7
due to isoimmunization (conditions classifiable to 773.0–773.2) 773.4
hypertensive 437.2
hypoglycemic 251.2
hypoxic (*see also* Damage, brain, anoxic)
ischemic (HIE) 768.7
infantile cystic necrotizing (congenital) 341.8
lead 984.9 *[323.71]*
leukopolio 330.0
metabolic (*see also* Delirium) 348.31
toxic 349.82
necrotizing
hemorrhagic ▶(acute)◀ 323.61
subacute 330.8
other specified type NEC 348.39
pellagrous 265.2
portal-systemic 572.2
postcontusional 310.2
posttraumatic 310.2
saturnine 984.9 *[323.71]*
septic 348.31
spongioform, subacute (viral) 046.19 ▲
subacute
necrotizing 330.8
spongioform 046.19 ▲
viral, spongioform 046.19 ▲
subcortical progressive (Schilder) 341.1
chronic (Binswanger's) 290.12
toxic 349.82
metabolic 349.82
traumatic (postconcussional) 310.2
current (*see also* Concussion, brain) 850.9
with skull fracture — *see* Fracture, skull, by site, with intracranial injury
vitamin B deficiency NEC 266.9
Wernicke's (superior hemorrhagic polioencephalitis) 265.1
Encephalorrhagia — *see also* Hemorrhage, brain 432.9
healed or old V12.54
late effect — *see* Late effect(s) (of) cerebrovascular disease
Encephalosis, posttraumatic 310.2
Enchondroma (M9220/0) — *see also* Neoplasm, bone, benign
multiple, congenital 756.4
Enchondromatosis (cartilaginous) (congenital) (multiple) 756.4
Enchondroses, multiple (cartilaginous) (congenital) 756.4
Encopresis — *see also* Incontinence, feces 787.6
nonorganic origin 307.7
Encounter for — *see also* Admission for
administrative purpose only V68.9
referral of patient without examination or treatment V68.81
specified purpose NEC V68.89
chemotherapy, antineoplastic V58.11
dialysis
extracorporeal (renal) V56.0
peritoneal V56.8
disability examination V68.01
end-of-life care V66.7
hospice care V66.7
immunotherapy, antineoplastic V58.12
palliative care V66.7
Encounter for — *see also* Admission for — *continued*
paternity testing V70.4
radiotherapy V58.0
respirator [ventilator] dependence during
mechanical failure V46.14
power failure V46.12
for weaning V46.13
screening mammogram NEC V76.12
for high-risk patient V76.11
terminal care V66.7
weaning from respirator [ventilator] V46.13
Encystment — *see* Cyst
Endamebiasis — *see* Amebiasis
Endamoeba — *see* Amebiasis
Endarteritis (bacterial, subacute) (infective) (septic) 447.6
brain, cerebral or cerebrospinal 437.4
late effect — *see* Late effect(s) (of) cerebrovascular disease
coronary (artery) — *see* Arteriosclerosis, coronary
deformans — *see* Arteriosclerosis
embolic (*see also* Embolism) 444.9
obliterans (*see also* Arteriosclerosis)
pulmonary 417.8
pulmonary 417.8
retina 362.18
senile — *see* Arteriosclerosis
syphilitic 093.89
brain or cerebral 094.89
congenital 090.5
spinal 094.89
tuberculous (*see also* Tuberculosis) 017.9 ☑
Endemic — *see* condition
Endocarditis (chronic) (indeterminate) (interstitial) ▶(marantic)◀ (nonbacterial thrombotic) (residual) (sclerotic) (sclerous) (senile) (valvular) 424.90
with
rheumatic fever (conditions classifiable to 390)
active — *see* Endocarditis, acute, rheumatic
inactive or quiescent (with chorea) 397.9
acute or subacute 421.9
rheumatic (aortic) (mitral) (pulmonary) (tricuspid) 391.1
with chorea (acute) (rheumatic) (Sydenham's) 392.0
aortic (heart) (nonrheumatic) (valve) 424.1
with
mitral (valve) disease 396.9
active or acute 391.1
with chorea (acute) (rheumatic) (Sydenham's) 392.0
bacterial 421.0
rheumatic fever (conditions classifiable to 390)
active — *see* Endocarditis, acute, rheumatic
inactive or quiescent (with chorea) 395.9
with mitral disease 396.9
acute or subacute 421.9
arteriosclerotic 424.1
congenital 746.89
hypertensive 424.1
rheumatic (chronic) (inactive) 395.9
with mitral (valve) disease 396.9
active or acute 391.1
with chorea (acute) (rheumatic) (Sydenham's) 392.0
active or acute 391.1
with chorea (acute) (rheumatic) (Sydenham's) 392.0
Endocarditis — *continued*
aortic — *continued*
specified cause, except rheumatic 424.1
syphilitic 093.22
arteriosclerotic or due to arteriosclerosis 424.99
atypical verrucous (Libman-Sacks) 710.0 *[424.91]*
bacterial (acute) (any valve) (chronic) (subacute) 421.0
blastomycotic 116.0 *[421.1]*
candidal 112.81
congenital 425.3
constrictive 421.0
Coxsackie 074.22
due to
blastomycosis 116.0 *[421.1]*
candidiasis 112.81
Coxsackie (virus) 074.22
disseminated lupus erythematosus 710.0 *[424.91]*
histoplasmosis (*see also* Histoplasmosis) 115.94
hypertension (benign) 424.99
moniliasis 112.81
prosthetic cardiac valve 996.61
Q fever 083.0 *[421.1]*
serratia marcescens 421.0
typhoid (fever) 002.0 *[421.1]*
fetal 425.3
gonococcal 098.84
hypertensive 424.99
infectious or infective (acute) (any valve) (chronic) (subacute) 421.0
lenta (acute) (any valve) (chronic) (subacute) 421.0
Libman-Sacks 710.0 *[424.91]*
Loeffler's (parietal fibroplastic) 421.0
malignant (acute) (any valve) (chronic) (subacute) 421.0
meningococcal 036.42
mitral (chronic) (double) (fibroid) (heart) (inactive) (valve) (with chorea) 394.9
with
aortic (valve) disease 396.9
active or acute 391.1
with chorea (acute) (rheumatic) (Sydenham's) 392.0
rheumatic fever (conditions classifiable to 390)
active — *see* Endocarditis, acute, rheumatic
inactive or quiescent (with chorea) 394.9
with aortic valve disease 396.9
active or acute 391.1
with chorea (acute) (rheumatic) (Sydenham's) 392.0
bacterial 421.0
arteriosclerotic 424.0
congenital 746.89
hypertensive 424.0
nonrheumatic 424.0
acute or subacute 421.9
syphilitic 093.21
monilial 112.81
mycotic (acute) (any valve) (chronic) (subacute) 421.0
pneumococcic (acute) (any valve) (chronic) (subacute) 421.0
pulmonary (chronic) (heart) (valve) 424.3
with
rheumatic fever (conditions classifiable to 390)
active — *see* Endocarditis, acute, rheumatic
inactive or quiescent (with chorea) 397.1
acute or subacute 421.9
rheumatic 391.1
Endocarditis — *continued*
pulmonary — *continued*
acute or subacute — *continued*
rheumatic — *continued*
with chorea (acute) (rheumatic) (Sydenham's) 392.0
arteriosclerotic or due to arteriosclerosis 424.3
congenital 746.09
hypertensive or due to hypertension (benign) 424.3
rheumatic (chronic) (inactive) (with chorea) 397.1
active or acute 391.1
with chorea (acute) (rheumatic) (Sydenham's) 392.0
syphilitic 093.24
purulent (acute) (any valve) (chronic) (subacute) 421.0
rheumatic (chronic) (inactive) (with chorea) 397.9
active or acute (aortic) (mitral) (pulmonary) (tricuspid) 391.1
with chorea (acute) (rheumatic) (Sydenham's) 392.0
septic (acute) (any valve) (chronic) (subacute) 421.0
specified cause, except rheumatic 424.99
streptococcal (acute) (any valve) (chronic) (subacute) 421.0
subacute — *see* Endocarditis, acute
suppurative (any valve) (acute) (chronic) (subacute) 421.0
syphilitic NEC 093.20
toxic (*see also* Endocarditis, acute) 421.9
tricuspid (chronic) (heart) (inactive) (rheumatic) (valve) (with chorea) 397.0
with
rheumatic fever (conditions classifiable to 390)
active — *see* Endocarditis, acute, rheumatic
inactive or quiescent (with chorea) 397.0
active or acute 391.1
with chorea (acute) (rheumatic) (Sydenham's) 392.0
arteriosclerotic 424.2
congenital 746.89
hypertensive 424.2
nonrheumatic 424.2
acute or subacute 421.9
specified cause, except rheumatic 424.2
syphilitic 093.23
tuberculous (*see also* Tuberculosis) 017.9 ☑ *[424.91]*
typhoid 002.0 *[421.1]*
ulcerative (acute) (any valve) (chronic) (subacute) 421.0
vegetative (acute) (any valve) (chronic) (subacute) 421.0
verrucous (acute) (any valve) (chronic) (subacute) NEC 710.0 *[424.91]*
nonbacterial 710.0 *[424.91]*
nonrheumatic 710.0 *[424.91]*
Endocardium, endocardial — *see also* condition
cushion defect 745.60
specified type NEC 745.69
Endocervicitis — *see also* Cervicitis 616.0
due to
intrauterine (contraceptive) device 996.65
gonorrheal (acute) 098.15
chronic or duration of 2 months or over 098.35
hyperplastic 616.0
syphilitic 095.8
trichomonal 131.09

Endocervicitis — *see also* Cervicitis — *continued*
tuberculous (*see also* Tuberculosis) 016.7 ☑
Endocrine — *see* condition
Endocrinopathy, pluriglandular 258.9
Endodontitis 522.0
End-of-life care V66.7
Endomastoiditis — *see also* Mastoiditis 383.9
Endometrioma 617.9
Endometriosis 617.9
appendix 617.5
bladder 617.8
bowel 617.5
broad ligament 617.3
cervix 617.0
colon 617.5
cul-de-sac (Douglas') 617.3
exocervix 617.0
fallopian tube 617.2
female genital organ NEC 617.8
gallbladder 617.8
in scar of skin 617.6
internal 617.0
intestine 617.5
lung 617.8
myometrium 617.0
ovary 617.1
parametrium 617.3
pelvic peritoneum 617.3
peritoneal (pelvic) 617.3
rectovaginal septum 617.4
rectum 617.5
round ligament 617.3
skin 617.6
specified site NEC 617.8
stromal (M8931/1) 236.0
umbilicus 617.8
uterus 617.0
internal 617.0
vagina 617.4
vulva 617.8
Endometritis (nonspecific) (purulent) (septic) (suppurative) 615.9
with
abortion — *see* Abortion, by type, with sepsis
ectopic pregnancy (*see also* categories 633.0–633.9) 639.0
molar pregnancy (*see also* categories 630–632) 639.0
acute 615.0
blennorrhagic 098.16
acute 098.16
chronic or duration of 2 months or over 098.36
cervix, cervical (*see also* Cervicitis) 616.0
hyperplastic 616.0
chronic 615.1
complicating pregnancy 670 ☑ ▲
affecting fetus or newborn 760.8
decidual 615.9
following
abortion 639.0
ectopic or molar pregnancy 639.0
gonorrheal (acute) 098.16
chronic or duration of 2 months or over 098.36
hyperplastic (*see also* Hyperplasia, endometrium) 621.30
cervix 616.0
polypoid — *see* Endometritis, hyperplastic
puerperal, postpartum, childbirth 670.0 ☑
senile (atrophic) 615.9
subacute 615.0
tuberculous (*see also* Tuberculosis) 016.7 ☑
Endometrium — *see* condition
Endomyocardiopathy, South African 425.2
Endomyocarditis — *see* Endocarditis
Endomyofibrosis 425.0
Endomyometritis — *see also* Endometritis 615.9
Endopericarditis — *see* Endocarditis
Endoperineuritis — *see* Disorder, nerve
Endophlebitis — *see also* Phlebitis 451.9
leg 451.2
deep (vessels) 451.19
superficial (vessels) 451.0
portal (vein) 572.1
retina 362.18
specified site NEC 451.89
syphilitic 093.89
Endophthalmia — *see also* Endophthalmitis 360.00
gonorrheal 098.42
Endophthalmitis (globe) (infective) (metastatic) (purulent) (subacute) 360.00
acute 360.01
bleb associated 379.63
chronic 360.03
parasitic 360.13
phacoanaphylactic 360.19
specified type NEC 360.19
sympathetic 360.11
Endosalpingioma (M9111/1) 236.2
Endosalpingiosis 629.89
Endosteitis — *see* Osteomyelitis
Endothelioma, bone (M9260/3) — *see* Neoplasm, bone, malignant
Endotheliosis 287.8
hemorrhagic infectional 287.8
Endotoxemia — code to condition
Endotoxic shock 785.52
Endotrachelitis — *see also* Cervicitis 616.0
Enema rash 692.89
Engelmann's disease (diaphyseal sclerosis) 756.9
Engel-von Recklinghausen disease or syndrome (osteitis fibrosa cystica) 252.01
English disease — *see also* Rickets 268.0
Engman's disease (infectious eczematoid dermatitis) 690.8
Engorgement
breast 611.79
newborn 778.7
puerperal, postpartum 676.2 ☑
liver 573.9
lung 514
pulmonary 514
retina, venous 362.37
stomach 536.8
venous, retina 362.37
Enlargement, enlarged — *see also* Hypertrophy
abdomen 789.3 ☑
adenoids 474.12
and tonsils 474.10
alveolar process or ridge 525.8
apertures of diaphragm (congenital) 756.6
blind spot, visual field 368.42
gingival 523.8
heart, cardiac (*see also* Hypertrophy, cardiac) 429.3
lacrimal gland, chronic 375.03
liver (*see also* Hypertrophy, liver) 789.1
lymph gland or node 785.6
orbit 376.46
organ or site, congenital NEC — *see* Anomaly, specified type NEC
parathyroid (gland) 252.01
pituitary fossa 793.0
prostate (simple) (soft) 600.00
with
other lower urinary tract symptoms (LUTS) 600.01
urinary
obstruction 600.01
retention 600.01
sella turcica 793.0
spleen (*see also* Splenomegaly) 789.2
Enlargement, enlarged — *see also* Hypertrophy — *continued*
spleen (*see also* Splenomegaly) — *continued*
congenital 759.0
thymus (congenital) (gland) 254.0
thyroid (gland) (*see also* Goiter) 240.9
tongue 529.8
tonsils 474.11
and adenoids 474.10
uterus 621.2
Enophthalmos 376.50
due to
atrophy of orbital tissue 376.51
surgery 376.52
trauma 376.52
Enostosis 526.89
Entamebiasis — *see* Amebiasis
Entamebic — *see* Amebiasis
Entanglement, umbilical cord(s) 663.3 ☑
with compression 663.2 ☑
affecting fetus or newborn 762.5
around neck with compression 663.1 ☑
twins in monoamniotic sac 663.2 ☑
Enteralgia 789.0 ☑
Enteric — *see* condition
Enteritis (acute) (catarrhal) (choleraic) (chronic) (congestive) (diarrheal) (exudative) (follicular) (hemorrhagic) (infantile) (lienteric) (noninfectious) (perforative) (phlegmonous) (presumed noninfectious) (pseudomembranous) 558.9
adaptive 564.9
aertrycke infection 003.0
allergic 558.3
amebic (*see also* Amebiasis) 006.9
with abscess — *see* Abscess, amebic
acute 006.0
with abscess — *see* Abscess, amebic
nondysenteric 006.2
chronic 006.1
with abscess — *see* Abscess, amebic
nondysenteric 006.2
nondysenteric 006.2
anaerobic (cocci) (gram-negative) (gram-positive) (mixed) NEC 008.46
bacillary NEC 004.9
bacterial NEC 008.5
specified NEC 008.49
Bacteroides (fragilis) (melaninogeniscus) (oralis) 008.46
Butyrivibrio (fibriosolvens) 008.46
Campylobacter 008.43
Candida 112.85
Chilomastix 007.8
choleriformis 001.1
chronic 558.9
ulcerative (*see also* Colitis, ulcerative) 556.9
cicatrizing (chronic) 555.0
Clostridium
botulinum 005.1
difficile 008.45
haemolyticum 008.46
novyi 008.46
perfringens (C) (F) 008.46
specified type NEC 008.46
coccidial 007.2
dietetic 558.9
due to
achylia gastrica 536.8
adenovirus 008.62
Acrobacter aerogenes 008.2
anaerobes (*see also* Enteritis, anaerobic) 008.46
Arizona (bacillus) 008.1
astrovirus 008.66
Bacillus coli — *see* Enteritis, E. coli
bacteria NEC 008.5
Enteritis — *continued*
due to — *continued*
bacteria — *continued*
specified NEC 008.49
Bacteroides (*see also* Enteritis, Bacteroides) 008.46
Butyrivibrio (fibriosolvens) 008.46
Calcivirus 008.65
Camplyobacter 008.43
Clostridium — *see* Enteritis, Clostridium
Cockle agent 008.64
Coxsackie (virus) 008.67
Ditchling agent 008.64
ECHO virus 008.67
Enterobacter aerogenes 008.2
enterococci 008.49
enterovirus NEC 008.67
Escherichia coli — *see* Enteritis, E. coli
Eubacterium 008.46
Fusobacterium (nucleatum) 008.46
gram-negative bacteria NEC 008.47
anaerobic NEC 008.46
Hawaii agent 008.63
irritating foods 558.9
Klebsiella aerogenes 008.47
Marin County agent 008.66
Montgomery County agent 008.63
Norwalk-like agent 008.63
Norwalk virus 008.63
Otofuke agent 008.63
Paracolobactrum arizonae 008.1
paracolon bacillus NEC 008.47
Arizona 008.1
Paramatta agent 008.64
Peptococcus 008.46
Peptostreptococcus 008.46
Proprionibacterium 008.46
Proteus (bacillus) (mirabilis) (morganii) 008.3
Pseudomonas aeruginosa 008.42
Rotavirus 008.61
Sapporo agent 008.63
small round virus (SRV) NEC 008.64
featureless NEC 008.63
structured NEC 008.63
Snow Mountain (SM) agent 008.63
specified
bacteria NEC 008.49
organism, nonbacterial NEC 008.8
virus NEC 008.69
Staphylococcus 008.41
Streptococcus 008.49
anaerobic 008.46
Taunton agent 008.63
Torovirus 008.69
Treponema 008.46
Veillonella 008.46
virus 008.8
specified type NEC 008.69
Wollan (W) agent 008.64
Yersinia enterocolitica 008.44
dysentery — *see* Dysentery
E. coli 008.00
enterohemorrhagic 008.04
enteroinvasive 008.03
enteropathogenic 008.01
enterotoxigenic 008.02
specified type NEC 008.09
el tor 001.1
embadomonial 007.8
eosinophilic 558.41 ●
epidemic 009.0
Eubacterium 008.46
fermentative 558.9
fulminant 557.0
Fusobacterium (nucleatum) 008.46
gangrenous (*see also* Enteritis, due to, by organism) 009.0
giardial 007.1
gram-negative bacteria NEC 008.47
anaerobic NEC 008.46

Enteritis — *continued*
- infectious NEC (*see also* Enteritis, due to, by organism) 009.0
  - presumed 009.1
- influenzal 487.8
- ischemic 557.9
  - acute 557.0
  - chronic 557.1
  - due to mesenteric artery insufficiency 557.1
- membranous 564.9
- mucous 564.9
- myxomembranous 564.9
- necrotic (*see also* Enteritis, due to, by organism) 009.0
- necroticans 005.2
- necrotizing of fetus or newborn ▶(*see also* Enterocolitis, necrotizing, newborn)◀ 777.50 ▲
- neurogenic 564.9
- newborn 777.8
  - necrotizing ▶(*see also* Enterocolitis, necrotizing, newborn)◀ 777.50 ▲
- parasitic NEC 129
- paratyphoid (fever) (*see also* Fever, paratyphoid) 002.9
- Peptococcus 008.46
- Peptostreptococcus 008.46
- Proprionibacterium 008.46
- protozoal NEC 007.9
- radiation 558.1
- regional (of) 555.9
  - intestine
    - large (bowel, colon, or rectum) 555.1
      - with small intestine 555.2
    - small (duodenum, ileum, or jejunum) 555.0
      - with large intestine 555.2
- Salmonella infection 003.0
- salmonellosis 003.0
- segmental (*see also* Enteritis, regional) 555.9
- septic (*see also* Enteritis, due to, by organism) 009.0
- Shigella 004.9
- simple 558.9
- spasmodic 564.9
- spastic 564.9
- staphylococcal 008.41
  - due to food 005.0
- streptococcal 008.49
  - anaerobic 008.46
- toxic 558.2
- Treponema (denticola) (macrodentium) 008.46
- trichomonal 007.3
- tuberculous (*see also* Tuberculosis) 014.8 ☑
- typhosa 002.0
- ulcerative (chronic) (*see also* Colitis, ulcerative) 556.9
- Veillonella 008.46
- viral 008.8
  - adenovirus 008.62
  - enterovirus 008.67
  - specified virus NEC 008.69
- Yersinia enterocolitica 008.44
- zymotic 009.0

Enteroarticular syndrome 099.3

Enterobiasis 127.4

Enterobius vermicularis 127.4

Enterocele — *see also* Hernia 553.9
- pelvis, pelvic (acquired) (congenital) 618.6
- vagina, vaginal (acquired) (congenital) 618.6

Enterocolitis — *see also* Enteritis
- fetus or newborn ▶(*see also* Enterocolitis, necrotizing, newborn)◀ 777.8
  - necrotizing 777.50 ▲
- fulminant 557.0
- granulomatous 555.2
- hemorrhagic (acute) 557.0
  - chronic 557.1
- necrotizing (acute) (membranous) 557.0
  - newborn 777.50 ●
    - with ●
      - perforation 777.53 ●
      - pneumatosis and perforation 777.53 ●
      - pneumatosis without perforation 777.52 ●
    - stage I 777.51 ●
    - stage II 777.52 ●
    - stage III 777.53 ●
- primary necrotizing ▶(*see also* Enterocolitis, necrotizing, newborn)◀ 777.50 ▲
- pseudomembranous 008.45
- radiation 558.1
  - newborn ▶(*see also* Enterocolitis, necrotizing, newborn)◀ 777.50 ▲
- ulcerative 556.0

Enterocystoma 751.5

Enterogastritis — *see* Enteritis

Enterogenous cyanosis 289.7

Enterolith, enterolithiasis (impaction) 560.39
- with hernia (*see also* Hernia, by site, with obstruction)
  - gangrenous — *see* Hernia, by site, with gangrene

Enteropathy 569.9
- exudative (of Gordon) 579.8
- gluten 579.0
- hemorrhagic, terminal 557.0
- protein-losing 579.8

Enteroperitonitis — *see also* Peritonitis 567.9

Enteroptosis 569.89

Enterorrhagia 578.9

Enterospasm 564.9
- psychogenic 306.4

Enterostenosis — *see also* Obstruction, intestine 560.9

Enterostomy status V44.4
- with complication 569.60

Enthesopathy 726.90
- ankle and tarsus 726.70
- elbow region 726.30
  - specified NEC 726.39
- hip 726.5
- knee 726.60
- peripheral NEC 726.8
- shoulder region 726.10
  - adhesive 726.0
- spinal 720.1
- wrist and carpus 726.4

Entrance, air into vein — *see* Embolism, air

Entrapment, nerve — *see* Neuropathy, entrapment

Entropion (eyelid) 374.00
- cicatricial 374.04
- congenital 743.62
- late effect of trachoma (healed) 139.1
- mechanical 374.02
- paralytic 374.02
- senile 374.01
- spastic 374.03

Enucleation of eye (current) (traumatic) 871.3

Enuresis 788.30
- habit disturbance 307.6
- nocturnal 788.36
  - psychogenic 307.6
- nonorganic origin 307.6
- psychogenic 307.6

Enzymopathy 277.9

Eosinopenia 288.59

Eosinophilia 288.3
- allergic 288.3
- hereditary 288.3
- idiopathic 288.3
- infiltrative 518.3
- Loeffler's 518.3
- myalgia syndrome 710.5
- pulmonary (tropical) 518.3
- secondary 288.3
- tropical 518.3

Eosinophilic — *see also* condition
- fasciitis 728.89
- granuloma (bone) 277.89
- infiltration lung 518.3

Ependymitis (acute) (cerebral) (chronic) (granular) — *see also* Meningitis 322.9

Ependymoblastoma (M9392/3)
- specified site — *see* Neoplasm, by site, malignant
- unspecified site 191.9

Ependymoma (epithelial) (malignant) (M9391/3)
- anaplastic type (M9392/3)
  - specified site — *see* Neoplasm, by site, malignant
  - unspecified site 191.9
- benign (M9391/0)
  - specified site — *see* Neoplasm, by site, benign
  - unspecified site 225.0
- myxopapillary (M9394/1) 237.5
- papillary (M9393/1) 237.5
- specified site — *see* Neoplasm, by site, malignant
- unspecified site 191.9

Ependymopathy 349.2
- spinal cord 349.2

Ephelides, ephelis 709.09

Ephemeral fever — *see also* Pyrexia 780.60 ▲

Epiblepharon (congenital) 743.62

Epicanthus, epicanthic fold (congenital) (eyelid) 743.63

Epicondylitis (elbow) (lateral) 726.32
- medial 726.31

Epicystitis — *see also* Cystitis 595.9

Epidemic — *see* condition

Epidermidalization, cervix — *see* condition

Epidermidization, cervix — *see* condition

Epidermis, epidermal — *see* condition

Epidermization, cervix — *see* condition

Epidermodysplasia verruciformis 078.19

Epidermoid
- cholesteatoma — *see* Cholesteatoma
- inclusion (*see also* Cyst, skin) 706.2

Epidermolysis
- acuta (combustiformis) (toxica) 695.15 ▲
- bullosa 757.39
- necroticans combustiformis 695.15 ▲
  - due to drug
    - correct substance properly administered 695.15 ▲
    - overdose or wrong substance given or taken 977.9
      - specified drug — *see* Table of Drugs and Chemicals

Epidermophytid — *see* Dermatophytosis

Epidermophytosis (infected) — *see* Dermatophytosis

Epidermosis, ear (middle) — *see also* Cholesteatoma 385.30

Epididymis — *see* condition

Epididymitis (nonvenereal) 604.90
- with abscess 604.0
- acute 604.99
- blennorrhagic (acute) 098.0
  - chronic or duration of 2 months or over 098.2
- caseous (*see also* Tuberculosis) 016.4 ☑
- chlamydial 099.54
- diphtheritic 032.89 *[604.91]*
- filarial 125.9 *[604.91]*
- gonococcal (acute) 098.0
  - chronic or duration of 2 months or over 098.2
- recurrent 604.99
- residual 604.99
- syphilitic 095.8 *[604.91]*
- tuberculous (*see also* Tuberculosis) 016.4 ☑

Epididymo-orchitis — *see also* Epididymitis 604.90
- with abscess 604.0
- chlamydial 099.54
- gonococcal (acute) 098.13
  - chronic or duration of 2 months or over 098.33

Epidural — *see* condition

Epigastritis — *see also* Gastritis 535.5 ☑

Epigastrium, epigastric — *see* condition

Epigastrocele — *see also* Hernia, epigastric 553.29

Epiglottiditis (acute) 464.30
- with obstruction 464.31
- chronic 476.1
- viral 464.30
  - with obstruction 464.31

Epiglottis — *see* condition

Epiglottitis (acute) 464.30
- with obstruction 464.31
- chronic 476.1
- viral 464.30
  - with obstruction 464.31

Epignathus 759.4

Epilepsia
- partialis continua (*see also* Epilepsy) 345.7 ☑
- procursiva (*see also* Epilepsy) 345.8 ☑

Epilepsy, epileptic (idiopathic) 345.9 ☑

> *Note — use the following fifth-digit subclassification with categories 345.0, 345.1, 345.4–345.9:*
>
> 0 *without mention of intractable epilepsy*
>
> 1 *with intractable epilepsy*

- abdominal 345.5 ☑
- absence (attack) 345.0 ☑
- akinetic 345.0 ☑
  - psychomotor 345.4 ☑
- automatism 345.4 ☑
- autonomic diencephalic 345.5 ☑
- brain 345.9 ☑
- Bravais-Jacksonian 345.5 ☑
- cerebral 345.9 ☑
- climacteric 345.9 ☑
- clonic 345.1 ☑
- clouded state 345.9 ☑
- coma 345.3
- communicating 345.4 ☑
- complicating pregnancy, childbirth, or the puerperium 649.4 ☑
- congenital 345.9 ☑
- convulsions 345.9 ☑
- cortical (focal) (motor) 345.5 ☑
- cursive (running) 345.8 ☑
- cysticercosis 123.1
- deterioration
  - with behavioral disturbance 345.9 ☑ *[294.11]*
  - without behavioral disturbance 345.9 ☑ *[294.10]*
- due to syphilis 094.89
- equivalent 345.5 ☑
- fit 345.9 ☑
- focal (motor) 345.5 ☑
- gelastic 345.8 ☑
- generalized 345.9 ☑
  - convulsive 345.1 ☑
  - flexion 345.1 ☑
  - nonconvulsive 345.0 ☑
- grand mal (idiopathic) 345.1 ☑
- Jacksonian (motor) (sensory) 345.5 ☑

Epilepsy, epileptic — *continued*
Kojevnikoff's, Kojevnikov's, Kojewnikoff's 345.7 ☑
laryngeal 786.2
limbic system 345.4 ☑
localization related (focal) (partial) and epileptic syndromes
with
complex partial seizures 345.4 ☑
simple partial seizures 345.5 ☑
major (motor) 345.1 ☑
minor 345.0 ☑
mixed (type) 345.9 ☑
motor partial 345.5 ☑
musicogenic 345.1 ☑
myoclonus, myoclonic 345.1 ☑
progressive (familial) 333.2
nonconvulsive, generalized 345.0 ☑
parasitic NEC 123.9
partial (focalized) 345.5 ☑
with
impairment of consciousness 345.4 ☑
memory and ideational disturbances 345.4 ☑
without impairment of consciousness 345.5 ☑
abdominal type 345.5 ☑
motor type 345.5 ☑
psychomotor type 345.4 ☑
psychosensory type 345.4 ☑
secondarily generalized 345.4 ☑
sensory type 345.5 ☑
somatomotor type 345.5 ☑
somatosensory type 345.5 ☑
temporal lobe type 345.4 ☑
visceral type 345.5 ☑
visual type 345.5 ☑
peripheral 345.9 ☑
petit mal 345.0 ☑
photokinetic 345.8 ☑
progressive myoclonic (familial) 333.2
psychic equivalent 345.5 ☑
psychomotor 345.4 ☑
psychosensory 345.4 ☑
reflex 345.1 ☑
seizure 345.9 ☑
senile 345.9 ☑
sensory-induced 345.5 ☑
sleep (*see also* Narcolepsy) 347.00
somatomotor type 345.5 ☑
somatosensory 345.5 ☑
specified type NEC 345.8 ☑
status (grand mal) 345.3
focal motor 345.7 ☑
petit mal 345.2
psychomotor 345.7 ☑
temporal lobe 345.7 ☑
symptomatic 345.9 ☑
temporal lobe 345.4 ☑
tonic (-clonic) 345.1 ☑
traumatic (injury unspecified) 907.0
injury specified — *see* Late, effect (of) specified injury
twilight 293.0
uncinate (gyrus) 345.4 ☑
Unverricht (-Lundborg) (familial myoclonic) 333.2
visceral 345.5 ☑
visual 345.5 ☑
Epileptiform
convulsions 780.39
seizure 780.39
Epiloia 759.5
Epimenorrhea 626.2
Epipharyngitis — *see also* Nasopharyngitis 460
Epiphora 375.20
due to
excess lacrimation 375.21
insufficient drainage 375.22
Epiphyseal arrest 733.91
femoral head 732.2
Epiphyseolysis, epiphysiolysis — *see also* Osteochondrosis 732.9
Epiphysitis — *see also* Osteochondrosis 732.9
juvenile 732.6
marginal (Scheuermann's) 732.0
os calcis 732.5
syphilitic (congenital) 090.0
vertebral (Scheuermann's) 732.0
Epiplocele — *see also* Hernia 553.9
Epiploitis — *see also* Peritonitis 567.9
Epiplosarcomphalocele — *see also* Hernia, umbilicus 553.1
Episcleritis 379.00
gouty 274.89 *[379.09]*
nodular 379.02
periodica fugax 379.01
angioneurotic — *see* Edema, angioneurotic
specified NEC 379.09
staphylococcal 379.00
suppurative 379.00
syphilitic 095.0
tuberculous (*see also* Tuberculosis) 017.3 ☑ *[379.09]*
Episode
brain (*see also* Disease, cerebrovascular, acute) 436
cerebral (*see also* Disease, cerebrovascular, acute) 436
depersonalization (in neurotic state) 300.6
hyporesponsive 780.09
psychotic (*see also* Psychosis) 298.9
organic, transient 293.9
schizophrenic (acute) NEC (*see also* Schizophrenia) 295.4 ☑
Epispadias
female 753.8
male 752.62
Episplenitis 289.59
Epistaxis (multiple) 784.7
hereditary 448.0
vicarious menstruation 625.8
Epithelioma (malignant) (M8011/3) — *see also* Neoplasm, by site, malignant
adenoides cysticum (M8100/0) — *see* Neoplasm, skin, benign
basal cell (M8090/3) — *see* Neoplasm, skin, malignant
benign (M8011/0) — *see* Neoplasm, by site, benign
Bowen's (M8081/2) — *see* Neoplasm, skin, in situ
calcifying (benign) (Malherbe's) (M8110/0) — *see* Neoplasm, skin, benign
external site — *see* Neoplasm, skin, malignant
intraepidermal, Jadassohn (M8096/0) — *see* Neoplasm, skin, benign
squamous cell (M8070/3) — *see* Neoplasm, by site, malignant
Epitheliopathy
pigment, retina 363.15
posterior multifocal placoid (acute) 363.15
Epithelium, epithelial — *see* condition
Epituberculosis (allergic) (with atelectasis) — *see also* Tuberculosis 010.8 ☑
Eponychia 757.5
Epstein's
nephrosis or syndrome (*see also* Nephrosis) 581.9
pearl (mouth) 528.4
Epstein-Barr infection (viral) 075
chronic 780.79 *[139.8]*
Epulis (giant cell) (gingiva) 523.8
Equinia 024
Equinovarus (congenital) 754.51
acquired 736.71
Equivalent
convulsive (abdominal) (*see also* Epilepsy) 345.5 ☑
Equivalent — *continued*
epileptic (psychic) (*see also* Epilepsy) 345.5 ☑
Erb's
disease 359.1
palsy, paralysis (birth) (brachial) (newborn) 767.6
spinal (spastic) syphilitic 094.89
pseudohypertrophic muscular dystrophy 359.1
Erb-Goldflam disease or syndrome 358.00
Erb (-Duchenne) paralysis (birth injury) (newborn) 767.6
Erdheim's syndrome (acromegalic macrospondylitis) 253.0
Erection, painful (persistent) 607.3
Ergosterol deficiency (vitamin D) 268.9
with
osteomalacia 268.2
rickets (*see also* Rickets) 268.0
Ergotism (ergotized grain) 988.2
from ergot used as drug (migraine therapy)
correct substance properly administered 349.82
overdose or wrong substance given or taken 975.0
Erichsen's disease (railway spine) 300.16
Erlacher-Blount syndrome (tibia vara) 732.4
Erosio interdigitalis blastomycetica 112.3
Erosion
arteriosclerotic plaque — *see* Arteriosclerosis, by site
artery NEC 447.2
without rupture 447.8
bone 733.99
bronchus 519.19
cartilage (joint) 733.99
cervix (uteri) (acquired) (chronic) (congenital) 622.0
with mention of cervicitis 616.0
cornea (recurrent) (*see also* Keratitis) 371.42
traumatic 918.1
dental (idiopathic) (occupational) 521.30
extending into
dentine 521.32
pulp 521.33
generalized 521.35
limited to enamel 521.31
localized 521.34
duodenum, postpyloric — *see* Ulcer, duodenum
esophagus 530.89
gastric 535.4 ☑
intestine 569.89
lymphatic vessel 457.8
pylorus, pyloric (ulcer) 535.4 ☑
sclera 379.16
spine, aneurysmal 094.89
spleen 289.59
stomach 535.4 ☑
teeth (idiopathic) (occupational) (*see also* Erosion, dental) 521.30
due to
medicine 521.30
persistent vomiting 521.30
urethra 599.84
uterus 621.8
vertebra 733.99
Erotomania 302.89
Clérambault's 297.8
Error
in diet 269.9
refractive 367.9
astigmatism (*see also* Astigmatism) 367.20
drug-induced 367.89
hypermetropia 367.0
hyperopia 367.0
myopia 367.1
Error — *continued*
refractive — *continued*
presbyopia 367.4
toxic 367.89
Eructation 787.3
nervous 306.4
psychogenic 306.4
Eruption
creeping 126.9
drug — *see* Dermatitis, due to, drug
Hutchinson, summer 692.72
Kaposi's varicelliform 054.0
napkin (psoriasiform) 691.0
polymorphous
light (sun) 692.72
other source 692.82
psoriasiform, napkin 691.0
recalcitrant pustular 694.8
ringed 695.89
skin (*see also* Dermatitis) 782.1
creeping (meaning hookworm) 126.9
due to
chemical(s) NEC 692.4
internal use 693.8
drug — *see* Dermatitis, due to, drug
prophylactic inoculation or vaccination against disease — *see* Dermatitis, due to, vaccine
smallpox vaccination NEC — *see* Dermatitis, due to, vaccine
erysipeloid 027.1
feigned 698.4
Hutchinson, summer 692.72
Kaposi's, varicelliform 054.0
vaccinia 999.0
lichenoid, axilla 698.3
polymorphous, due to light 692.72
toxic NEC 695.0
vesicular 709.8
teeth, tooth
accelerated 520.6
delayed 520.6
difficult 520.6
disturbance of 520.6
in abnormal sequence 520.6
incomplete 520.6
late 520.6
natal 520.6
neonatal 520.6
obstructed 520.6
partial 520.6
persistent primary 520.6
premature 520.6
prenatal 520.6
vesicular 709.8
Erysipelas (gangrenous) (infantile) (newborn) (phlegmonous) (suppurative) 035
external ear 035 *[380.13]*
puerperal, postpartum, childbirth 670.0 ☑
Erysipelatoid (Rosenbach's) 027.1
Erysipeloid (Rosenbach's) 027.1
Erythema, erythematous (generalized) 695.9
ab igne — *see* Burn, by site, first degree
annulare (centrifugum) (rheumaticum) 695.0
arthriticum epidemicum 026.1
brucellum (*see also* Brucellosis) 023.9
bullosum 695.19 ▲
caloricum — *see* Burn, by site, first degree
chronicum migrans 088.81
circinatum 695.19 ▲
diaper 691.0
due to
chemical (contact) NEC 692.4
internal 693.8
drug (internal use) 693.0
contact 692.3

Erythema, erythematous — *continued*
elevatum diutinum 695.89
endemic 265.2
epidemic, arthritic 026.1
figuratum perstans 695.0
gluteal 691.0
gyratum (perstans) (repens) 695.19 ▲
heat — *see* Burn, by site, first degree
ichthyosiforme congenitum 757.1
induratum (primary) (scrofulosorum) (*see also* Tuberculosis) 017.1 ☑
nontuberculous 695.2
infantum febrile 057.8
infectional NEC 695.9
infectiosum 057.0
inflammation NEC 695.9
intertrigo 695.89
iris 695.10 ▲
lupus (discoid) (localized) (*see also* Lupus, erythematosus) 695.4
marginatum 695.0
rheumaticum — *see* Fever, rheumatic
medicamentosum — *see* Dermatitis, due to, drug
migrans 529.1
chronicum 088.81
multiforme 695.10 ▲
bullosum 695.19 ▲
conjunctiva 695.19 ▲
exudativum (Hebra) 695.19 ▲
major 695.12 ●
minor 695.11 ●
pemphigoides 694.5
napkin 691.0
neonatorum 778.8
nodosum 695.2
tuberculous (*see also* Tuberculosis) 017.1 ☑
nummular, nummulare 695.19 ▲
palmar 695.0
palmaris hereditarium 695.0
pernio 991.5
perstans solare 692.72
rash, newborn 778.8
scarlatiniform (exfoliative) (recurrent) 695.0
simplex marginatum 057.8
solare (*see also* Sunburn) 692.71
streptogenes 696.5
toxic, toxicum NEC 695.0
newborn 778.8
tuberculous (primary) (*see also* Tuberculosis) 017.0 ☑
venenatum 695.0
Erythematosus — *see* condition
Erythematous — *see* condition
Erythermalgia (primary) 443.82
Erythralgia 443.82
Erythrasma 039.0
Erythredema 985.0
polyneuritica 985.0
polyneuropathy 985.0
Erythremia (acute) (M9841/3) 207.0 ☑
chronic (M9842/3) 207.1 ☑
secondary 289.0
Erythroblastopenia (acquired) 284.89
congenital 284.01
Erythroblastophthisis 284.01
Erythroblastosis (fetalis) (newborn) 773.2
due to
ABO
antibodies 773.1
incompatibility, maternal/fetal 773.1
isoimmunization 773.1
Rh
antibodies 773.0
incompatibility, maternal/fetal 773.0
isoimmunization 773.0
Erythrocyanosis (crurum) 443.89
Erythrocythemia — *see* Erythremia
Erythrocytopenia 285.9
Erythrocytosis (megalosplenic)
familial 289.6
oval, hereditary (*see also* Elliptocytosis) 282.1
secondary 289.0
stress 289.0
Erythroderma — *see also* Erythema 695.9
desquamativa (in infants) 695.89
exfoliative 695.89
ichthyosiform, congenital 757.1
infantum 695.89
maculopapular 696.2
neonatorum 778.8
psoriaticum 696.1
secondary 695.9
Erythrodysesthesia, palmar plantar (PPE) 693.0
Erythrogenesis imperfecta 284.09
Erythroleukemia (M9840/3) 207.0 ☑
Erythromelalgia 443.82
Erythromelia 701.8
Erythropenia 285.9
Erythrophagocytosis 289.9
Erythrophobia 300.23
Erythroplakia
oral mucosa 528.79
tongue 528.79
Erythroplasia (Queyrat) (M8080/2)
specified site — *see* Neoplasm, skin, in situ
unspecified site 233.5
Erythropoiesis, idiopathic ineffective 285.0
Escaped beats, heart 427.60
postoperative 997.1
Esoenteritis — *see* Enteritis
Esophagalgia 530.89
Esophagectasis 530.89
due to cardiospasm 530.0
Esophagismus 530.5
Esophagitis (alkaline) (chemical) (chronic) (infectional) (necrotic) (peptic) (postoperative) (regurgitant) 530.10
acute 530.12
candidal 112.84
eosinophilic 530.13 ●
reflux 530.11
specified NEC 530.19
tuberculous (*see also* Tuberculosis) 017.8 ☑
ulcerative 530.19
Esophagocele 530.6
Esophagodynia 530.89
Esophagomalacia 530.89
Esophagoptosis 530.89
Esophagospasm 530.5
Esophagostenosis 530.3
Esophagostomiasis 127.7
Esophagostomy
complication 530.87
infection 530.86
malfunctioning 530.87
mechanical 530.87
Esophagotracheal — *see* condition
Esophagus — *see* condition
Esophoria 378.41
convergence, excess 378.84
divergence, insufficiency 378.85
Esotropia (nonaccommodative) 378.00
accommodative 378.35
alternating 378.05
with
A pattern 378.06
specified noncomitancy NEC 378.08
V pattern 378.07
X pattern 378.08
Y pattern 378.08
intermittent 378.22
intermittent 378.20
alternating 378.22
monocular 378.21
monocular 378.01
Esotropia — *continued*
monocular — *continued*
with
A pattern 378.02
specified noncomitancy NEC 378.04
V pattern 378.03
X pattern 378.04
Y pattern 378.04
intermittent 378.21
Espundia 085.5
Essential — *see* condition
Esterapenia 289.89
Esthesioneuroblastoma (M9522/3) 160.0
Esthesioneurocytoma (M9521/3) 160.0
Esthesioneuroepithelioma (M9523/3) 160.0
Esthiomene 099.1
Estivo-autumnal
fever 084.0
malaria 084.0
Estrangement V61.09 ▲
Estriasis 134.0
Ethanolaminuria 270.8
Ethanolism — *see also* Alcoholism 303.9 ☑
Ether dependence, dependency — *see also* Dependence 304.6 ☑
Etherism — *see also* Dependence 304.6 ☑
Ethmoid, ethmoidal — *see* condition
Ethmoiditis (chronic) (nonpurulent) (purulent) — *see also* Sinusitis, ethmoidal 473.2
influenzal 487.1
Woakes' 471.1
Ethylism — *see also* Alcoholism 303.9 ☑
Eulenburg's disease (congenital paramyotonia) 359.29
Eunuchism 257.2
Eunuchoidism 257.2
hypogonadotropic 257.2
European blastomycosis 117.5
Eustachian — *see* condition
Euthyroidism 244.9
Euthyroid sick syndrome 790.94
Evaluation
fetal lung maturity 659.8 ☑
for suspected condition (*see also* Observation) V71.9
abuse V71.81
exposure
anthrax V71.82
biologic agent NEC V71.83
SARS V71.83
neglect V71.81
newborn — *see* Observation, suspected, condition, newborn
specified condition NEC V71.89
mental health V70.2
requested by authority V70.1
nursing care V63.8
social service V63.8
Evans' syndrome (thrombocytopenic purpura) 287.32
Eventration
colon into chest — *see* Hernia, diaphragm
diaphragm (congenital) 756.6
Eversion
bladder 596.8
cervix (uteri) 622.0
with mention of cervicitis 616.0
foot NEC 736.79
congenital 755.67
lacrimal punctum 375.51
punctum lacrimale (postinfectional) (senile) 375.51
ureter (meatus) 593.89
urethra (meatus) 599.84
uterus 618.1
complicating delivery 665.2 ☑
affecting fetus or newborn 763.89
puerperal, postpartum 674.8 ☑
Evidence
of malignancy
cytologic
without histologic confirmation
anus 796.76 ●
cervix 795.06 ●
vagina 795.16 ●
Evisceration
birth injury 767.8
bowel (congenital) — *see* Hernia, ventral
congenital (*see also* Hernia, ventral) 553.29
operative wound 998.32
traumatic NEC 869.1
eye 871.3
Evulsion — *see* Avulsion
Ewing's
angioendothelioma (M9260/3) — *see* Neoplasm, bone, malignant
sarcoma (M9260/3) — *see* Neoplasm, bone, malignant
tumor (M9260/3) — *see* Neoplasm, bone, malignant
Exaggerated lumbosacral angle (with impinging spine) 756.12
Examination (general) (routine) (of) (for) V70.9
allergy V72.7
annual V70.0
cardiovascular preoperative V72.81
cervical Papanicolaou smear V76.2
as a part of routine gynecological examination V72.31
to confirm findings of recent normal smear following initial abnormal smear V72.32
child care (routine) V20.2
clinical research investigation (normal control patient) (participant) V70.7
dental V72.2
developmental testing (child) (infant) V20.2
donor (potential) V70.8
ear V72.19
eye V72.0
following
accident (motor vehicle) V71.4
alleged rape or seduction (victim or culprit) V71.5
inflicted injury (victim or culprit) NEC V71.6
rape or seduction, alleged (victim or culprit) V71.5
treatment (for) V67.9
combined V67.6
fracture V67.4
involving high-risk medication NEC V67.51
mental disorder V67.3
specified condition NEC V67.59
follow-up (routine) (following) V67.9
cancer chemotherapy V67.2
chemotherapy V67.2
disease NEC V67.59
high-risk medication NEC V67.51
injury NEC V67.59
population survey V70.6
postpartum V24.2
psychiatric V67.3
psychotherapy V67.3
radiotherapy V67.1
specified surgery NEC V67.09
surgery V67.00
vaginal pap smear V67.01
gynecological V72.31
for contraceptive maintenance V25.40
intrauterine device V25.42
pill V25.41
specified method NEC V25.49
health (of)
armed forces personnel V70.5
checkup V70.0
child, routine V20.2

Examination — *continued*
health — *continued*
defined subpopulation NEC V70.5
inhabitants of institutions V70.5
occupational V70.5
pre-employment screening V70.5
preschool children V70.5
for admission to school V70.3
prisoners V70.5
for entrance into prison V70.3
prostitutes V70.5
refugees V70.5
school children V70.5
students V70.5
hearing V72.19
following failed hearing screening V72.11
infant V20.2
laboratory V72.6
lactating mother V24.1
medical (for) (of) V70.9
administrative purpose NEC V70.3
admission to
old age home V70.3
prison V70.3
school V70.3
adoption V70.3
armed forces personnel V70.5
at health care facility V70.0
camp V70.3
child, routine V20.2
clinical research (control) (normal comparison) (participant) V70.7
defined subpopulation NEC V70.5
donor (potential) V70.8
driving license V70.3
general V70.9
routine V70.0
specified reason NEC V70.8
immigration V70.3
inhabitants of institutions V70.5
insurance certification V70.3
marriage V70.3
medicolegal reasons V70.4
naturalization V70.3
occupational V70.5
population survey V70.6
pre-employment V70.5
preschool children V70.5
for admission to school V70.3
prison V70.3
prisoners V70.5
for entrance into prison V70.3
prostitutes V70.5
refugees V70.5
school children V70.5
specified reason NEC V70.8
sport competition V70.3
students V70.5
medicolegal reason V70.4
pelvic (annual) (periodic) V72.31
periodic (annual) (routine) V70.0
postpartum
immediately after delivery V24.0
routine follow-up V24.2
pregnancy (unconfirmed) (possible) V72.40
negative result V72.41
positive result V72.42
prenatal V22.1
first pregnancy V22.0
high-risk pregnancy V23.9
specified problem NEC V23.89
preoperative V72.84
cardiovascular V72.81
respiratory V72.82
specified NEC V72.83
preprocedural V72.84
cardiovascular V72.81
general physical V72.83
respiratory V72.82
specified NEC V72.83
psychiatric V70.2
follow-up not needing further care V67.3

Examination — *continued*
psychiatric — *continued*
requested by authority V70.1
radiological NEC V72.5
respiratory preoperative V72.82
screening — *see* Screening
sensitization V72.7
skin V72.7
hypersensitivity V72.7
special V72.9
specified type or reason NEC V72.85
preoperative V72.83
specified NEC V72.83
teeth V72.2
vaginal Papanicolaou smear V76.47
following hysterectomy for malignant condition V67.01
victim or culprit following
alleged rape or seduction V71.5
inflicted injury NEC V71.6
vision V72.0
well baby V20.2
Exanthem, exanthema — *see also* Rash 782.1
Boston 048
epidemic, with meningitis 048
lichenoid psoriasiform 696.2
subitum 058.10
due to
human herpesvirus 6 058.11
human herpesvirus 7 058.12
viral, virus NEC 057.9
specified type NEC 057.8
Excess, excessive, excessively
alcohol level in blood 790.3
carbohydrate tissue, localized 278.1
carotene (dietary) 278.3
cold 991.9
specified effect NEC 991.8
convergence 378.84
crying 780.95
of
adolescent 780.95
adult 780.95
baby 780.92
child 780.95
infant (baby) 780.92
newborn 780.92
development, breast 611.1
diaphoresis (*see also* Hyperhidrosis) 780.8
distance, interarch 524.28
divergence 378.85
drinking (alcohol) NEC (*see also* Abuse, drugs, nondependent) 305.0 ☑
continual (*see also* Alcoholism) 303.9 ☑
habitual (*see also* Alcoholism) 303.9 ☑
eating 783.6
eyelid fold (congenital) 743.62
fat 278.02
in heart (*see also* Degeneration, myocardial) 429.1
tissue, localized 278.1
foreskin 605
gas 787.3
gastrin 251.5
glucagon 251.4
heat (*see also* Heat) 992.9
horizontal
overjet 524.26
overlap 524.26
interarch distance 524.28
intermaxillary vertical dimension 524.37
interocclusal distance of teeth 524.37
large
colon 564.7
congenital 751.3
fetus or infant 766.0
with obstructed labor 660.1 ☑
affecting management of pregnancy 656.6 ☑
causing disproportion 653.5 ☑

Excess, excessive, excessively — *continued*
large — *continued*
newborn (weight of 4500 grams or more) 766.0
organ or site, congenital NEC — *see* Anomaly, specified type NEC
lid fold (congenital) 743.62
long
colon 751.5
organ or site, congenital NEC — *see* Anomaly, specified type NEC
umbilical cord (entangled)
affecting fetus or newborn 762.5
in pregnancy or childbirth 663.3 ☑
with compression 663.2 ☑
menstruation 626.2
number of teeth 520.1
causing crowding 524.31
nutrients (dietary) NEC 783.6
potassium (K) 276.7
salivation (*see also* Ptyalism) 527.7
secretion (*see also* Hypersecretion)
milk 676.6 ☑
sputum 786.4
sweat (*see also* Hyperhidrosis) 780.8
short
organ or site, congenital NEC — *see* Anomaly, specified type NEC
umbilical cord
affecting fetus or newborn 762.6
in pregnancy or childbirth 663.4 ☑
skin NEC 701.9
eyelid 743.62
acquired 374.30
sodium (Na) 276.0
spacing of teeth 524.32
sputum 786.4
sweating (*see also* Hyperhidrosis) 780.8
tearing (ducts) (eye) (*see also* Epiphora) 375.20
thirst 783.5
due to deprivation of water 994.3
tissue in reconstructed breast 612.0 ●
tuberosity 524.07
vitamin
A (dietary) 278.2
administered as drug (chronic) (prolonged excessive intake) 278.2
reaction to sudden overdose 963.5
D (dietary) 278.4
administered as drug (chronic) (prolonged excessive intake) 278.4
reaction to sudden overdose 963.5
weight 278.02
gain 783.1
of pregnancy 646.1 ☑
loss 783.21
Excitability, abnormal, under minor stress 309.29
Excitation
catatonic (*see also* Schizophrenia) 295.2 ☑
psychogenic 298.1
reactive (from emotional stress, psychological trauma) 298.1
Excitement
manic (*see also* Psychosis, affective) 296.0 ☑
recurrent episode 296.1 ☑
single episode 296.0 ☑
mental, reactive (from emotional stress, psychological trauma) 298.1

Excitement — *continued*
state, reactive (from emotional stress, psychological trauma) 298.1
Excluded pupils 364.76
Excoriation (traumatic) — *see also* Injury, superficial, by site 919.8
neurotic 698.4
Excyclophoria 378.44
Excyclotropia 378.33
Exencephalus, exencephaly 742.0
Exercise
breathing V57.0
remedial NEC V57.1
therapeutic NEC V57.1
Exfoliation
skin ●
due to erythematous condition 695.50 ●
involving (percent of body surface) ●
less than 10 percent 695.50 ●
10-19 percent 695.51 ●
20-29 percent 695.52 ●
30-39 percent 695.53 ●
40-49 percent 695.54 ●
50-59 percent 695.55 ●
60-69 percent 695.56 ●
70-79 percent 695.57 ●
80-89 percent 695.58 ●
90 percent or more 695.59 ●
teeth ●
due to systemic causes 525.0 ●
Exfoliative — *see also* condition
dermatitis 695.89
Exhaustion, exhaustive (physical NEC) 780.79
battle (*see also* Reaction, stress, acute) 308.9
cardiac (*see also* Failure, heart) 428.9
delirium (*see also* Reaction, stress, acute) 308.9
due to
cold 991.8
excessive exertion 994.5
exposure 994.4
overexertion 994.5 ●
fetus or newborn 779.89
heart (*see also* Failure, heart) 428.9
heat 992.5
due to
salt depletion 992.4
water depletion 992.3
manic (*see also* Psychosis, affective) 296.0 ☑
recurrent episode 296.1 ☑
single episode 296.0 ☑
maternal, complicating delivery 669.8 ☑
affecting fetus or newborn 763.89
mental 300.5
myocardium, myocardial (*see also* Failure, heart) 428.9
nervous 300.5
old age 797
postinfectional NEC 780.79
psychogenic 300.5
psychosis (*see also* Reaction, stress, acute) 308.9
senile 797
dementia 290.0
Exhibitionism (sexual) 302.4
Exomphalos 756.79
Exophoria 378.42
convergence, insufficiency 378.83
divergence, excess 378.85
Exophthalmic
cachexia 242.0 ☑
goiter 242.0 ☑
ophthalmoplegia 242.0 ☑ *[376.22]*
Exophthalmos 376.30
congenital 743.66
constant 376.31
endocrine NEC 259.9 *[376.22]*
hyperthyroidism 242.0 ☑ *[376.21]*
intermittent NEC 376.34

Index
Examination — Exophthalmos

☑ Additional Digit Required — Refer to the Tabular List for Digit Selection
Subterms under main terms may continue to next column or page
▶◀ Revised Text ● New Line ▲ Revised Code

- **Exophthalmos** — *continued*
  - malignant 242.0 ☑ *[376.21]*
  - pulsating 376.35
    - endocrine NEC 259.9 *[376.22]*
  - thyrotoxic 242.0 ☑ *[376.21]*
- **Exostosis** 726.91
  - cartilaginous (M9210/0) — *see* Neoplasm, bone, benign
  - congenital 756.4
  - ear canal, external 380.81
  - gonococcal 098.89
  - hip 726.5
  - intracranial 733.3
  - jaw (bone) 526.81
  - luxurians 728.11
  - multiple (cancellous) (congenital) (hereditary) 756.4
  - nasal bones 726.91
  - orbit, orbital 376.42
  - osteocartilaginous (M9210/0) — *see* Neoplasm, bone, benign
  - spine 721.8
    - with spondylosis — *see* Spondylosis
  - syphilitic 095.5
  - wrist 726.4
- **Exotropia** 378.10
  - alternating 378.15
    - with
      - A pattern 378.16
      - specified noncomitancy NEC 378.18
      - V pattern 378.17
      - X pattern 378.18
      - Y pattern 378.18
    - intermittent 378.24
  - intermittent 378.20
    - alternating 378.24
    - monocular 378.23
  - monocular 378.11
    - with
      - A pattern 378.12
      - specified noncomitancy NEC 378.14
      - V pattern 378.13
      - X pattern 378.14
      - Y pattern 378.14
    - intermittent 378.23
- **Explanation of**
  - investigation finding V65.4 ☑
  - medication V65.4 ☑
- **Exposure** 994.9
  - cold 991.9
    - specified effect NEC 991.8
  - effects of 994.9
  - exhaustion due to 994.4
  - to
    - AIDS virus V01.79
    - anthrax V01.81
    - aromatic ●
      - amines V87.11 ●
      - dyes V87.19 ●
    - arsenic V87.01 ●
    - asbestos V15.84
    - benzene V87.12 ●
    - body fluids (hazardous) V15.85
    - cholera V01.0
    - chromium compounds V87.09 ●
    - communicable disease V01.9
      - specified type NEC V01.89
    - dyes V87.2 ☑ ●
      - aromatic V87.19 ●
    - Escherichia coli (E. coli) V01.83
    - German measles V01.4
    - gonorrhea V01.6
    - hazardous
      - aromatic compounds NEC V87.19 ●
      - body fluids V15.85 ●
      - chemicals NEC V87.2 ☑ ●
      - metals V87.09 ●
      - substances V87.39 ●
    - HIV V01.79
    - human immunodeficiency virus V01.79
    - lead V15.86
- **Exposure** — *continued*
  - to — *continued*
    - meningococcus V01.84
    - mold V87.31 ●
    - nickel dust V87.09 ●
    - parasitic disease V01.89
    - poliomyelitis V01.2
    - polycyclic aromatic hydrocarbons V87.19 ●
    - potentially hazardous body fluids V15.85
    - rabies V01.5
    - rubella V01.4
    - SARS-associated coronavirus V01.82
    - smallpox V01.3
    - syphilis V01.6
    - tuberculosis V01.1
    - varicella V01.71
    - venereal disease V01.6
    - viral disease NEC V01.79
      - varicella V01.71
- **Exsanguination, fetal** 772.0
- **Exstrophy**
  - abdominal content 751.8
  - bladder (urinary) 753.5
- **Extensive** — *see* condition
- **Extra** — *see also* Accessory
  - rib 756.3
    - cervical 756.2
- **Extraction**
  - with hook 763.89
  - breech NEC 669.6 ☑
    - affecting fetus or newborn 763.0
  - cataract postsurgical V45.61
  - manual NEC 669.8 ☑
    - affecting fetus or newborn 763.89
- **Extrasystole** 427.60
  - atrial 427.61
  - postoperative 997.1
  - ventricular 427.69
- **Extrauterine gestation or pregnancy** — *see* Pregnancy, ectopic
- **Extravasation**
  - blood 459.0
    - lower extremity 459.0
  - chemotherapy, vesicant 998.81 ●
  - chyle into mesentery 457.8
  - pelvicalyceal 593.4
  - pyelosinus 593.4
  - urine 788.8
    - from ureter 788.8
  - vesicant ●
    - agent NEC 998.82 ●
    - chemotherapy 998.81 ●
- **Extremity** — *see* condition
- **Extrophy** — *see* Exstrophy
- **Extroversion**
  - bladder 753.5
  - uterus 618.1
    - complicating delivery 665.2 ☑
      - affecting fetus or newborn 763.89
    - postpartal (old) 618.1
- **Extruded tooth** 524.34
- **Extrusion**
  - alveolus and teeth 524.75
  - breast implant (prosthetic) 996.54
  - device, implant, or graft — *see* Complications, mechanical
  - eye implant (ball) (globe) 996.59
  - intervertebral disc — *see* Displacement, intervertebral disc
  - lacrimal gland 375.43
  - mesh (reinforcing) 996.59
  - ocular lens implant 996.53
  - prosthetic device NEC — *see* Complications, mechanical
  - vitreous 379.26
- **Exudate, pleura** — *see* Effusion, pleura
- **Exudates, retina** 362.82
- **Exudative** — *see* condition
- **Eye, eyeball, eyelid** — *see* condition
- **Eyestrain** 368.13
- **Eyeworm disease of Africa** 125.2

F

- **Faber's anemia or syndrome** (achlorhydric anemia) 280.9
- **Fabry's disease** (angiokeratoma corporis diffusum) 272.7
- **Face, facial** — *see* condition
- **Facet of cornea** 371.44
- **Faciocephalalgia, autonomic** — *see also* Neuropathy, peripheral, autonomic 337.9
- **Facioscapulohumeral myopathy** 359.1
- **Factitious disorder, illness** — *see* Illness, factitious
- **Factor**
  - deficiency — *see* Deficiency, factor
  - psychic, associated with diseases classified elsewhere 316
  - risk — *see* Problem
- **Fahr-Volhard disease** (malignant nephrosclerosis) 403.00
- **Failure, failed**
  - adenohypophyseal 253.2
  - attempted abortion (legal) (*see also* Abortion, failed) 638.9
  - bone marrow (anemia) 284.9
    - acquired (secondary) 284.89
    - congenital 284.09
    - idiopathic 284.9
  - cardiac (*see also* Failure, heart) 428.9
    - newborn 779.89
  - cardiorenal (chronic) 428.9
    - hypertensive (*see also* Hypertension, cardiorenal) 404.93
  - cardiorespiratory 799.1
    - specified during or due to a procedure 997.1
      - long-term effect of cardiac surgery 429.4
  - cardiovascular (chronic) 428.9
  - cerebrovascular 437.8
  - cervical dilatation in labor 661.0 ☑
    - affecting fetus or newborn 763.7
  - circulation, circulatory 799.89
    - fetus or newborn 779.89
    - peripheral 785.50
  - compensation — *see* Disease, heart
  - congestive (*see also* Failure, heart) 428.0
  - coronary (*see also* Insufficiency, coronary) 411.89
  - dental implant 525.79
    - due to
      - infection 525.71 ●
      - lack of attached gingiva 525.72
      - occlusal trauma (caused by poor prosthetic design) 525.72
      - parafunctional habits 525.72
      - periodontal infection (peri-implantitis) 525.72
      - poor oral hygiene 525.72
      - unintentional loading 525.71 ●
    - endosseous NEC 525.79
    - mechanical 525.73 ●
    - osseointegration 525.71
      - due to
        - complications of systemic disease 525.71
        - poor bone quality 525.71
        - premature loading 525.71 ●
        - following intentional prosthetic loading 525.72 ●
      - iatrogenic 525.71
      - prior to intentional prosthetic loading 525.71 ●
    - post-osseointegration
      - biological 525.72
        - iatrogenic 525.72
      - due to complications of systemic disease 525.72
      - mechanical 525.73
    - pre-integration 525.71
    - pre-osseointegration 525.71
  - dental prosthesis causing loss of dental implant 525.73
  - dental restoration
    - marginal integrity 525.61
- **Failure, failed** — *continued*
  - dental restoration — *continued*
    - periodontal anatomical integrity 525.65
  - descent of head (at term) 652.5 ☑
    - affecting fetus or newborn 763.1
    - in labor 660.0 ☑
      - affecting fetus or newborn 763.1
  - device, implant, or graft — *see* Complications, mechanical
  - engagement of head NEC 652.5 ☑
    - in labor 660.0 ☑
  - extrarenal 788.99 ▲
  - fetal head to enter pelvic brim 652.5 ☑
    - affecting fetus or newborn 763.1
    - in labor 660.0 ☑
      - affecting fetus or newborn 763.1
  - forceps NEC 660.7 ☑
    - affecting fetus or newborn 763.1
  - fusion (joint) (spinal) 996.49
  - growth in childhood 783.43
  - heart (acute) (sudden) 428.9
    - with
      - abortion — *see* Abortion, by type, with specified complication NEC
      - acute pulmonary edema (*see also* Failure, ventricular, left) 428.1
        - with congestion (*see also* Failure, heart) 428.0
      - decompensation (*see also* Failure, heart) 428.0
      - dilation — *see* Disease, heart
      - ectopic pregnancy (*see also* categories 633.0–633.9) 639.8
      - molar pregnancy (*see also* categories 630–632) 639.8
    - arteriosclerotic 440.9
    - combined left-right sided 428.0
    - combined systolic and diastolic 428.40
      - acute 428.41
      - acute on chronic 428.43
      - chronic 428.42
    - compensated (*see also* Failure, heart) 428.0
    - complicating
      - abortion — *see* Abortion, by type, with specified complication NEC
      - delivery (cesarean) (instrumental) 669.4 ☑
      - ectopic pregnancy (*see also* categories 633.0–633.9) 639.8
      - molar pregnancy (*see also* categories 630–632) 639.8
      - obstetric anesthesia or sedation 668.1 ☑
      - surgery 997.1
    - congestive (compensated) (decompensated) (*see also* Failure, heart) 428.0
      - with rheumatic fever (conditions classifiable to 390)
        - active 391.8
        - inactive or quiescent (with chorea) 398.91
      - fetus or newborn 779.89
      - hypertensive (*see also* Hypertension, heart) 402.91
        - with renal disease (*see also* Hypertension, cardiorenal) 404.91
          - with renal failure 404.93
        - benign 402.11
        - malignant 402.01
      - rheumatic (chronic) (inactive) (with chorea) 398.91
        - active or acute 391.8
          - with chorea (Sydenham's) 392.0

- **Failure, failed** — *continued*
  - heart — *continued*
    - decompensated (*see also* Failure, heart) 428.0
    - degenerative (*see also* Degeneration, myocardial) 429.1
    - diastolic 428.30
      - acute 428.31
      - acute on chronic 428.33
      - chronic 428.32
    - due to presence of (cardiac) prosthesis 429.4
    - fetus or newborn 779.89
    - following
      - abortion 639.8
      - cardiac surgery 429.4
      - ectopic or molar pregnancy 639.8
    - high output NEC 428.9
    - hypertensive (*see also* Hypertension, heart) 402.91
      - with renal disease (*see also* Hypertension, cardiorenal) 404.91
        - with renal failure 404.93
      - benign 402.11
      - malignant 402.01
    - left (ventricular) (*see also* Failure, ventricular, left) 428.1
      - with right-sided failure (see also Failure, heart) 428.0
    - low output (syndrome) NEC 428.9
    - organic — *see* Disease, heart
    - postoperative (immediate) 997.1
      - long term effect of cardiac surgery 429.4
    - rheumatic (chronic) (congestive) (inactive) 398.91
    - right (secondary to left heart failure, conditions classifiable to 428.1) (ventricular) (*see also* Failure, heart) 428.0
    - senile 797
    - specified during or due to a procedure 997.1
      - long-term effect of cardiac surgery 429.4
    - systolic 428.20
      - acute 428.21
      - acute on chronic 428.23
      - chronic 428.22
    - thyrotoxic (*see also* Thyrotoxicosis) 242.9 ☑ *[425.7]*
    - valvular — *see* Endocarditis
  - hepatic 572.8
    - acute 570
    - due to a procedure 997.4
  - hepatorenal 572.4
  - hypertensive heart (*see also* Hypertension, heart) 402.91
    - benign 402.11
    - malignant 402.01
  - induction (of labor) 659.1 ☑
    - abortion (legal) (*see also* Abortion, failed) 638.9
    - affecting fetus or newborn 763.89
    - by oxytocic drugs 659.1 ☑
    - instrumental 659.0 ☑
    - mechanical 659.0 ☑
    - medical 659.1 ☑
    - surgical 659.0 ☑
  - initial alveolar expansion, newborn 770.4
  - involution, thymus (gland) 254.8
  - kidney — *see* Failure, renal
  - lactation 676.4 ☑
  - Leydig's cell, adult 257.2
  - liver 572.8
    - acute 570
  - medullary 799.89
  - mitral — *see* Endocarditis, mitral
  - myocardium, myocardial (*see also* Failure, heart) 428.9
    - chronic (*see also* Failure, heart) 428.0

- **Failure, failed** — *continued*
  - myocardium, myocardial (*see also* Failure, heart) — *continued*
    - congestive (*see also* Failure, heart) 428.0
  - ovarian (primary) 256.39
    - iatrogenic 256.2
    - postablative 256.2
    - postirradiation 256.2
    - postsurgical 256.2
  - ovulation 628.0
  - prerenal 788.99 ▲
  - renal 586
    - with
      - abortion — *see* Abortion, by type, with renal failure
      - ectopic pregnancy (*see also* categories 633.0–633.9) 639.3
      - edema (*see also* Nephrosis) 581.9
      - hypertension (*see also* Hypertension, kidney) 403.91
      - hypertensive heart disease (conditions classifiable to 402) 404.92
        - with heart failure 404.93
        - benign 404.12
          - with heart failure 404.13
        - malignant 404.02
          - with heart failure 404.03
      - molar pregnancy (*see also* categories 630–632) 639.3
      - tubular necrosis (acute) 584.5
    - acute 584.9
      - with lesion of
        - necrosis
          - cortical (renal) 584.6
          - medullary (renal) (papillary) 584.7
          - tubular 584.5
        - specified pathology NEC 584.8
    - chronic 585.9
      - hypertensive or with hypertension (*see also* Hypertension, kidney) 403.91
    - due to a procedure 997.5
    - following
      - abortion 639.3
      - crushing 958.5
      - ectopic or molar pregnancy 639.3
      - labor and delivery (acute) 669.3 ☑
    - hypertensive (*see also* Hypertension, kidney) 403.91
    - puerperal, postpartum 669.3 ☑
  - respiration, respiratory 518.81
    - acute 518.81
    - acute and chronic 518.84
    - center 348.8
      - newborn 770.84
    - chronic 518.83
    - due to trauma, surgery or shock 518.5
    - newborn 770.84
  - rotation
    - cecum 751.4
    - colon 751.4
    - intestine 751.4
    - kidney 753.3
  - segmentation (*see also* Fusion)
    - fingers (*see also* Syndactylism, fingers) 755.11
    - toes (*see also* Syndactylism, toes) 755.13
  - seminiferous tubule, adult 257.2
  - senile (general) 797
    - with psychosis 290.20
  - testis, primary (seminal) 257.2
  - to progress 661.2 ☑
  - to thrive
    - adult 783.7
    - child 783.41
  - transplant 996.80

- **Failure, failed** — *continued*
  - transplant — *continued*
    - bone marrow 996.85
    - organ (immune or nonimmune cause) 996.80
      - bone marrow 996.85
      - heart 996.83
      - intestines 996.87
      - kidney 996.81
      - liver 996.82
      - lung 996.84
      - pancreas 996.86
      - specified NEC 996.89
    - skin 996.52
      - artificial 996.55
      - decellularized allodermis 996.55
      - temporary allograft or pigskin graft — omit code
  - trial of labor NEC 660.6 ☑
    - affecting fetus or newborn 763.1
  - tubal ligation 998.89
  - urinary 586
  - vacuum extraction
    - abortion — *see* Abortion, failed
    - delivery NEC 660.7 ☑
      - affecting fetus or newborn 763.1
  - vasectomy 998.89
  - ventouse NEC 660.7 ☑
    - affecting fetus or newborn 763.1
  - ventricular (*see also* Failure, heart) 428.9
    - left 428.1
      - with rheumatic fever (conditions classifiable to 390)
        - active 391.8
          - with chorea 392.0
        - inactive or quiescent (with chorea) 398.91
      - hypertensive (*see also* Hypertension, heart) 402.91
        - benign 402.11
        - malignant 402.01
      - rheumatic (chronic) (inactive) (with chorea) 398.91
        - active or acute 391.8
          - with chorea 392.0
    - right (*see also* Failure, heart) 428.0
  - vital centers, fetus or newborn 779.89
  - weight gain in childhood 783.41
- **Fainting** (fit) (spell) 780.2
- **Falciform hymen** 752.49
- **Fallen arches** 734
- **Falling, any organ or part** — *see* Prolapse
- **Fall, maternal, affecting fetus or newborn** 760.5
- **Fallopian**
  - insufflation
    - fertility testing V26.21
    - following sterilization reversal V26.22
  - tube — *see* condition
- **Fallot's**
  - pentalogy 745.2
  - tetrad or tetralogy 745.2
  - triad or trilogy 746.09
- **Fallout, radioactive** (adverse effect) NEC 990
- **False** — *see also* condition
  - bundle branch block 426.50
  - bursa 727.89
  - croup 478.75
  - joint 733.82
  - labor (pains) 644.1 ☑
  - opening, urinary, male 752.69
  - passage, urethra (prostatic) 599.4
  - positive
    - serological test for syphilis 795.6
    - Wassermann reaction 795.6
  - pregnancy 300.11
- **Family, familial** — *see also* condition
  - affected by ●
    - family member ●
      - currently on deployment (military) V61.01 ●

- **Family, familial** — *see also* condition — *continued*
  - affected by — *continued*
    - family member — *continued*
      - returned from deployment (military) (current or past conflict) V61.02 ●
  - disruption ▶(*see also* Disruption, family)◀ V61.09 ▲
  - estrangement V61.09 ●
  - hemophagocytic
    - lymphohistiocytosis 288.4
    - reticulosis 288.4
  - Li-Fraumeni (syndrome) V84.01
  - planning advice V25.09
    - natural
      - procreative V26.41
      - to avoid pregnancy V25.04
  - problem V61.9
    - specified circumstance NEC V61.8
  - retinoblastoma (syndrome) 190.5
- **Famine** 994.2
  - edema 262
- **Fanconi's anemia** (congenital pancytopenia) 284.09
- **Fanconi (-de Toni) (-Debré) syndrome** (cystinosis) 270.0
- **Farber (-Uzman) syndrome or disease** (disseminated lipogranulomatosis) 272.8
- **Farcin** 024
- **Farcy** 024
- **Farmers'**
  - lung 495.0
  - skin 692.74
- **Farsightedness** 367.0
- **Fascia** — *see* condition
- **Fasciculation** 781.0
- **Fasciculitis optica** 377.32
- **Fasciitis** 729.4
  - eosinophilic 728.89
  - necrotizing 728.86
  - nodular 728.79
  - perirenal 593.4
  - plantar 728.71
  - pseudosarcomatous 728.79
  - traumatic (old) NEC 728.79
    - current — *see* Sprain, by site
- **Fasciola hepatica infestation** 121.3
- **Fascioliasis** 121.3
- **Fasciolopsiasis** (small intestine) 121.4
- **Fasciolopsis** (small intestine) 121.4
- **Fast pulse** 785.0
- **Fat**
  - embolism (cerebral) (pulmonary) (systemic) 958.1
    - with
      - abortion — *see* Abortion, by type, with embolism
      - ectopic pregnancy (*see also* categories 633.0–633.9) 639.6
      - molar pregnancy (*see also* categories 630–632) 639.6
    - complicating delivery or puerperium 673.8 ☑
    - following
      - abortion 639.6
      - ectopic or molar pregnancy 639.6
    - in pregnancy, childbirth, or the puerperium 673.8 ☑
  - excessive 278.02
    - in heart (*see also* Degeneration, myocardial) 429.1
  - general 278.02
  - hernia, herniation 729.30
    - eyelid 374.34
    - knee 729.31
    - orbit 374.34
    - retro-orbital 374.34
    - retropatellar 729.31
    - specified site NEC 729.39
  - indigestion 579.8
  - in stool 792.1
  - localized (pad) 278.1

- **Fat** — *continued*
  - localized — *continued*
    - heart (*see also* Degeneration, myocardial) 429.1
    - knee 729.31
    - retropatellar 729.31
  - necrosis (*see also* Fatty, degeneration)
    - breast (aseptic) (segmental) 611.3
    - mesentery 567.82
    - omentum 567.82
    - peritoneum 567.82
  - pad 278.1
- **Fatal familial insomnia** (FFI) 046.72 ●
- **Fatal syncope** 798.1
- **Fatigue** 780.79
  - auditory deafness (*see also* Deafness) 389.9
  - chronic, syndrome 780.71
  - combat (*see also* Reaction, stress, acute) 308.9
  - during pregnancy 646.8 ☑
  - general 780.79
    - psychogenic 300.5
  - heat (transient) 992.6
  - muscle 729.89
  - myocardium (*see also* Failure, heart) 428.9
  - nervous 300.5
  - neurosis 300.5
  - operational 300.89
  - postural 729.89
  - posture 729.89
  - psychogenic (general) 300.5
  - senile 797
  - syndrome NEC 300.5
    - chronic 780.71
  - undue 780.79
  - voice 784.49
- **Fatness** 278.02
- **Fatty** — *see also* condition
  - apron 278.1
  - degeneration (diffuse) (general) NEC 272.8
    - localized — *see* Degeneration, by site, fatty
    - placenta — *see* Placenta, abnormal
  - heart (enlarged) (*see also* Degeneration, myocardial) 429.1
  - infiltration (diffuse) (general) (*see also* Degeneration, by site, fatty) 272.8
    - heart (enlarged) (*see also* Degeneration, myocardial) 429.1
  - liver 571.8
    - alcoholic 571.0
  - necrosis — *see* Degeneration, fatty
  - phanerosis 272.8
- **Fauces** — *see* condition
- **Fauchard's disease** (periodontitis) 523.40
- **Faucitis** 478.29
- **Faulty** — *see also* condition
  - position of teeth 524.30
- **Favism** (anemia) 282.2
- **Favre-Racouchot disease** (elastoidosis cutanea nodularis) 701.8
- **Favus** 110.9
  - beard 110.0
  - capitis 110.0
  - corporis 110.5
  - eyelid 110.8
  - foot 110.4
  - hand 110.2
  - scalp 110.0
  - specified site NEC 110.8
- **Feared complaint unfounded** V65.5
- **Fear, fearfulness** (complex) (reaction) 300.20
  - child 313.0
  - of
    - animals 300.29
    - closed spaces 300.29
    - crowds 300.29
    - eating in public 300.23
    - heights 300.29
    - open spaces 300.22
- **Fear, fearfulness** — *continued*
  - of — *continued*
    - open spaces — *continued*
      - with panic attacks 300.21
    - public speaking 300.23
    - streets 300.22
      - with panic attacks 300.21
    - travel 300.22
      - with panic attacks 300.21
    - washing in public 300.23
  - transient 308.0
- **Febricula** (continued) (simple) — *see also* Pyrexia 780.60 ▲
- **Febrile** — *see also* Pyrexia 780.60 ▲
  - convulsion (simple) 780.31
    - complex 780.32
  - seizure (simple) 780.31
    - atypical 780.32
    - complex 780.32
    - complicated 780.32
- **Febris** — *see also* Fever 780.60 ▲
  - aestiva (*see also* Fever, hay) 477.9
  - flava (*see also* Fever, yellow) 060.9
  - melitensis 023.0
  - pestis (*see also* Plague) 020.9
  - puerperalis 672.0 ☑
  - recurrens (*see also* Fever, relapsing) 087.9
    - pediculo vestimenti 087.0
  - rubra 034.1
  - typhoidea 002.0
  - typhosa 002.0
- **Fecal** — *see* condition
- **Fecalith** (impaction) 560.39
  - with hernia (*see also* Hernia, by site, with obstruction)
    - gangrenous — *see* Hernia, by site, with gangrene
  - appendix 543.9
  - congenital 777.1
- **Fede's disease** 529.0
- **Feeble-minded** 317
- **Feeble rapid pulse due to shock following injury** 958.4
- **Feeding**
  - faulty (elderly) (infant) 783.3
    - newborn 779.3
  - formula check V20.2
  - improper (elderly) (infant) 783.3
    - newborn 779.3
  - problem (elderly) (infant) 783.3
    - newborn 779.3
    - nonorganic origin 307.59
- **Feeling of foreign body in throat** 784.99
- **Feer's disease** 985.0
- **Feet** — *see* condition
- **Feigned illness** V65.2
- **Feil-Klippel syndrome** (brevicollis) 756.16
- **Feinmesser's** (hidrotic) **ectodermal dysplasia** 757.31
- **Felix's disease** (juvenile osteochondrosis, hip) 732.1
- **Felon** (any digit) (with lymphangitis) 681.01
  - herpetic 054.6
- **Felty's syndrome** (rheumatoid arthritis with splenomegaly and leukopenia) 714.1
- **Feminism in boys** 302.6
- **Feminization, testicular** 259.51 ▲
  - with pseudohermaphroditism, male 259.51 ▲
- **Femoral hernia** — *see* Hernia, femoral
- **Femora vara** 736.32
- **Femur, femoral** — *see* condition
- **Fenestrata placenta** — *see* Placenta, abnormal
- **Fenestration, fenestrated** — *see also* Imperfect, closure
  - aorta-pulmonary 745.0
  - aorticopulmonary 745.0
  - aortopulmonary 745.0
  - cusps, heart valve NEC 746.89
    - pulmonary 746.09
- **Fenestration, fenestrated** — *see also* Imperfect, closure — *continued*
  - hymen 752.49
  - pulmonic cusps 746.09
- **Fenwick's disease** 537.89
- **Fermentation** (gastric) (gastrointestinal) (stomach) 536.8
  - intestine 564.89
    - psychogenic 306.4
  - psychogenic 306.4
- **Fernell's disease** (aortic aneurysm) 441.9
- **Fertile eunuch syndrome** 257.2
- **Fertility, meaning multiparity** — *see* Multiparity
- **Fetal**
  - alcohol syndrome 760.71 ●
  - anemia 678.0 ☑ ●
  - thrombocytopenia 678.0 ☑ ●
  - twin to twin transfusion 678.0 ☑ ●
- **Fetalis uterus** 752.3
- **Fetid**
  - breath 784.99
  - sweat 705.89
- **Fetishism** 302.81
  - transvestic 302.3
- **Fetomaternal hemorrhage**
  - affecting management of pregnancy 656.0 ☑
  - fetus or newborn 772.0
- **Fetus, fetal** — *see also* condition
  - papyraceous 779.89
  - type lung tissue 770.4
- **Fever** 780.60 ▲
  - with chills 780.60 ▲
    - in malarial regions (*see also* Malaria) 084.6
  - abortus NEC 023.9
  - aden 061
  - African tick-borne 087.1
  - American
    - mountain tick 066.1
    - spotted 082.0
  - and ague (*see also* Malaria) 084.6
  - aphthous 078.4
  - arbovirus hemorrhagic 065.9
  - Assam 085.0
  - Australian A or Q 083.0
  - Bangkok hemorrhagic 065.4
  - biliary, Charcôt's intermittent — *see* Choledocholithiasis
  - bilious, hemoglobinuric 084.8
  - blackwater 084.8
  - blister 054.9
  - Bonvale Dam 780.79
  - boutonneuse 082.1
  - brain 323.9
    - late effect — *see* category 326
  - breakbone 061
  - Bullis 082.8
  - Bunyamwera 066.3
  - Burdwan 085.0
  - Bwamba (encephalitis) 066.3
  - Cameroon (*see also* Malaria) 084.6
  - Canton 081.9
  - catarrhal (acute) 460
    - chronic 472.0
  - cat-scratch 078.3
  - cerebral 323.9
    - late effect — *see* category 326
  - cerebrospinal (meningococcal) (*see also* Meningitis, cerebrospinal) 036.0
  - Chagres 084.0
  - Chandipura 066.8
  - changuinola 066.0
  - Charcôt's (biliary) (hepatic) (intermittent) — *see* Choledocholithiasis
  - Chikungunya (viral) 066.3
    - hemorrhagic 065.4
  - childbed 670.0 ☑
  - Chitral 066.0
  - Colombo (*see also* Fever, paratyphoid) 002.9
  - Colorado tick (virus) 066.1
- **Fever** — *continued*
  - congestive
    - malarial (*see also* Malaria) 084.6
    - remittent (*see also* Malaria) 084.6
  - Congo virus 065.0
  - continued 780.60 ▲
    - malarial 084.0
  - Corsican (*see also* Malaria) 084.6
  - Crimean hemorrhagic 065.0
  - Cyprus (*see also* Brucellosis) 023.9
  - dandy 061
  - deer fly (*see also* Tularemia) 021.9
  - dehydration, newborn 778.4
  - dengue (virus) 061
    - hemorrhagic 065.4
  - desert 114.0
  - due to heat 992.0
  - Dumdum 085.0
  - enteric 002.0
  - ephemeral (of unknown origin) (*see also* Pyrexia) 780.60 ▲
  - epidemic, hemorrhagic of the Far East 065.0
  - erysipelatous (*see also* Erysipelas) 035
  - estivo-autumnal (malarial) 084.0
  - etiocholanolone 277.31
  - famine (*see also* Fever, relapsing)
    - meaning typhus — *see* Typhus
  - Far Eastern hemorrhagic 065.0
  - five day 083.1
  - Fort Bragg 100.89
  - gastroenteric 002.0
  - gastromalarial (*see also* Malaria) 084.6
  - Gibraltar (*see also* Brucellosis) 023.9
  - glandular 075
  - Guama (viral) 066.3
  - Haverhill 026.1
  - hay (allergic) (with rhinitis) 477.9
    - with
      - asthma (bronchial) (*see also* Asthma) 493.0 ☑
    - due to
      - dander, animal (cat) (dog) 477.2
      - dust 477.8
      - fowl 477.8
      - hair, animal (cat) (dog) 477.2
      - pollen, any plant or tree 477.0
      - specified allergen other than pollen 477.8
  - heat (effects) 992.0
  - hematuric, bilious 084.8
  - hemoglobinuric (malarial) 084.8
    - bilious 084.8
  - hemorrhagic (arthropod-borne) NEC 065.9
    - with renal syndrome 078.6
    - arenaviral 078.7
    - Argentine 078.7
    - Bangkok 065.4
    - Bolivian 078.7
    - Central Asian 065.0
    - chikungunya 065.4
    - Crimean 065.0
    - dengue (virus) 065.4
    - Ebola 065.8
    - epidemic 078.6
      - of Far East 065.0
    - Far Eastern 065.0
    - Junin virus 078.7
    - Korean 078.6
    - Kyasanur forest 065.2
    - Machupo virus 078.7
    - mite-borne NEC 065.8
    - mosquito-borne 065.4
    - Omsk 065.1
    - Philippine 065.4
    - Russian (Yaroslav) 078.6
    - Singapore 065.4
    - Southeast Asia 065.4
    - Thailand 065.4
    - tick-borne NEC 065.3
  - hepatic (*see also* Cholecystitis) 575.8
    - intermittent (Charcôt's) — *see* Choledocholithiasis
  - herpetic (*see also* Herpes) 054.9
  - Hyalomma tick 065.0

☑ Additional Digit Required — Refer to the Tabular List for Digit Selection
Subterms under main terms may continue to next column or page
▶◀ Revised Text ● New Line ▲ Revised Code

Fever — *continued*
- icterohemorrhagic 100.0
- inanition 780.60 ▲
  - newborn 778.4
- in conditions classified elsewhere 780.61 ●
- infective NEC 136.9
- intermittent (bilious) (*see also* Malaria) 084.6
  - hepatic (Charcôt) — *see* Choledocholithiasis
  - of unknown origin (*see also* Pyrexia) 780.60 ▲
  - pernicious 084.0
- iodide
  - correct substance properly administered 780.60 ▲
  - overdose or wrong substance given or taken 975.5
- Japanese river 081.2
- jungle yellow 060.0
- Junin virus, hemorrhagic 078.7
- Katayama 120.2
- Kedani 081.2
- Kenya 082.1
- Korean hemorrhagic 078.6
- Lassa 078.89
- Lone Star 082.8
- lung — *see* Pneumonia
- Machupo virus, hemorrhagic 078.7
- malaria, malarial (*see also* Malaria) 084.6
- Malta (*see also* Brucellosis) 023.9
- Marseilles 082.1
- marsh (*see also* Malaria) 084.6
- Mayaro (viral) 066.3
- Mediterranean (*see also* Brucellosis) 023.9
  - familial 277.31
  - tick 082.1
- meningeal — *see* Meningitis
- metal fumes NEC 985.8
- Meuse 083.1
- Mexican — *see* Typhus, Mexican
- Mianeh 087.1
- miasmatic (*see also* Malaria) 084.6
- miliary 078.2
- milk, female 672.0 ☑
- mill 504
- mite-borne hemorrhagic 065.8
- Monday 504
- mosquito-borne NEC 066.3
  - hemorrhagic NEC 065.4
- mountain 066.1
  - meaning
    - Rocky Mountain spotted 082.0
    - undulant fever (*see also* Brucellosis) 023.9
  - tick (American) 066.1
- Mucambo (viral) 066.3
- mud 100.89
- Neapolitan (*see also* Brucellosis) 023.9
- neutropenic 288.00
- newborn (environmentally-induced) 778.4 ●
- nine-mile 083.0
- nonexanthematous tick 066.1
- North Asian tick-borne typhus 082.2
- Omsk hemorrhagic 065.1
- O'nyong-nyong (viral) 066.3
- Oropouche (viral) 066.3
- Oroya 088.0
- paludal (*see also* Malaria) 084.6
- Panama 084.0
- pappataci 066.0
- paratyphoid 002.9
  - A 002.1
  - B (Schottmüller's) 002.2
  - C (Hirschfeld) 002.3
- parrot 073.9
- periodic 277.31
- pernicious, acute 084.0
- persistent (of unknown origin) (*see also* Pyrexia) 780.60 ▲
- petechial 036.0
- pharyngoconjunctival 077.2

Fever — *continued*
- pharyngoconjunctival — *continued*
  - adenoviral type 3 077.2
- Philippine hemorrhagic 065.4
- phlebotomus 066.0
- Piry 066.8
- Pixuna (viral) 066.3
- Plasmodium ovale 084.3
- pleural (*see also* Pleurisy) 511.0
- pneumonic — *see* Pneumonia
- polymer fume 987.8
- postimmunization 780.63 ●
- postoperative 780.62 ▲
  - due to infection 998.59
- postvaccination 780.63 ●
- pretibial 100.89
- puerperal, postpartum 672.0 ☑
- putrid — *see* Septicemia
- pyemic — *see* Septicemia
- Q 083.0
  - with pneumonia 083.0 *[484.8]*
- quadrilateral 083.0
- quartan (malaria) 084.2
- Queensland (coastal) 083.0
  - seven-day 100.89
- Quintan (A) 083.1
- quotidian 084.0
- rabbit (*see also* Tularemia) 021.9
- rat-bite 026.9
  - due to
    - Spirillum minor or minus 026.0
    - Spirochaeta morsus muris 026.0
    - Streptobacillus moniliformis 026.1
- recurrent — *see* Fever, relapsing
- relapsing 087.9
  - Carter's (Asiatic) 087.0
  - Dutton's (West African) 087.1
  - Koch's 087.9
  - louse-borne (epidemic) 087.0
  - Novy's (American) 087.1
  - Obermeyer's (European) 087.0
  - spirillum NEC 087.9
  - tick-borne (endemic) 087.1
- remittent (bilious) (congestive) (gastric) (*see also* Malaria) 084.6
- rheumatic (active) (acute) (chronic) (subacute) 390
  - with heart involvement 391.9
    - carditis 391.9
    - endocarditis (aortic) (mitral) (pulmonary) (tricuspid) 391.1
    - multiple sites 391.8
    - myocarditis 391.2
    - pancarditis, acute 391.8
    - pericarditis 391.0
    - specified type NEC 391.8
    - valvulitis 391.1
  - cardiac hypertrophy 398.99
  - inactive or quiescent
    - with cardiac hypertrophy 398.99
    - carditis 398.90
    - endocarditis 397.9
      - aortic (valve) 395.9
        - with mitral (valve) disease 396.9
      - mitral (valve) 394.9
        - with aortic (valve) disease 396.9
      - pulmonary (valve) 397.1
      - tricuspid (valve) 397.0
    - heart conditions (classifiable to 429.3, 429.6, 429.9) 398.99
      - failure (congestive) (conditions classifiable to 428.0, 428.9) 398.91
    - left ventricular failure (conditions classifiable to 428.1) 398.91
    - myocardial degeneration (conditions classifiable to 429.1) 398.0

Fever — *continued*
- rheumatic — *continued*
  - inactive or quiescent — *continued*
    - myocarditis (conditions classifiable to 429.0) 398.0
    - pancarditis 398.99
    - pericarditis 393
- Rift Valley (viral) 066.3
- Rocky Mountain spotted 082.0
- rose 477.0
- Ross river (viral) 066.3
- Russian hemorrhagic 078.6
- sandfly 066.0
- San Joaquin (valley) 114.0
- São Paulo 082.0
- scarlet 034.1
- septic — *see* Septicemia
- seven-day 061
  - Japan 100.89
  - Queensland 100.89
- shin bone 083.1
- Singapore hemorrhagic 065.4
- solar 061
- sore 054.9
- South African tick-bite 087.1
- Southeast Asia hemorrhagic 065.4
- spinal — *see* Meningitis
- spirillary 026.0
- splenic (*see also* Anthrax) 022.9
- spotted (Rocky Mountain) 082.0
  - American 082.0
  - Brazilian 082.0
  - Colombian 082.0
  - meaning
    - cerebrospinal meningitis 036.0
    - typhus 082.9
- spring 309.23
- steroid
  - correct substance properly administered 780.60 ▲
  - overdose or wrong substance given or taken 962.0
- streptobacillary 026.1
- subtertian 084.0
- Sumatran mite 081.2
- sun 061
- swamp 100.89
- sweating 078.2
- swine 003.8
- sylvatic yellow 060.0
- Tahyna 062.5
- tertian — *see* Malaria, tertian
- Thailand hemorrhagic 065.4
- thermic 992.0
- three day 066.0
  - with Coxsackie exanthem 074.8
- tick
  - American mountain 066.1
  - Colorado 066.1
  - Kemerovo 066.1
  - Mediterranean 082.1
  - mountain 066.1
  - nonexanthematous 066.1
  - Quaranfil 066.1
- tick-bite NEC 066.1
- tick-borne NEC 066.1
  - hemorrhagic NEC 065.3
- transitory of newborn 778.4
- trench 083.1
- tsutsugamushi 081.2
- typhogastric 002.0
- typhoid (abortive) (ambulant) (any site) (hemorrhagic) (infection) (intermittent) (malignant) (rheumatic) 002.0
- typhomalarial (*see also* Malaria) 084.6
- typhus — *see* Typhus
- undulant (*see also* Brucellosis) 023.9
- unknown origin (*see also* Pyrexia) 780.60 ▲
- uremic — *see* Uremia
- uveoparotid 135
- valley (Coccidioidomycosis) 114.0
- Venezuelan equine 066.2
- Volhynian 083.1

Fever — *continued*
- Wesselsbron (viral) 066.3
- West
  - African 084.8
  - Nile (viral) 066.40
    - with
      - cranial nerve disorders 066.42
      - encephalitis 066.41
      - optic neuritis 066.42
      - other complications 066.49
      - other neurologic manifestations 066.42
      - polyradiculitis 066.42
- Whitmore's 025
- Wolhynian 083.1
- worm 128.9
- Yaroslav hemorrhagic 078.6
- yellow 060.9
  - jungle 060.0
  - sylvatic 060.0
  - urban 060.1
  - vaccination, prophylactic (against) V04.4
- Zika (viral) 066.3

Fibrillation
- atrial (established) (paroxysmal) 427.31
- auricular (atrial) (established) 427.31
- cardiac (ventricular) 427.41
- coronary (*see also* Infarct, myocardium) 410.9 ☑
- heart (ventricular) 427.41
- muscular 728.9
- postoperative 997.1
- ventricular 427.41

Fibrin
- ball or bodies, pleural (sac) 511.0
- chamber, anterior (eye) (gelatinous exudate) 364.04

Fibrinogenolysis (hemorrhagic) — *see* Fibrinolysis

Fibrinogenopenia (congenital) (hereditary) — *see also* Defect, coagulation 286.3
- acquired 286.6

Fibrinolysis (acquired) (hemorrhagic) (pathologic) 286.6
- with
  - abortion — *see* Abortion, by type, with hemorrhage, delayed or excessive
  - ectopic pregnancy (*see also* categories 633.0–633.9) 639.1
  - molar pregnancy (*see also* categories 630–632) 639.1
- antepartum or intrapartum 641.3 ☑
  - affecting fetus or newborn 762.1
- following
  - abortion 639.1
  - ectopic or molar pregnancy 639.1
- newborn, transient 776.2
- postpartum 666.3 ☑

Fibrinopenia (hereditary) — *see also* Defect, coagulation 286.3
- acquired 286.6

Fibrinopurulent — *see* condition

Fibrinous — *see* condition

Fibroadenoma (M9010/0)
- cellular intracanalicular (M9020/0) 217
- giant (intracanalicular) (M9020/0) 217
- intracanalicular (M9011/0)
  - cellular (M9020/0) 217
  - giant (M9020/0) 217
  - specified site — *see* Neoplasm, by site, benign
  - unspecified site 217
- juvenile (M9030/0) 217
- pericanicular (M9012/0)
  - specified site — *see* Neoplasm, by site, benign
  - unspecified site 217
- phyllodes (M9020/0) 217
- prostate 600.20

Fibroadenoma — *continued*
  prostate — *continued*
    with
      other lower urinary tract symptoms (LUTS) 600.21
      urinary
        obstruction 600.21
        retention 600.21
  specified site — *see* Neoplasm, by site, benign
  unspecified site 217
Fibroadenosis, breast (chronic) (cystic) (diffuse) (periodic) (segmental) 610.2
Fibroangioma (M9160/0) — *see also* Neoplasm, by site, benign
  juvenile (M9160/0)
    specified site — *see* Neoplasm, by site, benign
    unspecified site 210.7
Fibrocellulitis progressiva ossificans 728.11
Fibrochondrosarcoma (M9220/3) — *see* Neoplasm, cartilage, malignant
Fibrocystic
  disease 277.00
    bone NEC 733.29
    breast 610.1
    jaw 526.2
    kidney (congenital) 753.19
    liver 751.62
    lung 518.89
      congenital 748.4
    pancreas 277.00
  kidney (congenital) 753.19
Fibrodysplasia ossificans multiplex (progressiva) 728.11
Fibroelastosis (cordis) (endocardial) (endomyocardial) 425.3
Fibroid (tumor) (M8890/0) — *see also* Neoplasm, connective tissue, benign
  disease, lung (chronic) (*see also* Fibrosis, lung) 515
  heart (disease) (*see also* Myocarditis) 429.0
  induration, lung (chronic) (*see also* Fibrosis, lung) 515
  in pregnancy or childbirth 654.1 ☑
    affecting fetus or newborn 763.89
    causing obstructed labor 660.2 ☑
      affecting fetus or newborn 763.1
  liver — *see* Cirrhosis, liver
  lung (*see also* Fibrosis, lung) 515
  pneumonia (chronic) (*see also* Fibrosis, lung) 515
  uterus (M8890/0) (*see also* Leiomyoma, uterus) 218.9
Fibrolipoma (M8851/0) — *see also* Lipoma, by site 214.9
Fibroliposarcoma (M8850/3) — *see* Neoplasm, connective tissue, malignant
Fibroma (M8810/0) — *see also* Neoplasm, connective tissue, benign
  ameloblastic (M9330/0) 213.1
    upper jaw (bone) 213.0
  bone (nonossifying) 733.99
    ossifying (M9262/0) — *see* Neoplasm, bone, benign
  cementifying (M9274/0) — *see* Neoplasm, bone, benign
  chondromyxoid (M9241/0) — *see* Neoplasm, bone, benign
  desmoplastic (M8823/1) — *see* Neoplasm, connective tissue, uncertain behavior
  facial (M8813/0) — *see* Neoplasm, connective tissue, benign
  invasive (M8821/1) — *see* Neoplasm, connective tissue, uncertain behavior
  molle (M8851/0) (*see also* Lipoma, by site) 214.9
  myxoid (M8811/0) — *see* Neoplasm, connective tissue, benign

Fibroma — *see also* Neoplasm, connective tissue, benign — *continued*
  nasopharynx, nasopharyngeal (juvenile) (M9160/0) 210.7
  nonosteogenic (nonossifying) — *see* Dysplasia, fibrous
  odontogenic (M9321/0) 213.1
    upper jaw (bone) 213.0
  ossifying (M9262/0) — *see* Neoplasm, bone, benign
  periosteal (M8812/0) — *see* Neoplasm, bone, benign
  prostate 600.20
    with
      other lower urinary tract symptoms (LUTS) 600.21
      urinary
        obstruction 600.21
        retention 600.21
  soft (M8851/0) (*see also* Lipoma, by site) 214.9
Fibromatosis 728.79
  abdominal (M8822/1) — *see* Neoplasm, connective tissue, uncertain behavior
  aggressive (M8821/1) — *see* Neoplasm, connective tissue, uncertain behavior
  congenital generalized (CGF) 759.89
  Dupuytren's 728.6
  gingival 523.8
  plantar fascia 728.71
  proliferative 728.79
  pseudosarcomatous (proliferative) (subcutaneous) 728.79
  subcutaneous pseudosarcomatous (proliferative) 728.79
Fibromyalgia 729.1
Fibromyoma (M8890/0) — *see also* Neoplasm, connective tissue, benign
  uterus (corpus) (*see also* Leiomyoma, uterus) 218.9
    in pregnancy or childbirth 654.1 ☑
      affecting fetus or newborn 763.89
      causing obstructed labor 660.2 ☑
        affecting fetus or newborn 763.1
Fibromyositis — *see also* Myositis 729.1
  scapulohumeral 726.2
Fibromyxolipoma (M8852/0) — *see also* Lipoma, by site 214.9
Fibromyxoma (M8811/0) — *see* Neoplasm, connective tissue, benign
Fibromyxosarcoma (M8811/3) — *see* Neoplasm, connective tissue, malignant
Fibro-odontoma, ameloblastic (M9290/0) 213.1
  upper jaw (bone) 213.0
Fibro-osteoma (M9262/0) — *see* Neoplasm, bone, benign
Fibroplasia, retrolental ▶(*see also* Retinopathy of prematurity)◀ 362.21
Fibropurulent — *see* condition
Fibrosarcoma (M8810/3) — *see also* Neoplasm, connective tissue, malignant
  ameloblastic (M9330/3) 170.1
    upper jaw (bone) 170.0
  congenital (M8814/3) — *see* Neoplasm, connective tissue, malignant
  fascial (M8813/3) — *see* Neoplasm, connective tissue, malignant
  infantile (M8814/3) — *see* Neoplasm, connective tissue, malignant
  odontogenic (M9330/3) 170.1
    upper jaw (bone) 170.0
  periosteal (M8812/3) — *see* Neoplasm, bone, malignant

Fibrosclerosis
  breast 610.3
  corpora cavernosa (penis) 607.89
  familial multifocal NEC 710.8
  multifocal (idiopathic) NEC 710.8
  penis (corpora cavernosa) 607.89
Fibrosis, fibrotic
  adrenal (gland) 255.8
  alveolar (diffuse) 516.3
  amnion 658.8 ☑
  anal papillae 569.49
  anus 569.49
  appendix, appendiceal, noninflammatory 543.9
  arteriocapillary — *see* Arteriosclerosis
  bauxite (of lung) 503
  biliary 576.8
    due to Clonorchis sinensis 121.1
  bladder 596.8
    interstitial 595.1
    localized submucosal 595.1
    panmural 595.1
  bone, diffuse 756.59
  breast 610.3
  capillary (*see also* Arteriosclerosis)
    lung (chronic) (*see also* Fibrosis, lung) 515
  cardiac (*see also* Myocarditis) 429.0
  cervix 622.8
  chorion 658.8 ☑
  corpus cavernosum 607.89
  cystic (of pancreas) 277.00
    with
      manifestations
        gastrointestinal 277.03
        pulmonary 277.02
        specified NEC 277.09
      meconium ileus 277.01
      pulmonary exacerbation 277.02
  due to (presence of) any device, implant, or graft — *see* Complications, due to (presence of) any device, implant, or graft classified to 996.0–996.5 NEC
  ejaculatory duct 608.89
  endocardium (*see also* Endocarditis) 424.90
  endomyocardial (African) 425.0
  epididymis 608.89
  eye muscle 378.62
  graphite (of lung) 503
  heart (*see also* Myocarditis) 429.0
  hepatic (*see also* Cirrhosis, liver)
    due to Clonorchis sinensis 121.1
  hepatolienal — *see* Cirrhosis, liver
  hepatosplenic — *see* Cirrhosis, liver
  infrapatellar fat pad 729.31
  interstitial pulmonary, newborn 770.7
  intrascrotal 608.89
  kidney (*see also* Sclerosis, renal) 587
  liver — *see* Cirrhosis, liver
  lung (atrophic) (capillary) (chronic) (confluent) (massive) (perialveolar) (peribronchial) 515
    with
      anthracosilicosis (occupational) 500
      anthracosis (occupational) 500
      asbestosis (occupational) 501
      bagassosis (occupational) 495.1
      bauxite 503
      berylliosis (occupational) 503
      byssinosis (occupational) 504
      calcicosis (occupational) 502
      chalicosis (occupational) 502
      dust reticulation (occupational) 504
      farmers' lung 495.0
      gannister disease (occupational) 502
      graphite 503
      pneumonoconiosis (occupational) 505
      pneumosiderosis (occupational) 503
      siderosis (occupational) 503

Fibrosis, fibrotic — *continued*
  lung — *continued*
    with — *continued*
      silicosis (occupational) 502
      tuberculosis (*see also* Tuberculosis) 011.4 ☑
    diffuse (idiopathic) (interstitial) 516.3
    due to
      bauxite 503
      fumes or vapors (chemical) (inhalation) 506.4
      graphite 503
    following radiation 508.1
    postinflammatory 515
    silicotic (massive) (occupational) 502
    tuberculous (*see also* Tuberculosis) 011.4 ☑
  lymphatic gland 289.3
  median bar 600.90
    with
      other lower urinary tract symptoms (LUTS) 600.91
      urinary
        obstruction 600.91
        retention 600.91
  mediastinum (idiopathic) 519.3
  meninges 349.2
  muscle NEC 728.2
    iatrogenic (from injection) 999.9
  myocardium, myocardial (*see also* Myocarditis) 429.0
  oral submucous 528.8
  ovary 620.8
  oviduct 620.8
  pancreas 577.8
    cystic 277.00
      with
        manifestations
          gastrointestinal 277.03
          pulmonary 277.02
          specified NEC 277.09
        meconium ileus 277.01
        pulmonary exacerbation 277.02
  penis 607.89
  periappendiceal 543.9
  periarticular (*see also* Ankylosis) 718.5 ☑
  pericardium 423.1
  perineum, in pregnancy or childbirth 654.8 ☑
    affecting fetus or newborn 763.89
    causing obstructed labor 660.2 ☑
      affecting fetus or newborn 763.1
  perineural NEC 355.9
    foot 355.6
  periureteral 593.89
  placenta — *see* Placenta, abnormal
  pleura 511.0
  popliteal fat pad 729.31
  preretinal 362.56
  prostate (chronic) 600.90
    with
      other lower urinary tract symptoms (LUTS) 600.91
      urinary
        obstruction 600.91
        retention 600.91
  pulmonary (chronic) (*see also* Fibrosis, lung) 515
    alveolar capillary block 516.3
    interstitial
      diffuse (idiopathic) 516.3
      newborn 770.7
  radiation — *see* Effect, adverse, radiation
  rectal sphincter 569.49
  retroperitoneal, idiopathic 593.4
  sclerosing mesenteric (idiopathic) 567.82
  scrotum 608.89
  seminal vesicle 608.89
  senile 797
  skin NEC 709.2

Fibrosis, fibrotic — *continued*
spermatic cord 608.89
spleen 289.59
bilharzial (*see also* Schistosomiasis) 120.9
subepidermal nodular (M8832/0) — *see* Neoplasm, skin, benign
submucous NEC 709.2
oral 528.8
tongue 528.8
syncytium — *see* Placenta, abnormal
testis 608.89
chronic, due to syphilis 095.8
thymus (gland) 254.8
tunica vaginalis 608.89
ureter 593.89
urethra 599.84
uterus (nonneoplastic) 621.8
bilharzial (*see also* Schistosomiasis) 120.9
neoplastic (*see also* Leiomyoma, uterus) 218.9
vagina 623.8
valve, heart (*see also* Endocarditis) 424.90
vas deferens 608.89
vein 459.89
lower extremities 459.89
vesical 595.1
Fibrositis (periarticular) (rheumatoid) 729.0
humeroscapular region 726.2
nodular, chronic
Jaccoud's 714.4
rheumatoid 714.4
ossificans 728.11
scapulohumeral 726.2
Fibrothorax 511.0
Fibrotic — *see* Fibrosis
Fibrous — *see* condition
Fibroxanthoma (M8831/0) — *see also* Neoplasm, connective tissue, benign
atypical (M8831/1) — *see* Neoplasm, connective tissue, uncertain behavior
malignant (M8831/3) — *see* Neoplasm, connective tissue, malignant
Fibroxanthosarcoma (M8831/3) — *see* Neoplasm, connective tissue, malignant
Fiedler's
disease (leptospiral jaundice) 100.0
myocarditis or syndrome (acute isolated myocarditis) 422.91
Fiessinger-Leroy (-Reiter) syndrome 099.3
Fiessinger-Rendu syndrome (erythema muliforme exudativum) 695.19 ▲
Fifth disease (eruptive) 057.0
venereal 099.1
Filaria, filarial — *see* Infestation, filarial
Filariasis — *see also* Infestation, filarial 125.9
bancroftian 125.0
Brug's 125.1
due to
bancrofti 125.0
Brugia (Wuchereria) (malayi) 125.1
Loa loa 125.2
malayi 125.1
organism NEC 125.6
Wuchereria (bancrofti) 125.0
malayi 125.1
Malayan 125.1
ozzardi 125.5
specified type NEC 125.6
Filatoff's, Filatov's, Filatow's disease (infectious mononucleosis) 075
File-cutters' disease 984.9
specified type of lead — *see* Table of Drugs and Chemicals
Filling defect
biliary tract 793.3
Filling defect — *continued*
bladder 793.5
duodenum 793.4
gallbladder 793.3
gastrointestinal tract 793.4
intestine 793.4
kidney 793.5
stomach 793.4
ureter 793.5
Filtering bleb, eye (postglaucoma) (status) V45.69
with complication or rupture 997.99
postcataract extraction (complication) 997.99
Fimbrial cyst (congenital) 752.11
Fimbriated hymen 752.49
Financial problem affecting care V60.2
Findings, abnormal, without diagnosis (examination) (laboratory test) 796.4
17-ketosteroids, elevated 791.9
acetonuria 791.6
acid phosphatase 790.5
albumin-globulin ratio 790.99
albuminuria 791.0
alcohol in blood 790.3
alkaline phosphatase 790.5
amniotic fluid 792.3
amylase 790.5
anisocytosis 790.09
antenatal screening 796.5
anthrax, positive 795.31
antibody titers, elevated 795.79
anticardiolipin antibody 795.79
antigen-antibody reaction 795.79
antiphospholipid antibody 795.79
bacteriuria 791.9
ballistocardiogram 794.39
bicarbonate 276.9
bile in urine 791.4
bilirubin 277.4
bleeding time (prolonged) 790.92
blood culture, positive 790.7
blood gas level (arterial) 790.91
blood sugar level 790.29
high 790.29
fasting glucose 790.21
glucose tolerance test 790.22
low 251.2
calcium 275.40
cancer antigen 125 [CA 125] 795.82
carbonate 276.9
carcinoembryonic antigen [CEA] 795.81
casts, urine 791.7
catecholamines 791.9
cells, urine 791.7
cerebrospinal fluid (color) (content) (pressure) 792.0
cervical
high risk human papillomavirus (HPV) DNA test positive 795.05
low risk human papillomavirus (HPV) DNA test positive 795.09
chloride 276.9
cholesterol 272.9
high 272.0
with high triglycerides 272.2
chromosome analysis 795.2
chyluria 791.1
circulation time 794.39
cloudy dialysis effluent 792.5
cloudy urine 791.9
coagulation study 790.92
cobalt, blood 790.6
color of urine (unusual) NEC 791.9
copper, blood 790.6
C-reactive protein (CRP) 790.95
creatinine clearance 794.4 ●
crystals, urine 791.9
culture, positive NEC 795.39
blood 790.7
HIV V08
Findings, abnormal, without diagnosis — *continued*
culture, positive — *continued*
human immunodeficiency virus V08
nose 795.39
Staphylococcus — *see* Carrier (suspected) of, Staphylococcus ●
skin lesion NEC 795.39
spinal fluid 792.0
sputum 795.39
stool 792.1
throat 795.39
urine 791.9
viral
human immunodeficiency V08
wound 795.39
echocardiogram 793.2
echoencephalogram 794.01
echogram NEC — *see* Findings, abnormal, structure
electrocardiogram (ECG) (EKG) 794.31
electroencephalogram (EEG) 794.02
electrolyte level, urinary 791.9
electromyogram (EMG) 794.17
ocular 794.14
electro-oculogram (EOG) 794.12
electroretinogram (ERG) 794.11
enzymes, serum NEC 790.5
fibrinogen titer coagulation study 790.92
filling defect — *see* Filling defect
function study NEC 794.9
auditory 794.15
bladder 794.9
brain 794.00
cardiac 794.30
endocrine NEC 794.6
thyroid 794.5
kidney 794.4
liver 794.8
nervous system
central 794.00
peripheral 794.19
oculomotor 794.14
pancreas 794.9
placenta 794.9
pulmonary 794.2
retina 794.11
special senses 794.19
spleen 794.9
vestibular 794.16
gallbladder, nonvisualization 793.3
glucose 790.29
elevated
fasting 790.21
tolerance test 790.22
glycosuria 791.5
heart
shadow 793.2
sounds 785.3
hematinuria 791.2
hematocrit
drop (precipitous) 790.01
elevated 282.7
low 285.9
hematologic NEC 790.99
hematuria 599.70 ▲
hemoglobin
elevated 282.7
low 285.9
hemoglobinuria 791.2
histological NEC 795.4
hormones 259.9
immunoglobulins, elevated 795.79
indolacetic acid, elevated 791.9
iron 790.6
karyotype 795.2
ketonuria 791.6
lactic acid dehydrogenase (LDH) 790.4
lead 790.6
lipase 790.5
lipids NEC 272.9
lithium, blood 790.6
liver function test 790.6
Findings, abnormal, without diagnosis — *continued*
lung field (coin lesion) (shadow) 793.1
magnesium, blood 790.6
mammogram 793.80
calcification 793.89
calculus 793.89
microcalcification 793.81
mediastinal shift 793.2
melanin, urine 791.9
microbiologic NEC 795.39
mineral, blood NEC 790.6
myoglobinuria 791.3
nasal swab, anthrax 795.31
neonatal screening 796.6
nitrogen derivatives, blood 790.6
nonvisualization of gallbladder 793.3
nose culture, positive 795.39
odor of urine (unusual) NEC 791.9
oxygen saturation 790.91
Papanicolaou (smear) 796.9 ▲
anus 796.70 ●
with ●
atypical squamous cells ●
cannot exclude high grade squamous intraepithelial lesion (ASC-H) 796.72 ●
of undetermined significance (ASC-US) 796.71 ●
cytologic evidence of malignancy 796.76 ●
high grade squamous intraepithelial lesion (HGSIL) 796.74 ●
low grade squamous intraepithelial lesion (LGSIL) 796.73 ●
glandular 796.70 ●
specified finding NEC 796.79 ●
cervix 795.00
with
atypical squamous cells
cannot exclude high grade squamous intraepithelial lesion (ASC-H) 795.02
of undetermined significance (ASC-US) 795.01
cytologic evidence of malignancy 795.06
high grade squamous intraepithelial lesion (HGSIL) 795.04
low grade squamous intraepithelial lesion (LGSIL) 795.03
dyskaryotic 795.09
nonspecific finding NEC 795.09
other site 796.9 ▲
vagina 795.10 ●
with ●
atypical squamous cells ●
cannot exclude high grade squamous intraepithelial lesion (ASC-H) 795.12 ●
of undetermined significance (ASC-US) 795.11 ●
cytologic evidence of malignancy 795.16 ●
high grade squamous intraepithelial lesion (HGSIL) 795.14 ●
low grade squamous intraepithelial lesion (LGSIL) 795.13 ●
glandular 795.10 ●
specified NEC 795.19 ●
peritoneal fluid 792.9
phonocardiogram 794.39

Findings, abnormal, without diagnosis — *continued*
phosphorus 275.3
pleural fluid 792.9
pneumoencephalogram 793.0
PO_2-oxygen ratio 790.91
poikilocytosis 790.09
potassium
deficiency 276.8
excess 276.7
PPD 795.5
prostate specific antigen (PSA) 790.93
protein, serum NEC 790.99
proteinuria 791.0
prothrombin time (partial) (prolonged) (PT) (PTT) 790.92
pyuria 791.9
radiologic (x-ray) 793.99
abdomen 793.6
biliary tract 793.3
breast 793.89
abnormal mammogram NOS 793.80
mammographic
calcification 793.89
calculus 793.89
microcalcification 793.81
gastrointestinal tract 793.4
genitourinary organs 793.5
head 793.0
image test inconclusive due to excess body fat 793.91
intrathoracic organs NEC 793.2
lung 793.1
musculoskeletal 793.7
placenta 793.99
retroperitoneum 793.6
skin 793.99
skull 793.0
subcutaneous tissue 793.99
red blood cell 790.09
count 790.09
morphology 790.09
sickling 790.09
volume 790.09
saliva 792.4
scan NEC 794.9
bladder 794.9
bone 794.9
brain 794.09
kidney 794.4
liver 794.8
lung 794.2
pancreas 794.9
placental 794.9
spleen 794.9
thyroid 794.5
sedimentation rate, elevated 790.1
semen 792.2
serological (for)
human immunodeficiency virus (HIV)
inconclusive 795.71
positive V08
syphilis — *see* Findings, serology for syphilis
serology for syphilis
false positive 795.6
positive 097.1
false 795.6
follow-up of latent syphilis — *see* Syphilis, latent
only finding — *see* Syphilis, latent
serum 790.99
blood NEC 790.99
enzymes NEC 790.5
proteins 790.99
SGOT 790.4
SGPT 790.4
sickling of red blood cells 790.09
skin test, positive 795.79
tuberculin (without active tuberculosis) 795.5
sodium 790.6
deficiency 276.1

Findings, abnormal, without diagnosis — *continued*
sodium — *continued*
excess 276.0
spermatozoa 792.2
spinal fluid 792.0
culture, positive 792.0
sputum culture, positive 795.39
for acid-fast bacilli 795.39
stool NEC 792.1
bloody 578.1
occult 792.1
color 792.1
culture, positive 792.1
occult blood 792.1
stress test 794.39
structure, body (echogram) (thermogram) (ultrasound) (x-ray) NEC 793.99
abdomen 793.6
breast 793.89
abnormal mammogram 793.80
mammographic
calcification 793.89
calculus 793.89
microcalcification 793.81
gastrointestinal tract 793.4
genitourinary organs 793.5
head 793.0
echogram (ultrasound) 794.01
intrathoracic organs NEC 793.2
lung 793.1
musculoskeletal 793.7
placenta 793.99
retroperitoneum 793.6
skin 793.99
subcutaneous tissue NEC 793.99
synovial fluid 792.9
thermogram — *see* Findings, abnormal, structure
throat culture, positive 795.39
thyroid (function) 794.5
metabolism (rate) 794.5
scan 794.5
uptake 794.5
total proteins 790.99
toxicology (drugs) (heavy metals) 796.0
transaminase (level) 790.4
triglycerides 272.9
high 272.1
with high cholesterol 272.2
tuberculin skin test (without active tuberculosis) 795.5
tumor markers NEC 795.89
ultrasound (*see also* Findings, abnormal, structure)
cardiogram 793.2
uric acid, blood 790.6
urine, urinary constituents 791.9
acetone 791.6
albumin 791.0
bacteria 791.9
bile 791.4
blood 599.70 ▲
casts or cells 791.7
chyle 791.1
culture, positive 791.9
glucose 791.5
hemoglobin 791.2
ketone 791.6
protein 791.0
pus 791.9
sugar 791.5
vaginal
fluid 792.9 ●
high risk human papillomavirus (HPV) DNA test positive 795.15 ●
low risk human papillomavirus (HPV) DNA test positive 795.19 ●
vanillylmandelic acid, elevated 791.9
vectorcardiogram (VCG) 794.39
ventriculogram (cerebral) 793.0
VMA, elevated 791.9

Findings, abnormal, without diagnosis — *continued*
Wassermann reaction
false positive 795.6
positive 097.1
follow-up of latent syphilis — *see* Syphilis, latent
only finding — *see* Syphilis, latent
white blood cell 288.9
count 288.9
elevated 288.60
low 288.50
differential 288.9
morphology 288.9
wound culture 795.39
xerography 793.89
zinc, blood 790.6
Finger — *see* condition
Finnish type nephrosis (congenital) 759.89
Fire, St. Anthony's — *see also* Erysipelas 035
Fish
hook stomach 537.89
meal workers' lung 495.8
Fisher's syndrome 357.0
Fissure, fissured
abdominal wall (congenital) 756.79
anus, anal 565.0
congenital 751.5
buccal cavity 528.9
clitoris (congenital) 752.49
ear, lobule (congenital) 744.29
epiglottis (congenital) 748.3
larynx 478.79
congenital 748.3
lip 528.5
congenital (*see also* Cleft, lip) 749.10
nipple 611.2
puerperal, postpartum 676.1 ☑
palate (congenital) (*see also* Cleft, palate) 749.00
postanal 565.0
rectum 565.0
skin 709.8
streptococcal 686.9
spine (congenital) (*see also* Spina bifida) 741.9 ☑
sternum (congenital) 756.3
tongue (acquired) 529.5
congenital 750.13
Fistula (sinus) 686.9
abdomen (wall) 569.81
bladder 596.2
intestine 569.81
ureter 593.82
uterus 619.2
abdominorectal 569.81
abdominosigmoidal 569.81
abdominothoracic 510.0
abdominouterine 619.2
congenital 752.3
abdominovesical 596.2
accessory sinuses (*see also* Sinusitis) 473.9
actinomycotic — *see* Actinomycosis
alveolar
antrum (*see also* Sinusitis, maxillary) 473.0
process 522.7
anorectal 565.1
antrobuccal (*see also* Sinusitis, maxillary) 473.0
antrum (*see also* Sinusitis, maxillary) 473.0
anus, anal (infectional) (recurrent) 565.1
congenital 751.5
tuberculous (*see also* Tuberculosis) 014.8 ☑
aortic sinus 747.29
aortoduodenal 447.2
appendix, appendicular 543.9
arteriovenous (acquired) 447.0

Fistula — *continued*
arteriovenous — *continued*
brain 437.3
congenital 747.81
ruptured (*see also* Hemorrhage, subarachnoid) 430
ruptured (*see also* Hemorrhage, subarachnoid) 430
cerebral 437.3
congenital 747.81
congenital (peripheral) 747.60
brain — *see* Fistula, arteriovenous, brain, congenital
coronary 746.85
gastrointestinal 747.61
lower limb 747.64
pulmonary 747.3
renal 747.62
specified site NEC 747.69
upper limb 747.63
coronary 414.19
congenital 746.85
heart 414.19
pulmonary (vessels) 417.0
congenital 747.3
surgically created (for dialysis) V45.11 ▲
complication NEC 996.73
atherosclerosis — *see* Arteriosclerosis, extremities
embolism 996.74
infection or inflammation 996.62
mechanical 996.1
occlusion NEC 996.74
thrombus 996.74
traumatic — *see* Injury, blood vessel, by site
artery 447.2
aural 383.81
congenital 744.49
auricle 383.81
congenital 744.49
Bartholin's gland 619.8
bile duct (*see also* Fistula, biliary) 576.4
biliary (duct) (tract) 576.4
congenital 751.69
bladder (neck) (sphincter) 596.2
into seminal vesicle 596.2
bone 733.99
brain 348.8
arteriovenous — *see* Fistula, arteriovenous, brain
branchial (cleft) 744.41
branchiogenous 744.41
breast 611.0
puerperal, postpartum 675.1 ☑
bronchial 510.0
bronchocutaneous, bronchomediastinal, bronchopleural, bronchopleuromediastinal (infective) 510.0
tuberculous (*see also* Tuberculosis) 011.3 ☑
bronchoesophageal 530.89
congenital 750.3
buccal cavity (infective) 528.3
canal, ear 380.89
carotid-cavernous
congenital 747.81
with hemorrhage 430
traumatic 900.82
with hemorrhage (*see also* Hemorrhage, brain, traumatic) 853.0 ☑
late effect 908.3
cecosigmoidal 569.81
cecum 569.81
cerebrospinal (fluid) 349.81
cervical, lateral (congenital) 744.41
cervicoaural (congenital) 744.49
cervicosigmoidal 619.1
cervicovesical 619.0

Fistula — *continued*
cervix 619.8
chest (wall) 510.0
cholecystocolic (*see also* Fistula, gallbladder) 575.5
cholecystocolonic (*see also* Fistula, gallbladder) 575.5
cholecystoduodenal (*see also* Fistula, gallbladder) 575.5
cholecystoenteric (*see also* Fistula, gallbladder) 575.5
cholecystogastric (*see also* Fistula, gallbladder) 575.5
cholecystointestinal (*see also* Fistula, gallbladder) 575.5
choledochoduodenal 576.4
cholocolic (*see also* Fistula, gallbladder) 575.5
coccyx 685.1
with abscess 685.0
colon 569.81
colostomy 569.69
colovaginal (acquired) 619.1
common duct (bile duct) 576.4
congenital, NEC — *see* Anomaly, specified type NEC
cornea, causing hypotony 360.32
coronary, arteriovenous 414.19
congenital 746.85
costal region 510.0
cul-de-sac, Douglas' 619.8
cutaneous 686.9
cystic duct (*see also* Fistula, gallbladder) 575.5
congenital 751.69
dental 522.7
diaphragm 510.0
bronchovisceral 510.0
pleuroperitoneal 510.0
pulmonoperitoneal 510.0
duodenum 537.4
ear (canal) (external) 380.89
enterocolic 569.81
enterocutaneous 569.81
enteroenteric 569.81
entero-uterine 619.1
congenital 752.3
enterovaginal 619.1
congenital 752.49
enterovesical 596.1
epididymis 608.89
tuberculous (*see also* Tuberculosis) 016.4 ☑
esophagobronchial 530.89
congenital 750.3
esophagocutaneous 530.89
esophagopleurocutaneous 530.89
esophagotracheal 530.84
congenital 750.3
esophagus 530.89
congenital 750.4
ethmoid (*see also* Sinusitis, ethmoidal) 473.2
eyeball (cornea) (sclera) 360.32
eyelid 373.11
fallopian tube (external) 619.2
fecal 569.81
congenital 751.5
from periapical lesion 522.7
frontal sinus (*see also* Sinusitis, frontal) 473.1
gallbladder 575.5
with calculus, cholelithiasis, stones (*see also* Cholelithiasis) 574.2 ☑
congenital 751.69
gastric 537.4
gastrocolic 537.4
congenital 750.7
tuberculous (*see also* Tuberculosis) 014.8 ☑
gastroenterocolic 537.4
gastroesophageal 537.4
gastrojejunal 537.4
gastrojejunocolic 537.4

Fistula — *continued*
genital
organs
female 619.9
specified site NEC 619.8
male 608.89
tract-skin (female) 619.2
hepatopleural 510.0
hepatopulmonary 510.0
horseshoe 565.1
ileorectal 569.81
ileosigmoidal 569.81
ileostomy 569.69
ileovesical 596.1
ileum 569.81
in ano 565.1
tuberculous (*see also* Tuberculosis) 014.8 ☑
inner ear (*see also* Fistula, labyrinth) 386.40
intestine 569.81
intestinocolonic (abdominal) 569.81
intestinoureteral 593.82
intestinouterine 619.1
intestinovaginal 619.1
congenital 752.49
intestinovesical 596.1
involving female genital tract 619.9
digestive-genital 619.1
genital tract-skin 619.2
specified site NEC 619.8
urinary-genital 619.0
ischiorectal (fossa) 566
jejunostomy 569.69
jejunum 569.81
joint 719.80
ankle 719.87
elbow 719.82
foot 719.87
hand 719.84
hip 719.85
knee 719.86
multiple sites 719.89
pelvic region 719.85
shoulder (region) 719.81
specified site NEC 719.88
tuberculous — *see* Tuberculosis, joint
wrist 719.83
kidney 593.89
labium (majus) (minus) 619.8
labyrinth, labyrinthine NEC 386.40
combined sites 386.48
multiple sites 386.48
oval window 386.42
round window 386.41
semicircular canal 386.43
lacrimal, lachrymal (duct) (gland) (sac) 375.61
lacrimonasal duct 375.61
laryngotracheal 748.3
larynx 478.79
lip 528.5
congenital 750.25
lumbar, tuberculous (*see also* Tuberculosis) 015.0 ☑ *[730.8]* ☑
lung 510.0
lymphatic (node) (vessel) 457.8
mamillary 611.0
mammary (gland) 611.0
puerperal, postpartum 675.1 ☑
mastoid (process) (region) 383.1
maxillary (*see also* Sinusitis, maxillary) 473.0
mediastinal 510.0
mediastinobronchial 510.0
mediastinocutaneous 510.0
middle ear 385.89
mouth 528.3
nasal 478.19
sinus (*see also* Sinusitis) 473.9
nasopharynx 478.29
nipple — *see* Fistula, breast
nose 478.19
oral (cutaneous) 528.3

Fistula — *continued*
oral — *continued*
maxillary (*see also* Sinusitis, maxillary) 473.0
nasal (with cleft palate) (*see also* Cleft, palate) 749.00
orbit, orbital 376.10
oro-antral (*see also* Sinusitis, maxillary) 473.0
oval window (internal ear) 386.42
oviduct (external) 619.2
palate (hard) 526.89
soft 528.9
pancreatic 577.8
pancreaticoduodenal 577.8
parotid (gland) 527.4
region 528.3
pelvoabdominointestinal 569.81
penis 607.89
perianal 565.1
pericardium (pleura) (sac) (*see also* Pericarditis) 423.8
pericecal 569.81
perineal — *see* Fistula, perineum
perineorectal 569.81
perineosigmoidal 569.81
perineo-urethroscrotal 608.89
perineum, perineal (with urethral involvement) NEC 599.1
tuberculous (*see also* Tuberculosis) 017.9 ☑
ureter 593.82
perirectal 565.1
tuberculous (*see also* Tuberculosis) 014.8 ☑
peritoneum (*see also* Peritonitis) 567.22
periurethral 599.1
pharyngo-esophageal 478.29
pharynx 478.29
branchial cleft (congenital) 744.41
pilonidal (infected) (rectum) 685.1
with abscess 685.0
pleura, pleural, pleurocutaneous, pleuroperitoneal 510.0
stomach 510.0
tuberculous (*see also* Tuberculosis) 012.0 ☑
pleuropericardial 423.8
postauricular 383.81
postoperative, persistent 998.6
preauricular (congenital) 744.46
prostate 602.8
pulmonary 510.0
arteriovenous 417.0
congenital 747.3
tuberculous (*see also* Tuberculosis, pulmonary) 011.9 ☑
pulmonoperitoneal 510.0
rectolabial 619.1
rectosigmoid (intercommunicating) 569.81
rectoureteral 593.82
rectourethral 599.1
congenital 753.8
rectouterine 619.1
congenital 752.3
rectovaginal 619.1
congenital 752.49
old, postpartal 619.1
tuberculous (*see also* Tuberculosis) 014.8 ☑
rectovesical 596.1
congenital 753.8
rectovesicovaginal 619.1
rectovulvar 619.1
congenital 752.49
rectum (to skin) 565.1
tuberculous (*see also* Tuberculosis) 014.8 ☑
renal 593.89
retroauricular 383.81
round window (internal ear) 386.41
salivary duct or gland 527.4
congenital 750.24
sclera 360.32

Fistula — *continued*
scrotum (urinary) 608.89
tuberculous (*see also* Tuberculosis) 016.5 ☑
semicircular canals (internal ear) 386.43
sigmoid 569.81
vesicoabdominal 596.1
sigmoidovaginal 619.1
congenital 752.49
skin 686.9
ureter 593.82
vagina 619.2
sphenoidal sinus (*see also* Sinusitis, sphenoidal) 473.3
splenocolic 289.59
stercoral 569.81
stomach 537.4
sublingual gland 527.4
congenital 750.24
submaxillary
gland 527.4
congenital 750.24
region 528.3
thoracic 510.0
duct 457.8
thoracicoabdominal 510.0
thoracicogastric 510.0
thoracicointestinal 510.0
thoracoabdominal 510.0
thoracogastric 510.0
thorax 510.0
thyroglossal duct 759.2
thyroid 246.8
trachea (congenital) (external) (internal) 748.3
tracheoesophageal 530.84
congenital 750.3
following tracheostomy 519.09
traumatic
arteriovenous (*see also* Injury, blood vessel, by site) 904.9
brain — *see* Injury, intracranial
tuberculous — *see* Tuberculosis, by site
typhoid 002.0
umbilical 759.89
umbilico-urinary 753.8
urachal, urachus 753.7
ureter (persistent) 593.82
ureteroabdominal 593.82
ureterocervical 593.82
ureterorectal 593.82
ureterosigmoido-abdominal 593.82
ureterovaginal 619.0
ureterovesical 596.2
urethra 599.1
congenital 753.8
tuberculous (*see also* Tuberculosis) 016.3 ☑
urethroperineal 599.1
urethroperineovesical 596.2
urethrorectal 599.1
congenital 753.8
urethroscrotal 608.89
urethrovaginal 619.0
urethrovesical 596.2
urethrovesicovaginal 619.0
urinary (persistent) (recurrent) 599.1
uteroabdominal (anterior wall) 619.2
congenital 752.3
uteroenteric 619.1
uterofecal 619.1
uterointestinal 619.1
congenital 752.3
uterorectal 619.1
congenital 752.3
uteroureteric 619.0
uterovaginal 619.8
uterovesical 619.0
congenital 752.3
uterus 619.8
vagina (wall) 619.8
postpartal, old 619.8
vaginocutaneous (postpartal) 619.2
vaginoileal (acquired) 619.1

- **Fistula** — *continued*
  - vaginoperineal 619.2
  - vesical NEC 596.2
  - vesicoabdominal 596.2
  - vesicocervicovaginal 619.0
  - vesicocolic 596.1
  - vesicocutaneous 596.2
  - vesicoenteric 596.1
  - vesicointestinal 596.1
  - vesicometrorectal 619.1
  - vesicoperineal 596.2
  - vesicorectal 596.1
    - congenital 753.8
  - vesicosigmoidal 596.1
  - vesicosigmoidovaginal 619.1
  - vesicoureteral 596.2
  - vesicoureterovaginal 619.0
  - vesicourethral 596.2
  - vesicourethrorectal 596.1
  - vesicouterine 619.0
    - congenital 752.3
  - vesicovaginal 619.0
  - vulvorectal 619.1
    - congenital 752.49
- **Fit** 780.39
  - apoplectic (*see also* Disease, cerebrovascular, acute) 436
    - late effect — *see* Late effect(s) (of) cerebrovascular disease
  - epileptic (*see also* Epilepsy) 345.9 ☑
  - fainting 780.2
  - hysterical 300.11
  - newborn 779.0
- **Fitting** (of)
  - artificial
    - arm (complete) (partial) V52.0
    - breast V52.4
      - ● implant exchange (different material) (different size) V52.4
    - eye(s) V52.2
    - leg(s) (complete) (partial) V52.1
  - brain neuropacemaker V53.02
  - cardiac pacemaker V53.31
  - carotid sinus pacemaker V53.39
  - cerebral ventricle (communicating) shunt V53.01
  - colostomy belt V53.5
  - contact lenses V53.1
  - cystostomy device V53.6
  - defibrillator, automatic implantable cardiac V53.32
  - dentures V52.3
  - device, unspecified type V53.90
    - abdominal V53.5
    - cardiac
      - defibrillator, automatic implantable V53.32
      - pacemaker V53.31
      - specified NEC V53.39
    - cerebral ventricle (communicating) shunt V53.01
    - insulin pump V53.91
    - intrauterine contraceptive V25.1
    - nervous system V53.09
    - orthodontic V53.4
    - orthoptic V53.1
    - other device V53.99
    - prosthetic V52.9
      - breast V52.4
      - dental V52.3
      - eye V52.2
      - specified type NEC V52.8
    - special senses V53.09
    - substitution
      - auditory V53.09
      - nervous system V53.09
      - visual V53.09
    - urinary V53.6
  - diaphragm (contraceptive) V25.02
  - glasses (reading) V53.1
  - growth rod V54.02
  - hearing aid V53.2
  - ileostomy device V53.5
  - intestinal appliance or device NEC V53.5
- **Fitting** — *continued*
  - intrauterine contraceptive device V25.1
  - neuropacemaker (brain) (peripheral nerve) (spinal cord) V53.02
  - orthodontic device V53.4
  - orthopedic (device) V53.7
    - brace V53.7
    - cast V53.7
    - corset V53.7
    - shoes V53.7
  - pacemaker (cardiac) V53.31
    - brain V53.02
    - carotid sinus V53.39
    - peripheral nerve V53.02
    - spinal cord V53.02
  - prosthesis V52.9
    - arm (complete) (partial) V52.0
    - breast V52.4
      - ● implant exchange (different material) (different size) V52.4
    - dental V52.3
    - eye V52.2
    - leg (complete) (partial) V52.1
    - specified type NEC V52.8
  - spectacles V53.1
  - wheelchair V53.8
- **Fitz-Hugh and Curtis syndrome** 098.86
  - due to
    - Chlamydia trachomatis 099.56
    - Neisseria gonorrhoeae (gonococcal peritonitis) 098.86
- **Fitz's syndrome** (acute hemorrhagic pancreatitis) 577.0
- **Fixation**
  - joint — *see* Ankylosis
  - larynx 478.79
  - pupil 364.76
  - stapes 385.22
    - deafness (*see also* Deafness, conductive) 389.04
  - uterus (acquired) — *see* Malposition, uterus
  - vocal cord 478.5
- **Flaccid** — *see also* condition
  - foot 736.79
  - forearm 736.09
  - palate, congenital 750.26
- **Flail**
  - chest 807.4
    - newborn 767.3
  - joint (paralytic) 718.80
    - ankle 718.87
    - elbow 718.82
    - foot 718.87
    - hand 718.84
    - hip 718.85
    - knee 718.86
    - multiple sites 718.89
    - pelvic region 718.85
    - shoulder (region) 718.81
    - specified site NEC 718.88
    - wrist 718.83
- **Flajani (-Basedow) syndrome or disease** (exophthalmic goiter) 242.0 ☑
- **Flap, liver** 572.8
- **Flare, anterior chamber** (aqueous) (eye) 364.04
- **Flashback phenomena** (drug) (hallucinogenic) 292.89
- **Flat**
  - chamber (anterior) (eye) 360.34
  - chest, congenital 754.89
  - electroencephalogram (EEG) 348.8
  - foot (acquired) (fixed type) (painful) (postural) (spastic) 734
    - congenital 754.61
      - rocker bottom 754.61
      - vertical talus 754.61
    - rachitic 268.1
    - rocker bottom (congenital) 754.61
    - vertical talus, congenital 754.61
  - organ or site, congenital NEC — *see* Anomaly, specified type NEC
  - pelvis 738.6
- **Flat** — *continued*
  - pelvis — *continued*
    - with disproportion (fetopelvic) 653.2 ☑
      - affecting fetus or newborn 763.1
      - causing obstructed labor 660.1 ☑
        - affecting fetus or newborn 763.1
    - congenital 755.69
- **Flatau-Schilder disease** 341.1
- **Flattening**
  - head, femur 736.39
  - hip 736.39
  - lip (congenital) 744.89
  - nose (congenital) 754.0
    - acquired 738.0
- **Flatulence** 787.3
- **Flatus** 787.3
  - vaginalis 629.89
- **Flax dressers' disease** 504
- **Flea bite** — *see* Injury, superficial, by site
- **Fleischer (-Kayser) ring** (corneal pigmentation) 275.1 *[371.14]*
- **Fleischner's disease** 732.3
- **Fleshy mole** 631
- **Flexibilitas cerea** — *see also* Catalepsy 300.11
- **Flexion**
  - cervix — *see* Flexion, uterus
  - contracture, joint (*see also* Contraction, joint) 718.4 ☑
  - deformity, joint (*see also* Contraction, joint) 736.9
    - hip, congenital (*see also* Subluxation, congenital, hip) 754.32
  - uterus (*see also* Malposition, uterus) 621.6
- **Flexner's**
  - bacillus 004.1
  - diarrhea (ulcerative) 004.1
  - dysentery 004.1
- **Flexner-Boyd dysentery** 004.2
- **Flexure** — *see* condition
- **Floater, vitreous** 379.24
- **Floating**
  - cartilage (joint) (*see also* Disorder, cartilage, articular) 718.0 ☑
    - knee 717.6
  - gallbladder (congenital) 751.69
  - kidney 593.0
    - congenital 753.3
  - liver (congenital) 751.69
  - rib 756.3
  - spleen 289.59
- **Flooding** 626.2
- **Floor** — *see* condition
- **Floppy**
  - infant NEC 781.99
  - iris syndrome 364.81
  - valve syndrome (mitral) 424.0
- **Flu** — *see also* Influenza
  - gastric NEC 008.8
- **Fluctuating blood pressure** 796.4
- **Fluid**
  - abdomen 789.59
  - chest (*see also* Pleurisy, with effusion) 511.9
  - heart (*see also* Failure, heart) 428.0
  - joint (*see also* Effusion, joint) 719.0 ☑
  - loss (acute) 276.50
    - with
      - hypernatremia 276.0
      - hyponatremia 276.1
  - lung (*see also* Edema, lung)
    - encysted 511.89 ▲
  - peritoneal cavity 789.59
    - malignant 789.51
  - pleural cavity (*see also* Pleurisy, with effusion) 511.9
  - retention 276.6
- **Flukes** NEC — *see also* Infestation, fluke 121.9
  - blood NEC (*see also* Infestation, Schistosoma) 120.9
- **Flukes** — *see also* Infestation, fluke — *continued*
  - liver 121.3
- **Fluor** (albus) (vaginalis) 623.5
  - trichomonal (Trichomonas vaginalis) 131.00
- **Fluorosis** (dental) (chronic) 520.3
- **Flushing** 782.62
  - menopausal 627.2
- **Flush syndrome** 259.2
- **Flutter**
  - atrial or auricular 427.32
  - heart (ventricular) 427.42
    - atrial 427.32
  - impure 427.32
  - postoperative 997.1
  - ventricular 427.42
- **Flux** (bloody) (serosanguineous) 009.0
- **Focal** — *see* condition
- **Fochier's abscess** — *see* Abscess, by site
- **Focus, Assmann's** — *see also* Tuberculosis 011.0 ☑
- **Fogo selvagem** 694.4
- **Foix-Alajouanine syndrome** 336.1
- **Folds, anomalous** — *see also* Anomaly, specified type NEC
  - Bowman's membrane 371.31
  - Descemet's membrane 371.32
  - epicanthic 743.63
  - heart 746.89
  - posterior segment of eye, congenital 743.54
- **Folie à deux** 297.3
- **Follicle**
  - cervix (nabothian) (ruptured) 616.0
  - graafian, ruptured, with hemorrhage 620.0
  - nabothian 616.0
- **Folliclis** (primary) — *see also* Tuberculosis 017.0 ☑
- **Follicular** — *see also* condition
  - cyst (atretic) 620.0
- **Folliculitis** 704.8
  - abscedens et suffodiens 704.8
  - decalvans 704.09
  - gonorrheal (acute) 098.0
    - chronic or duration of 2 months or more 098.2
  - keloid, keloidalis 706.1
  - pustular 704.8
  - ulerythematosa reticulata 701.8
- **Folliculosis, conjunctival** 372.02
- **Følling's disease** (phenylketonuria) 270.1
- **Follow-up** (examination) (routine) (following) V67.9
  - cancer chemotherapy V67.2
  - chemotherapy V67.2
  - fracture V67.4
  - high-risk medication V67.51
  - injury NEC V67.59
  - postpartum
    - immediately after delivery V24.0
    - routine V24.2
  - psychiatric V67.3
  - psychotherapy V67.3
  - radiotherapy V67.1
  - specified condition NEC V67.59
  - specified surgery NEC V67.09
  - surgery V67.00
    - vaginal pap smear V67.01
  - treatment V67.9
    - combined NEC V67.6
    - fracture V67.4
    - involving high-risk medication NEC V67.51
    - mental disorder V67.3
    - specified NEC V67.59
- **Fong's syndrome** (hereditary osteoonychodysplasia) 756.89
- **Food**
  - allergy 693.1
  - anaphylactic shock — *see* Anaphylactic shock, due to, food

- **Food** — *continued*
  - asphyxia (from aspiration or inhalation) (*see also* Asphyxia, food) 933.1
  - choked on (*see also* Asphyxia, food) 933.1
  - deprivation 994.2
    - specified kind of food NEC 269.8
  - intoxication (*see also* Poisoning, food) 005.9
  - lack of 994.2
  - poisoning (*see also* Poisoning, food) 005.9
  - refusal or rejection NEC 307.59
  - strangulation or suffocation (*see also* Asphyxia, food) 933.1
  - toxemia (*see also* Poisoning, food) 005.9
- **Foot** — *see also* condition
  - and mouth disease 078.4
  - process disease 581.3
- **Foramen ovale** (nonclosure) (patent) (persistent) 745.5
- **Forbes-Albright syndrome** (nonpuerperal amenorrhea and lactation associated with pituitary tumor) 253.1
- **Forbes'(glycogen storage) disease** 271.0
- **Forced birth or delivery** NEC 669.8 ☑
  - affecting fetus or newborn NEC 763.89
- **Forceps**
  - delivery NEC 669.5 ☑
    - affecting fetus or newborn 763.2
- **Fordyce's disease** (ectopic sebaceous glands) (mouth) 750.26
- **Fordyce-Fox disease** (apocrine miliaria) 705.82
- **Forearm** — *see* condition
- **Foreign body**

> *Note — For foreign body with open wound, or other injury, see Wound, open, or the type of injury specified.*

  - accidentally left during a procedure 998.4
  - anterior chamber (eye) 871.6
    - magnetic 871.5
      - retained or old 360.51
    - retained or old 360.61
  - ciliary body (eye) 871.6
    - magnetic 871.5
      - retained or old 360.52
    - retained or old 360.62
  - entering through orifice (current) (old)
    - accessory sinus 932
    - air passage (upper) 933.0
      - lower 934.8
    - alimentary canal 938
    - alveolar process 935.0
    - antrum (Highmore) 932
    - anus 937
    - appendix 936
    - asphyxia due to (*see also* Asphyxia, food) 933.1
    - auditory canal 931
    - auricle 931
    - bladder 939.0
    - bronchioles 934.8
    - bronchus (main) 934.1
    - buccal cavity 935.0
    - canthus (inner) 930.1
    - cecum 936
    - cervix (canal) uterine 939.1
    - coil, ileocecal 936
    - colon 936
    - conjunctiva 930.1
    - conjunctival sac 930.1
    - cornea 930.0
    - digestive organ or tract NEC 938
    - duodenum 936
    - ear (external) 931
    - esophagus 935.1
    - eye (external) 930.9
      - combined sites 930.8
      - intraocular — *see* Foreign body, by site

Foreign body — *continued*
  - entering through orifice — *continued*
    - eye — *continued*
      - specified site NEC 930.8
    - eyeball 930.8
      - intraocular — *see* Foreign body, intraocular
    - eyelid 930.1
      - retained or old 374.86
    - frontal sinus 932
    - gastrointestinal tract 938
    - genitourinary tract 939.9
    - globe 930.8
      - penetrating 871.6
        - magnetic 871.5
          - retained or old 360.50
        - retained or old 360.60
    - gum 935.0
    - Highmore's antrum 932
    - hypopharynx 933.0
    - ileocecal coil 936
    - ileum 936
    - inspiration (of) 933.1
    - intestine (large) (small) 936
    - lacrimal apparatus, duct, gland, or sac 930.2
    - larynx 933.1
    - lung 934.8
    - maxillary sinus 932
    - mouth 935.0
    - nasal sinus 932
    - nasopharynx 933.0
    - nose (passage) 932
    - nostril 932
    - oral cavity 935.0
    - palate 935.0
    - penis 939.3
    - pharynx 933.0
    - pyriform sinus 933.0
    - rectosigmoid 937
      - junction 937
    - rectum 937
    - respiratory tract 934.9
      - specified part NEC 934.8
    - sclera 930.1
    - sinus 932
      - accessory 932
      - frontal 932
      - maxillary 932
      - nasal 932
      - pyriform 933.0
    - small intestine 936
    - stomach (hairball) 935.2
    - suffocation by (*see also* Asphyxia, food) 933.1
    - swallowed 938
      - tongue 933.0
    - tear ducts or glands 930.2
    - throat 933.0
    - tongue 935.0
      - swallowed 933.0
    - tonsil, tonsillar 933.0
      - fossa 933.0
    - trachea 934.0
    - ureter 939.0
    - urethra 939.0
    - uterus (any part) 939.1
    - vagina 939.2
    - vulva 939.2
    - wind pipe 934.0
  - feeling of, in throat 784.99
  - granuloma (old) 728.82
    - bone 733.99
    - in operative wound (inadvertently left) 998.4
      - due to surgical material intentionally left — *see* Complications, due to (presence of) any device, implant, or graft classified to 996.0–996.5 NEC
    - muscle 728.82
    - skin 709.4
    - soft tissue 709.4
    - subcutaneous tissue 709.4

Foreign body — *continued*
  - in
    - bone (residual) 733.99
    - open wound — *see* Wound, open, by site complicated
    - soft tissue (residual) 729.6
  - inadvertently left in operation wound (causing adhesions, obstruction, or perforation) 998.4
  - ingestion, ingested NEC 938
  - inhalation or inspiration (*see also* Asphyxia, food) 933.1
  - internal organ, not entering through an orifice — *see* Injury, internal, by site, with open wound
  - intraocular (nonmagnetic) 871.6
    - combined sites 871.6
      - magnetic 871.5
        - retained or old 360.59
      - retained or old 360.69
    - magnetic 871.5
      - retained or old 360.50
    - retained or old 360.60
    - specified site NEC 871.6
      - magnetic 871.5
        - retained or old 360.59
      - retained or old 360.69
  - iris (nonmagnetic) 871.6
    - magnetic 871.5
      - retained or old 360.52
    - retained or old 360.62
  - lens (nonmagnetic) 871.6
    - magnetic 871.5
      - retained or old 360.53
    - retained or old 360.63
  - lid, eye 930.1
  - ocular muscle 870.4
    - retained or old 376.6
  - old or residual
    - bone 733.99
    - eyelid 374.86
    - middle ear 385.83
    - muscle 729.6
      - ocular 376.6
    - retrobulbar 376.6
    - skin 729.6
      - with granuloma 709.4
    - soft tissue 729.6
      - with granuloma 709.4
    - subcutaneous tissue 729.6
      - with granuloma 709.4
  - operation wound, left accidentally 998.4
  - orbit 870.4
    - retained or old 376.6
  - posterior wall, eye 871.6
    - magnetic 871.5
      - retained or old 360.55
    - retained or old 360.65
  - respiratory tree 934.9
    - specified site NEC 934.8
  - retained (old) (nonmagnetic) (in)
    - anterior chamber (eye) 360.61
      - magnetic 360.51
    - ciliary body 360.62
      - magnetic 360.52
    - eyelid 374.86
    - globe 360.60
      - magnetic 360.50
    - intraocular 360.60
      - magnetic 360.50
      - specified site NEC 360.69
        - magnetic 360.59
    - iris 360.62
      - magnetic 360.52
    - lens 360.63
      - magnetic 360.53
    - muscle 729.6
    - orbit 376.6
    - posterior wall of globe 360.65
      - magnetic 360.55
    - retina 360.65
      - magnetic 360.55
    - retrobulbar 376.6
    - skin 729.6
      - with granuloma 709.4

Foreign body — *continued*
  - retained — *continued*
    - soft tissue 729.6
      - with granuloma 709.4
    - subcutaneous tissue 729.6
      - with granuloma 709.4
    - vitreous 360.64
      - magnetic 360.54
  - retina 871.6
    - magnetic 871.5
      - retained or old 360.55
    - retained or old 360.65
  - superficial, without major open wound (*see also* Injury, superficial, by site) 919.6
  - swallowed NEC 938
  - throat, feeling of 784.99
  - vitreous (humor) 871.6
    - magnetic 871.5
      - retained or old 360.54
    - retained or old 360.64
- **Forking, aqueduct of Sylvius** 742.3
  - with spina bifida (*see also* Spina bifida) 741.0 ☑
- **Formation**
  - bone in scar tissue (skin) 709.3
  - connective tissue in vitreous 379.25
  - Elschnig pearls (postcataract extraction) 366.51
  - hyaline in cornea 371.49
  - sequestrum in bone (due to infection) (*see also* Osteomyelitis) 730.1 ☑
  - valve
    - colon, congenital 751.5
    - ureter (congenital) 753.29
- **Formication** 782.0
- **Fort Bragg fever** 100.89
- **Fossa** — *see also* condition
  - pyriform — *see* condition
- **Foster-Kennedy syndrome** 377.04
- **Fothergill's**
  - disease, meaning scarlatina anginosa 034.1
  - neuralgia (*see also* Neuralgia, trigeminal) 350.1
- **Foul breath** 784.99
- **Found dead** (cause unknown) 798.9
- **Foundling** V20.0
- **Fournier's disease** (idiopathic gangrene) 608.83
- **Fourth**
  - cranial nerve — *see* condition
  - disease 057.8
  - molar 520.1
- **Foville's syndrome** 344.89
- **Fox's**
  - disease (apocrine miliaria) 705.82
  - impetigo (contagiosa) 684
- **Fox-Fordyce disease** (apocrine miliaria) 705.82

Fracture (abduction) (adduction) (avulsion) (compression) (crush) (dislocation) (oblique) (separation) (closed) 829.0

> *Note — For fracture of any of the following sites with fracture of other bones — see Fracture, multiple.*
>
> *"Closed" includes the following descriptions of fractures, with or without delayed healing, unless they are specified as open or compound:*
>
> | | |
> |---|---|
> | *comminuted* | *linear* |
> | *depressed* | *simple* |
> | *elevated* | *slipped epiphysis* |
> | *fissured* | *spiral* |
> | *greenstick* | *unspecified* |
> | *impacted* | |
>
> *"Open" includes the following descriptions of fractures, with or without delayed healing:*
>
> | | |
> |---|---|
> | *compound* | *puncture* |
> | *infected* | *with foreign body* |
> | *missile* | |
>
> *For late effect of fracture, see Late, effect, fracture, by site.*

- with
  - internal injuries in same region (conditions classifiable to 860–869) (*see also* Injury, internal, by site)
    - pelvic region — *see* Fracture, pelvis
- acetabulum (with visceral injury) (closed) 808.0
  - open 808.1
- acromion (process) (closed) 811.01
  - open 811.11
- alveolus (closed) 802.8
  - open 802.9
- ankle (malleolus) (closed) 824.8
  - bimalleolar (Dupuytren's) (Pott's) 824.4
    - open 824.5
  - bone 825.21
    - open 825.31
  - lateral malleolus only (fibular) 824.2
    - open 824.3
  - medial malleolus only (tibial) 824.0
    - open 824.1
  - open 824.9
  - pathologic 733.16
  - talus 825.21
    - open 825.31
  - trimalleolar 824.6
    - open 824.7
- antrum — *see* Fracture, skull, base
- arm (closed) 818.0
  - and leg(s) (any bones) 828.0
    - open 828.1
  - both (any bones) (with rib(s)) (with sternum) 819.0
    - open 819.1
  - lower 813.80
    - open 813.90
  - open 818.1
  - upper — *see* Fracture, humerus
- astragalus (closed) 825.21
  - open 825.31
- atlas — *see* Fracture, vertebra, cervical, first
- axis — *see* Fracture, vertebra, cervical, second
- back — *see* Fracture, vertebra, by site
- Barton's — *see* Fracture, radius, lower end
- basal (skull) — *see* Fracture, skull, base
- Bennett's (closed) 815.01
  - open 815.11
- bimalleolar (closed) 824.4
  - open 824.5
- bone (closed) NEC 829.0
  - birth injury NEC 767.3
  - open 829.1
  - pathologic NEC (*see also* Fracture, pathologic) 733.10
  - stress NEC (*see also* Fracture, stress) 733.95
- boot top — *see* Fracture, fibula
- boxers' — *see* Fracture, metacarpal bone(s)
- breast bone — *see* Fracture, sternum
- bucket handle (semilunar cartilage) — *see* Tear, meniscus
- burst — *see* Fracture, traumatic, by site
- bursting — *see* Fracture, phalanx, hand, distal
- calcaneus (closed) 825.0
  - open 825.1
- capitate (bone) (closed) 814.07
  - open 814.17
- capitellum (humerus) (closed) 812.49
  - open 812.59
- carpal bone(s) (wrist NEC) (closed) 814.00
  - open 814.10
  - specified site NEC 814.09
    - open 814.19
- cartilage, knee (semilunar) — *see* Tear, meniscus
- cervical — *see* Fracture, vertebra, cervical
- chauffeur's — *see* Fracture, ulna, lower end
- chisel — *see* Fracture, radius, upper end
- clavicle (interligamentous part) (closed) 810.00
  - acromial end 810.03
    - open 810.13
  - due to birth trauma 767.2
  - open 810.10
  - shaft (middle third) 810.02
    - open 810.12
  - sternal end 810.01
    - open 810.11
- clayshovelers' — *see* Fracture, vertebra, cervical
- coccyx (*see also* Fracture, vertebra, coccyx)
  - complicating delivery 665.6 ☑
- collar bone — *see* Fracture, clavicle
- Colles' (reversed) (closed) 813.41
  - open 813.51
- comminuted — *see* Fracture, by site
- compression (*see also* Fracture, by site)
  - nontraumatic — *see* Fracture, pathologic
- congenital 756.9
- coracoid process (closed) 811.02
  - open 811.12
- coronoid process (ulna) (closed) 813.02
  - mandible (closed) 802.23
    - open 802.33
  - open 813.12
- corpus cavernosum penis 959.13
- costochondral junction — *see* Fracture, rib
- costosternal junction — *see* Fracture, rib
- cranium — *see* Fracture, skull, by site
- cricoid cartilage (closed) 807.5
  - open 807.6
- cuboid (ankle) (closed) 825.23
  - open 825.33
- cuneiform
  - foot (closed) 825.24
    - open 825.34
  - wrist (closed) 814.03
    - open 814.13
- dental implant 525.73
- dental restorative material
  - with loss of material 525.64
  - without loss of material 525.63
- due to
  - birth injury — *see* Birth injury, fracture
  - gunshot — *see* Fracture, by site, open
  - neoplasm — *see* Fracture, pathologic
  - osteoporosis — *see* Fracture, pathologic
- Dupuytren's (ankle) (fibula) (closed) 824.4
  - open 824.5
  - radius 813.42
    - open 813.52
- Duverney's — *see* Fracture, ilium
- elbow (*see also* Fracture, humerus, lower end)
  - olecranon (process) (closed) 813.01
    - open 813.11
  - supracondylar (closed) 812.41
    - open 812.51
- ethmoid (bone) (sinus) — *see* Fracture, skull, base
- face bone(s) (closed) NEC 802.8
  - with
    - other bone(s) — *see* Fracture, multiple, skull
    - skull (*see also* Fracture, skull)
      - involving other bones — *see* Fracture, multiple, skull
  - open 802.9
- fatigue — *see* Fracture, march
- femur, femoral (closed) 821.00
  - cervicotrochanteric 820.03
    - open 820.13
  - condyles, epicondyles 821.21
    - open 821.31
  - distal end — *see* Fracture, femur, lower end
  - epiphysis (separation)
    - capital 820.01
      - open 820.11
    - head 820.01
      - open 820.11
    - lower 821.22
      - open 821.32
    - trochanteric 820.01
      - open 820.11
    - upper 820.01
      - open 820.11
  - head 820.09
    - open 820.19
  - lower end or extremity (distal end) (closed) 821.20
    - condyles, epicondyles 821.21
      - open 821.31
    - epiphysis (separation) 821.22
      - open 821.32
    - multiple sites 821.29
      - open 821.39
    - open 821.30
    - specified site NEC 821.29
      - open 821.39
    - supracondylar 821.23
      - open 821.33
    - T-shaped 821.21
      - open 821.31
  - neck (closed) 820.8
    - base (cervicotrochanteric) 820.03
      - open 820.13
    - extracapsular 820.20
      - open 820.30
    - intertrochanteric (section) 820.21
      - open 820.31
    - intracapsular 820.00
      - open 820.10
    - intratrochanteric 820.21
      - open 820.31
    - midcervical 820.02
      - open 820.12
    - open 820.9
    - pathologic 733.14
      - specified part NEC 733.15
    - specified site NEC 820.09
      - open 820.19
    - transcervical 820.02
      - open 820.12
    - transtrochanteric 820.20
      - open 820.30
  - open 821.10
  - pathologic 733.14
    - specified part NEC 733.15
  - peritrochanteric (section) 820.20
    - open 820.30
  - shaft (lower third) (middle third) (upper third) 821.01
    - open 821.11
  - subcapital 820.09
    - open 820.19
  - subtrochanteric (region) (section) 820.22
    - open 820.32
  - supracondylar 821.23
    - open 821.33
  - transepiphyseal 820.01
    - open 820.11
  - trochanter (greater) (lesser) (*see also* Fracture, femur, neck, by site) 820.20
    - open 820.30
  - T-shaped, into knee joint 821.21
    - open 821.31
  - upper end 820.8
    - open 820.9
- fibula (closed) 823.81
  - with tibia 823.82
    - open 823.92
  - distal end 824.8
    - open 824.9
  - epiphysis
    - lower 824.8
      - open 824.9
    - upper — *see* Fracture, fibula, upper end
  - head — *see* Fracture, fibula, upper end
  - involving ankle 824.2
    - open 824.3
  - lower end or extremity 824.8
    - open 824.9
  - malleolus (external) (lateral) 824.2
    - open 824.3
  - open NEC 823.91
  - pathologic 733.16
  - proximal end — *see* Fracture, fibula, upper end
  - shaft 823.21
    - with tibia 823.22
      - open 823.32
    - open 823.31
  - stress 733.93
  - torus 823.41
    - with tibia 823.42
  - upper end or extremity (epiphysis) (head) (proximal end) (styloid) 823.01
    - with tibia 823.02
      - open 823.12
    - open 823.11
- finger(s), of one hand (closed) (*see also* Fracture, phalanx, hand) 816.00
  - with
    - metacarpal bone(s), of same hand 817.0
      - open 817.1
    - thumb of same hand 816.03
      - open 816.13

- **Fracture** — *continued*
  - finger(s), of one hand (*see also* Fracture, phalanx, hand) — *continued*
    - open 816.10
  - foot, except toe(s) alone (closed) 825.20
    - open 825.30
  - forearm (closed) NEC 813.80
    - lower end (distal end) (lower epiphysis) 813.40
      - open 813.50
    - open 813.90
    - shaft 813.20
      - open 813.30
    - upper end (proximal end) (upper epiphysis) 813.00
      - open 813.10
  - fossa, anterior, middle, or posterior — *see* Fracture, skull, base
  - Fracture (abduction) (adduction) (avulsion) (compression) (crush) (dislocation) (oblique) (separation) (closed) 829.0
  - frontal (bone) (*see also* Fracture, skull, vault)
    - sinus — *see* Fracture, skull, base
  - Galeazzi's — *see* Fracture, radius, lower end
  - glenoid (cavity) (fossa) (scapula) (closed) 811.03
    - open 811.13
  - Gosselin's — *see* Fracture, ankle
  - greenstick — *see* Fracture, by site
  - grenade-throwers' — *see* Fracture, humerus, shaft
  - gutter — *see* Fracture, skull, vault
  - hamate (closed) 814.08
    - open 814.18
  - hand, one (closed) 815.00
    - carpals 814.00
      - open 814.10
      - specified site NEC 814.09
        - open 814.19
    - metacarpals 815.00
      - open 815.10
    - multiple, bones of one hand 817.0
      - open 817.1
    - open 815.10
    - phalanges (*see also* Fracture, phalanx, hand) 816.00
      - open 816.10
  - healing
    - aftercare (*see also* Aftercare, fracture) V54.89
    - change of cast V54.89
    - complications — *see* condition
    - convalescence V66.4
    - removal of
      - cast V54.89
      - fixation device
        - external V54.89
        - internal V54.01
  - heel bone (closed) 825.0
    - open 825.1
  - Hill-Sachs 812.09 ●
  - hip (closed) (*see also* Fracture, femur, neck) 820.8
    - open 820.9
    - pathologic 733.14
  - humerus (closed) 812.20
    - anatomical neck 812.02
      - open 812.12
    - articular process (*see also* Fracture humerus, condyle(s)) 812.44
      - open 812.54
    - capitellum 812.49
      - open 812.59
    - condyle(s) 812.44
      - lateral (external) 812.42
        - open 812.52
      - medial (internal epicondyle) 812.43
        - open 812.53
      - open 812.54
- **Fracture** — *continued*
  - humerus — *continued*
    - distal end — *see* Fracture, humerus, lower end
    - epiphysis
      - lower (*see also* Fracture, humerus, condyle(s)) 812.44
        - open 812.54
      - upper 812.09
        - open 812.19
    - external condyle 812.42
      - open 812.52
    - great tuberosity 812.03
      - open 812.13
    - head 812.09
      - open 812.19
    - internal epicondyle 812.43
      - open 812.53
    - lesser tuberosity 812.09
      - open 812.19
    - lower end or extremity (distal end) (*see also* Fracture, humerus, by site) 812.40
      - multiple sites NEC 812.49
        - open 812.59
      - open 812.50
      - specified site NEC 812.49
        - open 812.59
    - neck 812.01
      - open 812.11
    - open 812.30
    - pathologic 733.11
    - proximal end — *see* Fracture, humerus, upper end
    - shaft 812.21
      - open 812.31
    - supracondylar 812.41
      - open 812.51
    - surgical neck 812.01
      - open 812.11
    - trochlea 812.49
      - open 812.59
    - T-shaped 812.44
      - open 812.54
    - tuberosity — *see* Fracture, humerus, upper end
    - upper end or extremity (proximal end) (*see also* Fracture, humerus, by site) 812.00
      - open 812.10
      - specified site NEC 812.09
        - open 812.19
  - hyoid bone (closed) 807.5
    - open 807.6
  - hyperextension — *see* Fracture, radius, lower end
  - ilium (with visceral injury) (closed) 808.41
    - open 808.51
  - impaction, impacted — *see* Fracture, by site
  - incus — *see* Fracture, skull, base
  - innominate bone (with visceral injury) (closed) 808.49
    - open 808.59
  - instep, of one foot (closed) 825.20
    - with toe(s) of same foot 827.0
      - open 827.1
    - open 825.30
  - insufficiency — *see* Fracture, pathologic, by site
  - internal
    - ear — *see* Fracture, skull, base
    - semilunar cartilage, knee — *see* Tear, meniscus, medial
  - intertrochanteric — *see* Fracture, femur, neck, intertrochanteric
  - ischium (with visceral injury) (closed) 808.42
    - open 808.52
  - jaw (bone) (lower) (closed) (*see also* Fracture, mandible) 802.20
    - angle 802.25
      - open 802.35
    - open 802.30
- **Fracture** — *continued*
  - jaw (*see also* Fracture, mandible) — *continued*
    - upper — *see* Fracture, maxilla
  - knee
    - cap (closed) 822.0
      - open 822.1
    - cartilage (semilunar) — *see* Tear, meniscus
  - labyrinth (osseous) — *see* Fracture, skull, base
  - larynx (closed) 807.5
    - open 807.6
  - late effect — *see* Late, effects (of), fracture
  - Le Fort's — *see* Fracture, maxilla
  - leg (closed) 827.0
    - with rib(s) or sternum 828.0
      - open 828.1
    - both (any bones) 828.0
      - open 828.1
    - lower — *see* Fracture, tibia
    - open 827.1
    - upper — *see* Fracture, femur
  - limb
    - lower (multiple) (closed) NEC 827.0
      - open 827.1
    - upper (multiple) (closed) NEC 818.0
      - open 818.1
  - long bones, due to birth trauma — *see* Birth injury, fracture
  - lower end or extremity (anterior lip) (posterior) 824.8
    - open 824.9
  - lumbar — *see* Fracture, vertebra, lumbar
  - lunate bone (closed) 814.02
    - open 814.12
  - malar bone (closed) 802.4
    - open 802.5
  - Malgaigne's (closed) 808.43
    - open 808.53
  - malleolus (closed) 824.8
    - bimalleolar 824.4
      - open 824.5
    - lateral 824.2
      - and medial (*see also* Fracture, malleolus, bimalleolar)
        - with lip of tibia — *see* Fracture, malleolus, trimalleolar
      - open 824.3
    - medial (closed) 824.0
      - and lateral (*see also* Fracture, malleolus, bimalleolar)
        - with lip of tibia — *see* Fracture, malleolus, trimalleolar
      - open 824.1
    - open 824.9
    - trimalleolar (closed) 824.6
      - open 824.7
  - malleus — *see* Fracture, skull, base
  - malunion 733.81
  - mandible (closed) 802.20
    - angle 802.25
      - open 802.35
    - body 802.28
      - alveolar border 802.27
        - open 802.37
      - open 802.38
      - symphysis 802.26
        - open 802.36
    - condylar process 802.21
      - open 802.31
    - coronoid process 802.23
      - open 802.33
    - multiple sites 802.29
      - open 802.39
    - open 802.30
    - ramus NEC 802.24
      - open 802.34
    - subcondylar 802.22
      - open 802.32
  - manubrium — *see* Fracture, sternum
  - march 733.95
- **Fracture** — *continued*
  - march — *continued*
    - fibula 733.93
    - metatarsals 733.94
    - tibia 733.93
  - maxilla, maxillary (superior) (upper jaw) (closed) 802.4
    - inferior — *see* Fracture, mandible
    - open 802.5
  - meniscus, knee — *see* Tear, meniscus
  - metacarpus, metacarpal (bone(s)), of one hand (closed) 815.00
    - with phalanx, phalanges, hand (finger(s)) (thumb) of same hand 817.0
      - open 817.1
    - base 815.02
      - first metacarpal 815.01
        - open 815.11
      - open 815.12
      - thumb 815.01
        - open 815.11
    - multiple sites 815.09
      - open 815.19
    - neck 815.04
      - open 815.14
    - open 815.10
    - shaft 815.03
      - open 815.13
  - metatarsus, metatarsal (bone(s)), of one foot (closed) 825.25
    - with tarsal bone(s) 825.29
      - open 825.39
    - open 825.35
  - Monteggia's (closed) 813.03
    - open 813.13
  - Moore's — *see* Fracture, radius, lower end
    - multangular bone (closed)
      - larger 814.05
        - open 814.15
      - smaller 814.06
        - open 814.16
  - multiple (closed) 829.0

Note — Multiple fractures of sites classifiable to the same three- or four-digit category are coded to that category, except for sites classifiable to 810–818 or 820–827 in different limbs.

Multiple fractures of sites classifiable to different fourth-digit subdivisions within the same three-digit category should be dealt with according to coding rules.

Multiple fractures of sites classifiable to different three-digit categories (identifiable from the listing under "Fracture"), and of sites classifiable to 810–818 or 820–827 in different limbs should be coded according to the following list, which should be referred to in the following priority order: skull or face bones, pelvis or vertebral column, legs, arms.

    - arm (multiple bones in same arm except in hand alone) (sites classifiable to 810–817 with sites classifiable to a different three-digit category in 810–817 in same arm) (closed) 818.0
      - open 818.1
    - arms, both or arm(s) with rib(s) or sternum (sites classifiable to 810–818 with sites classifiable to same range of categories in other limb or to 807) (closed) 819.0
      - open 819.1
    - bones of trunk NEC (closed) 809.0
      - open 809.1
    - hand, metacarpal bone(s) with phalanx or phalanges of same hand (sites classifiable to 815 with sites classifiable to 816 in same hand) (closed) 817.0

- **Fracture** — *continued*
  - multiple — *continued*
    - hand, metacarpal bone(s) with phalanx or phalanges of same hand — *continued*
      - open 817.1
    - leg (multiple bones in same leg) (sites classifiable to 820–826 with sites classifiable to a different three-digit category in that range in same leg) (closed) 827.0
      - open 827.1
    - legs, both or leg(s) with arm(s), rib(s), or sternum (sites classifiable to 820–827 with sites classifiable to same range of categories in other leg or to 807 or 810–819) (closed) 828.0
      - open 828.1
    - open 829.1
    - pelvis with other bones except skull or face bones (sites classifiable to 808 with sites classifiable to 805–807 or 810–829) (closed) 809.0
      - open 809.1
    - skull, specified or unspecified bones, or face bone(s) with any other bone(s) (sites classifiable to 800–803 with sites classifiable to 805–829) (closed) 804.0 ☑

> *Note — Use the following fifth-digit subclassification with categories 800, 801, 803, and 804:*
>
> 0 *unspecified state of consciousness*
>
> 1 *with no loss of consciousness*
>
> 2 *with brief [less than one hour] loss of consciousness*
>
> 3 *with moderate [1–24 hours] loss of consciousness*
>
> 4 *with prolonged [more than 24 hours] loss of consciousness and return to pre-existing conscious level*
>
> 5 *with prolonged [more than 24 hours] loss of consciousness, without return to pre-existing conscious level*
>
> *Use fifth-digit 5 to designate when a patient is unconscious and dies before regaining consciousness, regardless of the duration of the loss of consciousness*
>
> 6 *with loss of consciousness of unspecified duration*
>
> 9 *with concussion, unspecified*

- with
  - contusion, cerebral 804.1 ☑
  - epidural hemorrhage 804.2 ☑
  - extradural hemorrhage 804.2 ☑
  - hemorrhage (intracranial) NEC 804.3 ☑
  - intracranial injury NEC 804.4 ☑
  - laceration, cerebral 804.1 ☑
  - subarachnoid hemorrhage 804.2 ☑
  - subdural hemorrhage 804.2 ☑
- open 804.5 ☑
  - with
    - contusion, cerebral 804.6 ☑
    - epidural hemorrhage 804.7 ☑

- **Fracture** — *continued*
  - multiple — *continued*
    - skull, specified or unspecified bones, or face bone(s) with any other bone(s) — *continued*
      - open — *continued*
        - with — *continued*
          - extradural hemorrhage 804.7 ☑
          - hemorrhage (intracranial) NEC 804.8 ☑
          - intracranial injury NEC 804.9 ☑
          - laceration, cerebral 804.6 ☑
          - subarachnoid hemorrhage 804.7 ☑
          - subdural hemorrhage 804.7 ☑
    - vertebral column with other bones, except skull or face bones (sites classifiable to 805 or 806 with sites classifiable to 807–808 or 810–829) (closed) 809.0
      - open 809.1
  - nasal (bone(s)) (closed) 802.0
    - open 802.1
    - sinus — *see* Fracture, skull, base
  - navicular
    - carpal (wrist) (closed) 814.01
      - open 814.11
    - tarsal (ankle) (closed) 825.22
      - open 825.32
  - neck — *see* Fracture, vertebra, cervical
  - neural arch — *see* Fracture, vertebra, by site
  - nonunion 733.82
  - nose, nasal, (bone) (septum) (closed) 802.0
    - open 802.1
  - occiput — *see* Fracture, skull, base
  - odontoid process — *see* Fracture, vertebra, cervical
  - olecranon (process) (ulna) (closed) 813.01
    - open 813.11
  - open 829.1
  - orbit, orbital (bone) (region) (closed) 802.8
    - floor (blow-out) 802.6
      - open 802.7
    - open 802.9
    - roof — *see* Fracture, skull, base
    - specified part NEC 802.8
      - open 802.9
  - os
    - calcis (closed) 825.0
      - open 825.1
    - magnum (closed) 814.07
      - open 814.17
    - pubis (with visceral injury) (closed) 808.2
      - open 808.3
    - triquetrum (closed) 814.03
      - open 814.13
  - osseous
    - auditory meatus — *see* Fracture, skull, base
    - labyrinth — *see* Fracture, skull, base
  - ossicles, auditory (incus) (malleus) (stapes) — *see* Fracture, skull, base
  - osteoporotic — *see* Fracture, pathologic
  - palate (closed) 802.8
    - open 802.9
  - paratrooper — *see* Fracture, tibia, lower end
  - parietal bone — *see* Fracture, skull, vault
  - parry — *see* Fracture, Monteggia's
  - patella (closed) 822.0

- **Fracture** — *continued*
  - patella — *continued*
    - open 822.1
  - pathologic (cause unknown) 733.10
    - ankle 733.16
    - femur (neck) 733.14
      - specified NEC 733.15
    - fibula 733.16
    - hip 733.14
    - humerus 733.11
    - radius (distal) 733.12
    - specified site NEC 733.19
    - tibia 733.16
    - ulna 733.12
    - vertebrae (collapse) 733.13
    - wrist 733.12
  - pedicle (of vertebral arch) — *see* Fracture, vertebra, by site
  - pelvis, pelvic (bone(s)) (with visceral injury) (closed) 808.8
    - multiple (with disruption of pelvic circle) 808.43
      - open 808.53
    - open 808.9
    - rim (closed) 808.49
      - open 808.59
  - peritrochanteric (closed) 820.20
    - open 820.30
  - phalanx, phalanges, of one
    - foot (closed) 826.0
      - with bone(s) of same lower limb 827.0
        - open 827.1
      - open 826.1
    - hand (closed) 816.00
      - with metacarpal bone(s) of same hand 817.0
        - open 817.1
      - distal 816.02
        - open 816.12
      - middle 816.01
        - open 816.11
      - multiple sites NEC 816.03
        - open 816.13
      - open 816.10
      - proximal 816.01
        - open 816.11
  - pisiform (closed) 814.04
    - open 814.14
  - pond — *see* Fracture, skull, vault
  - Pott's (closed) 824.4
    - open 824.5
  - prosthetic device, internal — *see* Complications, mechanical
  - pubis (with visceral injury) (closed) 808.2
    - open 808.3
  - Quervain's (closed) 814.01
    - open 814.11
  - radius (alone) (closed) 813.81
    - with ulna NEC 813.83
      - open 813.93
    - distal end — *see* Fracture, radius, lower end
    - epiphysis
      - lower — *see* Fracture, radius, lower end
      - upper — *see* Fracture, radius, upper end
    - head — *see* Fracture, radius, upper end
    - lower end or extremity (distal end) (lower epiphysis) 813.42
      - with ulna (lower end) 813.44
        - open 813.54
      - open 813.52
      - torus 813.45
    - neck — *see* Fracture, radius, upper end
    - open NEC 813.91
    - pathologic 733.12
    - proximal end — *see* Fracture, radius, upper end
    - shaft (closed) 813.21
      - with ulna (shaft) 813.23
        - open 813.33

- **Fracture** — *continued*
  - radius — *continued*
    - shaft — *continued*
      - open 813.31
    - upper end 813.07
      - with ulna (upper end) 813.08
        - open 813.18
      - epiphysis 813.05
        - open 813.15
      - head 813.05
        - open 813.15
      - multiple sites 813.07
        - open 813.17
      - neck 813.06
        - open 813.16
      - open 813.17
      - specified site NEC 813.07
        - open 813.17
  - ramus
    - inferior or superior (with visceral injury) (closed) 808.2
      - open 808.3
    - ischium — *see* Fracture, ischium
    - mandible 802.24
      - open 802.34
  - rib(s) (closed) 807.0 ☑

> *Note — Use the following fifth-digit subclassification with categories 807.0–807.1:*
>
> 0 *rib(s), unspecified*
>
> 1 *one rib*
>
> 2 *two ribs*
>
> 3 *three ribs*
>
> 4 *four ribs*
>
> 5 *five ribs*
>
> 6 *six ribs*
>
> 7 *seven ribs*
>
> 8 *eight or more ribs*
>
> 9 *multiple ribs, unspecified*

  - with flail chest (open) 807.4
  - open 807.1 ☑
- root, tooth 873.63
  - complicated 873.73
- sacrum — *see* Fracture, vertebra, sacrum
- scaphoid
  - ankle (closed) 825.22
    - open 825.32
  - wrist (closed) 814.01
    - open 814.11
- scapula (closed) 811.00
  - acromial, acromion (process) 811.01
    - open 811.11
  - body 811.09
    - open 811.19
  - coracoid process 811.02
    - open 811.12
  - glenoid (cavity) (fossa) 811.03
    - open 811.13
  - neck 811.03
    - open 811.13
  - open 811.10
- semilunar
  - bone, wrist (closed) 814.02
    - open 814.12
  - cartilage (interior) (knee) — *see* Tear, meniscus
- sesamoid bone — *see* Fracture, by site
- Shepherd's (closed) 825.21
  - open 825.31
- shoulder (*see also* Fracture, humerus, upper end)
  - blade — *see* Fracture, scapula
- silverfork — *see* Fracture, radius, lower end
- sinus (ethmoid) (frontal) (maxillary) (nasal) (sphenoidal) — *see* Fracture, skull, base
- Skillern's — *see* Fracture, radius, shaft

Fracture — *continued*
- skull (multiple NEC) (with face bones) (closed) 803.0 ☑

> *Note — Use the following fifth-digit subclassification with categories 800, 801, 803, and 804:*
>
> 0 *unspecified state of consciousness*
>
> 1 *with no loss of consciousness*
>
> 2 *with brief [less than one hour] loss of consciousness*
>
> 3 *with moderate [1-24 hours] loss of consciousness*
>
> 4 *with prolonged [more than 24 hours] loss of consciousness and return to pre-existing conscious level*
>
> 5 *with prolonged [more than 24 hours] loss of consciousness, without return to pre-existing conscious level*
>
> *Use fifth-digit 5 to designate when a patient is unconscious and dies before regaining consciousness, regardless of the duration of the loss of consciousness*
>
> 6 *with loss of consciousness of unspecified duration*
>
> 9 *with concussion, unspecified*

  - with
    - contusion, cerebral 803.1 ☑
    - epidural hemorrhage 803.2 ☑
    - extradural hemorrhage 803.2 ☑
    - hemorrhage (intracranial) NEC 803.3 ☑
    - intracranial injury NEC 803.4 ☑
    - laceration, cerebral 803.1 ☑
    - other bones — *see* Fracture, multiple, skull
    - subarachnoid hemorrhage 803.2 ☑
    - subdural hemorrhage 803.2 ☑
  - base (antrum) (ethmoid bone) (fossa) (internal ear) (nasal sinus) (occiput) (sphenoid) (temporal bone) (closed) 801.0 ☑
    - with
      - contusion, cerebral 801.1 ☑
      - epidural hemorrhage 801.2 ☑
      - extradural hemorrhage 801.2 ☑
      - hemorrhage (intracranial) NEC 801.3 ☑
      - intracranial injury NEC 801.4 ☑
      - laceration, cerebral 801.1 ☑
      - subarachnoid hemorrhage 801.2 ☑
      - subdural hemorrhage 801.2 ☑
    - open 801.5 ☑
      - with
        - contusion, cerebral 801.6 ☑
        - epidural hemorrhage 801.7 ☑
        - extradural hemorrhage 801.7 ☑
        - hemorrhage (intracranial) NEC 801.8 ☑
        - intracranial injury NEC 801.9 ☑

Fracture — *continued*
- skull — *continued*
  - base — *continued*
    - open — *continued*
      - with — *continued*
        - laceration, cerebral 801.6 ☑
        - subarachnoid hemorrhage 801.7 ☑
        - subdural hemorrhage 801.7 ☑
  - birth injury 767.3
  - face bones — *see* Fracture, face bones
  - open 803.5 ☑
    - with
      - contusion, cerebral 803.6 ☑
      - epidural hemorrhage 803.7 ☑
      - extradural hemorrhage 803.7 ☑
      - hemorrhage (intracranial) NEC 803.8 ☑
      - intracranial injury NEC 803.9 ☑
      - laceration, cerebral 803.6 ☑
      - subarachnoid hemorrhage 803.7 ☑
      - subdural hemorrhage 803.7 ☑
  - vault (frontal bone) (parietal bone) (vertex) (closed) 800.0 ☑
    - with
      - contusion, cerebral 800.1 ☑
      - epidural hemorrhage 800.2 ☑
      - extradural hemorrhage 800.2 ☑
      - hemorrhage (intracranial) NEC 800.3 ☑
      - intracranial injury NEC 800.4 ☑
      - laceration, cerebral 800.1 ☑
      - subarachnoid hemorrhage 800.2 ☑
      - subdural hemorrhage 800.2 ☑
    - open 800.5 ☑
      - with
        - contusion, cerebral 800.6 ☑
        - epidural hemorrhage 800.7 ☑
        - extradural hemorrhage 800.7 ☑
        - hemorrhage (intracranial) NEC 800.8 ☑
        - intracranial injury NEC 800.9 ☑
        - laceration, cerebral 800.6 ☑
        - subarachnoid hemorrhage 800.7 ☑
        - subdural hemorrhage 800.7 ☑
- Smith's 813.41
  - open 813.51
- sphenoid (bone) (sinus) — *see* Fracture, skull, base
- spine (*see also* Fracture, vertebra, by site due to birth trauma) 767.4
- spinous process — *see* Fracture, vertebra, by site
- spontaneous — *see* Fracture, pathologic
- sprinters' — *see* Fracture, ilium
- stapes — *see* Fracture, skull, base
- stave (*see also* Fracture, metacarpus, metacarpal bone(s))

Fracture — *continued*
- stave (*see also* Fracture, metacarpus, metacarpal bone(s)) — *continued*
  - spine — *see* Fracture, tibia, upper end
- sternum (closed) 807.2
  - with flail chest (open) 807.4
  - open 807.3
- Stieda's — *see* Fracture, femur, lower end
- stress 733.95
  - fibula 733.93
  - metatarsals 733.94
  - specified site NEC 733.95
  - tibia 733.93
- styloid process
  - metacarpal (closed) 815.02
    - open 815.12
  - radius — *see* Fracture, radius, lower end
  - temporal bone — *see* Fracture, skull, base
  - ulna — *see* Fracture, ulna, lower end
- supracondylar, elbow 812.41
  - open 812.51
- symphysis pubis (with visceral injury) (closed) 808.2
  - open 808.3
- talus (ankle bone) (closed) 825.21
  - open 825.31
- tarsus, tarsal bone(s) (with metatarsus) of one foot (closed) NEC 825.29
  - open 825.39
- temporal bone (styloid) — *see* Fracture, skull, base
- tendon — *see* Sprain, by site
- thigh — *see* Fracture, femur, shaft
- thumb (and finger(s)) of one hand (closed) (*see also* Fracture, phalanx, hand) 816.00
  - with metacarpal bone(s) of same hand 817.0
    - open 817.1
  - metacarpal(s) — *see* Fracture, metacarpus
  - open 816.10
- thyroid cartilage (closed) 807.5
  - open 807.6
- tibia (closed) 823.80
  - with fibula 823.82
    - open 823.92
  - condyles — *see* Fracture, tibia, upper end
  - distal end 824.8
    - open 824.9
  - epiphysis
    - lower 824.8
      - open 824.9
    - upper — *see* Fracture, tibia, upper end
  - head (involving knee joint) — *see* Fracture, tibia, upper end
  - intercondyloid eminence — *see* Fracture, tibia, upper end
  - involving ankle 824.0
    - open 824.9
  - lower end or extremity (anterior lip) (posterior lip) 824.8
    - open 824.9
  - malleolus (internal) (medial) 824.0
    - open 824.1
  - open NEC 823.90
  - pathologic 733.16
  - proximal end — *see* Fracture, tibia, upper end
  - shaft 823.20
    - with fibula 823.22
      - open 823.32
    - open 823.30
  - spine — *see* Fracture, tibia, upper end
  - stress 733.93
  - torus 823.40

Fracture — *continued*
- tibia — *continued*
  - torus — *continued*
    - with fibula 823.42
  - tuberosity — *see* Fracture, tibia, upper end
  - upper end or extremity (condyle) (epiphysis) (head) (spine) (proximal end) (tuberosity) 823.00
    - with fibula 823.02
      - open 823.12
    - open 823.10
- toe(s), of one foot (closed) 826.0
  - with bone(s) of same lower limb 827.0
    - open 827.1
  - open 826.1
- tooth (root) 873.63
  - complicated 873.73
- torus
  - fibula 823.41
    - with tibia 823.42
  - radius 813.45
  - tibia 823.40
    - with fibula 823.42
- trachea (closed) 807.5
  - open 807.6
- transverse process — *see* Fracture, vertebra, by site
- trapezium (closed) 814.05
  - open 814.15
- trapezoid bone (closed) 814.06
  - open 814.16
- trimalleolar (closed) 824.6
  - open 824.7
- triquetral (bone) (closed) 814.03
  - open 814.13
- trochanter (greater) (lesser) (closed) (*see also* Fracture, femur, neck, by site) 820.20
  - open 820.30
- trunk (bones) (closed) 809.0
  - open 809.1
- tuberosity (external) — *see* Fracture, by site
- ulna (alone) (closed) 813.82
  - with radius NEC 813.83
    - open 813.93
  - coronoid process (closed) 813.02
    - open 813.12
  - distal end — *see* Fracture, ulna, lower end
  - epiphysis
    - lower — *see* Fracture, ulna, lower end
    - upper — *see* Fracture, ulna, upper end
  - head — *see* Fracture, ulna, lower end
  - lower end (distal end) (head) (lower epiphysis) (styloid process) 813.43
    - with radius (lower end) 813.44
      - open 813.54
    - open 813.53
  - olecranon process (closed) 813.01
    - open 813.11
  - open NEC 813.92
  - pathologic 733.12
  - proximal end — *see* Fracture, ulna, upper end
  - shaft 813.22
    - with radius (shaft) 813.23
      - open 813.33
    - open 813.32
  - styloid process — *see* Fracture, ulna, lower end
  - transverse — *see* Fracture, ulna, by site
  - upper end (epiphysis) 813.04
    - with radius (upper end) 813.08
      - open 813.18
    - multiple sites 813.04
      - open 813.14
    - open 813.14

Fracture — *continued*
- ulna — *continued*
  - upper end — *continued*
    - specified site NEC 813.04
      - open 813.14
- unciform (closed) 814.08
  - open 814.18
- vertebra, vertebral (back) (body) (column) (neural arch) (pedicle) (spine) (spinous process) (transverse process) (closed) 805.8
  - with
    - hematomyelia — *see* Fracture, vertebra, by site, with spinal cord injury
    - injury to
      - cauda equina — *see* Fracture, vertebra, sacrum, with spinal cord injury
      - nerve — *see* Fracture, vertebra, by site, with spinal cord injury
    - paralysis — *see* Fracture, vertebra, by site, with spinal cord injury
    - paraplegia — *see* Fracture, vertebra, by site, with spinal cord injury
    - quadriplegia — *see* Fracture, vertebra, by site, with spinal cord injury
    - spinal concussion — *see* Fracture, vertebra, by site, with spinal cord injury
    - spinal cord injury (closed) NEC 806.8

> *Note — Use the following fifth-digit subclassification with categories 806.0–806.3:*
>
> *C_1–C_4 or unspecified level and D_1–D_6 (T_1–T_6) or unspecified level with*
>
> 0 *unspecified spinal cord injury*
> 1 *complete lesion of cord*
> 2 *anterior cord syndrome*
> 3 *central cord syndrome*
> 4 *specified injury NEC*
>
> *C_5–C_7 level and D_7–D_{12} level with:*
>
> 5 *unspecified spinal cord injury*
> 6 *complete lesion of cord*
> 7 *anterior cord syndrome*
> 8 *central cord syndrome*
> 9 *specified injury NEC*

-
  -
    -
      - cervical 806.0 ☑
        - open 806.1 ☑
      - dorsal, dorsolumbar 806.2 ☑
        - open 806.3 ☑
      - open 806.9
      - thoracic, thoracolumbar 806.2 ☑
        - open 806.3 ☑
  - atlanto-axial — *see* Fracture, vertebra, cervical
  - cervical (hangman) (teardrop) (closed) 805.00
    - with spinal cord injury — *see* Fracture, vertebra, with spinal cord injury, cervical
    - first (atlas) 805.01
      - open 805.11
    - second (axis) 805.02
      - open 805.12
    - third 805.03
      - open 805.13
    - fourth 805.04
      - open 805.14
    - fifth 805.05
      - open 805.15
    - sixth 805.06

Fracture — *continued*
- vertebra, vertebral — *continued*
  - cervical — *continued*
    - sixth — *continued*
      - open 805.16
    - seventh 805.07
      - open 805.17
    - multiple sites 805.08
      - open 805.18
    - open 805.10
  - chronic 733.13
  - coccyx (closed) 805.6
    - with spinal cord injury (closed) 806.60
      - cauda equina injury 806.62
        - complete lesion 806.61
          - open 806.71
        - open 806.72
      - open 806.70
      - specified type NEC 806.69
        - open 806.79
    - open 805.7
  - collapsed 733.13
  - compression, not due to trauma 733.13
  - dorsal (closed) 805.2
    - with spinal cord injury — *see* Fracture, vertebra, with spinal cord injury, dorsal
    - open 805.3
  - dorsolumbar (closed) 805.2
    - with spinal cord injury — *see* Fracture, vertebra, with spinal cord injury, dorsal
    - open 805.3
  - due to osteoporosis 733.13
  - fetus or newborn 767.4
  - lumbar (closed) 805.4
    - with spinal cord injury (closed) 806.4
      - open 806.5
    - open 805.5
  - nontraumatic 733.13
  - open NEC 805.9
  - pathologic (any site) 733.13
  - sacrum (closed) 805.6
    - with spinal cord injury 806.60
      - cauda equina injury 806.62
        - complete lesion 806.61
          - open 806.71
        - open 806.72
      - open 806.70
      - specified type NEC 806.69
        - open 806.79
    - open 805.7
  - site unspecified (closed) 805.8
    - with spinal cord injury (closed) 806.8
      - open 806.9
    - open 805.9
  - stress (any site) 733.95
  - thoracic (closed) 805.2
    - with spinal cord injury — *see* Fracture, vertebra, with spinal cord injury, thoracic
    - open 805.3
- vertex — *see* Fracture, skull, vault
- vomer (bone) 802.0
  - open 802.1
- Wagstaffe's — *see* Fracture, ankle
- wrist (closed) 814.00
  - open 814.10
  - pathologic 733.12
- xiphoid (process) — *see* Fracture, sternum
- zygoma (zygomatic arch) (closed) 802.4
  - open 802.5

Fragile X syndrome 759.83

Fragilitas
- crinium 704.2
- hair 704.2
- ossium 756.51
  - with blue sclera 756.51
- unguium 703.8
  - congenital 757.5

Fragility
- bone 756.51
  - with deafness and blue sclera 756.51
- capillary (hereditary) 287.8
- hair 704.2
- nails 703.8

Fragmentation — *see* Fracture, by site

Frailty 797 ●

Frambesia, frambesial (tropica) — *see also* Yaws 102.9
- initial lesion or ulcer 102.0
- primary 102.0

Frambeside
- gummatous 102.4
- of early yaws 102.2

Frambesioma 102.1

Franceschetti's syndrome (mandibulofacial dysostosis) 756.0

Francis' disease — *see also* Tularemia 021.9

Franklin's disease (heavy chain) 273.2

Frank's essential thrombocytopenia — *see also* Purpura, thrombocytopenic 287.39

Fraser's syndrome 759.89

Freckle 709.09
- malignant melanoma in (M8742/3) — *see* Melanoma
- melanotic (of Hutchinson) (M8742/2) — *see* Neoplasm, skin, in situ

Freeman-Sheldon syndrome 759.89

Freezing 991.9
- specified effect NEC 991.8

Freiberg's
- disease (osteochondrosis, second metatarsal) 732.5
- infraction of metatarsal head 732.5
- osteochondrosis 732.5

Frei's disease (climatic bubo) 099.1

Fremitus, friction, cardiac 785.3

Frenulum linguae 750.0

Frenum
- external os 752.49
- tongue 750.0

Frequency (urinary) NEC 788.41
- micturition 788.41
- nocturnal 788.43
- polyuria 788.42
- psychogenic 306.53

Frey's syndrome (auriculotemporal syndrome) 705.22

Friction
- burn (*see also* Injury, superficial, by site) 919.0
- fremitus, cardiac 785.3
- precordial 785.3
- sounds, chest 786.7

Friderichsen-Waterhouse syndrome or disease 036.3

Friedländer's
- B (bacillus) NEC (*see also* condition) 041.3
  - sepsis or septicemia 038.49
- disease (endarteritis obliterans) — *see* Arteriosclerosis

Friedreich's
- ataxia 334.0
- combined systemic disease 334.0
- disease 333.2
  - combined systemic 334.0
- myoclonia 333.2
- sclerosis (spinal cord) 334.0

Friedrich-Erb-Arnold syndrome (acropachyderma) 757.39

Frigidity 302.72
- psychic or psychogenic 302.72

Fröhlich's disease or syndrome (adiposogenital dystrophy) 253.8

Froin's syndrome 336.8

Frommel-Chiari syndrome 676.6 ☑

Frommel's disease 676.6 ☑

Frontal — *see also* condition
- lobe syndrome 310.0

Frostbite 991.3
- face 991.0

Frostbite — *continued*
- foot 991.2
- hand 991.1
- specified site NEC 991.3

Frotteurism 302.89

Frozen 991.9
- pelvis 620.8
- shoulder 726.0

Fructosemia 271.2

Fructosuria (benign) (essential) 271.2

Fuchs'
- black spot (myopic) 360.21
- corneal dystrophy (endothelial) 371.57
- heterochromic cyclitis 364.21

Fucosidosis 271.8

Fugue 780.99
- dissociative 300.13
- hysterical (dissociative) 300.13
- reaction to exceptional stress (transient) 308.1

Fukuhara syndrome 277.87

Fuller Albright's syndrome (osteitis fibrosa disseminata) 756.59

Fuller's earth disease 502

Fulminant, fulminating — *see* condition

Functional — see condition

Functioning
- borderline intellectual V62.89

Fundus — *see also* condition
- flavimaculatus 362.76

Fungemia 117.9

Fungus, fungous
- cerebral 348.8
- disease NEC 117.9
- infection — *see* Infection, fungus
- testis (*see also* Tuberculosis) 016.5 ☑ *[608.81]*

Funiculitis (acute) 608.4
- chronic 608.4
- endemic 608.4
- gonococcal (acute) 098.14
  - chronic or duration of 2 months or over 098.34
- tuberculous (*see also* Tuberculosis) 016.5 ☑

Funnel
- breast (acquired) 738.3
  - congenital 754.81
  - late effect of rickets 268.1
- chest (acquired) 738.3
  - congenital 754.81
  - late effect of rickets 268.1
- pelvis (acquired) 738.6
  - with disproportion (fetopelvic) 653.3 ☑
    - affecting fetus or newborn 763.1
    - causing obstructed labor 660.1 ☑
      - affecting fetus or newborn 763.1
  - congenital 755.69
  - tuberculous (*see also* Tuberculosis) 016.9 ☑

FUO — *see also* Pyrexia 780.60 ▲

Furfur 690.18
- microsporon 111.0

Furor, paroxysmal (idiopathic) — *see also* Epilepsy 345.8 ☑

Furriers' lung 495.8

Furrowed tongue 529.5
- congenital 750.13

Furrowing nail(s) (transverse) 703.8
- congenital 757.5

Furuncle 680.9
- abdominal wall 680.2
- ankle 680.6
- anus 680.5
- arm (any part, above wrist) 680.3
- auditory canal, external 680.0
- axilla 680.3
- back (any part) 680.2
- breast 680.2
- buttock 680.5
- chest wall 680.2
- corpus cavernosum 607.2
- ear (any part) 680.0

Furuncle — *continued*
eyelid 373.13
face (any part, except eye) 680.0
finger (any) 680.4
flank 680.2
foot (any part) 680.7
forearm 680.3
gluteal (region) 680.5
groin 680.2
hand (any part) 680.4
head (any part, except face) 680.8
heel 680.7
hip 680.6
kidney (*see also* Abscess, kidney) 590.2
knee 680.6
labium (majus) (minus) 616.4
lacrimal
gland (*see also* Dacryoadenitis) 375.00
passages (duct) (sac) (*see also* Dacryocystitis) 375.30
leg, any part except foot 680.6
malignant 022.0
multiple sites 680.9
neck 680.1
nose (external) (septum) 680.0
orbit 376.01
partes posteriores 680.5
pectoral region 680.2
penis 607.2
perineum 680.2
pinna 680.0
scalp (any part) 680.8

Furuncle — *continued*
scrotum 608.4
seminal vesicle 608.0
shoulder 680.3
skin NEC 680.9
specified site NEC 680.8
spermatic cord 608.4
temple (region) 680.0
testis 604.90
thigh 680.6
thumb 680.4
toe (any) 680.7
trunk 680.2
tunica vaginalis 608.4
umbilicus 680.2
upper arm 680.3
vas deferens 608.4
vulva 616.4
wrist 680.4

Furunculosis — *see also* Furuncle 680.9
external auditory meatus 680.0 *[380.13]*

Fusarium (infection) 118

Fusion, fused (congenital)
anal (with urogenital canal) 751.5
aorta and pulmonary artery 745.0
astragaloscaphoid 755.67
atria 745.5
atrium and ventricle 745.69
auditory canal 744.02
auricles, heart 745.5
binocular, with defective stereopsis 368.33
bone 756.9

Fusion, fused — *continued*
cervical spine — *see* Fusion, spine
choanal 748.0
commissure, mitral valve 746.5
cranial sutures, premature 756.0
cusps, heart valve NEC 746.89
mitral 746.5
tricuspid 746.89
ear ossicles 744.04
fingers (*see also* Syndactylism, fingers) 755.11
hymen 752.42
hymeno-urethral 599.89
causing obstructed labor 660.1 ☑
affecting fetus or newborn 763.1
joint (acquired) (*see also* Ankylosis)
congenital 755.8
kidneys (incomplete) 753.3
labium (majus) (minus) 752.49
larynx and trachea 748.3
limb 755.8
lower 755.69
upper 755.59
lobe, lung 748.5
lumbosacral (acquired) 724.6
congenital 756.15
surgical V45.4
nares (anterior) (posterior) 748.0
nose, nasal 748.0
nostril(s) 748.0
organ or site NEC — *see* Anomaly, specified type NEC
ossicles 756.9

Fusion, fused — *continued*
ossicles — *continued*
auditory 744.04
pulmonary valve segment 746.02
pulmonic cusps 746.02
ribs 756.3
sacroiliac (acquired) (joint) 724.6
congenital 755.69
surgical V45.4
skull, imperfect 756.0
spine (acquired) 724.9
arthrodesis status V45.4
congenital (vertebra) 756.15
postoperative status V45.4
sublingual duct with submaxillary duct at opening in mouth 750.26
talonavicular (bar) 755.67
teeth, tooth 520.2
testes 752.89
toes (*see also* Syndactylism, toes) 755.13
trachea and esophagus 750.3
twins 759.4
urethral-hymenal 599.89
vagina 752.49
valve cusps — *see* Fusion, cusps, heart valve
ventricles, heart 745.4
vertebra (arch) — *see* Fusion, spine
vulva 752.49

Fusospirillosis (mouth) (tongue) (tonsil) 101

Fussy infant (baby) 780.91

G

- **Gafsa boil** 085.1
- **Gain, weight** (abnormal) (excessive) — *see also* Weight, gain 783.1
- **Gaisböck's disease or syndrome** (polycythemia hypertonica) 289.0
- **Gait**
  - abnormality 781.2
    - hysterical 300.11
  - ataxic 781.2
    - hysterical 300.11
  - disturbance 781.2
    - hysterical 300.11
  - paralytic 781.2
  - scissor 781.2
  - spastic 781.2
  - staggering 781.2
    - hysterical 300.11
- **Galactocele** (breast) (infected) 611.5
  - puerperal, postpartum 676.8 ☑
- **Galactophoritis** 611.0
  - puerperal, postpartum 675.2 ☑
- **Galactorrhea** 676.6 ☑
  - not associated with childbirth 611.6
- **Galactosemia** (classic) (congenital) 271.1
- **Galactosuria** 271.1
- **Galacturia** 791.1
  - bilharziasis 120.0
- **Galen's vein** — *see* condition
- **Gallbladder** — *see also* condition
  - acute (*see also* Disease, gallbladder) 575.0
- **Gall duct** — *see* condition
- **Gallop rhythm** 427.89
- **Gallstone** (cholemic) (colic) (impacted) — *see also* Cholelithiasis
  - causing intestinal obstruction 560.31
- **Gambling, pathological** 312.31
- **Gammaloidosis** 277.39
- **Gammopathy** 273.9
  - macroglobulinemia 273.3
  - monoclonal (benign) (essential) (idiopathic) (with lymphoplasmacytic dyscrasia) 273.1
- **Gamna's disease** (siderotic splenomegaly) 289.51
- **Gampsodactylia** (congenital) 754.71
- **Gamstorp's disease** (adynamia episodica hereditaria) 359.3
- **Gandy-Nanta disease** (siderotic splenomegaly) 289.51
- **Gang activity, without manifest psychiatric disorder** V71.09
  - adolescent V71.02
  - adult V71.01
  - child V71.02
- **Gangliocytoma** (M9490/0) — *see* Neoplasm, connective tissue, benign
- **Ganglioglioma** (M9505/1) — *see* Neoplasm, by site, uncertain behavior
- **Ganglion** 727.43
  - joint 727.41
  - of yaws (early) (late) 102.6
  - periosteal (*see also* Periostitis) 730.3 ☑
  - tendon sheath (compound) (diffuse) 727.42
  - tuberculous (*see also* Tuberculosis) 015.9 ☑
- **Ganglioneuroblastoma** (M9490/3) — *see* Neoplasm, connective tissue, malignant
- **Ganglioneuroma** (M9490/0) — *see also* Neoplasm, connective tissue, benign
  - malignant (M9490/3) — *see* Neoplasm, connective tissue, malignant
- **Ganglioneuromatosis** (M9491/0) — *see* Neoplasm, connective tissue, benign
- **Ganglionitis**
  - fifth nerve (*see also* Neuralgia, trigeminal) 350.1
  - gasserian 350.1
- **Ganglionitis** — *continued*
  - geniculate 351.1
    - herpetic 053.11
    - newborn 767.5
  - herpes zoster 053.11
  - herpetic geniculate (Hunt's syndrome) 053.11
- **Gangliosidosis** 330.1
- **Gangosa** 102.5
- **Gangrene, gangrenous** (anemia) (artery) (cellulitis) (dermatitis) (dry) (infective) (moist) (pemphigus) (septic) (skin) (stasis) (ulcer) 785.4
  - with
    - arteriosclerosis (native artery) 440.24
      - bypass graft 440.30
        - autologous vein 440.31
        - nonautologous biological 440.32
    - diabetes (mellitus) 250.7 ☑ *[785.4]*
      - due to secondary diabetes ●
        249.7 ☑ *[785.4]* ●
  - abdomen (wall) 785.4
  - adenitis 683
  - alveolar 526.5
  - angina 462
    - diphtheritic 032.0
  - anus 569.49
  - appendices epiploicae — *see* Gangrene, mesentery
  - appendix — *see* Appendicitis, acute
  - arteriosclerotic — *see* Arteriosclerosis, with, gangrene
  - auricle 785.4
  - Bacillus welchii (*see also* Gangrene, gas) 040.0
  - bile duct (*see also* Cholangitis) 576.8
  - bladder 595.89
  - bowel — *see* Gangrene, intestine
  - cecum — *see* Gangrene, intestine
  - Clostridium perfringens or welchii (*see also* Gangrene, gas) 040.0
  - colon — *see* Gangrene, intestine
  - connective tissue 785.4
  - cornea 371.40
  - corpora cavernosa (infective) 607.2
    - noninfective 607.89
  - cutaneous, spreading 785.4
  - decubital (*see also* ▶Ulcer, pressure◀) 707.00 *[785.4]*
  - diabetic (any site) 250.7 ☑ *[785.4]*
    - due to secondary diabetes ●
      249.7 ☑ *[785.4]* ●
  - dropsical 785.4
  - emphysematous (*see also* Gangrene, gas) 040.0
  - epidemic (ergotized grain) 988.2
  - epididymis (infectional) (*see also* Epididymitis) 604.99
  - erysipelas (*see also* Erysipelas) 035
  - extremity (lower) (upper) 785.4
  - gallbladder or duct (*see also* Cholecystitis, acute) 575.0
  - gas (bacillus) 040.0
    - with
      - abortion — *see* Abortion, by type, with sepsis
      - ectopic pregnancy (*see also* categories 633.0–633.9) 639.0
      - molar pregnancy (*see also* categories 630–632) 639.0
    - following
      - abortion 639.0
      - ectopic or molar pregnancy 639.0
    - puerperal, postpartum, childbirth 670.0 ☑
  - glossitis 529.0
  - gum 523.8
  - hernia — *see* Hernia, by site, with gangrene
  - hospital noma 528.1
  - intestine, intestinal (acute) (hemorrhagic) (massive) 557.0
- **Gangrene, gangrenous** — *continued*
  - intestine, intestinal — *continued*
    - with
      - hernia — *see* Hernia, by site, with gangrene
      - mesenteric embolism or infarction 557.0
      - obstruction (*see also* Obstruction, intestine) 560.9
  - laryngitis 464.00
    - with obstruction 464.01
  - liver 573.8
  - lung 513.0
    - spirochetal 104.8
  - lymphangitis 457.2
  - Meleney's (cutaneous) 686.09
  - mesentery 557.0
    - with
      - embolism or infarction 557.0
      - intestinal obstruction (*see also* Obstruction, intestine) 560.9
  - mouth 528.1
  - noma 528.1
  - orchitis 604.90
  - ovary (*see also* Salpingo-oophoritis) 614.2
  - pancreas 577.0
  - penis (infectional) 607.2
    - noninfective 607.89
  - perineum 785.4
  - pharynx 462
  - pneumonia 513.0
  - Pott's 440.24
  - presenile 443.1
  - pulmonary 513.0
  - pulp, tooth 522.1
  - quinsy 475
  - Raynaud's (symmetric gangrene) 443.0 *[785.4]*
  - rectum 569.49
  - retropharyngeal 478.24
  - rupture — *see* Hernia, by site, with gangrene
  - scrotum 608.4
    - noninfective 608.83
  - senile 440.24
  - septic 034.0
  - septic 034.0
  - sore throat 462
  - spermatic cord 608.4
    - noninfective 608.89
  - spine 785.4
  - spirochetal NEC 104.8
  - spreading cutaneous 785.4
  - stomach 537.89
  - stomatitis 528.1
  - symmetrical 443.0 *[785.4]*
  - testis (infectional) (*see also* Orchitis) 604.99
    - noninfective 608.89
  - throat 462
    - diphtheritic 032.0
  - thyroid (gland) 246.8
  - tonsillitis (acute) 463
  - tooth (pulp) 522.1
  - tuberculous NEC (*see also* Tuberculosis) 011.9 ☑
  - tunica vaginalis 608.4
    - noninfective 608.89
  - umbilicus 785.4
  - uterus (*see also* Endometritis) 615.9
  - uvulitis 528.3
  - vas deferens 608.4
    - noninfective 608.89
  - vulva (*see also* Vulvitis) 616.10
- **Gannister disease** (occupational) 502
  - with tuberculosis — *see* Tuberculosis, pulmonary
- **Ganser's syndrome, hysterical** 300.16
- **Gardner-Diamond syndrome** (autoerythrocyte sensitization) 287.2
- **Gargoylism** 277.5
- **Garré's**
  - disease (*see also* Osteomyelitis) 730.1 ☑
- **Garré's** — *continued*
  - osteitis (sclerosing) (*see also* Osteomyelitis) 730.1 ☑
  - osteomyelitis (*see also* Osteomyelitis) 730.1 ☑
- **Garrod's pads, knuckle** 728.79
- **Gartner's duct**
  - cyst 752.41
  - persistent 752.41
- **Gas** 787.3
  - asphyxia, asphyxiation, inhalation, poisoning, suffocation NEC 987.9
    - specified gas — *see* Table of Drugs and Chemicals
  - bacillus gangrene or infection — *see* Gas, gangrene
  - cyst, mesentery 568.89
  - excessive 787.3
  - gangrene 040.0
    - with
      - abortion — *see* Abortion, by type, with sepsis
      - ectopic pregnancy (*see also* categories 633.0–633.9) 639.0
      - molar pregnancy (*see also* categories 630–632) 639.0
    - following
      - abortion 639.0
      - ectopic or molar pregnancy 639.0
    - puerperal, postpartum, childbirth 670.0 ☑
  - on stomach 787.3
  - pains 787.3
- **Gastradenitis** 535.0 ☑
- **Gastralgia** 536.8
  - psychogenic 307.89
- **Gastrectasis, gastrectasia** 536.1
  - psychogenic 306.4
- **Gastric** — *see* condition
- **Gastrinoma** (M8153/1)
  - malignant (M8153/3)
    - pancreas 157.4
    - specified site NEC — *see* Neoplasm, by site, malignant
    - unspecified site 157.4
  - specified site — *see* Neoplasm, by site, uncertain behavior
  - unspecified site 235.5
- **Gastritis** 535.5 ☑

> *Note — Use the following fifth-digit subclassification for category 535:*
>
> *0 without mention of hemorrhage*
>
> *1 with hemorrhage*

  - acute 535.0 ☑
  - alcoholic 535.3 ☑
  - allergic 535.4 ☑
  - antral 535.4 ☑
  - atrophic 535.1 ☑
  - atrophic-hyperplastic 535.1 ☑
  - bile-induced 535.4 ☑
  - catarrhal 535.0 ☑
  - chronic (atrophic) 535.1 ☑
  - cirrhotic 535.4 ☑
  - corrosive (acute) 535.4 ☑
  - dietetic 535.4 ☑
  - due to diet deficiency 269.9 *[535.4]* ☑
  - eosinophilic 535.7 ☑ ▲
  - erosive 535.4 ☑
  - follicular 535.4 ☑
    - chronic 535.1 ☑
  - giant hypertrophic 535.2 ☑
  - glandular 535.4 ☑
    - chronic 535.1 ☑
  - hypertrophic (mucosa) 535.2 ☑
    - chronic giant 211.1
  - irritant 535.4 ☑
  - nervous 306.4
  - phlegmonous 535.0 ☑
  - psychogenic 306.4
  - sclerotic 535.4 ☑
  - spastic 536.8

Gastritis — *continued*
subacute 535.0 ☑
superficial 535.4 ☑
suppurative 535.0 ☑
toxic 535.4 ☑
tuberculous (*see also* Tuberculosis) 017.9 ☑
Gastrocarcinoma (M8010/3) 151.9
Gastrocolic — *see* condition
Gastrocolitis — *see* Enteritis
Gastrodisciasis 121.8
Gastroduodenitis — *see also* Gastritis 535.5 ☑
catarrhal 535.0 ☑
infectional 535.0 ☑
virus, viral 008.8
specified type NEC 008.69
Gastrodynia 536.8
Gastroenteritis (acute) (catarrhal) (congestive) (hemorrhagic) (noninfectious) — *see also* Enteritis 558.9
aertrycke infection 003.0
allergic 558.3
chronic 558.9
ulcerative (*see also* Colitis, ulcerative) 556.9
dietetic 558.9
due to
antineoplastic chemotherapy 558.9 ●
food poisoning (*see also* Poisoning, food) 005.9
radiation 558.1
eosinophilic 558.41 ●
epidemic 009.0
functional 558.9
infectious (*see also* Enteritis, due to, by organism) 009.0
presumed 009.1
salmonella 003.0
septic (*see also* Enteritis, due to, by organism) 009.0
toxic 558.2
tuberculous (*see also* Tuberculosis) 014.8 ☑
ulcerative (*see also* Colitis, ulcerative) 556.9
viral NEC 008.8
specified type NEC 008.69
zymotic 009.0
Gastroenterocolitis — *see* Enteritis
Gastroenteropathy, protein-losing 579.8
Gastroenteroptosis 569.89
Gastroesophageal laceration-hemorrhage syndrome 530.7
Gastroesophagitis 530.19
Gastrohepatitis — *see also* Gastritis 535.5 ☑
Gastrointestinal — *see* condition
Gastrojejunal — *see* condition
Gastrojejunitis — *see also* Gastritis 535.5 ☑
Gastrojejunocolic — *see* condition
Gastroliths 537.89
Gastromalacia 537.89
Gastroparalysis 536.3
diabetic 250.6 ☑ *[536.3]*
due to secondary diabetes 249.6 ☑ *[536.3]* ●
Gastroparesis 536.3
diabetic 250.6 ☑ *[536.3]*
due to secondary diabetes 249.6 ☑ *[536.3]* ●
Gastropathy 537.9
congestive portal 537.89
erythematous 535.5 ☑
exudative 579.8
portal hypertensive 537.89
Gastroptosis 537.5
Gastrorrhagia 578.0
Gastrorrhea 536.8
psychogenic 306.4
Gastroschisis (congenital) 756.79
acquired 569.89
Gastrospasm (neurogenic) (reflex) 536.8
Gastrospasm — *continued*
neurotic 306.4
psychogenic 306.4
Gastrostaxis 578.0
Gastrostenosis 537.89
Gastrostomy
attention to V55.1
complication 536.40
specified type 536.49
infection 536.41
malfunctioning 536.42
status V44.1
Gastrosuccorrhea (continuous) (intermittent) 536.8
neurotic 306.4
psychogenic 306.4
Gaucher's
disease (adult) (cerebroside lipidosis) (infantile) 272.7
hepatomegaly 272.7
splenomegaly (cerebroside lipidosis) 272.7
GAVE (gastric antral vascular ectasia) 537.82
with hemorrhage 537.83
without hemorrhage 537.82
Gayet's disease (superior hemorrhagic polioencephalitis) 265.1
Gayet-Wernicke's syndrome (superior hemorrhagic polioencephalitis) 265.1
Gee (-Herter) (-Heubner) (-Thaysen) disease or syndrome (nontropical sprue) 579.0
Gélineau's syndrome — *see also* Narcolepsy 347.00
Gemination, teeth 520.2
Gemistocytoma (M9411/3)
specified site — *see* Neoplasm, by site, malignant
unspecified site 191.9
General, generalized — *see* condtion
Genetic
susceptibility to
MEN (multiple endocrine neoplasia) V84.81
neoplasia
multiple endocrine [MEN] V84.81
neoplasm
malignant, of
breast V84.01
endometrium V84.04
other V84.09
ovary V84.02
prostate V84.03
specified disease NEC V84.89
Genital — *see* condition
warts 078.11 ▲
Genito-anorectal syndrome 099.1
Genitourinary system — *see* condition
Genu
congenital 755.64
extrorsum (acquired) 736.42
congenital 755.64
late effects of rickets 268.1
introrsum (acquired) 736.41
congenital 755.64
late effects of rickets 268.1
rachitic (old) 268.1
recurvatum (acquired) 736.5
congenital 754.40
with dislocation of knee 754.41
late effects of rickets 268.1
valgum (acquired) (knock-knee) 736.41
congenital 755.64
late effects of rickets 268.1
varum (acquired) (bowleg) 736.42
congenital 755.64
late effect of rickets 268.1
Geographic tongue 529.1
Geophagia 307.52
Geotrichosis 117.9
intestine 117.9
lung 117.9
Geotrichosis — *continued*
mouth 117.9
Gephyrophobia 300.29
Gerbode defect 745.4
GERD (gastroesophageal reflux disease) 530.81 ●
Gerhardt's
disease (erythromelalgia) 443.82
syndrome (vocal cord paralysis) 478.30
Gerlier's disease (epidemic vertigo) 078.81
German measles 056.9
exposure to V01.4
Germinoblastoma (diffuse) (M9614/3) 202.8 ☑
follicular (M9692/3) 202.0 ☑
Germinoma (M9064/3) — *see* Neoplasm, by site, malignant
Gerontoxon 371.41
Gerstmann-Sträussler-Scheinker syndrome (GSS) 046.71 ●
Gerstmann's syndrome (finger agnosia) 784.69
Gestation (period) — *see also* Pregnancy
ectopic NEC (*see also* Pregnancy, ectopic) 633.90
with intrauterine pregnancy 633.91
Gestational proteinuria 646.2 ☑
with hypertension — *see* Toxemia, of pregnancy
Ghon tubercle primary infection — *see also* Tuberculosis 010.0 ☑
Ghost
teeth 520.4
vessels, cornea 370.64
Ghoul hand 102.3
Gianotti Crosti syndrome 057.8
due to known virus — *see* Infection, virus
due to unknown virus 057.8
Giant
cell
epulis 523.8
peripheral (gingiva) 523.8
tumor, tendon sheath 727.02
colon (congenital) 751.3
esophagus (congenital) 750.4
kidney 753.3
urticaria 995.1
hereditary 277.6
Giardia lamblia infestation 007.1
Giardiasis 007.1
Gibert's disease (pityriasis rosea) 696.3
Gibraltar fever — *see* Brucellosis
Giddiness 780.4
hysterical 300.11
psychogenic 306.9
Gierke's disease (glycogenosis I) 271.0
Gigantism (cerebral) (hypophyseal) (pituitary) 253.0
Gilbert's disease or cholemia (familial nonhemolytic jaundice) 277.4
Gilchrist's disease (North American blastomycosis) 116.0
Gilford (-Hutchinson) disease or syndrome (progeria) 259.8
Gilles de la Tourette's disease (motor-verbal tic) 307.23
Gillespie's syndrome (dysplasia oculodentodigitalis) 759.89
Gingivitis 523.10
acute 523.00
necrotizing 101
non-plaque induced 523.01
plaque induced 523.00
catarrhal 523.00
chronic 523.10
non-plaque induced 523.11
desquamative 523.10
expulsiva 523.40
hyperplastic 523.10
marginal, simple 523.10
necrotizing, acute 101
non-plaque induced 523.11
pellagrous 265.2
Gingivitis — *continued*
plaque induced 523.10
ulcerative 523.10
acute necrotizing 101
Vincent's 101
Gingivoglossitis 529.0
Gingivopericementitis 523.40
Gingivosis 523.10
Gingivostomatitis 523.10
herpetic 054.2
Giovannini's disease 117.9
GISA (glycopeptide intermediate staphylococcus aureus) V09.8 ☑
Glanders 024
Gland, glandular — *see* condition
Glanzmann (-Naegeli) disease or thrombasthenia 287.1
Glassblowers' disease 527.1
Glaucoma (capsular) (inflammatory) (noninflammatory) (primary) 365.9
with increased episcleral venous pressure 365.82
absolute 360.42
acute 365.22
narrow angle 365.22
secondary 365.60
angle closure 365.20
acute 365.22
chronic 365.23
intermittent 365.21
interval 365.21
residual stage 365.24
subacute 365.21
borderline 365.00
chronic 365.11
noncongestive 365.11
open angle 365.11
simple 365.11
closed angle — *see* Glaucoma, angle closure
congenital 743.20
associated with other eye anomalies 743.22
simple 743.21
congestive — *see* Glaucoma, narrow angle
corticosteroid-induced (glaucomatous stage) 365.31
residual stage 365.32
hemorrhagic 365.60
hypersecretion 365.81
infantile 365.14
congenital 743.20
associated with other eye anomalies 743.22
simple 743.21
in or with
aniridia 365.42 ▲
Axenfeld's anomaly 365.41 ▲
congenital syndromes NEC 759.89 *[365.44]*
disorder of lens NEC 365.59
iris
anomalies NEC 365.42 ▲
atrophy, essential 365.42 ▲
bombé 365.61 ▲
microcornea 365.43 ▲
neurofibromatosis 237.71 *[365.44]*
ocular
cysts NEC 365.64
disorders NEC 365.60
trauma 365.65
tumors NEC 365.64
pupillary block or seclusion 365.61 ▲
Rieger's anomaly or syndrome 365.41 ▲
seclusion of pupil 365.61 ▲
Sturge-Weber (-Dimitri) syndrome 759.6 *[365.44]*
systemic syndrome NEC 365.44
tumor of globe 365.64
vascular disorders NEC 365.63
juvenile 365.14
low tension 365.12
malignant 365.83

Glaucoma — *continued*
- narrow angle (primary) 365.20
  - acute 365.22
  - chronic 365.23
  - intermittent 365.21
  - interval 365.21
  - residual stage 365.24
  - subacute 365.21
- newborn 743.20
  - associated with other eye anomalies 743.22
  - simple 743.21
- noncongestive (chronic) 365.11
- nonobstructive (chronic) 365.11
- obstructive 365.60
  - due to lens changes 365.59
- open angle 365.10
  - with
    - borderline intraocular pressure 365.01
    - cupping of optic discs 365.01
  - primary 365.11
  - residual stage 365.15
- phacolytic 365.51
- pigmentary 365.13
- postinfectious 365.60
- pseudoexfoliation 365.52
- secondary NEC 365.60
- simple (chronic) 365.11
- simplex 365.11
- steroid responders 365.03
- suspect 365.00
- syphilitic 095.8
- traumatic NEC 365.65
  - newborn 767.8
- wide angle (*see also* Glaucoma, open angle) 365.10

Glaucomatous flecks (subcapsular) 366.31

Glazed tongue 529.4

Gleet 098.2

Glénard's disease or syndrome (enteroptosis) 569.89

Glinski-Simmonds syndrome (pituitary cachexia) 253.2

Glioblastoma (multiforme) (M9440/3)
- with sarcomatous component (M9442/3)
  - specified site — *see* Neoplasm, by site, malignant
  - unspecified site 191.9
- giant cell (M9441/3)
  - specified site — *see* Neoplasm, by site, malignant
  - unspecified site 191.9
- specified site — *see* Neoplasm, by site, malignant
- unspecified site 191.9

Glioma (malignant) (M9380/3)
- astrocytic (M9400/3)
  - specified site — *see* Neoplasm, by site, malignant
  - unspecified site 191.9
- mixed (M9382/3)
  - specified site — *see* Neoplasm, by site, malignant
  - unspecified site 191.9
- nose 748.1
- specified site NEC — *see* Neoplasm, by site, malignant
- subependymal (M9383/1) 237.5
- unspecified site 191.9

Gliomatosis cerebri (M9381/3) 191.0

Glioneuroma (M9505/1) — *see* Neoplasm, by site, uncertain behavior

Gliosarcoma (M9380/3)
- specified site — *see* Neoplasm, by site, malignant
- unspecified site 191.9

Gliosis (cerebral) 349.89
- spinal 336.0

Glisson's
- cirrhosis — *see* Cirrhosis, portal
- disease (*see also* Rickets) 268.0

Glissonitis 573.3

Globinuria 791.2

Globus 306.4
- hystericus 300.11

Glomangioma (M8712/0) — *see also* Hemangioma 228.00

Glomangiosarcoma (M8710/3) — *see* Neoplasm, connective tissue, malignant

Glomerular nephritis — *see also* Nephritis 583.9

Glomerulitis — *see also* Nephritis 583.9

Glomerulonephritis — *see also* Nephritis 583.9
- with
  - edema (*see also* Nephrosis) 581.9
  - lesion of
    - exudative nephritis 583.89
    - interstitial nephritis (diffuse) (focal) 583.89
    - necrotizing glomerulitis 583.4
      - acute 580.4
      - chronic 582.4
    - renal necrosis 583.9
      - cortical 583.6
      - medullary 583.7
    - specified pathology NEC 583.89
      - acute 580.89
      - chronic 582.89
  - necrosis, renal 583.9
    - cortical 583.6
    - medullary (papillary) 583.7
  - specified pathology or lesion NEC 583.89
- acute 580.9
  - with
    - exudative nephritis 580.89
    - interstitial nephritis (diffuse) (focal) 580.89
    - necrotizing glomerulitis 580.4
  - extracapillary with epithelial crescents 580.4
  - poststreptococcal 580.0
  - proliferative (diffuse) 580.0
  - rapidly progressive 580.4
  - specified pathology NEC 580.89
- arteriolar (*see also* Hypertension, kidney) 403.90
- arteriosclerotic (*see also* Hypertension, kidney) 403.90
- ascending (*see also* Pyelitis) 590.80
- basement membrane NEC 583.89
  - with
    - pulmonary hemorrhage (Goodpasture's syndrome) 446.21 *[583.81]*
- chronic 582.9
  - with
    - exudative nephritis 582.89
    - interstitial nephritis (diffuse) (focal) 582.89
    - necrotizing glomerulitis 582.4
    - specified pathology or lesion NEC 582.89
  - endothelial 582.2
  - extracapillary with epithelial crescents 582.4
  - hypocomplementemic persistent 582.2
  - lobular 582.2
  - membranoproliferative 582.2
  - membranous 582.1
    - and proliferative (mixed) 582.2
    - sclerosing 582.1
  - mesangiocapillary 582.2
  - mixed membranous and proliferative 582.2
  - proliferative (diffuse) 582.0
  - rapidly progressive 582.4
  - sclerosing 582.1
- cirrhotic — *see* Sclerosis, renal
- desquamative — *see* Nephrosis
- due to or associated with
  - amyloidosis 277.39 *[583.81]*
    - with nephrotic syndrome 277.39 *[581.81]*
    - chronic 277.39 *[582.81]*
  - diabetes mellitus 250.4 ☑ *[583.81]*

Glomerulonephritis — *see also* Nephritis — *continued*
- due to or associated with — *continued*
  - diabetes mellitus — *continued*
    - with nephrotic syndrome 250.4 ☑ *[581.81]*
      - due to secondary diabetes 249.4 ☑ *[581.81]* ●
    - due to secondary diabetes 249.4 ☑ *[581.81]* ●
  - diphtheria 032.89 *[580.81]*
  - gonococcal infection (acute) 098.19 *[583.81]*
    - chronic or duration of 2 months or over 098.39 *[583.81]*
  - infectious hepatitis 070.9 *[580.81]*
  - malaria (with nephrotic syndrome) 084.9 *[581.81]*
  - mumps 072.79 *[580.81]*
  - polyarteritis (nodosa) (with nephrotic syndrome) 446.0 *[581.81]*
  - specified pathology NEC 583.89
    - acute 580.89
    - chronic 582.89
  - streptotrichosis 039.8 *[583.81]*
  - subacute bacterial endocarditis 421.0 *[580.81]*
  - syphilis (late) 095.4
    - congenital 090.5 *[583.81]*
    - early 091.69 *[583.81]*
  - systemic lupus erythematosus 710.0 *[583.81]*
    - with nephrotic syndrome 710.0 *[581.81]*
    - chronic 710.0 *[582.81]*
  - tuberculosis (*see also* Tuberculosis) 016.0 ☑ *[583.81]*
  - typhoid fever 002.0 *[580.81]*
- extracapillary with epithelial crescents 583.4
  - acute 580.4
  - chronic 582.4
- exudative 583.89
  - acute 580.89
  - chronic 582.89
- focal (*see also* Nephritis) 583.9
  - embolic 580.4
- granular 582.89
- granulomatous 582.89
- hydremic (*see also* Nephrosis) 581.9
- hypocomplementemic persistent 583.2
  - with nephrotic syndrome 581.2
  - chronic 582.2
- immune complex NEC 583.89
- infective (*see also* Pyelitis) 590.80
- interstitial (diffuse) (focal) 583.89
  - with nephrotic syndrome 581.89
  - acute 580.89
  - chronic 582.89
- latent or quiescent 582.9
- lobular 583.2
  - with nephrotic syndrome 581.2
  - chronic 582.2
- membranoproliferative 583.2
  - with nephrotic syndrome 581.2
  - chronic 582.2
- membranous 583.1
  - with nephrotic syndrome 581.1
  - and proliferative (mixed) 583.2
    - with nephrotic syndrome 581.2
    - chronic 582.2
  - chronic 582.1
  - sclerosing 582.1
    - with nephrotic syndrome 581.1
- mesangiocapillary 583.2
  - with nephrotic syndrome 581.2
  - chronic 582.2
- minimal change 581.3
- mixed membranous and proliferative 583.2
  - with nephrotic syndrome 581.2
  - chronic 582.2
- necrotizing 583.4
  - acute 580.4

Glomerulonephritis — *see also* Nephritis — *continued*
- necrotizing — *continued*
  - chronic 582.4
- nephrotic (*see also* Nephrosis) 581.9
- old — *see* Glomerulonephritis, chronic
- parenchymatous 581.89
- poststreptococcal 580.0
- proliferative (diffuse) 583.0
  - with nephrotic syndrome 581.0
  - acute 580.0
  - chronic 582.0
- purulent (*see also* Pyelitis) 590.80
- quiescent — *see* Nephritis, chronic
- rapidly progressive 583.4
  - acute 580.4
  - chronic 582.4
- sclerosing membranous (chronic) 582.1
  - with nephrotic syndrome 581.1
- septic (*see also* Pyelitis) 590.80
- specified pathology or lesion NEC 583.89
  - with nephrotic syndrome 581.89
  - acute 580.89
  - chronic 582.89
- suppurative (acute) (disseminated) (*see also* Pyelitis) 590.80
- toxic — *see* Nephritis, acute
- tubal, tubular — *see* Nephrosis, tubular
- type II (Ellis) — *see* Nephrosis
- vascular — *see* Hypertension, kidney

Glomerulosclerosis — *see also* Sclerosis, renal 587
- focal 582.1
  - with nephrotic syndrome 581.1
- intercapillary (nodular) (with diabetes) 250.4 ☑ *[581.81]*
  - due to secondary diabetes 249.4 ☑ *[581.81]* ●

Glossagra 529.6

Glossalgia 529.6

Glossitis 529.0
- areata exfoliativa 529.1
- atrophic 529.4
- benign migratory 529.1
- gangrenous 529.0
- Hunter's 529.4
- median rhomboid 529.2
- Moeller's 529.4
- pellagrous 265.2

Glossocele 529.8

Glossodynia 529.6
- exfoliativa 529.4

Glossoncus 529.8

Glossophytia 529.3

Glossoplegia 529.8

Glossoptosis 529.8

Glossopyrosis 529.6

Glossotrichia 529.3

Glossy skin 701.9

Glottis — *see* condition

Glottitis — *see* Glossitis

Glucagonoma (M8152/0)
- malignant (M8152/3)
  - pancreas 157.4
  - specified site NEC — *see* Neoplasm, by site, malignant
  - unspecified site 157.4
- pancreas 211.7
- specified site NEC — *see* Neoplasm, by site, benign
- unspecified site 211.7

Glucoglycinuria 270.7

Glue ear syndrome 381.20

Glue sniffing (airplane glue) — *see also* Dependence 304.6 ☑

Glycinemia (with methylmalonic acidemia) 270.7

Glycinuria (renal) (with ketosis) 270.0

Glycogen
- infiltration (*see also* Disease, glycogen storage) 271.0
- storage disease (*see also* Disease, glycogen storage) 271.0

- **Glycogenosis** — *see also* Disease, glycogen storage 271.0
  - cardiac 271.0 *[425.7]*
  - Cori, types I-VII 271.0
  - diabetic, secondary 250.8 ☑ *[259.8]*
    - due to secondary diabetes 249.8 ☑ *[259.8]* ●
  - diffuse (with hepatic cirrhosis) 271.0
  - generalized 271.0
  - glucose-6-phosphatase deficiency 271.0
  - hepatophosphorylase deficiency 271.0
  - hepatorenal 271.0
  - myophosphorylase deficiency 271.0
- **Glycopenia** 251.2
- **Glycopeptide**
  - intermediate staphylococcus aureus (GISA) V09.8 ☑
  - resistant
    - enterococcus V09.8 ☑
    - staphylococcus aureus (GRSA) V09.8 ☑
- **Glycoprolinuria** 270.8
- **Glycosuria** 791.5
  - renal 271.4
- **Gnathostoma** (spinigerum) (infection) (infestation) 128.1
  - wandering swellings from 128.1
- **Gnathostomiasis** 128.1
- **Goiter** (adolescent) (colloid) (diffuse) (dipping) (due to iodine deficiency) (endemic) (euthyroid) (heart) (hyperplastic) (internal) (intrathoracic) (juvenile) (mixed type) (nonendemic) (parenchymatous) (plunging) (sporadic) (subclavicular) (substernal) 240.9
  - with
    - hyperthyroidism (recurrent) (*see also* Goiter, toxic) 242.0 ☑
    - thyrotoxicosis (*see also* Goiter, toxic) 242.0 ☑
  - adenomatous (*see also* Goiter, nodular) 241.9
  - cancerous (M8000/3) 193
  - complicating pregnancy, childbirth, or puerperium 648.1 ☑
  - congenital 246.1
  - cystic (*see also* Goiter, nodular) 241.9
  - due to enzyme defect in synthesis of thyroid hormone (butane-insoluble iodine) (coupling) (deiodinase) (iodide trapping or organification) (iodotyrosine dehalogenase) (peroxidase) 246.1
  - dyshormonogenic 246.1
  - exophthalmic (*see also* Goiter, toxic) 242.0 ☑
  - familial (with deaf-mutism) 243
  - fibrous 245.3
  - lingual 759.2
  - lymphadenoid 245.2
  - malignant (M8000/3) 193
  - multinodular (nontoxic) 241.1
    - toxic or with hyperthyroidism (*see also* Goiter, toxic) 242.2 ☑
  - nodular (nontoxic) 241.9
    - with
      - hyperthyroidism (*see also* Goiter, toxic) 242.3 ☑
      - thyrotoxicosis (*see also* Goiter, toxic) 242.3 ☑
    - endemic 241.9
    - exophthalmic (diffuse) (*see also* Goiter, toxic) 242.0 ☑
    - multinodular (nontoxic) 241.1
    - sporadic 241.9
    - toxic (*see also* Goiter, toxic) 242.3 ☑
    - uninodular (nontoxic) 241.0
  - nontoxic (nodular) 241.9
    - multinodular 241.1
    - uninodular 241.0
  - pulsating (*see also* Goiter, toxic) 242.0 ☑
  - simple 240.0

Goiter — *continued*
  - toxic 242.0 ☑

> *Note — Use the following fifth-digit subclassification with category 242:*
>
> 0 *without mention of thyrotoxic crisis or storm*
>
> 1 *with mention of thyrotoxic crisis or storm*

  - adenomatous 242.3 ☑
    - multinodular 242.2 ☑
    - uninodular 242.1 ☑
  - multinodular 242.2 ☑
  - nodular 242.3 ☑
    - multinodular 242.2 ☑
    - uninodular 242.1 ☑
  - uninodular 242.1 ☑
- uninodular (nontoxic) 241.0
  - toxic or with hyperthyroidism (*see also* Goiter, toxic) 242.1 ☑
- **Goldberg (-Maxwell) (-Morris) syndrome** (testicular feminization) 259.51 ▲
- **Goldblatt's**
  - hypertension 440.1
  - kidney 440.1
- **Goldenhar's syndrome** (oculoauriculovertebral dysplasia) 756.0
- **Goldflam-Erb disease or syndrome** 358.00
- **Goldscheider's disease** (epidermolysis bullosa) 757.39
- **Goldstein's disease** (familial hemorrhagic telangiectasia) 448.0
- **Golfer's elbow** 726.32
- **Goltz-Gorlin syndrome** (dermal hypoplasia) 757.39
- **Gonadoblastoma** (M9073/1)
  - specified site — *see* Neoplasm, by site uncertain behavior
  - unspecified site
    - female 236.2
    - male 236.4
- **Gonecystitis** — *see also* Vesiculitis 608.0
- **Gongylonemiasis** 125.6
  - mouth 125.6
- **Goniosynechiae** 364.73
- **Gonococcemia** 098.89
- **Gonococcus, gonococcal** (disease) (infection) — *see also* condition 098.0
  - anus 098.7
  - bursa 098.52
  - chronic NEC 098.2
  - complicating pregnancy, childbirth, or puerperium 647.1 ☑
    - affecting fetus or newborn 760.2
  - conjunctiva, conjunctivitis (neonatorum) 098.40
  - dermatosis 098.89
  - endocardium 098.84
  - epididymo-orchitis 098.13
    - chronic or duration of 2 months or over 098.33
  - eye (newborn) 098.40
  - fallopian tube (chronic) 098.37
    - acute 098.17
  - genitourinary (acute) (organ) (system) (tract) (*see also* Gonorrhea) 098.0
    - lower 098.0
      - chronic 098.2
    - upper 098.10
      - chronic 098.30
  - heart NEC 098.85
  - joint 098.50
  - keratoderma 098.81
  - keratosis (blennorrhagica) 098.81
  - lymphatic (gland) (node) 098.89
  - meninges 098.82
  - orchitis (acute) 098.13
    - chronic or duration of 2 months or over 098.33
  - pelvis (acute) 098.19

Gonococcus, gonococcal — *see also* condition — *continued*
  - pelvis — *continued*
    - chronic or duration of 2 months or over 098.39
  - pericarditis 098.83
  - peritonitis 098.86
  - pharyngitis 098.6
  - pharynx 098.6
  - proctitis 098.7
  - pyosalpinx (chronic) 098.37
    - acute 098.17
  - rectum 098.7
  - septicemia 098.89
  - skin 098.89
  - specified site NEC 098.89
  - synovitis 098.51
  - tendon sheath 098.51
  - throat 098.6
  - urethra (acute) 098.0
    - chronic or duration of 2 months or over 098.2
  - vulva (acute) 098.0
    - chronic or duration of 2 months or over 098.2
- **Gonocytoma** (M9073/1)
  - specified site — *see* Neoplasm, by site, uncertain behavior
  - unspecified site
    - female 236.2
    - male 236.4
- **Gonorrhea** 098.0
  - acute 098.0
  - Bartholin's gland (acute) 098.0
    - chronic or duration of 2 months or over 098.2
  - bladder (acute) 098.11
    - chronic or duration of 2 months or over 098.31
  - carrier (suspected of) V02.7
  - cervix (acute) 098.15
    - chronic or duration of 2 months or over 098.35
  - chronic 098.2
  - complicating pregnancy, childbirth, or puerperium 647.1 ☑
    - affecting fetus or newborn 760.2
  - conjunctiva, conjunctivitis (neonatorum) 098.40
  - contact V01.6
  - Cowper's gland (acute) 098.0
    - chronic or duration of 2 months or over 098.2
  - duration of two months or over 098.2
  - exposure to V01.6
  - fallopian tube (chronic) 098.37
    - acute 098.17
  - genitourinary (acute) (organ) (system) (tract) 098.0
    - chronic 098.2
    - duration of two months or over 098.2
  - kidney (acute) 098.19
    - chronic or duration of 2 months or over 098.39
  - ovary (acute) 098.19
    - chronic or duration of 2 months or over 098.39
  - pelvis (acute) 098.19
    - chronic or duration of 2 months or over 098.39
  - penis (acute) 098.0
    - chronic or duration of 2 months or over 098.2
  - prostate (acute) 098.12
    - chronic or duration of 2 months or over 098.32
  - seminal vesicle (acute) 098.14
    - chronic or duration of 2 months or over 098.34
  - specified site NEC — *see* Gonococcus
  - spermatic cord (acute) 098.14
    - chronic or duration of 2 months or over 098.34
  - urethra (acute) 098.0

Gonorrhea — *continued*
  - urethra — *continued*
    - chronic or duration of 2 months or over 098.2
  - vagina (acute) 098.0
    - chronic or duration of 2 months or over 098.2
  - vas deferens (acute) 098.14
    - chronic or duration of 2 months or over 098.34
  - vulva (acute) 098.0
    - chronic or duration of 2 months or over 098.2
- **Goodpasture's syndrome** (pneumorenal) 446.21
- **Good's syndrome** 279.06
- **Gopalan's syndrome** (burning feet) 266.2
- **Gordon's disease** (exudative enteropathy) 579.8
- **Gorlin-Chaudhry-Moss syndrome** 759.89
- **Gougerot-Blum syndrome** (pigmented purpuric lichenoid dermatitis) 709.1
- **Gougerot-Carteaud disease or syndrome** (confluent reticulate papillomatosis) 701.8
- **Gougerot-Hailey-Hailey disease** (benign familial chronic pemphigus) 757.39
- **Gougerot (-Houwer) -Sjögren syndrome** (keratoconjunctivitis sicca) 710.2
- **Gougerot's syndrome** (trisymptomatic) 709.1
- **Gouley's syndrome** (constrictive pericarditis) 423.2
- **Goundou** 102.6
- **Gout, gouty** 274.9
  - with specified manifestations NEC 274.89
  - arthritis (acute) 274.0
  - arthropathy 274.0
  - degeneration, heart 274.82
  - diathesis 274.9
  - eczema 274.89
  - episcleritis 274.89 *[379.09]*
  - external ear (tophus) 274.81
  - glomerulonephritis 274.10
  - iritis 274.89 *[364.11]*
  - joint 274.0
  - kidney 274.10
  - lead 984.9
    - specified type of lead — *see* Table of Drugs and Chemicals
  - nephritis 274.10
  - neuritis 274.89 *[357.4]*
  - phlebitis 274.89 *[451.9]*
  - rheumatic 714.0
  - saturnine 984.9
    - specified type of lead — *see* Table of Drugs and Chemicals
  - spondylitis 274.0
  - synovitis 274.0
  - syphilitic 095.8
  - tophi 274.0
    - ear 274.81
    - heart 274.82
    - specified site NEC 274.82
- **Gowers'**
  - muscular dystrophy 359.1
  - syndrome (vasovagal attack) 780.2
- **Gowers-Paton-Kennedy syndrome** 377.04
- **Gradenigo's syndrome** 383.02
- **Graft-versus-host disease** 279.50 ▲
  - bone marrow 996.85 ●
  - due to organ transplant NEC — *see* Complications, transplant, organ
- **Graham Steell's murmur** (pulmonic regurgitation) — *see also* Endocarditis, pulmonary 424.3
- **Grain-handlers' disease or lung** 495.8
- **Grain mite** (itch) 133.8
- **Grand**
  - mal (idiopathic) (*see also* Epilepsy) 345.1 ☑

☑ Additional Digit Required — Refer to the Tabular List for Digit Selection

Subterms under main terms may continue to next column or page

▶◀ Revised Text ● New Line ▲ Revised Code

Grand — *continued*
- mal (*see also* Epilepsy) — *continued*
  - hysteria of Charcôt 300.11
  - nonrecurrent or isolated 780.39
- multipara
  - affecting management of labor and delivery 659.4 ☑
  - status only (not pregnant) V61.5

Granite workers' lung 502

Granular — *see also* condition
- inflammation, pharynx 472.1
- kidney (contracting) (*see also* Sclerosis, renal) 587
- liver — *see* Cirrhosis, liver
- nephritis — *see* Nephritis

Granulation tissue, abnormal — *see also* Granuloma
- abnormal or excessive 701.5
- postmastoidectomy cavity 383.33
- postoperative 701.5
- skin 701.5

Granulocytopenia, granulocytopenic (primary) 288.00
- malignant 288.09

Granuloma NEC 686.1
- abdomen (wall) 568.89
  - skin (pyogenicum) 686.1
    - from residual foreign body 709.4
- annulare 695.89
- anus 569.49
- apical 522.6
- appendix 543.9
- aural 380.23
- beryllium (skin) 709.4
  - lung 503
- bone (*see also* Osteomyelitis) 730.1 ☑
  - eosinophilic 277.89
  - from residual foreign body 733.99
- canaliculus lacrimalis 375.81
- cerebral 348.8
- cholesterin, middle ear 385.82
- coccidioidal (progressive) 114.3
  - lung 114.4
  - meninges 114.2
  - primary (lung) 114.0
- colon 569.89
- conjunctiva 372.61
- dental 522.6
- ear, middle (cholesterin) 385.82
  - with otitis media — *see* Otitis media
- eosinophilic 277.89
  - bone 277.89
  - lung 277.89
  - oral mucosa 528.9
- exuberant 701.5
- eyelid 374.89
- facial
  - lethal midline 446.3
  - malignant 446.3
- faciale 701.8
- fissuratum (gum) 523.8
- foot NEC 686.1
- foreign body (in soft tissue) NEC 728.82
  - bone 733.99
  - in operative wound 998.4
  - muscle 728.82
  - skin 709.4
  - subcutaneous tissue 709.4
- fungoides 202.1 ☑
- gangraenescens 446.3
- giant cell (central) (jaw) (reparative) 526.3
  - gingiva 523.8
  - peripheral (gingiva) 523.8
- gland (lymph) 289.3
- Hodgkin's (M9661/3) 201.1 ☑
- ileum 569.89
- infectious NEC 136.9
- inguinale (Donovan) 099.2
  - venereal 099.2
- intestine 569.89
- iridocyclitis 364.10
- jaw (bone) 526.3

Granuloma — *continued*
- jaw — *continued*
  - reparative giant cell 526.3
- kidney (*see also* Infection, kidney) 590.9
- lacrimal sac 375.81
- larynx 478.79
- lethal midline 446.3
- lipid 277.89
- lipoid 277.89
- liver 572.8
- lung (infectious) (*see also* Fibrosis, lung) 515
  - coccidioidal 114.4
  - eosinophilic 277.89
- lymph gland 289.3
- Majocchi's 110.6
- malignant, face 446.3
- mandible 526.3
- mediastinum 519.3
- midline 446.3
- monilial 112.3
- muscle 728.82
  - from residual foreign body 728.82
- nasal sinus (*see also* Sinusitis) 473.9
- operation wound 998.59
  - foreign body 998.4
  - stitch (external) 998.89
    - internal wound 998.89
  - talc 998.7
- oral mucosa, eosinophilic or pyogenic 528.9
- orbit, orbital 376.11
- paracoccidioidal 116.1
- penis, venereal 099.2
- periapical 522.6
- peritoneum 568.89
  - due to ova of helminths NEC (*see also* Helminthiasis) 128.9
- postmastoidectomy cavity 383.33
- postoperative — *see* Granuloma, operation wound
- prostate 601.8
- pudendi (ulcerating) 099.2
- pudendorum (ulcerative) 099.2
- pulp, internal (tooth) 521.49
- pyogenic, pyogenicum (skin) 686.1
  - maxillary alveolar ridge 522.6
  - oral mucosa 528.9
- rectum 569.49
- reticulohistiocytic 277.89
- rubrum nasi 705.89
- sarcoid 135
- Schistosoma 120.9
- septic (skin) 686.1
- silica (skin) 709.4
- sinus (accessory) (infectional) (nasal) (*see also* Sinusitis) 473.9
- skin (pyogenicum) 686.1
  - from foreign body or material 709.4
- sperm 608.89
- spine
  - syphilitic (epidural) 094.89
  - tuberculous (*see also* Tuberculosis) 015.0 ☑ *[730.88]*
- stitch (postoperative) 998.89
  - internal wound 998.89
- suppurative (skin) 686.1
- suture (postoperative) 998.89
  - internal wound 998.89
- swimming pool 031.1
- talc 728.82
  - in operation wound 998.7
- telangiectaticum (skin) 686.1
- tracheostomy 519.09
- trichophyticum 110.6
- tropicum 102.4
- umbilicus 686.1
  - newborn 771.4
- urethra 599.84
- uveitis 364.10
- vagina 099.2
- venereum 099.2
- vocal cords 478.5
- Wegener's (necrotizing respiratory granulomatosis) 446.4

Granulomatosis NEC 686.1
- disciformis chronica et progressiva 709.3
- infantiseptica 771.2
- lipoid 277.89
- lipophagic, intestinal 040.2
- miliary 027.0
- necrotizing, respiratory 446.4
- progressive, septic 288.1
- Wegener's (necrotizing respiratory) 446.4

Granulomatous tissue — *see* Granuloma

Granulosis rubra nasi 705.89

Graphite fibrosis (of lung) 503

Graphospasm 300.89
- organic 333.84

Grating scapula 733.99

Gravel (urinary) — *see also* Calculus 592.9

Graves' disease (exophthalmic goiter) — *see also* Goiter, toxic 242.0 ☑

Gravis — *see* condition

Grawitz's tumor (hypernephroma) (M8312/3) 189.0

Grayness, hair (premature) 704.3
- congenital 757.4

Gray or grey syndrome (chloramphenicol) (newborn) 779.4

Greenfield's disease 330.0

Green sickness 280.9

Greenstick fracture — *see* Fracture, by site

Greig's syndrome (hypertelorism) 756.0

Grief 309.0

Griesinger's disease — *see also* Ancylostomiasis 126.9

Grinders'
- asthma 502
- lung 502
- phthisis (*see also* Tuberculosis) 011.4 ☑

Grinding, teeth 306.8

Grip
- Dabney's 074.1
- devil's 074.1

Grippe, grippal — *see also* Influenza
- Balkan 083.0
- intestinal 487.8
- summer 074.8

Grippy cold 487.1

Grisel's disease 723.5

Groin — *see* condition

Grooved
- nails (transverse) 703.8
- tongue 529.5
  - congenital 750.13

Ground itch 126.9

Growing pains, children 781.99

Growth (fungoid) (neoplastic) (new) (M8000/1) — *see also* Neoplasm, by site, unspecified nature
- adenoid (vegetative) 474.12
- benign (M8000/0) — *see* Neoplasm, by site, benign
- fetal, poor 764.9 ☑
  - affecting management of pregnancy 656.5 ☑
- malignant (M8000/3) — *see* Neoplasm, by site, malignant
- rapid, childhood V21.0
- secondary (M8000/6) — *see* Neoplasm, by site, malignant, secondary

GRSA (glycopeptide resistant staphylococcus aureus) V09.8 ☑

Gruber's hernia — *see* Hernia, Gruber's

Gruby's disease (tinea tonsurans) 110.0

● **GSS** (Gerstmann-Sträussler-Scheinker syndrome) 046.71 ●

G-trisomy 758.0

Guama fever 066.3

Gubler (-Millard) paralysis or syndrome 344.89

Guérin-Stern syndrome (arthrogryposis multiplex congenita) 754.89

Guertin's disease (electric chorea) 049.8

Guillain-Barré disease or syndrome 357.0

Guinea worms (infection) (infestation) 125.7

Guinon's disease (motor-verbal tic) 307.23

Gull and Sutton's disease — *see* Hypertension, kidney

Gull's disease (thyroid atrophy with myxedema) 244.8

Gum — *see* condition

Gumboil 522.7

Gumma (syphilitic) 095.9
- artery 093.89
  - cerebral or spinal 094.89
- bone 095.5
  - of yaws (late) 102.6
- brain 094.89
- cauda equina 094.89
- central nervous system NEC 094.9
- ciliary body 095.8 *[364.11]*
- congenital 090.5
  - testis 090.5
- eyelid 095.8 *[373.5]*
- heart 093.89
- intracranial 094.89
- iris 095.8 *[364.11]*
- kidney 095.4
- larynx 095.8
- leptomeninges 094.2
- liver 095.3
- meninges 094.2
- myocardium 093.82
- nasopharynx 095.8
- neurosyphilitic 094.9
- nose 095.8
- orbit 095.8
- palate (soft) 095.8
- penis 095.8
- pericardium 093.81
- pharynx 095.8
- pituitary 095.8
- scrofulous (see also Tuberculosis) 017.0 ☑
- skin 095.8
- specified site NEC 095.8
- spinal cord 094.89
- tongue 095.8
- tonsil 095.8
- trachea 095.8
- tuberculous (*see also* Tuberculosis) 017.0 ☑
- ulcerative due to yaws 102.4
- ureter 095.8
- yaws 102.4
  - bone 102.6

Gunn's syndrome (jaw-winking syndrome) 742.8

Gunshot wound — *see also* Wound, open, by site
- fracture — *see* Fracture, by site, open
- internal organs (abdomen, chest, or pelvis) — *see* Injury, internal, by site, with open wound
- intracranial — *see* Laceration, brain, with open intracranial wound

Günther's disease or syndrome (congenital erythropoietic porphyria) 277.1

Gustatory hallucination 780.1

Gynandrism 752.7

Gynandroblastoma (M8632/1)
- specified site — *see* Neoplasm, by site, uncertain behavior
- unspecified site
  - female 236.2
  - male 236.4

Gynandromorphism 752.7

Gynatresia (congenital) 752.49

Gynecoid pelvis, male 738.6

Gynecological examination V72.31
- for contraceptive maintenance V25.40

Gynecomastia 611.1

Gynephobia 300.29

Gyrate scalp 757.39

H

- **Haas' disease** (osteochondrosis head of humerus) 732.3
- **Habermann's disease** (acute parapsoriasis varioliformis) 696.2
- **Habit, habituation**
  - chorea 307.22
  - disturbance, child 307.9
  - drug (*see also* Dependence) 304.9 ☑
  - laxative (*see also* Abuse, drugs, nondependent) 305.9 ☑
  - spasm 307.20
    - chronic 307.22
    - transient (of childhood) 307.21
  - tic 307.20
    - chronic 307.22
    - transient (of childhood) 307.21
  - use of
    - nonprescribed drugs (*see also* Abuse, drugs, nondependent) 305.9 ☑
    - patent medicines (*see also* Abuse, drugs, nondependent) 305.9 ☑
  - vomiting 536.2
- **Hadfield-Clarke syndrome** (pancreatic infantilism) 577.8
- **Haff disease** 985.1
- **Hageman factor defect, deficiency, or disease** — *see also* Defect, coagulation 286.3
- **Haglund's disease** (osteochondrosis os tibiale externum) 732.5
- **Haglund-Läwen-Fründ syndrome** 717.89
- **Hagner's disease** (hypertrophic pulmonary osteoarthropathy) 731.2
- **Hag teeth, tooth** 524.39
- **Hailey-Hailey disease** (benign familial chronic pemphigus) 757.39
- **Hair** — *see also* condition
  - plucking 307.9
- **Hairball in stomach** 935.2
- **Hairy black tongue** 529.3
- **Half vertebra** 756.14
- **Halitosis** 784.99
- **Hallermann-Streiff syndrome** 756.0
- **Hallervorden-Spatz disease or syndrome** 333.0
- **Hallopeau's**
  - acrodermatitis (continua) 696.1
  - disease (lichen sclerosis et atrophicus) 701.0
- **Hallucination** (auditory) (gustatory) (olfactory) (tactile) 780.1
  - alcohol-induced 291.3
  - drug-induced 292.12
  - visual 368.16
- **Hallucinosis** 298.9
  - alcohol-induced (acute) 291.3
  - drug-induced 292.12
- **Hallus** — *see* Hallux
- **Hallux** 735.9
  - limitus 735.8
  - malleus (acquired) 735.3
  - rigidus (acquired) 735.2
    - congenital 755.66
    - late effects of rickets 268.1
  - valgus (acquired) 735.0
    - congenital 755.66
  - varus (acquired) 735.1
    - congenital 755.66
- **Halo, visual** 368.15
- **Hamartoblastoma** 759.6
- **Hamartoma** 759.6
  - epithelial (gingival), odontogenic, central, or peripheral (M9321/0) 213.1
    - upper jaw (bone) 213.0
  - vascular 757.32
- **Hamartosis, hamartoses** NEC 759.6
- **Hamman's disease or syndrome** (spontaneous mediastinal emphysema) 518.1
- **Hamman-Rich syndrome** (diffuse interstitial pulmonary fibrosis) 516.3
- **Hammer toe** (acquired) 735.4
  - congenital 755.66
  - late effects of rickets 268.1
- **Hand** — *see* condition
- **Hand-foot syndrome** 693.0
- **Hand-Schüller-Christian disease or syndrome** (chronic histiocytosis x) 277.89
- **Hanging** (asphyxia) (strangulation) (suffocation) 994.7
- **Hangnail** (finger) (with lymphangitis) 681.02
- **Hangover** (alcohol) — *see also* Abuse, drugs, nondependent 305.0 ☑
- **Hanot-Chauffard (-Troisier) syndrome** (bronze diabetes) 275.0
- **Hanot's cirrhosis or disease** — *see* Cirrhosis, biliary
- **Hansen's disease** (leprosy) 030.9
  - benign form 030.1
  - malignant form 030.0
- **Harada's disease or syndrome** 363.22
- **Hard chancre** 091.0
- **Hardening**
  - artery — *see* Arteriosclerosis
  - brain 348.8
  - liver 571.8
- **Hard firm prostate** 600.10
  - with
    - urinary
      - obstruction 600.11
      - retention 600.11
- **Harelip** — *see also* Cleft, lip 749.10
- **Hare's syndrome** (M8010/3) (carcinoma, pulmonary apex) 162.3
- **Harkavy's syndrome** 446.0
- **Harlequin** (fetus) 757.1
  - color change syndrome 779.89
- **Harley's disease** (intermittent hemoglobinuria) 283.2
- **Harris'**
  - lines 733.91
  - syndrome (organic hyperinsulinism) 251.1
- **Hart's disease or syndrome** (pellagra-cerebellar ataxia-renal aminoaciduria) 270.0
- **Hartmann's pouch** (abnormal sacculation of gallbladder neck) 575.8
  - of intestine V44.3
    - attention to V55.3
- **Hartnup disease** (pellagra-cerebellar ataxia-renal aminoaciduria) 270.0
- **Harvester lung** 495.0
- **Hashimoto's disease or struma** (struma lymphomatosa) 245.2
- **Hassall-Henle bodies** (corneal warts) 371.41
- **Haut mal** — *see also* Epilepsy 345.1 ☑
- **Haverhill fever** 026.1
- **Hawaiian wood rose dependence** 304.5 ☑
- **Hawkins' keloid** 701.4
- **Hay**
  - asthma (*see also* Asthma) 493.0 ☑
  - fever (allergic) (with rhinitis) 477.9
    - with asthma (bronchial) (*see also* Asthma) 493.0 ☑
    - allergic, due to grass, pollen, ragweed, or tree 477.0
    - conjunctivitis 372.05
    - due to
      - dander, animal (cat) (dog) 477.2
      - dust 477.8
      - fowl 477.8
      - hair, animal (cat) (dog) 477.2
      - pollen 477.0
      - specified allergen other than pollen 477.8
- **Hayem-Faber syndrome** (achlorhydric anemia) 280.9
- **Hayem-Widal syndrome** (acquired hemolytic jaundice) 283.9
- **Haygarth's nodosities** 715.04
- **Hazard-Crile tumor** (M8350/3) 193
- **Hb** (abnormal)
  - disease — *see* Disease, hemoglobin
  - trait — *see* Trait
- **H disease** 270.0
- **Head** — *see also* condition
  - banging 307.3
- **Headache** 784.0
  - allergic 339.00 ▲
  - associated with sexual activity 339.82 ●
  - cluster 339.00 ▲
    - chronic 339.02 ●
    - episodic 339.01 ●
  - daily ●
    - chronic 784.0 ●
    - new persistent (NPDH) 339.42 ●
  - drug induced 339.3 ●
  - due to
    - loss, spinal fluid 349.0
    - lumbar puncture 349.0
    - saddle block 349.0
  - emotional 307.81
  - histamine 339.00 ▲
  - hypnic 339.81 ●
  - lumbar puncture 349.0
  - medication overuse 339.3 ●
  - menopausal 627.2
  - menstrual 346.4 ☑ ●
  - migraine 346.9 ☑
  - nasal septum 784.0 ●
  - nonorganic origin 307.81
  - orgasmic 339.82 ●
  - postspinal 349.0
  - post-traumatic 339.20 ●
    - acute 339.21 ●
    - chronic 339.22 ●
  - premenstrual 346.4 ☑ ●
  - preorgasmic 339.82 ●
  - primary ●
    - cough 339.83 ●
    - exertional 339.84 ●
    - stabbing 339.85 ●
    - thunderclap 339.43 ●
  - psychogenic 307.81
  - psychophysiologic 307.81
  - rebound 339.3 ●
  - short lasting unilateral neuralgiform ● with conjunctival injection and ● tearing (SUNCT) 339.05 ●
  - sick 346.9 ☑ ▲
  - spinal 349.0
    - complicating labor and delivery 668.8 ☑
    - postpartum 668.8 ☑
  - spinal fluid loss 349.0
  - syndrome ●
    - cluster 339.00 ●
    - complicated NEC 339.44 ●
    - periodic in child or adolescent 346.2 ☑ ●
    - specified NEC 339.89 ●
  - tension 307.81
    - type 339.10 ●
      - chronic 339.11 ●
      - episodic 339.12 ●
  - vascular 784.0
    - migraine type 346.9 ☑
  - vasomotor 346.9 ☑
- **Health**
  - advice V65.4 ☑
  - audit V70.0
  - checkup V70.0
  - education V65.4 ☑
  - hazard (*see also* History of) V15.9
    - falling V15.88
    - specified cause NEC V15.89
  - instruction V65.4 ☑
  - services provided because (of)
    - boarding school residence V60.6
    - holiday relief for person providing home care V60.5
    - inadequate
      - housing V60.1
      - resources V60.2
    - lack of housing V60.0

Health — *continued*

  - services provided because — *continued*
    - no care available in home V60.4
    - person living alone V60.3
    - poverty V60.3
    - residence in institution V60.6
    - specified cause NEC V60.8
    - vacation relief for person providing home care V60.5
- **Healthy**
  - donor (*see also* Donor) V59.9
  - infant or child
    - accompanying sick mother V65.0
    - receiving care V20.1
  - person
    - accompanying sick relative V65.0
    - admitted for sterilization V25.2
    - receiving prophylactic inoculation or vaccination (*see also* Vaccination, prophylactic) V05.9
- **Hearing**
  - conservation and treatment V72.12
  - examination V72.19
    - following failed hearing screening V72.11
- **Heart** — *see* condition
- **Heartburn** 787.1
  - psychogenic 306.4
- **Heat** (effects) 992.9
  - apoplexy 992.0
  - burn (*see also* Burn, by site)
    - from sun (*see also* Sunburn) 692.71
  - collapse 992.1
  - cramps 992.2
  - dermatitis or eczema 692.89
  - edema 992.7
  - erythema — *see* Burn, by site
  - excessive 992.9
    - specified effect NEC 992.8
  - exhaustion 992.5
    - anhydrotic 992.3
    - due to
      - salt (and water) depletion 992.4
      - water depletion 992.3
  - fatigue (transient) 992.6
  - fever 992.0
  - hyperpyrexia 992.0
  - prickly 705.1
  - prostration — *see* Heat, exhaustion
  - pyrexia 992.0
  - rash 705.1
  - specified effect NEC 992.8
  - stroke 992.0
  - sunburn (*see also* Sunburn) 692.71
  - syncope 992.1
- **Heavy-chain disease** 273.2
- **Heavy-for-dates** (fetus or infant) 766.1
  - 4500 grams or more 766.0
  - exceptionally 766.0
- **Hebephrenia, hebephrenic** (acute) — *see also* Schizophrenia 295.1 ☑
  - dementia (praecox) (*see also* Schizophrenia) 295.1 ☑
  - schizophrenia (*see also* Schizophrenia) 295.1 ☑
- **Heberden's**
  - disease or nodes 715.04
  - syndrome (angina pectoris) 413.9
- **Hebra's disease**
  - dermatitis exfoliativa 695.89
  - erythema multiforme exudativum 695.19 ▲
  - pityriasis 695.89
    - maculata et circinata 696.3
    - rubra 695.89
      - pilaris 696.4
  - prurigo 698.2
- **Hebra, nose** 040.1
- **Hedinger's syndrome** (malignant carcinoid) 259.2
- **Heel** — *see* condition
- **Heerfordt's disease or syndrome** (uveoparotitis) 135
- **Hegglin's anomaly or syndrome** 288.2

- **Heidenhain's disease** 290.10
  - with dementia 290.10
- **Heilmeyer-Schöner disease** (M9842/3) 207.1 ☑
- **Heine-Medin disease** — *see also* Poliomyelitis 045.9 ☑
- **Heinz-body anemia, congenital** 282.7
- **Heller's disease or syndrome** (infantile psychosis) — *see also* Psychosis, childhood 299.1 ☑
- **H.E.L.L.P** 642.5 ☑
- **Helminthiasis** — *see also* Infestation, by specific parasite 128.9
  - Ancylostoma (*see also* Ancylostoma) 126.9
  - intestinal 127.9
    - mixed types (types classifiable to more than one of the categories 120.0–127.7) 127.8
    - specified type 127.7
  - mixed types (intestinal) (types classifiable to more than one of the categories 120.0–127.7) 127.8
  - Necator americanus 126.1
  - specified type NEC 128.8
  - Trichinella 124
- **Heloma** 700
- **Hemangioblastoma** (M9161/1) — *see also* Neoplasm, connective tissue, uncertain behavior
  - malignant (M9161/3) — *see* Neoplasm, connective tissue, malignant
- **Hemangioblastomatosis, cerebelloretinal** 759.6
- **Hemangioendothelioma** (M9130/1) — *see also* Neoplasm, by site, uncertain behavior
  - benign (M9130/0) 228.00
  - bone (diffuse) (M9130/3) — *see* Neoplasm, bone, malignant
  - malignant (M9130/3) — *see* Neoplasm, connective tissue, malignant
  - nervous system (M9130/0) 228.09
- **Hemangioendotheliosarcoma** (M9130/3) — *see* Neoplasm, connective tissue, malignant
- **Hemangiofibroma** (M9160/0) — *see* Neoplasm, by site, benign
- **Hemangiolipoma** (M8861/0) — *see* Lipoma
- **Hemangioma** (M9120/0) 228.00
  - arteriovenous (M9123/0) — *see* Hemangioma, by site
  - brain 228.02
  - capillary (M9131/0) — *see* Hemangioma, by site
  - cavernous (M9121/0) — *see* Hemangioma, by site
  - central nervous system NEC 228.09
  - choroid 228.09
  - heart 228.09
  - infantile (M9131/0) — *see* Hemangioma, by site
  - intra-abdominal structures 228.04
  - intracranial structures 228.02
  - intramuscular (M9132/0) — *see* Hemangioma, by site
  - iris 228.09
  - juvenile (M9131/0) — *see* Hemangioma, by site
  - malignant (M9120/3) — *see* Neoplasm, connective tissue, malignant
  - meninges 228.09
    - brain 228.02
    - spinal cord 228.09
  - peritoneum 228.04
  - placenta — *see* Placenta, abnormal
  - plexiform (M9131/0) — *see* Hemangioma, by site
  - racemose (M9123/0) — *see* Hemangioma, by site
  - retina 228.03
  - retroperitoneal tissue 228.04
- **Hemangioma** — *continued*
  - sclerosing (M8832/0) — *see* Neoplasm, skin, benign
  - simplex (M9131/0) — *see* Hemangioma, by site
  - skin and subcutaneous tissue 228.01
  - specified site NEC 228.09
  - spinal cord 228.09
  - venous (M9122/0) — *see* Hemangioma, by site
  - verrucous keratotic (M9142/0) — *see* Hemangioma, by site
- **Hemangiomatosis** (systemic) 757.32
  - involving single site — *see* Hemangioma
- **Hemangiopericytoma** (M9150/1) — *see also* Neoplasm, connective tissue, uncertain behavior
  - benign (M9150/0) — *see* Neoplasm, connective tissue, benign
  - malignant (M9150/3) — *see* Neoplasm, connective tissue, malignant
- **Hemangiosarcoma** (M9120/3) — *see* Neoplasm, connective tissue, malignant
- **Hemarthrosis** (nontraumatic) 719.10
  - ankle 719.17
  - elbow 719.12
  - foot 719.17
  - hand 719.14
  - hip 719.15
  - knee 719.16
  - multiple sites 719.19
  - pelvic region 719.15
  - shoulder (region) 719.11
  - specified site NEC 719.18
  - traumatic — *see* Sprain, by site
  - wrist 719.13
- **Hematemesis** 578.0
  - with ulcer — *see* Ulcer, by site, with hemorrhage
  - due to S. japonicum 120.2
  - Goldstein's (familial hemorrhagic telangiectasia) 448.0
  - newborn 772.4
    - due to swallowed maternal blood 777.3
- **Hematidrosis** 705.89
- **Hematinuria** — *see also* Hemoglobinuria 791.2
  - malarial 084.8
  - paroxysmal 283.2
- **Hematite miners' lung** 503
- **Hematobilia** 576.8
- **Hematocele** (congenital) (diffuse) (idiopathic) 608.83
  - broad ligament 620.7
  - canal of Nuck 629.0
  - cord, male 608.83
  - fallopian tube 620.8
  - female NEC 629.0
  - ischiorectal 569.89
  - male NEC 608.83
  - ovary 629.0
  - pelvis, pelvic
    - female 629.0
      - with ectopic pregnancy (*see also* Pregnancy, ectopic) 633.90
        - with intrauterine pregnancy 633.91
    - male 608.83
  - periuterine 629.0
  - retrouterine 629.0
  - scrotum 608.83
  - spermatic cord (diffuse) 608.83
  - testis 608.84
  - traumatic — *see* Injury, internal, pelvis
  - tunica vaginalis 608.83
  - uterine ligament 629.0
  - uterus 621.4
  - vagina 623.6
  - vulva 624.5
- **Hematocephalus** 742.4
- **Hematochezia** — *see also* Melena 578.1
- **Hematochyluria** — *see also* Infestation, filarial 125.9
- **Hematocolpos** 626.8
- **Hematocornea** 371.12
- **Hematogenous** — *see* condition
- **Hematoma** (skin surface intact) (traumatic) — *see also* Contusion

> *Note — Hematomas are coded according to origin and the nature and site of the hematoma or the accompanying injury. Hematomas of unspecified origin are coded as injuries of the sites involved, except:*
>
> (a) *hematomas of genital organs which are coded as diseases of the organ involved unless they complicate pregnancy or delivery*
>
> (b) *hematomas of the eye which are coded as diseases of the eye.*
>
> *For late effect of hematoma classifiable to 920–924 see Late, effect, contusion*

  - with
    - crush injury — *see* Crush
    - fracture — *see* Fracture, by site
    - injury of internal organs (*see also* Injury, internal, by site)
      - kidney — *see* Hematoma, kidney traumatic
      - liver — *see* Hematoma, liver, traumatic
      - spleen — *see* Hematoma, spleen
    - nerve injury — *see* Injury, nerve
    - open wound — *see* Wound, open, by site
    - skin surface intact — *see* Contusion
  - abdomen (wall) — *see* Contusion, abdomen
  - amnion 658.8 ☑
  - aorta, dissecting 441.00
    - abdominal 441.02
    - thoracic 441.01
    - thoracoabdominal 441.03
  - arterial (complicating trauma) 904.9
    - specified site — *see* Injury, blood vessel, by site
  - auricle (ear) 380.31
  - birth injury 767.8
    - skull 767.19
- **Hematoma** — *see also* Contusion — *continued*
  - brain (traumatic) 853.0 ☑

> *Note — Use the following fifth-digit subclassification with categories 851–854:*
>
> 0 *unspecified state of consciousness*
>
> 1 *with no loss of consciousness*
>
> 2 *with brief [less than one hour] loss of consciousness*
>
> 3 *with moderate [1–24 hours] loss of consciousness*
>
> 4 *with prolonged [more than 24 hours] loss of consciousness and return to pre-existing conscious level*
>
> 5 *with prolonged [more than 24 hours] loss of consciousness, without return to pre-existing conscious level*
>
> *Use fifth-digit 5 to designate when a patient is unconscious and dies before regaining consciousness, regardless of the duration of the loss of consciousness*
>
> 6 *with loss of consciousness of unspecified duration*
>
> 9 *with concussion, unspecified*

    - with
      - cerebral
        - contusion — *see* Contusion, brain
        - laceration — *see* Laceration, brain
      - open intracranial wound 853.1 ☑
      - skull fracture — *see* Fracture, skull, by site
    - extradural or epidural 852.4 ☑
      - with open intracranial wound 852.5 ☑
      - fetus or newborn 767.0
      - nontraumatic 432.0
    - fetus or newborn NEC 767.0
    - nontraumatic (*see also* Hemorrhage, brain) 431
      - epidural or extradural 432.0
      - newborn NEC 772.8
      - subarachnoid, arachnoid, or meningeal (*see also* Hemorrhage, subarachnoid) 430
      - subdural (*see also* Hemorrhage, subdural) 432.1
    - subarachnoid, arachnoid, or meningeal 852.0 ☑
      - with open intracranial wound 852.1 ☑
      - fetus or newborn 772.2
      - nontraumatic (*see also* Hemorrhage, subarachnoid) 430
    - subdural 852.2 ☑
      - with open intracranial wound 852.3 ☑
      - fetus or newborn (localized) 767.0
      - nontraumatic (*see also* Hemorrhage, subdural) 432.1
  - breast (nontraumatic) 611.89 ▲
  - broad ligament (nontraumatic) 620.7
    - complicating delivery 665.7 ☑
    - traumatic — *see* Injury, internal, broad ligament
  - calcified NEC 959.9
  - capitis 920
    - due to birth injury 767.19
    - newborn 767.19
  - cerebral — *see* Hematoma, brain
  - cesarean section wound 674.3 ☑
  - chorion — *see* Placenta, abnormal

Hematoma — *see also* Contusion — *continued*
complicating delivery (perineum) (vulva) 664.5 ☑
pelvic 665.7 ☑
vagina 665.7 ☑
corpus
cavernosum (nontraumatic) 607.82
luteum (nontraumatic) (ruptured) 620.1
dura (mater) — *see* Hematoma, brain, subdural
epididymis (nontraumatic) 608.83
epidural (traumatic) (*see also* Hematoma, brain, extradural)
spinal — *see* Injury, spinal, by site
episiotomy 674.3 ☑
external ear 380.31
extradural (*see also* Hematoma, brain, extradural)
fetus or newborn 767.0
nontraumatic 432.0
fetus or newborn 767.0
fallopian tube 620.8
genital organ (nontraumatic)
female NEC 629.89
male NEC 608.83
traumatic (external site) 922.4
internal — *see* Injury, internal, genital organ
graafian follicle (ruptured) 620.0
internal organs (abdomen, chest, or pelvis) (*see also* Injury, internal, by site)
kidney — *see* Hematoma, kidney, traumatic
liver — *see* Hematoma, liver, traumatic
spleen — *see* Hematoma, spleen
intracranial — *see* Hematoma, brain
kidney, cystic 593.81
traumatic 866.01
with open wound into cavity 866.11
labia (nontraumatic) 624.5
lingual (and other parts of neck, scalp, or face, except eye) 920
liver (subcapsular) 573.8
birth injury 767.8
fetus or newborn 767.8
traumatic NEC 864.01
with
laceration — *see* Laceration, liver
open wound into cavity 864.11
mediastinum — *see* Injury, internal, mediastinum
meninges, meningeal (brain) (*see also* Hematoma, brain, subarachnoid)
spinal — *see* Injury, spinal, by site
mesosalpinx (nontraumatic) 620.8
traumatic — *see* Injury, internal, pelvis
muscle (traumatic) — *see* Contusion, by site
nontraumatic 729.92 ●
nasal (septum) (and other part(s) of neck, scalp, or face, except eye) 920
obstetrical surgical wound 674.3 ☑
orbit, orbital (nontraumatic) 376.32
traumatic 921.2
ovary (corpus luteum) (nontraumatic) 620.1
traumatic — *see* Injury, internal, ovary
pelvis (female) (nontraumatic) 629.89
complicating delivery 665.7 ☑
male 608.83
traumatic (*see also* Injury, internal, pelvis)
specified organ NEC (*see also* Injury, internal, pelvis) 867.6

Hematoma — *see also* Contusion — *continued*
penis (nontraumatic) 607.82
pericranial (and neck, or face any part, except eye) 920
due to injury at birth 767.19
perineal wound (obstetrical) 674.3 ☑
complicating delivery 664.5 ☑
perirenal, cystic 593.81
pinna 380.31
placenta — *see* Placenta, abnormal
postoperative 998.12
retroperitoneal (nontraumatic) 568.81
traumatic — *see* Injury, internal, retroperitoneum
retropubic, male 568.81
scalp (and neck, or face any part, except eye) 920
fetus or newborn 767.19
scrotum (nontraumatic) 608.83
traumatic 922.4
seminal vesicle (nontraumatic) 608.83
traumatic — *see* Injury, internal, seminal, vesicle
soft tissue 729.92 ●
spermatic cord (*see also* Injury, internal, spermatic cord)
nontraumatic 608.83
spinal (cord) (meninges) (*see also* Injury, spinal, by site)
fetus or newborn 767.4
nontraumatic 336.1
spleen 865.01
with
laceration — *see* Laceration, spleen
open wound into cavity 865.11
sternocleidomastoid, birth injury 767.8
sternomastoid, birth injury 767.8
subarachnoid (*see also* Hematoma, brain, subarachnoid)
fetus or newborn 772.2
nontraumatic (*see also* Hemorrhage, subarachnoid) 430
newborn 772.2
subdural (*see also* Hematoma, brain, subdural)
fetus or newborn (localized) 767.0
nontraumatic (*see also* Hemorrhage, subdural) 432.1
subperiosteal (syndrome) 267
traumatic — *see* Hematoma, by site
superficial, fetus or newborn 772.6
syncytium — *see* Placenta, abnormal
testis (nontraumatic) 608.83
birth injury 767.8
traumatic 922.4
tunica vaginalis (nontraumatic) 608.83
umbilical cord 663.6 ☑
affecting fetus or newborn 762.6
uterine ligament (nontraumatic) 620.7
traumatic — *see* Injury, internal, pelvis
uterus 621.4
traumatic — *see* Injury, internal, pelvis
vagina (nontraumatic) (ruptured) 623.6
complicating delivery 665.7 ☑
traumatic 922.4
vas deferens (nontraumatic) 608.83
traumatic — *see* Injury, internal, vas deferens
vitreous 379.23
vocal cord 920
vulva (nontraumatic) 624.5
complicating delivery 664.5 ☑
fetus or newborn 767.8
traumatic 922.4
Hematometra 621.4
Hematomyelia 336.1

Hematomyelia — *continued*
with fracture of vertebra (*see also* Fracture, vertebra, by site, with spinal cord injury) 806.8
fetus or newborn 767.4
Hematomyelitis 323.9
late effect — *see* category 326
Hematoperitoneum — *see also* Hemoperitoneum 568.81
Hematopneumothorax — *see also* Hemothorax 511.89 ▲
Hematopoiesis, cyclic 288.02
Hematoporphyria (acquired) (congenital) 277.1
Hematoporphyrinuria (acquired) (congenital) 277.1
Hematorachis, hematorrhachis 336.1
fetus or newborn 767.4
Hematosalpinx 620.8
with
ectopic pregnancy (*see also* categories 633.0–633.9) 639.2
infectional (*see also* Salpingo-oophoritis) 614.2
molar pregnancy (*see also* categories 630–632) 639.2
Hematospermia 608.82
Hematothorax — *see also* Hemothorax 511.89 ▲
Hematotympanum 381.03
Hematuria (benign) (essential) (idiopathic) 599.70 ▲
due to S. hematobium 120.0
endemic 120.0
gross 599.71 ●
intermittent 599.70 ▲
malarial 084.8
microscopic 599.72 ●
paroxysmal 599.70 ▲
sulfonamide
correct substance properly administered 599.70 ▲
overdose or wrong substance given or taken 961.0
tropical (bilharziasis) 120.0
tuberculous (*see also* Tuberculosis) 016.9 ☑
Hematuric bilious fever 084.8
Hemeralopia 368.10
Hemiabiotrophy 799.89
Hemi-akinesia 781.8
Hemianalgesia — *see also* Disturbance, sensation 782.0
Hemianencephaly 740.0
Hemianesthesia — *see also* Disturbance, sensation 782.0
Hemianopia, hemianopsia (altitudinal) (homonymous) 368.46
binasal 368.47
bitemporal 368.47
heteronymous 368.47
syphilitic 095.8
Hemiasomatognosia 307.9
Hemiathetosis 781.0
Hemiatrophy 799.89
cerebellar 334.8
face 349.89
progressive 349.89
fascia 728.9
leg 728.2
tongue 529.8
Hemiballism (us) 333.5
Hemiblock (cardiac) (heart) (left) 426.2
Hemicardia 746.89
Hemicephalus, hemicephaly 740.0
Hemichorea 333.5
Hemicrania 346.9 ☑
congenital malformation 740.0
continua 339.41 ●
paroxysmal 339.03 ●
chronic 339.04 ●
episodic 339.03 ●
Hemidystrophy — *see* Hemiatrophy
Hemiectromelia 755.4
Hemihypalgesia — *see also* Disturbance, sensation 782.0

Hemihypertrophy (congenital) 759.89
cranial 756.0
Hemihypesthesia — *see also* Disturbance, sensation 782.0
Hemi-inattention 781.8
Hemimelia 755.4
lower limb 755.30
paraxial (complete) (incomplete) (intercalary) (terminal) 755.32
fibula 755.37
tibia 755.36
transverse (complete) (partial) 755.31
upper limb 755.20
paraxial (complete) (incomplete) (intercalary) (terminal) 755.22
radial 755.26
ulnar 755.27
transverse (complete) (partial) 755.21
Hemiparalysis — *see also* Hemiplegia 342.9 ☑
Hemiparesis — *see also* Hemiplegia 342.9 ☑
Hemiparesthesia — *see also* Disturbance, sensation 782.0
Hemiplegia 342.9 ☑
acute (*see also* Disease, cerebrovascular, acute) 436
alternans facialis 344.89
apoplectic (*see also* Disease, cerebrovascular, acute) 436
late effect or residual
affecting
dominant side 438.21
nondominant side 438.22
unspecified side 438.20
arteriosclerotic 437.0
late effect or residual
affecting
dominant side 438.21
nondominant side 438.22
unspecified side 438.20
ascending (spinal) NEC 344.89
attack (*see also* Disease, cerebrovascular, acute) 436
brain, cerebral (current episode) 437.8
congenital 343.1
cerebral — *see* Hemiplegia, brain
congenital (cerebral) (spastic) (spinal) 343.1
conversion neurosis (hysterical) 300.11
cortical — *see* Hemiplegia, brain
due to
arteriosclerosis 437.0
late effect or residual
affecting
dominant side 438.21
nondominant side 438.22
unspecified side 438.20
cerebrovascular lesion (*see also* Disease, cerebrovascular, acute) 436
late effect
affecting
dominant side 438.21
nondominant side 438.22
unspecified side 438.20
embolic (current) (*see also* Embolism, brain) 434.1 ☑
late effect
affecting
dominant side 438.21
nondominant side 438.22
unspecified side 438.20
flaccid 342.0 ☑
hypertensive (current episode) 437.8
infantile (postnatal) 343.4
late effect
birth injury, intracranial or spinal 343.4

Hemiplegia — *continued*
late effect — *continued*
cerebrovascular lesion — *see* Late effect(s) (of) cerebrovascular disease
viral encephalitis 139.0
middle alternating NEC 344.89
newborn NEC 767.0
seizure (current episode) (*see also* Disease, cerebrovascular, acute) 436
spastic 342.1 ☑
congenital or infantile 343.1
specified NEC 342.8 ☑
thrombotic (current) (*see also* Thrombosis, brain) 434.0 ☑
late effect — *see* Late effect(s) (of) cerebrovascular disease
Hemisection, spinal cord — *see* Fracture, vertebra, by site, with spinal cord injury
Hemispasm 781.0
facial 781.0
Hemispatial neglect 781.8
Hemisporosis 117.9
Hemitremor 781.0
Hemivertebra 756.14
Hemobilia 576.8
Hemocholecyst 575.8
Hemochromatosis (acquired) (diabetic) (hereditary) (liver) (myocardium) (primary idiopathic) (secondary) 275.0
with refractory anemia 238.72
Hemodialysis V56.0
Hemoglobin — *see also* condition
abnormal (disease) — *see* Disease, hemoglobin
AS genotype 282.5
fetal, hereditary persistence 282.7
high-oxygen-affinity 289.0
low NEC 285.9
S (Hb-S), heterozygous 282.5
Hemoglobinemia 283.2
due to blood transfusion NEC 999.89 ▲
bone marrow 996.85
paroxysmal 283.2
Hemoglobinopathy (mixed) — *see also* Disease, hemoglobin 282.7
with thalassemia 282.49
sickle-cell 282.60
with thalassemia (without crisis) 282.41
with
crisis 282.42
vaso-occlusive pain 282.42
Hemoglobinuria, hemoglobinuric 791.2
with anemia, hemolytic, acquired (chronic) NEC 283.2
cold (agglutinin) (paroxysmal) (with Raynaud's syndrome) 283.2
due to
exertion 283.2
hemolysis (from external causes) NEC 283.2
exercise 283.2
fever (malaria) 084.8
infantile 791.2
intermittent 283.2
malarial 084.8
march 283.2
nocturnal (paroxysmal) 283.2
paroxysmal (cold) (nocturnal) 283.2
Hemolymphangioma (M9175/0) 228.1
Hemolysis
fetal — *see* Jaundice, fetus or newborn
intravascular (disseminated) NEC 286.6
with
abortion — *see* Abortion, by type, with hemorrhage, delayed or excessive
Hemolysis — *continued*
intravascular — *continued*
with — *continued*
ectopic pregnancy (*see also* categories 633.0–633.9) 639.1
hemorrhage of pregnancy 641.3 ☑
affecting fetus or newborn 762.1
molar pregnancy (*see also* categories 630–632) 639.1
acute 283.2
following
abortion 639.1
ectopic or molar pregnancy 639.1
neonatal — *see* Jaundice, fetus or newborn
transfusion NEC 999.89 ▲
bone marrow 996.85
Hemolytic — *see also* condition
anemia — *see* Anemia, hemolytic
uremic syndrome 283.11
Hemometra 621.4
Hemopericardium (with effusion) 423.0
newborn 772.8
traumatic (*see also* Hemothorax, traumatic) 860.2
with open wound into thorax 860.3
Hemoperitoneum 568.81
infectional (*see also* Peritonitis) 567.29
traumatic — *see* Injury, internal, peritoneum
Hemophagocytic syndrome 288.4
infection-associated 288.4
Hemophilia (familial) (hereditary) 286.0
A 286.0
carrier (asymptomatic) V83.01
symptomatic V83.02
acquired 286.5
B (Leyden) 286.1
C 286.2
calcipriva (*see also* Fibrinolysis) 286.7
classical 286.0
nonfamilial 286.7
secondary 286.5
vascular 286.4
Hemophilus influenzae NEC 041.5
arachnoiditis (basic) (brain) (spinal) 320.0
late effect — *see* category 326
bronchopneumonia 482.2
cerebral ventriculitis 320.0
late effect — *see* category 326
cerebrospinal inflammation 320.0
late effect — *see* category 326
infection NEC 041.5
leptomeningitis 320.0
late effect — *see* category 326
meningitis (cerebral) (cerebrospinal) (spinal) 320.0
late effect — *see* category 326
meningomyelitis 320.0
late effect — *see* category 326
pachymeningitis (adhesive) (fibrous) (hemorrhagic) (hypertrophic) (spinal) 320.0
late effect — *see* category 326
pneumonia (broncho-) 482.2
Hemophthalmos 360.43
Hemopneumothorax — *see also* Hemothorax 511.89 ▲
traumatic 860.4
with open wound into thorax 860.5
Hemoptysis 786.3
due to Paragonimus (westermani) 121.2
newborn 770.3
tuberculous (*see also* Tuberculosis, pulmonary) 011.9 ☑
Hemorrhage, hemorrhagic (nontraumatic) 459.0
abdomen 459.0
accidental (antepartum) 641.2 ☑
affecting fetus or newborn 762.1
Hemorrhage, hemorrhagic — *continued*
adenoid 474.8
adrenal (capsule) (gland) (medulla) 255.41
newborn 772.5
after labor — *see* Hemorrhage, postpartum
alveolar
lung, newborn 770.3
process 525.8
alveolus 525.8
amputation stump (surgical) 998.11
secondary, delayed 997.69
anemia (chronic) 280.0
acute 285.1
antepartum — *see* Hemorrhage, pregnancy
anus (sphincter) 569.3
apoplexy (stroke) 432.9
arachnoid — *see* Hemorrhage, subarachnoid
artery NEC 459.0
brain (*see also* Hemorrhage, brain) 431
middle meningeal — *see* Hemorrhage, subarachnoid
basilar (ganglion) (*see also* Hemorrhage, brain) 431
bladder 596.8
blood dyscrasia 289.9
bowel 578.9
newborn 772.4
brain (miliary) (nontraumatic) 431
with
birth injury 767.0
arachnoid — *see* Hemorrhage, subarachnoid
due to
birth injury 767.0
rupture of aneurysm (congenital) (*see also* Hemorrhage, subarachnoid) 430
mycotic 431
syphilis 094.89
epidural or extradural — *see* Hemorrhage, extradural
fetus or newborn (anoxic) (hypoxic) (due to birth trauma) (nontraumatic) 767.0
intraventricular 772.10
grade I 772.11
grade II 772.12
grade III 772.13
grade IV 772.14
iatrogenic 997.02
postoperative 997.02
puerperal, postpartum, childbirth 674.0 ☑
stem 431
subarachnoid, arachnoid, or meningeal — *see* Hemorrhage, subarachnoid
subdural — *see* Hemorrhage, subdural
Hemorrhage, hemorrhagic — *continued*
brain — *continued*
traumatic NEC 853.0 ☑

Note — Use the following fifth-digit subclassification with categories 851–854:

0	*unspecified state of consciousness*
1	*with no loss of consciousness*
2	*with brief [less than one hour] loss of consciousness*
3	*with moderate [1–24 hours] loss of consciousness*
4	*with prolonged [more than 24 hours] loss of consciousness and return to pre-existing conscious level*
5	*with prolonged [more than 24 hours] loss of consciousness, without return to pre-existing conscious level*

Use fifth-digit 5 to designate when a patient is unconscious and dies before regaining consciousness, regardless of the duration of the loss of consciousness

6	*with loss of consciousness of unspecified duration*
9	*with concussion, unspecified*

with
cerebral
contusion — *see* Contusion, brain
laceration — *see* Laceration, brain
open intracranial wound 853.1 ☑
skull fracture — *see* Fracture, skull, by site
extradural or epidural 852.4 ☑
with open intracranial wound 852.5 ☑
subarachnoid 852.0 ☑
with open intracranial wound 852.1 ☑
subdural 852.2 ☑
with open intracranial wound 852.3 ☑
breast 611.79
bronchial tube — *see* Hemorrhage, lung
bronchopulmonary — *see* Hemorrhage, lung
bronchus (cause unknown) (*see also* Hemorrhage, lung) 786.3
bulbar (*see also* Hemorrhage, brain) 431
bursa 727.89
capillary 448.9
primary 287.8
capsular — *see* Hemorrhage, brain
cardiovascular 429.89
cecum 578.9
cephalic (*see also* Hemorrhage, brain) 431
cerebellar (*see also* Hemorrhage, brain) 431
cerebellum (*see also* Hemorrhage, brain) 431
cerebral (*see also* Hemorrhage, brain) 431
fetus or newborn (anoxic) (traumatic) 767.0
cerebromeningeal (*see also* Hemorrhage, brain) 431
cerebrospinal (*see also* Hemorrhage, brain) 431
cerebrovascular accident — *see* Hemorrhage, brain
cerebrum (*see also* Hemorrhage, brain) 431

Hemorrhage, hemorrhagic — continued
cervix (stump) (uteri) 622.8
cesarean section wound 674.3 ☑
chamber, anterior (eye) 364.41
childbirth — see Hemorrhage, complicating, delivery
choroid 363.61
expulsive 363.62
ciliary body 364.41
cochlea 386.8
colon — see Hemorrhage, intestine
complicating
delivery 641.9 ☑
affecting fetus or newborn 762.1
associated with
afibrinogenemia 641.3 ☑
affecting fetus or newborn 763.89
coagulation defect 641.3 ☑
affecting fetus or newborn 763.89
hyperfibrinolysis 641.3 ☑
affecting fetus or newborn 763.89
hypofibrinogenemia 641.3 ☑
affecting fetus or newborn 763.89
due to
low-lying placenta 641.1 ☑
affecting fetus or newborn 762.0
placenta previa 641.1 ☑
affecting fetus or newborn 762.0
premature separation of placenta 641.2 ☑
affecting fetus or newborn 762.1
retained
placenta 666.0 ☑
secundines 666.2 ☑
trauma 641.8 ☑
affecting fetus or newborn 763.89
uterine leiomyoma 641.8 ☑
affecting fetus or newborn 763.89
surgical procedure 998.11
complication(s)
of dental implant placement 525.71
concealed NEC 459.0
congenital 772.9
conjunctiva 372.72
newborn 772.8
cord, newborn 772.0
slipped ligature 772.3
stump 772.3
corpus luteum (ruptured) 620.1
cortical (see also Hemorrhage, brain) 431
cranial 432.9
cutaneous 782.7
newborn 772.6
cystitis — see Cystitis
cyst, pancreas 577.2
delayed
with
abortion — see Abortion, by type, with hemorrhage, delayed or excessive
ectopic pregnancy (see also categories 633.0–633.9) 639.1
molar pregnancy (see also categories 630–632) 639.1
following
abortion 639.1
ectopic or molar pregnancy 639.1
postpartum 666.2 ☑
diathesis (familial) 287.9
newborn 776.0
disease 287.9
newborn 776.0
specified type NEC 287.8

Hemorrhage, hemorrhagic — continued
disorder 287.9
due to intrinsic circulating anticoagulants 286.5
specified type NEC 287.8
due to
any device, implant or graft (presence of) classifiable to 996.0–996.5 — see Complications, due to (presence of) any device, implant, or graft classified to 996.0–996.5NEC
intrinsic circulating anticoagulant 286.5
duodenum, duodenal 537.89
ulcer — see Ulcer, duodenum, with hemorrhage
dura mater — see Hemorrhage, subdural
endotracheal — see Hemorrhage, lung
epicranial subaponeurotic (massive) 767.11
epidural — see Hemorrhage, extradural
episiotomy 674.3 ☑
esophagus 530.82
varix (see also Varix, esophagus, bleeding) 456.0
excessive
with
abortion — see Abortion, by type, with hemorrhage, delayed or excessive
ectopic pregnancy (see also categories 633.0–633.9) 639.1
molar pregnancy (see also categories 630–632) 639.1
following
abortion 639.1
ectopic or molar pregnancy 639.1
external 459.0
extradural (traumatic) (see also Hemorrhage, brain, traumatic, extradural)
birth injury 767.0
fetus or newborn (anoxic) (traumatic) 767.0
nontraumatic 432.0
eye 360.43
chamber (anterior) (aqueous) 364.41
fundus 362.81
eyelid 374.81
fallopian tube 620.8
fetomaternal 772.0
affecting management of pregnancy or puerperium 656.0 ☑
fetus, fetal 772.0
from
cut end of co-twin's cord 772.0
placenta 772.0
ruptured cord 772.0
vasa previa 772.0
into
co-twin 772.0
mother's circulation 772.0
affecting management of pregnancy or puerperium 656.0 ☑
fever (see also Fever, hemorrhagic) 065.9
with renal syndrome 078.6
arthropod-borne NEC 065.9
Bangkok 065.4
Crimean 065.0
dengue virus 065.4
epidemic 078.6
Junin virus 078.7
Korean 078.6
Machupo virus 078.7
mite-borne 065.8
mosquito-borne 065.4
Philippine 065.4

Hemorrhage, hemorrhagic — continued
fever (see also Fever, hemorrhagic) — continued
Russian (Yaroslav) 078.6
Singapore 065.4
southeast Asia 065.4
Thailand 065.4
tick-borne NEC 065.3
fibrinogenolysis (see also Fibrinolysis) 286.6
fibrinolytic (acquired) (see also Fibrinolysis) 286.6
fontanel 767.19
from tracheostomy stoma 519.09
fundus, eye 362.81
funis
affecting fetus or newborn 772.0
complicating delivery 663.8 ☑
gastric (see also Hemorrhage, stomach) 578.9
gastroenteric 578.9
newborn 772.4
gastrointestinal (tract) 578.9
newborn 772.4
genitourinary (tract) NEC 599.89
gingiva 523.8
globe 360.43
gravidarum — see Hemorrhage, pregnancy
gum 523.8
heart 429.89
hypopharyngeal (throat) 784.8
intermenstrual 626.6
irregular 626.6
regular 626.5
internal (organs) 459.0
capsule (see also Hemorrhage, brain) 431
ear 386.8
newborn 772.8
intestine 578.9
congenital 772.4
newborn 772.4
into
bladder wall 596.7
bursa 727.89
corpus luysii (see also Hemorrhage, brain) 431
intra-abdominal 459.0
during or following surgery 998.11
intra-alveolar, newborn (lung) 770.3
intracerebral (see also Hemorrhage, brain) 431
intracranial NEC 432.9
puerperal, postpartum, childbirth 674.0 ☑
traumatic — see Hemorrhage, brain, traumatic
intramedullary NEC 336.1
intraocular 360.43
intraoperative 998.11
intrapartum — see Hemorrhage, complicating, delivery
intrapelvic
female 629.89
male 459.0
intraperitoneal 459.0
intrapontine (see also Hemorrhage, brain) 431
intrauterine 621.4
complicating delivery — see Hemorrhage, complicating, delivery
in pregnancy or childbirth — see Hemorrhage, pregnancy
postpartum (see also Hemorrhage, postpartum) 666.1 ☑
intraventricular (see also Hemorrhage, brain) 431
fetus or newborn (anoxic) (traumatic) 772.10
grade I 772.11
grade II 772.12
grade III 772.13
grade IV 772.14
intravesical 596.7

Hemorrhage, hemorrhagic — continued
iris (postinfectional) (postinflammatory) (toxic) 364.41
joint (nontraumatic) 719.10
ankle 719.17
elbow 719.12
foot 719.17
forearm 719.13
hand 719.14
hip 719.15
knee 719.16
lower leg 719.16
multiple sites 719.19
pelvic region 719.15
shoulder (region) 719.11
specified site NEC 719.18
thigh 719.15
upper arm 719.12
wrist 719.13
kidney 593.81
knee (joint) 719.16
labyrinth 386.8
leg NEC 459.0
lenticular striate artery (see also Hemorrhage, brain) 431
ligature, vessel 998.11
liver 573.8
lower extremity NEC 459.0
lung 786.3
newborn 770.3
tuberculous (see also Tuberculosis, pulmonary) 011.9 ☑
malaria 084.8
marginal sinus 641.2 ☑
massive subaponeurotic, birth injury 767.11
maternal, affecting fetus or newborn 762.1
mediastinum 786.3
medulla (see also Hemorrhage, brain) 431
membrane (brain) (see also Hemorrhage, subarachnoid) 430
spinal cord — see Hemorrhage, spinal cord
meninges, meningeal (brain) (middle) (see also Hemorrhage, subarachnoid) 430
spinal cord — see Hemorrhage, spinal cord
mesentery 568.81
metritis 626.8
midbrain (see also Hemorrhage, brain) 431
mole 631
mouth 528.9
mucous membrane NEC 459.0
newborn 772.8
muscle 728.89
nail (subungual) 703.8
nasal turbinate 784.7
newborn 772.8
nasopharynx 478.29
navel, newborn 772.3
newborn 772.9
adrenal 772.5
alveolar (lung) 770.3
brain (anoxic) (hypoxic) (due to birth trauma) 767.0
cerebral (anoxic) (hypoxic) (due to birth trauma) 767.0
conjunctiva 772.8
cutaneous 772.6
diathesis 776.0
due to vitamin K deficiency 776.0
epicranial subaponeurotic (massive) 767.11
gastrointestinal 772.4
internal (organs) 772.8
intestines 772.4
intra-alveolar (lung) 770.3
intracranial (from any perinatal cause) 767.0
intraventricular (from any perinatal cause) 772.10

Hemorrhage, hemorrhagic — *continued*
- newborn — *continued*
  - intraventricular — *continued*
    - grade I 772.11
    - grade II 772.12
    - grade III 772.13
    - grade IV 772.14
  - lung 770.3
  - pulmonary (massive) 770.3
  - spinal cord, traumatic 767.4
  - stomach 772.4
  - subaponeurotic (massive) 767.11
  - subarachnoid (from any perinatal cause) 772.2
  - subconjunctival 772.8
  - subgaleal 767.11
  - umbilicus 772.0
    - slipped ligature 772.3
    - vasa previa 772.0
- nipple 611.79
- nose 784.7
  - newborn 772.8
- obstetrical surgical wound 674.3 ☑
- omentum 568.89
  - newborn 772.4
- optic nerve (sheath) 377.42
- orbit 376.32
- ovary 620.1
- oviduct 620.8
- pancreas 577.8
- parathyroid (gland) (spontaneous) 252.8
- parturition — *see* Hemorrhage, complicating, delivery
- penis 607.82
- pericardium, pericarditis 423.0
- perineal wound (obstetrical) 674.3 ☑
- peritoneum, peritoneal 459.0
- peritonsillar tissue 474.8
  - after operation on tonsils 998.11
  - due to infection 475
- petechial 782.7
- pituitary (gland) 253.8
- placenta NEC 641.9 ☑
  - affecting fetus or newborn 762.1
  - from surgical or instrumental damage 641.8 ☑
    - affecting fetus or newborn 762.1
  - previa 641.1 ☑
    - affecting fetus or newborn 762.0
- pleura — *see* Hemorrhage, lung
- polioencephalitis, superior 265.1
- polymyositis — *see* Polymyositis
- pons (*see also* Hemorrhage, brain) 431
- pontine (*see also* Hemorrhage, brain) 431
- popliteal 459.0
- postcoital 626.7
- postextraction (dental) 998.11
- postmenopausal 627.1
- postnasal 784.7
- postoperative 998.11
- postpartum (atonic) (following delivery of placenta) 666.1 ☑
  - delayed or secondary (after 24 hours) 666.2 ☑
  - retained placenta 666.0 ☑
  - third stage 666.0 ☑
- pregnancy (concealed) 641.9 ☑
  - accidental 641.2 ☑
    - affecting fetus or newborn 762.1
  - affecting fetus or newborn 762.1
  - before 22 completed weeks gestation 640.9 ☑
    - affecting fetus or newborn 762.1
  - due to
    - abruptio placenta 641.2 ☑
      - affecting fetus or newborn 762.1
    - afibrinogenemia or other coagulation defect (conditions classifiable to 286.0–286.9) 641.3 ☑
      - affecting fetus or newborn 762.1

Hemorrhage, hemorrhagic — *continued*
- pregnancy — *continued*
  - due to — *continued*
    - coagulation defect 641.3 ☑
      - affecting fetus or newborn 762.1
    - hyperfibrinolysis 641.3 ☑
      - affecting fetus or newborn 762.1
    - hypofibrinogenemia 641.3 ☑
      - affecting fetus or newborn 762.1
    - leiomyoma, uterus 641.8 ☑
      - affecting fetus or newborn 762.1
    - low-lying placenta 641.1 ☑
      - affecting fetus or newborn 762.1
    - marginal sinus (rupture) 641.2 ☑
      - affecting fetus or newborn 762.1
    - placenta previa 641.1 ☑
      - affecting fetus or newborn 762.0
    - premature separation of placenta (normally implanted) 641.2 ☑
      - affecting fetus or newborn 762.1
    - threatened abortion 640.0 ☑
      - affecting fetus or newborn 762.1
    - trauma 641.8 ☑
      - affecting fetus or newborn 762.1
  - early (before 22 completed weeks gestation) 640.9 ☑
    - affecting fetus or newborn 762.1
  - previous, affecting management of pregnancy or childbirth V23.49
  - unavoidable — *see* Hemorrhage, pregnancy, due to placenta previa
- prepartum (mother) — *see* Hemorrhage, pregnancy
- preretinal, cause unspecified 362.81
- prostate 602.1
- puerperal (*see also* Hemorrhage, postpartum) 666.1 ☑
- pulmonary (*see also* Hemorrhage, lung)
  - newborn (massive) 770.3
  - renal syndrome 446.21
- purpura (primary) (*see also* Purpura, thrombocytopenic) 287.39
- rectum (sphincter) 569.3
- recurring, following initial hemorrhage at time of injury 958.2
- renal 593.81
  - pulmonary syndrome 446.21
- respiratory tract (*see also* Hemorrhage, lung) 786.3
- retina, retinal (deep) (superficial) (vessels) 362.81
  - diabetic 250.5 ☑ *[362.01]*
    - due to secondary diabetes 249.5 ☑ *[362.01]* ●
  - due to birth injury 772.8
- retrobulbar 376.89
- retroperitoneal 459.0
- retroplacental (*see also* Placenta, separation) 641.2 ☑
- scalp 459.0
  - due to injury at birth 767.19
- scrotum 608.83
- secondary (nontraumatic) 459.0
  - following initial hemorrhage at time of injury 958.2
- seminal vesicle 608.83
- skin 782.7
  - newborn 772.6
- spermatic cord 608.83
- spinal (cord) 336.1

Hemorrhage, hemorrhagic — *continued*
- spinal — *continued*
  - aneurysm (ruptured) 336.1
    - syphilitic 094.89
  - due to birth injury 767.4
  - fetus or newborn 767.4
- spleen 289.59
- spontaneous NEC 459.0
  - petechial 782.7
- stomach 578.9
  - newborn 772.4
  - ulcer — *see* Ulcer, stomach, with hemorrhage
- subaponeurotic, newborn 767.11
  - massive (birth injury) 767.11
- subarachnoid (nontraumatic) 430
  - fetus or newborn (anoxic) (traumatic) 772.2
  - puerperal, postpartum, childbirth 674.0 ☑
  - traumatic — *see* Hemorrhage, brain, traumatic, subarachnoid
- subconjunctival 372.72
  - due to birth injury 772.8
  - newborn 772.8
- subcortical (*see also* Hemorrhage, brain) 431
- subcutaneous 782.7
- subdiaphragmatic 459.0
- subdural (nontraumatic) 432.1
  - due to birth injury 767.0
  - fetus or newborn (anoxic) (hypoxic) (due to birth trauma) 767.0
  - puerperal, postpartum, childbirth 674.0 ☑
  - spinal 336.1
  - traumatic — *see* Hemorrhage, brain, traumatic, subdural
- subgaleal 767.11
- subhyaloid 362.81
- subperiosteal 733.99
- subretinal 362.81
- subtentorial (*see also* Hemorrhage, subdural) 432.1
- subungual 703.8
  - due to blood dyscrasia 287.8
- suprarenal (capsule) (gland) 255.41
  - fetus or newborn 772.5
- tentorium (traumatic) (*see also* Hemorrhage, brain, traumatic)
  - fetus or newborn 767.0
  - nontraumatic — *see* Hemorrhage, subdural
- testis 608.83
- thigh 459.0
- third stage 666.0 ☑
- thorax — *see* Hemorrhage, lung
- throat 784.8
- thrombocythemia 238.71
- thymus (gland) 254.8
- thyroid (gland) 246.3
  - cyst 246.3
- tongue 529.8
- tonsil 474.8
  - postoperative 998.11
- tooth socket (postextraction) 998.11
- trachea — *see* Hemorrhage, lung
- traumatic (*see also* nature of injury)
  - brain — *see* Hemorrhage, brain, traumatic
  - recurring or secondary (following initial hemorrhage at time of injury) 958.2
- tuberculous NEC (*see also* Tuberculosis, pulmonary) 011.9 ☑
- tunica vaginalis 608.83
- ulcer — *see* Ulcer, by site, with hemorrhage
- umbilicus, umbilical cord 772.0
  - after birth, newborn 772.3
  - complicating delivery 663.8 ☑
    - affecting fetus or newborn 772.0
  - slipped ligature 772.3
  - stump 772.3

Hemorrhage, hemorrhagic — *continued*
- unavoidable (due to placenta previa) 641.1 ☑
  - affecting fetus or newborn 762.0
- upper extremity 459.0
- urethra (idiopathic) 599.84
- uterus, uterine (abnormal) 626.9
  - climacteric 627.0
  - complicating delivery — *see* Hemorrhage, complicating, delivery
  - due to
    - intrauterine contraceptive device 996.76
      - perforating uterus 996.32
  - functional or dysfunctional 626.8
  - in pregnancy — *see* Hemorrhage, pregnancy
  - intermenstrual 626.6
    - irregular 626.6
    - regular 626.5
  - postmenopausal 627.1
  - postpartum (*see also* Hemorrhage, postpartum) 666.1 ☑
  - prepubertal 626.8
  - pubertal 626.3
  - puerperal (immediate) 666.1 ☑
- vagina 623.8
- vasa previa 663.5 ☑
  - affecting fetus or newborn 772.0
- vas deferens 608.83
- ventricular (*see also* Hemorrhage, brain) 431
- vesical 596.8
- viscera 459.0
  - newborn 772.8
- vitreous (humor) (intraocular) 379.23
- vocal cord 478.5
- vulva 624.8

Hemorrhoids (anus) (rectum) (without complication) 455.6
- bleeding, prolapsed, strangulated, or ulcerated NEC 455.8
  - external 455.5
  - internal 455.2
- complicated NEC 455.8
- complicating pregnancy and puerperium 671.8 ☑
- external 455.3
  - with complication NEC 455.5
  - bleeding, prolapsed, strangulated, or ulcerated 455.5
  - thrombosed 455.4
- internal 455.0
  - with complication NEC 455.2
  - bleeding, prolapsed, strangulated, or ulcerated 455.2
  - thrombosed 455.1
- residual skin tag 455.9
- sentinel pile 455.9
- thrombosed NEC 455.7
  - external 455.4
  - internal 455.1

Hemosalpinx 620.8

Hemosiderosis 275.0
- dietary 275.0
- pulmonary (idiopathic) 275.0 *[516.1]*
- transfusion NEC 999.89 ▲
  - bone marrow 996.85

Hemospermia 608.82

Hemothorax 511.89 ▲
- bacterial, nontuberculous 511.1
- newborn 772.8
- nontuberculous 511.89 ▲
  - bacterial 511.1
- pneumococcal 511.1
- postoperative 998.11
- staphylococcal 511.1
- streptococcal 511.1
- traumatic 860.2
  - with
    - open wound into thorax 860.3
    - pneumothorax 860.4
      - with open wound into thorax 860.5

- **Hemothorax** — *continued*
  - tuberculous (*see also* Tuberculosis, pleura) 012.0 ☑
- **Hemotympanum** 385.89
- **Hench-Rosenberg syndrome** (palindromic arthritis) — *see also* Rheumatism, palindromic 719.3 ☑
- **Henle's warts** 371.41
- **Henoch (-Schönlein)**
  - disease or syndrome (allergic purpura) 287.0
  - purpura (allergic) 287.0
- **Henpue, henpuye** 102.6
- **Heparin-induced thrombocytopenia** (HIT) 289.84 ●
- **Heparitinuria** 277.5
- **Hepar lobatum** 095.3
- **Hepatalgia** 573.8
- **Hepatic** — *see also* condition
  - flexure syndrome 569.89
- **Hepatitis** 573.3
  - acute (*see also* Necrosis, liver) 570
    - alcoholic 571.1
    - infective 070.1
      - with hepatic coma 070.0
  - alcoholic 571.1
  - amebic — *see* Abscess, liver, amebic
  - anicteric (acute) — *see* Hepatitis, viral
  - antigen-associated (HAA) — *see* Hepatitis, viral, type B
  - Australian antigen (positive) — *see* Hepatitis, viral, type B
  - autoimmune 571.42 ▲
  - catarrhal (acute) 070.1
    - with hepatic coma 070.0
    - chronic 571.40
    - newborn 070.1
      - with hepatic coma 070.0
  - chemical 573.3
  - cholangiolitic 573.8
  - cholestatic 573.8
  - chronic 571.40
    - active 571.49
      - viral — *see* Hepatitis, viral
    - aggressive 571.49
    - persistent 571.41
    - viral — *see* Hepatitis, viral
  - cytomegalic inclusion virus 078.5 *[573.1]*
  - diffuse 573.3
  - "dirty needle" — *see* Hepatitis, viral
  - drug-induced 573.3
  - due to
    - Coxsackie 074.8 *[573.1]*
    - cytomegalic inclusion virus 078.5 *[573.1]*
    - infectious mononucleosis 075 *[573.1]*
    - malaria 084.9 *[573.2]*
    - mumps 072.71
    - secondary syphilis 091.62
    - toxoplasmosis (acquired) 130.5
      - congenital (active) 771.2
  - epidemic — *see* Hepatitis, viral, type A
  - fetus or newborn 774.4
  - fibrous (chronic) 571.49
    - acute 570
  - from injection, inoculation, or transfusion (blood) (other substance) (plasma) (serum) (onset within 8 months after administration) — *see* Hepatitis, viral
  - fulminant (viral) (*see also* Hepatitis, viral) 070.9
    - with hepatic coma 070.6
    - type A 070.1
      - with hepatic coma 070.0
    - type B — *see* Hepatitis, viral, type B
  - giant cell (neonatal) 774.4
  - hemorrhagic 573.8
  - history of
    - B V12.09
    - C V12.09

- **Hepatitis** — *continued*
  - homologous serum — *see* Hepatitis, viral
  - hypertrophic (chronic) 571.49
    - acute 570
  - infectious, infective (acute) (chronic) (subacute) 070.1
    - with hepatic coma 070.0
  - inoculation — *see* Hepatitis, viral
  - interstitial (chronic) 571.49
    - acute 570
  - lupoid 571.49
  - malarial 084.9 *[573.2]*
  - malignant (*see also* Necrosis, liver) 570
  - neonatal (toxic) 774.4
  - newborn 774.4
  - parenchymatous (acute) (*see also* Necrosis, liver) 570
  - peliosis 573.3
  - persistent, chronic 571.41
  - plasma cell 571.49
  - postimmunization — *see* Hepatitis, viral
  - postnecrotic 571.49
  - posttransfusion — *see* Hepatitis, viral
  - recurrent 571.49
  - septic 573.3
  - serum — *see* Hepatitis, viral
    - carrier (suspected of) V02.61
  - subacute (*see also* Necrosis, liver) 570
  - suppurative (diffuse) 572.0
  - syphilitic (late) 095.3
    - congenital (early) 090.0 *[573.2]*
      - late 090.5 *[573.2]*
    - secondary 091.62
  - toxic (noninfectious) 573.3
    - fetus or newborn 774.4
  - tuberculous (*see also* Tuberculosis) 017.9 ☑
  - viral (acute) (anicteric) (cholangiolitic) (cholestatic) (chronic) (subacute) 070.9
    - with hepatic coma 070.6
    - AU-SH type virus — *see* Hepatitis, viral, type B
    - Australian antigen — *see* Hepatitis, viral, type B
    - B-antigen — *see* Hepatitis, viral, type B
    - Coxsackie 074.8 *[573.1]*
    - cytomegalic inclusion 078.5 *[573.1]*
    - IH (virus) — *see* Hepatitis, viral, type A
    - infectious hepatitis virus — *see* Hepatitis, viral, type A
    - serum hepatitis virus — *see* Hepatitis, viral, type B
    - SH — *see* Hepatitis, viral, type B
    - specified type NEC 070.59
      - with hepatic coma 070.49
    - type A 070.1
      - with hepatic coma 070.0
    - type B (acute) 070.30
      - with
        - hepatic coma 070.20
          - with hepatitis delta 070.21
        - hepatitis delta 070.31
          - with hepatic coma 070.21
      - carrier status V02.61
      - chronic 070.32
        - with
          - hepatic coma 070.22
            - with hepatitis delta 070.23
          - hepatitis delta 070.33
            - with hepatic coma 070.23
    - type C
      - acute 070.51
        - with hepatic coma 070.41
      - carrier status V02.62
      - chronic 070.54
        - with hepatic coma 070.44
      - in remission 070.54

- **Hepatitis** — *continued*
  - viral — *continued*
    - type C — *continued*
      - unspecified 070.70
        - with hepatic coma 070.71
    - type delta (with hepatitis B carrier state) 070.52
      - with
        - active hepatitis B disease — *see* Hepatitis, viral, type B
        - hepatic coma 070.42
    - type E 070.53
      - with hepatic coma 070.43
    - vaccination and inoculation (prophylactic) V05.3
  - Waldenström's (lupoid hepatitis) 571.49
- **Hepatization, lung** (acute) — *see also* Pneumonia, lobar
  - chronic (*see also* Fibrosis, lung) 515
- **Hepatoblastoma** (M8970/3) 155.0
- **Hepatocarcinoma** (M8170/3) 155.0
- **Hepatocholangiocarcinoma** (M8180/3) 155.0
- **Hepatocholangioma, benign** (M8180/0) 211.5
- **Hepatocholangitis** 573.8
- **Hepatocystitis** — *see also* Cholecystitis 575.10
- **Hepatodystrophy** 570
- **Hepatolenticular degeneration** 275.1
- **Hepatolithiasis** — *see* Choledocholithiasis
- **Hepatoma** (malignant) (M8170/3) 155.0
  - benign (M8170/0) 211.5
  - congenital (M8970/3) 155.0
  - embryonal (M8970/3) 155.0
- **Hepatomegalia glycogenica diffusa** 271.0
- **Hepatomegaly** — *see also* Hypertrophy, liver 789.1
  - congenital 751.69
    - syphilitic 090.0
  - due to Clonorchis sinensis 121.1
  - Gaucher's 272.7
  - syphilitic (congenital) 090.0
- **Hepatoptosis** 573.8
- **Hepatorrhexis** 573.8
- **Hepatosis, toxic** 573.8
- **Hepatosplenomegaly** 571.8
  - due to S. japonicum 120.2
  - hyperlipemic (Bürger-Grutz type) 272.3
- **Herald patch** 696.3
- **Hereditary** — *see* condition
- **Heredodegeneration** 330.9
  - macular 362.70
- **Heredopathia atactica polyneuritiformis** 356.3
- **Heredosyphilis** — *see also* Syphilis, congenital 090.9
- **Hermaphroditism** (true) 752.7
  - with specified chromosomal anomaly — *see* Anomaly, chromosomes, sex
- **Hernia, hernial** (acquired) (recurrent) 553.9
  - with
    - gangrene (obstructed) NEC 551.9
    - obstruction NEC 552.9
      - and gangrene 551.9
  - abdomen (wall) — *see* Hernia, ventral
  - abdominal, specified site NEC 553.8
    - with
      - gangrene (obstructed) 551.8
      - obstruction 552.8
        - and gangrene 551.8
  - appendix 553.8
    - with
      - gangrene (obstructed) 551.8
      - obstruction 552.8
        - and gangrene 551.8
  - bilateral (inguinal) — *see* Hernia, inguinal

- **Hernia, hernial** — *continued*
  - bladder (sphincter)
    - congenital (female) (male) 756.71
    - female (*see also* Cystocele, female) 618.01
    - male 596.8
  - brain 348.4
    - congenital 742.0
  - broad ligament 553.8
  - cartilage, vertebral — *see* Displacement, intervertebral disc
  - cerebral 348.4
    - congenital 742.0
    - endaural 742.0
  - ciliary body 364.89
    - traumatic 871.1
  - colic 553.9
    - with
      - gangrene (obstructed) 551.9
      - obstruction 552.9
        - and gangrene 551.9
  - colon 553.9
    - with
      - gangrene (obstructed) 551.9
      - obstruction 552.9
        - and gangrene 551.9
  - colostomy (stoma) 569.69
  - Cooper's (retroperitoneal) 553.8
    - with
      - gangrene (obstructed) 551.8
      - obstruction 552.8
        - and gangrene 551.8
  - crural — *see* Hernia, femoral
  - diaphragm, diaphragmatic 553.3
    - with
      - gangrene (obstructed) 551.3
      - obstruction 552.3
        - and gangrene 551.3
    - congenital 756.6
    - due to gross defect of diaphragm 756.6
    - traumatic 862.0
      - with open wound into cavity 862.1
  - direct (inguinal) — *see* Hernia, inguinal
  - disc, intervertebral — *see* Displacement, intervertebral disc
  - diverticulum, intestine 553.9
    - with
      - gangrene (obstructed) 551.9
      - obstruction 552.9
        - and gangrene 551.9
  - double (inguinal) — *see* Hernia, inguinal
  - due to adhesion with obstruction 560.81
  - duodenojejunal 553.8
    - with
      - gangrene (obstructed) 551.8
      - obstruction 552.8
        - and gangrene 551.8
  - en glissade — *see* Hernia, inguinal
  - enterostomy (stoma) 569.69
  - epigastric 553.29
    - with
      - gangrene (obstruction) 551.29
      - obstruction 552.29
        - and gangrene 551.29
    - recurrent 553.21
      - with
        - gangrene (obstructed) 551.21
        - obstruction 552.21
          - and gangrene 551.21
  - esophageal hiatus (sliding) 553.3
    - with
      - gangrene (obstructed) 551.3
      - obstruction 552.3
        - and gangrene 551.3
    - congenital 750.6
  - external (inguinal) — *see* Hernia, inguinal
  - fallopian tube 620.4
  - fascia 728.89
  - fat 729.30
    - eyelid 374.34

- **Hernia, hernial** — *continued*
  - fat — *continued*
    - orbital 374.34
    - pad 729.30
      - eye, eyelid 374.34
      - knee 729.31
      - orbit 374.34
      - popliteal (space) 729.31
      - specified site NEC 729.39
  - femoral (unilateral) 553.00
    - with
      - gangrene (obstructed) 551.00
      - obstruction 552.00
        - with gangrene 551.00
    - bilateral 553.02
      - gangrenous (obstructed) 551.02
      - obstructed 552.02
        - with gangrene 551.02
      - recurrent 553.03
        - gangrenous (obstructed) 551.03
        - obstructed 552.03
          - with gangrene 551.03
    - recurrent (unilateral) 553.01
      - bilateral 553.03
        - gangrenous (obstructed) 551.03
        - obstructed 552.03
          - with gangrene 551.01
      - gangrenous (obstructed) 551.01
      - obstructed 552.01
        - with gangrene 551.01
  - foramen
    - Bochdalek 553.3
      - with
        - gangrene (obstructed) 551.3
        - obstruction 552.3
          - and gangrene 551.3
      - congenital 756.6
    - magnum 348.4
    - Morgagni, Morgagnian 553.3
      - with
        - gangrene 551.3
        - obstruction 552.3
          - and gangrene 551.3
      - congenital 756.6
  - funicular (umbilical) 553.1
    - with
      - gangrene (obstructed) 551.1
      - obstruction 552.1
        - and gangrene 551.1
    - spermatic cord — *see* Hernia, inguinal
  - gangrenous — *see* Hernia, by site, with gangrene
  - gastrointestinal tract 553.9
    - with
      - gangrene (obstructed) 551.9
      - obstruction 552.9
        - and gangrene 551.9
  - gluteal — *see* Hernia, femoral
  - Gruber's (internal mesogastric) 553.8
    - with
      - gangrene (obstructed) 551.8
      - obstruction 552.8
        - and gangrene 551.8
  - Hesselbach's 553.8
    - with
      - gangrene (obstructed) 551.8
      - obstruction 552.8
        - and gangrene 551.8
  - hiatal (esophageal) (sliding) 553.3
    - with
      - gangrene (obstructed) 551.3
      - obstruction 552.3
        - and gangrene 551.3
    - congenital 750.6
  - incarcerated (*see also* Hernia, by site, with obstruction) 552.9
    - gangrenous (*see also* Hernia, by site, with gangrene) 551.9
  - incisional 553.21
    - with
      - gangrene (obstructed) 551.21
      - obstruction 552.21
        - and gangrene 551.21

- **Hernia, hernial** — *continued*
  - incisional — *continued*
    - lumbar — *see* Hernia, lumbar
    - recurrent 553.21
      - with
        - gangrene (obstructed) 551.21
        - obstruction 552.21
          - and gangrene 551.21
  - indirect (inguinal) — *see* Hernia, inguinal
  - infantile — *see* Hernia, inguinal
  - infrapatellar fat pad 729.31
  - inguinal (direct) (double) (encysted) (external) (funicular) (indirect) (infantile) (internal) (interstitial) (oblique) (scrotal) (sliding) 550.9 ☑

Note — Use the following fifth-digit subclassification with category 550:

0	*unilateral or unspecified (not specified as recurrent)*
1	*unilateral or unspecified, recurrent*
2	*bilateral (not specified as recurrent)*
3	*bilateral, recurrent*

-
    - with
      - gangrene (obstructed) 550.0 ☑
      - obstruction 550.1 ☑
        - and gangrene 550.0 ☑
  - internal 553.8
    - with
      - gangrene (obstructed) 551.8
      - obstruction 552.8
        - and gangrene 551.8
    - inguinal — *see* Hernia, inguinal
  - interstitial 553.9
    - with
      - gangrene (obstructed) 551.9
      - obstruction 552.9
        - and gangrene 551.9
    - inguinal — *see* Hernia, inguinal
  - intervertebral cartilage or disc — *see* Displacement, intervertebral disc
  - intestine, intestinal 553.9
    - with
      - gangrene (obstructed) 551.9
      - obstruction 552.9
        - and gangrene 551.9
  - intra-abdominal 553.9
    - with
      - gangrene (obstructed) 551.9
      - obstruction 552.9
        - and gangrene 551.9
  - intraparietal 553.9
    - with
      - gangrene (obstructed) 551.9
      - obstruction 552.9
        - and gangrene 551.9
  - iris 364.89
    - traumatic 871.1
  - irreducible (*see also* Hernia, by site, with obstruction) 552.9
    - gangrenous (with obstruction) (*see also* Hernia, by site, with gangrene) 551.9
  - ischiatic 553.8
    - with
      - gangrene (obstructed) 551.8
      - obstruction 552.8
        - and gangrene 551.8
  - ischiorectal 553.8
    - with
      - gangrene (obstructed) 551.8
      - obstruction 552.8
        - and gangrene 551.8
  - lens 379.32
    - traumatic 871.1
  - linea
    - alba — *see* Hernia, epigastric
    - semilunaris — *see* Hernia, spigelian
  - Littre's (diverticular) 553.9

- **Hernia, hernial** — *continued*
  - Littre's — *continued*
    - with
      - gangrene (obstructed) 551.9
      - obstruction 552.9
        - and gangrene 551.9
  - lumbar 553.8
    - with
      - gangrene (obstructed) 551.8
      - obstruction 552.8
        - and gangrene 551.8
    - intervertebral disc 722.10
  - lung (subcutaneous) 518.89
    - congenital 748.69
  - mediastinum 519.3
  - mesenteric (internal) 553.8
    - with
      - gangrene (obstructed) 551.8
      - obstruction 552.8
        - and gangrene 551.8
  - mesocolon 553.8
    - with
      - gangrene (obstructed) 551.8
      - obstruction 552.8
        - and gangrene 551.8
  - muscle (sheath) 728.89
  - nucleus pulposus — *see* Displacement, intervertebral disc
  - oblique (inguinal) — *see* Hernia, inguinal
  - obstructive (*see also* Hernia, by site, with obstruction) 552.9
    - gangrenous (with obstruction) (*see also* Hernia, by site, with gangrene) 551.9
  - obturator 553.8
    - with
      - gangrene (obstructed) 551.8
      - obstruction 552.8
        - and gangrene 551.8
  - omental 553.8
    - with
      - gangrene (obstructed) 551.8
      - obstruction 552.8
        - and gangrene 551.8
  - orbital fat (pad) 374.34
  - ovary 620.4
  - oviduct 620.4
  - paracolostomy (stoma) 569.69
  - paraduodenal 553.8
    - with
      - gangrene (obstructed) 551.8
      - obstruction 552.8
        - and gangrene 551.8
  - paraesophageal 553.3
    - with
      - gangrene (obstructed) 551.3
      - obstruction 552.3
        - and gangrene 551.3
    - congenital 750.6
  - parahiatal 553.3
    - with
      - gangrene (obstructed) 551.3
      - obstruction 552.3
        - and gangrene 551.3
  - paraumbilical 553.1
    - with
      - gangrene (obstructed) 551.1
      - obstruction 552.1
        - and gangrene 551.1
  - parietal 553.9
    - with
      - gangrene (obstructed) 551.9
      - obstruction 552.9
        - and gangrene 551.9
  - perineal 553.8
    - with
      - gangrene (obstructed) 551.8
      - obstruction 552.8
        - and gangrene 551.8
  - peritoneal sac, lesser 553.8
    - with
      - gangrene (obstructed) 551.8
      - obstruction 552.8
        - and gangrene 551.8
  - popliteal fat pad 729.31

- **Hernia, hernial** — *continued*
  - postoperative 553.21
    - with
      - gangrene (obstructed) 551.21
      - obstruction 552.21
        - and gangrene 551.21
  - pregnant uterus 654.4 ☑
  - prevesical 596.8
  - properitoneal 553.8
    - with
      - gangrene (obstructed) 551.8
      - obstruction 552.8
        - and gangrene 551.8
  - pudendal 553.8
    - with
      - gangrene (obstructed) 551.8
      - obstruction 552.8
        - and gangrene 551.8
  - rectovaginal 618.6
  - retroperitoneal 553.8
    - with
      - gangrene (obstructed) 551.8
      - obstruction 552.8
        - and gangrene 551.8
  - Richter's (parietal) 553.9
    - with
      - gangrene (obstructed) 551.9
      - obstruction 552.9
        - and gangrene 551.9
  - Rieux's, Riex's (retrocecal) 553.8
    - with
      - gangrene (obstructed) 551.8
      - obstruction 552.8
        - and gangrene 551.8
  - sciatic 553.8
    - with
      - gangrene (obstructed) 551.8
      - obstruction 552.8
        - and gangrene 551.8
  - scrotum, scrotal — *see* Hernia, inguinal
  - sliding (inguinal) (*see also* Hernia, inguinal)
    - hiatus — *see* Hernia, hiatal
  - spigelian 553.29
    - with
      - gangrene (obstructed) 551.29
      - obstruction 552.29
        - and gangrene 551.29
  - spinal (*see also* Spina bifida) 741.9 ☑
    - with hydrocephalus 741.0 ☑
  - strangulated (*see also* Hernia, by site, with obstruction) 552.9
    - gangrenous (with obstruction) (*see also* Hernia, by site, with gangrene) 551.9
  - supraumbilicus (linea alba) — *see* Hernia, epigastric
  - tendon 727.9
  - testis (nontraumatic) 550.9 ☑
    - meaning
      - scrotal hernia 550.9 ☑
      - symptomatic late syphilis 095.8
  - Treitz's (fossa) 553.8
    - with
      - gangrene (obstructed) 551.8
      - obstruction 552.8
        - and gangrene 551.8
  - tunica
    - albuginea 608.89
    - vaginalis 752.89
  - umbilicus, umbilical 553.1
    - with
      - gangrene (obstructed) 551.1
      - obstruction 552.1
        - and gangrene 551.1
  - ureter 593.89
    - with obstruction 593.4
  - uterus 621.8
    - pregnant 654.4 ☑
  - vaginal (posterior) 618.6
  - Velpeau's (femoral) (*see also* Hernia, femoral) 553.00
  - ventral 553.20
    - with
      - gangrene (obstructed) 551.20

- **Hernia, hernial** — *continued*
  - ventral — *continued*
    - with — *continued*
      - obstruction 552.20
        - and gangrene 551.20
    - incisional 553.21
    - recurrent 553.21
      - with
        - gangrene (obstructed) 551.21
        - obstruction 552.21
          - and gangrene 551.21
  - vesical
    - congenital (female) (male) 756.71
    - female (*see also* Cystocele, female) 618.01
    - male 596.8
  - vitreous (into anterior chamber) 379.21
    - traumatic 871.1
- **Herniation** — *see also* Hernia
  - brain (stem) 348.4
  - cerebral 348.4
  - gastric mucosa (into duodenal bulb) 537.89
  - mediastinum 519.3
  - nucleus pulposus — *see* Displacement, intervertebral disc
- **Herpangina** 074.0
- **Herpes, herpetic** 054.9
  - auricularis (zoster) 053.71
    - simplex 054.73
  - blepharitis (zoster) 053.20
    - simplex 054.41
  - circinate 110.5
  - circinatus 110.5
    - bullous 694.5
  - conjunctiva (simplex) 054.43
    - zoster 053.21
  - cornea (simplex) 054.43
    - disciform (simplex) 054.43
    - zoster 053.21
  - encephalitis 054.3
  - eye (zoster) 053.29
    - simplex 054.40
  - eyelid (zoster) 053.20
    - simplex 054.41
  - febrilis 054.9
  - fever 054.9
  - geniculate ganglionitis 053.11
  - genital, genitalis 054.10
    - specified site NEC 054.19
  - gestationis 646.8 ☑
  - gingivostomatitis 054.2
  - iridocyclitis (simplex) 054.44
    - zoster 053.22
  - iris (any site) 695.10 ▲
  - iritis (simplex) 054.44
  - keratitis (simplex) 054.43
    - dendritic 054.42
    - disciform 054.43
    - interstitial 054.43
      - zoster 053.21
  - keratoconjunctivitis (simplex) 054.43
    - zoster 053.21
  - labialis 054.9
    - meningococcal 036.89
  - lip 054.9
  - meningitis (simplex) 054.72
    - zoster 053.0
  - ophthalmicus (zoster) 053.20
    - simplex 054.40
  - otitis externa (zoster) 053.71
    - simplex 054.73
  - penis 054.13
  - perianal 054.10
  - pharyngitis 054.79
  - progenitalis 054.10
  - scrotum 054.19
  - septicemia 054.5
  - simplex 054.9
    - complicated 054.8
      - ophthalmic 054.40
        - specified NEC 054.49
      - specified NEC 054.79
    - congenital 771.2
    - external ear 054.73
- **Herpes, herpetic** — *continued*
  - simplex — *continued*
    - keratitis 054.43
      - dendritic 054.42
    - meningitis 054.72
    - myelitis 054.74
    - neuritis 054.79
    - specified complication NEC 054.79
      - ophthalmic 054.49
    - visceral 054.71
  - stomatitis 054.2
  - tonsurans 110.0
    - maculosus (of Hebra) 696.3
  - visceral 054.71
  - vulva 054.12
  - vulvovaginitis 054.11
  - whitlow 054.6
  - zoster 053.9
    - auricularis 053.71
    - complicated 053.8
      - specified NEC 053.79
    - conjunctiva 053.21
    - cornea 053.21
    - ear 053.71
    - eye 053.29
    - geniculate 053.11
    - keratitis 053.21
      - interstitial 053.21
    - myelitis 053.14
    - neuritis 053.10
    - ophthalmicus(a) 053.20
    - oticus 053.71
    - otitis externa 053.71
    - specified complication NEC 053.79
    - specified site NEC 053.9
  - zosteriform, intermediate type 053.9
- **Herrick's**
  - anemia (hemoglobin S disease) 282.61
  - syndrome (hemoglobin S disease) 282.61
- **Hers' disease** (glycogenosis VI) 271.0
- **Herter (-Gee) disease or syndrome** (nontropical sprue) 579.0
- **Herter's infantilism** (nontropical sprue) 579.0
- **Herxheimer's disease** (diffuse idiopathic cutaneous atrophy) 701.8
- **Herxheimer's reaction** 995.0
- **Hesitancy, urinary** 788.64
- **Hesselbach's hernia** — *see* Hernia, Hesselbach's
- **Heterochromia** (congenital) 743.46
  - acquired 364.53
  - cataract 366.33
  - cyclitis 364.21
  - hair 704.3
  - iritis 364.21
  - retained metallic foreign body 360.62
    - magnetic 360.52
  - uveitis 364.21
- **Heterophoria** 378.40
  - alternating 378.45
  - vertical 378.43
- **Heterophyes, small intestine** 121.6
- **Heterophyiasis** 121.6
- **Heteropsia** 368.8
- **Heterotopia, heterotopic** — *see also* Malposition, congenital
  - cerebralis 742.4
  - pancreas, pancreatic 751.7
  - spinalis 742.59
- **Heterotropia** 378.30
  - intermittent 378.20
    - vertical 378.31
  - vertical (constant) (intermittent) 378.31
- **Heubner's disease** 094.89
- **Heubner-Herter disease or syndrome** (nontropical sprue) 579.0
- **Hexadactylism** 755.0 ☑
- **Heyd's syndrome** (hepatorenal) 572.4
- **HGSIL** (high grade squamous intraepithelial lesion) (cytologic finding) (Pap smear finding)
  - anus 796.74 ●
  - cervix 795.04 ●
- **HGSIL** — *continued*
  - cervix — *continued*
    - biopsy finding — code to CIN II or CIN III ● ●
  - vagina 795.14 ●
- **Hibernoma (M8880/0)** — *see* Lipoma
- **Hiccough** 786.8
  - epidemic 078.89
  - psychogenic 306.1
- **Hiccup** — *see also* Hiccough 786.8
- **Hicks (-Braxton) contractures** 644.1 ☑
- **Hidden penis** 752.65
- **Hidradenitis** (axillaris) (suppurative) 705.83
- **Hidradenoma** (nodular) (M8400/0) — *see also* Neoplasm, skin, benign
  - clear cell (M8402/0) — *see* Neoplasm, skin, benign
  - papillary (M8405/0) — *see* Neoplasm, skin, benign
- **Hidrocystoma** (M8404/0) — *see* Neoplasm, skin, benign
- **HIE** (hypoxic-ischemic encephalopathy) 768.7
- **High**
  - A_2 anemia 282.49
  - altitude effects 993.2
    - anoxia 993.2
    - on
      - ears 993.0
      - sinuses 993.1
    - polycythemia 289.0
  - arch
    - foot 755.67
    - palate 750.26
  - artery (arterial) tension (*see also* Hypertension) 401.9
    - without diagnosis of hypertension 796.2
  - basal metabolic rate (BMR) 794.7
  - blood pressure (*see also* Hypertension) 401.9
    - incidental reading (isolated) (nonspecific), no diagnosis of hypertension 796.2
  - cholesterol 272.0
    - with high triglycerides 272.2
  - compliance bladder 596.4
  - diaphragm (congenital) 756.6
  - frequency deafness (congenital) (regional) 389.8
  - head at term 652.5 ☑
    - affecting fetus or newborn 763.1
  - output failure (cardiac) (*see also* Failure, heart) 428.9
  - oxygen-affinity hemoglobin 289.0
  - palate 750.26
  - risk
    - behavior — *see* Problem
    - family situation V61.9
      - specified circumstance NEC V61.8
    - human papillomavirus (HPV) DNA test positive ● ●
      - anal 796.75 ●
      - cervical 795.05 ●
      - vaginal 795.15 ●
    - individual NEC V62.89
    - infant NEC V20.1
    - patient taking drugs (prescribed) V67.51
      - nonprescribed (*see also* Abuse, drugs, nondependent) 305.9 ☑
    - pregnancy V23.9
      - inadequate prenatal care V23.7
      - specified problem NEC V23.89
  - temperature (of unknown origin) (*see also* Pyrexia) 780.60 ▲
  - thoracic rib 756.3
  - triglycerides 272.1
    - with high cholesterol 272.2
- **Hildenbrand's disease** (typhus) 081.9
- **Hilger's syndrome** 337.09 ▲
- **Hill diarrhea** 579.1
- **Hilliard's lupus** — *see also* Tuberculosis 017.0 ☑
- **Hilum** — *see* condition
- **Hip** — *see* condition
- **Hippel's disease** (retinocerebral angiomatosis) 759.6
- **Hippus** 379.49
- **Hirschfeld's disease** (acute diabetes mellitus) — *see also* Diabetes 250.0 ☑
  - due to secondary diabetes 249.0 ☑ ●
- **Hirschsprung's disease or megacolon** (congenital) 751.3
- **Hirsuties** — *see also* Hypertrichosis 704.1
- **Hirsutism** — *see also* Hypertrichosis 704.1
- **Hirudiniasis** (external) (internal) 134.2
- **Hiss-Russell dysentery** 004.1
- **Histamine cephalgia** 339.00 ▲
- **Histidinemia** 270.5
- **Histidinuria** 270.5
- **Histiocytic syndromes** 288.4
- **Histiocytoma (M8832/0)** — *see also* Neoplasm, skin, benign
  - fibrous (M8830/0) (*see also* Neoplasm, skin, benign)
    - atypical (M8830/1) — *see* Neoplasm, connective tissue, uncertain behavior
    - malignant (M8830/3) — *see* Neoplasm, connective tissue, malignant
- **Histiocytosis** (acute) (chronic) (subacute) 277.89
  - acute differentiated progressive (M9722/3) 202.5 ☑
  - cholesterol 277.89
  - essential 277.89
  - lipid, lipoid (essential) 272.7
  - lipochrome (familial) 288.1
  - malignant (M9720/3) 202.3 ☑
  - X (chronic) 277.89
    - acute (progressive) (M9722/3) 202.5 ☑
- **Histoplasmosis** 115.90
  - with
    - endocarditis 115.94
    - meningitis 115.91
    - pericarditis 115.93
    - pneumonia 115.95
    - retinitis 115.92
    - specified manifestation NEC 115.99
  - African (due to Histoplasma duboisii) 115.10
    - with
      - endocarditis 115.14
      - meningitis 115.11
      - pericarditis 115.13
      - pneumonia 115.15
      - retinitis 115.12
      - specified manifestation NEC 115.19
  - American (due to Histoplasma capsulatum) 115.00
    - with
      - endocarditis 115.04
      - meningitis 115.01
      - pericarditis 115.03
      - pneumonia 115.05
      - retinitis 115.02
      - specified manifestation NEC 115.09
  - Darling's — *see* Histoplasmosis, American
  - large form (*see also* Histoplasmosis, African) 115.10
  - lung 115.05
  - small form (*see also* Histoplasmosis, American) 115.00
- **History** (personal) of
  - abuse
    - emotional V15.42
    - neglect V15.42
    - physical V15.41

History of — *continued*
abuse — *continued*
sexual V15.41
affective psychosis V11.1
alcoholism V11.3
specified as drinking problem (*see also* Abuse, drugs, nondependent) 305.0 ☑
allergy to
analgesic agent NEC V14.6
anesthetic NEC V14.4
antibiotic agent NEC V14.1
penicillin V14.0
anti-infective agent NEC V14.3
diathesis V15.09
drug V14.9
specified type NEC V14.8
eggs V15.03
food additives V15.05
insect bite V15.06
latex V15.07
medicinal agents V14.9
specified type NEC V14.8
milk products V15.02
narcotic agent NEC V14.5
nuts V15.05
peanuts V15.01
penicillin V14.0
radiographic dye V15.08
seafood V15.04
serum V14.7
specified food NEC V15.05
specified nonmedicinal agents NEC V15.09
spider bite V15.06
sulfa V14.2
sulfonamides V14.2
therapeutic agent NEC V15.09
vaccine V14.7
anemia V12.3
arrest, sudden cardiac V12.53
arthritis V13.4
attack, transient ischemic (TIA) V12.54
benign neoplasm of brain V12.41
blood disease V12.3
calculi, urinary V13.01
cardiovascular disease V12.50
myocardial infarction 412
chemotherapy, antineoplastic V87.41 ●
child abuse V15.41
cigarette smoking V15.82
circulatory system disease V12.50
myocardial infarction 412
congenital malformation V13.69
contraception V15.7
death, sudden, successfully resuscitated V12.53
deficit
prolonged reversible ischemic neurologic (PRIND) V12.54
reversible ischemic neurologic (RIND) V12.54
diathesis, allergic V15.09
digestive system disease V12.70
peptic ulcer V12.71
polyps, colonic V12.72
specified NEC V12.79
disease (of) V13.9
blood V12.3
blood-forming organs V12.3
cardiovascular system V12.50
circulatory system V12.50
specified NEC V12.59
digestive system V12.70
peptic ulcer V12.71
polyps, colonic V12.72
specified NEC V12.79
infectious V12.00
malaria V12.03
methicillin resistant Staphylococcus aureus (MRSA) V12.04 ●

History of — *continued*
disease — *continued*
infectious — *continued*
MRSA (methicillin resistant Staphylococcus aureus) V12.04 ●
poliomyelitis V12.02
specified NEC V12.09
tuberculosis V12.01
parasitic V12.00
specified NEC V12.09
respiratory system V12.60
pneumonia V12.61
specified NEC V12.69
skin V13.3
specified site NEC V13.8
subcutaneous tissue V13.3
trophoblastic V13.1
affecting management of pregnancy V23.1
disorder (of) V13.9
endocrine V12.2
genital system V13.29
hematological V12.3
immunity V12.2
mental V11.9
affective type V11.1
manic-depressive V11.1
neurosis V11.2
schizophrenia V11.0
specified type NEC V11.8
metabolic V12.2
musculoskeletal NEC V13.59 ▲
nervous system V12.40
specified type NEC V12.49
obstetric V13.29
affecting management of current pregnancy V23.49
pre-term labor V23.41
pre-term labor V13.21
sense organs V12.40
specified type NEC V12.49
specified site NEC V13.8
urinary system V13.00
calculi V13.01
infection V13.02
nephrotic syndrome V13.03
specified NEC V13.09
drug use
nonprescribed (*see also* Abuse, drugs, nondependent) 305.9 ☑
patent (*see also* Abuse, drugs, nondependent) 305.9 ☑
dysplasia
cervical (conditions classifiable to 622.10-622.12) V13.22
effect NEC of external cause V15.89
embolism (pulmonary) V12.51
emotional abuse V15.42
encephalitis V12.42
endocrine disorder V12.2
extracorporeal membrane oxygenation (ECMO) V15.87
falling V15.88
family
allergy V19.6
anemia V18.2
arteriosclerosis V17.49
arthritis V17.7
asthma V17.5
blindness V19.0
blood disorder NEC V18.3
cardiovascular disease V17.49
carrier, genetic disease V18.9
cerebrovascular disease V17.1
chronic respiratory condition NEC V17.6
colonic polyps V18.51
congenital anomalies V19.5
consanguinity V19.7
coronary artery disease V17.3
cystic fibrosis V18.19
deafness V19.2
diabetes mellitus V18.0
digestive disorders V18.59

History of — *continued*
family — *continued*
disease or disorder (of)
allergic V19.6
blood NEC V18.3
cardiovascular NEC V17.49
cerebrovascular V17.1
colonic polyps V18.51
coronary artery V17.3
death, sudden cardiac (SCD) V17.41
digestive V18.59
ear NEC V19.3
endocrine V18.19
multiple neoplasia [MEN] syndrome V18.11
eye NEC V19.1
genitourinary NEC V18.7
hypertensive V17.49
infectious V18.8
ischemic heart V17.3
kidney V18.69
polycystic V18.61
mental V17.0
metabolic V18.19
musculoskeletal NEC V17.89
osteoporosis V17.81
neurological NEC V17.2
parasitic V18.8
psychiatric condition V17.0
skin condition V19.4
ear disorder NEC V19.3
endocrine disease V18.19
multiple neoplasia [MEN] syndrome V18.11
epilepsy V17.2
eye disorder NEC V19.1
genetic disease carrier V18.9
genitourinary disease NEC V18.7
glomerulonephritis V18.69
gout V18.19
hay fever V17.6
hearing loss V19.2
hematopoietic neoplasia V16.7
Hodgkin's disease V16.7
Huntington's chorea V17.2
hydrocephalus V19.5
hypertension V17.49
infarction, myocardial V17.3
infectious disease V18.8
ischemic heart disease V17.3
kidney disease V18.69
polycystic V18.61
leukemia V16.6
lymphatic malignant neoplasia NEC V16.7
malignant neoplasm (of) NEC V16.9
anorectal V16.0
anus V16.0
appendix V16.0
bladder V16.52
bone V16.8
brain V16.8
breast V16.3
male V16.8
bronchus V16.1
cecum V16.0
cervix V16.49
colon V16.0
duodenum V16.0
esophagus V16.0
eye V16.8
gallbladder V16.0
gastrointestinal tract V16.0
genital organs V16.40
hemopoietic NEC V16.7
ileum V16.0
ilium V16.8
intestine V16.0
intrathoracic organs NEC V16.2
kidney V16.51
larynx V16.2
liver V16.0
lung V16.1
lymphatic NEC V16.7
ovary V16.41

History of — *continued*
family — *continued*
malignant neoplasm — *continued*
oviduct V16.41
pancreas V16.0
penis V16.49
prostate V16.42
rectum V16.0
respiratory organs NEC V16.2
skin V16.8
specified site NEC V16.8
stomach V16.0
testis V16.43
trachea V16.1
ureter V16.59
urethra V16.59
urinary organs V16.59
uterus V16.49
vagina V16.49
vulva V16.49
MEN (multiple endocrine neoplasia syndrome) V18.11
mental retardation V18.4
metabolic disease NEC V18.19
mongolism V19.5
monoclonal drug therapy V87.42 ●
multiple
endocrine neoplasia [MEN] syndrome V18.11
myeloma V16.7
musculoskeletal disease NEC V17.89
osteoporosis V17.81
myocardial infarction V17.3
nephritis V18.69
nephrosis V18.69
osteoporosis V17.81
parasitic disease V18.8
polycystic kidney disease V18.61
psychiatric disorder V17.0
psychosis V17.0
retardation, mental V18.4
retinitis pigmentosa V19.1
schizophrenia V17.0
skin conditions V19.4
specified condition NEC V19.8
stroke (cerebrovascular) V17.1
sudden cardiac death (SCD) V17.41
visual loss V19.0
fracture, healed ●
pathologic V13.51 ●
stress V13.52 ●
traumatic V15.51 ●
genital system disorder V13.29
pre-term labor V13.21
health hazard V15.9
falling V15.88
specified cause NEC V15.89
hepatitis
B V12.09
C V12.09
Hodgkin's disease V10.72
hypospadias V13.61
immunity disorder V12.2
infarction, cerebral, without residual deficits V12.54
infection
central nervous system V12.42
urinary (tract) V13.02
infectious disease V12.00
malaria V12.03
methicillin resistant Staphylococcus aureus (MRSA) V12.04 ●
MRSA (methicillin resistant Staphylococcus aureus) V12.04 ●
poliomyelitis V12.02
specified NEC V12.09
tuberculosis V12.01
injury NEC V15.59 ▲
insufficient prenatal care V23.7
in utero procedure ●
during pregnancy V15.21 ●
while a fetus V15.22 ●

History of — *continued*
- irradiation V15.3
- leukemia V10.60
  - lymphoid V10.61
  - monocytic V10.63
  - myeloid V10.62
  - specified type NEC V10.69
- little or no prenatal care V23.7
- low birth weight (*see also* Status, low birth weight) V21.30
- lymphosarcoma V10.71
- malaria V12.03
- malignant neoplasm (of) V10.9
  - accessory sinus V10.22
  - adrenal V10.88
  - anus V10.06
  - bile duct V10.09
  - bladder V10.51
  - bone V10.81
  - brain V10.85
  - breast V10.3
  - bronchus V10.11
  - cervix uteri V10.41
  - colon V10.05
  - connective tissue NEC V10.89
  - corpus uteri V10.42
  - digestive system V10.00
    - specified part NEC V10.09
  - duodenum V10.09
  - endocrine gland NEC V10.88
  - epididymis V10.48
  - esophagus V10.03
  - eye V10.84
  - fallopian tube V10.44
  - female genital organ V10.40
    - specified site NEC V10.44
  - gallbladder V10.09
  - gastrointestinal tract V10.00
  - gum V10.02
  - hematopoietic NEC V10.79
  - hypopharynx V10.02
  - ileum V10.09
  - intrathoracic organs NEC V10.20
  - jejunum V10.09
  - kidney V10.52
  - large intestine V10.05
  - larynx V10.21
  - lip V10.02
  - liver V10.07
  - lung V10.11
  - lymphatic NEC V10.79
  - lymph glands or nodes NEC V10.79
  - male genital organ V10.45
    - specified site NEC V10.49
  - mediastinum V10.29
  - melanoma (of skin) V10.82
  - middle ear V10.22
  - mouth V10.02
    - specified part NEC V10.02
  - nasal cavities V10.22
  - nasopharynx V10.02
  - nervous system NEC V10.86
  - nose V10.22
  - oropharynx V10.02
  - ovary V10.43
  - pancreas V10.09
  - parathyroid V10.88
  - penis V10.49
  - pharynx V10.02
  - pineal V10.88
  - pituitary V10.88
  - placenta V10.44
  - pleura V10.29
  - prostate V10.46
  - rectosigmoid junction V10.06
  - rectum V10.06
  - renal pelvis V10.53
  - respiratory organs NEC V10.20
  - salivary gland V10.02
  - skin V10.83
    - melanoma V10.82
  - small intestine NEC V10.09
  - soft tissue NEC V10.89
  - specified site NEC V10.89
  - stomach V10.04
  - testis V10.47

History of — *continued*
- malignant neoplasm — *continued*
  - thymus V10.29
  - thyroid V10.87
  - tongue V10.01
  - trachea V10.12
  - ureter V10.59
  - urethra V10.59
  - urinary organ V10.50
  - uterine adnexa V10.44
  - uterus V10.42
  - vagina V10.44
  - vulva V10.44
- manic-depressive psychosis V11.1
- meningitis V12.42
- mental disorder V11.9
  - affective type V11.1
  - manic-depressive V11.1
  - neurosis V11.2
  - schizophrenia V11.0
  - specified type NEC V11.8
- metabolic disorder V12.2
- methicillin resistant Staphylococcus aureus (MRSA) V12.04 ●
- MRSA (methicillin resistant Staphylococcus aureus) V12.04 ●
- musculoskeletal disorder NEC V13.59 ▲
- myocardial infarction 412
- neglect (emotional) V15.42
- nephrotic syndrome V13.03
- nervous system disorder V12.40
  - specified type NEC V12.49
- neurosis V11.2
- noncompliance with medical treatment V15.81
- nutritional deficiency V12.1
- obstetric disorder V13.29
  - affecting management of current pregnancy V23.49
    - pre-term labor V23.41
  - pre-term labor V13.21
- parasitic disease V12.00
  - specified NEC V12.09
- perinatal problems V13.7
  - low birth weight (*see also* Status, low birth weight) V21.30
- physical abuse V15.41
- poisoning V15.6
- poliomyelitis V12.02
- polyps, colonic V12.72
- poor obstetric V13.29
  - affecting management of current pregnancy V23.49
    - pre-term labor V23.41
  - pre-term labor V13.21
- prolonged reversible ischemic neurologic deficit (PRIND) V12.54
- psychiatric disorder V11.9
  - affective type V11.1
  - manic-depressive V11.1
  - neurosis V11.2
  - schizophrenia V11.0
  - specified type NEC V11.8
- psychological trauma V15.49
  - emotional abuse V15.42
  - neglect V15.42
  - physical abuse V15.41
  - rape V15.41
- psychoneurosis V11.2
- radiation therapy V15.3
- rape V15.41
- respiratory system disease V12.60
  - pneumonia V12.61
  - specified NEC V12.69
- reticulosarcoma V10.71
- return from military deployment V62.22 ●
- reversible ischemic neurologic deficit (RIND) V12.54
- schizophrenia V11.0
- skin disease V13.3
- smoking (tobacco) V15.82
- stroke without residual deficits V12.54
- subcutaneous tissue disease V13.3

History of — *continued*
- sudden
  - cardiac
    - arrest V12.53
    - death (successfully resuscitated) V12.53
- surgery to
  - great vessels V15.1
  - heart V15.1
    - in utero ●
      - during pregnancy V15.21 ●
      - while a fetus V15.22 ●
  - organs NEC V15.29 ▲
- syndrome, nephrotic V13.03
- therapy ●
  - antineoplastic drug V87.41 ●
  - drug NEC V87.49 ●
  - monoclonal drug V87.42 ●
- thrombophlebitis V12.52
- thrombosis V12.51
- tobacco use V15.82
- trophoblastic disease V13.1
  - affecting management of pregnancy V23.1
- tuberculosis V12.01
- ulcer, peptic V12.71
- urinary system disorder V13.00
  - calculi V13.01
  - infection V13.02
  - nephrotic syndrome V13.03
  - specified NEC V13.09

His-Werner disease (trench fever) 083.1

HIT (heparin-induced thrombocytopenia) 289.84 ●

Hives (bold) — *see also* Urticaria 708.9

HIV infection (disease) (illness) — *see* Human immunodeficiency virus (disease) (illness) (infection)

Hoarseness 784.49

Hobnail liver — *see* Cirrhosis, portal

Hobo, hoboism V60.0

Hodgkin's
- disease (M9650/3) 201.9 ☑
  - lymphocytic
    - depletion (M9653/3) 201.7 ☑
      - diffuse fibrosis (M9654/3) 201.7 ☑
      - reticular type (M9655/3) 201.7 ☑
    - predominance (M9651/3) 201.4 ☑
  - lymphocytic-histiocytic predominance (M9651/3) 201.4 ☑
  - mixed cellularity (M9652/3) 201.6 ☑
  - nodular sclerosis (M9656/3) 201.5 ☑
    - cellular phase (M9657/3) 201.5 ☑
- granuloma (M9661/3) 201.1 ☑
- lymphogranulomatosis (M9650/3) 201.9 ☑
- lymphoma (M9650/3) 201.9 ☑
- lymphosarcoma (M9650/3) 201.9 ☑
- paragranuloma (M9660/3) 201.0 ☑
- sarcoma (M9662/3) 201.2 ☑

Hodgson's disease (aneurysmal dilatation of aorta) 441.9
- ruptured 441.5

Hodi-potsy 111.0

Hoffa (-Kastert) disease or syndrome (liposynovitis prepatellaris) 272.8

Hoffmann-Bouveret syndrome (paroxysmal tachycardia) 427.2

Hoffman's syndrome 244.9 *[359.5]*

Hole
- macula 362.54
- optic disc, crater-like 377.22
- retina (macula) 362.54
  - round 361.31
    - with detachment 361.01

Holla disease — *see also* Spherocytosis 282.0

Holländer-Simons syndrome (progressive lipodystrophy) 272.6

Hollow foot (congenital) 754.71

Hollow foot — *continued*
- acquired 736.73

Holmes' syndrome (visual disorientation) 368.16

Holoprosencephaly 742.2
- due to
  - trisomy 13 758.1
  - trisomy 18 758.2

Holthouse's hernia — *see* Hernia, inguinal

Homesickness 309.89

Homocystinemia 270.4

Homocystinuria 270.4

Homologous serum jaundice (prophylactic) (therapeutic) — *see* Hepatitis, viral

Homosexuality — omit code
- ego-dystonic 302.0
- pedophilic 302.2
- problems with 302.0

Homozygous Hb-S disease 282.61

Honeycomb lung 518.89
- congenital 748.4

Hong Kong ear 117.3

HOOD (hereditary osteo-onychodysplasia) 756.89

Hooded
- clitoris 752.49
- penis 752.69

Hookworm (anemia) (disease) (infestation) — *see* Ancylostomiasis

Hoppe-Goldflam syndrome 358.00

Hordeolum (external) (eyelid) 373.11
- internal 373.12

Horn
- cutaneous 702.8
  - cheek 702.8
  - eyelid 702.8
  - penis 702.8
- iliac 756.89
- nail 703.8
  - congenital 757.5
- papillary 700

Horner's
- syndrome (*see also* Neuropathy, peripheral, autonomic) 337.9
  - traumatic 954.0
- teeth 520.4

Horseshoe kidney (congenital) 753.3

Horton's
- disease (temporal arteritis) 446.5
- headache or neuralgia 339.00 ▲

Hospice care V66.7

Hospitalism (in children) NEC 309.83

Hourglass contraction, contracture
- bladder 596.8
- gallbladder 575.2
  - congenital 751.69
- stomach 536.8
  - congenital 750.7
  - psychogenic 306.4
- uterus 661.4 ☑
  - affecting fetus or newborn 763.7

Household circumstance affecting care V60.9
- specified type NEC V60.8

Housemaid's knee 727.2

Housing circumstance affecting care V60.9
- specified type NEC V60.8

HTLV-I infection 079.51

HTLV-II infection 079.52

HTLV-III/LAV (disease) (illness) (infection) — *see* Human immunodeficiency virus (disease) (illness) (infection)

HTLV-III (disease) (illness) (infection) — *see* Human immunodeficiency virus (disease) (illness) (infection)

Huchard's disease (continued arterial hypertension) 401.9

Hudson-Stähli lines 371.11

Huguier's disease (uterine fibroma) 218.9

Human bite (open wound) — see also Wound, open, by site

- **Human bite** — see also Wound, open, by site — *continued*
  - intact skin surface — *see* Contusion
- **Human immunodeficiency virus** (disease) (illness) 042
  - infection V08
    - with symptoms, symptomatic 042
- **Human immunodeficiency virus-2 infection** 079.53
- **Human immunovirus** (disease) (illness) (infection) — *see* Human immunodeficiency virus (disease) (illness) (infection)
- **Human papillomavirus** 079.4
  - high risk, DNA test positive ●
    - anal 796.75 ●
    - cervical 795.05 ●
    - vaginal 795.15 ●
  - low risk, DNA test positive ●
    - anal 796.79 ●
    - cervical 795.09 ●
    - vaginal 795.19 ●
- **Human parvovirus** 079.83
- **Human T-cell lymphotrophic virus-I infection** 079.51
- **Human T-cell lymphotrophic virus-II infection** 079.52
- **Human T-cell lymphotrophic virus-III** (disease) (illness) (infection) — *see* Human immunodeficiency virus (disease) (illness) (infection)
- **Humpback** (acquired) 737.9
  - congenital 756.19
- **Hum, venous** — omit code
- **Hunchback** (acquired) 737.9
  - congenital 756.19
- **Hunger** 994.2
  - air, psychogenic 306.1
  - disease 251.1
- **Hungry bone syndrome** 275.5 ●
- **Hunner's ulcer** — *see also* Cystitis 595.1
- **Hunt's**
  - neuralgia 053.11
  - syndrome (herpetic geniculate ganglionitis) 053.11
    - dyssynergia cerebellaris myoclonica 334.2
- **Hunter's glossitis** 529.4
- **Hunterian chancre** 091.0
- **Hunter (-Hurler) syndrome** (mucopolysaccharidosis II) 277.5
- **Huntington's**
  - chorea 333.4
  - disease 333.4
- **Huppert's disease** (multiple myeloma) (M9730/3) 203.0 ☑
- **Hurler (-Hunter) disease or syndrome** (mucopolysaccharidosis II) 277.5
- **Hürthle cell**
  - adenocarcinoma (M8290/3) 193
  - adenoma (M8290/0) 226
  - carcinoma (M8290/3) 193
  - tumor (M8290/0) 226
- **Hutchinson's**
  - disease meaning
    - angioma serpiginosum 709.1
    - cheiropompholyx 705.81
    - prurigo estivalis 692.72
    - summer eruption, or summer prurigo 692.72
  - incisors 090.5
  - melanotic freckle (M8742/2) (*see also* Neoplasm, skin, in situ)
    - malignant melanoma in (M8742/3) — *see* Melanoma
  - teeth or incisors (congenital syphilis) 090.5
- **Hutchinson-Boeck disease or syndrome** (sarcoidosis) 135
- **Hutchinson-Gilford disease or syndrome** (progeria) 259.8
- **Hyaline**
  - degeneration (diffuse) (generalized) 728.9
    - localized — *see* Degeneration, by site
- **Hyaline** — *continued*
  - membrane (disease) (lung) (newborn) 769
- **Hyalinosis cutis et mucosae** 272.8
- **Hyalin plaque, sclera, senile** 379.16
- **Hyalitis** (asteroid) 379.22
  - syphilitic 095.8
- **Hydatid**
  - cyst or tumor (*see also* Echinococcus)
    - fallopian tube 752.11
  - mole — *see* Hydatidiform mole
  - Morgagni (congenital) 752.89
    - fallopian tube 752.11
- **Hydatidiform mole** (benign) (complicating pregnancy) (delivered) (undelivered) 630
  - invasive (M9100/1) 236.1
  - malignant (M9100/1) 236.1
  - previous, affecting management of pregnancy V23.1
- **Hydatidosis** — *see* Echinococcus
- **Hyde's disease** (prurigo nodularis) 698.3
- **Hydradenitis** 705.83
- **Hydradenoma** (M8400/0) — *see* Hidradenoma
- **Hydralazine lupus or syndrome**
  - correct substance properly administered 695.4
  - overdose or wrong substance given or taken 972.6
- **Hydramnios** 657.0 ☑
  - affecting fetus or newborn 761.3
- **Hydrancephaly** 742.3
  - with spina bifida (*see also* Spina bifida) 741.0 ☑
- **Hydranencephaly** 742.3
  - with spina bifida (*see also* Spina bifida) 741.0 ☑
- **Hydrargyrism** NEC 985.0
- **Hydrarthrosis** — *see also* Effusion, joint 719.0 ☑
  - gonococcal 098.50
  - intermittent (*see also* Rheumatism, palindromic) 719.3 ☑
  - of yaws (early) (late) 102.6
  - syphilitic 095.8
    - congenital 090.5
- **Hydremia** 285.9
- **Hydrencephalocele** (congenital) 742.0
- **Hydrencephalomeningocele** (congenital) 742.0
- **Hydroa** 694.0
  - aestivale 692.72
  - gestationis 646.8 ☑
  - herpetiformis 694.0
  - pruriginosa 694.0
  - vacciniforme 692.72
- **Hydroadenitis** 705.83
- **Hydrocalycosis** — *see also* Hydronephrosis 591
  - congenital 753.29
- **Hydrocalyx** — *see also* Hydronephrosis 591
- **Hydrocele** (calcified) (chylous) (idiopathic) (infantile) (inguinal canal) (recurrent) (senile) (spermatic cord) (testis) (tunica vaginalis) 603.9
  - canal of Nuck (female) 629.1
    - male 603.9
  - congenital 778.6
  - encysted 603.0
    - congenital 778.6
  - female NEC 629.89
  - infected 603.1
  - round ligament 629.89
  - specified type NEC 603.8
    - congenital 778.6
  - spinalis (*see also* Spina bifida) 741.9 ☑
  - vulva 624.8
- **Hydrocephalic fetus**
  - affecting management or pregnancy 655.0 ☑
  - causing disproportion 653.6 ☑
    - with obstructed labor 660.1 ☑
      - affecting fetus or newborn 763.1
- **Hydrocephalus** (acquired) (external) (internal) (malignant) (noncommunicating) (obstructive) (recurrent) 331.4
  - aqueduct of Sylvius stricture 742.3
    - with spina bifida (*see also* Spina bifida) 741.0 ☑
  - chronic 742.3
    - with spina bifida (*see also* Spina bifida) 741.0 ☑
  - communicating 331.3
  - congenital (external) (internal) 742.3
    - with spina bifida (*see also* Spina bifida) 741.0 ☑
  - due to
    - stricture of aqueduct of Sylvius 742.3
      - with spina bifida (*see also* Spina bifida) 741.0 ☑
    - toxoplasmosis (congenital) 771.2
  - fetal affecting management of pregnancy 655.0 ☑
  - foramen Magendie block (acquired) 331.3
    - congenital 742.3
      - with spina bifida (*see also* Spina bifida) 741.0 ☑
  - newborn 742.3
    - with spina bifida (*see also* Spina bifida) 741.0 ☑
  - normal pressure 331.5
    - idiopathic (INPH) 331.5
    - secondary 331.3
  - otitic 348.2
  - syphilitic, congenital 090.49
  - tuberculous (*see also* Tuberculosis) 013.8 ☑
- **Hydrocolpos** (congenital) 623.8
- **Hydrocystoma** (M8404/0) — *see* Neoplasm, skin, benign
- **Hydroencephalocele** (congenital) 742.0
- **Hydroencephalomeningocele** (congenital) 742.0
- **Hydrohematopneumothorax** — *see also* Hemothorax 511.89 ▲
- **Hydromeningitis** — *see* Meningitis
- **Hydromeningocele** (spinal) — *see also* Spina bifida 741.9 ☑
  - cranial 742.0
- **Hydrometra** 621.8
- **Hydrometrocolpos** 623.8
- **Hydromicrocephaly** 742.1
- **Hydromphalus** (congenital) (since birth) 757.39
- **Hydromyelia** 742.53
- **Hydromyelocele** — *see also* Spina bifida 741.9 ☑
- **Hydronephrosis** 591
  - atrophic 591
  - congenital 753.29
  - due to S. hematobium 120.0
  - early 591
  - functionless (infected) 591
  - infected 591
  - intermittent 591
  - primary 591
  - secondary 591
  - tuberculous (*see also* Tuberculosis) 016.0 ☑
- **Hydropericarditis** — *see also* Pericarditis 423.9
- **Hydropericardium** — *see also* Pericarditis 423.9
- **Hydroperitoneum** 789.59
- **Hydrophobia** 071
- **Hydrophthalmos** — *see also* Buphthalmia 743.20
- **Hydropneumohemothorax** — *see also* Hemothorax 511.89 ▲
- **Hydropneumopericarditis** — *see also* Pericarditis 423.9
- **Hydropneumopericardium** — *see also* Pericarditis 423.9
- **Hydropneumothorax** 511.89 ▲
  - nontuberculous 511.89 ▲
    - bacterial 511.1
- **Hydropneumothorax** — *continued*
    - pneumococcal 511.1
    - staphylococcal 511.1
    - streptococcal 511.1
  - traumatic 860.0
    - with open wound into thorax 860.1
  - tuberculous (*see also* Tuberculosis, pleura) 012.0 ☑
- **Hydrops** 782.3
  - abdominis 789.59
  - amnii (complicating pregnancy) (*see also* Hydramnios) 657.0 ☑
  - articulorum intermittens (*see also* Rheumatism, palindromic) 719.3 ☑
  - cardiac (*see also* Failure, heart) 428.0
  - congenital — *see* Hydrops, fetalis
  - endolymphatic (*see also* Disease, Ménière's) 386.00
  - fetal(is) or newborn 778.0
    - due to isoimmunization 773.3
    - not due to isoimmunization 778.0
  - gallbladder 575.3
  - idiopathic (fetus or newborn) 778.0
  - joint (see also Effusion, joint) 719.0 ☑
  - labyrinth (*see also* Disease, Ménière's) 386.00
  - meningeal NEC 331.4
  - nutritional 262
  - pericardium — *see* Pericarditis
  - pleura (*see also* Hydrothorax) 511.89 ▲
  - renal (*see also* Nephrosis) 581.9
  - spermatic cord (*see also* Hydrocele) 603.9
- **Hydropyonephrosis** — *see also* Pyelitis 590.80
  - chronic 590.00
- **Hydrorachis** 742.53
- **Hydrorrhea** (nasal) 478.19
  - gravidarum 658.1 ☑
  - pregnancy 658.1 ☑
- **Hydrosadenitis** 705.83
- **Hydrosalpinx** (fallopian tube) (follicularis) 614.1
- **Hydrothorax** (double) (pleural) 511.89 ▲
  - chylous (nonfilarial) 457.8
    - filaria (*see also* Infestation, filarial) 125.9
  - nontuberculous 511.89 ▲
    - bacterial 511.1
    - pneumococcal 511.1
    - staphylococcal 511.1
    - streptococcal 511.1
  - traumatic 862.29
    - with open wound into thorax 862.39
  - tuberculous (*see also* Tuberculosis, pleura) 012.0 ☑
- **Hydroureter** 593.5
  - congenital 753.22
- **Hydroureteronephrosis** — *see also* Hydronephrosis 591
- **Hydrourethra** 599.84
- **Hydroxykynureninuria** 270.2
- **Hydroxyprolinemia** 270.8
- **Hydroxyprolinuria** 270.8
- **Hygroma** (congenital) (cystic) (M9173/0) 228.1
  - prepatellar 727.3
  - subdural — *see* Hematoma, subdural
- **Hymen** — *see* condition
- **Hymenolepiasis** (diminuta) (infection) (infestation) (nana) 123.6
- **Hymenolepsis** (diminuta) (infection) (infestation) (nana) 123.6
- **Hypalgesia** — *see also* Disturbance, sensation 782.0
- **Hyperabduction syndrome** 447.8
- **Hyperacidity, gastric** 536.8
  - psychogenic 306.4
- **Hyperactive, hyperactivity** 314.01
  - basal cell, uterine cervix 622.10
  - bladder 596.51
  - bowel (syndrome) 564.9

☑ Additional Digit Required — Refer to the Tabular List for Digit Selection

Subterms under main terms may continue to next column or page

Hyperactive, hyperactivity — *continued*
bowel — *continued*
sounds 787.5
cervix epithelial (basal) 622.10
child 314.01
colon 564.9
gastrointestinal 536.8
psychogenic 306.4
intestine 564.9
labyrinth (unilateral) 386.51
with loss of labyrinthine reactivity 386.58
bilateral 386.52
nasal mucous membrane 478.19
stomach 536.8
thyroid (gland) (*see also* Thyrotoxicosis) 242.9 ☑
Hyperacusis 388.42
Hyperadrenalism (cortical) 255.3
medullary 255.6
Hyperadrenocorticism 255.3
congenital 255.2
iatrogenic
correct substance properly administered 255.3
overdose or wrong substance given or taken 962.0
Hyperaffectivity 301.11
Hyperaldosteronism (atypical) (hyperplastic) (normoaldosteronal) (normotensive) (primary) 255.10
secondary 255.14
Hyperalgesia — *see also* Disturbance, sensation 782.0
Hyperalimentation 783.6
carotene 278.3
specified NEC 278.8
vitamin A 278.2
vitamin D 278.4
Hyperaminoaciduria 270.9
arginine 270.6
citrulline 270.6
cystine 270.0
glycine 270.0
lysine 270.7
ornithine 270.6
renal (types I, II, III) 270.0
Hyperammonemia (congenital) 270.6
Hyperamnesia 780.99
Hyperamylasemia 790.5
Hyperaphia 782.0
Hyperazotemia 791.9
Hyperbetalipoproteinemia (acquired) (essential) (familial) (hereditary) (primary) (secondary) 272.0
with prebetalipoproteinemia 272.2
Hyperbilirubinemia 782.4
congenital 277.4
constitutional 277.4
neonatal (transient) (*see also* Jaundice, fetus or newborn) 774.6
of prematurity 774.2
Hyperbilirubinemica encephalopathia, newborn 774.7
due to isoimmunization 773.4
Hypercalcemia, hypercalcemic (idiopathic) 275.42
nephropathy 588.89
Hypercalcinuria 275.40
Hypercapnia 786.09
with mixed acid-based disorder 276.4
fetal, affecting newborn 770.89
Hypercarotinemia 278.3
Hypercementosis 521.5
Hyperchloremia 276.9
Hyperchlorhydria 536.8
neurotic 306.4
psychogenic 306.4
Hypercholesterinemia — *see* Hypercholesterolemia
Hypercholesterolemia 272.0
with hyperglyceridemia, endogenous 272.2
essential 272.0
familial 272.0
Hypercholesterolemia — *continued*
hereditary 272.0
primary 272.0
pure 272.0
Hypercholesterolosis 272.0
Hyperchylia gastrica 536.8
psychogenic 306.4
Hyperchylomicronemia (familial) (with hyperbetalipoproteinemia) 272.3
Hypercoagulation syndrome (primary) 289.81
secondary 289.82
Hypercorticosteronism
correct substance properly administered 255.3
overdose or wrong substance given or taken 962.0
Hypercortisonism
correct substance properly administered 255.3
overdose or wrong substance given or taken 962.0
Hyperdynamic beta-adrenergic state or syndrome (circulatory) 429.82
Hyperekplexia 759.89
Hyperelectrolytemia 276.9
Hyperemesis 536.2
arising during pregnancy — *see* Hyperemesis, gravidarum
gravidarum (mild) (before 22 completed weeks gestation) 643.0 ☑
with
carbohydrate depletion 643.1 ☑
dehydration 643.1 ☑
electrolyte imbalance 643.1 ☑
metabolic disturbance 643.1 ☑
affecting fetus or newborn 761.8
severe (with metabolic disturbance) 643.1 ☑
psychogenic 306.4
Hyperemia (acute) 780.99
anal mucosa 569.49
bladder 596.7
cerebral 437.8
conjunctiva 372.71
ear, internal, acute 386.30
enteric 564.89
eye 372.71
eyelid (active) (passive) 374.82
intestine 564.89
iris 364.41
kidney 593.81
labyrinth 386.30
liver (active) (passive) 573.8
lung 514
ovary 620.8
passive 780.99
pulmonary 514
renal 593.81
retina 362.89
spleen 289.59
stomach 537.89
Hyperesthesia (body surface) — *see also* Disturbance, sensation 782.0
larynx (reflex) 478.79
hysterical 300.11
pharynx (reflex) 478.29
Hyperestrinism 256.0
Hyperestrogenism 256.0
Hyperestrogenosis 256.0
Hyperexplexia 759.89
Hyperextension, joint 718.80
ankle 718.87
elbow 718.82
foot 718.87
hand 718.84
hip 718.85
knee 718.86
multiple sites 718.89
pelvic region 718.85
shoulder (region) 718.81
specified site NEC 718.88
wrist 718.83
Hyperfibrinolysis — *see* Fibrinolysis
Hyperfolliculinism 256.0
Hyperfructosemia 271.2
Hyperfunction
adrenal (cortex) 255.3
androgenic, acquired benign 255.3
medulla 255.6
virilism 255.2
corticoadrenal NEC 255.3
labyrinth — *see* Hyperactive, labyrinth
medulloadrenal 255.6
ovary 256.1
estrogen 256.0
pancreas 577.8
parathyroid (gland) 252.00
pituitary (anterior) (gland) (lobe) 253.1
testicular 257.0
Hypergammaglobulinemia 289.89
monoclonal, benign (BMH) 273.1
polyclonal 273.0
Waldenström's 273.0
Hyperglobulinemia 273.8
Hyperglycemia 790.29
maternal
affecting fetus or newborn 775.0
manifest diabetes in infant 775.1
postpancreatectomy (complete) (partial) 251.3
Hyperglyceridemia 272.1
endogenous 272.1
essential 272.1
familial 272.1
hereditary 272.1
mixed 272.3
pure 272.1
Hyperglycinemia 270.7
Hypergonadism
ovarian 256.1
testicular (infantile) (primary) 257.0
Hyperheparinemia — *see also* Circulating anticoagulants 286.5
Hyperhidrosis, hyperidrosis 705.21
axilla 705.21
face 705.21
focal (localized) 705.21
primary 705.21
axilla 705.21
face 705.21
palms 705.21
soles 705.21
secondary 705.22
axilla 705.22
face 705.22
palms 705.22
soles 705.22
generalized 780.8
palms 705.21
psychogenic 306.3
secondary 780.8
soles 705.21
Hyperhistidinemia 270.5
Hyperinsulinism (ectopic) (functional) (organic) NEC 251.1
iatrogenic 251.0
reactive 251.2
spontaneous 251.2
therapeutic misadventure (from administration of insulin) 962.3
Hyperiodemia 276.9
Hyperirritability (cerebral), in newborn 779.1
Hyperkalemia 276.7
Hyperkeratosis — *see also* Keratosis 701.1
cervix 622.2
congenital 757.39
cornea 371.89
due to yaws (early) (late) (palmar or plantar) 102.3
eccentrica 757.39
figurata centrifuga atrophica 757.39
follicularis 757.39
in cutem penetrans 701.1
limbic (cornea) 371.89
palmoplantaris climacterica 701.1
pinta (carate) 103.1
senile (with pruritus) 702.0
tongue 528.79
universalis congenita 757.1
Hyperkeratosis — *see also* Keratosis — *continued*
vagina 623.1
vocal cord 478.5
vulva 624.09
Hyperkinesia, hyperkinetic (disease) (reaction) (syndrome) 314.9
with
attention deficit — *see* Disorder, attention deficit
conduct disorder 314.2
developmental delay 314.1
simple disturbance of activity and attention 314.01
specified manifestation NEC 314.8
heart (disease) 429.82
of childhood or adolescence NEC 314.9
Hyperlacrimation — *see also* Epiphora 375.20
Hyperlipemia — *see also* Hyperlipidemia 272.4
Hyperlipidemia 272.4
carbohydrate-induced 272.1
combined 272.4
endogenous 272.1
exogenous 272.3
fat-induced 272.3
group
A 272.0
B 272.1
C 272.2
D 272.3
mixed 272.2
specified type NEC 272.4
Hyperlipidosis 272.7
hereditary 272.7
Hyperlipoproteinemia (acquired) (essential) (familial) (hereditary) (primary) (secondary) 272.4
Fredrickson type
I 272.3
IIa 272.0
IIb 272.2
III 272.2
IV 272.1
V 272.3
low-density-lipoid-type (LDL) 272.0
very-low-density-lipoid-type (VLDL) 272.1
Hyperlucent lung, unilateral 492.8
Hyperluteinization 256.1
Hyperlysinemia 270.7
Hypermagnesemia 275.2
neonatal 775.5
Hypermaturity (fetus or newborn)
post-term infant 766.21
prolonged gestation infant 766.22
Hypermenorrhea 626.2
Hypermetabolism 794.7
Hypermethioninemia 270.4
Hypermetropia (congenital) 367.0
Hypermobility
cecum 564.9
coccyx 724.71
colon 564.9
psychogenic 306.4
ileum 564.89
joint (acquired) 718.80
ankle 718.87
elbow 718.82
foot 718.87
hand 718.84
hip 718.85
knee 718.86
multiple sites 718.89
pelvic region 718.85
shoulder (region) 718.81
specified site NEC 718.88
wrist 718.83
kidney, congenital 753.3
meniscus (knee) 717.5
scapula 718.81
stomach 536.8
psychogenic 306.4
syndrome 728.5

☑ Additional Digit Required — Refer to the Tabular List for Digit Selection
Subterms under main terms may continue to next column or page

- **Hypermobility** — *continued*
  - testis, congenital 752.52
  - urethral 599.81
- **Hypermotility**
  - gastrointestinal 536.8
  - intestine 564.9
    - psychogenic 306.4
  - stomach 536.8
- **Hypernasality** 784.49
- **Hypernatremia** 276.0
  - with water depletion 276.0
- **Hypernephroma** (M8312/3) 189.0
- **Hyperopia** 367.0
- **Hyperorexia** 783.6
- **Hyperornithinemia** 270.6
- **Hyperosmia** — *see also* Disturbance, sensation 781.1
- **Hyperosmolality** 276.0
- **Hyperosteogenesis** 733.99
- **Hyperostosis** 733.99
  - calvarial 733.3
  - cortical 733.3
    - infantile 756.59
  - frontal, internal of skull 733.3
  - interna frontalis 733.3
  - monomelic 733.99
  - skull 733.3
    - congenital 756.0
  - vertebral 721.8
    - with spondylosis — *see* Spondylosis
    - ankylosing 721.6
- **Hyperovarianism** 256.1
- **Hyperovarism, hyperovaria** 256.1
- **Hyperoxaluria** (primary) 271.8
- **Hyperoxia** 987.8
- **Hyperparathyroidism** 252.00
  - ectopic 259.3
  - other 252.08
  - primary 252.01
  - secondary (of renal origin) 588.81
    - non-renal 252.02
  - tertiary 252.08
- **Hyperpathia** — *see also* Disturbance, sensation 782.0
  - psychogenic 307.80
- **Hyperperistalsis** 787.4
  - psychogenic 306.4
- **Hyperpermeability, capillary** 448.9
- **Hyperphagia** 783.6
- **Hyperphenylalaninemia** 270.1
- **Hyperphoria** 378.40
  - alternating 378.45
- **Hyperphosphatemia** 275.3
- **Hyperpiesia** — *see also* Hypertension 401.9
- **Hyperpiesis** — *see also* Hypertension 401.9
- **Hyperpigmentation** — *see* Pigmentation
- **Hyperpinealism** 259.8
- **Hyperpipecolatemia** 270.7
- **Hyperpituitarism** 253.1
- **Hyperplasia, hyperplastic**
  - adenoids (lymphoid tissue) 474.12
    - and tonsils 474.10
  - adrenal (capsule) (cortex) (gland) 255.8
    - with
      - sexual precocity (male) 255.2
      - virilism, adrenal 255.2
      - virilization (female) 255.2
    - congenital 255.2
    - due to excess ACTH (ectopic) (pituitary) 255.0
    - medulla 255.8
  - alpha cells (pancreatic)
    - with
      - gastrin excess 251.5
      - glucagon excess 251.4
  - appendix (lymphoid) 543.0
  - artery, fibromuscular NEC 447.8
    - carotid 447.8
    - renal 447.3
- **Hyperplasia, hyperplastic** — *continued*
  - bone 733.99
    - marrow 289.9
  - breast (*see also* Hypertrophy, breast) 611.1
  - carotid artery 447.8
  - cementation, cementum (teeth) (tooth) 521.5
  - cervical gland 785.6
  - cervix (uteri) 622.10
    - basal cell 622.10
    - congenital 752.49
    - endometrium 622.10
    - polypoid 622.10
  - chin 524.05
  - clitoris, congenital 752.49
  - dentin 521.5
  - endocervicitis 616.0
  - endometrium, endometrial (adenomatous) (atypical) (cystic) (glandular) (polypoid) (uterus) 621.30
    - with atypia 621.33
    - without atypia
      - complex 621.32
      - simple 621.31
    - cervix 622.10
  - epithelial 709.8
    - focal, oral, including tongue 528.79
    - mouth (focal) 528.79
    - nipple 611.89 ▲
    - skin 709.8
    - tongue (focal) 528.79
    - vaginal wall 623.0
  - erythroid 289.9
  - fascialis ossificans (progressiva) 728.11
  - fibromuscular, artery NEC 447.8
    - carotid 447.8
    - renal 447.3
  - genital
    - female 629.89
    - male 608.89
  - gingiva 523.8
  - glandularis
    - cystica uteri 621.30
    - endometrium (uterus) 621.30
    - interstitialis uteri 621.30
  - granulocytic 288.69
  - gum 523.8
  - hymen, congenital 752.49
  - islands of Langerhans 251.1
  - islet cell (pancreatic) 251.9
    - alpha cells
      - with excess
        - gastrin 251.5
        - glucagon 251.4
    - beta cells 251.1
  - juxtaglomerular (complex) (kidney) 593.89
  - kidney (congenital) 753.3
  - liver (congenital) 751.69
  - lymph node (gland) 785.6
  - lymphoid (diffuse) (nodular) 785.6
    - appendix 543.0
    - intestine 569.89
  - mandibular 524.02
    - alveolar 524.72
    - unilateral condylar 526.89
  - Marchand multiple nodular (liver) — *see* Cirrhosis, postnecrotic
  - maxillary 524.01
    - alveolar 524.71
  - medulla, adrenal 255.8
  - myometrium, myometrial 621.2
  - nose (lymphoid) (polypoid) 478.19
  - oral soft tissue (inflammatory) (irritative) (mucosa) NEC 528.9
    - gingiva 523.8
    - tongue 529.8
  - organ or site, congenital NEC — *see* Anomaly, specified type NEC
- **Hyperplasia, hyperplastic** — *continued*
  - ovary 620.8
  - palate, papillary 528.9
  - pancreatic islet cells 251.9
    - alpha
      - with excess
        - gastrin 251.5
        - glucagon 251.4
    - beta 251.1
  - parathyroid (gland) 252.01
  - persistent, vitreous (primary) 743.51
  - pharynx (lymphoid) 478.29
  - prostate 600.90
    - with
      - other lower urinary tract symptoms (LUTS) 600.91
      - urinary
        - obstruction 600.91
        - retention 600.91
    - adenofibromatous 600.20
      - with
        - other lower urinary tract symptoms (LUTS) 600.21
        - urinary
          - obstruction 600.21
          - retention 600.21
    - nodular 600.10
      - with
        - urinary
          - obstruction 600.11
          - retention 600.11
  - renal artery (fibromuscular) 447.3
  - reticuloendothelial (cell) 289.9
  - salivary gland (any) 527.1
  - Schimmelbusch's 610.1
  - suprarenal (capsule) (gland) 255.8
  - thymus (gland) (persistent) 254.0
  - thyroid (*see also* Goiter) 240.9
    - primary 242.0 ☑
    - secondary 242.2 ☑
  - tonsil (lymphoid tissue) 474.11
    - and adenoids 474.10
  - urethrovaginal 599.89
  - uterus, uterine (myometrium) 621.2
    - endometrium (*see also* Hyperplasia, endometrium) 621.30
  - vitreous (humor), primary persistent 743.51
  - vulva 624.3
  - zygoma 738.11
- **Hyperpnea** — *see also* Hyperventilation 786.01
- **Hyperpotassemia** 276.7
- **Hyperprebetalipoproteinemia** 272.1
  - with chylomicronemia 272.3
  - familial 272.1
- **Hyperprolactinemia** 253.1
- **Hyperprolinemia** 270.8
- **Hyperproteinemia** 273.8
- **Hyperprothrombinemia** 289.89
- **Hyperpselaphesia** 782.0
- **Hyperpyrexia** 780.60 ▲
  - heat (effects of) 992.0
  - malarial (*see also* Malaria) 084.6
  - malignant, due to anesthetic 995.86
  - rheumatic — *see* Fever, rheumatic
  - unknown origin (*see also* Pyrexia) 780.60 ▲
- **Hyperreactor, vascular** 780.2
- **Hyperreflexia** 796.1
  - bladder, autonomic 596.54
    - with cauda equina 344.61
  - detrusor 344.61
- **Hypersalivation** — *see also* Ptyalism 527.7
- **Hypersarcosinemia** 270.8
- **Hypersecretion**
  - ACTH 255.3
  - androgens (ovarian) 256.1
  - calcitonin 246.0
- **Hypersecretion** — *continued*
  - corticoadrenal 255.3
  - cortisol 255.0
  - estrogen 256.0
  - gastric 536.8
    - psychogenic 306.4
  - gastrin 251.5
  - glucagon 251.4
  - hormone
    - ACTH 255.3
    - anterior pituitary 253.1
    - growth NEC 253.0
    - ovarian androgen 256.1
    - testicular 257.0
    - thyroid stimulating 242.8 ☑
  - insulin — *see* Hyperinsulinism
  - lacrimal glands (*see also* Epiphora) 375.20
  - medulloadrenal 255.6
  - milk 676.6 ☑
  - ovarian androgens 256.1
  - pituitary (anterior) 253.1
  - salivary gland (any) 527.7
  - testicular hormones 257.0
  - thyrocalcitonin 246.0
  - upper respiratory 478.9
- **Hypersegmentation, hereditary** 288.2
  - eosinophils 288.2
  - neutrophil nuclei 288.2
- **Hypersensitive, hypersensitiveness, hypersensitivity** — *see also* Allergy
  - angiitis 446.20
    - specified NEC 446.29
  - carotid sinus 337.01 ▲
  - colon 564.9
    - psychogenic 306.4
  - DNA (deoxyribonucleic acid) NEC 287.2
  - drug (*see also* Allergy, drug) 995.27
  - esophagus 530.89
  - insect bites — *see* Injury, superficial, by site
  - labyrinth 386.58
  - pain (*see also* Disturbance, sensation) 782.0
  - pneumonitis NEC 495.9
  - reaction (*see also* Allergy) 995.3
    - upper respiratory tract NEC 478.8
  - stomach (allergic) (nonallergic) 536.8
    - psychogenic 306.4
- **Hypersomatotropism** (classic) 253.0
- **Hypersomnia, unspecified** 780.54
  - with sleep apnea, unspecified 780.53
  - alcohol induced 291.82
  - drug induced 292.85
  - due to
    - medical condition classified elsewhere 327.14
    - mental disorder 327.15
  - idiopathic
    - with long sleep time 327.11
    - without long sleep time 327.12
  - menstrual related 327.13
  - nonorganic origin 307.43
    - persistent (primary) 307.44
    - transient 307.43
  - organic 327.10
    - other 327.19
  - primary 307.44
  - recurrent 327.13
- **Hypersplenia** 289.4
- **Hypersplenism** 289.4
- **Hypersteatosis** 706.3
- **Hyperstimulation, ovarian** 256.1
- **Hypersuprarenalism** 255.3
- **Hypersusceptibility** — *see* Allergy
- **Hyper-TBG-nemia** 246.8
- **Hypertelorism** 756.0
  - orbit, orbital 376.41

	Malignant	Benign	Unspecified
Hypertension, hypertensive (arterial) (arteriolar) (crisis) (degeneration) (disease) (essential) (fluctuating) (idiopathic) (intermittent) (labile) (low renin) (orthostatic) (paroxysmal) (primary) (systemic) (uncontrolled) (vascular)	401.0	401.1	401.9
with			
chronic kidney disease			
stage I through stage IV, or unspecified	403.00	403.10	403.90
stage V or end stage renal disese	403.01	403.11	403.91
heart involvement (conditions classifiable to 429.0–429.3, 429.8, 429.9 due to hypertension) (*see also* Hypertension, heart)	402.00	402.10	402.90
with kidney involvement — *see* Hypertension, cardiorenal			
renal involvement (only conditions classifiable to 585, 586, 587) (excludes conditions classifiable to 584) (*see also* Hypertension, kidney)	403.00	403.10	403.90
with heart involvement — *see* Hypertension, cardiorenal			
failure (and sclerosis) (*see also* Hypertension, kidney)	403.01	403.11	403.91
sclerosis without failure (*see also* Hypertension, kidney)	403.00	403.10	403.90
accelerated (*see also* Hypertension, by type, malignant))	401.0	—	—
antepartum — *see* Hypertension, complicating pregnancy, childbirth, or the puerperium			
cardiorenal (disease)	404.00	404.10	404.90
with			
chronic kidney disease			
stage I through stage IV, or unspecified	404.00	404.10	404.90
and heart failure	404.01	404.11	404.91
stage V or end stage renal disease	404.02	404.12	404.92
and heart failure	404.03	404.13	404.93
heart failure	404.01	404.11	404.91
and chronic kidney disease	404.01	404.11	404.91
stage I through stage IV or unspecified	404.01	404.11	404.91
stave V or end stage renal disease	404.03	404.13	404.93
cardiovascular disease (arteriosclerotic) (sclerotic)	402.00	402.10	402.90
with			
heart failure	402.01	402.11	402.91
renal involvement (conditions classifiable to 403) (*see also* Hypertension, cardiorenal)	404.00	404.10	404.90
cardiovascular renal (disease) (sclerosis) (*see also* Hypertension, cardiorenal)	404.00	404.10	404.90
cerebrovascular disease NEC	437.2	437.2	437.2
complicating pregnancy, childbirth, or the puerperium	642.2	642.0	642.9
with			
albuminuria (and edema) (mild)	—	—	642.4
severe	—	—	642.5
chronic kidney disesae	642.2	642.2	642.2
and heart disease	642.2	642.2	642.2
edema (mild)	—	—	642.4
severe	—	—	642.5
heart disease	642.2	642.2	642.2
and chronic kidney disease	642.2	642.2	642.2
renal disease	642.2	642.2	642.2
and heart disease	642.2	642.2	642.2
chronic	642.2	642.0	642.0
with pre-eclampsia or eclampsia	642.7	642.7	642.7
fetus or newborn	760.0	760.0	760.0
essential	—	642.0	642.0
with pre-eclampsia or eclampsia	—	642.7	642.7
fetus or newborn	760.0	760.0	760.0
fetus or newborn	760.0	760.0	760.0
gestational	—	—	642.3
pre-existing	642.2	642.0	642.0
with pre-eclampsia or eclampsia	642.7	642.7	642.7
fetus or newborn	760.0	760.0	760.0
secondary to renal disease	642.1	642.1	642.1
with pre-eclampsia or eclampsia	642.7	642.7	642.7
fetus or newborn	760.0	760.0	760.0
transient	—	—	642.3
due to			
aldosteronism, primary	405.09	405.19	405.99
brain tumor	405.09	405.19	405.99
bulbar poliomyelitis	405.09	405.19	405.99
calculus			
kidney	405.09	405.19	405.99
ureter	405.09	405.19	405.99
coarctation, aorta	405.09	405.19	405.99
Cushing's disease	405.09	405.19	405.99
glomerulosclerosis (*see also* Hypertension, kidney)	403.00	403.10	403.90
periarteritis nodosa	405.09	405.19	405.99
pheochromocytoma	405.09	405.19	405.99
polycystic kidney(s)	405.09	405.19	405.99
polycythemia	405.09	405.19	405.99
porphyria	405.09	405.19	405.99
pyelonephritis	405.09	405.19	405.99
renal (artery)			
aneurysm	405.01	405.11	405.91

	Malignant	Benign	Unspecified
Hypertension, hypertensive — *continued*			
due to — *continued*			
renal — *continued*			
anomaly	405.01	405.11	405.91
embolism	405.01	405.11	405.91
fibromuscular hyperplasia	405.01	405.11	405.91
occlusion	405.01	405.11	405.91
stenosis	405.01	405.11	405.91
thrombosis	405.01	405.11	405.91
encephalopathy	437.2	437.2	437.2
gestational (transient) NEC	—	—	642.3
Goldblatt's	440.1	440.1	440.1
heart (disease) (conditions classifiable to 429.0–429.3, 429.8, 429.9 due to hypertension)	402.00	402.10	402.90
with heart failure	402.01	402.11	402.91
hypertensive kidney disease (conditions classifiable to 403) (*see also* Hypertension, cardiorenal)	404.00	404.10	404.90
renal sclerosis (*see also* Hypertension, cardiorenal)	404.00	404.10	404.90
intracranial, benign	—	348.2	—
intraocular	—	—	365.04
kidney	403.00	403.10	403.90
with			
chronic kidney disease			
stage I through stage IV, or unspecified	403.00	403.10	403.90
stage V or end stage renal disese	403.01	403.11	403.91
heart involvement (conditions classifiable to 429.0–429.3, 429.8, 429.9 due to hypertension) (*see also* Hypertension, cardiorenal)	404.00	404.10	404.90
hypertensive heart (disease) (conditions classifiable to 402) (*see also* Hypertension, cardiorenal)	404.00	404.10	404.90
lesser circulation	—	—	416.0
necrotizing	401.0	—	—
ocular	—	—	365.04
pancreatic duct — code to underlying condition ●			
with ●			
chronic pancreatitis ●	—	—	577.1
portal (due to chronic liver disease)	—	—	572.3
postoperative	—	—	997.91
psychogenic	—	—	306.2
puerperal, postpartum — *see* Hypertension, complicating pregnancy, childbirth, or the puerperium			
pulmonary (artery)	—	—	416.8
with cor pulmonale (chronic)	—	—	416.8
acute	—	—	415.0
idiopathic	—	—	416.0
primary	—	—	416.0
of newborn	—	—	747.83
secondary	—	—	416.8
renal (disease) (*see also* Hypertension, kidney)	403.00	403.10	403.90
renovascular NEC	405.01	405.11	405.91
secondary NEC	405.09	405.19	405.99
due to			
aldosteronism, primary	405.09	405.19	405.99
brain tumor	405.09	405.19	405.99
bulbar poliomyelitis	405.09	405.19	405.99
calculus			
kidney	405.09	405.19	405.99
ureter	405.09	405.19	405.99
coarctation, aorta	405.09	405.19	405.99
Cushing's disease	405.09	405.19	405.99
glomerulosclerosis (*see also* Hypertension, kidney)	403.00	403.10	403.90
periarteritis nodosa	405.09	405.19	405.99
pheochromocytoma	405.09	405.19	405.99
polycystic kidney(s)	405.09	405.19	405.99
polycythemia	405.09	405.19	405.99
porphyria	405.09	405.19	405.99
pyelonephritis	405.09	405.19	405.99
renal (artery)			
aneurysm	405.01	405.11	405.91
anomaly	405.01	405.11	405.91
embolism	405.01	405.11	405.91
fibromuscular hyperplasia	405.01	405.11	405.91
occlusion	405.01	405.11	405.91
stenosis	405.01	405.11	405.91
thrombosis	405.01	405.11	405.91
transient	—	—	796.2
of pregnancy	—	—	642.3
vascular degeneration	401.0	401.1	401.9
venous, chronic (asymptomatic) (idiopathic)	—	—	459.30
with			
complication, NEC	—	—	459.39
inflammation	—	—	459.32
with ulcer	—	—	459.33
ulcer	—	—	459.31
with inflammation	—	—	459.33

	Malignant	Benign	Unspecified
Hypertension, hypertensive — *continued*			
venous, chronic — *continued*			
due to			
deep vein thrombosis (*see also* Syndrome, postphlebetic)	—	—	459.10

Hyperthecosis, ovary 256.8
Hyperthermia (of unknown origin) — *see also* Pyrexia 780.60 ▲
malignant (due to anesthesia) 995.86
newborn 778.4
Hyperthymergasia — *see also* Psychosis, affective 296.0 ☑
reactive (from emotional stress, psychological trauma) 298.1
recurrent episode 296.1 ☑
single episode 296.0 ☑
Hyperthymism 254.8
Hyperthyroid (recurrent) — *see* Hyperthyroidism
Hyperthyroidism (latent) (preadult) (recurrent) (without goiter) 242.9 ☑

Note — Use the following fifth-digit subclassification with category 242:

0 without mention of thyrotoxic crisis or storm

1 with mention of thyrotoxic crisis or storm

with
goiter (diffuse) 242.0 ☑
adenomatous 242.3 ☑
multinodular 242.2 ☑
uninodular 242.1 ☑
nodular 242.3 ☑
multinodular 242.2 ☑
uninodular 242.1 ☑
thyroid nodule 242.1 ☑
complicating pregnancy, childbirth, or puerperium 648.1 ☑
neonatal (transient) 775.3
Hypertonia — *see* Hypertonicity
Hypertonicity
bladder 596.51
fetus or newborn 779.89
gastrointestinal (tract) 536.8
infancy 779.89
due to electrolyte imbalance 779.89
muscle 728.85
stomach 536.8
psychogenic 306.4
uterus, uterine (contractions) 661.4 ☑
affecting fetus or newborn 763.7
Hypertony — *see* Hypertonicity
Hypertransaminemia 790.4
Hypertrichosis 704.1
congenital 757.4
eyelid 374.54
lanuginosa 757.4
acquired 704.1
Hypertriglyceridemia, essential 272.1
Hypertrophy, hypertrophic
adenoids (infectional) 474.12
and tonsils (faucial) (infective) (lingual) (lymphoid) 474.10
adrenal 255.8
alveolar process or ridge 525.8
anal papillae 569.49
apocrine gland 705.82
artery NEC 447.8
carotid 447.8
congenital (peripheral) NEC 747.60
gastrointestinal 747.61
lower limb 747.64
renal 747.62
specified NEC 747.69
spinal 747.82
upper limb 747.63
renal 447.3
arthritis (chronic) (*see also* Osteoarthrosis) 715.9 ☑
spine (*see also* Spondylosis) 721.90
arytenoid 478.79
asymmetrical (heart) 429.9
auricular — *see* Hypertrophy, cardiac
Bartholin's gland 624.8
bile duct 576.8
bladder (sphincter) (trigone) 596.8
blind spot, visual field 368.42
bone 733.99
brain 348.8

Hypertrophy, hypertrophic — *continued*
breast 611.1
cystic 610.1
fetus or newborn 778.7
fibrocystic 610.1
massive pubertal 611.1
puerperal, postpartum 676.3 ☑
senile (parenchymatous) 611.1
cardiac (chronic) (idiopathic) 429.3
with
rheumatic fever (conditions classifiable to 390)
active 391.8
with chorea 392.0
inactive or quiescent (with chorea) 398.99
congenital NEC 746.89
fatty (*see also* Degeneration, myocardial) 429.1
hypertensive (*see also* Hypertension, heart) 402.90
rheumatic (with chorea) 398.99
active or acute 391.8
with chorea 392.0
valve (*see also* Endocarditis) 424.90
congenital NEC 746.89
cartilage 733.99
cecum 569.89
cervix (uteri) 622.6
congenital 752.49
elongation 622.6
clitoris (cirrhotic) 624.2
congenital 752.49
colon 569.89
congenital 751.3
conjunctiva, lymphoid 372.73
cornea 371.89
corpora cavernosa 607.89
duodenum 537.89
endometrium (uterus) (*see also* Hyperplasia, endometrium) 621.30
cervix 622.6
epididymis 608.89
esophageal hiatus (congenital) 756.6
with hernia — *see* Hernia, diaphragm
eyelid 374.30
falx, skull 733.99
fat pad 729.30
infrapatellar 729.31
knee 729.31
orbital 374.34
popliteal 729.31
prepatellar 729.31
retropatellar 729.31
specified site NEC 729.39
foot (congenital) 755.67
frenum, frenulum (tongue) 529.8
linguae 529.8
lip 528.5
gallbladder or cystic duct 575.8
gastric mucosa 535.2 ☑
gingiva 523.8
gland, glandular (general) NEC 785.6
gum (mucous membrane) 523.8
heart (idiopathic) (*see also* Hypertrophy, cardiac)
valve (*see also* Endocarditis)
congenital NEC 746.89
hemifacial 754.0
hepatic — *see* Hypertrophy, liver
hiatus (esophageal) 756.6
hilus gland 785.6
hymen, congenital 752.49
ileum 569.89
infrapatellar fat pad 729.31
intestine 569.89
jejunum 569.89
kidney (compensatory) 593.1
congenital 753.3
labial frenulum 528.5
labium (majus) (minus) 624.3
lacrimal gland, chronic 375.03
ligament 728.9

Hypertrophy, hypertrophic — *continued*
ligament — *continued*
spinal 724.8
linguae frenulum 529.8
lingual tonsil (infectional) 474.11
lip (frenum) 528.5
congenital 744.81
liver 789.1
acute 573.8
cirrhotic — *see* Cirrhosis, liver
congenital 751.69
fatty — *see* Fatty, liver
lymph gland 785.6
tuberculous — *see* Tuberculosis, lymph gland
mammary gland — *see* Hypertrophy, breast
maxillary frenulum 528.5
Meckel's diverticulum (congenital) 751.0
medial meniscus, acquired 717.3
median bar 600.90
with
other lower urinary tract symptoms (LUTS) 600.91
urinary
obstruction 600.91
retention 600.91
mediastinum 519.3
meibomian gland 373.2
meniscus, knee, congenital 755.64
metatarsal head 733.99
metatarsus 733.99
mouth 528.9
mucous membrane
alveolar process 523.8
nose 478.19
turbinate (nasal) 478.0
muscle 728.9
muscular coat, artery NEC 447.8
carotid 447.8
renal 447.3
myocardium (*see also* Hypertrophy, cardiac) 429.3
idiopathic 425.4
myometrium 621.2
nail 703.8
congenital 757.5
nasal 478.19
alae 478.19
bone 738.0
cartilage 478.19
mucous membrane (septum) 478.19
sinus (*see also* Sinusitis) 473.9
turbinate 478.0
nasopharynx, lymphoid (infectional) (tissue) (wall) 478.29
neck, uterus 622.6
nipple 611.1
normal aperture diaphragm (congenital) 756.6
nose (*see also* Hypertrophy, nasal) 478.19
orbit 376.46
organ or site, congenital NEC — *see* Anomaly, specified type NEC
osteoarthropathy (pulmonary) 731.2
ovary 620.8
palate (hard) 526.89
soft 528.9
pancreas (congenital) 751.7
papillae
anal 569.49
tongue 529.3
parathyroid (gland) 252.01
parotid gland 527.1
penis 607.89
phallus 607.89
female (clitoris) 624.2
pharyngeal tonsil 474.12
pharyngitis 472.1
pharynx 478.29
lymphoid (infectional) (tissue) (wall) 478.29

Hypertrophy, hypertrophic — *continued*
pituitary (fossa) (gland) 253.8
popliteal fat pad 729.31
preauricular (lymph) gland (Hampstead) 785.6
prepuce (congenital) 605
female 624.2
prostate (asymptomatic) (early) (recurrent) 600.90
with
other lower urinary tract symptlms (LUTS) 600.91
urinary
obstruction 600.91
retention 600.91
adenofibromatous 600.20
with
other lower urinary tract symptoms (LUTS) 600.21
urinary
obstruction 600.21
retention 600.21
benign 600.00
with
other lower urinary tract symptoms (LUTS) 600.01
urinary
obstruction 600.01
retention 600.01
congenital 752.89
pseudoedematous hypodermal 757.0
pseudomuscular 359.1
pylorus (muscle) (sphincter) 537.0
congenital 750.5
infantile 750.5
rectal sphincter 569.49
rectum 569.49
renal 593.1
rhinitis (turbinate) 472.0
salivary duct or gland 527.1
congenital 750.26
scaphoid (tarsal) 733.99
scar 701.4
scrotum 608.89
sella turcica 253.8
seminal vesicle 608.89
sigmoid 569.89
skin condition NEC 701.9
spermatic cord 608.89
spinal ligament 724.8
spleen — *see* Splenomegaly
spondylitis (spine) (*see also* Spondylosis) 721.90
stomach 537.89
subaortic stenosis (idiopathic) 425.1
sublingual gland 527.1
congenital 750.26
submaxillary gland 527.1
suprarenal (gland) 255.8
tendon 727.9
testis 608.89
congenital 752.89
thymic, thymus (congenital) (gland) 254.0
thyroid (gland) (*see also* Goiter) 240.9
primary 242.0 ☑
secondary 242.2 ☑
toe (congenital) 755.65
acquired 735.8
tongue 529.8
congenital 750.15
frenum 529.8
papillae (foliate) 529.3
tonsil (faucial) (infective) (lingual) (lymphoid) 474.11
with
adenoiditis 474.01
tonsillitis 474.00
and adenoiditis 474.02
and adenoids 474.10
tunica vaginalis 608.89
turbinate (mucous membrane) 478.0
ureter 593.89

Hypertrophy, hypertrophic — *continued*
- urethra 599.84
- uterus 621.2
  - puerperal, postpartum 674.8 ☑
- uvula 528.9
- vagina 623.8
- vas deferens 608.89
- vein 459.89
- ventricle, ventricular (heart) (left) (right) (*see also* Hypertrophy, cardiac)
  - congenital 746.89
  - due to hypertension (left) (right) (*see also* Hypertension, heart) 402.90
    - benign 402.10
    - malignant 402.00
  - right with ventricular septal defect, pulmonary stenosis or atresia, and dextraposition of aorta 745.2
- verumontanum 599.89
- vesical 596.8
- vocal cord 478.5
- vulva 624.3
  - stasis (nonfilarial) 624.3

Hypertropia (intermittent) (periodic) 378.31
Hypertyrosinemia 270.2
Hyperuricemia 790.6
Hypervalinemia 270.3
Hyperventilation (tetany) 786.01
- hysterical 300.11
- psychogenic 306.1
- syndrome 306.1

Hyperviscidosis 277.00
Hyperviscosity (of serum) (syndrome) NEC 273.3
- polycythemic 289.0
- sclerocythemic 282.8

Hypervitaminosis (dietary) NEC 278.8
- A (dietary) 278.2
- D (dietary) 278.4
- from excessive administration or use of vitamin preparations (chronic) 278.8
  - reaction to sudden overdose 963.5
  - vitamin A 278.2
    - reaction to sudden overdose 963.5
  - vitamin D 278.4
    - reaction to sudden overdose 963.5
  - vitamin K
    - correct substance properly administered 278.8
    - overdose or wrong substance given or taken 964.3

Hypervolemia 276.6
Hypesthesia — *see also* Disturbance, sensation 782.0
- cornea 371.81

Hyphema (anterior chamber) (ciliary body) (iris) 364.41
- traumatic 921.3

Hyphemia — *see* Hyphema
Hypoacidity, gastric 536.8
- psychogenic 306.4

Hypoactive labyrinth (function) — *see* Hypofunction, labyrinth
Hypoadrenalism 255.41
- tuberculous (*see also* Tuberculosis) 017.6 ☑

Hypoadrenocorticism 255.41
- pituitary 253.4

Hypoalbuminemia 273.8
Hypoaldosteronism 255.42
Hypoalphalipoproteinemia 272.5
Hypobarism 993.2
Hypobaropathy 993.2
Hypobetalipoproteinemia (familial) 272.5
Hypocalcemia 275.41
- cow's milk 775.4
- dietary 269.3

Hypocalcemia — *continued*
- neonatal 775.4
- phosphate-loading 775.4

Hypocalcification, teeth 520.4
Hypochloremia 276.9
Hypochlorhydria 536.8
- neurotic 306.4
- psychogenic 306.4

Hypocholesteremia 272.5
Hypochondria (reaction) 300.7
Hypochondriac 300.7
Hypochondriasis 300.7
Hypochromasia blood cells 280.9
Hypochromic anemia 280.9
- due to blood loss (chronic) 280.0
  - acute 285.1
- microcytic 280.9

Hypocoagulability — *see also* Defect, coagulation 286.9
Hypocomplementemia 279.8
Hypocythemia (progressive) 284.9
Hypodontia — *see also* Anodontia 520.0
Hypoeosinophilia 288.59
Hypoesthesia — *see also* Disturbance, sensation 782.0
- cornea 371.81
- tactile 782.0

Hypoestrinism 256.39
Hypoestrogenism 256.39
Hypoferremia 280.9
- due to blood loss (chronic) 280.0

Hypofertility
- female 628.9
- male 606.1

Hypofibrinogenemia 286.3
- acquired 286.6
- congenital 286.3

Hypofunction
- adrenal (gland) 255.41
  - cortex 255.41
  - medulla 255.5
  - specified NEC 255.5
- cerebral 331.9
- corticoadrenal NEC 255.41
- intestinal 564.89
- labyrinth (unilateral) 386.53
  - with loss of labyrinthine reactivity 386.55
  - bilateral 386.54
    - with loss of labyrinthine reactivity 386.56
- Leydig cell 257.2
- ovary 256.39
  - postablative 256.2
- pituitary (anterior) (gland) (lobe) 253.2
  - posterior 253.5
- testicular 257.2
  - iatrogenic 257.1
  - postablative 257.1
  - postirradiation 257.1
  - postsurgical 257.1

Hypogammaglobulinemia 279.00
- acquired primary 279.06
- non-sex-linked, congenital 279.06
- sporadic 279.06
- transient of infancy 279.09

Hypogenitalism (congenital) (female) (male) 752.89
- penis 752.69

Hypoglycemia (spontaneous) 251.2
- coma 251.0
  - diabetic 250.3 ☑
    - due to secondary diabetes 249.3 ☑ ●
- diabetic 250.8 ☑
  - due to secondary diabetes 249.8 ☑ ●
- due to insulin 251.0
  - therapeutic misadventure 962.3
- familial (idiopathic) 251.2
- following gastrointestinal surgery 579.3
- infantile (idiopathic) 251.2
- in infant of diabetic mother 775.0
- leucine-induced 270.3
- neonatal 775.6

Hypoglycemia — *continued*
- reactive 251.2
- specified NEC 251.1

Hypoglycemic shock 251.0
- diabetic 250.8 ☑
  - due to secondary diabetes 249.8 ☑ ●
- due to insulin 251.0
- functional (syndrome) 251.1

Hypogonadism
- female 256.39
- gonadotrophic (isolated) 253.4
- hypogonadotropic (isolated) (with anosmia) 253.4
- isolated 253.4
- male 257.2
  - hereditary familial (Reifenstein's syndrome) 259.52 ▲
- ovarian (primary) 256.39
- pituitary (secondary) 253.4
- testicular (primary) (secondary) 257.2

Hypohidrosis 705.0
Hypohidrotic ectodermal dysplasia 757.31
Hypoidrosis 705.0
Hypoinsulinemia, postsurgical 251.3
- postpancreatectomy (complete) (partial) 251.3

Hypokalemia 276.8
Hypokinesia 780.99
Hypoleukia splenica 289.4
Hypoleukocytosis 288.50
Hypolipidemia 272.5
Hypolipoproteinemia 272.5
Hypomagnesemia 275.2
- neonatal 775.4

Hypomania, hypomanic reaction — *see also* Psychosis, affective 296.0 ☑
- recurrent episode 296.1 ☑
- single episode 296.0 ☑

Hypomastia (congenital) 611.82 ▲
Hypomenorrhea 626.1
Hypometabolism 783.9
Hypomotility
- gastrointestinal tract 536.8
  - psychogenic 306.4
- intestine 564.89
  - psychogenic 306.4
- stomach 536.8
  - psychogenic 306.4

Hyponasality 784.49
Hyponatremia 276.1
Hypo-ovarianism 256.39
Hypo-ovarism 256.39
Hypoparathyroidism (idiopathic) (surgically induced) 252.1
- neonatal 775.4

Hypopharyngitis 462
Hypophoria 378.40
Hypophosphatasia 275.3
Hypophosphatemia (acquired) (congenital) (familial) 275.3
- renal 275.3

Hypophyseal, hypophysis — *see also* condition
- dwarfism 253.3
- gigantism 253.0
- syndrome 253.8

Hypophyseothalamic syndrome 253.8
Hypopiesis — *see* Hypotension
Hypopigmentation 709.00
- eyelid 374.53

Hypopinealism 259.8
Hypopituitarism (juvenile) (syndrome) 253.2
- due to
  - hormone therapy 253.7
  - hypophysectomy 253.7
  - radiotherapy 253.7
- postablative 253.7
- postpartum hemorrhage 253.2

Hypoplasia, hypoplasis 759.89
- adrenal (gland) 759.1
- alimentary tract 751.8
  - lower 751.2
  - upper 750.8

Hypoplasia, hypoplasis — *continued*
- anus, anal (canal) 751.2
- aorta 747.22
- aortic
  - arch (tubular) 747.10
  - orifice or valve with hypoplasia of ascending aorta and defective development of left ventricle (with mitral valve atresia) 746.7
- appendix 751.2
- areola 757.6
- arm (*see also* Absence, arm, congenital) 755.20
- artery (congenital) (peripheral) 747.60
  - brain 747.81
  - cerebral 747.81
  - coronary 746.85
  - gastrointestinal 747.61
  - lower limb 747.64
  - pulmonary 747.3
  - renal 747.62
  - retinal 743.58
  - specified NEC 747.69
  - spinal 747.82
  - umbilical 747.5
  - upper limb 747.63
- auditory canal 744.29
  - causing impairment of hearing 744.02
- biliary duct (common) or passage 751.61
- bladder 753.8
- bone NEC 756.9
  - face 756.0
  - malar 756.0
  - mandible 524.04
    - alveolar 524.74
  - marrow 284.9
    - acquired (secondary) 284.89
    - congenital 284.09
    - idiopathic 284.9
  - maxilla 524.03
    - alveolar 524.73
  - skull (*see also* Hypoplasia, skull) 756.0
- brain 742.1
  - gyri 742.2
  - specified part 742.2
- breast (areola) 611.82 ▲
- bronchus (tree) 748.3
- cardiac 746.89
  - valve — *see* Hypoplasia, heart, valve
  - vein 746.89
- carpus (*see also* Absence, carpal, congenital) 755.28
- cartilaginous 756.9
- cecum 751.2
- cementum 520.4
  - hereditary 520.5
- cephalic 742.1
- cerebellum 742.2
- cervix (uteri) 752.49
- chin 524.06
- clavicle 755.51
- coccyx 756.19
- colon 751.2
- corpus callosum 742.2
- cricoid cartilage 748.3
- dermal, focal (Goltz) 757.39
- digestive organ(s) or tract NEC 751.8
  - lower 751.2
  - upper 750.8
- ear 744.29
  - auricle 744.23
  - lobe 744.29
  - middle, except ossicles 744.03
    - ossicles 744.04
  - ossicles 744.04
- enamel of teeth (neonatal) (postnatal) (prenatal) 520.4
  - hereditary 520.5
- endocrine (gland) NEC 759.2
- endometrium 621.8
- epididymis 752.89

Hypoplasia, hypoplasis — *continued*
- epiglottis 748.3
- erythroid, congenital 284.01
- erythropoietic, chronic acquired 284.81
- esophagus 750.3
- Eustachian tube 744.24
- eye (*see also* Microphthalmos) 743.10
  - lid 743.62
- face 744.89
  - bone(s) 756.0
- fallopian tube 752.19
- femur (*see also* Absence, femur, congenital) 755.34
- fibula (*see also* Absence, fibula, congenital) 755.37
- finger (*see also* Absence, finger, congenital) 755.29
- focal dermal 757.39
- foot 755.31
- gallbladder 751.69
- genitalia, genital organ(s)
  - female 752.89
    - external 752.49
    - internal NEC 752.89
  - in adiposogenital dystrophy 253.8
  - male 752.89
    - penis 752.69
- glottis 748.3
- hair 757.4
- hand 755.21
- heart 746.89
  - left (complex) (syndrome) 746.7
  - valve NEC 746.89
    - pulmonary 746.01
- humerus (*see also* Absence, humerus, congenital) 755.24
- hymen 752.49
- intestine (small) 751.1
  - large 751.2
- iris 743.46
- jaw 524.09
- kidney(s) 753.0
- labium (majus) (minus) 752.49
- labyrinth, membranous 744.05
- lacrimal duct (apparatus) 743.65
- larynx 748.3
- leg (*see also* Absence, limb, congenital, lower) 755.30
- limb 755.4
  - lower (*see also* Absence, limb, congenital, lower) 755.30
  - upper (*see also* Absence, limb, congenital, upper) 755.20
- liver 751.69
- lung (lobe) 748.5
- mammary (areolar) 611.82 ▲
- mandibular 524.04
  - alveolar 524.74
  - unilateral condylar 526.89
- maxillary 524.03
  - alveolar 524.73
- medullary 284.9
- megakaryocytic 287.30
- metacarpus (*see also* Absence, metacarpal, congenital) 755.28
- metatarsus (*see also* Absence, metatarsal, congenital) 755.38
- muscle 756.89
  - eye 743.69
- myocardium (congenital) (Uhl's anomaly) 746.84
- nail(s) 757.5
- nasolacrimal duct 743.65
- nervous system NEC 742.8
- neural 742.8
- nose, nasal 748.1
- ophthalmic (*see also* Microphthalmos) 743.10
- optic nerve 377.43
- organ
  - of Corti 744.05
  - or site NEC — *see* Anomaly, by site
- osseous meatus (ear) 744.03

Hypoplasia, hypoplasis — *continued*
- ovary 752.0
- oviduct 752.19
- pancreas 751.7
- parathyroid (gland) 759.2
- parotid gland 750.26
- patella 755.64
- pelvis, pelvic girdle 755.69
- penis 752.69
- peripheral vascular system (congenital) NEC 747.60
  - gastrointestinal 747.61
  - lower limb 747.64
  - renal 747.62
  - specified NEC 747.69
  - spinal 747.82
  - upper limb 747.63
- pituitary (gland) 759.2
- pulmonary 748.5
  - arteriovenous 747.3
  - artery 747.3
  - valve 746.01
- punctum lacrimale 743.65
- radioulnar (*see also* Absence, radius, congenital, with ulna) 755.25
- radius (*see also* Absence, radius, congenital) 755.26
- rectum 751.2
- respiratory system NEC 748.9
- rib 756.3
- sacrum 756.19
- scapula 755.59
- shoulder girdle 755.59
- skin 757.39
- skull (bone) 756.0
  - with
    - anencephalus 740.0
    - encephalocele 742.0
    - hydrocephalus 742.3
      - with spina bifida (*see also* Spina bifida) 741.0 ☑
    - microcephalus 742.1
- spinal (cord) (ventral horn cell) 742.59
  - vessel 747.82
- spine 756.19
- spleen 759.0
- sternum 756.3
- tarsus (*see also* Absence, tarsal, congenital) 755.38
- testis, testicle 752.89
- thymus (gland) 279.11
- thyroid (gland) 243
  - cartilage 748.3
- tibiofibular (*see also* Absence, tibia, congenital, with fibula) 755.35
- toe (*see also* Absence, toe, congenital) 755.39
- tongue 750.16
- trachea (cartilage) (rings) 748.3
- Turner's (tooth) 520.4
- ulna (*see also* Absence, ulna, congenital) 755.27
- umbilical artery 747.5
- ureter 753.29
- uterus 752.3
- vagina 752.49
- vascular (peripheral) NEC (*see also* Hypoplasia, peripheral vascular system) 747.60
  - brain 747.81
- vein(s) (peripheral) NEC (*see also* Hypoplasia, peripheral vascular system) 747.60
  - brain 747.81
  - cardiac 746.89
  - great 747.49
  - portal 747.49
  - pulmonary 747.49
- vena cava (inferior) (superior) 747.49
- vertebra 756.19
- vulva 752.49
- zonule (ciliary) 743.39
- zygoma 738.12

Hypopotassemia 276.8

Hypoproaccelerinemia — *see also* Defect, coagulation 286.3

Hypoproconvertinemia (congenital) — *see also* Defect, coagulation 286.3

Hypoproteinemia (essential) (hypermetabolic) (idiopathic) 273.8

Hypoproteinosis 260

Hypoprothrombinemia (congenital) (hereditary) (idiopathic) — *see also* Defect, coagulation 286.3
- acquired 286.7
- newborn 776.3

Hypopselaphesia 782.0

Hypopyon (anterior chamber) (eye) 364.05
- iritis 364.05
- ulcer (cornea) 370.04

Hypopyrexia 780.99

Hyporeflex 796.1

Hyporeninemia, extreme 790.99
- in primary aldosteronism 255.10

Hyporesponsive episode 780.09

Hyposecretion
- ACTH 253.4
- ovary 256.39
  - postablative 256.2
- salivary gland (any) 527.7

Hyposegmentation of neutrophils, hereditary 288.2

Hyposiderinemia 280.9

Hyposmolality 276.1
- syndrome 276.1

Hyposomatotropism 253.3

Hyposomnia, unspecified — *see also* Insomnia 780.52
- with sleep apnea, unspecified 780.51

Hypospadias (male) 752.61
- female 753.8

Hypospermatogenesis 606.1

Hyposphagma 372.72

Hyposplenism 289.59

Hypostasis, pulmonary 514

Hypostatic — *see* condition

Hyposthenuria 593.89

Hyposuprarenalism 255.41

Hypo-TBG-nemia 246.8

Hypotension (arterial) (constitutional) 458.9
- chronic 458.1
- iatrogenic 458.29
- maternal, syndrome (following labor and delivery) 669.2 ☑
- of hemodialysis 458.21
- orthostatic (chronic) 458.0
  - dysautonomic-dyskinetic syndrome 333.0
- permanent idiopathic 458.1
- postoperative 458.29
- postural 458.0
- specified type NEC 458.8
- transient 796.3

Hypothermia (accidental) 991.6
- anesthetic 995.89
- associated with low environmental temperature 991.6 ●
- newborn NEC 778.3
- not associated with low environmental temperature 780.65 ▲

Hypothymergasia — *see also* Psychosis, affective 296.2 ☑
- recurrent episode 296.3 ☑
- single episode 296.2 ☑

Hypothyroidism (acquired) 244.9
- complicating pregnancy, childbirth, or puerperium 648.1 ☑
- congenital 243
- due to
  - ablation 244.1
    - radioactive iodine 244.1
    - surgical 244.0
  - iodine (administration) (ingestion) 244.2
    - radioactive 244.1
  - irradiation therapy 244.1

Hypothyroidism — *continued*
- due to — *continued*
  - p-aminosalicylic acid (PAS) 244.3
  - phenylbutazone 244.3
  - resorcinol 244.3
  - specified cause NEC 244.8
  - surgery 244.0
- goitrous (sporadic) 246.1
- iatrogenic NEC 244.3
- iodine 244.2
- pituitary 244.8
- postablative NEC 244.1
- postsurgical 244.0
- primary 244.9
- secondary NEC 244.8
- specified cause NEC 244.8
- sporadic goitrous 246.1

Hypotonia, hypotonicity, hypotony 781.3
- benign congenital 358.8
- bladder 596.4
- congenital 779.89
  - benign 358.8
- eye 360.30
  - due to
    - fistula 360.32
    - ocular disorder NEC 360.33
  - following loss of aqueous or vitreous 360.33
  - primary 360.31
- infantile muscular (benign) 359.0
- muscle 728.9
- uterus, uterine (contractions) — *see* Inertia, uterus

Hypotrichosis 704.09
- congenital 757.4
- lid (congenital) 757.4
  - acquired 374.55
- postinfectional NEC 704.09

Hypotropia 378.32

Hypoventilation 786.09
- congenital central alveolar syndrome 327.25
- idiopathic sleep related nonobstructive alveolar 327.24
- sleep related, in conditions classifiable elsewhere 327.26

Hypovitaminosis — *see also* Deficiency, vitamin 269.2

Hypovolemia 276.52
- surgical shock 998.0
- traumatic (shock) 958.4

Hypoxemia — *see also* Anoxia 799.02
- sleep related, in conditions classifiable elsewhere 327.26

Hypoxia — *see also* Anoxia 799.02
- cerebral 348.1
  - during or resulting from a procedure 997.01
  - newborn 770.88
    - mild or moderate 768.6
    - severe 768.5
- fetal, affecting newborn 770.88
- intrauterine — *see* Distress, fetal
- myocardial (*see also* Insufficiency, coronary) 411.89
  - arteriosclerotic — *see* Arteriosclerosis, coronary
- newborn 770.88
- sleep related 327.24

Hypoxic-ischemic encephalopathy (HIE) 768.7

Hypsarrhythmia — *see also* Epilepsy 345.6 ☑

Hysteralgia, pregnant uterus 646.8 ☑

Hysteria, hysterical 300.10
- anxiety 300.20
- Charcôt's gland 300.11
- conversion (any manifestation) 300.11
- dissociative type NEC 300.15
- psychosis, acute 298.1

Hysteroepilepsy 300.11

Hysterotomy, affecting fetus or newborn 763.89

I

Iatrogenic syndrome of excess cortisol 255.0
Iceland disease (epidemic neuromyasthenia) 049.8
Ichthyosis (congenita) 757.1
acquired 701.1
fetalis gravior 757.1
follicularis 757.1
hystrix 757.39
lamellar 757.1
lingual 528.6
palmaris and plantaris 757.39
simplex 757.1
vera 757.1
vulgaris 757.1
Ichthyotoxism 988.0
bacterial (*see also* Poisoning, food) 005.9
Icteroanemia, hemolytic (acquired) 283.9
congenital (*see also* Spherocytosis) 282.0
Icterus — *see also* Jaundice 782.4
catarrhal — *see* Icterus, infectious
conjunctiva 782.4
newborn 774.6
epidemic — *see* Icterus, infectious
febrilis — *see* Icterus, infectious
fetus or newborn — *see* Jaundice, fetus or newborn
gravis (*see also* Necrosis, liver) 570
complicating pregnancy 646.7 ☑
affecting fetus or newborn 760.8
fetus or newborn NEC 773.0
obstetrical 646.7 ☑
affecting fetus or newborn 760.8
hematogenous (acquired) 283.9
hemolytic (acquired) 283.9
congenital (*see also* Spherocytosis) 282.0
hemorrhagic (acute) 100.0
leptospiral 100.0
newborn 776.0
spirochetal 100.0
infectious 070.1
with hepatic coma 070.0
leptospiral 100.0
spirochetal 100.0
intermittens juvenilis 277.4
malignant (*see also* Necrosis, liver) 570
neonatorum (*see also* Jaundice, fetus or newborn) 774.6
pernicious (*see also* Necrosis, liver) 570
spirochetal 100.0
Ictus solaris, solis 992.0
Ideation
suicidal V62.84
Identity disorder 313.82
dissociative 300.14
gender role (child) 302.6
adult 302.85
psychosexual (child) 302.6
adult 302.85
Idioglossia 307.9
Idiopathic — *see* condition
Idiosyncrasy — *see also* Allergy 995.3
drug, medicinal substance, and biological — *see* Allergy, drug
Idiot, idiocy (congenital) 318.2
amaurotic (Bielschowsky) (-Jansky) (family) (infantile (late)) (juvenile (late)) (Vogt-Spielmeyer) 330.1
microcephalic 742.1
Mongolian 758.0
oxycephalic 756.0
Id reaction (due to bacteria) 692.89
IEED (involuntary emotional expression disorder) 310.8
IFIS (intraoperative floppy iris syndrome) 364.81
IgE asthma 493.0 ☑
Ileitis (chronic) — *see also* Enteritis 558.9
Ileitis — *see also* Enteritis — *continued*
infectious 009.0
noninfectious 558.9
regional (ulcerative) 555.0
with large intestine 555.2
segmental 555.0
with large intestine 555.2
terminal (ulcerative) 555.0
with large intestine 555.2
Ileocolitis — *see also* Enteritis 558.9
infectious 009.0
regional 555.2
ulcerative 556.1
Ileostomy status V44.2
with complication 569.60
Ileotyphus 002.0
Ileum — *see* condition
Ileus (adynamic) (bowel) (colon) (inhibitory) (intestine) (neurogenic) (paralytic) 560.1
arteriomesenteric duodenal 537.2
due to gallstone (in intestine) 560.31
duodenal, chronic 537.2
following gastrointestinal surgery 997.4
gallstone 560.31
mechanical (*see also* Obstruction, intestine) 560.9
meconium 777.1
due to cystic fibrosis 277.01
myxedema 564.89
postoperative 997.4
transitory, newborn 777.4
Iliac — *see* condition
Iliotibial band friction syndrome 728.89
Illegitimacy V61.6
Ill, louping 063.1
Illness — *see also* Disease
factitious 300.19
with
combined psychological and physical signs and symptoms 300.19
predominantly
physical signs and symptoms 300.19
psychological symptoms 300.16
chronic (with physical symptoms) 301.51
heart — *see* Disease, heart
manic-depressive (*see also* Psychosis, affective) 296.80
mental (*see also* Disorder, mental) 300.9
Imbalance 781.2
autonomic (*see also* Neuropathy, peripheral, autonomic) 337.9
electrolyte 276.9
with
abortion — *see* Abortion, by type, with metabolic disorder
ectopic pregnancy (*see also* categories 633.0–633.9) 639.4
hyperemesis gravidarum (before 22 completed weeks gestation) 643.1 ☑
molar pregnancy (*see also* categories 630–632) 639.4
following
abortion 639.4
ectopic or molar pregnancy 639.4
neonatal, transitory NEC 775.5
endocrine 259.9
eye muscle NEC 378.9
heterophoria — *see* Heterophoria
glomerulotubular NEC 593.89
hormone 259.9
hysterical (*see also* Hysteria) 300.10
labyrinth NEC 386.50
posture 729.90 ▲
Imbalance — *continued*
sympathetic (*see also* Neuropathy, peripheral, autonomic) 337.9
Imbecile, imbecility 318.0
moral 301.7
old age 290.9
senile 290.9
specified IQ — *see* IQ
unspecified IQ 318.0
Imbedding, intrauterine device 996.32
Imbibition, cholesterol (gallbladder) 575.6
Imerslund (-Gräsbeck) syndrome (anemia due to familial selective vitamin B_{12} malabsorption) 281.1
Iminoacidopathy 270.8
Iminoglycinuria, familial 270.8
Immature — *see also* Immaturity personality 301.89
Immaturity 765.1 ☑
extreme 765.0 ☑
fetus or infant light-for-dates — *see* Light-for-dates
lung, fetus or newborn 770.4
organ or site NEC — *see* Hypoplasia
pulmonary, fetus or newborn 770.4
reaction 301.89
sexual (female) (male) 259.0
Immersion 994.1
foot 991.4
hand 991.4
Immobile, immobility
complete ●
due to severe physical disability ●
or frailty 780.72 ●
intestine 564.89
joint — *see* Ankylosis
syndrome (paraplegic) 728.3
Immunization
ABO
affecting management of pregnancy 656.2 ☑
fetus or newborn 773.1
complication — *see* Complications, vaccination
Rh factor
affecting management of pregnancy 656.1 ☑
fetus or newborn 773.0
from transfusion 999.7
Immunodeficiency 279.3
with
adenosine-deaminase deficiency 279.2
defect, predominant
B-cell 279.00
T-cell 279.10
hyperimmunoglobulinemia 279.2
lymphopenia, hereditary 279.2
thrombocytopenia and eczema 279.12
thymic
aplasia 279.2
dysplasia 279.2
autosomal recessive, Swiss-type 279.2
common variable 279.06
severe combined (SCID) 279.2
to Rh factor
affecting management of pregnancy 656.1 ☑
fetus or newborn 773.0
X-linked, with increased IgM 279.05
Immunotherapy, prophylactic V07.2
antineoplastic V58.12
Impaction, impacted
bowel, colon, rectum 560.30
with hernia (*see also* Hernia, by site, with obstruction)
gangrenous — *see* Hernia, by site, with gangrene
by
calculus 560.39
gallstone 560.31
fecal 560.39
specified type NEC 560.39
calculus — *see* Calculus
Impaction, impacted — *continued*
cerumen (ear) (external) 380.4
cuspid 520.6
dental 520.6
fecal, feces 560.39
with hernia (*see also* Hernia, by site, with obstruction)
gangrenous — *see* Hernia, by site, with gangrene
fracture — *see* Fracture, by site
gallbladder — *see* Cholelithiasis
gallstone(s) — *see* Cholelithiasis
in intestine (any part) 560.31
intestine(s) 560.30
with hernia (*see also* Hernia, by site, with obstruction)
gangrenous — *see* Hernia, by site, with gangrene
by
calculus 560.39
gallstone 560.31
fecal 560.39
specified type NEC 560.39
intrauterine device (IUD) 996.32
molar 520.6
shoulder 660.4 ☑
affecting fetus or newborn 763.1
tooth, teeth 520.6
turbinate 733.99
Impaired, impairment (function)
arm V49.1
movement, involving
musculoskeletal system V49.1
nervous system V49.2
auditory discrimination 388.43
back V48.3
body (entire) V49.89
cognitive, mild, so stated 331.83
combined visual hearing V49.85
dual sensory V49.85
glucose
fasting 790.21
tolerance test (oral) 790.22
hearing (*see also* Deafness) 389.9
combined with visual impairment V49.85
heart — *see* Disease, heart
kidney (*see also* Disease, renal) 593.9
disorder resulting from 588.9
specified NEC 588.89
leg V49.1
movement, involving
musculoskeletal system V49.1
nervous system V49.2
limb V49.1
movement, involving
musculoskeletal system V49.1
nervous system V49.2
liver 573.8
mastication 524.9
mild cognitive, so stated 331.83
mobility
ear ossicles NEC 385.22
incostapedial joint 385.22
malleus 385.21
myocardium, myocardial (*see also* Insufficiency, myocardial) 428.0
neuromusculoskeletal NEC V49.89
back V48.3
head V48.2
limb V49.2
neck V48.3
spine V48.3
trunk V48.3
rectal sphincter 787.99
renal (*see also* Disease, renal) 593.9
disorder resulting from 588.9
specified NEC 588.89
spine V48.3
vision NEC 369.9
both eyes NEC 369.3
combined with hearing impairment V49.85
moderate 369.74
both eyes 369.25

- **Impaired, impairment** — *continued*
  - vision — *continued*
    - moderate — *continued*
      - both eyes — *continued*
        - with impairment of lesser eye (specified as)
          - blind, not further specified 369.15
          - low vision, not further specified 369.23
          - near-total 369.17
          - profound 369.18
          - severe 369.24
          - total 369.16
      - one eye 369.74
        - with vision of other eye (specified as)
          - near-normal 369.75
          - normal 369.76
    - near-total 369.64
      - both eyes 369.04
        - with impairment of lesser eye (specified as)
          - blind, not further specified 369.02
          - total 369.03
      - one eye 369.64
        - with vision of other eye (specified as)
          - near normal 369.65
          - normal 369.66
    - one eye 369.60
      - with low vision of other eye 369.10
    - profound 369.67
      - both eyes 369.08
        - with impairment of lesser eye (specified as)
          - blind, not further specified 369.05
          - near-total 369.07
          - total 369.06
      - one eye 369.67
        - with vision of other eye (specified as)
          - near-normal 369.68
          - normal 369.69
    - severe 369.71
      - both eyes 369.22
        - with impairment of lesser eye (specified as)
          - blind, not further specified 369.11
          - low vision, not further specified 369.21
          - near-total 369.13
          - profound 369.14
          - total 369.12
      - one eye 369.71
        - with vision of other eye (specified as)
          - near-normal 369.72
          - normal 369.73
    - total
      - both eyes 369.01
      - one eye 369.61
        - with vision of other eye (specified as)
          - near-normal 369.62
          - normal 369.63
- **Impaludism** — *see* Malaria
- **Impediment, speech** NEC 784.5
  - psychogenic 307.9
  - secondary to organic lesion 784.5
- **Impending**
  - cerebrovascular accident or attack 435.9
  - coronary syndrome 411.1
  - delirium tremens 291.0
  - myocardial infarction 411.1
- **Imperception, auditory** (acquired) (congenital) 389.9
- **Imperfect**
  - aeration, lung (newborn) 770.5
  - closure (congenital)
    - alimentary tract NEC 751.8
- **Imperfect** — *continued*
  - closure — *continued*
    - alimentary tract — *continued*
      - lower 751.5
      - upper 750.8
    - atrioventricular ostium 745.69
    - atrium (secundum) 745.5
      - primum 745.61
    - branchial cleft or sinus 744.41
    - choroid 743.59
    - cricoid cartilage 748.3
    - cusps, heart valve NEC 746.89
      - pulmonary 746.09
    - ductus
      - arteriosus 747.0
      - Botalli 747.0
    - ear drum 744.29
      - causing impairment of hearing 744.03
    - endocardial cushion 745.60
    - epiglottis 748.3
    - esophagus with communication to bronchus or trachea 750.3
    - Eustachian valve 746.89
    - eyelid 743.62
    - face, facial (*see also* Cleft, lip) 749.10
    - foramen
      - Botalli 745.5
      - ovale 745.5
    - genitalia, genital organ(s) or system
      - female 752.89
        - external 752.49
        - internal NEC 752.89
        - uterus 752.3
      - male 752.89
        - penis 752.69
    - glottis 748.3
    - heart valve (cusps) NEC 746.89
    - interatrial ostium or septum 745.5
    - interauricular ostium or septum 745.5
    - interventricular ostium or septum 745.4
    - iris 743.46
    - kidney 753.3
    - larynx 748.3
    - lens 743.36
    - lip (*see also* Cleft, lip) 749.10
    - nasal septum or sinus 748.1
    - nose 748.1
    - omphalomesenteric duct 751.0
    - optic nerve entry 743.57
    - organ or site NEC — *see* Anomaly, specified type, by site
    - ostium
      - interatrial 745.5
      - interauricular 745.5
      - interventricular 745.4
    - palate (*see also* Cleft, palate) 749.00
    - preauricular sinus 744.46
    - retina 743.56
    - roof of orbit 742.0
    - sclera 743.47
    - septum
      - aortic 745.0
      - aorticopulmonary 745.0
      - atrial (secundum) 745.5
        - primum 745.61
      - between aorta and pulmonary artery 745.0
      - heart 745.9
      - interatrial (secundum) 745.5
        - primum 745.61
      - interauricular (secundum) 745.5
        - primum 745.61
      - interventricular 745.4
        - with pulmonary stenosis or atresia, dextraposition of aorta, and hypertrophy of right ventricle 745.2
        - in tetralogy of Fallot 745.2
      - nasal 748.1
      - ventricular 745.4
- **Imperfect** — *continued*
  - closure — *continued*
    - septum — *continued*
      - ventricular — *continued*
        - with pulmonary stenosis or atresia, dextraposition of aorta, and hypertrophy of right ventricle 745.2
        - in tetralogy of Fallot 745.2
    - skull 756.0
      - with
        - anencephalus 740.0
        - encephalocele 742.0
        - hydrocephalus 742.3
          - with spina bifida (*see also* Spina bifida) 741.0 ☑
        - microcephalus 742.1
    - spine (with meningocele) (*see also* Spina bifida) 741.90
    - thyroid cartilage 748.3
    - trachea 748.3
    - tympanic membrane 744.29
      - causing impairment of hearing 744.03
    - uterus (with communication to bladder, intestine, or rectum) 752.3
    - uvula 749.02
      - with cleft lip (*see also* Cleft, palate, with cleft lip) 749.20
    - vitelline duct 751.0
  - development — *see* Anomaly, by site
  - erection 607.84
  - fusion — *see* Imperfect, closure
  - inflation lung (newborn) 770.5
  - intestinal canal 751.5
  - poise 729.90 ▲
  - rotation — *see* Malrotation
  - septum, ventricular 745.4
- **Imperfectly descended testis** 752.51
- **Imperforate** (congenital) — *see also* Atresia
  - anus 751.2
  - bile duct 751.61
  - cervix (uteri) 752.49
  - esophagus 750.3
  - hymen 752.42
  - intestine (small) 751.1
    - large 751.2
  - jejunum 751.1
  - pharynx 750.29
  - rectum 751.2
  - salivary duct 750.23
  - urethra 753.6
  - urinary meatus 753.6
  - vagina 752.49
- **Impervious** (congenital) — *see also* Atresia
  - anus 751.2
  - bile duct 751.61
  - esophagus 750.3
  - intestine (small) 751.1
    - large 751.5
  - rectum 751.2
  - urethra 753.6
- **Impetiginization of other dermatoses** 684
- **Impetigo** (any organism) (any site) (bullous) (circinate) (contagiosa) (neonatorum) (simplex) 684
  - Bockhart's (superficial folliculitis) 704.8
  - external ear 684 *[380.13]*
  - eyelid 684 *[373.5]*
  - Fox's (contagiosa) 684
  - furfuracea 696.5
  - herpetiformis 694.3
    - nonobstetrical 694.3
  - staphylococcal infection 684
  - ulcerative 686.8
  - vulgaris 684
- **Impingement, soft tissue between teeth** 524.89
- **Impingement, soft tissue between teeth** — *continued*
  - anterior 524.81
  - posterior 524.82
- **Implantation**
  - anomalous (*see also* Anomaly, specified type, by site)
    - ureter 753.4
  - cyst
    - external area or site (skin) NEC 709.8
    - iris 364.61
    - vagina 623.8
    - vulva 624.8
  - dermoid (cyst)
    - external area or site (skin) NEC 709.8
    - iris 364.61
    - vagina 623.8
    - vulva 624.8
  - placenta, low or marginal — *see* Placenta previa
- **Implant, endometrial** 617.9
- **Impotence** (sexual) 607.84
  - organic origin NEC 607.84
  - psychogenic 302.72
- **Impoverished blood** 285.9
- **Impression, basilar** 756.0
- **Imprisonment** V62.5
- **Improper**
  - development, infant 764.9 ☑
- **Improperly tied umbilical cord** (causing hemorrhage) 772.3
- **Impulses, obsessional** 300.3
- **Impulsive neurosis** 300.3
- **Inaction, kidney** — *see also* Disease, renal 593.9
- **Inactive** — *see* condition
- **Inadequate, inadequacy**
  - aesthetics of dental restoration 525.67
  - biologic 301.6
  - cardiac and renal — *see* Hypertension, cardiorenal
  - constitutional 301.6
  - development
    - child 783.40
    - fetus 764.9 ☑
      - affecting management of pregnancy 656.5 ☑
    - genitalia
      - after puberty NEC 259.0
      - congenital — *see* Hypoplasia, genitalia
    - lungs 748.5
    - organ or site NEC — *see* Hypoplasia, by site
  - dietary 269.9
  - distance, interarch 524.28
  - education V62.3
  - environment
    - economic problem V60.2
    - household condition NEC V60.1
    - poverty V60.2
    - unemployment V62.0
  - functional 301.6
  - household care, due to
    - family member
      - handicapped or ill V60.4
      - temporarily away from home V60.4
        - on vacation V60.5
    - technical defects in home V60.1
    - temporary absence from home of person rendering care V60.4
  - housing (heating) (space) V60.1
  - interarch distance 524.28
  - material resources V60.2
  - mental (*see also* Retardation, mental) 319
  - nervous system 799.2
  - personality 301.6
  - prenatal care in current pregnancy V23.7
  - pulmonary
    - function 786.09
      - newborn 770.89

- **Inadequate, inadequacy** — *continued*
  - pulmonary — *continued*
    - ventilation, newborn 770.89
  - respiration 786.09
    - newborn 770.89
  - sample
    - cytology ●
      - anal 796.78 ●
      - cervical 795.08 ●
      - vaginal 795.18 ●
  - social 301.6
- **Inanition** 263.9
  - with edema 262
  - due to
    - deprivation of food 994.2
    - malnutrition 263.9
  - fever 780.60 ▲
- **Inappropriate secretion**
  - ACTH 255.0
  - antidiuretic hormone (ADH) (excessive) 253.6
    - deficiency 253.5
  - ectopic hormone NEC 259.3
  - pituitary (posterior) 253.6
- **Inattention after or at birth** 995.52
- **Inborn errors of metabolism** — *see* Disorder, metabolism
- **Incarceration, incarcerated**
  - bubonocele (*see also* Hernia, inguinal, with obstruction)
    - gangrenous — *see* Hernia, inguinal, with gangrene
  - colon (by hernia) (*see also* Hernia, by site with obstruction)
    - gangrenous — *see* Hernia, by site, with gangrene
  - enterocele 552.9
    - gangrenous 551.9
  - epigastrocele 552.29
    - gangrenous 551.29
  - epiplocele 552.9
    - gangrenous 551.9
  - exomphalos 552.1
    - gangrenous 551.1
  - fallopian tube 620.8
  - hernia (*see also* Hernia, by site, with obstruction)
    - gangrenous — *see* Hernia, by site, with gangrene
  - iris, in wound 871.1
  - lens, in wound 871.1
  - merocele (*see also* Hernia, femoral, with obstruction) 552.00
  - omentum (by hernia) (*see also* Hernia, by site, with obstruction)
    - gangrenous — *see* Hernia, by site, with gangrene
  - omphalocele 756.79
  - rupture (meaning hernia) (*see also* Hernia, by site, with obstruction) 552.9
    - gangrenous (*see also* Hernia, by site, with gangrene) 551.9
  - sarcoepiplocele 552.9
    - gangrenous 551.9
  - sarcoepiplomphalocele 552.1
    - with gangrene 551.1
  - uterus 621.8
    - gravid 654.3 ☑
      - causing obstructed labor 660.2 ☑
        - affecting fetus or newborn 763.1
- **Incident, cerebrovascular** — *see also* Disease, cerebrovascular, acute 436
- **Incineration** (entire body) (from fire, conflagration, electricity, or lightning) — *see* Burn, multiple, specified sites
- **Incised wound**
  - external — *see* Wound, open, by site
  - internal organs (abdomen, chest, or pelvis) — *see* Injury, internal, by site, with open wound
- **Incision, incisional**
  - hernia — *see* Hernia, incisional
  - surgical, complication — *see* Complications, surgical procedures
  - traumatic
    - external — *see* Wound, open, by site
    - internal organs (abdomen, chest, or pelvis) — *see* Injury, internal, by site, with open wound
- **Inclusion**
  - azurophilic leukocytic 288.2
  - blennorrhea (neonatal) (newborn) 771.6
  - cyst — *see* Cyst, skin
  - gallbladder in liver (congenital) 751.69
- **Incompatibility**
  - ABO
    - affecting management of pregnancy 656.2 ☑
    - fetus or newborn 773.1
    - infusion or transfusion reaction 999.6
  - blood (group) (Duffy) (E) (K(ell)) (Kidd) (Lewis) (M) (N) (P) (S) NEC
    - affecting management of pregnancy 656.2 ☑
    - fetus or newborn 773.2
    - infusion or transfusion reaction 999.6
  - contour of existing restoration of tooth with oral health 525.65
  - marital V61.10
    - involving
      - divorce V61.03 ●
      - estrangement V61.09 ●
  - Rh (blood group) (factor)
    - affecting management of pregnancy 656.1 ☑
    - fetus or newborn 773.0
    - infusion or transfusion reaction 999.7
  - Rhesus — *see* Incompatibility, Rh
- **Incompetency, incompetence, incompetent**
  - annular
    - aortic (valve) (*see also* Insufficiency, aortic) 424.1
    - mitral (valve) (*see also* Insufficiency, mitral) 424.0
    - pulmonary valve (heart) (*see also* Endocarditis, pulmonary) 424.3
  - aortic (valve) (*see also* Insufficiency, aortic) 424.1
    - syphilitic 093.22
  - cardiac (orifice) 530.0
    - valve — *see* Endocarditis
  - cervix, cervical (os) 622.5
    - in pregnancy 654.5 ☑
      - affecting fetus or newborn 761.0
  - chronotropic 426.89 ●
    - with ●
      - autonomic dysfunction 337.9 ●
      - ischemic heart disease 414.9 ●
      - left ventricular dysfunction 337.9 ●
      - sinus node dysfunction 427.81 ●
  - esophagogastric (junction) (sphincter) 530.0
  - heart valve, congenital 746.89
  - mitral (valve) — *see* Insufficiency, mitral
  - papillary muscle (heart) 429.81
  - pelvic fundus
    - pubocervical tissue 618.81
    - rectovaginal tissue 618.82
  - pulmonary valve (heart) (*see also* Endocarditis, pulmonary) 424.3
    - congenital 746.09
  - tricuspid (annular) (rheumatic) (valve) (*see also* Endocarditis, tricuspid) 397.0
  - valvular — *see* Endocarditis
- **Incompetency, incompetence, incompetent** — *continued*
  - vein, venous (saphenous) (varicose) (*see also* Varicose, vein) 454.9
  - velopharyngeal (closure)
    - acquired 528.9
    - congenital 750.29
- **Incomplete** — *see also* condition
  - bladder emptying 788.21
  - expansion lungs (newborn) 770.5
  - gestation (liveborn) — *see* Immaturity
  - rotation — *see* Malrotation
- **Incontinence** 788.30
  - without sensory awareness 788.34
  - anal sphincter 787.6
  - continuous leakage 788.37
  - feces 787.6
    - due to hysteria 300.11
    - nonorganic origin 307.7
  - hysterical 300.11
  - mixed (male) (female) (urge and stress) 788.33
  - overflow 788.38
  - paradoxical 788.39
  - rectal 787.6
  - specified NEC 788.39
  - stress (female) 625.6
    - male NEC 788.32
  - urethral sphincter 599.84
  - urge 788.31
    - and stress (male) (female) 788.33
  - urine 788.30
    - active 788.30
    - due to ●
      - cognitive impairment 788.91 ●
      - immobility 788.91 ●
      - severe physical disability 788.91 ●
    - functional 788.91 ●
    - male 788.30
      - stress 788.32
        - and urge 788.33
    - neurogenic 788.39
    - nonorganic origin 307.6
    - stress (female) 625.6
      - male NEC 788.32
    - urge 788.31
      - and stress 788.33
- **Incontinentia pigmenti** 757.33
- **Incoordinate**
  - uterus (action) (contractions) 661.4 ☑
    - affecting fetus or newborn 763.7
- **Incoordination**
  - esophageal-pharyngeal (newborn) 787.24
  - muscular 781.3
  - papillary muscle 429.81
- **Increase, increased**
  - abnormal, in development 783.9
  - androgens (ovarian) 256.1
  - anticoagulants (antithrombin) (anti-VIIIa) (anti-IXa) (anti-Xa) (anti-XIa) 286.5
    - postpartum 666.3 ☑
  - cold sense (*see also* Disturbance, sensation) 782.0
  - estrogen 256.0
  - function
    - adrenal (cortex) 255.3
      - medulla 255.6
    - pituitary (anterior) (gland) (lobe) 253.1
      - posterior 253.6
  - heat sense (*see also* Disturbance, sensation) 782.0
  - intracranial pressure 781.99
    - injury at birth 767.8
  - light reflex of retina 362.13
  - permeability, capillary 448.9
  - pressure
    - intracranial 781.99
      - injury at birth 767.8
    - intraocular 365.00
  - pulsations 785.9
  - pulse pressure 785.9
  - sphericity, lens 743.36
- **Increase, increased** — *continued*
  - splenic activity 289.4
  - venous pressure 459.89
    - portal 572.3
- **Incrustation, cornea, lead or zinc** 930.0
- **Incyclophoria** 378.44
- **Incyclotropia** 378.33
- **Indeterminate sex** 752.7
- **India rubber skin** 756.83
- **Indicanuria** 270.2
- **Indigestion** (bilious) (functional) 536.8
  - acid 536.8
  - catarrhal 536.8
  - due to decomposed food NEC 005.9
  - fat 579.8
  - nervous 306.4
  - psychogenic 306.4
- **Indirect** — *see* condition
- **Indolent bubo** NEC 099.8
- **Induced**
  - abortion — *see* Abortion, induced
  - birth, affecting fetus or newborn 763.89
  - delivery — *see* Delivery
  - labor — *see* Delivery
- **Induration, indurated**
  - brain 348.8
  - breast (fibrous) 611.79
    - puerperal, postpartum 676.3 ☑
  - broad ligament 620.8
  - chancre 091.0
    - anus 091.1
    - congenital 090.0
    - extragenital NEC 091.2
  - corpora cavernosa (penis) (plastic) 607.89
  - liver (chronic) 573.8
    - acute 573.8
  - lung (black) (brown) (chronic) (fibroid) (*see also* Fibrosis, lung) 515
    - essential brown 275.0 *[516.1]*
  - penile 607.89
  - phlebitic — *see* Phlebitis
  - skin 782.8
  - stomach 537.89
- **Induratio penis plastica** 607.89
- **Industrial** — *see* condition
- **Inebriety** — *see also* Abuse, drugs, nondependent 305.0 ☑
- **Inefficiency**
  - kidney (*see also* Disease, renal) 593.9
  - thyroid (acquired) (gland) 244.9
- **Inelasticity, skin** 782.8
- **Inequality, leg** (acquired) (length) 736.81
  - congenital 755.30
- **Inertia**
  - bladder 596.4
    - neurogenic 596.54
      - with cauda equina syndrome 344.61
  - stomach 536.8
    - psychogenic 306.4
  - uterus, uterine 661.2 ☑
    - affecting fetus or newborn 763.7
    - primary 661.0 ☑
    - secondary 661.1 ☑
  - vesical 596.4
    - neurogenic 596.54
      - with cauda equina 344.61
- **Infant** — *see also* condition
  - excessive crying of 780.92
  - fussy (baby) 780.91
  - held for adoption V68.89
  - newborn — *see* Newborn
  - post-term (gestation period over 40 completed weeks to 42 completed weeks) 766.21
  - prolonged gestation of (period over 42 completed weeks) 766.22
  - syndrome of diabetic mother 775.0
- **"Infant Hercules" syndrome** 255.2
- **Infantile** — *see also* condition
  - genitalia, genitals 259.0
    - in pregnancy or childbirth NEC 654.4 ☑

- **Infantile** — *see also* condition — *continued*
  - genitalia, genitals — *continued*
    - in pregnancy or childbirth — *continued*
      - affecting fetus or newborn 763.89
      - causing obstructed labor 660.2 ☑
        - affecting fetus or newborn 763.1
  - heart 746.9
  - kidney 753.3
  - lack of care 995.52
  - macula degeneration 362.75
  - melanodontia 521.05
  - os, uterus (*see also* Infantile, genitalia) 259.0
  - pelvis 738.6
    - with disproportion (fetopelvic) 653.1 ☑
      - affecting fetus or newborn 763.1
      - causing obstructed labor 660.1 ☑
        - affecting fetus or newborn 763.1
  - penis 259.0
  - testis 257.2
  - uterus (*see also* Infantile, genitalia) 259.0
  - vulva 752.49
- **Infantilism** 259.9
  - with dwarfism (hypophyseal) 253.3
  - Brissaud's (infantile myxedema) 244.9
  - celiac 579.0
  - Herter's (nontropical sprue) 579.0
  - hypophyseal 253.3
  - hypothalamic (with obesity) 253.8
  - idiopathic 259.9
  - intestinal 579.0
  - pancreatic 577.8
  - pituitary 253.3
  - renal 588.0
  - sexual (with obesity) 259.0
- **Infants, healthy liveborn** — *see* Newborn
- **Infarct, infarction**
  - adrenal (capsule) (gland) 255.41
  - amnion 658.8 ☑
  - anterior (with contiguous portion of intraventricular septum) NEC (*see also* Infarct, myocardium) 410.1 ☑
  - appendices epiploicae 557.0
  - bowel 557.0
  - brain (stem) 434.91
    - embolic (*see also* Embolism, brain) 434.11
    - healed or old without residuals V12.54
    - iatrogenic 997.02
    - lacunar 434.91
    - late effect — *see* Late effect(s) (of) cerebrovascular disease
    - postoperative 997.02
    - puerperal, postpartum, childbirth 674.0 ☑
    - thrombotic (*see also* Thrombosis, brain) 434.01
  - breast 611.89 ▲
  - Brewer's (kidney) 593.81
  - cardiac (*see also* Infarct, myocardium) 410.9 ☑
  - cerebellar (*see also* Infarct, brain) 434.91
    - embolic (*see also* Embolism, brain) 434.11
  - cerebral (*see also* Infarct, brain) 434.91
    - aborted 434.91
    - embolic (*see also* Embolism, brain) 434.11
    - thrombotic (*see also* Infarct, brain) 434.01
  - chorion 658.8 ☑

- **Infarct, infarction** — *continued*
  - colon (acute) (agnogenic) (embolic) (hemorrhagic) (nonocclusive) (nonthrombotic) (occlusive) (segmental) (thrombotic) (with gangrene) 557.0
  - coronary artery (*see also* Infarct, myocardium) 410.9 ☑
  - cortical 434.91
  - embolic (*see also* Embolism) 444.9
  - fallopian tube 620.8
  - gallbladder 575.8
  - heart (*see also* Infarct, myocardium) 410.9 ☑
  - hepatic 573.4
  - hypophysis (anterior lobe) 253.8
  - impending (myocardium) 411.1
  - intestine (acute) (agnogenic) (embolic) (hemorrhagic) (nonocclusive) (nonthrombotic) (occlusive) (thrombotic) (with gangrene) 557.0
  - kidney 593.81
  - lacunar 434.91
  - liver 573.4
  - lung (embolic) (thrombotic) 415.19
    - with
      - abortion — *see* Abortion, by type, with, embolism
      - ectopic pregnancy (*see also* categories 633.0–633.9) 639.6
      - molar pregnancy (*see also* categories 630–632) 639.6
    - following
      - abortion 639.6
      - ectopic or molar pregnancy 639.6
    - iatrogenic 415.11
    - in pregnancy, childbirth, or puerperium — *see* Embolism, obstetrical
    - postoperative 415.11
    - septic 415.12
  - lymph node or vessel 457.8
  - medullary (brain) — *see* Infarct, brain
  - meibomian gland (eyelid) 374.85
  - mesentery, mesenteric (embolic) (thrombotic) (with gangrene) 557.0
  - midbrain — *see* Infarct, brain
  - myocardium, myocardial (acute or with a stated duration of 8 weeks or less) (with hypertension) 410.9 ☑

> *Note — Use the following fifth-digit subclassification with category 410:*
>
> 0 *episode unspecified*
>
> 1 *initial episode*
>
> 2 *subsequent episode without recurrence*

-
  -
    - with symptoms after 8 weeks from date of infarction 414.8
    - anterior (wall) (with contiguous portion of intraventricular septum) NEC 410.1 ☑
    - anteroapical (with contiguous portion of intraventricular septum) 410.1 ☑
    - anterolateral (wall) 410.0 ☑
    - anteroseptal (with contiguous portion of intraventricular septum) 410.1 ☑
    - apical-lateral 410.5 ☑
    - atrial 410.8 ☑
    - basal-lateral 410.5 ☑
    - chronic (with symptoms after 8 weeks from date of infarction) 414.8
    - diagnosed on ECG, but presenting no symptoms 412
    - diaphragmatic wall (with contiguous portion of intraventricular septum) 410.4 ☑

- **Infarct, infarction** — *continued*
  - myocardium, myocardial — *continued*
    - healed or old, currently presenting no symptoms 412
    - high lateral 410.5 ☑
    - impending 411.1
    - inferior (wall) (with contiguous portion of intraventricular septum) 410.4 ☑
    - inferolateral (wall) 410.2 ☑
    - inferoposterior wall 410.3 ☑
    - intraoperative 997.1
    - lateral wall 410.5 ☑
    - non-Q wave 410.7 ☑
    - non-ST elevation (NSTEMI)
    - nontransmural 410.7 ☑
    - papillary muscle 410.8 ☑
    - past (diagnosed on ECG or other special investigation, but currently presenting no symptoms) 412
      - with symptoms NEC 414.8
    - posterior (strictly) (true) (wall) 410.6 ☑
    - posterobasal 410.6 ☑
    - posteroinferior 410.3 ☑
    - posterolateral 410.5 ☑
    - postprocedural 997.1
    - previous, currently presenting no symptoms 412
    - Q wave (*see also* Infarct, myocardium, by site) 410.9 ☑
    - septal 410.8 ☑
    - specified site NEC 410.8 ☑
    - ST elevation (STEMI) 410.9 ☑
      - anterior (wall) 410.1 ☑
      - anterolateral (wall) 410.0 ☑
      - inferior (wall) 410.4 ☑
      - inferolateral (wall) 410.2 ☑
      - inferoposterior wall 410.3 ☑
      - lateral wall 410.5 ☑
      - posterior (strictly) (true) (wall) 410.6 ☑
      - specified site NEC 410.8 ☑
    - subendocardial 410.7 ☑
    - syphilitic 093.82
  - non-ST elevation myocardial infarction (NSTEMI) 410.7 ☑
  - nontransmural 410.7 ☑
  - omentum 557.0
  - ovary 620.8
  - pancreas 577.8
  - papillary muscle (*see also* Infarct, myocardium) 410.8 ☑
  - parathyroid gland 252.8
  - pituitary (gland) 253.8
  - placenta (complicating pregnancy) 656.7 ☑
    - affecting fetus or newborn 762.2
  - pontine — *see* Infarct, brain
  - posterior NEC (*see also* Infarct, myocardium) 410.6 ☑
  - prostate 602.8
  - pulmonary (artery) (hemorrhagic) (vein) 415.19
    - with
      - abortion — *see* Abortion, by type, with embolism
      - ectopic pregnancy (*see also* categories 633.0–633.9) 639.6
      - molar pregnancy (*see also* categories 630–632) 639.6
    - following
      - abortion 639.6
      - ectopic or molar pregnancy 639.6
    - iatrogenic 415.11
    - in pregnancy, childbirth, or puerperium — *see* Embolism, obstetrical
    - postoperative 415.11
    - septic 415.12
  - renal 593.81

- **Infarct, infarction** — *continued*
  - renal — *continued*
    - embolic or thrombotic 593.81
  - retina, retinal 362.84
    - with occlusion — *see* Occlusion, retina
  - spinal (acute) (cord) (embolic) (nonembolic) 336.1
  - spleen 289.59
    - embolic or thrombotic 444.89
  - subchorionic — *see* Infarct, placenta
  - subendocardial (*see also* Infarct, myocardium) 410.7 ☑
  - suprarenal (capsule) (gland) 255.41
  - syncytium — *see* Infarct, placenta
  - testis 608.83
  - thrombotic (*see also* Thrombosis) 453.9
    - artery, arterial — *see* Embolism
  - thyroid (gland) 246.3
  - ventricle (heart) (*see also* Infarct, myocardium) 410.9 ☑
- **Infecting** — *see* condition
- **Infection, infected, infective** (opportunistic) 136.9
  - with lymphangitis — *see* Lymphangitis
  - abortion — *see* Abortion, by type, with, sepsis
  - abscess (skin) — *see* Abscess, by site
  - Absidia 117.7
  - acanthamoeba 136.21 ●
  - Acanthocheilonema (perstans) 125.4
    - streptocerca 125.6
  - accessory sinus (chronic) (*see also* Sinusitis) 473.9
  - Achorion — *see* Dermatophytosis
  - Acremonium falciforme 117.4
  - acromioclavicular (joint) 711.91
  - actinobacillus
    - lignieresii 027.8
    - mallei 024
    - muris 026.1
  - actinomadura — *see* Actinomycosis
  - Actinomyces (israelii) (*see also* Actinomycosis)
    - muris-ratti 026.1
  - Actinomycetales (actinomadura) (Actinomyces) (Nocardia) (Streptomyces) — *see* Actinomycosis
  - actinomycotic NEC (*see also* Actinomycosis) 039.9
  - adenoid (chronic) 474.01
    - acute 463
    - and tonsil (chronic) 474.02
      - acute or subacute 463
  - adenovirus NEC 079.0
    - in diseases classified elsewhere — *see* category 079 ☑
    - unspecified nature or site 079.0
  - Aerobacter aerogenes NEC 041.85
    - enteritis 008.2
  - aerogenes capsulatus (*see also* Gangrene, gas) 040.0
  - aertrycke (*see also* Infection, Salmonella) 003.9
  - ajellomyces dermatitidis 116.0
  - alimentary canal NEC (*see also* Enteritis, due to, by organism) 009.0
  - Allescheria boydii 117.6
  - Alternaria 118
  - alveolus, alveolar (process) (pulpal origin) 522.4
  - ameba, amebic (histolytica) (*see also* Amebiasis) 006.9
    - acute 006.0
    - chronic 006.1
    - free-living 136.29 ▲
    - hartmanni 007.8
    - specified
      - site NEC 006.8
      - type NEC 007.8
  - amniotic fluid or cavity 658.4 ☑
    - affecting fetus or newborn 762.7
  - anaerobes (cocci) (gram-negative) (gram-positive) (mixed) NEC 041.84

Infection, infected, infective — *continued*
- anal canal 569.49
- Ancylostoma braziliense 126.2
- Angiostrongylus cantonensis 128.8
- anisakiasis 127.1
- Anisakis larva 127.1
- anthrax (*see also* Anthrax) 022.9
- antrum (chronic) (*see also* Sinusitis, maxillary) 473.0
- anus (papillae) (sphincter) 569.49
- arbor virus NEC 066.9
- arbovirus NEC 066.9
- argentophil-rod 027.0
- Ascaris lumbricoides 127.0
- ascomycetes 117.4
- Aspergillus (flavus) (fumigatus) (terreus) 117.3
- atypical
  - acid-fast (bacilli) (*see also* Mycobacterium, atypical) 031.9
  - mycobacteria (*see also* Mycobacterium, atypical) 031.9
- auditory meatus (circumscribed) (diffuse) (external) (*see also* Otitis, externa) 380.10
- auricle (ear) (*see also* Otitis, externa) 380.10
- axillary gland 683
- Babesiasis 088.82
- Babesiosis 088.82
- Bacillus NEC 041.89
  - abortus 023.1
  - anthracis (*see also* Anthrax) 022.9
  - cereus (food poisoning) 005.89
  - coli — *see* Infection, Escherichia coli
  - coliform NEC 041.85
  - Ducrey's (any location) 099.0
  - Flexner's 004.1
  - Friedländer's NEC 041.3
  - fusiformis 101
  - gas (gangrene) (*see also* Gangrene, gas) 040.0
  - mallei 024
  - melitensis 023.0
  - paratyphoid, paratyphosus 002.9
    - A 002.1
    - B 002.2
    - C 002.3
  - Schmorl's 040.3
  - Shiga 004.0
  - suipestifer (*see also* Infection, Salmonella) 003.9
  - swimming pool 031.1
  - typhosa 002.0
  - welchii (*see also* Gangrene, gas) 040.0
  - Whitmore's 025
- bacterial NEC 041.9
  - specified NEC 041.89
    - anaerobic NEC 041.84
    - gram-negative NEC 041.85
      - anaerobic NEC 041.84
- Bacterium
  - paratyphosum 002.9
    - A 002.1
    - B 002.2
    - C 002.3
  - typhosum 002.0
- Bacteroides (fragilis) (melaninogenicus) (oralis) NEC 041.82
- balantidium coli 007.0
- Bartholin's gland 616.89
- Basidiobolus 117.7
- Bedsonia 079.98
  - specified NEC 079.88
- bile duct 576.1
- bladder (*see also* Cystitis) 595.9
- Blastomyces, blastomycotic 116.0
  - brasiliensis 116.1
  - dermatitidis 116.0
  - European 117.5
  - loboi 116.2
  - North American 116.0
  - South American 116.1

Infection, infected, infective — *continued*
- bleb
  - postprocedural 379.60
    - stage 1 379.61
    - stage 2 379.62
    - stage 3 379.63
- blood stream — *see also* Septicemia
  - catheter-related (CRBSI) 999.31
- bone 730.9 ☑
  - specified — *see* Osteomyelitis
- Bordetella 033.9
  - bronchiseptica 033.8
  - parapertussis 033.1
  - pertussis 033.0
- Borrelia
  - bergdorfi 088.81
  - vincentii (mouth) (pharynx) (tonsil) 101
- bovine stomatitis 059.11 ●
- brain (*see also* Encephalitis) 323.9
  - late effect — *see* category 326
  - membranes (*see also* Meningitis) 322.9
  - septic 324.0
    - late effect — *see* category 326
    - meninges (*see also* Meningitis) 320.9
- branchial cyst 744.42
- breast 611.0
  - puerperal, postpartum 675.2 ☑
    - with nipple 675.9 ☑
      - specified type NEC 675.8 ☑
    - nonpurulent 675.2 ☑
    - purulent 675.1 ☑
- bronchus (*see also* Bronchitis) 490
  - fungus NEC 117.9
- Brucella 023.9
  - abortus 023.1
  - canis 023.3
  - melitensis 023.0
  - mixed 023.8
  - suis 023.2
- Brugia (Wuchereria) malayi 125.1
- bursa — *see* Bursitis
- buttocks (skin) 686.9
- Candida (albicans) (tropicalis) (*see also* Candidiasis) 112.9
  - congenital 771.7
- Candiru 136.8
- Capillaria
  - hepatica 128.8
  - philippinensis 127.5
- cartilage 733.99
- catheter-related bloodstream (CRBSI) 999.31
- cat liver fluke 121.0
- cellulitis — *see* Cellulitis, by site
- Cephalosporum falciforme 117.4
- Cercomonas hominis (intestinal) 007.3
- cerebrospinal (*see also* Meningitis) 322.9
  - late effect — *see* category 326
- cervical gland 683
- cervix (*see also* Cervicitis) 616.0
- cesarean section wound 674.3 ☑
- Chilomastix (intestinal) 007.8
- Chlamydia 079.98
  - specified NEC 079.88
- cholera (*see also* Cholera) 001.9
- chorionic plate 658.8 ☑
- Cladosporium
  - bantianum 117.8
  - carrionii 117.2
  - mansoni 111.1
  - trichoides 117.8
  - wernecki 111.1
- Clonorchis (sinensis) (liver) 121.1
- Clostridium (haemolyticum) (novyi) NEC 041.84
  - botulinum 005.1
  - histolyticum (*see also* Gangrene, gas) 040.0
  - oedematiens (*see also* Gangrene, gas) 040.0
  - perfringens 041.83

Infection, infected, infective — *continued*
- Clostridium — *continued*
  - perfringens — *continued*
    - due to food 005.2
  - septicum (*see also* Gangrene, gas) 040.0
  - sordellii (*see also* Gangrene, gas) 040.0
  - welchii (*see also* Gangrene, gas) 040.0
    - due to food 005.2
- Coccidioides (immitis) (*see also* Coccidioidomycosis) 114.9
- coccus NEC 041.89
- colon (*see also* Enteritis, due to, by organism) 009.0
  - bacillus — *see* Infection, Escherichia coli
- colostomy or enterostomy 569.61
- common duct 576.1
- complicating pregnancy, childbirth, or puerperium NEC 647.9 ☑
  - affecting fetus or newborn 760.2
- Condiobolus 117.7
- congenital NEC 771.89
  - Candida albicans 771.7
  - chronic 771.2
  - cytomegalovirus 771.1
  - hepatitis, viral 771.2
  - herpes simplex 771.2
  - listeriosis 771.2
  - malaria 771.2
  - poliomyelitis 771.2
  - rubella 771.0
  - toxoplasmosis 771.2
  - tuberculosis 771.2
  - urinary (tract) 771.82
  - vaccinia 771.2
- coronavirus 079.89
  - SARS-associated 079.82
- corpus luteum (*see also* Salpingo-oophoritis) 614.2
- Corynebacterium diphtheriae — *see* Diphtheria
- cotia virus 059.8 ●
- Coxsackie (*see also* Coxsackie) 079.2
  - endocardium 074.22
  - heart NEC 074.20
  - in diseases classified elsewhere — *see* category 079 ☑
  - meninges 047.0
  - myocardium 074.23
  - pericardium 074.21
  - pharynx 074.0
  - specified disease NEC 074.8
  - unspecified nature or site 079.2
- Cryptococcus neoformans 117.5
- Cryptosporidia 007.4
- Cunninghamella 117.7
- cyst — *see* Cyst
- Cysticercus cellulosae 123.1
- cytomegalovirus 078.5
  - congenital 771.1
- dental (pulpal origin) 522.4
- deuteromycetes 117.4
- Dicrocoelium dendriticum 121.8
- Dipetalonema (perstans) 125.4
  - streptocerca 125.6
- diphtherial — *see* Diphtheria
- Diphyllobothrium (adult) (latum) (pacificum) 123.4
  - larval 123.5
- Diplogonoporus (grandis) 123.8
- Dipylidium (caninum) 123.8
- Dirofilaria 125.6
- dog tapeworm 123.8
- Dracunculus medinensis 125.7
- Dreschlera 118
  - hawaiiensis 117.8
- Ducrey's bacillus (any site) 099.0
- due to or resulting from
  - central venous catheter 999.31

Infection, infected, infective — *continued*
- due to or resulting from — *continued*
  - device, implant, or graft (any) (presence of) — *see* Complications, infection and inflammation, due to (presence of) any device, implant, or graft classified to 996.0–996.5 NEC
  - injection, inoculation, infusion, transfusion, or vaccination (prophylactic) (therapeutic) 999.39
  - injury NEC — *see* Wound, open, by site, complicated
  - surgery 998.59
- duodenum 535.6 ☑
- ear (*see also* Otitis)
  - external (*see also* Otitis, externa) 380.10
  - inner (*see also* Labyrinthitis) 386.30
  - middle — *see* Otitis, media
- Eaton's agent NEC 041.81
- Eberthella typhosa 002.0
- Ebola 078.89
- echinococcosis 122.9
- Echinococcus (*see also* Echinococcus) 122.9
- Echinostoma 121.8
- ECHO virus 079.1
  - in diseases classified elsewhere — *see* category 079 ☑
  - unspecified nature or site 079.1
- Ehrlichiosis 082.40
  - chaffeensis 082.41
  - specified type NEC 082.49
- Endamoeba — *see* Infection, ameba
- endocardium (*see also* Endocarditis) 421.0
- endocervix (*see also* Cervicitis) 616.0
- Entamoeba — *see* Infection, ameba
- enteric (*see also* Enteritis, due to, by organism) 009.0
- Enterobacter aerogenes NEC 041.85
- Enterobacter sakazakii 041.85
- Enterobius vermicularis 127.4
- enterococcus NEC 041.04
- enterovirus NEC 079.89
  - central nervous system NEC 048
  - enteritis 008.67
  - meningitis 047.9
- Entomophthora 117.7
- Epidermophyton — *see* Dermatophytosis
- epidermophytosis — *see* Dermatophytosis
- episiotomy 674.3 ☑
- Epstein-Barr virus 075
  - chronic 780.79 *[139.8]*
- erysipeloid 027.1
- Erysipelothrix (insidiosa) (rhusiopathiae) 027.1
- erythema infectiosum 057.0
- Escherichia coli NEC 041.4
  - enteritis — *see* Enteritis, E. coli
  - generalized 038.42
  - intestinal — *see* Enteritis, E. coli
- esophagostomy 530.86
- ethmoidal (chronic) (sinus) (*see also* Sinusitis, ethmoidal) 473.2
- Eubacterium 041.84
- Eustachian tube (ear) 381.50
  - acute 381.51
  - chronic 381.52
- exanthema subitum (*see also* Exanthem subitum) 058.10
- external auditory canal (meatus) (*see also* Otitis, externa) 380.10
- eye NEC 360.00
- eyelid 373.9
  - specified NEC 373.8
- fallopian tube (*see also* Salpingo-oophoritis) 614.2

Infection, infected, infective — *continued*
- fascia 728.89
- Fasciola
  - gigantica 121.3
  - hepatica 121.3
- Fasciolopsis (buski) 121.4
- fetus (intra-amniotic) — *see* Infection, congenital
- filarial — *see* Infestation, filarial
- finger (skin) 686.9
  - abscess (with lymphangitis) 681.00
    - pulp 681.01
  - cellulitis (with lymphangitis) 681.00
  - distal closed space (with lymphangitis) 681.00
  - nail 681.02
    - fungus 110.1
- fish tapeworm 123.4
  - larval 123.5
- flagellate, intestinal 007.9
- fluke — *see* Infestation, fluke
- focal
  - teeth (pulpal origin) 522.4
  - tonsils 474.00
    - and adenoids 474.02
- Fonsecaea
  - compactum 117.2
  - pedrosoi 117.2
- food (*see also* Poisoning, food) 005.9
- foot (skin) 686.9
  - fungus 110.4
- Francisella tularensis (*see also* Tularemia) 021.9
- frontal sinus (chronic) (*see also* Sinusitis, frontal) 473.1
- fungus NEC 117.9
  - beard 110.0
  - body 110.5
  - dermatiacious NEC 117.8
  - foot 110.4
  - groin 110.3
  - hand 110.2
  - nail 110.1
  - pathogenic to compromised host only 118
  - perianal (area) 110.3
  - scalp 110.0
  - scrotum 110.8
  - skin 111.9
    - foot 110.4
    - hand 110.2
  - toenails 110.1
  - trachea 117.9
- Fusarium 118
- Fusobacterium 041.84
- gallbladder (*see also* Cholecystitis, acute) 575.0
- Gardnerella vaginalis 041.89
- gas bacillus (*see also* Gas, gangrene) 040.0
- gastric (*see also* Gastritis) 535.5 ☑
- Gastrodiscoides hominis 121.8
- gastroenteric (*see also* Enteritis, due to, by organism) 009.0
- gastrointestinal (*see also* Enteritis, due to, by organism) 009.0
- gastrostomy 536.41
- generalized NEC (*see also* Septicemia) 038.9
- genital organ or tract NEC
  - female 614.9
    - with
      - abortion — *see* Abortion, by type, with sepsis
      - ectopic pregnancy (*see also* categories 633.0–633.9) 639.0
      - molar pregnancy (*see also* categories 630–632) 639.0
    - complicating pregnancy 646.6 ☑
      - affecting fetus or newborn 760.8

Infection, infected, infective — *continued*
- genital organ or tract — *continued*
  - female — *continued*
    - following
      - abortion 639.0
      - ectopic or molar pregnancy 639.0
    - puerperal, postpartum, childbirth 670.0 ☑
      - minor or localized 646.6 ☑
        - affecting fetus or newborn 760.8
  - male 608.4
- genitourinary tract NEC 599.0
- Ghon tubercle, primary (*see also* Tuberculosis) 010.0 ☑
- Giardia lamblia 007.1
- gingival (chronic) 523.10
  - acute 523.00
  - Vincent's 101
- glanders 024
- Glenosporopsis amazonica 116.2
- Gnathostoma spinigerum 128.1
- Gongylonema 125.6
- gonococcal NEC (*see also* Gonococcus) 098.0
- gram-negative bacilli NEC 041.85
  - anaerobic 041.84
- guinea worm 125.7
- gum (*see also* Infection, gingival) 523.10
- Hantavirus 079.81
- heart 429.89
- Helicobacter pylori (H. pylori) 041.86
- helminths NEC 128.9
  - intestinal 127.9
    - mixed (types classifiable to more than one category in 120.0–127.7) 127.8
    - specified type NEC 127.7
  - specified type NEC 128.8
- Hemophilus influenzae NEC 041.5
  - generalized 038.41
- herpes (simplex) (*see also* Herpes, simplex) 054.9
  - congenital 771.2
  - zoster (*see also* Herpes, zoster) 053.9
    - eye NEC 053.29
- Heterophyes heterophyes 121.6
- Histoplasma (*see also* Histoplasmosis) 115.90
  - capsulatum (*see also* Histoplasmosis, American) 115.00
  - duboisii (*see also* Histoplasmosis, African) 115.10
- HIV V08
  - with symptoms, symptomatic 042
- hookworm (*see also* Ancylostomiasis) 126.9
- human herpesvirus NEC 058.89
- human herpesvirus 6 058.81
- human herpesvirus 7 058.82
- human herpesvirus 8 058.89
- human immunodeficiency virus V08
  - with symptoms, symptomatic 042
- human papillomavirus 079.4
- hydrocele 603.1
- hydronephrosis 591
- Hymenolepis 123.6
- hypopharynx 478.29
- inguinal glands 683
  - due to soft chancre 099.0
- intestine, intestinal (*see also* Enteritis, due to, by organism) 009.0
- intrauterine (*see also* Endometritis) 615.9
  - complicating delivery 646.6 ☑
- isospora belli or hominis 007.2
- Japanese B encephalitis 062.0
- jaw (bone) (acute) (chronic) (lower) (subacute) (upper) 526.4
- joint — *see* Arthritis, infectious or infective

Infection, infected, infective — *continued*
- Kaposi's sarcoma-associated herpesvirus 058.89
- kidney (cortex) (hematogenous) 590.9
  - with
    - abortion — *see* Abortion, by type, with urinary tract infection
    - calculus 592.0
    - ectopic pregnancy (*see also* categories 633.0–633.9) 639.8
    - molar pregnancy (*see also* categories 630–632) 639.8
  - complicating pregnancy or puerperium 646.6 ☑
    - affecting fetus or newborn 760.1
  - following
    - abortion 639.8
    - ectopic or molar pregnancy 639.8
  - pelvis and ureter 590.3
- Klebsiella pneumoniae NEC 041.3
- knee (skin) NEC 686.9
  - joint — *see* Arthritis, infectious
- Koch's (*see also* Tuberculosis, pulmonary) 011.9 ☑
- labia (majora) (minora) (*see also* Vulvitis) 616.10
- lacrimal
  - gland (*see also* Dacryoadenitis) 375.00
  - passages (duct) (sac) (*see also* Dacryocystitis) 375.30
- larynx NEC 478.79
- leg (skin) NEC 686.9
- Leishmania (*see also* Leishmaniasis) 085.9
  - braziliensis 085.5
  - donovani 085.0
  - ethiopica 085.3
  - furunculosa 085.1
  - infantum 085.0
  - mexicana 085.4
  - tropica (minor) 085.1
    - major 085.2
- Leptosphaeria senegalensis 117.4
- leptospira (*see also* Leptospirosis) 100.9
  - Australis 100.89
  - Bataviae 100.89
  - pyrogenes 100.89
  - specified type NEC 100.89
- leptospirochetal NEC (*see also* Leptospirosis) 100.9
- Leptothrix — *see* Actinomycosis
- Listeria monocytogenes (listeriosis) 027.0
  - congenital 771.2
- liver fluke — *see* Infestation, fluke, liver
- Loa loa 125.2
  - eyelid 125.2 *[373.6]*
- Loboa loboi 116.2
- local, skin (staphylococcal) (streptococcal) NEC 686.9
  - abscess — *see* Abscess, by site
  - cellulitis — *see* Cellulitis, by site
  - ulcer (*see also* Ulcer, skin) 707.9
- Loefflerella
  - mallei 024
  - whitmori 025
- lung 518.89
  - atypical Mycobacterium 031.0
    - tuberculous (*see also* Tuberculosis, pulmonary) 011.9 ☑
  - basilar 518.89
  - chronic 518.89
  - fungus NEC 117.9
  - spirochetal 104.8
  - virus — *see* Pneumonia, virus
- lymph gland (axillary) (cervical) (inguinal) 683
  - mesenteric 289.2

Infection, infected, infective — *continued*
- lymphoid tissue, base of tongue or posterior pharynx, NEC 474.00
- madurella
  - grisea 117.4
  - mycetomii 117.4
- major
  - with
    - abortion — *see* Abortion, by type, with sepsis
    - ectopic pregnancy (*see also* categories 633.0–633.9) 639.0
    - molar pregnancy (*see also* categories 630–632) 639.0
  - following
    - abortion 639.0
    - ectopic or molar pregnancy 639.0
  - puerperal, postpartum, childbirth 670.0 ☑
- Malassezia furfur 111.0
- Malleomyces
  - mallei 024
  - pseudomallei 025
- mammary gland 611.0
  - puerperal, postpartum 675.2 ☑
- Mansonella (ozzardi) 125.5
- mastoid (suppurative) — *see* Mastoiditis
- maxilla, maxillary 526.4
  - sinus (chronic) (*see also* Sinusitis, maxillary) 473.0
- mediastinum 519.2
- medina 125.7
- meibomian
  - cyst 373.12
  - gland 373.12
- melioidosis 025
- meninges (*see also* Meningitis) 320.9
- meningococcal (*see also* condition) 036.9
  - brain 036.1
  - cerebrospinal 036.0
  - endocardium 036.42
  - generalized 036.2
  - meninges 036.0
  - meningococcemia 036.2
  - specified site NEC 036.89
- mesenteric lymph nodes or glands NEC 289.2
- Metagonimus 121.5
- metatarsophalangeal 711.97
- methicillin ●
  - resistant Staphylococcus aureus (MRSA) 041.12 ●
  - susceptible Staphylococcus aureus (MSSA) 041.11 ●
- microorganism resistant to drugs — *see* Resistance (to), drugs by microorganisms
- Microsporidia 136.8
- microsporum, microsporic — *see* Dermatophytosis
- Mima polymorpha NEC 041.85
- mixed flora NEC 041.89
- Monilia (*see also* Candidiasis) 112.9
  - neonatal 771.7
- monkeypox 059.01 ▲
- Monosporium apiospermum 117.6
- mouth (focus) NEC 528.9
  - parasitic 136.9
- MRSA (methicillin resistant Staphylococcus aureus) 041.12 ●
- MSSA (methicillin susceptible Staphylococcus aureus) 041.11 ●
- Mucor 117.7
- muscle NEC 728.89
- mycelium NEC 117.9
- mycetoma
  - actinomycotic NEC (*see also* Actinomycosis) 039.9
  - mycotic NEC 117.4

☑ Additional Digit Required — Refer to the Tabular List for Digit Selection

Subterms under main terms may continue to next column or page

▶◀ Revised Text ● New Line ▲ Revised Code

Infection, infected, infective — *continued*
- Mycobacterium, mycobacterial (*see also* Mycobacterium) 031.9
- Mycoplasma NEC 041.81
- mycotic NEC 117.9
  - pathogenic to compromised host only 118
  - skin NEC 111.9
  - systemic 117.9
- myocardium NEC 422.90
- nail (chronic) (with lymphangitis) 681.9
  - finger 681.02
    - fungus 110.1
  - ingrowing 703.0
  - toe 681.11
    - fungus 110.1
- nasal sinus (chronic) (*see also* Sinusitis) 473.9
- nasopharynx (chronic) 478.29
  - acute 460
- navel 686.9
  - newborn 771.4
- Neisserian — *see* Gonococcus
- Neotestudina rosatii 117.4
- newborn, generalized 771.89
- nipple 611.0
  - puerperal, postpartum 675.0 ☑
    - with breast 675.9 ☑
      - specified type NEC 675.8 ☑
- Nocardia — *see* Actinomycosis
- nose 478.19
- nostril 478.19
- obstetrical surgical wound 674.3 ☑
- Oesophagostomum (apiostomum) 127.7
- Oestrus ovis 134.0
- Oidium albicans (*see also* Candidiasis) 112.9
- Onchocerca (volvulus) 125.3
  - eye 125.3 *[360.13]*
  - eyelid 125.3 *[373.6]*
- operation wound 998.59
- Opisthorchis (felineus) (tenuicollis) (viverrini) 121.0
- orbit 376.00
  - chronic 376.10
- orthopoxvirus 059.00 ●
  - specified NEC 059.09 ●
- ovary (*see also* Salpingo-oophoritis) 614.2
- Oxyuris vermicularis 127.4
- pancreas 577.0
- Paracoccidioides brasiliensis 116.1
- Paragonimus (westermani) 121.2
- parainfluenza virus 079.89
- parameningococcus NEC 036.9
  - with meningitis 036.0
- parapoxvirus 059.10 ●
  - specified NEC 059.19 ●
- parasitic NEC 136.9
- paratyphoid 002.9
  - type A 002.1
  - type B 002.2
  - type C 002.3
- paraurethral ducts 597.89
- parotid gland 527.2
- Pasteurella NEC 027.2
  - multocida (cat-bite) (dog-bite) 027.2
  - pestis (*see also* Plague) 020.9
  - pseudotuberculosis 027.2
  - septica (cat-bite) (dog-bite) 027.2
  - tularensis (*see also* Tularemia) 021.9
- pelvic, female (*see also* Disease, pelvis, inflammatory) 614.9
- penis (glans) (retention) NEC 607.2
  - herpetic 054.13
- Peptococcus 041.84
- Peptostreptococcus 041.84
- periapical (pulpal origin) 522.4
- peridental 523.30
- perineal wound (obstetrical) 674.3 ☑
- periodontal 523.31
- periorbital 376.00

Infection, infected, infective — *continued*
- periorbital — *continued*
  - chronic 376.10
- perirectal 569.49
- perirenal (*see also* Infection, kidney) 590.9
- peritoneal (*see also* Peritonitis) 567.9
- periureteral 593.89
- periurethral 597.89
- Petriellidium boydii 117.6
- pharynx 478.29
  - Coxsackie virus 074.0
  - phlegmonous 462
  - posterior, lymphoid 474.00
- Phialophora
  - gougerotii 117.8
  - jeanselmei 117.8
  - verrucosa 117.2
- Piedraia hortai 111.3
- pinna, acute 380.11
- pinta 103.9
  - intermediate 103.1
  - late 103.2
  - mixed 103.3
  - primary 103.0
- pinworm 127.4
- pityrosporum furfur 111.0
- pleuropneumonia-like organisms NEC (PPLO) 041.81
- pneumococcal NEC 041.2
  - generalized (purulent) 038.2
- Pneumococcus NEC 041.2
- postoperative wound 998.59
- posttraumatic NEC 958.3
- postvaccinal 999.39
- poxvirus 059.9 ●
  - specified NEC 059.8 ●
- prepuce NEC 607.1
- Proprionibacterium 041.84
- prostate (capsule) (*see also* Prostatitis) 601.9
- Proteus (mirabilis) (morganii) (vulgaris) NEC 041.6
  - enteritis 008.3
- protozoal NEC 136.8
  - intestinal NEC 007.9
- Pseudomonas NEC 041.7
  - mallei 024
  - pneumonia 482.1
  - pseudomallei 025
- psittacosis 073.9
- puerperal, postpartum (major) 670.0 ☑
  - minor 646.6 ☑
- pulmonary — *see* Infection, lung
- purulent — *see* Abscess
- putrid, generalized — *see* Septicemia
- pyemic — *see* Septicemia
- Pyrenochaeta romeroi 117.4
- Q fever 083.0
- rabies 071
- rectum (sphincter) 569.49
- renal (*see also* Infection, kidney) 590.9
  - pelvis and ureter 590.3
- resistant to drugs — *see* Resistance (to), drugs by microorganisms
- respiratory 519.8
  - chronic 519.8
  - influenzal (acute) (upper) 487.1
  - lung 518.89
  - rhinovirus 460
  - syncytial virus 079.6
  - upper (acute) (infectious) NEC 465.9
    - with flu, grippe, or influenza 487.1
    - influenzal 487.1
    - multiple sites NEC 465.8
    - streptococcal 034.0
    - viral NEC 465.9
- respiratory syncytial virus (RSV) 079.6

Infection, infected, infective — *continued*
- resulting from presence of shunt or other internal prosthetic device — *see* Complications, infection and inflammation, due to (presence of) any device, implant, or graft classified to 996.0–996.5 NEC
- retroperitoneal 567.39
- retrovirus 079.50
  - human immunodeficiency virus type 2 [HIV2] 079.53
  - human T-cell lymphotrophic virus type I [HTLV-I] 079.51
  - human T-cell lymphotrophic virus type II [HTLV-II] 079.52
  - specified NEC 079.59
- Rhinocladium 117.1
- Rhinosporidium — *see* beri 117.0
- rhinovirus
  - in diseases classified elsewhere — *see* category 079 ☑
  - unspecified nature or site 079.3
- Rhizopus 117.7
- rickettsial 083.9
- rickettsialpox 083.2
- rubella (*see also* Rubella) 056.9
  - congenital 771.0
- Saccharomyces (*see also* Candidiasis) 112.9
- Saksenaea 117.7
- salivary duct or gland (any) 527.2
- Salmonella (aertrycke) (callinarum) (choleraesuis) (enteritidis) (suipestifer) (typhimurium) 003.9
  - with
    - arthritis 003.23
    - gastroenteritis 003.0
    - localized infection 003.20
      - specified type NEC 003.29
    - meningitis 003.21
    - osteomyelitis 003.24
    - pneumonia 003.22
    - septicemia 003.1
    - specified manifestation NEC 003.8
  - due to food (poisoning) (any serotype) (*see also* Poisoning, food, due to, Salmonella)
  - hirschfeldii 002.3
  - localized 003.20
    - specified type NEC 003.29
  - paratyphi 002.9
    - A 002.1
    - B 002.2
    - C 002.3
  - schottmuelleri 002.2
  - specified type NEC 003.8
  - typhi 002.0
  - typhosa 002.0
- saprophytic 136.8
- Sarcocystis, lindemanni 136.5
- SARS-associated coronavirus 079.82
- scabies 133.0
- Schistosoma — *see* Infestation, Schistosoma
- Schmorl's bacillus 040.3
- scratch or other superficial injury — *see* Injury, superficial, by site
- scrotum (acute) NEC 608.4
- sealpox 059.12 ●
- secondary, burn or open wound (dislocation) (fracture) 958.3
- seminal vesicle (*see also* Vesiculitis) 608.0
- septic
  - generalized — *see* Septicemia
  - localized, skin (*see also* Abscess) 682.9
- septicemic — *see* Septicemia
- seroma 998.51
- Serratia (marcescens) 041.85
  - generalized 038.44
- sheep liver fluke 121.3

Infection, infected, infective — *continued*
- Shigella 004.9
  - boydii 004.2
  - dysenteriae 004.0
  - flexneri 004.1
  - group
    - A 004.0
    - B 004.1
    - C 004.2
    - D 004.3
  - Schmitz (-Stutzer) 004.0
  - schmitzii 004.0
  - Shiga 004.0
  - sonnei 004.3
  - specified type NEC 004.8
- Sin Nombre virus 079.81
- sinus (*see also* Sinusitis) 473.9
  - pilonidal 685.1
    - with abscess 685.0
  - skin NEC 686.9
- Skene's duct or gland (*see also* Urethritis) 597.89
- skin (local) (staphylococcal) (streptococcal) NEC 686.9
  - abscess — *see* Abscess, by site
  - cellulitis — *see* Cellulitis, by site
  - due to fungus 111.9
    - specified type NEC 111.8
  - mycotic 111.9
    - specified type NEC 111.8
  - ulcer (*see also* Ulcer, skin) 707.9
- slow virus 046.9
  - specified condition NEC 046.8
- Sparganum (mansoni) (proliferum) 123.5
- spermatic cord NEC 608.4
- sphenoidal (chronic) (sinus) (*see also* Sinusitis, sphenoidal) 473.3
- Spherophorus necrophorus 040.3
- spinal cord NEC (*see also* Encephalitis) 323.9
  - abscess 324.1
    - late effect — *see* category 326
  - late effect — *see* category 326
  - meninges — *see* Meningitis
  - streptococcal 320.2
- Spirillum
  - minus or minor 026.0
  - morsus muris 026.0
  - obermeieri 087.0
- spirochetal NEC 104.9
  - lung 104.8
  - specified nature or site NEC 104.8
- spleen 289.59
- Sporothrix schenckii 117.1
- Sporotrichum (schenckii) 117.1
- Sporozoa 136.8
- staphylococcal NEC 041.10
  - aureus 041.11
    - methicillin ●
      - resistant (MRSA) 041.12 ●
      - susceptible (MSSA) 041.11 ●
  - food poisoning 005.0
  - generalized (purulent) 038.10
    - aureus 038.11
      - methicillin ●
        - resistant 038.12 ●
        - susceptible 038.11 ●
    - specified organism NEC 038.19
  - pneumonia 482.40
    - aureus 482.41
      - methicillin ●
        - resistant (MRSA) 482.42 ●
        - susceptible (MSSA) 482.41 ●
      - MRSA (methicillin resistant Staphylococcus aureus) 482.42 ●
      - MSSA (methicillin susceptible Staphylococcus aureus) 482.41 ●
    - specified type NEC 482.49
  - septicemia 038.10
    - aureus 038.11

Infection, infected, infective — *continued*
- staphylococcal — *continued*
  - septicemia — *continued*
    - aureus — *continued*
      - methicillin ●
        - resistant (MRSA) 038.12 ●
        - susceptible (MSSA) 038.11 ●
      - MRSA (methicillin resistant Staphylococcus aureus) 038.12 ●
      - MSSA (methicillin susceptible Staphylococcus aureus) 038.11 ●
      - specified organism NEC 038.19
  - specified NEC 041.19
- steatoma 706.2
- Stellantchasmus falcatus 121.6
- Streptobacillus moniliformis 026.1
- streptococcal NEC 041.00
  - generalized (purulent) 038.0
  - Group
    - A 041.01
    - B 041.02
    - C 041.03
    - D [enterococcus] 041.04
    - G 041.05
  - pneumonia — *see* Pneumonia, streptococcal
  - septicemia 038.0
  - sore throat 034.0
  - specified NEC 041.09
- Streptomyces — *see* Actinomycosis
- streptotrichosis — *see* Actinomycosis
- Strongyloides (stercoralis) 127.2
- stump (amputation) (posttraumatic) (surgical) 997.62
  - traumatic — *see* Amputation, traumatic, by site, complicated
- subcutaneous tissue, local NEC 686.9
- submaxillary region 528.9
- suipestifer (*see also* Infection, Salmonella) 003.9
- swimming pool bacillus 031.1
- syphilitic — *see* Syphilis
- systemic — *see* Septicemia
- Taenia — *see* Infestation, Taenia
- Taeniarhynchus saginatus 123.2
- tanapox 059.21 ●
- tapeworm — *see* Infestation, tapeworm
- tendon (sheath) 727.89
- Ternidens diminutus 127.7
- testis (*see also* Orchitis) 604.90
- thigh (skin) 686.9
- threadworm 127.4
- throat 478.29
  - pneumococcal 462
  - staphylococcal 462
  - streptococcal 034.0
  - viral NEC (*see also* Pharyngitis) 462
- thumb (skin) 686.9
  - abscess (with lymphangitis) 681.00
    - pulp 681.01
  - cellulitis (with lymphangitis) 681.00
  - nail 681.02
- thyroglossal duct 529.8
- toe (skin) 686.9
  - abscess (with lymphangitis) 681.10
  - cellulitis (with lymphangitis) 681.10
  - nail 681.11
    - fungus 110.1
- tongue NEC 529.0
  - parasitic 112.0
- tonsil (faucial) (lingual) (pharyngeal) 474.00
  - acute or subacute 463
  - and adenoid 474.02
  - tag 474.00
- tooth, teeth 522.4
  - periapical (pulpal origin) 522.4

Infection, infected, infective — *continued*
- tooth, teeth — *continued*
  - peridental 523.30
  - periodontal 523.31
  - pulp 522.0
  - socket 526.5
- TORCH — *see* Infection, congenital ● NEC ●
  - without active infection 760.2 ●
- Torula histolytica 117.5
- Toxocara (cani) (cati) (felis) 128.0
- Toxoplasma gondii (*see also* Toxoplasmosis) 130.9
- trachea, chronic 491.8
  - fungus 117.9
- traumatic NEC 958.3
- trematode NEC 121.9
- trench fever 083.1
- Treponema
  - denticola 041.84
  - macrodenticum 041.84
  - pallidum (*see also* Syphilis) 097.9
- Trichinella (spiralis) 124
- Trichomonas 131.9
  - bladder 131.09
  - cervix 131.09
  - hominis 007.3
  - intestine 007.3
  - prostate 131.03
  - specified site NEC 131.8
  - urethra 131.02
  - urogenitalis 131.00
  - vagina 131.01
  - vulva 131.01
- Trichophyton, trichophytid — *see* Dermatophytosis
- Trichosporon (beigelii) cutaneum 111.2
- Trichostrongylus 127.6
- Trichuris (trichiuria) 127.3
- Trombicula (irritans) 133.8
- Trypanosoma (*see also* Trypanosomiasis) 086.9
  - cruzi 086.2
- tubal (*see also* Salpingo-oophoritis) 614.2
- tuberculous NEC (*see also* Tuberculosis) 011.9 ☑
- tubo-ovarian (*see also* Salpingo-oophoritis) 614.2
- tunica vaginalis 608.4
- tympanic membrane — *see* Myringitis
- typhoid (abortive) (ambulant) (bacillus) 002.0
- typhus 081.9
  - flea-borne (endemic) 081.0
  - louse-borne (epidemic) 080
  - mite-borne 081.2
  - recrudescent 081.1
  - tick-borne 082.9
    - African 082.1
    - North Asian 082.2
- umbilicus (septic) 686.9
  - newborn NEC 771.4
- ureter 593.89
- urethra (*see also* Urethritis) 597.80
- urinary (tract) NEC 599.0
  - with
    - abortion — *see* Abortion, by type, with urinary tract infection
    - ectopic pregnancy (*see also* categories 633.0–633.9) 639.8
    - molar pregnancy (*see also* categories 630–632) 639.8
  - candidal 112.2
  - complicating pregnancy, childbirth, or puerperium 646.6 ☑
    - affecting fetus or newborn 760.1
    - asymptomatic 646.5 ☑
      - affecting fetus or newborn 760.1
  - diplococcal (acute) 098.0
    - chronic 098.2

Infection, infected, infective — *continued*
- urinary — *continued*
  - due to Trichomonas (vaginalis) 131.00
  - following
    - abortion 639.8
    - ectopic or molar pregnancy 639.8
  - gonococcal (acute) 098.0
    - chronic or duration of 2 months or over 098.2
  - newborn 771.82
  - trichomonal 131.00
  - tuberculous (*see also* Tuberculosis) 016.3 ☑
- uterus, uterine (*see also* Endometritis) 615.9
- utriculus masculinus NEC 597.89
- vaccination 999.39
- vagina (granulation tissue) (wall) (*see also* Vaginitis) 616.10
- varicella 052.9
- varicose veins — *see* Varicose, veins
- variola 050.9
  - major 050.0
  - minor 050.1
- vas deferens NEC 608.4
- Veillonella 041.84
- verumontanum 597.89
- vesical (*see also* Cystitis) 595.9
- Vibrio
  - cholerae 001.0
    - El Tor 001.1
  - parahaemolyticus (food poisoning) 005.4
  - vulnificus 041.85
- Vincent's (gums) (mouth) (tonsil) 101
- vaccination 999.39
- virus, viral 079.99
  - adenovirus
    - in diseases classified elsewhere — *see* category 079 ☑
    - unspecified nature or site 079.0
  - central nervous system NEC 049.9
    - enterovirus 048
      - meningitis 047.9
        - specified type NEC 047.8
    - slow virus 046.9
      - specified condition NEC 046.8
  - chest 519.8
  - conjunctivitis 077.99
    - specified type NEC 077.8
  - coronavirus 079.89
    - SARS-associated 079.82
  - Coxsackie (*see also* Infection, Coxsackie) 079.2
  - Ebola 065.8
  - ECHO
    - in diseases classified elsewhere — *see* category 079 ☑
    - unspecified nature or site 079.1
  - encephalitis 049.9
    - arthropod-borne NEC 064
    - tick-borne 063.9
      - specified type NEC 063.8
  - enteritis NEC (*see also* Enteritis, viral) 008.8
  - exanthem NEC 057.9
  - Hantavirus 079.81
  - human papilloma 079.4
  - in diseases classified elsewhere — *see* category 079 ☑
  - intestine (*see also* Enteritis, viral) 008.8
  - lung — *see* Pneumonia, viral
  - respiratory syncytial (RSV) 079.6
  - retrovirus 079.50
  - rhinovirus
    - in diseases classified elsewhere — *see* category 079 ☑
    - unspecified nature or site 079.3
  - salivary gland disease 078.5
  - slow 046.9

Infection, infected, infective — *continued*
- virus, viral — *continued*
  - slow — *continued*
    - specified condition NEC 046.8
  - specified type NEC 079.89
    - in diseases classified elsewhere — *see* category 079 ☑
  - unspecified nature or site 079.99
  - warts 078.10
    - specified NEC 078.19 ●
  - yaba monkey tumor 059.22 ●
- vulva (*see also* Vulvitis) 616.10
- whipworm 127.3
- Whitmore's bacillus 025
- wound (local) (posttraumatic) NEC 958.3
  - with
    - dislocation — *see* Dislocation, by site, open
    - fracture — *see* Fracture, by site, open
    - open wound — *see* Wound, open, by site, complicated
  - postoperative 998.59
  - surgical 998.59
- Wuchereria 125.0
  - bancrofti 125.0
  - malayi 125.1
- yaba monkey tumor virus 059.22 ●
- yatapoxvirus 059.20 ●
- yaws — *see* Yaws
- yeast (*see also* Candidiasis) 112.9
- yellow fever (*see also* Fever, yellow) 060.9
- Yersinia pestis (*see also* Plague) 020.9
- Zeis' gland 373.12
- zoonotic bacterial NEC 027.9
- Zopfia senegalensis 117.4

Infective, infectious — *see* condition

Inferiority complex 301.9
- constitutional psychopathic 301.9

Infertility
- female 628.9
  - age related 628.8
  - associated with
    - adhesions, peritubal 614.6 *[628.2]*
    - anomaly
      - cervical mucus 628.4
      - congenital
        - cervix 628.4
        - fallopian tube 628.2
        - uterus 628.3
        - vagina 628.4
    - anovulation 628.0
    - dysmucorrhea 628.4
    - endometritis, tuberculous (*see also* Tuberculosis) 016.7 ☑ *[628.3]*
    - Stein-Leventhal syndrome 256.4 *[628.0]*
  - due to
    - adiposogenital dystrophy 253.8 *[628.1]*
    - anterior pituitary disorder NEC 253.4 *[628.1]*
      - hyperfunction 253.1 *[628.1]*
    - cervical anomaly 628.4
    - fallopian tube anomaly 628.2
    - ovarian failure 256.39 *[628.0]*
    - Stein-Leventhal syndrome 256.4 *[628.0]*
    - uterine anomaly 628.3
    - vaginal anomaly 628.4
  - nonimplantation 628.3
  - origin
    - cervical 628.4
    - pituitary-hypothalamus NEC 253.8 *[628.1]*
      - anterior pituitary NEC 253.4 *[628.1]*
        - hyperfunction NEC 253.1 *[628.1]*
      - dwarfism 253.3 *[628.1]*

Infertility — *continued*
female — *continued*
origin — *continued*
pituitary-hypothalamus — *continued*
panhypopituitarism 253.2 *[628.1]*
specified NEC 628.8
tubal (block) (occlusion) (stenosis) 628.2
adhesions 614.6 *[628.2]*
uterine 628.3
vaginal 628.4
previous, requiring supervision of pregnancy V23.0
male 606.9
absolute 606.0
due to
azoospermia 606.0
drug therapy 606.8
extratesticular cause NEC 606.8
germinal cell
aplasia 606.0
desquamation 606.1
hypospermatogenesis 606.1
infection 606.8
obstruction, afferent ducts 606.8
oligospermia 606.1
radiation 606.8
spermatogenic arrest (complete) 606.0
incomplete 606.1
systemic disease 606.8

Infestation 134.9
Acanthocheilonema (perstans) 125.4
streptocerca 125.6
Acariasis 133.9
demodex folliculorum 133.8
Sarcoptes scabiei 133.0
trombiculae 133.8
Agamofilaria streptocerca 125.6
Ancylostoma, Ankylostoma 126.9
americanum 126.1
braziliense 126.2
canium 126.8
ceylanicum 126.3
duodenale 126.0
new world 126.1
old world 126.0
Angiostrongylus cantonensis 128.8
anisakiasis 127.1
Anisakis larva 127.1
arthropod NEC 134.1
Ascaris lumbricoides 127.0
Bacillus fusiformis 101
Balantidium coli 007.0
beef tapeworm 123.2
Bothriocephalus (latus) 123.4
larval 123.5
broad tapeworm 123.4
larval 123.5
Brugia malayi 125.1
Candiru 136.8
Capillaria
hepatica 128.8
philippinensis 127.5
cat liver fluke 121.0
Cercomonas hominis (intestinal) 007.3
cestodes 123.9
specified type NEC 123.8
chigger 133.8
chigoe 134.1
Chilomastix 007.8
Clonorchis (sinensis) (liver) 121.1
coccidia 007.2
complicating pregnancy, childbirth, or puerperium 647.9 ☑
affecting fetus or newborn 760.8
Cysticercus cellulosae 123.1
Demodex folliculorum 133.8
Dermatobia (hominis) 134.0
Dibothriocephalus (latus) 123.4
larval 123.5
Dicrocoelium dendriticum 121.8

Infestation — *continued*
Diphyllobothrium (adult) (intestinal) (latum) (pacificum) 123.4
larval 123.5
Diplogonoporus (grandis) 123.8
Dipylidium (caninum) 123.8
Distoma hepaticum 121.3
dog tapeworm 123.8
Dracunculus medinensis 125.7
dragon worm 125.7
dwarf tapeworm 123.6
Echinococcus (*see also* Echinococcus) 122.9
Echinostoma ilocanum 121.8
Embadomonas 007.8
Endamoeba (histolytica) — *see* Infection, ameba
Entamoeba (histolytica) — *see* Infection, ameba
Enterobius vermicularis 127.4
Epidermophyton — *see* Dermatophytosis
eyeworm 125.2
Fasciola
gigantica 121.3
hepatica 121.3
Fasciolopsis (buski) (small intestine) 121.4
blood NEC (*see also* Schistosomiasis) 120.9
cat liver 121.0
filarial 125.9
due to
Acanthocheilonema (perstans) 125.4
streptocerca 125.6
Brugia (Wuchereria) malayi 125.1
Dracunculus medinensis 125.7
guinea worms 125.7
Mansonella (ozzardi) 125.5
Onchocerca volvulus 125.3
eye 125.3 *[360.13]*
eyelid 125.3 *[373.6]*
Wuchereria (bancrofti) 125.0
malayi 125.1
specified type NEC 125.6
fish tapeworm 123.4
larval 123.5
fluke 121.9
intestinal (giant) 121.4
liver (sheep) 121.3
cat 121.0
Chinese 121.1
clonorchiasis 121.1
fascioliasis 121.3
Oriental 121.1
lung (oriental) 121.2
sheep liver 121.3
fly larva 134.0
Gasterophilus (intestinalis) 134.0
Gastrodiscoides hominis 121.8
Giardia lamblia 007.1
Gnathostoma (spinigerum) 128.1
Gongylonema 125.6
guinea worm 125.7
helminth NEC 128.9
intestinal 127.9
mixed (types classifiable to more than one category in 120.0–127.7) 127.8
specified type NEC 127.7
specified type NEC 128.8
Heterophyes heterophyes (small intestine) 121.6
hookworm (*see also* Infestation, ancylostoma) 126.9
Hymenolepis (diminuta) (nana) 123.6
intestinal NEC 129
leeches (aquatic) (land) 134.2
Leishmania — *see* Leishmaniasis
lice (*see also* Infestation, pediculus) 132.9
Linguatulidae, linguatula (pentastoma) (serrata) 134.1

Infestation — *continued*
Loa loa 125.2
eyelid 125.2 *[373.6]*
louse (*see also* Infestation, pediculus) 132.9
body 132.1
head 132.0
pubic 132.2
maggots 134.0
Mansonella (ozzardi) 125.5
medina 125.7
Metagonimus yokogawai (small intestine) 121.5
Microfilaria streptocerca 125.3
eye 125.3 *[360.13]*
eyelid 125.3 *[373.6]*
Microsporon furfur 111.0
microsporum — *see* Dermatophytosis
mites 133.9
scabic 133.0
specified type NEC 133.8
monilia (albicans) (*see also* Candidiasis) 112.9
vagina 112.1
vulva 112.1
mouth 112.0
Necator americanus 126.1
nematode (intestinal) 127.9
Ancylostoma (*see also* Ancylostoma) 126.9
Ascaris lumbricoides 127.0
conjunctiva NEC 128.9
Dioctophyma 128.8
Enterobius vermicularis 127.4
Gnathostoma spinigerum 128.1
Oesophagostomum (apiostomum) 127.7
Physaloptera 127.4
specified type NEC 127.7
Strongyloides stercoralis 127.2
Ternidens diminutus 127.7
Trichinella spiralis 124
Trichostrongylus 127.6
Trichuris (trichiuria) 127.3
Oesophagostomum (apiostomum) 127.7
Oestrus ovis 134.0
Onchocerca (volvulus) 125.3
eye 125.3 *[360.13]*
eyelid 125.3 *[373.6]*
Opisthorchis (felineus) (tenuicollis) (viverrini) 121.0
Oxyuris vermicularis 127.4
Paragonimus (westermani) 121.2
parasite, parasitic NEC 136.9
eyelid 134.9 *[373.6]*
intestinal 129
mouth 112.0
orbit 376.13
skin 134.9
tongue 112.0
pediculus 132.9
capitis (humanus) (any site) 132.0
corporis (humanus) (any site) 132.1
eyelid 132.0 *[373.6]*
mixed (classifiable to more than one category in 132.0–132.2) 132.3
pubis (any site) 132.2
phthirus (pubis) (any site) 132.2
with any infestation classifiable to 132.0, 132.1 and 132.3
pinworm 127.4
pork tapeworm (adult) 123.0
protozoal NEC 136.8
pubic louse 132.2
rat tapeworm 123.6
red bug 133.8
roundworm (large) NEC 127.0
sand flea 134.1
saprophytic NEC 136.8
Sarcoptes scabiei 133.0
scabies 133.0
Schistosoma 120.9
bovis 120.8
cercariae 120.3

Infestation — *continued*
Schistosoma — *continued*
hematobium 120.0
intercalatum 120.8
japonicum 120.2
mansoni 120.1
mattheii 120.8
specified
site — *see* Schistosomiasis
type NEC 120.8
spindale 120.8
screw worms 134.0
skin NEC 134.9
Sparganum (mansoni) (proliferum) 123.5
larval 123.5
specified type NEC 134.8
Spirometra larvae 123.5
Sporozoa NEC 136.8
Stellantchasmus falcatus 121.6
Strongyloides 127.2
Strongylus (gibsoni) 127.7
Taenia 123.3
diminuta 123.6
Echinococcus (*see also* Echinococcus) 122.9
mediocanellata 123.2
nana 123.6
saginata (mediocanellata) 123.2
solium (intestinal form) 123.0
larval form 123.1
Taeniarhynchus saginatus 123.2
tapeworm 123.9
beef 123.2
broad 123.4
larval 123.5
dog 123.8
dwarf 123.6
fish 123.4
larval 123.5
pork 123.0
rat 123.6
Ternidens diminutus 127.7
Tetranychus molestissimus 133.8
threadworm 127.4
tongue 112.0
Toxocara (cani) (cati) (felis) 128.0
trematode(s) NEC 121.9
Trichina spiralis 124
Trichinella spiralis 124
Trichocephalus 127.3
Trichomonas 131.9
bladder 131.09
cervix 131.09
intestine 007.3
prostate 131.03
specified site NEC 131.8
urethra (female) (male) 131.02
urogenital 131.00
vagina 131.01
vulva 131.01
Trichophyton — *see* Dermatophytosis
Trichostrongylus instabilis 127.6
Trichuris (trichiuria) 127.3
Trombicula (irritans) 133.8
Trypanosoma — *see* Trypanosomiasis
Tunga penetrans 134.1
Uncinaria americana 126.1
whipworm 127.3
worms NEC 128.9
intestinal 127.9
Wuchereria 125.0
bancrofti 125.0
malayi 125.1

Infiltrate, infiltration
with an iron compound 275.0
amyloid (any site) (generalized) 277.39
calcareous (muscle) NEC 275.49
localized — *see* Degeneration, by site
calcium salt (muscle) 275.49
chemotherapy, vesicant 998.81 ●
corneal (*see also* Edema, cornea) 371.20
cyclid 373.9
fatty (diffuse) (generalized) 272.8

Infiltrate, infiltration — *continued*
fatty — *continued*
localized — *see* Degeneration, by site, fatty
glycogen, glycogenic (*see also* Disease, glycogen storage) 271.0
heart, cardiac
fatty (*see also* Degeneration, myocardial) 429.1
glycogenic 271.0 *[425.7]*
inflammatory in vitreous 379.29
kidney (*see also* Disease, renal) 593.9
leukemic (M9800/3) — *see* Leukemia
liver 573.8
fatty — *see* Fatty, liver
glycogen (*see also* Disease, glycogen storage) 271.0
lung (*see also* Infiltrate, pulmonary) 518.3
eosinophilic 518.3
x-ray finding only 793.1
lymphatic (*see also* Leukemia, lymphatic) 204.9 ☑
gland, pigmentary 289.3
muscle, fatty 728.9
myelogenous (*see also* Leukemia, myeloid) 205.9 ☑
myocardium, myocardial
fatty (*see also* Degeneration, myocardial) 429.1
glycogenic 271.0 *[425.7]*
pulmonary 518.3
with
eosinophilia 518.3
pneumonia — *see* Pneumonia, by type
x-ray finding only 793.1
Ranke's primary (*see also* Tuberculosis) 010.0 ☑
skin, lymphocytic (benign) 709.8
thymus (gland) (fatty) 254.8
urine 788.8
vesicant ●
agent NEC 998.82 ●
chemotherapy 998.81 ●
vitreous humor 379.29
Infirmity 799.89
senile 797
Inflammation, inflamed, inflammatory (with exudation)
abducens (nerve) 378.54
accessory sinus (chronic) (*see also* Sinusitis) 473.9
adrenal (gland) 255.8
alimentary canal — *see* Enteritis
alveoli (teeth) 526.5
scorbutic 267
amnion — *see* Amnionitis
anal canal 569.49
antrum (chronic) (*see also* Sinusitis, maxillary) 473.0
anus 569.49
appendix (*see also* Appendicitis) 541
arachnoid — *see* Meningitis
areola 611.0
puerperal, postpartum 675.0 ☑
areolar tissue NEC 686.9
artery — *see* Arteritis
auditory meatus (external) (*see also* Otitis, externa) 380.10
Bartholin's gland 616.89
bile duct or passage 576.1
bladder (*see also* Cystitis) 595.9
bleb
postprocedural 379.60
stage 1 379.61
stage 2 379.62
stage 3 379.63
bone — *see* Osteomyelitis
bowel (*see also* Enteritis) 558.9
brain (*see also* Encephalitis) 323.9
late effect — *see* category 326
membrane — *see* Meningitis
breast 611.0
puerperal, postpartum 675.2 ☑

Inflammation, inflamed, inflammatory — *continued*
broad ligament (*see also* Disease, pelvis, inflammatory) 614.4
acute 614.3
bronchus — *see* Bronchitis
bursa — *see* Bursitis
capsule
liver 573.3
spleen 289.59
catarrhal (*see also* Catarrh) 460
vagina 616.10
cecum (*see also* Appendicitis) 541
cerebral (*see also* Encephalitis) 323.9
late effect — *see* category 326
membrane — *see* Meningitis
cerebrospinal (*see also* Meningitis) 322.9
late effect — *see* category 326
meningococcal 036.0
tuberculous (*see also* Tuberculosis) 013.6 ☑
cervix (uteri) (*see also* Cervicitis) 616.0
chest 519.9
choroid NEC (*see also* Choroiditis) 363.20
cicatrix (tissue) — *see* Cicatrix
colon (*see also* Enteritis) 558.9
granulomatous 555.1
newborn 558.9
connective tissue (diffuse) NEC 728.9
cornea (*see also* Keratitis) 370.9
with ulcer (*see also* Ulcer, cornea) 370.00
corpora cavernosa (penis) 607.2
cranial nerve — *see* Disorder, nerve, cranial
diarrhea — *see* Diarrhea
disc (intervertebral) (space) 722.90
cervical, cervicothoracic 722.91
lumbar, lumbosacral 722.93
thoracic, thoracolumbar 722.92
Douglas' cul-de-sac or pouch (chronic) (*see also* Disease, pelvis, inflammatory) 614.4
acute 614.3
due to (presence of) any device, implant, or graft classifiable to 996.0–996.5 — *see* Complications, infection and inflammation, due to (presence of) any device, implant, or graft classified to 996.0–996.5 NEC
duodenum 535.6 ☑
dura mater — *see* Meningitis
ear (*see also* Otitis)
external (*see also* Otitis, externa) 380.10
inner (*see also* Labyrinthitis) 386.30
middle — *see* Otitis media
esophagus 530.10
ethmoidal (chronic) (sinus) (*see also* Sinusitis, ethmoidal) 473.2
Eustachian tube (catarrhal) 381.50
acute 381.51
chronic 381.52
extrarectal 569.49
eye 379.99
eyelid 373.9
specified NEC 373.8
fallopian tube (*see also* Salpingo-oophoritis) 614.2
fascia 728.9
fetal membranes (acute) 658.4 ☑
affecting fetus or newborn 762.7
follicular, pharynx 472.1
frontal (chronic) (sinus) (*see also* Sinusitis, frontal) 473.1
gallbladder (*see also* Cholecystitis, acute) 575.0
gall duct (*see also* Cholecystitis) 575.10
gastrointestinal (*see also* Enteritis) 558.9

Inflammation, inflamed, inflammatory — *continued*
genital organ (diffuse) (internal)
female 614.9
with
abortion — *see* Abortion, by type, with sepsis
ectopic pregnancy (*see also* categories 633.0–633.9) 639.0
molar pregnancy (*see also* categories 630–632) 639.0
complicating pregnancy, childbirth, or puerperium 646.6 ☑
affecting fetus or newborn 760.8
following
abortion 639.0
ectopic or molar pregnancy 639.0
male 608.4
gland (lymph) (*see also* Lymphadenitis) 289.3
glottis (*see also* Laryngitis) 464.00
with obstruction 464.01
granular, pharynx 472.1
gum 523.10
heart (*see also* Carditis) 429.89
hepatic duct 576.8
hernial sac — *see* Hernia, by site
ileum (*see also* Enteritis) 558.9
terminal or regional 555.0
with large intestine 555.2
intervertebral disc 722.90
cervical, cervicothoracic 722.91
lumbar, lumbosacral 722.93
thoracic, thoracolumbar 722.92
intestine (*see also* Enteritis) 558.9
jaw (acute) (bone) (chronic) (lower) (suppurative) (upper) 526.4
jejunum — *see* Enteritis
joint NEC (*see also* Arthritis) 716.9 ☑
sacroiliac 720.2
kidney (*see also* Nephritis) 583.9
knee (joint) 716.66
tuberculous (active) (*see also* Tuberculosis) 015.2 ☑
labium (majus) (minus) (*see also* Vulvitis) 616.10
lacrimal
gland (*see also* Dacryoadenitis) 375.00
passages (duct) (sac) (*see also* Dacryocystitis) 375.30
larynx (*see also* Laryngitis) 464.00
with obstruction 464.01
diphtheritic 032.3
leg NEC 686.9
lip 528.5
liver (capsule) (*see also* Hepatitis) 573.3
acute 570
chronic 571.40
suppurative 572.0
lung (acute) (*see also* Pneumonia) 486
chronic (interstitial) 518.89
lymphatic vessel (*see also* Lymphangitis) 457.2
lymph node or gland (*see also* Lymphadenitis) 289.3
mammary gland 611.0
puerperal, postpartum 675.2 ☑
maxilla, maxillary 526.4
sinus (chronic) (*see also* Sinusitis, maxillary) 473.0
membranes of brain or spinal cord — *see* Meningitis
meninges — *see* Meningitis
mouth 528.00
muscle 728.9
myocardium (*see also* Myocarditis) 429.0
nasal sinus (chronic) (*see also* Sinusitis) 473.9

Inflammation, inflamed, inflammatory — *continued*
nasopharynx — *see* Nasopharyngitis
navel 686.9
newborn NEC 771.4
nerve NEC 729.2
nipple 611.0
puerperal, postpartum 675.0 ☑
nose 478.19
suppurative 472.0
oculomotor nerve 378.51
optic nerve 377.30
orbit (chronic) 376.10
acute 376.00
chronic 376.10
ovary (*see also* Salpingo-oophoritis) 614.2
oviduct (*see also* Salpingo-oophoritis) 614.2
pancreas — *see* Pancreatitis
parametrium (chronic) (*see also* Disease, pelvis, inflammatory) 614.4
acute 614.3
parotid region 686.9
gland 527.2
pelvis, female (*see also* Disease, pelvis, inflammatory) 614.9
penis (corpora cavernosa) 607.2
perianal 569.49
pericardium (*see also* Pericarditis) 423.9
perineum (female) (male) 686.9
perirectal 569.49
peritoneum (*see also* Peritonitis) 567.9
periuterine (*see also* Disease, pelvis, inflammatory) 614.9
perivesical (*see also* Cystitis) 595.9
petrous bone (*see also* Petrositis) 383.20
pharynx (*see also* Pharyngitis) 462
follicular 472.1
granular 472.1
pia mater — *see* Meningitis
pleura — *see* Pleurisy
postmastoidectomy cavity 383.30
chronic 383.33
prostate (*see also* Prostatitis) 601.9
rectosigmoid — *see* Rectosigmoiditis
rectum (*see also* Proctitis) 569.49
respiratory, upper (*see also* Infection, respiratory, upper) 465.9
chronic, due to external agent — *see* Condition, respiratory, chronic, due to, external agent
due to
fumes or vapors (chemical) (inhalation) 506.2
radiation 508.1
retina (*see also* Retinitis) 363.20
retrocecal (*see also* Appendicitis) 541
retroperitoneal (*see also* Peritonitis) 567.9
salivary duct or gland (any) (suppurative) 527.2
scorbutic, alveoli, teeth 267
scrotum 608.4
sigmoid — *see* Enteritis
sinus (*see also* Sinusitis) 473.9
Skene's duct or gland (*see also* Urethritis) 597.89
skin 686.9
spermatic cord 608.4
sphenoidal (sinus) (*see also* Sinusitis, sphenoidal) 473.3
spinal
cord (*see also* Encephalitis) 323.9
late effect — *see* category 326
membrane — *see* Meningitis
nerve — *see* Disorder, nerve
spine (*see also* Spondylitis) 720.9
spleen (capsule) 289.59
stomach — *see* Gastritis
stricture, rectum 569.49
subcutaneous tissue NEC 686.9

Inflammation, inflamed, inflammatory — *continued*
  suprarenal (gland) 255.8
  synovial (fringe) (membrane) — *see* Bursitis
  tendon (sheath) NEC 726.90
  testis (*see also* Orchitis) 604.90
  thigh 686.9
  throat (*see also* Sore throat) 462
  thymus (gland) 254.8
  thyroid (gland) (*see also* Thyroiditis) 245.9
  tongue 529.0
  tonsil — *see* Tonsillitis
  trachea — *see* Tracheitis
  trochlear nerve 378.53
  tubal (*see also* Salpingo-oophoritis) 614.2
  tuberculous NEC (*see also* Tuberculosis) 011.9 ☑
  tubo-ovarian (*see also* Salpingo-oophoritis) 614.2
  tunica vaginalis 608.4
  tympanic membrane — *see* Myringitis
  umbilicus, umbilical 686.9
    newborn NEC 771.4
  uterine ligament (*see also* Disease, pelvis, inflammatory) 614.4
    acute 614.3
  uterus (catarrhal) (*see also* Endometritis) 615.9
  uveal tract (anterior) (*see also* Iridocyclitis) 364.3
    posterior — *see* Chorioretinitis
    sympathetic 360.11
  vagina (*see also* Vaginitis) 616.10
  vas deferens 608.4
  vein (*see also* Phlebitis) 451.9
    thrombotic 451.9
      cerebral (*see also* Thrombosis, brain) 434.0 ☑
      leg 451.2
        deep (vessels) NEC 451.19
        superficial (vessels) 451.0
      lower extremity 451.2
        deep (vessels) NEC 451.19
        superficial (vessels) 451.0
  vocal cord 478.5
  vulva (*see also* Vulvitis) 616.10
Inflation, lung imperfect (newborn) 770.5
Influenza, influenzal 487.1
  with
    bronchitis 487.1
    bronchopneumonia 487.0
    cold (any type) 487.1
    digestive manifestations 487.8
    hemoptysis 487.1
    involvement of
      gastrointestinal tract 487.8
      nervous system 487.8
    laryngitis 487.1
    manifestations NEC 487.8
      respiratory 487.1
        pneumonia 487.0
    pharyngitis 487.1
    pneumonia (any form classifiable to 480–483, 485–486) 487.0
    respiratory manifestations NEC 487.1
    sinusitis 487.1
    sore throat 487.1
    tonsillitis 487.1
    tracheitis 487.1
    upper respiratory infection (acute) 487.1
  abdominal 487.8
  Asian 487.1
  bronchial 487.1
  bronchopneumonia 487.0
  catarrhal 487.1
  due to identified avian influenza virus 488
  epidemic 487.1
  gastric 487.8
  intestinal 487.8

Influenza, influenzal — *continued*
  laryngitis 487.1
  maternal affecting fetus or newborn 760.2
    manifest influenza in infant 771.2
  pharyngitis 487.1
  pneumonia (any form) 487.0
  respiratory (upper) 487.1
  stomach 487.8
  vaccination, prophylactic (against) V04.81
Influenza-like disease 487.1
Infraction, Freiberg's (metatarsal head) 732.5
Infraeruption, teeth 524.34
Infusion complication, misadventure, or reaction — *see* Complication, infusion
Ingestion
  chemical — *see* Table of Drugs and Chemicals
  drug or medicinal substance
    overdose or wrong substance given or taken 977.9
      specified drug — *see* Table of Drugs and Chemicals
  foreign body NEC (*see also* Foreign body) 938
Ingrowing
  hair 704.8
  nail (finger) (toe) (infected) 703.0
Inguinal — *see also* condition
  testis 752.51
Inhalation
  carbon monoxide 986
  flame
    lung 947.1
    mouth 947.0
  food or foreign body (*see also* Asphyxia, food or foreign body) 933.1
  gas, fumes, or vapor (noxious) 987.9
    specified agent — *see* Table of Drugs and Chemicals
  liquid or vomitus (*see also* Asphyxia, food or foreign body) 933.1
    lower respiratory tract NEC 934.9
  meconium (fetus or newborn) 770.11
    with respiratory symptoms 770.12
  mucus (*see also* Asphyxia, mucus) 933.1
  oil (causing suffocation) (*see also* Asphyxia, food or foreign body) 933.1
  pneumonia — *see* Pneumonia, aspiration
  smoke 987.9
  steam 987.9
  stomach contents or secretions (*see also* Asphyxia, food or foreign body) 933.1
    in labor and delivery 668.0 ☑
Inhibition, inhibited
  academic as adjustment reaction 309.23
  orgasm
    female 302.73
    male 302.74
  sexual
    desire 302.71
    excitement 302.72
  work as adjustment reaction 309.23
Inhibitor, systemic lupus erythematosus (presence of) 286.5
Iniencephalus, iniencephaly 740.2
Injected eye 372.74

Injury 959.9

> *Note — For abrasion, insect bite (nonvenomous), blister, or scratch, see Injury, superficial.*
>
> *For laceration, traumatic rupture, tear, or penetrating wound of internal organs, such as heart, lung, liver, kidney, pelvic organs, whether or not accompanied by open wound in the same region, see Injury, internal.*
>
> *For nerve injury, see Injury, nerve.*
>
> *For late effect of injuries classifiable to 850–854, 860–869, 900–919, 950–959, see Late, effect, injury, by type.*

  abdomen, abdominal (viscera) (*see also* Injury, internal, abdomen)
    muscle or wall 959.12
  acoustic, resulting in deafness 951.5
  adenoid 959.09
  adrenal (gland) — *see* Injury, internal, adrenal
  alveolar (process) 959.09
  ankle (and foot) (and knee) (and leg, except thigh) 959.7
  anterior chamber, eye 921.3
  anus 959.19
  aorta (thoracic) 901.0
    abdominal 902.0
  appendix — *see* Injury, internal, appendix
  arm, upper (and shoulder) 959.2
  artery (complicating trauma) (*see also* Injury, blood vessel, by site) 904.9
    cerebral or meningeal (*see also* Hemorrhage, brain, traumatic, subarachnoid) 852.0 ☑
  auditory canal (external) (meatus) 959.09
  auricle, auris, ear 959.09
  axilla 959.2
  back 959.19
  bile duct — *see* Injury, internal, bile duct
  birth (*see also* Birth, injury)
    canal NEC, complicating delivery 665.9 ☑
  bladder (sphincter) — *see* Injury, internal, bladder
  blast (air) (hydraulic) (immersion) (underwater) NEC 869.0
    with open wound into cavity NEC 869.1
    abdomen or thorax — *see* Injury, internal, by site
    brain — *see* Concussion, brain
    ear (acoustic nerve trauma) 951.5
      with perforation of tympanic membrane — *see* Wound, open, ear, drum
  blood vessel NEC 904.9
    abdomen 902.9
      multiple 902.87
      specified NEC 902.89
    aorta (thoracic) 901.0
      abdominal 902.0
    arm NEC 903.9
    axillary 903.00
      artery 903.01
      vein 903.02
    azygos vein 901.89
    basilic vein 903.1
    brachial (artery) (vein) 903.1
    bronchial 901.89
    carotid artery 900.00
      common 900.01
      external 900.02
      internal 900.03
    celiac artery 902.20
      specified branch NEC 902.24
    cephalic vein (arm) 903.1
    colica dextra 902.26
    cystic
      artery 902.24

Injury — *continued*
  blood vessel — *continued*
    cystic — *continued*
      vein 902.39
    deep plantar 904.6
    digital (artery) (vein) 903.5
    due to accidental puncture or laceration during procedure 998.2
    extremity
      lower 904.8
        multiple 904.7
        specified NEC 904.7
      upper 903.9
        multiple 903.8
        specified NEC 903.8
    femoral
      artery (superficial) 904.1
        above profunda origin 904.0
        common 904.0
      vein 904.2
    gastric
      artery 902.21
      vein 902.39
    head 900.9
      intracranial — *see* Injury, intracranial
      multiple 900.82
      specified NEC 900.89
    hemiazygos vein 901.89
    hepatic
      artery 902.22
      vein 902.11
    hypogastric 902.59
      artery 902.51
      vein 902.52
    ileocolic
      artery 902.26
      vein 902.31
    iliac 902.50
      artery 902.53
      specified branch NEC 902.59
      vein 902.54
    innominate
      artery 901.1
      vein 901.3
    intercostal (artery) (vein) 901.81
    jugular vein (external) 900.81
      internal 900.1
    leg NEC 904.8
    mammary (artery) (vein) 901.82
    mesenteric
      artery 902.20
        inferior 902.27
        specified branch NEC 902.29
        superior (trunk) 902.25
          branches, primary 902.26
      vein 902.39
        inferior 902.32
        superior (and primary subdivisions) 902.31
    neck 900.9
      multiple 900.82
      specified NEC 900.89
    ovarian 902.89
      artery 902.81
      vein 902.82
    palmar artery 903.4
    pelvis 902.9
      multiple 902.87
      specified NEC 902.89
    plantar (deep) (artery) (vein) 904.6
    popliteal 904.40
      artery 904.41
      vein 904.42
    portal 902.33
    pulmonary 901.40
      artery 901.41
      vein 901.42
    radial (artery) (vein) 903.2
    renal 902.40
      artery 902.41
      specified NEC 902.49
      vein 902.42
    saphenous
      artery 904.7

- **Injury** — *continued*
  - blood vessel — *continued*
    - saphenous — *continued*
      - vein (greater) (lesser) 904.3
    - splenic
      - artery 902.23
      - vein 902.34
    - subclavian
      - artery 901.1
      - vein 901.3
    - suprarenal 902.49
    - thoracic 901.9
      - multiple 901.83
      - specified NEC 901.89
    - tibial 904.50
      - artery 904.50
        - anterior 904.51
        - posterior 904.53
      - vein 904.50
        - anterior 904.52
        - posterior 904.54
    - ulnar (artery) (vein) 903.3
    - uterine 902.59
      - artery 902.55
      - vein 902.56
    - vena cava
      - inferior 902.10
        - specified branches NEC 902.19
      - superior 901.2
  - brachial plexus 953.4
    - newborn 767.6
  - brain NEC (*see also* Injury, intracranial) 854.0 ☑
  - breast 959.19
  - broad ligament — *see* Injury, internal, broad ligament
  - bronchus, bronchi — *see* Injury, internal, bronchus
  - brow 959.09
  - buttock 959.19
  - canthus, eye 921.1
  - cathode ray 990
  - cauda equina 952.4
    - with fracture, vertebra — *see* Fracture, vertebra, sacrum
  - cavernous sinus (*see also* Injury, intracranial) 854.0 ☑
  - cecum — *see* Injury, internal, cecum
  - celiac ganglion or plexus 954.1
  - cerebellum (*see also* Injury, intracranial) 854.0 ☑
  - cervix (uteri) — *see* Injury, internal, cervix
  - cheek 959.09
  - chest (*see also* Injury, internal, chest)
    - wall 959.11
  - childbirth (*see also* Birth, injury)
    - maternal NEC 665.9 ☑
  - chin 959.09
  - choroid (eye) 921.3
  - clitoris 959.14
  - coccyx 959.19
    - complicating delivery 665.6 ☑
  - colon — *see* Injury, internal, colon
  - common duct — *see* Injury, internal, common duct
  - conjunctiva 921.1
    - superficial 918.2
  - cord
    - spermatic — *see* Injury, internal, spermatic cord
    - spinal — *see* Injury, spinal, by site
  - cornea 921.3
    - abrasion 918.1
      - due to contact lens 371.82
    - penetrating — *see* Injury, eyeball, penetrating
    - superficial 918.1
      - due to contact lens 371.82
  - cortex (cerebral) (*see also* Injury, intracranial) 854.0 ☑
    - visual 950.3
  - costal region 959.11
  - costochondral 959.11

- **Injury** — *continued*
  - cranial
    - bones — *see* Fracture, skull, by site
    - cavity (*see also* Injury, intracranial) 854.0 ☑
    - nerve — *see* Injury, nerve, cranial
  - crushing — *see* Crush
  - cutaneous sensory nerve
    - lower limb 956.4
    - upper limb 955.5
  - deep tissue — *see* Contusion, by site ●
    - meaning pressure ulcer 707.25 ●
  - delivery (*see also* Birth, injury)
    - maternal NEC 665.9 ☑
  - Descemet's membrane — *see* Injury, eyeball, penetrating
  - diaphragm — *see* Injury, internal, diaphragm
  - diffuse axonal — *see* Injury, intracranial
  - duodenum — *see* Injury, internal, duodenum
  - ear (auricle) (canal) (drum) (external) 959.09
  - elbow (and forearm) (and wrist) 959.3
  - epididymis 959.14
  - epigastric region 959.12
  - epiglottis 959.09
  - epiphyseal, current — *see* Fracture, by site
  - esophagus — *see* Injury, internal, esophagus
  - Eustachian tube 959.09
  - extremity (lower) (upper) NEC 959.8
  - eye 921.9
    - penetrating eyeball — *see* Injury, eyeball, penetrating
    - superficial 918.9
  - eyeball 921.3
    - penetrating 871.7
      - with
        - partial loss (of intraocular tissue) 871.2
        - prolapse or exposure (of intraocular tissue) 871.1
      - without prolapse 871.0
      - foreign body (nonmagnetic) 871.6
        - magnetic 871.5
    - superficial 918.9
  - eyebrow 959.09
  - eyelid(s) 921.1
    - laceration — *see* Laceration, eyelid
    - superficial 918.0
  - face (and neck) 959.09
  - fallopian tube — *see* Injury, internal, fallopian tube
  - finger(s) (nail) 959.5
  - flank 959.19
  - foot (and ankle) (and knee) (and leg, except thigh) 959.7
  - forceps NEC 767.9
    - scalp 767.19
  - forearm (and elbow) (and wrist) 959.3
  - forehead 959.09
  - gallbladder — *see* Injury, internal, gallbladder
  - gasserian ganglion 951.2
  - gastrointestinal tract — *see* Injury, internal, gastrointestinal tract
  - genital organ(s)
    - with
      - abortion — *see* Abortion, by type, with, damage to pelvic organs
      - ectopic pregnancy (*see also* categories 633.0–633.9) 639.2
      - molar pregnancy (*see also* categories 630–632) 639.2
    - external 959.14
      - fracture of corpus cavernosum penis 959.13
    - following
      - abortion 639.2

- **Injury** — *continued*
  - genital organ(s) — *continued*
    - following — *continued*
      - ectopic or molar pregnancy 639.2
    - internal — *see* Injury, internal, genital organs
    - obstetrical trauma NEC 665.9 ☑
      - affecting fetus or newborn 763.89
  - gland
    - lacrimal 921.1
      - laceration 870.8
    - parathyroid 959.09
    - salivary 959.09
    - thyroid 959.09
  - globe (eye) (*see also* Injury, eyeball) 921.3
  - grease gun — *see* Wound, open, by site, complicated
  - groin 959.19
  - gum 959.09
  - hand(s) (except fingers) 959.4
  - head NEC 959.01
    - with
      - loss of consciousness 850.5
      - skull fracture — *see* Fracture, skull, by site
  - heart — *see* Injury, internal, heart
  - heel 959.7
  - hip (and thigh) 959.6
  - hymen 959.14
  - hyperextension (cervical) (vertebra) 847.0
  - ileum — *see* Injury, internal, ileum
  - iliac region 959.19
  - infrared rays NEC 990
  - instrumental (during surgery) 998.2
    - birth injury — *see* Birth, injury
    - nonsurgical (*see also* Injury, by site) 959.9
    - obstetrical 665.9 ☑
      - affecting fetus or newborn 763.89
      - bladder 665.5 ☑
      - cervix 665.3 ☑
      - high vaginal 665.4 ☑
      - perineal NEC 664.9 ☑
      - urethra 665.5 ☑
      - uterus 665.5 ☑
  - internal 869.0

> *Note — For injury of internal organ(s) by foreign body entering through a natural orifice (e.g., inhaled, ingested, or swallowed) — see Foreign body, entering through orifice.*
>
> *For internal injury of any of the following sites with internal injury of any other of the sites — see Injury, internal, multiple.*

-
  -
    - with
      - fracture
        - pelvis — *see* Fracture, pelvis
        - specified site, except pelvis — *see* Injury, internal, by site
      - open wound into cavity 869.1
    - abdomen, abdominal (viscera) NEC 868.00
      - with
        - fracture, pelvis — *see* Fracture, pelvis
          - open wound into cavity 868.10
        - specified site NEC 868.09
          - with open wound into cavity 868.19
    - adrenal (gland) 868.01
      - with open wound into cavity 868.11
    - aorta (thoracic) 901.0
      - abdominal 902.0
    - appendix 863.85
      - with open wound into cavity 863.95

- **Injury** — *continued*
  - internal — *continued*
    - bile duct 868.02
      - with open wound into cavity 868.12
    - bladder (sphincter) 867.0
      - with
        - abortion — *see* Abortion, by type, with damage to pelvic organs
        - ectopic pregnancy (*see also* categories 633.0–633.9) 639.2
        - molar pregnancy (*see also* categories 630–632) 639.2
        - open wound into cavity 867.1
      - following
        - abortion 639.2
        - ectopic or molar pregnancy 639.2
      - obstetrical trauma 665.5 ☑
        - affecting fetus or newborn 763.89
    - blood vessel — *see* Injury, blood vessel, by site
    - broad ligament 867.6
      - with open wound into cavity 867.7
    - bronchus, bronchi 862.21
      - with open wound into cavity 862.31
    - cecum 863.89
      - with open wound into cavity 863.99
    - cervix (uteri) 867.4
      - with
        - abortion — *see* Abortion, by type, with damage to pelvic organs
        - ectopic pregnancy (*see also* categories 633.0–633.9) 639.2
        - molar pregnancy (*see also* categories 630–632) 639.2
        - open wound into cavity 867.5
      - following
        - abortion 639.2
        - ectopic or molar pregnancy 639.2
      - obstetrical trauma 665.3 ☑
        - affecting fetus or newborn 763.89
    - chest (*see also* Injury, internal, intrathoracic organs) 862.8
      - with open wound into cavity 862.9
    - colon 863.40
      - with
        - open wound into cavity 863.50
        - rectum 863.46
          - with open wound into cavity 863.56
      - ascending (right) 863.41
        - with open wound into cavity 863.51
      - descending (left) 863.43
        - with open wound into cavity 863.53
      - multiple sites 863.46
        - with open wound into cavity 863.56
      - sigmoid 863.44
        - with open wound into cavity 863.54
      - specified site NEC 863.49
        - with open wound into cavity 863.59
      - transverse 863.42
        - with open wound into cavity 863.52
    - common duct 868.02
      - with open wound into cavity 868.12

Injury — *continued*
internal — *continued*
complicating delivery 665.9 ☑
affecting fetus or newborn 763.89
diaphragm 862.0
with open wound into cavity 862.1
duodenum 863.21
with open wound into cavity 863.31
esophagus (intrathoracic) 862.22
with open wound into cavity 862.32
cervical region 874.4
complicated 874.5
fallopian tube 867.6
with open wound into cavity 867.7
gallbladder 868.02
with open wound into cavity 868.12
gastrointestinal tract NEC 863.80
with open wound into cavity 863.90
genital organ NEC 867.6
with open wound into cavity 867.7
heart 861.00
with open wound into thorax 861.10
ileum 863.29
with open wound into cavity 863.39
intestine NEC 863.89
with open wound into cavity 863.99
large NEC 863.40
with open wound into cavity 863.50
small NEC 863.20
with open wound into cavity 863.30
intra-abdominal (organ) 868.00
with open wound into cavity 868.10
multiple sites 868.09
with open wound into cavity 868.19
specified site NEC 868.09
with open wound into cavity 868.19
intrathoracic organs (multiple) 862.8
with open wound into cavity 862.9
diaphragm (only) — *see* Injury, internal, diaphragm
heart (only) — *see* Injury, internal, heart
lung (only) — *see* Injury, internal, lung
specified site NEC 862.29
with open wound into cavity 862.39
intrauterine (*see also* Injury, internal, uterus) 867.4
with open wound into cavity 867.5
jejunum 863.29
with open wound into cavity 863.39
kidney (subcapsular) 866.00
with
disruption of parenchyma (complete) 866.03
with open wound into cavity 866.13
hematoma (without rupture of capsule) 866.01
with open wound into cavity 866.11
laceration 866.02
with open wound into cavity 866.12

Injury — *continued*
internal — *continued*
kidney — *continued*
with — *continued*
open wound into cavity 866.10
liver 864.00
with
contusion 864.01
with open wound into cavity 864.11
hematoma 864.01
with open wound into cavity 864.11
laceration 864.05
with open wound into cavity 864.15
major (disruption of hepatic parenchyma) 864.04
with open wound into cavity 864.14
minor (capsule only) 864.02
with open wound into cavity 864.12
moderate (involving parenchyma) 864.03
with open wound into cavity 864.13
multiple 864.04
stellate 864.04
with open wound into cavity 864.14
open wound into cavity 864.10
lung 861.20
with open wound into thorax 861.30
hemopneumothorax — *see* Hemopneumothorax, traumatic
hemothorax — *see* Hemothorax, traumatic
pneumohemothorax — *see* Pneumohemothorax, traumatic
pneumothorax — *see* Pneumothorax, traumatic
transfusion related, acute (TRALI) 518.7
mediastinum 862.29
with open wound into cavity 862.39
mesentery 863.89
with open wound into cavity 863.99
mesosalpinx 867.6
with open wound into cavity 867.7
multiple 869.0

Note — Multiple internal injuries of sites classifiable to the same three- or four-digit category should be classified to that category.

Multiple injuries classifiable to different fourth-digit subdivisions of 861 (heart and lung injuries) should be dealt with according to coding rules.

internal
with open wound into cavity 869.1
intra-abdominal organ (sites classifiable to 863–868)
with
intrathoracic organ(s) (sites classifiable to 861–862) 869.0
with open wound into cavity 869.1

Injury — *continued*
internal — *continued*
multiple — *continued*
intra-abdominal organ — *continued*
with — *continued*
other intra-abdominal organ(s) (sites classifiable to 863–868, except where classifiable to the same three-digit category) 868.09
with open wound into cavity 868.19
intrathoracic organ (sites classifiable to 861–862)
with
intra-abdominal organ(s) (sites classifiable to 863–868) 869.0
with open wound into cavity 869.1
other intrathoracic organ(s) (sites classifiable to 861–862, except where classifiable to the same three-digit category) 862.8
with open wound into cavity 862.9
myocardium — *see* Injury, internal, heart
ovary 867.6
with open wound into cavity 867.7
pancreas (multiple sites) 863.84
with open wound into cavity 863.94
body 863.82
with open wound into cavity 863.92
head 863.81
with open wound into cavity 863.91
tail 863.83
with open wound into cavity 863.93
pelvis, pelvic (organs) (viscera) 867.8
with
fracture, pelvis — *see* Fracture, pelvis
open wound into cavity 867.9
specified site NEC 867.6
with open wound into cavity 867.7
peritoneum 868.03
with open wound into cavity 868.13
pleura 862.29
with open wound into cavity 862.39
prostate 867.6
with open wound into cavity 867.7
rectum 863.45
with
colon 863.46
with open wound into cavity 863.56
open wound into cavity 863.55
retroperitoneum 868.04
with open wound into cavity 868.14
round ligament 867.6
with open wound into cavity 867.7
seminal vesicle 867.6
with open wound into cavity 867.7
spermatic cord 867.6
with open wound into cavity 867.7

Injury — *continued*
internal — *continued*
spermatic cord — *continued*
scrotal — *see* Wound, open, spermatic cord
spleen 865.00
with
disruption of parenchyma (massive) 865.04
with open wound into cavity 865.14
hematoma (without rupture of capsule) 865.01
with open wound into cavity 865.11
open wound into cavity 865.10
tear, capsular 865.02
with open wound into cavity 865.12
extending into parenchyma 865.03
with open wound into cavity 865.13
stomach 863.0
with open wound into cavity 863.1
suprarenal gland (multiple) 868.01
with open wound into cavity 868.11
thorax, thoracic (cavity) (organs) (multiple) (*see also* Injury, internal, intrathoracic organs) 862.8
with open wound into cavity 862.9
thymus (gland) 862.29
with open wound into cavity 862.39
trachea (intrathoracic) 862.29
with open wound into cavity 862.39
cervical region (*see also* Wound, open, trachea) 874.02
ureter 867.2
with open wound into cavity 867.3
urethra (sphincter) 867.0
with
abortion — *see* Abortion, by type, with damage to pelvic organs
ectopic pregnancy (*see also* categories 633.0–633.9) 639.2
molar pregnancy (*see also* categories 630–632) 639.2
open wound into cavity 867.1
following
abortion 639.2
ectopic or molar pregnancy 639.2
obstetrical trauma 665.5 ☑
affecting fetus or newborn 763.89
uterus 867.4
with
abortion — *see* Abortion, by type, with damage to pelvic organs
ectopic pregnancy (*see also* categories 633.0–633.9) 639.2
molar pregnancy (*see also* categories 630–632) 639.2
open wound into cavity 867.5
following
abortion 639.2
ectopic or molar pregnancy 639.2
obstetrical trauma NEC 665.5 ☑
affecting fetus or newborn 763.89
vas deferens 867.6

- **Injury** — *continued*
  - internal — *continued*
    - vas deferens — *continued*
      - with open wound into cavity 867.7
    - vesical (sphincter) 867.0
      - with open wound into cavity 867.1
    - viscera (abdominal) (*see also* Injury, internal, multiple) 868.00
      - with
        - fracture, pelvis — *see* Fracture, pelvis
        - open wound into cavity 868.10
      - thoracic NEC (*see also* Injury, internal, intrathoracic organs) 862.8
        - with open wound into cavity 862.9
  - interscapular region 959.19
  - intervertebral disc 959.19
  - intestine — *see* Injury, internal, intestine
  - intra-abdominal (organs) NEC — *see* Injury, internal, intra-abdominal
  - intracranial 854.0 ☑

> *Note — Use the following fifth-digit subclassification with categories 851–854:*
>
> 0 *unspecified state of consciousness*
>
> 1 *with no loss of consciousness*
>
> 2 *with brief [less than one hour] loss of consciousness*
>
> 3 *with moderate [1–24 hours] loss of consciousness*
>
> 4 *with prolonged [more than 24 hours] loss of consciousness and return to pre-existing conscious level*
>
> 5 *with prolonged [more than 24 hours] loss of consciousness, without return to pre-existing conscious level*
>
> *Use fifth-digit 5 to designate when a patient is unconscious and dies before regaining consciousness, regardless of the duration of the loss of consciousness*
>
> 6 *with loss of consciousness of unspecified duration*
>
> 9 *with concussion, unspecified*

-
  - intracranial (continued)
    - with
      - open intracranial wound 854.1 ☑
      - skull fracture — *see* Fracture, skull, by site
    - contusion 851.8 ☑
      - with open intracranial wound 851.9 ☑
      - brain stem 851.4 ☑
        - with open intracranial wound 851.5 ☑
      - cerebellum 851.4 ☑
        - with open intracranial wound 851.5 ☑
      - cortex (cerebral) 851.0 ☑
        - with open intracranial wound 851.2 ☑
    - hematoma — *see* Injury, intracranial, hemorrhage
    - hemorrhage 853.0 ☑
      - with
        - laceration — *see* Injury, intracranial, laceration
        - open intracranial wound 853.1 ☑
      - extradural 852.4 ☑
        - with open intracranial wound 852.5 ☑

- **Injury** — *continued*
  - intracranial — *continued*
    - hemorrhage — *continued*
      - subarachnoid 852.0 ☑
        - with open intracranial wound 852.1 ☑
      - subdural 852.2 ☑
        - with open intracranial wound 852.3 ☑
    - laceration 851.8 ☑
      - with open intracranial wound 851.9 ☑
      - brain stem 851.6 ☑
        - with open intracranial wound 851.7 ☑
      - cerebellum 851.6 ☑
        - with open intracranial wound 851.7 ☑
      - cortex (cerebral) 851.2 ☑
        - with open intracranial wound 851.3 ☑
  - intraocular — *see* Injury, eyeball, penetrating
  - intrathoracic organs (multiple) — *see* Injury, internal, intrathoracic organs
  - intrauterine — *see* Injury, internal, intrauterine
  - iris 921.3
    - penetrating — *see* Injury, eyeball, penetrating
  - jaw 959.09
  - jejunum — *see* Injury, internal, jejunum
  - joint NEC 959.9
    - old or residual 718.80
      - ankle 718.87
      - elbow 718.82
      - foot 718.87
      - hand 718.84
      - hip 718.85
      - knee 718.86
      - multiple sites 718.89
      - pelvic region 718.85
      - shoulder (region) 718.81
      - specified site NEC 718.88
      - wrist 718.83
  - kidney — *see* Injury, internal, kidney
    - acute (nontraumatic) 584.9 ●
  - knee (and ankle) (and foot) (and leg, except thigh) 959.7
  - labium (majus) (minus) 959.14
  - labyrinth, ear 959.09
  - lacrimal apparatus, gland, or sac 921.1
    - laceration 870.8
  - larynx 959.09
  - late effect — *see* Late, effects (of), injury
  - leg, except thigh (and ankle) (and foot) (and knee) 959.7
    - upper or thigh 959.6
  - lens, eye 921.3
    - penetrating — *see* Injury, eyeball, penetrating
  - lid, eye — *see* Injury, eyelid
  - lip 959.09
  - liver — *see* Injury, internal, liver
  - lobe, parietal — *see* Injury, intracranial
  - lumbar (region) 959.19
    - plexus 953.5
  - lumbosacral (region) 959.19
    - plexus 953.5
  - lung — *see* Injury, internal, lung
  - malar region 959.09
  - mastoid region 959.09
  - maternal, during pregnancy, affecting fetus or newborn 760.5
  - maxilla 959.09
  - mediastinum — *see* Injury, internal, mediastinum
  - membrane
    - brain (*see also* Injury, intracranial) 854.0 ☑
    - tympanic 959.09

- **Injury** — *continued*
  - meningeal artery — *see* Hemorrhage, brain, traumatic, subarachnoid
  - meninges (cerebral) — *see* Injury, intracranial
  - mesenteric
    - artery — *see* Injury, blood vessel, mesenteric, artery
    - plexus, inferior 954.1
    - vein — *see* Injury, blood vessel, mesenteric, vein
  - mesentery — *see* Injury, internal, mesentery
  - mesosalpinx — *see* Injury, internal, mesosalpinx
  - middle ear 959.09
  - midthoracic region 959.11
  - mouth 959.09
  - multiple (sites not classifiable to the same four-digit category in 959.0–959.7) 959.8
    - internal 869.0
      - with open wound into cavity 869.1
  - musculocutaneous nerve 955.4
  - nail
    - finger 959.5
    - toe 959.7
  - nasal (septum) (sinus) 959.09
  - nasopharynx 959.09
  - neck (and face) 959.09
  - nerve 957.9
    - abducens 951.3
    - abducent 951.3
    - accessory 951.6
    - acoustic 951.5
    - ankle and foot 956.9
    - anterior crural, femoral 956.1
    - arm (*see also* Injury, nerve, upper limb) 955.9
    - auditory 951.5
    - axillary 955.0
    - brachial plexus 953.4
    - cervical sympathetic 954.0
    - cranial 951.9
      - first or olfactory 951.8
      - second or optic 950.0
      - third or oculomotor 951.0
      - fourth or trochlear 951.1
      - fifth or trigeminal 951.2
      - sixth or abducens 951.3
      - seventh or facial 951.4
      - eighth, acoustic, or auditory 951.5
      - ninth or glossopharyngeal 951.8
      - tenth, pneumogastric, or vagus 951.8
      - eleventh or accessory 951.6
      - twelfth or hypoglossal 951.7
      - newborn 767.7
    - cutaneous sensory
      - lower limb 956.4
      - upper limb 955.5
    - digital (finger) 955.6
      - toe 956.5
    - facial 951.4
      - newborn 767.5
    - femoral 956.1
    - finger 955.9
    - foot and ankle 956.9
    - forearm 955.9
    - glossopharyngeal 951.8
    - hand and wrist 955.9
    - head and neck, superficial 957.0
    - hypoglossal 951.7
    - involving several parts of body 957.8
    - leg (*see also* Injury, nerve, lower limb) 956.9
    - lower limb 956.9
      - multiple 956.8
      - specified site NEC 956.5
    - lumbar plexus 953.5
    - lumbosacral plexus 953.5
    - median 955.1
      - forearm 955.1

- **Injury** — *continued*
  - nerve — *continued*
    - median — *continued*
      - wrist and hand 955.1
    - multiple (in several parts of body) (sites not classifiable to the same three-digit category) 957.8
    - musculocutaneous 955.4
    - musculospiral 955.3
      - upper arm 955.3
    - oculomotor 951.0
    - olfactory 951.8
    - optic 950.0
    - pelvic girdle 956.9
      - multiple sites 956.8
      - specified site NEC 956.5
    - peripheral 957.9
      - multiple (in several regions) (sites not classifiable to the same three-digit category) 957.8
      - specified site NEC 957.1
    - peroneal 956.3
      - ankle and foot 956.3
      - lower leg 956.3
    - plantar 956.5
    - plexus 957.9
      - celiac 954.1
      - mesenteric, inferior 954.1
      - spinal 953.9
        - brachial 953.4
        - lumbosacral 953.5
        - multiple sites 953.8
      - sympathetic NEC 954.1
    - pneumogastric 951.8
    - radial 955.3
      - wrist and hand 955.3
    - sacral plexus 953.5
    - sciatic 956.0
      - thigh 956.0
    - shoulder girdle 955.9
      - multiple 955.8
      - specified site NEC 955.7
    - specified site NEC 957.1
    - spinal 953.9
      - plexus — *see* Injury, nerve, plexus, spinal
      - root 953.9
        - cervical 953.0
        - dorsal 953.1
        - lumbar 953.2
        - multiple sites 953.8
        - sacral 953.3
    - splanchnic 954.1
    - sympathetic NEC 954.1
      - cervical 954.0
    - thigh 956.9
    - tibial 956.5
      - ankle and foot 956.2
      - lower leg 956.5
      - posterior 956.2
    - toe 956.9
    - trigeminal 951.2
    - trochlear 951.1
    - trunk, excluding shoulder and pelvic girdles 954.9
      - specified site NEC 954.8
      - sympathetic NEC 954.1
    - ulnar 955.2
      - forearm 955.2
      - wrist (and hand) 955.2
    - upper limb 955.9
      - multiple 955.8
      - specified site NEC 955.7
    - vagus 951.8
    - wrist and hand 955.9
  - nervous system, diffuse 957.8
  - nose (septum) 959.09
  - obstetrical NEC 665.9 ☑
    - affecting fetus or newborn 763.89
  - occipital (region) (scalp) 959.09
    - lobe (*see also* Injury, intracranial) 854.0 ☑
  - optic 950.9
    - chiasm 950.1

Injury — *continued*
optic — *continued*
cortex 950.3
nerve 950.0
pathways 950.2
orbit, orbital (region) 921.2
penetrating 870.3
with foreign body 870.4
ovary — *see* Injury, internal, ovary
paint-gun — *see* Wound, open, by site, complicated
palate (soft) 959.09
pancreas — *see* Injury, internal, pancreas
parathyroid (gland) 959.09
parietal (region) (scalp) 959.09
lobe — *see* Injury, intracranial
pelvic
floor 959.19
complicating delivery 664.1 ☑
affecting fetus or newborn 763.89
joint or ligament, complicating delivery 665.6 ☑
affecting fetus or newborn 763.89
organs (*see also* Injury, internal, pelvis)
with
abortion — *see* Abortion, by type, with damage to pelvic organs
ectopic pregnancy (*see also* categories 633.0–633.9) 639.2
molar pregnancy (*see also* categories 633.0–633.9) 639.2
following
abortion 639.2
ectopic or molar pregnancy 639.2
obstetrical trauma 665.5 ☑
affecting fetus or newborn 763.89
pelvis 959.19
penis 959.14
fracture of corpus cavernosum 959.13
perineum 959.14
peritoneum — *see* Injury, internal, peritoneum
periurethral tissue
with
abortion — *see* Abortion, by type, with damage to pelvic organs
ectopic pregnancy (*see also* categories 633.0–633.9) 639.2
molar pregnancy (*see also* categories 630–632) 639.2
complicating delivery 665.5 ☑
affecting fetus or newborn 763.89
following
abortion 639.2
ectopic or molar pregnancy 639.2
phalanges
foot 959.7
hand 959.5
pharynx 959.09
pleura — *see* Injury, internal, pleura
popliteal space 959.7
post-cardiac surgery (syndrome) 429.4
prepuce 959.14
prostate — *see* Injury, internal, prostate
pubic region 959.19
pudenda 959.14
radiation NEC 990
radioactive substance or radium NEC 990
rectovaginal septum 959.14
rectum — *see* Injury, internal, rectum

Injury — *continued*
retina 921.3
penetrating — *see* Injury, eyeball, penetrating
retroperitoneal — *see* Injury, internal, retroperitoneum
roentgen rays NEC 990
round ligament — *see* Injury, internal, round ligament
sacral (region) 959.19
plexus 953.5
sacroiliac ligament NEC 959.19
sacrum 959.19
salivary ducts or glands 959.09
scalp 959.09
due to birth trauma 767.19
fetus or newborn 767.19
scapular region 959.2
sclera 921.3
penetrating — *see* Injury, eyeball, penetrating
superficial 918.2
scrotum 959.14
seminal vesicle — *see* Injury, internal, seminal vesicle
shoulder (and upper arm) 959.2
sinus
cavernous (*see also* Injury, intracranial) 854.0 ☑
nasal 959.09
skeleton NEC, birth injury 767.3
skin NEC 959.9
skull — *see* Fracture, skull, by site
soft tissue (of external sites) (severe) — *see* Wound, open, by site
specified site NEC 959.8
spermatic cord — *see* Injury, internal, spermatic cord
spinal (cord) 952.9
with fracture, vertebra — *see* Fracture, vertebra, by site, with spinal cord injury
cervical (C_1-C_4) 952.00
with
anterior cord syndrome 952.02
central cord syndrome 952.03
complete lesion of cord 952.01
incomplete lesion NEC 952.04
posterior cord syndrome 952.04
C_5-C_7 level 952.05
with
anterior cord syndrome 952.07
central cord syndrome 952.08
complete lesion of cord 952.06
incomplete lesion NEC 952.09
posterior cord syndrome 952.09
specified type NEC 952.09
specified type NEC 952.04
dorsal (D_1-D_6) (T_1-T_6) (thoracic) 952.10
with
anterior cord syndrome 952.12
central cord syndrome 952.13
complete lesion of cord 952.11
incomplete lesion NEC 952.14
posterior cord syndrome 952.14
D_7-D_{12} level (T_7-T_{12}) 952.15
with
anterior cord syndrome 952.17

Injury — *continued*
spinal — *continued*
dorsal — *continued*
D_7-D_{12} level — *continued*
with — *continued*
central cord syndrome 952.18
complete lesion of cord 952.16
incomplete lesion NEC 952.19
posterior cord syndrome 952.19
specified type NEC 952.19
specified type NEC 952.14
lumbar 952.2
multiple sites 952.8
nerve (root) NEC — *see* Injury, nerve, spinal, root
plexus 953.9
brachial 953.4
lumbosacral 953.5
multiple sites 953.8
sacral 952.3
thoracic (*see also* Injury, spinal, dorsal) 952.10
spleen — *see* Injury, internal, spleen
stellate ganglion 954.1
sternal region 959.11
stomach — *see* Injury, internal, stomach
subconjunctival 921.1
subcutaneous 959.9
subdural — *see* Injury, intracranial
submaxillary region 959.09
submental region 959.09
subungual
fingers 959.5
toes 959.7
superficial 919 ☑

Note — Use the following fourth-digit subdivisions with categories 910–919:

0 *Abrasion or friction burn without mention of infection*

1 *Abrasion or friction burn, infected*

2 *Blister without mention of infection*

3 *Blister, infected*

4 *Insect bite, nonvenomous, without mention of infection*

5 *Insect bite, nonvenomous, infected*

6 *Superficial foreign body (splinter) without major open wound and without mention of infection*

7 *Superficial foreign body (splinter) without major open wound, infected*

8 *Other and unspecified superficial injury without mention of infection*

9 *Other and unspecified superficial injury, infected*

For late effects of superficial injury, see category 906.2.

abdomen, abdominal (muscle) (wall) (and other part(s) of trunk) 911 ☑
ankle (and hip, knee, leg, or thigh) 916 ☑
anus (and other part(s) of trunk) 911 ☑
arm 913 ☑
upper (and shoulder) 912 ☑
auditory canal (external) (meatus) (and other part(s) of face, neck, or scalp, except eye) 910 ☑
axilla (and upper arm) 912 ☑
back (and other part(s) of trunk) 911 ☑

Injury — *continued*
superficial — *continued*
breast (and other part(s) of trunk) 911 ☑
brow (and other part(s) of face, neck, or scalp, except eye) 910 ☑
buttock (and other part(s) of trunk) 911 ☑
canthus, eye 918.0
cheek(s) (and other part(s) of face, neck, or scalp, except eye) 910 ☑
chest wall (and other part(s) of trunk) 911 ☑
chin (and other part(s) of face, neck, or scalp, except eye) 910 ☑
clitoris (and other part(s) of trunk) 911 ☑
conjunctiva 918.2
cornea 918.1
due to contact lens 371.82
costal region (and other part(s) of trunk) 911 ☑
ear(s) (auricle) (canal) (drum) (external) (and other part(s) of face, neck, or scalp, except eye) 910 ☑
elbow (and forearm) (and wrist) 913 ☑
epididymis (and other part(s) of trunk) 911 ☑
epigastric region (and other part(s) of trunk) 911 ☑
epiglottis (and other part(s) of face, neck, or scalp, except eye) 910 ☑
eye(s) (and adnexa) NEC 918.9
eyelid(s) (and periocular area) 918.0
face (any part(s), except eye) (and neck or scalp) 910 ☑
finger(s) (nail) (any) 915 ☑
flank (and other part(s) of trunk) 911 ☑
foot (phalanges) (and toe(s)) 917 ☑
forearm (and elbow) (and wrist) 913 ☑
forehead (and other part(s) of face, neck, or scalp, except eye) 910 ☑
globe (eye) 918.9
groin (and other part(s) of trunk) 911 ☑
gum(s) (and other part(s) of face, neck, or scalp, except eye) 910 ☑
hand(s) (except fingers alone) 914 ☑
head (and other part(s) of face, neck, or scalp, except eye) 910 ☑
heel (and foot or toe) 917 ☑
hip (and ankle, knee, leg, or thigh) 916 ☑
iliac region (and other part(s) of trunk) 911 ☑
interscapular region (and other part(s) of trunk) 911 ☑
iris 918.9
knee (and ankle, hip, leg, or thigh) 916 ☑
labium (majus) (minus) (and other part(s) of trunk) 911 ☑
lacrimal (apparatus) (gland) (sac) 918.0
leg (lower) (upper) (and ankle, hip, knee, or thigh) 916 ☑
lip(s) (and other part(s) of face, neck, or scalp, except eye) 910 ☑
lower extremity (except foot) 916 ☑
lumbar region (and other part(s) of trunk) 911 ☑

- **Injury** — *continued*
  - superficial — *continued*
    - malar region (and other part(s) of face, neck, or scalp, except eye) 910 ☑
    - mastoid region (and other part(s) of face, neck, or scalp, except eye) 910 ☑
    - midthoracic region (and other part(s) of trunk) 911 ☑
    - mouth (and other part(s) of face, neck, or scalp, except eye) 910 ☑
    - multiple sites (not classifiable to the same three-digit category) 919 ☑
    - nasal (septum) (and other part(s) of face, neck, or scalp, except eye) 910 ☑
    - neck (and face or scalp, any part(s), except eye) 910 ☑
    - nose (septum) (and other part(s) of face, neck, or scalp, except eye) 910 ☑
    - occipital region (and other part(s) of face, neck, or scalp, except eye) 910 ☑
    - orbital region 918.0
    - palate (soft) (and other part(s) of face, neck, or scalp, except eye) 910 ☑
    - parietal region (and other part(s) of face, neck, or scalp, except eye) 910 ☑
    - penis (and other part(s) of trunk) 911 ☑
    - perineum (and other part(s) of trunk) 911 ☑
    - periocular area 918.0
    - pharynx (and other part(s) of face, neck, or scalp, except eye) 910 ☑
    - popliteal space (and ankle, hip, leg, or thigh) 916 ☑
    - prepuce (and other part(s) of trunk) 911 ☑
    - pubic region (and other part(s) of trunk) 911 ☑
    - pudenda (and other part(s) of trunk) 911 ☑
    - sacral region (and other part(s) of trunk) 911 ☑
    - salivary (ducts) (glands) (and other part(s) of face, neck, or scalp, except eye) 910 ☑
    - scalp (and other part(s) of face or neck, except eye) 910 ☑
    - scapular region (and upper arm) 912 ☑
    - sclera 918.2
    - scrotum (and other part(s) of trunk) 911 ☑
    - shoulder (and upper arm) 912 ☑
    - skin NEC 919 ☑
    - specified site(s) NEC 919 ☑
    - sternal region (and other part(s) of trunk) 911 ☑
    - subconjunctival 918.2
    - subcutaneous NEC 919 ☑
    - submaxillary region (and other part(s) of face, neck, or scalp, except eye) 910 ☑
    - submental region (and other part(s) of face, neck, or scalp, except eye) 910 ☑
    - supraclavicular fossa (and other part(s) of face, neck, or scalp, except eye) 910 ☑
    - supraorbital 918.0
    - temple (and other part(s) of face, neck, or scalp, except eye) 910 ☑
    - temporal region (and other part(s) of face, neck, or scalp, except eye) 910 ☑
    - testis (and other part(s) of trunk) 911 ☑
    - thigh (and ankle, hip, knee, or leg) 916 ☑
    - thorax, thoracic (external) (and other part(s) of trunk) 911 ☑
    - throat (and other part(s) of face, neck, or scalp, except eye) 910 ☑
    - thumb(s) (nail) 915 ☑
    - toe(s) (nail) (subungual) (and foot) 917 ☑
    - tongue (and other part(s) of face, neck, or scalp, except eye) 910 ☑
    - tooth, teeth (*see also* Abrasion, dental) 521.20
    - trunk (any part(s)) 911 ☑
    - tunica vaginalis 959.14
    - tympanum, tympanic membrane (and other part(s) of face, neck, or scalp, except eye) 910 ☑
    - upper extremity NEC 913 ☑
    - uvula (and other part(s) of face, neck, or scalp, except eye) 910 ☑
    - vagina (and other part(s) of trunk) 911 ☑
    - vulva (and other part(s) of trunk) 911 ☑
    - wrist (and elbow) (and forearm) 913 ☑
  - supraclavicular fossa 959.19
  - supraorbital 959.09
  - surgical complication (external or internal site) 998.2
  - symphysis pubis 959.19
    - complicating delivery 665.6 ☑
      - affecting fetus or newborn 763.89
  - temple 959.09
  - temporal region 959.09
  - testis 959.14
  - thigh (and hip) 959.6
  - thorax, thoracic (external) 959.11
    - cavity — *see* Injury, internal, thorax
    - internal — *see* Injury, internal, intrathoracic organs
  - throat 959.09
  - thumb(s) (nail) 959.5
  - thymus — *see* Injury, internal, thymus
  - thyroid (gland) 959.09
  - toe (nail) (any) 959.7
  - tongue 959.09
  - tonsil 959.09
  - tooth NEC 873.63
    - complicated 873.73
  - trachea — *see* Injury, internal, trachea
  - trunk 959.19
  - tunica vaginalis 959.14
  - tympanum, tympanic membrane 959.09
  - ultraviolet rays NEC 990
  - ureter — *see* Injury, internal, ureter
  - urethra (sphincter) — *see* Injury, internal, urethra
  - uterus — *see* Injury, internal, uterus
  - uvula 959.09
  - vagina 959.14
  - vascular — *see* Injury, blood vessel
  - vas deferens — *see* Injury, internal, vas deferens
  - vein (*see also* Injury, blood vessel, by site) 904.9
  - vena cava
    - inferior 902.10
    - superior 901.2
  - vesical (sphincter) — *see* Injury, internal, vesical
  - viscera (abdominal) — *see* Injury, internal, viscera
    - with fracture, pelvis — *see* Fracture, pelvis
  - visual 950.9
    - cortex 950.3
  - vitreous (humor) 871.2
  - vulva 959.14
  - whiplash (cervical spine) 847.0
  - wringer — *see* Crush, by site
  - wrist (and elbow) (and forearm) 959.3
  - x-ray NEC 990
- **Inoculation** — *see also* Vaccination
  - complication or reaction — *see* Complication, vaccination
- **INPH** (idiopathic normal pressure hydrocephalus) 331.5
- **Insanity, insane** — *see also* Psychosis 298.9
  - adolescent (*see also* Schizophrenia) 295.9 ☑
  - alternating (*see also* Psychosis, affective, circular) 296.7
  - confusional 298.9
    - acute 293.0
    - subacute 293.1
  - delusional 298.9
  - paralysis, general 094.1
    - progressive 094.1
  - paresis, general 094.1
  - senile 290.20
- **Insect**
  - bite — *see* Injury, superficial, by site
  - venomous, poisoning by 989.5
- **Insemination, artificial** V26.1
- **Insensitivity**
  - adrenocorticotropin hormone (ACTH) 255.41
  - androgen 259.50 ▲
    - complete 259.51 ●
    - partial 259.52 ▲
- **Insertion**
  - cord (umbilical) lateral or velamentous 663.8 ☑
    - affecting fetus or newborn 762.6
  - intrauterine contraceptive device V25.1
  - placenta, vicious — *see* Placenta, previa
  - subdermal implantable contraceptive V25.5
  - velamentous, umbilical cord 663.8 ☑
    - affecting fetus or newborn 762.6
- **Insolation** 992.0
  - meaning sunstroke 992.0
- **Insomnia, unspecified** 780.52
  - with sleep apnea, unspecified 780.51
  - adjustment 307.41
  - alcohol induced 291.82
  - behavioral, of childhood V69.5
  - drug induced 292.85
  - due to
    - medical condition classified elsewhere 327.01
    - mental disorder 327.02
  - fatal familial (FFI) 046.72 ●
  - idiopathic 307.42
  - nonorganic origin 307.41
    - persistent (primary) 307.42
    - transient 307.41
  - organic 327.00
    - other 327.09
  - paradoxical 307.42
  - primary 307.42
  - psychophysiological 307.42
  - subjective complaint 307.49
- **Inspiration**
  - food or foreign body (*see also* Asphyxia, food or foreign body) 933.1
  - mucus (*see also* Asphyxia, mucus) 933.1
- **Inspissated bile syndrome, newborn** 774.4
- **Instability**
  - detrusor 596.59
  - emotional (excessive) 301.3
  - joint (posttraumatic) 718.80
    - ankle 718.87
    - elbow 718.82
    - foot 718.87
    - hand 718.84
    - hip 718.85
    - knee 718.86
    - lumbosacral 724.6
    - multiple sites 718.89
    - pelvic region 718.85
    - sacroiliac 724.6
    - shoulder (region) 718.81
    - specified site NEC 718.88
    - wrist 718.83
  - lumbosacral 724.6
  - nervous 301.89
  - personality (emotional) 301.59
  - thyroid, paroxysmal 242.9 ☑
  - urethral 599.83
  - vasomotor 780.2
- **Insufficiency, insufficient**
  - accommodation 367.4
  - adrenal (gland) (acute) (chronic) 255.41
    - medulla 255.5
    - primary 255.41
    - specified site NEC 255.5
  - adrenocortical 255.41
  - anterior (occlusal) guidance 524.54
  - anus 569.49
  - aortic (valve) 424.1
    - with
      - mitral (valve) disease 396.1
        - insufficiency, incompetence, or regurgitation 396.3
        - stenosis or obstruction 396.1
      - stenosis or obstruction 424.1
        - with mitral (valve) disease 396.8
    - congenital 746.4
    - rheumatic 395.1
      - with
        - mitral (valve) disease 396.1
          - insufficiency, incompetence, or regurgitation 396.3
          - stenosis or obstruction 396.1
        - stenosis or obstruction 395.2
          - with mitral (valve) disease 396.8
    - specified cause NEC 424.1
    - syphilitic 093.22
  - arterial 447.1
    - basilar artery 435.0
    - carotid artery 435.8
    - cerebral 437.1
    - coronary (acute or subacute) 411.89
    - mesenteric 557.1
    - peripheral 443.9
    - precerebral 435.9
    - vertebral artery 435.1
    - vertebrobasilar 435.3
  - arteriovenous 459.9
  - basilar artery 435.0
  - biliary 575.8
  - cardiac (*see also* Insufficiency, myocardial) 428.0
    - complicating surgery 997.1
    - due to presence of (cardiac) prosthesis 429.4
    - postoperative 997.1
      - long-term effect of cardiac surgery 429.4
    - specified during or due to a procedure 997.1
      - long-term effect of cardiac surgery 429.4
  - cardiorenal (*see also* Hypertension, cardiorenal) 404.90
  - cardiovascular (*see also* Disease, cardiovascular) 429.2

Insufficiency, insufficient — *continued*
cardiovascular (*see also* Disease, cardiovascular) — *continued*
renal (*see also* Hypertension, cardiorenal) 404.90
carotid artery 435.8
cerebral (vascular) 437.9
cerebrovascular 437.9
with transient focal neurological signs and symptoms 435.9
acute 437.1
with transient focal neurological signs and symptoms 435.9
circulatory NEC 459.9
fetus or newborn 779.89
convergence 378.83
coronary (acute or subacute) 411.89
chronic or with a stated duration of over 8 weeks 414.8
corticoadrenal 255.41
dietary 269.9
divergence 378.85
food 994.2
gastroesophageal 530.89
gonadal
ovary 256.39
testis 257.2
gonadotropic hormone secretion 253.4
heart (*see also* Insufficiency, myocardial)
fetus or newborn 779.89
valve (*see also* Endocarditis) 424.90
congenital NEC 746.89
hepatic 573.8
idiopathic autonomic 333.0
interocclusal distance of teeth (ridge) 524.36
kidney
acute 593.9
chronic 585.9
labyrinth, labyrinthine (function) 386.53
bilateral 386.54
unilateral 386.53
lacrimal 375.15
liver 573.8
lung (acute) (*see also* Insufficiency, pulmonary) 518.82
following trauma, surgery, or shock 518.5
newborn 770.89
mental (congenital) (*see also* Retardation, mental) 319
mesenteric 557.1
mitral (valve) 424.0
with
aortic (valve) disease 396.3
insufficiency, incompetence, or regurgitation 396.3
stenosis or obstruction 396.2
obstruction or stenosis 394.2
with aortic valve disease 396.8
congenital 746.6
rheumatic 394.1
with
aortic (valve) disease 396.3
insufficiency, incompetence, or regurgitation 396.3
stenosis or obstruction 396.2
obstruction or stenosis 394.2
with aortic valve disease 396.8
active or acute 391.1
with chorea, rheumatic (Sydenham's) 392.0
specified cause, except rheumatic 424.0
muscle
heart — *see* Insufficiency, myocardial

Insufficiency, insufficient — *continued*
muscle — *continued*
ocular (*see also* Strabismus) 378.9
myocardial, myocardium (with arteriosclerosis) 428.0
with rheumatic fever (conditions classifiable to 390)
active, acute, or subacute 391.2
with chorea 392.0
inactive or quiescent (with chorea) 398.0
congenital 746.89
due to presence of (cardiac) prosthesis 429.4
fetus or newborn 779.89
following cardiac surgery 429.4
hypertensive (*see also* Hypertension, heart) 402.91
benign 402.11
malignant 402.01
postoperative 997.1
long-term effect of cardiac surgery 429.4
rheumatic 398.0
active, acute, or subacute 391.2
with chorea (Sydenham's) 392.0
syphilitic 093.82
nourishment 994.2
organic 799.89
ovary 256.39
postablative 256.2
pancreatic 577.8
parathyroid (gland) 252.1
peripheral vascular (arterial) 443.9
pituitary (anterior) 253.2
posterior 253.5
placental — *see* Placenta, insufficiency
platelets 287.5
prenatal care in current pregnancy V23.7
progressive pluriglandular 258.9
pseudocholinesterase 289.89
pulmonary (acute) 518.82
following
shock 518.5
surgery 518.5
trauma 518.5
newborn 770.89
valve (*see also* Endocarditis, pulmonary) 424.3
congenital 746.09
pyloric 537.0
renal 593.9
acute 593.9
chronic 585.9
due to a procedure 997.5
respiratory 786.09
acute 518.82
following shock, surgery, or trauma 518.5
newborn 770.89
rotation — *see* Malrotation
suprarenal 255.41
medulla 255.5
tarso-orbital fascia, congenital 743.66
tear film 375.15
testis 257.2
thyroid (gland) (acquired) (*see also* Hypothyroidism)
congenital 243
tricuspid (*see also* Endocarditis, tricuspid) 397.0
congenital 746.89
syphilitic 093.23
urethral sphincter 599.84
valve, valvular (heart) (*see also* Endocarditis) 424.90
vascular 459.9
intestine NEC 557.9
mesenteric 557.1
peripheral 443.9
renal (*see also* Hypertension, kidney) 403.90

Insufficiency, insufficient — *continued*
velopharyngeal
acquired 528.9
congenital 750.29
venous (peripheral) 459.81
ventricular — *see* Insufficiency, myocardial
vertebral artery 435.1
vertebrobasilar artery 435.3
weight gain during pregnancy 646.8 ☑
zinc 269.3
Insufflation
fallopian
fertility testing V26.21
following sterilization reversal V26.22
meconium 770.11
with respiratory symptoms 770.12
Insular — *see* condition
Insulinoma (M8151/0)
malignant (M8151/3)
pancreas 157.4
specified site — *see* Neoplasm, by site, malignant
unspecified site 157.4
pancreas 211.7
specified site — *see* Neoplasm, by site, benign
unspecified site 211.7
Insuloma — *see* Insulinoma
Insult
brain 437.9
acute 436
cerebral 437.9
acute 436
cerebrovascular 437.9
acute 436
vascular NEC 437.9
acute 436
Insurance examination (certification) V70.3
Intemperance — *see also* Alcoholism 303.9 ☑
Interception of pregnancy (menstrual extraction) V25.3
Interference
balancing side 524.56
non-working side 524.56
Intermenstrual
bleeding 626.6
irregular 626.6
regular 626.5
hemorrhage 626.6
irregular 626.6
regular 626.5
pain(s) 625.2
Intermittent — *see* condition
Internal — *see* condition
Interproximal wear 521.10
Interruption
aortic arch 747.11
bundle of His 426.50
fallopian tube (for sterilization) V25.2
phase-shift, sleep cycle 307.45
repeated REM-sleep 307.48
sleep
due to perceived environmental disturbances 307.48
phase-shift, of 24-hour sleep-wake cycle 307.45
repeated REM-sleep type 307.48
vas deferens (for sterilization) V25.2
Intersexuality 752.7
Interstitial — *see* condition
Intertrigo 695.89
labialis 528.5
Intervertebral disc — *see* condition
Intestine, intestinal — *see also* condition
flu 487.8
Intolerance
carbohydrate NEC 579.8

Intolerance — *continued*
cardiovascular exercise, with pain (at rest) (with less than ordinary activity) (with ordinary activity) V47.2
cold 780.99
dissacharide (hereditary) 271.3
drug
correct substance properly administered 995.27
wrong substance given or taken in error 977.9
specified drug — *see* Table of Drugs and Chemicals
effort 306.2
fat NEC 579.8
foods NEC 579.8
fructose (hereditary) 271.2
glucose (-galactose) (congenital) 271.3
gluten 579.0
lactose (hereditary) (infantile) 271.3
lysine (congenital) 270.7
milk NEC 579.8
protein (familial) 270.7
starch NEC 579.8
sucrose (-isomaltose) (congenital) 271.3
Intoxicated NEC — *see also* Alcoholism 305.0 ☑
Intoxication
acid 276.2
acute
alcoholic 305.0 ☑
with alcoholism 303.0 ☑
hangover effects 305.0 ☑
caffeine 305.9 ☑
hallucinogenic (*see also* Abuse, drugs, nondependent) 305.3 ☑
alcohol (acute) 305.0 ☑
with alcoholism 303.0 ☑
hangover effects 305.0 ☑
idiosyncratic 291.4
pathological 291.4
alimentary canal 558.2
ammonia (hepatic) 572.2
caffeine 305.9 ☑
chemical (*see also* Table of Drugs and Chemicals)
via placenta or breast milk 760.70
alcohol 760.71
anticonvulsants
antifungals
anti-infective agents 760.74
antimetabolics
cocaine 760.75
"crack" 760.75
hallucinogenic agents NEC 760.73
medicinal agents NEC 760.79
narcotics 760.72
obstetric anesthetic or analgesic drug 763.5
specified agent NEC 760.79
suspected, affecting management of pregnancy 655.5 ☑
cocaine, through placenta or breast milk 760.75
delirium
alcohol 291.0
drug 292.81
drug 292.89
with delirium 292.81
correct substance properly administered (*see also* Allergy, drug) 995.27
newborn 779.4
obstetric anesthetic or sedation 668.9 ☑
affecting fetus or newborn 763.5
overdose or wrong substance given or taken — *see* Table of Drugs and Chemicals
pathologic 292.2
specific to newborn 779.4

Index
Insufficiency, insufficient — Intoxication

Intoxication — *continued*
drug — *continued*
via placenta or breast milk 760.70
alcohol 760.71
anticonvulsants 760.77
antifungals 760.74
anti-infective agents 760.74
antimetabolics 760.78
cocaine 760.75
"crack" 760.75
hallucinogenic agents 760.73
medicinal agents NEC 760.79
narcotics 760.72
obstetric anesthetic or analgesic drug 763.5
specified agent NEC 760.79
suspected, affecting management of pregnancy 655.5 ☑
enteric — *see* Intoxication, intestinal
fetus or newborn, via placenta or breast milk 760.70
alcohol 760.71
anticonvulsants 760.77
antifungals 760.74
anti-infective agents 760.74
antimetabolics 760.78
cocaine 760.75
"crack" 760.75
hallucinogenic agents 760.73
medicinal agents NEC 760.79
narcotics 760.72
obstetric anesthetic or analgesic drug 763.5
specified agent NEC 760.79
suspected, affecting management of pregnancy 655.5 ☑
food — *see* Poisoning, food
gastrointestinal 558.2
hallucinogenic (acute) 305.3 ☑
hepatocerebral 572.2
idiosyncratic alcohol 291.4
intestinal 569.89
due to putrefaction of food 005.9
methyl alcohol (*see also* Alcoholism) 305.0 ☑
with alcoholism 303.0 ☑
non-foodborne due to toxins of Clostridium botulinum [C. botulinum] — *see* Botulism
pathologic 291.4
drug 292.2
potassium (K) 276.7
septic
with
abortion — *see* Abortion, by type, with sepsis
ectopic pregnancy (*see also* categories 633.0–633.9) 639.0
molar pregnancy (*see also* categories 630–632) 639.0
during labor 659.3 ☑
following
abortion 639.0
ectopic or molar pregnancy 639.0
generalized — *see* Septicemia
puerperal, postpartum, childbirth 670.0 ☑
serum (prophylactic) (therapeutic) 999.5
uremic — *see* Uremia
water 276.6
Intracranial — *see* condition
Intrahepatic gallbladder 751.69
Intraligamentous — *see also* condition
pregnancy — *see* Pregnancy, cornual
Intraocular — *see also* condition
sepsis 360.00
Intrathoracic — *see also* condition
kidney 753.3
stomach — *see* Hernia, diaphragm
Intrauterine contraceptive device
checking V25.42
insertion V25.1
Intrauterine contraceptive device — *continued*
in situ V45.51
management V25.42
prescription V25.02
repeat V25.42
reinsertion V25.42
removal V25.42
Intraventricular — *see* condition
Intrinsic deformity — *see* Deformity
Intruded tooth 524.34
Intrusion, repetitive, of sleep (due to environmental disturbances) (with atypical polysomnographic features) 307.48
Intumescent, lens (eye) NEC 366.9
senile 366.12
Intussusception (colon) (enteric) (intestine) (rectum) 560.0
appendix 543.9
congenital 751.5
fallopian tube 620.8
ileocecal 560.0
ileocolic 560.0
ureter (with obstruction) 593.4
Invagination
basilar 756.0
colon or intestine 560.0
Invalid (since birth) 799.89
Invalidism (chronic) 799.89
Inversion
albumin-globulin (A-G) ratio 273.8
bladder 596.8
cecum (*see also* Intussusception) 560.0
cervix 622.8
nipple 611.79
congenital 757.6
puerperal, postpartum 676.3 ☑
optic papilla 743.57
organ or site, congenital NEC — *see* Anomaly, specified type NEC
sleep rhythm 327.39
nonorganic origin 307.45
testis (congenital) 752.51
uterus (postinfectional) (postpartal, old) 621.7
chronic 621.7
complicating delivery 665.2 ☑
affecting fetus or newborn 763.89
vagina — *see* Prolapse, vagina
Investigation
allergens V72.7
clinical research (control) (normal comparison) (participant) V70.7
Inviability — *see* Immaturity
Involuntary movement, abnormal 781.0
Involution, involutional — *see also* condition
breast, cystic or fibrocystic 610.1
depression (*see also* Psychosis, affective) 296.2 ☑
recurrent episode 296.3 ☑
single episode 296.2 ☑
melancholia (*see also* Psychosis, affective) 296.2 ☑
recurrent episode 296.3 ☑
single episode 296.2 ☑
ovary, senile 620.3
paranoid state (reaction) 297.2
paraphrenia (climacteric) (menopause) 297.2
psychosis 298.8
thymus failure 254.8
IQ
under 20 318.2
20-34 318.1
35-49 318.0
50-70 317
IRDS 769
Irideremia 743.45
Iridis rubeosis 364.42
diabetic 250.5 ☑ *[364.42]*
Iridis rubeosis — *continued*
diabetic — *continued*
due to secondary diabetes ●
249.5 ☑ *[364.42]* ●
Iridochoroiditis (panuveitis) 360.12
Iridocyclitis NEC 364.3
acute 364.00
primary 364.01
recurrent 364.02
chronic 364.10
in
lepromatous leprosy 030.0 *[364.11]*
sarcoidosis 135 *[364.11]*
tuberculosis (*see also* Tuberculosis) 017.3 ☑ *[364.11]*
due to allergy 364.04
endogenous 364.01
gonococcal 098.41
granulomatous 364.10
herpetic (simplex) 054.44
zoster 053.22
hypopyon 364.05
lens induced 364.23
nongranulomatous 364.00
primary 364.01
recurrent 364.02
rheumatic 364.10
secondary 364.04
infectious 364.03
noninfectious 364.04
subacute 364.00
primary 364.01
recurrent 364.02
sympathetic 360.11
syphilitic (secondary) 091.52
tuberculous (chronic) (*see also* Tuberculosis) 017.3 ☑ *[364.11]*
Iridocyclochoroiditis (panuveitis) 360.12
Iridodialysis 364.76
Iridodonesis 364.89
Iridoplegia (complete) (partial) (reflex) 379.49
Iridoschisis 364.52
Iris — *see* condition
Iritis 364.3
acute 364.00
primary 364.01
recurrent 364.02
chronic 364.10
in
sarcoidosis 135 *[364.11]*
tuberculosis (*see also* Tuberculosis) 017.3 ☑ *[364.11]*
diabetic 250.5 ☑ *[364.42]*
due to secondary diabetes ●
249.5 ☑ *[364.42]* ●
due to
allergy 364.04
herpes simplex 054.44
leprosy 030.0 *[364.11]*
endogenous 364.01
gonococcal 098.41
gouty 274.89 *[364.11]*
granulomatous 364.10
hypopyon 364.05
lens induced 364.23
nongranulomatous 364.00
papulosa 095.8 *[364.11]*
primary 364.01
recurrent 364.02
rheumatic 364.10
secondary 364.04
infectious 364.03
noninfectious 364.04
subacute 364.00
primary 364.01
recurrent 364.02
sympathetic 360.11
syphilitic (secondary) 091.52
congenital 090.0 *[364.11]*
late 095.8 *[364.11]*
tuberculous (*see also* Tuberculosis) 017.3 ☑ *[364.11]*
uratic 274.89 *[364.11]*
Iron
deficiency anemia 280.9
metabolism disease 275.0
storage disease 275.0
Iron-miners' lung 503
Irradiated enamel (tooth, teeth) 521.89
Irradiation
burn — *see* Burn, by site
effects, adverse 990
Irreducible, irreducibility — *see* condition
Irregular, irregularity
action, heart 427.9
alveolar process 525.8
bleeding NEC 626.4
breathing 786.09
colon 569.89
contour
acquired 371.70
of cornea 743.41 ●
acquired 371.70 ●
reconstructed breast 612.0 ●
dentin in pulp 522.3
eye movements NEC 379.59
menstruation (cause unknown) 626.4
periods 626.4
prostate 602.9
pupil 364.75
respiratory 786.09
septum (nasal) 470
shape, organ or site, congenital NEC — *see* Distortion
sleep-wake rhythm (non-24-hour) 327.39
nonorganic origin 307.45
vertebra 733.99
Irritability (nervous) 799.2
bladder 596.8
neurogenic 596.54
with cauda equina syndrome 344.61
bowel (syndrome) 564.1
bronchial (*see also* Bronchitis) 490
cerebral, newborn 779.1
colon 564.1
psychogenic 306.4
duodenum 564.89
heart (psychogenic) 306.2
ileum 564.89
jejunum 564.89
myocardium 306.2
rectum 564.89
stomach 536.9
psychogenic 306.4
sympathetic (nervous system) (*see also* Neuropathy, peripheral, autonomic) 337.9
urethra 599.84
ventricular (heart) (psychogenic) 306.2
Irritable — *see* Irritability
Irritation
anus 569.49
axillary nerve 353.0
bladder 596.8
brachial plexus 353.0
brain (traumatic) (*see also* Injury, intracranial) 854.0 ☑
nontraumatic — *see* Encephalitis
bronchial (*see also* Bronchitis) 490
cerebral (traumatic) (*see also* Injury, intracranial) 854.0 ☑
nontraumatic — *see* Encephalitis
cervical plexus 353.2
cervix (*see also* Cervicitis) 616.0
choroid, sympathetic 360.11
cranial nerve — *see* Disorder, nerve, cranial
digestive tract 536.9
psychogenic 306.4
gastric 536.9
psychogenic 306.4
gastrointestinal (tract) 536.9
functional 536.9
psychogenic 306.4
globe, sympathetic 360.11
intestinal (bowel) 564.9

Irritation — *continued*
labyrinth 386.50
lumbosacral plexus 353.1
meninges (traumatic) (*see also* Injury, intracranial) 854.0 ☑
nontraumatic — *see* Meningitis
myocardium 306.2
nerve — *see* Disorder, nerve
nervous 799.2
nose 478.19
penis 607.89
perineum 709.9
peripheral
autonomic nervous system (*see also* Neuropathy, peripheral, autonomic) 337.9
nerve — *see* Disorder, nerve
peritoneum (*see also* Peritonitis) 567.9
pharynx 478.29
plantar nerve 355.6
spinal (cord) (traumatic) (*see also* Injury, spinal, by site)
nerve (*see also* Disorder, nerve)
root NEC 724.9
traumatic — *see* Injury, nerve, spinal
nontraumatic — *see* Myelitis
stomach 536.9
psychogenic 306.4
sympathetic nerve NEC (*see also* Neuropathy, peripheral, autonomic) 337.9
ulnar nerve 354.2
vagina 623.9
Isambert's disease 012.3 ☑
Ischemia, ischemic 459.9
basilar artery (with transient neurologic deficit) 435.0
bone NEC 733.40
bowel (transient) 557.9
acute 557.0
chronic 557.1
due to mesenteric artery insufficiency 557.1
brain (*see also* Ischemia, cerebral)
recurrent focal 435.9
cardiac (*see also* Ischemia, heart) 414.9
cardiomyopathy 414.8

Ischemia, ischemic — *continued*
carotid artery (with transient neurologic deficit) 435.8
cerebral (chronic) (generalized) 437.1
arteriosclerotic 437.0
intermittent (with transient neurologic deficit) 435.9
newborn 779.2
puerperal, postpartum, childbirth 674.0 ☑
recurrent focal (with transient neurologic deficit) 435.9
transient (with transient neurologic deficit) 435.9
colon 557.9
acute 557.0
chronic 557.1
due to mesenteric artery insufficiency 557.1
coronary (chronic) (*see also* Ischemia, heart) 414.9
heart (chronic or with a stated duration of over 8 weeks) 414.9
acute or with a stated duration of 8 weeks or less (*see also* Infarct, myocardium) 410.9 ☑
without myocardial infarction 411.89
with coronary (artery) occlusion 411.81
subacute 411.89
intestine (transient) 557.9
acute 557.0
chronic 557.1
due to mesenteric artery insufficiency 557.1
kidney 593.81
labyrinth 386.50
muscles, leg 728.89
myocardium, myocardial (chronic or with a stated duration of over 8 weeks) 414.8
acute (*see also* Infarct, myocardium) 410.9 ☑
without myocardial infarction 411.89
with coronary (artery) occlusion 411.81
renal 593.81
retina, retinal 362.84

Ischemia, ischemic — *continued*
small bowel 557.9
acute 557.0
chronic 557.1
due to mesenteric artery insufficiency 557.1
spinal cord 336.1
subendocardial (*see also* Insufficiency, coronary) 411.89
vertebral artery (with transient neurologic deficit) 435.1
Ischialgia — *see also* Sciatica 724.3
Ischiopagus 759.4
Ischium, ischial — *see* condition
Ischomenia 626.8
Ischuria 788.5
Iselin's disease or osteochondrosis 732.5
Islands of
parotid tissue in
lymph nodes 750.26
neck structures 750.26
submaxillary glands in
fascia 750.26
lymph nodes 750.26
neck muscles 750.26
Islet cell tumor, pancreas (M8150/0) 211.7
Isoimmunization NEC — *see also* Incompatibility 656.2 ☑
anti-E 656.2 ☑
fetus or newborn 773.2
ABO blood groups 773.1
Rhesus (Rh) factor 773.0
Isolation V07.0
social V62.4
Isosporosis 007.2
Issue
medical certificate NEC V68.09
cause of death V68.09
disability examination V68.01
fitness V68.09
incapacity V68.09
repeat prescription NEC V68.1
appliance V68.1
contraceptive V25.40
device NEC V25.49
intrauterine V25.42
specified type NEC V25.49
pill V25.41

Issue — *continued*
repeat prescription — *continued*
glasses V68.1
medicinal substance V68.1
Itch — *see also* Pruritus 698.9
bakers' 692.89
barbers' 110.0
bricklayers' 692.89
cheese 133.8
clam diggers' 120.3
coolie 126.9
copra 133.8
Cuban 050.1
dew 126.9
dhobie 110.3
eye 379.99
filarial (*see also* Infestation, filarial) 125.9
grain 133.8
grocers' 133.8
ground 126.9
harvest 133.8
jock 110.3
Malabar 110.9
beard 110.0
foot 110.4
scalp 110.0
meaning scabies 133.0
Norwegian 133.0
perianal 698.0
poultrymen's 133.8
sarcoptic 133.0
scrub 134.1
seven year V61.10
meaning scabies 133.0
straw 133.8
swimmers' 120.3
washerwoman's 692.4
water 120.3
winter 698.8
Itsenko-Cushing syndrome (pituitary basophilism) 255.0
Ivemark's syndrome (asplenia with congenital heart disease) 759.0
Ivory bones 756.52
Ixodes 134.8
Ixodiasis 134.8

J

- **Jaccoud's nodular fibrositis, chronic** (Jaccoud's syndrome) 714.4
- **Jackson's**
  - membrane 751.4
  - paralysis or syndrome 344.89
  - veil 751.4
- **Jacksonian**
  - epilepsy (*see also* Epilepsy) 345.5 ☑
  - seizures (focal) (*see also* Epilepsy) 345.5 ☑
- **Jacob's ulcer** (M8090/3) — *see* Neoplasm, skin, malignant, by site
- **Jacquet's dermatitis** (diaper dermatitis) 691.0
- **Jadassohn's**
  - blue nevus (M8780/0) — *see* Neoplasm, skin, benign
  - disease (maculopapular erythroderma) 696.2
  - intraepidermal epithelioma (M8096/0) — *see* Neoplasm, skin, benign
- **Jadassohn-Lewandowski syndrome** (pachyonychia congenita) 757.5
- **Jadassohn-Pellizari's disease** (anetoderma) 701.3
- **Jadassohn-Tièche nevus** (M8780/0) — *see* Neoplasm, skin, benign
- **Jaffe-Lichtenstein (-Uehlinger) syndrome** 252.01
- **Jahnke's syndrome** (encephalocutaneous angiomatosis) 759.6
- **Jakob-Creutzfeldt disease** ▶(CJD)◀ (syndrome) 046.19 ▲
  - with dementia
    - with behavioral disturbance 046.19 *[294.11]* ▲
    - without behavioral disturbance 046.19 *[294.10]* ▲
  - familial 046.19 ●
  - iatrogenic 046.19 ●
  - specified NEC 046.19 ●
  - sporadic 046.19 ●
  - variant (vCJD) 046.11 ●
    - with dementia ●
      - with behavioral disturbance 046.11 *[294.11]* ●
      - without behavioral disturbance 046.11 *[294.10]* ●
- **Jaksch (-Luzet) disease or syndrome** (pseudoleukemia infantum) 285.8
- **Jamaican**
  - neuropathy 349.82
  - paraplegic tropical ataxic-spastic syndrome 349.82
- **Janet's disease** (psychasthenia) 300.89
- **Janiceps** 759.4
- **Jansky-Bielschowsky amaurotic familial idiocy** 330.1
- **Japanese**
  - B type encephalitis 062.0
  - river fever 081.2
  - seven-day fever 100.89
- **Jaundice** (yellow) 782.4
  - acholuric (familial) (splenomegalic) (*see also* Spherocytosis) 282.0
    - acquired 283.9
  - breast milk 774.39
  - catarrhal (acute) 070.1
    - with hepatic coma 070.0
    - chronic 571.9
    - epidemic — *see* Jaundice, epidemic
  - cholestatic (benign) 782.4
  - chronic idiopathic 277.4
  - epidemic (catarrhal) 070.1
    - with hepatic coma 070.0
    - leptospiral 100.0
    - spirochetal 100.0
  - febrile (acute) 070.1
    - with hepatic coma 070.0
    - leptospiral 100.0
    - spirochetal 100.0
  - fetus or newborn 774.6

Jaundice — *continued*
  - fetus or newborn — *continued*
    - due to or associated with
      - ABO
        - absence or deficiency of enzyme system for bilirubin conjugation (congenital) 774.39
        - antibodies 773.1
        - blood group incompatibility NEC 773.2
        - breast milk inhibitors to conjugation 774.39
          - associated with preterm delivery 774.2
        - bruising 774.1
        - Crigler-Najjar syndrome 277.4 *[774.31]*
        - delayed conjugation 774.30
          - associated with preterm delivery 774.2
          - development 774.39
        - drugs or toxins transmitted from mother 774.1
        - G-6-PD deficiency 282.2 *[774.0]*
        - galactosemia 271.1 *[774.5]*
        - Gilbert's syndrome 277.4 *[774.31]*
        - hepatocellular damage 774.4
        - hereditary hemolytic anemia (*see also* Anemia, hemolytic) 282.9 *[774.0]*
        - hypothyroidism, congenital 243 *[774.31]*
        - incompatibility, maternal/fetal NEC 773.2
        - incompatibility, maternal/fetal 773.1
        - infection 774.1
        - inspissated bile syndrome 774.4
        - isoimmunization NEC 773.2
        - isoimmunization 773.1
        - mucoviscidosis 277.01 *[774.5]*
        - obliteration of bile duct, congenital 751.61 *[774.5]*
        - polycythemia 774.1
        - preterm delivery 774.2
        - red cell defect 282.9 *[774.0]*
        - Rh
          - antibodies 773.0
          - incompatibility, maternal/fetal 773.0
          - isoimmunization 773.0
        - spherocytosis (congenital) 282.0 *[774.0]*
        - swallowed maternal blood 774.1
    - physiological NEC 774.6
  - from injection, inoculation, infusion, or transfusion (blood) (plasma) (serum) (other substance) (onset within 8 months after administration) — *see* Hepatitis, viral
  - Gilbert's (familial nonhemolytic) 277.4
  - hematogenous 283.9
  - hemolytic (acquired) 283.9
    - congenital (*see also* Spherocytosis) 282.0
  - hemorrhagic (acute) 100.0
    - leptospiral 100.0
    - newborn 776.0
    - spirochetal 100.0
  - hepatocellular 573.8
  - homologous (serum) — *see* Hepatitis, viral
  - idiopathic, chronic 277.4
  - infectious (acute) (subacute) 070.1
    - with hepatic coma 070.0
    - leptospiral 100.0
    - spirochetal 100.0
  - leptospiral 100.0
  - malignant (*see also* Necrosis, liver) 570
  - newborn (physiological) (*see also* Jaundice, fetus or newborn) 774.6
  - nonhemolytic, congenital familial (Gilbert's) 277.4

Jaundice — *continued*
  - nuclear, newborn (*see also* Kernicterus of newborn) 774.7
  - obstructive NEC (*see also* Obstruction, biliary) 576.8
  - postimmunization — *see* Hepatitis, viral
  - posttransfusion — *see* Hepatitis, viral
  - regurgitation (*see also* Obstruction, biliary) 576.8
  - serum (homologous) (prophylactic) (therapeutic) — *see* Hepatitis, viral
  - spirochetal (hemorrhagic) 100.0
  - symptomatic 782.4
    - newborn 774.6
- **Jaw** — *see* condition
- **Jaw-blinking** 374.43
  - congenital 742.8
- **Jaw-winking phenomenon or syndrome** 742.8
- **Jealousy**
  - alcoholic 291.5
  - childhood 313.3
  - sibling 313.3
- **Jejunitis** — *see also* Enteritis 558.9
- **Jejunostomy status** V44.4
- **Jejunum, jejunal** — *see* condition
- **Jensen's disease** 363.05
- **Jericho boil** 085.1
- **Jerks, myoclonic** 333.2
- **Jervell-Lange-Nielsen syndrome** 426.82
- **Jeune's disease or syndrome** (asphyxiating thoracic dystrophy) 756.4
- **Jigger disease** 134.1
- **Job's syndrome** (chronic granulomatous disease) 288.1
- **Jod-Basedow phenomenon** 242.8 ☑
- **Johnson-Stevens disease** (erythema multiforme exudativum) 695.13 ▲
- **Joint** — *see also* condition
  - Charcôt's 094.0 *[713.5]*
  - false 733.82
  - flail — *see* Flail, joint
  - mice — *see* Loose, body, joint, by site
  - sinus to bone 730.9 ☑
  - von Gies' 095.8
- **Jordan's anomaly or syndrome** 288.2
- **Josephs-Diamond-Blackfan anemia** (congenital hypoplastic) 284.01
- **Joubert syndrome** 759.89
- **Jumpers' knee** 727.2
- **Jungle yellow fever** 060.0
- **Jüngling's disease** (sarcoidosis) 135
- **Junin virus hemorrhagic fever** 078.7
- **Juvenile** — *see also* condition
  - delinquent 312.9
    - group (*see also* Disturbance, conduct) 312.2 ☑
    - neurotic 312.4

K

- **Kabuki syndrome** 759.89
- **Kahler (-Bozzolo) disease** (multiple myeloma) (M9730/3) 203.0 ☑
- **Kakergasia** 300.9
- **Kakke** 265.0
- **Kala-azar** (Indian) (infantile) (Mediterranean) (Sudanese) 085.0
- **Kalischer's syndrome** (encephalocutaneous angiomatosis) 759.6
- **Kallmann's syndrome** (hypogonadotropic hypogonadism with anosmia) 253.4
- **Kanner's syndrome** (autism) — *see also* Psychosis, childhood 299.0 ☑
- **Kaolinosis** 502
- **Kaposi's**
  - disease 757.33
    - lichen ruber 696.4
      - acuminatus 696.4
      - moniliformis 697.8
    - xeroderma pigmentosum 757.33
  - sarcoma (M9140/3) 176.9
    - adipose tissue 176.1

Kaposi's — *continued*
  - sarcoma — *continued*
    - aponeurosis 176.1
    - artery 176.1
    - associated herpesvirus infection 058.89
    - blood vessel 176.1
    - bursa 176.1
    - connective tissue 176.1
    - external genitalia 176.8
    - fascia 176.1
    - fatty tissue 176.1
    - fibrous tissue 176.1
    - gastrointestinal tract NEC 176.3
    - ligament 176.1
    - lung 176.4
    - lymph
      - gland(s) 176.5
      - node(s) 176.5
    - lymphatic(s) NEC 176.1
    - muscle (skeletal) 176.1
    - oral cavity NEC 176.8
    - palate 176.2
    - scrotum 176.8
    - skin 176.0
    - soft tissue 176.1
    - specified site NEC 176.8
    - subcutaneous tissue 176.1
    - synovia 176.1
    - tendon (sheath) 176.1
    - vein 176.1
    - vessel 176.1
    - viscera NEC 176.9
    - vulva 176.8
  - varicelliform eruption 054.0
    - vaccinia 999.0
- **Kartagener's syndrome or triad** (sinusitis, bronchiectasis, situs inversus) 759.3
- **Kasabach-Merritt syndrome** (capillary hemangioma associated with thrombocytopenic purpura) 287.39
- **Kaschin-Beck disease** (endemic polyarthritis) — *see* Disease, Kaschin-Beck
- **Kast's syndrome** (dyschondroplasia with hemangiomas) 756.4
- **Katatonia** — *see* Catatonia
- **Katayama disease or fever** 120.2
- **Kathisophobia** 781.0
- **Kawasaki disease** 446.1
- **Kayser-Fleischer ring** (cornea) (pseudosclerosis) 275.1 *[371.14]*
- **Kaznelson's syndrome** (congenital hypoplastic anemia) 284.01
- **Kearns-Sayre syndrome** 277.87
- **Kedani fever** 081.2
- **Kelis** 701.4
- **Kelly (-Patterson) syndrome** (sideropenic dysphagia) 280.8
- **Keloid, cheloid** 701.4
  - Addison's (morphea) 701.0
  - cornea 371.00
  - Hawkins' 701.4
  - scar 701.4
- **Keloma** 701.4
- **Kenya fever** 082.1
- **Keratectasia** 371.71
  - congenital 743.41
- **Keratinization NEC**
  - alveolar ridge mucosa
    - excessive 528.72
    - minimal 528.71
- **Keratitis** (nodular) (nonulcerative) (simple) (zonular) NEC 370.9
  - with ulceration (*see also* Ulcer, cornea) 370.00
  - actinic 370.24
  - arborescens 054.42
  - areolar 370.22
  - bullosa 370.8
  - deep — *see* Keratitis, interstitial
  - dendritic(a) 054.42
  - desiccation 370.34
  - diffuse interstitial 370.52
  - disciform(is) 054.43

☑ Additional Digit Required — Refer to the Tabular List for Digit Selection

▽ Subterms under main terms may continue to next column or page

▶◀ Revised Text ● New Line ▲ Revised Code

Keratitis — *continued*
- disciform — *continued*
  - varicella 052.7 *[370.44]*
- epithelialis vernalis 372.13 *[370.32]*
- exposure 370.34
- filamentary 370.23
- gonococcal (congenital) (prenatal) 098.43
- herpes, herpetic (simplex) NEC 054.43
  - zoster 053.21
- hypopyon 370.04
- in
  - chickenpox 052.7 *[370.44]*
  - exanthema (*see also* Exanthem) 057.9 *[370.44]*
  - paravaccinia (*see also* Paravaccinia) 051.9 *[370.44]*
  - smallpox (*see also* Smallpox) 050.9 *[370.44]*
  - vernal conjunctivitis 372.13 *[370.32]*
- interstitial (nonsyphilitic) 370.50
  - with ulcer (*see also* Ulcer, cornea) 370.00
  - diffuse 370.52
  - herpes, herpetic (simplex) 054.43
    - zoster 053.21
  - syphilitic (congenital) (hereditary) 090.3
  - tuberculous (*see also* Tuberculosis) 017.3 ☑ *[370.59]*
- lagophthalmic 370.34
- macular 370.22
- neuroparalytic 370.35
- neurotrophic 370.35
- nummular 370.22
- oyster-shuckers' 370.8
- parenchymatous — *see* Keratitis, interstitial
- petrificans 370.8
- phlyctenular 370.31
- postmeasles 055.71
- punctata, punctate 370.21
  - leprosa 030.0 *[370.21]*
  - profunda 090.3
  - superficial (Thygeson's) 370.21
- purulent 370.8
- pustuliformis profunda 090.3
- rosacea 695.3 *[370.49]*
- sclerosing 370.54
- specified type NEC 370.8
- stellate 370.22
- striate 370.22
- superficial 370.20
  - with conjunctivitis (*see also* Keratoconjunctivitis) 370.40
  - punctate (Thygeson's) 370.21
- suppurative 370.8
- syphilitic (congenital) (prenatal) 090.3
- trachomatous 076.1
  - late effect 139.1
- tuberculous (phlyctenular) (see also Tuberculosis) 017.3 ☑ *[370.31]*
- ulcerated (*see also* Ulcer, cornea) 370.00
- vesicular 370.8
- welders' 370.24
- xerotic (*see also* Keratomalacia) 371.45
  - vitamin A deficiency 264.4

Keratoacanthoma 238.2

Keratocele 371.72

Keratoconjunctivitis — *see also* Keratitis 370.40
- adenovirus type 8 077.1
- epidemic 077.1
- exposure 370.34
- gonococcal 098.43
- herpetic (simplex) 054.43
  - zoster 053.21
- in
  - chickenpox 052.7 *[370.44]*
  - exanthema (*see also* Exanthem) 057.9 *[370.44]*
  - paravaccinia (*see also* Paravaccinia) 051.9 *[370.44]*

Keratoconjunctivitis — *see also* Keratitis — *continued*
- in — *continued*
  - smallpox (*see also* Smallpox) 050.9 *[370.44]*
- infectious 077.1
- neurotrophic 370.35
- phlyctenular 370.31
- postmeasles 055.71
- shipyard 077.1
- sicca (Sjögren's syndrome) 710.2
  - not in Sjögren's syndrome 370.33
- specified type NEC 370.49
- tuberculous (phlyctenular) (*see also* Tuberculosis) 017.3 ☑ *[370.31]*

Keratoconus 371.60
- acute hydrops 371.62
- congenital 743.41
- stable 371.61

Keratocyst (dental) 526.0

Keratoderma, keratodermia (congenital) (palmaris et plantaris) (symmetrical) 757.39
- acquired 701.1
- blennorrhagica 701.1
  - gonococcal 098.81
- climacterium 701.1
- eccentrica 757.39
- gonorrheal 098.81
- punctata 701.1
- tylodes, progressive 701.1

Keratodermatocele 371.72

Keratoglobus 371.70
- congenital 743.41
  - associated with buphthalmos 743.22

Keratohemia 371.12

Keratoiritis — *see also* Iridocyclitis 364.3
- syphilitic 090.3
- tuberculous (*see also* Tuberculosis) 017.3 ☑ *[364.11]*

Keratolysis exfoliativa (congenital) 757.39
- acquired 695.89
- neonatorum 757.39

Keratoma 701.1
- congenital 757.39
- malignum congenitale 757.1
- palmaris et plantaris hereditarium 757.39
- senile 702.0

Keratomalacia 371.45
- vitamin A deficiency 264.4

Keratomegaly 743.41

Keratomycosis 111.1
- nigricans (palmaris) 111.1

Keratopathy 371.40
- band (*see also* Keratitis) 371.43
- bullous (*see also* Keratitis) 371.23
- degenerative (*see also* Degeneration, cornea) 371.40
  - hereditary (*see also* Dystrophy, cornea) 371.50
- discrete colliquative 371.49

Keratoscleritis, tuberculous — *see also* Tuberculosis 017.3 ☑ *[370.31]*

Keratosis 701.1
- actinic 702.0
- arsenical 692.4
- blennorrhagica 701.1
  - gonococcal 098.81
- congenital (any type) 757.39
- ear (middle) (*see also* Cholesteatoma) 385.30
- female genital (external) 629.89
- follicularis 757.39
  - acquired 701.1
  - congenital (acneiformis) (Siemens') 757.39
  - spinulosa (decalvans) 757.39
  - vitamin A deficiency 264.8
- follicular, vitamin A deficiency 264.8
- gonococcal 098.81
- larynx, laryngeal 478.79
- male genital (external) 608.89

Keratosis — *continued*
- middle ear (*see also* Cholesteatoma) 385.30
- nigricans 701.2
  - congenital 757.39
- obturans 380.21
- oral epithelium
  - residual ridge mucosa
    - excessive 528.72
    - minimal 528.71
- palmaris et plantaris (symmetrical) 757.39
- penile 607.89
- pharyngeus 478.29
- pilaris 757.39
  - acquired 701.1
- punctata (palmaris et plantaris) 701.1
- scrotal 608.89
- seborrheic 702.19
  - inflamed 702.11
- senilis 702.0
- solar 702.0
- suprafollicularis 757.39
- tonsillaris 478.29
- vagina 623.1
- vegetans 757.39
- vitamin A deficiency 264.8

Kerato-uveitis — *see also* Iridocyclitis 364.3

Keraunoparalysis 994.0

Kerion (celsi) 110.0

Kernicterus of newborn (not due to isoimmunization) 774.7
- due to isoimmunization (conditions classifiable to 773.0–773.2) 773.4

Ketoacidosis 276.2
- diabetic 250.1 ☑
  - due to secondary diabetes 249.1 ☑ ●

Ketonuria 791.6
- branched-chain, intermittent 270.3

Ketosis 276.2
- diabetic 250.1 ☑
  - due to secondary diabetes 249.1 ☑ ●

Kidney — *see* condition

Kienböck's
- disease 732.3
  - adult 732.8
- osteochondrosis 732.3

Kimmelstiel (-Wilson) disease or syndrome (intercapillary glomerulosclerosis) 250.4 ☑ *[581.81]*
- due to secondary diabetes 249.4 ☑ *[581.81]* ●

Kink, kinking
- appendix 543.9
- artery 447.1
- cystic duct, congenital 751.61
- hair (acquired) 704.2
- ileum or intestine (*see also* Obstruction, intestine) 560.9
- Lane's (*see also* Obstruction, intestine) 560.9
- organ or site, congenital NEC — *see* Anomaly, specified type NEC, by site
- ureter (pelvic junction) 593.3
  - congenital 753.20
- vein(s) 459.2
  - caval 459.2
  - peripheral 459.2

Kinnier Wilson's disease (hepatolenticular degeneration) 275.1

Kissing
- osteophytes 721.5
- spine 721.5
- vertebra 721.5

Klauder's syndrome (erythema multiforme, exudativum) 695.19 ▲

Klebs' disease — *see also* Nephritis 583.9

Kleine-Levin syndrome 327.13

Klein-Waardenburg syndrome (ptosisepicanthus) 270.2

Kleptomania 312.32

Klinefelter's syndrome 758.7

Klinger's disease 446.4

Klippel's disease 723.8

Klippel-Feil disease or syndrome (brevicollis) 756.16

Klippel-Trenaunay syndrome 759.89

Klumpke (-Déjérine) palsy, paralysis (birth) (newborn) 767.6

Klüver-Bucy (-Terzian) syndrome 310.0

Knee — *see* condition

Knifegrinders' rot — *see also* Tuberculosis 011.4 ☑

Knock-knee (acquired) 736.41
- congenital 755.64

Knot
- intestinal, syndrome (volvulus) 560.2
- umbilical cord (true) 663.2 ☑
  - affecting fetus or newborn 762.5

Knots, surfer 919.8
- infected 919.9

Knotting (of)
- hair 704.2
- intestine 560.2

Knuckle pads (Garrod's) 728.79

Köbner's disease (epidermolysis bullosa) 757.39

Koch's
- infection (*see also* Tuberculosis, pulmonary) 011.9 ☑
- relapsing fever 087.9

Koch-Weeks conjunctivitis 372.03

Koenig-Wichman disease (pemphigus) 694.4

Köhler's disease (osteochondrosis) 732.5
- first (osteochondrosis juvenilis) 732.5
- second (Freiburg's infarction, metatarsal head) 732.5
- patellar 732.4
- tarsal navicular (bone) (osteoarthrosis juvenilis) 732.5

Köhler-Mouchet disease (osteoarthrosis juvenilis) 732.5

Köhler-Pellegrini-Stieda disease or syndrome (calcification, knee joint) 726.62

Koilonychia 703.8
- congenital 757.5

Kojevnikov's, Kojewnikoff's epilepsy — *see also* Epilepsy 345.7 ☑

König's
- disease (osteochondritis dissecans) 732.7
- syndrome 564.89

Koniophthisis — *see also* Tuberculosis 011.4 ☑

Koplik's spots 055.9

Kopp's asthma 254.8

Korean hemorrhagic fever 078.6

Korsakoff (-Wernicke) disease, psychosis, or syndrome (nonalcoholic) 294.0
- alcoholic 291.1

Korsakov's disease — *see* Korsakoff's disease

Korsakow's disease — *see* Korsakoff's disease

Kostmann's disease or syndrome (infantile genetic agranulocytosis) 288.01

Krabbe's
- disease (leukodystrophy) 330.0
- syndrome
  - congenital muscle hypoplasia 756.89
  - cutaneocerebral angioma 759.6

Kraepelin-Morel disease — *see also* Schizophrenia 295.9 ☑

Kraft-Weber-Dimitri disease 759.6

Kraurosis
- ani 569.49
- penis 607.0
- vagina 623.8
- vulva 624.09

Kreotoxism 005.9

Krukenberg's
- spindle 371.13

☑ Additional Digit Required — Refer to the Tabular List for Digit Selection

▼ Subterms under main terms may continue to next column or page

▶◀ Revised Text ● New Line ▲ Revised Code

- **Krukenberg's** — *continued*
  - tumor (M8490/6) 198.6
- **Kufs' disease** 330.1
- **Kugelberg-Welander disease** 335.11
- **Kuhnt-Junius degeneration or disease** 362.52
- **Kulchitsky's cell carcinoma** (carcinoid tumor of intestine) 259.2
- **Kümmell's disease or spondylitis** 721.7
- **Kundrat's disease** (lymphosarcoma) 200.1 ☑
- **Kunekune** — *see* Dermatophytosis
- **Kunkel syndrome** (lupoid hepatitis) 571.49
- **Kupffer cell sarcoma** (M9124/3) 155.0
- **Kuru** 046.0
- **Kussmaul's**
  - coma (diabetic) 250.3 ☑
    - due to secondary diabetes 249.3 ☑ ●
  - disease (polyarteritis nodosa) 446.0
  - respiration (air hunger) 786.09
- **Kwashiorkor** (marasmus type) 260
- **Kyasanur Forest disease** 065.2
- **Kyphoscoliosis, kyphoscoliotic** (acquired) — *see also* Scoliosis 737.30
  - congenital 756.19
  - due to radiation 737.33
  - heart (disease) 416.1
  - idiopathic 737.30
    - infantile
      - progressive 737.32
      - resolving 737.31
  - late effect of rickets 268.1 *[737.43]*
  - specified NEC 737.39
  - thoracogenic 737.34
  - tuberculous (*see also* Tuberculosis) 015.0 ☑ *[737.43]*
- **Kyphosis, kyphotic** (acquired) (postural) 737.10
  - adolescent postural 737.0
  - congenital 756.19
  - dorsalis juvenilis 732.0
  - due to or associated with
    - Charcôt-Marie-Tooth disease 356.1 *[737.41]*
    - mucopolysaccharidosis 277.5 *[737.41]*
    - neurofibromatosis 237.71 *[737.41]*
    - osteitis
      - deformans 731.0 *[737.41]*
      - fibrosa cystica 252.01 *[737.41]*
    - osteoporosis (*see also* Osteoporosis) 733.0 ☑ *[737.41]*
    - poliomyelitis (*see also* Poliomyelitis) 138 *[737.41]*
    - radiation 737.11
    - tuberculosis (*see also* Tuberculosis) 015.0 ☑ *[737.41]*
  - Kümmell's 721.7
  - late effect of rickets 268.1 *[737.41]*
  - Morquio-Brailsford type (spinal) 277.5 *[737.41]*
  - pelvis 738.6
  - postlaminectomy 737.12
  - specified cause NEC 737.19
  - syphilitic, congenital 090.5 *[737.41]*
  - tuberculous (*see also* Tuberculosis) 015.0 ☑ *[737.41]*
- **Kyrle's disease** (hyperkeratosis follicularis in cutem penetrans) 701.1

L

- **Labia, labium** — *see* condition
- **Labiated hymen** 752.49
- **Labile**
  - blood pressure 796.2
  - emotions, emotionality 301.3
  - vasomotor system 443.9
- **Labioglossal paralysis** 335.22
- **Labium leporinum** — *see also* Cleft, lip 749.10
- **Labor** — *see also* Delivery
  - with complications — *see* Delivery, complicated
  - abnormal NEC 661.9 ☑
- **Labor** — *see also* Delivery — *continued*
  - abnormal — *continued*
    - affecting fetus or newborn 763.7
  - arrested active phase 661.1 ☑
    - affecting fetus or newborn 763.7
  - desultory 661.2 ☑
    - affecting fetus or newborn 763.7
  - dyscoordinate 661.4 ☑
    - affecting fetus or newborn 763.7
  - early onset (22-36 weeks gestation) 644.2 ☑
  - failed
    - induction 659.1 ☑
      - mechanical 659.0 ☑
      - medical 659.1 ☑
      - surgical 659.0 ☑
    - trial (vaginal delivery) 660.6 ☑
  - false 644.1 ☑
  - forced or induced, affecting fetus or newborn 763.89
  - hypertonic 661.4 ☑
    - affecting fetus or newborn 763.7
  - hypotonic 661.2 ☑
    - affecting fetus or newborn 763.7
    - primary 661.0 ☑
      - affecting fetus or newborn 763.7
    - secondary 661.1 ☑
      - affecting fetus or newborn 763.7
  - incoordinate 661.4 ☑
    - affecting fetus or newborn 763.7
  - irregular 661.2 ☑
    - affecting fetus or newborn 763.7
  - long — *see* Labor, prolonged
  - missed (at or near term) 656.4 ☑
  - obstructed NEC 660.9 ☑
    - affecting fetus or newborn 763.1
    - due to female genital mutilation 660.8 ☑
    - specified cause NEC 660.8 ☑
      - affecting fetus or newborn 763.1
  - pains, spurious 644.1 ☑
  - precipitate 661.3 ☑
    - affecting fetus or newborn 763.6
  - premature 644.2 ☑
    - threatened 644.0 ☑
  - prolonged or protracted 662.1 ☑
    - first stage 662.0 ☑
      - affecting fetus or newborn 763.89
    - second stage 662.2 ☑
      - affecting fetus or newborn 763.89
    - affecting fetus or newborn 763.89
  - threatened NEC 644.1 ☑
  - undelivered 644.1 ☑
- **Labored breathing** — *see also* Hyperventilation 786.09
- **Labyrinthitis** (inner ear) (destructive) (latent) 386.30
  - circumscribed 386.32
  - diffuse 386.31
  - focal 386.32
  - purulent 386.33
  - serous 386.31
  - suppurative 386.33
  - syphilitic 095.8
  - toxic 386.34
  - viral 386.35
- **Laceration** — *see also* Wound, open, by site
  - accidental, complicating surgery 998.2
  - Achilles tendon 845.09
    - with open wound 892.2
  - anus (sphincter) 879.6
    - with
      - abortion — *see* Abortion, by type, with damage to pelvic organs
      - ectopic pregnancy (*see also* categories 633.0–633.9) 639.2
      - molar pregnancy (*see also* categories 630–632) 639.2
    - complicated 879.7
- **Laceration** — *see also* Wound, open, by site — *continued*
  - anus — *continued*
    - complicating delivery (healed) (old) 654.8 ☑
      - with laceration of anal or rectal mucosa 664.3 ☑
      - not associated with third-degree perineal laceration 664.6 ☑
    - following
      - abortion 639.2
      - ectopic or molar pregnancy 639.2
    - nontraumatic, nonpuerperal (healed) (old) 569.43
  - bladder (urinary)
    - with
      - abortion — *see* Abortion, by type, with damage to pelvic organs
      - ectopic pregnancy (*see also* categories 633.0–633.9) 639.2
      - molar pregnancy (*see also* categories 630–632) 639.2
    - following
      - abortion 639.2
      - ectopic or molar pregnancy 639.2
    - obstetrical trauma 665.5 ☑
  - blood vessel — *see* Injury, blood vessel, by site
  - bowel
    - with
      - abortion — *see* Abortion, by type, with damage to pelvic organs
      - ectopic pregnancy (*see also* categories 633.0–633.9) 639.2
      - molar pregnancy (*see also* categories 630–632) 639.2
    - following
      - abortion 639.2
      - ectopic or molar pregnancy 639.2
    - obstetrical trauma 665.5 ☑
  - brain (cerebral) (membrane) (with hemorrhage) 851.8 ☑

> *Note — Use the following fifth-digit subclassification with categories 851–854:*
>
> 0 *unspecified state of consciousness*
>
> 1 *with no loss of consciousness*
>
> 2 *with brief [less than one hour] loss of consciousness*
>
> 3 *with moderate [1–24 hours] loss of consciousness*
>
> 4 *with prolonged [more than 24 hours] loss of consciousness and return to pre-existing conscious level*
>
> 5 *with prolonged [more than 24 hours] loss of consciousness, without return to pre-existing conscious level*
>
> *Use fifth-digit 5 to designate when a patient is unconscious and dies before regaining consciousness, regardless of the duration of the loss of consciousness*
>
> 6 *with loss of consciousness of unspecified duration*
>
> 9 *with concussion, unspecified*

-
  -
    - with
      - open intracranial wound 851.9 ☑
      - skull fracture — *see* Fracture, skull, by site
    - cerebellum 851.6 ☑
- **Laceration** — *see also* Wound, open, by site — *continued*
  - brain — *continued*
    - cerebellum — *continued*
      - with open intracranial wound 851.7 ☑
    - cortex 851.2 ☑
      - with open intracranial wound 851.3 ☑
    - during birth 767.0
    - stem 851.6 ☑
      - with open intracranial wound 851.7 ☑
  - broad ligament
    - with
      - abortion — *see* Abortion, by type, with damage to pelvic organs
      - ectopic pregnancy (*see also* categories 633.0–633.9) 639.2
      - molar pregnancy (*see also* categories 630–632) 639.2
    - following
      - abortion 639.2
      - ectopic or molar pregnancy 639.2
    - nontraumatic 620.6
    - obstetrical trauma 665.6 ☑
    - syndrome (nontraumatic) 620.6
  - capsule, joint — *see* Sprain, by site
  - cardiac — *see* Laceration, heart
  - causing eversion of cervix uteri (old) 622.0
  - central, complicating delivery 664.4 ☑
  - cerebellum — *see* Laceration, brain, cerebellum
  - cerebral (*see also* Laceration, brain)
    - during birth 767.0
  - cervix (uteri)
    - with
      - abortion — *see* Abortion, by type, with damage to pelvic organs
      - ectopic pregnancy (*see also* categories 633.0–633.9) 639.2
      - molar pregnancy (*see also* categories 630–632) 639.2
    - following
      - abortion 639.2
      - ectopic or molar pregnancy 639.2
    - nonpuerperal, nontraumatic 622.3
    - obstetrical trauma (current) 665.3 ☑
    - old (postpartal) 622.3
    - traumatic — *see* Injury, internal, cervix
  - chordae heart 429.5
  - complicated 879.9
  - cornea — *see* Laceration, eyeball
    - superficial 918.1
  - cortex (cerebral) — *see* Laceration, brain, cortex
  - esophagus 530.89
  - eye(s) — *see* Laceration, ocular
  - eyeball NEC 871.4
    - with prolapse or exposure of intraocular tissue 871.1
    - penetrating — *see* Penetrating wound, eyeball
    - specified as without prolapse of intraocular tissue 871.0
  - eyelid NEC 870.8
    - full thickness 870.1
      - involving lacrimal passages 870.2
    - skin (and periocular area) 870.0
      - penetrating — *see* Penetrating wound, orbit
  - fourchette
    - with
      - abortion — *see* Abortion, by type, with damage to pelvic organs

Laceration — *see also* Wound, open, by site — *continued*
fourchette — *continued*
with — *continued*
ectopic pregnancy (*see also* categories 633.0–633.9) 639.2
molar pregnancy (*see also* categories 630–632) 639.2
complicating delivery 664.0 ☑
following
abortion 639.2
ectopic or molar pregnancy 639.2
heart (without penetration of heart chambers) 861.02
with
open wound into thorax 861.12
penetration of heart chambers 861.03
with open wound into thorax 861.13
hernial sac — *see* Hernia, by site
internal organ (abdomen) (chest) (pelvis) NEC — *see* Injury, internal, by site
NEC — *see* Injury, internal, by site
kidney (parenchyma) 866.02
with
complete disruption of parenchyma (rupture) 866.03
with open wound into cavity 866.13
open wound into cavity 866.12
labia
complicating delivery 664.0 ☑
ligament (*see also* Sprain, by site)
with open wound — *see* Wound, open, by site
liver 864.05
with open wound into cavity 864.15
major (disruption of hepatic parenchyma) 864.04
with open wound into cavity 864.14
minor (capsule only) 864.02
with open wound into cavity 864.12
moderate (involving parenchyma without major disruption) 864.03
with open wound into cavity 864.13
multiple 864.04
with open wound into cavity 864.14
stellate 864.04
with open wound into cavity 864.14
lung 861.22
with open wound into thorax 861.32
meninges — *see* Laceration, brain
meniscus (knee) (*see also* Tear, meniscus) 836.2
old 717.5
site other than knee (*see also* Sprain, by site)
old NEC (*see also* Disorder, cartilage, articular) 718.0 ☑
muscle (*see also* Sprain, by site)
with open wound — *see* Wound, open, by site
myocardium — *see* Laceration, heart
nerve — *see* Injury, nerve, by site
ocular NEC (*see also* Laceration, eyeball) 871.4
adnexa NEC 870.8
penetrating 870.3
with foreign body 870.4
orbit (eye) 870.8
penetrating 870.3
with foreign body 870.4

Laceration — *see also* Wound, open, by site — *continued*
pelvic
floor (muscles)
with
abortion — *see* Abortion, by type, with damage to pelvic organs
ectopic pregnancy (*see also* categories 633.0–633.9) 639.2
molar pregnancy (*see also* categories 630–632) 639.2
complicating delivery 664.1 ☑
following
abortion 639.2
ectopic or molar pregnancy 639.2
nonpuerperal 618.7
old (postpartal) 618.7
organ NEC
with
abortion — *see* Abortion, by type, with damage to pelvic organs
ectopic pregnancy (*see also* categories 633.0–633.9) 639.2
molar pregnancy (*see also* categories 630–632) 639.2
complicating delivery 665.5 ☑
affecting fetus or newborn 763.89
following
abortion 639.2
ectopic or molar pregnancy 639.2
obstetrical trauma 665.5 ☑
perineum, perineal (old) (postpartal) 618.7
with
abortion — *see* Abortion, by type, with damage to pelvic floor
ectopic pregnancy (*see also* categories 633.0–633.9) 639.2
molar pregnancy (*see also* categories 630–632) 639.2
complicating delivery 664.4 ☑
first degree 664.0 ☑
second degree 664.1 ☑
third degree 664.2 ☑
fourth degree 664.3 ☑
anal sphincter (healed) (old) 654.8 ☑
not associated with third-degree perineal laceration 664.6 ☑
sphincter (anal) (healed) (old) 654.8 ☑
not associated with third-degree perineal laceration 664.6 ☑
central 664.4 ☑
involving
anal sphincter 664.2 ☑
fourchette 664.0 ☑
hymen 664.0 ☑
labia 664.0 ☑
pelvic floor 664.1 ☑
perineal muscles 664.1 ☑
rectovaginal septum 664.2 ☑
with anal mucosa 664.3 ☑
skin 664.0 ☑
sphincter (anal) 664.2 ☑
with anal mucosa 664.3 ☑
vagina 664.0 ☑
vaginal muscles 664.1 ☑
vulva 664.0 ☑
secondary 674.2 ☑

Laceration — *see also* Wound, open, by site — *continued*
perineum, perineal — *continued*
following
abortion 639.2
ectopic or molar pregnancy 639.2
male 879.6
complicated 879.7
muscles, complicating delivery 664.1 ☑
nonpuerperal, current injury 879.6
complicated 879.7
secondary (postpartal) 674.2 ☑
peritoneum
with
abortion — *see* Abortion, by type, with damage to pelvic organs
ectopic pregnancy (*see also* categories 633.0–633.9) 639.2
molar pregnancy (*see also* categories 630–632) 639.2
following
abortion 639.2
ectopic or molar pregnancy 639.2
obstetrical trauma 665.5 ☑
periurethral tissue
with
abortion — *see* Abortion, by type, with damage to pelvic organs
ectopic pregnancy (*see also* categories 633.0–633.9) 639.2
molar pregnancy (*see also* categories 630–632) 639.2
following
abortion 639.2
ectopic or molar pregnancy 639.2
obstetrical trauma 665.5 ☑
rectovaginal (septum)
with
abortion — *see* Abortion, by type, with damage to pelvic organs
ectopic pregnancy (*see also* categories 633.0–633.9) 639.2
molar pregnancy (*see also* categories 630–632) 639.2
complicating delivery 665.4 ☑
with perineum 664.2 ☑
involving anal or rectal mucosa 664.3 ☑
following
abortion 639.2
ectopic or molar pregnancy 639.2
nonpuerperal 623.4
old (postpartal) 623.4
spinal cord (meninges) (*see also* Injury, spinal, by site)
due to injury at birth 767.4
fetus or newborn 767.4
spleen 865.09
with
disruption of parenchyma (massive) 865.04
with open wound into cavity 865.14
open wound into cavity 865.19
capsule (without disruption of parenchyma) 865.02
with open wound into cavity 865.12
parenchyma 865.03
with open wound into cavity 865.13
massive disruption (rupture) 865.04
with open wound into cavity 865.14

Laceration — *see also* Wound, open, by site — *continued*
tendon 848.9
with open wound — *see* Wound, open, by site
Achilles 845.09
with open wound 892.2
lower limb NEC 844.9
with open wound NEC 894.2
upper limb NEC 840.9
with open wound NEC 884.2
tentorium cerebelli — *see* Laceration, brain, cerebellum
tongue 873.64
complicated 873.74
urethra
with
abortion — *see* Abortion, by type, with damage to pelvic organs
ectopic pregnancy (*see also* categories 633.0–633.9) 639.2
molar pregnancy (*see also* categories 630–632) 639.2
following
abortion 639.2
ectopic or molar pregnancy 639.2
nonpuerperal, nontraumatic 599.84
obstetrical trauma 665.5 ☑
uterus
with
abortion — *see* Abortion, by type, with damage to pelvic organs
ectopic pregnancy (*see also* categories 633.0–633.9) 639.2
molar pregnancy (*see also* categories 630–632) 639.2
following
abortion 639.2
ectopic or molar pregnancy 639.2
nonpuerperal, nontraumatic 621.8
obstetrical trauma NEC 665.5 ☑
old (postpartal) 621.8
vagina
with
abortion — *see* Abortion, by type, with damage to pelvic organs
ectopic pregnancy (*see also* categories 633.0–633.9) 639.2
molar pregnancy (*see also* categories 630–632) 639.2
perineal involvement, complicating delivery 664.0 ☑
complicating delivery 665.4 ☑
first degree 664.0 ☑
second degree 664.1 ☑
third degree 664.2 ☑
fourth degree 664.3 ☑
high 665.4 ☑
muscles 664.1 ☑
sulcus 665.4 ☑
wall 665.4 ☑
following
abortion 639.2
ectopic or molar pregnancy 639.2
nonpuerperal, nontraumatic 623.4
old (postpartal) 623.4
valve, heart — *see* Endocarditis
vulva
with
abortion — *see* Abortion, by type, with damage to pelvic organs
ectopic pregnancy (*see also* categories 633.0–633.9) 639.2

- **Laceration** — *see also* Wound, open, by site — *continued*
  - vulva — *continued*
    - with — *continued*
      - molar pregnancy (*see also* categories 630–632) 639.2
    - complicating delivery 664.0 ☑
    - following
      - abortion 639.2
      - ectopic or molar pregnancy 639.2
    - nonpuerperal, nontraumatic 624.4
    - old (postpartal) 624.4
- **Lachrymal** — *see* condition
- **Lachrymonasal duct** — *see* condition
- **Lack of**
  - adequate intermaxillary vertical dimension 524.36
  - appetite (*see also* Anorexia) 783.0
  - care
    - in home V60.4
    - of adult 995.84
    - of infant (at or after birth) 995.52
  - coordination 781.3
  - development (*see also* Hypoplasia)
    - physiological in childhood 783.40
  - education V62.3
  - energy 780.79
  - financial resources V60.2
  - food 994.2
    - in environment V60.8
  - growth in childhood 783.43
  - heating V60.1
  - housing (permanent) (temporary) V60.0
    - adequate V60.1
  - material resources V60.2
  - medical attention 799.89
  - memory (*see also* Amnesia) 780.93
    - mild, following organic brain damage 310.1
  - ovulation 628.0
  - person able to render necessary care V60.4
  - physical exercise V69.0
  - physiologic development in childhood 783.40
  - posterior occlusal support 524.57
  - prenatal care in current pregnancy V23.7
  - shelter V60.0
  - sleep V69.4
  - water 994.3
- **Lacrimal** — *see* condition
- **Lacrimation, abnormal** — *see also* Epiphora 375.20
- **Lacrimonasal duct** — *see* condition
- **Lactation, lactating** (breast) (puerperal) (postpartum)
  - defective 676.4 ☑
  - disorder 676.9 ☑
    - specified type NEC 676.8 ☑
  - excessive 676.6 ☑
  - failed 676.4 ☑
  - mastitis NEC 675.2 ☑
  - mother (care and/or examination) V24.1
  - nonpuerperal 611.6
  - suppressed 676.5 ☑
- **Lacticemia** 271.3
  - excessive 276.2
- **Lactosuria** 271.3
- **Lacunar skull** 756.0
- **Laennec's cirrhosis** (alcoholic) 571.2
  - nonalcoholic 571.5
- **Lafora's disease** 333.2
- **Lagleyze-von Hippel disease** (retinocerebral angiomatosis) 759.6
- **Lag, lid** (nervous) 374.41
- **Lagophthalmos** (eyelid) (nervous) 374.20
  - cicatricial 374.23
  - keratitis (*see also* Keratitis) 370.34
  - mechanical 374.22
  - paralytic 374.21
- **La grippe** — *see* Influenza
- **Lahore sore** 085.1
- **Lakes, venous** (cerebral) 437.8
- **Laki-Lorand factor deficiency** — *see also* Defect, coagulation 286.3
- **Lalling** 307.9
- **Lambliasis** 007.1
- **Lame back** 724.5
- **Lancereaux's diabetes** (diabetes mellitus with marked emaciation) 250.8 ☑ *[261]*
  - due to secondary diabetes ●
    - 249.8 ☑ *[261]* ●
- **Landau-Kleffner syndrome** 345.8 ☑ ●
- **Landouzy-Déjérine dystrophy** (fascioscapulohumeral atrophy) 359.1
- **Landry's disease or paralysis** 357.0
- **Landry-Guillain-Barré syndrome** 357.0
- **Lane's**
  - band 751.4
  - disease 569.89
  - kink (*see also* Obstruction, intestine) 560.9
- **Langdon Down's syndrome** (mongolism) 758.0
- **Language abolition** 784.69
- **Lanugo** (persistent) 757.4
- **Laparoscopic surgical procedure converted to open procedure** V64.41
- **Lardaceous**
  - degeneration (any site) 277.39
  - disease 277.39
  - kidney 277.39 *[583.81]*
  - liver 277.39
- **Large**
  - baby (regardless of gestational age) 766.1
    - exceptionally (weight of 4500 grams or more) 766.0
    - of diabetic mother 775.0
  - ear 744.22
  - fetus (*see also* Oversize, fetus)
    - causing disproportion 653.5 ☑
      - with obstructed labor 660.1 ☑
  - for dates
    - fetus or newborn (regardless of gestational age) 766.1
      - affecting management of pregnancy 656.6 ☑
      - exceptionally (weight of 4500 grams or more) 766.0
  - physiological cup 743.57
  - stature 783.9
  - waxy liver 277.39
  - white kidney — *see* Nephrosis
- **Larsen-Johansson disease** (juvenile osteopathia patellae) 732.4
- **Larsen's syndrome** (flattened facies and multiple congenital dislocations) 755.8
- **Larva migrans**
  - cutaneous NEC 126.9
    - ancylostoma 126.9
  - of Diptera in vitreous 128.0
  - visceral NEC 128.0
- **Laryngeal** — *see also* condition 786.2
  - syncope 786.2
- **Laryngismus** (acute) (infectious) (stridulous) 478.75
  - congenital 748.3
  - diphtheritic 032.3
- **Laryngitis** (acute) (edematous) (fibrinous) (gangrenous) (infective) (infiltrative) (malignant) (membranous) (phlegmonous) (pneumococcal) (pseudomembranous) (septic) (subglottic) (suppurative) (ulcerative) (viral) 464.00
  - with
    - influenza, flu, or grippe 487.1
    - obstruction 464.01
    - tracheitis (*see also* Laryngotracheitis) 464.20
      - with obstruction 464.21
      - acute 464.20
        - with obstruction 464.21
      - chronic 476.1
  - atrophic 476.0
- **Laryngitis** — *continued*
  - Borrelia vincentii 101
  - catarrhal 476.0
  - chronic 476.0
    - with tracheitis (chronic) 476.1
    - due to external agent — *see* Condition, respiratory, chronic, due to
  - diphtheritic (membranous) 032.3
  - due to external agent — *see* Inflammation, respiratory, upper, due to
  - Hemophilus influenzae 464.00
    - with obstruction 464.01
  - H. influenzae 464.00
    - with obstruction 464.01
  - hypertrophic 476.0
  - influenzal 487.1
  - pachydermic 478.79
  - sicca 476.0
  - spasmodic 478.75
    - acute 464.00
      - with obstruction 464.01
  - streptococcal 034.0
  - stridulous 478.75
  - syphilitic 095.8
    - congenital 090.5
  - tuberculous (*see also* Tuberculosis, larynx) 012.3 ☑
  - Vincent's 101
- **Laryngocele** (congenital) (ventricular) 748.3
- **Laryngofissure** 478.79
  - congenital 748.3
- **Laryngomalacia** (congenital) 748.3
- **Laryngopharyngitis** (acute) 465.0
  - chronic 478.9
    - due to external agent — *see* Condition, respiratory, chronic, due to
  - due to external agent — *see* Inflammation, respiratory, upper, due to
  - septic 034.0
- **Laryngoplegia** — *see also* Paralysis, vocal cord 478.30
- **Laryngoptosis** 478.79
- **Laryngospasm** 478.75
  - due to external agent — *see* Condition, respiratory, acute, due to
- **Laryngostenosis** 478.74
  - congenital 748.3
- **Laryngotracheitis** (acute) (infectional) (viral) — *see also* Laryngitis 464.20
  - with obstruction 464.21
  - atrophic 476.1
  - Borrelia vincenti 101
  - catarrhal 476.1
  - chronic 476.1
    - due to external agent — *see* Condition, respiratory, chronic, due to
  - diphtheritic (membranous) 032.3
  - due to external agent — *see* Inflammation, respiratory, upper, due to
  - H. influenzae 464.20
    - with obstruction 464.21
  - hypertrophic 476.1
  - influenzal 487.1
  - pachydermic 478.75
  - sicca 476.1
  - spasmodic 478.75
    - acute 464.20
      - with obstruction 464.21
  - streptococcal 034.0
  - stridulous 478.75
  - syphilitic 095.8
    - congenital 090.5
  - tuberculous (*see also* Tuberculosis, larynx) 012.3 ☑
  - Vincent's 101
- **Laryngotracheobronchitis** — *see also* Bronchitis 490
  - acute 466.0
  - chronic 491.8
  - viral 466.0
- **Laryngotracheobronchopneumonitis** — *see* Pneumonia, broncho-
- **Larynx, laryngeal** — *see* condition
- **Lasègue's disease** (persecution mania) 297.9
- **Lassa fever** 078.89
- **Lassitude** — *see also* Weakness 780.79
- **Late** — *see also* condition
  - effect(s) (of) (*see also* condition)
    - abscess
      - intracranial or intraspinal (conditions classifiable to 324) — *see* category 326
    - adverse effect of drug, medicinal or biological substance 909.5
    - allergic reaction 909.9
    - amputation
      - postoperative (late) 997.60
      - traumatic (injury classifiable to 885–887 and 895–897) 905.9
    - burn (injury classifiable to 948–949) 906.9
      - extremities NEC (injury classifiable to 943 or 945) 906.7
        - hand or wrist (injury classifiable to 944) 906.6
      - eye (injury classifiable to 940) 906.5
      - face, head, and neck (injury classifiable to 941) 906.5
      - specified site NEC (injury classifiable to 942 and 946–947) 906.8
    - cerebrovascular disease (conditions classifiable to 430–437) 438.9
      - with
        - alterations of sensations 438.6
        - aphasia 438.11
        - apraxia 438.81
        - ataxia 438.84
        - cognitive deficits 438.0
        - disturbances of vision 438.7
        - dysphagia 438.82
        - dysphasia 438.12
        - facial droop 438.83
        - facial weakness 438.83
        - hemiplegia/hemiparesis
          - affecting
            - dominant side 438.21
            - nondominant side 438.22
            - unspecified side 438.20
        - monoplegia of lower limb
          - affecting
            - dominant side 438.41
            - nondominant side 438.42
            - unspecified side 438.40
        - monoplegia of upper limb
          - affecting
            - dominant side 438.31
            - nondominant side 438.32
            - unspecified side 438.30
        - paralytic syndrome NEC
          - affecting
            - bilateral 438.53
            - dominant side 438.51
            - nondominant side 438.52
            - unspecified side 438.50
        - speech and language deficit 438.10
          - specified type NEC 438.19
        - vertigo 438.85
      - specified type NEC 438.89
    - childbirth complication(s) 677
    - complication(s) of
      - childbirth 677
      - delivery 677
      - pregnancy 677

- **Late** — *see also* condition — *continued*
  - effect(s) (*see also* condition) — *continued*
    - complication(s) of — *continued*
      - puerperium 677
      - surgical and medical care (conditions classifiable to 996–999) 909.3
      - trauma (conditions classifiable to 958) 908.6
    - contusion (injury classifiable to 920–924) 906.3
    - crushing (injury classifiable to 925–929) 906.4
    - delivery complication(s) 677
    - dislocation (injury classifiable to 830–839) 905.6
    - encephalitis or encephalomyelitis (conditions classifiable to 323) — *see* category 326
      - in infectious diseases 139.8
        - viral (conditions classifiable to 049.8, 049.9, 062–064) 139.0
    - external cause NEC (conditions classifiable to 995) 909.9
      - certain conditions classifiable to categories 991-994 909.4
    - foreign body in orifice (injury classifiable to 930–939) 908.5
    - fracture (multiple) (injury classifiable to 828–829) 905.5
      - extremity
        - lower (injury classifiable to 821–827) 905.4
          - neck of femur (injury classifiable to 820) 905.3
        - upper (injury classifiable to 810–819) 905.2
      - face and skull (injury classifiable to 800–804) 905.0
      - skull and face (injury classifiable to 800–804) 905.0
      - spine and trunk (injury classifiable to 805 and 807–809) 905.1
        - with spinal cord lesion (injury classifiable to 806) 907.2
    - infection
      - pyogenic, intracranial — *see* category 326
    - infectious diseases (conditions classifiable to 001–136) NEC 139.8
    - injury (injury classifiable to 959) 908.9
      - blood vessel 908.3
        - abdomen and pelvis (injury classifiable to 902) 908.4
        - extremity (injury classifiable to 903–904) 908.3
        - head and neck (injury classifiable to 900) 908.3
        - intracranial (injury classifiable to 850–854) 907.0
          - with skull fracture 905.0
        - thorax (injury classifiable to 901) 908.4
      - internal organ NEC (injury classifiable to 867 and 869) 908.2
        - abdomen (injury classifiable to 863–866 and 868) 908.1
        - thorax (injury classifiable to 860–862) 908.0
      - intracranial (injury classifiable to 850–854) 907.0

- **Late** — *see also* condition — *continued*
  - effect(s) (*see also* condition) — *continued*
    - injury — *continued*
      - intracranial — *continued*
        - with skull fracture (injury classifiable to 800–801 and 803–804) 905.0
      - nerve NEC (injury classifiable to 957) 907.9
        - cranial (injury classifiable to 950–951) 907.1
        - peripheral NEC (injury classifiable to 957) 907.9
          - lower limb and pelvic girdle (injury classifiable to 956) 907.5
          - upper limb and shoulder girdle (injury classifiable to 955) 907.4
        - roots and plexus(es), spinal (injury classifiable to 953) 907.3
        - trunk (injury classifiable to 954) 907.3
      - spinal
        - cord (injury classifiable to 806 and 952) 907.2
        - nerve root(s) and plexus(es) (injury classifiable to 953) 907.3
      - superficial (injury classifiable to 910–919) 906.2
      - tendon (tendon injury classifiable to 840–848, 880–884 with .2, and 890–894 with .2) 905.8
    - meningitis
      - bacterial (conditions classifiable to 320) — *see* category 326
      - unspecified cause (conditions classifiable to 322) — *see* category 326
    - myelitis (*see also* Late, effect(s) (of), encephalitis) — *see* category 326
    - parasitic diseases (conditions classifiable to 001–136 NEC) 139.8
    - phlebitis or thrombophlebitis of intracranial venous sinuses (conditions classifiable to 325) — *see* category 326
    - poisoning due to drug, medicinal or biological substance (conditions classifiable to 960–979) 909.0
    - poliomyelitis, acute (conditions classifiable to 045) 138
    - pregnancy complication(s) 677
    - puerperal complication(s) 677
    - radiation (conditions classifiable to 990) 909.2
    - rickets 268.1
    - sprain and strain without mention of tendon injury (injury classifiable to 840–848, except tendon injury) 905.7
      - tendon involvement 905.8
    - toxic effect of
      - drug, medicinal or biological substance (conditions classifiable to 960–979) 909.0
      - nonmedical substance (conditions classifiable to 980–989) 909.1
    - trachoma (conditions classifiable to 076) 139.1
    - tuberculosis 137.0
      - bones and joints (conditions classifiable to 015) 137.3

- **Late** — *see also* condition — *continued*
  - effect(s) (*see also* condition) — *continued*
    - tuberculosis — *continued*
      - central nervous system (conditions classifiable to 013) 137.1
      - genitourinary (conditions classifiable to 016) 137.2
      - pulmonary (conditions classifiable to 010–012) 137.0
      - specified organs NEC (conditions classifiable to 014, 017–018) 137.4
    - viral encephalitis (conditions classifiable to 049.8, 049.9, 062–064) 139.0
    - wound, open
      - extremity (injury classifiable to 880–884 and 890–894, except .2) 906.1
        - tendon (injury classifiable to 880–884 with .2 and 890–894 with .2) 905.8
      - head, neck, and trunk (injury classifiable to 870–879) 906.0
  - infant
    - post-term (gestation period over 40 completed weeks to 42 completed weeks) 766.21
    - prolonged gestation (period over 42 completed weeks) 766.22
- **Latent** — *see* condition
- **Lateral** — *see* condition
- **Laterocession** — *see* Lateroversion
- **Lateroflexion** — *see* Lateroversion
- **Lateroversion**
  - cervix — *see* Lateroversion, uterus
  - uterus, uterine (cervix) (postinfectional) (postpartal, old) 621.6
    - congenital 752.3
    - in pregnancy or childbirth 654.4 ☑
      - affecting fetus or newborn 763.89
- **Lathyrism** 988.2
- **Launois-Bensaude's lipomatosis** 272.8
- **Launois-Cléret syndrome** (adiposogenital dystrophy) 253.8
- **Launois' syndrome** (pituitary gigantism) 253.0
- **Laurence-Moon-Biedl syndrome** (obesity, polydactyly, and mental retardation) 759.89
- **LAV** (disease) (illness) (infection) — *see* Human immunodeficiency virus (disease) (illness) (infection)
- **LAV/HTLV-III** (disease) (illness) (infection) — *see* Human immunodeficiency virus (disease) (illness) (infection)
- **Lawford's syndrome** (encephalocutaneous angiomatosis) 759.6
- **Laxative habit** — *see also* Abuse, drugs, nondependent 305.9 ☑
- **Lax, laxity** — *see also* Relaxation
  - ligament 728.4
  - skin (acquired) 701.8
    - congenital 756.83
- **Lazy leukocyte syndrome** 288.09
- **LCAD** (long chain/very long chain acyl CoA dehydrogenase deficiency, VLCAD) 277.85
- **LCHAD** (long chain 3-hydroxyacyl CoA dehydrogenase deficiency) 277.85
- **Lead** — *see also* condition
  - exposure to V15.86
  - incrustation of cornea 371.15
  - poisoning 984.9
    - specified type of lead — *see* Table of Drugs and Chemicals
- **Lead miners' lung** 503
- **Leakage**
  - amniotic fluid 658.1 ☑
    - with delayed delivery 658.2 ☑

- **Leakage** — *continued*
  - amniotic fluid — *continued*
    - affecting fetus or newborn 761.1
  - bile from drainage tube (T tube) 997.4
  - blood (microscopic), fetal, into maternal circulation 656.0 ☑
    - affecting management of pregnancy or puerperium 656.0 ☑
  - device, implant, or graft — *see* Complications, mechanical
  - spinal fluid at lumbar puncture site 997.09
  - urine, continuous 788.37
- **Leaky heart** — *see* Endocarditis
- **Learning defect, specific** NEC (strephosymbolia) 315.2
- **Leather bottle stomach** (M8142/3) 151.9
- **Leber's**
  - congenital amaurosis 362.76
  - optic atrophy (hereditary) 377.16
- **Lederer's anemia or disease** (acquired infectious hemolytic anemia) 283.19
- **Lederer-Brill syndrome** (acquired infectious hemolytic anemia) 283.19
- **Leeches** (aquatic) (land) 134.2
- **Left-sided neglect** 781.8
- **Leg** — *see* condition
- **Legal investigation** V62.5
- **Legg (-Calvé) -Perthes disease or syndrome** (osteochondrosis, femoral capital) 732.1
- **Legionnaires' disease** 482.84
- **Leigh's disease** 330.8
- **Leiner's disease** (exfoliative dermatitis) 695.89
- **Leiofibromyoma** (M8890/0) — *see also* Leiomyoma
  - uterus (cervix) (corpus) (*see also* Leiomyoma, uterus) 218.9
- **Leiomyoblastoma** (M8891/1) — *see* Neoplasm, connective tissue, uncertain behavior
- **Leiomyofibroma** (M8890/0) — *see also* Neoplasm, connective tissue, benign
  - uterus (cervix) (corpus) (*see also* Leiomyoma, uterus) 218.9
- **Leiomyoma** (M8890/0) — *see also* Neoplasm, connective tissue, benign
  - bizarre (M8893/0) — *see* Neoplasm, connective tissue, benign
  - cellular (M8892/1) — *see* Neoplasm, connective tissue, uncertain behavior
  - epithelioid (M8891/1) — *see* Neoplasm, connective tissue, uncertain behavior
  - prostate (polypoid) 600.20
    - with
      - other lower urinary tract symptoms (LUTS) 600.21
      - urinary
        - obstruction 600.21
        - retention 600.21
  - uterus (cervix) (corpus) 218.9
    - interstitial 218.1
    - intramural 218.1
    - submucous 218.0
    - subperitoneal 218.2
    - subserous 218.2
  - vascular (M8894/0) — *see* Neoplasm, connective tissue, benign
- **Leiomyomatosis** (intravascular) (M8890/1) — *see* Neoplasm, connective tissue, uncertain behavior
- **Leiomyosarcoma** (M8890/3) — *see also* Neoplasm, connective tissue, malignant
  - epithelioid (M8891/3) — *see* Neoplasm, connective tissue, malignant
- **Leishmaniasis** 085.9
  - American 085.5
    - cutaneous 085.4

- **Leishmaniasis** — *continued*
  - American — *continued*
    - mucocutaneous 085.5
  - Asian desert 085.2
  - Brazilian 085.5
  - cutaneous 085.9
    - acute necrotizing 085.2
    - American 085.4
    - Asian desert 085.2
    - diffuse 085.3
    - dry form 085.1
    - Ethiopian 085.3
    - eyelid 085.5 *[373.6]*
    - late 085.1
    - lepromatous 085.3
    - recurrent 085.1
    - rural 085.2
    - ulcerating 085.1
    - urban 085.1
    - wet form 085.2
    - zoonotic form 085.2
  - dermal (*see also* Leishmaniasis, cutaneous)
    - post kala-azar 085.0
  - eyelid 085.5 *[373.6]*
  - infantile 085.0
  - Mediterranean 085.0
  - mucocutaneous (American) 085.5
  - naso-oral 085.5
  - nasopharyngeal 085.5
  - Old World 085.1
  - tegumentaria diffusa 085.4
  - vaccination, prophylactic (against) V05.2
  - visceral (Indian) 085.0
- **Leishmanoid, dermal** — *see also* Leishmaniasis, cutaneous
  - post kala-azar 085.0
- **Leloir's disease** 695.4
- **Lemiere syndrome** 451.89
- **Lenegre's disease** 426.0
- **Lengthening, leg** 736.81
- **Lennox-Gastaut syndrome** 345.0 ☑
  - with tonic seizures 345.1 ☑
- **Lennox's syndrome** — *see also* Epilepsy 345.0 ☑
- **Lens** — *see* condition
- **Lenticonus** (anterior) (posterior) (congenital) 743.36
- **Lenticular degeneration, progressive** 275.1
- **Lentiglobus** (posterior) (congenital) 743.36
- **Lentigo** (congenital) 709.09
  - juvenile 709.09
  - Maligna (M8742/2) (*see also* Neoplasm, skin, in situ)
    - melanoma (M8742/3) — *see* Melanoma
  - senile 709.09
- **Leonine leprosy** 030.0
- **Leontiasis**
  - ossium 733.3
  - syphilitic 095.8
    - congenital 090.5
- **Léopold-Lévi's syndrome** (paroxysmal thyroid instability) 242.9 ☑
- **Lepore hemoglobin syndrome** 282.49
- **Lepothrix** 039.0
- **Lepra** 030.9
  - Willan's 696.1
- **Leprechaunism** 259.8
- **Lepromatous leprosy** 030.0
- **Leprosy** 030.9
  - anesthetic 030.1
  - beriberi 030.1
  - borderline (group B) (infiltrated) (neuritic) 030.3
  - cornea (*see also* Leprosy, by type) 030.9 *[371.89]*
  - dimorphous (group B) (infiltrated) (lepromatous) (neuritic) (tuberculoid) 030.3
  - eyelid 030.0 *[373.4]*
- **Leprosy** — *continued*
  - indeterminate (group I) (macular) (neuritic) (uncharacteristic) 030.2
  - leonine 030.0
  - lepromatous (diffuse) (infiltrated) (macular) (neuritic) (nodular) (type L) 030.0
  - macular (early) (neuritic) (simple) 030.2
  - maculoanesthetic 030.1
  - mixed 030.0
  - neuro 030.1
  - nodular 030.0
  - primary neuritic 030.3
  - specified type or group NEC 030.8
  - tubercular 030.1
  - tuberculoid (macular) (maculoanesthetic) (major) (minor) (neuritic) (type T) 030.1
- **Leptocytosis, hereditary** 282.49
- **Leptomeningitis** (chronic) (circumscribed) (hemorrhagic) (nonsuppurative) — *see also* Meningitis 322.9
  - aseptic 047.9
    - adenovirus 049.1
    - Coxsackie virus 047.0
    - ECHO virus 047.1
    - enterovirus 047.9
    - lymphocytic choriomeningitis 049.0
  - epidemic 036.0
  - late effect — *see* category 326
  - meningococcal 036.0
  - pneumococcal 320.1
  - syphilitic 094.2
  - tuberculous (*see also* Tuberculosis, meninges) 013.0 ☑
- **Leptomeningopathy** — *see also* Meningitis 322.9
- **Leptospiral** — *see* condition
- **Leptospirochetal** — *see* condition
- **Leptospirosis** 100.9
  - autumnalis 100.89
  - canicula 100.89
  - grippotyphosa 100.89
  - hebdomidis 100.89
  - icterohemorrhagica 100.0
  - nanukayami 100.89
  - pomona 100.89
  - Weil's disease 100.0
- **Leptothricosis** — *see* Actinomycosis
- **Leptothrix infestation** — *see* Actinomycosis
- **Leptotricosis** — *see* Actinomycosis
- **Leptus dermatitis** 133.8
- **Leriche's syndrome** (aortic bifurcation occlusion) 444.0
- **Léris pleonosteosis** 756.89
- **Léri-Weill syndrome** 756.59
- **Lermoyez's syndrome** — *see also* Disease, Ménière's 386.00
- **Lesbianism** — *omit code*
  - ego-dystonic 302.0
  - problems with 302.0
- **Lesch-Nyhan syndrome** (hypoxanthineguanine-phosphoribosyltransferase deficiency) 277.2
- **Lesion(s)**
  - abducens nerve 378.54
  - alveolar process 525.8
  - anorectal 569.49
  - aortic (valve) — *see* Endocarditis, aortic
  - auditory nerve 388.5
  - basal ganglion 333.90
  - bile duct (*see also* Disease, biliary) 576.8
  - bladder 596.9
  - bone 733.90
  - brachial plexus 353.0
  - brain 348.8
    - congenital 742.9
    - vascular (*see also* Lesion, cerebrovascular) 437.9
      - degenerative 437.1
- **Lesion(s)** — *continued*
  - brain — *continued*
    - vascular (*see also* Lesion, cerebrovascular) — *continued*
      - healed or old without residuals V12.54
      - hypertensive 437.2
      - late effect — *see* Late effect(s) (of) cerebrovascular disease
  - buccal 528.9
  - calcified — *see* Calcification
  - canthus 373.9
  - carate — *see* Pinta, lesions
  - cardia 537.89
  - cardiac — *see* also Disease, heart
    - congenital 746.9
    - valvular — *see* Endocarditis
  - cauda equina 344.60
    - with neurogenic bladder 344.61
  - cecum 569.89
  - cerebral — *see* Lesion, brain
  - cerebrovascular (*see also* Disease, cerebrovascular NEC) 437.9
    - degenerative 437.1
      - healed or old without residuals V12.54
    - hypertensive 437.2
    - specified type NEC 437.8
  - cervical root (nerve) NEC 353.2
  - chiasmal 377.54
    - associated with
      - inflammatory disorders 377.54
      - neoplasm NEC 377.52
        - pituitary 377.51
      - pituitary disorders 377.51
      - vascular disorders 377.53
  - chorda tympani 351.8
  - coin, lung 793.1
  - colon 569.89
  - congenital — *see* Anomaly
  - conjunctiva 372.9
  - coronary artery (*see also* Ischemia, heart) 414.9
  - cranial nerve 352.9
    - first 352.0
    - second 377.49
    - third
      - partial 378.51
      - total 378.52
    - fourth 378.53
    - fifth 350.9
    - sixth 378.54
    - seventh 351.9
    - eighth 388.5
    - ninth 352.2
    - tenth 352.3
    - eleventh 352.4
    - twelfth 352.5
  - cystic — *see* Cyst
  - degenerative — *see* Degeneration
  - dermal (skin) 709.9
  - Dieulafoy (hemorrhagic)
    - of
      - duodenum 537.84
      - intestine 569.86
      - stomach 537.84
  - duodenum 537.89
    - with obstruction 537.3
  - eyelid 373.9
  - gasserian ganglion 350.8
  - gastric 537.89
  - gastroduodenal 537.89
  - gastrointestinal 569.89
  - glossopharyngeal nerve 352.2
  - heart (organic) (*see also* Disease, heart)
    - vascular — *see* Disease, cardiovascular
  - helix (ear) 709.9
  - high grade myelodysplastic syndrome 238.73
  - hyperchromic, due to pinta (carate) 103.1
  - hyperkeratotic (*see also* Hyperkeratosis) 701.1
- **Lesion(s)** — *continued*
  - hypoglossal nerve 352.5
  - hypopharynx 478.29
  - hypothalamic 253.9
  - ileocecal coil 569.89
  - ileum 569.89
  - iliohypogastric nerve 355.79
  - ilioinguinal nerve 355.79
  - in continuity — *see* Injury, nerve, by site
  - inflammatory — *see* Inflammation
  - intestine 569.89
  - intracerebral — *see* Lesion, brain
  - intrachiasmal (optic) (*see also* Lesion, chiasmal) 377.54
  - intracranial, space-occupying NEC 784.2
  - joint 719.90
    - ankle 719.97
    - elbow 719.92
    - foot 719.97
    - hand 719.94
    - hip 719.95
    - knee 719.96
    - multiple sites 719.99
    - pelvic region 719.95
    - sacroiliac (old) 724.6
    - shoulder (region) 719.91
    - specified site NEC 719.98
    - wrist 719.93
  - keratotic (*see also* Keratosis) 701.1
  - kidney (*see also* Disease, renal) 593.9
  - laryngeal nerve (recurrent) 352.3
  - leonine 030.0
  - lip 528.5
  - liver 573.8
  - low grade myelodysplastic syndrome 238.72
  - lumbosacral
    - plexus 353.1
    - root (nerve) NEC 353.4
  - lung 518.89
    - coin 793.1
  - maxillary sinus 473.0
  - mitral — *see* Endocarditis, mitral
  - motor cortex 348.8
  - nerve (*see also* Disorder, nerve) 355.9
  - nervous system 349.9
    - congenital 742.9
  - nonallopathic NEC 739.9
    - in region (of)
      - abdomen 739.9
      - acromioclavicular 739.7
      - cervical, cervicothoracic 739.1
      - costochondral 739.8
      - costovertebral 739.8
      - extremity
        - lower 739.6
        - upper 739.7
      - head 739.0
      - hip 739.5
      - lower extremity 739.6
      - lumbar, lumbosacral 739.3
      - occipitocervical 739.0
      - pelvic 739.5
      - pubic 739.5
      - rib cage 739.8
      - sacral, sacrococcygeal, sacroiliac 739.4
      - sternochondral 739.8
      - sternoclavicular 739.7
      - thoracic, thoracolumbar 739.2
      - upper extremity 739.7
  - nose (internal) 478.19
  - obstructive — *see* Obstruction
  - obturator nerve 355.79
  - occlusive
    - artery — *see* Embolism, artery
  - organ or site NEC — *see* Disease, by site
  - osteolytic 733.90
  - paramacular, of retina 363.32
  - peptic 537.89
  - periodontal, due to traumatic occlusion 523.8
  - perirectal 569.49

- **Lesion(s)** — *continued*
  - peritoneum (granulomatous) 568.89
  - pigmented (skin) 709.00
  - pinta — *see* Pinta, lesions
  - polypoid — *see* Polyp
  - prechiasmal (optic) (*see also* Lesion, chiasmal) 377.54
  - primary (*see also* Syphilis, primary)
    - carate 103.0
    - pinta 103.0
    - yaws 102.0
  - pulmonary 518.89
    - valve (*see also* Endocarditis, pulmonary) 424.3
  - pylorus 537.89
  - radiation NEC 990
  - radium NEC 990
  - rectosigmoid 569.89
  - retina, retinal (*see also* Retinopathy)
    - vascular 362.17
  - retroperitoneal 568.89
  - romanus 720.1
  - sacroiliac (joint) 724.6
  - salivary gland 527.8
    - benign lymphoepithelial 527.8
  - saphenous nerve 355.79
  - secondary — *see* Syphilis, secondary
  - sigmoid 569.89
  - sinus (accessory) (nasal) (*see also* Sinusitis) 473.9
  - skin 709.9
    - suppurative 686.00
  - SLAP (superior glenoid labrum) 840.7
  - space-occupying, intracranial NEC 784.2
  - spinal cord 336.9
    - congenital 742.9
    - traumatic (complete) (incomplete) (transverse) (*see also* Injury, spinal, by site)
      - with
        - broken
          - back — *see* Fracture, vertebra, by site, with spinal cord injury
          - neck — *see* Fracture, vertebra, cervical, with spinal cord injury
        - fracture, vertebra — *see* Fracture, vertebra, by site, with spinal cord injury
  - spleen 289.50
  - stomach 537.89
  - superior glenoid labrum (SLAP) 840.7
  - syphilitic — *see* Syphilis
  - tertiary — *see* Syphilis, tertiary
  - thoracic root (nerve) 353.3
  - tonsillar fossa 474.9
  - tooth, teeth 525.8
    - white spot 521.01
  - traumatic NEC (*see also* nature and site of injury) 959.9
  - tricuspid (valve) — *see* Endocarditis, tricuspid
  - trigeminal nerve 350.9
  - ulcerated or ulcerative — *see* Ulcer
  - uterus NEC 621.9
  - vagina 623.8
  - vagus nerve 352.3
  - valvular — *see* Endocarditis
  - vascular 459.9
    - affecting central nervous system (*see also* Lesion, cerebrovascular) 437.9
    - following trauma (*see also* Injury, blood vessel, by site) 904.9
    - retina 362.17
    - traumatic — *see* Injury, blood vessel, by site
    - umbilical cord 663.6 ☑
      - affecting fetus or newborn 762.6
  - visual
    - cortex NEC (*see also* Disorder, visual, cortex) 377.73
    - pathway NEC (*see also* Disorder, visual, pathway) 377.63
  - warty — *see* Verruca
  - white spot, on teeth 521.01
  - x-ray NEC 990
- **Lethargic** — *see* condition
- **Lethargy** 780.79
- **Letterer-Siwe disease** (acute histiocytosis X) (M9722/3) 202.5 ☑
- **Leucinosis** 270.3
- **Leucocoria** 360.44
- **Leucosarcoma** (M9850/3) 207.8 ☑
- **Leukasmus** 270.2
- **Leukemia, leukemic** (congenital) (M9800/3) 208.9 ☑

> *Note – Use the following fifth-digit subclassification for categories 203–208:*
>
> *0 without mention of ▶having achieved◀ remission failed remission* ●
>
> *1 with remission*
>
> *2 in relapse* ●

  - acute NEC (M9801/3) 208.0 ☑
  - aleukemic NEC (M9804/3) 208.8 ☑
    - granulocytic (M9864/3) 205.8 ☑
  - basophilic (M9870/3) 205.1 ☑
  - blast (cell) (M9801/3) 208.0 ☑
  - blastic (M9801/3) 208.0 ☑
    - granulocytic (M9861/3) 205.0 ☑
  - chronic NEC (M9803/3) 208.1 ☑
  - compound (M9810/3) 207.8 ☑
  - eosinophilic (M9880/3) 205.1 ☑
  - giant cell (M9910/3) 207.2 ☑
  - granulocytic (M9860/3) 205.9 ☑
    - acute (M9861/3) 205.0 ☑
    - aleukemic (M9864/3) 205.8 ☑
    - blastic (M9861/3) 205.0 ☑
    - chronic (M9863/3) 205.1 ☑
    - subacute (M9862/3) 205.2 ☑
    - subleukemic (M9864/3) 205.8 ☑
  - hairy cell (M9940/3) 202.4 ☑
  - hemoblastic (M9801/3) 208.0 ☑
  - histiocytic (M9890/3) 206.9 ☑
  - lymphatic (M9820/3) 204.9 ☑
    - acute (M9821/3) 204.0 ☑
    - aleukemic (M9824/3) 204.8 ☑
    - chronic (M9823/3) 204.1 ☑
    - subacute (M9822/3) 204.2 ☑
    - subleukemic (M9824/3) 204.8 ☑
  - lymphoblastic (M9821/3) 204.0 ☑
  - lymphocytic (M9820/3) 204.9 ☑
    - acute (M9821/3) 204.0 ☑
    - aleukemic (M9824/3) 204.8 ☑
    - chronic (M9823/3) 204.1 ☑
    - subacute (M9822/3) 204.2 ☑
    - subleukemic (M9824/3) 204.8 ☑
  - lymphogenous (M9820/3) — *see* Leukemia, lymphoid
  - lymphoid (M9820/3) 204.9 ☑
    - acute (M9821/3) 204.0 ☑
    - aleukemic (M9824/3) 204.8 ☑
    - blastic (M9821/3) 204.0 ☑
    - chronic (M9823/3) 204.1 ☑
    - subacute (M9822/3) 204.2 ☑
    - subleukemic (M9824/3) 204.8 ☑
  - lymphosarcoma cell (M9850/3) 207.8 ☑
  - mast cell (M9900/3) 207.8 ☑
  - megakaryocytic (M9910/3) 207.2 ☑
  - megakaryocytoid (M9910/3) 207.2 ☑
  - mixed (cell) (M9810/3) 207.8 ☑
  - monoblastic (M9891/3) 206.0 ☑
  - monocytic (Schilling-type) (M9890/3) 206.9 ☑
    - acute (M9891/3) 206.0 ☑
    - aleukemic (M9894/3) 206.8 ☑
    - chronic (M9893/3) 206.1 ☑
    - Naegeli-type (M9863/3) 205.1 ☑
    - subacute (M9892/3) 206.2 ☑
    - subleukemic (M9894/3) 206.8 ☑
  - monocytoid (M9890/3) 206.9 ☑
    - acute (M9891/3) 206.0 ☑
    - aleukemic (M9894/3) 206.8 ☑
    - chronic (M9893/3) 206.1 ☑
    - myelogenous (M9863/3) 205.1 ☑
    - subacute (M9892/3) 206.2 ☑
    - subleukemic (M9894/3) 206.8 ☑
  - monomyelocytic (M9860/3) — *see* Leukemia, myelomonocytic
  - myeloblastic (M9861/3) 205.0 ☑
  - myelocytic (M9863/3) 205.1 ☑
    - acute (M9861/3) 205.0 ☑
  - myelogenous (M9860/3) 205.9 ☑
    - acute (M9861/3) 205.0 ☑
    - aleukemic (M9864/3) 205.8 ☑
    - chronic (M9863/3) 205.1 ☑
    - monocytoid (M9863/3) 205.1 ☑
    - subacute (M9862/3) 205.2 ☑
    - subleukemic (M9864) 205.8 ☑
  - myeloid (M9860/3) 205.9 ☑
    - acute (M9861/3) 205.0 ☑
    - aleukemic (M9864/3) 205.8 ☑
    - chronic (M9863/3) 205.1 ☑
    - subacute (M9862/3) 205.2 ☑
    - subleukemic (M9864/3) 205.8 ☑
  - myelomonocytic (M9860/3) 205.9 ☑
    - acute (M9861/3) 205.0 ☑
    - chronic (M9863/3) 205.1 ☑
  - Naegeli-type monocytic (M9863/3) 205.1 ☑
  - neutrophilic (M9865/3) 205.1 ☑
  - plasma cell (M9830/3) 203.1 ☑
  - plasmacytic (M9830/3) 203.1 ☑
  - prolymphocytic (M9825/3) — *see* Leukemia, lymphoid
  - promyelocytic, acute (M9866/3) 205.0 ☑
  - Schilling-type monocytic (M9890/3) — *see* Leukemia, monocytic
  - stem cell (M9801/3) 208.0 ☑
  - subacute NEC (M9802/3) 208.2 ☑
  - subleukemic NEC (M9804/3) 208.8 ☑
  - thrombocytic (M9910/3) 207.2 ☑
  - undifferentiated (M9801/3) 208.0 ☑
- **Leukemoid reaction** (basophilic) (lymphocytic) (monocytic) (myelocytic) (neutrophilic) 288.62
- **Leukoclastic vasculitis** 446.29
- **Leukocoria** 360.44
- **Leukocythemia** — *see* Leukemia
- **Leukocytopenia** 288.50
- **Leukocytosis** 288.60
  - basophilic 288.8
  - eosinophilic 288.3
  - lymphocytic 288.8
  - monocytic 288.8
  - neutrophilic 288.8
- **Leukoderma** 709.09
  - syphilitic 091.3
    - late 095.8
- **Leukodermia** — *see also* Leukoderma 709.09
- **Leukodystrophy** (cerebral) (globoid cell) (metachromatic) (progressive) (sudanophilic) 330.0
- **Leukoedema, mouth or tongue** 528.79
- **Leukoencephalitis**
  - acute hemorrhagic (postinfectious) NEC 136.9 *[323.61]*
    - postimmunization or postvaccinal 323.51
  - subacute sclerosing 046.2
    - van Bogaert's 046.2
  - van Bogaert's (sclerosing) 046.2
- **Leukoencephalopathy** — *see also* Encephalitis 323.9
  - acute necrotizing hemorrhagic (postinfectious) 136.9 *[323.61]*
    - postimmunization or postvaccinal 323.51
  - metachromatic 330.0
  - multifocal (progressive) 046.3
  - progressive multifocal 046.3
  - reversible, posterior 348.5 ●
- **Leukoerythroblastosis** 289.9
- **Leukoerythrosis** 289.0
- **Leukokeratosis** — *see also* Leukoplakia 702.8
  - mouth 528.6
  - nicotina palati 528.79
  - tongue 528.6
- **Leukokoria** 360.44
- **Leukokraurosis vulva, vulvae** 624.09
- **Leukolymphosarcoma** (M9850/3) 207.8 ☑
- **Leukoma** (cornea) (interfering with central vision) 371.03
  - adherent 371.04
- **Leukomalacia, periventricular** 779.7
- **Leukomelanopathy, hereditary** 288.2
- **Leukonychia** (punctata) (striata) 703.8
  - congenital 757.5
- **Leukopathia**
  - unguium 703.8
    - congenital 757.5
- **Leukopenia** 288.50
  - basophilic 288.59
  - cyclic 288.02
  - eosinophilic 288.59
  - familial 288.59
  - malignant (*see also* Agranulocytosis) 288.09
  - periodic 288.02
  - transitory neonatal 776.7
- **Leukopenic** — *see* condition
- **Leukoplakia** 702.8
  - anus 569.49
  - bladder (postinfectional) 596.8
  - buccal 528.6
  - cervix (uteri) 622.2
  - esophagus 530.83
  - gingiva 528.6
  - kidney (pelvis) 593.89
  - larynx 478.79
  - lip 528.6
  - mouth 528.6
  - oral soft tissue (including tongue) (mucosa) 528.6
  - palate 528.6
  - pelvis (kidney) 593.89
  - penis (infectional) 607.0
  - rectum 569.49
  - syphilitic 095.8
  - tongue 528.6
  - tonsil 478.29
  - ureter (postinfectional) 593.89
  - urethra (postinfectional) 599.84
  - uterus 621.8
  - vagina 623.1
  - vesical 596.8
  - vocal cords 478.5
  - vulva 624.09
- **Leukopolioencephalopathy** 330.0
- **Leukorrhea** (vagina) 623.5
  - due to trichomonas (vaginalis) 131.00
  - trichomonal (Trichomonas vaginalis) 131.00
- **Leukosarcoma** (M9850/3) 207.8 ☑
- **Leukosis** (M9800/3) — *see* Leukemia
- **Lev's disease or syndrome** (acquired complete heart block) 426.0
- **Levi's syndrome** (pituitary dwarfism) 253.3
- **Levocardia** (isolated) 746.87
  - with situs inversus 759.3
- **Levulosuria** 271.2
- **Lewandowski's disease** (primary) — *see also* Tuberculosis 017.0 ☑
- **Lewandowski-Lutz disease** (epidermodysplasia verruciformis) 078.19
- **Lewy body dementia** 331.82
- **Lewy body disease** 331.82
- **Leyden's disease** (periodic vomiting) 536.2
- **Leyden-Möbius dystrophy** 359.1

Leydig cell
  carcinoma (M8650/3)
    specified site — *see* Neoplasm, by site, malignant
    unspecified site
      female 183.0
      male 186.9
  tumor (M8650/1)
    benign (M8650/0)
      specified site — *see* Neoplasm, by site, benign
      unspecified site
        female 220
        male 222.0
    malignant (M8650/3)
      specified site — *see* Neoplasm, by site, malignant
      unspecified site
        female 183.0
        male 186.9
    specified site — *see* Neoplasm, by site, uncertain behavior
    unspecified site
      female 236.2
      male 236.4
Leydig-Sertoli cell tumor (M8631/0)
  specified site — *see* Neoplasm, by site, benign
  unspecified site
    female 220
    male 222.0
LGSIL (low grade squamous intraepithelial lesion)
  anus 796.73 ●
  cervix 795.03 ●
  vagina 795.13 ●
Liar, pathologic 301.7
Libman-Sacks disease or syndrome 710.0 *[424.91]*
Lice (infestation) 132.9
  body (pediculus corporis) 132.1
  crab 132.2
  head (pediculus capitis) 132.0
  mixed (classifiable to more than one of the categories 132.0–132.2) 132.3
  pubic (pediculus pubis) 132.2
Lichen 697.9
  albus 701.0
  annularis 695.89
  atrophicus 701.0
  corneus obtusus 698.3
  myxedematous 701.8
  nitidus 697.1
  pilaris 757.39
    acquired 701.1
  planopilaris 697.0
  planus (acute) (chronicus) (hypertrophic) (verrucous) 697.0
    morphoeicus 701.0
    sclerosus (et atrophicus) 701.0
  ruber 696.4
    acuminatus 696.4
    moniliformis 697.8
    obtusus corneus 698.3
    of Wilson 697.0
    planus 697.0
  sclerosus (et atrophicus) 701.0
  scrofulosus (primary) (*see also* Tuberculosis) 017.0 ☑
  simplex (Vidal's) 698.3
    chronicus 698.3
    circumscriptus 698.3
  spinulosus 757.39
    mycotic 117.9
  striata 697.8
  urticatus 698.2
Lichenification 698.3
  nodular 698.3
Lichenoides tuberculosis (primary) — *see also* Tuberculosis 017.0 ☑
Lichtheim's disease or syndrome (subacute combined sclerosis with pernicious anemia) 281.0 *[336.2]*
Lien migrans 289.59
Lientery — *see also* Diarrhea 787.91
Lientery — *see also* Diarrhea — *continued*
  infectious 009.2
Life circumstance problem NEC V62.89
Li-Fraumeni cancer syndrome V84.01
Ligament — *see* condition
Light-for-dates (infant) 764.0 ☑
  with signs of fetal malnutrition 764.1 ☑
  affecting management of pregnancy 656.5 ☑
Light-headedness 780.4
Lightning (effects) (shock) (stroke) (struck by) 994.0
  burn — *see* Burn, by site
  foot 266.2
Lightwood's disease or syndrome (renal tubular acidosis) 588.89
Lignac's disease (cystinosis) 270.0
Lignac (-Fanconi) syndrome (cystinosis) 270.0
Lignac (-de Toni) (-Fanconi) (-Debré) syndrome (cystinosis) 270.0
Ligneous thyroiditis 245.3
Likoff's syndrome (angina in menopausal women) 413.9
Limb — *see* condition
Limitation of joint motion — *see also* Stiffness, joint 719.5 ☑
  sacroiliac 724.6
Limit dextrinosis 271.0
Limited
  cardiac reserve — *see* Disease, heart
  duction, eye NEC 378.63
  mandibular range of motion 524.52
Lindau's disease (retinocerebral angiomatosis) 759.6
Lindau (-von Hippel) disease (angiomatosis retinocerebellosa) 759.6
Linea corneae senilis 371.41
Lines
  Beau's (transverse furrows on fingernails) 703.8
  Harris' 733.91
  Hudson-Stähli 371.11
  Stähli's 371.11
Lingua
  geographical 529.1
  nigra (villosa) 529.3
  plicata 529.5
    congenital 750.13
  tylosis 528.6
Lingual (tongue) — *see* also condition
  thyroid 759.2
Linitis (gastric) 535.4 ☑
  plastica (M8142/3) 151.9
Lioderma essentialis (cum melanosis et telangiectasia) 757.33
Lip — *see also* condition
  biting 528.9
Lipalgia 272.8
Lipedema — *see* Edema
Lipemia — *see also* Hyperlipidemia 272.4
  retina, retinalis 272.3
Lipidosis 272.7
  cephalin 272.7
  cerebral (infantile) (juvenile) (late) 330.1
  cerebroretinal 330.1 *[362.71]*
  cerebroside 272.7
  cerebrospinal 272.7
  chemically-induced 272.7
  cholesterol 272.7
  diabetic 250.8 ☑ *[272.7]*
    due to secondary diabetes 249.8 ☑ *[272.7]* ●
  dystopic (hereditary) 272.7
  glycolipid 272.7
  hepatosplenomegalic 272.3
  hereditary, dystopic 272.7
  sulfatide 330.0
Lipoadenoma (M8324/0) — *see* Neoplasm, by site, benign
Lipoblastoma (M8881/0) — *see* Lipoma, by site
Lipoblastomatosis (M8881/0) — *see* Lipoma, by site
Lipochondrodystrophy 277.5
Lipochrome histiocytosis (familial) 288.1
Lipodystrophia progressiva 272.6
Lipodystrophy (progressive) 272.6
  insulin 272.6
  intestinal 040.2
  mesenteric 567.82
Lipofibroma (M8851/0) — *see* Lipoma, by site
Lipoglycoproteinosis 272.8
Lipogranuloma, sclerosing 709.8
Lipogranulomatosis (disseminated) 272.8
  kidney 272.8
Lipoid — *see also* condition
  histiocytosis 272.7
    essential 272.7
  nephrosis (*see also* Nephrosis) 581.3
  proteinosis of Urbach 272.8
Lipoidemia — *see also* Hyperlipidemia 272.4
Lipoidosis — *see also* Lipidosis 272.7
Lipoma (M8850/0) 214.9
  breast (skin) 214.1
  face 214.0
  fetal (M8881/0) (*see also* Lipoma, by site)
    fat cell (M8880/0) — *see* Lipoma, by site
  infiltrating (M8856/0) — *see* Lipoma, by site
  intra-abdominal 214.3
  intramuscular (M8856/0) — *see* Lipoma, by site
  intrathoracic 214.2
  kidney 214.3
  mediastinum 214.2
  muscle 214.8
  peritoneum 214.3
  retroperitoneum 214.3
  skin 214.1
    face 214.0
  spermatic cord 214.4
  spindle cell (M8857/0) — *see* Lipoma, by site
  stomach 214.3
  subcutaneous tissue 214.1
    face 214.0
  thymus 214.2
  thyroid gland 214.2
Lipomatosis (dolorosa) 272.8
  epidural 214.8
  fetal (M8881/0) — *see* Lipoma, by site
  Launois-Bensaude's 272.8
Lipomyohemangioma (M8860/0)
  specified site — *see* Neoplasm, connective tissue, benign
  unspecified site 223.0
Lipomyoma (M8860/0)
  specified site — *see* Neoplasm, connective tissue, benign
  unspecified site 223.0
Lipomyxoma (M8852/0) — *see* Lipoma, by site
Lipomyxosarcoma (M8852/3) — *see* Neoplasm, connective tissue, malignant
Lipophagocytosis 289.89
Lipoproteinemia (alpha) 272.4
  broad-beta 272.2
  floating-beta 272.2
  hyper-pre-beta 272.1
Lipoproteinosis (Rössle-Urbach-Wiethe) 272.8
Liposarcoma (M8850/3) — *see also* Neoplasm, connective tissue, malignant
  differentiated type (M8851/3) — *see* Neoplasm, connective tissue, malignant
  embryonal (M8852/3) — *see* Neoplasm, connective tissue, malignant
Liposarcoma — *see also* Neoplasm, connective tissue, malignant — *continued*
  mixed type (M8855/3) — *see* Neoplasm, connective tissue, malignant
  myxoid (M8852/3) — *see* Neoplasm, connective tissue, malignant
  pleomorphic (M8854/3) — *see* Neoplasm, connective tissue, malignant
  round cell (M8853/3) — *see* Neoplasm, connective tissue, malignant
  well differentiated type (M8851/3) — *see* Neoplasm, connective tissue, malignant
Liposynovitis prepatellaris 272.8
Lipping
  cervix 622.0
  spine (*see also* Spondylosis) 721.90
  vertebra (*see also* Spondylosis) 721.90
Lip pits (mucus), congenital 750.25
Lipschütz disease or ulcer 616.50
Lipuria 791.1
  bilharziasis 120.0
Liquefaction, vitreous humor 379.21
Lisping 307.9
Lissauer's paralysis 094.1
Lissencephalia, lissencephaly 742.2
Listerellose 027.0
Listeriose 027.0
Listeriosis 027.0
  congenital 771.2
  fetal 771.2
  suspected fetal damage affecting management of pregnancy 655.4 ☑
Listlessness 780.79
Lithemia 790.6
Lithiasis — *see also* Calculus
  hepatic (duct) — *see* Choledocholithiasis
  urinary 592.9
Lithopedion 779.9
  affecting management of pregnancy 656.8 ☑
Lithosis (occupational) 502
  with tuberculosis — *see* Tuberculosis, pulmonary
Lithuria 791.9
Litigation V62.5
Little
  league elbow 718.82
  stroke syndrome 435.9
Little's disease — *see* Palsy, cerebral
Littre's
  gland — *see* condition
  hernia — *see* Hernia, Littre's
Littritis — *see also* Urethritis 597.89
Livedo 782.61
  annularis 782.61
  racemose 782.61
  reticularis 782.61
Live flesh 781.0
Liver — *see also* condition
  donor V59.6
Livida, asphyxia
  newborn 768.6
Living
  alone V60.3
    with handicapped person V60.4
Lloyd's syndrome 258.1
Loa loa 125.2
Loasis 125.2
Lobe, lobar — *see* condition
Lobo's disease or blastomycosis 116.2
Lobomycosis 116.2
Lobotomy syndrome 310.0
Lobstein's disease (brittle bones and blue sclera) 756.51
Lobster-claw hand 755.58
Lobulation (congenital) — *see also* Anomaly, specified type NEC, by site
  kidney, fetal 753.3

☑ Additional Digit Required — Refer to the Tabular List for Digit Selection
Subterms under main terms may continue to next column or page

Lobulation — *see also* Anomaly, specified type, by site — *continued*
liver, abnormal 751.69
spleen 759.0
Lobule, lobular — *see* condition
Local, localized — *see* condition
Locked bowel or intestine — *see also* Obstruction, intestine 560.9
Locked-in state 344.81
Locked twins 660.5 ☑
affecting fetus or newborn 763.1
Locking
joint (*see also* Derangement, joint) 718.90
knee 717.9
Lockjaw — *see also* Tetanus 037
Locomotor ataxia (progressive) 094.0
Löffler's
endocarditis 421.0
eosinophilia or syndrome 518.3
pneumonia 518.3
syndrome (eosinophilic pneumonitis) 518.3
Löfgren's syndrome (sarcoidosis) 135
Loiasis 125.2
eyelid 125.2 *[373.6]*
Loneliness V62.89
Lone star fever 082.8
Longitudinal stripes or grooves, nails 703.8
congenital 757.5
Long labor 662.1 ☑
affecting fetus or newborn 763.89
first stage 662.0 ☑
second stage 662.2 ☑
Long-term (current) **drug use** V58.69
antibiotics V58.62
anticoagulants V58.61
anti-inflammatories, non-steroidal (NSAID) V58.64
antiplatelets/antithrombotics V58.63
aspirin V58.66
high-risk medications NEC V58.69
insulin V58.67
methadone V58.69 ●
opiate analgesic V58.69 ●
pain killers V58.69
anti-inflammatories, non-steroidal (NSAID) V58.64
aspirin V58.66
steroids V58.65
tamoxifen V58.69
Loop
intestine (*see also* Volvulus) 560.2
intrascleral nerve 379.29
vascular on papilla (optic) 743.57
Loose — *see also* condition
body
in tendon sheath 727.82
joint 718.10
ankle 718.17
elbow 718.12
foot 718.17
hand 718.14
hip 718.15
knee 717.6
multiple sites 718.19
pelvic region 718.15
prosthetic implant — *see* Complications, mechanical
shoulder (region) 718.11
specified site NEC 718.18
wrist 718.13
cartilage (joint) (*see also* Loose, body, joint) 718.1 ☑
knee 717.6
facet (vertebral) 724.9
prosthetic implant — *see* Complications, mechanical
sesamoid, joint (*see also* Loose, body, joint) 718.1 ☑
tooth, teeth 525.8
Loosening epiphysis 732.9
Looser (-Debray) -Milkman syndrome (osteomalacia with pseudofractures) 268.2
Lop ear (deformity) 744.29
Lorain's disease or syndrome (pituitary dwarfism) 253.3
Lorain-Levi syndrome (pituitary dwarfism) 253.3
Lordosis (acquired) (postural) 737.20
congenital 754.2
due to or associated with
Charcôt-Marie-Tooth disease 356.1 *[737.42]*
mucopolysaccharidosis 277.5 *[737.42]*
neurofibromatosis 237.71 *[737.42]*
osteitis
deformans 731.0 *[737.42]*
fibrosa cystica 252.01 *[737.42]*
osteoporosis (*see also* Osteoporosis) 733.00 *[737.42]*
poliomyelitis (*see also* Poliomyelitis) 138 *[737.42]*
tuberculosis (*see also* Tuberculosis) 015.0 ☑ *[737.42]*
late effect of rickets 268.1 *[737.42]*
postlaminectomy 737.21
postsurgical NEC 737.22
rachitic 268.1 *[737.42]*
specified NEC 737.29
tuberculous (*see also* Tuberculosis) 015.0 ☑ *[737.42]*
Loss
appetite 783.0
hysterical 300.11
nonorganic origin 307.59
psychogenic 307.59
blood — *see* Hemorrhage
central vision 368.41
consciousness 780.09
transient 780.2
control, sphincter, rectum 787.6
nonorganic origin 307.7
ear ossicle, partial 385.24
elasticity, skin 782.8
extremity or member, traumatic, current — *see* Amputation, traumatic
fluid (acute) 276.50
with
hypernatremia 276.0
hyponatremia 276.1
fetus or newborn 775.5
hair 704.00
hearing (*see also* Deafness)
central 389.14
conductive (air) 389.00
with sensorineural hearing loss 389.20
bilateral 389.22
unilateral 389.21
bilateral 389.06
combined types 389.08
external ear 389.01
inner ear 389.04
middle ear 389.03
multiple types 389.08
tympanic membrane 389.02
unilateral 389.05
mixed conductive and sensorineural 389.20
bilateral 389.22
unilateral 389.21
mixed type 389.20
bilateral 389.22
unilateral 389.21
nerve
bilateral 389.12
unilateral 389.13
neural
bilateral 389.12
unilateral 389.13
noise-induced 388.12
perceptive NEC (*see also* Loss, hearing, sensorineural) 389.10
sensorineural 389.10
with conductive hearing loss 389.20
Loss — *continued*
hearing (*see also* Deafness) — *continued*
sensorineural — *continued*
with conductive hearing loss — *continued*
bilateral 389.22
unilateral 389.21
asymmetrical 389.16
bilateral 389.18
central 389.14
neural 389.12
bilateral 389.12
unilateral 389.13
sensory
bilateral 389.11
unilateral 389.17
unilateral 389.15
sensory
bilateral 389.11
unilateral 389.17
specified type NEC 389.8
sudden NEC 388.2
height 781.91
labyrinthine reactivity (unilateral) 386.55
bilateral 386.56
memory (*see also* Amnesia) 780.93
mild, following organic brain damage 310.1
mind (*see also* Psychosis) 298.9
occlusal vertical dimension 524.37
organ or part — *see* Absence, by site, acquired
sensation 782.0
sense of
smell (*see also* Disturbance, sensation) 781.1
taste (*see also* Disturbance, sensation) 781.1
touch (*see also* Disturbance, sensation) 781.1
sight (acquired) (complete) (congenital) — *see* Blindness
spinal fluid
headache 349.0
substance of
bone (*see also* Osteoporosis) 733.00
cartilage 733.99
ear 380.32
vitreous (humor) 379.26
tooth, teeth
acquired 525.10
due to
caries 525.13
extraction 525.10
periodontal disease 525.12
specified NEC 525.19
trauma 525.11
vision, visual (*see also* Blindness) 369.9
both eyes (*see also* Blindness, both eyes) 369.3
complete (*see also* Blindness, both eyes) 369.00
one eye 369.8
sudden 368.11
transient 368.12
vitreous 379.26
voice (*see also* Aphonia) 784.41
weight (cause unknown) 783.21
Lou Gehrig's disease 335.20
Louis-Bar syndrome (ataxia-telangiectasia) 334.8
Louping ill 063.1
Lousiness — *see* Lice
Low
back syndrome 724.2
basal metabolic rate (BMR) 794.7
birthweight 765.1 ☑
extreme (less than 1000 grams) 765.0 ☑
for gestational age 764.0 ☑
status (*see also* Status, low birth weight) V21.30
Low — *continued*
bladder compliance 596.52
blood pressure (*see also* Hypotension) 458.9
reading (incidental) (isolated) (nonspecific) 796.3
cardiac reserve — *see* Disease, heart
compliance bladder 596.52
frequency deafness — *see* Disorder, hearing
function (*see also* Hypofunction)
kidney (*see also* Disease, renal) 593.9
liver 573.9
hemoglobin 285.9
implantation, placenta — *see* Placenta, previa
insertion, placenta — *see* Placenta, previa
lying
kidney 593.0
organ or site, congenital — *see* Malposition, congenital
placenta — *see* Placenta, previa
output syndrome (cardiac) (*see also* Failure, heart) 428.9
platelets (blood) (*see also* Thrombocytopenia) 287.5
reserve, kidney (*see also* Disease, renal) 593.9
risk
human papillomavirus (HPA) DNA test positive ●
anal 796.79 ●
cervical 795.09 ●
vaginal 795.19 ●
salt syndrome 593.9
tension glaucoma 365.12
vision 369.9
both eyes 369.20
one eye 369.70
Lower extremity — *see* condition
Lowe (-Terrey-MacLachlan) syndrome (oculocerebrorenal dystrophy) 270.8
Lown (-Ganong) -Levine syndrome (short P-R interval, normal QRS complex, and paroxysmal supraventricular tachycardia) 426.81
LSD reaction — *see also* Abuse, drugs, nondependent 305.3 ☑
L-shaped kidney 753.3
Lucas-Championnière disease (fibrinous bronchitis) 466.0
Lucey-Driscoll syndrome (jaundice due to delayed conjugation) 774.30
Ludwig's
angina 528.3
disease (submaxillary cellulitis) 528.3
Lues (venerea), **luetic** — *see* Syphilis
Luetscher's syndrome (dehydration) 276.51
Lumbago 724.2
due to displacement, intervertebral disc 722.10
Lumbalgia 724.2
due to displacement, intervertebral disc 722.10
Lumbar — *see* condition
Lumbarization, vertebra 756.15
Lumbermen's itch 133.8
Lump — *see also* Mass
abdominal 789.3 ☑
breast 611.72
chest 786.6
epigastric 789.3 ☑
head 784.2
kidney 753.3
liver 789.1
lung 786.6
mediastinal 786.6
neck 784.2
nose or sinus 784.2
pelvic 789.3 ☑
skin 782.2

Lump — *see also* Mass — *continued*
- substernal 786.6
- throat 784.2
- umbilicus 789.3 ☑

Lunacy — *see also* Psychosis 298.9
Lunatomalacia 732.3
Lung — *see also* condition
- donor V59.8
- drug addict's 417.8
- mainliners' 417.8
- vanishing 492.0

Lupoid (miliary) **of Boeck** 135
Lupus 710.0
- anticoagulant 289.81
- Cazenave's (erythematosus) 695.4
- discoid (local) 695.4
- disseminated 710.0
- erythematodes (discoid) (local) 695.4
- erythematosus (discoid) (local) 695.4
  - disseminated 710.0
  - eyelid 373.34
  - systemic 710.0
    - with
      - encephalitis 710.0 *[323.81]*
      - lung involvement 710.0 *[517.8]*
    - inhibitor (presence of) 286.5
- exedens 017.0 ☑
- eyelid (*see also* Tuberculosis) 017.0 ☑ *[373.4]*
- Hilliard's 017.0 ☑
- hydralazine
  - correct substance properly administered 695.4
  - overdose or wrong substance given or taken 972.6
- miliaris disseminatus faciei 017.0 ☑
- nephritis 710.0 *[583.81]*
  - acute 710.0 *[580.81]*
  - chronic 710.0 *[582.81]*
- nontuberculous, not disseminated 695.4
- pernio (Besnier) 135
- tuberculous (*see also* Tuberculosis) 017.0 ☑
  - eyelid (*see also* Tuberculosis) 017.0 ☑ *[373.4]*
- vulgaris 017.0 ☑

Luschka's joint disease 721.90
Luteinoma (M8610/0) 220
Lutembacher's disease or syndrome (atrial septal defect with mitral stenosis) 745.5
Luteoma (M8610/0) 220
Lutz-Miescher disease (elastosis perforans serpiginosa) 701.1
Lutz-Splendore-de Almeida disease (Brazilian blastomycosis) 116.1
Luxatio
- bulbi due to birth injury 767.8
- coxae congenita (*see also* Dislocation, hip, congenital) 754.30
- erecta — *see* Dislocation, shoulder
- imperfecta — *see* Sprain, by site
- perinealis — *see* Dislocation, hip

Luxation — *see also* Dislocation, by site
- eyeball 360.81
  - due to birth injury 767.8
  - lateral 376.36
- genital organs (external) NEC — *see* Wound, open, genital organs
- globe (eye) 360.81
  - lateral 376.36
- lacrimal gland (postinfectional) 375.16
- lens (old) (partial) 379.32
  - congenital 743.37
    - syphilitic 090.49 *[379.32]*
  - Marfan's disease 090.49
  - spontaneous 379.32
- penis — *see* Wound, open, penis
- scrotum — *see* Wound, open, scrotum
- testis — *see* Wound, open, testis

L-xyloketosuria 271.8
Lycanthropy — *see also* Psychosis 298.9
Lyell's disease or syndrome (toxic epidermal necrolysis) 695.15 ▲
- due to drug
  - correct substance properly administered 695.15 ▲
  - overdose or wrong substance given or taken 977.9
    - specified drug — *see* Table of Drugs and Chemicals

Lyme disease 088.81
Lymph
- gland or node — *see* condition
- scrotum (*see also* Infestation, filarial) 125.9

Lymphadenitis 289.3
- with
  - abortion — *see* Abortion, by type, with sepsis
  - ectopic pregnancy (*see also* categories 633.0–633.9) 639.0
  - molar pregnancy (*see also* categories 630–632) 639.0
- acute 683
  - mesenteric 289.2
- any site, except mesenteric 289.3
  - acute 683
  - chronic 289.1
  - mesenteric (acute) (chronic) (nonspecific) (subacute) 289.2
  - subacute 289.1
    - mesenteric 289.2
- breast, puerperal, postpartum 675.2 ☑
- chancroidal (congenital) 099.0
- chronic 289.1
  - mesenteric 289.2
- dermatopathic 695.89
- due to
  - anthracosis (occupational) 500
  - Brugia (Wuchereria) malayi 125.1
  - diphtheria (toxin) 032.89
  - lymphogranuloma venereum 099.1
  - Wuchereria bancrofti 125.0
- following
  - abortion 639.0
  - ectopic or molar pregnancy 639.0
- generalized 289.3
- gonorrheal 098.89
- granulomatous 289.1
- infectional 683
- mesenteric (acute) (chronic) (nonspecific) (subacute) 289.2
  - due to Bacillus typhi 002.0
  - tuberculous (*see also* Tuberculosis) 014.8 ☑
- mycobacterial 031.8
- purulent 683
- pyogenic 683
- regional 078.3
- septic 683
- streptococcal 683
- subacute, unspecified site 289.1
- suppurative 683
- syphilitic (early) (secondary) 091.4
  - late 095.8
- tuberculous — *see* Tuberculosis, lymph gland
- venereal 099.1

Lymphadenoid goiter 245.2
Lymphadenopathy (general) 785.6
- due to toxoplasmosis (acquired) 130.7
  - congenital (active) 771.2

Lymphadenopathy-associated virus (disease) (illness) (infection) — *see* Human immunodeficiency virus (disease) (illness) (infection)
Lymphadenosis 785.6
- acute 075

Lymphangiectasis 457.1
- conjunctiva 372.89
- postinfectional 457.1
- scrotum 457.1

Lymphangiectatic elephantiasis, nonfilarial 457.1
Lymphangioendothelioma (M9170/0) 228.1
- malignant (M9170/3) — *see* Neoplasm, connective tissue, malignant

Lymphangioma (M9170/0) 228.1
- capillary (M9171/0) 228.1
- cavernous (M9172/0) 228.1
- cystic (M9173/0) 228.1
- malignant (M9170/3) — *see* Neoplasm, connective tissue, malignant

Lymphangiomyoma (M9174/0) 228.1
Lymphangiomyomatosis (M9174/1) — *see* Neoplasm, connective tissue, uncertain behavior
Lymphangiosarcoma (M9170/3) — *see* Neoplasm, connective tissue, malignant
Lymphangitis 457.2
- with
  - abortion — *see* Abortion, by type, with sepsis
  - abscess — *see* Abscess, by site
  - cellulitis — *see* Abscess, by site
  - ectopic pregnancy (*see also* categories 633.0–633.9) 639.0
  - molar pregnancy (*see also* categories 630–632) 639.0
- acute (with abscess or cellulitis) 682.9
  - specified site — *see* Abscess, by site
- breast, puerperal, postpartum 675.2 ☑
- chancroidal 099.0
- chronic (any site) 457.2
- due to
  - Brugia (Wuchereria) malayi 125.1
  - Wuchereria bancrofti 125.0
- following
  - abortion 639.0
  - ectopic or molar pregnancy 639.0
- gangrenous 457.2
- penis
  - acute 607.2
  - gonococcal (acute) 098.0
    - chronic or duration of 2 months or more 098.2
- puerperal, postpartum, childbirth 670.0 ☑
- strumous, tuberculous (*see also* Tuberculosis) 017.2 ☑
- subacute (any site) 457.2
- tuberculous — *see* Tuberculosis, lymph gland

Lymphatic (vessel) — *see* condition
Lymphatism 254.8
- scrofulous (*see also* Tuberculosis) 017.2 ☑

Lymphectasia 457.1
Lymphedema — *see also* Elephantiasis 457.1
- acquired (chronic) 457.1
- chronic hereditary 757.0
- congenital 757.0
- idiopathic hereditary 757.0
- praecox 457.1
- secondary 457.1
- surgical NEC 997.99
  - postmastectomy (syndrome) 457.0

Lymph-hemangioma (M9120/0) — *see* Hemangioma, by site
Lymphoblastic — *see* condition
Lymphoblastoma (diffuse) (M9630/3) 200.1 ☑
- giant follicular (M9690/3) 202.0 ☑
- macrofollicular (M9690/3) 202.0 ☑

Lymphoblastosis, acute benign 075
Lymphocele 457.8
Lymphocythemia 288.51
Lymphocytic — *see also* condition
- chorioencephalitis (acute) (serous) 049.0
- choriomeningitis (acute) (serous) 049.0

Lymphocytoma (diffuse) (malignant) (M9620/3) 200.1 ☑
Lymphocytomatosis (M9620/3) 200.1 ☑
Lymphocytopenia 288.51
Lymphocytosis (symptomatic) 288.61
- infectious (acute) 078.89

Lymphoepithelioma (M8082/3) — *see* Neoplasm, by site, malignant
Lymphogranuloma (malignant) (M9650/3) 201.9 ☑
- inguinale 099.1
- venereal (any site) 099.1
  - with stricture of rectum 099.1
- venereum 099.1

Lymphogranulomatosis (malignant) (M9650/3) 201.9 ☑
- benign (Boeck's sarcoid) (Schaumann's) 135
- Hodgkin's (M9650/3) 201.9 ☑

Lymphohistiocytosis, familial hemophagocytic 288.4
Lymphoid — *see* condition
Lympholeukoblastoma (M9850/3) 207.8 ☑
Lympholeukosarcoma (M9850/3) 207.8 ☑
Lymphoma (malignant) (M9590/3) 202.8 ☑

Note — Use the following fifth-digit subclassification with categories 200–202:

0 unspecified site, extranodal and solid organ sites
1 lymph nodes of head, face, and neck
2 intrathoracic lymph nodes
3 intra-abdominal lymph nodes
4 lymph nodes of axilla and upper limb
5 lymph nodes of inguinal region and lower limb
6 intrapelvic lymph nodes
7 spleen
8 lymph nodes of multiple sites

- benign (M9590/0) — *see* Neoplasm, by site, benign
- Burkitt's type (lymphoblastic) (undifferentiated) (M9750/3) 200.2 ☑
- Castleman's (mediastinal lymph node hyperplasia) 785.6
- centroblastic-centrocytic
  - diffuse (M9614/3) 202.8 ☑
  - follicular (M9692/3) 202.0 ☑
- centroblastic type (diffuse) (M9632/3) 202.8 ☑
  - follicular (M9697/3) 202.0 ☑
- centrocytic (M9622/3) 202.8 ☑
- compound (M9613/3) 200.8 ☑
- convoluted cell type (lymphoblastic) (M9602/3) 202.8 ☑
- diffuse NEC (M9590/3) 202.8 ☑
  - large B cell 202.8 ☑
- follicular (giant) (M9690/3) 202.0 ☑
  - center cell (diffuse) (M9615/3) 202.8 ☑
    - cleaved (diffuse) (M9623/3) 202.8 ☑
      - follicular (M9695/3) 202.0 ☑
    - non-cleaved (diffuse) (M9633/3) 202.8 ☑
      - follicular (M9698/3) 202.0 ☑
  - centroblastic-centrocytic (M9692/3) 202.0 ☑
  - centroblastic type (M9697/3) 202.0 ☑
  - lymphocytic
    - intermediate differentiation (M9694/3) 202.0 ☑
    - poorly differentiated (M9696/3) 202.0 ☑

Lymphoma — *continued*
- follicular — *continued*
  - mixed (cell type) (lymphocytic-histiocytic) (small cell and large cell) (M9691/3) 202.0 ☑
- germinocytic (M9622/3) 202.8 ☑
- giant, follicular or follicle (M9690/3) 202.0 ☑
- histiocytic (diffuse) (M9640/3) 200.0 ☑
  - nodular (M9642/3) 200.0 ☑
  - pleomorphic cell type (M9641/3) 200.0 ☑
- Hodgkin's (M9650/3) (*see also* Disease, Hodgkin's) 201.9 ☑
- immunoblastic (type) (M9612/3) 200.8 ☑
- large cell (M9640/3) 200.7 ☑
  - anaplastic 200.6 ☑
  - nodular (M9642/3) 200.0 ☑
  - pleomorphic cell type (M9641/3) 200.0 ☑
- lymphoblastic (diffuse) (M9630/3) 200.1 ☑
  - Burkitt's type (M9750/3) 200.2 ☑
  - convoluted cell type (M9602/3) 202.8 ☑
- lymphocytic (cell type) (diffuse) (M9620/3) 200.1 ☑
  - with plasmacytoid differentiation, diffuse (M9611/3) 200.8 ☑
  - intermediate differentiation (diffuse) (M9621/3) 200.1 ☑
    - follicular (M9694/3) 202.0 ☑
    - nodular (M9694/3) 202.0 ☑
  - nodular (M9690/3) 202.0 ☑
  - poorly differentiated (diffuse) (M9630/3) 200.1 ☑
    - follicular (M9696/3) 202.0 ☑
    - nodular (M9696/3) 202.0 ☑
  - well differentiated (diffuse) (M9620/3) 200.1 ☑
    - follicular (M9693/3) 202.0 ☑
    - nodular (M9693/3) 202.0 ☑
- lymphocytic-histiocytic, mixed (diffuse) (M9613/3) 200.8 ☑
  - follicular (M9691/3) 202.0 ☑
  - nodular (M9691/3) 202.0 ☑
- lymphoplasmacytoid type (M9611/3) 200.8 ☑
- lymphosarcoma type (M9610/3) 200.1 ☑
- macrofollicular (M9690/3) 202.0 ☑
- mantle cell 200.4 ☑
- marginal zone 200.3 ☑
  - extranodal B-cell 200.3 ☑
  - nodal B-cell 200.3 ☑
  - splenic B-cell 200.3 ☑
- mixed cell type (diffuse) (M9613/3) 200.8 ☑
  - follicular (M9691/3) 202.0 ☑
  - nodular (M9691/3) 202.0 ☑
- nodular (M9690/3) 202.0 ☑
  - histiocytic (M9642/3) 200.0 ☑
  - lymphocytic (M9690/3) 202.0 ☑
    - intermediate differentiation (M9694/3) 202.0 ☑
    - poorly differentiated (M9696/3) 202.0 ☑
  - mixed (cell type) (lymphocytic-histiocytic) (small cell and large cell) (M9691/3) 202.0 ☑
- non-Hodgkin's type NEC (M9591/3) 202.8 ☑
- peripheral T-cell 202.7 ☑
- primary central nervous system 200.5 ☑
- reticulum cell (type) (M9640/3) 200.0 ☑
- small cell and large cell, mixed (diffuse) (M9613/3) 200.8 ☑
  - follicular (M9691/3) 202.0 ☑
  - nodular (9691/3) 202.0 ☑
- stem cell (type) (M9601/3) 202.8 ☑
- T-cell 202.1 ☑

Lymphoma — *continued*
- T-cell — *continued*
  - peripheral 202.7 ☑
- undifferentiated (cell type) (non-Burkitt's) (M9600/3) 202.8 ☑
  - Burkitt's type (M9750/3) 200.2 ☑

Lymphomatosis (M9590/3) — *see also* Lymphoma
- granulomatous 099.1

Lymphopathia
- venereum 099.1
- veneris 099.1

Lymphopenia 288.51
- familial 279.2

Lymphoreticulosis, benign (of inoculation) 078.3

Lymphorrhea 457.8

Lymphosarcoma (M9610/3) 200.1 ☑
- diffuse (M9610/3) 200.1 ☑
  - with plasmacytoid differentiation (M9611/3) 200.8 ☑
  - lymphoplasmacytic (M9611/3) 200.8 ☑
- follicular (giant) (M9690/3) 202.0 ☑
  - lymphoblastic (M9696/3) 202.0 ☑
  - lymphocytic, intermediate differentiation (M9694/3) 202.0 ☑
  - mixed cell type (M9691/3) 202.0 ☑
- giant follicular (M9690/3) 202.0 ☑
- Hodgkin's (M9650/3) 201.9 ☑
- immunoblastic (M9612/3) 200.8 ☑
- lymphoblastic (diffuse) (M9630/3) 200.1 ☑
  - follicular (M9696/3) 202.0 ☑
  - nodular (M9696/3) 202.0 ☑
- lymphocytic (diffuse) (M9620/3) 200.1 ☑
  - intermediate differentiation (diffuse) (M9621/3) 200.1 ☑
    - follicular (M9694/3) 202.0 ☑
    - nodular (M9694/3) 202.0 ☑
- mixed cell type (diffuse) (M9613/3) 200.8 ☑
  - follicular (M9691/3) 202.0 ☑
  - nodular (M9691/3) 202.0 ☑
- nodular (M9690/3) 202.0 ☑
  - lymphoblastic (M9696/3) 202.0 ☑
  - lymphocytic, intermediate differentiation (M9694/3) 202.0 ☑
  - mixed cell type (M9691/3) 202.0 ☑
- prolymphocytic (M9631/3) 200.1 ☑
- reticulum cell (M9640/3) 200.0 ☑

Lymphostasis 457.8

Lypemania — *see also* Melancholia 296.2 ☑

Lyssa 071

M

Macacus ear 744.29

Maceration
- fetus (cause not stated) 779.9
- wet feet, tropical (syndrome) 991.4

Machado-Joseph disease 334.8

Machupo virus hemorrhagic fever 078.7

Macleod's syndrome (abnormal transradiancy, one lung) 492.8

Macrocephalia, macrocephaly 756.0

Macrocheilia (congenital) 744.81

Macrochilia (congenital) 744.81

Macrocolon (congenital) 751.3

Macrocornea 743.41
- associated with buphthalmos 743.22

Macrocytic — *see* condition

Macrocytosis 289.89

Macrodactylia, macrodactylism (fingers) (thumbs) 755.57
- toes 755.65

Macrodontia 520.2

Macroencephaly 742.4

Macrogenia 524.05

Macrogenitosomia (female) (male) (praecox) 255.2

Macrogingivae 523.8

Macroglobulinemia (essential) (idiopathic) (monoclonal) (primary) (syndrome) (Waldenström's) 273.3

Macroglossia (congenital) 750.15
- acquired 529.8

Macrognathia, macrognathism (congenital) 524.00
- mandibular 524.02
  - alveolar 524.72
- maxillary 524.01
  - alveolar 524.71

Macrogyria (congenital) 742.4

Macrohydrocephalus — *see also* Hydrocephalus 331.4

Macromastia — *see also* Hypertrophy, breast 611.1

Macrophage activation syndrome 288.4

Macropsia 368.14

Macrosigmoid 564.7
- congenital 751.3

Macrospondylitis, acromegalic 253.0

Macrostomia (congenital) 744.83

Macrotia (external ear) (congenital) 744.22

Macula
- cornea, corneal
  - congenital 743.43
    - interfering with vision 743.42
  - interfering with central vision 371.03
  - not interfering with central vision 371.02
- degeneration (*see also* Degeneration, macula) 362.50
  - hereditary (*see also* Dystrophy, retina) 362.70
- edema, cystoid 362.53

Maculae ceruleae 132.1

Macules and papules 709.8

Maculopathy, toxic 362.55

Madarosis 374.55

Madelung's
- deformity (radius) 755.54
- disease (lipomatosis) 272.8
- lipomatosis 272.8

Madness — *see also* Psychosis 298.9
- myxedema (acute) 293.0
  - subacute 293.1

Madura
- disease (actinomycotic) 039.9
  - mycotic 117.4
- foot (actinomycotic) 039.4
  - mycotic 117.4

Maduromycosis (actinomycotic) 039.9
- mycotic 117.4

Maffucci's syndrome (dyschondroplasia with hemangiomas) 756.4

Magenblase syndrome 306.4

Main en griffe (acquired) 736.06
- congenital 755.59

Maintenance
- chemotherapy regimen or treatment V58.11
- dialysis regimen or treatment
  - extracorporeal (renal) V56.0
  - peritoneal V56.8
  - renal V56.0
- drug therapy or regimen
  - chemotherapy, antineoplastic V58.11
  - immunotherapy, antineoplastic V58.12
- external fixation NEC V54.89
- radiotherapy V58.0
- traction NEC V54.89

Majocchi's
- disease (purpura annularis telangiectodes) 709.1
- granuloma 110.6

Major — *see* condition

Mal
- cerebral (idiopathic) (*see also* Epilepsy) 345.9 ☑
- comital (*see also* Epilepsy) 345.9 ☑
- de los pintos (*see also* Pinta) 103.9
- de Meleda 757.39

Mal — *continued*
- de mer 994.6
- lie — *see* Presentation, fetal
- perforant (*see also* Ulcer, lower extremity) 707.15

Malabar itch 110.9
- beard 110.0
- foot 110.4
- scalp 110.0

Malabsorption 579.9
- calcium 579.8
- carbohydrate 579.8
- disaccharide 271.3
- drug-induced 579.8
- due to bacterial overgrowth 579.8
- fat 579.8
- folate, congenital 281.2
- galactose 271.1
- glucose-galactose (congenital) 271.3
- intestinal 579.9
- isomaltose 271.3
- lactose (hereditary) 271.3
- methionine 270.4
- monosaccharide 271.8
- postgastrectomy 579.3
- postsurgical 579.3
- protein 579.8
- sucrose (-isomaltose) (congenital) 271.3
- syndrome 579.9
  - postgastrectomy 579.3
  - postsurgical 579.3

Malacia, bone 268.2
- juvenile (*see also* Rickets) 268.0
- Kienböck's (juvenile) (lunate) (wrist) 732.3
  - adult 732.8

Malacoplakia
- bladder 596.8
- colon 569.89
- pelvis (kidney) 593.89
- ureter 593.89
- urethra 599.84

Malacosteon 268.2
- juvenile (*see also* Rickets) 268.0

Maladaptation — *see* Maladjustment

Maladie de Roger 745.4

Maladjustment
- conjugal V61.10
  - involving
    - divorce V61.03 ●
    - estrangement V61.09 ●
- educational V62.3
- family V61.9
  - specified circumstance NEC V61.8
- marital V61.10
  - involving
    - divorce V61.03 ●
    - estrangement V61.09 ●
- occupational V62.29 ▲
  - current military deployment status V62.21 ●
- simple, adult (*see also* Reaction, adjustment) 309.9
- situational acute (*see also* Reaction, adjustment) 309.9
- social V62.4

Malaise 780.79

Malakoplakia — *see* Malacoplakia

Malaria, malarial (fever) 084.6
- algid 084.9
- any type, with
  - algid malaria 084.9
  - blackwater fever 084.8
  - fever
    - blackwater 084.8
    - hemoglobinuric (bilious) 084.8
  - hemoglobinuria, malarial 084.8
  - hepatitis 084.9 *[573.2]*
  - nephrosis 084.9 *[581.81]*
  - pernicious complication NEC 084.9
    - cardiac 084.9
    - cerebral 084.9
- cardiac 084.9
- carrier (suspected) of V02.9
- cerebral 084.9

Malaria, malarial — *continued*
complicating pregnancy, childbirth, or puerperium 647.4 ☑
congenital 771.2
congestion, congestive 084.6
brain 084.9
continued 084.0
estivo-autumnal 084.0
falciparum (malignant tertian) 084.0
hematinuria 084.8
hematuria 084.8
hemoglobinuria 084.8
hemorrhagic 084.6
induced (therapeutically) 084.7
accidental — *see* Malaria, by type
liver 084.9 *[573.2]*
malariae (quartan) 084.2
malignant (tertian) 084.0
mixed infections 084.5
monkey 084.4
ovale 084.3
pernicious, acute 084.0
Plasmodium, P.
falciparum 084.0
malariae 084.2
ovale 084.3
vivax 084.1
quartan 084.2
quotidian 084.0
recurrent 084.6
induced (therapeutically) 084.7
accidental — *see* Malaria, by type
remittent 084.6
specified types NEC 084.4
spleen 084.6
subtertian 084.0
tertian (benign) 084.1
malignant 084.0
tropical 084.0
typhoid 084.6
vivax (benign tertian) 084.1
Malassez's disease (testicular cyst) 608.89
Malassimilation 579.9
Maldescent, testis 752.51
Maldevelopment — *see also* Anomaly, by site
brain 742.9
colon 751.5
hip (joint) 755.63
congenital dislocation (*see also* Dislocation, hip, congenital) 754.30
mastoid process 756.0
middle ear, except ossicles 744.03
ossicles 744.04
newborn (not malformation) 764.9 ☑
ossicles, ear 744.04
spine 756.10
toe 755.66
Male type pelvis 755.69
with disproportion (fetopelvic) 653.2 ☑
affecting fetus or newborn 763.1
causing obstructed labor 660.1 ☑
affecting fetus or newborn 763.1
Malformation (congenital) — *see also* Anomaly
bone 756.9
bursa 756.9
Chiari
type I 348.4
type II (*see also* Spina bifida) 741.0 ☑
type III 742.0
type IV 742.2
circulatory system NEC 747.9
specified type NEC 747.89
cochlea 744.05
digestive system NEC 751.9
lower 751.5
specified type NEC 751.8
upper 750.9
eye 743.9
gum 750.9
heart NEC 746.9

Malformation — *see also* Anomaly — *continued*
heart — *continued*
specified type NEC 746.89
valve 746.9
internal ear 744.05
joint NEC 755.9
specified type NEC 755.8
Mondini's (congenital) (malformation, cochlea) 744.05
muscle 756.9
nervous system (central) 742.9
pelvic organs or tissues
in pregnancy or childbirth 654.9 ☑
affecting fetus or newborn 763.89
causing obstructed labor 660.2 ☑
affecting fetus or newborn 763.1
placenta (*see also* Placenta, abnormal) 656.7 ☑
respiratory organs 748.9
specified type NEC 748.8
Rieger's 743.44
sense organs NEC 742.9
specified type NEC 742.8
skin 757.9
specified type NEC 757.8
spinal cord 742.9
teeth, tooth NEC 520.9
tendon 756.9
throat 750.9
umbilical cord (complicating delivery) 663.9 ☑
affecting fetus or newborn 762.6
umbilicus 759.9
urinary system NEC 753.9
specified type NEC 753.8
venous — *see* Anomaly, vein ●
Malfunction — *see also* Dysfunction
arterial graft 996.1
cardiac pacemaker 996.01
catheter device — *see* Complications, mechanical, catheter
colostomy 569.62
valve 569.62
cystostomy 997.5
device, implant, or graft NEC — *see* Complications, mechanical
enteric stoma 569.62
enterostomy 569.62
esophagostomy 530.87
gastroenteric 536.8
gastrostomy 536.42
ileostomy
valve 569.62
nephrostomy 997.5
pacemaker — *see* Complications, mechanical, pacemaker
prosthetic device, internal — *see* Complications, mechanical
tracheostomy 519.02
valve
colostomy 569.62
ileostomy 569.62
vascular graft or shunt 996.1
Malgaigne's fracture (closed) 808.43
open 808.53
Malherbe's
calcifying epithelioma (M8110/0) — *see* Neoplasm, skin, benign
tumor (M8110/0) — *see* Neoplasm, skin, benign
Malibu disease 919.8
infected 919.9
Malignancy (M8000/3) — *see* Neoplasm, by site, malignant
Malignant — *see* condition
Malingerer, malingering V65.2
Mallet, finger (acquired) 736.1
congenital 755.59
late effect of rickets 268.1
Malleus 024
Mallory's bodies 034.1
Mallory-Weiss syndrome 530.7

Malnutrition (calorie) 263.9
complicating pregnancy 648.9 ☑
degree
first 263.1
second 263.0
third 262
mild 263.1
moderate 263.0
severe 261
protein-calorie 262
fetus 764.2 ☑
"light-for-dates" 764.1 ☑
following gastrointestinal surgery 579.3
intrauterine or fetal 764.2 ☑
fetus or infant "light-for-dates" 764.1 ☑
lack of care, or neglect (child) (infant) 995.52
adult 995.84
malignant 260
mild 263.1
moderate 263.0
protein 260
protein-calorie 263.9
severe 262
specified type NEC 263.8
severe 261
protein-calorie NEC 262
Malocclusion (teeth) 524.4
angle's class I 524.21
angle's class II 524.22
angle's class III 524.23
due to
abnormal swallowing 524.59
accessory teeth (causing crowding) 524.31
dentofacial abnormality NEC 524.89
impacted teeth (causing crowding) 520.6
missing teeth 524.30
mouth breathing 524.59
sleep postures 524.59
supernumerary teeth (causing crowding) 524.31
thumb sucking 524.59
tongue, lip, or finger habits 524.59
temporomandibular (joint) 524.69
Malposition
cardiac apex (congenital) 746.87
cervix — *see* Malposition, uterus
congenital
adrenal (gland) 759.1
alimentary tract 751.8
lower 751.5
upper 750.8
aorta 747.21
appendix 751.5
arterial trunk 747.29
artery (peripheral) NEC (*see also* Malposition, congenital, peripheral vascular system) 747.60
coronary 746.85
pulmonary 747.3
auditory canal 744.29
causing impairment of hearing 744.02
auricle (ear) 744.29
causing impairment of hearing 744.02
cervical 744.43
biliary duct or passage 751.69
bladder (mucosa) 753.8
exteriorized or extroverted 753.5
brachial plexus 742.8
brain tissue 742.4
breast 757.6
bronchus 748.3
cardiac apex 746.87
cecum 751.5
clavicle 755.51
colon 751.5
digestive organ or tract NEC 751.8
lower 751.5

Malposition — *continued*
congenital — *continued*
digestive organ or tract — *continued*
upper 750.8
ear (auricle) (external) 744.29
ossicles 744.04
endocrine (gland) NEC 759.2
epiglottis 748.3
Eustachian tube 744.24
eye 743.8
facial features 744.89
fallopian tube 752.19
finger(s) 755.59
supernumerary 755.01
foot 755.67
gallbladder 751.69
gastrointestinal tract 751.8
genitalia, genital organ(s) or tract
female 752.89
external 752.49
internal NEC 752.89
male 752.89
penis 752.69
scrotal transposition 752.81
glottis 748.3
hand 755.59
heart 746.87
dextrocardia 746.87
with complete transposition of viscera 759.3
hepatic duct 751.69
hip (joint) (*see also* Dislocation, hip, congenital) 754.30
intestine (large) (small) 751.5
with anomalous adhesions, fixation, or malrotation 751.4
joint NEC 755.8
kidney 753.3
larynx 748.3
limb 755.8
lower 755.69
upper 755.59
liver 751.69
lung (lobe) 748.69
nail(s) 757.5
nerve 742.8
nervous system NEC 742.8
nose, nasal (septum) 748.1
organ or site NEC — *see* Anomaly, specified type NEC, by site
ovary 752.0
pancreas 751.7
parathyroid (gland) 759.2
patella 755.64
peripheral vascular system 747.60
gastrointestinal 747.61
lower limb 747.64
renal 747.62
specified NEC 747.69
spinal 747.82
upper limb 747.63
pituitary (gland) 759.2
respiratory organ or system NEC 748.9
rib (cage) 756.3
supernumerary in cervical region 756.2
scapula 755.59
shoulder 755.59
spinal cord 742.59
spine 756.19
spleen 759.0
sternum 756.3
stomach 750.7
symphysis pubis 755.69
testis (undescended) 752.51
thymus (gland) 759.2
thyroid (gland) (tissue) 759.2
cartilage 748.3
toe(s) 755.66
supernumerary 755.02
tongue 750.19
trachea 748.3
uterus 752.3

Malposition — *continued*
congenital — *continued*
vein(s) (peripheral) NEC (*see also* Malposition, congenital, peripheral vascular system) 747.60
great 747.49
portal 747.49
pulmonary 747.49
vena cava (inferior) (superior) 747.49
device, implant, or graft — *see* Complications, mechanical
fetus NEC (*see also* Presentation, fetal) 652.9 ☑
with successful version 652.1 ☑
affecting fetus or newborn 763.1
before labor, affecting fetus or newborn 761.7
causing obstructed labor 660.0 ☑
in multiple gestation (one fetus or more) 652.6 ☑
with locking 660.5 ☑
causing obstructed labor 660.0 ☑
gallbladder (*see also* Disease, gallbladder) 575.8
gastrointestinal tract 569.89
congenital 751.8
heart (*see also* Malposition, congenital, heart) 746.87
intestine 569.89
congenital 751.5
pelvic organs or tissues
in pregnancy or childbirth 654.4 ☑
affecting fetus or newborn 763.89
causing obstructed labor 660.2 ☑
affecting fetus or newborn 763.1
placenta — *see* Placenta, previa
stomach 537.89
congenital 750.7
tooth, teeth 524.30
with impaction 520.6
uterus (acquired) (acute) (adherent) (any degree) (asymptomatic) (postinfectional) (postpartal, old) 621.6
anteflexion or anteversion (*see also* Anteversion, uterus) 621.6
congenital 752.3
flexion 621.6
lateral (*see also* Lateroversion, uterus) 621.6
in pregnancy or childbirth 654.4 ☑
affecting fetus or newborn 763.89
causing obstructed labor 660.2 ☑
affecting fetus or newborn 763.1
inversion 621.6
lateral (flexion) (version) (*see also* Lateroversion, uterus) 621.6
lateroflexion (*see also* Lateroversion, uterus) 621.6
lateroversion (*see also* Lateroversion, uterus) 621.6
retroflexion or retroversion (*see also* Retroversion, uterus) 621.6
Malposture 729.90 ▲
Malpresentation, fetus — *see also* Presentation, fetal 652.9 ☑
Malrotation
cecum 751.4
colon 751.4
intestine 751.4
kidney 753.3
MALT (mucosa associated lymphoid tissue) 200.3 ☑
Malta fever — *see also* Brucellosis 023.9
Maltosuria 271.3
Maltreatment (of)
adult 995.80
emotional 995.82
multiple forms 995.85
neglect (nutritional) 995.84
physical 995.81
psychological 995.82
sexual 995.83
child 995.50
emotional 995.51
multiple forms 995.59
neglect (nutritional) 995.52
physical 995.54
shaken infant syndrome 995.55
psychological 995.51
sexual 995.53
spouse (*see also* Maltreatment, adult) 995.80
Malt workers' lung 495.4
Malum coxae senilis 715.25
Malunion, fracture 733.81
Mammillitis — *see also* Mastitis 611.0
puerperal, postpartum 675.2 ☑
Mammitis — *see also* Mastitis 611.0
puerperal, postpartum 675.2 ☑
Mammographic
calcification 793.89
calculus 793.89
microcalcification 793.81
Mammoplasia 611.1
Management
contraceptive V25.9
specified type NEC V25.8
procreative V26.9
specified type NEC V26.89
Mangled NEC — *see also* nature and site of injury 959.9
Mania (monopolar) — *see also* Psychosis, affective 296.0 ☑
alcoholic (acute) (chronic) 291.9
Bell's — *see* Mania, chronic
chronic 296.0 ☑
recurrent episode 296.1 ☑
single episode 296.0 ☑
compulsive 300.3
delirious (acute) 296.0 ☑
recurrent episode 296.1 ☑
single episode 296.0 ☑
epileptic (*see also* Epilepsy) 345.4 ☑
hysterical 300.10
inhibited 296.89
puerperal (after delivery) 296.0 ☑
recurrent episode 296.1 ☑
single episode 296.0 ☑
recurrent episode 296.1 ☑
senile 290.8
single episode 296.0 ☑
stupor 296.89
stuporous 296.89
unproductive 296.89
Manic-depressive insanity, psychosis, reaction, or syndrome — *see also* Psychosis, affective 296.80
circular (alternating) 296.7
currently
depressed 296.5 ☑
episode unspecified 296.7
hypomanic, previously depressed 296.4 ☑
manic 296.4 ☑
mixed 296.6 ☑
depressed (type), depressive 296.2 ☑
atypical 296.82
recurrent episode 296.3 ☑
single episode 296.2 ☑
hypomanic 296.0 ☑
recurrent episode 296.1 ☑
single episode 296.0 ☑
manic 296.0 ☑
atypical 296.81
recurrent episode 296.1 ☑
single episode 296.0 ☑
mixed NEC 296.89
perplexed 296.89
stuporous 296.89
Manifestations, rheumatoid
lungs 714.81
pannus — *see* Arthritis, rheumatoid
subcutaneous nodules — *see* Arthritis, rheumatoid
Mankowsky's syndrome (familial dysplastic osteopathy) 731.2
Mannoheptulosuria 271.8
Mannosidosis 271.8
Manson's
disease (schistosomiasis) 120.1
pyosis (pemphigus contagiosus) 684
schistosomiasis 120.1
Mansonellosis 125.5
Manual — *see* condition
Maple bark disease 495.6
Maple bark-strippers' lung 495.6
Maple syrup (urine) disease or syndrome 270.3
Marable's syndrome (celiac artery compression) 447.4
Marasmus 261
brain 331.9
due to malnutrition 261
intestinal 569.89
nutritional 261
senile 797
tuberculous NEC (*see also* Tuberculosis) 011.9 ☑
Marble
bones 756.52
skin 782.61
Marburg disease (virus) 078.89
March
foot 733.94
hemoglobinuria 283.2
Marchand multiple nodular hyperplasia (liver) 571.5
Marchesani (-Weill) syndrome (brachymorphism and ectopia lentis) 759.89
Marchiafava (-Bignami) disease or syndrome 341.8
Marchiafava-Micheli syndrome (paroxysmal nocturnal hemoglobinuria) 283.2
Marcus Gunn's syndrome (jaw-winking syndrome) 742.8
Marfan's
congenital syphilis 090.49
disease 090.49
syndrome (arachnodactyly) 759.82
meaning congenital syphilis 090.49
with luxation of lens 090.49 *[379.32]*
Marginal
implantation, placenta — *see* Placenta, previa
placenta — *see* Placenta, previa
sinus (hemorrhage) (rupture) 641.2 ☑
affecting fetus or newborn 762.1
Marie's
cerebellar ataxia 334.2
syndrome (acromegaly) 253.0
Marie-Bamberger disease or syndrome (hypertrophic) (pulmonary) (secondary) 731.2
idiopathic (acropachyderma) 757.39
primary (acropachyderma) 757.39
Marie-Charcôt-Tooth neuropathic atrophy, muscle 356.1
Marie-Strümpell arthritis or disease (ankylosing spondylitis) 720.0
Marihuana, marijuana
abuse (*see also* Abuse, drugs, nondependent) 305.2 ☑
dependence (*see also* Dependence) 304.3 ☑
Marion's disease (bladder neck obstruction) 596.0
Marital conflict V61.10
Mark
port wine 757.32
raspberry 757.32
strawberry 757.32
stretch 701.3
Mark — *continued*
tattoo 709.09
Maroteaux-Lamy syndrome (mucopolysaccharidosis VI) 277.5
Marriage license examination V70.3
Marrow (bone)
arrest 284.9
megakaryocytic 287.30
poor function 289.9
Marseilles fever 082.1
Marshall's (hidrotic) **ectodermal dysplasia** 757.31
Marsh's disease (exophthalmic goiter) 242.0 ☑
Marsh fever — *see also* Malaria 084.6
Martin-Albright syndrome (pseudohypoparathyroidism) 275.49
Martin's disease 715.27
Martorell-Fabre syndrome (pulseless disease) 446.7
Masculinization, female , with adrenal hyperplasia 255.2
Masculinovoblastoma (M8670/0) 220
Masochism 302.83
Masons' lung 502
Mass
abdominal 789.3 ☑
anus 787.99
bone 733.90
breast 611.72
cheek 784.2
chest 786.6
cystic — *see* Cyst
ear 388.8
epigastric 789.3 ☑
eye 379.92
female genital organ 625.8
gum 784.2
head 784.2
intracranial 784.2
joint 719.60
ankle 719.67
elbow 719.62
foot 719.67
hand 719.64
hip 719.65
knee 719.66
multiple sites 719.69
pelvic region 719.65
shoulder (region) 719.61
specified site NEC 719.68
wrist 719.63
kidney (*see also* Disease, kidney) 593.9
lung 786.6
lymph node 785.6
malignant (M8000/3) — *see* Neoplasm, by site, malignant
mediastinal 786.6
mouth 784.2
muscle (limb) 729.89
neck 784.2
nose or sinus 784.2
palate 784.2
pelvis, pelvic 789.3 ☑
penis 607.89
perineum 625.8
rectum 787.99
scrotum 608.89
skin 782.2
specified organ NEC — *see* Disease of specified organ or site
splenic 789.2
substernal 786.6
thyroid (*see also* Goiter) 240.9
superficial (localized) 782.2
testes 608.89
throat 784.2
tongue 784.2
umbilicus 789.3 ☑
uterus 625.8
vagina 625.8
vulva 625.8
Massive — *see* condition
Mastalgia 611.71
psychogenic 307.89

Mast cell
disease 757.33
systemic (M9741/3) 202.6 ☑
leukemia (M9900/3) 207.8 ☑
sarcoma (M9742/3) 202.6 ☑
tumor (M9740/1) 238.5
malignant (M9740/3) 202.6 ☑
Masters-Allen syndrome 620.6
Mastitis (acute) (adolescent) (diffuse) (interstitial) (lobular) (nonpurperal) (nonsuppurative) (parenchymatous) (phlegmonous) (simple) (subacute) (suppurative) 611.0
chronic (cystic) (fibrocystic) 610.1
cystic 610.1
Schimmelbusch's type 610.1
fibrocystic 610.1
infective 611.0
lactational 675.2 ☑
lymphangitis 611.0
neonatal (noninfective) 778.7
infective 771.5
periductal 610.4
plasma cell 610.4
puerperalis 675.2 ☑
puerperal, postpartum, (interstitial) (nonpurulent) (parenchymatous) 675.2 ☑
purulent 675.1 ☑
stagnation 676.2 ☑
retromammary 611.0
puerperal, postpartum 675.1 ☑
submammary 611.0
puerperal, postpartum 675.1 ☑
Mastocytoma (M9740/1) 238.5
malignant (M9740/3) 202.6 ☑
Mastocytosis 757.33
malignant (M9741/3) 202.6 ☑
systemic (M9741/3) 202.6 ☑
Mastodynia 611.71
psychogenic 307.89
Mastoid — *see* condition
Mastoidalgia — *see also* Otalgia 388.70
Mastoiditis (coalescent) (hemorrhagic) (pneumococcal) (streptococcal) (suppurative) 383.9
acute or subacute 383.00
with
Gradenigo's syndrome 383.02
petrositis 383.02
specified complication NEC 383.02
subperiosteal abscess 383.01
chronic (necrotic) (recurrent) 383.1
tuberculous (*see also* Tuberculosis) 015.6 ☑
Mastopathy, mastopathia 611.9
chronica cystica 610.1
diffuse cystic 610.1
estrogenic 611.89 ▲
ovarian origin 611.89 ▲
Mastoplasia 611.1
Masturbation 307.9
Maternal condition, affecting fetus or newborn
acute yellow atrophy of liver 760.8
albuminuria 760.1
anesthesia or analgesia 763.5
blood loss 762.1
chorioamnionitis 762.7
circulatory disease, chronic (conditions classifiable to 390–459, 745–747) 760.3
congenital heart disease (conditions classifiable to 745–746) 760.3
cortical necrosis of kidney 760.1
death 761.6
diabetes mellitus 775.0
manifest diabetes in the infant 775.1
disease NEC 760.9
circulatory system, chronic (conditions classifiable to 390–459, 745–747) 760.3

Maternal condition, affecting fetus or newborn — *continued*
disease — *continued*
genitourinary system (conditions classifiable to 580–599) 760.1
respiratory (conditions classifiable to 490–519, 748) 760.3
eclampsia 760.0
hemorrhage NEC 762.1
hepatitis acute, malignant, or subacute 760.8
hyperemesis (gravidarum) 761.8
hypertension (arising during pregnancy) (conditions classifiable to 642) 760.0
infection
disease classifiable to 001-136 ☑, 760.2
genital tract NEC 760.8
urinary tract 760.1
influenza 760.2
manifest influenza in the infant 771.2
injury (conditions classifiable to 800–996) 760.5
malaria 760.2
manifest malaria in infant or fetus 771.2
malnutrition 760.4
necrosis of liver 760.8
nephritis (conditions classifiable to 580–583) 760.1
nephrosis (conditions classifiable to 581) 760.1
noxious substance transmitted via breast milk or placenta 760.70
alcohol 760.71
anticonvulsants 760.77
antifungals 760.74
anti-infective agents 760.74
antimetabolics 760.78
cocaine 760.75
"crack" 760.75
diethylstilbestrol [DES] 760.76
hallucinogenic agents 760.73
medicinal agents NEC 760.79
narcotics 760.72
obstetric anesthetic or analgesic drug 760.72
specified agent NEC 760.79
nutritional disorder (conditions classifiable to 260–269) 760.4
operation unrelated to current delivery ▶(*see also* Newborn, affected by)◀ 760.64 ▲
pre-eclampsia 760.0
pyelitis or pyelonephritis, arising during pregnancy (conditions classifiable to 590) 760.1
renal disease or failure 760.1
respiratory disease, chronic (conditions classifiable to 490–519, 748) 760.3
rheumatic heart disease (chronic) (conditions classifiable to 393–398) 760.3
rubella (conditions classifiable to 056) 760.2
manifest rubella in the infant or fetus 771.0
surgery unrelated to current delivery ▶(*see also* Newborn, affected by)◀ 760.64 ▲
to uterus or pelvic organs 760.64 ▲
syphilis (conditions classifiable to 090 097) 760.2
manifest syphilis in the infant or fetus 090.0
thrombophlebitis 760.3
toxemia (of pregnancy) 760.0
pre-eclamptic 760.0
toxoplasmosis (conditions classifiable to 130) 760.2

Maternal condition, affecting fetus or newborn — *continued*
toxoplasmosis — *continued*
manifest toxoplasmosis in the infant or fetus 771.2
transmission of chemical substance through the placenta 760.70
alcohol 760.71
anticonvulsants 760.77
antifungals 760.74
anti-infective 760.74
antimetabolics 760.78
cocaine 760.75
"crack" 760.75
diethylstilbestrol [DES] 760.76
hallucinogenic agents 760.73
narcotics 760.72
specified substance NEC 760.79
uremia 760.1
urinary tract conditions (conditions classifiable to 580–599) 760.1
vomiting (pernicious) (persistent) (vicious) 761.8
Maternity — *see* Delivery
Matheiu's disease (leptospiral jaundice) 100.0
Mauclaire's disease or osteochondrosis 732.3
Maxcy's disease 081.0
Maxilla, maxillary — *see* condition
May (-Hegglin) anomaly or syndrome 288.2
Mayaro fever 066.3
Mazoplasia 610.8
MBD (minimal brain dysfunction), child — *see also* Hyperkinesia 314.9
MCAD (medium chain acyl CoA dehydrogenase deficiency) 277.85
McArdle (-Schmid-Pearson) disease or syndrome (glycogenosis V) 271.0
McCune-Albright syndrome (osteitis fibrosa disseminata) 756.59
MCLS (mucocutaneous lymph node syndrome) 446.1
McQuarrie's syndrome (idiopathic familial hypoglycemia) 251.2
Measles (black) (hemorrhagic) (suppressed) 055.9
with
encephalitis 055.0
keratitis 055.71
keratoconjunctivitis 055.71
otitis media 055.2
pneumonia 055.1
complication 055.8
specified type NEC 055.79
encephalitis 055.0
French 056.9
German 056.9
keratitis 055.71
keratoconjunctivitis 055.71
liberty 056.9
otitis media 055.2
pneumonia 055.1
specified complications NEC 055.79
vaccination, prophylactic (against) V04.2
Meatitis, urethral — *see also* Urethritis 597.89
Meat poisoning — *see* Poisoning, food
Meatus, meatal — *see* condition
Meat-wrappers' asthma 506.9
Meckel's
diverticulitis 751.0
diverticulum (displaced) (hypertrophic) 751.0
Meconium
aspiration 770.11
with
pneumonia 770.12
pneumonitis 770.12
respiratory symptoms 770.12
below vocal cords 770.11
with respiratory symptoms 770.12
syndrome 770.12

Meconium — *continued*
delayed passage in newborn 777.1
ileus 777.1
due to cystic fibrosis 277.01
in liquor 792.3
noted during delivery 656.8 ☑
insufflation 770.11
with respiratory symptoms 770.12
obstruction
fetus or newborn 777.1
in mucoviscidosis 277.01
passage of 792.3
noted during delivery 763.84
peritonitis 777.6
plug syndrome (newborn) NEC 777.1
staining 779.84
Median — *see also* condition
arcuate ligament syndrome 447.4
bar (prostate) 600.90
with
other lower urinary tract symptoms (LUTS) 600.91
urinary
obstruction 600.91
retention 600.91
rhomboid glossitis 529.2
vesical orifice 600.90
with
other lower urinary tract symptoms (LUTS) 600.91
urinary
obstruction 600.91
retention 600.91
Mediastinal shift 793.2
Mediastinitis (acute) (chronic) 519.2
actinomycotic 039.8
syphilitic 095.8
tuberculous (*see also* Tuberculosis) 012.8 ☑
Mediastinopericarditis — *see also* Pericarditis 423.9
acute 420.90
chronic 423.8
rheumatic 393
rheumatic, chronic 393
Mediastinum, mediastinal — *see* condition
Medical services provided for — *see* Health, services provided because (of)
Medicine poisoning (by overdose) (wrong substance given or taken in error) 977.9
specified drug or substance — *see* Table of Drugs and Chemicals
Medin's disease (poliomyelitis) 045.9 ☑
Mediterranean
anemia (with other hemoglobinopathy) 282.49
disease or syndrome (hemipathic) 282.49
fever (*see also* Brucellosis) 023.9
familial 277.31
kala-azar 085.0
leishmaniasis 085.0
tick fever 082.1
Medulla — *see* condition
Medullary
cystic kidney 753.16
sponge kidney 753.17
Medullated fibers
optic (nerve) 743.57
retina 362.85
Medulloblastoma (M9470/3)
desmoplastic (M9471/3) 191.6
specified site — *see* Neoplasm, by site, malignant
unspecified site 191.6
Medulloepithelioma (M9501/3) — *see also* Neoplasm, by site, malignant
teratoid (M9502/3) — *see* Neoplasm, by site, malignant
Medullomyoblastoma (M9472/3)
specified site — *see* Neoplasm, by site, malignant
unspecified site 191.6

- **Meekeren-Ehlers-Danlos syndrome** 756.83
- **Megacaryocytic** — *see* condition
- **Megacolon** (acquired) (functional) (not Hirschsprung's disease) 564.7
  - aganglionic 751.3
  - congenital, congenitum 751.3
  - Hirschsprung's (disease) 751.3
  - psychogenic 306.4
  - toxic (*see also* Colitis, ulcerative) 556.9
- **Megaduodenum** 537.3
- **Megaesophagus** (functional) 530.0
  - congenital 750.4
- **Megakaryocytic** — *see* condition
- **Megalencephaly** 742.4
- **Megalerythema** (epidermicum) (infectiosum) 057.0
- **Megalia, cutis et ossium** 757.39
- **Megaloappendix** 751.5
- **Megalocephalus, megalocephaly** NEC 756.0
- **Megalocornea** 743.41
  - associated with buphthalmos 743.22
- **Megalocytic anemia** 281.9
- **Megalodactylia** (fingers) (thumbs) 755.57
  - toes 755.65
- **Megaloduodenum** 751.5
- **Megaloesophagus** (functional) 530.0
  - congenital 750.4
- **Megalogastria** (congenital) 750.7
- **Megalomania** 307.9
- **Megalophthalmos** 743.8
- **Megalopsia** 368.14
- **Megalosplenia** — *see also* Splenomegaly 789.2
- **Megaloureter** 593.89
  - congenital 753.22
- **Megarectum** 569.49
- **Megasigmoid** 564.7
  - congenital 751.3
- **Megaureter** 593.89
  - congenital 753.22
- **Megrim** 346.9 ☑
- **Meibomian**
  - cyst 373.2
    - infected 373.12
  - gland — *see* condition
  - infarct (eyelid) 374.85
  - stye 373.11
- **Meibomitis** 373.12
- **Meige**
  - -Milroy disease (chronic hereditary edema) 757.0
  - syndrome (blepharospasm-oromandibular dystonia) 333.82
- **Melalgia, nutritional** 266.2
- **Melancholia** — *see also* Psychosis, affective 296.90
  - climacteric 296.2 ☑
    - recurrent episode 296.3 ☑
    - single episode 296.2 ☑
  - hypochondriac 300.7
  - intermittent 296.2 ☑
    - recurrent episode 296.3 ☑
    - single episode 296.2 ☑
  - involutional 296.2 ☑
    - recurrent episode 296.3 ☑
    - single episode 296.2 ☑
  - menopausal 296.2 ☑
    - recurrent episode 296.3 ☑
    - single episode 296.2 ☑
  - puerperal 296.2 ☑
  - reactive (from emotional stress, psychological trauma) 298.0
  - recurrent 296.3 ☑
  - senile 290.21
  - stuporous 296.2 ☑
    - recurrent episode 296.3 ☑
    - single episode 296.2 ☑
- **Melanemia** 275.0
- **Melanoameloblastoma** (M9363/0) — *see* Neoplasm, bone, benign
- **Melanoblastoma** (M8720/3) — *see* Melanoma
- **Melanoblastosis**
  - Block-Sulzberger 757.33
  - cutis linearis sive systematisata 757.33
- **Melanocarcinoma** (M8720/3) — *see* Melanoma
- **Melanocytoma, eyeball** (M8726/0) 224.0
- **Melanoderma, melanodermia** 709.09
  - Addison's (primary adrenal insufficiency) 255.41
- **Melanodontia, infantile** 521.05
- **Melanodontoclasia** 521.05
- **Melanoepithelioma** (M8720/3) — *see* Melanoma
- **Melanoma** (malignant) (M8720/3) 172.9

> *Note — Except where otherwise indicated, the morphological varieties of melanoma in the list below should be coded by site as for "Melanoma (malignant)". Internal sites should be coded to malignant neoplasm of those sites.*

  - abdominal wall 172.5
  - ala nasi 172.3
  - amelanotic (M8730/3) — *see* Melanoma, by site
  - ankle 172.7
  - anus, anal 154.3
    - canal 154.2
  - arm 172.6
  - auditory canal (external) 172.2
  - auricle (ear) 172.2
  - auricular canal (external) 172.2
  - axilla 172.5
  - axillary fold 172.5
  - back 172.5
  - balloon cell (M8722/3) — *see* Melanoma, by site
  - benign (M8720/0) — *see* Neoplasm, skin, benign
  - breast (female) (male) 172.5
  - brow 172.3
  - buttock 172.5
  - canthus (eye) 172.1
  - cheek (external) 172.3
  - chest wall 172.5
  - chin 172.3
  - choroid 190.6
  - conjunctiva 190.3
  - ear (external) 172.2
  - epithelioid cell (M8771/3) (*see also* Melanoma, by site)
    - and spindle cell, mixed (M8775/3) — *see* Melanoma, by site
  - external meatus (ear) 172.2
  - eye 190.9
  - eyebrow 172.3
  - eyelid (lower) (upper) 172.1
  - face NEC 172.3
  - female genital organ (external) NEC 184.4
  - finger 172.6
  - flank 172.5
  - foot 172.7
  - forearm 172.6
  - forehead 172.3
  - foreskin 187.1
  - gluteal region 172.5
  - groin 172.5
  - hand 172.6
  - heel 172.7
  - helix 172.2
  - hip 172.7
  - in
    - giant pigmented nevus (M8761/3) — *see* Melanoma, by site
    - Hutchinson's melanotic freckle (M8742/3) — *see* Melanoma, by site
    - junctional nevus (M8740/3) — *see* Melanoma, by site
    - precancerous melanosis (M8741/3) — *see* Melanoma, by site
  - in situ — *see* Melanoma, by site ●
    - skin 172.9 ●
  - interscapular region 172.5

- **Melanoma** — *continued*
  - iris 190.0
  - jaw 172.3
  - juvenile (M8770/0) — *see* Neoplasm, skin, benign
  - knee 172.7
  - labium
    - majus 184.1
    - minus 184.2
  - lacrimal gland 190.2
  - leg 172.7
  - lip (lower) (upper) 172.0
  - liver 197.7
  - lower limb NEC 172.7
  - male genital organ (external) NEC 187.9
  - meatus, acoustic (external) 172.2
  - meibomian gland 172.1
  - metastatic
    - of or from specified site — *see* Melanoma, by site
    - site not of skin — *see* Neoplasm, by site, malignant, secondary
    - to specified site — *see* Neoplasm, by site, malignant, secondary
    - unspecified site 172.9
  - nail 172.9
    - finger 172.6
    - toe 172.7
  - neck 172.4
  - nodular (M8721/3) — *see* Melanoma, by site
  - nose, external 172.3
  - orbit 190.1
  - penis 187.4
  - perianal skin 172.5
  - perineum 172.5
  - pinna 172.2
  - popliteal (fossa) (space) 172.7
  - prepuce 187.1
  - pubes 172.5
  - pudendum 184.4
  - retina 190.5
  - scalp 172.4
  - scrotum 187.7
  - septum nasal (skin) 172.3
  - shoulder 172.6
  - skin NEC 172.8
    - in situ 172.9 ●
  - spindle cell (M8772/3) (*see also* Melanoma, by site)
    - type A (M8773/3) 190.0
    - type B (M8774/3) 190.0
  - submammary fold 172.5
  - superficial spreading (M8743/3) — *see* Melanoma, by site
  - temple 172.3
  - thigh 172.7
  - toe 172.7
  - trunk NEC 172.5
  - umbilicus 172.5
  - upper limb NEC 172.6
  - vagina vault 184.0
  - vulva 184.4
- **Melanoplakia** 528.9
- **Melanosarcoma** (M8720/3) — *see also* Melanoma
  - epithelioid cell (M8771/3) — *see* Melanoma
- **Melanosis** 709.09
  - addisonian (primary adrenal insufficiency) 255.41
    - tuberculous (*see also* Tuberculosis) 017.6 ☑
  - adrenal 255.41
  - colon 569.89
  - conjunctiva 372.55
    - congenital 743.49
  - corii degenerativa 757.33
  - cornea (presenile) (senile) 371.12
    - congenital 743.43
      - interfering with vision 743.42
  - eye 372.55
    - congenital 743.49
  - jute spinners' 709.09
  - lenticularis progressiva 757.33

- **Melanosis** — *continued*
  - liver 573.8
  - precancerous (M8741/2) (*see also* Neoplasm, skin, in situ)
    - malignant melanoma in (M8741/3) — *see* Melanoma
  - prenatal 743.43
    - interfering with vision 743.42
  - Riehl's 709.09
  - sclera 379.19
    - congenital 743.47
  - suprarenal 255.41
  - tar 709.09
  - toxic 709.09
- **Melanuria** 791.9
- **Melasma** 709.09
  - adrenal (gland) 255.41
  - suprarenal (gland) 255.41
- **MELAS syndrome** (mitochondrial encephalopathy, lactic acidosis and stroke-like episodes) 277.87
- **Melena** 578.1
  - due to
    - swallowed maternal blood 777.3
    - ulcer — *see* Ulcer, by site, with hemorrhage
  - newborn 772.4
    - due to swallowed maternal blood 777.3
- **Meleney's**
  - gangrene (cutaneous) 686.09
  - ulcer (chronic undermining) 686.09
- **Melioidosis** 025
- **Melitensis, febris** 023.0
- **Melitococcosis** 023.0
- **Melkersson (-Rosenthal) syndrome** 351.8
- **Mellitus, diabetes** — *see* Diabetes
- **Melorheostosis** (bone) (leri) 733.99
- **Meloschisis** 744.83
- **Melotia** 744.29
- **Membrana**
  - capsularis lentis posterior 743.39
  - epipapillaris 743.57
- **Membranacea placenta** — *see* Placenta, abnormal
- **Membranaceous uterus** 621.8
- **Membrane, membranous** — *see also* condition
  - folds, congenital — *see* Web
  - Jackson's 751.4
  - over face (causing asphyxia), fetus or newborn 768.9
  - premature rupture — *see* Rupture, membranes, premature
  - pupillary 364.74
    - persistent 743.46
  - retained (complicating delivery) (with hemorrhage) 666.2 ☑
    - without hemorrhage 667.1 ☑
  - secondary (eye) 366.50
  - unruptured (causing asphyxia) 768.9
  - vitreous humor 379.25
- **Membranitis, fetal** 658.4 ☑
  - affecting fetus or newborn 762.7
- **Memory disturbance, loss or lack** — *see also* Amnesia 780.93
  - mild, following organic brain damage 310.1
- **MEN** (multiple endocrine neoplasia) (syndromes)
  - type I 258.01
  - type IIA 258.02
  - type IIB 258.03
- **Menadione** (vitamin K) **deficiency** 269.0
- **Menarche, precocious** 259.1
- **Mendacity, pathologic** 301.7
- **Mendelson's syndrome** (resulting from a procedure) 997.39 ▲
  - obstetric 668.0 ☑
- **Mende's syndrome** (ptosis-epicanthus) 270.2
- **Ménétrier's disease or syndrome** (hypertrophic gastritis) 535.2 ☑
- **Ménière's disease, syndrome, or vertigo** 386.00

Ménière's disease, syndrome, or vertigo — *continued*
cochlear 386.02
cochleovestibular 386.01
inactive 386.04
in remission 386.04
vestibular 386.03
Meninges, meningeal — *see* condition
Meningioma (M9530/0) — *see also* Neoplasm, meninges, benign
angioblastic (M9535/0) — *see* Neoplasm, meninges, benign
angiomatous (M9534/0) — *see* Neoplasm, meninges, benign
endotheliomatous (M9531/0) — *see* Neoplasm, meninges, benign
fibroblastic (M9532/0) — *see* Neoplasm, meninges, benign
fibrous (M9532/0) — *see* Neoplasm, meninges, benign
hemangioblastic (M9535/0) — *see* Neoplasm, meninges, benign
hemangiopericytic (M9536/0) — *see* Neoplasm, meninges, benign
malignant (M9530/3) — *see* Neoplasm, meninges, malignant
meningiothelial (M9531/0) — *see* Neoplasm, meninges, benign
meningotheliomatous (M9531/0) — *see* Neoplasm, meninges, benign
mixed (M9537/0) — *see* Neoplasm, meninges, benign
multiple (M9530/1) 237.6
papillary (M9538/1) 237.6
psammomatous (M9533/0) — *see* Neoplasm, meninges, benign
syncytial (M9531/0) — *see* Neoplasm, meninges, benign
transitional (M9537/0) — *see* Neoplasm, meninges, benign
Meningiomatosis (diffuse) (M9530/1) 237.6
Meningism — *see also* Meningismus 781.6
Meningismus (infectional) (pneumococcal) 781.6
due to serum or vaccine 997.09 *[321.8]*
influenzal NEC 487.8
Meningitis (basal) (basic) (basilar) (brain) (cerebral) (cervical) (congestive) (diffuse) (hemorrhagic) (infantile) (membranous) (metastatic) (nonspecific) (pontine) (progressive) (simple) (spinal) (subacute) (sympathetica) (toxic) 322.9
abacterial NEC (*see also* Meningitis, aseptic) 047.9
actinomycotic 039.8 *[320.7]*
adenoviral 049.1
Aerobacter aerogenes 320.82
anaerobes (cocci) (gram-negative) (gram-positive) (mixed) (NEC) 320.81
arbovirus NEC 066.9 *[321.2]*
specified type NEC 066.8 *[321.2]*
aseptic (acute) NEC 047.9
adenovirus 049.1
Coxsackie virus 047.0
due to
adenovirus 049.1
Coxsackie virus 047.0
ECHO virus 047.1
enterovirus 047.9
mumps 072.1
poliovirus (*see also* Poliomyelitis) 045.2 ☒ *[321.2]*
ECHO virus 047.1
herpes (simplex) virus 054.72
zoster 053.0
leptospiral 100.81
lymphocytic choriomeningitis 049.0
noninfective 322.0
Bacillus pyocyaneus 320.89
bacterial NEC 320.9
anaerobic 320.81
Meningitis — *continued*
bacterial — *continued*
gram-negative 320.82
anaerobic 320.81
Bacteroides (fragilis) (oralis) (melaninogenicus) 320.81
cancerous (M8000/6) 198.4
candidal 112.83
carcinomatous (M8010/6) 198.4
caseous (*see also* Tuberculosis, meninges) 013.0 ☒
cerebrospinal (acute) (chronic) (diplococcal) (endemic) (epidemic) (fulminant) (infectious) (malignant) (meningococcal) (sporadic) 036.0
carrier (suspected) of V02.59
chronic NEC 322.2
clear cerebrospinal fluid NEC 322.0
Clostridium (haemolyticum) (novyi) NEC 320.81
coccidioidomycosis 114.2
Coxsackie virus 047.0
cryptococcal 117.5 *[321.0]*
diplococcal 036.0
gram-negative 036.0
gram-positive 320.1
Diplococcus pneumoniae 320.1
due to
actinomycosis 039.8 *[320.7]*
adenovirus 049.1
coccidiomycosis 114.2
enterovirus 047.9
specified NEC 047.8
histoplasmosis (*see also* Histoplasmosis) 115.91
Listerosis 027.0 *[320.7]*
Lyme disease 088.81 *[320.7]*
moniliasis 112.83
mumps 072.1
neurosyphilis 094.2
nonbacterial organisms NEC 321.8
oidiomycosis 112.83
poliovirus (*see also* Poliomyelitis) 045.2 ☒ *[321.2]*
preventive immunization, inoculation, or vaccination 997.09 *[321.8]*
sarcoidosis 135 *[321.4]*
sporotrichosis 117.1 *[321.1]*
syphilis 094.2
acute 091.81
congenital 090.42
secondary 091.81
trypanosomiasis (*see also* Trypanosomiasis) 086.9 *[321.3]*
whooping cough 033.9 *[320.7]*
ECHO virus 047.1
E. coli 320.82
endothelial-leukocytic, benign, recurrent 047.9
Enterobacter aerogenes 320.82
enteroviral 047.9
specified type NEC 047.8
enterovirus 047.9
specified NEC 047.8
eosinophilic 322.1
epidemic NEC 036.0
Escherichia coli (E. coli) 320.82
Eubacterium 320.81
fibrinopurulent NEC 320.9
specified type NEC 320.89
Friedländer (bacillus) 320.82
fungal NEC 117.9 *[321.1]*
Fusobacterium 320.81
gonococcal 098.82
gram-negative bacteria NEC 320.82
anaerobic 320.81
cocci 036.0
specified NEC 320.82
gram-negative cocci NEC 036.0
specified NEC 320.82
gram-positive cocci NEC 320.9
herpes (simplex) virus 054.72
zoster 053.0
H. influenzae 320.0
Meningitis — *continued*
infectious NEC 320.9
influenzal 320.0
Klebsiella pneumoniae 320.82
late effect — *see* Late, effect, meningitis
leptospiral (aseptic) 100.81
Listerella (monocytogenes) 027.0 *[320.7]*
Listeria monocytogenes 027.0 *[320.7]*
lymphocytic (acute) (benign) (serous) 049.0
choriomeningitis virus 049.0
meningococcal (chronic) 036.0
Mima polymorpha 320.82
Mollaret's 047.9
monilial 112.83
mumps (virus) 072.1
mycotic NEC 117.9 *[321.1]*
Neisseria 036.0
neurosyphilis 094.2
nonbacterial NEC (*see also* Meningitis, aseptic) 047.9
nonpyogenic NEC 322.0
oidiomycosis 112.83
ossificans 349.2
Peptococcus 320.81
Peptostreptococcus 320.81
pneumococcal 320.1
poliovirus (*see also* Poliomyelitis) 045.2 ☒ *[321.2]*
Proprionibacterium 320.81
Proteus morganii 320.82
Pseudomonas (aeruginosa) (pyocyaneus) 320.82
purulent NEC 320.9
specified organism NEC 320.89
pyogenic NEC 320.9
specified organism NEC 320.89
Salmonella 003.21
septic NEC 320.9
specified organism NEC 320.89
serosa circumscripta NEC 322.0
serous NEC (*see also* Meningitis, aseptic) 047.9
lymphocytic 049.0
syndrome 348.2
Serratia (marcescens) 320.82
specified organism NEC 320.89
sporadic cerebrospinal 036.0
sporotrichosis 117.1 *[321.1]*
staphylococcal 320.3
sterile 997.09
streptococcal (acute) 320.2
suppurative 320.9
specified organism NEC 320.89
syphilitic 094.2
acute 091.81
congenital 090.42
secondary 091.81
torula 117.5 *[321.0]*
traumatic (complication of injury) 958.8
Treponema (denticola) (macrodenticum) 320.81
trypanosomiasis 086.1 *[321.3]*
tuberculous (*see also* Tuberculosis, meninges) 013.0 ☒
typhoid 002.0 *[320.7]*
Veillonella 320.81
Vibrio vulnificus 320.82
viral, virus NEC (*see also* Meningitis, aseptic) 047.9
Wallgren's (*see also* Meningitis, aseptic) 047.9
Meningocele (congenital) (spinal) — *see also* Spina bifida 741.9 ☒
acquired (traumatic) 349.2
cerebral 742.0
cranial 742.0
Meningocerebritis — *see* Meningoencephalitis
Meningococcemia (acute) (chronic) 036.2
Meningococcus, meningococcal — *see also* condition 036.9
Meningococcus, meningococcal — *see also* condition — *continued*
adrenalitis, hemorrhagic 036.3
carditis 036.40
carrier (suspected) of V02.59
cerebrospinal fever 036.0
encephalitis 036.1
endocarditis 036.42
exposure to V01.84
infection NEC 036.9
meningitis (cerebrospinal) 036.0
myocarditis 036.43
optic neuritis 036.81
pericarditis 036.41
septicemia (chronic) 036.2
Meningoencephalitis — *see also* Encephalitis 323.9
acute NEC 048
bacterial, purulent, pyogenic, or septic — *see* Meningitis
chronic NEC 094.1
diffuse NEC 094.1
diphasic 063.2
due to
actinomycosis 039.8 *[320.7]*
blastomycosis NEC (*see also* Blastomycosis) 116.0 *[323.41]*
free-living amebae 136.29 ▲
Listeria monocytogenes 027.0 *[320.7]*
Lyme disease 088.81 *[320.7]*
mumps 072.2
Naegleria (amebae) (gruberi) (organisms) 136.29 ▲
rubella 056.01
sporotrichosis 117.1 *[321.1]*
toxoplasmosis (acquired) 130.0
congenital (active) 771.2 *[323.41]*
Trypanosoma 086.1 *[323.2]*
epidemic 036.0
herpes 054.3
herpetic 054.3
H. influenzae 320.0
infectious (acute) 048
influenzal 320.0
late effect — *see* category 326
Listeria monocytogenes 027.0 *[320.7]*
lymphocytic (serous) 049.0
mumps 072.2
parasitic NEC 123.9 *[323.41]*
pneumococcal 320.1
primary amebic 136.29 ▲
rubella 056.01
serous 048
lymphocytic 049.0
specific 094.2
staphylococcal 320.3
streptococcal 320.2
syphilitic 094.2
toxic NEC 989.9 *[323.71]*
due to
carbon tetrachloride ▶(vapor)◀ 987.8 *[323.71]*
hydroxyquinoline derivatives poisoning 961.3 *[323.71]*
lead 984.9 *[323.71]*
mercury 985.0 *[323.71]*
thallium 985.8 *[323.71]*
toxoplasmosis (acquired) 130.0
trypanosomic 086.1 *[323.2]*
tuberculous (*see also* Tuberculosis, meninges) 013.0 ☒
virus NEC 048
Meningoencephalocele 742.0
syphilitic 094.89
congenital 090.49
Meningoencephalomyelitis — *see also* Meningoencephalitis 323.9
acute NEC 048
disseminated (postinfectious) 136.9 *[323.61]*
postimmunization or postvaccination 323.51
due to
actinomycosis 039.8 *[320.7]*

Meningoencephalomyelitis — *see also* Meningoencephalitis — *continued*
due to — *continued*
torula 117.5 *[323.41]*
toxoplasma or toxoplasmosis (acquired) 130.0
congenital (active) 771.2 *[323.41]*
late effect — *see* category 326
Meningoencephalomyelopathy — *see also* Meningoencephalomyelitis 349.9
Meningoencephalopathy — *see also* Meningoencephalitis 348.39
Meningoencephalopoliomyelitis — *see also* Poliomyelitis, bulbar 045.0 ☑
late effect 138
Meningomyelitis — *see also* Meningoencephalitis 323.9
blastomycotic NEC (*see also* Blastomycosis) 116.0 *[323.41]*
due to
actinomycosis 039.8 *[320.7]*
blastomycosis (*see also* Blastomycosis) 116.0 *[323.41]*
Meningococcus 036.0
sporotrichosis 117.1 *[323.41]*
torula 117.5 *[323.41]*
late effect — *see* category 326
lethargic 049.8
meningococcal 036.0
syphilitic 094.2
tuberculous (*see also* Tuberculosis, meninges) 013.0 ☑
Meningomyelocele — *see also* Spina bifida 741.9 ☑
syphilitic 094.89
Meningomyeloneuritis — *see* Meningoencephalitis
Meningoradiculitis — *see* Meningitis
Meningovascular — *see* condition
Meniscocytosis 282.60
Menkes' syndrome — *see* Syndrome, Menkes'
Menolipsis 626.0
Menometrorrhagia 626.2
Menopause, menopausal (symptoms) (syndrome) 627.2
arthritis (any site) NEC 716.3 ☑
artificial 627.4
bleeding 627.0
crisis 627.2
depression (*see also* Psychosis, affective) 296.2 ☑
agitated 296.2 ☑
recurrent episode 296.3 ☑
single episode 296.2 ☑
psychotic 296.2 ☑
recurrent episode 296.3 ☑
single episode 296.2 ☑
recurrent episode 296.3 ☑
single episode 296.2 ☑
melancholia (*see also* Psychosis, affective) 296.2 ☑
recurrent episode 296.3 ☑
single episode 296.2 ☑
paranoid state 297.2
paraphrenia 297.2
postsurgical 627.4
premature 256.31
postirradiation 256.2
postsurgical 256.2
psychoneurosis 627.2
psychosis NEC 298.8
surgical 627.4
toxic polyarthritis NEC 716.39
Menorrhagia (primary) 626.2
climacteric 627.0
menopausal 627.0
postclimacteric 627.1
postmenopausal 627.1
preclimacteric 627.0
premenopausal 627.0
puberty (menses retained) 626.3
Menorrhalgia 625.3
Menoschesis 626.8
Menostaxis 626.2
Menses, retention 626.8
Menstrual — *see also* Menstruation
cycle, irregular 626.4
disorders NEC 626.9
extraction V25.3
fluid, retained 626.8
molimen 625.4
period, normal V65.5
regulation V25.3
Menstruation
absent 626.0
anovulatory 628.0
delayed 626.8
difficult 625.3
disorder 626.9
psychogenic 306.52
specified NEC 626.8
during pregnancy 640.8 ☑
excessive 626.2
frequent 626.2
infrequent 626.1
irregular 626.4
latent 626.8
membranous 626.8
painful (primary) (secondary) 625.3
psychogenic 306.52
passage of clots 626.2
precocious 626.8
protracted 626.8
retained 626.8
retrograde 626.8
scanty 626.1
suppression 626.8
vicarious (nasal) 625.8
Mentagra — *see also* Sycosis 704.8
Mental — *see also* condition
deficiency (*see also* Retardation, mental) 319
deterioration (*see also* Psychosis) 298.9
disorder (*see also* Disorder, mental) 300.9
exhaustion 300.5
insufficiency (congenital) (*see also* Retardation, mental) 319
observation without need for further medical care NEC V71.09
retardation (*see also* Retardation, mental) 319
subnormality (*see also* Retardation, mental) 319
mild 317
moderate 318.0
profound 318.2
severe 318.1
upset (*see also* Disorder, mental) 300.9
Meralgia paresthetica 355.1
Mercurial — *see* condition
Mercurialism NEC 985.0
Merergasia 300.9
Merkel cell tumor — *see* Neoplasm, by site, malignant
Merocele — *see also* Hernia, femoral 553.00
Meromelia 755.4
lower limb 755.30
intercalary 755.32
femur 755.34
tibiofibular (complete) (incomplete) 755.33
fibula 755.37
metatarsal(s) 755.38
tarsal(s) 755.38
tibia 755.36
tibiofibular 755.35
terminal (complete) (partial) (transverse) 755.31
longitudinal 755.32
metatarsal(s) 755.38
phalange(s) 755.39
tarsal(s) 755.38
transverse 755.31
upper limb 755.20
Meromelia — *continued*
upper limb — *continued*
intercalary 755.22
carpal(s) 755.28
humeral 755.24
radioulnar (complete) (incomplete) 755.23
metacarpal(s) 755.28
phalange(s) 755.29
radial 755.26
radioulnar 755.25
ulnar 755.27
terminal (complete) (partial) (transverse) 755.21
longitudinal 755.22
carpal(s) 755.28
metacarpal(s) 755.28
phalange(s) 755.29
transverse 755.21
Merosmia 781.1
MERRF syndrome (myoclonus with epilepsy and with ragged red fibers) 277.87
Merycism — *see also* Vomiting
psychogenic 307.53
Merzbacher-Pelizaeus disease 330.0
Mesaortitis — *see* Aortitis
Mesarteritis — *see* Arteritis
Mesencephalitis — *see also* Encephalitis 323.9
late effect — *see* category 326
Mesenchymoma (M8990/1) — *see also* Neoplasm, connective tissue, uncertain behavior
benign (M8990/0) — *see* Neoplasm, connective tissue, benign
malignant (M8990/3) — *see* Neoplasm, connective tissue, malignant
Mesenteritis
retractile 567.82
sclerosing 567.82
Mesentery, mesenteric — *see* condition
Mesiodens, mesiodentes 520.1
causing crowding 524.31
Mesio-occlusion 524.23
Mesocardia (with asplenia) 746.87
Mesocolon — *see* condition
Mesonephroma (malignant) (M9110/3) — *see also* Neoplasm, by site, malignant
benign (M9110/0) — *see* Neoplasm, by site, benign
Mesophlebitis — *see* Phlebitis
Mesostromal dysgenesis 743.51
Mesothelioma (malignant) (M9050/3) — *see also* Neoplasm, by site, malignant
benign (M9050/0) — *see* Neoplasm, by site, benign
biphasic type (M9053/3) (*see also* Neoplasm, by site, malignant)
benign (M9053/0) — *see* Neoplasm, by site, benign
epithelioid (M9052/3) (*see also* Neoplasm, by site, malignant)
benign (M9052/0) — *see* Neoplasm, by site, benign
fibrous (M9051/3) (*see also* Neoplasm, by site, malignant)
benign (M9051/0) — *see* Neoplasm, by site, benign
Metabolic syndrome 277.7
Metabolism disorder 277.9
specified type NEC 277.89
Metagonimiasis 121.5
Metagonimus infestation (small intestine) 121.5
Metal
pigmentation (skin) 709.00
polishers' disease 502
Metalliferous miners' lung 503
Metamorphopsia 368.14
Metaplasia
bone, in skin 709.3
breast 611.89 ▲
Metaplasia — *continued*
cervix — *omit code*
endometrium (squamous) 621.8
esophagus 530.85
intestinal, of gastric mucosa 537.89
kidney (pelvis) (squamous) (*see also* Disease, renal) 593.89
myelogenous 289.89
myeloid 289.89
agnogenic 238.76
megakaryocytic 238.76
spleen 289.59
squamous cell
amnion 658.8 ☑
bladder 596.8
cervix — *see* condition
trachea 519.19
tracheobronchial tree 519.19
uterus 621.8
cervix — *see* condition
Metastasis, metastatic
abscess — *see* Abscess
calcification 275.40
cancer, neoplasm, or disease
from specified site (M8000/3) — *see* Neoplasm, by site, malignant
to specified site (M8000/6) — *see* Neoplasm, by site, secondary
deposits (in) (M8000/6) — *see* Neoplasm, by site, secondary
pneumonia 038.8 *[484.8]*
spread (to) (M8000/6) — *see* Neoplasm, by site, secondary
Metatarsalgia 726.70
anterior 355.6
due to Freiberg's disease 732.5
Morton's 355.6
Metatarsus, metatarsal — *see also* condition
abductus valgus (congenital) 754.60
adductus varus (congenital) 754.53
primus varus 754.52
valgus (adductus) (congenital) 754.60
varus (abductus) (congenital) 754.53
primus 754.52
Methadone use 304.00 ●
Methemoglobinemia 289.7
acquired (with sulfhemoglobinemia) 289.7
congenital 289.7
enzymatic 289.7
Hb-M disease 289.7
hereditary 289.7
toxic 289.7
Methemoglobinuria — *see also* Hemoglobinuria 791.2
Methicillin
resistant staphyloccocus aureus (MRSA) 041.12 ●
colonization V02.54 ●
personal history of V12.04 ●
susceptible staphylococcus aureus (MSSA) 041.11 ●
colonization V02.53 ●
Methioninemia 270.4
Metritis (catarrhal) (septic) (suppurative) — *see also* Endometritis 615.9
blennorrhagic 098.16
chronic or duration of 2 months or over 098.36
cervical (*see also* Cervicitis) 616.0
gonococcal 098.16
chronic or duration of 2 months or over 098.36
hemorrhagic 626.8
puerperal, postpartum, childbirth 670.0 ☑
tuberculous (*see also* Tuberculosis) 016.7 ☑
Metropathia hemorrhagica 626.8
Metroperitonitis — *see also* Peritonitis, pelvic, female 614.5
Metrorrhagia 626.6
arising during pregnancy — *see* Hemorrhage, pregnancy

Metrorrhagia — *continued*
  postpartum NEC 666.2 ☑
  primary 626.6
  psychogenic 306.59
  puerperal 666.2 ☑
Metrorrhexis — *see* Rupture, uterus
Metrosalpingitis — *see also* Salpingo-oophoritis 614.2
Metrostaxis 626.6
Metrovaginitis — *see also* Endometritis 615.9
  gonococcal (acute) 098.16
    chronic or duration of 2 months or over 098.36
Mexican fever — *see* Typhus, Mexican
Meyenburg-Altherr-Uehlinger syndrome 733.99
Meyer-Schwickerath and Weyers syndrome (dysplasia oculodentodigitalis) 759.89
Meynert's amentia (nonalcoholic) 294.0
  alcoholic 291.1
Mibelli's disease 757.39
Mice, joint — *see also* Loose, body, joint 718.1 ☑
  knee 717.6
Micheli-Rietti syndrome (thalassemia minor) 282.49
Michotte's syndrome 721.5
Micrencephalon, micrencephaly 742.1
Microalbuminuria 791.0
Microaneurysm, retina 362.14
  diabetic 250.5 ☑ *[362.01]*
    due to secondary diabetes 249.5 ☑ *[362.01]* ●
Microangiopathy 443.9
  diabetic (peripheral) 250.7 ☑ *[443.81]*
    due to secondary diabetes 249.7 ☑ *[443.81]* ●
    retinal 250.5 ☑ *[362.01]*
      due to secondary diabetes 249.5 ☑ *[362.01]* ●
  peripheral 443.9
    diabetic 250.7 ☑ *[443.81]*
      due to secondary diabetes 249.7 ☑ *[443.81]* ●
  retinal 362.18
    diabetic 250.5 ☑ *[362.01]*
      due to secondary diabetes 249.5 ☑ *[362.01]* ●
  thrombotic 446.6
    Moschcowitz's (thrombotic thrombocytopenic purpura) 446.6
Microcalcification, mammographic 793.81
Microcephalus, microcephalic, microcephaly 742.1
  due to toxoplasmosis (congenital) 771.2
Microcheilia 744.82
Microcolon (congenital) 751.5
Microcornea (congenital) 743.41
Microcytic — *see* condition
Microdeletions NEC 758.33
Microdontia 520.2
Microdrepanocytosis (thalassemia-Hb-S disease) 282.49
Microembolism
  atherothrombotic — *see* Atheroembolism
  retina 362.33
Microencephalon 742.1
Microfilaria streptocerca infestation 125.3
Microgastria (congenital) 750.7
Microgenia 524.06
Microgenitalia (congenital) 752.89
  penis 752.64
Microglioma (M9710/3)
  specified site — *see* Neoplasm, by site, malignant
  unspecified site 191.9
Microglossia (congenital) 750.16
Micrognathia, micrognathism (congenital) 524.00
  mandibular 524.04
Micrognathia, micrognathism — *continued*
  mandibular — *continued*
    alveolar 524.74
  maxillary 524.03
    alveolar 524.73
Microgyria (congenital) 742.2
Microinfarct, heart — *see also* Insufficiency, coronary 411.89
Microlithiasis, alveolar, pulmonary 516.2
Micromastia 611.82 ●
Micromyelia (congenital) 742.59
Micropenis 752.64
Microphakia (congenital) 743.36
Microphthalmia (congenital) — *see also* Microphthalmos 743.10
Microphthalmos (congenital) 743.10
  associated with eye and adnexal anomalies NEC 743.12
  due to toxoplasmosis (congenital) 771.2
  isolated 743.11
  simple 743.11
  syndrome 759.89
Micropsia 368.14
Microsporidiosis 136.8
Microsporon furfur infestation 111.0
Microsporosis — *see also* Dermatophytosis 110.9
  nigra 111.1
Microstomia (congenital) 744.84
Microthelia 757.6
Microthromboembolism — *see* Embolism
Microtia (congenital) (external ear) 744.23
Microtropia 378.34
Micturition
  disorder NEC 788.69
    psychogenic 306.53
  frequency 788.41
    psychogenic 306.53
  nocturnal 788.43
  painful 788.1
    psychogenic 306.53
Middle
  ear — *see* condition
  lobe (right) syndrome 518.0
Midplane — *see* condition
Miescher's disease 709.3
  cheilitis 351.8
  granulomatosis disciformis 709.3
Miescher-Leder syndrome or granulomatosis 709.3
Mieten's syndrome 759.89
Migraine (idiopathic) 346.9 ☑

> Note — The following fifth digit subclassification is for use with category 346: ●
>
> 0 without mention of intractable migraine without mention of status migrainosus ●
>
> 1 with intractable migraine, so stated, without mention of status migrainosus ●
>
> 2 without mention of intractable migraine with status migrainosus ●
>
> 3 with intractable migraine, so stated, with status migrainosus ●

  with aura ▶(acute-onset) (without headache) (prolonged) (typical)◀ 346.0 ☑
  without aura 346.1 ☑ ●
    chronic 346.7 ☑ ●
    transformed 346.7 ☑ ●
  abdominal (syndrome) 346.2 ☑
  allergic (histamine) 346.2 ☑
  atypical 346.8 ☑ ▲
  basilar 346.0 ☑ ▲
Migraine — *continued*
  chronic without aura 346.7 ☑ ●
  classic▶(al)◀ 346.0 ☑
  common 346.1 ☑
  hemiplegic 346.3 ☑ ▲
    familial 346.3 ☑ ●
    sporadic 346.3 ☑ ●
  lower-half 339.00 ▲
  menstrual 346.4 ☑ ▲
  menstrually related 346.4 ☑ ●
  ophthalmic 346.8 ☑
  ophthalmoplegic 346.2 ☑ ▲
  premenstrual 346.4 ☑ ●
  pure menstrual 346.4 ☑ ●
  retinal 346.0 ☑ ▲
  specified form NEC 346.8 ☑ ●
  transformed without aura 346.7 ☑ ●
  variant 346.2 ☑
Migrant, social V60.0
Migratory, migrating — *see also* condition
  person V60.0
  testis, congenital 752.52
Mikulicz's disease or syndrome (dryness of mouth, absent or decreased lacrimation) 527.1
Milian atrophia blanche 701.3
Miliaria (crystallina) (rubra) (tropicalis) 705.1
  apocrine 705.82
Miliary — *see* condition
Milium — *see also* Cyst, sebaceous 706.2
  colloid 709.3
  eyelid 374.84
Milk
  crust 690.11
  excess secretion 676.6 ☑
  fever, female 672.0 ☑
  poisoning 988.8
  retention 676.2 ☑
  sickness 988.8
  spots 423.1
Milkers' nodes 051.1
Milk-leg (deep vessels) 671.4 ☑
  complicating pregnancy 671.3 ☑
  nonpuerperal 451.19
  puerperal, postpartum, childbirth 671.4 ☑
Milkman (-Looser) disease or syndrome (osteomalacia with pseudofractures) 268.2
Milky urine — *see also* Chyluria 791.1
Millar's asthma (laryngismus stridulus) 478.75
Millard-Gubler-Foville paralysis 344.89
Millard-Gubler paralysis or syndrome 344.89
Miller-Dieker syndrome 758.33
Miller's disease (osteomalacia) 268.2
Miller Fisher's syndrome 357.0
Milles' syndrome (encephalocutaneous angiomatosis) 759.6
Mills' disease 335.29
Millstone makers' asthma or lung 502
Milroy's disease (chronic hereditary edema) 757.0
Miners' — *see also* condition
  asthma 500
  elbow 727.2
  knee 727.2
  lung 500
  nystagmus 300.89
  phthisis (*see also* Tuberculosis) 011.4 ☑
  tuberculosis (see also Tuberculosis) 011.4 ☑
Minkowski-Chauffard syndrome — *see also* Spherocytosis 282.0
Minor — *see* condition
Minor's disease 336.1
Minot's disease (hemorrhagic disease, newborn) 776.0
Minot-von Willebrand (-Jürgens) disease or syndrome (angiohemophilia) 286.4
Minus (and plus) hand (intrinsic) 736.09
Miosis (persistent) (pupil) 379.42
Mirizzi's syndrome (hepatic duct stenosis) — *see also* Obstruction, biliary 576.2
  with calculus, cholelithiasis, or stones — *see* Choledocholithiasis
Mirror writing 315.09
  secondary to organic lesion 784.69
Misadventure (prophylactic) (therapeutic) — *see also* Complications 999.9
  administration of insulin 962.3
  infusion — *see* Complications, infusion
  local applications (of fomentations, plasters, etc.) 999.9
    burn or scald — *see* Burn, by site
  medical care (early) (late) NEC 999.9
    adverse effect of drugs or chemicals — *see* Table of Drugs and Chemicals
    burn or scald — *see* Burn, by site
  radiation NEC 990
  radiotherapy NEC 990
  surgical procedure (early) (late) — *see* Complications, surgical procedure
  transfusion — *see* Complications, transfusion
  vaccination or other immunological procedure — *see* Complications, vaccination
Misanthropy 301.7
Miscarriage — *see* Abortion, spontaneous
Mischief, malicious, child — *see also* Disturbance, conduct 312.0 ☑
Misdirection
  aqueous 365.83
Mismanagement, feeding 783.3
Misplaced, misplacement
  kidney (*see also* Disease, renal) 593.0
    congenital 753.3
  organ or site, congenital NEC — *see* Malposition, congenital
Missed
  abortion 632
  delivery (at or near term) 656.4 ☑
  labor (at or near term) 656.4 ☑
Misshapen reconstructed breast 612.0 ●
Missing — *see also* Absence
  teeth (acquired) 525.10
    congenital (see also Anodontia) 520.0
    due to
      caries 525.13
      extraction 525.10
      periodontal disease 525.12
      specified NEC 525.19
      trauma 525.11
  vertebrae (congenital) 756.13
Misuse of drugs NEC — *see also* Abuse, drug, nondependent 305.9 ☑
Mitchell's disease (erythromelalgia) 443.82
Mite(s)
  diarrhea 133.8
  grain (itch) 133.8
  hair follicle (itch) 133.8
  in sputum 133.8
Mitochondrial encephalopathy, lactic acidosis and stroke-like episodes (MELAS syndrome) 277.87
Mitochondrial neurogastrointestinal encephalopathy syndrome (MNGIE) 277.87
Mitral — *see* condition
Mittelschmerz 625.2
Mixed — *see* condition
Mljet disease (mal de Meleda) 757.39
Mobile, mobility
  cecum 751.4
  coccyx 733.99
  excessive — *see* Hypermobility
  gallbladder 751.69
  kidney 593.0

Index

Metrorrhagia — Mobile, mobility

☑ Additional Digit Required — Refer to the Tabular List for Digit Selection

Subterms under main terms may continue to next column or page

▶◀ Revised Text ● New Line ▲ Revised Code

Mobile, mobility — *continued*
- kidney — *continued*
  - congenital 753.3
- organ or site, congenital NEC — *see* Malposition, congenital
- spleen 289.59

Mobitz heart block (atrioventricular) 426.10
- type I (Wenckebach's) 426.13
- type II 426.12

Möbius'
- disease 346.2 ☑ ▲
- syndrome
  - congenital oculofacial paralysis 352.6
  - ophthalmoplegic migraine 346.2 ☑ ▲

Moeller(-Barlow) disease (infantile scurvy) 267
- glossitis 529.4

Mohr's syndrome (types I and II) 759.89

Mola destruens (M9100/1) 236.1

Molarization, premolars 520.2

Molar pregnancy 631
- hydatidiform (delivered) (undelivered) 630

Molding, head (during birth) — *omit code*

Mold(s) in vitreous 117.9

Mole (pigmented) (M8720/0) — *see also* Neoplasm, skin, benign
- blood 631
- Breus' 631
- cancerous (M8720/3) — *see* Melanoma
- carneous 631
- destructive (M9100/1) 236.1
- ectopic — *see* Pregnancy, ectopic
- fleshy 631
- hemorrhagic 631
- hydatid, hydatidiform (benign) (complicating pregnancy) (delivered) (undelivered) (*see also* Hydatidiform mole) 630
  - invasive (M9100/1) 236.1
  - malignant (M9100/1) 236.1
  - previous, affecting management of pregnancy V23.1
- invasive (hydatidiform) (M9100/1) 236.1
- malignant
  - meaning
    - malignant hydatidiform mole (9100/1) 236.1
    - melanoma (M8720/3) — *see* Melanoma
- nonpigmented (M8730/0) — *see* Neoplasm, skin, benign
- pregnancy NEC 631
- skin (M8720/0) — *see* Neoplasm, skin, benign
- tubal — *see* Pregnancy, tubal
- vesicular (*see also* Hydatidiform mole) 630

Molimen, molimina (menstrual) 625.4

Mollaret's meningitis 047.9

Mollities (cerebellar) (cerebral) 437.8
- ossium 268.2

Molluscum
- contagiosum 078.0
- epitheliale 078.0
- fibrosum (M8851/0) — *see* Lipoma, by site
- pendulum (M8851/0) — *see* Lipoma, by site

Mönckeberg's arteriosclerosis, degeneration, disease, or sclerosis — *see also* Arteriosclerosis, extremities 440.20

Monday fever 504

Monday morning dyspnea or asthma 504

Mondini's malformation (cochlea) 744.05

Mondor's disease (thrombophlebitis of breast) 451.89

Mongolian, mongolianism, mongolism, mongoloid 758.0
- spot 757.33

Monilethrix (congenital) 757.4

Monilia infestation — *see* Candidiasis

Moniliasis — *see also* Candidiasis
- neonatal 771.7
- vulvovaginitis 112.1

Monkeypox 059.01 ▲

Monoarthritis 716.60
- ankle 716.67
- arm 716.62
  - lower (and wrist) 716.63
  - upper (and elbow) 716.62
- foot (and ankle) 716.67
- forearm (and wrist) 716.63
- hand 716.64
- leg 716.66
  - lower 716.66
  - upper 716.65
- pelvic region (hip) (thigh) 716.65
- shoulder (region) 716.61
- specified site NEC 716.68

Monoblastic — *see* condition

Monochromatism (cone) (rod) 368.54

Monocytic — *see* condition

Monocytopenia 288.59

Monocytosis (symptomatic) 288.63

Monofixation syndrome 378.34

Monomania — *see also* Psychosis 298.9

Mononeuritis 355.9
- cranial nerve — *see* Disorder, nerve, cranial
- femoral nerve 355.2
- lateral
  - cutaneous nerve of thigh 355.1
  - popliteal nerve 355.3
- lower limb 355.8
  - specified nerve NEC 355.79
- medial popliteal nerve 355.4
- median nerve 354.1
- multiplex 354.5
- plantar nerve 355.6
- posterior tibial nerve 355.5
- radial nerve 354.3
- sciatic nerve 355.0
- ulnar nerve 354.2
- upper limb 354.9
  - specified nerve NEC 354.8
- vestibular 388.5

Mononeuropathy — *see also* Mononeuritis 355.9
- diabetic NEC 250.6 ☑ *[355.9]*
  - due to secondary diabetes 249.6 ☑ *[355.9]* ●
  - lower limb 250.6 ☑ *[355.8]*
    - due to secondary diabetes 249.6 ☑ *[355.8]* ●
  - upper limb 250.6 ☑ *[354.9]*
    - due to secondary diabetes 249.6 ☑ *[354.9]* ●
- iliohypogastric nerve 355.79
- ilioinguinal nerve 355.79
- obturator nerve 355.79
- saphenous nerve 355.79

Mononucleosis, infectious 075
- with hepatitis 075 *[573.1]*

Monoplegia 344.5
- brain (current episode) (*see also* Paralysis, brain) 437.8
  - fetus or newborn 767.8
- cerebral (current episode) (*see also* Paralysis, brain) 437.8
- congenital or infantile (cerebral) (spastic) (spinal) 343.3
- embolic (current) (*see also* Embolism, brain) 434.1 ☑
  - late effect — *see* Late effect(s) (of) cerebrovascular disease
- infantile (cerebral) (spastic) (spinal) 343.3
- lower limb 344.30
  - affecting
    - dominant side 344.31
    - nondominant side 344.32
  - due to late effect of cerebrovascular accident — *see* Late effect(s) (of) cerebrovascular accident
- newborn 767.8
- psychogenic 306.0
  - specified as conversion reaction 300.11
- thrombotic (current) (*see also* Thrombosis, brain) 434.0 ☑
  - late effect — *see* Late effect(s) (of) cerebrovascular disease
- transient 781.4
- upper limb 344.40
  - affecting
    - dominant side 344.41
    - nondominant side 344.42
  - due to late effect of cerebrovascular accident — *see* Late effect(s) (of) cerebrovascular accident

Monorchism, monorchidism 752.89

Monteggia's fracture (closed) 813.03
- open 813.13

Mood swings
- brief compensatory 296.99
- rebound 296.99

Mooren's ulcer (cornea) 370.07

Moore's syndrome — *see also* Epilepsy 345.5 ☑

Mooser bodies 081.0

Mooser-Neill reaction 081.0

Moral
- deficiency 301.7
- imbecility 301.7

Morax-Axenfeld conjunctivitis 372.03

Morbilli — *see also* Measles 055.9

Morbus
- anglicus, anglorum 268.0
- Beigel 111.2
- caducus (*see also* Epilepsy) 345.9 ☑
- caeruleus 746.89
- celiacus 579.0
- comitialis (see also Epilepsy) 345.9 ☑
- cordis (*see also* Disease, heart)
  - valvulorum — *see* Endocarditis
- coxae 719.95
  - tuberculous (*see also* Tuberculosis) 015.1 ☑
- hemorrhagicus neonatorum 776.0
- maculosus neonatorum 772.6
- renum 593.0
- senilis (*see also* Osteoarthrosis) 715.9 ☑

Morel-Kraepelin disease — *see also* Schizophrenia 295.9 ☑

Morel-Moore syndrome (hyperostosis frontalis interna) 733.3

Morel-Morgagni syndrome (hyperostosis frontalis interna) 733.3

Morgagni
- cyst, organ, hydatid, or appendage 752.89
  - fallopian tube 752.11
- disease or syndrome (hyperostosis frontalis interna) 733.3

Morgagni-Adams-Stokes syndrome (syncope with heart block) 426.9

Morgagni-Stewart-Morel syndrome (hyperostosis frontalis interna) 733.3

Moria — *see also* Psychosis 298.9

Morning sickness 643.0 ☑

Moron 317

Morphea (guttate) (linear) 701.0

Morphine dependence — *see also* Dependence 304.0 ☑

Morphinism — *see also* Dependence 304.0 ☑

Morphinomania — *see also* Dependence 304.0 ☑

Morphoea 701.0

Morquio (-Brailsford) (-Ullrich) disease or syndrome (mucopolysaccharidosis IV) 277.5
- kyphosis 277.5

Morris syndrome (testicular feminization) 259.51 ▲

Morsus humanus (open wound) — *see also* Wound, open, by site
- skin surface intact — *see* Contusion

Mortification (dry) (moist) — *see also* Gangrene 785.4

Morton's
- disease 355.6
- foot 355.6
  - metatarsalgia (syndrome) 355.6
  - neuralgia 355.6
  - neuroma 355.6
  - syndrome (metatarsalgia) (neuralgia) 355.6
- toe 355.6

Morvan's disease 336.0

Mosaicism, mosaic (chromosomal) 758.9
- autosomal 758.5
- sex 758.81

Moschcowitz's syndrome (thrombotic thrombocytopenic purpura) 446.6

Mother yaw 102.0

Motion sickness (from travel, any vehicle) (from roundabouts or swings) 994.6

Mottled teeth (enamel) (endemic) (nonendemic) 520.3

Mottling enamel (endemic) (nonendemic) (teeth) 520.3

Mouchet's disease 732.5

Mould(s) (in vitreous) 117.9

Moulders'
- bronchitis 502
- tuberculosis (*see also* Tuberculosis) 011.4 ☑

Mounier-Kuhn syndrome 748.3
- with
  - acute exacerbation 494.1
  - bronchiectasis 494.0
    - with (acute) exacerbation 494.1
- acquired 519.19
  - with bronchiectasis 494.0
    - with (acute) exacerbation 494.1

Mountain
- fever — *see* Fever, mountain
- sickness 993.2
  - with polycythemia, acquired 289.0
  - acute 289.0
- tick fever 066.1

Mouse, joint — *see also* Loose, body, joint 718.1 ☑
- knee 717.6

Mouth — *see* condition

Movable
- coccyx 724.71
- kidney (*see also* Disease, renal) 593.0
  - congenital 753.3
- organ or site, congenital NEC — *see* Malposition, congenital
- spleen 289.59

Movement
- abnormal (dystonic) (involuntary) 781.0
- decreased fetal 655.7 ☑
- paradoxical facial 374.43

Moya Moya disease 437.5

Mozart's ear 744.29

MRSA (▶methicillin-resistant◀ staphylococcus aureus) 041.12 ▲
- colonization V02.54 ●
- personal history of V12.04 ●

MSSA (methicillin susceptible staphylococcus aureus) 041.11 ●
- colonization V02.53 ●

Mucha's disease (acute parapsoriasis varioliformis) 696.2

Mucha-Haberman syndrome (acute parapsoriasis varioliformis) 696.2

Mu-chain disease 273.2

Mucinosis (cutaneous) (papular) 701.8

Mucocele
- appendix 543.9
- buccal cavity 528.9
- gallbladder (*see also* Disease, gallbladder) 575.3

☑ Additional Digit Required — Refer to the Tabular List for Digit Selection

Subterms under main terms may continue to next column or page

▶◀ Revised Text ● New Line ▲ Revised Code

Mucocele — *continued*
lacrimal sac 375.43
orbit (eye) 376.81
salivary gland (any) 527.6
sinus (accessory) (nasal) 478.19
turbinate (bone) (middle) (nasal) 478.19
uterus 621.8
Mucocutaneous lymph node syndrome (acute) (febrile) (infantile) 446.1
Mucoenteritis 564.9
Mucolipidosis I, II, III 272.7
Mucopolysaccharidosis (types 1-6) 277.5
cardiopathy 277.5 *[425.7]*
Mucormycosis (lung) 117.7
Mucosa associated lymphoid tissue (MALT) 200.3 ☑
Mucositis — *see also* Inflammation, by site 528.00
cervix (ulcerative) 616.81
due to
antineoplastic therapy (ulcerative) 528.01
other drugs (ulcerative) 528.02
specified NEC 528.09
gastrointestinal (ulcerative) 538
nasal (ulcerative) 478.11
necroticans agranulocytica (*see also* Agranulocytosis) 288.09
ulcerative 528.00
vagina (ulcerative) 616.81
vulva (ulcerative) 616.81
Mucous — *see also* condition
patches (syphilitic) 091.3
congenital 090.0
Mucoviscidosis 277.00
with meconium obstruction 277.01
Mucus
asphyxia or suffocation (*see also* Asphyxia, mucus) 933.1
newborn 770.18
in stool 792.1
plug (*see also* Asphyxia, mucus) 933.1
aspiration, of newborn 770.17
tracheobronchial 519.19
newborn 770.18
Muguet 112.0
Mulberry molars 090.5
Müllerian mixed tumor (M8950/3) — *see* Neoplasm, by site, malignant
Multicystic kidney 753.19
Multilobed placenta — *see* Placenta, abnormal
Multinodular prostate 600.10
with
urinary
obstruction 600.11
retention 600.11
Multiparity V61.5
affecting
fetus or newborn 763.89
management of
labor and delivery 659.4 ☑
pregnancy V23.3
requiring contraceptive management (*see also* Contraception) V25.9
Multipartita placenta — *see* Placenta, abnormal
Multiple, multiplex — *see also* condition
birth
affecting fetus or newborn 761.5
healthy liveborn — *see* Newborn, multiple
digits (congenital) 755.00
fingers 755.01
toes 755.02
organ or site NEC — *see* Accessory
personality 300.14
renal arteries 747.62
Mumps 072.9
with complication 072.8
specified type NEC 072.79
encephalitis 072.2
hepatitis 072.71
meningitis (aseptic) 072.1

Mumps — *continued*
meningoencephalitis 072.2
oophoritis 072.79
orchitis 072.0
pancreatitis 072.3
polyneuropathy 072.72
vaccination, prophylactic (against) V04.6
Mumu — *see also* Infestation, filarial 125.9
Münchausen syndrome 301.51
Münchmeyer's disease or syndrome (exostosis luxurians) 728.11
Mural — *see* condition
Murmur (cardiac) (heart) (nonorganic) (organic) 785.2
abdominal 787.5
aortic (valve) (*see also* Endocarditis, aortic) 424.1
benign — *omit code*
cardiorespiratory 785.2
diastolic — *see* condition
Flint (*see also* Endocarditis, aortic) 424.1
functional — *omit code*
Graham Steell (pulmonic regurgitation) (*see also* Endocarditis, pulmonary) 424.3
innocent — *omit code*
insignificant — *omit code*
midsystolic 785.2
mitral (valve) — *see* Stenosis, mitral
physiologic — *see* condition
presystolic, mitral — *see* Insufficiency, mitral
pulmonic (valve) (*see also* Endocarditis, pulmonary) 424.3
Still's (vibratory) — *omit code*
systolic (valvular) — *see* condition
tricuspid (valve) — *see* Endocarditis, tricuspid
undiagnosed 785.2
valvular — *see* condition
vibratory — *omit code*
Murri's disease (intermittent hemoglobinuria) 283.2
Muscae volitantes 379.24
Muscle, muscular — *see* condition
Musculoneuralgia 729.1
Mushrooming hip 718.95
Mushroom workers' (pickers') lung 495.5
Mutation
factor V leiden 289.81
prothrombin gene 289.81
Mutism — *see also* Aphasia 784.3
akinetic 784.3
deaf (acquired) (congenital) 389.7
hysterical 300.11
selective (elective) 313.23
adjustment reaction 309.83
Myà's disease (congenital dilation, colon) 751.3
Myalgia (intercostal) 729.1
eosinophilia syndrome 710.5
epidemic 074.1
cervical 078.89
psychogenic 307.89
traumatic NEC 959.9
Myasthenia 358.00
cordis — *see* Failure, heart
gravis 358.00
with exacerbation (acute) 358.01
in crisis 358.01
neonatal 775.2
pseudoparalytica 358.00
stomach 536.8
psychogenic 306.4
syndrome
in
botulism 005.1 *[358.1]*
diabetes mellitus
250.6 ☑ *[358.1]*
due to secondary diabetes ●
249.6 ☑ *[358.1]* ●

Myasthenia — *continued*
syndrome — *continued*
in — *continued*
hypothyroidism (*see also* Hypothyroidism) 244.9 *[358.1]*
malignant neoplasm NEC 199.1 *[358.1]*
pernicious anemia 281.0 *[358.1]*
thyrotoxicosis (*see also* Thyrotoxicosis) 242.9 ☑ *[358.1]*
Myasthenic 728.87
Mycelium infection NEC 117.9
Mycetismus 988.1
Mycetoma (actinomycotic) 039.9
bone 039.8
mycotic 117.4
foot 039.4
mycotic 117.4
madurae 039.9
mycotic 117.4
maduromycotic 039.9
mycotic 117.4
mycotic 117.4
nocardial 039.9
Mycobacteriosis — *see* Mycobacterium
Mycobacterium, mycobacterial (infection) 031.9
acid-fast (bacilli) 031.9
anonymous (*see also* Mycobacterium, atypical) 031.9
atypical (acid-fast bacilli) 031.9
cutaneous 031.1
pulmonary 031.0
tuberculous (*see also* Tuberculosis, pulmonary) 011.9 ☑
specified site NEC 031.8
avium 031.0
intracellulare complex bacteremia (MAC) 031.2
balnei 031.1
Battey 031.0
cutaneous 031.1
disseminated 031.2
avium-intracellulare complex (DMAC) 031.2
fortuitum 031.0
intracellulare (battey bacillus) 031.0
kakerifu 031.8
kansasii 031.0
kasongo 031.8
leprae — *see* Leprosy
luciflavum 031.0
marinum 031.1
pulmonary 031.0
tuberculous (*see also* Tuberculosis, pulmonary) 011.9 ☑
scrofulaceum 031.1
tuberculosis (human, bovine) (*see also* Tuberculosis)
avian type 031.0
ulcerans 031.1
xenopi 031.0
Mycosis, mycotic 117.9
cutaneous NEC 111.9
ear 111.8 *[380.15]*
fungoides (M9700/3) 202.1 ☑
mouth 112.0
pharynx 117.9
skin NEC 111.9
stomatitis 112.0
systemic NEC 117.9
tonsil 117.9
vagina, vaginitis 112.1
Mydriasis (persistent) (pupil) 379.43
Myelatelia 742.59
Myelinoclasis, perivascular, acute (postinfectious) NEC 136.9 *[323.61]*
postimmunization or postvaccinal 323.51
Myelinosis, central pontine 341.8
Myelitis (ascending) (cerebellar) (childhood) (chronic) (descending) (diffuse) (disseminated) (pressure) (progressive) (spinal cord) (subacute) — *see also* Encephalitis 323.9

Myelitis — *see also* Encephalitis — *continued*
acute (transverse) 341.20
idiopathic 341.22
in conditions classified elsewhere 341.21
due to
infection classified elsewhere 136.9 *[323.42]*
specified cause NEC 323.82
vaccination (any) 323.52
viral diseases classified elsewhere 323.02
herpes simplex 054.74
herpes zoster 053.14
late effect — *see* category 326
optic neuritis in 341.0
postchickenpox 052.2
postimmunization 323.52
postinfectious 136.9 *[323.63]*
postvaccinal 323.52
postvaricella 052.2
syphilitic (transverse) 094.89
toxic 989.9 *[323.72]*
transverse 323.82
acute 341.20
idiopathic 341.22
in conditions classified elsewhere 341.21
idiopathic 341.22
tuberculous (*see also* Tuberculosis) 013.6 ☑
virus 049.9
Myeloblastic — *see* condition
Myelocele — *see also* Spina bifida 741.9 ☑
with hydrocephalus 741.0 ☑
Myelocystocele — *see also* Spina bifida 741.9 ☑
Myelocytic — *see* condition
Myelocytoma 205.1 ☑
Myelodysplasia (spinal cord) 742.59
meaning myelodysplastic syndrome — *see* Syndrome, myelodysplastic
Myeloencephalitis — *see* Encephalitis
Myelofibrosis 289.83
with myeloid metaplasia 238.76
idiopathic (chronic) 238.76
megakaryocytic 238.79
primary 238.76
secondary 289.83
Myelogenous — *see* condition
Myeloid — *see* condition
Myelokathexis 288.09
Myeloleukodystrophy 330.0
Myelolipoma (M8870/0) — *see* Neoplasm, by site, benign
Myeloma (multiple) (plasma cell) (plasmacytic) (M9730/3) 203.0 ☑
monostotic (M9731/1) 238.6
solitary (M9731/1) 238.6
Myelomalacia 336.8
Myelomata, multiple (M9730/3) 203.0 ☑
Myelomatosis (M9730/3) 203.0 ☑
Myelomeningitis — *see* Meningoencephalitis
Myelomeningocele (spinal cord) — *see also* Spina bifida 741.9 ☑
fetal, causing fetopelvic disproportion 653.7 ☑
Myelo-osteo-musculodysplasia hereditaria 756.89
Myelopathic — *see* condition
Myelopathy (spinal cord) 336.9
cervical 721.1
diabetic 250.6 ☑ *[336.3]*
due to secondary diabetes ●
249.6 ☑ *[336.3]* ●
drug-induced 336.8
due to or with
carbon tetrachloride 987.8 *[323.72]*
degeneration or displacement, intervertebral disc 722.70
cervical, cervicothoracic 722.71

- **Myelopathy** — *continued*
  - due to or with — *continued*
    - degeneration or displacement, intervertebral disc — *continued*
      - lumbar, lumbosacral 722.73
      - thoracic, thoracolumbar 722.72
    - hydroxyquinoline derivatives 961.3 *[323.72]*
    - infection — *see* Encephalitis
    - intervertebral disc disorder 722.70
      - cervical, cervicothoracic 722.71
      - lumbar, lumbosacral 722.73
      - thoracic, thoracolumbar 722.72
    - lead 984.9 *[323.72]*
    - mercury 985.0 *[323.72]*
    - neoplastic disease (*see also* Neoplasm, by site) 239.9 *[336.3]*
    - pernicious anemia 281.0 *[336.3]*
    - spondylosis 721.91
      - cervical 721.1
      - lumbar, lumbosacral 721.42
      - thoracic 721.41
    - thallium 985.8 *[323.72]*
  - lumbar, lumbosacral 721.42
  - necrotic (subacute) 336.1
  - radiation-induced 336.8
  - spondylogenic NEC 721.91
    - cervical 721.1
    - lumbar, lumbosacral 721.42
    - thoracic 721.41
  - thoracic 721.41
  - toxic NEC 989.9 *[323.72]*
  - transverse (*see also* Myelitis) 323.82
  - vascular 336.1
- **Myelophthisis** 284.2
- **Myeloproliferative disease** (M9960/1) 238.79
- **Myeloradiculitis** — *see also* Polyneuropathy 357.0
- **Myeloradiculodysplasia** (spinal) 742.59
- **Myelosarcoma** (M9930/3) 205.3 ☑
- **Myelosclerosis** 289.89
  - with myeloid metaplasia (M9961/1) 238.76
  - disseminated, of nervous system 340
  - megakaryocytic (M9961/1) 238.79
- **Myelosis** (M9860/3) — *see also* Leukemia, myeloid 205.9 ☑
  - acute (M9861/3) 205.0 ☑
  - aleukemic (M9864/3) 205.8 ☑
  - chronic (M9863/3) 205.1 ☑
  - erythremic (M9840/3) 207.0 ☑
    - acute (M9841/3) 207.0 ☑
  - megakaryocytic (M9920/3) 207.2 ☑
  - nonleukemic (chronic) 288.8
  - subacute (M9862/3) 205.2 ☑
- **Myesthenia** — *see* Myasthenia
- **Myiasis** (cavernous) 134.0
  - orbit 134.0 *[376.13]*
- **Myoadenoma, prostate** 600.20
  - with
    - other lower urinary tract symptoms (LUTS) 600.21
    - urinary
      - obstruction 600.21
      - retention 600.21
- **Myoblastoma**
  - granular cell (M9580/0) (*see also* Neoplasm, connective tissue, benign)
    - malignant (M9580/3) — *see* Neoplasm, connective tissue, malignant
  - tongue (M9580/0) 210.1
- **Myocardial** — *see* condition
- **Myocardiopathy** (congestive) (constrictive) (familial) (hypertrophic nonobstructive) (idiopathic) (infiltrative) (obstructive) (primary) (restrictive) (sporadic) 425.4
  - alcoholic 425.5
  - amyloid 277.39 *[425.7]*
  - beriberi 265.0 *[425.7]*
  - cobalt-beer 425.5
- **Myocardiopathy** — *continued*
  - due to
    - amyloidosis 277.39 *[425.7]*
    - beriberi 265.0 *[425.7]*
    - cardiac glycogenosis 271.0 *[425.7]*
    - Chagas' disease 086.0
    - Friedreich's ataxia 334.0 *[425.8]*
    - influenza 487.8 *[425.8]*
    - mucopolysaccharidosis 277.5 *[425.7]*
    - myotonia atrophica 359.21 *[425.8]*
    - progressive muscular dystrophy 359.1 *[425.8]*
    - sarcoidosis 135 *[425.8]*
  - glycogen storage 271.0 *[425.7]*
  - hypertrophic obstructive 425.1
  - metabolic NEC 277.9 *[425.7]*
  - nutritional 269.9 *[425.7]*
  - obscure (African) 425.2
  - peripartum 674.5 ☑
  - postpartum 674.5 ☑
  - secondary 425.9
  - thyrotoxic (*see also* Thyrotoxicosis) 242.9 ☑ *[425.7]*
  - toxic NEC 425.9
- **Myocarditis** (fibroid) (interstitial) (old) (progressive) (senile) (with arteriosclerosis) 429.0
  - with
    - rheumatic fever (conditions classifiable to 390) 398.0
      - active (*see also* Myocarditis, acute, rheumatic) 391.2
      - inactive or quiescent (with chorea) 398.0
  - active (nonrheumatic) 422.90
    - rheumatic 391.2
      - with chorea (acute) (rheumatic) (Sydenham's) 392.0
  - acute or subacute (interstitial) 422.90
    - due to Streptococcus (beta-hemolytic) 391.2
    - idiopathic 422.91
    - rheumatic 391.2
      - with chorea (acute) (rheumatic) (Sydenham's) 392.0
    - specified type NEC 422.99
  - aseptic of newborn 074.23
  - bacterial (acute) 422.92
  - chagasic 086.0
  - chronic (interstitial) 429.0
  - congenital 746.89
  - constrictive 425.4
  - Coxsackie (virus) 074.23
  - diphtheritic 032.82
  - due to or in
    - Coxsackie (virus) 074.23
    - diphtheria 032.82
    - epidemic louse-borne typhus 080 *[422.0]*
    - influenza 487.8 *[422.0]*
    - Lyme disease 088.81 *[422.0]*
    - scarlet fever 034.1 *[422.0]*
    - toxoplasmosis (acquired) 130.3
    - tuberculosis (*see also* Tuberculosis) 017.9 ☑ *[422.0]*
    - typhoid 002.0 *[422.0]*
    - typhus NEC 081.9 *[422.0]*
  - eosinophilic 422.91
  - epidemic of newborn 074.23
  - Fiedler's (acute) (isolated) (subacute) 422.91
  - giant cell (acute) (subacute) 422.91
  - gonococcal 098.85
  - granulomatous (idiopathic) (isolated) (nonspecific) 422.91
  - hypertensive (*see also* Hypertension, heart) 402.90
  - idiopathic 422.91
    - granulomatous 422.91
  - infective 422.92
  - influenzal 487.8 *[422.0]*
  - isolated (diffuse) (granulomatous) 422.91
  - malignant 422.99
  - meningococcal 036.43
- **Myocarditis** — *continued*
  - nonrheumatic, active 422.90
  - parenchymatous 422.90
  - pneumococcal (acute) (subacute) 422.92
  - rheumatic (chronic) (inactive) (with chorea) 398.0
    - active or acute 391.2
      - with chorea (acute) (rheumatic) (Sydenham's) 392.0
  - septic 422.92
  - specific (giant cell) (productive) 422.91
  - staphylococcal (acute) (subacute) 422.92
  - suppurative 422.92
  - syphilitic (chronic) 093.82
  - toxic 422.93
    - rheumatic (*see also* Myocarditis, acute rheumatic) 391.2
  - tuberculous (*see also* Tuberculosis) 017.9 ☑ *[422.0]*
  - typhoid 002.0 *[422.0]*
  - valvular — *see* Endocarditis
  - viral, except Coxsackie 422.91
    - Coxsackie 074.23
    - of newborn (Coxsackie) 074.23
- **Myocardium, myocardial** — *see* condition
- **Myocardosis** — *see also* Cardiomyopathy 425.4
- **Myoclonia** (essential) 333.2
  - epileptica 333.2
  - Friedrich's 333.2
  - massive 333.2
- **Myoclonic**
  - epilepsy, familial (progressive) 333.2
  - jerks 333.2
- **Myoclonus** (familial essential) (multifocal) (simplex) 333.2
  - with epilepsy and with ragged red fibers (MERRF syndrome) 277.87
  - facial 351.8
  - massive (infantile) 333.2
  - pharyngeal 478.29
- **Myodiastasis** 728.84
- **Myoendocarditis** — *see also* Endocarditis
  - acute or subacute 421.9
- **Myoepithelioma** (M8982/0) — *see* Neoplasm, by site, benign
- **Myofascitis** (acute) 729.1
  - low back 724.2
- **Myofibroma** (M8890/0) — *see also* Neoplasm, connective tissue, benign
  - uterus (cervix) (corpus) (*see also* Leiomyoma) 218.9
- **Myofibromatosis**
  - infantile 759.89
- **Myofibrosis** 728.2
  - heart (*see also* Myocarditis) 429.0
  - humeroscapular region 726.2
  - scapulohumeral 726.2
- **Myofibrositis** — *see also* Myositis 729.1
  - scapulohumeral 726.2
- **Myogelosis** (occupational) 728.89
- **Myoglobinuria** 791.3
- **Myoglobulinuria, primary** 791.3
- **Myokymia** — *see also* Myoclonus
  - facial 351.8
- **Myolipoma** (M8860/0)
  - specified site — *see* Neoplasm, connective tissue, benign
  - unspecified site 223.0
- **Myoma** (M8895/0) — *see also* Neoplasm, connective tissue, benign
  - cervix (stump) (uterus) (*see also* Leiomyoma) 218.9
  - malignant (M8895/3) — *see* Neoplasm, connective tissue, malignant
  - prostate 600.20
    - with
      - other lower urinary tract symptoms (LUTS) 600.21
- **Myoma** — *see also* Neoplasm, connective tissue, benign — *continued*
  - prostate — *continued*
    - with — *continued*
      - urinary
        - obstruction 600.21
        - retention 600.21
  - uterus (cervix) (corpus) (*see also* Leiomyoma) 218.9
    - in pregnancy or childbirth 654.1 ☑
      - affecting fetus or newborn 763.89
      - causing obstructed labor 660.2 ☑
        - affecting fetus or newborn 763.1
- **Myomalacia** 728.9
  - cordis, heart (*see also* Degeneration, myocardial) 429.1
- **Myometritis** — *see also* Endometritis 615.9
- **Myometrium** — *see* condition
- **Myonecrosis, clostridial** 040.0
- **Myopathy** 359.9
  - alcoholic 359.4
  - amyloid 277.39 *[359.6]*
  - benign, congenital 359.0
  - central core 359.0
  - centronuclear 359.0
  - congenital (benign) 359.0
  - critical illness 359.81
  - distal 359.1
  - due to drugs 359.4
  - endocrine 259.9 *[359.5]*
    - specified type NEC 259.8 *[359.5]*
  - extraocular muscles 376.82
  - facioscapulohumeral 359.1
  - in
    - Addison's disease 255.41 *[359.5]*
    - amyloidosis 277.39 *[359.6]*
    - cretinism 243 *[359.5]*
    - Cushing's syndrome 255.0 *[359.5]*
    - disseminated lupus erythematosus 710.0 *[359.6]*
    - giant cell arteritis 446.5 *[359.6]*
    - hyperadrenocorticism NEC 255.3 *[359.5]*
    - hyperparathyroidism 252.01 *[359.5]*
    - hypopituitarism 253.2 *[359.5]*
    - hypothyroidism (*see also* Hypothyroidism) 244.9 *[359.5]*
    - malignant neoplasm NEC (M8000/3) 199.1 *[359.6]*
    - myxedema (*see also* Myxedema) 244.9 *[359.5]*
    - polyarteritis nodosa 446.0 *[359.6]*
    - rheumatoid arthritis 714.0 *[359.6]*
    - sarcoidosis 135 *[359.6]*
    - scleroderma 710.1 *[359.6]*
    - Sjögren's disease 710.2 *[359.6]*
    - thyrotoxicosis (*see also* Thyrotoxicosis) 242.9 ☑ *[359.5]*
  - inflammatory 359.89
  - intensive care (ICU) 359.81
  - limb-girdle 359.1
  - myotubular 359.0
  - necrotizing, acute 359.81
  - nemaline 359.0
  - ocular 359.1
  - oculopharyngeal 359.1
  - of critical illness 359.81
  - primary 359.89
  - progressive NEC 359.89
  - proximal myotonic (PROMM) 359.21
  - quadriplegic, acute 359.81
  - rod body 359.0
  - scapulohumeral 359.1
  - specified type NEC 359.89
  - toxic 359.4
- **Myopericarditis** — *see also* Pericarditis 423.9
- **Myopia** (axial) (congenital) (increased curvature or refraction, nucleus of lens) 367.1
  - degenerative, malignant 360.21

- **Myopia** — *continued*
  - malignant 360.21
  - progressive high (degenerative) 360.21
- **Myosarcoma** (M8895/3) — *see* Neoplasm, connective tissue, malignant
- **Myosis** (persistent) 379.42
  - stromal (endolymphatic) (M8931/1) 236.0
- **Myositis** 729.1
  - clostridial 040.0
  - due to posture 729.1
  - epidemic 074.1
  - fibrosa or fibrous (chronic) 728.2
    - Volkmann's (complicating trauma) 958.6
  - infective 728.0
  - interstitial 728.81
  - multiple — *see* Polymyositis
  - occupational 729.1
  - orbital, chronic 376.12
  - ossificans 728.12
    - circumscribed 728.12
    - progressive 728.11
    - traumatic 728.12
  - progressive fibrosing 728.11
  - purulent 728.0
  - rheumatic 729.1
  - rheumatoid 729.1
  - suppurative 728.0
  - syphilitic 095.6
  - traumatic (old) 729.1
- **Myospasia impulsiva** 307.23
- **Myotonia** (acquisita) (intermittens) 728.85
  - atrophica 359.21
  - congenita 359.22
    - acetazolamide responsive 359.22
    - dominant form 359.22
    - recessive form 359.22
  - drug-induced 359.24
  - dystrophica 359.21
  - fluctuans 359.29
  - levior 359.29
  - permanens 359.29
- **Myotonic pupil** 379.46
- **Myriapodiasis** 134.1
- **Myringitis**
  - with otitis media — *see* Otitis media
  - acute 384.00
    - specified type NEC 384.09
  - bullosa hemorrhagica 384.01
  - bullous 384.01
  - chronic 384.1
- **Mysophobia** 300.29
- **Mytilotoxism** 988.0
- **Myxadenitis labialis** 528.5
- **Myxedema** (adult) (idiocy) (infantile) (juvenile) (thyroid gland) — *see also* Hypothyroidism 244.9
  - circumscribed 242.9 ☑
  - congenital 243
  - cutis 701.8
  - localized (pretibial) 242.9 ☑
  - madness (acute) 293.0
    - subacute 293.1
  - papular 701.8
  - pituitary 244.8
  - postpartum 674.8 ☑
  - pretibial 242.9 ☑
  - primary 244.9
- **Myxochondrosarcoma** (M9220/3) — *see* Neoplasm, cartilage, malignant
- **Myxofibroma** (M8811/0) — *see also* Neoplasm, connective tissue, benign
  - odontogenic (M9320/0) 213.1
    - upper jaw (bone) 213.0
- **Myxofibrosarcoma** (M8811/3) — *see* Neoplasm, connective tissue, malignant
- **Myxolipoma** (M8852/0) — *see also* Lipoma, by site 214.9
- **Myxoliposarcoma** (M8852/3) — *see* Neoplasm, connective tissue, malignant
- **Myxoma** (M8840/0) — *see also* Neoplasm, connective tissue, benign
  - odontogenic (M9320/0) 213.1
    - upper jaw (bone) 213.0
- **Myxosarcoma** (M8840/3) — *see* Neoplasm, connective tissue, malignant

N

- **Naegeli's**
  - disease (hereditary hemorrhagic thrombasthenia) 287.1
  - leukemia, monocytic (M9863/3) 205.1 ☑
  - syndrome (incontinentia pigmenti) 757.33
- **Naffziger's syndrome** 353.0
- **Naga sore** — *see also* Ulcer, skin 707.9
- **Nägele's pelvis** 738.6
  - with disproportion (fetopelvic) 653.0 ☑
    - affecting fetus or newborn 763.1
    - causing obstructed labor 660.1 ☑
      - affecting fetus or newborn 763.1
- **Nager-de Reynier syndrome** (dysostosis mandibularis) 756.0
- **Nail** — *see also* condition
  - biting 307.9
  - patella syndrome (hereditary osteoonychodysplasia) 756.89
- **Nanism, nanosomia** — *see also* Dwarfism 259.4
  - hypophyseal 253.3
  - pituitary 253.3
  - renis, renalis 588.0
- **Nanukayami** 100.89
- **Napkin rash** 691.0
- **Narcissism** 301.81
- **Narcolepsy** 347.00
  - with cataplexy 347.01
  - in conditions classified elsewhere 347.10
    - with cataplexy 347.11
- **Narcosis**
  - carbon dioxide (respiratory) 786.09
  - due to drug
    - correct substance properly administered 780.09
    - overdose or wrong substance given or taken 977.9
      - specified drug — *see* Table of Drugs and Chemicals
- **Narcotism (chronic)** — *see also* Dependence 304.9 ☑
  - acute
    - correct substance properly administered 349.82
    - overdose or wrong substance given or taken 967.8
      - specified drug — *see* Table of Drugs and Chemicals
- **NARP** (ataxia and retinitis pigmentosa) 277.87
- **Narrow**
  - anterior chamber angle 365.02
  - pelvis (inlet) (outlet) — *see* Contraction, pelvis
- **Narrowing**
  - artery NEC 447.1
    - auditory, internal 433.8 ☑
    - basilar 433.0 ☑
      - with other precerebral artery 433.3 ☑
      - bilateral 433.3 ☑
    - carotid 433.1 ☑
      - with other precerebral artery 433.3 ☑
      - bilateral 433.3 ☑
    - cerebellar 433.8 ☑
    - choroidal 433.8 ☑
    - communicating posterior 433.8 ☑
    - coronary (*see also* Arteriosclerosis, coronary)
      - congenital 746.85
        - due to syphilis 090.5
    - hypophyseal 433.8 ☑
- **Narrowing** — *continued*
  - artery — *continued*
    - pontine 433.8 ☑
    - precerebral NEC 433.9 ☑
      - multiple or bilateral 433.3 ☑
      - specified NEC 433.8 ☑
    - vertebral 433.2 ☑
      - with other precerebral artery 433.3 ☑
      - bilateral 433.3 ☑
  - auditory canal (external) (*see also* Stricture, ear canal, acquired) 380.50
  - cerebral arteries 437.0
  - cicatricial — *see* Cicatrix
  - congenital — *see* Anomaly, congenital
  - coronary artery — *see* Narrowing, artery, coronary
  - ear, middle 385.22
  - Eustachian tube (*see also* Obstruction, Eustachian tube) 381.60
  - eyelid 374.46
    - congenital 743.62
  - intervertebral disc or space NEC — *see* Degeneration, intervertebral disc
  - joint space, hip 719.85
  - larynx 478.74
  - lids 374.46
    - congenital 743.62
  - mesenteric artery (with gangrene) 557.0
  - palate 524.89
  - palpebral fissure 374.46
  - retinal artery 362.13
  - ureter 593.3
  - urethra (*see also* Stricture, urethra) 598.9
- **Narrowness, abnormal, eyelid** 743.62
- **Nasal** — *see* condition
- **Nasolacrimal** — *see* condition
- **Nasopharyngeal** — *see also* condition
  - bursa 478.29
  - pituitary gland 759.2
  - torticollis 723.5
- **Nasopharyngitis** (acute) (infective) (subacute) 460
  - chronic 472.2
    - due to external agent — *see* Condition, respiratory, chronic, due to
  - due to external agent — *see* Condition, respiratory, due to
  - septic 034.0
  - streptococcal 034.0
  - suppurative (chronic) 472.2
  - ulcerative (chronic) 472.2
- **Nasopharynx, nasopharyngeal** — *see* condition
- **Natal tooth, teeth** 520.6
- **Nausea** — *see also* Vomiting 787.02
  - with vomiting 787.01
  - epidemic 078.82
  - gravidarum — *see* Hyperemesis, gravidarum
  - marina 994.6
- **Navel** — *see* condition
- **Neapolitan fever** — *see also* Brucellosis 023.9
- **Near drowning** 994.1 ●
- **Nearsightedness** 367.1
- **Near-syncope** 780.2
- **Nebécourt's syndrome** 253.3
- **Nebula, cornea** (eye) 371.01
  - congenital 743.43
    - interfering with vision 743.42
- **Necator americanus infestation** 126.1
- **Necatoriasis** 126.1
- **Neck** — *see* condition
- **Necrencephalus** — *see also* Softening, brain 437.8
- **Necrobacillosis** 040.3
- **Necrobiosis** 799.89
  - brain or cerebral (*see also* Softening, brain) 437.8
  - lipoidica 709.3
- **Necrobiosis** — *continued*
  - lipoidica — *continued*
    - diabeticorum 250.8 ☑ *[709.3]*
      - due to secondary diabetes ●
        249.8 ☑ *[709.3]* ●
- **Necrodermolysis** 695.15 ▲
- **Necrolysis, toxic epidermal** 695.15 ▲
  - due to drug
    - correct substance properly administered 695.15 ▲
    - overdose or wrong substance given or taken 977.9
      - specified drug — *see* Table of Drugs and Chemicals
  - Stevens-Johnson syndrome overlap ●
    (SJS-TEN overlap syndrome) ●
    695.14 ●
- **Necrophilia** 302.89
- **Necrosis, necrotic**
  - adrenal (capsule) (gland) 255.8
  - antrum, nasal sinus 478.19
  - aorta (hyaline) (*see also* Aneurysm, aorta) 441.9
    - cystic medial 441.00
      - abdominal 441.02
      - thoracic 441.01
      - thoracoabdominal 441.03
    - ruptured 441.5
  - arteritis 446.0
  - artery 447.5
  - aseptic, bone 733.40
    - femur (head) (neck) 733.42
      - medial condyle 733.43
    - humoral head 733.41
    - jaw 733.45
    - medial femoral condyle 733.43
    - specific site NEC 733.49
    - talus 733.44
  - avascular, bone NEC (*see also* Necrosis, aseptic, bone) 733.40
  - bladder (aseptic) (sphincter) 596.8
  - bone (*see also* Osteomyelitis) 730.1 ☑
    - acute 730.0 ☑
    - aseptic or avascular 733.40
      - femur (head) (neck) 733.42
        - medial condyle 733.43
      - humoral head 733.41
      - jaw 733.45
      - medial femoral condyle 733.43
      - specified site NEC 733.49
      - talus 733.44
    - ethmoid 478.19
    - ischemic 733.40
    - jaw 526.4
      - asceptic 733.45
    - marrow 289.89
    - Paget's (osteitis deformans) 731.0
    - tuberculous — *see* Tuberculosis, bone
  - brain (softening) (*see also* Softening, brain) 437.8
  - breast (aseptic) (fat) (segmental) 611.3
  - bronchus, bronchi 519.19
  - central nervous system NEC (*see also* Softening, brain) 437.8
  - cerebellar (*see also* Softening, brain) 437.8
  - cerebral (softening) (*see also* Softening, brain) 437.8
  - cerebrospinal (softening) (*see also* Softening, brain) 437.8
  - colon 557.0
  - cornea (*see also* Keratitis) 371.40
  - cortical, kidney 583.6
  - cystic medial (aorta) 441.00
    - abdominal 441.02
    - thoracic 441.01
    - thoracoabdominal 441.03
  - dental 521.09
    - pulp 522.1
  - due to swallowing corrosive substance — *see* Burn, by site
  - ear (ossicle) 385.24
  - esophagus 530.89
  - ethmoid (bone) 478.19

Necrosis, necrotic — *continued*
eyelid 374.50
fat, fatty (generalized) (*see also* Degeneration, fatty) 272.8
abdominal wall 567.82
breast (aseptic) (segmental) 611.3
intestine 569.89
localized — *see* Degeneration, by site, fatty
mesentery 567.82
omentum 567.82
pancreas 577.8
peritoneum 567.82
skin (subcutaneous) 709.3
newborn 778.1
femur (aseptic) (avascular) 733.42
head 733.42
medial condyle 733.43
neck 733.42
gallbladder (*see also* Cholecystitis, acute) 575.0
gangrenous 785.4
gastric 537.89
glottis 478.79
heart (myocardium) — *see* Infarct, myocardium
hepatic (*see also* Necrosis, liver) 570
hip (aseptic) (avascular) 733.42
intestine (acute) (hemorrhagic) (massive) 557.0
ischemic 785.4
jaw 526.4
asceptic 733.45
kidney (bilateral) 583.9
acute 584.9
cortical 583.6
acute 584.6
with
abortion — *see* Abortion, by type, with renal failure
ectopic pregnancy (*see also* categories 633.0–633.9) 639.3
molar pregnancy (*see also* categories 630–632) 639.3
complicating pregnancy 646.2 ☑
affecting fetus or newborn 760.1
following labor and delivery 669.3 ☑
medullary (papillary) (*see also* Pyelitis) 590.80
in
acute renal failure 584.7
nephritis, nephropathy 583.7

Necrosis, necrotic — *continued*
kidney — *continued*
papillary (*see also* Pyelitis) 590.80
in
acute renal failure 584.7
nephritis, nephropathy 583.7
tubular 584.5
with
abortion — *see* Abortion, by type, with renal failure
ectopic pregnancy (*see also* categories 633.0–633.9) 639.3
molar pregnancy (*see also* categories 630–632) 639.3
complicating
abortion 639.3
ectopic or molar pregnancy 639.3
pregnancy 646.2 ☑
affecting fetus or newborn 760.1
following labor and delivery 669.3 ☑
traumatic 958.5
larynx 478.79
liver (acute) (congenital) (diffuse) (massive) (subacute) 570
with
abortion — *see* Abortion, by type, with specified complication NEC
ectopic pregnancy (*see also* categories 633.0–633.9) 639.8
molar pregnancy (*see also* categories 630–632) 639.8
complicating pregnancy 646.7 ☑
affecting fetus or newborn 760.8
following
abortion 639.8
ectopic or molar pregnancy 639.8
obstetrical 646.7 ☑
postabortal 639.8
puerperal, postpartum 674.8 ☑
toxic 573.3
lung 513.0
lymphatic gland 683
mammary gland 611.3
mastoid (chronic) 383.1
mesentery 557.0
fat 567.82
mitral valve — *see* Insufficiency, mitral
myocardium, myocardial — *see* Infarct, myocardium

Necrosis, necrotic — *continued*
nose (septum) 478.19
omentum 557.0
with mesenteric infarction 557.0
fat 567.82
orbit, orbital 376.10
ossicles, ear (aseptic) 385.24
ovary (*see also* Salpingo-oophoritis) 614.2
pancreas (aseptic) (duct) (fat) 577.8
acute 577.0
infective 577.0
papillary, kidney (*see also* Pyelitis) 590.80
perineum 624.8
peritoneum 557.0
with mesenteric infarction 557.0
fat 567.82
pharynx 462
in granulocytopenia 288.09
phosphorus 983.9
pituitary (gland) (postpartum) (Sheehan) 253.2
placenta (*see also* Placenta, abnormal) 656.7 ☑
pneumonia 513.0
pulmonary 513.0
pulp (dental) 522.1
pylorus 537.89
radiation — *see* Necrosis, by site
radium — *see* Necrosis, by site
renal — *see* Necrosis, kidney
sclera 379.19
scrotum 608.89
skin or subcutaneous tissue 709.8
due to burn — see Burn, by site
gangrenous 785.4
spine, spinal (column) 730.18
acute 730.18
cord 336.1
spleen 289.59
stomach 537.89
stomatitis 528.1
subcutaneous fat 709.3
fetus or newborn 778.1
subendocardial — *see* Infarct, myocardium
suprarenal (capsule) (gland) 255.8
teeth, tooth 521.09
testis 608.89
thymus (gland) 254.8
tonsil 474.8
trachea 519.19
tuberculous NEC — *see* Tuberculosis
tubular (acute) (anoxic) (toxic) 584.5
due to a procedure 997.5
umbilical cord, affecting fetus or newborn 762.6

Necrosis, necrotic — *continued*
vagina 623.8
vertebra (lumbar) 730.18
acute 730.18
tuberculous (*see also* Tuberculosis) 015.0 ☑ *[730.8]* ☑
vesical (aseptic) (bladder) 596.8
vulva 624.8
x-ray — *see* Necrosis, by site
Necrospermia 606.0
Necrotizing angiitis 446.0
Negativism 301.7
Neglect (child) (newborn) NEC 995.52
adult 995.84
after or at birth 995.52
hemispatial 781.8
left-sided 781.8
sensory 781.8
visuospatial 781.8
Negri bodies 071
Neill-Dingwall syndrome (microcephaly and dwarfism) 759.89
Neisserian infection NEC — *see* Gonococcus
Nematodiasis NEC — *see also* Infestation, Nematode 127.9
ancylostoma (*see also* Ancylostomiasis) 126.9
Neoformans cryptococcus infection 117.5
Neonatal — *see also* condition
adrenoleukodystrophy 277.86
teeth, tooth 520.6
Neonatorum — *see* condition
Neoplasia
anal intraepithelial I [AIN I] (histologically confirmed) 569.44 ●
anal intraepithelial II [AIN II] (histologically confirmed) 569.44 ●
anal intraepithelial III [AIN III] 230.6 ●
anal canal 230.5 ●
multiple endocrine [MEN]
type I 258.01
type IIA 258.02
type IIB 258.03
vaginal intraepithelial I [VAIN I] 623.0
vaginal intraepithelial II [VAIN II] 623.0
vaginal intraepithelial III [VAIN III] 233.31
vulvular intraepithelial I [VIN I] 624.01
vulvular intraepithelial II [VIN II] 624.02
vulvular intraepithelial III [VIN III] 233.32

	Malignant					
	Primary	Secondary	Ca in situ	Benign	Uncertain Behavior	Unspecified
Neoplasm, neoplastic	199.1	199.1	234.9	229.9	238.9	239.9

Notes — 1. The list below gives the code numbers for neoplasms by anatomical site. For each site there are six possible code numbers according to whether the neoplasm in question is malignant, benign, in situ, of uncertain behavior, or of unspecified nature. The description of the neoplasm will often indicate which of the six columns is appropriate; e.g., malignant melanoma of skin, benign fibroadenoma of breast, carcinoma in situ of cervix uteri.

Where such descriptors are not present, the remainder of the Index should be consulted where guidance is given to the appropriate column for each morphological (histological) variety listed; e.g., Mesonephroma — see Neoplasm, malignant; Embryoma — see also Neoplasm, uncertain behavior; Disease, Bowen's — see Neoplasm, skin, in situ. However, the guidance in the Index can be overridden if one of the descriptors mentioned above is present; e.g., malignant adenoma of colon is coded to 153.9 and not to 211.3 as the adjective "malignant" overrides the Index entry "Adenoma — see also Neoplasm, benign."

*2. Sites marked with the sign * (e.g., face NEC*) should be classified to malignant neoplasm of skin of these sites if the variety of neoplasm is a squamous cell carcinoma or an epidermoid carcinoma, and to benign neoplasm of skin of these sites if the variety of neoplasm is a papilloma (any type).*

	Primary	Secondary	Ca in situ	Benign	Uncertain Behavior	Unspecified
abdomen, abdominal	195.2	198.89	234.8	229.8	238.8	239.8
cavity	195.2	198.89	234.8	229.8	238.8	239.8
organ	195.2	198.89	234.8	229.8	238.8	239.8
viscera	195.2	198.89	234.8	229.8	238.8	239.8
wall	173.5	198.2	232.5	216.5	238.2	239.2
connective tissue	171.5	198.89	—	215.5	238.1	239.2
abdominopelvic	195.8	198.89	234.8	229.8	238.8	239.8
accessory sinus — *see* Neoplasm, sinus						
acoustic nerve	192.0	198.4	—	225.1	237.9	239.7
acromion (process)	170.4	198.5	—	213.4	238.0	239.2
adenoid (pharynx) (tissue)	147.1	198.89	230.0	210.7	235.1	239.0
adipose tissue (*see also* Neoplasm, connective tissue)	171.9	198.89	—	215.9	238.1	239.2
adnexa (uterine)	183.9	198.82	233.39	221.8	236.3	239.5
adrenal (cortex) (gland) (medulla)	194.0	198.7	234.8	227.0	237.2	239.7
ala nasi (external)	173.3	198.2	232.3	216.3	238.2	239.2
alimentary canal or tract NEC	159.9	197.8	230.9	211.9	235.5	239.0
alveolar	143.9	198.89	230.0	210.4	235.1	239.0
mucosa	143.9	198.89	230.0	210.4	235.1	239.0
lower	143.1	198.89	230.0	210.4	235.1	239.0
upper	143.0	198.89	230.0	210.4	235.1	239.0
ridge or process	170.1	198.5	—	213.1	238.0	239.2
carcinoma	143.9	—	—	—	—	—
lower	143.1	—	—	—	—	—
upper	143.0	—	—	—	—	—
lower	170.1	198.5	—	213.1	238.0	239.2
mucosa	143.9	198.89	230.0	210.4	235.1	239.0
lower	143.1	198.89	230.0	210.4	235.1	239.0
upper	143.0	198.89	230.0	210.4	235.1	239.0
upper	170.0	198.5	—	213.0	238.0	239.2
sulcus	145.1	198.89	230.0	210.4	235.1	239.0
alveolus	143.9	198.89	230.0	210.4	235.1	239.0
lower	143.1	198.89	230.0	210.4	235.1	239.0
upper	143.0	198.89	230.0	210.4	235.1	239.0
ampulla of Vater	156.2	197.8	230.8	211.5	235.3	239.0
ankle NEC*	195.5	198.89	232.7	229.8	238.8	239.8
anorectum, anorectal (junction)	154.8	197.5	230.7	211.4	235.2	239.0
antecubital fossa or space*	195.4	198.89	232.6	229.8	238.8	239.8
antrum (Highmore) (maxillary)	160.2	197.3	231.8	212.0	235.9	239.1
pyloric	151.2	197.8	230.2	211.1	235.2	239.0
tympanicum	160.1	197.3	231.8	212.0	235.9	239.1
anus, anal	154.3	197.5	230.6	211.4	235.5	239.0
canal	154.2	197.5	230.5	211.4	235.5	239.0
contiguous sites with rectosigmoid junction or rectum	154.8	—	—	—	—	—
margin	173.5	198.2	232.5	216.5	238.2	239.2
skin	173.5	198.2	232.5	216.5	238.2	239.2
sphincter	154.2	197.5	230.5	211.4	235.5	239.0
aorta (thoracic)	171.4	198.89	—	215.4	238.1	239.2

	Malignant					
	Primary	Secondary	Ca in situ	Benign	Uncertain Behavior	Unspecified
Neoplasm, neoplastic — *continued*						
aorta — *continued*						
abdominal	171.5	198.89	—	215.5	238.1	239.2
aortic body	194.6	198.89	—	227.6	237.3	239.7
aponeurosis	171.9	198.89	—	215.9	238.1	239.2
palmar	171.2	198.89	—	215.2	238.1	239.2
plantar	171.3	198.89	—	215.3	238.1	239.2
appendix	153.5	197.5	230.3	211.3	235.2	239.0
arachnoid (cerebral)	192.1	198.4	—	225.2	237.6	239.7
spinal	192.3	198.4	—	225.4	237.6	239.7
areola (female)	174.0	198.81	233.0	217	238.3	239.3
male	175.0	198.81	233.0	217	238.3	239.3
arm NEC*	195.4	198.89	232.6	229.8	238.8	239.8
artery — *see* Neoplasm, connective tissue						
aryepiglottic fold	148.2	198.89	230.0	210.8	235.1	239.0
hypopharyngeal aspect	148.2	198.89	230.0	210.8	235.1	239.0
laryngeal aspect	161.1	197.3	231.0	212.1	235.6	239.1
marginal zone	148.2	198.89	230.0	210.8	235.1	239.0
arytenoid (cartilage)	161.3	197.3	231.0	212.1	235.6	239.1
fold — *see* Neoplasm, aryepiglottic						
associated with transplanted organ ●	199.2	—	—	—	—	—
atlas	170.2	198.5	—	213.2	238.0	239.2
atrium, cardiac	164.1	198.89	—	212.7	238.8	239.8
auditory						
canal (external) (skin)	173.2	198.2	232.2	216.2	238.2	239.2
internal	160.1	197.3	231.8	212.0	235.9	239.1
nerve	192.0	198.4	—	225.1	237.9	239.7
tube	160.1	197.3	231.8	212.0	235.9	239.1
Eustachian	160.1	197.3	231.8	212.0	235.9	239.1
opening	147.2	198.89	230.0	210.7	235.1	239.0
auricle, ear	173.2	198.2	232.2	216.2	238.2	239.2
cartilage	171.0	198.89	—	215.0	238.1	239.2
auricular canal (external)	173.2	198.2	232.2	216.2	238.2	239.2
internal	160.1	197.3	231.8	212.0	235.9	239.1
autonomic nerve or nervous system NEC	171.9	198.89	—	215.9	238.1	239.2
axilla, axillary	195.1	198.89	234.8	229.8	238.8	239.8
fold	173.5	198.2	232.5	216.5	238.2	239.2
back NEC*	195.8	198.89	232.5	229.8	238.8	239.8
Bartholin's gland	184.1	198.82	233.32	221.2	236.3	239.5
basal ganglia	191.0	198.3	—	225.0	237.5	239.6
basis pedunculi	191.7	198.3	—	225.0	237.5	239.6
bile or biliary (tract)	156.9	197.8	230.8	211.5	235.3	239.0
canaliculi (biliferi) (intrahepatic)	155.1	197.8	230.8	211.5	235.3	239.0
canals, interlobular	155.1	197.8	230.8	211.5	235.3	239.0
contiguous sites	156.8	—	—	—	—	—
duct or passage (common) (cystic) (extrahepatic)	156.1	197.8	230.8	211.5	235.3	239.0
contiguous sites with gallbladder	156.8	—	—	—	—	—
interlobular	155.1	197.8	230.8	211.5	235.3	239.0
intrahepatic	155.1	197.8	230.8	211.5	235.3	239.0
and extrahepatic	156.9	197.8	230.8	211.5	235.3	239.0
bladder (urinary)	188.9	198.1	233.7	223.3	236.7	239.4
contiguous sites	188.8	—	—	—	—	—
dome	188.1	198.1	233.7	223.3	236.7	239.4
neck	188.5	198.1	233.7	223.3	236.7	239.4
orifice	188.9	198.1	233.7	223.3	236.7	239.4
ureteric	188.6	198.1	233.7	223.3	236.7	239.4
urethral	188.5	198.1	233.7	223.3	236.7	239.4
sphincter	188.8	198.1	233.7	223.3	236.7	239.4
trigone	188.0	198.1	233.7	223.3	236.7	239.4
urachus	188.7	—	233.7	223.3	236.7	239.4
wall	188.9	198.1	233.7	223.3	236.7	239.4
anterior	188.3	198.1	233.7	223.3	236.7	239.4
lateral	188.2	198.1	233.7	223.3	236.7	239.4
posterior	188.4	198.1	233.7	223.3	236.7	239.4

	Malignant					
	Primary	Secondary	Ca in situ	Benign	Uncertain Behavior	Unspecified
Neoplasm, neoplastic — *continued*						
blood vessel — *see* Neoplasm, connective tissue						
bone (periosteum)	170.9	198.5	—	213.9	238.0	239.2

Note — Carcinomas and adenocarcinomas, of any type other than intraosseous or odontogenic, of the sites listed under "Neoplasm, bone" should be considered as constituting metastatic spread from an unspecified primary site and coded to 198.5 for morbidity coding.

	Primary	Secondary	Ca in situ	Benign	Uncertain Behavior	Unspecified
acetabulum	170.6	198.5	—	213.6	238.0	239.2
acromion (process)	170.4	198.5	—	213.4	238.0	239.2
ankle	170.8	198.5	—	213.8	238.0	239.2
arm NEC	170.4	198.5	—	213.4	238.0	239.2
astragalus	170.8	198.5	—	213.8	238.0	239.2
atlas	170.2	198.5	—	213.2	238.0	239.2
axis	170.2	198.5	—	213.2	238.0	239.2
back NEC	170.2	198.5	—	213.2	238.0	239.2
calcaneus	170.8	198.5	—	213.8	238.0	239.2
calvarium	170.0	198.5	—	213.0	238.0	239.2
carpus (any)	170.5	198.5	—	213.5	238.0	239.2
cartilage NEC	170.9	198.5	—	213.9	238.0	239.2
clavicle	170.3	198.5	—	213.3	238.0	239.2
clivus	170.0	198.5	—	213.0	238.0	239.2
coccygeal vertebra	170.6	198.5	—	213.6	238.0	239.2
coccyx	170.6	198.5	—	213.6	238.0	239.2
costal cartilage	170.3	198.5	—	213.3	238.0	239.2
costovertebral joint	170.3	198.5	—	213.3	238.0	239.2
cranial	170.0	198.5	—	213.0	238.0	239.2
cuboid	170.8	198.5	—	213.8	238.0	239.2
cuneiform	170.9	198.5	—	213.9	238.0	239.2
ankle	170.8	198.5	—	213.8	238.0	239.2
wrist	170.5	198.5	—	213.5	238.0	239.2
digital	170.9	198.5	—	213.9	238.0	239.2
finger	170.5	198.5	—	213.5	238.0	239.2
toe	170.8	198.5	—	213.8	238.0	239.2
elbow	170.4	198.5	—	213.4	238.0	239.2
ethmoid (labyrinth)	170.0	198.5	—	213.0	238.0	239.2
face	170.0	198.5	—	213.0	238.0	239.2
lower jaw	170.1	198.5	—	213.1	238.0	239.2
femur (any part)	170.7	198.5	—	213.7	238.0	239.2
fibula (any part)	170.7	198.5	—	213.7	238.0	239.2
finger (any)	170.5	198.5	—	213.5	238.0	239.2
foot	170.8	198.5	—	213.8	238.0	239.2
forearm	170.4	198.5	—	213.4	238.0	239.2
frontal	170.0	198.5	—	213.0	238.0	239.2
hand	170.5	198.5	—	213.5	238.0	239.2
heel	170.8	198.5	—	213.8	238.0	239.2
hip	170.6	198.5	—	213.6	238.0	239.2
humerus (any part)	170.4	198.5	—	213.4	238.0	239.2
hyoid	170.0	198.5	—	213.0	238.0	239.2
ilium	170.6	198.5	—	213.6	238.0	239.2
innominate	170.6	198.5	—	213.6	238.0	239.2
intervertebral cartilage or disc	170.2	198.5	—	213.2	238.0	239.2
ischium	170.6	198.5	—	213.6	238.0	239.2
jaw (lower)	170.1	198.5	—	213.1	238.0	239.2
upper	170.0	198.5	—	213.0	238.0	239.2
knee	170.7	198.5	—	213.7	238.0	239.2
leg NEC	170.7	198.5	—	213.7	238.0	239.2
limb NEC	170.9	198.5	—	213.9	238.0	239.2
lower (long bones)	170.7	198.5	—	213.7	238.0	239.2
short bones	170.8	198.5	—	213.8	238.0	239.2
upper (long bones)	170.4	198.5	—	213.4	238.0	239.2
short bones	170.5	198.5	—	213.5	238.0	239.2
long	170.9	198.5	—	213.9	238.0	239.2
lower limbs NEC	170.7	198.5	—	213.7	238.0	239.2
upper limbs NEC	170.4	198.5	—	213.4	238.0	239.2
malar	170.0	198.5	—	213.0	238.0	239.2
mandible	170.1	198.5	—	213.1	238.0	239.2
marrow NEC	202.9	198.5	—	—	—	238.79
mastoid	170.0	198.5	—	213.0	238.0	239.2
maxilla, maxillary (superior)	170.0	198.5	—	213.0	238.0	239.2
inferior	170.1	198.5	—	213.1	238.0	239.2
metacarpus (any)	170.5	198.5	—	213.5	238.0	239.2

	Malignant					
	Primary	Secondary	Ca in situ	Benign	Uncertain Behavior	Unspecified
Neoplasm, neoplastic — *continued*						
bone — *continued*						
metatarsus (any)	170.8	198.5	—	213.8	238.0	239.2
navicular (ankle)	170.8	198.5	—	213.8	238.0	239.2
hand	170.5	198.5	—	213.5	238.0	239.2
nose, nasal	170.0	198.5	—	213.0	238.0	239.2
occipital	170.0	198.5	—	213.0	238.0	239.2
orbit	170.0	198.5	—	213.0	238.0	239.2
parietal	170.0	198.5	—	213.0	238.0	239.2
patella	170.8	198.5	—	213.8	238.0	239.2
pelvic	170.6	198.5	—	213.6	238.0	239.2
phalanges	170.9	198.5	—	213.9	238.0	239.2
foot	170.8	198.5	—	213.8	238.0	239.2
hand	170.5	198.5	—	213.5	238.0	239.2
pubic	170.6	198.5	—	213.6	238.0	239.2
radius (any part)	170.4	198.5	—	213.4	238.0	239.2
rib	170.3	198.5	—	213.3	238.0	239.2
sacral vertebra	170.6	198.5	—	213.6	238.0	239.2
sacrum	170.6	198.5	—	213.6	238.0	239.2
scaphoid (of hand)	170.5	198.5	—	213.5	238.0	239.2
of ankle	170.8	198.5	—	213.8	238.0	239.2
scapula (any part)	170.4	198.5	—	213.4	238.0	239.2
sella turcica	170.0	198.5	—	213.0	238.0	239.2
short	170.9	198.5	—	213.9	238.0	239.2
lower limb	170.8	198.5	—	213.8	238.0	239.2
upper limb	170.5	198.5	—	213.5	238.0	239.2
shoulder	170.4	198.5	—	213.4	238.0	239.2
skeleton, skeletal NEC	170.9	198.5	—	213.9	238.0	239.2
skull	170.0	198.5	—	213.0	238.0	239.2
sphenoid	170.0	198.5	—	213.0	238.0	239.2
spine, spinal (column)	170.2	198.5	—	213.2	238.0	239.2
coccyx	170.6	198.5	—	213.6	238.0	239.2
sacrum	170.6	198.5	—	213.6	238.0	239.2
sternum	170.3	198.5	—	213.3	238.0	239.2
tarsus (any)	170.8	198.5	—	213.8	238.0	239.2
temporal	170.0	198.5	—	213.0	238.0	239.2
thumb	170.5	198.5	—	213.5	238.0	239.2
tibia (any part)	170.7	198.5	—	213.7	238.0	239.2
toe (any)	170.8	198.5	—	213.8	238.0	239.2
trapezium	170.5	198.5	—	213.5	238.0	239.2
trapezoid	170.5	198.5	—	213.5	238.0	239.2
turbinate	170.0	198.5	—	213.0	238.0	239.2
ulna (any part)	170.4	198.5	—	213.4	238.0	239.2
unciform	170.5	198.5	—	213.5	238.0	239.2
vertebra (column)	170.2	198.5	—	213.2	238.0	239.2
coccyx	170.6	198.5	—	213.6	238.0	239.2
sacrum	170.6	198.5	—	213.6	238.0	239.2
vomer	170.0	198.5	—	213.0	238.0	239.2
wrist	170.5	198.5	—	213.5	238.0	239.2
xiphoid process	170.3	198.5	—	213.3	238.0	239.2
zygomatic	170.0	198.5	—	213.0	238.0	239.2
book-leaf (mouth)	145.8	198.89	230.0	210.4	235.1	239.0
bowel — *see* Neoplasm, intestine						
brachial plexus	171.2	198.89	—	215.2	238.1	239.2
brain NEC	191.9	198.3	—	225.0	237.5	239.6
basal ganglia	191.0	198.3	—	225.0	237.5	239.6
cerebellopontine angle	191.6	198.3	—	225.0	237.5	239.6
cerebellum NOS	191.6	198.3	—	225.0	237.5	239.6
cerebrum	191.0	198.3	—	225.0	237.5	239.6
choroid plexus	191.5	198.3	—	225.0	237.5	239.6
contiguous sites	191.8	—	—	—	—	—
corpus callosum	191.8	198.3	—	225.0	237.5	239.6
corpus striatum	191.0	198.3	—	225.0	237.5	239.6
cortex (cerebral)	191.0	198.3	—	225.0	237.5	239.6
frontal lobe	191.1	198.3	—	225.0	237.5	239.6
globus pallidus	191.0	198.3	—	225.0	237.5	239.6
hippocampus	191.2	198.3	—	225.0	237.5	239.6
hypothalamus	191.0	198.3	—	225.0	237.5	239.6
internal capsule	191.0	198.3	—	225.0	237.5	239.6
medulla oblongata	191.7	198.3	—	225.0	237.5	239.6
meninges	192.1	198.4	—	225.2	237.6	239.7
midbrain	191.7	198.3	—	225.0	237.5	239.6
occipital lobe	191.4	198.3	—	225.0	237.5	239.6
parietal lobe	191.3	198.3	—	225.0	237.5	239.6

	Malignant					
	Primary	Secondary	Ca in situ	Benign	Uncertain Behavior	Unspecified
Neoplasm, neoplastic — *continued*						
brain — *continued*						
peduncle	191.7	198.3	—	225.0	237.5	239.6
pons	191.7	198.3	—	225.0	237.5	239.6
stem	191.7	198.3	—	225.0	237.5	239.6
tapetum	191.8	198.3	—	225.0	237.5	239.6
temporal lobe	191.2	198.3	—	225.0	237.5	239.6
thalamus	191.0	198.3	—	225.0	237.5	239.6
uncus	191.2	198.3	—	225.0	237.5	239.6
ventricle (floor)	191.5	198.3	—	225.0	237.5	239.6
branchial (cleft) (vestiges)	146.8	198.89	230.0	210.6	235.1	239.0
breast (connective tissue) (female) (glandular tissue) (soft parts)	174.9	198.81	233.0	217	238.3	239.3
areola	174.0	198.81	233.0	217	238.3	239.3
male	175.0	198.81	233.0	217	238.3	239.3
axillary tail	174.6	198.81	233.0	217	238.3	239.3
central portion	174.1	198.81	233.0	217	238.3	239.3
contiguous sites	174.8	—	—	—	—	—
ectopic sites	174.8	198.81	233.0	217	238.3	239.3
inner	174.8	198.81	233.0	217	238.3	239.3
lower	174.8	198.81	233.0	217	238.3	239.3
lower-inner quadrant	174.3	198.81	233.0	217	238.3	239.3
lower-outer quadrant	174.5	198.81	233.0	217	238.3	239.3
male	175.9	198.81	233.0	217	238.3	239.3
areola	175.0	198.81	233.0	217	238.3	239.3
ectopic tissue	175.9	198.81	233.0	217	238.3	239.3
nipple	175.0	198.81	233.0	217	238.3	239.3
mastectomy site (skin)	173.5	198.2	—	—	—	—
specified as breast tissue	174.8	198.81	—	—	—	—
midline	174.8	198.81	233.0	217	238.3	239.3
nipple	174.0	198.81	233.0	217	238.3	239.3
male	175.0	198.81	233.0	217	238.3	239.3
outer	174.8	198.81	233.0	217	238.3	239.3
skin	173.5	198.2	232.5	216.5	238.2	239.2
tail (axillary)	174.6	198.81	233.0	217	238.3	239.3
upper	174.8	198.81	233.0	217	238.3	239.3
upper-inner quadrant	174.2	198.81	233.0	217	238.3	239.3
upper-outer quadrant	174.4	198.81	233.0	217	238.3	239.3
broad ligament	183.3	198.82	233.39	221.0	236.3	239.5
bronchiogenic, bronchogenic (lung)	162.9	197.0	231.2	212.3	235.7	239.1
bronchiole	162.9	197.0	231.2	212.3	235.7	239.1
bronchus	162.9	197.0	231.2	212.3	235.7	239.1
carina	162.2	197.0	231.2	212.3	235.7	239.1
contiguous sites with lung or trachea	162.8	—	—	—	—	—
lower lobe of lung	162.5	197.0	231.2	212.3	235.7	239.1
main	162.2	197.0	231.2	212.3	235.7	239.1
middle lobe of lung	162.4	197.0	231.2	212.3	235.7	239.1
upper lobe of lung	162.3	197.0	231.2	212.3	235.7	239.1
brow	173.3	198.2	232.3	216.3	238.2	239.2
buccal (cavity)	145.9	198.89	230.0	210.4	235.1	239.0
commissure	145.0	198.89	230.0	210.4	235.1	239.0
groove (lower) (upper)	145.1	198.89	230.0	210.4	235.1	239.0
mucosa	145.0	198.89	230.0	210.4	235.1	239.0
sulcus (lower) (upper)	145.1	198.89	230.0	210.4	235.1	239.0
bulbourethral gland	189.3	198.1	233.9	223.81	236.99	239.5
bursa — *see* Neoplasm, connective tissue						
buttock NEC*	195.3	198.89	232.5	229.8	238.8	239.8
calf*	195.5	198.89	232.7	229.8	238.8	239.8
calvarium	170.0	198.5	—	213.0	238.0	239.2
calyx, renal	189.1	198.0	233.9	223.1	236.91	239.5
canal						
anal	154.2	197.5	230.5	211.4	235.5	239.0
auditory (external)	173.2	198.2	232.2	216.2	238.2	239.2
auricular (external)	173.2	198.2	232.2	216.2	238.2	239.2

	Malignant					
	Primary	Secondary	Ca in situ	Benign	Uncertain Behavior	Unspecified
Neoplasm, neoplastic — *continued*						
canaliculi, biliary (biliferi) (intrahepatic)	155.1	197.8	230.8	211.5	235.3	239.0
canthus (eye) (inner) (outer)	173.1	198.2	232.1	216.1	238.2	239.2
capillary — *see* Neoplasm, connective tissue						
caput coli	153.4	197.5	230.3	211.3	235.2	239.0
cardia (gastric)	151.0	197.8	230.2	211.1	235.2	239.0
cardiac orifice (stomach)	151.0	197.8	230.2	211.1	235.2	239.0
cardio-esophageal junction	151.0	197.8	230.2	211.1	235.2	239.0
cardio-esophagus	151.0	197.8	230.2	211.1	235.2	239.0
carina (bronchus)	162.2	197.0	231.2	212.3	235.7	239.1
carotid (artery)	171.0	198.89	—	215.0	238.1	239.2
body	194.5	198.89	—	227.5	237.3	239.7
carpus (any bone)	170.5	198.5	—	213.5	238.0	239.2
cartilage (articular) (joint) NEC (*see also* Neoplasm, bone)	170.9	198.5	—	213.9	238.0	239.2
arytenoid	161.3	197.3	231.0	212.1	235.6	239.1
auricular	171.0	198.89	—	215.0	238.1	239.2
bronchi	162.2	197.3	—	212.3	235.7	239.1
connective tissue — *see* Neoplasm, connective tissue						
costal	170.3	198.5	—	213.3	238.0	239.2
cricoid	161.3	197.3	231.0	212.1	235.6	239.1
cuneiform	161.3	197.3	231.0	212.1	235.6	239.1
ear (external)	171.0	198.89	—	215.0	238.1	239.2
ensiform	170.3	198.5	—	213.3	238.0	239.2
epiglottis	161.1	197.3	231.0	212.1	235.6	239.1
anterior surface	146.4	198.89	230.0	210.6	235.1	239.0
eyelid	171.0	198.89	—	215.0	238.1	239.2
intervertebral	170.2	198.5	—	213.2	238.0	239.2
larynx, laryngeal	161.3	197.3	231.0	212.1	235.6	239.1
nose, nasal	160.0	197.3	231.8	212.0	235.9	239.1
pinna	171.0	198.89	—	215.0	238.1	239.2
rib	170.3	198.5	—	213.3	238.0	239.2
semilunar (knee)	170.7	198.5	—	213.7	238.0	239.2
thyroid	161.3	197.3	231.0	212.1	235.6	239.1
trachea	162.0	197.3	231.1	212.2	235.7	239.1
cauda equina	192.2	198.3	—	225.3	237.5	239.7
cavity						
buccal	145.9	198.89	230.0	210.4	235.1	239.0
nasal	160.0	197.3	231.8	212.0	235.9	239.1
oral	145.9	198.89	230.0	210.4	235.1	239.0
peritoneal	158.9	197.6	—	211.8	235.4	239.0
tympanic	160.1	197.3	231.8	212.0	235.9	239.1
cecum	153.4	197.5	230.3	211.3	235.2	239.0
central						
nervous system — *see* Neoplasm, nervous system						
white matter	191.0	198.3	—	225.0	237.5	239.6
cerebellopontine (angle)	191.6	198.3	—	225.0	237.5	239.6
cerebellum, cerebellar	191.6	198.3	—	225.0	237.5	239.6
cerebrum, cerebral (cortex) (hemisphere) (white matter)	191.0	198.3	—	225.0	237.5	239.6
meninges	192.1	198.4	—	225.2	237.6	239.7
peduncle	191.7	198.3	—	225.0	237.5	239.6
ventricle (any)	191.5	198.3	—	225.0	237.5	239.6
cervical region	195.0	198.89	234.8	229.8	238.8	239.8
cervix (cervical) (uteri) (uterus)	180.9	198.82	233.1	219.0	236.0	239.5
canal	180.0	198.82	233.1	219.0	236.0	239.5
contiguous sites	180.8	—	—	—	—	—
endocervix (canal) (gland)	180.0	198.82	233.1	219.0	236.0	239.5
exocervix	180.1	198.82	233.1	219.0	236.0	239.5
external os	180.1	198.82	233.1	219.0	236.0	239.5
internal os	180.0	198.82	233.1	219.0	236.0	239.5
nabothian gland	180.0	198.82	233.1	219.0	236.0	239.5

	Malignant					
	Primary	Secondary	Ca in situ	Benign	Uncertain Behavior	Unspecified
Neoplasm, neoplastic — *continued*						
cervix — *continued*						
squamocolumnar junction	180.8	198.82	233.1	219.0	236.0	239.5
stump	180.8	198.82	233.1	219.0	236.0	239.5
cheek	195.0	198.89	234.8	229.8	238.8	239.8
external	173.3	198.2	232.3	216.3	238.2	239.2
inner aspect	145.0	198.89	230.0	210.4	235.1	239.0
internal	145.0	198.89	230.0	210.4	235.1	239.0
mucosa	145.0	198.89	230.0	210.4	235.1	239.0
chest (wall) NEC	195.1	198.89	234.8	229.8	238.8	239.8
chiasma opticum	192.0	198.4	—	225.1	237.9	239.7
chin	173.3	198.2	232.3	216.3	238.2	239.2
choana	147.3	198.89	230.0	210.7	235.1	239.0
cholangiole	155.1	197.8	230.8	211.5	235.3	239.0
choledochal duct	156.1	197.8	230.8	211.5	235.3	239.0
choroid	190.6	198.4	234.0	224.6	238.8	239.8
plexus	191.5	198.3	—	225.0	237.5	239.6
ciliary body	190.0	198.4	234.0	224.0	238.8	239.8
clavicle	170.3	198.5	—	213.3	238.0	239.2
clitoris	184.3	198.82	233.32	221.2	236.3	239.5
clivus	170.0	198.5	—	213.0	238.0	239.2
cloacogenic zone	154.8	197.5	230.7	211.4	235.5	239.0
coccygeal						
body or glomus	194.6	198.89	—	227.6	237.3	239.7
vertebra	170.6	198.5	—	213.6	238.0	239.2
coccyx	170.6	198.5	—	213.6	238.0	239.2
colon (*see also* Neoplasm, intestine, large)						
and rectum	154.0	197.5	230.4	211.4	235.2	239.0
columnella	173.3	198.2	232.3	216.3	238.2	239.2
column, spinal — *see* Neoplasm, spine						
commissure						
labial, lip	140.6	198.89	230.0	210.4	235.1	239.0
laryngeal	161.0	197.3	231.0	212.1	235.6	239.1
common (bile) duct	156.1	197.8	230.8	211.5	235.3	239.0
concha	173.2	198.2	232.2	216.2	238.2	239.2
nose	160.0	197.3	231.8	212.0	235.9	239.1
conjunctiva	190.3	198.4	234.0	224.3	238.8	239.8
connective tissue NEC	171.9	198.89	—	215.9	238.1	239.2

Note — For neoplasms of connective tissue (blood vessel, bursa, fascia, ligament, muscle, peripheral nerves, sympathetic and parasympathetic nerves and ganglia, synovia, tendon, etc.) or of morphological types that indicate connective tissue, code according to the list under "Neoplasm, connective tissue"; for sites that do not appear in this list, code to neoplasm of that site; e.g.,

liposarcoma, shoulder 171.2

leiomyosarcoma, stomach 151.9

neurofibroma, chest wall 215.4

Morphological types that indicate connective tissue appear in the proper place in the alphabetic index with the instruction "see Neoplasm, connective tissue..."

	Primary	Secondary	Ca in situ	Benign	Uncertain Behavior	Unspecified
abdomen	171.5	198.89	—	215.5	238.1	239.2
abdominal wall	171.5	198.89	—	215.5	238.1	239.2
ankle	171.3	198.89	—	215.3	238.1	239.2
antecubital fossa or space	171.2	198.89	—	215.2	238.1	239.2
arm	171.2	198.89	—	215.2	238.1	239.2
auricle (ear)	171.0	198.89	—	215.0	238.1	239.2
axilla	171.4	198.89	—	215.4	238.1	239.2
back	171.7	198.89	—	215.7	238.1	239.2
breast (female) (*see also* Neoplasm, breast)	174.9	198.81	233.0	217	238.3	239.3
male	175.9	198.81	233.0	217	238.3	239.3
buttock	171.6	198.89	—	215.6	238.1	239.2
calf	171.3	198.89	—	215.3	238.1	239.2
cervical region	171.0	198.89	—	215.0	238.1	239.2
cheek	171.0	198.89	—	215.0	238.1	239.2
chest (wall)	171.4	198.89	—	215.4	238.1	239.2
chin	171.0	198.89	—	215.0	238.1	239.2
contiguous sites	171.8	—	—	—	—	—
diaphragm	171.4	198.89	—	215.4	238.1	239.2
ear (external)	171.0	198.89	—	215.0	238.1	239.2
elbow	171.2	198.89	—	215.2	238.1	239.2

	Malignant					
	Primary	Secondary	Ca in situ	Benign	Uncertain Behavior	Unspecified
Neoplasm, neoplastic — *continued*						
connective tissue — *continued*						
extrarectal	171.6	198.89	—	215.6	238.1	239.2
extremity	171.8	198.89	—	215.8	238.1	239.2
lower	171.3	198.89	—	215.3	238.1	239.2
upper	171.2	198.89	—	215.2	238.1	239.2
eyelid	171.0	198.89	—	215.0	238.1	239.2
face	171.0	198.89	—	215.0	238.1	239.2
finger	171.2	198.89	—	215.2	238.1	239.2
flank	171.7	198.89	—	215.7	238.1	239.2
foot	171.3	198.89	—	215.3	238.1	239.2
forearm	171.2	198.89	—	215.2	238.1	239.2
forehead	171.0	198.89	—	215.0	238.1	239.2
gastric	171.5	198.89	—	215.5	238.1	—
gastrointestinal	171.5	198.89	—	215.5	238.1	—
gluteal region	171.6	198.89	—	215.6	238.1	239.2
great vessels NEC	171.4	198.89	—	215.4	238.1	239.2
groin	171.6	198.89	—	215.6	238.1	239.2
hand	171.2	198.89	—	215.2	238.1	239.2
head	171.0	198.89	—	215.0	238.1	239.2
heel	171.3	198.89	—	215.3	238.1	239.2
hip	171.3	198.89	—	215.3	238.1	239.2
hypochondrium	171.5	198.89	—	215.5	238.1	239.2
iliopsoas muscle	171.6	198.89	—	215.5	238.1	239.2
infraclavicular region	171.4	198.89	—	215.4	238.1	239.2
inguinal (canal) (region)	171.6	198.89	—	215.6	238.1	239.2
intestine	171.5	198.89	—	215.5	238.1	—
intrathoracic	171.4	198.89	—	215.4	238.1	239.2
ischorectal fossa	171.6	198.89	—	215.6	238.1	239.2
jaw	143.9	198.89	230.0	210.4	235.1	239.0
knee	171.3	198.89	—	215.3	238.1	239.2
leg	171.3	198.89	—	215.3	238.1	239.2
limb NEC	171.9	198.89	—	215.8	238.1	239.2
lower	171.3	198.89	—	215.3	238.1	239.2
upper	171.2	198.89	—	215.2	238.1	239.2
nates	171.6	198.89	—	215.6	238.1	239.2
neck	171.0	198.89	—	215.0	238.1	239.2
orbit	190.1	198.4	234.0	224.1	238.8	239.8
pararectal	171.6	198.89	—	215.6	238.1	239.2
para-urethral	171.6	198.89	—	215.6	238.1	239.2
paravaginal	171.6	198.89	—	215.6	238.1	239.2
pelvis (floor)	171.6	198.89	—	215.6	238.1	239.2
pelvo-abdominal	171.8	198.89	—	215.8	238.1	239.2
perineum	171.6	198.89	—	215.6	238.1	239.2
perirectal (tissue)	171.6	198.89	—	215.6	238.1	239.2
periurethral (tissue)	171.6	198.89	—	215.6	238.1	239.2
popliteal fossa or space	171.3	198.89	—	215.3	238.1	239.2
presacral	171.6	198.89	—	215.6	238.1	239.2
psoas muscle	171.5	198.89	—	215.5	238.1	239.2
pterygoid fossa	171.0	198.89	—	215.0	238.1	239.2
rectovaginal septum or wall	171.6	198.89	—	215.6	238.1	239.2
rectovesical	171.6	198.89	—	215.6	238.1	239.2
retroperitoneum	158.0	197.6	—	211.8	235.4	239.0
sacrococcygeal region	171.6	198.89	—	215.6	238.1	239.2
scalp	171.0	198.89	—	215.0	238.1	239.2
scapular region	171.4	198.89	—	215.4	238.1	239.2
shoulder	171.2	198.89	—	215.2	238.1	239.2
skin (dermis) NEC	173.9	198.2	232.9	216.9	238.2	239.2
stomach	171.5	198.89	—	215.5	238.1	—
submental	171.0	198.89	—	215.0	238.1	239.2
supraclavicular region	171.0	198.89	—	215.0	238.1	239.2
temple	171.0	198.89	—	215.0	238.1	239.2
temporal region	171.0	198.89	—	215.0	238.1	239.2
thigh	171.3	198.89	—	215.3	238.1	239.2
thoracic (duct) (wall)	171.4	198.89	—	215.4	238.1	239.2
thorax	171.4	198.89	—	215.4	238.1	239.2
thumb	171.2	198.89	—	215.2	238.1	239.2
toe	171.3	198.89	—	215.3	238.1	239.2
trunk	171.7	198.89	—	215.7	238.1	239.2
umbilicus	171.5	198.89	—	215.5	238.1	239.2

☑ Additional Digit Required — Refer to the Tabular List for Digit Selection

Subterms under main terms may continue to next column or page

▶◀ Revised Text ● New Line ▲ Revised Code

	Malignant					
	Primary	Secondary	Ca in situ	Benign	Uncertain Behavior	Unspecified
Neoplasm, neoplastic — *continued*						
connective tissue — *continued*						
vesicorectal	171.6	198.89	—	215.6	238.1	239.2
wrist	171.2	198.89	—	215.2	238.1	239.2
conus medullaris	192.2	198.3	—	225.3	237.5	239.7
cord (true) (vocal)	161.0	197.3	231.0	212.1	235.6	239.1
false	161.1	197.3	231.0	212.1	235.6	239.1
spermatic	187.6	198.82	233.6	222.8	236.6	239.5
spinal (cervical) (lumbar) (thoracic)	192.2	198.3	—	225.3	237.5	239.7
cornea (limbus)	190.4	198.4	234.0	224.4	238.8	239.8
corpus						
albicans	183.0	198.6	233.39	220	236.2	239.5
callosum, brain	191.8	198.3	—	225.0	237.5	239.6
cavernosum	187.3	198.82	233.5	222.1	236.6	239.5
gastric	151.4	197.8	230.2	211.1	235.2	239.0
penis	187.3	198.82	233.5	222.1	236.6	239.5
striatum, cerebrum	191.0	198.3	—	225.0	237.5	239.6
uteri	182.0	198.82	233.2	219.1	236.0	239.5
isthmus	182.1	198.82	233.2	219.1	236.0	239.5
cortex						
adrenal	194.0	198.7	234.8	227.0	237.2	239.7
cerebral	191.0	198.3	—	225.0	237.5	239.6
costal cartilage	170.3	198.5	—	213.3	238.0	239.2
costovertebral joint	170.3	198.5	—	213.3	238.0	239.2
Cowper's gland	189.3	198.1	233.9	223.81	236.99	239.5
cranial (fossa, any)	191.9	198.3	—	225.0	237.5	239.6
meninges	192.1	198.4	—	225.2	237.6	239.7
nerve (any)	192.0	198.4	—	225.1	237.9	239.7
craniobuccal pouch	194.3	198.89	234.8	227.3	237.0	239.7
craniopharyngeal (duct) (pouch)	194.3	198.89	234.8	227.3	237.0	239.7
cricoid	148.0	198.89	230.0	210.8	235.1	239.0
cartilage	161.3	197.3	231.0	212.1	235.6	239.1
cricopharynx	148.0	198.89	230.0	210.8	235.1	239.0
crypt of Morgagni	154.8	197.5	230.7	211.4	235.2	239.0
crystalline lens	190.0	198.4	234.0	224.0	238.8	239.8
cul-de-sac (Douglas')	158.8	197.6	—	211.8	235.4	239.0
cuneiform cartilage	161.3	197.3	231.0	212.1	235.6	239.1
cutaneous — *see* Neoplasm, skin						
cutis — *see* Neoplasm, skin						
cystic (bile) duct (common)	156.1	197.8	230.8	211.5	235.3	239.0
dermis — *see* Neoplasm, skin						
diaphragm	171.4	198.89	—	215.4	238.1	239.2
digestive organs, system, tube, or tract NEC	159.9	197.8	230.9	211.9	235.5	239.0
contiguous sites with peritoneum	159.8	—	—	—	—	—
disc, intervertebral	170.2	198.5	—	213.2	238.0	239.2
disease, generalized	199.0	199.0	234.9	229.9	238.9	199.0
disseminated	199.0	199.0	234.9	229.9	238.9	199.0
Douglas' cul-de-sac or pouch	158.8	197.6	—	211.8	235.4	239.0
duodenojejunal junction	152.8	197.4	230.7	211.2	235.2	239.0
duodenum	152.0	197.4	230.7	211.2	235.2	239.0
dura (cranial) (mater)	192.1	198.4	—	225.2	237.6	239.7
cerebral	192.1	198.4	—	225.2	237.6	239.7
spinal	192.3	198.4	—	225.4	237.6	239.7
ear (external)	173.2	198.2	232.2	216.2	238.2	239.2
auricle or auris	173.2	198.2	232.2	216.2	238.2	239.2
canal, external	173.2	198.2	232.2	216.2	238.2	239.2
cartilage	171.0	198.89	—	215.0	238.1	239.2
external meatus	173.2	198.2	232.2	216.2	238.2	239.2
inner	160.1	197.3	231.8	212.0	235.9	239.8
lobule	173.2	198.2	232.2	216.2	238.2	239.2
middle	160.1	197.3	231.8	212.0	235.9	239.8
contiguous sites with accessory sinuses or nasal cavities	160.8	—	—	—	—	—
skin	173.2	198.2	232.2	216.2	238.2	239.2

	Malignant					
	Primary	Secondary	Ca in situ	Benign	Uncertain Behavior	Unspecified
Neoplasm, neoplastic — *continued*						
earlobe	173.2	198.2	232.2	216.2	238.2	239.2
ejaculatory duct	187.8	198.82	233.6	222.8	236.6	239.5
elbow NEC*	195.4	198.89	232.6	229.8	238.8	239.8
endocardium	164.1	198.89	—	212.7	238.8	239.8
endocervix (canal) (gland)	180.0	198.82	233.1	219.0	236.0	239.5
endocrine gland NEC	194.9	198.89	—	227.9	237.4	239.7
pluriglandular NEC	194.8	198.89	234.8	227.8	237.4	239.7
endometrium (gland) (stroma)	182.0	198.82	233.2	219.1	236.0	239.5
ensiform cartilage	170.3	198.5	—	213.3	238.0	239.2
enteric — *see* Neoplasm, intestine						
ependyma (brain)	191.5	198.3	—	225.0	237.5	239.6
epicardium	164.1	198.89	—	212.7	238.8	239.8
epididymis	187.5	198.82	233.6	222.3	236.6	239.5
epidural	192.9	198.4	—	225.9	237.9	239.7
epiglottis	161.1	197.3	231.0	212.1	235.6	239.1
anterior aspect or surface	146.4	198.89	230.0	210.6	235.1	239.0
cartilage	161.3	197.3	231.0	212.1	235.6	239.1
free border (margin)	146.4	198.89	230.0	210.6	235.1	239.0
junctional region	146.5	198.89	230.0	210.6	235.1	239.0
posterior (laryngeal) surface	161.1	197.3	231.0	212.1	235.6	239.1
suprahyoid portion	161.1	197.3	231.0	212.1	235.6	239.1
esophagogastric junction	151.0	197.8	230.2	211.1	235.2	239.0
esophagus	150.9	197.8	230.1	211.0	235.5	239.0
abdominal	150.2	197.8	230.1	211.0	235.5	239.0
cervical	150.0	197.8	230.1	211.0	235.5	239.0
contiguous sites	150.8	—	—	—	—	—
distal (third)	150.5	197.8	230.1	211.0	235.5	239.0
lower (third)	150.5	197.8	230.1	211.0	235.5	239.0
middle (third)	150.4	197.8	230.1	211.0	235.5	239.0
proximal (third)	150.3	197.8	230.1	211.0	235.5	239.0
specified part NEC	150.8	197.8	230.1	211.0	235.5	239.0
thoracic	150.1	197.8	230.1	211.0	235.5	239.0
upper (third)	150.3	197.8	230.1	211.0	235.5	239.0
ethmoid (sinus)	160.3	197.3	231.8	212.0	235.9	239.1
bone or labyrinth	170.0	198.5	—	213.0	238.0	239.2
Eustachian tube	160.1	197.3	231.8	212.0	235.9	239.1
exocervix	180.1	198.82	233.1	219.0	236.0	239.5
external						
meatus (ear)	173.2	198.2	232.2	216.2	238.2	239.2
os, cervix uteri	180.1	198.82	233.1	219.0	236.0	239.5
extradural	192.9	198.4	—	225.9	237.9	239.7
extrahepatic (bile) duct	156.1	197.8	230.8	211.5	235.3	239.0
contiguous sites with gallbladder	156.8	—	—	—	—	—
extraocular muscle	190.1	198.4	234.0	224.1	238.8	239.8
extrarectal	195.3	198.89	234.8	229.8	238.8	239.8
extremity*	195.8	198.89	232.8	229.8	238.8	239.8
lower*	195.5	198.89	232.7	229.8	238.8	239.8
upper*	195.4	198.89	232.6	229.8	238.8	239.8
eye NEC	190.9	198.4	234.0	224.9	238.8	239.8
contiguous sites	190.8	—	—	—	—	—
specified sites NEC	190.8	198.4	234.0	224.8	238.8	239.8
eyeball	190.0	198.4	234.0	224.0	238.8	239.8
eyebrow	173.3	198.2	232.3	216.3	238.2	239.2
eyelid (lower) (skin) (upper)	173.1	198.2	232.1	216.1	238.2	239.2
cartilage	171.0	198.89	—	215.0	238.1	239.2
face NEC*	195.0	198.89	232.3	229.8	238.8	239.8
fallopian tube (accessory)	183.2	198.82	233.39	221.0	236.3	239.5
falx (cerebelli) (cerebri)	192.1	198.4	—	225.2	237.6	239.7
fascia (*see also* Neoplasm, connective tissue)						
palmar	171.2	198.89	—	215.2	238.1	239.2
plantar	171.3	198.89	—	215.3	238.1	239.2
fatty tissue — *see* Neoplasm, connective tissue						
fauces, faucial NEC	146.9	198.89	230.0	210.6	235.1	239.0

	Malignant					
	Primary	Secondary	Ca in situ	Benign	Uncertain Behavior	Unspecified
Neoplasm, neoplastic — *continued*						
fauces, faucial — *continued*						
pillars	146.2	198.89	230.0	210.6	235.1	239.0
tonsil	146.0	198.89	230.0	210.5	235.1	239.0
femur (any part)	170.7	198.5	—	213.7	238.0	239.2
fetal membrane	181	198.82	233.2	219.8	236.1	239.5
fibrous tissue — *see* Neoplasm, connective tissue						
fibula (any part)	170.7	198.5	—	213.7	238.0	239.2
filum terminale	192.2	198.3	—	225.3	237.5	239.7
finger NEC*	195.4	198.89	232.6	229.8	238.8	239.8
flank NEC*	195.8	198.89	232.5	229.8	238.8	239.8
follicle, nabothian	180.0	198.82	233.1	219.0	236.0	239.5
foot NEC*	195.5	198.89	232.7	229.8	238.8	239.8
forearm NEC*	195.4	198.89	232.6	229.8	238.8	239.8
forehead (skin)	173.3	198.2	232.3	216.3	238.2	239.2
foreskin	187.1	198.82	233.5	222.1	236.6	239.5
fornix						
pharyngeal	147.3	198.89	230.0	210.7	235.1	239.0
vagina	184.0	198.82	233.31	221.1	236.3	239.5
fossa (of)						
anterior (cranial)	191.9	198.3	—	225.0	237.5	239.6
cranial	191.9	198.3	—	225.0	237.5	239.6
ischiorectal	195.3	198.89	234.8	229.8	238.8	239.8
middle (cranial)	191.9	198.3	—	225.0	237.5	239.6
pituitary	194.3	198.89	234.8	227.3	237.0	239.7
posterior (cranial)	191.9	198.3	—	225.0	237.5	239.6
pterygoid	171.0	198.89	—	215.0	238.1	239.2
pyriform	148.1	198.89	230.0	210.8	235.1	239.0
Rosenmüller	147.2	198.89	230.0	210.7	235.1	239.0
tonsillar	146.1	198.89	230.0	210.6	235.1	239.0
fourchette	184.4	198.82	233.32	221.2	236.3	239.5
frenulum						
labii — *see* Neoplasm, lip, internal						
linguae	141.3	198.89	230.0	210.1	235.1	239.0
frontal						
bone	170.0	198.5	—	213.0	238.0	239.2
lobe, brain	191.1	198.3	—	225.0	237.5	239.6
meninges	192.1	198.4	—	225.2	237.6	239.7
pole	191.1	198.3	—	225.0	237.5	239.6
sinus	160.4	197.3	231.8	212.0	235.9	239.1
fundus						
stomach	151.3	197.8	230.2	211.1	235.2	239.0
uterus	182.0	198.82	233.2	219.1	236.0	239.5
gallbladder	156.0	197.8	230.8	211.5	235.3	239.0
contiguous sites with extrahepatic bile ducts	156.8	—	—	—	—	—
gall duct						
(extrahepatic)	156.1	197.8	230.8	211.5	235.3	239.0
intrahepatic	155.1	197.8	230.8	211.5	235.3	239.0
ganglia (*see also* Neoplasm, connective tissue)	171.9	198.89	—	215.9	238.1	239.2
basal	191.0	198.3	—	225.0	237.5	239.6
ganglion (*see also* Neoplasm, connective tissue)	171.9	198.89	—	215.9	238.1	239.2
cranial nerve	192.0	198.4	—	225.1	237.9	239.7
Gartner's duct	184.0	198.82	233.31	221.1	236.3	239.5
gastric — *see* Neoplasm, stomach						
gastrocolic	159.8	197.8	230.9	211.9	235.5	239.0
gastroesophageal junction	151.0	197.8	230.2	211.1	235.2	239.0
gastrointestinal (tract) NEC	159.9	197.8	230.9	211.9	235.5	239.0
generalized	199.0	199.0	234.9	229.9	238.9	199.0
genital organ or tract						
female NEC	184.9	198.82	233.39	221.9	236.3	239.5
contiguous sites	184.8	—	—	—	—	—
specified site NEC	184.8	198.82	233.39	221.8	236.3	239.5
male NEC	187.9	198.82	233.6	222.9	236.6	239.5
contiguous sites	187.8	—	—	—	—	—

	Malignant					
	Primary	Secondary	Ca in situ	Benign	Uncertain Behavior	Unspecified
Neoplasm, neoplastic — *continued*						
genital organ or tract — *continued*						
male — *continued*						
specified site NEC	187.8	198.82	233.6	222.8	236.6	239.5
genitourinary tract						
female	184.9	198.82	233.39	221.9	236.3	239.5
male	187.9	198.82	233.6	222.9	236.6	239.5
gingiva (alveolar) (marginal)	143.9	198.89	230.0	210.4	235.1	239.0
lower	143.1	198.89	230.0	210.4	235.1	239.0
mandibular	143.1	198.89	230.0	210.4	235.1	239.0
maxillary	143.0	198.89	230.0	210.4	235.1	239.0
upper	143.0	198.89	230.0	210.4	235.1	239.0
gland, glandular (lymphatic) (system) (*see also* Neoplasm, lymph gland)						
endocrine NEC	194.9	198.89	—	227.9	237.4	239.7
salivary — *see* Neoplasm, salivary, gland						
glans penis	187.2	198.82	233.5	222.1	236.6	239.5
globus pallidus	191.0	198.3	—	225.0	237.5	239.6
glomus						
coccygeal	194.6	198.89	—	227.6	237.3	239.7
jugularis	194.6	198.89	—	227.6	237.3	239.7
glosso-epiglottic fold(s)	146.4	198.89	230.0	210.6	235.1	239.0
glossopalatine fold	146.2	198.89	230.0	210.6	235.1	239.0
glossopharyngeal sulcus	146.1	198.89	230.0	210.6	235.1	239.0
glottis	161.0	197.3	231.0	212.1	235.6	239.1
gluteal region*	195.3	198.89	232.5	229.8	238.8	239.8
great vessels NEC	171.4	198.89	—	215.4	238.1	239.2
groin NEC	195.3	198.89	232.5	229.8	238.8	239.8
gum	143.9	198.89	230.0	210.4	235.1	239.0
contiguous sites	143.8	—	—	—	—	—
lower	143.1	198.89	230.0	210.4	235.1	239.0
upper	143.0	198.89	230.0	210.4	235.1	239.0
hand NEC*	195.4	198.89	232.6	229.8	238.8	239.8
head NEC*	195.0	198.89	232.4	229.8	238.8	239.8
heart	164.1	198.89	—	212.7	238.8	239.8
contiguous sites with mediastinum or thymus	164.8	—	—	—	—	—
heel NEC*	195.5	198.89	232.7	229.8	238.8	239.8
helix	173.2	198.2	232.2	216.2	238.2	239.2
hematopoietic, hemopoietic tissue NEC	202.8	198.89	—	—	—	238.79
hemisphere, cerebral	191.0	198.3	—	225.0	237.5	239.6
hemorrhoidal zone	154.2	197.5	230.5	211.4	235.5	239.0
hepatic	155.2	197.7	230.8	211.5	235.3	239.0
duct (bile)	156.1	197.8	230.8	211.5	235.3	239.0
flexure (colon)	153.0	197.5	230.3	211.3	235.2	239.0
primary	155.0	—	—	—	—	—
hilus of lung	162.2	197.0	231.2	212.3	235.7	239.1
hip NEC*	195.5	198.89	232.7	229.8	238.8	239.8
hippocampus, brain	191.2	198.3	—	225.0	237.5	239.6
humerus (any part)	170.4	198.5	—	213.4	238.0	239.2
hymen	184.0	198.82	233.31	221.1	236.3	239.5
hypopharynx, hypopharyngeal NEC	148.9	198.89	230.0	210.8	235.1	239.0
contiguous sites	148.8	—	—	—	—	—
postcricoid region	148.0	198.89	230.0	210.8	235.1	239.0
posterior wall	148.3	198.89	230.0	210.8	235.1	239.0
pyriform fossa (sinus)	148.1	198.89	230.0	210.8	235.1	239.0
specified site NEC	148.8	198.89	230.0	210.8	235.1	239.0
wall	148.9	198.89	230.0	210.8	235.1	239.0
posterior	148.3	198.89	230.0	210.8	235.1	239.0
hypophysis	194.3	198.89	234.8	227.3	237.0	239.7
hypothalamus	191.0	198.3	—	225.0	237.5	239.6
ileocecum, ileocecal (coil) (junction) (valve)	153.4	197.5	230.3	211.3	235.2	239.0
ileum	152.2	197.4	230.7	211.2	235.2	239.0

	Malignant					
	Primary	Secondary	Ca in situ	Benign	Uncertain Behavior	Unspecified
Neoplasm, neoplastic — *continued*						
ilium	170.6	198.5	—	213.6	238.0	239.2
immunoproliferative NEC	203.8	—	—	—	—	—
infraclavicular (region)*	195.1	198.89	232.5	229.8	238.8	239.8
inguinal (region)*	195.3	198.89	232.5	229.8	238.8	239.8
insula	191.0	198.3	—	225.0	237.5	239.6
insular tissue (pancreas)	157.4	197.8	230.9	211.7	235.5	239.0
brain	191.0	198.3	—	225.0	237.5	239.6
interarytenoid fold	148.2	198.89	230.0	210.8	235.1	239.0
hypopharyngeal aspect	148.2	198.89	230.0	210.8	235.1	239.0
laryngeal aspect	161.1	197.3	231.0	212.1	235.6	239.1
marginal zone	148.2	198.89	230.0	210.8	235.1	239.0
interdental papillae	143.9	198.89	230.0	210.4	235.1	239.0
lower	143.1	198.89	230.0	210.4	235.1	239.0
upper	143.0	198.89	230.0	210.4	235.1	239.0
internal						
capsule	191.0	198.3	—	225.0	237.5	239.6
os (cervix)	180.0	198.82	233.1	219.0	236.0	239.5
intervertebral cartilage or disc	170.2	198.5	—	213.2	238.0	239.2
intestine, intestinal	159.0	197.8	230.7	211.9	235.2	239.0
large	153.9	197.5	230.3	211.3	235.2	239.0
appendix	153.5	197.5	230.3	211.3	235.2	239.0
caput coli	153.4	197.5	230.3	211.3	235.2	239.0
cecum	153.4	197.5	230.3	211.3	235.2	239.0
colon	153.9	197.5	230.3	211.3	235.2	239.0
and rectum	154.0	197.5	230.4	211.4	235.2	239.0
ascending	153.6	197.5	230.3	211.3	235.2	239.0
caput	153.4	197.5	230.3	211.3	235.2	239.0
contiguous sites	153.8	—	—	—	—	—
descending	153.2	197.5	230.3	211.3	235.2	239.0
distal	153.2	197.5	230.3	211.3	235.2	239.0
left	153.2	197.5	230.3	211.3	235.2	239.0
pelvic	153.3	197.5	230.3	211.3	235.2	239.0
right	153.6	197.5	230.3	211.3	235.2	239.0
sigmoid (flexure)	153.3	197.5	230.3	211.3	235.2	239.0
transverse	153.1	197.5	230.3	211.3	235.2	239.0
contiguous sites	153.8	—	—	—	—	—
hepatic flexure	153.0	197.5	230.3	211.3	235.2	239.0
ileocecum, ileocecal (coil) (valve)	153.4	197.5	230.3	211.3	235.2	239.0
sigmoid flexure (lower) (upper)	153.3	197.5	230.3	211.3	235.2	239.0
splenic flexure	153.7	197.5	230.3	211.3	235.2	239.0
small	152.9	197.4	230.7	211.2	235.2	239.0
contiguous sites	152.8	—	—	—	—	—
duodenum	152.0	197.4	230.7	211.2	235.2	239.0
ileum	152.2	197.4	230.7	211.2	235.2	239.0
jejunum	152.1	197.4	230.7	211.2	235.2	239.0
tract NEC	159.0	197.8	230.7	211.9	235.2	239.0
intra-abdominal	195.2	198.89	234.8	229.8	238.8	239.8
intracranial NEC	191.9	198.3	—	225.0	237.5	239.6
intrahepatic (bile) duct	155.1	197.8	230.8	211.5	235.3	239.0
intraocular	190.0	198.4	234.0	224.0	238.8	239.8
intraorbital	190.1	198.4	234.0	224.1	238.8	239.8
intrasellar	194.3	198.89	234.8	227.3	237.0	239.7
intrathoracic (cavity) (organs NEC)	195.1	198.89	234.8	229.8	238.8	239.8
contiguous sites with respiratory organs	165.8	—	—	—	—	—
iris	190.0	198.4	234.0	224.0	238.8	239.8
ischiorectal (fossa)	195.3	198.89	234.8	229.8	238.8	239.8
ischium	170.6	198.5	—	213.6	238.0	239.2
island of Reil	191.0	198.3	—	225.0	237.5	239.6
islands or islets of Langerhans	157.4	197.8	230.9	211.7	235.5	239.0
isthmus uteri	182.1	198.82	233.2	219.1	236.0	239.5
jaw	195.0	198.89	234.8	229.8	238.8	239.8
bone	170.1	198.5	—	213.1	238.0	239.2
carcinoma	143.9	—	—	—	—	—

	Malignant					
	Primary	Secondary	Ca in situ	Benign	Uncertain Behavior	Unspecified
Neoplasm, neoplastic — *continued*						
jaw — *continued*						
bone — *continued*						
carcinoma — *continued*						
lower	143.1	—	—	—	—	—
upper	143.0	—	—	—	—	—
lower	170.1	198.5	—	213.1	238.0	239.2
upper	170.0	198.5	—	213.0	238.0	239.2
carcinoma (any type) (lower)(upper)	195.0	—	—	—	—	—
skin	173.3	198.2	232.3	216.3	238.2	239.2
soft tissues	143.9	198.89	230.0	210.4	235.1	239.0
lower	143.1	198.89	230.0	210.4	235.1	239.0
upper	143.0	198.89	230.0	210.4	235.1	239.0
jejunum	152.1	197.4	230.7	211.2	235.2	239.0
joint NEC (*see also* Neoplasm, bone)	170.9	198.5	—	213.9	238.0	239.2
acromioclavicular	170.4	198.5	—	213.4	238.0	239.2
bursa or synovial membrane — *see* Neoplasm, connective tissue						
costovertebral	170.3	198.5	—	213.3	238.0	239.2
sternocostal	170.3	198.5	—	213.3	238.0	239.2
temporomandibular	170.1	198.5	—	213.1	238.0	239.2
junction						
anorectal	154.8	197.5	230.7	211.4	235.5	239.0
cardioesophageal	151.0	197.8	230.2	211.1	235.2	239.0
esophagogastric	151.0	197.8	230.2	211.1	235.2	239.0
gastroesophageal	151.0	197.8	230.2	211.1	235.2	239.0
hard and soft palate	145.5	198.89	230.0	210.4	235.1	239.0
ileocecal	153.4	197.5	230.3	211.3	235.2	239.0
pelvirectal	154.0	197.5	230.4	211.4	235.2	239.0
pelviureteric	189.1	198.0	233.9	223.1	236.91	239.5
rectosigmoid	154.0	197.5	230.4	211.4	235.2	239.0
squamocolumnar, of cervix	180.8	198.82	233.1	219.0	236.0	239.5
kidney (parenchyma)	189.0	198.0	233.9	223.0	236.91	239.5
calyx	189.1	198.0	233.9	223.1	236.91	239.5
hilus	189.1	198.0	233.9	223.1	236.91	239.5
pelvis	189.1	198.0	233.9	223.1	236.91	239.5
knee NEC*	195.5	198.89	232.7	229.8	238.8	239.8
labia (skin)	184.4	198.82	233.32	221.2	236.3	239.5
majora	184.1	198.82	233.32	221.2	236.3	239.5
minora	184.2	198.82	233.32	221.2	236.3	239.5
labial (*see also* Neoplasm, lip)						
sulcus (lower) (upper)	145.1	198.89	230.0	210.4	235.1	239.0
labium (skin)	184.4	198.82	233.32	221.2	236.3	239.5
majus	184.1	198.82	233.32	221.2	236.3	239.5
minus	184.2	198.82	233.32	221.2	236.3	239.5
lacrimal						
canaliculi	190.7	198.4	234.0	224.7	238.8	239.8
duct (nasal)	190.7	198.4	234.0	224.7	238.8	239.8
gland	190.2	198.4	234.0	224.2	238.8	239.8
punctum	190.7	198.4	234.0	224.7	238.8	239.8
sac	190.7	198.4	234.0	224.7	238.8	239.8
Langerhans, islands or islets	157.4	197.8	230.9	211.7	235.5	239.0
laryngopharynx	148.9	198.89	230.0	210.8	235.1	239.0
larynx, laryngeal NEC	161.9	197.3	231.0	212.1	235.6	239.1
aryepiglottic fold	161.1	197.3	231.0	212.1	235.6	239.1
cartilage (arytenoid) (cricoid) (cuneiform) (thyroid)	161.3	197.3	231.0	212.1	235.6	239.1
commissure (anterior) (posterior)	161.0	197.3	231.0	212.1	235.6	239.1
contiguous sites	161.8	—	—	—	—	—
extrinsic NEC	161.1	197.3	231.0	212.1	235.6	239.1
meaning hypopharynx	148.9	198.89	230.0	210.8	235.1	239.0
interarytenoid fold	161.1	197.3	231.0	212.1	235.6	239.1
intrinsic	161.0	197.3	231.0	212.1	235.6	239.1
ventricular band	161.1	197.3	231.0	212.1	235.6	239.1
leg NEC*	195.5	198.89	232.7	229.8	238.8	239.8
lens, crystalline	190.0	198.4	234.0	224.0	238.8	239.8

☑ Additional Digit Required — Refer to the Tabular List for Digit Selection

Subterms under main terms may continue to next column or page

	Malignant					
	Primary	Secondary	Ca in situ	Benign	Uncertain Behavior	Unspecified
Neoplasm, neoplastic — *continued*						
lid (lower) (upper)	173.1	198.2	232.1	216.1	238.2	239.2
ligament (*see also* Neoplasm, connective tissue)						
broad	183.3	198.82	233.39	221.0	236.3	239.5
Mackenrodt's	183.8	198.82	233.39	221.8	236.3	239.5
non-uterine — *see* Neoplasm, connective tissue						
round	183.5	198.82	—	221.0	236.3	239.5
sacro-uterine	183.4	198.82	—	221.0	236.3	239.5
uterine	183.4	198.82	—	221.0	236.3	239.5
utero-ovarian	183.8	198.82	233.39	221.8	236.3	239.5
uterosacral	183.4	198.82	—	221.0	236.3	239.5
limb*	195.8	198.89	232.8	229.8	238.8	239.8
lower*	195.5	198.89	232.7	229.8	238.8	239.8
upper*	195.4	198.89	232.6	229.8	238.8	239.8
limbus of cornea	190.4	198.4	234.0	224.4	238.8	239.8
lingual NEC (*see also* Neoplasm, tongue)	141.9	198.89	230.0	210.1	235.1	239.0
lingula, lung	162.3	197.0	231.2	212.3	235.7	239.1
lip (external) (lipstick area) (vermillion border)	140.9	198.89	230.0	210.0	235.1	239.0
buccal aspect — *see* Neoplasm, lip, internal						
commissure	140.6	198.89	230.0	210.4	235.1	239.0
contiguous sites	140.8	—	—	—	—	—
with oral cavity or pharynx	149.8	—	—	—	—	—
frenulum — *see* Neoplasm, lip, internal						
inner aspect — *see* Neoplasm, lip, internal						
internal (buccal) (frenulum) (mucosa) (oral)	140.5	198.89	230.0	210.0	235.1	239.0
lower	140.4	198.89	230.0	210.0	235.1	239.0
upper	140.3	198.89	230.0	210.0	235.1	239.0
lower	140.1	198.89	230.0	210.0	235.1	239.0
internal (buccal) (frenulum) (mucosa) (oral)	140.4	198.89	230.0	210.0	235.1	239.0
mucosa — *see* Neoplasm, lip, internal						
oral aspect — *see* Neoplasm, lip, internal						
skin (commissure) (lower) (upper)	173.0	198.2	232.0	216.0	238.2	239.2
upper	140.0	198.89	230.0	210.0	235.1	239.0
internal (buccal) (frenulum) (mucosa) (oral)	140.3	198.89	230.0	210.0	235.1	239.0
liver	155.2	197.7	230.8	211.5	235.3	239.0
primary	155.0	—	—	—	—	—
lobe						
azygos	162.3	197.0	231.2	212.3	235.7	239.1
frontal	191.1	198.3	—	225.0	237.5	239.6
lower	162.5	197.0	231.2	212.3	235.7	239.1
middle	162.4	197.0	231.2	212.3	235.7	239.1
occipital	191.4	198.3	—	225.0	237.5	239.6
parietal	191.3	198.3	—	225.0	237.5	239.6
temporal	191.2	198.3	—	225.0	237.5	239.6
upper	162.3	197.0	231.2	212.3	235.7	239.1
lumbosacral plexus	171.6	198.4	—	215.6	238.1	239.2
lung	162.9	197.0	231.2	212.3	235.7	239.1
azygos lobe	162.3	197.0	231.2	212.3	235.7	239.1
carina	162.2	197.0	231.2	212.3	235.7	239.1

	Malignant					
	Primary	Secondary	Ca in situ	Benign	Uncertain Behavior	Unspecified
Neoplasm, neoplastic — *continued*						
lung — *continued*						
contiguous sites with bronchus or trachea	162.8	—	—	—	—	—
hilus	162.2	197.0	231.2	212.3	235.7	239.1
lingula	162.3	197.0	231.2	212.3	235.7	239.1
lobe NEC	162.9	197.0	231.2	212.3	235.7	239.1
lower lobe	162.5	197.0	231.2	212.3	235.7	239.1
main bronchus	162.2	197.0	231.2	212.3	235.7	239.1
middle lobe	162.4	197.0	231.2	212.3	235.7	239.1
upper lobe	162.3	197.0	231.2	212.3	235.7	239.1
lymph, lymphatic						
channel NEC (*see also* Neoplasm, connective tissue)	171.9	198.89	—	215.9	238.1	239.2
gland (secondary)	—	196.9	—	229.0	238.8	239.8
abdominal	—	196.2	—	229.0	238.8	239.8
aortic	—	196.2	—	229.0	238.8	239.8
arm	—	196.3	—	229.0	238.8	239.8
auricular (anterior) (posterior)	—	196.0	—	229.0	238.8	239.8
axilla, axillary	—	196.3	—	229.0	238.8	239.8
brachial	—	196.3	—	229.0	238.8	239.8
bronchial	—	196.1	—	229.0	238.8	239.8
bronchopulmonary	—	196.1	—	229.0	238.8	239.8
celiac	—	196.2	—	229.0	238.8	239.8
cervical	—	196.0	—	229.0	238.8	239.8
cervicofacial	—	196.0	—	229.0	238.8	239.8
Cloquet	—	196.5	—	229.0	238.8	239.8
colic	—	196.2	—	229.0	238.8	239.8
common duct	—	196.2	—	229.0	238.8	239.8
cubital	—	196.3	—	229.0	238.8	239.8
diaphragmatic	—	196.1	—	229.0	238.8	239.8
epigastric, inferior	—	196.6	—	229.0	238.8	239.8
epitrochlear	—	196.3	—	229.0	238.8	239.8
esophageal	—	196.1	—	229.0	238.8	239.8
face	—	196.0	—	229.0	238.8	239.8
femoral	—	196.5	—	229.0	238.8	239.8
gastric	—	196.2	—	229.0	238.8	239.8
groin	—	196.5	—	229.0	238.8	239.8
head	—	196.0	—	229.0	238.8	239.8
hepatic	—	196.2	—	229.0	238.8	239.8
hilar (pulmonary)	—	196.1	—	229.0	238.8	239.8
splenic	—	196.2	—	229.0	238.8	239.8
hypogastric	—	196.6	—	229.0	238.8	239.8
ileocolic	—	196.2	—	229.0	238.8	239.8
iliac	—	196.6	—	229.0	238.8	239.8
infraclavicular	—	196.3	—	229.0	238.8	239.8
inguina, inguinal	—	196.5	—	229.0	238.8	239.8
innominate	—	196.1	—	229.0	238.8	239.8
intercostal	—	196.1	—	229.0	238.8	239.8
intestinal	—	196.2	—	229.0	238.8	239.8
intra-abdominal	—	196.2	—	229.0	238.8	239.8
intrapelvic	—	196.6	—	229.0	238.8	239.8
intrathoracic	—	196.1	—	229.0	238.8	239.9
jugular	—	196.0	—	229.0	238.8	239.8
leg	—	196.5	—	229.0	238.8	239.8
limb						
lower	—	196.5	—	229.0	238.8	239.8
upper	—	196.3	—	229.0	238.8	239.8
lower limb	—	196.5	—	229.0	238.8	238.9
lumbar	—	196.2	—	229.0	238.8	239.8
mandibular	—	196.0	—	229.0	238.8	239.8
mediastinal	—	196.1	—	229.0	238.8	239.8
mesenteric (inferior) (superior)	—	196.2	—	229.0	238.8	239.8
midcolic	—	196.2	—	229.0	238.8	239.8
multiple sites in categories 196.0–196.6	—	196.8	—	229.0	238.8	239.8
neck	—	196.0	—	229.0	238.8	239.8
obturator	—	196.6	—	229.0	238.8	239.8
occipital	—	196.0	—	229.0	238.8	239.8
pancreatic	—	196.2	—	229.0	238.8	239.8
para-aortic	—	196.2	—	229.0	238.8	239.8

	Malignant					
	Primary	Secondary	Ca in situ	Benign	Uncertain Behavior	Unspecified
Neoplasm, neoplastic — *continued*						
lymph, lymphatic — *continued*						
gland — *continued*						
paracervical	—	196.6	—	229.0	238.8	239.8
parametrial	—	196.6	—	229.0	238.8	239.8
parasternal	—	196.1	—	229.0	238.8	239.8
parotid	—	196.0	—	229.0	238.8	239.8
pectoral	—	196.3	—	229.0	238.8	239.8
pelvic	—	196.6	—	229.0	238.8	239.8
peri-aortic	—	196.2	—	229.0	238.8	239.8
peripancreatic	—	196.2	—	229.0	238.8	239.8
popliteal	—	196.5	—	229.0	238.8	239.8
porta hepatis	—	196.2	—	229.0	238.8	239.8
portal	—	196.2	—	229.0	238.8	239.8
preauricular	—	196.0	—	229.0	238.8	239.8
prelaryngeal	—	196.0	—	229.0	238.8	239.8
presymphysial	—	196.6	—	229.0	238.8	239.8
pretracheal	—	196.0	—	229.0	238.8	239.8
primary (any site) NEC	202.9	—	—	—	—	—
pulmonary (hiler)	—	196.1	—	229.0	238.8	239.8
pyloric	—	196.2	—	229.0	238.8	239.8
retroperitoneal	—	196.2	—	229.0	238.8	239.8
retropharyngeal	—	196.0	—	229.0	238.8	239.8
Rosenmüller's	—	196.5	—	229.0	238.8	239.8
sacral	—	196.6	—	229.0	238.8	239.8
scalene	—	196.0	—	229.0	238.8	239.8
site NEC	—	196.9	—	229.0	238.8	239.8
splenic (hilar)	—	196.2	—	229.0	238.8	239.8
subclavicular	—	196.3	—	229.0	238.8	239.8
subinguinal	—	196.5	—	229.0	238.8	239.8
sublingual	—	196.0	—	229.0	238.8	239.8
submandibular	—	196.0	—	229.0	238.8	239.8
submaxillary	—	196.0	—	229.0	238.8	239.8
submental	—	196.0	—	229.0	238.8	239.8
subscapular	—	196.3	—	229.0	238.8	239.8
supraclavicular	—	196.0	—	229.0	238.8	239.8
thoracic	—	196.1	—	229.0	238.8	239.8
tibial	—	196.5	—	229.0	238.8	239.8
tracheal	—	196.1	—	229.0	238.8	239.8
tracheobronchial	—	196.1	—	229.0	238.8	239.8
upper limb	—	196.3	—	229.0	238.8	239.8
Virchow's	—	196.0	—	229.0	238.8	239.8
node (*see also* Neoplasm, lymph gland)						
primary NEC	202.9	—	—	—	—	—
vessel (*see also* Neoplasm, connective tissue)	171.9	198.89	—	215.9	238.1	239.2
Mackenrodt's ligament	183.8	198.82	233.39	221.0	236.3	239.5
malar	170.0	198.5	—	213.0	238.0	239.2
region — *see* Neoplasm, cheek						
mammary gland — *see* Neoplasm, breast						
mandible	170.1	198.5	—	213.1	238.0	239.2
alveolar						
mucosa ●	143.1	198.89	230.0	210.4	235.1	239.0
mucose	143.1	198.89	230.0	210.4	235.1	239.0
ridge or process	170.1	198.5	—	213.1	238.0	239.2
carcinoma	143.1	—	—	—	—	—
carcinoma	143.1	—	—	—	—	—
marrow (bone) NEC	202.9	198.5	—	—	—	238.79
mastectomy site (skin)	173.5	198.2	—	—	—	—
specified as breast tissue	174.8	198.81	—	—	—	—
mastoid (air cells) (antrum) (cavity)	160.1	197.3	231.8	212.0	235.9	239.1
bone or process	170.0	198.5	—	213.0	238.0	239.2
maxilla, maxillary (superior)	170.0	198.5	—	213.0	238.0	239.2
alveolar						
mucosa	143.0	198.89	230.0	210.4	235.1	239.0
ridge or process	170.0	198.5	—	213.0	238.0	239.2

	Malignant					
	Primary	Secondary	Ca in situ	Benign	Uncertain Behavior	Unspecified
Neoplasm, neoplastic — *continued*						
maxilla, maxillary — *continued*						
alveolar — *continued*						
ridge or process — *continued*						
carcinoma	143.0	—	—	—	—	—
antrum	160.2	197.3	231.8	212.0	235.9	239.1
carcinoma	143.0	—	—	—	—	—
inferior — *see* Neoplasm, mandible						
sinus	160.2	197.3	231.8	212.0	235.9	239.1
meatus						
external (ear)	173.2	198.2	232.2	216.2	238.2	239.2
Meckel's diverticulum	152.3	197.4	230.7	211.2	235.2	239.0
mediastinum, mediastinal	164.9	197.1	—	212.5	235.8	239.8
anterior	164.2	197.1	—	212.5	235.8	239.8
contiguous sites with heart and thymus	164.8	—	—	—	—	—
posterior	164.3	197.1	—	212.5	235.8	239.8
medulla						
adrenal	194.0	198.7	234.8	227.0	237.2	239.7
oblongata	191.7	198.3	—	225.0	237.5	239.6
meibomian gland	173.1	198.2	232.1	216.1	238.2	239.2
meninges (brain) (cerebral) (cranial) (intracranial)	192.1	198.4	—	225.2	237.6	239.7
spinal (cord)	192.3	198.4	—	225.4	237.6	239.7
meniscus, knee joint (lateral) (medial)	170.7	198.5	—	213.7	238.0	239.2
mesentery, mesenteric	158.8	197.6	—	211.8	235.4	239.0
mesoappendix	158.8	197.6	—	211.8	235.4	239.0
mesocolon	158.8	197.6	—	211.8	235.4	239.0
mesopharynx — *see* Neoplasm, oropharynx						
mesosalpinx	183.3	198.82	233.39	221.0	236.3	239.5
mesovarium	183.3	198.82	233.39	221.0	236.3	239.5
metacarpus (any bone)	170.5	198.5	—	213.5	238.0	239.2
metastatic NEC (*see also* Neoplasm, by site, secondary)	—	199.1	—	—	—	—
metatarsus (any bone)	170.8	198.5	—	213.8	238.0	239.2
midbrain	191.7	198.3	—	225.0	237.5	239.6
milk duct — *see* Neoplasm, breast						
mons						
pubis	184.4	198.82	233.32	221.2	236.3	239.5
veneris	184.4	198.82	233.32	221.2	236.3	239.5
motor tract	192.9	198.4	—	225.9	237.9	239.7
brain	191.9	198.3	—	225.0	237.5	239.6
spinal	192.2	198.3	—	225.3	237.5	239.7
mouth	145.9	198.89	230.0	210.4	235.1	239.0
contiguous sites	145.8	—	—	—	—	—
floor	144.9	198.89	230.0	210.3	235.1	239.0
anterior portion	144.0	198.89	230.0	210.3	235.1	239.0
contiguous sites	144.8	—	—	—	—	—
lateral portion	144.1	198.89	230.0	210.3	235.1	239.0
roof	145.5	198.89	230.0	210.4	235.1	239.0
specified part NEC	145.8	198.89	230.0	210.4	235.1	239.0
vestibule	145.1	198.89	230.0	210.4	235.1	239.0
mucosa						
alveolar (ridge or process)	143.9	198.89	230.0	210.4	235.1	239.0
lower	143.1	198.89	230.0	210.4	235.1	239.0
upper	143.0	198.89	230.0	210.4	235.1	239.0
buccal	145.0	198.89	230.0	210.4	235.1	239.0
cheek	145.0	198.89	230.0	210.4	235.1	239.0
lip — *see* Neoplasm, lip, internal						
nasal	160.0	197.3	231.8	212.0	235.9	239.1
oral	145.0	198.89	230.0	210.4	235.1	239.0
Müllerian duct						
female	184.8	198.82	233.39	221.8	236.3	239.5
male	187.8	198.82	233.6	222.8	236.6	239.5

	Malignant					
	Primary	Secondary	Ca in situ	Benign	Uncertain Behavior	Unspecified
Neoplasm, neoplastic — *continued*						
multiple sites NEC	199.0	199.0	234.9	229.9	238.9	199.0
muscle (*see also* Neoplasm, connective tissue)						
extraocular	190.1	198.4	234.0	224.1	238.8	239.8
myocardium	164.1	198.89	—	212.7	238.8	239.8
myometrium	182.0	198.82	233.2	219.1	236.0	239.5
myopericardium	164.1	198.89	—	212.7	238.8	239.8
nabothian gland (follicle)	180.0	198.82	233.1	219.0	236.0	239.5
nail	173.9	198.2	232.9	216.9	238.2	239.2
finger	173.6	198.2	232.6	216.6	238.2	239.2
toe	173.7	198.2	232.7	216.7	238.2	239.2
nares, naris (anterior) (posterior)	160.0	197.3	231.8	212.0	235.9	239.1
nasal — *see* Neoplasm, nose						
nasolabial groove	173.3	198.2	232.3	216.3	238.2	239.2
nasolacrimal duct	190.7	198.4	234.0	224.7	238.8	239.8
nasopharynx, nasopharyngeal	147.9	198.89	230.0	210.7	235.1	239.0
contiguous sites	147.8	—	—	—	—	—
floor	147.3	198.89	230.0	210.7	235.1	239.0
roof	147.0	198.89	230.0	210.7	235.1	239.0
specified site NEC	147.8	198.89	230.0	210.7	235.1	239.0
wall	147.9	198.89	230.0	210.7	235.1	239.0
anterior	147.3	198.89	230.0	210.7	235.1	239.0
lateral	147.2	198.89	230.0	210.7	235.1	239.0
posterior	147.1	198.89	230.0	210.7	235.1	239.0
superior	147.0	198.89	230.0	210.7	235.1	239.0
nates	173.5	198.2	232.5	216.5	238.2	239.2
neck NEC*	195.0	198.89	234.8	229.8	238.8	239.8
nerve (autonomic) (ganglion) (parasympathetic) (peripheral) (sympathetic) (*see also* Neoplasm, connective tissue)						
abducens	192.0	198.4	—	225.1	237.9	239.7
accessory (spinal)	192.0	198.4	—	225.1	237.9	239.7
acoustic	192.0	198.4	—	225.1	237.9	239.7
auditory	192.0	198.4	—	225.1	237.9	239.7
brachial	171.2	198.89	—	215.2	238.1	239.2
cranial (any)	192.0	198.4	—	225.1	237.9	239.7
facial	192.0	198.4	—	225.1	237.9	239.7
femoral	171.3	198.89	—	215.3	238.1	239.2
glossopharyngeal	192.0	198.4	—	225.1	237.9	239.7
hypoglossal	192.0	198.4	—	225.1	237.9	239.7
intercostal	171.4	198.89	—	215.4	238.1	239.2
lumbar	171.7	198.89	—	215.7	238.1	239.2
median	171.2	198.89	—	215.2	238.1	239.2
obturator	171.3	198.89	—	215.3	238.1	239.2
oculomotor	192.0	198.4	—	225.1	237.9	239.7
olfactory	192.0	198.4	—	225.1	237.9	239.7
optic	192.0	198.4	—	225.1	237.9	239.7
peripheral NEC	171.9	198.89	—	215.9	238.1	239.2
radial	171.2	198.89	—	215.2	238.1	239.2
sacral	171.6	198.89	—	215.6	238.1	239.2
sciatic	171.3	198.89	—	215.3	238.1	239.2
spinal NEC	171.9	198.89	—	215.9	238.1	239.2
trigeminal	192.0	198.4	—	225.1	237.9	239.7
trochlear	192.0	198.4	—	225.1	237.9	239.7
ulnar	171.2	198.89	—	215.2	238.1	239.2
vagus	192.0	198.4	—	225.1	237.9	239.7
nervous system (central) NEC	192.9	198.4	—	225.9	237.9	239.7
autonomic NEC	171.9	198.89	—	215.9	238.1	239.2
brain (*see also* Neoplasm, brain)						
membrane or meninges	192.1	198.4	—	225.2	237.6	239.7
contiguous sites	192.8	—	—	—	—	—
parasympathetic NEC	171.9	198.89	—	215.9	238.1	239.2
sympathetic NEC	171.9	198.89	—	215.9	238.1	239.2
nipple (female)	174.0	198.81	233.0	217	238.3	239.3
male	175.0	198.81	233.0	217	238.3	239.3
nose, nasal	195.0	198.89	234.8	229.8	238.8	239.8
Neoplasm, neoplastic — *continued*						
nose, nasal — *continued*						
ala (external)	173.3	198.2	232.3	216.3	238.2	239.2
bone	170.0	198.5	—	213.0	238.0	239.2
cartilage	160.0	197.3	231.8	212.0	235.9	239.1
cavity	160.0	197.3	231.8	212.0	235.9	239.1
contiguous sites with accessory sinuses or middle ear	160.8	—	—	—	—	—
choana	147.3	198.89	230.0	210.7	235.1	239.0
external (skin)	173.3	198.2	232.3	216.3	238.2	239.2
fossa	160.0	197.3	231.8	212.0	235.9	239.1
internal	160.0	197.3	231.8	212.0	235.9	239.1
mucosa	160.0	197.3	231.8	212.0	235.9	239.1
septum	160.0	197.3	231.8	212.0	235.9	239.1
posterior margin	147.3	198.89	230.0	210.7	235.1	239.0
sinus — *see* Neoplasm, sinus						
skin	173.3	198.2	232.3	216.3	238.2	239.2
turbinate (mucosa)	160.0	197.3	231.8	212.0	235.9	239.1
bone	170.0	198.5	—	213.0	238.0	239.2
vestibule	160.0	197.3	231.8	212.0	235.9	239.1
nostril	160.0	197.3	231.8	212.0	235.9	239.1
nucleus pulposus	170.2	198.5	—	213.2	238.0	239.2
occipital						
bone	170.0	198.5	—	213.0	238.0	239.2
lobe or pole, brain	191.4	198.3	—	225.0	237.5	239.6
odontogenic — *see* Neoplasm, jaw bone						
oesophagus — *see* Neoplasm, esophagus						
olfactory nerve or bulb	192.0	198.4	—	225.1	237.9	239.7
olive (brain)	191.7	198.3	—	225.0	237.5	239.6
omentum	158.8	197.6	—	211.8	235.4	239.0
operculum (brain)	191.0	198.3	—	225.0	237.5	239.6
optic nerve, chiasm, or tract	192.0	198.4	—	225.1	237.9	239.7
oral (cavity)	145.9	198.89	230.0	210.4	235.1	239.0
contiguous sites with lip or pharynx	149.8	—	—	—	—	—
ill-defined	149.9	198.89	230.0	210.4	235.1	239.0
mucosa	145.9	198.89	230.0	210.4	235.1	239.0
orbit	190.1	198.4	234.0	224.1	238.8	239.8
bone	170.0	198.5	—	213.0	238.0	239.2
eye	190.1	198.4	234.0	224.1	238.8	239.8
soft parts	190.1	198.4	234.0	224.1	238.8	239.8
organ of Zuckerkandl	194.6	198.89	—	227.6	237.3	239.7
oropharynx	146.9	198.89	230.0	210.6	235.1	239.0
branchial cleft (vestige)	146.8	198.89	230.0	210.6	235.1	239.0
contiguous sites	146.8	—	—	—	—	—
junctional region	146.5	198.89	230.0	210.6	235.1	239.0
lateral wall	146.6	198.89	230.0	210.6	235.1	239.0
pillars of fauces	146.2	198.89	230.0	210.6	235.1	239.0
posterior wall	146.7	198.89	230.0	210.6	235.1	239.0
specified part NEC	146.8	198.89	230.0	210.6	235.1	239.0
vallecula	146.3	198.89	230.0	210.6	235.1	239.0
os						
external	180.1	198.82	233.1	219.0	236.0	239.5
internal	180.0	198.82	233.1	219.0	236.0	239.5
ovary	183.0	198.6	233.39	220	236.2	239.5
oviduct	183.2	198.82	233.39	221.0	236.3	239.5
palate	145.5	198.89	230.0	210.4	235.1	239.0
hard	145.2	198.89	230.0	210.4	235.1	239.0
junction of hard and soft palate	145.5	198.89	230.0	210.4	235.1	239.0
soft	145.3	198.89	230.0	210.4	235.1	239.0
nasopharyngeal surface	147.3	198.89	230.0	210.7	235.1	239.0
posterior surface	147.3	198.89	230.0	210.7	235.1	239.0
superior surface	147.3	198.89	230.0	210.7	235.1	239.0
palatoglossal arch	146.2	198.89	230.0	210.6	235.1	239.0
palatopharyngeal arch	146.2	198.89	230.0	210.6	235.1	239.0
pallium	191.0	198.3	—	225.0	237.5	239.6
palpebra	173.1	198.2	232.1	216.1	238.2	239.2

	Malignant					
	Primary	Secondary	Ca in situ	Benign	Uncertain Behavior	Unspecified
Neoplasm, neoplastic — *continued*						
pancreas	157.9	197.8	230.9	211.6	235.5	239.0
body	157.1	197.8	230.9	211.6	235.5	239.0
contiguous sites	157.8	—	—	—	—	—
duct (of Santorini) (of Wirsung)	157.3	197.8	230.9	211.6	235.5	239.0
ectopic tissue	157.8	197.8	230.9	211.6	235.5	239.0
head	157.0	197.8	230.9	211.6	235.5	239.0
islet cells	157.4	197.8	230.9	211.7	235.5	239.0
neck	157.8	197.8	230.9	211.6	235.5	239.0
tail	157.2	197.8	230.9	211.6	235.5	239.0
para-aortic body	194.6	198.89	—	227.6	237.3	239.7
paraganglion NEC	194.6	198.89	—	227.6	237.3	239.7
parametrium	183.4	198.82	—	221.0	236.3	239.5
paranephric	158.0	197.6	—	211.8	235.4	239.0
pararectal	195.3	198.89	—	229.8	238.8	239.8
parasagittal (region)	195.0	198.89	234.8	229.8	238.8	239.8
parasellar	192.9	198.4	—	225.9	237.9	239.7
parathyroid (gland)	194.1	198.89	234.8	227.1	237.4	239.7
paraurethral	195.3	198.89	—	229.8	238.8	239.8
gland	189.4	198.1	233.9	223.89	236.99	239.5
paravaginal	195.3	198.89	—	229.8	238.8	239.8
parenchyma, kidney	189.0	198.0	233.9	223.0	236.91	239.5
parietal						
bone	170.0	198.5	—	213.0	238.0	239.2
lobe, brain	191.3	198.3	—	225.0	237.5	239.6
paroophoron	183.3	198.82	233.39	221.0	236.3	239.5
parotid (duct) (gland)	142.0	198.89	230.0	210.2	235.0	239.0
parovarium	183.3	198.82	233.39	221.0	236.3	239.5
patella	170.8	198.5	—	213.8	238.0	239.2
peduncle, cerebral	191.7	198.3	—	225.0	237.5	239.6
pelvirectal junction	154.0	197.5	230.4	211.4	235.2	239.0
pelvis, pelvic	195.3	198.89	234.8	229.8	238.8	239.8
bone	170.6	198.5	—	213.6	238.0	239.2
floor	195.3	198.89	234.8	229.8	238.8	239.8
renal	189.1	198.0	233.9	223.1	236.91	239.5
viscera	195.3	198.89	234.8	229.8	238.8	239.8
wall	195.3	198.89	234.8	229.8	238.8	239.8
pelvo-abdominal	195.8	198.89	234.8	229.8	238.8	239.8
penis	187.4	198.82	233.5	222.1	236.6	239.5
body	187.3	198.82	233.5	222.1	236.6	239.5
corpus (cavernosum)	187.3	198.82	233.5	222.1	236.6	239.5
glans	187.2	198.82	233.5	222.1	236.6	239.5
skin NEC	187.4	198.82	233.5	222.1	236.6	239.5
periadrenal (tissue)	158.0	197.6	—	211.8	235.4	239.0
perianal (skin)	173.5	198.2	232.5	216.5	238.2	239.2
pericardium	164.1	198.89	—	212.7	238.8	239.8
perinephric	158.0	197.6	—	211.8	235.4	239.0
perineum	195.3	198.89	234.8	229.8	238.8	239.8
periodontal tissue NEC	143.9	198.89	230.0	210.4	235.1	239.0
periosteum — *see* Neoplasm, bone						
peripancreatic	158.0	197.6	—	211.8	235.4	239.0
peripheral nerve NEC	171.9	198.89	—	215.9	238.1	239.2
perirectal (tissue)	195.3	198.89	—	229.8	238.8	239.8
perirenal (tissue)	158.0	197.6	—	211.8	235.4	239.0
peritoneum, peritoneal (cavity)	158.9	197.6	—	211.8	235.4	239.0
contiguous sites	158.8	—	—	—	—	—
with digestive organs	159.8	—	—	—	—	—
parietal	158.8	197.6	—	211.8	235.4	239.0
pelvic	158.8	197.6	—	211.8	235.4	239.0
specified part NEC	158.8	197.6	—	211.8	235.4	239.0
peritonsillar (tissue)	195.0	198.89	234.8	229.8	238.8	239.8
periurethral tissue	195.3	198.89	—	229.8	238.8	239.8
phalanges	170.9	198.5	—	213.9	238.0	239.2
foot	170.8	198.5		213.8	238.0	239.2
hand	170.5	198.5	—	213.5	238.0	239.2
pharynx, pharyngeal	149.0	198.89	230.0	210.9	235.1	239.0
bursa	147.1	198.89	230.0	210.7	235.1	239.0
fornix	147.3	198.89	230.0	210.7	235.1	239.0
recess	147.2	198.89	230.0	210.7	235.1	239.0
region	149.0	198.89	230.0	210.9	235.1	239.0
tonsil	147.1	198.89	230.0	210.7	235.1	239.0

	Malignant					
	Primary	Secondary	Ca in situ	Benign	Uncertain Behavior	Unspecified
Neoplasm, neoplastic — *continued*						
pharynx, pharyngeal — *continued*						
wall (lateral) (posterior)	149.0	198.89	230.0	210.9	235.1	239.0
pia mater (cerebral) (cranial)	192.1	198.4	—	225.2	237.6	239.7
spinal	192.3	198.4	—	225.4	237.6	239.7
pillars of fauces	146.2	198.89	230.0	210.6	235.1	239.0
pineal (body) (gland)	194.4	198.89	234.8	227.4	237.1	239.7
pinna (ear) NEC	173.2	198.2	232.2	216.2	238.2	239.2
cartilage	171.0	198.89	—	215.0	238.1	239.2
piriform fossa or sinus	148.1	198.89	230.0	210.8	235.1	239.0
pituitary (body) (fossa) (gland) (lobe)	194.3	198.89	234.8	227.3	237.0	239.7
placenta	181	198.82	233.2	219.8	236.1	239.5
pleura, pleural (cavity)	163.9	197.2	—	212.4	235.8	239.1
contiguous sites	163.8	—	—	—	—	—
parietal	163.0	197.2	—	212.4	235.8	239.1
visceral	163.1	197.2	—	212.4	235.8	239.1
plexus						
brachial	171.2	198.89	—	215.2	238.1	239.2
cervical	171.0	198.89	—	215.0	238.1	239.2
choroid	191.5	198.3	—	225.0	237.5	239.6
lumbosacral	171.6	198.89	—	215.6	238.1	239.2
sacral	171.6	198.89	—	215.6	238.1	239.2
pluri-endocrine	194.8	198.89	234.8	227.8	237.4	239.7
pole						
frontal	191.1	198.3	—	225.0	237.5	239.6
occipital	191.4	198.3	—	225.0	237.5	239.6
pons (varolii)	191.7	198.3	—	225.0	237.5	239.6
popliteal fossa or space*	195.5	198.89	234.8	229.8	238.8	239.8
postcricoid (region)	148.0	198.89	230.0	210.8	235.1	239.0
posterior fossa (cranial)	191.9	198.3	—	225.0	237.5	239.6
postnasal space	147.9	198.89	230.0	210.7	235.1	239.0
prepuce	187.1	198.82	233.5	222.1	236.6	239.5
prepylorus	151.1	197.8	230.2	211.1	235.2	239.0
presacral (region)	195.3	198.89	—	229.8	238.8	239.8
prostate (gland)	185	198.82	233.4	222.2	236.5	239.5
utricle	189.3	198.1	233.9	223.81	236.99	239.5
pterygoid fossa	171.0	198.89	—	215.0	238.1	239.2
pubic bone	170.6	198.5	—	213.6	238.0	239.2
pudenda, pudendum (female)	184.4	198.82	233.32	221.2	236.3	239.5
pulmonary	162.9	197.0	231.2	212.3	235.7	239.1
putamen	191.0	198.3	—	225.0	237.5	239.6
pyloric						
antrum	151.2	197.8	230.2	211.1	235.2	239.0
canal	151.1	197.8	230.2	211.1	235.2	239.0
pylorus	151.1	197.8	230.2	211.1	235.2	239.0
pyramid (brain)	191.7	198.3	—	225.0	237.5	239.6
pyriform fossa or sinus	148.1	198.89	230.0	210.8	235.1	239.0
radius (any part)	170.4	198.5	—	213.4	238.0	239.2
Rathke's pouch	194.3	198.89	234.8	227.3	237.0	239.7
rectosigmoid (colon) (junction)	154.0	197.5	230.4	211.4	235.2	239.0
contiguous sites with anus or rectum	154.8	—	—	—	—	—
rectouterine pouch	158.8	197.6	—	211.8	235.4	239.0
rectovaginal septum or wall	195.3	198.89	234.8	229.8	238.8	239.8
rectovesical septum	195.3	198.89	234.8	229.8	238.8	239.8
rectum (ampulla)	154.1	197.5	230.4	211.4	235.2	239.0
and colon	154.0	197.5	230.4	211.4	235.2	239.0
contiguous sites with anus or rectosigmoid junction	154.8	—	—	—	—	—
renal	189.0	198.0	233.9	223.0	236.91	239.5
calyx	189.1	198.0	233.9	223.1	236.91	239.5
hilus	189.1	198.0	233.9	223.1	236.91	239.5
parenchyma	189.0	198.0	233.9	223.0	236.91	239.5
pelvis	189.1	198.0	233.9	223.1	236.91	239.5
respiratory						

	Malignant					
	Primary	Secondary	Ca in situ	Benign	Uncertain Behavior	Unspecified
Neoplasm, neoplastic — *continued*						
respiratory — *continued*						
organs or system NEC	165.9	197.3	231.9	212.9	235.9	239.1
contiguous sites with intrathoracic organs	165.8	—	—	—	—	—
specified sites NEC	165.8	197.3	231.8	212.8	235.9	239.1
tract NEC	165.9	197.3	231.9	212.9	235.9	239.1
upper	165.0	197.3	231.9	212.9	235.9	239.1
retina	190.5	198.4	234.0	224.5	238.8	239.8
retrobulbar	190.1	198.4	—	224.1	238.8	239.8
retrocecal	158.0	197.6	—	211.8	235.4	239.0
retromolar (area) (triangle) (trigone)	145.6	198.89	230.0	210.4	235.1	239.0
retro-orbital	195.0	198.89	234.8	229.8	238.8	239.8
retroperitoneal (space) (tissue)	158.0	197.6	—	211.8	235.4	239.0
contiguous sites	158.8	—	—	—	—	—
retroperitoneum	158.0	197.6	—	211.8	235.4	239.0
contiguous sites	158.8	—	—	—	—	—
retropharyngeal	149.0	198.89	230.0	210.9	235.1	239.0
retrovesical (septum)	195.3	198.89	234.8	229.8	238.8	239.8
rhinencephalon	191.0	198.3	—	225.0	237.5	239.6
rib	170.3	198.5	—	213.3	238.0	239.2
Rosenmüller's fossa	147.2	198.89	230.0	210.7	235.1	239.0
round ligament	183.5	198.82	—	221.0	236.3	239.5
sacrococcyx, sacrococcygeal	170.6	198.5	—	213.6	238.0	239.2
region	195.3	198.89	234.8	229.8	238.8	239.8
sacrouterine ligament	183.4	198.82	—	221.0	236.3	239.5
sacrum, sacral (vertebra)	170.6	198.5	—	213.6	238.0	239.2
salivary gland or duct (major)	142.9	198.89	230.0	210.2	235.0	239.0
contiguous sites	142.8	—	—	—	—	—
minor NEC	145.9	198.89	230.0	210.4	235.1	239.0
parotid	142.0	198.89	230.0	210.2	235.0	239.0
pluriglandular	142.8	198.89	—	210.2	235.0	239.0
sublingual	142.2	198.89	230.0	210.2	235.0	239.0
submandibular	142.1	198.89	230.0	210.2	235.0	239.0
submaxillary	142.1	198.89	230.0	210.2	235.0	239.0
salpinx (uterine)	183.2	198.82	233.39	221.0	236.3	239.5
Santorini's duct	157.3	197.8	230.9	211.6	235.5	239.0
scalp	173.4	198.2	232.4	216.4	238.2	239.2
scapula (any part)	170.4	198.5	—	213.4	238.0	239.2
scapular region	195.1	198.89	234.8	229.8	238.8	239.8
scar NEC (*see also* Neoplasm, skin)	173.9	198.2	232.9	216.9	238.2	239.2
sciatic nerve	171.3	198.89	—	215.3	238.1	239.2
sclera	190.0	198.4	234.0	224.0	238.8	239.8
scrotum (skin)	187.7	198.82	—	222.4	236.6	239.5
sebaceous gland — *see* Neoplasm, skin						
sella turcica	194.3	198.89	234.8	227.3	237.0	239.7
bone	170.0	198.5	—	213.0	238.0	239.2
semilunar cartilage (knee)	170.7	198.5	—	213.7	238.0	239.2
seminal vesicle	187.8	198.82	233.6	222.8	236.6	239.5
septum						
nasal	160.0	197.3	231.8	212.0	235.9	239.1
posterior margin	147.3	198.89	230.0	210.7	235.1	239.0
rectovaginal	195.3	198.89	234.8	229.8	238.8	239.8
rectovesical	195.3	198.89	234.8	229.8	238.8	239.8
urethrovaginal	184.9	198.82	233.39	221.9	236.3	239.5
vesicovaginal	184.9	198.82	233.39	221.9	236.3	239.5
shoulder NEC*	195.4	198.89	232.6	229.8	238.8	239.8
sigmoid flexure (lower) (upper)	153.3	197.5	230.3	211.3	235.2	239.0
sinus (accessory)	160.9	197.3	231.8	212.0	235.9	239.1
bone (any)	170.0	198.5	—	213.0	238.0	239.2
contiguous sites with middle ear or nasal cavities	160.8	—	—	—	—	—
ethmoidal	160.3	197.3	231.8	212.0	235.9	239.1
frontal	160.4	197.3	231.8	212.0	235.9	239.1
maxillary	160.2	197.3	231.8	212.0	235.9	239.1

	Malignant					
	Primary	Secondary	Ca in situ	Benign	Uncertain Behavior	Unspecified
Neoplasm, neoplastic — *continued*						
sinus — *continued*						
nasal, paranasal NEC	160.9	197.3	231.8	212.0	235.9	239.1
pyriform	148.1	198.89	230.0	210.8	235.1	239.0
sphenoidal	160.5	197.3	231.8	212.0	235.9	239.1
skeleton, skeletal NEC	170.9	198.5	—	213.9	238.0	239.2
Skene's gland	189.4	198.1	233.9	223.89	236.99	239.5
skin NEC	173.9	198.2	232.9	216.9	238.2	239.2
abdominal wall	173.5	198.2	232.5	216.5	238.2	239.2
ala nasi	173.3	198.2	232.3	216.3	238.2	239.2
ankle	173.7	198.2	232.7	216.7	238.2	239.2
antecubital space	173.6	198.2	232.6	216.6	238.2	239.2
anus	173.5	198.2	232.5	216.5	238.2	239.2
arm	173.6	198.2	232.6	216.6	238.2	239.2
auditory canal (external)	173.2	198.2	232.2	216.2	238.2	239.2
auricle (ear)	173.2	198.2	232.2	216.2	238.2	239.2
auricular canal (external)	173.2	198.2	232.2	216.2	238.2	239.2
axilla, axillary fold	173.5	198.2	232.5	216.5	238.2	239.2
back	173.5	198.2	232.5	216.5	238.2	239.2
breast	173.5	198.2	232.5	216.5	238.2	239.2
brow	173.3	198.2	232.3	216.3	238.2	239.2
buttock	173.5	198.2	232.5	216.5	238.2	239.2
calf	173.7	198.2	232.7	216.7	238.2	239.2
canthus (eye) (inner) (outer)	173.1	198.2	232.1	216.1	238.2	239.2
cervical region	173.4	198.2	232.4	216.4	238.2	239.2
cheek (external)	173.3	198.2	232.3	216.3	238.2	239.2
chest (wall)	173.5	198.2	232.5	216.5	238.2	239.2
chin	173.3	198.2	232.3	216.3	238.2	239.2
clavicular area	173.5	198.2	232.5	216.5	238.2	239.2
clitoris	184.3	198.82	233.32	221.2	236.3	239.5
columnella	173.3	198.2	232.3	216.3	238.2	239.2
concha	173.2	198.2	232.2	216.2	238.2	239.2
contiguous sites	173.8	—	—	—	—	—
ear (external)	173.2	198.2	232.2	216.2	238.2	239.2
elbow	173.6	198.2	232.6	216.6	238.2	239.2
eyebrow	173.3	198.2	232.3	216.3	238.2	239.2
eyelid	173.1	198.2	232.1	—	238.2	239.2
face NEC	173.3	198.2	232.3	216.3	238.2	239.2
female genital organs (external)	184.4	198.82	233.30	221.2	236.3	239.5
clitoris	184.3	198.82	233.32	221.2	236.3	239.5
labium NEC	184.4	198.82	233.32	221.2	236.3	239.5
majus	184.1	198.82	233.32	221.2	236.3	239.5
minus	184.2	198.82	233.32	221.2	236.3	239.5
pudendum	184.4	198.82	233.32	221.2	236.3	239.5
vulva	184.4	198.82	233.32	221.2	236.3	239.5
finger	173.6	198.2	232.6	216.6	238.2	239.2
flank	173.5	198.2	232.5	216.5	238.2	239.2
foot	173.7	198.2	232.7	216.7	238.2	239.2
forearm	173.6	198.2	232.6	216.6	238.2	239.2
forehead	173.3	198.2	232.3	216.3	238.2	239.2
glabella	173.3	198.2	232.3	216.3	238.2	239.2
gluteal region	173.5	198.2	232.5	216.5	238.2	239.2
groin	173.5	198.2	232.5	216.5	238.2	239.2
hand	173.6	198.2	232.6	216.6	238.2	239.2
head NEC	173.4	198.2	232.4	216.4	238.2	239.2
heel	173.7	198.2	232.7	216.7	238.2	239.2
helix	173.2	198.2	—	216.2	238.2	239.2
hip	173.7	198.2	232.7	216.7	238.2	239.2
infraclavicular region	173.5	198.2	232.5	216.5	238.2	239.2
inguinal region	173.5	198.2	232.5	216.5	238.2	239.2
jaw	173.3	198.2	232.3	216.3	238.2	239.2
knee	173.7	198.2	232.7	216.7	238.2	239.2
labia						
majora	184.1	198.82	233.32	221.2	236.3	239.5
minora	184.2	198.82	233.32	221.2	236.3	239.5
leg	173.7	198.2	232.7	216.7	238.2	239.2
lid (lower) (upper)	—	198.2	232.1	216.1	238.2	239.2
limb NEC	173.9	198.2	232.9	216.9	238.2	239.5
lower	173.7	198.2	232.7	216.7	238.2	239.2
upper	173.6	198.2	232.6	216.6	238.2	239.2
lip (lower) (upper)	173.0	198.2	232.0	216.0	238.2	239.2

	Malignant					
	Primary	Secondary	Ca in situ	Benign	Uncertain Behavior	Unspecified
Neoplasm, neoplastic — *continued*						
skin — *continued*						
male genital organs	187.9	198.82	233.6	222.9	236.6	239.5
penis	187.4	198.82	233.5	222.1	236.6	239.5
prepuce	187.1	198.82	233.5	222.1	236.6	239.5
scrotum	187.7	198.82	233.6	222.4	236.6	239.5
mastectomy site	173.5	198.2	—	—	—	—
specified as breast tissue	174.8	198.81	—	—	—	—
meatus, acoustic (external)	173.2	198.2	232.2	216.2	238.2	239.2
nates	173.5	198.2	232.5	216.5	238.2	239.0
neck	173.4	198.2	232.4	216.4	238.2	239.2
nose (external)	173.3	198.2	232.3	216.3	238.2	239.2
palm	173.6	198.2	232.6	216.6	238.2	239.2
palpebra	173.1	198.2	232.1	216.1	238.2	239.2
penis NEC	187.4	198.82	233.5	222.1	236.6	239.5
perianal	173.5	198.2	232.5	216.5	238.2	239.2
perineum	173.5	198.2	232.5	216.5	238.2	239.2
pinna	173.2	198.2	232.2	216.2	238.2	239.2
plantar	173.7	198.2	232.7	216.7	238.2	239.2
popliteal fossa or space	173.7	198.2	232.7	216.7	238.2	239.2
prepuce	187.1	198.82	233.5	222.1	236.6	239.5
pubes	173.5	198.2	232.5	216.5	238.2	239.2
sacrococcygeal region	173.5	198.2	232.5	216.5	238.2	239.2
scalp	173.4	198.2	232.4	216.4	238.2	239.2
scapular region	173.5	198.2	232.5	216.5	238.2	239.2
scrotum	187.7	198.82	233.6	222.4	236.6	239.5
shoulder	173.6	198.2	232.6	216.6	238.2	239.2
sole (foot)	173.7	198.2	232.7	216.7	238.2	239.2
specified sites NEC	173.8	198.2	232.8	216.8	232.8	239.2
submammary fold	173.5	198.2	232.5	216.5	238.2	239.2
supraclavicular region	173.4	198.2	232.4	216.4	238.2	239.2
temple	173.3	198.2	232.3	216.3	238.2	239.2
thigh	173.7	198.2	232.7	216.7	238.2	239.2
thoracic wall	173.5	198.2	232.5	216.5	238.2	239.2
thumb	173.6	198.2	232.6	216.6	238.2	239.2
toe	173.7	198.2	232.7	216.7	238.2	239.2
tragus	173.2	198.2	232.2	216.2	238.2	239.2
trunk	173.5	198.2	232.5	216.5	238.2	239.2
umbilicus	173.5	198.2	232.5	216.5	238.2	239.2
vulva	184.4	198.82	233.32	221.2	236.3	239.5
wrist	173.6	198.2	232.6	216.6	238.2	239.2
skull	170.0	198.5	—	213.0	238.0	239.2
soft parts or tissues — *see* Neoplasm, connective tissue						
specified site NEC	195.8	198.89	234.8	229.8	238.8	239.8
specified site — *see* Neoplasm, skin						
spermatic cord	187.6	198.82	233.6	222.8	236.6	239.5
sphenoid	160.5	197.3	231.8	212.0	235.9	239.1
bone	170.0	198.5	—	213.0	238.0	239.2
sinus	160.5	197.3	231.8	212.0	235.9	239.1
sphincter						
anal	154.2	197.5	230.5	211.4	235.5	239.0
of Oddi	156.1	197.8	230.8	211.5	235.3	239.0
spine, spinal (column)	170.2	198.5	—	213.2	238.0	239.2
bulb	191.7	198.3	—	225.0	237.5	239.6
coccyx	170.6	198.5	—	213.6	238.0	239.2
cord (cervical) (lumbar) (sacral) (thoracic)	192.2	198.3	—	225.3	237.5	239.7
dura mater	192.3	198.4	—	225.4	237.6	239.7
lumbosacral	170.2	198.5	—	213.2	238.0	239.2
membrane	192.3	198.4	—	225.4	237.6	239.7
meninges	192.3	198.4	—	225.4	237.6	239.7
nerve (root)	171.9	198.89	—	215.9	238.1	239.2
pia mater	192.3	198.4	—	225.4	237.6	239.7
root	171.9	198.89	—	215.9	238.1	239.2
sacrum	170.6	198.5	—	213.6	238.0	239.2
spleen, splenic NEC	159.1	197.8	230.9	211.9	235.5	239.0
flexure (colon)	153.7	197.5	230.3	211.3	235.2	239.0
stem, brain	191.7	198.3	—	225.0	237.5	239.6
Stensen's duct	142.0	198.89	230.0	210.2	235.0	239.0
Neoplasm, neoplastic — *continued*						
sternum	170.3	198.5	—	213.3	238.0	239.2
stomach	151.9	197.8	230.2	211.1	235.2	239.0
antrum (pyloric)	151.2	197.8	230.2	211.1	235.2	239.0
body	151.4	197.8	230.2	211.1	235.2	239.0
cardia	151.0	197.8	230.2	211.1	235.2	239.0
cardiac orifice	151.0	197.8	230.2	211.1	235.2	239.0
contiguous sites	151.8	—	—	—	—	—
corpus	151.4	197.8	230.2	211.1	235.2	239.0
fundus	151.3	197.8	230.2	211.1	235.2	239.0
greater curvature NEC	151.6	197.8	230.2	211.1	235.2	239.0
lesser curvature NEC	151.5	197.8	230.2	211.1	235.2	239.0
prepylorus	151.1	197.8	230.2	211.1	235.2	239.0
pylorus	151.1	197.8	230.2	211.1	235.2	239.0
wall NEC	151.9	197.8	230.2	211.1	235.2	239.0
anterior NEC	151.8	197.8	230.2	211.1	235.2	239.0
posterior NEC	151.8	197.8	230.2	211.1	235.2	239.0
stroma, endometrial	182.0	198.82	233.2	219.1	236.0	239.5
stump, cervical	180.8	198.82	233.1	219.0	236.0	239.5
subcutaneous (nodule) (tissue) NEC — *see* Neoplasm, connective tissue						
subdural	192.1	198.4	—	225.2	237.6	239.7
subglottis, subglottic	161.2	197.3	231.0	212.1	235.6	239.1
sublingual	144.9	198.89	230.0	210.3	235.1	239.0
gland or duct	142.2	198.89	230.0	210.2	235.0	239.0
submandibular gland	142.1	198.89	230.0	210.2	235.0	239.0
submaxillary gland or duct	142.1	198.89	230.0	210.2	235.0	239.0
submental	195.0	198.89	234.8	229.8	238.8	239.8
subpleural	162.9	197.0	—	212.3	235.7	239.1
substernal	164.2	197.1	—	212.5	235.8	239.8
sudoriferous, sudoriparous gland, site unspecified	173.9	198.2	232.9	216.9	238.2	239.2
specified site — *see* Neoplasm, skin						
supraclavicular region	195.0	198.89	234.8	229.8	238.8	239.8
supraglottis	161.1	197.3	231.0	212.1	235.6	239.1
suprarenal (capsule) (cortex) (gland) (medulla)	194.0	198.7	234.8	227.0	237.2	239.7
suprasellar (region)	191.9	198.3	—	225.0	237.5	239.6
sweat gland (apocrine) (eccrine), site unspecified	173.9	198.2	232.9	216.9	238.2	239.2
sympathetic nerve or nervous system NEC	171.9	198.89	—	215.9	238.1	239.2
symphysis pubis	170.6	198.5	—	213.6	238.0	239.2
synovial membrane — *see* Neoplasm, connective tissue						
tapetum, brain	191.8	198.3	—	225.0	237.5	239.6
tarsus (any bone)	170.8	198.5	—	213.8	238.0	239.2
temple (skin)	173.3	198.2	232.3	216.3	238.2	239.2
temporal						
bone	170.0	198.5	—	213.0	238.0	239.2
lobe or pole	191.2	198.3	—	225.0	237.5	239.6
region	195.0	198.89	234.8	229.8	238.8	239.8
skin	173.3	198.2	232.3	216.3	238.2	239.2
tendon (sheath) — *see* Neoplasm, connective tissue						
tentorium (cerebelli)	192.1	198.4	—	225.2	237.6	239.7
testis, testes (descended) (scrotal)	186.9	198.82	233.6	222.0	236.4	239.5
ectopic	186.0	198.82	233.6	222.0	236.4	239.5
retained	186.0	198.82	233.6	222.0	236.4	239.5
undescended	186.0	198.82	233.6	222.0	236.4	239.5
thalamus	191.0	198.3	—	225.0	237.5	239.6
thigh NEC*	195.5	198.89	234.8	229.8	238.8	239.8
thorax, thoracic (cavity) (organs NEC)	195.1	198.89	234.8	229.8	238.8	239.8
duct	171.4	198.89	—	215.4	238.1	239.2
wall NEC	195.1	198.89	234.8	229.8	238.8	239.8

	Malignant					
	Primary	Secondary	Ca in situ	Benign	Uncertain Behavior	Unspecified
Neoplasm, neoplastic — *continued*						
throat	149.0	198.89	230.0	210.9	235.1	239.0
thumb NEC*	195.4	198.89	232.6	229.8	238.8	239.8
thymus (gland)	164.0	198.89	—	212.6	235.8	239.8
contiguous sites with heart and mediastinum	164.8	—	—	—	—	—
thyroglossal duct	193	198.89	234.8	226	237.4	239.7
thyroid (gland)	193	198.89	234.8	226	237.4	239.7
cartilage	161.3	197.3	231.0	212.1	235.6	239.1
tibia (any part)	170.7	198.5	—	213.7	238.0	239.2
toe NEC*	195.5	198.89	232.7	229.8	238.8	239.8
tongue	141.9	198.89	230.0	210.1	235.1	239.0
anterior (two-thirds) NEC	141.4	198.89	230.0	210.1	235.1	239.0
dorsal surface	141.1	198.89	230.0	210.1	235.1	239.0
ventral surface	141.3	198.89	230.0	210.1	235.1	239.0
base (dorsal surface)	141.0	198.89	230.0	210.1	235.1	239.0
border (lateral)	141.2	198.89	230.0	210.1	235.1	239.0
contiguous sites	141.8	—	—	—	—	—
dorsal surface NEC	141.1	198.89	230.0	210.1	235.1	239.0
fixed part NEC	141.0	198.89	230.0	210.1	235.1	239.0
foreamen cecum	141.1	198.89	230.0	210.1	235.1	239.0
frenulum linguae	141.3	198.89	230.0	210.1	235.1	239.0
junctional zone	141.5	198.89	230.0	210.1	235.1	239.0
margin (lateral)	141.2	198.89	230.0	210.1	235.1	239.0
midline NEC	141.1	198.89	230.0	210.1	235.1	239.0
mobile part NEC	141.4	198.89	230.0	210.1	235.1	239.0
posterior (third)	141.0	198.89	230.0	210.1	235.1	239.0
root	141.0	198.89	230.0	210.1	235.1	239.0
surface (dorsal)	141.1	198.89	230.0	210.1	235.1	239.0
base	141.0	198.89	230.0	210.1	235.1	239.0
ventral	141.3	198.89	230.0	210.1	235.1	239.0
tip	141.2	198.89	230.0	210.1	235.1	239.0
tonsil	141.6	198.89	230.0	210.1	235.1	239.0
tonsil	146.0	198.89	230.0	210.5	235.1	239.0
fauces, faucial	146.0	198.89	230.0	210.5	235.1	239.0
lingual	141.6	198.89	230.0	210.1	235.1	239.0
palatine	146.0	198.89	230.0	210.5	235.1	239.0
pharyngeal	147.1	198.89	230.0	210.7	235.1	239.0
pillar (anterior) (posterior)	146.2	198.89	230.0	210.6	235.1	239.0
tonsillar fossa	146.1	198.89	230.0	210.6	235.1	239.0
tooth socket NEC	143.9	198.89	230.0	210.4	235.1	239.0
trachea (cartilage) (mucosa)	162.0	197.3	231.1	212.2	235.7	239.1
contiguous sites with bronchus or lung	162.8	—	—	—	—	—
tracheobronchial	162.8	197.3	231.1	212.2	235.7	239.1
contiguous sites with lung	162.8	—	—	—	—	—
tragus	173.2	198.2	232.2	216.2	238.2	239.2
trunk NEC*	195.8	198.89	232.5	229.8	238.8	239.8
tubo-ovarian	183.8	198.82	233.39	221.8	236.3	239.5
tunica vaginalis	187.8	198.82	233.6	222.8	236.6	239.5
turbinate (bone)	170.0	198.5	—	213.0	238.0	239.2
nasal	160.0	197.3	231.8	212.0	235.9	239.1
tympanic cavity	160.1	197.3	231.8	212.0	235.9	239.1
ulna (any part)	170.4	198.5	—	213.4	238.0	239.2
umbilicus, umbilical	173.5	198.2	232.5	216.5	238.2	239.2
uncus, brain	191.2	198.3	—	225.0	237.5	239.6
unknown site or unspecified	199.1	199.1	234.9	229.9	238.9	239.9
urachus	188.7	198.1	233.7	223.3	236.7	239.4
ureter-bladder junction)	188.6	198.1	233.7	223.3	236.7	239.4
ureter, ureteral	189.2	198.1	233.9	223.2	236.91	239.5
orifice (bladder)	188.6	198.1	233.7	223.3	236.7	239.4
urethra, urethral (gland)	189.3	198.1	233.9	223.81	236.99	239.5
orifice, internal	188.5	198.1	233.7	223.3	236.7	239.4
urethrovaginal (septum)	184.9	198.82	233.39	221.9	236.3	239.5
urinary organ or system NEC	189.9	198.1	233.9	223.9	236.99	239.5

	Malignant					
	Primary	Secondary	Ca in situ	Benign	Uncertain Behavior	Unspecified
Neoplasm, neoplastic — *continued*						
urinary organ or system — *continued*						
bladder — *see* Neoplasm, bladder						
contiguous sites	189.8	—	—	—	—	—
specified sites NEC	189.8	198.1	233.9	223.89	236.99	239.5
utero-ovarian	183.8	198.82	233.39	221.8	236.3	239.5
ligament	183.3	198.82	—	221.0	236.3	239.5
uterosacral ligament	183.4	198.82	—	221.0	236.3	239.5
uterus, uteri, uterine	179	198.82	233.2	219.9	236.0	239.5
adnexa NEC	183.9	198.82	233.39	221.8	236.3	239.5
contiguous sites	183.8	—	—	—	—	—
body	182.0	198.82	233.2	219.1	236.0	239.5
contiguous sites	182.8	—	—	—	—	—
cervix	180.9	198.82	233.1	219.0	236.0	239.5
cornu	182.0	198.82	233.2	219.1	236.0	239.5
corpus	182.0	198.82	233.2	219.1	236.0	239.5
endocervix (canal) (gland)	180.0	198.82	233.1	219.0	236.0	239.5
endometrium	182.0	198.82	233.2	219.1	236.0	239.5
exocervix	180.1	198.82	233.1	219.0	236.0	239.5
external os	180.1	198.82	233.1	219.0	236.0	239.5
fundus	182.0	198.82	233.2	219.1	236.0	239.5
internal os	180.0	198.82	233.1	219.0	236.0	239.5
isthmus	182.1	198.82	233.2	219.1	236.0	239.5
ligament	183.4	198.82	—	221.0	236.3	239.5
broad	183.3	198.82	233.39	221.0	236.3	239.5
round	183.5	198.82	—	221.0	236.3	239.5
lower segment	182.1	198.82	233.2	219.1	236.0	239.5
myometrium	182.0	198.82	233.2	219.1	236.0	239.5
squamocolumnar junction	180.8	198.82	233.1	219.0	236.0	239.5
tube	183.2	198.82	233.39	221.0	236.3	239.5
utricle, prostatic	189.3	198.1	233.9	223.81	236.99	239.5
uveal tract	190.0	198.4	234.0	224.0	238.8	239.8
uvula	145.4	198.89	230.0	210.4	235.1	239.0
vagina, vaginal (fornix) (vault) (wall)	184.0	198.82	233.31	221.1	236.3	239.5
vaginovesical	184.9	198.82	233.39	221.9	236.3	239.5
septum	184.9 ▲	198.82	233.39	221.9	236.3	239.5
vallecula (epiglottis)	146.3	198.89	230.0	210.6	235.1	239.0
vascular — *see* Neoplasm, connective tissue						
vas deferens	187.6	198.82	233.6	222.8	236.6	239.5
Vater's ampulla	156.2	197.8	230.8	211.5	235.3	239.0
vein, venous — *see* Neoplasm, connective tissue						
vena cava (abdominal) (inferior)	171.5	198.89	—	215.5	238.1	239.2
superior	171.4	198.89	—	215.4	238.1	239.2
ventricle (cerebral) (floor) (fourth) (lateral) (third)	191.5	198.3	—	225.0	237.5	239.6
cardiac (left) (right)	164.1	198.89	—	212.7	238.8	239.8
ventricular band of larynx	161.1	197.3	231.0	212.1	235.6	239.1
ventriculus — see Neoplasm, stomach						
vermillion border — *see* Neoplasm, lip						
vermis, cerebellum	191.6	198.3	—	225.0	237.5	239.6
vertebra (column)	170.2	198.5	—	213.2	238.0	239.2
coccyx	170.6	198.5	—	213.6	238.0	239.2
sacrum	170.6	198.5	—	213.6	238.0	239.2
vesical — *see* Neoplasm, bladder						
vesicle, seminal	187.8	198.82	233.6	222.8	236.6	239.5
vesicocervical tissue	184.9	198.82	233.39	221.9	236.3	239.5
vesicorectal	195.3	198.89	234.8	229.8	238.8	239.8
vesicovaginal	184.9	198.82	233.39	221.9	236.3	239.5
septum	184.9	198.82	233.39	221.9	236.3	239.5
vessel (blood) — *see* Neoplasm, connective tissue						
vestibular gland, greater	184.1	198.82	233.32	221.2	236.3	239.5

☑ Additional Digit Required — Refer to the Tabular List for Digit Selection

Subterms under main terms may continue to next column or page

▶◀ Revised Text ● New Line ▲ Revised Code

	Malignant					
	Primary	Secondary	Ca in situ	Benign	Uncertain Behavior	Unspecified
Neoplasm, neoplastic — *continued*						
vestibule						
mouth	145.1	198.89	230.0	210.4	235.1	239.0
nose	160.0	197.3	231.8	212.0	235.9	239.1
Virchow's gland	—	196.0	—	229.0	238.8	239.8
viscera NEC	195.8	198.89	234.8	229.8	238.8	239.8
vocal cords (true)	161.0	197.3	231.0	212.1	235.6	239.1
false	161.1	197.3	231.0	212.1	235.6	239.1
vomer	170.0	198.5	—	213.0	238.0	239.2
vulva	184.4	198.82	233.32	221.2	236.3	239.5
vulvovaginal gland	184.4	198.82	233.32	221.2	236.3	239.5
Waldeyer's ring	149.1	198.89	230.0	210.9	235.1	239.0
Wharton's duct	142.1	198.89	230.0	210.2	235.0	239.0
white matter (central) (cerebral)	191.0	198.3	—	225.0	237.5	239.6
windpipe	162.0	197.3	231.1	212.2	235.7	239.1
Wirsung's duct	157.3	197.8	230.9	211.6	235.5	239.0
wolffian (body) (duct)						
female	184.8	198.82	233.39	221.8	236.3	239.5
male	187.8	198.82	233.6	222.8	236.6	239.5
womb — *see* Neoplasm, uterus						
wrist NEC*	195.4	198.89	232.6	229.8	238.8	239.8
xiphoid process	170.3	198.5	—	213.3	238.0	239.2
Zuckerkandl's organ	194.6	198.89	—	227.6	237.3	239.7

Neovascularization
choroid 362.16
ciliary body 364.42
cornea 370.60
deep 370.63
localized 370.61
iris 364.42
retina 362.16
subretinal 362.16
Nephralgia 788.0
Nephritis, nephritic (albuminuric) (azotemic) (congenital) (degenerative) (diffuse) (disseminated) (epithelial) (familial) (focal) (granulomatous) (hemorrhagic) (infantile) (nonsuppurative, excretory) (uremic) 583.9
with
edema — *see* Nephrosis
lesion of
glomerulonephritis
hypocomplementemic persistent 583.2
with nephrotic syndrome 581.2
chronic 582.2
lobular 583.2
with nephrotic syndrome 581.2
chronic 582.2
membranoproliferative 583.2
with nephrotic syndrome 581.2
chronic 582.2
membranous 583.1
with nephrotic syndrome 581.1
chronic 582.1
mesangiocapillary 583.2
with nephrotic syndrome 581.2
chronic 582.2
mixed membranous and proliferative 583.2
with nephrotic syndrome 581.2
chronic 582.2
proliferative (diffuse) 583.0
with nephrotic syndrome 581.0
acute 580.0
chronic 582.0
rapidly progressive 583.4
acute 580.4
chronic 582.4
interstitial nephritis (diffuse) (focal) 583.89
with nephrotic syndrome 581.89
acute 580.89
chronic 582.89
necrotizing glomerulitis 583.4
acute 580.4
chronic 582.4
renal necrosis 583.9
cortical 583.6
medullary 583.7
specified pathology NEC 583.89
with nephrotic syndrome 581.89
acute 580.89
chronic 582.89
necrosis, renal 583.9
cortical 583.6
medullary (papillary) 583.7
nephrotic syndrome (*see also* Nephrosis) 581.9
papillary necrosis 583.7
specified pathology NEC 583.89
acute 580.9
extracapillary with epithelial crescents 580.4
hypertensive (*see also* Hypertension, kidney) 403.90
necrotizing 580.4
poststreptococcal 580.0

Nephritis, nephritic — *continued*
acute — *continued*
proliferative (diffuse) 580.0
rapidly progressive 580.4
specified pathology NEC 580.89
amyloid 277.39 *[583.81]*
chronic 277.39 *[582.81]*
arteriolar (*see also* Hypertension, kidney) 403.90
arteriosclerotic (*see also* Hypertension, kidney) 403.90
ascending (*see also* Pyelitis) 590.80
atrophic 582.9
basement membrane NEC 583.89
with
pulmonary hemorrhage (Goodpasture's syndrome) 446.21 *[583.81]*
calculous, calculus 592.0
cardiac (*see also* Hypertension, kidney) 403.90
cardiovascular (*see also* Hypertension, kidney) 403.90
chronic 582.9
arteriosclerotic (*see also* Hypertension, kidney) 403.90
hypertensive (*see also* Hypertension, kidney) 403.90
cirrhotic (*see also* Sclerosis, renal) 587
complicating pregnancy, childbirth, or puerperium 646.2 ☑
with hypertension 642.1 ☑
affecting fetus or newborn 760.0
affecting fetus or newborn 760.1
croupous 580.9
desquamative — *see* Nephrosis
due to
amyloidosis 277.39 *[583.81]*
chronic 277.39 *[582.81]*
arteriosclerosis (*see also* Hypertension, kidney) 403.90
diabetes mellitus 250.4 ☑ *[583.81]*
with nephrotic syndrome 250.4 ☑ *[581.81]*
due to secondary diabetes ●
249.4 ☑ *[581.81]* ●
due to secondary diabetes ●
249.4 ☑ *[581.81]* ●
diphtheria 032.89 *[580.81]*
gonococcal infection (acute) 098.19 *[583.81]*
chronic or duration of 2 months or over 098.39 *[583.81]*
gout 274.10
infectious hepatitis 070.9 *[580.81]*
mumps 072.79 *[580.81]*
specified kidney pathology NEC 583.89
acute 580.89
chronic 582.89
streptotrichosis 039.8 *[583.81]*
subacute bacterial endocarditis 421.0 *[580.81]*
systemic lupus erythematosus 710.0 *[583.81]*
chronic 710.0 *[582.81]*
typhoid fever 002.0 *[580.81]*
endothelial 582.2
end stage (chronic) (terminal) NEC 585.6
epimembranous 581.1
exudative 583.89
with nephrotic syndrome 581.89
acute 580.89
chronic 582.89
gonococcal (acute) 098.19 *[583.81]*
chronic or duration of 2 months or over 098.39 *[583.81]*
gouty 274.10
hereditary (Alport's syndrome) 759.89
hydremic — *see* Nephrosis
hypertensive (*see also* Hypertension, kidney) 403.90
hypocomplementemic persistent 583.2
with nephrotic syndrome 581.2
chronic 582.2

Nephritis, nephritic — *continued*
immune complex NEC 583.89
infective (*see also* Pyelitis) 590.80
interstitial (diffuse) (focal) 583.89
with nephrotic syndrome 581.89
acute 580.89
chronic 582.89
latent or quiescent — *see* Nephritis, chronic
lead 984.9
specified type of lead — *see* Table of Drugs and Chemicals
lobular 583.2
with nephrotic syndrome 581.2
chronic 582.2
lupus 710.0 *[583.81]*
acute 710.0 *[580.81]*
chronic 710.0 *[582.81]*
membranoproliferative 583.2
with nephrotic syndrome 581.2
chronic 582.2
membranous 583.1
with nephrotic syndrome 581.1
chronic 582.1
mesangiocapillary 583.2
with nephrotic syndrome 581.2
chronic 582.2
minimal change 581.3
mixed membranous and proliferative 583.2
with nephrotic syndrome 581.2
chronic 582.2
necrotic, necrotizing 583.4
acute 580.4
chronic 582.4
nephrotic — *see* Nephrosis
old — *see* Nephritis, chronic
parenchymatous 581.89
polycystic 753.12
adult type (APKD) 753.13
autosomal dominant 753.13
autosomal recessive 753.14
childhood type (CPKD) 753.14
infantile type 753.14
poststreptococcal 580.0
pregnancy — *see* Nephritis, complicating pregnancy
proliferative 583.0
with nephrotic syndrome 581.0
acute 580.0
chronic 582.0
purulent (*see also* Pyelitis) 590.80
rapidly progressive 583.4
acute 580.4
chronic 582.4
salt-losing or salt-wasting (*see also* Disease, renal) 593.9
saturnine 984.9
specified type of lead — *see* Table of Drugs and Chemicals
septic (*see also* Pyelitis) 590.80
specified pathology NEC 583.89
acute 580.89
chronic 582.89
staphylococcal (*see also* Pyelitis) 590.80
streptotrichosis 039.8 *[583.81]*
subacute (*see also* Nephrosis) 581.9
suppurative (*see also* Pyelitis) 590.80
syphilitic (late) 095.4
congenital 090.5 *[583.81]*
early 091.69 *[583.81]*
terminal (chronic) (end-stage) NEC 585.6
toxic — *see* Nephritis, acute
tubal, tubular — *see* Nephrosis, tubular
tuberculous (*see also* Tuberculosis) 016.0 ☑ *[583.81]*
type II (Ellis) — *see* Nephrosis
vascular — *see* Hypertension, kidney
war 580.9
Nephroblastoma (M8960/3) 189.0
epithelial (M8961/3) 189.0
mesenchymal (M8962/3) 189.0
Nephrocalcinosis 275.49

Nephrocystitis, pustular — *see also* Pyelitis 590.80
Nephrolithiasis (congenital) (pelvis) (recurrent) 592.0
uric acid 274.11
Nephroma (M8960/3) 189.0
mesoblastic (M8960/1) 236.9 ☑
Nephronephritis — *see also* Nephrosis 581.9
Nephronopthisis 753.16
Nephropathy — *see also* Nephritis 583.9
with
exudative nephritis 583.89
interstitial nephritis (diffuse) (focal) 583.89
medullary necrosis 583.7
necrosis 583.9
cortical 583.6
medullary or papillary 583.7
papillary necrosis 583.7
specified lesion or cause NEC 583.89
analgesic 583.89
with medullary necrosis, acute 584.7
arteriolar (*see also* Hypertension, kidney) 403.90
arteriosclerotic (*see also* Hypertension, kidney) 403.90
complicating pregnancy 646.2 ☑
diabetic 250.4 ☑ *[583.81]*
due to secondary diabetes ●
249.4 ☑ *[581.81]* ●
gouty 274.10
specified type NEC 274.19
hereditary amyloid 277.31
hypercalcemic 588.89
hypertensive (*see also* Hypertension, kidney) 403.90
hypokalemic (vacuolar) 588.89
IgA 583.9
obstructive 593.89
congenital 753.20
phenacetin 584.7
phosphate-losing 588.0
potassium depletion 588.89
proliferative (*see also* Nephritis, proliferative) 583.0
protein-losing 588.89
salt-losing or salt-wasting (*see also* Disease, renal) 593.9
sickle-cell (*see also* Disease, sickle-cell) 282.60 *[583.81]*
toxic 584.5
vasomotor 584.5
water-losing 588.89
Nephroptosis — *see also* Disease, renal 593.0
congenital (displaced) 753.3
Nephropyosis — *see also* Abscess, kidney 590.2
Nephrorrhagia 593.81
Nephrosclerosis (arteriolar) (arteriosclerotic) (chronic) (hyaline) — *see also* Hypertension, kidney 403.90
gouty 274.10
hyperplastic (arteriolar) (*see also* Hypertension, kidney) 403.90
senile (*see also* Sclerosis, renal) 587
Nephrosis, nephrotic (Epstein's) (syndrome) 581.9
with
lesion of
focal glomerulosclerosis 581.1
glomerulonephritis
endothelial 581.2
hypocomplementemic persistent 581.2
lobular 581.2
membranoproliferative 581.2
membranous 581.1
mesangiocapillary 581.2
minimal change 581.3
mixed membranous and proliferative 581.2
proliferative 581.0

- **Nephrosis, nephrotic** — *continued*
  - with — *continued*
    - lesion of — *continued*
      - segmental hyalinosis 581.1
      - specified pathology NEC 581.89
  - acute — *see* Nephrosis, tubular
  - anoxic — *see* Nephrosis, tubular
  - arteriosclerotic (*see also* Hypertension, kidney) 403.90
  - chemical — *see* Nephrosis, tubular
  - cholemic 572.4
  - complicating pregnancy, childbirth, or puerperium — *see* Nephritis, complicating pregnancy
  - diabetic 250.4 ☑ *[581.81]*
    - due to secondary diabetes ●
      - 249.4 ☑ *[581.81]* ●
  - Finnish type (congenital) 759.89
  - hemoglobinuric — *see* Nephrosis, tubular
  - in
    - amyloidosis 277.39 *[581.81]*
    - diabetes mellitus 250.4 ☑ *[581.81]*
      - due to secondary diabetes ●
        - 249.4 ☑ *[581.81]* ●
    - epidemic hemorrhagic fever 078.6
    - malaria 084.9 *[581.81]*
    - polyarteritis 446.0 *[581.81]*
    - systemic lupus erythematosus 710.0 *[581.81]*
  - ischemic — *see* Nephrosis, tubular
  - lipoid 581.3
  - lower nephron — *see* Nephrosis, tubular
  - lupoid 710.0 *[581.81]*
  - lupus 710.0 *[581.81]*
  - malarial 084.9 *[581.81]*
  - minimal change 581.3
  - necrotizing — *see* Nephrosis, tubular
  - osmotic (sucrose) 588.89
  - polyarteritic 446.0 *[581.81]*
  - radiation 581.9
  - specified lesion or cause NEC 581.89
  - syphilitic 095.4
  - toxic — *see* Nephrosis, tubular
  - tubular (acute) 584.5
    - due to a procedure 997.5
    - radiation 581.9
- **Nephrosonephritis hemorrhagic** (endemic) 078.6
- **Nephrostomy status** V44.6
  - with complication 997.5
- **Nerve** — *see* condition
- **Nerves** 799.2
- **Nervous** — *see also* condition 799.2
  - breakdown 300.9
  - heart 306.2
  - stomach 306.4
  - tension 799.2
- **Nervousness** 799.2
- **Nesidioblastoma** (M8150/0)
  - pancreas 211.7
  - specified site NEC — *see* Neoplasm, by site, benign
  - unspecified site 211.7
- **Netherton's syndrome** (ichthyosiform erythroderma) 757.1
- **Nettle rash** 708.8
- **Nettleship's disease** (urticaria pigmentosa) 757.33
- **Neumann's disease** (pemphigus vegetans) 694.4
- **Neuralgia, neuralgic** (acute) — *see also* Neuritis 729.2
  - accessory (nerve) 352.4
  - acoustic (nerve) 388.5
  - ankle 355.8
  - anterior crural 355.8
  - anus 787.99
  - arm 723.4
  - auditory (nerve) 388.5
  - axilla 353.0
  - bladder 788.1
  - brachial 723.4
  - brain — *see* Disorder, nerve, cranial
  - broad ligament 625.9
- **Neuralgia, neuralgic** — *see also* Neuritis — *continued*
  - cerebral — *see* Disorder, nerve, cranial
  - ciliary 339.00 ▲
  - cranial nerve (*see also* Disorder, nerve, cranial)
    - fifth or trigeminal (*see also* Neuralgia, trigeminal) 350.1
  - ear 388.71
    - middle 352.1
  - facial 351.8
  - finger 354.9
  - flank 355.8
  - foot 355.8
  - forearm 354.9
  - Fothergill's (*see also* Neuralgia, trigeminal) 350.1
    - postherpetic 053.12
  - glossopharyngeal (nerve) 352.1
  - groin 355.8
  - hand 354.9
  - heel 355.8
  - Horton's 339.00 ▲
  - Hunt's 053.11
  - hypoglossal (nerve) 352.5
  - iliac region 355.8
  - infraorbital (*see also* Neuralgia, trigeminal) 350.1
  - inguinal 355.8
  - intercostal (nerve) 353.8
    - postherpetic 053.19
  - jaw 352.1
  - kidney 788.0
  - knee 355.8
  - loin 355.8
  - malarial (*see also* Malaria) 084.6
  - mastoid 385.89
  - maxilla 352.1
  - median thenar 354.1
  - metatarsal 355.6
  - middle ear 352.1
  - migrainous 339.00 ▲
  - Morton's 355.6
  - nerve, cranial — *see* Disorder, nerve, cranial
  - nose 352.0
  - occipital 723.8
  - olfactory (nerve) 352.0
  - ophthalmic 377.30
    - postherpetic 053.19
  - optic (nerve) 377.30
  - penis 607.9
  - perineum 355.8
  - pleura 511.0
  - postherpetic NEC 053.19
    - geniculate ganglion 053.11
    - ophthalmic 053.19
    - trifacial 053.12
    - trigeminal 053.12
  - pubic region 355.8
  - radial (nerve) 723.4
  - rectum 787.99
  - sacroiliac joint 724.3
  - sciatic (nerve) 724.3
  - scrotum 608.9
  - seminal vesicle 608.9
  - shoulder 354.9
  - Sluder's 337.09 ▲
  - specified nerve NEC — *see* Disorder, nerve
  - spermatic cord 608.9
  - sphenopalatine (ganglion) 337.09 ▲
  - subscapular (nerve) 723.4
  - suprascapular (nerve) 723.4
  - testis 608.89
  - thenar (median) 354.1
  - thigh 355.8
  - tongue 352.5
  - trifacial (nerve) (*see also* Neuralgia, trigeminal) 350.1
  - trigeminal (nerve) 350.1
    - postherpetic 053.12
  - tympanic plexus 388.71
  - ulnar (nerve) 723.4
  - vagus (nerve) 352.3
- **Neuralgia, neuralgic** — *see also* Neuritis — *continued*
  - wrist 354.9
  - writers' 300.89
    - organic 333.84
- **Neurapraxia** — *see* Injury, nerve, by site
- **Neurasthenia** 300.5
  - cardiac 306.2
  - gastric 306.4
  - heart 306.2
  - postfebrile 780.79
  - postviral 780.79
- **Neurilemmoma** (M9560/0) — *see also* Neoplasm, connective tissue, benign
  - acoustic (nerve) 225.1
  - malignant (M9560/3) (*see also* Neoplasm, connective tissue, malignant)
    - acoustic (nerve) 192.0
- **Neurilemmosarcoma** (M9560/3) — *see* Neoplasm, connective tissue, malignant
- **Neurilemoma** — *see* Neurilemmoma
- **Neurinoma** (M9560/0) — *see* Neurilemmoma
- **Neurinomatosis** (M9560/1) — *see also* Neoplasm, connective tissue, uncertain behavior
  - centralis 759.5
- **Neuritis** — *see also* Neuralgia 729.2
  - abducens (nerve) 378.54
  - accessory (nerve) 352.4
  - acoustic (nerve) 388.5
    - syphilitic 094.86
  - alcoholic 357.5
    - with psychosis 291.1
  - amyloid, any site 277.39 *[357.4]*
  - anterior crural 355.8
  - arising during pregnancy 646.4 ☑
  - arm 723.4
  - ascending 355.2
  - auditory (nerve) 388.5
  - brachial (nerve) NEC 723.4
    - due to displacement, intervertebral disc 722.0
  - cervical 723.4
  - chest (wall) 353.8
  - costal region 353.8
  - cranial nerve (*see also* Disorder, nerve, cranial)
    - first or olfactory 352.0
    - second or optic 377.30
    - third or oculomotor 378.52
    - fourth or trochlear 378.53
    - fifth or trigeminal (*see also* Neuralgia, trigeminal) 350.1
    - sixth or abducens 378.54
    - seventh or facial 351.8
      - newborn 767.5
    - eighth or acoustic 388.5
    - ninth or glossopharyngeal 352.1
    - tenth or vagus 352.3
    - eleventh or accessory 352.4
    - twelfth or hypoglossal 352.5
  - Déjérine-Sottas 356.0
  - diabetic 250.6 ☑ *[357.2]*
    - due to secondary diabetes ●
      - 249.6 ☑ *[357.2]* ●
  - diphtheritic 032.89 *[357.4]*
  - due to
    - beriberi 265.0 *[357.4]*
    - displacement, prolapse, protrusion, or rupture of intervertebral disc 722.2
      - cervical 722.0
      - lumbar, lumbosacral 722.10
      - thoracic, thoracolumbar 722.11
    - herniation, nucleus pulposus 722.2
      - cervical 722.0
      - lumbar, lumbosacral 722.10
      - thoracic, thoracolumbar 722.11
  - endemic 265.0 *[357.4]*
  - facial (nerve) 351.8
    - newborn 767.5
- **Neuritis** — *see also* Neuralgia — *continued*
  - general — *see* Polyneuropathy
  - geniculate ganglion 351.1
    - due to herpes 053.11
  - glossopharyngeal (nerve) 352.1
  - gouty 274.89 *[357.4]*
  - hypoglossal (nerve) 352.5
  - ilioinguinal (nerve) 355.8
  - in diseases classified elsewhere — *see* Polyneuropathy, in
  - infectious (multiple) 357.0
  - intercostal (nerve) 353.8
  - interstitial hypertrophic progressive NEC 356.9
  - leg 355.8
  - lumbosacral NEC 724.4
  - median (nerve) 354.1
    - thenar 354.1
  - multiple (acute) (infective) 356.9
    - endemic 265.0 *[357.4]*
  - multiplex endemica 265.0 *[357.4]*
  - nerve root (*see also* Radiculitis) 729.2
  - oculomotor (nerve) 378.52
  - olfactory (nerve) 352.0
  - optic (nerve) 377.30
    - in myelitis 341.0
    - meningococcal 036.81
  - pelvic 355.8
  - peripheral (nerve) (*see also* Neuropathy, peripheral)
    - complicating pregnancy or puerperium 646.4 ☑
    - specified nerve NEC — *see* Mononeuritis
  - pneumogastric (nerve) 352.3
  - postchickenpox 052.7
  - postherpetic 053.19
  - progressive hypertrophic interstitial NEC 356.9
  - puerperal, postpartum 646.4 ☑
  - radial (nerve) 723.4
  - retrobulbar 377.32
    - syphilitic 094.85
  - rheumatic (chronic) 729.2
  - sacral region 355.8
  - sciatic (nerve) 724.3
    - due to displacement of intervertebral disc 722.10
  - serum 999.5
  - specified nerve NEC — *see* Disorder, nerve
  - spinal (nerve) 355.9
    - root (*see also* Radiculitis) 729.2
  - subscapular (nerve) 723.4
  - suprascapular (nerve) 723.4
  - syphilitic 095.8
  - thenar (median) 354.1
  - thoracic NEC 724.4
  - toxic NEC 357.7
  - trochlear (nerve) 378.53
  - ulnar (nerve) 723.4
  - vagus (nerve) 352.3
- **Neuroangiomatosis, encephalofacial** 759.6
- **Neuroastrocytoma** (M9505/1) — *see* Neoplasm, by site, uncertain behavior
- **Neuro-avitaminosis** 269.2
- **Neuroblastoma** (M9500/3)
  - olfactory (M9522/3) 160.0
  - specified site — *see* Neoplasm, by site, malignant
  - unspecified site 194.0
- **Neurochorioretinitis** — *see also* Chorioretinitis 363.20
- **Neurocirculatory asthenia** 306.2
- **Neurocytoma** (M9506/0) — *see* Neoplasm, by site, benign
- **Neurodermatitis** (circumscribed) (circumscripta) (local) 698.3
  - atopic 691.8
  - diffuse (Brocq) 691.8
  - disseminated 691.8
  - nodulosa 698.3

☑ Additional Digit Required — Refer to the Tabular List for Digit Selection

Subterms under main terms may continue to next column or page

▶◀ Revised Text ● New Line ▲ Revised Code

Neuroencephalomyelopathy, optic 341.0
Neuroendocrine tumor — *see* Tumor, neuroendocrine ●
Neuroepithelioma (M9503/3) — *see also* Neoplasm, by site, malignant
- olfactory (M9521/3) 160.0

Neurofibroma (M9540/0) — *see also* Neoplasm, connective tissue, benign
- melanotic (M9541/0) — *see* Neoplasm, connective tissue, benign
- multiple (M9540/1) 237.70
  - type 1 237.71
  - type 2 237.72
- plexiform (M9550/0) — *see* Neoplasm, connective tissue, benign

Neurofibromatosis (multiple) (M9540/1) 237.70
- acoustic 237.72
- malignant (M9540/3) — *see* Neoplasm, connective tissue, malignant
- type 1 237.71
- type 2 237.72
- von Recklinghausen's 237.71

Neurofibrosarcoma (M9540/3) — *see* Neoplasm, connective tissue, malignant
Neurogenic — *see also* condition
- bladder (atonic) (automatic) (autonomic) (flaccid) (hypertonic) (hypotonic) (inertia) (infranuclear) (irritable) (motor) (nonreflex) (nuclear) (paralysis) (reflex) (sensory) (spastic) (supranuclear) (uninhibited) 596.54
  - with cauda equina syndrome 344.61
- bowel 564.81
- heart 306.2

Neuroglioma (M9505/1) — *see* Neoplasm, by site, uncertain behavior
Neurolabyrinthitis (of Dix and Hallpike) 386.12
Neurolathyrism 988.2
Neuroleprosy 030.1
Neuroleptic malignant syndrome 333.92
Neurolipomatosis 272.8
Neuroma (M9570/0) — *see also* Neoplasm, connective tissue, benign
- acoustic (nerve) (M9560/0) 225.1
- amputation (traumatic) (*see also* Injury, nerve, by site)
  - surgical complication (late) 997.61
- appendix 211.3
- auditory nerve 225.1
- digital 355.6
  - toe 355.6
- interdigital (toe) 355.6
- intermetatarsal 355.6
- Morton's 355.6
- multiple 237.70
  - type 1 237.71
  - type 2 237.72
- nonneoplastic 355.9
  - arm NEC 354.9
  - leg NEC 355.8
  - lower extremity NEC 355.8
  - specified site NEC — *see* Mononeuritis, by site
  - upper extremity NEC 354.9
- optic (nerve) 225.1
- plantar 355.6
- plexiform (M9550/0) — *see* Neoplasm, connective tissue, benign
- surgical (nonneoplastic) 355.9
  - arm NEC 354.9
  - leg NEC 355.8
  - lower extremity NEC 355.8
  - upper extremity NEC 354.9
- traumatic (*see also* Injury, nerve, by site)
  - old — *see* Neuroma, nonneoplastic

Neuromyalgia 729.1
Neuromyasthenia (epidemic) 049.8
Neuromyelitis 341.8
- ascending 357.0
- optica 341.0

Neuromyopathy NEC 358.9
Neuromyositis 729.1
Neuronevus (M8725/0) — *see* Neoplasm, skin, benign
Neuronitis 357.0
- ascending (acute) 355.2
- vestibular 386.12

Neuroparalytic — *see* condition
Neuropathy, neuropathic — *see also* Disorder, nerve 355.9
- acute motor 357.82
- alcoholic 357.5
  - with psychosis 291.1
- arm NEC 354.9
- ataxia and retinitis pigmentosa (NARP syndrome) 277.87
- autonomic (peripheral) — *see* Neuropathy, peripheral, autonomic
- axillary nerve 353.0
- brachial plexus 353.0
- cervical plexus 353.2
- chronic
  - progressive segmentally demyelinating 357.89
  - relapsing demyelinating 357.89
- congenital sensory 356.2
- Déjérine-Sottas 356.0
- diabetic 250.6 ☑ *[357.2]*
  - due to secondary diabetes 249.6 ☑ *[357.2]* ●
- entrapment 355.9
  - iliohypogastric nerve 355.79
  - ilioinguinal nerve 355.79
  - lateral cutaneous nerve of thigh 355.1
  - median nerve 354.0
  - obturator nerve 355.79
  - peroneal nerve 355.3
  - posterior tibial nerve 355.5
  - saphenous nerve 355.79
  - ulnar nerve 354.2
- facial nerve 351.9
- hereditary 356.9
  - peripheral 356.0
  - sensory (radicular) 356.2
- hypertrophic
  - Charcôt-Marie-Tooth 356.1
  - Déjérine-Sottas 356.0
  - interstitial 356.9
  - Refsum 356.3
- intercostal nerve 354.8
- ischemic — *see* Disorder, nerve
- Jamaican (ginger) 357.7
- leg NEC 355.8
- lower extremity NEC 355.8
- lumbar plexus 353.1
- median nerve 354.1
- motor
  - acute 357.82
- multiple (acute) (chronic) (*see also* Polyneuropathy) 356.9
- optic 377.39
  - ischemic 377.41
  - nutritional 377.33
  - toxic 377.34
- peripheral (nerve) (*see also* Polyneuropathy) 356.9
  - arm NEC 354.9
  - autonomic 337.9
    - amyloid 277.39 *[337.1]*
    - idiopathic 337.00 ▲
    - in
      - amyloidosis 277.39 *[337.1]*
      - diabetes (mellitus) 250.6 ☑ *[337.1]*
        - due to secondary diabetes 249.6 ☑ *[337.1]* ●
      - diseases classified elsewhere 337.1
      - gout 274.89 *[337.1]*

Neuropathy, neuropathic — *see also* Disorder, nerve — *continued*
- peripheral (*see also* Polyneuropathy) — *continued*
  - autonomic — *continued*
    - in — *continued*
      - hyperthyroidism 242.9 ☑ *[337.1]*
  - due to
    - antitetanus serum 357.6
    - arsenic 357.7
    - drugs 357.6
    - lead 357.7
    - organophosphate compounds 357.7
    - toxic agent NEC 357.7
  - hereditary 356.0
  - idiopathic 356.9
    - progressive 356.4
    - specified type NEC 356.8
  - in diseases classified elsewhere — *see* Polyneuropathy, in
  - leg NEC 355.8
  - lower extremity NEC 355.8
  - upper extremity NEC 354.9
- plantar nerves 355.6
- progressive hypertrophic interstitial 356.9
- radicular NEC 729.2
  - brachial 723.4
  - cervical NEC 723.4
  - hereditary sensory 356.2
  - lumbar 724.4
  - lumbosacral 724.4
  - thoracic NEC 724.4
- sacral plexus 353.1
- sciatic 355.0
- spinal nerve NEC 355.9
  - root (*see also* Radiculitis) 729.2
- toxic 357.7
- trigeminal sensory 350.8
- ulnar nerve 354.2
- upper extremity NEC 354.9
- uremic 585.9 *[357.4]*
- vitamin B_{12} 266.2 *[357.4]*
  - with anemia (pernicious) 281.0 *[357.4]*
    - due to dietary deficiency 281.1 *[357.4]*

Neurophthisis — *see also* Disorder, nerve
- diabetic 250.6 ☑ *[357.2]*
  - due to secondary diabetes 249.6 ☑ *[357.2]* ●
- peripheral 356.9

Neuropraxia — *see* Injury, nerve
Neuroretinitis 363.05
- syphilitic 094.85

Neurosarcoma (M9540/3) — *see* Neoplasm, connective tissue, malignant
Neurosclerosis — *see* Disorder, nerve
Neurosis, neurotic 300.9
- accident 300.16
- anancastic, anankastic 300.3
- anxiety (state) 300.00
  - generalized 300.02
  - panic type 300.01
- asthenic 300.5
- bladder 306.53
- cardiac (reflex) 306.2
- cardiovascular 306.2
- climacteric, unspecified type 627.2
- colon 306.4
- compensation 300.16
- compulsive, compulsion 300.3
- conversion 300.11
- craft 300.89
- cutaneous 306.3
- depersonalization 300.6
- depressive (reaction) (type) 300.4
- endocrine 306.6
- environmental 300.89
- fatigue 300.5
- functional (*see also* Disorder, psychosomatic) 306.9

Neurosis, neurotic — *continued*
- gastric 306.4
- gastrointestinal 306.4
- genitourinary 306.50
- heart 306.2
- hypochondriacal 300.7
- hysterical 300.10
  - conversion type 300.11
  - dissociative type 300.15
- impulsive 300.3
- incoordination 306.0
  - larynx 306.1
  - vocal cord 306.1
- intestine 306.4
- larynx 306.1
  - hysterical 300.11
  - sensory 306.1
- menopause, unspecified type 627.2
- mixed NEC 300.89
- musculoskeletal 306.0
- obsessional 300.3
  - phobia 300.3
- obsessive-compulsive 300.3
- occupational 300.89
- ocular 306.7
- oral 307.0
- organ (*see also* Disorder, psychosomatic) 306.9
- pharynx 306.1
- phobic 300.20
- posttraumatic (acute) (situational) 309.81
  - chronic 309.81
- psychasthenic (type) 300.89
- railroad 300.16
- rectum 306.4
- respiratory 306.1
- rumination 306.4
- senile 300.89
- sexual 302.70
- situational 300.89
- specified type NEC 300.89
- state 300.9
  - with depersonalization episode 300.6
- stomach 306.4
- vasomotor 306.2
- visceral 306.4
- war 300.16

Neurospongioblastosis diffusa 759.5
Neurosyphilis (arrested) (early) (inactive) (late) (latent) (recurrent) 094.9
- with ataxia (cerebellar) (locomotor) (spastic) (spinal) 094.0
- acute meningitis 094.2
- aneurysm 094.89
- arachnoid (adhesive) 094.2
- arteritis (any artery) 094.89
- asymptomatic 094.3
- congenital 090.40
- dura (mater) 094.89
- general paresis 094.1
- gumma 094.9
- hemorrhagic 094.9
- juvenile (asymptomatic) (meningeal) 090.40
- leptomeninges (aseptic) 094.2
- meningeal 094.2
- meninges (adhesive) 094.2
- meningovascular (diffuse) 094.2
- optic atrophy 094.84
- parenchymatous (degenerative) 094.1
- paresis (*see also* Paresis, general) 094.1
- paretic (*see also* Paresis, general) 094.1
- relapse 094.9
- remission in (sustained) 094.9
- serological 094.3
- specified nature or site NEC 094.89
- tabes (dorsalis) 094.0
  - juvenile 090.40
- tabetic 094.0
  - juvenile 090.40
- taboparesis 094.1
  - juvenile 090.40

Neurosyphilis — *continued*
- thrombosis 094.89
- vascular 094.89

Neurotic — *see also* Neurosis 300.9
- excoriation 698.4
  - psychogenic 306.3

Neurotmesis — *see* Injury, nerve, by site
Neurotoxemia — *see* Toxemia
Neutro-occlusion 524.21
Neutropenia, neutropenic (idiopathic) (pernicious) (primary) 288.00
- chronic 288.09
  - hypoplastic 288.09
- congenital (nontransient) 288.01
- cyclic 288.02
- drug induced 288.03
- due to infection 288.04
- fever 288.00
- genetic 288.01
- immune 288.09
- infantile 288.01
- malignant 288.09
- neonatal, transitory (isoimmune) (maternal transfer) 776.7
- periodic 288.02
- splenic 289.53
- splenomegaly 289.53
- toxic 288.09

Neutrophilia, hereditary giant 288.2
Nevocarcinoma (M8720/3) — *see* Melanoma
Nevus (M8720/0) — *see also* Neoplasm, skin, benign

> *Note — Except where otherwise indicated, varieties of nevus in the list below that are followed by a morphology code number (M----/0) should be coded by site as for "Neoplasm, skin, benign."*

- acanthotic 702.8
- achromic (M8730/0)
- amelanotic (M8730/0)
- anemic, anemicus 709.09
- angiomatous (M9120/0) (*see also* Hemangioma) 228.00
- araneus 448.1
- avasculosus 709.09
- balloon cell (M8722/0)
- bathing trunk (M8761/1) 238.2
- blue (M8780/0)
  - cellular (M8790/0)
  - giant (M8790/0)
  - Jadassohn's (M8780/0)
  - malignant (M8780/3) — *see* Melanoma
- capillary (M9131/0) (*see also* Hemangioma) 228.00
- cavernous (M9121/0) (*see also* Hemangioma) 228.00
- cellular (M8720/0)
  - blue (M8790/0)
- comedonicus 757.33
- compound (M8760/0)
- conjunctiva (M8720/0) 224.3
- dermal (M8750/0)
  - and epidermal (M8760/0)
- epithelioid cell (and spindle cell) (M8770/0)
- flammeus 757.32
  - osteohypertrophic 759.89
- hairy (M8720/0)
- halo (M8723/0)
- hemangiomatous (M9120/0) (*see also* Hemangioma) 228.00
- intradermal (M8750/0)
- intraepidermal (M8740/0)
- involuting (M8724/0)
- Jadassohn's (blue) (M8780/0)
- junction, junctional (M8740/0)
  - malignant melanoma in (M8740/3) — *see* Melanoma
- juvenile (M8770/0)
- lymphatic (M9170/0) 228.1
- magnocellular (M8726/0)
  - specified site — *see* Neoplasm, by site, benign
  - unspecified site 224.0

Nevus — *see also* Neoplasm, skin, benign — *continued*
- malignant (M8720/3) — *see* Melanoma
- meaning hemangioma (M9120/0) (*see also* Hemangioma) 228.00
- melanotic (pigmented) (M8720/0)
- multiplex 759.5
- nonneoplastic 448.1
- nonpigmented (M8730/0)
- nonvascular (M8720/0)
- oral mucosa, white sponge 750.26
- osteohypertrophic, flammeus 759.89
- papillaris (M8720/0)
- papillomatosus (M8720/0)
- pigmented (M8720/0)
  - giant (M8761/1) (*see also* Neoplasm, skin, uncertain behavior)
    - malignant melanoma in (M8761/3) — *see* Melanoma
  - systematicus 757.33
- pilosus (M8720/0)
- port wine 757.32
- sanguineous 757.32
- sebaceous (senile) 702.8
- senile 448.1
- spider 448.1
- spindle cell (and epithelioid cell) (M8770/0)
- stellar 448.1
- strawberry 757.32
- syringocystadenomatous papilliferous (M8406/0)
- unius lateris 757.33
- Unna's 757.32
- vascular 757.32
- verrucous 757.33
- white sponge (oral mucosa) 750.26

Newborn (infant) (liveborn)
- affected by
  - amniocentesis 760.61 ●
  - maternal abuse of drugs (gestational) (via placenta) (via breast milk) (*see also* Noxious, substances transmitted through placenta or breast milk (affecting fetus or newborn)) 760.70 ●
    - methamphetamine(s) 760.72 ●
  - procedure ●
    - amniocentesis 760.61 ●
    - in utero NEC 760.62 ●
    - surgical on mother ●
      - during pregnancy NEC 760.63 ●
      - previous not associated with pregnancy 760.64 ●
- apnea 770.81
  - obstructive 770.82
  - specified NEC 770.82
- breast buds 779.89 ●
- cardiomyopathy 425.4
  - congenital 425.3
- convulsion 779.0
- electrolyte imbalance NEC (transitory) 775.5
- fever (environmentally-induced) 778.4 ●
- gestation
  - 24 completed weeks 765.22
  - 25-26 completed weeks 765.23
  - 27-28 completed weeks 765.24
  - 29-30 completed weeks 765.25
  - 31-32 completed weeks 765.26
  - 33-34 completed weeks 765.27
  - 35-36 completed weeks 765.28
  - 37 or more completed weeks 765.29
  - less than 24 completed weeks 765.21
  - unspecified completed weeks 765.20
- infection 771.89

Newborn — *continued*
- infection — *continued*
  - candida 771.7
  - mastitis 771.5
  - specified NEC 771.89
  - urinary tract 771.82
- mastitis 771.5
- multiple NEC
  - born in hospital (without mention of cesarean delivery or section) V37.00
    - with cesarean delivery or section V37.01
  - born outside hospital
    - hospitalized V37.1
    - not hospitalized V37.2
  - mates all liveborn
    - born in hospital (without mention of cesarean delivery or section) V34.00
      - with cesarean delivery or section V34.01
    - born outside hospital
      - hospitalized V34.1
      - not hospitalized V34.2
  - mates all stillborn
    - born in hospital (without mention of cesarean delivery or section) V35.00
      - with cesarean delivery or section V35.01
    - born outside hospital
      - hospitalized V35.1
      - not hospitalized V35.2
  - mates liveborn and stillborn
    - born in hospital (without mention of cesarean delivery or section) V36.00
      - with cesarean delivery or section V36.01
    - born outside hospital
      - hospitalized V36.1
      - not hospitalized V36.2
- omphalitis 771.4
- seizure 779.0
- sepsis 771.81
- single
  - born in hospital (without mention of cesarean delivery or section) V30.00
    - with cesarean delivery or section V30.01
  - born outside hospital
    - hospitalized V30.1
    - not hospitalized V30.2
- specified condition NEC 779.89
- twin NEC
  - born in hospital (without mention of cesarean delivery or section) V33.00
    - with cesarean delivery or section V33.01
  - born outside hospital
    - hospitalized V33.1
    - not hospitalized V33.2
  - mate liveborn
    - born in hospital V31.0 ☑
    - born outside hospital
      - hospitalized V31.1
      - not hospitalized V31.2
  - mate stillborn
    - born in hospital V32.0 ☑
    - born outside hospital
      - hospitalized V32.1
      - not hospitalized V32.2
- unspecified as to single or multiple birth
  - born in hospital (without mention of cesarean delivery or section) V39.00
    - with cesarean delivery or section V39.01
  - born outside hospital
    - hospitalized V39.1
    - not hospitalized V39.2

Newcastle's conjunctivitis or disease 077.8
Nezelof's syndrome (pure alymphocytosis) 279.13
Niacin (amide) **deficiency** 265.2
Nicolas-Durand-Favre disease (climatic bubo) 099.1
Nicolas-Favre disease (climatic bubo) 099.1
Nicotinic acid (amide) **deficiency** 265.2
Niemann-Pick disease (lipid histiocytosis) (splenomegaly) 272.7
Night
- blindness (*see also* Blindness, night) 368.60
  - congenital 368.61
  - vitamin A deficiency 264.5
- cramps 729.82
- sweats 780.8
- terrors, child 307.46

Nightmare 307.47
- REM-sleep type 307.47

Nipple — *see* condition
Nisbet's chancre 099.0
Nishimoto (-Takeuchi) disease 437.5
Nitritoid crisis or reaction — *see* Crisis, nitritoid
Nitrogen retention, extrarenal 788.99 ▲
Nitrosohemoglobinemia 289.89
Njovera 104.0
No
- diagnosis 799.9
- disease (found) V71.9
- room at the inn V65.0

Nocardiasis — *see* Nocardiosis
Nocardiosis 039.9
- with pneumonia 039.1
- lung 039.1
- specified type NEC 039.8

Nocturia 788.43
- psychogenic 306.53

Nocturnal — *see also* condition
- dyspnea (paroxysmal) 786.09
- emissions 608.89
- enuresis 788.36
  - psychogenic 307.6
- frequency (micturition) 788.43
  - psychogenic 306.53

Nodal rhythm disorder 427.89
Nodding of head 781.0
Node(s) — *see also* Nodule(s)
- Heberden's 715.04
- larynx 478.79
- lymph — *see* condition
- milkers' 051.1
- Osler's 421.0
- rheumatic 729.89
- Schmorl's 722.30
  - lumbar, lumbosacral 722.32
  - specified region NEC 722.39
  - thoracic, thoracolumbar 722.31
- singers' 478.5
- skin NEC 782.2
- tuberculous — *see* Tuberculosis, lymph gland
- vocal cords 478.5

Nodosities, Haygarth's 715.04
Nodule(s), nodular
- actinomycotic (*see also* Actinomycosis) 039.9
- arthritic — *see* Arthritis, nodosa
- breast 793.89 ●
- cutaneous 782.2
- Haygarth's 715.04
- inflammatory — *see* Inflammation
- juxta-articular 102.7
  - syphilitic 095.7
  - yaws 102.7
- larynx 478.79
- lung, solitary 518.89
  - emphysematous 492.8
- milkers' 051.1
- prostate 600.10

Nodule(s), nodular — *continued*
prostate — *continued*
with
urinary
obstruction 600.11
retention 600.11
retrocardiac 785.9 ●
rheumatic 729.89
rheumatoid — *see* Arthritis, rheumatoid
scrotum (inflammatory) 608.4
singers' 478.5
skin NEC 782.2
solitary, lung 518.89
emphysematous 492.8
subcutaneous 782.2
thyroid (gland) (nontoxic) (uninodular) 241.0
with
hyperthyroidism 242.1 ☑
thyrotoxicosis 242.1 ☑
toxic or with hyperthyroidism 242.1 ☑
vocal cords 478.5
Noma (gangrenous) (hospital) (infective) 528.1
auricle (*see also* Gangrene) 785.4
mouth 528.1
pudendi (*see also* Vulvitis) 616.10
vulvae (*see also* Vulvitis) 616.10
Nomadism V60.0
Non-adherence
artificial skin graft 996.55
decellularized allodermis graft 996.55
Non-autoimmune hemolytic anemia NEC 283.10
Nonclosure — *see also* Imperfect, closure
ductus
arteriosus 747.0
Botalli 747.0
Eustachian valve 746.89
foramen
Botalli 745.5
ovale 745.5
Noncompliance with medical treatment V15.81
renal dialysis V45.12 ●
Nondescent (congenital) — *see also* Malposition, congenital
cecum 751.4
colon 751.4
testis 752.51
Nondevelopment
brain 742.1
specified part 742.2
heart 746.89
organ or site, congenital NEC — *see* Hypoplasia
Nonengagement
head NEC 652.5 ☑
in labor 660.1 ☑
affecting fetus or newborn 763.1
Nonexanthematous tick fever 066.1
Nonexpansion, lung (newborn) NEC 770.4
Nonfunctioning
cystic duct (*see also* Disease, gallbladder) 575.8
gallbladder (*see also* Disease, gallbladder) 575.8
kidney (*see also* Disease, renal) 593.9
labyrinth 386.58
Nonhealing
stump (surgical) 997.69
wound, surgical 998.83
Nonimplantation of ovum, causing infertility 628.3
Noninsufflation, fallopian tube 628.2
Nonne-Milroy-Meige syndrome (chronic hereditary edema) 757.0
Nonovulation 628.0
Nonpatent fallopian tube 628.2
Nonpneumatization, lung NEC 770.4
Nonreflex bladder 596.54
with cauda equina 344.61
Nonretention of food — *see* Vomiting
Nonrotation — *see* Malrotation
Nonsecretion, urine — *see also* Anuria 788.5
newborn 753.3
Nonunion
fracture 733.82
organ or site, congenital NEC — *see* Imperfect, closure
symphysis pubis, congenital 755.69
top sacrum, congenital 756.19
Nonviability 765.0 ☑
Nonvisualization, gallbladder 793.3
Nonvitalized tooth 522.9
Non-working side interference 524.56
Normal
delivery — *see* category 650
menses V65.5
state (feared complaint unfounded) V65.5
Normoblastosis 289.89
Normocytic anemia (infectional) 285.9
due to blood loss (chronic) 280.0
acute 285.1
Norrie's disease (congenital) (progressive oculoacousticocerebral degeneration) 743.8
North American blastomycosis 116.0
Norwegian itch 133.0
Nosebleed 784.7
Nose, nasal — *see* condition
Nosomania 298.9
Nosophobia 300.29
Nostalgia 309.89
Notched lip, congenital — *see also* Cleft, lip 749.10
Notching nose, congenital (tip) 748.1
Notch of iris 743.46
Nothnagel's
syndrome 378.52
vasomotor acroparesthesia 443.89
Novy's relapsing fever (American) 087.1
Noxious
foodstuffs, poisoning by
fish 988.0
fungi 988.1
mushrooms 988.1
plants (food) 988.2
shellfish 988.0
specified type NEC 988.8
toadstool 988.1
substances transmitted through placenta or breast milk (affecting fetus or newborn) 760.70
acetretin 760.78
alcohol 760.71
aminopterin 760.78
antiandrogens 760.79
anticonvulsant 760.77
antifungal 760.74
anti-infective agents 760.74
antimetabolic 760.78
atorvastatin 760.78
carbamazepine 760.77
cocaine 760.75
"crack" 760.75
diethylstilbestrol (DES) 760.76
divalproex sodium 760.77
endocrine disrupting chemicals 760.79
estrogens 760.79
etretinate 760.78
fluconazole 760.74
fluvastatin 760.78
hallucinogenic agents NEC 760.73
hormones 760.79
lithium 760.79
lovastatin 760.78
medicinal agents NEC 760.79
methotrexate 760.78
misoprostil 760.79
narcotics 760.72
obstetric anesthetic or analgesic 763.5
phenobarbital 760.77
phenytoin 760.77
pravastatin 760.78
progestins 760.79
retinoic acid 760.78
Noxious — *continued*
substances transmitted through placenta or breast milk — *continued*
simvastatin 760.78
solvents 760.79
specified agent NEC 760.79
statins 760.78
suspected, affecting management of pregnancy 655.5 ☑
tetracycline 760.74
thalidomide 760.79
trimethadione 760.77
valproate 760.77
valproic acid 760.77
vitamin A 760.78
NPDH (new persistent daily headache) 339.42 ●
Nuchal hitch (arm) 652.8 ☑
Nucleus pulposus — *see* condition
Numbness 782.0
Nuns' knee 727.2
Nursemaid's
elbow 832.0 ☑
shoulder 831.0 ☑
Nutmeg liver 573.8
Nutrition, deficient or insufficient (particular kind of food) 269.9
due to
insufficient food 994.2
lack of
care (child) (infant) 995.52
adult 995.84
food 994.2
Nyctalopia — *see also* Blindness, night 368.60
vitamin A deficiency 264.5
Nycturia 788.43
psychogenic 306.53
Nymphomania 302.89
Nystagmus 379.50
associated with vestibular system disorders 379.54
benign paroxysmal positional 386.11
central positional 386.2
congenital 379.51
deprivation 379.53
dissociated 379.55
latent 379.52
miners' 300.89
positional
benign paroxysmal 386.11
central 386.2
specified NEC 379.56
vestibular 379.54
visual deprivation 379.53

O

Oasthouse urine disease 270.2

Obermeyer's relapsing fever (European) 087.0

Obesity (constitutional) (exogenous) (familial) (nutritional) (simple) 278.00
- adrenal 255.8
- complicating pregnancy, childbirth, or puerperium 649.1 ☑
- due to hyperalimentation 278.00
- endocrine NEC 259.9
- endogenous 259.9
- Fröhlich's (adiposogenital dystrophy) 253.8
- glandular NEC 259.9
- hypothyroid (*see also* Hypothyroidism) 244.9
- morbid 278.01
- of pregnancy 649.1 ☑
- pituitary 253.8
- severe 278.01
- thyroid (*see also* Hypothyroidism) 244.9

Oblique — *see also* condition
- lie before labor, affecting fetus or newborn 761.7

Obliquity, pelvis 738.6

Obliteration
- abdominal aorta 446.7
- appendix (lumen) 543.9
- artery 447.1
- ascending aorta 446.7
- bile ducts 576.8
  - with calculus, choledocholithiasis, or stones — *see* Choledocholithiasis
  - congenital 751.61
    - jaundice from 751.61 *[774.5]*
- common duct 576.8
  - with calculus, choledocholithiasis, or stones — *see* Choledocholithiasis
  - congenital 751.61
- cystic duct 575.8
  - with calculus, choledocholithiasis, or stones — *see* Choledocholithiasis
- disease, arteriolar 447.1
- endometrium 621.8
- eye, anterior chamber 360.34
- fallopian tube 628.2
- lymphatic vessel 457.1
  - postmastectomy 457.0
- organ or site, congenital NEC — *see* Atresia
- placental blood vessels — *see* Placenta, abnormal
- supra-aortic branches 446.7
- ureter 593.89
- urethra 599.84
- vein 459.9
- vestibule (oral) 525.8

Observation (for) V71.9
- without need for further medical care V71.9
- accident NEC V71.4
  - at work V71.3
- criminal assault V71.6
- deleterious agent ingestion V71.89
- disease V71.9
  - cardiovascular V71.7
  - heart V71.7
  - mental V71.09
  - specified condition NEC V71.89
- foreign body ingestion V71.89
- growth and development variations V21.8
- injuries (accidental) V71.4
  - inflicted NEC V71.6
    - during alleged rape or seduction V71.5
- malignant neoplasm, suspected V71.1
- postpartum
  - immediately after delivery V24.0
  - routine follow-up V24.2

Observation — *continued*
- pregnancy
  - high-risk V23.9
    - specified problem NEC V23.89
  - normal (without complication) V22.1
    - with nonobstetric complication V22.2
    - first V22.0
- rape or seduction, alleged V71.5
  - injury during V71.5
- suicide attempt, alleged V71.89
- suspected (undiagnosed) (unproven)
  - abuse V71.81
  - cardiovascular disease V71.7
  - child or wife battering victim V71.6
  - concussion (cerebral) V71.6
  - condition NEC V71.89
    - infant — *see* Observation, suspected, condition, newborn
    - maternal and fetal ●
      - amniotic cavity and membrane problem V89.01 ●
      - cervical shortening V89.05 ●
      - fetal anomaly V89.03 ●
      - fetal growth problem V89.04 ●
      - oligohydramnios V89.01 ●
      - other specified problem NEC V89.09 ●
      - placental problem V89.02 ●
      - polyhydramnios V89.01 ●
    - newborn V29.9
      - cardiovascular disease V29.8
      - congenital anomaly V29.8
      - genetic V29.3
      - infectious V29.0
      - ingestion foreign object V29.8
      - injury V29.8
      - metabolic V29.3
      - neoplasm V29.8
      - neurological V29.1
      - poison, poisoning V29.8
      - respiratory V29.2
      - specified NEC V29.8
  - exposure
    - anthrax V71.82
    - biologic agent NEC V71.83
    - SARS V71.83
  - infectious disease not requiring isolation V71.89
  - malignant neoplasm V71.1
  - mental disorder V71.09
  - neglect V71.81
  - neoplasm
    - benign V71.89
    - malignant V71.1
  - specified condition NEC V71.89
  - tuberculosis V71.2
- tuberculosis, suspected V71.2

Obsession, obsessional 300.3
- ideas and mental images 300.3
- impulses 300.3
- neurosis 300.3
- phobia 300.3
- psychasthenia 300.3
- ruminations 300.3
- state 300.3
- syndrome 300.3

Obsessive-compulsive 300.3
- neurosis 300.3
- personality 301.4
- reaction 300.3

Obstetrical trauma NEC (complicating delivery) 665.9 ☑
- with
  - abortion — *see* Abortion, by type, with damage to pelvic organs
  - ectopic pregnancy (*see also* categories 633.0–633.9) 639.2
  - molar pregnancy (*see also* categories 630–632) 639.2
- affecting fetus or newborn 763.89

Obstetrical trauma — *continued*
- following
  - abortion 639.2
  - ectopic or molar pregnancy 639.2

Obstipation — *see also* Constipation 564.00
- psychogenic 306.4

Obstruction, obstructed, obstructive
- airway NEC 519.8
  - with
    - allergic alveolitis NEC 495.9
    - asthma NEC (*see also* Asthma) 493.9 ☑
    - bronchiectasis 494.0
      - with acute exacerbation 494.1
    - bronchitis (chronic) (*see also* Bronchitis, with, obstruction) 491.20
    - emphysema NEC 492.8
  - chronic 496
    - with
      - allergic alveolitis NEC 495.5
      - asthma NEC (*see also* Asthma) 493.2 ☑
      - bronchiectasis 494.0
        - with acute exacerbation 494.1
      - bronchitis (chronic) (*see also* Bronchitis, with, obstruction) 491.20
      - emphysema NEC 492.8
  - due to
    - bronchospasm 519.11
    - foreign body 934.9
    - inhalation of fumes or vapors 506.9
    - laryngospasm 478.75
- alimentary canal (*see also* Obstruction, intestine) 560.9
- ampulla of Vater 576.2
  - with calculus, cholelithiasis, or stones — *see* Choledocholithiasis
- aortic (heart) (valve) (*see also* Stenosis, aortic) 424.1
  - rheumatic (*see also* Stenosis, aortic, rheumatic) 395.0
- aortoiliac 444.0
- aqueduct of Sylvius 331.4
  - congenital 742.3
    - with spina bifida (*see also* Spina bifida) 741.0 ☑
- Arnold-Chiari (*see also* Spina bifida) 741.0 ☑
- artery (*see also* Embolism, artery) 444.9
  - basilar (complete) (partial) (*see also* Occlusion, artery, basilar) 433.0 ☑
  - carotid (complete) (partial) (*see also* Occlusion, artery, carotid) 433.1 ☑
  - precerebral — *see* Occlusion, artery, precerebral NEC
  - retinal (central) (*see also* Occlusion, retina) 362.30
  - vertebral (complete) (partial) (*see also* Occlusion, artery, vertebral) 433.2 ☑
- asthma (chronic) (with obstructive pulmonary disease) 493.2 ☑
- band (intestinal) 560.81
- bile duct or passage (*see also* Obstruction, biliary) 576.2
  - congenital 751.61
    - jaundice from 751.61 *[774.5]*
- biliary (duct) (tract) 576.2
  - with calculus 574.51
    - with cholecystitis (chronic) 574.41
      - acute 574.31
  - congenital 751.61
    - jaundice from 751.61 *[774.5]*
  - gallbladder 575.2
    - with calculus 574.21

Obstruction, obstructed, obstructive — *continued*
- biliary — *continued*
  - gallbladder — *continued*
    - with calculus — *continued*
      - with cholecystitis (chronic) 574.11
        - acute 574.01
- bladder neck (acquired) 596.0
  - congenital 753.6
- bowel (*see also* Obstruction, intestine) 560.9
- bronchus 519.19
- canal, ear (*see also* Stricture, ear canal, acquired) 380.50
- cardia 537.89
- caval veins (inferior) (superior) 459.2
- cecum (*see also* Obstruction, intestine) 560.9
- circulatory 459.9
- colon (*see also* Obstruction, intestine) 560.9
  - sympathicotonic 560.89
- common duct (*see also* Obstruction, biliary) 576.2
  - congenital 751.61
- coronary (artery) (heart) (*see also* Arteriosclerosis, coronary)
  - acute (*see also* Infarct, myocardium) 410.9 ☑
    - without myocardial infarction 411.81
- cystic duct (*see also* Obstruction, gallbladder) 575.2
  - congenital 751.61
- device, implant, or graft — *see* Complications, due to (presence of) any device, implant, or graft classified to 996.0–996.5 NEC
- due to foreign body accidentally left in operation wound 998.4
- duodenum 537.3
  - congenital 751.1
  - due to
    - compression NEC 537.3
    - cyst 537.3
    - intrinsic lesion or disease NEC 537.3
    - scarring 537.3
    - torsion 537.3
    - ulcer 532.91
    - volvulus 537.3
- ejaculatory duct 608.89
- endocardium 424.90
  - arteriosclerotic 424.99
  - specified cause, except rheumatic 424.99
- esophagus 530.3
- eustachian tube (complete) (partial) 381.60
  - cartilaginous
    - extrinsic 381.63
    - intrinsic 381.62
  - due to
    - cholesteatoma 381.61
    - osseous lesion NEC 381.61
    - polyp 381.61
  - osseous 381.61
- fallopian tube (bilateral) 628.2
- fecal 560.39
  - with hernia (*see also* Hernia, by site, with obstruction)
    - gangrenous — *see* Hernia, by site, with gangrene
- foramen of Monro (congenital) 742.3
  - with spina bifida (*see also* Spina bifida) 741.0 ☑
- foreign body — *see* Foreign body
- gallbladder 575.2
  - with calculus, cholelithiasis, or stones 574.21
    - with cholecystitis (chronic) 574.11
      - acute 574.01
  - congenital 751.69
    - jaundice from 751.69 *[774.5]*

Obstruction, obstructed, obstructive — *continued*
- gastric outlet 537.0
- gastrointestinal (*see also* Obstruction, intestine) 560.9
- glottis 478.79
- hepatic 573.8
  - duct (*see also* Obstruction, biliary) 576.2
    - congenital 751.61
- icterus (*see also* Obstruction, biliary) 576.8
  - congenital 751.61
- ileocecal coil (*see also* Obstruction, intestine) 560.9
- ileum (*see also* Obstruction, intestine) 560.9
- iliofemoral (artery) 444.81
- internal anastomosis — *see* Complications, mechanical, graft
- intestine (mechanical) (neurogenic) (paroxysmal) (postinfectional) (reflex) 560.9
  - with
    - adhesions (intestinal) (peritoneal) 560.81
    - hernia (*see also* Hernia, by site, with obstruction)
      - gangrenous — *see* Hernia, by site, with gangrene
  - adynamic (*see also* Ileus) 560.1
  - by gallstone 560.31
  - congenital or infantile (small) 751.1
    - large 751.2
  - due to
    - Ascaris lumbricoides 127.0
    - mural thickening 560.89
    - procedure 997.4
      - involving urinary tract 997.5
  - impaction 560.39
  - infantile — *see* Obstruction, intestine, congenital
  - newborn
    - due to
      - fecaliths 777.1
      - inspissated milk 777.2
      - meconium (plug) 777.1
        - in mucoviscidosis 277.01
    - transitory 777.4
  - specified cause NEC 560.89
  - transitory, newborn 777.4
  - volvulus 560.2
- intracardiac ball valve prosthesis 996.02
- jaundice (*see also* Obstruction, biliary) 576.8
  - congenital 751.61
- jejunum (*see also* Obstruction, intestine) 560.9
- kidney 593.89
- labor 660.9 ☑
  - affecting fetus or newborn 763.1
  - by
    - bony pelvis (conditions classifiable to 653.0–653.9) 660.1 ☑
    - deep transverse arrest 660.3 ☑
    - impacted shoulder 660.4 ☑
    - locked twins 660.5 ☑
    - malposition (fetus) (conditions classifiable to 652.0–652.9) 660.0 ☑
      - head during labor 660.3 ☑
    - persistent occipitoposterior position 660.3 ☑
    - soft tissue, pelvic (conditions classifiable to 654.0–654.9) 660.2 ☑
- lacrimal
  - canaliculi 375.53
  - congenital 743.65
  - punctum 375.52
  - sac 375.54
- lacrimonasal duct 375.56
  - congenital 743.65
  - neonatal 375.55
- lacteal, with steatorrhea 579.2
- laryngitis (*see also* Laryngitis) 464.01
- larynx 478.79
  - congenital 748.3
- liver 573.8
  - cirrhotic (*see also* Cirrhosis, liver) 571.5
- lung 518.89
  - with
    - asthma — *see* Asthma
    - bronchitis (chronic) 491.20
    - emphysema NEC 492.8
  - airway, chronic 496
  - chronic NEC 496
    - with
      - asthma (chronic) (obstructive) 493.2 ☑
  - disease, chronic 496
    - with
      - asthma (chronic) (obstructive) 493.2 ☑
  - emphysematous 492.8
- lymphatic 457.1
- meconium
  - fetus or newborn 777.1
    - in mucoviscidosis 277.01
  - newborn due to fecaliths 777.1
- mediastinum 519.3
- mitral (rheumatic) — *see* Stenosis, mitral
- nasal 478.19
  - duct 375.56
    - neonatal 375.55
  - sinus — *see* Sinusitis
- nasolacrimal duct 375.56
  - congenital 743.65
  - neonatal 375.55
- nasopharynx 478.29
- nose 478.19
- organ or site, congenital NEC — *see* Atresia
- pancreatic duct 577.8
- parotid gland 527.8
- pelviureteral junction (*see also* Obstruction, ureter) 593.4
- pharynx 478.29
- portal (circulation) (vein) 452
- prostate 600.90
  - with
    - other lower urinary tract symptoms (LUTS) 600.91
    - urinary
      - obstruction 600.91
      - retention 600.91
  - valve (urinary) 596.0
- pulmonary
  - valve (heart) (*see also* Endocarditis, pulmonary) 424.3
  - vein, isolated 747.49
- pyemic — *see* Septicemia
- pylorus (acquired) 537.0
  - congenital 750.5
  - infantile 750.5
- rectosigmoid (*see also* Obstruction, intestine) 560.9
- rectum 569.49
- renal 593.89
- respiratory 519.8
  - chronic 496
- retinal (artery) (vein) (central) (*see also* Occlusion, retina) 362.30
- salivary duct (any) 527.8
  - with calculus 527.5
- sigmoid (*see also* Obstruction, intestine) 560.9
- sinus (accessory) (nasal) (*see also* Sinusitis) 473.9
- Stensen's duct 527.8
- stomach 537.89
  - acute 536.1
  - congenital 750.7
- submaxillary gland 527.8
  - with calculus 527.5
- thoracic duct 457.1
- thrombotic — *see* Thrombosis
- tooth eruption 520.6
- trachea 519.19
- tracheostomy airway 519.09
- tricuspid — *see* Endocarditis, tricuspid
- upper respiratory, congenital 748.8
- ureter (functional) 593.4
  - congenital 753.20
  - due to calculus 592.1
- ureteropelvic junction, congenital 753.21
- ureterovesical junction, congenital 753.22
- urethra 599.60
  - congenital 753.6
- urinary (moderate) 599.60
  - organ or tract (lower) 599.60
    - due to
      - benign prostatic hypertrophy (BPH) - see category 600
    - specified NEC 599.69
      - due to
        - benign prostatic hypertrophy (BPH) — see category 600
  - prostatic valve 596.0
- uropathy 599.60
- uterus 621.8
- vagina 623.2
- valvular — *see* Endocarditis
- vascular graft or shunt 996.1
  - atherosclerosis — *see* Arteriosclerosis, coronary
  - embolism 996.74
  - occlusion NEC 996.74
  - thrombus 996.74
- vein, venous 459.2
  - caval (inferior) (superior) 459.2
  - thrombotic — *see* Thrombosis
- vena cava (inferior) (superior) 459.2
- ventricular shunt 996.2
- vesical 596.0
- vesicourethral orifice 596.0
- vessel NEC 459.9

Obturator — *see* condition

Occlusal
- plane deviation 524.76
- wear, teeth 521.10

Occlusion
- anus 569.49
  - congenital 751.2
  - infantile 751.2
- aortoiliac (chronic) 444.0
- aqueduct of Sylvius 331.4
  - congenital 742.3
    - with spina bifida (*see also* Spina bifida) 741.0 ☑
- arteries of extremities, lower 444.22
  - without thrombus or embolus (*see also* Arteriosclerosis, extremities) 440.20
  - due to stricture or stenosis 447.1
  - upper 444.21
    - without thrombus or embolus (*see also* Arteriosclerosis, extremities) 440.20
    - due to stricture or stenosis 447.1
- artery NEC (*see also* Embolism, artery) 444.9
  - auditory, internal 433.8 ☑
  - basilar 433.0 ☑
    - with other precerebral artery 433.3 ☑
    - bilateral 433.3 ☑
  - brain or cerebral (*see also* Infarct, brain) 434.9 ☑
  - carotid 433.1 ☑
    - with other precerebral artery 433.3 ☑
    - bilateral 433.3 ☑

Occlusion — *continued*
- artery (*see also* Embolism, artery) — *continued*
  - cerebellar (anterior inferior) (posterior inferior) (superior) 433.8 ☑
  - cerebral (*see also* Infarct, brain) 434.9 ☑
  - choroidal (anterior) 433.8 ☑
  - chronic total
    - coronary 414.2
    - extremity(ies) 440.4
  - communicating posterior 433.8 ☑
  - complete
    - coronary 414.2
    - extremity(ies) 440.4
  - coronary (thrombotic) (*see also* Infarct, myocardium) 410.9 ☑
    - acute 410.9 ☑
      - without myocardial infarction 411.81
    - chronic total 414.2
    - complete 414.2
    - healed or old 412
    - total 414.2
  - extremity(ies)
    - chronic total 440.4
    - complete 440.4
    - total 440.4
  - hypophyseal 433.8 ☑
  - iliac (artery) 444.81
  - mesenteric (embolic) (thrombotic) (with gangrene) 557.0
  - pontine 433.8 ☑
  - precerebral NEC 433.9 ☑
    - late effect — *see* Late effect(s) (of) cerebrovascular disease
    - multiple or bilateral 433.3 ☑
    - puerperal, postpartum, childbirth 674.0 ☑
    - specified NEC 433.8 ☑
  - renal 593.81
  - retinal — *see* Occlusion, retina, artery
  - spinal 433.8 ☑
  - vertebral 433.2 ☑
    - with other precerebral artery 433.3 ☑
    - bilateral 433.3 ☑
- basilar (artery) — *see* Occlusion, artery, basilar
- bile duct (any) (*see also* Obstruction, biliary) 576.2
- bowel (*see also* Obstruction, intestine) 560.9
- brain (artery) (vascular) (*see also* Infarct, brain) 434.9 ☑
- breast (duct) 611.89 ▲
- carotid (artery) (common) (internal) — *see* Occlusion, artery, carotid
- cerebellar (anterior inferior) (artery) (posterior inferior) (superior) 433.8 ☑
- cerebral (artery) (*see also* Infarct, brain) 434.9 ☑
- cerebrovascular (*see also* Infarct, brain) 434.9 ☑
  - diffuse 437.0
- cervical canal (*see also* Stricture, cervix) 622.4
  - by falciparum malaria 084.0
- cervix (uteri) (*see also* Stricture, cervix) 622.4
- choanal 748.0
- choroidal (artery) 433.8 ☑
- colon (*see also* Obstruction, intestine) 560.9
- communicating posterior artery 433.8 ☑
- coronary (artery) (thrombotic) (*see also* Infarct, myocardium) 410.9 ☑
  - without myocardial infarction 411.81
  - acute 410.9 ☑

☑ Additional Digit Required — Refer to the Tabular List for Digit Selection

Subterms under main terms may continue to next column or page

▶◀ Revised Text ● New Line ▲ Revised Code

Occlusion — *continued*
- coronary (*see also* Infarct, myocardium) — *continued*
  - acute — *continued*
    - without myocardial infarction 411.81
  - healed or old 412
- cystic duct (*see also* Obstruction, gallbladder) 575.2
  - congenital 751.69
- disto
  - division I 524.22
  - division II 524.22
- embolic — *see* Embolism
- fallopian tube 628.2
  - congenital 752.19
- gallbladder (*see also* Obstruction, gallbladder) 575.2
  - congenital 751.69
    - jaundice from 751.69 *[774.5]*
- gingiva, traumatic 523.8
- hymen 623.3
  - congenital 752.42
- hypophyseal (artery) 433.8 ☑
- iliac artery 444.81
- intestine (*see also* Obstruction, intestine) 560.9
- kidney 593.89
- lacrimal apparatus — *see* Stenosis, lacrimal
- lung 518.89
- lymph or lymphatic channel 457.1
- mammary duct 611.89 ▲
- mesenteric artery (embolic) (thrombotic) (with gangrene) 557.0
- nose 478.1 ☑
  - congenital 748.0
- organ or site, congenital NEC — *see* Atresia
- oviduct 628.2
  - congenital 752.19
- periodontal, traumatic 523.8
- peripheral arteries (lower extremity) 444.22
  - without thrombus or embolus (*see also* Arteriosclerosis, extremities) 440.20
  - due to stricture or stenosis 447.1
  - upper extremity 444.21
    - without thrombus or embolus (*see also* Arteriosclerosis, extremities) 440.20
    - due to stricture or stenosis 447.1
- pontine (artery) 433.8 ☑
- posterior lingual, of mandibular teeth 524.29
- precerebral artery — *see* Occlusion, artery, precerebral NEC
- puncta lacrimalia 375.52
- pupil 364.74
- pylorus (*see also* Stricture, pylorus) 537.0
- renal artery 593.81
- retina, retinal (vascular) 362.30
  - artery, arterial 362.30
    - branch 362.32
    - central (total) 362.31
    - partial 362.33
    - transient 362.34
    - tributary 362.32
  - vein 362.30
    - branch 362.36
    - central (total) 362.35
    - incipient 362.37
    - partial 362.37
    - tributary 362.36
- spinal artery 433.8 ☑
- stent
  - coronary 996.72
- teeth (mandibular) (posterior lingual) 524.29
- thoracic duct 457.1
- tubal 628.2
- ureter (complete) (partial) 593.4
  - congenital 753.29

Occlusion — *continued*
- urethra (*see also* Stricture, urethra) 598.9
  - congenital 753.6
- uterus 621.8
- vagina 623.2
- vascular NEC 459.9
- vein — *see* Thrombosis
- vena cava (inferior) (superior) 453.2
- ventricle (brain) NEC 331.4
- vertebral (artery) — *see* Occlusion, artery, vertebral
- vessel (blood) NEC 459.9
- vulva 624.8

Occlusio pupillae 364.74

Occupational
- problems NEC V62.29 ▲
- therapy V57.21

Ochlophobia 300.29

Ochronosis (alkaptonuric) (congenital) (endogenous) 270.2
- with chloasma of eyelid 270.2

Ocular muscle — *see also* condition
- myopathy 359.1
- torticollis 781.93

Oculoauriculovertebral dysplasia 756.0

Oculogyric
- crisis or disturbance 378.87
  - psychogenic 306.7

Oculomotor syndrome 378.81

Oddi's sphincter spasm 576.5

Odelberg's disease (juvenile osteochondrosis) 732.1

Odontalgia 525.9

Odontoameloblastoma (M9311/0) 213.1
- upper jaw (bone) 213.0

Odontoclasia 521.05

Odontoclasis 873.63
- complicated 873.73

Odontodysplasia, regional 520.4

Odontogenesis imperfecta 520.5

Odontoma (M9280/0) 213.1
- ameloblastic (M9311/0) 213.1
  - upper jaw (bone) 213.0
- calcified (M9280/0) 213.1
  - upper jaw (bone) 213.0
- complex (M9282/0) 213.1
  - upper jaw (bone) 213.0
- compound (M9281/0) 213.1
  - upper jaw (bone) 213.0
- fibroameloblastic (M9290/0) 213.1
  - upper jaw (bone) 213.0
- follicular 526.0
- upper jaw (bone) 213.0

Odontomyelitis (closed) (open) 522.0

Odontonecrosis 521.09

Odontorrhagia 525.8

Odontosarcoma, ameloblastic (M9290/3) 170.1
- upper jaw (bone) 170.0

Odynophagia 787.20

Oesophagostomiasis 127.7

Oesophagostomum infestation 127.7

Oestriasis 134.0

Ogilvie's syndrome (sympathicotonic colon obstruction) 560.89

Oguchi's disease (retina) 368.61

Ohara's disease — *see also* Tularemia 021.9

Oidiomycosis — *see also* Candidiasis 112.9

Oidiomycotic meningitis 112.83

Oidium albicans infection — *see also* Candidiasis 112.9

Old age 797
- dementia (of) 290.0

Olfactory — *see* condition

Oligemia 285.9

Oligergasia — *see also* Retardation, mental 319

Oligoamnios 658.0 ☑
- affecting fetus or newborn 761.2

Oligoastrocytoma, mixed (M9382/3)
- specified site — *see* Neoplasm, by site, malignant
- unspecified site 191.9

Oligocythemia 285.9

Oligodendroblastoma (M9460/3)
- specified site — *see* Neoplasm, by site, malignant
- unspecified site 191.9

Oligodendroglioma (M9450/3)
- anaplastic type (M9451/3)
  - specified site — *see* Neoplasm, by site, malignant
  - unspecified site 191.9
- specified site — *see* Neoplasm, by site, malignant
- unspecified site 191.9

Oligodendroma — *see* Oligodendroglioma

Oligodontia — *see also* Anodontia 520.0

Oligoencephalon 742.1

Oligohydramnios 658.0 ☑
- affecting fetus or newborn 761.2
- due to premature rupture of membranes 658.1 ☑
  - affecting fetus or newborn 761.2

Oligohydrosis 705.0

Oligomenorrhea 626.1

Oligophrenia — *see also* Retardation, mental 319
- phenylpyruvic 270.1

Oligospermia 606.1

Oligotrichia 704.09
- congenita 757.4

Oliguria 788.5
- with
  - abortion — *see* Abortion, by type, with renal failure
  - ectopic pregnancy (*see also* categories 633.0–633.9) 639.3
  - molar pregnancy (*see also* categories 630–632) 639.3
- complicating
  - abortion 639.3
  - ectopic or molar pregnancy 639.3
  - pregnancy 646.2 ☑
    - with hypertension — *see* Toxemia, of pregnancy
- due to a procedure 997.5
- following labor and delivery 669.3 ☑
- heart or cardiac — *see* Failure, heart
- puerperal, postpartum 669.3 ☑
- specified due to a procedure 997.5

Ollier's disease (chondrodysplasia) 756.4

Omentitis — *see also* Peritonitis 567.9

Omentocele — *see also* Hernia, omental 553.8

Omentum, omental — *see* condition

Omphalitis (congenital) (newborn) 771.4
- not of newborn 686.9
- tetanus 771.3

Omphalocele 756.79

Omphalomesenteric duct, persistent 751.0

Omphalorrhagia, newborn 772.3

Omsk hemorrhagic fever 065.1

Onanism 307.9

Onchocerciasis 125.3
- eye 125.3 *[360.13]*

Onchocercosis 125.3

Oncocytoma (M8290/0) — *see* Neoplasm, by site, benign

Ondine's curse 348.8

Oneirophrenia — *see also* Schizophrenia 295.4 ☑

Onychauxis 703.8
- congenital 757.5

Onychia (with lymphangitis) 681.9
- dermatophytic 110.1
- finger 681.02
- toe 681.11

Onychitis (with lymphangitis) 681.9
- finger 681.02
- toe 681.11

Onychocryptosis 703.0

Onychodystrophy 703.8
- congenital 757.5

Onychogryphosis 703.8

Onychogryposis 703.8

Onycholysis 703.8

Onychomadesis 703.8

Onychomalacia 703.8

Onychomycosis 110.1
- finger 110.1
- toe 110.1

Onycho-osteodysplasia 756.89

Onychophagy 307.9

Onychoptosis 703.8

Onychorrhexis 703.8
- congenital 757.5

Onychoschizia 703.8

Onychotrophia — *see also* Atrophy, nail 703.8

O'nyong-nyong fever 066.3

Onyxis (finger) (toe) 703.0

Onyxitis (with lymphangitis) 681.9
- finger 681.02
- toe 681.11

Oocyte (egg) (ovum)
- donor V59.70
  - over age 35 V59.73
    - anonymous recipient V59.73
    - designated recipient V59.74
  - under age 35 V59.71
    - anonymous recipient V59.71
    - designated recipient V59.72

Oophoritis (cystic) (infectional) (interstitial) — *see also* Salpingo-oophoritis 614.2
- complicating pregnancy 646.6 ☑
- fetal (acute) 752.0
- gonococcal (acute) 098.19
  - chronic or duration of 2 months or over 098.39
- tuberculous (*see also* Tuberculosis) 016.6 ☑

Opacity, opacities
- cornea 371.00
  - central 371.03
  - congenital 743.43
    - interfering with vision 743.42
  - degenerative (*see also* Degeneration, cornea) 371.40
  - hereditary (*see also* Dystrophy, cornea) 371.50
  - inflammatory (*see also* Keratitis) 370.9
  - late effect of trachoma (healed) 139.1
  - minor 371.01
  - peripheral 371.02
- enamel (fluoride) (nonfluoride) (teeth) 520.3
- lens (*see also* Cataract) 366.9
- snowball 379.22
- vitreous (humor) 379.24
  - congenital 743.51

Opalescent dentin (hereditary) 520.5

Open, opening
- abnormal, organ or site, congenital — *see* Imperfect, closure
- angle with
  - borderline intraocular pressure 365.01
  - cupping of discs 365.01
- bite
  - anterior 524.24
  - posterior 524.25
- false — *see* Imperfect, closure
- margin on tooth restoration 525.61
- restoration margins 525.61
- wound — *see* Wound, open, by site

Operation
- causing mutilation of fetus 763.89
- destructive, on live fetus, to facilitate birth 763.89
- for delivery, fetus or newborn 763.89
- maternal, unrelated to current delivery, affecting fetus or newborn ▶(*see also* Newborn, affected by)◀ 760.64 ▲

Operational fatigue 300.89

Operative — *see* condition

Operculitis (chronic) 523.40
- acute 523.30

Operculum, retina 361.32

- **Operculum, retina** — *continued*
  - with detachment 361.01
- **Ophiasis** 704.01
- **Ophthalmia** — *see also* Conjunctivitis 372.30
  - actinic rays 370.24
  - allergic (acute) 372.05
    - chronic 372.14
  - blennorrhagic (neonatorum) 098.40
  - catarrhal 372.03
  - diphtheritic 032.81
  - Egyptian 076.1
  - electric, electrica 370.24
  - gonococcal (neonatorum) 098.40
  - metastatic 360.11
  - migraine 346.8 ☑
  - neonatorum, newborn 771.6
    - gonococcal 098.40
  - nodosa 360.14
  - phlyctenular 370.31
    - with ulcer (*see also* Ulcer, cornea) 370.00
  - sympathetic 360.11
- **Ophthalmitis** — *see* Ophthalmia
- **Ophthalmocele** (congenital) 743.66
- **Ophthalmoneuromyelitis** 341.0
- **Ophthalmopathy, infiltrative with thyrotoxicosis** 242.0 ☑
- **Ophthalmoplegia** — *see also* Strabismus 378.9
  - anterior internuclear 378.86
  - ataxia-areflexia syndrome 357.0
  - bilateral 378.9
  - diabetic 250.5 ☑ *[378.86]*
    - due to secondary diabetes ●
      - 249.5 ☑ *[378.86]* ●
  - exophthalmic 242.0 ☑ *[376.22]*
  - external 378.55
    - progressive 378.72
    - total 378.56
  - internal (complete) (total) 367.52
  - internuclear 378.86
  - migraine 346.2 ☑ ▲
  - painful 378.55
  - Parinaud's 378.81
  - progressive external 378.72
  - supranuclear, progressive 333.0
  - total (external) 378.56
    - internal 367.52
  - unilateral 378.9
- **Opisthognathism** 524.00
- **Opisthorchiasis** (felineus) (tenuicollis) (viverrini) 121.0
- **Opisthotonos, opisthotonus** 781.0
- **Opitz's disease** (congestive splenomegaly) 289.51
- **Opiumism** — *see also* Dependence 304.0 ☑
- **Oppenheim's disease** 358.8
- **Oppenheim-Urbach disease or syndrome** (necrobiosis lipoidica diabeticorum) 250.8 ☑ *[709.3]*
  - due to secondary diabetes ●
    - 249.8 ☑ *[709.3]* ●
- **Opsoclonia** 379.59
- **Optic nerve** — *see* condition
- **Orbit** — *see* condition
- **Orchioblastoma** (M9071/3) 186.9
- **Orchitis** (nonspecific) (septic) 604.90
  - with abscess 604.0
  - blennorrhagic (acute) 098.13
    - chronic or duration of 2 months or over 098.33
  - diphtheritic 032.89 *[604.91]*
  - filarial 125.9 *[604.91]*
  - gangrenous 604.99
  - gonococcal (acute) 098.13
    - chronic or duration of 2 months or over 098.33
  - mumps 072.0
  - parotidea 072.0
  - suppurative 604.99
  - syphilitic 095.8 *[604.91]*
  - tuberculous (*see also* Tuberculosis) 016.5 ☑ *[608.81]*
- **Orf** 051.2
- **Organic** — *see also* condition
  - heart — *see* Disease, heart
  - insufficiency 799.89
- **Oriental**
  - bilharziasis 120.2
  - schistosomiasis 120.2
  - sore 085.1
- **Orientation**
  - ego-dystonic sexual 302.0
- **Orifice** — *see* condition
- **Origin, both great vessels from right ventricle** 745.11
- **Ormond's disease or syndrome** 593.4
- **Ornithosis** 073.9
  - with
    - complication 073.8
      - specified NEC 073.7
    - pneumonia 073.0
      - pneumonitis (lobular) 073.0
- **Orodigitofacial dysostosis** 759.89
- **Oropouche fever** 066.3
- **Orotaciduria, oroticaciduria** (congenital) (hereditary) (pyrimidine deficiency) 281.4
- **Oroya fever** 088.0
- **Orthodontics** V58.5
  - adjustment V53.4
  - aftercare V58.5
  - fitting V53.4
- **Orthopnea** 786.02
- **Orthoptic training** V57.4
- **Osgood-Schlatter**
  - disease 732.4
  - osteochondrosis 732.4
- **Osler's**
  - disease (M9950/1) (polycythemia vera) 238.4
  - nodes 421.0
- **Osler-Rendu disease** (familial hemorrhagic telangiectasia) 448.0
- **Osler-Vaquez disease** (M9950/1) (polycythemia vera) 238.4
- **Osler-Weber-Rendu syndrome** (familial hemorrhagic telangiectasia) 448.0
- **Osmidrosis** 705.89
- **Osseous** — *see* condition
- **Ossification**
  - artery — *see* Arteriosclerosis
  - auricle (ear) 380.39
  - bronchus 519.19
  - cardiac (*see also* Degeneration, myocardial) 429.1
  - cartilage (senile) 733.99
  - coronary (artery) — *see* Arteriosclerosis, coronary
  - diaphragm 728.10
  - ear 380.39
    - middle (*see also* Otosclerosis) 387.9
  - falx cerebri 349.2
  - fascia 728.10
  - fontanel
    - defective or delayed 756.0
    - premature 756.0
  - heart (*see also* Degeneration, myocardial) 429.1
    - valve — *see* Endocarditis
  - larynx 478.79
  - ligament
    - posterior longitudinal 724.8
      - cervical 723.7
  - meninges (cerebral) 349.2
    - spinal 336.8
  - multiple, eccentric centers 733.99
  - muscle 728.10
    - heterotopic, postoperative 728.13
  - myocardium, myocardial (*see also* Degeneration, myocardial) 429.1
  - penis 607.81
  - periarticular 728.89
  - sclera 379.16
  - tendon 727.82
  - trachea 519.19
  - tympanic membrane (*see also* Tympanosclerosis) 385.00
  - vitreous (humor) 360.44
- **Osteitis** — *see also* Osteomyelitis 730.2 ☑
  - acute 730.0 ☑
  - alveolar 526.5
  - chronic 730.1 ☑
  - condensans (ilii) 733.5
  - deformans (Paget's) 731.0
    - due to or associated with malignant neoplasm (*see also* Neoplasm, bone, malignant) 170.9 *[731.1]*
  - due to yaws 102.6
  - fibrosa NEC 733.29
    - cystica (generalisata) 252.01
    - disseminata 756.59
    - osteoplastica 252.01
  - fragilitans 756.51
  - Garré's (sclerosing) 730.1 ☑
  - infectious (acute) (subacute) 730.0 ☑
    - chronic or old 730.1 ☑
  - jaw (acute) (chronic) (lower) (neonatal) (suppurative) (upper) 526.4
  - parathyroid 252.01
  - petrous bone (*see also* Petrositis) 383.20
  - pubis 733.5
  - sclerotic, nonsuppurative 730.1 ☑
  - syphilitic 095.5
  - tuberculosa
    - cystica (of Jüngling) 135
    - multiplex cystoides 135
- **Osteoarthritica spondylitis** (spine) — *see also* Spondylosis 721.90
- **Osteoarthritis** — *see also* Osteoarthrosis 715.9 ☑
  - distal interphalangeal 715.9 ☑
  - hyperplastic 731.2
  - interspinalis (*see also* Spondylosis) 721.90
  - spine, spinal NEC (*see also* Spondylosis) 721.90
- **Osteoarthropathy** — *see also* Osteoarthrosis 715.9 ☑
  - chronic idiopathic hypertrophic 757.39
  - familial idiopathic 757.39
  - hypertrophic pulmonary 731.2
    - secondary 731.2
  - idiopathic hypertrophic 757.39
  - primary hypertrophic 731.2
  - pulmonary hypertrophic 731.2
  - secondary hypertrophic 731.2
- **Osteoarthrosis** (degenerative) (hypertrophic) (rheumatoid) 715.9 ☑

> *Note — Use the following fifth-digit subclassification with category 715:*
>
> 0 *site unspecified*
> 1 *shoulder region*
> 2 *upper arm*
> 3 *forearm*
> 4 *hand*
> 5 *pelvic region and thigh*
> 6 *lower leg*
> 7 *ankle and foot*
> 8 *other specified sites except spine*
> 9 *multiple sites*

  - Deformans alkaptonurica 270.2
  - generalized 715.09
  - juvenilis (Köhler's) 732.5
  - localized 715.3 ☑
    - idiopathic 715.1 ☑
    - primary 715.1 ☑
    - secondary 715.2 ☑
  - multiple sites, not specified as generalized 715.89
  - polyarticular 715.09
  - spine (*see also* Spondylosis) 721.90
  - temporomandibular joint 524.69
- **Osteoblastoma** (M9200/0) — *see* Neoplasm, bone, benign
- **Osteochondritis** — *see also* Osteochondrosis 732.9
  - dissecans 732.7
    - hip 732.7
  - ischiopubica 732.1
  - multiple 756.59
  - syphilitic (congenital) 090.0
- **Osteochondrodermodysplasia** 756.59
- **Osteochondrodystrophy** 277.5
  - deformans 277.5
  - familial 277.5
  - fetalis 756.4
- **Osteochondrolysis** 732.7
- **Osteochondroma** (M9210/0) — *see also* Neoplasm, bone, benign
  - multiple, congenital 756.4
- **Osteochondromatosis** (M9210/1) 238.0
  - synovial 727.82
- **Osteochondromyxosarcoma** (M9180/3) — *see* Neoplasm, bone, malignant
- **Osteochondropathy** NEC 732.9
- **Osteochondrosarcoma** (M9180/3) — *see* Neoplasm, bone, malignant
- **Osteochondrosis** 732.9
  - acetabulum 732.1
  - adult spine 732.8
  - astragalus 732.5
  - Blount's 732.4
  - Buchanan's (juvenile osteochondrosis of iliac crest) 732.1
  - Buchman's (juvenile osteochondrosis) 732.1
  - Burns' 732.3
  - calcaneus 732.5
  - capitular epiphysis (femur) 732.1
  - carpal
    - lunate (wrist) 732.3
    - scaphoid 732.3
  - coxae juvenilis 732.1
  - deformans juvenilis (coxae) (hip) 732.1
    - Scheuermann's 732.0
    - spine 732.0
    - tibia 732.4
    - vertebra 732.0
  - Diaz's (astragalus) 732.5
  - dissecans (knee) (shoulder) 732.7
  - femoral capital epiphysis 732.1
  - femur (head) (juvenile) 732.1
  - foot (juvenile) 732.5
  - Freiberg's (disease) (second metatarsal) 732.5
  - Haas' 732.3
  - Haglund's (os tibiale externum) 732.5
  - hand (juvenile) 732.3
  - head of
    - femur 732.1
    - humerus (juvenile) 732.3
  - hip (juvenile) 732.1
  - humerus (juvenile) 732.3
  - iliac crest (juvenile) 732.1
  - ilium (juvenile) 732.1
  - ischiopubic synchondrosis 732.1
  - Iselin's (osteochondrosis fifth metatarsal) 732.5
  - juvenile, juvenilis 732.6
    - arm 732.3
    - capital femoral epiphysis 732.1
    - capitellum humeri 732.3
    - capitular epiphysis 732.1
    - carpal scaphoid 732.3
    - clavicle, sternal epiphysis 732.6
    - coxae 732.1
    - deformans 732.1
    - foot 732.5
    - hand 732.3
    - hip and pelvis 732.1
    - lower extremity, except foot 732.4
    - lunate, wrist 732.3
    - medial cuneiform bone 732.5
    - metatarsal (head) 732.5
    - metatarsophalangeal 732.5
    - navicular, ankle 732.5
    - patella 732.4
    - primary patellar center (of Köhler) 732.4
    - specified site NEC 732.6

- **Osteochondrosis** — *continued*
  - juvenile, juvenilis — *continued*
    - spine 732.0
    - tarsal scaphoid 732.5
    - tibia (epiphysis) (tuberosity) 732.4
    - upper extremity 732.3
    - vertebra (body) (Calvé) 732.0
      - epiphyseal plates (of Scheuermann) 732.0
  - Kienböck's (disease) 732.3
  - Köhler's (disease) (navicular, ankle) 732.5
    - patellar 732.4
    - tarsal navicular 732.5
  - Legg-Calvé-Perthes (disease) 732.1
  - lower extremity (juvenile) 732.4
  - lunate bone 732.3
  - Mauclaire's 732.3
  - metacarpal heads (of Mauclaire) 732.3
  - metatarsal (fifth) (head) (second) 732.5
  - navicular, ankle 732.5
  - os calcis 732.5
  - Osgood-Schlatter 732.4
  - os tibiale externum 732.5
  - Panner's 732.3
  - patella (juvenile) 732.4
  - patellar center
    - primary (of Köhler) 732.4
    - secondary (of Sinding-Larsen) 732.4
  - pelvis (juvenile) 732.1
  - Pierson's 732.1
  - radial head (juvenile) 732.3
  - Scheuermann's 732.0
  - Sever's (calcaneum) 732.5
  - Sinding-Larsen (secondary patellar center) 732.4
  - spine (juvenile) 732.0
    - adult 732.8
  - symphysis pubis (of Pierson) (juvenile) 732.1
  - syphilitic (congenital) 090.0
  - tarsal (navicular) (scaphoid) 732.5
  - tibia (proximal) (tubercle) 732.4
  - tuberculous — *see* Tuberculosis, bone
  - ulna 732.3
  - upper extremity (juvenile) 732.3
  - van Neck's (juvenile osteochondrosis) 732.1
  - vertebral (juvenile) 732.0
    - adult 732.8
- **Osteoclastoma** (M9250/1) 238.0
  - malignant (M9250/3) — *see* Neoplasm, bone, malignant
- **Osteocopic pain** 733.90
- **Osteodynia** 733.90
- **Osteodystrophy**
  - azotemic 588.0
  - chronica deformans hypertrophica 731.0
  - congenital 756.50
    - specified type NEC 756.59
  - deformans 731.0
  - fibrosa localisata 731.0
  - parathyroid 252.01
  - renal 588.0
- **Osteofibroma** (M9262/0) — *see* Neoplasm, bone, benign
- **Osteofibrosarcoma** (M9182/3) — *see* Neoplasm, bone, malignant
- **Osteogenesis imperfecta** 756.51
- **Osteogenic** — *see* condition
- **Osteoma** (M9180/0) — *see also* Neoplasm, bone, benign
  - osteoid (M9191/0) (*see also* Neoplasm, bone, benign)
    - giant (M9200/0) — *see* Neoplasm, bone, benign
- **Osteomalacia** 268.2
  - chronica deformans hypertrophica 731.0
  - due to vitamin D deficiency 268.2
  - infantile (*see also* Rickets) 268.0
  - juvenile (*see also* Rickets) 268.0
  - pelvis 268.2
  - vitamin D-resistant 275.3
- **Osteomalacic bone** 268.2
- **Osteomalacosis** 268.2
- **Osteomyelitis** (general) (infective) (localized) (neonatal) (purulent) (pyogenic) (septic) (staphylococcal) (streptococcal) (suppurative) (with periostitis) 730.2 ☑

> *Note — Use the following fifth-digit subclassification with category 730:*
>
> *0 site unspecified*
> *1 shoulder region*
> *2 upper arm*
> *3 forearm*
> *4 hand*
> *5 pelvic region and thigh*
> *6 lower leg*
> *7 ankle and foot*
> *8 other specified sites*
> *9 multiple sites*

  - acute or subacute 730.0 ☑
  - chronic or old 730.1 ☑
  - due to or associated with
    - diabetes mellitus 250.8 ☑ *[731.8]*
      - due to secondary diabetes 249.8 ☑ *[731.8]* ●
    - tuberculosis (*see also* Tuberculosis, bone) 015.9 ☑ *[730.8]* ☑
      - limb bones 015.5 ☑ *[730.8]* ☑
      - specified bones NEC 015.7 ☑ *[730.8]* ☑
      - spine 015.0 ☑ *[730.8]* ☑
    - typhoid 002.0 *[730.8]* ☑
  - Garré's 730.1 ☑
  - jaw (acute) (chronic) (lower) (neonatal) (suppurative) (upper) 526.4
  - nonsuppurating 730.1 ☑
  - orbital 376.03
  - petrous bone (*see also* Petrositis) 383.20
  - Salmonella 003.24
  - sclerosing, nonsuppurative 730.1 ☑
  - sicca 730.1 ☑
  - syphilitic 095.5
    - congenital 090.0 *[730.8]* ☑
  - tuberculous — *see* Tuberculosis, bone
  - typhoid 002.0 *[730.8]* ☑
- **Osteomyelofibrosis** 289.89
- **Osteomyelosclerosis** 289.89
- **Osteonecrosis** 733.40
  - meaning osteomyelitis 730.1 ☑
- **Osteo-onycho-arthro dysplasia** 756.89
- **Osteo-onychodysplasia, hereditary** 756.89
- **Osteopathia**
  - condensans disseminata 756.53
  - hyperostotica multiplex infantilis 756.59
  - hypertrophica toxica 731.2
  - striata 756.4
- **Osteopathy resulting from poliomyelitis** — *see also* Poliomyelitis 045.9 ☑ *[730.7]* ☑
  - familial dysplastic 731.2
- **Osteopecilia** 756.53
- **Osteopenia** 733.90
  - borderline 733.90 ●
- **Osteoperiostitis** — *see also* Osteomyelitis 730.2 ☑
  - ossificans toxica 731.2
  - toxica ossificans 731.2
- **Osteopetrosis** (familial) 756.52
- **Osteophyte** — *see* Exostosis
- **Osteophytosis** — *see* Exostosis
- **Osteopoikilosis** 756.53
- **Osteoporosis** (generalized) 733.00
  - circumscripta 731.0
  - disuse 733.03
  - drug-induced 733.09
  - idiopathic 733.02
  - postmenopausal 733.01
- **Osteoporosis** — *continued*
  - posttraumatic 733.7
  - screening V82.81
  - senile 733.01
  - specified type NEC 733.09
- **Osteoporosis-osteomalacia syndrome** 268.2
- **Osteopsathyrosis** 756.51
- **Osteoradionecrosis, jaw** 526.89
- **Osteosarcoma** (M9180/3) — *see also* Neoplasm, bone, malignant
  - chondroblastic (M9181/3) — *see* Neoplasm, bone, malignant
  - fibroblastic (M9182/3) — *see* Neoplasm, bone, malignant
  - in Paget's disease of bone (M9184/3) — *see* Neoplasm, bone, malignant
  - juxtacortical (M9190/3) — *see* Neoplasm, bone, malignant
  - parosteal (M9190/3) — *see* Neoplasm, bone, malignant
  - telangiectatic (M9183/3) — *see* Neoplasm, bone, malignant
- **Osteosclerosis** 756.52
  - fragilis (generalisata) 756.52
- **Osteosclerotic anemia** 289.89
- **Osteosis**
  - acromegaloid 757.39
  - cutis 709.3
  - parathyroid 252.01
  - renal fibrocystic 588.0
- **Österreicher-Turner syndrome** 756.89
- **Ostium**
  - atrioventriculare commune 745.69
  - primum (arteriosum) (defect) (persistent) 745.61
  - secundum (arteriosum) (defect) (patent) (persistent) 745.5
- **Ostrum-Furst syndrome** 756.59
- **Os, uterus** — *see* condition
- **Otalgia** 388.70
  - otogenic 388.71
  - referred 388.72
- **Othematoma** 380.31
- **Otitic hydrocephalus** 348.2
- **Otitis** 382.9
  - with effusion 381.4
    - purulent 382.4
    - secretory 381.4
    - serous 381.4
    - suppurative 382.4
  - acute 382.9
  - adhesive (*see also* Adhesions, middle ear) 385.10
  - chronic 382.9
    - with effusion 381.3
    - mucoid, mucous (simple) 381.20
    - purulent 382.3
    - secretory 381.3
    - serous 381.10
    - suppurative 382.3
  - diffuse parasitic 136.8
  - externa (acute) (diffuse) (hemorrhagica) 380.10
    - actinic 380.22
    - candidal 112.82
    - chemical 380.22
    - chronic 380.23
      - mycotic — *see* Otitis, externa, mycotic
      - specified type NEC 380.23
    - circumscribed 380.10
    - contact 380.22
    - due to
      - erysipelas 035 *[380.13]*
      - impetigo 684 *[380.13]*
      - seborrheic dermatitis 690.10 *[380.13]*
    - eczematoid 380.22
    - furuncular 680.0 *[380.13]*
    - infective 380.10
      - chronic 380.16
    - malignant 380.14
    - mycotic (chronic) 380.15
- **Otitis** — *continued*
  - externa — *continued*
    - mycotic — *continued*
      - due to
        - aspergillosis 117.3 *[380.15]*
        - moniliasis 112.82
        - otomycosis 111.8 *[380.15]*
    - reactive 380.22
    - specified type NEC 380.22
    - tropical 111.8 *[380.15]*
  - insidiosa (*see also* Otosclerosis) 387.9
  - interna (*see also* Labyrinthitis) 386.30
  - media (hemorrhagic) (staphylococcal) (streptococcal) 382.9
    - acute 382.9
      - with effusion 381.00
      - allergic 381.04
        - mucoid 381.05
        - sanguineous 381.06
        - serous 381.04
      - catarrhal 381.00
      - exudative 381.00
      - mucoid 381.02
        - allergic 381.05
      - necrotizing 382.00
        - with spontaneous rupture of ear drum 382.01
        - in
          - influenza 487.8 *[382.02]*
          - measles 055.2
          - scarlet fever 034.1 *[382.02]*
      - nonsuppurative 381.00
      - purulent 382.00
        - with spontaneous rupture of ear drum 382.01
      - sanguineous 381.03
        - allergic 381.06
      - secretory 381.01
      - seromucinous 381.02
      - serous 381.01
        - allergic 381.04
      - suppurative 382.00
        - with spontaneous rupture of ear drum 382.01
        - due to
          - influenza 487.8 *[382.02]*
          - scarlet fever 034.1 *[382.02]*
      - transudative 381.00
    - adhesive (*see also* Adhesions, middle ear) 385.10
    - allergic 381.4
      - acute 381.04
        - mucoid 381.05
        - sanguineous 381.06
        - serous 381.04
      - chronic 381.3
    - catarrhal 381.4
      - acute 381.00
      - chronic (simple) 381.10
    - chronic 382.9
      - with effusion 381.3
      - adhesive (*see also* Adhesions, middle ear) 385.10
      - allergic 381.3
      - atticoantral, suppurative (with posterior or superior marginal perforation of ear drum) 382.2
      - benign suppurative (with anterior perforation of ear drum) 382.1
      - catarrhal 381.10
      - exudative 381.3
      - mucinous 381.20
      - mucoid, mucous (simple) 381.20
      - mucosanguineous 381.29
      - nonsuppurative 381.3
      - purulent 382.3
      - secretory 381.3
      - seromucinous 381.3
      - serosanguineous 381.19
      - serous (simple) 381.10
      - suppurative 382.3

Otitis — *continued*
media — *continued*
chronic — *continued*
suppurative — *continued*
atticoantral (with posterior or superior marginal perforation of ear drum) 382.2
benign (with anterior perforation of ear drum) 382.1
tuberculous (*see also* Tuberculosis) 017.4 ☑
tubotympanic 382.1
transudative 381.3
exudative 381.4
acute 381.00
chronic 381.3
fibrotic (*see also* Adhesions, middle ear) 385.10
mucoid, mucous 381.4
acute 381.02
chronic (simple) 381.20
mucosanguineous, chronic 381.29
nonsuppurative 381.4
acute 381.00
chronic 381.3
postmeasles 055.2
purulent 382.4
acute 382.00
with spontaneous rupture of ear drum 382.01
chronic 382.3
sanguineous, acute 381.03
allergic 381.06
secretory 381.4
acute or subacute 381.01
chronic 381.3
seromucinous 381.4
acute or subacute 381.02
chronic 381.3
serosanguineous, chronic 381.19
serous 381.4
acute or subacute 381.01
chronic (simple) 381.10
subacute — *see* Otitis, media, acute
suppurative 382.4
acute 382.00
with spontaneous rupture of ear drum 382.01
chronic 382.3
atticoantral 382.2
benign 382.1
tuberculous (*see also* Tuberculosis) 017.4 ☑
tubotympanic 382.1
transudative 381.4
acute 381.00
chronic 381.3
tuberculous (*see also* Tuberculosis) 017.4 ☑
postmeasles 055.2
Otoconia 386.8
Otolith syndrome 386.19
Otomycosis 111.8 *[380.15]*
in
aspergillosis 117.3 *[380.15]*
moniliasis 112.82
Otopathy 388.9
Otoporosis — *see also* Otosclerosis 387.9
Otorrhagia 388.69
traumatic — *see* nature of injury
Otorrhea 388.60
blood 388.69
cerebrospinal (fluid) 388.61
Otosclerosis (general) 387.9
cochlear (endosteal) 387.2
involving
otic capsule 387.2
oval window
nonobliterative 387.0
obliterative 387.1
round window 387.2
nonobliterative 387.0
obliterative 387.1
specified type NEC 387.8
Otospongiosis — *see also* Otosclerosis 387.9
Otto's disease or pelvis 715.35
Outburst, aggressive — *see also* Disturbance, conduct 312.0 ☑
in children or adolescents 313.9
Outcome of delivery
multiple birth NEC V27.9
all liveborn V27.5
all stillborn V27.7
some liveborn V27.6
unspecified V27.9
single V27.9
liveborn V27.0
stillborn V27.1
twins V27.9
both liveborn V27.2
both stillborn V27.4
one liveborn, one stillborn V27.3
Outlet — *see also* condition
syndrome (thoracic) 353.0
Outstanding ears (bilateral) 744.29
Ovalocytosis (congenital) (hereditary) — *see also* Elliptocytosis 282.1
Ovarian — *see also* condition
pregnancy — *see* Pregnancy, ovarian
remnant syndrome 620.8
vein syndrome 593.4
Ovaritis (cystic) — *see also* Salpingo-oophoritis 614.2
Ovary, ovarian — *see* condition
Overactive — *see also* Hyperfunction
bladder 596.51
eye muscle (*see also* Strabismus) 378.9
hypothalamus 253.8
thyroid (*see also* Thyrotoxicosis) 242.9 ☑
Overactivity, child 314.01
Overbite (deep) (excessive) (horizontal) (vertical) 524.29
Overbreathing — *see also* Hyperventilation 786.01
Overconscientious personality 301.4
Overdevelopment — *see also* Hypertrophy
breast (female) (male) 611.1
nasal bones 738.0
prostate, congenital 752.89
Overdistention — *see* Distention
Overdose overdosage (drug) 977.9
specified drug or substance — *see* Table of Drugs and Chemicals
Overeating 783.6
nonorganic origin 307.51
Overexertion (effects) (exhaustion) 994.5
Overexposure (effects) 994.9
exhaustion 994.4
Overfeeding — *see also* Overeating 783.6
Overfill, endodontic 526.62
Overgrowth, bone NEC 733.99
Overhanging
tooth restoration 525.62
unrepairable, dental restorative materials 525.62
Overheated (effects) (places) — *see* Heat
Overinhibited child 313.0
Overjet 524.29
excessive horizontal 524.26
Overlaid, overlying (suffocation) 994.7
Overlap
excessive horizontal 524.26
Overlapping toe (acquired) 735.8
congenital (fifth toe) 755.66
Overload
fluid 276.6
potassium (K) 276.7
sodium (Na) 276.0
Overnutrition — *see also* Hyperalimentation 783.6
Overproduction — *see also* Hypersecretion
ACTH 255.3
cortisol 255.0
growth hormone 253.0
Overproduction — *see also* Hypersecretion — *continued*
thyroid-stimulating hormone (TSH) 242.8 ☑
Overriding
aorta 747.21
finger (acquired) 736.29
congenital 755.59
toe (acquired) 735.8
congenital 755.66
Oversize
fetus (weight of 4500 grams or more) 766.0
affecting management of pregnancy 656.6 ☑
causing disproportion 653.5 ☑
with obstructed labor 660.1 ☑
affecting fetus or newborn 763.1
Overstimulation, ovarian 256.1
Overstrained 780.79
heart — *see* Hypertrophy, cardiac
Overweight — *see also* Obesity 278.02
Overwork 780.79
Oviduct — *see* condition
Ovotestis 752.7
Ovulation (cycle)
failure or lack of 628.0
pain 625.2
Ovum
blighted 631
donor V59.70
over age 35 V59.73
anonymous recipient V59.73
designated recipient V59.74
under age 35 V59.71
anonymous recipient V59.71
designated recipient V59.72
dropsical 631
pathologic 631
Owren's disease or syndrome (parahemophilia) — *see also* Defect, coagulation 286.3
Oxalosis 271.8
Oxaluria 271.8
Ox heart — *see* Hypertrophy, cardiac
OX syndrome 758.6
Oxycephaly, oxycephalic 756.0
syphilitic, congenital 090.0
Oxyuriasis 127.4
Oxyuris vermicularis (infestation) 127.4
Ozena 472.0

P

Pacemaker syndrome 429.4
Pachyderma, pachydermia 701.8
laryngis 478.5
laryngitis 478.79
larynx (verrucosa) 478.79
Pachydermatitis 701.8
Pachydermatocele (congenital) 757.39
acquired 701.8
Pachydermatosis 701.8
Pachydermoperiostitis
secondary 731.2
Pachydermoperiostosis
primary idiopathic 757.39
secondary 731.2
Pachymeningitis (adhesive) (basal) (brain) (cerebral) (cervical) (chronic) (circumscribed) (external) (fibrous) (hemorrhagic) (hypertrophic) (internal) (purulent) (spinal) (suppurative) — *see also* Meningitis 322.9
gonococcal 098.82
Pachyonychia (congenital) 757.5
acquired 703.8
Pachyperiosteodermia
primary or idiopathic 757.39
secondary 731.2
Pachyperiostosis
primary or idiopathic 757.39
secondary 731.2
Pacinian tumor (M9507/0) — *see* Neoplasm, skin, benign
Pads, knuckle or Garrod's 728.79
Paget's disease (osteitis deformans) 731.0
with infiltrating duct carcinoma of the breast (M8541/3) — *see* Neoplasm, breast, malignant
bone 731.0
osteosarcoma in (M9184/3) — *see* Neoplasm, bone, malignant
breast (M8540/3) 174.0
extramammary (M8542/3) (*see also* Neoplasm, skin, malignant)
anus 154.3
skin 173.5
malignant (M8540/3)
breast 174.0
specified site NEC (M8542/3) — *see* Neoplasm, skin, malignant
unspecified site 174.0
mammary (M8540/3) 174.0
necrosis of bone 731.0
nipple (M8540/3) 174.0
osteitis deformans 731.0
Paget-Schroetter syndrome (intermittent venous claudication) 453.8
Pain(s) (*see also* Painful) 780.96
abdominal 789.0 ☑
acute 338.19
due to trauma 338.11
postoperative 338.18
post-thoracotomy 338.12
adnexa (uteri) 625.9
alimentary, due to vascular insufficiency 557.9
anginoid (*see also* Pain, precordial) 786.51
anus 569.42
arch 729.5
arm 729.5
axillary 729.5
back (postural) 724.5
low 724.2
psychogenic 307.89
bile duct 576.9
bladder 788.99 ▲
bone 733.90
breast 611.71
psychogenic 307.89
broad ligament 625.9
cancer associated 338.3
cartilage NEC 733.90
cecum 789.0 ☑
cervicobrachial 723.3
chest (central) 786.50
atypical 786.59
midsternal 786.51
musculoskeletal 786.59
noncardiac 786.59
substernal 786.51
wall (anterior) 786.52
chronic 338.29
associated with significant psychosocial dysfunction 338.4
due to trauma 338.21
postoperative 338.28
post-thoracotomy 338.22
syndrome 338.4
coccyx 724.79
colon 789.0 ☑
common duct 576.9
coronary — *see* Angina
costochondral 786.52
diaphragm 786.52
due to (presence of) any device, implant, or graft classifiable to 996.0–996.5 — *see* Complications, due to (presence of) any device, implant, or graft classified to 996.0–996.5 NEC
malignancy (primary) (secondary) 338.3
ear (*see also* Otalgia) 388.70
epigastric, epigastrium 789.06
extremity (lower) (upper) 729.5
eye 379.91
face, facial 784.0

Pain(s) (*see also* Painful) — *continued*
face, facial — *continued*
atypical 350.2
nerve 351.8
false (labor) 644.1 ☑
female genital organ NEC 625.9
psychogenic 307.89
finger 729.5
flank 789.0 ☑
foot 729.5
gallbladder 575.9
gas (intestinal) 787.3
gastric 536.8
generalized 780.96
genital organ
female 625.9
male 608.9
psychogenic 307.89
groin 789.0 ☑
growing 781.99
hand 729.5
head (*see also* Headache) 784.0
heart (see also Pain, precordial) 786.51
infraorbital (*see also* Neuralgia, trigeminal) 350.1
intermenstrual 625.2
jaw 526.9
joint 719.40
ankle 719.47
elbow 719.42
foot 719.47
hand 719.44
hip 719.45
knee 719.46
multiple sites 719.49
pelvic region 719.45
psychogenic 307.89
shoulder (region) 719.41
specified site NEC 719.48
wrist 719.43
kidney 788.0
labor, false or spurious 644.1 ☑
laryngeal 784.1
leg 729.5
limb 729.5
low back 724.2
lumbar region 724.2
mastoid (*see also* Otalgia) 388.70
maxilla 526.9
menstrual 625.3
metacarpophalangeal (joint) 719.44
metatarsophalangeal (joint) 719.47
mouth 528.9
muscle 729.1
intercostal 786.59
musculoskeletal (see also Pain, by site) 729.1
nasal 478.19
nasopharynx 478.29
neck NEC 723.1
psychogenic 307.89
neoplasm related (acute) (chronic) 338.3
nerve NEC 729.2
neuromuscular 729.1
nose 478.19
ocular 379.91
ophthalmic 379.91
orbital region 379.91
osteocopic 733.90
ovary 625.9
psychogenic 307.89
over heart (*see also* Pain, precordial) 786.51
ovulation 625.2
pelvic (female) 625.9
male NEC 789.0 ☑
psychogenic 307.89
psychogenic 307.89
penis 607.9
psychogenic 307.89
pericardial (*see also* Pain, precordial) 786.51
perineum
female 625.9

Pain(s) (*see also* Painful) — *continued*
perineum — *continued*
male 608.9
pharynx 478.29
pleura, pleural, pleuritic 786.52
postoperative 338.18
acute 338.18
chronic 338.28
post-thoracotomy 338.12
acute 338.12
chronic 338.22
preauricular 388.70
precordial (region) 786.51
psychogenic 307.89
premenstrual 625.4
psychogenic 307.80
cardiovascular system 307.89
gastrointestinal system 307.89
genitourinary system 307.89
heart 307.89
musculoskeletal system 307.89
respiratory system 307.89
skin 306.3
radicular (spinal) (*see also* Radiculitis) 729.2
rectum 569.42
respiration 786.52
retrosternal 786.51
rheumatic NEC 729.0
muscular 729.1
rib 786.50
root (spinal) (*see also* Radiculitis) 729.2
round ligament (stretch) 625.9
sacroiliac 724.6
sciatic 724.3
scrotum 608.9
psychogenic 307.89
seminal vesicle 608.9
sinus 478.19
skin 782.0
spermatic cord 608.9
spinal root (*see also* Radiculitis) 729.2
stomach 536.8
psychogenic 307.89
substernal 786.51
temporomandibular (joint) 524.62
temporomaxillary joint 524.62
testis 608.9
psychogenic 307.89
thoracic spine 724.1
with radicular and visceral pain 724.4
throat 784.1
tibia 733.90
toe 729.5
tongue 529.6
tooth 525.9
total hip replacement 996.77
total knee replacement 996.77
trigeminal (*see also* Neuralgia, trigeminal) 350.1
tumor associated 338.3
umbilicus 789.05
ureter 788.0
urinary (organ) (system) 788.0
uterus 625.9
psychogenic 307.89
vagina 625.9
vertebrogenic (syndrome) 724.5
vesical 788.99 ▲
vulva 625.9
xiphoid 733.90
Painful — *see also* Pain
arc syndrome 726.19
coitus
female 625.0
male 608.89
psychogenic 302.76
ejaculation (semen) 608.89
psychogenic 302.79
erection 607.3
feet syndrome 266.2
menstruation 625.3
psychogenic 306.52
micturition 788.1

Painful — *see also* Pain — *continued*
ophthalmoplegia 378.55
respiration 786.52
scar NEC 709.2
urination 788.1
wire sutures 998.89
Painters' colic 984.9
specified type of lead — *see* Table of Drugs and Chemicals
Palate — *see* condition
Palatoplegia 528.9
Palatoschisis — *see also* Cleft, palate 749.00
Palilalia 784.69
Palindromic arthritis — *see also* Rheumatism, palindromic 719.3 ☑
Palliative care V66.7
Pallor 782.61
temporal, optic disc 377.15
Palmar — *see also* condition
fascia — *see* condition
Palpable
cecum 569.89
kidney 593.89
liver 573.9
lymph nodes 785.6
ovary 620.8
prostate 602.9
spleen (*see also* Splenomegaly) 789.2
uterus 625.8
Palpitation (heart) 785.1
psychogenic 306.2
Palsy — *see also* Paralysis 344.9
atrophic diffuse 335.20
Bell's 351.0
newborn 767.5
birth 767.7
brachial plexus 353.0
fetus or newborn 767.6
brain (*see also* Palsy, cerebral)
noncongenital or noninfantile 344.89
late effect — *see* Late effect(s) (of) cerebrovascular disease
syphilitic 094.89
congenital 090.49
bulbar (chronic) (progressive) 335.22
pseudo NEC 335.23
supranuclear NEC 344.8 ☑
cerebral (congenital) (infantile) (spastic) 343.9
athetoid 333.71
diplegic 343.0
late effect — *see* Late effect(s) (of) cerebrovascular disease
hemiplegic 343.1
monoplegic 343.3
noncongenital or noninfantile 437.8
late effect — *see* Late effect(s) (of) cerebrovascular disease
paraplegic 343.0
quadriplegic 343.2
spastic, not congenital or infantile 344.89
syphilitic 094.89
congenital 090.49
tetraplegic 343.2
cranial nerve (*see also* Disorder, nerve, cranial)
multiple 352.6
creeping 335.21
divers' 993.3
Erb's (birth injury) 767.6
facial 351.0
newborn 767.5
glossopharyngeal 352.2
Klumpke (-Déjérine) 767.6
lead 984.9
specified type of lead — *see* Table of Drugs and Chemicals
median nerve (tardy) 354.0
peroneal nerve (acute) (tardy) 355.3

Palsy — *see also* Paralysis — *continued*
progressive supranuclear 333.0
pseudobulbar NEC 335.23
radial nerve (acute) 354.3
seventh nerve 351.0
newborn 767.5
shaking (*see also* Parkinsonism) 332.0
spastic (cerebral) (spinal) 343.9
hemiplegic 343.1
specified nerve NEC — *see* Disorder, nerve
supranuclear NEC 356.8
progressive 333.0
ulnar nerve (tardy) 354.2
wasting 335.21
Paltauf-Sternberg disease 201.9 ☑
Paludism — *see* Malaria
Panama fever 084.0
Panaris (with lymphangitis) 681.9
finger 681.02
toe 681.11
Panaritium (with lymphangitis) 681.9
finger 681.02
toe 681.11
Panarteritis (nodosa) 446.0
brain or cerebral 437.4
Pancake heart 793.2
with cor pulmonale (chronic) 416.9
Pancarditis (acute) (chronic) 429.89
with
rheumatic
fever (active) (acute) (chronic) (subacute) 391.8
inactive or quiescent 398.99
rheumatic, acute 391.8
chronic or inactive 398.99
Pancoast's syndrome or tumor (carcinoma, pulmonary apex) (M8010/3) 162.3
Pancoast-Tobias syndrome (M8010/3) (carcinoma, pulmonary apex) 162.3
Pancolitis 556.6
Pancreas, pancreatic — *see* condition
Pancreatitis 577.0
acute (edematous) (hemorrhagic) (recurrent) 577.0
annular 577.0
apoplectic 577.0
calcerceous 577.0
chronic (infectious) 577.1
recurrent 577.1
cystic 577.2
fibrous 577.8
gangrenous 577.0
hemorrhagic (acute) 577.0
interstitial (chronic) 577.1
acute 577.0
malignant 577.0
mumps 072.3
painless 577.1
recurrent 577.1
relapsing 577.1
subacute 577.0
suppurative 577.0
syphilitic 095.8
Pancreatolithiasis 577.8
Pancytolysis 289.9
Pancytopenia (acquired) 284.1
with malformations 284.09
congenital 284.09
Panencephalitis — *see also* Encephalitis
subacute, sclerosing 046.2
Panhematopenia 284.81
congenital 284.09
constitutional 284.09
splenic, primary 289.4
Panhemocytopenia 284.81
congenital 284.09
constitutional 284.09
Panhypogonadism 257.2
Panhypopituitarism 253.2
prepubertal 253.3
Panic (attack) (state) 300.01
reaction to exceptional stress (transient) 308.0

Panmyelopathy, familial constitutional 284.09
Panmyelophthisis 284.2
- acquired (secondary) 284.81
- congenital 284.2
- idiopathic 284.9

Panmyelosis (acute) (M9951/1) 238.79
Panner's disease 732.3
- capitellum humeri 732.3
- head of humerus 732.3
- tarsal navicular (bone) (osteochondrosis) 732.5

Panneuritis endemica 265.0 *[357.4]*
Panniculitis 729.30
- back 724.8
- knee 729.31
- mesenteric 567.82
- neck 723.6
- nodular, nonsuppurative 729.30
- sacral 724.8
- specified site NEC 729.39

Panniculus adiposus (abdominal) 278.1
Pannus (corneal) 370.62
- abdominal (symptomatic) 278.1
- allergic eczematous 370.62
- degenerativus 370.62
- keratic 370.62
- rheumatoid — *see* Arthritis, rheumatoid
- trachomatosus, trachomatous (active) 076.1 *[370.62]*
  - late effect 139.1

Panophthalmitis 360.02
Panotitis — *see* Otitis media
Pansinusitis (chronic) (hyperplastic) (nonpurulent) (purulent) 473.8
- acute 461.8
- due to fungus NEC 117.9
- tuberculous (*see also* Tuberculosis) 012.8 ☑

Panuveitis 360.12
- sympathetic 360.11

Panvalvular disease — *see* Endocarditis, mitral
Papageienkrankheit 073.9
Papanicolaou smear
- anus 796.70 ●
  - with ●
    - atypical squamous cells ●
      - cannot exclude high grade squamous intraepithelial lesion (ASC-H) 796.72 ●
      - of undetermined significance (ASC-US) 796.71 ●
    - cytologic evidence of malignancy 796.76 ●
    - high grade squamous intraepithelial lesion (HGSIL) 796.74 ●
    - low grade squamous intraepithelial lesion (LGSIL) 796.73 ●
  - glandular 796.70 ●
  - specified finding NEC 796.79 ●
  - unsatisfactory cytology 796.78 ●
- cervix (screening test) V76.2
  - as part of gynecological examination V72.31
  - for suspected malignant neoplasm V76.2
    - no disease found V71.1
  - inadequate ▶cytology◀ sample 795.08
  - nonspecific abnormal finding 795.00
    - with
      - atypical squamous cells
        - cannot exclude high grade squamous intraepithelial lesion (ASC-H) 795.02
        - of undetermined significance (ASC-US) 795.01
      - cytologic evidence of malignancy 795.06
      - high grade squamous intraepithelial lesion (HGSIL) 795.04
      - low grade squamous intraepithelial lesion (LGSIL) 795.03
    - nonspecific finding NEC 795.09
    - to confirm findings of recent normal smear following initial abnormal smear V72.32
  - satisfactory smear but lacking transformation zone 795.07 ●
  - unsatisfactory ▶cervical cytology◀ 795.08
- other specified site (*see also* Screening, malignant neoplasm)
  - for suspected malignant neoplasm (*see also* Screening, malignant neoplasm)
    - no disease found V71.1
  - nonspecific abnormal finding 796.9 ▲
- vagina V76.47 ●
  - with ●
    - atypical squamous cells ●
      - cannot exclude high grade squamous intraepithelial lesion (ASC-H) 795.12 ●
      - of undetermined significance (ASC-US) 795.11 ●
    - cytologic evidence of malignancy 795.16 ●
    - high grade squamous intraepithelial lesion (HGSIL) 795.14 ●
    - low grade squamous intraepithelial lesion (LGSIL) 795.13 ●
  - abnormal NEC 795.19 ●
  - following hysterectomy for malignant condition V67.01
  - inadequate cytology sample 795.18 ●
  - unsatisfactory cytology 795.18 ●

Papilledema 377.00
- associated with
  - decreased ocular pressure 377.02
  - increased intracranial pressure 377.01
  - retinal disorder 377.03
- choked disc 377.00
- infectional 377.00

Papillitis 377.31
- anus 569.49
- chronic lingual 529.4
- necrotizing, kidney 584.7
- optic 377.31
- rectum 569.49
- renal, necrotizing 584.7
- tongue 529.0

Papilloma (M8050/0) — *see also* Neoplasm, by site, benign

> *Note — Except where otherwise indicated, the morphological varieties of papilloma in the list below should be coded by site as for "Neoplasm, benign."*

- acuminatum (female) (male) 078.11
- bladder (urinary) (transitional cell) (M8120/1) 236.7
  - benign (M8120/0) 223.3
- choroid plexus (M9390/0) 225.0
  - anaplastic type (M9390/3) 191.5
  - malignant (M9390/3) 191.5
- ductal (M8503/0)
- dyskeratotic (M8052/0)
- epidermoid (M8052/0)
- hyperkeratotic (M8052/0)
- intracystic (M8504/0)
- intraductal (M8503/0)
- inverted (M8053/0)
- keratotic (M8052/0)
- parakeratotic (M8052/0)
- pinta (primary) 103.0
- renal pelvis (transitional cell) (M8120/1) 236.99
  - benign (M8120/0) 223.1
- Schneiderian (M8121/0)
  - specified site — *see* Neoplasm, by site, benign
  - unspecified site 212.0
- serous surface (M8461/0)
  - borderline malignancy (M8461/1)
    - specified site — *see* Neoplasm, by site, uncertain behavior
    - unspecified site 236.2
  - specified site — *see* Neoplasm, by site, benign
  - unspecified site 220
- squamous (cell) (M8052/0)
- transitional (cell) (M8120/0)
  - bladder (urinary) (M8120/1) 236.7
  - inverted type (M8121/1) — *see* Neoplasm, by site, uncertain behavior
  - renal pelvis (M8120/1) 236.91
  - ureter (M8120/1) 236.91
- ureter (transitional cell) (M8120/1) 236.91
  - benign (M8120/0) 223.2
- urothelial (M8120/1) — *see* Neoplasm, by site, uncertain behavior
- verrucous (M8051/0)
- villous (M8261/1) — *see* Neoplasm, by site, uncertain behavior
- yaws, plantar or palmar 102.1

Papillomata, multiple, of yaws 102.1
Papillomatosis (M8060/0) — *see also* Neoplasm, by site, benign
- confluent and reticulate 701.8
- cutaneous 701.8
- ductal, breast 610.1
- Gougerot-Carteaud (confluent reticulate) 701.8
- intraductal (diffuse) (M8505/0) — *see* Neoplasm, by site, benign
- subareolar duct (M8506/0) 217

Papillon-Léage and Psaume syndrome (orodigitofacial dysostosis) 759.89
Papule 709.8
- carate (primary) 103.0
- fibrous, of nose (M8724/0) 216.3
- pinta (primary) 103.0

Papulosis, malignant 447.8
Papyraceous fetus 779.89
- complicating pregnancy 646.0 ☑

Paracephalus 759.7
Parachute mitral valve 746.5
Paracoccidioidomycosis 116.1
- mucocutaneous-lymphangitic 116.1
- pulmonary 116.1
- visceral 116.1

Paracoccidiomycosis — *see* Paracoccidioidomycosis
Paracusis 388.40
Paradentosis 523.5
Paradoxical facial movements 374.43
Paraffinoma 999.9
Paraganglioma (M8680/1)
- adrenal (M8700/0) 227.0
  - malignant (M8700/3) 194.0
- aortic body (M8691/1) 237.3
  - malignant (M8691/3) 194.6
- carotid body (M8692/1) 237.3
  - malignant (M8692/3) 194.5
- chromaffin (M8700/0) (*see also* Neoplasm, by site, benign)
  - malignant (M8700/3) — *see* Neoplasm, by site, malignant
- extra-adrenal (M8693/1)
  - malignant (M8693/3)
    - specified site — *see* Neoplasm, by site, malignant
    - unspecified site 194.6
  - specified site — *see* Neoplasm, by site, uncertain behavior
  - unspecified site 237.3
- glomus jugulare (M8690/1) 237.3
  - malignant (M8690/3) 194.6
- jugular (M8690/1) 237.3
  - malignant (M8680/3)
    - specified site — *see* Neoplasm, by site, malignant
    - unspecified site 194.6
- nonchromaffin (M8693/1)
  - malignant (M8693/3)
    - specified site — *see* Neoplasm, by site, malignant
    - unspecified site 194.6
  - specified site — *see* Neoplasm, by site, uncertain behavior
  - unspecified site 237.3
- parasympathetic (M8682/1)
  - specified site — *see* Neoplasm, by site, uncertain behavior
  - unspecified site 237.3
- specified site — *see* Neoplasm, by site, uncertain behavior
- sympathetic (M8681/1)
  - specified site — *see* Neoplasm, by site, uncertain behavior
  - unspecified site 237.3
- unspecified site 237.3

Parageusia 781.1
- psychogenic 306.7

Paragonimiasis 121.2
Paragranuloma, Hodgkin's (M9660/3) 201.0 ☑
Parahemophilia — *see also* Defect, coagulation 286.3
Parakeratosis 690.8
- psoriasiformis 696.2
- variegata 696.2

Paralysis, paralytic (complete) (incomplete) 344.9
- with
  - broken
    - back — *see* Fracture, vertebra, by site, with spinal cord injury
    - neck — *see* Fracture, vertebra, cervical, with spinal cord injury
  - fracture, vertebra — *see* Fracture, vertebra, by site, with spinal cord injury
  - syphilis 094.89
- abdomen and back muscles 355.9
- abdominal muscles 355.9
- abducens (nerve) 378.54
- abductor 355.9
  - lower extremity 355.8
  - upper extremity 354.9
- accessory nerve 352.4
- accommodation 367.51
  - hysterical 300.11
- acoustic nerve 388.5
- agitans 332.0
  - arteriosclerotic 332.0
- alternating 344.89
  - oculomotor 344.89
- amyotrophic 335.20
- ankle 355.8
- anterior serratus 355.9
- anus (sphincter) 569.49
- apoplectic (current episode) (*see also* Disease, cerebrovascular, acute) 436
  - late effect — *see* Late effect(s) (of) cerebrovascular disease

☑ Additional Digit Required — Refer to the Tabular List for Digit Selection

▽ Subterms under main terms may continue to next column or page

Paralysis, paralytic — *continued*
- arm 344.40
  - affecting
    - dominant side 344.41
    - nondominant side 344.42
  - both 344.2
  - hysterical 300.11
  - late effect — *see* Late effect(s) (of) cerebrovascular disease
  - psychogenic 306.0
    - transient 781.4
    - traumatic NEC (*see also* Injury, nerve, upper limb) 955.9
- arteriosclerotic (current episode) 437.0
  - late effect — *see* Late effect(s) (of) cerebrovascular disease
- ascending (spinal), acute 357.0
- associated, nuclear 344.89
- asthenic bulbar 358.00
- ataxic NEC 334.9
  - general 094.1
- athetoid 333.71
- atrophic 356.9
  - infantile, acute (*see also* Poliomyelitis, with paralysis) 045.1 ☑
  - muscle NEC 355.9
  - progressive 335.21
  - spinal (acute) (*see also* Poliomyelitis, with paralysis) 045.1 ☑
- attack (*see also* Disease, cerebrovascular, acute) 436
- axillary 353.0
- Babinski-Nageotte's 344.89
- Bell's 351.0
  - newborn 767.5
- Benedikt's 344.89
- birth (injury) 767.7
  - brain 767.0
  - intracranial 767.0
  - spinal cord 767.4
- bladder (sphincter) 596.53
  - neurogenic 596.54
    - with cauda equina syndrome 344.61
  - puerperal, postpartum, childbirth 665.5 ☑
  - sensory 596.54
    - with cauda equina 344.61
  - spastic 596.54
    - with cauda equina 344.61
- bowel, colon, or intestine (*see also* Ileus) 560.1
- brachial plexus 353.0
  - due to birth injury 767.6
  - newborn 767.6
- brain
  - congenital — *see* Palsy, cerebral
  - current episode 437.8
  - diplegia 344.2
  - hemiplegia 342.9 ☑
    - late effect — *see* Late effect(s) (of) cerebrovascular disease
  - infantile — *see* Palsy, cerebral
  - late effect — *see* Late effect(s) (of) cerebrovascular disease
  - monoplegia (*see also* Monoplegia)
    - late effect — *see* Late effect(s) (of) cerebrovascular disease
  - paraplegia 344.1
  - quadriplegia — *see* Quadriplegia
  - syphilitic, congenital 090.49
  - triplegia 344.89
- bronchi 519.19
- Brown-Séquard's 344.89
- bulbar (chronic) (progressive) 335.22
  - infantile (*see also* Poliomyelitis, bulbar) 045.0 ☑
  - poliomyelitic (*see also* Poliomyelitis, bulbar) 045.0 ☑
  - pseudo 335.23
  - supranuclear 344.89
- bulbospinal 358.00
- cardiac (*see also* Failure, heart) 428.9

Paralysis, paralytic — *continued*
- cerebral
  - current episode 437.8
  - spastic, infantile — *see* Palsy, cerebral
- cerebrocerebellar 437.8
  - diplegic infantile 343.0
- cervical
  - plexus 353.2
  - sympathetic NEC 337.09 ▲
- Céstan-Chenais 344.89
- Charcôt-Marie-Tooth type 356.1
- childhood — *see* Palsy, cerebral
- Clark's 343.9
- colon (*see also* Ileus) 560.1
- compressed air 993.3
- compression
  - arm NEC 354.9
  - cerebral — *see* Paralysis, brain
  - leg NEC 355.8
  - lower extremity NEC 355.8
  - upper extremity NEC 354.9
- congenital (cerebral) (spastic) (spinal) — *see* Palsy, cerebral
- conjugate movement (of eye) 378.81
  - cortical (nuclear) (supranuclear) 378.81
- convergence 378.83
- cordis (*see also* Failure, heart) 428.9
- cortical (*see also* Paralysis, brain) 437.8
- cranial or cerebral nerve (*see also* Disorder, nerve, cranial) 352.9
- creeping 335.21
- crossed leg 344.89
- crutch 953.4
- deglutition 784.99
  - hysterical 300.11
- dementia 094.1
- descending (spinal) NEC 335.9
- diaphragm (flaccid) 519.4
  - due to accidental section of phrenic nerve during procedure 998.2
- digestive organs NEC 564.89
- diplegic — *see* Diplegia
- divergence (nuclear) 378.85
- divers' 993.3
- Duchenne's 335.22
- due to intracranial or spinal birth injury — *see* Palsy, cerebral
- embolic (current episode) (*see also* Embolism, brain) 434.1 ☑
  - late effect — *see* Late effect(s) (of) cerebrovascular disease
- enteric (*see also* Ileus) 560.1
  - with hernia — *see* Hernia, by site, with obstruction
- Erb (-Duchenne) (birth) (newborn) 767.6
- Erb's syphilitic spastic spinal 094.89
- esophagus 530.89
- essential, infancy (*see also* Poliomyelitis) 045.9 ☑
- extremity
  - lower — *see* Paralysis, leg
  - spastic (hereditary) 343.3
    - noncongenital or noninfantile 344.1
  - transient (cause unknown) 781.4
  - upper — *see* Paralysis, arm
- eye muscle (extrinsic) 378.55
  - intrinsic 367.51
- facial (nerve) 351.0
  - birth injury 767.5
  - congenital 767.5
  - following operation NEC 998.2
  - newborn 767.5
- familial 359.3
  - periodic 359.3
  - spastic 334.1
- fauces 478.29
- finger NEC 354.9
- foot NEC 355.8
- gait 781.2
- gastric nerve 352.3

Paralysis, paralytic — *continued*
- gaze 378.81
- general 094.1
  - ataxic 094.1
  - insane 094.1
  - juvenile 090.40
  - progressive 094.1
  - tabetic 094.1
- glossopharyngeal (nerve) 352.2
- glottis (*see also* Paralysis, vocal cord) 478.30
- gluteal 353.4
- Gubler (-Millard) 344.89
- hand 354.9
  - hysterical 300.11
  - psychogenic 306.0
- heart (*see also* Failure, heart) 428.9
- hemifacial, progressive 349.89
- hemiplegic — *see* Hemiplegia
- hyperkalemic periodic (familial) 359.3
- hypertensive (current episode) 437.8
- hypoglossal (nerve) 352.5
- hypokalemic periodic 359.3
- Hyrtl's sphincter (rectum) 569.49
- hysterical 300.11
- ileus (*see also* Ileus) 560.1
- infantile (*see also* Poliomyelitis) 045.9 ☑
  - atrophic acute 045.1 ☑
  - bulbar 045.0 ☑
  - cerebral — *see* Palsy, cerebral
  - paralytic 045.1 ☑
  - progressive acute 045.9 ☑
  - spastic — *see* Palsy, cerebral
  - spinal 045.9 ☑
- infective (*see also* Poliomyelitis) 045.9 ☑
- inferior nuclear 344.9
- insane, general or progressive 094.1
- internuclear 378.86
- interosseous 355.9
- intestine (*see also* Ileus) 560.1
- intracranial (current episode) (*see also* Paralysis, brain) 437.8
  - due to birth injury 767.0
- iris 379.49
  - due to diphtheria (toxin) 032.81 *[379.49]*
- ischemic, Volkmann's (complicating trauma) 958.6
- isolated sleep, recurrent
- Jackson's 344.89
- jake 357.7
- Jamaica ginger (jake) 357.7
- juvenile general 090.40
- Klumpke (-Déjérine) (birth) (newborn) 767.6
- labioglossal (laryngeal) (pharyngeal) 335.22
- Landry's 357.0
- laryngeal nerve (recurrent) (superior) (*see also* Paralysis, vocal cord) 478.30
- larynx (*see also* Paralysis, vocal cord) 478.30
  - due to diphtheria (toxin) 032.3
- late effect
  - due to
    - birth injury, brain or spinal (cord) — *see* Palsy, cerebral
    - edema, brain or cerebral — *see* Paralysis, brain
    - lesion
      - late effect — *see* Late effect(s) (of) cerebrovascular disease
      - spinal (cord) — *see* Paralysis, spinal
- lateral 335.24
- lead 984.9
  - specified type of lead — *see* Table of Drugs and Chemicals
- left side — *see* Hemiplegia
- leg 344.30

Paralysis, paralytic — *continued*
- leg — *continued*
  - affecting
    - dominant side 344.31
    - nondominant side 344.32
  - both (*see also* Paraplegia) 344.1
  - crossed 344.89
  - hysterical 300.11
  - psychogenic 306.0
  - transient or transitory 781.4
    - traumatic NEC (*see also* Injury, nerve, lower limb) 956.9
- levator palpebrae superioris 374.31
- limb NEC 344.5
  - all four — *see* Quadriplegia
  - quadriplegia — *see* Quadriplegia
- lip 528.5
- Lissauer's 094.1
- local 355.9
- lower limb (*see also* Paralysis, leg)
  - both (*see also* Paraplegia) 344.1
- lung 518.89
  - newborn 770.89
- median nerve 354.1
- medullary (tegmental) 344.89
- mesencephalic NEC 344.89
  - tegmental 344.89
- middle alternating 344.89
- Millard-Gubler-Foville 344.89
- monoplegic — *see* Monoplegia
- motor NEC 344.9
  - cerebral — *see* Paralysis, brain
  - spinal — *see* Paralysis, spinal
- multiple
  - cerebral — *see* Paralysis, brain
  - spinal — *see* Paralysis, spinal
- muscle (flaccid) 359.9
  - due to nerve lesion NEC 355.9
  - eye (extrinsic) 378.55
    - intrinsic 367.51
    - oblique 378.51
  - iris sphincter 364.89
  - ischemic (complicating trauma) (Volkmann's) 958.6
  - pseudohypertrophic 359.1
- muscular (atrophic) 359.9
  - progressive 335.21
- musculocutaneous nerve 354.9
- musculospiral 354.9
- nerve (*see also* Disorder, nerve)
  - third or oculomotor (partial) 378.51
    - total 378.52
  - fourth or trochlear 378.53
  - sixth or abducens 378.54
  - seventh or facial 351.0
    - birth injury 767.5
    - due to
      - injection NEC 999.9
      - operation NEC 997.09
    - newborn 767.5
  - accessory 352.4
  - auditory 388.5
  - birth injury 767.7
  - cranial or cerebral (*see also* Disorder, nerve, cranial) 352.9
  - facial 351.0
    - birth injury 767.5
    - newborn 767.5
  - laryngeal (*see also* Paralysis, vocal cord) 478.30
  - newborn 767.7
  - phrenic 354.8
    - newborn 767.7
  - radial 354.3
    - birth injury 767.6
    - newborn 767.6
  - syphilitic 094.89
  - traumatic NEC (*see also* Injury, nerve, by site) 957.9
  - trigeminal 350.9
  - ulnar 354.2
- newborn NEC 767.0
- normokalemic periodic 359.3
- obstetrical, newborn 767.7
- ocular 378.9
- oculofacial, congenital 352.6

Paralysis, paralytic — *continued*
oculomotor (nerve) (partial) 378.51
alternating 344.89
external bilateral 378.55
total 378.52
olfactory nerve 352.0
palate 528.9
palatopharyngolaryngeal 352.6
paratrigeminal 350.9
periodic (familial) (hyperkalemic) (hypokalemic) (normokalemic) (potassium sensitive) (secondary) 359.3
peripheral
autonomic nervous system — *see* Neuropathy, peripheral, autonomic
nerve NEC 355.9
peroneal (nerve) 355.3
pharynx 478.29
phrenic nerve 354.8
plantar nerves 355.6
pneumogastric nerve 352.3
poliomyelitis (current) (*see also* Poliomyelitis, with paralysis) 045.1 ☑
bulbar 045.0 ☑
popliteal nerve 355.3
pressure (*see also* Neuropathy, entrapment) 355.9
progressive 335.21
atrophic 335.21
bulbar 335.22
general 094.1
hemifacial 349.89
infantile, acute (*see also* Poliomyelitis) 045.9 ☑
multiple 335.20
pseudobulbar 335.23
pseudohypertrophic 359.1
muscle 359.1
psychogenic 306.0
pupil, pupillary 379.49
quadriceps 355.8
quadriplegic (*see also* Quadriplegia) 344.0 ☑
radial nerve 354.3
birth injury 767.6
rectum (sphincter) 569.49
rectus muscle (eye) 378.55
recurrent
isolated sleep 327.43
laryngeal nerve (*see also* Paralysis, vocal cord) 478.30
respiratory (muscle) (system) (tract) 786.09
center NEC 344.89
fetus or newborn 770.87
congenital 768.9
newborn 768.9
right side — *see* Hemiplegia
Saturday night 354.3
saturnine 984.9
specified type of lead — *see* Table of Drugs and Chemicals
sciatic nerve 355.0
secondary — *see* Paralysis, late effect
seizure (cerebral) (current episode) (*see also* Disease, cerebrovascular, acute) 436
late effect — *see* Late effect(s) (of) cerebrovascular disease
senile NEC 344.9
serratus magnus 355.9
shaking (*see also* Parkinsonism) 332.0
shock (*see also* Disease, cerebrovascular, acute) 436
late effect — *see* Late effect(s) (of) cerebrovascular disease
shoulder 354.9
soft palate 528.9
spasmodic — *see* Paralysis, spastic
spastic 344.9
cerebral infantile — *see* Palsy, cerebral

Paralysis, paralytic — *continued*
spastic — *continued*
congenital (cerebral) — *see* Palsy, cerebral
familial 334.1
hereditary 334.1
infantile 343.9
noncongenital or noninfantile, cerebral 344.9
syphilitic 094.0
spinal 094.89
sphincter, bladder (*see also* Paralysis, bladder) 596.53
spinal (cord) NEC 344.1
accessory nerve 352.4
acute (*see also* Poliomyelitis) 045.9 ☑
ascending acute 357.0
atrophic (acute) (*see also* Poliomyelitis, with paralysis) 045.1 ☑
spastic, syphilitic 094.89
congenital NEC 343.9
hemiplegic — *see* Hemiplegia
hereditary 336.8
infantile (*see also* Poliomyelitis) 045.9 ☑
late effect NEC 344.89
monoplegic — *see* Monoplegia
nerve 355.9
progressive 335.10
quadriplegic — *see* Quadriplegia
spastic NEC 343.9
traumatic — *see* Injury, spinal, by site
sternomastoid 352.4
stomach 536.3
diabetic 250.6 ☑ *[536.3]*
due to secondary diabetes 249.6 ☑ *[536.3]* ●
nerve (nondiabetic) 352.3
stroke (current episode) — *see* Infarct, brain
late effect — *see* Late effect(s) (of) cerebrovascular disease
subscapularis 354.8
superior nuclear NEC 334.9
supranuclear 356.8
sympathetic
cervical NEC 337.09 ▲
nerve NEC (*see also* Neuropathy, peripheral, autonomic) 337.9
nervous system — *see* Neuropathy, peripheral, autonomic
syndrome 344.9
specified NEC 344.89
syphilitic spastic spinal (Erb's) 094.89
tabetic general 094.1
thigh 355.8
throat 478.29
diphtheritic 032.0
muscle 478.29
thrombotic (current episode) (*see also* Thrombosis, brain) 434.0 ☑
late effect — *see* Late effect(s) (of) cerebrovascular disease
thumb NEC 354.9
tick (-bite) 989.5
Todd's (postepileptic transitory paralysis) 344.89
toe 355.6
tongue 529.8
transient
arm or leg NEC 781.4
traumatic NEC (*see also* Injury, nerve, by site) 957.9
trapezius 352.4
traumatic, transient NEC (*see also* Injury, nerve, by site) 957.9
trembling (*see also* Parkinsonism) 332.0
triceps brachii 354.9
trigeminal nerve 350.9
trochlear nerve 378.53
ulnar nerve 354.2
upper limb (*see also* Paralysis, arm)
both (*see also* Diplegia) 344.2

Paralysis, paralytic — *continued*
uremic — *see* Uremia
uveoparotitic 135
uvula 528.9
hysterical 300.11
postdiphtheritic 032.0
vagus nerve 352.3
vasomotor NEC 337.9
velum palati 528.9
vesical (*see also* Paralysis, bladder) 596.53
vestibular nerve 388.5
visual field, psychic 368.16
vocal cord 478.30
bilateral (partial) 478.33
complete 478.34
complete (bilateral) 478.34
unilateral (partial) 478.31
complete 478.32
Volkmann's (complicating trauma) 958.6
wasting 335.21
Weber's 344.89
wrist NEC 354.9
Paramedial orifice, urethrovesical 753.8
Paramenia 626.9
Parametritis (chronic) — *see also* Disease, pelvis, inflammatory 614.4
acute 614.3
puerperal, postpartum, childbirth 670.0 ☑
Parametrium, parametric — *see* condition
Paramnesia — *see also* Amnesia 780.93
Paramolar 520.1
causing crowding 524.31
Paramyloidosis 277.30
Paramyoclonus multiplex 333.2
Paramyotonia 359.29
congenita (of von Eulenburg) 359.29
Paraneoplastic syndrome — *see* condition
Parangi — *see also* Yaws 102.9
Paranoia 297.1
alcoholic 291.5
querulans 297.8
senile 290.20
Paranoid
dementia (*see also* Schizophrenia) 295.3 ☑
praecox (acute) 295.3 ☑
senile 290.20
personality 301.0
psychosis 297.9
alcoholic 291.5
climacteric 297.2
drug-induced 292.11
involutional 297.2
menopausal 297.2
protracted reactive 298.4
psychogenic 298.4
acute 298.3
senile 290.20
reaction (chronic) 297.9
acute 298.3
schizophrenia (acute) (*see also* Schizophrenia) 295.3 ☑
state 297.9
alcohol-induced 291.5
climacteric 297.2
drug-induced 292.11
due to or associated with
arteriosclerosis (cerebrovascular) 290.42
presenile brain disease 290.12
senile brain disease 290.20
involutional 297.2
menopausal 297.2
senile 290.20
simple 297.0
specified type NEC 297.8
tendencies 301.0
traits 301.0
trends 301.0
type, psychopathic personality 301.0

Paraparesis — *see also* Paraplegia 344.1
Paraphasia 784.3
Paraphilia — *see also* Deviation, sexual 302.9
Paraphimosis (congenital) 605
chancroidal 099.0
Paraphrenia, paraphrenic (late) 297.2
climacteric 297.2
dementia (*see also* Schizophrenia) 295.3 ☑
involutional 297.2
menopausal 297.2
schizophrenia (acute) (*see also* Schizophrenia) 295.3 ☑
Paraplegia 344.1
with
broken back — *see* Fracture, vertebra, by site, with spinal cord injury
fracture, vertebra — *see* Fracture, vertebra, by site, with spinal cord injury
ataxic — *see* Degeneration, combined, spinal cord
brain (current episode) (*see also* Paralysis, brain) 437.8
cerebral (current episode) (*see also* Paralysis, brain) 437.8
congenital or infantile (cerebral) (spastic) (spinal) 343.0
cortical — *see* Paralysis, brain
familial spastic 334.1
functional (hysterical) 300.11
hysterical 300.11
infantile 343.0
late effect 344.1
Pott's (*see also* Tuberculosis) 015.0 ☑ *[730.88]*
psychogenic 306.0
spastic
Erb's spinal 094.89
hereditary 334.1
not infantile or congenital 344.1
spinal (cord)
traumatic NEC — *see* Injury, spinal, by site
syphilitic (spastic) 094.89
traumatic NEC — *see* Injury, spinal, by site
Paraproteinemia 273.2
benign (familial) 273.1
monoclonal 273.1
secondary to malignant or inflammatory disease 273.1
Parapsoriasis 696.2
en plaques 696.2
guttata 696.2
lichenoides chronica 696.2
retiformis 696.2
varioliformis (acuta) 696.2
Parascarlatina 057.8
Parasitic — *see also* condition
disease NEC (*see also* Infestation, parasitic) 136.9
contact V01.89
exposure to V01.89
intestinal NEC 129
skin NEC 134.9
stomatitis 112.0
sycosis 110.0
beard 110.0
scalp 110.0
twin 759.4
Parasitism NEC 136.9
intestinal NEC 129
skin NEC 134.9
specified — *see* Infestation
Parasitophobia 300.29
Parasomnia 307.47
alcohol induced 291.82
drug induced 292.85
nonorganic origin 307.47
organic 327.40
in conditions classified elsewhere 327.44
other 327.49

Paraspadias 752.69
Paraspasm facialis 351.8
Parathyroid gland — *see* condition
Parathyroiditis (autoimmune) 252.1
Parathyroprival tetany 252.1
Paratrachoma 077.0
Paratyphilitis — *see also* Appendicitis 541
Paratyphoid (fever) — *see* Fever, paratyphoid
Paratyphus — *see* Fever, paratyphoid
Paraurethral duct 753.8
Para-urethritis 597.89
  gonococcal (acute) 098.0
    chronic or duration of 2 months or over 098.2
Paravaccinia NEC 051.9
  milkers' node 051.1
Paravaginitis — *see also* Vaginitis 616.10
Parencephalitis — *see also* Encephalitis 323.9
  late effect — *see* category 326
Parergasia 298.9
Paresis — *see also* Paralysis 344.9
  accommodation 367.51
  bladder (spastic) (sphincter) (*see also* Paralysis, bladder) 596.53
    tabetic 094.0
  bowel, colon, or intestine (*see also* Ileus) 560.1
  brain or cerebral — *see* Paralysis, brain
  extrinsic muscle, eye 378.55
  general 094.1
    arrested 094.1
    brain 094.1
    cerebral 094.1
    insane 094.1
    juvenile 090.40
      remission 090.49
    progressive 094.1
    remission (sustained) 094.1
    tabetic 094.1
  heart (*see also* Failure, heart) 428.9
  infantile (*see also* Poliomyelitis) 045.9 ☑
  insane 094.1
  juvenile 090.40
  late effect — *see* Paralysis, late effect
  luetic (general) 094.1
  peripheral progressive 356.9
  pseudohypertrophic 359.1
  senile NEC 344.9
  stomach 536.3
    diabetic 250.6 ☑ *[536.3]*
      due to secondary diabetes ●
        249.6 ☑ *[536.3]* ●
  syphilitic (general) 094.1
    congenital 090.40
  transient, limb 781.4
  vesical (sphincter) NEC 596.53
Paresthesia — *see also* Disturbance, sensation 782.0
  Berger's (paresthesia of lower limb) 782.0
  Bernhardt 355.1
  Magnan's 782.0
Paretic — *see* condition
Parinaud's
  conjunctivitis 372.02
  oculoglandular syndrome 372.02
  ophthalmoplegia 378.81
  syndrome (paralysis of conjugate upward gaze) 378.81
Parkes Weber and Dimitri syndrome (encephalocutaneous angiomatosis) 759.6
Parkinson's disease, syndrome, or tremor — *see* Parkinsonism
Parkinsonism (arteriosclerotic) (idiopathic) (primary) 332.0
  associated with orthostatic hypotension (idiopathic) (symptomatic) 333.0
  due to drugs 332.1
Parkinsonism — *continued*
  neuroleptic-induced 332.1
  secondary 332.1
  syphilitic 094.82
Parodontitis 523.40
Parodontosis 523.5
Paronychia (with lymphangitis) 681.9
  candidal (chronic) 112.3
  chronic 681.9
    candidal 112.3
    finger 681.02
    toe 681.11
  finger 681.02
  toe 681.11
  tuberculous (primary) (*see also* Tuberculosis) 017.0 ☑
Parorexia NEC 307.52
  hysterical 300.11
Parosmia 781.1
  psychogenic 306.7
Parotid gland — *see* condition
Parotiditis — *see also* Parotitis 527.2
  epidemic 072.9
  infectious 072.9
Parotitis 527.2
  allergic 527.2
  chronic 527.2
  epidemic (*see also* Mumps) 072.9
  infectious (*see also* Mumps) 072.9
  noninfectious 527.2
  nonspecific toxic 527.2
  not mumps 527.2
  postoperative 527.2
  purulent 527.2
  septic 527.2
  suppurative (acute) 527.2
  surgical 527.2
  toxic 527.2
Paroxysmal — *see also* condition
  dyspnea (nocturnal) 786.09
Parrot's disease (syphilitic osteochondritis) 090.0
Parrot fever 073.9
Parry's disease or syndrome (exophthalmic goiter) 242.0 ☑
Parry-Romberg syndrome 349.89
Parsonage-Aldren-Turner syndrome 353.5
Parsonage-Turner syndrome 353.5
Parson's disease (exophthalmic goiter) 242.0 ☑
Pars planitis 363.21
Particolored infant 757.39
Parturition — *see* Delivery
Parvovirus 079.83
  B19 079.83
  human 079.83
Passage
  false, urethra 599.4
  meconium noted during delivery 763.84
  of sounds or bougies (*see also* Attention to artificial opening) V55.9
Passive — *see* condition
Pasteurella septica 027.2
Pasteurellosis — *see also* Infection, Pasteurella 027.2
PAT (paroxysmal atrial tachycardia) 427.0
Patau's syndrome (trisomy D1) 758.1
Patch
  herald 696.3
Patches
  mucous (syphilitic) 091.3
    congenital 090.0
  smokers' (mouth) 528.6
Patellar — *see* condition
Patellofemoral syndrome 719.46
Patent — *see also* Imperfect closure
  atrioventricular ostium 745.69
  canal of Nuck 752.41
  cervix 622.5
    complicating pregnancy 654.5 ☑
      affecting fetus or newborn 761.0
  ductus arteriosus or Botalli 747.0
Patent — *see also* Imperfect closure — *continued*
  Eustachian
    tube 381.7
    valve 746.89
  foramen
    Botalli 745.5
    ovale 745.5
  interauricular septum 745.5
  interventricular septum 745.4
  omphalomesenteric duct 751.0
  os (uteri) — *see* Patent, cervix
  ostium secundum 745.5
  urachus 753.7
  vitelline duct 751.0
Paternity testing V70.4
Paterson-Kelly syndrome or web (sideropenic dysphagia) 280.8
Paterson (-Brown) (-Kelly) syndrome (sideropenic dysphagia) 280.8
Paterson's syndrome (sideropenic dysphagia) 280.8
Pathologic, pathological — *see also* condition
  asphyxia 799.01
  drunkenness 291.4
  emotionality 301.3
  fracture — *see* Fracture, pathologic
  liar 301.7
  personality 301.9
  resorption, tooth 521.40
    external 521.42
    internal 521.41
    specified NEC 521.49
  sexuality (*see also* Deviation, sexual) 302.9
Pathology (of) — *see also* Disease
  periradicular, associated with previous endodontic treatment 526.69
Patterned motor discharge, idiopathic — *see also* Epilepsy 345.5 ☑
Patulous — *see also* Patent
  anus 569.49
  Eustachian tube 381.7
Pause, sinoatrial 427.81
Pavor nocturnus 307.46
Pavy's disease 593.6
Paxton's disease (white piedra) 111.2
Payr's disease or syndrome (splenic flexure syndrome) 569.89
PBA (pseudobulbar affect) 310.8
Pearls
  Elschnig 366.51
  enamel 520.2
Pearl-workers' disease (chronic osteomyelitis) — *see also* Osteomyelitis 730.1 ☑
Pectenitis 569.49
Pectenosis 569.49
Pectoral — *see* condition
Pectus
  carinatum (congenital) 754.82
    acquired 738.3
    rachitic (*see also* Rickets) 268.0
  excavatum (congenital) 754.81
    acquired 738.3
    rachitic (*see also* Rickets) 268.0
  recurvatum (congenital) 754.81
    acquired 738.3
Pedatrophia 261
Pederosis 302.2
Pediculosis (infestation) 132.9
  capitis (head louse) (any site) 132.0
  corporis (body louse) (any site) 132.1
  eyelid 132.0 *[373.6]*
  mixed (classifiable to more than one category in 132.0–132.2) 132.3
  pubis (pubic louse) (any site) 132.2
  vestimenti 132.1
  vulvae 132.2
Pediculus (infestation) — *see* Pediculosis
Pedophilia 302.2
Peg-shaped teeth 520.2
Pelade 704.01
Pel's crisis 094.0
Pel-Ebstein disease — *see* Disease, Hodgkin's
Pelger-Huët anomaly or syndrome (hereditary hyposegmentation) 288.2
Peliosis (rheumatica) 287.0
Pelizaeus-Merzbacher
  disease 330.0
  sclerosis, diffuse cerebral 330.0
Pellagra (alcoholic or with alcoholism) 265.2
  with polyneuropathy 265.2 *[357.4]*
Pellagra-cerebellar-ataxia-renal aminoaciduria syndrome 270.0
Pellegrini's disease (calcification, knee joint) 726.62
Pellegrini (-Stieda) disease or syndrome (calcification, knee joint) 726.62
Pellizzi's syndrome (pineal) 259.8
Pelvic — *see also* condition
  congestion-fibrosis syndrome 625.5
  kidney 753.3
Pelvioectasis 591
Pelviolithiasis 592.0
Pelviperitonitis
  female (*see also* Peritonitis, pelvic, female) 614.5
  male (*see also* Peritonitis) 567.21
Pelvis, pelvic — *see also* condition or type
  infantile 738.6
  Nägele's 738.6
  obliquity 738.6
  Robert's 755.69
Pemphigoid 694.5
  benign, mucous membrane 694.60
    with ocular involvement 694.61
  bullous 694.5
  cicatricial 694.60
    with ocular involvement 694.61
  juvenile 694.2
Pemphigus 694.4
  benign 694.5
    chronic familial 757.39
  Brazilian 694.4
  circinatus 694.0
  congenital, traumatic 757.39
  conjunctiva 694.61
  contagiosus 684
  erythematodes 694.4
  erythematosus 694.4
  foliaceus 694.4
  frambesiodes 694.4
  gangrenous (*see also* Gangrene) 785.4
  malignant 694.4
  neonatorum, newborn 684
  ocular 694.61
  papillaris 694.4
  seborrheic 694.4
  South American 694.4
  syphilitic (congenital) 090.0
  vegetans 694.4
  vulgaris 694.4
  wildfire 694.4
Pendred's syndrome (familial goiter with deaf-mutism) 243
Pendulous
  abdomen 701.9
    in pregnancy or childbirth 654.4 ☑
      affecting fetus or newborn 763.89
  breast 611.89 ▲
Penetrating wound — *see also* Wound, open, by site
  with internal injury — *see* Injury, internal, by site, with open wound
  eyeball 871.7
    with foreign body (nonmagnetic) 871.6
      magnetic 871.5
  ocular (*see also* Penetrating wound, eyeball) 871.7
    adnexa 870.3
      with foreign body 870.4
    orbit 870.3

Index

Paraspadias — Penetrating wound

Penetrating wound — *see also* Wound, open, by site — *continued*
orbit — *continued*
with foreign body 870.4
Penetration, pregnant uterus by instrument
with
abortion — *see* Abortion, by type, with damage to pelvic organs
ectopic pregnancy (*see also* categories 633.0–633.9) 639.2
molar pregnancy (*see also* categories 630–632) 639.2
complication of delivery 665.1 ☑
affecting fetus or newborn 763.89
following
abortion 639.2
ectopic or molar pregnancy 639.2
Penfield's syndrome — *see also* Epilepsy 345.5 ☑
Penicilliosis of lung 117.3
Penis — *see* condition
Penitis 607.2
Pentalogy (of Fallot) 745.2
Penta X syndrome 758.81
Pentosuria (benign) (essential) 271.8
Peptic acid disease 536.8
Peregrinating patient V65.2
Perforated — *see* Perforation
Perforation, perforative (nontraumatic)
antrum (*see also* Sinusitis, maxillary) 473.0
appendix 540.0
with peritoneal abscess 540.1
atrial septum, multiple 745.5
attic, ear 384.22
healed 384.81
bile duct, except cystic (*see also* Disease, biliary) 576.3
cystic 575.4
bladder (urinary) 596.6
with
abortion — *see* Abortion, by type, with damage to pelvic organs
ectopic pregnancy (*see also* categories 633.0–633.9) 639.2
molar pregnancy (*see also* categories 630–632) 639.2
following
abortion 639.2
ectopic or molar pregnancy 639.2
obstetrical trauma 665.5 ☑
bowel 569.83
with
abortion — *see* Abortion, by type, with damage to pelvic organs
ectopic pregnancy (*see also* categories 633.0–633.9) 639.2
molar pregnancy (*see also* categories 630–632) 639.2
fetus or newborn 777.6
following
abortion 639.2
ectopic or molar pregnancy 639.2
obstetrical trauma 665.5 ☑
broad ligament
with
abortion — *see* Abortion, by type, with damage to pelvic organs
ectopic pregnancy (*see also* categories 633.0–633.9) 639.2
molar pregnancy (*see also* categories 630–632) 639.2
following
abortion 639.2
ectopic or molar pregnancy 639.2
obstetrical trauma 665.6 ☑

Perforation, perforative — *continued*
by
device, implant, or graft — *see* Complications, mechanical
foreign body left accidentally in operation wound 998.4
instrument (any) during a procedure, accidental 998.2
cecum 540.0
with peritoneal abscess 540.1
cervix (uteri) (*see also* Injury, internal, cervix)
with
abortion — *see* Abortion, by type, with damage to pelvic organs
ectopic pregnancy (*see also* categories 633.0–633.9) 639.2
molar pregnancy (*see also* categories 630–632) 639.2
following
abortion 639.2
ectopic or molar pregnancy 639.2
obstetrical trauma 665.3 ☑
colon 569.83
common duct (bile) 576.3
cornea (*see also* Ulcer, cornea) 370.00
due to ulceration 370.06
cystic duct 575.4
diverticulum (*see also* Diverticula) 562.10
small intestine 562.00
duodenum, duodenal (ulcer) — *see* Ulcer, duodenum, with perforation
ear drum — *see* Perforation, tympanum
enteritis — *see* Enteritis
esophagus 530.4
ethmoidal sinus (*see also* Sinusitis, ethmoidal) 473.2
foreign body (external site) (*see also* Wound, open, by site, complicated)
internal site, by ingested object — *see* Foreign body
frontal sinus (*see also* Sinusitis, frontal) 473.1
gallbladder or duct (*see also* Disease, gallbladder) 575.4
gastric (ulcer) — *see* Ulcer, stomach, with perforation
heart valve — *see* Endocarditis
ileum (*see also* Perforation, intestine) 569.83
instrumental
external — *see* Wound, open, by site
pregnant uterus, complicating delivery 665.9 ☑
surgical (accidental) (blood vessel) (nerve) (organ) 998.2
intestine 569.83
with
abortion — *see* Abortion, by type, with damage to pelvic organs
ectopic pregnancy (*see also* categories 633.0–633.9) 639.2
molar pregnancy (*see also* categories 630–632) 639.2
fetus or newborn 777.6
obstetrical trauma 665.5 ☑
ulcerative NEC 569.83
jejunum, jejunal 569.83
ulcer — *see* Ulcer, gastrojejunal, with perforation
mastoid (antrum) (cell) 383.89
maxillary sinus (*see also* Sinusitis, maxillary) 473.0
membrana tympani — *see* Perforation, tympanum

Perforation, perforative — *continued*
nasal
septum 478.19
congenital 748.1
syphilitic 095.8
sinus (*see also* Sinusitis) 473.9
congenital 748.1
palate (hard) 526.89
soft 528.9
syphilitic 095.8
syphilitic 095.8
palatine vault 526.89
syphilitic 095.8
congenital 090.5
pelvic
floor
with
abortion — *see* Abortion, by type, with damage to pelvic organs
ectopic pregnancy (*see also* categories 633.0–633.9) 639.2
molar pregnancy (*see also* categories 630–632) 639.2
obstetrical trauma 664.1 ☑
organ
with
abortion — *see* Abortion, by type, with damage to pelvic organs
ectopic pregnancy (*see also* categories 633.0–633.9) 639.2
molar pregnancy (*see also* categories 630–632) 639.2
following
abortion 639.2
ectopic or molar pregnancy 639.2
obstetrical trauma 665.5 ☑
perineum — *see* Laceration, perineum
periurethral tissue
with
abortion — *see* Abortion, by type, with damage to pelvic organs
ectopic pregnancy (*see also* categories 630–632) 639.2
molar pregnancy (*see also* categories 630–632) 639.2
pharynx 478.29
pylorus, pyloric (ulcer) — *see* Ulcer, stomach, with perforation
rectum 569.49
root canal space 526.61
sigmoid 569.83
sinus (accessory) (chronic) (nasal) (*see also* Sinusitis) 473.9
sphenoidal sinus (*see also* Sinusitis, sphenoidal) 473.3
stomach (due to ulcer) — *see* Ulcer, stomach, with perforation
surgical (accidental) (by instrument) (blood vessel) (nerve) (organ) 998.2
traumatic
external — *see* Wound, open, by site
eye (*see also* Penetrating wound, ocular) 871.7
internal organ — *see* Injury, internal, by site
tympanum (membrane) (persistent posttraumatic) (postinflammatory) 384.20
with
otitis media — *see* Otitis media
attic 384.22
central 384.21
healed 384.81
marginal NEC 384.23
multiple 384.24
pars flaccida 384.22

Perforation, perforative — *continued*
tympanum — *continued*
total 384.25
traumatic — *see* Wound, open, ear, drum
typhoid, gastrointestinal 002.0
ulcer — *see* Ulcer, by site, with perforation
ureter 593.89
urethra
with
abortion — *see* Abortion, by type, with damage to pelvic organs
ectopic pregnancy (*see also* categories 633.0–633.9) 639.2
molar pregnancy (*see also* categories 630–632) 639.2
following
abortion 639.2
ectopic or molar pregnancy 639.2
obstetrical trauma 665.5 ☑
uterus (*see also* Injury, internal, uterus)
with
abortion — *see* Abortion, by type, with damage to pelvic organs
ectopic pregnancy (*see also* categories 633.0–633.9) 639.2
molar pregnancy (*see also* categories 630–632) 639.2
by intrauterine contraceptive device 996.32
following
abortion 639.2
ectopic or molar pregnancy 639.2
obstetrical trauma — *see* Injury, internal, uterus, obstetrical trauma
uvula 528.9
syphilitic 095.8
vagina — *see* Laceration, vagina
viscus NEC 799.89
traumatic 868.00
with open wound into cavity 868.10
Periadenitis mucosa necrotica recurrens 528.2
Periangiitis 446.0
Periantritis 535.4 ☑
Periappendicitis (acute) — *see also* Appendicitis 541
Periarteritis (disseminated) (infectious) (necrotizing) (nodosa) 446.0
Periarthritis (joint) 726.90
Duplay's 726.2
gonococcal 098.50
humeroscapularis 726.2
scapulohumeral 726.2
shoulder 726.2
wrist 726.4
Periarthrosis (angioneural) — *see* Periarthritis
Peribronchitis 491.9
tuberculous (*see also* Tuberculosis) 011.3 ☑
Pericapsulitis, adhesive (shoulder) 726.0
Pericarditis (granular) (with decompensation) (with effusion) 423.9
with
rheumatic fever (conditions classifiable to 390)
active (*see also* Pericarditis, rheumatic) 391.0
inactive or quiescent 393
actinomycotic 039.8 *[420.0]*
acute (nonrheumatic) 420.90
with chorea (acute) (rheumatic) (Sydenham's) 392.0
bacterial 420.99

Pericarditis — *continued*
- acute — *continued*
  - benign 420.91
  - hemorrhagic 420.90
  - idiopathic 420.91
  - infective 420.90
  - nonspecific 420.91
  - rheumatic 391.0
    - with chorea (acute) (rheumatic) (Sydenham's) 392.0
  - sicca 420.90
  - viral 420.91
- adhesive or adherent (external) (internal) 423.1
  - acute — *see* Pericarditis, acute
  - rheumatic (external) (internal) 393
- amebic 006.8 *[420.0]*
- bacterial (acute) (subacute) (with serous or seropurulent effusion) 420.99
- calcareous 423.2
- cholesterol (chronic) 423.8
  - acute 420.90
- chronic (nonrheumatic) 423.8
  - rheumatic 393
- constrictive 423.2
- Coxsackie 074.21
- due to
  - actinomycosis 039.8 *[420.0]*
  - amebiasis 006.8 *[420.0]*
  - Coxsackie (virus) 074.21
  - histoplasmosis (*see also* Histoplasmosis) 115.93
  - nocardiosis 039.8 *[420.0]*
  - tuberculosis (*see also* Tuberculosis) 017.9 ☑ *[420.0]*
- fibrinocaseous (*see also* Tuberculosis) 017.9 ☑ *[420.0]*
- fibrinopurulent 420.99
- fibrinous — *see* Pericarditis, rheumatic
- fibropurulent 420.99
- fibrous 423.1
- gonococcal 098.83
- hemorrhagic 423.0
- idiopathic (acute) 420.91
- infective (acute) 420.90
- meningococcal 036.41
- neoplastic (chronic) 423.8
  - acute 420.90
- nonspecific 420.91
- obliterans, obliterating 423.1
- plastic 423.1
- pneumococcal (acute) 420.99
- postinfarction 411.0
- purulent (acute) 420.99
- rheumatic (active) (acute) (with effusion) (with pneumonia) 391.0
  - with chorea (acute) (rheumatic) (Sydenham's) 392.0
  - chronic or inactive (with chorea) 393
- septic (acute) 420.99
- serofibrinous — *see* Pericarditis, rheumatic
- staphylococcal (acute) 420.99
- streptococcal (acute) 420.99
- suppurative (acute) 420.99
- syphilitic 093.81
- tuberculous (acute) (chronic) (*see also* Tuberculosis) 017.9 ☑ *[420.0]*
- uremic 585.9 *[420.0]*
- viral (acute) 420.91

Pericardium, pericardial — *see* condition

Pericellulitis — *see also* Cellulitis 682.9

Pericementitis 523.40
- acute 523.30
- chronic (suppurative) 523.40

Pericholecystitis — *see also* Cholecystitis 575.10

Perichondritis
- auricle 380.00
  - acute 380.01
  - chronic 380.02
- bronchus 491.9

Perichondritis — *continued*
- ear (external) 380.00
  - acute 380.01
  - chronic 380.02
- larynx 478.71
  - syphilitic 095.8
  - typhoid 002.0 *[478.71]*
- nose 478.19
- pinna 380.00
  - acute 380.01
  - chronic 380.02
- trachea 478.9

Periclasia 523.5

Pericolitis 569.89

Pericoronitis (chronic) 523.40
- acute 523.33 ▲

Pericystitis — *see also* Cystitis 595.9

Pericytoma (M9150/1) — *see also* Neoplasm, connective tissue, uncertain behavior
- benign (M9150/0) — *see* Neoplasm, connective tissue, benign
- malignant (M9150/3) — *see* Neoplasm, connective tissue, malignant

Peridacryocystitis, acute 375.32

Peridiverticulitis — *see also* Diverticulitis 562.11

Periduodenitis 535.6 ☑

Periendocarditis — *see also* Endocarditis 424.90
- acute or subacute 421.9

Periepididymitis — *see also* Epididymitis 604.90

Perifolliculitis (abscedens) 704.8
- capitis, abscedens et suffodiens 704.8
- dissecting, scalp 704.8
- scalp 704.8
- superficial pustular 704.8

Perigastritis (acute) 535.0 ☑

Perigastrojejunitis (acute) 535.0 ☑

Perihepatitis (acute) 573.3
- chlamydial 099.56
- gonococcal 098.86

Peri-ileitis (subacute) 569.89

Perilabyrinthitis (acute) — *see* Labyrinthitis

Perimeningitis — *see* Meningitis

Perimetritis — *see also* Endometritis 615.9

Perimetrosalpingitis — *see also* Salpingo-oophoritis 614.2

Perineocele 618.05

Perinephric — *see* condition

Perinephritic — *see* condition

Perinephritis — *see also* Infection, kidney 590.9
- purulent (*see also* Abscess, kidney) 590.2

Perineum, perineal — *see* condition

Perineuritis NEC 729.2

Periodic — *see also* condition
- disease (familial) 277.31
- edema 995.1
  - hereditary 277.6
- fever 277.31
- headache syndromes in child or adolescent 346.2 ☑ ●
- limb movement disorder 327.51
- paralysis (familial) 359.3
- peritonitis 277.31
- polyserositis 277.31
- somnolence (*see also* Narcolepsy) 347.00

Periodontal
- cyst 522.8
- pocket 523.8

Periodontitis (chronic) (complex) (compound) (simplex) 523.40
- acute 523.33
- aggressive 523.30
  - generalized 523.32
  - localized 523.31
- apical 522.6
  - acute (pulpal origin) 522.4
- generalized 523.42

Periodontitis — *continued*
- localized 523.41

Periodontoclasia 523.5

Periodontosis 523.5

Periods — *see also* Menstruation
- heavy 626.2
- irregular 626.4

Perionychia (with lymphangitis) 681.9
- finger 681.02
- toe 681.11

Perioophoritis — *see also* Salpingo-oophoritis 614.2

Periorchitis — *see also* Orchitis 604.90

Periosteum, periosteal — *see* condition

Periostitis (circumscribed) (diffuse) (infective) 730.3 ☑

> *Note — Use the following fifth-digit subclassification with category 730:*
>
> *0 site unspecified*
> *1 shoulder region*
> *2 upper arm*
> *3 forearm*
> *4 hand*
> *5 pelvic region and thigh*
> *6 lower leg*
> *7 ankle and foot*
> *8 other specified sites*
> *9 multiple sites*

- with osteomyelitis (*see also* Osteomyelitis) 730.2 ☑
  - acute or subacute 730.0 ☑
  - chronic or old 730.1 ☑
- albuminosa, albuminosus 730.3 ☑
- alveolar 526.5
- alveolodental 526.5
- dental 526.5
- gonorrheal 098.89
- hyperplastica, generalized 731.2
- jaw (lower) (upper) 526.4
- monomelic 733.99
- orbital 376.02
- syphilitic 095.5
  - congenital 090.0 *[730.8]* ☑
  - secondary 091.61
- tuberculous (*see also* Tuberculosis, bone) 015.9 ☑ *[730.8]* ☑
- yaws (early) (hypertrophic) (late) 102.6

Periostosis — *see also* Periostitis 730.3 ☑
- with osteomyelitis (*see also* Osteomyelitis) 730.2 ☑
  - acute or subacute 730.0 ☑
  - chronic or old 730.1 ☑
- hyperplastic 756.59

Peripartum cardiomyopathy 674.5 ☑

Periphlebitis — *see also* Phlebitis 451.9
- lower extremity 451.2
  - deep (vessels) 451.19
  - superficial (vessels) 451.0
- portal 572.1
- retina 362.18
- superficial (vessels) 451.0
- tuberculous (*see also* Tuberculosis) 017.9 ☑
  - retina 017.3 ☑ *[362.18]*

Peripneumonia — *see* Pneumonia

Periproctitis 569.49

Periprostatitis — *see also* Prostatitis 601.9

Perirectal — *see* condition

Perirenal — *see* condition

Perisalpingitis — *see also* Salpingo-oophoritis 614.2

Perisigmoiditis 569.89

Perisplenitis (infectional) 289.59

Perispondylitis — *see* Spondylitis

Peristalsis reversed or visible 787.4

Peritendinitis — *see also* Tenosynovitis 726.90
- adhesive (shoulder) 726.0

Perithelioma (M9150/1) — *see* Pericytoma

Peritoneum, peritoneal — *see also* condition
- equilibration test V56.32

Peritonitis (acute) (adhesive) (fibrinous) (hemorrhagic) (idiopathic) (localized) (perforative) (primary) (with adhesions) (with effusion) 567.9
- with or following
  - abortion — *see* Abortion, by type, with sepsis
  - abscess 567.21
  - appendicitis 540.0
    - with peritoneal abscess 540.1
  - ectopic pregnancy (*see also* categories 633.0–633.9) 639.0
  - molar pregnancy (*see also* categories 630–632) 639.0
- aseptic 998.7
- bacterial 567.29
  - spontaneous 567.23
- bile, biliary 567.81
- chemical 998.7
- chlamydial 099.56
- chronic proliferative 567.89
- congenital NEC 777.6
- diaphragmatic 567.22
- diffuse NEC 567.29
- diphtheritic 032.83
- disseminated NEC 567.29
- due to
  - bile 567.81
  - foreign
    - body or object accidentally left during a procedure (instrument) (sponge) (swab) 998.4
    - substance accidentally left during a procedure (chemical) (powder) (talc) 998.7
  - talc 998.7
  - urine 567.89
- fibrinopurulent 567.29
- fibrinous 567.29
- fibrocaseous (*see also* Tuberculosis) 014.0 ☑
- fibropurulent 567.29
- general, generalized (acute) 567.21
- gonococcal 098.86
- in infective disease NEC 136.9 *[567.0]*
- meconium (newborn) 777.6
- pancreatic 577.8
- paroxysmal, benign 277.31
- pelvic
  - female (acute) 614.5
    - chronic NEC 614.7
      - with adhesions 614.6
    - puerperal, postpartum, childbirth 670.0 ☑
  - male (acute) 567.21
- periodic (familial) 277.31
- phlegmonous 567.29
- pneumococcal 567.1
- postabortal 639.0
- proliferative, chronic 567.89
- puerperal, postpartum, childbirth 670.0 ☑
- purulent 567.29
- septic 567.29
- spontaneous bacterial 567.23
- staphylococcal 567.29
- streptococcal 567.29
- subdiaphragmatic 567.29
- subphrenic 567.29
- suppurative 567.29
- syphilitic 095.2
  - congenital 090.0 *[567.0]*
- talc 998.7
- tuberculous (*see also* Tuberculosis) 014.0 ☑
- urine 567.89

Peritonsillar — *see* condition

Peritonsillitis 475

Perityphlitis — *see also* Appendicitis 541

Periureteritis 593.89
Periurethral — *see* condition
Periurethritis (gangrenous) 597.89
Periuterine — *see* condition
Perivaginitis — *see also* Vaginitis 616.10
Perivasculitis, retinal 362.18
Perivasitis (chronic) 608.4
Periventricular leukomalacia 779.7
Perivesiculitis (seminal) — *see also* Vesiculitis 608.0
Perlèche 686.8
  due to
    moniliasis 112.0
    riboflavin deficiency 266.0
Pernicious — *see* condition
Pernio, perniosis 991.5
Persecution
  delusion 297.9
  social V62.4
Perseveration (tonic) 784.69
Persistence, persistent (congenital) 759.89
  anal membrane 751.2
  arteria stapedia 744.04
  atrioventricular canal 745.69
  bloody ejaculate 792.2
  branchial cleft 744.41
  bulbus cordis in left ventricle 745.8
  canal of Cloquet 743.51
  capsule (opaque) 743.51
  cilioretinal artery or vein 743.51
  cloaca 751.5
  communication — *see* Fistula, congenital
  convolutions
    aortic arch 747.21
    fallopian tube 752.19
    oviduct 752.19
    uterine tube 752.19
  double aortic arch 747.21
  ductus
    arteriosus 747.0
    Botalli 747.0
  fetal
    circulation 747.83
    form of cervix (uteri) 752.49
    hemoglobin (hereditary) ("Swiss variety") 282.7
    pulmonary hypertension 747.83
  foramen
    Botalli 745.5
    ovale 745.5
  Gartner's duct 752.41
  hemoglobin, fetal (hereditary) (HPFH) 282.7
  hyaloid
    artery (generally incomplete) 743.51
    system 743.51
  hymen (tag)
    in pregnancy or childbirth 654.8 ☑
      causing obstructed labor 660.2 ☑
  lanugo 757.4
  left
    posterior cardinal vein 747.49
    root with right arch of aorta 747.21
    superior vena cava 747.49
  Meckel's diverticulum 751.0
  mesonephric duct 752.89
    fallopian tube 752.11
  mucosal disease (middle ear) (with posterior or superior marginal perforation of ear drum) 382.2
  nail(s), anomalous 757.5
  occiput, anterior or posterior 660.3 ☑
    fetus or newborn 763.1
  omphalomesenteric duct 751.0
  organ or site NEC — *see* Anomaly, specified type NEC
  ostium
    atrioventriculare commune 745.69
    primum 745.61
    secundum 745.5
  ovarian rests in fallopian tube 752.19

Persistence, persistent — *continued*
  pancreatic tissue in intestinal tract 751.5
  primary (deciduous)
    teeth 520.6
    vitreous hyperplasia 743.51
  pulmonary hypertension 747.83
  pupillary membrane 743.46
    iris 743.46
  Rhesus (Rh) titer 999.7
  right aortic arch 747.21
  sinus
    urogenitalis 752.89
    venosus with imperfect incorporation in right auricle 747.49
  thymus (gland) 254.8
    hyperplasia 254.0
  thyroglossal duct 759.2
  thyrolingual duct 759.2
  truncus arteriosus or communis 745.0
  tunica vasculosa lentis 743.39
  umbilical sinus 753.7
  urachus 753.7
  vegetative state 780.03
  vitelline duct 751.0
  wolffian duct 752.89
Person (with)
  admitted for clinical research, as participant or control subject V70.7
  affected by ●
    family member ●
      currently on deployment (military) V61.01 ●
      returned from deployment (military) (current or past conflict) V61.02 ●
  awaiting admission to adequate facility elsewhere V63.2
    undergoing social agency investigation V63.8
  concern (normal) about sick person in family V61.49
  consulting on behalf of another V65.19
    pediatric pre-birth visit for expectant mother V65.11
  currently deployed in theater or in support of military war, peacekeeping and humanitarian operations V62.21 ●
  feared
    complaint in whom no diagnosis was made V65.5
    condition not demonstrated V65.5
  feigning illness V65.2
  healthy, accompanying sick person V65.0
  history of military war, peacekeeping and humanitarian deployment (current or past conflict) V62.22 ●
  living (in)
    without
      adequate
        financial resources V60.2
        housing (heating) (space) V60.1
      housing (permanent) (temporary) V60.0
      material resources V60.2
      person able to render necessary care V60.4
      shelter V60.0
    alone V60.3
    boarding school V60.6
    residence remote from hospital or medical care facility V63.0
    residential institution V60.6
  medical services in home not available V63.1
  on waiting list V63.2
    undergoing social agency investigation V63.8
  sick or handicapped in family V61.49
  "worried well" V65.5

Personality
  affective 301.10
  aggressive 301.3
  amoral 301.7
  anancastic, anankastic 301.4
  antisocial 301.7
  asocial 301.7
  asthenic 301.6
  avoidant 301.82
  borderline 301.83
  change 310.1
  compulsive 301.4
  cycloid 301.13
  cyclothymic 301.13
  dependent 301.6
  depressive (chronic) 301.12
  disorder, disturbance NEC 301.9
    with
      antisocial disturbance 301.7
      pattern disturbance NEC 301.9
      sociopathic disturbance 301.7
      trait disturbance 301.9
  dual 300.14
  dyssocial 301.7
  eccentric 301.89
    "haltlose" type 301.89
  emotionally unstable 301.59
  epileptoid 301.3
  explosive 301.3
  fanatic 301.0
  histrionic 301.50
  hyperthymic 301.11
  hypomanic 301.11
  hypothymic 301.12
  hysterical 301.50
  immature 301.89
  inadequate 301.6
  labile 301.59
  masochistic 301.89
  morally defective 301.7
  multiple 300.14
  narcissistic 301.81
  obsessional 301.4
  obsessive-compulsive 301.4
  overconscientious 301.4
  paranoid 301.0
  passive (-dependent) 301.6
  passive-aggressive 301.84
  pathologic NEC 301.9
  pattern defect or disturbance 301.9
  pseudosocial 301.7
  psychoinfantile 301.59
  psychoneurotic NEC 301.89
  psychopathic 301.9
    with
      amoral trend 301.7
      antisocial trend 301.7
      asocial trend 301.7
      pathologic sexuality (*see also* Deviation, sexual) 302.9
    mixed types 301.9
  schizoid 301.20
  type A 301.4
  unstable (emotional) 301.59
Perthes' disease (capital femoral osteochondrosis) 732.1
Pertussis — *see also* Whooping cough 033.9
  vaccination, prophylactic (against) V03.6
Peruvian wart 088.0
Perversion, perverted
  appetite 307.52
    hysterical 300.11
  function
    pineal gland 259.8
    pituitary gland 253.9
      anterior lobe
        deficient 253.2
        excessive 253.1
      posterior lobe 253.6
    placenta — *see* Placenta, abnormal
  sense of smell or taste 781.1
    psychogenic 306.7
  sexual (*see also* Deviation, sexual) 302.9

Pervious, congenital — *see also* Imperfect, closure
  ductus arteriosus 747.0
Pes (congenital) — *see also* Talipes 754.70
  abductus (congenital) 754.60
    acquired 736.79
  acquired NEC 736.79
    planus 734
  adductus (congenital) 754.79
    acquired 736.79
  cavus 754.71
    acquired 736.73
  planovalgus (congenital) 754.69
    acquired 736.79
  planus (acquired) (any degree) 734
    congenital 754.61
    rachitic 268.1
  valgus (congenital) 754.61
    acquired 736.79
  varus (congenital) 754.50
    acquired 736.79
Pest — *see also* Plague 020.9
Pestis — *see also* Plague 020.9
  bubonica 020.0
  fulminans 020.0
  minor 020.8
  pneumonica — *see* Plague, pneumonic
Petechial
  fever 036.0
  typhus 081.9
Petechia, petechiae 782.7
  fetus or newborn 772.6
Petges-Cléjat or Petges-Clégat syndrome (poikilodermatomyositis) 710.3
Petit's
  disease (*see also* Hernia, lumbar) 553.8
Petit mal (idiopathic) — *see also* Epilepsy 345.0 ☑
  status 345.2
Petrellidosis 117.6
Petrositis 383.20
  acute 383.21
  chronic 383.22
Peutz-Jeghers disease or syndrome 759.6
Peyronie's disease 607.85
Pfeiffer's disease 075
Phacentocele 379.32
  traumatic 921.3
Phacoanaphylaxis 360.19
Phacocele (old) 379.32
  traumatic 921.3
Phaehyphomycosis 117.8
Phagedena (dry) (moist) — *see also* Gangrene 785.4
  arteriosclerotic 440.24
  geometric 686.09
  penis 607.89
  senile 440.2 ☑ *[785.4]*
  sloughing 785.4
  tropical (*see also* Ulcer, skin) 707.9
  vulva 616.50
Phagedenic — *see also* condition
  abscess (*see also* Abscess)
    chancroid 099.0
  bubo NEC 099.8
  chancre 099.0
  ulcer (tropical) (*see also* Ulcer, skin) 707.9
Phagomania 307.52
Phakoma 362.89
Phantom limb (syndrome) 353.6
Pharyngeal — *see also* condition
  arch remnant 744.41
  pouch syndrome 279.11
Pharyngitis (acute) (catarrhal) (gangrenous) (infective) (malignant) (membranous) (phlegmonous) (pneumococcal) (pseudomembranous) (simple) (staphylococcal) (subacute) (suppurative) (ulcerative) (viral) 462
  with influenza, flu, or grippe 487.1

Pharyngitis — *continued*
aphthous 074.0
atrophic 472.1
chlamydial 099.51
chronic 472.1
Coxsackie virus 074.0
diphtheritic (membranous) 032.0
follicular 472.1
fusospirochetal 101
gonococcal 098.6
granular (chronic) 472.1
herpetic 054.79
hypertrophic 472.1
infectional, chronic 472.1
influenzal 487.1
lymphonodular, acute 074.8
septic 034.0
streptococcal 034.0
tuberculous (*see also* Tuberculosis) 012.8 ☑
vesicular 074.0
Pharyngoconjunctival fever 077.2
Pharyngoconjunctivitis, viral 077.2
Pharyngolaryngitis (acute) 465.0
chronic 478.9
septic 034.0
Pharyngoplegia 478.29
Pharyngotonsillitis 465.8
tuberculous 012.8 ☑
Pharyngotracheitis (acute) 465.8
chronic 478.9
Pharynx, pharyngeal — *see* condition
Phase of life problem NEC V62.89
Phenomenon
Arthus' 995.21
flashback (drug) 292.89
jaw-winking 742.8
Jod-Basedow 242.8 ☑
L. E. cell 710.0
lupus erythematosus cell 710.0
Pelger-Huët (hereditary hyposegmentation) 288.2
Raynaud's (paroxysmal digital cyanosis) (secondary) 443.0
Reilly's (*see also* Neuropathy, peripheral, autonomic) 337.9
vasomotor 780.2
vasospastic 443.9
vasovagal 780.2
Wenckebach's, heart block (second degree) 426.13
Phenylketonuria (PKU) 270.1
Phenylpyruvicaciduria 270.1
Pheochromoblastoma (M8700/3)
specified site — *see* Neoplasm, by site, malignant
unspecified site 194.0
Pheochromocytoma (M8700/0)
malignant (M8700/3)
specified site — *see* Neoplasm, by site, malignant
unspecified site 194.0
specified site — *see* Neoplasm, by site, benign
unspecified site 227.0
Phimosis (congenital) 605
chancroidal 099.0
due to infection 605
Phlebectasia — *see also* Varicose, vein 454.9
congenital NEC 747.60
esophagus (*see also* Varix, esophagus) 456.1
with hemorrhage (*see also* Varix, esophagus, bleeding) 456.0
Phlebitis (infective) (pyemic) (septic) (suppurative) 451.9
antecubital vein 451.82
arm NEC 451.84
axillary vein 451.89
basilic vein 451.82
deep 451.83
superficial 451.82
axillary vein 451.89
basilic vein 451.82
blue 451.9
Phlebitis — *continued*
brachial vein 451.83
breast, superficial 451.89
cavernous (venous) sinus — *see* Phlebitis, intracranial sinus
cephalic vein 451.82
cerebral (venous) sinus — *see* Phlebitis, intracranial sinus
chest wall, superficial 451.89
complicating pregnancy or puerperium 671.9 ☑
affecting fetus or newborn 760.3
cranial (venous) sinus — *see* Phlebitis, intracranial sinus
deep (vessels) 451.19
femoral vein 451.11
specified vessel NEC 451.19
due to implanted device — *see* Complications, due to (presence of) any device, implant, or graft classified to 996.0–996.5 NEC
during or resulting from a procedure 997.2
femoral vein (deep) (superficial) 451.11
femoropopliteal 451.19
following infusion, perfusion, or transfusion 999.2
gouty 274.89 *[451.9]*
hepatic veins 451.89
iliac vein 451.81
iliofemoral 451.11
intracranial sinus (any) (venous) 325
late effect — *see* category 326
nonpyogenic 437.6
in pregnancy or puerperium 671.5 ☑
jugular vein 451.89
lateral (venous) sinus — *see* Phlebitis, intracranial sinus
leg 451.2
deep (vessels) 451.19
femoral vein 451.11
specified vessel NEC 451.19
superficial (vessels) 451.0
femoral vein 451.11
longitudinal sinus — *see* Phlebitis, intracranial sinus
lower extremity 451.2
deep (vessels) 451.19
femoral vein 451.11
specified vessel NEC 451.19
migrans, migrating (superficial) 453.1
superficial (vessels) 451.0
femoral vein 451.11
pelvic
with
abortion — *see* Abortion, by type, with sepsis
ectopic pregnancy (*see also* categories 633.0–633.9) 639.0
molar pregnancy (*see also* categories 630–632) 639.0
following
abortion 639.0
ectopic or molar pregnancy 639.0
puerperal, postpartum 671.4 ☑
popliteal vein 451.19
portal (vein) 572.1
postoperative 997.2
pregnancy 671.9 ☑
deep 671.3 ☑
specified type NEC 671.5 ☑
superficial 671.2 ☑
puerperal, postpartum, childbirth 671.9 ☑
deep 671.4 ☑
lower extremities 671.2 ☑
pelvis 671.4 ☑
specified site NEC 671.5 ☑
superficial 671.2 ☑
radial vein 451.83
retina 362.18
saphenous (great) (long) 451.0
Phlebitis — *continued*
saphenous — *continued*
accessory or small 451.0
sinus (meninges) — *see* Phlebitis, intracranial sinus
specified site NEC 451.89
subclavian vein 451.89
syphilitic 093.89
tibial vein 451.19
ulcer, ulcerative 451.9
leg 451.2
deep (vessels) 451.19
femoral vein 451.11
specified vessel NEC 451.19
superficial (vessels) 451.0
femoral vein 451.11
lower extremity 451.2
deep (vessels) 451.19
femoral vein 451.11
specified vessel NEC 451.19
superficial (vessels) 451.0
ulnar vein 451.83
umbilicus 451.89
upper extremity (*see also* Phlebitis, arm)
deep (veins) 451.83
brachial vein 451.83
radial vein 451.83
ulnar vein 451.83
superficial (veins) 451.82
antecubital vein 451.82
basilica vein 451.82
cephalic vein 451.82
uterus (septic) (*see also* Endometritis) 615.9
varicose (leg) (lower extremity) (*see also* Varicose, vein) 454.1
Phlebofibrosis 459.89
Phleboliths 459.89
Phlebosclerosis 459.89
Phlebothrombosis — *see* Thrombosis
Phlebotomus fever 066.0
Phlegmasia
alba dolens (deep vessels) 451.19
complicating pregnancy 671.3 ☑
nonpuerperal 451.19
puerperal, postpartum, childbirth 671.4 ☑
cerulea dolens 451.19
Phlegm, choked on 933.1
Phlegmon — *see also* Abscess 682.9
erysipelatous (*see also* Erysipelas) 035
iliac 682.2
fossa 540.1
throat 478.29
Phlegmonous — *see* condition
Phlyctenulosis (allergic) (keratoconjunctivitis) (nontuberculous) 370.31
cornea 370.31
with ulcer (*see also* Ulcer, cornea) 370.00
tuberculous (*see also* Tuberculosis) 017.3 ☑ *[370.31]*
Phobia, phobic (reaction) 300.20
animal 300.29
isolated NEC 300.29
obsessional 300.3
simple NEC 300.29
social 300.23
specified NEC 300.29
state 300.20
Phocas' disease 610.1
Phocomelia 755.4
lower limb 755.32
complete 755.33
distal 755.35
proximal 755.34
upper limb 755.22
complete 755.23
distal 755.25
proximal 755.24
Phoria — *see also* Heterophoria 378.40
Phosphate-losing tubular disorder 588.0
Phosphatemia 275.3
Phosphaturia 275.3
Photoallergic response 692.72
Photocoproporphyria 277.1
Photodermatitis (sun) 692.72
light other than sun 692.82
Photokeratitis 370.24
Photo-ophthalmia 370.24
Photophobia 368.13
Photopsia 368.15
Photoretinitis 363.31
Photoretinopathy 363.31
Photosensitiveness (sun) 692.72
light other than sun 692.82
Photosensitization (skin) (sun) 692.72
light other than sun 692.82
Phototoxic response 692.72
Phrenitis 323.9
Phrynoderma 264.8
Phthiriasis (pubis) (any site) 132.2
with any infestation classifiable to 132.0, 132.1, 132.3
Phthirus infestation — *see* Phthiriasis
Phthisis — *see also* Tuberculosis 011.9 ☑
bulbi (infectional) 360.41
colliers' 011.4 ☑
cornea 371.05
eyeball (due to infection) 360.41
millstone makers' 011.4 ☑
miners' 011.4 ☑
potters' 011.4 ☑
sandblasters' 011.4 ☑
stonemasons' 011.4 ☑
Phycomycosis 117.7
Physalopteriasis 127.7
Physical therapy NEC V57.1
breathing exercises V57.0
Physiological cup, optic papilla
borderline, glaucoma suspect 365.00
enlarged 377.14
glaucomatous 377.14
Phytobezoar 938
intestine 936
stomach 935.2
Pian — *see also* Yaws 102.9
Pianoma 102.1
Piarhemia, piarrhemia — *see also* Hyperlipemia 272.4
bilharziasis 120.9
Pica 307.52
hysterical 300.11
Pick's
cerebral atrophy 331.11
with dementia
with behavioral disturbance 331.11 *[294.11]*
without behavioral disturbance 331.11 *[294.10]*
disease
brain 331.11
dementia in
with behavioral disturbance 331.11 *[294.11]*
without behavioral disturbance 331.11 *[294.10]*
lipid histiocytosis 272.7
liver (pericardial pseudocirrhosis of liver) 423.2
pericardium (pericardial pseudocirrhosis of liver) 423.2
polyserositis (pericardial pseudocirrhosis of liver) 423.2
syndrome
heart (pericardial pseudocirrhosis of liver) 423.2
liver (pericardial pseudocirrhosis of liver) 423.2
tubular adenoma (M8640/0)
specified site — *see* Neoplasm, by site, benign
unspecified site
female 220
male 222.0
Pick-Herxheimer syndrome (diffuse idiopathic cutaneous atrophy) 701.8
Pick-Niemann disease (lipid histiocytosis) 272.7

Pickwickian syndrome (cardiopulmonary obesity) 278.8
Piebaldism, classic 709.09
Piedra 111.2
  beard 111.2
    black 111.3
    white 111.2
  black 111.3
  scalp 111.3
    black 111.3
    white 111.2
  white 111.2
Pierre Marie-Bamberger syndrome (hypertrophic pulmonary osteoarthropathy) 731.2
Pierre Marie's syndrome (pulmonary hypertrophic osteoarthropathy) 731.2
Pierre Mauriac's syndrome (diabetes-dwarfism-obesity) 258.1
Pierre Robin deformity or syndrome (congenital) 756.0
Pierson's disease or osteochondrosis 732.1
Pigeon
  breast or chest (acquired) 738.3
    congenital 754.82
    rachitic (*see also* Rickets) 268.0
  breeders' disease or lung 495.2
  fanciers' disease or lung 495.2
  toe 735.8
Pigmentation (abnormal) 709.00
  anomaly 709.00
    congenital 757.33
    specified NEC 709.09
  conjunctiva 372.55
  cornea 371.10
    anterior 371.11
    posterior 371.13
    stromal 371.12
  lids (congenital) 757.33
    acquired 374.52
  limbus corneae 371.10
  metals 709.00
  optic papilla, congenital 743.57
  retina (congenital) (grouped) (nevoid) 743.53
    acquired 362.74
  scrotum, congenital 757.33
Piles — *see* Hemorrhoids
Pili
  annulati or torti (congenital) 757.4
  incarnati 704.8
Pill roller hand (intrinsic) 736.09
Pilomatrixoma (M8110/0) — *see* Neoplasm, skin, benign
Pilonidal — *see* condition
Pimple 709.8
PIN I (prostatic intraepithelial neoplasia I) 602.3
PIN II (prostatic intraepithelial neoplasia II) 602.3
PIN III (prostatic intraepithelial neoplasia III) 233.4
Pinched nerve — *see* Neuropathy, entrapment
Pineal body or gland — *see* condition
Pinealoblastoma (M9362/3) 194.4
Pinealoma (M9360/1) 237.1
  malignant (M9360/3) 194.4
Pineoblastoma (M9362/3) 194.4
Pineocytoma (M9361/1) 237.1
Pinguecula 372.51
Pingueculitis 372.34 ●
Pinhole meatus — *see also* Stricture, urethra 598.9
Pink
  disease 985.0
  eye 372.03
  puffer 492.8
Pinkus' disease (lichen nitidus) 697.1
Pinpoint
  meatus (*see also* Stricture, urethra) 598.9
  os uteri (*see also* Stricture, cervix) 622.4
Pinselhaare (congenital) 757.4
Pinta 103.9
  cardiovascular lesions 103.2
  chancre (primary) 103.0
  erythematous plaques 103.1
  hyperchromic lesions 103.1
  hyperkeratosis 103.1
  lesions 103.9
    cardiovascular 103.2
    hyperchromic 103.1
    intermediate 103.1
    late 103.2
    mixed 103.3
    primary 103.0
    skin (achromic) (cicatricial) (dyschromic) 103.2
      hyperchromic 103.1
      mixed (achromic and hyperchromic) 103.3
  papule (primary) 103.0
  skin lesions (achromic) (cicatricial) (dyschromic) 103.2
    hyperchromic 103.1
    mixed (achromic and hyperchromic) 103.3
  vitiligo 103.2
Pintid 103.0
Pinworms (disease) (infection) (infestation) 127.4
Piry fever 066.8
Pistol wound — *see* Gunshot wound
Pitchers' elbow 718.82
Pithecoid pelvis 755.69
  with disproportion (fetopelvic) 653.2 ☑
    affecting fetus or newborn 763.1
    causing obstructed labor 660.1 ☑
Pithiatism 300.11
Pit, lip (mucus), **congenital** 750.25
Pitted — *see also* Pitting
  teeth 520.4
Pitting (edema) — *see also* Edema 782.3
  lip 782.3
  nail 703.8
    congenital 757.5
Pituitary gland — *see* condition
Pituitary snuff-takers' disease 495.8
Pityriasis 696.5
  alba 696.5
  capitis 690.11
  circinata (et maculata) 696.3
  Hebra's (exfoliative dermatitis) 695.89
  lichenoides et varioliformis 696.2
  maculata (et circinata) 696.3
  nigra 111.1
  pilaris 757.39
    acquired 701.1
    Hebra's 696.4
  rosea 696.3
  rotunda 696.3
  rubra (Hebra) 695.89
    pilaris 696.4
  sicca 690.18
  simplex 690.18
  specified type NEC 696.5
  streptogenes 696.5
  versicolor 111.0
    scrotal 111.0
Placenta, placental
  ablatio 641.2 ☑
    affecting fetus or newborn 762.1
  abnormal, abnormality 656.7 ☑
    with hemorrhage 641.8 ☑
      affecting fetus or newborn 762.1
    affecting fetus or newborn 762.2
  abruptio 641.2 ☑
    affecting fetus or newborn 762.1
  accessory lobe — *see* Placenta, abnormal
  accreta (without hemorrhage) 667.0 ☑
    with hemorrhage 666.0 ☑
  adherent (without hemorrhage) 667.0 ☑
    with hemorrhage 666.0 ☑
  apoplexy — *see* Placenta, separation
  battledore — *see* Placenta, abnormal
  bilobate — *see* Placenta, abnormal
Placenta, placental — *continued*
  bipartita — *see* Placenta, abnormal
  carneous mole 631
  centralis — *see* Placenta, previa
  circumvallata — *see* Placenta, abnormal
  cyst (amniotic) — *see* Placenta, abnormal
  deficiency — *see* Placenta, insufficiency
  degeneration — *see* Placenta, insufficiency
  detachment (partial) (premature) (with hemorrhage) 641.2 ☑
    affecting fetus or newborn 762.1
  dimidiata — *see* Placenta, abnormal
  disease 656.7 ☑
    affecting fetus or newborn 762.2
  duplex — *see* Placenta, abnormal
  dysfunction — *see* Placenta, insufficiency
  fenestrata — *see* Placenta, abnormal
  fibrosis — *see* Placenta, abnormal
  fleshy mole 631
  hematoma — *see* Placenta, abnormal
  hemorrhage NEC — *see* Placenta, separation
  hormone disturbance or malfunction — *see* Placenta, abnormal
  hyperplasia — *see* Placenta, abnormal
  increta (without hemorrhage) 667.0 ☑
    with hemorrhage 666.0 ☑
  infarction 656.7 ☑
    affecting fetus or newborn 762.2
  insertion, vicious — *see* Placenta, previa
  insufficiency
    affecting
      fetus or newborn 762.2
      management of pregnancy 656.5 ☑
  lateral — *see* Placenta, previa
  low implantation or insertion — *see* Placenta, previa
  low-lying — *see* Placenta, previa
  malformation — *see* Placenta, abnormal
  malposition — *see* Placenta, previa
  marginalis, marginata — *see* Placenta, previa
  marginal sinus (hemorrhage) (rupture) 641.2 ☑
    affecting fetus or newborn 762.1
  membranacea — *see* Placenta, abnormal
  multilobed — *see* Placenta, abnormal
  multipartita — *see* Placenta, abnormal
  necrosis — *see* Placenta, abnormal
  percreta (without hemorrhage) 667.0 ☑
    with hemorrhage 666.0 ☑
  polyp 674.4 ☑
  previa (central) (centralis) (complete) (lateral) (marginal) (marginalis) (partial) (partialis) (total) (with hemorrhage) 641.1 ☑
    without hemorrhage (before labor and delivery) (during pregnancy) 641.0 ☑
    affecting fetus or newborn 762.0
    noted
      before labor, without hemorrhage (with cesarean delivery) 641.0 ☑
      during pregnancy (without hemorrhage) 641.0 ☑
  retention (with hemorrhage) 666.0 ☑
    without hemorrhage 667.0 ☑
    fragments, complicating puerperium (delayed hemorrhage) 666.2 ☑
      without hemorrhage 667.1 ☑
    postpartum, puerperal 666.2 ☑
  separation (normally implanted) (partial) (premature) (with hemorrhage) 641.2 ☑
Placenta, placental — *continued*
  separation — *continued*
    affecting fetus or newborn 762.1
  septuplex — *see* Placenta, abnormal
  small — *see* Placenta, insufficiency
  softening (premature) — *see* Placenta, abnormal
  spuria — *see* Placenta, abnormal
  succenturiata — *see* Placenta, abnormal
  syphilitic 095.8
  transfusion syndromes 762.3
  transmission of chemical substance — *see* Absorption, chemical, through placenta
  trapped (with hemorrhage) 666.0 ☑
    without hemorrhage 667.0 ☑
  trilobate — *see* Placenta, abnormal
  tripartita — *see* Placenta, abnormal
  triplex — *see* Placenta, abnormal
  varicose vessel — *see* Placenta, abnormal
  vicious insertion — *see* Placenta, previa
Placentitis
  affecting fetus or newborn 762.7
  complicating pregnancy 658.4 ☑
Plagiocephaly (skull) 754.0
Plague 020.9
  abortive 020.8
  ambulatory 020.8
  bubonic 020.0
  cellulocutaneous 020.1
  lymphatic gland 020.0
  pneumonic 020.5
    primary 020.3
    secondary 020.4
  pulmonary — *see* Plague, pneumonic
  pulmonic — *see* Plague, pneumonic
  septicemic 020.2
  tonsillar 020.9
    septicemic 020.2
  vaccination, prophylactic (against) V03.3
Planning, family V25.09
  contraception V25.9
  natural
    procreative V26.41
    to avoid pregnancy V25.04
  procreation V26.49
    natural V26.41
Plaque
  artery, arterial — *see* Arteriosclerosis
  calcareous — *see* Calcification
  Hollenhorst's (retinal) 362.33
  tongue 528.6
Plasma cell myeloma 203.0 ☑
Plasmacytoma, plasmocytoma (solitary) (M9731/1) 238.6
  benign (M9731/0) — *see* Neoplasm, by site, benign
  malignant (M9731/3) 203.8 ☑
Plasmacytopenia 288.59
Plasmacytosis 288.64
Plaster ulcer — *see also* ▶Ulcer, pressure◀ 707.00
Plateau iris syndrome 364.82 ●
Platybasia 756.0
Platyonychia (congenital) 757.5
  acquired 703.8
Platypelloid pelvis 738.6
  with disproportion (fetopelvic) 653.2 ☑
    affecting fetus or newborn 763.1
    causing obstructed labor 660.1 ☑
      affecting fetus or newborn 763.1
  congenital 755.69
Platyspondylia 756.19
Plethora 782.62
  newborn 776.4
Pleuralgia 786.52
Pleura, pleural — *see* condition

- **Pleurisy** (acute) (adhesive) (chronic) (costal) (diaphragmatic) (double) (dry) (fetid) (fibrinous) (fibrous) (interlobar) (latent) (lung) (old) (plastic) (primary) (residual) (sicca) (sterile) (subacute) (unresolved) (with adherent pleura) 511.0
  - with
    - effusion (without mention of cause) 511.9
      - bacterial, nontuberculous 511.1
      - nontuberculous NEC 511.9
        - bacterial 511.1
      - pneumococcal 511.1
      - specified type NEC 511.89 ▲
      - staphylococcal 511.1
      - streptococcal 511.1
      - tuberculous (*see also* Tuberculosis, pleura) 012.0 ☑
        - primary, progressive 010.1 ☑
    - influenza, flu, or grippe 487.1
    - tuberculosis — *see* Pleurisy, tuberculous
  - encysted 511.89 ▲
  - exudative (*see also* Pleurisy, with effusion) 511.9
    - bacterial, nontuberculous 511.1
  - fibrinopurulent 510.9
    - with fistula 510.0
  - fibropurulent 510.9
    - with fistula 510.0
  - hemorrhagic 511.89 ▲
  - influenzal 487.1
  - pneumococcal 511.0
    - with effusion 511.1
  - purulent 510.9
    - with fistula 510.0
  - septic 510.9
    - with fistula 510.0
  - serofibrinous (*see also* Pleurisy, with effusion) 511.9
    - bacterial, nontuberculous 511.1
  - seropurulent 510.9
    - with fistula 510.0
  - serous (*see also* Pleurisy, with effusion) 511.9
    - bacterial, nontuberculous 511.1
  - staphylococcal 511.0
    - with effusion 511.1
  - streptococcal 511.0
    - with effusion 511.1
  - suppurative 510.9
    - with fistula 510.0
  - traumatic (post) (current) 862.29
    - with open wound into cavity 862.39
  - tuberculous (with effusion) (*see also* Tuberculosis, pleura) 012.0 ☑
    - primary, progressive 010.1 ☑
- **Pleuritis sicca** — *see* Pleurisy
- **Pleurobronchopneumonia** — *see also* Pneumonia, broncho- 485
- **Pleurodynia** 786.52
  - epidemic 074.1
  - viral 074.1
- **Pleurohepatitis** 573.8
- **Pleuropericarditis** — *see also* Pericarditis 423.9
  - acute 420.90
- **Pleuropneumonia** (acute) (bilateral) (double) (septic) — *see also* Pneumonia 486
  - chronic (*see also* Fibrosis, lung) 515
- **Pleurorrhea** — *see also* Hydrothorax 511.89 ▲
- **Plexitis, brachial** 353.0
- **Plica**
  - knee 727.83
  - polonica 132.0
  - syndrome 727.83
  - tonsil 474.8
- **Plicae dysphonia ventricularis** 784.49
- **Plicated tongue** 529.5
  - congenital 750.13
- **Plug**
  - bronchus NEC 519.19
- **Plug** — *continued*
  - meconium (newborn) NEC 777.1
  - mucus — *see* Mucus, plug
- **Plumbism** 984.9
  - specified type of lead — *see* Table of Drugs and Chemicals
- **Plummer's disease** (toxic nodular goiter) 242.3 ☑
- **Plummer-Vinson syndrome** (sideropenic dysphagia) 280.8
- **Pluricarential syndrome of infancy** 260
- **Plurideficiency syndrome of infancy** 260
- **Plus (and minus) hand** (intrinsic) 736.09
- **PMDD** (premenstrual dysphoric disorder) 625.4
- **PMS** 625.4
- **Pneumathemia — see Air, embolism, by type**
- **Pneumatic drill or hammer disease** 994.9
- **Pneumatocele** (lung) 518.89
  - intracranial 348.8
  - tension 492.0
- **Pneumatosis**
  - cystoides intestinalis 569.89
  - peritonei 568.89
  - pulmonum 492.8
- **Pneumaturia** 599.84
- **Pneumoblastoma** (M8981/3) — *see* Neoplasm, lung, malignant
- **Pneumocephalus** 348.8
- **Pneumococcemia** 038.2
- **Pneumococcus, pneumococcal** — *see* condition
- **Pneumoconiosis** (due to) (inhalation of) 505
  - aluminum 503
  - asbestos 501
  - bagasse 495.1
  - bauxite 503
  - beryllium 503
  - carbon electrode makers' 503
  - coal
    - miners' (simple) 500
    - workers' (simple) 500
  - cotton dust 504
  - diatomite fibrosis 502
  - dust NEC 504
    - inorganic 503
    - lime 502
    - marble 502
    - organic NEC 504
  - fumes or vapors (from silo) 506.9
  - graphite 503
  - hard metal 503
  - mica 502
  - moldy hay 495.0
  - rheumatoid 714.81
  - silica NEC 502
    - and carbon 500
  - silicate NEC 502
  - talc 502
- **Pneumocystis carinii pneumonia** 136.3
- **Pneumocystis jiroveci pneumonia** 136.3
- **Pneumocystosis** 136.3
  - with pneumonia 136.3
- **Pneumoenteritis** 025
- **Pneumohemopericardium** — *see also* Pericarditis 423.9
- **Pneumohemothorax** — *see also* Hemothorax 511.89 ▲
  - traumatic 860.4
    - with open wound into thorax 860.5
- **Pneumohydropericardium** — *see also* Pericarditis 423.9
- **Pneumohydrothorax** — *see also* Hydrothorax 511.89 ▲
- **Pneumomediastinum** 518.1
  - congenital 770.2
  - fetus or newborn 770.2
- **Pneumomycosis** 117.9
- **Pneumonia** (acute) (Alpenstich) (benign) (bilateral) (brain) (cerebral) (circumscribed) (congestive) (creeping) (delayed resolution) (double) (epidemic) (fever) (flash) (fulminant) (fungoid) (granulomatous) (hemorrhagic) (incipient) (infantile) (infectious) (infiltration) (insular) (intermittent) (latent) (lobe) (migratory) (newborn) (organized) (overwhelming) (primary) (progressive) (pseudolobar) (purulent) (resolved) (secondary) (senile) (septic) (suppurative) (terminal) (true) (unresolved) (vesicular) 486
  - with influenza, flu, or grippe 487.0
  - adenoviral 480.0
  - adynamic 514
  - alba 090.0
  - allergic 518.3
  - alveolar — *see* Pneumonia, lobar
  - anaerobes 482.81
  - anthrax 022.1 *[484.5]*
  - apex, apical — *see* Pneumonia, lobar
  - ascaris 127.0 *[484.8]*
  - aspiration 507.0
    - due to
      - aspiration of microorganisms
        - bacterial 482.9
          - specified type NEC 482.89
        - specified organism NEC 483.8
          - bacterial NEC 482.89
        - viral 480.9
          - specified type NEC 480.8
      - food (regurgitated) 507.0
      - gastric secretions 507.0
      - milk 507.0
      - oils, essences 507.1
      - solids, liquids NEC 507.8
      - vomitus 507.0
    - fetal 770.18
      - due to
        - blood 770.16
        - clear amniotic fluid 770.14
        - meconium 770.12
        - postnatal stomach contents 770.86
    - newborn 770.18
      - due to
        - blood 770.16
        - clear amniotic fluid 770.14
        - meconium 770.12
        - postnatal stomach contents 770.86
  - asthenic 514
  - atypical (disseminated) (focal) (primary) 486
    - with influenza 487.0
  - bacillus 482.9
    - specified type NEC 482.89
  - bacterial 482.9
    - specified type NEC 482.89
  - Bacteroides (fragilis) (oralis) (melaninogenicus) 482.81
  - basal, basic, basilar — *see* Pneumonia, lobar
  - bronchiolitis obliterans organized (BOOP) 516.8 ●
  - broncho-, bronchial (confluent) (croupous) (diffuse) (disseminated) (hemorrhagic) (involving lobes) (lobar) (terminal) 485
    - with influenza 487.0
    - allergic 518.3
    - aspiration (*see also* Pneumonia, aspiration) 507.0
    - bacterial 482.9
      - specified type NEC 482.89
    - capillary 466.19
      - with bronchospasm or obstruction 466.19
    - chronic (*see also* Fibrosis, lung) 515
    - congenital (infective) 770.0
    - diplococcal 481
- **Pneumonia** — *continued*
  - broncho-, bronchial — *continued*
    - Eaton's agent 483.0
    - Escherichia coli (E. coli) 482.82
    - Friedländer's bacillus 482.0
    - Hemophilus influenzae 482.2
    - hiberno-vernal 083.0 *[484.8]*
    - hypostatic 514
    - influenzal 487.0
    - inhalation (*see also* Pneumonia, aspiration) 507.0
      - due to fumes or vapors (chemical) 506.0
    - Klebsiella 482.0
    - lipid 507.1
      - endogenous 516.8
    - Mycoplasma (pneumoniae) 483.0
    - ornithosis 073.0
    - pleuropneumonia-like organisms (PPLO) 483.0
    - pneumococcal 481
    - Proteus 482.83
    - Pseudomonas 482.1
    - specified organism NEC 483.8
      - bacterial NEC 482.89
    - staphylococcal 482.40
      - aureus 482.41
        - methicillin ●
          - resistant (MRSA) 482.42 ●
          - susceptible (MSSA) 482.41 ●
      - specified type NEC 482.49
    - streptococcal — *see* Pneumonia, streptococcal
    - typhoid 002.0 *[484.8]*
    - viral, virus (*see also* Pneumonia, viral) 480.9
  - Butyrivibrio (fibriosolvens) 482.81
  - Candida 112.4
  - capillary 466.19
    - with bronchospasm or obstruction 466.19
  - caseous (*see also* Tuberculosis) 011.6 ☑
  - catarrhal — *see* Pneumonia, broncho-
  - central — *see* Pneumonia, lobar
  - Chlamydia, chlamydial 483.1
    - pneumoniae 483.1
    - psittaci 073.0
    - specified type NEC 483.1
    - trachomatis 483.1
  - cholesterol 516.8
  - chronic (*see also* Fibrosis, lung) 515
  - cirrhotic (chronic) (*see also* Fibrosis, lung) 515
  - Clostridium (haemolyticum) (novyi) NEC 482.81
  - confluent — *see* Pneumonia, broncho-
  - congenital (infective) 770.0
    - aspiration 770.18
  - croupous — *see* Pneumonia, lobar
  - cytomegalic inclusion 078.5 *[484.1]*
  - deglutition (*see also* Pneumonia, aspiration) 507.0
  - desquamative interstitial 516.8
  - diffuse — *see* Pneumonia, broncho-
  - diplococcal, diplococcus (broncho-) (lobar) 481
  - disseminated (focal) — *see* Pneumonia, broncho-
  - due to
    - adenovirus 480.0
    - anaerobes 482.81
    - Bacterium anitratum 482.83
    - Chlamydia, chlamydial 483.1
      - pneumoniae 483.1
      - psittaci 073.0
      - specified type NEC 483.1
      - trachomatis 483.1
    - coccidioidomycosis 114.0
    - Diplococcus (pneumoniae) 481
    - Eaton's agent 483.0
    - Escherichia coli (E. coli) 482.82
    - Friedländer's bacillus 482.0
    - fumes or vapors (chemical) (inhalation) 506.0

- **Pneumonia** — *continued*
  - due to — *continued*
    - fungus NEC 117.9 *[484.7]*
      - coccidioidomycosis 114.0
    - Hemophilus influenzae (H. influenzae) 482.2
    - Herellea 482.83
    - influenza 487.0
    - Klebsiella pneumoniae 482.0
    - Mycoplasma (pneumoniae) 483.0
    - parainfluenza virus 480.2
    - pleuropneumonia-like organism (PPLO) 483.0
    - Pneumococcus 481
    - Pneumocystis carinii 136.3
    - Pneumocystis jiroveci 136.3
    - Proteus 482.83
    - Pseudomonas 482.1
    - respiratory syncytial virus 480.1
    - rickettsia 083.9 *[484.8]*
    - SARS-associated coronavirus 480.3
    - specified
      - bacteria NEC 482.89
      - organism NEC 483.8
      - virus NEC 480.8
    - Staphylococcus 482.40
      - aureus 482.41
        - methicillin ●
          - resistant (MRSA) 482.42 ●
          - susceptible (MSSA) 482.41 ●
      - specified type NEC 482.49
    - Streptococcus (*see also* Pneumonia, streptococcal)
      - pneumoniae 481
    - virus (*see also* Pneumonia, viral) 480.9
      - SARS-associated coronavirus 480.3
  - Eaton's agent 483.0
  - embolic, embolism — (*see* Embolism, pulmonary
  - eosinophilic 518.3
  - Escherichia coli (E. coli) 482.82
  - Eubacterium 482.81
  - fibrinous — *see* Pneumonia, lobar
  - fibroid (chronic) (*see also* Fibrosis, lung) 515
  - fibrous (*see also* Fibrosis, lung) 515
  - Friedländer's bacillus 482.0
  - Fusobacterium (nucleatum) 482.81
  - gangrenous 513.0
  - giant cell (*see also* Pneumonia, viral) 480.9
  - gram-negative bacteria NEC 482.83
    - anaerobic 482.81
  - grippal 487.0
  - Hemophilus influenzae (bronchial) (lobar) 482.2
  - hypostatic (broncho-) (lobar) 514
  - in
    - actinomycosis 039.1
    - anthrax 022.1 *[484.5]*
    - aspergillosis 117.3 *[484.6]*
    - candidiasis 112.4
    - coccidioidomycosis 114.0
    - cytomegalic inclusion disease 078.5 *[484.1]*
    - histoplasmosis (*see also* Histoplasmosis) 115.95
    - infectious disease NEC 136.9 *[484.8]*
    - measles 055.1
    - mycosis, systemic NEC 117.9 *[484.7]*
    - nocardiasis, nocardiosis 039.1
    - ornithosis 073.0
    - pneumocystosis 136.3
    - psittacosis 073.0
    - Q fever 083.0 *[484.8]*
    - salmonellosis 003.22
    - toxoplasmosis 130.4
    - tularemia 021.2
    - typhoid (fever) 002.0 *[484.8]*
    - varicella 052.1

- **Pneumonia** — *continued*
  - in — *continued*
    - whooping cough (*see also* Whooping cough) 033.9 *[484.3]*
  - infective, acquired prenatally 770.0
  - influenzal (broncho) (lobar) (virus) 487.0
  - inhalation (*see also* Pneumonia, aspiration) 507.0
    - fumes or vapors (chemical) 506.0
  - interstitial 516.8
    - with influenzal 487.0
    - acute 136.3
    - chronic (*see also* Fibrosis, lung) 515
    - desquamative 516.8
    - hypostatic 514
    - lipoid 507.1
    - lymphoid 516.8
    - plasma cell 136.3
    - Pseudomonas 482.1
  - intrauterine (infective) 770.0
    - aspiration 770.18
      - blood 770.16
      - clear amniotic fluid 770.14
      - meconium 770.12
      - postnatal stomach contents 770.86
  - Klebsiella pneumoniae 482.0
  - Legionnaires' 482.84
  - lipid, lipoid (exogenous) (interstitial) 507.1
    - endogenous 516.8
  - lobar (diplococcal) (disseminated) (double) (interstitial) (pneumococcal, any type) 481
    - with influenza 487.0
    - bacterial 482.9
      - specified type NEC 482.89
    - chronic (*see also* Fibrosis, lung) 515
    - Escherichia coli (E. coli) 482.82
    - Friedländer's bacillus 482.0
    - Hemophilus influenzae (H. influenzae) 482.2
    - hypostatic 514
    - influenzal 487.0
    - Klebsiella 482.0
    - ornithosis 073.0
    - Proteus 482.83
    - Pseudomonas 482.1
    - psittacosis 073.0
    - specified organism NEC 483.8
      - bacterial NEC 482.89
    - staphylococcal 482.40
      - aureus 482.41
        - methicillin ●
          - resistant (MRSA) 482.42 ●
          - susceptible (MSSA) 482.41 ●
      - specified type NEC 482.49
    - streptococcal — *see* Pneumonia, streptococcal
    - viral, virus (*see also* Pneumonia, viral) 480.9
  - lobular (confluent) — *see* Pneumonia, broncho-
  - Löffler's 518.3
  - massive — *see* Pneumonia, lobar
  - meconium aspiration 770.12
  - metastatic NEC 038.8 *[484.8]*
  - methicillin resistant Staphylococcus aureus (MRSA) 482.42 ●
  - methicillin susceptible Staphylococcus aureus (MSSA) 482.41 ●
  - MRSA (methicillin resistant Staphylococcus aureus) 482.42 ●
  - MSSA (methicillin susceptible Staphylococcus aureus) 482.41 ●
  - Mycoplasma (pneumoniae) 483.0
  - necrotic 513.0
  - nitrogen dioxide 506.9
  - orthostatic 514
  - parainfluenza virus 480.2

- **Pneumonia** — *continued*
  - parenchymatous (*see also* Fibrosis, lung) 515
  - passive 514
  - patchy — *see* Pneumonia, broncho-
  - Peptococcus 482.81
  - Peptostreptococcus 482.81
  - plasma cell 136.3
  - pleurolobar — see Pneumonia, lobar
  - pleuropneumonia-like organism (PPLO) 483.0
  - pneumococcal (broncho) (lobar) 481
  - Pneumocystis (carinii) (jiroveci) 136.3
  - postinfectional NEC 136.9 *[484.8]*
  - postmeasles 055.1
  - postoperative 997.39 ▲
  - primary atypical 486
  - Proprionibacterium 482.81
  - Proteus 482.83
  - Pseudomonas 482.1
  - psittacosis 073.0
  - radiation 508.0
  - respiratory syncytial virus 480.1
  - resulting from a procedure 997.39 ▲
  - rheumatic 390 *[517.1]*
  - Salmonella 003.22
  - SARS-associated coronavirus 480.3
  - segmented, segmental — *see* Pneumonia, broncho-
  - Serratia (marcescens) 482.83
  - specified
    - bacteria NEC 482.89
    - organism NEC 483.8
    - virus NEC 480.8
  - spirochetal 104.8 *[484.8]*
  - staphylococcal (broncho) (lobar) 482.40
    - aureus 482.41
      - methicillin ●
        - resistant 482.42 ●
        - susceptible (MSSA) 482.41 ●
    - specified type NEC 482.49
  - static, stasis 514
  - streptococcal (broncho) (lobar) NEC 482.30
    - Group
      - A 482.31
      - B 482.32
      - specified NEC 482.39
    - pneumoniae 481
    - specified type NEC 482.39
  - Streptococcus pneumoniae 481
  - traumatic (complication) (early) (secondary) 958.8
  - tuberculous (any) (*see also* Tuberculosis) 011.6 ☑
  - tularemic 021.2
  - TWAR agent 483.1
  - varicella 052.1
  - Veillonella 482.81
  - ventilator associated 997.31 ▲
  - viral, virus (broncho) (interstitial) (lobar) 480.9
    - with influenza, flu, or grippe 487.0
    - adenoviral 480.0
    - parainfluenza 480.2
    - respiratory syncytial 480.1
    - SARS-associated coronavirus 480.3
    - specified type NEC 480.8
  - white (congenital) 090.0
- **Pneumonic** — *see* condition
- **Pneumonitis** (acute) (primary) — *see also* Pneumonia 486
  - allergic 495.9
    - specified type NEC 495.8
  - aspiration 507.0
    - due to fumes or gases 506.0
    - fetal 770.18
      - due to
        - blood 770.16
        - clear amniotic fluid 770.14
        - meconium 770.12
        - postnatal stomach contents 770.86
    - newborn 770.18

- **Pneumonitis** — *see also* Pneumonia — *continued*
  - aspiration — *continued*
    - newborn — *continued*
      - due to
        - blood 770.16
        - clear amniotic fluid 770.14
        - meconium 770.12
        - postnatal stomach contents 770.86
    - obstetric 668.0 ☑
  - chemical 506.0
    - due to fumes or gases 506.0
  - cholesterol 516.8
  - chronic (*see also* Fibrosis, lung) 515
  - congenital rubella 771.0
  - crack 506.0
  - due to
    - crack (cocaine) 506.0
    - fumes or vapors 506.0
    - inhalation
      - food (regurgitated), milk, vomitus 507.0
      - oils, essences 507.1
      - saliva 507.0
      - solids, liquids NEC 507.8
    - toxoplasmosis (acquired) 130.4
      - congenital (active) 771.2 *[484.8]*
  - eosinophilic 518.3
  - fetal aspiration 770.18
    - due to
      - blood 770.16
      - clear amniotic fluid 770.14
      - meconium 770.12
      - postnatal stomach contents 770.86
  - hypersensitivity 495.9
  - interstitial (chronic) (*see also* Fibrosis, lung) 515
    - lymphoid 516.8
  - lymphoid, interstitial 516.8
  - meconium aspiration 770.12
  - postanesthetic
    - correct substance properly administered 507.0
    - obstetric 668.0 ☑
    - overdose or wrong substance given 968.4
      - specified anesthetic — *see* Table of Drugs and Chemicals
  - postoperative 997.3 ☑
    - obstetric 668.0 ☑
  - radiation 508.0
  - rubella, congenital 771.0
  - "ventilation" 495.7
  - wood-dust 495.8
- **Pneumonoconiosis** — *see* Pneumoconiosis
- **Pneumoparotid** 527.8
- **Pneumopathy** NEC 518.89
  - alveolar 516.9
    - specified NEC 516.8
  - due to dust NEC 504
  - parietoalveolar 516.9
    - specified condition NEC 516.8
- **Pneumopericarditis** — *see also* Pericarditis 423.9
  - acute 420.90
- **Pneumopericardium** — *see also* Pericarditis
  - congenital 770.2
  - fetus or newborn 770.2
  - traumatic (post) (*see also* Pneumothorax, traumatic) 860.0
    - with open wound into thorax 860.1
- **Pneumoperitoneum** 568.89
  - fetus or newborn 770.2
- **Pneumophagia** (psychogenic) 306.4
- **Pneumopleurisy, pneumopleuritis** — *see also* Pneumonia 486
- **Pneumopyopericardium** 420.99
- **Pneumopyothorax** — *see also* Pyopneumothorax 510.9
  - with fistula 510.0
- **Pneumorrhagia** 786.3
  - newborn 770.3

Pneumorrhagia — *continued*
tuberculous (*see also* Tuberculosis, pulmonary) 011.9 ☑
Pneumosiderosis (occupational) 503
Pneumothorax (acute) (chronic) 512.8
congenital 770.2
due to operative injury of chest wall or lung 512.1
accidental puncture or laceration 512.1
fetus or newborn 770.2
iatrogenic 512.1
postoperative 512.1
spontaneous 512.8
fetus or newborn 770.2
tension 512.0
sucking 512.8
iatrogenic 512.1
postoperative 512.1
tense valvular, infectional 512.0
tension 512.0
iatrogenic 512.1
postoperative 512.1
spontaneous 512.0
traumatic 860.0
with
hemothorax 860.4
with open wound into thorax 860.5
open wound into thorax 860.1
tuberculous (*see also* Tuberculosis) 011.7 ☑
Pocket(s)
endocardial (*see also* Endocarditis) 424.90
periodontal 523.8
Podagra 274.9
Podencephalus 759.89
Poikilocytosis 790.09
Poikiloderma 709.09
Civatte's 709.09
congenital 757.33
vasculare atrophicans 696.2
Poikilodermatomyositis 710.3
Pointed ear 744.29
Poise imperfect 729.90 ▲
Poisoned — *see* Poisoning
Poisoning (acute) — *see also* Table of Drugs and Chemicals
Bacillus, B.
aertrycke (*see also* Infection, Salmonella) 003.9
botulinus 005.1
cholerae (suis) (*see also* Infection, Salmonella) 003.9
paratyphosus (*see also* Infection, Salmonella) 003.9
suipestifer (*see also* Infection, Salmonella) 003.9
bacterial toxins NEC 005.9
berries, noxious 988.2
blood (general) — *see* Septicemia
botulism 005.1
bread, moldy, mouldy — *see* Poisoning, food
Ciguatera 988.0
damaged meat — *see* Poisoning, food
death-cap (Amanita phalloides) (Amanita verna) 988.1
decomposed food — *see* Poisoning, food
diseased food — *see* Poisoning, food
drug — *see* Table of Drugs and Chemicals
epidemic, fish, meat, or other food — *see* Poisoning, food
fava bean 282.2
fish (bacterial) (*see also* Poisoning, food)
noxious 988.0
food (acute) (bacterial) (diseased) (infected) NEC 005.9
Poisoning — *see also* Table of Drugs and Chemicals — *continued*
food — *continued*
due to
bacillus
aertrycke (*see also* Poisoning, food, due to Salmonella) 003.9
botulinus 005.1
cereus 005.89
choleraesuis (*see also* Poisoning, food, due to Salmonella) 003.9
paratyphosus (*see also* Poisoning, food, due to Salmonella) 003.9
suipestifer (*see also* Poisoning, food, due to Salmonella) 003.9
Clostridium 005.3
botulinum 005.1
perfringens 005.2
welchii 005.2
Salmonella (aertrycke) (callinarum) (choleraesuis) (enteritidis) (paratyphi) (suipestifer) 003.9
with
gastroenteritis 003.0
localized infection(s) (*see also* Infection, Salmonella) 003.20
septicemia 003.1
specified manifestation NEC 003.8
specified bacterium NEC 005.89
Staphylococcus 005.0
Streptococcus 005.89
Vibrio parahaemolyticus 005.4
Vibrio vulnificus 005.81
noxious or naturally toxic 988.0
berries 988.2
fish 988.0
mushroom 988.1
plants NEC 988.2
ice cream — *see* Poisoning, food
ichthyotoxism (bacterial) 005.9
kreotoxism, food 005.9
malarial — *see* Malaria
meat — *see* Poisoning, food
mushroom (noxious) 988.1
mussel (*see also* Poisoning, food)
noxious 988.0
noxious foodstuffs (*see also* Poisoning, food, noxious) 988.9
specified type NEC 988.8
plants, noxious 988.2
pork (*see also* Poisoning, food)
specified NEC 988.8
Trichinosis 124
ptomaine — *see* Poisoning, food
putrefaction, food — *see* Poisoning, food
radiation 508.0
Salmonella (*see also* Infection, Salmonella) 003.9
sausage (*see also* Poisoning, food)
Trichinosis 124
saxitoxin 988.0
shellfish (*see also* Poisoning, food)
noxious (amnesic) (azaspiracid) (diarrheic) (neurotoxic) (paralytic) 988.0
Staphylococcus, food 005.0
toxic, from disease NEC 799.89
truffles — *see* Poisoning, food
uremic — *see* Uremia
uric acid 274.9
water 276.6
Poison ivy, oak, sumac or other plant dermatitis 692.6
Poker spine 720.0
Policeman's disease 729.2
Polioencephalitis (acute) (bulbar) — *see also* Poliomyelitis, bulbar 045.0 ☑
inferior 335.22
Polioencephalitis — *see also* Poliomyelitis, bulbar — *continued*
influenzal 487.8
superior hemorrhagic (acute) (Wernicke's) 265.1
Wernicke's (superior hemorrhagic) 265.1
Polioencephalomyelitis (acute) (anterior) (bulbar) — *see also* Polioencephalitis 045.0 ☑
Polioencephalopathy, superior hemorrhagic 265.1
with
beriberi 265.0
pellagra 265.2
Poliomeningoencephalitis — *see* Meningoencephalitis
Poliomyelitis (acute) (anterior) (epidemic) 045.9 ☑

Note — Use the following fifth-digit subclassification with category 045:

0	*poliovirus, unspecified type*
1	*poliovirus, type I*
2	*poliovirus, type II*
3	*poliovirus, type III*

with
paralysis 045.1 ☑
bulbar 045.0 ☑
abortive 045.2 ☑
ascending 045.9 ☑
progressive 045.9 ☑
bulbar 045.0 ☑
cerebral 045.0 ☑
chronic 335.21
congenital 771.2
contact V01.2
deformities 138
exposure to V01.2
late effect 138
nonepidemic 045.9 ☑
nonparalytic 045.2 ☑
old with deformity 138
posterior, acute 053.19
residual 138
sequelae 138
spinal, acute 045.9 ☑
syphilitic (chronic) 094.89
vaccination, prophylactic (against) V04.0
Poliosis (eyebrow) (eyelashes) 704.3
circumscripta (congenital) 757.4
acquired 704.3
congenital 757.4
Pollakiuria 788.41
psychogenic 306.53
Pollinosis 477.0
Pollitzer's disease (hidradenitis suppurativa) 705.83
Polyadenitis — *see also* Adenitis 289.3
malignant 020.0
Polyalgia 729.90 ▲
Polyangiitis (essential) 446.0
Polyarteritis (nodosa) (renal) 446.0
Polyarthralgia 719.49
psychogenic 306.0
Polyarthritis, polyarthropathy NEC 716.59
due to or associated with other specified conditions — *see* Arthritis, due to or associated with
endemic (*see also* Disease, Kaschin-Beck) 716.0 ☑
inflammatory 714.9
specified type NEC 714.89
juvenile (chronic) 714.30
acute 714.31
migratory — *see* Fever, rheumatic
rheumatic 714.0
fever (acute) — *see* Fever, rheumatic
Polycarential syndrome of infancy 260
Polychondritis (atrophic) (chronic) (relapsing) 733.99
Polycoria 743.46
Polycystic (congenital) (disease) 759.89
degeneration, kidney — *see* Polycystic, kidney
kidney (congenital) 753.12
adult type (APKD) 753.13
autosomal dominant 753.13
autosomal recessive 753.14
childhood type (CPKD) 753.14
infantile type 753.14
liver 751.62
lung 518.89
congenital 748.4
ovary, ovaries 256.4
spleen 759.0
Polycythemia (primary) (rubra) (vera) (M9950/1) 238.4
acquired 289.0
benign 289.0
familial 289.6
due to
donor twin 776.4
fall in plasma volume 289.0
high altitude 289.0
maternal-fetal transfusion 776.4
stress 289.0
emotional 289.0
erythropoietin 289.0
familial (benign) 289.6
Gaisböck's (hypertonica) 289.0
high altitude 289.0
hypertonica 289.0
hypoxemic 289.0
neonatorum 776.4
nephrogenous 289.0
relative 289.0
secondary 289.0
spurious 289.0
stress 289.0
Polycytosis cryptogenica 289.0
Polydactylism, polydactyly 755.00
fingers 755.01
toes 755.02
Polydipsia 783.5
Polydystrophic oligophrenia 277.5
Polyembryoma (M9072/3) — *see* Neoplasm, by site, malignant
Polygalactia 676.6 ☑
Polyglandular
deficiency 258.9
dyscrasia 258.9
dysfunction 258.9
syndrome 258.8
Polyhydramnios — *see also* Hydramnios 657.0 ☑
Polymastia 757.6
Polymenorrhea 626.2
Polymicrogyria 742.2
Polymyalgia 725
arteritica 446.5
rheumatica 725
Polymyositis (acute) (chronic) (hemorrhagic) 710.4
with involvement of
lung 710.4 *[517.8]*
skin 710.3
ossificans (generalisata) (progressiva) 728.19
Wagner's (dermatomyositis) 710.3
Polyneuritis, polyneuritic — *see also* Polyneuropathy 356.9
alcoholic 357.5
with psychosis 291.1
cranialis 352.6
demyelinating, chronic inflammatory (CIDP) 357.81
diabetic 250.6 ☑ *[357.2]*
due to secondary diabetes 249.6 ☑ *[357.2]* ●
due to lack of vitamin NEC 269.2 *[357.4]*
endemic 265.0 *[357.4]*
erythredema 985.0
febrile 357.0

Polyneuritis, polyneuritic — *see also* Polyneuropathy — *continued*
hereditary ataxic 356.3
idiopathic, acute 357.0
infective (acute) 357.0
nutritional 269.9 *[357.4]*
postinfectious 357.0
Polyneuropathy (peripheral) 356.9
alcoholic 357.5
amyloid 277.39 *[357.4]*
arsenical 357.7
critical illness 357.82
demyelinating, chronic inflammatory (CIDP) 357.81
diabetic 250.6 ☑ *[357.2]*
due to secondary diabetes 249.6 ☑ *[357.2]* ●
due to
antitetanus serum 357.6
arsenic 357.7
drug or medicinal substance 357.6
correct substance properly administered 357.6
overdose or wrong substance given or taken 977.9
specified drug — *see* Table of Drugs and Chemicals
lack of vitamin NEC 269.2 *[357.4]*
lead 357.7
organophosphate compounds 357.7
pellagra 265.2 *[357.4]*
porphyria 277.1 *[357.4]*
serum 357.6
toxic agent NEC 357.7
hereditary 356.0
idiopathic 356.9
progressive 356.4
in
amyloidosis 277.39 *[357.4]*
avitaminosis 269.2 *[357.4]*
specified NEC 269.1 *[357.4]*
beriberi 265.0 *[357.4]*
collagen vascular disease NEC 710.9 *[357.1]*
deficiency
B-complex NEC 266.2 *[357.4]*
vitamin B 266.1 *[357.4]*
vitamin B6 266.9 *[357.4]*
diabetes 250.6 ☑ *[357.2]*
due to secondary diabetes 249.6 ☑ *[357.2]* ●
diphtheria (*see also* Diphtheria) 032.89 *[357.4]*
disseminated lupus erythematosus 710.0 *[357.1]*
herpes zoster 053.13
hypoglycemia 251.2 *[357.4]*
malignant neoplasm (M8000/3) NEC 199.1 *[357.3]*
mumps 072.72
pellagra 265.2 *[357.4]*
polyarteritis nodosa 446.0 *[357.1]*
porphyria 277.1 *[357.4]*
rheumatoid arthritis 714.0 *[357.1]*
sarcoidosis 135 *[357.4]*
uremia 585.9 *[357.4]*
lead 357.7
nutritional 269.9 *[357.4]*
specified NEC 269.8 *[357.4]*
postherpetic 053.13
progressive 356.4
sensory (hereditary) 356.2
specified NEC 356.8
Polyonychia 757.5
Polyopia 368.2
refractive 368.15
Polyorchism, polyorchidism (three testes) 752.89
Polyorrhymenitis (peritoneal) — *see also* Polyserositis 568.82
pericardial 423.2
Polyostotic fibrous dysplasia 756.54
Polyotia 744.1
Polyphagia 783.6
Polypoid — *see* condition
Polyposis — *see also* Polyp
coli (adenomatous) (M8220/0) 211.3
adenocarcinoma in (M8220/3) 153.9
carcinoma in (M8220/3) 153.9
familial (M8220/0) 211.3
intestinal (adenomatous) (M8220/0) 211.3
multiple (M8221/0) — *see* Neoplasm, by site, benign
Polyp, polypus

Note — Polyps of organs or sites that do not appear in the list below should be coded to the residual category for diseases of the organ or site concerned.

accessory sinus 471.8
adenoid tissue 471.0
adenomatous (M8210/0) (*see also* Neoplasm, by site, benign)
adenocarcinoma in (M8210/3) — *see* Neoplasm, by site, malignant
carcinoma in (M8210/3) — *see* Neoplasm, by site, malignant
multiple (M8221/0) — *see* Neoplasm, by site, benign
antrum 471.8
anus, anal (canal) (nonadenomatous) 569.0
adenomatous 211.4
Bartholin's gland 624.6
bladder (M8120/1) 236.7
broad ligament 620.8
cervix (uteri) 622.7
adenomatous 219.0
in pregnancy or childbirth 654.6 ☑
affecting fetus or newborn 763.89
causing obstructed labor 660.2 ☑
mucous 622.7
nonneoplastic 622.7
choanal 471.0
cholesterol 575.6
clitoris 624.6
colon (M8210/0) (*see also* Polyp, adenomatous) 211.3
corpus uteri 621.0
dental 522.0
ear (middle) 385.30
endometrium 621.0
ethmoidal (sinus) 471.8
fallopian tube 620.8
female genital organs NEC 624.8
frontal (sinus) 471.8
gallbladder 575.6
gingiva 523.8
gum 523.8
labia 624.6
larynx (mucous) 478.4
malignant (M8000/3) — *see* Neoplasm, by site, malignant
maxillary (sinus) 471.8
middle ear 385.30
myometrium 621.0
nares
anterior 471.9
posterior 471.0
nasal (mucous) 471.9
cavity 471.0
septum 471.9
nasopharyngeal 471.0
neoplastic (M8210/0) — *see* Neoplasm, by site, benign
nose (mucous) 471.9
oviduct 620.8
paratubal 620.8
pharynx 478.29
congenital 750.29
placenta, placental 674.4 ☑
prostate 600.20
with
other lower urinary tract symptoms (LUTS) 600.21
Polyp, polypus — *continued*
prostate — *continued*
with — *continued*
urinary
obstruction 600.21
retention 600.21
pudenda 624.6
pulp (dental) 522.0
rectosigmoid 211.4
rectum (nonadenomatous) 569.0
adenomatous 211.4
septum (nasal) 471.9
sinus (accessory) (ethmoidal) (frontal) (maxillary) (sphenoidal) 471.8
sphenoidal (sinus) 471.8
stomach (M8210/0) 211.1
tube, fallopian 620.8
turbinate, mucous membrane 471.8
ureter 593.89
urethra 599.3
uterine
ligament 620.8
tube 620.8
uterus (body) (corpus) (mucous) 621.0
in pregnancy or childbirth 654.1 ☑
affecting fetus or newborn 763.89
causing obstructed labor 660.2 ☑
vagina 623.7
vocal cord (mucous) 478.4
vulva 624.6
Polyradiculitis (acute) 357.0
Polyradiculoneuropathy (acute) (segmentally demyelinating) 357.0
Polysarcia 278.00
Polyserositis (peritoneal) 568.82
due to pericarditis 423.2
paroxysmal (familial) 277.31
pericardial 423.2
periodic (familial) 277.31
pleural — *see* Pleurisy
recurrent 277.31
tuberculous (*see also* Tuberculosis, polyserositis) 018.9 ☑
Polysialia 527.7
Polysplenia syndrome 759.0
Polythelia 757.6
Polytrichia — *see also* Hypertrichosis 704.1
Polyunguia (congenital) 757.5
acquired 703.8
Polyuria 788.42
Pompe's disease (glycogenosis II) 271.0
Pompholyx 705.81
Poncet's disease (tuberculous rheumatism) — *see also* Tuberculosis 015.9 ☑
Pond fracture — *see* Fracture, skull, vault
Ponos 085.0
Pons, pontine — *see* condition
Poor
aesthetics of existing restoration of tooth 525.67
contractions, labor 661.2 ☑
affecting fetus or newborn 763.7
fetal growth NEC 764.9 ☑
affecting management of pregnancy 656.5 ☑
incorporation
artificial skin graft 996.55
decellularized allodermis graft 996.55
obstetrical history V13.29
affecting management of current pregnancy V23.49
pre-term labor V23.41
pre-term labor V13.21
sucking reflex (newborn) 796.1
vision NEC 369.9
Poradenitis, nostras 099.1
Porencephaly (congenital) (developmental) (true) 742.4
acquired 348.0
nondevelopmental 348.0
Porencephaly — *continued*
traumatic (post) 310.2
Porocephaliasis 134.1
Porokeratosis 757.39
disseminated superficial actinic (DSAP) 692.75
Poroma, eccrine (M8402/0) — *see* Neoplasm, skin, benign
Porphyria (acute) (congenital) (constitutional) (erythropoietic) (familial) (hepatica) (idiopathic) (idiosyncratic) (intermittent) (latent) (mixed hepatic) (photosensitive) (South African genetic) (Swedish) 277.1
acquired 277.1
cutaneatarda
hereditaria 277.1
symptomatica 277.1
due to drugs
correct substance properly administered 277.1
overdose or wrong substance given or taken 977.9
specified drug — *see* Table of Drugs and Chemicals
secondary 277.1
toxic NEC 277.1
variegata 277.1
Porphyrinuria (acquired) (congenital) (secondary) 277.1
Porphyruria (acquired) (congenital) 277.1
Portal — *see* condition
Port wine nevus or mark 757.32
Posadas-Wernicke disease 114.9
Position
fetus, abnormal (*see also* Presentation, fetal) 652.9 ☑
teeth, faulty (*see also* Anomaly, position tooth) 524.30
Positive
culture (nonspecific) 795.39
AIDS virus V08
blood 790.7
HIV V08
human immunodeficiency virus V08
nose 795.39
Staphylococcus — *see* Carrier (suspected) of, Staphylococcus ●
skin lesion NEC 795.39
spinal fluid 792.0
sputum 795.39
stool 792.1
throat 795.39
urine 791.9
wound 795.39
findings, anthrax 795.31
HIV V08
human immunodeficiency virus (HIV) V08
PPD 795.5
serology
AIDS virus V08
inconclusive 795.71
HIV V08
inconclusive 795.71
human immunodeficiency virus (HIV) V08
inconclusive 795.71
syphilis 097.1
with signs or symptoms — *see* Syphilis, by site and stage
false 795.6
skin test 795.7 ☑
tuberculin (without active tuberculosis) 795.5
VDRL 097.1
with signs or symptoms — *see* Syphilis, by site and stage
false 795.6
Wassermann reaction 097.1
false 795.6
Postcardiotomy syndrome 429.4
Postcaval ureter 753.4
Postcholecystectomy syndrome 576.0

- **Postclimacteric bleeding** 627.1
- **Postcommissurotomy syndrome** 429.4
- **Postconcussional syndrome** 310.2
- **Postcontusional syndrome** 310.2
- **Postcricoid region** — *see* condition
- **Post-dates** (pregnancy) — *see* Pregnancy
- **Postencephalitic** — *see also* condition
  - syndrome 310.8
- **Posterior** — *see* condition
- **Posterolateral sclerosis** (spinal cord) — *see* Degeneration, combined
- **Postexanthematous** — *see* condition
- **Postfebrile** — *see* condition
- **Postgastrectomy dumping syndrome** 564.2
- **Posthemiplegic chorea** 344.89
- **Posthemorrhagic anemia** (chronic) 280.0
  - acute 285.1
  - newborn 776.5
- **Posthepatitis syndrome** 780.79
- **Postherpetic neuralgia** (intercostal) (syndrome) (zoster) 053.19
  - geniculate ganglion 053.11
  - ophthalmica 053.19
  - trigeminal 053.12
- **Posthitis** 607.1
- **Postimmunization complication or reaction** — *see* Complications, vaccination
- **Postinfectious** — *see* condition
- **Postinfluenzal syndrome** 780.79
- **Postlaminectomy syndrome** 722.80
  - cervical, cervicothoracic 722.81
  - kyphosis 737.12
  - lumbar, lumbosacral 722.83
  - thoracic, thoracolumbar 722.82
- **Postleukotomy syndrome** 310.0
- **Postlobectomy syndrome** 310.0
- **Postmastectomy lymphedema** (syndrome) 457.0
- **Postmaturity, postmature** (fetus or newborn) (gestation period over 42 completed weeks) 766.22
  - affecting management of pregnancy
    - post-term pregnancy 645.1 ☑
    - prolonged pregnancy 645.2 ☑
  - syndrome 766.22
- **Postmeasles** — *see also* condition
  - complication 055.8
    - specified NEC 055.79
- **Postmenopausal**
  - endometrium (atrophic) 627.8
    - suppurative (see also Endometritis) 615.9
  - hormone replacement therapy V07.4
  - status (age related) (natural) V49.81
- **Postnasal drip** 784.91
- **Postnatal** — *see* condition
- **Postoperative** — *see also* condition
  - confusion state 293.9
  - psychosis 293.9
  - status NEC (*see also* Status (post)) V45.89
- **Postpancreatectomy hyperglycemia** 251.3
- **Postpartum** — *see also* condition
  - anemia 648.2 ☑
  - cardiomyopathy 674.5 ☑
  - observation
    - immediately after delivery V24.0
    - routine follow-up V24.2
- **Postperfusion syndrome** NEC 999.89 ▲
  - bone marrow 996.85
- **Postpoliomyelitic** — *see* condition
- **Postsurgery status** NEC — *see also* Status (post V45.89
- **Post-term** (pregnancy) 645.1 ☑
  - infant (gestation period over 40 completed weeks to 42 completed weeks) 766.21
- ● **Post-transplant lymphoproliferative disorder (PTLD)** 238.77 ●
- **Posttraumatic** — *see* condition
- **Posttraumatic brain syndrome, nonpsychotic** 310.2
- **Post-traumatic stress disorder** (PTSD) 309.81
- **Post-typhoid abscess** 002.0
- **Postures, hysterical** 300.11
- **Postvaccinal reaction or complication** — *see* Complications, vaccination
- **Postvagotomy syndrome** 564.2
- **Postvalvulotomy syndrome** 429.4
- **Postvasectomy sperm count** V25.8
- **Potain's disease** (pulmonary edema) 514
- **Potain's syndrome** (gastrectasis with dyspepsia) 536.1
- **Pott's**
  - curvature (spinal) (*see also* Tuberculosis) 015.0 ☑ *[737.43]*
  - disease or paraplegia (*see also* Tuberculosis) 015.0 ☑ *[730.88]*
  - fracture (closed) 824.4
    - open 824.5
  - gangrene 440.24
  - osteomyelitis (*see also* Tuberculosis) 015.0 ☑ *[730.88]*
  - spinal curvature (*see also* Tuberculosis) 015.0 ☑ *[737.43]*
  - tumor, puffy (*see also* Osteomyelitis) 730.2 ☑
- **Potter's**
  - asthma 502
  - disease 753.0
  - facies 754.0
  - lung 502
  - syndrome (with renal agenesis) 753.0
- **Pouch**
  - bronchus 748.3
  - Douglas' — *see* condition
  - esophagus, esophageal (congenital) 750.4
    - acquired 530.6
  - gastric 537.1
  - Hartmann's (abnormal sacculation of gallbladder neck) 575.8
    - of intestine V44.3
      - attention to V55.3
  - pharynx, pharyngeal (congenital) 750.27
- **Poulet's disease** 714.2
- **Poultrymen's itch** 133.8
- **Poverty** V60.2
- **PPE** (palmar plantar erythrodysesthesia) 693.0
- **Prader-Labhart-Willi-Fanconi syndrome** (hypogenital dystrophy with diabetic tendency) 759.81
- **Prader-Willi syndrome** (hypogenital dystrophy with diabetic tendency) 759.81
- **Preachers' voice** 784.49
- **Pre-AIDS** — *see* Human immunodeficiency virus (disease) (illness) (infection)
- **Preauricular appendage** 744.1
- **Prebetalipoproteinemia** (acquired) (essential) (familial) (hereditary) (primary) (secondary) 272.1
  - with chylomicronemia 272.3
- **Precipitate labor** 661.3 ☑
  - affecting fetus or newborn 763.6
- **Preclimacteric bleeding** 627.0
  - menorrhagia 627.0
- **Precocious**
  - adrenarche 259.1
  - menarche 259.1
  - menstruation 626.8
  - pubarche 259.1
  - puberty NEC 259.1
  - sexual development NEC 259.1
  - thelarche 259.1
- **Precocity, sexual** (constitutional) (cryptogenic) (female) (idiopathic) (male) NEC 259.1
  - with adrenal hyperplasia 255.2
- **Precordial pain** 786.51
  - psychogenic 307.89
- **Predeciduous teeth** 520.2
- **Prediabetes, prediabetic** 790.29
- **Prediabetes, prediabetic** — *continued*
  - complicating pregnancy, childbirth, or puerperium 648.8 ☑
  - fetus or newborn 775.89
- **Predislocation status of hip, at birth** — *see also* Subluxation, congenital, hip 754.32
- **Preeclampsia** (mild) 642.4 ☑
  - with pre-existing hypertension 642.7 ☑
  - affecting fetus or newborn 760.0
  - severe 642.5 ☑
  - superimposed on pre-existing hypertensive disease 642.7 ☑
- **Preeruptive color change, teeth, tooth** 520.8
- **Preexcitation** 426.7
  - atrioventricular conduction 426.7
  - ventricular 426.7
- **Preglaucoma** 365.00
- **Pregnancy** (single) (uterine) (without sickness) V22.2

Note — Use the following fifth-digit subclassification with categories 640–▶649◀, 651–676:

0	*unspecified as to episode of care*
1	*delivered, with or without mention of antepartum condition*
2	*delivered, with mention of postpartum complication*
3	*antepartum condition or complication*
4	*postpartum condition or complication*

  - abdominal (ectopic) 633.00
    - with intrauterine pregnancy 633.01
    - affecting fetus or newborn 761.4
  - abnormal NEC 646.9 ☑
  - ampullar — *see* Pregnancy, tubal
  - broad ligament — *see* Pregnancy, cornual
  - cervical — *see* Pregnancy, cornual
  - combined (extrauterine and intrauterine) — *see* Pregnancy, cornual
  - complicated (by)
    - abnormal, abnormality NEC 646.9 ☑
      - cervix 654.6 ☑
      - cord (umbilical) 663.9 ☑
      - glucose tolerance (conditions classifiable to 790.21–790.29) 648.8 ☑
      - pelvic organs or tissues NEC 654.9 ☑
      - pelvis (bony) 653.0 ☑
      - perineum or vulva 654.8 ☑
      - placenta, placental (vessel) 656.7 ☑
      - position
        - cervix 654.4 ☑
        - placenta 641.1 ☑
          - without hemorrhage 641.0 ☑
        - uterus 654.4 ☑
      - size, fetus 653.5 ☑
      - uterus (congenital) 654.0 ☑
    - abscess or cellulitis
      - bladder 646.6 ☑
      - genitourinary tract (conditions classifiable to 590, 595, 597, 599.0, 614.0–614.5, 614.7–614.9, 615) 646.6 ☑
      - kidney 646.6 ☑
      - urinary tract NEC 646.6 ☑
    - adhesion, pelvic peritoneal 648.9 ☑
    - air embolism 673.0 ☑
    - albuminuria 646.2 ☑
      - with hypertension — *see* Toxemia, of pregnancy
    - amnionitis 658.4 ☑

Pregnancy — *continued*
  - complicated — *continued*
    - amniotic fluid embolism 673.1 ☑
    - anemia (conditions classifiable to 280–285) 648.2 ☑
    - appendicitis 648.9 ☑
    - atrophy, yellow (acute) (liver) (subacute) 646.7 ☑
    - bacilluria, asymptomatic 646.5 ☑
    - bacteriuria, asymptomatic 646.5 ☑
    - bariatric surgery status 649.2 ☑
    - bicornis or bicornuate uterus 654.0 ☑
    - biliary problems 646.8 ☑
    - bone and joint disorders (conditions classifiable to 720–724 or conditions affecting lower limbs classifiable to 711–719, 725–738) 648.7 ☑
    - breech presentation (buttocks) (complete) (frank) 652.2 ☑
      - with successful version 652.1 ☑
    - cardiovascular disease (conditions classifiable to 390–398, 410–429) 648.6 ☑
      - congenital (conditions classifiable to 745–747) 648.5 ☑
    - cerebrovascular disorders (conditions classifiable to 430–434, 436–437) 674.0 ☑
    - cervicitis (conditions classifiable to 616.0) 646.6 ☑
    - chloasma (gravidarum) 646.8 ☑
    - cholelithiasis 646.8 ☑
    - chorea (gravidarum) — *see* Eclampsia, pregnancy
    - coagulation defect 649.3 ☑
    - conjoined twins 678.1 ☑ ●
    - contraction, pelvis (general) 653.1 ☑
      - inlet 653.2 ☑
      - outlet 653.3 ☑
    - convulsions (eclamptic) (uremic) 642.6 ☑
      - with pre-existing hypertension 642.7 ☑
    - current disease or condition (nonobstetric)
      - abnormal glucose tolerance 648.8 ☑
      - anemia 648.2 ☑
      - bone and joint (lower limb) 648.7 ☑
      - cardiovascular 648.6 ☑
        - congenital 648.5 ☑
      - cerebrovascular 674.0 ☑
      - diabetes ▶(conditions classifiable to 249 and 250)◀ 648.0 ☑
      - drug dependence 648.3 ☑
      - female genital mutilation 648.9 ☑
      - genital organ or tract 646.6 ☑
      - gonorrheal 647.1 ☑
      - hypertensive 642.2 ☑
        - chronic kidney 642.2 ☑
        - renal 642.1 ☑
      - infectious 647.9 ☑
        - specified type NEC 647.8 ☑
      - liver 646.7 ☑
      - malarial 647.4 ☑
      - nutritional deficiency 648.9 ☑
      - parasitic NEC 647.8 ☑
      - periodontal disease 648.9 ☑
      - renal 646.2 ☑
        - hypertensive 642.1 ☑
      - rubella 647.5 ☑
      - specified condition NEC 648.9 ☑
      - syphilitic 647.0 ☑
      - thyroid 648.1 ☑
      - tuberculous 647.3 ☑
      - urinary 646.6 ☑
      - venereal 647.2 ☑
      - viral NEC 647.6 ☑

☑ Additional Digit Required — Refer to the Tabular List for Digit Selection

Subterms under main terms may continue to next column or page

▶◀ Revised Text ● New Line ▲ Revised Code

- **Pregnancy** — *continued*
  - complicated — *continued*
    - cystitis 646.6 ☑
    - cystocele 654.4 ☑
    - death of fetus (near term) 656.4 ☑
      - early pregnancy (before 22 completed weeks gestation) 632
    - deciduitis 646.6 ☑
    - decreased fetal movements 655.7 ☑
    - diabetes (mellitus) (conditions classifiable to ▶249 and◀ 250) 648.0 ☑
    - disorders of liver 646.7 ☑
    - displacement, uterus NEC 654.4 ☑
    - disproportion — *see* Disproportion
    - double uterus 654.0 ☑
    - drug dependence (conditions classifiable to 304) 648.3 ☑
    - dysplasia, cervix 654.6 ☑
    - early onset of delivery (spontaneous) 644.2 ☑
    - eclampsia, eclamptic (coma) (convulsions) (delirium) (nephritis) (uremia) 642.6 ☑
      - with pre-existing hypertension 642.7 ☑
    - edema 646.1 ☑
      - with hypertension — *see* Toxemia, of pregnancy
    - effusion, amniotic fluid 658.1 ☑
      - delayed delivery following 658.2 ☑
    - embolism
      - air 673.0 ☑
      - amniotic fluid 673.1 ☑
      - blood-clot 673.2 ☑
      - cerebral 674.0 ☑
      - pulmonary NEC 673.2 ☑
      - pyemic 673.3 ☑
      - septic 673.3 ☑
    - emesis (gravidarum) — *see* Pregnancy, complicated, vomiting
    - endometritis (conditions classifiable to 615.0–615.9) 670 ☑
      - decidual 646.6 ☑
    - epilepsy 649.4 ☑
    - excessive weight gain NEC 646.1 ☑
    - face presentation 652.4 ☑
    - failure, fetal head to enter pelvic brim 652.5 ☑
    - false labor (pains) 644.1 ☑
    - fatigue 646.8 ☑
    - fatty metamorphosis of liver 646.7 ☑
    - female genital mutilation 648.9 ☑
    - fetal
      - conjoined twins 678.1 ☑ ●
      - death (near term) 656.4 ☑
        - early (before 22 completed weeks gestation) 632
      - deformity 653.7 ☑
      - distress 656.8 ☑
      - reduction of multiple fetuses reduced to single fetus 651.7 ☑
    - fibroid (tumor) (uterus) 654.1 ☑
    - footling presentation 652.8 ☑
      - with successful version 652.1 ☑
    - gallbladder disease 646.8 ☑
    - gastric banding status 649.2 ☑
    - gastric bypass status for obesity
    - goiter 648.1 ☑
    - gonococcal infection (conditions classifiable to 098) 647.1 ☑
    - gonorrhea (conditions classifiable to 098) 647.1 ☑
    - hemorrhage 641.9 ☑
      - accidental 641.2 ☑
      - before 22 completed weeks gestation NEC 640.9 ☑
      - cerebrovascular 674.0 ☑

- **Pregnancy** — *continued*
  - complicated — *continued*
    - hemorrhage — *continued*
      - due to
        - afibrinogenemia or other coagulation defect (conditions classifiable to 286.0–286.9) 641.3 ☑
        - leiomyoma, uterine 641.8 ☑
        - marginal sinus (rupture) 641.2 ☑
        - premature separation, placenta 641.2 ☑
        - trauma 641.8 ☑
      - early (before 22 completed weeks gestation) 640.9 ☑
      - threatened abortion 640.0 ☑
      - unavoidable 641.1 ☑
    - hepatitis (acute) (malignant) (subacute) 646.7 ☑
      - viral 647.6 ☑
    - herniation of uterus 654.4 ☑
    - high head at term 652.5 ☑
    - hydatidiform mole (delivered) (undelivered) 630
    - hydramnios 657.0 ☑
    - hydrocephalic fetus 653.6 ☑
    - hydrops amnii 657.0 ☑
    - hydrorrhea 658.1 ☑
    - hyperemesis (gravidarum) — *see* Hyperemesis, gravidarum
    - hypertension — *see* Hypertension, complicating pregnancy
    - hypertensive
      - chronic kidney disease 642.2 ☑
      - heart and chronic kidney disease 642.2 ☑
      - heart and renal disease 642.2 ☑
      - heart disease 642.2 ☑
      - renal disease 642.2 ☑
    - hypertensive heart and chronic kidney disease 642.2 ☑
    - hyperthyroidism 648.1 ☑
    - hypothyroidism 648.1 ☑
    - hysteralgia 646.8 ☑
    - icterus gravis 646.7 ☑
    - incarceration, uterus 654.3 ☑
    - incompetent cervix (os) 654.5 ☑
    - infection 647.9 ☑
      - amniotic fluid 658.4 ☑
      - bladder 646.6 ☑
      - genital organ (conditions classifiable to 614.0–614.5, 614.7–614.9, 615) 646.6 ☑
      - kidney (conditions classifiable to 590.0–590.9) 646.6 ☑
      - urinary (tract) 646.6 ☑
        - asymptomatic 646.5 ☑
    - infective and parasitic diseases NEC 647.8 ☑
    - inflammation
      - bladder 646.6 ☑
      - genital organ (conditions classifiable to 614.0–614.5, 614.7–614.9, 615) 646.6 ☑
      - urinary tract NEC 646.6 ☑
    - insufficient weight gain 646.8 ☑
    - intrauterine fetal death (near term) NEC 656.4 ☑
      - early (before 22 completed weeks' gestation) 632
    - malaria (conditions classifiable to 084) 647.4 ☑
    - malformation, uterus (congenital) 654.0 ☑
    - malnutrition (conditions classifiable to 260–269) 648.9 ☑
    - malposition
      - fetus — *see* Pregnancy, complicated, malpresentation
      - uterus or cervix 654.4 ☑
    - malpresentation 652.9 ☑
      - with successful version 652.1 ☑

- **Pregnancy** — *continued*
  - complicated — *continued*
    - malpresentation — *continued*
      - in multiple gestation 652.6 ☑
      - specified type NEC 652.8 ☑
    - marginal sinus hemorrhage or rupture 641.2 ☑
    - maternal drug abuse 648.4 ☑ ●
    - maternal obesity syndrome 646.1 ☑
    - menstruation 640.8 ☑
    - mental disorders (conditions classifiable to 290–303, 305.0, 305.2-305.9, 306–316, 317–319) 648.4 ☑
    - mentum presentation 652.4 ☑
    - missed
      - abortion 632
      - delivery (at or near term) 656.4 ☑
      - labor (at or near term) 656.4 ☑
    - necrosis
      - genital organ or tract (conditions classifiable to 614.0–614.5, 614.7–614.9, 615) 646.6 ☑
      - liver (conditions classifiable to 570) 646.7 ☑
      - renal, cortical 646.2 ☑
    - nephritis or nephrosis (conditions classifiable to 580–589) 646.2 ☑
      - with hypertension 642.1 ☑
    - nephropathy NEC 646.2 ☑
    - neuritis (peripheral) 646.4 ☑
    - nutritional deficiency (conditions classifiable to 260–269) 648.9 ☑
    - obesity 649.1 ☑
      - surgery status 649.2 ☑
    - oblique lie or presentation 652.3 ☑
      - with successful version 652.1 ☑
    - obstetrical trauma NEC 665.9 ☑
    - oligohydramnios NEC 658.0 ☑
    - onset of contractions before 37 weeks 644.0 ☑
    - oversize fetus 653.5 ☑
    - papyraceous fetus 646.0 ☑
    - patent cervix 654.5 ☑
    - pelvic inflammatory disease (conditions classifiable to 614.0–614.5, 614.7–614.9, 615) 646.6 ☑
    - pelvic peritoneal adhesion 648.9 ☑
    - placenta, placental
      - abnormality 656.7 ☑
      - abruptio or ablatio 641.2 ☑
      - detachment 641.2 ☑
      - disease 656.7 ☑
      - infarct 656.7 ☑
      - low implantation 641.1 ☑
        - without hemorrhage 641.0 ☑
      - malformation 656.7 ☑
      - malposition 641.1 ☑
        - without hemorrhage 641.0 ☑
      - marginal sinus hemorrhage 641.2 ☑
      - previa 641.1 ☑
        - without hemorrhage 641.0 ☑
      - separation (premature) (undelivered) 641.2 ☑
    - placentitis 658.4 ☑
    - polyhydramnios 657.0 ☑
    - postmaturity
      - post-term 645.1 ☑
      - prolonged 645.2 ☑
    - prediabetes 648.8 ☑
    - pre-eclampsia (mild) 642.4 ☑
      - severe 642.5 ☑
      - superimposed on pre-existing hypertensive disease 642.7 ☑
    - premature rupture of membranes 658.1 ☑

- **Pregnancy** — *continued*
  - complicated — *continued*
    - premature rupture of membranes — *continued*
      - with delayed delivery 658.2 ☑
    - previous
      - infertility V23.0
      - in utero procedure during previous pregnancy V23.86 ●
      - nonobstetric condition V23.89
      - poor obstetrical history V23.49
      - premature delivery V23.41
      - trophoblastic disease (conditions classifiable to 630) V23.1
    - prolapse, uterus 654.4 ☑
    - proteinuria (gestational) 646.2 ☑
      - with hypertension — *see* Toxemia, of pregnancy
    - pruritus (neurogenic) 646.8 ☑
    - psychosis or psychoneurosis 648.4 ☑
    - ptyalism 646.8 ☑
    - pyelitis (conditions classifiable to 590.0–590.9) 646.6 ☑
    - renal disease or failure NEC 646.2 ☑
      - with secondary hypertension 642.1 ☑
      - hypertensive 642.2 ☑
    - retention, retained dead ovum 631
    - retroversion, uterus 654.3 ☑
    - Rh immunization, incompatibility, or sensitization 656.1 ☑
    - rubella (conditions classifiable to 056) 647.5 ☑
    - rupture
      - amnion (premature) 658.1 ☑
        - with delayed delivery 658.2 ☑
      - marginal sinus (hemorrhage) 641.2 ☑
      - membranes (premature) 658.1 ☑
        - with delayed delivery 658.2 ☑
      - uterus (before onset of labor) 665.0 ☑
    - salivation (excessive) 646.8 ☑
    - salpingo-oophoritis (conditions classifiable to 614.0–614.2) 646.6 ☑
    - septicemia (conditions classifiable to 038.0–038.9) 647.8 ☑
      - postpartum 670.0 ☑
      - puerperal 670.0 ☑
    - smoking 649.0 ☑
    - spasms, uterus (abnormal) 646.8 ☑
    - specified condition NEC 646.8 ☑
    - spotting 649.5 ☑
    - spurious labor pains 644.1 ☑
    - status post
      - bariatric surgery 649.2 ☑
      - gastric banding 649.2 ☑
      - gastric bypass for obesity 649.2 ☑
      - obesity surgery 649.2 ☑
    - superfecundation 651.9 ☑
    - superfetation 651.9 ☑
    - syphilis (conditions classifiable to 090–097) 647.0 ☑
    - threatened
      - abortion 640.0 ☑
      - premature delivery 644.2 ☑
      - premature labor 644.0 ☑
    - thrombophlebitis (superficial) 671.2 ☑
      - deep 671.3 ☑
    - thrombosis 671.9 ☑
      - venous (superficial) 671.2 ☑
        - deep 671.3 ☑

- **Pregnancy** — *continued*
  - complicated — *continued*
    - thyroid dysfunction (conditions classifiable to 240–246) 648.1 ☑
    - thyroiditis 648.1 ☑
    - thyrotoxicosis 648.1 ☑
    - tobacco use disorder 649.0 ☑
    - torsion of uterus 654.4 ☑
    - toxemia — *see* Toxemia, of pregnancy
    - transverse lie or presentation 652.3 ☑
      - with successful version 652.1 ☑
    - trauma 648.9 ☑
      - obstetrical 665.9 ☑
    - tuberculosis (conditions classifiable to 010–018) 647.3 ☑
    - tumor
      - cervix 654.6 ☑
      - ovary 654.4 ☑
      - pelvic organs or tissue NEC 654.4 ☑
      - uterus (body) 654.1 ☑
        - cervix 654.6 ☑
      - vagina 654.7 ☑
      - vulva 654.8 ☑
    - unstable lie 652.0 ☑
    - uremia — *see* Pregnancy, complicated, renal disease
    - urethritis 646.6 ☑
    - vaginitis or vulvitis (conditions classifiable to 616.1) 646.6 ☑
    - varicose
      - placental vessels 656.7 ☑
      - veins (legs) 671.0 ☑
        - perineum 671.1 ☑
        - vulva 671.1 ☑
    - varicosity, labia or vulva 671.1 ☑
    - venereal disease NEC (conditions classifiable to 099) 647.2 ☑
    - viral disease NEC (conditions classifiable to 042, 050–055, 057–079, ▶795.05, 795.15, 796.75◀) 647.6 ☑
    - vomiting (incoercible) (pernicious) (persistent) (uncontrollable) (vicious) 643.9 ☑
      - due to organic disease or other cause 643.8 ☑
      - early — *see* Hyperemesis, gravidarum
      - late (after 22 completed weeks gestation) 643.2 ☑
    - young maternal age 659.8 ☑
  - complications NEC 646.9 ☑
  - cornual 633.80
    - with intrauterine pregnancy 633.81
    - affecting fetus or newborn 761.4
  - death, maternal NEC 646.9 ☑
  - delivered — *see* Delivery
  - ectopic (ruptured) NEC 633.90
    - with intrauterine pregnancy 633.91
    - abdominal — *see* Pregnancy, abdominal
    - affecting fetus or newborn 761.4
    - combined (extrauterine and intrauterine) — *see* Pregnancy, cornual
    - ovarian — *see* Pregnancy, ovarian
    - specified type NEC 633.80
      - with intrauterine pregnancy 633.81
      - affecting fetus or newborn 761.4
    - tubal — *see* Pregnancy, tubal
  - examination, pregnancy
    - negative result V72.41
    - not confirmed V72.40
    - positive result V72.42
  - extrauterine — *see* Pregnancy, ectopic
  - fallopian — *see* Pregnancy, tubal
  - false 300.11
    - labor (pains) 644.1 ☑
  - fatigue 646.8 ☑
  - illegitimate V61.6

- **Pregnancy** — *continued*
  - incidental finding V22.2
  - in double uterus 654.0 ☑
  - interstitial — *see* Pregnancy, cornual
  - intraligamentous — *see* Pregnancy, cornual
  - intramural — *see* Pregnancy, cornual
  - intraperitoneal — *see* Pregnancy, abdominal
  - isthmian — *see* Pregnancy, tubal
  - management affected by
    - abnormal, abnormality
      - fetus (suspected) 655.9 ☑
        - specified NEC 655.8 ☑
      - placenta 656.7 ☑
    - advanced maternal age NEC 659.6 ☑
      - multigravida 659.6 ☑
      - primigravida 659.5 ☑
    - antibodies (maternal)
      - anti-c 656.1 ☑
      - anti-d 656.1 ☑
      - anti-e 656.1 ☑
      - blood group (ABO) 656.2 ☑
        - Rh(esus) 656.1 ☑
    - appendicitis 648.9 ☑
    - bariatric surgery status 649.2 ☑
    - coagulation defect 649.3 ☑
    - elderly multigravida 659.6 ☑
    - elderly primigravida 659.5 ☑
    - epilepsy 649.4 ☑
    - fetal (suspected)
      - abnormality 655.9 ☑
        - abdominal 655.8 ☑ ●
        - acid-base balance 656.8 ☑
        - cardiovascular 655.8 ☑ ●
        - facial 655.8 ☑ ●
        - gastrointestinal 655.8 ☑ ●
        - gentourinary 655.8 ☑ ●
        - heart rate or rhythm 659.7 ☑
        - limb 655.8 ☑ ●
        - specified NEC 655.8 ☑
      - acidemia 656.3 ☑
      - anencephaly 655.0 ☑
      - aneuploidy 655.1 ☑ ●
      - bradycardia 659.7 ☑
      - central nervous system malformation 655.0 ☑
      - chromosomal abnormalities (conditions classifiable to 758.0–758.9) 655.1 ☑
      - damage from
        - drugs 655.5 ☑
          - obstetric, anesthetic, or sedative 655.5 ☑
        - environmental toxins 655.8 ☑
        - intrauterine contraceptive device 655.8 ☑
        - maternal
          - alcohol addiction 655.4 ☑
          - disease NEC 655.4 ☑
          - drug use 655.5 ☑
          - listeriosis 655.4 ☑
          - rubella 655.3 ☑
          - toxoplasmosis 655.4 ☑
          - viral infection 655.3 ☑
        - radiation 655.6 ☑
      - death (near term) 656.4 ☑
        - early (before 22 completed weeks' gestation) 632
      - distress 656.8 ☑
      - excessive growth 656.6 ☑
      - fetal-maternal hemorrhage 656.0 ☑
      - growth retardation 656.5 ☑
      - hereditary disease 655.2 ☑
      - hereditary disease in family (possibly) affecting fetus 655.2 ☑
      - hydrocephalus 655.0 ☑
      - incompatibility, blood groups (ABO) 656.2 ☑
      - intrauterine death 656.4 ☑
      - poor growth 656.5 ☑

- **Pregnancy** — *continued*
  - management affected by — *continued*
    - fetal — *continued*
      - Rh(esus) 656.1 ☑
      - spina bifida (with myelomeningocele) 655.0 ☑
    - gastric banding status 649.2 ☑
    - gastric bypass status for obesity 649.2 ☑
    - insufficient prenatal care V23.7
    - intrauterine death 656.4 ☑
    - isoimmunization (ABO) 656.2 ☑
      - Rh(esus) 656.1 ☑
    - large-for-dates fetus 656.6 ☑
    - light-for-dates fetus 656.5 ☑
    - meconium in liquor 656.8 ☑
    - mental disorder (conditions classifiable to 290–303, 305.0, 305.2–305.9, 306–316, 317–319) 648.4 ☑
    - multiparity (grand) 659.4 ☑
    - obesity 649.1 ☑
      - surgery status 649.2 ☑
    - poor obstetric history V23.49
      - pre-term labor V23.41
    - postmaturity
      - post-term 645.1 ☑
      - prolonged 645.2 ☑
    - post-term pregnancy 645.1 ☑
    - previous
      - abortion V23.2
        - habitual 646.3 ☑
      - cesarean delivery 654.2 ☑
      - difficult delivery V23.49
      - forceps delivery V23.49
      - habitual abortions 646.3 ☑
      - hemorrhage, antepartum or postpartum V23.49
      - hydatidiform mole V23.1
      - infertility V23.0
      - in utero procedure during previous pregnancy V23.86 ●
      - malignancy NEC V23.89
      - nonobstetrical conditions V23.8 ☑
      - premature delivery V23.41
      - trophoblastic disease (conditions in 630) V23.1
      - vesicular mole V23.1
    - prolonged pregnancy 645.2 ☑
    - small-for-dates fetus 656.5 ☑
    - smoking 649.0 ☑
    - spotting 649.5 ☑
    - suspected conditions not found ●
      - amniotic cavity and membrane problem V89.01 ●
      - cervical shortening V89.05 ●
      - fetal anomaly V89.03 ●
      - fetal growth problem V89.04 ●
      - oligohydramnios V89.01 ●
      - other specified problem NEC V89.09 ●
      - placental problem V89.02 ●
      - polyhydramnios V89.01 ●
    - tobacco use disorder 649.0 ☑
    - young maternal age 659.8 ☑
  - maternal death NEC 646.9 ☑
  - mesometric (mural) — *see* Pregnancy, cornual
  - molar 631
    - hydatidiform (*see also* Hydatidiform mole) 630
      - previous, affecting management of pregnancy V23.1
    - previous, affecting management of pregnancy V23.49
  - multiple NEC 651.9 ☑
    - with fetal loss and retention of one or more fetus(es) 651.6 ☑
    - affecting fetus or newborn 761.5
    - following (elective) fetal reduction 651.7 ☑

- **Pregnancy** — *continued*
  - multiple — *continued*
    - specified type NEC 651.8 ☑
      - with fetal loss and retention of one or more fetus(es) 651.6 ☑
      - following (elective) fetal reduction 651.7 ☑
  - mural — *see* Pregnancy, cornual
  - observation NEC V22.1
    - first pregnancy V22.0
    - high-risk V23.9
      - specified problem NEC V23.89
  - ovarian 633.20
    - with intrauterine pregnancy 633.21
    - affecting fetus or newborn 761.4
  - possible, not (yet) confirmed V72.40
  - postmature
    - post-term 645.1 ☑
    - prolonged 645.2 ☑
  - post-term 645.1 ☑
  - prenatal care only V22.1
    - first pregnancy V22.0
    - high-risk V23.9
      - specified problem NEC V23.89
  - prolonged 645.2 ☑
  - quadruplet NEC 651.2 ☑
    - with fetal loss and retention of one or more fetus(es) 651.5 ☑
    - affecting fetus or newborn 761.5
    - following (elective) fetal reduction 651.7 ☑
  - quintuplet NEC 651.8 ☑
    - with fetal loss and retention of one or more fetus(es) 651.6 ☑
    - affecting fetus or newborn 761.5
    - following (elective) fetal reduction 651.7 ☑
  - resulting from ●
    - assisted reproductive technology V23.85 ●
    - in vitro fertilization V23.85 ●
  - sextuplet NEC 651.8 ☑
    - with fetal loss and retention of one or more fetus(es) 651.6 ☑
    - affecting fetus or newborn 761.5
    - following (elective) fetal reduction 651.7 ☑
  - spurious 300.11
  - superfecundation NEC 651.9 ☑
    - with fetal loss and retention of one or more fetus(es) 651.6 ☑
    - following (elective) fetal reduction 651.7 ☑
  - superfetation NEC 651.9 ☑
    - with fetal loss and retention of one or more fetus(es) 651.6 ☑
    - following (elective) fetal reduction 651.7 ☑
  - supervision (of) (for) (*see also* Pregnancy, management affected by)
    - elderly
      - multigravida V23.82
      - primigravida V23.81
    - high-risk V23.9
      - insufficient prenatal care V23.7
      - specified problem NEC V23.89
    - multiparity V23.3
    - normal NEC V22.1
      - first V22.0
    - poor
      - obstetric history V23.49
        - pre-term labor V23.41
      - reproductive history V23.5
    - previous
      - abortion V23.2
      - hydatidiform mole V23.1
      - infertility V23.0
      - neonatal death V23.5
      - stillbirth V23.5
      - trophoblastic disease V23.1
      - vesicular mole V23.1
    - specified problem NEC V23.89
    - young
      - multigravida V23.84
      - primigravida V23.83

- **Pregnancy** — *continued*
  - triplet NEC 651.1 ☑
    - with fetal loss and retention of one or more fetus(es) 651.4 ☑
    - affecting fetus or newborn 761.5
    - following (elective) fetal reduction 651.7 ☑
  - tubal (with rupture) 633.10
    - with intrauterine pregnancy 633.11
    - affecting fetus or newborn 761.4
  - twin NEC 651.0 ☑
    - with fetal loss and retention of one fetus 651.3 ☑
    - affecting fetus or newborn 761.5
    - conjoined 678.1 ☑ ●
    - following (elective) fetal reduction 651.7 ☑
  - unconfirmed V72.40
  - undelivered (no other diagnosis) V22.2
    - with false labor 644.1 ☑
    - high-risk V23.9
      - specified problem NEC V23.89
  - unwanted NEC V61.7
- **Pregnant uterus** — *see* condition
- **Preiser's disease** (osteoporosis) 733.09
- **Prekwashiorkor** 260
- **Preleukemia** 238.75
- **Preluxation of hip, congenital** — *see also* Subluxation, congenital, hip 754.32
- **Premature** — *see also* condition
  - beats (nodal) 427.60
    - atrial 427.61
    - auricular 427.61
    - postoperative 997.1
    - specified type NEC 427.69
    - supraventricular 427.61
    - ventricular 427.69
  - birth NEC 765.1 ☑
  - closure
    - cranial suture 756.0
    - fontanel 756.0
    - foramen ovale 745.8
  - contractions 427.60
    - atrial 427.61
    - auricular 427.61
    - auriculoventricular 427.61
    - heart (extrasystole) 427.60
    - junctional 427.60
    - nodal 427.60
    - postoperative 997.1
    - ventricular 427.69
  - ejaculation 302.75
  - infant NEC 765.1 ☑
    - excessive 765.0 ☑
    - light-for-dates — *see* Light-for-dates
  - labor 644.2 ☑
    - threatened 644.0 ☑
  - lungs 770.4
  - menopause 256.31
  - puberty 259.1
  - rupture of membranes or amnion 658.1 ☑
    - affecting fetus or newborn 761.1
    - delayed delivery following 658.2 ☑
  - senility (syndrome) 259.8
  - separation, placenta (partial) — *see* Placenta, separation
  - ventricular systole 427.69
- **Prematurity** NEC 765.1 ☑
  - extreme 765.0 ☑
- **Premenstrual syndrome** 625.4
- **Premenstrual tension** 625.4
- **Premolarization, cuspids** 520.2
- **Premyeloma** 273.1
- **Prenatal**
  - care, normal pregnancy V22.1
    - first V22.0
  - death, cause unknown — *see* Death, fetus
  - screening — *see* Antenatal, screening
  - teeth 520.6
- **Prepartum** — *see* condition
- **Preponderance, left or right ventricular** 429.3
- **Prepuce** — *see* condition
- **PRES** (posterior reversible encephalopathy syndrome) 348.39
- **Presbycardia** 797
  - hypertensive (*see also* Hypertension, heart) 402.90
- **Presbycusis** 388.01
- **Presbyesophagus** 530.89
- **Presbyophrenia** 310.1
- **Presbyopia** 367.4
- **Prescription of contraceptives** NEC V25.02
  - diaphragm V25.02
  - oral (pill) V25.01
    - emergency V25.03
    - postcoital V25.03
    - repeat V25.41
  - repeat V25.40
    - oral (pill) V25.41
- **Presenile** — *see also* condition
  - aging 259.8
  - dementia (*see also* Dementia, presenile) 290.10
- **Presenility** 259.8
- **Presentation, fetal**
  - abnormal 652.9 ☑
    - with successful version 652.1 ☑
    - before labor, affecting fetus or newborn 761.7
    - causing obstructed labor 660.0 ☑
      - affecting fetus or newborn, any, except breech 763.1
    - in multiple gestation (one or more) 652.6 ☑
    - specified NEC 652.8 ☑
  - arm 652.7 ☑
    - causing obstructed labor 660.0 ☑
  - breech (buttocks) (complete) (frank) 652.2 ☑
    - with successful version 652.1 ☑
      - before labor, affecting fetus or newborn 761.7
    - before labor, affecting fetus or newborn 761.7
  - brow 652.4 ☑
    - causing obstructed labor 660.0 ☑
  - buttocks 652.2 ☑
  - chin 652.4 ☑
  - complete 652.2 ☑
  - compound 652.8 ☑
  - cord 663.0 ☑
  - extended head 652.4 ☑
  - face 652.4 ☑
    - to pubes 652.8 ☑
  - footling 652.8 ☑
  - frank 652.2 ☑
  - hand, leg, or foot NEC 652.8 ☑
  - incomplete 652.8 ☑
  - mentum 652.4 ☑
  - multiple gestation (one fetus or more) 652.6 ☑
  - oblique 652.3 ☑
    - with successful version 652.1 ☑
  - shoulder 652.8 ☑
    - affecting fetus or newborn 763.1
  - transverse 652.3 ☑
    - with successful version 652.1 ☑
  - umbilical cord 663.0 ☑
  - unstable 652.0 ☑
- **Prespondylolisthesis** (congenital) (lumbosacral) 756.11
- **Pressure**
  - area, skin ulcer (*see also* ▶Ulcer, pressure◀) 707.00
  - atrophy, spine 733.99
  - birth, fetus or newborn NEC 767.9
  - brachial plexus 353.0
  - brain 348.4
    - injury at birth 767.0
  - cerebral — *see* Pressure, brain
  - chest 786.59
  - cone, tentorial 348.4
    - injury at birth 767.0
  - funis — *see* Compression, umbilical cord
- **Pressure** — *continued*
  - hyposystolic (*see also* Hypotension) 458.9
  - increased
    - intracranial 781.99
      - due to
        - benign intracranial hypertension 348.2
        - hydrocephalus — *see* hydrocephalus
        - injury at birth 767.8
    - intraocular 365.00
  - lumbosacral plexus 353.1
  - mediastinum 519.3
  - necrosis (chronic) (skin) (*see also* Decubitus) 707.00
  - nerve — *see* Compression, nerve
  - paralysis (*see also* Neuropathy, entrapment) 355.9
  - pre-ulcer skin changes limited to ● persistent focal erythema (*see* ● *also* Ulcer, pressure) 707.21 ●
  - sore (chronic) (*see also* ▶Ulcer, pressure◀) 707.00
  - spinal cord 336.9
  - ulcer (chronic) (*see also* ▶Ulcer, pressure◀) 707.00
  - umbilical cord — *see* Compression, umbilical cord
  - venous, increased 459.89
- **Pre-syncope** 780.2
- **Preterm infant NEC** 765.1 ☑
  - extreme 765.0 ☑
- **Priapism** (penis) 607.3
- **Prickling sensation** — *see also* Disturbance, sensation 782.0
- **Prickly heat** 705.1
- **Primary** — *see* condition
- **Primigravida, elderly**
  - affecting
    - fetus or newborn 763.89
    - management of pregnancy, labor, and delivery 659.5 ☑
- **Primipara, old**
  - affecting
    - fetus or newborn 763.89
    - management of pregnancy, labor, and delivery 659.5 ☑
- **Primula dermatitis** 692.6
- **Primus varus** (bilateral) (metatarsus) 754.52
- **PRIND** (prolonged reversible ischemic neurologic deficit) 434.91
  - history of (personal) V12.54
- **Pringle's disease** (tuberous sclerosis) 759.5
- **Prinzmetal's angina** 413.1
- **Prinzmetal-Massumi syndrome** (anterior chest wall) 786.52
- **Prizefighter ear** 738.7
- **Problem** (with) V49.9
  - academic V62.3
  - acculturation V62.4
  - adopted child V61.29
  - aged
    - in-law V61.3
    - parent V61.3
    - person NEC V61.8
  - alcoholism in family V61.41
  - anger reaction (*see also* Disturbance, conduct) 312.0 ☑
  - behavioral V40.9
    - specified NEC V40.3
  - behavior, child 312.9
  - betting V69.3
  - cardiorespiratory NEC V47.2
  - career choice V62.29 ▲
  - care of sick or handicapped person in family or household V61.49
  - communication V40.1
  - conscience regarding medical care V62.6
  - delinquency (juvenile) 312.9
  - diet, inappropriate V69.1
  - digestive NEC V47.3
  - ear NEC V41.3
- **Problem** — *continued*
  - eating habits, inappropriate V69.1
  - economic V60.2
    - affecting care V60.9
      - specified type NEC V60.8
  - educational V62.3
  - enuresis, child 307.6
  - exercise, lack of V69.0
  - eye NEC V41.1
  - family V61.9
    - specified circumstance NEC V61.8
  - fear reaction, child 313.0
  - feeding (elderly) (infant) 783.3
    - newborn 779.3
    - nonorganic 307.59
  - fetal, affecting management of pregnancy 656.9 ☑
    - specified type NEC 656.8 ☑
  - financial V60.2
  - foster child V61.29
    - specified NEC V41.8
  - functional V41.9
    - specified type NEC V41.8
  - gambling V69.3
  - genital NEC V47.5
  - head V48.9
    - deficiency V48.0
    - disfigurement V48.6
    - mechanical V48.2
    - motor V48.2
    - movement of V48.2
    - sensory V48.4
    - specified condition NEC V48.8
  - hearing V41.2
  - high-risk sexual behavior V69.2
  - identity 313.82
  - influencing health status NEC V49.89
  - internal organ NEC V47.9
    - deficiency V47.0
    - mechanical or motor V47.1
  - interpersonal NEC V62.81
  - jealousy, child 313.3
  - learning V40.0
  - legal V62.5
  - life circumstance NEC V62.89
  - lifestyle V69.9
    - specified NEC V69.8
  - limb V49.9
    - deficiency V49.0
    - disfigurement V49.4
    - mechanical V49.1
    - motor V49.2
    - movement, involving
      - musculoskeletal system V49.1
      - nervous system V49.2
    - sensory V49.3
    - specified condition NEC V49.5
  - litigation V62.5
  - living alone V60.3
  - loneliness NEC V62.89
  - marital V61.10
    - involving
      - divorce V61.03 ▲
      - estrangement V61.09 ▲
      - psychosexual disorder 302.9
      - sexual function V41.7
    - relationship V61.10
  - mastication V41.6
  - medical care, within family V61.49
  - mental V40.9
    - specified NEC V40.2
  - mental hygiene, adult V40.9
  - multiparity V61.5
  - nail biting, child 307.9
  - neck V48.9
    - deficiency V48.1
    - disfigurement V48.7
    - mechanical V48.3
    - motor V48.3
    - movement V48.3
    - sensory V48.5
    - specified condition NEC V48.8
  - neurological NEC 781.99
  - none (feared complaint unfounded) V65.5
  - occupational V62.29 ▲

- **Problem** — *continued*
  - parent-child V61.20
    - relationship V61.20
  - partner V61.10
    - relationship V61.10
  - personal NEC V62.89
    - interpersonal conflict NEC V62.81
  - personality (*see also* Disorder, personality) 301.9
  - phase of life V62.89
  - placenta, affecting management of pregnancy 656.9 ☑
    - specified type NEC 656.8 ☑
  - poverty V60.2
  - presence of sick or handicapped person in family or household V61.49
  - psychiatric 300.9
  - psychosocial V62.9
    - specified type NEC V62.89
  - relational NEC V62.81
  - relationship, childhood 313.3
  - religious or spiritual belief
    - other than medical care V62.89
    - regarding medical care V62.6
  - self-damaging behavior V69.8
  - sexual
    - behavior, high-risk V69.2
    - function NEC V41.7
  - sibling
    - relational V61.8
    - relationship V61.8
  - sight V41.0
  - sleep disorder, child 307.40
  - sleep, lack of V69.4
  - smell V41.5
  - speech V40.1
  - spite reaction, child (*see also* Disturbance, conduct) 312.0 ☑
  - spoiled child reaction (*see also* Disturbance, conduct) 312.1 ☑
  - swallowing V41.6
  - tantrum, child (*see also* Disturbance, conduct) 312.1 ☑
  - taste V41.5
  - thumb sucking, child 307.9
  - tic (child) 307.21
  - trunk V48.9
    - deficiency V48.1
    - disfigurement V48.7
    - mechanical V48.3
    - motor V48.3
    - movement V48.3
    - sensory V48.5
    - specified condition NEC V48.8
  - unemployment V62.0
  - urinary NEC V47.4
  - voice production V41.4
- **Procedure** (surgical) **not done** NEC V64.3
  - because of
    - contraindication V64.1
    - patient's decision V64.2
      - for reasons of conscience or religion V62.6
    - specified reason NEC V64.3
- **Procidentia**
  - anus (sphincter) 569.1
  - rectum (sphincter) 569.1
  - stomach 537.89
  - uteri 618.1
- **Proctalgia** 569.42
  - fugax 564.6
  - spasmodic 564.6
    - psychogenic 307.89
- **Proctitis** 569.49
  - amebic 006.8
  - chlamydial 099.52
  - gonococcal 098.7
  - granulomatous 555.1
  - idiopathic 556.2
    - with ulcerative sigmoiditis 556.3
  - tuberculous (*see also* Tuberculosis) 014.8 ☑
  - ulcerative (chronic) (nonspecific) 556.2
    - with ulcerative sigmoiditis 556.3
- **Proctocele**
  - female (without uterine prolapse) 618.04
    - with uterine prolapse 618.4
      - complete 618.3
      - incomplete 618.2
  - male 569.49
- **Proctocolitis, idiopathic** 556.2
  - with ulcerative sigmoiditis 556.3
- **Proctoptosis** 569.1
- **Proctosigmoiditis** 569.89
  - ulcerative (chronic) 556.3
- **Proctospasm** 564.6
  - psychogenic 306.4
- **Prodromal-AIDS** — *see* Human immunodeficiency virus (disease) (illness) (infection)
- **Profichet's disease or syndrome** 729.90 ▲
- **Progeria** (adultorum) (syndrome) 259.8
- **Prognathism** (mandibular) (maxillary) 524.00
- **Progonoma** (melanotic) (M9363/0) — *see* Neoplasm, by site, benign
- **Progressive** — *see* condition
- **Prolapse, prolapsed**
  - anus, anal (canal) (sphincter) 569.1
  - arm or hand, complicating delivery 652.7 ☑
    - causing obstructed labor 660.0 ☑
      - affecting fetus or newborn 763.1
    - fetus or newborn 763.1
  - bladder (acquired) (mucosa) (sphincter)
    - congenital (female) (male) 756.71
    - female (*see also* Cystocele, female) 618.01
    - male 596.8
  - breast implant (prosthetic) 996.54
  - cecostomy 569.69
  - cecum 569.89
  - cervix, cervical (hypertrophied) 618.1
    - anterior lip, obstructing labor 660.2 ☑
      - affecting fetus or newborn 763.1
    - congenital 752.49
    - postpartal (old) 618.1
    - stump 618.84
  - ciliary body 871.1
  - colon (pedunculated) 569.89
  - colostomy 569.69
  - conjunctiva 372.73
  - cord — *see* Prolapse, umbilical cord
  - disc (intervertebral) — *see* Displacement, intervertebral disc
  - duodenum 537.89
  - eye implant (orbital) 996.59
    - lens (ocular) 996.53
  - fallopian tube 620.4
  - fetal extremity, complicating delivery 652.8 ☑
    - causing obstructed labor 660.0 ☑
    - fetus or newborn 763.1
  - funis — *see* Prolapse, umbilical cord
  - gastric (mucosa) 537.89
  - genital, female 618.9
    - specified NEC 618.89
  - globe 360.81
  - ileostomy bud 569.69
  - intervertebral disc — *see* Displacement, intervertebral disc
  - intestine (small) 569.89
  - iris 364.89
    - traumatic 871.1
  - kidney (*see also* Disease, renal) 593.0
    - congenital 753.3
  - laryngeal muscles or ventricle 478.79
  - leg, complicating delivery 652.8 ☑
    - causing obstructed labor 660.0 ☑
    - fetus or newborn 763.1
  - liver 573.8
  - meatus urinarius 599.5
  - mitral valve 424.0
  - ocular lens implant 996.53
  - organ or site, congenital NEC — *see* Malposition, congenital
- **Prolapse, prolapsed** — *continued*
  - ovary 620.4
  - pelvic (floor), female 618.89
  - perineum, female 618.89
  - pregnant uterus 654.4 ☑
  - rectum (mucosa) (sphincter) 569.1
    - due to Trichuris trichiuria 127.3
  - spleen 289.59
  - stomach 537.89
  - umbilical cord
    - affecting fetus or newborn 762.4
    - complicating delivery 663.0 ☑
  - ureter 593.89
    - with obstruction 593.4
  - ureterovesical orifice 593.89
  - urethra (acquired) (infected) (mucosa) 599.5
    - congenital 753.8
  - uterovaginal 618.4
    - complete 618.3
    - incomplete 618.2
    - specified NEC 618.89
  - uterus (first degree) (second degree) (third degree) (complete) (without vaginal wall prolapse) 618.1
    - with mention of vaginal wall prolapse — *see* Prolapse, uterovaginal
    - congenital 752.3
    - in pregnancy or childbirth 654.4 ☑
      - affecting fetus or newborn 763.1
      - causing obstructed labor 660.2 ☑
        - affecting fetus or newborn 763.1
    - postpartal (old) 618.1
  - uveal 871.1
  - vagina (anterior) (posterior) (vault) (wall) (without uterine prolapse) 618.00
    - with uterine prolapse 618.4
      - complete 618.3
      - incomplete 618.2
    - paravaginal 618.02
    - posthysterectomy 618.5
    - specified NEC 618.09
  - vitreous (humor) 379.26
    - traumatic 871.1
  - womb — *see* Prolapse, uterus
- **Prolapsus, female** 618.9
- **Proliferative** — *see* condition
- **Prolinemia** 270.8
- **Prolinuria** 270.8
- **Prolonged, prolongation**
  - bleeding time (*see also* Defect, coagulation) 790.92
    - "idiopathic" (in von Willebrand's disease) 286.4
  - coagulation time (*see also* Defect, coagulation) 790.92
  - gestation syndrome 766.22
  - labor 662.1 ☑
    - affecting fetus or newborn 763.89
    - first stage 662.0 ☑
    - second stage 662.2 ☑
  - pregnancy 645.2 ☑
  - PR interval 426.11
  - prothrombin time (*see also* Defect, coagulation) 790.92
  - QT interval 794.31
    - syndrome 426.82
  - rupture of membranes (24 hours or more prior to onset of labor) 658.2 ☑
  - uterine contractions in labor 661.4 ☑
    - affecting fetus or newborn 763.7
- **Prominauris** 744.29
- **Prominence**
  - auricle (ear) (congenital) 744.29
    - acquired 380.32
  - ischial spine or sacral promontory
    - with disproportion (fetopelvic) 653.3 ☑
      - affecting fetus or newborn 763.1
      - causing obstructed labor 660.1 ☑
- **Prominence** — *continued*
  - ischial spine or sacral promontory — *continued*
    - with disproportion — *continued*
      - causing obstructed labor — *continued*
        - affecting fetus or newborn 763.1
  - nose (congenital) 748.1
    - acquired 738.0
- **PROMM** (proximal myotonic myotonia) 359.21
- **Pronation**
  - ankle 736.79
  - foot 736.79
    - congenital 755.67
- **Prophylactic**
  - administration of
    - agents affecting estrogen receptors and estrogen levels NEC V07.59 ●
      - anastrozole (Arimidex) V07.52 ●
      - aromatase inhibitors V07.52 ●
      - estrogen receptor downregulators V07.59 ●
      - exemestar (Aromasin) V07.52 ●
      - fulvestrant (Faslodex) V07.59 ●
      - gonadotropin-releasing hormone (GnRH) agonist V07.59 ●
      - goserelin acetate (Zoladex) V07.59 ●
      - letrozole (Femara) V07.52 ●
      - leuprolide acetate (leuprorelin) (Lupron) V07.59 ●
      - megestrol acetate (Megace) V07.59 ●
      - raloxifene (Evista) V07.51 ●
      - selective estrogen receptor modulators (SERMs) V07.51 ●
      - tamoxifen (Nolvadex) V07.51 ●
      - toremifene (Fareston) V07.51 ●
    - antibiotics V07.39
    - antitoxin, any V07.2
    - antivenin V07.2
    - chemotherapeutic agent NEC V07.39
      - fluoride V07.31
    - diphtheria antitoxin V07.2
    - drug V07.39
    - gamma globulin V07.2
    - immune sera (gamma globulin) V07.2
    - RhoGAM V07.2
    - tetanus antitoxin V07.2
  - chemotherapy NEC V07.39
    - fluoride V07.31
  - hormone replacement (postmenopausal) V07.4
  - immunotherapy V07.2
  - measure V07.9
    - specified type NEC V07.8
  - medication V07.39
  - postmenopausal hormone replacement V07.4
  - sterilization V25.2
- **Proptosis** (ocular) — *see also* Exophthalmos 376.30
  - thyroid 242.0 ☑
- **Propulsion**
  - eyeball 360.81
- **Prosecution, anxiety concerning** V62.5
- **Prosopagnosia** 368.16 ●
- **Prostate, prostatic** — *see* condition
- **Prostatism** 600.90
  - with
    - other lower urinary tract symptoms (LUTS) 600.91
    - urinary
      - obstruction 600.91
      - retention 600.91
- **Prostatitis** (congestive) (suppurative) 601.9
  - acute 601.0
  - cavitary 601.8

Prostatitis — *continued*
chlamydial 099.54
chronic 601.1
diverticular 601.8
due to Trichomonas (vaginalis) 131.03
fibrous 600.90
with
other lower urinary tract symptoms (LUTS) 600.91
urinary
obstruction 600.91
retention 600.91
gonococcal (acute) 098.12
chronic or duration of 2 months or over 098.32
granulomatous 601.8
hypertrophic 600.00
with
other lower urinary tract symptoms (LUTS) 600.01
urinary
obstruction 600.01
retention 600.01
specified type NEC 601.8
subacute 601.1
trichomonal 131.03
tuberculous (*see also* Tuberculosis) 016.5 ☑ *[601.4]*
Prostatocystitis 601.3
Prostatorrhea 602.8
Prostatoseminovesiculitis, trichomonal 131.03
Prostration 780.79
heat 992.5
anhydrotic 992.3
due to
salt (and water) depletion 992.4
water depletion 992.3
nervous 300.5
newborn 779.89
senile 797
Protanomaly 368.51
Protanopia (anomalous trichromat) (complete) (incomplete) 368.51
Protection (against) (from) — *see* Prophylactic
Protein
deficiency 260
malnutrition 260
sickness (prophylactic) (therapeutic) 999.5
Proteinemia 790.99
Proteinosis
alveolar, lung or pulmonary 516.0
lipid 272.8
lipoid (of Urbach) 272.8
Proteinuria — *see also* Albuminuria 791.0
Bence-Jones NEC 791.0
gestational 646.2 ☑
with hypertension — *see* Toxemia, of pregnancy
orthostatic 593.6
postural 593.6
Proteolysis, pathologic 286.6
Protocoproporphyria 277.1
Protoporphyria (erythrohepatic) (erythropoietic) 277.1
Protrusio acetabuli 718.65
Protrusion
acetabulum (into pelvis) 718.65
device, implant, or graft — *see* Complications, mechanical
ear, congenital 744.29
intervertebral disc — *see* Displacement, intervertebral disc
nucleus pulposus — *see* Displacement, intervertebral disc
Proud flesh 701.5
Prune belly (syndrome) 756.71
Prurigo (ferox) (gravis) (Hebra's) (hebrae) (mitis) (simplex) 698.2
agria 698.3
asthma syndrome 691.8
Besnier's (atopic dermatitis) (infantile eczema) 691.8

Prurigo — *continued*
eczematodes allergicum 691.8
estivalis (Hutchinson's) 692.72
Hutchinson's 692.72
nodularis 698.3
psychogenic 306.3
Pruritus, pruritic 698.9
ani 698.0
psychogenic 306.3
conditions NEC 698.9
psychogenic 306.3
due to Onchocerca volvulus 125.3
ear 698.9
essential 698.9
genital organ(s) 698.1
psychogenic 306.3
gravidarum 646.8 ☑
hiemalis 698.8
neurogenic (any site) 306.3
perianal 698.0
psychogenic (any site) 306.3
scrotum 698.1
psychogenic 306.3
senile, senilis 698.8
Trichomonas 131.9
vulva, vulvae 698.1
psychogenic 306.3
Psammocarcinoma (M8140/3) — *see* Neoplasm, by site, malignant
Pseudarthrosis, pseudoarthrosis (bone) 733.82
joint following fusion V45.4
Pseudoacanthosis
nigricans 701.8
Pseudoaneurysm — *see* Aneurysm
Pseudoangina (pectoris) — *see* Angina
Pseudoangioma 452
Pseudo-Argyll-Robertson pupil 379.45
Pseudoarteriosus 747.89
Pseudoarthrosis — *see* Pseudarthrosis
Pseudoataxia 799.89
Pseudobulbar affect (PBA) 310.8
Pseudobursa 727.89
Pseudocholera 025
Pseudochromidrosis 705.89
Pseudocirrhosis, liver, pericardial 423.2
Pseudocoarctation 747.21
Pseudocowpox 051.1
Pseudocoxalgia 732.1
Pseudocroup 478.75
Pseudocyesis 300.11
Pseudocyst
lung 518.89
pancreas 577.2
retina 361.19
Pseudodementia 300.16
Pseudoelephantiasis neuroarthritica 757.0
Pseudoemphysema 518.89
Pseudoencephalitis
superior (acute) hemorrhagic 265.1
Pseudoerosion cervix, congenital 752.49
Pseudoexfoliation, lens capsule 366.11
Pseudofracture (idiopathic) (multiple) (spontaneous) (symmetrical) 268.2
Pseudoglanders 025
Pseudoglioma 360.44
Pseudogout — *see* Chondrocalcinosis
Pseudohallucination 780.1
Pseudohemianesthesia 782.0
Pseudohemophilia (Bernuth's) (hereditary) (typeB) 286.4
type A 287.8
vascular 287.8
Pseudohermaphroditism 752.7
with chromosomal anomaly — *see* Anomaly, chromosomal
adrenal 255.2
female (without adrenocortical disorder) 752.7
with adrenocortical disorder 255.2
adrenal 255.2
male (without gonadal disorder) 752.7

Pseudohermaphroditism — *continued*
male — *continued*
with
adrenocortical disorder 255.2
cleft scrotum 752.7
feminizing testis 259.51 ▲
gonadal disorder 257.9
adrenal 255.2
Pseudohole, macula 362.54
Pseudo-Hurler's disease (mucolipidosis III) 272.7
Pseudohydrocephalus 348.2
Pseudohypertrophic muscular dystrophy (Erb's) 359.1
Pseudohypertrophy, muscle 359.1
Pseudohypoparathyroidism 275.49
Pseudoinfluenza 487.1
Pseudoinsomnia 307.49
Pseudoleukemia 288.8
infantile 285.8
Pseudomembranous — *see* condition
Pseudomeningocele (cerebral) (infective) 349.2
postprocedural 997.01
spinal 349.2
Pseudomenstruation 626.8
Pseudomucinous
cyst (ovary) (M8470/0) 220
peritoneum 568.89
Pseudomyeloma 273.1
Pseudomyxoma peritonei (M8480/6) 197.6
Pseudoneuritis optic (nerve) 377.24
papilla 377.24
congenital 743.57
Pseudoneuroma — *see* Injury, nerve, by site
Pseudo-obstruction
intestine (chronic) (idiopathic) (intermittent secondary) (primary) 564.89
acute 560.89
Pseudopapilledema 377.24
Pseudoparalysis
arm or leg 781.4
atonic, congenital 358.8
Pseudopelade 704.09
Pseudophakia V43.1
Pseudopolycythemia 289.0
Pseudopolyposis, colon 556.4
Pseudoporencephaly 348.0
Pseudopseudohypoparathyroidism 275.49
Pseudopsychosis 300.16
Pseudopterygium 372.52
Pseudoptosis (eyelid) 374.34
Pseudorabies 078.89
Pseudoretinitis, pigmentosa 362.65
Pseudorickets 588.0
senile (Pozzi's) 731.0
Pseudorubella 057.8
Pseudoscarlatina 057.8
Pseudosclerema 778.1
Pseudosclerosis (brain)
Jakob's 046.19 ▲
of Westphal (-Strümpell) (hepatolenticular degeneration) 275.1
spastic 046.19 ▲
with dementia
with behavioral disturbance 046.19 *[294.11]* ▲
without behavioral disturbance 046.19 *[294.10]* ▲
Pseudoseizure 780.39
non-psychiatric 780.39
psychiatric 300.11
Pseudotabes 799.89
diabetic 250.6 ☑ *[337.1]*
due to secondary diabetes ●
249.6 ☑ *[337.1]* ●
Pseudotetanus — *see also* Convulsions 780.39
Pseudotetany 781.7
hysterical 300.11
Pseudothalassemia 285.0

Pseudotrichinosis 710.3
Pseudotruncus arteriosus 747.29
Pseudotuberculosis, pasteurella (infection) 027.2
Pseudotumor
cerebri 348.2
orbit (inflammatory) 376.11
Pseudo-Turner's syndrome 759.89
Pseudoxanthoma elasticum 757.39
Psilosis (sprue) (tropical) 579.1
Monilia 112.89
nontropical 579.0
not sprue 704.00
Psittacosis 073.9
Psoitis 728.89
Psora NEC 696.1
Psoriasis 696.1
any type, except arthropathic 696.1
arthritic, arthropathic 696.0
buccal 528.6
flexural 696.1
follicularis 696.1
guttate 696.1
inverse 696.1
mouth 528.6
nummularis 696.1
psychogenic 316 *[696.1]*
punctata 696.1
pustular 696.1
rupioides 696.1
vulgaris 696.1
Psorospermiasis 136.4
Psorospermosis 136.4
follicularis (vegetans) 757.39
Psychalgia 307.80
Psychasthenia 300.89
compulsive 300.3
mixed compulsive states 300.3
obsession 300.3
Psychiatric disorder or problem NEC 300.9
Psychogenic — *see also* condition
factors associated with physical conditions 316
Psychoneurosis, psychoneurotic — *see also* Neurosis 300.9
anxiety (state) 300.00
climacteric 627.2
compensation 300.16
compulsion 300.3
conversion hysteria 300.11
depersonalization 300.6
depressive type 300.4
dissociative hysteria 300.15
hypochondriacal 300.7
hysteria 300.10
conversion type 300.11
dissociative type 300.15
mixed NEC 300.89
neurasthenic 300.5
obsessional 300.3
obsessive-compulsive 300.3
occupational 300.89
personality NEC 301.89
phobia 300.20
senile NEC 300.89
Psychopathic — *see also* condition
constitution, posttraumatic 310.2
with psychosis 293.9
personality 301.9
amoral trends 301.7
antisocial trends 301.7
asocial trends 301.7
mixed types 301.7
state 301.9
Psychopathy, sexual — *see also* Deviation, sexual 302.9
Psychophysiologic, psychophysiological condition — *see* Reaction, psychophysiologic
Psychose passionelle 297.8
Psychosexual identity disorder 302.6
adult-life 302.85
childhood 302.6
Psychosis 298.9
acute hysterical 298.1

Psychosis — *continued*
- affecting management of pregnancy, childbirth, or puerperium 648.4 ☑
- affective (*see also* Disorder, mood) 296.90

> *Note — Use the following fifth-digit subclassification with categories 296.0–296.6:*
> - *0 unspecified*
> - *1 mild*
> - *2 moderate*
> - *3 severe, without mention of psychotic behavior*
> - *4 severe, specified as with psychotic behavior*
> - *5 in partial or unspecified remission*
> - *6 in full remission*

  - drug-induced 292.84
  - due to or associated with physical condition 293.83
  - involutional 293.83
    - recurrent episode 296.3 ☑
    - single episode 296.2 ☑
  - manic-depressive 296.80
    - circular (alternating) 296.7
      - currently depressed 296.5 ☑
      - currently manic 296.4 ☑
    - depressed type 296.2 ☑
      - atypical 296.82
      - recurrent episode 296.3 ☑
      - single episode 296.2 ☑
    - manic 296.0 ☑
      - atypical 296.81
      - recurrent episode 296.1 ☑
      - single episode 296.0 ☑
    - mixed type NEC 296.89
    - specified type NEC 296.89
  - senile 290.21
  - specified type NEC 296.99
- alcoholic 291.9
  - with
    - anxiety 291.89
    - delirium tremens 291.0
    - delusions 291.5
    - dementia 291.2
    - hallucinosis 291.3
    - jealousy 291.5
    - mood disturbance 291.89
    - paranoia 291.5
    - persisting amnesia 291.1
    - sexual dysfunction 291.89
    - sleep disturbance 291.89
  - amnestic confabulatory 291.1
  - delirium tremens 291.0
  - hallucinosis 291.3
  - Korsakoff's, Korsakov's, Korsakow's 291.1
  - paranoid type 291.5
  - pathological intoxication 291.4
  - polyneuritic 291.1
  - specified type NEC 291.89
- alternating (*see also* Psychosis, manic-depressive, circular) 296.7
- anergastic (*see also* Psychosis, organic) 294.9
- arteriosclerotic 290.40
  - with
    - acute confusional state 290.41
    - delirium 290.41
    - delusions 290.42
    - depressed mood 290.43
  - depressed type 290.43
  - paranoid type 290.42
  - simple type 290.40
  - uncomplicated 290.40
- atypical 298.9
  - depressive 296.82
  - manic 296.81
- borderline (schizophrenia) (*see also* Schizophrenia) 295.5 ☑

Psychosis — *continued*
- borderline (*see also* Schizophrenia) — *continued*
  - of childhood (*see also* Psychosis, childhood) 299.8 ☑
  - prepubertal 299.8 ☑
- brief reactive 298.8
- childhood, with origin specific to 299.9 ☑

> *Note — Use the following fifth-digit subclassification with category 299:*
> - *0 current or active state*
> - *1 residual state*

  - atypical 299.8 ☑
  - specified type NEC 299.8 ☑
- circular (*see also* Psychosis, manic-depressive, circular) 296.7
- climacteric (*see also* Psychosis, involutional) 298.8
- confusional 298.9
  - acute 293.0
  - reactive 298.2
  - subacute 293.1
- depressive (*see also* Psychosis, affective) 296.2 ☑
  - atypical 296.82
  - involutional 296.2 ☑
    - with hypomania (bipolar II) 296.89
    - recurrent episode 296.3 ☑
    - single episode 296.2 ☑
  - psychogenic 298.0
  - reactive (emotional stress) (psychological trauma) 298.0
  - recurrent episode 296.3 ☑
    - with hypomania (bipolar II) 296.89
  - single episode 296.2 ☑
- disintegrative, childhood (*see also* Psychosis, childhood) 299.1 ☑
- drug 292.9
  - with
    - affective syndrome 292.84
    - amnestic syndrome 292.83
    - anxiety 292.89
    - delirium 292.81
      - withdrawal 292.0
    - delusions 292.11
    - dementia 292.82
    - depressive state 292.84
    - hallucinations 292.12
    - hallucinosis 292.12
    - mood disorder 292.84
    - mood disturbance 292.84
    - organic personality syndrome NEC 292.89
    - sexual dysfunction 292.89
    - sleep disturbance 292.89
    - withdrawal syndrome (and delirium) 292.0
  - affective syndrome 292.84
  - delusions 292.11
  - hallucinatory state 292.12
  - hallucinosis 292.12
  - paranoid state 292.11
  - specified type NEC 292.89
  - withdrawal syndrome (and delirium) 292.0
- due to or associated with physical condition (*see also* Psychosis, organic) 293.9
- epileptic NEC 294.8
- excitation (psychogenic) (reactive) 298.1
- exhaustive (*see also* Reaction, stress, acute) 308.9
- hypomanic (*see also* Psychosis, affective) 296.0 ☑
  - recurrent episode 296.1 ☑
  - single episode 296.0 ☑
- hysterical 298.8
  - acute 298.1

Psychosis — *continued*
- in
  - conditions classified elsewhere
    - with
      - delusions 293.81
      - hallucinations 293.82
  - pregnancy, childbirth, or puerperium 648.4 ☑
- incipient 298.8
  - schizophrenic (*see also* Schizophrenia) 295.5 ☑
- induced 297.3
- infantile (*see also* Psychosis, childhood) 299.0 ☑
- infective 293.9
  - acute 293.0
  - subacute 293.1
- interactional (childhood) (*see also* Psychosis, childhood) 299.1 ☑
- involutional 298.8
  - depressive (*see also* Psychosis, affective) 296.2 ☑
    - recurrent episode 296.3 ☑
    - single episode 296.2 ☑
  - melancholic 296.2 ☑
    - recurrent episode 296.3 ☑
    - single episode 296.2 ☑
  - paranoid state 297.2
  - paraphrenia 297.2
- Korsakoff's, Korakov's, Korsakow's (nonalcoholic) 294.0
  - alcoholic 291.1
- mania (phase) (*see also* Psychosis, affective) 296.0 ☑
  - recurrent episode 296.1 ☑
  - single episode 296.0 ☑
- manic (*see also* Psychosis, affective) 296.0 ☑
  - atypical 296.81
  - recurrent episode 296.1 ☑
  - single episode 296.0 ☑
- manic-depressive 296.80
  - circular 296.7
    - currently
      - depressed 296.5 ☑
      - manic 296.4 ☑
    - mixed 296.6 ☑
  - depressive 296.2 ☑
    - recurrent episode 296.3 ☑
      - with hypomania (bipolar II) 296.89
    - single episode 296.2 ☑
  - hypomanic 296.0 ☑
    - recurrent episode 296.1 ☑
    - single episode 296.0 ☑
  - manic 296.0 ☑
    - atypical 296.81
    - recurrent episode 296.1 ☑
    - single episode 296.0 ☑
  - mixed NEC 296.89
  - perplexed 296.89
  - stuporous 296.89
- menopausal (*see also* Psychosis, involutional) 298.8
- mixed schizophrenic and affective (*see also* Schizophrenia) 295.7 ☑
- multi-infarct (cerebrovascular) (*see also* Psychosis, arteriosclerotic) 290.40
- organic NEC 294.9
  - due to or associated with
    - addiction
      - alcohol (*see also* Psychosis, alcoholic) 291.9
      - drug (*see also* Psychosis, drug) 292.9
    - alcohol intoxication, acute (*see also* Psychosis, alcoholic) 291.9
    - alcoholism (*see also* Psychosis, alcoholic) 291.9
    - arteriosclerosis (cerebral) (*see also* Psychosis, arteriosclerotic) 290.40

Psychosis — *continued*
- organic — *continued*
  - due to or associated with — *continued*
    - cerebrovascular disease
      - acute (psychosis) 293.0
      - arteriosclerotic (*see also* Psychosis, arteriosclerotic) 290.40
    - childbirth — *see* Psychosis, puerperal
    - dependence
      - alcohol (*see also* Psychosis, alcoholic) 291.9
      - drug 292.9
    - disease
      - alcoholic liver (*see also* Psychosis, alcoholic) 291.9
      - brain
        - arteriosclerotic (*see also* Psychosis, arteriosclerotic) 290.40
      - cerebrovascular
        - acute (psychosis) 293.0
        - arteriosclerotic (*see also* Psychosis, arteriosclerotic) 290.40
      - endocrine or metabolic 293.9
        - acute (psychosis) 293.0
        - subacute (psychosis) 293.1
      - Jakob-Creutzfeldt 046.19 ▲
        - with behavioral disturbance 046.19 *[294.11]* ▲
        - without behavioral disturbance 046.19 *[294.10]* ▲
        - familial 046.19 ●
        - iatrogenic 046.19 ●
        - specified NEC 046.19 ●
        - sporadic 046.19 ●
        - variant 046.11 ●
          - with dementia ●
            - with behavioral disturbance 046.11 *[294.11]* ●
            - without behavioral disturbance 046.11 *[294.10]* ●
      - liver, alcoholic (*see also* Psychosis, alcoholic) 291.9
    - disorder
      - cerebrovascular
        - acute (psychosis) 293.0
      - endocrine or metabolic 293.9
        - acute (psychosis) 293.0
        - subacute (psychosis) 293.1
    - epilepsy
      - with behavioral disturbance 345.9 ☑ *[294.11]*
      - without behavioral disturbance 345.9 ☑ *[294.10]*
      - transient (acute) 293.0
    - Huntington's chorea
      - with behavioral disturbance 333.4 *[294.11]*
      - without behavioral disturbance 333.4 *[294.10]*
    - infection
      - brain 293.9
        - acute (psychosis) 293.0
        - chronic 294.8
        - subacute (psychosis) 293.1
      - intracranial NEC 293.9
        - acute (psychosis) 293.0
        - chronic 294.8
        - subacute (psychosis) 293.1

- **Psychosis** — *continued*
  - organic — *continued*
    - due to or associated with — *continued*
      - intoxication
        - alcoholic (acute) (*see also* Psychosis, alcoholic) 291.9
          - pathological 291.4
        - drug (*see also* Psychosis, drug) 292.2
      - ischemia
        - cerebrovascular (generalized) (*see also* Psychosis, arteriosclerotic) 290.40
      - Jakob-Creutzfeldt disease (syndrome) 046.19 ▲
        - with behavioral disturbance 046.19 *[294.11]* ▲
        - without behavioral disturbance 046.19 *[294.10]* ▲
        - variant 046.11 ●
          - with dementia ●
            - with behavioral disturbance 046.11 *[294.11]* ●
            - without behavioral disturbance 046.11 *[294.10]* ●
      - multiple sclerosis
        - with behavioral disturbance 340 *[294.11]*
        - without behavioral disturbance 340 *[294.10]*
      - physical condition NEC 293.9
        - with
          - delusions 293.81
          - hallucinations 293.82
      - presenility 290.10
      - puerperium — *see* Psychosis, puerperal
      - sclerosis, multiple
        - with behavioral disturbance 340 *[294.11]*
        - without behavioral disturbance 340 *[294.10]*
      - senility 290.20
      - status epilepticus
        - with behavioral disturbance 345.3 *[294.11]*
        - without behavioral disturbance 345.3 *[294.10]*
      - trauma
        - brain (birth) (from electrical current) (surgical) 293.9
          - acute (psychosis) 293.0
          - chronic 294.8
          - subacute (psychosis) 293.1
          - unspecified physical condition 293.9
            - with
              - delusion 293.81
              - hallucinations 293.82
    - infective 293.9
      - acute (psychosis) 293.0
      - subacute 293.1
    - posttraumatic 293.9
      - acute 293.0
      - subacute 293.1
    - specified type NEC 294.8
    - transient 293.9
      - with
        - anxiety 293.84
        - delusions 293.81
        - depression 293.83
        - hallucinations 293.82
      - depressive type 293.83
      - hallucinatory type 293.82
      - paranoid type 293.81
      - specified type NEC 293.89
  - paranoic 297.1
  - paranoid (chronic) 297.9

- **Psychosis** — *continued*
  - paranoid — *continued*
    - alcoholic 291.5
    - chronic 297.1
    - climacteric 297.2
    - involutional 297.2
    - menopausal 297.2
    - protracted reactive 298.4
    - psychogenic 298.4
      - acute 298.3
    - schizophrenic (*see also* Schizophrenia) 295.3 ☑
    - senile 290.20
  - paroxysmal 298.9
    - senile 290.20
  - polyneuritic, alcoholic 291.1
  - postoperative 293.9
  - postpartum — *see* Psychosis, puerperal
  - prepsychotic (*see also* Schizophrenia) 295.5 ☑
  - presbyophrenic (type) 290.8
  - presenile (*see also* Dementia, presenile) 290.10
  - prison 300.16
  - psychogenic 298.8
    - depressive 298.0
    - paranoid 298.4
      - acute 298.3
  - puerperal
    - specified type — *see* categories 295-298 ☑
    - unspecified type 293.89
      - acute 293.0
      - chronic 293.89
      - subacute 293.1
  - reactive (emotional stress) (psychological trauma) 298.8
    - brief 298.8
    - confusion 298.2
    - depressive 298.0
    - excitation 298.1
  - schizo-affective (depressed) (excited) (*see also* Schizophrenia) 295.7 ☑
  - schizophrenia, schizophrenic (*see also* Schizophrenia) 295.9 ☑
    - borderline type 295.5 ☑
      - of childhood (*see also* Psychosis, childhood) 299.8 ☑
    - catatonic (excited) (withdrawn) 295.2 ☑
    - childhood type (*see also* Psychosis, childhood) 299.9 ☑
    - hebephrenic 295.1 ☑
    - incipient 295.5 ☑
    - latent 295.5 ☑
    - paranoid 295.3 ☑
    - prepsychotic 295.5 ☑
    - prodromal 295.5 ☑
    - pseudoneurotic 295.5 ☑
    - pseudopsychopathic 295.5 ☑
    - schizophreniform 295.4 ☑
    - simple 295.0 ☑
    - undifferentiated type 295.9 ☑
  - schizophreniform 295.4 ☑
  - senile NEC 290.20
    - with
      - delusional features 290.20
      - depressive features 290.21
    - depressed type 290.21
    - paranoid type 290.20
    - simple deterioration 290.20
    - specified type — *see* categories 295-298 ☑
  - shared 297.3
  - situational (reactive) 298.8
  - symbiotic (childhood) (*see also* Psychosis, childhood) 299.1 ☑
  - toxic (acute) 293.9
- **Psychotic** — *see also* condition 298.9
  - episode 298.9
    - due to or associated with physical conditions (*see also* Psychosis, organic) 293.9
- **Pterygium** (eye) 372.40

- **Pterygium** — *continued*
  - central 372.43
  - colli 744.5
  - double 372.44
  - peripheral (stationary) 372.41
    - progressive 372.42
  - recurrent 372.45
- **Ptilosis** 374.55
- **PTLD** (post-transplant lymphoproliferative disorder) 238.77 ●
- **Ptomaine** (poisoning) — *see also* Poisoning, food 005.9
- **Ptosis** (adiposa) 374.30
  - breast 611.81 ▲
  - cecum 569.89
  - colon 569.89
  - congenital (eyelid) 743.61
    - specified site NEC — *see* Anomaly, specified type NEC
  - epicanthus syndrome 270.2
  - eyelid 374.30
    - congenital 743.61
    - mechanical 374.33
    - myogenic 374.32
    - paralytic 374.31
  - gastric 537.5
  - intestine 569.89
  - kidney (*see also* Disease, renal) 593.0
    - congenital 753.3
  - liver 573.8
  - renal (*see also* Disease, renal) 593.0
    - congenital 753.3
  - splanchnic 569.89
  - spleen 289.59
  - stomach 537.5
  - viscera 569.89
- **PTSD** (Post-traumatic stress disorder) 309.81
- **Ptyalism** 527.7
  - hysterical 300.11
  - periodic 527.2
  - pregnancy 646.8 ☑
  - psychogenic 306.4
- **Ptyalolithiasis** 527.5
- **Pubalgia** 848.8
- **Pubarche, precocious** 259.1
- **Pubertas praecox** 259.1
- **Puberty** V21.1
  - abnormal 259.9
  - bleeding 626.3
  - delayed 259.0
  - precocious (constitutional) (cryptogenic) (idiopathic) NEC 259.1
    - due to
      - adrenal
        - cortical hyperfunction 255.2
        - hyperplasia 255.2
      - cortical hyperfunction 255.2
      - ovarian hyperfunction 256.1
        - estrogen 256.0
      - pineal tumor 259.8
      - testicular hyperfunction 257.0
  - premature 259.1
    - due to
      - adrenal cortical hyperfunction 255.2
      - pineal tumor 259.8
      - pituitary (anterior) hyperfunction 253.1
- **Puckering, macula** 362.56
- **Pudenda, pudendum** — *see* condition
- **Puente's disease** (simple glandular cheilitis) 528.5
- **Puerperal**
  - abscess
    - areola 675.1 ☑
    - Bartholin's gland 646.6 ☑
    - breast 675.1 ☑
    - cervix (uteri) 670.0 ☑
    - fallopian tube 670.0 ☑
    - genital organ 670.0 ☑
    - kidney 646.6 ☑
    - mammary 675.1 ☑
    - mesosalpinx 670.0 ☑
    - nabothian 646.6 ☑
    - nipple 675.0 ☑

- **Puerperal** — *continued*
  - abscess — *continued*
    - ovary, ovarian 670.0 ☑
    - oviduct 670.0 ☑
    - parametric 670.0 ☑
    - para-uterine 670.0 ☑
    - pelvic 670.0 ☑
    - perimetric 670.0 ☑
    - periuterine 670.0 ☑
    - retro-uterine 670.0 ☑
    - subareolar 675.1 ☑
    - suprapelvic 670.0 ☑
    - tubal (ruptured) 670.0 ☑
    - tubo-ovarian 670.0 ☑
    - urinary tract NEC 646.6 ☑
    - uterine, uterus 670.0 ☑
    - vagina (wall) 646.6 ☑
    - vaginorectal 646.6 ☑
    - vulvovaginal gland 646.6 ☑
  - accident 674.9 ☑
  - adnexitis 670.0 ☑
  - afibrinogenemia, or other coagulation defect 666.3 ☑
  - albuminuria (acute) (subacute) 646.2 ☑
    - pre-eclamptic 642.4 ☑
  - anemia (conditions classifiable to 280–285) 648.2 ☑
  - anuria 669.3 ☑
  - apoplexy 674.0 ☑
  - asymptomatic bacteriuria 646.5 ☑
  - atrophy, breast 676.3 ☑
  - blood dyscrasia 666.3 ☑
  - caked breast 676.2 ☑
  - cardiomyopathy 674.5 ☑
  - cellulitis — *see* Puerperal, abscess
  - cerebrovascular disorder (conditions classifiable to 430–434, 436–437) 674.0 ☑
  - cervicitis (conditions classifiable to 616.0) 646.6 ☑
  - coagulopathy (any) 666.3 ☑
  - complications 674.9 ☑
    - specified type NEC 674.8 ☑
  - convulsions (eclamptic) (uremic) 642.6 ☑
    - with pre-existing hypertension 642.7 ☑
  - cracked nipple 676.1 ☑
  - cystitis 646.6 ☑
  - cystopyelitis 646.6 ☑
  - deciduitis (acute) 670.0 ☑
  - delirium NEC 293.9
  - diabetes (mellitus) (conditions classifiable to ▶249 and◀ 250) 648.0 ☑
  - disease 674.9 ☑
    - breast NEC 676.3 ☑
    - cerebrovascular (acute) 674.0 ☑
    - nonobstetric NEC (*see also* Pregnancy, complicated, current disease or condition) 648.9 ☑
    - pelvis inflammatory 670.0 ☑
    - renal NEC 646.2 ☑
    - tubo-ovarian 670.0 ☑
    - Valsuani's (progressive pernicious anemia) 648.2 ☑
  - disorder
    - lactation 676.9 ☑
      - specified type NEC 676.8 ☑
    - nonobstetric NEC (*see also* Pregnancy, complicated, current disease or condition) 648.9 ☑
  - disruption
    - cesarean wound 674.1 ☑
    - episiotomy wound 674.2 ☑
    - perineal laceration wound 674.2 ☑
  - drug dependence (conditions classifiable to 304) 648.3 ☑
  - eclampsia 642.6 ☑
    - with pre-existing hypertension 642.7 ☑
  - embolism (pulmonary) 673.2 ☑
    - air 673.0 ☑

- **Puerperal** — *continued*
  - embolism — *continued*
    - amniotic fluid 673.1 ☑
    - blood-clot 673.2 ☑
    - brain or cerebral 674.0 ☑
    - cardiac 674.8 ☑
    - fat 673.8 ☑
    - intracranial sinus (venous) 671.5 ☑
    - pyemic 673.3 ☑
    - septic 673.3 ☑
    - spinal cord 671.5 ☑
  - endometritis (conditions classifiable to 615.0–615.9) 670.0 ☑
  - endophlebitis — *see* Puerperal, phlebitis
  - endotrachelitis 646.6 ☑
  - engorgement, breasts 676.2 ☑
  - erysipelas 670.0 ☑
  - failure
    - lactation 676.4 ☑
    - renal, acute 669.3 ☑
  - fever 670.0 ☑
    - meaning pyrexia (of unknown origin) 672.0 ☑
    - meaning sepsis 670.0 ☑
  - fissure, nipple 676.1 ☑
  - fistula
    - breast 675.1 ☑
    - mammary gland 675.1 ☑
    - nipple 675.0 ☑
  - galactophoritis 675.2 ☑
  - galactorrhea 676.6 ☑
  - gangrene
    - gas 670.0 ☑
    - uterus 670.0 ☑
  - gonorrhea (conditions classifiable to 098) 647.1 ☑
  - hematoma, subdural 674.0 ☑
  - hematosalpinx, infectional 670.0 ☑
  - hemiplegia, cerebral 674.0 ☑
  - hemorrhage 666.1 ☑
    - brain 674.0 ☑
    - bulbar 674.0 ☑
    - cerebellar 674.0 ☑
    - cerebral 674.0 ☑
    - cortical 674.0 ☑
    - delayed (after 24 hours) (uterine) 666.2 ☑
    - extradural 674.0 ☑
    - internal capsule 674.0 ☑
    - intracranial 674.0 ☑
    - intrapontine 674.0 ☑
    - meningeal 674.0 ☑
    - pontine 674.0 ☑
    - subarachnoid 674.0 ☑
    - subcortical 674.0 ☑
    - subdural 674.0 ☑
    - uterine, delayed 666.2 ☑
    - ventricular 674.0 ☑
  - hemorrhoids 671.8 ☑
  - hepatorenal syndrome 674.8 ☑
  - hypertrophy
    - breast 676.3 ☑
    - mammary gland 676.3 ☑
  - induration breast (fibrous) 676.3 ☑
  - infarction
    - lung — *see* Puerperal, embolism
    - pulmonary — *see* Puerperal, embolism
  - infection
    - Bartholin's gland 646.6 ☑
    - breast 675.2 ☑
      - with nipple 675.9 ☑
        - specified type NEC 675.8 ☑
    - cervix 646.6 ☑
    - endocervix 646.6 ☑
    - fallopian tube 670.0 ☑
    - generalized 670.0 ☑
    - genital tract (major) 670.0 ☑
      - minor or localized 646.6 ☑
    - kidney (bacillus coli) 646.6 ☑
    - mammary gland 675.2 ☑
      - with nipple 675.9 ☑
- **Puerperal** — *continued*
  - infection — *continued*
    - mammary gland — *continued*
      - with nipple — *continued*
        - specified type NEC 675.8 ☑
    - nipple 675.0 ☑
      - with breast 675.9 ☑
        - specified type NEC 675.8 ☑
    - ovary 670.0 ☑
    - pelvic 670.0 ☑
    - peritoneum 670.0 ☑
    - renal 646.6 ☑
    - tubo-ovarian 670.0 ☑
    - urinary (tract) NEC 646.6 ☑
      - asymptomatic 646.5 ☑
    - uterus, uterine 670.0 ☑
    - vagina 646.6 ☑
  - inflammation (*see also* Puerperal, infection)
    - areola 675.1 ☑
    - Bartholin's gland 646.6 ☑
    - breast 675.2 ☑
    - broad ligament 670.0 ☑
    - cervix (uteri) 646.6 ☑
    - fallopian tube 670.0 ☑
    - genital organs 670.0 ☑
      - localized 646.6 ☑
    - mammary gland 675.2 ☑
    - nipple 675.0 ☑
    - ovary 670.0 ☑
    - oviduct 670.0 ☑
    - pelvis 670.0 ☑
    - periuterine 670.0 ☑
    - tubal 670.0 ☑
    - vagina 646.6 ☑
    - vein — *see* Puerperal, phlebitis
  - inversion, nipple 676.3 ☑
  - ischemia, cerebral 674.0 ☑
  - lymphangitis 670.0 ☑
    - breast 675.2 ☑
  - malaria (conditions classifiable to 084) 647.4 ☑
  - malnutrition 648.9 ☑
  - mammillitis 675.0 ☑
  - mammitis 675.2 ☑
  - mania 296.0 ☑
    - recurrent episode 296.1 ☑
    - single episode 296.0 ☑
  - mastitis 675.2 ☑
    - purulent 675.1 ☑
    - retromammary 675.1 ☑
    - submammary 675.1 ☑
  - melancholia 296.2 ☑
    - recurrent episode 296.3 ☑
    - single episode 296.2 ☑
  - mental disorder (conditions classifiable to 290–303, 305.0, 305.2–305.9, 306–316, 317–319) 648.4 ☑
  - metritis (septic) (suppurative) 670.0 ☑
  - metroperitonitis 670.0 ☑
  - metrorrhagia 666.2 ☑
  - metrosalpingitis 670.0 ☑
  - metrovaginitis 670.0 ☑
  - milk leg 671.4 ☑
  - monoplegia, cerebral 674.0 ☑
  - necrosis
    - kidney, tubular 669.3 ☑
    - liver (acute) (subacute) (conditions classifiable to 570) 674.8 ☑
    - ovary 670.0 ☑
    - renal cortex 669.3 ☑
  - nephritis or nephrosis (conditions classifiable to 580–589) 646.2 ☑
    - with hypertension 642.1 ☑
  - nutritional deficiency (conditions classifiable to 260–269) 648.9 ☑
  - occlusion, precerebral artery 674.0 ☑
  - oliguria 669.3 ☑
  - oophoritis 670.0 ☑
  - ovaritis 670.0 ☑
  - paralysis
    - bladder (sphincter) 665.5 ☑
    - cerebral 674.0 ☑
- **Puerperal** — *continued*
  - paralytic stroke 674.0 ☑
  - parametritis 670.0 ☑
  - paravaginitis 646.6 ☑
  - pelviperitonitis 670.0 ☑
  - perimetritis 670.0 ☑
  - perimetrosalpingitis 670.0 ☑
  - perinephritis 646.6 ☑
  - perioophoritis 670.0 ☑
  - periphlebitis — *see* Puerperal, phlebitis
  - perisalpingitis 670.0 ☑
  - peritoneal infection 670.0 ☑
  - peritonitis (pelvic) 670.0 ☑
  - perivaginitis 646.6 ☑
  - phlebitis 671.9 ☑
    - deep 671.4 ☑
    - intracranial sinus (venous) 671.5 ☑
    - pelvic 671.4 ☑
    - specified site NEC 671.5 ☑
    - superficial 671.2 ☑
  - phlegmasia alba dolens 671.4 ☑
  - placental polyp 674.4 ☑
  - pneumonia, embolic — *see* Puerperal, embolism
  - prediabetes 648.8 ☑
  - pre-eclampsia (mild) 642.4 ☑
    - with pre-existing hypertension 642.7 ☑
    - severe 642.5 ☑
  - psychosis, unspecified (*see also* Psychosis, puerperal) 293.89
  - pyelitis 646.6 ☑
  - pyelocystitis 646.6 ☑
  - pyelohydronephrosis 646.6 ☑
  - pyelonephritis 646.6 ☑
  - pyelonephrosis 646.6 ☑
  - pyemia 670.0 ☑
  - pyocystitis 646.6 ☑
  - pyohemia 670.0 ☑
  - pyometra 670.0 ☑
  - pyonephritis 646.6 ☑
  - pyonephrosis 646.6 ☑
  - pyo-oophoritis 670.0 ☑
  - pyosalpingitis 670.0 ☑
  - pyosalpinx 670.0 ☑
  - pyrexia (of unknown origin) 672.0 ☑
  - renal
    - disease NEC 646.2 ☑
    - failure, acute 669.3 ☑
  - retention
    - decidua (fragments) (with delayed hemorrhage) 666.2 ☑
      - without hemorrhage 667.1 ☑
    - placenta (fragments) (with delayed hemorrhage) 666.2 ☑
      - without hemorrhage 667.1 ☑
    - secundines (fragments) (with delayed hemorrhage) 666.2 ☑
      - without hemorrhage 667.1 ☑
  - retracted nipple 676.0 ☑
  - rubella (conditions classifiable to 056) 647.5 ☑
  - salpingitis 670.0 ☑
  - salpingo-oophoritis 670.0 ☑
  - salpingo-ovaritis 670.0 ☑
  - salpingoperitonitis 670.0 ☑
  - sapremia 670.0 ☑
  - secondary perineal tear 674.2 ☑
  - sepsis (pelvic) 670.0 ☑
  - septicemia 670.0 ☑
  - subinvolution (uterus) 674.8 ☑
  - sudden death (cause unknown) 674.9 ☑
  - suppuration — *see* Puerperal, abscess
  - syphilis (conditions classifiable to 090–097) 647.0 ☑
  - tetanus 670.0 ☑
  - thelitis 675.0 ☑
  - thrombocytopenia 666.3 ☑
  - thrombophlebitis (superficial) 671.2 ☑
    - deep 671.4 ☑
    - pelvic 671.4 ☑
- **Puerperal** — *continued*
  - thrombophlebitis — *continued*
    - specified site NEC 671.5 ☑
  - thrombosis (venous) — *see* Thrombosis, puerperal
  - thyroid dysfunction (conditions classifiable to 240–246) 648.1 ☑
  - toxemia (*see also* Toxemia, of pregnancy) 642.4 ☑
    - eclamptic 642.6 ☑
      - with pre-existing hypertension 642.7 ☑
    - pre-eclamptic (mild) 642.4 ☑
      - with
        - convulsions 642.6 ☑
        - pre-existing hypertension 642.7 ☑
      - severe 642.5 ☑
  - tuberculosis (conditions classifiable to 010–018) 647.3 ☑
  - uremia 669.3 ☑
  - vaginitis (conditions classifiable to 616.1) 646.6 ☑
  - varicose veins (legs) 671.0 ☑
    - vulva or perineum 671.1 ☑
  - vulvitis (conditions classifiable to 616.1) 646.6 ☑
  - vulvovaginitis (conditions classifiable to 616.1) 646.6 ☑
  - white leg 671.4 ☑
- **Pulled muscle** — *see* Sprain, by site
- **Pulmolithiasis** 518.89
- **Pulmonary** — *see* condition
- **Pulmonitis** (unknown etiology) 486
- **Pulpitis** (acute) (anachoretic) (chronic) (hyperplastic) (putrescent) (suppurative) (ulcerative) 522.0
- **Pulpless tooth** 522.9
- **Pulse**
  - alternating 427.89
    - psychogenic 306.2
  - bigeminal 427.89
  - fast 785.0
  - feeble, rapid, due to shock following injury 958.4
  - rapid 785.0
  - slow 427.89
  - strong 785.9
  - trigeminal 427.89
  - water-hammer (*see also* Insufficiency, aortic) 424.1
  - weak 785.9
- **Pulseless disease** 446.7
- **Pulsus**
  - alternans or trigeminy 427.89
    - psychogenic 306.2
- **Punch drunk** 310.2
- **Puncta lacrimalia occlusion** 375.52
- **Punctiform hymen** 752.49
- **Puncture** (traumatic) — *see also* Wound, open, by site
  - accidental, complicating surgery 998.2
  - bladder, nontraumatic 596.6
  - by
    - device, implant, or graft — *see* Complications, mechanical
    - foreign body
      - internal organs (*see also* Injury, internal, by site)
        - by ingested object — *see* Foreign body
      - left accidentally in operation wound 998.4
    - instrument (any) during a procedure, accidental 998.2
  - internal organs, abdomen, chest, or pelvis — *see* Injury, internal, by site
  - kidney, nontraumatic 593.89
- **Pupil** — *see* condition
- **Pupillary membrane** 364.74
  - persistent 743.46
- **Pupillotonia** 379.46
  - pseudotabetic 379.46
- **Purpura** 287.2
  - abdominal 287.0

Purpura — *continued*
allergic 287.0
anaphylactoid 287.0
annularis telangiectodes 709.1
arthritic 287.0
autoerythrocyte sensitization 287.2
autoimmune 287.0
bacterial 287.0
Bateman's (senile) 287.2
capillary fragility (hereditary) (idiopathic) 287.8
cryoglobulinemic 273.2
devil's pinches 287.2
fibrinolytic (*see also* Fibrinolysis) 286.6
fulminans, fulminous 286.6
gangrenous 287.0
hemorrhagic (*see also* Purpura, thrombocytopenic) 287.39
nodular 272.7
nonthrombocytopenic 287.0
thrombocytopenic 287.39
Henoch's (purpura nervosa) 287.0
Henoch-Schönlein (allergic) 287.0
hypergammaglobulinemic (benign primary) (Waldenström's) 273.0
idiopathic 287.31
nonthrombocytopenic 287.0
thrombocytopenic 287.31
immune thrombocytopenic 287.31
infectious 287.0
malignant 287.0
neonatorum 772.6
nervosa 287.0
newborn NEC 772.6
nonthrombocytopenic 287.2
hemorrhagic 287.0
idiopathic 287.0
nonthrombopenic 287.2
peliosis rheumatica 287.0
pigmentaria, progressiva 709.09
posttransfusion 287.4
primary 287.0
primitive 287.0
red cell membrane sensitivity 287.2
rheumatica 287.0
Schönlein (-Henoch) (allergic) 287.0
scorbutic 267
senile 287.2
simplex 287.2
symptomatica 287.0
telangiectasia annularis 709.1
thrombocytopenic (*see also* Thrombocytopenia) 287.30
congenital 287.33
essential 287.30
hereditary 287.31
idiopathic 287.31
immune 287.31
neonatal, transitory (*see also* Thrombocytopenia, neonatal transitory) 776.1
primary 287.30
puerperal, postpartum 666.3 ☑
thrombotic 446.6
thrombohemolytic (*see also* Fibrinolysis) 286.6
thrombopenic (*see also* Thrombocytopenia) 287.30
congenital 287.33
essential 287.30
thrombotic 446.6
thrombocytic 446.6
thrombocytopenic 446.6
toxic 287.0
variolosa 050.0
vascular 287.0
visceral symptoms 287.0
Werlhof's (*see also* Purpura, thrombocytopenic) 287.39
Purpuric spots 782.7
Purulent — *see* condition
Pus
absorption, general — *see* Septicemia
in
stool 792.1
Pus — *continued*
in — *continued*
urine 791.9
tube (rupture) (*see also* Salpingo-oophoritis) 614.2
Pustular rash 782.1
Pustule 686.9
malignant 022.0
nonmalignant 686.9
Putnam-Dana syndrome (subacute combined sclerosis with pernicious anemia) 281.0 *[336.2]*
Putnam's disease (subacute combined sclerosis with pernicious anemia) 281.0 *[336.2]*
Putrefaction, intestinal 569.89
Putrescent pulp (dental) 522.1
Pyarthritis — *see* Pyarthrosis
Pyarthrosis — *see also* Arthritis, pyogenic 711.0 ☑
tuberculous — *see* Tuberculosis, joint
Pycnoepilepsy, pycnolepsy (idiopathic) — *see also* Epilepsy 345.0 ☑
Pyelectasia 593.89
Pyelectasis 593.89
Pyelitis (congenital) (uremic) 590.80
with
abortion — *see* Abortion, by type, with specified complication NEC
contracted kidney 590.00
ectopic pregnancy (*see also* categories 633.0–633.9) 639.8
molar pregnancy (*see also* categories 630–632) 639.8
acute 590.10
with renal medullary necrosis 590.11
chronic 590.00
with
renal medullary necrosis 590.01
complicating pregnancy, childbirth, or puerperium 646.6 ☑
affecting fetus or newborn 760.1
cystica 590.3
following
abortion 639.8
ectopic or molar pregnancy 639.8
gonococcal 098.19
chronic or duration of 2 months or over 098.39
tuberculous (*see also* Tuberculosis) 016.0 ☑ *[590.81]*
Pyelocaliectasis 593.89
Pyelocystitis — *see also* Pyelitis 590.80
Pyelohydronephrosis 591
Pyelonephritis — *see also* Pyelitis 590.80
acute 590.10
with renal medullary necrosis 590.11
chronic 590.00
syphilitic (late) 095.4
tuberculous (*see also* Tuberculosis) 016.0 ☑ *[590.81]*
Pyelonephrosis — *see also* Pyelitis 590.80
chronic 590.00
Pyelophlebitis 451.89
Pyelo-ureteritis cystica 590.3
Pyemia, pyemic (purulent) — *see also* Septicemia 038.9
abscess — *see* Abscess
arthritis (*see also* Arthritis, pyogenic) 711.0 ☑
Bacillus coli 038.42
embolism (*see also* Septicemia) 415.12
fever 038.9
infection 038.9
joint (*see also* Arthritis, pyogenic) 711.0 ☑
liver 572.1
meningococcal 036.2
newborn 771.81
phlebitis — *see* Phlebitis
Pyemia, pyemic — *see also* Septicemia — *continued*
pneumococcal 038.2
portal 572.1
postvaccinal 999.39
specified organism NEC 038.8
staphylococcal 038.10
aureus 038.11
methicillin ●
resistant 038.12 ●
susceptible 038.11 ●
specified organism NEC 038.19
streptococcal 038.0
tuberculous — *see* Tuberculosis, miliary
Pygopagus 759.4
Pykno-epilepsy, pyknolepsy (idiopathic) — *see also* Epilepsy 345.0 ☑
Pyle (-Cohn) disease (craniometaphyseal dysplasia) 756.89
Pylephlebitis (suppurative) 572.1
Pylethrombophlebitis 572.1
Pylethrombosis 572.1
Pyloritis — *see also* Gastritis 535.5 ☑
Pylorospasm (reflex) 537.81
congenital or infantile 750.5
neurotic 306.4
newborn 750.5
psychogenic 306.4
Pylorus, pyloric — *see* condition
Pyoarthrosis — *see* Pyarthrosis
Pyocele
mastoid 383.00
sinus (accessory) (nasal) (*see also* Sinusitis) 473.9
turbinate (bone) 473.9
urethra (*see also* Urethritis) 597.0
Pyococcal dermatitis 686.00
Pyococcide, skin 686.00
Pyocolpos — *see also* Vaginitis 616.10
Pyocyaneus dermatitis 686.09
Pyocystitis — *see also* Cystitis 595.9
Pyoderma, pyodermia 686.00
gangrenosum 686.01
specified type NEC 686.09
vegetans 686.8
Pyodermatitis 686.00
vegetans 686.8
Pyogenic — *see* condition
Pyohemia — *see* Septicemia
Pyohydronephrosis — *see also* Pyelitis 590.80
Pyometra 615.9
Pyometritis — *see also* Endometritis 615.9
Pyometrium — *see also* Endometritis 615.9
Pyomyositis 728.0
ossificans 728.19
tropical (bungpagga) 040.81
Pyonephritis — *see also* Pyelitis 590.80
chronic 590.00
Pyonephrosis (congenital) — *see also* Pyelitis 590.80
acute 590.10
Pyo-oophoritis — *see also* Salpingo-oophoritis 614.2
Pyo-ovarium — *see also* Salpingo-oophoritis 614.2
Pyopericarditis 420.99
Pyopericardium 420.99
Pyophlebitis — *see* Phlebitis
Pyopneumopericardium 420.99
Pyopneumothorax (infectional) 510.9
with fistula 510.0
subdiaphragmatic (*see also* Peritonitis) 567.29
subphrenic (*see also* Peritonitis) 567.29
tuberculous (*see also* Tuberculosis, pleura) 012.0 ☑
Pyorrhea (alveolar) (alveolaris) 523.40
degenerative 523.5
Pyosalpingitis — *see also* Salpingo-oophoritis 614.2
Pyosalpinx — *see also* Salpingo-oophoritis 614.2
Pyosepticemia — *see* Septicemia
Pyosis
Corlett's (impetigo) 684
Manson's (pemphigus contagiosus) 684
Pyothorax 510.9
with fistula 510.0
tuberculous (*see also* Tuberculosis, pleura) 012.0 ☑
Pyoureter 593.89
tuberculous (*see also* Tuberculosis) 016.2 ☑
Pyramidopallidonigral syndrome 332.0
Pyrexia (of unknown origin) (P.U.O.) 780.60 ▲
atmospheric 992.0
during labor 659.2 ☑
environmentally-induced newborn 778.4
heat 992.0
newborn, environmentally-induced 778.4
puerperal 672.0 ☑
Pyroglobulinemia 273.8
Pyromania 312.33
Pyrosis 787.1
Pyrroloporphyria 277.1
Pyuria (bacterial) 791.9

Q

Q fever 083.0
with pneumonia 083.0 *[484.8]*
Quadricuspid aortic valve 746.89
Quadrilateral fever 083.0
Quadriparesis — *see* Quadriplegia
meaning muscle weakness 728.87
Quadriplegia 344.00
with fracture, vertebra (process) — *see* Fracture, vertebra, cervical, with spinal cord injury
brain (current episode) 437.8
C1-C4
complete 344.01
incomplete 344.02
C5-C7
complete 344.03
incomplete 344.04
cerebral (current episode) 437.8
congenital or infantile (cerebral) (spastic) (spinal) 343.2
cortical 437.8
embolic (current episode) (*see also* Embolism, brain) 434.1 ☑
functional 780.72 ●
infantile (cerebral) (spastic) (spinal) 343.2
newborn NEC 767.0
specified NEC 344.09
thrombotic (current episode) (*see also* Thrombosis, brain) 434.0 ☑
traumatic — *see* Injury, spinal, cervical
Quadruplet
affected by maternal complications of pregnancy 761.5
healthy liveborn — *see* Newborn, multiple
pregnancy (complicating delivery) NEC 651.8 ☑
with fetal loss and retention of one or more fetus(es) 651.5 ☑
following (elective) fetal reduction 651.7 ☑
Quarrelsomeness 301.3
Quartan
fever 084.2
malaria (fever) 084.2
Queensland fever 083.0
coastal 083.0
seven-day 100.89
Quervain's disease 727.04
thyroid (subacute granulomatous thyroiditis) 245.1

Queyrat's erythroplasia (M8080/2)
- specified site — *see* Neoplasm, skin, in situ
- unspecified site 233.5

Quincke's disease or edema — *see* Edema, angioneurotic

Quinquaud's disease (acne decalvans) 704.09

Quinsy (gangrenous) 475

Quintan fever 083.1

Quintuplet
- affected by maternal complications of pregnancy 761.5
- healthy liveborn — *see* Newborn, multiple
- pregnancy (complicating delivery) NEC 651.2 ☑
  - with fetal loss and retention of one or more fetus(es) 651.6 ☑
  - following (elective) fetal reduction 651.7 ☑

Quotidian
- fever 084.0
- malaria (fever) 084.0

R

Rabbia 071

Rabbit fever — *see also* Tularemia 021.9

Rabies 071
- contact V01.5
- exposure to V01.5
- inoculation V04.5
  - reaction — *see* Complications, vaccination
- vaccination, prophylactic (against) V04.5

Rachischisis — *see also* Spina bifida 741.9 ☑

Rachitic — *see also* condition
- deformities of spine 268.1
- pelvis 268.1
  - with disproportion (fetopelvic) 653.2 ☑
    - affecting fetus or newborn 763.1
    - causing obstructed labor 660.1 ☑
      - affecting fetus or newborn 763.1

Rachitis, rachitism — *see* also Rickets
- acute 268.0
- fetalis 756.4
- renalis 588.0
- tarda 268.0

Racket nail 757.5

Radial nerve — *see* condition

Radiation effects or sickness — *see also* Effect, adverse, radiation
- cataract 366.46
- dermatitis 692.82
  - sunburn (*see also* Sunburn) 692.71

Radiculitis (pressure) (vertebrogenic) 729.2
- accessory nerve 723.4
- anterior crural 724.4
- arm 723.4
- brachial 723.4
- cervical NEC 723.4
- due to displacement of intervertebral disc — *see* Neuritis, due to, displacement intervertebral disc
- leg 724.4
- lumbar NEC 724.4
- lumbosacral 724.4
- rheumatic 729.2
- syphilitic 094.89
- thoracic (with visceral pain) 724.4

Radiculomyelitis 357.0
- toxic, due to
  - Clostridium tetani 037
  - Corynebacterium diphtheriae 032.89

Radiculopathy — *see also* Radiculitis 729.2

Radioactive substances, adverse effect — *see* Effect, adverse, radioactive substance

Radiodermal burns (acute) (chronic) (occupational) — *see* Burn, by site

Radiodermatitis 692.82

Radionecrosis — *see* Effect, adverse, radiation

Radiotherapy session V58.0

Radium, adverse effect — *see* Effect, adverse, radioactive substance

Raeder-Harbitz syndrome (pulseless disease) 446.7

Rage — *see also* Disturbance, conduct 312.0 ☑
- meaning rabies 071

Rag sorters' disease 022.1

Raillietiniasis 123.8

Railroad neurosis 300.16

Railway spine 300.16

Raised — *see* Elevation

Raiva 071

Rake teeth, tooth 524.39

Rales 786.7

Ramifying renal pelvis 753.3

Ramsay Hunt syndrome (herpetic geniculate ganglionitis) 053.11
- meaning dyssynergia cerebellaris myoclonica 334.2

Ranke's primary infiltration — *see also* Tuberculosis 010.0 ☑

Ranula 527.6
- congenital 750.26

Rape
- adult 995.83
- alleged, observation or examination V71.5
- child 995.53

Rapid
- feeble pulse, due to shock, following injury 958.4
- heart (beat) 785.0
  - psychogenic 306.2
- respiration 786.06
  - psychogenic 306.1
- second stage (delivery) 661.3 ☑
  - affecting fetus or newborn 763.6
- time-zone change syndrome 327.35

Rarefaction, bone 733.99

Rash 782.1
- canker 034.1
- diaper 691.0
- drug (internal use) 693.0
  - contact 692.3
- ECHO 9 virus 078.89
- enema 692.89
- food (*see also* Allergy, food) 693.1
- heat 705.1
- napkin 691.0
- nettle 708.8
- pustular 782.1
- rose 782.1
  - epidemic 056.9
  - of infants 057.8
- scarlet 034.1
- serum (prophylactic) (therapeutic) 999.5
- toxic 782.1
- wandering tongue 529.1

Rasmussen's aneurysm — *see also* Tuberculosis 011.2 ☑

Rat-bite fever 026.9
- due to Streptobacillus moniliformis 026.1
- spirochetal (morsus muris) 026.0

Rathke's pouch tumor (M9350/1) 237.0

Raymond (-Céstan) syndrome 433.8 ☑

Raynaud's
- disease or syndrome (paroxysmal digital cyanosis) 443.0
- gangrene (symmetric) 443.0 *[785.4]*
- phenomenon (paroxysmal digital cyanosis) (secondary) 443.0

RDS 769

Reaction
- acute situational maladjustment (*see also* Reaction, adjustment) 309.9
- adaptation (*see also* Reaction, adjustment) 309.9
- adjustment 309.9
  - with
    - anxious mood 309.24
      - with depressed mood 309.28
    - conduct disturbance 309.3
      - combined with disturbance of emotions 309.4
    - depressed mood 309.0
      - brief 309.0
        - with anxious mood 309.28
      - prolonged 309.1
    - elective mutism 309.83
    - mixed emotions and conduct 309.4
    - mutism, elective 309.83
    - physical symptoms 309.82
    - predominant disturbance (of)
      - conduct 309.3
      - emotions NEC 309.29
        - mixed 309.28
      - mixed, emotions and conduct 309.4
      - specified type NEC 309.89
    - specific academic or work inhibition 309.23
    - withdrawal 309.83
  - depressive 309.0
    - with conduct disturbance 309.4
    - brief 309.0
    - prolonged 309.1
  - specified type NEC 309.89
- adverse food NEC 995.7
- affective (*see also* Psychosis, affective) 296.90
  - specified type NEC 296.99
- aggressive 301.3
  - unsocialized (*see also* Disturbance, conduct) 312.0 ☑
- allergic (*see also* Allergy) 995.3
  - drug, medicinal substance, and biological — *see* Allergy, drug
  - food — *see* Allergy, food
  - serum 999.5
- anaphylactic — *see* Shock, anaphylactic
- anesthesia — *see* Anesthesia, complication
- anger 312.0 ☑
- antisocial 301.7
- antitoxin (prophylactic) (therapeutic) — *see* Complications, vaccination
- anxiety 300.00
- Arthus 995.21
- asthenic 300.5
- compulsive 300.3
- conversion (anesthetic) (autonomic) (hyperkinetic) (mixed paralytic) (paresthetic) 300.11
- deoxyribonuclease (DNA) (DNase) hypersensitivity NEC 287.2
- depressive 300.4
  - acute 309.0
  - affective (*see also* Psychosis, affective) 296.2 ☑
    - recurrent episode 296.3 ☑
    - single episode 296.2 ☑
  - brief 309.0
  - manic (*see also* Psychosis, affective) 296.80
  - neurotic 300.4
  - psychoneurotic 300.4
  - psychotic 298.0
- dissociative 300.15
- drug NEC (*see also* Table of Drugs and Chemicals) 995.20
  - allergic (*see also* Allergy, drug) 995.27

Reaction — *continued*
- drug (*see also* Table of Drugs and Chemicals) — *continued*
  - correct substance properly administered 995.20
  - obstetric anesthetic or analgesic NEC 668.9 ☑
    - affecting fetus or newborn 763.5
    - specified drug — *see* Table of Drugs and Chemicals
  - overdose or poisoning 977.9
    - specified drug — *see* Table of Drugs and Chemicals
  - specific to newborn 779.4
  - transmitted via placenta or breast milk — *see* Absorption, drug, through placenta
  - withdrawal NEC 292.0
    - infant of dependent mother 779.5
  - wrong substance given or taken in error 977.9
    - specified drug — *see* Table of Drugs and Chemicals
- dyssocial 301.7
- dystonic, acute, due to drugs 333.72
- erysipeloid 027.1
- fear 300.20
  - child 313.0
- fluid loss, cerebrospinal 349.0
- food (*see also* Allergy, food)
  - adverse NEC 995.7
  - anaphylactic shock — *see* Anaphylactic shock, due to, food
- foreign
  - body NEC 728.82
    - in operative wound (inadvertently left) 998.4
      - due to surgical material intentionally left — *see* Complications, due to (presence of) any device, implant, or graft classified to 996.0–996.5 NEC
  - substance accidentally left during a procedure (chemical) (powder) (talc) 998.7
    - body or object (instrument) (sponge) (swab) 998.4
- graft-versus-host (GVH) 279.50 ▲
- grief (acute) (brief) 309.0
  - prolonged 309.1
- gross stress (*see also* Reaction, stress, acute) 308.9
- group delinquent (*see also* Disturbance, conduct) 312.2 ☑
- Herxheimer's 995.0
- hyperkinetic (*see also* Hyperkinesia) 314.9
- hypochondriacal 300.7
- hypoglycemic, due to insulin 251.0
  - therapeutic misadventure 962.3
- hypomanic (*see also* Psychosis, affective) 296.0 ☑
  - recurrent episode 296.1 ☑
  - single episode 296.0 ☑
- hysterical 300.10
  - conversion type 300.11
  - dissociative 300.15
- id (bacterial cause) 692.89
- immaturity NEC 301.89
  - aggressive 301.3
  - emotional instability 301.59
- immunization — *see* Complications, vaccination
- incompatibility
  - blood group (ABO) (infusion) (transfusion) 999.6
  - Rh (factor) (infusion) (transfusion) 999.7
- inflammatory — *see* Infection
- infusion — *see* Complications, infusion
- inoculation (immune serum) — *see* Complications, vaccination

Reaction — *continued*
- insulin 995.23
- involutional
  - paranoid 297.2
  - psychotic (*see also* Psychosis, affective, depressive) 296.2 ☑
- leukemoid (basophilic) (lymphocytic) (monocytic) (myelocytic) (neutrophilic) 288.62
- LSD (*see also* Abuse, drugs, nondependent) 305.3 ☑
- lumbar puncture 349.0
- manic-depressive (*see also* Psychosis, affective) 296.80
  - depressed 296.2 ☑
    - recurrent episode 296.3 ☑
    - single episode 296.2 ☑
  - hypomanic 296.0 ☑
- neurasthenic 300.5
- neurogenic (*see also* Neurosis) 300.9
- neurotic NEC 300.9
- neurotic-depressive 300.4
- nitritoid — *see* Crisis, nitritoid
- obsessive compulsive 300.3
- organic 293.9
  - acute 293.0
  - subacute 293.1
- overanxious, child or adolescent 313.0
- paranoid (chronic) 297.9
  - acute 298.3
  - climacteric 297.2
  - involutional 297.2
  - menopausal 297.2
  - senile 290.20
  - simple 297.0
- passive
  - aggressive 301.84
  - dependency 301.6
- personality (*see also* Disorder, personality) 301.9
- phobic 300.20
- postradiation — *see* Effect, adverse, radiation
- psychogenic NEC 300.9
- psychoneurotic (*see also* Neurosis) 300.9
  - anxiety 300.00
  - compulsive 300.3
  - conversion 300.11
  - depersonalization 300.6
  - depressive 300.4
  - dissociative 300.15
  - hypochondriacal 300.7
  - hysterical 300.10
    - conversion type 300.11
    - dissociative type 300.15
  - neurasthenic 300.5
  - obsessive 300.3
  - obsessive-compulsive 300.3
  - phobic 300.20
  - tension state 300.9
- psychophysiologic NEC (*see also* Disorder, psychosomatic) 306.9
  - cardiovascular 306.2
  - digestive 306.4
  - endocrine 306.6
  - gastrointestinal 306.4
  - genitourinary 306.50
  - heart 306.2
  - hemic 306.8
  - intestinal (large) (small) 306.4
  - laryngeal 306.1
  - lymphatic 306.8
  - musculoskeletal 306.0
  - pharyngeal 306.1
  - respiratory 306.1
  - skin 306.3
  - special sense organs 306.7
- psychosomatic (*see also* Disorder, psychosomatic) 306.9
- psychotic (*see also* Psychosis) 298.9
  - depressive 298.0
  - due to or associated with physical condition (*see also* Psychosis, organic) 293.9
  - involutional (*see also* Psychosis, affective) 296.2 ☑
    - recurrent episode 296.3 ☑
    - single episode 296.2 ☑
- pupillary (myotonic) (tonic) 379.46
- radiation — *see* Effect, adverse, radiation
- runaway (*see also* Disturbance, conduct)
  - socialized 312.2 ☑
  - undersocialized, unsocialized 312.1 ☑
- scarlet fever toxin — *see* Complications, vaccination
- schizophrenic (*see also* Schizophrenia) 295.9 ☑
  - latent 295.5 ☑
- serological for syphilis — *see* Serology for syphilis
- serum (prophylactic) (therapeutic) 999.5
  - immediate 999.4
- situational (*see also* Reaction, adjustment) 309.9
  - acute, to stress 308.3
  - adjustment (*see also* Reaction, adjustment) 309.9
- somatization (*see also* Disorder, psychosomatic) 306.9
- spinal puncture 349.0
- spite, child (*see also* Disturbance, conduct) 312.0 ☑
- stress, acute 308.9
  - with predominant disturbance (of)
    - consciousness 308.1
    - emotions 308.0
    - mixed 308.4
    - psychomotor 308.2
    - specified type NEC 308.3
  - bone or cartilage — *see* Fracture, stress
- surgical procedure — *see* Complications, surgical procedure
- tetanus antitoxin — *see* Complications, vaccination
- toxin-antitoxin — *see* Complications, vaccination
- transfusion (blood) (bone marrow) (lymphocytes) (allergic) — *see* Complications, transfusion
- tuberculin skin test, nonspecific (without active tuberculosis) 795.5
  - positive (without active tuberculosis) 795.5
- ultraviolet — *see* Effect, adverse, ultraviolet
- undersocialized, unsocialized (*see also* Disturbance, conduct)
  - aggressive (type) 312.0 ☑
  - unaggressive (type) 312.1 ☑
- vaccination (any) — *see* Complications, vaccination
- white graft (skin) 996.52
- withdrawing, child or adolescent 313.22
- x-ray — *see* Effect, adverse, x-rays

Reactive depression — *see also* Reaction, depressive 300.4
- neurotic 300.4
- psychoneurotic 300.4
- psychotic 298.0

Rebound tenderness 789.6 ☑

Recalcitrant patient V15.81

Recanalization, thrombus — *see* Thrombosis

Recession, receding
- chamber angle (eye) 364.77
- chin 524.06
- gingival (postinfective) (postoperative) 523.20
  - generalized 523.25
  - localized 523.24
  - minimal 523.21
  - moderate 523.22
  - severe 523.23

Recklinghausen-Applebaum disease (hemochromatosis) 275.0

Recklinghausen's disease (M9540/1) 237.71
- bones (osteitis fibrosa cystica) 252.01

Reclus' disease (cystic) 610.1

Recrudescent typhus (fever) 081.1

Recruitment, auditory 388.44

Rectalgia 569.42

Rectitis 569.49

Rectocele
- female (without uterine prolapse) 618.04
  - with uterine prolapse 618.4
    - complete 618.3
    - incomplete 618.2
- in pregnancy or childbirth 654.4 ☑
  - causing obstructed labor 660.2 ☑
    - affecting fetus or newborn 763.1
- male 569.49
- vagina, vaginal (outlet) 618.04

Rectosigmoiditis 569.89
- ulcerative (chronic) 556.3

Rectosigmoid junction — *see* condition

Rectourethral — *see* condition

Rectovaginal — *see* condition

Rectovesical — *see* condition

Rectum, rectal — *see* condition

Recurrent — *see* condition

Red bugs 133.8

Red cedar asthma 495.8

Redness
- conjunctiva 379.93
- eye 379.93
- nose 478.19

Reduced ventilatory or vital capacity 794.2

Reduction
- function
  - kidney (*see also* Disease, renal) 593.9
  - liver 573.8
- ventilatory capacity 794.2
- vital capacity 794.2

Redundant, redundancy
- abdomen 701.9
- anus 751.5
- cardia 537.89
- clitoris 624.2
- colon (congenital) 751.5
- foreskin (congenital) 605
- intestine 751.5
- labia 624.3
- organ or site, congenital NEC — *see* Accessory
- panniculus (abdominal) 278.1
- prepuce (congenital) 605
- pylorus 537.89
- rectum 751.5
- scrotum 608.89
- sigmoid 751.5
- skin (of face) 701.9
  - eyelids 374.30
- stomach 537.89
- uvula 528.9
- vagina 623.8

Reduplication — *see* Duplication

Referral
- adoption (agency) V68.89
- nursing care V63.8
- patient without examination or treatment V68.81
- social services V63.8

Reflex — *see also* condition
- blink, deficient 374.45
- hyperactive gag 478.29
- neurogenic bladder NEC 596.54
  - atonic 596.54
    - with cauda equina syndrome 344.61
- vasoconstriction 443.9
- vasovagal 780.2

Reflux 530.81 ▲
- acid 530.81 ●
- esophageal 530.81
  - with esophagitis 530.11
- esophagitis 530.11
- gastroesophageal 530.81
- mitral — *see* Insufficiency, mitral
- ureteral — *see* Reflux, vesicoureteral
- vesicoureteral 593.70
  - with
    - reflux nephropathy 593.73
      - bilateral 593.72
      - unilateral 593.71

Reformed gallbladder 576.0

Reforming, artificial openings — *see also* Attention to, artificial, opening V55.9

Refractive error — *see also* Error, refractive 367.9

Refsum's disease or syndrome (heredopathia atactica polyneuritiformis) 356.3

Refusal of
- food 307.59
  - hysterical 300.11
- treatment because of, due to
  - patient's decision NEC V64.2
  - reason of conscience or religion V62.6

Regaud
- tumor (M8082/3) — *see* Neoplasm, nasopharynx, malignant
- type carcinoma (M8082/3) — *see* Neoplasm, nasopharynx, malignant

Regional — *see* condition

Regulation feeding (elderly) (infant) 783.3
- newborn 779.3

Regurgitated
- food, choked on 933.1
- stomach contents, choked on 933.1

Regurgitation 787.03
- aortic (valve) (*see also* Insufficiency, aortic) 424.1
  - congenital 746.4
  - syphilitic 093.22
- food (*see also* Vomiting)
  - with reswallowing — *see* Rumination
  - newborn 779.3
- gastric contents — *see* Vomiting
- heart — *see* Endocarditis
- mitral (valve) (*see also* Insufficiency, mitral)
  - congenital 746.6
- myocardial — *see* Endocarditis
- pulmonary (heart) (valve) (*see also* Endocarditis, pulmonary) 424.3
- stomach — *see* Vomiting
- tricuspid — *see* Endocarditis, tricuspid
- valve, valvular — *see* Endocarditis
- vesicoureteral — *see* Reflux, vesicoureteral

Rehabilitation V57.9
- multiple types V57.89
- occupational V57.21
- specified type NEC V57.89
- speech V57.3
- vocational V57.22

Reichmann's disease or syndrome (gastrosuccorrhea) 536.8

Reifenstein's syndrome (hereditary familial hypogonadism, male) 259.52 ▲

Reilly's syndrome or phenomenon — *see also* Neuropathy, peripheral, autonomic 337.9

Reimann's periodic disease 277.31

Reinsertion, contraceptive device V25.42

Reiter's disease, syndrome, or urethritis 099.3 *[711.1]* ☑
Rejection
food, hysterical 300.11
transplant 996.80
bone marrow 996.85
corneal 996.51
organ (immune or nonimmune cause) 996.80
bone marrow 996.85
heart 996.83
intestines 996.87
kidney 996.81
liver 996.82
lung 996.84
pancreas 996.86
specified NEC 996.89
skin 996.52
artificial 996.55
decellularized allodermis 996.55
Relapsing fever 087.9
Carter's (Asiatic) 087.0
Dutton's (West African) 087.1
Koch's 087.9
louse-borne (epidemic) 087.0
Novy's (American) 087.1
Obermeyer's (European) 087.0
Spirillum 087.9
tick-borne (endemic) 087.1
Relaxation
anus (sphincter) 569.49
due to hysteria 300.11
arch (foot) 734
congenital 754.61
back ligaments 728.4
bladder (sphincter) 596.59
cardio-esophageal 530.89
cervix (*see also* Incompetency, cervix) 622.5
diaphragm 519.4
inguinal rings — *see* Hernia, inguinal
joint (capsule) (ligament) (paralytic) (*see also* Derangement, joint) 718.90
congenital 755.8
lumbosacral joint 724.6
pelvic floor 618.89
pelvis 618.89
perineum 618.89
posture 729.90 ▲
rectum (sphincter) 569.49
sacroiliac (joint) 724.6
scrotum 608.89
urethra (sphincter) 599.84
uterus (outlet) 618.89
vagina (outlet) 618.89
vesical 596.59
Remains
canal of Cloquet 743.51
capsule (opaque) 743.51
Remittent fever (malarial) 084.6
Remnant
canal of Cloquet 743.51
capsule (opaque) 743.51
cervix, cervical stump (acquired) (postoperative) 622.8
cystic duct, postcholecystectomy 576.0
fingernail 703.8
congenital 757.5
meniscus, knee 717.5
thyroglossal duct 759.2
tonsil 474.8
infected 474.00
urachus 753.7
Remote effect of cancer — *see* condition
Removal (of)
catheter (urinary) (indwelling) V53.6
from artificial opening — *see* Attention to, artificial, opening
non-vascular V58.82
vascular V58.81
cerebral ventricle (communicating) shunt V53.01
device (*see also* Fitting (of))
Removal — *continued*
device (*see also* Fitting) — *continued*
contraceptive V25.42
fixation
external V54.89
internal V54.01
traction V54.89
drains V58.49
dressing
wound V58.30
nonsurgical V58.30
surgical V58.31
ileostomy V55.2
Kirschner wire V54.89
nonvascular catheter V58.82
pin V54.01
plaster cast V54.89
plate (fracture) V54.01
rod V54.01
screw V54.01
splint, external V54.89
staples V58.32
subdermal implantable contraceptive V25.43
sutures V58.32
traction device, external V54.89
vascular catheter V58.81
wound packing V58.30
nonsurgical V58.30
surgical V58.31
Ren
arcuatus 753.3
mobile, mobilis (*see also* Disease, renal) 593.0
congenital 753.3
unguliformis 753.3
Renal — *see also* condition
glomerulohyalinosis-diabetic syndrome 250.4 ☑ *[581.81]*
due to secondary diabetes ●
249.4 ☑ *[581.81]* ●
Rendu-Osler-Weber disease or syndrome (familial hemorrhagic telangiectasia) 448.0
Reninoma (M8361/1) 236.91
Rénon-Delille syndrome 253.8
Repair
pelvic floor, previous, in pregnancy or childbirth 654.4 ☑
affecting fetus or newborn 763.89
scarred tissue V51.8 ▲
Replacement by artificial or mechanical device or prosthesis of — *see also* Fitting (of
artificial skin V43.83
bladder V43.5
blood vessel V43.4
breast V43.82
eye globe V43.0
heart
with
assist device V43.21
fully implantable artificial heart V43.22
valve V43.3
intestine V43.89
joint V43.60
ankle V43.66
elbow V43.62
finger V43.69
hip (partial) (total) V43.64
knee V43.65
shoulder V43.61
specified NEC V43.69
wrist V43.63
kidney V43.89
larynx V43.81
lens V43.1
limb(s) V43.7
liver V43.89
lung V43.89
organ NEC V43.89
pancreas V43.89
skin (artificial) V43.83
tissue NEC V43.89
Reprogramming
cardiac pacemaker V53.31
Request for expert evidence V68.2
Reserve, decreased or low
cardiac — *see* Disease, heart
kidney (*see also* Disease, renal) 593.9
Residual — *see also* condition
bladder 596.8
foreign body — *see* Retention, foreign body
state, schizophrenic (*see also* Schizophrenia) 295.6 ☑
urine 788.69
Resistance, resistant (to)
activated protein C 289.81

Note — use the following subclassification for categories V09.5, V09.7, V09.8, V09.9:

0 without mention of resistance to multiple drugs

1 with resistance to multiple drugs

V09.5 quinolones and fluoroquinolones

V09.7 antimycobacterial agents

V09.8 specified drugs NEC

V09.9 unspecified drugs

drugs by microorganisms V09.9 ☑
Amikacin V09.4
aminoglycosides V09.4
Amodiaquine V09.5 ☑
Amoxicillin V09.0
Ampicillin V09.0
antimycobacterial agents V09.7 ☑
Azithromycin V09.2
Azlocillin V09.0
Aztreonam V09.1
Bacampicillin V09.0
Bacitracin V09.8 ☑
Benznidazole V09.8 ☑
B-lactam antibiotics V09.1
Capreomycin V09.7 ☑
Carbenicillin V09.0
Cefaclor V09.1
Cefadroxil V09.1
Cefamandole V09.1
Cefatetan V09.1
Cefazolin V09.1
Cefixime V09.1
Cefonicid V09.1
Cefoperazone V09.1
Ceforanide V09.1
Cefotaxime V09.1
Cefoxitin V09.1
Ceftazidime V09.1
Ceftizoxime V09.1
Ceftriaxone V09.1
Cefuroxime V09.1
Cephalexin V09.1
Cephaloglycin V09.1
Cephaloridine V09.1
Cephalosporins V09.1
Cephalothin V09.1
Cephapirin V09.1
Cephradine V09.1
Chloramphenicol V09.8 ☑
Chloraquine V09.5 ☑
Chlorguanide V09.8 ☑
Chlorproguanil V09.8 ☑
Chlortetracyline V09.3
Cinoxacin V09.5 ☑
Ciprofloxacin V09.5 ☑
Clarithromycin V09.2
Clindamycin V09.8 ☑
Clioquinol V09.5 ☑
Clofazimine V09.7 ☑
Cloxacillin V09.0
Cyclacillin V09.0
Cycloserine V09.7 ☑
Dapsone [DZ] V09.7 ☑
Demeclocycline V09.3
Dicloxacillin V09.0
Resistance, resistant — *continued*
drugs by microorganisms — *continued*
Doxycycline V09.3
Enoxacin V09.5 ☑
Erythromycin V09.2
Ethambutol [EMB] V09.7 ☑
Ethionamide [ETA] V09.7 ☑
fluoroquinolones V09.5 ☑
Gentamicin V09.4
Halofantrine V09.8 ☑
Imipenem V09.1
Iodoquinol V09.5 ☑
Isoniazid [INH] V09.7 ☑
Kanamycin V09.4
macrolides V09.2
Mafenide V09.6
MDRO (multiple drug resistant organisms) NOS V09.91
Mefloquine V09.8 ☑
Melasoprol V09.8 ☑
Methacycline V09.3
Methenamine V09.8 ☑
Methicillin ▶— *see* Infection, Methicillin◀ V09.0
Metronidazole V09.8 ☑
Mezlocillin V09.0
Minocycline V09.3
multiple drug resistant organisms NOS V09.91
Nafcillin V09.0
Nalidixic acid V09.5 ☑
Natamycin V09.2
Neomycin V09.4
Netilmicin V09.4
Nimorazole V09.8 ☑
Nitrofurantoin V09.8 ☑
Nitrofurtimox V09.8 ☑
Norfloxacin V09.5 ☑
Nystatin V09.2
Ofloxacin V09.5 ☑
Oleandomycin V09.2
Oxacillin V09.0
Oxytetracycline V09.3
Para-amino salicylic acid [PAS] V09.7 ☑
Paromomycin V09.4
Penicillin (G) (V) (VK) V09.0
penicillins V09.0
Pentamidine V09.8 ☑
Piperacillin V09.0
Primaquine V09.5 ☑
Proguanil V09.8 ☑
Pyrazinamide [PZA] V09.7 ☑
Pyrimethamine/Sulfalene V09.8 ☑
Pyrimethamine/Sulfodoxine V09.8 ☑
Quinacrine V09.5 ☑
Quinidine V09.8 ☑
Quinine V09.8 ☑
quinolones V09.5 ☑
Rifabutin V09.7 ☑
Rifampin [RIF] V09.7 ☑
Rifamycin V09.7 ☑
Rolitetracycline V09.3
specified drugs NEC V09.8 ☑
Spectinomycin V09.8 ☑
Spiramycin V09.2
Streptomycin [SM] V09.4
Sulfacetamide V09.6
Sulfacytine V09.6
Sulfadiazine V09.6
Sulfadoxine V09.6
Sulfamethoxazole V09.6
Sulfapyridine V09.6
Sulfasalizine V09.6
Sulfasoxazole V09.6
sulfonamides V09.6
Sulfoxone V09.7 ☑
tetracycline V09.3
tetracyclines V09.3
Thiamphenicol V09.8 ☑
Ticarcillin V09.0
Tinidazole V09.8 ☑
Tobramycin V09.4

Resistance, resistant — *continued*
- drugs by microorganisms — *continued*
  - Triamphenicol V09.8 ☑
  - Trimethoprim V09.8 ☑
  - Vancomycin V09.8 ☑
- insulin 277.7
- thyroid hormone 246.8

Resorption
- biliary 576.8
  - purulent or putrid (*see also* Cholecystitis) 576.8
- dental (roots) 521.40
  - alveoli 525.8
  - pathological
    - external 521.42
    - internal 521.41
    - specified NEC 521.49
- septic — *see* Septicemia
- teeth (roots) 521.40
  - pathological
    - external 521.42
    - internal 521.41
    - specified NEC 521.49

Respiration
- asymmetrical 786.09
- bronchial 786.09
- Cheyne-Stokes (periodic respiration) 786.04
- decreased, due to shock following injury 958.4
- disorder of 786.00
  - psychogenic 306.1
  - specified NEC 786.09
- failure 518.81
  - acute 518.81
  - acute and chronic 518.84
  - chronic 518.83
  - newborn 770.84
- insufficiency 786.09
  - acute 518.82
  - newborn NEC 770.89
- Kussmaul (air hunger) 786.09
- painful 786.52
- periodic 786.09
  - high altitude 327.22
- poor 786.09
  - newborn NEC 770.89
- sighing 786.7
  - psychogenic 306.1
- wheezing 786.07

Respiratory — *see also* condition
- distress 786.09
  - acute 518.82
  - fetus or newborn NEC 770.89
  - syndrome (newborn) 769
    - adult (following shock, surgery, or trauma) 518.5
      - specified NEC 518.82
- failure 518.81
  - acute 518.81
  - acute and chronic 518.84
  - chronic 518.83

Respiratory syncytial virus (RSV) 079.6
- bronchiolitis 466.11
- pneumonia 480.1
- vaccination, prophylactic (against) V04.82

Response
- photoallergic 692.72
- phototoxic 692.72

Restless legs syndrome (RLS) 333.94

Restlessness 799.2

Restoration of organ continuity from previous sterilization (tuboplasty) (vasoplasty) V26.0

Rest, rests
- mesonephric duct 752.89
  - fallopian tube 752.11
- ovarian, in fallopian tubes 752.19
- wolffian duct 752.89

Restriction of housing space V60.1

Restzustand, schizophrenic — *see also* Schizophrenia 295.6 ☑

Retained — *see* Retention

Retardation
- development, developmental, specific (*see also* Disorder, development, specific) 315.9
  - learning, specific 315.2
    - arithmetical 315.1
    - language (skills) 315.31
      - expressive 315.31
      - mixed receptive-expressive 315.32
    - mathematics 315.1
    - reading 315.00
      - phonological 315.39
    - written expression 315.2
  - motor 315.4
- endochondral bone growth 733.91
- growth (physical) in childhood 783.43
  - due to malnutrition 263.2
  - fetal (intrauterine) 764.9 ☑
    - affecting management of pregnancy 656.5 ☑
- intrauterine growth 764.9 ☑
  - affecting management of pregnancy 656.5 ☑
- mental 319
  - borderline V62.89
  - mild, IQ 50-70 317
  - moderate, IQ 35-49 318.0
  - profound, IQ under 20 318.2
  - severe, IQ 20-34 318.1
- motor, specific 315.4
- physical 783.43
  - child 783.43
  - due to malnutrition 263.2
  - fetus (intrauterine) 764.9 ☑
    - affecting management of pregnancy 656.5 ☑
- psychomotor NEC 307.9
- reading 315.00

Retching — *see* Vomiting

Retention, retained
- bladder (*see also* Retention, urine) 788.20
  - psychogenic 306.53
- carbon dioxide 276.2
- cholelithiasis 997.4 ●
- cyst — *see* Cyst
- dead
  - fetus (after 22 completed weeks gestation) 656.4 ☑
    - early fetal death (before 22 completed weeks gestation) 632
  - ovum 631
- decidua (following delivery) (fragments) (with hemorrhage) 666.2 ☑
  - without hemorrhage 667.1 ☑
- deciduous tooth 520.6
- dental root 525.3
- fecal (*see also* Constipation) 564.00
- fluid 276.6
- foreign body (*see also* Foreign body, retained)
  - bone 733.99
  - current trauma — *see* Foreign body, by site or type
  - middle ear 385.83
  - muscle 729.6
  - soft tissue NEC 729.6
- gallstones 997.4 ●
- gastric 536.8
- membranes (following delivery) (with hemorrhage) 666.2 ☑
  - with abortion — *see* Abortion, by type
  - without hemorrhage 667.1 ☑
- menses 626.8
- milk (puerperal) 676.2 ☑
- nitrogen, extrarenal 788.99 ▲
- placenta (total) (with hemorrhage) 666.0 ☑
  - with abortion — *see* Abortion, by type
  - without hemorrhage 667.0 ☑
  - portions or fragments 666.2 ☑
    - without hemorrhage 667.1 ☑

Retention, retained — *continued*
- products of conception
  - early pregnancy (fetal death before 22 completed weeks gestation) 632
  - following
    - abortion — *see* Abortion, by type
    - delivery 666.2 ☑
      - with hemorrhage 666.2 ☑
      - without hemorrhage 667.1 ☑
- secundines (following delivery) (with hemorrhage) 666.2 ☑
  - with abortion — *see* Abortion, by type
  - without hemorrhage 667.1 ☑
  - complicating puerperium (delayed hemorrhage) 666.2 ☑
- smegma, clitoris 624.8
- urine NEC 788.20
  - bladder, incomplete emptying 788.21
    - due to
      - benign prostatic hypertrophy (BPH) — see category 600
  - due to
    - benign prostatic hypertrophy (BPH) — see category 600
  - psychogenic 306.53
  - specified NEC 788.29
- water (in tissue) (*see also* Edema) 782.3

Reticulation, dust (occupational) 504

Reticulocytosis NEC 790.99

Reticuloendotheliosis
- acute infantile (M9722/3) 202.5 ☑
- leukemic (M9940/3) 202.4 ☑
- malignant (M9720/3) 202.3 ☑
- nonlipid (M9722/3) 202.5 ☑

Reticulohistiocytoma (giant cell) 277.89

Reticulohistiocytosis, multicentric 272.8

Reticulolymphosarcoma (diffuse) (M9613/3) 200.8 ☑
- follicular (M9691/3) 202.0 ☑
- nodular (M9691/3) 202.0 ☑

Reticulosarcoma (M9640/3) 200.0 ☑
- nodular (M9642/3) 200.0 ☑
- pleomorphic cell type (M9641/3) 200.0 ☑

Reticulosis (skin)
- acute of infancy (M9722/3) 202.5 ☑
- familial hemophagocytic 288.4
- histiocytic medullary (M9721/3) 202.3 ☑
- lipomelanotic 695.89
- malignant (M9720/3) 202.3 ☑
- Sézary's (M9701/3) 202.2 ☑

Retina, retinal — *see* condition

Retinitis — *see also* Chorioretinitis 363.20
- albuminurica 585.9 *[363.10]*
- arteriosclerotic 440.8 *[362.13]*
- central angiospastic 362.41
- Coat's 362.12
- diabetic 250.5 ☑ *[362.01]*
  - due to secondary diabetes 249.5 ☑ *[362.01]* ●
- disciformis 362.52
- disseminated 363.10
  - metastatic 363.14
  - neurosyphilitic 094.83
  - pigment epitheliopathy 363.15
- exudative 362.12
- focal 363.00
  - in histoplasmosis 115.92
    - capsulatum 115.02
    - duboisii 115.12
  - juxtapapillary 363.05
  - macular 363.06
  - paramacular 363.06
  - peripheral 363.08
  - posterior pole NEC 363.07
- gravidarum 646.8 ☑
- hemorrhagica externa 362.12

Retinitis — *see also* Chorioretinitis — *continued*
- juxtapapillary (Jensen's) 363.05
- luetic — *see* Retinitis, syphilitic
- metastatic 363.14
- pigmentosa 362.74
- proliferans 362.29
- proliferating 362.29
- punctata albescens 362.76
- renal 585.9 *[363.13]*
- syphilitic (secondary) 091.51
  - congenital 090.0 *[363.13]*
  - early 091.51
  - late 095.8 *[363.13]*
- syphilitica, central, recurrent 095.8 *[363.13]*
- tuberculous (*see also* Tuberculous) 017.3 ☑ *[363.13]*

Retinoblastoma (M9510/3) 190.5
- differentiated type (M9511/3) 190.5
- undifferentiated type (M9512/3) 190.5

Retinochoroiditis — *see also* Chorioretinitis 363.20
- central angiospastic 362.41
- disseminated 363.10
  - metastatic 363.14
  - neurosyphilitic 094.83
  - pigment epitheliopathy 363.15
  - syphilitic 094.83
- due to toxoplasmosis (acquired) (focal) 130.2
- focal 363.00
  - in histoplasmosis 115.92
    - capsulatum 115.02
    - duboisii 115.12
  - juxtapapillary (Jensen's) 363.05
  - macular 363.06
  - paramacular 363.06
  - peripheral 363.08
  - posterior pole NEC 363.07
- juxtapapillaris 363.05
- syphilitic (disseminated) 094.83

Retinopathy (background) 362.10
- arteriosclerotic 440.8 *[362.13]*
- atherosclerotic 440.8 *[362.13]*
- central serous 362.41
- circinate 362.10
- Coat's 362.12
- diabetic 250.5 ☑ *[362.01]*
  - due to secondary diabetes 249.5 ☑ *[362.01]* ●
  - nonproliferative 250.5 ☑ *[362.03]*
    - due to secondary diabetes 249.5 ☑ *[362.03]* ●
    - mild 250.5 ☑ *[362.04]*
      - due to secondary diabetes 249.5 ☑ *[362.04]* ●
    - moderate 250.5 ☑ *[362.05]*
      - due to secondary diabetes 249.5 ☑ *[362.05]* ●
    - severe 250.5 ☑ *[362.06]*
      - due to secondary diabetes 249.5 ☑ *[362.06]* ●
  - proliferative 250.5 ☑ *[362.02]*
    - due to secondary diabetes 249.5 ☑ *[362.02]* ●
- exudative 362.12
- hypertensive 362.11
- nonproliferative
  - diabetic 250.5 ☑ *[362.03]*
    - due to secondary diabetes 249.5 ☑ *[362.03]* ●
    - mild 250.5 ☑ *[362.04]*
      - due to secondary diabetes 249.5 ☑ *[362.04]* ●
    - moderate 250.5 ☑ *[362.05]*
      - due to secondary diabetes 249.5 ☑ *[362.05]* ●
    - severe 250.5 ☑ *[362.06]*
      - due to secondary diabetes 249.5 ☑ *[362.06]* ●
- of prematurity 362.20 ▲
  - cicatricial 362.21 ●
  - stage ●
    - 0 362.22 ●
    - 1 362.23 ●

Retinopathy — *continued*
of prematurity — *continued*
stage — *continued*
2 362.24 ●
3 362.25 ●
4 362.26 ●
5 362.27 ●
pigmentary, congenital 362.74
proliferative 362.29
diabetic 250.5 ☑ *[362.02]*
due to secondary diabetes 249.5 ☑ *[362.02]* ●
sickle-cell 282.60 *[362.29]*
solar 363.31
Retinoschisis 361.10
bullous 361.12
congenital 743.56
flat 361.11
juvenile 362.73
Retractile testis 752.52
Retraction
cervix — *see* Retraction, uterus
drum (membrane) 384.82
eyelid 374.41
finger 736.29
head 781.0
lid 374.41
lung 518.89
mediastinum 519.3
nipple 611.79
congenital 757.6
puerperal, postpartum 676.0 ☑
palmar fascia 728.6
pleura (*see also* Pleurisy) 511.0
ring, uterus (Bandl's) (pathological) 661.4 ☑
affecting fetus or newborn 763.7
sternum (congenital) 756.3
acquired 738.3
during respiration 786.9
substernal 738.3
supraclavicular 738.8
syndrome (Duane's) 378.71
uterus 621.6
valve (heart) — *see* Endocarditis
Retrobulbar — *see* condition
Retrocaval ureter 753.4
Retrocecal — *see also* condition
appendix (congenital) 751.5
Retrocession — *see* Retroversion
Retrodisplacement — *see* Retroversion
Retroflection, retroflexion — *see* Retroversion
Retrognathia, retrognathism (mandibular) (maxillary) 524.10
Retrograde
ejaculation 608.87
menstruation 626.8
Retroiliac ureter 753.4
Retroperineal — *see* condition
Retroperitoneal — *see* condition
Retroperitonitis 567.39
Retropharyngeal — *see* condition
Retroplacental — *see* condition
Retroposition — *see* Retroversion
Retrosternal thyroid (congenital) 759.2
Retroversion, retroverted
cervix — *see* Retroversion, uterus
female NEC (*see also* Retroversion, uterus) 621.6
iris 364.70
testis (congenital) 752.51
uterus, uterine (acquired) (acute) (adherent) (any degree) (asymptomatic) (cervix) (postinfectional) (postpartal, old) 621.6
congenital 752.3
in pregnancy or childbirth 654.3 ☑
affecting fetus or newborn 763.89
causing obstructed labor 660.2 ☑
affecting fetus or newborn 763.1
Retrusion, premaxilla (developmental) 524.04
Rett's syndrome 330.8
Reverse, reversed
peristalsis 787.4
Reye-Sheehan syndrome (postpartum pituitary necrosis) 253.2
Reye's syndrome 331.81
Rh (factor)
hemolytic disease 773.0
incompatibility, immunization, or sensitization
affecting management of pregnancy 656.1 ☑
fetus or newborn 773.0
transfusion reaction 999.7
negative mother, affecting fetus or newborn 773.0
titer elevated 999.7
transfusion reaction 999.7
Rhabdomyolysis (idiopathic) 728.88
Rhabdomyoma (M8900/0) — *see also* Neoplasm, connective tissue, benign
adult (M8904/0) — *see* Neoplasm, connective tissue, benign
fetal (M8903/0) — *see* Neoplasm, connective tissue, benign
glycogenic (M8904/0) — *see* Neoplasm, connective tissue, benign
Rhabdomyosarcoma (M8900/3) — *see also* Neoplasm, connective tissue, malignant
alveolar (M8920/3) — *see* Neoplasm, connective tissue, malignant
embryonal (M8910/3) — *see* Neoplasm, connective tissue, malignant
mixed type (M8902/3) — *see* Neoplasm, connective tissue, malignant
pleomorphic (M8901/3) — *see* Neoplasm, connective tissue, malignant
Rhabdosarcoma (M8900/3) — *see* Rhabdomyosarcoma
Rhesus (factor) (Rh) incompatibility — *see* Rh, incompatibility
Rheumaticosis — *see* Rheumatism
Rheumatism, rheumatic (acute NEC) 729.0
adherent pericardium 393
arthritis
acute or subacute — *see* Fever, rheumatic
chronic 714.0
spine 720.0
articular (chronic) NEC (*see also* Arthritis) 716.9 ☑
acute or subacute — *see* Fever, rheumatic
back 724.9
blennorrhagic 098.59
carditis — *see* Disease, heart, rheumatic
cerebral — *see* Fever, rheumatic
chorea (acute) — *see* Chorea, rheumatic
chronic NEC 729.0
coronary arteritis 391.9
chronic 398.99
degeneration, myocardium (*see also* Degeneration, myocardium, with rheumatic fever) 398.0
desert 114.0
febrile — *see* Fever, rheumatic
fever — *see* Fever, rheumatic
gonococcal 098.59
gout 274.0
heart
disease (*see also* Disease, heart, rheumatic) 398.90
failure (chronic) (congestive) (inactive) 398.91
hemopericardium — *see* Rheumatic, pericarditis
hydropericardium — *see* Rheumatic, pericarditis
Rheumatism, rheumatic — *continued*
inflammatory (acute) (chronic) (subacute) — *see* Fever, rheumatic
intercostal 729.0
meaning Tietze's disease 733.6
joint (chronic) NEC (*see also* Arthritis) 716.9 ☑
acute — *see* Fever, rheumatic
mediastinopericarditis — *see* Rheumatic, pericarditis
muscular 729.0
myocardial degeneration (*see also* Degeneration, myocardium, with rheumatic fever) 398.0
myocarditis (chronic) (inactive) (with chorea) 398.0
active or acute 391.2
with chorea (acute) (rheumatic) (Sydenham's) 392.0
myositis 729.1
neck 724.9
neuralgic 729.0
neuritis (acute) (chronic) 729.2
neuromuscular 729.0
nodose — *see* Arthritis, nodosa
nonarticular 729.0
palindromic 719.30
ankle 719.37
elbow 719.32
foot 719.37
hand 719.34
hip 719.35
knee 719.36
multiple sites 719.39
pelvic region 719.35
shoulder (region) 719.31
specified site NEC 719.38
wrist 719.33
pancarditis, acute 391.8
with chorea (acute) (rheumatic) (Sydenham's) 392.0
chronic or inactive 398.99
pericarditis (active) (acute) (with effusion) (with pneumonia) 391.0
with chorea (acute) (rheumatic) (Sydenham's) 392.0
chronic or inactive 393
pericardium — *see* Rheumatic, pericarditis
pleuropericarditis — *see* Rheumatic, pericarditis
pneumonia 390 *[517.1]*
pneumonitis 390 *[517.1]*
pneumopericarditis — *see* Rheumatic, pericarditis
polyarthritis
acute or subacute — *see* Fever, rheumatic
chronic 714.0
polyarticular NEC (*see also* Arthritis) 716.9 ☑
psychogenic 306.0
radiculitis 729.2
sciatic 724.3
septic — *see* Fever, rheumatic
spine 724.9
subacute NEC 729.0
torticollis 723.5
tuberculous NEC (*see also* Tuberculosis) 015.9 ☑
typhoid fever 002.0
Rheumatoid — *see also* condition
lungs 714.81
Rhinitis (atrophic) (catarrhal) (chronic) (croupous) (fibrinous) (hyperplastic) (hypertrophic) (membranous) (purulent) (suppurative) (ulcerative) 472.0
with
hay fever (*see also* Fever, hay) 477.9
with asthma (bronchial) 493.0 ☑
sore throat — *see* Nasopharyngitis
acute 460
Rhinitis — *continued*
allergic (nonseasonal) (seasonal) (*see also* Fever, hay) 477.9
with asthma (*see also* Asthma) 493.0 ☑
due to food 477.1
granulomatous 472.0
infective 460
obstructive 472.0
pneumococcal 460
syphilitic 095.8
congenital 090.0
tuberculous (*see also* Tuberculosis) 012.8 ☑
vasomotor (*see also* Fever, hay) 477.9
Rhinoantritis (chronic) 473.0
acute 461.0
Rhinodacryolith 375.57
Rhinolalia (aperta) (clausa) (open) 784.49
Rhinolith 478.19
nasal sinus (*see also* Sinusitis) 473.9
Rhinomegaly 478.19
Rhinopharyngitis (acute) (subacute) — *see also* Nasopharyngitis 460
chronic 472.2
destructive ulcerating 102.5
mutilans 102.5
Rhinophyma 695.3
Rhinorrhea 478.19
cerebrospinal (fluid) 349.81
paroxysmal (*see also* Fever, hay) 477.9
spasmodic (*see also* Fever, hay) 477.9
Rhinosalpingitis 381.50
acute 381.51
chronic 381.52
Rhinoscleroma 040.1
Rhinosporidiosis 117.0
Rhinovirus infection 079.3
Rhizomelic chrondrodysplasia punctata 277.86
Rhizomelique, pseudopolyarthritic 446.5
Rhoads and Bomford anemia (refractory) 238.72
Rhus
diversiloba dermatitis 692.6
radicans dermatitis 692.6
toxicodendron dermatitis 692.6
venenata dermatitis 692.6
verniciflua dermatitis 692.6
Rhythm
atrioventricular nodal 427.89
disorder 427.9
coronary sinus 427.89
ectopic 427.89
nodal 427.89
escape 427.89
heart, abnormal 427.9
fetus or newborn — *see* Abnormal, heart rate
idioventricular 426.89
accelerated 427.89
nodal 427.89
sleep, inversion 327.39
nonorganic origin 307.45
Rhytidosis facialis 701.8
Rib — *see also* condition
cervical 756.2
Riboflavin deficiency 266.0
Rice bodies — *see also* Loose, body, joint 718.1 ☑
knee 717.6
Richter's hernia — *see* Hernia, Richter's
Ricinism 988.2
Rickets (active) (acute) (adolescent) (adult) (chest wall) (congenital) (current) (infantile) (intestinal) 268.0
celiac 579.0
fetal 756.4
hemorrhagic 267
hypophosphatemic with nephrotic-glycosuric dwarfism 270.0
kidney 588.0
late effect 268.1
renal 588.0

- **Rickets** — *continued*
  - scurvy 267
  - vitamin D-resistant 275.3
- **Rickettsial disease** 083.9
  - specified type NEC 083.8
- **Rickettsialpox** 083.2
- **Rickettsiosis** NEC 083.9
  - specified type NEC 083.8
  - tick-borne 082.9
    - specified type NEC 082.8
  - vesicular 083.2
- **Ricord's chancre** 091.0
- **Riddoch's syndrome** (visual disorientation) 368.16
- **Rider's**
  - bone 733.99
  - chancre 091.0
- **Ridge, alveolus** — *see also* condition
  - edentulous
    - atrophy 525.20
      - mandible 525.20
        - minimal 525.21
        - moderate 525.22
        - severe 525.23
      - maxilla 525.20
        - minimal 525.24
        - moderate 525.25
        - severe 525.26
  - flabby 525.20
- **Ridged ear** 744.29
- **Riedel's**
  - disease (ligneous thyroiditis) 245.3
  - lobe, liver 751.69
  - struma (ligneous thyroiditis) 245.3
  - thyroiditis (ligneous) 245.3
- **Rieger's anomaly or syndrome** (mesodermal dysgenesis, anterior ocular segment) 743.44
- **Riehl's melanosis** 709.09
- **Rietti-Greppi-Micheli anemia or syndrome** 282.49
- **Rieux's hernia** — *see* Hernia, Rieux's
- **Rift Valley fever** 066.3
- **Riga's disease** (cachectic aphthae) 529.0
- **Riga-Fede disease** (cachectic aphthae) 529.0
- **Riggs' disease** (compound periodontitis) 523.40
- **Right middle lobe syndrome** 518.0
- **Rigid, rigidity** — *see also* condition
  - abdominal 789.4 ☑
  - articular, multiple congenital 754.89
  - back 724.8
  - cervix uteri
    - in pregnancy or childbirth 654.6 ☑
      - affecting fetus or newborn 763.89
      - causing obstructed labor 660.2 ☑
        - affecting fetus or newborn 763.1
  - hymen (acquired) (congenital) 623.3
  - nuchal 781.6
  - pelvic floor
    - in pregnancy or childbirth 654.4 ☑
      - affecting fetus or newborn 763.89
      - causing obstructed labor 660.2 ☑
        - affecting fetus or newborn 763.1
  - perineum or vulva
    - in pregnancy or childbirth 654.8 ☑
      - affecting fetus or newborn 763.89
      - causing obstructed labor 660.2 ☑
        - affecting fetus or newborn 763.1
  - spine 724.8
  - vagina
    - in pregnancy or childbirth 654.7 ☑
      - affecting fetus or newborn 763.89
      - causing obstructed labor 660.2 ☑
- **Rigid, rigidity** — *see also* condition — *continued*
  - vagina — *continued*
    - in pregnancy or childbirth — *continued*
      - causing obstructed labor — *continued*
        - affecting fetus or newborn 763.1
- **Rigors** 780.99
- **Riley-Day syndrome** (familial dysautonomia) 742.8
- **RIND** (reversible ischemic neurological deficit) 434.91
  - history of (personal) V12.54
- **Ring(s)**
  - aorta 747.21
  - Bandl's, complicating delivery 661.4 ☑
    - affecting fetus or newborn 763.7
  - contraction, complicating delivery 661.4 ☑
    - affecting fetus or newborn 763.7
  - esophageal (congenital) 750.3
  - Fleischer (-Kayser) (cornea) 275.1 *[371.14]*
  - hymenal, tight (acquired) (congenital) 623.3
  - Kayser-Fleischer (cornea) 275.1 *[371.14]*
  - retraction, uterus, pathological 661.4 ☑
    - affecting fetus or newborn 763.7
  - Schatzki's (esophagus) (congenital) (lower) 750.3
    - acquired 530.3
  - Soemmering's 366.51
  - trachea, abnormal 748.3
  - vascular (congenital) 747.21
  - Vossius' 921.3
    - late effect 366.21
- **Ringed hair** (congenital) 757.4
- **Ringing in the ear** — *see also* Tinnitus 388.30
- **Ringworm** 110.9
  - beard 110.0
  - body 110.5
  - Burmese 110.9
  - corporeal 110.5
  - foot 110.4
  - groin 110.3
  - hand 110.2
  - honeycomb 110.0
  - nails 110.1
  - perianal (area) 110.3
  - scalp 110.0
  - specified site NEC 110.8
  - Tokelau 110.5
- **Rise, venous pressure** 459.89
- **Risk**
  - factor — *see* Problem
  - falling
  - suicidal 300.9
- **Ritter's disease** (dermatitis exfoliativa neonatorum) 695.81
- **Rivalry, sibling** 313.3
- **Rivalta's disease** (cervicofacial actinomycosis) 039.3
- **River blindness** 125.3 *[360.13]*
- **Robert's pelvis** 755.69
  - with disproportion (fetopelvic) 653.0 ☑
    - affecting fetus or newborn 763.1
    - causing obstructed labor 660.1 ☑
      - affecting fetus or newborn 763.1
- **Robinson's** (hidrotic) **ectodermal dysplasia** 757.31
- **Robin's syndrome** 756.0
- **Robles' disease** (onchocerciasis) 125.3 *[360.13]*
- **Rochalimea** — *see* Rickettsial disease
- **Rocky Mountain fever** (spotted) 082.0
- **Rodent ulcer** (M8090/3) — *see also* Neoplasm, skin, malignant
  - cornea 370.07
- **Roentgen ray, adverse effect** — *see* Effect, adverse, x-ray
- **Roetheln** 056.9
- **Roger's disease** (congenital interventricular septal defect) 745.4
- **Rokitansky's**
  - disease (*see also* Necrosis, liver) 570
  - tumor 620.2
- **Rokitansky-Aschoff sinuses** (mucosal outpouching of gallbladder) — *see also* Disease, gallbladder 575.8
- **Rokitansky-Kuster-Hauser syndrome** (congenital absence vagina) 752.49
- **Rollet's chancre** (syphilitic) 091.0
- **Rolling of head** 781.0
- **Romano-Ward syndrome** (prolonged QT interval syndrome) 426.82
- **Romanus lesion** 720.1
- **Romberg's disease or syndrome** 349.89
- **Roof, mouth** — *see* condition
- **Rosacea** 695.3
  - acne 695.3
  - keratitis 695.3 *[370.49]*
- **Rosary, rachitic** 268.0
- **Rose**
  - cold 477.0
  - fever 477.0
  - rash 782.1
    - epidemic 056.9
    - of infants 057.8
- **Rosenbach's erysipelatoid or erysipeloid** 027.1
- **Rosen-Castleman-Liebow syndrome** (pulmonary proteinosis) 516.0
- **Rosenthal's disease** (factor XI deficiency) 286.2
- **Roseola** 057.8
  - infantum, infantilis (*see also* Exanthem subitum) 058.10
- **Rossbach's disease** (hyperchlorhydria) 536.8
  - psychogenic 306.4
- **Rössle-Urbach-Wiethe lipoproteinosis** 272.8
- **Ross river fever** 066.3
- **Rostan's asthma** (cardiac) — *see also* Failure, ventricular, left 428.1
- **Rot**
  - Barcoo (*see also* Ulcer, skin) 707.9
  - knife-grinders' (*see also* Tuberculosis) 011.4 ☑
- **Rotation**
  - anomalous, incomplete or insufficient — *see* Malrotation
  - cecum (congenital) 751.4
  - colon (congenital) 751.4
  - manual, affecting fetus or newborn 763.89
  - spine, incomplete or insufficient 737.8
  - tooth, teeth 524.35
  - vertebra, incomplete or insufficient 737.8
- **Rot-Bernhardt disease** 355.1
- **Röteln** 056.9
- **Roth-Bernhardt disease or syndrome** 355.1
- **Roth's disease or meralgia** 355.1
- **Rothmund (-Thomson) syndrome** 757.33
- **Rotor's disease or syndrome** (idiopathic hyperbilirubinemia) 277.4
- **Rotundum ulcus** — *see* Ulcer, stomach
- **Round**
  - back (with wedging of vertebrae) 737.10
    - late effect of rickets 268.1
  - hole, retina 361.31
    - with detachment 361.01
  - ulcer (stomach) — *see* Ulcer, stomach
  - worms (infestation) (large) NEC 127.0
- **Roussy-Lévy syndrome** 334.3
- **Routine postpartum follow-up** V24.2
- **Roy (-Jutras) syndrome** (acropachyderma) 757.39
- **Rubella** (German measles) 056.9
  - complicating pregnancy, childbirth, or puerperium 647.5 ☑
  - complication 056.8
    - neurological 056.00
- **Rubella** — *continued*
  - complication — *continued*
    - neurological — *continued*
      - encephalomyelitis 056.01
      - specified type NEC 056.09
    - specified type NEC 056.79
  - congenital 771.0
  - contact V01.4
  - exposure to V01.4
  - maternal
    - with suspected fetal damage affecting management of pregnancy 655.3 ☑
    - affecting fetus or newborn 760.2
      - manifest rubella in infant 771.0
  - specified complications NEC 056.79
  - vaccination, prophylactic (against) V04.3
- **Rubeola** (measles) — *see also* Measles 055.9
  - complicated 055.8
  - meaning rubella (*see also* Rubella) 056.9
  - scarlatinosis 057.8
- **Rubeosis iridis** 364.42
  - diabetica 250.5 ☑ *[364.42]*
    - due to secondary diabetes 249.5 ☑ *[364.42]* ●
- **Rubinstein-Taybi's syndrome** (brachydactylia, short stature and mental retardation) 759.89
- **Rudimentary** (congenital) — *see also* Agenesis
  - arm 755.22
  - bone 756.9
  - cervix uteri 752.49
  - eye (*see also* Microphthalmos) 743.10
  - fallopian tube 752.19
  - leg 755.32
  - lobule of ear 744.21
  - patella 755.64
  - respiratory organs in thoracopagus 759.4
  - tracheal bronchus 748.3
  - uterine horn 752.3
  - uterus 752.3
    - in male 752.7
    - solid or with cavity 752.3
  - vagina 752.49
- **Rud's syndrome** (mental deficiency, epilepsy, and infantilism) 759.89
- **Ruiter-Pompen (-Wyers) syndrome** (angiokeratoma corporis diffusum) 272.7
- **Ruled out condition** — *see also* Observation, suspected V71.9
- **Rumination** — *see also* Vomiting
  - disorder 307.53
  - neurotic 300.3
  - obsessional 300.3
  - psychogenic 307.53
- **Runaway reaction** — *see also* Disturbance, conduct
  - socialized 312.2 ☑
  - undersocialized, unsocialized 312.1 ☑
- **Runeberg's disease** (progressive pernicious anemia) 281.0
- **Runge's syndrome** (postmaturity) 766.22
- **Runny nose** 784.99
- **Rupia** 091.3
  - congenital 090.0
  - tertiary 095.9
- **Rupture, ruptured** 553.9
  - abdominal viscera NEC 799.89
    - obstetrical trauma 665.5 ☑
  - abscess (spontaneous) — *see* Abscess, by site
  - amnion — *see* Rupture, membranes
  - aneurysm — *see* Aneurysm
  - anus (sphincter) — *see* Laceration, anus
  - aorta, aortic 441.5
    - abdominal 441.3
    - arch 441.1
    - ascending 441.1

☑ Additional Digit Required — Refer to the Tabular List for Digit Selection
Subterms under main terms may continue to next column or page

Rupture, ruptured — *continued*
- aorta, aortic — *continued*
  - descending 441.5
    - abdominal 441.3
    - thoracic 441.1
  - syphilitic 093.0
  - thoracoabdominal 441.6
  - thorax, thoracic 441.1
  - transverse 441.1
  - traumatic (thoracic) 901.0
    - abdominal 902.0
  - valve or cusp (*see also* Endocarditis, aortic) 424.1
- appendix (with peritonitis) 540.0
  - with peritoneal abscess 540.1
  - traumatic — *see* Injury, internal, gastrointestinal tract
- arteriovenous fistula, brain (congenital) 430
- artery 447.2
  - brain (*see also* Hemorrhage, brain) 431
  - coronary (*see also* Infarct, myocardium) 410.9 ☑
  - heart (*see also* Infarct, myocardium) 410.9 ☑
  - pulmonary 417.8
  - traumatic (complication) (*see also* Injury, blood vessel, by site) 904.9
- bile duct, except cystic (*see also* Disease, biliary) 576.3
  - cystic 575.4
  - traumatic — *see* Injury, internal, intra-abdominal
- bladder (sphincter) 596.6
  - with
    - abortion — *see* Abortion, by type, with damage to pelvic organs
    - ectopic pregnancy (*see also* categories 633.0–633.9) 639.2
    - molar pregnancy (*see also* categories 630–632) 639.2
  - following
    - abortion 639.2
    - ectopic or molar pregnancy 639.2
  - nontraumatic 596.6
  - obstetrical trauma 665.5 ☑
  - spontaneous 596.6
  - traumatic — *see* Injury, internal, bladder
- blood vessel (*see also* Hemorrhage) 459.0
  - brain (*see also* Hemorrhage, brain) 431
  - heart (*see also* Infarct, myocardium) 410.9 ☑
  - traumatic (complication) (*see also* Injury, blood vessel, by site) 904.9
- bone — *see* Fracture, by site
- bowel 569.89
  - traumatic — *see* Injury, internal, intestine
- Bowman's membrane 371.31
- brain
  - aneurysm (congenital) (*see also* Hemorrhage, subarachnoid) 430
    - late effect — *see* Late effect(s) (of) cerebrovascular disease
    - syphilitic 094.87
  - hemorrhagic (*see also* Hemorrhage, brain) 431
  - injury at birth 767.0
  - syphilitic 094.89
- capillaries 448.9
- cardiac (*see also* Infarct, myocardium) 410.9 ☑
- cartilage (articular) (current) (*see also* Sprain, by site)
  - knee — *see* Tear, meniscus

Rupture, ruptured — *continued*
- cartilage (*see also* Sprain, by site) — *continued*
  - semilunar — *see* Tear, meniscus
- cecum (with peritonitis) 540.0
  - with peritoneal abscess 540.1
  - traumatic 863.89
    - with open wound into cavity 863.99
- cerebral aneurysm (congenital) (*see also* Hemorrhage, subarachnoid) 430
  - late effect — *see* Late effect(s) (of) cerebrovascular disease
- cervix (uteri)
  - with
    - abortion — *see* Abortion, by type, with damage to pelvic organs
    - ectopic pregnancy (*see also* categories 633.0–633.9) 639.2
    - molar pregnancy (*see also* categories 630–632) 639.2
  - following
    - abortion 639.2
    - ectopic or molar pregnancy 639.2
  - obstetrical trauma 665.3 ☑
  - traumatic — *see* Injury, internal, cervix
- chordae tendineae 429.5
- choroid (direct) (indirect) (traumatic) 363.63
- circle of Willis (*see also* Hemorrhage, subarachnoid) 430
  - late effect — *see* Late effect(s) (of) cerebrovascular disease
- colon 569.89
  - traumatic — *see* Injury, internal, colon
- cornea (traumatic) (*see also* Rupture, eye)
  - due to ulcer 370.00
- coronary (artery) (thrombotic) (*see also* Infarct, myocardium) 410.9 ☑
- corpus luteum (infected) (ovary) 620.1
- cyst — *see* Cyst
- cystic duct (*see also* Disease, gallbladder) 575.4
- Descemet's membrane 371.33
  - traumatic — *see* Rupture, eye
- diaphragm (*see also* Hernia, diaphragm)
  - traumatic — *see* Injury, internal, diaphragm
- diverticulum
  - bladder 596.3
  - intestine (large) (*see also* Diverticula) 562.10
    - small 562.00
- duodenal stump 537.89
- duodenum (ulcer) — *see* Ulcer, duodenum, with perforation
- ear drum (*see also* Perforation, tympanum) 384.20
  - with otitis media — *see* Otitis media
  - traumatic — *see* Wound, open, ear
- esophagus 530.4
  - traumatic 862.22
    - with open wound into cavity 862.32
    - cervical region — *see* Wound, open, esophagus
- eye (without prolapse of intraocular tissue) 871.0
  - with
    - exposure of intraocular tissue 871.1
    - partial loss of intraocular tissue 871.2
    - prolapse of intraocular tissue 871.1
  - due to burn 940.5
- fallopian tube 620.8

Rupture, ruptured — *continued*
- fallopian tube — *continued*
  - due to pregnancy — *see* Pregnancy, tubal
  - traumatic — *see* Injury, internal, fallopian tube
- fontanel 767.3
- free wall (ventricle) (*see also* Infarct, myocardium) 410.9 ☑
- gallbladder or duct (*see also* Disease, gallbladder) 575.4
  - traumatic — *see* Injury, internal, gallbladder
- gastric (*see also* Rupture, stomach) 537.89
  - vessel 459.0
- globe (eye) (traumatic) — *see* Rupture, eye
- graafian follicle (hematoma) 620.0
- heart (auricle) (ventricle) (*see also* Infarct, myocardium) 410.9 ☑
  - infectional 422.90
  - traumatic — *see* Rupture, myocardium, traumatic
- hymen 623.8
- internal
  - organ, traumatic (*see also* Injury, internal, by site)
    - heart — *see* Rupture, myocardium, traumatic
    - kidney — *see* Rupture, kidney
    - liver — *see* Rupture, liver
    - spleen — *see* Rupture, spleen, traumatic
  - semilunar cartilage — *see* Tear, meniscus
- intervertebral disc — *see* Displacement, intervertebral disc
  - traumatic (current) — *see* Dislocation, vertebra
- intestine 569.89
  - traumatic — *see* Injury, internal, intestine
- intracranial, birth injury 767.0
- iris 364.76
  - traumatic — *see* Rupture, eye
- joint capsule — *see* Sprain, by site
- kidney (traumatic) 866.03
  - with open wound into cavity 866.13
  - due to birth injury 767.8
  - nontraumatic 593.89
- lacrimal apparatus (traumatic) 870.2
- lens (traumatic) 366.20
- ligament (*see also* Sprain, by site)
  - with open wound — *see* Wound, open, by site
  - old (*see also* Disorder, cartilage, articular) 718.0 ☑
- liver (traumatic) 864.04
  - with open wound into cavity 864.14
  - due to birth injury 767.8
  - nontraumatic 573.8
- lymphatic (node) (vessel) 457.8
- marginal sinus (placental) (with hemorrhage) 641.2 ☑
  - affecting fetus or newborn 762.1
- meaning hernia — *see* Hernia
- membrana tympani (*see also* Perforation, tympanum) 384.20
  - with otitis media — *see* Otitis media
  - traumatic — *see* Wound, open, ear
- membranes (spontaneous)
  - artificial
    - delayed delivery following 658.3 ☑
      - affecting fetus or newborn 761.1
    - fetus or newborn 761.1
  - delayed delivery following 658.2 ☑
    - affecting fetus or newborn 761.1
  - premature (less than 24 hours prior to onset of labor) 658.1 ☑
    - affecting fetus or newborn 761.1

Rupture, ruptured — *continued*
- membranes — *continued*
  - premature — *continued*
    - delayed delivery following 658.2 ☑
      - affecting fetus or newborn 761.1
- meningeal artery (*see also* Hemorrhage, subarachnoid) 430
  - late effect — *see* Late effect(s) (of) cerebrovascular disease
- meniscus (knee) (*see also* Tear, meniscus)
  - old (*see also* Derangement, meniscus) 717.5
    - site other than knee — *see* Disorder, cartilage, articular
  - site other than knee — *see* Sprain, by site
- mesentery 568.89
  - traumatic — *see* Injury, internal, mesentery
- mitral — *see* Insufficiency, mitral
- muscle (traumatic) NEC (*see also* Sprain, by site)
  - with open wound — *see* Wound, open, by site
  - nontraumatic 728.83
- musculotendinous cuff (nontraumatic) (shoulder) 840.4
- mycotic aneurysm, causing cerebral hemorrhage (*see also* Hemorrhage, subarachnoid) 430
  - late effect — *see* Late effect(s) (of) cerebrovascular disease
- myocardium, myocardial (*see also* Infarct, myocardium) 410.9 ☑
  - traumatic 861.03
    - with open wound into thorax 861.13
- nontraumatic (meaning hernia) (*see also* Hernia, by site) 553.9
- obstructed (*see also* Hernia, by site, with obstruction) 552.9
  - gangrenous (*see also* Hernia, by site, with gangrene) 551.9
- operation wound ▶(*see also* Dehiscence)◀ 998.32
  - internal 998.31
- ovary, ovarian 620.8
  - corpus luteum 620.1
  - follicle (graafian) 620.0
- oviduct 620.8
  - due to pregnancy — *see* Pregnancy, tubal
- pancreas 577.8
  - traumatic — *see* Injury, internal, pancreas
- papillary muscle (ventricular) 429.6
- pelvic
  - floor, complicating delivery 664.1 ☑
  - organ NEC — *see* Injury, pelvic, organs
- penis (traumatic) — *see* Wound, open, penis
- perineum 624.8
  - during delivery (*see also* Laceration, perineum, complicating delivery) 664.4 ☑
- pharynx (nontraumatic) (spontaneous) 478.29
- pregnant uterus (before onset of labor) 665.0 ☑
- prostate (traumatic) — *see* Injury, internal, prostate
- pulmonary
  - artery 417.8
  - valve (heart) (*see also* Endocarditis, pulmonary) 424.3
  - vein 417.8
  - vessel 417.8
- pupil, sphincter 364.75
- pus tube (*see also* Salpingo-oophoritis) 614.2

Rupture, ruptured — *continued*
pyosalpinx (*see also* Salpingo-oophoritis) 614.2
rectum 569.49
traumatic — *see* Injury, internal, rectum
retina, retinal (traumatic) (without detachment) 361.30
with detachment (*see also* Detachment, retina, with retinal defect) 361.00
rotator cuff (capsule) (traumatic) 840.4
nontraumatic, complete 727.61
sclera 871.0
semilunar cartilage, knee (*see also* Tear, meniscus) 836.2
old (*see also* Derangement, meniscus) 717.5
septum (cardiac) 410.8 ☑
sigmoid 569.89
traumatic — *see* Injury, internal, colon, sigmoid
sinus of Valsalva 747.29
spinal cord (*see also* Injury, spinal, by site)
due to injury at birth 767.4
fetus or newborn 767.4
syphilitic 094.89
traumatic (*see also* Injury, spinal, by site)
with fracture — *see* Fracture, vertebra, by site, with spinal cord injury
spleen 289.59
congenital 767.8
due to injury at birth 767.8
malarial 084.9
nontraumatic 289.59
spontaneous 289.59
traumatic 865.04
with open wound into cavity 865.14
splenic vein 459.0
stomach 537.89
due to injury at birth 767.8
traumatic — *see* Injury, internal, stomach
ulcer — *see* Ulcer, stomach, with perforation
synovium 727.50
specified site NEC 727.59
tendon (traumatic) (*see also* Sprain, by site)

Rupture, ruptured — *continued*
tendon (*see also* Sprain, by site) — *continued*
with open wound — *see* Wound, open, by site
Achilles 845.09
nontraumatic 727.67
ankle 845.09
nontraumatic 727.68
biceps (long bead) 840.8
nontraumatic 727.62
foot 845.10
interphalangeal (joint) 845.13
metatarsophalangeal (joint) 845.12
nontraumatic 727.68
specified site NEC 845.19
tarsometatarsal (joint) 845.11
hand 842.10
carpometacarpal (joint) 842.11
interphalangeal (joint) 842.13
metacarpophalangeal (joint) 842.12
nontraumatic 727.63
extensors 727.63
flexors 727.64
specified site NEC 842.19
nontraumatic 727.60
specified site NEC 727.69
patellar 844.8
nontraumatic 727.66
quadriceps 844.8
nontraumatic 727.65
rotator cuff (capsule) 840.4
nontraumatic, complete 727.61
wrist 842.00
carpal (joint) 842.01
nontraumatic 727.63
extensors 727.63
flexors 727.64
radiocarpal (joint) (ligament) 842.02
radioulnar (joint), distal 842.09
specified site NEC 842.09
testis (traumatic) 878.2
complicated 878.3
due to syphilis 095.8
thoracic duct 457.8
tonsil 474.8
traumatic
with open wound — *see* Wound, open, by site
aorta — *see* Rupture, aorta, traumatic

Rupture, ruptured — *continued*
traumatic — *continued*
ear drum — *see* Wound, open, ear, drum
external site — *see* Wound, open, by site
eye 871.2
globe (eye) — *see* Wound, open, eyeball
internal organ (abdomen, chest, or pelvis) (*see also* Injury, internal, by site)
heart — *see* Rupture, myocardium, traumatic
kidney — *see* Rupture, kidney
liver — *see* Rupture, liver
spleen — *see* Rupture, spleen, traumatic
ligament, muscle, or tendon (*see also* Sprain, by site)
with open wound — *see* Wound, open, by site
meaning hernia — *see* Hernia
tricuspid (heart) (valve) — *see* Endocarditis, tricuspid
tube, tubal 620.8
abscess (*see also* Salpingo-oophoritis) 614.2
due to pregnancy — *see* Pregnancy, tubal
tympanum, tympanic (membrane) (*see also* Perforation, tympanum) 384.20
with otitis media — *see* Otitis media
traumatic — *see* Wound, open, ear, drum
umbilical cord 663.8 ☑
fetus or newborn 772.0
ureter (traumatic) (*see also* Injury, internal, ureter) 867.2
nontraumatic 593.89
urethra 599.84
with
abortion — *see* Abortion, by type, with damage to pelvic organs
ectopic pregnancy (*see also* categories 633.0–633.9) 639.2
molar pregnancy (*see also* categories 630–632) 639.2
following
abortion 639.2

Rupture, ruptured — *continued*
urethra — *continued*
following — *continued*
ectopic or molar pregnancy 639.2
obstetrical trauma 665.5 ☑
traumatic — *see* Injury, internal urethra
uterosacral ligament 620.8
uterus (traumatic) (*see also* Injury, internal uterus)
affecting fetus or newborn 763.89
during labor 665.1 ☑
nonpuerperal, nontraumatic 621.8
nontraumatic 621.8
pregnant (during labor) 665.1 ☑
before labor 665.0 ☑
vagina 878.6
complicated 878.7
complicating delivery — *see* Laceration, vagina, complicating delivery
valve, valvular (heart) — *see* Endocarditis
varicose vein — *see* Varicose, vein
varix — *see* Varix
vena cava 459.0
ventricle (free wall) (left) (*see also* Infarct, myocardium) 410.9 ☑
vesical (urinary) 596.6
traumatic — *see* Injury, internal, bladder
vessel (blood) 459.0
pulmonary 417.8
viscus 799.89
vulva 878.4
complicated 878.5
complicating delivery 664.0 ☑
Russell's dwarf (uterine dwarfism and craniofacial dysostosis) 759.89
Russell's dysentery 004.8
Russell (-Silver) syndrome (congenital hemihypertrophy and short stature) 759.89
Russian spring-summer type encephalitis 063.0
Rust's disease (tuberculous spondylitis) 015.0 ☑ *[720.81]*
Rustitskii's disease (multiple myeloma) (M9730/3) 203.0 ☑
Ruysch's disease (Hirschsprung's disease) 751.3
Rytand-Lipsitch syndrome (complete atrioventricular block) 426.0

S

Saber
shin 090.5
tibia 090.5
Saccharomyces infection — *see also* Candidiasis 112.9
Saccharopinuria 270.7
Saccular — *see* condition
Sacculation
aorta (nonsyphilitic) (*see also* Aneurysm, aorta) 441.9
ruptured 441.5
syphilitic 093.0
bladder 596.3
colon 569.89
intralaryngeal (congenital) (ventricular) 748.3
larynx (congenital) (ventricular) 748.3
organ or site, congenital — *see* Distortion
pregnant uterus, complicating delivery 654.4 ☑
affecting fetus or newborn 763.1
causing obstructed labor 660.2 ☑
affecting fetus or newborn 763.1
rectosigmoid 569.89
sigmoid 569.89
ureter 593.89
urethra 599.2
vesical 596.3
Sachs (-Tay) disease (amaurotic familial idiocy) 330.1
Sacks-Libman disease 710.0 *[424.91]*
Sac, lacrimal — *see* condition
Sacralgia 724.6
Sacralization
fifth lumbar vertebra 756.15
incomplete (vertebra) 756.15
Sacrodynia 724.6
Sacroiliac joint — *see* condition
Sacroiliitis NEC 720.2
Sacrum — *see* condition
Saddle
back 737.8
embolus, aorta 444.0
nose 738.0
congenital 754.0
due to syphilis 090.5
Sadism (sexual) 302.84
Saemisch's ulcer 370.04
Saenger's syndrome 379.46
Sago spleen 277.39
Sailors' skin 692.74
Saint
Anthony's fire (*see also* Erysipelas) 035
Guy's dance — *see* Chorea
Louis-type encephalitis 062.3
triad (*see also* Hernia, diaphragm) 553.3
Vitus' dance — *see* Chorea
Salicylism
correct substance properly administered 535.4 ☑
overdose or wrong substance given or taken 965.1
Salivary duct or gland — *see also* condition
virus disease 078.5
Salivation (excessive) — *see also* Ptyalism 527.7
Salmonella (aertrycke) (choleraesuis) (enteritidis) (gallinarum) (suipestifer) (typhimurium) — *see also* Infection, Salmonella 003.9
arthritis 003.23
carrier (suspected) of V02.3
meningitis 003.21
osteomyelitis 003.24
pneumonia 003.22
septicemia 003.1
typhosa 002.0
carrier (suspected) of V02.1
Salmonellosis 003.0
Salmonellosis — *continued*
with pneumonia 003.22
Salpingitis (catarrhal) (fallopian tube) (nodular) (pseudofollicular) (purulent) (septic) — *see also* Salpingo-oophoritis 614.2
ear 381.50
acute 381.51
chronic 381.52
Eustachian (tube) 381.50
acute 381.51
chronic 381.52
follicularis 614.1
gonococcal (chronic) 098.37
acute 098.17
interstitial, chronic 614.1
isthmica nodosa 614.1
old — *see* Salpingo-oophoritis, chronic
puerperal, postpartum, childbirth 670.0 ☑
specific (chronic) 098.37
acute 098.17
tuberculous (acute) (chronic) (*see also* Tuberculosis) 016.6 ☑
venereal (chronic) 098.37
acute 098.17
Salpingocele 620.4
Salpingo-oophoritis (catarrhal) (purulent) (ruptured) (septic) (suppurative) 614.2
acute 614.0
with
abortion — *see* Abortion, by type, with sepsis
ectopic pregnancy (*see also* categories 633.0–633.9) 639.0
molar pregnancy (*see also* categories 630–632) 639.0
following
abortion 639.0
ectopic or molar pregnancy 639.0
gonococcal 098.17
puerperal, postpartum, childbirth 670.0 ☑
tuberculous (*see also* Tuberculosis) 016.6 ☑
chronic 614.1
gonococcal 098.37
tuberculous (see also Tuberculosis) 016.6 ☑
complicating pregnancy 646.6 ☑
affecting fetus or newborn 760.8
gonococcal (chronic) 098.37
acute 098.17
old — *see* Salpingo-oophoritis, chronic
puerperal 670.0 ☑
specific — *see* Salpingo-oophoritis, gonococcal
subacute (*see also* Salpingo-oophoritis, acute) 614.0
tuberculous (acute) (chronic) (*see also* Tuberculosis) 016.6 ☑
venereal — *see* Salpingo-oophoritis, gonococcal
Salpingo-ovaritis — *see also* Salpingo-oophoritis 614.2
Salpingoperitonitis — *see also* Salpingo-oophoritis 614.2
Salt-losing
nephritis (*see also* Disease, renal) 593.9
syndrome (*see also* Disease, renal) 593.9
Salt-rheum — *see also* Eczema 692.9
Salzmann's nodular dystrophy 371.46
Sampling ●
chorionic villus V28.89 ●
Sampson's cyst or tumor 617.1
Sandblasters'
asthma 502
lung 502
Sander's disease (paranoia) 297.1
Sandfly fever 066.0
Sandhoff's disease 330.1
Sanfilippo's syndrome (mucopolysaccharidosis III) 277.5
Sanger-Brown's ataxia 334.2
San Joaquin Valley fever 114.0
Sao Paulo fever or typhus 082.0
Saponification, mesenteric 567.89
Sapremia — *see* Septicemia
Sarcocele (benign)
syphilitic 095.8
congenital 090.5
Sarcoepiplocele — *see also* Hernia 553.9
Sarcoepiplomphalocele — *see also* Hernia, umbilicus 553.1
Sarcoid (any site) 135
with lung involvement 135 *[517.8]*
Boeck's 135
Darier-Roussy 135
Spiegler-Fendt 686.8
Sarcoidosis 135
cardiac 135 *[425.8]*
lung 135 *[517.8]*
Sarcoma (M8800/3) — *see also* Neoplasm, connective tissue, malignant
alveolar soft part (M9581/3) — *see* Neoplasm, connective tissue, malignant
ameloblastic (M9330/3) 170.1
upper jaw (bone) 170.0
botryoid (M8910/3) — *see* Neoplasm, connective tissue, malignant
botryoides (M8910/3) — *see* Neoplasm, connective tissue, malignant
cerebellar (M9480/3) 191.6
circumscribed (arachnoidal) (M9471/3) 191.6
circumscribed (arachnoidal) cerebellar (M9471/3) 191.6
clear cell, of tendons and aponeuroses (M9044/3) — *see* Neoplasm, connective tissue, malignant
embryonal (M8991/3) — *see* Neoplasm, connective tissue, malignant
endometrial (stromal) (M8930/3) 182.0
isthmus 182.1
endothelial (M9130/3) (*see also* Neoplasm, connective tissue, malignant)
bone (M9260/3) — *see* Neoplasm, bone, malignant
epithelioid cell (M8804/3) — *see* Neoplasm, connective tissue, malignant
Ewing's (M9260/3) — *see* Neoplasm, bone, malignant
follicular dendritic cell 202.9 ☑
germinoblastic (diffuse) (M9632/3) 202.8 ☑
follicular (M9697/3) 202.0 ☑
giant cell (M8802/3) (*see also* Neoplasm, connective tissue, malignant)
bone (M9250/3) — *see* Neoplasm, bone, malignant
glomoid (M8710/3) — *see* Neoplasm, connective tissue, malignant
granulocytic (M9930/3) 205.3 ☑
hemangioendothelial (M9130/3) — *see* Neoplasm, connective tissue, malignant
hemorrhagic, multiple (M9140/3) — *see* Kaposi's, sarcoma
Hodgkin's (M9662/3) 201.2 ☑
immunoblastic (M9612/3) 200.8 ☑
interdigitating dendritic cell 202.9 ☑
Kaposi's (M9140/3) — *see* Kaposi's, sarcoma
Kupffer cell (M9124/3) 155.0
Langerhans cell 202.9 ☑
leptomeningeal (M9530/3) — *see* Neoplasm, meninges, malignant
Sarcoma — *see also* Neoplasm, connective tissue, malignant — *continued*
lymphangioendothelial (M9170/3) — *see* Neoplasm, connective tissue, malignant
lymphoblastic (M9630/3) 200.1 ☑
lymphocytic (M9620/3) 200.1 ☑
mast cell (M9740/3) 202.6 ☑
melanotic (M8720/3) — *see* Melanoma
meningeal (M9530/3) — *see* Neoplasm, meninges, malignant
meningothelial (M9530/3) — *see* Neoplasm, meninges, malignant
mesenchymal (M8800/3) (*see also* Neoplasm, connective tissue, malignant)
mixed (M8990/3) — *see* Neoplasm, connective tissue, malignant
mesothelial (M9050/3) — *see* Neoplasm, by site, malignant
monstrocellular (M9481/3)
specified site — *see* Neoplasm, by site, malignant
unspecified site 191.9
myeloid (M9930/3) 205.3 ☑
neurogenic (M9540/3) — *see* Neoplasm, connective tissue, malignant
odontogenic (M9270/3) 170.1
upper jaw (bone) 170.0
osteoblastic (M9180/3) — *see* Neoplasm, bone, malignant
osteogenic (M9180/3) (*see also* Neoplasm, bone, malignant)
juxtacortical (M9190/3) — *see* Neoplasm, bone, malignant
periosteal (M9190/3) — *see* Neoplasm, bone, malignant
periosteal (M8812/3) (*see also* Neoplasm, bone, malignant)
osteogenic (M9190/3) — *see* Neoplasm, bone, malignant
plasma cell (M9731/3) 203.8 ☑
pleomorphic cell (M8802/3) — *see* Neoplasm, connective tissue, malignant
reticuloendothelial (M9720/3) 202.3 ☑
reticulum cell (M9640/3) 200.0 ☑
nodular (M9642/3) 200.0 ☑
pleomorphic cell type (M9641/3) 200.0 ☑
round cell (M8803/3) — *see* Neoplasm, connective tissue, malignant
small cell (M8803/3) — *see* Neoplasm, connective tissue, malignant
spindle cell (M8801/3) — *see* Neoplasm, connective tissue, malignant
stromal (endometrial) (M8930/3) 182.0
isthmus 182.1
synovial (M9040/3) (*see also* Neoplasm, connective tissue, malignant)
biphasic type (M9043/3) — *see* Neoplasm, connective tissue, malignant
epithelioid cell type (M9042/3) — *see* Neoplasm, connective tissue, malignant
spindle cell type (M9041/3) — *see* Neoplasm, connective tissue, malignant
Sarcomatosis
meningeal (M9539/3) — *see* Neoplasm, meninges, malignant
specified site NEC (M8800/3) — *see* Neoplasm, connective tissue, malignant
unspecified site (M8800/6) 171.9
Sarcosinemia 270.8
Sarcosporidiosis 136.5
Satiety, early 780.94

- **Satisfactory smear but lacking transformation zone** ●
  - anal 796.77 ●
  - cervical 795.07 ●
- **Saturnine** — *see* condition
- **Saturnism** 984.9
  - specified type of lead — *see* Table of Drugs and Chemicals
- **Satyriasis** 302.89
- **Sauriasis** — *see* Ichthyosis
- **Sauriderma** 757.39
- **Sauriosis** — *see* Ichthyosis
- **Savill's disease** (epidemic exfoliative dermatitis) 695.89
- **SBE** (subacute bacterial endocarditis) 421.0
- **Scabies** (any site) 133.0
- **Scabs** 782.8
- **Scaglietti-Dagnini syndrome** (acromegalic macrospondylitis) 253.0
- **Scald, scalded** — *see also* Burn, by site
  - skin syndrome 695.81 ▲
- **Scalenus anticus (anterior) syndrome** 353.0
- **Scales** 782.8
- **Scalp** — *see* condition
- **Scaphocephaly** 756.0
- **Scaphoiditis, tarsal** 732.5
- **Scapulalgia** 733.90
- **Scapulohumeral myopathy** 359.1
- **Scarabiasis** 134.1
- **Scarlatina** 034.1
  - anginosa 034.1
  - maligna 034.1
  - myocarditis, acute 034.1 *[422.0]*
    - old (*see also* Myocarditis) 429.0
  - otitis media 034.1 *[382.02]*
  - ulcerosa 034.1
- **Scarlatinella** 057.8
- **Scarlet fever** (albuminuria) (angina) (convulsions) (lesions of lid) (rash) 034.1
- **Scar, scarring** — *see also* Cicatrix 709.2
  - adherent 709.2
  - atrophic 709.2
  - cervix
    - in pregnancy or childbirth 654.6 ☑
      - affecting fetus or newborn 763.89
      - causing obstructed labor 660.2 ☑
        - affecting fetus or newborn 763.1
  - cheloid 701.4
  - chorioretinal 363.30
    - disseminated 363.35
    - macular 363.32
    - peripheral 363.34
    - posterior pole NEC 363.33
  - choroid (*see also* Scar, chorioretinal) 363.30
  - compression, pericardial 423.9
  - congenital 757.39
  - conjunctiva 372.64
  - cornea 371.00
    - xerophthalmic 264.6
  - due to previous cesarean delivery, complicating pregnancy or childbirth 654.2 ☑
    - affecting fetus or newborn 763.89
  - duodenal (bulb) (cap) 537.3
  - hypertrophic 701.4
  - keloid 701.4
  - labia 624.4
  - lung (base) 518.89
  - macula 363.32
    - disseminated 363.35
    - peripheral 363.34
  - muscle 728.89
  - myocardium, myocardial 412
  - painful 709.2
  - papillary muscle 429.81
  - posterior pole NEC 363.33
    - macular — *see* Scar, macula
  - postnecrotic (hepatic) (liver) 571.9
  - psychic V15.49

- **Scar, scarring** — *see also* Cicatrix — *continued*
  - retina (*see also* Scar, chorioretinal) 363.30
  - trachea 478.9
  - uterus 621.8
    - in pregnancy or childbirth NEC 654.9 ☑
      - affecting fetus or newborn 763.89
      - due to previous cesarean delivery 654.2 ☑
  - vulva 624.4
- **Schamberg's disease, dermatitis, or dermatosis** (progressive pigmentary dermatosis) 709.09
- **Schatzki's ring** (esophagus) (lower) (congenital) 750.3
  - acquired 530.3
- **Schaufenster krankheit** 413.9
- **Schaumann's**
  - benign lymphogranulomatosis 135
  - disease (sarcoidosis) 135
  - syndrome (sarcoidosis) 135
- **Scheie's syndrome** (mucopolysaccharidosis IS) 277.5
- **Schenck's disease** (sporotrichosis) 117.1
- **Scheuermann's disease or osteochondrosis** 732.0
- **Scheuthauer-Marie-Sainton syndrome** (cleidocranialis dysostosis) 755.59
- **Schilder (-Flatau) disease** 341.1
- **Schilling-type monocytic leukemia** (M9890/3) 206.9 ☑
- **Schimmelbusch's disease, cystic mastitis, or hyperplasia** 610.1
- **Schirmer's syndrome** (encephalocutaneous angiomatosis) 759.6
- **Schistocelia** 756.79
- **Schistoglossia** 750.13
- **Schistosoma infestation** — *see* Infestation, Schistosoma
- **Schistosomiasis** 120.9
  - Asiatic 120.2
  - bladder 120.0
  - chestermani 120.8
  - colon 120.1
  - cutaneous 120.3
  - due to
    - S. hematobium 120.0
    - S. japonicum 120.2
    - S. mansoni 120.1
    - S. mattheii 120.8
  - eastern 120.2
  - genitourinary tract 120.0
  - intestinal 120.1
  - lung 120.2
  - Manson's (intestinal) 120.1
  - Oriental 120.2
  - pulmonary 120.2
  - specified type NEC 120.8
  - vesical 120.0
- **Schizencephaly** 742.4
- **Schizo-affective psychosis** — *see also* Schizophrenia 295.7 ☑
- **Schizodontia** 520.2
- **Schizoid personality** 301.20
  - introverted 301.21
  - schizotypal 301.22
- **Schizophrenia, schizophrenic** (reaction) 295.9 ☑

> *Note — Use the following fifth-digit subclassification with category 295:*
>
> 0 *unspecified*
>
> 1 *subchronic*
>
> 2 *chronic*
>
> 3 *subchronic with acute exacerbation*
>
> 4 *chronic with acute exacerbation*
>
> 5 *in remission*

  - acute (attack) NEC 295.8 ☑
    - episode 295.4 ☑
  - atypical form 295.8 ☑

- **Schizophrenia, schizophrenic** — *continued*
  - borderline 295.5 ☑
  - catalepsy 295.2 ☑
  - catatonic (type) (acute) (excited) (withdrawn) 295.2 ☑
  - childhood (type) (*see also* Psychosis, childhood) 299.9 ☑
  - chronic NEC 295.6 ☑
  - coenesthesiopathic 295.8 ☑
  - cyclic (type) 295.7 ☑
  - disorganized (type) 295.1 ☑
  - flexibilitas cerea 295.2 ☑
  - hebephrenic (type) (acute) 295.1 ☑
  - incipient 295.5 ☑
  - latent 295.5 ☑
  - paranoid (type) (acute) 295.3 ☑
  - paraphrenic (acute) 295.3 ☑
  - prepsychotic 295.5 ☑
  - primary (acute) 295.0 ☑
  - prodromal 295.5 ☑
  - pseudoneurotic 295.5 ☑
  - pseudopsychopathic 295.5 ☑
  - reaction 295.9 ☑
  - residual type (state) 295.6 ☑
  - restzustand 295.6 ☑
  - schizo-affective (type) (depressed) (excited) 295.7 ☑
  - schizophreniform type 295.4 ☑
  - simple (type) (acute) 295.0 ☑
  - simplex (acute) 295.0 ☑
  - specified type NEC 295.8 ☑
  - syndrome of childhood NEC (*see also* Psychosis, childhood) 299.9 ☑
  - undifferentiated type 295.9 ☑
    - acute 295.8 ☑
    - chronic 295.6 ☑
- **Schizothymia** 301.20
  - introverted 301.21
  - schizotypal 301.22
- **Schlafkrankheit** 086.5
- **Schlatter-Osgood disease** (osteochondrosis, tibial tubercle) 732.4
- **Schlatter's tibia** (osteochondrosis) 732.4
- **Schloffer's tumor** — *see also* Peritonitis 567.29
- **Schmidt's syndrome**
  - sphallo-pharyngo-laryngeal hemiplegia 352.6
  - thyroid-adrenocortical insufficiency 258.1
  - vagoaccessory 352.6
- **Schmincke**
  - carcinoma (M8082/3) — *see* Neoplasm, nasopharynx, malignant
  - tumor (M8082/3) — *see* Neoplasm, nasopharynx, malignant
- **Schmitz (-Stutzer) dysentery** 004.0
- **Schmorl's disease or nodes** 722.30
  - lumbar, lumbosacral 722.32
  - specified region NEC 722.39
  - thoracic, thoracolumbar 722.31
- **Schneiderian**
  - carcinoma (M8121/3)
    - specified site — *see* Neoplasm, by site, malignant
    - unspecified site 160.0
  - papilloma (M8121/0)
    - specified site — *see* Neoplasm, by site, benign
    - unspecified site 212.0
- **Schneider's syndrome** 047.9
- **Schnitzler syndrome** 273.1
- **Schoffer's tumor** — *see also* Peritonitis 567.29
- **Scholte's syndrome** (malignant carcinoid) 259.2
- **Scholz's disease** 330.0
- **Scholz (-Bielschowsky-Henneberg) syndrome** 330.0
- **Schönlein (-Henoch) disease** (primary) (purpura) (rheumatic) 287.0
- **School examination** V70.3
- **Schottmüller's disease** — *see also* Fever, paratyphoid 002.9

- **Schroeder's syndrome** (endocrine-hypertensive) 255.3
- **Schüller-Christian disease or syndrome** (chronic histiocytosis X) 277.89
- **Schultz's disease or syndrome** (agranulocytosis) 288.09
- **Schultze's acroparesthesia, simple** 443.89
- **Schwalbe-Ziehen-Oppenheimer disease** 333.6
- **Schwannoma** (M9560/0) — *see also* Neoplasm, connective tissue, benign
  - malignant (M9560/3) — *see* Neoplasm, connective tissue, malignant
- **Schwartz-Bartter syndrome** (inappropriate secretion of antidiuretic hormone) 253.6
- **Schwartz (-Jampel) syndrome** 359.23
- **Schweninger-Buzzi disease** (macular atrophy) 701.3
- **Sciatic** — *see* condition
- **Sciatica** (infectional) 724.3
  - due to
    - displacement of intervertebral disc 722.10
    - herniation, nucleus pulposus 722.10
  - wallet 724.3
- **Scimitar syndrome** (anomalous venous drainage, right lung to inferior vena cava) 747.49
- **Sclera** — *see* condition
- **Sclerectasia** 379.11
- **Scleredema**
  - adultorum 710.1
  - Buschke's 710.1
  - newborn 778.1
- **Sclerema**
  - adiposum (newborn) 778.1
  - adultorum 710.1
  - edematosum (newborn) 778.1
  - neonatorum 778.1
  - newborn 778.1
- **Scleriasis** — *see* Scleroderma
- **Scleritis** 379.00
  - with corneal involvement 379.05
  - anterior (annular) (localized) 379.03
  - brawny 379.06
  - granulomatous 379.09
  - posterior 379.07
  - specified NEC 379.09
  - suppurative 379.09
  - syphilitic 095.0
  - tuberculous (nodular) (*see also* Tuberculosis) 017.3 ☑ *[379.09]*
- **Sclerochoroiditis** — *see also* Scleritis 379.00
- **Scleroconjunctivitis** — *see also* Scleritis 379.00
- **Sclerocystic ovary** (syndrome) 256.4
- **Sclerodactylia** 701.0
- **Scleroderma, sclerodermia** (acrosclerotic) (diffuse) (generalized) (progressive) (pulmonary) 710.1
  - circumscribed 701.0
  - linear 701.0
  - localized (linear) 701.0
  - newborn 778.1
- **Sclerokeratitis** 379.05
  - meaning sclerosing keratitis 370.54
  - tuberculous (*see also* Tuberculosis) 017.3 ☑ *[379.09]*
- **Scleromalacia**
  - multiple 731.0
  - perforans 379.04
- **Scleroma, trachea** 040.1
- **Scleromyxedema** 701.8
- **Scleroperikeratitis** 379.05
- **Sclerose en plaques** 340
- **Sclerosis, sclerotic**
  - adrenal (gland) 255.8
  - Alzheimer's 331.0
    - with dementia — *see* Alzheimer's, dementia

Sclerosis, sclerotic — *continued*
amyotrophic (lateral) 335.20
annularis fibrosi
aortic 424.1
mitral 424.0
aorta, aortic 440.0
valve (*see also* Endocarditis, aortic) 424.1
artery, arterial, arteriolar, arteriovascular — *see* Arteriosclerosis
ascending multiple 340
Baló's (concentric) 341.1
basilar — *see* Sclerosis, brain
bone (localized) NEC 733.99
brain (general) (lobular) 341.9
Alzheimer's — *see* Alzheimer's, dementia
artery, arterial 437.0
atrophic lobar 331.0
with dementia
with behavioral disturbance 331.0 *[294.11]*
without behavioral disturbance 331.0 *[294.10]*
diffuse 341.1
familial (chronic) (infantile) 330.0
infantile (chronic) (familial) 330.0
Pelizaeus-Merzbacher type 330.0
disseminated 340
hereditary 334.2
infantile (degenerative) (diffuse) 330.0
insular 340
Krabbe's 330.0
miliary 340
multiple 340
Pelizaeus-Merzbacher 330.0
progressive familial 330.0
senile 437.0
tuberous 759.5
bulbar, progressive 340
bundle of His 426.50
left 426.3
right 426.4
cardiac — *see* Arteriosclerosis, coronary
cardiorenal (*see also* Hypertension, cardiorenal) 404.90
cardiovascular (*see also* Disease, cardiovascular) 429.2
renal (*see also* Hypertension, cardiorenal) 404.90
centrolobar, familial 330.0
cerebellar — *see* Sclerosis, brain
cerebral — *see* Sclerosis, brain
cerebrospinal 340
disseminated 340
multiple 340
cerebrovascular 437.0
choroid 363.40
diffuse 363.56
combined (spinal cord) (*see also* Degeneration, combined)
multiple 340
concentric, Baló's 341.1
cornea 370.54
coronary (artery) — *see* Arteriosclerosis, coronary
corpus cavernosum
female 624.8
male 607.89
Dewitzky's
aortic 424.1
mitral 424.0
diffuse NEC 341.1
disease, heart — *see* Arteriosclerosis, coronary
disseminated 340
dorsal 340
dorsolateral (spinal cord) — *see* Degeneration, combined
endometrium 621.8
extrapyramidal 333.90

Sclerosis, sclerotic — *continued*
eye, nuclear (senile) 366.16
Friedreich's (spinal cord) 334.0
funicular (spermatic cord) 608.89
gastritis 535.4 ☑
general (vascular) — *see* Arteriosclerosis
gland (lymphatic) 457.8
hepatic 571.9
hereditary
cerebellar 334.2
spinal 334.0
idiopathic cortical (Garré's) (*see also* Osteomyelitis) 730.1 ☑
ilium, piriform 733.5
insular 340
pancreas 251.8
Islands of Langerhans 251.8
kidney — *see* Sclerosis, renal
larynx 478.79
lateral 335.24
amyotrophic 335.20
descending 335.24
primary 335.24
spinal 335.24
liver 571.9
lobar, atrophic (of brain) 331.0
with dementia
with behavioral disturbance 331.0 *[294.11]*
without behavioral disturbance 331.0 *[294.10]*
lung (*see also* Fibrosis, lung) 515
mastoid 383.1
mitral — *see* Endocarditis, mitral
Mönckeberg's (medial) (*see also* Arteriosclerosis, extremities) 440.20
multiple (brain stem) (cerebral) (generalized) (spinal cord) 340
myocardium, myocardial — *see* Arteriosclerosis, coronary
nuclear (senile), eye 366.16
ovary 620.8
pancreas 577.8
penis 607.89
peripheral arteries (*see also* Arteriosclerosis, extremities) 440.20
plaques 340
pluriglandular 258.8
polyglandular 258.8
posterior (spinal cord) (syphilitic) 094.0
posterolateral (spinal cord) — *see* Degeneration, combined
prepuce 607.89
primary lateral 335.24
progressive systemic 710.1
pulmonary (*see also* Fibrosis, lung) 515
artery 416.0
valve (heart) (*see also* Endocarditis, pulmonary) 424.3
renal 587
with
cystine storage disease 270.0
hypertension (*see also* Hypertension, kidney) 403.90
hypertensive heart disease (conditions classifiable to 402) (*see also* Hypertension, cardiorenal) 404.90
arteriolar (hyaline) (*see also* Hypertension, kidney) 403.90
hyperplastic (*see also* Hypertension, kidney) 403.90
retina (senile) (vascular) 362.17
rheumatic
aortic valve 395.9
mitral valve 394.9
Schilder's 341.1
senile — *see* Arteriosclerosis
spinal (cord) (general) (progressive) (transverse) 336.8
ascending 357.0
combined (*see also* Degeneration, combined)

Sclerosis, sclerotic — *continued*
spinal — *continued*
combined (*see also* Degeneration, combined) — *continued*
multiple 340
syphilitic 094.89
disseminated 340
dorsolateral — *see* Degeneration, combined
hereditary (Friedreich's) (mixed form) 334.0
lateral (amyotrophic) 335.24
multiple 340
posterior (syphilitic) 094.0
stomach 537.89
subendocardial, congenital 425.3
systemic (progressive) 710.1
with lung involvement 710.1 *[517.2]*
tricuspid (heart) (valve) — *see* Endocarditis, tricuspid
tuberous (brain) 759.5
tympanic membrane (*see also* Tympanosclerosis) 385.00
valve, valvular (heart) — *see* Endocarditis
vascular — *see* Arteriosclerosis
vein 459.89
Sclerotenonitis 379.07
Sclerotitis — *see also* Scleritis 379.00
syphilitic 095.0
tuberculous (*see also* Tuberculosis) 017.3 ☑ *[379.09]*
Scoliosis (acquired) (postural) 737.30
congenital 754.2
due to or associated with
Charcôt-Marie-Tooth disease 356.1 *[737.43]*
mucopolysaccharidosis 277.5 *[737.43]*
neurofibromatosis 237.71 *[737.43]*
osteitis
deformans 731.0 *[737.43]*
fibrosa cystica 252.01 *[737.43]*
osteoporosis (*see also* Osteoporosis) 733.00 *[737.43]*
poliomyelitis 138 *[737.43]*
radiation 737.33
tuberculosis (*see also* Tuberculosis) 015.0 ☑ *[737.43]*
idiopathic 737.30
infantile
progressive 737.32
resolving 737.31
paralytic 737.39
rachitic 268.1
sciatic 724.3
specified NEC 737.39
thoracogenic 737.34
tuberculous (*see also* Tuberculosis) 015.0 ☑ *[737.43]*
Scoliotic pelvis 738.6
with disproportion (fetopelvic) 653.0 ☑
affecting fetus or newborn 763.1
causing obstructed labor 660.1 ☑
affecting fetus or newborn 763.1
Scorbutus, scorbutic 267
anemia 281.8
Scotoma (ring) 368.44
arcuate 368.43
Bjerrum 368.43
blind spot area 368.42
central 368.41
centrocecal 368.41
paracecal 368.42
paracentral 368.41
scintillating 368.12
Seidel 368.43
Scratch — *see* Injury, superficial, by site
Scratchy throat 784.99
Screening (for) V82.9
alcoholism V79.1
anemia, deficiency NEC V78.1
iron V78.0
anomaly, congenital V82.89
antenatal, of mother V28.9

Screening — *continued*
antenatal, of mother — *continued*
alphafetoprotein levels, raised V28.1
based on amniocentesis V28.2
chromosomal anomalies V28.0
raised alphafetoprotein levels V28.1
fetal growth retardation using ultrasonics V28.4
ultrasonics V28.4
genomic V28.89 ●
isoimmunization V28.5
malformations using ultrasonics V28.3
proteomic V28.89 ●
raised alphafetoprotein levels V28.1
risk ●
pre-term labor V28.82 ●
specified condition NEC V28.89 ▲
Streptococcus B V28.6
arterial hypertension V81.1
arthropod-borne viral disease NEC V73.5
asymptomatic bacteriuria V81.5
bacterial
and spirochetal sexually transmitted diseases V74.5
conjunctivitis V74.4
disease V74.9
sexually transmitted V74.5
specified condition NEC V74.8
bacteriuria, asymptomatic V81.5
blood disorder NEC V78.9
specified type NEC V78.8
bronchitis, chronic V81.3
brucellosis V74.8
cancer — *see* Screening, malignant neoplasm
cardiovascular disease NEC V81.2
cataract V80.2
Chagas' disease V75.3
chemical poisoning V82.5
cholera V74.0
cholesterol level V77.91
chromosomal
anomalies
by amniocentesis, antenatal V28.0
maternal postnatal V82.4
athletes V70.3
condition
cardiovascular NEC V81.2
eye NEC V80.2
genitourinary NEC V81.6
neurological V80.0
respiratory NEC V81.4
skin V82.0
specified NEC V82.89
congenital
anomaly V82.89
eye V80.2
dislocation of hip V82.3
eye condition or disease V80.2
conjunctivitis, bacterial V74.4
contamination NEC (*see also* Poisoning) V82.5
coronary artery disease V81.0
cystic fibrosis V77.6
deficiency anemia NEC V78.1
iron V78.0
dengue fever V73.5
depression V79.0
developmental handicap V79.9
in early childhood V79.3
specified type NEC V79.8
diabetes mellitus V77.1
diphtheria V74.3
disease or disorder V82.9
bacterial V74.9
specified NEC V74.8
blood V78.9
specified type NEC V78.8
blood-forming organ V78.9
specified type NEC V78.8

- **Screening** — *continued*
  - disease or disorder — *continued*
    - cardiovascular NEC V81.2
      - hypertensive V81.1
      - ischemic V81.0
    - Chagas' V75.3
    - chlamydial V73.98
      - specified NEC V73.88
    - ear NEC V80.3
    - endocrine NEC V77.99
    - eye NEC V80.2
    - genitourinary NEC V81.6
    - heart NEC V81.2
      - hypertensive V81.1
      - ischemic V81.0
    - HPV (human papillomavirus) V73.81
    - human papillomavirus V73.81
    - immunity NEC V77.99
    - infectious NEC V75.9
    - lipoid NEC V77.91
    - mental V79.9
      - specified type NEC V79.8
    - metabolic NEC V77.99
      - inborn NEC V77.7
    - neurological V80.0
    - nutritional NEC V77.99
    - rheumatic NEC V82.2
    - rickettsial V75.0
    - sexually transmitted V74.5
      - bacterial V74.5
      - spirochetal V74.5
    - sickle-cell V78.2
      - trait V78.2
    - specified type NEC V82.89
    - thyroid V77.0
    - vascular NEC V81.2
      - ischemic V81.0
    - venereal V74.5
    - viral V73.99
      - arthropod-borne NEC V73.5
      - specified type NEC V73.89
  - dislocation of hip, congenital V82.3
  - drugs in athletes V70.3
  - elevated titer V82.9 ●
  - emphysema (chronic) V81.3
  - encephalitis, viral (mosquito or tick borne) V73.5
  - endocrine disorder NEC V77.99
  - eye disorder NEC V80.2
    - congenital V80.2
  - fever
    - dengue V73.5
    - hemorrhagic V73.5
    - yellow V73.4
  - filariasis V75.6
  - galactosemia V77.4
  - genetic V82.79
    - disease carrier status V82.71
  - genitourinary condition NEC V81.6
  - glaucoma V80.1
  - gonorrhea V74.5
  - gout V77.5
  - Hansen's disease V74.2
  - heart disease NEC V81.2
    - hypertensive V81.1
    - ischemic V81.0
  - heavy metal poisoning V82.5
  - helminthiasis, intestinal V75.7
  - hematopoietic malignancy V76.89
  - hemoglobinopathies NEC V78.3
  - hemorrhagic fever V73.5
  - Hodgkin's disease V76.89
  - hormones in athletes V70.3
  - HPV (human papillomavirus) V73.81
  - human papillomavirus (HPV) V73.81
  - hypercholesterolemia V77.91
  - hyperlipdemia V77.91
  - hypertension V81.1
  - immunity disorder NEC V77.99
  - inborn errors of metabolism NEC V77.7
  - infection
    - bacterial V74.9
      - specified type NEC V74.8
    - mycotic V75.4

- **Screening** — *continued*
  - infection — *continued*
    - parasitic NEC V75.8
  - infectious disease V75.9
    - specified type NEC V75.8
  - ingestion of radioactive substance V82.5
  - intestinal helminthiasis V75.7
  - iron deficiency anemia V78.0
  - ischemic heart disease V81.0
  - lead poisoning V82.5
  - leishmaniasis V75.2
  - leprosy V74.2
  - leptospirosis V74.8
  - leukemia V76.89
  - lipoid disorder NEC V77.91
  - lymphoma V76.89
  - malaria V75.1
  - malignant neoplasm (of) V76.9
    - bladder V76.3
    - blood V76.89
    - breast V76.10
      - mammogram NEC V76.12
        - for high-risk patient V76.11
      - specified type NEC V76.19
    - cervix V76.2
    - colon V76.51
    - colorectal V76.51
    - hematopoietic system V76.89
    - intestine V76.50
      - colon V76.51
      - small V76.52
    - lung V76.0
    - lymph (glands) V76.89
    - nervous system V76.81
    - oral cavity V76.42
    - other specified neoplasm NEC V76.89
    - ovary V76.46
    - prostate V76.44
    - rectum V76.41
    - respiratory organs V76.0
    - skin V76.43
    - specified sites NEC V76.49
    - testis V76.45
    - vagina V76.47
      - following hysterectomy for malignant condition V67.01
  - malnutrition V77.2
  - mammogram NEC V76.12
    - for high-risk patient V76.11
  - maternal postnatal chromosomal anomalies V82.4
  - measles V73.2
  - mental
    - disorder V79.9
      - specified type NEC V79.8
    - retardation V79.2
  - metabolic disorder NEC V77.99
  - metabolic errors, inborn V77.7
  - mucoviscidosis V77.6
  - multiphasic V82.6
  - mycosis V75.4
  - mycotic infection V75.4
  - nephropathy V81.5
  - neurological condition V80.0
  - nutritional disorder V77.99
  - obesity V77.8
  - osteoporosis V82.81
  - parasitic infection NEC V75.8
  - phenylketonuria V77.3
  - plague V74.8
  - poisoning
    - chemical NEC V82.5
    - contaminated water supply V82.5
      - heavy metal V82.5
  - poliomyelitis V73.0
  - postnatal chromosomal anomalies, maternal V82.4
  - prenatal — *see* Screening, antenatal
  - pulmonary tuberculosis V74.1
  - radiation exposure V82.5
  - renal disease V81.5
  - respiratory condition NEC V81.4
  - rheumatic disorder NEC V82.2
  - rheumatoid arthritis V82.1

- **Screening** — *continued*
  - rickettsial disease V75.0
  - rubella V73.3
  - schistosomiasis V75.5
  - senile macular lesions of eye V80.2
  - sexually transmitted diseases V74.5
    - bacterial V74.5
    - spirochetal V74.5
  - sickle-cell anemia, disease, or trait V78.2
  - skin condition V82.0
  - sleeping sickness V75.3
  - smallpox V73.1
  - special V82.9
    - specified condition NEC V82.89
  - specified type NEC V82.89
  - spirochetal disease V74.9
    - sexually transmitted V74.5
    - specified type NEC V74.8
  - stimulants in athletes V70.3
  - syphilis V74.5
  - tetanus V74.8
  - thyroid disorder V77.0
  - trachoma V73.6
  - trypanosomiasis V75.3
  - tuberculosis, pulmonary V74.1
  - venereal disease V74.5
  - viral encephalitis
    - mosquito-borne V73.5
    - tick-borne V73.5
  - whooping cough V74.8
  - worms, intestinal V75.7
  - yaws V74.6
  - yellow fever V73.4
- **Scrofula** — *see also* Tuberculosis 017.2 ☑
- **Scrofulide** (primary) — *see also* Tuberculosis 017.0 ☑
- **Scrofuloderma, scrofulodermia** (any site) (primary) — *see also* Tuberculosis 017.0 ☑
- **Scrofulosis** (universal) — *see also* Tuberculosis 017.2 ☑
- **Scrofulosis lichen** (primary) — *see also* Tuberculosis 017.0 ☑
- **Scrofulous** — *see* condition
- **Scrotal tongue** 529.5
  - congenital 750.13
- **Scrotum** — *see* condition
- **Scurvy** (gum) (infantile) (rickets) (scorbutic) 267
- **Sea-blue histiocyte syndrome** 272.7
- **Seabright-Bantam syndrome** (pseudohypoparathyroidism) 275.49
- **Sealpox** 059.12 ●
- **Seasickness** 994.6
- **Seatworm** 127.4
- **Sebaceous**
  - cyst (*see also* Cyst, sebaceous) 706.2
  - gland disease NEC 706.9
- **Sebocystomatosis** 706.2
- **Seborrhea, seborrheic** 706.3
  - adiposa 706.3
  - capitis 690.11
  - congestiva 695.4
  - corporis 706.3
  - dermatitis 690.10
    - infantile 690.12
  - diathesis in infants 695.89
  - eczema 690.18
    - infantile 690.12
  - keratosis 702.19
    - inflamed 702.11
  - nigricans 705.89
  - sicca 690.18
  - wart 702.19
    - inflamed 702.11
- **Seckel's syndrome** 759.89
- **Seclusion pupil** 364.74
- **Seclusiveness, child** 313.22
- **Secondary** — *see also* condition
  - neoplasm — *see* Neoplasm, by site, malignant, secondary
- **Secretan's disease or syndrome** (posttraumatic edema) 782.3

- **Secretion**
  - antidiuretic hormone, inappropriate (syndrome) 253.6
  - catecholamine, by pheochromocytoma 255.6
  - hormone
    - antidiuretic, inappropriate (syndrome) 253.6
    - by
      - carcinoid tumor 259.2
      - pheochromocytoma 255.6
    - ectopic NEC 259.3
  - urinary
    - excessive 788.42
    - suppression 788.5
- **Section**
  - cesarean
    - affecting fetus or newborn 763.4
    - post mortem, affecting fetus or newborn 761.6
    - previous, in pregnancy or childbirth 654.2 ☑
      - affecting fetus or newborn 763.89
  - nerve, traumatic — *see* Injury, nerve, by site
- **Seeligmann's syndrome** (ichthyosis congenita) 757.1
- **Segmentation, incomplete** (congenital) — *see also* Fusion
  - bone NEC 756.9
  - lumbosacral (joint) 756.15
  - vertebra 756.15
    - lumbosacral 756.15
- **Seizure(s)** 780.39
  - akinetic (idiopathic) (*see also* Epilepsy) 345.0 ☑
    - psychomotor 345.4 ☑
  - apoplexy, apoplectic (*see also* Disease, cerebrovascular, acute) 436
  - atonic (*see also* Epilepsy) 345.0 ☑
  - autonomic 300.11
  - brain or cerebral (*see also* Disease, cerebrovascular, acute) 436
  - convulsive (*see also* Convulsions) 780.39
  - cortical (focal) (motor) (*see also* Epilepsy) 345.5 ☑
  - due to stroke 438.89
  - epilepsy, epileptic (cryptogenic) (*see also* Epilepsy) 345.9 ☑
  - epileptiform, epileptoid 780.39
    - focal (*see also* Epilepsy) 345.5 ☑
  - febrile (simple) 780.31
    - with status epilepticus 345.3
    - atypical 780.32
    - complex 780.32
    - complicated 780.32
  - heart — *see* Disease, heart
  - hysterical 300.11
  - Jacksonian (focal) (*see also* Epilepsy) 345.5 ☑
    - motor type 345.5 ☑
    - sensory type 345.5 ☑
  - migraine triggered 346.0 ☑ ●
  - newborn 779.0
  - paralysis (*see also* Disease, cerebrovascular, acute) 436
  - recurrent 345.9 ☑
    - epileptic — *see* Epilepsy
  - repetitive 780.39
    - epileptic — *see* Epilepsy
  - salaam (*see also* Epilepsy) 345.6 ☑
  - uncinate (*see also* Epilepsy) 345.4 ☑
- **Self-mutilation** 300.9
- **Semicoma** 780.09
- **Semiconsciousness** 780.09
- **Seminal**
  - vesicle — *see* condition
  - vesiculitis (*see also* Vesiculitis) 608.0
- **Seminoma** (M9061/3)
  - anaplastic type (M9062/3)
    - specified site — *see* Neoplasm, by site, malignant
    - unspecified site 186.9

Seminoma — *continued*
  specified site — *see* Neoplasm, by site, malignant
  spermatocytic (M9063/3)
    specified site — *see* Neoplasm, by site, malignant
    unspecified site 186.9
  unspecified site 186.9
Semliki Forest encephalitis 062.8
Senear-Usher disease or syndrome (pemphigus erythematosus) 694.4
Senecio jacobae dermatitis 692.6
Senectus 797
Senescence 797
Senile — *see also* condition 797
  cervix (atrophic) 622.8
  degenerative atrophy, skin 701.3
  endometrium (atrophic) 621.8
  fallopian tube (atrophic) 620.3
  heart (failure) 797
  lung 492.8
  ovary (atrophic) 620.3
  syndrome 259.8
  vagina, vaginitis (atrophic) 627.3
  wart 702.0
Senility 797
  with
    acute confusional state 290.3
    delirium 290.3
    mental changes 290.9
    psychosis NEC (*see also* Psychosis, senile) 290.20
  premature (syndrome) 259.8
Sensation
  burning (*see also* Disturbance, sensation) 782.0
    tongue 529.6
  choking 784.99
  loss of (*see also* Disturbance, sensation) 782.0
  prickling (*see also* Disturbance, sensation) 782.0
  tingling (*see also* Disturbance, sensation) 782.0
Sense loss (touch) — *see also* Disturbance, sensation 782.0
  smell 781.1
  taste 781.1
Sensibility disturbance NEC (cortical) (deep) (vibratory) — *see also* Disturbance, sensation 782.0
Sensitive dentine 521.89
Sensitiver Beziehungswahn 297.8
Sensitivity, sensitization — *see also* Allergy
  autoerythrocyte 287.2
  carotid sinus 337.01 ▲
  child (excessive) 313.21
  cold, autoimmune 283.0
  methemoglobin 289.7
  suxamethonium 289.89
  tuberculin, without clinical or radiological symptoms 795.5
Sensory
  extinction 781.8
  neglect 781.8
Separation
  acromioclavicular — *see* Dislocation, acromioclavicular
  anxiety, abnormal 309.21
  apophysis, traumatic — *see* Fracture, by site
  choroid 363.70
    hemorrhagic 363.72
    serous 363.71
  costochondral (simple) (traumatic) — *see* Dislocation, costochondral
  delayed
    umbilical cord 779.83
  epiphysis, epiphyseal
    nontraumatic 732.9
      upper femoral 732.2
    traumatic — *see* Fracture, by site
  fracture — *see* Fracture, by site
  infundibulum cardiac from right ventricle by a partition 746.83
Separation — *continued*
  joint (current) (traumatic) — *see* Dislocation, by site
  placenta (normally implanted) — *see* Placenta, separation
  pubic bone, obstetrical trauma 665.6 ☑
  retina, retinal (*see also* Detachment, retina) 361.9
    layers 362.40
      sensory (*see also* Retinoschisis) 361.10
    pigment epithelium (exudative) 362.42
      hemorrhagic 362.43
  sternoclavicular (traumatic) — *see* Dislocation, sternoclavicular
  symphysis pubis, obstetrical trauma 665.6 ☑
  tracheal ring, incomplete (congenital) 748.3
Sepsis (generalized) 995.91
  with
    abortion — *see* Abortion, by type, with sepsis
    acute organ dysfunction 995.92
    ectopic pregnancy (*see also* categories 633.0–633.9) 639.0
    molar pregnancy (*see also* categories 630–632) 639.0
    multiple organ dysfunction (MOD) 995.92
  buccal 528.3
  complicating labor 659.3 ☑
  dental (pulpal origin) 522.4
  female genital organ NEC 614.9
  fetus (intrauterine) 771.81
  following
    abortion 639.0
    ectopic or molar pregnancy 639.0
    infusion, perfusion, or transfusion 999.39
  Friedländer's 038.49
  intraocular 360.00
  localized
    in operation wound 998.59
    skin (*see also* Abscess) 682.9
  malleus 024
  nadir 038.9
  newborn (organism unspecified) NEC 771.81
  oral 528.3
  puerperal, postpartum, childbirth (pelvic) 670.0 ☑
  resulting from infusion, injection, transfusion, or vaccination 999.39
  severe 995.92
  skin, localized (*see also* Abscess) 682.9
  umbilical (newborn) (organism unspecified) 771.89
  tetanus 771.3
  urinary 599.0
    meaning sepsis 995.91
    meaning urinary tract infection 599.0
Septate — *see also* Septum
Septic — *see also* condition
  adenoids 474.01
    and tonsils 474.02
  arm (with lymphangitis) 682.3
  embolus — *see* Embolism
  finger (with lymphangitis) 681.00
  foot (with lymphangitis) 682.7
  gallbladder (*see also* Cholecystitis) 575.8
  hand (with lymphangitis) 682.4
  joint (*see also* Arthritis, septic) 711.0 ☑
  kidney (*see also* Infection, kidney) 590.9
  leg (with lymphangitis) 682.6
  mouth 528.3
  nail 681.9
    finger 681.02
Septic — *see also* condition — *continued*
  nail — *continued*
    toe 681.11
  shock (endotoxic) 785.52
  sore (*see also* Abscess) 682.9
    throat 034.0
      milk-borne 034.0
      streptococcal 034.0
  spleen (acute) 289.59
  teeth (pulpal origin) 522.4
  throat 034.0
  thrombus — *see* Thrombosis
  toe (with lymphangitis) 681.10
  tonsils 474.00
    and adenoids 474.02
  umbilical cord (newborn) (organism unspecified) 771.89
  uterus (*see also* Endometritis) 615.9
Septicemia, septicemic (generalized) (suppurative) 038.9
  with
    abortion — *see* Abortion, by type, with sepsis
    ectopic pregnancy (*see also* categories 633.0–633.9) 639.0
    molar pregnancy (*see also* categories 630–632) 639.0
  Aerobacter aerogenes 038.49
  anaerobic 038.3
  anthrax 022.3
  Bacillus coli 038.42
  Bacteroides 038.3
  Clostridium 038.3
  complicating labor 659.3 ☑
  cryptogenic 038.9
  enteric gram-negative bacilli 038.40
  Enterobacter aerogenes 038.49
  Erysipelothrix (insidiosa) (rhusiopathiae) 027.1
  Escherichia coli 038.42
  following
    abortion 639.0
    ectopic or molar pregnancy 639.0
    infusion, injection, transfusion, or vaccination 999.39
  Friedländer's (bacillus) 038.49
  gangrenous 038.9
  gonococcal 098.89
  gram-negative (organism) 038.40
    anaerobic 038.3
  Hemophilus influenzae 038.41
  herpes (simplex) 054.5
  herpetic 054.5
  Listeria monocytogenes 027.0
  meningeal — *see* Meningitis
  meningococcal (chronic) (fulminating) 036.2
  methicillin ●
    resistant Staphylococcus aureus (MRSA) 038.12 ●
    susceptible Staphylococcus aureus (MSSA) 038.11 ●
  MRSA (methicillin resistant Staphylococcus aureus) 038.12 ●
  MSSA (methicillin susceptible Staphylococcus aureus) 038.11 ●
  navel, newborn (organism unspecified) 771.89
  newborn (organism unspecified) 771.81
  plague 020.2
  pneumococcal 038.2
  postabortal 639.0
  postoperative 998.59
  Proteus vulgaris 038.49
  Pseudomonas (aeruginosa) 038.43
  puerperal, postpartum 670.0 ☑
  Salmonella (aertrycke) (callinarum) (choleraesuis) (enteritidis) (suipestifer) 003.1
  Serratia 038.44
  Shigella (*see also* Dysentery, bacillary) 004.9
  specified organism NEC 038.8
Septicemia, septicemic — *continued*
  staphylococcal 038.10
    aureus 038.11
      methicillin ●
        resistant (MRSA) 038.12 ●
        susceptible (MSSA) 038.11 ●
    specified organism NEC 038.19
  streptococcal (anaerobic) 038.0
  Streptococcus pneumoniae 038.2
  suipestifer 003.1
  umbilicus, newborn (organism unspecified) 771.89
  viral 079.99
  Yersinia enterocolitica 038.49
Septum, septate (congenital) — *see also* Anomaly, specified type NEC
  anal 751.2
  aqueduct of Sylvius 742.3
    with spina bifida (*see also* Spina bifida) 741.0 ☑
  hymen 752.49
  uterus (*see also* Double, uterus) 752.2
  vagina 752.49
    in pregnancy or childbirth 654.7 ☑
      affecting fetus or newborn 763.89
      causing obstructed labor 660.2 ☑
        affecting fetus or newborn 763.1
Sequestration
  lung (congenital) (extralobar) (intralobar) 748.5
  orbit 376.10
  pulmonary artery (congenital) 747.3
  splenic 289.52
Sequestrum
  bone (*see also* Osteomyelitis) 730.1 ☑
    jaw 526.4
  dental 525.8
  jaw bone 526.4
  sinus (accessory) (nasal) (*see also* Sinusitis) 473.9
    maxillary 473.0
Sequoiosis asthma 495.8
Serology for syphilis
  doubtful
    with signs or symptoms — *see* Syphilis, by site and stage
    follow-up of latent syphilis — *see* Syphilis, latent
  false positive 795.6
  negative, with signs or symptoms — *see* Syphilis, by site and stage
  positive 097.1
    with signs or symptoms — *see* Syphilis, by site and stage
    false 795.6
    follow-up of latent syphilis — *see* Syphilis, latent
    only finding — *see* Syphilis, latent
  reactivated 097.1
Seroma (postoperative) (non-infected) 998.13
  infected 998.51
  post-traumatic 729.91 ●
Seropurulent — *see* condition
Serositis, multiple 569.89
  pericardial 423.2
  peritoneal 568.82
  pleural — *see* Pleurisy
Serotonin syndrome 333.99
Serous — *see* condition
Sertoli cell
  adenoma (M8640/0)
    specified site — *see* Neoplasm, by site, benign
    unspecified site
      female 220
      male 222.0
  carcinoma (M8640/3)
    specified site — *see* Neoplasm, by site, malignant
    unspecified site 186.9
  syndrome (germinal aplasia) 606.0

Sertoli cell — *continued*
tumor (M8640/0)
with lipid storage (M8641/0)
specified site — *see* Neoplasm, by site, benign
unspecified site
female 220
male 222.0
specified site — *see* Neoplasm, by site, benign
unspecified site
female 220
male 222.0
Sertoli-Leydig cell tumor (M8631/0)
specified site — *see* Neoplasm, by site, benign
unspecified site
female 220
male 222.0
Serum
allergy, allergic reaction 999.5
shock 999.4
arthritis 999.5 *[713.6]*
complication or reaction NEC 999.5
disease NEC 999.5
hepatitis 070.3 ☑
intoxication 999.5
jaundice (homologous) — *see* Hepatitis, viral, type B
neuritis 999.5
poisoning NEC 999.5
rash NEC 999.5
reaction NEC 999.5
sickness NEC 999.5
Sesamoiditis 733.99
Seven-day fever 061
of
Japan 100.89
Queensland 100.89
Sever's disease or osteochondrosis (calcaneum) 732.5
Sex chromosome mosaics 758.81
Sex reassignment surgery status (*see also* Trans-sexualism 302.50
Sextuplet
affected by maternal complications of pregnancy 761.5
healthy liveborn — *see* Newborn, multiple
pregnancy (complicating delivery) NEC 651.8 ☑
with fetal loss and retention of one or more fetus(es) 651.6 ☑
following (elective) fetal reduction 651.7 ☑
Sexual
anesthesia 302.72
deviation (*see also* Deviation, sexual) 302.9
disorder (*see also* Deviation, sexual) 302.9
frigidity (female) 302.72
function, disorder of (psychogenic) 302.70
specified type NEC 302.79
immaturity (female) (male) 259.0
impotence 607.84
organic origin NEC 607.84
psychogenic 302.72
precocity (constitutional) (cryptogenic) (female) (idiopathic) (male) NEC 259.1
with adrenal hyperplasia 255.2
sadism 302.84
Sexuality, pathological — *see also* Deviation, sexual 302.9
Sézary's disease, reticulosis, or syndrome (M9701/3) 202.2 ☑
Shadow, lung 793.1
Shaken infant syndrome 995.55
Shaking
head (tremor) 781.0
palsy or paralysis (*see also* Parkinsonism) 332.0
Shallowness, acetabulum 736.39
Shaver's disease or syndrome (bauxite pneumoconiosis) 503
Shearing
artificial skin graft 996.55
decellularized allodermis graft 996.55
Sheath (tendon) — *see* condition
Shedding
nail 703.8
teeth, premature, primary (deciduous) 520.6
Sheehan's disease or syndrome (postpartum pituitary necrosis) 253.2
Shelf, rectal 569.49
Shell
shock (current) (*see also* Reaction, stress, acute) 308.9
lasting state 300.16
teeth 520.5
Shield kidney 753.3
Shifting
pacemaker 427.89
sleep-work schedule (affecting sleep) 327.36
Shift, mediastinal 793.2
Shiga's
bacillus 004.0
dysentery 004.0
Shigella (dysentery) — *see also* Dysentery, bacillary 004.9
carrier (suspected) of V02.3
Shigellosis — *see also* Dysentery, bacillary 004.9
Shingles — *see also* Herpes, zoster 053.9
eye NEC 053.29
Shin splints 844.9
Shipyard eye or disease 077.1
Shirodkar suture, in pregnancy 654.5 ☑
Shock 785.50
with
abortion — *see* Abortion, by type, with shock
ectopic pregnancy (*see also* categories 633.0–633.9) 639.5
molar pregnancy (*see also* categories 630–632) 639.5
allergic — *see* Shock, anaphylactic
anaclitic 309.21
anaphylactic 995.0
chemical — *see* Table of Drugs and Chemicals
correct medicinal substance properly administered 995.0
drug or medicinal substance
correct substance properly administered 995.0
overdose or wrong substance given or taken 977.9
specified drug — *see* Table of Drugs and Chemicals
following sting(s) 989.5
food — *see* Anaphylactic shock, due to, food
immunization 999.4
serum 999.4
anaphylactoid — *see* Shock, anaphylactic
anesthetic
correct substance properly administered 995.4
overdose or wrong substance given 968.4
specified anesthetic — *see* Table of Drugs and Chemicals
birth, fetus or newborn NEC 779.89
cardiogenic 785.51
chemical substance — *see* Table of Drugs and Chemicals
circulatory 785.59
complicating
abortion — *see* Abortion, by type, with shock
ectopic pregnancy (*see also* categories 633.0–633.9) 639.5
labor and delivery 669.1 ☑
Shock — *continued*
complicating — *continued*
molar pregnancy (*see also* categories 630–632) 639.5
culture 309.29
due to
drug 995.0
correct substance properly administered 995.0
overdose or wrong substance given or taken 977.9
specified drug — *see* Table of Drugs and Chemicals
food — *see* Anaphylactic shock, due to, food
during labor and delivery 669.1 ☑
electric 994.8
from electroshock gun (taser) ●
994.8 ●
endotoxic 785.52
due to surgical procedure 998.0
following
abortion 639.5
ectopic or molar pregnancy 639.5
injury (immediate) (delayed) 958.4
labor and delivery 669.1 ☑
gram-negative 785.52
hematogenic 785.59
hemorrhagic
due to
disease 785.59
surgery (intraoperative) (postoperative) 998.0
trauma 958.4
hypovolemic NEC 785.59
surgical 998.0
traumatic 958.4
insulin 251.0
therapeutic misadventure 962.3
kidney 584.5
traumatic (following crushing) 958.5
lightning 994.0
lung 518.5
nervous (*see also* Reaction, stress, acute) 308.9
obstetric 669.1 ☑
with
abortion — *see* Abortion, by type, with shock
ectopic pregnancy (*see also* categories 633.0–633.9) 639.5
molar pregnancy (*see also* categories 630–632) 639.5
following
abortion 639.5
ectopic or molar pregnancy 639.5
paralysis, paralytic (*see also* Disease, cerebrovascular, acute) 436
late effect — *see* Late effect(s) (of) cerebrovascular disease
pleural (surgical) 998.0
due to trauma 958.4
postoperative 998.0
with
abortion — *see* Abortion, by type, with shock
ectopic pregnancy (*see also* categories 633.0–633.9) 639.5
molar pregnancy (*see also* categories 630–632) 639.5
following
abortion 639.5
ectopic or molar pregnancy 639.5
psychic (*see also* Reaction, stress, acute) 308.9
past history (of) V15.49
psychogenic (*see also* Reaction, stress, acute) 308.9
septic 785.52
Shock — *continued*
septic — *continued*
with
abortion — *see* Abortion, by type, with shock
ectopic pregnancy (*see also* categories 633.0–633.9) 639.5
molar pregnancy (*see also* categories 630–632) 639.5
due to
surgical procedure 998.0
transfusion NEC 999.8 ☑
bone marrow 996.85
following
abortion 639.5
ectopic or molar pregnancy 639.5
surgical procedure 998.0
transfusion NEC 999.8 ☑
bone marrow 996.85
spinal (*see also* Injury, spinal, by site)
with spinal bone injury — *see* Fracture, vertebra, by site, with spinal cord injury
surgical 998.0
therapeutic misadventure NEC (*see also* Complications) 998.89
thyroxin 962.7
toxic 040.82
transfusion — *see* Complications, transfusion
traumatic (immediate) (delayed) 958.4
Shoemakers' chest 738.3
Short, shortening, shortness
Achilles tendon (acquired) 727.81
arm 736.89
congenital 755.20
back 737.9
bowel syndrome 579.3
breath 786.05
cervical, cervix 649.7 ☑ ●
gravid uterus 649.7 ☑ ●
non-gravid uterus 622.5 ●
acquired 622.5 ●
congenital 752.49 ●
chain acyl CoA dehydrogenase deficiency (SCAD) 277.85
common bile duct, congenital 751.69
cord (umbilical) 663.4 ☑
affecting fetus or newborn 762.6
cystic duct, congenital 751.69
esophagus (congenital) 750.4
femur (acquired) 736.81
congenital 755.34
frenulum linguae 750.0
frenum, lingual 750.0
hamstrings 727.81
hip (acquired) 736.39
congenital 755.63
leg (acquired) 736.81
congenital 755.30
metatarsus (congenital) 754.79
acquired 736.79
organ or site, congenital NEC — *see* Distortion
palate (congenital) 750.26
P-R interval syndrome 426.81
radius (acquired) 736.09
congenital 755.26
round ligament 629.89
sleeper 307.49
stature, constitutional (hereditary) (idiopathic) 783.43
tendon 727.81
Achilles (acquired) 727.81
congenital 754.79
congenital 756.89
thigh (acquired) 736.81
congenital 755.34
tibialis anticus 727.81
umbilical cord 663.4 ☑
affecting fetus or newborn 762.6
urethra 599.84
uvula (congenital) 750.26
vagina 623.8

Shortsightedness 367.1
Shoshin (acute fulminating beriberi) 265.0
Shoulder — *see* condition
Shovel-shaped incisors 520.2
Shower, thromboembolic — *see* Embolism
Shunt (status)
aortocoronary bypass V45.81
arterial-venous (dialysis) V45.11 ▲
arteriovenous, pulmonary (acquired) 417.0
congenital 747.3
traumatic (complication) 901.40
cerebral ventricle (communicating) in situ V45.2
coronary artery bypass V45.81
surgical, prosthetic, with complications — *see* Complications, shunt
vascular NEC V45.89
Shutdown
renal 586
with
abortion — *see* Abortion, by type, with renal failure
ectopic pregnancy (*see also* categories 633.0–633.9) 639.3
molar pregnancy (*see also* categories 630–632) 639.3
complicating
abortion 639.3
ectopic or molar pregnancy 639.3
following labor and delivery 669.3 ☑
Shwachman's syndrome 288.02
Shy-Drager syndrome (orthostatic hypotension with multisystem degeneration) 333.0
Sialadenitis (any gland) (chronic) (suppurative) 527.2
epidemic — *see* Mumps
Sialadenosis, periodic 527.2
Sialaporia 527.7
Sialectasia 527.8
Sialitis 527.2
Sialoadenitis — *see also* Sialadenitis 527.2
Sialoangitis 527.2
Sialodochitis (fibrinosa) 527.2
Sialodocholithiasis 527.5
Sialolithiasis 527.5
Sialorrhea — *see also* Ptyalism 527.7
periodic 527.2
Sialosis 527.8
rheumatic 710.2
Siamese twin 759.4
complicating pregnancy 678.1 ☑ ●
Sicard's syndrome 352.6
Sicca syndrome (keratoconjunctivitis) 710.2
Sick 799.9
cilia syndrome 759.89
or handicapped person in family V61.49
Sickle-cell
anemia (see also Disease, sickle-cell) 282.60
disease (see also Disease, sickle-cell) 282.60
hemoglobin
C disease (without crisis) 282.63
with
crisis 282.64
vaso-occlusive pain 282.64
D disease (without crisis) 282.68
with crisis 282.69
E disease (without crisis) 282.68
with crisis 282.69
thalassemia (without crisis) 282.41
with
crisis 282.42
vaso-occlusive pain 282.42
trait 282.5
Sicklemia — *see also* Disease, sickle-cell 282.60
trait 282.5
Sickness
air (travel) 994.6
airplane 994.6
alpine 993.2
altitude 993.2
Andes 993.2
aviators' 993.2
balloon 993.2
car 994.6
compressed air 993.3
decompression 993.3
green 280.9
harvest 100.89
milk 988.8
morning 643.0 ☑
motion 994.6
mountain 993.2
acute 289.0
protein (*see also* Complications, vaccination) 999.5
radiation NEC 990
roundabout (motion) 994.6
sea 994.6
serum NEC 999.5
sleeping (African) 086.5
by Trypanosoma 086.5
gambiense 086.3
rhodesiense 086.4
Gambian 086.3
late effect 139.8
Rhodesian 086.4
sweating 078.2
swing (motion) 994.6
train (railway) (travel) 994.6
travel (any vehicle) 994.6
Sick sinus syndrome 427.81
Sideropenia — *see also* Anemia, iron deficiency 280.9
Siderosis (lung) (occupational) 503
cornea 371.15
eye (bulbi) (vitreous) 360.23
lens 360.23
Siegal-Cattan-Mamou disease (periodic) 277.31
Siemens' syndrome
ectodermal dysplasia 757.31
keratosis follicularis spinulosa (decalvans) 757.39
Sighing respiration 786.7
Sigmoid
flexure — *see* condition
kidney 753.3
Sigmoiditis — *see* Enteritis
Silfverskiöld's syndrome 756.50
Silicosis, silicotic (complicated) (occupational) (simple) 502
fibrosis, lung (confluent) (massive) (occupational) 502
non-nodular 503
pulmonum 502
Silicotuberculosis — *see also* Tuberculosis 011.4 ☑
Silo fillers' disease 506.9
Silver's syndrome (congenital hemihypertrophy and short stature) 759.89
Silver wire arteries, retina 362.13
Silvestroni-Bianco syndrome (thalassemia minima) 282.49
Simian crease 757.2
Simmonds' cachexia or disease (pituitary cachexia) 253.2
Simons' disease or syndrome (progressive lipodystrophy) 272.6
Simple, simplex — *see* condition
Sinding-Larsen disease (juvenile osteopathia patellae) 732.4
Singapore hemorrhagic fever 065.4
Singers' node or nodule 478.5
Single
atrium 745.69
coronary artery 746.85
umbilical artery 747.5
Single — *continued*
ventricle 745.3
Singultus 786.8
epidemicus 078.89
Sinus — *see also* Fistula
abdominal 569.81
arrest 426.6
arrhythmia 427.89
bradycardia 427.89
chronic 427.81
branchial cleft (external) (internal) 744.41
coccygeal (infected) 685.1
with abscess 685.0
dental 522.7
dermal (congenital) 685.1
with abscess 685.0
draining — *see* Fistula
infected, skin NEC 686.9
marginal, ruptured or bleeding 641.2 ☑
affecting fetus or newborn 762.1
pause 426.6
pericranii 742.0
pilonidal (infected) (rectum) 685.1
with abscess 685.0
preauricular 744.46
rectovaginal 619.1
sacrococcygeal (dermoid) (infected) 685.1
with abscess 685.0
skin
infected NEC 686.9
noninfected — *see* Ulcer, skin
tachycardia 427.89
tarsi syndrome 726.79
testis 608.89
tract (postinfectional) — *see* Fistula
urachus 753.7
Sinuses, Rokitansky-Aschoff — *see also* Disease, gallbladder 575.8
Sinusitis (accessory) (nasal) (hyperplastic) (nonpurulent) (purulent) (chronic) 473.9
with influenza, flu, or grippe 487.1
acute 461.9
ethmoidal 461.2
frontal 461.1
maxillary 461.0
specified type NEC 461.8
sphenoidal 461.3
allergic (*see also* Fever, hay) 477.9
antrum — *see* Sinusitis, maxillary
due to
fungus, any sinus 117.9
high altitude 993.1
ethmoidal 473.2
acute 461.2
frontal 473.1
acute 461.1
influenzal 487.1 ▲
maxillary 473.0
acute 461.0
specified site NEC 473.8
sphenoidal 473.3
acute 461.3
syphilitic, any sinus 095.8
tuberculous, any sinus (*see also* Tuberculosis) 012.8 ☑
Sinusitis-bronchiectasis-situs inversus (syndrome) (triad) 759.3
Sioloangitis 527.2
Sipple's syndrome (medullary thyroid carcinoma-pheochromocytoma) 258.02
Sirenomelia 759.89
Siriasis 992.0
Sirkari's disease 085.0
SIRS (systemic inflammatory response syndrome) 995.90
due to
infectious process 995.91
with acute organ dysfunction 995.92
non-infectious process 995.93
SIRS — *continued*
due to — *continued*
non-infectious process — *continued*
with acute organ dysfunction 995.94
Siti 104.0
Sitophobia 300.29
Situational
disturbance (transient) (*see also* Reaction, adjustment) 309.9
acute 308.3
maladjustment, acute (*see also* Reaction, adjustment) 309.9
reaction (*see also* Reaction, adjustment) 309.9
acute 308.3
Situation, psychiatric 300.9
Situs inversus or transversus 759.3
abdominalis 759.3
thoracis 759.3
Sixth disease
due to
human herpesvirus 6 058.11
human herpesvirus 7 058.12
Sjögren-Larsson syndrome (ichthyosis congenita) 757.1
Sjögren (-Gougerot) syndrome or disease (keratoconjunctivitis sicca) 710.2
with lung involvement 710.2 *[517.8]*
SJS-TEN (Stevens-Johnson syndrome - toxic epidermal necrolysis overlap syndrome) 695.14 ● ● ●
Skeletal — *see* condition
Skene's gland — *see* condition
Skenitis — *see also* Urethritis 597.89
gonorrheal (acute) 098.0
chronic or duration of 2 months or over 098.2
Skerljevo 104.0
Skevas-Zerfus disease 989.5
Skin — *see also* condition
donor V59.1
hidebound 710.9
SLAP lesion (superior glenoid labrum) 840.7
Slate-dressers' lung 502
Slate-miners' lung 502
Sleep
deprivation V69.4
disorder 780.50
with apnea — *see* Apnea, sleep
child 307.40
movement, unspecified 780.58
nonorganic origin 307.40
specified type NEC 307.49
disturbance 780.50
with apnea — *see* Apnea, sleep
nonorganic origin 307.40
specified type NEC 307.49
drunkenness 307.47
movement disorder, unspecified 780.58
paroxysmal (*see also* Narcolepsy) 347.00
related movement disorder, unspecified 780.58
rhythm inversion 327.39
nonorganic origin 307.45
walking 307.46
hysterical 300.13
Sleeping sickness 086.5
late effect 139.8
Sleeplessness — *see also* Insomnia 780.52
menopausal 627.2
nonorganic origin 307.41
Slipped, slipping
epiphysis (postinfectional) 732.9
traumatic (old) 732.9
current — *see* Fracture, by site
upper femoral (nontraumatic) 732.2
intervertebral disc — *see* Displacement, intervertebral disc

- **Slipped, slipping** — *continued*
  - ligature, umbilical 772.3
  - patella 717.89
  - rib 733.99
  - sacroiliac joint 724.6
  - tendon 727.9
  - ulnar nerve, nontraumatic 354.2
  - vertebra NEC (*see also* Spondylolisthesis) 756.12
- **Slocumb's syndrome** 255.3
- **Sloughing** (multiple) (skin) 686.9
  - abscess — *see* Abscess, by site
  - appendix 543.9
  - bladder 596.8
  - fascia 728.9
  - graft — *see* Complications, graft
  - phagedena (*see also* Gangrene) 785.4
  - reattached extremity (*see also* Complications, reattached extremity) 996.90
  - rectum 569.49
  - scrotum 608.89
  - tendon 727.9
  - transplanted organ (*see also* Rejection, transplant, organ, by site) 996.80
  - ulcer (*see also* Ulcer, skin) 707.9
- **Slow**
  - feeding newborn 779.3
  - fetal, growth NEC 764.9 ☑
    - affecting management of pregnancy 656.5 ☑
- **Slowing**
  - heart 427.89
  - urinary stream 788.62
- **Sluder's neuralgia or syndrome** 337.09 ▲
- **Slurred, slurring, speech** 784.5
- **Small-for-dates** — *see also* Light-for-dates 764.0 ☑
  - affecting management of pregnancy 656.5 ☑
- **Smallpox** 050.9
  - contact V01.3
  - exposure to V01.3
  - hemorrhagic (pustular) 050.0
  - malignant 050.0
  - modified 050.2
  - vaccination
    - complications — *see* Complications, vaccination
    - prophylactic (against) V04.1
- **Small, smallness**
  - cardiac reserve — *see* Disease, heart
  - for dates
    - fetus or newborn 764.0 ☑
      - with malnutrition 764.1 ☑
        - affecting management of pregnancy 656.5 ☑
    - infant, term 764.0 ☑
      - with malnutrition 764.1 ☑
      - affecting management of pregnancy 656.5 ☑
  - introitus, vagina 623.3
  - kidney, unknown cause 589.9
    - bilateral 589.1
    - unilateral 589.0
  - ovary 620.8
  - pelvis
    - with disproportion (fetopelvic) 653.1 ☑
      - affecting fetus or newborn 763.1
    - causing obstructed labor 660.1 ☑
      - affecting fetus or newborn 763.1
  - placenta — *see* Placenta, insufficiency
  - uterus 621.8
  - white kidney 582.9
- **Smith's fracture** (separation) (closed) 813.41
  - open 813.51
- **Smith-Lemli Opitz syndrome** (cerebrohepatorenal syndrome) 759.89
- **Smith-Magenis syndrome** 758.33
- **Smith-Strang disease** (oasthouse urine) 270.2
- **Smokers'**
  - bronchitis 491.0
  - cough 491.0
  - syndrome (*see also* Abuse, drugs, nondependent) 305.1
  - throat 472.1
  - tongue 528.6
- **Smoking complicating pregnancy, childbirth, or the puerperium** 649.0 ☑
- **Smothering spells** 786.09
- **Snaggle teeth, tooth** 524.39
- **Snapping**
  - finger 727.05
  - hip 719.65
  - jaw 524.69
    - temporomandibular joint sounds on opening or closing 524.64
  - knee 717.9
  - thumb 727.05
- **Sneddon-Wilkinson disease or syndrome** (subcorneal pustular dermatosis) 694.1
- **Sneezing** 784.99
  - intractable 478.19
- **Sniffing**
  - cocaine (*see also* Dependence) 304.2 ☑
  - ether (*see also* Dependence) 304.6 ☑
  - glue (airplane) (*see also* Dependence) 304.6 ☑
- **Snoring** 786.09
- **Snow blindness** 370.24
- **Snuffles** (nonsyphilitic) 460
  - syphilitic (infant) 090.0
- **Social migrant** V60.0
- **Sodoku** 026.0
- **Soemmering's ring** 366.51
- **Soft** — *see also* condition
  - enlarged prostate 600.00
    - with
      - other lower urinary tract symptoms (LUTS) 600.01
      - urinary
        - obstruction 600.01
        - retention 600.01
  - nails 703.8
- **Softening**
  - bone 268.2
  - brain (necrotic) (progressive) 434.9 ☑
    - arteriosclerotic 437.0
    - congenital 742.4
    - embolic (*see also* Embolism, brain) 434.1 ☑
    - hemorrhagic (*see also* Hemorrhage, brain) 431
    - occlusive 434.9 ☑
    - thrombotic (*see also* Thrombosis, brain) 434.0 ☑
  - cartilage 733.92
  - cerebellar — *see* Softening, brain
  - cerebral — *see* Softening, brain
  - cerebrospinal — *see* Softening, brain
  - myocardial, heart (*see also* Degeneration, myocardial) 429.1
  - nails 703.8
  - spinal cord 336.8
  - stomach 537.89
- **Solar fever** 061
- **Soldier's**
  - heart 306.2
  - patches 423.1
- **Solitary**
  - cyst
    - bone 733.21
    - kidney 593.2
  - kidney (congenital) 753.0
  - tubercle, brain (*see also* Tuberculosis, brain) 013.2 ☑
  - ulcer, bladder 596.8
- **Somatization reaction, somatic reaction** — *see also* Disorder, psychosomatic 306.9
  - disorder 300.81
- **Somatoform disorder** 300.82
  - atypical 300.82
- **Somatoform disorder** — *continued*
  - severe 300.81
  - undifferentiated 300.82
- **Somnambulism** 307.46
  - hysterical 300.13
- **Somnolence** 780.09
  - nonorganic origin 307.43
  - periodic 349.89
- **Sonne dysentery** 004.3
- **Soor** 112.0
- **Sore**
  - Delhi 085.1
  - desert (*see also* Ulcer, skin) 707.9
  - eye 379.99
  - Lahore 085.1
  - mouth 528.9
    - canker 528.2
    - due to dentures 528.9
  - muscle 729.1
  - Naga (*see also* Ulcer, skin) 707.9
  - oriental 085.1
  - pressure (*see also* ▶Ulcer, pressure◀) 707.00
    - with gangrene (*see also* ▶Ulcer, pressure◀) 707.00 *[785.4]*
  - skin NEC 709.9
  - soft 099.0
  - throat 462
    - with influenza, flu, or grippe 487.1
    - acute 462
    - chronic 472.1
    - clergyman's 784.49
    - coxsackie (virus) 074.0
    - diphtheritic 032.0
    - epidemic 034.0
    - gangrenous 462
    - herpetic 054.79
    - influenzal 487.1
    - malignant 462
    - purulent 462
    - putrid 462
    - septic 034.0
    - streptococcal (ulcerative) 034.0
    - ulcerated 462
    - viral NEC 462
      - Coxsackie 074.0
  - tropical (*see also* Ulcer, skin) 707.9
  - veldt (*see also* Ulcer, skin) 707.9
- **Sotos' syndrome** (cerebral gigantism) 253.0
- **Sounds**
  - friction, pleural 786.7
  - succussion, chest 786.7
  - temporomandibular joint
    - on opening or closing 524.64
- **South African cardiomyopathy syndrome** 425.2
- **South American**
  - blastomycosis 116.1
  - trypanosomiasis — *see* Trypanosomiasis
- **Southeast Asian hemorrhagic fever** 065.4
- **Spacing, teeth, abnormal** 524.30
  - excessive 524.32
- **Spade-like hand** (congenital) 754.89
- **Spading nail** 703.8
  - congenital 757.5
- **Spanemia** 285.9
- **Spanish collar** 605
- **Sparganosis** 123.5
- **Spasmodic** — *see* condition
- **Spasmophilia** — *see also* Tetany 781.7
- **Spasm, spastic, spasticity** — *see also* condition 781.0
  - accommodation 367.53
  - ampulla of Vater (*see also* Disease, gallbladder) 576.8
  - anus, ani (sphincter) (reflex) 564.6
    - psychogenic 306.4
  - artery NEC 443.9
    - basilar 435.0
    - carotid 435.8
    - cerebral 435.9
      - specified artery NEC 435.8
- **Spasm, spastic, spasticity** — *see also* condition — *continued*
  - artery — *continued*
    - retinal (*see also* Occlusion, retinal, artery) 362.30
    - vertebral 435.1
    - vertebrobasilar 435.3
  - Bell's 351.0
  - bladder (sphincter, external or internal) 596.8
  - bowel 564.9
    - psychogenic 306.4
  - bronchus, bronchiole 519.11
  - cardia 530.0
  - cardiac — *see* Angina
  - carpopedal (*see also* Tetany) 781.7
  - cecum 564.9
    - psychogenic 306.4
  - cerebral (arteries) (vascular) 435.9
    - specified artery NEC 435.8
  - cerebrovascular 435.9
  - cervix, complicating delivery 661.4 ☑
    - affecting fetus or newborn 763.7
  - ciliary body (of accommodation) 367.53
  - colon 564.1
    - psychogenic 306.4
  - common duct (*see also* Disease, biliary) 576.8
  - compulsive 307.22
  - conjugate 378.82
  - convergence 378.84
  - coronary (artery) — *see* Angina
  - diaphragm (reflex) 786.8
    - psychogenic 306.1
  - duodenum, duodenal (bulb) 564.89
  - esophagus (diffuse) 530.5
    - psychogenic 306.4
  - facial 351.8
  - fallopian tube 620.8
  - gait 781.2
  - gastrointestinal (tract) 536.8
    - psychogenic 306.4
  - glottis 478.75
    - hysterical 300.11
    - psychogenic 306.1
      - specified as conversion reaction 300.11
    - reflex through recurrent laryngeal nerve 478.75
  - habit 307.20
    - chronic 307.22
    - transient (of childhood) 307.21
  - heart — *see* Angina
  - hourglass — *see* Contraction, hourglass
  - hysterical 300.11
  - infantile (*see also* Epilepsy) 345.6 ☑
  - internal oblique, eye 378.51
  - intestinal 564.9
    - psychogenic 306.4
  - larynx, laryngeal 478.75
    - hysterical 300.11
    - psychogenic 306.1
      - specified as conversion reaction 300.11
  - levator palpebrae superioris 333.81
  - lightning (*see also* Epilepsy) 345.6 ☑
  - mobile 781.0
  - muscle 728.85
    - back 724.8
    - psychogenic 306.0
  - nerve, trigeminal 350.1
  - nervous 306.0
  - nodding 307.3
    - infantile (*see also* Epilepsy) 345.6 ☑
  - occupational 300.89
  - oculogyric 378.87
  - ophthalmic artery 362.30
  - orbicularis 781.0
  - perineal 625.8
  - peroneo-extensor (*see also* Flat, foot) 734
  - pharynx (reflex) 478.29
    - hysterical 300.11

- **Spasm, spastic, spasticity** — *see also* condition — *continued*
  - pharynx — *continued*
    - psychogenic 306.1
      - specified as conversion reaction 300.11
  - pregnant uterus, complicating delivery 661.4 ☑
  - psychogenic 306.0
  - pylorus 537.81
    - adult hypertrophic 537.0
    - congenital or infantile 750.5
    - psychogenic 306.4
  - rectum (sphincter) 564.6
    - psychogenic 306.4
  - retinal artery NEC (*see also* Occlusion, retina, artery) 362.30
  - sacroiliac 724.6
  - salaam (infantile) (*see also* Epilepsy) 345.6 ☑
  - saltatory 781.0
  - sigmoid 564.9
    - psychogenic 306.4
  - sphincter of Oddi (*see also* Disease, gallbladder) 576.5
  - stomach 536.8
    - neurotic 306.4
  - throat 478.29
    - hysterical 300.11
    - psychogenic 306.1
      - specified as conversion reaction 300.11
  - tic 307.20
    - chronic 307.22
    - transient (of childhood) 307.21
  - tongue 529.8
  - torsion 333.6
  - trigeminal nerve 350.1
    - postherpetic 053.12
  - ureter 593.89
  - urethra (sphincter) 599.84
  - uterus 625.8
    - complicating labor 661.4 ☑
      - affecting fetus or newborn 763.7
  - vagina 625.1
    - psychogenic 306.51
  - vascular NEC 443.9
  - vasomotor NEC 443.9
  - vein NEC 459.89
  - vesical (sphincter, external or internal) 596.8
  - viscera 789.0 ☑
- **Spasmus nutans** 307.3
- **Spastic** — *see also* Spasm
  - child 343.9
- **Spasticity** — *see also* Spasm
  - cerebral, child 343.9
- **Speakers' throat** 784.49
- **Specific, specified** — *see* condition
- **Speech**
  - defect, disorder, disturbance, impediment NEC 784.5
    - psychogenic 307.9
  - therapy V57.3
- **Spells** 780.39
  - breath-holding 786.9
- **Spencer's disease** (epidemic vomiting) 078.82
- **Spens' syndrome** (syncope with heart block) 426.9
- **Spermatic cord** — *see* condition
- **Spermatocele** 608.1
  - congenital 752.89
- **Spermatocystitis** 608.4
- **Spermatocytoma** (M9063/3)
  - specified site — *see* Neoplasm, by site, malignant
  - unspecified site 186.9
- **Spermatorrhea** 608.89
- **Sperm counts**
  - fertility testing V26.21
  - following sterilization reversal V26.22
  - postvasectomy V25.8
- **Sphacelus** — *see also* Gangrene 785.4
- **Sphenoidal** — *see* condition
- **Sphenoiditis** (chronic) — *see also* Sinusitis, sphenoidal 473.3
- **Sphenopalatine ganglion neuralgia** 337.09 ▲
- **Sphericity, increased, lens** 743.36
- **Spherocytosis** (congenital) (familial) (hereditary) 282.0
  - hemoglobin disease 282.7
  - sickle-cell (disease) 282.60
- **Spherophakia** 743.36
- **Sphincter** — *see* condition
- **Sphincteritis, sphincter of Oddi** — *see also* Cholecystitis 576.8
- **Sphingolipidosis** 272.7
- **Sphingolipodystrophy** 272.7
- **Sphingomyelinosis** 272.7
- **Spicule tooth** 520.2
- **Spider**
  - finger 755.59
  - nevus 448.1
  - vascular 448.1
- **Spiegler-Fendt sarcoid** 686.8
- **Spielmeyer-Stock disease** 330.1
- **Spielmeyer-Vogt disease** 330.1
- **Spina bifida** (aperta) 741.9 ☑

> *Note — Use the following fifth-digit subclassification with category 741:*
>
> 0 *unspecified region*
>
> 1 *cervical region*
>
> 2 *dorsal [thoracic} region*
>
> 3 *lumbar region*

  - with hydrocephalus 741.0 ☑
    - fetal (suspected), affecting management of pregnancy 655.0 ☑
  - occulta 756.17
- **Spindle, Krukenberg's** 371.13
- **Spine, spinal** — *see* condition
- **Spiradenoma** (eccrine) (M8403/0) — *see* Neoplasm, skin, benign
- **Spirillosis** NEC — *see also* Fever, relapsing 087.9
- **Spirillum minus** 026.0
- **Spirillum obermeieri infection** 087.0
- **Spirochetal** — *see* condition
- **Spirochetosis** 104.9
  - arthritic, arthritica 104.9 *[711.8]* ☑
  - bronchopulmonary 104.8
  - icterohemorrhagica 100.0
  - lung 104.8
- **Spitting blood** — *see also* Hemoptysis 786.3
- **Splanchnomegaly** 569.89
- **Splanchnoptosis** 569.89
- **Spleen, splenic** — *see also* condition
  - agenesis 759.0
  - flexure syndrome 569.89
  - neutropenia syndrome 289.53
  - sequestration syndrome 289.52
- **Splenectasis** — *see also* Splenomegaly 789.2
- **Splenitis** (interstitial) (malignant) (nonspecific) 289.59
  - malarial (*see also* Malaria) 084.6
  - tuberculous (*see also* Tuberculosis) 017.7 ☑
- **Splenocele** 289.59
- **Splenomegalia** — *see* Splenomegaly
- **Splenomegalic** — *see* condition
- **Splenomegaly** 789.2
  - Bengal 789.2
  - cirrhotic 289.51
  - congenital 759.0
  - congestive, chronic 289.51
  - cryptogenic 789.2
  - Egyptian 120.1
  - Gaucher's (cerebroside lipidosis) 272.7
  - idiopathic 789.2
  - malarial (*see also* Malaria) 084.6
  - neutropenic 289.53
  - Niemann-Pick (lipid histiocytosis) 272.7
  - siderotic 289.51
  - syphilitic 095.8
    - congenital 090.0
- **Splenomegaly** — *continued*
  - tropical (Bengal) (idiopathic) 789.2
- **Splenopathy** 289.50
- **Splenopneumonia** — *see* Pneumonia
- **Splenoptosis** 289.59
- **Splinter** — *see* Injury, superficial, by site
- **Split, splitting**
  - heart sounds 427.89
  - lip, congenital (*see also* Cleft, lip) 749.10
  - nails 703.8
  - urinary stream 788.61
- **Spoiled child reaction** — *see also* Disturbance, conduct 312.1 ☑
- **Spondylarthritis** — *see also* Spondylosis 721.90
- **Spondylarthrosis** — *see also* Spondylosis 721.90
- **Spondylitis** 720.9
  - ankylopoietica 720.0
  - ankylosing (chronic) 720.0
  - atrophic 720.9
    - ligamentous 720.9
  - chronic (traumatic) (*see also* Spondylosis) 721.90
  - deformans (chronic) (*see also* Spondylosis) 721.90
  - gonococcal 098.53
  - gouty 274.0
  - hypertrophic (*see also* Spondylosis) 721.90
  - infectious NEC 720.9
  - juvenile (adolescent) 720.0
  - Kümmell's 721.7
  - Marie-Strümpell (ankylosing) 720.0
  - muscularis 720.9
  - ossificans ligamentosa 721.6
  - osteoarthritica (*see also* Spondylosis) 721.90
  - posttraumatic 721.7
  - proliferative 720.0
  - rheumatoid 720.0
  - rhizomelica 720.0
  - sacroiliac NEC 720.2
  - senescent (*see also* Spondylosis) 721.90
  - senile (*see also* Spondylosis) 721.90
  - static (*see also* Spondylosis) 721.90
  - traumatic (chronic) (*see also* Spondylosis) 721.90
  - tuberculous (*see also* Tuberculosis) 015.0 ☑ *[720.81]*
  - typhosa 002.0 *[720.81]*
- **Spondyloarthrosis** — *see also* Spondylosis 721.90
- **Spondylolisthesis** (congenital) (lumbosacral) 756.12
  - with disproportion (fetopelvic) 653.3 ☑
    - affecting fetus or newborn 763.1
    - causing obstructed labor 660.1 ☑
      - affecting fetus or newborn 763.1
  - acquired 738.4
  - degenerative 738.4
  - traumatic 738.4
    - acute (lumbar) — *see* Fracture, vertebra, lumbar
      - site other than lumbosacral — *see* Fracture, vertebra, by site
- **Spondylolysis** (congenital) 756.11
  - acquired 738.4
  - cervical 756.19
  - lumbosacral region 756.11
    - with disproportion (fetopelvic) 653.3 ☑
      - affecting fetus or newborn 763.1
      - causing obstructed labor 660.1 ☑
        - affecting fetus or newborn 763.1
- **Spondylopathy**
  - inflammatory 720.9
    - specified type NEC 720.89
  - traumatic 721.7
- **Spondylose rhizomelique** 720.0
- **Spondylosis** 721.90
- **Spondylosis** — *continued*
  - with
    - disproportion 653.3 ☑
      - affecting fetus or newborn 763.1
      - causing obstructed labor 660.1 ☑
        - affecting fetus or newborn 763.1
    - myelopathy NEC 721.91
  - cervical, cervicodorsal 721.0
    - with myelopathy 721.1
  - inflammatory 720.9
  - lumbar, lumbosacral 721.3
    - with myelopathy 721.42
  - sacral 721.3
    - with myelopathy 721.42
  - thoracic 721.2
    - with myelopathy 721.41
  - traumatic 721.7
- **Sponge**
  - divers' disease 989.5
  - inadvertently left in operation wound 998.4
  - kidney (medullary) 753.17
- **Spongioblastoma** (M9422/3)
  - multiforme (M9440/3)
    - specified site — *see* Neoplasm, by site, malignant
    - unspecified site 191.9
  - polare (M9423/3)
    - specified site — *see* Neoplasm, by site, malignant
    - unspecified site 191.9
  - primitive polar (M9443/3)
    - specified site — *see* Neoplasm, by site, malignant
    - unspecified site 191.9
  - specified site — *see* Neoplasm, by site, malignant
  - unspecified site 191.9
- **Spongiocytoma** (M9400/3)
  - specified site — *see* Neoplasm, by site, malignant
  - unspecified site 191.9
- **Spongioneuroblastoma** (M9504/3) — *see* Neoplasm, by site, malignant
- **Spontaneous** — *see also* condition
  - fracture — *see* Fracture, pathologic
- **Spoon nail** 703.8
  - congenital 757.5
- **Sporadic** — *see* condition
- **Sporotrichosis** (bones) (cutaneous) (disseminated) (epidermal) (lymphatic) (lymphocutaneous) (mucous membranes) (pulmonary) (skeletal) (visceral) 117.1
- **Sporotrichum schenckii infection** 117.1
- **Spots, spotting**
  - atrophic (skin) 701.3
  - Bitôt's (in the young child) 264.1
  - café au lait 709.09
  - cayenne pepper 448.1
  - complicating pregnancy 649.5 ☑
  - cotton wool (retina) 362.83
  - de Morgan's (senile angiomas) 448.1
  - Fúchs' black (myopic) 360.21
  - intermenstrual
    - irregular 626.6
    - regular 626.5
  - interpalpebral 372.53
  - Koplik's 055.9
  - liver 709.09
  - Mongolian (pigmented) 757.33
  - of pregnancy 649.5 ☑ ▲
  - purpuric 782.7
  - ruby 448.1
- **Spotted fever** — *see* Fever, spotted
- **Sprain, strain** (joint) (ligament) (muscle) (tendon) 848.9
  - abdominal wall (muscle) 848.8
  - Achilles tendon 845.09
  - acromioclavicular 840.0
  - ankle 845.00
    - and foot 845.00
  - anterior longitudinal, cervical 847.0

Sprain, strain — *continued*
- arm 840.9
  - upper 840.9
    - and shoulder 840.9
- astragalus 845.00
- atlanto-axial 847.0
- atlanto-occipital 847.0
- atlas 847.0
- axis 847.0
- back (*see also* Sprain, spine) 847.9
- breast bone 848.40
- broad ligament — *see* Injury, internal, broad ligament
- calcaneofibular 845.02
- carpal 842.01
- carpometacarpal 842.11
- cartilage
  - costal, without mention of injury to sternum 848.3
    - involving sternum 848.42
  - ear 848.8
  - knee 844.9
    - with current tear (*see also* Tear, meniscus) 836.2
  - semilunar (knee) 844.8
    - with current tear (*see also* Tear, meniscus) 836.2
  - septal, nose 848.0
  - thyroid region 848.2
  - xiphoid 848.49
- cervical, cervicodorsal, cervicothoracic 847.0
- chondrocostal, without mention of injury to sternum 848.3
  - involving sternum 848.42
- chondrosternal 848.42
- chronic (joint) — *see* Derangement, joint
- clavicle 840.9
- coccyx 847.4
- collar bone 840.9
- collateral, knee (medial) (tibial) 844.1
  - lateral (fibular) 844.0
  - recurrent or old 717.89
    - lateral 717.81
    - medial 717.82
- coracoacromial 840.8
- coracoclavicular 840.1
- coracohumeral 840.2
- coracoid (process) 840.9
- coronary, knee 844.8
- costal cartilage, without mention of injury to sternum 848.3
  - involving sternum 848.42
- cricoarytenoid articulation 848.2
- cricothyroid articulation 848.2
- cruciate
  - knee 844.2
  - old 717.89
    - anterior 717.83
    - posterior 717.84
- deltoid
  - ankle 845.01
  - shoulder 840.8
- dorsal (spine) 847.1
- ear cartilage 848.8
- elbow 841.9
  - and forearm 841.9
  - specified site NEC 841.8
- femur (proximal end) 843.9
  - distal end 844.9
- fibula (proximal end) 844.9
  - distal end 845.00
- fibulocalcaneal 845.02
- finger(s) 842.10
- foot 845.10
  - and ankle 845.00
- forearm 841.9
  - and elbow 841.9
  - specified site NEC 841.8
- glenoid (shoulder) (*see also* SLAP lesion) 840.8
- hand 842.10
- hip 843.9
  - and thigh 843.9
- humerus (proximal end) 840.9

Sprain, strain — *continued*
- humerus — *continued*
  - distal end 841.9
- iliofemoral 843.0
- infraspinatus 840.3
- innominate
  - acetabulum 843.9
  - pubic junction 848.5
  - sacral junction 846.1
- internal
  - collateral, ankle 845.01
  - semilunar cartilage 844.8
    - with current tear (*see also* Tear, meniscus) 836.2
    - old 717.5
- interphalangeal
  - finger 842.13
  - toe 845.13
- ischiocapsular 843.1
- jaw (cartilage) (meniscus) 848.1
  - old 524.69
- knee 844.9
  - and leg 844.9
  - old 717.5
    - collateral
      - lateral 717.81
      - medial 717.82
    - cruciate
      - anterior 717.83
      - posterior 717.84
- late effect — *see* Late, effects (of), sprain
- lateral collateral, knee 844.0
  - old 717.81
- leg 844.9
  - and knee 844.9
- ligamentum teres femoris 843.8
- low back 846.9
- lumbar (spine) 847.2
- lumbosacral 846.0
  - chronic or old 724.6
- mandible 848.1
  - old 524.69
- maxilla 848.1
- medial collateral, knee 844.1
  - old 717.82
- meniscus
  - jaw 848.1
    - old 524.69
  - knee 844.8
    - with current tear (*see also* Tear, meniscus) 836.2
    - old 717.5
  - mandible 848.1
    - old 524.69
  - specified site NEC 848.8
- metacarpal 842.10
  - distal 842.12
  - proximal 842.11
- metacarpophalangeal 842.12
- metatarsal 845.10
- metatarsophalangeal 845.12
- midcarpal 842.19
- midtarsal 845.19
- multiple sites, except fingers alone or toes alone 848.8
- neck 847.0
- nose (septal cartilage) 848.0
- occiput from atlas 847.0
- old — *see* Derangement, joint
- orbicular, hip 843.8
- patella(r) 844.8
  - old 717.89
- pelvis 848.5
- phalanx
  - finger 842.10
  - toe 845.10
- radiocarpal 842.02
- radiohumeral 841.2
- radioulnar 841.9
  - distal 842.09
- radius, radial (proximal end) 841.9
  - and ulna 841.9
    - distal 842.09
  - collateral 841.0
  - distal end 842.00

Sprain, strain — *continued*
- recurrent — *see* Sprain, by site
- rib (cage), without mention of injury to sternum 848.3
  - involving sternum 848.42
- rotator cuff (capsule) 840.4
- round ligament (*see also* Injury, internal, round ligament)
  - femur 843.8
- sacral (spine) 847.3
- sacrococcygeal 847.3
- sacroiliac (region) 846.9
  - chronic or old 724.6
  - ligament 846.1
  - specified site NEC 846.8
- sacrospinatus 846.2
- sacrospinous 846.2
- sacrotuberous 846.3
- scaphoid bone, ankle 845.00
- scapula(r) 840.9
- semilunar cartilage (knee) 844.8
  - with current tear (*see also* Tear, meniscus) 836.2
  - old 717.5
- septal cartilage (nose) 848.0
- shoulder 840.9
  - and arm, upper 840.9
  - blade 840.9
- specified site NEC 848.8
- spine 847.9
  - cervical 847.0
  - coccyx 847.4
  - dorsal 847.1
  - lumbar 847.2
  - lumbosacral 846.0
    - chronic or old 724.6
  - sacral 847.3
  - sacroiliac (*see also* Sprain, sacroiliac) 846.9
    - chronic or old 724.6
  - thoracic 847.1
- sternoclavicular 848.41
- sternum 848.40
- subglenoid (*see also* SLAP lesion) 840.8
- subscapularis 840.5
- supraspinatus 840.6
- symphysis
  - jaw 848.1
    - old 524.69
  - mandibular 848.1
    - old 524.69
  - pubis 848.5
- talofibular 845.09
- tarsal 845.10
- tarsometatarsal 845.11
- temporomandibular 848.1
  - old 524.69
- teres
  - ligamentum femoris 843.8
  - major or minor 840.8
- thigh (proximal end) 843.9
  - and hip 843.9
  - distal end 844.9
- thoracic (spine) 847.1
- thorax 848.8
- thumb 842.10
- thyroid cartilage or region 848.2
- tibia (proximal end) 844.9
  - distal end 845.00
- tibiofibular
  - distal 845.03
  - superior 844.3
- toe(s) 845.10
- trachea 848.8
- trapezoid 840.8
- ulna, ulnar (proximal end) 841.9
  - collateral 841.1
  - distal end 842.00
- ulnohumeral 841.3
- vertebrae (*see also* Sprain, spine) 847.9
  - cervical, cervicodorsal, cervicothoracic 847.0
- wrist (cuneiform) (scaphoid) (semilunar) 842.00

Sprain, strain — *continued*
- xiphoid cartilage 848.49

Sprengel's deformity (congenital) 755.52

Spring fever 309.23

Sprue 579.1
- celiac 579.0
- idiopathic 579.0
- meaning thrush 112.0
- nontropical 579.0
- tropical 579.1

Spur — *see also* Exostosis
- bone 726.91
  - calcaneal 726.73
- calcaneal 726.73
- iliac crest 726.5
- nose (septum) 478.19
  - bone 726.91
- septal 478.19

Spuria placenta — *see* Placenta, abnormal

Spurway's syndrome (brittle bones and blue sclera) 756.51

Sputum, abnormal (amount) (color) (excessive) (odor) (purulent) 786.4
- bloody 786.3

Squamous — *see also* condition
- cell metaplasia
  - bladder 596.8
  - cervix — *see* condition
- epithelium in
  - cervical canal (congenital) 752.49
  - uterine mucosa (congenital) 752.3
- metaplasia
  - bladder 596.8
  - cervix — *see* condition

Squashed nose 738.0
- congenital 754.0

Squeeze, divers' 993.3

Squint — *see also* Strabismus 378.9
- accommodative (*see also* Esotropia) 378.00
- concomitant (*see also* Heterotropia) 378.30

Stab — *see also* Wound, open, by site
- internal organs — *see* Injury, internal, by site, with open wound

Staggering gait 781.2
- hysterical 300.11

Staghorn calculus 592.0

Stain, staining
- meconium 779.84
- port wine 757.32
- tooth, teeth (hard tissues) 521.7
  - due to
    - accretions 523.6
    - deposits (betel) (black) (green) (materia alba) (orange) (tobacco) 523.6
    - metals (copper) (silver) 521.7
    - nicotine 523.6
    - pulpal bleeding 521.7
    - tobacco 523.6

Stälh's
- ear 744.29
- pigment line (cornea) 371.11

Stälhi's pigment lines (cornea) 371.11

Stammering 307.0

Standstill
- atrial 426.6
- auricular 426.6
- cardiac (*see also* Arrest, cardiac) 427.5
- sinoatrial 426.6
- sinus 426.6
- ventricular (*see also* Arrest, cardiac) 427.5

Stannosis 503

Stanton's disease (melioidosis) 025

Staphylitis (acute) (catarrhal) (chronic) (gangrenous) (membranous) (suppurative) (ulcerative) 528.3

Staphylococcemia 038.10
- aureus 038.11
- specified organism NEC 038.19

Staphylococcus, staphylococcal — *see* condition

Staphyloderma (skin) 686.00

Staphyloma 379.11
- anterior, localized 379.14
- ciliary 379.11
- cornea 371.73
- equatorial 379.13
- posterior 379.12
- posticum 379.12
- ring 379.15
- sclera NEC 379.11

Starch eating 307.52

Stargardt's disease 362.75

Starvation (inanition) (due to lack of food) 994.2
- edema 262
- voluntary NEC 307.1

Stasis
- bile (duct) (*see also* Disease, biliary) 576.8
- bronchus (*see also* Bronchitis) 490
- cardiac (*see also* Failure, heart) 428.0
- cecum 564.89
- colon 564.89
- dermatitis (*see also* Varix, with stasis dermatitis) 454.1
- duodenal 536.8
- eczema (*see also* Varix, with stasis dermatitis) 454.1
- edema (*see also* Hypertension, venous) 459.30
- foot 991.4
- gastric 536.3
- ileocecal coil 564.89
- ileum 564.89
- intestinal 564.89
- jejunum 564.89
- kidney 586
- liver 571.9
  - cirrhotic — *see* Cirrhosis, liver
- lymphatic 457.8
- pneumonia 514
- portal 571.9
- pulmonary 514
- rectal 564.89
- renal 586
  - tubular 584.5
- stomach 536.3
- ulcer
  - with varicose veins 454.0
  - without varicose veins 459.81
- urine NEC (*see also* Retention, urine) 788.20
- venous 459.81

State
- affective and paranoid, mixed, organic psychotic 294.8
- agitated 307.9
  - acute reaction to stress 308.2
- anxiety (neurotic) (*see also* Anxiety) 300.00
  - specified type NEC 300.09
- apprehension (*see also* Anxiety) 300.00
  - specified type NEC 300.09
- climacteric, female 627.2
  - following induced menopause 627.4
- clouded
  - epileptic (*see also* Epilepsy) 345.9 ☑
  - paroxysmal (idiopathic) (*see also* Epilepsy) 345.9 ☑
- compulsive (mixed) (with obsession) 300.3
- confusional 298.9
  - acute 293.0
    - with
      - arteriosclerotic dementia 290.41
      - presenile brain disease 290.11
      - senility 290.3
    - alcoholic 291.0
    - drug-induced 292.81
  - epileptic 293.0
  - postoperative 293.9

State — *continued*
- confusional — *continued*
  - reactive (emotional stress) (psychological trauma) 298.2
  - subacute 293.1
- constitutional psychopathic 301.9
- convulsive (*see also* Convulsions) 780.39
- depressive NEC 311
  - induced by drug 292.84
  - neurotic 300.4
- dissociative 300.15
- hallucinatory 780.1
  - induced by drug 292.12
- hypercoagulable (primary) 289.81
  - secondary 289.82
- hyperdynamic beta-adrenergic circulatory 429.82
- locked-in 344.81
- menopausal 627.2
  - artificial 627.4
  - following induced menopause 627.4
- neurotic NEC 300.9
  - with depersonalization episode 300.6
- obsessional 300.3
- oneiroid (*see also* Schizophrenia) 295.4 ☑
- panic 300.01
- paranoid 297.9
  - alcohol-induced 291.5
  - arteriosclerotic 290.42
  - climacteric 297.2
  - drug-induced 292.11
  - in
    - presenile brain disease 290.12
    - senile brain disease 290.20
  - involutional 297.2
  - menopausal 297.2
  - senile 290.20
  - simple 297.0
- postleukotomy 310.0
- pregnant (*see also* Pregnancy) V22.2
- psychogenic, twilight 298.2
- psychotic, organic (*see also* Psychosis, organic) 294.9
  - mixed paranoid and affective 294.8
  - senile or presenile NEC 290.9
  - transient NEC 293.9
    - with
      - anxiety 293.84
      - delusions 293.81
      - depression 293.83
      - hallucinations 293.82
- residual schizophrenic (*see also* Schizophrenia) 295.6 ☑
- tension (*see also* Anxiety) 300.9
- transient organic psychotic 293.9
  - anxiety type 293.84
  - depressive type 293.83
  - hallucinatory type 293.83
  - paranoid type 293.81
  - specified type NEC 293.89
- twilight
  - epileptic 293.0
  - psychogenic 298.2
- vegetative (persistent) 780.03

Status (post)
- absence
  - epileptic (*see also* Epilepsy) 345.2
  - of organ, acquired (postsurgical) — *see* Absence, by site, acquired
- administration of tPA(rtPA) in a different institution within the last 24 hours prior to admission to facility V45.88 ●
- anastomosis of intestine (for bypass) V45.3
- anginosus 413.9
- angioplasty, percutaneous transluminal coronary V45.82
- ankle prosthesis V43.66
- aortocoronary bypass or shunt V45.81
- arthrodesis V45.4

Status — *continued*
- artificially induced condition NEC V45.89
- artificial opening (of) V44.9
  - gastrointestinal tract NEC V44.4
  - specified site NEC V44.8
  - urinary tract NEC V44.6
  - vagina V44.7
- aspirator V46.0
- asthmaticus (*see also* Asthma) 493.9 ☑
- awaiting organ transplant V49.83
- bariatric surgery V45.86
  - complicating pregnancy, childbirth, or the puerperium 649.2 ☑
- bed confinement V49.84
- breast
  - correction V43.82 ●
  - implant removal V45.83 ●
  - reconstruction V43.82 ●
- cardiac
  - device (in situ) V45.00
    - carotid sinus V45.09
      - fitting or adjustment V53.39
    - defibrillator, automatic implantable V45.02
    - pacemaker V45.01
      - fitting or adjustment V53.31
- carotid sinus stimulator V45.09
- cataract extraction V45.61
- chemotherapy V66.2
  - current V58.69
- circumcision, female 629.20
- clitorectomy (female genital mutilation type I) 629.21
  - with excision of labia minora (female genital mutilation type II) 629.22
- colonization — *see* Carrier (suspected) of ●
- colostomy V44.3
- contraceptive device V45.59
  - intrauterine V45.51
  - subdermal V45.52
- convulsivus idiopathicus (*see also* Epilepsy) 345.3
- coronary artery bypass or shunt V45.81
- current military deployment status V62.21 ●
- cutting
  - female genital 629.20
    - specified NEC 629.29
    - type I 629.21
    - type II 629.22
    - type III 629.23
    - type IV 629.29
- cystostomy V44.50
  - appendico-vesicostomy V44.52
  - cutaneous-vesicostomy V44.51
  - specified type NEC V44.59
- defibrillator, automatic implantable cardiac V45.02
- dental crowns V45.84
- dental fillings V45.84
- dental restoration V45.84
- dental sealant V49.82
- dialysis (hemo) (peritoneal) V45.11 ▲
- donor V59.9
- drug therapy or regimen V67.59
  - high-risk medication NEC V67.51
- elbow prosthesis V43.62
- enterostomy V44.4
- epileptic, epilepticus (absence) (grand mal) (*see also* Epilepsy) 345.3
  - focal motor 345.7 ☑
  - partial 345.7 ☑
  - petit mal 345.2
  - psychomotor 345.7 ☑
  - temporal lobe 345.7 ☑
- estrogen receptor
  - negative [ER-] V86.1
  - positive [ER+] V86.0
- eye (adnexa) surgery V45.69

Status — *continued*
- female genital
  - cutting 629.20
    - specified NEC 629.29
    - type I 629.21
    - type II 629.22
    - type III 629.23
    - type IV 629.29
  - mutilation 629.20
    - type I 629.21
    - type II 629.22
    - type III 629.23
    - type IV 629.29
- filtering bleb (eye) (postglaucoma) V45.69
  - with rupture or complication 997.99
  - postcataract extraction (complication) 997.99
- finger joint prosthesis V43.69
- gastric
  - banding V45.86
    - complicating pregnancy, childbirth, or the puerperium 649.2 ☑
  - bypass for obesity V45.86
    - complicating pregnancy, childbirth, or the puerperium 649.2 ☑
- gastrostomy V44.1
- grand mal 345.3
- heart valve prosthesis V43.3
- hemodialysis V45.11 ▲
- hip prosthesis (joint) (partial) (total) V43.64
- hysterectomy V88.01 ●
  - partial with remaining cervical stump V88.02 ●
  - total V88.01 ●
- ileostomy V44.2
- infibulation (female genital mutilation type III) 629.23
- insulin pump V45.85
- intestinal bypass V45.3
- intrauterine contraceptive device V45.51
- jejunostomy V44.4
- knee joint prosthesis V43.65
- lacunaris 437.8
- lacunosis 437.8
- low birth weight V21.30
  - less than 500 grams V21.31
  - 1000–1499 grams V21.33
  - 1500–1999 grams V21.34
  - 2000–2500 grams V21.35
  - 500–999 grams V21.32
- lymphaticus 254.8
- malignant neoplasm, ablated or excised — *see* History, malignant neoplasm
- marmoratus 333.79
- mutilation, female 629.20
  - type I 629.21
  - type II 629.22
  - type III 629.23
  - type IV 629.29
- nephrostomy V44.6
- neuropacemaker NEC V45.89
  - brain V45.89
  - carotid sinus V45.09
  - neurologic NEC V45.89
- obesity surgery V45.86
  - compliating pregnancy, childbirth, or the puerperium 649.2 ☑
- organ replacement
  - by artificial or mechanical device or prosthesis of
    - artery V43.4
    - artificial skin V43.83
    - bladder V43.5
    - blood vessel V43.4
    - breast V43.82
    - eye globe V43.0
    - heart
      - assist device V43.21

Status — *continued*
- organ replacement — *continued*
  - by artificial or mechanical device or prosthesis of — *continued*
    - heart — *continued*
      - fully implantable artificial heart V43.22
      - valve V43.3
    - intestine V43.89
    - joint V43.60
      - ankle V43.66
      - elbow V43.62
      - finger V43.69
      - hip (partial) (total) V43.64
      - knee V43.65
      - shoulder V43.61
      - specified NEC V43.69
      - wrist V43.63
    - kidney V43.89
    - larynx V43.81
    - lens V43.1
    - limb(s) V43.7
    - liver V43.89
    - lung V43.89
    - organ NEC V43.89
    - pancreas V43.89
    - skin (artificial) V43.83
    - tissue NEC V43.89
    - vein V43.4
  - by organ transplant (heterologous) (homologous) — *see* Status, transplant
- pacemaker
  - brain V45.89
  - cardiac V45.01
  - carotid sinus V45.09
  - neurologic NEC V45.89
  - specified site NEC V45.89
- percutaneous transluminal coronary angioplasty V45.82
- peritoneal dialysis V45.11 ▲
- petit mal 345.2
- postcommotio cerebri 310.2
- postmenopausal (age related) (natural) V49.81
- postoperative NEC V45.89
- postpartum NEC V24.2
  - care immediately following delivery V24.0
  - routine follow-up V24.2
- postsurgical NEC V45.89
- renal dialysis V45.11 ▲
  - noncompliance V45.12 ●
- respirator [ventilator] V46.11
  - encounter
    - during
      - mechanical failure V46.14
      - power failure V46.12
    - for weaning V46.13
- reversed jejunal transposition (for bypass) V45.3
- sex reassignment surgery (*see also* Trans-sexualism) 302.50
- shoulder prosthesis V43.61
- shunt
  - aortocoronary bypass V45.81
  - arteriovenous (for dialysis) V45.11 ▲
  - cerebrospinal fluid V45.2
  - vascular NEC V45.89
    - aortocoronary (bypass) V45.81
  - ventricular (communicating) (for drainage) V45.2
- sterilization
  - tubal ligation V26.51
  - vasectomy V26.52
- subdermal contraceptive device V45.52
- thymicolymphaticus 254.8
- thymicus 254.8
- thymolymphaticus 254.8
- tooth extraction 525.10
- tracheostomy V44.0
- transplant
  - blood vessel V42.89

Status — *continued*
- transplant — *continued*
  - bone V42.4
    - marrow V42.81
  - cornea V42.5
  - heart V42.1
    - valve V42.2
  - intestine V42.84
  - kidney V42.0
  - liver V42.7
  - lung V42.6
  - organ V42.9
    - removal (due to complication, failure, rejection or infection) V45.87 ●
    - specified site NEC V42.89
  - pancreas V42.83
  - peripheral stem cells V42.82
  - skin V42.3
  - stem cells, peripheral V42.82
  - tissue V42.9
    - specified type NEC V42.89
  - vessel, blood V42.89
- tubal ligation V26.51
- ureterostomy V44.6
- urethrostomy V44.6
- vagina, artificial V44.7
- vascular shunt NEC V45.89
  - aortocoronary (bypass) V45.81
- vasectomy V26.52
- ventilator [respirator] V46.11
  - encounter
    - during
      - mechanical failure V46.14
      - power failure V46.12
    - for weaning V46.13
- wheelchair confinement V46.3 ●
- wrist prosthesis V43.63

Stave fracture — *see* Fracture, metacarpus, metacarpal bone(s)

Steal
- subclavian artery 435.2
- vertebral artery 435.1

Stealing, solitary, child problem — *see also* Disturbance, conduct 312.1 ☑

Steam burn — *see* Burn, by site

Steatocystoma multiplex 706.2

Steatoma (infected) 706.2
- eyelid (cystic) 374.84
  - infected 373.13

Steatorrhea (chronic) 579.8
- with lacteal obstruction 579.2
- idiopathic 579.0
  - adult 579.0
  - infantile 579.0
- pancreatic 579.4
- primary 579.0
- secondary 579.8
- specified cause NEC 579.8
- tropical 579.1

Steatosis 272.8
- heart (*see also* Degeneration, myocardial) 429.1
- kidney 593.89
- liver 571.8

Steele-Richardson (-Olszewski) Syndrome 333.0

Steinbrocker's syndrome — *see also* Neuropathy, peripheral, autonomic 337.9

Steinert's disease 359.21

Stein-Leventhal syndrome (polycystic ovary) 256.4

Stein's syndrome (polycystic ovary) 256.4

STEMI (ST elevation myocardial infarction — *see also* — Infarct, myocardium, ST elevation 410.9 ☑

Stenocardia — *see also* Angina 413.9

Stenocephaly 756.0

Stenosis (cicatricial) — *see also* Stricture
- ampulla of Vater 576.2
  - with calculus, cholelithiasis, or stones — *see* Choledocholithiasis
- anus, anal (canal) (sphincter) 569.2

Stenosis — *see also* Stricture — *continued*
- anus, anal — *continued*
  - congenital 751.2
- aorta (ascending) 747.22
  - arch 747.10
  - arteriosclerotic 440.0
  - calcified 440.0
- aortic (valve) 424.1
  - with
    - mitral (valve)
      - insufficiency or incompetence 396.2
      - stenosis or obstruction 396.0
  - atypical 396.0
  - congenital 746.3
  - rheumatic 395.0
    - with
      - insufficiency, incompetency or regurgitation 395.2
        - with mitral (valve) disease 396.8
      - mitral (valve)
        - disease (stenosis) 396.0
        - insufficiency or incompetence 396.2
        - stenosis or obstruction 396.0
  - specified cause, except rheumatic 424.1
  - syphilitic 093.22
- aqueduct of Sylvius (congenital) 742.3
  - with spina bifida (*see also* Spina bifida) 741.0 ☑
  - acquired 331.4
- artery NEC (*see also* Arteriosclerosis) 447.1
  - basilar — *see* Narrowing, artery, basilar
  - carotid (common) (internal) — *see* Narrowing, artery, carotid
  - celiac 447.4
  - cerebral 437.0
    - due to
      - embolism (*see also* Embolism, brain) 434.1 ☑
      - thrombus (*see also* Thrombosis, brain) 434.0 ☑
  - extremities 440.20
  - precerebral — *see* Narrowing, artery, precerebral
  - pulmonary (congenital) 747.3
    - acquired 417.8
  - renal 440.1
  - vertebral — *see* Narrowing, artery, vertebral
- bile duct or biliary passage (*see also* Obstruction, biliary) 576.2
  - congenital 751.61
- bladder neck (acquired) 596.0
  - congenital 753.6
- brain 348.8
- bronchus 519.19
  - syphilitic 095.8
- cardia (stomach) 537.89
  - congenital 750.7
- cardiovascular (*see also* Disease, cardiovascular) 429.2
- carotid artery — *see* Narrowing, artery, carotid
- cervix, cervical (canal) 622.4
  - congenital 752.49
  - in pregnancy or childbirth 654.6 ☑
    - affecting fetus or newborn 763.89
    - causing obstructed labor 660.2 ☑
      - affecting fetus or newborn 763.1
- colon (*see also* Obstruction, intestine) 560.9
  - congenital 751.2
- colostomy 569.62
- common bile duct (*see also* Obstruction, biliary) 576.2
  - congenital 751.61

Stenosis — *see also* Stricture — *continued*
- coronary (artery) — *see* Arteriosclerosis, coronary
- cystic duct (*see also* Obstruction, gallbladder) 575.2
  - congenital 751.61
- due to (presence of) any device, implant, or graft classifiable to 996.0–996.5 — *see* Complications, due to (presence of) any device, implant, or graft classified to 996.0–996.5 NEC
- duodenum 537.3
  - congenital 751.1
- ejaculatory duct NEC 608.89
- endocervical os — *see* Stenosis, cervix
- enterostomy 569.62
- esophagostomy 530.87
- esophagus 530.3
  - congenital 750.3
  - syphilitic 095.8
    - congenital 090.5
- external ear canal 380.50
  - secondary to
    - inflammation 380.53
    - surgery 380.52
    - trauma 380.51
- gallbladder (*see also* Obstruction, gallbladder) 575.2
- glottis 478.74
- heart valve (acquired) (*see also* Endocarditis)
  - congenital NEC 746.89
    - aortic 746.3
    - mitral 746.5
    - pulmonary 746.02
    - tricuspid 746.1
- hepatic duct (*see also* Obstruction, biliary) 576.2
- hymen 623.3
- hypertrophic subaortic (idiopathic) 425.1
- infundibulum cardiac 746.83
- intestine (*see also* Obstruction, intestine) 560.9
  - congenital (small) 751.1
    - large 751.2
- lacrimal
  - canaliculi 375.53
  - duct 375.56
    - congenital 743.65
  - punctum 375.52
    - congenital 743.65
  - sac 375.54
    - congenital 743.65
- lacrimonasal duct 375.56
  - congenital 743.65
  - neonatal 375.55
- larynx 478.74
  - congenital 748.3
  - syphilitic 095.8
    - congenital 090.5
- mitral (valve) (chronic) (inactive) 394.0
  - with
    - aortic (valve)
      - disease (insufficiency) 396.1
      - insufficiency or incompetence 396.1
      - stenosis or obstruction 396.0
    - incompetency, insufficiency or regurgitation 394.2
      - with aortic valve disease 396.8
  - active or acute 391.1
    - with chorea (acute) (rheumatic) (Sydenham's) 392.0
  - congenital 746.5
  - specified cause, except rheumatic 424.0
  - syphilitic 093.21
- myocardium, myocardial (*see also* Degeneration, myocardial) 429.1
  - hypertrophic subaortic (idiopathic) 425.1
- nares (anterior) (posterior) 478.19

Stenosis — *see also* Stricture — *continued*
nares — *continued*
congenital 748.0
nasal duct 375.56
congenital 743.65
nasolacrimal duct 375.56
congenital 743.65
neonatal 375.55
organ or site, congenital NEC — *see* Atresia
papilla of Vater 576.2
with calculus, cholelithiasis, or stones — *see* Choledocholithiasis
pulmonary (artery) (congenital) 747.3
with ventricular septal defect, dextraposition of aorta and hypertrophy of right ventricle 745.2
acquired 417.8
infundibular 746.83
in tetralogy of Fallot 745.2
subvalvular 746.83
valve (*see also* Endocarditis, pulmonary) 424.3
congenital 746.02
vein 747.49
acquired 417.8
vessel NEC 417.8
pulmonic (congenital) 746.02
infundibular 746.83
subvalvular 746.83
pylorus (hypertrophic) 537.0
adult 537.0
congenital 750.5
infantile 750.5
rectum (sphincter) (*see also* Stricture, rectum) 569.2
renal artery 440.1
salivary duct (any) 527.8
sphincter of Oddi (*see also* Obstruction, biliary) 576.2
spinal 724.00
cervical 723.0
lumbar, lumbosacral 724.02
nerve (root) NEC 724.9
specified region NEC 724.09
thoracic, thoracolumbar 724.01
stomach, hourglass 537.6
subaortic 746.81
hypertrophic (idiopathic) 425.1
supra (valvular)-aortic 747.22
trachea 519.19
congenital 748.3
syphilitic 095.8
tuberculous (*see also* Tuberculosis) 012.8 ☑
tracheostomy 519.02
tricuspid (valve) (*see also* Endocarditis, tricuspid) 397.0
congenital 746.1
nonrheumatic 424.2
tubal 628.2
ureter (*see also* Stricture, ureter) 593.3
congenital 753.29
urethra (*see also* Stricture, urethra) 598.9
vagina 623.2
congenital 752.49
in pregnancy or childbirth 654.7 ☑
affecting fetus or newborn 763.89
causing obstructed labor 660.2 ☑
affecting fetus or newborn 763.1
valve (cardiac) (heart) (*see also* Endocarditis) 424.90
congenital NEC 746.89
aortic 746.3
mitral 746.5
pulmonary 746.02
tricuspid 746.1
urethra 753.6
Stenosis — *see also* Stricture — *continued*
valvular (*see also* Endocarditis) 424.90
congenital NEC 746.89
urethra 753.6
vascular graft or shunt 996.1
atherosclerosis — *see* Arteriosclerosis, extremities
embolism 996.74
occlusion NEC 996.74
thrombus 996.74
vena cava (inferior) (superior) 459.2
congenital 747.49
ventricular shunt 996.2
vulva 624.8
Stercolith — *see also* Fecalith 560.39
appendix 543.9
Stercoraceous, stercoral ulcer 569.82
anus or rectum 569.41
Stereopsis, defective
with fusion 368.33
without fusion 368.32
Stereotypes NEC 307.3
Sterility
female — *see* Infertility, female
male (*see also* Infertility, male) 606.9
Sterilization, admission for V25.2
status
tubal ligation V26.51
vasectomy V26.52
Sternalgia — *see also* Angina 413.9
Sternopagus 759.4
Sternum bifidum 756.3
Sternutation 784.99
Steroid
effects (adverse) (iatrogenic)
cushingoid
correct substance properly administered 255.0
overdose or wrong substance given or taken 962.0
diabetes — ▶*see* Diabetes, secondary◀
correct substance properly administered 251.8
overdose or wrong substance given or taken 962.0
due to
correct substance properly administered 255.8
overdose or wrong substance given or taken 962.0
fever
correct substance properly administered 780.60 ▲
overdose or wrong substance given or taken 962.0
withdrawal
correct substance properly administered 255.41
overdose or wrong substance given or taken 962.0
responder 365.03
Stevens-Johnson disease or syndrome (erythema multiforme exudativum) 695.13 ▲
toxic epidermal necrolysis overlap ●
(SJS-TEN overlap syndrome) ●
695.14 ●
Stewart-Morel syndrome (hyperostosis frontalis interna) 733.3
Sticker's disease (erythema infectiosum) 057.0
Stickler syndrome 759.89
Sticky eye 372.03
Stieda's disease (calcification, knee joint) 726.62
Stiff
back 724.8
neck (*see also* Torticollis) 723.5
Stiff-baby 759.89
Stiff-man syndrome 333.91
Stiffness, joint NEC 719.50
ankle 719.57
back 724.8
Stiffness, joint — *continued*
elbow 719.52
finger 719.54
hip 719.55
knee 719.56
multiple sites 719.59
sacroiliac 724.6
shoulder 719.51
specified site NEC 719.58
spine 724.9
surgical fusion V45.4
wrist 719.53
Stigmata, congenital syphilis 090.5
Stillbirth, stillborn NEC 779.9
Still's disease or syndrome 714.30
adult onset 714.2 ●
Stiller's disease (asthenia) 780.79
Still-Felty syndrome (rheumatoid arthritis with splenomegaly and leukopenia) 714.1
Stilling-Türk-Duane syndrome (ocular retraction syndrome) 378.71
Stimulation, ovary 256.1
Sting (animal) (bee) (fish) (insect) (jellyfish) (Portuguese man-o-war) (wasp) (venomous) 989.5
anaphylactic shock or reaction 989.5
plant 692.6
Stippled epiphyses 756.59
Stitch
abscess 998.59
burst (in external operation wound) ▶(*see also* Dehiscence)◀ 998.32
internal 998.31
in back 724.5
Stojano's (subcostal) **syndrome** 098.86
Stokes-Adams syndrome (syncope with heart block) 426.9
Stokes' disease (exophthalmic goiter) 242.0 ☑
Stokvis' (-Talma) disease (enterogenous cyanosis) 289.7
Stomach — *see* condition
Stoma malfunction
colostomy 569.62
cystostomy 997.5
enterostomy 569.62
esophagostomy 530.87
gastrostomy 536.42
ileostomy 569.62
nephrostomy 997.5
tracheostomy 519.02
ureterostomy 997.5
Stomatitis 528.00
angular 528.5
due to dietary or vitamin deficiency 266.0
aphthous 528.2
bovine 059.11 ●
candidal 112.0
catarrhal 528.00
denture 528.9
diphtheritic (membranous) 032.0
due to
dietary deficiency 266.0
thrush 112.0
vitamin deficiency 266.0
epidemic 078.4
epizootic 078.4
follicular 528.00
gangrenous 528.1
herpetic 054.2
herpetiformis 528.2
malignant 528.00
membranous acute 528.00
monilial 112.0
mycotic 112.0
necrotic 528.1
ulcerative 101
necrotizing ulcerative 101
parasitic 112.0
septic 528.00
specified NEC 528.09
spirochetal 101
suppurative (acute) 528.00
ulcerative 528.00
Stomatitis — *continued*
ulcerative — *continued*
necrotizing 101
ulceromembranous 101
vesicular 528.00
with exanthem 074.3
Vincent's 101
Stomatocytosis 282.8
Stomatomycosis 112.0
Stomatorrhagia 528.9
Stone(s) — *see also* Calculus
bladder 594.1
diverticulum 594.0
cystine 270.0
heart syndrome (*see also* Failure, ventricular, left) 428.1
kidney 592.0
prostate 602.0
pulp (dental) 522.2
renal 592.0
salivary duct or gland (any) 527.5
ureter 592.1
urethra (impacted) 594.2
urinary (duct) (impacted) (passage) 592.9
bladder 594.1
diverticulum 594.0
lower tract NEC 594.9
specified site 594.8
xanthine 277.2
Stonecutters' lung 502
tuberculous (*see also* Tuberculosis) 011.4 ☑
Stonemasons'
asthma, disease, or lung 502
tuberculous (*see also* Tuberculosis) 011.4 ☑
phthisis (*see also* Tuberculosis) 011.4 ☑
Stoppage
bowel (*see also* Obstruction, intestine) 560.9
heart (*see also* Arrest, cardiac) 427.5
intestine (*see also* Obstruction, intestine) 560.9
urine NEC (*see also* Retention, urine) 788.20
Storm, thyroid (apathetic) — *see also* Thyrotoxicosis 242.9 ☑
Strabismus (alternating) (congenital) (nonparalytic) 378.9
concomitant (*see also* Heterotropia) 378.30
convergent (*see also* Esotropia) 378.00
divergent (*see also* Exotropia) 378.10
convergent (*see also* Esotropia) 378.00
divergent (*see also* Exotropia) 378.10
due to adhesions, scars — *see* Strabismus, mechanical
in neuromuscular disorder NEC 378.73
intermittent 378.20
vertical 378.31
latent 378.40
convergent (esophoria) 378.41
divergent (exophoria) 378.42
vertical 378.43
mechanical 378.60
due to
Brown's tendon sheath syndrome 378.61
specified musculofascial disorder NEC 378.62
paralytic 378.50
third or oculomotor nerve (partial) 378.51
total 378.52
fourth or trochlear nerve 378.53
sixth or abducens nerve 378.54
specified type NEC 378.73
vertical (hypertropia) 378.31
Strain — *see also* Sprain, by site
eye NEC 368.13
heart — *see* Disease, heart

- **Strain** — *see also* Sprain, by site — *continued*
  - meaning gonorrhea — *see* Gonorrhea
  - on urination 788.65
  - physical NEC V62.89
  - postural 729.90 ▲
  - psychological NEC V62.89
- **Strands**
  - conjunctiva 372.62
  - vitreous humor 379.25
- **Strangulation, strangulated** 994.7
  - appendix 543.9
  - asphyxiation or suffocation by 994.7
  - bladder neck 596.0
  - bowel — *see* Strangulation, intestine
  - colon — *see* Strangulation, intestine
  - cord (umbilical) — *see* Compression, umbilical cord
  - due to birth injury 767.8
  - food or foreign body (*see also* Asphyxia, food) 933.1
  - hemorrhoids 455.8
    - external 455.5
    - internal 455.2
  - hernia (*see also* Hernia, by site, with obstruction)
    - gangrenous — *see* Hernia, by site, with gangrene
  - intestine (large) (small) 560.2
    - with hernia (*see also* Hernia, by site, with obstruction)
      - gangrenous — *see* Hernia, by site, with gangrene
    - congenital (small) 751.1
      - large 751.2
  - mesentery 560.2
  - mucus (*see also* Asphyxia, mucus) 933.1
    - newborn 770.18
  - omentum 560.2
  - organ or site, congenital NEC — *see* Atresia
  - ovary 620.8
    - due to hernia 620.4
  - penis 607.89
    - foreign body 939.3
  - rupture (*see also* Hernia, by site, with obstruction) 552.9
    - gangrenous (*see also* Hernia, by site, with gangrene) 551.9
  - stomach, due to hernia (*see also* Hernia, by site, with obstruction) 552.9
    - with gangrene (*see also* Hernia, by site, with gangrene) 551.9
  - umbilical cord — *see* Compression, umbilical cord
  - vesicourethral orifice 596.0
- **Strangury** 788.1
- **Strawberry**
  - gallbladder (*see also* Disease, gallbladder) 575.6
  - mark 757.32
  - tongue (red) (white) 529.3
- **Straw itch** 133.8
- **Streak, ovarian** 752.0
- **Strephosymbolia** 315.01
  - secondary to organic lesion 784.69
- **Streptobacillary fever** 026.1
- **Streptobacillus moniliformis** 026.1
- **Streptococcemia** 038.0
- **Streptococcicosis** — *see* Infection, streptococcal
- **Streptococcus, streptococcal** — *see* condition
- **Streptoderma** 686.00
- **Streptomycosis** — *see* Actinomycosis
- **Streptothricosis** — *see* Actinomycosis
- **Streptothrix** — *see* Actinomycosis
- **Streptotrichosis** — *see* Actinomycosis
- **Stress** 308.9
  - fracture — *see* Fracture, stress
  - polycythemia 289.0
  - reaction (gross) (*see also* Reaction, stress, acute) 308.9
- **Stretching, nerve** — *see* Injury, nerve, by site
- **Striae** (albicantes) (atrophicae) (cutis distensae) (distensae) 701.3
- **Striations of nails** 703.8
- **Stricture** — *see also* Stenosis 799.89
  - ampulla of Vater 576.2
    - with calculus, cholelithiasis, or stones — *see* Choledocholithiasis
  - anus (sphincter) 569.2
    - congenital 751.2
    - infantile 751.2
  - aorta (ascending) 747.22
    - arch 747.10
    - arteriosclerotic 440.0
    - calcified 440.0
  - aortic (valve) (*see also* Stenosis, aortic) 424.1
    - congenital 746.3
  - aqueduct of Sylvius (congenital) 742.3
    - with spina bifida (*see also* Spina bifida) 741.0 ☑
    - acquired 331.4
  - artery 447.1
    - basilar — *see* Narrowing, artery, basilar
    - carotid (common) (internal) — *see* Narrowing, artery, carotid
    - celiac 447.4
    - cerebral 437.0
      - congenital 747.81
      - due to
        - embolism (*see also* Embolism, brain) 434.1 ☑
        - thrombus (*see also* Thrombosis, brain) 434.0 ☑
    - congenital (peripheral) 747.60
      - cerebral 747.81
      - coronary 746.85
      - gastrointestinal 747.61
      - lower limb 747.64
      - renal 747.62
      - retinal 743.58
      - specified NEC 747.69
      - spinal 747.82
      - umbilical 747.5
      - upper limb 747.63
    - coronary — *see* Arteriosclerosis, coronary
      - congenital 746.85
    - precerebral — *see* Narrowing, artery, precerebral NEC
    - pulmonary (congenital) 747.3
      - acquired 417.8
    - renal 440.1
    - vertebral — *see* Narrowing, artery, vertebral
  - auditory canal (congenital) (external) 744.02
    - acquired (*see also* Stricture, ear canal, acquired) 380.50
  - bile duct or passage (any) (postoperative) (*see also* Obstruction, biliary) 576.2
    - congenital 751.61
  - bladder 596.8
    - congenital 753.6
    - neck 596.0
      - congenital 753.6
  - bowel (*see also* Obstruction, intestine) 560.9
  - brain 348.8
  - bronchus 519.19
    - syphilitic 095.8
  - cardia (stomach) 537.89
    - congenital 750.7
  - cardiac (*see also* Disease, heart)
    - orifice (stomach) 537.89
  - cardiovascular (*see also* Disease, cardiovascular) 429.2
  - carotid artery — *see* Narrowing, artery, carotid
  - cecum (*see also* Obstruction, intestine) 560.9
  - cervix, cervical (canal) 622.4

- **Stricture** — *see also* Stenosis — *continued*
  - cervix, cervical — *continued*
    - congenital 752.49
    - in pregnancy or childbirth 654.6 ☑
      - affecting fetus or newborn 763.89
      - causing obstructed labor 660.2 ☑
        - affecting fetus or newborn 763.1
  - colon (*see also* Obstruction, intestine) 560.9
    - congenital 751.2
  - colostomy 569.62
  - common bile duct (*see also* Obstruction, biliary) 576.2
    - congenital 751.61
  - coronary (artery) — *see* Arteriosclerosis, coronary
    - congenital 746.85
  - cystic duct (*see also* Obstruction, gallbladder) 575.2
    - congenital 751.61
  - cystostomy 997.5
  - digestive organs NEC, congenital 751.8
  - duodenum 537.3
    - congenital 751.1
  - ear canal (external) (congenital) 744.02
    - acquired 380.50
      - secondary to
        - inflammation 380.53
        - surgery 380.52
        - trauma 380.51
  - ejaculatory duct 608.85
  - enterostomy 569.62
  - esophagostomy 530.87
  - esophagus (corrosive) (peptic) 530.3
    - congenital 750.3
    - syphilitic 095.8
      - congenital 090.5
  - eustachian tube (*see also* Obstruction, Eustachian tube) 381.60
    - congenital 744.24
  - fallopian tube 628.2
    - gonococcal (chronic) 098.37
      - acute 098.17
    - tuberculous (*see also* Tuberculosis) 016.6 ☑
  - gallbladder (*see also* Obstruction, gallbladder) 575.2
    - congenital 751.69
  - glottis 478.74
  - heart (*see also* Disease, heart)
    - congenital NEC 746.89
    - valve (*see also* Endocarditis)
      - congenital NEC 746.89
        - aortic 746.3
        - mitral 746.5
        - pulmonary 746.02
        - tricuspid 746.1
  - hepatic duct (*see also* Obstruction, biliary) 576.2
  - hourglass, of stomach 537.6
  - hymen 623.3
  - hypopharynx 478.29
  - intestine (*see also* Obstruction, intestine) 560.9
    - congenital (small) 751.1
      - large 751.2
    - ischemic 557.1
  - lacrimal
    - canaliculi 375.53
      - congenital 743.65
    - punctum 375.52
      - congenital 743.65
    - sac 375.54
      - congenital 743.65
  - lacrimonasal duct 375.56
    - congenital 743.65
    - neonatal 375.55
  - larynx 478.79
    - congenital 748.3
    - syphilitic 095.8

- **Stricture** — *see also* Stenosis — *continued*
  - larynx — *continued*
    - syphilitic — *continued*
      - congenital 090.5
  - lung 518.89
  - meatus
    - ear (congenital) 744.02
      - acquired (*see also* Stricture, ear canal, acquired) 380.50
    - osseous (congenital) (ear) 744.03
      - acquired (*see also* Stricture, ear canal, acquired) 380.50
    - urinarius (*see also* Stricture, urethra) 598.9
      - congenital 753.6
  - mitral (valve) (*see also* Stenosis, mitral) 394.0
    - congenital 746.5
    - specified cause, except rheumatic 424.0
  - myocardium, myocardial (*see also* Degeneration, myocardial) 429.1
    - hypertrophic subaortic (idiopathic) 425.1
  - nares (anterior) (posterior) 478.19
    - congenital 748.0
  - nasal duct 375.56
    - congenital 743.65
    - neonatal 375.55
  - nasolacrimal duct 375.56
    - congenital 743.65
    - neonatal 375.55
  - nasopharynx 478.29
    - syphilitic 095.8
  - nephrostomy 997.5
  - nose 478.19
    - congenital 748.0
  - nostril (anterior) (posterior) 478.19
    - congenital 748.0
  - organ or site, congenital NEC — *see* Atresia
  - osseous meatus (congenital) (ear) 744.03
    - acquired (*see also* Stricture, ear canal, acquired) 380.50
  - os uteri (*see also* Stricture, cervix) 622.4
  - oviduct — *see* Stricture, fallopian tube
  - pelviureteric junction 593.3
  - pharynx (dilation) 478.29
  - prostate 602.8
  - pulmonary, pulmonic
    - artery (congenital) 747.3
      - acquired 417.8
      - noncongenital 417.8
    - infundibulum (congenital) 746.83
    - valve (*see also* Endocarditis, pulmonary) 424.3
      - congenital 746.02
    - vein (congenital) 747.49
      - acquired 417.8
    - vessel NEC 417.8
  - punctum lacrimale 375.52
    - congenital 743.65
  - pylorus (hypertrophic) 537.0
    - adult 537.0
    - congenital 750.5
    - infantile 750.5
  - rectosigmoid 569.89
  - rectum (sphincter) 569.2
    - congenital 751.2
    - due to
      - chemical burn 947.3
      - irradiation 569.2
      - lymphogranuloma venereum 099.1
    - gonococcal 098.7
    - inflammatory 099.1
    - syphilitic 095.8
    - tuberculous (*see also* Tuberculosis) 014.8 ☑
  - renal artery 440.1
  - salivary duct or gland (any) 527.8
  - sigmoid (flexure) (*see also* Obstruction, intestine) 560.9

- **Stricture** — *see also* Stenosis — *continued*
  - spermatic cord 608.85
  - stoma (following) (of)
    - colostomy 569.62
    - cystostomy 997.5
    - enterostomy 569.62
    - esophagostomy 530.87
    - gastrostomy 536.42
    - ileostomy 569.62
    - nephrostomy 997.5
    - tracheostomy 519.02
    - ureterostomy 997.5
  - stomach 537.89
    - congenital 750.7
    - hourglass 537.6
  - subaortic 746.81
    - hypertrophic (acquired) (idiopathic) 425.1
  - subglottic 478.74
  - syphilitic NEC 095.8
  - tendon (sheath) 727.81
  - trachea 519.19
    - congenital 748.3
    - syphilitic 095.8
    - tuberculous (*see also* Tuberculosis) 012.8 ☑
  - tracheostomy 519.02
  - tricuspid (valve) (*see also* Endocarditis, tricuspid) 397.0
    - congenital 746.1
    - nonrheumatic 424.2
  - tunica vaginalis 608.85
  - ureter (postoperative) 593.3
    - congenital 753.29
    - tuberculous (*see also* Tuberculosis) 016.2 ☑
  - ureteropelvic junction 593.3
    - congenital 753.21
  - ureterovesical orifice 593.3
    - congenital 753.22
  - urethra (anterior) (meatal) (organic) (posterior) (spasmodic) 598.9
    - associated with schistosomiasis (*see also* Schistosomiasis) 120.9 *[598.01]*
    - congenital (valvular) 753.6
    - due to
      - infection 598.00
        - syphilis 095.8 *[598.01]*
      - trauma 598.1
    - gonococcal 098.2 *[598.01]*
    - gonorrheal 098.2 *[598.01]*
    - infective 598.00
    - late effect of injury 598.1
    - postcatheterization 598.2
    - postobstetric 598.1
    - postoperative 598.2
    - specified cause NEC 598.8
    - syphilitic 095.8 *[598.01]*
    - traumatic 598.1
    - valvular, congenital 753.6
  - urinary meatus (*see also* Stricture, urethra) 598.9
    - congenital 753.6
  - uterus, uterine 621.5
    - os (external) (internal) — *see* Stricture, cervix
  - vagina (outlet) 623.2
    - congenital 752.49
  - valve (cardiac) (heart) (*see also* Endocarditis) 424.90
    - congenital (cardiac) (heart) NEC 746.89
      - aortic 746.3
      - mitral 746.5
      - pulmonary 746.02
      - tricuspid 746.1
      - urethra 753.6
  - valvular (*see also* Endocarditis) 424.90
  - vascular graft or shunt 996.1
    - atherosclerosis — see Arteriosclerosis, extremities
    - embolism 996.74
    - occlusion NEC 996.74
- **Stricture** — *see also* Stenosis — *continued*
  - vascular graft or shunt — *continued*
    - thrombus 996.74
  - vas deferens 608.85
    - congenital 752.89
  - vein 459.2
  - vena cava (inferior) (superior) NEC 459.2
    - congenital 747.49
  - ventricular shunt 996.2
  - vesicourethral orifice 596.0
    - congenital 753.6
  - vulva (acquired) 624.8
- **Stridor** 786.1
  - congenital (larynx) 748.3
- **Stridulous** — *see* condition
- **Strippling of nails** 703.8
- **Stroke** 434.91
  - apoplectic (*see also* Disease, cerebrovascular, acute) 436
  - brain — *see* Infarct, brain
  - embolic 434.11
  - epileptic — *see* Epilepsy
  - healed or old V12.54
  - heart — *see* Disease, heart
  - heat 992.0
  - hemorrhagic — see Hemorrhage, brain
  - iatrogenic 997.02
  - in evolution 434.91
  - ischemic 434.91
  - late effect — *see* Late effect(s) (of) cerebrovascular disease
  - lightning 994.0
  - paralytic — *see* Infarct, brain
  - postoperative 997.02
  - progressive 435.9
  - thrombotic 434.01
- **Stromatosis, endometrial** (M8931/1) 236.0
- **Strong pulse** 785.9
- **Strongyloides stercoralis infestation** 127.2
- **Strongyloidiasis** 127.2
- **Strongyloidosis** 127.2
- **Strongylus** (gibsoni) infestation 127.7
- **Strophulus** (newborn) 779.89
  - pruriginosus 698.2
- **Struck by lightning** 994.0
- **Struma** — *see also* Goiter 240.9
  - fibrosa 245.3
  - Hashimoto (struma lymphomatosa) 245.2
  - lymphomatosa 245.2
  - nodosa (simplex) 241.9
    - endemic 241.9
    - multinodular 241.1
    - sporadic 241.9
    - toxic or with hyperthyroidism 242.3 ☑
      - multinodular 242.2 ☑
      - uninodular 242.1 ☑
    - toxicosa 242.3 ☑
      - multinodular 242.2 ☑
      - uninodular 242.1 ☑
    - uninodular 241.0
  - ovarii (M9090/0) 220
    - and carcinoid (M9091/1) 236.2
    - malignant (M9090/3) 183.0
  - Riedel's (ligneous thyroiditis) 245.3
  - scrofulous (*see also* Tuberculosis) 017.2 ☑
  - tuberculous (*see also* Tuberculosis) 017.2 ☑
    - abscess 017.2 ☑
    - adenitis 017.2 ☑
    - lymphangitis 017.2 ☑
    - ulcer 017.2 ☑
- **Strumipriva cachexia** — *see also* Hypothyroidism 244.9
- **Strümpell-Marie disease or spine** (ankylosing spondylitis) 720.0
- **Strümpell-Westphal pseudosclerosis** (hepatolenticular degeneration) 275.1
- **Stuart's disease** (congenital factor X deficiency) — *see also* Defect, coagulation 286.3
- **Stuart-Prower factor deficiency** (congenital factor X deficiency) — *see also* Defect, coagulation 286.3
- **Students' elbow** 727.2
- **Stuffy nose** 478.19
- **Stump** — *see also* Amputation
  - cervix, cervical (healed) 622.8
- **Stupor** 780.09
  - catatonic (*see also* Schizophrenia) 295.2 ☑
  - circular (*see also* Psychosis, manic-depressive, circular) 296.7
  - manic 296.89
  - manic-depressive (*see also* Psychosis, affective) 296.89
  - mental (anergic) (delusional) 298.9
  - psychogenic 298.8
  - reaction to exceptional stress (transient) 308.2
  - traumatic NEC (*see also* Injury, intracranial)
    - with spinal (cord)
      - lesion — *see* Injury, spinal, by site
      - shock — *see* Injury, spinal, by site
- **Sturge (-Weber) (-Dimitri) disease or syndrome** (encephalocutaneous angiomatosis) 759.6
- **Sturge-Kalischer-Weber syndrome** (encephalocutaneous angiomatosis) 759.6
- **Stuttering** 307.0
- **Sty, stye** 373.11
  - external 373.11
  - internal 373.12
  - meibomian 373.12
- **Subacidity, gastric** 536.8
  - psychogenic 306.4
- **Subacute** — *see* condition
- **Subarachnoid** — *see* condition
- **Subclavian steal syndrome** 435.2
- **Subcortical** — *see* condition
- **Subcostal syndrome** 098.86
  - nerve compression 354.8
- **Subcutaneous, subcuticular** — *see* condition
- **Subdelirium** 293.1
- **Subdural** — *see* condition
- **Subendocardium** — *see* condition
- **Subependymoma** (M9383/1) 237.5
- **Suberosis** 495.3
- **Subglossitis** — *see* Glossitis
- **Subhemophilia** 286.0
- **Subinvolution** (uterus) 621.1
  - breast (postlactational) (postpartum) 611.89 ▲
  - chronic 621.1
  - puerperal, postpartum 674.8 ☑
- **Sublingual** — *see* condition
- **Sublinguitis** 527.2
- **Subluxation** — *see also* Dislocation, by site
  - congenital NEC (*see also* Malposition, congenital)
    - hip (unilateral) 754.32
      - with dislocation of other hip 754.35
      - bilateral 754.33
    - joint
      - lower limb 755.69
      - shoulder 755.59
      - upper limb 755.59
    - lower limb (joint) 755.69
    - shoulder (joint) 755.59
    - upper limb (joint) 755.59
  - lens 379.32
    - anterior 379.33
    - posterior 379.34
  - rotary, cervical region of spine — *see* Fracture, vertebra, cervical
- **Submaxillary** — *see* condition
- **Submersion** (fatal) (nonfatal) 994.1
- **Submissiveness** (undue), in child 313.0
- **Submucous** — *see* condition
- **Subnormal, subnormality**
  - accommodation (*see also* Disorder, accommodation) 367.9
  - mental (*see also* Retardation, mental) 319
    - mild 317
    - moderate 318.0
    - profound 318.2
    - severe 318.1
  - temperature (accidental) 991.6
    - not associated with low environmental temperature 780.99
- **Subphrenic** — *see* condition
- **Subscapular nerve** — *see* condition
- **Subseptus uterus** 752.3
- **Subsiding appendicitis** 542
- **Substernal thyroid** — *see also* Goiter 240.9
  - congenital 759.2
- **Substitution disorder** 300.11
- **Subtentorial** — *see* condition
- **Subtertian**
  - fever 084.0
  - malaria (fever) 084.0
- **Subthyroidism** (acquired) — *see also* Hypothyroidism 244.9
  - congenital 243
- **Succenturiata placenta** — *see* Placenta, abnormal
- **Succussion sounds, chest** 786.7
- **Sucking thumb, child** 307.9
- **Sudamen** 705.1
- **Sudamina** 705.1
- **Sudanese kala-azar** 085.0
- **Sudden**
  - death, cause unknown (less than 24 hours) 798.1
    - cardiac (SCD)
      - family history of V17.41
      - personal history of, successfully resuscitated V12.53
    - during childbirth 669.9 ☑
    - infant 798.0
    - puerperal, postpartum 674.9 ☑
  - hearing loss NEC 388.2
  - heart failure (*see also* Failure, heart) 428.9
  - infant death syndrome 798.0
- **Sudeck's atrophy, disease, or syndrome** 733.7
- **SUDS** (sudden unexplained death) 798.2
- **Suffocation** — *see also* Asphyxia 799.01
  - by
    - bed clothes 994.7
    - bunny bag 994.7
    - cave-in 994.7
    - constriction 994.7
    - drowning 994.1
    - inhalation
      - food or foreign body (*see also* Asphyxia, food or foreign body) 933.1
      - oil or gasoline (*see also* Asphyxia, food or foreign body) 933.1
    - overlying 994.7
    - plastic bag 994.7
    - pressure 994.7
    - strangulation 994.7
  - during birth 768.1
  - mechanical 994.7
- **Sugar**
  - blood
    - high 790.29
    - low 251.2
  - in urine 791.5
- **Suicide, suicidal** (attempted)
  - by poisoning — *see* Table of Drugs and Chemicals
  - ideation V62.84
  - risk 300.9
  - tendencies 300.9
  - trauma NEC (*see also* nature and site of injury) 959.9

☑ Additional Digit Required — Refer to the Tabular List for Digit Selection

Subterms under main terms may continue to next column or page

- **Suipestifer infection** — *see also* Infection, Salmonella 003.9
- **Sulfatidosis** 330.0
- **Sulfhemoglobinemia, sulphemoglobinemia** (acquired) (congenital) 289.7
- **Sumatran mite fever** 081.2
- **Summer** — *see* condition
- **Sunburn** 692.71
  - first degree 692.71
  - second degree 692.76
  - third degree 692.77
  - dermatitis 692.71
  - due to
    - other ultraviolet radiation 692.82
    - tanning bed 692.82
- **SUNCT** (short lasting unilateral neuralgiform headache with conjunctival injection and tearing) 339.05 ●
- **Sunken**
  - acetabulum 718.85
  - fontanels 756.0
- **Sunstroke** 992.0
- **Superfecundation** 651.9 ☑
  - with fetal loss and retention of one or more fetus(es) 651.6 ☑
  - following (elective) fetal reduction 651.7 ☑
- **Superfetation** 651.9 ☑
  - with fetal loss and retention of one or more fetus(es) 651.6 ☑
  - following (elective) fetal reduction 651.7 ☑
- **Superinvolution uterus** 621.8
- **Supernumerary** (congenital)
  - aortic cusps 746.89
  - auditory ossicles 744.04
  - bone 756.9
  - breast 757.6
  - carpal bones 755.56
  - cusps, heart valve NEC 746.89
    - mitral 746.5
    - pulmonary 746.09
  - digit(s) 755.00
    - finger 755.01
    - toe 755.02
  - ear (lobule) 744.1
  - fallopian tube 752.19
  - finger 755.01
  - hymen 752.49
  - kidney 753.3
  - lacrimal glands 743.64
  - lacrimonasal duct 743.65
  - lobule (ear) 744.1
  - mitral cusps 746.5
  - muscle 756.82
  - nipples 757.6
  - organ or site NEC — *see* Accessory
  - ossicles, auditory 744.04
  - ovary 752.0
  - oviduct 752.19
  - pulmonic cusps 746.09
  - rib 756.3
    - cervical or first 756.2
      - syndrome 756.2
  - roots (of teeth) 520.2
  - spinal vertebra 756.19
  - spleen 759.0
  - tarsal bones 755.67
  - teeth 520.1
    - causing crowding 524.31
  - testis 752.89
  - thumb 755.01
  - toe 755.02
  - uterus 752.2
  - vagina 752.49
  - vertebra 756.19
- **Supervision** (of)
  - contraceptive method previously prescribed V25.40
    - intrauterine device V25.42
    - oral contraceptive (pill) V25.41
    - specified type NEC V25.49
    - subdermal implantable contraceptive V25.43
  - dietary (for) V65.3
    - allergy (food) V65.3
- **Supervision** — *continued*
  - dietary — *continued*
    - colitis V65.3
    - diabetes mellitus V65.3
    - food allergy intolerance V65.3
    - gastritis V65.3
    - hypercholesterolemia V65.3
    - hypoglycemia V65.3
    - intolerance (food) V65.3
    - obesity V65.3
    - specified NEC V65.3
  - lactation V24.1
  - pregnancy — *see* Pregnancy, supervision of
- **Supplemental teeth** 520.1
  - causing crowding 524.31
- **Suppression**
  - binocular vision 368.31
  - lactation 676.5 ☑
  - menstruation 626.8
  - ovarian secretion 256.39
  - renal 586
  - urinary secretion 788.5
  - urine 788.5
- **Suppuration, suppurative** — *see also* condition
  - accessory sinus (chronic) (*see also* Sinusitis) 473.9
  - adrenal gland 255.8
  - antrum (chronic) (*see also* Sinusitis, maxillary) 473.0
  - bladder (*see also* Cystitis) 595.89
  - bowel 569.89
  - brain 324.0
    - late effect 326
  - breast 611.0
    - puerperal, postpartum 675.1 ☑
  - dental periosteum 526.5
  - diffuse (skin) 686.00
  - ear (middle) (*see also* Otitis media) 382.4
    - external (*see also* Otitis, externa) 380.10
    - internal 386.33
  - ethmoidal (sinus) (chronic) (*see also* Sinusitis, ethmoidal) 473.2
  - fallopian tube (*see also* Salpingo-oophoritis) 614.2
  - frontal (sinus) (chronic) (*see also* Sinusitis, frontal) 473.1
  - gallbladder (*see also* Cholecystitis, acute) 575.0
  - gum 523.30
  - hernial sac — *see* Hernia, by site
  - intestine 569.89
  - joint (*see also* Arthritis, suppurative) 711.0 ☑
  - labyrinthine 386.33
  - lung 513.0
  - mammary gland 611.0
    - puerperal, postpartum 675.1 ☑
  - maxilla, maxillary 526.4
    - sinus (chronic) (*see also* Sinusitis, maxillary) 473.0
  - muscle 728.0
  - nasal sinus (chronic) (*see also* Sinusitis) 473.9
  - pancreas 577.0
  - parotid gland 527.2
  - pelvis, pelvic
    - female (*see also* Disease, pelvis, inflammatory) 614.4
      - acute 614.3
    - male (*see also* Peritonitis) 567.21
  - pericranial (*see also* Osteomyelitis) 730.2 ☑
  - salivary duct or gland (any) 527.2
  - sinus (nasal) (*see also* Sinusitis) 473.9
  - sphenoidal (sinus) (chronic) (*see also* Sinusitis, sphenoidal) 473.3
  - thymus (gland) 254.1
  - thyroid (gland) 245.0
  - tonsil 474.8
  - uterus (*see also* Endometritis) 615.9
  - vagina 616.10
- **Suppuration, suppurative** — *see also* condition — *continued*
  - wound (*see also* Wound, open, by site, complicated)
    - dislocation — *see* Dislocation, by site, compound
    - fracture — *see* Fracture, by site, open
    - scratch or other superficial injury — *see* Injury, superficial, by site
- **Supraeruption, teeth** 524.34
- **Supraglottitis** 464.50
  - with obstruction 464.51
- **Suprapubic drainage** 596.8
- **Suprarenal** (gland) — *see* condition
- **Suprascapular nerve** — *see* condition
- **Suprasellar** — *see* condition
- **Supraspinatus syndrome** 726.10
- **Surfer knots** 919.8
  - infected 919.9
- **Surgery**
  - cosmetic NEC V50.1
    - breast reconstruction following mastectomy V51.0 ●
    - following healed injury or operation V51.8
    - hair transplant V50.0
  - elective V50.9
    - breast
      - augmentation or reduction V50.1 ●
      - reconstruction following mastectomy V51.0 ●
    - circumcision, ritual or routine (in absence of medical indication) V50.2
    - cosmetic NEC V50.1
    - ear piercing V50.3
    - face-lift V50.1
    - following healed injury or operation V51.8 ▲
    - hair transplant V50.0
  - not done because of
    - contraindication V64.1
    - patient's decision V64.2
    - specified reason NEC V64.3
  - plastic
    - breast
      - augmentation or reduction V50.1 ●
      - reconstruction following mastectomy V51.0 ●
    - cosmetic V50.1
    - face-lift V50.1
    - following healed injury or operation V51.8 ▲
    - repair of scarred tissue (following healed injury or operation) V51.8 ▲
    - specified type NEC V50.8
  - previous, in pregnancy or childbirth
    - cervix 654.6 ☑
      - affecting fetus or newborn ▶(*see also* Newborn, affected by)◀ 760.63 ▲
      - causing obstructed labor 660.2 ☑
        - affecting fetus or newborn 763.1
    - pelvic soft tissues NEC 654.9 ☑
      - affecting fetus or newborn ▶(*see also* Newborn, affected by)◀ 760.63 ▲
      - causing obstructed labor 660.2 ☑
        - affecting fetus or newborn 763.1
    - perineum or vulva 654.8 ☑
    - uterus NEC 654.9 ☑
      - affecting fetus or newborn ▶(*see also* Newborn, affected by)◀ 760.63 ▲
      - causing obstructed labor 660.2 ☑
- **Surgery** — *continued*
  - previous, in pregnancy or childbirth — *continued*
    - uterus — *continued*
      - causing obstructed labor — *continued*
        - affecting fetus or newborn 763.1
      - due to previous cesarean delivery 654.2 ☑
    - vagina 654.7 ☑
- **Surgical**
  - abortion — *see* Abortion, legal
  - emphysema 998.81
  - kidney (*see also* Pyelitis) 590.80
  - operation NEC 799.9
  - procedures, complication or misadventure — *see* Complications, surgical procedure
  - shock 998.0
- **Survey** ●
  - fetal anatomic V28.81 ●
- **Susceptibility**
  - genetic
    - to
      - MEN (multiple endocrine neoplasia) V84.81
      - neoplasia
        - multiple endocrine [MEN] V84.81
      - neoplasm
        - malignant, of
          - breast V84.01
          - endometrium V84.04
          - other V84.09
          - ovary V84.02
          - prostate V84.03
      - specified disease V84.89
- **Suspected condition, ruled out** — *see also* Observation, suspected V71.9
  - specified condition NEC V71.89
- **Suspended uterus, in pregnancy or childbirth** 654.4 ☑
  - affecting fetus or newborn 763.89
  - causing obstructed labor 660.2 ☑
    - affecting fetus or newborn 763.1
- **Sutton and Gull's disease** (arteriolar nephrosclerosis) — *see also* Hypertension, kidney 403.90
- **Sutton's disease** 709.09
- **Suture**
  - burst (in external operation wound) ▶(*see also* Dehiscence)◀ 998.32
    - internal 998.31
  - inadvertently left in operation wound 998.4
  - removal V58.32
  - Shirodkar, in pregnancy (with or without cervical incompetence) 654.5 ☑
- **Swab inadvertently left in operation wound** 998.4
- **Swallowed, swallowing**
  - difficulty (*see also* Dysphagia) 787.20
  - foreign body NEC (*see also* Foreign body) 938
- **Swamp fever** 100.89
- **Swan neck hand** (intrinsic) 736.09
- **Sweat(s), sweating**
  - disease or sickness 078.2
  - excessive (*see also* Hyperhidrosis) 780.8
  - fetid 705.89
  - fever 078.2
  - gland disease 705.9
    - specified type NEC 705.89
  - miliary 078.2
  - night 780.8
- **Sweeley-Klionsky disease** (angiokeratoma corporis diffusum) 272.7
- **Sweet's syndrome** (acute febrile neutrophilic dermatosis) 695.89
- **Swelling** 782.3
  - abdominal (not referable to specific organ) 789.3 ☑
  - adrenal gland, cloudy 255.8

Swelling — *continued*
ankle 719.07
anus 787.99
arm 729.81
breast 611.72
Calabar 125.2
cervical gland 785.6
cheek 784.2
chest 786.6
ear 388.8
epigastric 789.3 ☑
extremity (lower) (upper) 729.81
eye 379.92
female genital organ 625.8
finger 729.81
foot 729.81
glands 785.6
gum 784.2
hand 729.81
head 784.2
inflammatory — *see* Inflammation
joint (*see also* Effusion, joint) 719.0 ☑
tuberculous — *see* Tuberculosis, joint
kidney, cloudy 593.89
leg 729.81
limb 729.81
liver 573.8
lung 786.6
lymph nodes 785.6
mediastinal 786.6
mouth 784.2
muscle (limb) 729.81
neck 784.2
nose or sinus 784.2
palate 784.2
pelvis 789.3 ☑
penis 607.83
perineum 625.8
rectum 787.99
scrotum 608.86
skin 782.2
splenic (*see also* Splenomegaly) 789.2
substernal 786.6
superficial, localized (skin) 782.2
testicle 608.86
throat 784.2
toe 729.81
tongue 784.2
tubular (*see also* Disease, renal) 593.9
umbilicus 789.3 ☑
uterus 625.8
vagina 625.8
vulva 625.8
wandering, due to Gnathostoma (spinigerum) 128.1
white — *see* Tuberculosis, arthritis
Swift's disease 985.0
Swimmers'
ear (acute) 380.12
itch 120.3
Swimming in the head 780.4
Swollen — *see also* Swelling
glands 785.6
Swyer-James syndrome (unilateral hyperlucent lung) 492.8
Swyer's syndrome (XY pure gonadal dysgenesis) 752.7
Sycosis 704.8
barbae (not parasitic) 704.8
contagiosa 110.0
lupoid 704.8
mycotic 110.0
parasitic 110.0
vulgaris 704.8
Sydenham's chorea — *see* Chorea, Sydenham's
Sylvatic yellow fever 060.0
Sylvest's disease (epidemic pleurodynia) 074.1
Symblepharon 372.63
congenital 743.62
Symonds' syndrome 348.2
Sympathetic — *see* condition
Sympatheticotonia — *see also* Neuropathy, peripheral, autonomic 337.9
Sympathicoblastoma (M9500/3)
specified site — *see* Neoplasm, by site, malignant
unspecified site 194.0
Sympathicogonioma (M9500/3) — *see* Sympathicoblastoma
Sympathoblastoma (M9500/3) — *see* Sympathicoblastoma
Sympathogonioma (M9500/3) — *see* Sympathicoblastoma
Symphalangy — *see also* Syndactylism 755.10
Symptoms, specified (general) NEC 780.99
abdomen NEC 789.9
bone NEC 733.90
breast NEC 611.79
cardiac NEC 785.9
cardiovascular NEC 785.9
chest NEC 786.9
development NEC 783.9
digestive system NEC 787.99
eye NEC 379.99
gastrointestinal tract NEC 787.99
genital organs NEC
female 625.9
male 608.9
head and neck NEC 784.99
heart NEC 785.9
joint NEC 719.60
ankle 719.67
elbow 719.62
foot 719.67
hand 719.64
hip 719.65
knee 719.66
multiple sites 719.69
pelvic region 719.65
shoulder (region) 719.61
specified site NEC 719.68
wrist 719.63
larynx NEC 784.99
limbs NEC 729.89
lymphatic system NEC 785.9
menopausal 627.2
metabolism NEC 783.9
mouth NEC 528.9
muscle NEC 728.9
musculoskeletal NEC 781.99
limbs NEC 729.89
nervous system NEC 781.99
neurotic NEC 300.9
nutrition, metabolism, and development NEC 783.9
pelvis NEC 789.9
female 625.9
peritoneum NEC 789.9
respiratory system NEC 786.9
skin and integument NEC 782.9
subcutaneous tissue NEC 782.9
throat NEC 784.99
tonsil NEC 784.99
urinary system NEC 788.99 ▲
vascular NEC 785.9
Sympus 759.89
Synarthrosis 719.80
ankle 719.87
elbow 719.82
foot 719.87
hand 719.84
hip 719.85
knee 719.86
multiple sites 719.89
pelvic region 719.85
shoulder (region) 719.81
specified site NEC 719.88
wrist 719.83
Syncephalus 759.4
Synchondrosis 756.9
abnormal (congenital) 756.9
ischiopubic (van Neck's) 732.1
Synchysis (senile) (vitreous humor) 379.21
scintillans 379.22
Syncope (near) (pre-) 780.2
anginosa 413.9
Syncope — *continued*
bradycardia 427.89
cardiac 780.2
carotid sinus 337.01 ▲
complicating delivery 669.2 ☑
due to lumbar puncture 349.0
fatal 798.1
heart 780.2
heat 992.1
laryngeal 786.2
tussive 786.2
vasoconstriction 780.2
vasodepressor 780.2
vasomotor 780.2
vasovagal 780.2
Syncytial infarct — *see* Placenta, abnormal
Syndactylism, syndactyly (multiple sites) 755.10
fingers (without fusion of bone) 755.11
with fusion of bone 755.12
toes (without fusion of bone) 755.13
with fusion of bone 755.14
Syndrome — *see also* Disease
with 5q deletion 238.74
5q minus 238.74
abdominal
acute 789.0 ☑
migraine 346.2 ☑
muscle deficiency 756.79
Abercrombie's (amyloid degeneration) 277.39
abnormal innervation 374.43
abstinence
alcohol 291.81
drug 292.0
Abt-Letterer-Siwe (acute histiocytosis X) (M9722/3) 202.5 ☑
Achard-Thiers (adrenogenital) 255.2
acid pulmonary aspiration 997.39 ▲
obstetric (Mendelson's) 668.0 ☑
acquired immune deficiency 042
acquired immunodeficiency 042
acrocephalosyndactylism 755.55
acute abdominal 789.0 ☑
acute chest 517.3
acute coronary 411.1
Adair-Dighton (brittle bones and blue sclera, deafness) 756.51
Adams-Stokes (-Morgagni) (syncope with heart block) 426.9
Addisonian 255.41
Adie (-Holmes) (pupil) 379.46
adiposogenital 253.8
adrenal
hemorrhage 036.3
meningococcic 036.3
adrenocortical 255.3
adrenogenital (acquired) (congenital) 255.2
feminizing 255.2
iatrogenic 760.79
virilism (acquired) (congenital) 255.2
affective organic NEC 293.89
drug-induced 292.84
afferent loop NEC 537.89
African macroglobulinemia 273.3
Ahumada-Del Castillo (nonpuerperal galactorrhea and amenorrhea) 253.1
air blast concussion — *see* Injury, internal, by site
Alagille 759.89
Albright (-Martin) (pseudohypoparathyroidism) 275.49
Albright-McCune-Sternberg (osteitis fibrosa disseminata) 756.59
alcohol withdrawal 291.81
Alder's (leukocyte granulation anomaly) 288.2
Aldrich (-Wiskott) (eczema-thrombocytopenia) 279.12
Alibert-Bazin (mycosis fungoides) (M9700/3) 202.1 ☑
Syndrome — *see also* Disease — *continued*
Alice in Wonderland 293.89
alien hand 781.8 ●
Allen-Masters 620.6
Alligator baby (ichthyosis congenita) 757.1
Alport's (hereditary hematuria-nephropathy-deafness) 759.89
Alvarez (transient cerebral ischemia) 435.9
alveolar capillary block 516.3
Alzheimer's 331.0
with dementia — *see* Alzheimer's, dementia
amnestic (confabulatory) 294.0
alcohol-induced persisting 291.1
drug-induced 292.83
posttraumatic 294.0
amotivational 292.89
amyostatic 275.1
amyotrophic lateral sclerosis 335.20
androgen insensitivity 259.51 ▲
partial 259.52 ●
Angelman 759.89
angina (*see also* Angina) 413.9
ankyloglossia superior 750.0
anterior
chest wall 786.52
compartment (tibial) 958.8
spinal artery 433.8 ☑
compression 721.1
tibial (compartment) 958.8
antibody deficiency 279.00
agammaglobulinemic 279.00
congenital 279.04
hypogammaglobulinemic 279.00
anticardiolipin antibody 289.81 ▲
antimongolism 758.39
antiphospholipid antibody 289.81 ▲
Anton (-Babinski) (hemiasomatognosia) 307.9
anxiety (*see also* Anxiety) 300.00
organic 293.84
aortic
arch 446.7
bifurcation (occlusion) 444.0
ring 747.21
Apert's (acrocephalosyndactyly) 755.55
Apert-Gallais (adrenogenital) 255.2
aphasia-apraxia-alexia 784.69
apical ballooning 429.83
"approximate answers" 300.16
arcuate ligament (-celiac axis) 447.4
arcus aortae 446.7
arc welders' 370.24
argentaffin, argintaffinoma 259.2
Argonz-Del Castillo (nonpuerperal galactorrhea and amenorrhea) 253.1
Argyll Robertson's (syphilitic) 094.89
nonsyphilitic 379.45
Armenian 277.31
arm-shoulder (*see also* Neuropathy, peripheral, autonomic) 337.9
Arnold-Chiari (*see also* Spina bifida) 741.0 ☑
type I 348.4
type II 741.0 ☑
type III 742.0
type IV 742.2
Arrillaga-Ayerza (pulmonary artery sclerosis with pulmonary hypertension) 416.0
arteriomesenteric duodenum occlusion 537.89
arteriovenous steal 996.73
arteritis, young female (obliterative brachiocephalic) 446.7
aseptic meningitis — *see* Meningitis, aseptic
Asherman's 621.5
Asperger's 299.8 ☑
asphyctic (*see also* Anxiety) 300.00

Syndrome — *see also* Disease — *continued*
aspiration, of newborn (massive) 770.18
meconium 770.12
ataxia-telangiectasia 334.8
Audry's (acropachyderma) 757.39
auriculotemporal 350.8
autosomal (*see also* Abnormal, autosomes NEC)
deletion 758.39
5p 758.31
22q11.2 758.32
Avellis' 344.89
Axenfeld's 743.44
Ayerza (-Arrillaga) (pulmonary artery sclerosis with pulmonary hypertension) 416.0
Baader's (erythema multiforme exudativum) 695.19 ▲
Baastrup's 721.5
Babinski (-Vaquez) (cardiovascular syphilis) 093.89
Babinski-Fröhlich (adiposogenital dystrophy) 253.8
Babinski-Nageotte 344.89
Bagratuni's (temporal arteritis) 446.5
Bakwin-Krida (craniometaphyseal dysplasia) 756.89
Balint's (psychic paralysis of visual disorientation) 368.16
Ballantyne (-Runge) (postmaturity) 766.22
ballooning posterior leaflet 424.0
Banti's — *see* Cirrhosis, liver
Bardet-Biedl (obesity, polydactyly, and mental retardation) 759.89
Bard-Pic's (carcinoma, head of pancreas) 157.0
Barlow's (mitral valve prolapse) 424.0
Barlow (-Möller) (infantile scurvy) 267
Baron Munchausen's 301.51
Barré-Guillain 357.0
Barré-Liéou (posterior cervical sympathetic) 723.2
Barrett's (chronic peptic ulcer of esophagus) 530.85
Bársony-Polgár (corkscrew esophagus) 530.5
Bársony-Teschendorf (corkscrew esophagus) 530.5
Barth 759.89
Bartter's (secondary hyperaldosteronism with juxtaglomerular hyperplasia) 255.13
Basedow's (exophthalmic goiter) 242.0 ☑
basilar artery 435.0
basofrontal 377.04
Bassen-Kornzweig (abetalipoproteinemia) 272.5
Batten-Steinert 359.21
battered
adult 995.81
baby or child 995.54
spouse 995.81
Baumgarten-Cruveilhier (cirrhosis of liver) 571.5
Beals 759.82
Bearn-Kunkel (-Slater) (lupoid hepatitis) 571.49
Beau's (*see also* Degeneration, myocardial) 429.1
Bechterew-Strümpell-Marie (ankylosing spondylitis) 720.0
Beck's (anterior spinal artery occlusion) 433.8 ☑
Beckwith (-Wiedemann) 759.89
Behçet's 136.1
Bekhterev-Strümpell-Marie (ankylosing spondylitis) 720.0
Benedikt's 344.89
Béquez César (-Steinbrinck-Chédiak-Higashi) (congenital gigantism of peroxidase granules) 288.2

Syndrome — *see also* Disease — *continued*
Bernard-Horner (*see also* Neuropathy, peripheral, autonomic) 337.9
Bernard-Sergent (acute adrenocortical insufficiency) 255.41
Bernhardt-Roth 355.1
Bernheim's (*see also* Failure, heart) 428.0
Bertolotti's (sacralization of fifth lumbar vertebra) 756.15
Besnier-Boeck-Schaumann (sarcoidosis) 135
Bianchi's (aphasia-apraxia-alexia syndrome) 784.69
Biedl-Bardet (obesity, polydactyly, and mental retardation) 759.89
Biemond's (obesity, polydactyly, and mental retardation) 759.89
big spleen 289.4
bilateral polycystic ovarian 256.4
Bing-Horton's 339.00 ▲
Biörck (-Thorson) (malignant carcinoid) 259.2
Birt-Hogg-Dube 759.89 ●
Blackfan-Diamond (congenital hypoplastic anemia) 284.01
black lung 500
black widow spider bite 989.5
bladder neck (*see also* Incontinence, urine) 788.30
blast (concussion) — *see* Blast, injury
blind loop (postoperative) 579.2
Bloch-Siemens (incontinentia pigmenti) 757.33
Bloch-Sulzberger (incontinentia pigmenti) 757.33
Bloom (-Machacek) (-Torre) 757.39
Blount-Barber (tibia vara) 732.4
blue
bloater 491.20
with
acute bronchitis 491.22
exacerbation (acute) 491.21
diaper 270.0
drum 381.02
sclera 756.51
toe 445.02
Boder-Sedgwick (ataxia-telangiectasia) 334.8
Boerhaave's (spontaneous esophageal rupture) 530.4
Bonnevie-Ullrich 758.6
Bonnier's 386.19
Borjeson-Forssman-Lehmann 759.89
Bouillaud's (rheumatic heart disease) 391.9
Bourneville (-Pringle) (tuberous sclerosis) 759.5
Bouveret (-Hoffmann) (paroxysmal tachycardia) 427.2
brachial plexus 353.0
Brachman-de Lange (Amsterdam dwarf, mental retardation, and brachycephaly) 759.89
bradycardia-tachycardia 427.81
Brailsford-Morquio (dystrophy) (mucopolysaccharidosis IV) 277.5
brain (acute) (chronic) (nonpsychotic) (organic) (with behavioral reaction) (with neurotic reaction) 310.9
with
presenile brain disease (*see also* Dementia, presenile) 290.10
psychosis, psychotic reaction (*see also* Psychosis, organic) 294.9
chronic alcoholic 291.2
congenital (*see also* Retardation, mental) 319
postcontusional 310.2
posttraumatic
nonpsychotic 310.2
psychotic 293.9

Syndrome — *see also* Disease — *continued*
brain — *continued*
posttraumatic — *continued*
psychotic — *continued*
acute 293.0
chronic (*see also* Psychosis, organic) 294.8
subacute 293.1
psycho-organic (*see also* Syndrome, psycho-organic) 310.9
psychotic (*see also* Psychosis, organic) 294.9
senile (*see also* Dementia, senile) 290.0
branchial arch 744.41
Brandt's (acrodermatitis enteropathica) 686.8
Brennemann's 289.2
Briquet's 300.81
Brissaud-Meige (infantile myxedema) 244.9
broad ligament laceration 620.6
Brock's (atelectasis due to enlarged lymph nodes) 518.0
broken heart 429.83
Brown-Séquard 344.89
brown spot 756.59
Brown's tendon sheath 378.61
Brugada 746.89
Brugsch's (acropachyderma) 757.39
bubbly lung 770.7
Buchem's (hyperostosis corticalis) 733.3
Budd-Chiari (hepatic vein thrombosis) 453.0
Büdinger-Ludloff-Läwen 717.89
bulbar 335.22
lateral (*see also* Disease, cerebrovascular, acute) 436
Bullis fever 082.8
bundle of Kent (anomalous atrioventricular excitation) 426.7
Bürger-Grütz (essential familial hyperlipemia) 272.3
Burke's (pancreatic insufficiency and chronic neutropenia) 577.8
Burnett's (milk-alkali) 275.42
Burnier's (hypophyseal dwarfism) 253.3
burning feet 266.2
Bywaters' 958.5
Caffey's (infantile cortical hyperostosis) 756.59
Calvé-Legg-Perthes (osteochrondrosis, femoral capital) 732.1
Caplan (-Colinet) syndrome 714.81
capsular thrombosis (*see also* Thrombosis, brain) 434.0 ☑
carbohydrate-deficient glycoprotein (CDGS) 271.8
carcinogenic thrombophlebitis 453.1
carcinoid 259.2
cardiac asthma (*see also* Failure, ventricular, left) 428.1
cardiacos negros 416.0
cardiopulmonary obesity 278.8
cardiorenal (*see also* Hypertension, cardiorenal) 404.90
cardiorespiratory distress (idiopathic), newborn 769
cardiovascular renal (*see also* Hypertension, cardiorenal) 404.90
cardiovasorenal 272.7
Carini's (ichthyosis congenita) 757.1
carotid
artery (internal) 435.8
body or sinus 337.01 ▲
carpal tunnel 354.0
Carpenter's 759.89
Cassidy (-Scholte) (malignant carcinoid) 259.2
cat-cry 758.31
cauda equina 344.60
causalgia 355.9

Syndrome — *see also* Disease — *continued*
causalgia — *continued*
lower limb 355.71
upper limb 354.4
cavernous sinus 437.6
celiac 579.0
artery compression 447.4
axis 447.4
central pain 338.0
cerebellomedullary malformation (*see also* Spina bifida) 741.0 ☑
cerebral gigantism 253.0
cerebrohepatorenal 759.89
cervical (root) (spine) NEC 723.8
disc 722.71
posterior, sympathetic 723.2
rib 353.0
sympathetic paralysis 337.09 ▲
traumatic (acute) NEC 847.0
cervicobrachial (diffuse) 723.3
cervicocranial 723.2
cervicodorsal outlet 353.2
Céstan's 344.89
Céstan (-Raymond) 433.8 ☑
Céstan-Chenais 344.89
chancriform 114.1
Charcôt's (intermittent claudication) 443.9
angina cruris 443.9
due to atherosclerosis 440.21
Charcôt-Marie-Tooth 356.1
Charcôt-Weiss-Baker 337.01 ▲
CHARGE association 759.89
Cheadle (-Möller) (-Barlow) (infantile scurvy) 267
Chédiak-Higashi (-Steinbrinck) (congenital gigantism of peroxidase granules) 288.2
chest wall 786.52
Chiari's (hepatic vein thrombosis) 453.0
Chiari-Frommel 676.6 ☑
chiasmatic 368.41
Chilaiditi's (subphrenic displacement, colon) 751.4
chondroectodermal dysplasia 756.55
chorea-athetosis-agitans 275.1
Christian's (chronic histiocytosis X) 277.89
chromosome 4 short arm deletion 758.39
chronic pain 338.4
Churg-Strauss 446.4
Clarke-Hadfield (pancreatic infantilism) 577.8
Claude's 352.6
Claude Bernard-Horner (*see also* Neuropathy, peripheral, autonomic) 337.9
Clérambault's
automatism 348.8
erotomania 297.8
Clifford's (postmaturity) 766.22
climacteric 627.2
Clouston's (hidrotic ectodermal dysplasia) 757.31
clumsiness 315.4
Cockayne's (microencephaly and dwarfism) 759.89
Cockayne-Weber (epidermolysis bullosa) 757.39
Coffin-Lowry 759.89
Cogan's (nonsyphilitic interstitial keratitis) 370.52
cold injury (newborn) 778.2
Collet (-Sicard) 352.6
combined immunity deficiency 279.2
compartment(al) (anterior) (deep) (posterior) 958.8
nontraumatic
abdomen 729.73
arm 729.71
buttock 729.72
fingers 729.71
foot 729.72

Syndrome — *see also* Disease — *continued*
compartment — *continued*
nontraumatic — *continued*
forearm 729.71
hand 729.71
hip 729.72
leg 729.72
lower extremity 729.72
shoulder 729.71
specified site NEC 729.79
thigh 729.72
toes 729.72
upper extremity 729.71
wrist 729.71
post-surgical (*see also* Syndrome, compartment, non-traumatic) 998.89 ●
traumatic 958.90
adomen 958.93
arm 958.91
buttock 958.92
fingers 958.91
foot 958.92
forearm 958.91
hand 958.91
hip 958.92
leg 958.92
lower extremity 958.92
shoulder 958.91
specified site NEC 958.99
thigh 958.92
tibial 958.92
toes 958.92
upper extremity 958.91
wrist 958.91
complex regional pain — *see also* Dystrophy, sympathetic ●
type I — *see* Dystrophy, sympathetic (posttraumatic) (reflex) ●
type II — *see* Causalgia ●
compression 958.5
cauda equina 344.60
with neurogenic bladder 344.61
concussion 310.2
congenital
affecting more than one system 759.7
specified type NEC 759.89
congenital central alveolar hypoventilation 327.25
facial diplegia 352.6
muscular hypertrophy-cerebral 759.89
congestion-fibrosis (pelvic) 625.5
conjunctivourethrosynovial 099.3
Conn (-Louis) (primary aldosteronism) 255.12
Conradi (-Hünermann) (chondrodysplasia calcificans congenita) 756.59
conus medullaris 336.8
Cooke-Apert-Gallais (adrenogenital) 255.2
Cornelia de Lange's (Amsterdam dwarf, mental retardation, and brachycephaly) 759.8 ☑
coronary insufficiency or intermediate 411.1
cor pulmonale 416.9
corticosexual 255.2
Costen's (complex) 524.60
costochondral junction 733.6
costoclavicular 353.0
costovertebral 253.0
Cotard's (paranoia) 297.1
Cowden 759.6
craniovertebral 723.2
Creutzfeldt-Jakob 046.19 ▲
with dementia
with behavioral disturbance 046.19 *[294.11]* ▲
without behavioral disturbance 046.19 *[294.10]* ▲
variant 046.11 ●

Syndrome — *see also* Disease — *continued*
Creutzfeldt-Jakob — *continued*
variant — *continued*
with dementia ●
with behavioral disturbance 046.11 *[294.11]* ●
without behavioral disturbance 046.11 *[294.10]* ●
crib death 798.0
cricopharyngeal 787.20
cri-du-chat 758.31
Crigler-Najjar (congenital hyperbilirubinemia) 277.4
crocodile tears 351.8
Cronkhite-Canada 211.3
croup 464.4
CRST (cutaneous systemic sclerosis) 710.1
crush 958.5
crushed lung (*see also* Injury, internal, lung) 861.20
Cruveilhier-Baumgarten (cirrhosis of liver) 571.5
cubital tunnel 354.2
Cuiffini-Pancoast (M8010/3) (carcinoma, pulmonary apex) 162.3
Curschmann (-Batten) (-Steinert) 359.21
Cushing's (iatrogenic) (idiopathic) (pituitary basophilism) (pituitary-dependent) 255.0
overdose or wrong substance given or taken 962.0
Cyriax's (slipping rib) 733.99
cystic duct stump 576.0
Da Costa's (neurocirculatory asthenia) 306.2
Dameshek's (erythroblastic anemia) 282.49
Dana-Putnam (subacute combined sclerosis with pernicious anemia) 281.0 *[336.2]*
Danbolt (-Closs) (acrodermatitis enteropathica) 686.8
Dandy-Walker (atresia, foramen of Magendie) 742.3
with spina bifida (*see also* Spina bifida) 741.0 ☑
Danlos' 756.83
Davies-Colley (slipping rib) 733.99
dead fetus 641.3 ☑
defeminization 255.2
defibrination (*see also* Fibrinolysis) 286.6
Degos' 447.8
Deiters' nucleus 386.19
Déjérine-Roussy 338.0
Déjérine-Thomas 333.0
de Lange's (Amsterdam dwarf, mental retardation, and brachycephaly) (Cornelia) 759.89
Del Castillo's (germinal aplasia) 606.0
deletion chromosomes 758.39
delusional
induced by drug 292.11
dementia-aphonia, of childhood (*see also* Psychosis, childhood) 299.1 ☑
demyelinating NEC 341.9
denial visual hallucination 307.9
depersonalization 300.6
de Quervain's 259.51 ●
Dercum's (adiposis dolorosa) 272.8
de Toni-Fanconi (-Debré) (cystinosis) 270.0
diabetes-dwarfism-obesity (juvenile) 258.1
diabetes mellitus-hypertension-nephrosis 250.4 ☑ *[581.81]*
due to secondary diabetes 249.4 ☑ *[581.81]* ●
diabetes mellitus in newborn infant 775.1

Syndrome — *see also* Disease — *continued*
diabetes-nephrosis 250.4 ☑ *[581.81]*
due to secondary diabetes 249.4 ☑ *[581.81]* ●
diabetic amyotrophy 250.6 ☑ *[353.5]*
due to secondary diabetes 249.6 ☑ *[353.5]* ●
Diamond-Blackfan (congenital hypoplastic anemia) 284.01
Diamond-Gardener (autoerythrocyte sensitization) 287.2
DIC (diffuse or disseminated intravascular coagulopathy) (*see also* Fibrinolysis) 286.6
diencephalohypophyseal NEC 253.8
diffuse cervicobrachial 723.3
diffuse obstructive pulmonary 496
DiGeorge's (thymic hypoplasia) 279.11
Dighton's 756.51
Di Guglielmo's (erythremic myelosis) (M9841/3) 207.0 ☑
disequilibrium 276.9
disseminated platelet thrombosis 446.6
Ditthomska 307.81
Doan-Wisemann (primary splenic neutropenia) 289.53
Döhle body-panmyelopathic 288.2
Donohue's (leprechaunism) 259.8
dorsolateral medullary (*see also* Disease, cerebrovascular, acute) 436
double athetosis 333.71
double whammy 360.81
Down's (mongolism) 758.0
Dresbach's (elliptocytosis) 282.1
Dressler's (postmyocardial infarction) 411.0
hemoglobinuria 283.2
postcardiotomy 429.4
drug withdrawal, infant, of dependent mother 779.5
dry skin 701.1
eye 375.15
DSAP (disseminated superficial actinic porokeratosis) 692.75
Duane's (retraction) 378.71
Duane-Stilling-Türk (ocular retraction syndrome) 378.71
Dubin-Johnson (constitutional hyperbilirubinemia) 277.4
Dubin-Sprinz (constitutional hyperbilirubinemia) 277.4
Duchenne's 335.22
due to abnormality
autosomal NEC (*see also* Abnormal, autosomes NEC) 758.5
13 758.1
18 758.2
21 or 22 758.0
D1 758.1
E3 758.2
G 758.0
chromosomal 758.89
sex 758.81
dumping 564.2
nonsurgical 536.8
Duplay's 726.2
Dupré's (meningism) 781.6
Dyke-Young (acquired macrocytic hemolytic anemia) 283.9
dyspraxia 315.4
dystocia, dystrophia 654.9 ☑
Eagle-Barret 756.71
Eales' 362.18
Eaton-Lambert (*see also* Neoplasm, by site, malignant) 199.1 *[358.1]*
Ebstein's (downward displacement, tricuspid valve into right ventricle) 746.2
ectopic ACTH secretion 255.0
eczema-thrombocytopenia 279.12
Eddowes' (brittle bones and blue sclera) 756.51
Edwards' 758.2

Syndrome — *see also* Disease — *continued*
efferent loop 537.89
effort (aviators') (psychogenic) 306.2
Ehlers-Danlos 756.83
Eisenmenger's (ventricular septal defect) 745.4
Ekbom's (restless legs) 333.94
Ekman's (brittle bones and blue sclera) 756.51
electric feet 266.2
Elephant man 237.71
Ellison-Zollinger (gastric hypersecretion with pancreatic islet cell tumor) 251.5
Ellis-van Creveld (chondroectodermal dysplasia) 756.55
embryonic fixation 270.2
empty sella (turcica) 253.8
endocrine-hypertensive 255.3
Engel-von Recklinghausen (osteitis fibrosa cystica) 252.01
enteroarticular 099.3
entrapment — *see* Neuropathy, entrapment
eosinophilia myalgia 710.5
epidemic vomiting 078.82
Epstein's — *see* Nephrosis
Erb (-Oppenheim)-Goldflam 358.00
Erdheim's (acromegalic macrospondylitis) 253.0
Erlacher-Blount (tibia vara) 732.4
erythrocyte fragmentation 283.19
euthyroid sick 790.94
Evans' (thrombocytopenic purpura) 287.32
excess cortisol, iatrogenic 255.0
exhaustion 300.5
extrapyramidal 333.90
eyelid-malar-mandible 756.0
eye retraction 378.71
Faber's (achlorhydric anemia) 280.9
Fabry (-Anderson) (angiokeratoma corporis diffusum) 272.7
facet 724.8
Fallot's 745.2
falx (*see also* Hemorrhage, brain) 431
familial eczema-thrombocytopenia 279.12
Fanconi (-de Toni) (-Debré) (cystinosis) 270.0
Fanconi's (anemia) (congenital pancytopenia) 284.09
Farber (-Uzman) (disseminated lipogranulomatosis) 272.8
fatigue NEC 300.5
chronic 780.71
faulty bowel habit (idiopathic megacolon) 564.7
FDH (focal dermal hypoplasia) 757.39
fecal reservoir 560.39
Feil-Klippel (brevicollis) 756.16
Felty's (rheumatoid arthritis with splenomegaly and leukopenia) 714.1
fertile eunuch 257.2
fetal alcohol 760.71
late effect 760.71
fibrillation-flutter 427.32
fibrositis (periarticular) 729.0
Fiedler's (acute isolated myocarditis) 422.91
Fiessinger-Leroy (-Reiter) 099.3
Fiessinger-Rendu (erythema multiforme exudativum) 695.19 ▲
first arch 756.0
Fisher's 357.0
fish odor 270.8
Fitz's (acute hemorrhagic pancreatitis) 577.0
Fitz-Hugh and Curtis 098.86
due to
Chlamydia trachomatis 099.56
Neisseria gonorrhoeae (gonococcal peritonitis) 098.86

Syndrome — *see also* Disease — *continued*
Flajani (-Basedow) (exophthalmic goiter) 242.0 ☑
flat back ●
acquired 737.29 ●
postprocedural 738.5 ●
floppy
infant 781.99
iris 364.81
valve (mitral) 424.0
flush 259.2
Foix-Alajouanine 336.1
Fong's (hereditary osteo-onychodysplasia) 756.89
foramen magnum 348.4
Forbes-Albright (nonpuerperal amenorrhea and lactation associated with pituitary tumor) 253.1
Foster-Kennedy 377.04
Foville's (peduncular) 344.89
fragile X 759.83
Franceschetti's (mandibulofacial dysostosis) 756.0
Fraser's 759.89
Freeman-Sheldon 759.89
Frey's (auriculotemporal) 705.22
Friderichsen-Waterhouse 036.3
Friedrich-Erb-Arnold (acropachyderma) 757.39
Fröhlich's (adiposogenital dystrophy) 253.8
Froin's 336.8
Frommel-Chiari 676.6 ☑
frontal lobe 310.0
Fukuhara 277.87
Fuller Albright's (osteitis fibrosa disseminata) 756.59
functional
bowel 564.9
prepubertal castrate 752.89
Gaisböck's (polycythemia hypertonica) 289.0
ganglion (basal, brain) 333.90
geniculi 351.1
Ganser's, hysterical 300.16
Gardner-Diamond (autoerythrocyte sensitization) 287.2
gastroesophageal junction 530.0
gastroesophageal laceration-hemorrhage 530.7
gastrojejunal loop obstruction 537.89
Gayet-Wernicke's (superior hemorrhagic polioencephalitis) 265.1
Gee-Herter-Heubner (nontropical sprue) 579.0
Gélineau's (*see also* Narcolepsy) 347.00
genito-anorectal 099.1
Gerhardt's (vocal cord paralysis) 478.30
Gerstmann's (finger agnosia) 784.69
Gerstmann-Sträussler-Scheinker (GSS) 046.71 ●
Gianotti Crosti 057.8
due to known virus — *see* Infection, virus
due to unknown virus 057.8
Gilbert's 277.4
Gilford (-Hutchinson) (progeria) 259.8
Gilles de la Tourette's 307.23
Gillespie's (dysplasia oculodentodigitalis) 759.89
Glénard's (enteroptosis) 569.89
Glinski-Simmonds (pituitary cachexia) 253.2
glucuronyl transferase 277.4
glue ear 381.20
Goldberg (-Maxwell) (-Morris) (testicular feminization) 259.51 ▲
Goldenhar's (oculoauriculovertebral dysplasia) 756.0
Goldflam-Erb 358.00
Goltz-Gorlin (dermal hypoplasia) 757.39
Good's 279.06

Syndrome — *see also* Disease — *continued*
Goodpasture's (pneumorenal) 446.21
Gopalan's (burning feet) 266.2
Gorlin-Chaudhry-Moss 759.89
Gougerot-Blum (pigmented purpuric lichenoid dermatitis) 709.1
Gougerot-Carteaud (confluent reticulate papillomatosis) 701.8
Gougerot (-Houwer)-Sjögren (keratoconjunctivitis sicca) 710.2
Gouley's (constrictive pericarditis) 423.2
Gowers' (vasovagal attack) 780.2
Gowers-Paton-Kennedy 377.04
Gradenigo's 383.02
gray or grey (chloramphenicol) (newborn) 779.4
Greig's (hypertelorism) 756.0
GSS (Gerstmann-Sträussler-Scheinker) 046.71 ●
Gubler-Millard 344.89
Guérin-Stern (arthrogryposis multiplex congenita) 754.89
Guillain-Barré (-Strohl) 357.0
Gunn's (jaw-winking syndrome) 742.8
Günther's (congenital erythropoietic porphyria) 277.1
gustatory sweating 350.8
H_3O 759.81
Hadfield-Clarke (pancreatic infantilism) 577.8
Haglund-Läwen-Fründ 717.89
hairless women 257.8
hair tourniquet (*see also* Injury, superficial, by site)
finger 915.8
infected 915.9
penis 911.8
infected 911.9
toe 917.8
infected 917.9
Hallermann-Streiff 756.0
Hallervorden-Spatz 333.0
Hamman's (spontaneous mediastinal emphysema) 518.1
Hamman-Rich (diffuse interstitial pulmonary fibrosis) 516.3
hand-foot 693.0
Hand-Schüller-Christian (chronic histiocytosis X) 277.89
Hanot-Chauffard (-Troisier) (bronze diabetes) 275.0
Harada's 363.22
Hare's (M8010/3) (carcinoma, pulmonary apex) 162.3
Harkavy's 446.0
harlequin color change 779.89
Harris' (organic hyperinsulinism) 251.1
Hart's (pellagra-cerebellar ataxia-renal aminoaciduria) 270.0
Hayem-Faber (achlorhydric anemia) 280.9
Hayem-Widal (acquired hemolytic jaundice) 283.9
headache — *see* Headache, syndrome ●
Heberden's (angina pectoris) 413.9
Hedinger's (malignant carcinoid) 259.2
Hegglin's 288.2
Heller's (infantile psychosis) (*see also* Psychosis, childhood) 299.1 ☑
H.E.L.L.P 642.5 ☑
hemolytic-uremic (adult) (child) 283.11
hemophagocytic 288.4
infection-associated 288.4
Hench-Rosenberg (palindromic arthritis) (*see also* Rheumatism, palindromic) 719.3 ☑
Henoch-Schönlein (allergic purpura) 287.0
hepatic flexure 569.89
hepatorenal 572.4
due to a procedure 997.4

Syndrome — *see also* Disease — *continued*
hepatorenal — *continued*
following delivery 674.8 ☑
hepatourologic 572.4
Herrick's (hemoglobin S disease) 282.61
Herter (-Gee) (nontropical sprue) 579.0
Heubner-Herter (nontropical sprue) 579.0
Heyd's (hepatorenal) 572.4
HHHO 759.81
high grade myelodysplastic 238.73
with 5q deletion 238.73
Hilger's 337.09 ▲
histocytic 288.4
Hoffa (-Kastert) (liposynovitis prepatellaris) 272.8
Hoffmann's 244.9 *[359.5]*
Hoffmann-Bouveret (paroxysmal tachycardia) 427.2
Hoffmann-Werdnig 335.0
Holländer-Simons (progressive lipodystrophy) 272.6
Holmes' (visual disorientation) 368.16
Holmes-Adie 379.46
Hoppe-Goldflam 358.00
Horner's (*see also* Neuropathy, peripheral, autonomic) 337.9
traumatic — *see* Injury, nerve, cervical sympathetic
hospital addiction 301.51
hungry bone 275.5 ●
Hunt's (herpetic geniculate ganglionitis) 053.11
dyssynergia cerebellaris myoclonica 334.2
Hunter (-Hurler) (mucopolysaccharidosis II) 277.5
hunterian glossitis 529.4
Hurler (-Hunter) (mucopolysaccharidosis II) 277.5
Hutchinson-Boeck (sarcoidosis) 135
Hutchinson-Gilford (progeria) 259.8
Hutchinson's incisors or teeth 090.5
hydralazine
correct substance properly administered 695.4
overdose or wrong substance given or taken 972.6
hydraulic concussion (abdomen) (*see also* Injury, internal, abdomen) 868.00
hyperabduction 447.8
hyperactive bowel 564.9
hyperaldosteronism with hypokalemic alkalosis (Bartter's) 255.13
hypercalcemic 275.42
hypercoagulation NEC 289.89
hypereosinophilic (idiopathic) 288.3
hyperkalemic 276.7
hyperkinetic (*see also* Hyperkinesia)
heart 429.82
hyperlipemia-hemolytic anemia-icterus 571.1
hypermobility 728.5
hypernatremia 276.0
hyperosmolarity 276.0
hyperperfusion 997.01
hypersomnia-bulimia 349.89
hypersplenic 289.4
hypersympathetic (*see also* Neuropathy, peripheral, autonomic) 337.9
hypertransfusion, newborn 776.4
hyperventilation, psychogenic 306.1
hyperviscosity (of serum) NEC 273.3
polycythemic 289.0
sclerothymic 282.8
hypoglycemic (familial) (neonatal) 251.2
functional 251.1
hypokalemic 276.8
hypophyseal 253.8
hypophyseothalamic 253.8
hypopituitarism 253.2

Syndrome — *see also* Disease — *continued*
hypoplastic left heart 746.7
hypopotassemia 276.8
hyposmolality 276.1
hypotension, maternal 669.2 ☑
hypothenar hammer 443.89
hypotonia-hypomentia-hypogonadism-obesity 759.81
ICF (intravascular coagulation-fibrinolysis) (*see also* Fibrinolysis) 286.6
idiopathic cardiorespiratory distress, newborn 769
idiopathic nephrotic (infantile) 581.9
iliotibial band 728.89
Imerslund (-Gräsbeck) (anemia due to familial selective vitamin B_{12} malabsorption) 281.1
immobility (paraplegic) 728.3
immunity deficiency, combined 279.2
impending coronary 411.1
impingement
shoulder 726.2
vertebral bodies 724.4
inappropriate secretion of antidiuretic hormone (ADH) 253.6
incomplete
mandibulofacial 756.0
infant
death, sudden (SIDS) 798.0
Hercules 255.2
of diabetic mother 775.0
shaken 995.55
infantilism 253.3
inferior vena cava 459.2
influenza-like 487.1
inspissated bile, newborn 774.4
insufficient sleep 307.44
intermediate coronary (artery) 411.1
internal carotid artery (*see also* Occlusion, artery, carotid) 433.1 ☑
interspinous ligament 724.8
intestinal
carcinoid 259.2
gas 787.3
knot 560.2
intraoperative floppy iris (IFIS) 364.81
intravascular
coagulation-fibrinolysis (ICF) (*see also* Fibrinolysis) 286.6
coagulopathy (*see also* Fibrinolysis) 286.6
inverted Marfan's 759.89
IRDS (idiopathic respiratory distress, newborn) 769
irritable
bowel 564.1
heart 306.2
weakness 300.5
ischemic bowel (transient) 557.9
chronic 557.1
due to mesenteric artery insufficiency 557.1
Itsenko-Cushing (pituitary basophilism) 255.0
IVC (intravascular coagulopathy) (*see also* Fibrinolysis) 286.6
Ivemark's (asplenia with congenital heart disease) 759.0
Jaccoud's 714.4
Jackson's 344.89
Jadassohn-Lewandowski (pachyonchia congenita) 757.5
Jaffe-Lichtenstein (-Uehlinger) 252.01
Jahnke's (encephalocutaneous angiomatosis) 759.6
Jakob-Creutzfeldt 046.19
with dementia
with behavioral disturbance 046.19 *[294.11]* ▲
without behavioral disturbance 046.19 *[294.10]* ▲
variant 046.11 ●

☑ Additional Digit Required — Refer to the Tabular List for Digit Selection
Subterms under main terms may continue to next column or page

▶◀ Revised Text ● New Line ▲ Revised Code

Syndrome — *see also* Disease — *continued*
Jakob-Creutzfeldt — *continued*
variant — *continued*
with dementia ●
with behavioral disturbance ●
046.11 *[294.11]* ●
without behavioral disturbance ●
046.11 *[294.10]* ●
Jaksch's (pseudoleukemia infantum) 285.8
Jaksch-Hayem (-Luzet) (pseudoleukemia infantum) 285.8
jaw-winking 742.8
jejunal 564.2
Jervell-Lange-Nielsen 426.82
jet lag 327.35
Jeune's (asphyxiating thoracic dystrophy of newborn) 756.4
Job's (chronic granulomatous disease) 288.1
Jordan's 288.2
Joseph-Diamond-Blackfan (congenital hypoplastic anemia) 284.01
Joubert 759.89
jugular foramen 352.6
Kabuki 759.89
Kahler's (multiple myeloma) (M9730/3) 203.0 ☑
Kalischer's (encephalocutaneous angiomatosis) 759.6
Kallmann's (hypogonadotropic hypogonadism with anosmia) 253.4
Kanner's (autism) (*see also* Psychosis, childhood) 299.0 ☑
Kartagener's (sinusitis, bronchiectasis, situs inversus) 759.3
Kasabach-Merritt (capillary hemangioma associated with thrombocytopenic purpura) 287.39
Kast's (dyschondroplasia with hemangiomas) 756.4
Kaznelson's (congenital hypoplastic anemia) 284.01
Kearns-Sayre 277.87
Kelly's (sideropenic dysphagia) 280.8
Kimmelstiel-Wilson (intercapillary glomerulosclerosis)
250.4 ☑ *[581.81]*
due to secondary diabetes ●
249.4 ☑ *[581.81]* ●
Klauder's (erythema multiforme exudativum) 695.19 ▲
Kleine-Levin 327.13
Klein-Waardenburg (ptosis-epicanthus) 270.2
Klinefelter's 758.7
Klippel-Feil (brevicollis) 756.16
Klippel-Trenaunay 759.89
Klumpke (-Déjérine) (injury to brachial plexus at birth) 767.6
Klüver-Bucy (-Terzian) 310.0
Köhler-Pellegrini-Stieda (calcification, knee joint) 726.62
König's 564.89
Korsakoff's (nonalcoholic) 294.0
Korsakoff (-Wernicke) (nonalcoholic) 294.0
alcoholic 291.1
alcoholic 291.1
Kostmann's (infantile genetic agranulocytosis) 288.01
Krabbe's
congenital muscle hypoplasia 756.89
cutaneocerebral angioma 759.6
Kunkel (lupoid hepatitis) 571.49
labyrinthine 386.50
laceration, broad ligament 620.6
Landau-Kleffner 345.8 ☑ ●
Langdon Down (mongolism) 758.0
Larsen's (flattened facies and multiple congenital dislocations) 755.8

Syndrome — *see also* Disease — *continued*
lateral
cutaneous nerve of thigh 355.1
medullary (*see also* Disease, cerebrovascular acute) 436
Launois' (pituitary gigantism) 253.0
Launois-Cléret (adiposogenital dystrophy) 253.8
Laurence-Moon (-Bardet)-Biedl (obesity, polydactyly, and mental retardation) 759.89
Lawford's (encephalocutaneous angiomatosis) 759.6
lazy
leukocyte 288.09
posture 728.3
Lederer-Brill (acquired infectious hemolytic anemia) 283.19
Legg-Calvé-Perthes (osteochondrosis capital femoral) 732.1
Lemiere 451.89
Lennox's (*see also* Epilepsy) 345.0 ☑
Lennox-Gastaut syndrome 345.0 ☑
with tonic seizures 345.1 ☑
lenticular 275.1
Léopold-Lévi's (paroxysmal thyroid instability) 242.9 ☑
Lepore hemoglobin 282.49
Leriche's (aortic bifurcation occlusion) 444.0
Léri-Weill 756.59
Lermoyez's (*see also* Disease, Ménière's) 386.00
Lesch-Nyhan (hypoxanthine-guanine-phosphoribosyltransferase deficiency) 277.2
leukoencephalopathy, reversible, ●
posterior 348.5 ●
Lev's (acquired complete heart block) 426.0
Levi's (pituitary dwarfism) 253.3
Lévy-Roussy 334.3
Lichtheim's (subacute combined sclerosis with pernicious anemia) 281.0 *[336.2]*
Li-Fraumeni V84.01
Lightwood's (renal tubular acidosis) 588.89
Lignac (-de Toni) (-Fanconi) (-Debré) (cystinosis) 270.0
Likoff's (angina in menopausal women) 413.9
liver-kidney 572.4
Lloyd's 258.1
lobotomy 310.0
Löffler's (eosinophilic pneumonitis) 518.3
Löfgren's (sarcoidosis) 135
long arm 18 or 21 deletion 758.39
Looser (-Debray)-Milkman (osteomalacia with pseudofractures) 268.2
Lorain-Levi (pituitary dwarfism) 253.3
Louis-Bar (ataxia-telangiectasia) 334.8
low
atmospheric pressure 993.2
back 724.2
psychogenic 306.0
output (cardiac) (*see also* Failure, heart) 428.9
Lowe's (oculocerebrorenal dystrophy) 270.8
lower radicular, newborn 767.4
Lowe-Terrey-MacLachlan (oculocerebrorenal dystrophy) 270.8
Lown (-Ganong)-Levine (short P-R interval, normal QRS complex, and supraventricular tachycardia) 426.81
Lucey-Driscoll (jaundice due to delayed conjugation) 774.30
Luetscher's (dehydration) 276.51
lumbar vertebral 724.4
Lutembacher's (atrial septal defect with mitral stenosis) 745.5

Syndrome — *see also* Disease — *continued*
Lyell's (toxic epidermal necrolysis) 695.15 ▲
due to drug
correct substance properly administered 695.15 ▲
overdose or wrong substance given or taken 977.9
specified drug — *see* Table of Drugs and Chemicals
MacLeod's 492.8
macrogenitosomia praecox 259.8
macroglobulinemia 273.3
macrophage activation 288.4
Maffucci's (dyschondroplasia with hemangiomas) 756.4
Magenblase 306.4
magnesium-deficiency 781.7
malabsorption 579.9
postsurgical 579.3
spinal fluid 331.3
Mal de Debarquement 780.4
malignant carcinoid 259.2
Mallory-Weiss 530.7
mandibulofacial dysostosis 756.0
manic-depressive (*see also* Psychosis, affective) 296.80
Mankowsky's (familial dysplastic osteopathy) 731.2
maple syrup (urine) 270.3
Marable's (celiac artery compression) 447.4
Marchesani (-Weill) (brachymorphism and ectopia lentis) 759.89
Marchiafava-Bignami 341.8
Marchiafava-Micheli (paroxysmal nocturnal hemoglobinuria) 283.2
Marcus Gunn's (jaw-winking syndrome) 742.8
Marfan's (arachnodactyly) 759.82
meaning congenital syphilis 090.49
with luxation of lens 090.49 *[379.32]*
Marie's (acromegaly) 253.0
primary or idiopathic (acropachyderma) 757.39
secondary (hypertrophic pulmonary osteoarthropathy) 731.2
Markus-Adie 379.46
Maroteaux-Lamy (mucopolysaccharidosis VI) 277.5
Martin's 715.27
Martin-Albright (pseudohypoparathyroidism) 275.49
Martorell-Fabré (pulseless disease) 446.7
massive aspiration of newborn 770.18
Masters-Allen 620.6
mastocytosis 757.33
maternal hypotension 669.2 ☑
maternal obesity 646.1 ☑
May (-Hegglin) 288.2
McArdle (-Schmid) (-Pearson) (glycogenosis V) 271.0
McCune-Albright (osteitis fibrosa disseminata) 756.59
McQuarrie's (idiopathic familial hypoglycemia) 251.2
meconium
aspiration 770.12
plug (newborn) NEC 777.1
median arcuate ligament 447.4
mediastinal fibrosis 519.3
Meekeren-Ehlers-Danlos 756.83
Meige (blepharospasm-oromandibular dystonia) 333.82
-Milroy (chronic hereditary edema) 757.0
MELAS (mitochondrial encephalopathy, lactic acidosis and stroke-like episodes) 277.87
Melkersson (-Rosenthal) 351.8

Syndrome — *see also* Disease — *continued*
MEN (multiple endocrine neoplasia)
type I 258.01
type IIA 258.02
type IIB 258.03
Mende's (ptosis-epicanthus) 270.2
Mendelson's (resulting from a procedure) 997.39 ▲
during labor 668.0 ☑
obstetric 668.0 ☑
Ménétrier's (hypertrophic gastritis) 535.2 ☑
Ménière's (*see also* Disease, Ménière's) 386.00
meningo-eruptive 047.1
Menkes' 759.89
glutamic acid 759.89
maple syrup (urine) disease 270.3
menopause 627.2
postartificial 627.4
menstruation 625.4
MERRF (myoclonus with epilepsy and with ragged red fibers) 277.87
mesenteric
artery, superior 557.1
vascular insufficiency (with gangrene) 557.1
metabolic 277.7
metastatic carcinoid 259.2
Meyenburg-Altherr-Uehlinger 733.99
Meyer-Schwickerath and Weyers (dysplasia oculodentodigitalis) 759.89
Micheli-Rietti (thalassemia minor) 282.49
Michotte's 721.5
micrognathia-glossoptosis 756.0
microphthalmos (congenital) 759.89
midbrain 348.8
middle
lobe (lung) (right) 518.0
radicular 353.0
Miescher's
familial acanthosis nigricans 701.2
granulomatosis disciformis 709.3
Mieten's 759.89
migraine 346.0 ☑
Mikity-Wilson (pulmonary dysmaturity) 770.7
Mikulicz's (dryness of mouth, absent or decreased lacrimation) 527.1
milk alkali (milk drinkers') 275.42
Milkman (-Looser) (osteomalacia with pseudofractures) 268.2
Millard-Gubler 344.89
Miller-Dieker 758.33
Miller Fisher's 357.0
Milles' (encephalocutaneous angiomatosis) 759.6
Minkowski-Chauffard (*see also* Spherocytosis) 282.0
Mirizzi's (hepatic duct stenosis) 576.2
with calculus, cholelithiasis, or stones — *see* Choledocholithiasis
mitochondrial neurogastrointestinal encephalopathy (MNGIE) 277.87
mitral
click (-murmur) 785.2
valve prolapse 424.0
MNGIE (mitochondrial neurogastrointestinal encephalopathy) 277.87
Möbius'
congenital oculofacial paralysis 352.6
ophthalmoplegic migraine 346.2 ☑ ▲
Mohr's (types I and II) 759.89
monofixation 378.34
Moore's (*see also* Epilepsy) 345.5 ☑
Morel-Moore (hyperostosis frontalis interna) 733.3
Morel-Morgagni (hyperostosis frontalis interna) 733.3

Syndrome — *see also* Disease — *continued*
Morgagni (-Stewart-Morel) (hyperostosis frontalis interna) 733.3
Morgagni-Adams-Stokes (syncope with heart block) 426.9
Morquio (-Brailsford) (-Ullrich) (mucopolysaccharidosis IV) 277.5
Morris (testicular feminization) 259.51 ▲
Morton's (foot) (metatarsalgia) (metatarsal neuralgia) (neuralgia) (neuroma) (toe) 355.6
Moschcowitz (-Singer-Symmers) (thrombotic thrombocytopenic purpura) 446.6
Mounier-Kuhn 748.3
with
acute exacerbation 494.1
bronchiectasis 494.0
with (acute) exacerbation 494.1
acquired 519.19
with bronchiectasis 494.0
with (acute) exacerbation 494.1
Mucha-Haberman (acute parapsoriasis varioliformis) 696.2
mucocutaneous lymph node (acute) (febrile) (infantile) (MCLS) 446.1
multiple
deficiency 260
endocrine neoplasia (MEN)
type I 258.01
type IIA 258.02
type IIB 258.03
operations 301.51
Munchausen's 301.51
Münchmeyer's (exostosis luxurians) 728.11
Murchison-Sanderson — *see* Disease, Hodgkin's
myasthenic — *see* Myasthenia, syndrome
myelodysplastic 238.75
with 5q deletion 238.74
high grade with 5q deletion 238.73
therapy-related 289.83 ●
myeloproliferative (chronic) (M9960/1) 238.79
myofascial pain NEC 729.1
Naffziger's 353.0
Nager-de Reynier (dysostosis mandibularis) 756.0
nail-patella (hereditary osteo-onychodysplasia) 756.89
NARP (neuropathy, ataxia and retinitis pigmentosa) 277.87
Nebécourt's 253.3
Neill-Dingwall (microencephaly and dwarfism) 759.89
nephrotic (*see also* Nephrosis) 581.9
diabetic 250.4 ☑ *[581.81]*
due to secondary diabetes ●
249.4 ☑ *[581.81]* ●
Netherton's (ichthyosiform erythroderma) 757.1
neurocutaneous 759.6
neuroleptic malignant 333.92
Nezelof's (pure alymphocytosis) 279.13
Niemann-Pick (lipid histiocytosis) 272.7
Nonne-Milroy-Meige (chronic hereditary edema) 757.0
nonsense 300.16
Noonan's 759.89
Nothnagel's
ophthalmoplegia-cerebellar ataxia 378.52
vasomotor acroparesthesia 443.89
nucleus ambiguous-hypoglossal 352.6
OAV (oculoauriculovertebral dysplasia) 756.0
obsessional 300.3
oculocutaneous 364.24
oculomotor 378.81

Syndrome — *see also* Disease — *continued*
oculourethroarticular 099.3
Ogilvie's (sympathicotonic colon obstruction) 560.89
ophthalmoplegia-cerebellar ataxia 378.52
Oppenheim-Urbach (necrobiosis lipoidica diabeticorum) 250.8 ☑ *[709.3]*
due to secondary diabetes ●
249.8 ☑ *[709.3]* ●
oral-facial-digital 759.89
organic
affective NEC 293.83
drug-induced 292.84
anxiety 293.84
delusional 293.81
alcohol-induced 291.5
drug-induced 292.11
due to or associated with
arteriosclerosis 290.42
presenile brain disease 290.12
senility 290.20
depressive 293.83
drug-induced 292.84
due to or associated with
arteriosclerosis 290.43
presenile brain disease 290.13
senile brain disease 290.21
hallucinosis 293.82
drug-induced 292.84
organic affective 293.83
induced by drug 292.84
organic personality 310.1
induced by drug 292.89
Ormond's 593.4
orodigitofacial 759.89
orthostatic hypotensive-dysautonomic dyskinetic 333.0
Osler-Weber-Rendu (familial hemorrhagic telangiectasia) 448.0
osteodermopathic hyperostosis 757.39
osteoporosis-osteomalacia 268.2
Österreicher-Turner (hereditary osteo-onychodysplasia) 756.89
os trigonum 755.69 ●
Ostrum-Furst 756.59
otolith 386.19
otopalatodigital 759.89
outlet (thoracic) 353.0
ovarian remnant 620.8
Owren's (*see also* Defect, coagulation) 286.3
OX 758.6
pacemaker 429.4
Paget-Schroetter (intermittent venous claudication) 453.8
pain (*see also* Pain)
central 338.0
chronic 338.4
complex regional 355.9 ●
type I 337.20 ●
lower limb 337.22 ●
specified site NEC 337.29 ●
upper limb 337.21 ●
type II ●
lower limb 355.71 ●
upper limb 354.4 ●
myelopathic 338.0
thalamic (hyperesthetic) 338.0
painful
apicocostal vertebral (M8010/3) 162.3
arc 726.19
bruising 287.2
feet 266.2
Pancoast's (carcinoma, pulmonary apex) (M8010/3) 162.3
panhypopituitary (postpartum) 253.2
papillary muscle 429.81
with myocardial infarction 410.8 ☑
Papillon-Léage and Psaume (orodigitofacial dysostosis) 759.89

Syndrome — *see also* Disease — *continued*
parabiotic (transfusion)
donor (twin) 772.0
recipient (twin) 776.4
paralysis agitans 332.0
paralytic 344.9
specified type NEC 344.89
paraneoplastic — *see* condition
Parinaud's (paralysis of conjugate upward gaze) 378.81
oculoglandular 372.02
Parkes Weber and Dimitri (encephalocutaneous angiomatosis) 759.6
Parkinson's (*see also* Parkinsonism) 332.0
parkinsonian (*see also* Parkinsonism) 332.0
Parry's (exophthalmic goiter) 242.0 ☑
Parry-Romberg 349.89
Parsonage-Aldren-Turner 353.5
Parsonage-Turner 353.5
Patau's (trisomy D1) 758.1
patella clunk 719.66
patellofemoral 719.46
Paterson (-Brown) (-Kelly) (sideropenic dysphagia) 280.8
Payr's (splenic flexure syndrome) 569.89
pectoral girdle 447.8
pectoralis minor 447.8
Pelger-Huët (hereditary hyposegmentation) 288.2
pellagra-cerebellar ataxia-renal aminoaciduria 270.0
pellagroid 265.2
Pellegrini-Stieda 726.62
Pellizzi's (pineal) 259.8
pelvic congestion (-fibrosis) 625.5
Pendred's (familial goiter with deafmutism) 243
Penfield's (*see also* Epilepsy) 345.5 ☑
Penta X 758.81
peptic ulcer — *see* Ulcer, peptic 533.9 ☑
perabduction 447.8
periodic 277.31
periurethral fibrosis 593.4
persistent fetal circulation 747.83
Petges-Cléjat (poikilodermatomyositis) 710.3
Peutz-Jeghers 759.6
Pfeiffer (acrocephalosyndactyly) 755.55
phantom limb 353.6
pharyngeal pouch 279.11
Pick's (pericardial pseudocirrhosis of liver) 423.2
heart 423.2
liver 423.2
Pick-Herxheimer (diffuse idiopathic cutaneous atrophy) 701.8
Pickwickian (cardiopulmonary obesity) 278.8
PIE (pulmonary infiltration with eosinophilia) 518.3
Pierre Marie-Bamberger (hypertrophic pulmonary osteoarthropathy) 731.2
Pierre Mauriac's (diabetes-dwarfism-obesity) 258.1
Pierre Robin 756.0
pigment dispersion, iris 364.53
pineal 259.8
pink puffer 492.8
pituitary 253.0
placental
dysfunction 762.2
insufficiency 762.2
transfusion 762.3
plantar fascia 728.71
plateau iris 364.82 ●
plica knee 727.83
Plummer-Vinson (sideropenic dysphagia) 280.8
pluricarential of infancy 260

Syndrome — *see also* Disease — *continued*
plurideficiency of infancy 260
pluriglandular (compensatory) 258.8
polycarential of infancy 260
polyglandular 258.8
polysplenia 759.0
pontine 433.8 ☑
popliteal
artery entrapment 447.8
web 756.89
postartificial menopause 627.4
postcardiac injury
postcardiotomy 429.4
postmyocardial infarction 411.0
postcardiotomy 429.4
postcholecystectomy 576.0
postcommissurotomy 429.4
postconcussional 310.2
postcontusional 310.2
postencephalitic 310.8
posterior
cervical sympathetic 723.2
fossa compression 348.4
inferior cerebellar artery (*see also* Disease, cerebrovascular, acute) 436
reversible encephalopathy (PRES) 348.39
postgastrectomy (dumping) 564.2
post-gastric surgery 564.2
posthepatitis 780.79
postherpetic (neuralgia) (zoster) 053.19
geniculate ganglion 053.11
ophthalmica 053.19
postimmunization — *see* Complications, vaccination
postinfarction 411.0
postinfluenza (asthenia) 780.79
postirradiation 990
postlaminectomy 722.80
cervical, cervicothoracic 722.81
lumbar, lumbosacral 722.83
thoracic, thoracolumbar 722.82
postleukotomy 310.0
postlobotomy 310.0
postmastectomy lymphedema 457.0
postmature (of newborn) 766.22
postmyocardial infarction 411.0
postoperative NEC 998.9
blind loop 579.2
postpartum panhypopituitary 253.2
postperfusion NEC 999.89 ▲
bone marrow 996.85
postpericardiotomy 429.4
postphlebitic (asymptomatic) 459.10
with
complications NEC 459.19
inflammation 459.12
and ulcer 459.13
stasis dermatitis 459.12
with ulcer 459.13
ulcer 459.11
with inflammation 459.13
postpolio (myelitis) 138
postvagotomy 564.2
postvalvulotomy 429.4
postviral (asthenia) NEC 780.79
Potain's (gastrectasis with dyspepsia) 536.1
potassium intoxication 276.7
Potter's 753.0
Prader (-Labhart) -Willi (-Fanconi) 759.81
preinfarction 411.1
preleukemic 238.75
premature senility 259.8
premenstrual 625.4
premenstrual tension 625.4
pre ulcer 536.9
Prinzmetal-Massumi (anterior chest wall syndrome) 786.52
Profichet's 729.90 ▲
progeria 259.8

Syndrome — *see also* Disease — *continued*
- progressive pallidal degeneration 333.0
- prolonged gestation 766.22
- Proteus (dermal hypoplasia) 757.39
- prune belly 756.71
- prurigo-asthma 691.8
- pseudocarpal tunnel (sublimis) 354.0
- pseudohermaphroditism-virilism-hirsutism 255.2
- pseudoparalytica 358.00
- pseudo-Turner's 759.89
- psycho-organic 293.9
  - acute 293.0
  - anxiety type 293.84
  - depressive type 293.83
  - hallucinatory type 293.82
  - nonpsychotic severity 310.1
    - specified focal (partial) NEC 310.8
  - paranoid type 293.81
  - specified type NEC 293.89
  - subacute 293.1
- pterygolymphangiectasia 758.6
- ptosis-epicanthus 270.2
- pulmonary
  - arteriosclerosis 416.0
  - hypoperfusion (idiopathic) 769
  - renal (hemorrhagic) 446.21
- pulseless 446.7
- Putnam-Dana (subacute combined sclerosis with pernicious anemia) 281.0 *[336.2]*
- pyloroduodenal 537.89
- pyramidopallidonigral 332.0
- pyriformis 355.0
- QT interval prolongation 426.82
- radicular NEC 729.2
  - lower limbs 724.4
  - upper limbs 723.4
    - newborn 767.4
- Raeder-Harbitz (pulseless disease) 446.7
- Ramsay Hunt's
  - dyssynergia cerebellaris myoclonica 334.2
  - herpetic geniculate ganglionitis 053.11
- rapid time-zone change 327.35
- Raymond (-Céstan) 433.8 ☑
- Raynaud's (paroxysmal digital cyanosis) 443.0
- RDS (respiratory distress syndrome, newborn) 769
- Refsum's (heredopathia atactica polyneuritiformis) 356.3
- Reichmann's (gastrosuccorrhea) 536.8
- Reifenstein's (hereditary familial hypogonadism, male) 259.52 ▲
- Reilly's (*see also* Neuropathy, peripheral, autonomic) 337.9
- Reiter's 099.3
- renal glomerulohyalinosis-diabetic 250.4 ☑ *[581.81]*
  - due to secondary diabetes 249.4 ☑ *[581.81]* ●
- Rendu-Osler-Weber (familial hemorrhagic telangiectasia) 448.0
- renofacial (congenital biliary fibroangiomatosis) 753.0
- Rénon-Delille 253.8
- respiratory distress (idiopathic) (newborn) 769
  - adult (following shock, surgery, or trauma) 518.5
    - specified NEC 518.82
  - type II 770.6
- restless legs (RLS) 333.94
- retinoblastoma (familial) 190.5
- retraction (Duane's) 378.71
- retroperitoneal fibrosis 593.4
- retroviral seroconversion (acute) V08
- Rett's 330.8
- Reye's 331.81
- Reye-Sheehan (postpartum pituitary necrosis) 253.2
- Riddoch's (visual disorientation) 368.16
- Ridley's (*see also* Failure, ventricular, left) 428.1
- Rieger's (mesodermal dysgenesis, anterior ocular segment) 743.44
- Rietti-Greppi-Micheli (thalassemia minor) 282.49
- right ventricular obstruction — *see* Failure, heart
- Riley-Day (familial dysautonomia) 742.8
- Robin's 756.0
- Rokitansky-Kuster-Hauser (congenital absence, vagina) 752.49
- Romano-Ward (prolonged QT interval syndrome) 426.82
- Romberg's 349.89
- Rosen-Castleman-Liebow (pulmonary proteinosis) 516.0
- rotator cuff, shoulder 726.10
- Roth's 355.1
- Rothmund's (congenital poikiloderma) 757.33
- Rotor's (idiopathic hyperbilirubinemia) 277.4
- Roussy-Lévy 334.3
- Roy (-Jutras) (acropachyderma) 757.39
- rubella (congenital) 771.0
- Rubinstein-Taybi's (brachydactylia, short stature, and mental retardation) 759.89
- Rud's (mental deficiency, epilepsy, and infantilism) 759.89
- Ruiter-Pompen (-Wyers) (angiokeratoma corporis diffusum) 272.7
- Runge's (postmaturity) 766.22
- Russell (-Silver) (congenital hemihypertrophy and short stature) 759.89
- Rytand-Lipsitch (complete atrioventricular block) 426.0
- sacralization-scoliosis-sciatica 756.15
- sacroiliac 724.6
- Saenger's 379.46
- salt
  - depletion (*see also* Disease, renal) 593.9
    - due to heat NEC 992.8
      - causing heat exhaustion or prostration 992.4
  - low (*see also* Disease, renal) 593.9
- salt-losing (*see also* Disease, renal) 593.9
- Sanfilippo's (mucopolysaccharidosis III) 277.5
- Scaglietti-Dagnini (acromegalic macrospondylitis) 253.0
- scalded skin 695.81 ▲
- scalenus anticus (anterior) 353.0
- scapulocostal 354.8
- scapuloperoneal 359.1
- scapulovertebral 723.4
- Schaumann's (sarcoidosis) 135
- Scheie's (mucopolysaccharidosis IS) 277.5
- Scheuthauer-Marie-Sainton (cleidocranialis dysostosis) 755.59
- Schirmer's (encephalocutaneous angiomatosis) 759.6
- schizophrenic, of childhood NEC (*see also* Psychosis, childhood) 299.9 ☑
- Schmidt's
  - sphallo-pharyngo-laryngeal hemiplegia 352.6
  - thyroid-adrenocortical insufficiency 258.1
  - vagoaccessory 352.6
- Schneider's 047.9
- Schnitzler 273.1
- Scholte's (malignant carcinoid) 259.2
- Scholz (-Bielschowsky-Henneberg) 330.0
- Schroeder's (endocrine-hypertensive) 255.3
- Schüller-Christian (chronic histiocytosis X) 277.89
- Schultz's (agranulocytosis) 288.09
- Schwartz (-Jampel) 359.23
- Schwartz-Bartter (inappropriate secretion of antidiuretic hormone) 253.6
- Scimitar (anomalous venous drainage, right lung to inferior vena cava) 747.49
- sclerocystic ovary 256.4
- sea-blue histiocyte 272.7
- Seabright-Bantam (pseudohypoparathyroidism) 275.49
- Seckel's 759.89
- Secretan's (posttraumatic edema) 782.3
- secretoinhibitor (keratoconjunctivitis sicca) 710.2
- Seeligmann's (ichthyosis congenita) 757.1
- Senear-Usher (pemphigus erythematosus) 694.4
- senilism 259.8
- seroconversion, retroviral (acute) V08
- serotonin 333.99
- serous meningitis 348.2
- Sertoli cell (germinal aplasia) 606.0
- sex chromosome mosaic 758.81
- Sézary's (reticulosis) (M9701/3) 202.2 ☑
- shaken infant 995.55
- Shaver's (bauxite pneumoconiosis) 503
- Sheehan's (postpartum pituitary necrosis) 253.2
- shock (traumatic) 958.4
  - kidney 584.5
    - following crush injury 958.5
  - lung 518.5
  - neurogenic 308.9
  - psychic 308.9
- Shone's 746.84 ●
- short
  - bowel 579.3
  - P-R interval 426.81
- shoulder-arm (*see also* Neuropathy, peripheral, autonomic) 337.9
- shoulder-girdle 723.4
- shoulder-hand (*see also* Neuropathy, peripheral, autonomic) 337.9
- Shwachman's 288.02
- Shy-Drager (orthostatic hypotension with multisystem degeneration) 333.0
- Sicard's 352.6
- sicca (keratoconjunctivitis) 710.2
- sick
  - cell 276.1
  - cilia 759.89
  - sinus 427.81
- sideropenic 280.8
- Siemens'
  - ectodermal dysplasia 757.31
  - keratosis follicularis spinulosa (decalvans) 757.39
- Silfverskiöld's (osteochondrodystrophy, extremities) 756.50
- Silver's (congenital hemihypertrophy and short stature) 759.89
- Silvestroni-Bianco (thalassemia minima) 282.49
- Simons' (progressive lipodystrophy) 272.6
- sinusitis-bronchiectasis-situs inversus 759.3
- sinus tarsi 726.79
- Sipple's (medullary thyroid carcinoma-pheochromocytoma) 258.02
- Sjögren (-Gougerot) (keratoconjunctivitis sicca) 710.2
  - with lung involvement 710.2 *[517.8]*
- Sjögren-Larsson (ichthyosis congenita) 757.1
- SJS-TEN (Stevens-Johnson syndrome - toxic epidermal necrolysis overlap) 695.14 ●
- Slocumb's 255.3
- Sluder's 337.09 ▲
- Smith-Lemli-Opitz (cerebrohepatorenal syndrome) 759.89
- Smith-Magenis 758.33
- smokers' 305.1
- Sneddon-Wilkinson (subcorneal pustular dermatosis) 694.1
- Sotos' (cerebral gigantism) 253.0
- South African cardiomyopathy 425.2
- spasmodic
  - upward movement, eye(s) 378.82
  - winking 307.20
- Spens' (syncope with heart block) 426.9
- spherophakia-brachymorphia 759.89
- spinal cord injury (*see also* Injury, spinal, by site)
  - with fracture, vertebra — *see* Fracture, vertebra, by site, with spinal cord injury
  - cervical — *see* Injury, spinal, cervical
  - fluid malabsorption (acquired) 331.3
- splenic
  - agenesis 759.0
  - flexure 569.89
  - neutropenia 289.53
  - sequestration 289.52
- Spurway's (brittle bones and blue sclera) 756.51
- staphylococcal scalded skin 695.81 ▲
- Stein's (polycystic ovary) 256.4
- Steinbrocker's (*see also* Neuropathy, peripheral, autonomic) 337.9
- Stein-Leventhal (polycystic ovary) 256.4
- Stevens-Johnson (erythema multiforme exudativum) 695.13 ▲
  - toxic epidermal necrolysis overlap (SJS-TEN overlap syndrome) 695.14 ●
- Stewart-Morel (hyperostosis frontalis interna) 733.3
- Stickler 759.89
- stiff-baby 759.89
- stiff-man 333.91
- Still's (juvenile rheumatoid arthritis) 714.30
- Still-Felty (rheumatoid arthritis with splenomegaly and leukopenia) 714.1
- Stilling-Türk-Duane (ocular retraction syndrome) 378.71
- Stojano's (subcostal) 098.86
- Stokes (-Adams) (syncope with heart block) 426.9
- Stokvis-Talma (enterogenous cyanosis) 289.7
- stone heart (*see also* Failure, ventricular, left) 428.1
- straight-back 756.19
- stroke (*see also* Disease, cerebrovascular, acute) 436
  - little 435.9
- Sturge-Kalischer-Weber (encephalotrigeminal angiomatosis) 759.6
- Sturge-Weber (-Dimitri) (encephalocutaneous angiomatosis) 759.6
- subclavian-carotid obstruction (chronic) 446.7
- subclavian steal 435.2

- **Syndrome** — *see also* Disease — *continued*
  - subcoracoid-pectoralis minor 447.8
  - subcostal 098.86
    - nerve compression 354.8
  - subperiosteal hematoma 267
  - subphrenic interposition 751.4
  - sudden infant death (SIDS) 798.0
  - Sudeck's 733.7
  - Sudeck-Leriche 733.7
  - superior
    - cerebellar artery (*see also* Disease, cerebrovascular, acute) 436
    - mesenteric artery 557.1
    - pulmonary sulcus (tumor) (M8010/3) 162.3
    - vena cava 459.2
  - suprarenal cortical 255.3
  - supraspinatus 726.10
  - Susac 348.39 ●
  - swallowed blood 777.3
  - sweat retention 705.1
  - Sweet's (acute febrile neutrophilic dermatosis) 695.89
  - Swyer's (XY pure gonadal dysgenesis) 752.7
  - Swyer-James (unilateral hyperlucent lung) 492.8
  - Symonds' 348.2
  - sympathetic
    - cervical paralysis 337.09 ▲
    - pelvic 625.5
  - syndactylic oxycephaly 755.55
  - syphilitic-cardiovascular 093.89
  - systemic
    - fibrosclerosing 710.8
    - inflammatory response (SIRS) 995.90
      - due to
        - infectious process 995.91
          - with acute organ dysfunction 995.92
        - non-infectious process 995.93
          - with acute organ dysfunction 995.94
  - systolic click (-murmur) 785.2
  - Tabagism 305.1
  - tachycardia-bradycardia 427.81
  - Takayasu (-Onishi) (pulseless disease) 446.7
  - Takotsubo 429.83
  - Tapia's 352.6
  - tarsal tunnel 355.5
  - Taussig-Bing (transposition, aorta and overriding pulmonary artery) 745.11
  - Taybi's (otopalatodigital) 759.89
  - Taylor's 625.5
  - teething 520.7
  - tegmental 344.89
  - telangiectasis-pigmentation-cataract 757.33
  - temporal 383.02
    - lobectomy behavior 310.0
  - temporomandibular joint-pain-dysfunction [TMJ] NEC 524.60
    - specified NEC 524.69
  - Terry's ▶(*see also* Retinopathy of prematurity)◀ 362.21
  - testicular feminization 259.51 ▲
  - testis, nonvirilizing 257.8
  - tethered (spinal) cord 742.59
  - thalamic 338.0
  - Thibierge-Weissenbach (cutaneous systemic sclerosis) 710.1
  - Thiele 724.6
  - thoracic outlet (compression) 353.0
  - thoracogenous rheumatic (hypertrophic pulmonary osteoarthropathy) 731.2
  - Thorn's (*see also* Disease, renal) 593.9
  - Thorson-Biörck (malignant carcinoid) 259.2
  - thrombopenia-hemangioma 287.39
  - thyroid-adrenocortical insufficiency 258.1
  - Tietze's 733.6
  - time-zone (rapid) 327.35
  - Tobias' (carcinoma, pulmonary apex) (M8010/3) 162.3
  - toilet seat 926.0
  - Tolosa-Hunt 378.55
  - Toni-Fanconi (cystinosis) 270.0
  - Touraine's (hereditary osteo-onychodysplasia) 756.89
  - Touraine-Solente-Golé (acropachyderma) 757.39
  - toxic
    - oil 710.5
    - shock 040.82
  - transfusion
    - fetal-maternal 772.0
    - twin
      - donor (infant) 772.0
      - recipient (infant) 776.4
  - transient left ventricular apical ballooning 429.83
  - Treacher Collins' (incomplete mandibulofacial dysostosis) 756.0
  - trigeminal plate 259.8
  - triple X female 758.81
  - trisomy NEC 758.5
    - 13 or D_1 758.1
    - 16-18 or E 758.2
    - 18 or E_3 758.2
    - 20 758.5
    - 21 or G (mongolism) 758.0
    - 22 or G (mongolism) 758.0
    - G 758.0
  - Troisier-Hanot-Chauffard (bronze diabetes) 275.0
  - tropical wet feet 991.4
  - Trousseau's (thrombophlebitis migrans visceral cancer) 453.1
  - Türk's (ocular retraction syndrome) 378.71
  - Turner's 758.6
  - Turner-Varny 758.6
  - Twiddler's (due to) ●
    - automatic implantable defibrillator 996.04 ●
    - pacemaker 996.01 ●
  - twin-to-twin transfusion 762.3
    - recipient twin 776.4
  - Uehlinger's (acropachyderma) 757.39
  - Ullrich (-Bonnevie) (-Turner) 758.6
  - Ullrich-Feichtiger 759.89
  - underwater blast injury (abdominal) (*see also* Injury, internal, abdomen) 868.00
  - universal joint, cervix 620.6
  - Unverricht (-Lundborg) 333.2
  - Unverricht-Wagner (dermatomyositis) 710.3
  - upward gaze 378.81
  - Urbach-Oppenheim (necrobiosis lipoidica diabeticorum) 250.8 ☑ *[709.3]*
    - due to secondary diabetes 249.8 ☑ *[709.3]* ●
  - Urbach-Wiethe (lipoid proteinosis) 272.8
  - uremia, chronic 585.9
  - urethral 597.81
  - urethro-oculoarticular 099.3
  - urethro-oculosynovial 099.3
  - urohepatic 572.4
  - uveocutaneous 364.24
  - uveomeningeal, uveomeningitis 363.22
  - vagohypoglossal 352.6
  - vagovagal 780.2
  - van Buchem's (hyperostosis corticalis) 733.3
  - van der Hoeve's (brittle bones and blue sclera, deafness) 756.51
  - van der Hoeve-Halbertsma-Waardenburg (ptosis-epicanthus) 270.2
  - van der Hoeve-Waardenburg-Gualdi (ptosis-epicanthus) 270.2
  - vanishing twin 651.33
  - van Neck-Odelberg (juvenile osteochondrosis) 732.1
  - vascular splanchnic 557.0
  - vasomotor 443.9
  - vasovagal 780.2
  - VATER 759.89
  - Velo-cardio-facial 758.32
  - vena cava (inferior) (superior) (obstruction) 459.2
  - Verbiest's (claudicatio intermittens spinalis) 435.1
  - Vernet's 352.6
  - vertebral
    - artery 435.1
      - compression 721.1
    - lumbar 724.4
    - steal 435.1
  - vertebrogenic (pain) 724.5
  - vertiginous NEC 386.9
  - video display tube 723.8
  - Villaret's 352.6
  - Vinson-Plummer (sideropenic dysphagia) 280.8
  - virilizing adrenocortical hyperplasia, congenital 255.2
  - virus, viral 079.99
  - visceral larval migrans 128.0
  - visual disorientation 368.16
  - vitamin B_6 deficiency 266.1
  - vitreous touch 997.99
  - Vogt's (corpus striatum) 333.71
  - Vogt-Koyanagi 364.24
  - Volkmann's 958.6
  - von Bechterew-Strümpell (ankylosing spondylitis) 720.0
  - von Graefe's 378.72
  - von Hippel-Lindau (angiomatosis retinocerebellosa) 759.6
  - von Schroetter's (intermittent venous claudication) 453.8
  - von Willebrand (-Jürgens) (angiohemophilia) 286.4
  - Waardenburg-Klein (ptosis epicanthus) 270.2
  - Wagner (-Unverricht) (dermatomyositis) 710.3
  - Waldenström's (macroglobulinemia) 273.3
  - Waldenström-Kjellberg (sideropenic dysphagia) 280.8
  - Wallenberg's (posterior inferior cerebellar artery) (*see also* Disease, cerebrovascular, acute) 436
  - Waterhouse (-Friderichsen) 036.3
  - water retention 276.6
  - Weber's 344.89
  - Weber-Christian (nodular nonsuppurative panniculitis) 729.30
  - Weber-Cockayne (epidermolysis bullosa) 757.39
  - Weber-Dimitri (encephalocutaneous angiomatosis) 759.6
  - Weber-Gubler 344.89
  - Weber-Leyden 344.89
  - Weber-Osler (familial hemorrhagic telangiectasia) 448.0
  - Wegener's (necrotizing respiratory granulomatosis) 446.4
  - Weill-Marchesani (brachymorphism and ectopia lentis) 759.89
  - Weingarten's (tropical eosinophilia) 518.3
  - Weiss-Baker (carotid sinus syncope) 337.01 ▲
  - Weissenbach-Thibierge (cutaneous systemic sclerosis) 710.1
  - Werdnig-Hoffmann 335.0
  - Werlhof-Wichmann (*see also* Purpura, thrombocytopenic) 287.39
  - Wermer's (polyendocrine adenomatosis) 258.01
  - Werner's (progeria adultorum) 259.8
  - Wernicke's (nonalcoholic) (superior hemorrhagic polioencephalitis) 265.1
  - Wernicke-Korsakoff (nonalcoholic) 294.0
    - alcoholic 291.1
  - Westphal-Strümpell (hepatolenticular degeneration) 275.1
  - wet
    - brain (alcoholic) 303.9 ☑
    - feet (maceration) (tropical) 991.4
    - lung
      - adult 518.5
      - newborn 770.6
  - whiplash 847.0
  - Whipple's (intestinal lipodystrophy) 040.2
  - "whistling face" (craniocarpotarsal dystrophy) 759.89
  - Widal (-Abrami) (acquired hemolytic jaundice) 283.9
  - Wilkie's 557.1
  - Wilkinson-Sneddon (subcorneal pustular dermatosis) 694.1
  - Willan-Plumbe (psoriasis) 696.1
  - Willebrand (-Jürgens) (angiohemophilia) 286.4
  - Willi-Prader (hypogenital dystrophy with diabetic tendency) 759.81
  - Wilson's (hepatolenticular degeneration) 275.1
  - Wilson-Mikity 770.7
  - Wiskott-Aldrich (eczema-thrombocytopenia) 279.12
  - withdrawal
    - alcohol 291.81
    - drug 292.0
      - infant of dependent mother 779.5
  - Woakes' (ethmoiditis) 471.1
  - Wolff-Parkinson-White (anomalous atrioventricular excitation) 426.7
  - Wright's (hyperabduction) 447.8
  - X
    - cardiac 413.9
    - dysmetabolic 277.7
  - xiphoidalgia 733.99
  - XO 758.6
  - XXX 758.81
  - XXXXY 758.81
  - XXY 758.7
  - yellow vernix (placental dysfunction) 762.2
  - Zahorsky's 074.0
  - Zellweger 277.86
  - Zieve's (jaundice, hyperlipemia and hemolytic anemia) 571.1
  - Zollinger-Ellison (gastric hypersecretion with pancreatic islet cell tumor) 251.5
  - Zuelzer-Ogden (nutritional megaloblastic anemia) 281.2
- **Synechia** (iris) (pupil) 364.70
  - anterior 364.72
    - peripheral 364.73
  - intrauterine (traumatic) 621.5
  - posterior 364.71
  - vulvae, congenital 752.49
- **Synesthesia** — *see also* Disturbance, sensation 782.0
- **Synodontia** 520.2
- **Synophthalmus** 759.89
- **Synorchidism** 752.89
- **Synorchism** 752.89
- **Synostosis** (congenital) 756.59
  - astragaloscaphoid 755.67
  - radioulnar 755.53
  - talonavicular (bar) 755.67
  - tarsal 755.67
- **Synovial** — *see* condition

☑ Additional Digit Required — Refer to the Tabular List for Digit Selection

▼ Subterms under main terms may continue to next column or page

▶◀ Revised Text ● New Line ▲ Revised Code

- **Synovioma** (M9040/3) — *see also* Neoplasm, connective tissue, malignant
  - benign (M9040/0) — *see* Neoplasm, connective tissue, benign
- **Synoviosarcoma** (M9040/3) — *see* Neoplasm, connective tissue, malignant
- **Synovitis** ▶(*see also* Tenosynovitis)◀ 727.00
  - chronic crepitant, wrist 727.2
  - due to crystals — *see* Arthritis, due to crystals
  - gonococcal 098.51
  - gouty 274.0
  - specified NEC 727.09 ●
  - syphilitic 095.7
    - congenital 090.0
  - traumatic, current — *see* Sprain, by site
  - tuberculous — *see* Tuberculosis, synovitis
  - villonodular 719.20
    - ankle 719.27
    - elbow 719.22
    - foot 719.27
    - hand 719.24
    - hip 719.25
    - knee 719.26
    - multiple sites 719.29
    - pelvic region 719.25
    - shoulder (region) 719.21
    - specified site NEC 719.28
    - wrist 719.23
- **Syphilide** 091.3
  - congenital 090.0
  - newborn 090.0
  - tubercular 095.8
    - congenital 090.0
- **Syphilis, syphilitic** (acquired) 097.9
  - with lung involvement 095.1
  - abdomen (late) 095.2
  - acoustic nerve 094.86
  - adenopathy (secondary) 091.4
  - adrenal (gland) 095.8
    - with cortical hypofunction 095.8
  - age under 2 years NEC (*see also* Syphilis, congenital) 090.9
    - acquired 097.9
  - alopecia (secondary) 091.82
  - anemia 095.8
  - aneurysm (artery) (ruptured) 093.89
    - aorta 093.0
    - central nervous system 094.89
    - congenital 090.5
  - anus 095.8
    - primary 091.1
    - secondary 091.3
  - aorta, aortic (arch) (abdominal) (insufficiency) (pulmonary) (regurgitation) (stenosis) (thoracic) 093.89
    - aneurysm 093.0
  - arachnoid (adhesive) 094.2
  - artery 093.89
    - cerebral 094.89
    - spinal 094.89
  - arthropathy (neurogenic) (tabetic) 094.0 *[713.5]*
  - asymptomatic — *see* Syphilis, latent
  - ataxia, locomotor (progressive) 094.0
  - atrophoderma maculatum 091.3
  - auricular fibrillation 093.89
  - Bell's palsy 094.89
  - bladder 095.8
  - bone 095.5
    - secondary 091.61
  - brain 094.89
  - breast 095.8
  - bronchus 095.8
  - bubo 091.0
  - bulbar palsy 094.89
  - bursa (late) 095.7
  - cardiac decompensation 093.89
  - cardiovascular (early) (late) (primary) (secondary) (tertiary) 093.9
    - specified type and site NEC 093.89

- **Syphilis, syphilitic** — *continued*
  - causing death under 2 years of age (*see also* Syphilis, congenital) 090.9
    - stated to be acquired NEC 097.9
  - central nervous system (any site) (early) (late) (latent) (primary) (recurrent) (relapse) (secondary) (tertiary) 094.9
    - with
      - ataxia 094.0
      - paralysis, general 094.1
        - juvenile 090.40
      - paresis (general) 094.1
        - juvenile 090.40
      - tabes (dorsalis) 094.0
        - juvenile 090.40
      - taboparesis 094.1
        - juvenile 090.40
    - aneurysm (ruptured) 094.87
    - congenital 090.40
    - juvenile 090.40
    - remission in (sustained) 094.9
    - serology doubtful, negative, or positive 094.9
    - specified nature or site NEC 094.89
    - vascular 094.89
  - cerebral 094.89
    - meningovascular 094.2
    - nerves 094.89
    - sclerosis 094.89
    - thrombosis 094.89
  - cerebrospinal 094.89
    - tabetic 094.0
  - cerebrovascular 094.89
  - cervix 095.8
  - chancre (multiple) 091.0
    - extragenital 091.2
    - Rollet's 091.2
  - Charcôt's joint 094.0 *[713.5]*
  - choked disc 094.89 *[377.00]*
  - chorioretinitis 091.51
    - congenital 090.0 *[363.13]*
    - late 094.83
  - choroiditis 091.51
    - congenital 090.0 *[363.13]*
    - late 094.83
    - prenatal 090.0 *[363.13]*
  - choroidoretinitis (secondary) 091.51
    - congenital 090.0 *[363.13]*
    - late 094.83
  - ciliary body (secondary) 091.52
    - late 095.8 *[364.11]*
  - colon (late) 095.8
  - combined sclerosis 094.89
  - complicating pregnancy, childbirth or puerperium 647.0 ☑
    - affecting fetus or newborn 760.2
  - condyloma (latum) 091.3
  - congenital 090.9
    - with
      - encephalitis 090.41
      - paresis (general) 090.40
      - tabes (dorsalis) 090.40
      - taboparesis 090.40
    - chorioretinitis, choroiditis 090.0 *[363.13]*
    - early or less than 2 years after birth NEC 090.2
      - with manifestations 090.0
      - latent (without manifestations) 090.1
        - negative spinal fluid test 090.1
        - serology, positive 090.1
      - symptomatic 090.0
    - interstitial keratitis 090.3
    - juvenile neurosyphilis 090.40
    - late or 2 years or more after birth NEC 090.7
      - chorioretinitis, choroiditis 090.5 *[363.13]*
      - interstitial keratitis 090.3
      - juvenile neurosyphilis NEC 090.40

- **Syphilis, syphilitic** — *continued*
  - congenital — *continued*
    - late or 2 years or more after birth — *continued*
      - latent (without manifestations) 090.6
        - negative spinal fluid test 090.6
        - serology, positive 090.6
      - symptomatic or with manifestations NEC 090.5
        - interstitial keratitis 090.3
  - conjugal 097.9
    - tabes 094.0
  - conjunctiva 095.8 *[372.10]*
  - contact V01.6
  - cord, bladder 094.0
  - cornea, late 095.8 *[370.59]*
  - coronary (artery) 093.89
    - sclerosis 093.89
  - coryza 095.8
    - congenital 090.0
  - cranial nerve 094.89
  - cutaneous — *see* Syphilis, skin
  - dacryocystitis 095.8
  - degeneration, spinal cord 094.89
  - d'emblée 095.8
  - dementia 094.1
    - paralytica 094.1
      - juvenilis 090.40
  - destruction of bone 095.5
  - dilatation, aorta 093.0
  - due to blood transfusion 097.9
  - dura mater 094.89
  - ear 095.8
    - inner 095.8
      - nerve (eighth) 094.86
      - neurorecurrence 094.86
  - early NEC 091.0
    - cardiovascular 093.9
    - central nervous system 094.9
      - paresis 094.1
      - tabes 094.0
    - latent (without manifestations) (less than 2 years after infection) 092.9
      - negative spinal fluid test 092.9
      - serological relapse following treatment 092.0
      - serology positive 092.9
    - paresis 094.1
    - relapse (treated, untreated) 091.7
    - skin 091.3
    - symptomatic NEC 091.89
      - extragenital chancre 091.2
      - primary, except extragenital chancre 091.0
      - secondary (*see also* Syphilis, secondary) 091.3
        - relapse (treated, untreated) 091.7
    - tabes 094.0
    - ulcer 091.3
  - eighth nerve 094.86
  - endemic, nonvenereal 104.0
  - endocarditis 093.20
    - aortic 093.22
    - mitral 093.21
    - pulmonary 093.24
    - tricuspid 093.23
  - epididymis (late) 095.8
  - epiglottis 095.8
  - epiphysitis (congenital) 090.0
  - esophagus 095.8
  - Eustachian tube 095.8
  - exposure to V01.6
  - eye 095.8 *[363.13]*
    - neuromuscular mechanism 094.85
  - eyelid 095.8 *[373.5]*
    - with gumma 095.8 *[373.5]*
    - ptosis 094.89
  - fallopian tube 095.8
  - fracture 095.5
  - gallbladder (late) 095.8
  - gastric 095.8
    - crisis 094.0

- **Syphilis, syphilitic** — *continued*
  - gastric — *continued*
    - polyposis 095.8
  - general 097.9
    - paralysis 094.1
      - juvenile 090.40
  - genital (primary) 091.0
  - glaucoma 095.8
  - gumma (late) NEC 095.9
    - cardiovascular system 093.9
    - central nervous system 094.9
    - congenital 090.5
    - heart or artery 093.89
  - heart 093.89
    - block 093.89
    - decompensation 093.89
    - disease 093.89
    - failure 093.89
    - valve (*see also* Syphilis, endocarditis) 093.20
  - hemianesthesia 094.89
  - hemianopsia 095.8
  - hemiparesis 094.89
  - hemiplegia 094.89
  - hepatic artery 093.89
  - hepatitis 095.3
  - hepatomegaly 095.3
    - congenital 090.0
  - hereditaria tarda (*see also* Syphilis, congenital, late) 090.7
  - hereditary (*see also* Syphilis, congenital) 090.9
    - interstitial keratitis 090.3
  - Hutchinson's teeth 090.5
  - hyalitis 095.8
  - inactive — *see* Syphilis, latent
  - infantum NEC (*see also* Syphilis, congenital) 090.9
  - inherited — *see* Syphilis, congenital
  - internal ear 095.8
  - intestine (late) 095.8
  - iris, iritis (secondary) 091.52
    - late 095.8 *[364.11]*
  - joint (late) 095.8
  - keratitis (congenital) (early) (interstitial) (late) (parenchymatous) (punctata profunda) 090.3
  - kidney 095.4
  - lacrimal apparatus 095.8
  - laryngeal paralysis 095.8
  - larynx 095.8
  - late 097.0
    - cardiovascular 093.9
    - central nervous system 094.9
    - latent or 2 years or more after infection (without manifestations) 096
      - negative spinal fluid test 096
      - serology positive 096
    - paresis 094.1
    - specified site NEC 095.8
    - symptomatic or with symptoms 095.9
    - tabes 094.0
  - latent 097.1
    - central nervous system 094.9
    - date of infection unspecified 097.1
    - early or less than 2 years after infection 092.9
    - late or 2 years or more after infection 096
    - serology
      - doubtful
        - follow-up of latent syphilis 097.1
          - central nervous system 094.9
          - date of infection unspecified 097.1
          - early or less than 2 years after infection 092.9
          - late or 2 years or more after infection 096
      - positive, only finding 097.1
        - date of infection unspecified 097.1

Index

Syphilis, syphilitic — Tabardillo

T

Tabes, tabetic
with
central nervous system syphilis 094.0
Charcôt's joint 094.0 *[713.5]*
cord bladder 094.0
crisis, viscera (any) 094.0
paralysis, general 094.1
paresis (general) 094.1
perforating ulcer 094.0
arthropathy 094.0 *[713.5]*
bladder 094.0
bone 094.0
cerebrospinal 094.0
congenital 090.40
conjugal 094.0
dorsalis 094.0
neurosyphilis 094.0
early 094.0
juvenile 090.40
latent 094.0
mesenterica (*see also* Tuberculosis) 014.8 ☑
paralysis insane, general 094.1
peripheral (nonsyphilitic) 799.89
spasmodic 094.0
not dorsal or dorsalis 343.9
syphilis (cerebrospinal) 094.0
Taboparalysis 094.1
Taboparesis (remission) 094.1
with
Charcôt's joint 094.1 *[713.5]*
cord bladder 094.1
perforating ulcer 094.1
juvenile 090.40
Tache noir 923.20
Tachyalimentation 579.3
Tachyarrhythmia, tachyrhythmia — *see also* Tachycardia
paroxysmal with sinus bradycardia 427.81
Tachycardia 785.0
atrial 427.89
auricular 427.89
AV nodal re-entry (re-entrant) 427.89
junctional ectopic 427.0
newborn 779.82
nodal 427.89
nonparoxysmal atrioventricular 426.89
nonparoxysmal atrioventricular (nodal) 426.89
nonsustained 427.2 ●
paroxysmal 427.2
with sinus bradycardia 427.81
atrial (PAT) 427.0
psychogenic 316 *[427.0]*
atrioventricular (AV) 427.0
psychogenic 316 *[427.0]*
essential 427.2
junctional 427.0
nodal 427.0
psychogenic 316 *[427.2]*
atrial 316 *[427.0]*
supraventricular 316 *[427.0]*
ventricular 316 *[427.1]*
supraventricular 427.0
psychogenic 316 *[427.0]*
ventricular 427.1
psychogenic 316 *[427.1]*
postoperative 997.1
psychogenic 306.2
sick sinus 427.81
sinoauricular 427.89
sinus 427.89
supraventricular 427.89
sustained 427.2 ●
supraventricular 427.0 ●
ventricular 427.1 ●
ventricular (paroxysmal) 427.1
psychogenic 316 *[427.1]*
Tachygastria 536.8
Tachypnea 786.06
hysterical 300.11
newborn (idiopathic) (transitory) 770.6
psychogenic 306.1

Tachypnea — *continued*
transitory, of newborn 770.6
Taenia (infection) (infestation) — *see also* Infestation, taenia 123.3
diminuta 123.6
echinococcal infestation (*see also* Echinococcus) 122.9
nana 123.6
saginata infestation 123.2
solium (intestinal form) 123.0
larval form 123.1
Taeniasis (intestine) — *see also* Infestation, taenia 123.3
saginata 123.2
solium 123.0
Taenzer's disease 757.4
Tag (hypertrophied skin) (infected) 701.9
adenoid 474.8
anus 455.9
endocardial (*see also* Endocarditis) 424.90
hemorrhoidal 455.9
hymen 623.8
perineal 624.8
preauricular 744.1
rectum 455.9
sentinel 455.9
skin 701.9
accessory 757.39
anus 455.9
congenital 757.39
preauricular 744.1
rectum 455.9
tonsil 474.8
urethra, urethral 599.84
vulva 624.8
Tahyna fever 062.5
Takayasu (-Onishi) disease or syndrome (pulseless disease) 446.7
Takotsubo syndrome 429.83
Talc granuloma 728.82
in operation wound 998.7
Talcosis 502
Talipes (congenital) 754.70
acquired NEC 736.79
planus 734
asymmetric 754.79
acquired 736.79
calcaneovalgus 754.62
acquired 736.76
calcaneovarus 754.59
acquired 736.76
calcaneus 754.79
acquired 736.76
cavovarus 754.59
acquired 736.75
cavus 754.71
acquired 736.73
equinovalgus 754.69
acquired 736.72
equinovarus 754.51
acquired 736.71
equinus 754.79
acquired, NEC 736.72
percavus 754.71
acquired 736.73
planovalgus 754.69
acquired 736.79
planus (acquired) (any degree) 734
congenital 754.61
due to rickets 268.1
valgus 754.60
acquired 736.79
varus 754.50
acquired 736.79
Talma's disease 728.85
Talon noir 924.20
hand 923.20
heel 924.20
toe 924.3
Tamponade heart (Rose's) — *see also* Pericarditis 423.3
Tanapox 059.21 ▲
Tangier disease (familial high-density lipoprotein deficiency) 272.5
Tank ear 380.12

Tantrum (childhood) — *see also* Disturbance, conduct 312.1 ☑
Tapeworm (infection) (infestation) — *see also* Infestation, tapeworm 123.9
Tapia's syndrome 352.6
Tarantism 297.8
Target-oval cell anemia 282.49
Tarlov's cyst 355.9
Tarral-Besnier disease (pityriasis rubra pilaris) 696.4
Tarsalgia 729.2
Tarsal tunnel syndrome 355.5
Tarsitis (eyelid) 373.00
syphilitic 095.8 *[373.00]*
tuberculous (*see also* Tuberculosis) 017.0 ☑ *[373.4]*
Tartar (teeth) 523.6
Tattoo (mark) 709.09
Taurodontism 520.2
Taussig-Bing defect, heart, or syndrome (transposition, aorta and overriding pulmonary artery) 745.11
Taybi's syndrome (otopalatodigital) 759.89
Tay's choroiditis 363.41
Taylor's
disease (diffuse idiopathic cutaneous atrophy) 701.8
syndrome 625.5
Tay-Sachs
amaurotic familial idiocy 330.1
disease 330.1
Tear stone 375.57
Tear, torn (traumatic) — *see also* Wound, open, by site
anus, anal (sphincter) 863.89
with open wound in cavity 863.99
complicating delivery (healed) (old) 654.8 ☑
with mucosa 664.3 ☑
not associated with third-degree perineal laceration 664.6 ☑
nontraumatic, nonpuerperal (healed) (old) 569.43
articular cartilage, old (*see also* Disorder, cartilage, articular) 718.0 ☑
bladder
with
abortion — *see* Abortion, by type, with damage to pelvic organs
ectopic pregnancy (*see also* categories 633.0–633.9) 639.2
molar pregnancy (*see also* categories 630–632) 639.2
following
abortion 639.2
ectopic or molar pregnancy 639.2
obstetrical trauma 665.5 ☑
bowel
with
abortion — *see* Abortion, by type, with damage to pelvic organs
ectopic pregnancy (*see also* categories 633.0–633.9) 639.2
molar pregnancy (*see also* categories 630–632) 639.2
following
abortion 639.2
ectopic or molar pregnancy 639.2
obstetrical trauma 665.5 ☑
broad ligament
with
abortion — *see* Abortion, by type, with damage to pelvic organs
ectopic pregnancy (*see also* categories 633.0–633.9) 639.2

Tear, torn — *see also* Wound, open, by site — *continued*
broad ligament — *continued*
with — *continued*
molar pregnancy (*see also* categories 630–632) 639.2
following
abortion 639.2
ectopic or molar pregnancy 639.2
obstetrical trauma 665.6 ☑
bucket handle (knee) (meniscus) — *see* Tear, meniscus
capsule
joint — *see* Sprain, by site
spleen — *see* Laceration, spleen, capsule
cartilage (*see also* Sprain, by site)
articular, old (*see also* Disorder, cartilage, articular) 718.0 ☑
knee — *see* Tear, meniscus
semilunar (knee) (current injury) — *see* Tear, meniscus
cervix
with
abortion — *see* Abortion, by type, with damage to pelvic organs
ectopic pregnancy (*see also* categories 633.0–633.9) 639.2
molar pregnancy (*see also* categories 630–632) 639.2
following
abortion 639.2
ectopic or molar pregnancy 639.2
obstetrical trauma (current) 665.3 ☑
old 622.3
dural 349.31 ▲
accidental puncture or laceration ●
during a procedure 349.31 ●
incidental (inadvertent) 349.31 ●
nontraumatic NEC 349.39 ●
internal organ (abdomen, chest, or pelvis) — *see* Injury, internal, by site
ligament (*see also* Sprain, by site)
with open wound — *see* Wound, open by site
meniscus (knee) (current injury) 836.2
bucket handle 836.0
old 717.0
lateral 836.1
anterior horn 836.1
old 717.42
bucket handle 836.1
old 717.41
old 717.40
posterior horn 836.1
old 717.43
specified site NEC 836.1
old 717.49
medial 836.0
anterior horn 836.0
old 717.1
bucket handle 836.0
old 717.0
old 717.3
posterior horn 836.0
old 717.2
old NEC 717.5
site other than knee — *see* Sprain, by site
muscle (*see also* Sprain, by site)
with open wound — *see* Wound, open by site
pelvic
floor, complicating delivery 664.1 ☑
organ NEC
with
abortion — *see* Abortion, by type, with damage to pelvic organs

- **Tear, torn** — *see also* Wound, open, by site — *continued*
  - pelvic — *continued*
    - organ — *continued*
      - with — *continued*
        - ectopic pregnancy (*see also* categories 633.0–633.9) 639.2
        - molar pregnancy (*see also* categories 630–632) 639.2
      - following
        - abortion 639.2
        - ectopic or molar pregnancy 639.2
      - obstetrical trauma 665.5 ☑
  - perineum (*see also* Laceration, perineum)
    - obstetrical trauma 665.5 ☑
  - periurethral tissue
    - with
      - abortion — *see* Abortion, by type, with damage to pelvic organs
      - ectopic pregnancy (*see also* categories 633.0–633.9) 639.2
      - molar pregnancy (*see also* categories 630–632) 639.2
    - following
      - abortion 639.2
      - ectopic or molar pregnancy 639.2
    - obstetrical trauma 665.5 ☑
  - rectovaginal septum — *see* Laceration, rectovaginal septum
  - retina, retinal (recent) (with detachment) 361.00
    - without detachment 361.30
    - dialysis (juvenile) (with detachment) 361.04
    - giant (with detachment) 361.03
    - horseshoe (without detachment) 361.32
    - multiple (with detachment) 361.02
      - without detachment 361.33
    - old
      - delimited (partial) 361.06
      - partial 361.06
      - total or subtotal 361.07
    - partial (without detachment)
      - giant 361.03
      - multiple defects 361.02
      - old (delimited) 361.06
      - single defect 361.01
    - round hole (without detachment) 361.31
    - single defect (with detachment) 361.01
    - total or subtotal (recent) 361.05
      - old 361.07
  - rotator cuff (traumatic) 840.4
    - current injury 840.4
    - degenerative 726.10
    - nontraumatic 727.61
  - semilunar cartilage, knee (*see also* Tear, meniscus) 836.2
    - old 717.5
  - tendon (*see also* Sprain, by site)
    - with open wound — *see* Wound, open by site
  - tentorial, at birth 767.0
  - umbilical cord
    - affecting fetus or newborn 772.0
    - complicating delivery 663.8 ☑
  - urethra
    - with
      - abortion — *see* Abortion, by type, with damage to pelvic organs
      - ectopic pregnancy (*see also* categories 633.0–633.9) 639.2
      - molar pregnancy (*see also* categories 630–632) 639.2
- **Tear, torn** — *see also* Wound, open, by site — *continued*
  - urethra — *continued*
    - following
      - abortion 639.2
      - ectopic or molar pregnancy 639.2
    - obstetrical trauma 665.5 ☑
  - uterus — *see* Injury, internal, uterus
  - vagina — *see* Laceration, vagina
  - vessel, from catheter 998.2
  - vulva, complicating delivery 664.0 ☑
- **Teething** 520.7
  - syndrome 520.7
- **Teeth, tooth** — *see also* condition
  - grinding 306.8
  - prenatal 520.6
- **Tegmental syndrome** 344.89
- **Telangiectasia, telangiectasis** (verrucous) 448.9
  - ataxic (cerebellar) 334.8
  - familial 448.0
  - hemorrhagic, hereditary (congenital) (senile) 448.0
  - hereditary hemorrhagic 448.0
  - retina 362.15
  - spider 448.1
- **Telecanthus** (congenital) 743.63
- **Telescoped bowel or intestine** — *see also* Intussusception 560.0
- **Teletherapy, adverse effect** NEC 990
- **Telogen effluvium** 704.02
- **Temperature**
  - body, high (of unknown origin) (*see also* Pyrexia) 780.60 ▲
  - cold, trauma from 991.9
    - newborn 778.2
    - specified effect NEC 991.8
  - high
    - body (of unknown origin) (*see also* Pyrexia) 780.60 ▲
    - trauma from — *see* Heat
- **Temper tantrum** (childhood) — *see also* Disturbance, conduct 312.1 ☑
- **Temple** — *see* condition
- **Temporal** — *see also* condition
  - lobe syndrome 310.0
- **Temporomandibular joint-pain-dysfunction syndrome** 524.60
- **Temporosphenoidal** — *see* condition
- **Tendency**
  - bleeding (*see also* Defect, coagulation) 286.9
  - homosexual, ego-dystonic 302.0
  - paranoid 301.0
  - suicide 300.9
- **Tenderness**
  - abdominal (generalized) (localized) 789.6 ☑
  - rebound 789.6 ☑
  - skin 782.0
- **Tendinitis, tendonitis** — *see also* Tenosynovitis 726.90
  - Achilles 726.71
  - adhesive 726.90
    - shoulder 726.0
  - calcific 727.82
    - shoulder 726.11
  - gluteal 726.5
  - patellar 726.64
  - peroneal 726.79
  - pes anserinus 726.61
  - psoas 726.5
  - tibialis (anterior) (posterior) 726.72
  - trochanteric 726.5
- **Tendon** — *see* condition
- **Tendosynovitis** — *see* Tenosynovitis
- **Tendovaginitis** — *see* Tenosynovitis
- **Tenesmus** 787.99
  - rectal 787.99
  - vesical 788.99 ▲
- **Tenia** — *see* Taenia
- **Teniasis** — *see* Taeniasis
- **Tennis elbow** 726.32
- **Tenonitis** — *see also* Tenosynovitis
  - eye (capsule) 376.04
- **Tenontosynovitis** — *see* Tenosynovitis
- **Tenontothecitis** — *see* Tenosynovitis
- **Tenophyte** 727.9
- **Tenosynovitis** ▶(*see also* Synovitis)◀ 727.00
  - adhesive 726.90
    - shoulder 726.0
  - ankle 727.06
  - bicipital (calcifying) 726.12
  - buttock 727.09
  - due to crystals — *see* Arthritis, due to crystals
  - elbow 727.09
  - finger 727.05
  - foot 727.06
  - gonococcal 098.51
  - hand 727.05
  - hip 727.09
  - knee 727.09
  - radial styloid 727.04
  - shoulder 726.10
    - adhesive 726.0
  - specified NEC 727.09 ●
  - spine 720.1
  - supraspinatus 726.10
  - toe 727.06
  - tuberculous — *see* Tuberculosis, tenosynovitis
  - wrist 727.05
- **Tenovaginitis** — *see* Tenosynovitis
- **Tension**
  - arterial, high (*see also* Hypertension) 401.9
    - without diagnosis of hypertension 796.2
  - headache 307.81
  - intraocular (elevated) 365.00
  - nervous 799.2
  - ocular (elevated) 365.00
  - pneumothorax 512.0
    - iatrogenic 512.1
    - postoperative 512.1
    - spontaneous 512.0
  - premenstrual 625.4
  - state 300.9
- **Tentorium** — *see* condition
- **Teratencephalus** 759.89
- **Teratism** 759.7
- **Teratoblastoma** (malignant) (M9080/3) — *see* Neoplasm, by site, malignant
- **Teratocarcinoma** (M9081/3) — *see also* Neoplasm, by site, malignant
  - liver 155.0
- **Teratoma** (solid) (M9080/1) — *see also* Neoplasm, by site, uncertain behavior
  - adult (cystic) (M9080/0) — *see* Neoplasm, by site, benign
  - and embryonal carcinoma, mixed (M9081/3) — *see* Neoplasm, by site, malignant
  - benign (M9080/0) — *see* Neoplasm, by site, benign
  - combined with choriocarcinoma (M9101/3) — *see* Neoplasm, by site, malignant
  - cystic (adult) (M9080/0) — *see* Neoplasm, by site, benign
  - differentiated type (M9080/0) — *see* Neoplasm, by site, benign
  - embryonal (M9080/3) (*see also* Neoplasm, by site, malignant)
    - liver 155.0
  - fetal
    - sacral, causing fetopelvic disproportion 653.7 ☑
  - immature (M9080/3) — *see* Neoplasm, by site, malignant
  - liver (M9080/3) 155.0
    - adult, benign, cystic, differentiated type or mature (M9080/0) 211.5
  - malignant (M9080/3) (*see also* Neoplasm, by site, malignant)
    - anaplastic type (M9082/3) — *see* Neoplasm, by site, malignant
- **Teratoma** — *see also* Neoplasm, by site, uncertain behavior — *continued*
  - malignant (*see also* Neoplasm, by site, malignant) — *continued*
    - intermediate type (M9083/3) — *see* Neoplasm, by site, malignant
    - liver (M9080/3) 155.0
    - trophoblastic (M9102/3)
      - specified site — *see* Neoplasm, by site, malignant
      - unspecified site 186.9
    - undifferentiated type (M9082/3) — *see* Neoplasm, by site, malignant
  - mature (M9080/0) — *see* Neoplasm, by site, benign
    - malignant (M9080/3) — *see* Neoplasm, by site, malignant
  - ovary (M9080/0) 220
    - embryonal, immature, or malignant (M9080/3) 183.0
  - suprasellar (M9080/3) — *see* Neoplasm, by site, malignant
  - testis (M9080/3) 186.9
    - adult, benign, cystic, differentiated type or mature (M9080/0) 222.0
    - undescended 186.0
- **Terminal care** V66.7
- **Termination**
  - anomalous (*see also* Malposition, congenital)
    - portal vein 747.49
    - right pulmonary vein 747.42
  - pregnancy (legal) (therapeutic) — *see* Abortion, legal 635.9 ☑
    - fetus NEC 779.6
    - illegal (*see also* Abortion, illegal) 636.9 ☑
- **Ternidens diminutus infestation** 127.7
- **Terrors, night** (child) 307.46
- **Terry's syndrome** ▶(*see also* Retinopathy of prematurity)◀ 362.21
- **Tertiary** — *see* condition
- **Tessellated fundus, retina** (tigroid) 362.89
- **Test(s)**
  - adequacy
    - hemodialysis V56.31
    - peritoneal dialysis V56.32
  - AIDS virus V72.6
  - allergen V72.7
  - bacterial disease NEC (*see also* Screening, by name of disease) V74.9
  - basal metabolic rate V72.6
  - blood-alcohol V70.4
  - blood-drug V70.4
    - for therapeutic drug monitoring V58.83
  - blood typing V72.86
    - Rh typing V72.86
  - developmental, infant or child V20.2
  - Dick V74.8
  - fertility V26.21
  - genetic
    - female V26.32
    - for genetic disease carrier status
      - female V26.31
      - male V26.34
    - male V26.39
  - hearing V72.19
    - following failed hearing screening V72.11
  - HIV V72.6
  - human immunodeficiency virus V72.6
  - Kveim V82.89
  - laboratory V72.6
    - for medicolegal reason V70.4
  - male partner of habitual aborter V26.35
  - Mantoux (for tuberculosis) V74.1
  - mycotic organism V75.4
  - nuchal translucency V28.89 ●
  - parasitic agent NEC V75.8
  - paternity V70.4

☑ Additional Digit Required — Refer to the Tabular List for Digit Selection

Subterms under main terms may continue to next column or page

▶◀ Revised Text ● New Line ▲ Revised Code

Test(s) — *continued*
- peritoneal equilibration V56.32
- pregnancy
  - negative result V72.41
  - positive result V72.42
    - first pregnancy V72.42
  - unconfirmed V72.40
- preoperative V72.84
  - cardiovascular V72.81
  - respiratory V72.82
  - specified NEC V72.83
- procreative management NEC V26.29
  - genetic disease carrier status
    - female V26.31
    - male V26.34
- Rh typing V72.86
- sarcoidosis V82.89
- Schick V74.3
- Schultz-Charlton V74.8
- skin, diagnostic
  - allergy V72.7
  - bacterial agent NEC (*see also* Screening, by name of disease) V74.9
  - Dick V74.8
  - hypersensitivity V72.7
  - Kveim V82.89
  - Mantoux V74.1
  - mycotic organism V75.4
  - parasitic agent NEC V75.8
  - sarcoidosis V82.89
  - Schick V74.3
  - Schultz-Charlton V74.8
  - tuberculin V74.1
- specified type NEC V72.85
- tuberculin V74.1
- vision V72.0
- Wassermann
  - positive (*see also* Serology for syphilis, positive) 097.1
    - false 795.6

Testicle, testicular, testis — *see also* condition
- feminization (syndrome) 259.51 ▲

Tetanus, tetanic (cephalic) (convulsions) 037
- with
  - abortion — *see* Abortion, by type, with sepsis
  - ectopic pregnancy (*see also* categories 633.0–633.9) 639.0
  - molar pregnancy — *see* categories 630–632 639.0
- following
  - abortion 639.0
  - ectopic or molar pregnancy 639.0
- inoculation V03.7
  - reaction (due to serum) — *see* Complications, vaccination
- neonatorum 771.3
- puerperal, postpartum, childbirth 670.0 ☑

Tetany, tetanic 781.7
- alkalosis 276.3
- associated with rickets 268.0
- convulsions 781.7
  - hysterical 300.11
- functional (hysterical) 300.11
- hyperkinetic 781.7
  - hysterical 300.11
- hyperpnea 786.01
  - hysterical 300.11
  - psychogenic 306.1
- hyperventilation 786.01
  - hysterical 300.11
  - psychogenic 306.1
- hypocalcemic, neonatal 775.4
- hysterical 300.11
- neonatal 775.4
- parathyroid (gland) 252.1
- parathyroprival 252.1
- postoperative 252.1
- postthyroidectomy 252.1
- pseudotetany 781.7
  - hysterical 300.11
- psychogenic 306.1

Tetany, tetanic — *continued*
- psychogenic — *continued*
  - specified as conversion reaction 300.11

Tetralogy of Fallot 745.2

Tetraplegia — *see* Quadriplegia

Thailand hemorrhagic fever 065.4

Thalassanemia 282.49

Thalassemia (alpha) (beta) (disease) (Hb-C) (Hb-D) (Hb-E) (Hb-H) (Hb-I) (high fetal gene) (high fetal hemoglobin) (intermedia) (major) (minima) (minor) (mixed) (trait) (with other hemoglobinopathy) 282.49
- Hb-S (without crisis) 282.41
  - with
    - crisis 282.42
    - vaso-occlusive pain 282.42
- sickle-cell (without crisis) 282.41
  - with
    - crisis 282.42
    - vaso-occlusive pain 282.42

Thalassemic variants 282.49

Thaysen-Gee disease (nontropical sprue) 579.0

Thecoma (M8600/0) 220
- malignant (M8600/3) 183.0

Thelarche, precocious 259.1

Thelitis 611.0
- puerperal, postpartum 675.0 ☑

Therapeutic — *see* condition

Therapy V57.9
- blood transfusion, without reported diagnosis V58.2
- breathing V57.0
- chemotherapy, antineoplastic V58.11
  - fluoride V07.31
  - prophylactic NEC V07.39
- dialysis (intermittent) (treatment)
  - extracorporeal V56.0
  - peritoneal V56.8
  - renal V56.0
  - specified type NEC V56.8
- exercise NEC V57.1
  - breathing V57.0
- extracorporeal dialysis (renal) V56.0
- fluoride prophylaxis V07.31
- hemodialysis V56.0
- hormone replacement (postmenopausal) V07.4
- immunotherapy antineoplastic V58.12
- long term oxygen therapy V46.2
- occupational V57.21
- orthoptic V57.4
- orthotic V57.81
- peritoneal dialysis V56.8
- physical NEC V57.1
- postmenopausal hormone replacement V07.4
- radiation V58.0
- speech V57.3
- vocational V57.22

Thermalgesia 782.0

Thermalgia 782.0

Thermanalgesia 782.0

Thermanesthesia 782.0

Thermic — *see* condition

Thermography (abnormal) 793.99
- breast 793.89

Thermoplegia 992.0

Thesaurismosis
- amyloid 277.39
- bilirubin 277.4
- calcium 275.40
- cystine 270.0
- glycogen (*see also* Disease, glycogen storage) 271.0
- kerasin 272.7
- lipoid 272.7
- melanin 255.41
- phosphatide 272.7
- urate 274.9

Thiaminic deficiency 265.1
- with beriberi 265.0

Thibierge-Weissenbach syndrome (cutaneous systemic sclerosis) 710.1

Thickened endometrium 793.5

Thickening
- bone 733.99
  - extremity 733.99
- breast 611.79
- hymen 623.3
- larynx 478.79
- nail 703.8
  - congenital 757.5
- periosteal 733.99
- pleura (*see also* Pleurisy) 511.0
- skin 782.8
- subepiglottic 478.79
- tongue 529.8
- valve, heart — *see* Endocarditis

Thiele syndrome 724.6

Thigh — *see* condition

Thinning vertebra — *see also* Osteoporosis 733.00

Thirst, excessive 783.5
- due to deprivation of water 994.3

Thomsen's disease 359.22

Thomson's disease (congenital poikiloderma) 757.33

Thoracic — *see also* condition
- kidney 753.3
- outlet syndrome 353.0
- stomach — *see* Hernia, diaphragm

Thoracogastroschisis (congenital) 759.89

Thoracopagus 759.4

Thoracoschisis 756.3

Thoracoscopic surgical procedure converted to open procedure V64.42

Thorax — *see* condition

Thorn's syndrome — *see also* Disease, renal 593.9

Thornwaldt's, Tornwaldt's
- bursitis (pharyngeal) 478.29
- cyst 478.26
- disease (pharyngeal bursitis) 478.29

Thorson-Biörck syndrome (malignant carcinoid) 259.2

Threadworm (infection) (infestation) 127.4

Threatened
- abortion or miscarriage 640.0 ☑
  - with subsequent abortion (*see also* Abortion, spontaneous) 634.9 ☑
  - affecting fetus 762.1
- labor 644.1 ☑
  - affecting fetus or newborn 761.8
  - premature 644.0 ☑
- miscarriage 640.0 ☑
  - affecting fetus 762.1
- premature
  - delivery 644.2 ☑
    - affecting fetus or newborn 761.8
  - labor 644.0 ☑
    - before 22 completed weeks gestation 640.0 ☑

Three-day fever 066.0

Threshers' lung 495.0

Thrix annulata (congenital) 757.4

Throat — *see* condition

Thrombasthenia (Glanzmann's) (hemorrhagic) (hereditary) 287.1

Thromboangiitis 443.1
- obliterans (general) 443.1
  - cerebral 437.1
  - vessels
    - brain 437.1
    - spinal cord 437.1

Thromboarteritis — *see* Arteritis

Thromboasthenia (Glanzmann's) (hemorrhagic) (hereditary) 287.1

Thrombocytasthenia (Glanzmann's) 287.1

Thrombocythemia (primary) (M9962/1) 238.71
- essential 238.71
- hemorrhagic 238.71
- idiopathic (hemorrhagic) (M9962/1) 238.71

Thrombocytopathy (dystrophic) (granulopenic) 287.1

Thrombocytopenia, thrombocytopenic 287.5
- with
  - absent radii (TAR) syndrome
  - giant hemangioma
- amegakaryocytic, congenital 287.33
- congenital 287.33
- cyclic 287.39
- dilutional 287.4
- due to
  - drugs 287.4
  - extracorporeal circulation of blood 287.4
  - massive blood transfusion 287.4
  - platelet alloimmunization 287.4
- essential 287.30
- fetal 678.0 ☑ ●
- heparin-induced (HIT) 289.84 ●
- hereditary 287.33
- Kasabach-Merritt 287.39
- neonatal, transitory 776.1
  - due to
    - exchange transfusion 776.1
    - idiopathic maternal thrombocytopenia 776.1
    - isoimmunization 776.1
- primary 287.30
- puerperal, postpartum 666.3 ☑
- purpura (*see also* Purpura, thrombocytopenic) 287.30
  - thrombotic 446.6
- secondary 287.4
- sex-linked 287.39

Thrombocytosis 238.71
- essential 238.71
- primary 238.71

Thromboembolism — *see* Embolism

Thrombopathy (Bernard-Soulier) 287.1
- constitutional 286.4
- Willebrand-Jürgens (angiohemophilia) 286.4

Thrombopenia — *see also* Thrombocytopenia 287.5

Thrombophlebitis 451.9
- antecubital vein 451.82
- antepartum (superficial) 671.2 ☑
  - affecting fetus or newborn 760.3
  - deep 671.3 ☑
- arm 451.89
  - deep 451.83
  - superficial 451.82
- breast, superficial 451.89
- cavernous (venous) sinus — *see* Thrombophlebitis, intracranial venous sinus
- cephalic vein 451.82
- cerebral (sinus) (vein) 325
  - late effect — *see* category 326
  - nonpyogenic 437.6
    - in pregnancy or puerperium 671.5 ☑
    - late effect — *see* Late effect(s) (of) cerebrovascular disease
- due to implanted device — *see* Complications, due to (presence of) any device, implant or graft classified to 996.0–996.5 NEC
- during or resulting from a procedure NEC 997.2
- femoral 451.11
- femoropopliteal 451.19
- following infusion, perfusion, or transfusion 999.2
- hepatic (vein) 451.89
- idiopathic, recurrent 453.1
- iliac vein 451.81
- iliofemoral 451.11
- intracranial venous sinus (any) 325
  - late effect — *see* category 326
  - nonpyogenic 437.6
    - in pregnancy or puerperium 671.5 ☑

- **Thrombophlebitis** — *continued*
  - intracranial venous sinus — *continued*
    - nonpyogenic — *continued*
      - late effect — *see* Late effect(s) (of) cerebrovascular disease
  - jugular vein 451.89
  - lateral (venous) sinus — *see* Thrombophlebitis, intracranial venous sinus
  - leg 451.2
    - deep (vessels) 451.19
      - femoral vein 451.11
      - specified vessel NEC 451.19
    - superficial (vessels) 451.0
      - femoral vein 451.11
  - longitudinal (venous) sinus — *see* Thrombophlebitis, intracranial venous sinus
  - lower extremity 451.2
    - deep (vessels) 451.19
      - femoral vein 451.11
      - specified vessel NEC 451.19
    - superficial (vessels) 451.0
  - migrans, migrating 453.1
  - pelvic
    - with
      - abortion — *see* Abortion, by type, with sepsis
      - ectopic pregnancy (*see also* categories 633.0–633.9) 639.0
      - molar pregnancy (*see also* categories 630–632) 639.0
    - following
      - abortion 639.0
      - ectopic or molar pregnancy 639.0
    - puerperal 671.4 ☑
  - popliteal vein 451.19
  - portal (vein) 572.1
  - postoperative 997.2
  - pregnancy (superficial) 671.2 ☑
    - affecting fetus or newborn 760.3
    - deep 671.3 ☑
  - puerperal, postpartum, childbirth (extremities) (superficial) 671.2 ☑
    - deep 671.4 ☑
    - pelvic 671.4 ☑
    - specified site NEC 671.5 ☑
  - radial vein 451.83
  - saphenous (greater) (lesser) 451.0
  - sinus (intracranial) — *see* Thrombophlebitis, intracranial venous sinus
    - specified site NEC 451.89
    - tibial vein 451.19
- **Thrombosis, thrombotic** (marantic) (multiple) (progressive) (vein) (vessel) 453.9
  - with childbirth or during the puerperium — *see* Thrombosis, puerperal, postpartum
  - antepartum — *see* Thrombosis, pregnancy
  - aorta, aortic 444.1
    - abdominal 444.0
    - bifurcation 444.0
    - saddle 444.0
    - terminal 444.0
    - thoracic 444.1
    - valve — *see* Endocarditis, aortic
  - apoplexy (*see also* Thrombosis, brain) 434.0 ☑
    - late effect — *see* Late effect(s) (of) cerebrovascular disease
  - appendix, septic — *see* Appendicitis, acute
  - arteriolar-capillary platelet, disseminated 446.6
  - artery, arteries (postinfectional) 444.9
    - auditory, internal 433.8 ☑
    - basilar (*see also* Occlusion, artery, basilar) 433.0 ☑
- **Thrombosis, thrombotic** — *continued*
  - artery, arteries — *continued*
    - carotid (common) (internal) (*see also* Occlusion, artery, carotid) 433.1 ☑
      - with other precerebral artery 433.3 ☑
    - cerebellar (anterior inferior) (posterior inferior) (superior) 433.8 ☑
    - cerebral (*see also* Thrombosis, brain) 434.0 ☑
    - choroidal (anterior) 433.8 ☑
    - communicating posterior 433.8 ☑
    - coronary (*see also* Infarct, myocardium) 410.9 ☑
      - without myocardial infarction 411.81
      - due to syphilis 093.89
      - healed or specified as old 412
    - extremities 444.22
      - lower 444.22
      - upper 444.21
    - femoral 444.22
    - hepatic 444.89
    - hypophyseal 433.8 ☑
    - meningeal, anterior or posterior 433.8 ☑
    - mesenteric (with gangrene) 557.0
    - ophthalmic (*see also* Occlusion, retina) 362.30
    - pontine 433.8 ☑
    - popliteal 444.22
    - precerebral — *see* Occlusion, artery, precerebral NEC
    - pulmonary 415.19
      - iatrogenic 415.11
      - postoperative 415.11
      - septic 415.12
    - renal 593.81
    - retinal (*see also* Occlusion, retina) 362.30
    - specified site NEC 444.89
    - spinal, anterior or posterior 433.8 ☑
    - traumatic (complication) (early) (*see also* Injury, blood vessel, by site) 904.9
    - vertebral (*see also* Occlusion, artery, vertebral) 433.2 ☑
      - with other precerebral artery 433.3 ☑
  - atrial (endocardial) 424.90
    - without endocarditis 429.89
    - due to syphilis 093.89
  - auricular (*see also* Infarct, myocardium) 410.9 ☑
  - axillary (vein) 453.8
  - basilar (artery) (*see also* Occlusion, artery, basilar) 433.0 ☑
  - bland NEC 453.9
  - brain (artery) (stem) 434.0 ☑
    - due to syphilis 094.89
    - iatrogenic 997.02
    - late effect — *see* Late effect(s) (of) cerebrovascular disease
    - postoperative 997.02
    - puerperal, postpartum, childbirth 674.0 ☑
    - sinus (*see also* Thrombosis, intracranial venous sinus) 325
  - capillary 448.9
    - arteriolar, generalized 446.6
  - cardiac (*see also* Infarct, myocardium) 410.9 ☑
    - due to syphilis 093.89
    - healed or specified as old 412
    - valve — *see* Endocarditis
  - carotid (artery) (common) (internal) (*see also* Occlusion, artery, carotid) 433.1 ☑
    - with other precerebral artery 433.3 ☑
- **Thrombosis, thrombotic** — *continued*
  - cavernous sinus (venous) — *see* Thrombosis, intracranial venous sinus
  - cerebellar artery (anterior inferior) (posterior inferior) (superior) 433.8 ☑
    - late effect — *see* Late effect(s) (of) cerebrovascular disease
  - cerebral (arteries) (*see also* Thrombosis, brain) 434.0 ☑
    - late effect — *see* Late effect(s) (of) cerebrovascular disese
  - coronary (artery) (*see also* Infarct, myocardium) 410.9 ☑
    - without myocardial infarction 411.81
    - due to syphilis 093.89
    - healed or specified as old 412
  - corpus cavernosum 607.82
  - cortical (*see also* Thrombosis, brain) 434.0 ☑
  - due to (presence of) any device, implant, or graft classifiable to 996.0–996.5 — *see* Complications, due to (presence of) any device, implant, or graft classified to 996.0–996.5 NEC
  - effort 453.8
  - endocardial — *see* Infarct, myocardium
  - eye (*see also* Occlusion, retina) 362.30
  - femoral (vein) 453.8
    - with inflammation or phlebitis 451.11
    - artery 444.22
    - deep 453.41
  - genital organ, male 608.83
  - heart (chamber) (*see also* Infarct, myocardium) 410.9 ☑
  - hepatic (vein) 453.0
    - artery 444.89
    - infectional or septic 572.1
  - iliac (vein) 453.8
    - with inflammation or phlebitis 451.81
    - artery (common) (external) (internal) 444.81
  - inflammation, vein — *see* Thrombophlebitis
  - internal carotid artery (*see also* Occlusion, artery, carotid) 433.1 ☑
    - with other precerebral artery 433.3 ☑
  - intestine (with gangrene) 557.0
  - intracranial (*see also* Thrombosis, brain) 434.0 ☑
    - venous sinus (any) 325
      - nonpyogenic origin 437.6
        - in pregnancy or puerperium 671.5 ☑
  - intramural (*see also* Infarct, myocardium) 410.9 ☑
    - without
      - cardiac condition 429.89
      - coronary artery disease 429.89
      - myocardial infarction 429.89
    - healed or specified as old 412
  - jugular (bulb) 453.8
  - kidney 593.81
    - artery 593.81
  - lateral sinus (venous) — *see* Thrombosis, intracranial venous sinus
  - leg 453.8
    - with inflammation or phlebitis — *see* Thrombophlebitis
    - deep (vessels) 453.40
      - lower (distal) 453.42
      - upper (proximal) 453.41
    - superficial (vessels) 453.8
  - liver (venous) 453.0
    - artery 444.89
    - infectional or septic 572.1
    - portal vein 452
- **Thrombosis, thrombotic** — *continued*
  - longitudinal sinus (venous) — *see* Thrombosis, intracranial venous sinus
  - lower extremity 453.8
    - deep vessels 453.40
      - calf 453.42
      - distal (lower leg) 453.42
      - femoral 453.41
      - iliac 453.41
      - lower leg 453.42
      - peroneal 453.42
      - popliteal 453.41
      - proximal (upper leg) 453.41
      - thigh 453.41
      - tibial 453.42
  - lung 415.19
    - iatrogenic 415.11
    - postoperative 415.11
    - septic 415.12
  - marantic, dural sinus 437.6
  - meninges (brain) (*see also* Thrombosis, brain) 434.0 ☑
  - mesenteric (artery) (with gangrene) 557.0
    - vein (inferior) (superior) 557.0
  - mitral — see Insufficiency, mitral
  - mural (heart chamber) (*see also* Infarct, myocardium) 410.9 ☑
    - without
      - cardiac condition 429.89
      - coronary artery disease 429.89
      - myocardial infarction 429.89
    - due to syphilis 093.89
    - following myocardial infarction 429.79
    - healed or specified as old 412
  - omentum (with gangrene) 557.0
  - ophthalmic (artery) (*see also* Occlusion, retina) 362.30
  - pampiniform plexus (male) 608.83
    - female 620.8
  - parietal (*see also* Infarct, myocardium) 410.9 ☑
  - penis, penile 607.82
  - peripheral arteries 444.22
    - lower 444.22
    - upper 444.21
  - platelet 446.6
  - portal 452
    - due to syphilis 093.89
    - infectional or septic 572.1
  - precerebral artery (*see also* Occlusion, artery, precerebral NEC)
  - pregnancy 671.9 ☑
    - deep (vein) 671.3 ☑
    - superficial (vein) 671.2 ☑
  - puerperal, postpartum, childbirth 671.9 ☑
    - brain (artery) 674.0 ☑
      - venous 671.5 ☑
    - cardiac 674.8 ☑
    - cerebral (artery) 674.0 ☑
      - venous 671.5 ☑
    - deep (vein) 671.4 ☑
    - intracranial sinus (nonpyogenic) (venous) 671.5 ☑
    - pelvic 671.4 ☑
    - pulmonary (artery) 673.2 ☑
    - specified site NEC 671.5 ☑
    - superficial 671.2 ☑
  - pulmonary (artery) (vein) 415.19
    - iatrogenic 415.11
    - postoperative 415.11
    - septic 415.12
  - renal (artery) 593.81
    - vein 453.3
  - resulting from presence of shunt or other internal prosthetic device — *see* Complications, due to (presence of) any device, implant, or graft classified to 996.0–996.5 NEC
  - retina, retinal (artery) 362.30
    - arterial branch 362.32

Thrombosis, thrombotic — *continued*
retina, retinal — *continued*
central 362.31
partial 362.33
vein
central 362.35
tributary (branch) 362.36
scrotum 608.83
seminal vesicle 608.83
sigmoid (venous) sinus — *see* Thrombosis, intracranial venous sinus 325
silent NEC 453.9
sinus, intracranial (venous) (any) (*see also* Thrombosis, intracranial venous sinus) 325
softening, brain (*see also* Thrombosis, brain) 434.0 ☑
specified site NEC 453.8
spermatic cord 608.83
spinal cord 336.1
due to syphilis 094.89
in pregnancy or puerperium 671.5 ☑
pyogenic origin 324.1
late effect — *see* category 326
spleen, splenic 289.59
artery 444.89
testis 608.83
traumatic (complication) (early) (*see also* Injury, blood vessel, by site) 904.9
tricuspid — *see* Endocarditis, tricuspid
tumor — see Neoplasm, by site
tunica vaginalis 608.83
umbilical cord (vessels) 663.6 ☑
affecting fetus or newborn 762.6
vas deferens 608.83
vein
deep 453.40
lower extremity — see Thrombosis, lower extremity
vena cava (inferior) (superior) 453.2
Thrombus — *see* Thrombosis
Thrush 112.0
newborn 771.7
Thumb — *see also* condition
gamekeeper's 842.12
sucking (child problem) 307.9
Thygeson's superficial punctate keratitis 370.21
Thymergasia — *see also* Psychosis, affective 296.80
Thymitis 254.8
Thymoma (benign) (M8580/0) 212.6
malignant (M8580/3) 164.0
Thymus, thymic (gland) — *see* condition
Thyrocele — *see also* Goiter 240.9
Thyroglossal — *see also* condition
cyst 759.2
duct, persistent 759.2
Thyroid (body) (gland) — *see also* condition
hormone resistance 246.8
lingual 759.2
Thyroiditis 245.9
acute (pyogenic) (suppurative) 245.0
nonsuppurative 245.0
autoimmune 245.2
chronic (nonspecific) (sclerosing) 245.8
fibrous 245.3
lymphadenoid 245.2
lymphocytic 245.2
lymphoid 245.2
complicating pregnancy, childbirth, or puerperium 648.1 ☑
de Quervain's (subacute granulomatous) 245.1
fibrous (chronic) 245.3
giant (cell) (follicular) 245.1
granulomatous (de Quervain's) (subacute) 245.1
Hashimoto's (struma lymphomatosa) 245.2
Thyroiditis — *continued*
iatrogenic 245.4
invasive (fibrous) 245.3
ligneous 245.3
lymphocytic (chronic) 245.2
lymphoid 245.2
lymphomatous 245.2
pseudotuberculous 245.1
pyogenic 245.0
radiation 245.4
Riedel's (ligneous) 245.3
subacute 245.1
suppurative 245.0
tuberculous (*see also* Tuberculosis) 017.5 ☑
viral 245.1
woody 245.3
Thyrolingual duct, persistent 759.2
Thyromegaly 240.9
Thyrotoxic
crisis or storm (*see also* Thyrotoxicosis) 242.9 ☑
heart failure (*see also* Thyrotoxicosis) 242.9 ☑ *[425.7]*
Thyrotoxicosis 242.9 ☑

Note — Use the following fifth-digit subclassification with category 242:

0 without mention of thyrotoxic crisis or storm

1 with mention of thyrotoxic crisis or storm

with
goiter (diffuse) 242.0 ☑
adenomatous 242.3 ☑
multinodular 242.2 ☑
uninodular 242.1 ☑
nodular 242.3 ☑
multinodular 242.2 ☑
uninodular 242.1 ☑
infiltrative
dermopathy 242.0 ☑
ophthalmopathy 242.0 ☑
thyroid acropachy 242.0 ☑
complicating pregnancy, childbirth, or puerperium 648.1 ☑
due to
ectopic thyroid nodule 242.4 ☑
ingestion of (excessive) thyroid material 242.8 ☑
specified cause NEC 242.8 ☑
factitia 242.8 ☑
heart 242.9 ☑ *[425.7]*
neonatal (transient) 775.3
TIA (transient ischemic attack) 435.9
with transient neurologic deficit 435.9
late effect — *see* Late effect(s) (of) cerebrovascular disease
Tibia vara 732.4
Tic 307.20
breathing 307.20
child problem 307.21
compulsive 307.22
convulsive 307.20
degenerative (generalized) (localized) 333.3
facial 351.8
douloureux (*see also* Neuralgia, trigeminal) 350.1
atypical 350.2
habit 307.20
chronic (motor or vocal) 307.22
transient (of childhood) 307.21
lid 307.20
transient (of childhood) 307.21
motor-verbal 307.23
occupational 300.89
orbicularis 307.20
transient (of childhood) 307.21
organic origin 333.3
postchoreic — *see* Chorea
psychogenic 307.20
compulsive 307.22
salaam 781.0
spasm 307.20
Tic — *continued*
spasm — *continued*
chronic (motor or vocal) 307.22
transient (of childhood) 307.21
Tick-bite fever NEC 066.1
African 087.1
Colorado (virus) 066.1
Rocky Mountain 082.0
Tick (-borne) fever NEC 066.1
American mountain 066.1
Colorado 066.1
hemorrhagic NEC 065.3
Crimean 065.0
Kyasanur Forest 065.2
Omsk 065.1
mountain 066.1
nonexanthematous 066.1
Tick paralysis 989.5
Tics and spasms, compulsive 307.22
Tietze's disease or syndrome 733.6
Tight, tightness
anus 564.89
chest 786.59
fascia (lata) 728.9
foreskin (congenital) 605
hymen 623.3
introitus (acquired) (congenital) 623.3
rectal sphincter 564.89
tendon 727.81
Achilles (heel) 727.81
urethral sphincter 598.9
Tilting vertebra 737.9
Timidity, child 313.21
Tinea (intersecta) (tarsi) 110.9
amiantacea 110.0
asbestina 110.0
barbae 110.0
beard 110.0
black dot 110.0
blanca 111.2
capitis 110.0
corporis 110.5
cruris 110.3
decalvans 704.09
flava 111.0
foot 110.4
furfuracea 111.0
imbricata (Tokelau) 110.5
lepothrix 039.0
manuum 110.2
microsporic (*see also* Dermatophytosis) 110.9
nigra 111.1
nodosa 111.2
pedis 110.4
scalp 110.0
specified site NEC 110.8
sycosis 110.0
tonsurans 110.0
trichophytic (*see also* Dermatophytosis) 110.9
unguium 110.1
versicolor 111.0
Tingling sensation — *see also* Disturbance, sensation 782.0
Tin-miners' lung 503
Tinnitus (aurium) 388.30
audible 388.32
objective 388.32
subjective 388.31
Tipped, teeth 524.33
Tipping
pelvis 738.6
with disproportion (fetopelvic) 653.0 ☑
affecting fetus or newborn 763.1
causing obstructed labor 660.1 ☑
affecting fetus or newborn 763.1
teeth 524.33
Tiredness 780.79
Tissue — *see* condition
Tobacco
abuse (affecting health) NEC (*see also* Abuse, drugs, nondependent) 305.1
heart 989.84
use disorder complicating pregnancy, childbirth, or the puerperium 649.0 ☑
Tobias' syndrome (carcinoma, pulmonary apex) (M8010/3) 162.3
Tocopherol deficiency 269.1
Todd's
cirrhosis — *see* Cirrhosis, biliary
paralysis (postepileptic transitory paralysis) 344.89
Toe — *see* condition
Toilet, artificial opening — *see also* Attention to, artificial, opening V55.9
Tokelau ringworm 110.5
Tollwut 071
Tolosa-Hunt syndrome 378.55
Tommaselli's disease
correct substance properly administered 599.70 ▲
overdose or wrong substance given or taken 961.4
Tongue — *see also* condition
worms 134.1
Tongue tie 750.0
Tonic pupil 379.46
Toni-Fanconi syndrome (cystinosis) 270.0
Tonsil — *see* condition
Tonsillitis (acute) (catarrhal) (croupous) (follicular) (gangrenous) (infective) (lacunar) (lingual) (malignant) (membranous) (phlegmonous) (pneumococcal) (pseudomembranous) (purulent) (septic) (staphylococcal) (subacute) (suppurative) (toxic) (ulcerative) (vesicular) (viral) 463
with influenza, flu, or grippe 487.1
chronic 474.00
diphtheritic (membranous) 032.0
hypertrophic 474.00
influenzal 487.1
parenchymatous 475
streptococcal 034.0
tuberculous (*see also* Tuberculosis) 012.8 ☑
Vincent's 101
Tonsillopharyngitis 465.8
Toothache 525.9
Tooth, teeth — *see* condition
Topagnosis 782.0
Tophi (gouty) 274.0
ear 274.81
heart 274.82
specified site NEC 274.82
TORCH infection — *see also* Infection, ●
congenital 760.2 ●
Torn — *see* Tear, torn
Tornwaldt's bursitis (disease) (pharyngeal bursitis) 478.29
cyst 478.26
Torpid liver 573.9
Torsion
accessory tube 620.5
adnexa (female) 620.5
aorta (congenital) 747.29
acquired 447.1
appendix
epididymis 608.24
testis 608.23
bile duct 576.8
with calculus, choledocholithiasis or stones — *see* Choledocholithiasis
congenital 751.69
bowel, colon, or intestine 560.2
cervix — *see* Malposition, uterus
duodenum 537.3
dystonia — *see* Dystonia, torsion
epididymis 608.24

- **Torsion** — *continued*
  - epididymis — *continued*
    - appendix 608.24
  - fallopian tube 620.5
  - gallbladder (*see also* Disease, gallbladder) 575.8
    - congenital 751.69
  - gastric 537.89
  - hydatid of Morgagni (female) 620.5
  - kidney (pedicle) 593.89
  - Meckel's diverticulum (congenital) 751.0
  - mesentery 560.2
  - omentum 560.2
  - organ or site, congenital NEC — *see* Anomaly, specified type NEC
  - ovary (pedicle) 620.5
    - congenital 752.0
  - oviduct 620.5
  - penis 607.89
    - congenital 752.69
  - renal 593.89
  - spasm — *see* Dystonia, torsion
  - spermatic cord 608.22
    - extravaginal 608.21
    - intravaginal 608.22
  - spleen 289.59
  - testicle, testis 608.20
    - appendix 608.23
  - tibia 736.89
  - umbilical cord — *see* Compression, umbilical cord
  - uterus (*see also* Malposition, uterus) 621.6
- **Torticollis** (intermittent) (spastic) 723.5
  - congenital 754.1
    - sternomastoid 754.1
  - due to birth injury 767.8
  - hysterical 300.11
  - ocular 781.93
  - psychogenic 306.0
    - specified as conversion reaction 300.11
  - rheumatic 723.5
  - rheumatoid 714.0
  - spasmodic 333.83
  - traumatic, current NEC 847.0
- **Tortuous**
  - artery 447.1
  - fallopian tube 752.19
  - organ or site, congenital NEC — *see* Distortion
  - renal vessel (congenital) 747.62
  - retina vessel (congenital) 743.58
    - acquired 362.17
  - ureter 593.4
  - urethra 599.84
  - vein — *see* Varicose, vein
- **Torula, torular** (infection) 117.5
  - histolytica 117.5
  - lung 117.5
- **Torulosis** 117.5
- **Torus**
  - fracture
    - fibula 823.41
      - with tibia 823.42
    - radius 813.45
    - tibia 823.40
      - with fibula 823.42
  - mandibularis 526.81
  - palatinus 526.81
- **Touch, vitreous** 997.99
- **Touraine-Solente-Golé syndrome** (acropachyderma) 757.39
- **Touraine's syndrome** (hereditary osteo-onychodysplasia) 756.89
- **Tourette's disease** (motor-verbal tic) 307.23
- **Tower skull** 756.0
  - with exophthalmos 756.0
- **Toxemia** 799.89
  - with
    - abortion — *see* Abortion, by type, with toxemia
  - bacterial — *see* Septicemia
  - biliary (*see also* Disease, biliary) 576.8
- **Toxemia** — *continued*
  - burn — *see* Burn, by site
  - congenital NEC 779.89
  - eclamptic 642.6 ☑
    - with pre-existing hypertension 642.7 ☑
  - erysipelatous (*see also* Erysipelas) 035
  - fatigue 799.89
  - fetus or newborn NEC 779.89
  - food (*see also* Poisoning, food) 005.9
  - gastric 537.89
  - gastrointestinal 558.2
  - intestinal 558.2
  - kidney (*see also* Disease, renal) 593.9
  - lung 518.89
  - malarial NEC (*see also* Malaria) 084.6
  - maternal (of pregnancy), affecting fetus or newborn 760.0
  - myocardial — *see* Myocarditis, toxic
  - of pregnancy (mild) (pre-eclamptic) 642.4 ☑
    - with
      - convulsions 642.6 ☑
      - pre-existing hypertension 642.7 ☑
    - affecting fetus or newborn 760.0
    - severe 642.5 ☑
  - pre-eclamptic — *see* Toxemia, of pregnancy
  - puerperal, postpartum — *see* Toxemia, of pregnancy
  - pulmonary 518.89
  - renal (*see also* Disease, renal) 593.9
  - septic (*see also* Septicemia) 038.9
  - small intestine 558.2
  - staphylococcal 038.10
    - aureus 038.11
    - due to food 005.0
    - specified organism NEC 038.19
  - stasis 799.89
  - stomach 537.89
  - uremic (*see also* Uremia) 586
  - urinary 586
- **Toxemica cerebropathia psychica** (nonalcoholic) 294.0
  - alcoholic 291.1
- **Toxic** (poisoning) — *see also* condition
  - from drug or poison — *see* Table of Drugs and Chemicals
  - oil syndrome 710.5
  - shock syndrome 040.82
  - thyroid (gland) (*see also* Thyrotoxicosis) 242.9 ☑
- **Toxicemia** — *see* Toxemia
- **Toxicity**
  - dilantin
    - asymptomatic 796.0
    - symptomatic — *see* Table of Drugs and Chemicals
  - drug
    - asymptomatic 796.0
    - symptomatic — *see* Table of Drugs and Chemicals
  - fava bean 282.2
  - from drug or poison
    - asymptomatic 796.0
    - symptomatic — *see* Table of Drugs and Chemicals
- **Toxicosis** — *see also* Toxemia 799.89
  - capillary, hemorrhagic 287.0
- **Toxinfection** 799.89
  - gastrointestinal 558.2
- **Toxocariasis** 128.0
- **Toxoplasma infection, generalized** 130.9
- **Toxoplasmosis** (acquired) 130.9
  - with pneumonia 130.4
  - congenital, active 771.2
  - disseminated (multisystemic) 130.8
  - maternal
    - with suspected damage to fetus affecting management of pregnancy 655.4 ☑
      - affecting fetus or newborn 760.2
        - manifest toxoplasmosis in fetus or newborn 771.2
- **Toxoplasmosis** — *continued*
  - multiple sites 130.8
  - multisystemic disseminated 130.8
  - specified site NEC 130.7
- **Trabeculation, bladder** 596.8
- **Trachea** — *see* condition
- **Tracheitis** (acute) (catarrhal) (infantile) (membranous) (plastic) (pneumococcal) (septic) (suppurative) (viral) 464.10
  - with
    - bronchitis 490
      - acute or subacute 466.0
      - chronic 491.8
      - tuberculosis — *see* Tuberculosis, pulmonary
    - laryngitis (acute) 464.20
      - with obstruction 464.21
      - chronic 476.1
      - tuberculous (*see also* Tuberculosis, larynx) 012.3 ☑
    - obstruction 464.11
  - chronic 491.8
    - with
      - bronchitis (chronic) 491.8
      - laryngitis (chronic) 476.1
    - due to external agent — *see* Condition, respiratory, chronic, due to
  - diphtheritic (membranous) 032.3
    - due to external agent — *see* Inflammation, respiratory, upper, due to
  - edematous 464.11
  - influenzal 487.1
  - streptococcal 034.0
  - syphilitic 095.8
  - tuberculous (*see also* Tuberculosis) 012.8 ☑
- **Trachelitis** (nonvenereal) — *see also* Cervicitis 616.0
  - trichomonal 131.09
- **Tracheobronchial** — *see* condition
- **Tracheobronchitis** — *see also* Bronchitis 490
  - acute or subacute 466.0
    - with bronchospasm or obstruction 466.0
  - chronic 491.8
  - influenzal 487.1
  - senile 491.8
- **Tracheobronchomegaly** (congenital) 748.3
  - with bronchiectasis 494.0
    - with (acute) exacerbation 494.1
  - acquired 519.19
    - with bronchiectasis 494.0
      - with (acute) exacerbation 494.1
- **Tracheobronchopneumonitis** — *see* Pneumonia, broncho
- **Tracheocele** (external) (internal) 519.19
  - congenital 748.3
- **Tracheomalacia** 519.19
  - congenital 748.3
- **Tracheopharyngitis** (acute) 465.8
  - chronic 478.9
    - due to external agent — *see* Condition, respiratory, chronic, due to
  - due to external agent — *see* Inflammation, respiratory, upper, due to
- **Tracheostenosis** 519.19
  - congenital 748.3
- **Tracheostomy**
  - attention to V55.0
  - complication 519.00
  - granuloma 519.09
  - hemorrhage 519.09
  - infection 519.01
  - malfunctioning 519.02
  - obstruction 519.09
  - sepsis 519.01
  - status V44.0
  - stenosis 519.02
- **Trachoma, trachomatous** 076.9
  - active (stage) 076.1
- **Trachoma, trachomatous** — *continued*
  - contraction of conjunctiva 076.1
  - dubium 076.0
  - healed or late effect 139.1
  - initial (stage) 076.0
  - Türck's (chronic catarrhal laryngitis) 476.0
- **Trachyphonia** 784.49
- **Training**
  - insulin pump V65.46
  - orthoptic V57.4
  - orthotic V57.81
- **Train sickness** 994.6
- **Trait**
  - hemoglobin
    - abnormal NEC 282.7
      - with thalassemia 282.49
    - C (*see also* Disease, hemoglobin, C) 282.7
      - with elliptocytosis 282.7
    - S (Hb-S) 282.5
  - Lepore 282.49
    - with other abnormal hemoglobin NEC 282.49
  - paranoid 301.0
  - sickle-cell 282.5
    - with
      - elliptocytosis 282.5
      - spherocytosis 282.5
- **Traits, paranoid** 301.0
- **Tramp** V60.0
- **Trance** 780.09
  - hysterical 300.13
- **Transaminasemia** 790.4
- **Transfusion, blood**
  - without reported diagnosis V58.2
  - donor V59.01
    - stem cells V59.02
  - fetal twin to twin 678.0 ☑ ●
  - incompatible 999.6
  - reaction or complication — *see* Complications, transfusion
  - related acute lung injury (TRALI) 518.7
  - syndrome
    - fetomaternal 772.0
    - twin-to-twin
      - blood loss (donor twin) 772.0
      - recipient twin 776.4
  - twin to twin fetal 678.0 ☑ ●
- **Transient** — *see also* condition
  - alteration of awareness 780.02
  - blindness 368.12
  - deafness (ischemic) 388.02
  - global amnesia 437.7
  - person (homeless) NEC V60.0
- **Transitional, lumbosacral joint of vertebra** 756.19
- **Translocation**
  - autosomes NEC 758.5
    - 13-15 758.1
    - 16-18 758.2
    - 21 or 22 758.0
    - balanced in normal individual 758.4
    - D_1 758.1
    - E_3 758.2
    - G 758.0
  - balanced autosomal in normal individual 758.4
  - chromosomes NEC 758.89
  - Down's syndrome 758.0
- **Translucency, iris** 364.53
- **Transmission of chemical substances through the placenta** (affecting fetus or newborn) 760.70
  - alcohol 760.71
  - anticonvulsants 760.77
  - antifungals 760.74
  - anti-infective agents 760.74
  - antimetabolics 760.78
  - cocaine 760.75
  - "crack" 760.75
  - diethylstilbestrol [DES] 760.76
  - hallucinogenic agents 760.73

Transmission of chemical substances through the placenta — *continued*
medicinal agents NEC 760.79
narcotics 760.72
obstetric anesthetic or analgesic drug 763.5
specified agent NEC 760.79
suspected, affecting management of pregnancy 655.5 ☑
Transplant(ed)
bone V42.4
marrow V42.81
complication (*see also* Complications, due to (presence of) any device, implant, or graft classified to 996.0–996.5 NEC)
bone marrow 996.85
corneal graft NEC 996.79
infection or inflammation 996.69
reaction 996.51
rejection 996.51
organ (failure) (immune or nonimmune cause) (infection) (rejection) 996.80
bone marrow 996.85
heart 996.83
intestines 996.87
kidney 996.81
liver 996.82
lung 996.84
pancreas 996.86
specified NEC 996.89
previously removed due to complication, failure, rejection or infection V45.87 ●
removal status V45.87 ●
skin NEC 996.79
infection or inflammation 996.69
rejection 996.52
artificial 996.55
decellularized allodermis 996.55
cornea V42.5
hair V50.0
heart V42.1
valve V42.2
intestine V42.84
kidney V42.0
liver V42.7
lung V42.6
organ V42.9
specified NEC V42.89
pancreas V42.83
peripheral stem cells V42.82
skin V42.3
stem cells, peripheral V42.82
tissue V42.9
specified NEC V42.89
Transplants, ovarian, endometrial 617.1
Transposed — *see* Transposition
Transposition (congenital) — *see also* Malposition, congenital
abdominal viscera 759.3
aorta (dextra) 745.11
appendix 751.5
arterial trunk 745.10
colon 751.5
great vessels (complete) 745.10
both originating from right ventricle 745.11
corrected 745.12
double outlet right ventricle 745.11
incomplete 745.11
partial 745.11
specified type NEC 745.19
heart 746.87
with complete transposition of viscera 759.3
intestine (large) (small) 751.5
pulmonary veins 747.49
reversed jejunal (for bypass) (status) V45.3
Transposition — *see also* Malposition, congenital — *continued*
scrotal 752.81
stomach 750.7
with general transposition of viscera 759.3
teeth, tooth 524.30
vessels (complete) 745.10
partial 745.11
viscera (abdominal) (thoracic) 759.3
Trans-sexualism 302.50
with
asexual history 302.51
heterosexual history 302.53
homosexual history 302.52
Transverse — *see also* condition
arrest (deep), in labor 660.3 ☑
affecting fetus or newborn 763.1
lie 652.3 ☑
before labor, affecting fetus or newborn 761.7
causing obstructed labor 660.0 ☑
affecting fetus or newborn 763.1
during labor, affecting fetus or newborn 763.1
Transvestism, transvestitism (transvestic fetishism) 302.3
Trapped placenta (with hemorrhage) 666.0 ☑
without hemorrhage 667.0 ☑
Traumatic — *see* condition
Trauma, traumatism — *see also* Injury, by site 959.9
birth — *see* Birth, injury NEC
causing hemorrhage of pregnancy or delivery 641.8 ☑
complicating
abortion — *see* Abortion, by type, with damage to pelvic organs
ectopic pregnancy (*see also* categories 633.0–633.9) 639.2
molar pregnancy (*see also* categories 630–632) 639.2
during delivery NEC 665.9 ☑
following
abortion 639.2
ectopic or molar pregnancy 639.2
maternal, during pregnancy, affecting fetus or newborn 760.5
neuroma — *see* Injury, nerve, by site
previous major, affecting management of pregnancy, childbirth, or puerperium V23.89
psychic (current) (*see also* Reaction, adjustment)
previous (history) V15.49
psychologic, previous (affecting health) V15.49
transient paralysis — *see* Injury, nerve, by site
Treacher Collins' syndrome (incomplete facial dysostosis) 756.0
Treitz's hernia — *see* Hernia, Treitz's
Trematode infestation NEC 121.9
Trematodiasis NEC 121.9
Trembles 988.8
Trembling paralysis — *see also* Parkinsonism 332.0
Tremor 781.0
essential (benign) 333.1
familial 333.1
flapping (liver) 572.8
hereditary 333.1
hysterical 300.11
intention 333.1
medication-induced postural 333.1
mercurial 985.0
muscle 728.85
Parkinson's (*see also* Parkinsonism) 332.0
psychogenic 306.0
specified as conversion reaction 300.11
senilis 797
specified type NEC 333.1
Trench
fever 083.1
foot 991.4
mouth 101
nephritis — *see* Nephritis, acute
Treponema pallidum infection — *see also* Syphilis 097.9
Treponematosis 102.9
due to
T. pallidum — *see* Syphilis
T. pertenue (yaws) (*see also* Yaws) 102.9
Triad
Kartagener's 759.3
Reiter's (complete) (incomplete) 099.3
Saint's (*see also* Hernia, diaphragm) 553.3
Trichiasis 704.2
cicatricial 704.2
eyelid 374.05
with entropion (*see also* Entropion) 374.00
Trichinella spiralis (infection) (infestation) 124
Trichinelliasis 124
Trichinellosis 124
Trichiniasis 124
Trichinosis 124
Trichobezoar 938
intestine 936
stomach 935.2
Trichocephaliasis 127.3
Trichocephalosis 127.3
Trichocephalus infestation 127.3
Trichoclasis 704.2
Trichoepithelioma (M8100/0) — *see also* Neoplasm, skin, benign
breast 217
genital organ NEC — *see* Neoplasm, by site, benign
malignant (M8100/3) — *see* Neoplasm, skin, malignant
Trichofolliculoma (M8101/0) — *see* Neoplasm, skin, benign
Tricholemmoma (M8102/0) — *see* Neoplasm, skin, benign
Trichomatosis 704.2
Trichomoniasis 131.9
bladder 131.09
cervix 131.09
intestinal 007.3
prostate 131.03
seminal vesicle 131.09
specified site NEC 131.8
urethra 131.02
urogenitalis 131.00
vagina 131.01
vulva 131.01
vulvovaginal 131.01
Trichomycosis 039.0
axillaris 039.0
nodosa 111.2
nodularis 111.2
rubra 039.0
Trichonocardiosis (axillaris) (palmellina) 039.0
Trichonodosis 704.2
Trichophytide — *see* Dermatophytosis
Trichophytid, trichophyton infection — *see also* Dermatophytosis 110.9
Trichophytobezoar 938
intestine 936
stomach 935.2
Trichophytosis — *see* Dermatophytosis
Trichoptilosis 704.2
Trichorrhexis (nodosa) 704.2
Trichosporosis nodosa 111.2
Trichostasis spinulosa (congenital) 757.4
Trichostrongyliasis (small intestine) 127.6
Trichostrongylosis 127.6
Trichostrongylus (instabilis) infection 127.6
Trichotillomania 312.39
Trichromat, anomalous (congenital) 368.59
Trichromatopsia, anomalous (congenital) 368.59
Trichuriasis 127.3
Trichuris trichiuria (any site) (infection) (infestation) 127.3
Tricuspid (valve) — *see* condition
Trifid — *see also* Accessory
kidney (pelvis) 753.3
tongue 750.13
Trigeminal neuralgia — *see also* Neuralgia, trigeminal 350.1
Trigeminoencephaloangiomatosis 759.6
Trigeminy 427.89
postoperative 997.1
Trigger finger (acquired) 727.03
congenital 756.89
Trigonitis (bladder) (chronic) (pseudomembranous) 595.3
tuberculous (*see also* Tuberculosis) 016.1 ☑
Trigonocephaly 756.0
Trihexosidosis 272.7
Trilobate placenta — *see* Placenta, abnormal
Trilocular heart 745.8
Trimethylaminuria 270.8
Tripartita placenta — *see* Placenta, abnormal
Triple — *see also* Accessory
kidneys 753.3
uteri 752.2
X female 758.81
Triplegia 344.89
congenital or infantile 343.8
Triplet
affected by maternal complications of pregnancy 761.5
healthy liveborn — *see* Newborn, multiple
pregnancy (complicating delivery) NEC 651.1 ☑
with fetal loss and retention of one or more fetus(es) 651.4 ☑
following (elective) fetal reduction 651.7 ☑
Triplex placenta — *see* Placenta, abnormal
Triplication — *see* Accessory
Trismus 781.0
neonatorum 771.3
newborn 771.3
Trisomy (syndrome) NEC 758.5
13 (partial) 758.1
16-18 758.2
18 (partial) 758.2
21 (partial) 758.0
22 758.0
autosomes NEC 758.5
D_1 758.1
E_3 758.2
G (group) 758.0
group D_1 758.1
group E 758.2
group G 758.0
Tritanomaly 368.53
Tritanopia 368.53
Troisier-Hanot-Chauffard syndrome (bronze diabetes) 275.0
Trombidiosis 133.8
Trophedema (hereditary) 757.0
congenital 757.0
Trophoblastic disease — *see also* Hydatidiform mole 630
previous, affecting management of pregnancy V23.1
Tropholymphedema 757.0
Trophoneurosis NEC 356.9
arm NEC 354.9
disseminated 710.1
facial 349.89
leg NEC 355.8
lower extremity NEC 355.8
upper extremity NEC 354.9

☑ Additional Digit Required — Refer to the Tabular List for Digit Selection
Subterms under main terms may continue to next column or page

Tropical — *see also* condition
maceration feet (syndrome) 991.4
wet foot (syndrome) 991.4
Trouble — *see also* Disease
bowel 569.9
heart — *see* Disease, heart
intestine 569.9
kidney (*see also* Disease, renal) 593.9
nervous 799.2
sinus (*see also* Sinusitis) 473.9
Trousseau's syndrome (thrombophlebitis migrans) 453.1
Truancy, childhood — *see also* Disturbance, conduct
socialized 312.2 ☑
undersocialized, unsocialized 312.1 ☑
Truncus
arteriosus (persistent) 745.0
common 745.0
communis 745.0
Trunk — *see* condition
Trychophytide — *see* Dermatophytosis
Trypanosoma infestation — *see* Trypanosomiasis
Trypanosomiasis 086.9
with meningoencephalitis 086.9 *[323.2]*
African 086.5
due to Trypanosoma 086.5
gambiense 086.3
rhodesiense 086.4
American 086.2
with
heart involvement 086.0
other organ involvement 086.1
without mention of organ involvement 086.2
Brazilian — *see* Trypanosomiasis, American
Chagas' — *see* Trypanosomiasis, American
due to Trypanosoma
cruzi — *see* Trypanosomiasis, American
gambiense 086.3
rhodesiense 086.4
gambiensis, Gambian 086.3
North American — *see* Trypanosomiasis, American
rhodesiensis, Rhodesian 086.4
South American — *see* Trypanosomiasis, American
T-shaped incisors 520.2
Tsutsugamushi fever 081.2
Tubercle — *see also* Tuberculosis
brain, solitary 013.2 ☑
Darwin's 744.29
epithelioid noncaseating 135
Ghon, primary infection 010.0 ☑
Tuberculid, tuberculide (indurating) (lichenoid) (miliary) (papulonecrotic) (primary) (skin) (subcutaneous) — *see also* Tuberculosis 017.0 ☑
Tuberculoma — *see also* Tuberculosis
brain (any part) 013.2 ☑
meninges (cerebral) (spinal) 013.1 ☑
spinal cord 013.4 ☑
Tuberculosis, tubercular, tuberculous (calcification) (calcified) (caseous) (chromogenic acid-fast bacilli) (congenital) (degeneration) (disease) (fibrocaseous) (fistula) (gangrene) (interstitial) (isolated circumscribed lesions) (necrosis) (parenchymatous) (ulcerative) 011.9 ☑

> *Note — Use the following fifth-digit subclassification with categories 010–018:*
>
> 0 *unspecified*
>
> 1 *bacteriological or histological examination not done*
>
> 2 *bacteriological or histological examination unknown (at present)*
>
> 3 *tubercle bacilli found (in sputum) by microscopy*
>
> 4 *tubercle bacilli not found (in sputum) by microscopy, but found by bacterial culture*
>
> 5 *tubercle bacilli not found by bacteriological exam–ination, but tuberculosis confirmed histologically*
>
> 6 *tubercle bacilli not found by bacteriological or histological examination, but tuberculosis confirmed by other methods [inoculation of animals]*
>
> *For tuberculous conditions specified as late effects or sequelae, see category 137.*

abdomen 014.8 ☑
lymph gland 014.8 ☑
abscess 011.9 ☑
arm 017.9 ☑
bone (*see also* Osteomyelitis, due to, tuberculosis) 015.9 ☑ *[730.8]* ☑
hip 015.1 ☑ *[730.85]*
knee 015.2 ☑ *[730.86]*
sacrum 015.0 ☑ *[730.88]*
specified site NEC 015.7 ☑ *[730.88]*
spinal 015.0 ☑ *[730.88]*
vertebra 015.0 ☑ *[730.88]*
brain 013.3 ☑
breast 017.9 ☑
Cowper's gland 016.5 ☑
dura (mater) 013.8 ☑
brain 013.3 ☑
spinal cord 013.5 ☑
epidural 013.8 ☑
brain 013.3 ☑
spinal cord 013.5 ☑
frontal sinus — *see* Tuberculosis, sinus
genital organs NEC 016.9 ☑
female 016.7 ☑
male 016.5 ☑
genitourinary NEC 016.9 ☑
gland (lymphatic) — *see* Tuberculosis, lymph gland
hip 015.1 ☑
iliopsoas 015.0 ☑ *[730.88]*
intestine 014.8 ☑
ischiorectal 014.8 ☑
joint 015.9 ☑
hip 015.1 ☑
knee 015.2 ☑
specified joint NEC 015.8 ☑
vertebral 015.0 ☑ *[730.88]*
kidney 016.0 ☑ *[590.81]*
knee 015.2 ☑
lumbar 015.0 ☑ *[730.88]*
lung 011.2 ☑
primary, progressive 010.8 ☑
meninges (cerebral) (spinal) 013.0 ☑
pelvic 016.9 ☑

Tuberculosis, tubercular, tuberculous — *continued*
abscess — *continued*
pelvic — *continued*
female 016.7 ☑
male 016.5 ☑
perianal 014.8 ☑
fistula 014.8 ☑
perinephritic 016.0 ☑ *[590.81]*
perineum 017.9 ☑
perirectal 014.8 ☑
psoas 015.0 ☑ *[730.88]*
rectum 014.8 ☑
retropharyngeal 012.8 ☑
sacrum 015.0 ☑ *[730.88]*
scrofulous 017.2 ☑
scrotum 016.5 ☑
skin 017.0 ☑
primary 017.0 ☑
spinal cord 013.5 ☑
spine or vertebra (column) 015.0 ☑ *[730.88]*
strumous 017.2 ☑
subdiaphragmatic 014.8 ☑
testis 016.5 ☑
thigh 017.9 ☑
urinary 016.3 ☑
kidney 016.0 ☑ *[590.81]*
uterus 016.7 ☑
accessory sinus — *see* Tuberculosis, sinus
Addison's disease 017.6 ☑
adenitis (*see also* Tuberculosis, lymph gland) 017.2 ☑
adenoids 012.8 ☑
adenopathy (*see also* Tuberculosis, lymph gland) 017.2 ☑
tracheobronchial 012.1 ☑
primary progressive 010.8 ☑
adherent pericardium 017.9 ☑ *[420.0]*
adnexa (uteri) 016.7 ☑
adrenal (capsule) (gland) 017.6 ☑
air passage NEC 012.8 ☑
alimentary canal 014.8 ☑
anemia 017.9 ☑
ankle (joint) 015.8 ☑
bone 015.5 ☑ *[730.87]*
anus 014.8 ☑
apex (*see also* Tuberculosis, pulmonary) 011.9 ☑
apical (*see also* Tuberculosis, pulmonary) 011.9 ☑
appendicitis 014.8 ☑
appendix 014.8 ☑
arachnoid 013.0 ☑
artery 017.9 ☑
arthritis (chronic) (synovial) 015.9 ☑ *[711.40]*
ankle 015.8 ☑ *[730.87]*
hip 015.1 ☑ *[711.45]*
knee 015.2 ☑ *[711.46]*
specified site NEC 015.8 ☑ *[711.48]*
spine or vertebra (column) 015.0 ☑ *[720.81]*
wrist 015.8 ☑ *[730.83]*
articular — *see* Tuberculosis, joint
ascites 014.0 ☑
asthma (*see also* Tuberculosis, pulmonary) 011.9 ☑
axilla, axillary 017.2 ☑
gland 017.2 ☑
bilateral (*see also* Tuberculosis, pulmonary) 011.9 ☑
bladder 016.1 ☑
bone (*see also* Osteomyelitis, due to, tuberculosis) 015.9 ☑ *[730.8]* ☑
hip 015.1 ☑ *[730.85]*
knee 015.2 ☑ *[730.86]*
limb NEC 015.5 ☑ *[730.88]*
sacrum 015.0 ☑ *[730.88]*
specified site NEC 015.7 ☑ *[730.88]*
spinal or vertebral column 015.0 ☑ *[730.88]*
bowel 014.8 ☑

Tuberculosis, tubercular, tuberculous — *continued*
bowel — *continued*
miliary 018.9 ☑
brain 013.2 ☑
breast 017.9 ☑
broad ligament 016.7 ☑
bronchi, bronchial, bronchus 011.3 ☑
ectasia, ectasis 011.5 ☑
fistula 011.3 ☑
primary, progressive 010.8 ☑
gland 012.1 ☑
primary, progressive 010.8 ☑
isolated 012.2 ☑
lymph gland or node 012.1 ☑
primary, progressive 010.8 ☑
bronchiectasis 011.5 ☑
bronchitis 011.3 ☑
bronchopleural 012.0 ☑
bronchopneumonia, bronchopneumonic 011.6 ☑
bronchorrhagia 011.3 ☑
bronchotracheal 011.3 ☑
isolated 012.2 ☑
bronchus — *see* Tuberculosis, bronchi
bronze disease (Addison's) 017.6 ☑
buccal cavity 017.9 ☑
bulbourethral gland 016.5 ☑
bursa (*see also* Tuberculosis, joint) 015.9 ☑
cachexia NEC (*see also* Tuberculosis, pulmonary) 011.9 ☑
cardiomyopathy 017.9 ☑ *[425.8]*
caries (*see also* Tuberculosis, bone) 015.9 ☑ *[730.8]* ☑
cartilage (*see also* Tuberculosis, bone) 015.9 ☑ *[730.8]* ☑
intervertebral 015.0 ☑ *[730.88]*
catarrhal (*see also* Tuberculosis, pulmonary) 011.9 ☑
cecum 014.8 ☑
cellular tissue (primary) 017.0 ☑
cellulitis (primary) 017.0 ☑
central nervous system 013.9 ☑
specified site NEC 013.8 ☑
cerebellum (current) 013.2 ☑
cerebral (current) 013.2 ☑
meninges 013.0 ☑
cerebrospinal 013.6 ☑
meninges 013.0 ☑
cerebrum (current) 013.2 ☑
cervical 017.2 ☑
gland 017.2 ☑
lymph nodes 017.2 ☑
cervicitis (uteri) 016.7 ☑
cervix 016.7 ☑
chest (*see also* Tuberculosis, pulmonary) 011.9 ☑
childhood type or first infection 010.0 ☑
choroid 017.3 ☑ *[363.13]*
choroiditis 017.3 ☑ *[363.13]*
ciliary body 017.3 ☑ *[364.11]*
colitis 014.8 ☑
colliers' 011.4 ☑
colliquativa (primary) 017.0 ☑
colon 014.8 ☑
ulceration 014.8 ☑
complex, primary 010.0 ☑
complicating pregnancy, childbirth, or puerperium 647.3 ☑
affecting fetus or newborn 760.2
congenital 771.2
conjunctiva 017.3 ☑ *[370.31]*
connective tissue 017.9 ☑
bone — *see* Tuberculosis, bone
contact V01.1
converter (tuberculin skin test) (without disease) 795.5
cornea (ulcer) 017.3 ☑ *[370.31]*
Cowper's gland 016.5 ☑
coxae 015.1 ☑ *[730.85]*
coxalgia 015.1 ☑ *[730.85]*
cul-de-sac of Douglas 014.8 ☑

Tuberculosis, tubercular, tuberculous — *continued*
- curvature, spine 015.0 ☑ *[737.40]*
- cutis (colliquativa) (primary) 017.0 ☑
- cystitis 016.1 ☑
- cyst, ovary 016.6 ☑
- dacryocystitis 017.3 ☑ *[375.32]*
- dactylitis 015.5 ☑
- diarrhea 014.8 ☑
- diffuse (*see also* Tuberculosis, miliary) 018.9 ☑
  - lung — *see* Tuberculosis, pulmonary
  - meninges 013.0 ☑
- digestive tract 014.8 ☑
- disseminated (*see also* Tuberculosis, miliary) 018.9 ☑
  - meninges 013.0 ☑
- duodenum 014.8 ☑
- dura (mater) 013.9 ☑
  - abscess 013.8 ☑
    - cerebral 013.3 ☑
    - spinal 013.5 ☑
- dysentery 014.8 ☑
- ear (inner) (middle) 017.4 ☑
  - bone 015.6 ☑
  - external (primary) 017.0 ☑
  - skin (primary) 017.0 ☑
- elbow 015.8 ☑
- emphysema — *see* Tuberculosis, pulmonary
- empyema 012.0 ☑
- encephalitis 013.6 ☑
- endarteritis 017.9 ☑
- endocarditis (any valve) 017.9 ☑ *[424.91]*
- endocardium (any valve) 017.9 ☑ *[424.91]*
- endocrine glands NEC 017.9 ☑
- endometrium 016.7 ☑
- enteric, enterica 014.8 ☑
- enteritis 014.8 ☑
- enterocolitis 014.8 ☑
- epididymis 016.4 ☑
- epididymitis 016.4 ☑
- epidural abscess 013.8 ☑
  - brain 013.3 ☑
  - spinal cord 013.5 ☑
- epiglottis 012.3 ☑
- episcleritis 017.3 ☑ *[379.00]*
- erythema (induratum) (nodosum) (primary) 017.1 ☑
- esophagus 017.8 ☑
- Eustachian tube 017.4 ☑
- exposure to V01.1
- exudative 012.0 ☑
  - primary, progressive 010.1 ☑
- eye 017.3 ☑
- eyelid (primary) 017.0 ☑
  - lupus 017.0 ☑ *[373.4]*
- fallopian tube 016.6 ☑
- fascia 017.9 ☑
- fauces 012.8 ☑
- finger 017.9 ☑
- first infection 010.0 ☑
- fistula, perirectal 014.8 ☑
- Florida 011.6 ☑
- foot 017.9 ☑
- funnel pelvis 137.3
- gallbladder 017.9 ☑
- galloping (*see also* Tuberculosis, pulmonary) 011.9 ☑
- ganglionic 015.9 ☑
- gastritis 017.9 ☑
- gastrocolic fistula 014.8 ☑
- gastroenteritis 014.8 ☑
- gastrointestinal tract 014.8 ☑
- general, generalized 018.9 ☑
  - acute 018.0 ☑
  - chronic 018.8 ☑
- genital organs NEC 016.9 ☑
  - female 016.7 ☑
  - male 016.5 ☑
- genitourinary NEC 016.9 ☑

Tuberculosis, tubercular, tuberculous — *continued*
- genu 015.2 ☑
- glandulae suprarenalis 017.6 ☑
- glandular, general 017.2 ☑
- glottis 012.3 ☑
- grinders' 011.4 ☑
- groin 017.2 ☑
- gum 017.9 ☑
- hand 017.9 ☑
- heart 017.9 ☑ *[425.8]*
- hematogenous — *see* Tuberculosis, miliary
- hemoptysis (*see also* Tuberculosis, pulmonary) 011.9 ☑
- hemorrhage NEC (*see also* Tuberculosis, pulmonary) 011.9 ☑
- hemothorax 012.0 ☑
- hepatitis 017.9 ☑
- hilar lymph nodes 012.1 ☑
  - primary, progressive 010.8 ☑
- hip (disease) (joint) 015.1 ☑
  - bone 015.1 ☑ *[730.85]*
- hydrocephalus 013.8 ☑
- hydropneumothorax 012.0 ☑
- hydrothorax 012.0 ☑
- hypoadrenalism 017.6 ☑
- hypopharynx 012.8 ☑
- ileocecal (hyperplastic) 014.8 ☑
- ileocolitis 014.8 ☑
- ileum 014.8 ☑
- iliac spine (superior) 015.0 ☑ *[730.88]*
- incipient NEC (*see also* Tuberculosis, pulmonary) 011.9 ☑
- indurativa (primary) 017.1 ☑
- infantile 010.0 ☑
- infection NEC 011.9 ☑
  - without clinical manifestation 010.0 ☑
- infraclavicular gland 017.2 ☑
- inguinal gland 017.2 ☑
- inguinalis 017.2 ☑
- intestine (any part) 014.8 ☑
- iris 017.3 ☑ *[364.11]*
- iritis 017.3 ☑ *[364.11]*
- ischiorectal 014.8 ☑
- jaw 015.7 ☑ *[730.88]*
- jejunum 014.8 ☑
- joint 015.9 ☑
  - hip 015.1 ☑
  - knee 015.2 ☑
  - specified site NEC 015.8 ☑
  - vertebral 015.0 ☑ *[730.88]*
- keratitis 017.3 ☑ *[370.31]*
  - interstitial 017.3 ☑ *[370.59]*
- keratoconjunctivitis 017.3 ☑ *[370.31]*
- kidney 016.0 ☑
- knee (joint) 015.2 ☑
- kyphoscoliosis 015.0 ☑ *[737.43]*
- kyphosis 015.0 ☑ *[737.41]*
- lacrimal apparatus, gland 017.3 ☑
- laryngitis 012.3 ☑
- larynx 012.3 ☑
- leptomeninges, leptomeningitis (cerebral) (spinal) 013.0 ☑
- lichenoides (primary) 017.0 ☑
- linguae 017.9 ☑
- lip 017.9 ☑
- liver 017.9 ☑
- lordosis 015.0 ☑ *[737.42]*
- lung — *see* Tuberculosis, pulmonary
- luposa 017.0 ☑
  - eyelid 017.0 ☑ *[373.4]*
- lymphadenitis — *see* Tuberculosis, lymph gland
- lymphangitis — *see* Tuberculosis, lymph gland
- lymphatic (gland) (vessel) — *see* Tuberculosis, lymph gland
- lymph gland or node (peripheral) 017.2 ☑
  - abdomen 014.8 ☑
  - bronchial 012.1 ☑
    - primary, progressive 010.8 ☑

Tuberculosis, tubercular, tuberculous — *continued*
- lymph gland or node — *continued*
  - cervical 017.2 ☑
  - hilar 012.1 ☑
    - primary, progressive 010.8 ☑
  - intrathoracic 012.1 ☑
    - primary, progressive 010.8 ☑
  - mediastinal 012.1 ☑
    - primary, progressive 010.8 ☑
  - mesenteric 014.8 ☑
  - peripheral 017.2 ☑
  - retroperitoneal 014.8 ☑
  - tracheobronchial 012.1 ☑
    - primary, progressive 010.8 ☑
- malignant NEC (*see also* Tuberculosis, pulmonary) 011.9 ☑
- mammary gland 017.9 ☑
- marasmus NEC (*see also* Tuberculosis, pulmonary) 011.9 ☑
- mastoiditis 015.6 ☑
- maternal, affecting fetus or newborn 760.2
- mediastinal (lymph) gland or node 012.1 ☑
  - primary, progressive 010.8 ☑
- mediastinitis 012.8 ☑
  - primary, progressive 010.8 ☑
- mediastinopericarditis 017.9 ☑ *[420.0]*
- mediastinum 012.8 ☑
  - primary, progressive 010.8 ☑
- medulla 013.9 ☑
  - brain 013.2 ☑
  - spinal cord 013.4 ☑
- melanosis, Addisonian 017.6 ☑
- membrane, brain 013.0 ☑
- meninges (cerebral) (spinal) 013.0 ☑
- meningitis (basilar) (brain) (cerebral) (cerebrospinal) (spinal) 013.0 ☑
- meningoencephalitis 013.0 ☑
- mesentery, mesenteric 014.8 ☑
  - lymph gland or node 014.8 ☑
- miliary (any site) 018.9 ☑
  - acute 018.0 ☑
  - chronic 018.8 ☑
  - specified type NEC 018.8 ☑
- millstone makers' 011.4 ☑
- miners' 011.4 ☑
- moulders' 011.4 ☑
- mouth 017.9 ☑
- multiple 018.9 ☑
  - acute 018.0 ☑
  - chronic 018.8 ☑
- muscle 017.9 ☑
- myelitis 013.6 ☑
- myocarditis 017.9 ☑ *[422.0]*
- myocardium 017.9 ☑ *[422.0]*
- nasal (passage) (sinus) 012.8 ☑
- nasopharynx 012.8 ☑
- neck gland 017.2 ☑
- nephritis 016.0 ☑ *[583.81]*
- nerve 017.9 ☑
- nose (septum) 012.8 ☑
- ocular 017.3 ☑
- old NEC 137.0
  - without residuals V12.01
- omentum 014.8 ☑
- oophoritis (acute) (chronic) 016.6 ☑
- optic 017.3 ☑ *[377.39]*
  - nerve trunk 017.3 ☑ *[377.39]*
  - papilla, papillae 017.3 ☑ *[377.39]*
- orbit 017.3 ☑
- orchitis 016.5 ☑ *[608.81]*
- organ, specified NEC 017.9 ☑
- orificialis (primary) 017.0 ☑
- osseous (*see also* Tuberculosis, bone) 015.9 ☑ *[730.8]* ☑
- osteitis (*see also* Tuberculosis, bone) 015.9 ☑ *[730.8]* ☑
- osteomyelitis (*see also* Tuberculosis, bone) 015.9 ☑ *[730.8]* ☑
- otitis (media) 017.4 ☑
- ovaritis (acute) (chronic) 016.6 ☑
- ovary (acute) (chronic) 016.6 ☑

Tuberculosis, tubercular, tuberculous — *continued*
- oviducts (acute) (chronic) 016.6 ☑
- pachymeningitis 013.0 ☑
- palate (soft) 017.9 ☑
- pancreas 017.9 ☑
- papulonecrotic (primary) 017.0 ☑
- parathyroid glands 017.9 ☑
- paronychia (primary) 017.0 ☑
- parotid gland or region 017.9 ☑
- pelvic organ NEC 016.9 ☑
  - female 016.7 ☑
  - male 016.5 ☑
- pelvis (bony) 015.7 ☑ *[730.85]*
- penis 016.5 ☑
- peribronchitis 011.3 ☑
- pericarditis 017.9 ☑ *[420.0]*
- pericardium 017.9 ☑ *[420.0]*
- perichondritis, larynx 012.3 ☑
- perineum 017.9 ☑
- periostitis (*see also* Tuberculosis, bone) 015.9 ☑ *[730.8]* ☑
- periphlebitis 017.9 ☑
  - eye vessel 017.3 ☑ *[362.18]*
  - retina 017.3 ☑ *[362.18]*
- perirectal fistula 014.8 ☑
- peritoneal gland 014.8 ☑
- peritoneum 014.0 ☑
- peritonitis 014.0 ☑
- pernicious NEC (*see also* Tuberculosis, pulmonary) 011.9 ☑
- pharyngitis 012.8 ☑
- pharynx 012.8 ☑
- phlyctenulosis (conjunctiva) 017.3 ☑ *[370.31]*
- phthisis NEC (*see also* Tuberculosis, pulmonary) 011.9 ☑
- pituitary gland 017.9 ☑
- placenta 016.7 ☑
- pleura, pleural, pleurisy, pleuritis (fibrinous) (obliterative) (purulent) (simple plastic) (with effusion) 012.0 ☑
  - primary, progressive 010.1 ☑
- pneumonia, pneumonic 011.6 ☑
- pneumothorax 011.7 ☑
- polyserositis 018.9 ☑
  - acute 018.0 ☑
  - chronic 018.8 ☑
- potters' 011.4 ☑
- prepuce 016.5 ☑
- primary 010.9 ☑
  - complex 010.0 ☑
  - complicated 010.8 ☑
    - with pleurisy or effusion 010.1 ☑
  - progressive 010.8 ☑
    - with pleurisy or effusion 010.1 ☑
  - skin 017.0 ☑
- proctitis 014.8 ☑
- prostate 016.5 ☑ *[601.4]*
- prostatitis 016.5 ☑ *[601.4]*
- pulmonaris (*see also* Tuberculosis, pulmonary) 011.9 ☑
- pulmonary (artery) (incipient) (malignant) (multiple round foci) (pernicious) (reinfection stage) 011.9 ☑
  - cavitated or with cavitation 011.2 ☑
    - primary, progressive 010.8 ☑
  - childhood type or first infection 010.0 ☑
  - chromogenic acid-fast bacilli 795.39
  - fibrosis or fibrotic 011.4 ☑
  - infiltrative 011.0 ☑
    - primary, progressive 010.9 ☑
  - nodular 011.1 ☑
  - specified NEC 011.8 ☑
  - sputum positive only 795.39
  - status following surgical collapse of lung NEC 011.9 ☑

Tuberculosis, tubercular, tuberculous — *continued*
- pyelitis 016.0 ☑ *[590.81]*
- pyelonephritis 016.0 ☑ *[590.81]*
- pyemia — *see* Tuberculosis, miliary
- pyonephrosis 016.0 ☑
- pyopneumothorax 012.0 ☑
- pyothorax 012.0 ☑
- rectum (with abscess) 014.8 ☑
  - fistula 014.8 ☑
- reinfection stage (*see also* Tuberculosis, pulmonary) 011.9 ☑
- renal 016.0 ☑
- renis 016.0 ☑
- reproductive organ 016.7 ☑
- respiratory NEC (*see also* Tuberculosis, pulmonary) 011.9 ☑
  - specified site NEC 012.8 ☑
- retina 017.3 ☑ *[363.13]*
- retroperitoneal (lymph gland or node) 014.8 ☑
  - gland 014.8 ☑
- retropharyngeal abscess 012.8 ☑
- rheumatism 015.9 ☑
- rhinitis 012.8 ☑
- sacroiliac (joint) 015.8 ☑
- sacrum 015.0 ☑ *[730.88]*
- salivary gland 017.9 ☑
- salpingitis (acute) (chronic) 016.6 ☑
- sandblasters' 011.4 ☑
- sclera 017.3 ☑ *[379.09]*
- scoliosis 015.0 ☑ *[737.43]*
- scrofulous 017.2 ☑
- scrotum 016.5 ☑
- seminal tract or vesicle 016.5 ☑ *[608.81]*
- senile NEC (*see also* Tuberculosis, pulmonary) 011.9 ☑
- septic NEC (*see also* Tuberculosis, miliary) 018.9 ☑
- shoulder 015.8 ☑
  - blade 015.7 ☑ *[730.8]* ☑
- sigmoid 014.8 ☑
- sinus (accessory) (nasal) 012.8 ☑
  - bone 015.7 ☑ *[730.88]*
  - epididymis 016.4 ☑
- skeletal NEC (*see also* Osteomyelitis, due to tuberculosis) 015.9 ☑ *[730.8]* ☑
- skin (any site) (primary) 017.0 ☑
- small intestine 014.8 ☑
- soft palate 017.9 ☑
- spermatic cord 016.5 ☑
- spinal
  - column 015.0 ☑ *[730.88]*
  - cord 013.4 ☑
  - disease 015.0 ☑ *[730.88]*
  - medulla 013.4 ☑
  - membrane 013.0 ☑
  - meninges 013.0 ☑
- spine 015.0 ☑ *[730.88]*
- spleen 017.7 ☑
- splenitis 017.7 ☑
- spondylitis 015.0 ☑ *[720.81]*
- spontaneous pneumothorax — *see* Tuberculosis, pulmonary
- sternoclavicular joint 015.8 ☑
- stomach 017.9 ☑
- stonemasons' 011.4 ☑
- struma 017.2 ☑
- subcutaneous tissue (cellular) (primary) 017.0 ☑
- subcutis (primary) 017.0 ☑
- subdeltoid bursa 017.9 ☑
- submaxillary 017.9 ☑
  - region 017.9 ☑
- supraclavicular gland 017.2 ☑
- suprarenal (capsule) (gland) 017.6 ☑
- swelling, joint (*see also* Tuberculosis, joint) 015.9 ☑
- symphysis pubis 015.7 ☑ *[730.88]*
- synovitis 015.9 ☑ *[727.01]*
  - hip 015.1 ☑ *[727.01]*
  - knee 015.2 ☑ *[727.01]*

Tuberculosis, tubercular, tuberculous — *continued*
- synovitis — *continued*
  - specified site NEC 015.8 ☑ *[727.01]*
  - spine or vertebra 015.0 ☑ *[727.01]*
- systemic — *see* Tuberculosis, miliary
- tarsitis (eyelid) 017.0 ☑ *[373.4]*
  - ankle (bone) 015.5 ☑ *[730.87]*
- tendon (sheath) — *see* Tuberculosis, tenosynovitis
- tenosynovitis 015.9 ☑ *[727.01]*
  - hip 015.1 ☑ *[727.01]*
  - knee 015.2 ☑ *[727.01]*
  - specified site NEC 015.8 ☑ *[727.01]*
  - spine or vertebra 015.0 ☑ *[727.01]*
- testis 016.5 ☑ *[608.81]*
- throat 012.8 ☑
- thymus gland 017.9 ☑
- thyroid gland 017.5 ☑
- toe 017.9 ☑
- tongue 017.9 ☑
- tonsil (lingual) 012.8 ☑
- tonsillitis 012.8 ☑
- trachea, tracheal 012.8 ☑
  - gland 012.1 ☑
    - primary, progressive 010.8 ☑
  - isolated 012.2 ☑
- tracheobronchial 011.3 ☑
  - glandular 012.1 ☑
    - primary, progressive 010.8 ☑
  - isolated 012.2 ☑
  - lymph gland or node 012.1 ☑
    - primary, progressive 010.8 ☑
- tubal 016.6 ☑
- tunica vaginalis 016.5 ☑
- typhlitis 014.8 ☑
- ulcer (primary) (skin) 017.0 ☑
  - bowel or intestine 014.8 ☑
  - specified site NEC — *see* Tuberculosis, by site
- unspecified site — *see* Tuberculosis, pulmonary
- ureter 016.2 ☑
- urethra, urethral 016.3 ☑
- urinary organ or tract 016.3 ☑
  - kidney 016.0 ☑
- uterus 016.7 ☑
- uveal tract 017.3 ☑ *[363.13]*
- uvula 017.9 ☑
- vaccination, prophylactic (against) V03.2
- vagina 016.7 ☑
- vas deferens 016.5 ☑
- vein 017.9 ☑
- verruca (primary) 017.0 ☑
- verrucosa (cutis) (primary) 017.0 ☑
- vertebra (column) 015.0 ☑ *[730.88]*
- vesiculitis 016.5 ☑ *[608.81]*
- viscera NEC 014.8 ☑
- vulva 016.7 ☑ *[616.51]*
- wrist (joint) 015.8 ☑
  - bone 015.5 ☑ *[730.83]*

Tuberculum
- auriculae 744.29
- occlusal 520.2
- paramolare 520.2

Tuberosity
- jaw, excessive 524.07
- maxillary, entire 524.07

Tuberous sclerosis (brain) 759.5

Tube, tubal, tubular — *see also* condition
- ligation, admission for V25.2

Tubo-ovarian — *see* condition

Tuboplasty, after previous sterilization V26.0

Tubotympanitis 381.10

Tularemia 021.9
- with
  - conjunctivitis 021.3
  - pneumonia 021.2
- bronchopneumonic 021.2
- conjunctivitis 021.3
- cryptogenic 021.1
- disseminated 021.8

Tularemia — *continued*
- enteric 021.1
- generalized 021.8
- glandular 021.8
- intestinal 021.1
- oculoglandular 021.3
- ophthalmic 021.3
- pneumonia 021.2
- pulmonary 021.2
- specified NEC 021.8
- typhoidal 021.1
- ulceroglandular 021.0
- vaccination, prophylactic (against) V03.4

Tularensis conjunctivitis 021.3

Tumefaction — *see also* Swelling
- liver (*see also* Hypertrophy, liver) 789.1

Tumor (M8000/1) — *see also* Neoplasm, by site, unspecified nature
- Abrikossov's (M9580/0) (*see also* Neoplasm, connective tissue, benign)
  - malignant (M9580/3) — *see* Neoplasm, connective tissue, malignant
- acinar cell (M8550/1) — *see* Neoplasm, by site, uncertain behavior
- acinic cell (M8550/1) — *see* Neoplasm, by site, uncertain behavior
- adenomatoid (M9054/0) (*see also* Neoplasm, by site, benign)
  - odontogenic (M9300/0) 213.1
    - upper jaw (bone) 213.0
- adnexal (skin) (M8390/0) — *see* Neoplasm, skin, benign
- adrenal
  - cortical (benign) (M8370/0) 227.0
    - malignant (M8370/3) 194.0
  - rest (M8671/0) — *see* Neoplasm, by site, benign
- alpha cell (M8152/0)
  - malignant (M8152/3)
    - pancreas 157.4
    - specified site NEC — *see* Neoplasm, by site, malignant
    - unspecified site 157.4
  - pancreas 211.7
  - specified site NEC — *see* Neoplasm, by site, benign
  - unspecified site 211.7
- aneurysmal (*see also* Aneurysm) 442.9
- aortic body (M8691/1) 237.3
  - malignant (M8691/3) 194.6
- argentaffin (M8241/1) — *see* Neoplasm, by site, uncertain behavior
- basal cell (M8090/1) (*see also* Neoplasm, skin, uncertain behavior)
- benign (M8000/0) — *see* Neoplasm, by site, benign
- beta cell (M8151/0)
  - malignant (M8151/3)
    - pancreas 157.4
    - specified site — *see* Neoplasm, by site, malignant
    - unspecified site 157.4
  - pancreas 211.7
  - specified site NEC — *see* Neoplasm, by site, benign
  - unspecified site 211.7
- blood — *see* Hematoma
- Brenner (M9000/0) 220
  - borderline malignancy (M9000/1) 236.2
  - malignant (M9000/3) 183.0
  - proliferating (M9000/1) 236.2
- Brooke's (M8100/0) — *see* Neoplasm, skin, benign
- brown fat (M8880/0) — *see* Lipoma, by site
- Burkitt's (M9750/3) 200.2 ☑
- calcifying epithelial odontogenic (M9340/0) 213.1

Tumor — *see also* Neoplasm, by site, unspecified nature — *continued*
- calcifying epithelial odontogenic — *continued*
  - upper jaw (bone) 213.0
- carcinoid (M8240/1) 209.60 ▲
  - benign 209.60 ●
    - appendix 209.51 ●
    - ascending colon 209.53 ●
    - bronchus 209.61 ●
    - cecum 209.52 ●
    - colon 209.50 ●
    - descending colon 209.55 ●
    - duodenum 209.41 ●
    - foregut 209.65 ●
    - hindgut 209.67 ●
    - ileum 209.43 ●
    - jejunum 209.42 ●
    - kidney 209.64 ●
    - large intestine 209.50 ●
    - lung 209.61 ●
    - midgut 209.66 ●
    - rectum 209.57 ●
    - sigmoid colon 209.56 ●
    - small intestine 209.40 ●
    - specified NEC 209.69 ●
    - stomach 209.63 ●
    - thymus 209.62 ●
    - transverse colon 209.54 ●
  - malignant (of) 209.20 ●
    - appendix 209.11 ●
    - ascending colon 209.13 ●
    - bronchus 209.21 ●
    - cecum 209.12 ●
    - colon 209.10 ●
    - descending colon 209.15 ●
    - duodenum 209.01 ●
    - foregut 209.25 ●
    - hindgut 209.27 ●
    - ileum 209.03 ●
    - jejunum 209.02 ●
    - kidney 209.24 ●
    - large intestine 209.10 ●
    - lung 209.21 ●
    - midgut 209.26 ●
    - rectum 209.17 ●
    - sigmoid colon 209.16 ●
    - small intestine 209.00 ●
    - specified NEC 209.29 ●
    - stomach 209.23 ●
    - thymus 209.22 ●
    - transverse colon 209.14 ●
- carotid body (M8692/1) 237.3
  - malignant (M8692/3) 194.5
- Castleman's (mediastinal lymph node hyperplasia) 785.6
- cells (M8001/1) (*see also* Neoplasm, by site, unspecified nature)
  - benign (M8001/0) — *see* Neoplasm, by site, benign
  - malignant (M8001/3) — *see* Neoplasm, by site, malignant
  - uncertain whether benign or malignant (M8001/1) — *see* Neoplasm, by site, uncertain nature
- cervix
  - in pregnancy or childbirth 654.6 ☑
    - affecting fetus or newborn 763.89
    - causing obstructed labor 660.2 ☑
      - affecting fetus or newborn 763.1
- chondromatous giant cell (M9230/0) — *see* Neoplasm, bone, benign
- chromaffin (M8700/0) (*see also* Neoplasm, by site, benign)
  - malignant (M8700/3) — *see* Neoplasm, by site, malignant
- Cock's peculiar 706.2
- Codman's (benign chondroblastoma) (M9230/0) — *see* Neoplasm, bone, benign
- dentigerous, mixed (M9282/0) 213.1
  - upper jaw (bone) 213.0

Tumor — *see also* Neoplasm, by site, unspecified nature — *continued*
dermoid (M9084/0) — *see* Neoplasm, by site, benign
with malignant transformation (M9084/3) 183.0
desmoid (extra-abdominal) (M8821/1) (*see also* Neoplasm, connective tissue, uncertain behavior)
abdominal (M8822/1) — *see* Neoplasm, connective tissue, uncertain behavior
embryonal (mixed) (M9080/1) (*see also* Neoplasm, by site, uncertain behavior)
liver (M9080/3) 155.0
endodermal sinus (M9071/3)
specified site — *see* Neoplasm, by site, malignant
unspecified site
female 183.0
male 186.9
epithelial
benign (M8010/0) — *see* Neoplasm, by site, benign
malignant (M8010/3) — *see* Neoplasm, by site, malignant
Ewing's (M9260/3) — *see* Neoplasm, bone, malignant
fatty — *see* Lipoma
fetal, causing disproportion 653.7 ☑
causing obstructed labor 660.1 ☑
fibroid (M8890/0) — *see* Leiomyoma
G cell (M8153/1)
malignant (M8153/3)
pancreas 157.4
specified site NEC — *see* Neoplasm, by site, malignant
unspecified site 157.4
specified site — *see* Neoplasm, by site, uncertain behavior
unspecified site 235.5
giant cell (type) (M8003/1) (*see also* Neoplasm, by site, unspecified nature)
bone (M9250/1) 238.0
malignant (M9250/3) — *see* Neoplasm, bone, malignant
chondromatous (M9230/0) — *see* Neoplasm, bone, benign
malignant (M8003/3) — *see* Neoplasm, by site, malignant
peripheral (gingiva) 523.8
soft parts (M9251/1) (*see also* Neoplasm, connective tissue, uncertain behavior)
malignant (M9251/3) — *see* Neoplasm, connective tissue, malignant
tendon sheath 727.02
glomus (M8711/0) (*see also* Hemangioma, by site)
jugulare (M8690/1) 237.3
malignant (M8690/3) 194.6
gonadal stromal (M8590/1) — *see* Neoplasm, by site, uncertain behavior
granular cell (M9580/0) (*see also* Neoplasm, connective tissue, benign)
malignant (M9580/3) — *see* Neoplasm, connective tissue, malignant
granulosa cell (M8620/1) 236.2
malignant (M8620/3) 183.0
granulosa cell-theca cell (M8621/1) 236.2
malignant (M8621/3) 183.0
Grawitz's (hypernephroma) (M8312/3) 189.0
hazard-crile (M8350/3) 193
hemorrhoidal — *see* Hemorrhoids
hilar cell (M8660/0) 220
Hürthle cell (benign) (M8290/0) 226
malignant (M8290/3) 193

Tumor — *see also* Neoplasm, by site, unspecified nature — *continued*
hydatid (*see also* Echinococcus) 122.9
hypernephroid (M8311/1) (*see also* Neoplasm, by site, uncertain behavior)
interstitial cell (M8650/1) (*see also* Neoplasm, by site, uncertain behavior)
benign (M8650/0) — *see* Neoplasm, by site, benign
malignant (M8650/3) — *see* Neoplasm, by site, malignant
islet cell (M8150/0)
malignant (M8150/3)
pancreas 157.4
specified site — *see* Neoplasm, by site, malignant
unspecified site 157.4
pancreas 211.7
specified site NEC — *see* Neoplasm, by site, benign
unspecified site 211.7
juxtaglomerular (M8361/1) 236.91
Krukenberg's (M8490/6) 198.6
Leydig cell (M8650/1)
benign (M8650/0)
specified site — *see* Neoplasm, by site, benign
unspecified site
female 220
male 222.0
malignant (M8650/3)
specified site — *see* Neoplasm, by site, malignant
unspecified site
female 183.0
male 186.9
specified site — *see* Neoplasm, by site, uncertain behavior
unspecified site
female 236.2
male 236.4
lipid cell, ovary (M8670/0) 220
lipoid cell, ovary (M8670/0) 220
lymphomatous, benign (M9590/0) (*see also* Neoplasm, by site, benign)
Malherbe's (M8110/0) — *see* Neoplasm, skin, benign
malignant (M8000/3) (*see also* Neoplasm, by site, malignant)
fusiform cell (type) (M8004/3) — *see* Neoplasm, by site, malignant
giant cell (type) (M8003/3) — *see* Neoplasm, by site, malignant
mixed NEC (M8940/3) — *see* Neoplasm, by site, malignant
small cell (type) (M8002/3) — *see* Neoplasm, by site, malignant
spindle cell (type) (M8004/3) — *see* Neoplasm, by site, malignant
mast cell (M9740/1) 238.5
malignant (M9740/3) 202.6 ☑
melanotic, neuroectodermal (M9363/0) — *see* Neoplasm, by site, benign
Merkel cell — *see* Neoplasm, by site, malignant
mesenchymal
malignant (M8800/3) — *see* Neoplasm, connective tissue, malignant
mixed (M8990/1) — *see* Neoplasm, connective tissue, uncertain behavior
mesodermal, mixed (M8951/3) (*see also* Neoplasm, by site, malignant)
liver 155.0
mesonephric (M9110/1) (*see also* Neoplasm, by site, uncertain behavior)
malignant (M9110/3) — *see* Neoplasm, by site, malignant

Tumor — *see also* Neoplasm, by site, unspecified nature — *continued*
metastatic
from specified site (M8000/3) — *see* Neoplasm, by site, malignant
to specified site (M8000/6) — *see* Neoplasm, by site, malignant, secondary
mixed NEC (M8940/0) (*see also* Neoplasm, by site, benign)
malignant (M8940/3) — *see* Neoplasm, by site, malignant
mucocarcinoid, malignant (M8243/3) — *see* Neoplasm, by site, malignant
mucoepidermoid (M8430/1) — *see* Neoplasm, by site, uncertain behavior
Müllerian, mixed (M8950/3) — *see* Neoplasm, by site, malignant
myoepithelial (M8982/0) — *see* Neoplasm, by site, benign
neuroendocrine 209.60 ●
malignant poorly differentiated 209.30 ●
neurogenic olfactory (M9520/3) 160.0
nonencapsulated sclerosing (M8350/3) 193
odontogenic (M9270/1) 238.0
adenomatoid (M9300/0) 213.1
upper jaw (bone) 213.0
benign (M9270/0) 213.1
upper jaw (bone) 213.0
calcifying epithelial (M9340/0) 213.1
upper jaw (bone) 213.0
malignant (M9270/3) 170.1
upper jaw (bone) 170.0
squamous (M9312/0) 213.1
upper jaw (bone) 213.0
ovarian stromal (M8590/1) 236.2
ovary
in pregnancy or childbirth 654.4 ☑
affecting fetus or newborn 763.89
causing obstructed labor 660.2 ☑
affecting fetus or newborn 763.1
pacinian (M9507/0) — *see* Neoplasm, skin, benign
Pancoast's (M8010/3) 162.3
papillary — *see* Papilloma
pelvic, in pregnancy or childbirth 654.9 ☑
affecting fetus or newborn 763.89
causing obstructed labor 660.2 ☑
affecting fetus or newborn 763.1
phantom 300.11
plasma cell (M9731/1) 238.6
benign (M9731/0) — *see* Neoplasm, by site, benign
malignant (M9731/3) 203.8 ☑
polyvesicular vitelline (M9071/3)
specified site — *see* Neoplasm, by site, malignant
unspecified site
female 183.0
male 186.9
Pott's puffy (*see also* Osteomyelitis) 730.2 ☑
Rathke's pouch (M9350/1) 237.0
regaud's (M8082/3) — *see* Neoplasm, nasopharynx, malignant
rete cell (M8140/0) 222.0
retinal anlage (M9363/0) — *see* Neoplasm, by site, benign
Rokitansky's 620.2
salivary gland type, mixed (M8940/0) (*see also* Neoplasm, by site, benign)
malignant (M8940/3) — *see* Neoplasm, by site, malignant
Sampson's 617.1
Schloffer's (*see also* Peritonitis) 567.29

Tumor — *see also* Neoplasm, by site, unspecified nature — *continued*
Schmincke (M8082/3) — *see* Neoplasm, nasopharynx, malignant
sebaceous (*see also* Cyst, sebaceous) 706.2
secondary (M8000/6) — *see* Neoplasm, by site, secondary
Sertoli cell (M8640/0)
with lipid storage (M8641/0)
specified site — *see* Neoplasm, by site, benign
unspecified site
female 220
male 222.0
specified site — *see* Neoplasm, by site, benign
unspecified site
female 220
male 222.0
Sertoli-Leydig cell (M8631/0)
specified site, — *see* Neoplasm, by site, benign
unspecified site
female 220
male 222.0
sex cord (-stromal) (M8590/1) — *see* Neoplasm, by site, uncertain behavior
skin appendage (M8390/0) — *see* Neoplasm, skin, benign
soft tissue
benign (M8800/0) — *see* Neoplasm, connective tissue, benign
malignant (M8800/3) — *see* Neoplasm, connective tissue, malignant
sternomastoid 754.1
stromal
abdomen
benign 215.5
malignant ▶NEC◀ 171.5
uncertain behavior 238.1
digestive system 238.1
benign 215.5
malignant ▶NEC◀ 171.5
uncertain behavior 238.1
gastric 238.1
benign 215.5
malignant 151.9 ▲
uncertain behavior 238.1
gastrointestinal 238.1
benign 215.5
malignant ▶NEC◀ 171.5
uncertain behavior 238.1
intestine (small) 238.1
benign 215.5
malignant 152.9 ▲
uncertain behavior 238.1
stomach 238.1
benign 215.5
malignant 151.9 ▲
uncertain behavior 238.1
superior sulcus (lung) (pulmonary) (syndrome) (M8010/3) 162.3
suprasulcus (M8010/3) 162.3
sweat gland (M8400/1) (*see also* Neoplasm, skin, uncertain behavior)
benign (M8400/0) — *see* Neoplasm, skin, benign
malignant (M8400/3) — *see* Neoplasm, skin, malignant
syphilitic brain 094.89
congenital 090.49
testicular stromal (M8590/1) 236.4
theca cell (M8600/0) 220
theca cell-granulosa cell (M8621/1) 236.2
theca-lutein (M8610/0) 220
turban (M8200/0) 216.4
uterus
in pregnancy or childbirth 654.1 ☑
affecting fetus or newborn 763.89

- **Tumor** — *see also* Neoplasm, by site, unspecified nature — *continued*
  - uterus — *continued*
    - in pregnancy or childbirth — *continued*
      - causing obstructed labor 660.2 ☑
        - affecting fetus or newborn 763.1
  - vagina
    - in pregnancy or childbirth 654.7 ☑
      - affecting fetus or newborn 763.89
      - causing obstructed labor 660.2 ☑
        - affecting fetus or newborn 763.1
  - varicose (*see also* Varicose, vein) 454.9
  - von Recklinghausen's (M9540/1) 237.71
  - vulva
    - in pregnancy or childbirth 654.8 ☑
      - affecting fetus or newborn 763.89
      - causing obstructed labor 660.2 ☑
        - affecting fetus or newborn 763.1
  - Warthin's (salivary gland) (M8561/0) 210.2
  - white (*see also* Tuberculosis, arthritis)
  - White-Darier 757.39
  - Wilms' (nephroblastoma) (M8960/3) 189.0
  - yolk sac (M9071/3)
    - specified site — *see* Neoplasm, by site, malignant
    - unspecified site
      - female 183.0
      - male 186.9
- **Tumorlet (M8040/1)** — *see* Neoplasm, by site, uncertain behavior
- **Tungiasis** 134.1
- **Tunica vasculosa lentis** 743.39
- **Tunnel vision** 368.45
- **Turban tumor** (M8200/0) 216.4
- **Türck's trachoma** (chronic catarrhal laryngitis) 476.0
- **Türk's syndrome** (ocular retraction syndrome) 378.71
- **Turner's**
  - hypoplasia (tooth) 520.4
  - syndrome 758.6
  - tooth 520.4
- **Turner-Kieser syndrome** (hereditary osteo-onychodysplasia) 756.89
- **Turner-Varny syndrome** 758.6
- **Turricephaly** 756.0
- **Tussis convulsiva** — *see also* Whooping cough 033.9
- **Twiddler's syndrome** (due to) ●
  - automatic implantable defibrillator 996.04 ●
  - pacemaker 996.01 ●
- **Twin**
  - affected by maternal complications of pregnancy 761.5
  - conjoined 759.4
  - fetal 678.1 ☑ ●
  - healthy liveborn — *see* Newborn, twin
  - pregnancy (complicating delivery) NEC 651.0 ☑
    - with fetal loss and retention of one fetus 651.3 ☑
    - conjoined 678.1 ☑ ●
    - following (elective) fetal reduction
- **Twinning, teeth** 520.2
- **Twist, twisted**
  - bowel, colon, or intestine 560.2
  - hair (congenital) 757.4
  - mesentery 560.2
  - omentum 560.2
  - organ or site, congenital NEC — *see* Anomaly, specified type NEC
  - ovarian pedicle 620.5
    - congenital 752.0
- **Twist, twisted** — *continued*
  - umbilical cord — *see* Compression, umbilical cord
- **Twitch** 781.0
- **Tylosis** 700
  - buccalis 528.6
  - gingiva 523.8
  - linguae 528.6
  - palmaris et plantaris 757.39
- **Tympanism** 787.3
- **Tympanites** (abdominal) (intestine) 787.3
- **Tympanitis** — *see* Myringitis
- **Tympanosclerosis** 385.00
  - involving
    - combined sites NEC 385.09
      - with tympanic membrane 385.03
    - tympanic membrane 385.01
      - with ossicles 385.02
        - and middle ear 385.03
- **Tympanum** — *see* condition
- **Tympany**
  - abdomen 787.3
  - chest 786.7
- **Typhlitis** — *see also* Appendicitis 541
- **Typhoenteritis** 002.0
- **Typhogastric fever** 002.0
- **Typhoid** (abortive) (ambulant) (any site) (fever) (hemorrhagic) (infection) (intermittent) (malignant) (rheumatic) 002.0
  - with pneumonia 002.0 *[484.8]*
  - abdominal 002.0
  - carrier (suspected) of V02.1
  - cholecystitis (current) 002.0
  - clinical (Widal and blood test negative) 002.0
  - endocarditis 002.0 *[421.1]*
  - inoculation reaction — *see* Complications, vaccination
  - meningitis 002.0 *[320.7]*
  - mesenteric lymph nodes 002.0
  - myocarditis 002.0 *[422.0]*
  - osteomyelitis (*see also* Osteomyelitis, due to, typhoid) 002.0 *[730.8]* ☑
  - perichondritis, larynx 002.0 *[478.71]*
  - pneumonia 002.0 *[484.8]*
  - spine 002.0 *[720.81]*
  - ulcer (perforating) 002.0
  - vaccination, prophylactic (against) V03.1
  - Widal negative 002.0
- **Typhomalaria** (fever) — *see also* Malaria 084.6
- **Typhomania** 002.0
- **Typhoperitonitis** 002.0
- **Typhus** (fever) 081.9
  - abdominal, abdominalis 002.0
  - African tick 082.1
  - amarillic (*see also* Fever, Yellow) 060.9
  - brain 081.9
  - cerebral 081.9
  - classical 080
  - endemic (flea-borne) 081.0
  - epidemic (louse-borne) 080
  - exanthematic NEC 080
  - exanthematicus SAI 080
    - brillii SAI 081.1
    - Mexicanus SAI 081.0
    - pediculo vestimenti causa 080
    - typhus murinus 081.0
  - flea-borne 081.0
  - Indian tick 082.1
  - Kenya tick 082.1
  - louse-borne 080
  - Mexican 081.0
    - flea-borne 081.0
    - louse-borne 080
    - tabardillo 080
  - mite-borne 081.2
  - murine 081.0
  - North Asian tick-borne 082.2
  - petechial 081.9
  - Queensland tick 082.3
  - rat 081.0
  - recrudescent 081.1
- **Typhus** — *continued*
  - recurrent (*see also* Fever, relapsing) 087.9
  - São Paulo 082.0
  - scrub (China) (India) (Malaya) (New Guinea) 081.2
  - shop (of Malaya) 081.0
  - Siberian tick 082.2
  - tick-borne NEC 082.9
  - tropical 081.2
  - vaccination, prophylactic (against) V05.8
- **Tyrosinemia** 270.2
  - neonatal 775.89
- **Tyrosinosis** (Medes) (Sakai) 270.2
- **Tyrosinuria** 270.2
- **Tyrosyluria** 270.2

U

- **Uehlinger's syndrome** (acropachyderma) 757.39
- **Uhl's anomaly or disease** (hypoplasia of myocardium, right ventricle) 746.84
- **Ulcerosa scarlatina** 034.1
- **Ulcer, ulcerated, ulcerating, ulceration, ulcerative** 707.9
  - with gangrene 707.9 *[785.4]*
  - abdomen (wall) (*see also* Ulcer, skin) 707.8
  - ala, nose 478.19
  - alveolar process 526.5
  - amebic (intestine) 006.9
    - skin 006.6
  - anastomotic — *see* Ulcer, gastrojejunal
  - anorectal 569.41
  - antral — *see* Ulcer, stomach
  - anus (sphincter) (solitary) 569.41
    - varicose — *see* Varicose, ulcer, anus
  - aorta — *see* Aneuysm
  - aphthous (oral) (recurrent) 528.2
    - genital organ(s)
      - female 616.50
      - male 608.89
    - mouth 528.2
  - arm (*see also* Ulcer, skin) 707.8
  - arteriosclerotic plaque — *see* Arteriosclerosis, by site
  - artery NEC 447.2
    - without rupture 447.8
  - atrophic NEC — *see* Ulcer, skin
  - Barrett's (chronic peptic ulcer of esophagus) 530.85
  - bile duct 576.8
  - bladder (solitary) (sphincter) 596.8
    - bilharzial (*see also* Schistosomiasis) 120.9 *[595.4]*
    - submucosal (*see also* Cystitis) 595.1
    - tuberculous (*see also* Tuberculosis) 016.1 ☑
  - bleeding NEC — *see* Ulcer, peptic, with hemorrhage
  - bone 730.9 ☑
  - bowel (*see also* Ulcer, intestine) 569.82
  - breast 611.0
  - bronchitis 491.8
  - bronchus 519.19
  - buccal (cavity) (traumatic) 528.9
  - burn (acute) — *see* Ulcer, duodenum
  - Buruli 031.1
  - buttock (*see also* Ulcer, skin) 707.8
    - decubitus (*see also* Ulcer, ▶pressure◀) 707.00
  - cancerous (M8000/3) — *see* Neoplasm, by site, malignant
  - cardia — *see* Ulcer, stomach
  - cardio-esophageal (peptic) 530.20
    - with bleeding 530.21
  - cecum (*see also* Ulcer, intestine) 569.82
  - cervix (uteri) (trophic) 622.0
    - with mention of cervicitis 616.0
- **Ulcer, ulcerated, ulcerating, ulceration, ulcerative** — *continued*
  - chancroidal 099.0
  - chest (wall) (*see also* Ulcer, skin) 707.8
  - Chiclero 085.4
  - chin (pyogenic) (*see also* Ulcer, skin) 707.8
  - chronic (cause unknown) (*see also* Ulcer, skin)
    - penis 607.89
  - Cochin-China 085.1
  - colitis — *see* Colitis, ulcerative
  - colon (*see also* Ulcer, intestine) 569.82
  - conjunctiva (acute) (postinfectional) 372.00
  - cornea (infectional) 370.00
    - with perforation 370.06
    - annular 370.02
    - catarrhal 370.01
    - central 370.03
    - dendritic 054.42
    - marginal 370.01
    - mycotic 370.05
    - phlyctenular, tuberculous (*see also* Tuberculosis) 017.3 ☑ *[370.31]*
    - ring 370.02
    - rodent 370.07
    - serpent, serpiginous 370.04
    - superficial marginal 370.01
    - tuberculous (*see also* Tuberculosis) 017.3 ☑ *[370.31]*
  - corpus cavernosum (chronic) 607.89
  - crural — *see* Ulcer, lower extremity
  - Curling's — *see* Ulcer, duodenum
  - Cushing's — *see* Ulcer, peptic
  - cystitis (interstitial) 595.1
  - decubitus (unspecified site) ▶(*see also* Ulcer, pressure)◀ 707.00
    - with gangrene 707.00 *[785.4]*
    - ankle 707.06
    - back
      - lower 707.03
      - upper 707.02
    - buttock 707.05
    - elbow 707.01
    - head 707.09
    - heel 707.07
    - hip 707.04
    - other site 707.09
    - sacrum 707.03
    - shoulder blades 707.02
  - dendritic 054.42
  - diabetes, diabetic (mellitus) 250.8 ☑ *[707.9]*
    - due to secondary diabetes ●
      - 249.8 ☑ *[707.9]* ●
    - lower limb 250.8 ☑ *[707.10]*
      - ankle 250.8 ☑ *[707.13]*
        - due to secondary diabetes ●
          - 249.8 ☑ *[707.13]* ●
      - calf 250.8 ☑ *[707.12]*
        - due to secondary diabetes ●
          - 249.8 ☑ *[707.12]* ●
      - due to secondary diabetes ●
        - 249.8 ☑ *[707.10]* ●
      - foot 250.8 ☑ *[707.15]*
        - due to secondary diabetes ●
          - 249.8 ☑ *[707.15]* ●
      - heel 250.8 ☑ *[707.14]*
        - due to secondary diabetes ●
          - 249.8 ☑ *[707.14]* ●
      - knee 250.8 ☑ *[707.19]*
        - due to secondary diabetes ●
          - 249.8 ☑ *[707.19]* ●
      - specified site NEC 250.8 ☑ *[707.19]*
        - due to secondary diabetes ●
          - 249.8 ☑ *[707.19]* ●
      - thigh 250.8 ☑ *[707.11]*
        - due to secondary diabetes ●
          - 249.8 ☑ *[707.11]* ●
      - toes 250.8 ☑ *[707.15]*
        - due to secondary diabetes ●
          - 249.8 ☑ *[707.15]* ●

Ulcer, ulcerated, ulcerating, ulceration, ulcerative — *continued*
  diabetes, diabetic — *continued*
    specified site NEC 250.8 ☑ *[707.8]*
      due to secondary diabetes 249.8 ☑ *[707.8]* ●
  Dieulafoy — *see* Lesion, Dieulafoy
  due to
    infection NEC — *see* Ulcer, skin
    radiation, radium — *see* Ulcer, by site
    trophic disturbance (any region) — *see* Ulcer, skin
    x-ray — *see* Ulcer, by site
  duodenum, duodenal (eroded) (peptic) 532.9 ☑

Note — Use the following fifth-digit subclassification with categories 531–534:

0 without mention of obstruction

1 with obstruction

    with
      hemorrhage (chronic) 532.4 ☑
        and perforation 532.6 ☑
      perforation (chronic) 532.5 ☑
        and hemorrhage 532.6 ☑
    acute 532.3 ☑
      with
        hemorrhage 532.0 ☑
          and perforation 532.2 ☑
        perforation 532.1 ☑
          and hemorrhage 532.2 ☑
    bleeding (recurrent) — *see* Ulcer, duodenum, with hemorrhage
    chronic 532.7 ☑
      with
        hemorrhage 532.4 ☑
          and perforation 532.6 ☑
        perforation 532.5 ☑
          and hemorrhage 532.6 ☑
    penetrating — *see* Ulcer, duodenum, with perforation
    perforating — *see* Ulcer, duodenum, with perforation
  dysenteric NEC 009.0
  elusive 595.1
  endocarditis (any valve) (acute) (chronic) (subacute) 421.0
  enteritis — *see* Colitis, ulcerative
  enterocolitis 556.0
  epiglottis 478.79
  esophagus (peptic) 530.20
    with bleeding 530.21
    due to ingestion
      aspirin 530.20
      chemicals 530.20
      medicinal agents 530.20
    fungal 530.20
    infectional 530.20
    varicose (*see also* Varix, esophagus) 456.1
      bleeding (*see also* Varix, esophagus, bleeding) 456.0
  eye NEC 360.00
    dendritic 054.42
  eyelid (region) 373.01
  face (*see also* Ulcer, skin) 707.8
  fauces 478.29
  Fenwick (-Hunner) (solitary) (*see also* Cystitis) 595.1
  fistulous NEC — *see* Ulcer, skin
  foot (indolent) (*see also* Ulcer, lower extremity) 707.15
    perforating 707.15
      leprous 030.1
      syphilitic 094.0
    trophic 707.15
    varicose 454.0
      inflamed or infected 454.2
  frambesial, initial or primary 102.0
  gallbladder or duct 575.8
  gall duct 576.8
  gangrenous (*see also* Gangrene) 785.4
  gastric — *see* Ulcer, stomach
  gastrocolic — *see* Ulcer, gastrojejunal
  gastroduodenal — *see* Ulcer, peptic
  gastroesophageal — *see* Ulcer, stomach
  gastrohepatic — *see* Ulcer, stomach
  gastrointestinal — *see* Ulcer, gastrojejunal
  gastrojejunal (eroded) (peptic) 534.9 ☑

Note — Use the following fifth-digit subclassification with categories 531–534:

0 without mention of obstruction

1 with obstruction

    with
      hemorrhage (chronic) 534.4 ☑
        and perforation 534.6 ☑
      perforation 534.5 ☑
        and hemorrhage 534.6 ☑
    acute 534.3 ☑
      with
        hemorrhage 534.0 ☑
          and perforation 534.2 ☑
        perforation 534.1 ☑
          and hemorrhage 534.2 ☑
    bleeding (recurrent) — *see* Ulcer, gastrojejunal, with hemorrhage
    chronic 534.7 ☑
      with
        hemorrhage 534.4 ☑
          and perforation 534.6 ☑
        perforation 534.5 ☑
          and hemorrhage 534.6 ☑
    penetrating — *see* Ulcer, gastrojejunal, with perforation
    perforating — *see* Ulcer, gastrojejunal, with perforation
  gastrojejunocolic — *see* Ulcer, gastrojejunal
  genital organ
    female 629.89
    male 608.89
  gingiva 523.8
  gingivitis 523.10
  glottis 478.79
  granuloma of pudenda 099.2
  groin (*see also* Ulcer, skin) 707.8
  gum 523.8
  gumma, due to yaws 102.4
  hand (*see also* Ulcer, skin) 707.8
  hard palate 528.9
  heel (*see also* Ulcer, lower extremity) 707.14
    decubitus (*see also* Ulcer, ▶pressure◀) 707.07
  hemorrhoids 455.8
    external 455.5
    internal 455.2
  hip (*see also* Ulcer, skin) 707.8
    decubitus (*see also* Ulcer, ▶pressure◀) 707.04
  Hunner's 595.1
  hypopharynx 478.29
  hypopyon (chronic) (subacute) 370.04
  hypostaticum — *see* Ulcer, varicose
  ileocolitis 556.1
  ileum (*see also* Ulcer, intestine) 569.82
  intestine, intestinal 569.82
    with perforation 569.83
    amebic 006.9
    duodenal — *see* Ulcer, duodenum
    granulocytopenic (with hemorrhage) 288.09
    marginal 569.82
    perforating 569.83
    small, primary 569.82
    stercoraceous 569.82
    stercoral 569.82
    tuberculous (*see also* Tuberculosis) 014.8 ☑
    typhoid (fever) 002.0
    varicose 456.8
  ischemic 707.9
    lower extremity (*see also* Ulcer, lower extremity) 707.10
      ankle 707.13
      calf 707.12
      foot 707.15
      heel 707.14
      knee 707.19
      specified site NEC 707.19
      thigh 707.11
      toes 707.15
  jejunum, jejunal — *see* Ulcer, gastrojejunal
  keratitis (*see also* Ulcer, cornea) 370.00
  knee — *see* Ulcer, lower extremity
  labium (majus) (minus) 616.50
  laryngitis (*see also* Laryngitis) 464.00
    with obstruction 464.01
  larynx (aphthous) (contact) 478.79
    diphtheritic 032.3
  leg — *see* Ulcer, lower extremity
  lip 528.5
  Lipschütz's 616.50
  lower extremity (atrophic) (chronic) (neurogenic) (perforating) (pyogenic) (trophic) (tropical) 707.10
    with gangrene (*see also* Ulcer, lower extremity) 707.10 *[785.4]*
      arteriosclerotic 440.24
    ankle 707.13
    arteriosclerotic 440.23
      with gangrene 440.24
    calf 707.12
    decubitus ▶(*see also* Ulcer, pressure)◀ 707.00
      with gangrene 707.00 *[785.4]*
      ankle 707.06
      buttock 707.05
      heel 707.07
      hip 707.04
    foot 707.15
    heel 707.14
    knee 707.19
    specified site NEC 707.19
    thigh 707.11
    toes 707.15
    varicose 454.0
      inflamed or infected 454.2
  luetic — *see* Ulcer, syphilitic
  lung 518.89
    tuberculous (*see also* Tuberculosis) 011.2 ☑
  malignant (M8000/3) — *see* Neoplasm, by site, malignant
  marginal NEC — *see* Ulcer, gastrojejunal
  meatus (urinarius) 597.89
  Meckel's diverticulum 751.0
  Meleney's (chronic undermining) 686.09
  Mooren's (cornea) 370.07
  mouth (traumatic) 528.9
  mycobacterial (skin) 031.1
  nasopharynx 478.29
  navel cord (newborn) 771.4
  neck (*see also* Ulcer, skin) 707.8
    uterus 622.0
  neurogenic NEC — *see* Ulcer, skin
  nose, nasal (infectional) (passage) 478.19
    septum 478.19
      varicose 456.8
    skin — *see* Ulcer, skin
    spirochetal NEC 104.8
  oral mucosa (traumatic) 528.9
  palate (soft) 528.9
  penetrating NEC — *see* Ulcer, peptic, with perforation
  penis (chronic) 607.89
  peptic (site unspecified) 533.9 ☑

Note — Use the following fifth-digit subclassification with categories 531–534:

0 without mention of obstruction

1 with obstruction

    with
      hemorrhage 533.4 ☑
        and perforation 533.6 ☑
      perforation (chronic) 533.5 ☑
        and hemorrhage 533.6 ☑
    acute 533.3 ☑
      with
        hemorrhage 533.0 ☑
          and perforation 533.2 ☑
        perforation 533.1 ☑
          and hemorrhage 533.2 ☑
    bleeding (recurrent) — *see* Ulcer, peptic, with hemorrhage
    chronic 533.7 ☑
      with
        hemorrhage 533.4 ☑
          and perforation 533.6 ☑
        perforation 533.5 ☑
          and hemorrhage 533.6 ☑
    penetrating — *see* Ulcer, peptic, with perforation
  perforating NEC (*see also* Ulcer, peptic, with perforation) 533.5 ☑
    skin 707.9
  perineum (*see also* Ulcer, skin) 707.8
  peritonsillar 474.8
  phagedenic (tropical) NEC — *see* Ulcer, skin
  pharynx 478.29
  phlebitis — *see* Phlebitis
  plaster (*see also* Ulcer, ▶pressure◀) 707.00
  popliteal space — *see* Ulcer, lower extremity
  postpyloric — *see* Ulcer, duodenum
  prepuce 607.89
  prepyloric — *see* Ulcer, stomach
  pressure 707.00 ●
    with ●
      abrasion, blister, partial thickness skin loss involving epidermis and/or dermis 707.22 ●
      full thickness skin loss involving damage or necrosis of subcutaneous tissue 707.23 ●
      gangrene 707.00 *[785.4]* ●
      necrosis of soft tissue through to underlying muscle, tendon, or bone 707.24 ●
    ankle 707.06 ●
    back ●
      lower 707.03 ●
      upper 707.02 ●
    buttock 707.05 ●
    elbow 707.01 ●
    head 707.09 ●
    healed — omit code ●
    healing — code to Ulcer, pressure, by stage ●
    heel 707.07 ●
    hip 707.04 ●
    other site 707.09 ●
    sacrum 707.03 ●
    shoulder blades 707.02 ●
    stage ●
      I (healing) 707.21 ●
      II (healing) 707.22 ●
      III (healing) 707.23 ●
      IV (healing) 707.24 ●
      unspecified (healing) 707.20 ●
    unstageable 707.25 ●
  primary of intestine 569.82
    with perforation 569.83
  proctitis 556.2

Ulcer, ulcerated, ulcerating, ulceration, ulcerative — *continued*
- proctitis — *continued*
  - with ulcerative sigmoiditis 556.3
- prostate 601.8
- pseudopeptic — *see* Ulcer, peptic
- pyloric — *see* Ulcer, stomach
- rectosigmoid 569.82
  - with perforation 569.83
- rectum (sphincter) (solitary) 569.41
  - stercoraceous, stercoral 569.41
  - varicose — *see* Varicose, ulcer, anus
- retina (*see also* Chorioretinitis) 363.20
- rodent (M8090/3) (*see also* Neoplasm, skin, malignant)
  - cornea 370.07
- round — *see* Ulcer, stomach
- sacrum (region) (*see also* Ulcer, skin) 707.8
- Saemisch's 370.04
- scalp (*see also* Ulcer, skin) 707.8
- sclera 379.09
- scrofulous (*see also* Tuberculosis) 017.2 ☑
- scrotum 608.89
  - tuberculous (*see also* Tuberculosis) 016.5 ☑
  - varicose 456.4
- seminal vesicle 608.89
- sigmoid 569.82
  - with perforation 569.83
- skin (atrophic) (chronic) (neurogenic) (non-healing) (perforating) (pyogenic) (trophic) 707.9
  - with gangrene 707.9 *[785.4]*
  - amebic 006.6
  - decubitus (*see also* Ulcer, ▶pressure◀) 707.00
    - with gangrene 707.00 *[785.4]*
  - in granulocytopenia 288.09
  - lower extremity (*see also* Ulcer, lower extremity) 707.10
    - with gangrene 707.10 *[785.4]*
      - arteriosclerotic 440.24
    - ankle 707.13
    - arteriosclerotic 440.23
      - with gangrene 440.24
    - calf 707.12
    - foot 707.15
    - heel 707.14
    - knee 707.19
    - specified site NEC 707.19
    - thigh 707.11
    - toes 707.15
  - mycobacterial 031.1
  - syphilitic (early) (secondary) 091.3
  - tuberculous (primary) (*see also* Tuberculosis) 017.0 ☑
  - varicose — *see* Ulcer, varicose
- sloughing NEC — *see* Ulcer, skin
- soft palate 528.9
- solitary, anus or rectum (sphincter) 569.41
- sore throat 462
  - streptococcal 034.0
- spermatic cord 608.89
- spine (tuberculous) 015.0 ☑ *[730.88]*
- stasis (leg) (venous) 454.0
  - with varicose veins 454.0
  - without varicose veins 459.81
  - inflamed or infected 454.2
- stercoral, stercoraceous 569.82
  - with perforation 569.83
  - anus or rectum 569.41
- stomach (eroded) (peptic) (round) 531.9 ☑

Note — Use the following fifth-digit subclassification with categories 531–534:

0	*without mention of obstruction*
1	*with obstruction*

  - with
    - hemorrhage 531.4 ☑

Ulcer, ulcerated, ulcerating, ulceration, ulcerative — *continued*
- stomach — *continued*
  - with — *continued*
    - hemorrhage — *continued*
      - and perforation 531.6 ☑
    - perforation (chronic) 531.5 ☑
      - and hemorrhage 531.6 ☑
  - acute 531.3 ☑
    - with
      - hemorrhage 531.0 ☑
        - and perforation 531.2 ☑
      - perforation 531.1 ☑
        - and hemorrhage 531.2 ☑
  - bleeding (recurrent) — *see* Ulcer, stomach, with hemorrhage
  - chronic 531.7 ☑
    - with
      - hemorrhage 531.4 ☑
        - and perforation 531.6 ☑
      - perforation 531.5 ☑
        - and hemorrhage 531.6 ☑
  - penetrating — *see* Ulcer, stomach, with perforation
  - perforating — *see* Ulcer, stomach, with perforation
- stoma, stomal — *see* Ulcer, gastrojejunal
- stomatitis 528.00
- stress — *see* Ulcer, peptic
- strumous (tuberculous) (*see also* Tuberculosis) 017.2 ☑
- submental (*see also* Ulcer, skin) 707.8
- submucosal, bladder 595.1
- syphilitic (any site) (early) (secondary) 091.3
  - late 095.9
  - perforating 095.9
    - foot 094.0
- testis 608.89
- thigh — *see* Ulcer, lower extremity
- throat 478.29
  - diphtheritic 032.0
- toe — *see* Ulcer, lower extremity
- tongue (traumatic) 529.0
- tonsil 474.8
  - diphtheritic 032.0
- trachea 519.19
- trophic — *see* Ulcer, skin
- tropical NEC (*see also* Ulcer, skin) 707.9
- tuberculous — *see* Tuberculosis, ulcer
- tunica vaginalis 608.89
- turbinate 730.9 ☑
- typhoid (fever) 002.0
  - perforating 002.0
- umbilicus (newborn) 771.4
- unspecified site NEC — *see* Ulcer, skin
- urethra (meatus) (*see also* Urethritis) 597.89
- uterus 621.8
  - cervix 622.0
    - with mention of cervicitis 616.0
  - neck 622.0
    - with mention of cervicitis 616.0
- vagina 616.89
- valve, heart 421.0
- varicose (lower extremity, any part) 454.0
  - anus — *see* Varicose, ulcer, anus
  - broad ligament 456.5
  - esophagus (*see also* Varix, esophagus) 456.1
    - bleeding (*see also* Varix, esophagus, bleeding) 456.0
  - inflamed or infected 454.2
  - nasal septum 456.8
  - perineum 456.6
  - rectum — *see* Varicose, ulcer, anus
  - scrotum 456.4
  - specified site NEC 456.8
  - sublingual 456.3
  - vulva 456.6
- vas deferens 608.89
- vesical (*see also* Ulcer, bladder) 596.8

Ulcer, ulcerated, ulcerating, ulceration, ulcerative — *continued*
- vulva (acute) (infectional) 616.50
  - Behçet's syndrome 136.1 *[616.51]*
  - herpetic 054.12
  - tuberculous 016.7 ☑ *[616.51]*
- vulvobuccal, recurring 616.50
- x-ray — *see* Ulcer, by site
- yaws 102.4

Ulcus — *see also* Ulcer
- cutis tuberculosum (*see also* Tuberculosis) 017.0 ☑
- duodeni — *see* Ulcer, duodenum
- durum 091.0
  - extragenital 091.2
- gastrojejunale — *see* Ulcer, gastrojejunal
- hypostaticum — *see* Ulcer, varicose
- molle (cutis) (skin) 099.0
- serpens corneae (pneumococcal) 370.04
- ventriculi — *see* Ulcer, stomach

Ulegyria 742.4

Ulerythema
- acneiforma 701.8
- centrifugum 695.4
- ophryogenes 757.4

Ullrich-Feichtiger syndrome 759.89

Ullrich (-Bonnevie) (-Turner) syndrome 758.6

Ulnar — *see* condition

Ulorrhagia 523.8

Ulorrhea 523.8

Umbilicus, umbilical — *see also* condition
- cord necrosis, affecting fetus or newborn 762.6

Unacceptable
- existing dental restoration
  - contours 525.65
  - morphology 525.65

Unavailability of medical facilities (at) V63.9
- due to
  - investigation by social service agency V63.8
  - lack of services at home V63.1
  - remoteness from facility V63.0
  - waiting list V63.2
- home V63.1
- outpatient clinic V63.0
- specified reason NEC V63.8

Uncinaria americana infestation 126.1

Uncinariasis — *see also* Ancylostomiasis 126.9

Unconscious, unconsciousness 780.09

Underdevelopment — *see also* Undeveloped
- sexual 259.0

Underfill, endodontic 526.63

Undernourishment 269.9

Undernutrition 269.9

Under observation — *see* Observation

Underweight 783.22
- for gestational age — *see* Light-for-dates

Underwood's disease (sclerema neonatorum) 778.1

Undescended — *see also* Malposition, congenital
- cecum 751.4
- colon 751.4
- testis 752.51

Undetermined diagnosis or cause 799.9

Undeveloped, undevelopment — *see also* Hypoplasia
- brain (congenital) 742.1
- cerebral (congenital) 742.1
- fetus or newborn 764.9 ☑
- heart 746.89
- lung 748.5
- testis 257.2
- uterus 259.0

Undiagnosed (disease) 799.9

Undulant fever — *see also* Brucellosis 023.9

Unemployment, anxiety concerning V62.0

Unequal leg (acquired) (length) 736.81
- congenital 755.30

Unerupted teeth, tooth 520.6

Unextracted dental root 525.3

Unguis incarnatus 703.0

Unicornis uterus 752.3

Unicorporeus uterus 752.3

Uniformis uterus 752.3

Unilateral — *see also* condition
- development, breast 611.89 ▲
- organ or site, congenital NEC — *see* Agenesis
- vagina 752.49

Unilateralis uterus 752.3

Unilocular heart 745.8

Uninhibited bladder 596.54
- with cauda equina syndrome 344.61
- neurogenic — *see also* Neurogenic, bladder 596.54

Union, abnormal — *see also* Fusion
- divided tendon 727.89
- larynx and trachea 748.3

Universal
- joint, cervix 620.6
- mesentery 751.4

Unknown
- cause of death 799.9
- diagnosis 799.9

Unna's disease (seborrheic dermatitis) 690.10

Unresponsiveness, adrenocorticotropin (ACTH) 255.41

Unsatisfactory
- cytology smear ●
  - anal 796.78 ●
  - cervical 795.08 ●
  - vaginal 795.18 ●
- restoration, tooth (existing) 525.60
  - specified NEC 525.69

Unsoundness of mind — *see also* Psychosis 298.9

Unspecified cause of death 799.9

Unstable
- back NEC 724.9
- colon 569.89
- joint — *see* Instability, joint
- lie 652.0 ☑
  - affecting fetus or newborn (before labor) 761.7
  - causing obstructed labor 660.0 ☑
    - affecting fetus or newborn 763.1
- lumbosacral joint (congenital) 756.19
  - acquired 724.6
- sacroiliac 724.6
- spine NEC 724.9

Untruthfulness, child problem — *see also* Disturbance, conduct 312.0 ☑

Unverricht (-Lundborg) disease, syndrome, or epilepsy 333.2

Unverricht-Wagner syndrome (dermatomyositis) 710.3

Upper respiratory — *see* condition

Upset
- gastric 536.8
  - psychogenic 306.4
- gastrointestinal 536.8
  - psychogenic 306.4
  - virus (*see also* Enteritis, viral) 008.8
- intestinal (large) (small) 564.9
  - psychogenic 306.4
- menstruation 626.9
- mental 300.9
- stomach 536.8
  - psychogenic 306.4

Urachus — *see also* condition
- patent 753.7
- persistent 753.7

Uratic arthritis 274.0

Urbach's lipoid proteinosis 272.8

Urbach-Oppenheim disease or syndrome (necrobiosis lipoidica diabeticorum) 250.8 ☑ *[709.3]*

☑ Additional Digit Required — Refer to the Tabular List for Digit Selection

Subterms under main terms may continue to next column or page

▶◀ Revised Text ● New Line ▲ Revised Code

Urbach-Oppenheim disease or syndrome — *continued*
due to secondary diabetes ●
249.8 ☑ *[709.3]* ●
Urbach-Wiethe disease or syndrome (lipoid proteinosis) 272.8
Urban yellow fever 060.1
Urea, blood, high — *see* Uremia
Uremia, uremic (absorption) (amaurosis) (amblyopia) (aphasia) (apoplexy) (coma) (delirium) (dementia) (dropsy) (dyspnea) (fever) (intoxication) (mania) (paralysis) (poisoning) (toxemia) (vomiting) 586
with
abortion — *see* Abortion, by type, with renal failure
ectopic pregnancy (*see also* categories 633.0–633.9) 639.3
hypertension (*see also* Hypertension, kidney) 403.91
molar pregnancy (*see also* categories 630–632) 639.3
chronic 585.9
complicating
abortion 639.3
ectopic or molar pregnancy 639.3
hypertension (*see also* Hypertension, kidney) 403.91
labor and delivery 669.3 ☑
congenital 779.89
extrarenal 788.99 ▲
hypertensive (chronic) (*see also* Hypertension, kidney) 403.91
maternal NEC, affecting fetus or newborn 760.1
neuropathy 585.9 *[357.4]*
pericarditis 585.9 *[420.0]*
prerenal 788.99 ▲
pyelitic (*see also* Pyelitis) 590.80
Ureteralgia 788.0
Ureterectasis 593.89
Ureteritis 593.89
cystica 590.3
due to calculus 592.1
gonococcal (acute) 098.19
chronic or duration of 2 months or over 098.39
nonspecific 593.89
Ureterocele (acquired) 593.89
congenital 753.23
Ureterolith 592.1
Ureterolithiasis 592.1
Ureterostomy status V44.6
with complication 997.5
Ureter, ureteral — *see* condition
Urethralgia 788.99 ▲
Urethra, urethral — *see* condition
Urethritis (abacterial) (acute) (allergic) (anterior) (chronic) (nonvenereal) (posterior) (recurrent) (simple) (subacute) (ulcerative) (undifferentiated) 597.80
diplococcal (acute) 098.0
chronic or duration of 2 months or over 098.2
due to Trichomonas (vaginalis) 131.02
gonococcal (acute) 098.0

Urethritis — *continued*
gonococcal — *continued*
chronic or duration of 2 months or over 098.2
nongonococcal (sexually transmitted) 099.40
Chlamydia trachomatis 099.41
Reiter's 099.3
specified organism NEC 099.49
nonspecific (sexually transmitted) (*see also* Urethritis, nongonococcal) 099.40
not sexually transmitted 597.80
Reiter's 099.3
trichomonal or due to Trichomonas (vaginalis) 131.02
tuberculous (*see also* Tuberculosis) 016.3 ☑
venereal NEC (*see also* Urethritis, nongonococcal) 099.40
Urethrocele
female 618.03
with uterine prolapse 618.4
complete 618.3
incomplete 618.2
male 599.5
Urethrolithiasis 594.2
Urethro-oculoarticular syndrome 099.3
Urethro-oculosynovial syndrome 099.3
Urethrorectal — *see* condition
Urethrorrhagia 599.84
Urethrorrhea 788.7
Urethrostomy status V44.6
with complication 997.5
Urethrotrigonitis 595.3
Urethrovaginal — *see* condition
Urhidrosis, uridrosis 705.89
Uric acid
diathesis 274.9
in blood 790.6
Uricacidemia 790.6
Uricemia 790.6
Uricosuria 791.9
Urination
frequent 788.41
painful 788.1
urgency 788.63
Urinemia — *see* Uremia
Urine, urinary — *see also* condition
abnormality NEC 788.69
blood in (*see also* Hematuria) 599.70 ▲
discharge, excessive 788.42
enuresis 788.30
nonorganic origin 307.6
extravasation 788.8
frequency 788.41
hesitancy 788.64
incontinence 788.30
active 788.30
female 788.30
stress 625.6
and urge 788.33
male 788.30
stress 788.32
and urge 788.33
mixed (stress and urge) 788.33
neurogenic 788.39
nonorganic origin 307.6

Urine, urinary — *see also* condition — *continued*
incontinence — *continued*
overflow 788.38
stress (female) 625.6
male NEC 788.32
intermittent stream 788.61
pus in 791.9
retention or stasis NEC 788.20
bladder, incomplete emptying 788.21
psychogenic 306.53
specified NEC 788.29
secretion
deficient 788.5
excessive 788.42
frequency 788.41
strain 788.65
stream
intermittent 788.61
slowing 788.62
splitting 788.61
weak 788.62
urgency 788.63
Urinoma NEC 599.9
bladder 596.8
kidney 593.89
renal 593.89
ureter 593.89
urethra 599.84
Uroarthritis, infectious 099.3
Urodialysis 788.5
Urolithiasis 592.9
Uronephrosis 593.89
Uropathy 599.9
obstructive 599.60
Urosepsis 599.0
meaning sepsis 995.91
meaning urinary tract infection 599.0
Urticaria 708.9
with angioneurotic edema 995.1
hereditary 277.6
allergic 708.0
cholinergic 708.5
chronic 708.8
cold, familial 708.2
dermatographic 708.3
due to
cold or heat 708.2
drugs 708.0
food 708.0
inhalants 708.0
plants 708.8
serum 999.5
factitial 708.3
giant 995.1
hereditary 277.6
gigantea 995.1
hereditary 277.6
idiopathic 708.1
larynx 995.1
hereditary 277.6
neonatorum 778.8
nonallergic 708.1
papulosa (Hebra) 698.2
perstans hemorrhagica 757.39
pigmentosa 757.33
recurrent periodic 708.8
serum 999.5

Urticaria — *continued*
solare 692.72
specified type NEC 708.8
thermal (cold) (heat) 708.2
vibratory 708.4
Urticarioides acarodermatitis 133.9
Use of
methadone 304.00 ●
nonprescribed drugs (*see also* Abuse, drugs, nondependent) 305.9 ☑
patent medicines (*see also* Abuse, drugs, nondependent) 305.9 ☑
Usher-Senear disease (pemphigus erythematosus) 694.4
Uta 085.5
Uterine size-date discrepancy 649.6 ☑
Uteromegaly 621.2
Uterovaginal — *see* condition
Uterovesical — *see* condition
Uterus — *see* condition
Utriculitis (utriculus prostaticus) 597.89
Uveal — *see* condition
Uveitis (anterior) — *see also* Iridocyclitis 364.3
acute or subacute 364.00
due to or associated with
gonococcal infection 098.41
herpes (simplex) 054.44
zoster 053.22
primary 364.01
recurrent 364.02
secondary (noninfectious) 364.04
infectious 364.03
allergic 360.11
chronic 364.10
due to or associated with
sarcoidosis 135 *[364.11]*
tuberculosis (*see also* Tuberculosis) 017.3 ☑ *[364.11]*
due to
operation 360.11
toxoplasmosis (acquired) 130.2
congenital (active) 771.2
granulomatous 364.10
heterochromic 364.21
lens-induced 364.23
nongranulomatous 364.00
posterior 363.20
disseminated — *see* Chorioretinitis, disseminated
focal — *see* Chorioretinitis, focal
recurrent 364.02
sympathetic 360.11
syphilitic (secondary) 091.50
congenital 090.0 *[363.13]*
late 095.8 *[363.13]*
tuberculous (*see also* Tuberculosis) 017.3 ☑ *[364.11]*
Uveoencephalitis 363.22
Uveokeratitis — *see also* Iridocyclitis 364.3
Uveoparotid fever 135
Uveoparotitis 135
Uvula — *see* condition
Uvulitis (acute) (catarrhal) (chronic) (gangrenous) (membranous) (suppurative) (ulcerative) 528.3

V

Vaccination
complication or reaction — *see* Complications, vaccination
delayed V64.00 ●
not carried out V64.00
because of
acute illness V64.01
allergy to vaccine or component V64.04
caregiver refusal V64.05
chronic illness V64.02
guardian refusal V64.05
immune compromised state V64.03
parent refusal V64.05
patient had disease being vaccinated against V64.08
patient refusal V64.06
reason NEC V64.09
religious reasons V64.07
prophylactic (against) V05.9
arthropod-borne viral
disease NEC V05.1
encephalitis V05.0
chickenpox V05.4
cholera (alone) V03.0
with typhoid-paratyphoid (cholera + TAB) V06.0
common cold V04.7
diphtheria (alone) V03.5
with
poliomyelitis (DTP+ polio) V06.3
tetanus V06.5
pertussis combined (DTP) (DTaP) V06.1
typhoid-paratyphoid (DTP + TAB) V06.2
disease (single) NEC V05.9
bacterial NEC V03.9
specified type NEC V03.89
combination NEC V06.9
specified type NEC V06.8
specified type NEC V05.8
encephalitis, viral, arthropod-borne V05.0
Hemophilus influenzae, type B [Hib] V03.81
hepatitis, viral V05.3
influenza V04.81
with
Streptococcus pneumoniae [pneumococcus] V06.6
leishmaniasis V05.2
measles (alone) V04.2
with mumps-rubella (MMR) V06.4
mumps (alone) V04.6
with measles and rubella (MMR) V06.4
pertussis alone V03.6
plague V03.3
poliomyelitis V04.0
with diphtheria-tetanus-pertussis (DTP + polio) V06.3
rabies V04.5
respiratory syncytial virus (RSV) V04.82
rubella (alone) V04.3
with measles and mumps (MMR) V06.4
smallpox V04.1
Streptococcus pneumoniae [pneumococcus] V03.82
with
influenza V06.6
tetanus toxoid (alone) V03.7
with diphtheria [Td] [DT] V06.5
with
pertussis (DTP) (DTaP) V06.1
with poliomyelitis (DTP+polio) V06.3
tuberculosis (BCG) V03.2

Vaccination — *continued*
prophylactic — *continued*
tularemia V03.4
typhoid-paratyphoid (TAB) (alone) V03.1
with diphtheria-tetanus-pertussis (TAB + DTP) V06.2
varicella V05.4
viral
disease NEC V04.89
encephalitis, arthropod-borne V05.0
hepatitis V05.3
yellow fever V04.4
Vaccinia (generalized) 999.0
without vaccination 051.02 ▲
congenital 771.2
conjunctiva 999.39
eyelids 999.0 *[373.5]*
localized 999.39
nose 999.39
not from vaccination 051.02 ▲
eyelid 051.02 *[373.5]* ▲
sine vaccinatione 051.02 ▲
Vacuum
extraction of fetus or newborn 763.3
in sinus (accessory) (nasal) (*see also* Sinusitis) 473.9
Vagabond V60.0
Vagabondage V60.0
Vagabonds' disease 132.1
Vaginalitis (tunica) 608.4
Vagina, vaginal — *see* ▶*also*◀ condition
high risk human papillomavirus (HPV) DNA test positive 795.15 ●
low risk human papillomavirus (HPV) DNA test positive 795.19 ●
Vaginismus (reflex) 625.1
functional 306.51
hysterical 300.11
psychogenic 306.51
Vaginitis (acute) (chronic) (circumscribed) (diffuse) (emphysematous) (Hemophilus vaginalis) (nonspecific) (nonvenereal) (ulcerative) 616.10
with
abortion — *see* Abortion, by type, with sepsis
ectopic pregnancy (*see also* categories 633.0–633.9) 639.0
molar pregnancy (*see also* categories 630–632) 639.0
adhesive, congenital 752.49
atrophic, postmenopausal 627.3
bacterial 616.10
blennorrhagic (acute) 098.0
chronic or duration of 2 months or over 098.2
candidal 112.1
chlamydial 099.53
complicating pregnancy or puerperium 646.6 ☑
affecting fetus or newborn 760.8
congenital (adhesive) 752.49
due to
C. albicans 112.1
Trichomonas (vaginalis) 131.01
following
abortion 639.0
ectopic or molar pregnancy 639.0
gonococcal (acute) 098.0
chronic or duration of 2 months or over 098.2
granuloma 099.2
Monilia 112.1
mycotic 112.1
pinworm 127.4 *[616.11]*
postirradiation 616.10
postmenopausal atrophic 627.3
senile (atrophic) 627.3
syphilitic (early) 091.0
late 095.8
trichomonal 131.01
tuberculous (*see also* Tuberculosis) 016.7 ☑
venereal NEC 099.8

Vaginosis — *see* Vaginitis
Vagotonia 352.3
Vagrancy V60.0
VAIN I (vaginal intraepithelial neoplasia I) 623.0
VAIN II (vaginal intraepithelial neoplasia II) 623.0
VAIN III (vaginal intraepithelial neoplasia III) 233.31
Vallecula — *see* condition
Valley fever 114.0
Valsuani's disease (progressive pernicious anemia, puerperal) 648.2 ☑
Valve, valvular (formation) — *see also* condition
cerebral ventricle (communicating) in situ V45.2
cervix, internal os 752.49
colon 751.5
congenital NEC — *see* Atresia
formation, congenital NEC — *see* Atresia
heart defect — *see* Anomaly, heart, valve
ureter 753.29
pelvic junction 753.21
vesical orifice 753.22
urethra 753.6
Valvulitis (chronic) — *see also* Endocarditis 424.90
rheumatic (chronic) (inactive) (with chorea) 397.9
active or acute (aortic) (mitral) (pulmonary) (tricuspid) 391.1
syphilitic NEC 093.20
aortic 093.22
mitral 093.21
pulmonary 093.24
tricuspid 093.23
Valvulopathy — *see* Endocarditis
van Bogaert-Nijssen (-Peiffer) disease 330.0
van Bogaert's leukoencephalitis (sclerosing) (subacute) 046.2
van Buchem's syndrome (hyperostosis corticalis) 733.3
Vancomycin (glycopeptide)
intermediate staphylococcus aureus (VISA/GISA) V09.8 ☑
resistant
enterococcus (VRE) V09.8 ☑
staphylococcus aureus (VRSA/GRSA) V09.8 ☑
van Creveld-von Gierke disease (glycogenosis I) 271.0
van den Bergh's disease (enterogenous cyanosis) 289.7
van der Hoeve-Halbertsma-Waardenburg syndrome (ptosis-epicanthus) 270.2
van der Hoeve-Waardenburg-Gualdi syndrome (ptosis epicanthus) 270.2
van der Hoeve's syndrome (brittle bones and blue sclera, deafness) 756.51
Vanillism 692.89
Vanishing lung 492.0
Vanishing twin 651.33
van Neck (-Odelberg) disease or syndrome (juvenile osteochondrosis) 732.1
Vapor asphyxia or suffocation NEC 987.9
specified agent — *see* Table of Drugs and Chemicals
Vaquez's disease (M9950/1) 238.4
Vaquez-Osler disease (polycythemia vera) (M9950/1) 238.4
Variance, lethal ball, prosthetic heart valve 996.02
Variants, thalassemic 282.49
Variations in hair color 704.3
Varicella 052.9
with
complication 052.8
specified NEC 052.7

Varicella — *continued*
with — *continued*
pneumonia 052.1
vaccination and inoculation (prophylactic) V05.4
exposure to V01.71
vaccination and inoculation (against) (prophylactic) V05.4
Varices — *see* Varix
Varicocele (scrotum) (thrombosed) 456.4
ovary 456.5
perineum 456.6
spermatic cord (ulcerated) 456.4
Varicose
aneurysm (ruptured) (*see also* Aneurysm) 442.9
dermatitis (lower extremity) — *see* Varicose, vein, inflamed or infected
eczema — *see* Varicose, vein
phlebitis — *see* Varicose, vein, inflamed or infected
placental vessel — *see* Placenta, abnormal
tumor — *see* Varicose, vein
ulcer (lower extremity, any part) 454.0
anus 455.8
external 455.5
internal 455.2
esophagus (*see also* Varix, esophagus) 456.1
bleeding (*see also* Varix, esophagus, bleeding) 456.0
inflamed or infected 454.2
nasal septum 456.8
perineum 456.6
rectum — *see* Varicose, ulcer, anus
scrotum 456.4
specified site NEC 456.8
vein (lower extremity) (ruptured) (*see also* Varix) 454.9
with
complications NEC 454.8
edema 454.8
inflammation or infection 454.1
ulcerated 454.2
pain 454.8
stasis dermatitis 454.1
with ulcer 454.2
swelling 454.8
ulcer 454.0
inflamed or infected 454.2
anus — *see* Hemorrhoids
broad ligament 456.5
congenital (peripheral) 747.60
gastrointestinal 747.61
lower limb 747.64
renal 747.62
specified NEC 747.69
upper limb 747.63
esophagus (ulcerated) (*see also* Varix, esophagus) 456.1
bleeding (*see also* Varix, esophagus, bleeding) 456.0
inflamed or infected 454.1
with ulcer 454.2
in pregnancy or puerperium 671.0 ☑
vulva or perineum 671.1 ☑
nasal septum (with ulcer) 456.8
pelvis 456.5
perineum 456.6
in pregnancy, childbirth, or puerperium 671.1 ☑
rectum — *see* Hemorrhoids
scrotum (ulcerated) 456.4
specified site NEC 456.8
sublingual 456.3
ulcerated 454.0
inflamed or infected 454.2
umbilical cord, affecting fetus or newborn 762.6
urethra 456.8
vulva 456.6
in pregnancy, childbirth, or puerperium 671.1 ☑

- **Varicose** — *continued*
  - vessel (*see also* Varix)
    - placenta — *see* Placenta, abnormal
- **Varicosis, varicosities, varicosity** — *see also* Varix 454.9
- **Variola** 050.9
  - hemorrhagic (pustular) 050.0
  - major 050.0
  - minor 050.1
  - modified 050.2
- **Varioloid** 050.2
- **Variolosa, purpura** 050.0
- **Varix** (lower extremity) (ruptured) 454.9
  - with
    - complications NEC 454.8
    - edema 454.8
    - inflammation or infection 454.1
      - with ulcer 454.2
    - pain 454.8
    - stasis dermatitis 454.1
      - with ulcer 454.2
    - swelling 454.8
    - ulcer 454.0
      - with inflammation or infection 454.2
  - aneurysmal (*see also* Aneurysm) 442.9
  - anus — *see* Hemorrhoids
  - arteriovenous (congenital) (peripheral) NEC 747.60
    - gastrointestinal 747.61
    - lower limb 747.64
    - renal 747.62
    - specified NEC 747.69
    - spinal 747.82
    - upper limb 747.63
  - bladder 456.5
  - broad ligament 456.5
  - congenital (peripheral) 747.60
  - esophagus (ulcerated) 456.1
    - bleeding 456.0
      - in
        - cirrhosis of liver 571.5 *[456.20]*
        - portal hypertension 572.3 *[456.20]*
    - congenital 747.69
      - in
        - cirrhosis of liver 571.5 *[456.21]*
          - with bleeding 571.5 *[456.20]*
        - portal hypertension 572.3 *[456.21]*
          - with bleeding 572.3 *[456.20]*
  - gastric 456.8
  - inflamed or infected 454.1
    - ulcerated 454.2
  - in pregnancy or puerperium 671.0 ☑
    - perineum 671.1 ☑
    - vulva 671.1 ☑
  - labia (majora) 456.6
  - orbit 456.8
    - congenital 747.69
  - ovary 456.5
  - papillary 448.1
  - pelvis 456.5
  - perineum 456.6
    - in pregnancy or puerperium 671.1 ☑
  - pharynx 456.8
  - placenta — *see* Placenta, abnormal
  - prostate 456.8
  - rectum — *see* Hemorrhoids
  - renal papilla 456.8
  - retina 362.17
  - scrotum (ulcerated) 456.4
  - sigmoid colon 456.8
  - specified site NEC 456.8
  - spinal (cord) (vessels) 456.8
  - spleen, splenic (vein) (with phlebolith) 456.8
  - sublingual 456.3
  - ulcerated 454.0
    - inflamed or infected 454.2
- **Varix** — *continued*
  - umbilical cord, affecting fetus or newborn 762.6
  - uterine ligament 456.5
  - vocal cord 456.8
  - vulva 456.6
    - in pregnancy, childbirth, or puerperium 671.1 ☑
- **Vasa previa** 663.5 ☑
  - affecting fetus or newborn 762.6
  - hemorrhage from, affecting fetus or newborn 772.0
- **Vascular** — *see also* condition
  - loop on papilla (optic) 743.57
  - sheathing, retina 362.13
  - spasm 443.9
  - spider 448.1
- **Vascularity, pulmonary, congenital** 747.3
- **Vascularization**
  - choroid 362.16
  - cornea 370.60
    - deep 370.63
    - localized 370.61
  - retina 362.16
  - subretinal 362.16
- **Vasculitis** 447.6
  - allergic 287.0
  - cryoglobulinemic 273.2
  - disseminated 447.6
  - kidney 447.8
  - leukocytoclastic 446.29
  - nodular 695.2
  - retinal 362.18
  - rheumatic — *see* Fever, rheumatic
- **Vasculopathy**
  - cardiac allograft 996.83
- **Vas deferens** — *see* condition
- **Vas deferentitis** 608.4
- **Vasectomy, admission for** V25.2
- **Vasitis** 608.4
  - nodosa 608.4
  - scrotum 608.4
  - spermatic cord 608.4
  - testis 608.4
  - tuberculous (*see also* Tuberculosis) 016.5 ☑
  - tunica vaginalis 608.4
  - vas deferens 608.4
- **Vasodilation** 443.9
- **Vasomotor** — *see* condition
- **Vasoplasty, after previous sterilization** V26.0
- **Vasoplegia, splanchnic** — *see also* Neuropathy, peripheral, autonomic 337.9
- **Vasospasm** 443.9
  - cerebral (artery) 435.9
    - with transient neurologic deficit 435.9
  - coronary 413.1
  - nerve
    - arm NEC 354.9
    - autonomic 337.9
    - brachial plexus 353.0
    - cervical plexus 353.2
    - leg NEC 355.8
    - lower extremity NEC 355.8
    - peripheral NEC 355.9
    - spinal NEC 355.9
    - sympathetic 337.9
    - upper extremity NEC 354.9
  - peripheral NEC 443.9
  - retina (artery) (*see also* Occlusion, retinal, artery) 362.30
- **Vasospastic** — *see* condition
- **Vasovagal attack** (paroxysmal) 780.2
  - psychogenic 306.2
- **Vater's ampulla** — *see* condition
- **VATER syndrome** 759.89
- **vCJD** (variant Creutzfeldt-Jakob disease) 046.11 ●
- **Vegetation, vegetative**
  - adenoid (nasal fossa) 474.2
  - consciousness (persistent) 780.03
- **Vegetation, vegetative** — *continued*
  - endocarditis (acute) (any valve) (chronic) (subacute) 421.0
  - heart (mycotic) (valve) 421.0
  - state (persistent) 780.03
- **Veil**
  - Jackson's 751.4
  - over face (causing asphyxia) 768.9
- **Vein, venous** — *see* condition
- **Veldt sore** — *see also* Ulcer, skin 707.9
- **Velo-cardio-facial syndrome** 758.32
- **Velpeau's hernia** — *see* Hernia, femoral
- **Venereal**
  - balanitis NEC 099.8
  - bubo 099.1
  - disease 099.9
    - specified nature or type NEC 099.8
  - granuloma inguinale 099.2
  - lymphogranuloma (Durand-Nicolas-Favre), any site 099.1
  - salpingitis 098.37
  - urethritis (*see also* Urethritis, nongonococcal) 099.40
  - vaginitis NEC 099.8
  - warts 078.11 ▲
- **Vengefulness, in child** — *see also* Disturbance, conduct 312.0 ☑
- **Venofibrosis** 459.89
- **Venom, venomous**
  - bite or sting (animal or insect) 989.5
  - poisoning 989.5
- **Venous** — *see* condition
- **Ventouse delivery** NEC 669.5 ☑
  - affecting fetus or newborn 763.3
- **Ventral** — *see* condition
- **Ventricle, ventricular** — *see also* condition
  - escape 427.69
  - standstill (*see also* Arrest, cardiac) 427.5
- **Ventriculitis, cerebral** — *see also* Meningitis 322.9
- **Ventriculostomy status** V45.2
- **Verbiest's syndrome** (claudicatio intermittens spinalis) 435.1
- **Vernet's syndrome** 352.6
- **Verneuil's disease** (syphilitic bursitis) 095.7
- **Verruca** (filiformis) 078.10
  - acuminata (any site) 078.11
  - necrogenica (primary) (*see also* Tuberculosis) 017.0 ☑
  - peruana 088.0
  - peruviana 088.0
  - plana (juvenilis) 078.19
  - plantaris 078.12 ▲
  - seborrheica 702.19
    - inflamed 702.11
  - senilis 702.0
  - tuberculosa (primary) (*see also* Tuberculosis) 017.0 ☑
  - venereal 078.11 ▲
  - viral 078.10
    - specified NEC 078.19 ●
  - vulgaris 078.10 ●
- **Verrucosities** — *see also* Verruca 078.10
- **Verrucous endocarditis** (acute) (any valve) (chronic) (subacute) 710.0 *[424.91]*
  - nonbacterial 710.0 *[424.91]*
- **Verruga**
  - peruana 088.0
  - peruviana 088.0
- **Verse's disease** (calcinosis intervertebralis) 275.49 *[722.90]*
- **Version**
  - before labor, affecting fetus or newborn 761.7
  - cephalic (correcting previous malposition) 652.1 ☑
    - affecting fetus or newborn 763.1
  - cervix — *see* Version, uterus
  - uterus (postinfectional) (postpartal, old) (*see also* Malposition, uterus) 621.6
    - forward — *see* Anteversion, uterus
- **Version** — *continued*
  - uterus (*see also* Malposition, uterus) — *continued*
    - lateral — *see* Lateroversion, uterus
- **Vertebra, vertebral** — *see* condition
- **Vertigo** 780.4
  - auditory 386.19
  - aural 386.19
  - benign paroxysmal positional 386.11
  - central origin 386.2
  - cerebral 386.2
  - Dix and Hallpike (epidemic) 386.12
  - endemic paralytic 078.81
  - epidemic 078.81
    - Dix and Hallpike 386.12
    - Gerlier's 078.81
    - Pedersen's 386.12
    - vestibular neuronitis 386.12
  - epileptic — *see* Epilepsy
  - Gerlier's (epidemic) 078.81
  - hysterical 300.11
  - labyrinthine 386.10
  - laryngeal 786.2
  - malignant positional 386.2
  - Ménière's (*see also* Disease, Ménière's) 386.00
  - menopausal 627.2
  - otogenic 386.19
  - paralytic 078.81
  - paroxysmal positional, benign 386.11
  - Pedersen's (epidemic) 386.12
  - peripheral 386.10
    - specified type NEC 386.19
  - positional
    - benign paroxysmal 386.11
    - malignant 386.2
- **Verumontanitis** (chronic) — *see also* Urethritis 597.89
- **Vesania** — *see also* Psychosis 298.9
- **Vesical** — *see* condition
- **Vesicle**
  - cutaneous 709.8
  - seminal — *see* condition
  - skin 709.8
- **Vesicocolic** — *see* condition
- **Vesicoperineal** — *see* condition
- **Vesicorectal** — *see* condition
- **Vesicourethrorectal** — *see* condition
- **Vesicovaginal** — *see* condition
- **Vesicular** — *see* condition
- **Vesiculitis** (seminal) 608.0
  - amebic 006.8
  - gonorrheal (acute) 098.14
    - chronic or duration of 2 months or over 098.34
  - trichomonal 131.09
  - tuberculous (*see also* Tuberculosis) 016.5 ☑ *[608.81]*
- **Vestibulitis** (ear) — *see also* Labyrinthitis 386.30
  - nose (external) 478.19
  - vulvar 625.71 ▲
- **Vestibulopathy, acute peripheral** (recurrent) 386.12
- **Vestige, vestigial** — *see also* Persistence
  - branchial 744.41
  - structures in vitreous 743.51
- **Vibriosis NEC** 027.9
- **Vidal's disease** (lichen simplex chronicus) 698.3
- **Video display tube syndrome** 723.8
- **Vienna-type encephalitis** 049.8
- **Villaret's syndrome** 352.6
- **Villous** — *see* condition
- **VIN I** (vulvar intraepithelial neoplasia I) 624.01
- **VIN II** (vulvar intraepithelial neoplasia II) 624.02
- **VIN III** (vulvar intraepithelial neoplasia III) 233.32
- **Vincent's**
  - angina 101
  - bronchitis 101
  - disease 101
  - gingivitis 101
  - infection (any site) 101

☑ Additional Digit Required — Refer to the Tabular List for Digit Selection

▽ Subterms under main terms may continue to next column or page

▶◀ Revised Text ● New Line ▲ Revised Code

Vincent's — *continued*
  laryngitis 101
  stomatitis 101
  tonsillitis 101
Vinson-Plummer syndrome (sideropenic dysphagia) 280.8
Viosterol deficiency — *see also* Deficiency, calciferol 268.9
Virchow's disease 733.99
Viremia 790.8
Virilism (adrenal) (female) NEC 255.2
  with
    3-beta-hydroxysteroid dehydrogenase defect 255.2
    11-hydroxylase defect 255.2
    21-hydroxylase defect 255.2
    adrenal
      hyperplasia 255.2
      insufficiency (congenital) 255.2
    cortical hyperfunction 255.2
Virilization (female) (suprarenal) — *see also* Virilism 255.2
  isosexual 256.4
Virulent bubo 099.0
Virus, viral — *see also* condition
  infection NEC (*see also* Infection, viral) 079.99
  septicemia 079.99
  yaba monkey tumor 059.22 ●
VISA (vancomycin intermediate staphylococcus aureus) V09.8 ☑
Viscera, visceral — *see* condition
Visceroptosis 569.89
Visible peristalsis 787.4
Vision, visual
  binocular, suppression 368.31
  blurred, blurring 368.8
    hysterical 300.11
  defect, defective (*see also* Impaired, vision) 369.9
  disorientation (syndrome) 368.16
  disturbance NEC (*see also* Disturbance, vision) 368.9
    hysterical 300.11
  examination V72.0
  field, limitation 368.40
  fusion, with defective steropsis 368.33
  hallucinations 368.16
  halos 368.16
  loss 369.9
    both eyes (*see also* Blindness, both eyes) 369.3
    complete (*see also* Blindness, both eyes) 369.00
    one eye 369.8
    sudden 368.16
  low (both eyes) 369.20
    one eye (other eye normal) (*see also* Impaired, vision) 369.70
      blindness, other eye 369.10
  perception, simultaneous without fusion 368.32
  tunnel 368.45
Vitality, lack or want of 780.79
  newborn 779.89
Vitamin deficiency NEC — *see also* Deficiency, vitamin 269.2
Vitelline duct, persistent 751.0
Vitiligo 709.01
  due to pinta (carate) 103.2
  eyelid 374.53
  vulva 624.8
Vitium cordis — *see* Disease, heart
Vitreous — *see also* condition
  touch syndrome 997.99
VLCAD (long chain/very long chain acyl CoA dehydrogenase deficiency, LCAD) 277.85
Vocal cord — *see* condition
Vocational rehabilitation V57.22
Vogt's (Cecile) disease or syndrome 333.7 ☑
Vogt-Koyanagi syndrome 364.24
Vogt-Spielmeyer disease (amaurotic familial idiocy) 330.1
Voice
  change (*see also* Dysphonia) 784.49
  loss (*see also* Aphonia) 784.41
Volhard-Fahr disease (malignant nephrosclerosis) 403.00
Volhynian fever 083.1
Volkmann's ischemic contracture or paralysis (complicating trauma) 958.6
Voluntary starvation 307.1
Volvulus (bowel) (colon) (intestine) 560.2
  with
    hernia (*see also* Hernia, by site, with obstruction)
      gangrenous — *see* Hernia, by site, with gangrene
    perforation 560.2
  congenital 751.5
  duodenum 537.3
  fallopian tube 620.5
  oviduct 620.5
  stomach (due to absence of gastrocolic ligament) 537.89
Vomiting 787.03
  with nausea 787.01
  allergic 535.4 ☑
  asphyxia 933.1
  bilious (cause unknown) 787.0 ☑
    following gastrointestinal surgery 564.3
  blood (*see also* Hematemesis) 578.0
  causing asphyxia, choking, or suffocation (*see also* Asphyxia, food) 933.1
  cyclical 536.2
    associated with migraine 346.2 ☑●
    psychogenic 306.4
  epidemic 078.82
  fecal matter 569.89
  following gastrointestinal surgery 564.3
  functional 536.8
    psychogenic 306.4
  habit 536.2
  hysterical 300.11
  nervous 306.4
  neurotic 306.4
  newborn 779.3
  of or complicating pregnancy 643.9 ☑
    due to
      organic disease 643.8 ☑
      specific cause NEC 643.8 ☑
    early — *see* Hyperemesis, gravidarum
    late (after 22 completed weeks of gestation) 643.2 ☑
  pernicious or persistent 536.2
    complicating pregnancy — *see* Hyperemesis, gravidarum
    psychogenic 306.4
  physiological 787.0 ☑
  psychic 306.4
  psychogenic 307.54
  stercoral 569.89
  uncontrollable 536.2
    psychogenic 306.4
  uremic — *see* Uremia
  winter 078.82
von Bechterew (-Strumpell) disease or syndrome (ankylosing spondylitis) 720.0
von Bezold's abscess 383.01
von Economo's disease (encephalitis lethargica) 049.8
von Eulenburg's disease (congenital paramyotonia) 359.29
von Gierke's disease (glycogenosis I) 271.0
von Gies' joint 095.8
von Graefe's disease or syndrome 378.72
von Hippel (-Lindau) disease or syndrome (retinocerebral angiomatosis) 759.6
von Jaksch's anemia or disease (pseudoleukemia infantum) 285.8
von Recklinghausen-Applebaum disease (hemochromatosis) 275.0
von Recklinghausen's
  disease or syndrome (nerves) (skin) (M9540/1) 237.71
    bones (osteitis fibrosa cystica) 252.01
  tumor (M9540/1) 237.71
von Schroetter's syndrome (intermittent venous claudication) 453.8
von Willebrand (-Jürgens) (-Minot) disease or syndrome (angiohemophilia) 286.4
von Zambusch's disease (lichen sclerosus et atrophicus) 701.0
Voorhoeve's disease or dyschondroplasia 756.4
Vossius' ring 921.3
  late effect 366.21
Voyeurism 302.82
VRE (vancomycin resistant enterococcus) V09.8 ☑
Vrolik's disease (osteogenesis imperfecta) 756.51
VRSA (vancomycin resistant staphylococcus aureus) V09.8 ☑
Vulva — *see* condition
Vulvismus 625.1
Vulvitis (acute) (allergic) (chronic) (gangrenous) (hypertrophic) (intertriginous) 616.10
  with
    abortion — *see* Abortion, by type, with sepsis
    ectopic pregnancy (*see also* categories 633.0–633.9) 639.0
    molar pregnancy (*see also* categories 630–632) 639.0
  adhesive, congenital 752.49
  blennorrhagic (acute) 098.0
    chronic or duration of 2 months or over 098.2
  chlamydial 099.53
  complicating pregnancy or puerperium 646.6 ☑
  due to Ducrey's bacillus 099.0
  following
    abortion 639.0
    ectopic or molar pregnancy 639.0
  gonococcal (acute) 098.0
    chronic or duration of 2 months or over 098.2
  herpetic 054.11
  leukoplakic 624.09
  monilial 112.1
  puerperal, postpartum, childbirth 646.6 ☑
  syphilitic (early) 091.0
    late 095.8
  trichomonal 131.01
Vulvodynia 625.70 ▲
  specified NEC 625.79 ●
Vulvorectal — *see* condition
Vulvovaginitis — *see also* Vulvitis 616.10
  amebic 006.8
  chlamydial 099.53
  gonococcal (acute) 098.0
    chronic or duration of 2 months or over 098.2
  herpetic 054.11
  monilial 112.1
  trichomonal (Trichomonas vaginalis) 131.01
Watermelon stomach 537.82
  with hemorrhage 537.83
  without hemorrhage 537.82

W

Waardenburg-Klein syndrome (ptosis-epicanthus) 270.2
Waardenburg's syndrome 756.89
  meaning ptosis-epicanthus 270.2
Wagner's disease (colloid milium) 709.3
Wagner (-Unverricht) syndrome (dermatomyositis) 710.3
Waiting list, person on V63.2
  undergoing social agency investigation V63.8
Wakefulness disorder — *see also* Hypersomnia 780.54
  nonorganic origin 307.43
Waldenström's
  disease (osteochondrosis, capital femoral) 732.1
  hepatitis (lupoid hepatitis) 571.49
  hypergammaglobulinemia 273.0
  macroglobulinemia 273.3
  purpura, hypergammaglobulinemic 273.0
  syndrome (macroglobulinemia) 273.3
Waldenström-Kjellberg syndrome (sideropenic dysphagia) 280.8
Walking
  difficulty 719.7
    psychogenic 307.9
  sleep 307.46
    hysterical 300.13
Wall, abdominal — *see* condition
Wallenberg's syndrome (posterior inferior cerebellar artery) — *see also* Disease, cerebrovascular, acute 436
Wallgren's
  disease (obstruction of splenic vein with collateral circulation) 459.89
  meningitis (*see also* Meningitis, aseptic) 047.9
Wandering
  acetabulum 736.39
  gallbladder 751.69
  kidney, congenital 753.3
  organ or site, congenital NEC — *see* Malposition, congenital
  pacemaker (atrial) (heart) 427.89
  spleen 289.59
Wardrop's disease (with lymphangitis) 681.9
  finger 681.02
  toe 681.11
War neurosis 300.16
Wart (digitate) (filiform) (infectious) (viral) 078.10
  common 078.19 ●
  external genital organs (venereal) 078.11 ▲
  fig 078.19
  flat 078.19 ●
  genital 078.11 ●
  Hassall-Henle's (of cornea) 371.41
  Henle's (of cornea) 371.41
  juvenile 078.19
  moist 078.10
  Peruvian 088.0
  plantar 078.12 ▲
  prosector (*see also* Tuberculosis) 017.0 ☑
  seborrheic 702.19
    inflamed 702.11
  senile 702.0
  specified NEC 078.19
  syphilitic 091.3
  tuberculous (*see also* Tuberculosis) 017.0 ☑
  venereal (female) (male) 078.11 ▲
Warthin's tumor (salivary gland) (M8561/0) 210.2
Washerwoman's itch 692.4
Wassilieff's disease (leptospiral jaundice) 100.0
Wasting
  disease 799.4
    due to malnutrition 261
  extreme (due to malnutrition) 261
  muscular NEC 728.2
  palsy, paralysis 335.21
  pelvic muscle 618.83
Water
  clefts 366.12
  deprivation of 994.3

- **Water** — *continued*
  - in joint (*see also* Effusion, joint) 719.0 ☑
  - intoxication 276.6
  - itch 120.3
  - lack of 994.3
  - loading 276.6
  - on
    - brain — *see* Hydrocephalus
    - chest 511.89 ▲
  - poisoning 276.6
- **Waterbrash** 787.1
- **Water-hammer pulse** — *see also* Insufficiency, aortic 424.1
- **Waterhouse (-Friderichsen) disease or syndrome** 036.3
- **Water-losing nephritis** 588.89
- **Wax in ear** 380.4
- **Waxy**
  - degeneration, any site 277.39
  - disease 277.39
  - kidney 277.39 *[583.81]*
  - liver (large) 277.39
  - spleen 277.39
- **Weak, weakness** (generalized) 780.79
  - arches (acquired) 734
    - congenital 754.61
  - bladder sphincter 596.59
  - congenital 779.89
  - eye muscle — *see* Strabismus
  - facial 781.94
  - foot (double) — *see* Weak, arches
  - heart, cardiac (*see also* Failure, heart) 428.9
    - congenital 746.9
  - mind 317
  - muscle (generalized) 728.87
  - myocardium (*see also* Failure, heart) 428.9
  - newborn 779.89
  - pelvic fundus
    - pubocervical tissue 618.81
    - rectovaginal tissue 618.82
  - pulse 785.9
  - senile 797
  - urinary stream 788.62
  - valvular — *see* Endocarditis
- **Wear, worn, tooth, teeth** (approximal) (hard tissues) (interproximal) (occlusal) — *see also* Attrition, teeth 521.10
- **Weather, weathered**
  - effects of
    - cold NEC 991.9
      - specified effect NEC 991.8
    - hot (*see also* Heat) 992.9
  - skin 692.74
- **Weber-Christian disease or syndrome** (nodular nonsuppurative panniculitis) 729.30
- **Weber-Cockayne syndrome** (epidermolysis bullosa) 757.39
- **Weber-Dimitri syndrome** 759.6
- **Weber-Gubler syndrome** 344.89
- **Weber-Leyden syndrome** 344.89
- **Weber-Osler syndrome** (familial hemorrhagic telangiectasia) 448.0
- **Weber's paralysis or syndrome** 344.89
- **Web, webbed** (congenital) — *see also* Anomaly, specified type NEC
  - canthus 743.63
  - digits (*see also* Syndactylism) 755.10
  - duodenal 751.5
  - esophagus 750.3
  - fingers (*see also* Syndactylism, fingers) 755.11
  - larynx (glottic) (subglottic) 748.2
  - neck (pterygium colli) 744.5
  - Paterson-Kelly (sideropenic dysphagia) 280.8
  - popliteal syndrome 756.89
  - toes (*see also* Syndactylism, toes) 755.13
- **Wedge-shaped or wedging vertebra** — *see also* Osteoporosis 733.00
- **Wegener's granulomatosis or syndrome** 446.4
- **Wegner's disease** (syphilitic osteochondritis) 090.0
- **Weight**
  - gain (abnormal) (excessive) 783.1
    - during pregnancy 646.1 ☑
      - insufficient 646.8 ☑
  - less than 1000 grams at birth 765.0 ☑
  - loss (cause unknown) 783.21
- **Weightlessness** 994.9
- **Weil's disease** (leptospiral jaundice) 100.0
- **Weill-Marchesani syndrome** (brachymorphism and ectopia lentis) 759.89
- **Weingarten's syndrome** (tropical eosinophilia) 518.3
- **Weir Mitchell's disease** (erythromelalgia) 443.82
- **Weiss-Baker syndrome** (carotid sinus syncope) 337.01 ▲
- **Weissenbach-Thibierge syndrome** (cutaneous systemic sclerosis) 710.1
- **Wen** — *see also* Cyst, sebaceous 706.2
- **Wenckebach's phenomenon, heart block** (second degree) 426.13
- **Werdnig-Hoffmann syndrome** (muscular atrophy) 335.0
- **Werlhof-Wichmann syndrome** — *see also* Purpura, thrombocytopenic 287.39
- **Werlhof's disease** — *see also* Purpura, thrombocytopenic 287.39
- **Wermer's syndrome or disease** (polyendocrine adenomatosis) 258.01
- **Werner's disease or syndrome** (progeria adultorum) 259.8
- **Werner-His disease** (trench fever) 083.1
- **Werner-Schultz disease** (agranulocytosis) 288.09
- **Wernicke's encephalopathy, disease, or syndrome** (superior hemorrhagic polioencephalitis) 265.1
- **Wernicke-Korsakoff syndrome or psychosis** (nonalcoholic) 294.0
  - alcoholic 291.1
- **Wernicke-Posadas disease** — *see also* Coccidioidomycosis 114.9
- **Wesselsbron fever** 066.3
- **West African fever** 084.8
- **West Nile**
  - encephalitis 066.41
  - encephalomyelitis 066.41
  - fever 066.40
    - with
      - cranial nerve disorders 066.42
      - encephalitis 066.41
      - optic neuritis 066.42
      - other complications 066.49
      - other neurologic manifestations 066.42
      - polyradiculitis 066.42
  - virus 066.40
- **Westphal-Strümpell syndrome** (hepatolenticular degeneration) 275.1
- **Wet**
  - brain (alcoholic) (*see also* Alcoholism) 303.9 ☑
  - feet, tropical (syndrome) (maceration) 991.4
  - lung (syndrome)
    - adult 518.5
    - newborn 770.6
- **Wharton's duct** — *see* condition
- **Wheal** 709.8
- **Wheelchair confinement status** V46.3 ●
- **Wheezing** 786.07
- **Whiplash injury or syndrome** 847.0
- **Whipple's disease or syndrome** (intestinal lipodystrophy) 040.2
- **Whipworm** 127.3
- **"Whistling face" syndrome** (craniocarpotarsal dystrophy) 759.89
- **White** — *see also* condition
- **White** — *see also* condition — *continued*
  - kidney
    - large — *see* Nephrosis
    - small 582.9
  - leg, puerperal, postpartum, childbirth 671.4 ☑
    - nonpuerperal 451.19
  - mouth 112.0
  - patches of mouth 528.6
  - sponge nevus of oral mucosa 750.26
  - spot lesions, teeth 521.01
- **White's disease** (congenital) (keratosis follicularis) 757.39
- **Whitehead** 706.2
- **Whitlow** (with lymphangitis) 681.01
  - herpetic 054.6
- **Whitmore's disease or fever** (melioidosis) 025
- **Whooping cough** 033.9
  - with pneumonia 033.9 *[484.3]*
  - due to
    - Bordetella
      - bronchoseptica 033.8
        - with pneumonia 033.8 *[484.3]*
      - parapertussis 033.1
        - with pneumonia 033.1 *[484.3]*
      - pertussis 033.0
        - with pneumonia 033.0 *[484.3]*
    - specified organism NEC 033.8
      - with pneumonia 033.8 *[484.3]*
  - vaccination, prophylactic (against) V03.6
- **Wichmann's asthma** (laryngismus stridulus) 478.75
- **Widal (-Abrami) syndrome** (acquired hemolytic jaundice) 283.9
- **Widening aorta** — *see also* Aneurysm, aorta 441.9
  - ruptured 441.5
- **Wilkie's disease or syndrome** 557.1
- **Wilkinson-Sneddon disease or syndrome** (subcorneal pustular dermatosis) 694.1
- **Willan's lepra** 696.1
- **Willan-Plumbe syndrome** (psoriasis) 696.1
- **Willebrand (-Jürgens) syndrome or thrombopathy** (angiohemophilia) 286.4
- **Willi-Prader syndrome** (hypogenital dystrophy with diabetic tendency) 759.81
- **Willis' disease** (diabetes mellitus) — *see also* Diabetes 250.0 ☑
  - due to secondary diabetes 249.0 ☑ ●
- **Wilms' tumor or neoplasm** (nephroblastoma) (M8960/3) 189.0
- **Wilson's**
  - disease or syndrome (hepatolenticular degeneration) 275.1
  - hepatolenticular degeneration 275.1
  - lichen ruber 697.0
- **Wilson-Brocq disease** (dermatitis exfoliativa) 695.89
- **Wilson-Mikity syndrome** 770.7
- **Window** — *see also* Imperfect, closure
  - aorticopulmonary 745.0
- **Winged scapula** 736.89
- **Winter** — *see also* condition
  - vomiting disease 078.82
- **Wise's disease** 696.2
- **Wiskott-Aldrich syndrome** (eczema-thrombocytopenia) 279.12
- **Withdrawal symptoms, syndrome**
  - alcohol 291.81
    - delirium (acute) 291.0
      - chronic 291.1
      - newborn 760.71
  - drug or narcotic 292.0
  - newborn, infant of dependent mother 779.5
- **Withdrawal symptoms, syndrome** — *continued*
  - steroid NEC
    - correct substance properly administered 255.41
    - overdose or wrong substance given or taken 962.0
- **Withdrawing reaction, child or adolescent** 313.22
- **Witts' anemia** (achlorhydric anemia) 280.9
- **Witzelsucht** 301.9
- **Woakes' syndrome** (ethmoiditis) 471.1
- **Wohlfart-Kugelberg-Welander disease** 335.11
- **Woillez's disease** (acute idiopathic pulmonary congestion) 518.5
- **Wolff-Parkinson-White syndrome** (anomalous atrioventricular excitation) 426.7
- **Wolhynian fever** 083.1
- **Wolman's disease** (primary familial xanthomatosis) 272.7
- **Wood asthma** 495.8
- **Woolly, wooly hair** (congenital) (nevus) 757.4
- **Wool-sorters' disease** 022.1
- **Word**
  - blindness (congenital) (developmental) 315.01
    - secondary to organic lesion 784.61
  - deafness (secondary to organic lesion) 784.69
    - developmental 315.31
- **Worm(s)** (colic) (fever) (infection) (infestation) — *see also* Infestation 128.9
  - guinea 125.7
  - in intestine NEC 127.9
- **Worm-eaten soles** 102.3
- **Worn out** — *see also* Exhaustion 780.79
  - joint prosthesis (*see also* Complications, mechanical, device NEC, prosthetic NEC, joint) 996.46 ●
- **"Worried well"** V65.5
- **Wound, open** (by cutting or piercing instrument) (by firearms) (cut) (dissection) (incised) (laceration) (penetration) (perforating) (puncture) (with initial hemorrhage, not internal) 879.8

> *Note — For fracture with open wound, see Fracture.*
>
> *For laceration, traumatic rupture, tear or penetrating wound of internal organs, such as heart, lung, liver, kidney, pelvic organs, etc., whether or not accompanied by open wound or fracture in the same region, see Injury, internal.*
>
> *For contused wound, see Contusion. For crush injury, see Crush. For abrasion, insect bite (nonvenomous), blister, or scratch, see Injury, superficial.*
>
> *Complicated includes wounds with:*
>
> *delayed healing*
>
> *delayed treatment*
>
> *foreign body*
>
> *primary infection*
>
> *For late effect of open wound, see Late, effect, wound, open, by site.*

  - abdomen, abdominal (external) (muscle) 879.2
    - complicated 879.3
    - wall (anterior) 879.2
      - complicated 879.3
      - lateral 879.4
        - complicated 879.5
  - alveolar (process) 873.62
    - complicated 873.72
  - ankle 891.0
    - with tendon involvement 891.2
    - complicated 891.1

Wound, open — *continued*
anterior chamber, eye (*see also* Wound, open, intraocular) 871.9
anus 879.6
complicated 879.7
arm 884.0
with tendon involvement 884.2
complicated 884.1
forearm 881.00
with tendon involvement 881.20
complicated 881.10
multiple sites — *see* Wound, open, multiple, upper limb
upper 880.03
with tendon involvement 880.23
complicated 880.13
multiple sites (with axillary or shoulder regions) 880.09
with tendon involvement 880.29
complicated 880.19
artery — *see* Injury, blood vessel, by site
auditory
canal (external) (meatus) 872.02
complicated 872.12
ossicles (incus) (malleus) (stapes) 872.62
complicated 872.72
auricle, ear 872.01
complicated 872.11
axilla 880.02
with tendon involvement 880.22
complicated 880.12
with tendon involvement 880.29
involving other sites of upper arm 880.09
complicated 880.19
back 876.0
complicated 876.1
bladder — *see* Injury, internal, bladder
blood vessel — *see* Injury, blood vessel, by site
brain — *see* Injury, intracranial, with open intracranial wound
breast 879.0
complicated 879.1
brow 873.42
complicated 873.52
buccal mucosa 873.61
complicated 873.71
buttock 877.0
complicated 877.1
calf 891.0
with tendon involvement 891.2
complicated 891.1
canaliculus lacrimalis 870.8
with laceration of eyelid 870.2
canthus, eye 870.8
laceration — *see* Laceration, eyelid
cavernous sinus — *see* Injury, intracranial
cerebellum — *see* Injury, intracranial
cervical esophagus 874.4
complicated 874.5
cervix — *see* Injury, internal, cervix
cheek(s) (external) 873.41
complicated 873.51
internal 873.61
complicated 873.71
chest (wall) (external) 875.0
complicated 875.1
chin 873.44
complicated 873.54
choroid 363.63
ciliary body (eye) (*see also* Wound, open, intraocular) 871.9
clitoris 878.8
complicated 878.9
cochlea 872.64
complicated 872.74
complicated 879.9
conjunctiva — *see* Wound, open, intraocular

Wound, open — *continued*
cornea (nonpenetrating) (*see also* Wound, open, intraocular) 871.9
costal region 875.0
complicated 875.1
Descemet's membrane (*see also* Wound, open, intraocular) 871.9
digit(s)
foot 893.0
with tendon involvement 893.2
complicated 893.1
hand 883.0
with tendon involvement 883.2
complicated 883.1
drumhead, ear 872.61
complicated 872.71
ear 872.8
canal 872.02
complicated 872.12
complicated 872.9
drum 872.61
complicated 872.71
external 872.00
complicated 872.10
multiple sites 872.69
complicated 872.79
ossicles (incus) (malleus) (stapes) 872.62
complicated 872.72
specified part NEC 872.69
complicated 872.79
elbow 881.01
with tendon involvement 881.21
complicated 881.11
epididymis 878.2
complicated 878.3
epigastric region 879.2
complicated 879.3
epiglottis 874.01
complicated 874.11
esophagus (cervical) 874.4
complicated 874.5
thoracic — *see* Injury, internal, esophagus
Eustachian tube 872.63
complicated 872.73
extremity
lower (multiple) NEC 894.0
with tendon involvement 894.2
complicated 894.1
upper (multiple) NEC 884.0
with tendon involvement 884.2
complicated 884.1
eye(s) (globe) — *see* Wound, open, intraocular
eyeball NEC 871.9
laceration (*see also* Laceration, eyeball) 871.4
penetrating (*see also* Penetrating wound, eyeball) 871.7
eyebrow 873.42
complicated 873.52
eyelid NEC 870.8
laceration — *see* Laceration, eyelid
face 873.40
complicated 873.50
multiple sites 873.49
complicated 873.59
specified part NEC 873.49
complicated 873.59
fallopian tube — *see* Injury, internal, fallopian tube
finger(s) (nail) (subungual) 883.0
with tendon involvement 883.2
complicated 883.1
flank 879.4
complicated 879.5
foot (any part except toe(s) alone) 892.0
with tendon involvement 892.2
complicated 892.1
forearm 881.00
with tendon involvement 881.20
complicated 881.10
forehead 873.42
complicated 873.52

Wound, open — *continued*
genital organs (external) NEC 878.8
complicated 878.9
internal — *see* Injury, internal, by site
globe (eye) (*see also* Wound, open, eyeball) 871.9
groin 879.4
complicated 879.5
gum(s) 873.62
complicated 873.72
hand (except finger(s) alone) 882.0
with tendon involvement 882.2
complicated 882.1
head NEC 873.8
with intracranial injury — *see* Injury, intracranial
due to or associated with skull fracture — *see* Fracture, skull
complicated 873.9
scalp — *see* Wound, open, scalp
heel 892.0
with tendon involvement 892.2
complicated 892.1
high-velocity (grease gun) — *see* Wound, open, complicated, by site
hip 890.0
with tendon involvement 890.2
complicated 890.1
hymen 878.6
complicated 878.7
hypochondrium 879.4
complicated 879.5
hypogastric region 879.2
complicated 879.3
iliac (region) 879.4
complicated 879.5
incidental to
dislocation — *see* Dislocation, open, by site
fracture — *see* Fracture, open, by site
intracranial injury — *see* Injury, intracranial, with open intracranial wound
nerve injury — *see* Injury, nerve, by site
inguinal region 879.4
complicated 879.5
instep 892.0
with tendon involvement 892.2
complicated 892.1
interscapular region 876.0
complicated 876.1
intracranial — *see* Injury, intracranial, with open intracranial wound
intraocular 871.9
with
partial loss (of intraocular tissue) 871.2
prolapse or exposure (of intraocular tissue) 871.1
without prolapse (of intraocular tissue) 871.0
laceration (*see also* Laceration, eyeball) 871.4
penetrating 871.7
with foreign body (nonmagnetic) 871.6
magnetic 871.5
iris (*see also* Wound, open, eyeball) 871.9
jaw (fracture not involved) 873.44
with fracture — *see* Fracture, jaw
complicated 873.54
knee 891.0
with tendon involvement 891.2
complicated 891.1
labium (majus) (minus) 878.4
complicated 878.5
lacrimal apparatus, gland, or sac 870.8
with laceration of eyelid 870.2
larynx 874.01

Wound, open — *continued*
larynx — *continued*
with trachea 874.00
complicated 874.10
complicated 874.11
leg (multiple) 891.0
with tendon involvement 891.2
complicated 891.1
lower 891.0
with tendon involvement 891.2
complicated 891.1
thigh 890.0
with tendon involvement 890.2
complicated 890.1
upper 890.0
with tendon involvement 890.2
complicated 890.1
lens (eye) (alone) (*see also* Cataract, traumatic) 366.20
with involvement of other eye structures — *see* Wound, open, eyeball
limb
lower (multiple) NEC 894.0
with tendon involvement 894.2
complicated 894.1
upper (multiple) NEC 884.0
with tendon involvement 884.2
complicated 884.1
lip 873.43
complicated 873.53
loin 876.0
complicated 876.1
lumbar region 876.0
complicated 876.1
malar region 873.41
complicated 873.51
mastoid region 873.49
complicated 873.59
mediastinum — *see* Injury, internal, mediastinum
midthoracic region 875.0
complicated 875.1
mouth 873.60
complicated 873.70
floor 873.64
complicated 873.74
multiple sites 873.69
complicated 873.79
specified site NEC 873.69
complicated 873.79
multiple, unspecified site(s) 879.8

Note — Multiple open wounds of sites classifiable to the same four-digit category should be classified to that category unless they are in different limbs.

Multiple open wounds of sites classifiable to different four-digit categories, or to different limbs, should be coded separately.

complicated 879.9
lower limb(s) (one or both) (sites classifiable to more than one three-digit category in 890 to 893) 894.0
with tendon involvement 894.2
complicated 894.1
upper limb(s) (one or both) (sites classifiable to more than one three-digit category in 880 to 883) 884.0
with tendon involvement 884.2
complicated 884.1
muscle — *see* Sprain, by site
nail
finger(s) 883.0
complicated 883.1
thumb 883.0
complicated 883.1
toe(s) 893.0
complicated 893.1
nape (neck) 874.8
complicated 874.9
specified part NEC 874.8
complicated 874.9

Wound, open — *continued*
nasal (*see also* Wound, open, nose)
cavity 873.22
complicated 873.32
septum 873.21
complicated 873.31
sinuses 873.23
complicated 873.33
nasopharynx 873.22
complicated 873.32
neck 874.8
complicated 874.9
nape 874.8
complicated 874.9
specified part NEC 874.8
complicated 874.9
nerve — *see* Injury, nerve, by site
non-healing surgical 998.83
nose 873.20
complicated 873.30
multiple sites 873.29
complicated 873.39
septum 873.21
complicated 873.31
sinuses 873.23
complicated 873.33
occipital region — *see* Wound, open, scalp
ocular NEC 871.9
adnexa 870.9
specified region NEC 870.8
laceration (*see also* Laceration, ocular) 871.4
muscle (extraocular) 870.3
with foreign body 870.4
eyelid 870.1
intraocular — *see* Wound, open, eyeball
penetrating (*see also* Penetrating wound, ocular) 871.7
orbit 870.8
penetrating 870.3
with foreign body 870.4
orbital region 870.9
ovary — *see* Injury, internal, pelvic organs
palate 873.65
complicated 873.75
palm 882.0
with tendon involvement 882.2
complicated 882.1
parathyroid (gland) 874.2
complicated 874.3
parietal region — *see* Wound, open, scalp
pelvic floor or region 879.6
complicated 879.7
penis 878.0
complicated 878.1
perineum 879.6
complicated 879.7
periocular area 870.8
laceration of skin 870.0
pharynx 874.4
complicated 874.5
pinna 872.01
complicated 872.11
popliteal space 891.0
with tendon involvement 891.2
complicated 891.1
prepuce 878.0
complicated 878.1
pubic region 879.2
complicated 879.3
pudenda 878.8
complicated 878.9
rectovaginal septum 878.8
complicated 878.9
sacral region 877.0
complicated 877.1
sacroiliac region 877.0
complicated 877.1
salivary (ducts) (glands) 873.69
complicated 873.79
scalp 873.0
complicated 873.1

Wound, open — *continued*
scalpel, fetus or newborn 767.8
scapular region 880.01
with tendon involvement 880.21
complicated 880.11
involving other sites of upper arm 880.09
with tendon involvement 880.29
complicated 880.19
sclera (*see also* Wound, open, intraocular) 871.9
scrotum 878.2
complicated 878.3
seminal vesicle — *see* Injury, internal, pelvic organs
shin 891.0
with tendon involvement 891.2
complicated 891.1
shoulder 880.00
with tendon involvement 880.20
complicated 880.10
involving other sites of upper arm 880.09
with tendon involvement 880.29
complicated 880.19
skin NEC 879.8
complicated 879.9
skull (*see also* Injury, intracranial, with open intracranial wound)
with skull fracture — *see* Fracture, skull
spermatic cord (scrotal) 878.2
complicated 878.3
pelvic region — *see* Injury, internal, spermatic cord
spinal cord — *see* Injury, spinal
sternal region 875.0
complicated 875.1
subconjunctival — *see* Wound, open, intraocular
subcutaneous NEC 879.8
complicated 879.9
submaxillary region 873.44
complicated 873.54
submental region 873.44
complicated 873.54
subungual
finger(s) (thumb) — *see* Wound, open, finger
toe(s) — *see* Wound, open, toe
supraclavicular region 874.8
complicated 874.9
supraorbital 873.42
complicated 873.52
surgical, non-healing 998.83
temple 873.49
complicated 873.59
temporal region 873.49
complicated 873.59
testis 878.2
complicated 878.3
thigh 890.0
with tendon involvement 890.2
complicated 890.1
thorax, thoracic (external) 875.0
complicated 875.1
throat 874.8
complicated 874.9
thumb (nail) (subungual) 883.0
with tendon involvement 883.2
complicated 883.1
thyroid (gland) 874.2
complicated 874.3
toe(s) (nail) (subungual) 893.0
with tendon involvement 893.2
complicated 893.1
tongue 873.64
complicated 873.74
tonsil — *see* Wound, open, neck
trachea (cervical region) 874.02
with larynx 874.00
complicated 874.10
complicated 874.12
intrathoracic — *see* Injury, internal, trachea
trunk (multiple) NEC 879.6

Wound, open — *continued*
trunk — *continued*
complicated 879.7
specified site NEC 879.6
complicated 879.7
tunica vaginalis 878.2
complicated 878.3
tympanic membrane 872.61
complicated 872.71
tympanum 872.61
complicated 872.71
umbilical region 879.2
complicated 879.3
ureter — *see* Injury, internal, ureter
urethra — *see* Injury, internal, urethra
uterus — *see* Injury, internal, uterus
uvula 873.69
complicated 873.79
vagina 878.6
complicated 878.7
vas deferens — *see* Injury, internal, vas deferens
vitreous (humor) 871.2
vulva 878.4
complicated 878.5
wrist 881.02
with tendon involvement 881.22
complicated 881.12
Wright's syndrome (hyperabduction) 447.8
pneumonia 390 *[517.1]*
Wringer injury — *see* Crush injury, by site
Wrinkling of skin 701.8
Wrist — *see also* condition
drop (acquired) 736.05
Wrong drug (given in error) NEC 977.9
specified drug or substance — *see* Table of Drugs and Chemicals
Wry neck — *see also* Torticollis
congenital 754.1
Wuchereria infestation 125.0
bancrofti 125.0
Brugia malayi 125.1
malayi 125.1
Wuchereriasis 125.0
Wuchereriosis 125.0
Wucherende struma langhans (M8332/3) 193

X

Xanthelasma 272.2
eyelid 272.2 *[374.51]*
palpebrarum 272.2 *[374.51]*
Xanthelasmatosis (essential) 272.2
Xanthelasmoidea 757.33
Xanthine stones 277.2
Xanthinuria 277.2
Xanthofibroma (M8831/0) — *see* Neoplasm, connective tissue, benign
Xanthoma(s), xanthomatosis 272.2
with
hyperlipoproteinemia
type I 272.3
type III 272.2
type IV 272.1
type V 272.3
bone 272.7
craniohypophyseal 277.89
cutaneotendinous 272.7
diabeticorum 250.8 ☑ *[272.2]*
due to secondary diabetes 249.8 ☑ *[272.7]* ●
disseminatum 272.7
eruptive 272.2
eyelid 272.2 *[374.51]*
familial 272.7
hereditary 272.7
hypercholesterinemic 272.0
hypercholesterolemic 272.0
hyperlipemic 272.4
hyperlipidemic 272.4
infantile 272.7
joint 272.7
juvenile 272.7

Xanthoma(s), xanthomatosis — *continued*
multiple 272.7
multiplex 272.7
primary familial 272.7
tendon (sheath) 272.7
tuberosum 272.2
tuberous 272.2
tubo-eruptive 272.2
Xanthosis 709.09
surgical 998.81
Xenophobia 300.29
Xeroderma (congenital) 757.39
acquired 701.1
eyelid 373.33
eyelid 373.33
pigmentosum 757.33
vitamin A deficiency 264.8
Xerophthalmia 372.53
vitamin A deficiency 264.7
Xerosis
conjunctiva 372.53
with Bitôt's spot 372.53
vitamin A deficiency 264.1
vitamin A deficiency 264.0
cornea 371.40
with corneal ulceration 370.00
vitamin A deficiency 264.3
vitamin A deficiency 264.2
cutis 706.8
skin 706.8
Xerostomia 527.7
Xiphodynia 733.90
Xiphoidalgia 733.90
Xiphoiditis 733.99
Xiphopagus 759.4
XO syndrome 758.6
X-ray
effects, adverse, NEC 990
of chest
for suspected tuberculosis V71.2
routine V72.5
XXX syndrome 758.81
XXXXY syndrome 758.81
XXY syndrome 758.7
Xyloketosuria 271.8
Xylosuria 271.8
Xylulosuria 271.8
XYY syndrome 758.81

Y

Yaba monkey tumor virus 059.22 ●
Yawning 786.09
psychogenic 306.1
Yaws 102.9
bone or joint lesions 102.6
butter 102.1
chancre 102.0
cutaneous, less than five years after infection 102.2
early (cutaneous) (macular) (maculopapular) (micropapular) (papular) 102.2
frambeside 102.2
skin lesions NEC 102.2
eyelid 102.9 *[373.4]*
ganglion 102.6
gangosis, gangosa 102.5
gumma, gummata 102.4
bone 102.6
gummatous
frambeside 102.4
osteitis 102.6
periostitis 102.6
hydrarthrosis 102.6
hyperkeratosis (early) (late) (palmar) (plantar) 102.3
initial lesions 102.0
joint lesions 102.6
juxta-articular nodules 102.7
late nodular (ulcerated) 102.4
latent (without clinical manifestations) (with positive serology) 102.8
mother 102.0
mucosal 102.7
multiple papillomata 102.1

Yaws — *continued*
nodular, late (ulcerated) 102.4
osteitis 102.6
papilloma, papillomata (palmar) (plantar) 102.1
periostitis (hypertrophic) 102.6
ulcers 102.4
wet crab 102.1
Yeast infection — *see also* Candidiasis 112.9
Yellow
atrophy (liver) 570
chronic 571.8
Yellow — *continued*
atrophy — *continued*
resulting from administration of blood, plasma, scrum, or other biological substance (within 8 months of administration) — *see* Hepatitis, viral
fever — *see* Fever, yellow
jack (*see also* Fever, yellow) 060.9
jaundice (*see also* Jaundice) 782.4
vernix syndrome 762.2
Yersinia septica 027.8

Z

Zagari's disease (xerostomia) 527.7
Zahorsky's disease (exanthema subitum) (*see also* Exanthem subitum) 058.10
syndrome (herpangina) 074.0
Zellweger syndrome 277.86
Zenker's diverticulum (esophagus) 530.6
Ziehen-Oppenheim disease 333.6
Zieve's syndrome (jaundice, hyperlipemia, and hemolytic anemia) 571.1
Zika fever 066.3
Zollinger-Ellison syndrome (gastric hypersecretion with pancreatic islet cell tumor) 251.5
Zona — *see also* Herpes, zoster 053.9
Zoophilia (erotica) 302.1
Zoophobia 300.29
Zoster (herpes) — *see also* Herpes, zoster 053.9
Zuelzer (-Ogden) anemia or syndrome (nutritional megaloblastic anemia) 281.2
Zygodactyly — *see also* Syndactylism 755.10
Zygomycosis 117.7
Zymotic — *see* condition

SECTION 2

Alphabetic Index to Poisoning and External Causes of Adverse Effects of Drugs and Other Chemical Substances

TABLE OF DRUGS AND CHEMICALS

This table contains a classification of drugs and other chemical substances to identify poisoning states and external causes of adverse effects.

Each of the listed substances in the table is assigned a code according to the poisoning classification (960-989). These codes are used when there is a statement of poisoning, overdose, wrong substance given or taken, or intoxication.

The table also contains a listing of external causes of adverse effects. An adverse effect is a pathologic manifestation due to ingestion or exposure to drugs or other chemical substances (e.g., dermatitis, hypersensitivity reaction, aspirin gastritis). The adverse effect is to be identified by the appropriate code found in Section 1, Index to Diseases and Injuries. An external cause code can then be used to identify the circumstances involved. The table headings pertaining to external causes are defined below:

Accidental poisoning (E850-E869) — accidental overdose of drug, wrong substance given or taken, drug taken inadvertently, accidents in the usage of drugs and biologicals in medical and surgical procedures, and to show external causes of poisonings classifiable to 980-989.

Therapeutic use (E930-E949) — a correct substance properly administered in therapeutic or prophylactic dosage as the external cause of adverse effects.

Suicide attempt (E950-E952) — instances in which self-inflicted injuries or poisonings are involved.

Assault (E961-E962) — injury or poisoning inflicted by another person with the intent to injure or kill.

Undetermined (E980-E982) — to be used when the intent of the poisoning or injury cannot be determined whether it was intentional or accidental.

The American Hospital Formulary Service list numbers are included in the table to help classify new drugs not identified in the table by name. The AHFS list numbers are keyed to the continually revised American Hospital Formulary Service (AHFS).* These listings are found in the table under the main term **Drug**.

Excluded from the table are radium and other radioactive substances. The classification of adverse effects and complications pertaining to these substances will be found in Section 1, Index to Diseases and Injuries, and Section 3, Index to External Causes of Injuries.

Although certain substances are indexed with one or more subentries, the majority are listed according to one use or state. It is recognized that many substances may be used in various ways, in medicine and in industry, and may cause adverse effects whatever the state of the agent (solid, liquid, or fumes arising from a liquid). In cases in which the reported data indicates a use or state not in the table, or which is clearly different from the one listed, an attempt should be made to classify the substance in the form which most nearly expresses the reported facts.

*American Hospital Formulary Service, 2 vol. (Washington, D.C.: American Society of Hospital Pharmacists, 1959-)

	Poisoning	External Cause (E-Code) Accident	Therapeutic Use	Suicide Attempt	Assault	Undetermined
1-propanol	980.3	E860.4	—	E950.9	E962.1	E980.9
2-propanol	980.2	E860.3	—	E950.9	E962.1	E980.9
2, 4-D (dichlorophenoxyacetic acid)	989.4	E863.5	—	E950.6	E962.1	E980.7
2, 4-toluene diisocyanate	983.0	E864.0	—	E950.7	E962.1	E980.6
2, 4, 5-T (trichlorophenoxyacetic acid)	989.2	E863.5	—	E950.6	E962.1	E980.7
14-hydroxydihydromorphinone	965.09	E850.2	E935.2	E950.0	E962.0	E980.0
ABOB	961.7	E857	E931.7	E950.4	E962.0	E980.4
Abrus (seed)	988.2	E865.3	—	E950.9	E962.1	E980.9
Absinthe	980.0	E860.1	—	E950.9	E962.1	E980.9
beverage	980.0	E860.0	—	E950.9	E962.1	E980.9
Acenocoumarin, acenocoumarol	964.2	E858.2	E934.2	E950.4	E962.0	E980.4
Acepromazine	969.1	E853.0	E939.1	E950.3	E962.0	E980.3
Acetal	982.8	E862.4	—	E950.9	E962.1	E980.9
Acetaldehyde (vapor)	987.8	E869.8	—	E952.8	E962.2	E982.8
liquid	989.89	E866.8	—	E950.9	E962.1	E980.9
Acetaminophen	965.4	E850.4	E935.4	E950.0	E962.0	E980.0
Acetaminosalol	965.1	E850.3	E935.3	E950.0	E962.0	E980.0
Acetanilid(e)	965.4	E850.4	E935.4	E950.0	E962.0	E980.0
Acetarsol, acetarsone	961.1	E857	E931.1	E950.4	E962.0	E980.4
Acetazolamide	974.2	E858.5	E944.2	E950.4	E962.0	E980.4
Acetic						
acid	983.1	E864.1	—	E950.7	E962.1	E980.6
with sodium acetate (ointment)	976.3	E858.7	E946.3	E950.4	E962.0	E980.4
irrigating solution	974.5	E858.5	E944.5	E950.4	E962.0	E980.4
lotion	976.2	E858.7	E946.2	E950.4	E962.0	E980.4
anhydride	983.1	E864.1	—	E950.7	E962.1	E980.6
ether (vapor)	982.8	E862.4	—	E950.9	E962.1	E980.9
Acetohexamide	962.3	E858.0	E932.3	E950.4	E962.0	E980.4
Acetomenaphthone	964.3	E858.2	E934.3	E950.4	E962.0	E980.4
Acetomorphine	965.01	E850.0	E935.0	E950.0	E962.0	E980.0
Acetone (oils) (vapor)	982.8	E862.4	—	E950.9	E962.1	E980.9
Acetophenazine (maleate)	969.1	E853.0	E939.1	E950.3	E962.0	E980.3
Acetophenetidin	965.4	E850.4	E935.4	E950.0	E962.0	E980.0
Acetophenone	982.0	E862.4	—	E950.9	E962.1	E980.9
Acetorphine	965.09	E850.2	E935.2	E950.0	E962.0	E980.0
Acetosulfone (sodium)	961.8	E857	E931.8	E950.4	E962.0	E980.4
Acetrizoate (sodium)	977.8	E858.8	E947.8	E950.4	E962.0	E980.4
Acetylcarbromal	967.3	E852.2	E937.3	E950.2	E962.0	E980.2
Acetylcholine (chloride)	971.0	E855.3	E941.0	E950.4	E962.0	E980.4
Acetylcysteine	975.5	E858.6	E945.5	E950.4	E962.0	E980.4
Acetyldigitoxin	972.1	E858.3	E942.1	E950.4	E962.0	E980.4
Acetyldihydrocodeine	965.09	E850.2	E935.2	E950.0	E962.0	E980.0
Acetyldihydrocodeinone	965.09	E850.2	E935.2	E950.0	E962.0	E980.0
Acetylene (gas) (industrial)	987.1	E868.1	—	E951.8	E962.2	E981.8
incomplete combustion of — see Carbon monoxide, fuel, utility						
tetrachloride (vapor)	982.3	E862.4	—	E950.9	E962.1	E980.9
Acetyliodosalicylic acid	965.1	E850.3	E935.3	E950.0	E962.0	E980.0
Acetylphenylhydrazine	965.8	E850.8	E935.8	E950.0	E962.0	E980.0
Acetylsalicylic acid	965.1	E850.3	E935.3	E950.0	E962.0	E980.0
Achromycin	960.4	E856	E930.4	E950.4	E962.0	E980.4
ophthalmic preparation	976.5	E858.7	E946.5	E950.4	E962.0	E980.4
topical NEC	976.0	E858.7	E946.0	E950.4	E962.0	E980.4
Acidifying agents	963.2	E858.1	E933.2	E950.4	E962.0	E980.4
Acids (corrosive) NEC	983.1	E864.1	—	E950.7	E962.1	E980.6
Aconite (wild)	988.2	E865.4	—	E950.9	E962.1	E980.9
Aconitine (liniment)	976.8	E858.7	E946.8	E950.4	E962.0	E980.4
Aconitum ferox	988.2	E865.4	—	E950.9	E962.1	E980.9
Acridine	983.0	E864.0	—	E950.7	E962.1	E980.6
vapor	987.8	E869.8	—	E952.8	E962.2	E982.8
Acriflavine	961.9	E857	E931.9	E950.4	E962.0	E980.4
Acrisorcin	976.0	E858.7	E946.0	E950.4	E962.0	E980.4
Acrolein (gas)	987.8	E869.8	—	E952.8	E962.2	E982.8
liquid	989.89	E866.8	—	E950.9	E962.1	E980.9
Actaea spicata	988.2	E865.4	—	E950.9	E962.1	E980.9
Acterol	961.5	E857	E931.5	E950.4	E962.0	E980.4
ACTH	962.4	E858.0	E932.4	E950.4	E962.0	E980.4
Acthar	962.4	E858.0	E932.4	E950.4	E962.0	E980.4
Actinomycin (C) (D)	960.7	E856	E930.7	E950.4	E962.0	E980.4
Adalin (acetyl)	967.3	E852.2	E937.3	E950.2	E962.0	E980.2
Adenosine (phosphate)	977.8	E858.8	E947.8	E950.4	E962.0	E980.4
ADH	962.5	E858.0	E932.5	E950.4	E962.0	E980.4
Adhesives	989.89	E866.6	—	E950.9	E962.1	E980.9
Adicillin	960.0	E856	E930.0	E950.4	E962.0	E980.4
Adiphenine	975.1	E855.6	E945.1	E950.4	E962.0	E980.4
Adjunct, pharmaceutical	977.4	E858.8	E947.4	E950.4	E962.0	E980.4
Adrenal (extract, cortex or medulla) (glucocorticoids) (hormones) (mineralocorticoids)	962.0	E858.0	E932.0	E950.4	E962.0	E980.4
ENT agent	976.6	E858.7	E946.6	E950.4	E962.0	E980.4
ophthalmic preparation	976.5	E858.7	E946.5	E950.4	E962.0	E980.4
topical NEC	976.0	E858.7	E946.0	E950.4	E962.0	E980.4
Adrenalin	971.2	E855.5	E941.2	E950.4	E962.0	E980.4
Adrenergic blocking agents	971.3	E855.6	E941.3	E950.4	E962.0	E980.4
Adrenergics	971.2	E855.5	E941.2	E950.4	E962.0	E980.4
Adrenochrome (derivatives)	972.8	E858.3	E942.8	E950.4	E962.0	E980.4
Adrenocorticotropic hormone	962.4	E858.0	E932.4	E950.4	E962.0	E980.4
Adrenocorticotropin	962.4	E858.0	E932.4	E950.4	E962.0	E980.4
Adriamycin	960.7	E856	E930.7	E950.4	E962.0	E980.4
Aerosol spray — see Sprays						
Aerosporin	960.8	E856	E930.8	E950.4	E962.0	E980.4
ENT agent	976.6	E858.7	E946.6	E950.4	E962.0	E980.4
ophthalmic preparation	976.5	E858.7	E946.5	E950.4	E962.0	E980.4
topical NEC	976.0	E858.7	E946.0	E950.4	E962.0	E980.4
Aethusa cynapium	988.2	E865.4	—	E950.9	E962.1	E980.9
Afghanistan black	969.6	E854.1	E939.6	E950.3	E962.0	E980.3
Aflatoxin	989.7	E865.9	—	E950.9	E962.1	E980.9
African boxwood	988.2	E865.4	—	E950.9	E962.1	E980.9
Agar (-agar)	973.3	E858.4	E943.3	E950.4	E962.0	E980.4
Agricultural agent NEC	989.89	E863.9	—	E950.6	E962.1	E980.7
Agrypnal	967.0	E851	E937.0	E950.1	E962.0	—
Air contaminant(s), source or type not specified	987.9	E869.9	—	E952.9	E962.2	E982.9
specified type — see specific substance						
Akee	988.2	E865.4	—	E950.9	E962.1	E980.9
Akrinol	976.0	E858.7	E946.0	E950.4	E962.0	E980.4
Alantolactone	961.6	E857	E931.6	E950.4	E962.0	E980.4
Albamycin	960.8	E856	E930.8	E950.4	E962.0	E980.4
Albumin (normal human serum)	964.7	E858.2	E934.7	E950.4	E962.0	E980.4
Albuterol	975.7	E858.6	E945.7	E950.4	E962.0	E980.4
Alcohol	980.9	E860.9	—	E950.9	E962.1	E980.9
absolute	980.0	E860.1	—	E950.9	E962.1	E980.9
beverage	980.0	E860.0	E947.8	E950.9	E962.1	E980.9
amyl	980.3	E860.4	—	E950.9	E962.1	E980.9
antifreeze	980.1	E860.2	—	E950.9	E962.1	E980.9
butyl	980.3	E860.4	—	E950.9	E962.1	E980.9
dehydrated	980.0	E860.1	—	E950.9	E862.1	E980.9
beverage	980.0	E860.0	E947.8	E950.9	E962.1	E980.9
denatured	980.0	E860.1	—	E950.9	E962.1	E980.9
deterrents	977.3	E858.8	E947.3	E950.4	E962.0	E980.4
diagnostic (gastric function)	977.8	E858.8	E947.8	E950.4	E962.0	E980.4
ethyl	980.0	E860.1	—	E950.9	E962.1	E980.9
beverage	980.0	E860.0	E947.8	E950.9	E962.1	E980.9
grain	980.0	E860.1	—	E950.9	E962.1	E980.9
beverage	980.0	E860.0	E947.8	E950.9	E962.1	E980.9
industrial	980.9	E860.9	—	E950.9	E962.1	E980.9
isopropyl	980.2	E860.3	—	E950.9	E962.1	E980.9
methyl	980.1	E860.2	—	E950.9	E962.1	E980.9
preparation for consumption	980.0	E860.0	E947.8	E950.9	E962.1	E980.9
propyl	980.3	E860.4	—	E950.9	E962.1	E980.9
secondary	980.2	E860.3	—	E950.9	E962.1	E980.9
radiator	980.1	E860.2	—	E950.9	E962.1	E980.9
rubbing	980.2	E860.3	—	E950.9	E962.1	E980.9
specified type NEC	980.8	E860.8	—	E950.9	E962.1	E980.9
surgical	980.9	E860.9	—	E950.9	E962.1	E980.9
vapor (from any type of alcohol)	987.8	E869.8	—	E952.8	E962.2	E982.8
wood	980.1	E860.2	—	E950.9	E962.1	E980.9
Alcuronium chloride	975.2	E858.6	E945.2	E950.4	E962.0	E980.4
Aldactone	974.4	E858.5	E944.4	E950.4	E962.0	E980.4
Aldicarb	989.3	E863.2	—	E950.6	E962.1	E980.7
Aldomet	972.6	E858.3	E942.6	E950.4	E962.0	E980.4
Aldosterone	962.0	E858.0	E932.0	E950.4	E962.0	E980.4
Aldrin (dust)	989.2	E863.0	—	E950.6	E962.1	E980.7
Algeldrate	973.0	E858.4	E943.0	E950.4	E962.0	E980.4
Alidase	963.4	E858.1	E933.4	E950.4	E962.0	E980.4
Aliphatic thiocyanates	989.0	E866.8	—	E950.9	E962.1	E980.9
Alkaline antiseptic solution (aromatic)	976.6	E858.7	E946.6	E950.4	E962.0	E980.4

	Poisoning	External Cause (E-Code)				
		Accident	Therapeutic Use	Suicide Attempt	Assault	Undetermined
Alkalinizing agents (medicinal)	963.3	E858.1	E933.3	E950.4	E962.0	E980.4
Alkalis, caustic	983.2	E864.2	—	E950.7	E962.1	E980.6
Alkalizing agents (medicinal)	963.3	E858.1	E933.3	E950.4	E962.0	E980.4
Alka-seltzer	965.1	E850.3	E935.3	E950.0	E962.0	E980.0
Alkavervir	972.6	E858.3	E942.6	E950.4	E962.0	E980.4
Allegron	969.0	E854.0	E939.0	E950.3	E962.0	E980.3
Alleve — Naproxen						
Allobarbital, allobarbitone	967.0	E851	E937.0	E950.1	E962.0	E980.1
Allopurinol	974.7	E858.5	E944.7	E950.4	E962.0	E980.4
Allylestrenol	962.2	E858.0	E932.2	E950.4	E962.0	E980.4
Allylisopropylacetylurea	967.8	E852.8	E937.8	E950.2	E962.0	E980.2
Allylisopropylmalonylurea	967.0	E851	E937.0	E950.1	E962.0	E980.1
Allyltribromide	967.3	E852.2	E937.3	E950.2	E962.0	E980.2
Aloe, aloes, aloin	973.1	E858.4	E943.1	E950.4	E962.0	E980.4
Alosetron	973.8	E858.4	E943.8	E950.4	E962.0	E980.4
Aloxidone	966.0	E855.0	E936.0	E950.4	E962.0	E980.4
Aloxiprin	965.1	E850.3	E935.3	E950.0	E962.0	E980.0
Alpha-1 blockers	971.3	E855.6	E941.3	E950.4	E962.0	E980.4
Alpha amylase	963.4	E858.1	E933.4	E950.4	E962.0	E980.4
Alphaprodine (hydrochloride)	965.09	E850.2	E935.2	E950.0	E962.0	E980.0
Alpha tocopherol	963.5	E858.1	E933.5	E950.4	E962.0	E980.4
Alseroxylon	972.6	E858.3	E942.6	E950.4	E962.0	E980.4
Alum (ammonium) (potassium)	983.2	E864.2	—	E950.7	E962.1	E980.6
medicinal (astringent) NEC	976.2	E858.7	E946.2	E950.4	E962.0	E980.4
Aluminium, aluminum (gel) (hydroxide)	973.0	E858.4	E943.0	E950.4	E962.0	E980.4
acetate solution	976.2	E858.7	E946.2	E950.4	E962.0	E980.4
aspirin	965.1	E850.3	E935.3	E950.0	E962.0	E980.0
carbonate	973.0	E858.4	E943.0	E950.4	E962.0	E980.4
glycinate	973.0	E858.4	E943.0	E950.4	E962.0	E980.4
nicotinate	972.2	E858.3	E942.2	E950.4	E962.0	E980.4
ointment (surgical) (topical)	976.3	E858.7	E946.3	E950.4	E962.0	E980.4
phosphate	973.0	E858.4	E943.0	E950.4	E962.0	E980.4
subacetate	976.2	E858.7	E946.2	E950.4	E962.0	E980.4
topical NEC	976.3	E858.7	E946.3	E950.4	E962.0	E980.4
Alurate	967.0	E851	E937.0	E950.1	E962.0	E980.1
Alverine (citrate)	975.1	E858.6	E945.1	E950.4	E962.0	E980.4
Alvodine	965.09	E850.2	E935.2	E950.0	E962.0	E980.0
Amanita phalloides	988.1	E865.5	—	E950.9	E962.1	E980.9
Amantadine (hydrochloride)	966.4	E855.0	E936.4	E950.4	E962.0	E980.4
Ambazone	961.9	E857	E931.9	E950.4	E962.0	E980.4
Ambenonium	971.0	E855.3	E941.0	E950.4	E962.0	E980.4
Ambutonium bromide	971.1	E855.4	E941.1	E950.4	E962.0	E980.4
Ametazole	977.8	E858.8	E947.8	E950.4	E962.0	E980.4
Amethocaine (infiltration) (topical)	968.5	E855.2	E938.5	E950.4	E962.0	E980.4
nerve block (peripheral) (plexus)	968.6	E855.2	E938.6	E950.4	E962.0	E980.4
spinal	968.7	E855.2	E938.7	E950.4	E962.0	E980.4
Amethopterin	963.1	E858.1	E933.1	E950.4	E962.0	E980.4
Amfepramone	977.0	E858.8	E947.0	E950.4	E962.0	E980.4
Amidon	965.02	E850.1	E935.1	E950.0	E962.0	E980.0
Amidopyrine	965.5	E850.5	E935.5	E950.0	E962.0	E980.0
Aminacrine	976.0	E858.7	E946.0	E950.4	E962.0	E980.4
Aminitrozole	961.5	E857	E931.5	E950.4	E962.0	E980.4
Aminoacetic acid	974.5	E858.5	E944.5	E950.4	E962.0	E980.4
Amino acids	974.5	E858.5	E944.5	E950.4	E962.0	E980.4
Aminocaproic acid	964.4	E858.2	E934.4	E950.4	E962.0	E980.4
Aminoethylisothiourium	963.8	E858.1	E933.8	E950.4	E962.0	E980.4
Aminoglutethimide	966.3	E855.0	E936.3	E950.4	E962.0	E980.4
Aminometradine	974.3	E858.5	E944.3	E950.4	E962.0	E980.4
Aminopentamide	971.1	E855.4	E941.1	E950.4	E962.0	E980.4
Aminophenazone	965.5	E850.5	E935.5	E950.0	E962.0	E980.0
Aminophenol	983.0	E864.0	—	E950.7	E962.1	E980.6
Aminophenylpyridone	969.5	E853.8	E939.5	E950.3	E962.0	E980.3
Aminophyllin	975.7	E858.6	E945.7	E950.4	E962.0	E980.4
Aminopterin	963.1	E858.1	E933.1	E950.4	E962.0	E980.4
Aminopyrine	965.5	E850.5	E935.5	E950.0	E962.0	E980.0
Aminosalicylic acid	961.8	E857	E931.8	E950.4	E962.0	E980.4
Amiphenazole	970.1	E854.3	E940.1	E950.4	E962.0	E980.4
Amiquinsin	972.6	E858.3	E942.6	E950.4	E962.0	E980.4
Amisometradine	974.3	E858.5	E944.3	E950.4	E962.0	E980.4
Amitriptyline	969.0	E854.0	E939.0	E950.3	E962.0	E980.3
Ammonia (fumes) (gas) (vapor)	987.8	E869.8	—	E952.8	E962.2	E982.8
liquid (household) NEC	983.2	E861.4	—	E950.7	E962.1	E980.6
Ammonia — *continued*						
spirit, aromatic	970.8	E854.3	E940.8	E950.4	E962.0	E980.4
Ammoniated mercury	976.0	E858.7	E946.0	E950.4	E962.0	E980.4
Ammonium						
carbonate	983.2	E864.2	—	E950.7	E962.1	E980.6
chloride (acidifying agent)	963.2	E858.1	E933.2	E950.4	E962.0	E980.4
expectorant	975.5	E858.6	E945.5	E950.4	E962.0	E980.4
compounds (household) NEC	983.2	E861.4	—	E950.7	E962.1	E980.6
fumes (any usage)	987.8	E869.8	—	E952.8	E962.2	E982.8
industrial	983.2	E864.2	—	E950.7	E962.1	E980.6
ichthyosulfonate	976.4	E858.7	E946.4	E950.4	E962.0	E980.4
mandelate	961.9	E857	E931.9	E950.4	E962.0	E980.4
Amobarbital	967.0	E851	E937.0	E950.1	E962.0	E980.1
Amodiaquin(e)	961.4	E857	E931.4	E950.4	E962.0	E980.4
Amopyroquin(e)	961.4	E857	E931.4	E950.4	E962.0	E980.4
Amphenidone	969.5	E853.8	E939.5	E950.3	E962.0	E980.3
Amphetamine	969.7	E854.2	E939.7	E950.3	E962.0	E980.3
Amphomycin	960.8	E856	E930.8	E950.4	E962.0	E980.4
Amphotericin B	960.1	E856	E930.1	E950.4	E962.0	E980.4
topical	976.0	E858.7	E946.0	E950.4	E962.0	E980.4
Ampicillin	960.0	E856	E930.0	E950.4	E962.0	E980.4
Amprotropine	971.1	E855.4	E941.1	E950.4	E962.0	E980.4
Amygdalin	977.8	E858.8	E947.8	E950.4	E962.0	E980.4
Amyl						
acetate (vapor)	982.8	E862.4	—	E950.9	E962.1	E980.9
alcohol	980.3	E860.4	—	E950.9	E962.1	E980.9
nitrite (medicinal)	972.4	E858.3	E942.4	E950.4	E962.0	E980.4
Amylase (alpha)	963.4	E858.1	E933.4	E950.4	E962.0	E980.4
Amylene hydrate	980.8	E860.8	—	E950.9	E962.1	E980.9
Amylobarbitone	967.0	E851	E937.0	E950.1	E962.0	E980.1
Amylocaine	968.9	E855.2	E938.9	E950.4	E962.0	E980.4
infiltration (subcutaneous)	968.5	E855.2	E938.5	E950.4	E962.0	E980.4
nerve block (peripheral) (plexus)	968.6	E855.2	E938.6	E950.4	E962.0	E980.4
spinal	968.7	E855.2	E938.7	E950.4	E962.0	E980.4
topical (surface)	968.5	E855.2	E938.5	E950.4	E962.0	E980.4
Amytal (sodium)	967.0	E851	E937.0	E950.1	E962.0	E980.1
Analeptics	970.0	E854.3	E940.0	E950.4	E962.0	E980.4
Analgesics	965.9	E850.9	E935.9	E950.0	E962.0	E980.0
aromatic NEC	965.4	E850.4	E935.4	E950.0	E962.0	E980.0
non-narcotic NEC	965.7	E850.7	E935.7	E950.0	E962.0	E980.0
specified NEC	965.8	E850.8	E935.8	E950.0	E962.0	E980.0
Anamirta cocculus	988.2	E865.3	—	E950.9	E962.1	E980.9
Ancillin	960.0	E856	E930.0	E950.4	E962.0	E980.4
Androgens (anabolic congeners)	962.1	E858.0	E932.1	E950.4	E962.0	E980.4
Androstalone	962.1	E858.0	E932.1	E950.4	E962.0	E980.4
Androsterone	962.1	E858.0	E932.1	E950.4	E962.0	E980.4
Anemone pulsatilla	988.2	E865.4	—	E950.9	E962.1	E980.9
Anesthesia, anesthetic (general) NEC	968.4	E855.1	E938.4	E950.4	E962.0	E980.4
block (nerve) (plexus)	968.6	E855.2	E938.6	E950.4	E962.0	E980.4
gaseous NEC	968.2	E855.1	E938.2	E950.4	E962.0	E980.4
halogenated hydrocarbon derivatives NEC	968.2	E855.1	E938.2	E950.4	E962.0	E980.4
infiltration (intradermal) (subcutaneous) (submucosal)	968.5	E855.2	E938.5	E950.4	E962.0	E980.4
intravenous	968.3	E855.1	E938.3	E950.4	E962.0	E980.4
local NEC	968.9	E855.2	E938.9	E950.4	E962.0	E980.4
nerve blocking (peripheral) (plexus)	968.6	E855.2	E938.6	E950.4	E962.0	E980.4
rectal NEC	968.3	E855.1	E938.3	E950.4	E962.0	E980.4
spinal	968.7	E855.2	E938.7	E950.4	E962.0	E980.4
surface	968.5	E855.2	E938.5	E950.4	E962.0	E980.4
topical	968.5	E855.2	E938.5	E950.4	E962.0	E980.4
Aneurine	963.5	E858.1	E933.5	E950.4	E962.0	E980.4
Anginine — *see* Glyceryl trinitrate						
Angio-Conray	977.8	E858.8	E947.8	E950.4	E962.0	E980.4
Angiotensin	971.2	E855.5	E941.2	E950.4	E962.0	E980.4
Anhydrohydroxyprogesterone	962.2	E858.0	E932.2	E950.4	E962.0	E980.4
Anhydron	974.3	E858.5	E944.3	E950.4	E962.0	E980.4
Anileridine	965.09	E850.2	E935.2	E950.0	E962.0	E980.0
Aniline (dye) (liquid)	983.0	E864.0	—	E950.7	E962.1	E980.6
analgesic	965.4	E850.4	E935.4	E950.0	E962.0	E980.0
derivatives, therapeutic NEC	965.4	E850.4	E935.4	E950.0	E962.0	E980.0
vapor	987.8	E869.8	—	E952.8	E962.2	E982.8
Aniscoropine	971.1	E855.4	E941.1	E950.4	E962.0	E980.4

		External Cause (E-Code)				
	Poisoning	Accident	Therapeutic Use	Suicide Attempt	Assault	Undetermined
Anisindione	964.2	E858.2	E934.2	E950.4	E962.0	E980.4
Anorexic agents	977.0	E858.8	E947.0	E950.4	E962.0	E980.4
Ant (bite) (sting)	—	E905.5	—	E950.9	E962.1	E980.9
Antabuse	977.3	E858.8	E947.3	E950.4	E962.0	E980.4
Antacids	973.0	E858.4	E943.0	E950.4	E962.0	E980.4
Antazoline	963.0	E858.1	E933.0	E950.4	E962.0	E980.4
Anthralin	976.4	E858.7	E946.4	E950.4	E962.0	E980.4
Anthramycin	960.7	E856	E930.7	E950.4	E962.0	E980.4
Antiadrenergics	971.3	E855.6	E941.3	E950.4	E962.0	E980.4
Antiallergic agents	963.0	E858.1	E933.0	E950.4	E962.0	E980.4
Antianemic agents NEC	964.1	E858.2	E934.1	E950.4	E962.0	E980.4
Antiaris toxicaria	988.2	E865.4	—	E950.9	E962.1	E980.9
Antiarteriosclerotic agents	972.2	E858.3	E942.2	E950.4	E962.0	E980.4
Antiasthmatics	975.7	E858.6	E945.7	E950.4	E962.0	E980.4
Antibiotics	960.9	E856	E930.9	E950.4	E962.0	E980.4
antifungal	960.1	E856	E930.1	E950.4	E962.0	E980.4
antimycobacterial	960.6	E856	E930.6	E950.4	E962.0	E980.4
antineoplastic	960.7	E856	E930.7	E950.4	E962.0	E980.4
cephalosporin (group)	960.5	E856	E930.5	E950.4	E962.0	E980.4
chloramphenicol (group)	960.2	E856	E930.2	E950.4	E962.0	E980.4
macrolides	960.3	E856	E930.3	E950.4	E962.0	E980.4
specified NEC	960.8	E856	E930.8	E950.4	E962.0	E980.4
tetracycline (group)	960.4	E856	E930.4	E950.4	E962.0	E980.4
Anticancer agents NEC	963.1	E858.1	E933.1	E950.4	E962.0	E980.4
antibiotics	960.7	E856	E930.7	E950.4	E962.0	E980.4
Anticholinergics	971.1	E855.4	E941.1	E950.4	E962.0	E980.4
Anticholinesterase (organophosphorus) (reversible)	971.0	E855.3	E941.0	E950.4	E962.0	E980.4
Anticoagulants	964.2	E858.2	E934.2	E950.4	E962.0	E980.4
antagonists	964.5	E858.2	E934.5	E950.4	E962.0	E980.4
Anti-common cold agents NEC	975.6	E858.6	E945.6	E950.4	E962.0	E980.4
Anticonvulsants NEC	966.3	E855.0	E936.3	E950.4	E962.0	E980.4
Antidepressants	969.0	E854.0	E939.0	E950.3	E962.0	E980.3
Antidiabetic agents	962.3	E858.0	E932.3	E950.4	E962.0	E980.4
Antidiarrheal agents	973.5	E858.4	E943.5	E950.4	E962.0	E980.4
Antidiuretic hormone	962.5	E858.0	E932.5	E950.4	E962.0	E980.4
Antidotes NEC	977.2	E858.8	E947.2	E950.4	E962.0	E980.4
Antiemetic agents	963.0	E858.1	E933.0	E950.4	E962.0	E980.4
Antiepilepsy agent NEC	966.3	E855.0	E936.3	E950.4	E962.0	E980.4
Antifertility pills	962.2	E858.0	E932.2	E950.4	E962.0	E980.4
Antiflatulents	973.8	E858.4	E943.8	E950.4	E962.0	E980.4
Antifreeze	989.89	E866.8	—	E950.9	E962.1	E980.9
alcohol	980.1	E860.2	—	E950.9	E962.1	E980.9
ethylene glycol	982.8	E862.4	—	E950.9	E962.1	E980.9
Antifungals (nonmedicinal) (sprays)	989.4	E863.6	—	E950.6	E962.1	E980.7
medicinal NEC	961.9	E857	E931.9	E950.4	E962.0	E980.4
antibiotic	960.1	E856	E930.1	E950.4	E962.0	E980.4
topical	976.0	E858.7	E946.0	E950.4	E962.0	E980.4
Antigastric secretion agents	973.0	E858.4	E943.0	E950.4	E962.0	E980.4
Antihelmintics	961.6	E857	E931.6	E950.4	E962.0	E980.4
Antihemophilic factor (human)	964.7	E858.2	E934.7	E950.4	E962.0	E980.4
Antihistamine	963.0	E858.1	E933.0	E950.4	E962.0	E980.4
Antihypertensive agents NEC	972.6	E858.3	E942.6	E950.4	E962.0	E980.4
Anti-infectives NEC	961.9	E857	E931.9	E950.4	E962.0	E980.4
antibiotics	960.9	E856	E930.9	E950.4	E962.0	E980.4
specified NEC	960.8	E856	E930.8	E950.4	E962.0	E980.4
antihelmintic	961.6	E857	E931.6	E950.4	E962.0	E980.4
antimalarial	961.4	E857	E931.4	E950.4	E962.0	E980.4
antimycobacterial NEC	961.8	E857	E931.8	E950.4	E962.0	E980.4
antibiotics	960.6	E856	E930.6	E950.4	E962.0	E980.4
antiprotozoal NEC	961.5	E857	E931.5	E950.4	E962.0	—
blood	961.4	E857	E931.4	E950.4	E962.0	E980.4
antiviral	961.7	E857	E931.7	E950.4	E962.0	E980.4
arsenical	961.1	E857	E931.1	E950.4	E962.0	E980.4
ENT agents	976.6	E858.7	E946.6	E950.4	E962.0	E980.4
heavy metals NEC	961.2	E857	E931.2	E950.4	E962.0	E980.4
local	976.0	E858.7	E946.0	E950.4	E962.0	E980.4
ophthalmic preparation	976.5	E858.7	E946.5	E950.4	E962.0	E980.4
topical NEC	976.0	E858.7	E946.0	E950.4	E962.0	E980.4
Anti-inflammatory agents (topical)	976.0	E858.7	E946.0	E950.4	E962.0	E980.4
Antiknock (tetraethyl lead)	984.1	E862.1	—	E950.9	—	E980.9
Antilipemics	972.2	E858.3	E942.2	E950.4	E962.0	E980.4
Antimalarials	961.4	E857	E931.4	E950.4	E962.0	E980.4
Antimony (compounds) (vapor) NEC	985.4	E866.2	—	E950.9	E962.1	E980.9
anti-infectives	961.2	E857	E931.2	E950.4	E962.0	E980.4
pesticides (vapor)	985.4	E863.4	—	E950.6	E962.2	E980.7
potassium tartrate	961.2	E857	E931.2	E950.4	E962.0	E980.4
tartrated	961.2	E857	E931.2	E950.4	E962.0	E980.4
Antimuscarinic agents	971.1	E855.4	E941.1	E950.4	E962.0	E980.4
Antimycobacterials NEC	961.8	E857	E931.8	E950.4	E962.0	E980.4
antibiotics	960.6	E856	E930.6	E950.4	E962.0	E980.4
Antineoplastic agents	963.1	E858.1	E933.1	E950.4	E962.0	E980.4
antibiotics	960.7	E856	E930.7	E950.4	E962.0	E980.4
Anti-Parkinsonism agents	966.4	E855.0	E936.4	E950.4	E962.0	E980.4
Antiphlogistics	965.69	E850.6	E935.6	E950.0	E962.0	E980.0
Antiprotozoals NEC	961.5	E857	E931.5	E950.4	E962.0	E980.4
blood	961.4	E857	E931.4	E950.4	E962.0	E980.4
Antipruritics (local)	976.1	E858.7	E946.1	E950.4	E962.0	E980.4
Antipsychotic agents NEC	969.3	E853.8	E939.3	E950.3	E962.0	E980.3
Antipyretics	965.9	E850.9	E935.9	E950.0	E962.0	E980.0
specified NEC	965.8	E850.8	E935.8	E950.0	E962.0	E980.0
Antipyrine	965.5	E850.5	E935.5	E950.0	E962.0	E980.0
Antirabies serum (equine)	979.9	E858.8	E949.9	E950.4	E962.0	E980.4
Antirheumatics	965.69	E850.6	E935.6	E950.0	E962.0	E980.0
Antiseborrheics	976.4	E858.7	E946.4	E950.4	E962.0	E980.4
Antiseptics (external) (medicinal)	976.0	E858.7	E946.0	E950.4	E962.0	E980.4
Antistine	963.0	E858.1	E933.0	E950.4	E962.0	E980.4
Antithyroid agents	962.8	E858.0	E932.8	E950.4	E962.0	E980.4
Antitoxin, any	979.9	E858.8	E949.9	E950.4	E962.0	E980.4
Antituberculars	961.8	E857	E931.8	E950.4	E962.0	E980.4
antibiotics	960.6	E856	E930.6	E950.4	E962.0	E980.4
Antitussives	975.4	E858.6	E945.4	E950.4	E962.0	E980.4
Antivaricose agents (sclerosing)	972.7	E858.3	E942.7	E950.4	E962.0	E980.4
Antivenin (crotaline) (spider-bite)	979.9	E858.8	E949.9	E950.4	E962.0	E980.4
Antivert	963.0	E858.1	E933.0	E950.4	E962.0	E980.4
Antivirals NEC	961.7	E857	E931.7	E950.4	E962.0	E980.4
Ant poisons — *see* Pesticides						
Antrol	989.4	E863.4	—	E950.6	E962.1	E980.7
fungicide	989.4	E863.6	—	E950.6	E962.1	E980.7
Apomorphine hydrochloride (emetic)	973.6	E858.4	E943.6	E950.4	E962.0	E980.4
Appetite depressants, central	977.0	E858.8	E947.0	E950.4	E962.0	E980.4
Apresoline	972.6	E858.3	E942.6	E950.4	E962.0	E980.4
Aprobarbital, aprobarbitone	967.0	E851	E937.0	E950.1	E962.0	E980.1
Apronalide	967.8	E852.8	E937.8	E950.2	E962.0	E980.2
Aqua fortis	983.1	E864.1	—	E950.7	E962.1	E980.6
Arachis oil (topical)	976.3	E858.7	E946.3	E950.4	E962.0	E980.4
cathartic	973.2	E858.4	E943.2	E950.4	E962.0	E980.4
Aralen	961.4	E857	E931.4	E950.4	E962.0	E980.4
Arginine salts	974.5	E858.5	E944.5	E950.4	E962.0	E980.4
Argyrol	976.0	E858.7	E946.0	E950.4	E962.0	E980.4
ENT agent	976.6	E858.7	E946.6	E950.4	E962.0	E980.4
ophthalmic preparation	976.5	E858.7	E946.5	E950.4	E962.0	E980.4
Aristocort	962.0	E858.0	E932.0	E950.4	E962.0	E980.4
ENT agent	976.6	E858.7	E946.6	E950.4	E962.0	E980.4
ophthalmic preparation	976.5	E858.7	E946.5	E950.4	E962.0	E980.4
topical NEC	976.0	E858.7	E946.0	E950.4	E962.0	E980.4
Aromatics, corrosive	983.0	E864.0	—	E950.7	E962.1	E980.6
disinfectants	983.0	E861.4	—	E950.7	E962.1	E980.6
Arsenate of lead (insecticide)	985.1	E863.4	—	E950.8	E962.1	E980.8
herbicide	985.1	E863.5	—	E950.8	E962.1	E980.8
Arsenic, arsenicals (compounds) (dust) (fumes) (vapor) NEC	985.1	E866.3	—	E950.8	E962.1	E980.8
anti-infectives	961.1	E857	E931.1	E950.4	E962.0	E980.4
pesticide (dust) (fumes)	985.1	E863.4	—	E950.8	E962.1	E980.8
Arsine (gas)	985.1	E866.3	—	E950.8	E962.1	E980.8
Arsphenamine (silver)	961.1	E857	E931.1	E950.4	E962.0	E980.4
Arsthinol	961.1	E857	E931.1	E950.4	E962.0	E980.4
Artane	971.1	E855.4	E941.1	E950.4	E962.0	E980.4
Arthropod (venomous) NEC	989.5	E905.5	—	E950.9	E962.1	E980.9
Asbestos	989.81	E866.8	—	E950.9	E962.1	E980.9
Ascaridole	961.6	E857	E931.6	E950.4	E962.0	E980.4
Ascorbic acid	963.5	E858.1	E933.5	E950.4	E962.0	E980.4
Asiaticoside	976.0	E858.7	E946.0	E950.4	E962.0	E980.4
Aspidium (oleoresin)	961.6	E857	E931.6	E950.4	E962.0	E980.4

		External Cause (E-Code)				
	Poisoning	Accident	Therapeutic Use	Suicide Attempt	Assault	Undetermined
Aspirin	965.1	E850.3	E935.3	E950.0	E962.0	E980.0
Astringents (local)	976.2	E858.7	E946.2	E950.4	E962.0	E980.4
Atabrine	961.3	E857	E931.3	E950.4	E962.0	E980.4
Ataractics	969.5	E853.8	E939.5	E950.3	E962.0	E980.3
Atonia drug, intestinal	973.3	E858.4	E943.3	E950.4	E962.0	E980.4
Atophan	974.7	E858.5	E944.7	E950.4	E962.0	E980.4
Atropine	971.1	E855.4	E941.1	E950.4	E962.0	E980.4
Attapulgite	973.5	E858.4	E943.5	E950.4	E962.0	E980.4
Attenuvax	979.4	E858.8	E949.4	E950.4	E962.0	E980.4
Aureomycin	960.4	E856	E930.4	E950.4	E962.0	E980.4
ophthalmic preparation	976.5	E858.7	E946.5	E950.4	E962.0	E980.4
topical NEC	976.0	E858.7	E946.0	E950.4	E962.0	E980.4
Aurothioglucose	965.69	E850.6	E935.6	E950.0	E962.0	E980.0
Aurothioglycanide	965.69	E850.6	E935.6	E950.0	E962.0	E980.0
Aurothiomalate	965.69	E850.6	E935.6	E950.0	E962.0	E980.0
Automobile fuel	981	E862.1	—	E950.9	E962.1	E980.9
Autonomic nervous system agents NEC	971.9	E855.9	E941.9	E950.4	E962.0	E980.4
Avlosulfon	961.8	E857	E931.8	E950.4	E962.0	E980.4
Avomine	967.8	E852.8	E937.8	E950.2	E962.0	E980.2
Azacyclonol	969.5	E853.8	E939.5	E950.3	E962.0	E980.3
Azapetine	971.3	E855.6	E941.3	E950.4	E962.0	E980.4
Azaribine	963.1	E858.1	E933.1	E950.4	E962.0	E980.4
Azaserine	960.7	E856	E930.7	E950.4	E962.0	E980.4
Azathioprine	963.1	E858.1	E933.1	E950.4	E962.0	E980.4
Azosulfamide	961.0	E857	E931.0	E950.4	E962.0	E980.4
Azulfidine	961.0	E857	E931.0	E950.4	E962.0	E980.4
Azuresin	977.8	E858.8	E947.8	E950.4	E962.0	E980.4
Bacimycin	976.0	E858.7	E946.0	E950.4	E962.0	E980.4
ophthalmic preparation	976.5	E858.7	E946.5	E950.4	E962.0	E980.4
Bacitracin	960.8	E856	E930.8	E950.4	E962.0	E980.4
ENT agent	976.6	E858.7	E946.6	E950.4	E962.0	E980.4
ophthalmic preparation	976.5	E858.7	E946.5	E950.4	E962.0	E980.4
topical NEC	976.0	E858.7	E946.0	E950.4	E962.0	E980.4
Baking soda	963.3	E858.1	E933.3	E950.4	E962.0	E980.4
BAL	963.8	E858.1	E933.8	E950.4	E962.0	E980.4
Bamethan (sulfate)	972.5	E858.3	E942.5	E950.4	E962.0	E980.4
Bamipine	963.0	E858.1	E933.0	E950.4	E962.0	E980.4
Baneberry	988.2	E865.4	—	E950.9	E962.1	E980.9
Banewort	988.2	E865.4	—	E950.9	E962.1	E980.9
Barbenyl	967.0	E851	E937.0	E950.1	E962.0	E980.1
Barbital, barbitone	967.0	E851	E937.0	E950.1	E962.0	E980.1
Barbiturates, barbituric acid	967.0	E851	E937.0	E950.1	E962.0	E980.1
anesthetic (intravenous)	968.3	E855.1	E938.3	E950.4	E962.0	E980.4
Barium (carbonate) (chloride) (sulfate)	985.8	E866.4	—	E950.9	E962.1	E980.9
diagnostic agent	977.8	E858.8	E947.8	E950.4	E962.0	E980.4
pesticide	985.8	E863.4	—	E950.6	E962.1	E980.7
rodenticide	985.8	E863.7	—	E950.6	E962.1	E980.7
Barrier cream	976.3	E858.7	E946.3	E950.4	E962.0	E980.4
Battery acid or fluid	983.1	E864.1	—	E950.7	E962.1	E980.6
Bay rum	980.8	E860.8	—	E950.9	E962.1	E980.9
BCG vaccine	978.0	E858.8	E948.0	E950.4	E962.0	E980.4
Bearsfoot	988.2	E865.4	—	E950.9	E962.1	E980.9
Beclamide	966.3	E855.0	E936.3	E950.4	E962.0	E980.4
Bee (sting) (venom)	989.5	E905.3	—	E950.9	E962.1	E980.9
Belladonna (alkaloids)	971.1	E855.4	E941.1	E950.4	E962.0	E980.4
Bemegride	970.0	E854.3	E940.0	E950.4	E962.0	E980.4
Benactyzine	969.8	E855.8	E939.8	E950.3	E962.0	E980.3
Benadryl	963.0	E858.1	E933.0	E950.4	E962.0	E980.4
Bendrofluazide	974.3	E858.5	E944.3	E950.4	E962.0	E980.4
Bendroflumethiazide	974.3	E858.5	E944.3	E950.4	E962.0	E980.4
Benemid	974.7	E858.5	E944.7	E950.4	E962.0	E980.4
Benethamine penicillin G	960.0	E856	E930.0	E950.4	E962.0	E980.4
Benisone	976.0	E858.7	E946.0	E950.4	E962.0	E980.4
Benoquin	976.8	E858.7	E946.8	E950.4	E962.0	E980.4
Benoxinate	968.5	E855.2	E938.5	E950.4	E962.0	E980.4
Bentonite	976.3	E858.7	E946.3	E950.4	E962.0	E980.4
Benzalkonium (chloride)	976.0	E858.7	E946.0	E950.4	E962.0	E980.4
ophthalmic preparation	976.5	E858.7	E946.5	E950.4	E962.0	E980.4
Benzamidosalicylate (calcium)	961.8	E857	E931.8	E950.4	E962.0	E980.4
Benzathine penicillin	960.0	E856	E930.0	E950.4	E962.0	E980.4
Benzcarbimine	963.1	E858.1	E933.1	E950.4	E962.0	E980.4
Benzedrex	971.2	E855.5	E941.2	E950.4	E962.0	E980.4
Benzedrine (amphetamine)	969.7	E854.2	E939.7	E950.3	E962.0	E980.3
Benzene (acetyl) (dimethyl) (methyl) (solvent) (vapor)	982.0	E862.4	—	E950.9	E962.1	E980.9
hexachloride (gamma) (insecticide) (vapor)	989.2	E863.0	—	E950.6	E962.1	E980.7
Benzethonium	976.0	E858.7	E946.0	E950.4	E962.0	E980.4
Benzhexol (chloride)	966.4	E855.0	E936.4	E950.4	E962.0	E980.4
Benzilonium	971.1	E855.4	E941.1	E950.4	E962.0	E980.4
Benzin(e) — *see* Ligroin						
Benziodarone	972.4	E858.3	E942.4	E950.4	E962.0	E980.4
Benzocaine	968.5	E855.2	E938.5	E950.4	E962.0	E980.4
Benzodiapin	969.4	E853.2	E939.4	E950.3	E962.0	E980.3
Benzodiazepines (tranquilizers) NEC	969.4	E853.2	E939.4	E950.3	E962.0	E980.3
Benzoic acid (with salicylic acid) (anti-infective)	976.0	E858.7	E946.0	E950.4	E962.0	E980.4
Benzoin	976.3	E858.7	E946.3	E950.4	E962.0	E980.4
Benzol (vapor)	982.0	E862.4	—	E950.9	E962.1	E980.9
Benzomorphan	965.09	E850.2	E935.2	E950.0	E962.0	E980.0
Benzonatate	975.4	E858.6	E945.4	E950.4	E962.0	E980.4
Benzothiadiazides	974.3	E858.5	E944.3	E950.4	E962.0	E980.4
Benzoylpas	961.8	E857	E931.8	E950.4	E962.0	E980.4
Benzperidol	969.5	E853.8	E939.5	E950.3	E962.0	E980.3
Benzphetamine	977.0	E858.8	E947.0	E950.4	E962.0	E980.4
Benzpyrinium	971.0	E855.3	E941.0	E950.4	E962.0	E980.4
Benzquinamide	963.0	E858.1	E933.0	E950.4	E962.0	E980.4
Benzthiazide	974.3	E858.5	E944.3	E950.4	E962.0	E980.4
Benztropine	971.1	E855.4	E941.1	E950.4	E962.0	E980.4
Benzyl						
acetate	982.8	E862.4	—	E950.9	E962.1	E980.9
benzoate (anti-infective)	976.0	E858.7	E946.0	E950.4	E962.0	E980.4
morphine	965.09	E850.2	E935.2	E950.0	E962.0	E980.0
penicillin	960.0	E856	E930.0	E950.4	E962.0	E980.4
Bephenium hydroxynapthoate	961.6	E857	E931.6	E950.4	E962.0	E980.4
Bergamot oil	989.89	E866.8	—	E950.9	E962.1	E980.9
Berries, poisonous	988.2	E865.3	—	E950.9	E962.1	E980.9
Beryllium (compounds) (fumes)	985.3	E866.4	—	E950.9	E962.1	E980.9
Beta-carotene	976.3	E858.7	E946.3	E950.4	E962.0	E980.4
Beta-Chlor	967.1	E852.0	E937.1	E950.2	E962.0	E980.2
Betamethasone	962.0	E858.0	E932.0	E950.4	E962.0	E980.4
topical	976.0	E858.7	E946.0	E950.4	E962.0	E980.4
Betazole	977.8	E858.8	E947.8	E950.4	E962.0	E980.4
Bethanechol	971.0	E855.3	E941.0	E950.4	E962.0	E980.4
Bethanidine	972.6	E858.3	E942.6	E950.4	E962.0	E980.4
Betula oil	976.3	E858.7	E946.3	E950.4	E962.0	E980.4
Bhang	969.6	E854.1	E939.6	E950.3	E962.0	E980.3
Bialamicol	961.5	E857	E931.5	E950.4	E962.0	E980.4
Bichloride of mercury — *see* Mercury, chloride						
Bichromates (calcium) (crystals) (potassium) (sodium)	983.9	E864.3	—	E950.7	E962.1	E980.6
fumes	987.8	E869.8	—	E952.8	E962.2	E982.8
Biguanide derivatives, oral	962.3	E858.0	E932.3	E950.4	E962.0	E980.4
Biligrafin	977.8	E858.8	E947.8	E950.4	E962.0	E980.4
Bilopaque	977.8	E858.8	E947.8	E950.4	E962.0	E980.4
Bioflavonoids	972.8	E858.3	E942.8	E950.4	E962.0	E980.4
Biological substance NEC	979.9	E858.8	E949.9	E950.4	E962.0	E980.4
Biperiden	966.4	E855.0	E936.4	E950.4	E962.0	E980.4
Bisacodyl	973.1	E858.4	E943.1	E950.4	E962.0	E980.4
Bishydroxycoumarin	964.2	E858.2	E934.2	E950.4	E962.0	E980.4
Bismarsen	961.1	E857	E931.1	E950.4	E962.0	E980.4
Bismuth (compounds) NEC	985.8	E866.4	—	E950.9	E962.1	E980.9
anti-infectives	961.2	E857	E931.2	E950.4	E962.0	E980.4
subcarbonate	973.5	E858.4	E943.5	E950.4	E962.0	E980.4
sulfarsphenamine	961.1	E857	E931.1	E950.4	E962.0	E980.4
Bisphosphonates						
intravenous	963.1	E858.1	E933.7	E950.4	E962.0	E980.4
oral	963.1	E858.1	E933.6	E950.4	E962.0	E980.4
Bithionol	961.6	E857	E931.6	E950.4	E962.0	E980.4
Bitter almond oil	989.0	E866.8	—	E950.9	E962.1	E980.9
Bittersweet	988.2	E865.4	—	E950.9	E962.1	E930.9
Black						
flag	989.4	E863.4	—	E950.6	E962.1	E980.7
henbane	988.2	E865.4	—	E950.9	E962.1	E980.9
leaf (40)	989.4	E863.4	—	E950.6	E962.1	E980.7
widow spider (bite)	989.5	E905.1	—	E950.9	E962.1	E980.9
antivenin	979.9	E858.8	E949.9	E950.4	E962.0	E980.4
Blast furnace gas (carbon monoxide from)	986	E868.8	—	E952.1	E962.2	E982.1
Bleach NEC	983.9	E864.3	—	E950.7	E962.1	E980.6
Bleaching solutions	983.9	E864.3	—	E950.7	E962.1	E980.6
Bleomycin (sulfate)	960.7	E856	E930.7	E950.4	E962.0	E980.4

		External Cause (E-Code)				
	Poisoning	Accident	Therapeutic Use	Suicide Attempt	Assault	Undetermined
Blockain	968.9	E855.2	E938.9	E950.4	E962.0	E980.4
infiltration (subcutaneous)	968.5	E855.2	E938.5	E950.4	E962.0	E980.4
nerve block (peripheral) (plexus)	968.6	E855.2	E938.6	E950.4	E962.0	E980.4
topical (surface)	968.5	E855.2	E938.5	E950.4	E962.0	E980.4
Blood (derivatives) (natural) (plasma) (whole)	964.7	E858.2	E934.7	E950.4	E962.0	E980.4
affecting agent	964.9	E858.2	E934.9	E950.4	E962.0	E980.4
specified NEC	964.8	E858.2	E934.8	E950.4	E962.0	E980.4
substitute (macromolecular)	964.8	E858.2	E934.8	E950.4	E962.0	E980.4
Blue velvet	965.09	E850.2	E935.2	E950.0	E962.0	E980.0
Bone meal	989.89	E866.5	—	E950.9	E962.1	E980.9
Bonine	963.0	E858.1	E933.0	E950.4	E962.0	E980.4
Boracic acid	976.0	E858.7	E946.0	E950.4	E962.0	E980.4
ENT agent	976.6	E858.7	E946.6	E950.4	E962.0	E980.4
ophthalmic preparation	976.5	E858.7	E946.5	E950.4	E962.0	E980.4
Borate (cleanser) (sodium)	989.6	E861.3	—	E950.9	E962.1	E980.9
Borax (cleanser)	989.6	E861.3	—	E950.9	E962.1	E980.9
Boric acid	976.0	E858.7	E946.0	E950.4	E962.0	E980.4
ENT agent	976.6	E858.7	E946.6	E950.4	E962.0	E980.4
ophthalmic preparation	976.5	E858.7	E946.5	E950.4	E962.0	E980.4
Boron hydride NEC	989.89	E866.8	—	E950.9	E962.1	E980.9
fumes or gas	987.8	E869.8	—	E952.8	E962.2	E982.8
Botox	975.3	E858.6	E945.3	E950.4	E962.0	E980.4
Brake fluid vapor	987.8	E869.8	—	E952.8	E962.2	E982.8
Brass (compounds) (fumes)	985.8	E866.4	—	E950.9	E962.1	E980.9
Brasso	981	E861.3	—	E950.9	E962.1	E980.9
Bretylium (tosylate)	972.6	E858.3	E942.6	E950.4	E962.0	E980.4
Brevital (sodium)	968.3	E855.1	E938.3	E950.4	E962.0	E980.4
British antilewisite	963.8	E858.1	E933.8	E950.4	E962.0	E980.4
Bromal (hydrate)	967.3	E852.2	E937.3	E950.2	E962.0	E980.2
Bromelains	963.4	E858.1	E933.4	E950.4	E962.0	E980.4
Bromides NEC	967.3	E852.2	E937.3	E950.2	E962.0	E980.2
Bromine (vapor)	987.8	E869.8	—	E952.8	E962.2	E982.8
compounds (medicinal)	967.3	E852.2	E937.3	E950.2	E962.0	E980.2
Bromisovalum	967.3	E852.2	E937.3	E950.2	E962.0	E980.2
Bromobenzyl cyanide	987.5	E869.3	—	E952.8	E962.2	E982.8
Bromodiphenhydramine	963.0	E858.1	E933.0	E950.4	E962.0	E980.4
Bromoform	967.3	E852.2	E937.3	E950.2	E962.0	E980.2
Bromophenol blue reagent	977.8	E858.8	E947.8	E950.4	E962.0	E980.4
Bromosalicylhydroxamic acid	961.8	E857	E931.8	E950.4	E962.0	E980.4
Bromo-seltzer	965.4	E850.4	E935.4	E950.0	E962.0	E980.0
Brompheniramine	963.0	E858.1	E933.0	E950.4	E962.0	E980.4
Bromural	967.3	E852.2	E937.3	E950.2	E962.0	E980.2
Brown spider (bite) (venom)	989.5	E905.1	—	E950.9	E962.1	E980.9
Brucia	988.2	E865.3	—	E950.9	E962.1	E980.9
Brucine	989.1	E863.7	—	E950.6	E962.1	E980.7
Brunswick green — *see* Copper						
Bruten — *see* Ibuprofen						
Bryonia (alba) (dioica)	988.2	E865.4	—	E950.9	E962.1	E980.9
Buclizine	969.5	E853.8	E939.5	E950.3	E962.0	E980.3
Bufferin	965.1	E850.3	E935.3	E950.0	E962.0	E980.0
Bufotenine	969.6	E854.1	E939.6	E950.3	E962.0	E980.3
Buphenine	971.2	E855.5	E941.2	E950.4	E962.0	E980.4
Bupivacaine	968.9	E855.2	E938.9	E950.4	E962.0	E980.4
infiltration (subcutaneous)	968.5	E855.2	E938.5	E950.4	E962.0	E980.4
nerve block (peripheral) (plexus)	968.6	E855.2	E938.6	E950.4	E962.0	E980.4
Busulfan	963.1	E858.1	E933.1	E950.4	E962.0	E980.4
Butabarbital (sodium)	967.0	E851	E937.0	E950.1	E962.0	E980.1
Butabarbitone	967.0	E851	E937.0	E950.1	E962.0	E980.1
Butabarpal	967.0	E851	E937.0	E950.1	E962.0	E980.1
Butacaine	968.5	E855.2	E938.5	E950.4	E962.0	E980.4
Butallylonal	967.0	E851	E937.0	E950.1	E962.0	E980.1
Butane (distributed in mobile container)	987.0	E868.0	—	E951.1	E962.2	E981.1
distributed through pipes	987.0	E867	—	E951.0	E962.2	E981.0
incomplete combustion of — *see* Carbon monoxide, butane						
Butanol	980.3	E860.4	—	E950.9	E962.1	E980.9
Butanone	982.8	E862.4	—	E950.9	E962.1	E980.9
Butaperazine	969.1	E853.0	E939.1	E950.3	E962.0	E980.3
Butazolidin	965.5	E850.5	E935.5	E950.0	E962.0	E980.0
Butethal	967.0	E851	E937.0	E950.1	E962.0	E980.1
Butethamate	971.1	E855.4	E941.1	E950.4	E962.0	E980.4
Buthalitone (sodium)	968.3	E855.1	E938.3	E950.4	E962.0	E980.4
Butisol (sodium)	967.0	E851	E937.0	E950.1	E962.0	E980.1
Butobarbital, butobarbitone	967.0	E851	E937.0	E950.1	E962.0	E980.1
Butriptyline	969.0	E854.0	E939.0	E950.3	E962.0	E980.3
Buttercups	988.2	E865.4	—	E950.9	E962.1	E980.9
Butter of antimony — *see* Antimony						
Butyl						
acetate (secondary)	982.8	E862.4	—	E950.9	E962.1	E980.9
alcohol	980.3	E860.4	—	E950.9	E962.1	E980.9
carbinol	980.8	E860.8	—	E950.9	E962.1	E980.9
carbitol	982.8	E862.4	—	E950.9	E962.1	E980.9
cellosolve	982.8	E862.4	—	E950.9	E962.1	E980.9
chloral (hydrate)	967.1	E852.0	E937.1	E950.2	E962.0	E980.2
formate	982.8	E862.4	—	E950.9	E962.1	E980.9
scopolammonium bromide	971.1	E855.4	E941.1	E950.4	E962.0	E980.4
Butyn	968.5	E855.2	E938.5	E950.4	E962.0	E980.4
Butyrophenone (-based tranquilizers)	969.2	E853.1	E939.2	E950.3	E962.0	E980.3
Cacodyl, cacodylic acid — *see* Arsenic						
Cactinomycin	960.7	E856	E930.7	E950.4	E962.0	E980.4
Cade oil	976.4	E858.7	E946.4	E950.4	E962.0	E980.4
Cadmium (chloride) (compounds) (dust) (fumes) (oxide)	985.5	E866.4	—	E950.9	E962.1	E980.9
sulfide (medicinal) NEC	976.4	E858.7	E946.4	E950.4	E962.0	E980.4
Caffeine	969.7	E854.2	E939.7	E950.3	E962.0	E980.3
Calabar bean	988.2	E865.4	—	E950.9	E962.1	E980.9
Caladium seguinium	988.2	E865.4	—	E950.9	E962.1	E980.9
Calamine (liniment) (lotion)	976.3	E858.7	E946.3	E950.4	E962.0	E980.4
Calciferol	963.5	E858.1	E933.5	E950.4	E962.0	E980.4
Calcium (salts) NEC	974.5	E858.5	E944.5	E950.4	E962.0	E980.4
acetylsalicylate	965.1	E850.3	E935.3	E950.0	E962.0	E980.0
benzamidosalicylate	961.8	E857	E931.8	E950.4	E962.0	E980.4
carbaspirin	965.1	E850.3	E935.3	E950.0	E962.0	E980.0
carbimide (citrated)	977.3	E858.8	E947.3	E950.4	E962.0	E980.4
carbonate (antacid)	973.0	E858.4	E943.0	E950.4	E962.0	E980.4
cyanide (citrated)	977.3	E858.8	E947.3	E950.4	E962.0	E980.4
dioctyl sulfosuccinate	973.2	E858.4	E943.2	E950.4	E962.0	E980.4
disodium edathamil	963.8	E858.1	E933.8	E950.4	E962.0	E980.4
disodium edetate	963.8	E858.1	E933.8	E950.4	E962.0	E980.4
EDTA	963.8	E858.1	E933.8	E950.4	E962.0	E980.4
hydrate, hydroxide	983.2	E864.2	—	E950.7	E962.1	E980.6
mandelate	961.9	E857	E931.9	E950.4	E962.0	E980.4
oxide	983.2	E864.2	—	E950.7	E962.1	E980.6
Calomel — see Mercury, chloride						
Caloric agents NEC	974.5	E858.5	E944.5	E950.4	E962.0	E980.4
Calusterone	963.1	E858.1	E933.1	E950.4	E962.0	E980.4
Camoquin	961.4	E857	E931.4	E950.4	E962.0	E980.4
Camphor (oil)	976.1	E858.7	E946.1	E950.4	E962.0	E980.4
Candeptin	976.0	E858.7	E946.0	E950.4	E962.0	E980.4
Candicidin	976.0	E858.7	E946.0	E950.4	E962.0	E980.4
Cannabinols	969.6	E854.1	E939.6	E950.3	E962.0	E980.3
Cannabis (derivatives) (indica) (sativa)	969.6	E854.1	E939.6	E950.3	E962.0	E980.3
Canned heat	980.1	E860.2	—	E950.9	E962.1	E980.9
Cantharides, cantharidin, cantharis	976.8	E858.7	E946.8	E950.4	E962.0	E980.4
Capillary agents	972.8	E858.3	E942.8	E950.4	E962.0	E980.4
Capreomycin	960.6	E856	E930.6	E950.4	E962.0	E980.4
Captodiame, captodiamine	969.5	E853.8	E939.5	E950.3	E962.0	E980.3
Caramiphen (hydrochloride)	971.1	E855.4	E941.1	E950.4	E962.0	E980.4
Carbachol	971.0	E855.3	E941.0	E950.4	E962.0	E980.4
Carbacrylamine resins	974.5	E858.5	E944.5	E950.4	E962.0	E980.4
Carbamate (sedative)	967.8	E852.8	E937.8	E950.2	E962.0	E980.2
herbicide	989.3	E863.5	—	E950.6	E962.1	E980.7
insecticide	989.3	E863.2	—	E950.6	E962.1	E980.7
Carbamazepine	966.3	E855.0	E936.3	E950.4	E962.0	E980.4
Carbamic esters	967.8	E852.8	E937.8	E950.2	E962.0	E980.2
Carbamide	974.4	E858.5	E944.4	E950.4	E962.0	E980.4
topical	976.8	E858.7	E946.8	E950.4	E962.0	E980.4
Carbamylcholine chloride	971.0	E855.3	E941.0	E950.4	E962.0	E980.4
Carbarsone	961.1	E857	E931.1	E950.4	E962.0	E980.4
Carbaryl	989.3	E863.2	—	E950.6	E962.1	E980.7
Carbaspirin	965.1	E850.3	E935.3	E950.0	E962.0	E980.0
Carbazochrome	972.8	E858.3	E942.8	E950.4	E962.0	E980.4
Carbenicillin	960.0	E856	E930.0	E950.4	E962.0	E980.4
Carbenoxolone	973.8	E858.4	E943.8	E950.4	E962.0	E980.4
Carbetapentane	975.4	E858.6	E945.4	E950.4	E962.0	E980.4
Carbimazole	962.8	E858.0	E932.8	E950.4	E962.0	E980.4
Carbinol	980.1	E860.2	—	E950.9	E962.1	E980.9

☑ Additional Digit Required — Refer to the Tabular List for Digit Selection

Subterms under main terms may continue to next column or page

▶◀ Revised Text ● New Line ▲ Revised Code

		External Cause (E-Code)				
	Poisoning	**Accident**	**Therapeutic Use**	**Suicide Attempt**	**Assault**	**Undetermined**
Carbinoxamine	963.0	E858.1	E933.0	E950.4	E962.0	E980.4
Carbitol	982.8	E862.4	—	E950.9	E962.1	E980.9
Carbocaine	968.9	E855.2	E938.9	E950.4	E962.0	E980.4
infiltration (subcutaneous)	968.5	E855.2	E938.5	E950.4	E962.0	E980.4
nerve block (peripheral) (plexus)	968.6	E855.2	E938.6	E950.4	E962.0	E980.4
topical (surface)	968.5	E855.2	E938.5	E950.4	E962.0	E980.4
Carbol-fuchsin solution	976.0	E858.7	E946.0	E950.4	E962.0	E980.4
Carbolic acid — *see also* Phenol)	983.0	E864.0	—	E950.7	E962.1	E980.6
Carbomycin	960.8	E856	E930.8	E950.4	E962.0	E980.4
Carbon						
bisulfide (liquid) (vapor)	982.2	E862.4	—	E950.9	E962.1	E980.9
dioxide (gas)	987.8	E869.8	—	E952.8	E962.2	E982.8
disulfide (liquid) (vapor)	982.2	E862.4	—	E950.9	E962.1	E980.9
monoxide (from incomplete combustion of) (in) NEC	986	E868.9	—	E952.1	E962.2	E982.1
blast furnace gas	986	E868.8	—	E952.1	E962.2	E982.1
butane (distributed in mobile container)	986	E868.0	—	E951.1	E962.2	E981.1
distributed through pipes	986	E867	—	E951.0	E962.2	E981.0
charcoal fumes	986	E868.3	—	E952.1	E962.2	E982.1
coal						
gas (piped)	986	E867	—	E951.0	E962.2	E981.0
solid (in domestic stoves, fireplaces)	986	E868.3	—	E952.1	E962.2	E982.1
coke (in domestic stoves, fireplaces)	986	E868.3	—	E952.1	E962.2	E982.1
exhaust gas (motor) not in transit	986	E868.2	—	E952.0	E962.2	E982.0
combustion engine, any not in watercraft	986	E868.2	—	E952.0	E962.2	E982.0
farm tractor, not in transit	986	E868.2	—	E952.0	E962.2	E982.0
gas engine	986	E868.2	—	E952.0	E962.2	E982.0
motor pump	986	E868.2	—	E952.0	E962.2	E982.0
motor vehicle, not in transit	986	E868.2	—	E952.0	E962.2	E982.0
fuel (in domestic use)	986	E868.3	—	E952.1	E962.2	E982.1
gas (piped)	986	E867	—	E951.0	E962.2	E981.0
in mobile container	986	E868.0	—	E951.1	E962.2	E981.1
utility	986	E868.1	—	E951.8	E962.2	E981.1
in mobile container	986	E868.0	—	E951.1	E962.2	E981.1
piped (natural)	986	E867	—	E951.0	E962.2	E981.0
illuminating gas	986	E868.1	—	E951.8	E962.2	E981.8
industrial fuels or gases, any	986	E868.8	—	E952.1	E962.2	E982.1
kerosene (in domestic stoves, fireplaces)	986	E868.3	—	E952.1	E962.2	E982.1
kiln gas or vapor	986	E868.8	—	E952.1	E962.2	E982.1
motor exhaust gas, not in transit	986	E868.2	—	E952.0	E962.2	E982.0
piped gas (manufactured) (natural)	986	E867	—	E951.0	E962.2	E981.0
producer gas	986	E868.8	—	E952.1	E962.2	E982.1
propane (distributed in mobile container)	986	E868.0	—	E951.1	E962.2	E981.1
distributed through pipes	986	E867	—	E951.0	E962.2	E981.0
specified source NEC	986	E868.8	—	E952.1	E962.2	E982.1
stove gas	986	E868.1	—	E951.8	E962.2	E981.8
piped	986	E867	—	E951.0	E962.2	E981.0
utility gas	986	E868.1	—	E951.8	E962.2	E981.8
piped	986	E867	—	E951.0	E962.2	E981.0
water gas	986	E868.1	—	E951.8	E962.2	E981.8
wood (in domestic stoves, fireplaces)	986	E868.3	—	E952.1	E962.2	E982.1
tetrachloride (vapor) NEC	987.8	E869.8	—	E952.8	E962.2	E982.8
liquid (cleansing agent) NEC	982.1	E861.3	—	E950.9	E962.1	E980.9
solvent	982.1	E862.4	—	E950.9	E962.1	E980.9
Carbonic acid (gas)	987.8	E869.8	—	E952.8	E962.2	E982.8
anhydrase inhibitors	974.2	E858.5	E944.2	E950.4	E962.0	E980.4
Carbowax	976.3	E858.7	E946.3	E950.4	E962.0	E980.4
Carbrital	967.0	E851	E937.0	E950.1	E962.0	E980.1
Carbromal (derivatives)	967.3	E852.2	E937.3	E950.2	E962.0	E980.2
Cardiac						
depressants	972.0	E858.3	E942.0	E950.4	E962.0	E980.4
rhythm regulators	972.0	E858.3	E942.0	E950.4	E962.0	E980.4
Cardiografin	977.8	E858.8	E947.8	E950.4	E962.0	E980.4

		External Cause (E-Code)				
	Poisoning	**Accident**	**Therapeutic Use**	**Suicide Attempt**	**Assault**	**Undetermined**
Cardio-green	977.8	E858.8	E947.8	E950.4	E962.0	E980.4
Cardiotonic glycosides	972.1	E858.3	E942.1	E950.4	E962.0	E980.4
Cardiovascular agents NEC	972.9	E858.3	E942.9	E950.4	E962.0	E980.4
Cardrase	974.2	E858.5	E944.2	E950.4	E962.0	E980.4
Carfusin	976.0	E858.7	E946.0	E950.4	E962.0	E980.4
Carisoprodol	968.0	E855.1	E938.0	E950.4	E962.0	E980.4
Carmustine	963.1	E858.1	E933.1	E950.4	E962.0	E980.4
Carotene	963.5	E858.1	E933.5	E950.4	E962.0	E980.4
Carphenazine (maleate)	969.1	E853.0	E939.1	E950.3	E962.0	E980.3
Carter's Little Pills	973.1	E858.4	E943.1	E950.4	E962.0	E980.4
Cascara (sagrada)	973.1	E858.4	E943.1	E950.4	E962.0	E980.4
Cassava	988.2	E865.4	—	E950.9	E962.1	E980.9
Castellani's paint	976.0	E858.7	E946.0	E950.4	E962.0	E980.4
Castor						
bean	988.2	E865.3	—	E950.9	E962.1	E980.9
oil	973.1	E858.4	E943.1	E950.4	E962.0	E980.4
Caterpillar (sting)	989.5	E905.5	—	E950.9	E962.1	E980.9
Catha (edulis)	970.8	E854.3	E940.8	E950.4	E962.0	E980.4
Cathartics NEC	973.3	E858.4	E943.3	E950.4	E962.0	E980.4
contact	973.1	E858.4	E943.1	E950.4	E962.0	E980.4
emollient	973.2	E858.4	E943.2	E950.4	E962.0	E980.4
intestinal irritants	973.1	E858.4	E943.1	E950.4	E962.0	E980.4
saline	973.3	E858.4	E943.3	E950.4	E962.0	E980.4
Cathomycin	960.8	E856	E930.8	E950.4	E962.0	E980.4
Caustic(s)	983.9	E864.4	—	E950.7	E962.1	E980.6
alkali	983.2	E864.2	—	E950.7	E962.1	E980.6
hydroxide	983.2	E864.2	—	E950.7	E962.1	E980.6
potash	983.2	E864.2	—	E950.7	E962.1	E980.6
soda	983.2	E864.2	—	E950.7	E962.1	E980.6
specified NEC	983.9	E864.3	—	E950.7	E962.1	E980.6
Ceepryn	976.0	E858.7	E946.0	E950.4	E962.0	E980.4
ENT agent	976.6	E858.7	E946.6	E950.4	E962.0	E980.4
lozenges	976.6	E858.7	E946.6	E950.4	E962.0	E980.4
Celestone	962.0	E858.0	E932.0	E950.4	E962.0	E980.4
topical	976.0	E858.7	E946.0	E950.4	E962.0	E980.4
Cellosolve	982.8	E862.4	—	E950.9	E962.1	E980.9
Cell stimulants and proliferants	976.8	E858.7	E946.8	E950.4	E962.0	E980.4
Cellulose derivatives, cathartic	973.3	E858.4	E943.3	E950.4	E962.0	E980.4
nitrates (topical)	976.3	E858.7	E946.3	E950.4	E962.0	E980.4
Centipede (bite)	989.5	E905.4	—	E950.9	E962.1	E980.9
Central nervous system						
depressants	968.4	E855.1	E938.4	E950.4	E962.0	E980.4
anesthetic (general) NEC	968.4	E855.1	E938.4	E950.4	E962.0	E980.4
gases NEC	968.2	E855.1	E938.2	E950.4	E962.0	E980.4
intravenous	968.3	E855.1	E938.3	E950.4	E962.0	E980.4
barbiturates	967.0	E851	E937.0	E950.1	E962.0	E980.1
bromides	967.3	E852.2	E937.3	E950.2	E962.0	E980.2
cannabis sativa	969.6	E854.1	E939.6	E950.3	E962.0	E980.3
chloral hydrate	967.1	E852.0	E937.1	E950.2	E962.0	E980.2
hallucinogenics	969.6	E854.1	E939.6	E950.3	E962.0	E980.3
hypnotics	967.9	E852.9	E937.9	E950.2	E962.0	E980.2
specified NEC	967.8	E852.8	E937.8	E950.2	E962.0	E980.2
muscle relaxants	968.0	E855.1	E938.0	E950.4	E962.0	E980.4
paraldehyde	967.2	E852.1	E937.2	E950.2	E962.0	E980.2
sedatives	967.9	E852.9	E937.9	E950.2	E962.0	E980.2
mixed NEC	967.6	E852.5	E937.6	E950.2	E962.0	E980.2
specified NEC	967.8	E852.8	E937.8	E950.2	E962.0	E980.2
muscle-tone depressants	—	—	—	—	—	E980.4
stimulants	970.9	E854.3	E940.9	E950.4	E962.0	E980.4
amphetamines	969.7	E854.2	E939.7	E950.3	E962.0	E980.3
analeptics	970.0	E854.3	E940.0	E950.4	E962.0	E980.4
antidepressants	969.0	E854.0	E939.0	E950.3	E962.0	E980.3
opiate antagonists	970.1	E854.3	E940.0	E950.4	E962.0	E980.4
specified NEC	970.8	E854.3	E940.8	E950.4	E962.0	E980.4
Cephalexin	960.5	E856	E930.5	E950.4	E962.0	E980.4
Cephaloglycin	960.5	E856	E930.5	E950.4	E962.0	E980.4
Cephaloridine	960.5	E856	E930.5	E950.4	E962.0	E980.4
Cephalosporins NEC	960.5	E856	E930.5	E950.4	E962.0	E980.4
N (adicillin)	960.0	E856	E930.0	E950.4	E962.0	E980.4
Cephalothin (sodium)	960.5	E856	E930.5	E950.4	E962.0	E980.4
Cerbera (odallam)	988.2	E865.4	—	E950.9	E962.1	E980.9
Cerberin	972.1	E858.3	E942.1	E950.4	E962.0	E980.4
Cerebral stimulants	970.9	E854.3	E940.9	E950.4	E962.0	E980.4
psychotherapeutic	969.7	E854.2	E939.7	E950.3	E962.0	E980.3
specified NEC	970.8	E854.3	E940.8	E950.4	E962.0	E980.4
Cetalkonium (chloride)	976.0	E858.7	E946.0	E950.4	E962.0	E980.4
Cetoxime	963.0	E858.1	E933.0	E950.4	E962.0	E980.4
Cetrimide	976.2	E858.7	E946.2	E950.4	E962.0	E980.4

		External Cause (E-Code)				
	Poisoning	Accident	Therapeutic Use	Suicide Attempt	Assault	Undetermined
Cetylpyridinium	976.0	E858.7	E946.0	E950.4	E962.0	E980.4
ENT agent	976.6	E858.7	E946.6	E950.4	E962.0	E980.4
lozenges	976.6	E858.7	E946.6	E950.4	E962.0	E980.4
Cevadilla — see Sabadilla						
Cevitamic acid	963.5	E858.1	E933.5	E950.4	E962.0	E980.4
Chalk, precipitated	973.0	E858.4	E943.0	E950.4	E962.0	E980.4
Charcoal						
fumes (carbon monoxide)	986	E868.3	—	E952.1	E962.2	E982.1
industrial	986	E868.8	—	E952.1	E962.2	E982.1
medicinal (activated)	973.0	E858.4	E943.0	E950.4	E962.0	E980.4
Chelating agents NEC	977.2	E858.8	E947.2	E950.4	E962.0	E980.4
Chelidonium majus	988.2	E865.4	—	E950.9	E962.1	E980.9
Chemical substance	989.9	E866.9	—	E950.9	E962.1	E980.9
specified NEC	989.89	E866.8	—	E950.9	E962.1	E980.9
Chemotherapy, antineoplastic	963.1	E858.1	E933.1	E950.4	E962.0	E980.4
Chenopodium (oil)	961.6	E857	E931.6	E950.4	E962.0	E980.4
Cherry laurel	988.2	E865.4	—	E950.9	E962.1	E980.9
Chiniofon	961.3	E857	E931.3	E950.4	E962.0	E980.4
Chlophedianol	975.4	E858.6	E945.4	E950.4	E962.0	E980.4
Chloral (betaine) (formamide) (hydrate)	967.1	E852.0	E937.1	E950.2	E962.0	E980.2
Chloralamide	967.1	E852.0	E937.1	E950.2	E962.0	E980.2
Chlorambucil	963.1	E858.1	E933.1	E950.4	E962.0	E980.4
Chloramphenicol	960.2	E856	E930.2	E950.4	E962.0	E980.4
ENT agent	976.6	E858.7	E946.6	E950.4	E962.0	E980.4
ophthalmic preparation	976.5	E858.7	E946.5	E950.4	E962.0	E980.4
topical NEC	976.0	E858.7	E946.0	E950.4	E962.0	E980.4
Chlorate(s) (potassium) (sodium) NEC	983.9	E864.3	—	E950.7	E962.1	E980.6
herbicides	989.4	E863.5	—	E950.6	E962.1	E980.7
Chlorcylizine	963.0	E858.1	E933.0	E950.4	E962.0	E980.4
Chlordan(e) (dust)	989.2	E863.0	—	E950.6	E962.1	E980.7
Chlordantoin	976.0	E858.7	E946.0	E950.4	E962.0	E980.4
Chlordiazepoxide	969.4	E853.2	E939.4	E950.3	E962.0	E980.3
Chloresium	976.8	E858.7	E946.8	E950.4	E962.0	E980.4
Chlorethiazol	967.1	E852.0	E937.1	E950.2	E962.0	E980.2
Chlorethyl — *see* Ethyl, chloride						
Chloretone	967.1	E852.0	E937.1	E950.2	E962.0	E980.2
Chlorex	982.3	E862.4	—	E950.9	E962.1	E980.9
Chlorhexadol	967.1	E852.0	E937.1	E950.2	E962.0	E980.2
Chlorhexidine (hydrochloride)	976.0	E858.7	E946.0	E950.4	E962.0	E980.4
Chlorhydroxyquinolin	976.0	E858.7	E946.0	E950.4	E962.0	E980.4
Chloride of lime (bleach)	983.9	E864.3	—	E950.7	E962.1	E980.6
Chlorinated						
camphene	989.2	E863.0	—	E950.6	E962.1	E980.7
diphenyl	989.89	E866.8	—	E950.9	E962.1	E980.9
hydrocarbons NEC	989.2	E863.0	—	E950.6	E962.1	E980.7
solvent	982.3	E862.4	—	E950.9	E962.1	E980.9
lime (bleach)	983.9	E864.3	—	E950.7	E962.1	E980.6
naphthalene — see Naphthalene						
pesticides NEC	989.2	E863.0	—	E950.6	E962.1	E980.7
soda — see Sodium, hypochlorite						
Chlorine (fumes) (gas)	987.6	E869.8	—	E952.8	E962.2	E982.8
bleach	983.9	E864.3	—	E950.7	E962.1	E980.6
compounds NEC	983.9	E864.3	—	E950.7	E962.1	E980.6
disinfectant	983.9	E861.4	—	E950.7	E962.1	E980.6
releasing agents NEC	983.9	E864.3	—	E950.7	E962.1	E980.6
Chlorisondamine	972.3	E858.3	E942.3	E950.4	E962.0	E980.4
Chlormadinone	962.2	E858.0	E932.2	E950.4	E962.0	E980.4
Chlormerodrin	974.0	E858.5	E944.0	E950.4	E962.0	E980.4
Chlormethiazole	967.1	E852.0	E937.1	E950.2	E962.0	E980.2
Chlormethylenecycline	960.4	E856	E930.4	E950.4	E962.0	E980.4
Chlormezanone	969.5	E853.8	E939.5	E950.3	E962.0	E980.3
Chloroacetophenone	987.5	E869.3	—	E952.8	E962.2	E982.8
Chloroaniline	983.0	E864.0	—	E950.7	E962.1	E980.6
Chlorobenzene, chlorobenzol	982.0	E862.4	—	E950.9	E962.1	E980.9
Chlorobutanol	967.1	E852.0	E937.1	E950.2	E962.0	E980.2
Chlorodinitrobenzene	983.0	E864.0	—	E950.7	E962.1	E980.6
dust or vapor	987.8	E869.8	—	E952.8	E962.2	E982.8
Chloroethane — see Ethyl, chloride						
Chloroform (fumes) (vapor)	987.8	E869.8	—	E952.8	E962.2	E982.8
anesthetic (gas)	968.2	E855.1	E938.2	E950.4	E962.0	E980.4
liquid NEC	968.4	E855.1	E938.4	E950.4	E962.0	E980.4
solvent	982.3	E862.4	—	E950.9	E962.1	E980.9
Chloroguanide	961.4	E857	E931.4	E950.4	E962.0	E980.4

		External Cause (E-Code)				
	Poisoning	Accident	Therapeutic Use	Suicide Attempt	Assault	Undetermined
Chloromycetin	960.2	E856	E930.2	E950.4	E962.0	E980.4
ENT agent	976.6	E858.7	E946.6	E950.4	E962.0	E980.4
ophthalmic preparation	976.5	E858.7	E946.5	E950.4	E962.0	E980.4
otic solution	976.6	E858.7	E946.6	E950.4	E962.0	E980.4
topical NEC	976.0	E858.7	E946.0	E950.4	E962.0	E980.4
Chloronitrobenzene	983.0	E864.0	—	E950.7	E962.1	E980.6
dust or vapor	987.8	E869.8	—	E952.8	E962.2	E982.8
Chlorophenol	983.0	E864.0	—	E950.7	E962.1	E980.6
Chlorophenothane	989.2	E863.0	—	E950.6	E962.1	E980.7
Chlorophyll (derivatives)	976.8	E858.7	E946.8	E950.4	E962.0	E980.4
Chloropicrin (fumes)	987.8	E869.8	—	E952.8	E962.2	E982.8
fumigant	989.4	E863.8	—	E950.6	E962.1	E980.7
fungicide	989.4	E863.6	—	E950.6	E962.1	E980.7
pesticide (fumes)	989.4	E863.4	—	E950.6	E962.1	E980.7
Chloroprocaine	968.9	E855.2	E938.9	E950.4	E962.0	E980.4
infiltration (subcutaneous)	968.5	E855.2	E938.5	E950.4	E962.0	E980.4
nerve block (peripheral) (plexus)	968.6	E855.2	E938.6	E950.4	E962.0	E980.4
Chloroptic	976.5	E858.7	E946.5	E950.4	E962.0	E980.4
Chloropurine	963.1	E858.1	E933.1	E950.4	E962.0	E980.4
Chloroquine (hydrochloride) (phosphate)	961.4	E857	E931.4	E950.4	E962.0	E980.4
Chlorothen	963.0	E858.1	E933.0	E950.4	E962.0	E980.4
Chlorothiazide	974.3	E858.5	E944.3	E950.4	E962.0	E980.4
Chlorotrianisene	962.2	E858.0	E932.2	E950.4	E962.0	E980.4
Chlorovinyldichloroarsine	985.1	E866.3	—	E950.8	E962.1	E980.8
Chloroxylenol	976.0	E858.7	E946.0	E950.4	E962.0	E980.4
Chlorphenesin (carbamate)	968.0	E855.1	E938.0	E950.4	E962.0	E980.4
topical (antifungal)	976.0	E858.7	E946.0	E950.4	E962.0	E980.4
Chlorpheniramine	963.0	E858.1	E933.0	E950.4	E962.0	E980.4
Chlorphenoxamine	966.4	E855.0	E936.4	E950.4	E962.0	E980.4
Chlorphentermine	977.0	E858.8	E947.0	E950.4	E962.0	E980.4
Chlorproguanil	961.4	E857	E931.4	E950.4	E962.0	E980.4
Chlorpromazine	969.1	E853.0	E939.1	E950.3	E962.0	E980.3
Chlorpropamide	962.3	E858.0	E932.3	E950.4	E962.0	E980.4
Chlorprothixene	969.3	E853.8	E939.3	E950.3	E962.0	E980.3
Chlorquinaldol	976.0	E858.7	E946.0	E950.4	E962.0	E980.4
Chlortetracycline	960.4	E856	E930.4	E950.4	E962.0	E980.4
Chlorthalidone	974.4	E858.5	E944.4	E950.4	E962.0	E980.4
Chlortrianisene	962.2	E858.0	E932.2	E950.4	E962.0	E980.4
Chlor-Trimeton	963.0	E858.1	E933.0	E950.4	E962.0	E980.4
Chlorzoxazone	968.0	E855.1	E938.0	E950.4	E962.0	E980.4
Choke damp	987.8	E869.8	—	E952.8	E962.2	E982.8
Cholebrine	977.8	E858.8	E947.8	E950.4	E962.0	E980.4
Cholera vaccine	978.2	E858.8	E948.2	E950.4	E962.0	E980.4
Cholesterol-lowering agents	972.2	E858.3	E942.2	E950.4	E962.0	E980.4
Cholestyramine (resin)	972.2	E858.3	E942.2	E950.4	E962.0	E980.4
Cholic acid	973.4	E858.4	E943.4	E950.4	E962.0	E980.4
Choline						
dihydrogen citrate	977.1	E858.8	E947.1	E950.4	E962.0	E980.4
salicylate	965.1	E850.3	E935.3	E950.0	E962.0	E980.0
theophyllinate	974.1	E858.5	E944.1	E950.4	E962.0	E980.4
Cholinergics	971.0	E855.3	E941.0	E950.4	E962.0	E980.4
Cholografin	977.8	E858.8	E947.8	E950.4	E962.0	E980.4
Chorionic gonadotropin	962.4	E858.0	E932.4	E950.4	E962.0	E980.4
Chromates	983.9	E864.3	—	E950.7	E962.1	E980.6
dust or mist	987.8	E869.8	—	E952.8	E962.2	E982.8
lead	984.0	E866.0	—	E950.9	E962.1	E980.9
paint	984.0	E861.5	—	E950.9	E962.1	E980.9
Chromic acid	983.9	E864.3	—	E950.7	E962.1	E980.6
dust or mist	987.8	E869.8	—	E952.8	E962.2	E982.8
Chromium	985.6	E866.4	—	E950.9	E962.1	E980.9
compounds — see Chromates						
Chromonar	972.4	E858.3	E942.4	E950.4	E962.0	E980.4
Chromyl chloride	983.9	E864.3	—	E950.7	E962.1	E980.6
Chrysarobin (ointment)	976.4	E858.7	E946.4	E950.4	E962.0	E980.4
Chrysazin	973.1	E858.4	E943.1	E950.4	E962.0	E980.4
Chymar	963.4	E858.1	E933.4	E950.4	E962.0	E980.4
ophthalmic preparation	976.5	E858.7	E946.5	E950.4	E962.0	E980.4
Chymotrypsin	963.4	E858.1	E933.4	E950.4	E962.0	E980.4
ophthalmic preparation	976.5	E858.7	E946.5	E950.4	E962.0	E980.4
Cicuta maculata or virosa	988.2	E865.4	—	E950.9	E962.1	E980.9
Cigarette lighter fluid	981	E862.1	—	E950.9	E962.1	E980.9
Cinchocaine (spinal)	968.7	E855.2	E938.7	E950.4	E962.0	E980.4
topical (surface)	968.5	E855.2	E938.5	E950.4	E962.0	E980.4
Cinchona	961.4	E857	E931.4	E950.4	E962.0	E980.4
Cinchonine alkaloids	961.4	E857	E931.4	E950.4	E962.0	E980.4
Cinchophen	974.7	E858.5	E944.7	E950.4	E962.0	E980.4
Cinnarizine	963.0	E858.1	E933.0	E950.4	E962.0	E980.4
Citanest	968.9	E855.2	E938.9	E950.4	E962.0	E980.4

	Poisoning	External Cause (E-Code) Accident	Therapeutic Use	Suicide Attempt	Assault	Undetermined
Citanest — *continued*						
infiltration (subcutaneous)	968.5	E855.2	E938.5	E950.4	E962.0	E980.4
nerve block (peripheral) (plexus)	968.6	E855.2	E938.6	E950.4	E962.0	E980.4
Citric acid	989.89	E866.8	—	E950.9	E962.1	E980.9
Citrovorum factor	964.1	E858.2	E934.1	E950.4	E962.0	E980.4
Claviceps purpurea	988.2	E865.4	—	E950.9	E962.1	E980.9
Cleaner, cleansing agent NEC	989.89	E861.3	—	E950.9	E962.1	E980.9
of paint or varnish	982.8	E862.9	—	E950.9	E962.1	E980.9
Clematis vitalba	988.2	E865.4	—	E950.9	E962.1	E980.9
Clemizole	963.0	E858.1	E933.0	E950.4	E962.0	E980.4
penicillin	960.0	E856	E930.0	E950.4	E962.0	E980.4
Clidinium	971.1	E855.4	E941.1	E950.4	E962.0	E980.4
Clindamycin	960.8	E856	E930.8	E950.4	E962.0	E980.4
Cliradon	965.09	E850.2	E935.2	E950.0	E962.0	E980.0
Clocortolone	962.0	E858.0	E932.0	E950.4	E962.0	E980.4
Clofedanol	975.4	E858.6	E945.4	E950.4	E962.0	E980.4
Clofibrate	972.2	E858.3	E942.2	E950.4	E962.0	E980.4
Clomethiazole	967.1	E852.0	E937.1	E950.2	E962.0	E980.2
Clomiphene	977.8	E858.8	E947.8	E950.4	E962.0	E980.4
Clonazepam	969.4	E853.2	E939.4	E950.3	E962.0	E980.3
Clonidine	972.6	E858.3	E942.6	E950.4	E962.0	E980.4
Clopamide	974.3	E858.5	E944.3	E950.4	E962.0	E980.4
Clorazepate	969.4	E853.2	E939.4	E950.3	E962.0	E980.3
Clorexolone	974.4	E858.5	E944.4	E950.4	E962.0	E980.4
Clorox (bleach)	983.9	E864.3	—	E950.7	E962.1	E980.6
Clortermine	977.0	E858.8	E947.0	E950.4	E962.0	E980.4
Clotrimazole	976.0	E858.7	E946.0	E950.4	E962.0	E980.4
Cloxacillin	960.0	E856	E930.0	E950.4	E962.0	E980.4
Coagulants NEC	964.5	E858.2	E934.5	E950.4	E962.0	E980.4
Coal (carbon monoxide from) — *see also* Carbon, monoxide, coal						
oil — see Kerosene						
tar NEC	983.0	E864.0	—	E950.7	E962.1	E980.6
fumes	987.8	E869.8	—	E952.8	E962.2	E982.8
medicinal (ointment)	976.4	E858.7	E946.4	E950.4	E962.0	E980.4
analgesics NEC	965.5	E850.5	E935.5	E950.0	E962.0	E980.0
naphtha (solvent)	981	E862.0	—	E950.9	E962.1	E980.9
Cobalt (fumes) (industrial)	985.8	E866.4	—	E950.9	E962.1	E980.9
Cobra (venom)	989.5	E905.0	—	E950.9	E962.1	E980.9
Coca (leaf)	970.8	E854.3	E940.8	E950.4	E962.0	E980.4
Cocaine (hydrochloride) (salt)	970.8	E854.3	E940.8	E950.4	E962.0	E980.4
topical anesthetic	968.5	E855.2	E938.5	E950.4	E962.0	E980.4
Coccidioidin	977.8	E858.8	E947.8	E950.4	E962.0	E980.4
Cocculus indicus	988.2	E865.3	—	E950.9	E962.1	E980.9
Cochineal	989.89	E866.8	—	E950.9	E962.1	E980.9
medicinal products	977.4	E858.8	E947.4	E950.4	E962.0	E980.4
Codeine	965.09	E850.2	E935.2	E950.0	E962.0	E980.0
Coffee	989.89	E866.8	—	E950.9	E962.1	E980.9
Cogentin	971.1	E855.4	E941.1	E950.4	E962.0	E980.4
Coke fumes or gas (carbon monoxide)	986	E868.3	—	E952.1	E962.2	E982.1
industrial use	986	E868.8	—	E952.1	E962.2	E982.1
Colace	973.2	E858.4	E943.2	E950.4	E962.0	E980.4
Colchicine	974.7	E858.5	E944.7	E950.4	E962.0	E980.4
Colchicum	988.2	E865.3	—	E950.9	E962.1	E980.9
Cold cream	976.3	E858.7	E946.3	E950.4	E962.0	E980.4
Colestipol	972.2	E858.3	E942.2	E950.4	E962.0	E980.4
Colistimethate	960.8	E856	E930.8	E950.4	E962.0	E980.4
Colistin	960.8	E856	E930.8	E950.4	E962.0	E980.4
Collagen	977.8	E866.8	E947.8	E950.9	E962.1	E980.9
Collagenase	976.8	E858.7	E946.8	E950.4	E962.0	E980.4
Collodion (flexible)	976.3	E858.7	E946.3	E950.4	E962.0	E980.4
Colocynth	973.1	E858.4	E943.1	E950.4	E962.0	E980.4
Coloring matter — *see* Dye(s)						
Combustion gas — see Carbon, monoxide						
Compazine	969.1	E853.0	E939.1	E950.3	E962.0	E980.3
Compound						
42 (warfarin)	989.4	E863.7		E950.6	E962.1	E980.7
269 (endrin)	989.2	E863.0	—	E950.6	E962.1	E980.7
497 (dieldrin)	989.2	E863.0	—	E950.6	E962.1	E980.7
1080 (sodium fluoroacetate)	989.4	E863.7	—	E950.6	E962.1	E980.7
3422 (parathion)	989.3	E863.1	—	E950.6	E962.1	E980.7
3911 (phorate)	989.3	E863.1	—	E950.6	E962.1	E980.7
3956 (toxaphene)	989.2	E863.0	—	E950.6	E962.1	E980.7
4049 (malathion)	989.3	E863.1	—	E950.6	E962.1	E980.7

	Poisoning	External Cause (E-Code) Accident	Therapeutic Use	Suicide Attempt	Assault	Undetermined
Compound — *continued*						
4124 (dicapthon)	989.4	E863.4	—	E950.6	E962.1	E980.7
E (cortisone)	962.0	E858.0	E932.0	E950.4	E962.0	E980.4
F (hydrocortisone)	962.0	E858.0	E932.0	E950.4	E962.0	E980.4
Congo red	977.8	E858.8	E947.8	E950.4	E962.0	E980.4
Coniine, conine	965.7	E850.7	E935.7	E950.0	E962.0	E980.0
Conium (maculatum)	988.2	E865.4	—	E950.9	E962.1	E980.9
Conjugated estrogens (equine)	962.2	E858.0	E932.2	E950.4	E962.0	E980.4
Contac	975.6	E858.6	E945.6	E950.4	E962.0	E980.4
Contact lens solution	976.5	E858.7	E946.5	E950.4	E962.0	E980.4
Contraceptives (oral)	962.2	E858.0	E932.2	E950.4	E962.0	E980.4
vaginal	976.8	E858.7	E946.8	E950.4	E962.0	E980.4
Contrast media (roentgenographic)	977.8	E858.8	E947.8	E950.4	E962.0	E980.4
Convallaria majalis	988.2	E865.4	—	E950.9	E962.1	E980.9
Copper (dust) (fumes) (salts) NEC	985.8	E866.4	—	E950.9	E962.1	E980.9
arsenate, arsenite	985.1	E866.3	—	E950.8	E962.1	E980.8
insecticide	985.1	E863.4	—	E950.8	E962.1	E980.8
emetic	973.6	E858.4	E943.6	E950.4	E962.0	E980.4
fungicide	985.8	E863.6	—	E950.6	E962.1	E980.7
insecticide	985.8	E863.4	—	E950.6	E962.1	E980.7
oleate	976.0	E858.7	E946.0	E950.4	E962.0	E980.4
sulfate	983.9	E864.3	—	E950.7	E962.1	E980.6
cupric	973.6	E858.4	E943.6	E950.4	E962.0	E980.4
cuprous	983.9	E864.3	—	E950.7	E962.1	E980.6
fungicide	983.9	E863.6	—	E950.7	E962.1	E980.6
Copperhead snake (bite) (venom)	989.5	E905.0	—	E950.9	E962.1	E980.9
Coral (sting)	989.5	E905.6	—	E950.9	E962.1	E980.9
snake (bite) (venom)	989.5	E905.0	—	E950.9	E962.1	E980.9
Cordran	976.0	E858.7	E946.0	E950.4	E962.0	E980.4
Corn cures	976.4	E858.7	E946.4	E950.4	E962.0	E980.4
Cornhusker's lotion	976.3	E858.7	E946.3	E950.4	E962.0	E980.4
Corn starch	976.3	E858.7	E946.3	E950.4	E962.0	E980.4
Corrosive	983.9	E864.4	—	E950.7	E962.1	E980.6
acids NEC	983.1	E864.1	—	E950.7	E962.1	E980.6
aromatics	983.0	E864.0	—	E950.7	E962.1	E980.6
disinfectant	983.0	E861.4	—	E950.7	E962.1	E980.6
fumes NEC	987.9	E869.9	—	E952.9	E962.2	E982.9
specified NEC	983.9	E864.3	—	E950.7	E962.1	E980.6
sublimate — see Mercury, chloride						
Cortate	962.0	E858.0	E932.0	E950.4	E962.0	E980.4
Cort-Dome	962.0	E858.0	E932.0	E950.4	E962.0	E980.4
ENT agent	976.6	E858.7	E946.6	E950.4	E962.0	E980.4
ophthalmic preparation	976.5	E858.7	E946.5	E950.4	E962.0	E980.4
topical NEC	976.0	E858.7	E946.0	E950.4	E962.0	E980.4
Cortef	962.0	E858.0	E932.0	E950.4	E962.0	E980.4
ENT agent	976.6	E858.7	E946.6	E950.4	E962.0	E980.4
ophthalmic preparation	976.5	E858.7	E946.5	E950.4	E962.0	E980.4
topical NEC	976.0	E858.7	E946.0	E950.4	E962.0	E980.4
Corticosteroids (fluorinated)	962.0	E858.0	E932.0	E950.4	E962.0	E980.4
ENT agent	976.6	E858.7	E946.6	E950.4	E962.0	E980.4
ophthalmic preparation	976.5	E858.7	E946.5	E950.4	E962.0	E980.4
topical NEC	976.0	E858.7	E946.0	E950.4	E962.0	E980.4
Corticotropin	962.4	E858.0	E932.4	E950.4	E962.0	E980.4
Cortisol	962.0	E858.0	E932.0	E950.4	E962.0	E980.4
ENT agent	976.6	E858.7	E946.6	E950.4	E962.0	E980.4
ophthalmic preparation	976.5	E858.7	E946.5	E950.4	E962.0	E980.4
topical NEC	976.0	E858.7	E946.0	E950.4	E962.0	E980.4
Cortisone derivatives (acetate)	962.0	E858.0	E932.0	E950.4	E962.0	E980.4
ENT agent	976.6	E858.7	E946.6	E950.4	E962.0	E980.4
ophthalmic preparation	976.5	E858.7	E946.5	E950.4	E962.0	E980.4
topical NEC	976.0	E858.7	E946.0	E950.4	E962.0	E980.4
Cortogen	962.0	E858.0	E932.0	E950.4	E962.0	E980.4
ENT agent	976.6	E858.7	E946.6	E950.4	E962.0	E980.4
ophthalmic preparation	976.5	E858.7	E946.5	E950.4	E962.0	E980.4
Cortone	962.0	E858.0	E932.0	E950.4	E962.0	E980.4
ENT agent	976.6	E858.7	E946.6	E950.4	E962.0	E980.4
ophthalmic preparation	976.5	E858.7	E946.5	E950.4	E962.0	E980.4
Cortril	962.0	E858.0	E932.0	E950.4	E962.0	E980.4
ENT agent	976.6	E858.7	E946.6	E950.4	E962.0	E980.4
ophthalmic preparation	976.5	E858.7	E946.5	E950.4	E962.0	E980.4
topical NEC	976.0	E858.7	E946.0	E950.4	E962.0	E980.4
Cosmetics	989.89	E866.7	—	E950.9	E962.1	E980.9
Cosyntropin	977.8	E858.8	E947.8	E950.4	E962.0	E980.4
Cotarnine	964.5	E858.2	E934.5	E950.4	E962.0	E980.4

		External Cause (E-Code)				
	Poisoning	Accident	Therapeutic Use	Suicide Attempt	Assault	Undetermined
Cottonseed oil	976.3	E858.7	E946.3	E950.4	E962.0	E980.4
Cough mixtures (antitussives)	975.4	E858.6	E945.4	E950.4	E962.0	E980.4
containing opiates	965.09	E850.2	E935.2	E950.0	E962.0	E980.0
expectorants	975.5	E858.6	E945.5	E950.4	E962.0	E980.4
Coumadin	964.2	E858.2	E934.2	E950.4	E962.0	E980.4
rodenticide	989.4	E863.7	—	E950.6	E962.1	E980.7
Coumarin	964.2	E858.2	E934.2	E950.4	E962.0	E980.4
Coumetarol	964.2	E858.2	E934.2	E950.4	E962.0	E980.4
Cowbane	988.2	E865.4	—	E950.9	E962.1	E980.9
Cozyme	963.5	E858.1	E933.5	E950.4	E962.0	E980.4
Crack	970.8	E854.3	E940.8	E950.4	E962.0	E980.4
Creolin	983.0	E864.0	—	E950.7	E962.1	E980.6
disinfectant	983.0	E861.4	—	E950.7	E962.1	E980.6
Creosol (compound)	983.0	E864.0	—	E950.7	E962.1	E980.6
Creosote (beechwood) (coal tar)	983.0	E864.0	—	E950.7	E962.1	E980.6
medicinal (expectorant)	975.5	E858.6	E945.5	E950.4	E962.0	E980.4
syrup	975.5	E858.6	E945.5	E950.4	E962.0	E980.4
Cresol	983.0	E864.0	—	E950.7	E962.1	E980.6
disinfectant	983.0	E861.4	—	E950.7	E962.1	E980.6
Cresylic acid	983.0	E864.0	—	E950.7	E962.1	E980.6
Cropropamide	965.7	E850.7	E935.7	E950.0	E962.0	E980.0
with crotethamide	970.0	E854.3	E940.0	E950.4	E962.0	E980.4
Crotamiton	976.0	E858.7	E946.0	E950.4	E962.0	E980.4
Crotethamide	965.7	E850.7	E935.7	E950.0	E962.0	E980.0
with cropropamide	970.0	E854.3	E940.0	E950.4	E962.0	E980.4
Croton (oil)	973.1	E858.4	E943.1	E950.4	E962.0	E980.4
chloral	967.1	E852.0	E937.1	E950.2	E962.0	E980.2
Crude oil	981	E862.1	—	E950.9	E962.1	E980.9
Cryogenine	965.8	E850.8	E935.8	E950.0	E962.0	E980.0
Cryolite (pesticide)	989.4	E863.4	—	E950.6	E962.1	E980.7
Cryptenamine	972.6	E858.3	E942.6	E950.4	E962.0	E980.4
Crystal violet	976.0	E858.7	E946.0	E950.4	E962.0	E980.4
Cuckoopint	988.2	E865.4	—	E950.9	E962.1	E980.9
Cumetharol	964.2	E858.2	E934.2	E950.4	E962.0	E980.4
Cupric sulfate	973.6	E858.4	E943.6	E950.4	E962.0	E980.4
Cuprous sulfate	983.9	E864.3	—	E950.7	E962.1	E980.6
Curare, curarine	975.2	E858.6	E945.2	E950.4	E962.0	E980.4
Cyanic acid — *see* Cyanide(s)						
Cyanide(s) (compounds) (hydrogen) (potassium) (sodium) NEC	989.0	E866.8	—	E950.9	E962.1	E980.9
dust or gas (inhalation) NEC	987.7	E869.8	—	E952.8	E962.2	E982.8
fumigant	989.0	E863.8	—	E950.6	E962.1	E980.7
mercuric — see Mercury						
pesticide (dust) (fumes)	989.0	E863.4	—	E950.6	E962.1	E980.7
Cyanocobalamin	964.1	E858.2	E934.1	E950.4	E962.0	E980.4
Cyanogen (chloride) (gas) NEC	987.8	E869.8	—	E952.8	E962.2	E982.8
Cyclaine	968.5	E855.2	E938.5	E950.4	E962.0	E980.4
Cyclamen europaeum	988.2	E865.4	—	E950.9	E962.1	E980.9
Cyclandelate	972.5	E858.3	E942.5	E950.4	E962.0	E980.4
Cyclazocine	965.09	E850.2	E935.2	E950.0	E962.0	E980.0
Cyclizine	963.0	E858.1	E933.0	E950.4	E962.0	E980.4
Cyclobarbital, cyclobarbitone	967.0	E851	E937.0	E950.1	E962.0	E980.1
Cycloguanil	961.4	E857	E931.4	E950.4	E962.0	E980.4
Cyclohexane	982.0	E862.4	—	E950.9	E962.1	E980.9
Cyclohexanol	980.8	E860.8	—	E950.9	E962.1	E980.9
Cyclohexanone	982.8	E862.4	—	E950.9	E962.1	E980.9
Cyclomethycaine	968.5	E855.2	E938.5	E950.4	E962.0	E980.4
Cyclopentamine	971.2	E855.5	E941.2	E950.4	E962.0	E980.4
Cyclopenthiazide	974.3	E858.5	E944.3	E950.4	E962.0	E980.4
Cyclopentolate	971.1	E855.4	E941.1	E950.4	E962.0	E980.4
Cyclophosphamide	963.1	E858.1	E933.1	E950.4	E962.0	E980.4
Cyclopropane	968.2	E855.1	E938.2	E950.4	E962.0	E980.4
Cycloserine	960.6	E856	E930.6	E950.4	E962.0	E980.4
Cyclothiazide	974.3	E858.5	E944.3	E950.4	E962.0	E980.4
Cycrimine	966.4	E855.0	E936.4	E950.4	E962.0	E980.4
Cymarin	972.1	E858.3	E942.1	E950.4	E962.0	E980.4
Cyproheptadine	963.0	E858.1	E933.0	E950.4	E962.0	E980.4
Cyprolidol	969.0	E854.0	E939.0	E950.3	E962.0	E980.3
Cytarabine	963.1	E858.1	E933.1	E950.4	E962.0	E980.4
Cytisus						
laburnum	988.2	E865.4	—	E950.9	E962.1	E980.9
scoparius	988.2	E865.4	—	E950.9	E962.1	E980.9
Cytomel	962.7	E858.0	E932.7	E950.4	E962.0	E980.4
Cytosine (antineoplastic)	963.1	E858.1	E933.1	E950.4	E962.0	E980.4
Cytoxan	963.1	E858.1	E933.1	E950.4	E962.0	E980.4

		External Cause (E-Code)				
	Poisoning	Accident	Therapeutic Use	Suicide Attempt	Assault	Undetermined
Dacarbazine	963.1	E858.1	E933.1	E950.4	E962.0	E980.4
Dactinomycin	960.7	E856	E930.7	E950.4	E962.0	E980.4
DADPS	961.8	E857	E931.8	E950.4	E962.0	E980.4
Dakin's solution (external)	976.0	E858.7	E946.0	E950.4	E962.0	E980.4
Dalmane	969.4	E853.2	E939.4	E950.3	E962.0	E980.3
DAM	977.2	E858.8	E947.2	E950.4	E962.0	E980.4
Danilone	964.2	E858.2	E934.2	E950.4	E962.0	E980.4
Danthron	973.1	E858.4	E943.1	E950.4	E962.0	E980.4
Dantrolene	975.2	E858.6	E945.2	E950.4	E962.0	E980.4
Daphne (gnidium) (mezereum)	988.2	E865.4	—	E950.9	E962.1	E980.9
berry	988.2	E865.3	—	E950.9	E962.1	E980.9
Dapsone	961.8	E857	E931.8	E950.4	E962.0	E980.4
Daraprim	961.4	E857	E931.4	E950.4	E962.0	E980.4
Darnel	988.2	E865.3	—	E950.9	E962.1	E980.9
Darvon	965.8	E850.8	E935.8	E950.0	E962.0	E980.0
Daunorubicin	960.7	E856	E930.7	E950.4	E962.0	E980.4
DBI	962.3	E858.0	E932.3	E950.4	E962.0	E980.4
D-Con (rodenticide)	989.4	E863.7	—	E950.6	E962.1	E980.7
DDS	961.8	E857	E931.8	E950.4	E962.0	E980.4
DDT	989.2	E863.0	—	E950.6	E962.1	E980.7
Deadly nightshade	988.2	E865.4	—	E950.9	E962.1	E980.9
berry	988.2	E865.3	—	E950.9	E962.1	E980.9
Deanol	969.7	E854.2	E939.7	E950.3	E962.0	E980.3
Debrisoquine	972.6	E858.3	E942.6	E950.4	E962.0	E980.4
Decaborane	989.89	E866.8	—	E950.9	E962.1	E980.9
fumes	987.8	E869.8	—	E952.8	E962.2	E982.8
Decadron	962.0	E858.0	E932.0	E950.4	E962.0	E980.4
ENT agent	976.6	E858.7	E946.6	E950.4	E962.0	E980.4
ophthalmic preparation	976.5	E858.7	E946.5	E950.4	E962.0	E980.4
topical NEC	976.0	E858.7	E946.0	E950.4	E962.0	E980.4
Decahydronaphthalene	982.0	E862.4	—	E950.9	E962.1	E980.9
Decalin	982.0	E862.4	—	E950.9	E962.1	E980.9
Decamethonium	975.2	E858.6	E945.2	E950.4	E962.0	E980.4
Decholin	973.4	E858.4	E943.4	E950.4	E962.0	E980.4
sodium (diagnostic)	977.8	E858.8	E947.8	E950.4	E962.0	E980.4
Declomycin	960.4	E856	E930.4	E950.4	E962.0	E980.4
Deferoxamine	963.8	E858.1	E933.8	E950.4	E962.0	E980.4
Dehydrocholic acid	973.4	E858.4	E943.4	E950.4	E962.0	E980.4
DeKalin	982.0	E862.4	—	E950.9	E962.1	E980.9
Delalutin	962.2	E858.0	E932.2	E950.4	E962.0	E980.4
Delphinium	988.2	E865.3	—	E950.9	E962.1	E980.9
Deltasone	962.0	E858.0	E932.0	E950.4	E962.0	E980.4
Deltra	962.0	E858.0	E932.0	E950.4	E962.0	E980.4
Delvinal	967.0	E851	E937.0	E950.1	E962.0	E980.1
Demecarium (bromide)	971.0	E855.3	E941.0	E950.4	E962.0	E980.4
Demeclocycline	960.4	E856	E930.4	E950.4	E962.0	E980.4
Demecolcine	963.1	E858.1	E933.1	E950.4	E962.0	E980.4
Demelanizing agents	976.8	E858.7	E946.8	E950.4	E962.0	E980.4
Demerol	965.09	E850.2	E935.2	E950.0	E962.0	E980.0
Demethylchlortetracycline	960.4	E856	E930.4	E950.4	E962.0	E980.4
Demethyltetracycline	960.4	E856	E930.4	E950.4	E962.0	E980.4
Demeton	989.3	E863.1	—	E950.6	E962.1	E980.7
Demulcents	976.3	E858.7	E946.3	E950.4	E962.0	E980.4
Demulen	962.2	E858.0	E932.2	E950.4	E962.0	E980.4
Denatured alcohol	980.0	E860.1	—	E950.9	E962.1	E980.9
Dendrid	976.5	E858.7	E946.5	E950.4	E962.0	E980.4
Dental agents, topical	976.7	E858.7	E946.7	E950.4	E962.0	E980.4
Deodorant spray (feminine hygiene)	976.8	E858.7	E946.8	E950.4	E962.0	E980.4
Deoxyribonuclease	963.4	E858.1	E933.4	E950.4	E962.0	E980.4
Depressants						
appetite, central	977.0	E858.8	E947.0	E950.4	E962.0	E980.4
cardiac	972.0	E858.3	E942.0	E950.4	E962.0	E980.4
central nervous system (anesthetic)	968.4	E855.1	E938.4	E950.4	E962.0	E980.4
psychotherapeutic	969.5	E853.9	E939.5	E950.3	E962.0	E980.3
Dequalinium	976.0	E858.7	E946.0	E950.4	E962.0	E980.4
Dermolate	976.2	E858.7	E946.2	E950.4	E962.0	E980.4
DES	962.2	E858.0	E932.2	E950.4	E962.0	E980.4
Desenex	976.0	E858.7	E946.0	E950.4	E962.0	E980.4
Deserpidine	972.6	E858.3	E942.6	E950.4	E962.0	E980.4
Desipramine	969.0	E854.0	E939.0	E950.3	E962.0	E980.3
Deslanoside	972.1	E858.3	E942.1	E950.4	E962.0	E980.4
Desocodeine	965.09	E850.2	E935.2	E950.0	E962.0	E980.0
Desomorphine	965.09	E850.2	E935.2	E950.0	E962.0	E980.0
Desonide	976.0	E858.7	E946.0	E950.4	E962.0	E980.4
Desoxycorticosterone derivatives	962.0	E858.0	E932.0	E950.4	E962.0	E980.4
Desoxyephedrine	969.7	E854.2	E939.7	E950.3	E962.0	E980.3
DET	969.6	E854.1	E939.6	E950.3	E962.0	E980.3

		External Cause (E-Code)				
	Poisoning	Accident	Therapeutic Use	Suicide Attempt	Assault	Undetermined
Detergents (ingested)						
(synthetic)	989.6	E861.0	—	E950.9	E962.1	E980.9
ENT agent	976.6	E858.7	E946.6	E950.4	E962.0	E980.4
external medication	976.2	E858.7	E946.2	E950.4	E962.0	E980.4
ophthalmic preparation	976.5	E858.7	E946.5	E950.4	E962.0	E980.4
topical NEC	976.0	E858.7	E946.0	E950.4	E962.0	E980.4
Deterrent, alcohol	977.3	E858.8	E947.3	E950.4	E962.0	E980.4
Detrothyronine	962.7	E858.0	E932.7	E950.4	E962.0	E980.4
Dettol (external medication)	976.0	E858.7	E946.0	E950.4	E962.0	E980.4
Dexamethasone	962.0	E858.0	E932.0	E950.4	E962.0	E980.4
Dexamphetamine	969.7	E854.2	E939.7	E950.3	E962.0	E980.3
Dexedrine	969.7	E854.2	E939.7	E950.3	E962.0	E980.3
Dexpanthenol	963.5	E858.1	E933.5	E950.4	E962.0	E980.4
Dextran	964.8	E858.2	E934.8	E950.4	E962.0	E980.4
Dextriferron	964.0	E858.2	E934.0	E950.4	E962.0	E980.4
Dextroamphetamine	969.7	E854.2	E939.7	E950.3	E962.0	E980.3
Dextro calcium						
pantothenate	963.5	E858.1	E933.5	E950.4	E962.0	E980.4
Dextromethorphan	975.4	E858.6	E945.4	E950.4	E962.0	E980.4
Dextromoramide	965.09	E850.2	E935.2	E950.0	E962.0	E980.0
Dextro pantothenyl						
alcohol	963.5	E858.1	E933.5	E950.4	E962.0	E980.4
topical	976.8	E858.7	E946.8	E950.4	E962.0	E980.4
Dextropropoxyphene						
(hydrochloride)	965.8	E850.8	E935.8	E950.0	E962.0	E980.0
Dextrorphan	965.09	E850.2	E935.2	E950.0	E962.0	E980.0
Dextrose NEC	974.5	E858.5	E944.5	E950.4	E962.0	E980.4
Dextrothyroxin	962.7	E858.0	E932.7	E950.4	E962.0	E980.4
DFP	971.0	E855.3	E941.0	E950.4	E962.0	E980.4
DHE-45	972.9	E858.3	E942.9	E950.4	E962.0	E980.4
Diabinese	962.3	E858.0	E932.3	E950.4	E962.0	E980.4
Diacetyl monoxime	977.2	E858.8	E947.2	E950.4	E962.0	E980.4
Diacetylmorphine	965.01	E850.0	E935.0	E950.0	E962.0	E980.0
Diagnostic agents	977.8	E858.8	E947.8	E950.4	E962.0	E980.4
Dial (soap)	976.2	E858.7	E946.2	E950.4	E962.0	E980.4
sedative	967.0	E851	E937.0	E950.1	E962.0	E980.1
Diallylbarbituric acid	967.0	E851	E937.0	E950.1	E962.0	E980.1
Diaminodiphenylsulfone	961.8	E857	E931.8	E950.4	E962.0	E980.4
Diamorphine	965.01	E850.0	E935.0	E950.0	E962.0	E980.0
Diamox	974.2	E858.5	E944.2	E950.4	E962.0	E980.4
Diamthazole	976.0	E858.7	E946.0	E950.4	E962.0	E980.4
Diaphenylsulfone	961.8	E857	E931.8	E950.4	E962.0	E980.4
Diasone (sodium)	961.8	E857	E931.8	E950.4	E962.0	E980.4
Diazepam	969.4	E853.2	E939.4	E950.3	E962.0	E980.3
Diazinon	989.3	E863.1	—	E950.6	E962.1	E980.7
Diazomethane (gas)	987.8	E869.8	—	E952.8	E962.2	E982.8
Diazoxide	972.5	E858.3	E942.5	E950.4	E962.0	E980.4
Dibenamine	971.3	E855.6	E941.3	E950.4	E962.0	E980.4
Dibenzheptropine	963.0	E858.1	E933.0	E950.4	E962.0	E980.4
Dibenzyline	971.3	E855.6	E941.3	E950.4	E962.0	E980.4
Diborane (gas)	987.8	E869.8	—	E952.8	E962.2	E982.8
Dibromomannitol	963.1	E858.1	E933.1	E950.4	E962.0	E980.4
Dibucaine (spinal)	968.7	E855.2	E938.7	E950.4	E962.0	E980.4
topical (surface)	968.5	E855.2	E938.5	E950.4	E962.0	E980.4
Dibunate sodium	975.4	E858.6	E945.4	E950.4	E962.0	E980.4
Dibutoline	971.1	E855.4	E941.1	E950.4	E962.0	E980.4
Dicapthon	989.4	E863.4	—	E950.6	E962.1	E980.7
Dichloralphenazone	967.1	E852.0	E937.1	E950.2	E962.0	E980.2
Dichlorodifluoromethane	987.4	E869.2	—	E952.8	E962.2	E982.8
Dichloroethane	982.3	E862.4	—	E950.9	E962.1	E980.9
Dichloroethylene	982.3	E862.4	—	E950.9	E962.1	E980.9
Dichloroethyl sulfide	987.8	E869.8	—	E952.8	E962.2	E982.8
Dichlorohydrin	982.3	E862.4	—	E950.9	E962.1	E980.9
Dichloromethane (solvent)						
(vapor)	982.3	E862.4	—	E950.9	E962.1	E980.9
Dichlorophen(e)	961.6	E857	E931.6	E950.4	E962.0	E980.4
Dichlorphenamide	974.2	E858.5	E944.2	E950.4	E962.0	E980.4
Dichlorvos	989.3	E863.1	—	E950.6	E962.1	E980.7
Diclofenac sodium	965.69	E850.6	E935.6	E950.0	E962.0	E980.0
Dicoumarin, dicumarol	964.2	E858.2	E934.2	E950.4	E962.0	E980.4
Dicyanogen (gas)	987.8	E869.8	—	E952.8	E962.2	E982.8
Dicyclomine	971.1	E855.4	E941.1	E950.4	E962.0	E980.4
Dieldrin (vapor)	989.2	E863.0	—	E950.6	E962.1	E980.7
Dienestrol	962.2	E858.0	E932.2	E950.4	E962.0	E980.4
Dietetics	977.0	E858.8	E947.0	E950.4	E962.0	E980.4
Diethazine	966.4	E855.0	E936.4	E950.4	E962.0	E980.4
Diethyl						
barbituric acid	967.0	E851	E937.0	E950.1	E962.0	E980.1
carbamazine	961.6	E857	E931.6	E950.4	E962.0	E980.4
carbinol	980.8	E860.8	—	E950.9	E962.1	E980.9
carbonate	982.8	E862.4	—	E950.9	E962.1	E980.9
Diethyl — *continued*						
dioxide	982.8	E862.4	—	E950.9	E962.1	E980.9
ether (vapor) — see ther(s)						
glycol (monoacetate) (monoethyl						
ether)	982.8	E862.4	—	E950.9	E962.1	E980.9
propion	977.0	E858.8	E947.0	E950.4	E962.0	E980.4
stilbestrol	962.2	E858.0	E932.2	E950.4	E962.0	E980.4
Diethylene						
Diethylsulfone-diethylmethane	967.8	E852.8	E937.8	E950.2	E962.0	E980.2
Difencloxazine	965.09	E850.2	E935.2	E950.0	E962.0	E980.0
Diffusin	963.4	E858.1	E933.4	E950.4	E962.0	E980.4
Diflos	971.0	E855.3	E941.0	E950.4	E962.0	E980.4
Digestants	973.4	E858.4	E943.4	E950.4	E962.0	E980.4
Digitalin(e)	972.1	E858.3	E942.1	E950.4	E962.0	E980.4
Digitalis glycosides	972.1	E858.3	E942.1	E950.4	E962.0	E980.4
Digitoxin	972.1	E858.3	E942.1	E950.4	E962.0	E980.4
Digoxin	972.1	E858.3	E942.1	E950.4	E962.0	E980.4
Dihydrocodeine	965.09	E850.2	E935.2	E950.0	E962.0	E980.0
Dihydrocodeinone	965.09	E850.2	E935.2	E950.0	E962.0	E980.0
Dihydroergocristine	972.9	E858.3	E942.9	E950.4	E962.0	E980.4
Dihydroergotamine	972.9	E858.3	E942.9	E950.4	E962.0	E980.4
Dihydroergotoxine	972.9	E858.3	E942.9	E950.4	E962.0	E980.4
Dihydrohydroxycodeinone	965.09	E850.2	E935.2	E950.0	E962.0	E980.0
Dihydrohydroxymorphinone	965.09	E850.2	E935.2	E950.0	E962.0	E980.0
Dihydroisocodeine	965.09	E850.2	E935.2	E950.0	E962.0	E980.0
Dihydromorphine	965.09	E850.2	E935.2	E950.0	E962.0	E980.0
Dihydromorphinone	965.09	E850.2	E935.2	E950.0	E962.0	E980.0
Dihydrostreptomycin	960.6	E856	E930.6	E950.4	E962.0	E980.4
Dihydrotachysterol	962.6	E858.0	E932.6	E950.4	E962.0	E980.4
Dihydroxyanthraquinone	973.1	E858.4	E943.1	E950.4	E962.0	E980.4
Dihydroxycodeinone	965.09	E850.2	E935.2	E950.0	E962.0	E980.0
Diiodohydroxyquin	961.3	E857	E931.3	E950.4	E962.0	E980.4
topical	976.0	E858.7	E946.0	E950.4	E962.0	E980.4
Diiodohydroxyquinoline	961.3	E857	E931.3	E950.4	E962.0	E980.4
Dilantin	966.1	E855.0	E936.1	E950.4	E962.0	E980.4
Dilaudid	965.09	E850.2	E935.2	E950.0	E962.0	E980.0
Diloxanide	961.5	E857	E931.5	E950.4	E962.0	E980.4
Dimefline	970.0	E854.3	E940.0	E950.4	E962.0	E980.4
Dimenhydrinate	963.0	E858.1	E933.0	E950.4	E962.0	E980.4
Dimercaprol	963.8	E858.1	E933.8	E950.4	E962.0	E980.4
Dimercaptopropanol	963.8	E858.1	E933.8	E950.4	E962.0	E980.4
Dimetane	963.0	E858.1	E933.0	E950.4	E962.0	E980.4
Dimethicone	976.3	E858.7	E946.3	E950.4	E962.0	E980.4
Dimethindene	963.0	E858.1	E933.0	E950.4	E962.0	E980.4
Dimethisoquin	968.5	E855.2	E938.5	E950.4	E962.0	E980.4
Dimethisterone	962.2	E858.0	E932.2	E950.4	E962.0	E980.4
Dimethoxanate	975.4	E858.6	E945.4	E950.4	E962.0	E980.4
Dimethyl						
arsine, arsinic acid — see Arsenic						
carbinol	980.2	E860.3	—	E950.9	E962.1	E980.9
diguanide	962.3	E858.0	E932.3	E950.4	E962.0	E980.4
ketone	982.8	E862.4	—	E950.9	E962.1	E980.9
vapor	987.8	E869.8	—	E952.8	E962.2	E982.8
meperidine	965.09	E850.2	E935.2	E950.0	E962.0	E980.0
parathion	989.3	E863.1	—	E950.6	E962.1	E980.7
polysiloxane	973.8	E858.4	E943.8	E950.4	E962.0	E980.4
sulfate (fumes)	987.8	E869.8	—	E952.8	E962.2	E982.8
liquid	983.9	E864.3	—	E950.7	E962.1	E980.6
sulfoxide NEC	982.8	E862.4	—	E950.9	E962.1	E980.9
medicinal	976.4	E858.7	E946.4	E950.4	E962.0	E980.4
triptamine	969.6	E854.1	E939.6	E950.3	E962.0	E980.3
tubocurarine	975.2	E858.6	E945.2	E950.4	E962.0	E980.4
Dindevan	964.2	E858.2	E934.2	E950.4	E962.0	E980.4
Dinitrobenzene	983.0	E864.0	—	E950.7	E962.1	E980.6
vapor	987.8	E869.8	—	E952.8	E962.2	E982.8
Dinitro (-ortho-) cresol						
(herbicide) (spray)	989.4	E863.5	—	E950.6	E962.1	E980.7
insecticide	989.4	E863.4	—	E950.6	E962.1	E980.7
Dinitro-orthocresol						
(herbicide)	989.4	E863.5	—	E950.6	E962.1	E980.7
insecticide	989.4	E863.4	—	E950.6	E962.1	E980.7
Dinitrophenol (herbicide)						
(spray)	989.4	E863.5	—	E950.6	E962.1	E980.7
insecticide	989.4	E863.4	—	E950.6	E962.1	E980.7
Dinoprost	975.0	E858.6	E945.0	E950.4	E962.0	E980.4
Dioctyl sulfosuccinate (calcium)						
(sodium)	973.2	E858.4	E943.2	E950.4	E962.0	E980.4
Diodoquin	961.3	E857	E931.3	E950.4	E962.0	E980.4
Dione derivatives NEC	966.3	E855.0	E936.3	E950.4	E962.0	E980.4
Dionin	965.09	E850.2	E935.2	E950.0	E962.0	E980.0

☑ Additional Digit Required — Refer to the Tabular List for Digit Selection

Subterms under main terms may continue to next column or page

		External Cause (E-Code)				
	Poisoning	Accident	Therapeutic Use	Suicide Attempt	Assault	Undetermined
Dioxane	982.8	E862.4	—	E950.9	E962.1	E980.9
Dioxin — *see* Herbicide						
Dioxyline	972.5	E858.3	E942.5	E950.4	E962.0	E980.4
Dipentene	982.8	E862.4	—	E950.9	E962.1	E980.9
Diphemanil	971.1	E855.4	E941.1	E950.4	E962.0	E980.4
Diphenadione	964.2	E858.2	E934.2	E950.4	E962.0	E980.4
Diphenhydramine	963.0	E858.1	E933.0	E950.4	E962.0	E980.4
Diphenidol	963.0	E858.1	E933.0	E950.4	E962.0	E980.4
Diphenoxylate	973.5	E858.4	E943.5	E950.4	E962.0	E980.4
Diphenylchloroarsine	985.1	E866.3	—	E950.8	E962.1	E980.8
Diphenylhydantoin (sodium)	966.1	E855.0	E936.1	E950.4	E962.0	E980.4
Diphenylpyraline	963.0	E858.1	E933.0	E950.4	E962.0	E980.4
Diphtheria						
antitoxin	979.9	E858.8	E949.9	E950.4	E962.0	E980.4
toxoid	978.5	E858.8	E948.5	E950.4	E962.0	E980.4
with tetanus toxoid	978.9	E858.8	E948.9	E950.4	E962.0	E980.4
with pertussis component	978.6	E858.8	E948.6	E950.4	E962.0	E980.4
vaccine	978.5	E858.8	E948.5	E950.4	E962.0	E980.4
Dipipanone	965.09	E850.2	E935.2	E950.0	E962.0	E980.0
Diplovax	979.5	E858.8	E949.5	E950.4	E962.0	E980.4
Diprophylline	975.1	E858.6	E945.1	E950.4	E962.0	E980.4
Dipyridamole	972.4	E858.3	E942.4	E950.4	E962.0	E980.4
Dipyrone	965.5	E850.5	E935.5	E950.0	E962.0	E980.0
Diquat	989.4	E863.5	—	E950.6	E962.1	E980.7
Disinfectant NEC	983.9	E861.4	—	E950.7	E962.1	E980.6
alkaline	983.2	E861.4	—	E950.7	E962.1	E980.6
aromatic	983.0	E861.4	—	E950.7	E962.1	E980.6
Disipal	966.4	E855.0	E936.4	E950.4	E962.0	E980.4
Disodium edetate	963.8	E858.1	E933.8	E950.4	E962.0	E980.4
Disulfamide	974.4	E858.5	E944.4	E950.4	E962.0	E980.4
Disulfanilamide	961.0	E857	E931.0	E950.4	E962.0	E980.4
Disulfiram	977.3	E858.8	E947.3	E950.4	E962.0	E980.4
Dithiazanine	961.6	E857	E931.6	E950.4	E962.0	E980.4
Dithioglycerol	963.8	E858.1	E933.8	E950.4	E962.0	E980.4
Dithranol	976.4	E858.7	E946.4	E950.4	E962.0	E980.4
Diucardin	974.3	E858.5	E944.3	E950.4	E962.0	E980.4
Diupres	974.3	E858.5	E944.3	E950.4	E962.0	E980.4
Diuretics NEC	974.4	E858.5	E944.4	E950.4	E962.0	E980.4
carbonic acid anhydrase inhibitors	974.2	E858.5	E944.2	E950.4	E962.0	E980.4
mercurial	974.0	E858.5	E944.0	E950.4	E962.0	E980.4
osmotic	974.4	E858.5	E944.4	E950.4	E962.0	E980.4
purine derivatives	974.1	E858.5	E944.1	E950.4	E962.0	E980.4
saluretic	974.3	E858.5	E944.3	E950.4	E962.0	E980.4
Diuril	974.3	E858.5	E944.3	E950.4	E962.0	E980.4
Divinyl ether	968.2	E855.1	E938.2	E950.4	E962.0	E980.4
D-lysergic acid diethylamide	969.6	E854.1	E939.6	E950.3	E962.0	E980.3
DMCT	960.4	E856	E930.4	E950.4	E962.0	E980.4
DMSO	982.8	E862.4	—	E950.9	E962.1	E980.9
DMT	969.6	E854.1	E939.6	E950.3	E962.0	E980.3
DNOC	989.4	E863.5	—	E950.6	E962.1	E980.7
DOCA	962.0	E858.0	E932.0	E950.4	E962.0	E980.4
Dolophine	965.02	E850.1	E935.1	E950.0	E962.0	E980.0
Doloxene	965.8	E850.8	E935.8	E950.0	E962.0	E980.0
DOM	969.6	E854.1	E939.6	E950.3	E962.0	E980.3
Domestic gas — *see* Gas, utility						
Domiphen (bromide) (lozenges)	976.6	E858.7	E946.6	E950.4	E962.0	E980.4
Dopa (levo)	966.4	E855.0	E936.4	E950.4	E962.0	E980.4
Dopamine	971.2	E855.5	E941.2	E950.4	E962.0	E980.4
Doriden	967.5	E852.4	E937.5	E950.2	E962.0	E980.2
Dormiral	967.0	E851	E937.0	E950.1	E962.0	E980.1
Dormison	967.8	E852.8	E937.8	E950.2	E962.0	E980.2
Dornase	963.4	E858.1	E933.4	E950.4	E962.0	E980.4
Dorsacaine	968.5	E855.2	E938.5	E950.4	E962.0	E980.4
Dothiepin hydrochloride	969.0	E854.0	E939.0	E950.3	E962.0	E980.3
Doxapram	970.0	E854.3	E940.0	E950.4	E962.0	E980.4
Doxepin	969.0	E854.0	E939.0	E950.3	E962.0	E980.3
Doxorubicin	960.7	E856	E930.7	E950.4	E962.0	E980.4
Doxycycline	960.4	E856	E930.4	E950.4	E962.0	E980.4
Doxylamine	963.0	E858.1	E933.0	E950.4	E962.0	E980.4
Dramamine	963.0	E858.1	E933.0	E950.4	E962.0	E980.4
Drano (drain cleaner)	983.2	E864.2	—	E950.7	E962.1	E980.6
Dromoran	965.09	E850.2	E935.2	E950.0	E962.0	E980.0
Dromostanolone	962.1	E858.0	E932.1	E950.4	E962.0	E980.4
Droperidol	969.2	E853.1	E939.2	E950.3	E962.0	E980.3
Drotrecogin alfa	964.2	E858.2	E934.2	E950.4	E962.0	E980.4
Drug	977.9	E858.9	E947.9	E950.5	E962.0	E980.5

		External Cause (E-Code)				
	Poisoning	Accident	Therapeutic Use	Suicide Attempt	Assault	Undetermined
Drug — *continued*						
AHFS List						
4:00 antihistamine drugs	963.0	E858.1	E933.0	E950.4	E962.0	E980.4
8:04 amebacides	961.5	E857	E931.5	E950.4	E962.0	E980.4
arsenical anti-infectives	961.1	E857	E931.1	E950.4	E962.0	E980.4
quinoline derivatives	961.3	E857	E931.3	E950.4	E962.0	E980.4
8:08 anthelmintics	961.6	E857	E931.6	E950.4	E962.0	E980.4
quinoline derivatives	961.3	E857	E931.3	E950.4	E962.0	E980.4
8:12.04 antifungal antibiotics	960.1	E856	E930.1	E950.4	E962.0	E980.4
8:12.06 cephalosporins	960.5	E856	E930.5	E950.4	E962.0	E980.4
8:12.08 chloramphenicol	960.2	E856	E930.2	E950.4	E962.0	E980.4
8:12.12 erythromycins	960.3	E856	E930.3	E950.4	E962.0	E980.4
8:12.16 penicillins	960.0	E856	E930.0	E950.4	E962.0	E980.4
8:12.20 streptomycins	960.6	E856	E930.6	E950.4	E962.0	E980.4
8:12.24 tetracyclines	960.4	E856	E930.4	E950.4	E962.0	E980.4
8:12.28 other antibiotics	960.8	E856	E930.8	E950.4	E962.0	E980.4
antimycobacterial	960.6	E856	E930.6	E950.4	E962.0	E980.4
macrolides	960.3	E856	E930.3	E950.4	E962.0	E980.4
8:16 antituberculars	961.8	E857	E931.8	E950.4	E962.0	E980.4
antibiotics	960.6	E856	E930.6	E950.4	E962.0	E980.4
8:18 antivirals	961.7	E857	E931.7	E950.4	E962.0	E980.4
8:20 plasmodicides (antimalarials)	961.4	E857	E931.4	E950.4	E962.0	E980.4
8:24 sulfonamides	961.0	E857	E931.0	E950.4	E962.0	E980.4
8:26 sulfones	961.8	E857	E931.8	E950.4	E962.0	E980.4
8:28 treponemicides	961.2	E857	E931.2	E950.4	E962.0	E980.4
8:32 trichomonacides	961.5	E857	E931.5	E950.4	E962.0	E980.4
nitrofuran derivatives	961.9	E857	E931.9	E950.4	E962.0	E980.4
quinoline derivatives	961.3	E857	E931.3	E950.4	E962.0	E980.4
8:36 urinary germicides	961.9	E857	E931.9	E950.4	E962.0	E980.4
quinoline derivatives	961.3	E857	E931.3	E950.4	E962.0	E980.4
8:40 other anti-infectives	961.9	E857	E931.9	E950.4	E962.0	E980.4
10:00 antineoplastic agents	963.1	E858.1	E933.1	E950.4	E962.0	E980.4
antibiotics	960.7	E856	E930.7	E950.4	E962.0	E980.4
progestogens	962.2	E858.0	E932.2	E950.4	E962.0	E980.4
12:04 parasympathomimetic (cholinergic) agents	971.0	E855.3	E941.0	E950.4	E962.0	E980.4
12:08 parasympatholytic (cholinergic-blocking) agents	971.1	E855.4	E941.1	E950.4	E962.0	E980.4
12:12 Sympathomimetic (adrenergic) agents	971.2	E855.5	E941.2	E950.4	E962.0	E980.4
12:16 sympatholytic (adrenergic-blocking) agents	971.3	E855.6	E941.3	E950.4	E962.0	E980.4
12:20 skeletal muscle relaxants						
central nervous system muscle-tone depressants	968.0	E855.1	E938.0	E950.4	E962.0	E980.4
myoneural blocking agents	975.2	E858.6	E945.2	E950.4	E962.0	E980.4
16:00 blood derivatives	964.7	E858.2	E934.7	E950.4	E962.0	E980.4
20:04.04 iron preparations	964.0	E858.2	E934.0	E950.4	E962.0	E980.4
20:04.08 liver and stomach preparations	964.1	E858.2	E934.1	E950.4	E962.0	E980.4
20:04 antianemia drugs	964.1	E858.2	E934.1	E950.4	E962.0	E980.4
20:12.04 anticoagulants	964.2	E858.2	E934.2	E950.4	E962.0	E980.4
20:12.08 antiheparin agents	964.5	E858.2	E934.5	E950.4	E962.0	E980.4
20:12.12 coagulants	964.5	E858.2	E934.5	E950.4	E962.0	E980.4
20:12.16 hemostatics NEC	964.5	E858.2	E934.5	E950.4	E962.0	E980.4
capillary active drugs	972.8	E858.3	E942.8	E950.4	E962.0	E980.4
24:04 cardiac drugs	972.9	E858.3	E942.9	E950.4	E962.0	E980.4
cardiotonic agents	972.1	E858.3	E942.1	E950.4	E962.0	E980.4
rhythm regulators	972.0	E858.3	E942.0	E950.4	E962.0	E980.4
24:06 antilipemic agents	972.2	E858.3	E942.2	E950.4	E962.0	E980.4
thyroid derivatives	962.7	E858.0	E932.7	E950.4	E962.0	E980.4
24:08 hypotensive agents	972.6	E858.3	E942.6	E950.4	E962.0	E980.4
adrenergic blocking agents	971.3	E855.6	E941.3	E950.4	E962.0	E980.4
ganglion blocking agents	972.3	E858.3	E942.3	E950.4	E962.0	E980.4
vasodilators	972.5	E858.3	E942.5	E950.4	E962.0	E980.4
24:12 vasodilating agents NEC	972.5	E858.3	E942.5	E950.4	E962.0	E980.4
coronary	972.4	E858.3	E942.4	E950.4	E962.0	E980.4
nicotinic acid derivatives	972.2	E858.3	E942.2	E950.4	E962.0	E980.4
24:16 sclerosing agents	972.7	E858.3	E942.7	E950.4	E962.0	E980.4
28:04 general anesthetics	968.4	E855.1	E938.4	E950.4	E962.0	E980.4
gaseous anesthetics	968.2	E855.1	E938.2	E950.4	E962.0	E980.4
halothane	968.1	E855.1	E938.1	E950.4	E962.0	E980.4

		External Cause (E-Code)				
	Poisoning	Accident	Therapeutic Use	Suicide Attempt	Assault	Undetermined
Drug — *continued*						
28:04 general anesthetics — *continued*						
intravenous anesthetics	968.3	E855.1	E938.3	E950.4	E962.0	E980.4
28:08 analgesics and antipyretics	965.9	E850.9	E935.9	E950.0	E962.0	E980.0
antirheumatics	965.69	E850.6	E935.6	E950.0	E962.0	E980.0
aromatic analgesics	965.4	E850.4	E935.4	E950.0	E962.0	E980.0
non-narcotic NEC	965.7	E850.7	E935.7	E950.0	E962.0	E980.0
opium alkaloids	965.00	E850.2	E935.2	E950.0	E962.0	E980.0
heroin	965.01	E850.0	E935.0	E950.0	E962.0	E980.0
methadone	965.02	E850.1	E935.1	E950.0	E962.0	E980.0
specified type NEC	965.09	E850.2	E935.2	E950.0	E962.0	E980.0
pyrazole derivatives	965.5	E850.5	E935.5	E950.0	E962.0	E980.0
salicylates	965.1	E850.3	E935.3	E950.0	E962.0	E980.0
specified NEC	965.8	E850.8	E935.8	E950.0	E962.0	E980.0
28:10 narcotic antagonists	970.1	E854.3	E940.1	E950.4	E962.0	E980.4
28:12 anticonvulsants	966.3	E855.0	E936.3	E950.4	E962.0	E980.4
barbiturates	967.0	E851	E937.0	E950.1	E962.0	E980.1
benzodiazepine-based tranquilizers	969.4	E853.2	E939.4	E950.3	E962.0	E980.3
bromides	967.3	E852.2	E937.3	E950.2	E962.0	E980.2
hydantoin derivatives	966.1	E855.0	E936.1	E950.4	E962.0	E980.4
oxazolidine (derivatives)	966.0	E855.0	E936.0	E950.4	E962.0	E980.4
succinimides	966.2	E855.0	E936.2	E950.4	E962.0	E980.4
28:16.04 antidepressants	969.0	E854.0	E939.0	E950.3	E962.0	E980.3
28:16.08 tranquilizers	969.5	E853.9	E939.5	E950.3	E962.0	E980.3
benzodiazepine-based	969.4	E853.2	E939.4	E950.3	E962.0	E980.3
butyrophenone-based	969.2	E853.1	E939.2	E950.3	E962.0	E980.3
major NEC	969.3	E853.8	E939.3	E950.3	E962.0	E980.3
phenothiazine-based	969.1	E853.0	E939.1	E950.3	E962.0	E980.3
28:16.12 other psychotherapeutic agents	969.8	E855.8	E939.8	E950.3	E962.0	E980.3
28:20 respiratory and cerebral stimulants	970.9	E854.3	E940.9	E950.4	E962.0	E980.4
analeptics	970.0	E854.3	E940.0	E950.4	E962.0	E980.4
anorexigenic agents	977.0	E858.8	E947.0	E950.4	E962.0	E980.4
psychostimulants	969.7	E854.2	E939.7	E950.3	E962.0	E980.3
specified NEC	970.8	E854.3	E940.8	E950.4	E962.0	E980.4
28:24 sedatives and hypnotics	967.9	E852.9	E937.9	E950.2	E962.0	E980.2
barbiturates	967.0	E851	E937.0	E950.1	E962.0	E980.1
benzodiazepine-based tranquilizers	969.4	E853.2	E939.4	E950.3	E962.0	E980.3
chloral hydrate (group)	967.1	E852.0	E937.1	E950.2	E962.0	E980.2
glutethamide group	967.5	E852.4	E937.5	E950.2	E962.0	E980.2
intravenous anesthetics	968.3	E855.1	E938.3	E950.4	E962.0	E980.4
methaqualone (compounds)	967.4	E852.3	E937.4	E950.2	E962.0	E980.2
paraldehyde	967.2	E852.1	E937.2	E950.2	E962.0	E980.2
phenothiazine-based tranquilizers	969.1	E853.0	E939.1	E950.3	E962.0	E980.3
specified NEC	967.8	E852.8	E937.8	E950.2	E962.0	E980.2
thiobarbiturates	968.3	E855.1	E938.3	E950.4	E962.0	E980.4
tranquilizer NEC	969.5	E853.9	E939.5	E950.3	E962.0	E980.3
36:04 to 36:88 diagnostic agents	977.8	E858.8	E947.8	E950.4	E962.0	E980.4
40:00 electrolyte, caloric, and water balance agents NEC	974.5	E858.5	E944.5	E950.4	E962.0	E980.4
40:04 acidifying agents	963.2	E858.1	E933.2	E950.4	E962.0	E980.4
40:08 alkalinizing agents	963.3	E858.1	E933.3	E950.4	E962.0	E980.4
40:10 ammonia detoxicants	974.5	E858.5	E944.5	E950.4	E962.0	E980.4
40:12 replacement solutions	974.5	E858.5	E944.5	E950.4	E962.0	E980.4
plasma expanders	964.8	E858.2	E934.8	E950.4	E962.0	E980.4
40:16 sodium-removing resins	974.5	E858.5	E944.5	E950.4	E962.0	E980.4
40:18 potassium-removing resins	974.5	E858.5	E944.5	E950.4	E962.0	E980.4
40:20 caloric agents	974.5	E858.5	E944.5	E950.4	E962.0	E980.4
40:24 salt and sugar substitutes	974.5	E858.5	E944.5	E950.4	E962.0	E980.4
40:28 diuretics NEC	974.4	E858.5	E944.4	E950.4	E962.0	E980.4
carbonic acid anhydrase inhibitors	974.2	E858.5	E944.2	E950.4	E962.0	E980.4
mercurials	974.0	E858.5	E944.0	E950.4	E962.0	E980.4
purine derivatives	974.1	E858.5	E944.1	E950.4	E962.0	E980.4
saluretics	974.3	E858.5	E944.3	E950.4	E962.0	E980.4
thiazides	974.3	E858.5	E944.3	E950.4	E962.0	E980.4
40:36 irrigating solutions	974.5	E858.5	E944.5	E950.4	E962.0	E980.4
Drug — *continued*						
40:40 uricosuric agents	974.7	E858.5	E944.7	E950.4	E962.0	E980.4
44:00 enzymes	963.4	E858.1	E933.4	E950.4	E962.0	E980.4
fibrinolysis-affecting agents	964.4	E858.2	E934.4	E950.4	E962.0	E980.4
gastric agents	973.4	E858.4	E943.4	E950.4	E962.0	E980.4
48:00 expectorants and cough preparations						
antihistamine agents	963.0	E858.1	E933.0	E950.4	E962.0	E980.4
antitussives	975.4	E858.6	E945.4	E950.4	E962.0	E980.4
codeine derivatives	965.09	E850.2	E935.2	E950.0	E962.0	E980.0
expectorants	975.5	E858.6	E945.5	E950.4	E962.0	E980.4
narcotic agents NEC	965.09	E850.2	E935.2	E950.0	E962.0	E980.0
52:04.04 antibiotics (EENT)						
ENT agent	976.6	E858.7	E946.6	E950.4	E962.0	E980.4
ophthalmic preparation	976.5	E858.7	E946.5	E950.4	E962.0	E980.4
52:04.06 antivirals (EENT)						
ENT agent	976.6	E858.7	E946.6	E950.4	E962.0	E980.4
ophthalmic preparation	976.5	E858.7	E946.5	E950.4	E962.0	E980.4
52:04.08 sulfonamides (EENT)						
ENT agent	976.6	E858.7	E946.6	E950.4	E962.0	E980.4
ophthalmic preparation	976.5	E858.7	E946.5	E950.4	E962.0	E980.4
52:04.12 miscellaneous anti-infectives (EENT)						
ENT agent	976.6	E858.7	E946.6	E950.4	E962.0	E980.4
ophthalmic preparation	976.5	E858.7	E946.5	E950.4	E962.0	E980.4
52:04 anti-infectives (EENT)						
ENT agent	976.6	E858.7	E946.6	E950.4	E962.0	E980.4
ophthalmic preparation	976.5	E858.7	E946.5	E950.4	E962.0	E980.4
52:08 anti-inflammatory agents (EENT)						
ENT agent	976.6	E858.7	E946.6	E950.4	E962.0	E980.4
ophthalmic preparation	976.5	E858.7	E946.5	E950.4	E962.0	E980.4
52:10 carbonic anhydrase inhibitors	974.2	E858.5	E944.2	E950.4	E962.0	E980.4
52:12 contact lens solutions	976.5	E858.7	E946.5	E950.4	E962.0	E980.4
52:16 local anesthetics (EENT)	968.5	E855.2	E938.5	E950.4	E962.0	E980.4
52:20 miotics	971.0	E855.3	E941.0	E950.4	E962.0	E980.4
52:24 mydriatics						
adrenergics	971.2	E855.5	E941.2	E950.4	E962.0	E980.4
anticholinergics	971.1	E855.4	E941.1	E950.4	E962.0	E980.4
antimuscarinics	971.1	E855.4	E941.1	E950.4	E962.0	E980.4
parasympatholytics	971.1	E855.4	E941.1	E950.4	E962.0	E980.4
spasmolytics	971.1	E855.4	E941.1	E950.4	E962.0	E980.4
sympathomimetics	971.2	E855.5	E941.2	E950.4	E962.0	E980.4
52:28 mouth washes and gargles	976.6	E858.7	E946.6	E950.4	E962.0	E980.4
52:32 vasoconstrictors (EENT)	971.2	E855.5	E941.2	E950.4	E962.0	E980.4
52:36 unclassified agents (EENT)						
ENT agent	976.6	E858.7	E946.6	E950.4	E962.0	E980.4
ophthalmic preparation	976.5	E858.7	E946.5	E950.4	E962.0	E980.4
56:04 antacids and adsorbents	973.0	E858.4	E943.0	E950.4	E962.0	E980.4
56:08 antidiarrhea agents	973.5	E858.4	E943.5	E950.4	E962.0	E980.4
56:10 antiflatulents	973.8	E858.4	E943.8	E950.4	E962.0	E980.4
56:12 cathartics NEC	973.3	E858.4	E943.3	E950.4	E962.0	E980.4
emollients	973.2	E858.4	E943.2	E950.4	E962.0	E980.4
irritants	973.1	E858.4	E943.1	E950.4	E962.0	E980.4
56:16 digestants	973.4	E858.4	E943.4	E950.4	E962.0	E980.4
56:20 emetics and antiemetics						
antiemetics	963.0	E858.1	E933.0	E950.4	E962.0	E980.4
emetics	973.6	E858.4	E943.6	E950.4	E962.0	E980.4
56:24 lipotropic agents	977.1	E858.8	E947.1	E950.4	E962.0	E980.4
56:40 miscellaneous G.I. drugs	973.8	E858.4	E943.8	E950.4	E962.0	E980.4
60:00 gold compounds	965.69	E850.6	E935.6	E950.0	E962.0	E980.0
64:00 heavy metal antagonists	963.8	E858.1	E933.8	E950.4	E962.0	E980.4
68:04 adrenals	962.0	E858.0	E932.0	E950.4	E962.0	E980.4
68:08 androgens	962.1	E858.0	E932.1	E950.4	E962.0	E980.4
68:12 contraceptives, oral	962.2	E858.0	E932.2	E950.4	E962.0	E980.4
68:16 estrogens	962.2	E858.0	E932.2	E950.4	E962.0	E980.4
68:18 gonadotropins	962.4	E858.0	E932.4	E950.4	E962.0	E980.4
68:20.08 insulins	962.3	E858.0	E932.3	E950.4	E962.0	E980.4
68:20 insulins and antidiabetic agents	962.3	E858.0	E932.3	E950.4	E962.0	E980.4
68:24 parathyroid	962.6	E858.0	E932.6	E950.4	E962.0	E980.4
68:28 pituitary (posterior)	962.5	E858.0	E932.5	E950.4	E962.0	E980.4
anterior	962.4	E858.0	E932.4	E950.4	E962.0	E980.4

		External Cause (E-Code)				
	Poisoning	Accident	Therapeutic Use	Suicide Attempt	Assault	Undetermined
Drug — *continued*						
68:32 progestogens	962.2	E858.0	E932.2	E950.4	E962.0	E980.4
68:34 other corpus luteum hormones NEC	962.2	E858.0	E932.2	E950.4	E962.0	E980.4
68:36 thyroid and antithyroid						
antithyroid	962.8	E858.0	E932.8	E950.4	E962.0	E980.4
thyroid (derivatives)	962.7	E858.0	E932.7	E950.4	E962.0	E980.4
72:00 local anesthetics NEC	968.9	E855.2	E938.9	E950.4	E962.0	E980.4
infiltration (intradermal) (subcutaneous) (submucosal)	968.5	E855.2	E938.5	E950.4	E962.0	E980.4
nerve blocking (peripheral) (plexus) (regional)	968.6	E855.2	E938.6	E950.4	E962.0	E980.4
spinal	968.7	E855.2	E938.7	E950.4	E962.0	E980.4
topical (surface)	968.5	E855.2	E938.5	E950.4	E962.0	E980.4
76:00 oxytocics	975.0	E858.6	E945.0	E950.4	E962.0	E980.4
78:00 radioactive agents	990	—	—	—	—	—
80:04 serums NEC	979.9	E858.8	E949.9	E950.4	E962.0	E980.4
immune gamma globulin (human)	964.6	E858.2	E934.6	E950.4	E962.0	E980.4
80:08 toxoids NEC	978.8	E858.8	E948.8	E950.4	E962.0	E980.4
diphtheria	978.5	E858.8	E948.5	E950.4	E962.0	E980.4
and diphtheria	978.9	E858.8	E948.9	E950.4	E962.0	E980.4
with pertussis component	978.6	E858.8	E948.6	E950.4	E962.0	E980.4
and tetanus	978.9	E858.8	E948.9	E950.4	E962.0	E980.4
with pertussis component	978.6	E858.8	E948.6	E950.4	E962.0	E980.4
tetanus	978.4	E858.8	E948.4	E950.4	E962.0	E980.4
80:12 vaccines	979.9	E858.8	E949.9	E950.4	E962.0	E980.4
bacterial NEC	978.8	E858.8	E948.8	E950.4	E962.0	E980.4
with						
other bacterial components	978.9	E858.8	E948.9	E950.4	E962.0	E980.4
pertussis component	978.6	E858.8	E948.6	E950.4	E962.0	E980.4
viral and rickettsial components	979.7	E858.8	E949.7	E950.4	E962.0	E980.4
rickettsial NEC	979.6	E858.8	E949.6	E950.4	E962.0	E980.4
with						
bacterial component	979.7	E858.8	E949.7	E950.4	E962.0	E980.4
pertussis component	978.6	E858.8	E948.6	E950.4	E962.0	E980.4
viral component	979.7	E858.8	E949.7	E950.4	E962.0	E980.4
viral NEC	979.6	E858.8	E949.6	E950.4	E962.0	E980.4
with						
bacterial component	979.7	E858.8	E949.7	E950.4	E962.0	E980.4
pertussis component	978.6	E858.8	E948.6	E950.4	E962.0	E980.4
rickettsial component	979.7	E858.8	E949.7	E950.4	E962.0	E980.4
84:04.04 antibiotics (skin and mucous membrane)	976.0	E858.7	E946.0	E950.4	E962.0	E980.4
84:04.08 fungicides (skin and mucous membrane)	976.0	E858.7	E946.0	E950.4	E962.0	E980.4
84:04.12 scabicides and pediculicides (skin and mucous membrane)	976.0	E858.7	E946.0	E950.4	E962.0	E980.4
84:04.16 miscellaneous local anti-infectives (skin and mucous membrane)	976.0	E858.7	E946.0	E950.4	E962.0	E980.4
84:06 anti-inflammatory agents (skin and mucous membrane)	976.0	E858.7	E946.0	E950.4	E962.0	E980.4
84:08 antipruritics and local anesthetics						
antipruritics	976.1	E858.7	E946.1	E950.4	E962.0	E980.4
local anesthetics	968.5	E855.2	E938.5	E950.4	E962.0	E980.4
84:12 astringents	976.2	E858.7	E946.2	E950.4	E962.0	E980.4
84:16 cell stimulants and proliferants	976.8	E858.7	E946.8	E950.4	E962.0	E980.4
84:20 detergents	976.2	E858.7	E946.2	E950.4	E962.0	E980.4
84:24 emollients, demulcents, and protectants	976.3	E858.7	E946.3	E950.4	E962.0	E980.4
84:28 keratolytic agents	976.4	E858.7	E946.4	E950.4	E962.0	E980.4
84:32 keratoplastic agents	976.4	E858.7	E946.4	E950.4	E962.0	E980.4
84:36 miscellaneous agents (skin and mucous membrane)	976.8	E858.7	E946.8	E950.4	E962.0	E980.4

		External Cause (E-Code)				
	Poisoning	Accident	Therapeutic Use	Suicide Attempt	Assault	Undetermined
Drug — *continued*						
86:00 spasmolytic agents	975.1	E858.6	E945.1	E950.4	E962.0	E980.4
antiasthmatics	975.7	E858.6	E945.7	E950.4	E962.0	E980.4
papaverine	972.5	E858.3	E942.5	E950.4	E962.0	E980.4
theophylline	974.1	E858.5	E944.1	E950.4	E962.0	E980.4
88:04 vitamin A	963.5	E858.1	E933.5	E950.4	E962.0	E980.4
88:08 vitamin B complex	963.5	E858.1	E933.5	E950.4	E962.0	E980.4
hematopoietic vitamin	964.1	E858.2	E934.1	E950.4	E962.0	E980.4
nicotinic acid derivatives	972.2	E858.3	E942.2	E950.4	E962.0	E980.4
88:12 vitamin C	963.5	E858.1	E933.5	E950.4	E962.0	E980.4
88:16 vitamin D	963.5	E858.1	E933.5	E950.4	E962.0	E980.4
88:20 vitamin E	963.5	E858.1	E933.5	E950.4	E962.0	E980.4
88:24 vitamin K activity	964.3	E858.2	E934.3	E950.4	E962.0	E980.4
88:28 multivitamin preparations	963.5	E858.1	E933.5	E950.4	E962.0	E980.4
92:00 unclassified therapeutic agents	977.8	E858.8	E947.8	E950.4	E962.0	E980.4
specified NEC	977.8	E858.8	E947.8	E950.4	E962.0	E980.4
Duboisine	971.1	E855.4	E941.1	E950.4	E962.0	E980.4
Dulcolax	973.1	E858.4	E943.1	E950.4	E962.0	E980.4
Duponol (C) (EP)	976.2	E858.7	E946.2	E950.4	E962.0	E980.4
Durabolin	962.1	E858.0	E932.1	E950.4	E962.0	E980.4
Dyclone	968.5	E855.2	E938.5	E950.4	E962.0	E980.4
Dyclonine	968.5	E855.2	E938.5	E950.4	E962.0	E980.4
Dydrogesterone	962.2	E858.0	E932.2	E950.4	E962.0	E980.4
Dyes NEC	989.89	E866.8	—	E950.9	E962.1	E980.9
diagnostic agents	977.8	E858.8	E947.8	E950.4	E962.0	E980.4
pharmaceutical NEC	977.4	E858.8	E947.4	E950.4	E962.0	E980.4
Dyfols	971.0	E855.3	E941.0	E950.4	E962.0	E980.4
Dymelor	962.3	E858.0	E932.3	E950.4	E962.0	E980.4
Dynamite	989.89	E866.8	—	E950.9	E962.1	E980.9
fumes	987.8	E869.8	—	E952.8	E962.2	E982.8
Dyphylline	975.1	E858.6	E945.1	E950.4	E962.0	E980.4
Ear preparations	976.6	E858.7	E946.6	E950.4	E962.0	E980.4
Echothiopate, ecothiopate	971.0	E855.3	E941.0	E950.4	E962.0	E980.4
Ecstasy	969.7	E854.2	E939.7	E950.3	E962.0	E980.3
Ectylurea	967.8	E852.8	E937.8	E950.2	E962.0	E980.2
Edathamil disodium	963.8	E858.1	E933.8	E950.4	E962.0	E980.4
Edecrin	974.4	E858.5	E944.4	E950.4	E962.0	E980.4
Edetate, disodium (calcium)	963.8	E858.1	E933.8	E950.4	E962.0	E980.4
Edrophonium	971.0	E855.3	E941.0	E950.4	E962.0	E980.4
Elase	976.8	E858.7	E946.8	E950.4	E962.0	E980.4
Elaterium	973.1	E858.4	E943.1	E950.4	E962.0	E980.4
Elder	988.2	E865.4	—	E950.9	E962.1	E980.9
berry (unripe)	988.2	E865.3	—	E950.9	E962.1	E980.9
Electrolytes NEC	974.5	E858.5	E944.5	E950.4	E962.0	E980.4
Electrolytic agent NEC	974.5	E858.5	E944.5	E950.4	E962.0	E980.4
Embramine	963.0	E858.1	E933.0	E950.4	E962.0	E980.4
Emetics	973.6	E858.4	E943.6	E950.4	E962.0	E980.4
Emetine (hydrochloride)	961.5	E857	E931.5	E950.4	E962.0	E980.4
Emollients	976.3	E858.7	E946.3	E950.4	E962.0	E980.4
Emylcamate	969.5	E853.8	E939.5	E950.3	E962.0	E980.3
Encyprate	969.0	E854.0	E939.0	E950.3	E962.0	E980.3
Endocaine	968.5	E855.2	E938.5	E950.4	E962.0	E980.4
Endrin	989.2	E863.0	—	E950.6	E962.1	E980.7
Enflurane	968.2	E855.1	E938.2	E950.4	E962.0	E980.4
Enovid	962.2	E858.0	E932.2	E950.4	E962.0	E980.4
ENT preparations (anti-infectives)	976.6	E858.7	E946.6	E950.4	E962.0	E980.4
Enzodase	963.4	E858.1	E933.4	E950.4	E962.0	E980.4
Enzymes NEC	963.4	E858.1	E933.4	E950.4	E962.0	E980.4
Epanutin	966.1	E855.0	E936.1	E950.4	E962.0	E980.4
Ephedra (tincture)	971.2	E855.5	E941.2	E950.4	E962.0	E980.4
Ephedrine	971.2	E855.5	E941.2	E950.4	E962.0	E980.4
Epiestriol	962.2	E858.0	E932.2	E950.4	E962.0	E980.4
Epilim — see Sodium valproate						
Epinephrine	971.2	E855.5	E941.2	E950.4	E962.0	E980.4
Epsom salt	973.3	E858.4	E943.3	E950.4	E962.0	E980.4
Equanil	969.5	E853.8	E939.5	E950.3	E962.0	E980.3
Equisetum (diuretic)	974.4	E858.5	E944.4	E950.4	E962.0	E980.4
Ergometrine	975.0	E858.6	E945.0	E950.4	E962.0	E980.4
Ergonovine	975.0	E858.6	E945.0	E950.4	E962.0	E980.4
Ergot NEC	988.2	E865.4	—	E950.9	E962.1	E980.9
medicinal (alkaloids)	975.0	E858.6	E945.0	E950.4	E962.0	E980.4
Ergotamine (tartrate) (for migraine) NEC	972.9	E858.3	E942.9	E950.4	E962.0	E980.4
Ergotrate	975.0	E858.6	E945.0	E950.4	E962.0	E980.4
Erythrityl tetranitrate	972.4	E858.3	E942.4	E950.4	E962.0	E980.4
Erythrol tetranitrate	972.4	E858.3	E942.4	E950.4	E962.0	E980.4
Erythromycin	960.3	E856	E930.3	E950.4	E962.0	E980.4
ophthalmic preparation	976.5	E858.7	E946.5	E950.4	E962.0	E980.4

		External Cause (E-Code)				
	Poisoning	Accident	Therapeutic Use	Suicide Attempt	Assault	Undetermined
Erythromycin — *continued*						
topical NEC	976.0	E858.7	E946.0	E950.4	E962.0	E980.4
Eserine	971.0	E855.3	E941.0	E950.4	E962.0	E980.4
Eskabarb	967.0	E851	E937.0	E950.1	E962.0	E980.1
Eskalith	969.8	E855.8	E939.8	E950.3	E962.0	E980.3
Estradiol (cypionate) (dipropionate) (valerate)	962.2	E858.0	E932.2	E950.4	E962.0	E980.4
Estriol	962.2	E858.0	E932.2	E950.4	E962.0	E980.4
Estrogens (with progestogens)	962.2	E858.0	E932.2	E950.4	E962.0	E980.4
Estrone	962.2	E858.0	E932.2	E950.4	E962.0	E980.4
Etafedrine	971.2	E855.5	E941.2	E950.4	E962.0	E980.4
Ethacrynate sodium	974.4	E858.5	E944.4	E950.4	E962.0	E980.4
Ethacrynic acid	974.4	E858.5	E944.4	E950.4	E962.0	E980.4
Ethambutol	961.8	E857	E931.8	E950.4	E962.0	E980.4
Ethamide	974.2	E858.5	E944.2	E950.4	E962.0	E980.4
Ethamivan	970.0	E854.3	E940.0	E950.4	E962.0	E980.4
Ethamsylate	964.5	E858.2	E934.5	E950.4	E962.0	E980.4
Ethanol	980.0	E860.1	—	E950.9	E962.1	E980.9
beverage	980.0	E860.0	—	E950.9	E962.1	E980.9
Ethchlorvynol	967.8	E852.8	E937.8	E950.2	E962.0	E980.2
Ethebenecid	974.7	E858.5	E944.7	E950.4	E962.0	E980.4
Ether(s) (diethyl) (ethyl) (vapor)	987.8	E869.8	—	E952.8	E962.2	E982.8
anesthetic	968.2	E855.1	E938.2	E950.4	E962.0	E980.4
petroleum — see Ligroin						
solvent	982.8	E862.4	—	E950.9	E962.1	E980.9
Ethidine chloride (vapor)	987.8	E869.8	—	E952.8	E962.2	E982.8
liquid (solvent)	982.3	E862.4	—	E950.9	E962.1	E980.9
Ethinamate	967.8	E852.8	E937.8	E950.2	E962.0	E980.2
Ethinylestradiol	962.2	E858.0	E932.2	E950.4	E962.0	E980.4
Ethionamide	961.8	E857	E931.8	E950.4	E962.0	E980.4
Ethisterone	962.2	E858.0	E932.2	E950.4	E962.0	E980.4
Ethobral	967.0	E851	E937.0	E950.1	E962.0	E980.1
Ethocaine (infiltration) (topical)	968.5	E855.2	E938.5	E950.4	E962.0	E980.4
nerve block (peripheral) (plexus)	968.6	E855.2	E938.6	E950.4	E962.0	E980.4
spinal	968.7	E855.2	E938.7	E950.4	E962.0	E980.4
Ethoheptazine (citrate)	965.7	E850.7	E935.7	E950.0	E962.0	E980.0
Ethopropazine	966.4	E855.0	E936.4	E950.4	E962.0	E980.4
Ethosuximide	966.2	E855.0	E936.2	E950.4	E962.0	E980.4
Ethotoin	966.1	E855.0	E936.1	E950.4	E962.0	E980.4
Ethoxazene	961.9	E857	E931.9	E950.4	E962.0	E980.4
Ethoxzolamide	974.2	E858.5	E944.2	E950.4	E962.0	E980.4
Ethyl						
acetate (vapor)	982.8	E862.4	—	E950.9	E962.1	E980.9
alcohol	980.0	E860.1	—	E950.9	E962.1	E980.9
beverage	980.0	E860.0	—	E950.9	E962.1	E980.9
aldehyde (vapor)	987.8	E869.8	—	E952.8	E962.2	E982.8
liquid	989.89	E866.8	—	E950.9	E962.1	E980.9
aminobenzoate	968.5	E855.2	E938.5	E950.4	E962.0	E980.4
biscoumacetate	964.2	E858.2	E934.2	E950.4	E962.0	E980.4
bromide (anesthetic)	968.2	E855.1	E938.2	E950.4	E962.0	E980.4
carbamate (antineoplastic)	963.1	E858.1	E933.1	E950.4	E962.0	E980.4
carbinol	980.3	E860.4	—	E950.9	E962.1	E980.9
chaulmoograte	961.8	E857	E931.8	E950.4	E962.0	E980.4
chloride (vapor)	987.8	E869.8	—	E952.8	E962.2	E982.8
anesthetic (local)	968.5	E855.2	E938.5	E950.4	E962.0	E980.4
inhaled	968.2	E855.1	E938.2	E950.4	E962.0	E980.4
solvent	982.3	E862.4	—	E950.9	E962.1	E980.9
estranol	962.1	E858.0	E932.1	E950.4	E962.0	E980.4
ether — see Ether(s)						
formate (solvent) NEC	982.8	E862.4	—	E950.9	E962.1	E980.9
iodoacetate	987.5	E869.3	—	E952.8	E962.2	E982.8
lactate (solvent) NEC	982.8	E862.4	—	E950.9	E962.1	E980.9
methylcarbinol	980.8	E860.8	—	E950.9	E962.1	E980.9
morphine	965.09	E850.2	E935.2	E950.0	E962.0	E980.0
Ethylene (gas)	987.1	E869.8	—	E952.8	E962.2	E982.8
anesthetic (general)	968.2	E855.1	E938.2	E950.4	E962.0	E980.4
chlorohydrin (vapor)	982.3	E862.4	—	E950.9	E962.1	E980.9
dichloride (vapor)	982.3	E862.4	—	E950.9	E962.1	E980.9
glycol(s) (any) (vapor)	982.8	E862.4	—	E950.9	E962.1	E980.9
Ethylidene						
chloride NEC	982.3	E862.4	—	E950.9	E962.1	E980.9
diethyl ether	982.8	E862.4	—	E950.9	E962.1	E980.9
Ethynodiol	962.2	E858.0	E932.2	E950.4	E962.0	E980.4
Etidocaine	968.9	E855.2	E938.9	E950.4	E962.0	E980.4
infiltration (subcutaneous)	968.5	E855.2	E938.5	E950.4	E962.0	E980.4
nerve (peripheral) (plexus)	968.6	E855.2	E938.6	E950.4	E962.0	E980.4
Etilfen	967.0	E851	E937.0	E950.1	E962.0	E980.1
Etomide	965.7	E850.7	E935.7	E950.0	E962.0	E980.0
Etorphine	965.09	E850.2	E935.2	E950.0	E962.0	E980.0
Etoval	967.0	E851	E937.0	E950.1	E962.0	E980.1
Etryptamine	969.0	E854.0	E939.0	E950.3	E962.0	E980.3
Eucaine	968.5	E855.2	E938.5	E950.4	E962.0	E980.4
Eucalyptus (oil) NEC	975.5	E858.6	E945.5	E950.4	E962.0	E980.4
Eucatropine	971.1	E855.4	E941.1	E950.4	E962.0	E980.4
Eucodal	965.09	E850.2	E935.2	E950.0	E962.0	E980.0
Euneryl	967.0	E851	E937.0	E950.1	E962.0	E980.1
Euphthalmine	971.1	E855.4	E941.1	E950.4	E962.0	E980.4
Eurax	976.0	E858.7	E946.0	E950.4	E962.0	E980.4
Euresol	976.4	E858.7	E946.4	E950.4	E962.0	E980.4
Euthroid	962.7	E858.0	E932.7	E950.4	E962.0	E980.4
Evans blue	977.8	E858.8	E947.8	E950.4	E962.0	E980.4
Evipal	967.0	E851	E937.0	E950.1	E962.0	E980.1
sodium	968.3	E855.1	E938.3	E950.4	E962.0	E980.4
Evipan	967.0	E851	E937.0	E950.1	E962.0	E980.1
sodium	968.3	E855.1	E938.3	E950.4	E962.0	E980.4
Exalgin	965.4	E850.4	E935.4	E950.0	E962.0	E980.0
Excipients, pharmaceutical	977.4	E858.8	E947.4	E950.4	E962.0	E980.4
Exhaust gas — *see* Carbon, monoxide						
Ex-Lax (phenolphthalein)	973.1	E858.4	E943.1	E950.4	E962.0	E980.4
Expectorants	975.5	E858.6	E945.5	E950.4	E962.0	E980.4
External medications (skin) (mucous membrane)	976.9	E858.7	E946.9	E950.4	E962.0	E980.4
dental agent	976.7	E858.7	E946.7	E950.4	E962.0	E980.4
ENT agent	976.6	E858.7	E946.6	E950.4	E962.0	E980.4
ophthalmic preparation	976.5	E858.7	E946.5	E950.4	E962.0	E980.4
specified NEC	976.8	E858.7	E946.8	E950.4	E962.0	E980.4
Eye agents (anti-infective)	976.5	E858.7	E946.5	E950.4	E962.0	E980.4
Factor IX complex (human)	964.5	E858.2	E934.5	E950.4	E962.0	E980.4
Fecal softeners	973.2	E858.4	E943.2	E950.4	E962.0	E980.4
Fenbutrazate	977.0	E858.8	E947.0	E950.4	E962.0	E980.4
Fencamfamin	970.8	E854.3	E940.8	E950.4	E962.0	E980.4
Fenfluramine	977.0	E858.8	E947.0	E950.4	E962.0	E980.4
Fenoprofen	965.61	E850.6	E935.6	E950.0	E962.0	E980.0
Fentanyl	965.09	E850.2	E935.2	E950.0	E962.0	E980.0
Fentazin	969.1	E853.0	E939.1	E950.3	E962.0	E980.3
Fenticlor, fentichlor	976.0	E858.7	E946.0	E950.4	E962.0	E980.4
Fer de lance (bite) (venom)	989.5	E905.0	—	E950.9	E962.1	E980.9
Ferric — *see* Iron						
Ferrocholinate	964.0	E858.2	E934.0	E950.4	E962.0	E980.4
Ferrous fumerate, gluconate, lactate, salt NEC, sulfate (medicinal)	964.0	E858.2	E934.0	E950.4	E962.0	E980.4
Ferrum — see Iron						
Fertilizers NEC	989.89	E866.5	—	E950.9	E962.1	E980.4
with herbicide mixture	989.4	E863.5	—	E950.6	E962.1	E980.7
Fibrinogen (human)	964.7	E858.2	E934.7	E950.4	E962.0	E980.4
Fibrinolysin	964.4	E858.2	E934.4	E950.4	E962.0	E980.4
Fibrinolysis-affecting agents	964.4	E858.2	E934.4	E950.4	E962.0	E980.4
Filix mas	961.6	E857	E931.6	E950.4	E962.0	E980.4
Fiorinal	965.1	E850.3	E935.3	E950.0	E962.0	E980.0
Fire damp	987.1	E869.8	—	E952.8	E962.2	E982.8
Fish, nonbacterial or noxious	988.0	E865.2	—	E950.9	E962.1	E980.9
shell	988.0	E865.1	—	E950.9	E962.1	E980.9
Flagyl	961.5	E857	E931.5	E950.4	E962.0	E980.4
Flavoxate	975.1	E858.6	E945.1	E950.4	E962.0	E980.4
Flaxedil	975.2	E858.6	E945.2	E950.4	E962.0	E980.4
Flaxseed (medicinal)	976.3	E858.7	E946.3	E950.4	E962.0	E980.4
Flomax	971.3	E855.6	E941.3	E950.4	E962.0	E980.4
Florantyrone	973.4	E858.4	E943.4	E950.4	E962.0	E980.4
Floraquin	961.3	E857	E931.3	E950.4	E962.0	E980.4
Florinef	962.0	E858.0	E932.0	E950.4	E962.0	E980.4
ENT agent	976.6	E858.7	E946.6	E950.4	E962.0	E980.4
ophthalmic preparation	976.5	E858.7	E946.5	E950.4	E962.0	E980.4
topical NEC	976.0	E858.7	E946.0	E950.4	E962.0	E980.4
Flowers of sulfur	976.4	E858.7	E946.4	E950.4	E962.0	E980.4
Floxuridine	963.1	E858.1	E933.1	E950.4	E962.0	E980.4
Flucytosine	961.9	E857	E931.9	E950.4	E962.0	E980.4
Fludrocortisone	962.0	E858.0	E932.0	E950.4	E962.0	E980.4
ENT agent	976.6	E858.7	E946.6	E950.4	E962.0	E980.4
ophthalmic preparation	976.5	E858.7	E946.5	E950.4	E962.0	E980.4
topical NEC	976.0	E858.7	E946.0	E950.4	E962.0	E980.4
Flumethasone	976.0	E858.7	E946.0	E950.4	E962.0	E980.4
Flumethiazide	974.3	E858.5	E944.3	E950.4	E962.0	E980.4
Flumidin	961.7	E857	E931.7	E950.4	E962.0	E980.4

	Poisoning	External Cause (E-Code) Accident	Therapeutic Use	Suicide Attempt	Assault	Undetermined
Flunitrazepam	969.4	E853.2	E939.4	E950.3	E962.0	E980.3
Fluocinolone	976.0	E858.7	E946.0	E950.4	E962.0	E980.4
Fluocortolone	962.0	E858.0	E932.0	E950.4	E962.0	E980.4
Fluohydrocortisone	962.0	E858.0	E932.0	E950.4	E962.0	E980.4
ENT agent	976.6	E858.7	E946.6	E950.4	E962.0	E980.4
ophthalmic preparation	976.5	E858.7	E946.5	E950.4	E962.0	E980.4
topical NEC	976.0	E858.7	E946.0	E950.4	E962.0	E980.4
Fluonid	976.0	E858.7	E946.0	E950.4	E962.0	E980.4
Fluopromazine	969.1	E853.0	E939.1	E950.3	E962.0	E980.3
Fluoracetate	989.4	E863.7	—	E950.6	E962.1	E980.7
Fluorescein (sodium)	977.8	E858.8	E947.8	E950.4	E962.0	E980.4
Fluoride(s) (pesticides) (sodium) NEC	989.4	E863.4	—	E950.6	E962.1	E980.7
hydrogen — see Hydrofluoric acid						
medicinal	976.7	E858.7	E946.7	E950.4	E962.0	E980.4
not pesticide NEC	983.9	E864.4	—	E950.7	E962.1	E980.6
stannous	976.7	E858.7	E946.7	E950.4	E962.0	E980.4
Fluorinated corticosteroids	962.0	E858.0	E932.0	E950.4	E962.0	E980.4
Fluorine (compounds) (gas)	987.8	E869.8	—	E952.8	E962.2	E982.8
salt — see Fluoride(s)						
Fluoristan	976.7	E858.7	E946.7	E950.4	E962.0	E980.4
Fluoroacetate	989.4	E863.7	—	E950.6	E962.1	E980.7
Fluorodeoxyuridine	963.1	E858.1	E933.1	E950.4	E962.0	E980.4
Fluorometholone (topical) NEC	976.0	E858.7	E946.0	E950.4	E962.0	E980.4
ophthalmic preparation	976.5	E858.7	E946.5	E950.4	E962.0	E980.4
Fluorouracil	963.1	E858.1	E933.1	E950.4	E962.0	E980.4
Fluothane	968.1	E855.1	E938.1	E950.4	E962.0	E980.4
Fluoxetine hydrochloride	969.0	E854.0	E939.0	E950.3	E962.0	E980.3
Fluoxymesterone	962.1	E858.0	E932.1	E950.4	E962.0	E980.4
Fluphenazine	969.1	E853.0	E939.1	E950.3	E962.0	E980.3
Fluprednisolone	962.0	E858.0	E932.0	E950.4	E962.0	E980.4
Flurandrenolide	976.0	E858.7	E946.0	E950.4	E962.0	E980.4
Flurazepam (hydrochloride)	969.4	E853.2	E939.4	E950.3	E962.0	E980.3
Flurbiprofen	965.61	E850.6	E935.6	E950.0	E962.0	E980.0
Flurobate	976.0	E858.7	E946.0	E950.4	E962.0	E980.4
Flurothyl	969.8	E855.8	E939.8	E950.3	E962.0	E980.3
Fluroxene	968.2	E855.1	E938.2	E950.4	E962.0	E980.4
Folacin	964.1	E858.2	E934.1	E950.4	E962.0	E980.4
Folic acid	964.1	E858.2	E934.1	E950.4	E962.0	E980.4
Follicle stimulating hormone	962.4	E858.0	E932.4	E950.4	E962.0	E980.4
Food, foodstuffs, nonbacterial or noxious	988.9	E865.9	—	E950.9	E962.1	E980.9
berries, seeds	988.2	E865.3	—	E950.9	E962.1	E980.9
fish	988.0	E865.2	—	E950.9	E962.1	E980.9
mushrooms	988.1	E865.5	—	E950.9	E962.1	E980.9
plants	988.2	E865.9	—	E950.9	E962.1	E980.9
specified type NEC	988.2	E865.4	—	E950.9	E962.1	E980.9
shellfish	988.0	E865.1	—	E950.9	E962.1	E980.9
specified NEC	988.8	E865.8	—	E950.9	E962.1	E980.9
Fool's parsley	988.2	E865.4	—	E950.9	E962.1	E980.9
Formaldehyde (solution)	989.89	E861.4	—	E950.9	E962.1	E980.9
fungicide	989.4	E863.6	—	E950.6	E962.1	E980.7
gas or vapor	987.8	E869.8	—	E952.8	E962.2	E982.8
Formalin	989.89	E861.4	—	E950.9	E962.1	E980.9
fungicide	989.4	E863.6	—	E950.6	E962.1	E980.7
vapor	987.8	E869.8	—	E952.8	E962.2	E982.8
Formic acid	983.1	E864.1	—	E950.7	E962.1	E980.6
automobile	981	E862.1	—	E950.9	E962.1	E980.9
exhaust gas, not in transit	986	E868.2	—	E952.0	E962.2	E982.0
vapor NEC	987.1	E869.8	—	E952.8	E962.2	E982.8
gas (domestic use) (*see also* Carbon, monoxide, fuel) utility	987.1	E868.1	—	E951.8	E962.2	E981.8
incomplete combustion of — see Carbon, monoxide, fuel, utility						
in mobile container	987.0	E868.0	—	E951.1	E962.2	E981.1
piped (natural)	987.1	E867	—	E951.0	E962.2	E981.0
industrial, incomplete combustion	986	E868.3	—	E952.1	E962.2	E982.1
vapor	987.8	E869.8	—	E952.8	E962.2	E982.8
Fowler's solution	985.1	E866.3	—	E950.8	E962.1	E980.8
Foxglove	988.2	E865.4	—	E950.9	E962.1	E980.9
Fox green	977.8	E858.8	E947.8	E950.4	E962.0	E980.4
Framycetin	960.8	E856	E930.8	E950.4	E962.0	E980.4
Frangula (extract)	973.1	E858.4	E943.1	E950.4	E962.0	E980.4

	Poisoning	External Cause (E-Code) Accident	Therapeutic Use	Suicide Attempt	Assault	Undetermined
Frei antigen	977.8	E858.8	E947.8	E950.4	E962.0	E980.4
Freons	987.4	E869.2	—	E952.8	E962.2	E982.8
Fructose	974.5	E858.5	E944.5	E950.4	E962.0	E980.4
Frusemide	974.4	E858.5	E944.4	E950.4	E962.0	E980.4
FSH	962.4	E858.0	E932.4	E950.4	E962.0	E980.4
Fuel						
Fugillin	960.8	E856	E930.8	E950.4	E962.0	E980.4
Fulminate of mercury	985.0	E866.1	—	E950.9	E962.1	E980.9
Fulvicin	960.1	E856	E930.1	E950.4	E962.0	E980.4
Fumadil	960.8	E856	E930.8	E950.4	E962.0	E980.4
Fumagillin	960.8	E856	E930.8	E950.4	E962.0	E980.4
Fumes (from)	987.9	E869.9	—	E952.9	E962.2	E982.9
carbon monoxide — see Carbon, monoxide						
charcoal (domestic use)	986	E868.3	—	E952.1	E962.2	E982.1
chloroform — see Chloroform						
coke (in domestic stoves, fireplaces)	986	E868.3	—	E952.1	E962.2	E982.1
corrosive NEC	987.8	E869.8	—	E952.8	E962.2	E982.8
ether — see Ether(s)						
freons	987.4	E869.2	—	E952.8	E962.2	E982.8
hydrocarbons	987.1	E869.8	—	E952.8	E962.2	E982.8
petroleum (liquefied)	987.0	E868.0	—	E951.1	E962.2	E981.1
distributed through pipes (pure or mixed with air)	987.0	E867	—	E951.0	E962.2	E981.0
lead — see Lead						
metals — see specified metal						
nitrogen dioxide	987.2	E869.0	—	E952.8	E962.2	E982.8
pesticides — see Pesticides						
petroleum (liquefied)	987.0	E868.0	—	E951.1	E962.2	E981.1
distributed through pipes (pure or mixed with air)	987.0	E867	—	E951.0	E962.2	E981.0
polyester	987.8	E869.8	—	E952.8	E962.2	E982.8
specified, source other (*see also* substance specified)	987.8	E869.8	—	E952.8	E962.2	E982.8
sulfur dioxide	987.3	E869.1	—	E952.8	E962.2	E982.8
Fumigants	989.4	E863.8	—	E950.6	E962.1	E980.7
Fungicides — *see also* Antifungals	989.4	E863.6	—	E950.6	E962.1	E980.7
Fungi, noxious, used as food	988.1	E865.5	—	E950.9	E962.1	E980.9
Fungizone	960.1	E856	E930.1	E950.4	E962.0	E980.4
topical	976.0	E858.7	E946.0	E950.4	E962.0	E980.4
Furacin	976.0	E858.7	E946.0	E950.4	E962.0	E980.4
Furadantin	961.9	E857	E931.9	E950.4	E962.0	E980.4
Furazolidone	961.9	E857	E931.9	E950.4	E962.0	E980.4
Furnace (coal burning) (domestic), gas from	986	E868.3	—	E952.1	E962.2	E982.1
industrial	986	E868.8	—	E952.1	E962.2	E982.1
Furniture polish	989.89	E861.2	—	E950.9	E962.1	E980.9
Furosemide	974.4	E858.5	E944.4	E950.4	E962.0	E980.4
Furoxone	961.9	E857	E931.9	E950.4	E962.0	E980.4
Fusel oil (amyl) (butyl) (propyl)	980.3	E860.4	—	E950.9	E962.1	E980.9
Fusidic acid	960.8	E856	E930.8	E950.4	E962.0	E980.4
Gallamine	975.2	E858.6	E945.2	E950.4	E962.0	E980.4
Gallotannic acid	976.2	E858.7	E946.2	E950.4	E962.0	E980.4
Gamboge	973.1	E858.4	E943.1	E950.4	E962.0	E980.4
Gamimune	964.6	E858.2	E934.6	E950.4	E962.0	E980.4
Gamma-benzene hexachloride (vapor)	989.2	E863.0	—	E950.6	E962.1	E980.7
Gamma globulin	964.6	E858.2	E934.6	E950.4	E962.0	E980.4
Gamma hydroxy butyrate (GHB)	968.4	E855.1	E938.4	E950.4	E962.0	E980.4
Gamulin	964.6	E858.2	E934.6	E950.4	E962.0	E980.4
Ganglionic blocking agents	972.3	E858.3	E942.3	E950.4	E962.0	E980.4
Ganja	969.6	E854.1	E939.6	E950.3	E962.0	E980.3
Garamycin	960.8	E856	E930.8	E950.4	E962.0	E980.4
ophthalmic preparation	976.5	E858.7	E946.5	E950.4	E962.0	E980.4
topical NEC	976.0	E858.7	E946.0	E950.4	E962.0	E980.4
Gardenal	967.0	E851	E937.0	E950.1	E962.0	E980.1
Gardepanyl	967.0	E851	E937.0	E950.1	E962.0	E980.1
Gas	987.9	E869.9	—	E952.9	E962.2	E982.9
acetylene	987.1	E868.1	—	E951.8	E962.2	E981.8
incomplete combustion of — see Carbon, monoxide, fuel, utility						
air contaminants, source or type not specified	987.9	E869.9	—	E952.9	E962.2	E982.9

		External Cause (E-Code)				
	Poisoning	Accident	Therapeutic Use	Suicide Attempt	Assault	Undetermined
Gas — *continued*						
anesthetic (general) NEC	968.2	E855.1	E938.2	E950.4	E962.0	E980.4
blast furnace	986	E868.8	—	E952.1	E962.2	E982.1
butane — see Butane						
carbon monoxide — see Carbon, monoxide						
chlorine	987.6	E869.8	—	E952.8	E962.2	E982.8
coal — see Carbon, monoxide, coal						
cyanide	987.7	E869.8	—	E952.8	E962.2	E982.8
dicyanogen	987.8	E869.8	—	E952.8	E962.2	E982.8
domestic — see Gas, utility						
exhaust — see Carbon, monoxide, exhaust gas						
from wood- or coal-burning stove or fireplace	986	E868.3	—	E952.1	E962.2	E982.1
fuel (domestic use) (*see also* Carbon, monoxide, fuel)						
industrial use	986	E868.8	—	E952.1	E962.2	E982.1
utility	987.1	E868.1	—	E951.8	E962.2	E981.8
incomplete combustion of — see Carbon, monoxide, fuel, utility						
in mobile container	987.0	E868.0	—	E951.1	E962.2	E981.1
piped (natural)	987.1	E867	—	E951.0	E962.2	E981.0
garage	986	E868.2	—	E952.0	E962.2	E982.0
hydrocarbon NEC	987.1	E869.8	—	E952.8	E962.2	E982.8
incomplete combustion of — see Carbon, monoxide, fuel, utility						
liquefied (mobile container)	987.0	E868.0	—	E951.1	E962.2	E981.1
piped	987.0	E867	—	E951.0	E962.2	E981.0
hydrocyanic acid	987.7	E869.8	—	E952.8	E962.2	E982.8
illuminating — see Gas, utility						
incomplete combustion, any — see Carbon, monoxide						
kiln	986	E868.8	—	E952.1	E962.2	E982.1
lacrimogenic	987.5	E869.3	—	E952.8	E962.2	E982.8
marsh	987.1	E869.8	—	E952.8	E962.2	E982.8
motor exhaust, not in transit	986	E868.8	—	E952.1	E962.2	E982.1
mustard — see Mustard, gas						
natural	987.1	E867	—	E951.0	E962.2	E981.0
nerve (war)	987.9	E869.9	—	E952.9	E962.2	E982.9
oils	981	E862.1	—	E950.9	E962.1	E980.9
petroleum (liquefied) (distributed in mobile containers)	987.0	E868.0	—	E951.1	E962.2	E981.1
piped (pure or mixed with air)	987.0	E867	—	E951.1	E962.2	E981.1
piped (manufactured) (natural) NEC	987.1	E867	—	E951.0	E962.2	E981.0
producer	986	E868.8	—	E952.1	E962.2	E982.1
propane — see Propane						
refrigerant (freon)	987.4	E869.2	—	E952.8	E962.2	E982.8
not freon	987.9	E869.9	—	E952.9	E962.2	E982.9
sewer	987.8	E869.8	—	E952.8	E962.2	E982.8
specified source NEC (see also substance specified)	987.8	E869.8	—	E952.8	E962.2	E982.8
stove — see Gas, utility						
tear	987.5	E869.3	—	E952.8	E962.2	E982.8
utility (for cooking, heating, or lighting) (piped) NEC	987.1	E868.1	—	E951.8	E962.2	E981.8
incomplete combustion of — see Carbon, monoxide, fuel, utilty						
in mobile container	987.0	E868.0	—	E951.1	E962.2	E981.1
piped (natural)	987.1	E867	—	E951.0	E962.2	E981.0
water	987.1	E868.1	—	E951.8	E962.2	E981.8
incomplete combustion of — see Carbon, monoxide, fuel, utility						
Gaseous substance — see Gas						
Gasoline, gasolene	981	E862.1	—	E950.9	E962.1	E980.9
vapor	987.1	E869.8	—	E952.8	E962.2	E982.8
Gastric enzymes	973.4	E858.4	E943.4	E950.4	E962.0	E980.4
Gastrografin	977.8	E858.8	E947.8	E950.4	E962.0	E980.4
Gastrointestinal agents	973.9	E858.4	E943.9	E950.4	E962.0	E980.4
specified NEC	973.8	E858.4	E943.8	E950.4	E962.0	E980.4
Gaultheria procumbens	988.2	E865.4	—	E950.9	E962.1	E980.9
Gelatin (intravenous)	964.8	E858.2	E934.8	E950.4	E962.0	E980.4
absorbable (sponge)	964.5	E858.2	E934.5	E950.4	E962.0	E980.4

		External Cause (E-Code)				
	Poisoning	Accident	Therapeutic Use	Suicide Attempt	Assault	Undetermined
Gelfilm	976.8	E858.7	E946.8	E950.4	E962.0	E980.4
Gelfoam	964.5	E858.2	E934.5	E950.4	E962.0	E980.4
Gelsemine	970.8	E854.3	E940.8	E950.4	E962.0	E980.4
Gelsemium (sempervirens)	988.2	E865.4	—	E950.9	E962.1	E980.9
Gemonil	967.0	E851	E937.0	E950.1	E962.0	E980.1
Gentamicin	960.8	E856	E930.8	E950.4	E962.0	E980.4
ophthalmic preparation	976.5	E858.7	E946.5	E950.4	E962.0	E980.4
topical NEC	976.0	E858.7	E946.0	E950.4	E962.0	E980.4
Gentian violet	976.0	E858.7	E946.0	E950.4	E962.0	E980.4
Gexane	976.0	E858.7	E946.0	E950.4	E962.0	E980.4
Gila monster (venom)	989.5	E905.0	—	E950.9	E962.1	E980.9
Ginger, Jamaica	989.89	E866.8	—	E950.9	E962.1	E980.9
Gitalin	972.1	E858.3	E942.1	E950.4	E962.0	E980.4
Gitoxin	972.1	E858.3	E942.1	E950.4	E962.0	E980.4
Glandular extract (medicinal) NEC	977.9	E858.9	E947.9	E950.5	E962.0	E980.5
Glaucarubin	961.5	E857	E931.5	E950.4	E962.0	E980.4
Globin zinc insulin	962.3	E858.0	E932.3	E950.4	E962.0	E980.4
Glucagon	962.3	E858.0	E932.3	E950.4	E962.0	E980.4
Glucochloral	967.1	E852.0	E937.1	E950.2	E962.0	E980.2
Glucocorticoids	962.0	E858.0	E932.0	E950.4	E962.0	E980.4
Glucose	974.5	E858.5	E944.5	E950.4	E962.0	E980.4
oxidase reagent	977.8	E858.8	E947.8	E950.4	E962.0	E980.4
Glucosulfone sodium	961.8	E857	E931.8	E950.4	E962.0	E980.4
Glue(s)	989.89	E866.6	—	E950.9	E962.1	E980.9
Glutamic acid (hydrochloride)	973.4	E858.4	E943.4	E950.4	E962.0	E980.4
Glutaraldehyde	989.89	E861.4	—	E950.9	E962.1	E980.9
Glutathione	963.8	E858.1	E933.8	E950.4	E962.0	E980.4
Glutethimide (group)	967.5	E852.4	E937.5	E950.2	E962.0	E980.2
Glycerin (lotion)	976.3	E858.7	E946.3	E950.4	E962.0	E980.4
Glycerol (topical)	976.3	E858.7	E946.3	E950.4	E962.0	E980.4
Glyceryl						
guaiacolate	975.5	E858.6	E945.5	E950.4	E962.0	E980.4
triacetate (topical)	976.0	E858.7	E946.0	E950.4	E962.0	E980.4
trinitrate	972.4	E858.3	E942.4	E950.4	E962.0	E980.4
Glycine	974.5	E858.5	E944.5	E950.4	E962.0	E980.4
Glycobiarsol	961.1	E857	E931.1	E950.4	E962.0	E980.4
Glycols (ether)	982.8	E862.4	—	E950.9	E962.1	E980.9
Glycopyrrolate	971.1	E855.4	E941.1	E950.4	E962.0	E980.4
Glymidine	962.3	E858.0	E932.3	E950.4	E962.0	E980.4
Gold (compounds) (salts)	965.69	E850.6	E935.6	E950.0	E962.0	E980.0
Golden sulfide of antimony	985.4	E866.2	—	E950.9	E962.1	E980.9
Goldylocks	988.2	E865.4	—	E950.9	E962.1	E980.9
Gonadal tissue extract	962.9	E858.0	E932.9	E950.4	E962.0	E980.4
beverage	980.0	E860.0	—	E950.9	E962.1	E980.9
female	962.2	E858.0	E932.2	E950.4	E962.0	E980.4
male	962.1	E858.0	E932.1	E950.4	E962.0	E980.4
Gonadotropin	962.4	E858.0	E932.4	E950.4	E962.0	E980.4
Grain alcohol	980.0	E860.1	—	E950.9	E962.1	E980.9
Gramicidin	960.8	E856	E930.8	E950.4	E962.0	E980.4
Gratiola officinalis	988.2	E865.4	—	E950.9	E962.1	E980.9
Grease	989.89	E866.8	—	E950.9	E962.1	E980.9
Green hellebore	988.2	E865.4	—	E950.9	E962.1	E980.9
Green soap	976.2	E858.7	E946.2	E950.4	E962.0	E980.4
Grifulvin	960.1	E856	E930.1	E950.4	E962.0	E980.4
Griseofulvin	960.1	E856	E930.1	E950.4	E962.0	E980.4
Growth hormone	962.4	E858.0	E932.4	E950.4	E962.0	E980.4
Guaiacol	975.5	E858.6	E945.5	E950.4	E962.0	E980.4
Guaiac reagent	977.8	E858.8	E947.8	E950.4	E962.0	E980.4
Guaifenesin	975.5	E858.6	E945.5	E950.4	E962.0	E980.4
Guaiphenesin	975.5	E858.6	E945.5	E950.4	E962.0	E980.4
Guanatol	961.4	E857	E931.4	E950.4	E962.0	E980.4
Guanethidine	972.6	E858.3	E942.6	E950.4	E962.0	E980.4
Guano	989.89	E866.5	—	E950.9	E962.1	E980.9
Guanochlor	972.6	E858.3	E942.6	E950.4	E962.0	E980.4
Guanoctine	972.6	E858.3	E942.6	E950.4	E962.0	E980.4
Guanoxan	972.6	E858.3	E942.6	E950.4	E962.0	E980.4
Hair treatment agent NEC	976.4	E858.7	E946.4	E950.4	E962.0	E980.4
Halcinonide	976.0	E858.7	E946.0	E950.4	E962.0	E980.4
Halethazole	976.0	E858.7	E946.0	E950.4	E962.0	E980.4
Hallucinogens	969.6	E854.1	E939.6	E950.3	E962.0	E980.3
Haloperidol	969.2	E853.1	E939.2	E950.3	E962.0	E980.3
Haloprogin	976.0	E858.7	E946.0	E950.4	E962.0	E980.4
Halotex	976.0	E858.7	E946.0	E950.4	E962.0	E980.4
Halothane	968.1	E855.1	E938.1	E950.4	E962.0	E980.4
Halquinols	976.0	E858.7	E946.0	E950.4	E962.0	E980.4
Hand sanitizer ●	976.0	E858.7	E946.0	E950.4	E962.0	E980.4
Harmonyl	972.6	E858.3	E942.6	E950.4	E962.0	E980.4
Hartmann's solution	974.5	E858.5	E944.5	E950.4	E962.0	E980.4

		External Cause (E-Code)				
	Poisoning	Accident	Therapeutic Use	Suicide Attempt	Assault	Undetermined
Hashish	969.6	E854.1	E939.6	E950.3	E962.0	E980.3
Hawaiian wood rose seeds	969.6	E854.1	E939.6	E950.3	E962.0	E980.3
Headache cures, drugs, powders NEC	977.9	E858.9	E947.9	E950.5	E962.0	E980.9
Heavenly Blue (morning glory)	969.6	E854.1	E939.6	E950.3	E962.0	E980.3
Heavy metal antagonists	963.8	E858.1	E933.8	E950.4	E962.0	E980.4
anti-infectives	961.2	E857	E931.2	E950.4	E962.0	E980.4
Hedaquinium	976.0	E858.7	E946.0	E950.4	E962.0	E980.4
Hedge hyssop	988.2	E865.4	—	E950.9	E962.1	E980.9
Heet	976.8	E858.7	E946.8	E950.4	E962.0	E980.4
Helenin	961.6	E857	E931.6	E950.4	E962.0	E980.4
Hellebore (black) (green) (white)	988.2	E865.4	—	E950.9	E962.1	E980.9
Hemlock	988.2	E865.4	—	E950.9	E962.1	E980.9
Hemostatics	964.5	E858.2	E934.5	E950.4	E962.0	E980.4
capillary active drugs	972.8	E858.3	E942.8	E950.4	E962.0	E980.4
Henbane	988.2	E865.4	—	E950.9	E962.1	E980.9
Heparin (sodium)	964.2	E858.2	E934.2	E950.4	E962.0	E980.4
Heptabarbital, heptabarbitone	967.0	E851	E937.0	E950.1	E962.0	E980.1
Heptachlor	989.2	E863.0	—	E950.6	E962.1	E980.7
Heptalgin	965.09	E850.2	E935.2	E950.0	E962.0	E980.0
Herbicides	989.4	E863.5	—	E950.6	E962.1	E980.7
Heroin	965.01	E850.0	E935.0	E950.0	E962.0	E980.0
Herplex	976.5	E858.7	E946.5	E950.4	E962.0	E980.4
HES	964.8	E858.2	E934.8	E950.4	E962.0	E980.4
Hetastarch	964.8	E858.2	E934.8	E950.4	E962.0	E980.4
Hexachlorocyclohexane	989.2	E863.0	—	E950.6	E962.1	E980.7
Hexachlorophene	976.2	E858.7	E946.2	E950.4	E962.0	E980.4
Hexadimethrine (bromide)	964.5	E858.2	E934.5	E950.4	E962.0	E980.4
Hexafluorenium	975.2	E858.6	E945.2	E950.4	E962.0	E980.4
Hexa-germ	976.2	E858.7	E946.2	E950.4	E962.0	E980.4
Hexahydrophenol	980.8	E860.8	—	E950.9	E962.1	E980.9
Hexalin	980.8	E860.8	—	E950.9	E962.1	E980.9
Hexamethonium	972.3	E858.3	E942.3	E950.4	E962.0	E980.4
Hexamethyleneamine	961.9	E857	E931.9	E950.4	E962.0	E980.4
Hexamine	961.9	E857	E931.9	E950.4	E962.0	E980.4
Hexanone	982.8	E862.4	—	E950.9	E962.1	E980.9
Hexapropymate	967.8	E852.8	E937.8	E950.2	E962.0	E980.2
Hexestrol	962.2	E858.0	E932.2	E950.4	E962.0	E980.4
Hexethal (sodium)	967.0	E851	E937.0	E950.1	E962.0	E980.1
Hexetidine	976.0	E858.7	E946.0	E950.4	E962.0	E980.4
Hexobarbital, hexobarbitone	967.0	E851	E937.0	E950.1	E962.0	E980.1
sodium (anesthetic)	968.3	E855.1	E938.3	E950.4	E962.0	E980.4
soluble	968.3	E855.1	E938.3	E950.4	E962.0	E980.4
Hexocyclium	971.1	E855.4	E941.1	E950.4	E962.0	E980.4
Hexoestrol	962.2	E858.0	E932.2	E950.4	E962.0	E980.4
Hexone	982.8	E862.4	—	E950.9	E962.1	E980.9
Hexylcaine	968.5	E855.2	E938.5	E950.4	E962.0	E980.4
Hexylresorcinol	961.6	E857	E931.6	E950.4	E962.0	E980.4
Hinkle's pills	973.1	E858.4	E943.1	E950.4	E962.0	E980.4
Histalog	977.8	E858.8	E947.8	E950.4	E962.0	E980.4
Histamine (phosphate)	972.5	E858.3	E942.5	E950.4	E962.0	E980.4
Histoplasmin	977.8	E858.8	E947.8	E950.4	E962.0	E980.4
Holly berries	988.2	E865.3	—	E950.9	E962.1	E980.9
Homatropine	971.1	E855.4	E941.1	E950.4	E962.0	E980.4
Homo-tet	964.6	E858.2	E934.6	E950.4	E962.0	E980.4
Hormones (synthetic substitute) NEC	962.9	E858.0	E932.9	E950.4	E962.0	E980.4
adrenal cortical steroids	962.0	E858.0	E932.0	E950.4	E962.0	E980.4
antidiabetic agents	962.3	E858.0	E932.3	E950.4	E962.0	E980.4
follicle stimulating	962.4	E858.0	E932.4	E950.4	E962.0	E980.4
gonadotropic	962.4	E858.0	E932.4	E950.4	E962.0	E980.4
growth	962.4	E858.0	E932.4	E950.4	E962.0	E980.4
ovarian (substitutes)	962.2	E858.0	E932.2	E950.4	E962.0	E980.4
parathyroid (derivatives)	962.6	E858.0	E932.6	E950.4	E962.0	E980.4
pituitary (posterior)	962.5	E858.0	E932.5	E950.4	E962.0	E980.4
anterior	962.4	E858.0	E932.4	E950.4	E962.0	E980.4
thyroid (derivative)	962.7	E858.0	E932.7	E950.4	E962.0	E980.4
Hornet (sting)	989.5	E905.3	—	E950.9	E962.1	E980.9
Horticulture agent NEC	989.4	E863.9	—	E950.6	E962.1	E980.7
Hyaluronidase	963.4	E858.1	E933.4	E950.4	E962.0	E980.4
Hyazyme	963.4	E858.1	E933.4	E950.4	E962.0	E980.4
Hycodan	965.09	E850.2	E935.2	E950.0	E962.0	E980.0
Hydantoin derivatives	966.1	E855.0	E936.1	E950.4	E962.0	E980.4
Hydeltra	962.0	E858.0	E932.0	E950.4	E962.0	E980.4
Hydergine	971.3	E855.6	E941.3	E950.4	E962.0	E980.4
Hydrabamine penicillin	960.0	E856	E930.0	E950.4	E962.0	E980.4
Hydralazine, hydrallazine	972.6	E858.3	E942.6	E950.4	E962.0	E980.4
Hydrargaphen	976.0	E858.7	E946.0	E950.4	E962.0	E980.4
Hydrazine	983.9	E864.3	—	E950.7	E962.1	E980.6
Hydriodic acid	975.5	E858.6	E945.5	E950.4	E962.0	E980.4
Hydrocarbon gas	987.1	E869.8	—	E952.8	E962.2	E982.8
incomplete combustion of — see Carbon, monoxide, fuel, utility						
liquefied (mobile container)	987.0	E868.0	—	E951.1	E962.2	E981.1
piped (natural)	987.0	E867	—	E951.0	E962.2	E981.0
Hydrochloric acid (liquid)	983.1	E864.1	—	E950.7	E962.1	E980.6
medicinal	973.4	E858.4	E943.4	E950.4	E962.0	E980.4
vapor	987.8	E869.8	—	E952.8	E962.2	E982.8
Hydrochlorothiazide	974.3	E858.5	E944.3	E950.4	E962.0	E980.4
Hydrocodone	965.09	E850.2	E935.2	E950.0	E962.0	E980.0
Hydrocortisone	962.0	E858.0	E932.0	E950.4	E962.0	E980.4
ENT agent	976.6	E858.7	E946.6	E950.4	E962.0	E980.4
ophthalmic preparation	976.5	E858.7	E946.5	E950.4	E962.0	E980.4
topical NEC	976.0	E858.7	E946.0	E950.4	E962.0	E980.4
Hydrocortone	962.0	E858.0	E932.0	E950.4	E962.0	E980.4
ENT agent	976.6	E858.7	E946.6	E950.4	E962.0	E980.4
ophthalmic preparation	976.5	E858.7	E946.5	E950.4	E962.0	E980.4
topical NEC	976.0	E858.7	E946.0	E950.4	E962.0	E980.4
Hydrocyanic acid — see Cyanide(s)						
Hydroflumethiazide	974.3	E858.5	E944.3	E950.4	E962.0	E980.4
Hydrofluoric acid (liquid)	983.1	E864.1	—	E950.7	E962.1	E980.6
vapor	987.8	E869.8	—	E952.8	E962.2	E982.8
Hydrogen	987.8	E869.8	—	E952.8	E962.2	E982.8
arsenide	985.1	E866.3	—	E950.8	E962.1	E980.8
arseniureted	985.1	E866.3	—	E950.8	E962.1	E980.8
cyanide (salts)	989.0	E866.8	—	E950.9	E962.1	E980.9
gas	987.7	E869.8	—	E952.8	E962.2	E982.8
fluoride (liquid)	983.1	E864.1	—	E950.7	E962.1	E980.6
vapor	987.8	E869.8	—	E952.8	E962.2	E982.8
peroxide (solution)	976.6	E858.7	E946.6	E950.4	E962.0	E980.4
phosphureted	987.8	E869.8	—	E952.8	E962.2	E982.8
sulfide (gas)	987.8	E869.8	—	E952.8	E962.2	E982.8
arseniureted	985.1	E866.3	—	E950.8	E962.1	E980.8
sulfureted	987.8	E869.8	—	E952.8	E962.2	E982.8
Hydromorphinol	965.09	E850.2	E935.2	E950.0	E962.0	E980.0
Hydromorphinone	965.09	E850.2	E935.2	E950.0	E962.0	E980.0
Hydromorphone	965.09	E850.2	E935.2	E950.0	E962.0	E980.0
Hydromox	974.3	E858.5	E944.3	E950.4	E962.0	E980.4
Hydrophilic lotion	976.3	E858.7	E946.3	E950.4	E962.0	E980.4
Hydroquinone	983.0	E864.0	—	E950.7	E962.1	E980.6
vapor	987.8	E869.8	—	E952.8	E962.2	E982.8
Hydrosulfuric acid (gas)	987.8	E869.8	—	E952.8	E962.2	E982.8
Hydrous wool fat (lotion)	976.3	E858.7	E946.3	E950.4	E962.0	E980.4
Hydroxide, caustic	983.2	E864.2	—	E950.7	E962.1	E980.6
Hydroxocobalamin	964.1	E858.2	E934.1	E950.4	E962.0	E980.4
Hydroxyamphetamine	971.2	E855.5	E941.2	E950.4	E962.0	E980.4
Hydroxychloroquine	961.4	E857	E931.4	E950.4	E962.0	E980.4
Hydroxydihydrocodeinone	965.09	E850.2	E935.2	E950.0	E962.0	E980.0
Hydroxyethyl starch	964.8	E858.2	E934.8	E950.4	E962.0	E980.4
Hydroxyphenamate	969.5	E853.8	E939.5	E950.3	E962.0	E980.3
Hydroxyphenylbutazone	965.5	E850.5	E935.5	E950.0	E962.0	E980.0
Hydroxyprogesterone	962.2	E858.0	E932.2	E950.4	E962.0	E980.4
Hydroxyquinoline derivatives	961.3	E857	E931.3	E950.4	E962.0	E980.4
Hydroxystilbamidine	961.5	E857	E931.5	E950.4	E962.0	E980.4
Hydroxyurea	963.1	E858.1	E933.1	E950.4	E962.0	E980.4
Hydroxyzine	969.5	E853.8	E939.5	E950.3	E962.0	E980.3
Hyoscine (hydrobromide)	971.1	E855.4	E941.1	E950.4	E962.0	E980.4
Hyoscyamine	971.1	E855.4	E941.1	E950.4	E962.0	E980.4
Hyoscyamus (albus) (niger)	988.2	E865.4	—	E950.9	E962.1	E980.9
Hypaque	977.8	E858.8	E947.8	E950.4	E962.0	E980.4
Hypertussis	964.6	E858.2	E934.6	E950.4	E962.0	E980.4
Hypnotics NEC	967.9	E852.9	E937.9	E950.2	E962.0	E980.2
Hypochlorites — *see* Sodium, hypochlorite						
Hypotensive agents NEC	972.6	E858.3	E942.6	E950.4	E962.0	E980.4
Ibufenac	965.69	E850.6	E935.6	E950.0	E962.0	E980.0
Ibuprofen	965.61	E850.6	E935.6	E950.0	E962.0	E980.0
ICG	977.8	E858.8	E947.8	E950.4	E962.0	E980.4
Ichthammol	976.4	E858.7	E946.4	E950.4	E962.0	E980.4
Ichthyol	976.4	E858.7	E946.4	E950.4	E962.0	E980.4
Idoxuridine	976.5	E858.7	E946.5	E950.4	E962.0	E980.4
IDU	976.5	E858.7	E946.5	E950.4	E962.0	E980.4
Iletin	962.3	E858.0	E932.3	E950.4	E962.0	E980.4

		External Cause (E-Code)				
	Poisoning	Accident	Therapeutic Use	Suicide Attempt	Assault	Undetermined
Ilex	988.2	E865.4	—	E950.9	E962.1	E980.9
Illuminating gas — see Gas, utility						
Ilopan	963.5	E858.1	E933.5	E950.4	E962.0	E980.4
Ilotycin	960.3	E856	E930.3	E950.4	E962.0	E980.4
ophthalmic preparation	976.5	E858.7	E946.5	E950.4	E962.0	E980.4
topical NEC	976.0	E858.7	E946.0	E950.4	E962.0	E980.4
Imipramine	969.0	E854.0	E939.0	E950.3	E962.0	E980.3
Immu-G	964.6	E858.2	E934.6	E950.4	E962.0	E980.4
Immuglobin	964.6	E858.2	E934.6	E950.4	E962.0	E980.4
Immune serum globulin	964.6	E858.2	E934.6	E950.4	E962.0	E980.4
Immunosuppressive agents	963.1	E858.1	E933.1	E950.4	E962.0	E980.4
Immu-tetanus	964.6	E858.2	E934.6	E950.4	E962.0	E980.4
Indandione (derivatives)	964.2	E858.2	E934.2	E950.4	E962.0	E980.4
Inderal	972.0	E858.3	E942.0	E950.4	E962.0	E980.4
Indian						
hemp	969.6	E854.1	E939.6	E950.3	E962.0	E980.3
tobacco	988.2	E865.4	—	E950.9	E962.1	E980.9
Indigo carmine	977.8	E858.8	E947.8	E950.4	E962.0	E980.4
Indocin	965.69	E850.6	E935.6	E950.0	E962.0	E980.0
Indocyanine green	977.8	E858.8	E947.8	E950.4	E962.0	E980.4
Indomethacin	965.69	E850.6	E935.6	E950.0	E962.0	E980.0
Industrial						
alcohol	980.9	E860.9	—	E950.9	E962.1	E980.9
fumes	987.8	E869.8	—	E952.8	E962.2	E982.8
solvents (fumes) (vapors)	982.8	E862.9	—	E950.9	E962.1	E980.9
Influenza vaccine	979.6	E858.8	E949.6	E950.4	E962.0	E982.8
Ingested substances NEC	989.9	E866.9	—	E950.9	E962.1	E980.9
INH (isoniazid)	961.8	E857	E931.8	E950.4	E962.0	E980.4
Inhalation, gas (noxious) — *see* Gas						
Ink	989.89	E866.8	—	E950.9	E962.1	E980.9
Innovar	967.6	E852.5	E937.6	E950.2	E962.0	E980.2
Inositol niacinate	972.2	E858.3	E942.2	E950.4	E962.0	E980.4
Inproquone	963.1	E858.1	E933.1	E950.4	E962.0	E980.4
Insecticides — *see also* Pesticides	989.4	E863.4	—	E950.6	E962.1	E980.7
chlorinated	989.2	E863.0	—	E950.6	E962.1	E980.7
mixtures	989.4	E863.3	—	E950.6	E962.1	E980.7
organochlorine (compounds)	989.2	E863.0	—	E950.6	E962.1	E980.7
organophosphorus (compounds)	989.3	E863.1	—	E950.6	E962.1	E980.7
Insect (sting), venomous	989.5	E905.5	—	E950.9	E962.1	E980.9
Insular tissue extract	962.3	E858.0	E932.3	E950.4	E962.0	E980.4
Insulin (amorphous) (globin) (isophane) (Lente) (NPH) (protamine) (Semilente) (Ultralente) (zinc)	962.3	E858.0	E932.3	E950.4	E962.0	E980.4
Intranarcon	968.3	E855.1	E938.3	E950.4	E962.0	E980.4
Inulin	977.8	E858.8	E947.8	E950.4	E962.0	E980.4
Invert sugar	974.5	E858.5	E944.5	E950.4	E962.0	E980.4
Inza — *see* Naproxen						
Iodide NEC — *see also* Iodine	976.0	E858.7	E946.0	E950.4	E962.0	E980.4
mercury (ointment)	976.0	E858.7	E946.0	E950.4	E962.0	E980.4
methylate	976.0	E858.7	E946.0	E950.4	E962.0	E980.4
potassium (expectorant) NEC	975.5	E858.6	E945.5	E950.4	E962.0	E980.4
Iodinated glycerol	975.5	E858.6	E945.5	E950.4	E962.0	E980.4
Iodine (antiseptic, external) (tincture) NEC	976.0	E858.7	E946.0	E950.4	E962.0	E980.4
diagnostic	977.8	E858.8	E947.8	E950.4	E962.0	E980.4
for thyroid conditions (antithyroid)	962.8	E858.0	E932.8	E950.4	E962.0	E980.4
vapor	987.8	E869.8	—	E952.8	E962.2	E982.8
Iodized oil	977.8	E858.8	E947.8	E950.4	E962.0	E980.4
Iodobismitol	961.2	E857	E931.2	E950.4	E962.0	E980.4
Iodochlorhydroxyquin	961.3	E857	E931.3	E950.4	E962.0	E980.4
topical	976.0	E858.7	E946.0	E950.4	E962.0	E980.4
Iodoform	976.0	E858.7	E946.0	E950.4	E962.0	E980.4
Iodopanoic acid	977.8	E858.8	E947.8	E950.4	E962.0	E980.4
Iodophthalein	977.8	E858.8	E947.8	E950.4	E962.0	E980.4
Ion exchange resins	974.5	E858.5	E944.5	E950.4	E962.0	E980.4
Iopanoic acid	977.8	E858.8	E947.8	E950.4	E962.0	E980.4
Iophendylate	977.8	E858.8	E947.8	E950.4	E962.0	E980.4
Iothiouracil	962.8	E858.0	E932.8	E950.4	E962.0	E980.4
Ipecac	973.6	E858.4	E943.6	E950.4	E962.0	E980.4
Ipecacuanha	973.6	E858.4	E943.6	E950.4	E962.0	E980.4
Ipodate	977.8	E858.8	E947.8	E950.4	E962.0	E980.4

		External Cause (E-Code)				
	Poisoning	Accident	Therapeutic Use	Suicide Attempt	Assault	Undetermined
Ipral	967.0	E851	E937.0	E950.1	E962.0	E980.1
Ipratropium	975.1	E858.6	E945.1	E950.4	E962.0	E980.4
Iproniazid	969.0	E854.0	E939.0	E950.3	E962.0	E980.3
Iron (compounds) (medicinal) (preparations)	964.0	E858.2	E934.0	E950.4	E962.0	E980.4
dextran	964.0	E858.2	E934.0	E950.4	E962.0	E980.4
nonmedicinal (dust) (fumes) NEC	985.8	E866.4	—	E950.9	E962.1	E980.9
Irritant drug	977.9	E858.9	E947.9	E950.5	E962.0	E980.5
Ismelin	972.6	E858.3	E942.6	E950.4	E962.0	E980.4
Isoamyl nitrite	972.4	E858.3	E942.4	E950.4	E962.0	E980.4
Isobutyl acetate	982.8	E862.4	—	E950.9	E962.1	E980.9
Isocarboxazid	969.0	E854.0	E939.0	E950.3	E962.0	E980.3
Isoephedrine	971.2	E855.5	E941.2	E950.4	E962.0	E980.4
Isoetharine	971.2	E855.5	E941.2	E950.4	E962.0	E980.4
Isofluorophate	971.0	E855.3	E941.0	E950.4	E962.0	E980.4
Isoniazid (INH)	961.8	E857	E931.8	E950.4	E962.0	E980.4
Isopentaquine	961.4	E857	E931.4	E950.4	E962.0	E980.4
Isophane insulin	962.3	E858.0	E932.3	E950.4	E962.0	E980.4
Isopregnenone	962.2	E858.0	E932.2	E950.4	E962.0	E980.4
Isoprenaline	971.2	E855.5	E941.2	E950.4	E962.0	E980.4
Isopropamide	971.1	E855.4	E941.1	E950.4	E962.0	E980.4
Isopropanol	980.2	E860.3	—	E950.9	E962.1	E980.9
topical (germicide)	976.0	E858.7	E946.0	E950.4	E962.0	E980.4
Isopropyl						
acetate	982.8	E862.4	—	E950.9	E962.1	E980.9
alcohol	980.2	E860.3	—	E950.9	E962.1	E980.9
topical (germicide)	976.0	E858.7	E946.0	E950.4	E962.0	E980.4
ether	982.8	E862.4	—	E950.9	E962.1	E980.9
Isoproterenol	971.2	E855.5	E941.2	E950.4	E962.0	E980.4
Isosorbide dinitrate	972.4	E858.3	E942.4	E950.4	E962.0	E980.4
Isothipendyl	963.0	E858.1	E933.0	E950.4	E962.0	E980.4
Isoxazolyl penicillin	960.0	E856	E930.0	E950.4	E962.0	E980.4
Isoxsuprine hydrochloride	972.5	E858.3	E942.5	E950.4	E962.0	E980.4
I-thyroxine sodium	962.7	E858.0	E932.7	E950.4	E962.0	E980.4
Jaborandi (pilocarpus) (extract)	971.0	E855.3	E941.0	E950.4	E962.0	E980.4
Jalap	973.1	E858.4	E943.1	E950.4	E962.0	E980.4
Jamaica						
dogwood (bark)	965.7	E850.7	E935.7	E950.0	E962.0	E980.0
ginger	989.89	E866.8	—	E950.9	E962.1	E980.9
Jatropha	988.2	E865.4	—	E950.9	E962.1	E980.9
curcas	988.2	E865.3	—	E950.9	E962.1	E980.9
Jectofer	964.0	E858.2	E934.0	E950.4	E962.0	E980.4
Jellyfish (sting)	989.5	E905.6	—	E950.9	E962.1	E980.9
Jequirity (bean)	988.2	E865.3	—	E950.9	E962.1	E980.9
Jimson weed	988.2	E865.4	—	E950.9	E962.1	E980.9
seeds	988.2	E865.3	—	E950.9	E962.1	E980.9
Juniper tar (oil) (ointment)	976.4	E858.7	E946.4	E950.4	E962.0	E980.4
Kallikrein	972.5	E858.3	E942.5	E950.4	E962.0	E980.4
Kanamycin	960.6	E856	E930.6	E950.4	E962.0	E980.4
Kantrex	960.6	E856	E930.6	E950.4	E962.0	E980.4
Kaolin	973.5	E858.4	E943.5	E950.4	E962.0	E980.4
Karaya (gum)	973.3	E858.4	E943.3	E950.4	E962.0	E980.4
Kemithal	968.3	E855.1	E938.3	E950.4	E962.0	E980.4
Kenacort	962.0	E858.0	E932.0	E950.4	E962.0	E980.4
Keratolytics	976.4	E858.7	E946.4	E950.4	E962.0	E980.4
Keratoplastics	976.4	E858.7	E946.4	E950.4	E962.0	E980.4
Kerosene, kerosine (fuel) (solvent) NEC	981	E862.1	—	E950.9	E962.1	E980.9
insecticide	981	E863.4	—	E950.6	E962.1	E980.7
vapor	987.1	E869.8	—	E952.8	E962.2	E982.8
Ketamine	968.3	E855.1	E938.3	E950.4	E962.0	E980.4
Ketobemidone	965.09	E850.2	E935.2	E950.0	E962.0	E980.0
Ketols	982.8	E862.4	—	E950.9	E962.1	E980.9
Ketone oils	982.8	E862.4	—	E950.9	E962.1	E980.9
Ketoprofen	965.61	E850.6	E935.6	E950.0	E962.0	E980.0
Kiln gas or vapor (carbon monoxide)	986	E868.8	—	E952.1	E962.2	E982.1
Konsyl	973.3	E858.4	E943.3	E950.4	E962.0	E980.4
Kosam seed	988.2	E865.3	—	E950.9	E962.1	E980.9
Krait (venom)	989.5	E905.0	—	E950.9	E962.1	E980.9
Kwell (insecticide)	989.2	E863.0	—	E950.6	E962.1	E980.7
anti-infective (topical)	976.0	E858.7	E946.0	E950.4	E962.0	E980.4
Laburnum (flowers) (seeds)	988.2	E865.3	—	E950.9	E962.1	E980.9
leaves	988.2	E865.4	—	E950.9	E962.1	E980.9
Lacquers	989.89	E861.6	—	E950.9	E962.1	E980.9
Lacrimogenic gas	987.5	E869.3	—	E952.8	E962.2	E982.8
Lactic acid	983.1	E864.1	—	E950.7	E962.1	E980.6
Lactobacillus acidophilus	973.5	E858.4	E943.5	E950.4	E962.0	E980.4
Lactoflavin	963.5	E858.1	E933.5	E950.4	E962.0	E980.4

		External Cause (E-Code)				
	Poisoning	Accident	Therapeutic Use	Suicide Attempt	Assault	Undeter-mined
Lactuca (virosa) (extract)	967.8	E852.8	E937.8	E950.2	E962.0	E980.2
Lactucarium	967.8	E852.8	E937.8	E950.2	E962.0	E980.2
Laevulose	974.5	E858.5	E944.5	E950.4	E962.0	E980.4
Lanatoside (C)	972.1	E858.3	E942.1	E950.4	E962.0	E980.4
Lanolin (lotion)	976.3	E858.7	E946.3	E950.4	E962.0	E980.4
Largactil	969.1	E853.0	E939.1	E950.3	E962.0	E980.3
Larkspur	988.2	E865.3	—	E950.9	E962.1	E980.9
Laroxyl	969.0	E854.0	E939.0	E950.3	E962.0	E980.3
Lasix	974.4	E858.5	E944.4	E950.4	E962.0	E980.4
Latex	989.82	E866.8	—	E950.9	E962.1	E980.9
Lathyrus (seed)	988.2	E865.3	—	E950.9	E962.1	E980.9
Laudanum	965.09	E850.2	E935.2	E950.0	E962.0	E980.0
Laudexium	975.2	E858.6	E945.2	E950.4	E962.0	E980.4
Laurel, black or cherry	988.2	E865.4	—	E950.9	E962.1	E980.9
Laurolinium	976.0	E858.7	E946.0	E950.4	E962.0	E980.4
Lauryl sulfoacetate	976.2	E858.7	E946.2	E950.4	E962.0	E980.4
Laxatives NEC	973.3	E858.4	E943.3	E950.4	E962.0	E980.4
emollient	973.2	E858.4	E943.2	E950.4	E962.0	E980.4
L-dopa	966.4	E855.0	E936.4	E950.4	E962.0	E980.4
Lead (dust) (fumes) (vapor) NEC	984.9	E866.0	—	E950.9	E962.1	E980.9
acetate (dust)	984.1	E866.0	—	E950.9	E962.1	E980.9
anti-infectives	961.2	E857	E931.2	E950.4	E962.0	E980.4
antiknock compound (tetraethyl)	984.1	E862.1	—	E950.9	E962.1	E980.9
arsenate, arsenite (dust) (insecticide) (vapor)	985.1	E863.4	—	E950.8	E962.1	E980.8
herbicide	985.1	E863.5	—	E950.8	E962.1	E980.8
carbonate	984.0	E866.0	—	E950.9	E962.1	E980.9
paint	984.0	E861.5	—	E950.9	E962.1	E980.9
chromate	984.0	E866.0	—	E950.9	E962.1	E980.9
paint	984.0	E861.5	—	E950.9	E962.1	E980.9
dioxide	984.0	E866.0	—	E950.9	E962.1	E980.9
inorganic (compound)	984.0	E866.0	—	E950.9	E962.1	E980.9
paint	984.0	E861.5	—	E950.9	E962.1	E980.9
iodide	984.0	E866.0	—	E950.9	E962.1	E980.9
pigment (paint)	984.0	E861.5	—	E950.9	E962.1	E980.9
monoxide (dust)	984.0	E866.0	—	E950.9	E962.1	E980.9
paint	984.0	E861.5	—	E950.9	E962.1	E980.9
organic	984.1	E866.0	—	E950.9	E962.1	E980.9
oxide	984.0	E866.0	—	E950.9	E962.1	E980.9
paint	984.0	E861.5	—	E950.9	E962.1	E980.9
paint	984.0	E861.5	—	E950.9	E962.1	E980.9
salts	984.0	E866.0	—	E950.9	E962.1	E980.9
specified compound NEC	984.8	E866.0	—	E950.9	E962.1	E980.9
tetra-ethyl	984.1	E862.1	—	E950.9	E962.1	E980.9
Lebanese red	969.6	E854.1	E939.6	E950.3	E962.0	E980.3
Lente Iletin (insulin)	962.3	E858.0	E932.3	E950.4	E962.0	E980.4
Leptazol	970.0	E854.3	E940.0	E950.4	E962.0	E980.4
Leritine	965.09	E850.2	E935.2	E950.0	E962.0	E980.0
Letter	962.7	E858.0	E932.7	E950.4	E962.0	E980.4
Lettuce opium	967.8	E852.8	E937.8	E950.2	E962.0	E980.2
Leucovorin (factor)	964.1	E858.2	E934.1	E950.4	E962.0	E980.4
Leukeran	963.1	E858.1	E933.1	E950.4	E962.0	E980.4
Levalbuterol	975.7	E858.6	E945.7	E950.4	E962.0	E980.4
Levallorphan	970.1	E854.3	E940.1	E950.4	E962.0	E980.4
Levanil	967.8	E852.8	E937.8	E950.2	E962.0	E980.2
Levarterenol	971.2	E855.5	E941.2	E950.4	E962.0	E980.4
Levodopa	966.4	E855.0	E936.4	E950.4	E962.0	E980.4
Levo-dromoran	965.09	E850.2	E935.2	E950.0	E962.0	E980.0
Levoid	962.7	E858.0	E932.7	E950.4	E962.0	E980.4
Levo-iso-methadone	965.02	E850.1	E935.1	E950.0	E962.0	E980.0
Levomepromazine	967.8	E852.8	E937.8	E950.2	E962.0	E980.2
Levoprome	967.8	E852.8	E937.8	E950.2	E962.0	E980.2
Levopropoxyphene	975.4	E858.6	E945.4	E950.4	E962.0	E980.4
Levorphan, levophanol	965.09	E850.2	E935.2	E950.0	E962.0	E980.0
Levothyroxine (sodium)	962.7	E858.0	E932.7	E950.4	E962.0	E980.4
Levsin	971.1	E855.4	E941.1	E950.4	E962.0	E980.4
Levulose	974.5	E858.5	E944.5	E950.4	E962.0	E980.4
Lewisite (gas)	985.1	E866.3	—	E950.8	E962.1	E980.8
Librium	969.4	E853.2	E939.4	E950.3	E962.0	E980.3
Lidex	976.0	E858.7	E946.0	E950.4	E962.0	E980.4
Lidocaine (infiltration) (topical)	968.5	E855.2	E938.5	E950.4	E962.0	E980.4
nerve block (peripheral) (plexus)	968.6	E855.2	E938.6	E950.4	E962.0	E980.4
spinal	968.7	E855.2	E938.7	E950.4	E962.0	E980.4
Lighter fluid	981	E862.1	—	E950.9	E962.1	E980.9
Lignocaine (infiltration) (topical)	968.5	E855.2	E938.5	E950.4	E962.0	E980.4
Lignocaine — *continued*						
nerve block (peripheral) (plexus)	968.6	E855.2	E938.6	E950.4	E962.0	E980.4
spinal	968.7	E855.2	E938.7	E950.4	E962.0	E980.4
Ligroin(e) (solvent)	981	E862.0	—	E950.9	E962.1	E980.9
vapor	987.1	E869.8	—	E952.8	E962.2	E982.8
Ligustrum vulgare	988.2	E865.3	—	E950.9	E962.1	E980.9
Lily of the valley	988.2	E865.4	—	E950.9	E962.1	E980.9
Lime (chloride)	983.2	E864.2	—	E950.7	E962.1	E980.6
solution, sulferated	976.4	E858.7	E946.4	E950.4	E962.0	E980.4
Limonene	982.8	E862.4	—	E950.9	E962.1	E980.9
Lincomycin	960.8	E856	E930.8	E950.4	E962.0	E980.4
Lindane (insecticide) (vapor)	989.2	E863.0	—	E950.6	E962.1	E980.7
anti-infective (topical)	976.0	E858.7	E946.0	E950.4	E962.0	E980.4
Liniments NEC	976.9	E858.7	E946.9	E950.4	E962.0	E980.4
Linoleic acid	972.2	E858.3	E942.2	E950.4	E962.0	E980.4
Liothyronine	962.7	E858.0	E932.7	E950.4	E962.0	E980.4
Liotrix	962.7	E858.0	E932.7	E950.4	E962.0	E980.4
Lipancreatin	973.4	E858.4	E943.4	E950.4	E962.0	E980.4
Lipo-Lutin	962.2	E858.0	E932.2	E950.4	E962.0	E980.4
Lipotropic agents	977.1	E858.8	E947.1	E950.4	E962.0	E980.4
Liquefied petroleum gases	987.0	E868.0	—	E951.1	E962.2	E981.1
piped (pure or mixed with air)	987.0	E867	—	E951.0	E962.2	E981.0
Liquid petrolatum	973.2	E858.4	E943.2	E950.4	E962.0	E980.4
substance	989.9	E866.9	—	E950.9	E962.1	E980.9
specified NEC	989.89	E866.8	—	E950.9	E962.1	E980.9
Lirugen	979.4	E858.8	E949.4	E950.4	E962.0	E980.4
Lithane	969.8	E855.8	E939.8	E950.3	E962.0	E980.3
Lithium	985.8	E866.4	—	E950.9	E962.1	E980.9
carbonate	969.8	E855.8	E939.8	E950.3	E962.0	E980.3
Lithonate	969.8	E855.8	E939.8	E950.3	E962.0	E980.3
Liver (extract) (injection) (preparations)	964.1	E858.2	E934.1	E950.4	E962.0	E980.4
Lizard (bite) (venom)	989.5	E905.0	—	E950.9	E962.1	E980.9
LMD	964.8	E858.2	E934.8	E950.4	E962.0	E980.4
Lobelia	988.2	E865.4	—	E950.9	E962.1	E980.9
Lobeline	970.0	E854.3	E940.0	E950.4	E962.0	E980.4
Locorten	976.0	E858.7	E946.0	E950.4	E962.0	E980.4
Lolium temulentum	988.2	E865.3	—	E950.9	E962.1	E980.9
Lomotil	973.5	E858.4	E943.5	E950.4	E962.0	E980.4
Lomustine	963.1	E858.1	E933.1	E950.4	E962.0	E980.4
Lophophora williamsii	969.6	E854.1	E939.6	E950.3	E962.0	E980.3
Lorazepam	969.4	E853.2	E939.4	E950.3	E962.0	E980.3
Lotions NEC	976.9	E858.7	E946.9	E950.4	E962.0	E980.4
Lotronex	973.8	E858.4	E943.8	E950.4	E962.0	E980.4
Lotusate	967.0	E851	E937.0	E950.1	E962.0	E980.1
Lowila	976.2	E858.7	E946.2	E950.4	E962.0	E980.4
Loxapine	969.3	E853.8	E939.3	E950.3	E962.0	E980.3
Lozenges (throat)	976.6	E858.7	E946.6	E950.4	E962.0	E980.4
LSD (25)	969.6	E854.1	E939.6	E950.3	E962.0	E980.3
L-Tryptophan — *see* amino acid						
Lubricating oil NEC	981	E862.2	—	E950.9	E962.1	E980.9
Lucanthone	961.6	E857	E931.6	E950.4	E962.0	E980.4
Luminal	967.0	E851	E937.0	E950.1	E962.0	E980.1
Lung irritant (gas) NEC	987.9	E869.9	—	E952.9	E962.2	E982.9
Lutocylol	962.2	E858.0	E932.2	E950.4	E962.0	E980.4
Lutromone	962.2	E858.0	E932.2	E950.4	E962.0	E980.4
Lututrin	975.0	E858.6	E945.0	E950.4	E962.0	E980.4
Lye (concentrated)	983.2	E864.2	—	E950.7	E962.1	E980.6
Lygranum (skin test)	977.8	E858.8	E947.8	E950.4	E962.0	E980.4
Lymecycline	960.4	E856	E930.4	E950.4	E962.0	E980.4
Lymphogranuloma venereum antigen	977.8	E858.8	E947.8	E950.4	E962.0	E980.4
Lynestrenol	962.2	E858.0	E932.2	E950.4	E962.0	E980.4
Lyovac Sodium Edecrin	974.4	E858.5	E944.4	E950.4	E962.0	E980.4
Lypressin	962.5	E858.0	E932.5	E950.4	E962.0	E980.4
Lysergic acid (amide) (diethylamide)	969.6	E854.1	E939.6	E950.3	E962.0	E980.3
Lysergide	969.6	E854.1	E939.6	E950.3	E962.0	E980.3
Lysine vasopressin	962.5	E858.0	E932.5	E950.4	E962.0	E980.4
Lysol	983.0	E864.0	—	E950.7	E962.1	E980.6
Lytta (vitatta)	976.8	E858.7	E946.8	E950.4	E962.0	E980.4
Mace	987.5	E869.3	—	E952.8	E962.2	E982.8
Macrolides (antibiotics)	960.3	E856	E930.3	E950.4	E962.0	E980.4
Mafenide	976.0	E858.7	E946.0	E950.4	E962.0	E980.4
Magaldrate	973.0	E858.4	E943.0	E950.4	E962.0	E980.4
Magic mushroom	969.6	E854.1	E939.6	E950.3	E962.0	E980.3
Magnamycin	960.8	E856	E930.8	E950.4	E962.0	E980.4
Magnesia magma	973.0	E858.4	E943.0	E950.4	E962.0	E980.4

		External Cause (E-Code)				
	Poisoning	Accident	Therapeutic Use	Suicide Attempt	Assault	Undetermined
Magnesium (compounds) (fumes) NEC	985.8	E866.4	—	E950.9	E962.1	E980.9
antacid	973.0	E858.4	E943.0	E950.4	E962.0	E980.4
carbonate	973.0	E858.4	E943.0	E950.4	E962.0	E980.4
cathartic	973.3	E858.4	E943.3	E950.4	E962.0	E980.4
citrate	973.3	E858.4	E943.3	E950.4	E962.0	E980.4
hydroxide	973.0	E858.4	E943.0	E950.4	E962.0	E980.4
oxide	973.0	E858.4	E943.0	E950.4	E962.0	E980.4
sulfate (oral)	973.3	E858.4	E943.3	E950.4	E962.0	E980.4
intravenous	966.3	E855.0	E936.3	E950.4	E962.0	E980.4
trisilicate	973.0	E858.4	E943.0	E950.4	E962.0	E980.4
Malathion (insecticide)	989.3	E863.1	—	E950.6	E962.1	E980.7
Male fern (oleoresin)	961.6	E857	E931.6	E950.4	E962.0	E980.4
Mandelic acid	961.9	E857	E931.9	E950.4	E962.0	E980.4
Manganese compounds (fumes) NEC	985.2	E866.4	—	E950.9	E962.1	E980.9
Mannitol (diuretic) (medicinal) NEC	974.4	E858.5	E944.4	E950.4	E962.0	E980.4
hexanitrate	972.4	E858.3	E942.4	E950.4	E962.0	E980.4
mustard	963.1	E858.1	E933.1	E950.4	E962.0	E980.4
Mannomustine	963.1	E858.1	E933.1	E950.4	E962.0	E980.4
MAO inhibitors	969.0	E854.0	E939.0	E950.3	E962.0	E980.3
Mapharsen	961.1	E857	E931.1	E950.4	E962.0	E980.4
Marcaine	968.9	E855.2	E938.9	E950.4	E962.0	E980.4
infiltration (subcutaneous)	968.5	E855.2	E938.5	E950.4	E962.0	E980.4
nerve block (peripheral) (plexus)	968.6	E855.2	E938.6	E950.4	E962.0	E980.4
Marezine	963.0	E858.1	E933.0	E950.4	E962.0	E980.4
Marihuana, marijuana (derivatives)	969.6	E854.1	E939.6	E950.3	E962.0	E980.3
Marine animals or plants (sting)	989.5	E905.6	—	E950.9	E962.1	E980.9
Marplan	969.0	E854.0	E939.0	E950.3	E962.0	E980.3
Marsh gas	987.1	E869.8	—	E952.8	E962.2	E982.8
Marsilid	969.0	E854.0	E939.0	E950.3	E962.0	E980.3
Matulane	963.1	E858.1	E933.1	E950.4	E962.0	E980.4
Mazindol	977.0	E858.8	E947.0	E950.4	E962.0	E980.4
MDMA	969.7	E854.2	E939.7	E950.3	E962.0	E980.3
Meadow saffron	988.2	E865.3	—	E950.9	E962.1	E980.9
Measles vaccine	979.4	E858.8	E949.4	E950.4	E962.0	E980.4
Meat, noxious or nonbacterial	988.8	E865.0	—	E950.9	E962.1	E980.9
Mebanazine	969.0	E854.0	E939.0	E950.3	E962.0	E980.3
Mebaral	967.0	E851	E937.0	E950.1	E962.0	E980.1
Mebendazole	961.6	E857	E931.6	E950.4	E962.0	E980.4
Mebeverine	975.1	E858.6	E945.1	E950.4	E962.0	E980.4
Mebhydroline	963.0	E858.1	E933.0	E950.4	E962.0	E980.4
Mebrophenhydramine	963.0	E858.1	E933.0	E950.4	E962.0	E980.4
Mebutamate	969.5	E853.8	E939.5	E950.3	E962.0	E980.3
Mecamylamine (chloride)	972.3	E858.3	E942.3	E950.4	E962.0	E980.4
Mechlorethamine hydrochloride	963.1	E858.1	E933.1	E950.4	E962.0	E980.4
Meclizene (hydrochloride)	963.0	E858.1	E933.0	E950.4	E962.0	E980.4
Meclofenoxate	970.0	E854.3	E940.0	E950.4	E962.0	E980.4
Meclozine (hydrochloride)	963.0	E858.1	E933.0	E950.4	E962.0	E980.4
Medazepam	969.4	E853.2	E939.4	E950.3	E962.0	E980.3
Medicine, medicinal substance	977.9	E858.9	E947.9	E950.5	E962.0	E980.5
specified NEC	977.8	E858.8	E947.8	E950.4	E962.0	E980.4
Medinal	967.0	E851	E937.0	E950.1	E962.0	E980.1
Medomin	967.0	E851	E937.0	E950.1	E962.0	E980.1
Medroxyprogesterone	962.2	E858.0	E932.2	E950.4	E962.0	E980.4
Medrysone	976.5	E858.7	E946.5	E950.4	E962.0	E980.4
Mefenamic acid	965.7	E850.7	E935.7	E950.0	E962.0	E980.0
Megahallucinogen	969.6	E854.1	E939.6	E950.3	E962.0	E980.3
Megestrol	962.2	E858.0	E932.2	E950.4	E962.0	E980.4
Meglumine	977.8	E858.8	E947.8	E950.4	E962.0	E980.4
Meladinin	976.3	E858.7	E946.3	E950.4	E962.0	E980.4
Melanizing agents	976.3	E858.7	E946.3	E950.4	E962.0	E980.4
Melarsoprol	961.1	E857	E931.1	E950.4	E962.0	E980.4
Melia azedarach	988.2	E865.3	—	E950.9	E962.1	E980.9
Mellaril	969.1	E853.0	E939.1	E950.3	E962.0	E980.3
Meloxine	976.3	E858.7	E946.3	E950.4	E962.0	E980.4
Melphalan	963.1	E858.1	E933.1	E950.4	E962.0	E980.4
Menadiol sodium diphosphate	964.3	E858.2	E934.3	E950.4	E962.0	E980.4
Menadione (sodium bisulfite)	964.3	E858.2	E934.3	E950.4	E962.0	E980.4
Menaphthone	964.3	E858.2	E934.3	E950.4	E962.0	E980.4
Meningococcal vaccine	978.8	E858.8	E948.8	E950.4	E962.0	E980.4
Menningovax-C	978.8	E858.8	E948.8	E950.4	E962.0	E980.4
Menotropins	962.4	E858.0	E932.4	E950.4	E962.0	E980.4
Menthol NEC	976.1	E858.7	E946.1	E950.4	E962.0	E980.4
Mepacrine	961.3	E857	E931.3	E950.4	E962.0	E980.4
Meparfynol	967.8	E852.8	E937.8	E950.2	E962.0	E980.2
Mepazine	969.1	E853.0	E939.1	E950.3	E962.0	E980.3
Mepenzolate	971.1	E855.4	E941.1	E950.4	E962.0	E980.4
Meperidine	965.09	E850.2	E935.2	E950.0	E962.0	E980.0
Mephenamin(e)	966.4	E855.0	E936.4	E950.4	E962.0	E980.4
Mephenesin (carbamate)	968.0	E855.1	E938.0	E950.4	E962.0	E980.4
Mephenoxalone	969.5	E853.8	E939.5	E950.3	E962.0	E980.3
Mephentermine	971.2	E855.5	E941.2	E950.4	E962.0	E980.4
Mephenytoin	966.1	E855.0	E936.1	E950.4	E962.0	E980.4
Mephobarbital	967.0	E851	E937.0	E950.1	E962.0	E980.1
Mepiperphenidol	971.1	E855.4	E941.1	E950.4	E962.0	E980.4
Mepivacaine	968.9	E855.2	E938.9	E950.4	E962.0	E980.4
infiltration (subcutaneous)	968.5	E855.2	E938.5	E950.4	E962.0	E980.4
nerve block (peripheral) (plexus)	968.6	E855.2	E938.6	E950.4	E962.0	E980.4
topical (surface)	968.5	E855.2	E938.5	E950.4	E962.0	E980.4
Meprednisone	962.0	E858.0	E932.0	E950.4	E962.0	E980.4
Meprobam	969.5	E853.8	E939.5	E950.3	E962.0	E980.3
Meprobamate	969.5	E853.8	E939.5	E950.3	E962.0	E980.3
Mepyramine (maleate)	963.0	E858.1	E933.0	E950.4	E962.0	E980.4
Meralluride	974.0	E858.5	E944.0	E950.4	E962.0	E980.4
Merbaphen	974.0	E858.5	E944.0	E950.4	E962.0	E980.4
Merbromin	976.0	E858.7	E946.0	E950.4	E962.0	E980.4
Mercaptomerin	974.0	E858.5	E944.0	E950.4	E962.0	E980.4
Mercaptopurine	963.1	E858.1	E933.1	E950.4	E962.0	E980.4
Mercumatilin	974.0	E858.5	E944.0	E950.4	E962.0	E980.4
Mercuramide	974.0	E858.5	E944.0	E950.4	E962.0	E980.4
Mercuranin	976.0	E858.7	E946.0	E950.4	E962.0	E980.4
Mercurochrome	976.0	E858.7	E946.0	E950.4	E962.0	E980.4
Mercury, mercuric, mercurous (compounds) (cyanide) (fumes) (nonmedicinal) (vapor) NEC	985.0	E866.1	—	E950.9	E962.1	E980.9
ammoniated	976.0	E858.7	E946.0	E950.4	E962.0	E980.4
anti-infective	961.2	E857	E931.2	E950.4	E962.0	E980.4
topical	976.0	E858.7	E946.0	E950.4	E962.0	E980.4
chloride (antiseptic) NEC	976.0	E858.7	E946.0	E950.4	E962.0	E980.4
fungicide	985.0	E863.6	—	E950.6	E962.1	E980.7
diuretic compounds	974.0	E858.5	E944.0	E950.4	E962.0	E980.4
fungicide	985.0	E863.6	—	E950.6	E962.1	E980.7
organic (fungicide)	985.0	E863.6	—	E950.6	E962.1	E980.7
Merethoxylline	974.0	E858.5	E944.0	E950.4	E962.0	E980.4
Mersalyl	974.0	E858.5	E944.0	E950.4	E962.0	E980.4
Merthiolate (topical)	976.0	E858.7	E946.0	E950.4	E962.0	E980.4
ophthalmic preparation	976.5	E858.7	E946.5	E950.4	E962.0	E980.4
Meruvax	979.4	E858.8	E949.4	E950.4	E962.0	E980.4
Mescal buttons	969.6	E854.1	E939.6	E950.3	E962.0	E980.3
Mescaline (salts)	969.6	E854.1	E939.6	E950.3	E962.0	E980.3
Mesoridazine besylate	969.1	E853.0	E939.1	E950.3	E962.0	E980.3
Mestanolone	962.1	E858.0	E932.1	E950.4	E962.0	E980.4
Mestranol	962.2	E858.0	E932.2	E950.4	E962.0	E980.4
Metacresylacetate	976.0	E858.7	E946.0	E950.4	E962.0	E980.4
Metaldehyde (snail killer) NEC	989.4	E863.4	—	E950.6	E962.1	E980.7
Metals (heavy) (nonmedicinal) NEC	985.9	E866.4	—	E950.9	E962.1	E980.9
dust, fumes, or vapor NEC	985.9	E866.4	—	E950.9	E962.1	E980.9
light NEC	985.9	E866.4	—	E950.9	E962.1	E980.9
dust, fumes, or vapor NEC	985.9	E866.4	—	E950.9	E962.1	E980.9
pesticides (dust) (vapor)	985.9	E863.4	—	E950.6	E962.1	E980.7
Metamucil	973.3	E858.4	E943.3	E950.4	E962.0	E980.4
Metaphen	976.0	E858.7	E946.0	E950.4	E962.0	E980.4
Metaproterenol	975.1	E858.6	E945.1	E950.4	E962.0	E980.4
Metaraminol	972.8	E858.3	E942.8	E950.4	E962.0	E980.4
Metaxalone	968.0	E855.1	E938.0	E950.4	E962.0	E980.4
Metformin	962.3	E858.0	E932.3	E950.4	E962.0	E980.4
Methacycline	960.4	E856	E930.4	E950.4	E962.0	E980.4
Methadone	965.02	E850.1	E935.1	E950.0	E962.0	E980.0
Methallenestril	962.2	E858.0	E932.2	E950.4	E962.0	E980.4
Methamphetamine	969.7	E854.2	E939.7	E950.3	E962.0	E980.3
Methandienone	962.1	E858.0	E932.1	E950.4	E962.0	E980.4
Methandriol	962.1	E858.0	E932.1	E950.4	E962.0	E980.4
Methandrostenolone	962.1	E858.0	E932.1	E950.4	E962.0	E980.4
Methane gas	987.1	E869.8	—	E952.8	E962.2	E982.8
Methanol	980.1	E860.2	—	E950.9	E962.1	E980.9
vapor	987.8	E869.8	—	E952.8	E962.2	E982.8
Methantheline	971.1	E855.4	E941.1	E950.4	E962.0	E980.4

		External Cause (E-Code)				
	Poisoning	Accident	Therapeutic Use	Suicide Attempt	Assault	Undetermined
Methaphenilene	963.0	E858.1	E933.0	E950.4	E962.0	E980.4
Methapyrilene	963.0	E858.1	E933.0	E950.4	E962.0	E980.4
Methaqualone (compounds)	967.4	E852.3	E937.4	E950.2	E962.0	E980.2
Metharbital, metharbitone	967.0	E851	E937.0	E950.1	E962.0	E980.1
Methazolamide	974.2	E858.5	E944.2	E950.4	E962.0	E980.4
Methdilazine	963.0	E858.1	E933.0	E950.4	E962.0	E980.4
Methedrine	969.7	E854.2	E939.7	E950.3	E962.0	E980.3
Methenamine (mandelate)	961.9	E857	E931.9	E950.4	E962.0	E980.4
Methenolone	962.1	E858.0	E932.1	E950.4	E962.0	E980.4
Methergine	975.0	E858.6	E945.0	E950.4	E962.0	E980.4
Methiacil	962.8	E858.0	E932.8	E950.4	E962.0	E980.4
Methicillin (sodium)	960.0	E856	E930.0	E950.4	E962.0	E980.4
Methimazole	962.8	E858.0	E932.8	E950.4	E962.0	E980.4
Methionine	977.1	E858.8	E947.1	E950.4	E962.0	E980.4
Methisazone	961.7	E857	E931.7	E950.4	E962.0	E980.4
Methitural	967.0	E851	E937.0	E950.1	E962.0	E980.1
Methixene	971.1	E855.4	E941.1	E950.4	E962.0	E980.4
Methobarbital, methobarbitone	967.0	E851	E937.0	E950.1	E962.0	E980.1
Methocarbamol	968.0	E855.1	E938.0	E950.4	E962.0	E980.4
Methohexital, methohexitone (sodium)	968.3	E855.1	E938.3	E950.4	E962.0	E980.4
Methoin	966.1	E855.0	E936.1	E950.4	E962.0	E980.4
Methopholine	965.7	E850.7	E935.7	E950.0	E962.0	E980.0
Methorate	975.4	E858.6	E945.4	E950.4	E962.0	E980.4
Methoserpidine	972.6	E858.3	E942.6	E950.4	E962.0	E980.4
Methotrexate	963.1	E858.1	E933.1	E950.4	E962.0	E980.4
Methotrimeprazine	967.8	E852.8	E937.8	E950.2	E962.0	E980.2
Methoxa-Dome	976.3	E858.7	E946.3	E950.4	E962.0	E980.4
Methoxamine	971.2	E855.5	E941.2	E950.4	E962.0	E980.4
Methoxsalen	976.3	E858.7	E946.3	E950.4	E962.0	E980.4
Methoxybenzyl penicillin	960.0	E856	E930.0	E950.4	E962.0	E980.4
Methoxychlor	989.2	E863.0	—	E950.6	E962.1	E980.7
Methoxyflurane	968.2	E855.1	E938.2	E950.4	E962.0	E980.4
Methoxyphenamine	971.2	E855.5	E941.2	E950.4	E962.0	E980.4
Methoxypromazine	969.1	E853.0	E939.1	E950.3	E962.0	E980.3
Methoxypsoralen	976.3	E858.7	E946.3	E950.4	E962.0	E980.4
Methscopolamine (bromide)	971.1	E855.4	E941.1	E950.4	E962.0	E980.4
Methsuximide	966.2	E855.0	E936.2	E950.4	E962.0	E980.4
Methyclothiazide	974.3	E858.5	E944.3	E950.4	E962.0	E980.4
Methyl						
acetate	982.8	E862.4	—	E950.9	E962.1	E980.9
acetone	982.8	E862.4	—	E950.9	E962.1	E980.9
alcohol	980.1	E860.2	—	E950.9	E962.1	E980.9
amphetamine	969.7	E854.2	E939.7	E950.3	E962.0	E980.3
androstanolone	962.1	E858.0	E932.1	E950.4	E962.0	E980.4
atropine	971.1	E855.4	E941.1	E950.4	E962.0	E980.4
benzene	982.0	E862.4	—	E950.9	E962.1	E980.9
bromide (gas)	987.8	E869.8	—	E952.8	E962.2	E982.8
fumigant	987.8	E863.8	—	E950.6	E962.2	E980.7
butanol	980.8	E860.8	—	E950.9	E962.1	E980.9
carbinol	980.1	E860.2	—	E950.9	E962.1	E980.9
cellosolve	982.8	E862.4	—	E950.9	E962.1	E980.9
cellulose	973.3	E858.4	E943.3	E950.4	E962.0	E980.4
chloride (gas)	987.8	E869.8	—	E952.8	E962.2	E982.8
cyclohexane	982.8	E862.4	—	E950.9	E962.1	E980.9
cyclohexanone	982.8	E862.4	—	E950.9	E962.1	E980.9
dihydromorphinone	965.09	E850.2	E935.2	E950.0	E962.0	E980.0
ergometrine	975.0	E858.6	E945.0	E950.4	E962.0	E980.4
ergonovine	975.0	E858.6	E945.0	E950.4	E962.0	E980.4
ethyl ketone	982.8	E862.4	—	E950.9	E962.1	E980.9
hydrazine	983.9	E864.3	—	E950.7	E962.1	E980.6
isobutyl ketone	982.8	E862.4	—	E950.9	E962.1	E980.9
morphine NEC	965.09	E850.2	E935.2	E950.0	E962.0	E980.0
parafynol	967.8	E852.8	E937.8	E950.2	E962.0	E980.2
parathion	989.3	E863.1	—	E950.6	E962.1	E980.7
pentynol NEC	967.8	E852.8	E937.8	E950.2	E962.0	E980.2
peridol	969.2	E853.1	E939.2	E950.3	E962.0	E980.3
phenidate	969.7	E854.2	E939.7	E950.3	E962.0	E980.3
prednisolone	962.0	E858.0	E932.0	E950.4	E962.0	E980.4
ENT agent	976.6	E858.7	E946.6	E950.4	E962.0	E980.4
ophthalmic preparation	976.5	E858.7	E946.5	E950.4	E962.0	E980.4
topical NEC	976.0	E858.7	E946.0	E950.4	E962.0	E980.4
propylcarbinol	980.8	E860.8	—	E950.9	E962.1	E980.9
rosaniline NEC	976.0	E858.7	E946.0	E950.4	E962.0	E980.4
salicylate NEC	976.3	E858.7	E946.3	E950.4	E962.0	E980.4
sulfate (fumes)	987.8	E869.8	—	E952.8	E962.2	E982.8
liquid	983.9	E864.3	—	E950.7	E962.1	E980.6
sulfonal	967.8	E852.8	E937.8	E950.2	E962.0	E980.2
testosterone	962.1	E858.0	E932.1	E950.4	E962.0	E980.4

		External Cause (E-Code)				
	Poisoning	Accident	Therapeutic Use	Suicide Attempt	Assault	Undetermined
Methyl — *continued*						
thiouracil	962.8	E858.0	E932.8	E950.4	E962.0	E980.4
Methylated spirit	980.0	E860.1	—	E950.9	E962.1	E980.9
Methyldopa	972.6	E858.3	E942.6	E950.4	E962.0	E980.4
Methylene						
blue	961.9	E857	E931.9	E950.4	E962.0	E980.4
chloride or dichloride (solvent) NEC	982.3	E862.4	—	E950.9	E962.1	E980.9
Methylhexabital	967.0	E851	E937.0	E950.1	E962.0	E980.1
Methylparaben (ophthalmic)	976.5	E858.7	E946.5	E950.4	E962.0	E980.4
Methyprylon	967.5	E852.4	E937.5	E950.2	E962.0	E980.2
Methysergide	971.3	E855.6	E941.3	E950.4	E962.0	E980.4
Metoclopramide	963.0	E858.1	E933.0	E950.4	E962.0	E980.4
Metofoline	965.7	E850.7	E935.7	E950.0	E962.0	E980.0
Metopon	965.09	E850.2	E935.2	E950.0	E962.0	E980.0
Metronidazole	961.5	E857	E931.5	E950.4	E962.0	E980.4
Metycaine	968.9	E855.2	E938.9	E950.4	E962.0	E980.4
infiltration (subcutaneous)	968.5	E855.2	E938.5	E950.4	E962.0	E980.4
nerve block (peripheral) (plexus)	968.6	E855.2	E938.6	E950.4	E962.0	E980.4
topical (surface)	968.5	E855.2	E938.5	E950.4	E962.0	E980.4
Metyrapone	977.8	E858.8	E947.8	E950.4	E962.0	E980.4
Mevinphos	989.3	E863.1	—	E950.6	E962.1	E980.7
Mezereon (berries)	988.2	E865.3	—	E950.9	E962.1	E980.9
Micatin	976.0	E858.7	E946.0	E950.4	E962.0	E980.4
Miconazole	976.0	E858.7	E946.0	E950.4	E962.0	E980.4
Midol	965.1	E850.3	E935.3	E950.0	E962.0	E980.0
Mifepristone	962.9	E858.0	E932.9	E950.4	E962.0	E980.4
Milk of magnesia	973.0	E858.4	E943.0	E950.4	E962.0	E980.4
Millipede (tropical) (venomous)	989.5	E905.4	—	E950.9	E962.1	E980.9
Miltown	969.5	E853.8	E939.5	E950.3	E962.0	E980.3
Mineral						
oil (medicinal)	973.2	E858.4	E943.2	E950.4	E962.0	E980.4
nonmedicinal	981	E862.1	—	E950.9	E962.1	E980.9
topical	976.3	E858.7	E946.3	E950.4	E962.0	E980.4
salts NEC	974.6	E858.5	E944.6	E950.4	E962.0	E980.4
spirits	981	E862.0	—	E950.9	E962.1	E980.9
Minocycline	960.4	E856	E930.4	E950.4	E962.0	E980.4
Mithramycin (antineoplastic)	960.7	E856	E930.7	E950.4	E962.0	E980.4
Mitobronitol	963.1	E858.1	E933.1	E950.4	E962.0	E980.4
Mitomycin (antineoplastic)	960.7	E856	E930.7	E950.4	E962.0	E980.4
Mitotane	963.1	E858.1	E933.1	E950.4	E962.0	E980.4
Moderil	972.6	E858.3	E942.6	E950.4	E962.0	E980.4
Mogadon — *see* Nitrazepam						
Molindone	969.3	E853.8	E939.3	E950.3	E962.0	E980.3
Monistat	976.0	E858.7	E946.0	E950.4	E962.0	E980.4
Monkshood	988.2	E865.4	—	E950.9	E962.1	E980.9
Monoamine oxidase inhibitors	969.0	E854.0	E939.0	E950.3	E962.0	E980.3
Monochlorobenzene	982.0	E862.4	—	E950.9	E962.1	E980.9
Monosodium glutamate	989.89	E866.8	—	E950.9	E962.1	E980.9
Monoxide, carbon — *see* Carbon, monoxide						
Moperone	969.2	E853.1	E939.2	E950.3	E962.0	E980.3
Morning glory seeds	969.6	E854.1	E939.6	E950.3	E962.0	E980.3
Moroxydine (hydrochloride)	961.7	E857	E931.7	E950.4	E962.0	E980.4
Morphazinamide	961.8	E857	E931.8	E950.4	E962.0	E980.4
Morphinans	965.09	E850.2	E935.2	E950.0	E962.0	E980.0
Morphine NEC	965.09	E850.2	E935.2	E950.0	E962.0	E980.0
antagonists	970.1	E854.3	E940.1	E950.4	E962.0	E980.4
Morpholinylethylmorphine	965.09	E850.2	E935.2	E950.0	E962.0	E980.0
Morrhuate sodium	972.7	E858.3	E942.7	E950.4	E962.0	E980.4
Moth balls — *see also* Pesticides	989.4	E863.4	—	E950.6	E962.1	E980.7
naphthalene	983.0	E863.4	—	E950.7	E962.1	E980.6
Motor exhaust gas — see Carbon, monoxide, exhaust gas						
Mouth wash	976.6	E858.7	E946.6	E950.4	E962.0	E980.4
Mucolytic agent	975.5	E858.6	E945.5	E950.4	E962.0	E980.4
Mucomyst	975.5	E858.6	E945.5	E950.4	E962.0	E980.4
Mucous membrane agents (external)	976.9	E858.7	E946.9	E950.4	E962.0	E980.4
specified NEC	976.8	E858.7	E946.8	E950.4	E962.0	E980.4
Mumps						
immune globulin (human)	964.6	E858.2	E934.6	E950.4	E962.0	E980.4
skin test antigen	977.8	E858.8	E947.8	E950.4	E962.0	E980.4
vaccine	979.6	E858.8	E949.6	E950.4	E962.0	E980.4

	Poisoning	External Cause (E-Code)				
		Accident	Therapeutic Use	Suicide Attempt	Assault	Undeter-mined
Mumpsvax	979.6	E858.8	E949.6	E950.4	E962.0	E980.4
Muriatic acid — *see* Hydrochloric acid						
Muscarine	971.0	E855.3	E941.0	E950.4	E962.0	E980.4
Muscle affecting agents NEC	975.3	E858.6	E945.3	E950.4	E962.0	E980.4
oxytocic	975.0	E858.6	E945.0	E950.4	E962.0	E980.4
relaxants	975.3	E858.6	E945.3	E950.4	E962.0	E980.4
central nervous system	968.0	E855.1	E938.0	E950.4	E962.0	E980.4
skeletal	975.2	E858.6	E945.2	E950.4	E962.0	E980.4
smooth	975.1	E858.6	E945.1	E950.4	E962.0	E980.4
Mushrooms, noxious	988.1	E865.5	—	E950.9	E962.1	E980.9
Mussel, noxious	988.0	E865.1	—	E950.9	E962.1	E980.9
Mustard (emetic)	973.6	E858.4	E943.6	E950.4	E962.0	E980.4
gas	987.8	E869.8	—	E952.8	E962.2	E982.8
nitrogen	963.1	E858.1	E933.1	E950.4	E962.0	E980.4
Mustine	963.1	E858.1	E933.1	E950.4	E962.0	E980.4
M-vac	979.4	E858.8	E949.4	E950.4	E962.0	E980.4
Mycifradin	960.8	E856	E930.8	E950.4	E962.0	E980.4
topical	976.0	E858.7	E946.0	E950.4	E962.0	E980.4
Mycitracin	960.8	E856	E930.8	E950.4	E962.0	E980.4
ophthalmic preparation	976.5	E858.7	E946.5	E950.4	E962.0	E980.4
Mycostatin	960.1	E856	E930.1	E950.4	E962.0	E980.4
topical	976.0	E858.7	E946.0	E950.4	E962.0	E980.4
Mydriacyl	971.1	E855.4	E941.1	E950.4	E962.0	E980.4
Myelobromal	963.1	E858.1	E933.1	E950.4	E962.0	E980.4
Myleran	963.1	E858.1	E933.1	E950.4	E962.0	E980.4
Myochrysin(e)	965.69	E850.6	E935.6	E950.0	E962.0	E980.0
Myoneural blocking agents	975.2	E858.6	E945.2	E950.4	E962.0	E980.4
Myristica fragrans	988.2	E865.3	—	E950.9	E962.1	E980.9
Myristicin	988.2	E865.3	—	E950.9	E962.1	E980.9
Mysoline	966.3	E855.0	E936.3	E950.4	E962.0	E980.4
Nafcillin (sodium)	960.0	E856	E930.0	E950.4	E962.0	E980.4
Nail polish remover	982.8	E862.4	—	E950.9	E962.1	E908.9
Nalidixic acid	961.9	E857	E931.9	E950.4	E962.0	E980.4
Nalorphine	970.1	E854.3	E940.1	E950.4	E962.0	E980.4
Naloxone	970.1	E854.3	E940.1	E950.4	E962.0	E980.4
Nandrolone (decanoate) (phenpropioate)	962.1	E858.0	E932.1	E950.4	E962.0	E980.4
Naphazoline	971.2	E855.5	E941.2	E950.4	E962.0	E980.4
Naphtha (painter's) (petroleum)	981	E862.0	—	E950.9	E962.1	E980.9
solvent	981	E862.0	—	E950.9	E962.1	E980.9
vapor	987.1	E869.8	—	E952.8	E962.2	E982.8
Naphthalene (chlorinated)	983.0	E864.0	—	E950.7	E962.1	E980.6
insecticide or moth repellent	983.0	E863.4	—	E950.7	E962.1	E980.6
vapor	987.8	E869.8	—	E952.8	E962.2	E982.8
Naphthol	983.0	E864.0	—	E950.7	E962.1	E980.6
Naphthylamine	983.0	E864.0	—	E950.7	E962.1	E980.6
Naprosyn — see Naproxen						
Naproxen	965.61	E850.6	E935.6	E950.0	E962.0	E980.0
Narcotic (drug)	967.9	E852.9	E937.9	E950.2	E962.0	E980.2
analgesic NEC	965.8	E850.8	E935.8	E950.0	E962.0	E980.0
antagonist	970.1	E854.3	E940.1	E950.4	E962.0	E980.4
specified NEC	967.8	E852.8	E937.8	E950.2	E962.0	E980.2
Narcotine	975.4	E858.6	E945.4	E950.4	E962.0	E980.4
Nardil	969.0	E854.0	E939.0	E950.3	E962.0	E980.3
Natrium cyanide — see Cyanide(s)						
Natural						
blood (product)	964.7	E858.2	E934.7	E950.4	E962.0	E980.4
gas (piped)	987.1	E867	—	E951.0	E962.2	E981.0
incomplete combustion	986	E867	—	E951.0	E962.2	E981.0
Nealbarbital, nealbarbitone	967.0	E851	E937.0	E950.1	E962.0	E980.1
Nectadon	975.4	E858.6	E945.4	E950.4	E962.0	E980.4
Nematocyst (sting)	989.5	E905.6	—	E950.9	E962.1	E980.9
Nembutal	967.0	E851	E937.0	E950.1	E962.0	E980.1
Neoarsphenamine	961.1	E857	E931.1	E950.4	E962.0	E980.4
Neocinchophen	974.7	E858.5	E944.7	E950.4	E962.0	E980.4
Neomycin	960.8	E856	E930.8	E950.4	E962.0	E980.4
ENT agent	976.6	E858.7	E946.6	E950.4	E962.0	E980.4
ophthalmic preparation	976.5	E858.7	E946.5	E950.4	E962.0	E980.4
topical NEC	976.0	E858.7	E946.0	E950.4	E962.0	E980.4
Neonal	967.0	E851	E937.0	E950.1	E962.0	E980.1
Neoprontosil	961.0	E857	E931.0	E950.4	E962.0	E980.4
Neosalvarsan	961.1	E857	E931.1	E950.4	E962.0	E980.4
Neosilversalvarsan	961.1	E857	E931.1	E950.4	E962.0	E980.4
Neosporin	960.8	E856	E930.8	E950.4	E962.0	E980.4

	Poisoning	External Cause (E-Code)				
		Accident	Therapeutic Use	Suicide Attempt	Assault	Undeter-mined
Neosporin — *continued*						
ENT agent	976.6	E858.7	E946.6	E950.4	E962.0	E980.4
opthalmic preparation	976.5	E858.7	E946.5	E950.4	E962.0	E980.4
topical NEC	976.0	E858.7	E946.0	E950.4	E962.0	E980.4
Neostigmine	971.0	E855.3	E941.0	E950.4	E962.0	E980.4
Neraval	967.0	E851	E937.0	E950.1	E962.0	E980.1
Neravan	967.0	E851	E937.0	E950.1	E962.0	E980.1
Nerium oleander	988.2	E865.4	—	E950.9	E962.1	E980.9
Nerve gases (war)	987.9	E869.9	—	E952.9	E962.2	E982.9
Nesacaine	968.9	E855.2	E938.9	E950.4	E962.0	E980.4
infiltration (subcutaneous)	968.5	E855.2	E938.5	E950.4	E962.0	E980.4
nerve block (peripheral) (plexus)	968.6	E855.2	E938.6	E950.4	E962.0	E980.4
Neurobarb	967.0	E851	E937.0	E950.1	E962.0	E980.1
Neuroleptics NEC	969.3	E853.8	E939.3	E950.3	E962.0	E980.3
Neuroprotective agent	977.8	E858.8	E947.8	E950.4	E962.0	E980.4
Neutral spirits	980.0	E860.1	—	E950.9	E962.1	E980.9
beverage	980.0	E860.0	—	E950.9	E962.1	E980.9
Niacin, niacinamide	972.2	E858.3	E942.2	E950.4	E962.0	E980.4
Nialamide	969.0	E854.0	E939.0	E950.3	E962.0	E980.3
Nickle (carbonyl) (compounds) (fumes) (tetracarbonyl) (vapor)	985.8	E866.4	—	E950.9	E962.1	E980.9
Niclosamide	961.6	E857	E931.6	E950.4	E962.0	E980.4
Nicomorphine	965.09	E850.2	E935.2	E950.0	E962.0	E980.0
Nicotinamide	972.2	E858.3	E942.2	E950.4	E962.0	E980.4
Nicotine (insecticide) (spray) (sulfate) NEC	989.4	E863.4	—	E950.6	E962.1	E980.7
not insecticide	989.89	E866.8	—	E950.9	E962.1	E980.9
Nicotinic acid (derivatives)	972.2	E858.3	E942.2	E950.4	E962.0	E980.4
Nicotinyl alcohol	972.2	E858.3	E942.2	E950.4	E962.0	E980.4
Nicoumalone	964.2	E858.2	E934.2	E950.4	E962.0	E980.4
Nifenazone	965.5	E850.5	E935.5	E950.0	E962.0	E980.0
Nifuraldezone	961.9	E857	E931.9	E950.4	E962.0	E980.4
Nightshade (deadly)	988.2	E865.4	—	E950.9	E962.1	E980.9
Nikethamide	970.0	E854.3	E940.0	E950.4	E962.0	E980.4
Nilstat	960.1	E856	E930.1	E950.4	E962.0	E980.4
topical	976.0	E858.7	E946.0	E950.4	E962.0	E980.4
Nimodipine	977.8	E858.8	E947.8	E950.4	E962.0	E980.4
Niridazole	961.6	E857	E931.6	E950.4	E962.0	E980.4
Nisentil	965.09	E850.2	E935.2	E950.0	E962.0	E980.0
Nitrates	972.4	E858.3	E942.4	E950.4	E962.0	E980.4
Nitrazepam	969.4	E853.2	E939.4	E950.3	E962.0	E980.3
Nitric						
acid (liquid)	983.1	E864.1	—	E950.7	E962.1	E980.6
vapor	987.8	E869.8	—	E952.8	E962.2	E982.8
oxide (gas)	987.2	E869.0	—	E952.8	E962.2	E982.8
Nitrite, amyl (medicinal) (vapor)	972.4	E858.3	E942.4	E950.4	E962.0	E980.4
Nitroaniline	983.0	E864.0	—	E950.7	E962.1	E980.6
vapor	987.8	E869.8	—	E952.8	E962.2	E982.8
Nitrobenzene, nitrobenzol	983.0	E864.0	—	E950.7	E962.1	E980.6
vapor	987.8	E869.8	—	E952.8	E962.2	E982.8
Nitrocellulose	976.3	E858.7	E946.3	E950.4	E962.0	E980.4
Nitrofuran derivatives	961.9	E857	E931.9	E950.4	E962.0	E980.4
Nitrofurantoin	961.9	E857	E931.9	E950.4	E962.0	E980.4
Nitrofurazone	976.0	E858.7	E946.0	E950.4	E962.0	E980.4
Nitrogen (dioxide) (gas) (oxide)	987.2	E869.0	—	E952.8	E962.2	E982.8
mustard (antineoplastic)	963.1	E858.1	E933.1	E950.4	E962.0	E980.4
nonmedicinal	989.89	E866.8	—	E950.9	E962.1	E980.9
fumes	987.8	E869.8	—	E952.8	E962.2	E982.8
Nitroglycerin, nitroglycerol (medicinal)	972.4	E858.3	E942.4	E950.4	E962.0	E980.4
Nitrohydrochloric acid	983.1	E864.1	—	E950.7	E962.1	E980.6
Nitromersol	976.0	E858.7	E946.0	E950.4	E962.0	E980.4
Nitronaphthalene	983.0	E864.0	—	E950.7	E962.2	E980.6
Nitrophenol	983.0	E864.0	—	E950.7	E962.2	E980.6
Nitrothiazol	961.6	E857	E931.6	E950.4	E962.0	E980.4
Nitrotoluene, nitrotoluol	983.0	E864.0	—	E950.7	E962.1	E980.6
vapor	987.8	E869.8	—	E952.8	E962.2	E982.8
Nitrous	968.2	E855.1	E938.2	E950.4	E962.0	E980.4
acid (liquid)	983.1	E864.1	—	E950.7	E962.1	E980.6
fumes	987.2	E869.0	—	E952.8	E962.2	E982.8
oxide (anesthetic) NEC	968.2	E855.1	E938.2	E950.4	E962.0	E980.4
Nitrozone	976.0	E858.7	E946.0	E950.4	E962.0	E980.4
Noctec	967.1	E852.0	E937.1	E950.2	E962.0	E980.2
Noludar	967.5	E852.4	E937.5	E950.2	E962.0	E980.2
Noptil	967.0	E851	E937.0	E950.1	E962.0	E980.1
Noradrenalin	971.2	E855.5	E941.2	E950.4	E962.0	E980.4
Noramidopyrine	965.5	E850.5	E935.5	E950.0	E962.0	E980.0

	Poisoning	External Cause (E-Code)				
		Accident	Therapeutic Use	Suicide Attempt	Assault	Undetermined
Norepinephrine	971.2	E855.5	E941.2	E950.4	E962.0	E980.4
Norethandrolone	962.1	E858.0	E932.1	E950.4	E962.0	E980.4
Norethindrone	962.2	E858.0	E932.2	E950.4	E962.0	E980.4
Norethisterone	962.2	E858.0	E932.2	E950.4	E962.0	E980.4
Norethynodrel	962.2	E858.0	E932.2	E950.4	E962.0	E980.4
Norlestrin	962.2	E858.0	E932.2	E950.4	E962.0	E980.4
Norlutin	962.2	E858.0	E932.2	E950.4	E962.0	E980.4
Normison — see Benzodiazepines						
Normorphine	965.09	E850.2	E935.2	E950.0	E962.0	E980.0
Nortriptyline	969.0	E854.0	E939.0	E950.3	E962.0	E980.3
Noscapine	975.4	E858.6	E945.4	E950.4	E962.0	E980.4
Nose preparations	976.6	E858.7	E946.6	E950.4	E962.0	E980.4
Novobiocin	960.8	E856	E930.8	E950.4	E962.0	E980.4
Novocain (infiltration) (topical)	968.5	E855.2	E938.5	E950.4	E962.0	E980.4
nerve block (peripheral) (plexus)	968.6	E855.2	E938.6	E950.4	E962.0	E980.4
spinal	968.7	E855.2	E938.7	E950.4	E962.0	E980.4
Noxythiolin	961.9	E857	E931.9	E950.4	E962.0	E980.4
NPH Iletin (insulin)	962.3	E858.0	E932.3	E950.4	E962.0	E980.4
Numorphan	965.09	E850.2	E935.2	E950.0	E962.0	E980.0
Nunol	967.0	E851	E937.0	E950.1	E962.0	E980.1
Nupercaine (spinal anesthetic)	968.7	E855.2	E938.7	E950.4	E962.0	E980.4
topical (surface)	968.5	E855.2	E938.5	E950.4	E962.0	E980.4
Nutmeg oil (liniment)	976.3	E858.7	E946.3	E950.4	E962.0	E980.4
Nux vomica	989.1	E863.7	—	E950.6	E962.1	E980.7
Nydrazid	961.8	E857	E931.8	E950.4	E962.0	E980.4
Nylidrin	971.2	E855.5	E941.2	E950.4	E962.0	E980.4
Nystatin	960.1	E856	E930.1	E950.4	E962.0	E980.4
topical	976.0	E858.7	E946.0	E950.4	E962.0	E980.4
Nytol	963.0	E858.1	E933.0	E950.4	E962.0	E980.4
Oblivion	967.8	E852.8	E937.8	E950.2	E962.0	E980.2
Octyl nitrite	972.4	E858.3	E942.4	E950.4	E962.0	E980.4
Oestradiol (cypionate) (dipropionate) (valerate)	962.2	E858.0	E932.2	E950.4	E962.0	E980.4
Oestriol	962.2	E858.0	E932.2	E950.4	E962.0	E980.4
Oestrone	962.2	E858.0	E932.2	E950.4	E962.0	E980.4
Oil (of) NEC	989.89	E866.8	—	E950.9	E962.1	E980.9
bitter almond	989.0	E866.8	—	E950.9	E962.1	E980.9
camphor	976.1	E858.7	E946.1	E950.4	E962.0	E980.4
colors	989.89	E861.6	—	E950.9	E962.1	E980.9
fumes	987.8	E869.8	—	E952.8	E962.2	E982.8
lubricating	981	E862.2	—	E950.9	E962.1	E980.9
specified source, other — see substance specified						
vitriol (liquid)	983.1	E864.1	—	E950.7	E962.1	E980.6
fumes	987.8	E869.8	—	E952.8	E962.2	E982.8
wintergreen (bitter) NEC	976.3	E858.7	E946.3	E950.4	E962.0	E980.4
Ointments NEC	976.9	E858.7	E946.9	E950.4	E962.0	E980.4
Oleander	988.2	E865.4	—	E950.9	E962.1	E980.9
Oleandomycin	960.3	E856	E930.3	E950.4	E962.0	E980.4
Oleovitamin A	963.5	E858.1	E933.5	E950.4	E962.0	E980.4
Oleum ricini	973.1	E858.4	E943.1	E950.4	E962.0	E980.4
Olive oil (medicinal) NEC	973.2	E858.4	E943.2	E950.4	E962.0	E980.4
OMPA	989.3	E863.1	—	E950.6	E962.1	E980.7
Oncovin	963.1	E858.1	E933.1	E950.4	E962.0	E980.4
Ophthaine	968.5	E855.2	E938.5	E950.4	E962.0	E980.4
Ophthetic	968.5	E855.2	E938.5	E950.4	E962.0	E980.4
Opiates, opioids, opium NEC	965.00	E850.2	E935.2	E950.0	E962.0	E980.0
antagonists	970.1	E854.3	E940.1	E950.4	E962.0	E980.4
Oracon	962.2	E858.0	E932.2	E950.4	E962.0	E980.4
Oragrafin	977.8	E858.8	E947.8	E950.4	E962.0	E980.4
Oral contraceptives	962.2	E858.0	E932.2	E950.4	E962.0	E980.4
Orciprenaline	975.1	E858.6	E945.1	E950.4	E962.0	E980.4
Organidin	975.5	E858.6	E945.5	E950.4	E962.0	E980.4
Organophosphates	989.3	E863.1	—	E950.6	E962.1	E980.7
Orimune	979.5	E858.8	E949.5	E950.4	E962.0	E980.4
Orinase	962.3	E858.0	E932.3	E950.4	E962.0	E980.4
Orphenadrine	966.4	E855.0	E936.4	E950.4	E962.0	E980.4
Ortal (sodium)	967.0	E851	E937.0	E950.1	E962.0	E980.1
Orthoboric acid	976.0	E858.7	E946.0	E950.4	E962.0	E980.4
ENT agent	976.6	E858.7	E946.6	E950.4	E962.0	E980.4
ophthalmic preparation	976.5	E858.7	E946.5	E950.4	E962.0	E980.4
Orthocaine	968.5	E855.2	E938.5	E950.4	E962.0	E980.4
Ortho-Novum	962.2	E858.0	E932.2	E950.4	E962.0	E980.4
Orthotolidine (reagent)	977.8	E858.8	E947.8	E950.4	E962.0	E980.4
Osmic acid (liquid)	983.1	E864.1	—	E950.7	E962.1	E980.6
fumes	987.8	E869.8	—	E952.8	E962.2	E982.8
Osmotic diuretics	974.4	E858.5	E944.4	E950.4	E962.0	E980.4
Ouabain	972.1	E858.3	E942.1	E950.4	E962.0	E980.4
Ovarian hormones (synthetic substitutes)	962.2	E858.0	E932.2	E950.4	E962.0	E980.4
Ovral	962.2	E858.0	E932.2	E950.4	E962.0	E980.4
Ovulation suppressants	962.2	E858.0	E932.2	E950.4	E962.0	E980.4
Ovulen	962.2	E858.0	E932.2	E950.4	E962.0	E980.4
Oxacillin (sodium)	960.0	E856	E930.0	E950.4	E962.0	E980.4
Oxalic acid	983.1	E864.1	—	E950.7	E962.1	E980.6
Oxanamide	969.5	E853.8	E939.5	E950.3	E962.0	E980.3
Oxandrolone	962.1	E858.0	E932.1	E950.4	E962.0	E980.4
Oxaprozin	965.61	E850.6	E935.6	E950.0	E962.0	E980.0
Oxazepam	969.4	E853.2	E939.4	E950.3	E962.0	E980.3
Oxazolidine derivatives	966.0	E855.0	E936.0	E950.4	E962.0	E980.4
Ox bile extract	973.4	E858.4	E943.4	E950.4	E962.0	E980.4
Oxedrine	971.2	E855.5	E941.2	E950.4	E962.0	E980.4
Oxeladin	975.4	E858.6	E945.4	E950.4	E962.0	E980.4
Oxethazaine NEC	968.5	E855.2	E938.5	E950.4	E962.0	E980.4
Oxidizing agents NEC	983.9	E864.3	—	E950.7	E962.1	E980.6
Oxolinic acid	961.3	E857	E931.3	E950.4	E962.0	E980.4
Oxophenarsine	961.1	E857	E931.1	E950.4	E962.0	E980.4
Oxsoralen	976.3	E858.7	E946.3	E950.4	E962.0	E980.4
Oxtriphylline	975.7	E858.6	E945.7	E950.4	E962.0	E980.4
Oxybuprocaine	968.5	E855.2	E938.5	E950.4	E962.0	E980.4
Oxybutynin	975.1	E858.6	E945.1	E950.4	E962.0	E980.4
Oxycodone	965.09	E850.2	E935.2	E950.0	E962.0	E980.0
Oxygen	987.8	E869.8	—	E952.8	E962.2	E982.8
Oxylone	976.0	E858.7	E946.0	E950.4	E962.0	E980.4
ophthalmic preparation	976.5	E858.7	E946.5	E950.4	E962.0	E980.4
Oxymesterone	962.1	E858.0	E932.1	E950.4	E962.0	E980.4
Oxymetazoline	971.2	E855.5	E941.2	E950.4	E962.0	E980.4
Oxymetholone	962.1	E858.0	E932.1	E950.4	E962.0	E980.4
Oxymorphone	965.09	E850.2	E935.2	E950.0	E962.0	E980.0
Oxypertine	969.0	E854.0	E939.0	E950.3	E962.0	E980.3
Oxyphenbutazone	965.5	E850.5	E935.5	E950.0	E962.0	E980.0
Oxyphencyclimine	971.1	E855.4	E941.1	E950.4	E962.0	E980.4
Oxyphenisatin	973.1	E858.4	E943.1	E950.4	E962.0	E980.4
Oxyphenonium	971.1	E855.4	E941.1	E950.4	E962.0	E980.4
Oxyquinoline	961.3	E857	E931.3	E950.4	E962.0	E980.4
Oxytetracycline	960.4	E856	E930.4	E950.4	E962.0	E980.4
Oxytocics	975.0	E858.6	E945.0	E950.4	E962.0	E980.4
Oxytocin	975.0	E858.6	E945.0	E950.4	E962.0	E980.4
Ozone	987.8	E869.8	—	E952.8	E962.2	E982.8
PABA	976.3	E858.7	E946.3	E950.4	E962.0	E980.4
Packed red cells	964.7	E858.2	E934.7	E950.4	E962.0	E980.4
Paint NEC	989.89	E861.6	—	E950.9	E962.1	E980.9
cleaner	982.8	E862.9	—	E950.9	E962.1	E980.9
fumes NEC	987.8	E869.8	—	E952.8	E962.1	E982.8
lead (fumes)	984.0	E861.5	—	E950.9	E962.1	E980.9
solvent NEC	982.8	E862.9	—	E950.9	E962.1	E980.9
stripper	982.8	E862.9	—	E950.9	E962.1	E980.9
Palfium	965.09	E850.2	E935.2	E950.0	E962.0	E980.0
Palivizumab	979.9	E858.8	E949.6	E950.4	E962.0	E980.4
Paludrine	961.4	E857	E931.4	E950.4	E962.0	E980.4
PAM	977.2	E855.8	E947.2	E950.4	E962.0	E980.4
Pamaquine (naphthoate)	961.4	E857	E931.4	E950.4	E962.0	E980.4
Pamprin	965.1	E850.3	E935.3	E950.0	E962.0	E980.0
Panadol	965.4	E850.4	E935.4	E950.0	E962.0	E980.0
Pancreatic dornase (mucolytic)	963.4	E858.1	E933.4	E950.4	E962.0	E980.4
Pancreatin	973.4	E858.4	E943.4	E950.4	E962.0	E980.4
Pancrelipase	973.4	E858.4	E943.4	E950.4	E962.0	E980.4
Pangamic acid	963.5	E858.1	E933.5	E950.4	E962.0	E980.4
Panthenol	963.5	E858.1	E933.5	E950.4	E962.0	E980.4
topical	976.8	E858.7	E946.8	E950.4	E962.0	E980.4
Pantopaque	977.8	E858.8	E947.8	E950.4	E962.0	E980.4
Pantopon	965.00	E850.2	E935.2	E950.0	E962.0	E980.0
Pantothenic acid	963.5	E858.1	E933.5	E950.4	E962.0	E980.4
Panwarfin	964.2	E858.2	E934.2	E950.4	E962.0	E980.4
Papain	973.4	E858.4	E943.4	E950.4	E962.0	E980.4
Papaverine	972.5	E858.3	E942.5	E950.4	E962.0	E980.4
Para-aminobenzoic acid	976.3	E858.7	E946.3	E950.4	E962.0	E980.4
Para-aminophenol derivatives	965.4	E850.4	E935.4	E950.0	E962.0	E980.0
Para-aminosalicylic acid (derivatives)	961.8	E857	E931.8	E950.4	E962.0	E980.4
Paracetaldehyde (medicinal)	967.2	E852.1	E937.2	E950.2	E962.0	E980.2
Paracetamol	965.4	E850.4	E935.4	E950.0	E962.0	E980.0
Paracodin	965.09	E850.2	E935.2	E950.0	E962.0	E980.0
Paradione	966.0	E855.0	E936.0	E950.4	E962.0	E980.4

	Poisoning	External Cause (E-Code)				
		Accident	Therapeutic Use	Suicide Attempt	Assault	Undetermined
Paraffin(s) (wax)	981	E862.3	—	E950.9	E962.1	E980.9
liquid (medicinal)	973.2	E858.4	E943.2	E950.4	E962.0	E980.4
nonmedicinal (oil)	981	E962.1	—	E950.9	E962.1	E980.9
Paraldehyde (medicinal)	967.2	E852.1	E937.2	E950.2	E962.0	E980.2
Paramethadione	966.0	E855.0	E936.0	E950.4	E962.0	E980.4
Paramethasone	962.0	E858.0	E932.0	E950.4	E962.0	E980.4
Paraquat	989.4	E863.5	—	E950.6	E962.1	E980.7
Parasympatholytics	971.1	E855.4	E941.1	E950.4	E962.0	E980.4
Parasympathomimetics	971.0	E855.3	E941.0	E950.4	E962.0	E980.4
Parathion	989.3	E863.1	—	E950.6	E962.1	E980.7
Parathormone	962.6	E858.0	E932.6	E950.4	E962.0	E980.4
Parathyroid (derivatives)	962.6	E858.0	E932.6	E950.4	E962.0	E980.4
Paratyphoid vaccine	978.1	E858.8	E948.1	E950.4	E962.0	E980.4
Paredrine	971.2	E855.5	E941.2	E950.4	E962.0	E980.4
Paregoric	965.00	E850.2	E935.2	E950.0	E962.0	E980.0
Pargyline	972.3	E858.3	E942.3	E950.4	E962.0	E980.4
Paris green	985.1	E866.3	—	E950.8	E962.1	E980.8
insecticide	985.1	E863.4	—	E950.8	E962.1	E980.8
Parnate	969.0	E854.0	E939.0	E950.3	E962.0	E980.3
Paromomycin	960.8	E856	E930.8	E950.4	E962.0	E980.4
Paroxypropione	963.1	E858.1	E933.1	E950.4	E962.0	E980.4
Parzone	965.09	E850.2	E935.2	E950.0	E962.0	E980.0
PAS	961.8	E857	E931.8	E950.4	E962.0	E980.4
PCBs	981	E862.3	—	E950.9	E962.1	E980.9
PCP (pentachlorophenol)	989.4	E863.6	—	E950.6	E962.1	E980.7
herbicide	989.4	E863.5	—	E950.6	E962.1	E980.7
insecticide	989.4	E863.4	—	E950.6	E962.1	E980.7
phencyclidine	968.3	E855.1	E938.3	E950.4	E962.0	E980.4
Peach kernel oil (emulsion)	973.2	E858.4	E943.2	E950.4	E962.0	E980.4
Peanut oil (emulsion) NEC	973.2	E858.4	E943.2	E950.4	E962.0	E980.4
topical	976.3	E858.7	E946.3	E950.4	E962.0	E980.4
Pearly Gates (morning glory seeds)	969.6	E854.1	E939.6	E950.3	E962.0	E980.3
Pecazine	969.1	E853.0	E939.1	E950.3	E962.0	E980.3
Pecilocin	960.1	E856	E930.1	E950.4	E962.0	E980.4
Pectin (with kaolin) NEC	973.5	E858.4	E943.5	E950.4	E962.0	E980.4
Pelletierine tannate	961.6	E857	E931.6	E950.4	E962.0	E980.4
Pemoline	969.7	E854.2	E939.7	E950.3	E962.0	E980.3
Pempidine	972.3	E858.3	E942.3	E950.4	E962.0	E980.4
Penamecillin	960.0	E856	E930.0	E950.4	E962.0	E980.4
Penethamate hydriodide	960.0	E856	E930.0	E950.4	E962.0	E980.4
Penicillamine	963.8	E858.1	E933.8	E950.4	E962.0	E980.4
Penicillin (any type)	960.0	E856	E930.0	E950.4	E962.0	E980.4
Penicillinase	963.4	E858.1	E933.4	E950.4	E962.0	E980.4
Pentachlorophenol (fungicide)	989.4	E863.6	—	E950.6	E962.1	E980.7
herbicide	989.4	E863.5	—	E950.6	E962.1	E980.7
insecticide	989.4	E863.4	—	E950.6	E962.1	E980.7
Pentaerythritol	972.4	E858.3	E942.4	E950.4	E962.0	E980.4
chloral	967.1	E852.0	E937.1	E950.2	E962.0	E980.2
tetranitrate NEC	972.4	E858.3	E942.4	E950.4	E962.0	E980.4
Pentagastrin	977.8	E858.8	E947.8	E950.4	E962.0	E980.4
Pentalin	982.3	E862.4	—	E950.9	E962.1	E980.9
Pentamethonium (bromide)	972.3	E858.3	E942.3	E950.4	E962.0	E980.4
Pentamidine	961.5	E857	E931.5	E950.4	E962.0	E980.4
Pentanol	980.8	E860.8		E950.9	E962.1	E980.9
Pentaquine	961.4	E857	E931.4	E950.4	E962.0	E980.4
Pentazocine	965.8	E850.8	E935.8	E950.0	E962.0	E980.0
Penthienate	971.1	E855.4	E941.1	E950.4	E962.0	E980.4
Pentobarbital, pentobarbitone (sodium)	967.0	E851	E937.0	E950.1	E962.0	E980.1
Pentolinium (tartrate)	972.3	E858.3	E942.3	E950.4	E962.0	E980.4
Pentothal	968.3	E855.1	E938.3	E950.4	E962.0	E980.4
Pentylenetetrazol	970.0	E854.3	E940.0	E950.4	E962.0	E980.4
Pentylsalicylamide	961.8	E857	E931.8	E950.4	E962.0	E980.4
Pepsin	973.4	E858.4	E943.4	E950.4	E962.0	E980.4
Peptavlon	977.8	E858.8	E947.8	E950.4	E962.0	E980.4
Percaine (spinal)	968.7	E855.2	E938.7	E950.4	E962.0	E980.4
topical (surface)	968.5	E855.2	E938.5	E950.4	E962.0	E980.4
Perchloroethylene (vapor)	982.3	E862.4	—	E950.9	E962.1	E980.9
medicinal	961.6	E857	E931.6	E950.4	E962.0	E980.4
Percodan	965.09	E850.2	E935.2	E950.0	E962.0	E980.0
Percogesic	965.09	E850.2	E935.2	E950.0	E962.0	E980.0
Percorten	962.0	E858.0	E932.0	E950.4	E962.0	E980.4
Pergonal	962.4	E858.0	E932.4	E950.4	E962.0	E980.4
Perhexiline	972.4	E858.3	E942.4	E950.4	E962.0	E980.4
Periactin	963.0	E858.1	E933.0	E950.4	E962.0	E980.4
Periclor	967.1	E852.0	E937.1	E950.2	E962.0	E980.2
Pericyazine	969.1	E853.0	E939.1	E950.3	E962.0	E980.3
Peritrate	972.4	E858.3	E942.4	E950.4	E962.0	E980.4
Permanganates NEC	983.9	E864.3	—	E950.7	E962.1	E980.6
Permanganates — *continued*						
potassium (topical)	976.0	E858.7	E946.0	E950.4	E962.0	E980.4
Pernocton	967.0	E851	E937.0	E950.1	E962.0	E980.1
Pernoston	967.0	E851	E937.0	E950.1	E962.0	E980.1
Peronin(e)	965.09	E850.2	E935.2	E950.0	E962.0	E980.0
Perphenazine	969.1	E853.0	E939.1	E950.3	E962.0	E980.3
Pertofrane	969.0	E854.0	E939.0	E950.3	E962.0	E980.3
Pertussis						
immune serum (human)	964.6	E858.2	E934.6	E950.4	E962.0	E980.4
vaccine (with diphtheria toxoid) (with tetanus toxoid)	978.6	E858.8	E948.6	E950.4	E962.0	E980.4
Peruvian balsam	976.8	E858.7	E946.8	E950.4	E962.0	E980.4
Pesticides (dust) (fumes) (vapor)	989.4	E863.4	—	E950.6	E962.1	E980.7
arsenic	985.1	E863.4	—	E950.8	E962.1	E980.8
chlorinated	989.2	E863.0	—	E950.6	E962.1	E980.7
cyanide	989.0	E863.4	—	E950.6	E962.1	E980.7
kerosene	981	E863.4	—	E950.6	E962.1	E980.7
mixture (of compounds)	989.4	E863.3	—	E950.6	E962.1	E980.7
naphthalene	983.0	E863.4	—	E950.7	E962.1	E980.6
organochlorine (compounds)	989.2	E863.0	—	E950.6	E962.1	E980.7
petroleum (distillate) (products) NEC	981	E863.4	—	E950.6	E962.1	E980.7
specified ingredient NEC	989.4	E863.4	—	E950.6	E962.1	E980.7
strychnine	989.1	E863.4	—	E950.6	E962.1	E980.7
thallium	985.8	E863.7	—	E950.6	E962.1	E980.7
Pethidine (hydrochloride)	965.09	E850.2	E935.2	E950.0	E962.0	E980.0
Petrichloral	967.1	E852.0	E937.1	E950.2	E962.0	E980.2
Petrol	981	E862.1	—	E950.9	E962.1	E980.9
vapor	987.1	E869.8	—	E952.8	E962.2	E982.8
Petrolatum (jelly) (ointment)	976.3	E858.7	E946.3	E950.4	E962.0	E980.4
hydrophilic	976.3	E858.7	E946.3	E950.4	E962.0	E980.4
liquid	973.2	E858.4	E943.2	E950.4	E962.0	E980.4
topical	976.3	E858.7	E946.3	E950.4	E962.0	E980.4
nonmedicinal	981	E862.1	—	E950.9	E962.1	E980.9
Petroleum (cleaners) (fuels) (products) NEC	981	E862.1	—	E950.9	E962.1	E980.9
benzin(e) — see Ligroin						
ether — see Ligroin						
jelly — see Petrolatum						
naphtha — see Ligroin						
pesticide	981	E863.4	—	E950.6	E962.1	E980.7
solids	981	E862.3	—	E950.9	E962.1	E980.9
solvents	981	E862.0	—	E950.9	E962.1	E980.9
vapor	987.1	E869.8	—	E952.8	E962.2	E982.8
Peyote	969.6	E854.1	E939.6	E950.3	E962.0	E980.3
Phanodorm, phanodorn	967.0	E851	E937.0	E950.1	E962.0	E980.1
Phanquinone, phanquone	961.5	E857	E931.5	E950.4	E962.0	E980.4
Pharmaceutical excipient or adjunct	977.4	E858.8	E947.4	E950.4	E962.0	E980.4
Phenacemide	966.3	E855.0	E936.3	E950.4	E962.0	E980.4
Phenacetin	965.4	E850.4	E935.4	E950.0	E962.0	E980.0
Phenadoxone	965.09	E850.2	E935.2	E950.0	E962.0	E980.0
Phenaglycodol	969.5	E853.8	E939.5	E950.3	E962.0	E980.3
Phenantoin	966.1	E855.0	E936.1	E950.4	E962.0	E980.4
Phenaphthazine reagent	977.8	E858.8	E947.8	E950.4	E962.0	E980.4
Phenazocine	965.09	E850.2	E935.2	E950.0	E962.0	E980.0
Phenazone	965.5	E850.5	E935.5	E950.0	E962.0	E980.0
Phenazopyridine	976.1	E858.7	E946.1	E950.4	E962.0	E980.4
Phenbenicillin	960.0	E856	E930.0	E950.4	E962.0	E980.4
Phenbutrazate	977.0	E858.8	E947.0	E950.4	E962.0	E980.4
Phencyclidine	968.3	E855.1	E938.3	E950.4	E962.0	E980.4
Phendimetrazine	977.0	E858.8	E947.0	E950.4	E962.0	E980.4
Phenelzine	969.0	E854.0	E939.0	E950.3	E962.0	E980.3
Phenergan	967.8	E852.8	E937.8	E950.2	E962.0	E980.2
Phenethicillin (potassium)	960.0	E856	E930.0	E950.4	E962.0	E980.4
Phenetsal	965.1	E850.3	E935.3	E950.0	E962.0	E980.0
Pheneturide	966.3	E855.0	E936.3	E950.4	E962.0	E980.4
Phenformin	962.3	E858.0	E932.3	E950.4	E962.0	E980.4
Phenglutarimide	971.1	E855.4	E941.1	E950.4	E962.0	E980.4
Phenicarbazide	965.8	E850.8	E935.8	E950.0	E962.0	E980.0
Phenindamine (tartrate)	963.0	E858.1	E933.0	E950.4	E962.0	E980.4
Phenindione	964.2	E858.2	E934.2	E950.4	E962.0	E980.4
Pheniprazine	969.0	E854.0	E939.0	E950.3	E962.0	E980.3
Pheniramine (maleate)	963.0	E858.1	E933.0	E950.4	E962.0	E980.4
Phenmetrazine	977.0	E858.8	E947.0	E950.4	E962.0	E980.4
Phenobal	967.0	E851	E937.0	E950.1	E962.0	E980.1
Phenobarbital	967.0	E851	E937.0	E950.1	E962.0	E980.1
Phenobarbitone	967.0	E851	E937.0	E950.1	E962.0	E980.1
Phenoctide	976.0	E858.7	E946.0	E950.4	E962.0	E980.4

	Poisoning	External Cause (E-Code) Accident	Therapeutic Use	Suicide Attempt	Assault	Undetermined
Phenol (derivatives) NEC	983.0	E864.0	—	E950.7	E962.1	E980.6
disinfectant	983.0	E864.0	—	E950.7	E962.1	E980.6
pesticide	989.4	E863.4	—	E950.6	E962.1	E980.7
red	977.8	E858.8	E947.8	E950.4	E962.0	E980.4
Phenolphthalein	973.1	E858.4	E943.1	E950.4	E962.0	E980.4
Phenolsulfonphthalein	977.8	E858.8	E947.8	E950.4	E962.0	E980.4
Phenomorphan	965.09	E850.2	E935.2	E950.0	E962.0	E980.0
Phenonyl	967.0	E851	E937.0	E950.1	E962.0	E980.1
Phenoperidine	965.09	E850.2	E935.2	E950.0	E962.0	E980.0
Phenoquin	974.7	E858.5	E944.7	E950.4	E962.0	E980.4
Phenothiazines (tranquilizers) NEC	969.1	E853.0	E939.1	E950.3	E962.0	E980.3
insecticide	989.3	E863.4	—	E950.6	E962.1	E980.7
Phenoxybenzamine	971.3	E855.6	E941.3	E950.4	E962.0	E980.4
Phenoxymethyl penicillin	960.0	E856	E930.0	E950.4	E962.0	E980.4
Phenprocoumon	964.2	E858.2	E934.2	E950.4	E962.0	E980.4
Phensuximide	966.2	E855.0	E936.2	E950.4	E962.0	E980.4
Phentermine	977.0	E858.8	E947.0	E950.4	E962.0	E980.4
Phentolamine	971.3	E855.6	E941.3	E950.4	E962.0	E980.4
Phenyl						
butazone	965.5	E850.5	E935.5	E950.0	E962.0	E980.0
enediamine	983.0	E864.0	—	E950.7	E962.1	E980.6
hydrazine	983.0	E864.0	—	E950.7	E962.1	E980.6
antineoplastic	963.1	E858.1	E933.1	E950.4	E962.0	E980.4
mercuric compounds — see Mercury						
salicylate	976.3	E858.7	E946.3	E950.4	E962.0	E980.4
Phenylephrin	971.2	E855.5	E941.2	E950.4	E962.0	E980.4
Phenylethylbiguanide	962.3	E858.0	E932.3	E950.4	E962.0	E980.4
Phenylpropanolamine	971.2	E855.5	E941.2	E950.4	E962.0	E980.4
Phenylsulfthion	989.3	E863.1	—	E950.6	E962.1	E980.7
Phenyramidol, phenyramidon	965.7	E850.7	E935.7	E950.0	E962.0	E980.0
Phenytoin	966.1	E855.0	E936.1	E950.4	E962.0	E980.4
pHisoHex	976.2	E858.7	E946.2	E950.4	E962.0	E980.4
Pholcodine	965.09	E850.2	E935.2	E950.0	E962.0	E980.0
Phorate	989.3	E863.1	—	E950.6	E962.1	E980.7
Phosdrin	989.3	E863.1	—	E950.6	E962.1	E980.7
Phosgene (gas)	987.8	E869.8	—	E952.8	E962.2	E982.8
Phosphate (tricresyl)	989.89	E866.8	—	E950.9	E962.1	E980.9
organic	989.3	E863.1	—	E950.6	E962.1	E980.7
solvent	982.8	E862.4	—	E950.9	E926.1	E980.9
Phosphine	987.8	E869.8	—	E952.8	E962.2	E982.8
fumigant	987.8	E863.8	—	E950.6	E962.2	E980.7
Phospholine	971.0	E855.3	E941.0	E950.4	E962.0	E980.4
Phosphoric acid	983.1	E864.1	—	E950.7	E962.1	E980.6
Phosphorus (compounds) NEC	983.9	E864.3	—	E950.7	E962.1	E980.6
rodenticide	983.9	E863.7	—	E950.7	E962.1	E980.6
Phthalimidoglutarimide	967.8	E852.8	E937.8	E950.2	E962.0	E980.2
Phthalylsulfathiazole	961.0	E857	E931.0	E950.4	E962.0	E980.4
Phylloquinone	964.3	E858.2	E934.3	E950.4	E962.0	E980.4
Physeptone	965.02	E850.1	E935.1	E950.0	E962.0	E980.0
Physostigma venenosum	988.2	E865.4	—	E950.9	E962.1	E980.9
Physostigmine	971.0	E855.3	E941.0	E950.4	E962.0	E980.4
Phytolacca decandra	988.2	E865.4	—	E950.9	E962.1	E980.9
Phytomenadione	964.3	E858.2	E934.3	E950.4	E962.0	E980.4
Phytonadione	964.3	E858.2	E934.3	E950.4	E962.0	E980.4
Picric (acid)	983.0	E864.0	—	E950.7	E962.1	E980.6
Picrotoxin	970.0	E854.3	E940.0	E950.4	E962.0	E980.4
Pilocarpine	971.0	E855.3	E941.0	E950.4	E962.0	E980.4
Pilocarpus (jaborandi) extract	971.0	E855.3	E941.0	E950.4	E962.0	E980.4
Pimaricin	960.1	E856	E930.1	E950.4	E962.0	E980.4
Piminodine	965.09	E850.2	E935.2	E950.0	E962.0	E980.0
Pine oil, pinesol (disinfectant)	983.9	E861.4	—	E950.7	E962.1	E980.6
Pinkroot	961.6	E857	E931.6	E950.4	E962.0	E980.4
Pipadone	965.09	E850.2	E935.2	E950.0	E962.0	E980.0
Pipamazine	963.0	E858.1	E933.0	E950.4	E962.0	E980.4
Pipazethate	975.4	E858.6	E945.4	E950.4	E962.0	E980.4
Pipenzolate	971.1	E855.4	E941.1	E950.4	E962.0	E980.4
Piperacetazine	969.1	E853.0	E939.1	E950.3	E962.0	E980.3
Piperazine NEC	961.6	E857	E931.6	E950.4	E962.0	E980.4
estrone sulfate	962.2	E858.0	E932.2	E950.4	E962.0	E980.4
Piper cubeba	988.2	E865.4	—	E950.9	E962.1	E980.9
Piperidione	975.4	E858.6	E945.4	E950.4	E962.0	E980.4
Piperidolate	971.1	E855.4	E941.1	E950.4	E962.0	E980.4
Piperocaine	968.9	E855.2	E938.9	E950.4	E962.0	E980.4
infiltration (subcutaneous)	968.5	E855.2	E938.5	E950.4	E962.0	E980.4
Piperocaine — *continued*						
nerve block (peripheral) (plexus)	968.6	E855.2	E938.6	E950.4	E962.0	E980.4
topical (surface)	968.5	E855.2	E938.5	E950.4	E962.0	E980.4
Pipobroman	963.1	E858.1	E933.1	E950.4	E962.0	E980.4
Pipradrol	970.8	E854.3	E940.8	E950.4	E962.0	E980.4
Piscidia (bark) (erythrina)	965.7	E850.7	E935.7	E950.0	E962.0	E980.0
Pitch	983.0	E864.0	—	E950.7	E962.1	E980.6
Pitkin's solution	968.7	E855.2	E938.7	E950.4	E962.0	E980.4
Pitocin	975.0	E858.6	E945.0	E950.4	E962.0	E980.4
Pitressin (tannate)	962.5	E858.0	E932.5	E950.4	E962.0	E980.4
Pituitary extracts (posterior)	962.5	E858.0	E932.5	E950.4	E962.0	E980.4
anterior	962.4	E858.0	E932.4	E950.4	E962.0	E980.4
Pituitrin	962.5	E858.0	E932.5	E950.4	E962.0	E980.4
Placental extract	962.9	E858.0	E932.9	E950.4	E962.0	E980.4
Placidyl	967.8	E852.8	E937.8	E950.2	E962.0	E980.2
Plague vaccine	978.3	E858.8	E948.3	E950.4	E962.0	E980.4
Plant foods or fertilizers NEC	989.89	E866.5	—	E950.9	E962.1	E980.9
mixed with herbicides	989.4	E863.5	—	E950.6	E962.1	E980.7
Plants, noxious, used as food	988.2	E865.9	—	E950.9	E962.1	E980.9
berries and seeds	988.2	E865.3	—	E950.9	E962.1	E980.9
specified type NEC	988.2	E865.4	—	E950.9	E962.1	E980.9
Plasma (blood)	964.7	E858.2	E934.7	E950.4	E962.0	E980.4
expanders	964.8	E858.2	E934.8	E950.4	E962.0	E980.4
Plasmanate	964.7	E858.2	E934.7	E950.4	E962.0	E980.4
Plegicil	969.1	E853.0	E939.1	E950.3	E962.0	E980.3
Podophyllin	976.4	E858.7	E946.4	E950.4	E962.0	E980.4
Podophyllum resin	976.4	E858.7	E946.4	E950.4	E962.0	E980.4
Poison NEC	989.9	E866.9	—	E950.9	E962.1	E980.9
Poisonous berries	988.2	E865.3	—	E950.9	E962.1	E980.9
Pokeweed (any part)	988.2	E865.4	—	E950.9	E962.1	E980.9
Poldine	971.1	E855.4	E941.1	E950.4	E962.0	E980.4
Poliomyelitis vaccine	979.5	E858.8	E949.5	E950.4	E962.0	E980.4
Poliovirus vaccine	979.5	E858.8	E949.5	E950.4	E962.0	E980.4
Polish (car) (floor) (furniture) (metal) (silver)	989.89	E861.2	—	E950.9	E962.1	E980.9
abrasive	989.89	E861.3	—	E950.9	E962.1	E980.9
porcelain	989.89	E861.3	—	E950.9	E962.1	E980.9
Poloxalkol	973.2	E858.4	E943.2	E950.4	E962.0	E980.4
Polyaminostyrene resins	974.5	E858.5	E944.5	E950.4	E962.0	E980.4
Polychlorinated biphenyl — *see* PCBs						
Polycycline	960.4	E856	E930.4	E950.4	E962.0	E980.4
Polyester resin hardener	982.8	E862.4	—	E950.9	E962.1	E980.9
fumes	987.8	E869.8	—	E952.8	E962.2	E982.8
Polyestradiol (phosphate)	962.2	E858.0	E932.2	E950.4	E962.0	E980.4
Polyethanolamine alkyl sulfate	976.2	E858.7	E946.2	E950.4	E962.0	E980.4
Polyethylene glycol	976.3	E858.7	E946.3	E950.4	E962.0	E980.4
Polyferose	964.0	E858.2	E934.0	E950.4	E962.0	E980.4
Polymyxin B	960.8	E856	E930.8	E950.4	E962.0	E980.4
ENT agent	976.6	E858.7	E946.6	E950.4	E962.0	E980.4
ophthalmic preparation	976.5	E858.7	E946.5	E950.4	E962.0	E980.4
topical NEC	976.0	E858.7	E946.0	E950.4	E962.0	E980.4
Polynoxylin(e)	976.0	E858.7	E946.0	E950.4	E962.0	E980.4
Polyoxymethyleneurea	976.0	E858.7	E946.0	E950.4	E962.0	E980.4
Polytetrafluoroethylene (inhaled)	987.8	E869.8	—	E952.8	E962.2	E982.8
Polythiazide	974.3	E858.5	E944.3	E950.4	E962.0	E980.4
Polyvinylpyrrolidone	964.8	E858.2	E934.8	E950.4	E962.0	E980.4
Pontocaine (hydrochloride) (infiltration) (topical)	968.5	E855.2	E938.5	E950.4	E962.0	E980.4
nerve block (peripheral) (plexus)	968.6	E855.2	E938.6	E950.4	E962.0	E980.4
spinal	968.7	E855.2	E938.7	E950.4	E962.0	E980.4
Pot	969.6	E854.1	E939.6	E950.3	E962.0	E980.3
Potash (caustic)	983.2	E864.2	—	E950.7	E962.1	E980.6
Potassic saline injection (lactated)	974.5	E858.5	E944.5	E950.4	E962.0	E980.4
Potassium (salts) NEC	974.5	E858.5	E944.5	E950.4	E962.0	E980.4
aminosalicylate	961.8	E857	E931.8	E950.4	E962.0	E980.4
arsenite (solution)	985.1	E866.3	—	E950.8	E962.1	E980.8
bichromate	983.9	E864.3	—	E950.7	E962.1	E980.6
bisulfate	983.9	E864.3	—	E950.7	E962.1	E980.6
bromide (medicinal) NEC	967.3	E852.2	E937.3	E950.2	E962.0	E980.2
carbonate	983.2	E864.2	—	E950.7	E962.1	E980.6
chlorate NEC	983.9	E864.3	—	E950.7	E962.1	E980.6
cyanide — see Cyanide						

		External Cause (E-Code)				
	Poisoning	Accident	Therapeutic Use	Suicide Attempt	Assault	Undetermined
Potassium (salts) — *continued*						
hydroxide	983.2	E864.2	—	E950.7	E962.1	E980.6
iodide (expectorant) NEC	975.5	E858.6	E945.5	E950.4	E962.0	E980.4
nitrate	989.89	E866.8	—	E950.9	E962.1	E980.9
oxalate	983.9	E864.3	—	E950.7	E962.1	E980.6
perchlorate NEC	977.8	E858.8	E947.8	E950.4	E962.0	E980.4
antithyroid	962.8	E858.0	E932.8	E950.4	E962.0	E980.4
permanganate	976.0	E858.7	E946.0	E950.4	E962.0	E980.4
nonmedicinal	983.9	E864.3	—	E950.7	E962.1	E980.6
Povidone-iodine (anti-infective) NEC	976.0	E858.7	E946.0	E950.4	E962.0	E980.4
Practolol	972.0	E858.3	E942.0	E950.4	E962.0	E980.4
Pralidoxime (chloride)	977.2	E858.8	E947.2	E950.4	E962.0	E980.4
Pramoxine	968.5	E855.2	E938.5	E950.4	E962.0	E980.4
Prazosin	972.6	E858.3	E942.6	E950.4	E962.0	E980.4
Prednisolone	962.0	E858.0	E932.0	E950.4	E962.0	E980.4
ENT agent	976.6	E858.7	E946.6	E950.4	E962.0	E980.4
ophthalmic preparation	976.5	E858.7	E946.5	E950.4	E962.0	E980.4
topical NEC	976.0	E858.7	E946.0	E950.4	E962.0	E980.4
Prednisone	962.0	E858.0	E932.0	E950.4	E962.0	E980.4
Pregnanediol	962.2	E858.0	E932.2	E950.4	E962.0	E980.4
Pregneninolone	962.2	E858.0	E932.2	E950.4	E962.0	E980.4
Preludin	977.0	E858.8	E947.0	E950.4	E962.0	E980.4
Premarin	962.2	E858.0	E932.2	E950.4	E962.0	E980.4
Prenylamine	972.4	E858.3	E942.4	E950.4	E962.0	E980.4
Preparation H	976.8	E858.7	E946.8	E950.4	E962.0	E980.4
Preservatives	989.89	E866.8	—	E950.9	E962.1	E980.9
Pride of China	988.2	E865.3	—	E950.9	E962.1	E980.9
Prilocaine	968.9	E855.2	E938.9	E950.4	E962.0	E980.4
infiltration (subcutaneous)	968.5	E855.2	E938.5	E950.4	E962.0	E980.4
nerve block (peripheral) (plexus)	968.6	E855.2	E938.6	E950.4	E962.0	E980.4
Primaquine	961.4	E857	E931.4	E950.4	E962.0	E980.4
Primidone	966.3	E855.0	E936.3	E950.4	E962.0	E980.4
Primula (veris)	988.2	E865.4	—	E950.9	E962.1	E980.9
Prinadol	965.09	E850.2	E935.2	E950.0	E962.0	E980.0
Priscol, Priscoline	971.3	E855.6	E941.3	E950.4	E962.0	E980.4
Privet	988.2	E865.4	—	E950.9	E962.1	E980.9
Privine	971.2	E855.5	E941.2	E950.4	E962.0	E980.4
Pro-Banthine	971.1	E855.4	E941.1	E950.4	E962.0	E980.4
Probarbital	967.0	E851	E937.0	E950.1	E962.0	E980.1
Probenecid	974.7	E858.5	E944.7	E950.4	E962.0	E980.4
Procainamide (hydrochloride)	972.0	E858.3	E942.0	E950.4	E962.0	E980.4
Procaine (hydrochloride) (infiltration) (topical)	968.5	E855.2	E938.5	E950.4	E962.0	E980.4
nerve block (peripheral) (plexus)	968.6	E855.2	E938.6	E950.4	E962.0	E980.4
penicillin G	960.0	E856	E930.0	E950.4	E962.0	E980.4
spinal	968.7	E855.2	E938.7	E950.4	E962.0	E980.4
Procalmidol	969.5	E853.8	E939.5	E950.3	E962.0	E980.3
Procarbazine	963.1	E858.1	E933.1	E950.4	E962.0	E980.4
Prochlorperazine	969.1	E853.0	E939.1	E950.3	E962.0	E980.3
Procyclidine	966.4	E855.0	E936.4	E950.4	E962.0	E980.4
Producer gas	986	E868.8	—	E952.1	E962.2	E982.1
Profenamine	966.4	E855.0	E936.4	E950.4	E962.0	E980.4
Profenil	975.1	E858.6	E945.1	E950.4	E962.0	E980.4
Progesterones	962.2	E858.0	E932.2	E950.4	E962.0	E980.4
Progestin	962.2	E858.0	E932.2	E950.4	E962.0	E980.4
Progestogens (with estrogens)	962.2	E858.0	E932.2	E950.4	E962.0	E980.4
Progestone	962.2	E858.0	E932.2	E950.4	E962.0	E980.4
Proguanil	961.4	E857	E931.4	E950.4	E962.0	E980.4
Prolactin	962.4	E858.0	E932.4	E950.4	E962.0	E980.4
Proloid	962.7	E858.0	E932.7	E950.4	E962.0	E980.4
Proluton	962.2	E858.0	E932.2	E950.4	E962.0	E980.4
Promacetin	961.8	E857	E931.8	E950.4	E962.0	E980.4
Promazine	969.1	E853.0	E939.1	E950.3	E962.0	E980.3
Promedol	965.09	E850.2	E935.2	E950.0	E962.0	E980.0
Promethazine	967.8	E852.8	E937.8	E950.2	E962.0	E980.2
Promin	961.8	E857	E931.8	E950.4	E962.0	E980.4
Pronestyl (hydrochloride)	972.0	E858.3	E942.0	E950.4	E962.0	E980.4
Pronetalol, pronethalol	972.0	E858.3	E942.0	E950.4	E962.0	E980.4
Prontosil	961.0	E857	E931.0	E950.4	E962.0	E980.4
Propamidine isethionate	961.5	E857	E931.5	E950.4	E962.0	E980.4
Propanal (medicinal)	967.8	E852.8	E937.8	E950.2	E962.0	E980.2
Propane (gas) (distributed in mobile container)	987.0	E868.0	—	E951.1	E962.2	E981.1
distributed through pipes	987.0	E867	—	E951.0	E962.2	E981.0
incomplete combustion of — see Carbon monoxide, Propane						
Propanidid	968.3	E855.1	E938.3	E950.4	E962.0	E980.4
Propanol	980.3	E860.4	—	E950.9	E962.1	E980.9
Propantheline	971.1	E855.4	E941.1	E950.4	E962.0	E980.4
Proparacaine	968.5	E855.2	E938.5	E950.4	E962.0	E980.4
Propatyl nitrate	972.4	E858.3	E942.4	E950.4	E962.0	E980.4
Propicillin	960.0	E856	E930.0	E950.4	E962.0	E980.4
Propiolactone (vapor)	987.8	E869.8	—	E952.8	E962.2	E982.8
Propiomazine	967.8	E852.8	E937.8	E950.2	E962.0	E980.2
Propionaldehyde (medicinal)	967.8	E852.8	E937.8	E950.2	E962.0	E980.2
Propionate compound	976.0	E858.7	E946.0	E950.4	E962.0	E980.4
Propion gel	976.0	E858.7	E946.0	E950.4	E962.0	E980.4
Propitocaine	968.9	E855.2	E938.9	E950.4	E962.0	E980.4
infiltration (subcutaneous)	968.5	E855.2	E938.5	E950.4	E962.0	E980.4
nerve block (peripheral) (plexus)	968.6	E855.2	E938.6	E950.4	E962.0	E980.4
Propoxur	989.3	E863.2	—	E950.6	E962.1	E980.7
Propoxycaine	968.9	E855.2	E938.9	E950.4	E962.0	E980.4
infiltration (subcutaneous)	968.5	E855.2	E938.5	E950.4	E962.0	E980.4
nerve block (peripheral) (plexus)	968.6	E855.2	E938.6	E950.4	E962.0	E980.4
topical (surface)	968.5	E855.2	E938.5	E950.4	E962.0	E980.4
Propoxyphene (hydrochloride)	965.8	E850.8	E935.8	E950.0	E962.0	E980.0
Propranolol	972.0	E858.3	E942.0	E950.4	E962.0	E980.4
Propyl						
alcohol	980.3	E860.4	—	E950.9	E962.1	E980.9
carbinol	980.3	E860.4	—	E950.9	E962.1	E980.9
hexadrine	971.2	E855.5	E941.2	E950.4	E962.0	E980.4
iodone	977.8	E858.8	E947.8	E950.4	E962.0	E980.4
thiouracil	962.8	E858.0	E932.8	E950.4	E962.0	E980.4
Propylene	987.1	E869.8	—	E952.8	E962.2	E982.8
Propylparaben (ophthalmic)	976.5	E858.7	E946.5	E950.4	E962.0	E980.4
Proscillaridin	972.1	E858.3	E942.1	E950.4	E962.0	E980.4
Prostaglandins	975.0	E858.6	E945.0	E950.4	E962.0	E980.4
Prostigmin	971.0	E855.3	E941.0	E950.4	E962.0	E980.4
Protamine (sulfate)	964.5	E858.2	E934.5	E950.4	E962.0	E980.4
zinc insulin	962.3	E858.0	E932.3	E950.4	E962.0	E980.4
Protectants (topical)	976.3	E858.7	E946.3	E950.4	E962.0	E980.4
Protein hydrolysate	974.5	E858.5	E944.5	E950.4	E962.0	E980.4
Prothiaden — *see* Dothiepin hydrochloride						
Prothionamide	961.8	E857	E931.8	E950.4	E962.0	E980.4
Prothipendyl	969.5	E853.8	E939.5	E950.3	E962.0	E980.3
Protokylol	971.2	E855.5	E941.2	E950.4	E962.0	E980.4
Protopam	977.2	E858.8	E947.2	E950.4	E962.0	E980.4
Protoveratrine(s) (A) (B)	972.6	E858.3	E942.6	E950.4	E962.0	E980.4
Protriptyline	969.0	E854.0	E939.0	E950.3	E962.0	E980.3
Provera	962.2	E858.0	E932.2	E950.4	E962.0	E980.4
Provitamin A	963.5	E858.1	E933.5	E950.4	E962.0	E980.4
Proxymetacaine	968.5	E855.2	E938.5	E950.4	E962.0	E980.4
Proxyphylline	975.1	E858.6	E945.1	E950.4	E962.0	E980.4
Prozac — *see* Fluoxetine hydrochloride						
Prunus						
laurocerasus	988.2	E865.4	—	E950.9	E962.1	E980.9
virginiana	988.2	E865.4	—	E950.9	E962.1	E980.9
Prussic acid	989.0	E866.8	—	E950.9	E962.1	E980.9
vapor	987.7	E869.8	—	E952.8	E962.2	E982.8
Pseudoephedrine	971.2	E855.5	E941.2	E950.4	E962.0	E980.4
Psilocin	969.6	E854.1	E939.6	E950.3	E962.0	E980.3
Psilocybin	969.6	E854.1	E939.6	E950.3	E962.0	E980.3
PSP	977.8	E858.8	E947.8	E950.4	E962.0	E980.4
Psychedelic agents	969.6	E854.1	E939.6	E950.3	E962.0	E980.3
Psychodysleptics	969.6	E854.1	E939.6	E950.3	E962.0	E980.3
Psychostimulants	969.7	E854.2	E939.7	E950.3	E962.0	E980.3
Psychotherapeutic agents	969.9	E855.9	E939.9	E950.3	E962.0	E980.3
antidepressants	969.0	E854.0	E939.0	E950.3	E962.0	E980.3
specified NEC	969.8	E855.8	E939.8	E950.3	E962.0	E980.3
tranquilizers NEC	969.5	E853.9	E939.5	E950.3	E962.0	E980.3
Psychotomimetic agents	969.6	E854.1	E939.6	E950.3	E962.0	E980.3
Psychotropic agents	969.9	E854.8	E939.9	E950.3	E962.0	E980.3
specified NEC	969.8	E854.8	E939.8	E950.3	E962.0	E980.3
Psyllium	973.3	E858.4	E943.3	E950.4	E962.0	E980.4
Pteroylglutamic acid	964.1	E858.2	E934.1	E950.4	E962.0	E980.4
Pteroyltriglutamate	963.1	E858.1	E933.1	E950.4	E962.0	E980.4
PTFE	987.8	E869.8	—	E952.8	E962.2	E982.8
Pulsatilla	988.2	E865.4	—	E950.9	E962.1	E980.9
Purex (bleach)	983.9	E864.3	—	E950.7	E962.1	E980.6
Purine diuretics	974.1	E858.5	E944.1	E950.4	E962.0	E980.4

		External Cause (E-Code)				
	Poisoning	Accident	Therapeutic Use	Suicide Attempt	Assault	Undetermined
Purinethol	963.1	E858.1	E933.1	E950.4	E962.0	E980.4
PVP	964.8	E858.2	E934.8	E950.4	E962.0	E980.4
Pyrabital	965.7	E850.7	E935.7	E950.0	E962.0	E980.0
Pyramidon	965.5	E850.5	E935.5	E950.0	E962.0	E980.0
Pyrantel (pamoate)	961.6	E857	E931.6	E950.4	E962.0	E980.4
Pyrathiazine	963.0	E858.1	E933.0	E950.4	E962.0	E980.4
Pyrazinamide	961.8	E857	E931.8	E950.4	E962.0	E980.4
Pyrazinoic acid (amide)	961.8	E857	E931.8	E950.4	E962.0	E980.4
Pyrazole (derivatives)	965.5	E850.5	E935.5	E950.0	E962.0	E980.0
Pyrazolone (analgesics)	965.5	E850.5	E935.5	E950.0	E962.0	E980.0
Pyrethrins, pyrethrum	989.4	E863.4	—	E950.6	E962.1	E980.7
Pyribenzamine	963.0	E858.1	E933.0	E950.4	E962.0	E980.4
Pyridine (liquid) (vapor)	982.0	E862.4	—	E950.9	E962.1	E980.9
aldoxime chloride	977.2	E858.8	E947.2	E950.4	E962.0	E980.4
Pyridium	976.1	E858.7	E946.1	E950.4	E962.0	E980.4
Pyridostigmine	971.0	E855.3	E941.0	E950.4	E962.0	E980.4
Pyridoxine	963.5	E858.1	E933.5	E950.4	E962.0	E980.4
Pyrilamine	963.0	E858.1	E933.0	E950.4	E962.0	E980.4
Pyrimethamine	961.4	E857	E931.4	E950.4	E962.0	E980.4
Pyrogallic acid	983.0	E864.0	—	E950.7	E962.1	E980.6
Pyroxylin	976.3	E858.7	E946.3	E950.4	E962.0	E980.4
Pyrrobutamine	963.0	E858.1	E933.0	E950.4	E962.0	E980.4
Pyrrocitine	968.5	E855.2	E938.5	E950.4	E962.0	E980.4
Pyrvinium (pamoate)	961.6	E857	E931.6	E950.4	E962.0	E980.4
PZI	962.3	E858.0	E932.3	E950.4	E962.0	E980.4
Quaalude	967.4	E852.3	E937.4	E950.2	E962.0	E980.2
Quaternary ammonium derivatives	971.1	E855.4	E941.1	E950.4	E962.0	E980.4
Quicklime	983.2	E864.2	—	E950.7	E962.1	E980.6
Quinacrine	961.3	E857	E931.3	E950.4	E962.0	E980.4
Quinaglute	972.0	E858.3	E942.0	E950.4	E962.0	E980.4
Quinalbarbitone	967.0	E851	E937.0	E950.1	E962.0	E980.1
Quinestradiol	962.2	E858.0	E932.2	E950.4	E962.0	E980.4
Quinethazone	974.3	E858.5	E944.3	E950.4	E962.0	E980.4
Quinidine (gluconate) (polygalacturonate) (salts) (sulfate)	972.0	E858.3	E942.0	E950.4	E962.0	E980.4
Quinine	961.4	E857	E931.4	E950.4	E962.0	E980.4
Quiniobine	961.3	E857	E931.3	E950.4	E962.0	E980.4
Quinolines	961.3	E857	E931.3	E950.4	E962.0	E980.4
Quotane	968.5	E855.2	E938.5	E950.4	E962.0	E980.4
Rabies						
immune globulin (human)	964.6	E858.2	E934.6	E950.4	E962.0	E980.4
vaccine	979.1	E858.8	E949.1	E950.4	E962.0	E980.4
Racemoramide	965.09	E850.2	E935.2	E950.0	E962.0	E980.0
Racemorphan	965.09	E850.2	E935.2	E950.0	E962.0	E980.0
Radiator alcohol	980.1	E860.2	—	E950.9	E962.1	E980.9
Radio-opaque (drugs) (materials)	977.8	E858.8	E947.8	E950.4	E962.0	E980.4
Ranunculus	988.2	E865.4	—	E950.9	E962.1	E980.9
Rat poison	989.4	E863.7	—	E950.6	E962.1	E980.7
Rattlesnake (venom)	989.5	E905.0	—	E950.9	E962.1	E980.9
Raudixin	972.6	E858.3	E942.6	E950.4	E962.0	E980.4
Rautensin	972.6	E858.3	E942.6	E950.4	E962.0	E980.4
Rautina	972.6	E858.3	E942.6	E950.4	E962.0	E980.4
Rautotal	972.6	E858.3	E942.6	E950.4	E962.0	E980.4
Rauwiloid	972.6	E858.3	E942.6	E950.4	E962.0	E980.4
Rauwoldin	972.6	E858.3	E942.6	E950.4	E962.0	E980.4
Rauwolfia (alkaloids)	972.6	E858.3	E942.6	E950.4	E962.0	E980.4
Realgar	985.1	E866.3	—	E950.8	E962.1	E980.8
Red cells, packed	964.7	E858.2	E934.7	E950.4	E962.0	E980.4
Reducing agents, industrial NEC	983.9	E864.3	—	E950.7	E962.1	E980.6
Refrigerant gas (freon)	987.4	E869.2	—	E952.8	E962.2	E982.8
central nervous system	968.0	E855.1	E938.0	E950.4	E962.0	E980.4
not freon	987.9	E869.9	—	E952.9	E962.2	E982.9
Regroton	974.4	E858.5	E944.4	E950.4	E962.0	E980.4
Rela	968.0	E855.1	E938.0	E950.4	E962.0	E980.4
Relaxants, skeletal muscle (autonomic)	975.2	E858.6	E945.2	E950.4	E962.0	E980.4
Renese	974.3	E858.5	E944.3	E950.4	E962.0	E980.4
Renografin	977.8	E858.8	E947.8	E950.4	E962.0	E980.4
Replacement solutions	974.5	E858.5	E944.5	E950.4	E962.0	E980.4
Rescinnamine	972.6	E858.3	E942.6	E950.4	E962.0	E980.4
Reserpine	972.6	E858.3	E942.6	E950.4	E962.0	E980.4
Resorcin, resorcinol	976.4	E858.7	E946.4	E950.4	E962.0	E980.4
Respaire	975.5	E858.6	E945.5	E950.4	E962.0	E980.4
Respiratory agents NEC	975.8	E858.6	E945.8	E950.4	E962.0	E980.4
Retinoic acid	976.8	E858.7	E946.8	E950.4	E962.0	E980.4
Retinol	963.5	E858.1	E933.5	E950.4	E962.0	E980.4
Rh (D) immune globulin (human)	964.6	E858.2	E934.6	E950.4	E962.0	E980.4
Rhodine	965.1	E850.3	E935.3	E950.0	E962.0	E980.0
RhoGAM	964.6	E858.2	E934.6	E950.4	E962.0	E980.4
Riboflavin	963.5	E858.1	E933.5	E950.4	E962.0	E980.4
Ricin	989.89	E866.8	—	E950.9	E962.1	E980.9
Ricinus communis	988.2	E865.3	—	E950.9	E962.1	E980.9
Rickettsial vaccine NEC	979.6	E858.8	E949.6	E950.4	E962.0	E980.4
with viral and bacterial vaccine	979.7	E858.8	E949.7	E950.4	E962.0	E980.4
Rifampin	960.6	E856	E930.6	E950.4	E962.0	E980.4
Rimifon	961.8	E857	E931.8	E950.4	E962.0	E980.4
Ringer's injection (lactated)	974.5	E858.5	E944.5	E950.4	E962.0	E980.4
Ristocetin	960.8	E856	E930.8	E950.4	E962.0	E980.4
Ritalin	969.7	E854.2	E939.7	E950.3	E962.0	E980.3
Roach killers — *see* Pesticides						
Rocky Mountain spotted fever vaccine	979.6	E858.8	E949.6	E950.4	E962.0	E980.4
Rodenticides	989.4	E863.7	—	E950.6	E962.1	E980.7
Rohypnol	969.4	E853.2	E939.4	E950.3	E962.0	E980.3
Rolaids	973.0	E858.4	E943.0	E950.4	E962.0	E980.4
Rolitetracycline	960.4	E856	E930.4	E950.4	E962.0	E980.4
Romilar	975.4	E858.6	E945.4	E950.4	E962.0	E980.4
Rose water ointment	976.3	E858.7	E946.3	E950.4	E962.0	E980.4
Rosuvastatin calcium	972.1	E858.3	E942.2	E950.4	E962.0	E980.4
Rotenone	989.4	E863.7	—	E950.6	E962.1	E980.7
Rotoxamine	963.0	E858.1	E933.0	E950.4	E962.0	E980.4
Rough-on-rats	989.4	E863.7	—	E950.6	E962.1	E980.7
RU486	962.9	E858.0	E932.9	E950.4	E962.0	E980.4
Rubbing alcohol	980.2	E860.3	—	E950.9	E962.1	E980.9
Rubella virus vaccine	979.4	E858.8	E949.4	E950.4	E962.0	E980.4
Rubelogen	979.4	E858.8	E949.4	E950.4	E962.0	E980.4
Rubeovax	979.4	E858.8	E949.4	E950.4	E962.0	E980.4
Rubidomycin	960.7	E856	E930.7	E950.4	E962.0	E980.4
Rue	988.2	E865.4	—	E950.9	E962.1	E980.9
Ruta	988.2	E865.4	—	E950.9	E962.1	E980.9
Sabadilla (medicinal)	976.0	E858.7	E946.0	E950.4	E962.0	E980.4
pesticide	989.4	E863.4	—	E950.6	E962.1	E980.7
Sabin oral vaccine	979.5	E858.8	E949.5	E950.4	E962.0	E980.4
Saccharated iron oxide	964.0	E858.2	E934.0	E950.4	E962.0	E980.4
Saccharin	974.5	E858.5	E944.5	E950.4	E962.0	E980.4
Safflower oil	972.2	E858.3	E942.2	E950.4	E962.0	E980.4
Salbutamol sulfate	975.7	E858.6	E945.7	E950.4	E962.0	E980.4
Salicylamide	965.1	E850.3	E935.3	E950.0	E962.0	E980.0
Salicylate(s)	965.1	E850.3	E935.3	E950.0	E962.0	E980.0
methyl	976.3	E858.7	E946.3	E950.4	E962.0	E980.4
theobromine calcium	974.1	E858.5	E944.1	E950.4	E962.0	E980.4
Salicylazosulfapyridine	961.0	E857	E931.0	E950.4	E962.0	E980.4
Salicylhydroxamic acid	976.0	E858.7	E946.0	E950.4	E962.0	E980.4
Salicylic acid (keratolytic) NEC	976.4	E858.7	E946.4	E950.4	E962.0	E980.4
congeners	965.1	E850.3	E935.3	E950.0	E962.0	E980.0
salts	965.1	E850.3	E935.3	E950.0	E962.0	E980.0
Saliniazid	961.8	E857	E931.8	E950.4	E962.0	E980.4
Salol	976.3	E858.7	E946.3	E950.4	E962.0	E980.4
Salt (substitute) NEC	974.5	E858.5	E944.5	E950.4	E962.0	E980.4
Saluretics	974.3	E858.5	E944.3	E950.4	E962.0	E980.4
Saluron	974.3	E858.5	E944.3	E950.4	E962.0	E980.4
Salvarsan 606 (neosilver) (silver)	961.1	E857	E931.1	E950.4	E962.0	E980.4
Sambucus canadensis	988.2	E865.4	—	E950.9	E962.1	E980.9
berry	988.2	E865.3	—	E950.9	E962.1	E980.9
Sandril	972.6	E858.3	E942.6	E950.4	E962.0	E980.4
Sanguinaria canadensis	988.2	E865.4	—	E950.9	E962.1	E980.9
Saniflush (cleaner)	983.9	E861.3	—	E950.7	E962.1	E980.6
Santonin	961.6	E857	E931.6	E950.4	E962.0	E980.4
Santyl	976.8	E858.7	E946.8	E950.4	E962.0	E980.4
Sarkomycin	960.7	E856	E930.7	E950.4	E962.0	E980.4
Saroten	969.0	E854.0	E939.0	E950.3	E962.0	E980.3
Saturnine — *see* Lead						
Savin (oil)	976.4	E858.7	E946.4	E950.4	E962.0	E980.4
Scammony	973.1	E858.4	E943.1	E950.4	E962.0	E980.4
Scarlet red	976.8	E858.7	E946.8	E950.4	E962.0	E980.4
Scheele's green	985.1	E866.3	—	E950.8	E962.1	E980.8
insecticide	985.1	E863.4	—	E950.8	E962.1	E980.8
Schradan	989.3	E863.1	—	E950.6	E962.1	E980.7
Schweinfurt(h) green	985.1	E866.3	—	E950.8	E962.1	E980.8
insecticide	985.1	E863.4	—	E950.8	E962.1	E980.8
Scilla — see Squill						
Sclerosing agents	972.7	E858.3	E942.7	E950.4	E962.0	E980.4

☑ Additional Digit Required — Refer to the Tabular List for Digit Selection

▽ Subterms under main terms may continue to next column or page

▶◀ Revised Text ● New Line ▲ Revised Code

	Poisoning	External Cause (E-Code) Accident	Therapeutic Use	Suicide Attempt	Assault	Undetermined
Scopolamine	971.1	E855.4	E941.1	E950.4	E962.0	E980.4
Scouring powder	989.89	E861.3	—	E950.9	E962.1	E980.9
Sea						
anemone (sting)	989.5	E905.6	—	E950.9	E962.1	E980.9
cucumber (sting)	989.5	E905.6	—	E950.9	E962.1	E980.9
snake (bite) (venom)	989.5	E905.0	—	E950.9	E962.1	E980.9
urchin spine (puncture)	989.5	E905.6	—	E950.9	E962.1	E980.9
Secbutabarbital	967.0	E851	E937.0	E950.1	E962.0	E980.1
Secbutabarbitone	967.0	E851	E937.0	E950.1	E962.0	E980.1
Secobarbital	967.0	E851	E937.0	E950.1	E962.0	E980.1
Seconal	967.0	E851	E937.0	E950.1	E962.0	E980.1
Secretin	977.8	E858.8	E947.8	E950.4	E962.0	E980.4
Sedatives, nonbarbiturate	967.9	E852.9	E937.9	E950.2	E962.0	E980.2
specified NEC	967.8	E852.8	E937.8	E950.2	E962.0	E980.2
Sedormid	967.8	E852.8	E937.8	E950.2	E962.0	E980.2
Seed (plant)	988.2	E865.3	—	E950.9	E962.1	E980.9
disinfectant or dressing	989.89	E866.5	—	E950.9	E962.1	E980.9
Selenium (fumes) NEC	985.8	E866.4	—	E950.9	E962.1	E980.9
disulfide or sulfide	976.4	E858.7	E946.4	E950.4	E962.0	E980.4
Selsun	976.4	E858.7	E946.4	E950.4	E962.0	E980.4
Senna	973.1	E858.4	E943.1	E950.4	E962.0	E980.4
Septisol	976.2	E858.7	E946.2	E950.4	E962.0	E980.4
Serax	969.4	E853.2	E939.4	E950.3	E962.0	E980.3
Serenesil	967.8	E852.8	E937.8	E950.2	E962.0	E980.2
Serenium (hydrochloride)	961.9	E857	E931.9	E950.4	E962.0	E980.4
Serepax — *see* Oxazepam						
Sernyl	968.3	E855.1	E938.3	E950.4	E962.0	E980.4
Serotonin	977.8	E858.8	E947.8	E950.4	E962.0	E980.4
Serpasil	972.6	E858.3	E942.6	E950.4	E962.0	E980.4
Sewer gas	987.8	E869.8	—	E952.8	E962.2	E982.8
Shampoo	989.6	E861.0	—	E950.9	E962.1	E980.9
Shellfish, nonbacterial or noxious	988.0	E865.1	—	E950.9	E962.1	E980.9
Silicones NEC	989.83	E866.8	E947.8	E950.9	E962.1	E980.9
Silvadene	976.0	E858.7	E946.0	E950.4	E962.0	E980.4
Silver (compound) (medicinal) NEC	976.0	E858.7	E946.0	E950.4	E962.0	E980.4
anti-infectives	976.0	E858.7	E946.0	E950.4	E962.0	E980.4
arsphenamine	961.1	E857	E931.1	E950.4	E962.0	E980.4
nitrate	976.0	E858.7	E946.0	E950.4	E962.0	E980.4
ophthalmic preparation	976.5	E858.7	E946.5	E950.4	E962.0	E980.4
toughened (keratolytic)	976.4	E858.7	E946.4	E950.4	E962.0	E980.4
nonmedicinal (dust)	985.8	E866.4	—	E950.9	E962.1	E980.9
protein (mild) (strong)	976.0	E858.7	E946.0	E950.4	E962.0	E980.4
salvarsan	961.1	E857	E931.1	E950.4	E962.0	E980.4
Simethicone	973.8	E858.4	E943.8	E950.4	E962.0	E980.4
Sinequan	969.0	E854.0	E939.0	E950.3	E962.0	E980.3
Singoserp	972.6	E858.3	E942.6	E950.4	E962.0	E980.4
Sintrom	964.2	E858.2	E934.2	E950.4	E962.0	E980.4
Sitosterols	972.2	E858.3	E942.2	E950.4	E962.0	E980.4
Skeletal muscle relaxants	975.2	E858.6	E945.2	E950.4	E962.0	E980.4
Skin						
agents (external)	976.9	E858.7	E946.9	E950.4	E962.0	E980.4
specified NEC	976.8	E858.7	E946.8	E950.4	E962.0	E980.4
test antigen	977.8	E858.8	E947.8	E950.4	E962.0	E980.4
Sleep-eze	963.0	E858.1	E933.0	E950.4	E962.0	E980.4
Sleeping draught (drug) (pill) (tablet)	967.9	E852.9	E937.9	E950.2	E962.0	E980.2
Smallpox vaccine	979.0	E858.8	E949.0	E950.4	E962.0	E980.4
Smelter fumes NEC	985.9	E866.4	—	E950.9	E962.1	E980.9
Smog	987.3	E869.1	—	E952.8	E962.2	E982.8
Smoke NEC	987.9	E869.9	—	E952.9	E962.2	E982.9
Smooth muscle relaxant	975.1	E858.6	E945.1	E950.4	E962.0	E980.4
Snail killer	989.4	E863.4	—	E950.6	E962.1	E980.7
Snake (bite) (venom)	989.5	E905.0	—	E950.9	E962.1	E980.9
Snuff	989.89	E866.8	—	E950.9	E962.1	E980.9
Soap (powder) (product)	989.6	E861.1	—	E950.9	E962.1	E980.9
bicarb	963.3	E858.1	E933.3	E950.4	E962.0	E980.4
chlorinated — see Sodium, hypochlorite						
medicinal, soft	976.2	E858.7	E946.2	E950.4	E962.0	E980.4
Soda (caustic)	983.2	E864.2	—	E950.7	E962.1	E980.6
Sodium						
acetosulfone	961.8	E857	E931.8	E950.4	E962.0	E980.4
acetrizoate	977.8	E858.8	E947.8	E950.4	E962.0	E980.4
amytal	967.0	E851	E937.0	E950.1	E962.0	E980.1
arsenate — see Arsenic						
bicarbonate	963.3	E858.1	E933.3	E950.4	E962.0	E980.4
bichromate	983.9	E864.3	—	E950.7	E962.1	E980.6
biphosphate	963.2	E858.1	E933.2	E950.4	E962.0	E980.4
bisulfate	983.9	E864.3	—	E950.7	E962.1	E980.6
Sodium — *continued*						
borate (cleanser)	989.6	E861.3	—	E950.9	E962.1	E980.9
bromide NEC	967.3	E852.2	E937.3	E950.2	E962.0	E980.2
cacodylate (nonmedicinal) NEC	978.8	E858.8	E948.8	E950.4	E962.0	E980.4
anti-infective	961.1	E857	E931.1	E950.4	E962.0	E980.4
herbicide	989.4	E863.5	—	E950.6	E962.1	E980.7
calcium edetate	963.8	E858.1	E933.8	E950.4	E962.0	E980.4
carbonate NEC	983.2	E864.2	—	E950.7	E962.1	E980.6
chlorate NEC	983.9	E864.3	—	E950.7	E962.1	E980.6
herbicide	983.9	E863.5	—	E950.7	E962.1	E980.6
chloride NEC	974.5	E858.5	E944.5	E950.4	E962.0	E980.4
chromate	983.9	E864.3	—	E950.7	E962.1	E980.6
citrate	963.3	E858.1	E933.3	E950.4	E962.0	E980.4
cyanide — see Cyanide(s)						
cyclamate	974.5	E858.5	E944.5	E950.4	E962.0	E980.4
diatrizoate	977.8	E858.8	E947.8	E950.4	E962.0	E980.4
dibunate	975.4	E858.6	E945.4	E950.4	E962.0	E980.4
dioctyl sulfosuccinate	973.2	E858.4	E943.2	E950.4	E962.0	E980.4
edetate	963.8	E858.1	E933.8	E950.4	E962.0	E980.4
ethacrynate	974.4	E858.5	E944.4	E950.4	E962.0	E980.4
fluoracetate (dust) (rodenticide)	989.4	E863.7	—	E950.6	E962.1	E980.7
fluoride — see Fluoride(s)						
free salt	974.5	E858.5	E944.5	E950.4	E962.0	E980.4
glucosulfone	961.8	E857	E931.8	E950.4	E962.0	E980.4
hydroxide	983.2	E864.2	—	E950.7	E962.1	E980.6
hypochlorite (bleach) NEC	983.9	E864.3	—	E950.7	E962.1	E980.6
disinfectant	983.9	E861.4	—	E950.7	E962.1	E980.6
medicinal (anti-infective) (external)	976.0	E858.7	E946.0	E950.4	E962.0	E980.4
vapor	987.8	E869.8	—	E952.8	E962.2	E982.8
hyposulfite	976.0	E858.7	E946.0	E950.4	E962.0	E980.4
indigotindisulfonate	977.8	E858.8	E947.8	E950.4	E962.0	E980.4
iodide	977.8	E858.8	E947.8	E950.4	E962.0	E980.4
iothalamate	977.8	E858.8	E947.8	E950.4	E962.0	E980.4
iron edetate	964.0	E858.2	E934.0	E950.4	E962.0	E980.4
lactate	963.3	E858.1	E933.3	E950.4	E962.0	E980.4
lauryl sulfate	976.2	E858.7	E946.2	E950.4	E962.0	E980.4
L-triiodothyronine	962.7	E858.0	E932.7	E950.4	E962.0	E980.4
metrizoate	977.8	E858.8	E947.8	E950.4	E962.0	E980.4
monofluoracetate (dust) (rodenticide)	989.4	E863.7	—	E950.6	E962.1	E980.7
morrhuate	972.7	E858.3	E942.7	E950.4	E962.0	E980.4
nafcillin	960.0	E856	E930.0	E950.4	E962.0	E980.4
nitrate (oxidizing agent)	983.9	E864.3	—	E950.7	E962.1	E980.6
nitrite (medicinal)	972.4	E858.3	E942.4	E950.4	E962.0	E980.4
nitroferricyanide	972.6	E858.3	E942.6	E950.4	E962.0	E980.4
nitroprusside	972.6	E858.3	E942.6	E950.4	E962.0	E980.4
para-aminohippurate	977.8	E858.8	E947.8	E950.4	E962.0	E980.4
perborate (nonmedicinal) NEC	989.89	E866.8	—	E950.9	E962.1	E980.9
medicinal	976.6	E858.7	E946.6	E950.4	E962.0	E980.4
soap	989.6	E861.1	—	E950.9	E962.1	E980.9
percarbonate — see Sodium, perborate						
phosphate	973.3	E858.4	E943.3	E950.4	E962.0	E980.4
polystyrene sulfonate	974.5	E858.5	E944.5	E950.4	E962.0	E980.4
propionate	976.0	E858.7	E946.0	E950.4	E962.0	E980.4
psylliate	972.7	E858.3	E942.7	E950.4	E962.0	E980.4
removing resins	974.5	E858.5	E944.5	E950.4	E962.0	E980.4
salicylate	965.1	E850.3	E935.3	E950.0	E962.0	E980.0
sulfate	973.3	E858.4	E943.3	E950.4	E962.0	E980.4
sulfoxone	961.8	E857	E931.8	E950.4	E962.0	E980.4
tetradecyl sulfate	972.7	E858.3	E942.7	E950.4	E962.0	E980.4
thiopental	968.3	E855.1	E938.3	E950.4	E962.0	E980.4
thiosalicylate	965.1	E850.3	E935.3	E950.0	E962.0	E980.0
thiosulfate	976.0	E858.7	E946.0	E950.4	E962.0	E980.4
tolbutamide	977.8	E858.8	E947.8	E950.4	E962.0	E980.4
tyropanoate	977.8	E858.8	E947.8	E950.4	E962.0	E980.4
valproate	966.3	E855.0	E936.3	E950.4	E962.0	E980.4
Solanine	977.8	E858.8	E947.8	E950.4	E962.0	E980.4
Solanum dulcamara	988.2	E865.4	—	E950.9	E962.1	E980.9
Solapsone	961.8	E857	E931.8	E950.4	E962.0	E980.4
Solasulfone	961.8	E857	E931.8	E950.4	E962.0	E980.4
Soldering fluid	983.1	E864.1	—	E950.7	E962.1	E980.6
Solid substance	989.9	E866.9	—	E950.9	E962.1	E980.9
specified NEC	989.9	E866.8	—	E950.9	E962.1	E980.9
Solvents, industrial	982.8	E862.9	—	E950.9	E962.1	E980.9
naphtha	981	E862.0	—	E950.9	E962.1	E980.9
petroleum	981	E862.0	—	E950.9	E962.1	E980.9
specified NEC	982.8	E862.4	—	E950.9	E962.1	E980.9

	Poisoning	External Cause (E-Code)				
		Accident	Therapeutic Use	Suicide Attempt	Assault	Undetermined
Soma	968.0	E855.1	E938.0	E950.4	E962.0	E980.4
Somatotropin	962.4	E858.0	E932.4	E950.4	E962.0	E980.4
Sominex	963.0	E858.1	E933.0	E950.4	E962.0	E980.4
Somnos	967.1	E852.0	E937.1	E950.2	E962.0	E980.2
Somonal	967.0	E851	E937.0	E950.1	E962.0	E980.1
Soneryl	967.0	E851	E937.0	E950.1	E962.0	E980.1
Soothing syrup	977.9	E858.9	E947.9	E950.5	E962.0	E980.5
Sopor	967.4	E852.3	E937.4	E950.2	E962.0	E980.2
Soporific drug	967.9	E852.9	E937.9	E950.2	E962.0	E980.2
specified type NEC	967.8	E852.8	E937.8	E950.2	E962.0	E980.2
Sorbitol NEC	977.4	E858.8	E947.4	E950.4	E962.0	E980.4
Sotradecol	972.7	E858.3	E942.7	E950.4	E962.0	E980.4
Spacoline	975.1	E858.6	E945.1	E950.4	E962.0	E980.4
Spanish fly	976.8	E858.7	E946.8	E950.4	E962.0	E980.4
Sparine	969.1	E853.0	E939.1	E950.3	E962.0	E980.3
Sparteine	975.0	E858.6	E945.0	E950.4	E962.0	E980.4
Spasmolytics	975.1	E858.6	E945.1	E950.4	E962.0	E980.4
anticholinergics	971.1	E855.4	E941.1	E950.4	E962.0	E980.4
Spectinomycin	960.8	E856	E930.8	E950.4	E962.0	E980.4
Speed	969.7	E854.2	E939.7	E950.3	E962.0	E980.3
Spermicides	976.8	E858.7	E946.8	E950.4	E962.0	E980.4
Spider (bite) (venom)	989.5	E905.1	—	E950.9	E962.1	E980.9
antivenin	979.9	E858.8	E949.9	E950.4	E962.0	E980.4
Spigelia (root)	961.6	E857	E931.6	E950.4	E962.0	E980.4
Spiperone	969.2	E853.1	E939.2	E950.3	E962.0	E980.3
Spiramycin	960.3	E856	E930.3	E950.4	E962.0	E980.4
Spirilene	969.5	E853.8	E939.5	E950.3	E962.0	E980.3
Spirit(s) (neutral) NEC	980.0	E860.1	—	E950.9	E962.1	E980.9
beverage	980.0	E860.0	—	E950.9	E962.1	E980.9
industrial	980.9	E860.9	—	E950.9	E962.1	E980.9
mineral	981	E862.0	—	E950.9	E962.1	E980.9
of salt — see Hydrochloric acid						
surgical	980.9	E860.9	—	E950.9	E962.1	E980.9
Spironolactone	974.4	E858.5	E944.4	E950.4	E962.0	E980.4
Sponge, absorbable (gelatin)	964.5	E858.2	E934.5	E950.4	E962.0	E980.4
Sporostacin	976.0	E858.7	E946.0	E950.4	E962.0	E980.4
Sprays (aerosol)	989.89	E866.8	—	E950.9	E962.1	E980.9
cosmetic	989.89	E866.7	—	E950.9	E962.1	E980.9
medicinal NEC	977.9	E858.9	E947.9	E950.5	E962.0	E980.5
pesticides — see Pesticides						
specified content — see substance specified						
Spurge flax	988.2	E865.4	—	E950.9	E962.1	E980.9
Spurges	988.2	E865.4	—	E950.9	E962.1	E980.9
Squill (expectorant) NEC	975.5	E858.6	E945.5	E950.4	E962.0	E980.4
rat poison	989.4	E863.7	—	E950.6	E962.1	E980.7
Squirting cucumber (cathartic)	973.1	E858.4	E943.1	E950.4	E962.0	E980.4
Stains	989.89	E866.8	—	E950.9	E962.1	E980.9
Stannous — *see also* Tin						
fluoride	976.7	E858.7	E946.7	E950.4	E962.0	E980.4
Stanolone	962.1	E858.0	E932.1	E950.4	E962.0	E980.4
Stanozolol	962.1	E858.0	E932.1	E950.4	E962.0	E980.4
Staphisagria or stavesacre (pediculicide)	976.0	E858.7	E946.0	E950.4	E962.0	E980.4
Stelazine	969.1	E853.0	E939.1	E950.3	E962.0	E980.3
Stemetil	969.1	E853.0	E939.1	E950.3	E962.0	E980.3
Sterculia (cathartic) (gum)	973.3	E858.4	E943.3	E950.4	E962.0	E980.4
Sternutator gas	987.8	E869.8	—	E952.8	E962.2	E982.8
Steroids NEC	962.0	E858.0	E932.0	E950.4	E962.0	E980.4
ENT agent	976.6	E858.7	E946.6	E950.4	E962.0	E980.4
ophthalmic preparation	976.5	E858.7	E946.5	E950.4	E962.0	E980.4
topical NEC	976.0	E858.7	E946.0	E950.4	E962.0	E980.4
Stibine	985.8	E866.4	—	E950.9	E962.1	E980.9
Stibophen	961.2	E857	E931.2	E950.4	E962.0	E980.4
Stilbamide, stilbamidine	961.5	E857	E931.5	E950.4	E962.0	E980.4
Stilbestrol	962.2	E858.0	E932.2	E950.4	E962.0	E980.4
Stimulants (central nervous system)	970.9	E854.3	E940.9	E950.4	E962.0	E980.4
analeptics	970.0	E854.3	E940.0	E950.4	E962.0	E980.4
opiate antagonist	970.1	E854.3	E940.1	E950.4	E962.0	E980.4
psychotherapeutic NEC	969.0	E854.0	E939.0	E950.3	E962.0	E980.3
specified NEC	970.8	E854.3	E940.8	E950.4	E962.0	E980.4
Storage batteries (acid) (cells)	983.1	E864.1	—	E950.7	E962.1	E980.6
Stovaine	968.9	E855.2	E938.9	E950.4	E962.0	E980.4
infiltration (subcutaneous)	968.5	E855.2	E938.5	E950.4	E962.0	E980.4
nerve block (peripheral) (plexus)	968.6	E855.2	E938.6	E950.4	E962.0	E980.4
spinal	968.7	E855.2	E938.7	E950.4	E962.0	E980.4
Stovaine — *continued*						
topical (surface)	968.5	E855.2	E938.5	E950.4	E962.0	E980.4
Stovarsal	961.1	E857	E931.1	E950.4	E962.0	E980.4
Stove gas — *see* Gas, utility						
Stoxil	976.5	E858.7	E946.5	E950.4	E962.0	E980.4
STP	969.6	E854.1	E939.6	E950.3	E962.0	E980.3
Stramonium (medicinal) NEC	971.1	E855.4	E941.1	E950.4	E962.0	E980.4
natural state	988.2	E865.4	—	E950.9	E962.1	E980.9
Streptodornase	964.4	E858.2	E934.4	E950.4	E962.0	E980.4
Streptoduocin	960.6	E856	E930.6	E950.4	E962.0	E980.4
Streptokinase	964.4	E858.2	E934.4	E950.4	E962.0	E980.4
Streptomycin	960.6	E856	E930.6	E950.4	E962.0	E980.4
Streptozocin	960.7	E856	E930.7	E950.4	E962.0	E980.4
Stripper (paint) (solvent)	982.8	E862.9	—	E950.9	E962.1	E980.9
Strobane	989.2	E863.0	—	E950.6	E962.1	E980.7
Strophanthin	972.1	E858.3	E942.1	E950.4	E962.0	E980.4
Strophanthus hispidus or kombe	988.2	E865.4	—	E950.9	E962.1	E980.9
Strychnine (rodenticide) (salts)	989.1	E863.7	—	E950.6	E962.1	E980.7
medicinal NEC	970.8	E854.3	E940.8	E950.4	E962.0	E980.4
Strychnos (ignatii) — see Strychnine						
Styramate	968.0	E855.1	E938.0	E950.4	E962.0	E980.4
Styrene	983.0	E864.0	—	E950.7	E962.1	E980.6
Succinimide (anticonvulsant)	966.2	E855.0	E936.2	E950.4	E962.0	E980.4
mercuric — see Mercury						
Succinylcholine	975.2	E858.6	E945.2	E950.4	E962.0	E980.4
Succinylsulfathiazole	961.0	E857	E931.0	E950.4	E962.0	E980.4
Sucrose	974.5	E858.5	E944.5	E950.4	E962.0	E980.4
Sulfacetamide	961.0	E857	E931.0	E950.4	E962.0	E980.4
ophthalmic preparation	976.5	E858.7	E946.5	E950.4	E962.0	E980.4
Sulfachlorpyridazine	961.0	E857	E931.0	E950.4	E962.0	E980.4
Sulfacytine	961.0	E857	E931.0	E950.4	E962.0	E980.4
Sulfadiazine	961.0	E857	E931.0	E950.4	E962.0	E980.4
silver (topical)	976.0	E858.7	E946.0	E950.4	E962.0	E980.4
Sulfadimethoxine	961.0	E857	E931.0	E950.4	E962.0	E980.4
Sulfadimidine	961.0	E857	E931.0	E950.4	E962.0	E980.4
Sulfaethidole	961.0	E857	E931.0	E950.4	E962.0	E980.4
Sulfafurazole	961.0	E857	E931.0	E950.4	E962.0	E980.4
Sulfaguanidine	961.0	E857	E931.0	E950.4	E962.0	E980.4
Sulfamerazine	961.0	E857	E931.0	E950.4	E962.0	E980.4
Sulfameter	961.0	E857	E931.0	E950.4	E962.0	E980.4
Sulfamethizole	961.0	E857	E931.0	E950.4	E962.0	E980.4
Sulfamethoxazole	961.0	E857	E931.0	E950.4	E962.0	E980.4
Sulfamethoxydiazine	961.0	E857	E931.0	E950.4	E962.0	E980.4
Sulfamethoxypyridazine	961.0	E857	E931.0	E950.4	E962.0	E980.4
Sulfamethylthiazole	961.0	E857	E931.0	E950.4	E962.0	E980.4
Sulfamylon	976.0	E858.7	E946.0	E950.4	E962.0	E980.4
Sulfan blue (diagnostic dye)	977.8	E858.8	E947.8	E950.4	E962.0	E980.4
Sulfanilamide	961.0	E857	E931.0	E950.4	E962.0	E980.4
Sulfanilylguanidine	961.0	E857	E931.0	E950.4	E962.0	E980.4
Sulfaphenazole	961.0	E857	E931.0	E950.4	E962.0	E980.4
Sulfaphenylthiazole	961.0	E857	E931.0	E950.4	E962.0	E980.4
Sulfaproxyline	961.0	E857	E931.0	E950.4	E962.0	E980.4
Sulfapyridine	961.0	E857	E931.0	E950.4	E962.0	E980.4
Sulfapyrimidine	961.0	E857	E931.0	E950.4	E962.0	E980.4
Sulfarsphenamine	961.1	E857	E931.1	E950.4	E962.0	E980.4
Sulfasalazine	961.0	E857	E931.0	E950.4	E962.0	E980.4
Sulfasomizole	961.0	E857	E931.0	E950.4	E962.0	E980.4
Sulfasuxidine	961.0	E857	E931.0	E950.4	E962.0	E980.4
Sulfinpyrazone	974.7	E858.5	E944.7	E950.4	E962.0	E980.4
Sulfisoxazole	961.0	E857	E931.0	E950.4	E962.0	E980.4
ophthalmic preparation	976.5	E858.7	E946.5	E950.4	E962.0	E980.4
Sulfomyxin	960.8	E856	E930.8	E950.4	E962.0	E980.4
Sulfonal	967.8	E852.8	E937.8	E950.2	E962.0	E980.2
Sulfonamides (mixtures)	961.0	E857	E931.0	E950.4	E962.0	E980.4
Sulfones	961.8	E857	E931.8	E950.4	E962.0	E980.4
Sulfonethylmethane	967.8	E852.8	E937.8	E950.2	E962.0	E980.2
Sulfonmethane	967.8	E852.8	E937.8	E950.2	E962.0	E980.2
Sulfonphthal, sulfonphthol	977.8	E858.8	E947.8	E950.4	E962.0	E980.4
Sulfonylurea derivatives, oral	962.3	E858.0	E932.3	E950.4	E962.0	E980.4
Sulfoxone	961.8	E857	E931.8	E950.4	E962.0	E980.4
Sulfur, sulfureted, sulfuric, sulfurous, sulfuryl (compounds) NEC	989.89	E866.8	—	E950.9	E962.1	E980.9
acid	983.1	E864.1	—	E950.7	E962.1	E980.6
dioxide	987.3	E869.1	—	E952.8	E962.2	E982.8

		External Cause (E-Code)				
	Poisoning	Accident	Therapeutic Use	Suicide Attempt	Assault	Undetermined
Sulfur, sulfureted, sulfuric, sulfurous, sulfuryl (compounds) — *continued*						
ether — see Ether(s)						
hydrogen	987.8	E869.8	—	E952.8	E962.2	E982.8
medicinal (keratolytic) (ointment) NEC	976.4	E858.7	E946.4	E950.4	E962.0	E980.4
pesticide (vapor)	989.4	E863.4	—	E950.6	E962.1	E980.7
vapor NEC	987.8	E869.8	—	E952.8	E962.2	E982.8
Sulkowitch's reagent	977.8	E858.8	E947.8	E950.4	E962.0	E980.4
Sulphadione	961.8	E857	E931.8	E950.4	E962.0	E980.4
Sulph — *see also* Sulf-						
Sulthiame, sultiame	966.3	E855.0	E936.3	E950.4	E962.0	E980.4
Superinone	975.5	E858.6	E945.5	E950.4	E962.0	E980.4
Suramin	961.5	E857	E931.5	E950.4	E962.0	E980.4
Surfacaine	968.5	E855.2	E938.5	E950.4	E962.0	E980.4
Surital	968.3	E855.1	E938.3	E950.4	E962.0	E980.4
Sutilains	976.8	E858.7	E946.8	E950.4	E962.0	E980.4
Suxamethonium (bromide) (chloride) (iodide)	975.2	E858.6	E945.2	E950.4	E962.0	E980.4
Suxethonium (bromide)	975.2	E858.6	E945.2	E950.4	E962.0	E980.4
Sweet oil (birch)	976.3	E858.7	E946.3	E950.4	E962.0	E980.4
Sym-dichloroethyl ether	982.3	E862.4	—	E950.9	E962.1	E980.9
Sympatholytics	971.3	E855.6	E941.3	E950.4	E962.0	E980.4
Sympathomimetics	971.2	E855.5	E941.2	E950.4	E962.0	E980.4
Synagis	979.6	E858.8	E949.6	E950.4	E962.0	E980.4
Synalar	976.0	E858.7	E946.0	E950.4	E962.0	E980.4
Synthroid	962.7	E858.0	E932.7	E950.4	E962.0	E980.4
Syntocinon	975.0	E858.6	E945.0	E950.4	E962.0	E950.4
Syrosingopine	972.6	E858.3	E942.6	E950.4	E962.0	E980.4
Systemic agents (primarily)	963.9	E858.1	E933.9	E950.4	E962.0	E980.4
specified NEC	963.8	E858.1	E933.8	E950.4	E962.0	E980.4
Tablets — *see also* specified substance	977.9	E858.9	E947.9	E950.5	E962.0	E980.5
Tace	962.2	E858.0	E932.2	E950.4	E962.0	E980.4
Tacrine	971.0	E855.3	E941.0	E950.4	E962.0	E980.4
Talbutal	967.0	E851	E937.0	E950.1	E962.0	E980.1
Talc	976.3	E858.7	E946.3	E950.4	E962.0	E980.4
Talcum	976.3	E858.7	E946.3	E950.4	E962.0	E980.4
Tamsulosin	971.3	E855.6	E941.3	E950.4	E962.0	E980.4
Tandearil, tanderil	965.5	E850.5	E935.5	E950.0	E962.0	E980.0
Tannic acid	983.1	E864.1	—	E950.7	E962.1	E980.6
medicinal (astringent)	976.2	E858.7	E946.2	E950.4	E962.0	E980.4
Tannin — see Tannic acid						
Tansy	988.2	E865.4	—	E950.9	E962.1	E980.9
TAO	960.3	E856	E930.3	E950.4	E962.0	E980.4
Tapazole	962.8	E858.0	E932.8	E950.4	E962.0	E980.4
Tar NEC	983.0	E864.0	—	E950.7	E962.1	E980.6
camphor — see Naphthalene						
fumes	987.8	E869.8	—	E952.8	E962.2	E982.8
Taractan	969.3	E853.8	E939.3	E950.3	E962.0	E980.3
Tarantula (venomous)	989.5	E905.1	—	E950.9	E962.1	E980.9
Tartar emetic (anti-infective)	961.2	E857	E931.2	E950.4	E962.0	E980.4
Tartaric acid	983.1	E864.1	—	E950.7	E962.1	E980.6
Tartrated antimony (anti-infective)	961.2	E857	E931.2	E950.4	E962.0	E980.4
TCA — *see* Trichloroacetic acid						
TDI	983.0	E864.0	—	E950.7	E962.1	E980.6
vapor	987.8	E869.8	—	E952.8	E962.2	E982.8
Tear gas	987.5	E869.3	—	E952.8	E962.2	E982.8
Teclothiazide	974.3	E858.5	E944.3	E950.4	E962.0	E980.4
Tegretol	966.3	E855.0	E936.3	E950.4	E962.0	E980.4
Telepaque	977.8	E858.8	E947.8	E950.4	E962.0	E980.4
Tellurium	985.8	E866.4	—	E950.9	E962.1	E980.9
fumes	985.8	E866.4	—	E950.9	E962.1	E980.9
TEM	963.1	E858.1	E933.1	E950.4	E962.0	E980.4
Temazepan — see Benzodiazepines						
TEPA	963.1	E858.1	E933.1	E950.4	E962.0	E980.4
TEPP	989.3	E863.1	—	E950.6	E962.1	E980.7
Terbutaline	971.2	E855.5	E941.2	E950.4	E962.0	E980.4
Teroxalene	961.6	E857	E931.6	E950.4	E962.0	E980.4
Terpin hydrate	975.5	E858.6	E945.5	E950.4	E962.0	E980.4
Terramycin	960.4	E856	E930.4	E950.4	E962.0	E980.4
Tessalon	975.4	E858.6	E945.4	E950.4	E962.0	E980.4
Testosterone	962.1	E858.0	E932.1	E950.4	E962.0	E980.4
Tetanus (vaccine)	978.4	E858.8	E948.4	E950.4	E962.0	E980.4
antitoxin	979.9	E858.8	E949.9	E950.4	E962.0	E980.4
immune globulin (human)	964.6	E858.2	E934.6	E950.4	E962.0	E980.4
toxoid	978.4	E858.8	E948.4	E950.4	E962.0	E980.4
Tetanus — *continued*						
toxoid — *continued*						
with diphtheria toxoid	978.9	E858.8	E948.9	E950.4	E962.0	E980.4
with pertussis	978.6	E858.8	E948.6	E950.4	E962.0	E980.4
Tetrabenazine	969.5	E853.8	E939.5	E950.3	E962.0	E980.3
Tetracaine (infiltration) (topical)	968.5	E855.2	E938.5	E950.4	E962.0	E980.4
nerve block (peripheral) (plexus)	968.6	E855.2	E938.6	E950.4	E962.0	E980.4
spinal	968.7	E855.2	E938.7	E950.4	E962.0	E980.4
Tetrachlorethylene — see Tetrachloroethylene						
Tetrachlormethiazide	974.3	E858.5	E944.3	E950.4	E962.0	E980.4
Tetrachloroethane (liquid) (vapor)	982.3	E862.4	—	E950.9	E962.1	E980.9
paint or varnish	982.3	E861.6	—	E950.9	E962.1	E980.9
Tetrachloroethylene (liquid) (vapor)	982.3	E862.4	—	E950.9	E962.1	E980.9
medicinal	961.6	E857	E931.6	E950.4	E962.0	E980.4
Tetrachloromethane — see Carbon, tetrachloride						
Tetracycline	960.4	E856	E930.4	E950.4	E962.0	E980.4
ophthalmic preparation	976.5	E858.7	E946.5	E950.4	E962.0	E980.4
topical NEC	976.0	E858.7	E946.0	E950.4	E962.0	E980.4
Tetraethylammonium chloride	972.3	E858.3	E942.3	E950.4	E962.0	E980.4
Tetraethyl lead (antiknock compound)	984.1	E862.1	—	E950.9	E962.1	E980.9
Tetraethyl pyrophosphate	989.3	E863.1	—	E950.6	E962.1	E980.7
Tetraethylthiuram disulfide	977.3	E858.8	E947.3	E950.4	E962.0	E980.4
Tetrahydroaminoacridine	971.0	E855.3	E941.0	E950.4	E962.0	E980.4
Tetrahydrocannabinol	969.6	E854.1	E939.6	E950.3	E962.0	E980.3
Tetrahydronaphthalene	982.0	E862.4	—	E950.9	E962.1	E980.9
Tetrahydrozoline	971.2	E855.5	E941.2	E950.4	E962.0	E980.4
Tetralin	982.0	E862.4	—	E950.9	E962.1	E980.9
Tetramethylthiuram (disulfide) NEC	989.4	E863.6	—	E950.6	E962.1	E980.7
medicinal	976.2	E858.7	E946.2	E950.4	E962.0	E980.4
Tetronal	967.8	E852.8	E937.8	E950.2	E962.0	E980.2
Tetryl	983.0	E864.0	—	E950.7	E962.1	E980.6
Thalidomide	967.8	E852.8	E937.8	E950.2	E962.0	E980.2
Thallium (compounds) (dust) NEC	985.8	E866.4	—	E950.9	E962.1	E980.9
pesticide (rodenticide)	985.8	E863.7	—	E950.6	E962.1	E980.7
THC	969.6	E854.1	E939.6	E950.3	E962.0	E980.3
Thebacon	965.09	E850.2	E935.2	E950.0	E962.0	E980.0
Thebaine	965.09	E850.2	E935.2	E950.0	E962.0	E980.0
Theobromine (calcium salicylate)	974.1	E858.5	E944.1	E950.4	E962.0	E980.4
Theophylline (diuretic)	974.1	E858.5	E944.1	E950.4	E962.0	E980.4
ethylenediamine	975.7	E858.6	E945.7	E950.4	E962.0	E980.4
Thiabendazole	961.6	E857	E931.6	E950.4	E962.0	E980.4
Thialbarbital, thialbarbitone	968.3	E855.1	E938.3	E950.4	E962.0	E980.4
Thiamine	963.5	E858.1	E933.5	E950.4	E962.0	E980.4
Thiamylal (sodium)	968.3	E855.1	E938.3	E950.4	E962.0	E980.4
Thiazesim	969.0	E854.0	E939.0	E950.3	E962.0	E980.3
Thiazides (diuretics)	974.3	E858.5	E944.3	E950.4	E962.0	E980.4
Thiethylperazine	963.0	E858.1	E933.0	E950.4	E962.0	E980.4
Thimerosal (topical)	976.0	E858.7	E946.0	E950.4	E962.0	E980.4
ophthalmic preparation	976.5	E858.7	E946.5	E950.4	E962.0	E980.4
Thioacetazone	961.8	E857	E931.8	E950.4	E962.0	E980.4
Thiobarbiturates	968.3	E855.1	E938.3	E950.4	E962.0	E980.4
Thiobismol	961.2	E857	E931.2	E950.4	E962.0	E980.4
Thiocarbamide	962.8	E858.0	E932.8	E950.4	E962.0	E980.4
Thiocarbarsone	961.1	E857	E931.1	E950.4	E962.0	E980.4
Thiocarlide	961.8	E857	E931.8	E950.4	E962.0	E980.4
Thioguanine	963.1	E858.1	E933.1	E950.4	E962.0	E980.4
Thiomercaptomerin	974.0	E858.5	E944.0	E950.4	E962.0	E980.4
Thiomerin	974.0	E858.5	E944.0	E950.4	E962.0	E980.4
Thiopental, thiopentone (sodium)	968.3	E855.1	E938.3	E950.4	E962.0	E980.4
Thiopropazate	969.1	E853.0	E939.1	E950.3	E962.0	E980.3
Thioproperazine	969.1	E853.0	E939.1	E950.3	E962.0	E980.3
Thioridazine	969.1	E853.0	E939.1	E950.3	E962.0	E980.3
Thio-TEPA, thiotepa	963.1	E858.1	E933.1	E950.4	E962.0	E980.4
Thiothixene	969.3	E853.8	E939.3	E950.3	E962.0	E980.3
Thiouracil	962.8	E858.0	E932.8	E950.4	E962.0	E980.4
Thiourea	962.8	E858.0	E932.8	E950.4	E962.0	E980.4
Thiphenamil	971.1	E855.4	E941.1	E950.4	E962.0	E980.4

☑ Additional Digit Required — Refer to the Tabular List for Digit Selection

Subterms under main terms may continue to next column or page

Substance	Poisoning	External Cause (E-Code)				
		Accident	Therapeutic Use	Suicide Attempt	Assault	Undetermined
Thiram NEC	989.4	E863.6	—	E950.6	E962.1	E980.7
medicinal	976.2	E858.7	E946.2	E950.4	E962.0	E980.4
Thonzylamine	963.0	E858.1	E933.0	E950.4	E962.0	E980.4
Thorazine	969.1	E853.0	E939.1	E950.3	E962.0	E980.3
Thornapple	988.2	E865.4	—	E950.9	E962.1	E980.9
Throat preparation (lozenges) NEC	976.6	E858.7	E946.6	E950.4	E962.0	E980.4
Thrombin	964.5	E858.2	E934.5	E950.4	E962.0	E980.4
Thrombolysin	964.4	E858.2	E934.4	E950.4	E962.0	E980.4
Thymol	983.0	E864.0	—	E950.7	E962.1	E980.6
Thymus extract	962.9	E858.0	E932.9	E950.4	E962.0	E980.4
Thyroglobulin	962.7	E858.0	E932.7	E950.4	E962.0	E980.4
Thyroid (derivatives) (extract)	962.7	E858.0	E932.7	E950.4	E962.0	E980.4
Thyrolar	962.7	E858.0	E932.7	E950.4	E962.0	E980.4
Thyrothrophin, thyrotropin	977.8	E858.8	E947.8	E950.4	E962.0	E980.4
Thyroxin(e)	962.7	E858.0	E932.7	E950.4	E962.0	E980.4
Tigan	963.0	E858.1	E933.0	E950.4	E962.0	E980.4
Tigloidine	968.0	E855.1	E938.0	E950.4	E962.0	E980.4
Tin (chloride) (dust) (oxide) NEC	985.8	E866.4	—	E950.9	E962.1	E980.9
anti-infectives	961.2	E857	E931.2	E950.4	E962.0	E980.4
Tinactin	976.0	E858.7	E946.0	E950.4	E962.0	E980.4
Tincture, iodine — *see* Iodine						
Tindal	969.1	E853.0	E939.1	E950.3	E962.0	E980.3
Titanium (compounds) (vapor)	985.8	E866.4	—	E950.9	E962.1	E980.9
ointment	976.3	E858.7	E946.3	E950.4	E962.0	E980.4
Titroid	962.7	E858.0	E932.7	E950.4	E962.0	E980.4
TMTD — *see* Tetramethylthiuram disulfide						
TNT	989.89	E866.8	—	E950.9	E962.1	E980.9
fumes	987.8	E869.8	—	E952.8	E962.2	E982.8
Toadstool	988.1	E865.5	—	E950.9	E962.1	E980.9
Tobacco NEC	989.84	E866.8	—	E950.9	E962.1	E980.9
Indian	988.2	E865.4	—	E950.9	E962.1	E980.9
smoke, second-hand	987.8	E869.4	—	—	—	—
Tocopherol	963.5	E858.1	E933.5	E950.4	E962.0	E980.4
Tocosamine	975.0	E858.6	E945.0	E950.4	E962.0	E980.4
Tofranil	969.0	E854.0	E939.0	E950.3	E962.0	E980.3
Toilet deodorizer	989.89	E866.8	—	E950.9	E962.1	E980.9
Tolazamide	962.3	E858.0	E932.3	E950.4	E962.0	E980.4
Tolazoline	971.3	E855.6	E941.3	E950.4	E962.0	E980.4
Tolbutamide	962.3	E858.0	E932.3	E950.4	E962.0	E980.4
sodium	977.8	E858.8	E947.8	E950.4	E962.0	E980.4
Tolmetin	965.69	E850.6	E935.6	E950.0	E962.0	E980.0
Tolnaftate	976.0	E858.7	E946.0	E950.4	E962.0	E980.4
Tolpropamine	976.1	E858.7	E946.1	E950.4	E962.0	E980.4
Tolserol	968.0	E855.1	E938.0	E950.4	E962.0	E980.4
Toluene (liquid) (vapor)	982.0	E862.4	—	E950.9	E962.1	E980.9
diisocyanate	983.0	E864.0	—	E950.7	E962.1	E980.6
Toluidine	983.0	E864.0	—	E950.7	E962.1	E980.6
vapor	987.8	E869.8	—	E952.8	E962.2	E982.8
Toluol (liquid) (vapor)	982.0	E862.4	—	E950.9	E962.1	E980.9
Tolylene-2, 4-diisocyanate	983.0	E864.0	—	E950.7	E962.1	E980.6
Tonics, cardiac	972.1	E858.3	E942.1	E950.4	E962.0	E980.4
Toxaphene (dust) (spray)	989.2	E863.0	—	E950.6	E962.1	E980.7
Toxoids NEC	978.8	E858.8	E948.8	E950.4	E962.0	E980.4
Tractor fuel NEC	981	E862.1	—	E950.9	E962.1	E980.9
Tragacanth	973.3	E858.4	E943.3	E950.4	E962.0	E980.4
Tramazoline	971.2	E855.5	E941.2	E950.4	E962.0	E980.4
Tranquilizers	969.5	E853.9	E939.5	E950.3	E962.0	E980.3
benzodiazepine-based	969.4	E853.2	E939.4	E950.3	E962.0	E980.3
butyrophenone-based	969.2	E853.1	E939.2	E950.3	E962.0	E980.3
major NEC	969.3	E853.8	E939.3	E950.3	E962.0	E980.3
phenothiazine-based	969.1	E853.0	E939.1	E950.3	E962.0	E980.3
specified NEC	969.5	E853.8	E939.5	E950.3	E962.0	E980.3
Trantoin	961.9	E857	E931.9	E950.4	E962.0	E980.4
Tranxene	969.4	E853.2	E939.4	E950.3	E962.0	E980.3
Tranylcypromine (sulfate)	969.0	E854.0	E939.0	E950.3	E962.0	E980.3
Trasentine	975.1	E858.6	E945.1	E950.4	E962.0	E980.4
Travert	974.5	E858.5	E944.5	E950.4	E962.0	E980.4
Trecator	961.8	E857	E931.8	E950.4	E962.0	E980.4
Tretinoin	976.8	E858.7	E946.8	E950.4	E962.0	E980.4
Triacetin	976.0	E858.7	E946.0	E950.4	E962.0	E980.4
Triacetyloleandomycin	960.3	E856	E930.3	E950.4	E962.0	E980.4
Triamcinolone	962.0	E858.0	E932.0	E950.4	E962.0	E980.4
ENT agent	976.6	E858.7	E946.6	E950.4	E962.0	E980.4
medicinal (keratolytic)	976.4	E858.7	E946.4	E950.4	E962.0	E980.4
ophthalmic preparation	976.5	E858.7	E946.5	E950.4	E962.0	E980.4
Triamcinolone — *continued*						
topical NEC	976.0	E858.7	E946.0	E950.4	E962.0	E980.4
Triamterene	974.4	E858.5	E944.4	E950.4	E962.0	E980.4
Triaziquone	963.1	E858.1	E933.1	E950.4	E962.0	E980.4
Tribromacetaldehyde	967.3	E852.2	E937.3	E950.2	E962.0	E980.2
Tribromoethanol	968.2	E855.1	E938.2	E950.4	E962.0	E980.4
Tribromomethane	967.3	E852.2	E937.3	E950.2	E962.0	E980.2
Trichlorethane	982.3	E862.4	—	E950.9	E962.1	E980.9
Trichlormethiazide	974.3	E858.5	E944.3	E950.4	E962.0	E980.4
Trichloroacetic acid	983.1	E864.1	—	E950.7	E962.1	E980.6
Trichloroethanol	967.1	E852.0	E937.1	E950.2	E962.0	E980.2
Trichloroethylene (liquid) (vapor)	982.3	E862.4	—	E950.9	E962.1	E980.9
anesthetic (gas)	968.2	E855.1	E938.2	E950.4	E962.0	E980.4
Trichloroethyl phosphate	967.1	E852.0	E937.1	E950.2	E962.0	E980.2
Trichlorofluoromethane NEC	987.4	E869.2	—	E952.8	E962.2	E982.8
Trichlorotriethylamine	963.1	E858.1	E933.1	E950.4	E962.0	E980.4
Trichomonacides NEC	961.5	E857	E931.5	E950.4	E962.0	E980.4
Trichomycin	960.1	E856	E930.1	E950.4	E962.0	E980.4
Triclofos	967.1	E852.0	E937.1	E950.2	E962.0	E980.2
Tricresyl phosphate	989.89	E866.8	—	E950.9	E962.1	E980.9
solvent	982.8	E862.4	—	E950.9	E962.1	E980.9
Tricyclamol	966.4	E855.0	E936.4	E950.4	E962.0	E980.4
Tridesilon	976.0	E858.7	E946.0	E950.4	E962.0	E980.4
Tridihexethyl	971.1	E855.4	E941.1	E950.4	E962.0	E980.4
Tridione	966.0	E855.0	E936.0	E950.4	E962.0	E980.4
Triethanolamine NEC	983.2	E864.2	—	E950.7	E962.1	E980.6
detergent	983.2	E861.0	—	E950.7	E962.1	E980.6
trinitrate	972.4	E858.3	E942.4	E950.4	E962.0	E980.4
Triethanomelamine	963.1	E858.1	E933.1	E950.4	E962.0	E980.4
Triethylene melamine	963.1	E858.1	E933.1	E950.4	E962.0	E980.4
Triethylenephosphoramide	963.1	E858.1	E933.1	E950.4	E962.0	E980.4
Triethylenethiophosphoramide	963.1	E858.1	E933.1	E950.4	E962.0	E980.4
Trifluoperazine	969.1	E853.0	E939.1	E950.3	E962.0	E980.3
Trifluperidol	969.2	E853.1	E939.2	E950.3	E962.0	E980.3
Triflupromazine	969.1	E853.0	E939.1	E950.3	E962.0	E980.3
Trihexyphenidyl	971.1	E855.4	E941.1	E950.4	E962.0	E980.4
Triiodothyronine	962.7	E858.0	E932.7	E950.4	E962.0	E980.4
Trilene	968.2	E855.1	E938.2	E950.4	E962.0	E980.4
Trimeprazine	963.0	E858.1	E933.0	E950.4	E962.0	E980.4
Trimetazidine	972.4	E858.3	E942.4	E950.4	E962.0	E980.4
Trimethadione	966.0	E855.0	E936.0	E950.4	E962.0	E980.4
Trimethaphan	972.3	E858.3	E942.3	E950.4	E962.0	E980.4
Trimethidinium	972.3	E858.3	E942.3	E950.4	E962.0	E980.4
Trimethobenzamide	963.0	E858.1	E933.0	E950.4	E962.0	E980.4
Trimethylcarbinol	980.8	E860.8	—	E950.9	E962.1	E980.9
Trimethylpsoralen	976.3	E858.7	E946.3	E950.4	E962.0	E980.4
Trimeton	963.0	E858.1	E933.0	E950.4	E962.0	E980.4
Trimipramine	969.0	E854.0	E939.0	E950.3	E962.0	E980.3
Trimustine	963.1	E858.1	E933.1	E950.4	E962.0	E980.4
Trinitrin	972.4	E858.3	E942.4	E950.4	E962.0	E980.4
Trinitrophenol	983.0	E864.0	—	E950.7	E962.1	E980.6
Trinitrotoluene	989.89	E866.8	—	E950.9	E962.1	E980.9
fumes	987.8	E869.8	—	E952.8	E962.2	E982.8
Trional	967.8	E852.8	E937.8	E950.2	E962.0	E980.2
Trioxide of arsenic — *see* Arsenic						
Trioxsalen	976.3	E858.7	E946.3	E950.4	E962.0	E980.4
Tripelennamine	963.0	E858.1	E933.0	E950.4	E962.0	E980.4
Triperidol	969.2	E853.1	E939.2	E950.3	E962.0	E980.3
Triprolidine	963.0	E858.1	E933.0	E950.4	E962.0	E980.4
Trisoralen	976.3	E858.7	E946.3	E950.4	E962.0	E980.4
Troleandomycin	960.3	E856	E930.3	E950.4	E962.0	E980.4
Trolnitrate (phosphate)	972.4	E858.3	E942.4	E950.4	E962.0	E980.4
Trometamol	963.3	E858.1	E933.3	E950.4	E962.0	E980.4
Tromethamine	963.3	E858.1	E933.3	E950.4	E962.0	E980.4
Tronothane	968.5	E855.2	E938.5	E950.4	E962.0	E980.4
Tropicamide	971.1	E855.4	E941.1	E950.4	E962.0	E980.4
Troxidone	966.0	E855.0	E936.0	E950.4	E962.0	E980.4
Tryparsamide	961.1	E857	E931.1	E950.4	E962.0	E980.4
Trypsin	963.4	E858.1	E933.4	E950.4	E962.0	E980.4
Tryptizol	969.0	E854.0	E939.0	E950.3	E962.0	E980.3
Tuaminoheptane	971.2	E855.5	E941.2	E950.4	E962.0	E980.4
Tuberculin (old)	977.8	E858.8	E947.8	E950.4	E962.0	E980.4
Tubocurare	975.2	E858.6	E945.2	E950.4	E962.0	E980.4
Tubocurarine	975.2	E858.6	E945.2	E950.4	E962.0	E980.4
Turkish green	969.6	E854.1	E939.6	E950.3	E962.0	E980.3
Turpentine (spirits of) (liquid) (vapor)	982.8	E862.4	—	E950.9	E962.1	E980.9
Tybamate	969.5	E853.8	E939.5	E950.3	E962.0	E980.3

		External Cause (E-Code)				
	Poisoning	Accident	Therapeutic Use	Suicide Attempt	Assault	Undetermined
Tyloxapol	975.5	E858.6	E945.5	E950.4	E962.0	E980.4
Tymazoline	971.2	E855.5	E941.2	E950.4	E962.0	E980.4
Typhoid vaccine	978.1	E858.8	E948.1	E950.4	E962.0	E980.4
Typhus vaccine	979.2	E858.8	E949.2	E950.4	E962.0	E980.4
Tyrothricin	976.0	E858.7	E946.0	E950.4	E962.0	E980.4
ENT agent	976.6	E858.7	E946.6	E950.4	E962.0	E980.4
ophthalmic preparation	976.5	E858.7	E946.5	E950.4	E962.0	E980.4
Undecenoic acid	976.0	E858.7	E946.0	E950.4	E962.0	E980.4
Undecylenic acid	976.0	E858.7	E946.0	E950.4	E962.0	E980.4
Unna's boot	976.3	E858.7	E946.3	E950.4	E962.0	E980.4
Uracil mustard	963.1	E858.1	E933.1	E950.4	E962.0	E980.4
Uramustine	963.1	E858.1	E933.1	E950.4	E962.0	E980.4
Urari	975.2	E858.6	E945.2	E950.4	E962.0	E980.4
Urea	974.4	E858.5	E944.4	E950.4	E962.0	E980.4
topical	976.8	E858.7	E946.8	E950.4	E962.0	E980.4
Urethan(e) (antineoplastic)	963.1	E858.1	E933.1	E950.4	E962.0	E980.4
Urginea (maritima) (scilla) — *see* Squill						
Uric acid metabolism agents NEC	974.7	E858.5	E944.7	E950.4	E962.0	E980.4
Urokinase	964.4	E858.2	E934.4	E950.4	E962.0	E980.4
Urokon	977.8	E858.8	E947.8	E950.4	E962.0	E980.4
Urotropin	961.9	E857	E931.9	E950.4	E962.0	E980.4
Urtica	988.2	E865.4	—	E950.9	E962.1	E980.9
Utility gas — *see* Gas, utility						
Vaccine NEC	979.9	E858.8	E949.9	E950.4	E962.0	E980.4
bacterial NEC	978.8	E858.8	E948.8	E950.4	E962.0	E980.4
with						
other bacterial component	978.9	E858.8	E948.9	E950.4	E962.0	E980.4
pertussis component	978.6	E858.8	E948.6	E950.4	E962.0	E980.4
viral-rickettsial component	979.7	E858.8	E949.7	E950.4	E962.0	E980.4
mixed NEC	978.9	E858.8	E948.9	E950.4	E962.0	E980.4
BCG	978.0	E858.8	E948.0	E950.4	E962.0	E980.4
cholera	978.2	E858.8	E948.2	E950.4	E962.0	E980.4
diphtheria	978.5	E858.8	E948.5	E950.4	E962.0	E980.4
influenza	979.6	E858.8	E949.6	E950.4	E962.0	E980.4
measles	979.4	E858.8	E949.4	E950.4	E962.0	E980.4
meningococcal	978.8	E858.8	E948.8	E950.4	E962.0	E980.4
mumps	979.6	E858.8	E949.6	E950.4	E962.0	E980.4
paratyphoid	978.1	E858.8	E948.1	E950.4	E962.0	E980.4
pertussis (with diphtheria toxoid) (with tetanus toxoid)	978.6	E858.8	E948.6	E950.4	E962.0	E980.4
plague	978.3	E858.8	E948.3	E950.4	E962.0	E980.4
poliomyelitis	979.5	E858.8	E949.5	E950.4	E962.0	E980.4
poliovirus	979.5	E858.8	E949.5	E950.4	E962.0	E980.4
rabies	979.1	E858.8	E949.1	E950.4	E962.0	E980.4
respiratory syncytial virus	979.6	E858.8	E949.6	E950.4	E962.0	E980.4
rickettsial NEC	979.6	E858.8	E949.6	E950.4	E962.0	E980.4
with						
bacterial component	979.7	E858.8	E949.7	E950.4	E962.0	E980.4
pertussis component	978.6	E858.8	E948.6	E950.4	E962.0	E980.4
viral component	979.7	E858.8	E949.7	E950.4	E962.0	E980.4
Rocky mountain spotted fever	979.6	E858.8	E949.6	E950.4	E962.0	E980.4
rotavirus	979.6	E858.8	E949.6	E950.4	E962.0	E980.4
rubella virus	979.4	E858.8	E949.4	E950.4	E962.0	E980.4
sabin oral	979.5	E858.8	E949.5	E950.4	E962.0	E980.4
smallpox	979.0	E858.8	E949.0	E950.4	E962.0	E980.4
tetanus	978.4	E858.8	E948.4	E950.4	E962.0	E980.4
typhoid	978.1	E858.8	E948.1	E950.4	E962.0	E980.4
typhus	979.2	E858.8	E949.2	E950.4	E962.0	E980.4
viral NEC	979.6	E858.8	E949.6	E950.4	E962.0	E980.4
with						
bacterial component	979.7	E858.8	E949.7	E950.4	E962.0	E980.4
pertussis component	978.6	E858.8	E948.6	E950.4	E962.0	E980.4
rickettsial component	979.7	E858.8	E949.7	E950.4	E962.0	E980.4
yellow fever	979.3	E858.8	E949.3	E950.4	E962.0	E980.4
Vaccinia immune globulin (human)	964.6	E858.2	E934.6	E950.4	E962.0	E980.4
Vaginal contraceptives	976.8	E858.7	E946.8	E950.4	E962.0	E980.4
Valethamate	971.1	E855.4	E941.1	E950.4	E962.0	E980.4
Valisone	976.0	E858.7	E946.0	E950.4	E962.0	E980.4
Valium	969.4	E853.2	E939.4	E950.3	E962.0	E980.3
Valmid	967.8	E852.8	E937.8	E950.2	E962.0	E980.2
Vanadium	985.8	E866.4	—	E950.9	E962.1	E980.9
Vancomycin	960.8	E856	E930.8	E950.4	E962.0	E980.4
Vapor — *see also* Gas	987.9	E869.9	—	E952.9	E962.2	E982.9
kiln (carbon monoxide)	986	E868.8	—	E952.1	E962.2	E982.1
lead — see Lead						
Vapor — *see also* Gas — *continued*						
specified source NEC (see also specific substance)	987.8	E869.8	—	E952.8	E962.2	E982.8
Varidase	964.4	E858.2	E934.4	E950.4	E962.0	E980.4
Varnish	989.89	E861.6	—	E950.9	E962.1	E980.9
cleaner	982.8	E862.9	—	E950.9	E962.1	E980.9
Vaseline	976.3	E858.7	E946.3	E950.4	E962.0	E980.4
Vasodilan	972.5	E858.3	E942.5	E950.4	E962.0	E980.4
Vasodilators NEC	972.5	E858.3	E942.5	E950.4	E962.0	E980.4
coronary	972.4	E858.3	E942.4	E950.4	E962.0	E980.4
Vasopressin	962.5	E858.0	E932.5	E950.4	E962.0	E980.4
Vasopressor drugs	962.5	E858.0	E932.5	E950.4	E962.0	E980.4
Venom, venomous (bite) (sting)	989.5	E905.9	—	E950.9	E962.1	E980.9
arthropod NEC	989.5	E905.5	—	E950.9	E962.1	E980.9
bee	989.5	E905.3	—	E950.9	E962.1	E980.9
centipede	989.5	E905.4	—	E950.9	E962.1	E980.9
hornet	989.5	E905.3	—	E950.9	E962.1	E980.9
lizard	989.5	E905.0	—	E950.9	E962.1	E980.9
marine animals or plants	989.5	E905.6	—	E950.9	E962.1	E980.9
millipede (tropical)	989.5	E905.4	—	E950.9	E962.1	E980.9
plant NEC	989.5	E905.7	—	E950.9	E962.1	E980.9
marine	989.5	E905.6	—	E950.9	E962.1	E980.9
scorpion	989.5	E905.2	—	E950.9	E962.1	E980.9
snake	989.5	E905.0	—	E950.9	E962.1	E980.9
specified NEC	989.5	E905.8	—	E950.9	E962.1	E980.9
spider	989.5	E905.1	—	E950.9	E962.1	E980.9
wasp	989.5	E905.3	—	E950.9	E962.1	E980.9
Ventolin — *see* Salbutamol sulfate						
Veramon	967.0	E851	E937.0	E950.1	E962.0	E980.1
Veratrum						
album	988.2	E865.4	—	E950.9	E962.1	E980.9
alkaloids	972.6	E858.3	E942.6	E950.4	E962.0	E980.4
viride	988.2	E865.4	—	E950.9	E962.1	E980.9
Verdigris — *see also* Copper	985.8	E866.4	—	E950.9	E962.1	E980.9
Veronal	967.0	E851	E937.0	E950.1	E962.0	E980.1
Veroxil	961.6	E857	E931.6	E950.4	E962.0	E980.4
Versidyne	965.7	E850.7	E935.7	E950.0	E962.0	E980.0
Viagra	972.5	E858.3	E942.5	E950.4	E962.0	E980.4
Vienna						
green	985.1	E866.3	—	E950.8	E962.1	E980.8
insecticide	985.1	E863.4	—	E950.6	E962.1	E980.7
red	989.89	E866.8	—	E950.9	E962.1	E980.9
pharmaceutical dye	977.4	E858.8	E947.4	E950.4	E962.0	E980.4
Vinbarbital, vinbarbitone	967.0	E851	E937.0	E950.1	E962.0	E980.1
Vinblastine	963.1	E858.1	E933.1	E950.4	E962.0	E980.4
Vincristine	963.1	E858.1	E933.1	E950.4	E962.0	E980.4
Vinesthene, vinethene	968.2	E855.1	E938.2	E950.4	E962.0	E980.4
Vinyl						
bital	967.0	E851	E937.0	E950.1	E962.0	E980.1
ether	968.2	E855.1	E938.2	E950.4	E962.0	E980.4
Vioform	961.3	E857	E931.3	E950.4	E962.0	E980.4
topical	976.0	E858.7	E946.0	E930.4	E962.0	E980.4
Viomycin	960.6	E856	E930.6	E950.4	E962.0	E980.4
Viosterol	963.5	E858.1	E933.5	E950.4	E962.0	E980.4
Viper (venom)	989.5	E905.0	—	E950.9	E962.1	E980.9
Viprynium (embonate)	961.6	E857	E931.6	E950.4	E962.0	E980.4
Virugon	961.7	E857	E931.7	E950.4	E962.0	E980.4
Visine	976.5	E858.7	E946.5	E950.4	E962.0	E980.4
Vitamins NEC	963.5	E858.1	E933.5	E950.4	E962.0	E980.4
B_{12}	964.1	E858.2	E934.1	E950.4	E962.0	E980.4
hematopoietic	964.1	E858.2	E934.1	E950.4	E962.0	E980.4
K	964.3	E858.2	E934.3	E950.4	E962.0	E980.4
Vleminckx's solution	976.4	E858.7	E946.4	E950.4	E962.0	E980.4
Voltaren — *see* Diclofenac sodium						
Warfarin (potassium) (sodium)	964.2	E858.2	E934.2	E950.4	E962.0	E980.4
rodenticide	989.4	E863.7	—	E950.6	E962.1	E980.7
Wasp (sting)	989.5	E905.3	—	E950.9	E962.1	E980.9
Water						
balance agents NEC	974.5	E858.5	E944.5	E950.4	E962.0	E980.4
gas	987.1	E868.1	—	E951.8	E962.2	E981.8
incomplete combustion of — see Carbon, monoxide, fuel, utility						
hemlock	988.2	E865.4	—	E950.9	E962.1	E980.9
moccasin (venom)	989.5	E905.0	—	E950.9	E962.1	E980.9

		External Cause (E-Code)				
	Poisoning	Accident	Therapeutic Use	Suicide Attempt	Assault	Undetermined
Wax (paraffin) (petroleum)	981	E862.3	—	E950.9	E962.1	E980.9
automobile	989.89	E861.2	—	E950.9	E962.1	E980.9
floor	981	E862.0	—	E950.9	E962.1	E980.9
Weed killers NEC	989.4	E863.5	—	E950.6	E962.1	E980.7
Welldorm	967.1	E852.0	E937.1	E950.2	E962.0	E980.2
White						
arsenic — see Arsenic						
hellebore	988.2	E865.4	—	E950.9	E962.1	E980.9
lotion (keratolytic)	976.4	E858.7	E946.4	E950.4	E962.0	E980.4
spirit	981	E862.0	—	E950.9	E962.1	E980.9
Whitewashes	989.89	E861.6	—	E950.9	E962.1	E980.9
Whole blood	964.7	E858.2	E934.7	E950.4	E962.0	E980.4
Wild						
black cherry	988.2	E865.4	—	E950.9	E962.1	E980.9
poisonous plants NEC	988.2	E865.4	—	E950.9	E962.1	E980.9
Window cleaning fluid	989.89	E861.3	—	E950.9	E962.1	E980.9
Wintergreen (oil)	976.3	E858.7	E946.3	E950.4	E962.0	E980.4
Witch hazel	976.2	E858.7	E946.2	E950.4	E962.0	E980.4
Wood						
alcohol	980.1	E860.2	—	E950.9	E962.1	E980.9
spirit	980.1	E860.2	—	E950.9	E962.1	E980.9
Woorali	975.2	E858.6	E945.2	E950.4	E962.0	E980.4
Wormseed, American	961.6	E857	E931.6	E950.4	E962.0	E980.4
Xanthine diuretics	974.1	E858.5	E944.1	E950.4	E962.0	E980.4
Xanthocillin	960.0	E856	E930.0	E950.4	E962.0	E980.4
Xanthotoxin	976.3	E858.7	E946.3	E950.4	E962.0	E980.4
Xigris	964.2	E858.2	E934.2	E950.4	E962.0	E980.4
Xylene (liquid) (vapor)	982.0	E862.4	—	E950.9	E962.1	E980.9
Xylocaine (infiltration) (topical)	968.5	E855.2	E938.5	E950.4	E962.0	E980.4
nerve block (peripheral) (plexus)	968.6	E855.2	E938.6	E950.4	E962.0	E980.4
spinal	968.7	E855.2	E938.7	E950.4	E962.0	E980.4
Xylol (liquid) (vapor)	982.0	E862.4	—	E950.9	E962.1	E980.9
Xylometazoline	971.2	E855.5	E941.2	E950.4	E962.0	E980.4
Yellow						
fever vaccine	979.3	E858.8	E949.3	E950.4	E962.0	E980.4
jasmine	988.2	E865.4	—	E950.9	E962.1	E980.9
Yew	988.2	E865.4	—	E950.9	E962.1	E980.9
Zactane	965.7	E850.7	E935.7	E950.0	E962.0	E980.0
Zaroxolyn	974.3	E858.5	E944.3	E950.4	E962.0	E980.4
Zephiran (topical)	976.0	E858.7	E946.0	E950.4	E962.0	E980.4
ophthalmic preparation	976.5	E858.7	E946.5	E950.4	E962.0	E980.4
Zerone	980.1	E860.2	—	E950.9	E962.1	E980.9
Zinc (compounds) (fumes) (salts) (vapor) NEC	985.8	E866.4	—	E950.9	E962.1	E980.9
anti-infectives	976.0	E858.7	E946.0	E950.4	E962.0	E980.4
antivaricose	972.7	E858.3	E942.7	E950.4	E962.0	E980.4
bacitracin	976.0	E858.7	E946.0	E950.4	E962.0	E980.4
chloride	976.2	E858.7	E946.2	E950.4	E962.0	E980.4
gelatin	976.3	E858.7	E946.3	E950.4	E962.0	E980.4
oxide	976.3	E858.7	E946.3	E950.4	E962.0	E980.4
peroxide	976.0	E858.7	E946.0	E950.4	E962.0	E980.4
pesticides	985.8	E863.4	—	E950.6	E962.1	E980.7
phosphide (rodenticide)	985.8	E863.7	—	E950.6	E962.1	E980.7
stearate	976.3	E858.7	E946.3	E950.4	E962.0	E980.4
sulfate (antivaricose)	972.7	E858.3	E942.7	E950.4	E962.0	E980.4
ENT agent	976.6	E858.7	E946.6	E950.4	E962.0	E980.4
ophthalmic solution	976.5	E858.7	E946.5	E950.4	E962.0	E980.4
topical NEC	976.0	E858.7	E946.0	E950.4	E962.0	E980.4
undecylenate	976.0	E858.7	E946.0	E950.4	E962.0	E980.4
Zovant	964.2	E858.2	E934.2	E950.4	E962.0	E980.4
Zoxazolamine	968.0	E855.1	E938.0	E950.4	E962.0	E980.4
Zygadenus (venenosus)	988.2	E865.4	—	E950.9	E962.1	E980.9

SECTION 3

Alphabetic Index to External Causes of Injury and Poisoning (E Code)

This section contains the index to the codes which classify environmental events, circumstances, and other conditions as the cause of injury and other adverse effects. Where a code from the section Supplementary Classification of External Causes of Injury and Poisoning (E800-E999) is applicable, it is intended that the E code shall be used in addition to a code from the main body of the classification, Chapters 1 to 17.

The alphabetic index to the E codes is organized by main terms which describe the accident, circumstance, event, or specific agent which caused the injury or other adverse effect.

Note — Transport accidents (E800-E848) include accidents involving:

aircraft and spacecraft (E840-E845)

watercraft (E830-E838)

motor vehicle (E810-E825)

railway (E800-E807)

other road vehicles (E826-E829)

For definitions and examples related to transport accidents — see Volume 1 code categories E800-E848.

The fourth-digit subdivisions for use with categories E800-E848 to identify the injured person are found at the end of this section.

For identifying the place in which an accident or poisoning occurred (circumstances classifiable to categories E850-E869 and E880-E928) — see the listing in this section under "Accident, occurring."

See the Table of Drugs and Chemicals (Section 2 of this volume) for identifying the specific agent involved in drug overdose or a wrong substance given or taken in error, and for intoxication or poisoning by a drug or other chemical substance.

The specific adverse effect, reaction, or localized toxic effect to a correct drug or substance properly administered in therapeutic or prophylactic dosage should be classified according to the nature of the adverse effect (e.g., allergy, dermatitis, tachycardia) listed in Section 1 of this volume.

A

Abandonment
causing exposure to weather conditions — *see* Exposure
child, with intent to injure or kill E968.4
helpless person, infant, newborn E904.0
with intent to injure or kill E968.4
Abortion, criminal, injury to child E968.8
Abuse (alleged) (suspected)
adult
by
child E967.4
ex-partner E967.3
ex-spouse E967.3
father E967.0
grandchild E967.7
grandparent E967.6
mother E967.2
non-related caregiver E967.8
other relative E967.7
other specified person E967.1
partner E967.3
sibling E967.5
spouse E967.3
stepfather E967.0
stepmother E967.2
unspecified person E967.9
child
by
boyfriend of parent or guardian E967.0
child E967.4
father E967.0
female partner of parent or guardian E967.2
girlfriend of parent or guardian E967.2
grandchild E967.7
grandparent E967.6
male partner of parent or guardian E967.0
mother E967.2
non-related caregiver E967.8
other relative E967.7
other specified person(s) E967.1
sibling E967.5
stepfather E967.0
stepmother E967.2
unspecified person E967.9
Accident (to) E928.9
aircraft (in transit) (powered) E841 ☑
at landing, take-off E840 ☑
due to, caused by cataclysm — *see* categories E908 ☑, E909 ☑
late effect of E929.1
unpowered (*see also* Collision, aircraft, unpowered) E842 ☑
while alighting, boarding E843 ☑
amphibious vehicle
on
land — *see* Accident, motor vehicle
water — *see* Accident, watercraft
animal-drawn vehicle NEC E827 ☑
animal, ridden NEC E828 ☑
balloon (*see also* Collision, aircraft, unpowered) E842 ☑
caused by, due to
abrasive wheel (metalworking) E919.3
animal NEC E906.9
being ridden (in sport or transport) E828 ☑
avalanche NEC E909.2
band saw E919.4
bench saw E919.4
bore, earth-drilling or mining (land) (seabed) E919.1
bulldozer E919.7

Accident (to) — *continued*
caused by, due to — *continued*
cataclysmic
earth surface movement or eruption E909.9
storm E908.9
chain
hoist E919.2
agricultural operations E919.0
mining operations E919.1
saw E920.1
circular saw E919.4
cold (excessive) (*see also* Cold, exposure to) E901.9
combine E919.0
conflagration — *see* Conflagration
corrosive liquid, substance NEC E924.1
cotton gin E919.8
crane E919.2
agricultural operations E919.0
mining operations E919.1
cutting or piercing instrument (*see also* Cut) E920.9
dairy equipment E919.8
derrick E919.2
agricultural operations E919.0
mining operations E919.1
drill E920.1
earth (land) (seabed) E919.1
hand (powered) E920.1
not powered E920.4
metalworking E919.3
woodworking E919.4
earth(-)
drilling machine E919.1
moving machine E919.7
scraping machine E919.7
electric
current (*see also* Electric shock) E925.9
motor (*see also* Accident, machine, by type of machine)
current (of) — *see* Electric shock
elevator (building) (grain) E919.2
agricultural operations E919.0
mining operations E919.1
environmental factors NEC E928.9
excavating machine E919.7
explosive material (*see also* Explosion) E923.9
farm machine E919.0
firearm missile — *see* Shooting
fire, flames (*see also* Fire)
conflagration — *see* Conflagration
forging (metalworking) machine E919.3
forklift (truck) E919.2
agricultural operations E919.0
mining operations E919.1
gas turbine E919.5
harvester E919.0
hay derrick, mower, or rake E919.0
heat (excessive) (*see also* Heat) E900.9
hoist (*see also* Accident, caused by, due to, lift) E919.2
chain — *see* Accident, caused by, due to, chain
shaft E919.1
hot
liquid E924.0
caustic or corrosive E924.1
object (not producing fire or flames) E924.8
substance E924.9
caustic or corrosive E924.1
liquid (metal) NEC E924.0
specified type NEC E924.8
human bite E928.3
ignition — *see* Ignition
internal combustion engine E919.5
landslide NEC E909.2

Accident (to) — *continued*
caused by, due to — *continued*
lathe (metalworking) E919.3
turnings E920.8
woodworking E919.4
lift, lifting (appliances) E919.2
agricultural operations E919.0
mining operations E919.1
shaft E919.1
lightning NEC E907
machine, machinery (*see also* Accident, machine)
drilling, metal E919.3
manufacturing, for manufacture of
beverages E919.8
clothing E919.8
foodstuffs E919.8
paper E919.8
textiles E919.8
milling, metal E919.3
moulding E919.4
power press, metal E919.3
printing E919.8
rolling mill, metal E919.3
sawing, metal E919.3
specified type NEC E919.8
spinning E919.8
weaving E919.8
natural factor NEC E928.9
overhead plane E919.4
plane E920.4
overhead E919.4
powered
hand tool NEC E920.1
saw E919.4
hand E920.1
printing machine E919.8
pulley (block) E919.2
agricultural operations E919.0
mining operations E919.1
transmission E919.6
radial saw E919.4
radiation — *see* Radiation
reaper E919.0
road scraper E919.7
when in transport under its own power — *see* categories E810-E825 ☑
roller coaster E919.8
sander E919.4
saw E920.4
band E919.4
bench E919.4
chain E920.1
circular E919.4
hand E920.4
powered E920.1
powered, except hand E919.4
radial E919.4
sawing machine, metal E919.3
shaft
hoist E919.1
lift E919.1
transmission E919.6
shears E920.4
hand E920.4
powered E920.1
mechanical E919.3
shovel E920.4
steam E919.7
spinning machine E919.8
steam (*see also* Burning, steam)
engine E919.5
shovel E919.7
thresher E919.0
thunderbolt NEC E907
tractor E919.0
when in transport under its own power — *see* categories E810-E825 ☑
transmission belt, cable, chain, gear, pinion, pulley, shaft E919.6
turbine (gas) (water driven) E919.5
under-cutter E919.1

Accident (to) — *continued*
caused by, due to — *continued*
weaving machine E919.8
winch E919.2
agricultural operations E919.0
mining operations E919.1
diving E883.0
with insufficient air supply E913.2
glider (hang) (*see also* Collision, aircraft, unpowered) E842 ☑
hovercraft
on
land — *see* Accident, motor vehicle
water — *see* Accident, watercraft
ice yacht (*see also* Accident, vehicle NEC) E848
in
medical, surgical procedure
as, or due to misadventure — *see* Misadventure
causing an abnormal reaction or later complication without mention of misadventure — *see* Reaction, abnormal
kite carrying a person (*see also* Collision, involving aircraft, unpowered) E842 ☑
land yacht (*see also* Accident, vehicle NEC) E848
late effect of — *see* Late effect
launching pad E845 ☑
machine, machinery (*see also* Accident, caused by, due to, by specific type of machine) E919.9
agricultural including animal-powered E919.0
earth-drilling E919.1
earth moving or scraping E919.7
excavating E919.7
involving transport under own power on highway or transport vehicle — *see* categories E810-E825 ☑, E840-E845 ☑
lifting (appliances) E919.2
metalworking E919.3
mining E919.1
prime movers, except electric motors E919.5
electric motors — *see* Accident, machine, by specific type of machine
recreational E919.8
specified type NEC E919.8
transmission E919.6
watercraft (deck) (engine room) (galley) (laundry) (loading) E836 ☑
woodworking or forming E919.4
motor vehicle (on public highway) (traffic) E819 ☑
due to cataclysm — *see* categories E908 ☑, E909 ☑
involving
collision (*see also* Collision, motor vehicle) E812 ☑
nontraffic, not on public highway — *see* categories E820-E825 ☑
not involving collision — *see* categories E816-E819 ☑
nonmotor vehicle NEC E829 ☑
nonroad — *see* Accident, vehicle NEC
road, except pedal cycle, animal-drawn vehicle, or animal being ridden E829 ☑
nonroad vehicle NEC — *see* Accident, vehicle NEC
not elsewhere classifiable involving
cable car (not on rails) E847
on rails E829 ☑
coal car in mine E846

Accident (to) — *continued*
not elsewhere classifiable involving — *continued*
hand truck — *see* Accident, vehicle NEC
logging car E846
sled(ge), meaning snow or ice vehicle E848
tram, mine or quarry E846
truck
mine or quarry E846
self-propelled, industrial E846
station baggage E846
tub, mine or quarry E846
vehicle NEC E848
snow and ice E848
used only on industrial premises E846
wheelbarrow E848
occurring (at) (in)
apartment E849.0
baseball field, diamond E849.4
construction site, any E849.3
dock E849.8
yard E849.3
dormitory E849.7
factory (building) (premises) E849.3
farm E849.1
buildings E849.1
house E849.0
football field E849.4
forest E849.8
garage (place of work) E849.3
private (home) E849.0
gravel pit E849.2
gymnasium E849.4
highway E849.5
home (private) (residential) E849.0
institutional E849.7
hospital E849.7
hotel E849.6
house (private) (residential) E849.0
movie E849.6
public E849.6
institution, residential E849.7
jail E849.7
mine E849.2
motel E849.6
movie house E849.6
office (building) E849.6
orphanage E849.7
park (public) E849.4
mobile home E849.8
trailer E849.8
parking lot or place E849.8
place
industrial NEC E849.3
parking E849.8
public E849.8
specified place NEC E849.5
recreational NEC E849.4
sport NEC E849.4
playground (park) (school) E849.4
prison E849.6
public building NEC E849.6
quarry E849.2
railway
line NEC E849.8
yard E849.3
residence
home (private) E849.0
resort (beach) (lake) (mountain) (seashore) (vacation) E849.4
restaurant E849.6
sand pit E849.2
school (building) (private) (public) (state) E849.6
reform E849.7
riding E849.4
seashore E849.8
resort E849.4
shop (place of work) E849.3
commercial E849.6
skating rink E849.4
sports palace E849.4
stadium E849.4

Accident (to) — *continued*
occurring — *continued*
store E849.6
street E849.5
swimming pool (public) E849.4
private home or garden E849.0
tennis court, public E849.4
theatre, theater E849.6
trailer court E849.8
tunnel E849.8
under construction E849.2
warehouse E849.3
yard
dock E849.3
industrial E849.3
private (home) E849.0
railway E849.3
off-road type motor vehicle (not on public highway) NEC E821 ☑
on public highway — *see* categories E810-E819 ☑
pedal cycle E826 ☑
railway E807 ☑
due to cataclysm — *see* categories E908 ☑, E909 ☑
involving
avalanche E909.2
burning by engine, locomotive, train (*see also* Explosion, railway engine) E803 ☑
collision (*see also* Collision, railway) E800 ☑
derailment (*see also* Derailment, railway) E802 ☑
explosion (*see also* Explosion, railway engine) E803 ☑
fall (*see also* Fall, from, railway rolling stock) E804 ☑
fire (*see also* Explosion, railway engine) E803 ☑
hitting by, being struck by
object falling in, on, from, rolling stock, train, vehicle E806 ☑
rolling stock, train, vehicle E805 ☑
overturning, railway rolling stock, train, vehicle (*see also* Derailment, railway) E802 ☑
running off rails, railway (*see also* Derailment, railway) E802 ☑
specified circumstances NEC E806 ☑
train or vehicle hit by
avalanche E909.2
falling object (earth, rock, tree) E806 ☑
due to cataclysm — *see* categories E908 ☑, E909 ☑
landslide E909.2
roller skate E885.1
scooter (nonmotorized) E885.0
skateboard E885.2
ski(ing) E885.3
jump E884.9
lift or tow (with chair or gondola) E847
snowboard E885.4
snow vehicle, motor driven (not on public highway) E820 ☑
on public highway — *see* categories E810-E819 ☑
spacecraft E845 ☑
specified cause NEC E928.8
street car E829 ☑
traffic NEC E819 ☑
vehicle NEC (with pedestrian) E848
battery powered
airport passenger vehicle E846
truck (baggage) (mail) E846

Accident (to) — *continued*
vehicle — *continued*
powered commercial or industrial (with other vehicle or object within commercial or industrial premises) E846
watercraft E838 ☑
with
drowning or submersion resulting from
accident other than to watercraft E832 ☑
accident to watercraft E830 ☑
injury, except drowning or submersion, resulting from
accident other than to watercraft — *see* categories E833-E838 ☑
accident to watercraft E831 ☑
due to, caused by cataclysm — *see* categories E908 ☑, E909 ☑
machinery E836 ☑
Acid throwing E961
Acosta syndrome E902.0
Aeroneurosis E902.1
Aero-otitis media — *see* Effects of, air pressure
Aerosinusitis — *see* Effects of, air pressure
After-effect, late — *see* Late effect
Air
blast
in
terrorism E979.2
war operations E993
embolism (traumatic) NEC E928.9
in
infusion or transfusion E874.1
perfusion E874.2
sickness E903
Alpine sickness E902.0
Altitude sickness — *see* Effects of, air pressure
Anaphylactic shock, anaphylaxis — *see also* Table of Drugs and Chemicals E947.9
due to bite or sting (venomous) — *see* Bite, venomous
Andes disease E902.0
Apoplexy
heat — *see* Heat
Arachnidism E905.1
Arson E968.0
Asphyxia, asphyxiation
by
chemical
in
terrorism E979.7
war operations E997.2
explosion — *see* Explosion
food (bone) (regurgitated food) (seed) E911
foreign object, except food E912
fumes
in
terrorism (chemical weapons) E979.7
war operations E997.2
gas (*see also* Table of Drugs and Chemicals)
in
terrorism E979.7
war operations E997.2
legal
execution E978
intervention (tear) E972
tear E972
mechanical means (*see also* Suffocation) E913.9
from
conflagration — *see* Conflagration
fire (*see also* Fire) E899
in
terrorism E979.3

Asphyxia, asphyxiation — *continued*
from — *continued*
fire (*see also* Fire) — *continued*
in — *continued*
war operations E990.9
ignition — *see* Ignition
Aspiration
foreign body — *see* Foreign body, aspiration
mucus, not of newborn (with asphyxia, obstruction respiratory passage, suffocation) E912
phlegm (with asphyxia, obstruction respiratory passage, suffocation) E912
vomitus (with asphyxia, obstruction respiratory passage, suffocation) (*see also* Foreign body, aspiration, food) E911
Assassination (attempt) — *see also* Assault E968.9
Assault (homicidal) (by) (in) E968.9
acid E961
swallowed E962.1
air gun E968.6
BB gun E968.6
bite NEC E968.8
of human being E968.7
bomb ((placed in) car or house) E965.8
antipersonnel E965.5
letter E965.7
petrol E965.6
brawl (hand) (fists) (foot) E960.0
burning, burns (by fire) E968.0
acid E961
swallowed E962.1
caustic, corrosive substance E961
swallowed E962.1
chemical from swallowing caustic, corrosive substance NEC E962.1
hot liquid E968.3
scalding E968.3
vitriol E961
swallowed E962.1
caustic, corrosive substance E961
swallowed E962.1
cut, any part of body E966
dagger E966
drowning E964
explosive(s) E965.9
bomb (*see also* Assault, bomb) E965.8
dynamite E965.8
fight (hand) (fists) (foot) E960.0
with weapon E968.9
blunt or thrown E968.2
cutting or piercing E966
firearm — *see* Shooting, homicide
fire E968.0
firearm(s) — *see* Shooting, homicide
garrotting E963
gunshot (wound) — *see* Shooting, homicide
hanging E963
injury NEC E968.9
knife E966
late effect of E969
ligature E963
poisoning E962.9
drugs or medicinals E962.0
gas(es) or vapors, except drugs and medicinals E962.2
solid or liquid substances, except drugs and medicinals E962.1
puncture, any part of body E966
pushing
before moving object, train, vehicle E968.5
from high place E968.1
rape E960.1
scalding E968.3
shooting — *see* Shooting, homicide
sodomy E960.1
stab, any part of body E966

Assault — *continued*
- strangulation E963
- submersion E964
- suffocation E963
- transport vehicle E968.5
- violence NEC E968.9
- vitriol E961
  - swallowed E962.1
- weapon E968.9
  - blunt or thrown E968.2
  - cutting or piercing E966
  - firearm — *see* Shooting, homicide
- wound E968.9
  - cutting E966
  - gunshot — *see* Shooting, homicide
  - knife E966
  - piercing E966
  - puncture E966
  - stab E966

Attack by animal NEC E906.9

Avalanche E909.2
- falling on or hitting
  - motor vehicle (in motion) (on public highway) E909.2
  - railway train E909.2

Aviators' disease E902.1

B

Barotitis, barodontalgia, barosinusitis, barotrauma (otitic) (sinus) — *see* Effects of, air pressure

Battered
- baby or child (syndrome) — *see* Abuse, child; category E967 ☑
- person other than baby or child — *see* Assault

Bayonet wound — *see also* Cut, by bayonet E920.3
- in
  - legal intervention E974
  - terrorism E979.8
  - war operations E995

Bean in nose E912

Bed set on fire NEC E898.0

Beheading (by guillotine)
- homicide E966
- legal execution E978

Bending, injury in E927.8 ▲

Bends E902.0

Bite
- animal NEC E906.5
  - other specified (except arthropod) E906.3
  - venomous NEC E905.9
- arthropod (nonvenomous) NEC E906.4
  - venomous — *see* Sting
- black widow spider E905.1
- cat E906.3
- centipede E905.4
- cobra E905.0
- copperhead snake E905.0
- coral snake E905.0
- dog E906.0
- fer de lance E905.0
- gila monster E905.0
- human being
  - accidental E928.3
  - assault E968.7
- insect (nonvenomous) E906.4
  - venomous — *see* Sting
- krait E905.0
- late effect of — *see* Late effect
- lizard E906.2
  - venomous E905.0
- mamba E905.0
- marine animal
  - nonvenomous E906.3
    - snake E906.2
  - venomous E905.6
    - snake E905.0
- millipede E906.4
  - venomous E905.4
- moray eel E906.3
- rat E906.1
- rattlesnake E905.0
- rodent, except rat E906.3
- serpent — *see* Bite, snake
- shark E906.3
- snake (venomous) E905.0
  - nonvenomous E906.2
  - sea E905.0
- spider E905.1
  - nonvenomous E906.4
- tarantula (venomous) E905.1
- venomous NEC E905.9
  - by specific animal — *see category* E905 ☑
- viper E905.0
- water moccasin E905.0

Blast (air)
- from nuclear explosion E996
- in
  - terrorism E979.2
    - from nuclear explosion E979.5
    - underwater E979.0
  - war operations E993
    - from nuclear explosion E996
    - underwater E992

Blizzard E908.3

Blow E928.9
- by law-enforcing agent, police (on duty) E975
  - with blunt object (baton) (nightstick) (stave) (truncheon) E973

Blowing up — *see also* Explosion E923.9

Brawl (hand) (fists) (foot) E960.0

Breakage (accidental)
- cable of cable car not on rails E847
- ladder (causing fall) E881.0
- part (any) of
  - animal-drawn vehicle E827 ☑
  - ladder (causing fall) E881.0
  - motor vehicle
    - in motion (on public highway) E818 ☑
      - not on public highway E825 ☑
  - nonmotor road vehicle, except animal-drawn vehicle or pedal cycle E829 ☑
  - off-road type motor vehicle (not on public highway) NEC E821 ☑
    - on public highway E818 ☑
  - pedal cycle E826 ☑
  - scaffolding (causing fall) E881.1
  - snow vehicle, motor-driven (not on public highway) E820 ☑
    - on public highway E818 ☑
  - vehicle NEC — *see* Accident, vehicle

Broken
- glass
  - fall on E888.0
  - injury by E920.8
- power line (causing electric shock) E925.1

Bumping against, into (accidentally)
- object (moving) E917.9
  - caused by crowd E917.1
    - with subsequent fall E917.6
  - furniture E917.3
    - with subsequent fall E917.7
  - in
    - running water E917.2
    - sports E917.0
      - with subsequent fall E917.5
  - stationary E917.4
    - with subsequent fall E917.8
- person(s) E917.9
  - with fall E886.9
    - in sports E886.0
  - as, or caused by, a crowd E917.1
    - with subsequent fall E917.6
  - in sports E917.0
    - with fall E886.0

Burning, burns (accidental) (by) (from) (on) E899
- acid (any kind) E924.1
  - swallowed — *see* Table of Drugs and Chemicals
- bedclothes (*see also* Fire, specified NEC) E898.0
- blowlamp (*see also* Fire, specified NEC) E898.1
- blowtorch (*see also* Fire, specified NEC) E898.1
- boat, ship, watercraft — *see* categories E830 ☑, E831 ☑, E837 ☑
- bonfire (controlled) E897
  - uncontrolled E892
- candle (*see also* Fire, specified NEC) E898.1
- caustic liquid, substance E924.1
  - swallowed — *see* Table of Drugs and Chemicals
- chemical E924.1
  - from swallowing caustic, corrosive substance — *see* Table of Drugs and Chemicals
  - in
    - terrorism E979.7
    - war operations E997.2
- cigar(s) or cigarette(s) (*see also* Fire, specified NEC) E898.1
- clothes, clothing, nightdress — *see* Ignition, clothes
  - with conflagration — *see* Conflagration
- conflagration — *see* Conflagration
- corrosive liquid, substance E924.1
  - swallowed — *see* Table of Drugs and Chemicals
- electric current (*see also* Electric shock) E925.9
- fire, flames (*see also* Fire) E899
- flare, Verey pistol E922.8
- heat
  - from appliance (electrical) E924.8
  - in local application, or packing during medical or surgical procedure E873.5
- homicide (attempt) (*see also* Assault, burning) E968.0
- hot
  - liquid E924.0
    - caustic or corrosive E924.1
  - object (not producing fire or flames) E924.8
  - substance E924.9
    - caustic or corrosive E924.1
    - liquid (metal) NEC E924.0
    - specified type NEC E924.8
  - tap water E924.2
- ignition (*see also* Ignition)
  - clothes, clothing, nightdress (*see also* Ignition, clothes)
    - with conflagration — *see* Conflagration
  - highly inflammable material (benzine) (fat) (gasoline) (kerosene) (paraffin) (petrol) E894
- in
  - terrorism E979.3
    - from nuclear explosion E979.5
    - petrol bomb E979.3
  - war operations (from fire-producing device or conventional weapon) E990.9
    - from nuclear explosion E996
    - petrol bomb E990.0
- inflicted by other person
  - stated as
    - homicidal, intentional (*see also* Assault, burning) E968.0
    - undetermined whether accidental or intentional (*see also* Burn, stated as undetermined whether accidental or intentional) E988.1
- internal, from swallowed caustic, corrosive liquid, substance — *see* Table of Drugs and Chemicals
- lamp (*see also* Fire, specified NEC) E898.1
- late effect of NEC E929.4
- lighter (cigar) (cigarette) (*see also* Fire, specified NEC) E898.1
- lightning E907
- liquid (boiling) (hot) (molten) E924.0
  - caustic, corrosive (external) E924.1
    - swallowed — *see* Table of Drugs and Chemicals
- local application of externally applied substance in medical or surgical care E873.5
- machinery — *see* Accident, machine
- matches (*see also* Fire, specified NEC) E898.1
- medicament, externally applied E873.5
- metal, molten E924.0
- object (hot) E924.8
  - producing fire or flames — *see* Fire
- oven (electric) (gas) E924.8
- pipe (smoking) (*see also* Fire, specified NEC) E898.1
- radiation — *see* Radiation
- railway engine, locomotive, train (*see also* Explosion, railway engine) E803 ☑
- self-inflicted (unspecified whether accidental or intentional) E988.1
  - caustic or corrosive substance NEC E988.7
  - stated as intentional, purposeful E958.1
    - caustic or corrosive substance NEC E958.7
  - stated as undetermined whether accidental or intentional E988.1
    - caustic or corrosive substance NEC E988.7
- steam E924.0
  - pipe E924.8
- substance (hot) E924.9
  - boiling or molten E924.0
  - caustic, corrosive (external) E924.1
    - swallowed — *see* Table of Drugs and Chemicals
- suicidal (attempt) NEC E958.1
  - caustic substance E958.7
  - late effect of E959
- tanning bed E926.2
- therapeutic misadventure
  - overdose of radiation E873.2
- torch, welding (*see also* Fire, specified NEC) E898.1
- trash fire (*see also* Burning, bonfire) E897
- vapor E924.0
- vitriol E924.1
- x-rays E926.3
  - in medical, surgical procedure — *see* Misadventure, failure, in dosage, radiation

Butted by animal E906.8

C

Cachexia, lead or saturnine E866.0
- from pesticide NEC (*see also* Table of Drugs and Chemicals) E863.4

Caisson disease E902.2

Capital punishment (any means) E978

Car sickness E903

Casualty (not due to war) NEC E928.9
- terrorism E979.8
- war (*see also* War operations) E995

Cat
- bite E906.3
- scratch E906.8

Cataclysmic (any injury)
- earth surface movement or eruption E909.9
  - specified type NEC E909.8
- storm or flood resulting from storm E908.9
  - specified type NEC E909.8

Catching fire — *see* Ignition

- **Caught**
  - between
    - objects (moving) (stationary and moving) E918
      - and machinery — *see* Accident, machine
  - by cable car, not on rails E847
  - in
    - machinery (moving parts of) — *see*, Accident, machine
    - object E918
- **Cave-in** (causing asphyxia, suffocation (by pressure)) — *see also* Suffocation, due to, cave-in E913.3
  - with injury other than asphyxia or suffocation E916
    - with asphyxia or suffocation (*see also* Suffocation, due to, cave-in) E913.3
  - struck or crushed by E916
    - with asphyxia or suffocation (*see also* Suffocation, due to, cave-in) E913.3
- **Change(s) in air pressure** — *see also* Effects of, air pressure
  - sudden, in aircraft (ascent) (descent) (causing aeroneurosis or aviators' disease) E902.1
- **Chilblains** E901.0
  - due to manmade conditions E901.1
- **Choking** (on) (any object except food or vomitus) E912
  - apple E911
  - bone E911
  - food, any type (regurgitated) E911
  - mucus or phlegm E912
  - seed E911
- **Civil insurrection** — *see* War operations
- **Cloudburst** E908.8
- **Cold, exposure to** (accidental) (excessive) (extreme) (place) E901.9
  - causing chilblains or immersion foot E901.0
  - due to
    - manmade conditions E901.1
    - specified cause NEC E901.8
    - weather (conditions) E901.0
  - late effect of NEC E929.5
  - self-inflicted (undetermined whether accidental or intentional) E988.3
    - suicidal E958.3
  - suicide E958.3
- **Colic, lead, painter's, or saturnine** — *see* category E866 ☑
- **Collapse**
  - building E916
    - burning (uncontrolled fire) E891.8
      - in terrorism E979.3
      - private E890.8
  - dam E909.3
  - due to heat — *see* Heat
  - machinery — *see* Accident, machine or vehicle
  - man-made structure E909.3
  - postoperative NEC E878.9
  - structure
    - burning (uncontrolled fire) NEC E891.8
      - in terrorism E979.3
- **Collision** (accidental)

> *Note — In the case of collisions between different types of vehicles, persons and objects, priority in classification is in the following order:*
>
> *Aircraft*
>
> *Watercraft*
>
> *Motor vehicle*
>
> *Railway vehicle*
>
> *Pedal cycle*
>
> *Animal-drawn vehicle*
>
> *Animal being ridden*
>
> *Streetcar or other nonmotor road vehicle*
>
> *Other vehicle*
>
> *Pedestrian or person using pedestrian conveyance*
>
> *Object (except where falling from or set in motion by vehicle etc. listed above)*
>
> *In the listing below, the combinations are listed only under the vehicle etc. having priority. For definitions, see Supplementary Classification of External Causes of Injury and Poisoning (E800-E999).*

  - aircraft (with object or vehicle) (fixed) (movable) (moving) E841 ☑
    - with
      - person (while landing, taking off) (without accident to aircraft) E844 ☑
    - powered (in transit) (with unpowered aircraft) E841 ☑
      - while landing, taking off E840 ☑
    - unpowered E842 ☑
    - while landing, taking off E840 ☑
  - animal being ridden (in sport or transport) E828 ☑
    - and
      - animal (being ridden) (herded) (unattended) E828 ☑
      - nonmotor road vehicle, except pedal cycle or animal-drawn vehicle E828 ☑
      - object (fallen) (fixed) (movable) (moving) not falling from or set in motion by vehicle of higher priority E828 ☑
      - pedestrian (conveyance or vehicle) E828 ☑
  - animal-drawn vehicle E827 ☑
    - and
      - animal (being ridden) (herded) (unattended) E827 ☑
      - nonmotor road vehicle, except pedal cycle E827 ☑
      - object (fallen) (fixed) (movable) (moving) not falling from or set in motion by vehicle of higher priority E827 ☑
      - pedestrian (conveyance or vehicle) E827 ☑
      - streetcar E827 ☑
  - motor vehicle (on public highway) (traffic accident) E812 ☑
    - after leaving, running off, public highway (without antecedent collision) (without re-entry) E816 ☑
      - with antecedent collision on public highway — *see* categories E810-E815 ☑
      - with re-entrance collision with another motor vehicle E811 ☑
    - and
      - abutment (bridge) (overpass) E815 ☑

Collision — *continued*
  - motor vehicle — *continued*
    - and — *continued*
      - animal (herded) (unattended) E815 ☑
        - carrying person, property E813 ☑
      - animal-drawn vehicle E813 ☑
      - another motor vehicle (abandoned) (disabled) (parked) (stalled) (stopped) E812 ☑
        - with, involving re-entrance (on same roadway) (across median strip) E811 ☑
      - any object, person, or vehicle off the public highway resulting from a noncollision motor vehicle nontraffic accident E816 ☑
      - avalanche, fallen or not moving E815 ☑
        - falling E909.2
      - boundary fence E815 ☑
      - culvert E815 ☑
      - fallen
        - stone E815 ☑
        - tree E815 ☑
      - guard post or guard rail E815 ☑
      - inter-highway divider E815 ☑
      - landslide, fallen or not moving E815 ☑
        - moving E909 ☑
      - machinery (road) E815 ☑
      - nonmotor road vehicle NEC E813 ☑
      - object (any object, person, or vehicle off the public highway resulting from a noncollision motor vehicle nontraffic accident) E815 ☑
        - off, normally not on, public highway resulting from a noncollision motor vehicle traffic accident E816 ☑
      - pedal cycle E813 ☑
      - pedestrian (conveyance) E814 ☑
      - person (using pedestrian conveyance) E814 ☑
      - post or pole (lamp) (light) (signal) (telephone) (utility) E815 ☑
      - railway rolling stock, train, vehicle E810 ☑
      - safety island E815 ☑
      - street car E813 ☑
      - traffic signal, sign, or marker (temporary) E815 ☑
      - tree E815 ☑
      - tricycle E813 ☑
      - wall of cut made for road E815 ☑
    - due to cataclysm — *see* categories E908 ☑, E909 ☑
    - not on public highway, nontraffic accident E822 ☑
      - and
        - animal (carrying person, property) (herded) (unattended) E822 ☑
        - animal-drawn vehicle E822 ☑
        - another motor vehicle (moving), except off-road motor vehicle E822 ☑
          - stationary E823 ☑
        - avalanche, fallen, not moving E823 ☑
          - moving E909.2
        - landslide, fallen, not moving E823 ☑
          - moving E909.2

Collision — *continued*
  - motor vehicle — *continued*
    - not on public highway, nontraffic accident — *continued*
      - and — *continued*
        - nonmotor vehicle (moving) E822 ☑
          - stationary E823 ☑
        - object (fallen) (normally) (fixed) (movable but not in motion) (stationary) E823 ☑
          - moving, except when falling from, set in motion by, aircraft or cataclysm E822 ☑
        - pedal cycle (moving) E822 ☑
          - stationary E823 ☑
        - pedestrian (conveyance) E822 ☑
        - person (using pedestrian conveyance) E822 ☑
        - railway rolling stock, train, vehicle (moving) E822 ☑
          - stationary E823 ☑
        - road vehicle (any) (moving) E822 ☑
          - stationary E823 ☑
        - tricycle (moving) E822 ☑
          - stationary E823 ☑
  - off-road type motor vehicle (not on public highway) E821 ☑
    - and
      - animal (being ridden) (-drawn vehicle) E821 ☑
      - another off-road motor vehicle, except snow vehicle E821 ☑
      - other motor vehicle, not on public highway E821 ☑
      - other object or vehicle NEC, fixed or movable, not set in motion by aircraft, motor vehicle on highway, or snow vehicle, motor driven E821 ☑
      - pedal cycle E821 ☑
      - pedestrian (conveyance) E821 ☑
      - railway train E821 ☑
    - on public highway — *see* Collision, motor vehicle
  - pedal cycle E826 ☑
    - and
      - animal (carrying person, property) (herded) (unherded) E826 ☑
      - animal-drawn vehicle E826 ☑
      - another pedal cycle E826 ☑
      - nonmotor road vehicle E826 ☑
      - object (fallen) (fixed) (movable) (moving) not falling from or set in motion by aircraft, motor vehicle, or railway train NEC E826 ☑
      - pedestrian (conveyance) E826 ☑
      - person (using pedestrian conveyance) E826 ☑
      - street car E826 ☑
  - pedestrian(s) (conveyance) E917.9
    - with fall E886.9
      - in sports E886.0
    - and
      - crowd, human stampede E917.1
        - with subsequent fall E917.6
      - furniture E917.3
        - with subsequent fall E917.7
      - machinery — *see* Accident, machine
      - object (fallen) (moving) not falling from NEC, fixed or set in motion by any vehicle classifiable to E800-E848 ☑, E917.9

Collision — *continued*
pedestrian(s) — *continued*
and — *continued*
object not falling from, fixed or set in motion by any vehicle classifiable to — *continued*
with subsequent fall E917.6
caused by a crowd E917.1
with subsequent fall E917.6
furniture E917.3
with subsequent fall E917.7
in
running water E917.2
with drowning or submersion — *see* Submersion
sports E917.0
with subsequent fall E917.5
stationary E917.4
with subsequent fall E917.8
vehicle, nonmotor, nonroad E848
in
running water E917.2
with drowning or submersion — *see* Submersion
sports E917.0
with fall E886.0
person(s) (using pedestrian conveyance) (*see also* Collision, pedestrian) E917.9
railway (rolling stock) (train) (vehicle) (with (subsequent) derailment, explosion, fall or fire) E800 ☑
with antecedent derailment E802 ☑
and
animal (carrying person) (herded) (unattended) E801 ☑
another railway train or vehicle E800 ☑
buffers E801 ☑
fallen tree on railway E801 ☑
farm machinery, nonmotor (in transport) (stationary) E801 ☑
gates E801 ☑
nonmotor vehicle E801 ☑
object (fallen) (fixed) (movable) (moving) not falling from, set in motion by, aircraft or motor vehicle NEC E801 ☑
pedal cycle E801 ☑
pedestrian (conveyance) E805 ☑
person (using pedestrian conveyance) E805 ☑
platform E801 ☑
rock on railway E801 ☑
street car E801 ☑
snow vehicle, motor-driven (not on public highway) E820 ☑
and
animal (being ridden) (-drawn vehicle) E820 ☑
another off-road motor vehicle E820 ☑
other motor vehicle, not on public highway E820 ☑
other object or vehicle NEC, fixed or movable, not set in motion by aircraft or motor vehicle on highway E820 ☑
pedal cycle E820 ☑
pedestrian (conveyance) E820 ☑
railway train E820 ☑
on public highway — *see* Collision, motor vehicle
street car(s) E829 ☑

Collision — *continued*
street car(s) — *continued*
and
animal, herded, not being ridden, unattended E829 ☑
nonmotor road vehicle NEC E829 ☑
object (fallen) (fixed) (movable) (moving) not falling from or set in motion by aircraft, animal-drawn vehicle, animal being ridden, motor vehicle, pedal cycle, or railway train E829 ☑
pedestrian (conveyance) E829 ☑
person (using pedestrian conveyance) E829 ☑
vehicle
animal-drawn — *see* Collision, animal-drawn vehicle
motor — *see* Collision, motor vehicle
nonmotor
nonroad E848
and
another nonmotor, nonroad vehicle E848
object (fallen) (fixed) (movable) (moving) not falling from or set in motion by aircraft, animal-drawn vehicle, animal being ridden, motor vehicle, nonmotor road vehicle, pedal cycle, railway train, or streetcar E848
road, except animal being ridden, animal-drawn vehicle, or pedal cycle E829 ☑
and
animal, herded, not being ridden, unattended E829 ☑
another nonmotor road vehicle, except animal being ridden, animal-drawn vehicle, or pedal cycle E829 ☑
object (fallen) (fixed) (movable) (moving) not falling from or set in motion by, aircraft, animal-drawn vehicle, animal being ridden, motor vehicle, pedal cycle, or railway train E829 ☑
pedestrian (conveyance) E829 ☑
person (using pedestrian conveyance) E829 ☑
vehicle, nonmotor, nonroad E829 ☑
watercraft E838 ☑
and
person swimming or water skiing E838 ☑
causing
drowning, submersion E830 ☑
injury except drowning, submersion E831 ☑
Combustion, spontaneous — *see* Ignition
Complication of medical or surgical procedure or treatment
as an abnormal reaction — *see* Reaction, abnormal
delayed, without mention of misadventure — *see* Reaction, abnormal
due to misadventure — *see* Misadventure

Compression
divers' squeeze E902.2
trachea by
food E911
foreign body, except food E912
Conflagration
building or structure, except private dwelling (barn) (church) (convalescent or residential home) (factory) (farm outbuilding) (hospital) (hotel) (institution) (educational) (domitory) (residential) (school) (shop) (store) (theater) E891.9
with or causing (injury due to)
accident or injury NEC E891.9
specified circumstance NEC E891.8
burns, burning E891.3
carbon monoxide E891.2
fumes E891.2
polyvinylchloride (PVC) or similar material E891.1
smoke E891.2
causing explosion E891.0
in terrorism E979.3
not in building or structure E892
private dwelling (apartment) (boarding house) (camping place) (caravan) (farmhouse) (home (private)) (house) (lodging house) (private garage) (rooming house) (tenement) E890.9
with or causing (injury due to)
accident or injury NEC E890.9
specified circumstance NEC E890.8
burns, burning E890.3
carbon monoxide E890.2
fumes E890.2
polyvinylchloride (PVC) or similar material E890.1
smoke E890.2
causing explosion E890.0
Constriction, external
caused by
hair E928.4
other object E928.5
Contact with
dry ice E901.1
liquid air, hydrogen, nitrogen E901.1
Cramp(s)
Heat — *see* Heat
swimmers (*see also* category E910) E910.2
not in recreation or sport E910.3
Cranking (car) (truck) (bus) (engine), injury by E917.9
Crash
aircraft (in transit) (powered) E841 ☑
at landing, take-off E840 ☑
in
terrorism E979.1
war operations E994
on runway NEC E840 ☑
stated as
homicidal E968.8
suicidal E958.6
undetermined whether accidental or intentional E988.6
unpowered E842 ☑
glider E842 ☑
motor vehicle (*see also* Accident, motor vehicle)
homicidal E968.5
suicidal E958.5
undetermined whether accidental or intentional E988.5
Crushed (accidentally) E928.9
between
boat(s), ship(s), watercraft (and dock or pier) (without accident to watercraft) E838 ☑

Crushed — *continued*
between — *continued*
boat(s), ship(s), watercraft — *continued*
after accident to, or collision, watercraft E831 ☑
objects (moving) (stationary and moving) E918
by
avalanche NEC E909.2
boat, ship, watercraft after accident to, collision, watercraft E831 ☑
cave-in E916
with asphyxiation or suffocation (*see also* Suffocation, due to, cave-in) E913.3
crowd, human stampede E917.1
falling
aircraft (*see also* Accident, aircraft) E841 ☑
in
terrorism E979.1
war operations E994
earth, material E916
with asphyxiation or suffocation (*see also* Suffocation, due to, cave-in) E913.3
object E916
on ship, watercraft E838 ☑
while loading, unloading watercraft E838 ☑
landslide NEC E909.2
lifeboat after abandoning ship E831 ☑
machinery — *see* Accident, machine
railway rolling stock, train, vehicle (part of) E805 ☑
street car E829 ☑
vehicle NEC — *see* Accident, vehicle NEC
in
machinery — *see* Accident, machine
object E918
transport accident — *see* categories E800-E848 ☑
late effect of NEC E929.9
Cut, cutting (any part of body) (accidental) E920.9
by
arrow E920.8
axe E920.4
bayonet (*see also* Bayonet wound) E920.3
blender E920.2
broken glass E920.8
following fall E888.0
can opener E920.4
powered E920.2
chisel E920.4
circular saw E919.4
cutting or piercing instrument (*see also* category) E920 ☑
following fall E888.0
late effect of E929.8
dagger E920.3
dart E920.8
drill — *see* Accident, caused by drill
edge of stiff paper E920.8
electric
beater E920.2
fan E920.2
knife E920.2
mixer E920.2
fork E920.4
garden fork E920.4
hand saw or tool (not powered) E920.4
powered E920.1
hedge clipper E920.4
powered E920.1
hoe E920.4

Cut, cutting — *continued*
by — *continued*
ice pick E920.4
knife E920.3
electric E920.2
lathe turnings E920.8
lawn mower E920.4
powered E920.0
riding E919.8
machine — *see* Accident, machine
meat
grinder E919.8
slicer E919.8
nails E920.8
needle E920.4
hypodermic E920.5
object, edged, pointed, sharp — *see* category E920 ☑
following fall E888.0
paper cutter E920.4
piercing instrument (*see also* category) E920 ☑
late effect of E929.8
pitchfork E920.4
powered
can opener E920.2
garden cultivator E920.1
riding E919.8
hand saw E920.1
hand tool NEC E920.1
hedge clipper E920.1
household appliance or implement E920.2
lawn mower (hand) E920.0
riding E919.8
rivet gun E920.1
staple gun E920.1
rake E920.4
saw
circular E919.4
hand E920.4
scissors E920.4
screwdriver E920.4
sewing machine (electric) (powered) E920.2
not powered E920.4
shears E920.4
shovel E920.4
spade E920.4
splinters E920.8
sword E920.3
tin can lid E920.8
wood slivers E920.8
homicide (attempt) E966
inflicted by other person
stated as
intentional, homicidal E966
undetermined whether accidental or intentional E986
late effect of NEC E929.8
legal
execution E978
intervention E974
self-inflicted (unspecified whether accidental or intentional) E986
stated as intentional, purposeful E956
stated as undetermined whether accidental or intentional E986
suicidal (attempt) E956
terrorism E979.8
war operations E995
Cyclone E908.1

D

Death due to injury occurring one year or more previous — *see* Late effect
Decapitation (accidental circumstances) NEC E928.9
homicidal E966
legal execution (by guillotine) E978
Deprivation — *see also* Privation
homicidal intent E968.4
Derailment (accidental)
railway (rolling stock) (train) (vehicle) (with subsequent collision) E802 ☑
with
collision (antecedent) (*see also* Collision, railway) E800 ☑
explosion (subsequent) (without antecedent collision) E802 ☑
antecedent collision E803 ☑
fall (without collision (antecedent)) E802 ☑
fire (without collision (antecedent)) E802 ☑
street car E829 ☑
Descent
parachute (voluntary) (without accident to aircraft) E844 ☑
due to accident to aircraft — *see* categories E840-E842 ☑
Desertion
child, with intent to injure or kill E968.4
helpless person, infant, newborn E904.0
with intent to injure or kill E968.4
Destitution — *see* Privation
Disability, late effect or sequela of injury — *see* Late effect
Disease
Andes E902.0
aviators' E902.1
caisson E902.2
range E902.0
Divers' disease, palsy, paralysis, squeeze E902.0
Dog bite E906.0
Dragged by
cable car (not on rails) E847
on rails E829 ☑
motor vehicle (on highway) E814 ☑
not on highway, nontraffic accident E825 ☑
street car E829 ☑
Drinking poison (accidental) — *see* Table of Drugs and Chemicals
Drowning — *see* Submersion
Dust in eye E914

E

Earth falling (on) (with asphyxia or suffocation (by pressure)) — *see also* Suffocation, due to, cave-in E913.3
as, or due to, a cataclysm (involving any transport vehicle) — *see* categories E908 ☑, E909 ☑
not due to cataclysmic action E913.3
motor vehicle (in motion) (on public highway) E813 ☑
not on public highway E825 ☑
nonmotor road vehicle NEC E829 ☑
pedal cycle E826 ☑
railway rolling stock, train, vehicle E806 ☑
street car E829 ☑
struck or crushed by E916
with asphyxiation or suffocation E913.3
with injury other than asphyxia, suffocation E916
Earthquake (any injury) E909.0
Effect(s) (adverse) of
air pressure E902.9
at high altitude E902.9
in aircraft E902.1
residence or prolonged visit (causing conditions classifiable to E902.0) E902.0
due to
diving E902.2
specified cause NEC E902.8
in aircraft E902.1
Effect(s) (adverse) of — *continued*
cold, excessive (exposure to) (*see also* Cold, exposure to) E901.9
heat (excessive) (*see also* Heat) E900.9
hot
place — *see* Heat
weather E900.0
insulation — *see* Heat
late — *see* Late effect of
motion E903
nuclear explosion or weapon
in
terrorism E979.5
war operations (blast) (fireball) (heat) (radiation) (direct) (secondary) E996
radiation — *see* Radiation
terrorism, secondary E979.9
travel E903
Electric shock, electrocution (accidental) (from exposed wire, faulty appliance, high voltage cable, live rail, open socket) (by) (in) E925.9
appliance or wiring
domestic E925.0
factory E925.2
farm (building) E925.8
house E925.0
home E925.0
industrial (conductor) (control apparatus) (transformer) E925.2
outdoors E925.8
public building E925.8
residential institution E925.8
school E925.8
specified place NEC E925.8
caused by other person
stated as
intentional, homicidal E968.8
undetermined whether accidental or intentional E988.4
electric power generating plant, distribution station E925.1
electroshock gun (taser) (stun gun) ● E925.8 ●
caused by other person E968.8 ●
legal intervention E975 ●
stated as accidental E925.8 ●
stated as intentional E968.8 ●
due to legal intervention E975 ●
stated as intentional self-harm (suicidal attempt) E958.4 ●
stated as undetermined whether accidental or intentional E988.4 ●
suicide (attempt) E958.4 ●
homicidal (attempt) E968.8
legal execution E978
lightning E907
machinery E925.9
domestic E925.0
factory E925.2
farm E925.8
home E925.0
misadventure in medical or surgical procedure
in electroshock therapy E873.4
self-inflicted (undetermined whether accidental or intentional) E988.4
stated as intentional E958.4
stated as undetermined whether accidental or intentional E988.4
suicidal (attempt) E958.4
transmission line E925.1
Electrocution — *see* Electric shock
Embolism
air (traumatic) NEC — *see* Air, embolism
Encephalitis
lead or saturnine E866.0
from pesticide NEC E863.4
Entanglement
in
bedclothes, causing suffocation E913.0
wheel of pedal cycle E826 ☑
Entry of foreign body, material, any — *see* Foreign body
Execution, legal (any method) E978
Exertion, excessive physical, from prolonged activity E927.2 ●
Exhaustion
cold — *see* Cold, exposure to
due to excessive exertion E927.8 ▲
heat — *see* Heat
Explosion (accidental) (in) (of) (on) E923.9
acetylene E923.2
aerosol can E921.8
aircraft (in transit) (powered) E841 ☑
at landing, take-off E840 ☑
in
terrorism E979.1
war operations E994
unpowered E842 ☑
air tank (compressed) (in machinery) E921.1
anesthetic gas in operating theatre E923.2
automobile tire NEC E921.8
causing transport accident — *see* categories E810-E825 ☑
blasting (cap) (materials) E923.1
boiler (machinery), not on transport vehicle E921.0
steamship — *see* Explosion, watercraft
bomb E923.8
in
terrorism E979.2
war operations E993
after cessation of hostilities E998
atom, hydrogen or nuclear E996
injury by fragments from E991.9
antipersonnel bomb E991.3
butane E923.2
caused by
other person
stated as
intentional, homicidal — *see* Assault, explosive
undetermined whether accidental or homicidal E985.5
coal gas E923.2
detonator E923.1
dynamite E923.1
explosive (material) NEC E923.9
gas(es) E923.2
missile E923.8
in
terrorism E979.2
war operations E993
injury by fragments from E991.9
antipersonnel bomb E991.3
used in blasting operations E923.1
fire-damp E923.2
fireworks E923.0
gas E923.2
cylinder (in machinery) E921.1
pressure tank (in machinery) E921.1
gasoline (fumes) (tank) not in moving motor vehicle E923.2
grain store (military) (munitions) E923.8
grenade E923.8
in
terrorism E979.2
war operations E993

- **Explosion** — *continued*
  - grenade — *continued*
    - in — *continued*
      - war operations — *continued*
        - injury by fragments from E991.9
  - homicide (attempt) — *see* Assault, explosive
  - hot water heater, tank (in machinery) E921.0
  - in mine (of explosive gases) NEC E923.2
  - late effect of NEC E929.8
  - machinery (*see also* Accident, machine)
    - pressure vessel — *see* Explosion, pressure vessel
  - methane E923.2
  - missile E923.8
    - in
      - terrorism E979.2
      - war operations E993
        - injury by fragments from E991.9
  - motor vehicle (part of)
    - in motion (on public highway) E818 ☑
      - not on public highway E825 ☑
  - munitions (dump) (factory) E923.8
    - in
      - terrorism E979.2
      - war operations E993
  - of mine E923.8
    - in
      - terrorism
        - at sea or in harbor E979.0
        - land E979.2
        - marine E979.0
      - war operations
        - after cessation of hostilities E998
        - at sea or in harbor E992
        - land E993
          - after cessation of hostilities E998
          - injury by fragments from E991.9
        - marine E992
  - own weapons
    - in
      - terrorism (*see also* Suicide) E979.2
      - war operations E993
        - injury by fragments from E991.9
          - antipersonnel bomb E991.3
  - pressure
    - cooker E921.8
    - gas tank (in machinery) E921.1
    - vessel (in machinery) E921.9
      - on transport vehicle — *see* categories E800-E848 ☑
      - specified type NEC E921.8
  - propane E923.2
  - railway engine, locomotive, train (boiler) (with subsequent collision, derailment, fall) E803 ☑
    - with
      - collision (antecedent) (*see also* Collision, railway) E800 ☑
      - derailment (antecedent) E802 ☑
      - fire (without antecedent collision or derailment) E803 ☑
  - secondary fire resulting from — *see* Fire
  - self-inflicted (unspecified whether accidental or intentional) E985.5
    - stated as intentional, purposeful E955.5
  - shell (artillery) E923.8
    - in
      - terrorism E979.2
      - war operations E993
        - injury by fragments from E991.9

- **Explosion** — *continued*
  - stated as undetermined whether caused accidentally or purposely inflicted E985.5
  - steam or water lines (in machinery) E921.0
  - suicide (attempted) E955.5
  - terrorism — *see* Terrorism, explosion
  - torpedo E923.8
    - in
      - terrorism E979.0
      - war operations E992
  - transport accident — *see* categories E800-E848
  - war operations — *see* War operations, explosion
  - watercraft (boiler) E837 ☑
    - causing drowning, submersion (after jumping from watercraft) E830 ☑
- **Exposure** (weather) (conditions) (rain) (wind) E904.3
  - with homicidal intent E968.4
  - environmental
    - to
      - algae bloom E928.6
      - blue-green algae bloom E928.6
      - brown tide E928.6
      - cyanobacteria bloom E928.6
      - Florida red tide E928.6
      - harmful alage
        - and toxins E928.6
        - bloom E928.6
      - ▶pfiesteria◀ piscicida E928.6
      - red tide E928.6
  - excessive E904.3
    - cold (*see also* Cold, exposure to) E901.9
      - self-inflicted — *see* Cold, exposure to, self-inflicted
    - heat (*see also* Heat) E900.9
  - helpless person, infant, newborn due to abandonment or neglect E904.0
  - noise E928.1
  - prolonged in deep-freeze unit or refrigerator E901.1
  - radiation — *see* Radiation
  - resulting from transport accident — *see* categories E800-E848 ☑
  - smoke from, due to
    - fire — *see* Fire
    - tobacco, second-hand E869.4
  - vibration E928.2

F

- **Fallen on by**
  - animal (horse) (not being ridden) E906.8
    - being ridden (in sport or transport) E828 ☑
- **Fall, falling** (accidental) E888.9
  - building E916
    - burning E891.8
      - private E890.8
  - down
    - escalator E880.0
    - ladder E881.0
      - in boat, ship, watercraft E833 ☑
    - staircase E880.9
    - stairs, steps — *see* Fall, from, stairs
  - earth (with asphyxia or suffocation (by pressure)) (*see also* Earth, falling) E913.3
  - from, off
    - aircraft (at landing, take-off) (in-transit) (while alighting, boarding) E843 ☑
      - resulting from accident to aircraft — *see* categories E840-E842 ☑
    - animal (in sport or transport) E828 ☑
    - animal-drawn vehicle E827 ☑
    - balcony E882

- **Fall, falling** — *continued*
  - from, off — *continued*
    - bed E884.4
    - bicycle E826 ☑
    - boat, ship, watercraft (into water) E832 ☑
      - after accident to, collision, fire on E830 ☑
        - and subsequently struck by (part of) boat E831 ☑
      - and subsequently struck by (part of) while alighting, boat E831 ☑
      - burning, crushed, sinking E830 ☑
        - and subsequently struck by (part of) boat E831 ☑
    - bridge E882
    - building E882
      - burning (uncontrolled fire) E891.8
        - in terrorism E979.3
      - private E890.8
    - bunk in boat, ship, watercraft E834 ☑
      - due to accident to watercraft E831 ☑
    - cable car (not on rails) E847
      - on rails E829 ☑
    - car — *see* Fall from motor vehicle
    - chair E884.2
    - cliff E884.1
    - commode E884.6
    - curb (sidewalk) E880.1
    - elevation aboard ship E834 ☑
      - due to accident to ship E831 ☑
    - embankment E884.9
    - escalator E880.0
    - fire escape E882
    - flagpole E882
    - furniture NEC E884.5
    - gangplank (into water) (*see also* Fall, from, boat) E832 ☑
      - to deck, dock E834 ☑
    - hammock on ship E834 ☑
      - due to accident to watercraft E831 ☑
    - haystack E884.9
    - heelies E885.1 ●
    - high place NEC E884.9
      - stated as undetermined whether accidental or intentional — *see* Jumping, from, high place
    - horse (in sport or transport) E828 ☑
    - in-line skates E885.1
    - ladder E881.0
      - in boat, ship, watercraft E833 ☑
        - due to accident to watercraft E831 ☑
    - machinery (*see also* Accident, machine)
      - not in operation E884.9
    - motor vehicle (in motion) (on public highway) E818 ☑
      - not on public highway E825 ☑
        - stationary, except while alighting, boarding, entering, leaving E884.9
        - while alighting, boarding, entering, leaving E824 ☑
      - stationary, except while alighting, boarding, entering, leaving E884.9
      - while alighting, boarding, entering, leaving, except off-road type motor vehicle E817 ☑
        - off-road type — *see* Fall, from, off-road type motor vehicle

- **Fall, falling** — *continued*
  - from, off — *continued*
    - nonmotor road vehicle (while alighting, boarding) NEC E829 ☑
      - stationary, except while alighting, boarding, entering, leaving E884.9
    - off road type motor vehicle (not on public highway) NEC E821 ☑
      - on public highway E818 ☑
        - while alighting, boarding, entering, leaving E817 ☑
      - snow vehicle — *see* Fall from snow vehicle, motor-driven
    - one
      - deck to another on ship E834 ☑
        - due to accident to ship E831 ☑
      - level to another NEC E884.9
        - boat, ship, or watercraft E834 ☑
          - due to accident to watercraft E831 ☑
    - pedal cycle E826 ☑
    - playground equipment E884.0
    - railway rolling stock, train, vehicle (while alighting, boarding) E804 ☑
      - with
        - collision (*see also* Collision, railway) E800 ☑
        - derailment (*see also* Derailment, railway) E802 ☑
        - explosion (*see also* Explosion, railway engine) E803 ☑
    - rigging (aboard ship) E834 ☑
      - due to accident to watercraft E831 ☑
    - roller skates E885.1
    - scaffolding E881.1
    - scooter (nonmotorized) E885.0
    - sidewalk (curb) E880.1
      - moving E885.9
    - skateboard E885.2
    - skis E885.3
    - snowboard E885.4
    - snow vehicle, motor-driven (not on public highway) E820 ☑
      - on public highway E818 ☑
        - while alighting, boarding, entering, leaving E817 ☑
    - stairs, steps E880.9
      - boat, ship, watercraft E833 ☑
        - due to accident to watercraft E831 ☑
      - motor bus, motor vehicle — *see* Fall, from, motor vehicle, while alighting, boarding
      - street car E829 ☑
    - stationary vehicle NEC E884.9
    - stepladder E881.0
    - street car (while boarding, alighting) E829 ☑
      - stationary, except while boarding or alighting E884.9
    - structure NEC E882
      - burning (uncontrolled fire) E891.8
        - in terrorism E979.3
    - table E884.9
    - toilet E884.6
    - tower E882
    - tree E884.9
    - turret E882
    - vehicle NEC (*see also* Accident, vehicle NEC)
      - stationary E884.9
    - viaduct E882
    - wall E882
    - wheelchair E884.3
    - wheelies E885.1 ●

Fall, falling — *continued*
  from, off — *continued*
    window E882
  in, on
    aircraft (at landing, take-off) (in-transit) E843 ☑
      resulting from accident to aircraft — *see* categories E840-E842 ☑
    boat, ship, watercraft E835 ☑
      due to accident to watercraft E831 ☑
      one level to another NEC E834 ☑
      on ladder, stairs E833 ☑
    cutting or piercing instrument or machine E888.0
    deck (of boat, ship, watercraft) E835 ☑
      due to accident to watercraft E831 ☑
    escalator E880.0
    gangplank E835 ☑
    glass, broken E888.0
    knife E888.0
    ladder E881.0
      in boat, ship, watercraft E833 ☑
        due to accident to watercraft E831 ☑
    object
      edged, pointed or sharp E888.0
      other E888.1
    pitchfork E888.0
    railway rolling stock, train, vehicle (while alighting, boarding) E804 ☑
      with
        collision (*see also* Collision, railway) E800 ☑
        derailment (*see also* Derailment, railway) E802 ☑
        explosion (see also Explosion, railway engine) E803 ☑
    scaffolding E881.1
    scissors E888.0
    staircase, stairs, steps (*see also* Fall, from, stairs) E880.9
    street car E829 ☑
    water transport (*see also* Fall, in, boat) E835 ☑
  into
    cavity E883.9
    dock E883.9
      from boat, ship, watercraft (*see also* Fall, from, boat) E832 ☑
    hold (of ship) E834 ☑
      due to accident to watercraft E831 ☑
    hole E883.9
    manhole E883.2
    moving part of machinery — *see* Accident, machine
    opening in surface NEC E883.9
    pit E883.9
    quarry E883.9
    shaft E883.9
    storm drain E883.2
    tank E883.9
    water (with drowning or submersion) E910.9
    well E883.1
  late effect of NEC E929.3
  object (*see also* Hit by, object, falling) E916
  other E888.8
  over
    animal E885.9
    cliff E884.1
    embankment E884.9
    small object E885.9
  overboard (*see also* Fall, from, boat) E832 ☑
  resulting in striking against object E888.1

Fall, falling — *continued*
  resulting in striking against object — *continued*
    sharp E888.0
  rock E916
  same level NEC E888.9
    aircraft (any kind) E843 ☑
      resulting from accident to aircraft — *see* categories E840-E842 ☑
    boat, ship, watercraft E835 ☑
      due to accident to, collision, watercraft E831 ☑
    from
      collision, pushing, shoving, by or with other person(s) E886.9
        as, or caused by, a crowd E917.6
        in sports E886.0
      in-line skates E885.1
      roller skates E885.1
      scooter (nonmotorized) E885.0
      skateboard E885.2
      slipping stumbling, tripping E885 ☑
      snowboard E885.4
  snowslide E916
    as avalanche E909.2
  stone E916
  through
    hatch (on ship) E834 ☑
      due to accident to watercraft E831 ☑
    roof E882
    window E882
  timber E916
  while alighting from, boarding, entering, leaving
    aircraft (any kind) E843 ☑
    motor bus, motor vehicle — *see* Fall, from, motor vehicle, while alighting, boarding
    nonmotor road vehicle NEC E829 ☑
    railway train E804 ☑
    street car E829 ☑
Fell or jumped from high place, so stated — *see* Jumping, from, high place
Felo-de-se — *see also* Suicide E958.9
Fever
  heat — *see* Heat
  thermic — *see* Heat
Fight (hand) (fist) (foot) — *see also* Assault, fight E960.0
Fire (accidental) (caused by great heat from appliance (electrical), hot object or hot substance) (secondary, resulting from explosion) E899
  conflagration — *see* Conflagration
  controlled, normal (in brazier, fireplace, furnace, or stove) (charcoal) (coal) (coke) (electric) (gas) (wood)
    bonfire E897
    brazier, not in building or structure E897
    in building or structure, except private dwelling (barn) (church) (convalescent or residential home) (factory) (farm outbuilding) (hospital) (hotel) (institution (educational) (dormitory) (residential)) (private garage) (school) (shop) (store) (theatre) E896
    in private dwelling (apartment) (boarding house) (camping place) (caravan) (farmhouse) (home (private)) (house) (lodging house) (rooming house) (tenement) E895
    not in building or structure E897
    trash E897
  forest (uncontrolled) E892

Fire, hot object or hot substance — *continued*
  grass (uncontrolled) E892
  hay (uncontrolled) E892
  homicide (attempt) E968.0
    late effect of E969
  in, of, on, starting in E892
    aircraft (in transit) (powered) E841 ☑
      at landing, take-off E840 ☑
      stationary E892
      unpowered (balloon) (glider) E842 ☑
    balloon E842 ☑
    boat, ship, watercraft — *see* categories E830 ☑, E831 ☑, E837 ☑
    building or structure, except private dwelling (barn) (church) (convalescent or residential home) (factory) (farm outbuilding) (hospital) (hotel) (institution (educational) (dormitory) (residential)) (school) (shop) (store) (theatre) (*see also* Conflagration, building or structure, except private dwelling) E891.9
    forest (uncontrolled) E892
    glider E842 ☑
    grass (uncontrolled) E892
    hay (uncontrolled) E892
    lumber (uncontrolled) E892
    machinery — *see* Accident, machine
    mine (uncontrolled) E892
    motor vehicle (in motion) (on public highway) E818 ☑
      not on public highway E825 ☑
      stationary E892
    prairie (uncontrolled) E892
    private dwelling (apartment) (boarding house) (camping place) (caravan) (farmhouse) (home (private)) (house) (lodging house) (private garage) (rooming house) (tenement) (*see also* Conflagration, private dwelling) E890.9
    railway rolling stock, train, vehicle (*see also* Explosion, railway engine) E803 ☑
      stationary E892
    room NEC E898.1
    street car (in motion) E829 ☑
      stationary E892
    terrorism (by fire-producing device) E979.3
      fittings or furniture (burning building) (uncontrolled fire) E979.3
      from nuclear explosion E979.5
    transport vehicle, stationary NEC E892
    tunnel (uncontrolled) E892
    war operations (by fire-producing device or conventional weapon) E990.9
      from nuclear explosion E996
      petrol bomb E990.0
  late effect of NEC E929.4
  lumber (uncontrolled) E892
  mine (uncontrolled) E892
  prairie (uncontrolled) E892
  self-inflicted (unspecified whether accidental or intentional) E988.1
    stated as intentional, purposeful E958.1
  specified NEC E898.1
    with
      conflagration — *see* Conflagration
      ignition (of)
        clothing — *see* Ignition, clothes

Fire, hot object or hot substance — *continued*
  specified — *continued*
    with — *continued*
      ignition — *continued*
        highly inflammable material (benzine) (fat) (gasoline) (kerosene) (paraffin) (petrol) E894
  started by other person
    stated as
      with intent to injure or kill E968.0
      undetermined whether or not with intent to injure or kill E988.1
  suicide (attempted) E958.1
    late effect of E959
  tunnel (uncontrolled) E892
Fireball effects from nuclear explosion
  in
    terrorism E979.5
    war operations E996
Fireworks (explosion) E923.0
Flash burns from explosion — *see also* Explosion E923.9
Flood (any injury) (resulting from storm) E908.2
  caused by collapse of dam or manmade structure E909.3
Forced landing (aircraft) E840 ☑
Foreign body, object or material (entrance into) (accidental)
  air passage (causing injury) E915
    with asphyxia, obstruction, suffocation E912
      food or vomitus E911
    nose (with asphyxia, obstruction, suffocation) E912
      causing injury without asphyxia, obstruction, suffocation E915
  alimentary canal (causing injury) (with obstruction) E915
    with asphyxia, obstruction respiratory passage, suffocation E912
      food E911
    mouth E915
      with asphyxia, obstruction, suffocation E912
        food E911
    pharynx E915
      with asphyxia, obstruction, suffocation E912
        food E911
  aspiration (with asphyxia, obstruction respiratory passage, suffocation) E912
    causing injury without asphyxia, obstruction respiratory passage, suffocation E915
    food (regurgitated) (vomited) E911
      causing injury without asphyxia, obstruction respiratory passage, suffocation E915
    mucus (not of newborn) E912
    phlegm E912
  bladder (causing injury or obstruction) E915
  bronchus, bronchi — *see* Foreign body, air passages
  conjunctival sac E914
  digestive system — *see* Foreign body, alimentary canal
  ear (causing injury or obstruction) E915
  esophagus (causing injury or obstruction) (*see also* Foreign body, alimentary canal) E915
  eye (any part) E914
  eyelid E914
  hairball (stomach) (with obstruction) E915
  ingestion — *see* Foreign body, alimentary canal

Foreign body, object or material — *continued*
inhalation — *see* Foreign body, aspiration
intestine (causing injury or obstruction) E915
iris E914
lacrimal apparatus E914
larynx — *see* Foreign body, air passage
late effect of NEC E929.8
lung — *see* Foreign body, air passage
mouth — *see* Foreign body, alimentary canal, mouth
nasal passage — *see* Foreign body, air passage, nose
nose — *see* Foreign body, air passage, nose
ocular muscle E914
operation wound (left in) — *see* Misadventure, foreign object
orbit E914
pharynx — *see* Foreign body, alimentary canal, pharynx
rectum (causing injury or obstruction) E915
stomach (hairball) (causing injury or obstruction) E915
tear ducts or glands E914
trachea — *see* Foreign body, air passage
urethra (causing injury or obstruction) E915
vagina (causing injury or obstruction) E915
Found dead, injured
from exposure (to) — *see* Exposure
on
public highway E819 ☑
railway right of way E807 ☑
Fracture (circumstances unknown or unspecified) E887
due to specified external means — *see* manner of accident
late effect of NEC E929.3
occurring in water transport NEC E835 ☑
Freezing — *see* Cold, exposure to
Frostbite E901.0
due to manmade conditions E901.1
Frozen — *see* Cold, exposure to

G

Garrotting, homicidal (attempted) E963
Gored E906.8
Gunshot wound — *see also* Shooting E922.9

H

Hailstones, injury by E904.3
Hairball (stomach) (with obstruction) E915
Hanged himself — *see also* Hanging, self-inflicted E983.0
Hang gliding E842 ☑
Hanging (accidental) E913.8
caused by other person
in accidental circumstances E913.8
stated as
intentional, homicidal E963
undetermined whether accidental or intentional E983.0
homicide (attempt) E963
in bed or cradle E913.0
legal execution E978
self-inflicted (unspecified whether accidental or intentional) E983.0
in accidental circumstances E913.8
stated as intentional, purposeful E953.0
stated as undetermined whether accidental or intentional E983.0
suicidal (attempt) E953.0
Heat (apoplexy) (collapse) (cramps) (effects of) (excessive) (exhaustion) (fever) (prostration) (stroke) E900.9
due to
manmade conditions (as listed in E900.1, except boat, ship, watercraft) E900.1
weather (conditions) E900.0
from
electric heating appartus causing burning E924.8
nuclear explosion
in
terrorism E979.5
war operations E996
generated in, boiler, engine, evaporator, fire room of boat, ship, watercraft E838 ☑
inappropriate in local application or packing in medical or surgical procedure E873.5
late effect of NEC E989
Hemorrhage
delayed following medical or surgical treatment without mention of misadventure — *see* Reaction, abnormal
during medical or surgical treatment as misadventure — *see* Misadventure, cut
High
altitude, effects E902.9
level of radioactivity, effects — *see* Radiation
pressure effects (*see also* Effects of, air pressure)
from rapid descent in water (causing caisson or divers' disease, palsy, or paralysis) E902.2
temperature, effects — *see* Heat
Hit, hitting (accidental) by
aircraft (propeller) (without accident to aircraft) E844 ☑
unpowered E842 ☑
avalanche E909.2
being thrown against object in or part of
motor vehicle (in motion) (on public highway) E818 ☑
not on public highway E825 ☑
nonmotor road vehicle NEC E829 ☑
street car E829 ☑
boat, ship, watercraft
after fall from watercraft E838 ☑
damaged, involved in accident E831 ☑
while swimming, water skiing E838 ☑
bullet (*see also* Shooting) E922.9
from air gun E922.4
in
terrorism E979.4
war operations E991.2
rubber E991.0
flare, Verey pistol (*see also* Shooting) E922.8
hailstones E904.3
landslide E909.2
law-enforcing agent (on duty) E975
with blunt object (baton) (night stick) (stave) (truncheon) E973
machine — *see* Accident, machine
missile
firearm (*see also* Shooting) E922.9
in
terrorism — *see* Terrorism, missile
war operations — *see* War operations, missile
motor vehicle (on public highway) (traffic accident) E814 ☑
not on public highway, nontraffic accident E822 ☑
nonmotor road vehicle NEC E829 ☑
Hit, hitting by — *continued*
object
falling E916
from, in, on
aircraft E844 ☑
due to accident to aircraft — *see* categories E840-E842 ☑
unpowered E842 ☑
boat, ship, watercraft E838 ☑
due to accident to watercraft E831 ☑
building E916
burning (uncontrolled fire) E891.8
in terrorism E979.3
private E890.8
cataclysmic
earth surface movement or eruption E909.9
storm E908.9
cave-in E916
with asphyxiation or suffocation (*see also* Suffocation, due to, cave-in) E913.3
earthquake E909.0
motor vehicle (in motion) (on public highway) E818 ☑
not on public highway E825 ☑
stationary E916
nonmotor road vehicle NEC E829 ☑
pedal cycle E826 ☑
railway rolling stock, train, vehicle E806 ☑
street car E829 ☑
structure, burning NEC E891.8
vehicle, stationary E916
moving NEC — *see* Striking against, object
projected NEC — *see* Striking against, object
set in motion by
compressed air or gas, spring, striking, throwing — *see* Striking against, object
explosion — *see* Explosion
thrown into, on, or towards
motor vehicle (in motion) (on public highway) E818 ☑
not on public highway E825 ☑
nonmotor road vehicle NEC E829 ☑
pedal cycle E826 ☑
street car E829 ☑
off-road type motor vehicle (not on public highway) E821 ☑
on public highway E814 ☑
other person(s) E917.9
with blunt or thrown object E917.9
in sports E917.0
with subsequent fall E917.5
intentionally, homicidal E968.2
as, or caused by, a crowd E917.1
with subsequent fall E917.6
in sports E917.0
pedal cycle E826 ☑
police (on duty) E975
with blunt object (baton) (nightstick) (stave) (truncheon) E973
railway, rolling stock, train, vehicle (part of) E805 ☑
shot — *see* Shooting
snow vehicle, motor-driven (not on public highway) E820 ☑
on public highway E814 ☑
street car E829 ☑
vehicle NEC — *see* Accident, vehicle NEC
Homicide, homicidal (attempt) (justifiable) — *see also* Assault E968.9
Hot
liquid, object, substance, accident caused by (*see also* Accident, caused by, hot, by type of substance)
late effect of E929.8
place, effects — *see* Heat
weather, effects E900.0
Humidity, causing problem E904.3
Hunger E904.1
resulting from
abandonment or neglect E904.0
transport accident — *see* categories E800-E848 ☑
Hurricane (any injury) E908.0
Hypobarism, hypobaropathy — *see* Effects of, air pressure
Hypothermia — *see* Cold, exposure to

I

Ictus
caloris — *see* Heat
solaris E900.0
Ignition (accidental)
anesthetic gas in operating theatre E923.2
bedclothes
with
conflagration — *see* Conflagration
ignition (of)
clothing — *see* Ignition, clothes
highly inflammable material (benzine) (fat) (gasoline) (kerosene) (paraffin) (petrol) E894
benzine E894
clothes, clothing (from controlled fire) (in building) E893.9
with conflagration — *see* Conflagration
from
bonfire E893.2
highly inflammable material E894
sources or material as listed in E893.8
trash fire E893.2
uncontrolled fire — *see* Conflagration
in
private dwelling E893.0
specified building or structure, except private dwelling E893.1
not in building or structure E893.2
explosive material — *see* Explosion
fat E894
gasoline E894
kerosene E894
material
explosive — *see* Explosion
highly inflammable E894
with conflagration — *see* Conflagration
with explosion E923.2
nightdress — *see* Ignition, clothes
paraffin E894
petrol E894
Immersion — *see* Submersion
Implantation of quills of porcupine E906.8
Inanition (from) E904.9
hunger — *see* Lack of, food
resulting from homicidal intent E968.4
thirst — *see* Lack of, water
Inattention after, at birth E904.0
homicidal, infanticidal intent E968.4
Infanticide — *see also* Assault

Ingestion
- foreign body (causing injury) (with obstruction) — *see* Foreign body, alimentary canal
- poisonous substance NEC — *see* Table of Drugs and Chemicals

Inhalation
- excessively cold substance, manmade E901.1
- foreign body — *see* Foreign body, aspiration
- liquid air, hydrogen, nitrogen E901.1
- mucus, not of newborn (with asphyxia, obstruction respiratory passage, suffocation) E912
- phlegm (with asphyxia, obstruction respiratory passage, suffocation) E912
- poisonous gas — *see* Table of Drugs and Chemicals
- smoke from, due to
  - fire — *see* Fire
  - tobacco, second-hand E869.4
- vomitus (with asphyxia, obstruction respiratory passage, suffocation) E911

Injury, injured (accidental(ly)) NEC E928.9
- by, caused by, from
  - air rifle (BB gun) E922.4
  - animal (not being ridden) NEC E906.9
    - being ridden (in sport or transport) E828 ☑
  - assault (*see also* Assault) E968.9
  - avalanche E909.2
  - bayonet (*see also* Bayonet wound) E920.3
  - being thrown against some part of, or object in
    - motor vehicle (in motion) (on public highway) E818 ☑
      - not on public highway E825 ☑
    - nonmotor road vehicle NEC E829 ☑
    - off-road motor vehicle NEC E821 ☑
    - railway train E806 ☑
    - snow vehicle, motor-driven E820 ☑
    - street car E829 ☑
  - bending E927.8 ▲
  - bite, human E928.3
  - broken glass E920.8
  - bullet — *see* Shooting
  - cave-in (*see also* Suffocation, due to, cave-in) E913.3
    - without asphyxiation or suffocation E916
    - earth surface movement or eruption E909.9
    - storm E908.9
  - cloudburst E908.8
  - cutting or piercing instrument (*see also* Cut) E920.9
  - cyclone E908.1
  - earthquake E909.0
  - earth surface movement or eruption E909.9
  - electric current (*see also* Electric shock) E925.9
  - explosion (*see also* Explosion) E923.9
  - fire — *see* Fire
  - flare, Verey pistol E922.8
  - flood E908.2
  - foreign body — *see* Foreign body
  - hailstones E904.3
  - hurricane E908.0
  - landslide E909.2
  - law-enforcing agent, police, in course of legal intervention — *see* Legal intervention
  - lightning E907

Injury, injured — *continued*
- by, caused by, from — *continued*
  - live rail or live wire — *see* Electric shock
  - machinery (*see also* Accident, machine)
    - aircraft, without accident to aircraft E844 ☑
    - boat, ship, watercraft (deck) (engine room) (galley) (laundry) (loading) E836 ☑
  - missile
    - explosive E923.8
    - firearm — *see* Shooting
    - in
      - terrorism — see Terrorism, missile
      - war operations — *see* War operations, missile
  - moving part of motor vehicle (in motion) (on public highway) E818 ☑
    - not on public highway, nontraffic accident E825 ☑
    - while alighting, boarding, entering, leaving — *see* Fall, from, motor vehicle, while alighting, boarding
  - nail E920.8
  - needle (sewing) E920.4
    - hypodermic E920.5
  - noise E928.1
  - object
    - fallen on
      - motor vehicle (in motion) (on public highway) E818 ☑
        - not on public highway E825 ☑
    - falling — *see* Hit by, object, falling
  - paintball gun E922.5
  - radiation — *see* Radiation
  - railway rolling stock, train, vehicle (part of) E805 ☑
    - door or window E806 ☑
  - rotating propeller, aircraft E844 ☑
  - rough landing of off-road type motor vehicle (after leaving ground or rough terrain) E821 ☑
    - snow vehicle E820 ☑
  - saber (*see also* Wound, saber) E920.3
  - shot — *see* Shooting
  - sound waves E928.1
  - splinter or sliver, wood E920.8
  - straining E927.8 ▲
  - street car (door) E829 ☑
  - suicide (attempt) E958.9
  - sword E920.3
  - terrorism — *see* Terrorism
  - third rail — *see* Electric shock
  - thunderbolt E907
  - tidal wave E909.4
    - caused by storm E908.0
  - tornado E908.1
  - torrential rain E908.2
  - twisting E927.8 ▲
  - vehicle NEC — *see* Accident, vehicle NEC
  - vibration E928.2
  - volcanic eruption E909.1
  - weapon burst, in war operations E993
  - weightlessness (in spacecraft, real or simulated) E928.0
  - wood splinter or sliver E920.8
- due to
  - civil insurrection — *see* War operations
    - occurring after cessation of hostilities E998
  - terrorism — see Terrorism

Injury, injured — *continued*
- due to — *continued*
  - war operations — *see* War operations
    - occurring after cessation of hostilities E998
- homicidal (*see also* Assault) E968.9
- inflicted (by)
  - in course of arrest (attempted), suppression of disturbance, maintenance of order, by law enforcing agents — *see* Legal intervention
  - law-enforcing agent (on duty) — *see* Legal intervention
  - other person
    - stated as
      - accidental E928.9
      - homicidal, intentional — *see* Assault
      - undetermined whether accidental or intentional — *see* Injury, stated as undetermined
  - police (on duty) — *see* Legal intervention
- in, on
  - civil insurrection — *see* War operations
  - fight E960.0
  - parachute descent (voluntary) (without accident to aircraft) E844 ☑
    - with accident to aircraft — *see* categories E840-E842 ☑
  - public highway E819 ☑
  - railway right of way E807 ☑
  - terrorism — *see* Terrorism
  - war operations — *see* War operations
- late effect of E929.9
- purposely (inflicted) by other person(s) — *see* Assault
- self-inflicted (unspecified whether accidental or intentional) E988.9
  - stated as
    - accidental E928.9
    - intentionally, purposely E958.9
- specified cause NEC E928.8
- stated as
  - hanging E983.0
  - knife E986
  - late effect of E989
  - puncture (any part of body) E986
  - shooting — *see* Shooting, stated as undetermined whether accidental or intentional
  - specified means NEC E988.8
  - stab (any part of body) E986
  - strangulation — *see* Suffocation, stated as undetermined whether accidental or intentional
  - submersion E984
  - suffocation — *see* Suffocation, stated as undetermined whether accidental or intentional
  - undetermined whether accidentally or purposely inflicted (by) E988.9
    - cut (any part of body) E986
    - cutting or piercing instrument (classifiable to E920) E986
    - drowning E984
    - explosive(s) (missile) E985.5
    - falling from high place E987.9
      - manmade structure, except residential E987.1
      - natural site E987.2
      - residential premises E987.0
- to child due to criminal abortion E968.8

Insufficient nourishment — *see also* Lack of, food

Insufficient nourishment — *see also* Lack of, food — *continued*
- homicidal intent E968.4

Insulation, effects — *see* Heat

Interruption of respiration by
- food lodged in esophagus E911
- foreign body, except food, in esophagus E912

Intervention, legal — *see* Legal intervention

Intoxication, drug or poison — *see* Table of Drugs and Chemicals

Irradiation — *see* Radiation

J

Jammed (accidentally)
- between objects (moving) (stationary and moving) E918
- in object E918

Jumped or fell from high place, so stated — *see* Jumping, from, high place, stated as
- in undetermined circumstances

Jumping
- before train, vehicle or other moving object (unspecified whether accidental or intentional) E988.0
  - stated as
    - intentional, purposeful E958.0
    - suicidal (attempt) E958.0
- from
  - aircraft
    - by parachute (voluntarily) (without accident to aircraft) E844 ☑
    - due to accident to aircraft — *see* categories E840-E842 ☑
  - boat, ship, watercraft (into water)
    - after accident to, fire on, watercraft E830 ☑
      - and subsequently struck by (part of) boat E831 ☑
    - burning, crushed, sinking E830 ☑
      - and subsequently struck by (part of) boat E831 ☑
    - voluntarily, without accident (to boat) with injury other than drowning or submersion E883.0
  - building (*see also* Jumping, from, high place)
    - burning (uncontrolled fire) E891.8
      - in terrorism E979.3
      - private E890.8
  - cable car (not on rails) E847
    - on rails E829 ☑
  - high place
    - in accidental circumstances or in sport — *see* categories E880-E884 ☑
    - stated as
      - with intent to injure self E957.9
        - man-made structures NEC E957.1
        - natural sites E957.2
        - residential premises E957.0
      - in undetermined circumstances E987.9
        - man-made structures NEC E987.1
        - natural sites E987.2
        - residential premises E987.0
      - suicidal (attempt) E957.9
        - man-made structures NEC E957.1
        - natural sites E957.1
        - residential premises E957.0
  - motor vehicle (in motion) (on public highway) — *see* Fall, from, motor vehicle

- **Jumping** — *continued*
  - from — *continued*
    - nonmotor road vehicle NEC E829 ☑
    - street car E829 ☑
    - structure (*see also* Jumping, from, high place)
      - burning NEC (uncontrolled fire) E891.8
        - in terrorism E979.3
  - into water
    - with injury other than drowning or submersion E883.0
      - drowning or submersion — *see* Submersion
    - from, off, watercraft — *see* Jumping, from, boat
- **Justifiable homicide** — *see* Assault

K

- **Kicked by**
  - animal E906.8
  - person(s) (accidentally) E917.9
    - with intent to injure or kill E960.0
    - as, or caused by a crowd E917.1
      - with subsequent fall E917.6
    - in fight E960.0
    - in sports E917.0
      - with subsequent fall E917.5
- **Kicking against**
  - object (moving) E917.9
    - in sports E917.0
      - with subsequent fall E917.5
    - stationary E917.4
      - with subsequent fall E917.8
  - person — *see* Striking against, person
- **Killed, killing** (accidentally) NEC — *see also* Injury E928.9
  - in
    - action — *see* War operations
    - brawl, fight (hand) (fists) (foot) E960.0
      - by weapon (*see also* Assault)
        - cutting, piercing E966
        - firearm — *see* Shooting, homicide
  - self
    - stated as
      - accident E928.9
      - suicide — *see* Suicide
    - unspecified whether accidental or suicidal E988.9
- **Knocked down** (accidentally) (by) NEC E928.9
  - animal (not being ridden) E906.8
    - being ridden (in sport or transport) E828 ☑
  - blast from explosion (*see also* Explosion) E923.9
  - crowd, human stampede E917.6
  - late effect of — *see* Late effect
  - person (accidentally) E917.9
    - in brawl, fight E960.0
    - in sports E917.5
  - transport vehicle — *see* vehicle involved under Hit by
  - while boxing E917.5

L

- **Laceration NEC** E928.9
- **Lack of**
  - air (refrigerator or closed place), suffocation by E913.2
  - care (helpless person) (infant) (newborn) E904.0
    - homicidal intent E968.4
  - food except as result of transport accident E904.1
    - helpless person, infant, newborn due to
      - abandonment or neglect E904.0
  - water except as result of transport accident E904.2
- **Lack of** — *continued*
  - water except as result of transport accident — *continued*
    - helpless person, infant, newborn due to
      - abandonment or neglect E904.0
- **Landslide** E909.2
  - falling on, hitting
    - motor vehicle (any) (in motion) (on or off public highway) E909.2
    - railway rolling stock, train, vehicle E909.2
- **Late effect of**
  - accident NEC (accident classifiable to E928.9) E929.9
    - specified NEC (accident classifiable to E910–E928.8) E929.8
  - assault E969
  - fall, accidental (accident classifiable to E880–E888) E929.3
  - fire, accident caused by (accident classifiable to E890–E899) E929.4
  - homicide, attempt (any means) E969
  - injury due to terrorism E999.1
  - injury undetermined whether accidentally or purposely inflicted (injury classifiable to E980–E988) E989
  - legal intervention (injury classifiable to E970–E976) E977
  - medical or surgical procedure, test or therapy
    - as, or resulting in, or from
      - abnormal or delayed reaction or complication — *see* Reaction, abnormal
      - misadventure — *see* Misadventure
  - motor vehicle accident (accident classifiable to E810–E825) E929.0
  - natural or environmental factor, accident due to (accident classifiable to E900–E909) E929.5
  - poisoning, accidental (accident classifiable to E850–E858, E860–E869) E929.2
  - suicide, attempt (any means) E959
  - transport accident NEC (accident classifiable to E800–E807, E826–E838, E840–E848) E929.1
  - war operations, injury due to (injury classifiable to E990–E998) E999.0
- **Launching pad accident** E845 ☑
- **Legal**
  - execution, any method E978
  - intervention (by) (injury from) E976
    - baton E973
    - bayonet E974
    - blow E975
    - blunt object (baton) (nightstick) (stave) (truncheon) E973
    - cutting or piercing instrument E974
    - dynamite E971
    - execution, any method E973
    - explosive(s) (shell) E971
    - firearm(s) E970
    - gas (asphyxiation) (poisoning) (tear) E972
    - grenade E971
    - late effect of E977
    - machine gun E970
    - manhandling E975
    - mortar bomb E971
    - nightstick E973
    - revolver E970
    - rifle E970
    - specified means NEC E975
    - stabbing E974
    - stave E973
    - truncheon E973
- **Lifting, injury in** E927.8 ▲
- **Lightning** (shock) (stroke) (struck by) E907
- **Liquid** (noncorrosive) in eye E914
  - corrosive E924.1
- **Loss of control**
  - motor vehicle (on public highway) (without antecedent collision) E816 ☑
    - with
      - antecedent collision on public highway — *see* Collision, motor vehicle
        - involving any object, person or vehicle not on public highway E816 ☑
        - not on public highway, nontraffic accident E825 ☑
          - with antecedent collision — *see* Collision, motor vehicle, not on public highway
        - on public highway — *see* Collision, motor vehicle
  - off-road type motor vehicle (not on public highway) E821 ☑
    - on public highway — *see* Loss of control, motor vehicle
  - snow vehicle, motor-driven (not on public highway) E820 ☑
    - on public highway — *see* Loss of control, motor vehicle
- **Lost at sea** E832 ☑
  - with accident to watercraft E830 ☑
  - in war operations E995
- **Low**
  - pressure, effects — *see* Effects of, air pressure
  - temperature, effects — *see* Cold, exposure to
- **Lying before train, vehicle or other moving object** (unspecified whether accidental or intentional) E988.0
  - stated as intentional, purposeful, suicidal (attempt) E958.0
- **Lynching** — *see also* Assault E968.9

M

- **Malfunction, atomic power plant in water transport** E838 ☑
- **Mangled (accidentally) NEC** E928.9
- **Manhandling** (in brawl, fight) E960.0
  - legal intervention E975
- **Manslaughter** (nonaccidental) — *see* Assault
- **Marble in nose** E912
- **Mauled by animal** E906.8
- **Medical procedure, complication of**
  - delayed or as an abnormal reaction without mention of misadventure — *see* Reaction, abnormal
  - due to or as a result of misadventure — *see* Misadventure
- **Melting of fittings and furniture in burning**
  - in terrorism E979.3
- **Minamata disease** E865.2
- **Misadventure(s) to patient(s) during surgical or medical care** E876.9
  - contaminated blood, fluid, drug or biological substance (presence of agents and toxins as listed in E875) E875.9
    - administered (by) NEC E875.9
      - infusion E875.0
      - injection E875.1
      - specified means NEC E875.2
      - transfusion E875.0
      - vaccination E875.1
  - cut, cutting, puncture, perforation or hemorrhage (accidental) (inadvertent) (inappropriate) (during) E870.9
    - aspiration of fluid or tissue (by puncture or catheterization, except heart) E870.5
- **Misadventure(s) to patient(s) during surgical or medical care** — *continued*
  - cut, cutting, puncture, perforation or hemorrhage — *continued*
    - biopsy E870.8
      - needle (aspirating) E870.5
    - blood sampling E870.5
    - catheterization E870.5
      - heart E870.6
    - dialysis (kidney) E870.2
    - endoscopic examination E870.4
    - enema E870.7
    - infusion E870.1
    - injection E870.3
    - lumbar puncture E870.5
    - needle biopsy E870.5
    - paracentesis, abdominal E870.5
    - perfusion E870.2
    - specified procedure NEC E870.8
    - surgical operation E870.0
    - thoracentesis E870.5
    - transfusion E870.1
    - vaccination E870.3
  - excessive amount of blood or other fluid during transfusion or infusion E873.0
  - failure
    - in dosage E873.9
      - electroshock therapy E873.4
      - inappropriate temperature (too hot or too cold) in local application and packing E873.5
      - infusion
        - excessive amount of fluid E873.0
        - incorrect dilution of fluid E873.1
      - insulin-shock therapy E873.4
      - nonadministration of necessary drug or medicinal E873.6
      - overdose (*see also* Overdose)
        - radiation, in therapy E873.2
      - radiation
        - inadvertent exposure of patient (receiving radiation for test or therapy) E873.3
          - not receiving radiation for test or therapy — *see* Radiation
        - overdose E873.2
      - specified procedure NEC E873.8
      - transfusion
        - excessive amount of blood E873.0
    - mechanical, of instrument or apparatus (during procedure) E874.9
      - aspiration of fluid or tissue (by puncture or catheterization, except of heart) E874.4
      - biopsy E874.8
        - needle (aspirating) E874.4
      - blood sampling E874.4
      - catheterization E874.4
        - heart E874.5
      - dialysis (kidney) E874.2
      - endoscopic examination E874.3
      - enema E874.8
      - infusion E874.1
      - injection E874.8
      - lumbar puncture E874.4
      - needle biopsy E874.4
      - paracentesis, abdominal E874.4
      - perfusion E874.2
      - specified procedure NEC E874.8
      - surgical operation E874.0
      - thoracentesis E874.4
      - transfusion E874.1
      - vaccination E874.8
    - sterile precautions (during procedure) E872.9

Poisoning — *see also* Table of Drugs and Chemicals — *continued*
- legal

Pressure, external, causing asphyxia, suffocation — *see also* Suffocation E913.9

Privation E904.9
- food (*see also* Lack of, food) E904.1
- helpless person, infant, newborn due to abandonment or neglect E904.0
- late effect of NEC E929.5
- resulting from transport accident — *see* categories E800-E848 ☑
- water (*see also* Lack of, water) E904.2

Projected objects, striking against or struck by — *see* Striking against, object

Prolonged stay in
- high altitude (causing conditions as listed in E902.0) E902.0
- weightless environment E928.0

Prostration
- heat — *see* Heat

Pulling, injury in E927.8 ▲

Puncture, puncturing — *see also* Cut E920.9
- by
  - plant thorns or spines E920.8
    - toxic reaction E905.7
      - marine or sea plants E905.6
  - sea-urchin spine E905.6

Pushing (injury in) (overexertion) E927.8 ▲
- by other person(s) (accidental) E917.9
  - with fall E886.9
    - in sports E886.0
  - as, or caused by, a crowd, human stampede E917.1
    - with subsequent fall E917.6
  - before moving vehicle or object
    - stated as
      - intentional, homicidal E968.5
      - undetemined whether accidental or intentional E988.8
  - from
    - high place
      - in accidental circum-stances — *see* categories E880-E884 ☑
      - stated as
        - intentional, homicidal E968.1
        - undetermined whether accidental or intentional E987.9
          - man-made structure, except residential E987.1
          - natural site E987.2
          - residential E987.0
    - motor vehicle (*see also* Fall, from, motor vehicle) E818 ☑
      - stated as
        - intentional, homicidal E968.5
        - undetermined whether accidental or intentional E988.8
  - in sports E917.0
    - with fall E886.0

R

Radiation (exposure to) E926.9
- abnormal reaction to medical test or therapy E879.2
- arc lamps E926.2
- atomic power plant (malfunction) NEC E926.9
  - in water transport E838 ☑
- electromagnetic, ionizing E926.3
- gamma rays E926.3

Radiation — *continued*
- in
  - terrorism (from or following nuclear explosion) (direct) (secondary) E979.5
    - laser E979.8
  - war operations (from or following nuclear explosion) (direct) (secondary) E996
    - laser(s) E997.0
  - water transport E838 ☑
- inadvertent exposure of patient (receiving test or therapy) E873.3
- infrared (heaters and lamps) E926.1
  - excessive heat E900.1
- ionized, ionizing (particles, artificially accelerated) E926.8
  - electromagnetic E926.3
- isotopes, radioactive — *see* Radiation, radioactive isotopes
- laser(s) E926.4
  - in
    - terrorism E979.8
    - war operations E997.0
  - misadventure in medical care — *see* Misadventure, failure, in dosage, radiation
- late effect of NEC E929.8
  - excessive heat from — *see* Heat
- light sources (visible) (ultraviolet) E926.2
- misadventure in medical or surgical procedure — *see* Misadventure, failure, in dosage, radiation
- overdose (in medical or surgical procedure) E873.2
- radar E926.0
- radioactive isotopes E926.5
  - atomic power plant malfunction E926.5
    - in water transport E838 ☑
  - misadventure in medical or surgical treatment — *see* Misadventure, failure, in dosage, radiation
- radiobiologicals — *see* Radiation, radioactive isotopes
- radiofrequency E926.0
- radiopharmaceuticals — *see* Radiation, radioactive isotopes
- radium NEC E926.9
- sun E926.2
  - excessive heat from E900.0
- tanning bed E926.2
- welding arc or torch E926.2
  - excessive heat from E900.1
- x-rays (hard) (soft) E926.3
  - misadventure in medical or surgical treatment — *see* Misadventure, failure, in dosage, radiation

Rape E960.1

Reaction, abnormal to or following (medical or surgical procedure) E879.9
- amputation (of limbs) E878.5
- anastomosis (arteriovenous) (blood vessel) (gastrojejunal) (skin) (tendon) (natural, artificial material, tissue) E878.2
  - external stoma, creation of E878.3
- aspiration (of fluid) E879.4
  - tissue E879.8
- biopsy E879.8
- blood
  - sampling E879.7
  - transfusion
    - procedure E879.8
- bypass — *see* Reaction, abnormal, anastomosis
- catheterization
  - cardiac E879.0
  - urinary E879.6
- colostomy E878.3
- cystostomy E878.3
- dialysis (kidney) E879.1

Reaction, abnormal to or following — *continued*
- drugs or biologicals — *see* Table of Drugs and Chemicals
- duodenostomy E878.3
- electroshock therapy E879.3
- formation of external stoma E878.3
- gastrostomy E878.3
- graft — *see* Reaction, abnormal, anastomosis
- hypothermia E879.8
- implant, implantation (of)
  - artificial
    - internal device (cardiac pacemaker) (electrodes in brain) (heart valve prosthesis) (orthopedic) E878.1
    - material or tissue (for anastomosis or bypass) E878.2
      - with creation of external stoma E878.3
  - natural tissues (for anastomosis or bypass) E878.2
    - with creation of external stoma E878.3
    - as transplantion — *see* Reaction, abnormal, transplant
- infusion
  - procedure E879.8
- injection
  - procedure E879.8
    - specific type of procedure) E879.9
- insertion of gastric or duodenal sound E879.5
- insulin-shock therapy E879.3
- lumbar puncture E879.4
- perfusion E879.1
- procedures other than surgical operation (*see also* Reaction, abnormal, by
  - specified procedure NEC E879.8
- radiological procedure or therapy E879.2
- removal of organ (partial) (total) NEC E878.6
  - with
    - anastomosis, bypass or graft E878.2
    - formation of external stoma E878.3
    - implant of artificial internal device E878.1
    - transplant(ation)
      - partial organ E878.4
      - whole organ E878.0
- sampling
  - blood E879.7
  - fluid NEC E879.4
  - tissue E879.8
- shock therapy E879.3
- surgical operation (*see also* Reaction, abnormal, by specified type of operation) E878.9
  - restorative NEC E878.4
    - with
      - anastomosis, bypass or graft E878.2
      - fomation of external stoma E878.3
      - implant(ation) — *see* Reaction, abnormal, implant
      - transplant(ation) — *see* Reaction, abnormal, transplant
  - specified operation NEC E878.8
- thoracentesis E879.4
- transfusion
  - procedure E879.8
- transplant, transplantation (heart) (kidney) (liver) E878.0
  - partial organ E878.4
- ureterostomy E878.3
- vaccination E879.8

Reduction in
- atmospheric pressure (*see also* Effects of, air pressure)
  - while surfacing from
    - deep water diving causing caisson or divers' disease, palsy or paralysis E902.2
    - underground E902.8

Residual (effect) — *see* Late effect

Rock falling on or hitting (accidentally)
- motor vehicle (in motion) (on public highway) E818 ☑
  - not on public highway E825 ☑
- nonmotor road vehicle NEC E829 ☑
- pedal cycle E826 ☑
- person E916
- railway rolling stock, train, vehicle E806 ☑

Running off, away
- animal (being ridden) (in sport or transport) E828 ☑
  - not being ridden E906.8
- animal-drawn vehicle E827 ☑
- rails, railway (*see also* Derailment) E802 ☑
- roadway
  - motor vehicle (without antecedent collision) E816 ☑
    - with
      - antecedent collision — *see* Collision motor vehicle
      - subsequent collision
        - involving any object, person or vehicle not on public highway E816 ☑
        - on public highway E811 ☑
    - nontraffic accident E825 ☑
      - with antecedent collision — *see* Collision, motor vehicle, not on public highway
  - nonmotor road vehicle NEC E829 ☑
  - pedal cycle E826 ☑

Run over (accidentally) (by)
- animal (not being ridden) E906.8
  - being ridden (in sport or transport) E828 ☑
- animal-drawn vehicle E827 ☑
- machinery — *see* Accident, machine
- motor vehicle (on public highway) — *see* Hit by, motor vehicle
- nonmotor road vehicle NEC E829 ☑
- railway train E805 ☑
- street car E829 ☑
- vehicle NEC E848

S

Saturnism E866.0
- from insecticide NEC E863.4

Scald, scalding (accidental) (by) (from) (in) E924.0
- acid — *see* Scald, caustic
- boiling tap water E924.2
- caustic or corrosive liquid, substance E924.1
  - swallowed — *see* Table of Drugs and Chemicals
- homicide (attempt) — *see* Assault, burning
- inflicted by other person
  - stated as
    - intentional or homicidal E968.3
    - undetermined whether accidental or intentional E988.2
- late effect of NEC E929.8
- liquid (boiling) (hot) E924.0
- local application of externally applied substance in medical or surgical care E873.5
- molten metal E924.0
- self-inflicted (unspecified whether accidental or intentional) E988.2

Scald, scalding — *continued*
self-inflicted — *continued*
stated as intentional, purposeful E958.2
stated as undetermined whether accidental or intentional E988.2
steam E924.0
tap water (boiling) E924.2
transport accident — *see* categories E800-E848 ☑
vapor E924.0
Scratch, cat E906.8
Sea
sickness E903
Self-mutilation — *see* Suicide
Sequelae (of)
in
terrorism E999.1
war operations E999.0
Shock
anaphylactic (*see also* Table of Drugs and Chemicals) E947.9
due to
bite (venomous) — *see* Bite, venomous NEC
sting — *see* Sting
electric (*see also* Electric shock) E925.9
from electric appliance or current (*see also* Electric shock) E925.9
Shooting, shot (accidental(ly)) E922.9
air gun E922.4
BB gun E922.4
hand gun (pistol) (revolver) E922.0
himself (*see also* Shooting, self-inflicted) E985.4
hand gun (pistol) (revolver) E985.0
military firearm, except hand gun E985.3
hand gun (pistol) (revolver) E985.0
rifle (hunting) E985.2
military E985.3
shotgun (automatic) E985.1
specified firearm NEC E985.4
Verey pistol E985.4
homicide (attempt) E965.4
air gun E968.6
BB gun E968.6
hand gun (pistol) (revolver) E965.0
military firearm, except hand gun E965.3
hand gun (pistol) (revolver) E965.0
paintball gun E965.4
rifle (hunting) E965.2
military E965.3
shotgun (automatic) E965.1
specified firearm NEC E965.4
Verey pistol E965.4
in
terrorism — *see* Terrorism, shooting
war operations — *see* War operations, shooting
inflicted by other person
in accidental circumstances E922.9
hand gun (pistol) (revolver) E922.0
military firearm, except hand gun E922.3
hand gun (pistol) (revolver) E922.0
rifle (hunting) E922.2
military E922.3
shotgun (automatic) E922.1
specified firearm NEC E922.8
Verey pistol E922.8
stated as
intentional, homicidal E965.4
hand gun (pistol) (revolver) E965.0
military firearm, except hand gun E965.3

Shooting, shot — *continued*
inflicted by other person — *continued*
stated as — *continued*
intentional, homicidal — *continued*
military firearm, except hand gun — *continued*
hand gun (pistol) (revolver) E965.0
paintball gun E965.4
rifle (hunting) E965.2
military E965.3
shotgun (automatic) E965.1
specified firearm E965.4
Verey pistol E965.4
undetermined whether accidental or intentional E985.4
air gun E985.6
BB gun E985.6
hand gun (pistol) (revolver) E985.0
military firearm, except hand gun E985.3
hand gun (pistol) (revolver) E985.0
paintball gun E985.7
rifle (hunting) E985.2
shotgun (automatic) E985.1
specified firearm NEC E985.4
Verey pistol E985.4
legal
execution E978
intervention E970
military firearm, except hand gun E922.3
hand gun (pistol) (revolver) E922.0
paintball gun E922.5
rifle (hunting) E922.2
military E922.3
self-inflicted (unspecified whether accidental or intentional) E985.4
air gun E985.6
BB gun E985.6
hand gun (pistol) (revolver) E985.0
military firearm, except hand gun E985.3
hand gun (pistol) (revolver) E985.0
paintball gun E985.7
rifle (hunting) E985.2
military E985.3
shotgun (automatic) E985.1
specified firearm NEC E985.4
stated as
accidental E922.9
hand gun (pistol) (revolver) E922.0
military firearm, except hand gun E922.3
hand gun (pistol) (revolver) E922.0
paintball gun E922.5
rifle (hunting) E922.2
military E922.3
shotgun (automatic) E922.1
specified firearm NEC E922.8
Verey pistol E922.8
intentional, purposeful E955.4
hand gun (pistol) (revolver) E955.0
military firearm, except hand gun E955.3
hand gun (pistol) (revolver) E955.0
paintball gun E955.7
rifle (hunting) E955.2
military E955.3
shotgun (automatic) E955.1
specified firearm NEC E955.4
Verey pistol E955.4
shotgun (automatic) E922.1
specified firearm NEC E922.8
stated as undetermined whether accidental or intentional E985.4
hand gun (pistol) (revolver) E985.0

Shooting, shot — *continued*
stated as undetermined whether accidental or intentional — *continued*
military firearm, except hand gun E985.3
hand gun (pistol) (revolver) E985.0
paintball gun E985.7
rifle (hunting) E985.2
military E985.3
shotgun (automatic) E985.1
specified firearm NEC E985.4
Verey pistol E985.4
suicidal (attempt) E955.4
air gun E955.6
BB gun E955.6
hand gun (pistol) (revolver) E955.0
military firearm, except hand gun E955.3
hand gun (pistol) (revolver) E955.0
paintball gun E955.7
rifle (hunting) E955.2
military E955.3
shotgun (automatic) E955.1
specified firearm NEC E955.4
Verey pistol E955.4
Verey pistol E922.8
Shoving (accidentally) by other person — *see also* Pushing by other person E917.9
Sickness
air E903
alpine E902.0
car E903
motion E903
mountain E902.0
sea E903
travel E903
Sinking (accidental)
boat, ship, watercraft (causing drowning, submersion) E830 ☑
causing injury except drowning, submersion E831 ☑
Siriasis E900.0
Skydiving E844 ☑
Slashed wrists — *see also* Cut, self-inflicted E986
Slipping (accidental)
on
deck (of boat, ship, watercraft) (icy) (oily) (wet) E835 ☑
ice E885.9
ladder of ship E833 ☑
due to accident to watercraft E831 ☑
mud E885.9
oil E885.9
snow E885.9
stairs of ship E833 ☑
due to accident to watercraft E831 ☑
surface
slippery E885 ☑
wet E885 ☑
Sliver, wood, injury by E920.8
Smothering, smothered — *see also* Suffocation E913.9
Smouldering building or structure in terrorism E979.3
Sodomy (assault) E960.1
Solid substance in eye (any part) or adnexa E914
Sound waves (causing injury) E928.1
Splinter, injury by E920.8
Stab, stabbing E966
accidental — *see* Cut
Starvation E904.1
helpless person, infant, newborn — *see* Lack of food
homicidal intent E968.4
late effect of NEC E929.5
resulting from accident connected with transport — *see* categories E800-E848 ☑

Stepped on
by
animal (not being ridden) E906.8
being ridden (in sport or transport) E828 ☑
crowd E917.1
person E917.9
in sports E917.0
in sports E917.0
Stepping on
object (moving) E917.9
in sports E917.0
with subsequent fall E917.5
stationary E917.4
with subsequent fall E917.8
person E917.9
as, or caused by a crowd E917.1
with subsequent fall E917.6
in sports E917.0
Sting E905.9
ant E905.5
bee E905.3
caterpillar E905.5
coral E905.6
hornet E905.3
insect NEC E905.5
jellyfish E905.6
marine animal or plant E905.6
nematocysts E905.6
scorpion E905.2
sea anemone E905.6
sea cucumber E905.6
wasp E905.3
yellow jacket E905.3
Storm E908.9
specified type NEC E908.8
Straining, injury in E927.8 ▲
Strangling — *see* Suffocation
Strangulation — *see* Suffocation
Strenuous movements (in recreational or other activities) E927.8 ▲
Striking against
bottom (when jumping or diving into water) E883.0
object (moving) E917.9
caused by crowd E917.1
with subsequent fall E917.6
furniture E917.3
with subsequent fall E917.7
in
running water E917.2
with drowning or submersion — *see* Submersion
sports E917.0
with subsequent fall E917.5
stationary E917.4
with subsequent fall E917.8
person(s) E917.9
with fall E886.9
in sports E886.0
as, or caused by, a crowd E917.1
with subsequent fall E917.6
in sports E917.0
with fall E886.0
Stroke
heat — *see* Heat
lightning E907
Struck by — *see also* Hit by
bullet
in
terrorism E979.4
war operations E991.2
rubber E991.0
lightning E907
missile
in terrorism — *see* Terrorism, missile
object
falling
from, in, on
building
burning (uncontrolled fire)
in terrorism E979.3
thunderbolt E907

Stumbling over animal, carpet, curb, rug or (small) object (with fall) E885.9
  without fall — *see* Striking against, object
Submersion (accidental) E910.8
  boat, ship, watercraft (causing drowning, submersion) E830 ☑
    causing injury except drowning, submersion E831 ☑
  by other person
    in accidental circumstances — *see* category E910 ☑
    intentional, homicidal E964
    stated as undetermined whether accidental or intentional E984
  due to
    accident
      machinery — *see* Accident, machine
      to boat, ship, watercraft E830 ☑
      transport — *see* categories E800-E848 ☑
    avalanche E909.2
    cataclysmic
      earth surface movement or eruption E909.9
      storm E908.9
    cloudburst E908.8
    cyclone E908.1
    fall
      from
        boat, ship, watercraft (not involved in accident) E832 ☑
          burning, crushed E830 ☑
          involved in accident, collision E830 ☑
        gangplank (into water) E832 ☑
      overboard NEC E832 ☑
    flood E908.2
    hurricane E908.0
    jumping into water E910.8
      from boat, ship, watercraft
        burning, crushed, sinking E830 ☑
        involved in accident, collision E830 ☑
        not involved in accident, for swim E910.2
      in recreational activity (without diving equipment) E910.2
        with or using diving equipment E910.1
      to rescue another person E910.3
  homicide (attempt) E964
  in
    bathtub E910.4
    specified activity, not sport, transport or recreational E910.3
    sport or recreational activity (without diving equipment) E910.2
      with or using diving equipment E910.1
      water skiing E910.0
    swimming pool NEC E910.8
    terrorism E979.8
    war operations E995
    water transport E832 ☑
      due to accident to boat, ship, watercraft E830 ☑
  landslide E909.2
    overturning boat, ship, watercraft E909.2
    sinking boat, ship, watercraft E909.2
    submersion boat, ship, watercraft E909.2
    tidal wave E909.4
      caused by storm E908.0
    torrential rain E908.2
  late effect of NEC E929.8

Submersion (accidental) — *continued*
  quenching tank E910.8
  self-inflicted (unspecified whether accidental or intentional) E984
    in accidental circumstances — *see* category E910 ☑
    stated as intentional, purposeful E954
  stated as undetermined whether accidental or intentional E984
  suicidal (attempted) E954
  while
    attempting rescue of another person E910.3
    engaged in
      marine salvage E910.3
      underwater construction or repairs E910.3
    fishing, not from boat E910.2
    hunting, not from boat E910.2
    ice skating E910.2
    pearl diving E910.3
    placing fishing nets E910.3
    playing in water E910.2
    scuba diving E910.1
      nonrecreational E910.3
    skin diving E910.1
    snorkel diving E910.2
    spear fishing underwater E910.1
    surfboarding E910.2
    swimming (swimming pool) E910.2
    wading (in water) E910.2
    water skiing E910.0
Sucked
  into
    jet (aircraft) E844 ☑
Suffocation (accidental) (by external means) (by pressure) (mechanical) E913.9
  caused by other person
    in accidental circumstances — *see category* E913 ☑
    stated as
      intentional, homicidal E963
      undetermined whether accidental or intentional E983.9
        by, in
          hanging E983.0
          plastic bag E983.1
          specified means NEC E983.8
  due to, by
    avalanche E909.2
    bedclothes E913.0
    bib E913.0
    blanket E913.0
    cave-in E913.3
      caused by cataclysmic earth surface movement or eruption E909.9
    conflagration — *see* Conflagration
    explosion — *see* Explosion
    falling earth, other substance E913.3
    fire — *see* Fire
    food, any type (ingestion) (inhalation) (regurgitated) (vomited) E911
    foreign body, except food (ingestion) (inhalation) E912
    ignition — *see* Ignition
    landslide E909.2
    machine(ry) — *see* Accident, machine
    material, object except food entering by nose or mouth, ingested, inhaled E912
    mucus (aspiration) (inhalation), not of newborn E912
    phlegm (aspiration) (inhalation) E912
    pillow E913.0
    plastic bag — *see* Suffocation, in, plastic bag
    sheet (plastic) E913.0

Suffocation — *continued*
  due to, by — *continued*
    specified means NEC E913.8
    vomitus (aspiration) (inhalation) E911
  homicidal (attempt) E963
  in
    airtight enclosed place E913.2
    baby carriage E913.0
    bed E913.0
    closed place E913.2
    cot, cradle E913.0
    perambulator E913.0
    plastic bag (in accidental circumstances) E913.1
      homicidal, purposely inflicted by other person E963
      self-inflicted (unspecified whether accidental or intentional) E983.1
        in accidental circumstances E913.1
        intentional, suicidal E953.1
      stated as undetermined whether accidentally or purposely inflicted E983.1
      suicidal, purposely self-inflicted E953.1
    refrigerator E913.2
  self-inflicted (*see also* Suffocation, stated as undetermined whether accidental or intentional) E953.9
    in accidental circumstances — *see* category E913 ☑
    stated as intentional, purposeful — *see* Suicide, suffocation
  stated as undetermined whether accidental or intentional E983.9
    by, in
      hanging E983.0
      plastic bag E983.1
      specified means NEC E983.8
  suicidal — *see* Suicide, suffocation
Suicide, suicidal (attempted) (by) E958.9
  burning, burns E958.1
  caustic substance E958.7
    poisoning E950.7
    swallowed E950.7
  cold, extreme E958.3
  cut (any part of body) E956
  cutting or piercing instrument (classifiable to E920) E956
  drowning E954
  electrocution E958.4
  explosive(s) (classifiable to E923) E955.5
  fire E958.1
  firearm (classifiable to E922) — *see* Shooting, suicidal
  hanging E953.0
  jumping
    before moving object, train, vehicle E958.0
    from high place — *see* Jumping, from, high place, stated as, suicidal
  knife E956
  late effect of E959
  motor vehicle, crashing of E958.5
  poisoning — *see* Table of Drugs and Chemicals
  puncture (any part of body) E956
  scald E958.2
  shooting — *see* Shooting, suicidal
  specified means NEC E958.8
  stab (any part of body) E956
  strangulation — *see* Suicide, suffocation
  submersion E954
  suffocation E953.9
    by, in
      hanging E953.0
      plastic bag E953.1
      specified means NEC E953.8
  wound NEC E958.9

Sunburn E926.2
Sunstroke E900.0
Supersonic waves (causing injury) E928.1
Surgical procedure, complication of
  delayed or as an abnormal reaction without mention of misadventure — *see* Reaction, abnormal
  due to or as a result of misadventure — *see* Misadventure
Swallowed, swallowing
  foreign body — *see* Foreign body, alimentary canal
  poison — *see* Table of Drugs and Chemicals
  substance
    caustic — *see* Table of Drugs and Chemicals
    corrosive — *see* Table of Drugs and Chemicals
    poisonous — *see* Table of Drugs and Chemicals
Swimmers cramp — *see also* category E910 E910.2
  not in recreation or sport E910.3
Syndrome, battered
  baby or child — *see* Abuse, child
  wife — *see* Assault

T

Tackle in sport E886.0
Terrorism (injury) (by) (in) E979.8
  air blast E979.2
  aircraft burned, destroyed, exploded, shot down E979.1
    used as a weapon E979.1
  anthrax E979.6
  asphyxia from
    chemical (weapons) E979.7
    fire, conflagration (caused by fire-producing device) E979.3
      from nuclear explosion E979.5
    gas or fumes E979.7
  bayonet E979.8
  biological agents E979.6
  blast (air) (effects) E979.2
    from nuclear explosion E979.5
    underwater E979.0
  bomb (antipersonnel) (mortar) (explosion) (fragments) E979.2
  bullet(s) (from carbine, machine gun, pistol, rifle, shotgun) E979.4
  burn from
    chemical E979.7
    fire, conflagration (caused by fire-producing device) E979.3
      from nuclear explosion E979.5
    gas E979.7
  burning aircraft E979.1
  chemical E979.7
  cholera E979.6
  conflagration E979.3
  crushed by falling aircraft E979.1
  depth-charge E979.0
  destruction of aircraft E979.1
  disability, as sequelae one year or more after injury E999.1
  drowning E979.8
  effect
    of nuclear weapon (direct) (secondary) E979.5
    secondary NEC E979.9
    sequelae E999.1
  explosion (artillery shell) (breech-block) (cannon block) E979.2
    aircraft E979.1
    bomb (antipersonnel) (mortar) E979.2
      nuclear (atom) (hydrogen) E979.5
    depth-charge E979.0
    grenade E979.2
    injury by fragments from E979.2
    land-mine E979.2
    marine weapon E979.0
    mine (land) E979.2

- **Terrorism** — *continued*
  - explosion — *continued*
    - mine — *continued*
      - at sea or in harbor E979.0
      - marine E979.0
    - missile (explosive) NEC E979.2
    - munitions (dump) (factory) E979.2
    - nuclear (weapon) E979.5
      - other direct and secondary effects of E979.5
    - sea-based artillery shell E979.0
    - torpedo E979.0
  - exposure to ionizing radiation from nuclear explosion E979.5
  - falling aircraft E979.1
  - firearms E979.4
  - fireball effects from nuclear explosion E979.5
  - fire or fire-producing device E979.3
  - fragments from artillery shell, bomb NEC, grenade, guided missile, land-mine, rocket, shell, shrapnel E979.2
  - gas or fumes E979.7
  - grenade (explosion) (fragments) E979.2
  - guided missile (explosion) (fragments) E979.2
    - nuclear E979.5
  - heat from nuclear explosion E979.5
  - hot substances E979.3
  - hydrogen cyanide E979.7
  - land-mine (explosion) (fragments) E979.2
  - laser(s) E979.8
  - late effect of E999.1
  - lewisite E979.7
  - lung irritant (chemical) (fumes) (gas) E979.7
  - marine mine E979.0
  - mine E979.2
    - at sea E979.0
    - in harbor E979.0
    - land (explosion) (fragments) E979.2
    - marine E979.0
  - missile (explosion) (fragments) (guided) E979.2
    - marine E979.0
    - nuclear weapons E979.5
  - mortar bomb (explosion) (fragments) E979.2
  - mustard gas E979.7
  - nerve gas E979.7
  - nuclear weapons E979.5
  - pellets (shotgun) E979.4
  - petrol bomb E979.3
  - phosgene E979.7
  - piercing object E979.8
  - poisoning (chemical) (fumes) (gas) E979.7
  - radiation, ionizing from nuclear explosion E979.5
  - rocket (explosion) (fragments) E979.2
  - saber, sabre E979.8
  - sarin E979.7
  - screening smoke E979.7
  - sequelae effect (of) E999.1
  - shell (aircraft) (artillery) (cannon) (land-based) (explosion) (fragments) E979.2
    - sea-based E979.0
  - shooting E979.4
    - bullet(s) E979.4
    - pellet(s) (rifle) (shotgun) E979.4
  - shrapnel E979.2
  - smallpox E979.7
  - stabbing object(s) E979.8
  - submersion E979.8
  - torpedo E979.0
  - underwater blast E979.0
  - vesicant (chemical) (fumes) (gas) E979.7
  - weapon burst E979.2
- **Thermic fever** E900.9
- **Thermoplegia** E900.9
- **Thirst** — *see also* Lack of water
- **Thirst** — *see also* Lack of water — *continued*
  - resulting from accident connected with transport — *see* categories E800-E848 ☑
- **Thrown** (accidently)
  - against object in or part of vehicle
    - by motion of vehicle
      - aircraft E844 ☑
      - boat, ship, watercraft E838 ☑
      - motor vehicle (on public highway) E818 ☑
        - not on public highway E825 ☑
        - off-road type (not on public highway) E821 ☑
          - on public highway E818 ☑
        - snow vehicle E820 ☑
          - on public highway E818 ☑
    - nonmotor road vehicle NEC E829 ☑
    - railway rolling stock, train, vehicle E806 ☑
    - street car E829 ☑
  - from
    - animal (being ridden) (in sport or transport) E828 ☑
    - high place, homicide (attempt) E968.1
    - machinery — *see* Accident, machine
    - vehicle NEC — *see* Accident, vehicle NEC
  - off — *see* Thrown, from
  - overboard (by motion of boat, ship, watercraft) E832 ☑
    - by accident to boat, ship, watercraft E830 ☑
- **Thunderbolt** NEC E907
- **Tidal wave** (any injury) E909.4
  - caused by storm E908.0
- **Took**
  - overdose of drug — *see* Table of Drugs and Chemicals
  - poison — *see* Table of Drugs and Chemicals
- **Tornado** (any injury) E908.1
- **Torrential rain** (any injury) E908.2
- **Traffic accident NEC** E819 ☑
- **Trampled by animal** E906.8
  - being ridden (in sport or transport) E828 ☑
- **Trapped** (accidently)
  - between
    - objects (moving) (stationary and moving) E918
  - by
    - door of
      - elevator E918
      - motor vehicle (on public highway) (while alighting, boarding) — *see* Fall, from, motor vehicle, while alighting
      - railway train (underground) E806 ☑
      - street car E829 ☑
      - subway train E806 ☑
  - in object E918
- **Trauma** ●
  - cumulative ●
    - from ●
      - repetitive ●
        - impact E927.4 ●
        - motion or movements E927.3 ●
  - sudden from strenuous movement E927.0 ●
- **Travel** (effects) E903
  - sickness E903
- **Tree**
  - falling on or hitting E916
    - motor vehicle (in motion) (on public highway) E818 ☑
- **Tree** — *continued*
  - falling on or hitting — *continued*
    - motor vehicle — *continued*
      - not on public highway E825 ☑
    - nonmotor road vehicle NEC E829 ☑
    - pedal cycle E826 ☑
    - person E916
    - railway rolling stock, train, vehicle E806 ☑
    - street car E829 ☑
- **Trench foot** E901.0
- **Tripping over animal, carpet, curb, rug, or small object** (with fall) E885 ☑
  - without fall — *see* Striking against, object
- **Tsunami** E909.4
- **Twisting, injury in** E927.8 ▲

V

- **Violence, nonaccidental** — *see also* Assault E968.9
- **Volcanic eruption** (any injury) E909.1
- **Vomitus in air passages** (with asphyxia, obstruction or suffocation) E911

W

- **War operations** (during hostilities) (injury) (by) (in) E995
  - after cessation of hostilities, injury due to E998
  - air blast E993
  - aircraft burned, destroyed, exploded, shot down E994
  - asphyxia from
    - chemical E997.2
    - fire, conflagration (caused by fire producing device or conventional weapon) E990.9
      - from nuclear explosion E996
      - petrol bomb E990.0
    - fumes E997.2
    - gas E997.2
  - battle wound NEC E995
  - bayonet E995
  - biological warfare agents E997.1
  - blast (air) (effects) E993
    - from nuclear explosion E996
    - underwater E992
  - bomb (mortar) (explosion) E993
    - after cessation of hostilities E998
    - fragments, injury by E991.9
      - antipersonnel E991.3
  - bullet(s) (from carbine, machine gun, pistol, rifle, shotgun) E991.2
    - rubber E991.0
  - burn from
    - chemical E997.2
    - fire, conflagration (caused by fire-producing device or conventional weapon) E990.9
      - from nuclear explosion E996
      - petrol bomb E990.0
    - gas E997.2
  - burning aircraft E994
  - chemical E997.2
  - chlorine E997.2
  - conventional warfare, specified form NEC E995
  - crushing by falling aircraft E994
  - depth charge E992
  - destruction of aircraft E994
  - disability as sequela one year or more after injury E999.0
  - drowning E995
  - effect (direct) (secondary) nuclear weapon E996
  - explosion (artillery shell) (breech block) (cannon shell) E993
    - after cessation of hostilities of bomb, mine placed in war E998
    - aircraft E994
    - bomb (mortar) E993
- **War operations** — *continued*
  - explosion — *continued*
    - bomb — *continued*
      - atom E996
      - hydrogen E996
      - injury by fragments from E991.9
        - antipersonnel E991.3
      - nuclear E996
    - depth charge E992
    - injury by fragments from E991.9
      - antipersonnel E991.3
    - marine weapon E992
    - mine
      - at sea or in harbor E992
      - land E993
        - injury by fragments from E991.9
      - marine E992
    - munitions (accidental) (being used in war) (dump) (factory) E993
    - nuclear (weapon) E996
    - own weapons (accidental) E993
      - injury by fragments from E991.9
        - antipersonnel E991.3
    - sea-based artillery shell E992
    - torpedo E992
  - exposure to ionizing radiation from nuclear explosion E996
  - falling aircraft E994
  - fireball effects from nuclear explosion E996
  - fire or fire-producing device E990.9
    - petrol bomb E990.0
  - fragments from
    - antipersonnel bomb E991.3
    - artillery shell, bomb NEC, grenade, guided missile, land mine, rocket, shell, shrapnel E991.9
  - fumes E997.2
  - gas E997.2
  - grenade (explosion) E993
    - fragments, injury by E991.9
  - guided missile (explosion) E993
    - fragments, injury by E991.9
    - nuclear E996
  - heat from nuclear explosion E996
  - injury due to, but occurring after cessation of hostilities E998
  - lacrimator (gas) (chemical) E997.2
  - land mine (explosion) E993
    - after cessation of hostilities E998
    - fragments, injury by E991.9
  - laser(s) E997.0
  - late effect of E999.0
  - lewisite E997.2
  - lung irritant (chemical) (fumes) (gas) E997.2
  - marine mine E992
  - mine
    - after cessation of hostilities E998
    - at sea E992
    - in harbor E992
    - land (explosion) E993
      - fragments, injury by E991.9
    - marine E992
  - missile (guided) (explosion) E993
    - fragments, injury by E991.9
    - marine E992
    - nuclear E996
  - mortar bomb (explosion) E993
    - fragments, injury by E991.9
  - mustard gas E997.2
  - nerve gas E997.2
  - phosgene E997.2
  - poisoning (chemical) (fumes) (gas) E997.2
  - radiation, ionizing from nuclear explosion E996
  - rocket (explosion) E993
    - fragments, injury by E991.9
  - saber, sabre E995
  - screening smoke E997.8

War operations — *continued*
- shell (aircraft) (artillery) (cannon) (land based) (explosion) E993
  - fragments, injury by E991.9
  - sea-based E992
- shooting E991.2
  - after cessation of hostilities E998
  - bullet(s) E991.2
    - rubber E991.0
  - pellet(s) (rifle) E991.1
  - shrapnel E991.9
  - submersion E995
  - torpedo E992
- unconventional warfare, except by nuclear weapon E997.9
  - biological (warfare) E997.1
  - gas, fumes, chemicals E997.2
  - laser(s) E997.0
  - specified type NEC E997.8
- underwater blast E992
- vesicant (chemical) (fumes) (gas) E997.2
- weapon burst E993

Washed
- away by flood — *see* Flood
- away by tidal wave — *see* Tidal wave
- off road by storm (transport vehicle) E908.9
- overboard E832 ☑

Weather exposure — *see also* Exposure
- cold E901.0
- hot E900.0

Weightlessness (causing injury) (effects of) (in spacecraft, real or simulated) E928.0

Wound (accidental) NEC — *see also* Injury E928.9
- battle (*see also* War operations) E995
- bayonet E920.3
  - in
    - legal intervention E974
    - war operations E995
- gunshot — *see* Shooting
- incised — *see* Cut
- saber, sabre E920.3
  - in war operations E995

Railway Accidents (E800-E807)

The following fourth-digit subdivisions are for use with categories E800-E807 to identify the injured person:

.0 **Railway employee**
Any person who by virtue of his employment in connection with a railway, whether by the railway company or not, is at increased risk of involvement in a railway accident, such as:
catering staff on train
postal staff on train
driver
railway fireman
guard
shunter
porter
sleeping car attendant

.1 **Passenger on railway**
Any authorized person traveling on a train, except a railway employee
EXCLUDES intending passenger waiting at station (.8)
unauthorized rider on railway vehicle (.8)

.2 **Pedestrian** See definition (r), E-Codes-2

.3 **Pedal cyclist** See definition (p), E-Codes-2

.8 **Other specified person** Intending passenger waiting at station
Unauthorized rider on railway vehicle

.9 **Unspecified person**

Motor Vehicle Traffic and Nontraffic Accidents (E810-E825)

The following fourth-digit subdivisions are for use with categories E810-E819 and E820-E825 to identify the injured person:

.0 **Driver of motor vehicle other than motorcycle** See definition (1), E-Codes-2

.1 **Passenger in motor vehicle other than motorcycle** See definition (1), E-Codes-2

.2 **Motorcyclist** See definition (1), E-Codes-2

.3 **Passenger on motorcycle** See definition (1), E-Codes-2

.4 **Occupant of streetcar**

.5 **Rider of animal; occupant of animal-drawn vehicle**

.6 **Pedal cyclist** See definition (p), E-Codes-2

.7 **Pedestrian** See definition (r), E-Codes-2

.8 **Other specified person**
Occupant of vehicle other than above
Person in railway train involved in accident
Unauthorized rider of motor vehicle

.9 **Unspecified person**

Other Road Vehicle Accidents (E826-E829)

(animal-drawn vehicle, streetcar, pedal cycle, and other nonmotor road vehicle accidents)

The following fourth-digit subdivisions are for use with categories E826-E829 to identify the injured person:

.0 **Pedestrian** See definition (r), E-Codes-2

.1 **Pedal cyclist** (does not apply to codes E827, E828, E829) See definition (p), E-Codes-2

.2 **Rider of animal** (does not apply to code E829)

.3 **Occupant of animal-drawn vehicle (does not apply to codes E828, E829)**

.4 **Occupant of streetcar**

.8 **Other specified person**

.9 **Unspecified person**

Water Transport Accidents (E830-E838)

The following fourth-digit subdivisions are for use with categories E830-E838 to identify the injured person:

.0 **Occupant of small boat, unpowered**

.1 **Occupant of small boat, powered** See definition (t), E-Codes-2
EXCLUDES water skier (.4)

.2 **Occupant of other watercraft — crew**
Persons:
engaged in operation of watercraft
providing passenger services [cabin attendants, ship's physician, catering personnel]
working on ship during voyage in other capacity [musician in band, operators of shops and beauty parlors]

.3 **Occupant of other watercraft — other than crew**
Passenger
Occupant of lifeboat, other than crew, after abandoning ship

.4 **Water skier**

.5 **Swimmer**

.6 **Dockers, stevedores**
Longshoreman employed on the dock in loading and unloading ships

.8 **Other specified person**
Immigration and custom officials on board ship
Persons:
accompanying passenger or member of crew visiting boat
Pilot (guiding ship into port)

.9 **Unspecified person**

Air and Space Transport Accidents (E840-E845)

The following fourth-digit subdivisions are for use with categories E840-E845 to identify the injured person:

.0 **Occupant of spacecraft**
Crew
Passenger (civilian)
(military)
Troops
} in military aircraft [air force] [army] [national guard] [navy]

.1 **Occupant of military aircraft, any**
EXCLUDES occupants of aircraft operated under jurisdiction of police departments (.5) parachutist (.7)

.2 **Crew of commercial aircraft (powered) in surface to surface transport**

.3 **Other occupant of commercial aircraft (powered) in surface to surface transport**
Flight personnel:
not part of crew
on familiarization flight Passenger on aircraft

.4 **Occupant of commercial aircraft (powered) in surface to air transport**
Occupant [crew] [passenger] of aircraft (powered) engaged in activities, such as:
air drops of emergency supplies
air drops of parachutists, except from military craft
crop dusting
lowering of construction material [bridge or telephone pole]
sky writing

.5 **Occupant of other powered aircraft**
Occupant [crew] [passenger] of aircraft (powered) engaged in activities, such as:
aerial spraying (crops)(fire retardants)
aerobatic flying
aircraft racing
rescue operation
storm surveillance
traffic suveillance
Occupant of private plane NOS

.6 **Occupant of unpowered aircraft, except parachutist**
Occupant of aircraft classifiable to E842

.7 **Parachutist (military)(other)**
Person making voluntary descent
person making descent after accident to aircraft (.1-.6)

.8 **Ground crew, airline employee**
Persons employed at airfields (civil)(military) or launching pads, not occupants of aircraft

.9 **Other person**

1. INFECTIOUS AND PARASITIC DISEASES (001-139)

Note: Categories for "late effects" of infectious and parasitic diseases are to be found at 137-139.

INCLUDES diseases generally recognized as communicable or transmissible as well as a few diseases of unknown but possibly infectious origin

EXCLUDES *acute respiratory infections (460-466)*
carrier or suspected carrier of infectious organism (V02.0-V02.9)
certain localized infections
influenza (487.0-487.8, 488)

INTESTINAL INFECTIOUS DISEASES (001-009)

EXCLUDES *helminthiases (120.0-129)*

✓4th **001 Cholera**

DEF: An acute infectious enteritis caused by a potent enterotoxin elaborated by *Vibrio cholerae*; the vibrio produces a toxin in the intestinal tract that changes the permeability of the mucosa leading to diarrhea and dehydration.

001.0 Due to Vibrio cholerae

001.1 Due to Vibrio cholerae el tor

001.9 Cholera, unspecified

✓4th **002 Typhoid and paratyphoid fevers**

DEF: Typhoid fever: an acute generalized illness caused by *Salmonella typhi*; notable clinical features are fever, headache, abdominal pain, cough, toxemia, leukopenia, abnormal pulse, rose spots on the skin, bacteremia, hyperplasia of intestinal lymph nodes, mesenteric lymphadenopathy, and Peyer's patches in the intestines.

DEF: Paratyphoid fever: a prolonged febrile illness, much like typhoid but usually less severe; caused by salmonella serotypes other than *S. typhi*, especially *S. enteritidis* serotypes paratyphi A and B and *S. choleraesuis*.

002.0 Typhoid fever
Typhoid (fever) (infection) [any site]

002.1 Paratyphoid fever A

002.2 Paratyphoid fever B

002.3 Paratyphoid fever C

002.9 Paratyphoid fever, unspecified

✓4th **003 Other salmonella infections**

INCLUDES infection or food poisoning by Salmonella [any serotype]

DEF: Infections caused by a genus of gram-negative, anaerobic bacteria of the family *Enterobacteriaceae*; affecting warm-blooded animals, like humans; major symptoms are enteric fevers, acute gastroenteritis and septicemia.

003.0 Salmonella gastroenteritis
Salmonellosis

003.1 Salmonella septicemia

✓5th **003.2 Localized salmonella infections**

003.20 Localized salmonella infection, unspecified

003.21 Salmonella meningitis

003.22 Salmonella pneumonia

003.23 Salmonella arthritis

003.24 Salmonella osteomyelitis

003.29 Other

003.8 Other specified salmonella infections

003.9 Salmonella infection, unspecified

✓4th **004 Shigellosis**

INCLUDES bacillary dysentery

DEF: Acute infectious dysentery caused by the genus *Shigella*, of the family *Enterobacteriaceae*; affecting the colon causing the release of blood-stained stools with accompanying tenesmus, abdominal cramps and fever.

004.0 Shigella dysenteriae
Infection by group A Shigella (Schmitz) (Shiga)

004.1 Shigella flexneri
Infection by group B Shigella

004.2 Shigella boydii
Infection by group C Shigella

004.3 Shigella sonnei
Infection by group D Shigella

004.8 Other specified Shigella infections

004.9 Shigellosis, unspecified

✓4th **005 Other food poisoning (bacterial)**

EXCLUDES *salmonella infections (003.0-003.9)*
toxic effect of:
food contaminants (989.7)
noxious foodstuffs (988.0-988.9)

DEF: Enteritis caused by ingesting contaminated foods and characterized by diarrhea, abdominal pain, vomiting; symptoms may be mild or life threatening.

005.0 Staphylococcal food poisoning
Staphylococcal toxemia specified as due to food

005.1 Botulism food poisoning
Botulism NOS
Food poisoning due to Clostridium botulinum

EXCLUDES *infant botulism (040.41)*
wound botulism (040.42)

005.2 Food poisoning due to Clostridium perfringens [C. welchii]
Enteritis necroticans

005.3 Food poisoning due to other Clostridia

005.4 Food poisoning due to Vibrio parahaemolyticus

✓5th **005.8 Other bacterial food poisoning**

EXCLUDES *salmonella food poisoning (003.0-003.9)*

005.81 Food poisoning due to Vibrio vulnificus

005.89 Other bacterial food poisoning
Food poisoning due to Bacillus cereus

005.9 Food posioning, unspecified

✓4th **006 Amebiasis**

INCLUDES infection due to Entamoeba histolytica

EXCLUDES *amebiasis due to organisms other than Entamoeba histolytica (007.8)*

DEF: Infection of the large intestine caused by *Entamoeba histolytica*; usually asymptomatic but symptoms may range from mild diarrhea to profound life-threatening dysentery. Extraintestinal complications include hepatic abscess, which may rupture into the lung, pericardium or abdomen, causing life-threatening infections.

006.0 Acute amebic dysentery without mention of abscess
Acute amebiasis

DEF: Sudden, severe *Entamoeba histolytica* infection causing bloody stools.

006.1 Chronic intestinal amebiasis without mention of abscess
Chronic:
amebiasis
amebic dysentery

006.2 Amebic nondysenteric colitis

DEF: *Entamoeba histolytica* infection with inflamed colon but no dysentery.

006.3 Amebic liver abscess
Hepatic amebiasis

006.4 Amebic lung abscess
Amebic abscess of lung (and liver)

006.5 Amebic brain abscess
Amebic abscess of brain (and liver) (and lung)

006.6 Amebic skin ulceration
Cutaneous amebiasis

✓4th ✓5th Additional Digit Required | Unspecified Code | Other Specified Code | Manifestation Code | ►◄ Revised Text | ● New Code | ▲ Revised Code Title

006.8 Amebic infection of other sites
Amebic:
appendicitis
balanitis
Ameboma

EXCLUDES *specific infections by free-living amebae ▶(136.21-136.29)◀*

006.9 Amebiasis, unspecified
Amebiasis NOS

✓4th 007 Other protozoal intestinal diseases

INCLUDES protozoal:
colitis
diarrhea
dysentery

007.0 Balantidiasis
Infection by Balantidium coli

007.1 Giardiasis
Infection by Giardia lamblia
Lambliasis

007.2 Coccidiosis
Infection by Isospora belli and Isospora hominis
Isosporiasis

007.3 Intestinal trichomoniasis
DEF: Colitis, diarrhea, or dysentery caused by the protozoa *Trichomonas.*

007.4 Cryptosporidiosis
AHA: 4Q, '97, 30
DEF: An intestinal infection by protozoan parasites causing intractable diarrhea in patients with AIDS and other immunosuppressed individuals.

007.5 Cyclosporiasis
AHA: 4Q, '00, 38
DEF: An infection of the small intestine by the protozoal organism, *Cyclospora caytenanesis,* spread to humans though ingestion of contaminated water or food. Symptoms include watery diarrhea with frequent explosive bowel movements, loss of appetite, loss of weight, bloating, increased gas, stomach cramps, nausea, vomiting, muscle aches, low grade fever, and fatigue.

007.8 Other specified protozoal intestinal diseases
Amebiasis due to organisms other than Entamoeba histolytica

007.9 Unspecified protozoal intestinal disease
Flagellate diarrhea
Protozoal dysentery NOS

✓4th 008 Intestinal infections due to other organisms

INCLUDES any condition classifiable to 009.0-009.3 with mention of the responsible organisms

EXCLUDES *food poisoning by these organisms (005.0-005.9)*

✓5th 008.0 Escherichia coli [E. coli]
AHA: 4Q, '92, 17

008.00 E. coli, unspecified
E. coli enteritis NOS

008.01 Enteropathogenic E. coli
DEF: *E. coli* causing inflammation of intestines.

008.02 Enterotoxigenic E. coli
DEF: A toxic reaction to *E. coli* of the intestinal mucosa, causing voluminous watery secretions.

008.03 Enteroinvasive E. coli
DEF: *E. coli* infection penetrating intestinal mucosa.

008.04 Enterohemorrhagic E. coli
DEF: E. coli infection penetrating the intestinal mucosa, producing microscopic ulceration and bleeding.

008.09 Other intestinal E. coli infections

008.1 Arizona group of paracolon bacilli

008.2 Aerobacter aerogenes
Enterobacter aeogenes

008.3 Proteus (mirabilis) (morganii)

✓5th 008.4 Other specified bacteria
AHA: 4Q, '92, 18

008.41 Staphylococcus
Staphylococcal enterocolitis

008.42 Pseudomonas
AHA: 2Q, '89, 10

008.43 Campylobacter

008.44 Yersinia enterocolitica

008.45 Clostridium difficile
Pseudomembranous colitis
DEF: An overgrowth of a species of bacterium that is a part of the normal colon flora in human infants and sometimes in adults; produces a toxin that causes pseudomembranous enterocolitis.; typically is seen in patients undergoing antibiotic therapy.

008.46 Other anaerobes
Anaerobic enteritis NOS
Bacteroides (fragilis)
Gram-negative anaerobes

008.47 Other gram-negative bacteria
Gram-negative enteritis NOS

EXCLUDES *gram-negative anaerobes (008.46)*

008.49 Other
AHA: 2Q, '89, 10; 1Q, '88, 6

008.5 Bacterial enteritis, unspecified

✓5th 008.6 Enteritis due to specified virus
AHA: 4Q, '92, 18

008.61 Rotavirus

008.62 Adenovirus

008.63 Norwalk virus
Norwalk-like agent

008.64 Other small round viruses [SRVs]
Small round virus NOS

008.65 Calicivirus
DEF: Enteritis due to a subgroup of *Picornaviruses.*

008.66 Astrovirus

008.67 Enterovirus NEC
Coxsackie virus
Echovirus

EXCLUDES *poliovirus (045.0-045.9)*

008.69 Other viral enteritis
Torovirus
AHA: 1Q, '03, 10

008.8 Other organism, not elsewhere classified
Viral:
enteritis NOS
gastroenteritis

EXCLUDES *influenza with involvement of gastrointestinal tract (487.8)*

N Newborn Age: 0 P Pediatric Age: 0-17 M Maternity Age: 12-55 A Adult Age: 15-124

4th 009 Ill-defined intestinal infections

EXCLUDES *diarrheal disease or intestinal infection due to specified organism (001.0-008.8)*
diarrhea following gastrointestinal surgery (564.4)
intestinal malabsorption (579.0-579.9)
ischemic enteritis (557.0-557.9)
other noninfectious gastroenteritis and colitis (558.1-558.9)
regional enteritis (555.0-555.9)
ulcerative colitis (556)

009.0 Infectious colitis, enteritis, and gastroenteritis

Colitis, Enteritis, Gastroenteritis } septic

Dysentery:
NOS
catarrhal
hemorrhagic

AHA: 3Q, '99, 4

DEF: Colitis: An inflammation of mucous membranes of the colon.

DEF: Enteritis: An inflammation of mucous membranes of the small intestine.

DEF: Gastroenteritis: An inflammation of mucous membranes of stomach and intestines.

009.1 Colitis, enteritis, and gastroenteritis of presumed infectious origin

EXCLUDES *colitis NOS (558.9)*
enteritis NOS (558.9)
gastroenteritis NOS (558.9)

AHA: 3Q, '99, 6

009.2 Infectious diarrhea

Diarrhea:
dysenteric
epidemic
Infectious diarrheal disease NOS

009.3 Diarrhea of presumed infectious origin

EXCLUDES *diarrhea NOS (787.91)*

AHA: N-D, '87, 7

TUBERCULOSIS (010-018)

INCLUDES infection by Mycobacterium tuberculosis (human) (bovine)

EXCLUDES *congenital tuberculosis (771.2)*
late effects of tuberculosis (137.0-137.4)

The following fifth digit subclassification is for use with categories 010-018:

0 unspecified
1 bacteriological or histological examination not done
2 bacteriological or histological examination unknown (at present)
3 tubercle bacilli found (in sputum) by microscopy
4 tubercle bacilli not found (in sputum) by microscopy, but found by bacterial culture
5 tubercle bacilli not found by bacteriological examination, but tuberculosis confirmed histologically
6 tubercle bacilli not found by bacteriological or histological examination but tuberculosis confirmed by other methods [inoculation of animals]

DEF: An infection by *Mycobacterium tuberculosis* causing the formation of small, rounded nodules, called tubercles, that can disseminate throughout the body via lymph and blood vessels. Localized tuberculosis is most often seen in the lungs.

4th 010 Primary tuberculous infection

DEF: Tuberculosis of the lungs occurring when the patient is first infected.

§ 5th **010.0 Primary tuberculous infection**
[0-6]
EXCLUDES *nonspecific reaction to tuberculin skin test without active tuberculosis (795.5)*
positive PPD (795.5)
positive tuberculin skin test without active tuberculosis (795.5)

DEF: Hilar or paratracheal lymph node enlargement in pulmonary tuberculosis.

§ 5th **010.1 Tuberculous pleurisy in primary progressive tuberculosis**
[0-6]
DEF: Inflammation and exudation in the lining of the tubercular lung.

§ 5th **010.8 Other primary progressive tuberculosis**
[0-6]
EXCLUDES *tuberculous erythema nodosum (017.1)*

§ 5th **010.9 Primary tuberculous infection, unspecified**
[0-6]

4th 011 Pulmonary tuberculosis

Use additional code to identify any associated silicosis (502)

§ 5th **011.0 Tuberculosis of lung, infiltrative**
[0-6]

§ 5th **011.1 Tuberculosis of lung, nodular**
[0-6]

§ 5th **011.2 Tuberculosis of lung with cavitation**
[0-6]

§ 5th **011.3 Tuberculosis of bronchus**
[0-6]
EXCLUDES *isolated bronchial tuberculosis (012.2)*

§ 5th **011.4 Tuberculous fibrosis of lung**
[0-6]

§ 5th **011.5 Tuberculous bronchiectasis**
[0-6]

§ 5th **011.6 Tuberculous pneumonia [any form]**
[0-6]
DEF: Inflammatory pulmonary reaction to tuberculous cells.

§ 5th **011.7 Tuberculous pneumothorax**
[0-6]
DEF: Spontaneous rupture of damaged tuberculous pulmonary tissue.

§ 5th **011.8 Other specified pulmonary tuberculosis**
[0-6]

§ 5th **011.9 Pulmonary tuberculosis, unspecified**
[0-6]
Respiratory tuberculosis NOS
Tuberculosis of lung NOS

4th 012 Other respiratory tuberculosis

EXCLUDES *respiratory tuberculosis, unspecified (011.9)*

§ 5th **012.0 Tuberculous pleurisy**
[0-6]
Tuberculosis of pleura
Tuberculous empyema
Tuberculous hydrothorax

EXCLUDES *pleurisy with effusion without mention of cause (511.9)*
tuberculous pleurisy in primary progressive tuberculosis (010.1)

DEF: Inflammation and exudation in the lining of the tubercular lung.

§ 5th **012.1 Tuberculosis of intrathoracic lymph nodes**
[0-6]
Tuberculosis of lymph nodes:
hilar
mediastinal
tracheobronchial
Tuberculous tracheobronchial adenopathy

EXCLUDES *that specified as primary (010.0-010.9)*

§ 5th **012.2 Isolated tracheal or bronchial tuberculosis**
[0-6]

§ 5th **012.3 Tuberculous laryngitis**
[0-6]
Tuberculosis of glottis

§ Requires fifth-digit. Valid digits are in [brackets] under each code. See beginning of section 010-018 for codes and definitions.

§ 5th **012.8 Other specified respiratory tuberculosis**
[0-6]
Tuberculosis of:
mediastinum
nasopharynx
nose (septum)
sinus [any nasal]

4th **013 Tuberculosis of meninges and central nervous system**

§ 5th **013.0 Tuberculous meningitis**
[0-6]
Tuberculosis of meninges (cerebral) (spinal)
Tuberculous:
leptomeningitis
meningoencephalitis

EXCLUDES *tuberculoma of meninges (013.1)*

§ 5th **013.1 Tuberculoma of meninges**
[0-6]

§ 5th **013.2 Tuberculoma of brain**
[0-6]
Tuberculosis of brain (current disease)

§ 5th **013.3 Tuberculous abscess of brain**
[0-6]

§ 5th **013.4 Tuberculoma of spinal cord**
[0-6]

§ 5th **013.5 Tuberculous abscess of spinal cord**
[0-6]

§ 5th **013.6 Tuberculous encephalitis or myelitis**
[0-6]

§ 5th **013.8 Other specified tuberculosis of central nervous system**
[0-6]

§ 5th **013.9 Unspecified tuberculosis of central nervous system**
[0-6]
Tuberculosis of central nervous system NOS

4th **014 Tuberculosis of intestines, peritoneum, and mesenteric glands**

§ 5th **014.0 Tuberculous peritonitis**
[0-6]
Tuberculous ascites

DEF: Tuberculous inflammation of the membrane lining the abdomen.

§ 5th **014.8 Other**
[0-6]
Tuberculosis (of):
anus
intestine (large) (small)
mesenteric glands
rectum
retroperitoneal (lymph nodes)
Tuberculous enteritis

4th **015 Tuberculosis of bones and joints**

Use additional code to identify manifestation, as:
tuberculous:
arthropathy (711.4)
necrosis of bone (730.8)
osteitis (730.8)
osteomyelitis (730.8)
synovitis (727.01)
tenosynovitis (727.01)

§ 5th **015.0 Vertebral column**
[0-6]
Pott's disease

Use additional code to identify manifestation, as:
curvature of spine [Pott's] (737.4)
kyphosis (737.4)
spondylitis (720.81)

§ 5th **015.1 Hip**
[0-6]

§ 5th **015.2 Knee**
[0-6]

§ 5th **015.5 Limb bones**
[0-6]
Tuberculous dactylitis

§ 5th **015.6 Mastoid**
[0-6]
Tuberculous mastoiditis

§ 5th **015.7 Other specified bone**
[0-6]

§ 5th **015.8 Other specified joint**
[0-6]

§ 5th **015.9 Tuberculosis of unspecified bones and joints**
[0-6]

4th **016 Tuberculosis of genitourinary system**

§ 5th **016.0 Kidney**
[0-6]
Renal tuberculosis

Use additional code to identify manifestation, as:
tuberculous:
nephropathy (583.81)
pyelitis (590.81)
pyelonephritis (590.81)

§ 5th **016.1 Bladder**
[0-6]

§ 5th **016.2 Ureter**
[0-6]

§ 5th **016.3 Other urinary organs**
[0-6]

§ 5th **016.4 Epididymis** ♂
[0-6]

§ 5th **016.5 Other male genital organs** ♂
[0-6]
Use additional code to identify manifestation, as:
tuberculosis of:
prostate (601.4)
seminal vesicle (608.81)
testis (608.81)

§ 5th **016.6 Tuberculous oophoritis and salpingitis** ♀
[0-6]

§ 5th **016.7 Other female genital organs** ♀
[0-6]
Tuberculous:
cervicitis
endometritis

§ 5th **016.9 Genitourinary tuberculosis, unspecified**
[0-6]

4th **017 Tuberculosis of other organs**

§ 5th **017.0 Skin and subcutaneous cellular tissue**
[0-6]

Lupus:	Tuberculosis:
exedens	colliquativa
vulgaris	cutis
Scrofuloderma	lichenoides
	papulonecrotica
	verrucosa cutis

EXCLUDES *lupus erythematosus (695.4)*
disseminated (710.0)
lupus NOS (710.0)
nonspecific reaction to tuberculin skin test without active tuberculosis (795.5)
positive PPD (795.5)
positive tuberculin skin test without active tuberculosis (795.5)

§ 5th **017.1 Erythema nodosum with hypersensitivity reaction in tuberculosis**
[0-6]
Bazin's disease
Erythema:
induratum
nodosum, tuberculous
Tuberculosis indurativa

EXCLUDES *erythema nodosum NOS (695.2)*

DEF: Tender, inflammatory, bilateral nodules appearing on the shins and thought to be an allergic reaction to tuberculotoxin.

§ Requires fifth-digit. Valid digits are in [brackets] under each code. See beginning of section 010-018 for codes and definitions.

N Newborn Age: 0 P Pediatric Age: 0-17 M Maternity Age: 12-55 A Adult Age: 15-124

§ ✓5th **017.2 Peripheral lymph nodes**
[0-6]
Scrofula
Scrofulous abscess
Tuberculous adenitis

EXCLUDES *tuberculosis of lymph nodes:*
bronchial and mediastinal (012.1)
mesenteric and retroperitoneal (014.8)
tuberculous tracheobronchial adenopathy (012.1)

DEF: Scrofula: Old name for tuberculous cervical lymphadenitis.

§ ✓5th **017.3 Eye**
[0-6]
Use additional code to identify manifestation, as:
tuberculous:
chorioretinitis, disseminated (363.13)
episcleritis (379.09)
interstitial keratitis (370.59)
iridocyclitis, chronic (364.11)
keratoconjunctivitis (phlyctenular) (370.31)

§ ✓5th **017.4 Ear**
[0-6]
Tuberculosis of ear
Tuberculous otitis media

EXCLUDES *tuberculous mastoiditis (015.6)*

§ ✓5th **017.5 Thyroid gland**
[0-6]

§ ✓5th **017.6 Adrenal glands**
[0-6]
Addison's disease, tuberculous

§ ✓5th **017.7 Spleen**
[0-6]

§ ✓5th **017.8 Esophagus**
[0-6]

§ ✓5th **017.9 Other specified organs**
[0-6]
Use additional code to identify manifestation, as:
tuberculosis of:
endocardium [any valve] (424.91)
myocardium (422.0)
pericardium (420.0)

✓4th **018 Miliary tuberculosis**

INCLUDES tuberculosis:
disseminated
generalized
miliary, whether of a single specified site, multiple sites, or unspecified site
polyserositis

DEF: A form of tuberculosis caused by caseous material carried through the bloodstream planting seedlike tubercles in various body organs.

§ ✓5th **018.0 Acute miliary tuberculosis**
[0-6]

§ ✓5th **018.8 Other specified miliary tuberculosis**
[0-6]

§ ✓5th **018.9 Miliary tuberculosis, unspecified**
[0-6]

ZOONOTIC BACTERIAL DISEASES (020-027)

✓4th **020 Plague**

INCLUDES infection by Yersinia [Pasteurella] pestis

020.0 Bubonic

DEF: Most common acute and severe form of plague characterized by lymphadenopathy (buboes), chills, fever and headache.

020.1 Cellulocutaneous

DEF: Plague characterized by inflammation and necrosis of skin.

020.2 Septicemic

DEF: Plague characterized by massive infection in the bloodstream.

020.3 Primary pneumonic

DEF: Plague characterized by massive pulmonary infection.

020.4 Secondary pneumonic

DEF: Lung infection as a secondary complication of plague.

020.5 Pneumonic, unspecified

020.8 Other specified types of plague
Abortive plague
Ambulatory plague
Pestis minor

020.9 Plague, unspecified

✓4th **021 Tularemia**

INCLUDES deerfly fever
infection by Francisella [Pasteurella] tularensis
rabbit fever

DEF: A febrile disease transmitted by the bites of deer flies, fleas and ticks, by inhalations of aerosolized *F. tularensis* or by ingestion of contaminated food or water; patients quickly develop fever, chills, weakness, headache, backache and malaise.

021.0 Ulceroglandular tularemia

DEF: Lesions occur at the site *Francisella tularensis* organism enters body, usually the fingers or hands.

021.1 Enteric tularemia
Tularemia:
cryptogenic
intestinal
typhoidal

021.2 Pulmonary tularemia
Bronchopneumonic tularemia

021.3 Oculoglandular tularemia

DEF: Painful conjunctival infection by *Francisella tularensis* organism with possible corneal, preauricular lymph, or lacrimal involvement.

021.8 Other specified tularemia
Tularemia:
generalized or disseminated
glandular

021.9 Unspecified tularemia

✓4th **022 Anthrax**

AHA: 4Q '02, 70

DEF: An infectious bacterial disease usually transmitted by contact with infected animals or their discharges or products; it is classified by primary routes of inoculation as cutaneous, gastrointestinal and by inhalation.

022.0 Cutaneous anthrax
Malignant pustule

022.1 Pulmonary anthrax
Respiratory anthrax
Wool-sorters' disease

022.2 Gastrointestinal anthrax

022.3 Anthrax septicemia

022.8 Other specified manifestations of anthrax

022.9 Anthrax, unspecified

✓4th **023 Brucellosis**

INCLUDES fever:
Malta
Mediterranean
undulant

DEF: An infectious disease caused by gram-negative, aerobic coccobacilli organisms; it is transmitted to humans through contact with infected tissue or dairy products; fever, sweating, weakness and aching are symptoms of the disease.

023.0 Brucella melitensis

DEF: Infection from direct or indirect contact with infected sheep or goats.

023.1 Brucella abortus

DEF: Infection from direct or indirect contact with infected cattle.

023.2 Brucella suis

DEF: Infection from direct or indirect contact with infected swine.

§ Requires fifth-digit. Valid digits are in [brackets] under each code. See beginning of section 010-018 for codes and definitions.

023.3 Brucella canis

DEF: Infection from direct or indirect contact with infected dogs.

023.8 Other brucellosis

Infection by more than one organism

023.9 Brucellosis, unspecified

024 Glanders

Infection by:
  Actinobacillus mallei
  Malleomyces mallei
  Pseudomonas mallei
Farcy
Malleus

DEF: Equine infection causing mucosal inflammation and skin ulcers in humans.

025 Melioidosis

Infection by:
  Malleomyces pseudomallei
  Pseudomonas pseudomallei
  Whitmore's bacillus
Pseudoglanders

DEF: Rare infection caused by *Pseudomonas pseudomallei;* clinical symptoms range from localized infection to fatal septicemia.

✓4th **026 Rat-bite fever**

026.0 Spirillary fever

Rat-bite fever due to Spirillum minor [S. minus]
Sodoku

026.1 Streptobacillary fever

Epidemic arthritic erythema
Haverhill fever
Rat-bite fever due to Streptobacillus moniliformis

026.9 Unspecified rat-bite fever

✓4th **027 Other zoonotic bacterial diseases**

027.0 Listeriosis

Infection } by Listeria monocytogenes
Septicemia }

Use additional code to identify manifestation, as meningitis (320.7)

EXCLUDES *congenital listeriosis (771.2)*

027.1 Erysipelothrix infection

Erysipeloid (of Rosenbach)
Infection } by Erysipelothrix insidiosa [E. rhusiopathiae]
Septicemia }

DEF: Usually associated with handling of fish, meat, or poultry; symptoms range from localized inflammation to septicemia.

027.2 Pasteurellosis

Pasteurella pseudotuberculosis infection
Mesenteric adenitis } by Pasteurella multocida [P. septica]
Septic infection (cat bite) (dog bite) }

EXCLUDES *infection by:*
Francisella [Pasteurella] tularensis (021.0-021.9)
Yersinia [Pasteurella] pestis (020.0-020.9)

DEF: Swelling, abscesses, or septicemia from *Pasteurella multocida*, commonly transmitted to humans by a dog or cat scratch.

027.8 Other specified zoonotic bacterial diseases

027.9 Unspecified zoonotic bacterial disease

OTHER BACTERIAL DISEASES (030-041)

EXCLUDES *bacterial venereal diseases (098.0-099.9)*
bartonellosis (088.0)

✓4th **030 Leprosy**

INCLUDES Hansen's disease
infection by Mycobacterium leprae

030.0 Lepromatous [type L]

Lepromatous leprosy (macular) (diffuse) (infiltrated) (nodular) (neuritic)

DEF: Infectious, disseminated leprosy bacilli with lesions and deformities.

030.1 Tuberculoid [type T]

Tuberculoid leprosy (macular) (maculoanesthetic) (major) (minor) (neuritic)

DEF: Relatively benign, self-limiting leprosy with neuralgia and scales.

030.2 Indeterminate [group I]

Indeterminate [uncharacteristic] leprosy (macular) (neuritic)

DEF: Uncharacteristic leprosy, frequently an early manifestation.

030.3 Borderline [group B]

Borderline or dimorphous leprosy (infiltrated) (neuritic)

DEF: Transitional form of leprosy, neither lepromatous nor tuberculoid.

030.8 Other specified leprosy

030.9 Leprosy, unspecified

✓4th **031 Diseases due to other mycobacteria**

031.0 Pulmonary

Battey disease
Infection by Mycobacterium:
  avium
  intracellulare [Battey bacillus]
  kansasii

031.1 Cutaneous

Buruli ulcer
Infection by Mycobacterium:
  marinum [M. balnei]
  ulcerans

031.2 Disseminated

Disseminated mycobacterium avium-intracellulare complex (DMAC)
Mycobacterium avium-intracellulare complex (MAC) bacteremia

AHA: 4Q, '97, 31

DEF: Disseminated mycobacterium avium-intracellulare complex (DMAC): A serious systemic form of MAC commonly observed in patients in the late course of AIDS.

DEF: Mycobacterium avium-intracellulare complex (MAC) bacterium: Human pulmonary disease, lymphadenitis in children and systemic disease in immunocompromised individuals caused by a slow growing, gram-positive, aerobic organism.

031.8 Other specified mycobacterial diseases

031.9 Unspecified diseases due to mycobacteria

Atypical mycobacterium infection NOS

✓4th **032 Diphtheria**

INCLUDES infection by Corynebacterium diphtheriae

032.0 Faucial diphtheria

Membranous angina, diphtheritic

DEF: Diphtheria of the throat.

032.1 Nasopharyngeal diphtheria

032.2 Anterior nasal diphtheria

032.3 Laryngeal diphtheria

Laryngotracheitis, diphtheritic

✓5th **032.8 Other specified diphtheria**

032.81 Conjunctival diphtheria
Pseudomembranous diphtheritic conjunctivitis

032.82 Diphtheritic myocarditis

032.83 Diphtheritic peritonitis

032.84 Diphtheritic cystitis

032.85 Cutaneous diphtheria

032.89 Other

032.9 Diphtheria, unspecified

✓4th **033 Whooping cough**

INCLUDES pertussis

Use additional code to identify any associated pneumonia (484.3)

DEF: An acute, highly contagious respiratory tract infection caused by *Bordetella pertussis* and *B. bronchiseptica;* characteristic paroxysmal cough.

033.0 Bordetella pertussis [B. pertussis]

033.1 Bordetella parapertussis [B. parapertussis]

033.8 Whooping cough due to other specified organism
Bordetella bronchiseptica [B. bronchiseptica]

033.9 Whooping cough, unspecified organism

✓4th **034 Streptococcal sore throat and scarlet fever**

034.0 Streptococcal sore throat

Septic:	Streptococcal:
angina	angina
sore throat	laryngitis
	pharyngitis
	tonsillitis

034.1 Scarlet fever
Scarlatina

EXCLUDES *parascarlatina (057.8)*

DEF: Streptococcal infection and fever with red rash spreading from trunk.

035 Erysipelas

EXCLUDES *postpartum or puerperal erysipelas (670)*

DEF: An acute superficial cellulitis involving the dermal lymphatics; it is often caused by group A streptococci.

✓4th **036 Meningococcal infection**

036.0 Meningococcal meningitis
Cerebrospinal fever (meningococcal)
Meningitis:
cerebrospinal
epidemic

036.1 Meningococcal encephalitis

036.2 Meningococcemia
Meningococcal septicemia

036.3 Waterhouse-Friderichsen syndrome, meningococcal
Meningococcal hemorrhagic adrenalitis
Meningococcic adrenal syndrome
Waterhouse-Friderichsen syndrome NOS

✓5th **036.4 Meningococcal carditis**

036.40 Meningococcal carditis, unspecified

036.41 Meningococcal pericarditis

DEF: Meningococcal infection of the outer membrane of the heart.

036.42 Meningococcal endocarditis

DEF: Meningococcal infection of the membranes lining the cavities of the heart.

036.43 Meningococcal myocarditis

DEF: Meningococcal infection of the muscle of the heart.

✓5th **036.8 Other specified meningococcal infections**

036.81 Meningococcal optic neuritis

036.82 Meningococcal arthropathy

036.89 Other

036.9 Meningococcal infection, unspecified
Meningococcal infection NOS

037 Tetanus

EXCLUDES *tetanus:*
complicating:
abortion (634-638 with .0, 639.0)
ectopic or molar pregnancy (639.0)
neonatorum (771.3)
puerperal (670)

DEF: An acute, often fatal, infectious disease caused by the anaerobic, spore-forming bacillus *Clostridium tetani;* the bacillus most often enters the body through a contaminated wound, burns, surgical wounds, or cutaneous ulcers. Symptoms include lockjaw, spasms, seizures, and paralysis.

✓4th **038 Septicemia**

Use additional code for systemic inflammatory response syndrome (SIRS) (995.91-995.92)

EXCLUDES *bacteremia (790.7)*
during labor (659.3)
following ectopic or molar pregnancy (639.0)
following infusion, injection, transfusion, or vaccination (999.3)
postpartum, puerperal (670)
septicemia (sepsis) of newborn (771.81)
that complicating abortion (634-638 with .0, 639.0)

AHA: 2Q, '04, 16; 4Q, '88, 10; 3Q, '88, 12

DEF: A systemic disease associated with the presence and persistence of pathogenic microorganisms or their toxins in the blood.

038.0 Streptococcal septicemia

AHA: 4Q, '03, 79; 2Q, '96, 5

✓5th **038.1 Staphylococcal septicemia**

AHA: 4Q, '97, 32

038.10 Staphylococcal septicemia,unspecified

▲ **038.11 Methicillin susceptible Staphylococcus aureus septicemia**
▶MSSA septicemia
Staphylococcus aureus septicemia NOS◀

AHA: 1Q, '05, 7; 2Q, '00, 5; 4Q, '98, 42

● **038.12 Methicillin resistant Staphylococcus aureus septicemia**

038.19 Other staphylococcal septicemia

AHA: 2Q, '00, 5

038.2 Pneumococcal septicemia [Streptococcus pneumoniae septicemia]

AHA: 2Q, '96, 5; 1Q, '91, 13

038.3 Septicemia due to anaerobes
Septicemia due to bacteroides

EXCLUDES *gas gangrene (040.0)*
that due to anaerobic streptococci (038.0)

DEF: Infection of blood by microorganisms categorized as gram-negative by Gram's method of staining for identification of bacteria.

✓5th **038.4 Septicemia due to other gram-negative organisms**

DEF: Infection of blood by microorganisms categorized as gram-negative by Gram's method of staining for identification of bacteria.

038.40 Gram-negative organism, unspecified
Gram-negative septicemia NOS

038.41 Hemophilus influenzae [H. influenzae]

038.42 Escherichia coli [E. coli]

AHA: 4Q, '03, 73

038.43 Pseudomonas

038.44 Serratia

038.49 Other

038.8 Other specified septicemias

EXCLUDES *septicemia (due to):*
anthrax (022.3)
gonococcal (098.89)
herpetic (054.5)
meningococcal (036.2)
septicemic plague (020.2)

038.9 Unspecified septicemia

Septicemia NOS

EXCLUDES *bacteremia NOS (790.7)*

AHA: 4Q, '07, 97; 2Q, '05, 18-19; 2Q, '04, 16; 4Q, '03, 79; 2Q, '00, 3; 3Q, '99, 5, 9; 1Q, '98, 5; 3Q, '96, 16; 2Q, '96, 6

✓4th **039 Actinomycotic infections**

INCLUDES actinomycotic mycetoma
infection by Actinomycetales, such as species of Actinomyces, Actinomadura, Nocardia, Streptomyces
maduromycosis (actinomycotic)
schizomycetoma (actinomycotic)

DEF: Inflammatory lesions and abscesses at site of infection by *Actinomyces israelii.*

039.0 Cutaneous

Erythrasma
Trichomycosis axillaris

039.1 Pulmonary

Thoracic actinomycosis

039.2 Abdominal

039.3 Cervicofacial

039.4 Madura foot

EXCLUDES *madura foot due to mycotic infection (117.4)*

039.8 Of other specified sites

039.9 Of unspecified site

Actinomycosis NOS
Maduromycosis NOS
Nocardiosis NOS

✓4th **040 Other bacterial diseases**

EXCLUDES *bacteremia NOS (790.7)*
bacterial infection NOS (041.9)

040.0 Gas gangrene

Gas bacillus infection or gangrene
Infection by Clostridium:
histolyticum
oedematiens
perfringens [welchii]
septicum
sordellii
Malignant edema
Myonecrosis, clostridial
Myositis, clostridial

AHA: 1Q, '95, 11

040.1 Rhinoscleroma

DEF: Growths on the nose and nasopharynx caused by *Klebsiella rhinoscleromatis.*

040.2 Whipple's disease

Intestinal lipodystrophy

040.3 Necrobacillosis

AHA: 4Q, '07, 85

DEF: Infection with *Fusobacterium necrophorum* causing abscess or necrosis.

✓5th **040.4 Other specified botulism**

Non-foodborne intoxication due to toxins of Clostridium botulinum [C. botulinum]

EXCLUDES *botulism NOS (005.1)*
food poisoning due to toxins of Clostridium botulinum (005.1)

040.41 Infant botulism P

AHA: 4Q, '07, 60

DEF: Colonization of Clostridium botulinum spores in the large intestine; poisoning due to release of neurotoxins results in constipation; may progress to neuromuscular paralysis; affects infants of less than six months of age.

040.42 Wound botulism

Non-foodborne botulism NOS
Use additional code to identify complicated open wound

AHA: 4Q, '07, 60

✓5th **040.8 Other specified bacterial diseases**

040.81 Tropical pyomyositis

040.82 Toxic shock syndrome

Use additional code to identify the organism

AHA: 4Q, '02, 44

DEF: Syndrome caused by staphylococcal exotoxin that may rapidly progress to severe and intractable shock; symptoms include characteristic sunburn-like rash with peeling of skin on palms and soles, sudden onset high fever, vomiting, diarrhea, myalgia, and hypotension.

040.89 Other

AHA: N-D, '86, 7

✓4th **041 Bacterial infection in conditions classified elsewhere and of unspecified site**

Note: This category is provided to be used as an additional code to identify the bacterial agent in diseases classified elsewhere. This category will also be used to classify bacterial infections of unspecified nature or site.

EXCLUDES *septicemia (038.0-038.9)*

AHA: 2Q, '01, 12; J-A, '84, 19

✓5th **041.0 Streptococcus**

041.00 Streptococcus, unspecified

041.01 Group A

AHA: 1Q, '02, 3

041.02 Group B

041.03 Group C

041.04 Group D [Enterococcus]

041.05 Group G

041.09 Other Streptococcus

✓5th **041.1 Staphylococcus**

041.10 Staphylococcus, unspecified

AHA: 2Q, '06, 15

▲ **041.11 Methicillin susceptible Staphylococcus aureus**

▶MSSA
Staphylococcus aureus NOS◀

AHA: 2Q, '06, 16; 4Q, '03, 104, 106; 2Q, '01, 11; 4Q, '98, 42, 54; 4Q, '97, 32

● **041.12 Methicillin resistant Staphylococcus aureus**

Methicillin-resistant staphylococcus aureus (MRSA)

041.19 Other Staphylococcus

AHA: ▶2Q, '08, 3◀

041.2 Pneumococcus

041.3 Friedländer's bacillus
Infection by Klebsiella pneumoniae

041.4 Escherichia coli [E. coli]

041.5 Hemophilus influenzae [H. influenzae]

041.6 Proteus (mirabilis) (morganii)

041.7 Pseudomonas
AHA: 4Q, '02, 45

✓5th **041.8 Other specified bacterial infections**

041.81 Mycoplasma
Eaton's agent
Pleuropneumonia-like organisms [PPLO]

041.82 Bacteroides fragilis
DEF: Anaerobic gram-negative bacilli of the gastrointestinal tract; frequently implicated in intra-abdominal infection; commonly resistant to antibiotics.

041.83 Clostridium perfringens

041.84 Other anaerobes
Gram-negative anaerobes
EXCLUDES *Helicobacter pylori (041.86)*

041.85 Other gram-negative organisms
Aerobacter aerogenes
Gram-negative bacteria NOS
Mima polymorpha
Serratia
EXCLUDES *gram-negative anaerobes (041.84)*
AHA: 1Q, '95, 18

041.86 Helicobacter pylori [H. pylori]
AHA: 4Q, '95, 60

041.89 Other specified bacteria
AHA: 2Q, '06, 7; 2Q, '03, 7

041.9 Bacterial infection, unspecified
AHA: 2Q, '91, 9

HUMAN IMMUNODEFICIENCY VIRUS (HIV) INFECTION (042)

042 Human immunodeficiency virus [HIV] disease
Acquired immune deficiency syndrome
Acquired immunodeficiency syndrome
AIDS
AIDS-like syndrome
AIDS-related complex
ARC
HIV infection, symptomatic
Use additional code(s) to identify all manifestations of HIV
Use additional code to identify HIV-2 infection (079.53)
EXCLUDES *asymptomatic HIV infection status (V08)*
exposure to HIV virus (V01.79)
nonspecific serologic evidence of HIV (795.71)
AHA: 4Q, '07, 63; 3Q, '06, 15; 1Q, '05, 7; 2Q, '04, 11; 1Q, '04, 5; 1Q, '03, 15; 1Q, '99, 14; 4Q, '97, 30, 31; 1Q, '93, 21; 2Q, '92, 11; 3Q, '90, 17; J-A, '87, 8

POLIOMYELITIS AND OTHER NON-ARTHROPOD-BORNE VIRAL DISEASES ►AND PRION DISEASES◄ OF CENTRAL NERVOUS SYSTEM (045-049)

✓4th **045 Acute poliomyelitis**
EXCLUDES *late effects of acute poliomyelitis (138)*

The following fifth-digit subclassification is for use with category 045:
0 poliovirus, unspecified type
1 poliovirus type I
2 poliovirus type II
3 poliovirus type III

§ ✓5th **045.0 Acute paralytic poliomyelitis specified as bulbar**
[0-3]
Infantile paralysis (acute) } specified as bulbar
Poliomyelitis (acute) (anterior) } specified as bulbar
Polioencephalitis (acute) (bulbar)
Polioencephalomyelitis (acute) (anterior) (bulbar)
DEF: Acute paralytic infection occurring where the brain merges with the spinal cord; affecting breathing, swallowing, and heart rate.

§ ✓5th **045.1 Acute poliomyelitis with other paralysis**
[0-3]
Paralysis:
acute atrophic, spinal
infantile, paralytic
Poliomyelitis (acute) anterior epidemic } with paralysis except bulbar
DEF: Paralytic infection affecting peripheral or spinal nerves.

§ ✓5th **045.2 Acute nonparalytic poliomyelitis**
[0-3]
Poliomyelitis (acute) anterior epidemic } specified as nonparalytic
DEF: Nonparalytic infection causing pain, stiffness, and paresthesias.

§ ✓5th **045.9 Acute poliomyelitis, unspecified**
[0-3]
Infantile paralysis
Poliomyelitis (acute) anterior epidemic } unspecified whether paralytic or nonparalytic

▲ ✓4th **046 Slow virus infections and prion diseases of central nervous system**

046.0 Kuru
DEF: A chronic, progressive, fatal nervous system disorder; clinical symptoms include cerebellar ataxia, trembling, spasticity and progressive dementia.

✓5th **046.1 Jakob-Creutzfeldt disease**

● **046.11 Variant Creutzfeldt-Jakob disease**
vCJD

● **046.19 Other and unspecified Creutzfeldt-Jacob disease**
CJD
Familial Creutzfeldt-Jakob disease
Iatrogenic Creutzfeldt-Jakob disease
Jakob-Creutzfeldt disease, unspecified
Sporadic Creutzfeldt-Jakob disease
Subacute spongiform encephalopathy
EXCLUDES *variant Creutzfeldt-Jakob disease (vCJD) (046.11)*
DEF: Communicable, progressive spongiform encephalopathy thought to be caused by an infectious particle known as a "prion" (proteinaceous infection particle). This is a progressive, fatal disease manifested principally by mental deterioration.

046.2 Subacute sclerosing panencephalitis
Dawson's inclusion body encephalitis
Van Bogaert's sclerosing leukoencephalitis
DEF: Progressive viral infection causing cerebral dysfunction, blindness, dementia, and death (SSPE).

046.3 Progressive multifocal leukoencephalopathy
Multifocal leukoencephalopathy NOS
DEF: Infection affecting cerebral cortex in patients with weakened immune systems.

● ✓5th **046.7 Other specified prion diseases of central nervous system**
EXCLUDES *Creutzfeldt-Jakob disease (046.11-046.19)*
Jakob-Creutzfeldt disease (046.11-046.19)
kuru (046.0)
variant Creutzfeldt-Jakob disease (vCJD) (046.11)

§ Requires fifth-digit. Valid digits are in [brackets] under each code. See category 045 for codes and definitions.

● 046.71 **Gerstmann-Sträussler-Scheinker syndrome**
GSS syndrome

● 046.72 **Fatal familial insomnia**
FFI

● 046.79 **Other and unspecified prion disease of central nervous system**

046.8 **Other specified slow virus infection of central nervous system**

046.9 **Unspecified slow virus infection of central nervous system**

4th 047 Meningitis due to enterovirus

INCLUDES meningitis:
abacterial
aseptic
viral

EXCLUDES *meningitis due to:*
adenovirus (049.1)
arthropod-borne virus (060.0-066.9)
leptospira (100.81)
virus of:
herpes simplex (054.72)
herpes zoster (053.0)
lymphocytic choriomeningitis (049.0)
mumps (072.1)
poliomyelitis (045.0-045.9)
any other infection specifically classified elsewhere

AHA: J-F, '87, 6

047.0 **Coxsackie virus**

047.1 **ECHO virus**
Meningo-eruptive syndrome

047.8 **Other specified viral meningitis**

047.9 **Unspecified viral meningitis**
Viral meningitis NOS

048 **Other enterovirus diseases of central nervous system**
Boston exanthem

4th 049 Other non-arthropod-borne viral diseases of central nervous system

EXCLUDES *late effects of viral encephalitis (139.0)*

049.0 **Lymphocytic choriomeningitis**
Lymphocytic:
meningitis (serous) (benign)
meningoencephalitis (serous) (benign)

049.1 **Meningitis due to adenovirus**

DEF: Inflammation of lining of brain caused by Arenaviruses and usually occurring in adults in fall and winter months.

049.8 **Other specified non-arthropod-borne viral diseases of central nervous system**
Encephalitis:
acute:
inclusion body
necrotizing
epidemic
lethargica
Rio Bravo
von Economo's disease

EXCLUDES *human herpesvirus 6 encephalitis (058.21)*
other human herpesvirus encephalitis (058.29)

049.9 **Unspecified non-arthropod-borne viral diseases of central nervous system**
Viral encephalitis NOS

VIRAL DISEASES ACCOMPANIED BY EXANTHEM ▶(050-059)◀

EXCLUDES *arthropod-borne viral diseases (060.0-066.9)*
Boston exanthem (048)

4th 050 Smallpox

050.0 **Variola major**
Hemorrhagic (pustular) smallpox
Malignant smallpox
Purpura variolosa

DEF: Form of smallpox known for its high mortality; exists only in laboratories.

050.1 **Alastrim**
Variola minor

DEF: Mild form of smallpox known for its low mortality rate.

050.2 **Modified smallpox**
Varioloid

DEF: Mild form occurring in patients with history of infection or vaccination.

050.9 **Smallpox, unspecified**

4th 051 Cowpox and paravaccinia

▲ 5th 051.0 **Cowpox and vaccinia not from vaccination**

● 051.01 **Cowpox**

DEF: A disease contracted by milking infected cows; vesicles usually appear on the fingers, may spread to hands and adjacent areas and usually disappear without scarring; other associated features of the disease may include local edema, lymphangitis and regional lymphadenitis with or without fever.

● 051.02 **Vaccinia not from vaccination**

EXCLUDES *vaccinia (generalized) (from vaccination) (999.0)*

051.1 **Pseudocowpox**
Milkers' node

DEF: Hand lesions and mild fever in dairy workers caused by exposure to paravaccinia.

051.2 **Contagious pustular dermatitis**
Ecthyma contagiosum
Orf

DEF: Skin eruptions caused by exposure to poxvirus-infected sheep or goats.

051.9 **Paravaccinia, unspecified**

4th 052 Chickenpox

DEF: Contagious infection by *Varicella-zoster* virus causing rash with pustules and fever.

052.0 **Postvaricella encephalitis**
Postchickenpox encephalitis

052.1 **Varicella (hemorrhagic) pneumonitis**

052.2 **Postvaricella myelitis**
Postchickenpox myelitis

AHA: 4Q, '06, 58-63

052.7 **With other specified complications**

AHA: 1Q, '02, 3

052.8 **With unspecified complication**

052.9 **Varicella without mention of complication**
Chickenpox NOS
Varicella NOS

4th 053 Herpes zoster

INCLUDES shingles
zona

DEF: Self-limiting infection by *varicella-zoster* virus causing unilateral eruptions and neuralgia along affected nerves.

053.0 **With meningitis**

DEF: *Varicella-zoster* virus infection causing inflammation of the lining of the brain and/or spinal cord.

5th 053.1 **With other nervous system complications**

053.10 With unspecified nervous system complication

053.11 Geniculate herpes zoster
Herpetic geniculate ganglionitis
DEF: Unilateral eruptions and neuralgia along the facial nerve geniculum affecting face and outer and middle ear.

053.12 Postherpetic trigeminal neuralgia
DEF: Severe oral or nasal pain following a herpes zoster infection.

053.13 Postherpetic polyneuropathy
DEF: Multiple areas of pain following a herpes zoster infection.

053.14 Herpes zoster myelitis
AHA: 4Q, '06, 58-63

053.19 Other

✓5th **053.2 With ophthalmic complications**

053.20 Herpes zoster dermatitis of eyelid
Herpes zoster ophthalmicus

053.21 Herpes zoster keratoconjunctivitis

053.22 Herpes zoster iridocyclitis

053.29 Other

✓5th **053.7 With other specified complications**

053.71 Otitis externa due to herpes zoster

053.79 Other

053.8 With unspecified complication

053.9 Herpes zoster without mention of complication
Herpes zoster NOS

✓4th **054 Herpes simplex**

EXCLUDES *congenital herpes simplex (771.2)*

054.0 Eczema herpeticum
Kaposi's varicelliform eruption
DEF: Herpes simplex virus invading site of preexisting skin inflammation.

✓5th **054.1 Genital herpes**
AHA: J-F, '87, 15, 16

054.10 Genital herpes, unspecified
Herpes progenitalis

054.11 Herpetic vulvovaginitis ♀

054.12 Herpetic ulceration of vulva ♀

054.13 Herpetic infection of penis ♂

054.19 Other

054.2 Herpetic gingivostomatitis

054.3 Herpetic meningoencephalitis
Herpes encephalitis
Simian B disease

EXCLUDES *human herpesvirus 6 encephalitis (058.21)*
other human herpesvirus encephalitis (058.29)

DEF: Inflammation of the brain and its lining, caused by infection of herpes simplex 1 in adults and simplex 2 in newborns.

✓5th **054.4 With ophthalmic complications**

054.40 With unspecified ophthalmic complication

054.41 Herpes simplex dermatitis of eyelid

054.42 Dendritic keratitis

054.43 Herpes simplex disciform keratitis

054.44 Herpes simplex iridocyclitis

054.49 Other

054.5 Herpetic septicemia
AHA: 2Q, '00, 5

054.6 Herpetic whitlow
Herpetic felon
DEF: A primary infection of the terminal segment of a finger by herpes simplex; intense itching and pain start the disease, vesicles form, and tissue ultimately is destroyed.

✓5th **054.7 With other specified complications**

054.71 Visceral herpes simplex

054.72 Herpes simplex meningitis

054.73 Herpes simplex otitis externa

054.74 Herpes simplex myelitis
AHA: 4Q, '06, 58-63

054.79 Other

054.8 With unspecified complication

054.9 Herpes simplex without mention of complication

✓4th **055 Measles**

INCLUDES morbilli
rubeola

055.0 Postmeasles encephalitis

055.1 Postmeasles pneumonia

055.2 Postmeasles otitis media

✓5th **055.7 With other specified complications**

055.71 Measles keratoconjunctivitis
Measles keratitis

055.79 Other

055.8 With unspecified complication

055.9 Measles without mention of complication

✓4th **056 Rubella**

INCLUDES German measles
EXCLUDES *congenital rubella (771.0)*

DEF: Acute but usually benign togavirus infection causing fever, sore throat, and rash; associated with complications to fetus as a result of maternal infection.

✓5th **056.0 With neurological complications**

056.00 With unspecified neurological complication

056.01 Encephalomyelitis due to rubella
Encephalitis } due to rubella
Meningoencephalitis } due to rubella

056.09 Other

✓5th **056.7 With other specified complications**

056.71 Arthritis due to rubella

056.79 Other

056.8 With unspecified complications

056.9 Rubella without mention of complication

✓4th **057 Other viral exanthemata**
DEF: Skin eruptions or rashes and fever caused by viruses, including poxviruses.

057.0 Erythema infectiosum [fifth disease]
DEF: A moderately contagious, benign, epidemic disease, usually seen in children, and of probable viral etiology; a red macular rash appears on the face and may spread to the limbs and trunk.

057.8 Other specified viral exanthemata
Dukes (-Filatow) disease
Fourth disease
Parascarlatina
Pseudoscarlatina
EXCLUDES *exanthema subitum [sixth disease] (058.10-058.12)*
roseola infantum (058.10-058.12)

057.9 Viral exanthem, unspecified

4th 058 Other human herpesvirus
EXCLUDES *congenital herpes (771.2)*
cytomegalovirus (078.5)
Epstein-Barr virus (075)
herpes NOS (054.0-054.9)
herpes simplex (054.0-054.9)
herpes zoster (053.0-053.9)
human herpesvirus NOS (054.0-054.9)
human herpesvirus 1 (054.0-054.9)
human herpesvirus 2 (054.0-054.9)
human herpesvirus 3 (052.0-053.9)
human herpesvirus 4 (075)
human herpesvirus 5 (078.5)
varicella (052.0-052.9)
varicella-zoster virus (052.0-053.9)
AHA: 4Q, '07, 61

5th 058.1 Roseola infantum
Exanthema subitum [sixth disease]

058.10 Roseola infantum, unspecified P
Exanthema subitum [sixth disease], unspecified
AHA: 4Q, '07, 63

058.11 Roseola infantum due to human herpesvirus 6 P
Exanthema subitum [sixth disease] due to human herpesvirus 6

058.12 Roseola infantum due to human herpesvirus 7 P
Exanthema subitum [sixth disease] due to human herpesvirus 7

5th 058.2 Other human herpesvirus encephalitis
EXCLUDES *herpes encephalitis NOS (054.3)*
herpes simplex encephalitis (054.3)
human herpesvirus encephalitis NOS (054.3)
simian B herpesvirus encephalitis (054.3)

058.21 Human herpesvirus 6 encephalitis

058.29 Other human herpesvirus encephalitis
Human herpesvirus 7 encephalitis

5th 058.8 Other human herpesvirus infections

058.81 Human herpesvirus 6 infection

058.82 Human herpesvirus 7 infection

058.89 Other human herpesvirus infection
Human herpesvirus 8 infection
Kaposi's sarcoma-associated herpesvirus infection
AHA: 4Q, '07, 63

• **4th 059 Other poxvirus infections**
EXCLUDES *contagious pustular dermatitis (051.2)*
cowpox (051.01)
ecthyma contagiosum (051.2)
milker's nodule (051.1)
orf (051.2)
paravaccinia NOS (051.9)
pseudocowpox (051.1)
smallpox (050.0-050.9)
vaccinia (generalized) (from vaccination) (999.0)
vaccinia not from vaccination (051.02)

• **5th 059.0 Other orthopoxvirus infections**
• **059.00 Orthopoxvirus infection, unspecified**
• **059.01 Monkeypox**
• **059.09 Other orthopoxvirus infection**

• **5th 059.1 Other parapoxvirus infections**
• **059.10 Parapoxvirus infection, unspecified**
• **059.11 Bovine stomatitis**
• **059.12 Sealpox**
• **059.19 Other parapoxvirus infections**

• **5th 059.2 Yatapoxvirus infections**
• **059.20 Yatapoxvirus infection, unspecified**
• **059.21 Tanapox**
• **059.22 Yaba monkey tumor virus**

• **059.8 Other poxvirus infections**
• **059.9 Poxvirus infections, unspecified**

ARTHROPOD-BORNE VIRAL DISEASES (060-066)

Use additional code to identify any associated meningitis (321.2)
EXCLUDES *late effects of viral encephalitis (139.0)*

4th 060 Yellow fever
DEF: Fever and jaundice from infection by mosquito-borne virus of genus *Flavivirus.*

060.0 Sylvatic
Yellow fever: jungle
Yellow fever: sylvan
DEF: Yellow fever transmitted from animal to man, via mosquito.

060.1 Urban
DEF: Yellow fever transmitted from man to man, via mosquito.

060.9 Yellow fever, unspecified

061 Dengue
Breakbone fever
EXCLUDES *hemorrhagic fever caused by dengue virus (065.4)*
DEF: Acute, self-limiting infection by mosquito-borne virus characterized by fever and generalized aches.

4th 062 Mosquito-borne viral encephalitis

062.0 Japanese encephalitis
Japanese B encephalitis
DEF: Flavivirus causing inflammation of the brain, with a wide range of clinical manifestations.

062.1 Western equine encephalitis
DEF: Alphavirus WEE infection causing inflammation of the brain, found in areas west of the Mississippi; transmitted horse to mosquito to man.

062.2 Eastern equine encephalitis
EXCLUDES *Venezuelan equine encephalitis (066.2)*
DEF: Alphavirus EEE causing inflammation of the brain and spinal cord, found as far north as Canada and south into South America and Mexico; transmitted horse to mosquito to man.

062.3 St. Louis encephalitis
DEF: Epidemic form caused by Flavivirus and transmitted by mosquito, and characterized by fever, difficulty in speech, and headache.

062.4 Australian encephalitis
Australian arboencephalitis
Australian X disease
Murray Valley encephalitis
DEF: Flavivirus causing inflammation of the brain, occurring in Australia and New Guinea.

062.5 California virus encephalitis
Encephalitis:
California
La Crosse
Tahyna fever
DEF: Bunyamwere virus causing inflammation of the brain.

062.8 Other specified mosquito-borne viral encephalitis
Encephalitis by Ilheus virus
EXCLUDES *West Nile virus (066.40-066.49)*

062.9 Mosquito-borne viral encephalitis, unspecified

✓4th 063 Tick-borne viral encephalitis

INCLUDES diphasic meningoencephalitis

063.0 Russian spring-summer [taiga] encephalitis

063.1 Louping ill
DEF: Inflammation of brain caused by virus transmitted sheep to tick to man; incidence usually limited to British Isles.

063.2 Central European encephalitis
DEF: Inflammation of brain caused by virus transmitted by tick; limited to central Europe and presenting with two distinct phases.

063.8 Other specified tick-borne viral encephalitis
Langat encephalitis
Powassan encephalitis

063.9 Tick-borne viral encephalitis, unspecified

064 Viral encephalitis transmitted by other and unspecified arthropods

Arthropod-borne viral encephalitis, vector unknown
Negishi virus encephalitis
EXCLUDES *viral encephalitis NOS (049.9)*

✓4th 065 Arthropod-borne hemorrhagic fever

065.0 Crimean hemorrhagic fever [CHF Congo virus]
Central Asian hemorrhagic fever

065.1 Omsk hemorrhagic fever

065.2 Kyasanur Forest disease

065.3 Other tick-borne hemorrhagic fever

065.4 Mosquito-borne hemorrhagic fever
Chikungunya hemorrhagic fever
Dengue hemorrhagic fever
EXCLUDES *Chikungunya fever (066.3)*
dengue (061)
yellow fever (060.0-060.9)

065.8 Other specified arthropod-borne hemorrhagic fever
Mite-borne hemorrhagic fever

065.9 Arthropod-borne hemorrhagic fever, unspecified
Arbovirus hemorrhagic fever NOS

✓4th 066 Other arthropod-borne viral diseases

066.0 Phlebotomus fever
Changuinola fever
Sandfly fever
DEF: Sandfly-borne viral infection occurring in Asia, Mideast and South America.

066.1 Tick-borne fever
Nairobi sheep disease
Tick fever:
American mountain
Colorado
Kemerovo
Quaranfil

066.2 Venezuelan equine fever
Venezuelan equine encephalitis
DEF: Alphavirus VEE infection causing inflammation of the brain, usually limited to South America, Mexico, and Florida; transmitted horse to mosquito to man.

066.3 Other mosquito-borne fever
Fever (viral):
Bunyamwera
Bwamba
Chikungunya
Guama
Mayaro
Mucambo
O'Nyong-Nyong
Oropouche
Pixuna
Rift valley
Ross river
Wesselsbron
Zika
EXCLUDES *dengue (061)*
yellow fever (060.0-060.9)

✓5th 066.4 West Nile fever
AHA: 4Q, '02, 44
DEF: Mosquito-borne fever causing fatal inflammation of the brain, the lining of the brain, or of the lining of the brain and spinal cord.

066.40 West Nile fever, unspecified
West Nile fever NOS
West Nile fever without complications
West Nile virus NOS

066.41 West Nile fever with encephalitis
West Nile encephalitis
West Nile encephalomyelitis
AHA: 4Q, '04, 51

066.42 West Nile fever with other neurologic manifestation
Use additional code to specify the neurologic manifestation
AHA: 4Q, '04, 51

066.49 West Nile fever with other complications
Use additional code to specify the other conditions

066.8 Other specified arthropod-borne viral diseases
Chandipura fever
Piry fever

066.9 Arthropod-borne viral disease, unspecified
Arbovirus infection NOS

OTHER DISEASES DUE TO VIRUSES AND CHLAMYDIAE (070-079)

✓4th 070 Viral hepatitis

INCLUDES viral hepatitis (acute) (chronic)
EXCLUDES *cytomegalic inclusion virus hepatitis (078.5)*

The following fifth-digit subclassification is for use with categories 070.2 and 070.3:
- **0 acute or unspecified, without mention of hepatitis delta**
- **1 acute or unspecified, with hepatitis delta**
- **2 chronic, without mention of hepatitis delta**
- **3 chronic, with hepatitis delta**

AHA: 2Q,'07, 5
DEF: Hepatitis A: HAV infection is self-limiting with flulike symptoms; transmission, fecal-oral.
DEF: Hepatitis B: HBV infection can be chronic and systemic; transmission, bodily fluids.
DEF: Hepatitis C: HCV infection can be chronic and systemic; transmission, blood transfusion and unidentified agents.
DEF: Hepatitis D (delta): HDV occurs only in the presence of hepatitis B virus.
DEF: Hepatitis E: HEV is epidemic form; transmission and nature under investigation.

070.0 Viral hepatitis A with hepatic coma

070.1 Viral hepatitis A without mention of hepatic coma
Infectious hepatitis

§ ✓5th 070.2 Viral hepatitis B with hepatic coma
[0-3] AHA: 4Q, '91, 28; For code 070.20: 2Q, '07, 6

§ Requires fifth-digit. Valid digits are in [brackets] under each code. See category 070 for codes and definitions.

§ ✓5th **070.3 Viral hepatitis B without mention of hepatic coma**
[0-3]
Serum hepatitis
AHA: 1Q, '93, 28; 4Q, '91, 28

✓5th **070.4 Other specified viral hepatitis with hepatic coma**
AHA: 4Q, '91, 28

070.41 Acute hepatitis C with hepatic coma

070.42 Hepatitis delta without mention of active hepatitis B disease with hepatic coma
Hepatitis delta with hepatitis B carrier state

070.43 Hepatitis E with hepatic coma

070.44 Chronic hepatitis C with hepatic coma
AHA: 2Q,'07, 5

070.49 Other specified viral hepatitis with hepatic coma

✓5th **070.5 Other specified viral hepatitis without mention of hepatic coma**
AHA: 4Q, '91, 28

070.51 Acute hepatitis C without mention of hepatic coma

070.52 Hepatitis delta without mention of active hepatititis B disease or hepatic coma

070.53 Hepatitis E without mention of hepatic coma

070.54 Chronic hepatitis C without mention of hepatic coma
AHA: 3Q, '07, 7; 2Q, '06, 13

070.59 Other specified viral hepatitis without mention of hepatic coma

070.6 Unspecified viral hepatitis with hepatic coma
EXCLUDES *unspecified viral hepatitis C with hepatic coma (070.71)*

✓5th **070.7 Unspecified viral hepatitis C**

070.70 Unspecified viral hepatitis C without hepatic coma
Unspecified viral hepatitis C NOS
AHA: 4Q, '04, 52

070.71 Unspecified viral hepatitis C with hepatic coma
AHA: 4Q, '04, 52

070.9 Unspecified viral hepatitis without mention of hepatic coma
Viral hepatitis NOS
EXCLUDES *unspecified viral hepatitis C without hepatic coma (070.70)*

071 Rabies
Hydrophobia
Lyssa
DEF: Acute infectious disease of the CNS caused by a rhabdovirus; usually spread by virus-laden saliva from bites by infected animals; it progresses from fever, restlessness, and extreme excitability, to hydrophobia, seizures, confusion and death.

✓4th **072 Mumps**
DEF: Acute infectious disease caused by paramyxovirus; usually seen in children less than 15 years of age; salivary glands are typically enlarged, and other organs, such as testes, pancreas and meninges, are often involved.

072.0 Mumps orchitis ♂

072.1 Mumps meningitis

072.2 Mumps encephalitis
Mumps meningoencephalitis

072.3 Mumps pancreatitis

✓5th **072.7 Mumps with other specified complications**

072.71 Mumps hepatitis

072.72 Mumps polyneuropathy

072.79 Other

072.8 Mumps with unspecified complication

072.9 Mumps without mention of complication
Epidemic parotitis
Infectious parotitis

✓4th **073 Ornithosis**
INCLUDES parrot fever
psittacosis
DEF: *Chlamydia psittaci* infection often transmitted from birds to humans.

073.0 With pneumonia
Lobular pneumonitis due to ornithosis

073.7 With other specified complications

073.8 With unspecified complication

073.9 Ornithosis, unspecified

✓4th **074 Specific diseases due to Coxsackie virus**
EXCLUDES *Coxsackie virus:*
infection NOS (079.2)
meningitis (047.0)

074.0 Herpangina
Vesicular pharyngitis
DEF: Acute infectious coxsackie virus infection causing throat lesions, fever, and vomiting; generally affects children in summer.

074.1 Epidemic pleurodynia
Bornholm disease
Devil's grip
Epidemic:
myalgia
myositis
DEF: Paroxysmal pain in chest, accompanied by fever and usually limited to children and young adults; caused by coxsackie virus.

✓5th **074.2 Coxsackie carditis**

074.20 Coxsackie carditis, unspecified

074.21 Coxsackie pericarditis
DEF: Coxsackie infection of the outer lining of the heart.

074.22 Coxsackie endocarditis
DEF: Coxsackie infection within the heart's cavities.

074.23 Coxsackie myocarditis
Aseptic myocarditis of newborn
DEF: Coxsackie infection of the muscle of the heart.

074.3 Hand, foot, and mouth disease
Vesicular stomatitis and exanthem
DEF: Mild coxsackie infection causing lesions on hands, feet and oral mucosa, most commonly seen in preschool children.

074.8 Other specified diseases due to Coxsackie virus
Acute lymphonodular pharyngitis

075 Infectious mononucleosis
Glandular fever
Monocytic angina
Pfeiffer's disease
AHA: 3Q, '01, 13; M-A, '87, 8
DEF: Acute infection by Epstein-Barr virus causing fever, sore throat, enlarged lymph glands and spleen, and fatigue; usually seen in teens and young adults.

§ Requires fifth-digit. Valid digits are in [brackets] under each code. See category 070 for codes and definitions.

✓4th 076 Trachoma

EXCLUDES *late effect of trachoma (139.1)*

DEF: A chronic infectious disease of the cornea and conjunctiva caused by a strain of the bacteria *Chlamydia trachomatis;* the infection can cause photophobia, pain, excessive tearing and sometimes blindness.

076.0 Initial stage
Trachoma dubium

076.1 Active stage
Granular conjunctivitis (trachomatous)
Trachomatous:
follicular conjunctivitis
pannus

076.9 Trachoma, unspecified
Trachoma NOS

✓4th 077 Other diseases of conjunctiva due to viruses and Chlamydiae

EXCLUDES *ophthalmic complications of viral diseases classified elsewhere*

077.0 Inclusion conjunctivitis
Paratrachoma
Swimming pool conjunctivitis
EXCLUDES *inclusion blennorrhea (neonatal) (771.6)*
DEF: Pus in conjunctiva caused by *Chlamydiae trachomatis.*

077.1 Epidemic keratoconjunctivitis
Shipyard eye
DEF: Highly contagious corneal or conjunctival infection caused by adenovirus type 8; symptoms include inflammation and corneal infiltrates.

077.2 Pharyngoconjunctival fever
Viral pharyngoconjunctivitis

077.3 Other adenoviral conjunctivitis
Acute adenoviral follicular conjunctivitis

077.4 Epidemic hemorrhagic conjunctivitis
Apollo:
conjunctivitis
disease
Conjunctivitis due to enterovirus type 70
Hemorrhagic conjunctivitis (acute) (epidemic)

077.8 Other viral conjunctivitis
Newcastle conjunctivitis

✓5th 077.9 Unspecified diseases of conjunctiva due to viruses and Chlamydiae

077.98 Due to Chlamydiae

077.99 Due to viruses
Viral conjunctivitis NOS

✓4th 078 Other diseases due to viruses and Chlamydiae

EXCLUDES *viral infection NOS (079.0-079.9)*
viremia NOS (790.8)

078.0 Molluscum contagiosum
DEF: Benign poxvirus infection causing small bumps on the skin or conjunctiva; transmitted by close contact.

✓5th 078.1 Viral warts
Viral warts due to human papilloma virus
AHA: 2Q, '97, 9; 4Q, '93, 22
DEF: A keratotic papilloma of the epidermis caused by the human papilloma virus; the superficial vegetative lesions last for varying durations and eventually regress spontaneously.

078.10 Viral warts, unspecified
Verruca:
Vulgaris
Warts (infectious)

078.11 Condyloma acuminatum
▶Condyloma NOS
Genital warts NOS◀
DEF: Clusters of mucosa or epidermal lesions on external genitalia; viral infection is sexually transmitted.

● **078.12 Plantar wart**
Verruca plantaris

078.19 Other specified viral warts
▶Common wart
Flat wart
Verruca plana◀

078.2 Sweating fever
Miliary fever
Sweating disease
DEF: A viral infection characterized by profuse sweating; various papular, vesicular and other eruptions cause the blockage of sweat glands.

078.3 Cat-scratch disease
Benign lymphoreticulosis (of inoculation)
Cat-scratch fever

078.4 Foot and mouth disease
Aphthous fever
Epizootic:
aphthae
stomatitis
DEF: Ulcers on oral mucosa, legs, and feet after exposure to infected animal.

078.5 Cytomegaloviral disease
Cytomegalic inclusion disease
Salivary gland virus disease
Use additional code to identify manifestation, as:
cytomegalic inclusion virus:
hepatitis (573.1)
pneumonia (484.1)
EXCLUDES *congenital cytomegalovirus infection (771.1)*
AHA: 1Q, '03, 10; 3Q, '98, 4; 2Q, '93, 11; 1Q, '89, 9
DEF: A herpesvirus inclusion associated with serious disease morbidity including fever, leukopenia, pneumonia, retinitis, hepatitis and organ transplant; often leads to syndromes such as hepatomegaly, splenomegaly and thrombocytopenia; a common post-transplant complication for organ transplant recipients.

078.6 Hemorrhagic nephrosonephritis
Hemorrhagic fever:
epidemic
Korean
Russian
with renal syndrome
DEF: Viral infection causing kidney dysfunction and bleeding disorders.

078.7 Arenaviral hemorrhagic fever
Hemorrhagic fever:
Argentine
Bolivian
Hemorrhagic fever:
Junin virus
Machupo virus

✓5th 078.8 Other specified diseases due to viruses and Chlamydiae

EXCLUDES *epidemic diarrhea (009.2)*
lymphogranuloma venereum (099.1)

078.81 Epidemic vertigo

078.82 Epidemic vomiting syndrome
Winter vomiting disease

078.88 Other specified diseases due to Chlamydiae
AHA: 4Q, '96, 22

078.89 Other specified diseases due to viruses
Epidemic cervical myalgia
Marburg disease
Tanapox

✓4th 079 Viral and chlamydial infection in conditions classified elsewhere and of unspecified site

Note: This category is provided to be used as an additional code to identify the viral agent in diseases classifiable elsewhere. This category will also be used to classify virus infection of unspecified nature or site.

079.0 Adenovirus

079.1 ECHO virus

DEF: An "orphan" enteric RNA virus, certain serotypes of which are associated with human disease, especially aseptic meningitis.

079.2 Coxsackie virus

DEF: A heterogenous group of viruses associated with aseptic meningitis, myocarditis, pericarditis, and acute onset juvenile diabetes.

079.3 Rhinovirus

DEF: Rhinoviruses affect primarily the upper respiratory tract. Over 100 distinct types infect humans.

079.4 Human papillomavirus

AHA: 2Q, '97, 9; 4Q, '93, 22

DEF: Viral infection caused by the genus *Papillomavirus* causing cutaneous and genital warts, including verruca vulgaris and condyloma acuminatum; certain types are associated with cervical dysplasia, cancer and other genital malignancies.

✓5th **079.5 Retrovirus**

EXCLUDES *human immunodeficiency virus, type 1 [HIV-1] (042)*
human T-cell lymphotrophic virus, type III [HTLV-III] (042)
lymphadenopathy-associated virus [LAV] (042)

AHA: 4Q, '93, 22, 23

DEF: A large group of RNA viruses that carry reverse transcriptase and include the leukoviruses and lentiviruses.

079.50 Retrovirus, unspecified

079.51 Human T-cell lymphotrophic virus, type I [HTLV-I]

079.52 Human T-cell lymphotrophic virus, type II [HTLV-II]

079.53 Human immunodeficiency virus, type 2 [HIV-2]

079.59 Other specified retrovirus

079.6 Respiratory syncytial virus [RSV]]

AHA: 4Q, '96, 27, 28

DEF: The major respiratory pathogen of young children, causing severe bronchitis and bronchopneumonia, and minor infection in adults.

✓5th **079.8 Other specified viral and chlamydial infections**

AHA: 1Q, '88, 12

079.81 Hantavirus

AHA: 4Q, '95, 60

DEF: An infection caused by the Muerto Canyon virus whose primary rodent reservoir is the deer mouse Peromyscus maniculatus; commonly characterized by fever, myalgias, headache, cough and rapid respiratory decline.

079.82 SARS-associated coronavirus

AHA: ►4Q, '03, 46◄

DEF: A life-threatening respiratory disease described as severe acute respiratory syndrome (SARS); etiology coronavirus; most common presenting symptoms may range from mild to more severe forms of flu-like conditions; fever, chills, cough, headache, myalgia; diagnosis of SARS is based upon clinical, laboratory, and epidemiological criteria.

079.83 Parvovirus B19

Human parvovirus
Parvovirus NOS

EXCLUDES *erythema infectiosum [fifth disease] (057.0)*

AHA: ►4Q, '07, 64◄

DEF: ►The only known parvovirus to cause disease in humans; most common manifestation is erythema infectiosum; also associated with polyarthropathy, chronic anemia, red cell aplasia, and fetal hydrops.◄

079.88 Other specified chlamydial infection

079.89 Other specified viral infection

✓5th **079.9 Unspecified viral and chlamydial infections**

EXCLUDES *viremia NOS (790.8)*

079.98 Unspecified chlamydial infection

Chlamydial infections NOS

079.99 Unspecified viral infection

Viral infections NOS

RICKETTSIOSES AND OTHER ARTHROPOD-BORNE DISEASES (080-088)

EXCLUDES *arthropod-borne viral diseases (060.0-066.9)*

080 Louse-borne [epidemic] typhus

Typhus (fever):
classical
epidemic
exanthematic NOS
louse-borne

DEF: *Rickettsia prowazekii;* causes severe headache, rash, high fever.

✓4th **081 Other typhus**

081.0 Murine [endemic] typhus

Typhus (fever):
endemic
flea-borne

DEF: Milder typhus caused by *Rickettsia typhi (mooseri);* transmitted by rat flea.

081.1 Brill's disease

Brill-Zinsser disease
Recrudescent typhus (fever)

081.2 Scrub typhus

Japanese river fever
Kedani fever
Mite-borne typhus
Tsutsugamushi

DEF: Typhus caused by *Rickettsia tsutsugamushi* transmitted by chigger.

081.9 Typhus, unspecified

Typhus (fever) NOS

✓4th **082 Tick-borne rickettsioses**

082.0 Spotted fevers

Rocky mountain spotted fever
Sao Paulo fever

082.1 Boutonneuse fever

African tick typhus
India tick typhus
Kenya tick typhus
Marseilles fever
Mediterranean tick fever

082.2 North Asian tick fever

Siberian tick typhus

082.3 Queensland tick typhus

✓5th **082.4 Ehrlichiosis**

AHA: 3Q, '06, 11; 4Q, '00, 38

082.40 Ehrlichiosis, unspecified

082.41 Ehrlichiosis chaffeensis [E. chaffeensis]

DEF: A febrile illness caused by bacterial infection, also called human monocytic ehrlichiosis (HME). Causal organism is *Ehrlichia chaffeensis,* transmitted by the Lone Star tick, *Amblyomma americanum.* Symptoms include fever, chills, myalgia, nausea, vomiting, diarrhea, confusion, and severe headache occurring one week after a tick bite. Clinical findings are lymphadenopathy, rash, thrombocytopenia, leukopenia, and abnormal liver function tests.

082.49 Other ehrlichiosis

082.8 Other specified tick-borne rickettsioses
Lone star fever
AHA: 4Q, '99, 19

082.9 Tick-borne rickettsiosis, unspecified
Tick-borne typhus NOS

4th 083 Other rickettsioses

083.0 Q fever
DEF: Infection of *Coxiella burnettii* usually acquired through airborne organisms.

083.1 Trench fever
Quintan fever
Wolhynian fever

083.2 Rickettsialpox
Vesicular rickettsiosis
DEF: Infection of *Rickettsia akari* usually acquired through a mite bite.

083.8 Other specified rickettsioses

083.9 Rickettsiosis, unspecified

4th 084 Malaria

Note: Subcategories 084.0-084.6 exclude the listed conditions with mention of pernicious complications (084.8-084.9).

EXCLUDES *congenital malaria (771.2)*

DEF: Mosquito-borne disease causing high fever and prostration and cataloged by species of *Plasmodium: P. falciparum, P. malariae, P. ovale, and P. vivax.*

084.0 Falciparum malaria [malignant tertian]
Malaria (fever):
by Plasmodium falciparum
subtertian

084.1 Vivax malaria [benign tertian]
Malaria (fever) by Plasmodium vivax

084.2 Quartan malaria
Malaria (fever) by Plasmodium malariae
Malariae malaria

084.3 Ovale malaria
Malaria (fever) by Plasmodium ovale

084.4 Other malaria
Monkey malaria

084.5 Mixed malaria
Malaria (fever) by more than one parasite

084.6 Malaria, unspecified
Malaria (fever) NOS

084.7 Induced malaria
Therapeutically induced malaria
EXCLUDES *accidental infection from syringe, blood transfusion, etc. (084.0-084.6, above, according to parasite species)*
transmission from mother to child during delivery (771.2)

084.8 Blackwater fever
Hemoglobinuric:
fever (bilious)
malaria
Malarial hemoglobinuria
DEF: Severe hemic and renal complication of *Plasmodium falciparum* infection.

084.9 Other pernicious complications of malaria
Algid malaria
Cerebral malaria
Use additional code to identify complication, as:
malarial:
hepatitis (573.2)
nephrosis (581.81)

4th 085 Leishmaniasis

085.0 Visceral [kala-azar]
Dumdum fever
Infection by Leishmania:
donovani
infantum
Leishmaniasis:
dermal, post-kala-azar
Mediterranean
visceral (Indian)

085.1 Cutaneous, urban
Aleppo boil
Baghdad boil
Delhi boil
Infection by Leishmania tropica (minor)
Leishmaniasis, cutaneous:
dry form
late
recurrent
ulcerating
Oriental sore

085.2 Cutaneous, Asian desert
Infection by Leishmania tropica major
Leishmaniasis, cutaneous:
acute necrotizing
rural
wet form
zoonotic form

085.3 Cutaneous, Ethiopian
Infection by Leishmania ethiopica
Leishmaniasis, cutaneous:
diffuse
lepromatous

085.4 Cutaneous, American
Chiclero ulcer
Infection by Leishmania mexicana
Leishmaniasis tegumentaria diffusa

085.5 Mucocutaneous (American)
Espundia
Infection by Leishmania braziliensis
Uta

085.9 Leishmaniasis, unspecified

4th 086 Trypanosomiasis

Use additional code to identify manifestations, as:
trypanosomiasis:
encephalitis (323.2)
meningitis (321.3)

086.0 Chagas' disease with heart involvement
American trypanosomiasis } with heart involvement
Infection by Trypanosoma cruzi } with heart involvement
Any condition classifiable to 086.2 with heart involvement

086.1 Chagas' disease with other organ involvement
American trypanosomiasis } with involvement of organ other than heart
Infection by Trypanosoma cruzi } with involvement of organ other than heart
Any condition classifiable to 086.2 with involvement of organ other than heart

086.2 Chagas' disease without mention of organ involvement
American trypanosomiasis
Infection by Trypanosoma cruzi

086.3 Gambian trypanosomiasis
Gambian sleeping sickness
Infection by Trypanosoma gambiense

086.4 Rhodesian trypanosomiasis
Infection by Trypanosoma rhodesiense
Rhodesian sleeping sickness

086.5 African trypanosomiasis, unspecified
Sleeping sickness NOS

086.9 Trypanosomiasis, unspecified

4th 087 Relapsing fever

INCLUDES recurrent fever

DEF: Infection of *Borrelia;* symptoms are episodic and include fever and arthralgia.

087.0 Louse-borne

087.1 Tick-borne

087.9 Relapsing fever, unspecified

4th 088 Other arthropod-borne diseases

088.0 Bartonellosis

Carrión's disease
Oroya fever
Verruga peruana

5th 088.8 Other specified arthropod-borne diseases

088.81 Lyme disease

Erythema chronicum migrans

AHA: 4Q, '91, 15; 3Q, '90, 14; 2Q, '89, 10

DEF: A recurrent multisystem disorder caused by the spirochete *Borrelia burgdorferi* with the carrier being the tick *Ixodes dammini;* the disease begins with lesions of erythema chronicum migrans; it is followed by arthritis of the large joints, myalgia, malaise, and neurological and cardiac manifestations.

088.82 Babesiosis

Babesiasis

AHA: 4Q, '93, 23

DEF: A tick-borne disease caused by infection of *Babesia,* characterized by fever, malaise, listlessness, severe anemia and hemoglobinuria.

088.89 Other

088.9 Arthropod-borne disease, unspecified

SYPHILIS AND OTHER VENEREAL DISEASES (090-099)

EXCLUDES *nonvenereal endemic syphilis (104.0)*
urogenital trichomoniasis (131.0)

4th 090 Congenital syphilis

DEF: Infection by spirochete *Treponema pallidum* acquired in utero from the infected mother.

090.0 Early congenital syphilis, symptomatic

Congenital syphilitic:
- choroiditis
- coryza (chronic)
- hepatomegaly
- mucous patches
- periostitis

Congenital syphilitic:
- splenomegaly

Syphilitic (congenital):
- epiphysitis
- osteochondritis
- pemphigus

Any congenital syphilitic condition specified as early or manifest less than two years after birth

090.1 Early congenital syphilis, latent

Congenital syphilis without clinical manifestations, with positive serological reaction and negative spinal fluid test, less than two years after birth

090.2 Early congenital syphilis, unspecified

Congenital syphilis NOS, less than two years after birth

090.3 Syphilitic interstitial keratitis

Syphilitic keratitis:
- parenchymatous
- punctata profunda

EXCLUDES *interstitial keratitis NOS (370.50)*

5th 090.4 Juvenile neurosyphilis

Use additional code to identify any associated mental disorder

DEF: *Treponema pallidum* infection involving the nervous system.

090.40 Juvenile neurosyphilis, unspecified

Congenital neurosyphilis
Dementia paralytica juvenilis
Juvenile:
- general paresis
- tabes
- taboparesis

090.41 Congenital syphilitic encephalitis

DEF: Congenital *Treponema pallidum* infection involving the brain.

090.42 Congenital syphilitic meningitis

DEF: Congenital *Treponema pallidum* infection involving the lining of the brain and/or spinal cord.

090.49 Other

090.5 Other late congenital syphilis, symptomatic

Gumma due to congenital syphilis
Hutchinson's teeth
Syphilitic saddle nose

Any congenital syphilitic condition specified as late or manifest two years or more after birth

090.6 Late congenital syphilis, latent

Congenital syphilis without clinical manifestations, with positive serological reaction and negative spinal fluid test, two years or more after birth

090.7 Late congenital syphilis, unspecified

Congenital syphilis NOS, two years or more after birth

090.9 Congenital syphilis, unspecified

4th 091 Early syphilis, symptomatic

EXCLUDES *early cardiovascular syphilis (093.0-093.9)*
early neurosyphilis (094.0-094.9)

091.0 Genital syphilis (primary)

Genital chancre

DEF: Genital lesion at the site of initial infection by *Treponema pallidum.*

091.1 Primary anal syphilis

DEF: Anal lesion at the site of initial infection by *Treponema pallidum.*

091.2 Other primary syphilis

Primary syphilis of:
- breast
- fingers

Primary syphilis of:
- lip
- tonsils

DEF: Lesion at the site of initial infection by *Treponema pallidum.*

091.3 Secondary syphilis of skin or mucous membranes

Condyloma latum
Secondary syphilis of:
- anus
- mouth
- pharynx

Secondary syphilis of:
- skin
- tonsils
- vulva

DEF: Transitory or chronic lesions following initial syphilis infection.

091.4 Adenopathy due to secondary syphilis

Syphilitic adenopathy (secondary)
Syphilitic lymphadenitis (secondary)

5th 091.5 Uveitis due to secondary syphilis

091.50 Syphilitic uveitis, unspecified

091.51 Syphilitic chorioretinitis (secondary)

DEF: Inflammation of choroid and retina as a secondary infection.

091.52 Syphilitic iridocyclitis (secondary)
DEF: Inflammation of iris and ciliary body as a secondary infection.

091.6 Secondary syphilis of viscera and bone

091.61 Secondary syphilitic periostitis
DEF: Inflammation of outer layers of bone as a secondary infection.

091.62 Secondary syphilitic hepatitis
Secondary syphilis of liver

091.69 Other viscera

091.7 Secondary syphilis, relapse
Secondary syphilis, relapse (treated) (untreated)
DEF: Return of symptoms of syphilis following asymptomatic period.

091.8 Other forms of secondary syphilis

091.81 Acute syphilitic meningitis (secondary)
DEF: Sudden, severe inflammation of the lining of the brain and/or spinal cord as a secondary infection.

091.82 Syphilitic alopecia
DEF: Hair loss following initial syphilis infection.

091.89 Other

091.9 Unspecified secondary syphilis

092 Early syphilis, latent

INCLUDES syphilis (acquired) without clinical manifestations, with positive serological reaction and negative spinal fluid test, less than two years after infection

092.0 Early syphilis, latent, serological relapse after treatment

092.9 Early syphilis, latent, unspecified

093 Cardiovascular syphilis

093.0 Aneurysm of aorta, specified as syphilitic
Dilatation of aorta, specified as syphilitic

093.1 Syphilitic aortitis
DEF: Inflammation of the aorta – the main artery leading from the heart.

093.2 Syphilitic endocarditis
DEF: Inflammation of the tissues lining the cavities of the heart.

093.20 Valve, unspecified
Syphilitic ostial coronary disease

093.21 Mitral valve

093.22 Aortic valve
Syphilitic aortic incompetence or stenosis

093.23 Tricuspid valve

093.24 Pulmonary valve

093.8 Other specified cardiovascular syphilis

093.81 Syphilitic pericarditis
DEF: Inflammation of the outer lining of the heart.

093.82 Syphilitic myocarditis
DEF: Inflammation of the muscle of the heart.

093.89 Other

093.9 Cardiovascular syphilis, unspecified

094 Neurosyphilis
Use additional code to identify any associated mental disorder

094.0 Tabes dorsalis
Locomotor ataxia (progressive)
Posterior spinal sclerosis (syphilitic)
Tabetic neurosyphilis
Use additional code to identify manifestation, as:
neurogenic arthropathy [Charcot's joint disease] (713.5)
DEF: Progressive degeneration of nerves associated with long-term syphilis; causing pain, wasting away, incontinence, and ataxia.

094.1 General paresis
Dementia paralytica
General paralysis (of the insane) (progressive)
Paretic neurosyphilis
Taboparesis
DEF: Degeneration of brain associated with long-term syphilis, causing loss of brain function, progressive dementia, and paralysis.

094.2 Syphilitic meningitis
Meningovascular syphilis
EXCLUDES *acute syphilitic meningitis (secondary) (091.81)*
DEF: Inflammation of the lining of the brain and/or spinal cord.

094.3 Asymptomatic neurosyphilis

094.8 Other specified neurosyphilis

094.81 Syphilitic encephalitis

094.82 Syphilitic Parkinsonism
DEF: Decreased motor function, tremors, and muscular rigidity.

094.83 Syphilitic disseminated retinochoroiditis
DEF: Inflammation of retina and choroid due to neurosyphilis.

094.84 Syphilitic optic atrophy
DEF: Degeneration of the eye and its nerves due to neurosyphilis.

094.85 Syphilitic retrobulbar neuritis
DEF: Inflammation of the posterior optic nerve to neurosyphilis.

094.86 Syphilitic acoustic neuritis
DEF: Inflammation of acoustic nerve due to neurosyphilis.

094.87 Syphilitic ruptured cerebral aneurysm

094.89 Other

094.9 Neurosyphilis, unspecified
Gumma (syphilitic)
Syphilis (early) (late)
Syphiloma
} of central nervous system NOS

095 Other forms of late syphilis, with symptoms

INCLUDES gumma (syphilitic)
syphilis, late, tertiary, or unspecified stage

095.0 Syphilitic episcleritis

095.1 Syphilis of lung

095.2 Syphilitic peritonitis

095.3 Syphilis of liver

095.4 Syphilis of kidney

095.5 Syphilis of bone

095.6 Syphilis of muscle
Syphilitic myositis

095.7 Syphilis of synovium, tendon, and bursa
Syphilitic:
bursitis
synovitis

095.8 Other specified forms of late symptomatic syphilis

EXCLUDES *cardiovascular syphilis (093.0-093.9)*
neurosyphilis (094.0-094.9)

095.9 Late symptomatic syphilis, unspecified

096 Late syphilis, latent

Syphilis (acquired) without clinical manifestations, with positive serological reaction and negative spinal fluid test, two years or more after infection

4th 097 Other and unspecified syphilis

097.0 Late syphilis, unspecified

097.1 Latent syphilis, unspecified

Positive serological reaction for syphilis

097.9 Syphilis, unspecified

Syphilis (acquired) NOS

EXCLUDES *syphilis NOS causing death under two years of age (090.9)*

4th 098 Gonococcal infections

DEF: *Neisseria gonorrhoeae* infection generally acquired in utero or in sexual congress.

098.0 Acute, of lower genitourinary tract

Gonococcal:
- Bartholinitis (acute)
- urethritis (acute)
- vulvovaginitis (acute)

Gonorrhea (acute):
- NOS
- genitourinary (tract) NOS

5th 098.1 Acute, of upper genitourinary tract

098.10 Gonococcal infection (acute) of upper genitourinary tract, site unspecified

098.11 Gonococcal cystitis (acute) upper

Gonorrhea (acute) of bladder

098.12 Gonococcal prostatitis (acute) ♂

098.13 Gonococcal epididymo-orchitis (acute) ♂

Gonococcal orchitis (acute)

DEF: Acute inflammation of the testes.

098.14 Gonococcal seminal vesiculitis (acute) ♂

Gonorrhea (acute) of seminal vesicle

098.15 Gonococcal cervicitis (acute) ♀

Gonorrhea (acute) of cervix

098.16 Gonococcal endometritis (acute) ♀

Gonorrhea (acute) of uterus

098.17 Gonococcal salpingitis, specified as acute ♀

DEF: Acute inflammation of the fallopian tubes.

098.19 Other

098.2 Chronic, of lower genitourinary tract

Gonococcal:
- Bartholinitis
- urethritis
- vulvovaginitis

Gonorrhea:
- NOS
- genitourinary (tract)

} specified as chronic or with duration of two months or more

Any condition classifiable to 098.0 specified as chronic or with duration of two months or more

5th 098.3 Chronic, of upper genitourinary tract

INCLUDES any condition classifiable to 098.1 stated as chronic or with a duration of two months or more

098.30 Chronic gonococcal infection of upper genitourinary tract, site unspecified

098.31 Gonococcal cystitis, chronic

Gonorrhea of bladder, chronic

Any condition classifiable to 098.11, specified as chronic

098.32 Gonococcal prostatitis, chronic ♂

Any condition classifiable to 098.12, specified as chronic

098.33 Gonococcal epididymo-orchitis, chronic ♂

Chronic gonococcal orchitis

Any condition classifiable to 098.13, specified as chronic

DEF: Chronic inflammation of the testes.

098.34 Gonococcal seminal vesiculitis, chronic ♂

Gonorrhea of seminal vesicle, chronic

Any condition classifiable to 098.14, specified as chronic

098.35 Gonococcal cervicitis, chronic ♀

Gonorrhea of cervix, chronic

Any condition classifiable to 098.15, specified as chronic

098.36 Gonococcal endometritis, chronic ♀

Any condition classifiable to 098.16, specified as chronic

DEF: Chronic inflammation of the uterus.

098.37 Gonococcal salpingitis (chronic) ♀

DEF: Chronic inflammation of the fallopian tubes.

098.39 Other

5th 098.4 Gonococcal infection of eye

098.40 Gonococcal conjunctivitis (neonatorum)

Gonococcal ophthalmia (neonatorum)

DEF: Infection of conjunctiva present at birth.

098.41 Gonococcal iridocyclitis

DEF: Inflammation and infection of iris and ciliary body.

098.42 Gonococcal endophthalmia

DEF: Inflammation and infection of contents of eyeball.

098.43 Gonococcal keratitis

DEF: Inflammation and infection of the cornea.

098.49 Other

5th 098.5 Gonococcal infection of joint

098.50 Gonococcal arthritis

Gonococcal infection of joint NOS

098.51 Gonococcal synovitis and tenosynovitis

098.52 Gonococcal bursitis

DEF: Inflammation of the sac-like cavities in a joint.

098.53 Gonococcal spondylitis

098.59 Other

Gonococcal rheumatism

098.6 Gonococcal infection of pharynx

098.7 Gonococcal infection of anus and rectum

Gonococcal proctitis

5th 098.8 Gonococcal infection of other specified sites

098.81 Gonococcal keratosis (blennorrhagica)

DEF: Pustular skin lesions caused by *Neisseria gonorrhoeae.*

098.82 Gonococcal meningitis

DEF: Inflammation of lining of brain and/or spinal cord.

098.83 Gonococcal pericarditis

DEF: Inflammation of the outer lining of the heart.

098.84 Gonococcal endocarditis
DEF: Inflammation of tissues lining the cavities of heart.

098.85 Other gonococcal heart disease

098.86 Gonococcal peritonitis
DEF: Inflammation of the membrane lining the abdomen.

098.89 Other
Gonococcemia

✓4th **099 Other venereal diseases**

099.0 Chancroid
Bubo (inguinal):
chancroidal
due to Hemophilus ducreyi
Chancre:
Ducrey's
simple
soft
Ulcus molle (cutis)(skin)
DEF: A sexually transmitted disease caused by *Haemophilus ducreyi;* it is identified by a painful primary ulcer at the site of inoculation (usually external genitalia) with related lymphadenitis.

099.1 Lymphogranuloma venereum
Climatic or tropical bubo
(Durand-) Nicolas-Favre disease
Esthiomene
Lymphogranuloma inguinale
DEF: Sexually transmitted infection of *Chlamydia trachomatis* causing skin lesions.

099.2 Granuloma inguinale
Donovanosis
Granuloma pudendi (ulcerating)
Granuloma venereum
Pudendal ulcer
DEF: Chronic, sexually transmitted infection of *Calymmatobacterium granulomatis* causing progressive, anogenital skin ulcers.

099.3 Reiter's disease
Reiter's syndrome
Use additional code for associated:
arthropathy (711.1)
conjunctivitis (372.33)
DEF: A symptom complex of unknown etiology consisting of urethritis, conjunctivitis, arthritis and myocutaneous lesions. It occurs most commonly in young men and patients with HIV and may precede or follow AIDS. Also a form of reactive arthritis.

✓5th **099.4 Other nongonococcal urethritis [NGU]**

099.40 Unspecified
Nonspecific urethritis

099.41 Chlamydia trachomatis

099.49 Other specified organism

✓5th **099.5 Other venereal diseases due to Chlamydia trachomatis**
EXCLUDES *Chlamydia trachomatis infection of conjunctiva (076.0-076.9, 077.0, 077.9)*
Lymphogranuloma venereum (099.1)
DEF: Venereal diseases caused by *Chlamydia trachomatis* at other sites besides the urethra (e.g., pharynx, anus and rectum, conjunctiva and peritoneum).

099.50 Unspecified site

099.51 Pharynx

099.52 Anus and rectum

099.53 Lower genitourinary sites
Use additional code to specify site of infection, such as:
bladder (595.4)
cervix (616.0)
vagina and vulva (616.11)
EXCLUDES *urethra (099.41)*

099.54 Other genitourinary sites
Use additional code to specify site of infection, such as:
pelvic inflammatory disease NOS (614.9)
testis and epididymis (604.91)

099.55 Unspecified genitourinary site

099.56 Peritoneum
Perihepatitis

099.59 Other specified site

099.8 Other specified venereal diseases

099.9 Venereal disease, unspecified

OTHER SPIROCHETAL DISEASES (100-104)

✓4th **100 Leptospirosis**
DEF: An infection of any spirochete of the genus Leptospire in blood. This zoonosis is transmitted to humans most often by exposure with contaminated animal tissues or water and less often by contact with urine. Patients present with flulike symptoms, the most common being muscle aches involving the thighs and low back. Treatment is with hydration and antibiotics.

100.0 Leptospirosis icterohemorrhagica
Leptospiral or spirochetal jaundice (hemorrhagic)
Weil's disease

✓5th **100.8 Other specified leptospiral infections**

100.81 Leptospiral meningitis (aseptic)

100.89 Other
Fever:
Fort Bragg
pretibial
swamp
Infection by Leptospira:
australis
bataviae
pyrogenes

100.9 Leptospirosis, unspecified

101 Vincent's angina
Acute necrotizing ulcerative:
gingivitis
stomatitis
Fusospirochetal pharyngitis
Spirochetal stomatitis
Trench mouth
Vincent's:
gingivitis
infection [any site]
DEF: Painful ulceration with edema and hypermic patches of the oropharyngeal and throat membranes; it is caused by spreading of acute ulcerative gingivitis.

✓4th **102 Yaws**
INCLUDES frambesia
pian
DEF: An infectious, endemic, tropical disease caused by *Treponema pertenue;* it usually affects persons 15 years old or younger; a primary cutaneous lesion develops, then a granulomatous skin eruption, and occasionally lesions that destroy skin and bone.

102.0 Initial lesions
Chancre of yaws
Frambesia, initial or primary
Initial frambesial ulcer
Mother yaw

102.1 Multiple papillomata and wet crab yaws
Butter yaws
Frambesioma
Pianoma
Plantar or palmar papilloma of yaws

102.2 Other early skin lesions
Cutaneous yaws, less than five years after infection
Early yaws (cutaneous) (macular) (papular) (maculopapular) (micropapular)
Frambeside of early yaws

102.3 Hyperkeratosis
Ghoul hand
Hyperkeratosis, palmar or plantar (early) (late) due to yaws
Worm-eaten soles

DEF: Overgrowth of skin of palm of bottoms of feet, due to yaws.

102.4 Gummata and ulcers
Gummatous frambeside
Nodular late yaws (ulcerated)

DEF: Rubbery lesions and areas of dead skin caused by yaws.

102.5 Gangosa
Rhinopharyngitis mutilans

DEF: Massive, mutilating lesions of the nose and oral cavity caused by yaws.

102.6 Bone and joint lesions
Goundou, Gumma, bone, Gummatous osteitis or periostitis } of yaws (late)
Hydrarthrosis, Osteitis, Periostitis (hypertrophic) } of yaws (early) (late)

102.7 Other manifestations
Juxta-articular nodules of yaws
Mucosal yaws

102.8 Latent yaws
Yaws without clinical manifestations, with positive serology

102.9 Yaws, unspecified

✓4th **103 Pinta**

DEF: A chronic form of treponematosis, endemic in areas of tropical America; it is identified by the presence of red, violet, blue, coffee-colored or white spots on the skin.

103.0 Primary lesions
Chancre (primary), Papule (primary), Pintid } of pinta [carate]

103.1 Intermediate lesions
Erythematous plaques, Hyperchronic lesions, Hyperkeratosis } of pinta [carate]

103.2 Late lesions
Cardiovascular lesions
Skin lesions:
achromic
cicatricial
dyschromic
Vitiligo
} of pinta [carate]

103.3 Mixed lesions
Achromic and hyperchromic skin lesions of pinta [carate]

103.9 Pinta, unspecified

✓4th **104 Other spirochetal infection**

104.0 Nonvenereal endemic syphilis
Bejel
Njovera

DEF: *Treponema pallidum, T. pertenue, or T. caroteum* infection transmitted non-sexually, causing lesions on mucosa and skin.

104.8 Other specified spirochetal infections

EXCLUDES *relapsing fever (087.0-087.9)*
syphilis (090.0-097.9)

104.9 Spirochetal infection, unspecified

MYCOSES (110-118)

Use additional code to identify manifestation as:
arthropathy (711.6)
meningitis (321.0-321.1)
otitis externa (380.15)

EXCLUDES *infection by Actinomycetales, such as species of Actinomyces, Actinomadura, Nocardia, Streptomyces (039.0-039.9)*

✓4th **110 Dermatophytosis**

INCLUDES infection by species of Epidermophyton, Microsporum, and Trichophyton
tinea, any type except those in 111

DEF: Superficial infection of the skin caused by a parasitic fungus.

110.0 Of scalp and beard
Kerion
Sycosis, mycotic
Trichophytic tinea [black dot tinea], scalp

110.1 Of nail
Dermatophytic onychia
Onychomycosis
Tinea unguium

110.2 Of hand
Tinea manuum

110.3 Of groin and perianal area
Dhobie itch
Eczema marginatum
Tinea cruris

110.4 Of foot
Athlete's foot
Tinea pedis

110.5 Of the body
Herpes circinatus
Tinea imbricata [Tokelau]

110.6 Deep seated dermatophytosis
Granuloma trichophyticum
Majocchi's granuloma

110.8 Of other specified sites

110.9 Of unspecified site
Favus NOS
Microsporic tinea NOS
Ringworm NOS

✓4th **111 Dermatomycosis, other and unspecified**

111.0 Pityriasis versicolor
Infection by Malassezia [Pityrosporum] furfur
Tinea flava
Tinea versicolor

111.1 Tinea nigra
Infection by Cladosporium species
Keratomycosis nigricans
Microsporosis nigra
Pityriasis nigra
Tinea palmaris nigra

111.2 Tinea blanca
Infection by Trichosporon (beigelii) cutaneum
White piedra

111.3 Black piedra
Infection by Piedraia hortai

111.8 Other specified dermatomycoses

111.9 Dermatomycosis, unspecified

4th 112 Candidiasis

INCLUDES infection by Candida species
moniliasis

EXCLUDES *neonatal monilial infection (771.7)*

DEF: Fungal infection caused by *Candida*; usually seen in mucous membranes or skin.

112.0 Of mouth
Thrush (oral)

112.1 Of vulva and vagina ♀
Candidal vulvovaginitis
Monilial vulvovaginitis

112.2 Of other urogenital sites
Candidal balanitis
AHA: 4Q, '03, 105; 4Q, '96, 33

112.3 Of skin and nails
Candidal intertrigo
Candidal onychia
Candidal perionyxis [paronychia]

112.4 Of lung
Candidal pneumonia
AHA: 2Q, '98, 7

112.5 Disseminated
Systemic candidiasis
AHA: 2Q, '00, 5; 2Q, '89, 10

5th 112.8 Of other specified sites

112.81 Candidal endocarditis

112.82 Candidal otitis externa
Otomycosis in moniliasis

112.83 Candidal meningitis

112.84 Candidal esophagitis
AHA: 4Q, '92, 19

112.85 Candidal enteritis
AHA: 4Q, '92, 19

112.89 Other
AHA: 1Q, '92, 17; 3Q, '91, 20

112.9 Of unspecified site

4th 114 Coccidioidomycosis

INCLUDES infection by Coccidioides (immitis)
Posada-Wernicke disease

AHA: 4Q, '93, 23

DEF: A funqal disease caused by inhalation of dust particles containing arthrospores of *Coccidiodes immitis;* a self-limited respiratory infection; the primary form is known as San Joaquin fever, desert fever or valley fever.

114.0 Primary coccidioidomycosis (pulmonary)
Acute pulmonary coccidioidomycosis
Coccidioidomycotic pneumonitis
Desert rheumatism
Pulmonary coccidioidomycosis
San Joaquin Valley fever

DEF: Acute, self-limiting *Coccidioides immitis* infection of the lung.

114.1 Primary extrapulmonary coccidioidomycosis
Chancriform syndrome
Primary cutaneous coccidioidomycosis

DEF: Acute, self-limiting *Coccidioides immitis* infection in nonpulmonary site.

114.2 Coccidioidal meningitis

DEF: *Coccidioides immitis* infection of the lining of the brain and/or spinal cord.

114.3 Other forms of progressive coccidioidomycosis
Coccidioidal granuloma
Disseminated coccidioidomycosis

114.4 Chronic pulmonary coccidioidomycosis

114.5 Pulmonary coccidioidomycosis, unspecified

114.9 Coccidioidomycosis, unspecified

4th 115 Histoplasmosis

The following fifth-digit subclassification is for use with category 115:
0 without mention of manifestation
1 meningitis
2 retinitis
3 pericarditis
4 endocarditis
5 pneumonia
9 other

§ 5th **115.0 Infection by Histoplasma capsulatum**
[0-5, 9]
American histoplasmosis
Darling's disease
Reticuloendothelial cytomycosis
Small form histoplasmosis

DEF: Infection resulting from inhalation of fungal spores, causing acute pneumonia, an influenza-like illness, or a disseminated disease of the reticuloendothelial system. In immunocompromised patients it can reactivate, affecting lungs, meninges, heart, peritoneum and adrenals.

§ 5th **115.1 Infection by Histoplasma duboisii**
[0-5, 9]
African histoplasmosis
Large form histoplasmosis

§ 5th **115.9 Histoplasmosis, unspecified**
[0-5, 9]
Histoplasmosis NOS

4th 116 Blastomycotic infection

116.0 Blastomycosis
Blastomycotic dermatitis
Chicago disease
Cutaneous blastomycosis
Disseminated blastomycosis
Gilchrist's disease
Infection by Blastomyces [Ajellomyces] dermatitidis
North American blastomycosis
Primary pulmonary blastomycosis

116.1 Paracoccidioidomycosis
Brazilian blastomycosis
Infection by Paracoccidioides [Blastomyces] brasilicnsis
Lutz-Splendore-Almeida disease
Mucocutaneous-lymphangitic paracoccidioidomycosis
Pulmonary paracoccidioidomycosis
South American blastomycosis
Visceral paracoccidioidomycosis

116.2 Lobomycosis
Infections by Loboa [Blastomyces] loboi
Keloidal blastomycosis
Lobo's disease

4th 117 Other mycoses

117.0 Rhinosporidiosis
Infection by Rhinosporidium seeberi

117.1 Sporotrichosis
Cutaneous sporotrichosis
Disseminated sporotrichosis
Infection by Sporothrix [Sporotrichum] schenckii
Lymphocutaneous sporotrichosis
Pulmonary sporotrichosis
Sporotrichosis of the bones

117.2 Chromoblastomycosis
Chromomycosis
Infcction by Cladosporidium carrionii, Fonsecaea compactum, Fonsecaea pedrosoi, Phialophora verrucosa

117.3 Aspergillosis
Infection by Aspergillus species, mainly A. fumigatus, A. flavus group, A. terreus group
AHA: 4Q, '97, 40

§ Requires fifth-digit. Valid digits are in [brackets] under each code. See category 115 for codes and definitions.

117.4 Mycotic mycetomas
Infection by various genera and species of Ascomycetes and Deuteromycetes, such as Acremonium [Cephalosporium] falciforme, Neotestudina rosatii, Madurella grisea, Madurella mycetomii, Pyrenochaeta romeroi, Zopfia [Leptosphaeria] senegalensis
Madura foot, mycotic
Maduromycosis, mycotic
EXCLUDES *actinomycotic mycetomas (039.0-039.9)*

117.5 Cryptococcosis
Busse-Buschke's disease
European cryptococcosis
Infection by Cryptococcus neoformans
Pulmonary cryptococcosis
Systemic cryptococcosis
Torula

117.6 Allescheriosis [Petriellidosis]
Infections by Allescheria [Petriellidium] boydii [Monosporium apiospermum]
EXCLUDES *mycotic mycetoma (117.4)*

117.7 Zygomycosis [Phycomycosis or Mucormycosis]
Infection by species of Absidia, Basidiobolus, Conidiobolus, Cunninghamella, Entomophthora, Mucor, Rhizopus, Saksenaea

117.8 Infection by dematiacious fungi, [Phaehyphomycosis]
Infection by dematiacious fungi, such as Cladosporium trichoides [bantianum], Dreschlera hawaiiensis, Phialophora gougerotii, Phialophora jeanselmi

117.9 Other and unspecified mycoses

118 Opportunistic mycoses
Infection of skin, subcutaneous tissues, and/or organs by a wide variety of fungi generally considered to be pathogenic to compromised hosts only (e.g., infection by species of Alternaria, Dreschlera, Fusarium)
▶Use additional code to identify manifestation, such as: keratitis (370.8)◀

HELMINTHIASES (120-129)

✓4th **120 Schistosomiasis [bilharziasis]**
DEF: Infection caused by *Schistosoma*, a genus of flukes or trematode parasites.

120.0 Schistosoma haematobium
Vesical schistosomiasis NOS

120.1 Schistosoma mansoni
Intestinal schistosomiasis NOS

120.2 Schistosoma japonicum
Asiatic schistosomiasis NOS
Katayama disease or fever

120.3 Cutaneous
Cercarial dermatitis
Infection by cercariae of Schistosoma
Schistosome dermatitis
Swimmers' itch

120.8 Other specified schistosomiasis
Infection by Schistosoma:
- bovis
- intercalatum
- mattheii
- spindale

Schistosomiasis chestermani

120.9 Schistosomiasis, unspecified
Blood flukes NOS
Hemic distomiasis

✓4th **121 Other trematode infections**

121.0 Opisthorchiasis
Infection by:
- cat liver fluke
- Opisthorchis (felineus) (tenuicollis) (viverrini)

121.1 Clonorchiasis
Biliary cirrhosis due to clonorchiasis
Chinese liver fluke disease
Hepatic distomiasis due to Clonorchis sinensis
Oriental liver fluke disease

121.2 Paragonimiasis
Infection by Paragonimus
Lung fluke disease (oriental)
Pulmonary distomiasis

121.3 Fascioliasis
Infection by Fasciola:
- gigantica
- hepatica

Liver flukes NOS
Sheep liver fluke infection

121.4 Fasciolopsiasis
Infection by Fasciolopsis (buski)
Intestinal distomiasis

121.5 Metagonimiasis
Infection by Metagonimus yokogawai

121.6 Heterophyiasis
Infection by:
- Heterophyes heterophyes
- Stellantchasmus falcatus

121.8 Other specified trematode infections
Infection by:
- Dicrocoelium dendriticum
- Echinostoma ilocanum
- Gastrodiscoides hominis

121.9 Trematode infection, unspecified
Distomiasis NOS
Fluke disease NOS

✓4th **122 Echinococcosis**
INCLUDES echinococciasis
hydatid disease
hydatidosis

DEF: Infection caused by larval forms of tapeworms of the genus *Echinococcus.*

122.0 Echinococcus granulosus infection of liver
122.1 Echinococcus granulosus infection of lung
122.2 Echinococcus granulosus infection of thyroid
122.3 Echinococcus granulosus infection, other
122.4 Echinococcus granulosus infection,unspecified
122.5 Echinococcus multilocularis infection of liver
122.6 Echinococcus multilocularis infection, other
122.7 Echinococcus multilocularis infection, unspecified
122.8 Echinococcosis, unspecified, of liver
122.9 Echinococcosis, other and unspecified

✓4th **123 Other cestode infection**

123.0 Taenia solium infection, intestinal form
Pork tapeworm (adult) (infection)

123.1 Cysticercosis
Cysticerciasis
Infection by Cysticercus cellulosae [larval form of Taenia solium]
AHA: 2Q, '97, 8

123.2 Taenia saginata infection
Beef tapeworm (infection)
Infection by Taeniarhynchus saginatus

123.3 Taeniasis, unspecified

123.4 Diphyllobothriasis, intestinal
Diphyllobothrium (adult) (latum) (pacificum) infection
Fish tapeworm (infection)

123.5 Sparganosis [larval diphyllobothriasis]
Infection by:
- Diphyllobothrium larvae
- Sparganum (mansoni) (proliferum)
- Spirometra larvae

123.6 Hymenolepiasis
Dwarf tapeworm (infection)
Hymenolepis (diminuta) (nana) infection
Rat tapeworm (infection)

123.8 Other specified cestode infection
Diplogonoporus (grandis) } infection
Dipylidium (caninum) } infection
Dog tapeworm (infection)

123.9 Cestode infection, unspecified
Tapeworm (infection) NOS

124 Trichinosis
Trichinella spiralis infection
Trichinellosis
Trichiniasis

DEF: Infection by *Trichinella spiralis*, the smallest of the parasitic nematodes.

✓4th **125 Filarial infection and dracontiasis**

125.0 Bancroftian filariasis
Chyluria } due to Wuchereria bancrofti
Elephantiasis } due to Wuchereria bancrofti
Infection } due to Wuchereria bancrofti
Lymphadenitis } due to Wuchereria bancrofti
Lymphangitis } due to Wuchereria bancrofti
Wuchereriasis

125.1 Malayan filariasis
Brugia filariasis } due to Brugia [Wuchereria] malayi
Chyluria } due to Brugia [Wuchereria] malayi
Elephantiasis } due to Brugia [Wuchereria] malayi
Infection } due to Brugia [Wuchereria] malayi
Lymphadenitis } due to Brugia [Wuchereria] malayi
Lymphangitis } due to Brugia [Wuchereria] malayi

125.2 Loiasis
Eyeworm disease of Africa
Loa loa infection

125.3 Onchocerciasis
Onchocerca volvulus infection
Onchocercosis

125.4 Dipetalonemiasis
Infection by:
- Acanthocheilonema perstans
- Dipetalonema perstans

125.5 Mansonella ozzardi infection
Filariasis ozzardi

125.6 Other specified filariasis
Dirofilaria infection
Infection by:
- Acanthocheilonema streptocerca
- Dipetalonema streptocerca

125.7 Dracontiasis
Guinea-worm infection
Infection by Dracunculus medinensis

125.9 Unspecified filariasis

✓4th **126 Ancylostomiasis and necatoriasis**

INCLUDES cutaneous larva migrans due to Ancylostoma
hookworm (disease) (infection)
uncinariasis

126.0 Ancylostoma duodenale

126.1 Necator americanus

126.2 Ancylostoma braziliense

126.3 Ancylostoma ceylanicum

126.8 Other specified Ancylostoma

126.9 Ancylostomiasis and necatoriasis, unspecified
Creeping eruption NOS
Cutaneous larva migrans NOS

✓4th **127 Other intestinal helminthiases**

127.0 Ascariasis
Ascaridiasis
Infection by Ascaris lumbricoides
Roundworm infection

127.1 Anisakiasis
Infection by Anisakis larva

127.2 Strongyloidiasis
Infection by Strongyloides stercoralis

EXCLUDES *trichostrongyliasis (127.6)*

127.3 Trichuriasis
Infection by Trichuris trichiuria
Trichocephaliasis
Whipworm (disease) (infection)

127.4 Enterobiasis
Infection by Enterobius vermicularis
Oxyuriasis
Oxyuris vermicularis infection
Pinworm (disease) (infection)
Threadworm infection

127.5 Capillariasis
Infection by Capillaria philippinensis

EXCLUDES *infection by Capillaria hepatica (128.8)*

127.6 Trichostrongyliasis
Infection by Trichostrongylus species

127.7 Other specified intestinal helminthiasis
Infection by:
- Oesophagostomum apiostomum and related species
- Ternidens diminutus
- other specified intestinal helminth

Physalopteriasis

127.8 Mixed intestinal helminthiasis
Infection by intestinal helminths classified to more than one of the categories 120.0-127.7
Mixed helminthiasis NOS

127.9 Intestinal helminthiasis, unspecified

✓4th **128 Other and unspecified helminthiases**

128.0 Toxocariasis
Larva migrans visceralis
Toxocara (canis) (cati) infection
Visceral larva migrans syndrome

128.1 Gnathostomiasis
Infection by Gnathostoma spinigerum and related species

128.8 Other specified helminthiasis
Infection by:
- Angiostrongylus cantonensis
- Capillaria hepatica
- other specified helminth

128.9 Helminth infection, unspecified
Helminthiasis NOS
Worms NOS

129 Intestinal parasitism, unspecified

OTHER INFECTIOUS AND PARASITIC DISEASES (130–136)

✓4th **130 Toxoplasmosis**

INCLUDES infection by toxoplasma gondii
toxoplasmosis (acquired)

EXCLUDES *congenital toxoplasmosis (771.2)*

130.0 Meningoencephalitis due to toxoplasmosis
Encephalitis due to acquired toxoplasmosis

130.1 Conjunctivitis due to toxoplasmosis

130.2 Chorioretinitis due to toxoplasmosis
Focal retinochoroiditis due to acquired toxoplasmosis

130.3 Myocarditis due to toxoplasmosis

130.4 Pneumonitis due to toxoplasmosis

130.5 Hepatitis due to toxoplasmosis

130.7 Toxoplasmosis of other specified sites

130.8 Multisystemic disseminated toxoplasmosis
Toxoplasmosis of multiple sites

130.9 Toxoplasmosis, unspecified

131 Trichomoniasis
INCLUDES infection due to Trichomonas (vaginalis)

✓5th **131.0 Urogenital trichomoniasis**

131.00 Urogenital trichomoniasis, unspecified
Fluor (vaginalis) } trichomonal or due to Trichomonas (vaginalis)
Leukorrhea (vaginalis) } trichomonal or due to Trichomonas (vaginalis)

DEF: *Trichomonas vaginalis* infection of reproductive and urinary organs, transmitted through coitus.

131.01 Trichomonal vulvovaginitis ♀
Vaginitis, trichomonal or due to Trichomonas (vaginalis)

DEF: *Trichomonas vaginalis* infection of vulva and vagina; often asymptomatic, transmitted through coitus.

131.02 Trichomonal urethritis

DEF: *Trichomonas vaginalis* infection of the urethra.

131.03 Trichomonal prostatitis ♂

DEF: *Trichomonas vaginalis* infection of the prostate.

131.09 Other

131.8 Other specified sites
EXCLUDES *intestinal (007.3)*

131.9 Trichomoniasis, unspecified

✓4th **132 Pediculosis and phthirus infestation**

132.0 Pediculus capitis [head louse]

132.1 Pediculus corporis [body louse]

132.2 Phthirus pubis [pubic louse]
Pediculus pubis

132.3 Mixed infestation
Infestation classifiable to more than one of the categories 132.0-132.2

132.9 Pediculosis, unspecified

✓4th **133 Acariasis**

133.0 Scabies
Infestation by Sarcoptes scabiei
Norwegian scabies
Sarcoptic itch

133.8 Other acariasis
Chiggers
Infestation by:
- Demodex folliculorum
- Trombicula

133.9 Acariasis, unspecified
Infestation by mites NOS

✓4th **134 Other infestation**

134.0 Myiasis
Infestation by:
- Dermatobia (hominis)
- fly larvae
- Gasterophilus (intestinalis)
- maggots
- Oestrus ovis

134.1 Other arthropod infestation
Infestation by:
- chigoe
- sand flea
- Tunga penetrans

Jigger disease
Scarabiasis
Tungiasis

134.2 Hirudiniasis
Hirudiniasis (external) (internal)
Leeches (aquatic) (land)

134.8 Other specified infestations

134.9 Infestation, unspecified
Infestation (skin) NOS
Skin parasites NOS

135 Sarcoidosis
Besnier-Boeck-Schaumann disease
Lupoid (miliary) of Boeck
Lupus pernio (Besnier)
Lymphogranulomatosis, benign (Schaumann's)
Sarcoid (any site):
- NOS
- Boeck
- Darier-Roussy

Uveoparotid fever

DEF: A chronic, granulomatous reticulosis (abnormal increase in cells), affecting any organ or tissue; acute form has high rate of remission; chronic form is progressive.

✓4th **136 Other and unspecified infectious and parasitic diseases**

136.0 Ainhum
Dactylolysis spontanea

DEF: A disease affecting the toes, especially the fifth digit, and sometimes the fingers, especially seen in black adult males; it is characterized by a linear constriction around the affected digit leading to spontaneous amputation of the distal part of the digit.

136.1 Behçet's syndrome

DEF: A chronic inflammatory disorder of unknown etiology involving the small blood vessels; it is characterized by recurrent aphthous ulceration of the oral and pharyngeal mucous membranes and the genitalia, skin lesions, severe uvetis, retinal vascularitis and optic atrophy.

✓5th **136.2 Specific infections by free-living amebae**

● **136.21 Specific infection due to acanthamoeba**
Use additional code to identify manifestation, such as:
keratitis (370.8)

● **136.29 Other specific infections by free-living amebae**
Meningoencephalitis due to Naegleria

136.3 Pneumocystosis
Pneumonia due to Pneumocystis carinii
Pneumonia due to Pneumocystis jiroveci

AHA: 1Q, '05, 7; 1Q, '03, 15; N-D, '87, 5-6

DEF: *Pneumocystis carinii* fungus causing pneumonia in immunocompromised patients; a leading cause of death among AIDS patients.

136.4 Psorospermiasis

136.5 Sarcosporidiosis
Infection by Sarcocystis lindemanni

DEF: *Sarcocystis* infection causing muscle cysts of intestinal inflammation.

136.8 Other specified infectious and parasitic diseases
Candiru infestation

136.9 Unspecified infectious and parasitic diseases
Infectious disease NOS
Parasitic disease NOS

AHA: 2Q, '91, 8

LATE EFFECTS OF INFECTIOUS AND PARASITIC DISEASES (137-139)

✓4th 137 Late effects of tuberculosis

Note: This category is to be used to indicate conditions classifiable to 010-018 as the cause of late effects, which are themselves classified elsewhere. The "late effects" include those specified as such, as sequelae, or as due to old or inactive tuberculosis, without evidence of active disease.

137.0 Late effects of respiratory or unspecified tuberculosis

137.1 Late effects of central nervous system tuberculosis

137.2 Late effects of genitourinary tuberculosis

137.3 Late effects of tuberculosis of bones and joints

137.4 Late effects of tuberculosis of other specified organs

138 Late effects of acute poliomyelitis

Note: This category is to be used to indicate conditions classifiable to 045 as the cause of late effects, which are themselves classified elsewhere. The "late effects" include conditions specified as such, or as sequelae, or as due to old or inactive poliomyelitis, without evidence of active disease.

✓4th 139 Late effects of other infectious and parasitic diseases

Note: This category is to be used to indicate conditions classifiable to categories 001-009, 020-041, 046-136 as the cause of late effects, which are themselves classified elsewhere. The "late effects" include conditions specified as such; they also include sequela of diseases classifiable to the above categories if there is evidence that the disease itself is no longer present.

139.0 Late effects of viral encephalitis

Late effects of conditions classifiable to 049.8-049.9, 062-064

139.1 Late effects of trachoma

Late effects of conditions classifiable to 076

139.8 Late effects of other and unspecified infectious and parasitic diseases

AHA: 2Q, '06, 17; 4Q, '91, 15; 3Q, '90, 14; M-A, '87, 8

Infectious and Parasitic Diseases

137–139.8

2. NEOPLASMS (140-239)

Notes:

1. Content

This chapter contains the following broad groups:

140-195	Malignant neoplasms, stated or presumed to be primary, of specified sites, except of lymphatic and hematopoietic tissue
196-198	Malignant neoplasms, stated or presumed to be secondary, of specified sites
199	Malignant neoplasms, without specification of site
200-208	Malignant neoplasms, stated or presumed to be primary, of lymphatic and hematopoietic tissue
▶209	Neuroendocrine tumors◀
210-229	Benign neoplasms
230-234	Carcinoma in situ
235-238	Neoplasms of uncertain behavior [see Note, above category 235]
239	Neoplasms of unspecified nature

2. Functional activity

All neoplasms are classified in this chapter, whether or not functionally active. An additional code from Chapter 3 may be used to identify such functional activity associated with any neoplasm, e.g.:

catecholamine-producing malignant pheochromocytoma of adrenal:
code 194.0, additional code 255.6

basophil adenoma of pituitary with Cushing's syndrome:
code 227.3, additional code 255.0

3. Morphology [Histology]

For those wishing to identify the histological type of neoplasms, a comprehensive coded nomenclature, which comprises the morphology rubrics of the ICD-Oncology, is given in Appendix A.

4. Malignant neoplasms overlapping site boundaries

Categories 140-195 are for the classification of primary malignant neoplasms according to their point of origin. A malignant neoplasm that overlaps two or more subcategories within a three-digit rubric and whose point of origin cannot be determined should be classified to the subcategory .8 "Other."

For example, "carcinoma involving tip and ventral surface of tongue" should be assigned to 141.8. On the other hand, "carcinoma of tip of tongue, extending to involve the ventral surface" should be coded to 141.2, as the point of origin, the tip, is known. Three subcategories (149.8, 159.8, 165.8) have been provided for malignant neoplasms that overlap the boundaries of three-digit rubrics within certain systems.

Overlapping malignant neoplasms that cannot be classified as indicated above should be assigned to the appropriate subdivision of category 195 (Malignant neoplasm of other and ill-defined sites).

AHA: 2Q, '90, 7

DEF: An abnormal growth, such as a tumor. Morphology determines behavior, i.e., whether it will remain intact (benign) or spread to adjacent tissue (malignant). The term mass is not synonymous with neoplasm, as it is often used to describe cysts and thickenings such as those occurring with hematoma or infection.

MALIGNANT NEOPLASM OF LIP, ORAL CAVITY, AND PHARYNX (140-149)

EXCLUDES *carcinoma in situ (230.0)*

✓4th **140 Malignant neoplasm of lip**

EXCLUDES *skin of lip (173.0)*

140.0 Upper lip, vermilion border
Upper lip:
NOS
external
lipstick area

Lip

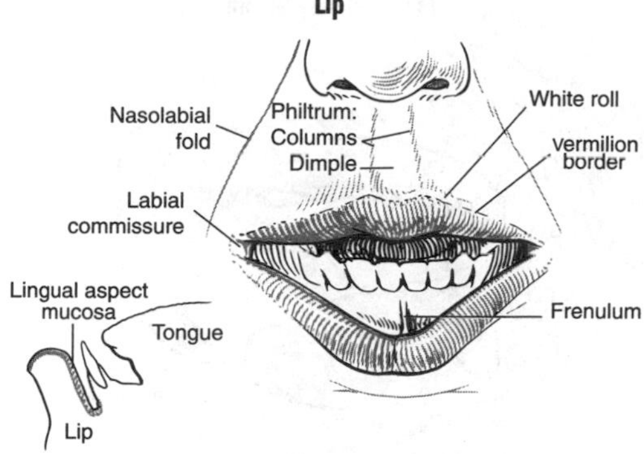

140.1 Lower lip, vermilion border
Lower lip:
NOS
external
lipstick area

140.3 Upper lip, inner aspect
Upper lip:
buccal aspect
frenulum
mucosa
oral aspect

140.4 Lower lip, inner aspect
Lower lip:
buccal aspect
frenulum
mucosa
oral aspect

140.5 Lip, unspecified, inner aspect
Lip, not specified whether upper or lower:
buccal aspect
frenulum
mucosa
oral aspect

140.6 Commissure of lip
Labial commissure

140.8 Other sites of lip
Malignant neoplasm of contiguous or overlapping sites of lip whose point of origin cannot be determined

140.9 Lip, unspecified, vermilion border
Lip, not specified as upper or lower:
NOS
external
lipstick area

✓4th **141 Malignant neoplasm of tongue**

141.0 Base of tongue
Dorsal surface of base of tongue
Fixed part of tongue NOS

AHA: 4Q, '06, 90

Tongue

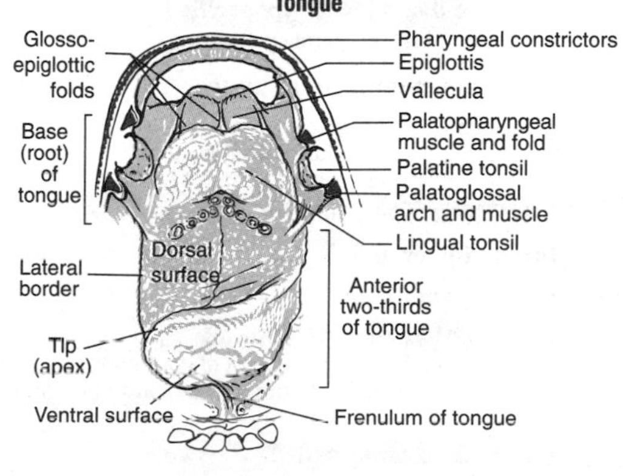

Main Salivary Glands

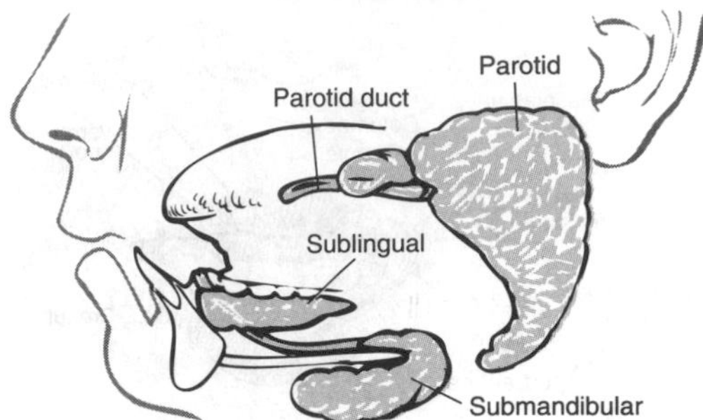

141.1 Dorsal surface of tongue
Anterior two-thirds of tongue, dorsal surface
Dorsal tongue NOS
Midline of tongue
EXCLUDES *dorsal surface of base of tongue (141.0)*

141.2 Tip and lateral border of tongue

141.3 Ventral surface of tongue
Anterior two-thirds of tongue, ventral surface
Frenulum linguae

141.4 Anterior two-thirds of tongue, part unspecified
Mobile part of tongue NOS

141.5 Junctional zone
Border of tongue at junction of fixed and mobile parts at insertion of anterior tonsillar pillar

141.6 Lingual tonsil

141.8 Other sites of tongue
Malignant neoplasm of contiguous or overlapping sites of tongue whose point of origin cannot be determined

141.9 Tongue, unspecified
Tongue NOS

✓4th 142 Malignant neoplasm of major salivary glands
INCLUDES salivary ducts
EXCLUDES *malignant neoplasm of minor salivary glands:*
NOS (145.9)
buccal mucosa (145.0)
soft palate (145.3)
tongue (141.0-141.9)
tonsil, palatine (146.0)

142.0 Parotid gland

142.1 Submandibular gland
Submaxillary gland

142.2 Sublingual gland

142.8 Other major salivary glands
Malignant neoplasm of contiguous or overlapping sites of salivary glands and ducts whose point of origin cannot be determined

142.9 Salivary gland, unspecified
Salivary gland (major) NOS

✓4th 143 Malignant neoplasm of gum
INCLUDES alveolar (ridge) mucosa
gingiva (alveolar) (marginal)
interdental papillae
EXCLUDES *malignant odontogenic neoplasms (170.0-170.1)*

143.0 Upper gum

143.1 Lower gum

143.8 Other sites of gum
Malignant neoplasm of contiguous or overlapping sites of gum whose point of origin cannot be determined

143.9 Gum, unspecified

Mouth

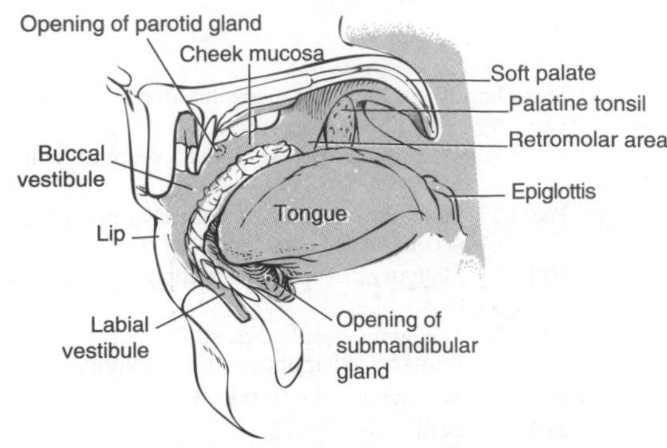

✓4th 144 Malignant neoplasm of floor of mouth

144.0 Anterior portion
Anterior to the premolar-canine junction

144.1 Lateral portion

144.8 Other sites of floor of mouth
Malignant neoplasm of contiguous or overlapping sites of floor of mouth whose point of origin cannot be determined

144.9 Floor of mouth, part unspecified

✓4th 145 Malignant neoplasm of other and unspecified parts of mouth
EXCLUDES *mucosa of lips (140.0-140.9)*

145.0 Cheek mucosa
Buccal mucosa
Cheek, inner aspect

145.1 Vestibule of mouth
Buccal sulcus (upper) (lower)
Labial sulcus (upper) (lower)

145.2 Hard palate

145.3 Soft palate
EXCLUDES *nasopharyngeal [posterior] [superior] surface of soft palate (147.3)*

145.4 Uvula

145.5 Palate, unspecified
Junction of hard and soft palate
Roof of mouth

145.6 Retromolar area

145.8 Other specified parts of mouth
Malignant neoplasm of contiguous or overlapping sites of mouth whose point of origin cannot be determined

145.9 Mouth, unspecified
Buccal cavity NOS
Minor salivary gland, unspecified site
Oral cavity NOS

✓4th 146 Malignant neoplasm of oropharynx

146.0 Tonsil
Tonsil:
NOS
faucial
palatine
EXCLUDES *lingual tonsil (141.6)*
pharyngeal tonsil (147.1)

AHA: S-O, '87, 8

146.1 Tonsillar fossa

146.2 Tonsillar pillars (anterior) (posterior)
Faucial pillar
Glossopalatine fold
Palatoglossal arch
Palatopharyngeal arch

Oropharynx

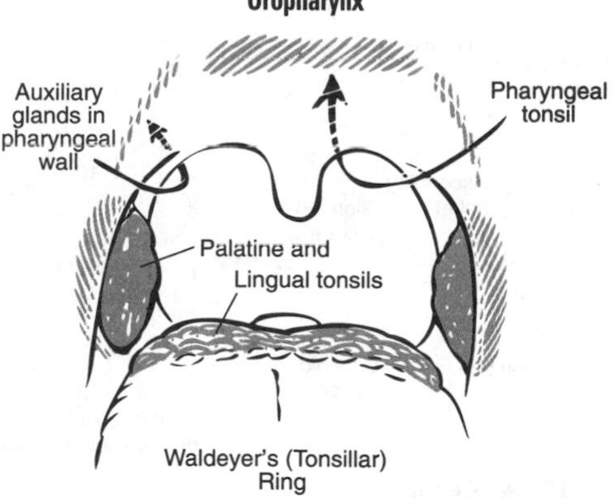

146.3 Vallecula
Anterior and medial surface of the pharyngoepiglottic fold

146.4 Anterior aspect of epiglottis
Epiglottis, free border [margin]
Glossoepiglottic fold(s)

EXCLUDES *epiglottis:*
NOS (161.1)
suprahyoid portion (161.1)

146.5 Junctional region
Junction of the free margin of the epiglottis, the aryepiglottic fold, and the pharyngoepiglottic fold

146.6 Lateral wall of oropharynx

146.7 Posterior wall of oropharynx

146.8 Other specified sites of oropharynx
Branchial cleft
Malignant neoplasm of contiguous or overlapping sites of oropharynx whose point of origin cannot be determined

146.9 Oropharynx, unspecified
AHA: 2Q, '02, 6

4th **147 Malignant neoplasm of nasopharynx**

147.0 Superior wall
Roof of nasopharynx

147.1 Posterior wall
Adenoid
Pharyngeal tonsil

147.2 Lateral wall
Fossa of Rosenmüller
Opening of auditory tube
Pharyngeal recess

147.3 Anterior wall
Floor of nasopharynx
Nasopharyngeal [posterior] [superior] surface of soft palate
Posterior margin of nasal septum and choanae

Nasopharynx

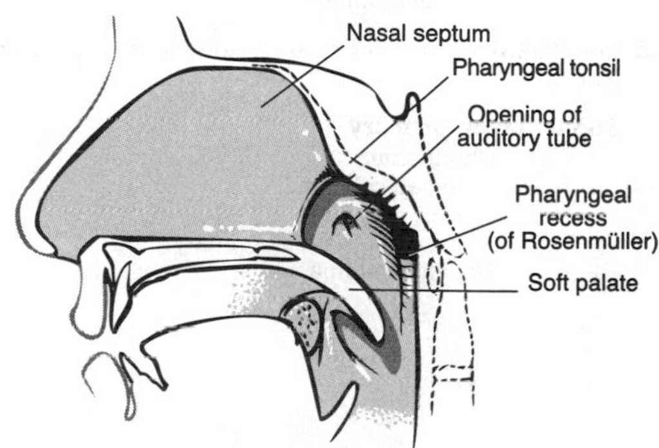

Hypopharynx

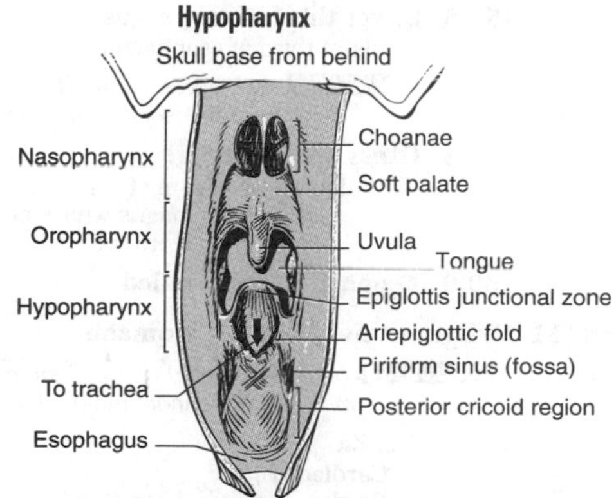

147.8 Other specified sites of nasopharynx
Malignant neoplasm of contiguous or overlapping sites of nasopharynx whose point of origin cannot be determined

147.9 Nasopharynx, unspecified
Nasopharyngeal wall NOS

4th **148 Malignant neoplasm of hypopharynx**

148.0 Postcricoid region

148.1 Pyriform sinus
Pyriform fossa

148.2 Aryepiglottic fold, hypopharyngeal aspect
Aryepiglottic fold or interarytenoid fold:
NOS
marginal zone

EXCLUDES *aryepiglottic fold or interarytenoid fold, laryngeal aspect (161.1)*

148.3 Posterior hypopharyngeal wall

148.8 Other specified sites of hypopharynx
Malignant neoplasm of contiguous or overlapping sites of hypopharynx whose point of origin cannot be determined

148.9 Hypopharynx, unspecified
Hypopharyngeal wall NOS
Hypopharynx NOS

4th **149 Malignant neoplasm of other and ill-defined sites within the lip, oral cavity, and pharynx**

149.0 Pharynx, unspecified

149.1 Waldeyer's ring

149.8 Other
Malignant neoplasms of lip, oral cavity, and pharynx whose point of origin cannot be assigned to any one of the categories 140-148

EXCLUDES *"book leaf" neoplasm [ventral surface of tongue and floor of mouth] (145.8)*

149.9 Ill-defined

MALIGNANT NEOPLASM OF DIGESTIVE ORGANS AND PERITONEUM (150-159)

EXCLUDES *carcinoma in situ (230.1-230.9)*

4th **150 Malignant neoplasm of esophagus**

150.0 Cervical esophagus

150.1 Thoracic esophagus

150.2 Abdominal esophagus

EXCLUDES *adenocarcinoma (151.0)*
cardio-esophageal junction (151.0)

150.3 Upper third of esophagus
Proximal third of esophagus

150.4 Middle third of esophagus

150.5 Lower third of esophagus
Distal third of esophagus
EXCLUDES *adenocarcinoma (151.0)*
cardio-esophageal junction (151.0)

150.8 Other specified part
Malignant neoplasm of contiguous or overlapping sites of esophagus whose point of origin cannot be determined

150.9 Esophagus, unspecified

4th 151 Malignant neoplasm of stomach
EXCLUDES ▶*benign carcinoid tumor of stomach (209.63)*
malignant carcinoid tumor of stomach (209.23)◀

151.0 Cardia
Cardiac orifice
Cardio-esophageal junction
EXCLUDES *squamous cell carcinoma (150.2, 150.5)*

151.1 Pylorus
Prepylorus
Pyloric canal

151.2 Pyloric antrum
Antrum of stomach NOS

151.3 Fundus of stomach

151.4 Body of stomach

151.5 Lesser curvature, unspecified
Lesser curvature, not classifiable to 151.1-151.4

151.6 Greater curvature, unspecified
Greater curvature, not classifiable to 151.0-151.4

151.8 Other specified sites of stomach
Anterior wall, not classifiable to 151.0-151.4
Posterior wall, not classifiable to 151.0-151.4
Malignant neoplasm of contiguous or overlapping sites of stomach whose point of origin cannot be determined

151.9 Stomach, unspecified
Carcinoma ventriculi
Gastric cancer
AHA: 2Q, '01, 17

4th 152 Malignant neoplasm of small intestine, including duodenum
EXCLUDES ▶*benign carcinoid tumor of small intestine and duodenum (209.40-209.43)*
malignant carcinoid tumor of small intestine and duodenum (209.00-209.03)◀

152.0 Duodenum

152.1 Jejunum

152.2 Ileum
EXCLUDES *ileocecal valve (153.4)*

152.3 Meckel's diverticulum

152.8 Other specified sites of small intestine
Duodenojejunal junction
Malignant neoplasm of contiguous or overlapping sites of small intestine whose point of origin cannot be determined

152.9 Small intestine, unspecified

4th 153 Malignant neoplasm of colon
EXCLUDES ▶*benign carcinoid tumor of colon (209.50-209.56)*
malignant carcinoid tumor of colon (209.10-209.16)◀

153.0 Hepatic flexure

153.1 Transverse colon

153.2 Descending colon
Left colon

153.3 Sigmoid colon
Sigmoid (flexure)
EXCLUDES *rectosigmoid junction (154.0)*

Colon

Anatomical distribution of large bowel cancers

153.4 Cecum
Ileocecal valve

153.5 Appendix

153.6 Ascending colon
Right colon

153.7 Splenic flexure

153.8 Other specified sites of large intestine
Malignant neoplasm of contiguous or overlapping sites of colon whose point of origin cannot be determined
EXCLUDES *ileocecal valve (153.4)*
rectosigmoid junction (154.0)

153.9 Colon, unspecified
Large intestine NOS

4th 154 Malignant neoplasm of rectum, rectosigmoid junction, and anus
EXCLUDES ▶*benign carcinoid tumor of rectum (209.57)*
malignant carcinoid tumor of rectum (209.17)◀

154.0 Rectosigmoid junction
Colon with rectum
Rectosigmoid (colon)

154.1 Rectum
Rectal ampulla

154.2 Anal canal
Anal sphincter
EXCLUDES *skin of anus (172.5, 173.5)*
AHA: 1Q, '01, 8

154.3 Anus, unspecified
EXCLUDES *anus:*
margin (172.5, 173.5)
skin (172.5, 173.5)
perianal skin (172.5, 173.5)

154.8 Other
Anorectum
Cloacogenic zone
Malignant neoplasm of contiguous or overlapping sites of rectum, rectosigmoid junction, and anus whose point of origin cannot be determined

4th 155 Malignant neoplasm of liver and intrahepatic bile ducts

155.0 Liver, primary
Carcinoma:
hepatocellular
liver cell
liver, specified as primary
Hepatoblastoma

155.1 Intrahepatic bile ducts
Canaliculi biliferi
Interlobular:
 bile ducts
 biliary canals
Intrahepatic:
 biliary passages
 canaliculi
 gall duct
EXCLUDES *hepatic duct (156.1)*

155.2 Liver, not specified as primary or secondary

✓4th 156 Malignant neoplasm of gallbladder and extrahepatic bile ducts

156.0 Gallbladder

156.1 Extrahepatic bile ducts
Biliary duct or passage NOS
Common bile duct
Cystic duct
Hepatic duct
Sphincter of Oddi

156.2 Ampulla of Vater
DEF: Malignant neoplasm in the area of dilation at the juncture of the common bile and pancreatic ducts near the opening into the lumen of the duodenum.

156.8 Other specified sites of gallbladder and extrahepatic bile ducts
Malignant neoplasm of contiguous or overlapping sites of gallbladder and extrahepatic bile ducts whose point of origin cannot be determined

156.9 Biliary tract, part unspecified
Malignant neoplasm involving both intrahepatic and extrahepatic bile ducts

✓4th 157 Malignant neoplasm of pancreas
AHA: ►4Q, '07, 72◄

157.0 Head of pancreas
AHA: 2Q, '05, 9; 4Q, '00, 40

157.1 Body of pancreas

157.2 Tail of pancreas

157.3 Pancreatic duct
Duct of:
 Santorini
 Wirsung

157.4 Islets of Langerhans
Islets of Langerhans, any part of pancreas
Use additional code to identify any functional activity
DEF: Malignant neoplasm within the structures of the pancreas that produce insulin, somatostatin and glucagon.

157.8 Other specified sites of pancreas
Ectopic pancreatic tissue
Malignant neoplasm of contiguous or overlapping sites of pancreas whose point of origin cannot be determined

157.9 Pancreas, part unspecified
AHA: 4Q, '89, 11

✓4th 158 Malignant neoplasm of retroperitoneum and peritoneum

158.0 Retroperitoneum
Periadrenal tissue
Perinephric tissue
Perirenal tissue
Retrocecal tissue

Retroperitoneum and Peritoneum

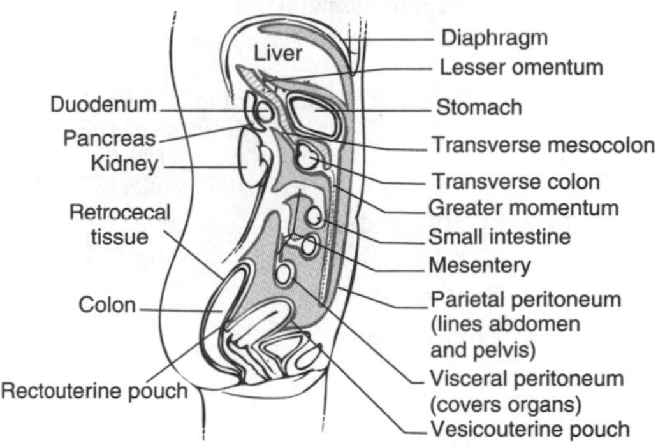

158.8 Specified parts of peritoneum
Cul-de-sac (of Douglas)
Malignant neoplasm of contiguous or overlapping sites of retroperitoneum and peritoneum whose point of origin cannot be determined
Mesentery
Mesocolon
Omentum
Peritoneum:
 parietal
 pelvic
Rectouterine pouch

158.9 Peritoneum, unspecified

✓4th 159 Malignant neoplasm of other and ill-defined sites within the digestive organs and peritoneum

159.0 Intestinal tract, part unspecified
Intestine NOS

159.1 Spleen, not elsewhere classified
Angiosarcoma } of spleen
Fibrosarcoma }
EXCLUDES *Hodgkin's disease (201.0-201.9)*
lymphosarcoma (200.1)
reticulosarcoma (200.0)

159.8 Other sites of digestive system and intra-abdominal organs
Malignant neoplasm of digestive organs and peritoneum whose point of origin cannot be assigned to any one of the categories 150-158
EXCLUDES *anus and rectum (154.8)*
cardio-esophageal junction (151.0)
colon and rectum (154.0)

159.9 Ill-defined
Alimentary canal or tract NOS
Gastrointestinal tract NOS
EXCLUDES *abdominal NOS (195.2)*
intra-abdominal NOS (195.2)

NEOPLASM OF RESPIRATORY AND INTRATHORACIC ORGANS (160-165)

EXCLUDES *carcinoma in situ (231.0-231.9)*

✓4th 160 Malignant neoplasm of nasal cavities, middle ear, and accessory sinuses

160.0 Nasal cavities
Cartilage of nose
Conchae, nasal
Internal nose
Septum of nose
Vestibule of nose
EXCLUDES *nasal bone (170.0)*
nose NOS (195.0)
olfactory bulb (192.0)
posterior margin of septum and choanae (147.3)
skin of nose (172.3, 173.3)
turbinates (170.0)

160.1 Auditory tube, middle ear, and mastoid air cells
Antrum tympanicum
Eustachian tube
Tympanic cavity

EXCLUDES *auditory canal (external) (172.2, 173.2)*
bone of ear (meatus) (170.0)
cartilage of ear (171.0)
ear (external) (skin) (172.2, 173.2)

160.2 Maxillary sinus
Antrum (Highmore) (maxillary)

160.3 Ethmoidal sinus

160.4 Frontal sinus

160.5 Sphenoidal sinus

160.8 Other
Malignant neoplasm of contiguous or overlapping sites of nasal cavities, middle ear, and accessory sinuses whose point of origin cannot be determined

160.9 Accessory sinus, unspecified

✓4th 161 Malignant neoplasm of larynx

161.0 Glottis
Intrinsic larynx
Laryngeal commissure (anterior) (posterior)
True vocal cord
Vocal cord NOS

161.1 Supraglottis
Aryepiglottic fold or interarytenoid fold, laryngeal aspect
Epiglottis (suprahyoid portion) NOS
Extrinsic larynx
False vocal cords
Posterior (laryngeal) surface of epiglottis
Ventricular bands

EXCLUDES *anterior aspect of epiglottis (146.4)*
aryepiglottic fold or interarytenoid fold:
NOS (148.2)
hypopharyngeal aspect (148.2)
marginal zone (148.2)

161.2 Subglottis

161.3 Laryngeal cartilages
Cartilage:
arytenoid
cricoid
Cartilage:
cuneiform
thyroid

161.8 Other specified sites of larynx
Malignant neoplasm of contiguous or overlapping sites of larynx whose point of origin cannot be determined

AHA: 3Q, '07, 7

161.9 Larynx, unspecified

✓4th 162 Malignant neoplasm of trachea, bronchus, and lung

EXCLUDES ▶*benign carcinoid tumor of bronchus (209.61)*
malignant carcinoid tumor of bronchus (209.21)◀

162.0 Trachea
Cartilage } of trachea
Mucosa } of trachea

162.2 Main bronchus
Carina
Hilus of lung

162.3 Upper lobe, bronchus or lung
AHA: 1Q, '04, 4

162.4 Middle lobe, bronchus or lung

162.5 Lower lobe, bronchus or lung

162.8 Other parts of bronchus or lung
Malignant neoplasm of contiguous or overlapping sites of bronchus or lung whose point of origin cannot be determined

AHA: 3Q, '06, 7

162.9 Bronchus and lung, unspecified
AHA: 3Q, '06, 14-15; 2Q, '97, 3; 4Q, '96, 48

✓4th 163 Malignant neoplasm of pleura

163.0 Parietal pleura

163.1 Visceral pleura

163.8 Other specified sites of pleura
Malignant neoplasm of contiguous or overlapping sites of pleura whose point of origin cannot be determined

163.9 Pleura, unspecified

✓4th 164 Malignant neoplasm of thymus, heart, and mediastinum

164.0 Thymus
EXCLUDES ▶*benign carcinoid tumor of the thymus (209.62)*
malignant carcinoid tumor of the thymus (209.22)◀

164.1 Heart
Endocardium
Epicardium
Myocardium
Pericardium

EXCLUDES *great vessels (171.4)*

164.2 Anterior mediastinum

164.3 Posterior mediastinum

164.8 Other
Malignant neoplasm of contiguous or overlapping sites of thymus, heart, and mediastinum whose point of origin cannot be determined

164.9 Mediastinum, part unspecified

✓4th 165 Malignant neoplasm of other and ill-defined sites within the respiratory system and intrathoracic organs

165.0 Upper respiratory tract, part unspecified

165.8 Other
Malignant neoplasm of respiratory and intrathoracic organs whose point of origin cannot be assigned to any one of the categories 160-164

165.9 Ill-defined sites within the respiratory system
Respiratory tract NOS

EXCLUDES *intrathoracic NOS (195.1)*
thoracic NOS (195.1)

MALIGNANT NEOPLASM OF BONE, CONNECTIVE TISSUE, SKIN, AND BREAST (170-176)

EXCLUDES *carcinoma in situ:*
breast (233.0)
skin (232.0-232.9)

✓4th 170 Malignant neoplasm of bone and articular cartilage

INCLUDES cartilage (articular) (joint)
periosteum

EXCLUDES *bone marrow NOS (202.9)*
cartilage:
ear (171.0)
eyelid (171.0)
larynx (161.3)
nose (160.0)
synovia (171.0-171.9)

AHA: 4Q, '06, 103

Skull

170.0 Bones of skull and face, except mandible

Bone:	Bone:
ethmoid	sphenoid
frontal	temporal
malar	zygomatic
nasal	Maxilla (superior)
occipital	Turbinate
orbital	Upper jaw bone
parietal	Vomer

EXCLUDES *carcinoma, any type except intraosseous or odontogenic:*
maxilla, maxillary (sinus) (160.2)
upper jaw bone (143.0)
jaw bone (lower) (170.1)

170.1 Mandible
Inferior maxilla
Jaw bone NOS
Lower jaw bone

EXCLUDES *carcinoma, any type except intraosseous or odontogenic:*
jaw bone NOS (143.9)
lower (143.1)
upper jaw bone (170.0)

170.2 Vertebral column, excluding sacrum and coccyx
Spinal column
Spine
Vertebra

EXCLUDES *sacrum and coccyx (170.6)*

170.3 Ribs, sternum, and clavicle
Costal cartilage
Costovertebral joint
Xiphoid process

170.4 Scapula and long bones of upper limb
Acromion
Bones NOS of upper limb
Humerus
Radius
Ulna

AHA: 2Q, '99, 9

170.5 Short bones of upper limb

Carpal	Scaphoid (of hand)
Cuneiform, wrist	Semilunar or lunate
Metacarpal	Trapezium
Navicular, of hand	Trapezoid
Phalanges of hand	Unciform
Pisiform	

170.6 Pelvic bones, sacrum, and coccyx
Coccygeal vertebra
Ilium
Ischium
Pubic bone
Sacral vertebra

170.7 Long bones of lower limb
Bones NOS of lower limb
Femur
Fibula
Tibia

170.8 Short bones of lower limb

Astragalus [talus]	Navicular (of ankle)
Calcaneus	Patella
Cuboid	Phalanges of foot
Cuneiform, ankle	Tarsal
Metatarsal	

170.9 Bone and articular cartilage, site unspecified

✓4th **171 Malignant neoplasm of connective and other soft tissue**

INCLUDES blood vessel
bursa
fascia
fat
ligament, except uterine
muscle
peripheral, sympathetic, and parasympathetic nerves and ganglia
synovia
tendon (sheath)

EXCLUDES *cartilage (of):*
articular (170.0-170.9)
larynx (161.3)
nose (160.0)
connective tissue:
breast (174.0-175.9)
▶*internal organs–code to malignant neoplasm of the site [e.g., leiomyosarcoma of stomach, 151.9]*◀
heart (164.1)
uterine ligament (183.4)

171.0 Head, face, and neck
Cartilage of:
ear
eyelid

AHA: 2Q, '99, 6

171.2 Upper limb, including shoulder
Arm
Finger
Forearm
Hand

171.3 Lower limb, including hip
Foot
Leg
Popliteal space
Thigh
Toe

171.4 Thorax
Axilla
Diaphragm
Great vessels

EXCLUDES *heart (164.1)*
mediastinum (164.2-164.9)
thymus (164.0)

171.5 Abdomen
Abdominal wall
Hypochondrium

EXCLUDES *peritoneum (158.8)*
retroperitoneum (158.0)

171.6 Pelvis
Buttock
Groin
Inguinal region
Perineum

EXCLUDES *pelvic peritoneum (158.8)*
retroperitoneum (158.0)
uterine ligament, any (183.3-183.5)

171.7 Trunk, unspecified
Back NOS
Flank NOS

171.8 **Other specified sites of connective and other soft tissue**
Malignant neoplasm of contiguous or overlapping sites of connective tissue whose point of origin cannot be determined

171.9 **Connective and other soft tissue, site unspecified**

✓4th **172 Malignant melanoma of skin**

INCLUDES melanocarcinoma
melanoma (skin) NOS
▶melanoma in situ of skin◀

EXCLUDES *skin of genital organs (184.0-184.9, 187.1-187.9)*
sites other than skin–code to malignant neoplasm of the site

DEF: Malignant neoplasm of melanocytes; most common in skin, may involve oral cavity, esophagus, anal canal, vagina, leptomeninges, or conjunctiva.

172.0 **Lip**
EXCLUDES *vermilion border of lip (140.0-140.1, 140.9)*

172.1 **Eyelid, including canthus**

172.2 **Ear and external auditory canal**
Auricle (ear)
Auricular canal, external
External [acoustic] meatus
Pinna

172.3 **Other and unspecified parts of face**
Cheek (external)
Chin
Eyebrow
Forehead
Nose, external
Temple

172.4 **Scalp and neck**

172.5 **Trunk, except scrotum**
Axilla
Breast
Buttock
Groin
Perianal skin
Perineum
Umbilicus
EXCLUDES *anal canal (154.2)*
anus NOS (154.3)
scrotum (187.7)

172.6 **Upper limb, including shoulder**
Arm
Finger
Forearm
Hand

172.7 **Lower limb, including hip**
Ankle
Foot
Heel
Knee
Leg
Popliteal area
Thigh
Toe

172.8 **Other specified sites of skin**
Malignant melanoma of contiguous or overlapping sites of skin whose point of origin cannot be determined

172.9 **Melanoma of skin, site unspecified**

✓4th **173 Other malignant neoplasm of skin**

INCLUDES malignant neoplasm of:
sebaceous glands
sudoriferous, sudoriparous glands
sweat glands

EXCLUDES *Kaposi's sarcoma (176.0-176.9)*
malignant melanoma of skin (172.0-172.9)
skin of genital organs (184.0-184.9, 187.1-187.9)

AHA: 1Q, '00, 18; 2Q, '96, 12

173.0 **Skin of lip**
EXCLUDES *vermilion border of lip (140.0-140.1, 140.9)*

173.1 **Eyelid, including canthus**
EXCLUDES *cartilage of eyelid (171.0)*

173.2 **Skin of ear and external auditory canal**
Auricle (ear)
Auricular canal, external
External meatus
Pinna
EXCLUDES *cartilage of ear (171.0)*

173.3 **Skin of other and unspecified parts of face**
Cheek, external
Chin
Eyebrow
Forehead
Nose, external
Temple
AHA: 1Q, '00, 3

173.4 **Scalp and skin of neck**

173.5 **Skin of trunk, except scrotum**
Axillary fold
Perianal skin
Skin of:
abdominal wall
anus
back
breast
buttock
chest wall
groin
perineum
Umbilicus
EXCLUDES *anal canal (154.2)*
anus NOS (154.3)
skin of scrotum (187.7)
AHA: 1Q, '01, 8

173.6 **Skin of upper limb, including shoulder**
Arm
Finger
Forearm
Hand

173.7 **Skin of lower limb, including hip**
Ankle
Foot
Heel
Knee
Leg
Popliteal area
Thigh
Toe

173.8 **Other specified sites of skin**
Malignant neoplasm of contiguous or overlapping sites of skin whose point of origin cannot be determined

173.9 **Skin, site unspecified**

✓4th **174 Malignant neoplasm of female breast**

Use additional code to identify estrogen receptor status (V86.0, V86.1)

INCLUDES breast (female)
connective tissue
soft parts
Paget's disease of:
breast
nipple

EXCLUDES *skin of breast (172.5, 173.5)*

AHA: 3Q, '97, 8; 4Q, '89, 11

174.0 **Nipple and areola** ♀

174.1 **Central portion** ♀

174.2 **Upper-inner quadrant** ♀

174.3 **Lower-inner quadrant** ♀

174.4 **Upper-outer quadrant** ♀
AHA: 1Q, '04, 3

174.5 **Lower-outer quadrant** ♀

174.6 **Axillary tail** ♀

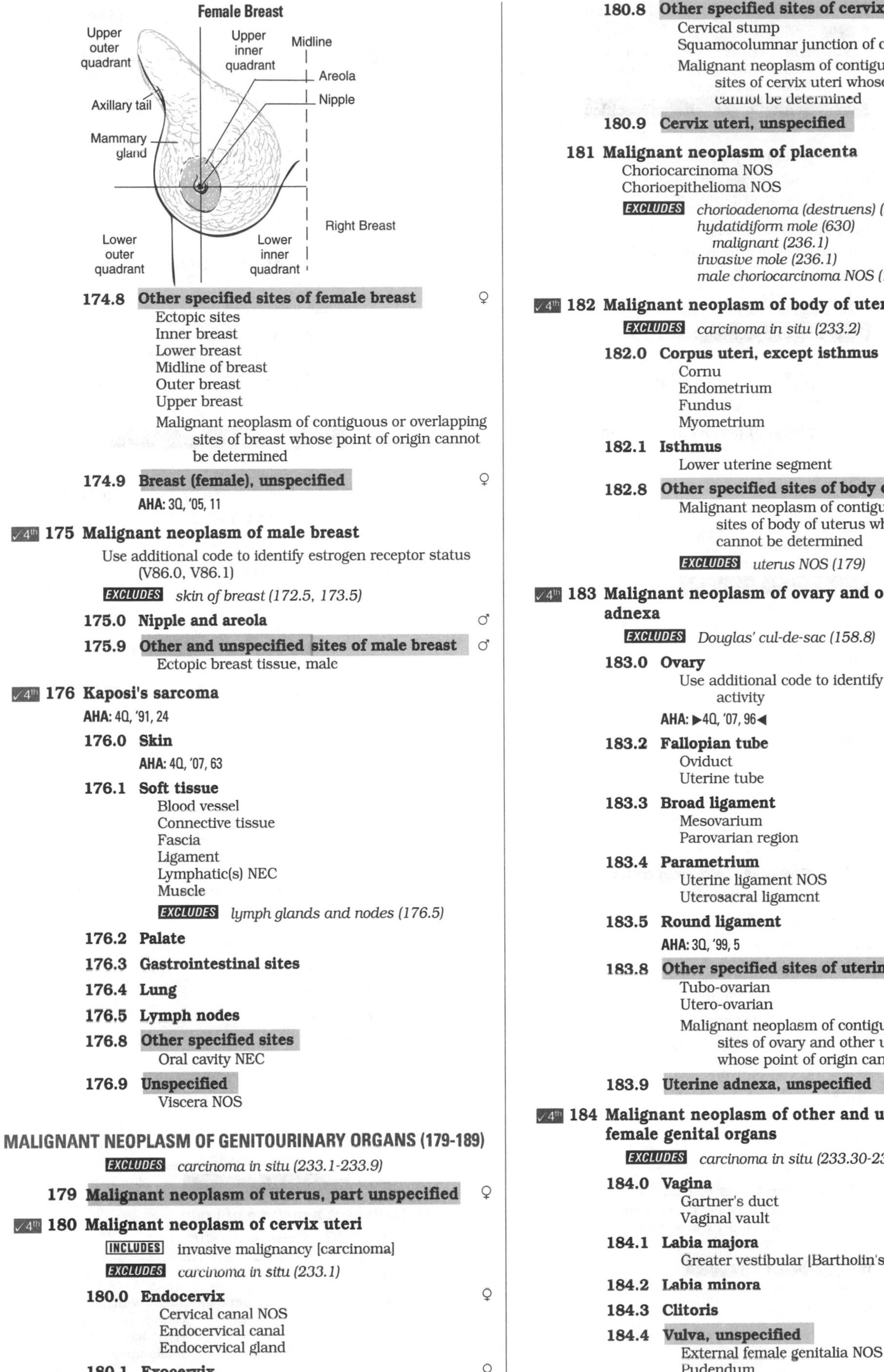

174.8 Other specified sites of female breast ♀
Ectopic sites
Inner breast
Lower breast
Midline of breast
Outer breast
Upper breast
Malignant neoplasm of contiguous or overlapping sites of breast whose point of origin cannot be determined

174.9 Breast (female), unspecified ♀
AHA: 3Q, '05, 11

✓4th **175 Malignant neoplasm of male breast**
Use additional code to identify estrogen receptor status (V86.0, V86.1)
EXCLUDES *skin of breast (172.5, 173.5)*

175.0 Nipple and areola ♂

175.9 Other and unspecified sites of male breast ♂
Ectopic breast tissue, male

✓4th **176 Kaposi's sarcoma**
AHA: 4Q, '91, 24

176.0 Skin
AHA: 4Q, '07, 63

176.1 Soft tissue
Blood vessel
Connective tissue
Fascia
Ligament
Lymphatic(s) NEC
Muscle
EXCLUDES *lymph glands and nodes (176.5)*

176.2 Palate

176.3 Gastrointestinal sites

176.4 Lung

176.5 Lymph nodes

176.8 Other specified sites
Oral cavity NEC

176.9 Unspecified
Viscera NOS

MALIGNANT NEOPLASM OF GENITOURINARY ORGANS (179-189)

EXCLUDES *carcinoma in situ (233.1-233.9)*

179 Malignant neoplasm of uterus, part unspecified ♀

✓4th **180 Malignant neoplasm of cervix uteri**
INCLUDES invasive malignancy [carcinoma]
EXCLUDES *carcinoma in situ (233.1)*

180.0 Endocervix ♀
Cervical canal NOS
Endocervical canal
Endocervical gland

180.1 Exocervix ♀

180.8 Other specified sites of cervix ♀
Cervical stump
Squamocolumnar junction of cervix
Malignant neoplasm of contiguous or overlapping sites of cervix uteri whose point of origin cannot be determined

180.9 Cervix uteri, unspecified ♀

181 Malignant neoplasm of placenta ♀
Choriocarcinoma NOS
Chorioepithelioma NOS
EXCLUDES *chorioadenoma (destruens) (236.1)*
hydatidiform mole (630)
malignant (236.1)
invasive mole (236.1)
male choriocarcinoma NOS (186.0-186.9)

✓4th **182 Malignant neoplasm of body of uterus**
EXCLUDES *carcinoma in situ (233.2)*

182.0 Corpus uteri, except isthmus ♀
Cornu
Endometrium
Fundus
Myometrium

182.1 Isthmus ♀
Lower uterine segment

182.8 Other specified sites of body of uterus ♀
Malignant neoplasm of contiguous or overlapping sites of body of uterus whose point of origin cannot be determined
EXCLUDES *uterus NOS (179)*

✓4th **183 Malignant neoplasm of ovary and other uterine adnexa**
EXCLUDES *Douglas' cul-de-sac (158.8)*

183.0 Ovary ♀
Use additional code to identify any functional activity
AHA: ►4Q, '07, 96◄

183.2 Fallopian tube ♀
Oviduct
Uterine tube

183.3 Broad ligament ♀
Mesovarium
Parovarian region

183.4 Parametrium ♀
Uterine ligament NOS
Uterosacral ligament

183.5 Round ligament ♀
AHA: 3Q, '99, 5

183.8 Other specified sites of uterine adnexa ♀
Tubo-ovarian
Utero-ovarian
Malignant neoplasm of contiguous or overlapping sites of ovary and other uterine adnexa whose point of origin cannot be determined

183.9 Uterine adnexa, unspecified ♀

✓4th **184 Malignant neoplasm of other and unspecified female genital organs**
EXCLUDES *carcinoma in situ (233.30-233.39)*

184.0 Vagina ♀
Gartner's duct
Vaginal vault

184.1 Labia majora ♀
Greater vestibular [Bartholin's] gland

184.2 Labia minora ♀

184.3 Clitoris ♀

184.4 Vulva, unspecified ♀
External female genitalia NOS
Pudendum

Neoplasms

184.8 Other specified sites of female genital organs ♀

Malignant neoplasm of contiguous or overlapping sites of female genital organs whose point of origin cannot be determined

184.9 Female genital organ, site unspecified ♀

Female genitourinary tract NOS

185 Malignant neoplasm of prostate ♂

EXCLUDES *seminal vesicles (187.8)*

AHA: 3Q, '03, 13; 3Q, '99, 5; 3Q, '92, 7

✓4th **186 Malignant neoplasm of testis**

Use additional code to identify any functional activity

186.0 Undescended testis ♂

Ectopic testis
Retained testis

186.9 Other and unspecified testis ♂

Testis:
NOS
descended
scrotal

✓4th **187 Malignant neoplasm of penis and other male genital organs**

187.1 Prepuce ♂

Foreskin

187.2 Glans penis ♂

187.3 Body of penis ♂

Corpus cavernosum

187.4 Penis, part unspecified ♂

Skin of penis NOS

187.5 Epididymis ♂

187.6 Spermatic cord ♂

Vas deferens

187.7 Scrotum ♂

Skin of scrotum

187.8 Other specified sites of male genital organs ♂

Seminal vesicle
Tunica vaginalis

Malignant neoplasm of contiguous or overlapping sites of penis and other male genital organs whose point of origin cannot be determined

187.9 Male genital organ, site unspecified ♂

Male genital organ or tract NOS

✓4th **188 Malignant neoplasm of bladder**

EXCLUDES *carcinoma in situ (233.7)*

188.0 Trigone of urinary bladder

188.1 Dome of urinary bladder

188.2 Lateral wall of urinary bladder

188.3 Anterior wall of urinary bladder

188.4 Posterior wall of urinary bladder

188.5 Bladder neck

Internal urethral orifice

188.6 Ureteric orifice

188.7 Urachus

188.8 Other specified sites of bladder

Malignant neoplasm of contiguous or overlapping sites of bladder whose point of origin cannot be determined

188.9 Bladder, part unspecified

Bladder wall NOS

AHA: 1Q, '00, 5

✓4th **189 Malignant neoplasm of kidney and other and unspecified urinary organs**

EXCLUDES ▶*benign carcinoid tumor of kidney (209.64)*
malignant carcinoid tumor of kidney (209.24)◀

189.0 Kidney, except pelvis

Kidney NOS
Kidney parenchyma

AHA: 2Q, '05, 4; 2Q, '04, 4

189.1 Renal pelvis

Renal calyces
Ureteropelvic junction

189.2 Ureter

EXCLUDES *ureteric orifice of bladder (188.6)*

189.3 Urethra

EXCLUDES *urethral orifice of bladder (188.5)*

189.4 Paraurethral glands

189.8 Other specified sites of urinary organs

Malignant neoplasm of contiguous or overlapping sites of kidney and other urinary organs whose point of origin cannot be determined

189.9 Urinary organ, site unspecified

Urinary system NOS

MALIGNANT NEOPLASM OF OTHER AND UNSPECIFIED SITES (190-199)

EXCLUDES *carcinoma in situ (234.0-234.9)*

✓4th **190 Malignant neoplasm of eye**

EXCLUDES *carcinoma in situ (234.0)*
eyelid (skin) (172.1, 173.1)
cartilage (171.0)
optic nerve (192.0)
orbital bone (170.0)

190.0 Eyeball, except conjunctiva, cornea, retina, and choroid

Ciliary body
Crystalline lens
Iris
Sclera
Uveal tract

190.1 Orbit

Connective tissue of orbit
Extraocular muscle
Retrobulbar

EXCLUDES *bone of orbit (170.0)*

190.2 Lacrimal gland

190.3 Conjunctiva

190.4 Cornea

190.5 Retina

190.6 Choroid

190.7 Lacrimal duct

Lacrimal sac
Nasolacrimal duct

190.8 Other specified sites of eye

Malignant neoplasm of contiguous or overlapping sites of eye whose point of origin cannot be determined

190.9 Eye, part unspecified

✓4th **191 Malignant neoplasm of brain**

EXCLUDES *cranial nerves (192.0)*
retrobulbar area (190.1)

AHA: 4Q, '07, 104

191.0 Cerebrum, except lobes and ventricles

Basal ganglia
Cerebral cortex
Corpus striatum
Globus pallidus
Hypothalamus
Thalamus

184.8–191.0

Brain and Meninges

Fourth ventricle
Cerebrum
Corpus callosum
Thalamus
Hypothalamus
Hypophysis
Cerebellum
Pons
Medulla oblongata
Midsagittal Section (between hemispheres)

191.1 Frontal lobe
AHA: 4Q, '05, 118

191.2 Temporal lobe
Hippocampus
Uncus
AHA: 4Q, '06, 123

191.3 Parietal lobe

191.4 Occipital lobe

191.5 Ventricles
Choroid plexus
Floor of ventricle

191.6 Cerebellum NOS
Cerebellopontine angle

191.7 Brain stem
Cerebral peduncle
Medulla oblongata
Midbrain
Pons

191.8 Other parts of brain
Corpus callosum
Tapetum
Malignant neoplasm of contiguous or overlapping sites of brain whose point of origin cannot be determined

191.9 Brain, unspecified
Cranial fossa NOS

4th 192 Malignant neoplasm of other and unspecified parts of nervous system

EXCLUDES *peripheral, sympathetic, and parasympathetic nerves and ganglia (171.0-171.9)*

192.0 Cranial nerves
Olfactory bulb

192.1 Cerebral meninges
Dura (mater)
Falx (cerebelli) (cerebri)
Meninges NOS
Tentorium

192.2 Spinal cord
Cauda equina

192.3 Spinal meninges

192.8 Other specified sites of nervous system
Malignant neoplasm of contiguous or overlapping sites of other parts of nervous system whose point of origin cannot be determined

192.9 Nervous system, part unspecified
Nervous system (central) NOS
EXCLUDES *meninges NOS (192.1)*

193 Malignant neoplasm of thyroid gland
Thyroglossal duct
Use additional code to identify any functional activity

4th 194 Malignant neoplasm of other endocrine glands and related structures

EXCLUDES *islets of Langerhans (157.4)*
▶neuroendocrine tumors (209.00-209.69)◀
ovary (183.0)
testis (186.0-186.9)
thymus (164.0)

194.0 Adrenal gland
Adrenal cortex
Adrenal medulla
Suprarenal gland

194.1 Parathyroid gland

194.3 Pituitary gland and craniopharyngeal duct
Craniobuccal pouch
Hypophysis
Rathke's pouch
Sella turcica
AHA: J-A, '85, 9

194.4 Pineal gland

194.5 Carotid body

194.6 Aortic body and other paraganglia
Coccygeal body
Glomus jugulare
Para-aortic body

194.8 Other
Pluriglandular involvement NOS
Note: If the sites of multiple involvements are known, they should be coded separately.

194.9 Endocrine gland, site unspecified

4th 195 Malignant neoplasm of other and ill-defined sites

INCLUDES malignant neoplasms of contiguous sites, not elsewhere classified, whose point of origin cannot be determined

EXCLUDES *malignant neoplasm:*
lymphatic and hematopoietic tissue (200.0-208.9)
secondary sites (196.0-198.8)
unspecified site (199.0-199.1)

195.0 Head, face, and neck
Cheek NOS
Jaw NOS
Nose NOS
Supraclavicular region NOS
AHA: 4Q, '03, 107

195.1 Thorax
Axilla
Chest (wall) NOS
Intrathoracic NOS

195.2 Abdomen
Intra-abdominal NOS
AHA: 2Q, '97, 3

195.3 Pelvis
Groin
Inguinal region NOS
Presacral region
Sacrococcygeal region
Sites overlapping systems within pelvis, as:
rectovaginal (septum)
rectovesical (septum)

195.4 Upper limb

195.5 Lower limb

195.8 Other specified sites
Back NOS
Flank NOS
Trunk NOS

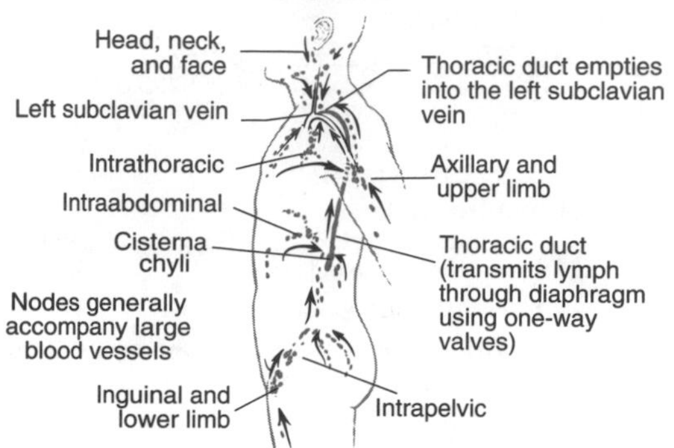

✓4th 196 Secondary and unspecified malignant neoplasm of lymph nodes

EXCLUDES *any malignant neoplasm of lymph nodes, specified as primary (200.0-202.9)*
Hodgkin's disease (201.0-201.9)
lymphosarcoma (200.1)
other forms of lymphoma (202.0-202.9)
reticulosarcoma (200.0)

AHA: 2Q, '92, 3; M-J, '85, 3

196.0 Lymph nodes of head, face, and neck
Cervical
Cervicofacial
Scalene
Supraclavicular
AHA: 3Q, '07, 7

196.1 Intrathoracic lymph nodes
Bronchopulmonary
Intercostal
Mediastinal
Tracheobronchial
AHA: 3Q, '06, 7

196.2 Intra-abdominal lymph nodes
Intestinal
Mesenteric
Retroperitoneal
AHA: 4Q, '03, 111

196.3 Lymph nodes of axilla and upper limb
Brachial
Epitrochlear
Infraclavicular
Pectoral

196.5 Lymph nodes of inguinal region and lower limb
Femoral
Groin
Popliteal
Tibial

196.6 Intrapelvic lymph nodes
Hypogastric
Iliac
Obturator
Parametrial

196.8 Lymph nodes of multiple sites

196.9 Site unspecified
Lymph nodes NOS

✓4th 197 Secondary malignant neoplasm of respiratory and digestive systems

EXCLUDES *lymph node metastasis (196.0-196.9)*

AHA: M-J, '85, 3

197.0 Lung
Bronchus
AHA: 1Q, '06, 4; 2Q, '99, 9

197.1 Mediastinum
AHA: 3Q, '06, 7

197.2 Pleura
AHA: ▶1Q, '08, 16;◀ 3Q, '07, 3; 4Q, '03, 110; 4Q, '89, 11

197.3 Other respiratory organs
Trachea

197.4 Small intestine, including duodenum

197.5 Large intestine and rectum

197.6 Retroperitoneum and peritoneum
AHA: 2Q, '04, 4; 4Q, '89, 11

197.7 Liver, specified as secondary
AHA: 1Q, '06, 4; 2Q, '05, 9

197.8 Other digestive organs and spleen
AHA: 2Q, '97, 3; 2Q, '92, 3

✓4th 198 Secondary malignant neoplasm of other specified sites

EXCLUDES *lymph node metastasis (196.0-196.9)*

AHA: M-J, '85, 3

198.0 Kidney

198.1 Other urinary organs

198.2 Skin
Skin of breast

198.3 Brain and spinal cord
AHA: 3Q, '07, 4; 3Q, '99, 7

198.4 Other parts of nervous system
Meninges (cerebral) (spinal)
AHA: J-F, '87, 7

198.5 Bone and bone marrow
AHA: 1Q, '07, 6; 4Q, '03, 110; 3Q, '99, 5; 2Q, '92, 3; 1Q, '91, 16; 4Q, '89, 10

198.6 Ovary ♀

198.7 Adrenal gland
Suprarenal gland

✓5th **198.8 Other specified sites**

198.81 Breast
EXCLUDES *skin of breast (198.2)*

198.82 Genital organs

198.89 Other
EXCLUDES *retroperitoneal lymph nodes (196.2)*
AHA: 2Q, '05, 4; 2Q, '97, 4

✓4th 199 Malignant neoplasm without specification of site

EXCLUDES ▶*malignant carcinoid tumor of unknown primary site (209.20)*
malignant neuroendocrine tumor, any site (209.30)
neuroendocrine carcinoma, any site (209.30)◀

199.0 Disseminated
Carcinomatosis
Generalized:
cancer
malignancy
Multiple cancer
} unspecified site (primary) (secondary)
AHA: 4Q, '89, 10

199.1 Other
Cancer
Carcinoma
Malignancy
} unspecified site (primary) (secondary)
AHA: 3Q, '06, 14-15; 1Q, '06, 4

● **199.2 Malignant neoplasm associated with transplanted organ**
Code first complication of transplanted organ (996.80-996.89)
Use additional code for specific malignancy site

MALIGNANT NEOPLASM OF LYMPHATIC AND HEMATOPOIETIC TISSUE (200-208)

EXCLUDES *secondary neoplasm of:*
bone marrow (198.5)
spleen (197.8)
secondary and unspecified neoplasm of lymph nodes (196.0-196.9)

The following fifth-digit subclassification is for use with categories 200-202:
0 unspecified site, extranodal and solid organ sites
1 lymph nodes of head, face, and neck
2 intrathoracic lymph nodes
3 intra-abdominal lymph nodes
4 lymph nodes of axilla and upper limb
5 lymph nodes of inguinal region and lower limb
6 intrapelvic lymph nodes
7 spleen
8 lymph nodes of multiple sites

✓4th **200 Lymphosarcoma and reticulosarcoma and other specified malignant tumors of lymphatic tissue**
AHA: 4Q, '07, 65; 2Q, '92, 3; N-D, '86, 5

§ ✓5th **200.0 Reticulosarcoma**
[0-8]
Lymphoma (malignant):
histiocytic (diffuse):
nodular
pleomorphic cell type
reticulum cell type
Reticulum cell sarcoma:
NOS
pleomorphic cell type
AHA: For Code 200.03: 3Q, '01, 12
DEF: Malignant lymphoma of primarily histolytic cells; commonly originates in reticuloendothelium of lymph nodes.

§ ✓5th **200.1 Lymphosarcoma**
[0-8]
Lymphoblastoma (diffuse)
Lymphoma (malignant):
lymphoblastic (diffuse)
lymphocytic (cell type) (diffuse)
lymphosarcoma type
Lymphosarcoma:
NOS
diffuse NOS
lymphoblastic (diffuse)
lymphocytic (diffuse)
prolymphocytic
EXCLUDES *lymphosarcoma:*
follicular or nodular (202.0)
mixed cell type (200.8)
lymphosarcoma cell leukemia (207.8)
DEF: Malignant lymphoma created from anaplastic lymphoid cells resembling lymphocytes or lymphoblasts.

§ ✓5th **200.2 Burkitt's tumor or lymphoma**
[0-8]
Malignant lymphoma, Burkitt's type
DEF: Large osteolytic lesion most common in jaw or as abdominal mass; usually found in central Africa but reported elsewhere.

§ ✓5th **200.3 Marginal zone lymphoma**
[0-8]
Extranodal marginal zone B-cell lymphoma
Mucosa associated lymphoid tissue [MALT]
Nodal marginal zone B-cell lymphoma
Splenic marginal zone B-cell lymphoma
AHA: 4Q, '07, 65

§ ✓5th **200.4 Mantle cell lymphoma**
[0-8] AHA: 4Q, '07, 65

§ ✓5th **200.5 Primary central nervous system lymphoma**
[0-8] AHA: 4Q, '07, 66

§ ✓5th **200.6 Anaplastic large cell lymphoma**
[0-8] AHA: 4Q, '07, 66

§ ✓5th **200.7 Large cell lymphoma**
[0-8] AHA: 4Q, '07, 66

§ ✓5th **200.8 Other named variants**
[0-8]
Lymphoma (malignant):
lymphoplasmacytoid type
mixed lymphocytic-histiocytic (diffuse)
Lymphosarcoma, mixed cell type (diffuse)
Reticulolymphosarcoma (diffuse)

✓4th **201 Hodgkin's disease**
AHA: 2Q, '92, 3; N-D, '86, 5
DEF: Painless, progressive enlargement of lymph nodes, spleen and general lymph tissue; symptoms include anorexia, lassitude, weight loss, fever, pruritis, night sweats, anemia.

§ ✓5th **201.0 Hodgkin's paragranuloma**
[0-8]

§ ✓5th **201.1 Hodgkin's granuloma**
[0-8] AHA: 2Q, '99, 7

§ ✓5th **201.2 Hodgkin's sarcoma**
[0-8]

§ ✓5th **201.4 Lymphocytic-histiocytic predominance**
[0-8]

§ ✓5th **201.5 Nodular sclerosis**
[0-8]
Hodgkin's disease, nodular sclerosis:
NOS
cellular phase

§ ✓5th **201.6 Mixed cellularity**
[0-8]

§ ✓5th **201.7 Lymphocytic depletion**
[0-8]
Hodgkin's disease, lymphocytic depletion:
NOS
diffuse fibrosis
reticular type

§ ✓5th **201.9 Hodgkin's disease, unspecified**
[0-8]
Hodgkin's:
disease NOS
lymphoma NOS
Malignant:
lymphogranuloma
lymphogranulomatosis

✓4th **202 Other malignant neoplasms of lymphoid and histiocytic tissue**
AHA: 2Q, '92, 3; N-D, '86, 5

§ ✓5th **202.0 Nodular lymphoma**
[0-8]
Brill-Symmers disease
Lymphoma:
follicular (giant)
lymphocytic, nodular
Lymphosarcoma:
follicular (giant)
nodular
DEF: Lymphomatous cells clustered into nodules within the lymph node; usually occurs in older adults and may involve all nodes and possibly extranodal sites.

§ ✓5th **202.1 Mycosis fungoides**
[0-8] AHA: 2Q, '92, 4
DEF: Type of cutaneous T-cell lymphoma; may evolve into generalized lymphoma; formerly thought to be of fungoid origin.

§ ✓5th **202.2 Sézary's disease**
[0-8] AHA: 2Q, '99, 7
DEF: Type of cutaneous T-cell lymphoma with erythroderma, intense pruritus, peripheral lymphadenopathy, abnormal hyperchromatic mononuclear cells in skin, lymph nodes and peripheral blood.

§ ✓5th **202.3 Malignant histiocytosis**
[0-8]
Histiocytic medullary reticulosis
Malignant:
reticuloendotheliosis
reticulosis

§ ✓5th **202.4 Leukemic reticuloendotheliosis**
[0-8]
Hairy-cell leukemia
DEF: Chronic leukemia with large, mononuclear cells with "hairy" appearance in marrow, spleen, liver, blood.

§ Requires fifth-digit. Valid digits are in [brackets] under each code. See beginning of section 200-208 for codes and definitions.

§ ✓5th **202.5 Letterer-Siwe disease**
[0-8]
Acute:
differentiated progressive histiocytosis
histiocytosis X (progressive)
infantile reticuloendotheliosis
reticulosis of infancy

EXCLUDES *Hand-Schüller-Christian disease (277.89)*
histiocytosis (acute) (chronic) (277.89)
histiocytosis X (chronic) (277.89)

DEF: A recessive reticuloendotheliosis of early childhood, with a hemorrhagic tendency, eczema-like skin eruption, hepatosplenomegaly, including lymph node enlargement, and progressive anemia; it is often a fatal disease with no established cause.

§ ✓5th **202.6 Malignant mast cell tumors**
[0-8]
Malignant:
mastocytoma
mastocytosis
Mast cell sarcoma
Systemic tissue mast cell disease

EXCLUDES *mast cell leukemia (207.8)*

§ ✓5th **202.7 Peripheral T-cell lymphoma**
[0-8] **AHA:** 4Q, '07, 66

§ ✓5th **202.8 Other lymphomas**
[0-8]
Lymphoma (malignant):
NOS
diffuse

EXCLUDES *benign lymphoma (229.0)*

AHA: 4Q, '06, 135; 2Q, '06, 20-21; 2Q, '92, 4;
For code 202.80: ▶1Q, '08, 16;◀ 3Q, '07, 3

§ ✓5th **202.9 Other and unspecified malignant neoplasms of lymphoid and histiocytic tissue**
[0-8]
Follicular dendritic cell sarcoma
Interdigitating dendritic cell sarcoma
Langerhans cell sarcoma
Malignant neoplasm of bone marrow NOS

✓4th **203 Multiple myeloma and immunoproliferative neoplasms**

AHA: 4Q, '91, 26

The following fifth-digit subclassification is for use with category 203:
▲ **0 without mention of having achieved remission**
▶Failed remission◀
1 in remission
● **2 in relapse**

§ ✓5th **203.0 Multiple myeloma**
[0-2]
Kahler's disease
Myelomatosis

EXCLUDES *solitary myeloma (238.6)*

AHA: 1Q, '96, 16; 4Q, '89, 10; **For code 203.00:** 2Q,'07, 8

§ ✓5th **203.1 Plasma cell leukemia**
[0-2]
Plasmacytic leukemia

AHA: 4Q, '91, 26; S-O, '86, 12

§ ✓5th **203.8 Other immunoproliferative neoplasms**
[0-2] **AHA:** 4Q, '90, 26; S-O, '86, 12

✓4th **204 Lymphoid leukemia**

INCLUDES leukemia:
lymphatic
lymphoblastic
lymphocytic
lymphogenous

AHA: 3Q, '93, 4

The following fifth-digit subclassification is for use with category 204:
▲ **0 without mention of having achieved remission**
▶Failed remission◀
1 in remission
● **2 in relapse**

§ ✓5th **204.0 Acute**
[0-2]
EXCLUDES *acute exacerbation of chronic lymphoid leukemia (204.1)*

AHA: 3Q, '99, 6

§ ✓5th **204.1 Chronic**
[0-2]

§ ✓5th **204.2 Subacute**
[0-2]

§ ✓5th **204.8 Other lymphoid leukemia**
[0-2]
Aleukemic leukemia:
lymphatic
lymphocytic
lymphoid

§ ✓5th **204.9 Unspecified lymphoid leukemia**
[0-2]

✓4th **205 Myeloid leukemia**

INCLUDES leukemia:
granulocytic
myeloblastic
myelocytic
myelogenous
myelomonocytic
myelosclerotic
myelosis

AHA: 3Q, '93, 3; 4Q, '91, 26; 4Q, '90, 3; M-J, '85, 18

The following fifth-digit subclassification is for use with category 205:
▲ **0 without mention of having achieved remission**
▶Failed remission◀
1 in remission
● **2 in relapse**

§ ✓5th **205.0 Acute**
[0-2]
Acute promyelocytic leukemia

EXCLUDES *acute exacerbation of chronic myeloid leukemia (205.1)*

AHA: 2Q, '06, 20-21

§ ✓5th **205.1 Chronic**
[0-2]
Eosinophilic leukemia
Neutrophilic leukemia

AHA: 1Q, '00, 6; J-A, '85, 13

§ ✓5th **205.2 Subacute**
[0-2]

§ ✓5th **205.3 Myeloid sarcoma**
[0-2]
Chloroma
Granulocytic sarcoma

§ ✓5th **205.8 Other myeloid leukemia**
[0-2]
Aleukemic leukemia:
granulocytic
myelogenous
myeloid
Aleukemic myelosis

§ ✓5th **205.9 Unspecified myeloid leukemia**
[0-2]

✓4th **206 Monocytic leukemia**

INCLUDES leukemia:
histiocytic
monoblastic
monocytoid

The following fifth-digit subclassification is for use with category 206:
▲ **0 without mention of having achieved remission**
▶Failed remission◀
1 in remission
● **2 in relapse**

§ ✓5th **206.0 Acute**
[0-2]
EXCLUDES *acute exacerbation of chronic monocytic leukemia (206.1)*

§ Requires fifth-digit. Valid digits are in [brackets] under each code. See appropriate category for codes and definitions.

N Newborn Age: 0 P Pediatric Age: 0-17 M Maternity Age: 12-55 A Adult Age: 15-124

§ ✓5th 206.1 **Chronic**
[0-2]

§ ✓5th 206.2 **Subacute**
[0-2]

§ ✓5th 206.8 **Other monocytic leukemia**
[0-2]
Aleukemic:
monocytic leukemia
monocytoid leukemia

§ ✓5th 206.9 **Unspecified monocytic leukemia**
[0-2]

✓4th **207 Other specified leukemia**

EXCLUDES *leukemic reticuloendotheliosis (202.4)*
plasma cell leukemia (203.1)

The following fifth-digit subclassification is for use with category 207:
▲ **0 without mention of having achieved remission**
▶Failed remission◀
1 in remission
● **2 in relapse**

§ ✓5th **207.0 Acute erythremia and erythroleukemia**
[0-2]
Acute erythremic myelosis
Di Guglielmo's disease
Erythremic myelosis

DEF: Erythremia: polycythemia vera.

DEF: Erythroleukemia: a malignant blood dyscrasia (a myeloproliferative disorder).

§ ✓5th **207.1 Chronic erythremia**
[0-2]
Heilmeyer-Schöner disease

§ ✓5th **207.2 Megakaryocytic leukemia**
[0-2]
Megakaryocytic myelosis
Thrombocytic leukemia

§ ✓5th **207.8 Other specified leukemia**
[0-2]
Lymphosarcoma cell leukemia

✓4th **208 Leukemia of unspecified cell type**

The following fifth-digit subclassification is for use with category 208:
▲ **0 without mention of having achieved remission**
▶Failed remission◀
1 in remission
● **2 in relapse**

§ ✓5th **208.0 Acute**
[0-2]
Acute leukemia NOS
Blast cell leukemia
Stem cell leukemia

EXCLUDES *acute exacerbation of chronic unspecified leukemia (208.1)*

§ ✓5th **208.1 Chronic**
[0-2]
Chronic leukemia NOS

§ ✓5th **208.2 Subacute**
[0-2]
Subacute leukemia NOS

§ ✓5th **208.8 Other leukemia of unspecified cell type**
[0-2]

§ ✓5th **208.9 Unspecified leukemia**
[0-2]
Leukemia NOS

▶NEUROENDOCRINE TUMORS (209)◀

● ✓4th **209 Neuroendocrine tumors**

Code first any associated multiple endocrine neoplasia syndrome (258.01-258.03)

Use additional code to identify associated endocrine syndrome, such as:
carcinoid syndrome (259.2)

EXCLUDES *pancreatic islet cell tumors (157.4)*

● ✓5th **209.0 Malignant carcinoid tumors of the small intestine**

● **209.00 Malignant carcinoid tumor of the small intestine, unspecified portion**

● **209.01 Malignant carcinoid tumor of the duodenum**

● **209.02 Malignant carcinoid tumor of the jejunum**

● **209.03 Malignant carcinoid tumor of the ileum**

● ✓5th **209.1 Malignant carcinoid tumors of the appendix, large intestine, and rectum**

● **209.10 Malignant carcinoid tumor of the large intestine, unspecified portion**
Malignant carcinoid tumor of the colon NOS

● **209.11 Malignant carcinoid tumor of the appendix**

● **209.12 Malignant carcinoid tumor of the cecum**

● **209.13 Malignant carcinoid tumor of the ascending colon**

● **209.14 Malignant carcinoid tumor of the transverse colon**

● **209.15 Malignant carcinoid tumor of the descending colon**

● **209.16 Malignant carcinoid tumor of the sigmoid colon**

● **209.17 Malignant carcinoid tumor of the rectum**

● ✓5th **209.2 Malignant carcinoid tumors of other and unspecified sites**

● **209.20 Malignant carcinoid tumor of unknown primary site**

● **209.21 Malignant carcinoid tumor of the bronchus and lung**

● **209.22 Malignant carcinoid tumor of the thymus**

● **209.23 Malignant carcinoid tumor of the stomach**

● **209.24 Malignant carcinoid tumor of the kidney**

● **209.25 Malignant carcinoid tumor of the foregut NOS**

● **209.26 Malignant carcinoid tumor of the midgut NOS**

● **209.27 Malignant carcinoid tumor of the hindgut NOS**

● **209.29 Malignant carcinoid tumors of other sites**

● ✓5th **209.3 Malignant poorly differentiated neuroendocrine tumors**

● **209.30 Malignant poorly differentiated neuroendocrine carcinoma, any site**
High grade neuroendocrine carcinoma, any site
Malignant poorly differentiated neuroendocrine tumor NOS

● ✓5th **209.4 Benign carcinoid tumors of the small intestine**

● **209.40 Benign carcinoid tumor of the small intestine, unspecified portion**

● **209.41 Benign carcinoid tumor of the duodenum**

● **209.42 Benign carcinoid tumor of the jejunum**

● **209.43 Benign carcinoid tumor of the ileum**

● ✓5th **209.5 Benign carcinoid tumors of the appendix, large intestine, and rectum**

● **209.50 Benign carcinoid tumor of the large intestine, unspecified portion**
Benign carcinoid tumor of the colon NOS

● **209.51 Benign carcinoid tumor of the appendix**

§ Requires fifth-digit. Valid digits are in [brackets] under each code. See appropriate category for codes and definitions.

● **209.52 Benign carcinoid tumor of the cecum**

● **209.53 Benign carcinoid tumor of the ascending colon**

● **209.54 Benign carcinoid tumor of the transverse colon**

● **209.55 Benign carcinoid tumor of the descending colon**

● **209.56 Benign carcinoid tumor of the sigmoid colon**

● **209.57 Benign carcinoid tumor of the rectum**

● ✓5th **209.6 Benign carcinoid tumors of other and unspecified sites**

● **209.60 Benign carcinoid tumor of unknown primary site**
Carcinoid tumor NOS
Neuroendocrine tumor NOS

● **209.61 Benign carcinoid tumor of the bronchus and lung**

● **209.62 Benign carcinoid tumor of the thymus**

● **209.63 Benign carcinoid tumor of the stomach**

● **209.64 Benign carcinoid tumor of the kidney**

● **209.65 Benign carcinoid tumor of the foregut NOS**

● **209.66 Benign carcinoid tumor of the midgut NOS**

● **209.67 Benign carcinoid tumor of the hindgut NOS**

● **209.69 Benign carcinoid tumors of other sites**

BENIGN NEOPLASMS (210-229)

✓4th **210 Benign neoplasm of lip, oral cavity, and pharynx**

EXCLUDES *cyst (of):*
jaw (526.0-526.2, 526.89)
oral soft tissue (528.4)
radicular (522.8)

210.0 Lip
Frenulum labii
Lip (inner aspect) (mucosa) (vermilion border)

EXCLUDES *labial commissure (210.4)*
skin of lip (216.0)

210.1 Tongue
Lingual tonsil

210.2 Major salivary glands
Gland:
parotid
sublingual
submandibular

EXCLUDES *benign neoplasms of minor salivary glands:*
NOS (210.4)
buccal mucosa (210.4)
lips (210.0)
palate (hard) (soft) (210.4)
tongue (210.1)
tonsil, palatine (210.5)

210.3 Floor of mouth

210.4 Other and unspecified parts of mouth
Gingiva
Gum (upper) (lower)
Labial commissure
Oral cavity NOS
Oral mucosa
Palate (hard) (soft)
Uvula

EXCLUDES *benign odontogenic neoplasms of bone (213.0-213.1)*
developmental odontogenic cysts (526.0)
mucosa of lips (210.0)
nasopharyngeal [posterior] [superior] surface of soft palate (210.7)

210.5 Tonsil
Tonsil (faucial) (palatine)

EXCLUDES *lingual tonsil (210.1)*
pharyngeal tonsil (210.7)
tonsillar:
fossa (210.6)
pillars (210.6)

210.6 Other parts of oropharynx
Branchial cleft or vestiges
Epiglottis, anterior aspect
Fauces NOS
Mesopharynx NOS
Tonsillar:
fossa
pillars
Vallecula

EXCLUDES *epiglottis:*
NOS (212.1)
suprahyoid portion (212.1)

210.7 Nasopharynx
Adenoid tissue
Lymphadenoid tissue
Pharyngeal tonsil
Posterior nasal septum

210.8 Hypopharynx
Arytenoid fold
Laryngopharynx
Postcricoidregion
Pyriform fossa

210.9 Pharynx, unspecified
Throat NOS

✓4th **211 Benign neoplasm of other parts of digestive system**

EXCLUDES *benign stromal tumors of digestive system (215.5)*

211.0 Esophagus

211.1 Stomach
Body, Cardia, Fundus } of stomach
Cardiac orifice
Pylorus

EXCLUDES ▶*benign carcinoid tumors of the stomach (209.63)*◀

211.2 Duodenum, jejunum, and ileum
Small intestine NOS

EXCLUDES *ampulla of Vater (211.5)*
▶*benign carcinoid tumors of the small intestine (209.40-209.43)*◀
ileocecal valve (211.3)

211.3 Colon
Appendix
Cecum
Ileocecal valve
Large intestine NOS

EXCLUDES ▶*benign carcinoid tumors of the large intestine (209.50-209.56)*◀
rectosigmoid junction (211.4)

AHA: 3Q, '05, 17; 2Q, '05, 16; 4Q, '01, 56

211.4 Rectum and anal canal
Anal canal or sphincter
Anus NOS
Rectosigmoid junction
EXCLUDES *anus:*
margin (216.5)
skin (216.5)
▶*benign carcinoid tumors of the rectum (209.57)*◀
perianal skin (216.5)

211.5 Liver and biliary passages
Ampulla of Vater
Common bile duct
Cystic duct
Gallbladder
Hepatic duct
Sphincter of Oddi

211.6 Pancreas, except islets of Langerhans

211.7 Islets of Langerhans
Islet cell tumor
Use additional code to identify any functional activity

211.8 Retroperitoneum and peritoneum
Mesentery
Mesocolon
Omentum
Retroperitoneal tissue

211.9 Other and unspecified site
Alimentary tract NOS
Digestive system NOS
Gastrointestinal tract NOS
Intestinal tract NOS
Intestine NOS
Spleen, not elsewhere classified

✓4th 212 Benign neoplasm of respiratory and intrathoracic organs

212.0 Nasal cavities, middle ear, and accessory sinuses
Cartilage of nose
Eustachian tube
Nares
Septum of nose
Sinus:
ethmoidal
frontal
maxillary
sphenoidal
EXCLUDES *auditory canal (external) (216.2)*
bone of:
ear (213.0)
nose [turbinates] (213.0)
cartilage of ear (215.0)
ear (external) (skin) (216.2)
nose NOS (229.8)
skin (216.3)
olfactory bulb (225.1)
polyp of:
accessory sinus (471.8)
ear (385.30-385.35)
nasal cavity (471.0)
posterior margin of septum and choanae (210.7)

212.1 Larynx
Cartilage:
arytenoid
cricoid
cuneiform
thyroid
Epiglottis (suprahyoid portion) NOS
Glottis
Vocal cords (false)(true)
EXCLUDES *epiglottis, anterior aspect (210.6)*
polyp of vocal cord or larynx (478.4)

212.2 Trachea

212.3 Bronchus and lung
Carina
Hilus of lung
EXCLUDES ▶*benign carcinoid tumors of bronchus and lung (209.61)*◀

212.4 Pleura

212.5 Mediastinum

212.6 Thymus
EXCLUDES ▶*benign carcinoid tumors of thymus (209.62)*◀

212.7 Heart
EXCLUDES *great vessels (215.4)*

212.8 Other specified sites

212.9 Site unspecified
Respiratory organ NOS
Upper respiratory tract NOS
EXCLUDES *intrathoracic NOS (229.8)*
thoracic NOS (229.8)

✓4th 213 Benign neoplasm of bone and articular cartilage
INCLUDES cartilage (articular) (joint)
periosteum
EXCLUDES *cartilage of:*
ear (215.0)
eyelid (215.0))
larynx (212.1)
nose (212.0)
exostosis NOS (726.91
synovia (215.0-215.9)

213.0 Bones of skull and face
EXCLUDES *lower jaw bone (213.1)*

213.1 Lower jaw bone

213.2 Vertebral column, excluding sacrum and coccyx

213.3 Ribs, sternum, and clavicle

213.4 Scapula and long bones of upper limb

213.5 Short bones of upper limb

213.6 Pelvic bones, sacrum, and coccyx

213.7 Long bones of lower limb

213.8 Short bones of lower limb

213.9 Bone and articular cartilage, site unspecified

✓4th 214 Lipoma
INCLUDES angiolipoma
fibrolipoma
hibernoma
lipoma (fetal) (infiltrating) (intramuscular)
myelolipoma
myxolipoma

DEF: Benign tumor frequently composed of mature fat cells; may occasionally be composed of fetal fat cells.

214.0 Skin and subcutaneous tissue of face

214.1 Other skin and subcutaneous tissue

214.2 Intrathoracic organs

214.3 Intra-abdominal organs

214.4 Spermatic cord ♂

214.8 Other specified sites
AHA: 3Q, '94, 7

214.9 Lipoma, unspecified site

✓4th 215 Other benign neoplasm of connective and other soft tissue

INCLUDES blood vessel
bursa
fascia
ligament
muscle
peripheral, sympathetic, and parasympathetic nerves and ganglia
synovia
tendon (sheath)

EXCLUDES *cartilage:*
articular (213.0-213.9)
larynx (212.1)
nose (212.0)
connective tissue of:
breast (217)
internal organ, except lipoma and hemangioma–code to benign neoplasm of the site
lipoma (214.0-214.9)

215.0 Head, face, and neck

215.2 Upper limb, including shoulder

215.3 Lower limb, including hip

215.4 Thorax

EXCLUDES *heart (212.7)*
mediastinum (212.5)
thymus (212.6)

215.5 Abdomen
Abdominal wall
Benign stromal tumors of abdomen
Hypochondrium

215.6 Pelvis
Buttock
Groin
Inguinal region
Perineum

EXCLUDES *uterine:*
leiomyoma (218.0-218.9)
ligament, any (221.0)

215.7 Trunk, unspecified
Back NOS
Flank NOS

215.8 Other specified sites

215.9 Site unspecified

✓4th 216 Benign neoplasm of skin

INCLUDES blue nevus
dermatofibroma
hydrocystoma
pigmented nevus
syringoadenoma
syringoma

EXCLUDES *skin of genital organs (221.0-222.9)*

AHA: 1Q, '00, 21

216.0 Skin of lip

EXCLUDES *vermilion border of lip (210.0)*

216.1 Eyelid, including canthus

EXCLUDES *cartilage of eyelid (215.0)*

216.2 Ear and external auditory canal
Auricle (ear)
Auricular canal, external
External meatus
Pinna

EXCLUDES *cartilage of ear (215.0)*

216.3 Skin of other and unspecified parts of face
Cheek, external
Eyebrow
Nose, external
Temple

216.4 Scalp and skin of neck

AHA: 3Q, '91, 12

216.5 Skin of trunk, except scrotum
Axillary fold
Perianal skin
Skin of:
abdominal wall
anus
back
breast
Skin of:
buttock
chest wall
groin
perineum
Umbilicus

EXCLUDES *anal canal (211.4)*
anus NOS (211.4)
skin of scrotum (222.4)

216.6 Skin of upper limb, including shoulder

216.7 Skin of lower limb, including hip

216.8 Other specified sites of skin

216.9 Skin, site unspecified

217 Benign neoplasm of breast
Breast (male) (female):
connective tissue
glandular tissue
soft parts

EXCLUDES *adenofibrosis (610.2)*
benign cyst of breast (610.0)
fibrocystic disease (610.1)
skin of breast (216.5)

AHA: 1Q, '00, 4

✓4th 218 Uterine leiomyoma

INCLUDES fibroid (bleeding) (uterine)
uterine:
fibromyoma
myoma

DEF: Benign tumor primarily derived from uterine smooth muscle tissue; may contain fibrous, fatty, or epithelial tissue; also called uterine fibroid or myoma.

218.0 Submucous leiomyoma of uterus ♀

218.1 Intramural leiomyoma of uterus ♀
Interstitial leiomyoma of uterus

218.2 Subserous leiomyoma of uterus ♀

218.9 Leiomyoma of uterus, unspecified ♀

AHA: 1Q, '03, 4

✓4th 219 Other benign neoplasm of uterus

219.0 Cervix uteri ♀

219.1 Corpus uteri ♀
Endometrium
Fundus
Myometrium

219.8 Other specified parts of uterus ♀

219.9 Uterus, part unspecified ♀

Types of Uterine Fibroids

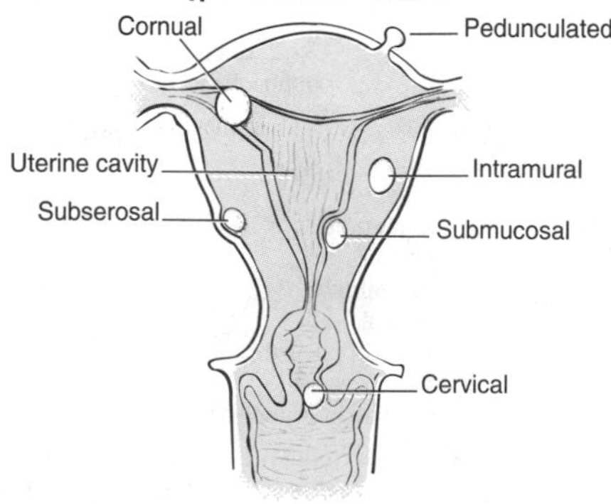

220 Benign neoplasm of ovary ♀

Use additional code to identify any functional activity (256.0-256.1)

EXCLUDES *cyst:*
corpus albicans (620.2)
corpus luteum (620.1)
endometrial (617.1)
follicular (atretic) (620.0)
graafian follicle (620.0)
ovarian NOS (620.2)
retention (620.2)

✓4th **221 Benign neoplasm of other female genital organs**

INCLUDES adenomatous polyp
benign teratoma

EXCLUDES *cyst:*
epoophoron (752.11)
fimbrial (752.11)
Gartner's duct (752.11)
parovarian (752.11)

221.0 Fallopian tube and uterine ligaments ♀
Oviduct
Parametruim
Uterine ligament (broad) (round) (uterosacral)
Uterine tube

221.1 Vagina ♀

221.2 Vulva ♀
Clitoris
External female genitalia NOS
Greater vestibular [Bartholin's] gland
Labia (majora) (minora)
Pudendum

EXCLUDES *Bartholin's (duct) (gland) cyst (616.2)*

221.8 Other specified sites of female genital organs ♀

221.9 Female genital organ, site unspecified ♀
Female genitourinary tract NOS

✓4th **222 Benign neoplasm of male genital organs**

222.0 Testis ♂
Use additional code to identify any functional activity

222.1 Penis ♂
Corpus cavernosum
Glans penis
Prepuce

222.2 Prostate ♂

EXCLUDES *adenomatous hyperplasia of prostate (600.20-600.21)*
prostatic:
adenoma (600.20-600.21)
enlargement (600.00-600.01)
hypertrophy (600.00-600.01)

222.3 Epididymis ♂

222.4 Scrotum ♂
Skin of scrotum

222.8 Other specified sites of male genital organs ♂
Seminal vesicle
Spermatic cord

222.9 Male genital organ, site unspecified ♂
Male genitourinary tract NOS

✓4th **223 Benign neoplasm of kidney and other urinary organs**

223.0 Kidney, except pelvis
Kidney NOS

EXCLUDES ▶*benign carcinoid tumors of kidney (209.64)*◀
renal:
calyces (223.1)
pelvis (223.1)

223.1 Renal pelvis

223.2 Ureter

EXCLUDES *ureteric orifice of bladder (223.3)*

223.3 Bladder

✓5th **223.8 Other specified sites of urinary organs**

223.81 Urethra

EXCLUDES *urethral orifice of bladder (223.3)*

223.89 Other
Paraurethral glands

223.9 Urinary organ, site unspecified
Urinary system NOS

✓4th **224 Benign neoplasm of eye**

EXCLUDES *cartilage of eyelid (215.0)*
eyelid (skin) (216.1)
optic nerve (225.1)
orbital bone (213.0)

224.0 Eyeball, except conjunctiva, cornea, retina, and choroid
Ciliary body
Iris
Sclera
Uveal tract

224.1 Orbit

EXCLUDES *bone of orbit (213.0)*

224.2 Lacrimal gland

224.3 Conjunctiva

224.4 Cornea

224.5 Retina

EXCLUDES *hemangioma of retina (228.03)*

224.6 Choroid

224.7 Lacrimal duct
Lacrimal sac
Nasolacrimal duct

224.8 Other specified parts of eye

224.9 Eye, part unspecified

✓4th **225 Benign neoplasm of brain and other parts of nervous system**

EXCLUDES *hemangioma (228.02)*
neurofibromatosis (237.7)
peripheral, sympathetic, and parasympathetic nerves and ganglia (215.0-215.9)
retrobulbar (224.1)

225.0 Brain

225.1 Cranial nerves
Acoustic neuroma

AHA: 4Q, '04, 113

225.2 Cerebral meninges
Meninges NOS
Meningioma (cerebral)

Eyeball

225.3 Spinal cord
Cauda equina

225.4 Spinal meninges
Spinal meningioma

225.8 Other specified sites of nervous system

225.9 Nervous system, part unspecified
Nervous system (central) NOS
EXCLUDES *meninges NOS (225.2)*

226 Benign neoplasm of thyroid glands
Use additional code to identify any functional activity

✓4th **227 Benign neoplasm of other endocrine glands and related structures**
Use additional code to identify any functional activity
EXCLUDES *ovary (220)*
pancreas (211.6)
testis (222.0)

227.0 Adrenal gland
Suprarenal gland

227.1 Parathyroid gland

227.3 Pituitary gland and craniopharyngeal duct (pouch)
Craniobuccal pouch
Hypophysis
Rathke's pouch
Sella turcica

227.4 Pineal gland
Pineal body

227.5 Carotid body

227.6 Aortic body and other paraganglia
Coccygeal body
Glomus jugulare
Para-aortic body
AHA: N-D, '84, 17

227.8 Other

227.9 Endocrine gland, site unspecified

✓4th **228 Hemangioma and lymphangioma, any site**
INCLUDES angioma (benign) (cavernous) (congenital) NOS
cavernous nevus
glomus tumor
hemangioma (benign) (congenital)
EXCLUDES *benign neoplasm of spleen, except hemangioma and lymphangioma (211.9)*
glomus jugulare (227.6)
nevus:
NOS (216.0-216.9)
blue or pigmented (216.0-216.9)
vascular (757.32)
AHA: 1Q, '00, 21

✓5th **228.0 Hemangioma, any site**
AHA: J-F, '85, 19
DEF: A common benign tumor usually occurring in infancy; composed of newly formed blood vessels due to malformation of angioblastic tissue.

228.00 Of unspecified site

228.01 Of skin and subcutaneous tissue

228.02 Of intracranial structures

228.03 Of retina

228.04 Of intra-abdominal structures
Peritoneum
Retroperitoneal tissue

228.09 Of other sites
Systemic angiomatosis
AHA: 3Q, '91, 20

228.1 Lymphangioma, any site
Congenital lymphangioma
Lymphatic nevus

✓4th **229 Benign neoplasm of other and unspecified sites**

229.0 Lymph nodes
EXCLUDES *lymphangioma (228.1)*

229.8 Other specified sites
Intrathoracic NOS
Thoracic NOS

229.9 Site unspecified

CARCINOMA IN SITU (230-234)

INCLUDES Bowen's disease
erythroplasia
Queyrat's erythroplasia
EXCLUDES *leukoplakia–see Alphabetic Index*
DEF: A neoplastic type; with tumor cells confined to epithelium of origin; without further invasion.

✓4th **230 Carcinoma in situ of digestive organs**

230.0 Lip, oral cavity, and pharynx
Gingiva
Hypopharynx
Mouth [any part]
Nasopharynx
Oropharynx
Salivary gland or duct
Tongue
EXCLUDES *aryepiglottic fold or interarytenoid fold, laryngeal aspect (231.0)*
epiglottis:
NOS (231.0)
suprahyoid portion (231.0)
skin of lip (232.0)

230.1 Esophagus

230.2 Stomach
Body, Cardia, Fundus } of stomach
Cardiac orifice
Pylorus

230.3 Colon
Appendix
Cecum
Ileocecal valve
Large intestine NOS
EXCLUDES *rectosigmoid junction (230.4)*

230.4 Rectum
Rectosigmoid junction

230.5 Anal canal
Anal sphincter

230.6 Anus, unspecified
EXCLUDES *anus:*
margin (232.5)
skin (232.5)
perianal skin (232.5)

230.7 Other and unspecified parts of intestine
Duodenum
Ileum
Jejunum
Small intestine NOS
EXCLUDES *ampulla of Vater (230.8)*

230.8 Liver and biliary system
Ampulla of Vater
Common bile duct
Cystic duct
Gallbladder
Hepatic duct
Sphincter of Oddi

230.9 Other and unspecified digestive organs
Digestive organ NOS
Gastrointestinal tract NOS
Pancreas
Spleen

✓4th 231 Carcinoma in situ of respiratory system

231.0 Larynx
Cartilage:
arytenoid
cricoid
cuneiform
thyroid
Epiglottis:
NOS
posterior surface
suprahyoid portion
Vocal cords (false)(true)
EXCLUDES *aryepiglottic fold or interarytenoid fold: NOS (230.0) hypopharyngeal aspect (230.0) marginal zone (230.0)*

231.1 Trachea

231.2 Bronchus and lung
Carina
Hilus of lung

231.8 Other specified parts of respiratory system
Accessory sinuses
Middle ear
Nasal cavities
Pleura
EXCLUDES *ear (external) (skin) (232.2) nose NOS (234.8) skin (232.3)*

231.9 Respiratory system, part unspecified
Respiratory organ NOS

✓4th 232 Carcinoma in situ of skin
INCLUDES pigment cells
EXCLUDES *▶melanoma in situ of skin (172.0-172.9)◀*

232.0 Skin of lip
EXCLUDES *vermilion border of lip (230.0)*

232.1 Eyelid, including canthus

232.2 Ear and external auditory canal

232.3 Skin of other and unspecified parts of face

232.4 Scalp and skin of neck

232.5 Skin of trunk, except scrotum
Anus, margin
Axillary fold
Perianal skin
Skin of:
abdominal wall
anus
back
Skin of:
breast
buttock
chest wall
groin
perineum
Umbilicus
EXCLUDES *anal canal (230.5) anus NOS (230.6) skin of genital organs (233.30-233.39, 233.5-233.6)*

232.6 Skin of upper limb, including shoulder

232.7 Skin of lower limb, including hip

232.8 Other specified sites of skin

232.9 Skin, site unspecified

✓4th 233 Carcinoma in situ of breast and genitourinary system

233.0 Breast
EXCLUDES *Paget's disease (174.0-174.9) skin of breast (232.5)*

233.1 Cervix uteri ♀
Adenocarcinoma in situ of cervix
Cervical intraepithelial glandular neoplasia, ▶grade III◀
Cervical intraepithelial neoplasia III [CIN III]
Severe dysplasia of cervix
EXCLUDES *cervical intraepithelial neoplasia II [CIN II] (622.12) cytologic evidence of malignancy without histologic confirmation (795.06) high grade squamous intraepithelial lesion (HGSIL) (795.04) moderate dysplasia of cervix (622.12)*
AHA: 3Q, '92, 7; 3Q, '92, 8; 1Q, '91, 11

233.2 Other and unspecified parts of uterus ♀

✓5th 233.3 Other and unspecified female genital organs
AHA: 4Q, '07, 67

233.30 Unspecified female genital organ ♀

233.31 Vagina ♀
Severe dysplasia of vagina
Vaginal intraepithelial neoplasia III [VAIN III]

233.32 Vulva ♀
Severe dysplasia of vulva
Vulvar intraepithelial neoplasia III [VIN III]

233.39 Other female genital organ ♀

233.4 Prostate ♂

233.5 Penis ♂

233.6 Other and unspecified male genital organs ♂

233.7 Bladder

233.9 Other and unspecified urinary organs

✓4th 234 Carcinoma in situ of other and unspecified sites

234.0 Eye
EXCLUDES *cartilage of eyelid (234.8) eyelid (skin) (232.1) optic nerve (234.8) orbital bone (234.8)*

234.8 Other specified sites
Endocrine gland [any]

234.9 Site unspecified
Carcinoma in situ NOS

NEOPLASMS OF UNCERTAIN BEHAVIOR (235-238)

Note: Categories 235–238 classify by site certain histomorphologically well-defined neoplasms, the subsequent behavior of which cannot be predicted from the present appearance.

✓4th 235 Neoplasm of uncertain behavior of digestive and respiratory systems
EXCLUDES *stromal tumors of uncertain behavior of digestive system (238.1)*

235.0 Major salivary glands
Gland:
parotid
sublingual
submandibular
EXCLUDES *minor salivary glands (235.1)*

235.1 Lip, oral cavity, and pharynx
Gingiva
Hypopharynx
Minor salivary glands
Mouth
Nasopharynx
Oropharynx
Tongue

EXCLUDES *aryepiglottic fold or interarytenoid fold, laryngeal aspect (235.6)*
epiglottis:
NOS (235.6)
suprahyoid portion (235.6)
skin of lip (238.2)

235.2 Stomach, intestines, and rectum

235.3 Liver and biliary passages
Ampulla of Vater
Bile ducts [any]
Gallbladder
Liver

235.4 Retroperitoneum and peritoneum

235.5 Other and unspecified digestive organs
Anal:
canal
sphincter
Anus NOS
Esophagus
Pancreas
Spleen

EXCLUDES *anus:*
margin (238.2)
skin (238.2)
perianal skin (238.2)

235.6 Larynx

EXCLUDES *aryepiglottic fold or interarytenoid fold:*
NOS (235.1)
hypopharyngeal aspect (235.1)
marginal zone (235.1)

235.7 Trachea, bronchus, and lung

235.8 Pleura, thymus, and mediastinum

235.9 Other and unspecified respiratory organs
Accessory sinuses
Middle ear
Nasal cavities
Respiratory organ NOS

EXCLUDES *ear (external) (skin) (238.2)*
nose (238.8)
skin (238.2)

✓4th **236 Neoplasm of uncertain behavior of genitourinary organs**

236.0 Uterus ♀

236.1 Placenta ♀
Chorioadenoma (destruens)
Invasive mole
Malignant hydatid(iform) mole

236.2 Ovary ♀
Use additional code to identify any functional activity

236.3 Other and unspecified female genital organs ♀

236.4 Testis ♂
Use additional code to identify any functional activity

236.5 Prostate ♂

236.6 Other and unspecified male genital organs ♂

236.7 Bladder

✓5th **236.9 Other and unspecified urinary organs**

236.90 Urinary organ, unspecified

236.91 Kidney and ureter

236.99 Other

✓4th **237 Neoplasm of uncertain behavior of endocrine glands and nervous system**

237.0 Pituitary gland and craniopharyngeal duct
Use additional code to identify any functional activity

237.1 Pineal gland

237.2 Adrenal gland
Suprarenal gland
Use additional code to identify any functional activity

237.3 Paragangliа
Aortic body
Carotid body
Coccygeal body
Glomus jugulare

AHA: N-D, '84, 17

237.4 Other and unspecified endocrine glands
Parathyroid gland
Thyroid gland

237.5 Brain and spinal cord

237.6 Meninges
Meninges:
NOS
cerebral
spinal

✓5th **237.7 Neurofibromatosis**
von Recklinghausen's disease

DEF: An inherited condition with developmental changes in the nervous system, muscles, bones and skin; multiple soft tumors (neurofibromas) distributed over the entire body.

237.70 Neurofibromatosis, unspecified

237.71 Neurofibromatosis, type 1 [von Recklinghausen's disease]

237.72 Neurofibromatosis, type 2 [acoustic neurofibromatosis]

DEF: Inherited condition with cutaneous lesions, benign tumors of peripheral nerves and bilateral 8th nerve masses.

237.9 Other and unspecified parts of nervous system
Cranial nerves

EXCLUDES *peripheral, sympathetic, and parasympathetic nerves and ganglia (238.1)*

✓4th **238 Neoplasm of uncertain behavior of other and unspecified sites and tissues**

238.0 Bone and articular cartilage

EXCLUDES *cartilage:*
ear (238.1)
eyelid (238.1)
larynx (235.6)
nose (235.9)
synovia (238.1)

AHA: 4Q, '04, 128

238.1 Connective and other soft tissue
Peripheral, sympathetic, and parasympathetic nerves and ganglia
Stromal tumors of digestive system

EXCLUDES *cartilage (of):*
articular (238.0)
larynx (235.6)
nose (235.9)
connective tissue of breast (238.3)

238.2 Skin

EXCLUDES *anus NOS (235.5)*
skin of genital organs (236.3, 236.6)
vermilion border of lip (235.1)

238.3 Breast

EXCLUDES *skin of breast (238.2)*

238.4 Polycythemia vera

DEF: Abnormal proliferation of all bone marrow elements, increased red cell mass and total blood volume; unknown etiology, frequently associated with splenomegaly, leukocytosis, and thrombocythemia.

238.5 Histiocytic and mast cells

Mast cell tumor NOS
Mastocytoma NOS

238.6 Plasma cells

Plasmacytoma NOS
Solitary myeloma

✓5th **238.7 Other lymphatic and hematopoietic tissues**

EXCLUDES *acute myelogenous leukemia (205.0)*
chronic myelomonocytic leukemia (205.1)
myelosclerosis NOS (289.89)
myelosis:
NOS (205.9)
megakaryocytic (207.2)

AHA: 3Q, '01, 13; 1Q, '97, 5; 2Q, '89, 8

238.71 Essential thrombocythemia

Essential hemorrhagic thrombocythemia
Essential thrombocytosis
Idiopathic (hemorrhagic) thrombocythemia
Primary thrombocytosis

AHA: 4Q, '06, 63-66

238.72 Low grade myelodysplastic syndrome lesions

Refractory anemia (RA)
Refractory anemia with ringed sideroblasts (RARS)
Refractory cytopenia with multilineage dysplasia (RCMD)
Refractory cytopenia with multilineage dysplasia and ringed sideroblasts (RCMD-RS)

AHA: 4Q, '06, 63-66

DEF: Refractory anemia (RA): Form of bone marrow disorder (myelodysplastic syndrome) that interferes with red blood cell production in the bone marrow; malignancy unresponsive to hematinics; characteristic normal or hypercellular marrow with abnormal erythrocyte development and reticulocytopenia.

238.73 High grade myelodysplastic syndrome lesions

Refractory anemia with excess blasts-1 (RAEB-1)
Refractory anemia with excess blasts-2 (RAEB-2)

AHA: 4Q, '06, 63-66

238.74 Myelodysplastic syndrome with 5q deletion

5q minus syndrome NOS

EXCLUDES *constitutional 5q deletion (758.39)*
high grade myelodysplastic syndrome with 5q deletion (238.73)

AHA: 4Q, '06, 63-66

238.75 Myelodysplastic syndrome, unspecified

AHA: 4Q, '06, 63-66

238.76 Myelofibrosis with myeloid metaplasia

Agnogenic myeloid metaplasia
Idiopathic myelofibrosis (chronic)
Myelosclerosis with myeloid metaplasia
Primary myelofibrosis

EXCLUDES *myelofibrosis NOS (289.83)*
myelophthisic anemia (284.2)
myelophthisis (284.2)
secondary myelofibrosis (289.83)

AHA: 4Q, '06, 63-66

● **238.77 Post-transplant lymphoproliferative disorder [PTLD]**

Code first complications of transplant (996.80-996.89)

238.79 Other lymphatic and hematopoietic tissues

Lymphoproliferative disease (chronic) NOS
Megakaryocytic myelosclerosis
Myeloproliferative disease (chronic) NOS
Panmyelosis (acute)

AHA: 4Q, '06, 63-66

238.8 Other specified sites

Eye
Heart

EXCLUDES *eyelid (skin) (238.2)*
cartilage (238.1)

238.9 Site unspecified

NEOPLASMS OF UNSPECIFIED NATURE (239)

✓4th **239 Neoplasms of unspecified nature**

Note: Category 239 classifies by site neoplasms of unspecified morphology and behavior. The term "mass,"unless otherwise stated, is not to be regarded as a neoplastic growth.

INCLUDES "growth" NOS
neoplasm NOS
new growth NOS
tumor NOS

239.0 Digestive system

EXCLUDES *anus:*
margin (239.2)
skin (239.2)
perianal skin (239.2)

239.1 Respiratory system

239.2 Bone, soft tissue, and skin

EXCLUDES *anal canal (239.0)*
anus NOS (239.0)
bone marrow (202.9)
cartilage:
larynx (239.1)
nose (239.1)
connective tissue of breast (239.3)
skin of genital organs (239.5)
vermilion border of lip (239.0)

239.3 Breast

EXCLUDES *skin of breast (239.2)*

239.4 Bladder

239.5 Other genitourinary organs

239.6 Brain

EXCLUDES *cerebral meninges (239.7)*
cranial nerves (239.7)

239.7 Endocrine glands and other parts of nervous system

EXCLUDES *peripheral, sympathetic, and parasympathetic nerves and ganglia (239.2)*

239.8 Other specified sites

EXCLUDES *eyelid (skin) (239.2)*
cartilage (239.2)
great vessels (239.2)
optic nerve (239.7)

239.9 Site unspecified

3. ENDOCRINE, NUTRITIONAL AND METABOLIC DISEASES, AND IMMUNITY DISORDERS (240-279)

EXCLUDES *endocrine and metabolic disturbances specific to the fetus and newborn (775.0-775.9)*

Note: All neoplasms, whether functionally active or not, are classified in Chapter 2. Codes in Chapter 3 (i.e., 242.8, 246.0, 251-253, 255-259) may be used to identify such functional activity associated with any neoplasm, or by ectopic endocrine tissue.

DISORDERS OF THYROID GLAND (240-246)

✓4th **240 Simple and unspecified goiter**

DEF: An enlarged thyroid gland often caused by an inadequate dietary intake of iodine.

240.0 Goiter, specified as simple

Any condition classifiable to 240.9, specified as simple

240.9 Goiter, unspecified

Enlargement of thyroid
Goiter or struma:
NOS
diffuse colloid
endemic
hyperplastic
nontoxic (diffuse)
parenchymatous
sporadic

EXCLUDES *congenital (dyshormonogenic) goiter (246.1)*

✓4th **241 Nontoxic nodular goiter**

EXCLUDES *adenoma of thyroid (226)*
cystadenoma of thyroid (226)

241.0 Nontoxic uninodular goiter

Thyroid nodule
Uninodular goiter (nontoxic)

DEF: Enlarged thyroid, commonly due to decreased thyroid production, with single nodule; no clinical hypothyroidism.

241.1 Nontoxic multinodular goiter

Multinodular goiter (nontoxic)

DEF: Enlarged thyroid, commonly due to decreased thyroid production with multiple nodules; no clinical hypothyroidism.

241.9 Unspecified nontoxic nodular goiter

Adenomatous goiter
Nodular goiter (nontoxic) NOS
Struma nodosa (simplex)

✓4th **242 Thyrotoxicosis with or without goiter**

EXCLUDES *neonatal thyrotoxicosis (775.3)*

DEF: A condition caused by excess quantities of thyroid hormones being introduced into the tissues

The following fifth-digit subclassification is for use with categories 242:
0 without mention of thyrotoxic crisis or storm
1 with mention of thyrotoxic crisis or storm

§ ✓5th **242.0 Toxic diffuse goiter**
[0-1]
Basedow's disease
Exophthalmic or toxic goiter NOS
Graves' disease
Primary thyroid hyperplasia

DEF: Diffuse thyroid enlargement accompanied by hyperthyroidism, bulging eyes, and dermopathy.

§ ✓5th **242.1 Toxic uninodular goiter**
[0-1]
Thyroid nodule } toxic or with hyperthyroidism
Uninodular goiter } toxic or with hyperthyroidism

DEF: Symptomatic hyperthyroidism with a single nodule on the enlarged thyroid gland. Abrupt onset of symptoms; including extreme nervousness, insomnia, weight loss, tremors, and psychosis or coma.

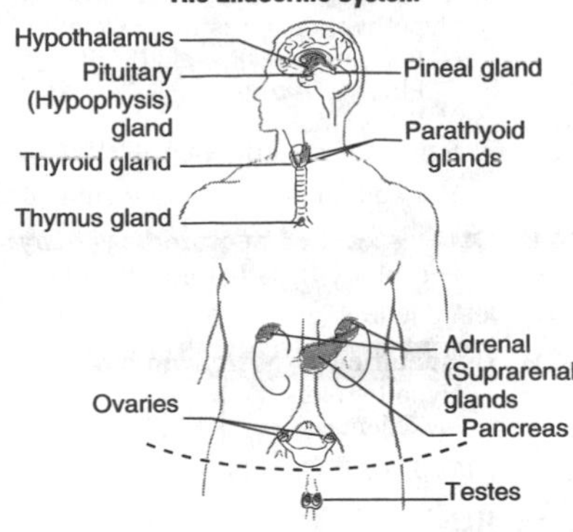

§ ✓5th **242.2 Toxic multinodular goiter**
[0-1]
Secondary thyroid hyperplasia

DEF: Symptomatic hyperthyroidism with multiple nodules on the enlarged thyroid gland. Abrupt onset of symptoms; including extreme nervousness, insomnia, weight loss, tremors, and psychosis or coma.

§ ✓5th **242.3 Toxic nodular goiter, unspecified**
[0-1]
Adenomatous goiter } toxic or with hyperthyroidism
Nodular goiter } toxic or with hyperthyroidism
Struma nodosa } toxic or with hyperthyroidism

Any condition classifiable to 241.9 specified as toxic or with hyperthyroidism

§ ✓5th **242.4 Thyrotoxicosis from ectopic thyroid nodule**
[0-1]

§ ✓5th **242.8 Thyrotoxicosis of other specified origin**
[0-1]
Overproduction of thyroid-stimulating hormone [TSH]
Thyrotoxicosis:
factitia from ingestion of excessive thyroid material

Use additional E code to identify cause, if drug-induced

§ ✓5th **242.9 Thyrotoxicosis without mention of goiter or other cause**
[0-1]
Hyperthyroidism NOS
Thyrotoxicosis NOS

243 Congenital hypothyroidism

Congenital thyroid insufficiency
Cretinism (athyrotic) (endemic)

Use additional code to identify associated mental retardation

EXCLUDES *congenital (dyshormonogenic) goiter (246.1)*

DEF: Underproduction of thyroid hormone present from birth.

✓4th **244 Acquired hypothyroidism**

INCLUDES athyroidism (acquired)
hypothyroidism (acquired)
myxedema (adult) (juvenile)
thyroid (gland) insufficiency (acquired)

244.0 Postsurgical hypothyroidism

DEF: Underproduction of thyroid hormone due to surgical removal of all or part of the thyroid gland.

244.1 Other postablative hypothyroidism

Hypothyroidism following therapy, such as irradiation

244.2 Iodine hypothyroidism

Hypothyroidism resulting from administration or ingestion of iodide

Use additional E code to identify drug

§ Requires fifth-digit. Valid digits are in [brackets] under each code. See category 242 for codes and definitions.

244.3 Other iatrogenic hypothyroidism
Hypothyroidism resulting from:
P-aminosalicylic acid [PAS]
Phenylbutazone
Resorcinol
Iatrogenic hypothyroidism NOS
Use additional E code to identify drug

244.8 Other specified acquired hypothyroidism
Secondary hypothyroidism NEC
AHA: J-A, '85, 9

244.9 Unspecified hypothyroidism
Hypothyroidism } primary or NOS
Myxedema }
AHA: 3Q, '99, 19; 4Q, '96, 29

4th 245 Thyroiditis

245.0 Acute thyroiditis
Abscess of thyroid
Thyroiditis:
nonsuppurative, acute
pyogenic
suppurative
Use additional code to identify organism
DEF: Inflamed thyroid caused by infection, with abscess and liquid puris.

245.1 Subacute thyroiditis
Thyroiditis:
de Quervain's
giant cell
granulomatous
viral
DEF: Inflammation of the thyroid, characterized by fever and painful enlargement of the thyroid gland, with granulomas in the gland.

245.2 Chronic lymphocytic thyroiditis
Hashimoto's disease
Struma lymphomatosa
Thyroiditis:
autoimmune
lymphocytic (chronic)
DEF: Autoimmune disease of thyroid; lymphocytes infiltrate the gland and thyroid antibodies are produced; women more often affected.

245.3 Chronic fibrous thyroiditis
Struma fibrosa
Thyroiditis:
invasive (fibrous)
ligneous
Riedel's
DEF: Persistent fibrosing inflammation of thyroid with adhesions to nearby structures; rare condition

245.4 Iatrogenic thyroiditis
Use additional code to identify cause
DEF: Thyroiditis resulting from treatment or intervention by physician or in a patient intervention setting.

245.8 Other and unspecified chronic thyroiditis
Chronic thyroiditis:
NOS
nonspecific

245.9 Thyroiditis, unspecified
Thyroiditis NOS

4th 246 Other disorders of thyroid

246.0 Disorders of thyrocalcitonin secretion
Hypersecretion of calcitonin or thyrocalcitonin

246.1 Dyshormonogenic goiter
Congenital (dyshormonogenic) goiter
Goiter due to enzyme defect in synthesis of thyroid hormone
Goitrous cretinism (sporadic)

246.2 Cyst of thyroid
EXCLUDES *cystadenoma of thyroid (226)*

246.3 Hemorrhage and infarction of thyroid

246.8 Other specified disorders of thyroid
Abnormality of thyroid-binding globulin
Atrophy of thyroid
Hyper-TBG-nemia
Hypo-TBG-nemia
AHA: 2Q, '06, 5

246.9 Unspecified disorder of thyroid

DISEASES OF OTHER ENDOCRINE GLANDS ▶(249-259)◀

● **4th 249 Secondary diabetes mellitus**
INCLUDES diabetes mellitus (due to) (in) (secondary) (with):
drug-induced or chemical induced
infection
Use additional code to identify any associated insulin use (V58.67)
EXCLUDES *gestational diabetes (648.8)*
hyperglycemia NOS (790.29)
neonatal diabetes mellitus (775.1)
nonclinical diabetes (790.29)
Type I diabetes – see category 250
Type II diabetes – see category 250

The following fifth-digit subclassification is for use with category 249:
0 not stated as uncontrolled, or unspecified
1 uncontrolled

● § 5th **249.0 Secondary diabetes mellitus without mention of complication**
[0-1]
Secondary diabetes mellitus without mention of complication or manifestation classifiable to 249.1-249.9
Secondary diabetes mellitus NOS

● § 5th **249.1 Secondary diabetes mellitus with ketoacidosis**
[0-1]
Secondary diabetes mellitus with diabetic acidosis without mention of coma
Secondary diabetes mellitus with diabetic ketosis without mention of coma

● § 5th **249.2 Secondary diabetes mellitus with hyperosmolarity**
[0-1]
Secondary diabetes mellitus with hyperosmolar (nonketotic) coma

● § 5th **249.3 Secondary diabetes mellitus with other coma**
[0-1]
Secondary diabetes mellitus with diabetic coma (with ketoacidosis)
Secondary diabetes mellitus with diabetic hypoglycemic coma
Secondary diabetes mellitus with insulin coma NOS
EXCLUDES *secondary diabetes mellitus with hyperosmolar coma (249.2)*

● § 5th **249.4 Secondary diabetes mellitus with renal manifestations**
[0-1]
Use additional code to identify manifestation, as:
chronic kidney disease (585.1-585.9)
diabetic nephropathy NOS (583.81)
diabetic nephrosis (581.81)
intercapillary glomerulosclerosis (581.81)
Kimmelstiel-Wilson syndrome (581.81)

● § 5th **249.5 Secondary diabetes mellitus with ophthalmic manifestations**
[0-1]
Use additional code to identify manifestation, as:
diabetic blindness (369.00-369.9)
diabetic cataract (366.41)
diabetic glaucoma (365.44)
diabetic macular edema (362.07)
diabetic retinal edema (362.07)
diabetic retinopathy (362.01-362.07)

§ Requires fifth-digit. Valid digits are in [brackets] under each code. See category 249 for codes and definitions.

● § ✓5th **249.6 Secondary diabetes mellitus with neurological manifestations**
[0-1]
Use additional code to identify manifestation, as:
diabetic amyotrophy (353.5)
diabetic gastroparalysis (536.3)
diabetic gastroparesis (536.3)
diabetic mononeuropathy (354.0-355.9)
diabetic neurogenic arthropathy (713.5)
diabetic peripheral autonomic neuropathy (337.1)
diabetic polyneuropathy (357.2)

● § ✓5th **249.7 Secondary diabetes mellitus with peripheral circulatory disorders**
[0-1]
Use additional code to identify manifestation, as:
diabetic gangrene (785.4)
diabetic peripheral angiopathy (443.81)

● § ✓5th **249.8 Secondary diabetes mellitus with other specified manifestations**
[0-1]
Secondary diabetic hypoglycemia in diabetes mellitus
Secondary hypoglycemic shock in diabetes mellitus
Use additional code to identify manifestation, as:
any associated ulceration (707.10-707.9)
diabetic bone changes (731.8)

● § ✓5th **249.9 Secondary diabetes mellitus with unspecified complication**
[0-1]

✓4th **250 Diabetes mellitus**

EXCLUDES *gestational diabetes (648.8)*
hyperglycemia NOS (790.29)
neonatal diabetes mellitus (775.1)
nonclinical diabetes (790.29)
▶*secondary diabetes (249.0-249.9)*◀

The following fifth-digit subclassification is for use with category 250:
0 type II or unspecified type, not state as uncontrolled
Fifth-digit 0 is for use for type II patients, even if the patient requires insulin
Use additional code, if applicable, for associated long-term (current) insulin use V58.67
1 type I [juvenile type], not stated as uncontrolled
2 type II or unspecified type, uncontrolled
Fifth-digit 2 is for use for type II patients, even if the patient requires insulin
Use additional code, if applicable, for associated long-term (current) insulin use V58.67
3 type I [juvenile type], uncontrolled

AHA: 4Q, '04, 56; 2Q, '04, 17; 2Q, '02, 13; 2Q,'01, 16; 2Q,'98, 15; 4Q, '97, 32; 2Q, '97, 14; 3Q, '96, 5; 4Q, '93, 19; 2Q, '92, 5; 3Q, '91, 3; 2Q, '90, 22; N-D, '85, 11

DEF: Diabetes mellitus: Inability to metabolize carbohydrates, proteins, and fats with insufficient secretion of insulin. Symptoms may be unremarkable, with long-term complications, involving kidneys, nerves, blood vessels, and eyes.

DEF: Uncontrolled diabetes: A nonspecific term indicating that the current treatment regimen does not keep the blood sugar level of a patient within acceptable levels.

§ ✓5th **250.0 Diabetes mellitus without mention of complication**
[0-3]
Diabetes mellitus without mention of complication or manifestation classifiable to 250.1-250.9
Diabetes (mellitus) NOS

AHA: 1Q, '06, 14; 4Q, '97, 32; 3Q, '91, 3, 12; N-D, '85, 11; **For code 250.00:** 1Q, '05, 15; 4Q, '04, 55; 4Q, '03, 105, 108; 2Q, '03, 16; 1Q, '02, 7, 11; **For code 250.01:** 4Q, '04, 55; 4Q, '03, 110; 2Q, '03, 6; **For code 250.02:** 1Q, '03, 5

§ ✓5th **250.1 Diabetes with ketoacidosis**
[0-3]
Diabetic:
acidosis } without mention of coma
ketosis }

AHA: 3Q, '91, 6; **For code 250.11:** 4Q, '03, 82; **For code 250.13:** 2Q, '06, 19-20

DEF: Diabetic hyperglycemic crisis causing ketone presence in body fluids.

§ ✓5th **250.2 Diabetes with hyperosmolarity**
[0-3]
Hyperosmolar (nonketotic) coma

AHA: 4Q, '93, 19; 3Q, '91, 7

§ ✓5th **250.3 Diabetes with other coma**
[0-3]
Diabetic coma (with ketoacidosis)
Diabetic hypoglycemic coma
Insulin coma NOS

EXCLUDES *diabetes with hyperosmolar coma (250.2)*

AHA: 3Q, '91, 7, 12

DEF: Coma (not hyperosmolar) caused by hyperglycemia or hypoglycemia as complication of diabetes.

§ ✓5th **250.4 Diabetes with renal manifestations**
[0-3]
Use additional code to identify manifestation, as:
chronic kidney disease (585.1-585.9)
diabetic:
nephropathy NOS (583.81)
nephrosis (581.81)
intercapillary glomerulosclerosis (581.81)
Kimmelstiel-Wilson syndrome (581.81)

AHA: 3Q, '91, 8, 12; S-O, '87, 9; S-O, '84, 3; **For code 250.40:** 1Q, '03, 20

§ ✓5th **250.5 Diabetes with ophthalmic manifestations**
[0-3]
Use additional code to identify manifestation, as:
diabetic:
blindness (369.00-369.9)
cataract (366.41)
glaucoma (365.44)
macular edema (362.07)
retinal edema (362.07)
retinopathy (362.01-362.07)

AHA: 4Q, '05, 65; 3Q, '91, 8; S-O, '85, 11; **For code 250.50:** 4Q, '05, 67

§ ✓5th **250.6 Diabetes with neurological manifestations**
[0-3]
Use additional code to identify manifestation, as:
diabetic:
amyotrophy ▶(353.5)◀
gastroparalysis (536.3)
gastroparesis (536.3)
mononeuropathy (354.0-355.9)
neurogenic arthropathy (713.5)
peripheral autonomic neuropathy (337.1)
polyneuropathy (357.2)

AHA: 2Q, '93, 6; 2Q, '92, 15; 3Q, '91, 9; N-D, '84, 9; **For code 250.60:** 4Q, '03, 105; **For code 250.61:** 2Q, '04, 7

§ ✓5th **250.7 Diabetes with peripheral circulatory disorders**
[0-3]
Use additional code to identify manifestation, as:
diabetic:
gangrene (785.4)
peripheral angiopathy (443.81)

AHA: 1Q, '96, 10; 3Q, '94, 5; 2Q, '94, 17; 3Q, '91, 10, 12; 3Q, '90, 15; **For code 250.70:** 1Q, '04, 14

DEF: Blood vessel damage or disease, usually in the feet, legs, or hands, as a complication of diabetes.

§ ✓5th **250.8 Diabetes with other specified manifestations**
[0-3]
Diabetic hypoglycemia ▶NOS◀
Hypoglycemic shock ▶NOS◀
Use additional code to identify manifestation, as:
any associated ulceration (707.10-707.9)
diabetic bone changes (731.8)

AHA: 4Q, '00, 44; 4Q, '97, 43; 2Q, '97, 16, 4Q, '93, 20; 3Q, '91, 10; **For code 250.80:** 1Q, '04, 14

§ ✓5th **250.9 Diabetes with unspecified complication**
[0-3]
AHA: 2Q, '92, 15; 3Q, '91, 7, 12

§ Requires fifth-digit. Valid digits are in [brackets] under each code. See appropriate category for codes and definitions.

✓4th ✓5th Additional Digit Required | Unspecified Code | Other Specified Code | Manifestation Code | ▶◀ Revised Text | ● New Code | ▲ Revised Code Title

✓4th 251 Other disorders of pancreatic internal secretion

251.0 Hypoglycemic coma
Iatrogenic hyperinsulinism
Non-diabetic insulin coma
Use additional E code to identify cause, if drug-induced
EXCLUDES *hypoglycemic coma in diabetes mellitus ▶(249.3, 250.3)◀*
AHA: M-A, '85, 8
DEF: Coma induced by low blood sugar in non-diabetic patient.

251.1 Other specified hypoglycemia
Hyperinsulinism:
NOS
ectopic
functional
Hyperplasia of pancreatic islet beta cells NOS
EXCLUDES *hypoglycemia:*
in diabetes mellitus ▶(249.8, 250.8)◀
in infant of diabetic mother (775.0)
hypoglycemic coma (251.0)
neonatal hypoglycemia (775.6)
Use additional E code to identify cause, if drug-induced.
AHA: 1Q, '03, 10
DEF: Excessive production of insulin by the pancreas; associated with obesity and insulin-producing tumors.

251.2 Hypoglycemia, unspecified
Hypoglycemia:
NOS
reactive
spontaneous
EXCLUDES *hypoglycemia:*
with coma (251.0)
in diabetes mellitus ▶(249.8, 250.8)◀
leucine-induced (270.3)
AHA: M-A, '85, 8

251.3 Postsurgical hypoinsulinemia
Hypoinsulinemia following complete or partial pancreatectomy
Postpancreatectomy hyperglycemia
AHA: 3Q, '91, 6

251.4 Abnormality of secretion of glucagon
Hyperplasia of pancreatic islet alpha cells with glucagon excess
DEF: Production malfunction of a pancreatic hormone secreted by cells of the islets of Langerhans.

251.5 Abnormality of secretion of gastrin
Hyperplasia of pancreatic alpha cells with gastrin excess
Zollinger-Ellison syndrome

251.8 Other specified disorders of pancreatic internal secretion
AHA: 2Q, '98, 15; 3Q, '91, 6

251.9 Unspecified disorder of pancreatic internal secretion
Islet cell hyperplasia NOS

✓4th 252 Disorders of parathyroid gland
EXCLUDES *▶hungry bone syndrome (275.5)◀*

✓5th 252.0 Hyperparathyroidism
EXCLUDES *ectopic hyperparathyroidism (259.3)*
DEF: Abnormally high secretion of parathyroid hormones causing bone deterioration, reduced renal function, kidney stones.

252.00 Hyperparathyroidism, unspecified

252.01 Primary hyperparathyroidism
Hyperplasia of parathyroid
DEF: Parathyroid dysfunction commonly caused by hyperplasia of two or more glands; characteristic hyper-calcemia and increased parathyroid hormone levels.

Dorsal View of Parathyroid Glands

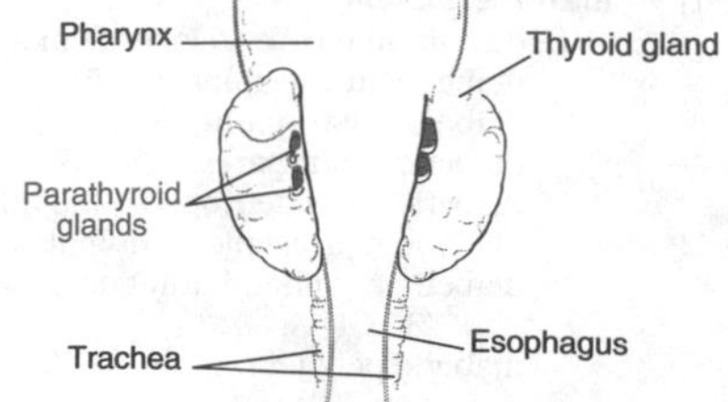

252.02 Secondary hyperparathyroidism, non-renal
EXCLUDES *secondary hyperparathyroidism (of renal origin) (588.81)*
AHA: 4Q, '04, 57-59
DEF: Underlying disease of nonrenal origin decreases blood levels of calcium causing the parathyroid to release increased levels of parathyroid hormone; para-thyroid hormone levels return to normal once underlying condition is treated and blood calcium levels are normal.

252.08 Other hyperparathyroidism
Tertiary hyperparathyroidism
DEF: Tertiary hyperparathyroidism: chronic secondary hyperparathyroidism leads to adenomatous parathyroid causing irreversible abnormal production of parathyroid hormone (PTH); PTH remains high after the serum calcium levels are brought under control.

252.1 Hypoparathyroidism
Parathyroiditis (autoimmune)
Tetany:
parathyroid
parathyroprival
EXCLUDES *pseudohypoparathyroidism (275.4)*
pseudopseudohypoparathyroidism (275.4)
tetany NOS (781.7)
transitory neonatal hypoparathyroidism (775.4)
DEF: Abnormally low secretion of parathyroid hormones which causes decreased calcium and increased phosphorus in the blood. Resulting in muscle cramps, tetany, urinary frequency and cataracts.

252.8 Other specified disorders of parathyroid gland
Cyst } of parathyroid
Hemorrhage }

252.9 Unspecified disorder of parathyroid gland

✓4th 253 Disorders of the pituitary gland and its hypothalamic control
INCLUDES the listed conditions whether the disorder is in the pituitary or the hypothalamus
EXCLUDES *Cushing's syndrome (255.0)*

253.0 Acromegaly and gigantism
Overproduction of growth hormone
DEF: Acromegaly: chronic, beginning in middle age; caused by hypersecretion of the pituitary growth hormone; produces enlarged parts of skeleton, especially the nose, ears, jaws, fingers and toes.
DEF: Gigantism: pituitary gigantism caused by excess growth of short flat bones; men may grow 78 to 80 inches tall.

253.1 Other and unspecified anterior pituitary hyperfunction
Forbes-Albright syndrome
EXCLUDES *overproduction of:*
ACTH (255.3)
thyroid-stimulating hormone [TSH] (242.8)
AHA: J-A, '85, 9
DEF: Spontaneous galactorrhea-amenorrhea syndrome unrelated to pregnancy; usually related to presence of pituitary tumor.

253.2 Panhypopituitarism
Cachexia, pituitary
Necrosis of pituitary (postpartum)
Pituitary insufficiency NOS
Sheehan's syndrome
Simmonds' disease
EXCLUDES *iatrogenic hypopituitarism (253.7)*
DEF: Damage to or absence of pituitary gland leading to impaired sexual function, weight loss, fatigue, bradycardia, hypotension, pallor, depression, and impaired growth in children; called Simmonds' disease if cachexia is prominent.

253.3 Pituitary dwarfism
Isolated deficiency of (human) growth hormone [HGH]
Lorain-Levi dwarfism
DEF: Dwarfism with infantile physical characteristics due to abnormally low secretion of growth hormone and gonadotropin deficiency.

253.4 Other anterior pituitary disorders
Isolated or partial deficiency of an anterior pituitary hormone, other than growth hormone
Prolactin deficiency
AHA: J-A, '85, 9

253.5 Diabetes insipidus
Vasopressin deficiency
EXCLUDES *nephrogenic diabetes insipidus (588.1)*
DEF: Metabolic disorder causing insufficient antidiuretic hormone release; symptoms include frequent urination, thirst, ravenous hunger, loss of weight, fatigue.

253.6 Other disorders of neurohypophysis
Syndrome of inappropriate secretion of antidiuretic hormone [ADH]
EXCLUDES *ectopic antidiuretic hormone secretion (259.3)*

253.7 Iatrogenic pituitary disorders
Hypopituitarism:
hormone-induced
hypophysectomy-induced
postablative
radiotherapy-induced
Use additional E code to identify cause
DEF: Pituitary dysfunction that results from drug therapy, radiation therapy, or surgery, causing mild to severe symptoms.

253.8 Other disorders of the pituitary and other syndromes of diencephalohypophyseal origin
Abscess of pituitary
Adiposogenital dystrophy
Cyst of Rathke's pouch
Fröhlich's syndrome
EXCLUDES *craniopharyngioma (237.0)*

253.9 Unspecified
Dyspituitarism

✓4th 254 Diseases of thymus gland
EXCLUDES *aplasia or dysplasia with immunodeficiency (279.2)*
hypoplasia with immunodeficiency (279.2)
myasthenia gravis (358.00-358.01)

254.0 Persistent hyperplasia of thymus
Hypertrophy of thymus
DEF: Continued abnormal growth of the twin lymphoid lobes that produce T lymphocytes.

254.1 Abscess of thymus

254.8 Other specified diseases of thymus gland
Astrophy } of thymus
Cyst } of thymus
EXCLUDES *thymoma (212.6)*

254.9 Unspecified disease of thymus gland

✓4th 255 Disorders of adrenal glands
INCLUDES the listed conditions whether the basic disorder is in the adrenals or is pituitary-induced

255.0 Cushing's syndrome
Adrenal hyperplasia due to excess ACTH
Cushing's syndrome:
NOS
iatrogenic
idiopathic
pituitary-dependent
Ectopic ACTH syndrome
Iatrogenic syndrome of excess cortisol
Overproduction of cortisol
Use additional E code to identify cause, if drug-induced
EXCLUDES *congenital adrenal hyperplasia (255.2)*
DEF: Due to adrenal cortisol oversecretion or glucocorticoid medications; may cause fatty tissue of the face, neck and body; osteoporosis and curvature of spine, hypertension, diabetes mellitus, female genitourinary problems, male impotence, degeneration of muscle tissues, weakness.

✓5th 255.1 Hyperaldosteronism
AHA: 4Q, '03, 48
DEF: Oversecretion of aldosterone causing fluid retention, hypertension.

255.10 Hyperaldosteronism, unspecified
Aldosteronism NOS
Primary aldosteronism, unspecified
EXCLUDES *Conn's syndrome (255.12)*

255.11 Glucocorticoid-remediable aldosteronism
Familial aldosteronism type I
EXCLUDES *Conn's syndrome (255.12)*
DEF: A rare autosomal dominant familial form of primary aldosteronism in which the secretion of aldosterone is under the influence of adrenocortiotrophic hormone (ACTH) rather than the renin-angiotensin mechanism; characterized by moderate hypersecretion of aldosterone and suppressed plasma renin activity rapidly reversed by administration of glucosteroids; symptoms include hypertension and mild hypokalemia.

255.12 Conn's syndrome
DEF: A type of primary aldosteronism caused by an adenoma of the glomerulosa cells in the adrenal cortex; presence of hypertension.

255.13 Bartter's syndrome
DEF: A cluster of symptoms caused by a defect in the ability of the kidney to reabsorb potassium; signs include alkalosis (hypokalemic alkalosis), increased aldosterone, increased plasma renin, and normal blood pressure; symptoms include muscle cramping, weakness, constipation, frequency of urination, and failure to grow; also known as urinary potassium wasting or juxtaglomerular cell hyperplasia.

255.14 Other secondary aldosteronism
AHA: 3Q, '06, 24

255.2 Adrenogenital disorders
Achard-Thiers syndrome
Adrenogenital syndromes, virilizing or feminizing, whether acquired or associated with congenital adrenal hyperplasia consequent on inborn enzyme defects in hormone synthesis
Congenital adrenal hyperplasia
Female adrenal pseudohermaphroditism
Male:
macrogenitosomia praecox
sexual precocity with adrenal hyperplasia
Virilization (female) (suprarenal)
EXCLUDES *adrenal hyperplasia due to excess ACTH (255.0)*
isosexual virilization (256.4)

255.3 Other corticoadrenal overactivity
Acquired benign adrenal androgenic overactivity
Overproduction of ACTH

5th **255.4 Corticoadrenal insufficiency**
EXCLUDES *tuberculous Addison's disease (017.6)*
AHA: 4Q, '07, 68; 3Q, '06, 24
DEF: Underproduction of adrenal hormones causing low blood pressure.

255.41 Glucocorticoid deficiency
Addisonian crisis
Addison's disease NOS
Adrenal atrophy (autoimmune)
Adrenal calcification
Adrenal crisis
Adrenal hemorrhage
Adrenal infarction
Adrenal insufficiency NOS
Combined glucocorticoid and mineralocorticoid deficiency
Corticoadrenal insufficiency NOS
AHA: 4Q, '07, 68, 69
DEF: Decreased function of the adrenal cortex resulting in insufficient production of glucocorticoid, the hormone regulating carbohydrate, fat, and protein metabolism; manifestations include hyponatremia, hyperpigmentation, orthostatic hypotension, anemia, loss of appetite, and malaise.

255.42 Mineralocorticoid deficiency
Hypoaldosteronism
EXCLUDES *combined glucocorticoid and mineralocorticoid deficiency (255.41)*
DEF: Decreased function of the adrenal cortex resulting in insufficient production of mineralocorticoid, the hormone regulating electrolyte and water balance; manifestations include hyponatremia, hyperkalemia, and mild acidosis.

255.5 Other adrenal hypofunction
Adrenal medullary insufficiency
EXCLUDES *Waterhouse-Friderichsen syndrome (meningococcal) (036.3)*

255.6 Medulloadrenal hyperfunction
Catecholamine secretion by pheochromocytoma

255.8 Other specified disorders of adrenal glands
Abnormality of cortisol-binding globulin

255.9 Unspecified disorder of adrenal glands

4th **256 Ovarian dysfunction**
AHA: 4Q, '00, 51

256.0 Hyperestrogenism ♀
DEF: Excess secretion of estrogen by the ovaries; characterized by ovaries containing multiple follicular cysts filled with serous fluid.

256.1 Other ovarian hyperfunction ♀
Hypersecretion of ovarian androgens
AHA: 3Q, '95, 15

256.2 Postablative ovarian failure ♀
Ovarian failure:
iatrogenic
postirradiation
postsurgical
Use additional code for states associated with artificial menopause (627.4)
EXCLUDES *acquired absence of ovary (V45.77)*
asymptomatic age-related (natural) postmenopausal status (V49.81)
AHA: 2Q, '02, 12
DEF: Failed ovarian function after medical or surgical intervention.

5th **256.3 Other ovarian failure**
Use additional code for states associated with natural menopause (627.2)
EXCLUDES *asymptomatic age-related (natural) postmenopausal status (V49.81)*
AHA: 4Q, '01, 41

256.31 Premature menopause A ♀
DEF: Permanent cessation of ovarian function before the age of 40 occuring naturally of unknown cause.

256.39 Other ovarian failure ♀
Delayed menarche
Ovarian hypofunction
Primary ovarian failure NOS

256.4 Polycystic ovaries ♀
Isosexual virilization
Stein-Leventhal syndrome
DEF: Multiple serous filled cysts of ovary; symptoms of infertility, hirsutism, oligomenorrhea or amenorrhea.

256.8 Other ovarian dysfunction ♀

256.9 Unspecified ovarian dysfunction ♀

4th **257 Testicular dysfunction**

257.0 Testicular hyperfunction ♂
Hypersecretion of testicular hormones

257.1 Postablative testicular hypofunction ♂
Testicular hypofunction:
iatrogenic
postirradiation
postsurgical

257.2 Other testicular hypofunction
Defective biosynthesis of testicular androgen
Eunuchoidism:
NOS
hypogonadotropic
Failure:
Leydig's cell, adult
seminiferous tubule, adult
Testicular hypogonadism
EXCLUDES *azoospermia (606.0)*

257.8 Other testicular dysfunction
EXCLUDES *androgen insensitivity syndromes ►(259.50-259.52)◄*

257.9 Unspecified testicular dysfunction ♂

✓4th 258 Polyglandular dysfunction and related disorders

✓5th 258.0 Polyglandular activity in multiple endocrine adenomatosis

Multiple endocrine neoplasia [MEN] syndromes

Use additional codes to identify any malignancies and other conditions associated with the syndromes

AHA: 4Q, '07, 70

258.01 Multiple endocrine neoplasia [MEN] type I

Wermer's syndrome

AHA: 4Q, '07, 70, 72

DEF: Wermer's syndrome: A rare hereditary condition characterized by the presence of adenomas or hyperplasia in more than one endocrine gland causing premature aging.

258.02 Multiple endocrine neoplasia [MEN] type IIA

Sipple's syndrome

DEF: Sipple's syndrome: A hereditary disorder caused by a defect in the RET gene that causes overactivity of the thyroid, adrenal, and parathyroid glands, resulting in neoplasm; commonly adrenal pheochromocytoma and thyroid medullary carcinoma.

258.03 Multiple endocrine neoplasia [MEN] type IIB

258.1 Other combinations of endocrine dysfunction

Lloyd's syndrome
Schmidt's syndrome

258.8 Other specified polyglandular dysfunction

258.9 Polyglandular dysfunction, unspecified

✓4th 259 Other endocrine disorders

259.0 Delay in sexual development and puberty, not elsewhere classified

Delayed puberty

259.1 Precocious sexual development and puberty, not elsewhere classified P

Sexual precocity:
- NOS
- constitutional
- cryptogenic
- idiopathic

259.2 Carcinoid syndrome

Hormone secretion by carcinoid tumors

DEF: Presence of carcinoid tumors that spread to liver; characterized by cyanotic flushing of skin, diarrhea, bronchospasm, acquired tricuspid and pulmonary stenosis, sudden drops in blood pressure, edema, ascites.

259.3 Ectopic hormone secretion, not elsewhere classified

Ectopic:
- antidiuretic hormone secretion [ADH]
- hyperparathyroidism

EXCLUDES *ectopic ACTH syndrome (255.0)*

AHA: N-D, '85, 4

259.4 Dwarfism, not elsewhere classified

Dwarfism:
- NOS
- constitutional

EXCLUDES *dwarfism:*
- *achondroplastic (756.4)*
- *intrauterine (759.7)*
- *nutritional (263.2)*
- *pituitary (253.3)*
- *renal (588.0)*

progeria (259.8)

✓5th 259.5 Androgen insensitivity syndrome

AHA: 4Q, '05, 53

DEF: X chromosome abnormality that prohibits the body from recognizing androgen; XY genotype with ambiguous genitalia.

● **259.50 Androgen insensitivity, unspecified**

● **259.51 Androgen insensitivity syndrome**

Complete androgen insensitivity
de Quervain's syndrome
Goldberg-Maxwell Syndrome

● **259.52 Partial androgen insensitivity**

Partial androgen insensitivity syndrome
Reifenstein syndrome

259.8 Other specified endocrine disorders

Pineal gland dysfunction
Progeria
Werner's syndrome

259.9 Unspecified endocrine disorder

Disturbance:
- endocrine NOS
- hormone NOS

Infantilism NOS

NUTRITIONAL DEFICIENCIES (260-269)

EXCLUDES *deficiency anemias (280.0-281.9)*

260 Kwashiorkor

Nutritional edema with dyspigmentation of skin and hair

DEF: Syndrome, particularly of children; excessive carbohydrate with inadequate protein intake, inhibited growth potential, anomalies in skin and hair pigmentation, edema and liver disease.

261 Nutritional marasmus

Nutritional atrophy
Severe calorie deficiency
Severe malnutrition NOS

AHA: 4Q, '07, 97; 3Q, '06, 14; 2Q, '06, 12

DEF: Protein-calorie malabsorption or malnutrition of children; characterized by tissue wasting, dehydration, and subcutaneous fat depletion; may occur with infectious disease; also called infantile atrophy.

262 Other severe, protein-calorie malnutrition

Nutritional edema without mention of dyspigmentation of skin and hair

AHA: 4Q, '92, 24; J-A, '85, 12

✓4th 263 Other and unspecified protein-calorie malnutrition

AHA: 4Q, '92, 24

263.0 Malnutrition of moderate degree

AHA: J-A, '85, 1

DEF: Malnutrition characterized by biochemical changes in electrolytes, lipids, blood plasma.

263.1 Malnutrition of mild degree

AHA: J-A, '85, 1

263.2 Arrested development following protein-calorie malnutrition

Nutritional dwarfism
Physical retardation due to malnutrition

263.8 Other protein-calorie malnutrition

263.9 Unspecified protein-calorie malnutrition

Dystrophy due to malnutrition
Malnutrition (calorie) NOS

EXCLUDES *nutritional deficiency NOS (269.9)*

AHA: 4Q, '03, 109; N-D, '84, 19

✓4th 264 Vitamin A deficiency

264.0 With conjunctival xerosis

DEF: Vitamin A deficiency with conjunctival dryness.

264.1 With conjunctival xerosis and Bitot's spot

Bitot's spot in the young child

DEF: Vitamin A deficiency with conjunctival dryness, superficial spots of keratinized epithelium.

264.2 With corneal xerosis

DEF: Vitamin A deficiency with corneal dryness.

264.3 With corneal ulceration and xerosis

DEF: Vitamin A deficiency with corneal dryness, epithelial ulceration.

264.4 With keratomalacia

DEF: Vitamin A deficiency creating corneal dryness; progresses to corneal insensitivity, softness, necrosis; usually bilateral.

264.5 With night blindness

DEF: Vitamin A deficiency causing vision failure in dim light.

264.6 With xerophthalmic scars of cornea

DEF: Vitamin A deficiency with corneal scars from dryness.

264.7 Other ocular manifestations of vitamin A deficiency

Xerophthalmia due to vitamin A deficiency

264.8 Other manifestations of vitamin A deficiency

Follicular keratosis } due to vitamin A deficiency
Xeroderma }

264.9 Unspecified vitamin A deficiency

Hypovitaminosis A NOS

✓4th 265 Thiamine and niacin deficiency states

265.0 Beriberi

DEF: Inadequate vitamin B_1 (thiamine) intake, affects heart and peripheral nerves; individual may become edematous and develop cardiac disease due to the excess fluid; alcoholics and people with a diet of excessive polished rice prone to the disease.

265.1 Other and unspecified manifestations of thiamine deficiency

Other vitamin B_1 deficiency states

265.2 Pellagra

Deficiency:
- niacin (-tryptophan)
- nicotinamide
- nicotinic acid
- vitamin PP

Pellagra (alcoholic)

DEF: Niacin deficiency causing dermatitis, inflammation of mucous membranes, diarrhea, and psychic disturbances.

✓4th 266 Deficiency of B-complex components

266.0 Ariboflavinosis

Riboflavin [vitamin B_2] deficiency

AHA: S-O, '86, 10

DEF: Vitamin B_2 (riboflavin) deficiency marked by swollen lips and tongue fissures, corneal vascularization, scaling lesions, and anemia.

266.1 Vitamin B_6 deficiency

Deficiency:
- pyridoxal
- pyridoxamine
- pyridoxine

Vitamin B_6 deficiency syndrome

EXCLUDES *vitamin B_6-responsive sideroblastic anemia (285.0)*

DEF: Vitamin B_6 deficiency causing skin, lip, and tongue disturbances, peripheral neuropathy; and convulsions in infants.

266.2 Other B-complex deficiencies

Deficiency:
- cyanocobalamin
- folic acid
- vitamin B_{12}

EXCLUDES *combined system disease with anemia (281.0-281.1)*
deficiency anemias (281.0-281.9)
subacute degeneration of spinal cord with anemia (281.0-281.1)

266.9 Unspecified vitamin B deficiency

267 Ascorbic acid deficiency

Deficiency of vitamin C
Scurvy

EXCLUDES *scorbutic anemia (281.8)*

DEF: Vitamin C deficiency causing swollen gums, myalgia, weight loss, and weakness.

✓4th 268 Vitamin D deficiency

EXCLUDES *vitamin D-resistant:*
osteomalacia (275.3)
rickets (275.3)

268.0 Rickets, active

EXCLUDES *celiac rickets (579.0)*
renal rickets (588.0)

DEF: Inadequate vitamin D intake, usually in pediatrics, that affects bones most involved with muscular action; may cause nodules on ends and sides of bones; delayed closure of fontanels in infants; symptoms may include muscle soreness, and profuse sweating.

268.1 Rickets, late effect

Any condition specified as due to rickets and stated to be a late effect or sequela of rickets

Code first the nature of late effect

DEF: Distorted or demineralized bones as a result of vitamin D deficiency.

268.2 Osteomalacia, unspecified

DEF: Softening of bones due to decrease in calcium; marked by pain, tenderness, muscular weakness, anorexia, and weight loss.

268.9 Unspecified vitamin D deficiency

Avitaminosis D

✓4th 269 Other nutritional deficiencies

269.0 Deficiency of vitamin K

EXCLUDES *deficiency of coagulation factor due to vitamin K deficiency (286.7)*
vitamin K deficiency of newborn (776.0)

269.1 Deficiency of other vitamins

Deficiency:
- vitamin E
- vitamin P

269.2 Unspecified vitamin deficiency

Multiple vitamin deficiency NOS

269.3 Mineral deficiency, not elsewhere classified

Deficiency:
- calcium, dietary
- iodine

EXCLUDES *deficiency:*
calcium NOS (275.4)
potassium (276.8)
sodium (276.1)

269.8 Other nutritional deficiency

EXCLUDES *adult failure to thrive (783.7)*
failure to thrive in childhood (783.41)
feeding problems (783.3)
newborn (779.3)

269.9 Unspecified nutritional deficiency

OTHER METABOLIC AND IMMUNITY DISORDERS (270-279)

Use additional code to identify any associated mental retardation

✓4th 270 Disorders of amino-acid transport and metabolism

EXCLUDES *abnormal findings without manifest disease (790.0-796.9)*
disorders of purine and pyrimidine metabolism (277.1-277.2)
gout (274.0-274.9)

270.0 Disturbances of amino-acid transport
Cystinosis
Cystinuria
Fanconi (-de Toni) (-Debré) syndrome
Glycinuria (renal)
Hartnup disease

270.1 Phenylketonuria [PKU]
Hyperphenylalaninemia

DEF: Inherited metabolic condition causing excess phenylpyruvic and other acids in urine; results in mental retardation, neurological manifestations, including spasticity and tremors, light pigmentation, eczema, and mousy odor.

270.2 Other disturbances of aromatic amino-acid metabolism
Albinism
Alkaptonuria
Alkaptonuric ochronosis
Disturbances of metabolismof tyrosine and tryptophan
Homogentisic acid defects
Hydroxykynureninuria
Hypertyrosinemia
Indicanuria
Kynureninase defects
Oasthouse urine disease
Ochronosis
Tyrosinosis
Tyrosinuria
Waardenburg syndrome

EXCLUDES *vitamin B_6-deficiency syndrome (266.1)*

AHA: 3Q, '99, 20

270.3 Disturbances of branched-chain amino-acid metabolism
Disturbances of metabolism of leucine, isoleucine, and valine
Hypervalinemia
Intermittent branched-chain ketonuria
Leucine-induced hypoglycemia
Leucinosis
Maple syrup urine disease

AHA: 3Q, '00, 8

270.4 Disturbances of sulphur-bearing amino-acid metabolism
Cystathioninemia
Cystathioninuria
Disturbances of metabolism of methionine, homocystine, and cystathionine
Homocystinuria
Hypermethioninemia
Methioninemia

AHA: 2Q, '07, 7;1Q, '04, 6

270.5 Disturbances of histidine metabolism
Carnosinemia
Histidinemia
Hyperhistidinemia
Imidazole aminoaciduria

270.6 Disorders of urea cycle metabolism
Argininosuccinic aciduria
Citrullinemia
Disorders of metabolism of ornithine, citrulline, argininosuccinic acid, arginine, and ammonia
Hyperammonemia
Hyperornithinemia

270.7 Other disturbances of straight-chain amino-acid metabolism
Glucoglycinuria
Glycinemia (with methyl-malonic acidemia)
Hyperglycinemia
Hyperlysinemia
Other disturbances of metabolism of glycine, threonine, serine, glutamine, and lysine
Pipecolic acidemia
Saccharopinuria

AHA: 3Q, '00, 8

270.8 Other specified disorders of amino-acid metabolism
Alaninemia
Ethanolaminuria
Glycoprolinuria
Hydroxyprolinemia
Hyperprolinemia
Iminoacidopathy
Prolinemia
Prolinuria
Sarcosinemia

270.9 Unspecified disorder of amino-acid metabolism

✓4th 271 Disorders of carbohydrate transport and metabolism

EXCLUDES *abnormality of secretion of glucagon (251.4)*
diabetes mellitus ►(249.0-249.9, 250.0-250.9)◄
hypoglycemia NOS (251.2)
mucopolysaccharidosis (277.5)

271.0 Glycogenosis
Amylopectinosis
Glucose-6-phosphatase deficiency
Glycogen storage disease
McArdle's disease
Pompe's disease
von Gierke's disease

AHA: 1Q, '98, 5

DEF: Excess glycogen storage; rare inherited trait affects liver, kidneys; causes various symptoms depending on type, though often weakness and muscle cramps.

271.1 Galactosemia
Galactose-1-phosphate uridyl transferase deficiency
Galactosuria

DEF: Any of three genetic disorders due to defective galactose metabolism; symptoms include failure to thrive in infancy, jaundice, liver and spleen damage, cataracts, and mental retardation.

271.2 Hereditary fructose intolerance
Essential benign fructosuria
Fructosemia

DEF: Chromosome recessive disorder of carbohydrate metabolism; in infants, occurs after dietary sugar introduced; characterized by enlarged spleen, yellowish cast to skin, and progressive inability to thrive.

271.3 Intestinal disaccharidase deficiencies and disaccharide malabsorption
Intolerance or malabsorption (congenital) (of):
glucose-galactose
lactose
sucrose-isomaltose

271.4 Renal glycosuria
Renal diabetes

DEF: Persistent abnormal levels of glucose in urine, with normal blood glucose levels; caused by failure of the renal tubules to reabsorb glucose.

271.8 Other specified disorders of carbohydrate transport and metabolism
Essential benign pentosuria
Fucosidosis
Glycolic aciduria
Hyperoxaluria (primary)
Mannosidosis
Oxalosis
Xylosuria
Xylulosuria

271.9 Unspecified disorder of carbohydrate transport and metabolism

Lipid Metabolism

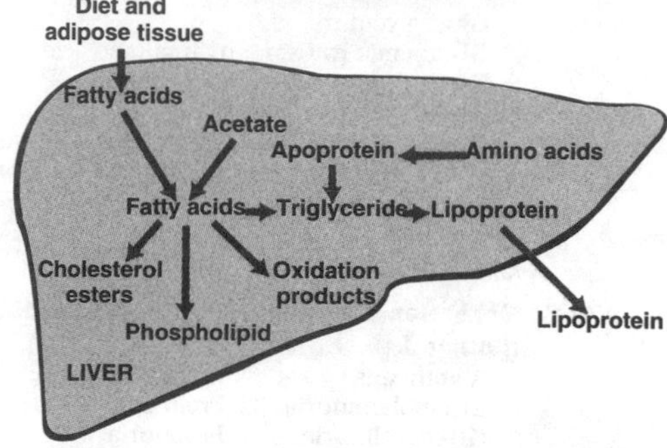

272 Disorders of lipoid metabolism

EXCLUDES *localized cerebral lipidoses (330.1)*

272.0 Pure hypercholesterolemia
- Familial hypercholesterolemia
- Fredrickson Type IIa hyperlipoproteinemia
- Hyperbetalipoproteinemia
- Hyperlipidemia, Group A
- Low-density-lipoid-type [LDL] hyperlipoproteinemia

AHA: 4Q, '05, 71

272.1 Pure hyperglyceridemia
- Endogenous hyperglyceridemia
- Fredrickson Type IV hyperlipoproteinemia
- Hyperlipidemia, Group B
- Hyperprebetalipoproteinemia
- Hypertriglyceridemia, essential
- Very-low-density-lipoid-type [VLDL] hyperlipoproteinemia

272.2 Mixed hyperlipidemia
- Broad- or floating-betalipoproteinemia
- Fredrickson Type IIb or III hyperlipoproteinemia
- Hypercholesterolemia with endogenous hyperglyceridemia
- Hyperbetalipoproteinemia with prebetalipoproteinemia
- Tubo-eruptive xanthoma
- Xanthoma tuberosum

DEF: Elevated levels of lipoprotein, a complex of fats and proteins, in blood due to inherited metabolic disorder.

272.3 Hyperchylomicronemia
- Bürger-Grütz syndrome
- Fredrickson type I or V hyperlipoproteinemia
- Hyperlipidemia, Group D
- Mixed hyperglyceridemia

272.4 Other and unspecified hyperlipidemia
- Alpha-lipoproteinemia
- Combined hyperlipidemia
- Hyperlipidemia NOS
- Hyperlipoproteinemia NOS

AHA: 1Q, '05, 17

DEF: Hyperlipoproteinemia: elevated levels of transient chylomicrons in the blood which are a form of lipoproteins which transport dietary cholesterol and triglycerides from the small intestine to the blood.

272.5 Lipoprotein deficiencies
- Abetalipoproteinemia
- Bassen-Kornzweig syndrome
- High-density lipoid deficiency
- Hypoalphalipoproteinemia
- Hypobetalipoproteinemia (familial)

DEF: Abnormally low levels of lipoprotein, a complex of fats and protein, in the blood.

272.6 Lipodystrophy
- Barraquer-Simons disease
- Progressive lipodystrophy
- Use additional E code to identify cause, if iatrogenic

EXCLUDES *intestinal lipodystrophy (040.2)*

DEF: Disturbance of fat metabolism resulting in loss of fatty tissue in some areas of the body.

272.7 Lipidoses
- Chemically-induced lipidosis
- Disease:
  - Anderson's
  - Fabry's
  - Gaucher's
  - I cell [mucolipidosis I]
  - lipoid storage NOS
  - Niemann-Pick
  - pseudo-Hurler's or mucolipdosis III
  - triglyceride storage, Type I or II
  - Wolman's or triglyceride storage, Type III
- Mucolipidosis II
- Primary familial xanthomatosis

EXCLUDES *cerebral lipidoses (330.1)*
Tay-Sachs disease (330.1)

DEF: Lysosomal storage diseases marked by an abnormal amount of lipids in reticuloendothelial cells.

272.8 Other disorders of lipoid metabolism
- Hoffa's disease or liposynovitis prepatellaris
- Launois-Bensaude's lipomatosis
- Lipoid dermatoarthritis

272.9 Unspecified disorder of lipoid metabolism

273 Disorders of plasma protein metabolism

EXCLUDES *agammaglobulinemia and hypogammaglobulinemia (279.0-279.2)*
coagulation defects (286.0-286.9)
hereditary hemolytic anemias (282.0-282.9)

273.0 Polyclonal hypergammaglobulinemia
- Hypergammaglobulinemic purpura:
  - benign primary
  - Waldenström's

DEF: Elevated blood levels of gamma globulins, frequently found in patients with chronic infectious diseases.

273.1 Monoclonal paraproteinemia
- Benign monoclonal hypergammaglobulinemia [BMH]
- Monoclonal gammopathy:
  - NOS
  - associated with lymphoplasmacytic dyscrasias
  - benign
- Paraproteinemia:
  - benign (familial)
  - secondary to malignant or inflammatory disease

DEF: Elevated blood levels of macroglobulins (plasma globulins of high weight); characterized by malignant neoplasms of bone marrow, spleen, liver, or lymph nodes; symptoms include weakness, fatigue, bleeding disorders, and vision problems.

273.2 Other paraproteinemias
- Cryoglobulinemic:
  - purpura
  - vasculitis
- Mixed cryoglobulinemia

AHA: ►2Q, '08, 17◄

273.3 Macroglobulinemia
- Macroglobulinemia (idiopathic) (primary)
- Waldenström's macroglobulinemia

273.4 Alpha-1-antitrypsin deficiency
- AAT deficiency

DEF: Disorder of plasma protein metabolism that results in a deficiency of Alpha-1-antitrypsin, an acute-phase reactive protein, released into the blood in response to infection or injury to protect tissue against the harmful effect of enzymes.

273.8 Other disorders of plasma protein metabolism
Abnormality of transport protein
Bisalbuminemia
AHA: 2Q, '98, 11

273.9 Unspecified disorder of plasma protein metabolism

✓4th **274 Gout**
EXCLUDES *lead gout (984.0-984.9)*
AHA: 2Q, '95, 4
DEF: Purine and pyrimidine metabolic disorders; manifested by hyperuricemia and recurrent acute inflammatory arthritis; monosodium urate or monohydrate crystals may be deposited in and around the joints, leading to joint destruction, and severe crippling.

274.0 Gouty arthropathy

✓5th **274.1 Gouty nephropathy**

274.10 Gouty nephropathy, unspecified
AHA: N-D, '85, 15

274.11 Uric acid nephrolithiasis
DEF: Sodium urate stones in the kidney.

274.19 Other

✓5th **274.8 Gout with other specified manifestations**

274.81 Gouty tophi of ear
DEF: Chalky sodium urate deposit in the ear due to gout; produces chronic inflammation of external ear.

274.82 Gouty tophi of other sites
Gouty tophi of heart

274.89 Other
Use additional code to identify manifestations, as:
gouty:
iritis (364.11)
neuritis (357.4)

274.9 Gout, unspecified

✓4th **275 Disorders of mineral metabolism**
EXCLUDES *abnormal findings without manifest disease (790.0-796.9)*

275.0 Disorders of iron metabolism
Bronzed diabetes
Hemochromatosis
Pigmentary cirrhosis (of liver)
EXCLUDES *anemia:*
iron deficiency (280.0-280.9)
sideroblastic (285.0)
AHA: 2Q, '97, 11

275.1 Disorders of copper metabolism
Hepatolenticular degeneration
Wilson's disease

275.2 Disorders of magnesium metabolism
Hypermagnesemia
Hypomagnesemia

275.3 Disorders of phosphorus metabolism
Familial hypophosphatemia
Hypophosphatasia
Vitamin D-resistant:
osteomalacia
rickets

✓5th **275.4 Disorders of calcium metabolism**
EXCLUDES ▶*hungry bone syndrome (275.5)*◀
parathyroid disorders (252.00-252.9)
vitamin D deficiency (268.0-268.9)
AHA: 4Q, '97, 33

275.40 Unspecified disorder of calcium metabolism

275.41 Hypocalcemia
AHA: 3Q, '07, 5
DEF: Abnormally decreased blood calcium level; symptoms include hyperactive deep tendon reflexes, muscle, abdominal cramps, and carpopedal spasm.

275.42 Hypercalcemia
AHA: 4Q, '03, 110
DEF: Abnormally increased blood calcium level; symptoms include muscle weakness, fatigue, nausea, depression, and constipation.

275.49 Other disorders of calcium metabolism
Nephrocalcinosis
Pseudohypoparathyroidism
Pseudopseudohypoparathyroidism
DEF: Nephrocalcinosis: calcium phosphate deposits in the tubules of the kidney with resultant renal insufficiency.
DEF: Pseudohypoparathyroidism: inherited disorder with signs and symptoms of hypoparathyroidism; caused by inadequate response to parathyroid hormone, not hormonal deficiency. Symptoms include muscle cramps, tetany, urinary frequency, blurred vision due to cataracts, and dry scaly skin.
DEF: Pseudopseudohypoparathyroidism: clinical manifestations of hypoparathyroidism without affecting blood calcium levels.

● **275.5 Hungry bone syndrome**

275.8 Other specified disorders of mineral metabolism

275.9 Unspecified disorder of mineral metabolism

✓4th **276 Disorders of fluid, electrolyte, and acid-base balance**
EXCLUDES *diabetes insipidus (253.5)*
familial periodic paralysis (359.3)

276.0 Hyperosmolality and/or hypernatremia
Sodium [Na] excess
Sodium [Na] overload

276.1 Hyposmolality and/or hyponatremia
Sodium [Na] deficiency

276.2 Acidosis
Acidosis:
NOS
lactic
metabolic
respiratory
EXCLUDES *diabetic acidosis* ▶*(249.1, 250.1)*◀
AHA: J-F, '87, 15
DEF: Disorder involves decrease of pH (hydrogen ion) concentration in blood and cellular tissues; caused by increase in acid and decrease in bicarbonate.

276.3 Alkalosis
Alkalosis:
NOS
metabolic
Alkalosis:
respiratory
DEF: Accumulation of base (non-acid part of salt), or loss of acid without relative loss of base in body fluids; caused by increased arterial plasma bicarbonate concentration or loss of carbon dioxide due to hyperventilation.

276.4 Mixed acid-base balance disorder
Hypercapnia with mixed acid-base disorder

✓5th **276.5 Volume depletion**
EXCLUDES *hypovolemic shock:*
postoperative (998.0)
traumatic (958.4)
AHA: 4Q, '05, 54; 2Q, '05, 9; 1Q, '03, 5, 22; 3Q, '02, 21; 4Q, '97, 30; 2Q, '88, 9

276.50 Volume depletion, unspecified
DEF: Depletion of total body water (dehydration) and/or contraction of total intravascular plasma (hypovolemia).

276.51 Dehydration

AHA: ▶1Q, '08, 10◀

DEF: Depletion of total body water; blood volume may be normal while fluid is pulled from other tissues.

276.52 Hypovolemia

Depletion of volume of plasma

DEF: Depletion of volume plasma; depletion of total blood volume.

276.6 Fluid overload

Fluid retention

EXCLUDES *ascites (789.51-789.59)*
localized edema (782.3)

AHA: 3Q, '07, 9; 4Q, '06, 136

276.7 Hyperpotassemia

Hyperkalemia
Potassium [K]:
excess
Potassium [K]:
intoxication
overload

AHA: 1Q, '05, 9; 2Q,'01, 12

DEF: Elevated blood levels of potassium; symptoms include abnormal EKG readings, weakness; related to defective renal excretion.

276.8 Hypopotassemia

Hypokalemia
Potassium [K] deficiency

DEF: Decreased blood levels of potassium; symptoms include neuromuscular disorders.

276.9 Electrolyte and fluid disorders not elsewhere classified

Electrolyte imbalance
Hyperchloremia
Hypochloremia

EXCLUDES *electrolyte imbalance:*
associated with hyperemesis gravidarum (643.1)
complicating labor and delivery (669.0)
following abortion and ectopic or molar pregnancy (634-638 with .4, 639.4)

AHA: J-F, '87, 15

✓4th **277 Other and unspecified disorders of metabolism**

✓5th **277.0 Cystic fibrosis**

Fibrocystic disease of the pancreas
Mucoviscidosis

AHA: 4Q, '90, 16; 3Q, '90, 18

DEF: Generalized, genetic disorder of infants, children, and young adults marked by exocrine gland dysfunction; characterized by chronic pulmonary disease with excess mucus production, pancreatic deficiency, high levels of electrolytes in the sweat.

277.00 Without mention of meconium ileus

Cystic fibrosis NOS

AHA: 2Q, '03, 12

277.01 With meconium ileus N

Meconium:
ileus (of newborn)
obstruction of intestine in mucoviscidosis

277.02 With pulmonary manifestations

Cystic fibrosis with pulmonary exacerbation

Use additional code to identify any infectious organism present, such as:
pseudomonas (041.7)

277.03 With gastrointestinal manifestations

EXCLUDES *with meconium ileus (277.01)*

AHA: 4Q, '02, 45

277.09 With other manifestations

277.1 Disorders of porphyrin metabolism

Hematoporphyria
Hematoporphyrinuria
Hereditary coproporphyria
Porphyria
Porphyrinuria
Protocoproporphyria
Protoporphyria
Pyrroloporphyria

277.2 Other disorders of purine and pyrimidine metabolism

Hypoxanthine-guanine-phosphoribosyltransferase deficiency [HG-PRT deficiency]
Lesch-Nyhan syndrome
Xanthinuria

EXCLUDES *gout (274.0-274.9)*
orotic aciduric anemia (281.4)

✓5th **277.3 Amyloidosis**

AHA: 1Q, '96, 16

DEF: Conditions of diverse etiologies characterized by the accumulation of insoluble fibrillar proteins (amyloid) in various organs and tissues of the body, compromising vital functions.

277.30 Amyloidosis, unspecified

Amyloidosis NOS

AHA: 4Q, '06, 66

277.31 Familial Mediterranean fever

Benign paroxysmal peritonitis
Hereditary amyloid nephropathy
Periodic familial polyserositis
Recurrent polyserositis

AHA: 4Q, '06, 66

DEF: Childhood or early-life onset of recurrent attacks characterized by high fevers with pain and inflammation of chest and abdominal cavities, skin and joints, also rash or vasculitis. Underlying cause is unknown, or possibly genetic, but may be precipitated by stress, trauma or exertion.

277.39 Other amyloidosis

Hereditary cardiac amyloidosis
Inherited systemic amyloidosis
Neuropathic (Portuguese) (Swiss) amyloidosis
Secondary amyloidosis

AHA: ▶2Q, '08, 8;◀ 4Q, '06, 66

277.4 Disorders of bilirubin excretion

Hyperbilirubinemia:
congenital
constitutional
Syndrome:
Crigler-Najjar
Dubin-Johnson
Gilbert's
Rotor's

EXCLUDES *hyperbilirubinemias specific to the perinatal period (774.0-774.7)*

277.5 Mucopolysaccharidosis

Gargoylism
Hunter's syndrome
Hurler's syndrome
Lipochondrodystrophy
Maroteaux-Lamy syndrome
Morquio-Brailsford disease
Osteochondrodystrophy
Sanfilippo's syndrome
Scheie's syndrome

DEF: Metabolism disorders evidenced by excretion of various mucopolysaccharides in urine and infiltration of these substances into connective tissue, with resulting various defects of bone, cartilage and connective tissue.

277.6 Other deficiencies of circulating enzymes

Hereditary angioedema

277.7 Dysmetabolic syndrome X

Use additional code for associated manifestation, such as:
cardiovascular disease (414.00-414.07)
obesity (278.00-278.01)

AHA: 4Q, '01, 42

DEF: A specific group of metabolic disorders that are related to the state of insulin resistance (decreased cellular response to insulin) without elevated blood sugars; often related to elevated cholesterol and triglycerides, obesity, cardiovascular disease, and high blood pressure.

✓5th **277.8 Other specified disorders of metabolism**

AHA: 4Q, '03, 50; 2Q, '01, 18; S-O, '87, 9

277.81 Primary carnitine deficiency

277.82 Carnitine deficiency due to inborn errors of metabolism

277.83 Iatrogenic carnitine deficiency

Carnitine deficiency due to:
hemodialysis
valproic acid therapy

277.84 Other secondary carnitine deficiency

277.85 Disorders of fatty acid oxidation

Carnitine palmitoyltransferase deficiencies (CPT1, CPT2)
Glutaric aciduria type II (type IIA, IIB, IIC)
Long chain 3-hydroxyacyl CoA dehydrogenase deficiency (LCHAD)
Long chain/very long chain acyl CoA dehydrogenase deficiency (LCAD, VLCAD)
Medium chain acyl CoA dehydrogenase deficiency (MCAD)
Short chain acyl CoA dehydrogenase deficiency (SCAD)

EXCLUDES *primary carnitine deficiency (277.81)*

277.86 Peroxisomal disorders

Adrenomyeloneuropathy
Neonatal adrenoleukodystrophy
Rhizomelic chrondrodysplasia punctata
X-linked adrenoleukodystrophy
Zellweger syndrome

EXCLUDES *infantile Refsum disease (356.3)*

277.87 Disorders of mitochondrial metabolism

Kearns-Sayre syndrome
Mitochondrial Encephalopathy, Lactic Acidosis and Stroke-like episodes (MELAS syndrome)
Mitochondrial Neurogastrointestinal Encephalopathy syndrome (MNGIE)
Myoclonus with Epilepsy and with Ragged Red Fibers (MERRF syndrome)
Neuropathy, Ataxia and Retinitis Pigmentosa (NARP syndrome)

Use additional code for associated conditions

EXCLUDES *disorders of pyruvate metabolism (271.8)*
Leber's optic atrophy (377.16)
Leigh's subacute necrotizing encephalopathy (330.8)
Reye's syndrome (331.81)

AHA: 4Q, '04, 62

277.89 Other specified disorders of metabolism

Hand-Schüller-Christian disease
Histiocytosis (acute) (chronic)
Histiocytosis X (chronic)

EXCLUDES *histiocytosis:*
acute differentiated progressive (202.5)
X, acute (progressive) (202.5)

277.9 Unspecified disorder of metabolism

Enzymopathy NOS

✓4th **278 Overweight, obesity and other hyperalimentation**

EXCLUDES *hyperalimentation NOS (783.6)*
poisoning by vitamins NOS (963.5)
polyphagia (783.6)

✓5th **278.0 Overweight and obesity**

Use additional code to identify Body Mass Index (BMI), if known (V85.0-V85.54)

EXCLUDES *adiposogenital dystrophy (253.8)*
obesity of endocrine origin NOS (259.9)

AHA: 4Q, '05, 97

278.00 Obesity, unspecified

Obesity NOS

AHA: 4Q, '01, 42; 1Q, '99, 5, 6

DEF: BMI (body mass index) between 30.0 and 38.9.

278.01 Morbid obesity

Severe obesity

AHA: 2Q, '06, 5-6; 3Q, '03, 6-8

DEF: Increased weight beyond limits of skeletal and physical requirements (125 percent or more over ideal body weight), as a result of excess fat in subcutaneous connective tissues.

DEF: BMI (body mass index) greater than 39.

278.02 Overweight

AHA: 4Q, '05, 55

DEF: BMI (body mass index) between 25 and 29.9.

278.1 Localized adiposity

Fat pad

AHA: 2Q, '06, 10

278.2 Hypervitaminosis A

278.3 Hypercarotinemia

DEF: Elevated blood carotene level due to ingesting excess carotenoids or the inability to convert carotenoids to vitamin A.

278.4 Hypervitaminosis D

DEF: Weakness, fatigue, loss of weight, and other symptoms resulting from ingesting excessive amounts of vitamin D.

278.8 Other hyperalimentation

✓4th **279 Disorders involving the immune mechanism**

✓5th **279.0 Deficiency of humoral immunity**

DEF: Inadequate immune response to bacterial infections with potential reinfection by viruses due to lack of circulating immunoglobulins (acquired antibodies).

279.00 Hypogammaglobulinemia, unspecified

Agammaglobulinemia NOS

279.01 Selective IgA immunodeficiency

279.02 Selective IgM immunodeficiency

279.03 Other selective immunoglobulin deficiencies

Selective deficiency of IgG

279.04 Congenital hypogammaglobulinemia

Agammaglobulinemia:
Bruton's type
X-linked

279.05 Immunodeficiency with increased IgM

Immunodeficiency with hyper-IgM:
autosomal recessive
X-linked

279.06 Common variable immunodeficiency

Dysgammaglobulinemia (acquired) (congenital) (primary)
Hypogammaglobulinemia:
acquired primary
congenital non-sex-linked
sporadic

279.09 Other
Transient hypogammaglobulinemia of infancy

✓5th **279.1 Deficiency of cell-mediated immunity**

279.10 Immunodeficiency with predominant T-cell defect, unspecified
AHA: S-O, '87, 10

279.11 DiGeorge's syndrome
Pharyngeal pouch syndrome
Thymic hypoplasia
DEF: Congenital disorder due to defective development of the third and fourth pharyngeal pouches; results in hypoplasia or aplasia of the thymus, parathyroid glands; related to congenital heart defects, anomalies of the great vessels, esophageal atresia, and abnormalities of facial structures.

279.12 Wiskott-Aldrich syndrome
DEF: A disease characterized by chronic conditions, such as eczema, suppurative otitis media and anemia; it results from an X-linked recessive gene and is classified as an immune deficiency syndrome.

279.13 Nezelof's syndrome
Cellular immunodeficiency with abnormal immunoglobulin deficiency
DEF: Immune system disorder characterized by a patholo-gical deficiency in cellular immunity and humoral anti-bodies resulting in inability to fight infectious diseases.

279.19 Other
EXCLUDES *ataxia-telangiectasia (334.8)*

279.2 Combined immunity deficiency
Agammaglobulinemia:
- autosomal recessive
- Swiss-type
- x-linked recessive

Severe combined immunodeficiency [SCID]
Thymic:
- alymophoplasia
- aplasia or dysplasia with immunodeficiency

EXCLUDES *thymic hypoplasia (279.11)*

DEF: Agammaglobulinemia: No immunoglobulins in the blood.
DEF: Thymic alymphoplasia: Severe combined immunodeficiency; result of failed lymphoid tissue development.

279.3 Unspecified immunity deficiency

279.4 Autoimmune disease, not elsewhere classified
Autoimmune disease NOS
EXCLUDES *transplant failure or rejection (996.80-996.89)*

● ✓5th **279.5 Graft-versus-host disease**
Code first underlying cause, such as:
- complication of transplanted organ (bone marrow) (996.80-996.89)
- complication of blood transfusion (999.8)

Use additional code to identify associated manifestations, such as:
- desquamative dermatitis (695.89)
- diarrhea (787.91)
- elevated bilirubin (782.4)
- hair loss (704.09)

● **279.50 Graft-versus-host disease, unspecified**
● **279.51 Acute graft-versus-host disease**
● **279.52 Chronic graft-versus-host disease**
● **279.53 Acute on chronic graft-versus-host disease**

279.8 Other specified disorders involving the immune mechanism
Single complement [C_1-C_9] deficiency or dysfunction

279.9 Unspecified disorder of immune mechanism
AHA: 3Q, '92, 13

4. DISEASES OF THE BLOOD AND BLOOD-FORMING ORGANS (280-289)

EXCLUDES *anemia complicating pregnancy or the puerperium (648.2)*

✓4th 280 Iron deficiency anemias

INCLUDES anemia:
- asiderotic
- hypochromic-microcytic
- sideropenic

EXCLUDES *familial microcytic anemia (282.49)*

280.0 Secondary to blood loss (chronic)
Normocytic anemia due to blood loss

EXCLUDES *acute posthemorrhagic anemia (285.1)*

AHA: 4Q, '93, 34

280.1 Secondary to inadequate dietary iron intake

280.8 Other specified iron deficiency anemias
Paterson-Kelly syndrome
Plummer-Vinson syndrome
Sideropenic dysphagia

280.9 Iron deficiency anemia, unspecified
Anemia:
- achlorhydric
- chlorotic
- idiopathic hypochromic
- iron [Fe] deficiency NOS

✓4th 281 Other deficiency anemias

281.0 Pernicious anemia
Anemia:
- Addison's
- Biermer's
- congenital pernicious

Congenital intrinsic factor [Castle's] deficiency

EXCLUDES *combined system disease without mention of anemia (266.2)*
subacute degeneration of spinal cord without mention of anemia (266.2)

AHA: N-D, '84, 1; S-O, '84, 16

DEF: Chronic progressive anemia due to Vitamin B12 malabsorption; caused by lack of a secretion known as intrinsic factor, which is produced by the gastric mucosa of the stomach.

281.1 Other vitamin B_{12} deficiency anemia
Anemia:
- vegan's
- vitamin B_{12} deficiency (dietary)
- due to selective vitamin B_{12} malabsorption with proteinuria

Syndrome:
- Imerslund's
- Imerslund-Gräsbeck

EXCLUDES *combined system disease without mention of anemia (266.2)*
subacute degeneration of spinal cord without mention of anemia (266.2)

281.2 Folate-deficiency anemia
Congenital folate malabsorption
Folate or folic acid deficiency anemia:
- NOS
- dietary
- drug-induced

Goat's milk anemia
Nutritional megaloblastic anemia (of infancy)

Use additional E code to identify drug

DEF: Macrocytic anemia resembles pernicious anemia but without absence of hydrochloric acid secretions; responsive to folic acid therapy.

281.3 Other specified megaloblastic anemias not elsewhere classified
Combined B_{12} and folate-deficiency anemia
Refractory megaloblastic anemia

DEF: Megaloblasts predominant in bone marrow with few normoblasts; rare familial type associated with proteinuria and genitourinary tract anomalies.

281.4 Protein-deficiency anemia
Amino-acid-deficiency anemia

281.8 Anemia associated with other specified nutritional deficiency
Scorbutic anemia

281.9 Unspecified deficiency anemia
Anemia:
- dimorphic
- macrocytic
- megaloblastic NOS
- nutritional NOS
- simple chronic

✓4th 282 Hereditary hemolytic anemias

DEF: Escalated rate of erythrocyte destruction; similar to all anemias, occurs when imbalance exists between blood loss and blood production.

282.0 Hereditary spherocytosis
Acholuric (familial) jaundice
Congenital hemolytic anemia (spherocytic)
Congenital spherocytosis
Minkowski-Chauffard syndrome
Spherocytosis (familial)

EXCLUDES *hemolytic anemia of newborn (773.0-773.5)*

DEF: Hereditary, chronic illness marked by abnormal red blood cell membrane; symptoms include enlarged spleen, jaundice; and anemia in severe cases.

282.1 Hereditary elliptocytosis
Elliptocytosis (congenital)
Ovalocytosis (congenital) (hereditary)

DEF: Genetic hemolytic anemia characterized by malformed, elliptical erythrocytes; there is increased destruction of red cells with resulting anemia.

282.2 Anemias due to disorders of glutathione metabolism
Anemia:
- 6-phosphogluconic dehydrogenase deficiency
- enzyme deficiency, drug-induced
- erythrocytic glutathione deficiency
- glucose-6-phosphate dehydrogenase [G-6-PD] deficiency
- glutathione-reductase deficiency
- hemolytic nonspherocytic (hereditary), type I

Disorder of pentose phosphate pathway
Favism

282.3 Other hemolytic anemias due to enzyme deficiency
Anemia:
- hemolytic nonspherocytic (hereditary), type II
- hexokinase deficiency
- pyruvate kinase [PK] deficiency
- triosephosphate isomerase deficiency

✓5th 282.4 Thalassemias

EXCLUDES *sickle-cell:*
disease (282.60-282.69)
trait (282.5)

AHA: 4Q, '03, 51

DEF: A group of inherited hemolytic disorders characterized by decreased production of at least one of the four polypeptide globin chains which results in defective hemoglobin synthesis; symptoms include severe anemia, expanded marrow spaces, transfusional and absorptive iron overload, impaired growth rate, thickened cranial bones, and pathologic fractures.

282.41 Sickle-cell thalassemia without crisis
Sickle-cell thalassemia NOS
Thalassemia Hb-S disease without crisis

282.42 Sickle-cell thalassemia with crisis
Sickle-cell thalassemia with vaso-occlusive pain
Thalassemia Hb-S disease with crisis
Use additional code for type of crisis, such as:
acute chest syndrome (517.3)
splenic sequestration (289.52)

282.49 Other thalassemia
Cooley's anemia
Hb-Bart's disease
Hereditary leptocytosis
Mediterranean anemia (with other hemoglobinopathy)
Microdrepanocytosis
Thalassemia (alpha) (beta) (intermedia) (major) (minima) (minor) (mixed) (trait) (with other hemoglobinopathy)
Thalassemia NOS

282.5 Sickle-cell trait
Hb-AS genotype
Hemoglobin S [Hb-S] trait
Heterozygous:
hemoglobin S
Hb-S

EXCLUDES *that with other hemoglobinopathy (282.60-282.69)*
that with thalassemia (282.49)

DEF: Heterozygous genetic makeup characterized by one gene for normal hemoglobin and one for sickle-cell hemoglobin; clinical disease rarely present.

✓5th **282.6 Sickle-cell disease**
Sickle-cell anemia

EXCLUDES *sickle-cell thalassemia (282.41-282.42)*
sickle-cell trait (282.5)

DEF: Inherited blood disorder; sickle-shaped red blood cells are hard and pointed, clogging blood flow; anemia characterized by, periodic episodes of pain, acute abdominal discomfort, skin ulcerations of the legs, increased infections; occurs primarily in persons of African descent.

282.60 Sickle-cell disease, unspecified
Sickle-cell anemia NOS
AHA: 2Q, '97, 11

282.61 Hb-SS disease without crisis

282.62 Hb-SS disease with crisis
Hb-SS disease with vaso-occlusive pain
Sickle-cell crisis NOS
Use additional code for type of crisis, such as:
acute chest syndrome (517.3)
splenic sequestration (289.52)
AHA: 4Q, '03, 56; 2Q, '98, 8; 2Q, '91, 15

282.63 Sickle-cell/Hb-C disease without crisis
Hb-S/Hb-C disease without crisis

282.64 Sickle-cell/Hb-C disease with crisis
Hb-S/Hb-C disease with crisis
Sickle-cell/Hb-C disease with vaso-occlusive pain
Use additional code for type of crisis, such as:
acute chest syndrome (517.3)
splenic sequestration (289.52)
AHA: 4Q, '03, 51

282.68 Other sickle-cell disease without crisis
Hb-S/Hb-D, Hb-S/Hb-E, Sickle-cell/Hb-D, Sickle-cell/Hb-E } diseases without crisis
AHA: 4Q, '03, 51

282.69 Other sickle-cell disease with crisis
Hb-S/Hb-D, Hb-S/Hb-E, Sickle-cell/Hb-D, Sickle-cell/Hb-E } diseases with crisis
Other sickle-cell disease with vaso-occlusive pain
Use additional code for type of crisis, such as:
acute chest syndrome (517.3)
splenic sequestration (289.52)

282.7 Other hemoglobinopathies
Abnormal hemoglobin NOS
Congenital Heinz-body anemia
Disease:
hemoglobin C [Hb-C]
hemoglobin D [Hb-D]
hemoglobin E [Hb-E]
hemoglobin Zurich [Hb-Zurich]
Hemoglobinopathy NOS
Hereditary persistence of fetal hemoglobin [HPFH]
Unstable hemoglobin hemolytic disease

EXCLUDES *familial polycythemia (289.6)*
hemoglobin M [Hb-M] disease (289.7)
high-oxygen-affinity hemoglobin (289.0)

DEF: Any disorder of hemoglobin due to alteration of molecular structure; may include overt anemia.

282.8 Other specified hereditary hemolytic anemias
Stomatocytosis

282.9 Hereditary hemolytic anemia, unspecified
Hereditary hemolytic anemia NOS

✓4th **283 Acquired hemolytic anemias**
AHA: N-D, '84, 1
DEF: Non-heriditary anemia characterized by premature destruction of red blood cells; caused by infectious organisms, poisons, and physical agents

283.0 Autoimmune hemolytic anemias
Autoimmune hemolytic disease (cold type) (warm type)
Chronic cold hemagglutinin disease
Cold agglutinin disease or hemoglobinuria
Hemolytic anemia:
cold type (secondary) (symptomatic)
drug-induced
warm type (secondary) (symptomatic)
Use additional E code to identify cause, if drug-induced

EXCLUDES *Evans' syndrome (287.32)*
hemolytic disease of newborn (773.0-773.5)

✓5th **283.1 Non-autoimmune hemolytic anemias**
Use additional E code to identify cause
AHA: 4Q, '93, 25
DEF: Hemolytic anemia and thrombocytopenia with acute renal failure; relatively rare condition; 50 percent of patients require renal dialysis.

283.10 Non-autoimmune hemolytic anemia, unspecified

283.11 Hemolytic-uremic syndrome

283.19 Other non-autoimmune hemolytic anemias
Hemolytic anemia:
mechanical
microangiopathic
toxic

283.2 Hemoglobinuria due to hemolysis from external causes
Acute intravascular hemolysis
Hemoglobinuria:
from exertion
march
paroxysmal (cold) (nocturnal)
due to other hemolysis
Marchiafava-Micheli syndrome
Use additional E code to identify cause

283.9 Acquired hemolytic anemia, unspecified
Acquired hemolytic anemia NOS
Chronic idiopathic hemolytic anemia

✓4th 284 Aplastic anemia and other bone marrow failure syndromes
AHA: 1Q, '91, 14; N-D, '84, 1; S-O, '84, 16
DEF: Bone marrow failure to produce the normal amount of blood components; generally non-responsive to usual therapy.

✓5th 284.0 Constitutional aplastic anemia
AHA: 1Q, '91, 14

284.01 Constitutional red blood cell aplasia
Aplasia, (pure) red cell:
congenital
of infants
primary
Blackfan-Diamond syndrome
Familial hypoplastic anemia
AHA: 4Q, '06, 67-69

284.09 Other constitutional aplastic anemia
Fanconi's anemia
Pancytopenia with malformations
AHA: 4Q, '06, 67-69

284.1 Pancytopenia
EXCLUDES *pancytopenia (due to) (with):*
aplastic anemia NOS (284.9)
bone marrow infiltration (284.2)
constitutional red blood cell aplasia (284.01)
drug induced (284.89)
hairy cell leukemia (202.4)
human immunodeficiency virus disease (042)
leukoerythroblastic anemia (284.2)
malformations (284.09)
myelodysplastic syndromes (238.72-238.75)
myeloproliferative disease (238.79)
other constitutional aplastic anemia (284.09)
AHA: 4Q, '06, 67-69

284.2 Myelophthisis
Leukoerythroblastic anemia
Myelophthisic anemia
Code first the underlying disorder, such as:
malignant neoplasm of breast (174.0-174.9, 175.0-175.9)
tuberculosis (015.0-015.9)
EXCLUDES *idiopathic myelofibrosis (238.76)*
myelofibrosis NOS (289.83)
myelofibrosis with myeloid metaplasia (238.76)
primary myelofibrosis (238.76)
secondary myelofibrosis (289.83)
AHA: 4Q, '06, 67-69
DEF: A secondary disease process involving replacement of normal hematopoeitic tissue in the bone marrow with abnormal tissue, such as fibrous tissue or tumors. Occurs with advanced-stage neoplasms, granulomatous diseases such as miliary tuberculosis, and other inflammatory or infectious diseases or in countries where access to medical care is not readily available.

✓5th 284.8 Other specified aplastic anemias
AHA: 4Q, '07, 72; 3Q, '05, 11; 1Q, '97, 5; 1Q, '92, 15; 1Q, '91, 14

284.81 Red cell aplasia (acquired) (adult) (with thymoma)
Red cell aplasia NOS

284.89 Other specified aplastic anemias
Aplastic anemia (due to):
chronic systemic disease
drugs
infection
radiation
toxic (paralytic)
Use additional E code to identify cause
AHA: ▶2Q, '08, 6◀

284.9 Aplastic anemia, unspecified
Anemia:
aplastic (idiopathic) NOS
aregenerative
hypoplastic NOS
nonregenerative
Medullary hypoplasia
EXCLUDES *refractory anemia (238.72)*

✓4th 285 Other and unspecified anemias
AHA: 1Q, '91, 14; N-D, '84, 1

285.0 Sideroblastic anemia
Anemia:
hypochromic with iron loading
sideroachrestic
sideroblastic:
acquired
congenital
hereditary
primary
secondary (drug-induced) (due to disease)
sex-linked hypochromic
vitamin B6-responsive
Pyridoxine-responsive (hypochromic) anemia
Use additional E code to identify cause, if drug induced
EXCLUDES *refractory sideroblastic anemia (238.72)*
DEF: Characterized by a disruption of final heme synthesis; results in iron overload of reticuloendothelial tissues.

285.1 Acute posthemorrhagic anemia
Anemia due to acute blood loss
EXCLUDES *anemia due to chronic blood loss (280.0)*
blood loss anemia NOS (280.0)
AHA: 1Q, '07, 19; 2Q, '92, 15

✓5th 285.2 Anemia of chronic disease
Anemia in chronic illness
AHA: 4Q, '00, 39

285.21 Anemia in chronic kidney disease
Anemia in end stage renal disease
Erythropoietin-resistant anemia (EPO resistant anemia)

285.22 Anemia in neoplastic disease

285.29 Anemia of other chronic disease
Anemia in other chronic illness

285.8 Other specified anemias
Anemia:
dyserythropoietic (congenital)
dyshematopoietic (congenital)
von Jaksch's
Infantile pseudoleukemia
AHA: 1Q, '91, 16

285.9 Anemia, unspecified
Anemia:
  NOS
  essential
  normocytic, not due to blood loss
  profound
  progressive
  secondary
Oligocythemia

EXCLUDES *anemia (due to):*
  blood loss:
    acute (285.1)
    chronic or unspecified (280.0)
  iron deficiency (280.0-280.9)

AHA: 1Q, '07, 19; 1Q, '02, 14; 2Q, '92, 16; M-A, '85, 13; N-D, '84, 1

✓4th 286 Coagulation defects

AHA: 2Q, '06, 17

286.0 Congenital factor VIII disorder
Antihemophilic globulin [AHG] deficiency
Factor VIII (functional)deficiency
Hemophilia:
  NOS
  A
  classical
  familial
  hereditary
Subhemophilia

EXCLUDES *factor VIII deficiency with vascular defect (286.4)*

DEF: Hereditary, sex-linked, results in missing antihemophilic globulin (AHG) (factor VIII); causes abnormal coagulation characterized by increased tendency to bleeding, large bruises of skin, soft tissue; may also be bleeding in mouth, nose, gastrointestinal tract; after childhood, hemorrhages in joints, resulting in swelling and impaired function.

286.1 Congenital factor IX disorder
Christmas disease
Deficiency:
  factor IX (functional)
  plasma thromboplastin component [PTC]
Hemophilia B

DEF: Deficiency of plasma thromboplastin component (PTC) (factor IX) and plasma thromboplastin antecedent (PTA); PTC deficiency clinically indistinguishable from classical hemophilia; PTA deficiency found in both sexes.

286.2 Congenital factor XI deficiency
Hemophilia C
Plasma thromboplastin antecedent [PTA] deficiency
Rosenthal's disease

286.3 Congenital deficiency of other clotting factors
Congenital afibrinogenemia
Deficiency:
  AC globulin factor:
    I [fibrinogen]
    II [prothrombin]
    V [labile]
    VII [stable]
    X [Stuart-Prower]
    XII [Hageman]
    XIII [fibrin stabilizing]
  Laki-Lorand factor
  proaccelerin
Disease
  Owren's
  Stuart-Prower
Dysfibrinogenemia (congenital)
Dysprothrombinemia (constitutional)
Hypoproconvertinemia
Hypoprothrombinemia (hereditary)
Parahemophilia

286.4 von Willebrand's disease
Angiohemophilia (A) (B)
Constitutional thrombopathy
Factor VIII deficiency with vascular defect
Pseudohemophilia type B
Vascular hemophilia
von Willebrand's (-Jürgens') disease

EXCLUDES *factor VIII deficiency:*
  NOS (286.0)
  with functional defect (286.0)
hereditary capillary fragility (287.8)

DEF: Abnormal blood coagulation caused by deficient blood Factor VII; congenital; symptoms include excess or prolonged bleeding, such as hemorrhage during menstruation, following birthing, or after surgical procedure.

286.5 Hemorrhagic disorder due to intrinsic circulating anticoagulants
Antithrombinemia
Antithromboplastinemia
Antithromboplastino-genemia
Hyperheparinemia
Increase in:
  anti-VIIIa
  anti-IXa
  anti-Xa
  anti-XIa
  antithrombin
Secondary hemophilia
Systemic lupus erythematosus [SLE] inhibitor

AHA: 3Q, '04, 7; No.5, '93, 16; 3Q, '92, 15; 3Q, '90, 14

286.6 Defibrination syndrome
Afibrinogenemia, acquired
Consumption coagulopathy
Diffuse or disseminated intravascular coagulation [DIC syndrome]
Fibrinolytic hemorrhage, acquired
Hemorrhagic fibrinogenolysis
Pathologic fibrinolysis
Purpura:
  fibrinolytic
  fulminans

EXCLUDES *that complicating:*
  abortion (634-638 with .1, 639.1)
  pregnancy or the puerperium (641.3, 666.3)
disseminated intravascular coagulation in newborn (776.2)

AHA: 4Q, '93, 29

DEF: Characterized by destruction of circulating fibrinogen; often precipitated by other conditions, such as injury, causing release of thromboplastic particles in blood stream.

286.7 Acquired coagulation factor deficiency
Deficiency of coagulation factor due to:
  liver disease
  vitamin K deficiency
Hypoprothrombinemia, acquired

Use additional E code to identify cause, if drug induced

EXCLUDES *vitamin K deficiency of newborn (776.0)*

AHA: 4Q, '93, 29

286.9 Other and unspecified coagulation defects
Defective coagulation NOS
Deficiency, coagulation factor NOS
Delay, coagulation
Disorder:
  coagulation
  hemostasis

EXCLUDES *abnormal coagulation profile (790.92)*
hemorrhagic disease of newborn (776.0)
that complicating:
  abortion (634-638 with .1, 639.1)
  pregnancy or the puerperium (641.3, 666.3)

AHA: 4Q, '99, 22; 4Q, '93, 29

287 Purpura and other hemorrhagic conditions

EXCLUDES *hemorrhagic thrombocythemia (238.79)*
purpura fulminans (286.6)

AHA: 1Q, '91, 14

287.0 Allergic purpura

Peliosis rheumatica
Purpura:
anaphylactoid
autoimmune
Henoch's
nonthrombocytopenic:
hemorrhagic
idiopathic
rheumatica
Schönlein-Henoch
vascular
Vasculitis, allergic

EXCLUDES *hemorrhagic purpura (287.39)*
purpura annularis telangiectodes (709.1)

DEF: Any hemorrhagic condition, thrombocytic or nonthrombocytopenic in origin, caused by a presumed allergic reaction.

287.1 Qualitative platelet defects

Thrombasthenia (hemorrhagic) (hereditary)
Thrombocytasthenia
Thrombocytopathy (dystrophic)
Thrombopathy (Bernard-Soulier)

EXCLUDES *von Willebrand's disease (286.4)*

287.2 Other nonthrombocytopenic purpuras

Purpura:
NOS
senile
simplex

287.3 Primary thrombocytopenia

EXCLUDES *thrombotic thrombocytopenic purpura (446.6)*
transient thrombocytopenia of newborn (776.1)

AHA: 4Q, '05, 56

DEF: Decrease in number of blood platelets in circulating blood and purpural skin hemorrhages.

287.30 Primary thrombocytopenia, unspecified

Megakaryocytic hypoplasia

287.31 Immune thrombocytopenic purpura

Idiopathic thrombocytopenic purpura
Tidal platelet dysgenesis

AHA: 4Q, '05, 57

DEF: Tidal platelet dysgenesis: Platelet counts fluctuate from normal to very low within periods of 20 to 40 days and may involve autoimmune platelet destruction.

287.32 Evans' syndrome

DEF: Combination of immunohemolytic anemia and autoimmune hemolytic anemia, sometimes with neutropenia.

287.33 Congenital and hereditary thrombocytopenic purpura

Congenital and hereditary thrombocytopenia
Thrombocytopenia with absent radii (TAR) syndrome

EXCLUDES *Wiskott-Aldrich syndrome (279.12)*

DEF: Thrombocytopenia with absent radii (TAR) syndrome: autosomal recessive syndrome characterized by thrombocytopenia and bilateral radial aplasia; manifestations include skeletal, gastrointestinal, hematologic, and cardiac system abnormalities.

287.39 Other primary thrombocytopenia

287.4 Secondary thrombocytopenia

Posttransfusion purpura
Thrombocytopenia (due to):
dilutional
drugs
extracorporeal circulation of blood
massive blood transfusion
platelet alloimmunization

Use additional E code to identify cause

EXCLUDES ▶*heparin-induced thrombocytopenia (HIT) (289.84)*◀
transient thrombocytopenia of newborn (776.1)

AHA: 4Q, '99, 22; 4Q '93, 29

DEF: Reduced number of platelets in circulating blood as consequence of an underlying disease or condition.

287.5 Thrombocytopenia, unspecified

287.8 Other specified hemorrhagic conditions

Capillary fragility (hereditary)
Vascular pseudohemophilia

287.9 Unspecified hemorrhagic conditions

Hemorrhagic diathesis (familial)

288 Diseases of white blood cells

EXCLUDES *leukemia (204.0-208.9)*

AHA: 4Q, '06, 69; 1Q, '91, 14

288.0 Neutropenia

Decreased absolute neutrophil count [ANC]

Use additional code for any associated:
fever ▶(780.61)◀
mucositis (478.11, 528.00-528.09, 538, 616.81)

EXCLUDES *neutropenic splenomegaly (289.53)*
transitory neonatal neutropenia (776.7)

AHA: 4Q, '06, 69-73; 3Q, '05, 11; 3Q, '99, 6; 2Q, '99, 9; 3Q, '96, 16; 2Q, '96, 6

DEF: Sudden, severe condition characterized by reduced number of white blood cells; results in sores in the throat, stomach or skin; symptoms include chills, fever; some drugs can bring on condition.

288.00 Neutropenia, unspecified

AHA: 4Q, '06, 69-73

288.01 Congenital neutropenia

Congenital agranulocytosis
Infantile genetic agranulocytosis
Kostmann's syndrome

AHA: 4Q, '06, 69-73

288.02 Cyclic neutropenia

Cyclic hematopoiesis
Periodic neutropenia

AHA: 4Q, '06, 69-73

288.03 Drug induced neutropenia

Use additional E code to identify drug

AHA: 4Q, '06, 69-73

288.04 Neutropenia due to infection

AHA: 4Q, '06, 69-73

288.09 Other neutropenia

Agranulocytosis
Neutropenia:
immune
toxic

AHA: 4Q, '06, 69-73

288.1 Functional disorders of polymorphonuclear neutrophils

Chronic (childhood) granulomatous disease
Congenital dysphagocytosis
Job's syndrome
Lipochrome histiocytosis (familial)
Progressive septic granulomatosis

288.2 Genetic anomalies of leukocytes
Anomaly (granulation) (gran ulocyte) or syndrome:
- Alder's (-Reilly)
- Chédiak-Steinbrinck (-Higashi)
- Jordan's
- May-Hegglin
- Pelger-Huet

Hereditary:
- hypersegmentation
- hyposegmentation
- leukomelanopathy

288.3 Eosinophilia
Eosinophilia:
- allergic
- hereditary
- idiopathic
- secondary

Eosinophilic leukocytosis

EXCLUDES *Löffler's syndrome (518.3)*
pulmonary eosinophilia (518.3)

AHA: 3Q, '00, 11

DEF: Elevated number of eosinophils in the blood; characteristic of allergic states and various parasitic infections.

288.4 Hemophagocytic syndromes
Familial hemophagocytic lymphohistiocytosis
Familial hemophagocytic reticulosis
Hemophagocytic syndrome, infection-associated
Histiocytic syndromes
Macrophage activation syndrome

AHA: 4Q, '06, 69-73

✓5th **288.5 Decreased white blood cell count**

EXCLUDES *neutropenia (288.01-288.09)*

288.50 Leukocytopenia, unspecified
Decreased leukocytes, unspecified
Decreased white blood cell count, unspecified
Leukopenia NOS

AHA: 4Q, '06, 69-73

288.51 Lymphocytopenia
Decreased lymphocytes

AHA: 4Q, '06, 69-73

288.59 Other decreased white blood cell count
Basophilic leukopenia
Eosinophilic leukopenia
Monocytopenia
Plasmacytopenia

AHA: 4Q, '06, 69-73

✓5th **288.6 Elevated white blood cell count**

EXCLUDES *eosinophilia (288.3)*

288.60 Leukocytosis, unspecified
Elevated leukocytes, unspecified
Elevated white blood cell count, unspecified

AHA: 4Q, '06, 69-73

288.61 Lymphocytosis (symptomatic)
Elevated lymphocytes

AHA: 4Q, '06, 69-73

288.62 Leukemoid reaction
Basophilic leukemoid reaction
Lymphocytic leukemoid reaction
Monocytic leukemoid reaction
Myelocytic leukemoid reaction
Neutrophilic leukemoid reaction

AHA: 4Q, '06, 69-73

288.63 Monocytosis (symptomatic)

EXCLUDES *infectious mononucleosis (075)*

AHA: 4Q, '06, 69-73

288.64 Plasmacytosis

AHA: 4Q, '06, 69-73

288.65 Basophilia

AHA: 4Q, '06, 69-73

288.66 Bandemia
Bandemia without diagnosis of specific infection

EXCLUDES *confirmed infection–code to infection*
leukemia (204.00-208.9)

AHA: ►4Q, '07, 73◄

DEF: ►Increase in early neutrophil cells, called band cells; may indicate infection.◄

288.69 Other elevated white blood cell count

AHA: 4Q, '06, 69-73

288.8 Other specified disease of white blood cells

EXCLUDES *decreased white blood cell counts (288.50-288.59)*
elevated white blood cell counts (288.60-288.69)
immunity disorders (279.0-279.9)

AHA: M-A, '87, 12

288.9 Unspecified disease of white blood cells

✓4th **289 Other diseases of blood and blood-forming organs**

289.0 Polycythemia, secondary
High-oxygen-affinity hemoglobin
Polycythemia:
- acquired
- benign
- due to:
  - fall in plasma volume
  - high altitude
- emotional
- erythropoietin
- hypoxemic
- nephrogenous
- relative
- spurious
- stress

EXCLUDES *polycythemia:*
neonatal (776.4)
primary (238.4)
vera (238.4)

DEF: Elevated number of red blood cells in circulating blood as result of reduced oxygen supply to the tissues.

289.1 Chronic lymphadenitis
Chronic:
- adenitis } any lymph node, except mesenteric
- lymphadenitis } any lymph node, except mesenteric

EXCLUDES *acute lymphadenitis (683)*
mesenteric (289.2)
enlarged glands NOS (785.6)

DEF: Persistent inflammation of lymph node tissue; origin of infection is usually elsewhere.

289.2 Nonspecific mesenteric lymphadenitis
Mesenteric lymphadenitis (acute) (chronic)

DEF: Inflammation of the lymph nodes in peritoneal fold that encases abdominal organs; disease resembles acute appendicitis; unknown etiology.

289.3 Lymphadenitis, unspecified, except mesenteric

AHA: 2Q, '92, 8

289.4 Hypersplenism
"Big spleen" syndrome
Dyssplenism
Hypersplenia

EXCLUDES *primary splenic neutropenia (289.53)*

DEF: An overactive spleen; it causes a deficiency of the peripheral blood components, an increase in bone marrow cells and sometimes a notable increase in the size of the spleen.

✓5th **289.5 Other diseases of spleen**

289.50 Disease of spleen, unspecified

289.51 Chronic congestive splenomegaly

289.52 Splenic sequestration

Code first sickle-cell disease in crisis (282.42, 282.62, 282.64, 282.69)

AHA: 4Q, '03, 51

DEF: Blood is entrapped in the spleen due to vessel occlusion; most often associated with sickle-cell disease; spleen becomes enlarged and there is a sharp drop in hemoglobin.

289.53 Neutropenic splenomegaly

AHA: 4Q, '06, 73

289.59 Other

Lien migrans
Perisplenitis
Splenic:
- abscess
- atrophy
- cyst
- fibrosis
- infarction
- rupture, nontraumatic

Splenitis
Wandering spleen

EXCLUDES *bilharzial splenic fibrosis (120.0-120.9)*
hepatolienal fibrosis (571.5)
splenomegaly NOS (789.2)

289.6 Familial polycythemia

Familial:
- benign polycythemia
- erythrocytosis

DEF: Elevated number of red blood cells.

289.7 Methemoglobinemia

Congenital NADH [DPNH]-methemoglobin-reductase deficiency
Hemoglobin M [Hb-M] disease
Methemoglobinemia:
- NOS
- acquired (with sulfhemoglobinemia)
- hereditary
- toxic

Stokvis' disease
Sulfhemoglobinemia

Use additional E code to identify cause

DEF: Presence in the blood of methemoglobin, a chemically altered form of hemoglobin; causes cyanosis, headache, dizziness, ataxia dyspnea, tachycardia, nausea, stupor, coma, and, rarely, death.

✓5th **289.8 Other specified diseases of blood and blood-forming organs**

AHA: 4Q, '03, 56; 1Q, '02, 16; 2Q, '89, 8; M-A, '87, 12

DEF: Hypercoagulable states: a group of inherited or acquired abnormalities of specific proteins and anticoagulant factors; also called thromboembolic states or thrombotic disorders, these disorders result in the abnormal development of blood clots.

289.81 Primary hypercoagulable state

Activated protein C resistance
Antithrombin III deficiency
Factor V Leiden mutation
Lupus anticoagulant
Protein C deficiency
Protein S deficiency
Prothrombin gene mutation

DEF: Activated protein C resistance: decreased effectiveness of protein C to degrade factor V, necessary to inhibit clotting cascade; also called Factor V Leiden mutation.

DEF: Antithrombin III deficiency: deficiency in plasma antithrombin III one of six naturally occurring antithrombins that limit coagulation.

DEF: Factor V Leiden mutation: also called activated protein C resistance.

DEF: Lupus anticoagulant: deficiency in a circulating anticoagulant that inhibits the conversion of prothrombin into thrombin; autoimmune antibodies induce procoagulant surfaces in platelets; also called anti-phospholipid syndrome.

DEF: Protein C deficiency: deficiency of activated protein C which functions to bring the blood-clotting process into balance; same outcome as factor V Leiden mutation.

DEF: Protein S deficiency: similar to protein C deficiency; protein S is a vitamin K dependent cofactor in the activation of protein C.

DEF: Prothrombin gene mutation: increased levels of prothrombin, or factor II, a plasma protein that is converted to thrombin, which acts upon fibrinogen to form the fibrin.

289.82 Secondary hypercoagulable state

EXCLUDES ▶*heparin-induced thrombocytopenia (HIT) (289.84)*◀

289.83 Myelofibrosis

Myelofibrosis NOS
Secondary myelofibrosis

Code first the underlying disorder, such as:
malignant neoplasm of breast (174.0-174.9, 175.0-175.9)

▶Use additional code for associated therapy-related myelodysplastic syndrome, if applicable (238.72, 238.73)

Use additional external cause code if due to anti neoplastic chemotherapy (E933.1)◀

EXCLUDES *idiopathic myelofibrosis (238.76)*
leukoerythroblastic anemia (284.2)
myelofibrosis with myeloid metaplasia (238.76)
myelophthisic anemia (284.2)
myelophthisis (284.2)
primary myelofibrosis (238.76)

AHA: 4Q, '06, 73

DEF: A progressive bone marrow disease characterized by the replacement of bone marrow with the overgrowth of neoplastic stem cells and fibrotic tissue, also progressive anemia and enlarged spleen.

● **289.84 Heparin-induced thrombocytopenia [HIT]**

289.89 Other specified diseases of blood and blood-forming organs

Hypergammaglobulinemia
Pseudocholinesterase deficiency

289.9 Unspecified diseases of blood and blood-forming organs

Blood dyscrasia NOS
Erythroid hyperplasia

AHA: M-A, '85, 14

5. MENTAL DISORDERS (290-319)

PSYCHOSES (290-299)

EXCLUDES *mental retardation (317-319)*

ORGANIC PSYCHOTIC CONDITIONS (290-294)

INCLUDES psychotic organic brain syndrome

EXCLUDES *nonpsychotic syndromes of organic etiology (310.0-310.9)*
psychoses classifiable to 295-298 and without impairment of orientation, comprehension, calculation, learning capacity, and judgment, but associated with physical disease, injury, or condition affecting the brain [eg., following childbirth] (295.0-298.8)

✓4th **290 Dementias**

Code first the associated neurological condition

EXCLUDES *dementia due to alcohol (291.0-291.2)*
dementia due to drugs (292.82)
dementia not classified as senile, presenile, or arteriosclerotic (294.10-294.11)
psychoses classifiable to 295-298 occurring in the senium without dementia or delirium (295.0-298.8)
senility with mental changes of nonpsychotic severity (310.1)
transient organic psychotic conditions (293.0-293.9)

290.0 Senile dementia, uncomplicated A

Senile dementia:
NOS
simple type

EXCLUDES *mild memory disturbances, not amounting to dementia, associated with senile brain disease (310.1)*
senile dementia with:
delirium or confusion (290.3)
delusional [paranoid] features (290.20)
depressive features (290.21)

AHA: 4Q, '99, 4

✓5th **290.1 Presenile dementia**

Brain syndrome with presenile brain disease

EXCLUDES *arteriosclerotic dementia (290.40-290.43)*
dementia associated with other cerebral conditions (294.10-294.11)

AHA: N-D, '84, 20

290.10 Presenile dementia, uncomplicated A

Presenile dementia:
NOS
simple type

290.11 Presenile dementia with delirium A

Presenile dementia with acute confusional state

AHA: 1Q, '88, 3

290.12 Presenile dementia with delusional features A

Presenile dementia, paranoid type

290.13 Presenile dementia with depressive features A

Presenile dementia, depressed type

✓5th **290.2 Senile dementia with delusional or depressive features**

EXCLUDES *senile dementia:*
NOS (290.0)
with delirium and/or confusion (290.3)

290.20 Senile dementia with delusional features A

Senile dementia, paranoid type
Senile psychosis NOS

290.21 Senile dementia with depressive features A

290.3 Senile dementia with delirium A

Senile dementia with acute confusional state

EXCLUDES *senile:*
dementia NOS (290.0)
psychosis NOS (290.20)

✓5th **290.4 Vascular dementia**

Multi-infarct dementia or psychosis

Use additional code to identify cerebral atherosclerosis (437.0)

EXCLUDES *suspected cases with no clear evidence of arteriosclerosis (290.9)*

AHA: 1Q, '88, 3

290.40 Vascular dementia, uncomplicated A

Arteriosclerotic dementia:
NOS
simple type

290.41 Vascular dementia with delirium A

Arteriosclerotic dementia with acute confusional state

290.42 Vascular dementia with delusions A

Arteriosclerotic dementia, paranoid type

290.43 Vascular dementia with depressed mood A

Arteriosclerotic dementia, depressed type

290.8 Other specified senile psychotic conditions

Presbyophrenic psychosis

290.9 Unspecified senile psychotic condition A

✓4th **291 Alcohol induced mental disorders**

EXCLUDES *alcoholism without psychosis (303.0-303.9)*

AHA: 1Q, '88, 3; S-O, '86, 3

291.0 Alcohol withdrawal delirium

Alcoholic delirium
Delirium tremens

EXCLUDES *alcohol withdrawal (291.81)*

AHA: 2Q, '91, 11

291.1 Alcohol induced persisting amnestic disorder

Alcoholic polyneuritic psychosis
Korsakoff's psychosis, alcoholic
Wernicke-Korsakoff syndrome (alcoholic)

AHA: 1Q, '88, 3

DEF: Prominent and lasting reduced memory span, disordered time appreciation and confabulation, occurring in alcoholics, as sequel to acute alcoholic psychosis.

291.2 Alcohol induced persisting dementia

Alcoholic dementia NOS
Alcoholism associated with dementia NOS
Chronic alcoholic brain syndrome

291.3 Alcohol induced psychotic disorder with hallucinations

Alcoholic:
hallucinosis (acute)
psychosis with hallucinosis

EXCLUDES *alcohol withdrawal with delirium (291.0)*
schizophrenia (295.0-295.9) and paranoid states (297.0-297.9) taking the form of chronic hallucinosis with clear consciousness in an alcoholic

AHA: 2Q, '91, 11

DEF: Psychosis lasting less than six months with slight or no clouding of consciousness in which auditory hallucinations predominate.

291.4 Idiosyncratic alcohol intoxication
Pathologic:
alcohol intoxication
drunkenness
EXCLUDES *acute alcohol intoxication (305.0)*
in alcoholism (303.0)
simple drunkenness (305.0)

DEF: Unique behavioral patterns, like belligerence, after intake of relatively small amounts of alcohol; behavior not due to excess consumption.

291.5 Alcohol induced psychotic disorder with delusions
Alcoholic:
paranoia
psychosis, paranoid type
EXCLUDES *nonalcoholic paranoid states (297.0-297.9)*
schizophrenia, paranoid type (295.3)

✓5th **291.8 Other specified alcohol induced mental disorders**
AHA: 3Q, '94, 13; J-A, '85, 10

291.81 Alcohol withdrawal
Alcohol:
abstinence syndrome or symptoms
withdrawal syndrome or symptoms
EXCLUDES *alcohol withdrawal:*
delirium (291.0)
hallucinosis (291.3)
delirium tremens (291.0)
AHA: 4Q, '96, 28; 2Q, '91, 11

291.82 Alcohol induced sleep disorders
Alcohol induced circadian rhythm sleep disorders
Alcohol induced hypersomnia
Alcohol induced insomnia
Alcohol induced parasomnia

291.89 Other
Alcohol induced anxiety disorder
Alcohol induced mood disorder
Alcohol induced sexual dysfunction

291.9 Unspecified alcohol induced mental disorders
Alcoholic:
mania NOS
psychosis NOS
Alcoholism (chronic) with psychosis
Alcohol related disorder NOS

✓4th **292 Drug induced mental disorders**
INCLUDES organic brain syndrome associated with consumption of drugs
Use additional code for any associated drug dependence (304.0-304.9)
Use additional E code to identify drug
AHA: 3Q, '04, 8; 2Q, '91, 11; S-O, '86, 3

292.0 Drug withdrawal
Drug:
abstinence syndrome or symptoms
withdrawal syndrome or symptoms
AHA: 1Q, '97, 12; 1Q, '88, 3

✓5th **292.1 Drug induced psychotic disorders**

292.11 Drug induced psychotic disorder with delusions
Paranoid state induced by drugs

292.12 Drug induced psychotic disorder with hallucinations
Hallucinatory state induced by drugs
EXCLUDES *states following LSD or other hallucinogens, lasting only a few days or less ["bad trips"] (305.3)*

292.2 Pathological drug intoxication
Drug reaction:
NOS
idiosyncratic
pathologic
} resulting in brief psychotic states
EXCLUDES *expected brief psychotic reactions to hallucinogens ["bad trips"] (305.3)*
physiological side-effects of drugs (e.g., dystonias)

✓5th **292.8 Other specified drug induced mental disorders**

292.81 Drug induced delirium
AHA: 1Q, '88, 3

292.82 Drug induced persisting dementia

292.83 Drug induced persisting amnestic disorder

292.84 Drug induced mood disorder
Depressive state induced by drugs

292.85 Drug induced sleep disorders
Drug induced circadian rhythm sleep disorder
Drug induced hypersomnia
Drug induced insomnia
Drug induced parasomnia

292.89 Other
Drug induced anxiety disorder
Drug induced organic personality syndrome
Drug induced sexual dysfunction
Drug intoxication

292.9 Unspecified drug induced mental disorder
Drug related disorder NOS
Organic psychosis NOS due to or associated with drugs

✓4th **293 Transient mental disorders due to conditions classified elsewhere**
INCLUDES transient organic mental disorders not associated with alcohol or drugs
Code first the associated physical or neurological condition
EXCLUDES *confusional state or delirium superimposed on senile dementia (290.3)*
dementia due to:
alcohol (291.0-291.9)
arteriosclerosis (290.40-290.43)
drugs (292.82)
senility (290.0)

293.0 Delirium due to conditions classified elsewhere
Acute:
confusional state
infective psychosis
organic reaction
posttraumatic organic psychosis
psycho-organic syndrome
Acute psychosis associated with endocrine, metabolic, or cerebrovascular disorder
Epileptic:
confusional state
twilight state
AHA: 1Q, '88, 3

293.1 Subacute delirium
Subacute:
confusional state
infective psychosis
organic reaction
posttraumatic organic psychosis
psycho-organic syndrome
psychosis associated with endocrine or metabolic disorder

✓5th **293.8 Other specified transient mental disorders due to conditions classified elsewhere**

293.81 Psychotic disorder with delusions in conditions classified elsewhere
Transient organic psychotic condition, paranoid type

293.82 Psychotic disorder with hallucinations in conditions classified elsewhere
Transient organic psychotic condition, hallucinatory type

293.83 Mood disorder in conditions classified elsewhere
Transient organic psychotic condition, depressive type

293.84 Anxiety disorder in conditions classified elsewhere
AHA: 4Q, '96, 29

293.89 Other
Catatonic disorder in conditions classified elsewhere

293.9 Unspecified transient mental disorder in conditions classified elsewhere
Organic psychosis:
infective NOS
posttraumatic NOS
transient NOS
Psycho-organic syndrome

✓4th **294 Persistent mental disorders due to conditions classified elsewhere**

INCLUDES organic psychotic brain syndromes (chronic), not elsewhere classified

AHA: M-A, '85, 12

294.0 Amnestic disorder in conditions classified elsewhere
Korsakoff's psychosis or syndrome (nonalcoholic)
Code first underlying condition
EXCLUDES *alcoholic:*
amnestic syndrome (291.1)
Korsakoff's psychosis (291.1)

✓5th **294.1 Dementia in conditions classified elsewhere**
Dementia of the Alzheimer's type
Code first any underlying physical condition, as:
dementia in:
Alzheimer's disease (331.0)
cerebral lipidoses (330.1)
dementia with Lewy bodies (331.82)
dementia with Parkinsonism (331.82)
epilepsy (345.0-345.9)
frontal dementia (331.19)
frontotemporal dementia (331.19)
general paresis [syphilis] (094.1)
hepatolenticular degeneration (275.1)
Huntington's chorea (333.4)
Jakob-Creutzfeldt disease (046.1)
multiple sclerosis (340)
Pick's disease of the brain (331.11)
polyarteritis nodosa (446.0)
syphilis (094.1)

EXCLUDES *dementia:*
arteriosclerotic (290.40-290.43)
presenile (290.10-290.13)
senile (290.0)
epileptic psychosis NOS (294.8)

AHA: 4Q, '00, 40; 1Q, '99, 14; N-D, '85, 5

294.10 Dementia in conditions classified elsewhere without behavioral disturbance
Dementia in conditions classified elsewhere NOS

294.11 Dementia in conditions classified elsewhere with behavioral disturbance
Aggressive behavior
Combative behavior
Violent behavior
Wandering off
AHA: 4Q, '00, 41

294.8 Other persistent mental disorders due to conditions classified elsewhere
Amnestic disorder NOS
Dementia NOS
Epileptic psychosis NOS
Mixed paranoid and affective organic psychotic states
Use additional code for associated epilepsy (345.0-345.9)
EXCLUDES *mild memory disturbances, not amounting to dementia (310.1)*
AHA: 3Q, '03, 14; 1Q, '88, 5

294.9 Unspecified persistent mental disorders due to conditions classified elsewhere
Cognitive disorder NOS
Organic psychosis (chronic)
AHA: 2Q, '07, 4

OTHER PSYCHOSES (295-299)

Use additional code to identify any associated physical disease, injury, or condition affecting the brain with psychoses classifiable to 295-298

✓4th **295 Schizophrenic disorders**

INCLUDES schizophrenia of the types described in 295.0-295.9 occurring in children

EXCLUDES *childhood type schizophrenia (299.9)*
infantile autism (299.0)

The following fifth-digit subclassification is for use with category 295:
0 unspecified
1 subchronic
2 chronic
3 subchronic with acute exacerbation
4 chronic with acute exacerbation
5 in remission

DEF: Group of disorders with disturbances in thought (delusions, hallucinations), mood (blunted, flattened, inappropriate affect), sense of self, relationship to world; also bizarre, purposeless behavior, repetitious activity, or inactivity.

§ ✓5th **295.0 Simple type**
[0-5]
Schizophrenia simplex
EXCLUDES *latent schizophrenia (295.5)*

§ ✓5th **295.1 Disorganized type**
[0-5]
Hebephrenia
Hebephrenic type schizophrenia
DEF: Inappropriate behavior; results in extreme incoherence and disorganization of time, place and sense of social appropriateness; withdrawal from routine social interaction may occur.

§ ✓5th **295.2 Catatonic type**
[0-5]
Catatonic (schizophrenia):
agitation
excitation
excited type
stupor
withdrawn type
Schizophrenic:
catalepsy
catatonia
flexibilitas cerea
DEF: Extreme changes in motor activity; one extreme is decreased response or reaction to the environment and the other is spontaneous activity.

§ Requires fifth-digit. Valid digits are in [brackets] under each code. See category 295 for codes and definitions.

§ ✓5th **295.3 Paranoid type**
[0-5]
Paraphrenic schizophrenia

EXCLUDES *involutional paranoid state (297.2)*
paranoia (297.1)
paraphrenia (297.2)

DEF: Preoccupied with delusional suspicions and auditory hallucinations related to single theme; usually hostile, grandiose, overly religious, occasionally hypochondriacal.

§ ✓5th **295.4 Schizophreniform disorder**
[0-5]
Oneirophrenia
Schizophreniform:
attack
psychosis, confusional type

EXCLUDES *acute forms of schizophrenia of:*
catatonic type (295.2)
hebephrenic type (295.1)
paranoid type (295.3)
simple type (295.0)
undifferentiated type (295.8)

§ ✓5th **295.5 Latent schizophrenia**
[0-5]
Latent schizophrenic reaction
Schizophrenia:
borderline
incipient
prepsychotic
prodromal
pseudoneurotic
pseudopsychopathic

EXCLUDES *schizoid personality (301.20-301.22)*

AHA: For code 295.50: 1Q, '06, 10

§ ✓5th **295.6 Residual type**
[0-5]
Chronic undifferentiated schizophrenia
Restzustand (schizophrenic)
Schizophrenic residual state

AHA: For code 295.62: 4Q, '06, 78

§ ✓5th **295.7 Schizoaffective disorder**
[0-5]
Cyclic schizophrenia
Mixed schizophrenic and affective psychosis
Schizo-affective psychosis
Schizophreniform psychosis, affective type

§ ✓5th **295.8 Other specified types of schizophrenia**
[0-5]
Acute (undifferentiated) schizophrenia
Atypical schizophrenia
Cenesthopathic schizophrenia

EXCLUDES *infantile autism (299.0)*

§ ✓5th **295.9 Unspecified schizophrenia**
[0-5]
Schizophrenia:
NOS
mixed NOS
undifferentiated NOS
undifferentiated type
Schizophrenic reaction NOS
Schizophreniform psychosis NOS

AHA: 3Q, '95, 6

✓4th **296 Episodic mood disorders**

INCLUDES episodic affective disorders

EXCLUDES *neurotic depression (300.4)*
reactive depressive psychosis (298.0)
reactive excitation (298.1)

The following fifth-digit subclassification is for use with categories 296.0-296.6:

0 unspecified
1 mild
2 moderate
3 severe, without mention of psychotic behavior
4 severe, specified as with psychotic behavior
5 in partial or unspecified remission
6 in full remission

AHA: M-A, '85, 14

§ ✓5th **296.0 Bipolar I disorder, single manic episode**
[0-6]
Hypomania (mild) NOS
Hypomanic psychosis
Mania (momopolar) NOS
Manic-depressive psychosis or reaction:
hypomanic
manic
} single episode or unspecified

EXCLUDES *circular type, if there was a previous attack of depression (296.4)*

DEF: Mood disorder identified by hyperactivity; may show extreme agitation or exaggerated excitability; speech and thought processes may be accelerated.

§ ✓5th **296.1 Manic disorder, recurrent episode**
[0-6]
Any condition classifiable to 296.0, stated to be recurrent

EXCLUDES *circular type, if there was a previous attack of depression (296.4)*

§ ✓5th **296.2 Major depressive disorder, single episode**
[0-6]
Depressive psychosis
Endogenous depression
Involutional melancholia
Manic-depressive psychosis or reaction, depressed type
Monopolar depression
Psychotic depression
} single episode or unspecified

EXCLUDES *circular type, if previous attack was of manic type (296.5)*
depression NOS (311)
reactive depression (neurotic) (300.4)
psychotic (298.0)

DEF: Mood disorder that produces depression; may exhibit as sadness, low self-esteem, or guilt feelings; other manifestations may be withdrawal from friends and family; interrupted sleep.

§ ✓5th **296.3 Major depressive disorder, recurrent episode**
[0-6]
Any condition classifiable to 296.2, stated to be recurrent

EXCLUDES *circular type, if previous attack was of manic type (296.5)*
depression NOS (311)
reactive depression (neurotic) (300.4)
psychotic (298.0)

§ ✓5th **296.4 Bipolar I disorder, most recent episode (or current) manic**
[0-6]
Bipolar disorder, now manic
Manic-depressive psychosis, circular type but currently manic

EXCLUDES *brief compensatory or rebound mood swings (296.99)*

§ ✓5th **296.5 Bipolar I disorder, most recent episode (or current) depressed**
[0-6]
Bipolar disorder, now depressed
Manic-depressive psychosis, circular type but currently depressed

EXCLUDES *brief compensatory or rebound mood swings (296.99)*

§ ✓5th **296.6 Bipolar I disorder, most recent episode (or current) mixed**
[0-6]
Manic-depressive psychosis, circular type, mixed

296.7 Bipolar I disorder, most recent episode (or current) unspecified
Atypical bipolar affective disorder NOS
Manic-depressive psychosis, circular type, current condition not specified as either manic or depressive

DEF: Manic-depressive disorder referred to as bipolar because of the mood range from manic to depressive.

§ Requires fifth-digit. Valid digits are in [brackets] under each code. See appropriate category for codes and definitions.

5th **296.8 Other and unspecified bipolar disorders**

296.80 Bipolar disorder, unspecified
Bipolar disorder NOS
Manic-depressive:
reaction NOS
syndrome NOS

296.81 Atypical manic disorder

296.82 Atypical depressive disorder

296.89 Other
Bipolar II disorder
Manic-depressive psychosis, mixed type

5th **296.9 Other and unspecified episodic mood disorder**
EXCLUDES *psychogenic affective psychoses (298.0-298.8)*

296.90 Unspecified episodic mood disorder
Affective psychosis NOS
Melancholia NOS
Mood disorder NOS
AHA: M-A, '85, 14

296.99 Other specified episodic mood disorder
Mood swings:
brief compensatory
rebound

4th **297 Delusional disorders**
INCLUDES paranoid disorders
EXCLUDES *acute paranoid reaction (298.3)*
alcoholic jealousy or paranoid state (291.5)
paranoid schizophrenia (295.3)

297.0 Paranoid state, simple

297.1 Delusional disorder
Chronic paranoid psychosis
Sander's disease
Systematized delusions
EXCLUDES *paranoid personality disorder (301.0)*

297.2 Paraphrenia
Involutional paranoid state
Late paraphrenia
Paraphrenia (involutional)
DEF: Paranoid schizophrenic disorder that persists over a prolonged period but does not distort personality despite persistent delusions.

297.3 Shared psychotic disorder
Folie à deux
Induced psychosis or paranoid disorder
DEF: Mental disorder two people share; first person with the delusional disorder convinces second person because of a close relationship and shared experiences to accept the delusions.

297.8 Other specified paranoid states
Paranoia querulans
Sensitiver Beziehungswahn
EXCLUDES *acute paranoid reaction or state (298.3)*
senile paranoid state (290.20)

297.9 Unspecified paranoid state
Paranoid:
disorder NOS
psychosis NOS
reaction NOS
state NOS
AHA: J-A, '85, 9

4th **298 Other nonorganic psychoses**
INCLUDES psychotic conditions due to or provoked by:
emotional stress
environmental factors as major part of etiology

298.0 Depressive type psychosis
Psychogenic depressive psychosis
Psychotic reactive depression
Reactive depressive psychosis
EXCLUDES *manic-depressive psychosis, depressed type (296.2-296.3)*
neurotic depression (300.4)
reactive depression NOS (300.4)

298.1 Excitative type psychosis
Acute hysterical psychosis
Psychogenic excitation
Reactive excitation
EXCLUDES *manic-depressive psychosis, manic type (296.0-296.1)*
DEF: Affective disorder similar to manic-depressive psychosis, in the manic phase, seemingly brought on by stress.

298.2 Reactive confusion
Psychogenic confusion
Psychogenic twilight state
EXCLUDES *acute confusional state (293.0)*
DEF: Confusion, disorientation, cloudiness in consciousness; brought on by severe emotional upheaval.

298.3 Acute paranoid reaction
Acute psychogenic paranoid psychosis
Bouffée délirante
EXCLUDES *paranoid states (297.0-297.9)*

298.4 Psychogenic paranoid psychosis
Protracted reactive paranoid psychosis

298.8 Other and unspecified reactive psychosis
Brief psychotic disorder
Brief reactive psychosis NOS
Hysterical psychosis
Psychogenic psychosis NOS
Psychogenic stupor
EXCLUDES *acute hysterical psychosis (298.1)*

298.9 Unspecified psychosis
Atypical psychosis
Psychosis NOS
Psychotic disorder NOS
AHA: 3Q, '06, 22

4th **299 Pervasive developmental disorders**
EXCLUDES *adult type psychoses occurring in childhood, as:*
affective disorders (296.0-296.9)
manic-depressive disorders (296.0-296.9)
schizophrenia (295.0-295.9)

The following fifth-digit subclassification is for use with category 299:
0 current or active state
1 residual state

§ 5th **299.0 Autistic disorder**
[0-1]
Childhood autism
Infantile psychosis
Kanner's syndrome
EXCLUDES *disintegrative psychosis (299.1)*
Heller's syndrome (299.1)
schizophrenic syndrome of childhood (299.9)
DEF: Severe mental disorder of children, results in impaired social behavior; abnormal development of communicative skills, appears to be unaware of the need for emotional support and offers little emotional response to family members.

§ 5th **299.1 Childhood disintegrative disorder**
[0-1]
Heller's syndrome
Use additional code to identify any associated neurological disorder
EXCLUDES *infantile autism (299.0)*
schizophrenic syndrome of childhood (299.9)
DEF: Mental disease of children identified by impaired development of reciprocal social skills, verbal and nonverbal communication skills, imaginative play.

§ Requires fifth-digit. Valid digits are in [brackets] under each code. See category 299 for codes and definitions.

§ ✓5th **299.8 Other specified pervasive developmental disorders**
[0-1]
Asperger's disorder
Atypical childhood psychosis
Borderline psychosis of childhood
EXCLUDES *simple stereotypes without psychotic disturbance (307.3)*

§ ✓5th **299.9 Unspecified pervasive developmental disorder**
[0-1]
Child psychosis NOS
Pervasive developmental disorder NOS
Schizophrenia, childhood type NOS
Schizophrenic syndrome of childhood NOS
EXCLUDES *schizophrenia of adult type occurring in childhood (295.0-295.9)*

NEUROTIC DISORDERS, PERSONALITY DISORDERS, AND OTHER NONPSYCHOTIC MENTAL DISORDERS (300-316)

✓4th **300 Anxiety, dissociative and somatoform disorders**

✓5th **300.0 Anxiety states**

EXCLUDES *anxiety in:*
acute stress reaction (308.0)
transient adjustment reaction (309.24)
neurasthenia (300.5)
psychophysiological disorders (306.0-306.9)
separation anxiety (309.21)

DEF: Mental disorder characterized by anxiety and avoidance be-havior not particularly related to any specific situation or stimulus; symptoms include emotional instability, apprehension, fatigue.

300.00 Anxiety state, unspecified
Anxiety:
neurosis
reaction
state (neurotic)
Atypical anxiety disorder
AHA: 1Q, '02, 6

300.01 Panic disorder without agoraphobia
Panic:
attack
state
EXCLUDES *panic disorder with agoraphobia (300.21)*
DEF: Neurotic disorder characterized by recurrent panic or anxiety, apprehension, fear or terror; symptoms include shortness of breath, palpitations, dizziness, faintness or shakiness; fear of dying may persist or fear of other morbid consequences.

300.02 Generalized anxiety disorder

300.09 Other

✓5th **300.1 Dissociative, conversion and factitious disorders**

EXCLUDES *adjustment reaction (309.0-309.9)*
anorexia nervosa (307.1)
gross stress reaction (308.0-308.9)
hysterical personality (301.50-301.59)
psychophysiologic disorders (306.0-306.9)

300.10 Hysteria, unspecified

300.11 Conversion disorder
Astasia-abasia, hysterical
Conversion hysteria or reaction
Hysterical:
blindness
deafness
paralysis
AHA: N-D, '85, 15
DEF: Mental disorder that impairs physical functions with no physiological basis; sensory motor symptoms include seizures, paralysis, temporary blindness; increase in stress or avoidance of unpleasant responsibilities may precipitate.

300.12 Dissociative amnesia
Hysterical amnesia

300.13 Dissociative fugue
Hysterical fugue
DEF: Dissociative hysteria; identified by loss of memory, flight from familiar surroundings; conscious activity is not associated with perception of surroundings, no later memory of episode.

300.14 Dissociative identity disorder

300.15 Dissociative disorder or reaction, unspecified
DEF: Hysterical neurotic episode; sudden but temporary changes in perceived identity, memory, consciousness, segregated memory patterns exist separate from dominant personality.

300.16 Factitious disorder with predominantly psychological signs and symptoms
Compensation neurosis
Ganser's syndrome, hysterical
DEF: A disorder characterized by the purposeful assumption of mental illness symptoms; the symptoms are not real, possibly representing what the patient imagines mental illness to be like, and are acted out more often when another person is present.

300.19 Other and unspecified factitious illness
Factitious disorder (with combined psychological and physical signs and symptoms) (with predominantly physical signs and symptoms) NOS
EXCLUDES *multiple operations or hospital addiction syndrome (301.51)*

✓5th **300.2 Phobic disorders**

EXCLUDES *anxiety state not associated with a specific situation or object (300.00-300.09)*
obsessional phobias (300.3)

300.20 Phobia, unspecified
Anxiety-hysteria NOS
Phobia NOS

300.21 Agoraphobia with panic disorder
Fear of:
open spaces } with panic attacks
streets } with panic attacks
travel } with panic attacks
Panic disorder with agoraphobia
EXCLUDES *agoraphobia without panic disorder (300.22)*
panic disorder without agoraphobia (300.01)

300.22 Agoraphobia without mention of panic attacks
Any condition classifiable to 300.21 without mention of panic attacks

§ Requires fifth-digit. Valid digits are in [brackets] under each code. See category 299 for codes and definitions.

300.23 Social phobia
Fear of:
eating in public
public speaking
washing in public

300.29 Other isolated or specific phobias
Acrophobia
Animal phobias
Claustrophobia
Fear of crowds

300.3 Obsessive-compulsive disorders
Anancastic neurosis
Compulsive neurosis
Obsessional phobia [any]

EXCLUDES *obsessive-compulsive symptoms occurring in:*
endogenous depression (296.2-296.3)
organic states (eg., encephalitis)
schizophrenia (295.0-295.9)

300.4 Dysthymic disorder
Anxiety depression
Depression with anxiety
Depressive reaction
Neurotic depressive state
Reactive depression

EXCLUDES *adjustment reaction with depressive symptoms (309.0-309.1)*
depression NOS (311)
manic-depressive psychosis, depressed type (296.2-296.3)
reactive depressive psychosis (298.0)

DEF: Depression without psychosis; less severe depression related to personal change or unexpected circumstances; also referred to as "reactional depression."

300.5 Neurasthenia
Fatigue neurosis
Nervous debility
Psychogenic:
asthenia
general fatigue

Use additional code to identify any associated physical disorder

EXCLUDES *anxiety state (300.00-300.09)*
neurotic depression (300.4)
psychophysiological disorders (306.0-306.9)
specific nonpsychotic mental disorders following organic brain damage (310.0-310.9)

DEF: Physical and mental symptoms caused primarily by what is known as mental exhaustion; symptoms include chronic weakness, fatigue.

300.6 Depersonalization disorder
Derealization (neurotic)
Neurotic state with depersonalization episode

EXCLUDES *depersonalization associated with:*
anxiety (300.00-300.09)
depression (300.4)
manic-depressive disorder or psychosis (296.0-296.9)
schizophrenia (295.0-295.9)

DEF: Dissociative disorder characterized by feelings of strangeness about self or body image; symptoms include dizziness, anxiety, fear of insanity, loss of reality of surroundings.

300.7 Hypochondriasis
Body dysmorphic disorder

EXCLUDES *hypochondriasis in:*
hysteria (300.10-300.19)
manic depressive psychosis, depressed type (296.2-296.3)
neurasthenia (300.5)
obsessional disorder (300.3)
schizophrenia (295.0-295.9)

✓5th **300.8 Somatoform disorders**

300.81 Somatization disorder
Briquet's disorder
Severe somatoform disorder

300.82 Undifferentiated somatoform disorder
Atypical somatoform disorder
Somatoform disorder NOS

AHA: 4Q, '96, 29

DEF: Disorders in which patients have symptoms that suggest an organic disease but no evidence of physical disorder after repeated testing.

300.89 Other somatoform disorders
Occupational neurosis, including writers' cramp
Psychasthenia
Psychasthenic neurosis

300.9 Unspecified nonpsychotic mental disorder
Psychoneurosis NOS

✓4th **301 Personality disorders**

INCLUDES character neurosis

Use additional code to identify any associated neurosis or psychosis, or physical condition

EXCLUDES *nonpsychotic personality disorder associated with organic brain syndromes (310.0-310.9)*

301.0 Paranoid personality disorder
Fanatic personality
Paranoid personality (disorder)
Paranoid traits

EXCLUDES *acute paranoid reaction (298.3)*
alcoholic paranoia (291.5)
paranoid schizophrenia (295.3)
paranoid states (297.0-297.9)

AHA: J-A, '85, 9

✓5th **301.1 Affective personality disorder**

EXCLUDES *affective psychotic disorders (296.0-296.9)*
neurasthenia (300.5)
neurotic depression (300.4)

301.10 Affective personality disorder, unspecified

301.11 Chronic hypomanic personality disorder
Chronic hypomanic disorder
Hypomanic personality

301.12 Chronic depressive personality disorder
Chronic depressive disorder
Depressive character or personality

301.13 Cyclothymic disorder
Cycloid personality
Cyclothymia
Cyclothymic personality

✓5th **301.2 Schizoid personality disorder**

EXCLUDES *schizophrenia (295.0-295.9)*

301.20 Schizoid personality disorder, unspecified

301.21 Introverted personality

301.22 Schizotypal personality disorder

301.3 Explosive personality disorder
Aggressive:
personality
reaction
Aggressiveness
Emotional instability (excessive)
Pathological emotionality
Quarrelsomeness

EXCLUDES *dyssocial personality (301.7)*
hysterical neurosis (300.10-300.19)

301.4 Obsessive-compulsive personality disorder
Anancastic personality
Obsessional personality
EXCLUDES *obsessive-compulsive disorder (300.3)*
phobic state (300.20-300.29)

✓5th **301.5 Histrionic personality disorder**
EXCLUDES *hysterical neurosis (300.10-300.19)*
DEF: Extreme emotional behavior, often theatrical; often concerned about own appeal; may demand attention, exhibit seductive behavior.

301.50 Histrionic personality disorder, unspecified
Hysterical personality NOS

301.51 Chronic factitious illness with physical symptoms
Hospital addiction syndrome
Multiple operations syndrome
Munchausen syndrome

301.59 Other histrionic personality disorder
Personality:
emotionally unstable
labile
psychoinfantile

301.6 Dependent personality disorder
Asthenic personality
Inadequate personality
Passive personality
EXCLUDES *neurasthenia (300.5)*
passive-aggressive personality (301.84)
DEF: Overwhelming feeling of helplessness; fears of abandonment may persist; difficulty in making personal decisions without confirmation by others; low self-esteem due to irrational sensitivity to criticism.

301.7 Antisocial personality disorder
Amoral personality
Asocial personality
Dyssocial personality
Personality disorder with predominantly sociopathic or asocial manifestation
EXCLUDES *disturbance of conduct without specifiable personality disorder (312.0-312.9)*
explosive personality (301.3)
AHA: S-0, '84, 16
DEF: Continuous antisocial behavior that violates rights of others; social traits include extreme aggression, total disregard for traditional social rules.

✓5th **301.8 Other personality disorders**

301.81 Narcissistic personality disorder
DEF: Grandiose fantasy or behavior, lack of social empathy, hypersensitive to the lack of others' judgment, exploits others; also sense of entitlement to have expectations met, need for continual admiration.

301.82 Avoidant personality disorder
DEF: Personality disorder marked by feelings of social inferiority; sensitivity to criticism, emotionally restrained due to fear of rejection.

301.83 Borderline personality disorder
DEF: Personality disorder characterized by unstable moods, self-image, and interpersonal relationships; uncontrolled anger, impulsive and self-destructive acts, fears of abandonment, feelings of emptiness and boredom, recurrent suicide threats or self-mutilation.

301.84 Passive-aggressive personality
DEF: Pattern of procrastination and refusal to meet standards; introduce own obstacles to success and exploit failure.

301.89 Other
Personality:
eccentric
"haltlose" type
immature
masochistic
psychoneurotic
EXCLUDES *psychoinfantile personality (301.59)*

301.9 Unspecified personality disorder
Pathological personality NOS
Personality disorder NOS
Psychopathic:
constitutional state
personality (disorder)

✓4th **302 Sexual and gender identity disorders**
EXCLUDES *sexual disorder manifest in:*
organic brain syndrome (290.0-294.9, 310.0-310.9)
psychosis (295.0-298.9)

302.0 Ego-dystonic sexual orientation
Ego-dystonic lesbianism
Sexual orientation conflict disorder
EXCLUDES *homosexual pedophilia (302.2)*

302.1 Zoophilia
Bestiality
DEF: A sociodeviant disorder marked by engaging in sexual intercourse with animals.

302.2 Pedophilia
DEF: A sociodeviant condition of adults characterized by sexual activity with children.

302.3 Transvestic fetishism
EXCLUDES *trans-sexualism (302.5)*
DEF: The desire to dress in clothing of opposite sex.

302.4 Exhibitionism
DEF: Sexual deviant behavior; exposure of genitals to strangers; behavior prompted by intense sexual urges and fantasies.

✓5th **302.5 Trans-sexualism**
Sex reassignment surgery status
EXCLUDES *transvestism (302.3)*
DEF: Gender identity disturbance; overwhelming desire to change anatomic sex, due to belief that individual is a member of the opposite sex.

302.50 With unspecified sexual history

302.51 With asexual history

302.52 With homosexual history

302.53 With heterosexual history

302.6 Gender identity disorder in children
Feminism in boys
Gender identity disorder NOS
EXCLUDES *gender identity disorder in adult (302.85)*
trans-sexualism (302.50-302.53)
transvestism (302.3)

✓5th **302.7 Psychosexual dysfunction**
EXCLUDES *impotence of organic origin (607.84)*
normal transient symptoms from ruptured hymen
transient or occasional failures of erection due to fatigue, anxiety, alcohol, or drugs

302.70 Psychosexual dysfunction, unspecified
Sexual dysfunction NOS

302.71 Hypoactive sexual desire disorder
EXCLUDES *decreased sexual desire NOS (799.81)*

302.72 With inhibited sexual excitement
Female sexual arousal disorder
Frigidity
Impotence
Male erectile disorder

302.73 Female orgasmic disorder ♀

302.74 Male orgasmic disorder ♂

302.75 Premature ejaculation ♂

302.76 Dyspareunia, psychogenic ♀
DEF: Difficult or painful sex due to psychosomatic state.

302.79 With other specified psychosexual dysfunctions
Sexual aversion disorder

✓5th **302.8 Other specified psychosexual disorders**

302.81 Fetishism
DEF: Psychosexual disorder noted for intense sexual urges and arousal precipitated by fantasies; use of inanimate objects, such as clothing, to stimulate sexual arousal, orgasm.

302.82 Voyeurism
DEF: Psychosexual disorder characterized by uncontrollable impulse to observe others, without their knowledge, who are nude or engaged in sexual activity.

302.83 Sexual masochism
DEF: Psychosexual disorder noted for need to achieve sexual gratification through humiliating or hurtful acts inflicted on self.

302.84 Sexual sadism
DEF: Psychosexual disorder noted for need to achieve sexual gratification through humiliating or hurtful acts inflicted on someone else.

302.85 Gender identity disorder in adolescents or adults
Use additional code to identify sex reassignment surgery status (302.5)
EXCLUDES *gender identity disorder NOS (302.6)*
gender identity disorder in children (302.6)

302.89 Other
Frotteurism
Nymphomania
Satyriasis

302.9 Unspecified psychosexual disorder
Paraphilia NOS
Pathologic sexuality NOS
Sexual deviation NOS
Sexual disorder NOS

✓4th **303 Alcohol dependence syndrome**
Use additional code to identify any associated condition, as:
alcoholic psychoses (291.0-291.9)
drug dependence (304.0-304.9)
physical complications of alcohol, such as:
cerebral degeneration (331.7)
cirrhosis of liver (571.2)
epilepsy (345.0-345.9)
gastritis (535.3)
hepatitis (571.1)
liver damage NOS (571.3)
EXCLUDES *drunkenness NOS (305.0)*

The following fifth-digit subclassification is for use with category 303:
0 unspecified
1 continuous
2 episodic
3 in remission

AHA: 3Q, '95, 6; 2Q, '91, 9; 4Q, '88, 8; S-O, '86, 3

§ ✓5th **303.0 Acute alcoholic intoxication**
[0-3]
Acute drunkenness in alcoholism

§ ✓5th **303.9 Other and unspecified alcohol dependence**
[0-3]
Chronic alcoholism
Dipsomania
AHA: 2Q, '02, 4; 2Q, '89, 9 ; **For code 303.90:** 2Q, '07, 6

✓4th **304 Drug dependence**
EXCLUDES *nondependent abuse of drugs (305.1-305.9)*

The following fifth-digit subclassification is for use with category 304:
0 unspecified
1 continuous
2 episodic
3 in remission

AHA: 2Q, '91, 10; 4Q, '88, 8; S-O, '86, 3

§ ✓5th **304.0 Opioid type dependence**
[0-3]
Heroin
Meperidine
Methadone
Morphine
Opium
Opium alkaloids and their derivatives
Synthetics with morphine-like effects
AHA: 2Q, '06, 7

§ ✓5th **304.1 Sedative, hypnotic or anxiolytic dependence**
[0-3]
Barbiturates
Nonbarbiturate sedatives and tranquilizers with a similar effect:
chlordiazepoxide
diazepam
glutethimide
meprobamate
methaqualone

§ ✓5th **304.2 Cocaine dependence**
[0-3]
Coca leaves and derivatives

§ ✓5th **304.3 Cannabis dependence**
[0-3]
Hashish
Hemp
Marihuana

§ ✓5th **304.4 Amphetamine and other psychostimulant dependence**
[0-3]
Methylphenidate
Phenmetrazine

§ ✓5th **304.5 Hallucinogen dependence**
[0-3]
Dimethyltryptamine [DMT]
Lysergic acid diethylamide [LSD] and derivatives
Mescaline
Psilocybin

§ ✓5th **304.6 Other specified drug dependence**
[0-3]
Absinthe addiction
Glue sniffing
Inhalant dependence
Phencyclidine dependence
EXCLUDES *tobacco dependence (305.1)*

§ ✓5th **304.7 Combinations of opioid type drug with any other**
[0-3]
AHA: M-A, '86, 12

§ ✓5th **304.8 Combinations of drug dependence excluding opioid type drug**
[0-3]
AHA: M-A, '86, 12

§ ✓5th **304.9 Unspecified drug dependence**
[0-3]
Drug addiction NOS
Drug dependence NOS
AHA: For code 304.90: 4Q, '03, 103

§ Requires fifth-digit. Valid digits are in [brackets] under each code. See appropriate category for codes and definitions.

✓4th ✓5th Additional Digit Required | Unspecified Code | Other Specified Code | Manifestation Code | ►◄ Revised Text | ● New Code | ▲ Revised Code Title

✓4th 305 Nondependent abuse of drugs

Note: Includes cases where a person, for whom no other diagnosis is possible, has come under medical care because of the maladaptive effect of a drug on which he is not dependent and that he has taken on his own initiative to the detriment of his health or social functioning.

EXCLUDES *alcohol dependence syndrome (303.0-303.9)*
drug dependence (304.0-304.9)
drug withdrawal syndrome (292.0)
poisoning by drugs or medicinal substances (960.0-979.9)

The following fifth-digit subclassification is for use with codes 305.0, 305.2-305.9:

0 unspecified
1 continuous
2 episodic
3 in remission

AHA: 2Q, '91, 10; 4Q, '88, 8; S-O, '86, 3

§ ✓5th **305.0 Alcohol abuse**
[0-3]
Drunkenness NOS
Excessive drinking of alcohol NOS
"Hangover" (alcohol)
Inebriety NOS

EXCLUDES *acute alcohol intoxication in alcoholism (303.0)*
alcoholic psychoses (291.0-291.9)

AHA: 3Q, '96, 16

305.1 Tobacco use disorder
Tobacco dependence

EXCLUDES *history of tobacco use (V15.82)*
smoking complicating pregnancy (649.0)
tobacco use disorder complicating pregnancy (649.0)

AHA: 2Q, '96, 10; N-D, '84, 12

§ ✓5th **305.2 Cannabis abuse**
[0-3]

§ ✓5th **305.3 Hallucinogen abuse**
[0-3]
Acute intoxication from hallucinogens ["bad trips"]
LSD reaction

§ ✓5th **305.4 Sedative, hypnotic or anxiolytic abuse**
[0-3]

§ ✓5th **305.5 Opioid abuse**
[0-3]

§ ✓5th **305.6 Cocaine abuse**
[0-3]
AHA: 1Q, '93, 25; For code 305.60: 1Q, '05, 6

§ ✓5th **305.7 Amphetamine or related acting sympathomimetic abuse**
[0-3]
AHA: For code 305.70: 2Q, '03, 10–11

§ ✓5th **305.8 Antidepressant type abuse**
[0-3]

§ ✓5th **305.9 Other, mixed, or unspecified drug abuse**
[0-3]
Caffeine intoxication
Inhalant abuse
"Laxative habit"
Misuse of drugs NOS
Nonprescribed use of drugs or patent medicinals
Phencyclidine abuse

AHA: 3Q, '99, 20

✓4th 306 Physiological malfunction arising from mental factors

INCLUDES psychogenic:
physical symptoms } not involving tissue damage
physiological manifestations } not involving tissue damage

EXCLUDES *hysteria (300.11-300.19)*
physical symptoms secondary to a psychiatric disorder classified elsewhere
psychic factors associated with physical conditions involving tissue damage classified elsewhere (316)
specific nonpsychotic mental disorders following organic brain damage (310.0-310.9)

DEF: Functional disturbances or interruptions due to mental or psychological causes; no tissue damage sustained in these conditions.

306.0 Musculoskeletal
Psychogenic paralysis
Psychogenic torticollis

EXCLUDES *Gilles de la Tourette's syndrome (307.23)*
paralysis as hysterical or conversion reaction (300.11)
tics (307.20-307.22)

306.1 Respiratory
Psychogenic:
air hunger
cough
hiccough
hyperventilation
yawning

EXCLUDES *psychogenic asthma (316 and 493.9)*

306.2 Cardiovascular
Cardiac neurosis
Cardiovascular neurosis
Neurocirculatory asthenia
Psychogenic cardiovascular disorder

EXCLUDES *psychogenic paroxysmal tachycardia (316 and 427.2)*

AHA: J-A, '85, 14

DEF: Neurocirculatory asthenia: functional nervous and circulatory irregularities with palpitations, dyspnea, fatigue, rapid pulse, precordial pain, fear of effort, discomfort during exercise, anxiety; also called DaCosta's syndrome, Effort syndrome, Irritable or Soldier's Heart.

306.3 Skin
Psychogenic pruritus

EXCLUDES *psychogenic:*
alopecia (316 and 704.00)
dermatitis (316 and 692.9)
eczema (316 and 691.8 or 692.9)
urticaria (316 and 708.0-708.9)

§ Requires fifth-digit. Valid digits are in [brackets] under each code. See category 305 for codes and definitions.

306.4 Gastrointestinal

Aerophagy
Cyclical vomiting, psychogenic
Diarrhea, psychogenic
Nervous gastritis
Psychogenic dyspepsia

EXCLUDES *cyclical vomiting NOS (536.2)*
▶associated with migraine (346.2)◀
globus hystericus (300.11)
mucous colitis (316 and 564.9)
psychogenic:
cardiospasm (316 and 530.0)
duodenal ulcer (316 and 532.0-532.9)
gastric ulcer (316 and 531.0-531.9)
peptic ulcer NOS (316 and 533.0-533.9)
vomiting NOS (307.54)

AHA: 2Q, '89, 11

DEF: Aerophagy: excess swallowing of air, usually unconscious; related to anxiety; results in distended abdomen or belching, often interpreted by the patient as a physical disorder.

✓5th **306.5 Genitourinary**

EXCLUDES *enuresis, psychogenic (307.6)*
frigidity (302.72)
impotence (302.72)
psychogenic dyspareunia (302.76)

306.50 Psychogenic genitourinary malfunction, unspecified

306.51 Psychogenic vaginismus ♀

Functional vaginismus

DEF: Psychogenic response resulting in painful contractions of vaginal canal muscles; can be severe enough to prevent sexual intercourse.

306.52 Psychogenic dysmenorrhea ♀

306.53 Psychogenic dysuria

306.59 Other

AHA: M-A, '87, 11

306.6 Endocrine

306.7 Organs of special sense

EXCLUDES *hysterical blindness or deafness (300.11)*
psychophysical visual disturbances (368.16)

306.8 Other specified psychophysiological malfunction

Bruxism
Teeth grinding

306.9 Unspecified psychophysiological malfunction

Psychophysiologic disorder NOS
Psychosomatic disorder NOS

✓4th **307 Special symptoms or syndromes, not elsewhere classified**

Note: This category is intended for use if the psychopathology is manifested by a single specific symptom or group of symptoms which is not part of an organic illness or other mental disorder classifiable elsewhere.

EXCLUDES *those due to mental disorders classified elsewhere*
those of organic origin

307.0 Stuttering

EXCLUDES *dysphasia (784.5)*
lisping or lalling (307.9)
retarded development of speech (315.31-315.39)

307.1 Anorexia nervosa

EXCLUDES *eating disturbance NOS (307.50)*
feeding problem (783.3)
of nonorganic origin (307.59)
loss of appetite (783.0)
of nonorganic origin (307.59)

AHA: 2Q, '06, 12; 4Q, '89, 11

✓5th **307.2 Tics**

EXCLUDES *nail-biting or thumb-sucking (307.9)*
stereotypes occurring in isolation (307.3)
tics of organic origin (333.3)

DEF: Involuntary muscle response usually confined to the face, shoulders.

307.20 Tic disorder, unspecified

Tic disorder NOS

307.21 Transient tic disorder

307.22 Chronic motor or vocal tic disorder

307.23 Tourette's disorder

Motor-verbal tic disorder

DEF: Syndrome of facial and vocal tics in childhood; progresses to spontaneous or involuntary jerking, obscene utterances, other uncontrollable actions considered inappropriate.

307.3 Stereotypic movement disorder

Body-rocking
Head banging
Spasmus nutans
Stereotypes NOS

EXCLUDES *tics (307.20-307.23)*
of organic origin (333.3)

✓5th **307.4 Specific disorders of sleep of nonorganic origin**

EXCLUDES *narcolepsy (347.00-347.11)*
organic hypersomnia (327.10-327.19)
organic insomnia (327.00-327.09)
those of unspecified cause (780.50-780.59)

307.40 Nonorganic sleep disorder, unspecified

307.41 Transient disorder of initiating or maintaining sleep

Adjustment insomnia
Hyposomnia, Insomnia, Sleeplessness } associated with intermittent emotional reactions or conflicts

307.42 Persistent disorder of initiating or maintaining sleep

Hyposomnia, insomnia, or sleeplessness associated with:
anxiety
conditioned arousal
depression (major) (minor)
psychosis
Idiopathic insomnia
Paradoxical insomnia
Primary insomnia
Psychophysiological insomnia

307.43 Transient disorder of initiating or maintaining wakefulness

Hypersomnia associated with acute or intermittent emotional reactions or conflicts

307.44 Persistent disorder of initiating or maintaining wakefulness

Hypersomnia associated with depression (major) (minor)
Insufficient sleep syndrome
Primary hypersomnia

EXCLUDES *sleep deprivation (V69.4)*

307.45 Circadian rhythm sleep disorder of nonorganic origin

307.46 Sleep arousal disorder
Night terror disorder
Night terrors
Sleep terror disorder
Sleepwalking
Somnambulism

DEF: Sleepwalking marked by extreme terror, panic, screaming, confusion; no recall of event upon arousal; term may refer to simply the act of sleepwalking.

307.47 Other dysfunctions of sleep stages or arousal from sleep
Nightmare disorder
Nightmares:
NOS
REM-sleep type
Sleep drunkenness

307.48 Repetitive intrusions of sleep
Repetitive intrusion of sleep with:
atypical polysomnographic features
environmental disturbances
repeated REM-sleep interruptions

307.49 Other
"Short-sleeper"
Subjective insomnia complaint

✓5th **307.5 Other and unspecified disorders of eating**

EXCLUDES *anorexia:*
nervosa (307.1)
of unspecified cause (783.0)
overeating, of unspecified cause (783.6)
vomiting:
NOS ▶(787.03)◀
cyclical (536.2)
▶associated with migraine (346.2)◀
psychogenic (306.4)

307.50 Eating disorder, unspecified
Eating disorder NOS

307.51 Bulimia nervosa
Overeating of nonorganic origin

DEF: Mental disorder commonly characterized by binge eating followed by self-induced vomiting; perceptions of being fat; and fear the inability to stop eating voluntarily.

307.52 Pica
Perverted appetite of nonorganic origin

DEF: Compulsive eating disorder characterized by craving for substances, other than food; such as paint chips or dirt.

307.53 Rumination disorder
Regurgitation, of nonorganic origin, of food with reswallowing

EXCLUDES *obsessional rumination (300.3)*

307.54 Psychogenic vomiting

307.59 Other
Feeding disorder of infancy or early childhood of nonorganic origin
Infantile feeding disturbances } of nonorganic origin
Loss of appetite } of nonorganic origin

307.6 Enuresis
Enuresis (primary) (secondary) of nonorganic origin

EXCLUDES *enuresis of unspecified cause (788.3)*

DEF: Involuntary urination past age of normal control; also called bedwetting; no trace to biological problem; focus on psychological issues.

307.7 Encopresis
Encopresis (continuous) (discontinuous) of nonorganic origin

EXCLUDES *encopresis of unspecified cause (787.6)*

DEF: Inability to control bowel movements; cause traced to psychological, not biological, problems.

✓5th **307.8 Pain disorders related to psychological factors**

307.80 Psychogenic pain, site unspecified

307.81 Tension headache

EXCLUDES *headache:*
NOS (784.0)
migraine (346.0-346.9)
▶syndromes (339.00-339.89)
tension type (339.10-339.12)◀

AHA: N-D, '85, 16

307.89 Other
Code first to type or site of pain

EXCLUDES *pain disorder exclusively attributed to psychological factors (307.80)*
psychogenic pain (307.80)

307.9 Other and unspecified special symptoms or syndromes, not elsewhere classified
Communication disorder NOS
Hair plucking
Lalling
Lisping
Masturbation
Nail-biting
Thumb-sucking

✓4th **308 Acute reaction to stress**

INCLUDES catastrophic stress
combat fatigue
gross stress reaction (acute)
transient disorders in response to exceptional physical or mental stress which usually subside within hours or days

EXCLUDES *adjustment reaction or disorder (309.0-309.9)*
chronic stress reaction (309.1-309.9)

308.0 Predominant disturbance of emotions
Anxiety } as acute reaction to exceptional [gross] stress
Emotional crisis } as acute reaction to exceptional [gross] stress
Panic state } as acute reaction to exceptional [gross] stress

308.1 Predominant disturbance of consciousness
Fugues as acute reaction to exceptional [gross] stress

308.2 Predominant psychomotor disturbance
Agitation states } as acute reaction to exceptional [gross] stress
Stupor } as acute reaction to exceptional [gross] stress

308.3 Other acute reactions to stress
Acute situational disturbance
Acute stress disorder

EXCLUDES *prolonged posttraumatic emotional disturbance (309.81)*

308.4 Mixed disorders as reaction to stress

308.9 Unspecified acute reaction to stress

✓4th **309 Adjustment reaction**

INCLUDES adjustment disorders
reaction (adjustment) to chronic stress

EXCLUDES *acute reaction to major stress (308.0-308.9)*
neurotic disorders (300.0-300.9)

309.0 Adjustment disorder with depressed mood
Grief reaction

EXCLUDES *affective psychoses (296.0-296.9)*
neurotic depression (300.4)
prolonged depressive reaction (309.1)
psychogenic depressive psychosis (298.0)

309.1 Prolonged depressive reaction

EXCLUDES *affective psychoses (296.0-296.9)*
brief depressive reaction (309.0)
neurotic depression (300.4)
psychogenic depressive psychosis (298.0)

✓5th **309.2 With predominant disturbance of other emotions**

309.21 Separation anxiety disorder

DEF: Abnormal apprehension by a child when physically separated from support environment; byproduct of abnormal symbiotic child-parent relationship.

309.22 Emancipation disorder of adolescence and early adult life

DEF: Adjustment reaction of late adolescence; conflict over independence from parental supervision; symptoms include difficulty in making decisions, increased reliance on parental advice, deliberate adoption of values in opposition of parents.

309.23 Specific academic or work inhibition

309.24 Adjustment disorder with anxiety

309.28 Adjustment disorder with mixed anxiety and depressed mood

Adjustment reaction with anxiety and depression

309.29 Other

Culture shock

309.3 Adjustment disorder with disturbance of conduct

Conduct disturbance } as adjustment reaction
Destructiveness }

EXCLUDES *destructiveness in child (312.9)*
disturbance of conduct NOS (312.9)
dyssocial behavior without manifest psychiatric disorder (V71.01-V71.02)
personality disorder with predominantly sociopathic or asocial manifestations (301.7)

309.4 Adjustment disorder with mixed disturbance of emotions and conduct

✓5th **309.8 Other specified adjustment reactions**

309.81 Posttraumatic stress disorder

Chronic posttraumatic stress disorder
Concentration camp syndrome
Posttraumatic stress disorder NOS
Post-traumatic stress disorder (PTSD)

EXCLUDES *acute stress disorder (308.3)*
posttraumatic brain syndrome:
nonpsychotic (310.2)
psychotic (293.0-293.9)

DEF: Preoccupation with traumatic events beyond normal experience; i.e., rape, personal assault, combat, natural disasters, accidents, torture precipitate disorder; also recurring flashbacks of trauma; symptoms include difficulty remembering, sleeping, or concentrating, and guilt feelings for surviving.

309.82 Adjustment reaction with physical symptoms

309.83 Adjustment reaction with withdrawal

Elective mutism as adjustment reaction
Hospitalism (in children) NOS

309.89 Other

309.9 Unspecified adjustment reaction

Adaptation reaction NOS
Adjustment reaction NOS

✓4th **310 Specific nonpsychotic mental disorders due to brain damage**

EXCLUDES *neuroses, personality disorders, or other nonpsychotic conditions occurring in a form similar to that seen with functional disorders but in association with a physical condition (300.0-300.9, 301.0-301.9)*

310.0 Frontal lobe syndrome

Lobotomy syndrome
Postleucotomy syndrome [state]

EXCLUDES *postcontusion syndrome (310.2)*

310.1 Personality change due to conditions classified elsewhere

Cognitive or personality change of other type, of nonpsychotic severity
Organic psychosyndrome of nonpsychotic severity
Presbyophrenia NOS
Senility with mental changes of nonpsychotic severity

EXCLUDES *memory loss of unknown cause (780.93)*

AHA: 2Q, '05, 6

DEF: Personality disorder caused by organic factors, such as brain lesions, head trauma, or cerebrovascular accident (CVA).

310.2 Postconcussion syndrome

Postcontusion syndrome or encephalopathy
Posttraumatic brain syndrome, nonpsychotic
Status postcommotio cerebri

▶Use additional code to identify associated post-traumatic headache, if applicable (339.20-339.22)◀

EXCLUDES *frontal lobe syndrome (310.0)*
postencephalitic syndrome (310.8)
any organic psychotic conditions following head injury (293.0-294.0)

AHA: 4Q, '90, 24

DEF: Nonpsychotic disorder due to brain trauma, causes symptoms unrelated to any disease process; symptoms include amnesia, serial headaches, rapid heartbeat, fatigue, disrupted sleep patterns, inability to concentrate.

310.8 Other specified nonpsychotic mental disorders following organic brain damage

Mild memory disturbance
Postencephalitic syndrome
Other focal (partial) organic psychosyndromes

310.9 Unspecified nonpsychotic mental disorder following organic brain damage

AHA: 4Q, '03, 103

311 Depressive disorder, not elsewhere classified

Depressive disorder NOS
Depressive state NOS
Depression NOS

EXCLUDES *acute reaction to major stress with depressive symptoms (308.0)*
affective personality disorder (301.10-301.13)
affective psychoses (296.0-296.9)
brief depressive reaction (309.0)
depressive states associated with stressful events (309.0-309.1)
disturbance of emotions specific to childhood and adolescence, with misery and unhappiness (313.1)
mixed adjustment reaction with depressive symptoms (309.4)
neurotic depression (300.4)
prolonged depressive adjustment reaction (309.1)
psychogenic depressive psychosis (298.0)

AHA: 4Q, '03, 75

Mental Disorders

309.1–311

✓4th 312 Disturbance of conduct, not elsewhere classified

EXCLUDES *adjustment reaction with disturbance of conduct (309.3)*
drug dependence (304.0-304.9)
dyssocial behavior without manifest psychiatric disorder (V71.01-V71.02)
personality disorder with predominantly sociopathic or asocial manifestations (301.7)
sexual deviations (302.0-302.9)

The following fifth-digit subclassification is for use with categories 312.0-312.2
- 0 **unspecified**
- 1 **mild**
- 2 **moderate**
- 3 **severe**

§ ✓5th **312.0 Undersocialized conduct disorder, aggressive type**
[0-3]
Aggressive outburst
Anger reaction
Unsocialized aggressive disorder

DEF: Mental condition identified by behaviors disrespectful of others' rights and of age-appropriate social norms or rules; symptoms include bullying, vandalism, verbal and physical abusiveness, lying, stealing, defiance.

§ ✓5th **312.1 Undersocialized conduct disorder, unaggressive type**
[0-3]
Childhood truancy, unsocialized
Solitary stealing
Tantrums

§ ✓5th **312.2 Socialized conduct disorder**
[0-3]
Childhood truancy, socialized
Group delinquency

EXCLUDES *gang activity without manifest psychiatric disorder (V71.01)*

✓5th **312.3 Disorders of impulse control, not elsewhere classified**

312.30 Impulse control disorder, unspecified

312.31 Pathological gambling

312.32 Kleptomania

312.33 Pyromania

312.34 Intermittent explosive disorder

312.35 Isolated explosive disorder

312.39 Other
Trichotillomania

312.4 Mixed disturbance of conduct and emotions
Neurotic delinquency

EXCLUDES *compulsive conduct disorder (312.3)*

✓5th **312.8 Other specified disturbances of conduct, not elsewhere classified**

312.81 Conduct disorder, childhood onset type

312.82 Conduct disorder, adolescent onset type

312.89 Other conduct disorder
Conduct disorder of unspecified onset

312.9 Unspecified disturbance of conduct
Delinquency (juvenile)
Disruptive behavior disorder NOS

✓4th 313 Disturbance of emotions specific to childhood and adolescence

EXCLUDES *adjustment reaction (309.0-309.9)*
emotional disorder of neurotic type (300.0-300.9)
masturbation, nail-biting, thumbsucking, and other isolated symptoms (307.0-307.9)

313.0 Overanxious disorder
Anxiety and fearfulness } of childhood and adolescence
Overanxious disorder }

EXCLUDES *abnormal separation anxiety (309.21)*
anxiety states (300.00-300.09)
hospitalism in children (309.83)
phobic state (300.20-300.29)

313.1 Misery and unhappiness disorder

EXCLUDES *depressive neurosis (300.4)*

✓5th **313.2 Sensitivity, shyness, and social withdrawal disorder**

EXCLUDES *infantile autism (299.0)*
schizoid personality (301.20-301.22)
schizophrenia (295.0-295.9)

313.21 Shyness disorder of childhood
Sensitivity reaction of childhood or adolescence

313.22 Introverted disorder of childhood
Social withdrawal } of childhood and adolescence
Withdrawal reaction }

313.23 Selective mutism

EXCLUDES *elective mutism as adjustment reaction (309.83)*

313.3 Relationship problems
Sibling jealousy

EXCLUDES *relationship problems associated with aggression, destruction, or other forms of conduct disturbance (312.0-312.9)*

✓5th **313.8 Other or mixed emotional disturbances of childhood or adolescence**

313.81 Oppositional defiant disorder

DEF: Mental disorder of children noted for pervasive opposition, defiance of authority.

313.82 Identity disorder
Identity problem

DEF: Distress of adolescents caused by inability to form acceptable self-identity; uncertainty about career choice, sexual orientation, moral values.

313.83 Academic underachievement disorder

313.89 Other P
Reactive attachment disorder of infancy or early childhood

313.9 Unspecified emotional disturbance of childhood or adolescence P
Mental disorder of infancy, childhood or adolescence NOS

✓4th 314 Hyperkinetic syndrome of childhood

EXCLUDES *hyperkinesis as symptom of underlying disorder–code the underlying disorder*

DEF: A behavioral disorder usually diagnosed at an early age; characterized by the inability to focus attention for a normal period of time.

✓5th **314.0 Attention deficit disorder**
Adult
Child

314.00 Without mention of hyperactivity
Predominantly inattentive type

AHA: 1Q, '97, 8

314.01 With hyperactivity
Combined type
Overactivity NOS
Predominantly hyperactive/impulsive type
Simple disturbance of attention with overactivity

AHA: 1Q, '97, 8

§ Requires fifth-digit. Valid digits are in [brackets] under each code. See category 312 for codes and definitions.

314.1 Hyperkinesis with developmental delay
Developmental disorder of hyperkinesis
Use additional code to identify any associated neurological disorder

314.2 Hyperkinetic conduct disorder
Hyperkinetic conduct disorder without developmental delay
EXCLUDES *hyperkinesis with significant delays in specific skills (314.1)*

314.8 Other specified manifestations of hyperkinetic syndrome

314.9 Unspecified hyperkinetic syndrome
Hyperkinetic reaction of childhood or adolescence NOS
Hyperkinetic syndrome NOS

4th 315 Specific delays in development
EXCLUDES *that due to a neurological disorder (320.0-389.9)*

5th 315.0 Specific reading disorder

315.00 Reading disorder, unspecified

315.01 Alexia
DEF: Lack of ability to understand written language; manifestation of aphasia.

315.02 Developmental dyslexia
DEF: Serious impairment of reading skills unexplained in relation to general intelligence and teaching processes; it can be inherited or congenital.

315.09 Other
Specific spelling difficulty

315.1 Mathematics disorder
Dyscalculia

315.2 Other specific learning difficulties
Disorder of written expression
EXCLUDES *specific arithmetical disorder (315.1)*
specific reading disorder (315.00-315.09)

5th 315.3 Developmental speech or language disorder

315.31 Expressive language disorder
Developmental aphasia
Word deafness
EXCLUDES *acquired aphasia (784.3)*
elective mutism (309.83, 313.0, 313.23)

315.32 Mixed receptive-expressive language disorder
Central auditory processing disorder
EXCLUDES *acquired auditory processing disorder (388.45)*

315.34 Speech and language developmental delay due to hearing loss
AHA: 4Q, '07, 80, 81

315.39 Other
Developmental articulation disorder
Dyslalia
Phonological disorder
EXCLUDES *lisping and lalling (307.9)*
stammering and stuttering (307.0)
AHA: 3Q, '07, 7

315.4 Developmental coordination disorder
Clumsiness syndrome
Dyspraxia syndrome
Specific motor development disorder

315.5 Mixed development disorder
AHA: 2Q, '02, 11

315.8 Other specified delays in development

315.9 Unspecified delay in development
Developmental disorder NOS
Learning disorder NOS

316 Psychic factors associated with diseases classified elsewhere
Psychologic factors in physical conditions classified elsewhere
Use additional code to identify the associated physical condition, as:
psychogenic:
asthma (493.9)
dermatitis (692.9)
duodenal ulcer (532.0-532.9)
eczema (691.8, 692.9)
gastric ulcer (531.0-531.9)
mucous colitis (564.9)
paroxysmal tachycardia (427.2)
ulcerative colitis (556)
urticaria (708.0-708.9)
psychosocial dwarfism (259.4)
EXCLUDES *physical symptoms and physiological malfunctions, not involving tissue damage, of mental origin (306.0-306.9)*

MENTAL RETARDATION (317-319)

Use additional code(s) to identify any associated psychiatric or physical condition(s)

317 Mild mental retardation
High-grade defect
IQ 50-70
Mild mental subnormality

4th 318 Other specified mental retardation

318.0 Moderate mental retardation
IQ 35-49
Moderate mental subnormality

318.1 Severe mental retardation
IQ 20-34
Severe mental subnormality

318.2 Profound mental retardation
IQ under 20
Profound mental subnormality

319 Unspecified mental retardation
Mental deficiency NOS
Mental subnormality NOS

6. DISEASES OF THE NERVOUS SYSTEM AND SENSE ORGANS (320-389)

INFLAMMATORY DISEASES OF THE CENTRAL NERVOUS SYSTEM (320-326)

✓4th **320 Bacterial meningitis**

INCLUDES arachnoiditis, leptomeningitis, meningitis, meningoencephalitis, meningomyelitis, pachymeningitis } bacterial

AHA: J-F, '87, 6

DEF: Bacterial infection causing inflammation of the lining of the brain and/or spinal cord.

320.0 Hemophilus meningitis
Meningitis due to Hemophilus influenzae [H. influenzae]

320.1 Pneumococcal meningitis

320.2 Streptococcal meningitis

320.3 Staphylococcal meningitis

320.7 Meningitis in other bacterial diseases classified elsewhere

Code first underlying disease, as:
actinomycosis (039.8)
listeriosis (027.0)
typhoid fever (002.0)
whooping cough (033.0-033.9)

EXCLUDES meningitis (in):
epidemic (036.0)
gonococcal (098.82)
meningococcal (036.0)
salmonellosis (003.21)
syphilis:
NOS (094.2)
congenital (090.42)
meningovascular (094.2)
secondary (091.81)
tuberculous (013.0)

✓5th **320.8 Meningitis due to other specified bacteria**

320.81 Anaerobic meningitis
Bacteroides (fragilis)
Gram-negative anaerobes

320.82 Meningitis due to gram-negative bacteria, not elsewhere classified
Aerobacter aerogenes pneumoniae
Escherichia coli [E. coli]
Friedländer bacillus
Klebsiella
Proteus morganii
Pseudomonas

EXCLUDES gram-negative anaerobes (320.81)

320.89 Meningitis due to other specified bacteria
Bacillus pyocyaneus

320.9 Meningitis due to unspecified bacterium
Meningitis:
bacterial NOS
purulent NOS
pyogenic NOS
suppurative NOS

✓4th **321 Meningitis due to other organisms**

INCLUDES arachnoiditis, leptomeningitis, meningitis, pachymeningitis } due to organisms other than bacterial

AHA: J-F, '87, 6

DEF: Infection causing inflammation of the lining of the brain and/or spinal cord, due to organisms other than bacteria.

321.0 Cryptococcal meningitis
Code first underlying disease (117.5)

321.1 Meningitis in other fungal diseases
Code first underlying disease (110.0-118)

EXCLUDES meningitis in:
candidiasis (112.83)
coccidioidomycosis (114.2)
histoplasmosis (115.01, 115.11, 115.91)

321.2 Meningitis due to viruses not elsewhere classified
Code first underlying disease, as:
meningitis due to arbovirus (060.0-066.9)

EXCLUDES meningitis (due to):
abacterial (047.0-047.9)
adenovirus (049.1)
aseptic NOS (047.9)
Coxsackie (virus)(047.0)
ECHO virus (047.1)
enterovirus (047.0-047.9)
herpes simplex virus (054.72)
herpes zoster virus (053.0)
lymphocytic choriomeningitis virus (049.0)
mumps (072.1)
viral NOS (047.9)
meningo-eruptive syndrome (047.1)

AHA: 4Q, '04, 51

321.3 Meningitis due to trypanosomiasis
Code first underlying disease (086.0-086.9)

321.4 Meningitis in sarcoidosis
Code first underlying disease (135)

321.8 Meningitis due to other nonbacterial organisms classified elsewhere
Code first underlying disease

EXCLUDES leptospiral meningitis (100.81)

✓4th **322 Meningitis of unspecified cause**

INCLUDES arachnoiditis, leptomeningitis, meningitis, pachymeningitis } with no organism specified as cause

AHA: J-F, '87, 6

DEF: Infection causing inflammation of the lining of the brain and/or spinal cord, due to unspecified cause.

322.0 Nonpyogenic meningitis
Meningitis with clear cerebrospinal fluid

322.1 Eosinophilic meningitis

322.2 Chronic meningitis

322.9 Meningitis, unspecified

✓4th 323 Encephalitis, myelitis, and encephalomyelitis

INCLUDES acute disseminated encephalomyelitis
meningoencephalitis, except bacterial
meningomyelitis, except bacterial
myelitis:
ascending
transverse

EXCLUDES *acute transverse myelitis NOS (341.20)*
acute transverse myelitis in conditions classified elsewhere (341.21)
bacterial:
meningoencephalitis (320.0-320.9)
meningomyelitis (320.0-320.9)
idiopathic transverse myelitis (341.22)

DEF: Encephalitis: inflammation of brain tissues.

DEF: Myelitis: inflammation of the spinal cord.

DEF: Encephalomyelitis: inflammation of brain and spinal cord.

✓5th 323.0 Encephalitis, myelitis, and encephalomyelitis in viral diseases classified elsewhere

Code first underlying disease, as:
cat-scratch disease (078.3)
infectious mononucleosis (075)
ornithosis (073.7)

323.01 Encephalitis and encephalomyelitis in viral diseases classified elsewhere

EXCLUDES *encephalitis (in):*
arthropod-borne viral (062.0-064)
herpes simplex (054.3)
mumps (072.2)
other viral diseases of central nervous system (049.8-049.9)
poliomyelitis (045.0-045.9)
rubella (056.01)
slow virus infections of central nervous system (046.0-046.9)
viral NOS (049.9)
West Nile (066.41)

AHA: 4Q, '06, 58-63

323.02 Myelitis in viral diseases classified elsewhere

EXCLUDES *myelitis (in):*
herpes simplex (054.74)
herpes zoster (053.14)
poliomyelitis (045.0-045.9)
rubella (056.01)
other viral diseases of central nervous system (049.8-049.9)

AHA: 4Q, '06, 58-63

323.1 Encephalitis, myelitis, and encephalomyelitis in rickettsial diseases classified elsewhere

Code first underlying disease (080-083.9)

DEF: Inflammation of the brain caused by rickettsial disease carried by louse, tick, or mite.

323.2 Encephalitis, myelitis, and encephalomyelitis in protozoal diseases classified elsewhere

Code first underlying disease, as:
malaria (084.0-084.9)
trypanosomiasis (086.0-086.9)

DEF: Inflammation of the brain caused by protozoal disease carried by mosquitoes and flies.

✓5th 323.4 Other encephalitis, myelitis, and encephalomyelitis due to infection classified elsewhere

Code first underlying disease

323.41 Other encephalitis and encephalomyelitis due to infection classified elsewhere

EXCLUDES *encephalitis (in):*
meningococcal (036.1)
syphilis:
NOS (094.81)
congenital (090.41)
toxoplasmosis (130.0)
tuberculosis (013.6)
meningoencephalitis due to free-living ameba [Naegleria] ►(136.29)◄

AHA: 4Q, '06, 58-63

323.42 Other myelitis due to infection classified elsewhere

EXCLUDES *myelitis (in):*
syphilis (094.89)
tuberculosis (013.6)

AHA: 4Q, '06, 58-63

✓5th 323.5 Encephalitis, myelitis, and encephalomyelitis following immunization procedures

Use additional E code to identify vaccine

323.51 Encephalitis and encephalomyelitis following immunization procedures

Encephalitis postimmunization or postvaccinal
Encephalomyelitis postimmunization or postvaccinal

AHA: 4Q, '06, 58-63

323.52 Myelitis following immunization procedures

Myelitis postimmunization or postvaccinal

AHA: 4Q, '06, 58-63

✓5th 323.6 Postinfectious encephalitis, myelitis, and encephalomyelitis

Code first underlying disease

DEF: Infection, inflammation of brain several weeks following the outbreak of a systemic infection.

323.61 Infectious acute disseminated encephalomyelitis [ADEM]

Acute necrotizing hemorrhagic encephalopathy

EXCLUDES *noninfectious acute disseminated encephalomyelitis (ADEM) (323.81)*

AHA: 4Q, '06, 58-63

323.62 Other postinfectious encephalitis and encephalomyelitis

EXCLUDES *encephalitis:*
postchickenpox (052.0)
postmeasles (055.0)

AHA: 4Q, '06, 58-63

323.63 Postinfectious myelitis

EXCLUDES *postchickenpox myelitis (052.2)*
herpes simplex myelitis (054.74)
herpes zoster myelitis (053.14)

AHA: 4Q, '06, 58-63

✓5th **323.7 Toxic encephalitis, myelitis, and encephalomyelitis**

Code first underlying cause, as:
carbon tetrachloride (982.1)
hydroxyquinoline derivatives (961.3)
lead (984.0-984.9)
mercury (985.0)
thallium (985.8)

AHA: 2Q, '97, 8

323.71 Toxic encephalitis and encephalomyelitis

AHA: 4Q, '06, 58-63

323.72 Toxic myelitis

AHA: 4Q, '06, 58-63

✓5th **323.8 Other causes of encephalitis, myelitis, and encephalomyelitis**

323.81 Other causes of encephalitis and encephalomyelitis
Noninfectious acute disseminated encephalomyelitis (ADEM)

AHA: 4Q, '06, 58-63

323.82 Other causes of myelitis
Transverse myelitis NOS

AHA: 4Q, '06, 58-63

323.9 Unspecified cause of encephalitis, myelitis, and encephalomyelitis

✓4th **324 Intracranial and intraspinal abscess**

324.0 Intracranial abscess
Abscess (embolic):
cerebellar
cerebral
Abscess (embolic) of brain [any part]:
epidural
extradural
otogenic
subdural

EXCLUDES *tuberculous (013.3)*

324.1 Intraspinal abscess
Abscess (embolic) of spinal cord [any part]:
epidural
extradural
subdural

EXCLUDES *tuberculous (013.5)*

324.9 Of unspecified site
Extradural or subdural abscess NOS

325 Phlebitis and thrombophlebitis of intracranial venous sinuses

Embolism; Endophlebitis; Phlebitis, septic or suppurative; Thrombophlebitis; Thrombosis } of cavernous, lateral or other intracranial or unspecified intracranial venous sinus

EXCLUDES *that specified as:*
complicating pregnancy, childbirth, or the puerperium (671.5)
of nonpyogenic origin (437.6)

DEF: Inflammation and formation of blood clot in a vein within the brain or its lining.

326 Late effects of intracranial abscess or pyogenic infection

Note: This category is to be used to indicate conditions whose primary classification is to 320-325 [excluding 320.7, 321.0-321.8, 323.01-323.42, 323.6-323.7] as the cause of late effects, themselves classifiable elsewhere. The "late effects" include conditions specified as such, or as sequelae, which may occur at any time after the resolution of the causal condition.

Use additional code to identify condition, as:
hydrocephalus (331.4)
paralysis (342.0-342.9, 344.0-344.9)

ORGANIC SLEEP DISORDERS (327)

✓4th **327 Organic sleep disorders**

AHA: 4Q, '05, 59-64

✓5th **327.0 Organic disorders of initiating and maintaining sleep [Organic insomnia]**

EXCLUDES *insomnia NOS (780.52)*
insomnia not due to a substance or known physiological condition (307.41-307.42)
insomnia with sleep apnea NOS (780.51)

327.00 Organic insomnia, unspecified

327.01 Insomnia due to medical condition classified elsewhere
Code first underlying condition
EXCLUDES *insomnia due to mental disorder (327.02)*

327.02 Insomnia due to mental disorder
Code first mental disorder
EXCLUDES *alcohol induced insomnia (291.82)*
drug induced insomnia (292.85)

327.09 Other organic insomnia

✓5th **327.1 Organic disorder of excessive somnolence [Organic hypersomnia]**

EXCLUDES *hypersomnia NOS (780.54)*
hypersomnia not due to a substance or known physiological condition (307.43-307.44)
hypersomnia with sleep apnea NOS (780.53)

327.10 Organic hypersomnia, unspecified

327.11 Idiopathic hypersomnia with long sleep time

327.12 Idiopathic hypersomnia without long sleep time

327.13 Recurrent hypersomnia
Kleine-Levin syndrome
Menstrual related hypersomnia

327.14 Hypersomnia due to medical condition classified elsewhere
Code first underlying condition
EXCLUDES *hypersomnia due to mental disorder (327.15)*

327.15 Hypersomnia due to mental disorder
Code first mental disorder
EXCLUDES *alcohol induced hypersomnia (291.82)*
drug induced hypersomnia (292.85)

327.19 Other organic hypersomnia

✓5th **327.2 Organic sleep apnea**

EXCLUDES *Cheyne-Stokes breathing (786.04)*
hypersomnia with sleep apnea NOS (780.53)
insomnia with sleep apnea NOS (780.51)
sleep apnea in newborn (770.81-770.82)
sleep apnea NOS (780.57)

327.20 Organic sleep apnea, unspecified

327.21 Primary central sleep apnea

327.22 High altitude periodic breathing

327.23 Obstructive sleep apnea (adult) (pediatric)

327.24 Idiopathic sleep related nonobstructive alveolar hypoventilation
Sleep related hypoxia

327.25 Congenital central alveolar hypoventilation syndrome

327.26 *Sleep related hypoventilation/ hypoxemia in conditions classifiable elsewhere*
Code first underlying condition

327.27 *Central sleep apnea in conditions classified elsewhere*
Code first underlying condition

327.29 Other organic sleep apnea

✓5th **327.3 Circadian rhythm sleep disorder**
Organic disorder of sleep wake cycle
Organic disorder of sleep wake schedule

EXCLUDES *alcohol induced circadian rhythm sleep disorder (291.82)*
circadian rhythm sleep disorder of nonorganic origin (307.45)
disruption of 24 hour sleep wake cycle NOS (780.55)
drug induced circadian rhythm sleep disorder (292.85)

327.30 Circadian rhythm sleep disorder, unspecified

327.31 Circadian rhythm sleep disorder, delayed sleep phase type

327.32 Circadian rhythm sleep disorder, advanced sleep phase type

327.33 Circadian rhythm sleep disorder, irregular sleep-wake type

327.34 Circadian rhythm sleep disorder, free-running type

327.35 Circadian rhythm sleep disorder, jet lag type

327.36 Circadian rhythm sleep disorder, shift work type

327.37 *Circadian rhythm sleep disorder in conditions classified elsewhere*
Code first underlying condition

327.39 Other circadian rhythm sleep disorder

✓5th **327.4 Organic parasomnia**

EXCLUDES *alcohol induced parasomnia (291.82)*
drug induced parasomnia (292.85)
parasomnia not due to a known physiological condition (307.47)

327.40 Organic parasomnia, unspecified

327.41 Confusional arousals

327.42 REM sleep behavior disorder

327.43 Recurrent isolated sleep paralysis

327.44 *Parasomnia in conditions classified elsewhere*
Code first underlying condition

327.49 Other organic parasomnia

✓5th **327.5 Organic sleep related movement disorders**

EXCLUDES *restless legs syndrome (333.94)*
sleep related movement disorder NOS (780.58)

327.51 Periodic limb movement disorder
Periodic limb movement sleep disorder

327.52 Sleep related leg cramps

327.53 Sleep related bruxism

327.59 Other organic sleep related movement disorders

327.8 Other organic sleep disorders

AHA: 2Q, '07, 6

HEREDITARY AND DEGENERATIVE DISEASES OF THE CENTRAL NERVOUS SYSTEM (330-337)

EXCLUDES *hepatolenticular degeneration (275.1)*
multiple sclerosis (340)
other demyelinating diseases of central nervous system (341.0-341.9)

✓4th **330 Cerebral degenerations usually manifest in childhood**

Use additional code to identify associated mental retardation

330.0 Leukodystrophy
Krabbe's disease
Leukodystrophy:
NOS
globoid cell
metachromatic
sudanophilic
Pelizaeus-Merzbacher disease
Sulfatide lipidosis

DEF: Hereditary disease of arylsulfatase or cerebroside sulfatase; characterized by a diffuse loss of myelin in CNS; infantile form causes blindness, motor disturbances, rigidity, mental deterioration and, occasionally, convulsions.

330.1 Cerebral lipidoses
Amaurotic (familial) idiocy
Disease:
Batten
Jansky-Bielschowsky
Kufs'
Spielmeyer-Vogt
Tay-Sachs
Gangliosidosis

DEF: Genetic disorder causing abnormal lipid accumulation in the reticuloendothelial cells of the brain.

330.2 *Cerebral degeneration in generalized lipidoses*
Code first underlying disease, as:
Fabry's disease (272.7)
Gaucher's disease (272.7)
Niemann-Pick disease (272.7)
sphingolipidosis (272.7)

330.3 *Cerebral degeneration of childhood in other diseases classified elsewhere*
Code first underlying disease, as:
Hunter's disease (277.5)
mucopolysaccharidosis (277.5)

330.8 Other specified cerebral degenerations in childhood
Alpers' disease or gray-matter degeneration
Infantile necrotizing encephalomyelopathy
Leigh's disease
Subacute necrotizing encephalopathy or encephalomyelopathy
AHA: N-D, '85, 5

330.9 Unspecified cerebral degeneration in childhood

✓4th 331 Other cerebral degenerations
Use additional code, where applicable, to identify ▶dementia:◀
with behavioral disturbance (294.11)
without behavioral disturbance (294.10)

331.0 Alzheimer's disease
AHA: 4Q, '00, 41; 4Q, '99, 7; N-D, '84, 20
DEF: Diffuse atrophy of cerebral cortex; causing a progressive decline in intellectual and physical functions, including memory loss, personality changes and profound dementia.

✓5th 331.1 Frontotemporal dementia
AHA: 4Q, '03, 57
DEF: Rare, progressive degenerative brain disease, similar to Alzheimer's; cortical atrophy affects the frontal and temporal lobes.

331.11 Pick's disease
DEF: A less common form of progressive frontotemporal dementia with asymmetrical atrophy of the frontal and temporal regions of the cerebral cortex including abnormal rounded brain cells called Pick cells together with the presence of abnormal staining of protein (called tau) within the cells, called Pick bodies; symptoms include prominent apathy, deterioration of social skills, behavioral changes such as disinhibition and restlessness, echolalia, impairment of language, memory, and intellect, increased carelessness, poor personal hygiene, and decreased attention span.

331.19 Other frontotemporal dementia
Frontal dementia

331.2 Senile degeneration of brain
EXCLUDES *senility NOS (797)*

331.3 Communicating hydrocephalus
Secondary normal pressure hydrocephalus
EXCLUDES *congenital hydrocephalus (742.3)*
idiopathic normal pressure hydrocephalus (331.5)
normal pressure hydrocephalus (331.5)
spina bifida with hydrocephalus (741.0)
AHA: S-O, '85, 12
DEF: Subarachnoid hemorrhage and meningitis causing excess buildup of cerebrospinal fluid in cavities due to nonabsorption of fluid back through fluid pathways.

331.4 Obstructive hydrocephalus
Acquired hydrocephalus NOS
EXCLUDES *congenital hydrocephalus (742.3)*
idiopathic normal pressure hydrocephalus (331.5)
normal pressure hydrocephalus (331.5)
spina bifida with hydrocephalus (741.0)
AHA: 4Q, '03, 106; 1Q, '99, 9
DEF: Obstruction of cerebrospinal fluid passage from brain into spinal canal.

331.5 Idiopathic normal pressure hydrocephalus [INPH]
Normal pressure hydrocephalus NOS
EXCLUDES *congenital hydrocephalus (742.3)*
secondary normal pressure hydrocephalus (331.3)
spina bifida with hydrocephalus (741.0)
AHA: 4Q, '07, 74
DEF: Abnormal increase of cerebrospinal fluid in the brain's ventricles; results in dementia, progressive mental impairment, gait disturbance, and impaired bladder control.

331.7 Cerebral degeneration in diseases classified elsewhere
Code first underlying disease, as:
alcoholism (303.0-303.9)
beriberi (265.0)
cerebrovascular disease (430-438)
congenital hydrocephalus (741.0, 742.3)
myxedema (244.0-244.9)
neoplastic disease (140.0-239.9)
vitamin B_{12} deficiency (266.2)
EXCLUDES *cerebral degeneration in:*
Jakob-Creutzfeldt disease (046.1)
progressive multifocal leukoencephalopathy (046.3)
subacute spongiform encephalopathy (046.1)

✓5th 331.8 Other cerebral degeneration

331.81 Reye's syndrome P
DEF: Rare childhood illness, often developed after a viral upper respiratory infection; characterized by vomiting, elevated serum transaminase, changes in liver and other viscera; symptoms may be followed by an encephalopathic phase with brain swelling, disturbances of consciousness and seizures; can be fatal.

331.82 Dementia with Lewy bodies
Dementia with Parkinsonism
Lewy body dementia
Lewy body disease
AHA: 4Q, '03, 57
DEF: A cerebral dementia with neurophysiologic changes including increased hippocampal volume, hypoperfusion in the occipital lobes, and beta amyloid deposits with neurofibrillarity tangles, atrophy of cortex and brainstem, hallmark neuropsychologic characteristics are fluctuating cognition with pronounced variation in attention and alertness; recurrent hallucinations; and parkinsonism.

331.83 Mild cognitive impairment, so stated
EXCLUDES *altered mental status (780.97)*
cerebral degeneration (331.0-331.9)
change in mental status (780.97)
cognitive deficits following (late effects of) cerebral hemorrhage or infarction (438.0)
cognitive impairment due to intracranial or head injury (850-854, 959.01)
cognitive impairment due to late effect of intracranial injury (907.0)
dementia (290.0-290.43, 294.8)
mild memory disturbance (310.8)
neurologic neglect syndrome (781.8)
personality change, nonpsychotic (310.1)
AHA: 4Q, '06, 75

331.89 Other
Cerebral ataxia

331.9 Cerebral degeneration, unspecified

4th 332 Parkinson's disease

EXCLUDES *dementia with Parkinsonism (331.82)*

332.0 Paralysis agitans

Parkinsonism or Parkinson's disease:
NOS
idiopathic
primary

AHA: M-A, '87, 7

DEF: Form of parkinsonism; progressive, occurs in senior years; characterized by masklike facial expression; condition affects ability to stand erect, walk smoothly; weakened muscles, also tremble and involuntarily movement.

332.1 Secondary Parkinsonism

Neuroleptic-induced Parkinsonism
Parkinsonism due to drugs

Use additional E code to identify drug, if drug-induced

EXCLUDES *Parkinsonism (in):*
Huntington's disease (333.4)
progressive supranuclear palsy (333.0)
Shy-Drager syndrome (333.0)
syphilitic (094.82)

4th 333 Other extrapyramidal disease and abnormal movement disorders

INCLUDES other forms of extrapyramidal, basal ganglia, or striatopallidal disease

EXCLUDES *abnormal movements of head NOS (781.0)*
sleep related movement disorders (327.51-327.59)

333.0 Other degenerative diseases of the basal ganglia

Atrophy or degeneration:
olivopontocerebellar [Déjérine-Thomas syndrome]
pigmentary pallidal [Hallervorden-Spatz disease]
striatonigral

Parkinsonian syndrome associated with:
idiopathic orthostatic hypotension
symptomatic orthostatic hypotension

Progressive supranuclear ophthalmoplegia
Shy-Drager syndrome

AHA: 3Q, '96, 8

333.1 Essential and other specified forms of tremor

Benign essential tremor
Familial tremor
Medication-induced postural tremor

Use additional E code to identify drug, if drug-induced

EXCLUDES *tremor NOS (781.0)*

333.2 Myoclonus

Familial essential myoclonus
Progressive myoclonic epilepsy
Unverricht-Lundborg disease

Use additional E code to identify drug, if drug-induced

AHA: 3Q, '97, 4; M-A, '87, 12

DEF: Spontaneous movements or contractions of muscles.

333.3 Tics of organic origin

Use additional E code to identify drug, if drug-induced

EXCLUDES *Gilles de la Tourette's syndrome (307.23)*
habit spasm (307.22)
tic NOS (307.20)

333.4 Huntington's chorea

DEF: Genetic disease characterized by chronic progressive men tal deterioration; dementia and death within 15 years of onset.

333.5 Other choreas

Hemiballism(us)
Paroxysmal choreo-athetosis

Use additional E code to identify drug, if drug-induced

EXCLUDES *Sydenham's or rheumatic chorea (392.0-392.9)*

333.6 Genetic torsion dystonia

Dystonia:
deformans progressiva
musculorum deformans
(Schwalbe-) Ziehen-Oppenheim disease

DEF: Sustained muscular contractions, causing twisting and repetitive movements that result in abnormal postures of trunk and limbs; etiology unknown.

5th 333.7 Acquired torsion dystonia

333.71 Athetoid cerebral palsy

Double athetosis (syndrome)
Vogt's disease

EXCLUDES *infantile cerebral palsy (343.0-343.9)*

AHA: 4Q, '06, 76-78

333.72 Acute dystonia due to drugs

Acute dystonic reaction due to drugs
Neuroleptic induced acute dystonia

Use additional E code to identify drug

EXCLUDES *blepharospasm due to drugs (333.85)*
orofacial dyskinesia due to drugs (333.85)
secondary Parkinsonism (332.1)
subacute dyskinesia due to drugs (333.85)
tardive dyskinesia (333.85)

AHA: 4Q, '06, 76-78

333.79 Other acquired torsion dystonia

AHA: 4Q, '06, 76-78

5th 333.8 Fragments of torsion dystonia

Use additional E code to identify drug, if drug-induced

333.81 Blepharospasm

EXCLUDES *blepharospasm due to drugs (333.85)*

DEF: Uncontrolled winking or blinking due to orbicularis oculi muscle spasm.

333.82 Orofacial dyskinesia

EXCLUDES *orofacial dyskinesia due to drugs (333.85)*

DEF: Uncontrolled movement of mouth or facial muscles.

333.83 Spasmodic torticollis

EXCLUDES *torticollis:*
NOS (723.5)
hysterical (300.11)
psychogenic (306.0)

DEF: Uncontrolled movement of head due to spasms of neck muscle.

333.84 Organic writers' cramp

EXCLUDES *pychogenic (300.89)*

333.85 Subacute dyskinesia due to drugs
Blepharospasm due to drugs
Orofacial dyskinesia due to drugs
Tardive dyskinesia
Use additional E code to identify drug
EXCLUDES *acute dystonia due to drugs (333.72)*
acute dystonic reaction due to drugs (333.72)
secondary Parkinsonism (332.1)
AHA: 4Q, '06, 76-78

333.89 Other

333.9 Other and unspecified extrapyramidal diseases and abnormal movement disorders

333.90 Unspecified extrapyramidal disease and abnormal movement disorder
Medication-induced movement disorders NOS
Use additional E code to identify drug, if drug-induced

333.91 Stiff-man syndrome

333.92 Neuroleptic malignant syndrome
Use additional E code to identify drug
EXCLUDES *neuroleptic induced Parkinsonism (332.1)*
AHA: 4Q, '94, 37

333.93 Benign shuddering attacks
AHA: 4Q, '94, 37

333.94 Restless legs syndrome [RLS]
AHA: 4Q, '06, 79
DEF: Neurological disorder of unknown etiology with an irresistible urge to move the legs, which may temporarily relieve the symptoms, is accompanied by motor restlessness and sensations of pain, burning, prickling, or tingling.

333.99 Other
Neuroleptic-induced acute akathisia
Use additional E code to identify drug, if drug-induced
AHA: 4Q, '04, 95; 2Q, '04, 12; 4Q, '94, 37

334 Spinocerebellar disease
EXCLUDES *olivopontocerebellar degeneration (333.0)*
peroneal muscular atrophy (356.1)

334.0 Friedreich's ataxia
DEF: Genetic recessive disease of children; sclerosis of dorsal, lateral spinal cord columns; characterized by ataxia, speech impairment, swaying and irregular movements, with muscle paralysis, especially of lower limbs.

334.1 Hereditary spastic paraplegia

334.2 Primary cerebellar degeneration
Cerebellar ataxia:
- Marie's
- Sanger-Brown

Dyssynergia cerebellaris myoclonica
Primary cerebellar degeneration:
- NOS
- hereditary
- sporadic

AHA: M-A, '87, 9

334.3 Other cerebellar ataxia
Cerebellar ataxia NOS
Use additional E code to identify drug, if drug-induced

334.4 Cerebellar ataxia in diseases classified elsewhere
Code first underlying disease, as:
- alcoholism (303.0-303.9)
- myxedema (244.0-244.9)
- neoplastic disease (140.0-239.9)

334.8 Other spinocerebellar diseases
Ataxia-telangiectasia [Louis-Bar syndrome]
Corticostriatal-spinal degeneration

334.9 Spinocerebellar disease, unspecified

335 Anterior horn cell disease

335.0 Werdnig-Hoffmann disease
Infantile spinal muscular atrophy
Progressive muscular atrophy of infancy
DEF: Spinal muscle atrophy manifested in prenatal period or shortly after birth; symptoms include hypotonia, atrophy of skeletal muscle; death occurs in infancy.

335.1 Spinal muscular atrophy

335.10 Spinal muscular atrophy, unspecified

335.11 Kugelberg-Welander disease
Spinal muscular atrophy:
- familial
- juvenile

DEF: Hereditary; juvenile muscle atrophy; appears during first two decades of life; due to lesions of anterior horns of spinal cord; includes wasting, diminution of lower body muscles and twitching.

335.19 Other
Adult spinal muscular atrophy

335.2 Motor neuron disease

335.20 Amyotrophic lateral sclerosis A
Motor neuron disease (bulbar) (mixed type)
AHA: 4Q, '95, 81

335.21 Progressive muscular atrophy
Duchenne-Aran muscular atrophy
Progressive muscular atrophy (pure)

335.22 Progressive bulbar palsy

335.23 Pseudobulbar palsy

335.24 Primary lateral sclerosis

335.29 Other

335.8 Other anterior horn cell diseases

335.9 Anterior horn cell disease, unspecified

336 Other diseases of spinal cord

336.0 Syringomyelia and syringobulbia
AHA: 1Q, '89, 10

336.1 Vascular myelopathies
Acute infarction of spinal cord (embolic) (nonembolic)
Arterial thrombosis of spinal cord
Edema of spinal cord
Hematomyelia
Subacute necrotic myelopathy

336.2 Subacute combined degeneration of spinal cord in diseases classified elsewhere
Code first underlying disease, as:
- pernicious anemia (281.0)
- other vitamin B_{12} deficiency anemia (281.1)
- vitamin B_{12} deficiency (266.2)

336.3 Myelopathy in other diseases classified elsewhere

Code first underlying disease, as:
myelopathy in neoplastic disease (140.0-239.9)

EXCLUDES *myelopathy in:*
intervertebral disc disorder (722.70-722.73)
spondylosis (721.1, 721.41-721.42, 721.91)

AHA: 3Q, '99, 5

336.8 Other myelopathy

Myelopathy:
drug-induced
radiation-induced

Use additonal E code to identify cause

336.9 Unspecified disease of spinal cord

Cord compression NOS
Myelopathy NOS

EXCLUDES *myelitis (323.02, 323.1, 323.2, 323.42, 323.52, 323.63, 323.72, 323.82, 323.9)*
spinal (canal) stenosis (723.0, 724.00-724.09)

✓4th **337 Disorders of the autonomic nervous system**

INCLUDES disorders of peripheral autonomic, sympathetic, parasympathetic, or vegetative system

EXCLUDES *familial dysautonomia [Riley-Day syndrome] (742.8)*

✓5th **337.0 Idiopathic peripheral autonomic neuropathy**

● **337.00 Idiopathic peripheral autonomic neuropathy, unspecified**

● **337.01 Carotid sinus syndrome**

Carotid sinus syncope

● **337.09 Other idiopathic peripheral autonomic neuropathy**

Cervical sympathetic dystrophy or paralysis

337.1 Peripheral autonomic neuropathy in disorders classified elsewhere

Code first underlying disease, as:
amyloidosis (277.30-277.39)
diabetes ►(249.6, 250.6)◄

AHA: 2Q, '93, 6; 3Q, '91, 9; N-D, '84, 9

✓5th **337.2 Reflex sympathetic dystrophy**

AHA: 4Q, '93, 24

DEF: Disturbance of the sympathetic nervous system evidenced by sweating, pain, pallor and edema following injury to nerves or blood vessels.

337.20 Reflex sympathetic dystrophy, unspecified

►Complex regional pain syndrome type I, unspecified◄

337.21 Reflex sympathetic dystrophy of the upper limb

►Complex regional pain syndrome type I of the upper limb◄

337.22 Reflex sympathetic dystrophy of the lower limb

►Complex regional pain syndrome type I of the lower limb◄

337.29 Reflex sympathetic dystrophy of other specified site

►Complex regional pain syndrome type I of other specified site◄

337.3 Autonomic dysreflexia

Use additional code to identify the cause, such as:
►pressure◄ ulcer (707.00-707.09)
fecal impaction (560.39)
urinary tract infection (599.0)

AHA: 4Q, '98, 37

DEF: Noxious stimuli evokes paroxysmal hypertension, bradycardia, excess sweating, headache, pilomotor responses, facial flushing, and nasal congestion due to uncontrolled parasympathetic nerve response; usually occurs in patients with spinal cord injury above major sympathetic outflow tract (T_6).

337.9 Unspecified disorder of autonomic nervous system

PAIN (338)

✓4th **338 Pain, not elsewhere classified**

Use additional code to identify:
pain associated with psychological factors (307.89)

EXCLUDES *generalized pain (780.96)*
►*headache syndromes (339.00-339.89)*◄
localized pain, unspecified type–code to pain by site
►*migraines (346.0-346.9)*◄
pain disorder exclusively attributed to psychological factors (307.80)
►*vulvar vestibulitis (625.71)*
vulvodynia (625.70-625.79)◄

AHA: 2Q, '07, 12

338.0 Central pain syndrome

Déjérine-Roussy syndrome
Myelopathic pain syndrome
Thalamic pain syndrome (hyperesthetic)

AHA: 4Q, '06, 79-81

✓5th **338.1 Acute pain**

338.11 Acute pain due to trauma

AHA: 1Q, '07, 7; 4Q, '06, 79-81

338.12 Acute post-thoracotomy pain

Post-thoracotomy pain NOS

AHA: 4Q, '06, 79-81

338.18 Other acute postoperative pain

Postoperative pain NOS

AHA: 2Q, '07, 11; 4Q, '06, 79-81

338.19 Other acute pain

EXCLUDES *neoplasm related acute pain (338.3)*

AHA: 2Q, '07, 11; 4Q, '06, 79-81

✓5th **338.2 Chronic pain**

EXCLUDES *causalgia (355.9)*
lower limb (355.71)
upper limb (354.4)
chronic pain syndrome (338.4)
myofascial pain syndrome (729.1)
neoplasm related chronic pain (338.3)
reflex sympathetic dystrophy (337.20-337.29)

338.21 Chronic pain due to trauma

AHA: 4Q, '06, 79-81

338.22 Chronic post-thoracotomy pain

AHA: 4Q, '06, 79-81

338.28 Other chronic postoperative pain

AHA: 4Q, '06, 79-81

338.29 Other chronic pain

AHA: 4Q, '06, 79-81

338.3 Neoplasm related pain (acute) (chronic)
Cancer associated pain
Pain due to malignancy (primary) (secondary)
Tumor associated pain
AHA: 2Q, '07, 11; 4Q, '06, 79-81

338.4 Chronic pain syndrome
Chronic pain associated with significant psychosocial dysfunction
AHA: 2Q, '07, 11; 4Q, '06, 79-81

►OTHER HEADACHE SYNDROMES (339)◄

● ✓4th **339 Other headache syndromes**
EXCLUDES *headache:*
NOS (784.0)
due to lumbar puncture (349.0)
migraine (346.0-346.9)

● ✓5th **339.0 Cluster headaches and other trigeminal autonomic cephalgias**
TACS

● **339.00 Cluster headache syndrome, unspecified**
Ciliary neuralgia
Cluster headache NOS
Histamine cephalgia
Lower half migraine
Migrainous neuralgia

● **339.01 Episodic cluster headache**

● **339.02 Chronic cluster headache**

● **339.03 Episodic paroxysmal hemicrania**
Paroxysmal hemicrania NOS

● **339.04 Chronic paroxysmal hemicrania**

● **339.05 Short lasting unilateral neuralgiform headache with conjunctival injection and tearing**
SUNCT

● **339.09 Other trigeminal autonomic cephalgias**

● ✓5th **339.1 Tension type headache**
EXCLUDES *tension headache NOS (307.81)*
tension headache related to psychological factors (307.81)

● **339.10 Tension type headache, unspecified**

● **339.11 Episodic tension type headache**

● **339.12 Chronic tension type headache**

● ✓5th **339.2 Post-traumatic headache**

● **339.20 Post-traumatic headache, unspecified**

● **339.21 Acute post-traumatic headache**

● **339.22 Chronic post-traumatic headache**

● ✓5th **339.3 Drug induced headache, not elsewhere classified**
Medication overuse headache
Rebound headache

● ✓5th **339.4 Complicated headache syndromes**

● **339.41 Hemicrania continua**

● **339.42 New daily persistent headache**
NDPH

● **339.43 Primary thunderclap headache**

● **339.44 Other complicated headache syndrome**

● ✓5th **339.8 Other specified headache syndromes**

● **339.81 Hypnic headache**

● **339.82 Headache associated with sexual activity**
Orgasmic headache
Preorgasmic headache

● **339.83 Primary cough headache**

● **339.84 Primary exertional headache**

● **339.85 Primary stabbing headache**

● **339.89 Other specified headache syndromes**

OTHER DISORDERS OF THE CENTRAL NERVOUS SYSTEM (340-349)

340 Multiple sclerosis
Disseminated or multiple sclerosis:
NOS
brain stem
cord
generalized

✓4th **341 Other demyelinating diseases of central nervous system**

341.0 Neuromyelitis optica

341.1 Schilder's disease
Baló's concentric sclerosis
Encephalitis periaxialis:
concentrica [Baló's]
diffusa [Schilder's]

DEF: Chronic leukoencephalopathy of children and adolescents; symptoms include blindness, deafness, bilateral spasticity and progressive mental deterioration.

✓5th **341.2 Acute (transverse) myelitis**
EXCLUDES *acute (transverse) myelitis (in) (due to):*
following immunization procedures (323.52)
infection classified elsewhere (323.42)
postinfectious (323.63)
protozoal diseases classified elsewhere (323.2)
rickettsial diseases classified elsewhere (323.1)
toxic (323.72)
viral diseases classified elsewhere (323.02)
transverse myelitis NOS (323.82)

341.20 Acute (transverse) myelitis NOS
AHA: 4Q, '06, 58-63

341.21 Acute (transverse) myelitis in conditions classified elsewhere
Code first underlying condition
AHA: 4Q, '06, 58-63

341.22 Idiopathic transverse myelitis
AHA: 4Q, '06, 58-63

341.8 Other demyelinating diseases of central nervous system
Central demyelination of corpus callosum
Central pontine myelinosis
Marchiafava (-Bignami) disease
AHA: N-D, '87, 6

341.9 Demyelinating disease of central nervous system, unspecified

✓4th **342 Hemiplegia and hemiparesis**
Note: This category is to be used when hemiplegia (complete) (incomplete) is reported without further specification, or is stated to be old or long-standing but of unspecified cause. The category is also for use in multiple coding to identify these types of hemiplegia resulting from any cause.

EXCLUDES *congenital (343.1)*
hemiplegia due to late effect of cerebrovascular accident (438.20-438.22)
infantile NOS (343.4)

The following fifth-diits are for use with codes 342.0-342.9:
0 affecting unspecified side
1 affecting dominant side
2 affecting nondominant side

AHA: 4Q, '94, 38

§ ✓5th **342.0 Flaccid hemiplegia**
[0-2]

§ ✓5th **342.1 Spastic hemiplegia**
[0-2]

§ Requires fifth-digit. Valid digits are in [brackets] under each code. See category 342 for codes and definitions.

§ 5th **342.8 Other specified hemiplegia**
[0-2]

§ 5th **342.9 Hemiplegia, unspecified**
[0-2] **AHA:** 3Q, '06, 5; 4Q, '98, 87

4th **343 Infantile cerebral palsy**

INCLUDES cerebral:
palsy NOS
spastic infantile paralysis
congenital spastic paralysis (cerebral)
Little's disease
paralysis (spastic) due to birth injury:
intracranial
spinal

EXCLUDES *athetoid cerebral palsy (333.71)*
hereditary cerebral paralysis, such as:
hereditary spastic paraplegia (334.1)
Vogt's disease (333.71)
spastic paralysis specified as noncongenital or noninfantile (344.0-344.9)

343.0 Diplegic
Congenital diplegia
Congenital paraplegia
DEF: Paralysis affecting both sides of the body simultaneously.

343.1 Hemiplegic
Congenital hemiplegia
EXCLUDES *infantile hemiplegia NOS (343.4)*

343.2 Quadriplegic
Tetraplegic

343.3 Monoplegic

343.4 Infantile hemiplegia
Infantile hemiplegia (postnatal) NOS

343.8 Other specified infantile cerebral palsy

343.9 Infantile cerebral palsy, unspecified
Cerebral palsy NOS
AHA: 4Q, '05, 89

4th **344 Other paralytic syndromes**

Note: This category is to be used when the listed conditions are reported without further specification or are stated to be old or long-standing but of unspecified cause. The category is also for use in multiple coding to identify these conditions resulting from any cause.

INCLUDES paralysis (complete) (incomplete), except as classifiable to 342 and 343

EXCLUDES *congenital or infantile cerebral palsy (343.0-343.9)*
hemiplegia (342.0-342.9)
congenital or infantile (343.1, 343.4)

5th **344.0 Quadriplegia and quadriparesis**

344.00 Quadriplegia unspecified
AHA: 4Q, '03, 103; 4Q, '98, 38

344.01 C_1-C_4 complete

344.02 C_1-C_4 incomplete

344.03 C_5-C_7 complete

344.04 C_5-C_7 incomplete

344.09 Other
AHA: 1Q, '01, 12; 4Q, '98, 39

344.1 Paraplegia
Paralysis of both lower limbs
Paraplegia (lower)
AHA: 4Q, '03, 110; M-A, '87, 10

344.2 Diplegia of upper limbs
Diplegia (upper)
Paralysis of both upper limbs

5th **344.3 Monoplegia of lower limb**
Paralysis of lower limb
EXCLUDES *monoplegia of lower limb due to late effect of cerebrovascular accident (438.40-438.42)*

344.30 Affecting unspecified side

344.31 Affecting dominant side

344.32 Affecting nondominant side

5th **344.4 Monoplegia of upper limb**
Paralysis of upper limb
EXCLUDES *monoplegia of upper limb due to late effect of cerebrovascular accident (438.30-438.32)*

344.40 Affecting unspecified side

344.41 Affecting dominant side

344.42 Affecting nondominant side

344.5 Unspecified monoplegia

5th **344.6 Cauda equina syndrome**
DEF: Dull pain and paresthesias in sacrum, perineum and bladder due to compression of spinal nerve roots; pain radiates down buttocks, back of thigh, calf of leg and into foot with prickling, burning sensations.

344.60 Without mention of neurogenic bladder

344.61 With neurogenic bladder
Acontractile bladder
Autonomic hyperreflexia of bladder
Cord bladder
Detrusor hyperreflexia
AHA: M-J, '87, 12; M-A, '87, 10

5th **344.8 Other specified paralytic syndromes**

344.81 Locked-in state
AHA: 4Q, '93, 24
DEF: State of consciousness where patients are paralyzed and unable to respond to environmental stimuli; patients have eye movements, and stimuli can enter the brain but patients cannot respond to stimuli.

344.89 Other specified paralytic syndrome
AHA: 2Q, '99, 4

344.9 Paralysis, unspecified

4th **345 Epilepsy and recurrent seizures**

The following fifth-digit subclassification is for use with categories 345.0, .1, .4-.9:
0 without mention of intractable eilepsy
1 with intractable epilepsy

EXCLUDES *progressive myoclonic epilepsy (333.2)*

AHA: 1Q, '93, 24; 2Q, '92, 8; 4Q, '92, 23
DEF: Brain disorder characterized by electrical-like disturbances; may include occasional impairment or loss of consciousness, abnormal motor phenomena and psychic or sensory disturbances.

§ 5th **345.0 Generalized nonconvulsive epilepsy**
[0-1] Absences:
atonic
typical
Minor epilepsy
Petit mal
Pykno-epilepsy
Seizures:
akinetic
atonic
AHA: For code 345.00: 1Q, '04, 18

§ Requires fifth-digit. Valid digits are in [brackets] under each code. See appropriate category for codes and definitions.

§ 5th **345.1 Generalized convulsive epilepsy**
[0-1]
Epileptic seizures:
clonic
myoclonic
tonic
tonic-clonic
Grand mal
Major epilepsy
EXCLUDES *convulsions:*
NOS (780.39)
infantile (780.39)
newborn (779.0)
infantile spasms (345.6)

AHA: 3Q, '97, 4

DEF: Convulsive seizures with tension of limbs (tonic) or rhythmic contractions (clonic).

345.2 Petit mal status
Epileptic absence status

DEF: Minor myoclonic spasms and sudden momentary loss of consciousness in epilepsy.

345.3 Grand mal status
Status epilepticus NOS
EXCLUDES *epilepsia partialis continua (345.7)*
status:
psychomotor (345.7)
temporal lobe (345.7)

AHA: 3Q, '05, 12

DEF: Sudden loss of consciousness followed by generalized convulsions in epilepsy.

§ 5th **345.4 Localization-related (focal) (partial) epilepsy and epileptic syndromes with complex partial seizures**
[0-1]
Epilepsy:
limbic system
partial:
secondarily generalized
with impairment of consciousness
with memory and ideational disturbances
psychomotor
psychosensory
temporal lobe
Epileptic automatism

§ 5th **345.5 Localization-related (focal) (partial) epilepsy and epileptic syndromes with simple partial seizures**
[0-1]
Epilepsy:
Bravais-Jacksonian NOS
focal (motor) NOS
Jacksonian NOS
motor partial
partial NOS:
without impairment of consciousness
sensory-induced
somatomotor
somatosensory
visceral
visual

§ 5th **345.6 Infantile spasms**
[0-1]
Hypsarrhythmia
Lightning spasms
Salaam attacks
EXCLUDES *salaam tic (781.0)*

AHA: N-D, '84, 12

§ 5th **345.7 Epilepsia partialis continua**
[0-1]
Kojevnikov's epilepsy

DEF: Continuous muscle contractions and relaxation; result of abnormal neural discharge.

§ 5th **345.8 Other forms of epilepsy and recurrent seizures**
[0-1]
Epilepsy:
cursive [running]
gelastic

§ 5th **345.9 Epilepsy, unspecified**
[0-1]
Epileptic convulsions, fits, or seizures NOS
Recurrent seizures NOS
Seizure disorder NOS
EXCLUDES *convulsion (convulsive) disorder (780.39)*
convulsive seizure or fit NOS (780.39)
recurrent convulsions (780.39)

AHA: ▶1Q, '08, 17;◀ N-D, '87, 12

4th **346 Migraine**
EXCLUDES ▶*headache:*
NOS (784.0)
syndromes (339.00-339.89)◀

The following fifth-digit subclassification is for use with category 346:
▲ **0 without mention of intractable migraine without mention of status migrainosus**
▲ **1 with intractable migraine, so stated without mention of status migrainosus**
● **2 without mention of intractable migraine with status migrainosus**
● **3 with intractable migraine, so stated, with status migrainosus**

DEF: Benign vascular headache of extreme pain; commonly associated with irritability, nausea, vomiting and often photophobia; premonitory visual hallucination of a crescent in the visual field (scotoma).

▲ § 5th **346.0 Migraine with aura**
[0-3]
▶Basilar migraine
Classic migraine◀
Migraine preceded or accompanied by transient focal neurological phenomena
▶Migraine triggered seizures
Migraine with acute-onset aura
Migraine with aura without headache (migraine equivalents)
Migraine with prolonged aura
Migraine with typical aura
Retinal migraine◀
EXCLUDES ▶*persistent migraine aura (346.5, 346.6)*◀

▲ § 5th **346.1 Migraine without aura**
[0-3]
▶Common migraine ◀

▲ § 5th **346.2 Variants of migraine, not elsewhere classified**
[0-3]
▶Abdominal migraine
Cyclical vomiting associated with migraine
Ophthalmoplegic migraine
Periodic headache syndromes in child or adolescent◀
EXCLUDES ▶*cyclical vomiting NOS (536.2)*
psychogenic cyclical vomiting (306.4)◀

● § 5th **346.3 Hemiplegic migraine**
[0-3]
Familial migraine
Sporadic migraine

● § 5th **346.4 Menstrual migraine** ♀
[0-3]
Menstrual headache
Menstrually related migraine
Premenstrual headache
Premenstrual migraine
Pure menstrual migraine

● § 5th **346.5 Persistent migraine aura without cerebral infarction**
[0-3]
Persistent migraine aura NOS

● § 5th **346.6 Persistent migraine aura with cerebral infarction**
[0-3]

● § 5th **346.7 Chronic migraine without aura**
[0-3]
Transformed migraine without aura

▲ § 5th **346.8 Other forms of migraine**
[0-3]

▲ § 5th **346.9 Migraine, unspecified**
[0-3]
AHA: N-D, '85, 16

§ Requires fifth-digit. Valid digits are in [brackets] under each code. See appropriate category for codes and definitions.

✓4th **347 Cataplexy and narcolepsy**

DEF: Cataplexy: Sudden onset of muscle weakness with loss of tone and strength; caused by aggressive or spontaneous emotions.

DEF: Narcolepsy: Brief, recurrent, uncontrollable episodes of sound sleep.

✓5th **347.0 Narcolepsy**

347.00 Without cataplexy
Narcolepsy NOS

347.01 With cataplexy

✓5th **347.1 Narcolepsy in conditions classified elsewhere**

Code first underlying condition

347.10 Without cataplexy

347.11 With cataplexy

✓4th **348 Other conditions of brain**

348.0 Cerebral cysts

Arachnoid cyst
Porencephalic cyst
Porencephaly, acquired
Pseudoporencephaly

EXCLUDES *porencephaly (congenital) (742.4)*

348.1 Anoxic brain damage

EXCLUDES *that occurring in:*
abortion (634-638 with .7, 639.8)
ectopic or molar pregnancy (639.8)
labor or delivery (668.2, 669.4)
that of newborn (767.0, 768.0-768.9, 772.1-772.2)

Use additional E code to identify cause

DEF: Brain injury due to lack of oxygen, other than birth trauma.

348.2 Benign intracranial hypertension

Pseudotumor cerebri

EXCLUDES *hypertensive encephalopathy (437.2)*

DEF: Elevated pressure in brain due to fluid retention in brain cavities.

✓5th **348.3 Encephalopathy, not elsewhere classified**

AHA: 4Q, '03, 58; 3Q, '97, 4

348.30 Encephalopathy, unspecified

348.31 Metabolic encephalopathy

Septic encephalopathy

EXCLUDES *toxic metabolic encephalopathy (349.82)*

348.39 Other encephalopathy

EXCLUDES *encephalopathy:*
alcoholic (291.2)
hepatic (572.2)
hypertensive (437.2)
toxic (349.82)

348.4 Compression of brain

Compression } brain (stem)
Herniation } brain (stem)

Posterior fossa compression syndrome

AHA: 4Q, '94, 37

DEF: Elevated pressure in brain due to blood clot, tumor, fracture, abscess, other condition.

Cranial Nerves

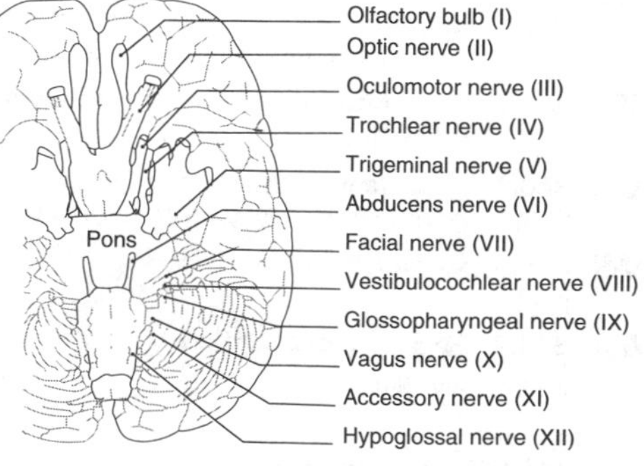

348.5 Cerebral edema

DEF: Elevated pressure in the brain due to fluid retention in brain tissues.

348.8 Other conditions of brain

Cerebral:
calcification
fungus

AHA: S-O, '87, 9

348.9 Unspecified condition of brain

✓4th **349 Other and unspecified disorders of the nervous system**

349.0 Reaction to spinal or lumbar puncture

Headache following lumbar puncture

AHA: 2Q, '99, 9; 3Q, '90, 18

349.1 Nervous system complications from surgically implanted device

EXCLUDES *immediate postoperative complications (997.00-997.09)*
mechanical complications of nervous system device (996.2)

349.2 Disorders of meninges, not elsewhere classified

Adhesions, meningeal (cerebral) (spinal)
Cyst, spinal meninges
Meningocele, acquired
Pseudomeningocele, acquired

AHA: 1Q, '06, 15; 2Q, '98, 18; 3Q, '94, 4

● ✓5th **349.3 Dural tear**

● **349.31 Accidental puncture or laceration of dura during a procedure**

Incidental (inadvertent) durotomy

● **349.39 Other dural tear**

✓5th **349.8 Other specified disorders of nervous system**

349.81 Cerebrospinal fluid rhinorrhea

EXCLUDES *cerebrospinal fluid otorrhea (388.61)*

DEF: Cerebrospinal fluid discharging from the nose; caused by fracture of frontal bone with tearing of dura mater and arachnoid.

349.82 Toxic encephalopathy

Toxic metabolic encephalopathy

Use additional E code to identify cause

AHA: 4Q, '93, 29

DEF: Brain tissue degeneration due to toxic substance.

349.89 Other

349.9 Unspecified disorders of nervous system

Disorder of nervous system (central) NOS

DISORDERS OF THE PERIPHERAL NERVOUS SYSTEM (350-359)

EXCLUDES *diseases of:*
acoustic [8th] nerve (388.5)
oculomotor [3rd, 4th, 6th] nerves (378.0-378.9)
optic [2nd] nerve (377.0-377.9)
peripheral autonomic nerves (337.0-337.9)
neuralgia } NOS or "rheumatic" (729.2)
neuritis } NOS or "rheumatic" (729.2)
radiculitis } NOS or "rheumatic" (729.2)
peripheral neuritis in pregnancy (646.4)

✓4th **350 Trigeminal nerve disorders**

INCLUDES disorders of 5th cranial nerve

350.1 Trigeminal neuralgia

Tic douloureux
Trifacial neuralgia
Trigeminal neuralgia NOS

EXCLUDES *postherpetic (053.12)*

Trigeminal and Facial Nerve Branches

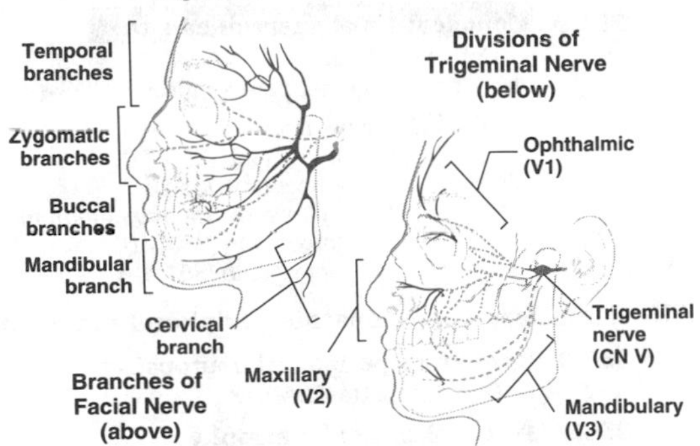

350.2 Atypical face pain

350.8 Other specified trigeminal nerve disorders

350.9 Trigeminal nerve disorder, unspecified

✓4th **351 Facial nerve disorders**

INCLUDES disorders of 7th cranial nerve

EXCLUDES *that in newborn (767.5)*

351.0 Bell's palsy

Facial palsy

DEF: Unilateral paralysis of face due to lesion on facial nerve; produces facial distortion.

351.1 Geniculate ganglionitis

Geniculate ganglionitis NOS

EXCLUDES *herpetic (053.11)*

DEF: Inflammation of tissue at bend in facial nerve.

351.8 Other facial nerve disorders

Facial myokymia
Melkersson's syndrome

AHA: 3Q, '02, 13

351.9 Facial nerve disorder, unspecified

✓4th **352 Disorders of other cranial nerves**

352.0 Disorders of olfactory [lst] nerve

352.1 Glossopharyngeal neuralgia

AHA: 2Q, '02, 8

DEF: Pain between throat and ear along petrosal and jugular ganglia.

352.2 Other disorders of glossopharyngeal [9th] nerve

352.3 Disorders of pneumogastric [10th] nerve

Disorders of vagal nerve

EXCLUDES *paralysis of vocal cords or larynx (478.30-478.34)*

DEF: Nerve disorder affecting ear, tongue, pharynx, larynx, esophagus, viscera and thorax.

352.4 Disorders of accessory [11th] nerve

DEF: Nerve disorder affecting palate, pharynx, larynx, thoracic viscera, sternocleidomastoid and trapezius muscles.

352.5 Disorders of hypoglossal [12th] nerve

DEF: Nerve disorder affecting tongue muscles.

352.6 Multiple cranial nerve palsies

Collet-Sicard syndrome
Polyneuritis cranialis

352.9 Unspecified disorder of cranial nerves

Peripheral Nervous System

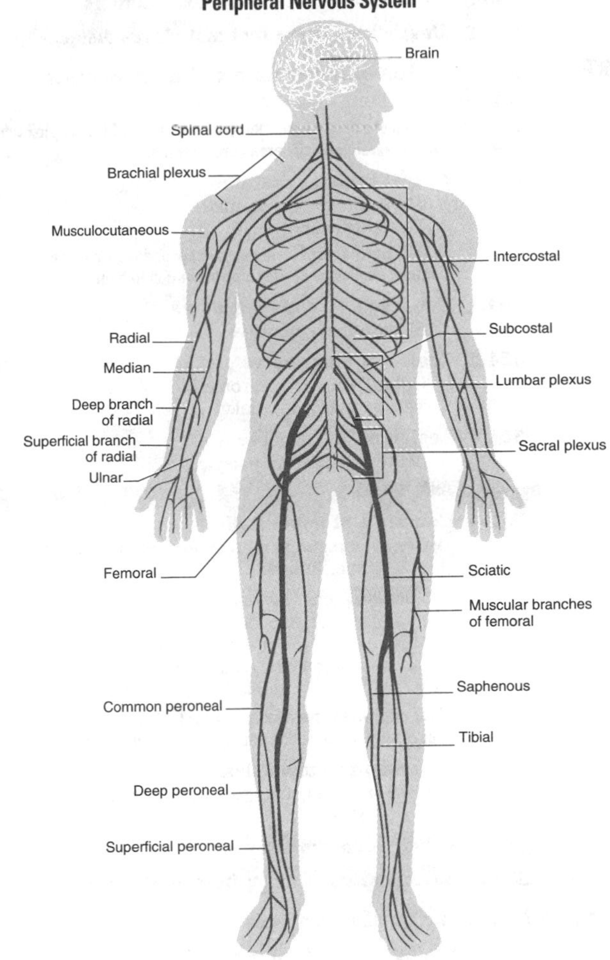

✓4th **353 Nerve root and plexus disorders**

EXCLUDES *conditions due to:*
intervertebral disc disorders (722.0-722.9)
spondylosis (720.0-721.9)
vertebrogenic disorders (723.0-724.9)

353.0 Brachial plexus lesions

Cervical rib syndrome
Costoclavicular syndrome
Scalenus anticus syndrome
Thoracic outlet syndrome

EXCLUDES *brachial neuritis or radiculitis NOS (723.4)*
that in newborn (767.6)

AHA: 3Q, '06, 12

DEF: Acquired disorder in tissue along nerves in shoulder; causes corresponding motor and sensory dysfunction.

353.1 Lumbosacral plexus lesions

DEF: Acquired disorder in tissue along nerves in lower back; causes corresponding motor and sensory dysfunction.

353.2 Cervical root lesions, not elsewhere classified

353.3 Thoracic root lesions, not elsewhere classified

353.4 Lumbosacral root lesions, not elsewhere classified

353.5 Neuralgic amyotrophy

Parsonage-Aldren-Turner syndrome

▶Code first any associated underlying disease, such as:
diabetes mellitus (249.6, 250.6)◀

353.6 Phantom limb (syndrome)

DEF: Abnormal tingling or a burning sensation, transient aches, and intermittent or continuous pain perceived as originating in the absent limb.

353.8 Other nerve root and plexus disorders

353.9 Unspecified nerve root and plexus disorder

✓4th **354 Mononeuritis of upper limb and mononeuritis multiplex**

DEF: Inflammation of a single nerve; known as mononeuritis multiplex when several nerves in unrelated body areas are affected.

354.0 Carpal tunnel syndrome
Median nerve entrapment
Partial thenar atrophy

DEF: Compression of median nerve by tendons; causes pain, tingling, numbness and burning sensation in hand.

354.1 Other lesion of median nerve
Median nerve neuritis

354.2 Lesion of ulnar nerve
Cubital tunnel syndrome
Tardy ulnar nerve palsy

354.3 Lesion of radial nerve
Acute radial nerve palsy

AHA: N-D, '87, 6

354.4 Causalgia of upper limb
▶Complex regional pain syndrome type II of the upper limb◀

EXCLUDES *causalgia:*
NOS (355.9)
lower limb (355.71)
▶complex regional pain syndrome type II of the lower limb (355.71)◀

DEF: Peripheral nerve damage, upper limb; usually due to injury; causes burning sensation and trophic skin changes.

354.5 Mononeuritis multiplex
Combinations of single conditions classifiable to 354 or 355

354.8 Other mononeuritis of upper limb

354.9 Mononeuritis of upper limb, unspecified

✓4th **355 Mononeuritis of lower limb**

355.0 Lesion of sciatic nerve

EXCLUDES *sciatica NOS (724.3)*

AHA: 2Q, '89, 12

DEF: Acquired disorder of sciatic nerve; causes motor and sensory dysfunction in back, buttock and leg.

355.1 Meralgia paresthetica
Lateral cutaneous femoral nerve of thigh compression or syndrome

DEF: Inguinal ligament entraps lateral femoral cutaneous nerve; causes tingling, pain and numbness along outer thigh.

355.2 Other lesion of femoral nerve

355.3 Lesion of lateral popliteal nerve
Lesion of common peroneal nerve

355.4 Lesion of medial popliteal nerve

355.5 Tarsal tunnel syndrome

DEF: Compressed, entrapped posterior tibial nerve; causes tingling, pain and numbness in sole of foot.

355.6 Lesion of plantar nerve
Morton's metatarsalgia, neuralgia, or neuroma

✓5th **355.7 Other mononeuritis of lower limb**

355.71 Causalgia of lower limb

EXCLUDES *causalgia:*
NOS (355.9)
upper limb (354.4)
▶complex regional pain syndrome of upper limb (354.4)◀

DEF: Dysfunction of lower limb peripheral nerve, usually due to injury; causes burning pain and trophic skin changes.

355.79 Other mononeuritis of lower limb

355.8 Mononeuritis of lower limb, unspecified

355.9 Mononeuritis of unspecified site
Causalgia NOS
▶Complex regional pain syndrome NOS◀

EXCLUDES *causalgia:*
lower limb (355.71)
upper limb (354.4)
▶complex regional pain syndrome:
lower limb (355.71)
upper limb (354.4)◀

✓4th **356 Hereditary and idiopathic peripheral neuropathy**

356.0 Hereditary peripheral neuropathy
Déjérine-Sottas disease

356.1 Peroneal muscular atrophy
Charcôt-Marie-Tooth disease
Neuropathic muscular atrophy

DEF: Genetic disorder, in muscles innervated by peroneal nerves; symptoms include muscle wasting in lower limbs and locomotor difficulties.

356.2 Hereditary sensory neuropathy

DEF: Inherited disorder in dorsal root ganglia, optic nerve, and cerebellum, causing sensory losses, shooting pains, and foot ulcers.

356.3 Refsum's disease
Heredopathia atactica polyneuritiformis

DEF: Genetic disorder of lipid metabolism; causes persistent, painful inflammation of nerves and retinitis pigmentosa.

356.4 Idiopathic progressive polyneuropathy

356.8 Other specified idiopathic peripheral neuropathy
Supranuclear paralysis

356.9 Unspecified

✓4th **357 Inflammatory and toxic neuropathy**

357.0 Acute infective polyneuritis
Guillain-Barré syndrome
Postinfectious polyneuritis

AHA: 2Q, '98, 12

DEF: Guillain-Barré syndrome: acute demyelinatry polyneuropathy preceded by viral illness (i.e., herpes, cytomegalovirus [CMV], Epstein-Barr virus [EBV]) or a bacterial illness; areflexic motor paralysis with mild sensory disturbance and acellular rise in spinal fluid protein.

357.1 Polyneuropathy in collagen vascular disease

Code first underlying disease, as:
disseminated lupus erythematosus (710.0)
polyarteritis nodosa (446.0)
rheumatoid arthritis (714.0)

357.2 Polyneuropathy in diabetes

Code first underlying disease ▶(249.6, 250.6)◀

AHA: 4Q, '03, 105; 2Q, '92, 15; 3Q, '91, 9

357.3 Polyneuropathy in malignant disease

Code first underlying disease (140.0-208.9)

357.4 *Polyneuropathy in other diseases classified elsewhere*

Code first underlying disease, as:
amyloidosis (277.30-277.39)
beriberi (265.0)
chronic uremia (585.9)
deficiency of B vitamins (266.0-266.9)
diphtheria (032.0-032.9)
hypoglycemia (251.2)
pellagra (265.2)
porphyria (277.1)
sarcoidosis (135)
uremia NOS (586)

EXCLUDES *polyneuropathy in:*
herpes zoster (053.13)
mumps (072.72)

AHA: ►2Q, '08, 8;◄ 2Q, '98, 15

357.5 Alcoholic polyneuropathy

357.6 Polyneuropathy due to drugs

Use additional E code to identify drug

357.7 Polyneuropathy due to other toxic agents

Use additional E code to identify toxic agent

✓5th **357.8 Other**

AHA: 4Q, '02, 47; 2Q, '98, 12

357.81 Chronic inflammatory demyelinating polyneuritis

DEF: Inflammation of peripheral nerves resulting in destruction of myelin sheath; associated with diabetes mellitus, dys-proteinemias, renal failure and malnutrition; symptoms in-clude tingling, numbness, burning pain, diminished tendon reflexes, weakness, and atrophy in lower extremities.

357.82 Critical illness polyneuropathy

Acute motor neuropathy

AHA: 4Q, '03, 111

DEF: An acute axonal neuropathy, both sensory and motor, that is associated with Systemic Inflammatory Response Syndrome (SIRS).

357.89 Other inflammatory and toxic neuropathy

357.9 Unspecified

✓4th **358 Myoneural disorders**

✓5th **358.0 Myasthenia gravis**

AHA: 4Q, '03, 59

DEF: Autoimmune disorder of acetylcholine at neuromuscular junction; causing fatigue of voluntary muscles.

358.00 Myasthenia gravis without (acute) exacerbation

Myasthenia gravis NOS

358.01 Myasthenia gravis with (acute) exacerbation

Myasthenia gravis in crisis

AHA: 4Q, '07, 109; 1Q, '05, 4; 4Q, '04, 139

358.1 Myasthenic syndromes in diseases classified elsewhere

Eaton-Lambert syndrome from stated cause classified elsewhere

Code first underlying disease, as:
botulism ►(005.1, 040.41-040.42)◄
hypothyroidism (244.0-244.9)
malignant neoplasm (140.0-208.9)
pernicious anemia (281.0)
thyrotoxicosis (242.0-242.9)

358.2 Toxic myoneural disorders

Use additional E code to identify toxic agent

358.8 Other specified myoneural disorders

358.9 Myoneural disorders, unspecified

AHA: 2Q, '02, 16

✓4th **359 Muscular dystrophies and other myopathies**

EXCLUDES *idiopathic polymyositis (710.4)*

359.0 Congenital hereditary muscular dystrophy

Benign congenital myopathy
Central core disease
Centronuclear myopathy
Myotubular myopathy
Nemaline body disease

EXCLUDES *arthrogryposis multiplex congenita (754.89)*

DEF: Genetic disorder; causing progressive or nonprogressive muscle weakness.

359.1 Hereditary progressive muscular dystrophy

Muscular dystrophy:	Muscular dystrophy:
NOS	Gower's
distal	Landouzy-Déjérine
Duchenne	limb-girdle
Erb's	ocular
fascioscapulohumeral	oculopharyngeal

DEF: Genetic degenerative, muscle disease; causes progressive weakness, wasting of muscle with no nerve involvement.

✓5th **359.2 Myotonic disorders**

EXCLUDES *periodic paralysis (359.3)*

AHA: 4Q, '07, 75

DEF: Impaired movement due to spasmatic, rigid muscles.

359.21 Myotonic muscular dystrophy

Dystrophia myotonica
Myotonia atrophica
Myotonic dystrophy
Proximal myotonic myopathy [PROMM]
Steinert's disease

359.22 Myotonia congenita

Acetazolamide responsive myotonia congenita
Dominant form [Thomsen's disease]
Recessive form [Becker's disease]

359.23 Myotonic chondrodystrophy

Congenital myotonic chondrodystrophy
Schwartz-Jampel disease

359.24 Drug induced myotonia

Use additional E code to identify drug

359.29 Other specified myotonic disorder

Myotonia fluctuans
Myotonia levior
Myotonia permanens
Paramyotonia congenita (of von Eulenburg)

359.3 Periodic paralysis

Familial periodic paralysis
Hypokalemic familial periodic paralysis
Hyperkalemic periodic paralysis
Hypokalemic periodic paralysis
Potassium sensitive periodic paralysis

EXCLUDES *paramyotonia congenita (of von Eulenburg) (359.29)*

DEF: Genetic disorder; characterized by rapidly progressive flaccid paralysis; attacks often occur after exercise or exposure to cold or dietary changes.

359.4 Toxic myopathy

Use additional E code to identify toxic agent

AHA: 1Q, '88, 5

DEF: Muscle disorder caused by toxic agent.

359.5 Myopathy in endocrine diseases classified elsewhere

Code first underlying disease, as:
Addison's disease (255.41)
Cushing's syndrome (255.0)
hypopituitarism (253.2)
myxedema (244.0-244.9)
thyrotoxicosis (242.0-242.9)

DEF: Muscle disorder secondary to dysfunction in hormone secretion.

359.6 Symptomatic inflammatory myopathy in diseases classified elsewhere

Code first underlying disease, as:
amyloidosis (277.30-277.39)
disseminated lupus erythematosus (710.0)
malignant neoplasm (140.0-208.9)
polyarteritis nodosa (446.0)
rheumatoid arthritis (714.0)
sarcoidosis (135)
scleroderma (710.1)
Sjögren's disease (710.2)

✓5th **359.8 Other myopathies**
AHA: 4Q, '02, 47; 3Q, '90, 17

359.81 Critical illness myopathy
Acute necrotizing myopathy
Acute quadriplegic myopathy
Intensive care (ICU) myopathy
Myopathy of critical illness

359.89 Other myopathies

359.9 Myopathy, unspecified

DISORDERS OF THE EYE AND ADNEXA (360-379)

▶Use additional external cause code, if applicable, to identify the cause of the eye condition◀

✓4th **360 Disorders of the globe**

INCLUDES disorders affecting multiple structures of eye

✓5th **360.0 Purulent endophthalmitis**

EXCLUDES *bleb associated endophthalmitis (379.63)*

360.00 Purulent endophthalmitis, unspecified

360.01 Acute endophthalmitis

360.02 Panophthalmitis

360.03 Chronic endophthalmitis

360.04 Vitreous abscess

✓5th **360.1 Other endophthalmitis**

EXCLUDES *bleb associated endophthalmitis (379.63)*

360.11 Sympathetic uveitis
DEF: Inflammation of vascular layer of uninjured eye; follows injury to other eye.

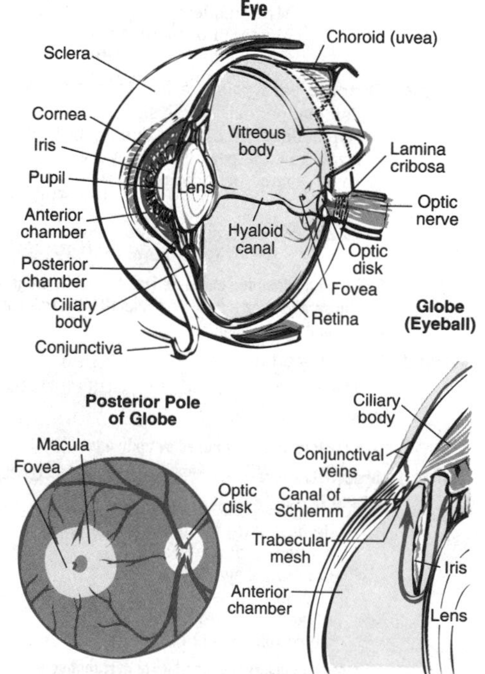

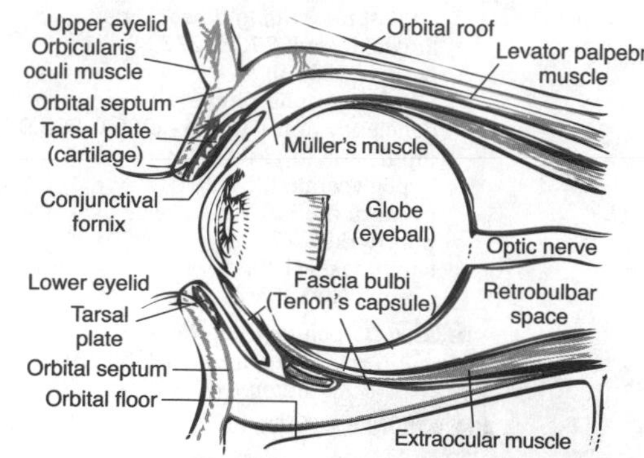

360.12 Panuveitis
DEF: Inflammation of entire vascular layer of eye, including choroid, iris and ciliary body.

360.13 Parasitic endophthalmitis NOS
DEF: Parasitic infection causing inflammation of the entire eye.

360.14 Ophthalmia nodosa
DEF: Conjunctival inflammation caused by embedded hairs.

360.19 Other
Phacoanaphylactic endophthalmitis

✓5th **360.2 Degenerative disorders of globe**
AHA: 3Q, '91, 3

360.20 Degenerative disorder of globe, unspecified

360.21 Progressive high (degenerative) myopia
Malignant myopia
DEF: Severe, progressive nearsightedness in adults, complicated by serious disease of the choroid; leads to retinal detachment and blindness.

360.23 Siderosis
DEF: Iron pigment deposits within tissue of eyeball; caused by high iron content of blood.

360.24 Other metallosis
Chalcosis
DEF: Metal deposits, other than iron, within eyeball tissues.

360.29 Other
EXCLUDES *xerophthalmia (264.7)*

✓5th **360.3 Hypotony of eye**

360.30 Hypotony, unspecified
DEF: Low osmotic pressure causing lack of tone, tension and strength.

360.31 Primary hypotony

360.32 Ocular fistula causing hypotony
DEF: Low intraocular pressure due to leak through abnormal passage.

360.33 Hypotony associated with other ocular disorders

360.34 Flat anterior chamber
DEF: Low pressure behind cornea, causing compression.

✓5th **360.4 Degenerated conditions of globe**

360.40 Degenerated globe or eye, unspecified

360.41 Blind hypotensive eye
Atrophy of globe
Phthisis bulbi
DEF: Vision loss due to extremely low intraocular pressure.

360.42 Blind hypertensive eye
Absolute glaucoma
DEF: Vision loss due to painful, high intraocular pressure.

360.43 Hemophthalmos, except current injury
EXCLUDES *traumatic (871.0-871.9, 921.0-921.9)*
DEF: Pool of blood within eyeball, not from current injury.

360.44 Leucocoria
DEF: Whitish mass or reflex in the pupil behind lens; also called cat's eye reflex; often indicative of retinoblastoma.

✓5th **360.5 Retained (old) intraocular foreign body, magnetic**
EXCLUDES *current penetrating injury with magnetic foreign body (871.5)*
retained (old) foreign body of orbit (376.6)

360.50 Foreign body, magnetic, intraocular, unspecified

360.51 Foreign body, magnetic, in anterior chamber

360.52 Foreign body, magnetic, in iris or ciliary body

360.53 Foreign body, magnetic, in lens

360.54 Foreign body, magnetic, in vitreous

360.55 Foreign body, magnetic, in posterior wall

360.59 Foreign body, magnetic, in other or multiple sites

✓5th **360.6 Retained (old) intraocular foreign body, nonmagnetic**
Retained (old) foreign body:
NOS
nonmagnetic
EXCLUDES *current penetrating injury with (nonmagnetic) foreign body (871.6)*
retained (old) foreign body in orbit (376.6)

360.60 Foreign body, intraocular, unspecified

360.61 Foreign body in anterior chamber

360.62 Foreign body in iris or ciliary body

360.63 Foreign body in lens

360.64 Foreign body in vitreous

360.65 Foreign body in posterior wall

360.69 Foreign body in other or multiple sites

✓5th **360.8 Other disorders of globe**

360.81 Luxation of globe
DEF: Displacement of eyeball.

360.89 Other

360.9 Unspecified disorder of globe

✓4th **361 Retinal detachments and defects**
DEF: Light-sensitive layer at back of eye, separates from blood supply; disrupting vision.

✓5th **361.0 Retinal detachment with retinal defect**
Rhegmatogenous retinal detachment
EXCLUDES *detachment of retinal pigment epithelium (362.42-362.43)*
retinal detachment (serous) (without defect) (361.2)

361.00 Retinal detachment with retinal defect, unspecified

361.01 Recent detachment, partial, with single defect

361.02 Recent detachment, partial, with multiple defects

361.03 Recent detachment, partial, with giant tear

361.04 Recent detachment, partial, with retinal dialysis
Dialysis (juvenile) of retina (with detachment)

361.05 Recent detachment, total or subtotal

361.06 Old detachment, partial
Delimited old retinal detachment

361.07 Old detachment, total or subtotal

✓5th **361.1 Retinoschisis and retinal cysts**
EXCLUDES *juvenile retinoschisis (362.73)*
microcystoid degeneration of retina (362.62)
parasitic cyst of retina (360.13)

361.10 Retinoschisis, unspecified
DEF: Separation of retina due to degenerative process of aging; should not be confused with acute retinal detachment.

361.11 Flat retinoschisis
DEF: Slow, progressive split of retinal sensory layers

361.12 Bullous retinoschisis
DEF: Fluid retention between split retinal sensory layers.

361.13 Primary retinal cysts

361.14 Secondary retinal cysts

361.19 Other
Pseudocyst of retina

361.2 Serous retinal detachment
Retinal detachment without retinal defect
EXCLUDES *central serous retinopathy (362.41)*
retinal pigment epithelium detachment (362.42-362.43)

✓5th **361.3 Retinal defects without detachment**
EXCLUDES *chorioretinal scars after surgery for detachment (363.30-363.35)*
peripheral retinal degeneration without defect (362.60-362.66)

361.30 Retinal defect, unspecified
Retinal break(s) NOS

361.31 Round hole of retina without detachment

361.32 Horseshoe tear of retina without detachment
Operculum of retina without mention of detachment

361.33 Multiple defects of retina without detachment

✓5th **361.8 Other forms of retinal detachment**

361.81 Traction detachment of retina
Traction detachment with vitreoretinal organization

361.89 Other
AHA: 3Q, '99, 12

361.9 Unspecified retinal detachment
AHA: N-D, '87, 10

✓4th **362 Other retinal disorders**

EXCLUDES *chorioretinal scars (363.30-363.35)*
chorioretinitis (363.0-363.2)

✓5th **362.0 Diabetic retinopathy**

Code first diabetes ▶(249.5, 250.5)◀

DEF: Retinal changes in diabetes of long duration; causes hemorrhages, microaneurysms, waxy deposits and proliferative noninflammatory degenerative disease of retina.

AHA: 4Q, '05, 65; 3Q, '91, 8

362.01 Background diabetic retinopathy
Diabetic retinal microaneurysms
Diabetic retinopathy NOS

362.02 Proliferative diabetic retinopathy
AHA: 3Q, '96, 5
DEF: Occurrence of the ischemic effects of vessel blockages result in neovascularization; new blood vessels begin to form to compensate for restricted blood flow; multiple areas of the retina and inner vitreous may be affected.

362.03 Nonproliferative diabetic retinopathy NOS

362.04 Mild nonproliferative diabetic retinopathy
DEF: Early stages of degenerative condition of the retina due to diabetes; microaneurysm formation; small balloon-like swelling of the retinal vessels.

362.05 Moderate nonproliferative diabetic retinopathy
DEF: Stage of degenerative condition of the retina due to diabetes with pronounced microaneurysms; vessel blockages can occur.

362.06 Severe nonproliferative diabetic retinopathy
AHA: 4Q, '05, 67
DEF: Stage of degenerative condition of the retina due to diabetes in which vascular breakdown in the retina results in multiple vascular blockages, or "beadings," intraretinal hemorrhages can be numerous.

362.07 Diabetic macular edema
Note: Code 362.07 must be used with a code for diabetic retinopathy (362.01-362.06)
Diabetic retinal edema
DEF: Leakage from retinal blood vessels causes swelling of the macula and impaired vision; exudates or plaques may develop in the posterior pole of the retina due to the breakdown of retinal vasculature.

✓5th **362.1 Other background retinopathy and retinal vascular changes**

362.10 Background retinopathy, unspecified
AHA: 1Q, '06, 12

362.11 Hypertensive retinopathy
AHA: 3Q, '90, 3
DEF: Retinal irregularities caused by systemic hypertension.

362.12 Exudative retinopathy
Coats' syndrome
AHA: 3Q, '99, 12

362.13 Changes in vascular appearance
Vascular sheathing of retina
Use additional code for any associated atherosclerosis (440.8)

362.14 Retinal microaneurysms NOS
DEF: Microscopic dilation of retinal vessels in nondiabetic.

362.15 Retinal telangiectasia
DEF: Dilation of blood vessels of the retina.

362.16 Retinal neovascularization NOS
Neovascularization:
- choroidal
- subretinal

DEF: New and abnormal vascular growth in the retina.

362.17 Other intraretinal microvascular abnormalities
Retinal sclerosis
Retinal varices

362.18 Retinal vasculitis
Eales' disease
Retinal:
- arteritis
- endarteritis
- perivasculitis
- phlebitis

DEF: Inflammation of retinal blood vessels.

✓5th **362.2 Other proliferative retinopathy**

● **362.20 Retinopathy of prematurity, unspecified**
Retinopathy of prematurity NOS

362.21 Retrolental fibroplasia
▶Cicatricial retinopathy of prematurity◀
DEF: Fibrous tissue in vitreous, from retina to lens, causing blindness; associated with premature infants requiring high amounts of oxygen.

● **362.22 Retinopathy of prematurity, stage 0**

● **362.23 Retinopathy of prematurity, stage 1**

● **362.24 Retinopathy of prematurity, stage 2**

● **362.25 Retinopathy of prematurity, stage 3**

● **362.26 Retinopathy of prematurity, stage 4**

● **362.27 Retinopathy of prematurity, stage 5**

362.29 Other nondiabetic proliferative retinopathy
AHA: 3Q, '96, 5

✓5th **362.3 Retinal vascular occlusion**

DEF: Obstructed blood flow to and from retina.

362.30 Retinal vascular occlusion, unspecified

362.31 Central retinal artery occlusion

362.32 Arterial branch occlusion

362.33 Partial arterial occlusion
Hollenhorst plaque
Retinal microembolism

362.34 Transient arterial occlusion
Amaurosis fugax
AHA: 1Q, '00, 16

362.35 Central retinal vein occlusion
AHA: 2Q, '93, 6

362.36 Venous tributary (branch) occlusion

362.37 Venous engorgement
Occlusion:
- incipient } of retinal vein
- partial } of retinal vein

✓5th **362.4 Separation of retinal layers**

EXCLUDES *retinal detachment (serous) (361.2)*
rhegmatogenous (361.00-361.07)

362.40 Retinal layer separation, unspecified

362.41 Central serous retinopathy
DEF: Serous-filled blister causing detachment of retina from pigment epithelium.

362.42 Serous detachment of retinal pigment epithelium
Exudative detachment of retinal pigment epithelium
DEF: Blister of fatty fluid causing detachment of retina from pigment epithelium.

362.43 Hemorrhagic detachment of retinal pigment epithelium

DEF: Blood-filled blister causing detachment of retina from pigment epithelium.

✓5th **362.5 Degeneration of macula and posterior pole**

EXCLUDES *degeneration of optic disc (377.21-377.24)*
hereditary retinal degeneration [dystrophy] (362.70-362.77)

362.50 Macular degeneration (senile), unspecified

362.51 Nonexudative senile macular degeneration
Senile macular degeneration:
atrophic
dry

362.52 Exudative senile macular degeneration
Kuhnt-Junius degeneration
Senile macular degeneration:
disciform
wet

DEF: Leakage in macular blood vessels with loss of visual acuity.

362.53 Cystoid macular degeneration
Cystoid macular edema

DEF: Retinal swelling and cyst formation in macula.

362.54 Macular cyst, hole, or pseudohole

362.55 Toxic maculopathy
Use additional E code to identify drug, if drug induced

362.56 Macular puckering
Preretinal fibrosis

362.57 Drusen (degenerative)

DEF: White, hyaline deposits on Bruch's membrane (lamina basalis choroideae).

✓5th **362.6 Peripheral retinal degenerations**

EXCLUDES *hereditary retinal degeneration [dystrophy] (362.70-362.77)*
retinal degeneration with retinal defect (361.00-361.07)

362.60 Peripheral retinal degeneration, unspecified

362.61 Paving stone degeneration

DEF: Degeneration of peripheral retina; causes thinning through which choroid is visible.

362.62 Microcystoid degeneration
Blessig's cysts
Iwanoff's cysts

362.63 Lattice degeneration
Palisade degeneration of retina

DEF: Degeneration of retina; often bilateral, usually benign; characterized by lines intersecting at irregular intervals in peripheral retina; retinal thinning and retinal holes may occur.

362.64 Senile reticular degeneration

DEF: Net-like appearance of retina; sign of degeneration.

362.65 Secondary pigmentary degeneration
Pseudoretinitis pigmentosa

362.66 Secondary vitreoretinal degenerations

✓5th **362.7 Hereditary retinal dystrophies**

DEF: Genetically induced progressive changes in retina.

362.70 Hereditary retinal dystrophy, unspecified

362.71 Retinal dystrophy in systemic or cerebroretinal lipidoses
Code first underlying disease, as:
cerebroretinal lipidoses (330.1)
systemic lipidoses (272.7)

362.72 Retinal dystrophy in other systemic disorders and syndromes
Code first underlying disease, as:
Bassen-Kornzweig syndrome (272.5)
Refsum's disease (356.3)

362.73 Vitreoretinal dystrophies
Juvenile retinoschisis

362.74 Pigmentary retinal dystrophy
Retinal dystrophy, albipunctate
Retinitis pigmentosa

362.75 Other dystrophies primarily involving the sensory retina
Progressive cone(-rod) dystrophy
Stargardt's disease

362.76 Dystrophies primarily involving the retinal pigment epithelium
Fundus flavimaculatus
Vitelliform dystrophy

362.77 Dystrophies primarily involving Bruch's membrane
Dystrophy:
hyaline
pseudoinflammatory foveal
Hereditary drusen

✓5th **362.8 Other retinal disorders**

EXCLUDES *chorioretinal inflammations (363.0-363.2)*
chorioretinal scars (363.30-363.35)

362.81 Retinal hemorrhage
Hemorrhage:
preretinal
retinal (deep) (superficial)
subretinal

AHA: 4Q, '96, 43

362.82 Retinal exudates and deposits

362.83 Retinal edema
Retinal:
cotton wool spots
edema (localized) (macular) (peripheral)

DEF: Retinal swelling due to fluid accumulation.

362.84 Retinal ischemia

DEF: Reduced retinal blood supply.

362.85 Retinal nerve fiber bundle defects

362.89 Other retinal disorders

362.9 Unspecified retinal disorder

✓4th **363 Chorioretinal inflammations, scars, and other disorders of choroid**

✓5th **363.0 Focal chorioretinitis and focal retinochoroiditis**

EXCLUDES *focal chorioretinitis or retinochoroiditis in:*
histoplasmosis (115.02, 115.12, 115.92)
toxoplasmosis (130.2)
congenital infection (771.2)

363.00 Focal chorioretinitis, unspecified
Focal:
choroiditis or chorioretinitis NOS
retinitis or retinochoroiditis NOS

363.01 Focal choroiditis and chorioretinitis, juxtapapillary

363.03 Focal choroiditis and chorioretinitis of other posterior pole

363.04 Focal choroiditis and chorioretinitis, peripheral

363.05 Focal retinitis and retinochoroiditis, juxtapapillary
Neuroretinitis

363.06 Focal retinitis and retinochoroiditis, macular or paramacular

363.07 Focal retinitis and retinochoroiditis of other posterior pole

363.08 Focal retinitis and retinochoroiditis, peripheral

✓5th **363.1 Disseminated chorioretinitis and disseminated retinochoroiditis**

EXCLUDES *disseminated choroiditis or chorioretinitis in secondary syphilis (091.51)*
neurosyphilitic disseminated retinitis or retinochoroiditis (094.83)
retinal (peri)vasculitis (362.18)

363.10 Disseminated chorioretinitis, unspecified
Disseminated:
choroiditis or chorioretinitis NOS
retinitis or retinochoroiditis NOS

363.11 Disseminated choroiditis and, chorioretinitis posterior pole

363.12 Disseminated choroiditis and chorioretinitis, peripheral

363.13 Disseminated choroiditis and chorioretinitis, generalized
Code first any underlying disease, as:
tuberculosis (017.3)

363.14 Disseminated retinitis and retinochoroiditis, metastatic

363.15 Disseminated retinitis and retinochoroiditis, pigment epitheliopathy
Acute posterior multifocal placoid pigment epitheliopathy
DEF: Widespread inflammation of retina and choroid; characterized by pigmented epithelium involvement.

✓5th **363.2 Other and unspecified forms of chorioretinitis and retinochoroiditis**

EXCLUDES *panophthalmitis (360.02)*
sympathetic uveitis (360.11)
uveitis NOS (364.3)

363.20 Chorioretinitis, unspecified
Choroiditis NOS
Retinitis NOS
Uveitis, posterior NOS

363.21 Pars planitis
Posterior cyclitis
DEF: Inflammation of peripheral retina and ciliary body; characterized by bands of white cells.

363.22 Harada's disease
DEF: Retinal detachment and bilateral widespread exudative choroiditis; symptoms include headache, vomiting, increased lymphocytes in cerebrospinal fluid; and temporary or permanent deafness may occur.

✓5th **363.3 Chorioretinal scars**
Scar (postinflammatory) (postsurgical) (posttraumatic):
choroid
retina

363.30 Chorioretinal scar, unspecified

363.31 Solar retinopathy
DEF: Retinal scarring caused by solar radiation.

363.32 Other macular scars

363.33 Other scars of posterior pole

363.34 Peripheral scars

363.35 Disseminated scars

✓5th **363.4 Choroidal degenerations**

363.40 Choroidal degeneration, unspecified
Choroidal sclerosis NOS

363.41 Senile atrophy of choroid
DEF: Wasting away of choroid; due to aging.

363.42 Diffuse secondary atrophy of choroid
DEF: Wasting away of choroid in systemic disease.

363.43 Angioid streaks of choroid
DEF: Degeneration of choroid; characterized by dark brown steaks radiating from optic disk; occurs with pseudoxanthoma, elasticum or Paget's disease.

✓5th **363.5 Hereditary choroidal dystrophies**
Hereditary choroidal atrophy:
partial [choriocapillaris]
total [all vessels]

363.50 Hereditary choroidal dystrophy or atrophy, unspecified

363.51 Circumpapillary dystrophy of choroid, partial

363.52 Circumpapillary dystrophy of choroid, total
Helicoid dystrophy of choroid

363.53 Central dystrophy of choroid, partial
Dystrophy, choroidal:
central areolar
circinate

363.54 Central choroidal atrophy, total
Dystrophy, choroidal:
central gyrate
serpiginous

363.55 Choroideremia
DEF: Hereditary choroid degeneration, occurs in first decade; characterized by constricted visual field and ultimately blindness in males; less debilitating in females.

363.56 Other diffuse or generalized dystrophy, partial
Diffuse choroidal sclerosis

363.57 Other diffuse or generalized dystrophy, total
Generalized gyrate atrophy, choroid

✓5th **363.6 Choroidal hemorrhage and rupture**

363.61 Choroidal hemorrhage, unspecified

363.62 Expulsive choroidal hemorrhage

363.63 Choroidal rupture

✓5th **363.7 Choroidal detachment**

363.70 Choroidal detachment, unspecified

363.71 Serous choroidal detachment
DEF: Detachment of choroid from sclera; due to blister of serous fluid.

363.72 Hemorrhagic choroidal detachment
DEF: Detachment of choroid from sclera; due to blood-filled blister.

363.8 Other disorders of choroid

363.9 Unspecified disorder of choroid

✓4th **364 Disorders of iris and ciliary body**

✓5th **364.0 Acute and subacute iridocyclitis**

Anterior uveitis, Cylitis, Iridocyclitis, Iritis } acute, subacute

EXCLUDES *gonococcal (098.41)*
herpes simplex (054.44)
herpes zoster (053.22)

364.00 Acute and subacute iridocyclitis, unspecified

364.01 Primary iridocyclitis

364.02 Recurrent iridocyclitis

364.03 Secondary iridocyclitis, infectious

364.04 Secondary iridocyclitis, noninfectious

Aqueous:
cells
fibrin
flare

364.05 Hypopyon

DEF: Accumulation of white blood cells between cornea and lens.

✓5th **364.1 Chronic iridocyclitis**

EXCLUDES *posterior cyclitis (363.21)*

364.10 Chronic iridocyclitis, unspecified

364.11 Chronic iridocyclitis in diseases classified elsewhere

Code first underlying disease, as:
sarcoidosis (135)
tuberculosis (017.3)

EXCLUDES *syphilitic iridocyclitis (091.52)*

DEF: Persistent inflammation of iris and ciliary body; due to underlying disease or condition.

✓5th **364.2 Certain types of iridocyclitis**

EXCLUDES *posterior cyclitis (363.21)*
sympathetic uveitis (360.11)

364.21 Fuchs' heterochromic cyclitis

DEF: Chronic cyclitis characterized by differences in the color of the two irises; the lighter iris appears in the inflamed eye.

364.22 Glaucomatocyclitic crises

DEF: One-sided form of secondary open angle glaucoma; recurrent, uncommon and of short duration; causes high intraocular pressure, rarely damage.

364.23 Lens-induced iridocyclitis

DEF: Inflammation of iris; due to immune reaction to proteins in lens following trauma or other lens abnormality.

364.24 Vogt-Koyanagi syndrome

DEF: Uveomeningitis with exudative iridocyclitis and choroiditis; causes depigmentation of hair and skin, detached retina; tinnitus and loss of hearing may occur.

364.3 Unspecified iridocyclitis

Uveitis NOS

✓5th **364.4 Vascular disorders of iris and ciliary body**

364.41 Hyphema

Hemorrhage of iris or ciliary body

DEF: Hemorrhage in anterior chamber; also called hyphemia or "blood shot" eyes.

364.42 Rubeosis iridis

Neovascularization of iris or ciliary body

DEF: Blood vessel and connective tissue formation on surface of iris; symptomatic of diabetic retinopathy, central retinal vein occlusion and retinal detachment.

✓5th **364.5 Degenerations of iris and ciliary body**

364.51 Essential or progressive iris atrophy

364.52 Iridoschisis

DEF: Splitting of the iris into two layers.

364.53 Pigmentary iris degeneration

Acquired heterochromia, Pigment dispersion syndrome, Translucency } of iris

364.54 Degeneration of pupillary margin

Atrophy of sphincter, Ectropion of pigment epithelium } of iris

364.55 Miotic cysts of pupillary margin

DEF: Serous-filled sacs in pupillary margin of iris.

364.56 Degenerative changes of chamber angle

364.57 Degenerative changes of ciliary body

364.59 Other iris atrophy

Iris atrophy (generalized) (sector shaped)

✓5th **364.6 Cysts of iris, ciliary body, and anterior chamber**

EXCLUDES *miotic pupillary cyst (364.55)*
parasitic cyst (360.13)

364.60 Idiopathic cysts

DEF: Fluid-filled sacs in iris or ciliary body; unknown etiology.

364.61 Implantation cysts

Epithelial down-growth, anterior chamber
Implantation cysts (surgical) (traumatic)

364.62 Exudative cysts of iris or anterior chamber

364.63 Primary cyst of pars plana

DEF: Fluid-filled sacs of outermost ciliary ring.

364.64 Exudative cyst of pars plana

DEF: Protein, fatty-filled sacs of outermost ciliary ring; due to fluid lead from blood vessels.

✓5th **364.7 Adhesions and disruptions of iris and ciliary body**

EXCLUDES *flat anterior chamber (360.34)*

364.70 Adhesions of iris, unspecified

Synechiae (iris) NOS

364.71 Posterior synechiae

DEF: Adhesion binding iris to lens.

364.72 Anterior synechiae

DEF: Adhesion binding the iris to cornea.

364.73 Goniosynechiae

Peripheral anterior synechiae

DEF: Adhesion binding the iris to cornea at the angle of the anterior chamber.

364.74 Pupillary membranes

Iris bombé
Pupillary:
occlusion
Pupillary:
seclusion

DEF: Membrane traversing the pupil and blocking vision.

364.75 Pupillary abnormalities

Deformed pupil
Ectopic pupil
Rupture of sphincter, pupil

364.76 Iridodialysis

DEF: Separation of the iris from the ciliary body base; due to trauma or surgical accident.

364.77 Recession of chamber angle

DEF: Receding of anterior chamber angle of the eye; restricts vision.

5th **364.8 Other disorders of iris and ciliary body**

AHA: 2Q, '07, 9

364.81 Floppy iris syndrome

Intraoperative floppy iris syndrome [IFIS]

Use additional E code to identify cause, such as:

sympatholytics [antiadrenergics] causing adverse effect in therapeutic use (E941.3)

AHA: 4Q, '07, 77, 79

DEF: Condition complicating cataract surgery for patients who have received alpha blocker treatment for urinary retention problems; iris dilator muscle fails to dilate, and the iris may billow or flap.

● **364.82 Plateau iris syndrome**

364.89 Other disorders of iris and ciliary body

Prolapse of iris NOS

EXCLUDES *prolapse of iris in recent wound (871.1)*

364.9 Unspecified disorder of iris and ciliary body

4th **365 Glaucoma**

EXCLUDES *blind hypertensive eye [absolute glaucoma] (360.42)*
congenital glaucoma (743.20-743.22)

DEF: Rise in intraocular pressure restricting blood flow; multiple causes.

5th **365.0 Borderline glaucoma [glaucoma suspect]**

AHA: 1Q, '90, 8

365.00 Preglaucoma, unspecified

365.01 Open angle with borderline findings

Open angle with:
borderline intraocular pressure
cupping of optic discs

DEF: Minor block of aqueous outflow from eye.

365.02 Anatomical narrow angle

365.03 Steroid responders

365.04 Ocular hypertension

DEF: High fluid pressure within eye; no apparent cause.

5th **365.1 Open-angle glaucoma**

365.10 Open-angle glaucoma, unspecified

Wide-angle glaucoma NOS

365.11 Primary open angle glaucoma

Chronic simple glaucoma

DEF: High intraocular pressure, despite free flow of aqueous.

365.12 Low tension glaucoma

365.13 Pigmentary glaucoma

DEF: High intraocular pressure; due to iris pigment granules blocking aqueous flow.

365.14 Glaucoma of childhood

Infantile or juvenile glaucoma

365.15 Residual stage of open angle glaucoma

5th **365.2 Primary angle-closure glaucoma**

365.20 Primary angle-closure glaucoma, unspecified

365.21 Intermittent angle-closure glaucoma

Angle-closure glaucoma:
interval
subacute

DEF: Recurring attacks of high intraocular pressure; due to blocked aqueous flow.

365.22 Acute angle-closure glaucoma

DEF: Sudden, severe rise in intraocular pressure due to blockage in aqueous drainage.

365.23 Chronic angle-closure glaucoma

AHA: 2Q, '98, 16

365.24 Residual stage of angle-closure glaucoma

5th **365.3 Corticosteroid-induced glaucoma**

DEF: Elevated intraocular pressure; due to long-term corticosteroid therapy.

365.31 Glaucomatous stage

365.32 Residual stage

5th **365.4 Glaucoma associated with congenital anomalies, dystrophies, and systemic syndromes**

365.41 Glaucoma associated with chamber angle anomalies

365.42 Glaucoma associated with anomalies of iris

365.43 Glaucoma associated with other anterior segment anomalies

365.44 Glaucoma associated with systemic syndromes

Code first associated disease, as
neurofibromatosis (237.7)
Sturge-Weber (-Dimitri) syndrome (759.6)

5th **365.5 Glaucoma associated with disorders of the lens**

365.51 Phacolytic glaucoma

DEF: Elevated intraocular pressure; due to lens protein blocking aqueous flow.

365.52 Pseudoexfoliation glaucoma

DEF: Glaucoma characterized by small grayish particles deposited on the lens.

365.59 Glaucoma associated with other lens disorders

5th **365.6 Glaucoma associated with other ocular disorders**

365.60 Glaucoma associated with unspecified ocular disorder

365.61 Glaucoma associated with pupillary block

DEF: Acute, open-angle glaucoma caused by mature cataract; aqueous flow is blocked by lens material and macrophages.

365.62 Glaucoma associated with ocular inflammations

365.63 Glaucoma associated with vascular disorders

365.64 Glaucoma associated with tumors or cysts

365.65 Glaucoma associated with ocular trauma

Aqueos Misdirection Syndrome

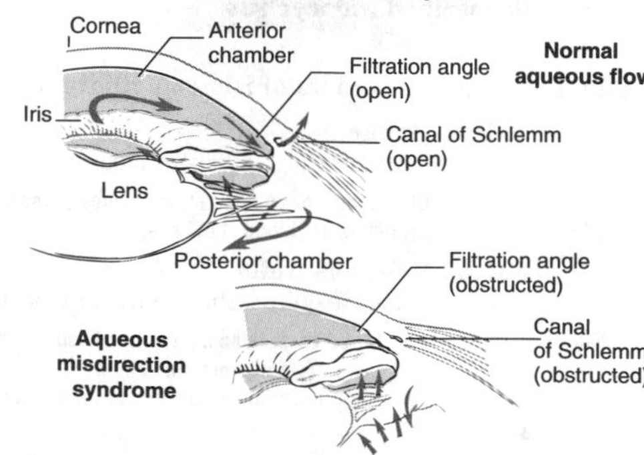

✓5th **365.8 Other specified forms of glaucoma**

365.81 Hypersecretion glaucoma

365.82 Glaucoma with increased episcleral venous pressure

365.83 Aqueous misdirection
Malignant glaucoma
AHA: 4Q, '02, 48
DEF: A form of glaucoma that occurs when aqueous humor flows into the posterior chamber of the eye (vitreous) rather than through the normal recycling channels into the anterior chamber.

365.89 Other specified glaucoma
AHA: 2Q, '98, 16

365.9 Unspecified glaucoma
AHA: 3Q, '03, 14; 2Q, '01, 16

✓4th **366 Cataract**
EXCLUDES *congenital cataract (743.30-743.34)*
DEF: A variety of conditions that create a cloudy, or calcified lens that obstructs vision.

✓5th **366.0 Infantile, juvenile, and presenile cataract**

366.00 Nonsenile cataract, unspecified

366.01 Anterior subcapsular polar cataract
DEF: Defect within the front, center lens surface.

366.02 Posterior subcapsular polar cataract
DEF: Defect within the rear, center lens surface.

366.03 Cortical, lamellar, or zonular cataract
DEF: Opacities radiating from center to edge of lens; appear as thin, concentric layers of lens.

366.04 Nuclear cataract

366.09 Other and combined forms of nonsenile cataract

✓5th **366.1 Senile cataract**
AHA: 3Q, '91, 9; S-0, '85, 10

366.10 Senile cataract, unspecified A
AHA: 1Q, '03, 5

366.11 Pseudoexfoliation of lens capsule A

366.12 Incipient cataract A
Cataract:
- coronary
- immature NOS
- punctate

Water clefts
DEF: Minor disorders of lens not affecting vision; due to aging.

366.13 Anterior subcapsular polar senile cataract A

366.14 Posterior subcapsular polar senile cataract A

366.15 Cortical senile cataract A

Cataract

Sclera
Trebeculae
Ciliary suspensory fibers
Lens
Posterior polar cataract
Cortical cataract
Cornea
Iris
Anterior polar cataract

366.16 Nuclear sclerosis A
Cataracta brunescens
Nuclear cataract
AHA: 4Q, '07, 79

366.17 Total or mature cataract A

366.18 Hypermature cataract A
Morgagni cataract

366.19 Other and combined forms of senile cataract A

✓5th **366.2 Traumatic cataract**

366.20 Traumatic cataract, unspecified

366.21 Localized traumatic opacities
Vossius' ring

366.22 Total traumatic cataract

366.23 Partially resolved traumatic cataract

✓5th **366.3 Cataract secondary to ocular disorders**

366.30 Cataracta complicata, unspecified

366.31 Glaucomatous flecks (subcapsular)
Code first underlying glaucoma (365.0-365.9)

366.32 Cataract in inflammatory disorders
Code first underlying condition, as:
chronic choroiditis (363.0-363.2)

366.33 Cataract with neovascularization
Code first underlying condition, as:
chronic iridocyclitis (364.10)

366.34 Cataract in degenerative disorders
Sunflower cataract
Code first underlying condition, as:
- chalcosis (360.24)
- degenerative myopia (360.21)
- pigmentary retinal dystrophy (362.74)

✓5th **366.4 Cataract associated with other disorders**

366.41 Diabetic cataract
Code first diabetes ▶*(249.5, 250.5)*◀
AHA:3Q, '91, 9; S-0, '85, 11

366.42 Tetanic cataract
Code first underlying disease, as:
- calcinosis (275.4)
- hypoparathyroidism (252.1)

366.43 Myotonic cataract
Code first underlying disorder ▶*(359.21, 359.23)*◀

366.44 Cataract associated with other syndromes
Code first underlying condition, as:
- craniofacial dysostosis (756.0)
- galactosemia (271.1)

366.45 Toxic cataract
Drug-induced cataract
Use additional E code to identify drug or other toxic substance

366.46 Cataract associated with radiation and other physical influences
Use additional E code to identify cause

✓5th **366.5 After-cataract**

366.50 After-cataract, unspecified
Secondary cataract NOS

366.51 Soemmering's ring
DEF: A donut-shaped lens remnant and a capsule behind the pupil as a result of cataract surgery or trauma.

366.52 Other after-cataract, not obscuring vision

366.53 After-cataract, obscuring vision

366.8 Other cataract
Calcification of lens

366.9 Unspecified cataract

✓4th **367 Disorders of refraction and accommodation**

367.0 Hypermetropia
Far-sightedness
Hyperopia
DEF: Refraction error, called also hyperopia, focal point is posterior to retina; abnormally short anteroposterior diameter or subnormal refractive power; causes farsightedness.

367.1 Myopia
Near-sightedness
DEF: Refraction error, focal point is anterior to retina; causes near-sightedness.

✓5th **367.2 Astigmatism**

367.20 Astigmatism, unspecified

367.21 Regular astigmatism

367.22 Irregular astigmatism

✓5th **367.3 Anisometropia and aniseikonia**

367.31 Anisometropia
DEF: Eyes with refractive powers that differ by at least one diopter.

367.32 Aniseikonia
DEF: Eyes with unequal retinal imaging; usually due to refractive error.

367.4 Presbyopia
DEF: Loss of crystalline lens elasticity; causes errors of accommodation; due to aging.

✓5th **367.5 Disorders of accommodation**

367.51 Paresis of accommodation
Cycloplegia
DEF: Partial paralysis of ciliary muscle; causing focus problems.

367.52 Total or complete internal ophthalmoplegia
DEF: Total paralysis of ciliary muscle; large pupil incapable of focus.

367.53 Spasm of accommodation
DEF: Abnormal contraction of ciliary muscle; causes focus problems.

✓5th **367.8 Other disorders of refraction and accommodation**

367.81 Transient refractive change

367.89 Other
Drug-induced } disorders of refraction
Toxic } and accommodation

367.9 Unspecified disorder of refraction and accommodation

✓4th **368 Visual disturbances**

EXCLUDES *electrophysiological disturbances (794.11-794.14)*

✓5th **368.0 Amblyopia ex anopsia**
DEF: Vision impaired due to disuse; esotropia often cause.

368.00 Amblyopia, unspecified

368.01 Strabismic amblyopia
Suppression amblyopia

368.02 Deprivation amblyopia
DEF: Decreased vision associated with suppressed retinal image of one eye.

368.03 Refractive amblyopia

✓5th **368.1 Subjective visual disturbances**

368.10 Subjective visual disturbance, unspecified

368.11 Sudden visual loss

368.12 Transient visual loss
Concentric fading
Scintillating scotoma

368.13 Visual discomfort
Asthenopia
Eye strain
Photophobia

368.14 Visual distortions of shape and size
Macropsia
Metamorphopsia
Micropsia

368.15 Other visual distortions and entoptic phenomena
Photopsia
Refractive:
- diplopia
- polyopia

Visual halos

368.16 Psychophysical visual disturbances
▶Prosopagnosia◀
Visual:
- agnosia
- disorientation syndrome
- hallucinations
- ▶object agnosia◀

368.2 Diplopia
Double vision

✓5th **368.3 Other disorders of binocular vision**

368.30 Binocular vision disorder, unspecified

368.31 Suppression of binocular vision

368.32 Simultaneous visual perception without fusion

368.33 Fusion with defective stereopsis
DEF: Faulty depth perception though normal ability to focus.

368.34 Abnormal retinal correspondence

✓5th **368.4 Visual field defects**

368.40 Visual field defect, unspecified

368.41 Scotoma involving central area
Scotoma:
- central
- centrocecal
- paracentral

DEF: Vision loss (blind spot) in central five degrees of visual field.

368.42 Scotoma of blind spot area
Enlarged:
- angioscotoma
- blind spot

Paracecal scotoma

368.43 Sector or arcuate defects
Scotoma:
- arcuate
- Bjerrum
- Seidel

DEF: Arc-shaped blind spot caused by retinal nerve damage.

368.44 Other localized visual field defect
Scotoma:
- NOS
- ring

Visual field defect:
- nasal step
- peripheral

368.45 Generalized contraction or constriction

368.46 Homonymous bilateral field defects
Hemianopsia (altitudinal) (homonymous)
Quadrant anopia
DEF: Disorders found in the corresponding vertical halves of the visual fields of both eyes.

368.47 Heteronymous bilateral field defects
Hemianopsia:
binasal
bitemporal
DEF: Disorders in the opposite halves of the visual fields of both eyes.

✓5th **368.5 Color vision deficiencies**
Color blindness

368.51 Protan defect
Protanomaly
Protanopia
DEF: Mild difficulty distinguishing green and red hues with shortened spectrum; sex-linked affecting one percent of males.

368.52 Deutan defect
Deuteranomaly
Deuteranopia
DEF: Male-only disorder; difficulty in distinguishing green and red, no shortened spectrum.

368.53 Tritan defect
Tritanomaly
Tritanopia
DEF: Difficulty in distinguishing blue and yellow; occurs often due to drugs, retinal detachment and central nervous system diseases.

368.54 Achromatopsia
Monochromatism (cone) (rod)
DEF: Complete color blindness; caused by disease, injury to retina, optic nerve or pathway.

368.55 Acquired color vision deficiencies

368.59 Other color vision deficiencies

✓5th **368.6 Night blindness**
Nyctalopia
DEF: Nyctalopia: disorder of vision in dim light or night blindness.

368.60 Night blindness, unspecified

368.61 Congenital night blindness
Hereditary night blindness
Oguchi's disease

368.62 Acquired night blindness
EXCLUDES *that due to vitamin A deficiency (264.5)*

368.63 Abnormal dark adaptation curve
Abnormal threshold } of cones or rods
Delayed adaptation } of cones or rods

368.69 Other night blindness

368.8 Other specified visual disturbances
Blurred vision NOS
AHA: 4Q, '02, 56

368.9 Unspecified visual disturbance
AHA: 3Q, '06, 22; 1Q, '04, 15

✓4th **369 Blindness and low vision**

Note: Visual impairment refers to a functional limitation of the eye (e.g., limited visual acuity or visual field). It should be distinguished from visual disability, indicating a limitation of the abilities of the individual (e.g., limited reading skills, vocational skills), and from visual handicap, indicating a limitation of personal and socioeconomic independence (e.g., limited mobility, limited employability).

The levels of impairment defined in the table on the next page are based on the recommendations of the WHO Study Group on Prevention of Blindness (Geneva, November 6-10, 1972; WHO Technical Report Series 518), and of the International Council of Ophthalmology (1976).

Note that definitions of blindness vary in different settings.

For international reporting WHO defines blindness as profound impairment. This definition can be applied to blindness of one eye (369.1, 369.6) and to blindness of the individual (369.0).

For determination of benefits in the U.S.A., the definition of legal blindness as severe impairment is often used. This definition applies to blindness of the individual only.

EXCLUDES *correctable impaired vision due to refractive errors (367.0-367.9)*

✓5th **369.0 Profound impairment, both eyes**

369.00 Impairment level not further specified
Blindness:
NOS according to WHO definition
both eyes

369.01 Better eye: total impairment; lesser eye: total impairment

369.02 Better eye: near-total impairment; lesser eye: not further specified

369.03 Better eye: near-total impairment; lesser eye: total impairment

369.04 Better eye: near-total impairment; lesser eye: near-total impairment

369.05 Better eye: profound impairment; lesser eye: not further specified

369.06 Better eye: profound impairment; lesser eye: total impairment

369.07 Better eye: profound impairment; lesser eye: near-total impairment

369.08 Better eye: profound impairment; lesser eye: profound impairment

✓4th **369.1 Moderate or severe impairment, better eye, profound impairment lesser eye**

369.10 Impairment level not further specified
Blindness, one eye, low vision other eye

369.11 Better eye: severe impairment; lesser eye: blind, not further specified

369.12 Better eye: severe impairment; lesser eye: total impairment

369.13 Better eye: severe impairment; lesser eye: near-total impairment

369.14 Better eye: severe impairment; lesser eye: profound impairment

369.15 Better eye: moderate impairment; lesser eye: blind, not further specified

369.16 Better eye: moderate impairment; lesser eye: total impairment

369.17 Better eye: moderate impairment; lesser eye: near-total impairment

369.18 Better eye: moderate impairment; lesser eye: profound impairment

✓5th **369.2 Moderate or severe impairment, both eyes**

369.20 Impairment level not further specified
Low vision, both eyes NOS

369.21 Better eye: severe impairment; lesser eye: not further specified

369.22 Better eye: severe impairment; lesser eye: severe impairment

369.23 Better eye: moderate impairment; lesser eye: not further specified

369.24 Better eye: moderate impairment; lesser eye: severe impairment

369.25 Better eye: moderate impairment; lesser eye: moderate impairment

369.3 Unqualified visual loss, both eyes

EXCLUDES *blindness NOS:*
legal [U.S.A. definition] (369.4)
WHO definition (369.00)

369.4 Legal blindness, as defined in U.S.A.
Blindness NOS according to U.S.A. definition

EXCLUDES *legal blindness with specification of impairment level (369.01-369.08, 369.11-369.14, 369.21-369.22)*

✓5th **369.6 Profound impairment, one eye**

369.60 Impairment level not further specified
Blindness, one eye

369.61 One eye: total impairment; other eye: not specified

369.62 One eye: total impairment; other eye: near normal vision

Classification: "legal"	Classification: WHO	LEVELS OF VISUAL IMPAIRMENT: Visual acuity and/or visual field limitation (whichever is worse)	Additional descriptors which may be encountered
	(NEAR-) NORMAL VISION	RANGE OF NORMAL VISION 20/10 20/13 20/16 20/20 20/25 2.0 1.6 1.25 1.0 0.8	
	(NEAR-) NORMAL VISION	NEAR-NORMAL VISION 20/30 20/40 20/50 20/60 0.7 0.6 0.5 0.4 0.3	
	LOW VISION	MODERATE VISUAL IMPAIRMENT 20/70 20/80 20/100 20/125 20/160 0.25 0.20 0.16 0.12	Moderate low vision
LEGAL BLINDNESS (U.S.A.) both eyes	LOW VISION	SEVERE VISUAL IMPAIRMENT 20/200 20/250 20/320 20/400 0.10 0.08 0.06 0.05 Visual field: 20 degrees or less	Severe low vision, "Legal" blindness
LEGAL BLINDNESS (U.S.A.) both eyes	BLINDNESS (WHO) one or both eyes	PROFOUND VISUAL IMPAIRMENT 20/500 20/630 20/800 20/1000 0.04 0.03 0.025 0.02 Count fingers at: less than 3m (10 ft.) Visual field: 10 degrees or less	Profound low vision, Moderate blindness
LEGAL BLINDNESS (U.S.A.) both eyes	BLINDNESS (WHO) one or both eyes	NEAR-TOTAL VISUAL IMPAIRMENT Visual acuity: less than 0.02 (20/1000) Count fingers at: 1m (3 ft.) or less Hand movements: 5m (15 ft.) or less Light projection, light perception Visual field: 5 degrees or less	Severe blindness Near-total blindness
LEGAL BLINDNESS (U.S.A.) both eyes	BLINDNESS (WHO) one or both eyes	TOTAL VISUAL IMPAIRMENT No light perception (NLP)	Total blindness

Visual acuity refers to best achievable acuity with correction.
Non-listed Snellen fractions may be classified by converting to the nearest decimal equivalent, e.g. 10/200 = 0.05, 6/30 = 0.20.
CF (count fingers) without designation of distance, may be classified to profound impairment.
HM (hand motion) without designation of distance, may be classified to near-total impairment.
Visual field measurements refer to the largest field diameter for a 1/100 white test object.

369.63 One eye: total impairment; other eye: normal vision

369.64 One eye: near-total impairment; other eye: not specified

369.65 One eye: near-total impairment; other eye: near-normal vision

369.66 One eye: near-total impairment; other eye: normal vision

369.67 One eye: profound impairment; other eye: not specified

369.68 One eye: profound impairment; other eye: near-normal vision

369.69 One eye: profound impairment; other eye: normal vision

✓5th **369.7 Moderate or severe impairment, one eye**

369.70 Impairment level not further specified
Low vision, one eye

369.71 One eye: severe impairment; other eye: not specified

369.72 One eye: severe impairment; other eye: near-normal vision

369.73 One eye: severe impairment; other eye: normal vision

369.74 One eye: moderate impairment; other eye: not specified

369.75 One eye: moderate impairment; other eye: near-normal vision

369.76 One eye: moderate impairment; other eye: normal vision

369.8 Unqualified visual loss, one eye

369.9 Unspecified visual loss
AHA: 4Q, '02, 114; 3Q, '02, 20

✓4th 370 Keratitis

✓5th **370.0 Corneal ulcer**

EXCLUDES *that due to vitamin A deficiency (264.3)*

370.00 Corneal ulcer, unspecified

370.01 Marginal corneal ulcer

370.02 Ring corneal ulcer

370.03 Central corneal ulcer

370.04 Hypopyon ulcer
Serpiginous ulcer
DEF: Corneal ulcer with an accumulation of pus in the eye's anterior chamber.

370.05 Mycotic corneal ulcer
DEF: Fungal infection causing corneal tissue loss.

370.06 Perforated corneal ulcer
DEF: Tissue loss through all layers of cornea.

370.07 Mooren's ulcer
DEF: Tissue loss, with chronic inflammation, at junction of cornea and sclera; seen in elderly.

✓5th **370.2 Superficial keratitis without conjunctivitis**

EXCLUDES *dendritic [herpes simplex] keratitis (054.42)*

370.20 Superficial keratitis, unspecified

370.21 Punctate keratitis
Thygeson's superficial punctate keratitis
DEF: Formation of cellular and fibrinous deposits (keratic precipitates) on posterior surface; deposits develop after injury or iridocyclitis.

370.22 Macular keratitis

Keratitis:
- areolar
- nummular

Keratitis:
- stellate
- striate

370.23 Filamentary keratitis

DEF: Keratitis characterized by twisted filaments of mucoid material on the cornea's surface.

370.24 Photokeratitis

Snow blindness
Welders' keratitis

AHA: 3Q, '96, 6

DEF: Painful, inflamed cornea; due to extended exposure to ultraviolet light.

✓5th **370.3 Certain types of keratoconjunctivitis**

370.31 Phlyctenular keratoconjunctivitis

Phlyctenulosis

Use additional code for any associated tuberculosis (017.3)

DEF: Miniature blister on conjunctiva or cornea; associated with tuberculosis and malnutrition disorders.

370.32 Limbar and corneal involvement in vernal conjunctivitis

Use additional code for vernal conjunctivitis (372.13)

DEF: Corneal itching and inflammation in conjunctivitis; often limited to lining of eyelids.

370.33 Keratoconjunctivitis sicca, not specified as Sjögren's

EXCLUDES *Sjögren's syndrome (710.2)*

DEF: Inflammation of conjunctiva and cornea; characterized by "horny" looking tissue and excess blood in these areas; decreased flow of lacrimal (tear) is a contributing factor.

370.34 Exposure keratoconjunctivitis

DEF: Incomplete closure of eyelid causing dry, inflamed eye.

370.35 Neurotrophic keratoconjunctivitis

✓5th **370.4 Other and unspecified keratoconjunctivitis**

370.40 Keratoconjunctivitis, unspecified

Superficial keratitis with conjunctivitis NOS

370.44 Keratitis or keratoconjunctivitis in exanthema

Code first underlying condition (050.0-052.9)

EXCLUDES *herpes simplex (054.43)*
herpes zoster (053.21)
measles (055.71)

370.49 Other

EXCLUDES *epidemic keratoconjunctivitis (077.1)*

✓5th **370.5 Interstitial and deep keratitis**

370.50 Interstitial keratitis, unspecified

370.52 Diffuse interstitial keratitis

Cogan's syndrome

DEF: Inflammation of cornea; with deposits in middle corneal layers; may obscure vision.

370.54 Sclerosing keratitis

DEF: Chronic corneal inflammation leading to opaque scarring.

370.55 Corneal abscess

DEF: Pocket of pus and inflammation on the cornea.

370.59 Other

EXCLUDES *disciform herpes simplex keratitis (054.43)*
syphilitic keratitis (090.3)

✓5th **370.6 Corneal neovascularization**

370.60 Corneal neovascularization, unspecified

370.61 Localized vascularization of cornea

DEF: Limited infiltration of cornea by new blood vessels.

370.62 Pannus (corneal)

AHA: 3Q, '02, 20

DEF: Buildup of superficial vascularization and granulated tissue under epithelium of cornea.

370.63 Deep vascularization of cornea

DEF: Deep infiltration of cornea by new blood vessels.

370.64 Ghost vessels (corneal)

370.8 Other forms of keratitis

▶Code first underlying condition, such as:
Acanthamoeba (136.21)
Fusarium (118)◀

AHA: 3Q, '94, 5

370.9 Unspecified keratitis

✓4th **371 Corneal opacity and other disorders of cornea**

✓5th **371.0 Corneal scars and opacities**

EXCLUDES *that due to vitamin A deficiency (264.6)*

371.00 Corneal opacity,

Corneal scar NOS

371.01 Minor opacity of cornea

Corneal nebula

371.02 Peripheral opacity of cornea

Corneal macula not interfering with central vision

371.03 Central opacity of cornea

Corneal:
leucoma } interfering with central vision
macula }

371.04 Adherent leucoma

DEF: Dense, opaque corneal growth adhering to the iris; also spelled as leukoma.

371.05 Phthisical cornea

Code first underlying tuberculosis (017.3)

✓5th **371.1 Corneal pigmentations and deposits**

371.10 Corneal deposit, unspecified

371.11 Anterior pigmentations

Stähli's lines

371.12 Stromal pigmentations

Hematocornea

371.13 Posterior pigmentations

Krukenberg spindle

371.14 Kayser-Fleischer ring

DEF: Copper deposits forming ring at outer edge of cornea; seen in Wilson's disease and other liver disorders.

371.15 Other deposits associated with metabolic disorders

371.16 Argentous deposits

DEF: Silver deposits in cornea.

✓5th **371.2 Corneal edema**

371.20 Corneal edema, unspecified

371.21 Idiopathic corneal edema

DEF: Corneal swelling and fluid retention of unknown cause.

371.22 Secondary corneal edema

DEF: Corneal swelling and fluid retention caused by an underlying disease, injury, or condition.

371.23 **Bullous keratopathy**

DEF: Corneal degeneration; characterized by recurring, rupturing epithelial "blisters;" ruptured blebs expose corneal nerves, cause great pain; occurs in glaucoma, iridocyclitis and Fuchs' epithelial dystrophy.

371.24 **Corneal edema due to wearing of contact lenses**

✓5th 371.3 **Changes of corneal membranes**

371.30 **Corneal membrane change, unspecified**

371.31 **Folds and rupture of Bowman's membrane**

371.32 **Folds in Descemet's membrane**

371.33 **Rupture in Descemet's membrane**

✓5th 371.4 **Corneal degenerations**

371.40 **Corneal degeneration, unspecified**

371.41 **Senile corneal changes**
Arcus senilis
Hassall-Henle bodies

371.42 **Recurrent erosion of cornea**

EXCLUDES *Mooren's ulcer (370.07)*

371.43 **Band-shaped keratopathy**

DEF: Horizontal bands of superficial corneal calcium deposits.

371.44 **Other calcerous degenerations of cornea**

371.45 **Keratomalacia NOS**

EXCLUDES *that due to vitamin A deficiency (264.4)*

DEF: Destruction of the cornea by keratinization of the epithelium with ulceration and perforation of the cornea; seen in cases of vitamin A deficiency.

371.46 **Nodular degeneration of cornea**
Salzmann's nodular dystrophy

371.48 **Peripheral degenerations of cornea**
Marginal degeneration of cornea [Terrien's]

371.49 **Other**
Discrete colliquative keratopathy

✓5th 371.5 **Hereditary corneal dystrophies**

DEF: Genetic disorder; leads to opacities, edema or lesions of cornea.

371.50 **Corneal dystrophy, unspecified**

371.51 **Juvenile epithelial corneal dystrophy**

371.52 **Other anterior corneal dystrophies**
Corneal dystrophy:
microscopic cystic
ring-like

371.53 **Granular corneal dystrophy**

371.54 **Lattice corneal dystrophy**

371.55 **Macular corneal dystrophy**

371.56 **Other stromal corneal dystrophies**
Crystalline corneal dystrophy

371.57 **Endothelial corneal dystrophy**
Combined corneal dystrophy
Cornea guttata
Fuchs' endothelial dystrophy

371.58 **Other posterior corneal dystrophies**
Polymorphous corneal dystrophy

✓5th 371.6 **Keratoconus**

DEF: Bilateral bulging protrusion of anterior cornea; often due to noninflammatory thinning.

371.60 **Keratoconus, unspecified**

371.61 **Keratoconus, stable condition**

371.62 **Keratoconus, acute hydrops**

✓5th 371.7 **Other corneal deformities**

371.70 **Corneal deformity, unspecified**

371.71 **Corneal ectasia**

DEF: Bulging protrusion of thinned, scarred cornea.

371.72 **Descemetocele**

DEF: Protrusion of Descemet's membrane into cornea.

371.73 **Corneal staphyloma**

DEF: Protrusion of cornea into adjacent tissue.

✓5th 371.8 **Other corneal disorders**

371.81 **Corneal anesthesia and hypoesthesia**

DEF: Decreased or absent sensitivity of cornea.

371.82 **Corneal disorder due to contact lens**

EXCLUDES *corneal edema due to contact lens (371.24)*

DEF: Contact lens wear causing cornea disorder, excluding swelling.

371.89 **Other**

AHA: 3Q, '99, 12

371.9 **Unspecified corneal disorder**

✓4th 372 **Disorders of conjunctiva**

EXCLUDES *keratoconjunctivitis (370.3-370.4)*

✓5th 372.0 **Acute conjunctivitis**

372.00 **Acute conjunctivitis, unspecified**

372.01 **Serous conjunctivitis, except viral**

EXCLUDES *viral conjunctivitis NOS (077.9)*

372.02 **Acute follicular conjunctivitis**
Conjunctival folliculosis NOS

EXCLUDES *conjunctivitis:*
adenoviral (acute follicular) (077.3)
epidemic hemorrhagic (077.4)
inclusion (077.0)
Newcastle (077.8)
epidemic keratoconjunctivitis (077.1)
pharyngoconjunctival fever (077.2)

DEF: Severe conjunctival inflammation with dense infiltrations of lymphoid tissues of inner eyelids; may be traced to a viral or chlamydial etiology.

372.03 **Other mucopurulent conjunctivitis**
Catarrhal conjunctivitis

EXCLUDES *blennorrhea neonatorum (gonococcal) (098.40)*
neonatal conjunctivitis(771.6)
ophthalmia neonatorum NOS (771.6)

372.04 **Pseudomembranous conjunctivitis**
Membranous conjunctivitis

EXCLUDES *diphtheritic conjunctivitis (032.81)*

DEF: Severe inflammation of conjunctiva; false membrane develops on inner surface of eyelid; membrane can be removed without harming epithelium, due to bacterial infections, toxic and allergic factors, and viral infections.

372.05 **Acute atopic conjunctivitis**

DEF: Sudden, severe conjunctivitis due to allergens.

✓5th 372.1 **Chronic conjunctivitis**

372.10 **Chronic conjunctivitis, unspecified**

372.11 **Simple chronic conjunctivitis**

372.12 Chronic follicular conjunctivitis

DEF: Persistent conjunctival inflammation with dense, localized infiltrations of lymphoid tissues of inner eyelids.

372.13 Vernal conjunctivitis

AHA: 3Q, '96, 8

372.14 Other chronic allergic conjunctivitis

AHA: 3Q, '96, 8

372.15 Parasitic conjunctivitis

Code first underlying disease, as:
filariasis (125.0-125.9)
mucocutaneous leishmaniasis (085.5)

5th **372.2 Blepharoconjunctivitis**

372.20 Blepharoconjunctivitis, unspecified

372.21 Angular blepharoconjunctivitis

DEF: Inflammation at junction of upper and lower eyelids; may block lacrimal secretions.

372.22 Contact blepharoconjunctivitis

5th **372.3 Other and unspecified conjunctivitis**

372.30 Conjunctivitis, unspecified

372.31 Rosacea conjunctivitis

Code first underlying rosacea dermatitis (695.3)

372.33 Conjunctivitis in mucocutaneous disease

Code first underlying disease, as:
erythema multiforme ▶(695.10-695.19)◀
Reiter's disease (099.3)

EXCLUDES *ocular pemphigoid (694.61)*

● **372.34 Pingueculitis**

372.39 Other

AHA: 2Q, '07, 9

5th **372.4 Pterygium**

EXCLUDES *pseudopterygium (372.52)*

DEF: Wedge-shaped, conjunctival thickening that advances from the inner corner of the eye toward the cornea.

372.40 Pterygium, unspecified

372.41 Peripheral pterygium, stationary

372.42 Peripheral pterygium, progressive

372.43 Central pterygium

372.44 Double pterygium

372.45 Recurrent pterygium

5th **372.5 Conjunctival degenerations and deposits**

372.50 Conjunctival degeneration, unspecified

372.51 Pinguecula

DEF: Proliferative spot on the bulbar conjunctiva located near the sclerocorneal junction, usually on the nasal side; it is seen in elderly people.

372.52 Pseudopterygium

DEF: Conjunctival scar joined to the cornea; it looks like a pterygium but is not attached to the tissue.

372.53 Conjunctival xerosis

EXCLUDES *conjunctival xerosis due to vitamin A deficiency (264.0, 264.1, 264.7)*

DEF: Dry conjunctiva due to vitamin A deficiency; related to Bitot's spots; may develop into xerophthalmia and keratomalacia.

372.54 Conjunctival concretions

DEF: Calculus or deposit on conjunctiva.

372.55 Conjunctival pigmentations

Conjunctival argyrosis

DEF: Color deposits in conjunctiva.

372.56 Conjunctival deposits

5th **372.6 Conjunctival scars**

372.61 Granuloma of conjunctiva

372.62 Localized adhesions and strands of conjunctiva

DEF: Abnormal fibrous connections in conjunctiva.

372.63 Symblepharon

Extensive adhesions of conjunctiva

DEF: Adhesion of the eyelids to the eyeball.

372.64 Scarring of conjunctiva

Contraction of eye socket (after enucleation)

5th **372.7 Conjunctival vascular disorders and cysts**

372.71 Hyperemia of conjunctiva

DEF: Conjunctival blood vessel congestion causing eye redness.

372.72 Conjunctival hemorrhage

Hyposphagma
Subconjunctival hemorrhage

372.73 Conjunctival edema

Chemosis of conjunctiva
Subconjunctival edema

DEF: Fluid retention and swelling in conjunctival tissue.

372.74 Vascular abnormalities of conjunctiva

Aneurysm(ata) of conjunctiva

372.75 Conjunctival cysts

DEF: Abnormal sacs of fluid in conjunctiva.

5th **372.8 Other disorders of conjunctiva**

372.81 Conjunctivochalasis

AHA: 4Q, '00, 41

DEF: Bilateral condition of redundant conjunctival tissue between globe and lower eyelid margin; may cover lower punctum, interferring with normal tearing.

372.89 Other disorders of conjunctiva

372.9 Unspecified disorder of conjunctiva

4th **373 Inflammation of eyelids**

5th **373.0 Blepharitis**

EXCLUDES *blepharoconjunctivitis (372.20-372.22)*

373.00 Blepharitis, unspecified

373.01 Ulcerative blepharitis

373.02 Squamous blepharitis

5th **373.1 Hordeolum and other deep inflammation of eyelid**

DEF: Purulent, localized, staphylococcal infection in sebaceous glands of eyelids.

373.11 Hordeolum externum

Hordeolum NOS   Stye

DEF: Infection of the oil glands in the eyelash follicles.

373.12 Hordeolum internum

Infection of meibomian gland

DEF: Infection of the oil gland of the eyelid margin.

373.13 Abscess of eyelid

Furuncle of eyelid

DEF: Inflamed pocket of pus on the eyelid.

373.2 Chalazion

Meibomian (gland) cyst

EXCLUDES *infected meibomian gland (373.12)*

DEF: Chronic inflammation of the meibomian gland, causing an eyelid mass.

✓5th **373.3 Noninfectious dermatoses of eyelid**

373.31 Eczematous dermatitis of eyelid

373.32 Contact and allergic dermatitis of eyelid

373.33 Xeroderma of eyelid

373.34 Discoid lupus erythematosus of eyelid

373.4 Infective dermatitis of eyelid of types resulting in deformity

Code first underlying disease, as:
leprosy (030.0-030.9)
lupus vulgaris (tuberculous) (017.0)
yaws (102.0-102.9)

373.5 Other infective dermatitis of eyelid

Code first underlying disease, as:
actinomycosis (039.3)
impetigo (684)
mycotic dermatitis (110.0-111.9)
vaccinia (051.0)
postvaccination (999.0)

EXCLUDES *herpes:*
simplex (054.41)
zoster (053.20)

373.6 Parasitic infestation of eyelid

Code first underlying disease, as:
leishmaniasis (085.0-085.9)
loiasis (125.2)
onchocerciasis (125.3)
pediculosis (132.0)

373.8 Other inflammations of eyelids

373.9 Unspecified inflammation of eyelid

✓4th **374 Other disorders of eyelids**

✓5th **374.0 Entropion and trichiasis of eyelid**

DEF: Entropion: turning inward of eyelid edge toward eyeball.

DEF: Trichiasis: ingrowing eyelashes marked by irritation with possible distortion of sight.

374.00 Entropion, unspecified

374.01 Senile entropion A

374.02 Mechanical entropion

374.03 Spastic entropion

374.04 Cicatricial entropion

374.05 Trichiasis without entropion

✓5th **374.1 Ectropion**

DEF: Turning outward (eversion) of eyelid edge; exposes palpebral conjunctiva; dryness irritation result.

374.10 Ectropion, unspecified

374.11 Senile ectropion A

374.12 Mechanical ectropion

374.13 Spastic ectropion

374.14 Cicatricial ectropion

✓5th **374.2 Lagophthalmos**

DEF: Incomplete closure of eyes; causes dry eye and other complications.

374.20 Lagophthalmos, unspecified

374.21 Paralytic lagophthalmos

374.22 Mechanical lagophthalmos

374.23 Cicatricial lagophthalmos

✓5th **374.3 Ptosis of eyelid**

374.30 Ptosis of eyelid, unspecified

AHA: 2Q, '96, 11

374.31 Paralytic ptosis

DEF: Drooping of upper eyelid due to nerve disorder.

Entropion and Ectropion

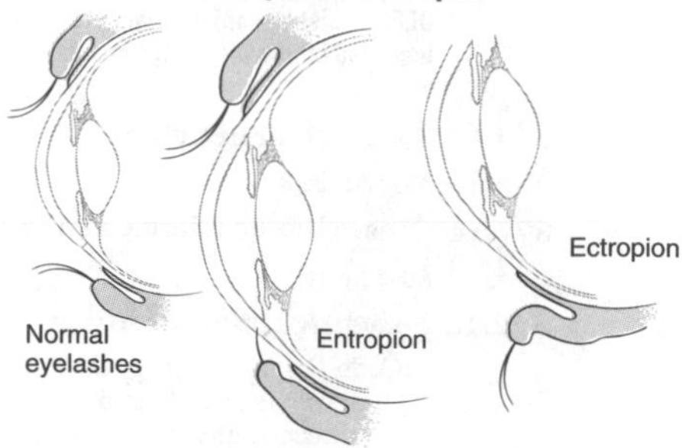

374.32 Myogenic ptosis

DEF: Drooping of upper eyelid due to muscle disorder.

374.33 Mechanical ptosis

DEF: Outside force causes drooping of upper eyelid.

374.34 Blepharochalasis

Pseudoptosis

DEF: Loss of elasticity, thickened or indurated skin of eyelids associated with recurrent episodes of idiopathic edema causing intracellular tissue atrophy.

✓5th **374.4 Other disorders affecting eyelid function**

EXCLUDES *blepharoclonus (333.81)*
blepharospasm (333.81)
facial nerve palsy (351.0)
third nerve palsy or paralysis (378.51-378.52)
tic (psychogenic) (307.20-307.23)
organic (333.3)

374.41 Lid retraction or lag

374.43 Abnormal innervation syndrome

Jaw-blinking
Paradoxical facial movements

374.44 Sensory disorders

374.45 Other sensorimotor disorders

Deficient blink reflex

374.46 Blepharophimosis

Ankyloblepharon

DEF: Narrowing of palpebral fissure horizontally; caused by laterally displaced inner canthi; either acquired or congenital.

✓5th **374.5 Degenerative disorders of eyelid and periocular area**

374.50 Degenerative disorder of eyelid, unspecified

374.51 Xanthelasma

Xanthoma (planum) (tuberosum) of eyelid
Code first underlying condition (272.0-272.9)

DEF: Fatty tumors of the eyelid linked to high fat content of blood.

374.52 Hyperpigmentation of eyelid

Chloasma
Dyspigmentation

DEF: Excess pigment of eyelid.

374.53 Hypopigmentation of eyelid

Vitiligo of eyelid

DEF: Lack of color pigment of the eyelid.

374.54 Hypertrichosis of eyelid

DEF: Excessive eyelash growth.

374.55 Hypotrichosis of eyelid

Madarosis of eyelid

DEF: Less than normal, or absent, eyelashes.

374.56 Other degenerative disorders of skin affecting eyelid

✓5th **374.8 Other disorders of eyelid**

374.81 Hemorrhage of eyelid

EXCLUDES *black eye (921.0)*

374.82 Edema of eyelid

Hyperemia of eyelid

DEF: Swelling and fluid retention in eyelid.

374.83 Elephantiasis of eyelid

DEF: Filarial disease causing dermatitis and enlargement of eyelid.

374.84 Cysts of eyelids

Sebaceous cyst of eyelid

374.85 Vascular anomalies of eyelid

374.86 Retained foreign body of eyelid

374.87 Dermatochalasis

DEF: Acquired form of connective tissue disorder associated with decreased elastic tissue and abnormal elastin formation resulting in loss of elasticity of the skin of the eyelid, generally associated with aging.

374.89 Other disorders of eyelid

374.9 Unspecified disorder of eyelid

✓4th **375 Disorders of lacrimal system**

✓5th **375.0 Dacryoadenitis**

375.00 Dacryoadenitis, unspecified

375.01 Acute dacryoadenitis

DEF: Severe, sudden inflammation of the lacrimal gland.

375.02 Chronic dacryoadenitis

DEF: Persistent inflammation of the lacrimal gland.

375.03 Chronic enlargement of lacrimal gland

✓5th **375.1 Other disorders of lacrimal gland**

375.11 Dacryops

DEF: Overproduction and constant flow of tears; may cause distended lacrimal duct.

375.12 Other lacrimal cysts and cystic degeneration

375.13 Primary lacrimal atrophy

375.14 Secondary lacrimal atrophy

DEF: Wasting away of the lacrimal gland due to another disease.

375.15 Tear film insufficiency, unspecified

Dry eye syndrome

AHA: 3Q, '96, 6

DEF: Eye dryness and irritation from insufficient tear production.

375.16 Dislocation of lacrimal gland

✓5th **375.2 Epiphora**

DEF: Abnormal development of tears due to stricture of lacrimal passages.

375.20 Epiphora, unspecified as to cause

375.21 Epiphora due to excess lacrimation

DEF: Tear overflow due to overproduction.

375.22 Epiphora due to insufficient drainage

DEF: Tear overflow due to blocked drainage.

✓5th **375.3 Acute and unspecified inflammation of lacrimal passages**

EXCLUDES *neonatal dacryocystitis (771.6)*

375.30 Dacryocystitis, unspecified

375.31 Acute canaliculitis, lacrimal

375.32 Acute dacryocystitis

Acute peridacryocystitis

Lacrimal System

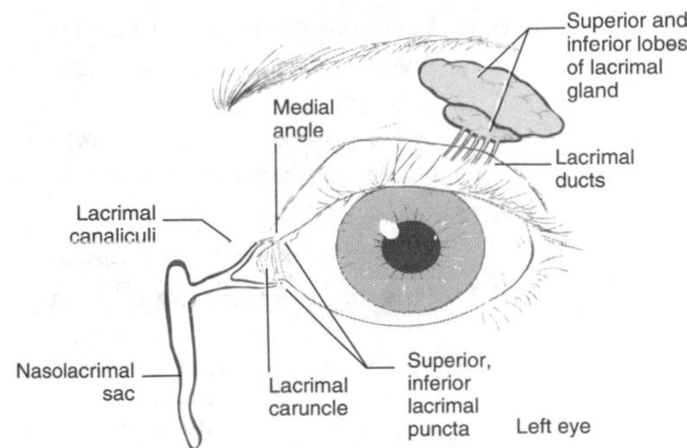

375.33 Phlegmonous dacryocystitis

DEF: Infection of the tear sac with pockets of pus.

✓5th **375.4 Chronic inflammation of lacrimal passages**

375.41 Chronic canaliculitis

375.42 Chronic dacryocystitis

375.43 Lacrimal mucocele

✓5th **375.5 Stenosis and insufficiency of lacrimal passages**

375.51 Eversion of lacrimal punctum

DEF: Abnormal turning outward of the tear duct.

375.52 Stenosis of lacrimal punctum

DEF: Abnormal narrowing of the tear duct.

375.53 Stenosis of lacrimal canaliculi

375.54 Stenosis of lacrimal sac

DEF: Abnormal narrowing of the tear sac.

375.55 Obstruction of nasolacrimal duct, neonatal

EXCLUDES *congenital anomaly of nasolacrimal duct (743.65)*

DEF: Acquired, abnormal obstruction of tear drainage system from the eye to the nose; in an infant.

375.56 Stenosis of nasolacrimal duct, acquired

375.57 Dacryolith

DEF: Concretion or stone anywhere in lacrimal system.

✓5th **375.6 Other changes of lacrimal passages**

375.61 Lacrimal fistula

DEF: Abnormal communication from the lacrimal system.

375.69 Other

✓5th **375.8 Other disorders of lacrimal system**

375.81 Granuloma of lacrimal passages

DEF: Abnormal nodules within lacrimal system.

375.89 Other

375.9 Unspecified disorder of lacrimal system

✓4th **376 Disorders of the orbit**

✓5th **376.0 Acute inflammation of orbit**

376.00 Acute inflammation of orbit, unspecified

376.01 Orbital cellulitis

Abscess of orbit

DEF: Infection of tissue between the orbital bone and eyeball.

376.02 Orbital periostitis

DEF: Inflammation of connective tissue covering the orbital bone.

376.03 Orbital osteomyelitis

DEF: Inflammation of the orbital bone.

376.04 Tenonitis

✓5th **376.1 Chronic inflammatory disorders of orbit**

376.10 Chronic inflammation of orbit, unspecified

376.11 Orbital granuloma
Pseudotumor (inflammatory) of orbit
DEF: Abnormal nodule between orbital bone and eyeball.

376.12 Orbital myositis
DEF: Painful inflammation of the muscles of the eye.

376.13 Parasitic infestation of orbit
Code first underlying disease, as:
hydatid infestation of orbit (122.3, 122.6, 122.9)
myiasis of orbit (134.0)

✓5th **376.2 Endocrine exophthalmos**
Code first underlying thyroid disorder (242.0-242.9)

376.21 Thyrotoxic exophthalmos
DEF: Painful inflammation of eye muscles.

376.22 Exophthalmic ophthalmoplegia
DEF: Inability to rotate eye as a result of bulging eyes.

✓5th **376.3 Other exophthalmic conditions**

376.30 Exophthalmos, unspecified
DEF: Abnormal protrusion of eyeball.

376.31 Constant exophthalmos
DEF: Continuous, abnormal protrusion or bulging of eyeball.

376.32 Orbital hemorrhage
DEF: Bleeding behind the eyeball, causing it to bulge forward.

376.33 Orbital edema or congestion
DEF: Fluid retention behind eyeball, causing forward bulge.

376.34 Intermittent exophthalmos

376.35 Pulsating exophthalmos
DEF: Bulge or protrusion; associated with a carotid-cavernous fistula.

376.36 Lateral displacement of globe
DEF: Abnormal displacement of the eyeball away from nose, toward temple.

✓5th **376.4 Deformity of orbit**

376.40 Deformity of orbit, unspecified

376.41 Hypertelorism of orbit
DEF: Abnormal increase in interorbital distance; associated with congenital facial deformities; may be accompanied by mental deficiency.

376.42 Exostosis of orbit
DEF: Abnormal bony growth of orbit.

376.43 Local deformities due to bone disease
DEF: Acquired abnormalities of orbit; due to bone disease.

376.44 Orbital deformities associated with craniofacial deformities

376.45 Atrophy of orbit
DEF: Wasting away of bone tissue of orbit.

376.46 Enlargement of orbit

376.47 Deformity due to trauma or surgery

✓5th **376.5 Enophthalmos**
DEF: Recession of eyeball deep into eye socket.

376.50 Enophthalmos, unspecified as to cause

376.51 Enophthalmos due to atrophy of orbital tissue

376.52 Enophthalmos due to trauma or surgery

376.6 Retained (old) foreign body following penetrating wound of orbit
Retrobulbar foreign body

✓5th **376.8 Other orbital disorders**

376.81 Orbital cysts
Encephalocele of orbit
AHA: 3Q, '99, 13

376.82 Myopathy of extraocular muscles
DEF: Disease in the muscles that control eyeball movement.

376.89 Other

376.9 Unspecified disorder of orbit

✓4th **377 Disorders of optic nerve and visual pathways**

✓5th **377.0 Papilledema**

377.00 Papilledema, unspecified

377.01 Papilledema associated with increased intracranial pressure

377.02 Papilledema associated with decreased ocular pressure

377.03 Papilledema associated with retinal disorder

377.04 Foster-Kennedy syndrome
DEF: Retrobulbar optic neuritis, central scotoma and optic atrophy; caused by tumors in frontal lobe of brain that press downward.

✓5th **377.1 Optic atrophy**

377.10 Optic atrophy, unspecified

377.11 Primary optic atrophy
EXCLUDES *neurosyphilitic optic atrophy (094.84)*

377.12 Postinflammatory optic atrophy
DEF: Adverse effect of inflammation causing wasting away of eye.

377.13 Optic atrophy associated with retinal dystrophies
DEF: Progressive changes in retinal tissue due to metabolic disorder causing wasting away of eye.

377.14 Glaucomatous atrophy [cupping] of optic disc

377.15 Partial optic atrophy
Temporal pallor of optic disc

377.16 Hereditary optic atrophy
Optic atrophy:
dominant hereditary
Leber's

✓5th **377.2 Other disorders of optic disc**

377.21 Drusen of optic disc

377.22 Crater-like holes of optic disc

377.23 Coloboma of optic disc
DEF: Ocular malformation caused by the failure of fetal fissure of optic stalk to close.

377.24 Pseudopapilledema

✓5th **377.3 Optic neuritis**
EXCLUDES *meningococcal optic neuritis (036.81)*

377.30 Optic neuritis, unspecified

377.31 Optic papillitis
DEF: Swelling and inflammation of the optic disc.

377.32 Retrobulbar neuritis (acute)
EXCLUDES *syphilitic retrobulbar neuritis (094.85)*
DEF: Inflammation of optic nerve immediately behind the eyeball.

377.33 Nutritional optic neuropathy
DEF: Malnutrition causing optic nerve disorder.

377.34 Toxic optic neuropathy
Toxic amblyopia
DEF: Toxic substance causing optic nerve disorder.

377.39 Other
EXCLUDES *ischemic optic neuropathy (377.41)*

✓5th **377.4 Other disorders of optic nerve**

377.41 Ischemic optic neuropathy
DEF: Decreased blood flow affecting optic nerve.

377.42 Hemorrhage in optic nerve sheaths
DEF: Bleeding in meningeal lining of optic nerve.

377.43 Optic nerve hypoplasia
AHA: 4Q, '06, 81

377.49 Other
Compression of optic nerve

✓5th **377.5 Disorders of optic chiasm**

377.51 Associated with pituitary neoplasms and disorders
DEF: Abnormal pituitary growth causing disruption in nerve chain from retina to brain.

377.52 Associated with other neoplasms
DEF: Abnormal growth, other than pituitary, causing disruption in nerve chain from retina to brain.

377.53 Associated with vascular disorders
DEF: Vascular disorder causing disruption in nerve chain from retina to brain.

377.54 Associated with inflammatory disorders
DEF: Inflammatory disease causing disruption in nerve chain from retina to brain.

✓5th **377.6 Disorders of other visual pathways**

377.61 Associated with neoplasms

377.62 Associated with vascular disorders

377.63 Associated with inflammatory disorders

✓5th **377.7 Disorders of visual cortex**
EXCLUDES *visual:*
agnosia (368.16)
hallucinations (368.16)
halos (368.15)

377.71 Associated with neoplasms

377.72 Associated with vascular disorders

377.73 Associated with inflammatory

377.75 Cortical blindness
DEF: Blindness due to brain disorder, rather than eye disorder.

377.9 Unspecified disorder of optic nerve and visual pathways

✓4th **378 Strabismus and other disorders of binocular eye movements**
EXCLUDES *nystagmus and other irregular eye movements (379.50-379.59)*
DEF: Misalignment of the eyes due to imbalance in extraocular muscles.

✓5th **378.0 Esotropia**
Convergent concomitant strabismus
EXCLUDES *intermittent esotropia (378.20-378.22)*
DEF: Visual axis deviation created by one eye fixing upon an image and the other eye deviating inward.

378.00 Esotropia, unspecified

378.01 Monocular esotropia

378.02 Monocular esotropia with A pattern

378.03 Monocular esotropia with V pattern

Eye Musculature

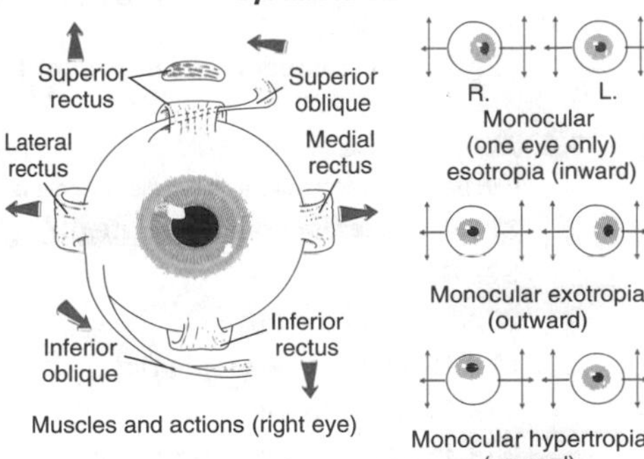

378.04 Monocular esotropia with other noncomitancies
Monocular esotropia with X or Y pattern

378.05 Alternating esotropia

378.06 Alternating esotropia with A pattern

378.07 Alternating esotropia with V pattern

378.08 Alternating esotropia with other noncomitancies
Alternating esotropia with X or Y pattern

✓5th **378.1 Exotropia**
Divergent concomitant strabismus
EXCLUDES *intermittent exotropia (378.20, 378.23-378.24)*
DEF: Visual axis deviation created by one eye fixing upon an image and the other eye deviating outward.

378.10 Exotropia, unspecified

378.11 Monocular exotropia

378.12 Monocular exotropia with A pattern

378.13 Monocular exotropia with V pattern

378.14 Monocular exotropia with other noncomitancies
Monocular exotropia with X or Y pattern

378.15 Alternating exotropia

378.16 Alternating exotropia with A pattern

378.17 Alternating exotropia with V pattern

378.18 Alternating exotropia with other noncomitancies
Alternating exotropia with X or Y pattern

✓5th **378.2 Intermittent heterotropia**
EXCLUDES *vertical heterotropia (intermittent) (378.31)*
DEF: Deviation of eyes seen only at intervals; it is also called strabismus.

378.20 Intermittent heterotropia, unspecified
Intermittent:
esotropia NOS
exotropia NOS

378.21 Intermittent esotropia, monocular

378.22 Intermittent esotropia, alternating

378.23 Intermittent exotropia, monocular

378.24 Intermittent exotropia, alternating

✓5th **378.3 Other and unspecified heterotropia**

378.30 Heterotropia, unspecified

378.31 Hypertropia
Vertical heterotropia (constant) (intermittent)

378.32 Hypotropia

378.33 Cyclotropia

378.34 **Monofixation syndrome**
Microtropia

378.35 **Accommodative component in esotropia**

✓5th 378.4 **Heterophoria**
DEF: Deviation occurring only when the other eye is covered.

378.40 **Heterophoria, unspecified**

378.41 **Esophoria**

378.42 **Exophoria**

378.43 **Vertical heterophoria**

378.44 **Cyclophoria**

378.45 **Alternating hyperphoria**

✓5th 378.5 **Paralytic strabismus**
DEF: Deviation of the eye due to nerve paralysis affecting muscle.

378.50 **Paralytic strabismus, unspecified**

378.51 **Third or oculomotor nerve palsy, partial**
AHA: 3Q, '91, 9

378.52 **Third or oculomotor nerve palsy, total**
AHA: 2Q, '89, 12

378.53 **Fourth or trochlear nerve palsy**
AHA: 2Q, '01, 21

378.54 **Sixth or abducens nerve palsy**
AHA: 2Q, '89, 12

378.55 **External ophthalmoplegia**

378.56 **Total ophthalmoplegia**

✓5th 378.6 **Mechanical strabismus**
DEF: Deviation of the eye due to an outside force upon the extraocular muscles.

378.60 **Mechanical strabismus, unspecified**

378.61 **Brown's (tendon) sheath syndrome**
DEF: Congenital or acquired shortening of the anterior sheath of the superior oblique muscle; the eye is unable to move upward and inward; it is usually unilateral.

378.62 **Mechanical strabismus from other musculofascial disorders**

378.63 **Limited duction associated with other conditions**

✓5th 378.7 **Other specified strabismus**

378.71 **Duane's syndrome**
DEF: Congenital, affects one eye; due to abnormal fibrous bands attached to rectus muscle; inability to abduct affected eye with retraction of globe.

378.72 **Progressive external ophthalmoplegia**
DEF: Paralysis progressing from one eye muscle to another.

378.73 **Strabismus in other neuromuscular disorders**

✓5th 378.8 **Other disorders of binocular eye movements**
EXCLUDES *nystagmus (379.50-379.56)*

378.81 **Palsy of conjugate gaze**
DEF: Paralysis progressing from one eye muscle to another.

378.82 **Spasm of conjugate gaze**
DEF: Muscle contractions impairing parallel movement of eye.

378.83 **Convergence insufficiency or palsy**

378.84 **Convergence excess or spasm**

378.85 **Anomalies of divergence**

378.86 **Internuclear ophthalmoplegia**
DEF: Eye movement anomaly due to brainstem lesion.

378.87 **Other dissociated deviation of eye movements**
Skew deviation

378.9 **Unspecified disorder of eye movements**
Ophthalmoplegia NOS
Strabismus NOS
AHA: 2Q, '01, 21

✓4th **379 Other disorders of eye**

✓5th 379.0 **Scleritis and episcleritis**
EXCLUDES *syphilitic episcleritis (095.0)*

379.00 **Scleritis, unspecified**
Episcleritis NOS

379.01 **Episcleritis periodica fugax**
DEF: Hyperemia (engorgement) of the sclera and overlying conjunctiva characterized by a sudden onset and short duration.

379.02 **Nodular episcleritis**
DEF: Inflammation of the outermost layer of the sclera, with formation of nodules.

379.03 **Anterior scleritis**

379.04 **Scleromalacia perforans**
DEF: Scleral thinning, softening and degeneration; seen with rheumatoid arthritis.

379.05 **Scleritis with corneal involvement**
Scleroperikeratitis

379.06 **Brawny scleritis**
DEF: Severe scleral inflammation with thickening corneal margins.

379.07 **Posterior scleritis**
Sclerotenonitis

379.09 **Other**
Scleral abscess

✓5th 379.1 **Other disorders of sclera**
EXCLUDES *blue sclera (743.47)*

379.11 **Scleral ectasia**
Scleral staphyloma NOS
DEF: Protrusion of the contents of the eyeball where the sclera has thinned.

379.12 **Staphyloma posticum**
DEF: Ring-shaped protrusion or bulging of sclera and uveal tissue at posterior pole of eye.

379.13 **Equatorial staphyloma**
DEF: Ring-shaped protrusion or bulging of sclera and uveal tissue midway between front and back of eye.

379.14 **Anterior staphyloma, localized**

379.15 **Ring staphyloma**

379.16 **Other degenerative disorders of sclera**

379.19 **Other**

✓5th 379.2 **Disorders of vitreous body**
DEF: Disorder of clear gel that fills space between retina and lens.

379.21 **Vitreous degeneration**
Vitreous:
  cavitation
  detachment
  liquefaction

379.22 **Crystalline deposits in vitreous**
Asteroid hyalitis
Synchysis scintillans

379.23 **Vitreous hemorrhage**
AHA: 3Q, '91, 15

379.24 Other vitreous opacities
Vitreous floaters

379.25 Vitreous membranes and strands

379.26 Vitreous prolapse
DEF: Slipping of vitreous from normal position.

379.29 Other disorders of vitreous
EXCLUDES *vitreous abscess (360.04)*
AHA: 1Q, '99, 11

✓5th **379.3 Aphakia and other disorders of lens**
EXCLUDES *after-cataract (366.50-366.53)*

379.31 Aphakia
EXCLUDES *cataract extraction status (V45.61)*
DEF: Absence of eye's crystalline lens.

379.32 Subluxation of lens

379.33 Anterior dislocation of lens
DEF: Lens displaced toward iris.

379.34 Posterior dislocation of lens
DEF: Lens displaced backward toward vitreous.

379.39 Other disorders of lens

✓5th **379.4 Anomalies of pupillary function**

379.40 Abnormal pupillary function, unspecified

379.41 Anisocoria
DEF: Unequal pupil diameter.

379.42 Miosis (persistent), not due to miotics
DEF: Abnormal contraction of pupil less than 2 mil.

379.43 Mydriasis (persistent), not due to mydriatics
DEF: Morbid dilation of pupil.

379.45 Argyll Robertson pupil, atypical
Argyll Robertson phenomenon or pupil, nonsyphilitic
EXCLUDES *Argyll Robertson pupil (syphilitic) (094.89)*
DEF: Failure of pupil to respond to light; affects both eyes; may be caused by diseases such as syphilis of the central nervous system or miosis.

379.46 Tonic pupillary reaction
Adie's pupil or syndrome

379.49 Other
Hippus
Pupillary paralysis

✓5th **379.5 Nystagmus and other irregular eye movements**

379.50 Nystagmus, unspecified
AHA: 4Q, '02, 68; 2Q, '01, 21
DEF: Involuntary, rapid, rhythmic movement of eyeball; vertical, horizontal, rotatory or mixed; cause may be congenital, acquired, physiological, neurological, myopathic, or due to ocular diseases.

379.51 Congenital nystagmus

379.52 Latent nystagmus

379.53 Visual deprivation nystagmus

379.54 Nystagmus associated with disorders of the vestibular system

379.55 Dissociated nystagmus

379.56 Other forms of nystagmus

379.57 Deficiencies of saccadic eye movements
Abnormal optokinetic response
DEF: Saccadic eye movements; small, rapid, involuntary movements by both eyes simultaneously, due to changing point of fixation on visualized object.

379.58 Deficiencies of smooth pursuit movements

379.59 Other irregularities of eye movements
Opsoclonus

✓5th **379.6 Inflammation (infection) of postprocedural bleb**
Postprocedural blebitis

379.60 Inflammation (infection) of postprocedural bleb, unspecified
AHA: 4Q, '06, 82

379.61 Inflammation (infection) of postprocedural bleb, stage 1
AHA: 4Q, '06, 82

379.62 Inflammation (infection) of postprocedural bleb, stage 2
AHA: 4Q, '06, 82

379.63 Inflammation (infection) of postprocedural bleb, stage 3
Bleb associated endophthalmitis
AHA: 4Q, '06, 82

379.8 Other specified disorders of eye and adnexa

✓5th **379.9 Unspecified disorder of eye and adnexa**

379.90 Disorder of eye, unspecified

379.91 Pain in or around eye

379.92 Swelling or mass of eye

379.93 Redness or discharge of eye

379.99 Other ill-defined disorders of eye
EXCLUDES *blurred vision NOS (368.8)*

DISEASES OF THE EAR AND MASTOID PROCESS (380-389)

▶Use additional external cause code, if applicable, to identify the cause of the ear condition◀

✓4th **380 Disorders of external ear**

✓5th **380.0 Perichondritis and chondritis of pinna**
Chondritis of auricle
Perichondritis of auricle

380.00 Perichondritis of pinna, unspecified

380.01 Acute perichondritis of pinna

380.02 Chronic perichondritis of pinna

380.03 Chondritis of pinna
AHA: 4Q, '04, 76
DEF: Infection that has progressed into the cartilage; presents as indurated and edematous skin over the pinna; vascular compromise occurs with tissue necrosis and deformity.

✓5th **380.1 Infective otitis externa**

380.10 Infective otitis externa, unspecified
Otitis externa (acute):
- NOS
- circumscribed
- diffuse
- hemorrhagica
- infective NOS

380.11 Acute infection of pinna
EXCLUDES *furuncular otitis externa (680.0)*

380.12 Acute swimmers' ear
Beach ear
Tank ear
DEF: Otitis externa due to swimming.

Ear and Mastoid Process

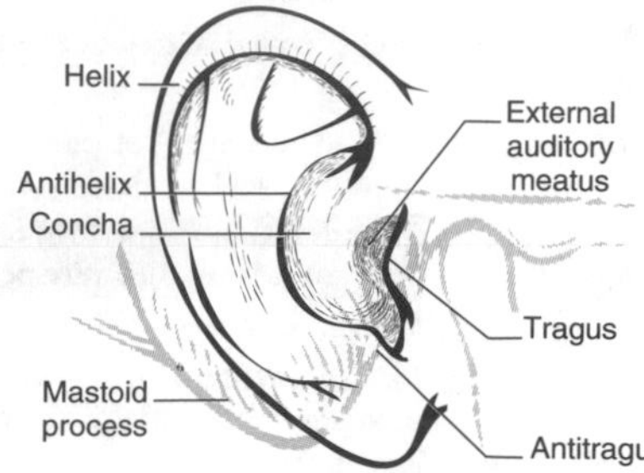

380.13* *Other acute infections of external ear

Code first underlying disease, as:
erysipelas (035)
impetigo (684)
seborrheic dermatitis (690.10-690.18)

EXCLUDES *herpes simplex (054.73)*
herpes zoster (053.71)

380.14 Malignant otitis externa

DEF: Severe necrotic otitis externa; due to bacteria.

380.15* *Chronic mycotic otitis externa

Code first underlying disease, as:
aspergillosis (117.3)
otomycosis NOS (111.9)

EXCLUDES *candidal otitis externa (112.82)*

380.16 Other chronic infective otitis externa

Chronic infective otitis externa NOS

✓5th **380.2 Other otitis externa**

380.21 Cholesteatoma of external ear

Keratosis obturans of external ear (canal)

EXCLUDES *cholesteatoma NOS (385.30-385.35)*
postmastoidectomy (383.32)

DEF: Cystlike mass filled with debris, including cholesterol; rare, congenital condition.

380.22 Other acute otitis externa

Acute otitis externa:
actinic
chemical
contact
eczematoid
reactive

380.23 Other chronic otitis externa

Chronic otitis externa NOS

✓5th **380.3 Noninfectious disorders of pinna**

380.30 Disorder of pinna, unspecified

380.31 Hematoma of auricle or pinna

380.32 Acquired deformities of auricle or pinna

EXCLUDES *cauliflower ear (738.7)*

AHA: 3Q, '03, 12

380.39 Other

EXCLUDES *gouty tophi of ear (274.81)*

380.4 Impacted cerumen

Wax in ear

✓5th **380.5 Acquired stenosis of external ear canal**

Collapse of external ear canal

380.50 Acquired stenosis of external ear canal, unspecified as to cause

380.51 Secondary to trauma

DEF: Narrowing of the external ear canal; due to trauma.

380.52 Secondary to surgery

DEF: Postsurgical narrowing of the external ear canal.

380.53 Secondary to inflammation

DEF: Narrowing of the external ear canal; due to chronic inflammation.

✓5th **380.8 Other disorders of external ear**

380.81 Exostosis of external ear canal

380.89 Other

380.9 Unspecified disorder of external ear

✓4th **381 Nonsuppurative otitis media and Eustachian tube disorders**

✓5th **381.0 Acute nonsuppurative otitis media**

Acute tubotympanic catarrh
Otitis media, acute or subacute:
catarrhal
exudative
transudative
with effusion

EXCLUDES *otitic barotrauma (993.0)*

381.00 Acute nonsuppurative otitis media, unspecified

381.01 Acute serous otitis media

Acute or subacute secretory otitis media

DEF: Sudden, severe infection of the middle ear.

381.02 Acute mucoid otitis media

Acute or subacute seromucinous otitis media
Blue drum syndrome

DEF: Sudden, severe infection of the middle ear, with mucous.

381.03 Acute sanguinous otitis media

DEF: Sudden, severe infection of the middle ear, with blood.

381.04 Acute allergic serous otitis media

381.05 Acute allergic mucoid otitis media

381.06 Acute allergic sanguinous otitis media

✓5th **381.1 Chronic serous otitis media**

Chronic tubotympanic catarrh

381.10 Chronic serous otitis media, simple or unspecified

DEF: Persistent infection of the middle ear, without pus.

381.19 Other

Serosanguinous chronic otitis media

✓5th **381.2 Chronic mucoid otitis media**

Glue ear

EXCLUDES *adhesive middle ear disease (385.10-385.19)*

DEF: Chronic condition; characterized by viscous fluid in middle ear; due to obstructed Eustachian tube.

381.20 Chronic mucoid otitis media, simple or unspecified

381.29 Other

Mucosanguinous chronic otitis media

381.3 Other and unspecified chronic nonsuppurative otitis media

Otitis media, chronic:
allergic
exudative
secretory

Otitis media, chronic:
seromucinous
transudative
with effusion

381.4 Nonsuppurative otitis media, not specified as acute or chronic

Otitis media:
allergic
catarrhal
exudative
mucoid

Otitis media:
secretory
seromucinous
serous
transudative
with effusion

✓5th **381.5 Eustachian salpingitis**

381.50 Eustachian salpingitis, unspecified

381.51 Acute Eustachian salpingitis

DEF: Sudden, severe inflammation of the Eustachian tube.

381.52 Chronic Eustachian salpingitis

DEF: Persistent inflammation of the Eustachian tube.

✓5th **381.6 Obstruction of Eustachian tube**

Stenosis } of Eustachian tube
Stricture }

381.60 Obstruction of Eustachian tube, unspecified

381.61 Osseous obstruction of Eustachian tube

Obstruction of Eustachian tube from cholesteatoma, polyp, or other osseous lesion

381.62 Intrinsic cartilaginous obstruction of Eustachian tube

DEF: Blockage of Eustachian tube; due to cartilage overgrowth.

381.63 Extrinsic cartilaginous obstruction of Eustachian tube

Compression of Eustachian tube

381.7 Patulous Eustachian tube

DEF: Distended, oversized Eustachian tube.

✓5th **381.8 Other disorders of Eustachian tube**

381.81 Dysfunction of Eustachian tube

381.89 Other

381.9 Unspecified Eustachian tube disorder

✓4th **382 Suppurative and unspecified otitis media**

✓5th **382.0 Acute suppurative otitis media**

Otitis media, acute:
necrotizing NOS
purulent

382.00 Acute suppurative otitis media without spontaneous rupture of ear drum

DEF: Sudden, severe inflammation of middle ear, with pus.

382.01 Acute suppurative otitis media with spontaneous rupture of ear drum

DEF: Sudden, severe inflammation of middle ear, with pressure tearing ear drum tissue.

382.02 Acute suppurative otitis media in diseases classified elsewhere

Code first underlying disease, as:
influenza (487.8)
scarlet fever (034.1)

EXCLUDES *postmeasles otitis (055.2)*

382.1 Chronic tubotympanic suppurative otitis media

Benign chronic suppurative ottis media } (with anterior perforation of ear drum)
Chronic tubotympanic disease }

DEF: Inflammation of tympanic cavity and auditory tube; with pus formation.

382.2 Chronic atticoantral suppurative otitis media

Chronic atticoantral disease } (with posterior or superior maginal perforation of ear drum)
Persistent mucosal disease }

DEF: Inflammation of upper tympanic membrane and mastoid antrum with pus formation.

382.3 Unspecified chronic suppurative otitis media

Chronic purulent otitis media

EXCLUDES *tuberculous otitis media (017.4)*

382.4 Unspecified suppurative otitis media

Purulent otitis media NOS

382.9 Unspecified otitis media

Otitis media:
NOS
acute NOS
chronic NOS

AHA: N-D, '84, 16

✓4th **383 Mastoiditis and related conditions**

✓5th **383.0 Acute mastoiditis**

Abscess of mastoid
Empyema of mastoid

383.00 Acute mastoiditis without complications

DEF: Sudden, severe inflammation of mastoid air cells.

383.01 Subperiosteal abscess of mastoid

DEF: Pocket of pus within the mastoid bone.

383.02 Acute mastoiditis with other complications

Gradenigo's syndrome

383.1 Chronic mastoiditis

Caries of mastoid
Fistula of mastoid

EXCLUDES *tuberculous mastoiditis (015.6)*

DEF: Persistent inflammation of the mastoid air cells.

✓5th **383.2 Petrositis**

Coalescing osteitis }
Inflammation } of pertrous bone
Osteomyelitis }

383.20 Petrositis, unspecified

383.21 Acute petrositis

DEF: Sudden, severe inflammation of dense bone behind the ear.

383.22 Chronic petrositis

DEF: Persistent inflammation of dense bone behind the ear.

✓5th **383.3 Complications following mastoidectomy**

383.30 Postmastoidectomy complication, unspecified

383.31 Mucosal cyst of postmastoidectomy cavity

DEF: Mucous-lined cyst cavity following removal of mastoid bone.

383.32 Recurrent cholesteatoma of postmastoidectomy cavity

DEF: Cystlike mass of cell debris in cavity following removal of mastoid bone.

383.33 Granulations of postmastoidectomy cavity

Chronic inflammation of postmastoidectomy cavity

DEF: Granular tissue in cavity following removal of mastoid bone.

✓5th **383.8 Other disorders of mastoid**

383.81 Postauricular fistula

DEF: Abnormal passage behind mastoid cavity.

383.89 Other

383.9 Unspecified mastoiditis

✓4th **384 Other disorders of tympanic membrane**

✓5th **384.0 Acute myringitis without mention of otitis media**

384.00 Acute myringitis, unspecified

Acute tympanitis NOS

DEF: Sudden, severe inflammation of ear drum.

384.01 Bullous myringitis
Myringitis bullosa hemorrhagica
DEF: Type of viral otitis media characterized by the appearance of serous or hemorrhagic blebs on the tympanic membrane.

384.09 Other

384.1 Chronic myringitis without mention of otitis media
Chronic tympanitis
DEF: Persistent inflammation of ear drum; with no evidence of middle ear infection.

✓5th **384.2 Perforation of tympanic membrane**
Perforation of ear drum:
NOS
persistent posttraumatic
postinflammatory
EXCLUDES *otitis media with perforation of tympanic membrane (382.00-382.9)*
traumatic perforation [current injury] (872.61)

384.20 Perforation of tympanic membrane, unspecified

384.21 Central perforation of tympanic membrane

384.22 Attic perforation of tympanic membrane
Pars flaccida

384.23 Other marginal perforation of tympanic membrane

384.24 Multiple perforations of tympanic membrane

384.25 Total perforation of tympanic membrane

✓5th **384.8 Other specified disorders of tympanic membrane**

384.81 Atrophic flaccid tympanic membrane
Healed perforation of ear drum

384.82 Atrophic nonflaccid tympanic membrane

384.9 Unspecified disorder of tympanic membrane

✓4th **385 Other disorders of middle ear and mastoid**
EXCLUDES *mastoiditis (383.0-383.9)*

✓5th **385.0 Tympanosclerosis**

385.00 Tympanosclerosis, unspecified as to involvement

385.01 Tympanosclerosis involving tympanic membrane only
DEF: Tough, fibrous tissue impeding functions of ear drum.

385.02 Tympanosclerosis involving tympanic membrane and ear ossicles
DEF: Tough, fibrous tissue impeding functions of middle ear bones (stapes, malleus, incus).

Middle and Inner Ear

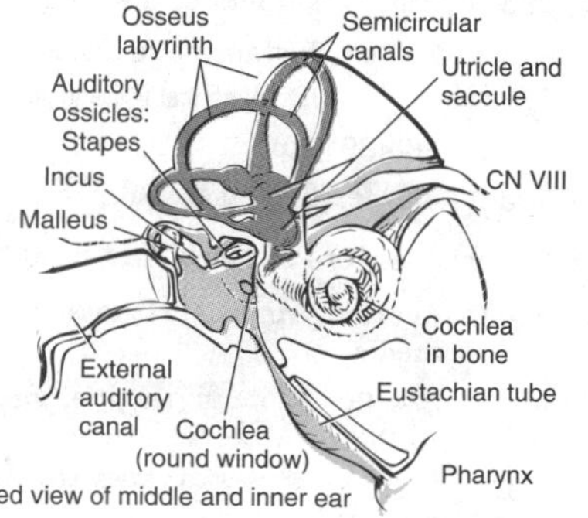

Exposed view of middle and inner ear

385.03 Tympanosclerosis involving tympanic membrane, ear ossicles, and middle ear
DEF: Tough, fibrous tissue impeding functions of ear drum, middle ear bones and middle ear canal.

385.09 Tympanosclerosis involving other combination of structures

✓5th **385.1 Adhesive middle ear disease**
Adhesive otitis
Otitis media:
chronic adhesive
fibrotic
EXCLUDES *glue ear (381.20-381.29)*
DEF: Adhesions of middle ear structures.

385.10 Adhesive middle ear disease, unspecified as to involvement

385.11 Adhesions of drum head to incus

385.12 Adhesions of drum head to stapes

385.13 Adhesions of drum head to promontorium

385.19 Other adhesions and combinations

✓5th **385.2 Other acquired abnormality of ear ossicles**

385.21 Impaired mobility of malleus
Ankylosis of malleus

385.22 Impaired mobility of other ear ossicles
Ankylosis of ear ossicles, except malleus

385.23 Discontinuity or dislocation of ear ossicles
DEF: Disruption in auditory chain; created by malleus, incus and stapes.

385.24 Partial loss or necrosis of ear ossicles
DEF: Tissue loss in malleus, incus and stapes.

✓5th **385.3 Cholesteatoma of middle ear and mastoid**
Cholesterosis, Epidermosis, Keratosis, Polyp } of (middle) ear
EXCLUDES *cholesteatoma:*
external ear canal (380.21)
recurrent of postmastoidectomy cavity (383.32)
DEF: Cystlike mass of middle ear and mastoid antrum filled with debris, including cholesterol.

385.30 Cholesteatoma, unspecified

385.31 Cholesteatoma of attic

385.32 Cholesteatoma of middle ear

385.33 Cholesteatoma of middle ear and mastoid
AHA: 3Q, '00, 10
DEF: Cystlike mass of cell debris in middle ear and mastoid air cells behind ear.

385.35 Diffuse cholesteatosis

Cholesteatoma

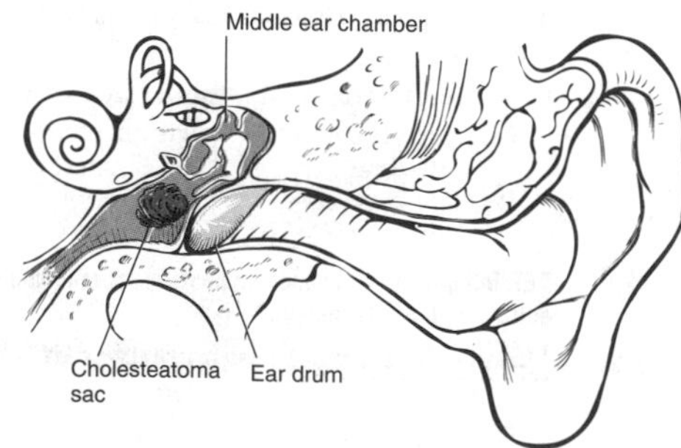

✓5th **385.8 Other disorders of middle ear and mastoid**

385.82 Cholesterin granuloma

DEF: Granuloma formed of fibrotic tissue; contains cholesterol crystals surrounded by foreign-body cells; found in the middle ear and mastoid area.

385.83 Retained foreign body of middle ear

AHA: 3Q, '94, 7; N-D, '87, 9

385.89 Other

385.9 Unspecified disorder of middle ear and mastoid

✓4th **386 Vertiginous syndromes and other disorders of vestibular system**

EXCLUDES *vertigo NOS (780.4)*

AHA: M-A, '85, 12

✓5th **386.0 Ménière's disease**

Endolymphatic hydrops
Lermoyez's syndrome
▶Ménière's◀ syndrome or vertigo

DEF: Distended membranous labyrinth of middle ear from endolymphatic hydrops; causes ischemia, failure of nerve function; hearing and balance dysfunction; symptoms include fluctuating deafness, ringing in ears and dizziness.

▲ **386.00 Ménière's disease, unspecified**

▶Ménière's◀ disease (active)

▲ **386.01 Active Ménière's disease, cochleovestibular**

▲ **386.02 Active Ménière's disease, cochlear**

▲ **386.03 Active Ménière's disease, vestibular**

▲ **386.04 Inactive Ménière's disease**

▶Ménière's◀ disease in remission

✓5th **386.1 Other and unspecified peripheral vertigo**

EXCLUDES *epidemic vertigo (078.81)*

386.10 Peripheral vertigo, unspecified

386.11 Benign paroxysmal positional vertigo

Benign paroxysmal positional nystagmus

386.12 Vestibular neuronitis

Acute (and recurrent) peripheral vestibulopathy

DEF: Transient benign vertigo, unknown cause; characterized by response to caloric stimulation on one side, nystagmus with rhythmic movement of eyes; normal auditory function present; occurs in young adults.

386.19 Other

Aural vertigo
Otogenic vertigo

386.2 Vertigo of central origin

Central positional nystagmus
Malignant positional vertigo

✓5th **386.3 Labyrinthitis**

386.30 Labyrinthitis, unspecified

386.31 Serous labyrinthitis

Diffuse labyrinthitis

DEF: Inflammation of labyrinth; with fluid buildup.

386.32 Circumscribed labyrinthitis

Focal labyrinthitis

386.33 Suppurative labyrinthitis

Purulent labyrinthitis

DEF: Inflammation of labyrinth; with pus.

386.34 Toxic labyrinthitis

DEF: Inflammation of labyrinth; due to toxic reaction.

386.35 Viral labyrinthitis

✓5th **386.4 Labyrinthine fistula**

386.40 Labyrinthine fistula, unspecified

386.41 Round window fistula

386.42 Oval window fistula

386.43 Semicircular canal fistula

386.48 Labyrinthine fistula of combined sites

✓5th **386.5 Labyrinthine dysfunction**

386.50 Labyrinthine dysfunction, unspecified

386.51 Hyperactive labyrinth, unilateral

DEF: Abnormal increased sensitivity of labyrinth to stimuli such as sound, pressure or gravitational change, affecting one ear.

386.52 Hyperactive labyrinth, bilateral

DEF: Abnormal increased sensitivity of labyrinth to stimuli such as sound, pressure or gravitational change, affecting both ears.

386.53 Hypoactive labyrinth, unilateral

DEF: Abnormal decreased sensitivity of labyrinth to stimuli such as sound, pressure or gravitational change, affecting one ear.

386.54 Hypoactive labyrinth, bilateral

DEF: Abnormal decreased sensitivity of labyrinth to stimuli such as sound, pressure or gravitational change, affecting both ears.

386.55 Loss of labyrinthine reactivity, unilateral

DEF: Decreased function of the labyrinth sensors, affecting one ear

386.56 Loss of labyrinthine reactivity, bilateral

DEF: Decreased function of the labyrinth sensors, affecting both ears

386.58 Other forms and combinations

386.8 Other disorders of labyrinth

386.9 Unspecified vertiginous syndromes and labyrinthine disorders

✓4th **387 Otosclerosis**

INCLUDES otospongiosis

DEF: Synonym for otospongiosis, spongy bone formation in the labyrinth bones of the ear; it causes progressive hearing impairment.

387.0 Otosclerosis involving oval window, nonobliterative

DEF: Tough, fibrous tissue impeding functions of oval window.

387.1 Otosclerosis involving oval window, obliterative

DEF: Tough, fibrous tissue blocking oval window.

387.2 Cochlear otosclerosis

Otosclerosis involving:
otic capsule
round window

DEF: Tough, fibrous tissue impeding functions of cochlea.

387.8 Other otosclerosis

387.9 Otosclerosis, unspecified

✓4th **388 Other disorders of ear**

✓5th **388.0 Degenerative and vascular disorders of ear**

388.00 Degenerative and vascular disorders, unspecified

388.01 Presbyacusis

DEF: Progressive, bilateral perceptive hearing loss caused by advancing age; it is also known as presbycusis.

388.02 Transient ischemic deafness

DEF: Restricted blood flow to auditory organs causing temporary hearing loss.

✓5th **388.1 Noise effects on inner ear**

388.10 Noise effects on inner ear, unspecified

388.11 Acoustic trauma (explosive) to ear

Otitic blast injury

388.12 Noise-induced hearing loss

388.2 Sudden hearing loss, unspecified

✓5th **388.3 Tinnitus**

DEF: Abnormal noises in ear; may be heard by others beside the affected individual; noises include ringing, clicking, roaring and buzzing.

388.30 Tinnitus, unspecified

388.31 Subjective tinnitus

388.32 Objective tinnitus

✓5th **388.4 Other abnormal auditory perception**

388.40 Abnormal auditory perception, unspecified

388.41 Diplacusis

DEF: Perception of a single auditory sound as two sounds at two different levels of intensity.

388.42 Hyperacusis

DEF: Exceptionally acute sense of hearing caused by such conditions as Bell's palsy; this term may also refer to painful sensitivity to sounds.

388.43 Impairment of auditory discrimination

DEF: Impaired ability to distinguish tone of sound.

388.44 Recruitment

DEF: Perception of abnormally increased loudness caused by a slight increase in sound intensity; it is a term used in audiology.

388.45 Acquired auditory processing disorder

Auditory processing disorder NOS

EXCLUDES *central auditory processing disorder (315.32)*

AHA: ▶4Q, '07, 79◀

DEF: ▶ Difficulty in recognizing and interpreting sounds; a failure of the brain to process auditory information; due to neurological problems due to injury, infection, and degenerative conditions.◀

388.5 Disorders of acoustic nerve

Acoustic neuritis

Degeneration } of acoustic or eighth nerve

Disorder } of acoustic or eighth nerve

EXCLUDES *acoustic neuroma (225.1)*
syphilitic acoustic neuritis (094.86)

AHA: M-A, '87, 8

✓5th **388.6 Otorrhea**

388.60 Otorrhea, unspecified

Discharging ear NOS

388.61 Cerebrospinal fluid otorrhea

EXCLUDES *cerebrospinal fluid rhinorrhea (349.81)*

DEF: Spinal fluid leakage from ear.

388.69 Other

Otorrhagia

✓5th **388.7 Otalgia**

388.70 Otalgia, unspecified

Earache NOS

388.71 Otogenic pain

388.72 Referred pain

388.8 Other disorders of ear

388.9 Unspecified disorder of ear

✓4th **389 Hearing loss**

✓5th **389.0 Conductive hearing loss**

Conductive deafness

EXCLUDES *mixed conductive and sensorineural hearing loss (389.20-389.22)*

AHA: ▶4Q, '07, 80;◀ 4Q, '89, 5

DEF: Dysfunction in sound-conducting structures of external or middle ear causing hearing loss.

389.00 Conductive hearing loss, unspecified

389.01 Conductive hearing loss, external ear

389.02 Conductive hearing loss, tympanic membrane

389.03 Conductive hearing loss, middle ear

389.04 Conductive hearing loss, inner ear

389.05 Conductive hearing loss, unilateral

389.06 Conductive hearing loss, bilateral

AHA: ▶4Q, '07, 81◀

389.08 Conductive hearing loss of combined types

✓5th **389.1 Sensorineural hearing loss**

Perceptive hearing loss or deafness

EXCLUDES *abnormal auditory perception (388.40-388.44)*
mixed conductive and sensorineural hearing loss (389.20-389.22)
psychogenic deafness (306.7)

AHA: ▶4Q, '07, 80;◀ 4Q, '89, 5

DEF: Nerve conduction causing hearing loss.

389.10 Sensorineural hearing loss, unspecified

AHA: 1Q, '93, 29

389.11 Sensory hearing loss, bilateral

389.12 Neural hearing loss, bilateral

389.13 Neural hearing loss, unilateral

389.14 Central hearing loss

389.15 Sensorineural hearing loss, unilateral

AHA: 4Q, '06, 84

389.16 Sensorineural hearing loss, asymmetrical

AHA: 4Q, '06, 84

389.17 Sensory hearing loss, unilateral

389.18 Sensorineural hearing loss, bilateral

AHA: 4Q, '06, 84

✓5th **389.2 Mixed conductive and sensorineural hearing loss**

Deafness or hearing loss of type classifiable to 389.00-389.08 with type classifiable to 389.10-389.18

AHA: ▶4Q, '07, 80◀

389.20 Mixed hearing loss, unspecified

389.21 Mixed hearing loss, unilateral

389.22 Mixed hearing loss, bilateral

389.7 Deaf, non-speaking, not elsewhere classifiable

389.8 Other specified forms of hearing loss

389.9 Unspecified hearing loss

Deafness NOS

AHA: 1Q, '04, 15

7. DISEASES OF THE CIRCULATORY SYSTEM (390-459)

ACUTE RHEUMATIC FEVER (390-392)

DEF: Febrile disease occurs mainly in children or young adults following throat infection by group A *streptococci;* symptoms include fever, joint pain, lesions of heart, blood vessels and joint connective tissue, abdominal pain, skin changes, and chorea.

390 Rheumatic fever without mention of heart involvement

Arthritis, rheumatic, acute or subacute
Rheumatic fever (active) (acute)
Rheumatism, articular, acute or subacute

EXCLUDES *that with heart involvement (391.0-391.9)*

4th 391 Rheumatic fever with heart involvement

EXCLUDES *chronic heart diseases of rheumatic origin ▶(393-398.99)◀ unless rheumatic fever is also present or there is evidence of recrudescence or activity of the rheumatic process*

391.0 Acute rheumatic pericarditis

Rheumatic:
- fever (active) (acute) with pericarditis
- pericarditis (acute)

Any condition classifiable to 390 with pericarditis

EXCLUDES *that not specified as rheumatic (420.0-420.9)*

DEF: Sudden, severe inflammation of heart lining due to rheumatic fever.

391.1 Acute rheumatic endocarditis

Rheumatic:
- endocarditis, acute
- fever (active) (acute) with endocarditis or valvulitis
- valvulitis acute

Any condition classifiable to 390 with endocarditis or valvulitis

DEF: Sudden, severe inflammation of heart cavities due to rheumatic fever.

391.2 Acute rheumatic myocarditis

Rheumatic fever (active) (acute) with myocarditis

Any condition classifiable to 390 with myocarditis

DEF: Sudden, severe inflammation of heart muscles due to rheumatic fever.

391.8 Other acute rheumatic heart disease

Rheumatic:
- fever (active) (acute) with other or multiple types of heart involvement
- pancarditis, acute

Any condition classifiable to 390 with other or multiple types of heart involvement

391.9 Acute rheumatic heart disease, unspecified

Rheumatic:
- carditis, acute
- fever (active) (acute) with unspecified type of heart involvement
- heart disease, active or acute

Any condition classifiable to 390 with unspecified type of heart involvement

4th 392 Rheumatic chorea

INCLUDES Sydenham's chorea

EXCLUDES *chorea:*
- *NOS (333.5)*
- *Huntington's (333.4)*

DEF: Childhood disease linked with rheumatic fever and streptococcal infections; symptoms include spasmodic, involuntary movements of limbs or facial muscles, psychic symptoms, and irritability.

392.0 With heart involvement

Rheumatic chorea with heart involvement of any type classifiable to 391

392.9 Without mention of heart involvement

CHRONIC RHEUMATIC HEART DISEASE (393-398)

393 Chronic rheumatic pericarditis

Adherent pericardium, rheumatic
Chronic rheumatic:
- mediastinopericarditis
- myopericarditis

EXCLUDES *pericarditis NOS or not specified as rheumatic (423.0-423.9)*

DEF: Persistent inflammation of heart lining due to rheumatic heart disease.

4th 394 Diseases of mitral valve

EXCLUDES *that with aortic valve involvement (396.0-396.9)*

394.0 Mitral stenosis

Mitral (valve):
- obstruction (rheumatic)
- stenosis NOS

DEF: Narrowing, of mitral valve between left atrium and left ventricle; due to rheumatic heart disease.

394.1 Rheumatic mitral insufficiency

Rheumatic mitral:
- incompetence
- regurgitation

EXCLUDES *that not specified as rheumatic (424.0)*

AHA: 2Q, '05, 14

DEF: Malfunction of mitral valve between left atrium and left ventricle; due to rheumatic heart disease.

394.2 Mitral stenosis with insufficiency

Mitral stenosis with incompetence or regurgitation

AHA: 1Q, '07, 11

DEF: A narrowing or stricture of the mitral valve situated between the left atrium and left ventricle. The stenosis interferes with blood flow from the atrium into the ventricle. If the valve does not completely close, it becomes insufficient (inadequate) and cannot prevent regurgitation (abnormal backward flow) into the atrium when the left ventricle contracts. This abnormal function is also called incompetence.

394.9 Other and unspecified mitral valve diseases

Mitral (valve):
- disease (chronic)
- failure

4th 395 Diseases of aortic valve

EXCLUDES *that not specified as rheumatic (424.1)*
that with mitral valve involvement (396.0-396.9)

395.0 Rheumatic aortic stenosis

Rheumatic aortic (valve) obstruction

AHA: 4Q, '88, 8

DEF: Narrowing of the aortic valve; results in backflow into ventricle; due to rheumatic heart disease.

395.1 Rheumatic aortic insufficiency

Rheumatic aortic:
- incompetence
- regurgitation

DEF: Malfunction of the aortic valve; results in backflow into left ventricle; due to rheumatic heart disease.

395.2 Rheumatic aortic stenosis with insufficiency

Rheumatic aortic stenosis with incompetence or regurgitation

DEF: Malfunction and narrowing, of the aortic valve; results in backflow into left ventricle; due to rheumatic heart disease.

395.9 Other and unspecified rheumatic aortic diseases

Rheumatic aortic (valve) disease

4th 396 Diseases of mitral and aortic valves

INCLUDES involvement of both mitral and aortic valves, whether specified as rheumatic or not

AHA: N-D, '87, 8

396.0 Mitral valve stenosis and aortic valve stenosis

Atypical aortic (valve) stenosis
Mitral and aortic (valve) obstruction (rheumatic)

396.1 Mitral valve stenosis and aortic valve insufficiency

396.2 Mitral valve insufficiency and aortic valve stenosis

AHA: 2Q, '00, 16

396.3 Mitral valve insufficiency and aortic valve insufficiency

Mitral and aortic (valve):
incompetence
regurgitation

396.8 Multiple involvement of mitral and aortic valves

Stenosis and insufficiency of mitral or aortic valve with stenosis or insufficiency, or both, of the other valve

396.9 Mitral and aortic valve diseases, unspecified

✓4th **397 Diseases of other endocardial structures**

397.0 Diseases of tricuspid valve

Tricuspid (valve) (rheumatic):
disease
insufficiency
obstruction
regurgitation
stenosis

AHA: 3Q, '06, 7; 2Q, '00, 16

DEF: Malfunction of the valve between right atrium and right ventricle; due to rheumatic heart disease.

397.1 Rheumatic diseases of pulmonary valve

EXCLUDES *that not specified as rheumatic (424.3)*

397.9 Rheumatic diseases of endocardium, valve unspecified

Rheumatic:
endocarditis (chronic)
valvulitis (chronic)

EXCLUDES *that not specified as rheumatic (424.90-424.99)*

✓4th **398 Other rheumatic heart disease**

398.0 Rheumatic myocarditis

Rheumatic degeneration of myocardium

EXCLUDES *myocarditis not specified as rheumatic (429.0)*

DEF: Chronic inflammation of heart muscle; due to rheumatic heart disease.

✓5th **398.9 Other and unspecified rheumatic heart diseases**

398.90 Rheumatic heart disease, unspecified

Rheumatic:
carditis
heart disease NOS

EXCLUDES *carditis not specified as rheumatic (429.89)*
heart disease NOS not specified as rheumatic (429.9)

Sections of Heart Muscle

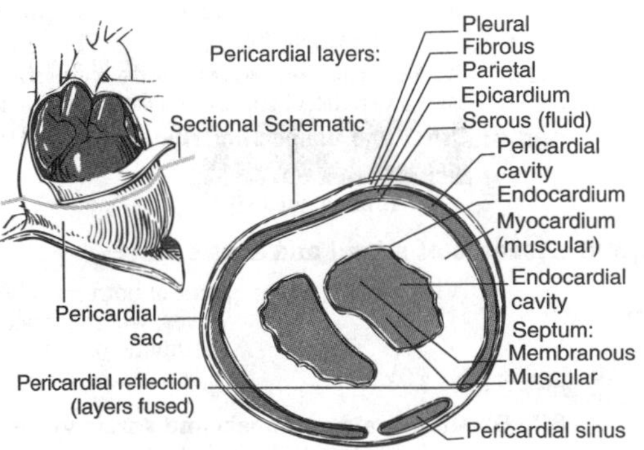

398.91 Rheumatic heart failure (congestive)

Rheumatic left ventricular failure

AHA: 2Q, '05, 14; 1Q, '95, 6; 3Q, '88, 3

DEF: Decreased cardiac output, edema and hypertension; due to rheumatic heart disease.

398.99 Other

HYPERTENSIVE DISEASE (401-405)

EXCLUDES *that complicating pregnancy, childbirth, or the puerperium (642.0-642.9)*
that involving coronary vessels (410.00-414.9)

AHA: 3Q, '90, 3; 2Q, '89, 12; S-O, '87, 9; J-A, '84, 11

✓4th **401 Essential hypertension**

INCLUDES high blood pressure
hyperpiesia
hyperpiesis
hypertension (arterial) (essential) (primary) (systemic)
hypertensive vascular:
degeneration
disease

EXCLUDES *elevated blood pressure without diagnosis of hypertension (796.2)*
pulmonary hypertension (416.0-416.9)
that involving vessels of:
brain (430-438)
eye (362.11)

AHA: 2Q, '92, 5

DEF: Hypertension that occurs without apparent organic cause; idiopathic.

401.0 Malignant

AHA: M-J, '85, 19

DEF: Severe high arterial blood pressure; results in necrosis in kidney, retina, etc.; hemorrhages occur and death commonly due to uremia or rupture of cerebral vessel.

401.1 Benign

DEF: Mildly elevated arterial blood pressure.

401.9 Unspecified

AHA: ▶2Q, '08, 16;◀ 4Q, '05, 71; 3Q, '05, 8; 4Q, '04, 78; 4Q, '03, 105, 108, 111; 3Q, '03, 14; 2Q, '03, 16; 4Q, '97, 37

✓4th **402 Hypertensive heart disease**

INCLUDES hypertensive:
cardiomegaly
cardiopathy
cardiovascular disease
heart (disease) (failure)
any condition classifiable to 429.0-429.3, 429.8, 429.9 due to hypertension

Use additional code to specify type of heart failure (428.0-428.43), if known

AHA: 4Q, '02, 49; 2Q, '93, 9; N-D, '84, 18

✓5th **402.0 Malignant**

402.00 Without heart failure

402.01 With heart failure

✓5th **402.1 Benign**

402.10 Without heart failure

402.11 With heart failure

✓5th **402.9 Unspecified**

402.90 Without heart failure

402.91 With heart failure

AHA: 4Q, '02, 52; 1Q, '93, 19; 2Q, '89, 12

✓4th 403 Hypertensive chronic kidney disease

INCLUDES arteriolar nephritis
arteriosclerosis of:
kidney
renal arterioles
arteriosclerotic nephritis (chronic) (interstitial)
hypertensive:
nephropathy
renal failure
uremia (chronic)
nephrosclerosis
renal sclerosis with hypertension
▶any condition classifiable to 585 with any condition classifiable to 401◀

EXCLUDES *acute renal failure (584.5-584.9)*
renal disease stated as not due to hypertension
renovascular hypertension (405.0-405.9 with fifth-digit 1)

The following fifth-digit subclassification is for use with category 403:
0 with chronic kidney disease stage I through stage IV, or unspecified
Use additional code to identify the stage of chronic kidney disease (585.1-585.4, 585.9)
1 with chronic kidney disease stage V or end stage renal disease
Use additional code to identify the stage of chronic kidney disease (585.5, 585.6)

AHA: 4Q, '06, 84-86; 4Q, '05, 68; 4Q, '92, 22; 2Q, '92, 5

§ ✓5th **403.0 Malignant**
[0-1]

§ ✓5th **403.1 Benign**
[0-1]

§ ✓5th **403.9 Unspecified**
[0-1] **AHA: For code 403.90:** ▶1Q, '08, 10;◀2Q, '07, 3; 4Q, '06, 86; **For code 403.91:** ▶1Q, '08, 7;◀ 4Q, '05, 69; 1Q, '04, 14; 1Q, '03, 20; 2Q, '01, 11; 3Q, '91, 8

✓4th 404 Hypertensive heart and chronic kidney disease

INCLUDES disease:
cardiorenal
cardiovascular renal
any condition classifiable to 402 with any condition classifiable to 403

Use additional code to specify type of heart failure (428.0-428.43), if known

The following fifth-digit subclassification is for use with category 404:
0 without heart failure and with chronic kidney disease stage I through stage IV, or unspecified
Use additional code to identify the stage of chronic kidney disease (585.1-585.4, 585.9)
1 with heart failure and with chronic kidney disease stage I through stage IV, or unspecified
Use additional code to identify the stage of chronic kidney disease (585.1-585.4, 585.9)
2 without heart failure and with chronic kidney disease stage V or end stage renal disease
Use additional code to identify the stage of chronic kidney disease (585.5, 585.6)
3 with heart failure and chronic kidney disease stage V or end stage renal disease
Use additional code to identify the stage of chronic kidney disease (585.5, 585.6)

AHA: 4Q, '06, 84-86; 4Q, '05, 68; 4Q, '02, 49; 3Q, '90, 3; J-A, '84, 14

§ ✓5th **404.0 Malignant**
[0-3]

§ ✓5th **404.1 Benign**
[0-3]

§ ✓5th **404.9 Unspecified**
[0-3]

✓4th 405 Secondary hypertension

AHA: 3Q, '90, 3; S-O, '87, 9, 11; J-A, '84, 14

DEF: High arterial blood pressure due to or with a variety of primary diseases, such as renal disorders, CNS disorders, endocrine, and vascular diseases.

✓5th **405.0 Malignant**
405.01 Renovascular
405.09 Other

✓5th **405.1 Benign**
405.11 Renovascular
405.19 Other

✓5th **405.9 Unspecified**
405.91 Renovascular
405.99 Other
AHA: 3Q, '00, 4

ISCHEMIC HEART DISEASE (410-414)

INCLUDES that with mention of hypertension

Use additional code to identify presence of hypertension (401.0-405.9)

AHA: 3Q, '91, 10; J-A, '84, 5

✓4th 410 Acute myocardial infarction

INCLUDES cardiac infarction
coronary (artery):
embolism
occlusion
rupture
thrombosis
infarction of heart, myocardium, or ventricle
rupture of heart, myocardium, or ventricle
ST elevation (STEMI) and non-ST elevation (NSTEMI) myocardial infarction
any condition classifiable to 414.1-414.9 specified as acute or with a stated duration of 8 weeks or less

The following fifth-digit subclassification is for use with category 410:
0 episode of care unspecified
Use when the source document does not contain sufficient information for the assigment of fifth-digit 1 or 2.
1 initial episode of care
Use fifth-digit 1 to designate the first episode of care (regardless of facility site) for a newly diagnosed myocardial infarction. The fifth-digit 1 is assigned regardless of the number of times a patient may be transferred during the initial episode of care.
2 subsequent episode of care
Use fifth-digit 2 to designate an episode of care following the initial episode when the patient is admitted for further observation, evaluation or treatment for a myocardial infarction that has received initial treatment, but is still less than 8 weeks old.

AHA: 2Q, '06, 9; 4Q, '05, 69; 3Q, '01, 21; 3Q, '98, 15; 4Q, '97, 37; 3Q, '95, 9; 4Q, 92, 24; 1Q, '92, 10; 3Q, '91, 18; 1Q, '91, 14; 3Q, '89, 3

DEF: A sudden insufficiency of blood supply to an area of the heart muscle; usually due to a coronary artery occlusion.

§ Requires fifth-digit. Valid digits are in [brackets] under each code. See appropriate category for codes and definitions.

Acute Myocardial Infarction

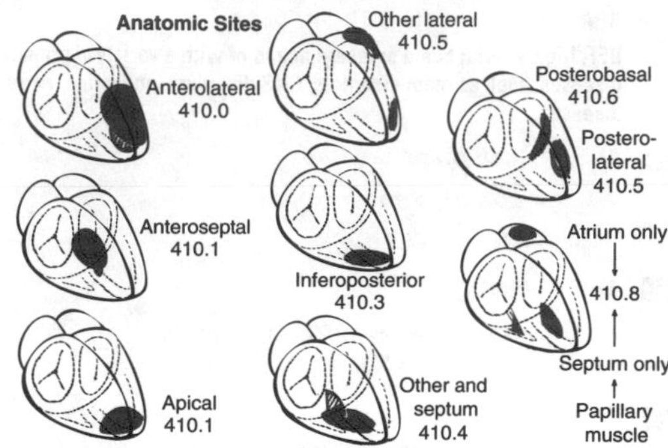

§ ✓5th **410.0 Of anterolateral wall**
[0-2]
ST elevation myocardial infarction (STEMI) of anterolateral wall

§ ✓5th **410.1 Of other anterior wall**
[0-2]
Infarction:
- anterior (wall) NOS, anteroapical, anteroseptal } (with contiguous portion of intraventricular septum)

ST elevation myocardial infarction (STEMI) of other anterior wall

AHA: For code 410.11: 3Q, '03, 10

§ ✓5th **410.2 Of inferolateral wall**
[0-2]
ST elevation myocardial infarction (STEMI) of inferolateral wall

§ ✓5th **410.3 Of inferoposterior wall**
[0-2]
ST elevation myocardial infarction (STEMI) of inferoposterior wall

§ ✓5th **410.4 Of other inferior wall**
[0-2]
Infarction:
- diaphragmatic wall NOS, inferior (wall) NOS } (with contiguous portion of intraventricular septum)

ST elevation myocardial infarction (STEMI) of other inferior wall

AHA: 1Q, '00, 7, 26; 4Q, '99, 9; 3Q, '97, 10;
For code 410.41: 2Q, '01, 8, 9

§ ✓5th **410.5 Of other lateral wall**
[0-2]
Infarction:
- apical-lateral
- basal-lateral
- high lateral
- posterolateral

ST elevation myocardial infarction (STEMI) of other lateral wall

§ ✓5th **410.6 True posterior wall infarction**
[0-2]
Infarction:
- posterobasal
- strictly posterior

ST elevation myocardial infarction (STEMI) of true posterior wall

§ ✓5th **410.7 Subendocardial infarction**
[0-2]
Non-ST elevation myocardial infarction (NSTEMI)
Nontransmural infarction

AHA: 1Q, '00, 7; **For code 410.71:** 4Q, '05, 71; 2Q, '05, 19

§ ✓5th **410.8 Of other specified sites**
[0-2]
Infarction of:
- atrium
- papillary muscle
- septum alone

ST elevation myocardial infarction (STEMI) of other specified sites

§ ✓5th **410.9 Unspecified site**
[0-2]
Acute myocardial infarction NOS
Coronary occlusion NOS
Myocardial infarction NOS

AHA: 1Q, '96, 17; 1Q, '92, 9; **For code 410.91:** 2Q, '05, 18; 3Q, '02, 5

✓4th **411 Other acute and subacute forms of ischemic heart disease**

AHA: 4Q, '94, 55; 3Q, '91, 24

411.0 Postmyocardial infarction syndrome
Dressler's syndrome

DEF: Complication developing several days/weeks after myocardial infarction; symptoms include fever, leukocytosis, chest pain, evi-dence of pericarditis, pleurisy, and pneumonitis; tendency to recur.

411.1 Intermediate coronary syndrome
Impending infarction
Preinfarction angina
Preinfarction syndrome
Unstable angina

EXCLUDES *angina (pectoris) (413.9)*
▶decubitus (413.0)◀

AHA: 3Q, '07, 9; 4Q, '05, 105; 2Q, '04, 3; 1Q, '03, 12; 3Q, '01, 15; 2Q, '01, 7, 9; 4Q, '98, 86; 2Q, '96, 10; 3Q, '91, 24; 1Q, '91, 14; 3Q, '90, 6; 4Q, '89, 10

DEF: A condition representing an intermediate stage between angina of effort and acute myocardial infarction. It is often documented by the physician as "unstable angina."

✓5th **411.8 Other**

AHA: 3Q, '91, 18; 3Q, '89, 4

411.81 Acute coronary occlusion without myocardial infarction
Acute coronary (artery):
- embolism, obstruction, occlusion, thrombosis } without or not resulting in myocardial infarction

EXCLUDES *obstruction without infarction due to atherosclerosis (414.00-414.07)*
occlusion without infarction due to atherosclerosis (414.00-414.07)

AHA: 3Q, '91, 24; 1Q, '91, 14

DEF: Interrupted blood flow to a portion of the heart; without tissue death.

411.89 Other
Coronary insufficiency (acute)
Subendocardial ischemia

AHA: 3Q, '01, 14; 1Q, '92, 9

412 Old myocardial infarction
Healed myocardial infarction
Past myocardial infarction diagnosed on ECG [EKG] or other special investigation, but currently presenting no symptoms

AHA: 2Q, '03, 10; 2Q, '01, 9; 3Q, '98, 15; 2Q, '91, 22; 3Q, '90, 7

✓4th **413 Angina pectoris**

DEF: Severe constricting pain in the chest, often radiating from the precordium to the left shoulder and down the arm, due to ischemia of the heart muscle; usually caused by coronary disease; pain is often precipitated by effort or excitement.

413.0 Angina decubitus
Nocturnal angina

DEF: Angina occurring only in the recumbent position.

413.1 Prinzmetal angina
Variant angina pectoris

AHA: 3Q, '06, 23

DEF Angina occurring when patient is recumbent; associated with ST-segment elevations.

§ Requires fifth-digit. Valid digits are in [brackets] under each code. See category 410 for codes and definitions.

413.9 Other and unspecified angina pectoris
Angina:
NOS
cardiac
of effort
Anginal syndrome
Status anginosus
Stenocardia
Syncope anginosa
EXCLUDES *preinfarction angina (411.1)*
AHA: ▶2Q, '08, 16;◀ 3Q, '02, 4; 3Q, '91, 16; 3Q, '90, 6

✓4th 414 Other forms of chronic ischemic heart disease
EXCLUDES *arteriosclerotic cardiovascular disease [ASCVD] (429.2)*
cardiovascular:
arteriosclerosis or sclerosis (429.2)
degeneration or disease (429.2)

✓5th 414.0 Coronary atherosclerosis
Arteriosclerotic heart disease [ASHD]
Atherosclerotic heart disease
Coronary (artery):
arteriosclerosis
arteritis or endarteritis
atheroma
sclerosis
stricture
Use additional code, if applicable, to identify chronic total occlusion of coronary artery (414.2)
EXCLUDES *embolism of graft (996.72)*
occlusion NOS of graft (996.72)
thrombus of graft (996.72)
AHA: 2Q, '97, 13; 2Q, '95, 17; 4Q, '94, 49; 2Q, '94, 13; 1Q, '94, 6; 3Q, '90, 7
DEF: A chronic condition marked by thickening and loss of elasticity of the coronary artery; caused by deposits of plaque containing cholesterol, lipoid material and lipophages.

414.00 Of unspecified type of vessel, native or graft A
AHA: 1Q, '04, 24; 2Q, '03, 16; 3Q, '01, 15; 4Q, '99, 4; 3Q, '97, 15; 4Q, '96, 31

414.01 Of native coronary artery A
AHA: ▶2Q, '08, 16;◀ 3Q, '06, 25; 4Q, '05, 71; 2Q, '04, 3; 4Q, '03, 108; 3Q, '03, 9, 14; 3Q, '02, 4-9; 3Q, '01, 15; 2Q, '01, 8, 9; 3Q, '97, 15; 2Q, '96, 10; 4Q, '96, 31
DEF: Plaque deposits in natural heart vessels.

414.02 Of autologous vein bypass graft A
DEF: Plaque deposit in grafted vein originating within patient.

414.03 Of nonautologous biological bypass graft A
DEF: Plaque deposits in grafted vessel originating outside patient.

414.04 Of artery bypass graft A
Internal mammary artery
AHA: 4Q, '96, 31
DEF: Plaque deposits in grafted artery originating within patient.

414.05 Of unspecified type of bypass graft A
Bypass graft NOS
AHA: 3Q, '97, 15; 4Q, '96, 31

414.06 Of native coronary artery of transplanted heart
AHA: 4Q, '03, 60; 4Q, '02, 53

414.07 Of bypass graft (artery) (vein) of transplanted heart A

Arteries of the Heart

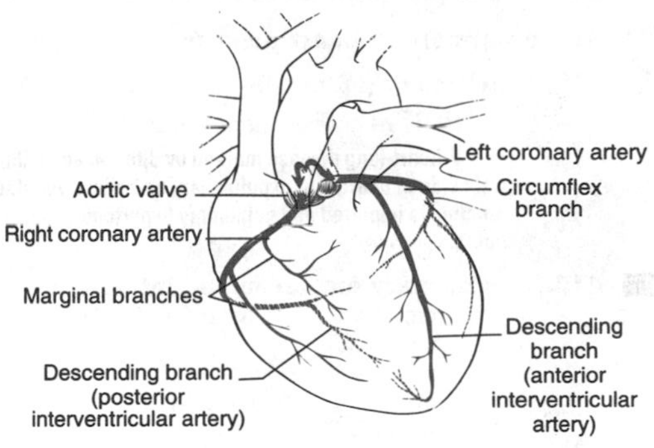

✓5th 414.1 Aneurysm and dissection of heart
AHA: 4Q, '02, 54

414.10 Aneurysm of heart (wall)
Aneurysm (arteriovenous):
mural
ventricular

414.11 Aneurysm of coronary vessels
Aneurysm (arteriovenous) of coronary vessels
AHA: 3Q, '03, 10; 1Q, '99, 17
DEF: Dilatation of all three-vessel wall layers forming a sac filled with blood.

414.12 Dissection of coronary artery
DEF: A tear in the intimal arterial wall of a coronary artery resulting in the sudden intrusion of blood within the layers of the wall.

414.19 Other aneurysm of heart
Arteriovenous fistula, acquired, of heart

414.2 Chronic total occlusion of coronary artery
Complete occlusion of coronary artery
Total occlusion of coronary artery
Code first coronary atherosclerosis (414.00-414.07)
EXCLUDES *acute coronary occlusion with myocardial infarction (410.00-410.92)*
acute coronary occlusion without myocardial infarction (411.81)
AHA: 4Q, '07, 82
DEF: Complete blockage of coronary artery due to plaque accumulation over an extended period of time; results in substantial reduction of blood flow.

● **414.3 Coronary atherosclerosis due to lipid rich plaque**
Code first coronary atherosclerosis (414.00-414.07)

414.8 Other specified forms of chronic ischemic heart disease
Chronic coronary insufficiency
Ischemia, myocardial (chronic)
Any condition classifiable to 410 specified as chronic, or presenting with symptoms after 8 weeks from date of infarction
EXCLUDES *coronary insufficiency (acute) (411.89)*
AHA: 3Q, '01, 15; 1Q, '92, 10; 3Q, '90, 7, 15; 2Q, '90, 19

414.9 Chronic ischemic heart disease, unspecified
Ischemic heart disease NOS

DISEASES OF PULMONARY CIRCULATION (415-417)

✓4th 415 Acute pulmonary heart disease

415.0 Acute cor pulmonale

EXCLUDES *cor pulmonale NOS (416.9)*

DEF: A heart-lung disease marked by dilation and failure of the right side of heart; due to pulmonary embolism; ventilatory function is impaired and pulmonary hypertension results within hours.

✓5th **415.1 Pulmonary embolism and infarction**

Pulmonary (artery) (vein):
- apoplexy
- embolism
- infarction (hemorrhagic)
- thrombosis

EXCLUDES *that complicating:*
- *abortion (634-638 with .6, 639.6)*
- *ectopic or molar pregnancy (639.6)*
- *pregnancy, childbirth, or the puerperium (673.0-673.8)*

AHA: 4Q, '90, 25

DEF: Embolism: Closure of the pulmonary artery or branch; due to thrombosis (blood clot).

DEF: Infarction: Necrosis of lung tissue; due to obstructed arterial blood supply, most often by pulmonary embolism.

415.11 Iatrogenic pulmonary embolism and infarction

►Use additional code for associated septic pulmonary embolism, if applicable, 415.12◄

AHA: 4Q, '95, 58

415.12 Septic pulmonary embolism

Septic embolism NOS

Code first underlying infection, such as:
- septicemia (038.0-038.9)

EXCLUDES *septic arterial embolism (449)*

AHA: 4Q, '07, 84-86

415.19 Other

✓4th 416 Chronic pulmonary heart disease

416.0 Primary pulmonary hypertension

Idiopathic pulmonary arteriosclerosis

Pulmonary hypertension (essential) (idiopathic) (primary)

DEF: A rare increase in pulmonary circulation, often resulting in right ventricular failure or fatal syncope.

416.1 Kyphoscoliotic heart disease

DEF: High blood pressure within the lungs as a result of curvature of the spine.

416.8 Other chronic pulmonary heart diseases

Pulmonary hypertension, secondary

416.9 Chronic pulmonary heart disease, unspecified

Chronic cardiopulmonary disease

Cor pulmonale (chronic) NOS

✓4th 417 Other diseases of pulmonary circulation

417.0 Arteriovenous fistula of pulmonary vessels

EXCLUDES *congenital arteriovenous fistula (747.3)*

DEF: Abnormal communication between blood vessels within lung.

417.1 Aneurysm of pulmonary artery

EXCLUDES *congenital aneurysm (747.3)*

417.8 Other specified diseases of pulmonary circulation

Pulmonary:
- arteritis
- endarteritis

Rupture } of pulmonary vessel
Stricture }

417.9 Unspecified disease of pulmonary circulation

OTHER FORMS OF HEART DISEASE (420-429)

✓4th 420 Acute pericarditis

INCLUDES acute:
- mediastinopericarditis
- myopericarditis
- pericardial effusion
- pleuropericarditis
- pneumopericarditis

EXCLUDES *acute rheumatic pericarditis (391.0)*
postmyocardial infarction syndrome [Dressler's] (411.0)

DEF: Inflammation of the pericardium (heart sac); pericardial friction rub results from this inflammation and is heard as a scratchy or leathery sound.

420.0 Acute pericarditis in diseases classified elsewhere

Code first underlying disease, as:
- actinomycosis (039.8)
- amebiasis (006.8)
- chronic uremia (585.9)
- nocardiosis (039.8)
- tuberculosis (017.9)
- uremia NOS (586)

EXCLUDES *pericarditis (acute) (in):*
- *Coxsackie (virus) (074.21)*
- *gonococcal (098.83)*
- *histoplasmosis (115.0-115.9 with fifth-digit 3)*
- *meningococcal infection (036.41)*
- *syphilitic (093.81)*

✓5th **420.9 Other and unspecified acute pericarditis**

420.90 Acute pericarditis, unspecified

Pericarditis (acute):
- NOS
- infective NOS
- sicca

AHA: 2Q, '89, 12

Anatomy

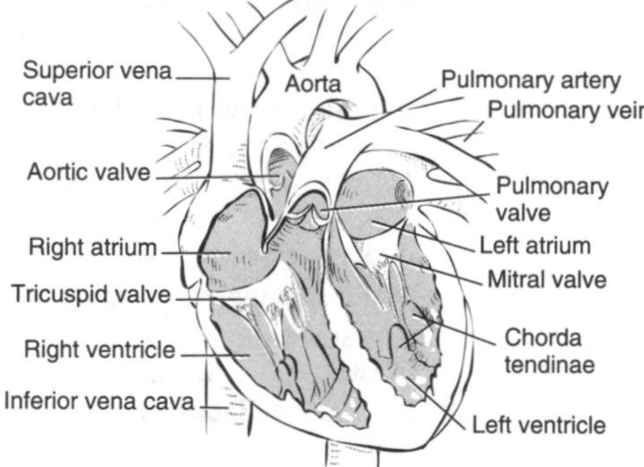

Blood Flow

420.91 Acute idiopathic pericarditis
Pericarditis, acute:
benign
nonspecific
viral

420.99 Other
Pericarditis (acute):
pneumococcal
purulent
staphylococcal
streptococcal
suppurative
Pneumopyopericardium
Pyopericardium
EXCLUDES *pericarditis in diseases classified elsewhere (420.0)*

✓4th 421 Acute and subacute endocarditis

DEF: Bacterial inflammation of the endocardium (intracardiac area); major symptoms include fever, fatigue, heart murmurs, splenomegaly, embolic episodes and areas of infarction.

421.0 Acute and subacute bacterial endocarditis
Endocarditis (acute)(chronic) (subacute):
bacterial
infective NOS
lenta
malignant
purulent
septic
ulcerative
vegetative
Infective aneurysm
Subacute bacterial endocarditis [SBE]
Use additional code to identify infectious organism [e.g., Streptococcus 041.0, Staphylococcus 041.1]
AHA: 1Q, '99, 12; 1Q, '91, 15

421.1 Acute and subacute infective endocarditis in diseases classified elsewhere
Code first underlying disease, as:
blastomycosis (116.0)
Q fever (083.0)
typhoid (fever) (002.0)
EXCLUDES *endocarditis (in):*
Coxsackie (virus) (074.22)
gonococcal (098.84)
histoplasmosis (115.0-115.9 with fifth-digit 4)
meningococcal infection (036.42)
monilial (112.81)

421.9 Acute endocarditis, unspecified
Endocarditis, Myoendocarditis, Periendocarditis } acute or subacute
EXCLUDES *acute rheumatic endocarditis (391.1)*

✓4th 422 Acute myocarditis

EXCLUDES *acute rheumatic myocarditis (391.2)*

DEF: Acute inflammation of the muscular walls of the heart (myocardium).

422.0 Acute myocarditis in diseases classified elsewhere
Code first underlying disease, as:
myocarditis (acute):
influenzal (487.8)
tuberculous (017.9)
EXCLUDES *myocarditis (acute) (due to):*
aseptic, of newborn (074.23)
Coxsackie (virus) (074.23)
diphtheritic (032.82)
meningococcal infection (036.43)
syphilitic (093.82)
toxoplasmosis (130.3)

✓5th 422.9 Other and unspecified acute myocarditis

422.90 Acute myocarditis, unspecified
Acute or subacute (interstitial) myocarditis

422.91 Idiopathic myocarditis
Myocarditis (acute or subacute):
Fiedler's
giant cell
isolated (diffuse) (granulomatous)
nonspecific granulomatous

422.92 Septic myocarditis
Myocarditis, acute or subacute:
pneumococcal
staphylococcal
Use additional code to identify infectious organism [e.g., Staphylococcus 041.1]
EXCLUDES *myocarditis, acute or subacute:*
in bacterial diseases classified elsewhere (422.0)
streptococcal (391.2)

422.93 Toxic myocarditis
DEF: Inflammation of the heart muscle due to an adverse reaction to certain drugs or chemicals reaching the heart through the bloodstream.

422.99 Other

✓4th 423 Other diseases of pericardium

EXCLUDES *that specified as rheumatic (393)*

423.0 Hemopericardium
DEF: Blood in the pericardial sac (pericardium).

423.1 Adhesive pericarditis
Adherent pericardium
Fibrosis of pericardium
Milk spots
Pericarditis:
adhesive
obliterative
Soldiers' patches
DEF: Two layers of serous pericardium adhere to each other by fibrous adhesions.

423.2 Constrictive pericarditis
Concato's disease
Pick's disease of heart (and liver)
DEF: Inflammation identified by a rigid, thickened and sometimes calcified pericardium; ventricles of the heart cannot be adequately filled and congestive heart failure may result.

423.3 Cardiac tamponade
Code first the underlying cause
AHA: ▶4Q, '07, 86, 87◀
DEF: ▶Life-threatening condition in which fluid or blood accumulates between the muscle of the heart (myocardium) and the outer sac (pericardium), resulting in compression of the heart, which decreases cardiac output.◀

▶Cardiac Tamponade◀

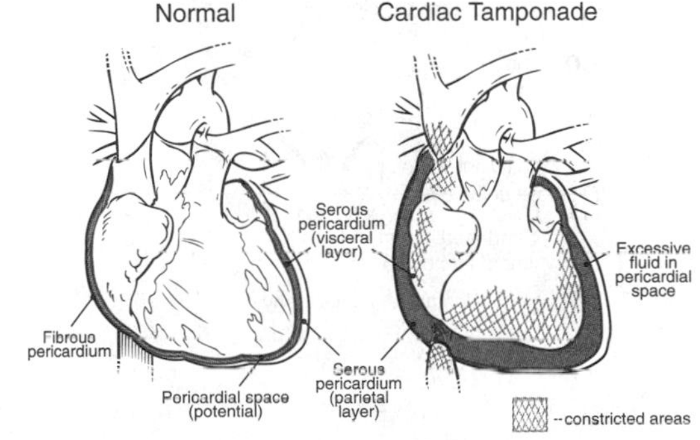

423.8 Other specified diseases of pericardium

Calcification } of pericardium
Fistula

AHA: 2Q, '89, 12

423.9 Unspecified disease of pericardium

AHA: 1Q, '07, 11

424 Other diseases of endocardium

EXCLUDES *bacterial endocarditis (421.0-421.9)*
rheumatic endocarditis (391.1, 394.0-397.9)
syphilitic endocarditis (093.20-093.24)

424.0 Mitral valve disorders

Mitral (valve):
incompetence } NOS of specified cause, except rheumatic
insufficiency
regurgitation

EXCLUDES *mitral (valve):*
disease (394.9)
failure (394.9)
stenosis (394.0)
the listed conditions:
specified as rheumatic (394.1)
unspecified as to cause but with mention of:
diseases of aortic valve (396.0-396.9)
mitral stenosis or obstruction (394.2)

AHA: 3Q, '06, 7; 2Q, '00, 16; 3Q, '98, 11; N-D, '87, 8; N-D, '84, 8

424.1 Aortic valve disorders

Aortic (valve):
incompetence } NOS of specified cause, except rheumatic
insufficiency
regurgitation
stenosis

EXCLUDES *hypertrophic subaortic stenosis (425.1)*
that specified as rheumatic (395.0-395.9)
that of unspecified cause but with mention of diseases of mitral valve (396.0-396.9)

AHA: 4Q, '88, 8; N-D, '87, 8

424.2 Tricuspid valve disorders, specified as nonrheumatic

Tricuspid valve:
incompetence } of specified cause, except rheumatic
insufficiency
regurgitation
stenosis

EXCLUDES *rheumatic or of unspecified cause (397.0)*

Heart Valve Disorders

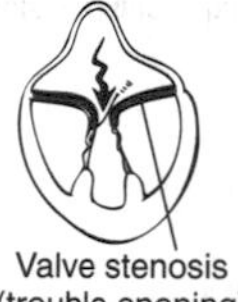

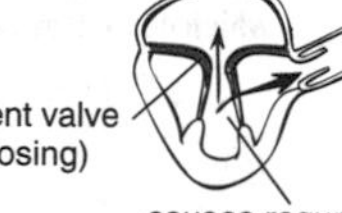

Insufficient valve (unable to close completely)
Shortened, fused chorda tendinae
Ventricular hypertrophy

Normal Heart Valve Function

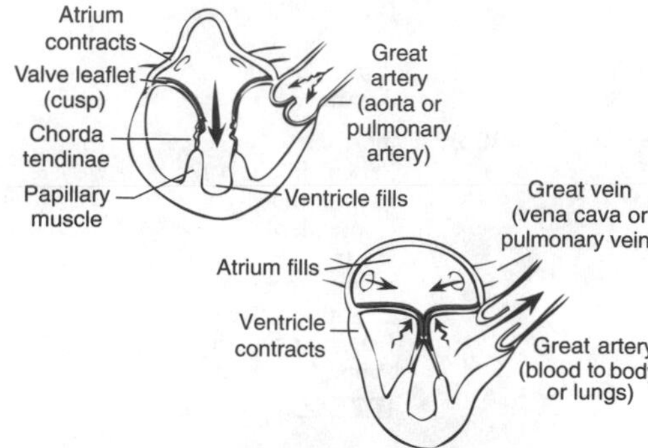

424.3 Pulmonary valve disorders

Pulmonic:
incompetence NOS
insufficiency NOS
regurgitation NOS
stenosis NOS

EXCLUDES *that specified as rheumatic (397.1)*

424.9 Endocarditis, valve unspecified

424.90 Endocarditis, valve unspecified, unspecified cause

Endocarditis (chronic):
NOS
nonbacterial thrombotic
Valvular:
incompetence } of unspecified valve, unspecified cause
insufficiency
regurgitation
stenosis
Valvulitis (chronic)

424.91 Endocarditis in diseases classified elsewhere

Code first underlying disease as:
atypical verrucous endocarditis [Libman-Sacks] (710.0)
disseminated lupus erythematosus (710.0)
tuberculosis (017.9)

EXCLUDES *syphilitic (093.20-093.24)*

424.99 Other

Any condition classifiable to 424.90 with specified cause, except rheumatic

EXCLUDES *endocardial fibroelastosis (425.3)*
that specified as rheumatic (397.9)

425 Cardiomyopathy

INCLUDES myocardiopathy

AHA: J-A, '85, 15

425.0 Endomyocardial fibrosis

425.1 Hypertrophic obstructive cardiomyopathy

Hypertrophic subaortic stenosis (idiopathic)

DEF: Cardiomyopathy marked by left ventricle hypertrophy, enlarged septum; results in obstructed blood flow.

425.2 Obscure cardiomyopathy of Africa

Becker's disease
Idiopathic mural endomyocardial disease

425.3 Endocardial fibroelastosis

Elastomyofibrosis

DEF: A condition marked by left ventricle hypertrophy and conversion of the endocardium into a thick fibroelastic coat; capacity of the ventricle may be reduced, but is often increased.

425.4 Other primary cardiomyopathies

Cardiomyopathy:
- NOS
- congestive
- constrictive
- familial
- hypertrophic

Cardiomyopathy:
- idiopathic
- nonobstructive
- obstructive
- restrictive

Cardiovascular collagenosis

AHA: 1Q, '07, 20; 2Q, '05, 14; 1Q, '00, 22; 4Q, '97, 55; 2Q, '90, 19

425.5 Alcoholic cardiomyopathy

AHA: S-O, '85, 15

DEF: Heart disease as result of excess alcohol consumption.

425.7 Nutritional and metabolic cardiomyopathy

Code first underlying disease, as:
- amyloidosis (277.30-277.39)
- beriberi (265.0)
- cardiac glycogenosis (271.0)
- mucopolysaccharidosis (277.5)
- thyrotoxicosis (242.0-242.9)

EXCLUDES *gouty tophi of heart (274.82)*

425.8 Cardiomyopathy in other diseases classified elsewhere

Code first underlying disease, as:
- Friedreich's ataxia (334.0)
- myotonia atrophica (359.21)
- progressive muscular dystrophy (359.1)
- sarcoidosis (135)

EXCLUDES *cardiomyopathy in Chagas' disease (086.0)*

AHA: 2Q, '93, 9

425.9 Secondary cardiomyopathy, unspecified

426 Conduction disorders

DEF: Disruption or disturbance in the electrical impulses that regulate heartbeats.

426.0 Atrioventricular block, complete

Third degree atrioventricular block

AHA: 2Q, '06, 14

426.1 Atrioventricular block, other and unspecified

AHA: 2Q, '06, 14

426.10 Atrioventricular block, unspecified

Atrioventricular [AV] block (incomplete) (partial)

426.11 First degree atrioventricular block

Incomplete atrioventricular block, first degree

Prolonged P-R interval NOS

AHA: 2Q, '06, 14

426.12 Mobitz (type) II atrioventricular block

Incomplete atrioventricular block:
- Mobitz (type) II
- second degree, Mobitz (type) II

AHA: 2Q, '06, 14

DEF: Impaired conduction of excitatory impulse from cardiac atrium to ventricle through AV node.

426.13 Other second degree atrioventricular block

Incomplete atrioventricular block:
- Mobitz (type) I [Wenckebach's]
- second degree:
  - NOS
  - Mobitz (type) I
- with 2:1 atrioventricular response [block]

Wenckebach's phenomenon

DEF: Wenckebach's phenomenon: impulses generated at constant rate to sinus node, P-R interval lengthens; results in cycle of ventricular inadequacy and shortened P-R interval; second-degree A-V block commonly called "Mobitz type 1."

Nerve Conduction of the Heart

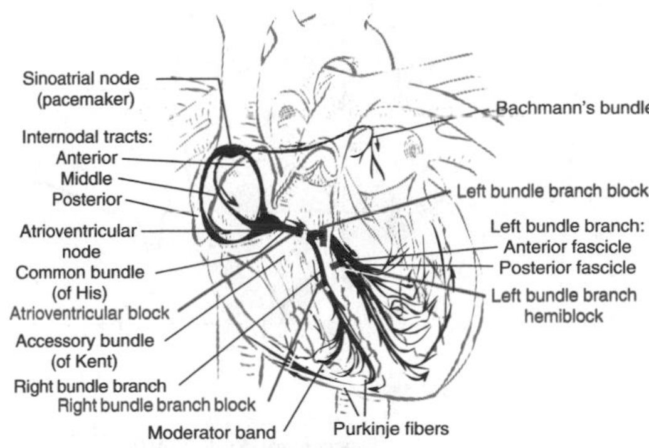

426.2 Left bundle branch hemiblock

Block:
- left anterior fascicular
- left posterior fascicular

426.3 Other left bundle branch block

Left bundle branch block:
- NOS
- anterior fascicular with posterior fascicular
- complete
- main stem

426.4 Right bundle branch block

AHA: 3Q, '00, 3

426.5 Bundle branch block, other and unspecified

426.50 Bundle branch block, unspecified

426.51 Right bundle branch block and left posterior fascicular block

426.52 Right bundle branch block and left anterior fascicular block

426.53 Other bilateral bundle branch block

Bifascicular block NOS

Bilateral bundle branch block NOS

Right bundle branch with left bundle branch block (incomplete) (main stem)

426.54 Trifascicular block

426.6 Other heart block

Intraventricular block:
- NOS
- diffuse
- myofibrillar

Sinoatrial block

Sinoauricular block

426.7 Anomalous atrioventricular excitation

Atrioventricular conduction:
- accelerated
- accessory
- pre-excitation

Ventricular pre-excitation

Wolff-Parkinson-White syndrome

DEF: Wolff-Parkinson-White: normal conduction pathway is bypassed; results in short P-R interval on EKG; tendency to supraventricular tachycardia.

426.8 Other specified conduction disorders

426.81 Lown-Ganong-Levine syndrome

Syndrome of short P-R interval, normal QRS complexes, and supraventricular tachycardias

426.82 Long QT syndrome

AHA: 4Q, '05, 72

DEF: Condition characterized by recurrent syncope, malignant arrhythmias, and sudden death; characteristic prolonged Q-T interval on electrocardiogram.

Normal and Long QT Electrocardiogram

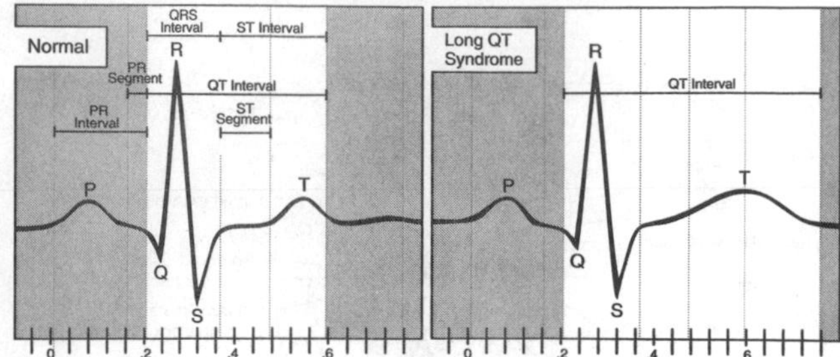

426.89 **Other**
Dissociation:
atrioventricular [AV]
interference
isorhythmic
Nonparoxysmal AV nodal tachycardia

426.9 **Conduction disorder, unspecified**
Heart block NOS
Stokes-Adams syndrome

✓4th **427 Cardiac dysrhythmias**

EXCLUDES *that complicating:*
abortion (634-638 with .7, 639.8)
ectopic or molar pregnancy (639.8)
labor or delivery (668.1, 669.4)

AHA: J-A, '85, 15

DEF: Disruption or disturbance in the rhythm of heartbeats.

427.0 **Paroxysmal supraventricular tachycardia**
Paroxysmal tachycardia:
atrial [PAT]
atrioventricular [AV]
junctional
nodal

DEF: Rapid atrial rhythm.

427.1 **Paroxysmal ventricular tachycardia**
Ventricular tachycardia (paroxysmal)

AHA: ▶1Q, '08, 14;◀ 2Q, '06, 15-16; 3Q, '95, 9; M-A, '86, 11

DEF: Rapid ventricular rhythm.

427.2 **Paroxysmal tachycardia, unspecified**
Bouveret-Hoffmann syndrome
Paroxysmal tachycardia:
NOS
essential

✓5th 427.3 **Atrial fibrillation and flutter**

427.31 **Atrial fibrillation**

AHA: 3Q, '05, 8; 4Q, '04, 78, 121; 3Q, '04, 7; 4Q, '03, 95, 105; 1Q, '03, 8; 2Q, '99, 17; 3Q, '95, 8

DEF: Irregular, rapid atrial contractions.

427.32 **Atrial flutter**

AHA: 4Q, '03, 94

DEF: Regular, rapid atrial contractions.

✓5th 427.4 **Ventricular fibrillation and flutter**

427.41 **Ventricular fibrillation**

AHA: 3Q, '02, 5

DEF: Irregular, rapid ventricular contractions.

427.42 **Ventricular flutter**

DEF: Regular, rapid, ventricular contractions.

427.5 **Cardiac arrest**
Cardiorespiratory arrest

AHA: 3Q,'02, 5; 2Q, '00, 12; 3Q, '95, 8; 2Q, '88, 8

✓5th 427.6 **Premature beats**

427.60 **Premature beats, unspecified**
Ectopic beats
Extrasystoles
Extrasystolic arrhythmia
Premature contractions or systoles NOS

427.61 **Supraventricular premature beats**
Atrial premature beats, contractions, or systoles

427.69 **Other**
Ventricular premature beats, contractions, or systoles

AHA: 4Q, '93, 42

✓5th 427.8 **Other specified cardiac dysrhythmias**

427.81 **Sinoatrial node dysfunction**
Sinus bradycardia:
persistent
severe
Syndrome:
sick sinus
tachycardia-bradycardia

EXCLUDES *sinus bradycardia NOS (427.89)*

AHA: 3Q, '00, 8

DEF: Complex cardiac arrhythmia; appears as severe sinus bradycardia, sinus bradycardia with tachycardia, or sinus bradycardia with atrioventricular block.

427.89 **Other**
Rhythm disorder:
coronary sinus
ectopic
nodal
Wandering (atrial) pacemaker

EXCLUDES *carotid sinus syncope (337.0)*
neonatal bradycardia (779.81)
neonatal tachycardia (779.82)
reflex bradycardia (337.0)
tachycardia NOS (785.0)

427.9 **Cardiac dysrhythmia, unspecified**
Arrhythmia (cardiac) NOS

AHA: 2Q, '89, 10

✓4th **428 Heart failure**

Code, if applicable, heart failure due to hypertension first (402.0-402.9, with fifth-digit 1 or 404.0-404.9 with fifth-digit 1 or 3)

EXCLUDES *following cardiac surgery (429.4)*
rheumatic (398.91)
that complicating:
abortion (634-638 with .7, 639.8)
ectopic or molar pregnancy (639.8)
labor or delivery (668.1, 669.4)

AHA: 4Q, '02, 49; 3Q, '98, 5; 2Q, '90, 16; 2Q, '90, 19; 2Q, '89, 10; 3Q, '88, 3

428.0 **Congestive heart failure, unspecified**
Congestive heart disease
Right heart failure (secondary to left heart failure)

EXCLUDES *fluid overload NOS (276.6)*

AHA: 3Q, '07, 9; 1Q, 07, 20; 3Q, '06, 7; 4Q, '05, 120; 3Q, '05, 8; 1Q, '05, 5, 9; 1Q, '05, 5, 9; 4Q, '04, 140; 3Q, '04, 7;4Q, '03, 109; 1Q, '03, 9; 4Q, '02, 52; 2Q, '01, 13; 4Q, '00, 48; 2Q, '00, 16; 1Q, '00, 22; 4Q, '99, 4; 1Q, '99, 11; 4Q, '97, 55; 3Q, '97, 10; 3Q, '96, 9; 3Q, '91, 18; 3Q, '91, 19; 2Q, '89, 12

DEF: Mechanical inadequacy; caused by inability of heart to pump and circulate blood; results in fluid collection in lungs, hypertension, congestion and edema of tissue.

428.1 **Left heart failure**
Acute edema of lung } with heart disease NOS or heart failure
Acute pulmonary edema } with heart disease NOS or heart failure
Cardiac asthma
Left ventricular failure

DEF: Mechanical inadequacy of left ventricle; causing fluid in lungs.

Echocardiography of Heart Failure

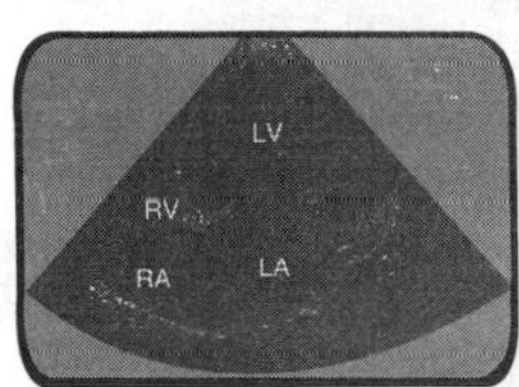

Four-chamber echocardiograms, two-dimensional views.
LV: Left ventricle
RV: Right ventricle
RA: Right atrium
LA: Left atrium

Systolic dysfunction with dilated LV

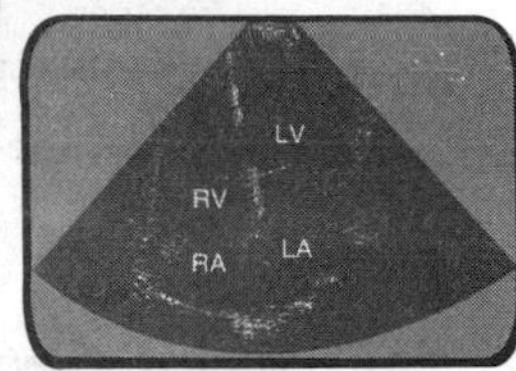

Diastolic dysfunction with LV hypertrophy

✓5th **428.2 Systolic heart failure**

EXCLUDES *combined systolic and diastolic heart failure (428.40-428.43)*

DEF: Heart failure due to a defect in expulsion of blood caused by an abnormality in systolic function, or ventricular contractile dysfunction.

428.20 Unspecified

428.21 Acute

428.22 Chronic

AHA: 4Q, '05, 120

428.23 Acute on chronic

AHA: 1Q, '03, 9

✓5th **428.3 Diastolic heart failure**

EXCLUDES *combined systolic and diastolic heart failure (428.40-428.43)*

DEF: Heart failure due to resistance to ventricular filling caused by an abnormality in the diastolic function.

428.30 Unspecified

AHA: 4Q, '02, 52

428.31 Acute

428.32 Chronic

428.33 Acute on chronic

AHA: 1Q, '07, 20

✓5th **428.4 Combined systolic and diastolic heart failure**

428.40 Unspecified

428.41 Acute

AHA: 4Q, '04, 140

428.42 Chronic

428.43 Acute on chronic

AHA: 3Q, '06, 7; 4Q, '02, 52

428.9 Heart failure, unspecified

Cardiac failure NOS
Heart failure NOS
Myocardial failure NOS
Weak heart

AHA: 2Q, '89, 10; N-D, '85, 14

✓4th **429 Ill-defined descriptions and complications of heart disease**

429.0 Myocarditis, unspecified

Myocarditis
NOS
chronic (interstitial
fibroid
senile
} (with mention of arteriosclerosis)

Use additional code to identify presence of arteriosclerosis

EXCLUDES *acute or subacute (422.0-422.9)*
rheumatic (398.0)
acute (391.2)
that due to hypertension (402.0-402.9)

429.1 Myocardial degeneration

Degeneration of heart or myocardium:
fatty
mural
muscular
Myocardial:
degeneration
disease
} (with mention of arteriosclerosis)

Use additional code to identify presence of arteriosclerosis

EXCLUDES *that due to hypertension (402.0-402.9)*

429.2 Cardiovascular disease, unspecified

Arteriosclerotic cardiovascular disease [ASCVD]
Cardiovascular arteriosclerosis
Cardiovascular:
degeneration
disease
sclerosis
} (with mention of arteriosclerosis)

Use additional code to identify presence of arteriosclerosis

EXCLUDES *that due to hypertension (402.0-402.9)*

429.3 Cardiomegaly

Cardiac:
dilatation
hypertrophy
Ventricular dilatation

EXCLUDES *that due to hypertension (402.0-402.9)*

429.4 Functional disturbances following cardiac surgery

Cardiac insufficiency
Heart failure
} following cardiac surgery or due to presthesis

Postcardiotomy syndrome
Postvalvulotomy syndrome

EXCLUDES *cardiac failure in the immediate postoperative period (997.1)*

AHA: 2Q, '02, 12; N-D, '85, 6

429.5 Rupture of chordae tendineae

DEF: Torn tissue, between heart valves and papillary muscles.

429.6 Rupture of papillary muscle

DEF: Torn muscle, between chordae tendineae and heart wall.

✓5th **429.7 Certain sequelae of myocardial infarction, not elsewhere classified**

Use additional code to identify the associated myocardial infarction:
with onset of 8 weeks or less (410.00-410.92)
with onset of more than 8 weeks (414.8)

EXCLUDES *congenital defects of heart (745, 746)*
coronary aneurysm (414.11)
disorders of papillary muscle (429.6, 429.81)
postmyocardial infarction syndrome (411.0)
rupture of chordae tendineae (429.5)

AHA: 3Q, '89, 5

429.71 Acquired cardiac septal defect A

EXCLUDES *acute septal infarction (410.00-410.92)*

DEF: Abnormal communication, between opposite heart chambers; due to defect of septum; not present at birth.

429.79 Other A

Mural thrombus (atrial) (ventricular), acquired, following myocardial infarction

AHA: 1Q, '92, 10

Circulatory System

5th **429.8 Other ill-defined heart diseases**

429.81 Other disorders of papillary muscle

Papillary muscle:
- atrophy
- degeneration
- dysfunction
- incompetence
- incoordination
- scarring

429.82 Hyperkinetic heart disease

DEF: Condition of unknown origin in young adults; marked by increased cardiac output at rest, increased rate of ventricular ejection; may lead to heart failure.

429.83 Takotsubo syndrome

Broken heart syndrome
Reversible left ventricular dysfunction following sudden emotional stress
Stress induced cardiomyopathy
Transient left ventricular apical ballooning syndrome

AHA: 4Q, '06, 87

429.89 Other

Carditis

EXCLUDES *that due to hypertension (402.0-402.9)*

AHA: 2Q, '06, 18; 3Q, '05, 14; 1Q, '92, 10

429.9 Heart disease, unspecified

Heart disease (organic) NOS
Morbus cordis NOS

EXCLUDES *that due to hypertension (402.0-402.9)*

AHA: 1Q, '93, 19

CEREBROVASCULAR DISEASE (430-438)

INCLUDES with mention of hypertension (conditions classifiable to 401-405)

Use additional code to identify presence of hypertension

EXCLUDES *any condition classifiable to 430-434, 436, 437 occurring during pregnancy, childbirth, or the puerperium, or specified as puerperal (674.0)*
iatrogenic cerebrovascular infarction or hemorrhage (997.02)

AHA: 1Q, '93, 27; 3Q, '91, 10; 3Q, '90, 3; 2Q, '89, 8; M-A, '85, 6

430 Subarachnoid hemorrhage

Meningeal hemorrhage
Ruptured:
- berry aneurysm
- (congenital) cerebral aneurysm NOS

EXCLUDES *syphilitic ruptured cerebral aneurysm (094.87)*

AHA: 4Q, '04, 77

DEF: Bleeding in space between brain and lining.

Berry Aneurysms

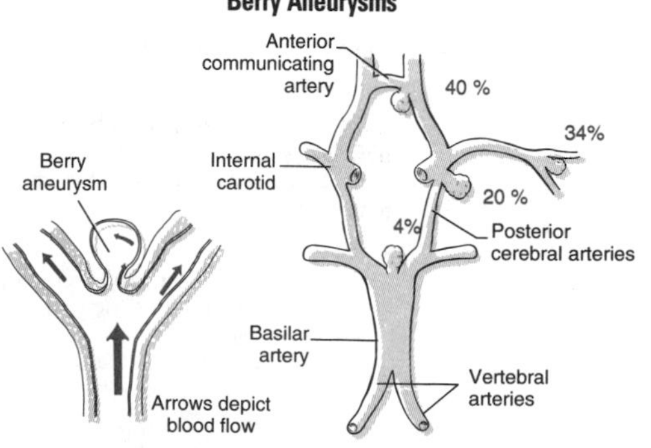

431 Intracerebral hemorrhage

Hemorrhage (of):
- basilar
- bulbar
- cerebellar
- cerebral
- cerebromeningeal
- cortical
- internal capsule
- intrapontine
- pontine
- subcortical
- ventricular

Rupture of blood vessel in brain

AHA: 3Q, '07, 4; 4Q, '04, 77

DEF: Bleeding within the brain.

4th **432 Other and unspecified intracranial hemorrhage**

AHA: 4Q, '04, 7

432.0 Nontraumatic extradural hemorrhage

Nontraumatic epidural hemorrhage

DEF: Bleeding, nontraumatic, between skull and brain lining.

432.1 Subdural hemorrhage

Subdural hematoma, nontraumatic

DEF: Bleeding, between outermost and other layers of brain lining.

432.9 Unspecified intracranial hemorrhage

Intracranial hemorrhage NOS

4th **433 Occlusion and stenosis of precerebral arteries**

INCLUDES embolism, narrowing, obstruction, thrombosis } of basilar, carotid, and vertebral arteries

►Use additional code, if applicable, to identify status post administration of tPA (rtPA) in a different facility within the last 24 hours prior to admission to current facility (V45.88)◄

EXCLUDES *insufficiency NOS of precerebral arteries (435.0-435.9)*

The following fifth-digit subclassification is for use with category 433:
0 without mention of cerebral infarction
1 with cerebral infarction

AHA: 2Q, '95, 14; 3Q, '90, 16

DEF: Blockage, stricture, arteries branching into brain.

§ 5th **433.0 Basilar artery**
[0-1]

§ 5th **433.1 Carotid artery**
[0-1] **AHA:** 1Q, '00, 16; **For code 433.10:** 1Q, '06, 17; 1Q, '02, 7, 10

§ 5th **433.2 Vertebral artery**
[0-1]

§ 5th **433.3 Multiple and bilateral**
[0-1] **AHA:** 2Q, '02, 19

§ 5th **433.8 Other specified precerebral artery**
[0-1]

§ 5th **433.9 Unspecified precerebral artery**
[0-1] Precerebral artery NOS

Cerebrovascular Arteries

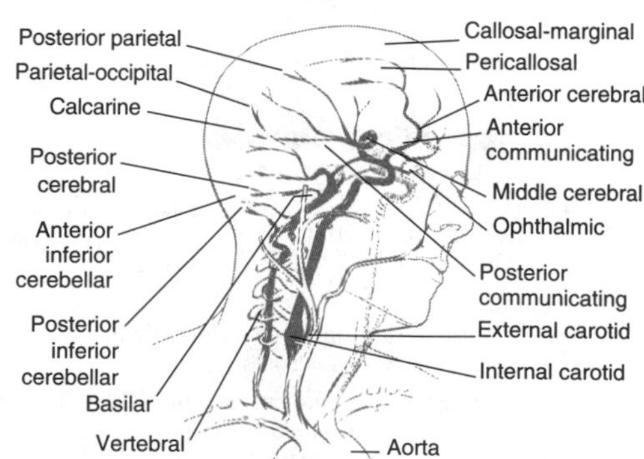

§ Requires fifth-digit. Valid digits are in [brackets] under each code. See appropriate category for codes and definitions.

4th 434 Occlusion of cerebral arteries

▶Use additional code, if applicable, to identify status post administration of tPA (rtPA) in a different facility within the last 24 hours prior to admission to current facility (V45.88)◀

The following fifth-digit subclassification is for use with category 434:
0 without mention of cerebral infarction
1 with cerebral infarction

AHA: 2Q, '95, 14

§ 5th **434.0 Cerebral thrombosis**
[0-1] Thrombosis of cerebral arteries
AHA: For code 434.01: 4Q, '04, 77

§ 5th **434.1 Cerebral embolism**
[0-1] AHA: For code 434.11: 4Q, '04, 77; 3Q, '97, 11

§ 5th **434.9 Cerebral artery occlusion, unspecified**
[0-1] AHA: For code 434.91: 3Q, '07, 9; 1Q, '07, 23; 4Q, '04, 77-78; 4Q, '98, 87

4th 435 Transient cerebral ischemia

INCLUDES cerebrovascular insufficiency (acute) with transient focal neurological signs and symptoms
insufficiency of basilar, carotid, and vertebral arteries
spasm of cerebral arteries

EXCLUDES *acute cerebrovascular insufficiency NOS (437.1)*
that due to any condition classifiable to 433 (433.0-433.9)

DEF: Temporary restriction of blood flow, to arteries branching into brain.

435.0 Basilar artery syndrome

435.1 Vertebral artery syndrome

435.2 Subclavian steal syndrome
DEF: Cerebrovascular insufficiency, due to occluded subclavian artery; symptoms include pain in mastoid and posterior head regions, flaccid paralysis of arm and diminished or absent radial pulse on affected side.

435.3 Vertebrobasilar artery syndrome
AHA: 4Q, '95, 60
DEF: Transient ischemic attack; due to brainstem dysfunction; symptoms include confusion, vertigo, binocular blindness, diplopia, unilateral or bilateral weakness and paresthesis of extremities.

435.8 Other specified transient cerebral ischemias

435.9 Unspecified transient cerebral ischemia
Impending cerebrovascular accident
Intermittent cerebral ischemia
Transient ischemic attack [TIA]
AHA: N-D, '85, 12

436 Acute, but ill-defined, cerebrovascular disease

Apoplexy, apoplectic:
NOS
attack
cerebral
seizure
Cerebral seizure

EXCLUDES *any condition classifiable to categories 430-435*
cerebrovascular accident (434.91)
CVA (ischemic) (434.91)
embolic (434.11)
hemorrhagic (430, 431, 432.0-432.9)
thrombotic (434.01)
postoperative cerebrovascular accident (997.02)
stroke (ischemic) (434.91)
embolic (434.11)
hemorrhagic (430, 431, 432.0-432.9)
thrombotic (434.01)

AHA: 4Q, '04, 77; 4Q, '99, 3

4th 437 Other and ill-defined cerebrovascular disease

437.0 Cerebral atherosclerosis A
Atheroma of cerebral arteries
Cerebral arteriosclerosis

437.1 Other generalized ischemic cerebrovascular disease
Acute cerebrovascular insufficiency NOS
Cerebral ischemia (chronic)

437.2 Hypertensive encephalopathy
AHA: J-A, '84, 14
DEF: Cerebral manifestations (such as visual disturbances and headache) due to high blood pressure.

437.3 Cerebral aneurysm, nonruptured
Internal carotid artery, intracranial portion
Internal carotid artery NOS
EXCLUDES *congenital cerebral aneurysm, nonruptured (747.81)*
internal carotid artery, extracranial portion (442.81)

437.4 Cerebral arteritis
AHA: 4Q, '99, 21
DEF: Inflammation of a cerebral artery or arteries.

437.5 Moyamoya disease
DEF: Cerebrovascular ischemia; vessels occlude and rupture causing tiny hemorrhages at base of brain; predominantly affects Japanese.

437.6 Nonpyogenic thrombosis of intracranial venous sinus
EXCLUDES *pyogenic (325)*

437.7 Transient global amnesia
AHA: 4Q, '92, 20
DEF: Episode of short-term memory loss, not often recurrent; pathogenesis unknown; with no signs or symptoms of neurological disorder.

437.8 Other

437.9 Unspecified
Cerebrovascular disease or lesion NOS

4th 438 Late effects of cerebrovascular disease

Note: This category is to be used to indicate conditions in 430-437 as the cause of late effects. The "late effects" include conditions specified as such, as sequelae, which may occur at any time after the onset of the causal condition.

EXCLUDES *personal history of:*
cerebral infarction without residual deficits (V12.54)
PRIND [Prolonged reversible ischemic neurologic deficit] (V12.54)
RIND [Reversible ischemic neurological deficit] (V12.54)
transient ischemic attack [TIA] (V12.54)

AHA: 3Q, '06, 3-4, 6; 4Q, '99, 4, 6, 7; 4Q, '98, 39, 88; 4Q, '97, 35, 37; 4Q, '92, 21;N-D,'86, 12; M-A, '86, 7

438.0 Cognitive deficits

5th **438.1 Speech and language deficits**

438.10 Speech and language deficit, unspecified

438.11 Aphasia
AHA: 4Q, '03, 105; 4Q, '97, 36
DEF: Impairment or absence of the ability to communicate by speech, writing or signs or to comprehend the spoken or written language due to disease or injury to the brain. Total aphasia is the loss of function of both sensory and motor areas of the brain.

§ Requires fifth-digit. Valid digits are in [brackets] under each code. See category 434 for codes and definitions.

438.12 Dysphasia

AHA: 4Q, '99, 3, 9

DEF: Impaired speech; marked by inability to sequence language.

438.19 Other speech and language deficits

✓5th **438.2 Hemiplegia/hemiparesis**

DEF: Paralysis of one side of the body.

438.20 Hemiplegia affecting unspecified side

AHA: ▶4Q, '07, 94;◀ 4Q, '03, 105; 4Q, '99, 3, 9

438.21 Hemiplegia affecting dominant side

438.22 Hemiplegia affecting nondominant side

AHA: 4Q, '03, 105; 1Q, '02, 16

✓5th **438.3 Monoplegia of upper limb**

DEF: Paralysis of one limb or one muscle group.

438.30 Monoplegia of upper limb affecting unspecified side

438.31 Monoplegia of upper limb affecting dominant side

438.32 Monoplegia of upper limb affecting nondominant side

✓5th **438.4 Monoplegia of lower limb**

438.40 Monoplegia of lower limb affecting unspecified side

438.41 Monoplegia of lower limb affecting dominant side

438.42 Monoplegia of lower limb affecting nondominant side

✓5th **438.5 Other paralytic syndrome**

Use additional code to identify type of paralytic syndrome, such as:
locked-in state (344.81)
quadriplegia (344.00-344.09)

EXCLUDES *late effects of cerebrovascular accident with:*
hemiplegia/hemiparesis (438.20-438.22)
monoplegia of lower limb (438.40-438.42)
monoplegia of upper limb (438.30-438.32)

438.50 Other paralytic syndrome affecting unspecified side

438.51 Other paralytic syndrome affecting dominant side

438.52 Other paralytic syndrome affecting nondominant side

438.53 Other paralytic syndrome, bilateral

AHA: 4Q, '98, 39

438.6 Alterations of sensations

Use additional code to identify the altered sensation

438.7 Disturbances of vision

Use additional code to identify the visual disturbance

AHA: 4Q, '02, 56

✓5th **438.8 Other late effects of cerebrovascular disease**

438.81 Apraxia

DEF: Inability to activate learned movements; no known sensory or motor impairment.

438.82 Dysphagia

Use additional code to identify the type of dysphagia, if known (787.20-787.29)

AHA: ▶4Q, '07, 94◀

DEF: Inability or difficulty in swallowing.

438.83 Facial weakness

Facial droop

438.84 Ataxia

AHA: 4Q, '02, 56

438.85 Vertigo

438.89 Other late effects of cerebrovascular disease

Use additional code to identify the late effect

AHA: 1Q, '05, 13; 4Q, '98, 39

438.9 Unspecified late effects of cerebrovascular disease

DISEASES OF ARTERIES, ARTERIOLES, AND CAPILLARIES (440-449)

✓4th **440 Atherosclerosis**

INCLUDES arteriolosclerosis
arteriosclerosis (obliterans) (senile)
arteriosclerotic vascular disease
atheroma
degeneration:
  arterial
  arteriovascular
  vascular
endarteritis deformans or obliterans
senile:
  arteritis
  endarteritis

EXCLUDES *atheroembolism (445.01-445.89)*
atherosclerosis of bypass graft of the extremities (440.30-440.32)

DEF: Stricture and reduced elasticity of an artery; due to plaque deposits.

440.0 Of aorta A

AHA: 2Q, '93, 7; 2Q, '93, 8; 4Q, '88, 8

440.1 Of renal artery A

EXCLUDES *atherosclerosis of renal arterioles (403.00-403.91)*

✓5th **440.2 Of native arteries of the extremities**

Use additional code, if applicable, to identify chronic total occlusion of artery of the extremities (440.4)

EXCLUDES *atherosclerosis of bypass graft of the extremities (440.30-440.32)*

AHA: 4Q, '94, 49; 4Q, '93, 27; 4Q, '92, 25; 3Q, '90, 15; M-A, '87, 6

440.20 Atherosclerosis of the extremities, unspecified A

440.21 Atherosclerosis of the extremities with intermittent claudication A

DEF: Atherosclerosis; marked by pain, tension and weakness after walking; no symptoms while at rest.

440.22 Atherosclerosis of the extremities with rest pain A

INCLUDES any condition classifiable to 440.21

DEF: Atherosclerosis, marked by pain, tension and weakness while at rest.

440.23 Atherosclerosis of the extremities with ulceration A

INCLUDES any condition classifiable to 440.21 and 440.22

Use additional code for any associated ulceration (707.10-707.9)

AHA: 4Q, '00, 44

Map of Major Arteries

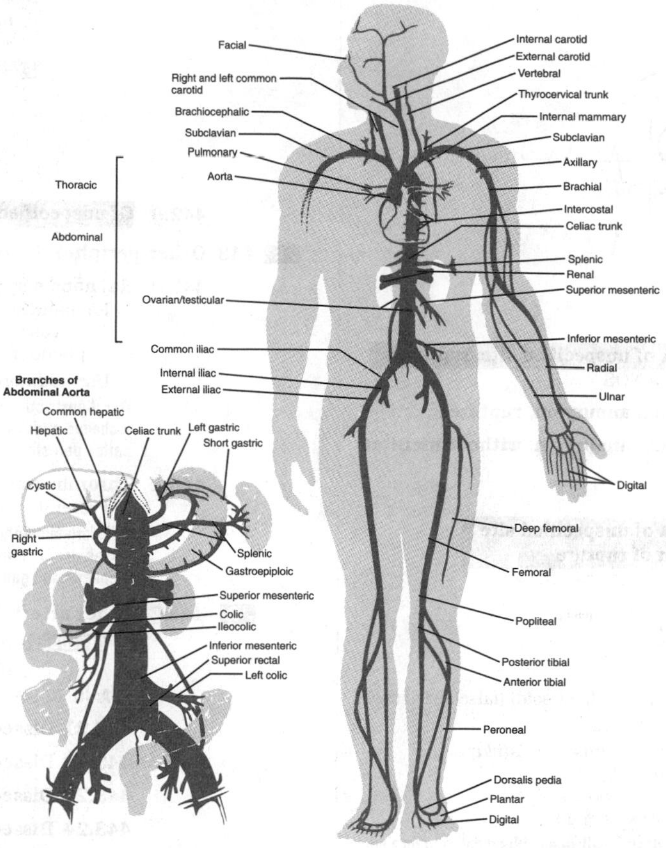

440.24 Atherosclerosis of the extremities with gangrene

INCLUDES any condition classifiable to 440.21, 440.22, and 440.23 with ischemic gangrene 785.4

Use additional code for any associated ulceration (707.10-707.9)

EXCLUDES *gas gangrene (040.0)*

AHA: 4Q, '03, 109; 3Q, '03, 14; 4Q, '95, 54; 1Q, '95, 11

440.29 Other A

5th **440.3 Of bypass graft of extremities**

EXCLUDES *atherosclerosis of native arteries of the extremities (440.21-440.24)*
embolism [occlusion NOS] [thrombus] of graft (996.74)

AHA: 4Q, '94, 49

440.30 Of unspecified graft A

440.31 Of autologous vein bypass graft A

440.32 Of nonautologous biological bypass graft A

440.4 Chronic total occlusion of artery of the extremities

Complete occlusion of artery of the extremities
Total occlusion of artery of the extremities

Code first atherosclerosis of arteries of the extremities (440.20-440.29, 440.30-440.32)

EXCLUDES *acute occlusion of artery of extremity (444.21-444.22)*

AHA: ▶4Q, '07, 82◀

440.8 Of other specified arteries A

EXCLUDES *basilar (433.0)*
carotid (433.1)
cerebral (437.0)
coronary (414.00-414.07)
mesenteric (557.1)
precerebral (433.0-433.9)
pulmonary (416.0)
vertebral (433.2)

440.9 Generalized and unspecified atherosclerosis A

Arteriosclerotic vascular disease NOS

EXCLUDES *arteriosclerotic cardiovascular disease [ASCVD] (429.2)*

4th **441 Aortic aneurysm and dissection**

EXCLUDES *syphilitic aortic aneurysm (093.0)*
traumatic aortic aneurysm (901.0, 902.0)

5th **441.0 Dissection of aorta**

AHA: 4Q, '89, 10

DEF: Dissection or splitting of wall of the aorta; due to blood entering through intimal tear or interstitial hemorrhage.

441.00 Unspecified site

441.01 Thoracic

AHA: ▶4Q, '07, 87◀

441.02 Abdominal

441.03 Thoracoabdominal

441.1 Thoracic aneurysm, ruptured

441.2 Thoracic aneurysm without mention of rupture

AHA: 3Q, '92, 10

441.3 Abdominal aneurysm, ruptured

441.4 Abdominal aneurysm without mention of rupture

AHA: 4Q, '00, 64; 1Q, '99, 15, 16, 17; 3Q, '92, 10

Thoracic and Abdominal Aortic Aneurysm

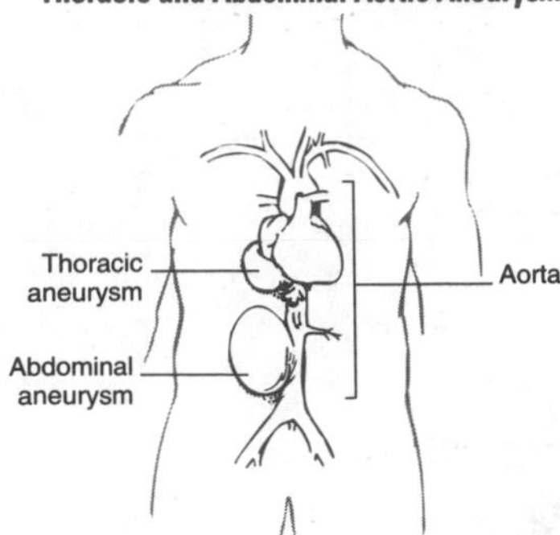

441.5 Aortic aneurysm of unspecified site, ruptured
Rupture of aorta NOS

441.6 Thoracoabdominal aneurysm, ruptured

441.7 Thoracoabdominal aneurysm, without mention of rupture
AHA: 2Q, '06, 16

441.9 Aortic aneurysm of unspecified site without mention of rupture
Aneurysm
Dilatation } of aorta
Hyaline necrosis

4th **442 Other aneurysm**
INCLUDES aneurysm (ruptured) (cirsoid) (false) (varicose)
aneurysmal varix
EXCLUDES *arteriovenous aneurysm or fistula:*
acquired (447.0)
congenital (747.60-747.69)
traumatic (900.0-904.9)

DEF: Dissection or splitting of arterial wall; due to blood entering through intimal tear or interstitial hemorrhage.

442.0 Of artery of upper extremity

442.1 Of renal artery

442.2 Of iliac artery
AHA: 1Q, '99, 16, 17

442.3 Of artery of lower extremity
Aneurysm:
femoral artery
popliteal artery
AHA: ▶2Q, '08, 13;◀ 3Q, '02, 24-26; 1Q, '99, 16

5th **442.8 Of other specified artery**

442.81 Artery of neck
Aneurysm of carotid artery (common) (external) (internal, extracranial portion)
EXCLUDES *internal carotid artery, intracranial portion (437.3)*

442.82 Subclavian artery

442.83 Splenic artery

442.84 Other visceral artery
Aneurysm:
celiac
gastroduodenal
gastroepiploic
hepatic } artery
pancreaticoduodenal
superior mesenteric

442.89 Other
Aneurysm:
mediastinal artery
spinal artery
EXCLUDES *cerebral (nonruptured) (437.3)*
congenital (747.81)
ruptured (430)
coronary (414.11)
heart (414.10)
pulmonary (417.1)

442.9 Of unspecified site

4th **443 Other peripheral vascular disease**

443.0 Raynaud's syndrome
Raynaud's:
disease
phenomenon (secondary)
Use additional code to identify gangrene (785.4)

DEF: Constriction of the arteries, due to cold or stress; bilateral ischemic attacks of fingers, toes, nose or ears; symptoms include pallor, paresthesia and pain; more common in females.

443.1 Thromboangiitis obliterans [Buerger's disease]
Presenile gangrene

DEF: Inflammatory disease of extremity blood vessels, mainly the lower; occurs primarily in young men and leads to tissue ischemia and gangrene.

5th **443.2 Other arterial dissection**
EXCLUDES *dissection of aorta (441.00-441.03)*
dissection of coronary arteries (414.12)
AHA: 4Q, '02, 54

443.21 Dissection of carotid artery

443.22 Dissection of iliac artery

443.23 Dissection of renal artery

443.24 Dissection of vertebral artery

443.29 Dissection of other artery

5th **443.8 Other specified peripheral vascular diseases**

443.81 Peripheral angiopathy in diseases classified elsewhere
Code first underlying disease, as:
diabetes mellitus ▶(249.7, 250.7)◀
AHA: 1Q, '04, 14; 3Q, '91, 10

443.82 Erythromelalgia
AHA: 4Q, '05, 73

DEF: Rare syndrome of paroxysmal vasodilation; maldistribution of blood flow causes redness, pain, increased skin temperature, and burning sensations in various parts of the body.

443.89 Other
Acrocyanosis
Acroparesthesia:
simple [Schultze's type]
vasomotor [Nothnagel's type]
Erythrocyanosis
EXCLUDES *chilblains (991.5)*
frostbite (991.0-991.3)
immersion foot (991.4)
AHA: 4Q, '07, 124

443.9 Peripheral vascular disease, unspecified
Intermittent claudication NOS
Peripheral:
angiopathy NOS
vascular disease NOS
Spasm of artery
EXCLUDES *atherosclerosis of the arteries of the extremities (440.20-440.22)*
spasm of cerebral artery (435.0-435.9)
AHA: 4Q, '92, 25; 3Q, '91, 10

Arterial Diseases and Disorders

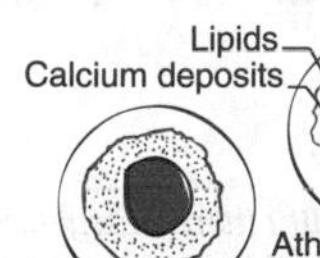
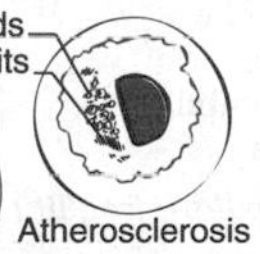
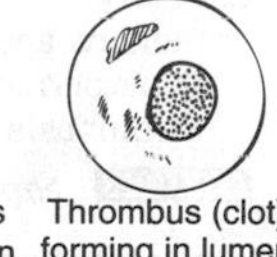

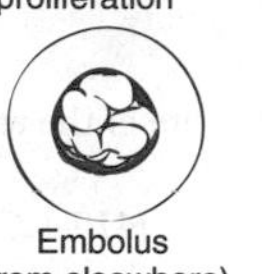
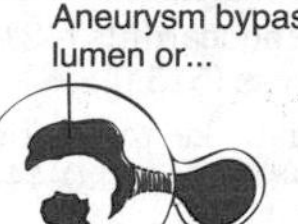

4th 444 Arterial embolism and thrombosis

INCLUDES infarction:
embolic
thrombotic
occlusion

EXCLUDES *atheroembolism (445.01-445.89)*
that complicating:
abortion (634-638 with .6, 639.6)
ectopic or molar pregnancy (639.6)
pregnancy, childbirth, or the pueperium (673.0-673.8)
septic arterial embolism (449)

AHA: 2Q, '92, 11; 4Q, '90, 27

444.0 Of abdominal aorta
Aortic bifurcation syndrome
Aortoiliac obstruction
Leriche's syndrome
Saddle embolus

AHA: 2Q, '93, 7; 4Q, '90, 27

444.1 Of thoracic aorta
Embolism or thrombosis of aorta (thoracic)

5th 444.2 Of arteries of the extremities

AHA: M A, '87, 6

444.21 Upper extremity

444.22 Lower extremity
Arterial embolism or thrombosis:
femoral
peripheral NOS
popliteal

EXCLUDES *iliofemoral (444.81)*

AHA: ▶4Q, '07, 85;◀ 3Q, '03, 10; 1Q, '03, 17; 3Q, '90, 16

5th 444.8 Of other specified artery

444.81 Iliac artery

AHA: 1Q, '03, 16

444.89 Other

EXCLUDES *basilar (433.0)*
carotid (433.1)
cerebral (434.0-434.9)
coronary (410.00-410.92)
mesenteric (557.0)
ophthalmic (362.30-362.34)
precerebral (433.0-433.9)
pulmonary (415.19)
renal (593.81)
retinal (362.30-362.34)
vertebral (433.2)

444.9 Of unspecified artery

4th 445 Atheroembolism

INCLUDES atherothrombotic microembolism
cholesterol embolism

AHA: 4Q, '02, 57

5th 445.0 Of extremities

445.01 Upper extremity

445.02 Lower extremity

5th 445.8 Of other sites

445.81 Kidney
Use additional code for any associated acute renal failure or chronic kidney disease (584, 585)

445.89 Other site

4th 446 Polyarteritis nodosa and allied conditions

446.0 Polyarteritis nodosa
Disseminated necrotizing periarteritis
Necrotizing angiitis
Panarteritis (nodosa)
Periarteritis (nodosa)

DEF: Inflammation of small and mid-size arteries; symptoms related to involved arteries in kidneys, muscles, gastrointestinal tract and heart; results in tissue death.

446.1 Acute febrile mucocutaneous lymph node syndrome [MCLS]
Kawasaki disease

DEF: Acute febrile disease of children; marked by erythema of conjunctiva and mucous membranes of upper respiratory tract, skin eruptions and edema.

5th 446.2 Hypersensitivity angiitis

EXCLUDES *antiglomerular basement membrane disease without pulmonary hemorrhage (583.89)*

446.20 Hypersensitivity angiitis, unspecified

446.21 Goodpasture's syndrome
Antiglomerular basement membrane antibody-mediated nephritis with pulmonary hemorrhage
Use additional code to identify renal disease (583.81)

DEF: Glomerulonephritis associated with hematuria, progresses rapidly; results in death from renal failure.

446.29 Other specified hypersensitivity angiitis

AHA: 1Q, '95, 3

446.3 Lethal midline granuloma
Malignant granuloma of face

AHA: 3Q, '00, 11

DEF: Granulomatous lesion; in nose or paranasal sinuses; often fatal; occurs chiefly in males.

446.4 Wegener's granulomatosis
Necrotizing respiratory granulomatosis
Wegener's syndrome

AHA: 3Q, '00, 11

DEF: A disease occurring mainly in men; marked by necrotizing granulomas and ulceration of the upper respiratory tract; underlying condition is a vasculitis affecting small vessels and is possibly due to an immune disorder.

446.5 Giant cell arteritis
Bagratuni's syndrome
Cranial arteritis
Horton's disease
Temporal arteritis

DEF: Inflammation of arteries; due to giant cells affecting carotid artery branches, resulting in occlusion; symptoms include fever, headache and neurological problems; occurs in elderly.

446.6 Thrombotic microangiopathy
Moschcowitz's syndrome
Thrombotic thrombocytopenic purpura

DEF: Blockage of small blood vessels; due to hyaline deposits; symptoms include purpura, CNS disorders; results in protracted disease or rapid death.

446.7 Takayasu's disease
Aortic arch arteritis
Pulseless disease
DEF: Progressive obliterative arteritis of brachiocephalic trunk, left subclavian, and left common carotid arteries above aortic arch; results in ischemia in brain, heart and arm; pulses impalpable in head, neck and arms; more common in young adult females.

✓4th 447 Other disorders of arteries and arterioles

447.0 Arteriovenous fistula, acquired
Arteriovenous aneurysm, acquired
EXCLUDES *cerebrovascular (437.3)*
coronary (414.19)
pulmonary (417.0)
surgically created arteriovenous shunt or fistula:
complication (996.1, 996.61-996.62)
status or presence ►(V45.11)◄
traumatic (900.0-904.9)
DEF: Communication between an artery and vein caused by error in healing.

447.1 Stricture of artery
AHA: 2Q, '93, 8; M-A, '87, 6

447.2 Rupture of artery
Erosion } of artery
Fistula, except arteriovenous } of artery
Ulcer } of artery
EXCLUDES *traumatic rupture of artery (900.0-904.9)*

447.3 Hyperplasia of renal artery
Fibromuscular hyperplasia of renal artery
DEF: Overgrowth of cells in muscular lining of renal artery.

447.4 Celiac artery compression syndrome
Celiac axis syndrome
Marable's syndrome

447.5 Necrosis of artery

447.6 Arteritis, unspecified
Aortitis NOS
Endarteritis NOS
EXCLUDES *arteritis, endarteritis:*
aortic arch (446.7)
cerebral (437.4)
coronary (414.00-414.07)
deformans (440.0-440.9)
obliterans (440.0-440.9)
pulmonary (417.8)
senile (440.0-440.9)
polyarteritis NOS (446.0)
syphilitic aortitis (093.1)
AHA: 1Q, '95, 3

447.8 Other specified disorders of arteries and arterioles
Fibromuscular hyperplasia of arteries, except renal

447.9 Unspecified disorders of arteries and arterioles

✓4th 448 Disease of capillaries

448.0 Hereditary hemorrhagic telangiectasia
Rendu-Osler-Weber disease
DEF: Genetic disease with onset after puberty; results in multiple telangiectases, dilated venules on skin and mucous membranes; recurrent bleeding may occur.

448.1 Nevus, non-neoplastic
Nevus:
araneus
senile
Nevus:
spider
stellar
EXCLUDES *neoplastic (216.0-216.9)*
port wine (757.32)
strawberry (757.32)
DEF: Enlarged or malformed blood vessels of skin; results in reddish swelling, skin patch, or birthmark.

448.9 Other and unspecified capillary diseases
Capillary:
hemorrhage
hyperpermeability
thrombosis
EXCLUDES *capillary fragility (hereditary) (287.8)*

449 Septic arterial embolism
Code first underlying infection, such as:
infective endocarditis (421.0)
lung abscess (513.0)
Use additional code to identify the site of the embolism (433.0-433.9, 444.0-444.9)
EXCLUDES *septic pulmonary embolism (415.12)*
AHA: 4Q, '07, 84-85

DISEASES OF VEINS AND LYMPHATICS, AND OTHER DISEASES OF CIRCULATORY SYSTEM (451-459)

✓4th 451 Phlebitis and thrombophlebitis
INCLUDES endophlebitis
inflammation, vein
periphlebitis
suppurative phlebitis
Use additional E code to identify drug, if drug-induced
EXCLUDES *that complicating:*
abortion (634-638 with .7, 639.8)
ectopic or molar pregnancy (639.8)
pregnancy, childbirth, or the puerperium (671.0-671.9)
that due to or following:
implant or catheter device (996.61-996.62)
infusion, perfusion, or transfusion (999.2)
AHA: 1Q, '92, 16
DEF: Inflammation of a vein (phlebitis) with formation of a thrombus (thrombophlebitis).

451.0 Of superficial vessels of lower extremities
Saphenous vein (greater) (lesser)
AHA: 3Q, '91, 16

✓5th 451.1 Of deep vessels of lower extremities
AHA: 3Q, '91, 16

451.11 Femoral vein (deep) (superficial)

451.19 Other
Femoropopliteal vein
Popliteal vein
Tibial vein

451.2 Of lower extremities, unspecified
AHA: 4Q, '04, 80

✓5th 451.8 Of other sites
EXCLUDES *intracranial venous sinus (325)*
nonpyogenic (437.6)
portal (vein) (572.1)

451.81 Iliac vein

451.82 Of superficial veins of upper extremities
Antecubital vein
Basilic vein
Cephalic vein

451.83 Of deep veins of upper extremities
Brachial vein
Radial vein
Ulnar vein

451.84 Of upper extremities, unspecified

451.89 Other
Axillary vein
Jugular vein
Subclavian vein
Thrombophlebitis of breast (Mondor's disease)

Map of Major Veins

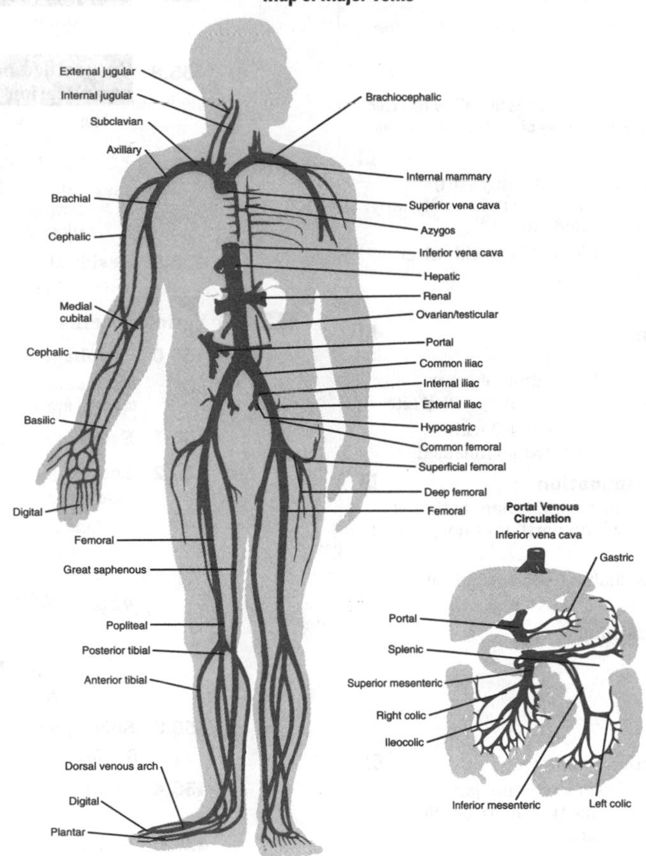

451.9 Of unspecified site

452 Portal vein thrombosis

Portal (vein) obstruction

EXCLUDES *hepatic vein thrombosis (453.0)*
phlebitis of portal vein (572.1)

DEF: Formation of a blood clot in main vein of liver.

✓4th **453 Other venous embolism and thrombosis**

EXCLUDES *that complicating:*
abortion (634-638 with .7, 639.8)
ectopic or molar pregnancy (639.8)
pregnancy, childbirth, or the puerperium (671.0-671.9)
that with inflammation, phlebitis, and thrombophlebitis (451.0-451.9)

AHA: 1Q, '92, 16

453.0 Budd-Chiari syndrome

Hepatic vein thrombosis

DEF: Thrombosis or other obstruction of hepatic vein; symptoms include enlarged liver, extensive collateral vessels, intractable ascites and severe portal hypertension.

453.1 Thrombophlebitis migrans

DEF: Slow, advancing thrombophlebitis; appearing first in one vein then another.

453.2 Of vena cava

453.3 Of renal vein

✓5th **453.4 Venous embolism and thrombosis of deep vessels of lower extremity**

453.40 Venous embolism and thrombosis of unspecified deep vessels of lower extremity

Deep vein thrombosis NOS
DVT NOS

453.41 Venous embolism and thrombosis of deep vessels of proximal lower extremity

Femoral
Iliac
Popliteal
Thigh
Upper leg NOS

AHA: 4Q, '04, 79

453.42 Venous embolism and thrombosis of deep vessels of distal lower extremity

Calf
Lower leg NOS
Peroneal
Tibial

453.8 Of other specified veins

EXCLUDES *cerebral (434.0-434.9)*
coronary (410.00-410.92)
intracranial venous sinus (325)
nonpyogenic (437.6)
mesenteric (557.0)
portal (452)
precerebral (433.0-433.9)
pulmonary (415.19)

AHA: 3Q, '91, 16; M-A, '87, 6

453.9 Of unspecified site

Embolism of vein
Thrombosis (vein)

✓4th 454 Varicose veins of lower extremities

EXCLUDES *that complicating pregnancy, childbirth, or the puerperium (671.0)*

AHA: 2Q, '91, 20

DEF: Dilated leg veins; due to incompetent vein valves that allow reversed blood flow and cause tissue erosion or weakness of wall; may be painful.

454.0 With ulcer A

Varicose ulcer (lower extremity, any part)
Varicose veins with ulcer of lower extremity [any part] or of unspecified site
Any condition classifiable to 454.9 with ulcer or specified as ulcerated

AHA: 4Q, '99, 18

454.1 With inflammation A

Stasis dermatitis
Varicose veins with inflammation of lower extremity [any part] or of unspecified site
Any condition classifiable to 454.9 with inflammation or specified as inflamed

454.2 With ulcer and inflammation A

Varicose veins with ulcer and inflammation of lower extremity [any part] or of unspecified site
Any condition classifiable to 454.9 with ulcer and inflammation

454.8 With other complications

Edema
Pain
Swelling

AHA: 4Q, '02, 58

454.9 Asymptomatic varicose veins A

Phlebectasia, Varicose veins, Varix } of lower extremity [any part] or of unspecified site
Varicose veins NOS

AHA: 4Q, '02, 58

✓4th 455 Hemorrhoids

INCLUDES hemorrhoids (anus) (rectum)
piles
varicose veins, anus or rectum

EXCLUDES *that complicating pregnancy, childbirth, or the puerperium (671.8)*

DEF: Varicose condition of external hemorrhoidal veins causing painful swellings at the anus.

455.0 Internal hemorrhoids without mention of complication

AHA: 3Q, '05, 17

455.1 Internal thrombosed hemorrhoids

455.2 Internal hemorrhoids with other complication

Internal hemorrhoids:
bleeding
prolapsed
strangulated
ulcerated

AHA: 3Q, '05, 17; 1Q, '03, 8

455.3 External hemorrhoids without mention of complication

AHA: 1Q, '07, 13; 3Q, '05, 17

455.4 External thrombosed hemorrhoids

455.5 External hemorrhoids with other complication

External hemorrhoids:
bleeding
prolapsed
strangulated
ulcerated

AHA: 3Q, '05, 17; 1Q, '03, 8

455.6 Unspecified hemorrhoids without mention of complication

Hemorrhoids NOS

455.7 Unspecified thrombosed hemorrhoids

Thrombosed hemorrhoids, unspecified whether internal or external

455.8 Unspecified hemorrhoids with other complication

Hemorrhoids, unspecified whether internal or external:
bleeding
prolapsed
strangulated
ulcerated

455.9 Residual hemorrhoidal skin tags

Skin tags, anus or rectum

✓4th 456 Varicose veins of other sites

456.0 Esophageal varices with bleeding

DEF: Distended, tortuous, veins of lower esophagus, usually due to portal hypertension.

456.1 Esophageal varices without mention of bleeding

✓5th 456.2 Esophageal varices in diseases classified elsewhere

Code first underlying cause, as:
cirrhosis of liver (571.0-571.9)
portal hypertension (572.3)

456.20 With bleeding

AHA: N-D, '85, 14

456.21 Without mention of bleeding

AHA: 3Q, '05, 15; 2Q, '02, 4

456.3 Sublingual varices

DEF: Distended, tortuous veins beneath tongue.

456.4 Scrotal varices ♂

Varicocele

456.5 Pelvic varices

Varices of broad ligament

456.6 Vulval varices ♀

Varices of perineum

EXCLUDES *that complicating pregnancy, childbirth, or the puerperium (671.1)*

456.8 Varices of other sites

Varicose veins of nasal septum (with ulcer)

EXCLUDES *placental varices (656.7)*
retinal varices (362.17)
varicose ulcer of unspecified site (454.0)
varicose veins of unspecified site (454.9)

AHA: 2Q, '02, 4

✓4th 457 Noninfectious disorders of lymphatic channels

457.0 Postmastectomy lymphedema syndrome A

Elephantiasis, Obliteration of lymphatic vessel } due to mastectomy

AHA: 2Q, '02, 12

DEF: Reduced lymphatic circulation following mastectomy; symptoms include swelling of the arm on the operative side.

457.1 Other lymphedema

Elephantiasis (nonfilarial) NOS
Lymphangiectasis
Lymphedema:
acquired (chronic)
praecox
secondary
Obliteration, lymphatic vessel

EXCLUDES *elephantiasis (nonfilarial):*
congenital (757.0)
eyelid (374.83)
vulva (624.8)

AHA: 3Q, '04, 5

DEF: Fluid retention due to reduced lymphatic circulation; due to other than mastectomy.

457.2 Lymphangitis
Lymphangitis:
NOS
chronic
subacute
EXCLUDES *acute lymphangitis (682.0-682.9)*

457.8 Other noninfectious disorders of lymphatic channels
Chylocele (nonfilarial)
Chylous:
ascites
cyst
Lymph node or vessel:
fistula
infarction
rupture
EXCLUDES *chylocele:*
filarial (125.0-125.9)
tunica vaginalis (nonfilarial) (608.84)
AHA: 1Q, '04, 5; 3Q, '03, 17

457.9 Unspecified noninfectious disorder of lymphatic channels

✓4th **458 Hypotension**
INCLUDES hypopiesis
EXCLUDES *cardiovascular collapse (785.50)*
maternal hypotension syndrome (669.2)
shock (785.50-785.59)
Shy-Drager syndrome (333.0)

458.0 Orthostatic hypotension
Hypotension:
orthostatic (chronic)
postural
AHA: 3Q, '00, 8; 3Q, '91, 9
DEF: Low blood pressure; occurs when standing.

458.1 Chronic hypotension
Permanent idiopathic hypotension
DEF: Persistent low blood pressure.

✓5th **458.2 Iatrogenic hypotension**
AHA: 4Q, '03, 60; 3Q, '02, 12; 4Q, '95, 57
DEF: Abnormally low blood pressure; due to medical treatment.

458.21 Hypotension of hemodialysis
Intra-dialytic hypotension
AHA: 4Q, '03, 61

458.29 Other iatrogenic hypotension
Postoperative hypotension

458.8 Other specified hypotension
AHA: 4Q, '97, 37

458.9 Hypotension, unspecified
Hypotension (arterial) NOS

✓4th **459 Other disorders of circulatory system**

459.0 Hemorrhage, unspecified
Rupture of blood vessel NOS
Spontaneous hemorrhage NEC
EXCLUDES *hemorrhage:*
gastrointestinal NOS (578.9)
in newborn NOS (772.9)
secondary or recurrent following trauma (958.2)
traumatic rupture of blood vessel (900.0-904.9)
▶*nontraumatic hematoma of soft tissue (729.92)*◀
AHA: 4Q, '90, 26

✓5th **459.1 Postphlebitic syndrome**
Chronic venous hypertension due to deep vein thrombosis
EXCLUDES *chronic venous hypertension without deep vein thrombosis (459.30-459.39)*
AHA: 4Q, '02, 58; 2Q, '91, 20
DEF: Various conditions following deep vein thrombosis; including edema, pain, stasis dermatitis, cellulitis, varicose veins and ulceration of the lower leg.

459.10 Postphlebitic syndrome without complications
Asymptomatic postphlebitic syndrome
Postphlebitic syndrome NOS

459.11 Postphlebitic syndrome with ulcer

459.12 Postphlebitic syndrome with inflammation

459.13 Postphlebitic syndrome with ulcer and inflammation

459.19 Postphlebitic syndrome with other complication

459.2 Compression of vein
Stricture of vein
Vena cava syndrome (inferior) (superior)

✓5th **459.3 Chronic venous hypertension (idiopathic)**
Stasis edema
EXCLUDES *chronic venous hypertension due to deep vein thrombosis (459.10-459.9)*
varicose veins (454.0-454.9)
AHA: 4Q, '02, 59

459.30 Chronic venous hypertension without complications
Asymptomatic chronic venous hypertension
Chronic venous hypertension NOS

459.31 Chronic venous hypertension with ulcer
AHA: 4Q, '02, 43

459.32 Chronic venous hypertension with inflammation

459.33 Chronic venous hypertension with ulcer and inflammation

459.39 Chronic venous hypertension with other complication

✓5th **459.8 Other specified disorders of circulatory system**

459.81 Venous (peripheral) insufficiency, unspecified
Chronic venous insufficiency NOS
Use additional code for any associated ulceration (707.10-707.9)
AHA: 3Q, '04, 5; 2Q, '91, 20; M-A, '87, 6
DEF: Insufficient drainage, venous blood, any part of body, results in edema or dermatosis.

459.89 Other
Collateral circulation (venous), any site
Phlebosclerosis
Venofibrosis

459.9 Unspecified circulatory system disorder

8. DISEASES OF THE RESPIRATORY SYSTEM (460-519)

Use additional code to identify infectious organism

ACUTE RESPIRATORY INFECTIONS (460-466)

EXCLUDES *pneumonia and influenza (480.0-488)*

460 Acute nasopharyngitis [common cold]

Coryza (acute)
Nasal catarrh, acute
Nasopharyngitis:
NOS
acute
infective NOS
Rhinitis:
acute
infective

EXCLUDES *nasopharyngitis, chronic (472.2)*
pharyngitis:
acute or unspecified (462)
chronic (472.1)
rhinitis:
allergic (477.0-477.9)
chronic or unspecified (472.0)
sore throat:
acute or unspecified (462)
chronic (472.1)

AHA: 1Q, '88, 12

DEF: Acute inflammation of mucous membranes; extends from nares to pharynx.

✓4th **461 Acute sinusitis**

INCLUDES abscess, empyema, infection, inflammation, suppuration } acute, of sinus (accessory) (nasal)

EXCLUDES *chronic or unspecified sinusitis (473.0-473.9)*

461.0 Maxillary
Acute antritis

461.1 Frontal

461.2 Ethmoidal

461.3 Sphenoidal

461.8 Other acute sinusitis
Acute pansinusitis

461.9 Acute sinusitis, unspecified
Acute sinusitis NOS

462 Acute pharyngitis

Acute sore throat NOS
Pharyngitis (acute):
NOS
gangrenous
infective
phlegmonous
pneumococcal
staphylococca
suppurative
ulcerative
Sore throat (viral) NOS
Viral pharyngitis

EXCLUDES *abscess:*
peritonsillar [quinsy] (475)
pharyngeal NOS (478.29)
retropharyngeal (478.24)
chronic pharyngitis (472.1)
infectious mononucleosis (075)
that specified as (due to):
Coxsackie (virus) (074.0)
gonococcus (098.6)
herpes simplex (054.79)
influenza (487.1)
septic (034.0)
streptococcal (034.0)

AHA: 4Q, '99, 26; S-O, '85, 8

Respiratory System

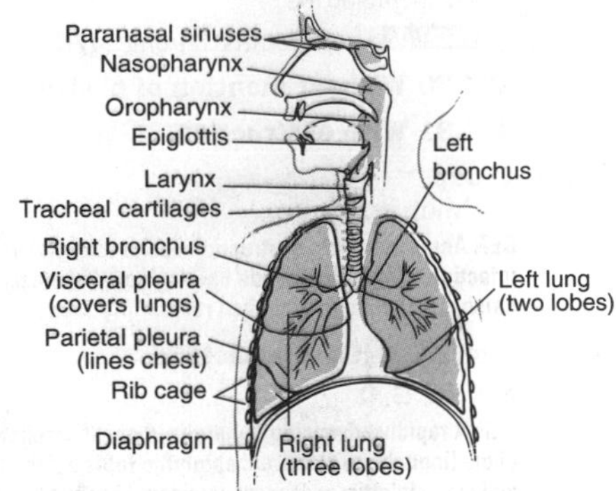

463 Acute tonsillitis

Tonsillitis (acute):
NOS
follicular
gangrenous
infective
pneumococcal
septic
staphylococcal
suppurative
ulcerative
viral

EXCLUDES *chronic tonsillitis (474.0)*
hypertrophy of tonsils (474.1)
peritonsillar abscess [quinsy] (475)
sore throat:
acute or NOS (462)
septic (034.0)
streptococcal tonsillitis (034.0)

AHA: N-D, '84, 16

✓4th **464 Acute laryngitis and tracheitis**

EXCLUDES *that associated with influenza (487.1)*
that due to Streptococcus (034.0)

✓5th **464.0 Acute laryngitis**
Laryngitis (acute):
NOS
edematous
Hemophilus influenzae [H. influenzae]
pneumococcal
septic
suppurative
ulcerative

EXCLUDES *chronic laryngitis (476.0-476.1)*
influenzal laryngitis (487.1)

AHA: 4Q, '01, 42

464.00 Without mention of obstruction

464.01 With obstruction

✓5th **464.1 Acute tracheitis**
Tracheitis (acute):
NOS
catarrhal
viral

EXCLUDES *chronic tracheitis (491.8)*

464.10 Without mention of obstruction

464.11 With obstruction

✓5th **464.2 Acute laryngotracheitis**
Laryngotracheitis (acute)
Tracheitis (acute) with laryngitis (acute)

EXCLUDES *chronic laryngotracheitis (476.1)*

464.20 Without mention of obstruction

464.21 With obstruction

5th **464.3 Acute epiglottitis**
Viral epiglottitis
EXCLUDES *epiglottitis, chronic (476.1)*

464.30 Without mention of obstruction

464.31 With obstruction

464.4 Croup
Croup syndrome
DEF: Acute laryngeal obstruction due to allergy, foreign body or infection; symptoms include barking cough, hoarseness and harsh, persistent high-pitched respiratory sound.

5th **464.5 Supraglottitis, unspecified**
AHA: 4Q, '01, 42
DEF: A rapidly advancing generalized upper respiratory infection of the lingual tonsillar area, epiglottic folds, false vocal cords, and the epiglottis; seen most commonly in children, but can affect people of any age.

464.50 Without mention of obstruction
AHA: 4Q, '01, 43

464.51 With obstruction

4th **465 Acute upper respiratory infections of multiple or unspecified sites**
EXCLUDES *upper respiratory infection due to:*
influenza (487.1)
Streptococcus (034.0)

465.0 Acute laryngopharyngitis
DEF: Acute infection of the vocal cords and pharynx.

465.8 Other multiple sites
Multiple URI
AHA: ▶4Q, '07, 85◀

465.9 Unspecified site
Acute URI NOS
Upper respiratory infection (acute)

4th **466 Acute bronchitis and bronchiolitis**
INCLUDES that with:
bronchospasm
obstruction

466.0 Acute bronchitis
Bronchitis, acute or subacute:
fibrinous
membranous
pneumococcal
purulent
septic
viral
with tracheitis
Croupous bronchitis
Tracheobronchitis, acute
EXCLUDES *acute bronchitis with chronic obstructive pulmonary disease (491.22)*
AHA: 4Q, '04, 137; 1Q, '04, 3; 4Q, '02, 46; 4Q, '96, 28; 4Q, '91, 24; 1Q, '88, 12
DEF: Acute inflammation of main branches of bronchial tree due to infectious or irritant agents; symptoms include cough with a varied production of sputum, fever, substernal soreness, and lung rales.

5th **466.1 Acute bronchiolitis**
Bronchiolitis (acute)
Capillary pneumonia
DEF: Acute inflammation of finer subdivisions of bronchial tree due to infectious or irritant agents; symptoms include cough with a varied production of sputum, fever, substernal soreness, and lung rales.

466.11 Acute bronchiolitis due to respiratory syncytial virus (RSV)
AHA: 1Q, '05, 10; 4Q, '96, 27

466.19 Acute bronchiolitis due to other infectious organisms
Use additional code to identify organism

OTHER DISEASES OF THE UPPER RESPIRATORY TRACT (470-478)

470 Deviated nasal septum
Deflected septum (nasal) (acquired)
EXCLUDES *congenital (754.0)*

4th **471 Nasal polyps**
EXCLUDES *adenomatous polyps (212.0)*

471.0 Polyp of nasal cavity
Polyp:
choanal
nasopharyngeal

471.1 Polypoid sinus degeneration
Woakes' syndrome or ethmoiditis

471.8 Other polyp of sinus
Polyp of sinus:
accessory
ethmoidal
maxillary
sphenoidal

471.9 Unspecified nasal polyp
Nasal polyp NOS

4th **472 Chronic pharyngitis and nasopharyngitis**

472.0 Chronic rhinitis
Ozena
Rhinitis:
NOS
atrophic
granulomatous
hypertrophic
obstructive
purulent
ulcerative
EXCLUDES *allergic rhinitis (477.0-477.9)*
DEF: Persistent inflammation of mucous membranes of nose.

472.1 Chronic pharyngitis
Chronic sore throat
Pharyngitis:
atrophic
granular (chronic)
hypertrophic

472.2 Chronic nasopharyngitis
EXCLUDES *acute or unspecified nasopharyngitis (460)*
DEF: Persistent inflammation of mucous membranes extending from nares to pharynx.

4th **473 Chronic sinusitis**
INCLUDES abscess / empyema / infection / suppuration } (chronic) of sinus (accessory) (nasal)
EXCLUDES *acute sinusitis (461.0-461.9)*

473.0 Maxillary
Antritis (chronic)

Upper Respiratory System

Paranasal sinuses drain into nose via ducts under nasal conchae
Frontal sinus
Olfactory bulb and nerves
Sphenoid sinus
Window in nasal septum reveals lateral nasal wall
Orifice of auditory tube
Nasal cavity from front
Naris
Soft palate
Nasal conchae
Epiglottis
Meati
Larynx
Vocal cords
Septum
Cricoid cartilage
Trachea

Paranasal Sinuses

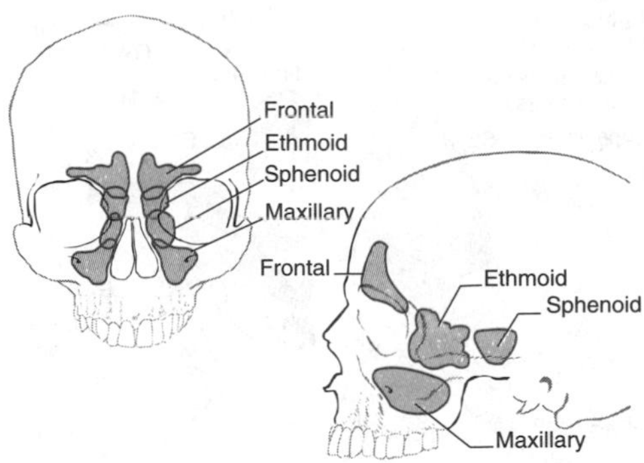

473.1 Frontal

473.2 Ethmoidal

EXCLUDES *Woakes' ethmoiditis (471.1)*

473.3 Sphenoidal

473.8 Other chronic sinusitis

Pansinusitis (chronic)

473.9 Unspecified sinusitis (chronic)

Sinusitis (chronic) NOS

✓4th 474 Chronic disease of tonsils and adenoids

✓5th 474.0 Chronic tonsillitis and adenoiditis

EXCLUDES *acute or unspecified tonsillitis (463)*

AHA: 4Q, '97, 38

474.00 Chronic tonsillitis

474.01 Chronic adenoiditis

474.02 Chronic tonsillitis and adenoiditis

✓5th 474.1 Hypertrophy of tonsils and adenoids

Enlargement / Hyperplasia / Hypertrophy } of tonsils or adenoids

EXCLUDES *that with:*
adenoiditis (474.01)
adenoiditis and tonsillitis (474.02)
tonsillitis (474.00)

474.10 Tonsils with adenoids

AHA: 2Q, '05, 16

474.11 Tonsils alone

474.12 Adenoids alone

474.2 Adenoid vegetations

DEF: Fungus-like growth of lymph tissue between the nares and pharynx.

474.8 Other chronic disease of tonsils and adenoids

Amygdalolith
Calculus, tonsil
Cicatrix of tonsil (and adenoid)
Tonsillar tag
Ulcer, tonsil

474.9 Unspecified chronic disease of tonsils and adenoids

Disease (chronic) of tonsils (and adenoids)

475 Peritonsillar abscess

Abscess of tonsil
Peritonsillar cellulitis
Quinsy

EXCLUDES *tonsillitis:*
acute or NOS (463)
chronic (474.0)

✓4th 476 Chronic laryngitis and laryngotracheitis

476.0 Chronic laryngitis

Laryngitis:
catarrhal
hypertrophic
sicca

476.1 Chronic laryngotracheitis

Laryngitis, chronic, with tracheitis (chronic)
Tracheitis, chronic, with laryngitis

EXCLUDES *chronic tracheitis (491.8)*
laryngitis and tracheitis, acute or unspecified (464.00-464.51)

✓4th 477 Allergic rhinitis

INCLUDES allergic rhinitis (nonseasonal) (seasonal)
hay fever
spasmodic rhinorrhea

EXCLUDES *allergic rhinitis with asthma (bronchial) (493.0)*

DEF: True immunoglobulin E (IgE)-mediated allergic reaction of nasal mucosa; seasonal (typical hay fever) or perennial (year-round allergens: dust, food, dander).

477.0 Due to pollen

Pollinosis

477.1 Due to food

AHA: 4Q, '00, 42

477.2 Due to animal (cat) (dog) hair and dander

477.8 Due to other allergen

477.9 Cause unspecified

AHA: 2Q, '97, 9

✓4th 478 Other diseases of upper respiratory tract

478.0 Hypertrophy of nasal turbinates

DEF: Overgrowth, enlargement of shell-shaped bones, in nasal cavity.

✓5th 478.1 Other diseases of nasal cavity and sinuses

EXCLUDES *varicose ulcer of nasal septum (456.8)*

478.11 Nasal mucositis (ulcerative)

Use additional E code to identify adverse effects of therapy, such as:
antineoplastic and immunosuppressive drugs (E930.7, E933.1)
radiation therapy (E879.2)

AHA: 4Q, '06, 88-90

478.19 Other diseases of nasal cavity and sinuses

Abscess / Necrosis / Ulcer } of nose (septum)

Cyst or mucocele of sinus (nasal)
Rhinolith

AHA: 4Q, '06, 88-90

✓5th 478.2 Other diseases of pharynx, not elsewhere classified

478.20 Unspecified disease of pharynx

478.21 Cellulitis of pharynx or nasopharynx

478.22 Parapharyngeal abscess

478.24 Retropharyngeal abscess

DEF: Purulent infection, behind pharynx and front of precerebral fascia.

478.25 Edema of pharynx or nasopharynx

478.26 Cyst of pharynx or nasopharynx

478.29 Other

Abscess of pharynx or nasopharynx

EXCLUDES *ulcerative pharyngitis (462)*

✓5th **478.3 Paralysis of vocal cords or larynx**

DEF: Loss of motor ability of vocal cords or larynx; due to nerve or muscle damage.

478.30 Paralysis, unspecified

Laryngoplegia
Paralysis of glottis

478.31 Unilateral, partial

478.32 Unilateral, complete

478.33 Bilateral, partial

478.34 Bilateral, complete

478.4 Polyp of vocal cord or larynx

EXCLUDES *adenomatous polyps (212.1)*

478.5 Other diseases of vocal cords

Abscess, Cellulitis, Granuloma, Leukoplakia } of vocal cords
Chorditis (fibrinous) (nodosa) (tuberosa)
Singers' nodes

478.6 Edema of larynx

Edema (of):
glottis
subglottic
supraglottic

✓5th **478.7 Other diseases of larynx, not elsewhere classified**

478.70 Unspecified disease of larynx

478.71 Cellulitis and perichondritis of larynx

DEF: Inflammation of deep soft tissues or lining of bone of the larynx.

478.74 Stenosis of larynx

478.75 Laryngeal spasm

Laryngismus (stridulus)

DEF: Involuntary muscle contraction of the larynx.

478.79 Other

Abscess, Necrosis, Obstruction, Pachyderma, Ulcer } of larynx

EXCLUDES *ulcerative laryngitis (464.00-464.01)*

AHA: 3Q, '91, 20

478.8 Upper respiratory tract hypersensitivity reaction, site unspecified

EXCLUDES *hypersensitivity reaction of lower respiratory tract, as:*
extrinsic allergic alveolitis (495.0-495.9)
pneumoconiosis (500-505)

478.9 Other and unspecified diseases of upper respiratory tract

Abscess, Cicatrix } of trachea

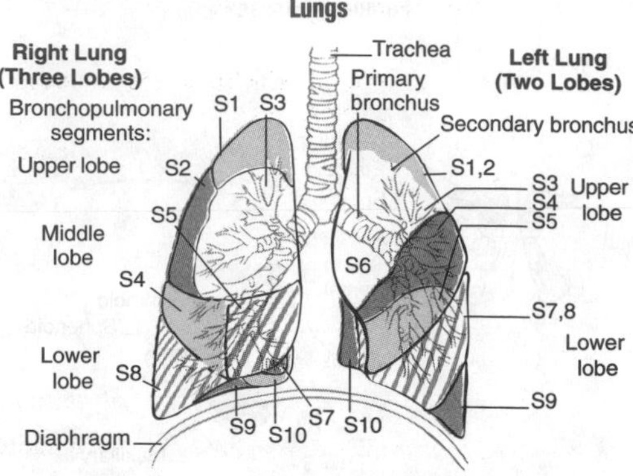

PNEUMONIA AND INFLUENZA (480-488)

EXCLUDES *pneumonia:*
allergic or eosinophilic (518.3)
aspiration:
NOS (507.0)
newborn (770.18)
solids and liquids (507.0-507.8)
congenital (770.0)
lipoid (507.1)
passive (514)
rheumatic (390)
►*ventilator-associated (997.31)*◄

✓4th **480 Viral pneumonia**

480.0 Pneumonia due to adenovirus

480.1 Pneumonia due to respiratory syncytial virus

AHA: 4Q, '96, 28; 1Q, '88, 12

480.2 Pneumonia due to parainfluenza virus

480.3 Pneumonia due to SARS-associated coronavirus

AHA: 4Q, '03, 46-47

DEF: A severe adult respiratory syndrome caused by the coronavirus, specified as inflammation of the lungs with consolidation.

480.8 Pneumonia due to other virus not elsewhere classified

EXCLUDES *congenital rubella pneumonitis (771.0)*
influenza with pneumonia, any form (487.0)
pneumonia complicating viral diseases classified elsewhere (484.1-484.8)

480.9 Viral pneumonia, unspecified

AHA: 3Q, '98, 5

481 Pneumococcal pneumonia [Streptococcus pneumoniae pneumonia]

Lobar pneumonia, organism unspecified

AHA: 2Q, '98, 7; 4Q, '92, 19; 1Q, '92, 18; 1Q, '91, 13; 1Q, '88, 13; M-A, '85, 6

✓4th **482 Other bacterial pneumonia**

AHA: 4Q, '93, 39

482.0 Pneumonia due to Klebsiella pneumoniae

482.1 Pneumonia due to Pseudomonas

482.2 Pneumonia due to Hemophilus influenzae [H. influenzae]

AHA: 2Q, '05, 19

✓5th **482.3 Pneumonia due to Streptococcus**

EXCLUDES *Streptococcus pneumoniae (481)*

AHA: 1Q, '88, 13

482.30 Streptococcus, unspecified

482.31 Group A

482.32 Group B

482.39 Other Streptococcus

✓5th **482.4 Pneumonia due to Staphylococcus**

AHA: 3Q, '91, 16

482.40 Pneumonia due to Staphylococcus, unspecified

▲ **482.41 Methicillin susceptible pneumonia due to Staphylococcus aureus**

▶Staphylococcus aureus
MSSA pneumonia
Pneumonia due to Staphylococcus aureus NOS◀

● **482.42 Methicillin resistant pneumonia due to Staphylococcus aureus**

482.49 Other Staphylococcus pneumonia

✓5th **482.8 Pneumonia due to other specified bacteria**

EXCLUDES *pneumonia, complicating infectious disease classified elsewhere (484.1-484.8)*

AHA: 3Q, '88, 11

482.81 Anaerobes

Bacteroides (melaninogenicus)
Gram-negative anaerobes

482.82 Escherichia coli [E. coli]

482.83 Other gram-negative bacteria

Gram-negative pneumonia NOS
Proteus
Serratia marcescens

EXCLUDES *gram-negative anaerobes (482.81)*
Legionnaires' disease (482.84)

AHA: 2Q, '98, 5; 3Q, '94, 9

482.84 Legionnaires' disease

AHA: 4Q, '97, 38

DEF: Severe and often fatal infection by Legionella pneumophilia; symptoms include high fever, gastrointestinal pain, headache, myalgia, dry cough, and pneumonia; transmitted airborne via air conditioning systems, humidifiers, water faucets, shower heads; not person-to-person contact.

482.89 Other specified bacteria

AHA: 2Q, '97, 6

482.9 Bacterial pneumonia unspecified

AHA: 2Q, '98, 6; 2Q, '97, 6; 1Q, '94, 17

✓4th **483 Pneumonia due to other specified organism**

AHA: N-D, '87, 5

483.0 Mycoplasma pneumoniae

Eaton's agent
Pleuropneumonia-like organism [PPLO]

483.1 Chlamydia

AHA: 4Q, '96, 31

483.8 Other specified organism

✓4th **484 Pneumonia in infectious diseases classified elsewhere**

EXCLUDES *influenza with pneumonia, any form (487.0)*

484.1 Pneumonia in cytomegalic inclusion disease

Code first underlying disease (078.5)

484.3 Pneumonia in whooping cough

Code first underlying disease (033.0-033.9)

484.5 Pneumonia in anthrax

Code first underlying disease (022.1)

484.6 Pneumonia in aspergillosis

Code first underlying disease (117.3)

AHA: 4Q, '97, 40

484.7 Pneumonia in other systemic mycoses

Code first underlying disease

EXCLUDES *pneumonia in:*
candidiasis (112.4)
coccidioidomycosis (114.0)
histoplasmosis (115.0-115.9 with fifth-digit 5)

484.8 Pneumonia in other infectious diseases classified elsewhere

Code first underlying disease, as:
Q fever (083.0)
typhoid fever (002.0)

EXCLUDES *pneumonia in:*
actinomycosis (039.1)
measles (055.1)
nocardiosis (039.1)
ornithosis (073.0)
Pneumocystis carinii (136.3)
salmonellosis (003.22)
toxoplasmosis (130.4)
tuberculosis (011.6)
tularemia (021.2)
varicella (052.1)

485 Bronchitis, not specified as acute or chronic

Bronchopneumonia:
hemorrhagic
terminal
Pleurobronchopneumonia
Pneumonia:
lobular
segmental

EXCLUDES *bronchiolitis (acute) (466.11-466.19)*
chronic (491.8)
lipoid pneumonia (507.1)

486 Pneumonia, organism unspecified

EXCLUDES *hypostatic or passive pneumonia (514)*
influenza with pneumonia, any form (487.0)
inhalation or aspiration pneumonia due to foreign materials (507.0-507.8)
pneumonitis due to fumes and vapors (506.0)

AHA: 4Q, '99, 6; 3Q, '99, 9; 3Q, '98, 7; 2Q, '98, 4, 5; 1Q, '98, 8; 3Q, '97, 9; 3Q, '94, 10; 3Q, '88, 11

✓4th **487 Influenza**

EXCLUDES *Hemophilus influenzae [H. influenzae]:*
infection NOS (041.5)
influenza due to identified avian influenza virus (488)
laryngitis (464.00-464.01)
meningitis (320.0)

487.0 With pneumonia

Influenza with pneumonia, any form
Influenzal:
bronchopneumonia
pneumonia

Use additional code to identify the type of pneumonia (480.0-480.9, 481, 482.0-482.9, 483.0-483.8, 485)

AHA: 1Q, '06, 18; 2Q, '05, 18

487.1 With other respiratory manifestations

Influenza NOS
Influenzal:
laryngitis
pharyngitis
respiratory infection (upper) (acute)

AHA: 1Q, '06, 18; 2Q, '05, 18; 4Q, '99, 26

487.8 With other manifestations

Encephalopathy due to influenza
Influenza with involvement of gastrointestinal tract

EXCLUDES *"intestinal flu" [viral gastroenteritis] (008.8)*

488 Influenza due to identified avian influenza virus

Note: Influenza caused by influenza viruses that normally infect only birds and, less commonly, other animals

EXCLUDES *influenza caused by other influenza viruses (487)*

AHA: ▶4Q, '07, 87◀

DEF:▶ Infection caused by contact with bird influenza viruses; results in flu-like symptoms that may progress to other severe and life-threatening complications.◀

CHRONIC OBSTRUCTIVE PULMONARY DISEASE AND ALLIED CONDITIONS (490-496)

AHA: 3Q, '88, 5

490 Bronchitis, not specified as acute or chronic

Bronchitis NOS:
- catarrhal
- with tracheitis NOS

Tracheobronchitis NOS

EXCLUDES *bronchitis:*
- *allergic NOS (493.9)*
- *asthmatic NOS (493.9)*
- *due to fumes and vapors (506.0)*

✓4th **491 Chronic bronchitis**

EXCLUDES *chronic obstructive asthma (493.2)*

491.0 Simple chronic bronchitis

Catarrhal bronchitis, chronic
Smokers' cough

491.1 Mucopurulent chronic bronchitis

Bronchitis (chronic) (recurrent):
- fetid
- mucopurulent
- purulent

AHA: 3Q, '88, 12

DEF: Chronic bronchial infection characterized by both mucus and pus secretions in the bronchial tree; recurs after asymptomatic periods; signs are coughing, expectoration and secondary changes in the lung.

✓5th **491.2 Obstructive chronic bronchitis**

Bronchitis:
- emphysematous
- obstructive (chronic) (diffuse)

Bronchitis with:
- chronic airway obstruction
- emphysema

EXCLUDES *asthmatic bronchitis (acute) NOS (493.9)*
chronic obstructive asthma (493.2)

AHA: 3Q, '97, 9; 4Q, '91, 25; 2Q, '91, 21

491.20 Without exacerbation

Emphysema with chronic bronchitis

AHA: 3Q, '97, 9

Bronchioli and Alveoli

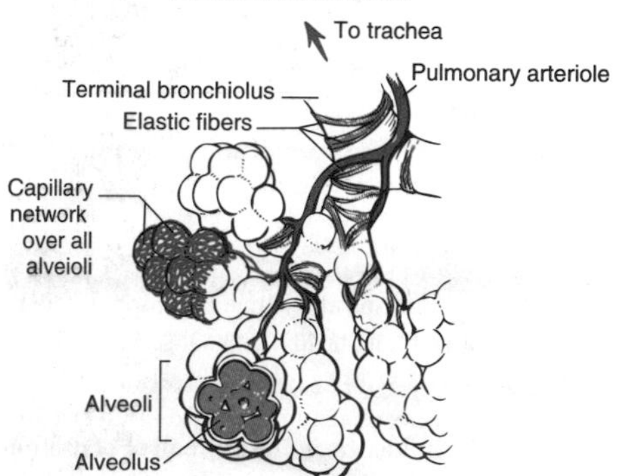

Interrelationship Between Chronic Airway Obstruction, Chronic Bronchitis, and Emphysema

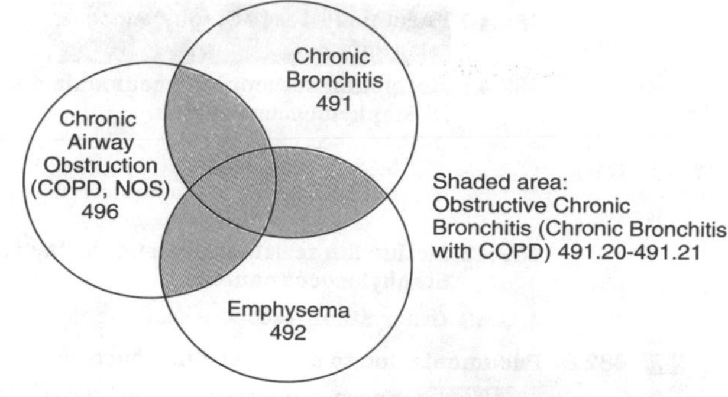

491.21 With (acute) exacerbation

Acute exacerbation of chronic obstructive pulmonary disease [COPD]
Decompensated chronic obstructive pulmonary disease [COPD]
Decompensated chronic obstructive pulmonary disease [COPD] with exacerbation

EXCLUDES *chronic obstructive asthma with acute exacerbation (493.22)*

AHA: 1Q, '04, 3; 3Q, '02, 18, 19; 4Q, '01, 43; 2Q, '96, 10

491.22 With acute bronchitis

AHA: 3Q, '06, 20; 4Q, '04, 82

491.8 Other chronic bronchitis

Chronic:
- tracheitis
- tracheobronchitis

491.9 Unspecified chronic bronchitis

✓4th **492 Emphysema**

AHA: 2Q, '91, 21

492.0 Emphysematous bleb

Giant bullous emphysema
Ruptured emphysematous bleb
Tension pneumatocele
Vanishing lung

AHA: 2Q, '93, 3

DEF: Formation of vesicle or bulla in emphysematous lung, more than one millimeter; contains serum or blood.

492.8 Other emphysema

Emphysema (lung or pulmonary):
- NOS
- centriacinar
- centrilobular
- obstructive
- panacinar
- panlobular
- unilateral
- vesicular

MacLeod's syndrome
Swyer-James syndrome
Unilateral hyperlucent lung

EXCLUDES *emphysema:*
- *with chronic bronchitis (491.20-491.22)*
- *compensatory (518.2)*
- *due to fumes and vapors (506.4)*
- *interstitial (518.1)*
  - *newborn (770.2)*
- *mediastinal (518.1)*
- *surgical (subcutaneous) (998.81)*
- *traumatic (958.7)*

AHA: 1Q, '05, 4; 4Q, '93, 41; J-A, '84, 17

✓4th **493 Asthma**

EXCLUDES *wheezing NOS (786.07)*

The following fifth-digit subclassification is for use with codes 493.0-493.2, 493.9:
0 unspecified
1 with status asthmaticus
2 with (acute) exacerbation

AHA: 4Q, '04, 137; 4Q, '03, 62; 4Q, '01, 43; 4Q, '00, 42; 1Q, '91, 13; 3Q, '88, 9; J-A, '85, 8; N-D, '84, 17

DEF: Status asthmaticus: severe, intractable episode of asthma unresponsive to normal therapeutic measures.

§ ✓5th **493.0 Extrinsic asthma**
[0-2]
Asthma:
allergic with stated cause
atopic
childhood
hay
platinum
Hay fever with asthma

EXCLUDES *asthma:*
allergic NOS (493.9)
detergent (507.8)
miners' (500)
wood (495.8)

DEF: Transient stricture of airway diameters of bronchi; due to environmental factor; also called allergic (bronchial) asthma.

§ ✓5th **493.1 Intrinsic asthma**
[0-2]
Late-onset asthma

AHA: 3Q, '88, 9; M-A, '85, 7

DEF: Transient stricture, of airway diameters of bronchi; due to pathophysiological disturbances.

§ ✓5th **493.2 Chronic obstructive asthma**
[0-2]
Asthma with chronic obstructive pulmonary disease [COPD]
Chronic asthmatic bronchitis

EXCLUDES *acute bronchitis (466.0)*
chronic obstructive bronchitis (491.20-491.22)

AHA: 2Q, '91, 21; 2Q, '90, 20; **For code 493.20:** 4Q, '03, 108; **For code 493.22:** 3Q, '06, 20

DEF: Persistent narrowing of airway diameters in the bronchial tree, restricting airflow and causing constant labored breathing.

✓5th **493.8 Other forms of asthma**

AHA: 4Q, '03, 62

493.81 Exercise induced bronchospasm

493.82 Cough variant asthma

§ ✓5th **493.9 Asthma, unspecified**
[0-2]
Asthma (bronchial) (allergic NOS)
Bronchitis:
allergic
asthmatic

AHA: 4Q, '97, 40, **For code 493.90:** 4Q, '04, 137; 4Q, '03, 108; 4Q, '99, 25; 1Q, '97, 7, **For code 493.91:** 1Q, '05, 5; **For code 493.92:** 1Q, '03, 9

✓4th **494 Bronchiectasis**

Bronchiectasis (fusiform) (postinfectious) (recurrent)
Bronchiolectasis

EXCLUDES *congenital (748.61)*
tuberculous bronchiectasis (current disease) (011.5)

AHA: 4Q, '00, 42

DEF: Dilation of bronchi; due to infection or chronic conditions; causes decreased lung capacity and recurrent infections of lungs.

494.0 Bronchiectasis without acute exacerbation

494.1 Bronchiectasis with acute exacerbation

✓4th **495 Extrinsic allergic alveolitis**

INCLUDES allergic alveolitis and pneumonitis due to inhaled organic dust particles of fungal, thermophilic actinomycete, or other origin

DEF: Pneumonitis due to particles inhaled into lung, often at workplace; symptoms include cough, chills, fever, increased heart and respiratory rates; develops within hours of exposure.

495.0 Farmers' lung

495.1 Bagassosis

495.2 Bird-fanciers' lung
Budgerigar-fanciers' disease or lung
Pigeon-fanciers' disease or lung

495.3 Suberosis
Cork-handlers' disease or lung

495.4 Malt workers' lung
Alveolitis due to Aspergillus clavatus

495.5 Mushroom workers' lung

495.6 Maple bark-strippers' lung
Alveolitis due to Cryptostroma corticale

495.7 "Ventilation" pneumonitis
Allergic alveolitis due to fungal, thermophilic actinomycete, and other organisms growing in ventilation [air conditioning] systems

495.8 Other specified allergic alveolitis and pneumonitis
Cheese-washers' lung
Coffee workers' lung
Fish-meal workers' lung
Furriers' lung
Grain-handlers' disease or lung
Pituitary snuff-takers' disease
Sequoiosis or red-cedar asthma
Wood asthma

495.9 Unspecified allergic alveolitis and pneumonitis
Alveolitis, allergic (extrinsic)
Hypersensitivity pneumonitis

496 Chronic airway obstruction, not elsewhere classified

Note: This code is not to be used with any code from categories 491-493

Chronic:
nonspecific lung disease
obstructive lung disease
obstructive pulmonary disease [COPD] NOS

EXCLUDES *chronic obstructive lung disease [COPD] specified (as) (with):*
allergic alveolitis (495.0-495.9)
asthma (493.20-493.22)
bronchiectasis (494.0-494.1)
bronchitis (491.20-491.22)
with emphysema (491.20-491.22)
decompensated (491.21)
emphysema (492.0-492.8)

AHA: 3Q, '07, 10; 4Q, '03, 109; 2Q, '00, 15; 2Q, '92, 16; 2Q, '91, 21; 3Q, '88, 56

PNEUMOCONIOSES AND OTHER LUNG DISEASES DUE TO EXTERNAL AGENTS (500-508)

DEF: Permanent deposits of particulate matter, within lungs; due to occupational or environmental exposure; results in chronic induration and fibrosis. (See specific listings in 500-508 code range)

500 Coal workers' pneumoconiosis A

Anthracosilicosis
Anthracosis
Black lung disease
Coal workers' lung
Miner's asthma

501 Asbestosis A

§ Requires fifth-digit. Valid digits are in [brackets] under each code. See category 493 for codes and definitions.

502 Pneumoconiosis due to other silica or silicates
Pneumoconiosis due to talc
Silicotic fibrosis (massive) of lung
Silicosis (simple) (complicated)

503 Pneumoconiosis due to other inorganic dust
Aluminosis (of lung)
Baritosis
Bauxite fibrosis (of lung)
Berylliosis
Graphite fibrosis (of lung)
Siderosis
Stannosis

504 Pneumonopathy due to inhalation of other dust
Byssinosis
Cannabinosis
Flax-dressers' disease
EXCLUDES *allergic alveolitis (495.0-495.9)*
asbestosis (501)
bagassosis (495.1)
farmers' lung (495.0)

505 Pneumoconiosis, unspecified

✓4th **506 Respiratory conditions due to chemical fumes and vapors**
Use additional E code to identify cause

506.0 Bronchitis and pneumonitis due to fumes and vapors
Chemical bronchitis (acute)

506.1 Acute pulmonary edema due to fumes and vapors
Chemical pulmonary edema (acute)
EXCLUDES *acute pulmonary edema NOS (518.4)*
chronic or unspecified pulmonary edema (514)
AHA: 3Q, '88, 4

506.2 Upper respiratory inflammation due to fumes and vapors
AHA: 3Q, '05, 10

506.3 Other acute and subacute respiratory conditions due to fumes and vapors

506.4 Chronic respiratory conditions due to fumes and vapors

Emphysema (diffuse) (chronic) Obliterative bronchiolitis (chronic) (subacute) Pulmonary fibrosis (chronic)	due to inhalation of chemical fumes and vapors

506.9 Unspecified respiratory conditions due to fumes and vapors
Silo-fillers' disease

✓4th **507 Pneumonitis due to solids and liquids**
EXCLUDES *fetal aspiration pneumonitis (770.18)*
AHA: 3Q, '91, 16

507.0 Due to inhalation of food or vomitus
Aspiration pneumonia (due to):
NOS
food (regurgitated)
gastric secretions
milk
saliva
vomitus
AHA: ▶1Q, '08, 18; ◀1Q, '89,10

507.1 Due to inhalation of oils and essences
Lipoid pneumonia (exogenous)
EXCLUDES *endogenous lipoid pneumonia (516.8)*

507.8 Due to other solids and liquids
Detergent asthma

✓4th **508 Respiratory conditions due to other and unspecified external agents**
Use additional E code to identify cause

508.0 Acute pulmonary manifestations due to radiation
Radiation pneumonitis
AHA: 2Q, '88, 4

508.1 Chronic and other pulmonary manifestations due to radiation
Fibrosis of lung following radiation

508.8 Respiratory conditions due to other specified external agents

508.9 Respiratory conditions due to unspecified external agent

OTHER DISEASES OF RESPIRATORY SYSTEM (510-519)

✓4th **510 Empyema**
Use additional code to identify infectious organism (041.0-041.9)
EXCLUDES *abscess of lung (513.0)*
DEF: Purulent infection; within pleural space.

510.0 With fistula
Fistula:
bronchocutaneous
bronchopleural
hepatopleural
mediastinal
pleural
thoracic
Any condition classifiable to 510.9 with fistula
DEF: Purulent infection of respiratory cavity; with communication from cavity to another structure.

510.9 Without mention of fistula
Abscess:
pleura
thorax
Empyema (chest) (lung) (pleura)
Fibrinopurulent pleurisy
Pleurisy:
purulent
septic
seropurulent
suppurative
Pyopneumothorax
Pyothorax
AHA: 4Q, '07, 113; 3Q, '94, 6

✓4th **511 Pleurisy**
EXCLUDES *pleurisy with mention of tuberculosis, current disease (012.0)*
DEF: Inflammation of serous membrane of lungs and lining of thoracic cavity; causes exudation in cavity or membrane surface.

511.0 Without mention of effusion or current tuberculosis
Adhesion, lung or pleura
Calcification of pleura
Pleurisy (acute) (sterile):
diaphragmatic
fibrinous
interlobar
Pleurisy:
NOS
pneumococcal
staphylococcal
streptococcal
Thickening of pleura
AHA: 3Q, '94, 5

511.1 With effusion, with mention of a bacterial cause other than tuberculosis
Pleurisy with effusion (exudative) (serous):
pneumococcal
staphylococcal
streptococcal
other specified nontuberculous bacterial cause

✓5th **511.8 Other specified forms of effusion, except tuberculous**
EXCLUDES *traumatic (860.2-860.5, 862.29, 862.39)*
AHA: 1Q, '97, 10

● **511.81 Malignant pleural effusion**
Code first malignant neoplasm, if known

● **511.89 Other specified forms of effusion, except tuberculous**
Encysted pleurisy
Hemopneumothorax
Hemothorax
Hydropneumothorax
Hydrothorax

511.9 Unspecified pleural effusion
Pleural effusion NOS
Pleurisy:
exudative
serofibrinous
serous
with effusion NOS
AHA: 2Q, '03, 7; 3Q, '91, 19; 4Q, '89, 11

✓4th **512 Pneumothorax**
DEF: Collapsed lung; due to gas or air in pleural space.

512.0 Spontaneous tension pneumothorax
AHA: 3Q, '94, 5
DEF: Leaking air from lung into lining causing collapse.

512.1 Iatrogenic pneumothorax
Postoperative pneumothorax
AHA: 4Q, '94, 40
DEF: Air trapped in the lining of the lung following surgery.

512.8 Other spontaneous pneumothorax
Pneumothorax:
NOS
acute
Pneumothorax:
chronic
EXCLUDES *pneumothorax:*
congenital (770.2)
traumatic (860.0-860.1, 860.4-860.5)
tuberculous, current disease (011.7)
AHA: 2Q, '93, 3

✓4th **513 Abscess of lung and mediastinum**

513.0 Abscess of lung
Abscess (multiple) of lung
Gangrenous or necrotic pneumonia
Pulmonary gangrene or necrosis
AHA: 4Q, '07, 85; 2Q, '98, 7

513.1 Abscess of mediastinum

514 Pulmonary congestion and hypostasis
Hypostatic:
bronchopneumonia
pneumonia
Passive pneumonia
Pulmonary congestion (chronic) (passive)
Pulmonary edema:
NOS
chronic
EXCLUDES *acute pulmonary edema:*
NOS (518.4)
with mention of heart disease or failure (428.1)
hypostatic pneumonia due to or specified as a specific type of pneumonia–code to the type of pneumonia (480.0-480.9, 481, 482.0-482.49, 483.0-483.8, 485, 486, 487.0)
AHA: 2Q, '98, 6; 3Q, '88, 5
DEF: Excessive retention of interstitial fluid in the lungs and pulmonary vessels; due to poor circulation.

515 Postinflammatory pulmonary fibrosis
Cirrhosis of lung
Fibrosis of lung (atrophic) (confluent) (massive) (perialveolar) (peribronchial)
Induration of lung
} chronic or unspecified

DEF: Fibrosis and scarring of the lungs due to inflammatory reaction.

✓4th **516 Other alveolar and parietoalveolar pneumonopathy**

516.0 Pulmonary alveolar proteinosis
DEF: Reduced ventilation; due to proteinaceous deposits on alveoli; symptoms include dyspnea, cough, chest pain, weakness, weight loss, and hemoptysis.

516.1 ***Idiopathic pulmonary hemosiderosis***
Code first underlying disease (275.0)
Essential brown induration of lung
DEF: Fibrosis of alveolar walls; marked by abnormal amounts hemosiderin in lungs; primarily affects children; symptoms include anemia, fluid in lungs, and blood in sputum; etiology unknown.

516.2 Pulmonary alveolar microlithiasis
DEF: Small calculi in pulmonary alveoli resembling sand-like particles on x-ray.

516.3 Idiopathic fibrosing alveolitis
Alveolar capillary block
Diffuse (idiopathic) (interstitial) pulmonary fibrosis
Hamman-Rich syndrome

516.8 Other specified alveolar and parietoalveolar pneumonopathies
Endogenous lipoid pneumonia
Interstitial pneumonia (desquamative) (lymphoid)
EXCLUDES *lipoid pneumonia, exogenous or unspecified (507.1)*
AHA:2Q, '06, 20; 1Q, '92, 12

516.9 Unspecified alveolar and parietoalveolar pneumonopathy

✓4th **517 Lung involvement in conditions classified elsewhere**
EXCLUDES *rheumatoid lung (714.81)*

517.1 ***Rheumatic pneumonia***
Code first underlying disease (390)

517.2 ***Lung involvement in systemic sclerosis***
Code first underlying disease (710.1)

517.3 ***Acute chest syndrome***
Code first sickle-cell disease in crisis (282.42, 282.62, 282.64, 282.69)
AHA: 4Q, '03, 51, 56

517.8 Lung involvement in other diseases classified elsewhere

Code first underlying disease, as:
amyloidosis (277.30-277.39)
polymyositis (710.4)
sarcoidosis (135)
Sjögren's disease (710.2)
systemic lupus erythematosus (710.0)

EXCLUDES *syphilis (095.1)*

AHA: 2Q, '03, 7

✓4th 518 Other diseases of lung

518.0 Pulmonary collapse
Atelectasis
Collapse of lung
Middle lobe syndrome

EXCLUDES *atelectasis:*
congenital (partial) (770.5)
primary (770.4)
tuberculous, current disease (011.8)

AHA: 4Q, '90, 25

518.1 Interstitial emphysema
Mediastinal emphysema

EXCLUDES *surgical (subcutaneous) emphysema (998.81)*
that in fetus or newborn (770.2)
traumatic emphysema (958.7)

DEF: Escaped air from the alveoli trapped in the interstices of the lung; trauma or cough may cause the disease.

518.2 Compensatory emphysema

DEF: Distention of all or part of the lung caused by disease processes or surgical intervention that decreased volume in another part of the lung; overcompensation reaction to the loss of capacity in another part of the lung.

518.3 Pulmonary eosinophilia
Eosinophilic asthma
Löffler's syndrome
Pneumonia:
allergic
eosinophilic
Tropical eosinophilia

DEF: Infiltration, into pulmonary parenchyma of eosinophilia; results in cough, fever, and dyspnea.

518.4 Acute edema of lung, unspecified
Acute pulmonary edema NOS
Pulmonary edema, postoperative

EXCLUDES *pulmonary edema:*
acute, with mention of heart disease or failure (428.1)
chronic or unspecified (514)
due to external agents (506.0-508.9)

DEF: Severe, sudden fluid retention within lung tissues.

518.5 Pulmonary insufficiency following trauma and surgery
Adult respiratory distress syndrome
Pulmonary insufficiency following:
shock
surgery
trauma
Shock lung

EXCLUDES *adult respiratory distress syndrome associated with other conditions (518.82)*
pneumonia:
aspiration (507.0)
hypostatic (514)
respiratory failure in other conditions (518.81, 518.83-518.84)

AHA: 4Q, '04, 139; 3Q, '88, 3; 3Q, '88, 7; S-O, '87, 1

518.6 Allergic bronchopulmonary aspergillosis

AHA: 4Q, '97, 39

DEF: Noninvasive hypersensitive reaction; due to allergic reaction to *Aspergillus fumigatus* (mold).

518.7 Transfusion related acute lung injury [TRALI]

AHA: 4Q, '06, 91

DEF: A relatively rare, but serious pulmonary complication of blood transfusion, with acute respiratory distress, noncardiogenic pulmonary edema, cyanosis, hypoxemia, hypotension, fever and chills.

✓5th 518.8 Other diseases of lung

518.81 Acute respiratory failure
Respiratory failure NOS

EXCLUDES *acute and chronic respiratory failure (518.84)*
acute respiratory distress (518.82)
chronic respiratory failure (518.83)
respiratory arrest (799.1)
respiratory failure, newborn (770.84)

AHA: ►1Q, '08, 18;◄ 3Q, '07, 6; 2Q, '06, 25; 4Q, '05, 96; 2Q, '05, 19; 1Q, '05, 3-8; 1Q, '05, 3–8; 4Q, '04, 139; 1Q, '03, 15; 4Q, '98, 41; 3Q, '91, 14; 2Q, '91, 3; 4Q, '90, 25; 2Q, '90, 20; 3Q, '88, 7; 3Q, '88, 10; S-O, '87, 1

518.82 Other pulmonary insufficiency, not elsewhere classified
Acute respiratory distress
Acute respiratory insufficiency
Adult respiratory distress syndrome NEC

EXCLUDES *adult respiratory distress syndrome associated with trauma and surgery (518.5)*
pulmonary insufficiency following trauma and surgery (518.5)
respiratory distress:
NOS (786.09)
newborn (770.89)
syndrome, newborn (769)
shock lung (518.5)

AHA: 4Q, '03, 105; 2Q, '91, 21; 3Q, '88, 7

518.83 Chronic respiratory failure

AHA: 4Q, '05, 96; 4Q, '03, 103, 111

518.84 Acute and chronic respiratory failure
Acute on chronic respiratory failure

518.89 Other diseases of lung, not elsewhere classified
Broncholithiasis
Calcification of lung
Lung disease NOS
Pulmolithiasis

AHA: 3Q, '90, 18; 4Q, '88, 6

DEF: Broncholithiasis: calculi in lumen of transbronchial tree.

DEF: Pulmolithiasis: calculi in lung.

✓4th 519 Other diseases of respiratory system

✓5th 519.0 Tracheostomy complications

519.00 Tracheostomy complication, unspecified

519.01 Infection of tracheostomy
Use additional code to identify type of infection, such as:
abscess or cellulitis of neck (682.1)
septicemia (038.0-038.9)
Use additional code to identify organism (041.00-041.9)

AHA: 4Q, '98, 41

519.02 Mechanical complication of tracheostomy
Tracheal stenosis due to tracheostomy

519.09 Other tracheostomy complications
Hemorrhage due to tracheostomy
Tracheoesophageal fistula due to tracheostomy

✓5th **519.1 Other diseases of trachea and bronchus, not elsewhere classified**
AHA: 3Q, '02, 18; 3Q, '88, 6

519.11 Acute bronchospasm
Bronchospasm NOS
EXCLUDES *acute bronchitis with bronchospasm (466.0)*
asthma (493.00-493.92)
exercise induced bronchospasm (493.81)
AHA: 4Q, '06, 92

519.19 Other diseases of trachea and bronchus
Calcification, Stenosis, Ulcer } of bronchus or trachea
AHA: 4Q, '06, 92

519.2 Mediastinitis
DEF: Inflammation of tissue between organs behind sternum.

519.3 Other diseases of mediastinum, not elsewhere classified
Fibrosis, Hernia, Retraction } of mediastinum

519.4 Disorders of diaphragm
Diaphragmitis
Paralysis of diaphragm
Relaxation of diaphragm
EXCLUDES *congenital defect of diaphragm (756.6)*
diaphragmatic hernia (551-553 with .3)
congenital (756.6)

519.8 Other diseases of respiratory system, not elsewhere classified
AHA: 4Q, '89, 12

519.9 Unspecified disease of respiratory system
Respiratory disease (chronic) NOS

9. DISEASES OF THE DIGESTIVE SYSTEM (520-579)

DISEASES OF ORAL CAVITY, SALIVARY GLANDS, AND JAWS (520-529)

4th 520 Disorders of tooth development and eruption

520.0 Anodontia

Absence of teeth (complete) (congenital) (partial)
Hypodontia
Oligodontia

EXCLUDES *acquired absence of teeth (525.10-525.19)*

520.1 Supernumerary teeth

Distomolar
Fourth molar
Mesiodens
Paramolar
Supplemental teeth

EXCLUDES *supernumerary roots (520.2)*

520.2 Abnormalities of size and form

Concrescence }
Fusion } of teeth
Gemination }

Dens evaginatus
Dens in dente
Dens invaginatus
Enamel pearls
Macrodontia
Microdontia
Peg-shaped [conical] teeth
Supernumerary roots
Taurodontism
Tuberculum paramolare

EXCLUDES *that due to congenital syphilis (090.5)*
tuberculum Carabelli, which is regarded as a normal variation

520.3 Mottled teeth

Mottling of enamel
Dental fluorosis
Nonfluoride enamel opacities

Digestive System

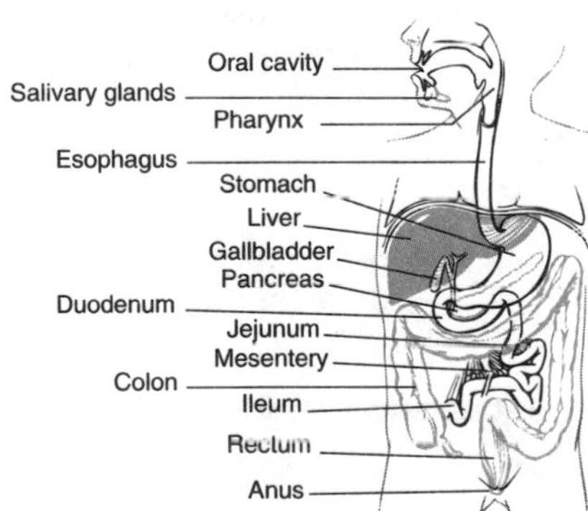

The Oral Cavity

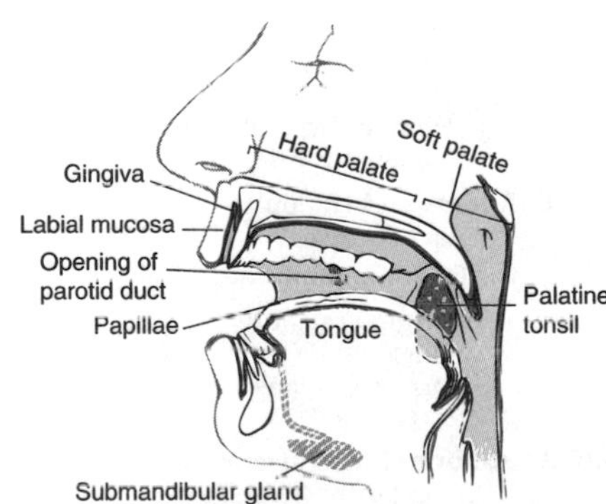

Teeth

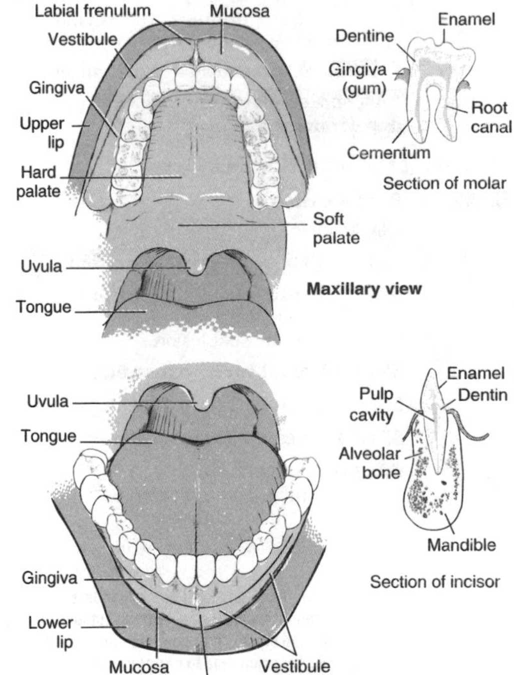

520.4 Disturbances of tooth formation

Aplasia and hypoplasia of cementum
Dilaceration of tooth
Enamel hypoplasia (neonatal) (postnatal) (prenatal)
Horner's teeth
Hypocalcification of teeth
Regional odontodysplasia
Turner's tooth

EXCLUDES *Hutchinson's teeth and mulberry molars in congenital syphilis (090.5)*
mottled teeth (520.3)

520.5 Hereditary disturbances in tooth structure, not elsewhere classified

Amelogensis }
Dentinogenesis } imperfecta
Odontogenesis }

Dentinal dysplasia
Shell teeth

520.6 Disturbances in tooth eruption

Teeth:
- embedded
- impacted
- natal
- neonatal
- prenatal
- primary [deciduous]:
  - persistent
  - shedding, premature

Tooth eruption:
- late
- obstructed
- premature

EXCLUDES *exfoliation of teeth (attributable to disease of surrounding tissues) (525.0-525.19)*

AHA: 1Q, '06, 18; 2Q, '05, 15

520.7 Teething syndrome

520.8 Other specified disorders of tooth development and eruption
Color changes during tooth formation
Pre-eruptive color changes
EXCLUDES *posteruptive color changes (521.7)*

520.9 Unspecified disorder of tooth development and eruption

✓4th 521 Diseases of hard tissues of teeth

✓5th 521.0 Dental caries
AHA: 4Q, '01, 44

521.00 Dental caries, unspecified

521.01 Dental caries limited to enamel
Initial caries
White spot lesion

521.02 Dental caries extending into dentine

521.03 Dental caries extending into pulp

521.04 Arrested dental caries

521.05 Odontoclasia
Infantile melanodontia
Melanodontoclasia
EXCLUDES *internal and external resorption of teeth (521.40-521.49)*
DEF: A pathological dental condition described as stained areas, loss of tooth substance, and hypoplasia linked to nutritional deficiencies during tooth development and to cariogenic oral conditions; synonyms are melanodontoclasia and infantile melanodontia.

521.06 Dental caries pit and fissure
Primary dental caries, pit and fissure origin

521.07 Dental caries of smooth surface
Primary dental caries, smooth surface origin

521.08 Dental caries of root surface
Primary dental caries, root surface

521.09 Other dental caries
AHA: 3Q, '02, 14

✓5th 521.1 Excessive attrition (approximal wear) (occlusal wear)

521.10 Excessive attrition, unspecified

521.11 Excessive attrition, limited to enamel

521.12 Excessive attrition, extending into dentine

521.13 Excessive attrition, extending into pulp

521.14 Excessive attrition, localized

521.15 Excessive attrition, generalized

✓5th 521.2 Abrasion
Abrasion:
dentifrice, habitual, occupational, ritual, traditional } of teeth
Wedge defect NOS } of teeth

521.20 Abrasion, unspecified

521.21 Abrasion, limited to enamel

521.22 Abrasion, extending into dentine

521.23 Abrasion, extending into pulp

521.24 Abrasion, localized

521.25 Abrasion, generalized

✓5th 521.3 Erosion
Erosion of teeth:
NOS
due to:
medicine
persistent vomiting
idiopathic
occupational

521.30 Erosion, unspecified

521.31 Erosion, limited to enamel

521.32 Erosion, extending into dentine

521.33 Erosion, extending into pulp

521.34 Erosion, localized

521.35 Erosion, generalized

✓5th 521.4 Pathological resorption
DEF: Loss of dentin and cementum due to disease process.

521.40 Pathological resorption, unspecified

521.41 Pathological resorption, internal

521.42 Pathological resorption, external

521.49 Other pathological resorption
Internal granuloma of pulp

521.5 Hypercementosis
Cementation hyperplasia
DEF: Excess deposits of cementum, on tooth root.

521.6 Ankylosis of teeth
DEF: Adhesion of tooth to surrounding bone.

521.7 Intrinsic posteruptive color changes
Staining [discoloration] of teeth:
NOS
due to:
drugs
metals
pulpal bleeding
EXCLUDES *accretions [deposits] on teeth (523.6)*
extrinsic color changes (523.6)
pre-eruptive color changes (520.8)

✓5th 521.8 Other specified diseases of hard tissues of teeth

521.81 Cracked tooth
EXCLUDES *asymptomatic craze lines in enamel — omit code*
broken tooth due to trauma (873.63, 873.73)
fractured tooth due to trauma (873.63, 873.73)

521.89 Other specified diseases of hard tissues of teeth
Irradiated enamel
Sensitive dentin

521.9 Unspecified disease of hard tissues of teeth

✓4th 522 Diseases of pulp and periapical tissues

522.0 Pulpitis
Pulpal:
abscess
polyp
Pulpitis:
acute
chronic (hyperplastic) (ulcerative)
suppurative

522.1 Necrosis of the pulp
Pulp gangrene
DEF: Death of pulp tissue.

522.2 Pulp degeneration
Denticles
Pulp calcifications
Pulp stones

522.3 Abnormal hard tissue formation in pulp
Secondary or irregular dentin

522.4 Acute apical periodontitis of pulpal origin
DEF: Severe inflammation of periodontal ligament due to pulpal inflammation or necrosis.

522.5 Periapical abscess without sinus
Abscess:
dental
dentoalveolar
EXCLUDES *periapical abscess with sinus (522.7)*

522.6 Chronic apical periodontitis
Apical or periapical granuloma
Apical periodontitis NOS

522.7 Periapical abscess with sinus
Fistula:
alveolar process
dental

522.8 Radicular cyst
Cyst:
apical (periodontal)
periapical
radiculodental
residual radicular
EXCLUDES *lateral developmental or lateral periodontal cyst (526.0)*
DEF: Cyst in tissue around tooth apex due to chronic infection of granuloma around root.

522.9 Other and unspecified diseases of pulp and periapical tissues

4th 523 Gingival and periodontal diseases

5th 523.0 Acute gingivitis
EXCLUDES *acute necrotizing ulcerative gingivitis (101)*
herpetic gingivostomatitis (054.2)

523.00 Acute gingivitis, plaque induced
Acute gingivitis NOS

523.01 Acute gingivitis, non-plaque induced

5th 523.1 Chronic gingivitis
Gingivitis (chronic):
desquamative
hyperplastic
simple marginal
ulcerative
EXCLUDES *herpetic gingivostomatitis (054.2)*

523.10 Chronic gingivitis, plaque induced
Chronic gingivitis NOS
Gingivitis NOS

523.11 Chronic gingivitis, non-plaque induced

5th 523.2 Gingival recession
Gingival recession (postinfective) (postoperative)

523.20 Gingival recession, unspecified

523.21 Gingival recession, minimal

523.22 Gingival recession, moderate

523.23 Gingival recession, severe

523.24 Gingival recession, localized

523.25 Gingival recession, generalized

5th 523.3 Aggressive and acute periodontitis
Acute:
pericementitis
pericoronitis
EXCLUDES *acute apical periodontitis (522.4)*
periapical abscess (522.5, 522.7)
DEF: Severe inflammation, of tissues supporting teeth.

523.30 Aggressive periodontitis, unspecified

523.31 Aggressive periodontitis, localized
Periodontal abscess

523.32 Aggressive periodontitis, generalized

523.33 Acute periodontitis

5th 523.4 Chronic periodontitis
Chronic pericoronitis
Pericementitis (chronic)
Periodontitis:
NOS
complex
simplex
EXCLUDES *chronic apical periodontitis (522.6)*

523.40 Chronic periodontitis, unspecified

523.41 Chronic periodontitis, localized

523.42 Chronic periodontitis, generalized

523.5 Periodontosis

523.6 Accretions on teeth
Dental calculus:
subgingival
supragingival
Deposits on teeth:
betel
materia alba
soft
tartar
tobacco
Extrinsic discoloration of teeth
EXCLUDES *intrinsic discoloration of teeth (521.7)*
DEF: Foreign material on tooth surface, usually plaque or calculus.

523.8 Other specified periodontal diseases
Giant cell:
epulis
peripheral granuloma
Gingival:
cysts
enlargement NOS
fibromatosis
Gingival polyp
Periodontal lesions due to traumatic occlusion
Peripheral giant cell granuloma
EXCLUDES *leukoplakia of gingiva (528.6)*

523.9 Unspecified gingival and periodontal disease
AHA: 3Q, '02, 14

4th 524 Dentofacial anomalies, including malocclusion

5th 524.0 Major anomalies of jaw size
EXCLUDES *hemifacial atrophy or hypertrophy (754.0)*
unilateral condylar hyperplasia or hypoplasia of mandible (526.89)

524.00 Unspecified anomaly
DEF: Unspecified deformity of jaw size.

524.01 Maxillary hyperplasia
DEF: Overgrowth or over development of upper jaw bone.

524.02 Mandibular hyperplasia
DEF: Overgrowth or over development of lower jaw bone.

524.03 Maxillary hypoplasia
DEF: Incomplete or underdeveloped, upper jaw bone.

524.04 Mandibular hypoplasia
DEF: Incomplete or underdeveloped, lower jaw bone.

524.05 Macrogenia
DEF: Enlarged, jaw, especially chin; affects bone, soft tissue, or both.

524.06 Microgenia
DEF: Underdeveloped mandible, characterized by an extremely small chin.

524.07 Excessive tuberosity of jaw
Entire maxillary tuberosity

524.09 Other specified anomaly

5th **524.1 Anomalies of relationship of jaw to cranial base**

524.10 Unspecified anomaly
Prognathism
Retrognathism
DEF: Prognathism: protrusion of lower jaw.
DEF: Retrognathism: jaw is located posteriorly to a normally positioned jaw; backward position of mandible.

524.11 Maxillary asymmetry
DEF: Absence of symmetry of maxilla.

524.12 Other jaw asymmetry

524.19 Other specified anomaly

5th **524.2 Anomalies of dental arch relationship**
Anomaly of dental arch
EXCLUDES *hemifacial atrophy or hypertrophy (754.0)*
soft tissue impingement (524.81-524.82)
unilateral condylar hyperplasia or hypoplasia of mandible (526.89)

524.20 Unspecified anomaly of dental arch relationship

524.21 Malocclusion, Angle's class I
Neutro-occlusion

524.22 Malocclusion, Angle's class II
Disto-occlusion Division I
Disto-occlusion Division II

524.23 Malocclusion, Angle's class III
Mesio-occlusion

524.24 Open anterior occlusal relationship
Anterior open bite

524.25 Open posterior occlusal relationship
Posterior open bite

524.26 Excessive horizontal overlap
Excessive horizontal overjet

524.27 Reverse articulation
Anterior articulation
Crossbite
Posterior articulation

524.28 Anomalies of interarch distance
Excessive interarch distance
Inadequate interarch distance

524.29 Other anomalies of dental arch relationship
Other anomalies of dental arch

Angle's Classification of Malocclusion

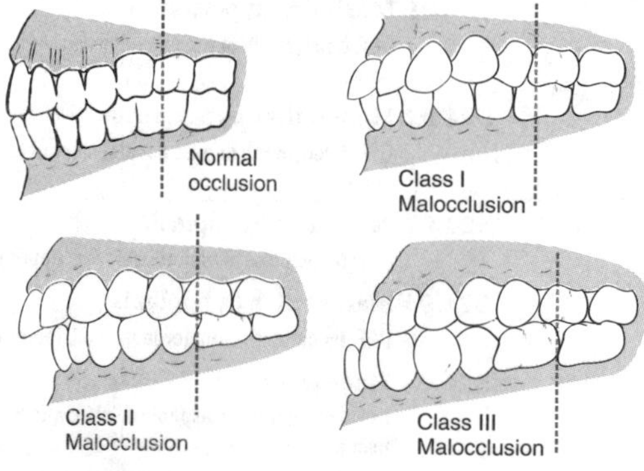

5th **524.3 Anomalies of tooth position of fully erupted teeth**
EXCLUDES *impacted or embedded teeth with abnormal position of such teeth or adjacent teeth (520.6)*

524.30 Unspecified anomaly of tooth position
Diastema of teeth NOS
Displacement of teeth NOS
Transposition of teeth NOS

524.31 Crowding of teeth

524.32 Excessive spacing of teeth

524.33 Horizontal displacement of teeth
Tipped teeth
Tipping of teeth

524.34 Vertical displacement of teeth
Extruded tooth
Infraeruption of teeth
Intruded tooth
Supraeruption of teeth

524.35 Rotation of tooth/teeth

524.36 Insufficient interocclusal distance of teeth (ridge)
Lack of adequate intermaxillary vertical dimension

524.37 Excessive interocclusal distance of teeth
Excessive intermaxillary vertical dimension
Loss of occlusal vertical dimension

524.39 Other anomalies of tooth position

524.4 Malocclusion, unspecified
DEF: Malposition of top and bottom teeth; interferes with chewing.

5th **524.5 Dentofacial functional abnormalities**

524.50 Dentofacial functional abnormality, unspecified

524.51 Abnormal jaw closure

524.52 Limited mandibular range of motion

524.53 Deviation in opening and closing of the mandible

524.54 Insufficient anterior guidance
Insufficient anterior occlusal guidance

524.55 Centric occlusion maximum intercuspation discrepancy
Centric occlusion of teeth discrepancy

524.56 Non-working side interference
Balancing side interference

524.57 Lack of posterior occlusal support

524.59 Other dentofacial functional abnormalities
Abnormal swallowing
Mouth breathing
Sleep postures
Tongue, lip, or finger habits

5th **524.6 Temporomandibular joint disorders**
EXCLUDES *current temporomandibular joint:*
dislocation (830.0-830.1)
strain (848.1)

524.60 Temporomandibular joint disorders, unspecified
Temporomandibular joint-pain-dysfunction syndrome [TMJ]

524.61 Adhesions and ankylosis (bony or fibrous)
DEF: Stiffening or union of temporomandibular joint due to bony or fibrous union across joint.

524.62 Arthralgia of temporomandibular joint
DEF: Pain in temporomandibular joint; not inflammatory in nature.

524.63 Articular disc disorder (reducing or non-reducing)

524.64 Temporomandibular joint sounds on opening and/or closing the jaw

524.69 Other specified temporomandibular joint disorders

✓5th **524.7 Dental alveolar anomalies**

524.70 Unspecified alveolar anomaly

524.71 Alveolar maxillary hyperplasia
DEF: Excessive tissue formation in the dental alveoli of upper jaw.

524.72 Alveolar mandibular hyperplasia
DEF: Excessive tissue formation in the dental alveoli of lower jaw.

524.73 Alveolar maxillary hypoplasia
DEF: Incomplete or underdeveloped, alveolar tissue of upper jaw.

524.74 Alveolar mandibular hypoplasia
DEF: Incomplete or underdeveloped, alveolar tissue of lower jaw.

524.75 Vertical displacement of alveolus and teeth
Extrusion of alveolus and teeth

524.76 Occlusal plane deviation

524.79 Other specified alveolar anomaly

✓5th **524.8 Other specified dentofacial anomalies**

524.81 Anterior soft tissue impingement

524.82 Posterior soft tissue impingement

524.89 Other specified dentofacial anomalies

524.9 Unspecified dentofacial anomalies

✓4th **525 Other diseases and conditions of the teeth and supporting structures**

525.0 Exfoliation of teeth due to systemic causes
DEF: Deterioration of teeth and surrounding structures due to systemic disease.

✓5th **525.1 Loss of teeth due to trauma, extraction, or periodontal disease**
Code first class of edentulism (525.40-525.44, 525.50-525.54)
AHA: 4Q, '05, 74; 4Q, '01, 44

525.10 Acquired absence of teeth, unspecified
Tooth extraction status, NOS

525.11 Loss of teeth due to trauma

525.12 Loss of teeth due to periodontal disease

525.13 Loss of teeth due to caries

525.19 Other loss of teeth

✓5th **525.2 Atrophy of edentulous alveolar ridge**

525.20 Unspecified atrophy of edentulous alveolar ridge
Atrophy of the mandible NOS
Atrophy of the maxilla NOS

525.21 Minimal atrophy of the mandible

525.22 Moderate atrophy of the mandible

525.23 Severe atrophy of the mandible

525.24 Minimal atrophy of the maxilla

525.25 Moderate atrophy of the maxilla

525.26 Severe atrophy of the maxilla

525.3 Retained dental root

✓5th **525.4 Complete edentulism**
Use additional code to identify cause of edentulism (525.10-525.19)
AHA: 4Q, '05, 74

525.40 Complete edentulism, unspecified
Edentulism NOS

525.41 Complete edentulism, class I

525.42 Complete edentulism, class II

525.43 Complete edentulism, class III

525.44 Complete edentulism, class IV

✓5th **525.5 Partial edentulism**
Use additional code to identify cause of edentulism (525.10-525.19)
AHA: 4Q, '05, 74

525.50 Partial edentulism, unspecified

525.51 Partial edentulism, class I

525.52 Partial edentulism, class II

525.53 Partial edentulism, class III

525.54 Partial edentulism, class IV

✓5th **525.6 Unsatisfactory restoration of tooth**
Defective bridge, crown, fillings
Defective dental restoration

EXCLUDES *dental restoration status (V45.84)*
unsatisfactory endodontic treatment (526.61-526.69)

525.60 Unspecified unsatisfactory restoration of tooth
Unspecified defective dental restoration

525.61 Open restoration margins
Dental restoration failure of marginal integrity
Open margin on tooth restoration

525.62 Unrepairable overhanging of dental restorative materials
Overhanging of tooth restoration

525.63 Fractured dental restorative material without loss of material

EXCLUDES *cracked tooth (521.81)*
fractured tooth (873.63, 873.73)

525.64 Fractured dental restorative material with loss of material

EXCLUDES *cracked tooth (521.81)*
fractured tooth (873.63, 873.73)

525.65 Contour of existing restoration of tooth biologically incompatible with oral health
Dental restoration failure of periodontal anatomical integrity
Unacceptable contours of existing restoration
Unacceptable morphology of existing restoration

525.66 Allergy to existing dental restorative material
Use additional code to identify the specific type of allergy

525.67 Poor aesthetics of existing restoration
Dental restoration aesthetically inadequate or displeasing

525.69 Other unsatisfactory restoration of existing tooth

✓5th **525.7 Endosseous dental implant failure**

525.71 Osseointegration failure of dental implant

►Failure of dental implant due to infection
Failure of dental implant due to unintentional loading
Failure of dental implant osseointegration due to premature loading
Failure of dental implant to osseointegrate prior to intentional prosthetic loading◄
Hemorrhagic complications of dental implant placement
Iatrogenic osseointegration failure of dental implant
Osseointegration failure of dental implant due to complications of systemic disease
Osseointegration failure of dental implant due to poor bone quality
Pre-integration failure of dental implant NOS
Pre-osseointegration failure of dental implant

525.72 Post-osseointegration biological failure of dental implant

Failure of dental implant due to lack of attached gingiva
Failure of dental implant due to occlusal trauma (caused by poor prosthetic design)
Failure of dental implant due to parafunctional habits
Failure of dental implant due to periodontal infection (peri-implantitis)
Failure of dental implant due to poor oral hygiene
►Failure of dental implant to osseointegrate following intentional prosthetic loading◄
Iatrogenic post-osseointegration failure of dental implant
Post-osseointegration failure of dental implant due to complications of systemic disease

525.73 Post-osseointegration mechanic failure of dental implant

Failure of dental prosthesis causing loss of dental implant
Fracture of dental implant
►Mechanical failure of dental implant NOS◄

EXCLUDES *cracked tooth (521.81)*
fractured dental restorative material with loss of material (525.64)
fractured dental restorative material without loss of material (525.63)
fractured tooth (873.63, 873.73)

525.79 Other endosseous dental implant failure

Dental implant failure NOS

525.8 Other specified disorders of the teeth and supporting structures

Enlargement of alveolar ridge NOS
Irregular alveolar process

525.9 Unspecified disorder of the teeth and supporting structures

✓4th **526 Diseases of the jaws**

526.0 Developmental odontogenic cysts

Cyst:
dentigerous
eruption
follicular
lateral developmental
lateral periodontal
primordial
Keratocyst

EXCLUDES *radicular cyst (522.8)*

526.1 Fissural cysts of jaw

Cyst:
globulomaxillary
incisor canal
median anterior maxillary
median palatal
nasopalatine
palatine of papilla

EXCLUDES *cysts of oral soft tissues (528.4)*

526.2 Other cysts of jaws

Cyst of jaw
NOS
aneurysmal
hemorrhagic
traumatic

526.3 Central giant cell (reparative) granuloma

EXCLUDES *peripheral giant cell granuloma (523.8)*

526.4 Inflammatory conditions

Abscess, Osteitis, Osteomyelitis (neonatal), Periostitis } of jaw (acute) (chronic) (suppurative)

Sequestrum of jaw bone

EXCLUDES *alveolar osteitis (526.5)*
osteonecrosis of jaw (733.45)

526.5 Alveolitis of jaw

Alveolar osteitis
Dry socket

DEF: Inflammation, of alveoli or tooth socket.

✓5th **526.6 Periradicular pathology associated with previous endodontic treatment**

526.61 Perforation of root canal space

526.62 Endodontic overfill

526.63 Endodontic underfill

526.69 Other periradicular pathology associated with previous endodontic treatment

✓5th **526.8 Other specified diseases of the jaws**

526.81 Exostosis of jaw

Torus mandibularis
Torus palatinus

DEF: Spur or bony outgrowth on the jaw.

526.89 Other

Cherubism, Fibrous dysplasia, Latent bone cyst, Osteoradionecrosis } of jaw(s)

Unilateral condylar hyperplasia or hypoplasia of mandible

526.9 Unspecified disease of the jaws

✓4th **527 Diseases of the salivary glands**

527.0 Atrophy

DEF: Wasting away, necrosis of salivary gland tissue.

527.1 Hypertrophy

DEF: Overgrowth or overdeveloped salivary gland tissue.

527.2 Sialoadenitis
Parotitis:
NOS
allergic
toxic
Sialoangitis
Sialodochitis
EXCLUDES *epidemic or infectious parotitis (072.0-072.9)*
uveoparotid fever (135)
DEF: Inflammation of salivary gland.

527.3 Abscess

527.4 Fistula
EXCLUDES *congenital fistula of salivary gland (750.24)*

527.5 Sialolithiasis
Calculus, Stone } of salivary gland or duct
Sialodocholithiasis

527.6 Mucocele
Mucous:
extravasation cyst of salivary gland
retention cyst of salivary gland
Ranula
DEF: Dilated salivary gland cavity filled with mucous.

527.7 Disturbance of salivary secretion
Hyposecretion
Ptyalism
Sialorrhea
Xerostomia

527.8 Other specified diseases of the salivary glands
Benign lymphoepithelial lesion of salivary gland
Sialectasia
Sialosis
Stenosis, Stricture } of salivary duct

527.9 Unspecified disease of the salivary glands

✓4th **528 Diseases of the oral soft tissues, excluding lesions specific for gingiva and tongue**

✓5th **528.0 Stomatitis and mucositis (ulcerative)**
EXCLUDES *cellulitis and abscess of mouth (528.3)*
diphtheritic stomatitis (032.0)
epizootic stomatitis (078.4)
gingivitis (523.0-523.1)
oral thrush (112.0)
Stevens-Johnson syndrome ►(695.13)◄
stomatitis:
acute necrotizing ulcerative (101)
aphthous (528.2)
gangrenous (528.1)
herpetic (054.2)
Vincent's (101)
AHA: 2Q, '99, 9
DEF: Stomatitis: Inflammation of oral mucosa; labial and buccal mucosa, tongue, palate, floor of the mouth, and gingivae.

528.00 Stomatitis and mucositis, unspecified
Mucositis NOS
Ulcerative mucositis NOS
Ulcerative stomatitis NOS
Vesicular stomatitis NOS
AHA: 4Q, '06, 88-90

528.01 Mucositis (ulcerative) due to antineoplastic therapy
Use additional E code to identify adverse effects of therapy, such as:
antineoplastic and immunosuppressive drugs (E930.7, E933.1)
radiation therapy (E879.2)
AHA: 4Q, '06, 88-90

528.02 Mucositis (ulcerative) due to other drugs
Use additional E code to identify drug
AHA: 4Q, '06, 88-90

528.09 Other stomatitis and mucositis (ulcerative)
AHA: 4Q, '06, 88-90

528.1 Cancrum oris
Gangrenous stomatitis
Noma
DEF: A severely gangrenous lesion of mouth due to fusospirochetal infection; destroys buccal, labial and facial tissues; can be fatal; found primarily in debilitated and malnourished children.

528.2 Oral aphthae
Aphthous stomatitis
Canker sore
Periadenitis mucosa necrotica recurrens
Recurrent aphthous ulcer
Stomatitis herpetiformis
EXCLUDES *herpetic stomatitis (054.2)*
DEF: Small oval or round ulcers of the mouth marked by a grayish exudate and a red halo effect.

528.3 Cellulitis and abscess
Cellulitis of mouth (floor)
Ludwig's angina
Oral fistula
EXCLUDES *abscess of tongue (529.0)*
cellulitis or abscess of lip (528.5)
fistula (of):
dental (522.7)
lip (528.5)
gingivitis (523.00-523.11)

528.4 Cysts
Dermoid cyst, Epidermoid cyst, Epstein's pearl, Lymphoepithelial cyst, Nasoalveolar cyst, Nasolabial cyst } of mouth
EXCLUDES *cyst:*
gingiva (523.8)
tongue (529.8)

528.5 Diseases of lips
Abscess, Cellulitis, Fistula, Hypertrophy } of lips
Cheilitis:
NOS
angular
Cheilodynia
Cheilosis
EXCLUDES *actinic cheilitis (692.79)*
congenital fistula of lip (750.25)
leukoplakia of lips (528.6)
AHA: S-O, '86, 10

528.6 Leukoplakia of oral mucosa, including tongue
Leukokeratosis of oral mucosa
Leukoplakia of:
gingiva
lips
tongue
EXCLUDES *carcinoma in situ (230.0, 232.0)*
leukokeratosis nicotina palati (528.79)
DEF: Thickened white patches of epithelium on mucous membranes of mouth.

✓5th **528.7 Other disturbances of oral epithelium, including tongue**

EXCLUDES *carcinoma in situ (230.0, 232.0)*
leukokeratosis NOS (702.8)

528.71 Minimal keratinized residual ridge mucosa
Minimal keratinization of alveolar ridge mucosa

528.72 Excessive keratinized residual ridge mucosa
Excessive keratinization of alveolar ridge mucosa

528.79 Other disturbances of oral epithelium, including tongue
Erythroplakia of mouth or tongue
Focal epithelial hyperplasia of mouth or tongue
Leukoedema of mouth or tongue
Leukokeratosis nicotina palate
Other oral epithelium disturbances

528.8 Oral submucosal fibrosis, including of tongue

528.9 Other and unspecified diseases of the oral soft tissues
Cheek and lip biting
Denture sore mouth
Denture stomatitis
Melanoplakia
Papillary hyperplasia of palate
Eosinophilic granuloma } of oral mucosa
Irritative hyperplasia } of oral mucosa
Pyogenic granuloma } of oral mucosa
Ulcer (traumatic) } of oral mucosa

✓4th **529 Diseases and other conditions of the tongue**

529.0 Glossitis
Abscess } of tongue
Ulceration (traumatic) } of tongue

EXCLUDES *glossitis:*
benign migratory (529.1)
Hunter's (529.4)
median rhomboid (529.2)
Moeller's (529.4)

529.1 Geographic tongue
Benign migratory glossitis
Glossitis areata exfoliativa

DEF: Chronic glossitis; marked by filiform papillae atrophy and inflammation; no known etiology.

529.2 Median rhomboid glossitis

DEF: A noninflammatory, congenital disease characterized by rhomboid-like lesions at the middle third of the tongue's dorsal surface.

529.3 Hypertrophy of tongue papillae
Black hairy tongue
Coated tongue
Hypertrophy of foliate papillae
Lingua villosa nigra

529.4 Atrophy of tongue papillae
Bald tongue
Glazed tongue
Glossitis:
Hunter's
Moeller's
Glossodynia exfoliativa
Smooth atrophic tongue

529.5 Plicated tongue
Fissured } tongue
Furrowed } tongue
Scrotal } tongue

EXCLUDES *fissure of tongue, congenital (750.13)*

DEF: Cracks, fissures or furrows, on dorsal surface of tongue.

529.6 Glossodynia
Glossopyrosis
Painful tongue

EXCLUDES *glossodynia exfoliativa (529.4)*

529.8 Other specified conditions of the tongue
Atrophy } (of) tongue
Crenated } (of) tongue
Enlargement } (of) tongue
Hypertrophy } (of) tongue
Glossocele
Glossoptosis

EXCLUDES *erythroplasia of tongue (528.79)*
leukoplakia of tongue (528.6)
macroglossia (congenital) (750.15)
microglossia (congenital) (750.16)
oral submucosal fibrosis (528.8)

529.9 Unspecified condition of the tongue

DISEASES OF ESOPHAGUS, STOMACH, AND DUODENUM (530-538)

✓4th **530 Diseases of esophagus**

EXCLUDES *esophageal varices (456.0-456.2)*

530.0 Achalasia and cardiospasm
Achalasia (of cardia)
Aperistalsis of esophagus
Megaesophagus

EXCLUDES *congenital cardiospasm (750.7)*

DEF: Failure of smooth muscle fibers to relax, at gastrointestinal junctures; such as esophagogastric sphincter when swallowing.

✓5th **530.1 Esophagitis**
Esophagitis:
chemical
peptic
postoperative
regurgitant

Use additional E code to identify cause, if induced by chemical

EXCLUDES *tuberculous esophagitis (017.8)*

AHA:4Q, '93, 27; 1Q, '92, 17; 3Q, '91, 20

530.10 Esophagitis, unspecified
▶Esophagitis NOS◀
AHA: 3Q, '05, 17

530.11 Reflux esophagitis
AHA: 4Q, '95, 82
DEF: Inflammation of lower esophagus; due to regurgitated gastric acid.

530.12 Acute esophagitis
AHA: 4Q, '01, 45
DEF: An acute inflammation of the mucous lining or submucosal coat of the esophagus.

● **530.13 Eosinophilic esophagitis**

530.19 Other esophagitis
▶Abscess of esophagus◀
AHA: 3Q, '01, 10

Esophagus

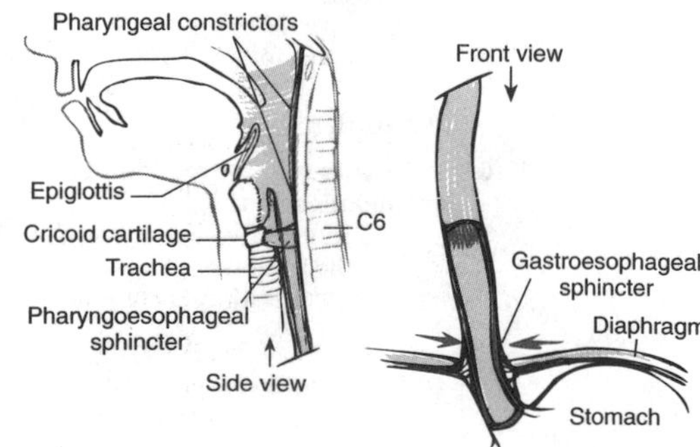

✓5th **530.2 Ulcer of esophagus**
Ulcer of esophagus:
fungal
peptic
Ulcer of esophagus due to ingestion of:
aspirin
chemicals
medicines
Use additional E code to identify cause, if induced by chemical or drug
AHA: 4Q, '03, 63

530.20 Ulcer of esophagus without bleeding
Ulcer of esophagus NOS

530.21 Ulcer of esophagus with bleeding
EXCLUDES *bleeding esophageal varices (456.0, 456.20)*

530.3 Stricture and stenosis of esophagus
Compression of esophagus
Obstruction of esophagus
EXCLUDES *congenital stricture of esophagus (750.3)*
AHA: 2Q, '01, 4; 2Q, '97, 3; 1Q, '88, 13

530.4 Perforation of esophagus
Rupture of esophagus
EXCLUDES *traumatic perforation of esophagus (862.22, 862.32, 874.4-874.5)*

530.5 Dyskinesia of esophagus
Corkscrew esophagus
Curling esophagus
Esophagospasm
Spasm of esophagus
EXCLUDES *cardiospasm (530.0)*
AHA: 1Q, '88, 13; N-D, '84, 19
DEF: Difficulty performing voluntary esophageal movements.

530.6 Diverticulum of esophagus, acquired
Diverticulum, acquired:
epiphrenic
pharyngoesophageal
pulsion
subdiaphragmatic
traction
Zenker's (hypopharyngeal)
Esophageal pouch, acquired
Esophagocele, acquired
EXCLUDES *congenital diverticulum of esophagus (750.4)*
AHA: J-F, '85, 3

530.7 Gastroesophageal laceration-hemorrhage syndrome
Mallory-Weiss syndrome
DEF: Laceration of distal esophagus and proximal stomach due to vomiting, hiccups or other sustained activity.

✓5th **530.8 Other specified disorders of esophagus**

530.81 Esophageal reflux
Gastroesophageal reflux
EXCLUDES *reflux esophagitis (530.11)*
AHA: 2Q, '01, 4; 1Q, '95, 7; 4Q, '92, 27
DEF: Regurgitation of the gastric contents into esophagus and possibly pharynx; where aspiration may occur between the vocal cords and down into the trachea.

530.82 Esophageal hemorrhage
EXCLUDES *hemorrhage due to esophageal varices (456.0-456.2)*
AHA: 1Q, '05, 17

530.83 Esophageal leukoplakia

530.84 Tracheoesophageal fistula
EXCLUDES *congenital tracheoesophageal fistula (750.3)*

530.85 Barrett's esophagus
AHA: 4Q, '03, 63
DEF: A metaplastic disorder in which specialized colum-nar epithelial cells replace the normal squamous epith-elial cells; an acquired condition secondary to chronic gastroesophageal reflux damage to the mucosa; assoc-iated with increased risk of developing adenocarcinoma.

530.86 Infection of esophagostomy
Use additional code to specify infection

530.87 Mechanical complication of esophagostomy
Malfunction of esophagostomy

530.89 Other
EXCLUDES *Paterson-Kelly syndrome (280.8)*

530.9 Unspecified disorder of esophagus

✓4th **531 Gastric ulcer**
INCLUDES ulcer (peptic):
prepyloric
pylorus
stomach
Use additional E code to identify drug, if drug-induced
EXCLUDES *peptic ulcer NOS (533.0-533.9)*

The following fifth-digit subclassification is for use with category 531:
0 without mention of obstruction
1 with obstruction

AHA: 1Q, '91, 15; 4Q, '90, 27
DEF: Destruction of tissue in lumen of stomach due to action of gastric acid and pepsin on gastric mucosa decreasing resistance to ulcers.

§ ✓5th **531.0 Acute with hemorrhage**
[0-1] **AHA:** N-D, '84, 15

§ ✓5th **531.1 Acute with perforation**
[0-1]

§ ✓5th **531.2 Acute with hemorrhage and perforation**
[0-1]

§ ✓5th **531.3 Acute without mention of hemorrhage or perforation**
[0-1]

§ ✓5th **531.4 Chronic or unspecified with hemorrhage**
[0-1] **AHA:** 4Q, '90, 22

§ ✓5th **531.5 Chronic or unspecified with perforation**
[0-1]

§ ✓5th **531.6 Chronic or unspecified with hemorrhage and perforation**
[0-1]

§ ✓5th **531.7 Chronic without mention of hemorrhage or perforation**
[0-1]

§ ✓5th **531.9 Unspecified as acute or chronic, without mention of hemorrhage or perforation**
[0-1]

Stomach

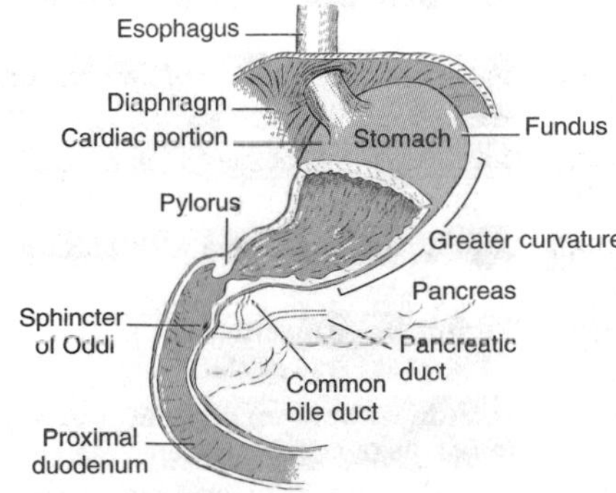

§ Requires fifth-digit. Valid digits are in [brackets] under each code. See category 531 for codes and definitions.

✓4th 532 Duodenal ulcer

INCLUDES erosion (acute) of duodenum
ulcer (peptic):
duodenum
postpyloric

Use additional E code to identify drug, if drug-induced

EXCLUDES *peptic ulcer NOS (533.0-533.9)*

The following fifth-digit subclassification is for use with category 532:
0 without mention of obstruction
1 with obstruction

AHA: 4Q, '90, 27; 1Q, '91, 15

DEF: Ulcers in duodenum due to action of gastric acid and pepsin on mucosa decreasing resistance to ulcers.

§ ✓5th **532.0 Acute with hemorrhage**
[0-1] AHA: 4Q, '90, 22

§ ✓5th **532.1 Acute with perforation**
[0-1]

§ ✓5th **532.2 Acute with hemorrhage and perforation**
[0-1]

§ ✓5th **532.3 Acute without mention of hemorrhage or perforation**
[0-1]

§ ✓5th **532.4 Chronic or unspecified with hemorrhage**
[0-1]

§ ✓5th **532.5 Chronic or unspecified with perforation**
[0-1]

§ ✓5th **532.6 Chronic or unspecified with hemorrhage and perforation**
[0-1]

§ ✓5th **532.7 Chronic without mention of hemorrhage or perforation**
[0-1]

§ ✓5th **532.9 Unspecified as acute or chronic, without mention of hemorrhage or perforation**
[0-1]

✓4th 533 Peptic ulcer, site unspecified

INCLUDES gastroduodenal ulcer NOS
peptic ulcer NOS
stress ulcer NOS

Use additional E code to identify drug, if drug-induced

EXCLUDES *peptic ulcer:*
duodenal (532.0-532.9)
gastric (531.0-531.9)

The following fifth-digit subclassification is for use with category 533:
0 without mention of obstruction
1 with obstruction

AHA: 1Q, '91, 15; 4Q, '90, 27

DEF: Ulcer of mucous membrane of esophagus, stomach or duodenum due to gastric acid secretion.

§ ✓5th **533.0 Acute with hemorrhage**
[0-1]

§ ✓5th **533.1 Acute with perforation**
[0-1]

§ ✓5th **533.2 Acute with hemorrhage and perforation**
[0-1]

§ ✓5th **533.3 Acute without mention of hemorrhage and perforation**
[0-1]

§ ✓5th **533.4 Chronic or unspecified with hemorrhage**
[0-1]

§ ✓5th **533.5 Chronic or unspecified with perforation**
[0-1]

§ ✓5th **533.6 Chronic or unspecified with hemorrhage and perforation**
[0-1]

§ ✓5th **533.7 Chronic without mention of hemorrhage or perforation**
[0-1]

§ ✓5th **533.9 Unspecified as acute or chronic, without mention of hemorrhage or perforation**
[0-1]

✓4th 534 Gastrojejunal ulcer

INCLUDES ulcer (peptic) or erosion:
anastomotic
gastrocolic
gastrointestinal
gastrojejunal
jejunal
marginal
stomal

EXCLUDES *primary ulcer of small intestine (569.82)*

The following fifth-digit subclassification is for use with category 534:
0 without mention of obstruction
1 with obstruction

AHA: 1Q, '91, 15; 4Q, '90, 27

§ ✓5th **534.0 Acute with hemorrhage**
[0-1]

§ ✓5th **534.1 Acute with perforation**
[0-1]

§ ✓5th **534.2 Acute with hemorrhage and perforation**
[0-1]

§ ✓5th **534.3 Acute without mention of hemorrhage or perforation**
[0-1]

§ ✓5th **534.4 Chronic or unspecified with hemorrhage**
[0-1]

§ ✓5th **534.5 Chronic or unspecified with perforation**
[0-1]

§ ✓5th **534.6 Chronic or unspecified with hemorrhage and perforation**
[0-1]

§ ✓5th **534.7 Chronic without mention of hemorrhage or perforation**
[0-1]

§ ✓5th **534.9 Unspecified as acute or chronic, without mention of hemorrhage or perforation**
[0-1]

✓4th 535 Gastritis and duodenitis

The following fifth-digit subclassification is for use with category 535:
0 without mention of obstruction
1 with obstruction

AHA: 2Q, '92, 9; 4Q, '91, 25

§ ✓5th **535.0 Acute gastritis**
[0-1] AHA: 2Q, '92, 8; N-D, '86, 9

§ ✓5th **535.1 Atrophic gastritis**
[0-1] Gastritis:
atrophic-hyperplastic
chronic (atrophic)

AHA: 1Q, '94, 18

DEF: Inflammation of stomach, with mucous membrane atrophy and peptic gland destruction.

§ ✓5th **535.2 Gastric mucosal hypertrophy**
[0-1] Hypertrophic gastritis

§ ✓5th **535.3 Alcoholic gastritis**
[0-1]

§ ✓5th **535.4 Other specified gastritis**
[0-1] Gastritis:
allergic
bile induced
irritant
superficial
toxic

EXCLUDES ►*eosinophilic gastritis (535.7)*◄

AHA: 4Q, '90, 27

§ Requires fifth-digit. Valid digits are in [brackets] under each code. See appropriate category for codes and definitions.

§ ✓5th **535.5 Unspecified gastritis and gastroduodenitis**
[0-1] **AHA: For code 535.50:** 3Q, '05, 17; 4Q, '99, 25

§ ✓5th **535.6 Duodenitis**
[0-1] **AHA: For code 535.60:** 3Q, '05, 17
DEF: Inflammation of intestine, between pylorus and jejunum.

● § ✓5th **535.7 Eosinophilic gastritis**
[0-1]

✓4th **536 Disorders of function of stomach**
EXCLUDES *functional disorders of stomach specified as psychogenic (306.4)*

536.0 Achlorhydria
DEF: Absence of gastric acid due to gastric mucosa atrophy; unresponsive to histamines; also known as gastric anacidity.

536.1 Acute dilatation of stomach
Acute distention of stomach

536.2 Persistent vomiting
▶Cyclical vomiting◀
Habit vomiting
Persistent vomiting [not of pregnancy]
Uncontrollable vomiting
EXCLUDES *excessive vomiting in pregnancy (643.0-643.9)*
vomiting NOS ▶(787.03)
cyclical, associated with migraine (346.2)◀

536.3 Gastroparesis
Gastroparalysis
Code first underlying disease, such as: diabetes mellitus ▶(249.6, 250.6)◀
AHA: 2Q, '04, 7; 2Q, '01, 4; 4Q, '94, 42
DEF: Slight degree of paralysis within muscular coat of stomach.

✓5th **536.4 Gastrostomy complications**
AHA: 4Q, '98, 42

536.40 Gastrostomy complication, unspecified

536.41 Infection of gastrostomy
Use additional code to specify type of infection, such as:
abscess or cellulitis of abdomen (682.2)
septicemia (038.0-038.9)
Use additional code to identify organism (041.00-041.9)
AHA: 4Q, '98, 42

536.42 Mechanical complication of gastrostomy

536.49 Other gastrostomy complications
AHA: 4Q, '98, 42

536.8 Dyspepsia and other specified disorders of function of stomach
Achylia gastrica
Hourglass contraction of stomach
Hyperacidity
Hyperchlorhydria
Hypochlorhydria
Indigestion
Tachygastria
EXCLUDES *achlorhydria (536.0)*
heartburn (787.1)
AHA: 2Q, '93, 6; 2Q, '89, 16; N-D, '84, 9

536.9 Unspecified functional disorder of stomach
Functional gastrointestinal:
disorder
disturbance
irritation

Duodenum

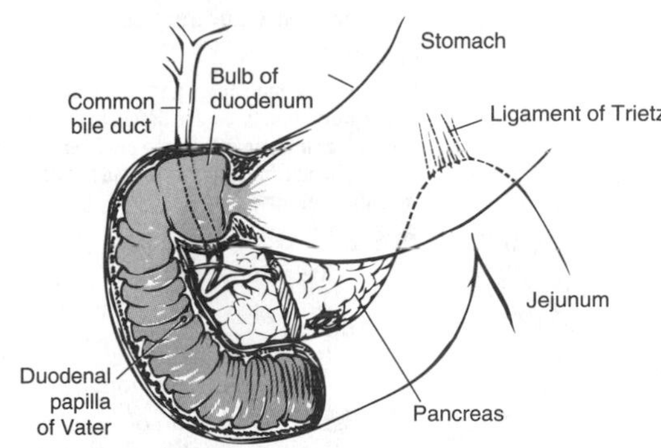

✓4th **537 Other disorders of stomach and duodenum**

537.0 Acquired hypertrophic pyloric stenosis
Constriction, Obstruction, Stricture } of pylorus, acquired or adult
EXCLUDES *congenital or infantile pyloric stenosis (750.5)*
AHA: 2Q, '01, 4; J-F, '85, 14

537.1 Gastric diverticulum
EXCLUDES *congenital diverticulum of stomach (750.7)*
AHA: J-F, '85, 4
DEF: Herniated sac or pouch, within stomach or duodenum.

537.2 Chronic duodenal ileus
DEF: Persistent obstruction between pylorus and jejunum.

537.3 Other obstruction of duodenum
Cicatrix, Stenosis, Stricture, Volvulus } of duodenum
EXCLUDES *congenital obstruction of duodenum (751.1)*

537.4 Fistula of stomach or duodenum
Gastrocolic fistula
Gastrojejunocolic fistula

537.5 Gastroptosis
DEF: Downward displacement of stomach.

537.6 Hourglass stricture or stenosis of stomach
Cascade stomach
EXCLUDES *congenital hourglass stomach (750.7)*
hourglass contraction of stomach (536.8)

✓5th **537.8 Other specified disorders of stomach and duodenum**
AHA: 4Q, '91, 25

537.81 Pylorospasm
EXCLUDES *congenital pylorospasm (750.5)*
DEF: Spasm of the pyloric sphincter.

537.82 Angiodysplasia of stomach and duodenum (without mention of hemorrhage)
AHA: 2Q, '07, 7; 3Q, '96, 10; 4Q, '90, 4

537.83 Angiodysplasia of stomach and duodenum with hemorrhage
AHA: 2Q, '07, 7
DEF: Bleeding of stomach and duodenum due to vascular abnormalities.

§ Requires fifth-digit. Valid digits are in [brackets] under each code. See category 535 for codes and definitions.

537.84 Dieulafoy lesion (hemorrhagic) of stomach and duodenum

AHA: 4Q, '02, 60

DEF: An abnormally large and convoluted submucosal artery protruding through a defect in the mucosa in the stomach or intestines that can erode the epithelium causing hemorrhaging; also called Dieulafoy's vascular malformation.

537.89 Other

Gastric or duodenal:
- prolapse
- rupture

Intestinal metaplasia of gastric mucosa
Passive congestion of stomach

EXCLUDES *diverticula of duodenum (562.00-562.01)*
gastrointestinal hemorrhage (578.0-578.9)

AHA: 3Q, '05, 15; N-D, '84, 7

537.9 Unspecified disorder of stomach and duodenum

538 Gastrointestinal mucositis (ulcerative)

Use additional E code to identify adverse effects of therapy, such as:
- antineoplastic and immunosuppressive drugs (E930.7, E933.1)
- radiation therapy (E879.2)

EXCLUDES *mucositis (ulcerative) of mouth and oral soft tissue (528.00- 528.09)*

AHA: 4Q, '06, 88-90

APPENDICITIS (540-543)

✓4th 540 Acute appendicitis

AHA: N-D, '84, 19

DEF: Inflammation of vermiform appendix due to fecal obstruction, neoplasm or foreign body of appendiceal lumen; causes infection, edema and infarction of appendiceal wall; may result in mural necrosis, and perforation.

540.0 With generalized peritonitis

Appendicitis (acute) with: perforation, peritonitis (generalized), rupture — fulminating, gangrenous, obstructive

Cecitis (acute) with perforation, peritonitis (generalized), rupture
Rupture of appendix

EXCLUDES *acute appendicitis with peritoneal abscess (540.1)*

540.1 With peritoneal abscess

Abscess of appendix
With generalized peritonitis

AHA: N-D, '84, 19

540.9 Without mention of peritonitis

Acute appendicitis without mention of perforation, peritonitis, or rupture:
- fulminating
- gangrenous
- inflamed
- obstructive

Acute cecitis without mention of perforation, peritonitis, or rupture

AHA: 1Q, '01, 15; 4Q, '97, 52

541 Appendicitis, unqualified

AHA: 2Q, '90, 26

542 Other appendicitis

Appendicitis:
- chronic
- recurrent
- relapsing
- subacute

EXCLUDES *hyperplasia (lymphoid) of appendix (543.0)*

AHA: 1Q, '01, 15

Appendix

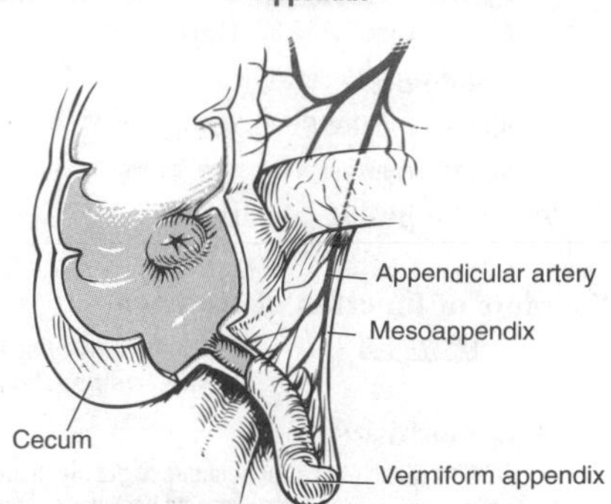

✓4th 543 Other diseases of appendix

543.0 Hyperplasia of appendix (lymphoid)

DEF: Proliferation of cells in appendix tissue.

543.9 Other and unspecified diseases of appendix

Appendicular or appendiceal:
- colic
- concretion
- fistula

Diverticulum, Fecalith, Intussusception, Mucocele, Stercolith — of appendix

HERNIA OF ABDOMINAL CAVITY (550-553)

INCLUDES hernia:
- acquired
- congenital, except diaphragmatic or hiatal

✓4th 550 Inguinal hernia

INCLUDES bubonocele
inguinal hernia (direct) (double) (indirect) (oblique) (sliding)
scrotal hernia

The following fifth-digit subclassification is for use with category 550:
- **0 unilateral or unspecified (not specified as recurrent)**
  Unilateral NOS
- **1 unilateral or unspecified, recurrent**
- **2 bilateral (not specified as recurrent)**
  Bilateral NOS
- **3 bilateral, recurrent**

AHA: N-D, '85, 12

DEF: Hernia protrusion of an abdominal organ or tissue through inguinal canal.

DEF: Indirect inguinal hernia: (external or oblique) leaves abdomen through deep inguinal ring, passes through inguinal canal lateral to the inferior epigastric artery.

DEF: Direct inguinal hernia: (internal) emerges between inferior epigastric artery and rectus muscle edge.

§ ✓5th **550.0 Inguinal hernia, with gangrene**
[0-3] Inguinal hernia with gangrene (and obstruction)

§ ✓5th **550.1 Inguinal hernia, with obstruction, without mention of gangrene**
[0-3] Inguinal hernia with mention of incarceration, irreducibility, or strangulation

§ ✓5th **550.9 Inguinal hernia, without mention of obstruction or gangrene**
[0-3] Inguinal hernia NOS

AHA: For code 550.91: 3Q, '03, 10; 1Q, '03, 4

§ Requires fifth-digit. Valid digits are in [brackets] under each code. See category 550 for codes and definitions.

Inguinal Hernias

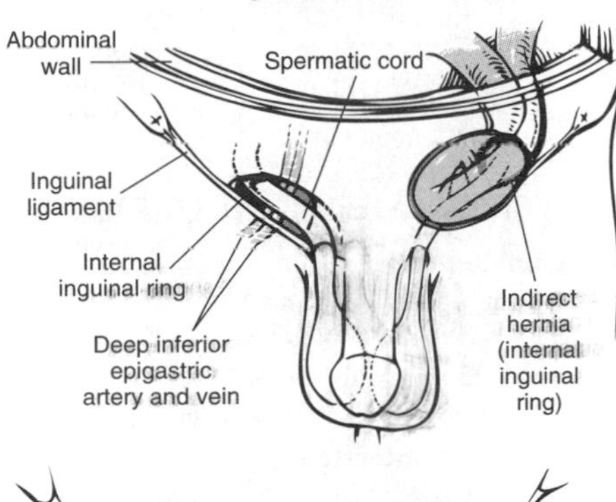

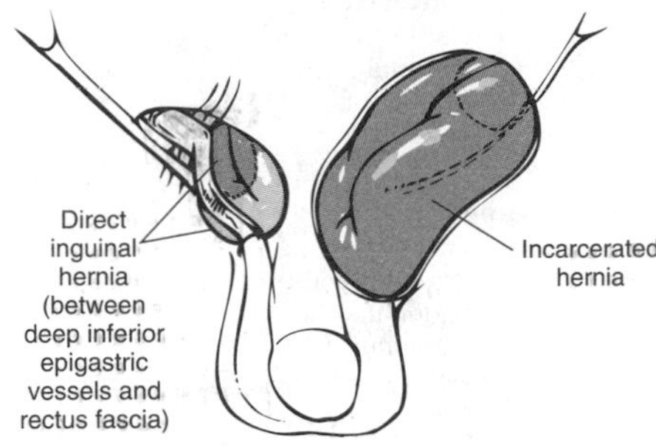

✓4th **551 Other hernia of abdominal cavity, with gangrene**

INCLUDES *that with gangrene (and obstruction)*

✓5th **551.0 Femoral hernia with gangrene**

551.00 Unilateral or unspecified (not specified as recurrent)
Femoral hernia NOS with gangrene

551.01 Unilateral or unspecified, recurrent

551.02 Bilateral (not specified as recurrent)

551.03 Bilateral, recurrent

551.1 Umbilical hernia with gangrene
Parumbilical hernia specified as gangrenous

✓5th **551.2 Ventral hernia with gangrene**

551.20 Ventral, unspecified, with gangrene

551.21 Incisional, with gangrene
Hernia:
postoperative } specified as
recurrent, ventral } gangrenous

551.29 Other
Epigastric hernia specified as gangrenous

551.3 Diaphragmatic hernia with gangrene
Hernia:
hiatal (esophageal) (sliding) } specified as
paraesophageal } gangrenous
Thoracic stomach

EXCLUDES *congenital diaphragmatic hernia (756.6)*

Hernias of Abdominal Cavity

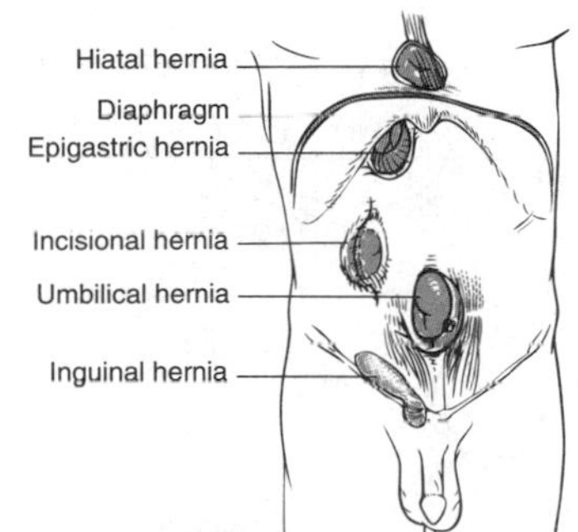

551.8 Hernia of other specified sites, with gangrene
Any condition classifiable to 553.8 if specified as gangrenous

551.9 Hernia of unspecified site, with gangrene
Any condition classifiable to 553.9 if specified as gangrenous

✓4th **552 Other hernia of abdominal cavity, with obstruction, but without mention of gangrene**

EXCLUDES *that with mention of gangrene (551.0-551.9)*

✓5th **552.0 Femoral hernia with obstruction**
Femoral hernia specified as incarcerated, irreducible, strangulated, or causing obstruction

552.00 Unilateral or unspecified (not specified as recurrent)

552.01 Unilateral or unspecified, recurrent

552.02 Bilateral (not specified as recurrent)

552.03 Bilateral, recurrent

552.1 Umbilical hernia with obstruction
Parumbilical hernia specified as incarcerated, irreducible, strangulated, or causing obstruction

✓5th **552.2 Ventral hernia with obstruction**
Ventral hernia specified as incarcerated, irreducible, strangulated, or causing obstruction

552.20 Ventral, unspecified, with obstruction

552.21 Incisional, with obstruction
Hernia:
postoperative } specified as incarcerated, irreducible,
recurrent, } strangulated, or causing
ventral } obstruction

AHA: 3Q, '03, 11

552.29 Other
Epigastric hernia specified as incarcerated, irreducible, strangulated, or causing obstruction

552.3 Diaphragmatic hernia with obstruction
Hernia:
hiatal (esophageal) (sliding) } specified as caracerated, irreducible,
paraesophageal } strangulated, or
Thoracic stomach } causing obstruction

EXCLUDES *congenital diaphragmatic hernia (756.6)*

552.8 Hernia of other specified sites, with obstruction
Any condition classifiable to 553.8 if specified as incarcerated, irreducible, strangulated, or causing obstruction

EXCLUDES *hernia due to adhesion with obstruction (560.81)*

AHA: 1Q, '04, 10

Femoral Hernia

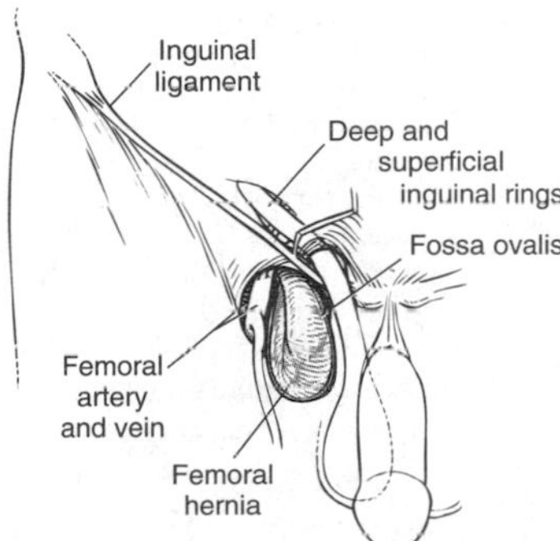

Digestive System

551–552.8

Diaphragmatic Hernias

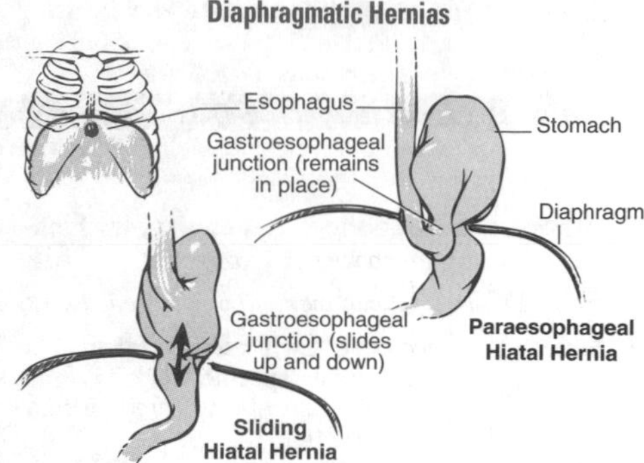

552.9 Hernia of unspecified site, with obstruction
Any condition classifiable to 553.9 if specified as incarcerated, irreducible, strangulated, or causing obstruction

✓4th **553 Other hernia of abdominal cavity without mention of obstruction or gangrene**

EXCLUDES *the listed conditions with mention of:*
gangrene (and obstruction) (551.0-551.9)
obstruction (552.0-552.9)

✓5th **553.0 Femoral hernia**

553.00 Unilateral or unspecified (not specified as recurrent)
Femoral hernia NOS

553.01 Unilateral or unspecified, recurrent

553.02 Bilateral (not specified as recurrent)

553.03 Bilateral, recurrent

553.1 Umbilical hernia
Parumbilical hernia

✓5th **553.2 Ventral hernia**

553.20 Ventral, unspecified
AHA: 2Q, '06, 10; 3Q, '03, 6

553.21 Incisional
Hernia:
postoperative
recurrent, ventral
AHA: 3Q, '03, 6

553.29 Other
Hernia:
epigastric
spigelian

553.3 Diaphragmatic hernia
Hernia:
hiatal (esophageal) (sliding)
paraesophageal
Thoracic stomach

EXCLUDES *congenital:*
diaphragmatic hernia (756.6)
hiatal hernia (750.6)
esophagocele (530.6)

AHA: 2Q, '01, 6; 1Q, '00, 6

553.8 Hernia of other specified sites
Hernia:
ischiatic
ischiorectal
lumbar
obturator
pudendal
retroperitoneal
sciatic
Other abdominal hernia of specified site

EXCLUDES *vaginal enterocele (618.6)*

553.9 Hernia of unspecified site
Enterocele
Epiplocele
Hernia:
NOS
interstitial
intestinal
intra-abdominal
Rupture (nontraumatic)
Sarcoepiplocele

NONINFECTIOUS ENTERITIS AND COLITIS (555-558)

✓4th **555 Regional enteritis**

INCLUDES Crohn's disease
Granulomatous enteritis

EXCLUDES *ulcerative colitis (556)*

DEF: Inflammation of intestine; classified to site.

555.0 Small intestine
Ileitis:
regional
segmental
terminal
Regional enteritis or Crohn's disease of:
duodenum
ileum
jejunum

555.1 Large intestine
Colitis:
granulmatous
regional
transmural
Regional enteritis or Crohn's disease of:
colon
large bowel
rectum
AHA: 3Q, '99, 8

555.2 Small intestine with large intestine
Regional ileocolitis
AHA: 1Q, '03, 18

555.9 Unspecified site
Crohn's disease NOS
Regional enteritis NOS
AHA: 2Q, '05, 11; 3Q, '99, 8; 4Q, '97, 42; 2Q, '97, 3

✓4th **556 Ulcerative colitis**

AHA: 3Q, '99, 8

DEF: Chronic inflammation of mucosal lining of intestinal tract; may be single area or entire colon.

556.0 Ulcerative (chronic) enterocolitis

556.1 Ulcerative (chronic) ileocolitis

556.2 Ulcerative (chronic) proctitis

556.3 Ulcerative (chronic) proctosigmoiditis

556.4 Pseudopolyposis of colon

556.5 Left-sided ulcerative (chronic) colitis

556.6 Universal ulcerative (chronic) colitis
Pancolitis

556.8 Other ulcerative colitis

556.9 Ulcerative colitis, unspecified
Ulcerative enteritis NOS
AHA: 1Q, '03, 10

Large Intestine

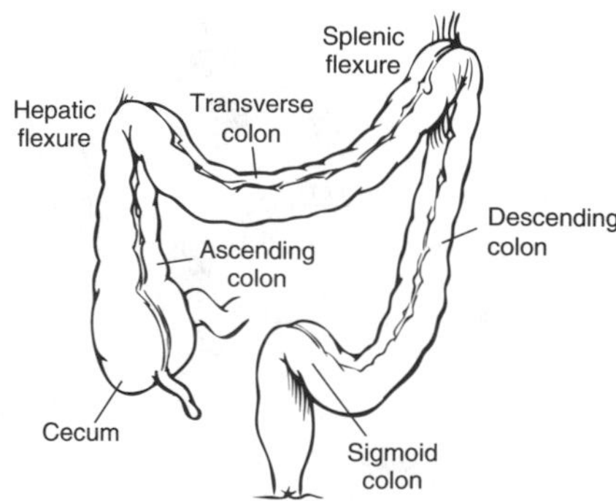

✓4th 557 Vascular insufficiency of intestine

EXCLUDES *necrotizing enterocolitis of the newborn ►(777.50-777.53)◄*

DEF: Inadequacy of intestinal vessels.

557.0 Acute vascular insufficiency of intestine

Acute:
- hemorrhagic enterocolitis
- ischemic colitis, enteritis, or enterocolitis
- massive necrosis of intestine

Bowel infarction
Embolism of mesenteric artery
Fulminant enterocolitis
Hemorrhagic necrosis of intestine
Infarction of appendices epiploicae
Intestinal gangrene
Intestinal infarction (acute) (agnogenic) (hemorrhagic) (nonocclusive)
Mesenteric infarction (embolic) (thrombotic)
Necrosis of intestine
Terminal hemorrhagic enteropathy
Thrombosis of mesenteric artery

AHA: ►2Q, '08, 15;◄ 4Q, '01, 53

557.1 Chronic vascular insufficiency of intestine

Angina, abdominal
Chronic ischemic colitis, enteritis, or enterocolitis
Ischemic stricture of intestine
Mesenteric:
- angina
- artery syndrome (superior)
- vascular insufficiency

AHA: 3Q, '96, 9; 4Q, '90, 4; N-D, '86, 11; N-D, '84, 7

557.9 Unspecified vascular insufficiency of intestine

Alimentary pain due to vascular insufficiency
Ischemic colitis, enteritis, or enterocolitis NOS

✓4th 558 Other and unspecified noninfectious gastroenteritis and colitis

EXCLUDES *infectious:*
- *colitis, enteritis, or gastroenteritis (009.0-009.1)*
- *diarrhea (009.2-009.3)*

558.1 Gastroenteritis and colitis due to radiation

Radiation enterocolitis

558.2 Toxic gastroenteritis and colitis

Use additional E code to identify cause

558.3 Allergic gastroenteritis and colitis

Use additional code to identify type of food allergy (V15.01-V15.05)

AHA: 1Q, '03, 12; 4Q, '00, 42

DEF: True immunoglobulin E (IgE)-mediated allergic reaction of the lining of the stomach, intestines, or colon to food proteins; causes nausea, vomiting, diarrhea, and abdominal cramping.

● ✓5th **558.4 Eosinophilic gastroenteritis and colitis**

● **558.41 Eosinophilic gastroenteritis**

Eosinophilic enteritis

● **558.42 Eosinophilic colitis**

558.9 Other and unspecified noninfectious gastroenteritis and colitis

Colitis Enteritis Gastroenteritis Ileitis Jejunitis Sigmoiditis	NOS, dietetic, or noninfectious

AHA: ►2Q, '08, 10; 1Q, '08, 10;◄ 3Q, '99, 4, 6; N-D, '87, 7

OTHER DISEASES OF INTESTINES AND PERITONEUM (560-569)

✓4th 560 Intestinal obstruction without mention of hernia

EXCLUDES
- *duodenum (537.2-537.3)*
- *inguinal hernia with obstruction (550.1)*
- *intestinal obstruction complicating hernia (552.0-552.9)*
- *mesenteric:*
  - *embolism (557.0)*
  - *infarction (557.0)*
  - *thrombosis (557.0)*
- *neonatal intestinal obstruction (277.01, 777.1-777.2, 777.4)*

560.0 Intussusception

Intussusception (colon) (intestine) (rectum)
Invagination of intestine or colon

EXCLUDES *intussusception of appendix (543.9)*

AHA: 4Q, '98, 82

DEF: Prolapse of a bowel section into adjacent section; occurs primarily in children; symptoms include paroxysmal pain, vomiting, presence of lower abdominal tumor and blood, and mucous passage from rectum.

560.1 Paralytic ileus

Adynamic ileus
Ileus (of intestine) (of bowel) (of colon)
Paralysis of intestine or colon

EXCLUDES *gallstone ileus (560.31)*

AHA: J-F, '87, 13

DEF: Obstruction of ileus due to inhibited bowel motility.

560.2 Volvulus

Knotting Strangulation Torsion Twist	if intestine, bowel, or colon

DEF: Entanglement of bowel; causes obstruction; may compromise bowel circulation.

✓5th **560.3 Impaction of intestine**

560.30 Impaction of intestine, unspecified

Impaction of colon

560.31 Gallstone ileus

Obstruction of intestine by gallstone

560.39 Other

Concretion of intestine
Enterolith
Fecal impaction

AHA: 4Q, '98, 38

✓5th **560.8 Other specified intestinal obstruction**

560.81 Intestinal or peritoneal adhesions with obstruction (postoperative) (postinfection)

EXCLUDES *adhesions without obstruction (568.0)*

AHA: 4Q, '95, 55; 3Q, '95, 6; N-D, '87, 9

DEF: Obstruction of peritoneum or intestine due to abnormal union of tissues.

560.89 Other

Acute pseudo-obstruction of intestine
Mural thickening causing obstruction

EXCLUDES *ischemic stricture of intestine (557.1)*

AHA: 2Q, '97, 3; 1Q, '88, 6

560.9 Unspecified intestinal obstruction

Enterostenosis

Obstruction Occlusion Stenosis Stricture	of intestine or colon

EXCLUDES *congenital stricture or stenosis of intestine (751.1-751.2)*

Digestive System

557–560.9

Volvulus and Diverticulitis

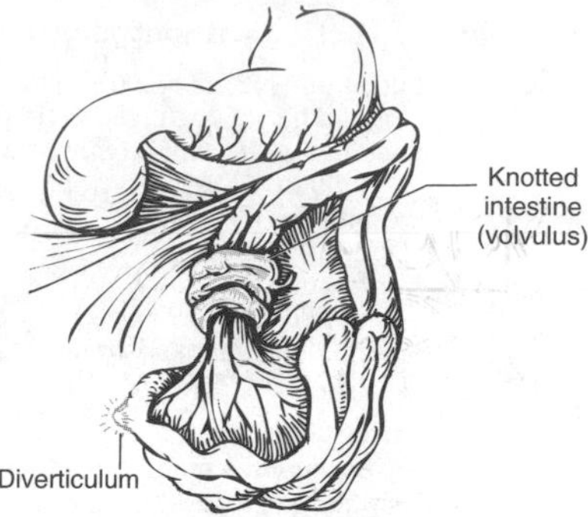

562 Diverticula of intestine

Use additional code to identify any associated:
peritonitis (567.0-567.9)

EXCLUDES *congenital diverticulum of colon (751.5)*
diverticulum of appendix (543.9)
Meckel's diverticulum (751.0)

AHA: 4Q, '91, 25; J-F, '85, 1

562.0 Small intestine

562.00 Diverticulosis of small intestine (without mention of hemorrhage)

Diverticulosis:
duodenum, ileum, jejunum } without mention of diverticulitis

DEF: Saclike herniations of mucous lining of small intestine.

562.01 Diverticulitis of small intestine (without mention of hemorrhage)

Diverticulitis (with diverticulosis):
duodenum
ileum
jejunum
small intestine

DEF: Inflamed saclike herniations of mucous lining of small intestine

562.02 Diverticulosis of small intestine with hemorrhage

562.03 Diverticulitis of small intestine with hemorrhage

562.1 Colon

562.10 Diverticulosis of colon (without mention of hemorrhage)

Diverticulosis:
NOS
intestine (large)
Diverticular disease (colon)
} without metion of diverticulitis

AHA: 3Q, '05, 17; 3Q, '02, 15; 4Q, '90, 21; J-F, '85, 5

DEF: Saclike herniations of mucous lining of large intestine.

562.11 Diverticulitis of colon (without mention of hemorrhage)

Diverticulitis (with diverticulosis):
NOS
colon
intestine (large)

AHA: 1Q, '96, 14; J-F, '85, 5

DEF: Inflamed saclike herniations of mucosal lining of large intestine.

562.12 Diverticulosis of colon with hemorrhage

562.13 Diverticulitis of colon with hemorrhage

564 Functional digestive disorders, not elsewhere classified

EXCLUDES *functional disorders of stomach (536.0-536.9)*
those specified as psychogenic (306.4)

564.0 Constipation

AHA: 4Q, '01, 45

564.00 Constipation, unspecified

564.01 Slow transit constipation

DEF: Delay in the transit of fecal material through the colon secondary to smooth muscle dysfunction or decreased peristaltic contractions along the colon: also called colonic inertia or delayed transit.

564.02 Outlet dysfunction constipation

DEF: Failure to relax the paradoxical contractions of the striated pelvic floor muscles during the attempted defecation.

564.09 Other constipation

564.1 Irritable bowel syndrome

Irritable colon
Spastic colon

AHA: 1Q, '88, 6

DEF: Functional gastrointestinal disorder (FGID); symptoms following meals include diarrhea, constipation, abdominal pain; other symptoms include bloating, gas, distended abdomen, nausea, vomiting, appetite loss, emotional distress, and depression.

564.2 Postgastric surgery syndromes

Dumping syndrome
Jejunal syndrome
Postgastrectomy syndrome
Postvagotomy syndrome

EXCLUDES *malnutrition following gastrointestinal surgery (579.3)*
postgastrojejunostomy ulcer (534.0-534.9)

AHA: 1Q, '95, 11

564.3 Vomiting following gastrointestinal surgery

Vomiting (bilious) following gastrointestinal surgery

564.4 Other postoperative functional disorders

Diarrhea following gastrointestinal surgery

EXCLUDES *colostomy and enterostomy complications (569.60-569.69)*

564.5 Functional diarrhea

EXCLUDES *diarrhea:*
NOS (787.91)
psychogenic (306.4)

DEF: Diarrhea with no detectable organic cause.

564.6 Anal spasm

Proctalgia fugax

564.7 Megacolon, other than Hirschsprung's

Dilatation of colon

EXCLUDES *megacolon:*
congenital [Hirschsprung's] (751.3)
toxic (556)

DEF: Enlarged colon; congenital or acquired; can occur acutely or become chronic.

564.8 Other specified functional disorders of intestine

EXCLUDES *malabsorption (579.0-579.9)*

AHA: 1Q, '88, 6

564.81 Neurogenic bowel

AHA: 1Q, '01, 12; 4Q, '98, 45

DEF: Disorder of bowel due to spinal cord lesion above conus medullaris; symptoms include precipitous micturition, nocturia, catheter intolerance, headache, sweating, nasal obstruction and spastic contractions.

564.89 Other functional disorders of intestine
Atony of colon
DEF: Absence of normal bowel tone or strength.

564.9 Unspecified functional disorder of intestine

✓4th 565 Anal fissure and fistula

565.0 Anal fissure
EXCLUDES *anal sphincter tear (healed) (non-traumatic) (old) (569.43)*
traumatic (863.89, 863.99)
DEF: Ulceration of cleft at anal mucosa; causes pain, itching, bleeding, infection, and sphincter spasm; may occur with hemorrhoids.

565.1 Anal fistula
Fistula:
anorectal
rectal
rectum to skin
EXCLUDES *fistula of rectum to internal organs–see Alphabetic Index*
ischiorectal fistula (566)
rectovaginal fistula (619.1)
AHA: 1Q, '07, 13
DEF: Abnormal opening on cutaneous surface near anus; may lack connection with rectum.

566 Abscess of anal and rectal regions
Abscess:
ischiorectal
perianal
perirectal
Cellulitis:
anal
perirectal
rectal
Ischiorectal fistula

✓4th 567 Peritonitis and retroperitoneal infections
EXCLUDES *peritonitis:*
benign paroxysmal (277.31)
pelvic, female (614.5, 614.7)
periodic familial (277.31)
puerperal (670)
with or following:
abortion (634-638 with .0, 639.0)
appendicitis (540.0-540.1)
ectopic or molar pregnancy (639.0)
DEF: Inflammation of the peritoneal cavity.

567.0 *Peritonitis in infectious diseases classified elsewhere*
Code first underlying disease
EXCLUDES *peritonitis:*
gonococcal (098.86)
syphilitic (095.2)
tuberculous (014.0)

567.1 Pneumococcal peritonitis

Anal Fistula and Abscess

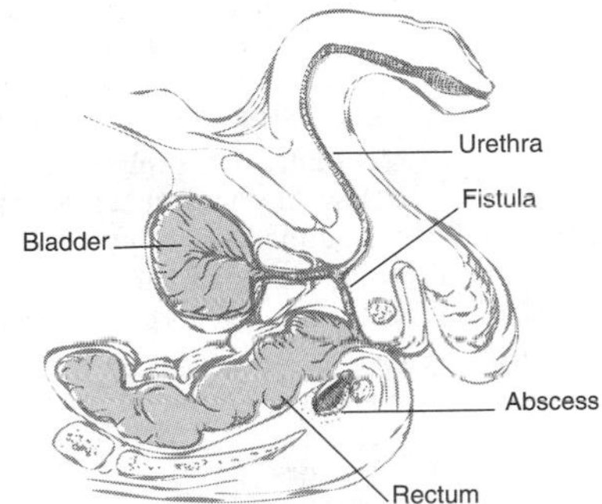

Psoas Muscle Abscess

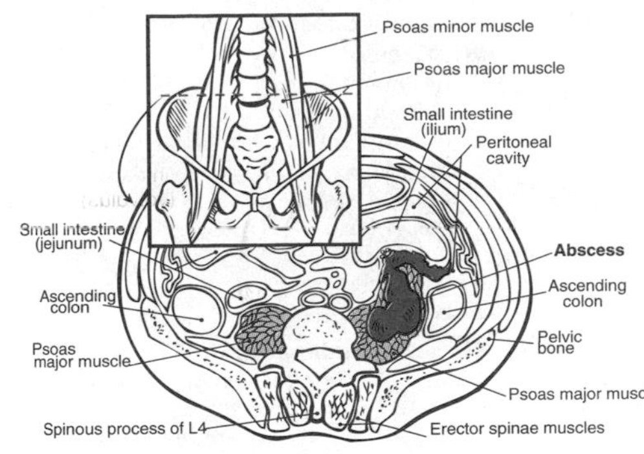

✓5th 567.2 Other suppurative peritonitis
AHA: 4Q, '05, 74; 2Q, '01, 11, 12; 3Q, '99, 9; 2Q, '98, 19

567.21 Peritonitis (acute) generalized
Pelvic peritonitis, male

567.22 Peritoneal abscess
Abscess (of):
abdominopelvic
mesenteric
omentum
peritoneum
retrocecal
subdiaphragmatic
subhepatic
subphrenic

567.23 Spontaneous bacterial peritonitis
EXCLUDES *bacterial peritonitis NOS (567.29)*

567.29 Other suppurative peritonitis
Subphrenic peritonitis

✓5th 567.3 Retroperitoneal infections
AHA: 4Q, '05, 74

567.31 Psoas muscle abscess
DEF: Infection that extends into or around the psoas muscle that connects the lumbar vertebrae to the femur.

567.38 Other retroperitoneal abscess
AHA: 4Q, '05, 77

567.39 Other retroperitoneal infections

✓5th 567.8 Other specified peritonitis
AHA: 4Q, '05, 74

567.81 Choleperitonitis
Peritonitis due to bile
DEF: Inflammation or infection due to presence of bile in the peritoneum resulting from rupture of the bile passages or gallbladder.

567.82 Sclerosing mesenteritis
Fat necrosis of peritoneum
(Idiopathic) sclerosing mesenteric fibrosis
Mesenteric lipodystrophy
Mesenteric panniculitis
Retractile mesenteritis
AHA: 4Q, '05, 77
DEF: Inflammatory processes involving the mesenteric fat; progresses to fibrosis and necrosis of tissue.

567.89 Other specified peritonitis
Chronic proliferative peritonitis
Mesenteric saponification
Peritonitis due to urine

567.9 Unspecified peritonitis
Peritonitis NOS
Peritonitis of unspecified cause
AHA: 1Q, '04, 10

✓4th **568 Other disorders of peritoneum**

568.0 Peritoneal adhesions (postoperative) (postinfection)

Adhesions (of):
abdominal (wall)
diaphragm
intestine
male pelvis
mesenteric
omentum
stomach
Adhesive bands

EXCLUDES *adhesions:*
pelvic, female (614.6)
with obstruction:
duodenum (537.3)
intestine (560.81)

AHA: 3Q, '03, 7, 11; 4Q, '95, 55; 3Q, '95, 7; S-O, '85, 11

DEF: Abnormal union of tissues in peritoneum.

✓5th **568.8 Other specified disorders of peritoneum**

568.81 Hemoperitoneum (nontraumatic)

568.82 Peritoneal effusion (chronic)

EXCLUDES *ascites NOS (789.51-789.59)*

DEF: Persistent leakage of fluid within peritoneal cavity.

568.89 Other

Peritoneal:
cyst
granuloma

568.9 Unspecified disorder of peritoneum

✓4th **569 Other disorders of intestine**

569.0 Anal and rectal polyp

Anal and rectal polyp NOS

EXCLUDES *adenomatous anal and rectal polyp (211.4)*

569.1 Rectal prolapse

Procidentia:
anus (sphincter)
rectum (sphincter)
Proctoptosis
Prolapse:
anal canal
rectal mucosa

EXCLUDES *prolapsed hemorrhoids (455.2, 455.5)*

569.2 Stenosis of rectum and anus

Stricture of anus (sphincter)

569.3 Hemorrhage of rectum and anus

EXCLUDES *gastrointestinal bleeding NOS (578.9)*
melena (578.1)

AHA: 3Q, '05, 17

Rectum and Anus

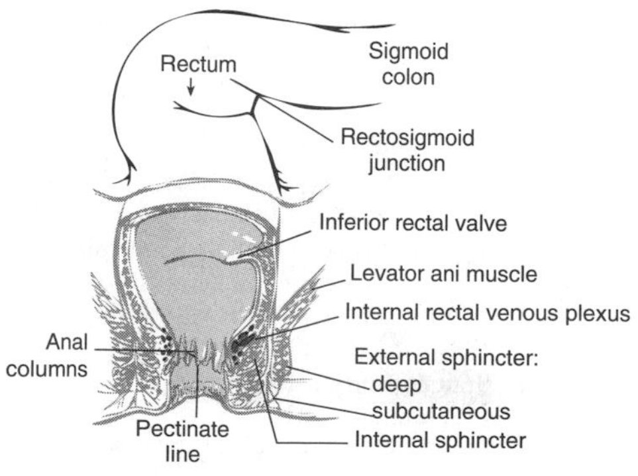

✓5th **569.4 Other specified disorders of rectum and anus**

569.41 Ulcer of anus and rectum

Solitary ulcer } of anus (sphincter) or rectum (sphincter)
Stercoral ulcer }

569.42 Anal or rectal pain

AHA: 1Q, '03, 8; 1Q, '96, 13

569.43 Anal sphincter tear (healed) (old)

Tear of anus, nontraumatic
Use additional code for any associated fecal incontinence (787.6)

EXCLUDES *anal fissure (565.0)*
anal sphincter tear (healed) (old) complicating delivery (654.8)

AHA: 4Q, '07, 88

● **569.44 Dysplasia of anus**

Anal intraepithelial neoplasia I and II (AIN I and II) (histologically confirmed)
Dysplasia of anus NOS
Mild and moderate dysplasia of anus (histologically confirmed)

EXCLUDES *abnormal results from anal cytologic examination without histologic confirmation (796.70-796.79)*
anal intraepithelial neoplasia III (230.5, 230.6)
carcinoma in situ of anus (230.5, 230.6)
HGSIL of anus (796.74)
severe dysplasia of anus (230.5, 230.6)

569.49 Other

Granuloma } of rectum (sphincter)
Rupture }
Hypertrophy of anal papillae
Proctitis NOS

EXCLUDES *fistula of rectum to:*
internal organs—see Alphabetic Index
skin (565.1)
hemorrhoids (455.0-455.9)
incontinence of sphincter ani (787.6)

569.5 Abscess of intestine

EXCLUDES *appendiceal abscess (540.1)*

✓5th **569.6 Colostomy and enterostomy complications**

AHA: 4Q, '95, 58

DEF: Complication in a surgically created opening, from intestine to surface skin.

569.60 Colostomy and enterostomy complication, unspecified

569.61 Infection of colostomy or enterostomy

Use additional code to identify organism (041.00-041.9)
Use additional code to specify type of infection, such as:
abscess or cellulitis of abdomen (682.2)
septicemia (038.0-038.9)

569.62 Mechanical complication of colostomy and enterostomy

Malfunction of colostomy and enterostomy

AHA: 2Q, '05, 11 ; 1Q, '03, 10; 4Q, '98, 44

569.69 Other complication

Fistula
Hernia
Prolapse

AHA: 3Q, '98, 16

✓5th **569.8 Other specified disorders of intestine**

AHA: 4Q, '91, 25

569.81 Fistula of intestine, excluding rectum and anus

Fistula:
abdominal wall
enterocolic
enteroenteric
ileorectal

EXCLUDES *fistula of intestine to internal organs–see Alphabetic Index*
persistent postoperative fistula (998.6)

AHA: 3Q, '99, 8

569.82 Ulceration of intestine

Primary ulcer of intestine
Ulceration of colon

EXCLUDES *that with perforation (569.83)*

569.83 Perforation of intestine

569.84 Angiodysplasia of intestine (without mention of hemorrhage)

AHA: 3Q, '96, 10; 4Q, '90, 4; 4Q, '90, 21

DEF: Small vascular abnormalities of the intestinal tract without bleeding problems.

569.85 Angiodysplasia of intestine with hemorrhage

AHA: 3Q, '96, 9

DEF: Small vascular abnormalities of the intestinal tract with bleeding problems.

569.86 Dieulafoy lesion (hemorrhagic) of intestine

AHA: 4Q, '02, 60-61

569.89 Other

Enteroptosis
Granuloma } of intestine
Prolapse }
Pericolitis
Perisigmoiditis
Visceroptosis

EXCLUDES *gangrene of intestine, mesentery, or omentum (557.0)*
hemorrhage of intestine NOS (578.9)
obstruction of intestine (560.0-560.9)

AHA: 3Q, '96, 9

569.9 Unspecified disorder of intestine

OTHER DISEASES OF DIGESTIVE SYSTEM (570-579)

570 Acute and subacute necrosis of liver

Acute hepatic failure
Acute or subacute hepatitis, not specified as infective
Necrosis of liver (acute) (diffuse) (massive) (subacute)
Parenchymatous degeneration of liver
Yellow atrophy (liver) (acute) (subacute)

EXCLUDES *icterus gravis of newborn (773.0-773.2)*
serum hepatitis (070.2-070.3)
that with:
abortion (634-638 with .7, 639.8)
ectopic or molar pregnancy (639.8)
pregnancy, childbirth, or the puerperium (646.7)
viral hepatitis (070.0-070.9)

AHA: 2Q, '05, 9; 1Q, '00, 22

✓4th **571 Chronic liver disease and cirrhosis**

571.0 Alcoholic fatty liver A

Liver

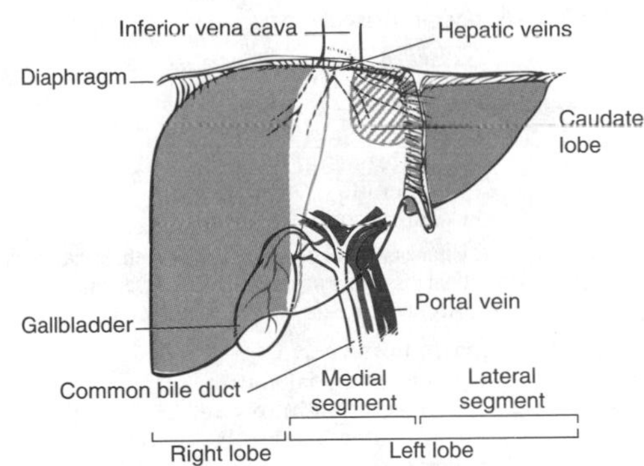

571.1 Acute alcoholic hepatitis A

Acute alcoholic liver disease

AHA: 2Q, '02, 4

571.2 Alcoholic cirrhosis of liver A

Florid cirrhosis
Laennec's cirrhosis (alcoholic)

AHA: 3Q, '07, 7; 2Q, '07, 6; 2Q, '02, 4; 1Q, '02, 3; N-D, '85, 14

DEF: Fibrosis and dysfunction, of liver; due to alcoholic liver disease.

571.3 Alcoholic liver damage, unspecified A

✓5th **571.4 Chronic hepatitis**

EXCLUDES *viral hepatitis (acute) (chronic) (070.0-070.9)*

571.40 Chronic hepatitis, unspecified

571.41 Chronic persistent hepatitis

● **571.42 Autoimmune hepatitis**

571.49 Other

Chronic hepatitis:
active
aggressive
Recurrent hepatitis

AHA: 3Q, '99, 19; N-D, '85, 14

571.5 Cirrhosis of liver without mention of alcohol

Cirrhosis of liver:
NOS
cryptogenic
macronodular
micronodular
posthepatitic
postnecrotic
Healed yellow atrophy (liver)
Portal cirrhosis

▶Code first, if applicable, viral hepatitis (acute) (chronic) (070.0-070.9)◀

AHA: 3Q, '07, 7; 2Q, '07, 5

DEF: Fibrosis and dysfunction of liver; not alcohol related.

571.6 Biliary cirrhosis

Chronic nonsuppurative destructive cholangitis
Cirrhosis:
cholangitic
cholestatic

571.8 Other chronic nonalcoholic liver disease

Chronic yellow atrophy (liver)
Fatty liver, without mention of alcohol

AHA: 2Q, '96, 12

571.9 Unspecified chronic liver disease without mention of alcohol

✓4th 572 Liver abscess and sequelae of chronic liver disease

572.0 Abscess of liver

EXCLUDES *amebic liver abscess (006.3)*

572.1 Portal pyemia

Phlebitis of portal vein
Portal thrombophlebitis
Pylephlebitis
Pylethrombophlebitis

DEF: Inflammation of portal vein or branches; may be due to intestinal disease; symptoms include fever, chills, jaundice, sweating, and abscess in various body parts.

572.2 Hepatic coma

Hepatic encephalopathy
Hepatocerebral intoxication
Portal-systemic encephalopathy

EXCLUDES *hepatic coma associated with viral hepatitis–see category 070*

AHA: 2Q, '07, 5; 2Q, '05, 9; 1Q, '02, 3; 3Q, '95, 14

572.3 Portal hypertension

AHA: 3Q, '05, 15

DEF: Abnormally high blood pressure in the portal vein.

572.4 Hepatorenal syndrome

EXCLUDES *that following delivery (674.8)*

AHA: 3Q, '93, 15

DEF: Hepatic and renal failure characterized by cirrhosis with ascites or obstructive jaundice, oliguria, and low sodium concentration.

572.8 Other sequelae of chronic liver disease

✓4th 573 Other disorders of liver

EXCLUDES *amyloid or lardaceous degeneration of liver (277.39)*
congenital cystic disease of liver (751.62)
glycogen infiltration of liver (271.0)
hepatomegaly NOS (789.1)
portal vein obstruction (452)

573.0 Chronic passive congestion of liver

DEF: Blood accumulation in liver tissue.

573.1 Hepatitis in viral diseases classified elsewhere

Code first underlying disease as:
Coxsackie virus disease (074.8)
cytomegalic inclusion virus disease (078.5)
infectious mononucleosis (075)

EXCLUDES *hepatitis (in):*
mumps (072.71)
viral (070.0-070.9)
yellow fever (060.0-060.9)

573.2 Hepatitis in other infectious diseases classified elsewhere

Code first underlying disease, as:
malaria (084.9)

EXCLUDES *hepatitis in:*
late syphilis (095.3)
secondary syphilis (091.62)
toxoplasmosis (130.5)

Gallbladder and Bile Ducts

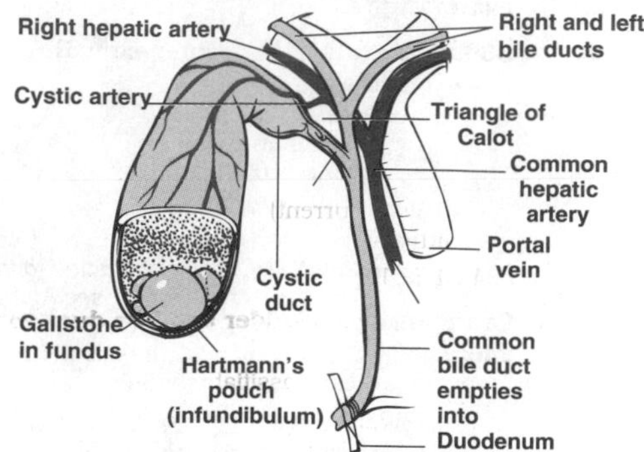

573.3 Hepatitis, unspecified

Toxic (noninfectious) hepatitis
Use additional E code to identify cause

AHA: 3Q, '98, 3, 4; 4Q, '90, 26

573.4 Hepatic infarction

573.8 Other specified disorders of liver

Hepatoptosis

573.9 Unspecified disorder of liver

✓4th 574 Cholelithiasis

The following fifth-digit subclassification is for use with category 574:
0 without mention of obstruction
1 with obstruction

✓5th 574.0 Calculus of gallbladder with acute cholecystitis
[0-1]

Billary calculus, Calculus of cystic duct, Cholelithiasis } with acute cholecystitis

Any condition classifiable to 574.2 with acute cholecystitis

AHA: 4Q, '96, 32

§ **✓5th 574.1 Calculus of gallbladder with other cholecystitis**
[0-1]

Billary calculus, Calculus of cystic duct, Cholelithiasis } with cholecystitis

Cholecystitis with cholelithiasis NOS
Any condition classifiable to 574.2 with cholecystitis (chronic)

AHA: 3Q, '99, 9; 4Q, '96, 32, 69; 2Q, '96, 13; **For code 574.10:** 1Q, '03, 5

§ **✓5th 574.2 Calculus of gallbladder without mention of cholecystitis**
[0-1]

Biliary:
calculus NOS
colic NOS
Calculus of cystic duct
Cholelithiasis NOS
Colic (recurrent) of gallbladder
Gallstone (impacted)

AHA: For code 574.20: 1Q, '88, 14

§ **✓5th 574.3 Calculus of bile duct with acute cholecystitis**
[0-1]

Calculus of bile duct (any), Choledocholithiasis } with acute cholecystitis

Any condition classifiable to 574.5 with acute cholecystitis

§ **✓5th 574.4 Calculus of bile duct with other cholecystitis**
[0-1]

Calculus of bile duct (any), Choledocholithiasis } with cholecystitis (chronic)

Any condition classifiable to 574.5 with cholecystitis (chronic)

§ Requires fifth-digit. Valid digits are in [brackets] under each code. See category 574 for codes and definitions.

§ ✓5th **574.5 Calculus of bile duct without mention of cholecystitis**
[0-1]
Calculus of:
bile duct [any]
common duct
hepatic duct
Choledocholithiasis
Hepatic:
colic (recurrent)
lithiasis
AHA: 3Q, '94, 11

§ ✓5th **574.6 Calculus of gallbladder and bile duct with acute cholecystitis**
[0-1]
Any condition classifiable to 574.0 and 574.3
AHA: 4Q, '96, 32

§ ✓5th **574.7 Calculus of gallbladder and bile duct with other cholecystitis**
[0-1]
Any condition classifiable to 574.1 and 574.4
AHA: 4Q, '96, 32

§ ✓5th **574.8 Calculus of gallbladder and bile duct with acute and chronic cholecystitis**
[0-1]
Any condition classifiable to 574.6 and 574.7
AHA: 4Q, '96, 32

§ ✓5th **574.9 Calculus of gallbladder and bile duct without cholecystitis**
[0-1]
Any condition classifiable to 574.2 and 574.5
AHA: 4Q, '96, 32

✓4th **575 Other disorders of gallbladder**

575.0 Acute cholecystitis

Abscess of gallbladder
Angiocholecystitis
Cholecystitis:
emphysematous (acute)
gangrenous
suppurative
Empyema of gallbladder
Gangrene of gallbladder
} without mention of calculus

EXCLUDES *that with:*
acute and chronic cholecystitis (575.12)
choledocholithiasis (574.3)
choledocholithiasis and cholelithiasis (574.6)
cholelithiasis (574.0)

AHA: 3Q, '91, 17

✓5th **575.1 Other cholecystitis**
Cholecystitis:
NOS
chronic
} without mention of calculus

EXCLUDES *that with:*
choledocholithiasis (574.4)
choledocholithiasis and cholelithiasis (574.8)
cholelithiasis (574.1)

AHA: 4Q, '96, 32

575.10 Cholecystitis, unspecified
Cholecystitis NOS

575.11 Chronic cholecystitis

575.12 Acute and chronic cholecystitis
AHA: 4Q, '97, 52; 4Q, '96, 32

575.2 Obstruction of gallbladder
Occlusion
Stenosis
Stricture
} of cystic duct or gallbladder without mention of calculus

EXCLUDES *that with calculus (574.0-574.2 with fifth-digit 1)*

575.3 Hydrops of gallbladder
Mucocele of gallbladder
AHA: 2Q, '89, 13
DEF: Serous fluid accumulation in bladder.

575.4 Perforation of gallbladder
Rupture of cystic duct or gallbladder

575.5 Fistula of gallbladder
Fistula:
cholecystoduodenal
cholecystoenteric

575.6 Cholesterolosis of gallbladder
Strawberry gallbladder
AHA: 4Q, '90, 17
DEF: Cholesterol deposits in gallbladder tissue.

575.8 Other specified disorders of gallbladder
Adhesions
Atrophy
Cyst
Hypertrophy
Nonfunctioning
Ulcer
} of cystic duct or gallbladder

Biliary dyskinesia

EXCLUDES *Hartmann's pouch of intestine (V44.3)*
nonvisualization of gallbladder (793.3)

AHA: 4Q, '90, 26; 2Q, '89, 13

575.9 Unspecified disorder of gallbladder

✓4th **576 Other disorders of biliary tract**

EXCLUDES *that involving the:*
cystic duct (575.0-575.9)
gallbladder (575.0-575.9)

576.0 Postcholecystectomy syndrome
AHA: 1Q, '88, 10
DEF: Jaundice or abdominal pain following cholecystectomy.

576.1 Cholangitis
Cholangitis:
NOS
acute
ascending
chronic
primary
Cholangitis:
recurrent
sclerosing
secondary
stenosing
suppurative
AHA: 2Q, '99, 13

576.2 Obstruction of bile duct
Occlusion
Stenosis
Stricture
} of bile duct, except cystic duct, without mention of calculus

EXCLUDES *congenital (751.61)*
that with calculus (574.3-574.5 with fifth-digit 1)

AHA: 3Q, '03, 17-18; 1Q, '01, 8; 2Q, '99, 13

576.3 Perforation of bile duct
Rupture of bile duct, except cystic duct

576.4 Fistula of bile duct
Choledochoduodenal fistula

576.5 Spasm of sphincter of Oddi

576.8 Other specified disorders of biliary tract
Adehesions
Atrophy
Cyst
Hypertrophy
Nonfunctioning
Ulcer
} of bile duct (any)

EXCLUDES *congenital choledochal cyst (751.69)*

AHA: 3Q, '03, 17; 2Q, '99, 14

576.9 Unspecified disorder of biliary tract

§ Requires fifth-digit. Valid digits are in [brackets] under each code. See category 574 for codes and definitions.

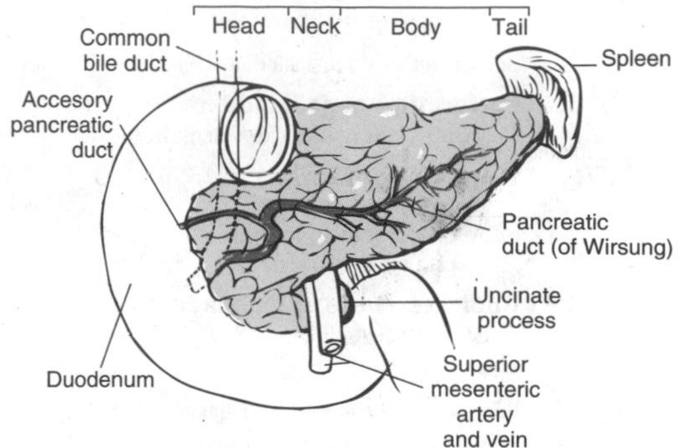

577 Diseases of pancreas

577.0 Acute pancreatitis
Abscess of pancreas
Necrosis of pancreas:
acute
infective
Pancreatitis:
NOS
acute (recurrent)
apoplectic
hemorrhagic
subacute
suppurative

EXCLUDES *mumps pancreatitis (072.3)*

AHA: 3Q, '99, 9; 2Q, '98, 19; 2Q, '96, 13; 2Q, '89, 9

577.1 Chronic pancreatitis
Chronic pancreatitis:
NOS
infectious
interstitial
Pancreatitis:
painless
recurrent
relapsing

AHA: 1Q, '01, 8; 2Q, '96, 13; 3Q, '94, 11

577.2 Cyst and pseudocyst of pancreas

577.8 Other specified diseases of pancreas
Atrophy, Calculus, Cirrhosis, Fibrosis } of pancreas
Pancreatic:
infantilism
necrosis:
NOS
aseptic
fat
Pancreatolithiasis

EXCLUDES *fibrocystic disease of pancreas (277.00-277.09)*
islet cell tumor of pancreas (211.7)
pancreatic steatorrhea (579.4)

AHA: 1Q, '01, 8

577.9 Unspecified disease of pancreas

578 Gastrointestinal hemorrhage

EXCLUDES *that with mention of:*
angiodysplasia of stomach and duodenum (537.83)
angiodysplasia of intestine (569.85)
diverticulitis, intestine:
large (562.13)
small (562.03)
diverticulosis, intestine:
large (562.12)
small (562.02)
gastritis and duodenitis (535.0-535.6)
ulcer:
duodenal, gastric, gastrojejunal or peptic (531.00-534.91)

AHA: 2Q, '92, 9; 4Q, '90, 20

578.0 Hematemesis
Vomiting of blood

AHA: 2Q, '02, 4

578.1 Blood in stool
Melena

EXCLUDES *melena of the newborn (772.4, 777.3)*
occult blood (792.1)

AHA: 2Q, '06, 17; 2Q, '92, 8

578.9 Hemorrhage of gastrointestinal tract, unspecified
Gastric hemorrhage
Intestinal hemorrhage

AHA: 4Q, '06, 91; 3Q, '05, 17; N-D, '86, 9

579 Intestinal malabsorption

579.0 Celiac disease
Celiac:
crisis
infantilism
rickets
Gee (-Herter) disease
Gluten enteropathy
Idiopathic steatorrhea
Nontropical sprue

DEF: Malabsorption syndrome due to gluten consumption; symptoms include fetid, bulky, frothy, oily stools; distended abdomen, gas, weight loss, asthenia, electrolyte depletion and vitamin B, D and K deficiency.

579.1 Tropical sprue
Sprue:
NOS
tropical
Tropical steatorrhea

DEF: Diarrhea, occurs in tropics; may be due to enteric infection and malnutrition.

579.2 Blind loop syndrome
Postoperative blind loop syndrome

DEF: Obstruction or impaired passage in small intestine due to alterations, from strictures or surgery; causes stasis, abnormal bacterial flora, diarrhea, weight loss, multiple vitamin deficiency, and megaloblastic anemia.

579.3 Other and unspecified postsurgical nonabsorption
Hypoglycemia, Malnutrition } following gastrointestinal surgery

AHA: 4Q, '03, 104

579.4 Pancreatic steatorrhea

DEF: Excess fat in feces due to absence of pancreatic juice in intestine.

579.8 Other specified intestinal malabsorption
Enteropathy:
exudative
protein-losing
Steatorrhea (chronic)

AHA: 1Q, '88, 6

579.9 Unspecified intestinal malabsorption
Malabsorption syndrome NOS

AHA: 4Q, '04, 59

10. DISEASES OF THE GENITOURINARY SYSTEM (580-629)

NEPHRITIS, NEPHROTIC SYNDROME, AND NEPHROSIS (580-589)

EXCLUDES *hypertensive chronic kidney disease (403.00-403.91, 404.00-404.93)*

✓4th **580 Acute glomerulonephritis**

INCLUDES acute nephritis

DEF: Acute, severe inflammation in tuft of capillaries that filter the kidneys.

580.0 With lesion of proliferative glomerulonephritis
Acute (diffuse) proliferative glomerulonephritis
Acute poststreptococcal glomerulonephritis

580.4 With lesion of rapidly progressive glomerulonephritis
Acute nephritis with lesion of necrotizing glomerulitis

DEF: Acute glomerulonephritis; progresses to ESRD with diffuse epithelial proliferation.

✓5th **580.8 With other specified pathological lesion in kidney**

580.81 Acute glomerulonephritis in diseases classified elsewhere
Code first underlying disease, as:
infectious hepatitis (070.0-070.9)
mumps (072.79)
subacute bacterial endocarditis (421.0)
typhoid fever (002.0)

580.89 Other
Glomerulonephritis, acute, with lesion of:
exudative nephritis
interstitial (diffuse) (focal) nephritis

580.9 Acute glomerulonephritis with unspecified pathological lesion in kidney
Glomerulonephritis
NOS
hemorrhagic
Nephritis
Nephropathy
} specified as acute

✓4th **581 Nephrotic syndrome**

DEF: Disease process marked by symptoms such as; extensive edema, notable proteinuria, hypoalbuminemia, and susceptibility to intercurrent infections.

581.0 With lesion of proliferative glomerulonephritis

581.1 With lesion of membranous glomerulonephritis
Epimembranous nephritis
Idiopathic membranous glomerular disease
Nephrotic syndrome with lesion of:
focal glomerulosclerosis
sclerosing membranous glomerulonephritis
segmental hyalinosis

581.2 With lesion of membranoproliferative glomerulonephritis
Nephrotic syndrome with lesion (of):
endothelial
hypocomplementemic persistent
lobular
mesangiocapillary
mixed membranous and proliferative
} glomerulonephritis

DEF: Glomerulonephritis combined with clinical features of nephrotic syndrome; characterized by uneven thickening of glomerular capillary walls and mesangial cell increase; slowly progresses to ESRD.

581.3 With lesion of minimal change glomerulonephritis
Foot process disease
Lipoid nephrosis
Minimal change:
glomerular disease
glomerulitis
nephrotic syndrome

AHA: 1Q, '07, 23

✓4th **581.8 With other specified pathological lesion in kidney**

581.81 Nephrotic syndrome in diseases classified elsewhere
Code first underlying disease, as:
amyloidosis (277.30-277.39)
diabetes mellitus ▶(249.4, 250.4)◀
tes mellitus (250.4)
malaria (084.9)
polyarteritis (446.0)
systemic lupus erythematosus (710.0)

EXCLUDES *nephrosis in epidemic hemorrhagic fever (078.6)*

AHA: 3Q, '91, 8, 12; S-O, '85, 3

581.89 Other
Glomerulonephritis with edema and lesion of:
exudative nephritis
interstitial (diffuse) (focal) nephritis

581.9 Nephrotic syndrome with unspecified pathological lesion in kidney
Glomerulonephritis with edema NOS
Nephritis:
nephrotic NOS
with edema NOS
Nephrosis NOS
Renal disease with edema NOS

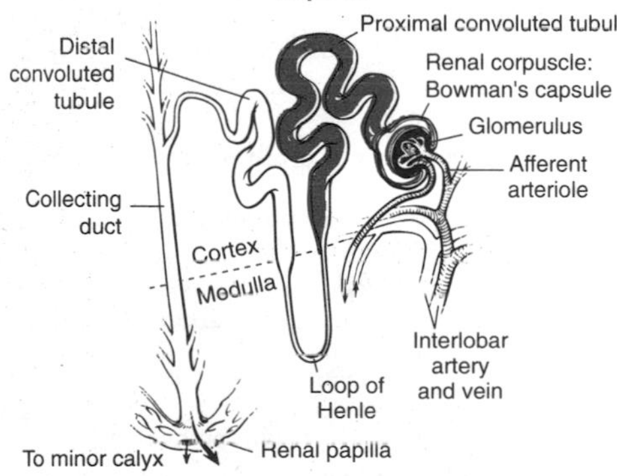

4th 582 Chronic glomerulonephritis

INCLUDES chronic nephritis

DEF: Slow progressive type of nephritis characterized by inflammation of the capillary loops in the glomeruli of the kidney, which leads to renal failure.

582.0 With lesion of proliferative glomerulonephritis
Chronic (diffuse) proliferative glomerulonephritis

582.1 With lesion of membranous glomerulonephritis
Chronic glomerulonephritis:
membranous
sclerosing
Focal glomerulosclerosis
Segmental hyalinosis

AHA: S-O, '84, 16

582.2 With lesion of membranoproliferative glomerulonephritis
Chronic glomerulonephritis:
endothelial
hypocomplementemic persistent
lobular
membranoproliferative
mesangiocapillary
mixed membranous and proliferative

DEF: Chronic glomerulonephritis with mesangial cell proliferation.

582.4 With lesion of rapidly progressive glomerulonephritis
Chronic nephritis with lesion of necrotizing glomerulitis

DEF: Chronic glomerulonephritis rapidly progresses to ESRD; marked by diffuse epithelial proliferation.

5th 582.8 With other specified pathological lesion in kidney

582.81 Chronic glomerulonephritis in diseases classified elsewhere
Code first underlying disease, as:
amyloidosis (277.30-277.39)
systemic lupus erythematosus (710.0)

582.89 Other
Chronic glomerulonephritis with lesion of:
exudative nephritis
interstitial (diffuse) (focal) nephritis

582.9 Chronic glomerulonephritis with unspecified pathological lesion in kidney
Glomerulonephritis:
NOS
hemorrhagic
Nephritis
Nephropathy
} specified as chronic

AHA: 2Q, '01, 12

4th 583 Nephritis and nephropathy, not specified as acute or chronic

INCLUDES "renal disease" so stated, not specified as acute or chronic but with stated pathology or cause

583.0 With lesion of proliferative glomerulonephritis
Proliferative:
glomerulonephritis (diffuse) NOS
nephritis NOS
nephropathy NOS

583.1 With lesion of membranous glomerulonephritis
Membranous:
glomerulonephritis NOS
nephritis NOS
Membranous nephropathy NOS

DEF: Kidney inflammation or dysfunction with deposits on glomerular capillary basement membranes.

583.2 With lesion of membranoproliferative glomerulonephritis
Membranoproliferative:
glomerulonephritis NOS
nephritis NOS
nephropathy NOS
Nephritis NOS, with lesion of:
hypocomplementemic persistent
lobular
mesangiocapillary
mixed membranous and proliferative
} glomerulonephritis

DEF: Kidney inflammation or dysfunction with mesangial cell proliferation.

583.4 With lesion of rapidly progressive glomerulonephritis
Necrotizing or rapidly progressive:
glomerulitis NOS
glomerulonephritis NOS
nephritis NOS
nephropathy NOS
Nephritis, unspecified, with lesion of necrotizing glomerulitis

DEF: Kidney inflammation or dysfunction; rapidly progresses to ESRD marked by diffuse epithelial proliferation.

583.6 With lesion of renal cortical necrosis
Nephritis, NOS
Nephropathy NS
} with (renal) cortical necrosis

Renal cortical necrosis NOS

583.7 With lesion of renal medullary necrosis
Nephritis, NOS
Nephropathy NOS
} with (renal) medullary [papillary] necrosis

5th 583.8 With other specified pathological lesion in kidney

583.81 Nephritis and nephropathy, not specified as acute or chronic, in diseases classified elsewhere
Code first underlying disease, as:
amyloidosis (277.30-277.39)
diabetes mellitus ►(249.4, 250.4)◄
gonococcal infection (098.19)
Goodpasture's syndrome (446.21)
systemic lupus erythematosus (710.0)
tuberculosis (016.0)

EXCLUDES *gouty nephropathy (274.10)*
syphilitic nephritis (095.4)

AHA: 2Q, '03, 7; 3Q, '91, 8; S-O, '85, 3

583.89 Other
Glomerulitis
Glomerulonephritis
Nephritis
Nephropathy
Renal disease
} with lesions of: exudative nephritis interstitial nephritis

583.9 With unspecified pathological lesion in kidney
Glomerulitis
Glomerulonephritis
Nephritis
Nephropathy
} NOS

EXCLUDES *nephropathy complicating pregnancy, labor, or the puerperium (642.0-642.9, 646.2)*
renal disease NOS with no stated cause (593.9)

4th 584 Acute renal failure

EXCLUDES *following labor and delivery (669.3)*
posttraumatic (958.5)
that complicating:
abortion (634-638 with .3, 639.3)
ectopic or molar pregnancy (639.3)

AHA: 1Q, '93, 18; 2Q, '92, 5; 4Q, '92, 22

DEF: State resulting from increasing urea and related substances from the blood (azotemia), often with urine output of less than 500 ml per day.

584.5 With lesion of tubular necrosis
Lower nephron nephrosis
Renal failure with (acute) tubular necrosis
Tubular necrosis:
NOS
acute

DEF: Acute decline in kidney efficiency with destruction of tubules.

584.6 With lesion of renal cortical necrosis

DEF: Acute decline in kidney efficiency with destruction of renal tissues that filter blood.

584.7 With lesion of renal medullary [papillary] necrosis
Necrotizing renal papillitis

DEF: Acute decline in kidney efficiency with destruction of renal tissues that collect urine.

584.8 With other specified pathological lesion in kidney

AHA: N-D, '85, 1

584.9 Acute renal failure, unspecified
▶Acute kidney injury (nontraumatic)◀

EXCLUDES ▶*traumatic kidney injury (866.00-866.13)*◀

AHA: 4Q, '07, 97; 2Q, '05, 18; 2Q, '03, 7; 1Q, '03, 22; 3Q, '02, 21, 28; 2Q, '01, 14; 1Q, '00, 22; 3Q, '96, 9; 4Q, '88, 1

4th 585 Chronic kidney disease [CKD]
Chronic uremia

Code first hypertensive chronic kidney disease, if applicable, (403.00-403.91, 404.00-404.93)

Use additional code to identify kidney transplant status, if applicable (V42.0)

Use additional code to identify manifestation as:
uremic:
neuropathy (357.4)
pericarditis (420.0)

AHA: 4Q, '06, 84-86; 4Q, '05, 68, 77; 1Q, '04, 5; 4Q, '03, 61, 111; 2Q, '03, 7; 2Q, '01, 12, 13; 1Q, '01, 3; 4Q, '98, 55; 3Q, '98, 6, 7; 2Q, '98, 20; 3Q, '96, 9; 1Q, '93, 18; 3Q, '91, 8; 4Q, '89, 1; N-D, '85, 15; S-O, '84, 3

585.1 Chronic kidney disease, Stage I

DEF: Some kidney damage; normal or slightly increased GFR (> 90).

585.2 Chronic kidney disease, Stage II (mild)

DEF: Kidney damage with mild decrease in GFR (60–89).

585.3 Chronic kidney disease, Stage III (moderate)

AHA: 4Q, '05, 69

DEF: Kidney damage with moderate decrease in GFR (30–59).

585.4 Chronic kidney disease, Stage IV (severe)

DEF: Kidney damage with severe decrease in GFR (15–29).

585.5 Chronic kidney disease, Stage V

EXCLUDES *chronic kidney disease, stage V requiring chronic dialysis (585.6)*

DEF: Kidney failure with GFR value of less than 15.

585.6 End stage renal disease
Chronic kidney disease requiring chronic dialysis

DEF: Federal government indicator of a stage V CKD patient undergoing treatment by dialysis or transplantation.

AHA: ▶1Q, '08, 7;◀ 4Q, '07, 86; 3Q, '07, 5, 9; 4Q, '06, 136; 4Q, '05, 79

585.9 Chronic kidney disease, unspecified
Chronic renal disease
Chronic renal failure NOS
Chronic renal insufficiency

AHA: ▶1Q, '08, 10;◀ 2Q, '07, 3; 4Q, '06, 86; 4Q, '05, 79

586 Renal failure, unspecified
Uremia NOS

EXCLUDES *following labor and delivery (669.3)*
posttraumatic renal failure (958.5)
that complicating:
abortion (634-638 with .3, 639.3)
ectopic or molar pregnancy (639.3)
uremia:
extrarenal (788.9)
prerenal (788.9)

AHA: 3Q, '98, 6; 1Q, '93, 18; 1Q, '88, 3

DEF: Renal failure: kidney functions cease; malfunction may be due to inability to excrete metabolized substances or retain level of electrolytes.

DEF: Uremia: excess urea, creatinine and other nitrogenous products of protein and amino acid metabolism in blood due to reduced excretory function in bilateral kidney disease; also called azotemia.

587 Renal sclerosis, unspecified
Atrophy of kidney
Contracted kidney
Renal:
cirrhosis
fibrosis

4th 588 Disorders resulting from impaired renal function

588.0 Renal osteodystrophy
Azotemic osteodystrophy
Phosphate-losing tubular disorders
Renal:
dwarfism
infantilism
rickets

DEF: Bone disorder that results in various bone diseases such as osteomalacia, osteoporosis or osteosclerosis; caused by impaired renal function, an abnormal level of phosphorus in the blood and impaired stimulation of the parathyroid.

588.1 Nephrogenic diabetes insipidus

EXCLUDES *diabetes insipidus NOS (253.5)*

DEF: Type of diabetes due to renal tubules inability to reabsorb water; not responsive to vasopressin; may develop into chronic renal insufficiency.

5th 588.8 Other specified disorders resulting from impaired renal function

EXCLUDES *secondary hypertension (405.0-405.9)*

588.81 Secondary hyperparathyroidism (of renal origin)
Secondary hyperparathyroidism NOS

AHA: 4Q, '04, 58-59

DEF: Parathyroid dysfunction caused by chronic renal failure; phosphate clearance is impaired, phosphate is released from bone, vitamin D is not produced, intestinal calcium absorption is low, and blood levels of calcium are lowered causing excessive production of parathyroid hormone.

588.89 Other specified disorders resulting from impaired renal function
Hypokalemic nephropathy

588.9 Unspecified disorder resulting from impaired renal function

4th 589 Small kidney of unknown cause

589.0 Unilateral small kidney

589.1 Bilateral small kidneys

589.9 Small kidney, unspecified

Genitourinary System

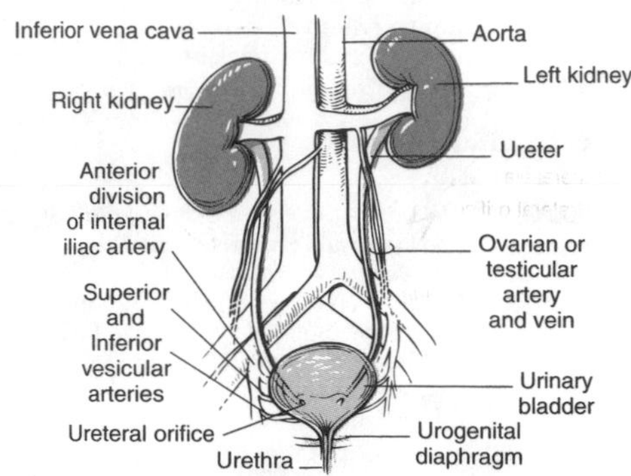

OTHER DISEASES OF URINARY SYSTEM (590-599)

✓4th **590 Infections of kidney**

Use additional code to identify organism, such as Escherichia coli [E. coli] (041.4)

✓5th **590.0 Chronic pyelonephritis**

Chronic pyelitis
Chronic pyonephrosis

Code if applicable, any casual condition first

590.00 Without lesion of renal medullary necrosis

590.01 With lesion of renal medullary necrosis

✓5th **590.1 Acute pyelonephritis**

Acute pyelitis
Acute pyonephrosis

590.10 Without lesion of renal medullary necrosis

590.11 With lesion of renal medullary necrosis

590.2 Renal and perinephric abscess

Abscess:
kidney
nephritic
perirenal
Carbuncle of kidney

590.3 Pyeloureteritis cystica

Infection of renal pelvis and ureter
Ureteritis cystica

DEF: Inflammation and formation of submucosal cysts in the kidney, pelvis, and ureter.

✓5th **590.8 Other pyelonephritis or pyonephrosis, not specified as acute or chronic**

590.80 Pyelonephritis, unspecified

Pyelitis NOS
Pyelonephritis NOS

AHA: 1Q, '98, 10; 4Q, '97, 40

590.81 Pyelitis or pyelonephritis in diseases classified elsewhere

Code first underlying disease, as:
tuberculosis (016.0)

590.9 Infection of kidney, unspecified

EXCLUDES *urinary tract infection NOS (599.0)*

591 Hydronephrosis

Hydrocalycosis
Hydronephrosis
Hydroureteronephrosis

EXCLUDES *congenital hydronephrosis (753.29)*
hydroureter (593.5)

AHA: 2Q, '98, 9

DEF: Distention of kidney and pelvis, with urine build-up due to ureteral obstruction; pyonephrosis may result.

✓4th **592 Calculus of kidney and ureter**

EXCLUDES *nephrocalcinosis (275.4)*

592.0 Calculus of kidney

Nephrolithiasis NOS
Renal calculus or stone
Staghorn calculus
Stone in kidney

EXCLUDES *uric acid nephrolithiasis (274.11)*

AHA: 1Q, '00, 4

592.1 Calculus of ureter

Ureteric stone
Ureterolithiasis

AHA: 2Q, '98, 9; 1Q, '98, 10; 1Q, '91, 11

592.9 Urinary calculus, unspecified

AHA: 1Q, '98, 10; 4Q, '97, 40

✓4th **593 Other disorders of kidney and ureter**

593.0 Nephroptosis

Floating kidney
Mobile kidney

593.1 Hypertrophy of kidney

593.2 Cyst of kidney, acquired

Cyst (multiple) (solitary) of kidney, not congenital
Peripelvic (lymphatic) cyst

EXCLUDES *calyceal or pyelogenic cyst of kidney (591)*
congenital cyst of kidney (753.1)
polycystic (disease of) kidney (753.1)

AHA: 4Q, '90, 3

DEF: Abnormal, fluid-filled sac in the kidney, not present at birth.

593.3 Stricture or kinking of ureter

Angulation } of ureter (post-operative)
Constriction } of ureter (post-operative)
Stricture of pelviureteric junction

AHA: 2Q, '98, 9

DEF: Stricture or knot in tube connecting kidney to bladder.

593.4 Other ureteric obstruction

Idiopathic retroperitoneal fibrosis
Occlusion NOS of ureter

EXCLUDES *that due to calculus (592.1)*

AHA: 2Q, '97, 4

593.5 Hydroureter

EXCLUDES *congenital hydroureter (753.22)*
hydroureteronephrosis (591)

593.6 Postural proteinuria

Benign postural proteinuria
Orthostatic proteinuria

EXCLUDES *proteinuria NOS (791.0)*

DEF: Excessive amounts of serum protein in the urine caused by the body position, e.g., orthostatic and lordotic.

✓5th **593.7 Vesicoureteral reflux**

AHA: 4Q, '94, 42

DEF: Backflow of urine, from bladder into ureter due to obstructed bladder neck.

593.70 Unspecified or without reflux nephropathy

593.71 With reflux nephropathy, unilateral

593.72 With reflux nephropathy, bilateral

593.73 With reflux nephropathy NOS

✓5th **593.8 Other specified disorders of kidney and ureter**

593.81 Vascular disorders of kidney

Renal (artery):
embolism
hemorrhage
thrombosis
Renal infarction

N Newborn Age: 0 P Pediatric Age: 0-17 M Maternity Age: 12-55 A Adult Age: 15-124

593.82 Ureteral fistula
Intestinoureteral fistula
EXCLUDES *fistula between ureter and female genital tract (619.0)*
DEF: Abnormal communication, between tube connecting kidney to bladder and another structure.

593.89 Other
Adhesions, kidney or ureter
Periureteritis
Polyp of ureter
Pyelectasia
Ureterocele
EXCLUDES *tuberculosis of ureter (016.2)*
ureteritis cystica (590.3)

593.9 Unspecified disorder of kidney and ureter
Acute renal disease
Acute renal insufficiency
Renal disease NOS
Salt-losing nephritis or syndrome
EXCLUDES *chronic renal insufficiency (585.9)*
cystic kidney disease (753.1)
nephropathy, so stated (583.0-583.9)
renal disease:
arising in pregnancy or the puerperium (642.1-642.2, 642.4-642.7, 646.2)
not specified as acute or chronic, but with stated pathology or cause (583.0-583.9)
AHA: 4Q, '05, 79; 1Q, '93, 17

✓4th 594 Calculus of lower urinary tract

594.0 Calculus in diverticulum of bladder
DEF: Stone or mineral deposit in abnormal sac on the bladder wall.

594.1 Other calculus in bladder
Urinary bladder stone
EXCLUDES *staghorn calculus (592.0)*
DEF: Stone or mineral deposit in bladder.

594.2 Calculus in urethra
DEF: Stone or mineral deposit in tube that empties urine from bladder.

594.8 Other lower urinary tract calculus
AHA: J-F, '85, 16

594.9 Calculus of lower urinary tract, unspecified
EXCLUDES *calculus of urinary tract NOS (592.9)*

✓4th 595 Cystitis

EXCLUDES *prostatocystitis (601.3)*
Use additional code to identify organism, such as Escherichia coli [E. coli] (041.4)

595.0 Acute cystitis
EXCLUDES *trigonitis (595.3)*
AHA: 2Q, '99, 15
DEF: Acute inflammation of bladder.

595.1 Chronic interstitial cystitis
Hunner's ulcer
Panmural fibrosis of bladder
Submucous cystitis
DEF: Inflamed lesion affecting bladder wall; symptoms include urinary frequency, pain on bladder filling, nocturia, and distended bladder.

595.2 Other chronic cystitis
Chronic cystitis NOS
Subacute cystitis
EXCLUDES *trigonitis (595.3)*
DEF: Persistent inflammation of bladder.

Bladder

Anterior View
Fundus
Left ureter
Right ureter
Lateral wall
Ureteral orifice
Trigone
Uvula of bladder
Urethra

Lateral View

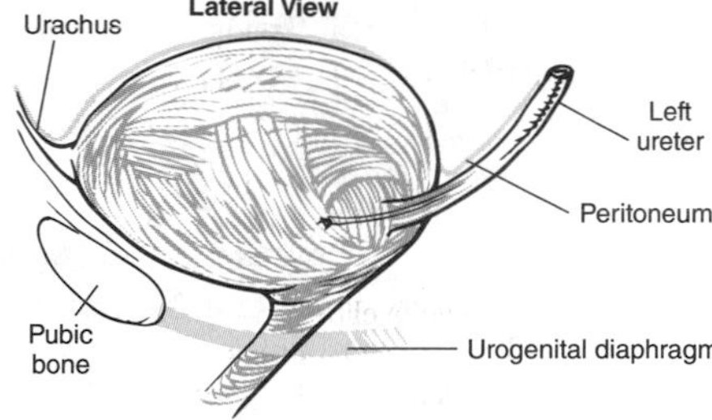

595.3 Trigonitis
Follicular cystitis
Trigonitis (acute) (chronic)
Urethrotrigonitis
DEF: Inflammation of the triangular area of the bladder called the trigonum vesicae.

595.4 Cystitis in diseases classified elsewhere
Code first underlying disease, as:
actinomycosis (039.8)
amebiasis (006.8)
bilharziasis (120.0-120.9)
Echinococcus infestation (122.3, 122.6)
EXCLUDES *cystitis:*
diphtheritic (032.84)
gonococcal (098.11, 098.31)
monilial (112.2)
trichomonal (131.09)
tuberculous (016.1)

✓5th 595.8 Other specified types of cystitis

595.81 Cystitis cystica
DEF: Inflammation of the bladder characterized by formation of multiple cysts.

595.82 Irradiation cystitis
Use additional E code to identify cause
DEF: Inflammation of the bladder due to effects of radiation.

595.89 Other
Abscess of bladder:
Cystitis:
bullous
emphysematous
glandularis

595.9 Cystitis, unspecified

596 Other disorders of bladder

Use additional code to identify urinary incontinence (625.6, 788.30-788.39)

AHA: M-A, '87, 10

596.0 Bladder neck obstruction

Contracture (acquired) / Obstruction (acquired) / Stenosis (acquired) } of bladder neck or vesicourethral orifice

EXCLUDES *congenital (753.6)*

AHA: 3Q, '02, 28; 2Q, '01, 14; N-D, '86, 10

DEF: Bladder outlet and vesicourethral obstruction; occurs more often in males as a consequence of benign prostatic hypertrophy or prostatic cancer; may also occur in either sex due to strictures, following radiation, cystoscopy, catheterization, injury, infection, blood clots, bladder cancer, impaction or disease compressing bladder neck.

596.1 Intestinovesical fistula

Fistula:
- enterovesical
- vesicocolic
- vesicoenteric
- vesicorectal

DEF: Abnormal communication, between intestine and bladder.

596.2 Vesical fistula, not elsewhere classified

Fistula:
- bladder NOS
- urethrovesical
- vesicocutaneous
- vesicoperineal

EXCLUDES *fistula between bladder and female genital tract (619.0)*

DEF: Abnormal communication between bladder and another structure.

596.3 Diverticulum of bladder

Diverticulitis / Diverticulum (acquired) (false) } of bladder

EXCLUDES *that with calculus in diverticulum of bladder (594.0)*

DEF: Abnormal pouch in bladder wall.

596.4 Atony of bladder

High compliance bladder

Hypotonicity / Inertia } of bladder

EXCLUDES *neurogenic bladder (596.54)*

DEF: Distended, bladder with loss of expulsive force; linked to CNS disease.

✓5th **596.5 Other functional disorders of bladder**

EXCLUDES *cauda equina syndrome with neurogenic bladder (344.61)*

596.51 Hypertonicity of bladder

Hyperactivity

Overactive bladder

DEF: Abnormal tension of muscular wall of bladder; may appear after surgery of voluntary nerve.

596.52 Low bladder compliance

DEF: Low bladder capacity; causes increased pressure and frequent urination.

596.53 Paralysis of bladder

DEF: Impaired bladder motor function due to nerve or muscle damage.

596.54 Neurogenic bladder NOS

AHA: 1Q, '01, 12

DEF: Unspecified dysfunctional bladder due to lesion of central, peripheral nervous system; may result in incontinence, residual urine retention, urinary infection, stones and renal failure.

596.55 Detrusor sphincter dyssynergia

DEF: Instability of the urinary bladder sphincter muscle associated with urinary incontinence.

596.59 Other functional disorder of bladder

Detrusor instability

DEF: Detrusor instability: instability of bladder; marked by uninhibited contractions often leading to incontinence.

596.6 Rupture of bladder, nontraumatic

596.7 Hemorrhage into bladder wall

Hyperemia of bladder

EXCLUDES *acute hemorrhagic cystitis (595.0)*

596.8 Other specified disorders of bladder

Bladder:
- calcified
- contracted
- hemorrhage
- hypertrophy

EXCLUDES *cystocele, female (618.01-618.02, 618.09, 618.2-618.4)*
hernia or prolapse of bladder, female (618.01-618.02, 618.09, 618.2-618.4)

AHA: J-F, '85, 8

596.9 Unspecified disorder of bladder

AHA: J-F, '85, 8

✓4th **597 Urethritis, not sexually transmitted, and urethral syndrome**

EXCLUDES *nonspecific urethritis, so stated (099.4)*

597.0 Urethral abscess

Abscess:
- periurethral
- urethral (gland)

Abscess of:
- bulbourethral gland
- Cowper's gland
- Littré's gland

Periurethral cellulitis

EXCLUDES *urethral caruncle (599.3)*

DEF: Pocket of pus in tube that empties urine from the bladder.

✓5th **597.8 Other urethritis**

597.80 Urethritis, unspecified

597.81 Urethral syndrome NOS

597.89 Other

Adenitis, Skene's glands

Cowperitis

Meatitis, urethral

Ulcer, urethra (meatus)

Verumontanitis

EXCLUDES *trichomonal (131.02)*

✓4th **598 Urethral stricture**

Use additional code to identify urinary incontinence (625.6, 788.30-788.39)

INCLUDES pinhole meatus
stricture of urinary meatus

EXCLUDES *congenital stricture of urethra and urinary meatus (753.6)*

DEF: Narrowing of tube that empties urine from bladder.

✓5th **598.0 Urethral stricture due to infection**

598.00 Due to unspecified infection

598.01 Due to infective diseases classified elsewhere

Code first underlying disease, as:
- gonococcal infection (098.2)
- schistosomiasis (120.0-120.9)
- syphilis (095.8)

598.1 Traumatic urethral stricture
Stricture of urethra:
late effect of injury
postobstetric
EXCLUDES *postoperative following surgery on genitourinary tract (598.2)*

598.2 Postoperative urethral stricture
Postcatheterization stricture of urethra
AHA: 3Q, '97, 6

598.8 Other specified causes of urethral stricture
AHA: N-D, '84, 9

598.9 Urethral stricture, unspecified

✓4th **599 Other disorders of urethra and urinary tract**

599.0 Urinary tract infection, site not specified
EXCLUDES *candidiasis of urinary tract (112.2)*
urinary tract infection of newborn (771.82)
Use additional code to identify organism, such as Escherichia coli [E. coli] (041.4)
AHA: 3Q, '05, 12; 2Q, '04, 13; 4Q, '03, 79; 4Q, '99, 6; 2Q, '99, 15;1Q, '98, 5; 2Q, '96, 7; 4Q, '96, 33; 2Q, '95, 7; 1Q, '92, 13

599.1 Urethral fistula
Fistula:
urethroperineal
urethrorectal
Urinary fistula NOS
EXCLUDES *fistula:*
urethroscrotal (608.89)
urethrovaginal (619.0)
urethrovesicovaginal (619.0)
AHA: 3Q, '97, 6

599.2 Urethral diverticulum
DEF: Abnormal pouch in urethral wall.

599.3 Urethral caruncle
Polyp of urethra

599.4 Urethral false passage
DEF: Abnormal opening in urethra due to surgery; trauma or disease.

599.5 Prolapsed urethral mucosa
Prolapse of urethra
Urethrocele
EXCLUDES *urethrocele, female (618.03, 618.09, 618.2-618.4)*

✓5th **599.6 Urinary obstruction**
Use additional code to identify urinary incontinence (625.6, 788.30-788.39)
EXCLUDES *obstructive nephropathy NOS (593.89)*
AHA: 4Q, '05, 80

599.60 Urinary obstruction, unspecified
Obstructive uropathy NOS
Urinary (tract) obstruction NOS

599.69 Urinary obstruction, not elsewhere classified
Code, if applicable, any causal condition first, such as:
hyperplasia of prostate (600.0-600.9 with fifth-digit 1)
AHA: 4Q, '06, 93

✓5th **599.7 Hematuria**
Hematuria (benign) (essential)
EXCLUDES *hemoglobinuria (791.2)*
AHA: 1Q, '00, 5; 3Q, '95, 8

● **599.70 Hematuria, unspecified**
● **599.71 Gross hematuria**
● **599.72 Microscopic hematuria**

✓5th **599.8 Other specified disorders of urethra and urinary tract**
Use additional code to identify urinary incontinence (625.6, 788.30-788.39), if present
EXCLUDES *symptoms and other conditions classifiable to 788.0-788.2, 788.4-788.9, 791.0-791.9*

599.81 Urethral hypermobility
DEF: Hyperactive urethra.

599.82 Intrinsic (urethral) sphincter deficiency [ISD]
AHA: 2Q, '96, 15
DEF: Malfunctioning urethral sphincter.

599.83 Urethral instability
DEF: Inconsistent functioning of urethra.

599.84 Other specified disorders of urethra
Rupture of urethra (nontraumatic)
Urethral:
cyst
granuloma
DEF: Rupture of urethra due to herniation or breaking down of tissue; not due to trauma.
DEF: Urethral cyst: abnormal sac in urethra; usually fluid filled.
DEF: Granuloma: inflammatory cells forming small nodules in urethra.

599.89 Other specified disorders of urinary tract

599.9 Unspecified disorder of urethra and urinary tract

DISEASES OF MALE GENITAL ORGANS (600-608)

✓4th **600 Hyperplasia of prostate**
INCLUDES enlarged prostate
AHA: 3Q, '05, 20; 4Q, '00, 43; 3Q, '94, 12; 3Q, '92, 7; N-D, '86, 10
DEF: Fibrostromal proliferation in periurethral glands, causes blood in urine; etiology unknown.

✓5th **600.0 Hypertrophy (benign) of prostate**
Benign prostatic hypertrophy
Enlargement of prostate
Smooth enlarged prostate
Soft enlarged prostate
AHA: 4Q, '06, 93-95; 3Q, '05, 20; 4Q, '03, 63; 1Q, '03, 6; 3Q, '02, 28; 2Q, '01, 14

600.00 Hypertrophy (benign) of prostate without urinary obstruction and other lower urinary tract symptoms [LUTS] A ♂
Hypertrophy (benign) of prostate NOS

600.01 Hypertrophy (benign) of prostate with urinary obstruction and other lower urinary tract symptoms [LUTS] A ♂
Hypertrophy (benign) of prostate with urinary retention
Use additional code to identify symptoms:
incomplete bladder emptying (788.21)
nocturia (788.43)
straining on urination (788.65)
urinary frequency (788.41)
urinary hesitancy (788.64)
urinary incontinence (788.30-788.39)
urinary obstruction (599.69)
urinary retention (788.20)
urinary urgency (788.63)
weak urinary stream (788.62)
AHA: 4Q, '06, 93-95; 4Q, '03, 64

Male Pelvic Organs

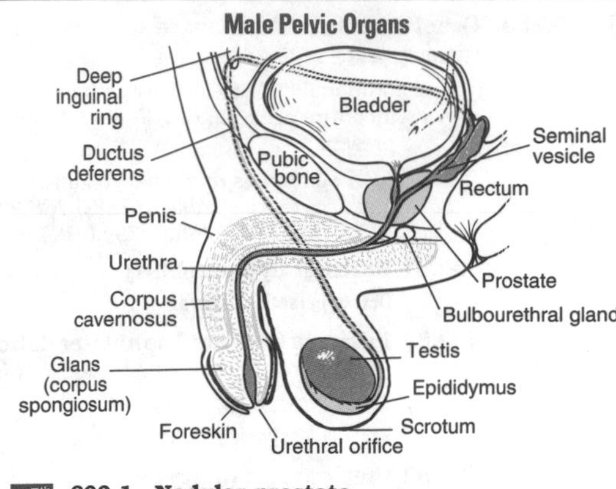

✓5th **600.1 Nodular prostate**
Hard, firm prostate
Multinodular prostate
EXCLUDES *malignant neoplasm of prostate (185)*
AHA: 4Q, '03, 63
DEF: Hard, firm nodule in prostate.

600.10 Nodular prostate without urinary obstruction A ♂
Nodular prostate NOS

600.11 Nodular prostate with urinary obstruction A ♂
Nodular prostate with urinary retention

✓5th **600.2 Benign localized hyperplasia of prostate**
Adenofibromatous hypertrophy of prostate
Adenoma of prostate
Fibroadenoma of prostate
Fibroma of prostate
Myoma of prostate
Polyp of prostate
EXCLUDES *benign neoplasms of prostate (222.2)*
hypertrophy of prostate (600.00-600.01)
malignant neoplasm of prostate (185)
AHA: 4Q, '06, 93-95; 4Q, '03, 63
DEF: Benign localized hyperplasia is a clearly defined epithelial tumor. Other terms used for this condition are adenofibromatous hypertrophy of prostate, adenoma of prostate, fibroadenoma of prostate, fibroma of prostate, myoma of prostate, and polyp of prostate.

600.20 Benign localized hyperplasia of prostate without urinary obstruction and other lower urinary tract symptoms [LUTS] A ♂
Benign localized hyperplasia of prostate NOS

600.21 Benign localized hyperplasia of prostate with urinary obstruction and other lower urinary tract symptoms [LUTS] A ♂
Benign localized hyperplasia of prostate with urinary retention
Use additional code to identify symptoms:
incomplete bladder emptying (788.21)
nocturia (788.43)
straining on urination (788.65)
urinary frequency (788.41)
urinary hesitancy (788.64)
urinary incontinence (788.30-788.39)
urinary obstruction (599.69)
urinary retention (788.20)
urinary urgency (788.63)
weak urinary stream (788.62)

600.3 Cyst of prostate A ♂
DEF: Sacs of fluid, which differentiate this from either nodular or adenomatous tumors.

✓5th **600.9 Hyperplasia of prostate, unspecified**
Median bar
Prostatic obstruction NOS
AHA: 4Q, '06, 93-95; 4Q, '03, 63

600.90 Hyperplasia of prostate, unspecified, without urinary obstruction and other lower urinary tract symptoms [LUTS] A ♂
Hyperplasia of prostate NOS

600.91 Hyperplasia of prostate, unspecified with urinary obstruction and other lower urinary tract symptoms [LUTS] A ♂
Hyperplasia of prostate, unspecified, with urinary retention
Use additional code to identify symptoms:
incomplete bladder emptying (788.21)
nocturia (788.43)
straining on urination (788.65)
urinary frequency (788.41)
urinary hesitancy (788.64)
urinary incontinence (788.30-788.39)
urinary obstruction (599.69)
urinary retention (788.20)
urinary urgency (788.63)
weak urinary stream (788.62)

✓4th **601 Inflammatory diseases of prostate**
Use additional code to identify organism, such as Staphylococcus (041.1), or Streptococcus (041.0)

601.0 Acute prostatitis A ♂

601.1 Chronic prostatitis A ♂

601.2 Abscess of prostate A ♂

601.3 Prostatocystitis A ♂

601.4 Prostatitis in diseases classified elsewhere A ♂
Code first underlying disease, as:
actinomycosis (039.8)
blastomycosis (116.0)
syphilis (095.8)
tuberculosis (016.5)
EXCLUDES *prostatitis:*
gonococcal (098.12, 098.32)
monilial (112.2)
trichomonal (131.03)

601.8 Other specified inflammatory diseases of prostate A ♂
Prostatitis:
cavitary
diverticular
granulomatous

601.9 Prostatitis, unspecified A ♂
Prostatitis NOS

✓4th **602 Other disorders of prostate**

602.0 Calculus of prostate A ♂
Prostatic stone
DEF: Stone or mineral deposit in prostate.

602.1 Congestion or hemorrhage of prostate A ♂
DEF: Bleeding or fluid collection in prostate.

602.2 Atrophy of prostate A ♂

Common Inguinal Canal Anomalies

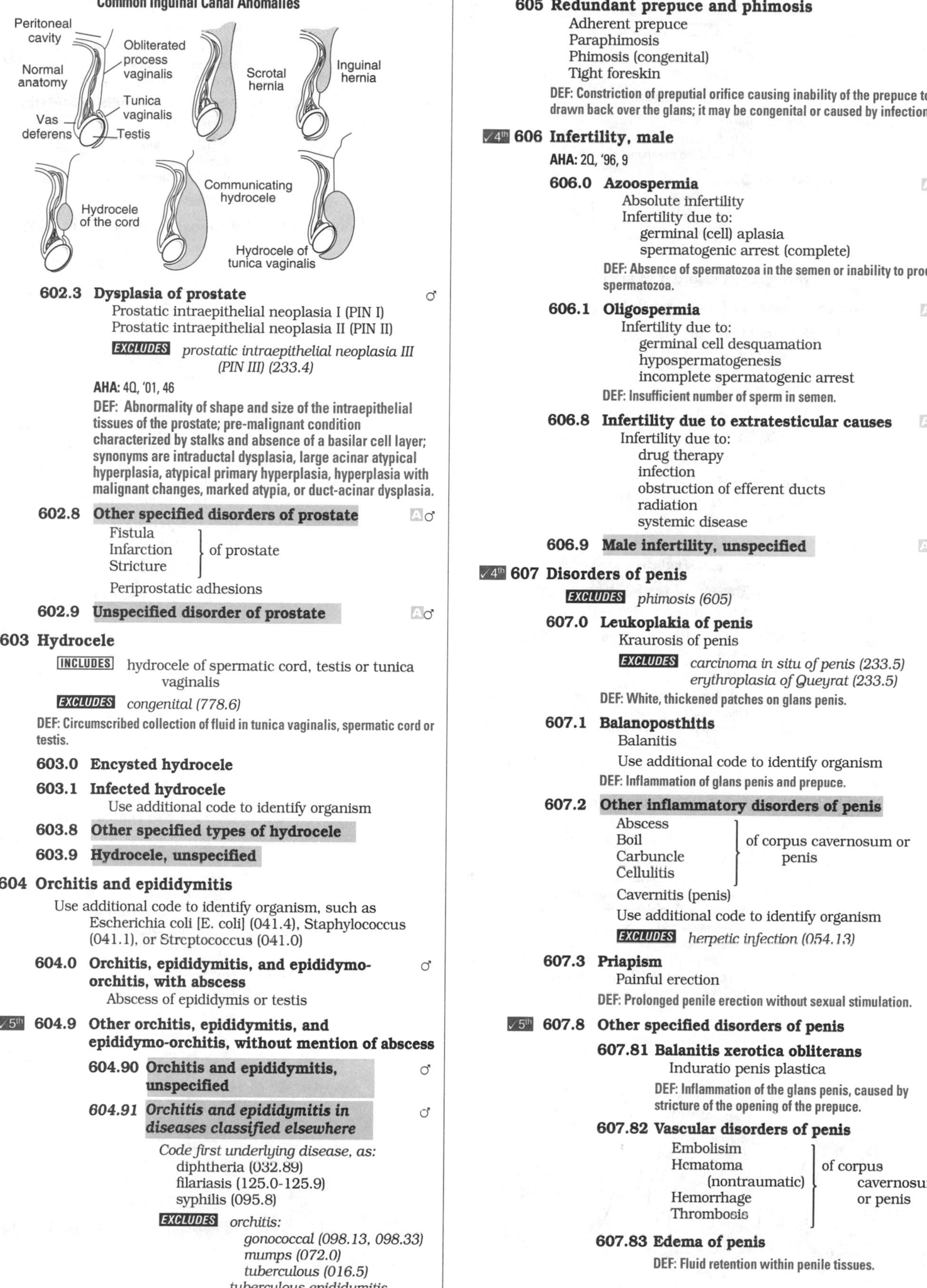

602.3 Dysplasia of prostate ♂
- Prostatic intraepithelial neoplasia I (PIN I)
- Prostatic intraepithelial neoplasia II (PIN II)

EXCLUDES *prostatic intraepithelial neoplasia III (PIN III) (233.4)*

AHA: 4Q, '01, 46

DEF: Abnormality of shape and size of the intraepithelial tissues of the prostate; pre-malignant condition characterized by stalks and absence of a basilar cell layer; synonyms are intraductal dysplasia, large acinar atypical hyperplasia, atypical primary hyperplasia, hyperplasia with malignant changes, marked atypia, or duct-acinar dysplasia.

602.8 Other specified disorders of prostate A ♂
- Fistula / Infarction / Stricture } of prostate
- Periprostatic adhesions

602.9 Unspecified disorder of prostate A ♂

✓4th **603 Hydrocele**

INCLUDES hydrocele of spermatic cord, testis or tunica vaginalis

EXCLUDES *congenital (778.6)*

DEF: Circumscribed collection of fluid in tunica vaginalis, spermatic cord or testis.

603.0 Encysted hydrocele

603.1 Infected hydrocele
- Use additional code to identify organism

603.8 Other specified types of hydrocele

603.9 Hydrocele, unspecified

✓4th **604 Orchitis and epididymitis**

Use additional code to identify organism, such as Escherichia coli [E. coli] (041.4), Staphylococcus (041.1), or Streptococcus (041.0)

604.0 Orchitis, epididymitis, and epididymo-orchitis, with abscess ♂
- Abscess of epididymis or testis

✓5th **604.9 Other orchitis, epididymitis, and epididymo-orchitis, without mention of abscess**

604.90 Orchitis and epididymitis, unspecified ♂

604.91 Orchitis and epididymitis in diseases classified elsewhere ♂

Code first underlying disease, as:
- diphtheria (032.89)
- filariasis (125.0-125.9)
- syphilis (095.8)

EXCLUDES *orchitis:*
- *gonococcal (098.13, 098.33)*
- *mumps (072.0)*
- *tuberculous (016.5)*
- *tuberculous epididymitis (016.4)*

604.99 Other ♂

605 Redundant prepuce and phimosis ♂
- Adherent prepuce
- Paraphimosis
- Phimosis (congenital)
- Tight foreskin

DEF: Constriction of preputial orifice causing inability of the prepuce to be drawn back over the glans; it may be congenital or caused by infection.

✓4th **606 Infertility, male**

AHA: 2Q, '96, 9

606.0 Azoospermia A ♂
- Absolute infertility
- Infertility due to:
  - germinal (cell) aplasia
  - spermatogenic arrest (complete)

DEF: Absence of spermatozoa in the semen or inability to produce spermatozoa.

606.1 Oligospermia A ♂
- Infertility due to:
  - germinal cell desquamation
  - hypospermatogenesis
  - incomplete spermatogenic arrest

DEF: Insufficient number of sperm in semen.

606.8 Infertility due to extratesticular causes A ♂
- Infertility due to:
  - drug therapy
  - infection
  - obstruction of efferent ducts
  - radiation
  - systemic disease

606.9 Male infertility, unspecified A ♂

✓4th **607 Disorders of penis**

EXCLUDES *phimosis (605)*

607.0 Leukoplakia of penis ♂
- Kraurosis of penis

EXCLUDES *carcinoma in situ of penis (233.5)*
erythroplasia of Queyrat (233.5)

DEF: White, thickened patches on glans penis.

607.1 Balanoposthitis ♂
- Balanitis
- Use additional code to identify organism

DEF: Inflammation of glans penis and prepuce.

607.2 Other inflammatory disorders of penis ♂
- Abscess / Boil / Carbuncle / Cellulitis } of corpus cavernosum or penis
- Cavernitis (penis)
- Use additional code to identify organism

EXCLUDES *herpetic infection (054.13)*

607.3 Priapism ♂
- Painful erection

DEF: Prolonged penile erection without sexual stimulation.

✓5th **607.8 Other specified disorders of penis**

607.81 Balanitis xerotica obliterans ♂
- Induratio penis plastica

DEF: Inflammation of the glans penis, caused by stricture of the opening of the prepuce.

607.82 Vascular disorders of penis ♂
- Embolism / Hematoma (nontraumatic) / Hemorrhage / Thrombosis } of corpus cavernosum or penis

607.83 Edema of penis ♂

DEF: Fluid retention within penile tissues.

607.84 Impotence of organic origin A ♂

EXCLUDES *nonorganic (302.72)*

AHA: 3Q, '91, 11

DEF: Physiological cause interfering with erection.

607.85 Peyronie's disease ♂

AHA: 4Q, '03, 64

DEF: A severe curvature of the erect penis due to fibrosis of the cavernous sheaths.

607.89 Other ♂

Atrophy, Fibrosis, Hypertrophy, Ulcer (chronic) } of corpus cavernosum or penis

607.9 Unspecified disorder of penis ♂

✓4th **608 Other disorders of male genital organs**

608.0 Seminal vesiculitis ♂

Abscess, Cellulitis } of seminal vesicle

Vesiculitis (seminal)

Use additional code to identify organism

EXCLUDES *gonococcal infection (098.14, 098.34)*

DEF: Inflammation of seminal vesicle.

608.1 Spermatocele ♂

DEF: Cystic enlargement of the epididymis or the testis; the cysts contain spermatozoa.

✓5th **608.2 Torsion of testis**

DEF: Twisted or rotated testis; may compromise blood flow.

608.20 Torsion of testis, unspecified ♂

AHA: 4Q, '06, 95

608.21 Extravaginal torsion of spermatic cord ♂

AHA: 4Q, '06, 95

DEF: Torsion of the spermatic cord just below the tunica vaginalis attachments. Often manifests in the neonatal period after having developed in utero. This type of torsion accounts for approximately 5% of all torsions. It is usually associated with high birth weight.

608.22 Intravaginal torsion of spermatic cord ♂

Torsion of spermatic cord NOS

AHA: 4Q, '06, 95

DEF: Torsion within the tunica vaginalis also called the "bell-clapper" anomaly. It usually occurs in older children, with peak incidence occurring at approximately 13 years of age. This type of torsion accounts for roughly 16% emergency room torsion encounters. Of note, the left testis is most frequently affected, with only 2% cases presenting as bilateral torsions.

Torsion of the Testis

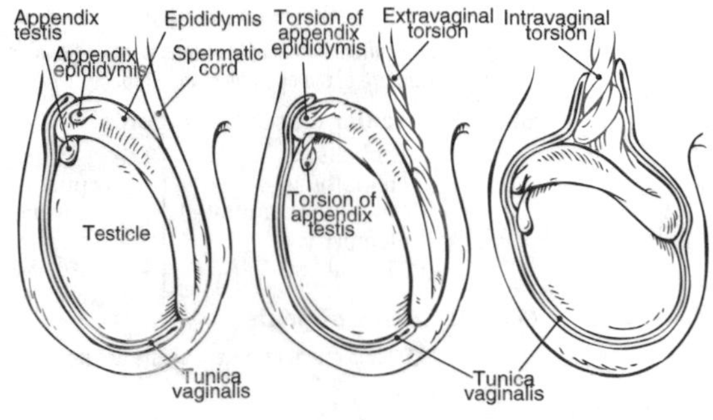

608.23 Torsion of appendix testis ♂

AHA: 4Q, '06, 95

DEF: Torsion of small solid projection of tissue on the upper outer surface of the testis (hydatid of Morgagni); a remnant of the embryologic mullerian duct.

608.24 Torsion of appendix epididymis ♂

AHA: 4Q, '06, 95

DEF: Torsion of small stalked appendage of the head of the epididymis (pedunculated hydatid); a detached embryologic efferent duct.

608.3 Atrophy of testis ♂

608.4 Other inflammatory disorders of male genital organs ♂

Abscess, Boil, Carbuncle, Cellulitis } of scrotum, spermatic cord, testis [except abscess], tunica vaginalis, or vas deferens

Vasitis

Use additional code to identify organism

EXCLUDES *abscess of testis (604.0)*

✓5th **608.8 Other specified disorders of male genital organs**

608.81 *Disorders of male genital organs in diseases classified elsewhere* ♂

Code first underlying disease, as:
filariasis (125.0-125.9)
tuberculosis (016.5)

608.82 Hematospermia ♂

AHA: 4Q, '01, 46

DEF: Presence of blood in the ejaculate; relatively common, affecting men of any age after puberty; cause is often difficult to determine since the semen originates in several organs, often the result of a viral or bacterial infection and inflammation.

608.83 Vascular disorders ♂

Hematoma (nontraumatic), Hemorrhage, Thrombosis } of seminal vessel, spermatic cord, testis, scrotum, tunica vaginalis, or vas deferens

Hematocele NOS, male

AHA: 4Q, '03, 110

608.84 Chylocele of tunica vaginalis ♂

DEF: Chylous effusion into tunica vaginalis; due to infusion of lymphatic fluids.

608.85 Stricture ♂

Stricture of:
spermatic cord
tunica vaginalis
vas deferens

608.86 Edema ♂

608.87 Retrograde ejaculation ♂

AHA: 4Q, '01, 46

DEF: Condition where the semen travels to the bladder rather than out through the urethra due to damaged nerves causing the bladder neck to remain open during ejaculation.

608.89 Other ♂

Atrophy, Fibrosis, Hypertrophy, Ulcer } of seminal vessel, spermatic cord, testis, scrotum, tunica vaginalis, or vas deferens

EXCLUDES *atrophy of testis (608.3)*

608.9 Unspecified disorder of male genital organs ♂

DISORDERS OF BREAST ▶(610-612)◀

✓4th 610 Benign mammary dysplasias

610.0 Solitary cyst of breast
Cyst (solitary) of breast

610.1 Diffuse cystic mastopathy A
Chronic cystic mastitis
Cystic breast
Fibrocystic disease of breast

AHA: 2Q, '06, 10

DEF: Extensive formation of nodular cysts in breast tissue; symptoms include tenderness, change in size and hyperplasia of ductal epithelium.

610.2 Fibroadenosis of breast
Fibroadenosis of breast:
NOS
chronic
cystic
diffuse
periodic
segmental

DEF: Non-neoplastic nodular condition of breast.

610.3 Fibrosclerosis of breast

DEF: Fibrous tissue in breast.

610.4 Mammary duct ectasia
Comedomastitis
Duct ectasia
Mastitis:
periductal
plasma cell

DEF: Atrophy of duct epithelium; causes distended collecting ducts of mammary gland; drying up of breast secretion, intraductal inflammation and periductal and interstitial chronic inflammatory reaction.

610.8 Other specified benign mammary dysplasias
Mazoplasia
Sebaceous cyst of breast

610.9 Benign mammary dysplasia, unspecified

✓4th 611 Other disorders of breast

EXCLUDES *that associated with lactation or the puerperium (675.0-676.9)*

611.0 Inflammatory disease of breast
Abscess (acute) (chronic) (nonpuerperal) of:
areola
breast
Mammillary fistula
Mastitis (acute) (subacute) (nonpuerperal):
NOS
infective
retromammary
submammary

EXCLUDES *carbuncle of breast (680.2)*
chronic cystic mastitis (610.1)
neonatal infective mastitis (771.5)
thrombophlebitis of breast [Mondor's disease] (451.89)

611.1 Hypertrophy of breast
Gynecomastia
Hypertrophy of breast:
NOS
massive pubertal

EXCLUDES ▶*breast engorgement in newborn (778.7)*
disproportion of reconstructed breast (612.1)◀

611.2 Fissure of nipple

611.3 Fat necrosis of breast
Fat necrosis (segmental) of breast
▶Code first breast necrosis due to breast graft (996.79)◀

DEF: Splitting of neutral fats in adipose tissue cells as a result of trauma; a firm circumscribed mass is then formed in the breast.

611.4 Atrophy of breast

611.5 Galactocele

DEF: Milk-filled cyst in breast; due to blocked duct.

611.6 Galactorrhea not associated with childbirth

DEF: Flow of milk not associated with childbirth or pregnancy.

✓5th **611.7 Signs and symptoms in breast**

611.71 Mastodynia
Pain in breast

611.72 Lump or mass in breast
AHA: 2Q, '03, 4-5

611.79 Other
Induration of breast
Inversion of nipple
Nipple discharge
Retraction of nipple

✓5th **611.8 Other specified disorders of breast**

● **611.81 Ptosis of breast**
EXCLUDES *ptosis of native breast in relation to reconstructed breast (612.1)*

● **611.82 Hypoplasia of breast**
Micromastia
EXCLUDES *hypoplasia of native breast in relation to reconstructed breast (612.1)*

● **611.83 Capsular contracture of breast implant**

● **611.89 Other specified disorders of breast**
Hematoma (nontraumatic) of breast
Infarction of breast
Occlusion of breast duct
Subinvolution of breast (postlactational) (postpartum)

611.9 Unspecified breast disorder

● ✓4th 612 Deformity and disproportion of reconstructed breast

● **612.0 Deformity of reconstructed breast**
Contour irregularity in reconstructed breast
Excess tissue in reconstructed breast
Misshapen reconstructed breast

● **612.1 Disproportion of reconstructed breast**
Breast asymmetry between native breast and reconstructed breast
Disproportion between native breast and reconstructed breast

INFLAMMATORY DISEASE OF FEMALE PELVIC ORGANS (614-616)

Use additional code to identify organism, such as Staphylococcus (041.1), or Streptococcus (041.0)

EXCLUDES *that associated with pregnancy, abortion, childbirth, or the puerperium (630-676.9)*

✓4th 614 Inflammatory disease of ovary, fallopian tube, pelvic cellular tissue, and peritoneum

EXCLUDES *endometritis (615.0-615.9)*
major infection following delivery (670)
that complicating:
abortion (634-638 with .0, 639.0)
ectopic or molar pregnancy (639.0)
pregnancy or labor (646.6)

614.0 Acute salpingitis and oophoritis ♀
Any condition classifiable to 614.2, specified as acute or subacute

DEF: Acute inflammation, of ovary and fallopian tube.

614.1 Chronic salpingitis and oophoritis ♀
Hydrosalpinx
Salpingitis:
follicularis
isthmica nodosa
Any condition classifiable to 614.2, specified as chronic

DEF: Persistent inflammation of ovary and fallopian tube.

614.2 Salpingitis and oophoritis not specified as acute, subacute, or chronic ♀
Abscess (of):
fallopian tube
ovary
tubo-ovarian
Oophoritis
Perioophoritis
Perisalpingitis
Pyosalpinx
Salpingitis
Salpingo-oophoritis
Tubo-ovarian inflammatory disease

EXCLUDES *gonococcal infection (chronic) (098.37)*
acute (098.17)
tuberculous (016.6)

AHA: 2Q, '91, 5

614.3 Acute parametritis and pelvic cellulitis ♀
Acute inflammatory pelvic disease
Any condition classifiable to 614.4, specified as acute

DEF: Parametritis: inflammation of the parametrium; pelvic cellulitis is a synonym for parametritis.

614.4 Chronic or unspecified parametritis and pelvic cellulitis ♀
Abscess (of):
broad ligament } chronic or NOS
parametrium }
pelvis, femal }
pouch of Douglas }
Chronic inflammatory pelvic disease
Pelvic cellulitis, female

EXCLUDES *tuberculous (016.7)*

614.5 Acute or unspecified pelvic peritonitis, female ♀

AHA: 4Q, '05, 74

614.6 Pelvic peritoneal adhesions, female (postoperative) (postinfection) ♀
Adhesions:
peritubal
tubo-ovarian
Use additional code to identify any associated infertility (628.2)

AHA: 3Q, '03, 6; 1Q, '03, 4; 3Q, '95, 7; 3Q, '94, 12

DEF: Fibrous scarring abnormally joining structures within abdomen.

614.7 Other chronic pelvic peritonitis, female ♀

EXCLUDES *tuberculous (016.7)*

614.8 Other specified inflammatory disease of female pelvic organs and tissues ♀

614.9 Unspecified inflammatory disease of female pelvic organs and tissues ♀
Pelvic infection or inflammation, female NOS
Pelvic inflammatory disease [PID]

✓4th 615 Inflammatory diseases of uterus, except cervix

EXCLUDES *following delivery (670)*
hyperplastic endometritis (621.30-621.33)
that complicating:
abortion (634-638 with .0, 639.0)
ectopic or molar pregnancy (639.0)
pregnancy or labor (646.6)

615.0 Acute ♀
Any condition classifiable to 615.9, specified as acute or subacute

615.1 Chronic ♀
Any condition classifiable to 615.9, specified as chronic

615.9 Unspecified inflammatory disease of uterus ♀
Endometritis
Endomyometritis
Intrauterine infection
Metritis
Myometritis
Perimetritis
Pyometra
Uterine abscess

✓4th 616 Inflammatory disease of cervix, vagina, and vulva

EXCLUDES *that complicating:*
abortion (634-638 with .0, 639.0)
ectopic or molar pregnancy (639.0)
pregnancy, childbirth, or the puerperium (646.6)

616.0 Cervicitis and endocervicitis ♀
Cervicitis } with or without mention of erosion or ectropion
Endocervicitis }
Nabothian (gland) cyst or follicle

EXCLUDES *erosion or ectropion without mention of cervicitis (622.0)*

✓5th 616.1 Vaginitis and vulvovaginitis

EXCLUDES ▶*vulvar vestibulitis (625.71)*◀

DEF: Inflammation or infection of vagina or external female genitalia.

616.10 Vaginitis and vulvovaginitis, unspecified ♀
Vaginitis:
NOS
postirradiation
Vulvitis NOS
Vulvovaginitis NOS
Use additional code to identify organism, such as Escherichia coli [E. coli] (041.4), Staphylococcus (041.1), or Streptococcus (041.0)

EXCLUDES *noninfective leukorrhea (623.5)*
postmenopausal or senile vaginitis (627.3)

616.11 Vaginitis and vulvovaginitis in diseases classified elsewhere ♀
Code first underlying disease, as:
pinworm vaginitis (127.4)

EXCLUDES *herpetic vulvovaginitis (054.11)*
monilial vulvovaginitis (112.1)
trichomonal vaginitis or vulvovaginitis (131.01)

616.2 Cyst of Bartholin's gland ♀
Bartholin's duct cyst

DEF: Fluid-filled sac within gland of vaginal orifice.

616.3 Abscess of Bartholin's gland ♀
Vulvovaginal gland abscess

616.4 Other abscess of vulva ♀
Abscess } of vulva
Carbuncle }
Furuncle }

✓5th 616.5 Ulceration of vulva

616.50 Ulceration of vulva, unspecified ♀
Ulcer NOS of vulva

Female Genitourinary System

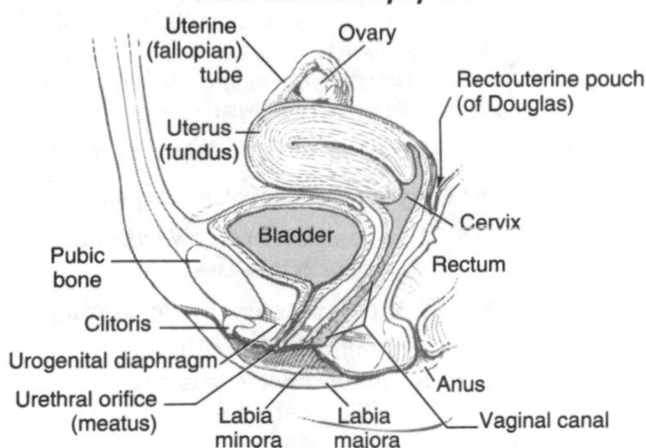

616.51 *Ulceration of vulva in diseases classified elsewhere* ♀

Code first underlying disease, as:
Behçet's syndrome (136.1)
tuberculosis (016.7)

EXCLUDES *vulvar ulcer (in):*
gonococcal (098.0)
herpes simplex (054.12)
syphilitic (091.0)

✓5th **616.8 Other specified inflammatory diseases of cervix,vagina, and vulva**

EXCLUDES *noninflammatory disorders of:*
cervix (622.0-622.9)
vagina (623.0-623.9)
vulva (624.0-624.9)

616.81 Mucositis (ulcerative) of cervix, vagina, and vulva ♀

Use additional E code to identify adverse effects of therapy, such as:
antineoplastic and immunosuppressive drugs (E930.7, E933.1)
radiation therapy (E879.2)

AHA: 4Q, '06, 88-90

616.89 Other inflammatory disease of cervix,vagina and vulva ♀

Caruncle, vagina or labium
Ulcer, vagina

AHA: 4Q, '06, 88-90

616.9 Unspecified inflammatory disease of cervix, vagina, and vulva ♀

OTHER DISORDERS OF FEMALE GENITAL TRACT (617-629)

✓4th **617 Endometriosis**

617.0 Endometriosis of uterus ♀

Adenomyosis
Endometriosis:
cervix
internal
myometrium

EXCLUDES *stromal endometriosis (236.0)*

AHA: 3Q, '92, 7

DEF: Aberrant uterine mucosal tissue; creating products of menses and inflamed uterine tissues.

617.1 Endometriosis of ovary ♀

Chocolate cyst of ovary
Endometrial cystoma of ovary

DEF: Aberrant uterine tissue; creating products of menses and inflamed ovarian tissues.

Common Sites of Endometriosis

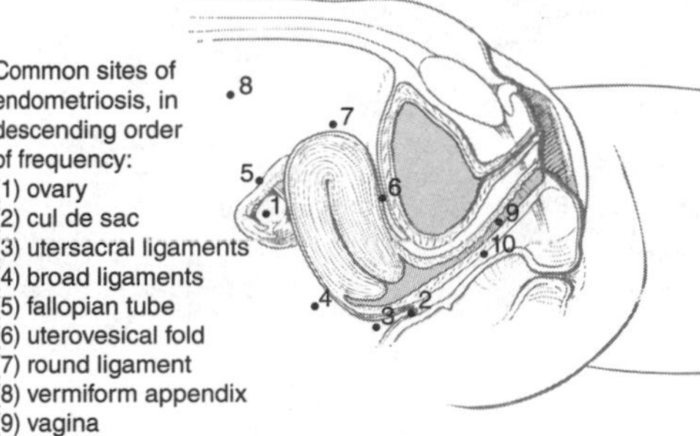

617.2 Endometriosis of fallopian tube ♀

DEF: Aberrant uterine tissue; creating products of menses and inflamed tissues of fallopian tubes.

617.3 Endometriosis of pelvic peritoneum ♀

Endometriosis:
broad ligament
cul-de-sac (Douglas')
parametrium
round ligament

DEF: Aberrant uterine tissue; creating products of menses and inflamed peritoneum tissues.

617.4 Endometriosis of rectovaginal septum and vagina ♀

DEF: Aberrant uterine tissue; creating products of menses and inflamed tissues in and behind vagina.

617.5 Endometriosis of intestine ♀

Endometriosis:
appendix
colon
rectum

DEF: Aberrant uterine tissue; creating products of menses and inflamed intestinal tissues.

617.6 Endometriosis in scar of skin ♀

617.8 Endometriosis of other specified sites ♀

Endometriosis:
bladder
lung
umbilicus
vulva

617.9 Endometriosis, site unspecified ♀

✓4th **618 Genital prolapse**

Use additional code to identify urinary incontinence (625.6, 788.31, 788.33-788.39)

EXCLUDES *that complicating pregnancy, labor, or delivery (654.4)*

✓5th **618.0 Prolapse of vaginal walls without mention of uterine prolapse**

EXCLUDES *that with uterine prolapse (618.2-618.4)*
enterocele (618.6)
vaginal vault prolapse following hysterectomy (618.5)

618.00 Unspecified prolapse of vaginal walls ♀

Vaginal prolapse NOS

Vaginal Midline Cystocele

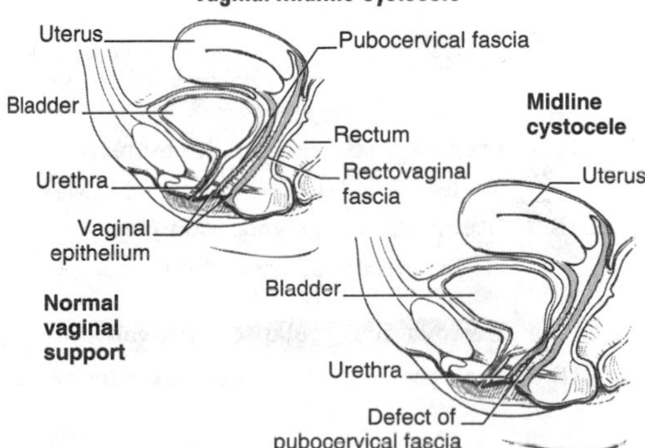

Vaginal Lateral Cystocele

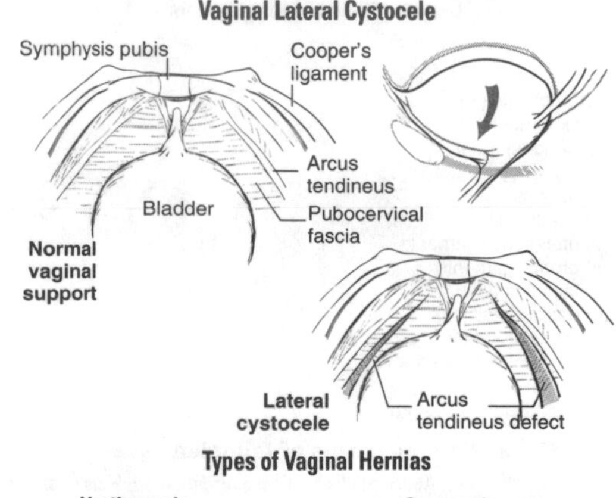

Types of Vaginal Hernias

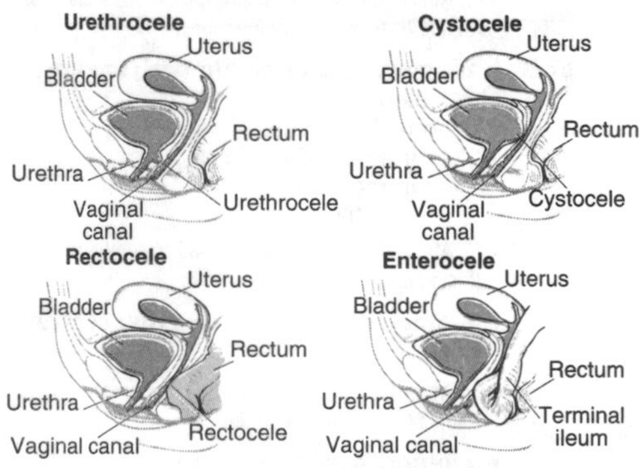

618.01 Cystocele, midline ♀
Cystocele NOS

DEF: Defect in the pubocervical fascia, the supportive layer of the bladder, causing bladder drop and herniated into the vagina along the midline.

618.02 Cystocele, lateral ♀
Paravaginal

DEF: Loss of support of the lateral attachment of the vagina at the arcus tendinous results in bladder drop; bladder herniates into the vagina laterally; also called paravaginal defect.

618.03 Urethrocele ♀

618.04 Rectocele ♀
Proctocele

618.05 Perineocele ♀

618.09 Other prolapse of vaginal walls without mention of uterine prolapse ♀
Cystourethrocele

618.1 Uterine prolapse without mention of vaginal wall prolapse ♀
Descensus uteri
Uterine prolapse:
- NOS
- complete
- first degree
- second degree
- third degree

EXCLUDES *that with mention of cystocele, urethrocele, or rectocele (618.2-618.4)*

618.2 Uterovaginal prolapse, incomplete ♀

DEF: Downward displacement of uterus downward into vagina.

618.3 Uterovaginal prolapse, complete ♀

DEF: Downward displacement of uterus exposed within external genitalia.

618.4 Uterovaginal prolapse, unspecified ♀

618.5 Prolapse of vaginal vault after hysterectomy ♀

618.6 Vaginal enterocele, congenital or acquired ♀
Pelvic enterocele, congenital or acquired

DEF: Vaginal vault hernia formed by the loop of the small intestine protruding into the rectal vaginal pouch; can also accompany uterine prolapse or follow hysterectomy.

618.7 Old laceration of muscles of pelvic floor ♀

✓5th **618.8 Other specified genital prolapse**

618.81 Incompetence or weakening of pubocervical tissue ♀

618.82 Incompetence or weakening of rectovaginal tissue ♀

618.83 Pelvic muscle wasting ♀
Disuse atrophy of pelvic muscles and anal sphincter

618.84 Cervical stump prolapse ♀
AHA: 4Q, '06, 97

618.89 Other specified genital prolapse ♀

618.9 Unspecified genital prolapse ♀

✓4th **619 Fistula involving female genital tract**

EXCLUDES *vesicorectal and intestinovesical fistula (596.1)*

619.0 Urinary-genital tract fistula, female ♀
Fistula:
- cervicovesical
- ureterovaginal
- urethrovaginal
- urethrovesicovaginal
- uteroureteric
- uterovesical
- vesicocervicovaginal
- vesicovaginal

619.1 Digestive-genital tract fistula, female ♀
Fistula:
- intestinouterine
- intestinovaginal
- rectovaginal
- rectovulval
- sigmoidovaginal
- uterorectal

619.2 Genital tract-skin fistula, female ♀
Fistula:
- uterus to abdominal wall
- vaginoperineal

619.8 Other specified fistulas involving female genital tract ♀
Fistula:
- cervix
- cul-de-sac (Douglas')
- uterus
- vagina

DEF: Abnormal communication between female reproductive tract and skin.

619.9 Unspecified fistula involving female genital tract ♀

✓4th **620 Noninflammatory disorders of ovary, fallopian tube, and broad ligament**

EXCLUDES *hydrosalpinx (614.1)*

620.0 Follicular cyst of ovary ♀
Cyst of graafian follicle

DEF: Fluid-filled, encapsulated cyst due to occluded follicle duct that secretes hormones into ovaries.

620.1 Corpus luteum cyst or hematoma ♀
Corpus luteum hemorrhage or rupture
Lutein cyst

DEF: Fluid-filled cyst due to serous developing from corpus luteum or clotted blood.

Uterus and Ovaries

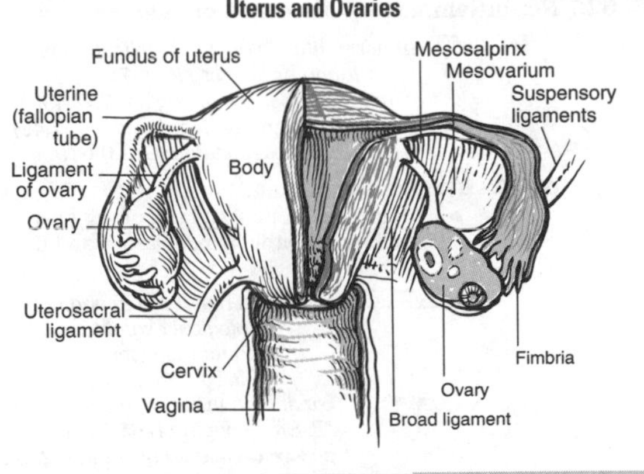

620.2 Other and unspecified ovarian cyst ♀
Cyst:
- NOS, corpus albicans, retention NOS, serous, theca-lutein } of ovary

Simple cystoma of ovary

EXCLUDES *cystadenoma (benign) (serous) (220)*
developmental cysts (752.0)
neoplastic cysts (220)
polycystic ovaries (256.4)
Stein-Leventhal syndrome (256.4)

620.3 Acquired atrophy of ovary and fallopian tube ♀
Senile involution of ovary

620.4 Prolapse or hernia of ovary and fallopian tube ♀
Displacement of ovary and fallopian tube
Salpingocele

620.5 Torsion of ovary, ovarian pedicle, or fallopian tube ♀
Torsion:
- accessory tube
- hydatid of Morgagni

620.6 Broad ligament laceration syndrome ♀
Masters-Allen syndrome

620.7 Hematoma of broad ligament ♀
Hematocele, broad ligament

DEF: Blood within peritoneal fold that supports uterus.

620.8 Other noninflammatory disorders of ovary, fallopian tube, and broad ligament ♀
Cyst, Polyp } of broad ligament or fallopian tube

Infarction, Rupture } of ovary or fallopian tube

Hematosalpinx

EXCLUDES *hematosalpinx in ectopic pregnancy (639.2)*
peritubal adhesions (614.6)
torsion of ovary, ovarian pedicle, or fallopian tube (620.5)

620.9 Unspecified noninflammatory disorder of ovary, fallopian tube, and broad ligament ♀

✓4th **621 Disorders of uterus, not elsewhere classified**

621.0 Polyp of corpus uteri ♀
Polyp:
- endometrium
- uterus NOS

EXCLUDES *cervical polyp NOS (622.7)*

621.1 Chronic subinvolution of uterus ♀
EXCLUDES *puerperal (674.8)*

AHA: 1Q, '91, 11

DEF: Abnormal size of uterus after delivery; the uterus does not return to its normal size after the birth of a child.

621.2 Hypertrophy of uterus ♀
Bulky or enlarged uterus

EXCLUDES *puerperal (674.8)*

✓5th **621.3 Endometrial hyperplasia**
Hyperplasia (adenomatous) (cystic) (glandular) of endometrium

DEF: Abnormal cystic overgrowth of endometrial tissue.

621.30 Endometrial hyperplasia, unspecified ♀
Endometrial hyperplasia NOS

621.31 Simple endometrial hyperplasia without atypia ♀

621.32 Complex endometrial hyperplasia without atypia ♀

621.33 Endometrial hyperplasia with atypia ♀

621.4 Hematometra ♀
Hemometra

EXCLUDES *that in congenital anomaly (752.2-752.3)*

DEF: Accumulated blood in uterus.

621.5 Intrauterine synechiae ♀
Adhesions of uterus
Band(s) of uterus

621.6 Malposition of uterus ♀
Anteversion, Retroflexion, Retroversion } of uterus

EXCLUDES *malposition complicating pregnancy, labor, or delivery (654.3-654.4)*
prolapse of uterus (618.1-618.4)

621.7 Chronic inversion of uterus ♀
EXCLUDES *current obstetrical trauma (665.2)*
prolapse of uterus (618.1-618.4)

621.8 Other specified disorders of uterus, not elsewhere classified ♀
Atrophy, acquired; Cyst; Fibrosis NOS; Old laceration (postpartum); Ulcer } of uterus

EXCLUDES *bilharzial fibrosis (120.0-120.9)*
endometriosis (617.0)
fistulas (619.0-619.8)
inflammatory diseases (615.0-615.9)

621.9 Unspecified disorder of uterus ♀

✓4th **622 Noninflammatory disorders of cervix**
EXCLUDES *abnormality of cervix complicating pregnancy, labor, or delivery (654.5-654.6)*
fistula (619.0-619.8)

622.0 Erosion and ectropion of cervix ♀
Eversion, Ulcer } of cervix

EXCLUDES *that in chronic cervicitis (616.0)*

DEF: Ulceration or turning outward of uterine cervix.

✓5th **622.1 Dysplasia of cervix (uteri)**

EXCLUDES *abnormal results from cervical cytologic examination without histologic confirmation (795.00-795.09)*
carcinoma in situ of cervix (233.1)
cervical intraepithelial neoplasia III [CIN III] (233.1)
▶*HGSIL of cervix (795.04)*◀

AHA: 1Q, '91, 11

DEF: Abnormal cell structures in portal between uterus and vagina.

622.10 Dysplasia of cervix, unspecified ♀
Anaplasia of cervix
Cervical atypism
Cervical dysplasia NOS

622.11 Mild dysplasia of cervix ♀
Cervical intraepithelial neoplasia I [CIN I]

622.12 Moderate dysplasia of cervix ♀
Cervical intraepithelial neoplasia II [CIN II]

EXCLUDES *carcinoma in situ of cervix (233.1)*
cervical intraepithelial neo-plasia III [CIN III] (233.1)
severe dysplasia (233.1)

622.2 Leukoplakia of cervix (uteri) ♀

EXCLUDES *carcinoma in situ of cervix (233.1)*

DEF: Thickened, white patches on portal between uterus and vagina.

622.3 Old laceration of cervix ♀

Adhesions } of cervix
Band(s) } of cervix
Cicatrix (postpartum) } of cervix

EXCLUDES *current obstetrical trauma (665.3)*

DEF: Scarring or other evidence of old wound on cervix.

622.4 Stricture and stenosis of cervix ♀

Atresia (acquired) } of cervix
Contracture } of cervix
Occlusion } of cervix
Pinpoint os uteri

EXCLUDES *congenital (752.49)*
that complicating labor (654.6)

622.5 Incompetence of cervix ♀

EXCLUDES *complicating pregnancy (654.5)*
that affecting fetus or newborn (761.0)

DEF: Inadequate functioning of cervix; marked by abnormal widening during pregnancy; causing miscarriage.

622.6 Hypertrophic elongation of cervix ♀

DEF: Overgrowth of cervix tissues extending down into vagina.

622.7 Mucous polyp of cervix ♀
Polyp NOS of cervix

EXCLUDES *adenomatous polyp of cervix (219.0)*

622.8 Other specified noninflammatory disorders of cervix ♀

Atrophy (senile) } of cervix
Cyst } of cervix
Fibrosis } of cervix
Hemorrhage } of cervix

EXCLUDES *endometriosis (617.0)*
fistula (619.0-619.8)
inflammatory diseases (616.0)

622.9 Unspecified noninflammatory disorder of cervix ♀

✓4th **623 Noninflammatory disorders of vagina**

EXCLUDES *abnormality of vagina complicating pregnancy, labor, or delivery (654.7)*
congenital absence of vagina (752.49)
congenital diaphragm or bands (752.49)
fistulas involving vagina (619.0-619.8)

623.0 Dysplasia of vagina ♀
▶Mild and moderate dysplasia of vagina◀
Vaginal intraepithelial neoplasia I and II [VAIN I and II]

EXCLUDES ▶*abnormal results from vaginal cytological examination without histologic confirmation (795.10-795.19)*◀
carcinoma in situ of vagina (233.31)
▶*HGSIL of vagina (795.14)*◀
severe dysplasia of vagina (233.31)
vaginal intraepithelial neoplasia III [VAIN III] (233.31)

623.1 Leukoplakia of vagina ♀

DEF: Thickened white patches on vaginal canal.

623.2 Stricture or atresia of vagina ♀
Adhesions (postoperative) (postradiation) of vagina
Occlusion of vagina
Stenosis, vagina
Use additional E code to identify any external cause

EXCLUDES *congenital atresia or stricture (752.49)*

623.3 Tight hymenal ring ♀

Rigid hymen } acquired or congenital
Tight hymenal ring } acquired or congenital
Tight introitus } acquired or congenital

EXCLUDES *imperforate hymen (752.42)*

623.4 Old vaginal laceration ♀

EXCLUDES *old laceration involving muscles of pelvic floor (618.7)*

DEF: Scarring or other evidence of old wound on vagina.

623.5 Leukorrhea, not specified as infective ♀
Leukorrhea NOS of vagina
Vaginal discharge NOS

EXCLUDES *trichomonal (131.00)*

DEF: Viscid whitish discharge, from vagina.

623.6 Vaginal hematoma ♀

EXCLUDES *current obstetrical trauma (665.7)*

623.7 Polyp of vagina ♀

623.8 Other specified noninflammatory disorders of vagina ♀

Cyst } of vagina
Hemorrhage } of vagina

623.9 Unspecified noninflammatory disorder of vagina ♀

✓4th **624 Noninflammatory disorders of vulva and perineum**

EXCLUDES *abnormality of vulva and perineum complicating pregnancy, labor, or delivery (654.8)*
condyloma acuminatum (078.1)
fistulas involving:
perineum – see Alphabetic Index
vulva (619.0-619.8)
vulval varices (456.6)
vulvar involvement in skin conditions (690-709.9)

✓5th **624.0 Dystrophy of vulva**

EXCLUDES *carcinoma in situ of vulva (233.32)*
severe dysplasia of vulva (233.32)
vulvar intraepithelial neoplasia III [VIN III] (233.32)

AHA: 4Q, '07, 90

624.01 **Vulvar intraepithelial neoplasia I [VIN I]** ♀
Mild dysplasia of vulva

624.02 **Vulvar intraepithelial neoplasia II [VIN II]** ♀
Moderate dysplasia of vulva
AHA: 4Q, '07, 91

624.09 **Other dystrophy of vulva** ♀
Kraurosis of vulva
Leukoplakia of vulva

624.1 **Atrophy of vulva** ♀

624.2 **Hypertrophy of clitoris** ♀
EXCLUDES *that in endocrine disorders (255.2, 256.1)*

624.3 **Hypertrophy of labia** ♀
Hypertrophy of vulva NOS
DEF: Overgrowth of fleshy folds on either side of vagina.

624.4 **Old laceration or scarring of vulva** ♀
DEF: Scarring or other evidence of old wound on external female genitalia.

624.5 **Hematoma of vulva** ♀
EXCLUDES *that complicating delivery (664.5)*
DEF: Blood in tissue of external genitalia.

624.6 **Polyp of labia and vulva** ♀

624.8 **Other specified noninflammatory disorders of vulva and perineum** ♀
Cyst, Edema, Stricture } of vulva
AHA: 1Q, '03, 13; 1Q, '95, 8

624.9 **Unspecified noninflammatory disorder of vulva and perineum** ♀

4th 625 **Pain and other symptoms associated with female genital organs**

625.0 **Dyspareunia** ♀
EXCLUDES *psychogenic dyspareunia (302.76)*
DEF: Difficult or painful sexual intercourse.

625.1 **Vaginismus** ♀
Colpospasm
Vulvismus
EXCLUDES *psychogenic vaginismus (306.51)*
DEF: Vaginal spasms; due to involuntary contraction of musculature; prevents intercourse.

625.2 **Mittelschmerz** ♀
Intermenstrual pain
Ovulation pain
DEF: Pain occurring between menstrual periods.

625.3 **Dysmenorrhea** ♀
Painful menstruation
EXCLUDES *psychogenic dysmenorrhea (306.52)*
AHA: 2Q, '94, 12

625.4 **Premenstrual tension syndromes** ♀
▶Menstrual molimen◀
Premenstrual dysphoric disorder
Premenstrual syndrome
Premenstrual tension NOS
EXCLUDES ▶*menstrual migraine (346.4)*◀
AHA: 4Q, '03, 116

625.5 **Pelvic congestion syndrome** ♀
Congestion-fibrosis syndrome
Taylor's syndrome
DEF: Excessive accumulation of blood in vessels of pelvis; may occur after orgasm; causes abnormal menstruation, lower back pain and vaginal discharge.

625.6 **Stress incontinence, female** ♀
EXCLUDES *mixed incontinence (788.33)*
stress incontinence, male (788.32)
DEF: Involuntary leakage of urine due to insufficient sphincter control; occurs upon sneezing, laughing, coughing, sudden movement or lifting.

● 5th 625.7 **Vulvodynia**

● 625.70 **Vulvodynia, unspecified** ♀
Vulvodynia NOS

● 625.71 **Vulvar vestibulitis** ♀

● 625.79 **Other vulvodynia** ♀

625.8 **Other specified symptoms associated with female genital organs** ♀
AHA: N-D, '85, 16

625.9 **Unspecified symptom associated with female genital organs** ♀
AHA: 4Q, '06, 110

4th 626 **Disorders of menstruation and other abnormal bleeding from female genital tract**
EXCLUDES *menopausal and premenopausal bleeding (627.0)*
pain and other symptoms associated with menstrual cycle (625.2-625.4)
postmenopausal bleeding (627.1)

626.0 **Absence of menstruation** ♀
Amenorrhea (primary) (secondary)

626.1 **Scanty or infrequent menstruation** ♀
Hypomenorrhea
Oligomenorrhea

626.2 **Excessive or frequent menstruation** ♀
Heavy periods
Menometrorrhagia
Menorrhagia
Plymenorrhea
EXCLUDES *premenopausal (627.0)*
that in puberty (626.3)

626.3 **Puberty bleeding** ♀
Excessive bleeding associated with onset of menstrual periods
Pubertal menorrhagia

626.4 **Irregular menstrual cycle** ♀
Irregular:
- bleeding NOS
- menstruation
- periods

626.5 **Ovulation bleeding** ♀
Regular intermenstrual bleeding

626.6 **Metrorrhagia** ♀
Bleeding unrelated to menstrual cycle
Irregular intermenstrual bleeding

626.7 **Postcoital bleeding** ♀
DEF: Bleeding from vagina after sexual intercourse.

626.8 **Other** ♀
Dysfunctional or functional uterine hemorrhage NOS
Menstruation:
- retained
- suppression of

626.9 **Unspecified** ♀

4th 627 **Menopausal and postmenopausal disorders**
EXCLUDES *asymptomatic age-related (natural) postmenopausal status (V49.81)*

627.0 **Premenopausal menorrhagia** ♀
Excessive bleeding associated with onset of menopause
Menorrhagia:
- climacteric
- menopausal
- preclimacteric

627.1 Postmenopausal bleeding ♀

627.2 Symptomatic menopausal or female climacteric states ♀

Symptoms, such as flushing, sleeplessness, headache, lack of concentration, associated with the menopause

627.3 Postmenopausal atrophic vaginitis ♀

Senile (atrophic) vaginitis

627.4 Symptomatic states associated with artificial menopause ♀

Postartificial menopause syndromes

Any condition classifiable to 627.1, 627.2, or 627.3 which follows induced menopause

DEF: Conditions arising after hysterectomy.

627.8 Other specified menopausal and postmenopausal disorders ♀

EXCLUDES *premature menopause NOS (256.31)*

627.9 Unspecified menopausal and postmenopausal disorder ♀

✓4th **628 Infertility, female**

INCLUDES primary and secondary sterility

AHA: 2Q, '96, 9; 1Q, '95, 7

DEF: Infertility: inability to conceive for at least one year with regular intercourse.

DEF: Primary infertility: occurring in patients who have never conceived.

DEF: Secondary infertility: occurring in patients who have previously conceived.

628.0 Associated with anovulation ♀

Anovulatory cycle

Use additional code for any associated Stein-Leventhal syndrome (256.4)

628.1 Of pituitary-hypothalamic origin ♀

Code first underlying cause, as:
adiposogenital dystrophy (253.8)
anterior pituitary disorder (253.0-253.4)

628.2 Of tubal origin ♀

Infertility associated with congenital anomaly of tube

Tubal:
block
occlusion
stenosis

Use additional code for any associated peritubal adhesions (614.6)

628.3 Of uterine origin ♀

Infertility associated with congenital anomaly of uterus

Nonimplantation

Use additional code for any associated tuberculous endometritis (016.7)

628.4 Of cervical or vaginal origin ♀

Infertility associated with:
anomaly of cervical mucus
congenital structural anomaly
dysmucorrhea

628.8 Of other specified origin ♀

628.9 Of unspecified origin ♀

✓4th **629 Other disorders of female genital organs**

629.0 Hematocele, female, not elsewhere classified ♀

EXCLUDES *hematocele or hematoma:*
broad ligament (620.7)
fallopian tube (620.8)
that associated with ectopic pregnancy (633.00-633.91)
uterus (621.4)
vagina (623.6)
vulva (624.5)

629.1 Hydrocele, canal of Nuck ♀

Cyst of canal of Nuck (acquired)

EXCLUDES *congenital (752.41)*

✓5th **629.2 Female genital mutilation status**

Female circumcision status
Female genital cutting

AHA: 4Q, '04, 88

629.20 Female genital mutilation status, unspecified ♀

Female genital cutting status, unspecified
Female genital mutilation status NOS

629.21 Female genital mutilation Type I status ♀

Clitorectomy status
Female genital cutting Type I status

DEF: Female genital mutilation involving clitorectomy, with part or all of the clitoris removed.

629.22 Female genital mutilation Type II status ♀

Clitorectomy with excision of labia minora status
Female genital cutting Type II status

AHA: 4Q, '04, 90

DEF: Female genital mutilation involving clitoris and the labia minora amputation.

629.23 Female genital mutilation Type III status ♀

Female genital cutting Type III status
Infibulation status

AHA: 4Q, '04, 90

DEF: Female genital mutilation involving removal, most or all of the labia minora excised, labia majora incised which is then made into a hood of skin over the urethral and vaginal opening.

629.29 Other female genital mutilation status ♀

Female genital cutting Type IV status
Female genital mutilation Type IV status
Other female genital cutting status

AHA: 4Q, '06, 97

✓5th **629.8 Other specified disorders of female genital organs**

629.81 Habitual aborter without current pregnancy ♀

EXCLUDES *habitual aborter with current pregnancy (646.3)*

AHA: 4Q, '06, 98

629.89 Other specified disorders of female genital organs ♀

AHA: 4Q, '06, 98

629.9 Unspecified disorder of female genital organs ♀

11. COMPLICATIONS OF PREGNANCY, CHILDBIRTH, AND THE PUERPERIUM ▸(630-679)◂

ECTOPIC AND MOLAR PREGNANCY (630-633)

Use additional code from category 639 to identify any complications

630 Hydatidiform mole M♀

Trophoblastic disease NOS
Vesicular mole

EXCLUDES *chorioadenoma (destruens) (236.1)*
chorionepithelioma (181)
malignant hydatidiform mole (236.1)

DEF: Abnormal product of pregnancy; marked by mass of cysts resembling bunch of grapes due to chorionic villi proliferation, and dissolution; must be surgically removed.

631 Other abnormal product of conception M♀

Blighted ovum
Mole:
NOS
carneous
fleshy
stone

632 Missed abortion M♀

Early fetal death before completion of 22 weeks' gestation with retention of dead fetus
Retained products of conception, not following spontaneous or induced abortion or delivery

EXCLUDES *failed induced abortion (638.0-638.9)*
fetal death (intrauterine) (late) (656.4)
missed delivery (656.4)
that with abnormal product of conception (630, 631)

AHA: 1Q, '01, 5

✓4th **633 Ectopic pregnancy**

INCLUDES ruptured ectopic pregnancy

AHA: 4Q, '02, 61
DEF: Fertilized egg develops outside uterus.

✓5th **633.0 Abdominal pregnancy**

Intraperitoneal pregnancy

633.00 Abdominal pregnancy without intrauterine pregnancy M♀

633.01 Abdominal pregnancy with intrauterine pregnancy M♀

✓5th **633.1 Tubal pregnancy**

Fallopian pregnancy
Rupture of (fallopian) tube due to pregnancy
Tubal abortion

AHA: 2Q, '90, 27

633.10 Tubal pregnancy without intrauterine pregnancy M♀

633.11 Tubal pregnancy with intrauterine pregnancy M♀

✓5th **633.2 Ovarian pregnancy**

633.20 Ovarian pregnancy without intrauterine pregnancy M♀

633.21 Ovarian pregnancy with intrauterine pregnancy M♀

✓5th **633.8 Other ectopic pregnancy**

Pregnancy:
cervical
combined
cornual
intraligamentous
mesometric
mural

633.80 Other ectopic pregnancy without intrauterine pregnancy M♀

633.81 Other ectopic pregnancy with intrauterine pregnancy M♀

✓5th **633.9 Unspecified ectopic pregnancy**

633.90 Unspecified ectopic pregnancy without intrauterine pregnancy M♀

633.91 Unspecified ectopic pregnancy with intrauterine pregnancy M♀

OTHER PREGNANCY WITH ABORTIVE OUTCOME (634-639)

The following fourth-digit subdivisions are for use with categories 634-638:

.0 Complicated by genital tract and pelvic infection
Endometritis
Salpingo-oophoritis
Sepsis NOS
Septicemia NOS
Any condition classifiable to 639.0 with condition classifiable to 634-638
EXCLUDES *urinary tract infection (634-638 with .7)*

.1 Complicated by delayed or excessive hemorrhage
Afibrinogenemia
Defibrination syndrome
Intravascular hemolysis
Any condition classifiable to 639.1 with condition classifiable to 634-638

.2 Complicated by damage to pelvic organs and tissues
Laceration, perforation, or tear of:
bladder
uterus
Any condition classifiable to 639.2 with condition classifiable to 634-638

.3 Complicated by renal failure
Oliguria
Uremia
Any condition classifiable to 639.3, with condition classifiable to 634-638

.4 Complicated by metabolic disorder
Electrolyte imbalance with conditions classfiable to 634-638

.5 Complicated by shock
Circulatory collapse
Shock (postoperative) (septic)
Any condition classifiable to 639.5 with condition classifiable to 634-638

.6 Complicated by embolism
Embolism:
NOS
amniotic fluid
pulmonary
Any condition classifiable to 639.6, with condition classifiable to 634-638

.7 With other specified complications
Cardiac arrest or failure
Urinary tract infection
Any condition classiable to 639.8 with condition classifiable to 634-638

.8 With unspecified complication

.9 Without mention of complication

Ectopic Pregnancy Sites

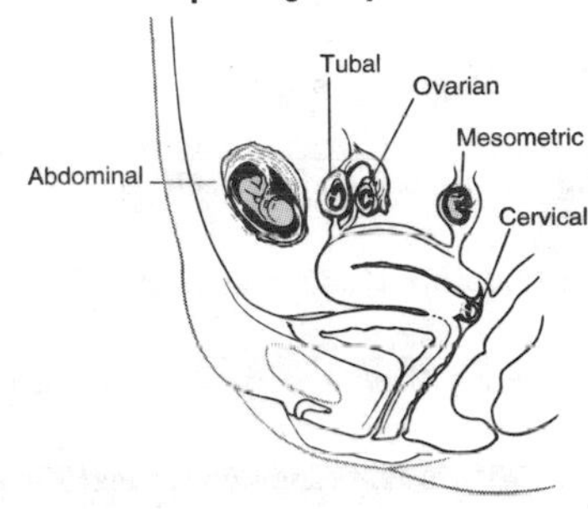

§ ✓4th 634 **Spontaneous abortion**

Requires fifth-digit to identify stage:
0 **unspecified**
1 **incomplete**
2 **complete**

INCLUDES miscarriage
spontaneous abortion

AHA: 2Q, '91, 16

DEF: Spontaneous premature expulsion of the products of conception from the uterus.

§§ ✓5th 634.0 **Complicated by genital tract and pelvic infection** [0-2] M♀

§§ ✓5th 634.1 **Complicated by delayed or excessive hemorrhage** [0-2] M♀
AHA: For Code 634.11: 1Q, '03, 6

§§ ✓5th 634.2 **Complicated by damage to pelvic organs or tissues** [0-2] M♀

§§ ✓5th 634.3 **Complicated by renal failure** [0-2] M♀

§§ ✓5th 634.4 **Complicated by metabolic disorder** [0-2] M♀

§§ ✓5th 634.5 **Complicated by shock** [0-2] M♀

§§ ✓5th 634.6 **Complicated by embolism** [0-2] M♀

§§ ✓5th 634.7 **With other specified complications** [0-2] M♀

§§ ✓5th 634.8 **With unspecified complication** [0-2] M♀

§§ ✓5th 634.9 **Without mention of complication** [0-2] M♀

§ ✓4th 635 **Legally induced abortion**

Requires fifth-digit to identify stage:
0 **unspecified**
1 **incomplete**
2 **complete**

INCLUDES abortion or termination of pregnancy:
elective
legal
therapeutic

EXCLUDES *menstrual extraction or regulation (V25.3)*

AHA: 2Q, '94, 14

DEF: Intentional expulsion of products of conception from uterus performed by medical professionals inside boundaries of law.

§§ ✓5th 635.0 **Complicated by genital tract and pelvic infection** [0-2] M♀

§§ ✓5th 635.1 **Complicated by delayed or excessive hemorrhage** [0-2] M♀

§§ ✓5th 635.2 **Complicated by damage to pelvic organs or tissues** [0-2] M♀

§§ ✓5th 635.3 **Complicated by renal failure** [0-2] M♀

§§ ✓5th 635.4 **Complicated by metabolic disorder** [0-2] M♀

§§ ✓5th 635.5 **Complicated by shock** [0-2] M♀

§§ ✓5th 635.6 **Complicated by embolism** [0-2] M♀

§§ ✓5th 635.7 **With other specified complications** [0-2] M♀

§§ ✓5th 635.8 **With unspecified complication** [0-2] M♀

§§ ✓5th 635.9 **Without mention of complication** [0-2] M♀
AHA: For code 635.92: 2Q, '94, 14

§ ✓4th 636 **Illegally induced abortion**

Requires fifth-digit to identify stage:
0 **unspecified**
1 **incomplete**
2 **complete**

INCLUDES abortion:
criminal
illegal
self-induced

DEF: Intentional expulsion of products of conception from uterus; outside boundaries of law.

§§ ✓5th 636.0 **Complicated by genital tract and pelvic infection** [0-2] M♀

§§ ✓5th 636.1 **Complicated by delayed or excessive hemorrhage** [0-2] M♀

§§ ✓5th 636.2 **Complicated by damage to pelvic organs or tissues** [0-2] M♀

§§ ✓5th 636.3 **Complicated by renal failure** [0-2] M♀

§§ ✓5th 636.4 **Complicated by metabolic disorder** [0-2] M♀

§§ ✓5th 636.5 **Complicated by shock** [0-2] M♀

§§ ✓5th 636.6 **Complicated by embolism** [0-2] M♀

§§ ✓5th 636.7 **With other specified complications** [0-2] M♀

§§ ✓5th 636.8 **With unspecified complication** [0-2] M♀

§§ ✓5th 636.9 **Without mention of complication** [0-2] M♀

§ ✓4th 637 **Unspecified abortion**

Requires fifth-digit to identify stage:
0 **unspecified**
1 **incomplete**
2 **complete**

INCLUDES abortion NOS
retained products of conception following abortion, not classifiable elsewhere

§§ ✓5th 637.0 **Complicated by genital tract and pelvic infection** [0-2] M♀

§§ ✓5th 637.1 **Complicated by delayed or excessive hemorrhage** [0-2] M♀

§§ ✓5th 637.2 **Complicated by damage to pelvic organs or tissues** [0-2] M♀

§§ ✓5th 637.3 **Complicated by renal failure** [0-2] M♀

§§ ✓5th 637.4 **Complicated by metabolic disorder** [0-2] M♀

§§ ✓5th 637.5 **Complicated by shock** [0-2] M♀

§§ ✓5th 637.6 **Complicated by embolism** [0-2] M♀

§§ ✓5th 637.7 **With other specified complications** [0-2] M♀

§§ ✓5th 637.8 **With unspecified complication** [0-2] M♀

§§ ✓5th 637.9 **Without mention of complication** [0-2] M♀

§ See beginning of section 634-639 for fourth-digit definitions.
§§ Requires fifth-digit. Valid digits are in [brackets] under each code. See appropriate category for codes and definitions.

§ ✓4th **638 Failed attempted abortion**

INCLUDES failure of attempted induction of (legal) abortion

EXCLUDES *incomplete abortion (634.0-637.9)*

DEF: Continued pregnancy despite an attempted legal abortion.

638.0 Complicated by genital tract and pelvic infection M ♀

638.1 Complicated by delayed or excessive hemorrhage M ♀

638.2 Complicated by damage to pelvic organs or tissues M ♀

638.3 Complicated by renal failure M ♀

638.4 Complicated by metabolic disorder M ♀

638.5 Complicated by shock M ♀

638.6 Complicated by embolism M ♀

638.7 With other specified complications M ♀

638.8 With unspecified complication M ♀

638.9 Without mention of complication M ♀

✓4th **639 Complications following abortion and ectopic and molar pregnancies**

Note: This category is provided for use when it is required to classify separately the complications classifiable to the fourth-digit level in categories 634-638; for example:

a) when the complication itself was responsible for an episode of medical care, the abortion, ectopic or molar pregnancy itself having been dealt with at a previous episode

b) when these conditions are immediate complications of ectopic or molar pregnancies classifiable to 630-633 where they cannot be identified at fourth-digit level.

639.0 Genital tract and pelvic infection M ♀

Endometritis
Parametritis
Pelvic peritonitis
Salpingitis
Salpingo-oophoritis
Sepsis NOS
Septicemia NOS
} following conditions classifiable to 630-638

EXCLUDES *urinary tract infection (639.8)*

639.1 Delayed or excessive hemorrhage M ♀

Afibrinogenemia
Defibrination syndrome
Intravascular
} following conditions classfiable to 630-638

639.2 Damage to pelvic organs and tissues M ♀

Laceration, perforation, or tear of:
bladder
bowel
broad ligament
cervix
periurethral tissue
uterus
vagina
} following conditions classifiable to 630-638

639.3 Renal failure M ♀

Oliguria
Renal:
failure (acute)
shutdown
tubular necrosis
Uremia
} following conditions classifiable to 630-638

639.4 Metabolic disorders M ♀

Electrolyte imbalance following conditions classifiable to 630-638

639.5 Shock M ♀

Circulatory collapse
Shock (postoperative) (septic)
} following conditions classifiable to 630-638

639.6 Embolism M ♀

Embolism:
NOS
air
amniotic fluid
blood-clot
fat
pulmonary
pyemic
septic
soap
} following conditions classifiable to 630-638

639.8 Other specified complications following abortion or ectopic and molar pregnancy M ♀

Acute yellow atrophy or necrosis of liver
Cardiac arrest or failure
Cerebral anoxia
Urinary tract infection
} following conditons classifiable to 630-638

639.9 Unspecified complication following abortion or ectopic and molar pregnancy M ♀

Complication(s) not further specified following conditions classifiable to 630-638

COMPLICATIONS MAINLY RELATED TO PREGNANCY (640-649)

INCLUDES the listed conditions even if they arose or were present during labor, delivery, or the puerperium

AHA: 2Q, '90, 11

The following fifth-digit subclassification is for use with categories 640-649 to denote the current episode of care. Valid fifth-digits are in [brackets] under each code.

0 unspecified as to episode of care or not applicable

1 delivered, with or without mention of antepartum condition

Antepartum condition with delivery
Delivery NOS (with mention of antepartum complication during current episode of care)
Intrapartum obstetric condition (with mention of antepartum complication during current episode of care)
Pregnancy, delivered (with mention of antepartum complication during current episode of care)

2 delivered, with mention of postpartum complication

Delivery with mention of puerperal complication during current episode of care

3 antepartum condition or complication

Antepartum obstetric condtion, not delivered during the current episode of care

4 postpartum condition of complication

Postpartum or puerperal obstetric condition or complication following delivery that occurred:
during previous episode of care
outside hospital, with subsequent admission for observation or care

✓4th **640 Hemorrhage in early pregnancy**

INCLUDES hemorrhage before completion of 22 weeks' gestation

§§ ✓5th **640.0 Threatened abortion** M ♀
[0,1,3] DEF: Bloody discharge during pregnancy; cervix may be dilated and pregnancy is threatened, but the pregnancy is not terminated.

§§ ✓5th **640.8 Other specified hemorrhage in early pregnancy** M ♀
[0,1,3]

§§ ✓5th **640.9 Unspecified hemorrhage in early pregnancy** M ♀
[0,1,3]

§ See beginning of section 634-639 for fourth-digit definitions

§§ Requires fifth-digit. Valid digits are in [brackets] under each code. See beginning of section 640-649 for codes and definitions.

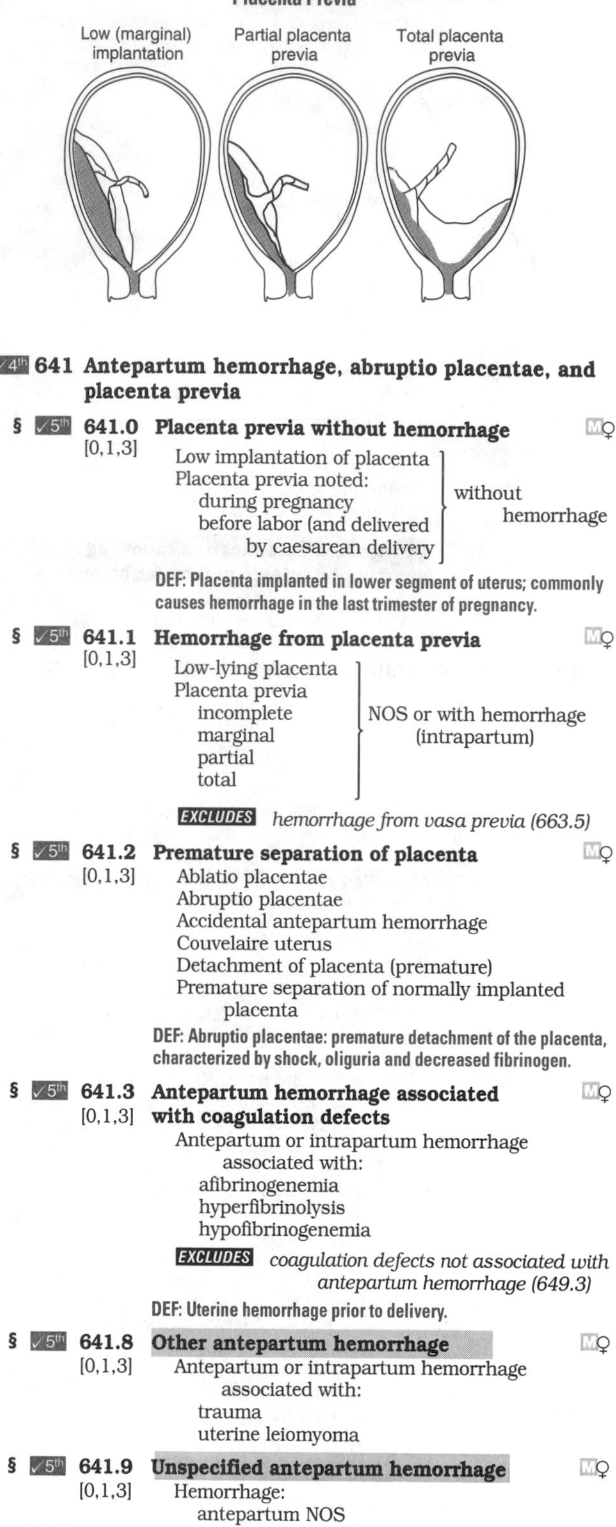

✓4th 641 Antepartum hemorrhage, abruptio placentae, and placenta previa

§ ✓5th **641.0 Placenta previa without hemorrhage** M♀
[0,1,3]
Low implantation of placenta
Placenta previa noted:
  during pregnancy
  before labor (and delivered by caesarean delivery)
} without hemorrhage

DEF: Placenta implanted in lower segment of uterus; commonly causes hemorrhage in the last trimester of pregnancy.

§ ✓5th **641.1 Hemorrhage from placenta previa** M♀
[0,1,3]
Low-lying placenta
Placenta previa
  incomplete
  marginal
  partial
  total
} NOS or with hemorrhage (intrapartum)

EXCLUDES *hemorrhage from vasa previa (663.5)*

§ ✓5th **641.2 Premature separation of placenta** M♀
[0,1,3]
Ablatio placentae
Abruptio placentae
Accidental antepartum hemorrhage
Couvelaire uterus
Detachment of placenta (premature)
Premature separation of normally implanted placenta

DEF: Abruptio placentae: premature detachment of the placenta, characterized by shock, oliguria and decreased fibrinogen.

§ ✓5th **641.3 Antepartum hemorrhage associated with coagulation defects** M♀
[0,1,3]
Antepartum or intrapartum hemorrhage associated with:
  afibrinogenemia
  hyperfibrinolysis
  hypofibrinogenemia

EXCLUDES *coagulation defects not associated with antepartum hemorrhage (649.3)*

DEF: Uterine hemorrhage prior to delivery.

§ ✓5th **641.8 Other antepartum hemorrhage** M♀
[0,1,3]
Antepartum or intrapartum hemorrhage associated with:
  trauma
  uterine leiomyoma

§ ✓5th **641.9 Unspecified antepartum hemorrhage** M♀
[0,1,3]
Hemorrhage:
  antepartum NOS
  intrapartum NOS
  of pregnancy NOS

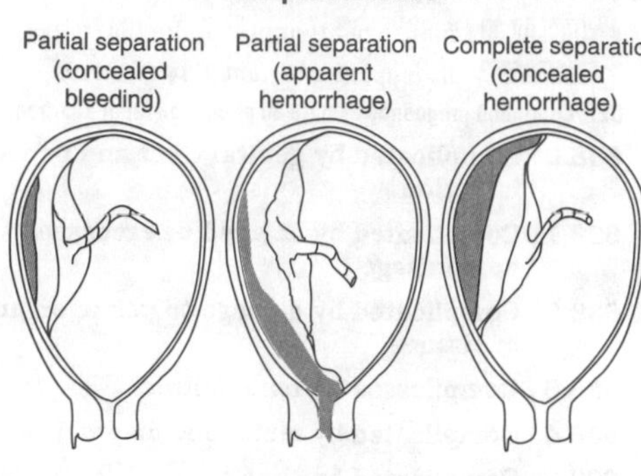

✓4th 642 Hypertension complicating pregnancy, childbirth, and the puerperium

§ ✓5th **642.0 Benign essential hypertension complicating pregnancy, childbirth, and the puerperium** M♀
[0-4]
Hypertension
  benign essential
  chronic NOS
  essential
  pre-existing NOS
} specified as complicating, or as reason for obstetric care during pregnancy, childbirth, or the puerperium

§ ✓5th **642.1 Hypertension secondary to renal disease, complicating pregnancy, childbirth, and the puerperium** M♀
[0-4]
Hypertension secondary to renal disease, specified as complicating, or as a reason for obstetric care during pregnancy, childbirth, or the puerperium

§ ✓5th **642.2 Other pre-existing hypertension complicating pregnancy, childbirth, and the puerperium** M♀
[0-4]
Hypertensive
  chronic kidney disease
  heart and chronic kidney disease
  heart disease
Malignant hypertension
} specified as complicating, or as a reason for obstetric care during pregnancy, childbirth, or the puerperium

§ ✓5th **642.3 Transient hypertension of pregnancy** M♀
[0-4]
Gestational hypertension
Transient hypertension, so described, in pregnancy, childbirth, or the puerperium

AHA: 3Q, '90, 4

§ ✓5th **642.4 Mild or unspecified pre-eclampsia** M♀
[0-4]
Hypertension in pregnancy, childbirth, or the puerperium, not specified as pre-existing, with either albuminuria or edema, or both; mild or unspecified
Pre-eclampsia:
  NOS
  mild
Toxemia (pre-eclamptic):
  NOS
  mild

EXCLUDES *albuminuria in pregnancy, without mention of hypertension (646.2)*
edema in pregnancy, without mention of hypertension (646.1)

§ ✓5th **642.5 Severe pre-eclampsia** M♀
[0-4]
Hypertension in pregnancy, childbirth, or the puerperium, not specified as pre-existing, with either albuminuria or edema, or both; specified as severe
Pre-eclampsia, severe
Toxemia (pre-eclamptic), severe

AHA: N-D, '85, 3

§ Requires fifth-digit. Valid digits are in [brackets] under each code. See beginning of section 640-649 for codes and definitions.

§ 5th **642.6 Eclampsia** M♀
[0-4]
Toxemia:
eclamptic
with convulsions

§ 5th **642.7 Pre-eclampsia or eclampsia superimposed on pre-existing hypertension** M♀
[0-4]
Conditions classifiable to 642.4-642.6, with conditions classifiable to 642.0-642.2

§ 5th **642.9 Unspecified hypertension complicating pregnancy, childbirth, or the puerperium** M♀
[0-4]
Hypertension NOS, without mention of albuminuria or edema, complicating pregnancy, childbirth, or the puerperium

4th **643 Excessive vomiting in pregnancy**

INCLUDES hyperemesis / vomiting: persistent / vicious } arising during pregnancy
hyperemesis gravidarum

§ 5th **643.0 Mild hyperemesis gravidarum** M♀
[0,1,3]
Hyperemesis gravidarum, mild or unspecified, starting before the end of the 22nd week of gestation
DEF: Detrimental vomiting and nausea.

§ 5th **643.1 Hyperemesis gravidarum with metabolic disturbance** M♀
[0,1,3]
Hyperemesis gravidarum, starting before the end of the 22nd week of gestation, with metabolic disturbance, such as:
carbohydrate depletion
dehydration
electrolyte imbalance

§ 5th **643.2 Late vomiting of pregnancy** M♀
[0,1,3]
Excessive vomiting starting after 22 completed weeks of gestation

§ 5th **643.8 Other vomiting complicating pregnancy** M♀
[0,1,3]
Vomiting due to organic disease or other cause, specified as complicating pregnancy, or as a reason for obstetric care during pregnancy
Use additional code to specify cause

§ 5th **643.9 Unspecified vomiting of pregnancy** M♀
[0,1,3]
Vomiting as a reason for care during pregnancy, length of gestation unspecified

4th **644 Early or threatened labor**

§ 5th **644.0 Threatened premature labor** M♀
[0,3]
Premature labor after 22 weeks, but before 37 completed weeks of gestation without delivery
EXCLUDES *that occurring before 22 completed weeks of gestation (640.0)*

§ 5th **644.1 Other threatened labor** M♀
[0,3]
False labor:
NOS / after 37 completed weeks of gestation } without delivery
Threatened labor NOS } without delivery

§ 5th **644.2 Early onset of delivery** M♀
[0,1]
Onset (spontaneous) of delivery / Premature labor with onset of delivery } before 37 completed weeks of gestation
AHA: 2Q, '91, 16

4th **645 Late pregnancy**
AHA: 4Q, '00, 43; 4Q, '91, 26

§ 5th **645.1 Post term pregnancy** M♀
[0,1,3]
Pregnancy over 40 completed weeks to 42 completed weeks gestation

§ 5th **645.2 Prolonged pregnancy** M♀
[0,1,3]
Pregnancy which has advanced beyond 42 completed weeks gestation

4th **646 Other complications of pregnancy, not elsewhere classified**
Use additional code(s) to further specify complication
AHA: 4Q, '95, 59

§ 5th **646.0 Papyraceous fetus** M♀
[0,1,3]
DEF: Fetus that dies in the second trimester of pregnancy and is retained in the uterus, with subsequent atrophy and mummification; commonly occurs in twin pregnancy, nonviable fetus becomes compressed by growth of living twin and exhibits parchment-like skin.

§ 5th **646.1 Edema or excessive weight gain in pregnancy, without mention of hypertension** M♀
[0-4]
Gestational edema
Maternal obesity syndrome
EXCLUDES *that with mention of hypertension (642.0-642.9)*

§ 5th **646.2 Unspecified renal disease in pregnancy, without mention of hypertension** M♀
[0-4]
Albuminuria / Nephropathy NOS / Renal disease NOS / Uremia } in pregnancy or the puerperium, without mention of hypertension
Gestational proteinuria
EXCLUDES *that with mention of hypertension (642.0-642.9)*

§ 5th **646.3 Habitual aborter** M♀
[0,1,3]
EXCLUDES *with current abortion (634.0-634.9)*
without current pregnancy (629.81)
DEF: Three or more consecutive spontaneous abortions.

§ 5th **646.4 Peripheral neuritis in pregnancy** M♀
[0-4]

§ 5th **646.5 Asymptomatic bacteriuria in pregnancy** M♀
[0-4]

§ 5th **646.6 Infections of genitourinary tract in pregnancy** M♀
[0-4]
Conditions classifiable to 590, 595, 597, 599.0, 616 complicating pregnancy, childbirth, or the puerperium
Conditions classifiable to 614.0-614.5, 614.7-614.9, 615 complicating pregnancy or labor
EXCLUDES *major puerperal infection (670)*
AHA: For code 646.63: 4Q, '04, 90

§ 5th **646.7 Liver disorders in pregnancy** M♀
[0,1,3]
Acute yellow atrophy of liver (obstetric) (true) / Icterus gravis / Necrosis of liver } of pregnancy
EXCLUDES *hepatorenal syndrome following delivery (674.8)*
viral hepatitis (647.6)

§ 5th **646.8 Other specified complications of pregnancy** M♀
[0-4]
Fatigue during pregnancy
Herpes gestationis
Insufficient weight gain of pregnancy
AHA: 3Q, '98, 16; J-F, '85, 15

§ 5th **646.9 Unspecified complication of pregnancy** M♀
[0,1,3]

§ Requires fifth-digit. Valid digits are in [brackets] under each code. See beginning of section 640-649 for codes and definitions.

4th 647 Infectious and parasitic conditions in the mother classifiable elsewhere, but complicating pregnancy, childbirth, or the puerperium

INCLUDES the listed conditions when complicating the pregnant state, aggravated by the pregnancy, or when a main reason for obstetric care

Use additional code(s) to further specify complication

EXCLUDES *those conditions in the mother known or suspected to have affected the fetus (655.0-655.9)*

§ 5th **647.0 Syphilis** M♀
[0-4] Conditions classifiable to 090-097

§ 5th **647.1 Gonorrhea** M♀
[0-4] Conditions classifiable to 098

§ 5th **647.2 Other venereal diseases** M♀
[0-4] Conditions classifiable to 099

§ 5th **647.3 Tuberculosis** M♀
[0-4] Conditions classifiable to 010-018

§ 5th **647.4 Malaria** M♀
[0-4] Conditions classifiable to 084

§ 5th **647.5 Rubella** M♀
[0-4] Conditions classifiable to 056

§ 5th **647.6 Other viral diseases** M♀
[0-4] Conditions classifiable to ▶042, 050-055, 057-079, 795.05, 795.15, 796.75◀

AHA: J-F, '85, 15

§ 5th **647.8 Other specified infectious and parasitic diseases** M♀
[0-4]

§ 5th **647.9 Unspecified infection or infestation** M♀
[0-4]

4th 648 Other current conditions in the mother classifiable elsewhere, but complicating pregnancy, childbirth, or the puerperium

INCLUDES the listed conditions when complicating the pregnant state, aggravated by the pregnancy, or when a main reason for obstetric care

Use additional code(s) to identify the condition

EXCLUDES *those conditions in the mother known or suspected to have affected the fetus ▶(655.0-655.9)◀*

§ 5th **648.0 Diabetes mellitus** M♀
[0-4] Conditions classifiable to ▶249, 250◀

EXCLUDES *gestational diabetes (648.8)*

AHA: 3Q, '91, 5, 11

§ 5th **648.1 Thyroid dysfunction** M♀
[0-4] Conditions classifiable to 240-246

§ 5th **648.2 Anemia** M♀
[0-4] Conditions classifiable to 280-285

AHA: For Code 648.22: 1Q, '02, 14

§ 5th **648.3 Drug dependence** M♀
[0-4] Conditions classifiable to 304

AHA: 2Q, '98, 13; 4Q, '88, 8

§ 5th **648.4 Mental disorders** M♀
[0-4] Conditions classifiable to 290-303, 305.0, 305.2-305.9, 306-316, 317-319

AHA: 2Q, '98, 13; 4Q, '95, 63

§ 5th **648.5 Congenital cardiovascular disorders** M♀
[0-4] Conditions classifiable to 745-747

§ 5th **648.6 Other cardiovascular diseases** M♀
[0-4] Conditions classifiable to 390-398, 410-429

EXCLUDES *cerebrovascular disorders in the puerperium (674.0)*
peripartum cardiomyopathy (674.5)
venous complications (671.0-671.9)

AHA: 3Q, '98, 11

§ 5th **648.7 Bone and joint disorders of back, pelvis, and lower limbs** M♀
[0-4] Conditions classifiable to 720-724, and those classifiable to 711-719 or 725-738, specified as affecting the lower limbs

§ 5th **648.8 Abnormal glucose tolerance** M♀
[0-4] Conditions classifiable to 790.21-790.29
Gestational diabetes

Use additional code, if applicable, for associated long-term (current) insulin use (V58.67)

AHA: 3Q, '91, 5; For code 648.83: 4Q, '04, 56

DEF: Glucose intolerance arising in pregnancy, resolving at end of pregnancy.

§ 5th **648.9 Other current conditions classifiable elsewhere** M♀
[0-4] Conditions classifiable to 440-459, ▶795.01-795.04, 795.06, 795.10-795.14, 795.16, 796.70-796.74, 796.76◀
Nutritional deficiencies [conditions classifiable to 260-269]

AHA: 3Q, '06, 14; 4Q, '04, 88; N-D, '87, 10; For code 648.91: 1Q, '02, 14; For code 648.93: 4Q, '04, 90

4th 649 Other conditions or status of the mother complicating pregnancy, childbirth, or the puerperium

AHA: 4Q, '06, 99

§ 5th **649.0 Tobacco use disorder complicating pregnancy, childbirth, or the puerperium** M♀
[0-4] Smoking complicating pregnancy, childbirth, or the puerperium

AHA: 4Q, '06, 99

§ 5th **649.1 Obesity complicating pregnancy, childbirth, or the puerperium** M♀
[0-4] Use additional code to identify the obesity (278.00, 278.01)

AHA: 4Q, '06, 99

§ 5th **649.2 Bariatric surgery status complicating pregnancy, childbirth, or the puerperium** M♀
[0-4] Gastric banding status complicating pregnancy, childbirth, or the puerperium
Gastric bypass status for obesity complicating pregnancy, childbirth, or the puerperium
Obesity surgery status complicating pregnancy, childbirth, or the puerperium

AHA: 4Q, '06, 99, 118

§ 5th **649.3 Coagulation defects complicating pregnancy, childbirth, or the puerperium** M♀
[0-4] Conditions classifiable to 286

Use additional code to identify the specific coagulation defect (286.0-286.9)

EXCLUDES *coagulation defects causing antepartum hemorrhage (641.3)*
postpartum coagulation defects (666.3)

AHA: 4Q, '06, 99

§ 5th **649.4 Epilepsy complicating pregnancy, childbirth, or the puerperium** M♀
[0-4] Conditions classifiable to 345

Use additional code to identify the specific type of epilepsy (345.00-345.91)

EXCLUDES *eclampsia (642.6)*

AHA: 4Q, '06, 99

§ Requires fifth-digit. Valid digits are in [brackets] under each code. See beginning of section 640-649 for codes and definitions.

§ 5th **649.5 Spotting complicating pregnancy** M♀
[0,1,3] EXCLUDES *antepartum hemorrhage (641.0-641.9)*
hemorrhage in early pregnancy (640.0-640.9)
AHA: 4Q, '06, 99

§ 5th **649.6 Uterine size date discrepancy** M♀
[0-4] EXCLUDES ▶*suspected problem with fetal growth not found (V89.04)*◀
AHA: 4Q, '06, 99

● § 5th **649.7 Cervical shortening** ♀
[0,1,3] EXCLUDES *suspected cervical shortening not found (V89.05)*

NORMAL DELIVERY, AND OTHER INDICATIONS FOR CARE IN PREGNANCY, LABOR, AND DELIVERY (650-659)

The following fifth-digit subclassification is for use with categories 651-659 to denote the current episode of care. Valid fifth-digits are in [brackets] under each code.
- **0 unspecified as to episode of care or not applicable**
- **1 delivered, with or without mention of antepartum condition**
- **2 delivered, with mention of postpartum complication**
- **3 antepartum condition or complication**
- **4 postpartum condition or complication**

650 Normal delivery M♀
Delivery requiring minimal or no assistance, with or without episiotomy, without fetal manipulation [e.g., rotation version] or instrumentation [forceps] of spontaneous, cephalic, vaginal, full-term, single, live-born infant. This code is for use as a single diagnosis code and is not to be used with any other code in the range 630-676.
Use additional code to indicate outcome of delivery (V27.0)
EXCLUDES *breech delivery (assisted) (spontaneous) NOS (652.2)*
delivery by vacuum extractor, forceps, cesarean section, or breech extraction, without specified complication (669.5-669.7)
AHA: 2Q, '02, 10; 3Q, '01, 12; 3Q, '00, 5; 4Q, '95, 28, 59

4th **651 Multiple gestation**

§ 5th **651.0 Twin pregnancy** M♀
[0,1,3] EXCLUDES ▶fetal conjoined twins (678.1)◀
AHA: 3Q, '06, 16

§ 5th **651.1 Triplet pregnancy** M♀
[0,1,3]

§ 5th **651.2 Quadruplet pregnancy** M♀
[0,1,3]

§ 5th **651.3 Twin pregnancy with fetal loss and retention of one fetus** M♀
[0,1,3]
Vanishing twin syndrome (651.33

§ 5th **651.4 Triplet pregnancy with fetal loss and retention of one or more fetus(es)** M♀
[0,1,3]

§ 5th **651.5 Quadruplet pregnancy with fetal loss and retention of one or more fetus(es)** M♀
[0,1,3]

§ 5th **651.6 Other multiple pregnancy with fetal loss and retention of one or more fetus(es)** M♀
[0,1,3]

§ 5th **651.7 Multiple gestation following (elective) fetal reduction** M♀
[0,1,3]
Fetal reduction of multiple fetuses reduced to single fetus
AHA: 3Q, '06, 18; For code 651.71: 4Q, '05, 81

§ 5th **651.8 Other specified multiple gestation** M♀
[0,1,3]

§ 5th **651.9 Unspecified multiple gestation** M♀
[0,1,3]

Malposition and Malpresentation

4th **652 Malposition and malpresentation of fetus**
Code first any associated obstructed labor (660.0)

§ 5th **652.0 Unstable lie** M♀
[0,1,3] DEF: Changing fetal position.

§ 5th **652.1 Breech or other malpresentation successfully converted to cephalic presentation** M♀
[0,1,3]
Cephalic version NOS

§ 5th **652.2 Breech presentation without mention of version** M♀
[0,1,3]
Breech delivery (assisted) (spontaneous) NOS
Buttocks presentation
Complete breech
Frank breech
EXCLUDES *footling presentation (652.8)*
incomplete breech (652.8)
DEF: Fetal presentation of buttocks or feet at birth canal.

§ 5th **652.3 Transverse or oblique presentation** M♀
[0,1,3]
Oblique lie
Transverse lie
EXCLUDES *transverse arrest of fetal head (660.3)*
DEF: Delivery of fetus, shoulder first.

§ 5th **652.4 Face or brow presentation** M♀
[0,1,3]
Mentum presentation

§ 5th **652.5 High head at term** M♀
[0,1,3]
Failure of head to enter pelvic brim

§ 5th **652.6 Multiple gestation with malpresentation of one fetus or more** M♀
[0,1,3]

§ 5th **652.7 Prolapsed arm** M♀
[0,1,3]

§ 5th **652.8 Other specified malposition or malpresentation** M♀
[0,1,3]
Compound presentation

§ 5th **652.9 Unspecified malposition or malpresentation** M♀
[0,1,3]

4th **653 Disproportion**
Code first any associated obstructed labor (660.1)

§ 5th **653.0 Major abnormality of bony pelvis, not further specified** M♀
[0,1,3]
Pelvic deformity NOS

§ 5th **653.1 Generally contracted pelvis** M♀
[0,1,3]
Contracted pelvis NOS

§ 5th **653.2 Inlet contraction of pelvis** M♀
[0,1,3]
Inlet contraction (pelvis)

§ 5th **653.3 Outlet contraction of pelvis** M♀
[0,1,3]
Outlet contraction (pelvis)

§ 5th **653.4 Fetopelvic disproportion** M♀
[0,1,3]
Cephalopelvic disproportion NOS
Disproportion of mixed maternal and fetal origin, with normally formed fetus

§ Requires fifth-digit. Valid digits are in [brackets] under each code. See beginning of section 640-649 for codes and definitions.

4th 5th Additional Digit Required | Unspecified Code | Other Specified Code | Manifestation Code | ▶◀ Revised Text | ● New Code | ▲ Revised Code Title

Cephalopelvic Disproportion

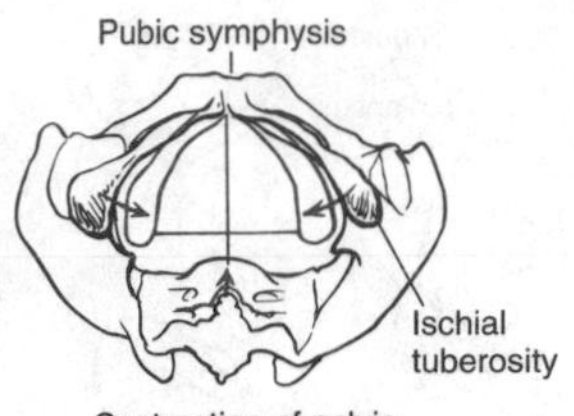

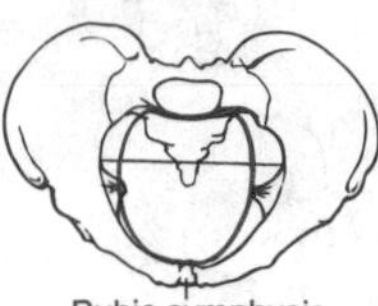

§ ✓5th **653.5 Unusually large fetus causing disproportion** M♀
[0,1,3]
Disproportion of fetal origin with normally formed fetus
Fetal disproportion NOS
EXCLUDES *that when the reason for medical care was concern for the fetus (656.6)*

§ ✓5th **653.6 Hydrocephalic fetus causing disproportion** M♀
[0,1,3]
EXCLUDES *that when the reason for medical care was concern for the fetus (655.0)*

§ ✓5th **653.7 Other fetal abnormality causing disproportion** M♀
[0,1,3]
Fetal:
- ascites
- hydrops
- myelomeningocele
- sacral teratoma
- tumor

EXCLUDES ▶*conjoined twins causing disproportion (678.1)*◀

§ ✓5th **653.8 Disproportion of other origin** M♀
[0,1,3]
EXCLUDES *shoulder (girdle) dystocia (660.4)*

§ ✓5th **653.9 Unspecified disproportion** M♀
[0,1,3]

✓4th **654 Abnormality of organs and soft tissues of pelvis**

INCLUDES the listed conditions during pregnancy, childbirth, or the puerperium

Code first any associated obstructed labor (660.2)

EXCLUDES *trauma to perineum and vulva complicating current delivery (664.0-664.9)*

§ ✓5th **654.0 Congenital abnormalities of uterus** M♀
[0-4]
Double uterus
Uterus bicornis

§ ✓5th **654.1 Tumors of body of uterus** M♀
[0-4]
Uterine fibroids

§ ✓5th **654.2 Previous cesarean delivery** M♀
[0,1,3]
Uterine scar from previous cesarean delivery
AHA: 1Q, '92, 8

§ ✓5th **654.3 Retroverted and incarcerated gravid uterus** M♀
[0-4]
DEF: Retroverted: tilted back uterus; no change in angle of longitudinal axis.
DEF: Incarcerated: immobile, fixed uterus.

§ ✓5th **654.4 Other abnormalities in shape or position of gravid uterus and of neighboring structures** M♀
[0-4]
Cystocele
Pelvic floor repair
Pendulous abdomen
Prolapse of gravid uterus
Rectocele
Rigid pelvic floor

§ ✓5th **654.5 Cervical incompetence** M♀
[0-4]
Presence of Shirodkar suture with or without mention of cervical incompetence
DEF: Abnormal cervix; tendency to dilate in second trimester; causes premature fetal expulsion.
DEF: Shirodkar suture: purse-string suture used to artificially close incompetent cervix.

§ ✓5th **654.6 Other congenital or acquired abnormality of cervix** M♀
[0-4]
Cicatricial cervix
Polyp of cervix
Previous surgery to cervix
Rigid cervix (uteri)
Stenosis or stricture of cervix
Tumor of cervix

§ ✓5th **654.7 Congenital or acquired abnormality of vagina** M♀
[0-4]
Previous surgery to vagina
Septate vagina
Stenosis of vagina (acquired) (congenital)
Stricture of vagina
Tumor of vagina

§ ✓5th **654.8 Congenital or acquired abnormality of vulva** M♀
[0-4]
Anal sphincter tear (healed) (old) complicating delivery
Fibrosis of perineum
Persistent hymen
Previous surgery to perineum or vulva
Rigid perineum
Tumor of vulva
EXCLUDES *anal sphincter tear (healed) (old) not associated with delivery (569.43)*
varicose veins of vulva (671.1)
AHA: 1Q, '03, 14

§ ✓5th **654.9 Other and unspecified** M♀
[0-4]
Uterine scar NEC

✓4th **655 Known or suspected fetal abnormality affecting management of mother**

INCLUDES the listed conditions in the fetus as a reason for observation or obstetrical care of the mother, or for termination of pregnancy

AHA: 3Q, '90, 4

§ ✓5th **655.0 Central nervous system malformation in fetus** M♀
[0,1,3]
Fetal or suspected fetal:
- anencephaly
- hydrocephalus
- spina bifida (with myelomeningocele)

§ ✓5th **655.1 Chromosomal abnormality in fetus** M♀
[0,1,3]

§ ✓5th **655.2 Hereditary disease in family possibly affecting fetus** M♀
[0,1,3]

§ ✓5th **655.3 Suspected damage to fetus from viral disease in the mother** M♀
[0,1,3]
Suspected damage to fetus from maternal rubella

§ ✓5th **655.4 Suspected damage to fetus from other disease in the mother** M♀
[0,1,3]
Suspected damage to fetus from maternal:
- alcohol addiction
- listeriosis
- toxoplasmosis

§ ✓5th **655.5 Suspected damage to fetus from drugs** M♀
[0,1,3]

§ ✓5th **655.6 Suspected damage to fetus from radiation** M♀
[0,1,3]

§ ✓5th **655.7 Decreased fetal movements** M♀
[0,1,3]
AHA: 4Q, '97, 41

§ Requires fifth-digit. Valid digits are in [brackets] under each code. See beginning of section 640-649 for codes and definitions.

§ ✓5th **655.8 Other known or suspected fetal abnormality, not elsewhere classified** M♀
[0,1,3]
Suspected damage to fetus from:
environmental toxins
intrauterine contraceptive device
AHA: 3Q, '06, 16, 18

§ ✓5th **655.9 Unspecified** M♀
[0,1,3]

▲ ✓4th **656 Other known or suspected fetal and placental problems affecting management of mother**
EXCLUDES ▶*fetal hematologic conditions (678.0)*
suspected placental problems not found (V89.02)◀

§ ✓5th **656.0 Fetal-maternal hemorrhage** M♀
[0,1,3]
Leakage (microscopic) of fetal blood into maternal circulation

§ ✓5th **656.1 Rhesus isoimmunization** M♀
[0,1,3]
Anti-D [Rh] antibodies
Rh incompatibility
DEF: Antibodies developing against Rh factor; mother with Rh negative develops antibodies against Rh positive fetus.

§ ✓5th **656.2 Isoimmunization from other and unspecified blood-group incompatibility** M♀
[0,1,3]
ABO isoimmunization
AHA: 4Q, '06, 135

§ ✓5th **656.3 Fetal distress** M♀
[0,1,3]
Fetal metabolic acidemia
EXCLUDES *abnormal fetal acid-base balance (656.8)*
abnormality in fetal heart rate or rhythm (659.7)
fetal bradycardia (659.7)
fetal tachycardia (659.7)
meconium in liquor (656.8)
AHA: N-D, '86, 4
DEF: Life-threatening disorder; fetal anoxia, hemolytic disease and other miscellaneous diseases cause fetal distress.

§ ✓5th **656.4 Intrauterine death** M♀
[0,1,3]
Fetal death:
NOS
after completion of 22 weeks' gestation
late
Missed delivery
EXCLUDES *missed abortion (632)*

§ ✓5th **656.5 Poor fetal growth** M♀
[0,1,3]
"Light-for-dates"
"Placental insufficiency"
"Small-for-dates"

§ ✓5th **656.6 Excessive fetal growth** M♀
[0,1,3]
"Large-for-dates"

§ ✓5th **656.7 Other placental conditions** M♀
[0,1,3]
Abnormal placenta
Placental infarct
EXCLUDES *placental polyp (674.4)*
placentitis (658.4)

§ ✓5th **656.8 Other specified fetal and placental problems** M♀
[0,1,3]
Abnormal acid base balance
Intrauterine acidosis
Lithopedian
Meconium in liquor
▶Subchorionic hematoma◀
DEF: Lithopedion: Calcified fetus; not expelled by mother.

§ ✓5th **656.9 Unspecified fetal and placental problem** M♀
[0,1,3]

✓4th **657 Polyhydramnios** M♀
[0,1,3] EXCLUDES ▶*suspected polyhydramnios not found (V89.01)*◀
§ ✓5th Use 0 as fourth-digit for this category
Hydramnios
AHA: 3Q, '06, 16; 4Q, '91, 26
DEF: Excess amniotic fluid.

✓4th **658 Other problems associated with amniotic cavity and membranes**
EXCLUDES *amniotic fluid embolism (673.1)*
▶*suspected problems with amniotic cavity and membranes not found (V89.01)*◀

§ ✓5th **658.0 Oligohydramnios** M♀
[0,1,3]
Oligohydramnios without mention of rupture of membranes
AHA: 3Q, '06, 16
DEF: Deficient amount of amniotic fluid.

§ ✓5th **658.1 Premature rupture of membranes** M♀
[0,1,3]
Rupture of amniotic sac less than 24 hours prior to the onset of labor
AHA: For code 658.13: 1Q, '01, 5; 4Q, '98, 77

§ ✓5th **658.2 Delayed delivery after spontaneous or unspecified rupture of membranes** M♀
[0,1,3]
Prolonged rupture of membranes NOS
Rupture of amniotic sac 24 hours or more prior to the onset of labor

§ ✓5th **658.3 Delayed delivery after artificial rupture of membranes** M♀
[0,1,3]

§ ✓5th **658.4 Infection of amniotic cavity** M♀
[0,1,3]
Amnionitis
Chorioamnionitis
Membranitis
Placentitis

§ ✓5th **658.8 Other** M♀
[0,1,3]
Amnion nodosum
Amniotic cyst

§ ✓5th **658.9 Unspecified** M♀
[0,1,3]

✓4th **659 Other indications for care or intervention related to labor and delivery, not elsewhere classified**

§ ✓5th **659.0 Failed mechanical induction** M♀
[0,1,3]
Failure of induction of labor by surgical or other instrumental methods

§ ✓5th **659.1 Failed medical or unspecified induction** M♀
[0,1,3]
Failed induction NOS
Failure of induction of labor by medical methods, such as oxytocic drugs

§ ✓5th **659.2 Maternal pyrexia during labor,unspecified** M♀
[0,1,3]
DEF: Fever during labor.

§ ✓5th **659.3 Generalized infection during labor** M♀
[0,1,3]
Septicemia during labor

§ ✓5th **659.4 Grand multiparity** M♀
[0,1,3]
EXCLUDES *supervision only, in pregnancy (V23.3)*
without current pregnancy (V61.5)
DEF: Having borne six or more children previously.

§ ✓5th **659.5 Elderly primigravida** M♀
[0,1,3]
First pregnancy in a woman who will be 35 years of age or older at expected date of delivery
EXCLUDES *supervision only, in pregnancy (V23.81)*
AHA: 3Q, '01, 12

§ ✓5th **659.6 Elderly multigravida** M♀
[0,1,3]
Second or more pregnancy in a woman who will be 35 years of age or older at expected date of delivery
EXCLUDES *elderly primigravida 659.5*
supervision only, in pregnancy (V23.82)
AHA: 3Q, '01, 12

§ Requires fifth-digit. Valid digits are in [brackets] under each code. See beginning of section 640-649 for codes and definitions.

§ 5th **659.7 Abnormality in fetal heart rate or rhythm** M♀
[0,1,3]
Depressed fetal heart tones
Fetal:
bradycardia
tachycardia
Fetal heart rate decelerations
Non-reassuring fetal heart rate or rhythm

AHA: 4Q, '98, 48

§ 5th **659.8 Other specified indications for care or intervention related to labor and delivery** M♀
[0,1,3]
Pregnancy in a female less than 16 years old at expected date of delivery
Very young maternal age

AHA: 3Q, '01, 12

§ 5th **659.9 Unspecified indication for care or intervention related to labor and delivery** M♀
[0,1,3]

COMPLICATIONS OCCURRING MAINLY IN THE COURSE OF LABOR AND DELIVERY (660-669)

The following fifth-digit subclassification is for use with categories 660-669 to denote the current episode of care. Valid fifth-digits are in [brackets] under each code.

- **0 unspecified as to episode of care or not applicable**
- **1 delivered, with or without mention of antepartum condition**
- **2 delivered, with mention of postpartum complication**
- **3 antepartum condition or complication**
- **4 postpartum condition or complication**

4th **660 Obstructed labor**

AHA: 3Q, '95, 10

§ 5th **660.0 Obstruction caused by malposition of fetus at onset of labor** M♀
[0,1,3]
Any condition classifiable to 652, causing obstruction during labor
Use additional code from 652.0-652.9 to identify condition

§ 5th **660.1 Obstruction by bony pelvis** M♀
[0,1,3]
Any condition classifiable to 653, causing obstruction during labor
Use additional code from 653.0-653.9 to identify condition

§ 5th **660.2 Obstruction by abnormal pelvic soft tissues** M♀
[0,1,3]
Prolapse of anterior lip of cervix
Any condition classifiable to 654, causing obstruction during labor
Use additional code from 654.0-654.9 to identify condition

§ 5th **660.3 Deep transverse arrest and persistent occipitoposterior position** M♀
[0,1,3]

§ 5th **660.4 Shoulder (girdle) dystocia** M♀
[0,1,3]
Impacted shoulders

DEF: Obstructed labor due to impacted fetal shoulders.

§ 5th **660.5 Locked twins** M♀
[0,1,3]

§ 5th **660.6 Failed trial of labor, unspecified** M♀
[0,1,3]
Failed trial of labor, without mention of condition or suspected condition

§ 5th **660.7 Failed forceps or vacuum extractor, unspecified** M♀
0,1,3]
Application of ventouse or forceps, without mention of condition

§ 5th **660.8 Other causes of obstructed labor** M♀
[0,1,3]
Use additional code to identify condition

AHA: 4Q, '04, 88

§ 5th **660.9 Unspecified obstructed labor** M♀
[0,1,3]
Dystocia:
NOS
fetal NOS
maternal NOS

4th **661 Abnormality of forces of labor**

§ 5th **661.0 Primary uterine inertia** M♀
[0,1,3]
Failure of cervical dilation
Hypotonic uterine dysfunction, primary
Prolonged latent phase of labor

DEF: Lack of efficient contractions during labor causing prolonged labor.

§ 5th **661.1 Secondary uterine inertia** M♀
[0,1,3]
Arrested active phase of labor
Hypotonic uterine dysfunction, secondary

§ 5th **661.2 Other and unspecified uterine inertia** M♀
[0,1,3]
Atony of uterus without hemorrhage
Desultory labor
Irregular labor
Poor contractions
Slow slope active phase of labor

EXCLUDES *atony of uterus with hemorrhage (666.1)*
postpartum atony of uterus without hemorrhage (669.8)

§ 5th **661.3 Precipitate labor** M♀
[0,1,3]
DEF: Rapid labor and delivery.

§ 5th **661.4 Hypertonic, incoordinate, or prolonged uterine contractions** M♀
[0,1,3]
Cervical spasm
Contraction ring (dystocia)
Dyscoordinate labor
Hourglass contraction of uterus
Hypertonic uterine dysfunction
Incoordinate uterine action
Retraction ring (Bandl's) (pathological)
Tetanic contractions
Uterine dystocia NOS
Uterine spasm

§ 5th **661.9 Unspecified abnormality of labor** M♀
[0,1,3]

4th **662 Long labor**

§ 5th **662.0 Prolonged first stage** M♀
[0,1,3]

§ 5th **662.1 Prolonged labor, unspecified** M♀
[0,1,3]

§ 5th **662.2 Prolonged second stage** M♀
[0,1,3]

§ 5th **662.3 Delayed delivery of second twin, triplet, etc.** M♀
[0,1,3]

4th **663 Umbilical cord complications**

§ 5th **663.0 Prolapse of cord** M♀
[0,1,3]
Presentation of cord

DEF: Abnormal presentation of fetus; marked by protruding umbilical cord during labor; can cause fetal death.

§ 5th **663.1 Cord around neck, with compression** M♀
[0,1,3]
Cord tightly around neck

§ 5th **663.2 Other and unspecified cord entanglement, with compression** M♀
[0,1,3]
Entanglement of cords of twins in mono-amniotic sac
Knot in cord (with compression)

§ 5th **663.3 Other and unspecified cord entanglement, without mention of compression** M♀
[0,1,3]

AHA: For code 663.31: 2Q, '03, 9

§ Requires fifth-digit. Valid digits are in [brackets] under each code. See beginning of section 640-649 for codes and definitions.

Perineal Lacerations

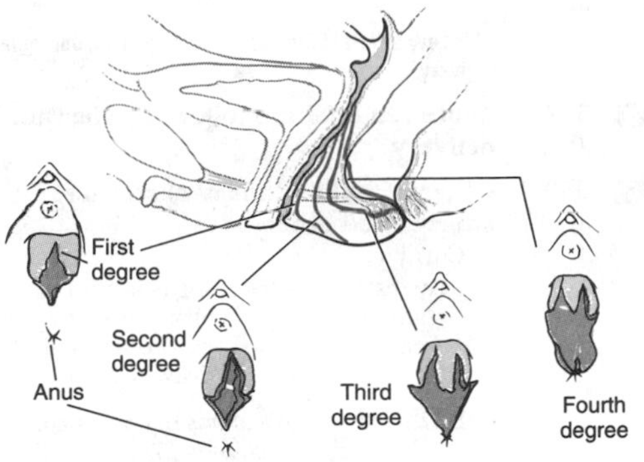

§ ✓5th **663.4 Short cord** M♀
[0,1,3]

§ ✓5th **663.5 Vasa previa** M♀
[0,1,3]

DEF: Abnormal presentation of fetus marked by blood vessels of umbilical cord in front of fetal head.

§ ✓5th **663.6 Vascular lesions of cord** M♀
[0,1,3]
Bruising of cord
Hematoma of cord
Thrombosis of vessels of cord

§ ✓5th **663.8 Other umbilical cord complications** M♀
[0,1,3]
Velamentous insertion of umbilical cord

§ ✓5th **663.9 Unspecified umbilical cord complication** M♀
[0,1,3]

✓4th 664 Trauma to perineum and vulva during delivery

INCLUDES damage from instruments
that from extension of episiotomy

AHA: 1Q, '92, 11; N-D, '84, 10

§ ✓5th **664.0 First-degree perineal laceration** M♀
[0,1,4]
Perineal laceration, rupture, or tear involving:
- fourchette
- hymen
- labia
- skin
- vagina
- vulva

§ ✓5th **664.1 Second-degree perineal laceration** M♀
[0,1,4]
Perineal laceration, rupture, or tear (following episiotomy) involving:
- pelvic floor
- perineal muscles
- vaginal muscles

EXCLUDES *that involving anal sphincter (664.2)*

§ ✓5th **664.2 Third-degree perineal laceration** M♀
[0,1,4]
Perineal laceration, rupture, or tear (following episiotomy) involving:
- anal sphincter
- rectovaginal septum
- sphincter NOS

EXCLUDES *anal sphincter tear during delivery not associated with third-degree perineal laceration (664.6)*
that with anal or rectal mucosal laceration (664.3)

§ ✓5th **664.3 Fourth-degree perineal laceration** M♀
[0,1,4]
Perineal laceration, rupture, or tear as classifiable to 664.2 and involving also:
- anal mucosa
- rectal mucosa

§ ✓5th **664.4 Unspecified perineal laceration** M♀
[0,1,4]
Central laceration

AHA: 1Q, '92, 8

§ ✓5th **664.5 Vulval and perineal hematoma** M♀
[0,1,4] AHA: N-D, '84, 10

§ ✓5th **664.6 Anal sphincter tear complicating delivery, not associated with third-degree perineal laceration** M♀
[0,1,4]

EXCLUDES *third-degree perineal laceration (664.2)*

AHA: For code 664.61: 4Q, '07, 88, 90

§ ✓5th **664.8 Other specified trauma to perineum and vulva** M♀
[0,1,4]

AHA: For code 664.81: 4Q, '07, 125

§ ✓5th **664.9 Unspecified trauma to perineum and vulva** M♀
[0,1,4]

✓4th 665 Other obstetrical trauma

INCLUDES damage from instruments

§ ✓5th **665.0 Rupture of uterus before onset of labor** M♀
[0,1,3]

§ ✓5th **665.1 Rupture of uterus during labor** M♀
[0,1]
Rupture of uterus NOS

§ ✓5th **665.2 Inversion of uterus** M♀
[0,2,4]

§ ✓5th **665.3 Laceration of cervix** M♀
[0,1,4]

§ ✓5th **665.4 High vaginal laceration** M♀
[0,1,4]
Laceration of vaginal wall or sulcus without mention of perineal laceration

§ ✓5th **665.5 Other injury to pelvic organs** M♀
[0,1,4]
Injury to:
- bladder
- urethra

AHA: M-A, '87, 10

§ ✓5th **665.6 Damage to pelvic joints and ligaments** M♀
[0,1,4]
Avulsion of inner symphyseal cartilage
Damage to coccyx
Separation of symphysis (pubis)

AHA: N-D, '84, 12

§ ✓5th **665.7 Pelvic hematoma** M♀
[0,1,2,4]
Hematoma of vagina

§ ✓5th **665.8 Other specified obstetrical trauma** M♀
[0-4]

§ ✓5th **665.9 Unspecified obstetrical trauma** M♀
[0-4]

✓4th 666 Postpartum hemorrhage

AHA: 1Q, '88, 14

§ ✓5th **666.0 Third-stage hemorrhage** M♀
[0,2,4]
Hemorrhage associated with retained, trapped, or adherent placenta
Retained placenta NOS

§ ✓5th **666.1 Other immediate postpartum hemorrhage** M♀
[0,2,4]
Atony of uterus with hemorrhage
Hemorrhage within the first 24 hours following delivery of placenta
Postpartum atony of uterus with hemorrhage
Postpartum hemorrhage (atonic) NOS

EXCLUDES *atony of uterus without hemorrhage (661.2)*
postpartum atony of uterus without hemorrhage (669.8)

§ Requires fifth-digit. Valid digits are in [brackets] under each code. See beginning of section 640-649 for codes and definitions.

✓4th ✓5th Additional Digit Required | Unspecified Code | Other Specified Code | Manifestation Code | ►◄ Revised Text | ● New Code | ▲ Revised Code Title

§ ✓5th **666.2 Delayed and secondary postpartum hemorrhage** M♀
[0,2,4]
Hemorrhage:
after the first 24 hours following delivery
associated with retained portions of placenta or membranes
Postpartum hemorrhage specified as delayed or secondary
Retained products of conception NOS, following delivery

§ ✓5th **666.3 Postpartum coagulation defects** M♀
[0,2,4]
Postpartum:
afibrinogenemia
fibrinolysis

✓4th **667 Retained placenta or membranes, without hemorrhage**
Requires fith digit; valid digits are in [brackets] under each code. See beginning of section 660-669 for definitions.
AHA: 1Q, '88, 14
DEF: Postpartum condition resulting from failure to expel placental membrane tissues due to failed contractions of uterine wall.

§ ✓5th **667.0 Retained placenta without hemorrhage** M♀
[0,2,4]
Placenta accreta } without hemorrhage
Retained placenta: } without hemorrhage
NOS
total

§ ✓5th **667.1 Retained portions of placenta or membranes,without hemorrhage** M♀
[0,2,4]
Retained products of conception following delivery, without hemorrhage

✓4th **668 Complications of the administration of anesthetic or other sedation in labor and delivery**
INCLUDES complications arising from the administration of a general or local anesthetic, analgesic, or other sedation in labor and delivery
EXCLUDES *reaction to spinal or lumbar puncture (349.0)*
spinal headache (349.0)
Use additional code(s) to further specify complication

§ ✓5th **668.0 Pulmonary complications** M♀
[0-4]
Inhalation (aspiration) of stomach contents or secretions } following anesthesia or other sedation in labor or delivery
Mendelson's syndrome
Pressure collapse of lung

§ ✓5th **668.1 Cardiac complications** M♀
[0-4]
Cardiac arrest or failure following anesthesia or other sedation in labor and delivery

§ ✓5th **668.2 Central nervous system complications** M♀
[0-4]
Cerebral anoxia following anesthesia or other sedation in labor and delivery

§ ✓5th **668.8 Other complications of anesthesia or other sedation in labor and delivery** M♀
[0-4]
AHA: 2Q, '99, 9

§ ✓5th **668.9 Unspecified complication of anesthesia and other sedation** M♀
[0-4]

✓4th **669 Other complications of labor and delivery, not elsewhere classified**

§ ✓5th **669.0 Maternal distress** M♀
[0-4]
Metabolic disturbance in labor and delivery

§ ✓5th **669.1 Shock during or following labor and delivery** M♀
[0-4]
Obstetric shock

§ ✓5th **669.2 Maternal hypotension syndrome** M♀
[0-4]
DEF: Low arterial blood pressure, in mother, during labor and delivery.

§ ✓5th **669.3 Acute renal failure following labor and delivery** M♀
[0,2,4]

§ ✓5th **669.4 Other complications of obstetrical surgery and procedures** M♀
[0-4]
Cardiac:
arrest } following cesarean or other obstetrical surgery or procedure, including delivery NOS
failure
Cerebral anoxia
EXCLUDES *complications of obstetrical surgical wounds (674.1-674.3)*

§ ✓5th **669.5 Forceps or vacuum extractor delivery without mention of indication** M♀
[0,1]
Delivery by ventouse, without mention of indication

§ ✓5th **669.6 Breech extraction, without mention of indication** M♀
[0,1]
EXCLUDES *breech delivery NOS (652.2)*

§ ✓5th **669.7 Cesarean delivery, without mention of indication** M♀
[0,1]
AHA: For code **669.71:** 1Q, '01, 11

§ ✓5th **669.8 Other complications of labor and delivery** M♀
[0-4]
AHA: 4Q, '06, 135

§ ✓5th **669.9 Unspecified complication of labor and delivery** M♀
[0-4]

COMPLICATIONS OF THE PUERPERIUM (670-677)

Note: Categories 671 and 673-676 include the listed conditions even if they occur during pregnancy or childbirth.

The following fifth-digit subclassification is for use with categories 670-676 to denote the current episode of care. Valid fifth-digits are in [brackets] under each code.
0 unspecified as to episode of care or not applicable
1 delivered, with or without mention of antepartum condition
2 delivered, with mention of postpartum complication
3 antepartum condition or complication
4 postpartum condition or complication

✓4th **670 Major puerperal infection** M♀
[0,2,4]

§ ✓5th Use 0 as fourth-digit for this category
Puerperal:
endometritis
fever (septic)
pelvic:
cellulitis
sepsis
peritonitis
pyemia
salpingitis
septicemia
EXCLUDES *infection following abortion (639.0)*
minor genital tract infection following delivery (646.6)
puerperal pyrexia NOS (672)
puerperal fever NOS (672)
puerperal pyrexia of unknown origin (672)
urinary tract infection following delivery (646.6)
AHA: 4Q, '91, 26; 2Q, '91, 7; **For code 670.02:** 3Q, '07, 8
DEF: Infection and inflammation, following childbirth.

§ Requires fifth-digit. Valid digits are in [brackets] under each code. See beginning of section 640-649 for codes and definitions.

4th 671 Venous complications in pregnancy and the puerperium

§ 5th **671.0 Varicose veins of legs** M ♀
[0-4]
Varicose veins NOS
DEF: Distended, tortuous veins on legs associated with pregnancy.

§ 5th **671.1 Varicose veins of vulva and perineum** M ♀
[0-4]
DEF: Distended, tortuous veins on external female genitalia associated with pregnancy.

§ 5th **671.2 Superficial thrombophlebitis** M ♀
[0-4]
Thrombophlebitis (superficial)

§ 5th **671.3 Deep phlebothrombosis, antepartum** M ♀
[0,1,3]
Deep vein thrombosis antepartum

§ 5th **671.4 Deep phlebothrombosis, postpartum** M ♀
[0,2,4]
Deep-vein thrombosis, postpartum
Pelvic thrombophlebitis, postpartum
Phlegmasia alba dolens (puerperal)

§ 5th **671.5 Other phlebitis and thrombosis** M ♀
[0-4]
Cerebral venous thrombosis
Thrombosis of intracranial venous sinus

§ 5th **671.8 Other venous complications** M ♀
[0-4]
Hemorrhoids

§ 5th **671.9 Unspecified venous complication** M ♀
[0-4]
Phlebitis NOS
Thrombosis NOS

4th 672 Pyrexia of unknown origin during [0,2,4] the puerperium M ♀

§ 5th Use 0 as fourth-digit for this category
Postpartum fever NOS
Puerperal fever NOS
Puerperal pyrexia NOS
AHA: 4Q, '91, 26
DEF: Fever of unknown origin experienced by the mother after childbirth.

4th 673 Obstetrical pulmonary embolism

INCLUDES pulmonary emboli in pregnancy, childbirth, or the puerperium, or specified as puerperal

EXCLUDES *embolism following abortion (639.6)*

§ 5th **673.0 Obstetrical air embolism** M ♀
[0-4]
DEF: Sudden blocking of pulmonary artery with air or nitrogen bubbles during puerperium.

§ 5th **673.1 Amniotic fluid embolism** M ♀
[0-4]
DEF: Sudden onset of pulmonary artery blockage from amniotic fluid entering the mother's circulation near the end of pregnancy due to strong uterine contractions.

§ 5th **673.2 Obstetrical blood-clot embolism** M ♀
[0-4]
Puerperal pulmonary embolism NOS
AHA: For code 673.24: 1Q, '05, 6
DEF: Blood clot blocking artery in the lung; associated with pregnancy.

§ 5th **673.3 Obstetrical pyemic and septic embolism** M ♀
[0-4]

§ 5th **673.8 Other pulmonary embolism** M ♀
[0-4]
Fat embolism

4th 674 Other and unspecified complications of the puerperium, not elsewhere classified

§ 5th **674.0 Cerebrovascular disorders in the puerperium** M ♀
[0-4]
Any condition classifiable to 430-434, 436-437 occurring during pregnancy, childbirth, or the puerperium, or specified as puerperal

EXCLUDES *intracranial venous sinus thrombosis (671.5)*

§ 5th **674.1 Disruption of cesarean wound** M ♀
[0,2,4]
Dehiscence or disruption of uterine wound

EXCLUDES *uterine rupture before onset of labor (665.0)*
uterine rupture during labor (665.1)

§ 5th **674.2 Disruption of perineal wound** M ♀
[0,2,4]
Breakdown of perineum
Disruption of wound of:
episiotomy
perineal laceration
Secondary perineal tear
AHA: For code 674.24: 1Q, '97, 9

§ 5th **674.3 Other complications of obstetrical surgical wounds** M ♀
[0,2,4]
Hematoma } of cesarean section or perineal wound
Hemorrhage }
Infection }

EXCLUDES *damage from instruments in delivery (664.0-665.9)*

AHA: 2Q, '91, 7

§ 5th **674.4 Placental polyp** M ♀
[0,2,4]

§ 5th **674.5 Peripartum cardiomyopathy** M ♀
[0-4]
Postpartum cardiomyopathy
AHA: 4Q, '03, 65
DEF: Any structural or functional abnormality of the ventricular myocardium, non-inflammatory disease of obscure or unknown etiology with onset during the postpartum period.

§ 5th **674.8 Other** M ♀
[0,2,4]
Hepatorenal syndrome, following delivery
Postpartum:
subinvolution of uterus
uterine hypertrophy
AHA: 3Q, '98, 16

§ 5th **674.9 Unspecified** M ♀
[0,2,4]
Sudden death of unknown cause during the puerperium

4th 675 Infections of the breast and nipple associated with childbirth

INCLUDES the listed conditions during pregnancy, childbirth, or the puerperium

§ 5th **675.0 Infections of nipple** M ♀
[0-4]
Abscess of nipple

§ 5th **675.1 Abscess of breast** M ♀
[0-4]
Abscess:
mammary
subareolar
submammary
purulent
retromammary
submammary

§ 5th **675.2 Nonpurulent mastitis** M ♀
[0-4]
Lymphangitis of breast
Mastitis:
NOS
interstitial
parenchymatous

§ 5th **675.8 Other specified infections of the breast and nipple** M ♀
[0-4]

§ Requires fifth-digit. Valid digits are in [brackets] under each code. See beginning of section 640-649 for codes and definitions.

Lactation Process: Ejection Reflex Arc

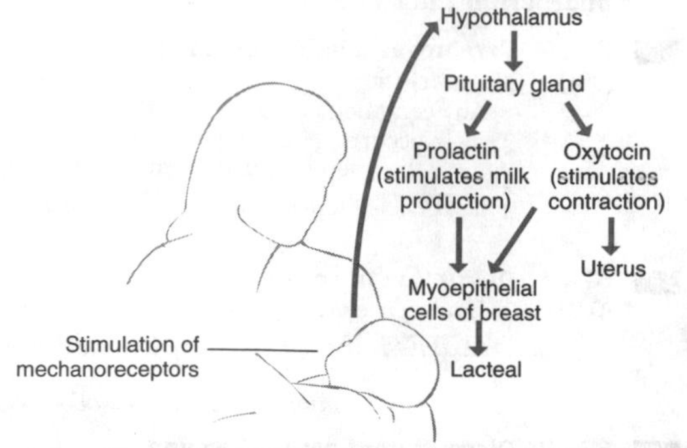

§ 5th **675.9 Unspecified infection of the breast and nipple** M♀
[0-4]

4th **676 Other disorders of the breast associated with childbirth and disorders of lactation**

INCLUDES the listed conditions during pregnancy, the puerperium, or lactation

§ 5th **676.0 Retracted nipple** M♀
[0-4]

§ 5th **676.1 Cracked nipple** M♀
[0-4] Fissure of nipple

§ 5th **676.2 Engorgement of breasts** M♀
[0-4]

DEF: Abnormal accumulation of milk in ducts of breast.

§ 5th **676.3 Other and unspecified disorder of breast** M♀
[0-4]

§ 5th **676.4 Failure of lactation** M♀
[0-4] Agalactia

DEF: Abrupt ceasing of milk secretion by breast.

§ 5th **676.5 Suppressed lactation** M♀
[0-4]

§ 5th **676.6 Galactorrhea** M♀
[0-4] EXCLUDES *galactorrhea not associated with childbirth (611.6)*

DEF: Excessive or persistent milk secretion by breast; may be in absence of nursing.

§ 5th **676.8 Other disorders of lactation** M♀
[0-4] Galactocele

DEF: Galactocele: Obstructed mammary gland, creating retention cyst, results in milk-filled cysts enlarging mammary gland.

§ 5th **676.9 Unspecified disorder of lactation** M♀
[0-4]

677 Late effect of complication of pregnancy, childbirth, and the puerperium ♀

Note: This category is to be used to indicate conditions in 632-648.9 and 651-676.9 as the cause of the late effect, themselves classifiable elsewhere. The "late effects" include conditions specified as such, or as sequelae, which may occur at any time after puerperium.

Code first any sequelae

AHA: 1Q, '97, 9; 4Q, '94, 42

▶OTHER MATERNAL AND FETAL COMPLICATIONS (678-679)◀

The following fifth-digit subclassification is for use with categories 678-679 to denote the current episode of care. Valid fifth-digits are in [brackets] under each code.

0 unspecified as to episode of care or not applicable
1 delivered, with or without mention of antepartum condition
2 delivered, with mention of postpartum complication
3 antepartum condition or complication
4 postpartum condition or complication

● 4th **678 Other fetal conditions**

● § 5th **678.0 Fetal hematologic conditions** M♀
[0,1,3] Fetal anemia
Fetal thrombocytopenia
Fetal twin to twin transfusion

EXCLUDES *fetal and neonatal hemorrhage (772.0-772.9)*
fetal hematologic disorders affecting newborn (776.0-776.9)
fetal-maternal hemorrhage (656.00-656.03)
isoimmunization incompatibility (656.10-656.13, 656.20-656.23)

● § 5th **678.1 Fetal conjoined twins** M♀
[0,1,3]

● 4th **679 Complications of in utero procedures**

● § 5th **679.0 Maternal complications from in utero procedure** M♀
[0-4]

EXCLUDES *maternal history of in utero procedure during previous pregnancy (V23.86)*

● § 5th **679.1 Fetal complications from in utero procedure** M♀
[0-4] Fetal complications from amniocentesis

EXCLUDES *newborn affected by in utero procedure (760.61-760.64)*

§ Requires fifth-digit. Valid digits are in [brackets] under each code. See beginning of section 640-649 for codes and definitions.

N Newborn Age: 0 P Pediatric Age: 0-17 M Maternity Age: 12-55 A Adult Age: 15-124

12. DISEASES OF THE SKIN AND SUBCUTANEOUS TISSUE (680-709)

INFECTIONS OF SKIN AND SUBCUTANEOUS TISSUE (680-686)

EXCLUDES *certain infections of skin classified under "Infectious and Parasitic Diseases," such as:*
erysipelas (035)
erysipeloid of Rosenbach (027.1)
herpes:
simplex (054.0-054.9)
zoster (053.0-053.9)
molluscum contagiosum (078.0)
viral warts (078.1)

4th **680 Carbuncle and furuncle**

INCLUDES boil
furunculosis

DEF: Carbuncle: necrotic boils in skin and subcutaneous tissue of neck or back mainly due to staphylococcal infection.

DEF: Furuncle: circumscribed inflammation of corium and subcutaneous tissue due to staphylococcal infection.

680.0 Face
Ear [any part]
Face [any part, except eye]
Nose (septum)
Temple (region)

EXCLUDES *eyelid (373.13)*
lacrimal apparatus (375.31)
orbit (376.01)

680.1 Neck

680.2 Trunk
Abdominal wall
Back [any part, except buttocks]
Breast
Chest wall
Flank
Groin
Pectoral region
Perineum
Umbilicus

EXCLUDES *buttocks (680.5)*
external genital organs:
female (616.4)
male (607.2, 608.4)

680.3 Upper arm and forearm
Arm [any part, except hand]
Axilla
Shoulder

680.4 Hand
Finger [any]
Thumb
Wrist

680.5 Buttock
Anus
Gluteal region

680.6 Leg, except foot
Ankle
Hip
Knee
Thigh

680.7 Foot
Heel
Toe

680.8 Other specified sites
Head [any part, except face]
Scalp

EXCLUDES *external genital organs:*
female (616.4)
male (607.2, 608.4)

680.9 Unspecified site
Boil NOS
Carbuncle NOS
Furuncle NOS

Skin and Subcutaneous Layer

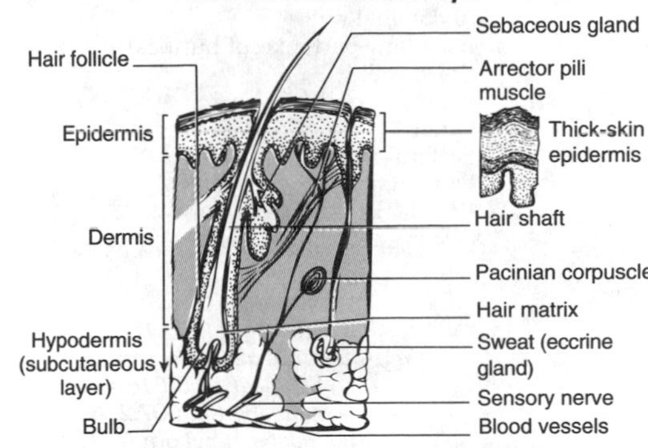

4th **681 Cellulitis and abscess of finger and toe**

INCLUDES that with lymphangitis

Use additional code to identify organism, such as Staphylococcus (041.1)

AHA: 2Q, '91, 5; J-F, '87, 12

DEF: Acute suppurative inflammation and edema in subcutaneous tissue or muscle of finger or toe.

5th **681.0 Finger**

681.00 Cellulitis and abscess, unspecified

681.01 Felon
Pulp abscess
Whitlow

EXCLUDES *herpetic whitlow (054.6)*

DEF: Painful abscess of fingertips caused by infection in the closed space of terminal phalanx.

681.02 Onychia and paronychia of finger
Panaritium } of finger
Perionychia } of finger

DEF: Onychia: inflammation of nail matrix; causes nail loss.

DEF: Paronychia: inflammation of tissue folds around nail.

5th **681.1 Toe**

681.10 Cellulitis and abscess, unspecified
AHA: 1Q, '05, 14

681.11 Onychia and paronychia of toe
Panaritium } of toe
Perionychia } of toe

681.9 Cellulitis and abscess of unspecified digit
Infection of nail NOS

4th **682 Other cellulitis and abscess**

INCLUDES abscess (acute) } (with lymphangitis) except of finger or toe
cellulitis (diffuse) } (with lymphangitis) except of finger or toe
lymphangitis, acute } (with lymphangitis) except of finger or toe

Use additional code to identify organism, such as Staphylococcus (041.1)

EXCLUDES *lymphangitis (chronic) (subacute) (457.2)*

AHA: 2Q, '91, 5; J-F, '87, 12; S-O, '85, 10

DEF: Cellulitis: Acute suppurative inflammation of deep subcutaneous tissue and sometimes muscle due to infection of wound, burn or other lesion.

682.0 Face
Cheek, external
Chin
Forehead
Nose, external
Submandibular
Temple (region)

EXCLUDES *ear [any part] (380.10-380.16)*
eyelid (373.13)
lacrimal apparatus (375.31)
lip (528.5)
mouth (528.3)
nose (internal) (478.1)
orbit (376.01)

682.1 Neck

682.2 Trunk
Abdominal wall
Back [any part, except buttock]
Chest wall
Flank
Groin
Pectoral region
Perineum
Umbilicus, except newborn
EXCLUDES *anal and rectal regions (566)*
breast:
NOS (611.0)
puerperal (675.1)
external genital organs:
female (616.3-616.4)
male (604.0, 607.2, 608.4)
umbilicus, newborn (771.4)
AHA: 4Q, '98, 42

682.3 Upper arm and forearm
Arm [any part, except hand]
Axilla
Shoulder
EXCLUDES *hand (682.4)*
AHA: 2Q, '03, 7

682.4 Hand, except fingers and thumb
Wrist
EXCLUDES *finger and thumb (681.00-681.02)*

682.5 Buttock
Gluteal region
EXCLUDES *anal and rectal regions (566)*

682.6 Leg, except foot
Ankle
Hip
Knee
Thigh
AHA: 3Q, '04, 5; 4Q, '03, 108

682.7 Foot, except toes
Heel
EXCLUDES *toe (681.10-681.11)*

682.8 Other specified sites
Head [except face]
Scalp
EXCLUDES *face (682.0)*

682.9 Unspecified site
Abscess NOS
Cellulitis NOS
Lymphangitis, acute NOS
EXCLUDES *lymphangitis NOS (457.2)*

Lymphatic System of Head and Neck

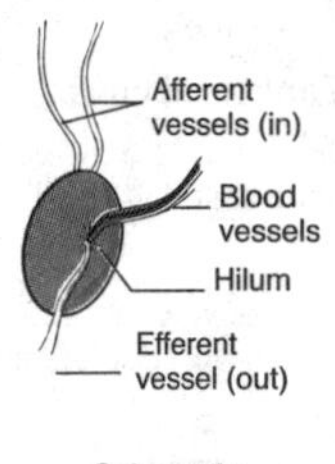

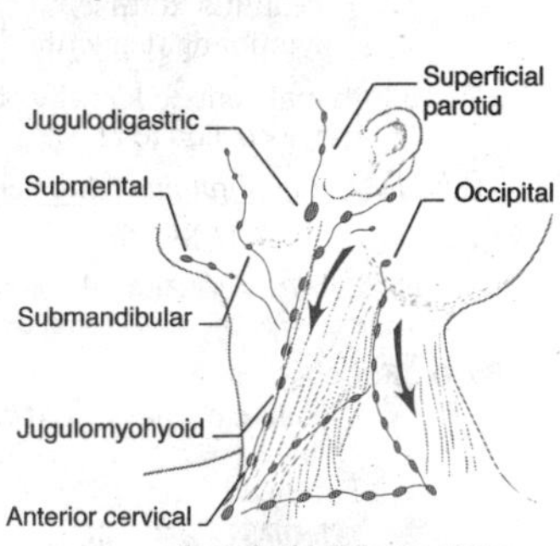

683 Acute lymphadenitis
Abscess (acute) / Adenitis, acute / Lymphadenitis, acute } lymph gland or node, except mesenteric
Use additional code to identify organism, such as Staphylococcus (041.1)
EXCLUDES *enlarged glands NOS (785.6)*
lymphadenitis:
chronic or subacute, except mesenteric (289.1)
mesenteric (acute) (chronic) (subacute) (289.2)
unspecified (289.3)

DEF: Acute inflammation of lymph nodes due to primary infection located elsewhere in the body.

684 Impetigo
Impetiginization of other dermatoses
Impetigo (contagiosa) [any site] [any organism]:
bullous
circinate
neonatorum
simplex
Pemphigus neonatorum
EXCLUDES *impetigo herpetiformis (694.3)*

DEF: Infectious skin disease commonly occurring in children; caused by group A streptococci or *Staphylococcus aureus;* skin lesions usually appear on the face and consist of subcorneal vesicles and bullae that burst and form yellow crusts.

✓4th **685 Pilonidal cyst**
INCLUDES fistula / sinus } coccygeal or pilonidal

DEF: Hair-containing cyst or sinus in the tissues of the sacrococcygeal area; often drains through opening at the postanal dimple.

685.0 With abscess

685.1 Without mention of abscess

✓4th **686 Other local infections of skin and subcutaneous tissue**
Use additional code to identify any infectious organism (041.0-041.8)

✓5th **686.0 Pyoderma**
Dermatitis:
purulent
septic
suppurative

DEF: Nonspecific purulent skin disease related most to furuncles, pustules, or possibly carbuncles.

686.00 Pyoderma, unspecified

686.01 Pyoderma gangrenosum
AHA: 4Q, '97, 42

DEF: Persistent debilitating skin disease, characterized by irregular, boggy, blue-red ulcerations, with central healing and undermined edges.

686.09 Other pyoderma

Stages of Pilonidal Disease

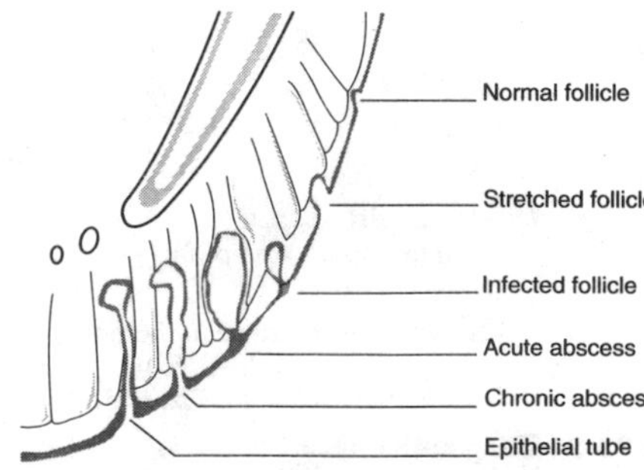

686.1 Pyogenic granuloma
Granuloma:
septic
suppurative
telangiectaticum
EXCLUDES *pyogenic granuloma of oral mucosa (528.9)*
DEF: Solitary polypoid capillary hemangioma often asociated with local irritation, trauma, and superimposed inflammation; located on the skin and gingival or oral mucosa.

686.8 Other specified local infections of skin and subcutaneous tissue
Bacterid (pustular)
Dermatitis vegetans
Ecthyma
Perlèche
EXCLUDES *dermatitis infectiosa eczematoides (690.8)*
panniculitis (729.30-729.39)

686.9 Unspecified local infection of skin and subcutaneous tissue
Fistula of skin NOS
Skin infection NOS
EXCLUDES *fistula to skin from internal organs – see Alphabetic Index*

OTHER INFLAMMATORY CONDITIONS OF SKIN AND SUBCUTANEOUS TISSUE (690-698)

EXCLUDES *panniculitis (729.30-729.39)*

✓4th 690 Erythematosquamous dermatosis
EXCLUDES *eczematous dermatitis of eyelid (373.31)*
parakeratosis variegata (696.2)
psoriasis (696.0-696.1)
seborrheic keratosis (702.11-702.19)

✓5th 690.1 Seborrheic dermatitis
AHA: 4Q, '95, 58

690.10 Seborrheic dermatitis, unspecified
Seborrheic dermatitis NOS

690.11 Seborrhea capitis P
Cradle cap

690.12 Seborrheic infantile dermatitis P

690.18 Other seborrheic dermatitis

690.8 Other erythematosquamous dermatosis

✓4th 691 Atopic dermatitis and related conditions
DEF: Atopic dermatitis: chronic, pruritic, inflammatory skin disorder found on the face and antecubital and popliteal fossae; noted in persons with a hereditary predisposition to pruritus, and often accompanied by allergic rhinitis, hay fever, asthma, and extreme itching; also called allergic dermatitis, allergic or atopic eczema, or disseminated neurodermatitis.

691.0 Diaper or napkin rash
Ammonia dermatitis
Diaper or napkin:
dermatitis
erythema
rash
Psoriasiform napkin eruption

691.8 Other atopic dermatitis and related conditions
Atopic dermatitis
Besnier's prurigo
Eczema:
atopic
flexural
intrinsic (allergic)
Neurodermatitis:
atopic
diffuse (of Brocq)

✓4th 692 Contact dermatitis and other eczema
INCLUDES dermatitis:
NOS
contact
occupational
venenata
eczema (acute) (chronic):
NOS
allergic
erythematous
occupational
EXCLUDES *allergy NOS (995.3)*
contact dermatitis of eyelids (373.32)
dermatitis due to substances taken internally (693.0-693.9)
eczema of external ear (380.22)
perioral dermatitis (695.3)
urticarial reactions (708.0-708.9, 995.1)
DEF: Contact dermatitis: acute or chronic dermatitis caused by initial irritant effect of a substance, or by prior sensitization to a substance coming once again in contact with skin.

692.0 Due to detergents

692.1 Due to oils and greases

692.2 Due to solvents
Dermatitis due to solvents of:
chlorocompound, cyclohexane, ester, glycol, hydrocarbon, ketone } group

692.3 Due to drugs and medicines in contact with skin
Dermatitis (allergic) (contact) due to:
arnica
fungicides
iodine
keratolytics
mercurials
neomycin
pediculocides
phenols
scabicides
any drug applied to skin
Dermatitis medicamentosa due to drug applied to skin
Use additional E code to identify drug
EXCLUDES *allergy NOS due to drugs (995.27)*
dermatitis due to ingested drugs (693.0)
dermatitis medicamentosa NOS (693.0)

692.4 Due to other chemical products
Dermatitis due to:
acids
adhesive plaster
alkalis
caustics
dichromate
insecticide
nylon
plastic
rubber
AHA: 2Q, '89, 16

692.5 Due to food in contact with skin
Dermatitis, contact, due to:
cereals
fish
flour
fruit
meat
milk
EXCLUDES *dermatitis due to:*
dyes (692.89)
ingested foods (693.1)
preservatives (692.89)

692.6 Due to plants [except food]
Dermatitis due to:
lacquer tree [Rhus verniciflua]
poison:
ivy [Rhus toxicodendron]
oak [Rhus diversiloba]
sumac [Rhus venenata]
vine [Rhus radicans]
primrose [Primula]
ragweed [Senecio jacobae]
other plants in contact with the skin

EXCLUDES *allergy NOS due to pollen (477.0)*
nettle rash (708.8)

✓5th **692.7 Due to solar radiation**

EXCLUDES *sunburn due to other ultraviolet radiation exposure (692.82)*

692.70 Unspecified dermatitis due to sun

692.71 Sunburn
First degree sunburn
Sunburn NOS

AHA: 4Q, '01, 47

692.72 Acute dermatitis due to solar radiation
Acute solar skin damage NOS
Berlogue dermatitis
Photoallergic response
Phototoxic response
Polymorphus light eruption

Use additional E code to identify drug, if drug induced

EXCLUDES *sunburn (692.71, 692.76-692.77)*

DEF: Berloque dermatitis: Phytophotodermatitis due to sun exposure after use of a product containing bergamot oil; causes red patches, which may turn brown.

DEF: Photoallergic response: Dermatitis due to hypersensitivity to the sun; causes papulovesicular, eczematous or exudative eruptions.

DEF: Phototoxic response: Chemically induced sensitivity to sun causes burn-like reaction, occasionally vesiculation and subsequent hyperpigmentation.

DEF: Polymorphous light eruption: Inflammatory skin eruptions due to sunlight exposure; eruptions differ in size and shape.

DEF: Acute solar skin damage (NOS): Rapid, unspecified injury to skin from sun.

692.73 Actinic reticuloid and actinic granuloma

DEF: Actinic reticuloid: Dermatosis aggravated by light, causes chronic eczema-like eruption on exposed skin which extends to other unexposed surfaces; occurs in the eldery.

DEF: Actinic granuloma: Inflammatory response of skin to sun causing small nodule of microphages.

692.74 Other chronic dermatitis due to solar radiation
Chronic solar skin damage NOS
Solar elastosis

EXCLUDES *actinic [solar] keratosis (702.0)*

DEF: Solar elastosis: Premature aging of skin of light-skinned people; causes inelasticity, thinning or thickening, wrinkling, dryness, scaling and hyperpigmentation.

DEF: Chronic solar skin damage (NOS): Chronic skin impairment due to exposure to the sun, not otherwise specified.

692.75 Disseminated superficial actinic porokeratosis [DSAP]

DEF: Autosomal dominant skin condition occurring in skin that has been overexposed to the sun. Primarily affects women over the age of 16; characterized by numerous superficial annular, keratotic, brownish-red spots or thickenings with depressed centers and sharp, ridged borders. High risk that condition will evolve into squamous cell carcinoma.

AHA: 4Q, '00, 43

692.76 Sunburn of second degree

AHA: 4Q, '01, 47

692.77 Sunburn of third degree

AHA: 4Q, '01, 47

692.79 Other dermatitis due to solar radiation
Hydroa aestivale
Photodermatitis } (due to sun)
Photosensitiveness } (due to sun)
Solar skin damage NOS

✓5th **692.8 Due to other specified agents**

692.81 Dermatitis due to cosmetics

692.82 Dermatitis due to other radiation
Infrared rays
Light, except from sun
Radiation NOS
Tanning bed
Ultraviolet rays, except from sun
X-rays

EXCLUDES *solar radiation (692.70-692.79)*

AHA: 4Q, '01, 47; 3Q, '00, 5

692.83 Dermatitis due to metals
Jewelry

692.84 Due to animal (cat) (dog) dander
Due to animal (cat) (dog) hair

692.89 Other
Dermatitis due to:
cold weather
dyes
hot weather
preservatives

EXCLUDES *allergy (NOS) (rhinitis) due to animal hair or dander (477.2)*
allergy to dust (477.8)
sunburn (692.71, 692.76-692.77)

692.9 Unspecified cause
Dermatitis:
NOS
contact NOS
venenata NOS
Eczema NOS

✓4th **693 Dermatitis due to substances taken internally**

EXCLUDES *adverse effect NOS of drugs and medicines (995.20)*
allergy NOS (995.3)
contact dermatitis (692.0-692.9)
urticarial reactions (708.0-708.9, 995.1)

DEF: Inflammation of skin due to ingested substance.

693.0 Due to drugs and medicines
Dermatitis medicamentosa NOS

Use additional E code to identify drug

EXCLUDES *that due to drugs in contact with skin (692.3)*

AHA: 2Q, '07, 8

693.1 Due to food

693.8 Due to other specified substances taken internally

693.9 Due to unspecified substance taken internally

EXCLUDES *dermatitis NOS (692.9)*

✓4th **694 Bullous dermatoses**

694.0 Dermatitis herpetiformis

Dermatosis herpetiformis
Duhring's disease
Hydroa herpetiformis

EXCLUDES *herpes gestationis (646.8)*
dermatitis herpetiformis:
juvenile (694.2)
senile (694.5)

DEF: Chronic, relapsing multisystem disease manifested most in the cutaneous system; seen as an extremely pruritic eruption of various combinations of lesions that frequently heal leaving hyperpigmentation or hypopigmentation and occasionally scarring; usually associated with an asymptomatic gluten-sensitive enteropathy, and immunogenic factors are believed to play a role in its origin.

694.1 Subcorneal pustular dermatosis

Sneddon-Wilkinson disease or syndrome

DEF: Chronic relapses of sterile pustular blebs beneath the horny skin layer of the trunk and skin folds; resembles dermatitis herpetiformis.

694.2 Juvenile dermatitis herpetiformis

Juvenile pemphigoid

694.3 Impetigo herpetiformis

DEF: Rare dermatosis associated with pregnancy; marked by itching pustules in third trimester, hypocalcemia, tetany, fever and lethargy; may result in maternal or fetal death.

694.4 Pemphigus

Pemphigus:
NOS
erythematosus
foliaceus
malignant
vegetans
vulgaris

EXCLUDES *pemphigus neonatorum (684)*

DEF: Chronic, relapsing, sometimes fatal skin diseases; causes vesicles, bullae; autoantibodies against intracellular connections cause acantholysis.

694.5 Pemphigoid

Benign pemphigus NOS
Bullous pemphigoid
Herpes circinatus bullosus
Senile dermatitis herpetiformis

✓5th **694.6 Benign mucous membrane pemphigoid**

Cicatricial pemphigoid
Mucosynechial atrophic bullous dermatitis

694.60 Without mention of ocular involvement

694.61 With ocular involvement

Ocular pemphigus

DEF: Mild self-limiting, subepidermal blistering of mucosa including the conjunctiva, seen predominantly in the elderly. It produces adhesions and scarring.

694.8 Other specified bullous dermatoses

EXCLUDES *herpes gestationis (646.8)*

694.9 Unspecified bullous dermatoses

✓4th **695 Erythematous conditions**

695.0 Toxic erythema

Erythema venenatum

✓5th **695.1 Erythema multiforme**

▶Use additional code to identify associated manifestations, such as:
arthropathy associated with dermatological disorders (713.3)
conjunctival edema (372.73)
conjunctivitis (372.04, 372.33)
corneal scars and opacities (371.00-371.05)
corneal ulcer (370.00-370.07)
edema of eyelid (374.82)
inflammation of eyelid (373.8)
keratoconjunctivitis sicca (370.33)
mechanical lagophthalmos (374.22)
mucositis (478.11, 528.00, 538, 616.81)
stomatitis (528.00)
symblepharon (372.63)

Use additional E-code to identify drug, if drug-induced

Use additional code to identify percentage of skin exfoliation (695.50-695.59)

EXCLUDES *(Staphylococcal) scalded skin syndrome (695.81)*◀

DEF: Symptom complex with a varied skin eruption pattern of macular, bullous, papular, nodose, or vesicular lesions on the neck, face, and legs; gastritis and rheumatic pains are also noticeable, first-seen symptoms; complex is secondary to a number of factors, including infections, ingestants, physical agents, malignancy and pregnancy.

● **695.10 Erythema multiforme, unspecified**

Erythema iris
Herpes iris

● **695.11 Erythema multiforme minor**

● **695.12 Erythema multiforme major**

● **695.13 Stevens-Johnson syndrome**

● **695.14 Stevens-Johnson syndrome-toxic epidermal necrolysis overlap syndrome**

SJS-TEN overlap syndrome

● **695.15 Toxic epidermal necrolysis**

Lyell's syndrome

● **695.19 Other erythema multiforme**

695.2 Erythema nodosum

EXCLUDES *tuberculous erythema nodosum (017.1)*

DEF: Panniculitis (an inflammatory reaction of the subcutaneous fat) of women, usually seen as a hypersensitivity reaction to various infections, drugs, sarcoidosis, and specific enteropathies; the acute stage is often associated with other symptoms, including fever, malaise, and arthralgia; the lesions are pink to blue in color, appear in crops as tender nodules and are found on the front of the legs below the knees.

695.3 Rosacea

Acne:
erythematosa
rosacea
Perioral dermatitis
Rhinophyma

DEF: Chronic skin disease, usually of the face, characterized by persistent erythema and sometimes by telangiectasis with acute episodes of edema, engorgement papules, and pustules.

695.4 Lupus erythematosus

Lupus:
erythematodes (discoid)
erythematosus (discoid), not disseminated

EXCLUDES *lupus (vulgaris) NOS (017.0)*
systemic [disseminated] lupus erythematosus (710.0)

DEF: Group of connective tissue disorders occurring as various cutaneous diseases of unknown origin; it primarily affects women between the ages of 20 and 40.

● ✓5th **695.5 Exfoliation due to erythematous conditions according to extent of body surface involved**

Code first erythematous condition causing exfoliation, such as:
- Ritter's disease (695.81)
- (Staphylococcal) scalded skin syndrome (695.81)
- Stevens-Johnson syndrome (695.13)
- Stevens-Johnson syndrome-toxic epidermal necrolysis overlap syndrome (695.14)
- toxic epidermal necrolysis (695.15)

● **695.50 Exfoliation due to erythematous condition involving less than 10 percent of body surface**

Exfoliation due to erythematous condition NOS

● **695.51 Exfoliation due to erythematous condition involving 10-19 percent of body surface**

● **695.52 Exfoliation due to erythematous condition involving 20-29 percent of body surface**

● **695.53 Exfoliation due to erythematous condition involving 30-39 percent of body surface**

● **695.54 Exfoliation due to erythematous condition involving 40-49 percent of body surface**

● **695.55 Exfoliation due to erythematous condition involving 50-59 percent of body surface**

● **695.56 Exfoliation due to erythematous condition involving 60-69 percent of body surface**

● **695.57 Exfoliation due to erythematous condition involving 70-79 percent of body surface**

● **695.58 Exfoliation due to erythematous condition involving 80-89 percent of body surface**

● **695.59 Exfoliation due to erythematous condition involving 90 percent or more of body surface**

✓5th **695.8 Other specified erythematous conditions**

695.81 Ritter's disease

Dermatitis exfoliativa neonatorum

▶(Staphylococcal) Scalded skin syndrome

Use additional code to identify percentage of skin exfoliation (695.50-695.59)◀

DEF: Infectious skin disease of infants and young children marked by eruptions ranging from a localized bullous type to widespread development of easily ruptured fine vesicles and bullae; results in exfoliation of large planes of skin and leaves raw areas.

695.89 Other

Erythema intertrigo
Intertrigo
Pityriasis rubra (Hebra)

EXCLUDES *mycotic intertrigo (111.0-111.9)*

AHA: S-O, '86, 10

695.9 Unspecified erythematous condition

Erythema NOS
Erythroderma (secondary)

✓4th **696 Psoriasis and similar disorders**

696.0 Psoriatic arthropathy

DEF: Psoriasis associated with inflammatory arthritis; often involves interphalangeal joints.

696.1 Other psoriasis

Acrodermatitis continua
Dermatitis repens
Psoriasis:
- NOS
- any type, except arthropathic

EXCLUDES *psoriatic arthropathy (696.0)*

696.2 Parapsoriasis

Parakeratosis variegata
Parapsoriasis lichenoides chronica
Pityriasis lichenoides et varioliformis

DEF: Erythrodermas similar to lichen, planus and psoriasis; symptoms include redness and itching; resistant to treatment.

696.3 Pityriasis rosea

Pityriasis circinata (et maculata)

DEF: Common, self-limited rash of unknown etiology marked by a solitary erythematous, salmon or fawn-colored herald plaque on the trunk, arms or thighs; followed by development of papular or macular lesions that tend to peel and form a scaly collarette.

696.4 Pityriasis rubra pilaris

Devergie's disease
Lichen ruber acuminatus

EXCLUDES *pityriasis rubra (Hebra) (695.89)*

DEF: Inflammatory disease of hair follicles; marked by firm, red lesions topped by horny plugs; may form patches; occurs on fingers elbows, knees.

696.5 Other and unspecified pityriasis

Pityriasis:
- NOS
- alba
- streptogenes

EXCLUDES *pityriasis:*
- *simplex (690.18)*
- *versicolor (111.0)*

696.8 Other

✓4th **697 Lichen**

EXCLUDES *lichen:*
- *obtusus corneus (698.3)*
- *pilaris (congenital) (757.39)*
- *ruber acuminatus (696.4)*
- *sclerosus et atrophicus (701.0)*
- *scrofulosus (017.0)*
- *simplex chronicus (698.3)*
- *spinulosus (congenital) (757.39)*
- *urticatus (698.2)*

697.0 Lichen planus

Lichen:
- planopilaris
- ruber planus

DEF: Inflammatory, pruritic skin disease; marked by angular, flat-top, violet-colored papules; may be acute and widespread or chronic and localized.

697.1 Lichen nitidus

Pinkus' disease

DEF: Chronic, inflammatory, usually asymptomatic skin disorder, characterized by numerous glistening, flat-topped, discrete, smooth, skin-colored micropapules most often on penis, lower abdomen, inner thighs, wrists, forearms, breasts and buttocks.

697.8 Other lichen, not elsewhere classified

Lichen:
- ruber moniliforme
- striata

697.9 Lichen, unspecified

✓4th **698 Pruritus and related conditions**

EXCLUDES *pruritus specified as psychogenic (306.3)*

DEF: Pruritus: Intense, persistent itching due to irritation of sensory nerve endings from organic or psychogenic causes.

698.0 Pruritus ani

Perianal itch

698.1 Pruritus of genital organs

698.2 Prurigo
Lichen urticatus
Prurigo:
NOS
Hebra's
mitis
simplex
Urticaria papulosa (Hebra)
EXCLUDES *prurigo nodularis (698.3)*

698.3 Lichenification and lichen simplex chronicus
Hyde's disease
Neurodermatitis (circumscripta) (local)
Prurigo nodularis
EXCLUDES *neurodermatitis, diffuse (of Brocq) (691.8)*
DEF: Lichenification: thickening of skin due to prolonged rubbing or scratching.
DEF: Lichen simplex chronicus: eczematous dermatitis, of face, neck, extremities, scrotum, vulva, and perianal region due to repeated itching, rubbing and scratching; spontaneous or evolves with other dermatoses.

698.4 Dermatitis factitia [artefacta]
Dermatitis ficta
Neurotic excoriation
Use additional code to identify any associated mental disorder
DEF: Various types of self-inflicted skin lesions characterized in appearance as an erythema to a gangrene.

698.8 Other specified pruritic conditions
Pruritus:
hiemalis
senilis
Winter itch

698.9 Unspecified pruritic disorder
Itch NOS
Pruritus NOS

OTHER DISEASES OF SKIN AND SUBCUTANEOUS TISSUE (700-709)

EXCLUDES *conditions confined to eyelids (373.0-374.9)*
congenital conditions of skin, hair, and nails (757.0-757.9)

700 Corns and callosities
Callus
Clavus
DEF: Corns: Conical or horny thickening of skin on toes, due to friction, pressure from shoes and hosiery; pain and inflammation may develop.
DEF: Callosities: Localized overgrowth (hyperplasia) of the horny epidermal layer due to pressure or friction.

✓4th **701 Other hypertrophic and atrophic conditions of skin**
EXCLUDES *dermatomyositis (710.3)*
hereditary edema of legs (757.0)
scleroderma (generalized) (710.1)

701.0 Circumscribed scleroderma
Addison's keloid
Dermatosclerosis, localized
Lichen sclerosus et atrophicus
Morphea
Scleroderma, circumscribed or localized
DEF: Thickened, hardened, skin and subcutaneous tissue; may involve musculoskeletal system.

701.1 Keratoderma, acquired
Acquired:
ichthyosis
keratoderma palmaris et plantaris
Elastosis perforans serpiginosa
Hyperkeratosis:
NOS
follicularis in cutem penetrans
palmoplantaris climacterica
Keratoderma:
climactericum
tylodes, progressive
Keratosis (blennorrhagica)
EXCLUDES *Darier's disease [keratosis follicularis] (congenital) (757.39)*
keratosis:
arsenical (692.4)
gonococcal (098.81)
AHA:4Q, '94, 48

701.2 Acquired acanthosis nigricans
Keratosis nigricans
DEF: Diffuse velvety hyperplasia of the spinous skin layer of the axilla and other body folds marked by gray, brown, or black pigmentation; in adult form it is often associated with an internal carcinoma (malignant acanthosis nigricans) in a benign, nevoid form it is relatively generalized; benign juvenile form with obesity is sometimes caused by an endocrine disturbance.

701.3 Striae atrophicae
Atrophic spots of skin
Atrophoderma maculatum
Atrophy blanche (of Milian)
Degenerative colloid atrophy
Senile degenerative atrophy
Striae distensae
DEF: Bands of atrophic, depressed, wrinkled skin associated with stretching of skin from pregnancy, obesity, or rapid growth during puberty.

701.4 Keloid scar
Cheloid
Hypertrophic scar
Keloid
DEF: Overgrowth of scar tissue due to excess amounts of collagen during connective tissue repair; occurs mainly on upper trunk, face.

701.5 Other abnormal granulation tissue
Excessive granulation

701.8 Other specified hypertrophic and atrophic conditions of skin
Acrodermatitis atrophicans chronica
Atrophia cutis senilis
Atrophoderma neuriticum
Confluent and reticulate papillomatosis
Cutis laxa senilis
Elastosis senilis
Folliculitis ulerythematosa reticulata
Gougerot-Carteaud syndrome or disease
AHA: ►1Q, '08, 7◄

701.9 Unspecified hypertrophic and atrophic conditions of skin
Atrophoderma
Skin tag

✓4th **702 Other dermatoses**
EXCLUDES *carcinoma in situ (232.0-232.9)*

702.0 Actinic keratosis
AHA: 1Q, '92, 18
DEF: Wart-like growth, red or skin-colored; may form a cutaneous horn.

✓5th **702.1 Seborrheic keratosis**
DEF: Common, benign, lightly pigmented, warty growth composed of basaloid cells.

702.11 Inflamed seborrheic keratosis
AHA: 4Q, '94, 48

702.19 **Other seborrheic keratosis**
Seborrheic keratosis NOS

702.8 **Other specified dermatoses**

✓4th **703 Diseases of nail**

EXCLUDES *congenital anomalies (757.5)*
onychia and paronychia (681.02, 681.11)

703.0 **Ingrowing nail**
Ingrowing nail with infection
Unguis incarnatus

EXCLUDES *infection, nail NOS (681.9)*

703.8 **Other specified diseases of nail**
Dystrophia unguium
Hypertrophy of nail
Koilonychia
Leukonychia (punctata) (striata)
Onychauxis
Onychogryposis
Onycholysis

703.9 **Unspecified disease of nail**

✓4th **704 Diseases of hair and hair follicles**

EXCLUDES *congenital anomalies (757.4)*

✓5th 704.0 **Alopecia**

EXCLUDES *madarosis (374.55)*
syphilitic alopecia (091.82)

DEF: Lack of hair, especially on scalp; often called baldness; may be partial or total; occurs at any age.

704.00 **Alopecia, unspecified**
Baldness
Loss of hair

704.01 **Alopecia areata**
Ophiasis

DEF: Alopecia areata: usually reversible, inflammatory, patchy hair loss found in beard or scalp.

DEF: Ophiasis: alopecia areata of children; marked by band around temporal and occipital scalp margins.

704.02 **Telogen effluvium**

DEF: Shedding of hair from premature telogen development in follicles due to stress, including shock, childbirth, surgery, drugs or weight loss.

704.09 **Other**
Folliculitis decalvans
Hypotrichosis:
NOS
postinfectional NOS
Pseudopelade

704.1 **Hirsutism**
Hypertrichosis:
NOS
lanuginosa, acquired
Polytrichia

EXCLUDES *hypertrichosis of eyelid (374.54)*

DEF: Excess hair growth; often in unexpected places and amounts.

704.2 **Abnormalities of the hair**
Atrophic hair
Clastothrix
Fragilitas crinium
Trichiasis:
NOS
cicatrical
Trichorrhexis (nodosa)

EXCLUDES *trichiasis of eyelid (374.05)*

704.3 **Variations in hair color**
Canities (premature)
Grayness, hair (premature)
Heterochromia of hair
Poliosis:
NOS
circumscripta, acquired

704.8 **Other specified diseases of hair and hair follicles**
Folliculitis:
NOS
abscedens et suffodiens
pustular
Perifolliculitis:
NOS
capitis abscedens et suffodiens
scalp
Sycosis:
NOS
barbae [not parasitic]
lupoid
vulgaris

704.9 **Unspecified disease of hair and hair follicles**

✓4th **705 Disorders of sweat glands**

705.0 **Anhidrosis**
Hypohidrosis
Oligohidrosis

DEF: Lack or deficiency of ability to sweat.

705.1 **Prickly heat**
Heat rash
Miliaria rubra (tropicalis)
Sudamina

✓5th 705.2 **Focal hyperhidrosis**

EXCLUDES *generalized (secondary) hyperhidrosis (780.8)*

705.21 **Primary focal hyperhidrosis**
Focal hyperhidrosis NOS
Hyperhidrosis NOS
Hyperhidrosis of:
axilla
face
palms
soles

AHA: 4Q, '04, 91

DEF: A rare condition that is a disorder of the sweat glands resulting in excessive production of sweat; occurs in the absence of any underlying or causative condition and is almost always focal, confined to one or more specific areas of the body.

705.22 **Secondary focal hyperhidrosis**
Frey's syndrome

AHA: 4Q, '04, 91

DEF: Secondary focal hyperhidrosis: a symptom of an underlying disease process resulting in excessive sweating beyond what the body requires to maintain thermal control, confined to one or more specific areas of the body.

DEF: Frey's syndrome: an auriculotemporal syndrome due to lesion on the parotid gland; characteristic redness and excessive sweating on the cheek in connection with eating.

✓5th 705.8 **Other specified disorders of sweat glands**

705.81 **Dyshidrosis**
Cheiropompholyx
Pompholyx

DEF: Vesicular eruption, on hands, feet causing itching and burning.

705.82 **Fox-Fordyce disease**

DEF: Chronic, usually pruritic disease chiefly of women evidenced by small follicular papular eruptions, especially in the axillary and pubic areas; develops from the closure and rupture of the affected apocrine glands' intraepidermal portion of the ducts.

705.83 **Hidradenitis**
Hidradenitis suppurativa

DEF: Inflamed sweat glands.

705.89 Other
Bromhidrosis
Chromhidrosis
Granulosis rubra nasi
Urhidrosis

EXCLUDES *generalized hyperhidrosis (780.8)*
hidrocystoma (216.0-216.9)

DEF: Bromhidrosis: foul-smelling axillary sweat due to decomposed bacteria.

DEF: Chromhidrosis: secretion of colored sweat.

DEF: Granulosis rubra nasi: ideopathic condition of children; causes redness, sweating around nose, face and chin; tends to end by puberty.

DEF: Urhidrosis: urinous substance, such as uric acid, in sweat; occurs in uremia.

705.9 Unspecified disorder of sweat glands
Disorder of sweat glands NOS

✓4th 706 Diseases of sebaceous glands

706.0 Acne varioliformis
Acne:
frontalis
necrotica

DEF: Rare form of acne characterized by persistent brown papulo-pustules usually on the brow and temporoparietal part of the scalp.

706.1 Other acne
Acne:
NOS
conglobata
cystic
pustular
vulgaris
Blackhead
Comedo

EXCLUDES *acne rosacea (695.3)*

706.2 Sebaceous cyst
Atheroma, skin
Keratin cyst
Wen

DEF: Benign epidermal cyst, contains sebum and keratin; presents as firm, circumscribed nodule.

706.3 Seborrhea

EXCLUDES *seborrhea:*
capitis (690.11)
sicca (690.18)
seborrheic
dermatitis (690.10)
keratosis (702.11-702.19)

DEF: Seborrheic dermatitis marked by excessive secretion of sebum; the sebum forms an oily coating, crusts, or scales on the skin; it is also called hyperseatosis.

706.8 Other specified diseases of sebaceous glands
Asteatosis (cutis)
Xerosis cutis

706.9 Unspecified disease of sebaceous glands

✓4th 707 Chronic ulcer of skin

INCLUDES non-infected sinus of skin
non-healing ulcer

EXCLUDES *varicose ulcer (454.0, 454.2)*

AHA: 4Q, '04, 92

▲ ✓5th **707.0 Pressure ulcer**
Bed sore
Decubitus ulcer
Plaster ulcer

▶Use additional code to identify pressure ulcer stage (707.20-707.25)◀

AHA: 1Q, '04, 14; 4Q, '03, 110; 4Q, '99, 20; 1Q, '96, 15; 3Q, '90, 15; N-D, '87, 9

▲ **707.00 Unspecified site**

Four Stages of Pressure Ulcers

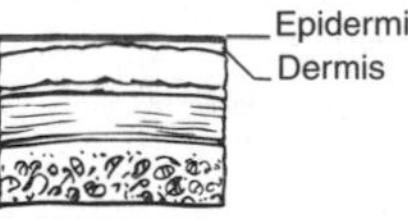

First Stage
Persistent focal erythema

Second Stage
Partial thickness skin loss involving epidermis, dermis, or both

Third Stage
Full thickness skin loss extending through subcutaneous tissue

Fourth Stage
Necrosis of soft tissue extending to muscle and bone

▲ **707.01 Elbow**

▲ **707.02 Upper back**
Shoulder blades

▲ **707.03 Lower back**
Sacrum

AHA: 1Q, '05, 16

▲ **707.04 Hip**

▲ **707.05 Buttock**

▲ **707.06 Ankle**

▲ **707.07 Heel**

AHA: 1Q, '05, 16

▲ **707.09 Other site**
Head

▲ ✓5th **707.1 Ulcer of lower limbs, except pressure ulcer**
Ulcer, chronic:
neurogenic } of lower limb
trophic }

Code, if applicable, any causal condition first:
atherosclerosis of the extremities with ulceration (440.23)
chronic venous hypertension with ulcer (459.31)
chronic venous hypertension with ulcer and inflammation (459.33)
diabetes mellitus ▶(249.80-249.81, 250.80-250.83)◀
postphlebitic syndrome with ulcer (459.11)
postphlebitic syndrome with ulcer and inflammation (459.13)

AHA: 4Q, '00, 44; 4Q, '99, 15

▲ **707.10 Ulcer of lower limb, unspecified**

AHA: 3Q, '04, 5; 4Q, '02, 43

▲ **707.11 Ulcer of thigh**

▲ **707.12 Ulcer of calf**

▲ **707.13 Ulcer of ankle**

▲ **707.14 Ulcer of heel and midfoot**
Plantar surface of midfoot

▲ **707.15 Ulcer of other part of foot**
Toes

▲ **707.19 Ulcer of other part of lower limb**

● ✓5th **707.2 Pressure ulcer stages**
Code first site of pressure ulcer (707.00-707.09)

● **707.20 Pressure ulcer, unspecified stage**
Healing pressure ulcer NOS
Healing pressure ulcer, unspecified stage

● **707.21 Pressure ulcer stage I**
Healing pressure ulcer, stage I
Pressure pre-ulcer skin changes limited to persistent focal erythema

● **707.22 Pressure ulcer stage II**
Healing pressure ulcer, stage II
Pressure ulcer with abrasion, blister, partial thickness skin loss involving epidermis and/or dermis

Cutaneous Lesions

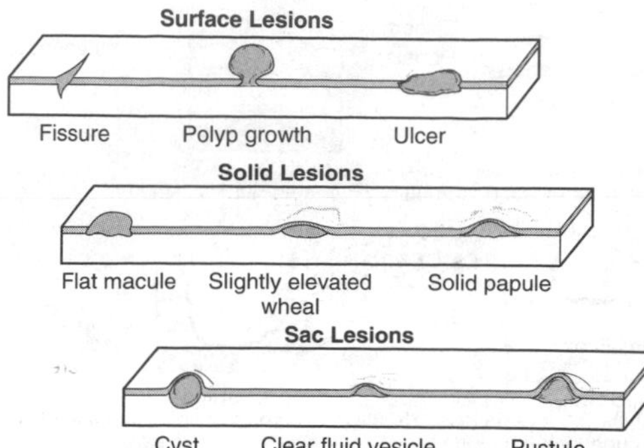

● **707.23 Pressure ulcer stage III**
Healing pressure ulcer, stage III
Pressure ulcer with full thickness skin loss involving damage or necrosis of subcutaneous tissue

● **707.24 Pressure ulcer stage IV**
Healing pressure ulcer, stage IV
Pressure ulcer with necrosis of soft tissues through to underlying muscle, tendon, or bone

● **707.25 Pressure ulcer, unstageable**

707.8 Chronic ulcer of other specified sites
Ulcer, chronic:
neurogenic } of other specified sites
trophic }

707.9 Chronic ulcer of unspecified site
Chronic ulcer NOS
Trophic ulcer NOS
Tropical ulcer NOS
Ulcer of skin NOS

✓4th **708 Urticaria**

EXCLUDES *edema:*
angioneurotic (995.1)
Quincke's (995.1)
hereditary angioedema (277.6)
urticaria:
giant (995.1)
papulosa (Hebra) (698.2)
pigmentosa (juvenile) (congenital) (757.33)

DEF: Skin disorder marked by raised edematous patches of skin or mucous membrane with intense itching; also called hives.

708.0 Allergic urticaria

708.1 Idiopathic urticaria

708.2 Urticaria due to cold and heat
Thermal urticaria

708.3 Dermatographic urticaria
Dermatographia
Factitial urticaria

708.4 Vibratory urticaria

708.5 Cholinergic urticaria

708.8 Other specified urticaria
Nettle rash
Urticaria:
chronic
recurrent periodic

708.9 Urticaria, unspecified
Hives NOS

✓4th **709 Other disorders of skin and subcutaneous tissue**

✓5th **709.0 Dyschromia**

EXCLUDES *albinism (270.2)*
pigmented nevus (216.0-216.9)
that of eyelid (374.52-374.53)

DEF: Pigment disorder of skin or hair.

709.00 Dyschromia, unspecified

709.01 Vitiligo

DEF: Persistent, progressive development of nonpigmented white patches on otherwise normal skin.

709.09 Other

709.1 Vascular disorders of skin
Angioma serpiginosum
Purpura (primary)annularis telangiectodes

709.2 Scar conditions and fibrosis of skin
Adherent scar (skin)
Cicatrix
Disfigurement (due to scar)
Fibrosis, skin NOS
Scar NOS

EXCLUDES *keloid scar (701.4)*

AHA: N-D, '84, 19

709.3 Degenerative skin disorders
Calcinosis:
circumscripta
cutis
Colloid milium
Degeneration, skin
Deposits, skin
Senile dermatosis NOS
Subcutaneous calcification

709.4 Foreign body granuloma of skin and subcutaneous tissue

EXCLUDES *residual foreign body without granuloma of skin and subcutaneous tissue (729.6)*
that of muscle (728.82)

709.8 Other specified disorders of skin
Epithelial hyperplasia
Menstrual dermatosis
Vesicular eruption

AHA: N-D, '87, 6

DEF: Epithelial hyperplasia: increased number of epitheleal cells.

DEF: Vesicular eruption: liquid-filled structures appearing through skin.

709.9 Unspecified disorder of skin and subcutaneous tissue
Dermatosis NOS

13. DISEASES OF THE MUSCULOSKELETAL SYSTEM AND CONNECTIVE TISSUE (710-739)

▶Use additional external cause code, if applicable, to identify the cause of the musculoskeletal condition◀

The following fifth-digit subclassification is for use with categories 711-712, 715-716, 718-719, and 730:

0 site unspecified

1 shoulder region
- Acromioclavicular joint(s)
- Clavicle
- Glenohumeral joint(s)
- Scapula
- Sternoclavicular joint(s)

2 upper arm
- Elbow joint
- Humerus

3 forearm
- Radius
- Ulna
- Wrist joint

4 hand
- Carpus
- Metacarpus
- Phalanges [fingers]

5 pelvic region and thigh
- Buttock
- Femur
- Hip (joint)

6 lower leg
- Fibula
- Knee joint
- Patella
- Tibia

7 ankle and foot
- Ankle joint
- Digits [toes]
- Metatarsus
- Phalanges, foot
- Tarsus
- Other joints in foot

8 other specified sites
- Head
- Neck
- Ribs
- Skull
- Trunk
- Vertebral column

9 multiple sites

ARTHROPATHIES AND RELATED DISORDERS (710-719)

EXCLUDES *disorders of spine (720.0-724.9)*

✓4th 710 Diffuse diseases of connective tissue

INCLUDES all collagen diseases whose effects are not mainly confined to a single system

EXCLUDES *those affecting mainly the cardiovascular system, i.e., polyarteritis nodosa and allied conditions (446.0-446.7)*

710.0 Systemic lupus erythematosus

Disseminated lupus erythematosus
Libman-Sacks disease

Use additional code to identify manifestation, as:
- endocarditis (424.91)
- nephritis (583.81)
  - chronic (582.81)
- nephrotic syndrome (581.81)

EXCLUDES *lupus erythematosus (discoid) NOS (695.4)*

AHA: 2Q, '03, 7-8; 2Q, '97, 8

DEF: A chronic multisystemic inflammatory disease affecting connective tissue; marked by anemia, leukopenia, muscle and joint pains, fever, rash of a butterfly pattern around cheeks and forehead area; of unknown etiology.

710.1 Systemic sclerosis

Acrosclerosis
CRST syndrome
Progressive systemic sclerosis
Scleroderma

Use additional code to identify manifestation, as:
- lung involvement (517.2)
- myopathy (359.6)

EXCLUDES *circumscribed scleroderma (701.0)*

AHA: 1Q, '88, 6

DEF: Systemic disease, involving excess fibrotic collagen build-up; symptoms include thickened skin; fibrotic degenerative changes in various organs; and vascular abnomalities; condition occurs more often in females.

Joint Structures

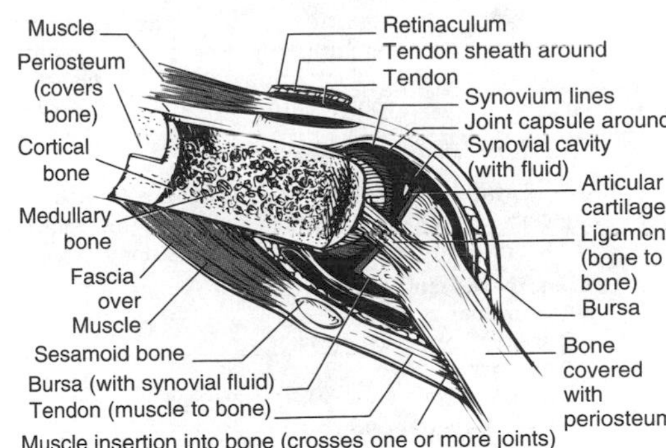

710.2 Sicca syndrome

Keratoconjunctivitis sicca
Sjögren's disease

DEF: Autoimmune disease; associated with keratoconjunctivitis, laryngopharyngitis, rhinitis, dry mouth, enlarged parotid gland, and chronic polyarthritis.

710.3 Dermatomyositis

Poikilodermatomyositis
Polymyositis with skin involvement

DEF: Polymyositis associated with flat-top purple papules on knuckles; marked by upper eyelid rash, edema of eyelids and orbit area, red rash on forehead, neck, shoulders, trunk and arms; symptoms include fever, weight loss aching muscles; visceral cancer (in individuals older than 40).

710.4 Polymyositis

DEF: Chronic, progressive, inflammatory skeletal muscle disease; causes weakness of limb girdles, neck, pharynx; may precede or follow scleroderma, Sjogren's disease, systemic lupus erythematosus, arthritis, or malignancy.

710.5 Eosinophilia myalgia syndrome

Toxic oil syndrome

Use additional E code to identify drug, if drug induced

AHA: 4Q, '92, 21

DEF: Eosinophilia myalgia syndrome (EMS): inflammatory, multisystem fibrosis; associated with ingesting elementary L-tryptophan; symptoms include myalgia, weak limbs and bulbar muscles, distal sensory loss, areflexia, arthralgia, cough, fever, fatigue, skin rashes, myopathy, and eosinophil counts greater than 1000/microliter.

DEF: Toxic oil syndrome: syndrome similar to EMS due to ingesting contaminated cooking oil.

710.8 Other specified diffuse diseases of connective tissue

Multifocal fibrosclerosis (idiopathic) NEC
Systemic fibrosclerosing syndrome

AHA: M-A, '87, 12

710.9 Unspecified diffuse connective tissue disease

Collagen disease NOS

4th 711 Arthropathy associated with infections

INCLUDES arthritis, arthropathy, polyarthritis, polyarthropathy } associated with conditions classifiable below

EXCLUDES *rheumatic fever (390)*

The following fifth-digit subclassification is for use with category 711; valid digits are in [brackets] under each code. See list at beginning of chapter for definitions.

0 site unspecified
1 shoulder region
2 upper arm
3 forearm
4 hand
5 pelvic region and thigh
6 lower leg
7 ankle and foot
8 other specified sites
9 multiple sites

AHA: 1Q, '92, 17

§ 5th **711.0 Pyogenic arthritis**
[0-9]
Arthritis or polyarthritis (due to):
coliform [Escherichia coli]
Hemophilus influenzae [H. influenzae]
pneumococcal
Pseudomonas
staphylococcal
streptococcal
Pyarthrosis

Use additional code to identify infectious organism (041.0-041.8)

AHA: 1Q, '92, 16; 1Q, '91, 15

DEF: Infectious arthritis caused by various bacteria; marked by inflamed synovial membranes, and purulent effusion in joints.

§ 5th ***711.1 Arthropathy associated with Reiter's disease and nonspecific urethritis***
[0-9]
Code first underlying disease as:
nonspecific urethritis (099.4)
Reiter's disease (099.3)

DEF: Reiter's disease: joint disease marked by diarrhea, urethritis, conjunctivitis, keratosis and arthritis; of unknown etiology; affects young males.

DEF: Urethritis: inflamed urethra.

§ 5th ***711.2 Arthropathy in Behçet's syndrome***
[0-9]
Code first underlying disease (136.1)

DEF: Behçet's syndrome: Chronic inflammatory disorder, of unknown etiology; affects small blood vessels; causes ulcers of oral and pharyngeal mucous membranes and genitalia, skin lesions, retinal vasculitis, optic atrophy and severe uveitis.

§ 5th ***711.3 Postdysenteric arthropathy***
[0-9]
Code first underlying disease as:
dysentery (009.0)
enteritis, infectious (008.0-009.3)
paratyphoid fever (002.1-002.9)
typhoid fever (002.0)

EXCLUDES *salmonella arthritis (003.23)*

§ 5th ***711.4 Arthropathy associated with other bacterial diseases***
[0-9]
Code first underlying disease as:
diseases classifiable to 010-040, 090-099, except as in 711.1, 711.3, and 713.5
leprosy (030.0-030.9)
tuberculosis (015.0-015.9)

EXCLUDES *gonococcal arthritis (098.50)*
meningococcal arthritis (036.82)

§ 5th ***711.5 Arthropathy associated with other viral diseases***
[0-9]
Code first underlying disease as:
diseases classifiable to 045-049, 050-079, 480, 487
O'nyong nyong (066.3)

EXCLUDES *that due to rubella (056.71)*

§ 5th ***711.6 Arthropathy associated with mycoses***
[0-9]
Code first underlying disease (110.0-118)

§ 5th ***711.7 Arthropathy associated with helminthiasis***
[0-9]
Code first underlying disease as:
filariasis (125.0-125.9)

§ 5th ***711.8 Arthropathy associated with other infectious and parasitic diseases***
[0-9]
Code first underlying disease as:
diseases classifiable to 080-088, 100-104, 130-136

EXCLUDES *arthropathy associated with sarcoidosis (713.7)*

AHA: 4Q, '91, 15; 3Q, '90, 14

§ 5th **711.9 Unspecified infective arthritis**
[0-9]
Infective arthritis or polyarthritis (acute) (chronic) (subacute) NOS

4th 712 Crystal arthropathies

INCLUDES crystal-induced arthritis and synovitis

EXCLUDES *gouty arthropathy (274.0)*

DEF: Joint disease due to urate crystal deposit in joints or synovial membranes.

The following fifth-digit subclassification is for use with category 712; valid digits are in [brackets] under each code. See list at beginning of chapter for definitions.

0 site unspecified
1 shoulder region
2 upper arm
3 forearm
4 hand
5 pelvic region and thigh
6 lower leg
7 ankle and foot
8 other specified sites
9 multiple sites

§ 5th ***712.1 Chondrocalcinosis due to dicalcium phosphate crystals***
[0-9]
Chondrocalcinosis due to dicalcium phosphate crystals (with other crystals)
Code first underlying disease (275.4)

§ 5th ***712.2 Chondrocalcinosis due to pyrophosphate crystals***
[0-9]
Code first underlying disease (275.4)

§ 5th ***712.3 Chondrocalcinosis, unspecified***
[0-9]
Code first underlying disease (275.4)

§ 5th **712.8 Other specified crystal arthropathies**
[0-9]

§ 5th **712.9 Unspecified crystal arthropathy**
[0-9]

§ Requires fifth-digit. Valid digits are in [brackets] under each code. See beginning of section 710-739 for codes and defintions.

✓4th 713 Arthropathy associated with other disorders classified elsewhere

INCLUDES arthritis, arthropathy, polyarthritis, polyarthropathy } associated with conditions classifiable below

713.0 *Arthropathy associated with other endocrine and metabolic disorders*

Code first underlying disease as:
acromegaly (253.0)
hemochromatosis (275.0)
hyperparathyroidism (252.00-252.08)
hypogammaglobulinemia (279.00-279.09)
hypothyroidism (243-244.9)
lipoid metabolism disorder (272.0-272.9)
ochronosis (270.2)

EXCLUDES *arthropathy associated with:*
amyloidosis (713.7)
crystal deposition disorders, except gout (712.1-712.9)
diabetic neuropathy (713.5)
gouty arthropathy (274.0)

713.1 *Arthropathy associated with gastrointestinal conditions other than infections*

Code first underlying disease as:
regional enteritis (555.0-555.9)
ulcerative colitis (556)

713.2 *Arthropathy associated with hematological disorders*

Code first underlying disease as:
hemoglobinopathy (282.4-282.7)
hemophilia (286.0-286.2)
leukemia (204.0-208.9)
malignant reticulosis (202.3)
multiple myelomatosis (203.0)

EXCLUDES *arthropathy associated with Henoch-Schönlein purpura (713.6)*

713.3 *Arthropathy associated with dermatological disorders*

Code first underlying disease as:
erythema multiforme ▶(695.10-695.19)◀
erythema nodosum (695.2)

EXCLUDES *psoriatic arthropathy (696.0)*

713.4 *Arthropathy associated with respiratory disorders*

Code first underlying disease as:
diseases classifiable to 490-519

EXCLUDES *arthropathy associated with respiratory infections (711.0, 711.4-711.8)*

713.5 *Arthropathy associated with neurological disorders*

Charcôt's arthropathy, Neuropathic arthritis } associated with diseases classifiable elsewhere

Code first underlying disease as:
neuropathic joint disease [Charcôt's joints]:
NOS (094.0)
diabetic ▶(249.6, 250.6)◀
syringomyelic (336.0)
tabetic [syphilitic] (094.0)

713.6 *Arthropathy associated with hypersensitivity reaction*

Code first underlying disease as:
Henoch (-Schönlein) purpura (287.0)
serum sickness (999.5)

EXCLUDES *allergic arthritis NOS (716.2)*

713.7 *Other general diseases with articular involvement*

Code first underlying disease as:
amyloidosis (277.30-277.39)
familial Mediterranean fever (277.31)
sarcoidosis (135)

AHA: 2Q, '97, 12

713.8 *Arthropathy associated with other condition classifiable elsewhere*

Code first underlying disease as:
conditions classifiable elsewhere except as in 711.1-711.8, 712, and 713.0-713.7

✓4th 714 Rheumatoid arthritis and other inflammatory polyarthropathies

EXCLUDES *rheumatic fever (390)*
rheumatoid arthritis of spine NOS (720.0)

AHA: 2Q, '95, 3

714.0 Rheumatoid arthritis

Arthritis or polyarthritis:
atrophic
rheumatic (chronic)

Use additional code to identify manifestation, as:
myopathy (359.6)
polyneuropathy (357.1)

EXCLUDES *juvenile rheumatoid arthritis NOS (714.30)*

AHA: 2Q, '06, 20; 1Q, '90, 5

DEF: Chronic systemic disease principally of joints, manifested by inflammatory changes in articular structures and synovial membranes, atrophy, and loss in bone density.

714.1 Felty's syndrome

Rheumatoid arthritis with splenoadenomegaly and leukopenia

DEF: Syndrome marked by rheumatoid arthritis, splenomegaly, leukopenia, pigmented spots on lower extremity skin, anemia, and thrombocytopenia.

714.2 Other rheumatoid arthritis with visceral or systemic involvement

Rheumatoid carditis

✓5th 714.3 Juvenile chronic polyarthritis

DEF: Rheumatoid arthritis of more than one joint; lasts longer than six weeks in age 17 or younger; symptoms include fever, erythematous rash, weight loss, lymphadenopathy, hepatosplenomegaly and pericarditis.

714.30 Polyarticular juvenile rheumatoid arthritis, chronic or unspecified

Juvenile rheumatoid arthritis NOS
Still's disease

714.31 Polyarticular juvenile rheumatoid arthritis, acute

714.32 Pauciarticular juvenile rheumatoid arthritis

714.33 Monoarticular juvenile rheumatoid arthritis

714.4 Chronic postrheumatic arthropathy

Chronic rheumatoid nodular fibrositis
Jaccoud's syndrome

DEF: Persistent joint disorder; follows previous rheumatic infection.

✓5th 714.8 Other specified inflammatory polyarthropathies

714.81 Rheumatoid lung

Caplan's syndrome
Diffuse interstitial rheumatoid disease of lung
Fibrosing alveolitis, rheumatoid

DEF: Lung disorders associated with rheumatoid arthritis.

714.89 Other

714.9 Unspecified inflammatory polyarthropathy
Inflammatory polyarthropathy or polyarthritis NOS
EXCLUDES *polyarthropathy NOS (716.5)*

✓4th 715 Osteoarthrosis and allied disorders
Note: Localized, in the subcategories below, includes bilateral involvement of the same site.
INCLUDES arthritis or polyarthritis:
degenerative
hypertrophic
degenerative joint disease
osteoarthritis
EXCLUDES *Marie-Strümpell spondylitis (720.0)*
osteoarthrosis [osteoarthritis] of spine (721.0-721.9)

The following fifth-digit subclassification is for use with category 715; valid digits are in [brackets] under each code. See list at beginning of chapter for definitions.
0 site unspecified
1 shoulder region
2 upper arm
3 forearm
4 hand
5 pelvic region and thigh
6 lower leg
7 ankle and foot
8 other specified sites
9 multiple sites

§ ✓5th **715.0 Osteoarthrosis, generalized**
[0,4,9] Degenerative joint disease, involving multiple joints
Primary generalized hypertrophic osteoarthrosis
DEF: Chronic noninflammatory arthritis; marked by degenerated articular cartilage and enlarged bone; symptoms include pain and stiffness with activity; occurs among elderly.

§ ✓5th **715.1 Osteoarthrosis, localized, primary**
[0-8] Localized osteoarthropathy, idiopathic

§ ✓5th **715.2 Osteoarthrosis, localized, secondary**
[0-8] Coxae malum senilis

§ ✓5th **715.3 Osteoarthrosis, localized, not specified whether primary or secondary**
[0-8] Otto's pelvis
AHA: For code 715.35: 3Q, '04, 12; 2Q, '04, 15; For code 715.36: 4Q, '03, 118; 2Q, '95, 5

§ ✓5th **715.8 Osteoarthrosis involving, or with mention of more than one site, but not specified as generalized**
[0,9]

§ ✓5th **715.9 Osteoarthrosis, unspecified whether generalized or localized**
[0-8]
AHA: For code 715.90: 2Q, '97, 12

✓4th 716 Other and unspecified arthropathies
EXCLUDES *cricoarytenoid arthropathy (478.79)*

The following fifth-digit subclassification is for use with category 716; valid digits are in [brackets] under each code. See list at beginning of chapter for definitions.
0 site unspecified
1 shoulder region
2 upper arm
3 forearm
4 hand
5 pelvic region and thigh
6 lower leg
7 ankle and foot
8 other specified sites
9 multiple sites

AHA: 2Q, '95, 3

§ ✓5th **716.0 Kaschin-Beck disease**
[0-9] Endemic polyarthritis
DEF: Chronic degenerative disease of spine and peripheral joints; occurs in eastern Siberian, northern Chinese, and Korean youth; may be a mycotoxicosis caused by eating cereals infected with fungus.

§ ✓5th **716.1 Traumatic arthropathy**
[0-9] AHA: For Code 716.11: 1Q, '02, 9

§ ✓5th **716.2 Allergic arthritis**
[0-9] EXCLUDES *arthritis associated with Henoch-Schönlein purpura or serum sickness (713.6)*

§ ✓5th **716.3 Climacteric arthritis** ♀
[0-9] Menopausal arthritis
DEF: Ovarian hormone deficiency; causes pain in small joints, shoulders, elbows or knees; affects females at menopause; also called arthropathia ovaripriva.

§ ✓5th **716.4 Transient arthropathy**
[0-9] EXCLUDES *palindromic rheumatism (719.3)*

§ ✓5th **716.5 Unspecified polyarthropathy or polyarthritis**
[0-9]

§ ✓5th **716.6 Unspecified monoarthritis**
[0-8] Coxitis

§ ✓5th **716.8 Other specified arthropathy**
[0-9]

§ ✓5th **716.9 Arthropathy, unspecified**
[0-9] Arthritis } (acute) (chronic) (subacute)
Arthropathy } (acute) (chronic) (subacute)
Articular rheumatism (chronic)
Inflammation of joint NOS

✓4th 717 Internal derangement of knee
INCLUDES degeneration, rupture, old, tear, old } of articular cartilage or meniscus of knee
EXCLUDES *acute derangement of knee (836.0-836.6)*
ankylosis (718.5)
contracture (718.4)
current injury (836.0-836.6)
deformity (736.4-736.6)
recurrent dislocation (718.3)

717.0 Old bucket handle tear of medial meniscus
Old bucket handle tear of unspecified cartilage

717.1 Derangement of anterior horn of medial meniscus

717.2 Derangement of posterior horn of medial meniscus

717.3 Other and unspecified derangement of medial meniscus
Degeneration of internal semilunar cartilage

Disruption and Tears of Meniscus

Bucket-handle

Flap-type

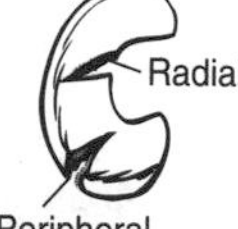

Peripheral

Horizontal cleavage

Vertical

Congenital discoid meniscus

§ Requires fifth-digit. Valid digits are in [brackets] under each code. See beginning of section 710-739 for codes and defintions.

N Newborn Age: 0 P Pediatric Age: 0-17 M Maternity Age: 12-55 A Adult Age: 15-124

Internal Derangements of Knee

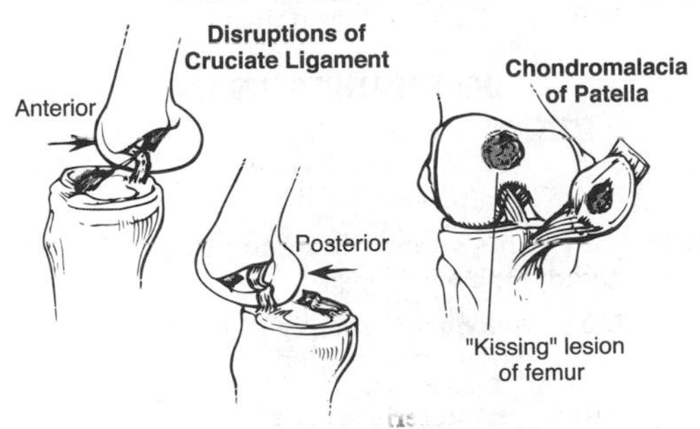

✓5th **717.4 Derangement of lateral meniscus**

717.40 Derangement of lateral meniscus, unspecified

717.41 Bucket handle tear of lateral meniscus

717.42 Derangement of anterior horn of lateral meniscus

717.43 Derangement of posterior horn of lateral meniscus

717.49 Other

717.5 Derangement of meniscus, not elsewhere classified

Congenital discoid meniscus
Cyst of semilunar cartilage
Derangement of semilunar cartilage NOS

717.6 Loose body in knee

Joint mice, knee
Rice bodies, knee (joint)

DEF: The presence in the joint synovial area of a small, frequently calcified, loose body created from synovial membrane, organized fibrin fragments of articular cartilage or arthritis osteophytes.

717.7 Chondromalacia of patella

Chondromalacia patellae
Degeneration [softening] of articular cartilage of patella

AHA: M-A, '85, 14; N-D, '84, 9

DEF: Softened patella cartilage.

✓5th **717.8 Other internal derangement of knee**

717.81 Old disruption of lateral collateral ligament

717.82 Old disruption of medial collateral ligament

717.83 Old disruption of anterior cruciate ligament

717.84 Old disruption of posterior cruciate ligament

717.85 Old disruption of other ligaments of knee

Capsular ligament of knee

717.89 Other

Old disruption of ligaments NOS

717.9 Unspecified internal derangement of knee

Derangement NOS of knee

✓4th **718 Other derangement of joint**

EXCLUDES *current injury (830.0-848.9)*
jaw (524.60-524.69)

The following fifth-digit subclassification is for use with category 718; valid digits are in [brackets] under each code. See list at beginning of chapter for definitions.

0 site unspecified
1 shoulder region
2 upper arm
3 forearm
4 hand
5 pelvic region and thigh
6 lower leg
7 ankle and foot
8 other specified sites
9 multiple sites

§ ✓5th **718.0 Articular cartilage disorder**
[0-5,7-9]
Meniscus:
disorder
rupture, old
tear, old
Old rupture of ligament(s) of joint NOS

EXCLUDES *articular cartilage disorder:*
in ochronosis (270.2)
knee (717.0-717.9)
chondrocalcinosis (275.4)
metastatic calcification (275.4)

§ ✓5th **718.1 Loose body in joint**
[0-5,7-9]
Joint mice

EXCLUDES *knee (717.6)*

AHA: For code 718.17: 2Q, '01, 15

DEF: Calcified loose bodies in synovial fluid; due to arthritic osteophytes.

§ ✓5th **718.2 Pathological dislocation**
[0-9]
Dislocation or displacement of joint, not recurrent and not current injury
Spontaneous dislocation (joint)

§ ✓5th **718.3 Recurrent dislocation of joint**
[0-9]
AHA: N-D, '87, 7

§ ✓5th **718.4 Contracture of joint**
[0-9]
AHA: 4Q, '98, 40

§ ✓5th **718.5 Ankylosis of joint**
[0-9]
Ankylosis of joint (fibrous) (osseous)

EXCLUDES *spine (724.9)*
stiffness of joint without mention of ankylosis (719.5)

DEF: Immobility and solidification, of joint; due to disease, injury or surgical procedure.

§ ✓5th **718.6 Unspecified intrapelvic protrusion of acetabulum**
[0,5]
Protrusio acetabuli, unspecified

DEF: Sinking of the floor of acetabulum; causing femoral head to protrude, limits hip movement; of unknown etiology.

Joint Derangements and Disorders

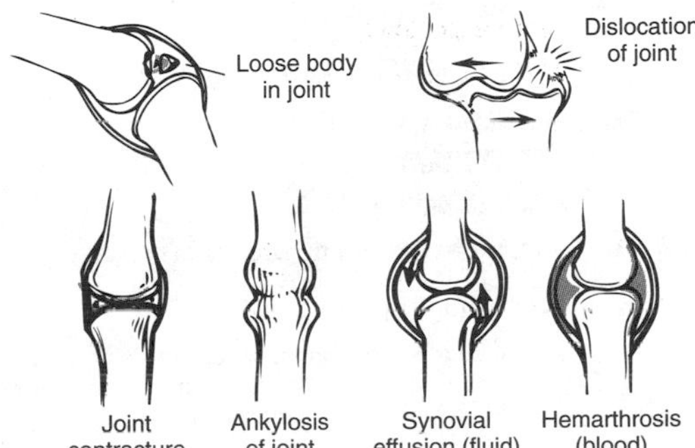

§ Requires fifth-digit. Valid digits are in [brackets] under each code. See beginning of section 710-739 for codes and defintions.

§ ✓5th **718.7 Developmental dislocation of joint**
[0-9]
EXCLUDES *congenital dislocation of joint (754.0-755.8)*
traumatic dislocation of joint (830-839)
AHA: 4Q, '01, 48

§ ✓5th **718.8 Other joint derangement, not elsewhere classified**
[0-9]
Flail joint (paralytic) Instability of joint
EXCLUDES *deformities classifiable to 736 (736.0-736.9)*
AHA: For code 718.81: 2Q, '00, 14

§ ✓5th **718.9 Unspecified derangement of joint**
[0-5,7-9] EXCLUDES *knee (717.9)*

✓4th **719 Other and unspecified disorders of joint**
EXCLUDES *jaw (524.60-524.69)*

The following fifth-digit subclassification is for use with codes 719.0-719.6, 719.8-719.9; valid digits are in [brackets] under each code. See list at beginning of chapter for definitions.

0 site unspecified
1 shoulder region
2 upper arm
3 forearm
4 hand
5 pelvic region and thigh
6 lower leg
7 ankle and foot
8 other specified sites
9 multiple sites

§ ✓5th **719.0 Effusion of joint**
[0-9]
Hydrarthrosis
Swelling of joint, with or without pain
EXCLUDES *intermittent hydrarthrosis (719.3)*

§ ✓5th **719.1 Hemarthrosis**
[0-9] EXCLUDES *current injury (840.0-848.9)*

§ ✓5th **719.2 Villonodular synovitis**
[0-9]
DEF: Overgrowth of synovial tissue, especially at knee joint; due to macrophage infiltration of giant cells in synovial villi and fibrous nodules.

§ ✓5th **719.3 Palindromic rheumatism**
[0-9]
Hench-Rosenberg syndrome
Intermittent hydrarthrosis
DEF: Recurrent episodes of afebrile arthritis and periarthritis marked by their complete disappearance after a few days or hours; causes swelling, redness, and disability usually affecting only one joint; no known cause; affects adults of either sex.

§ ✓5th **719.4 Pain in joint**
[0-9]
Arthralgia
AHA: For code 719.46: 1Q, '01, 3

§ ✓5th **719.5 Stiffness of joint, not elsewhere classified**
[0-9]

§ ✓5th **719.6 Other symptoms referable to joint**
[0-9]
Joint crepitus
Snapping hip
AHA: 1Q, '94, 15; For code 719.66: 2Q, '07, 6

719.7 Difficulty in walking
EXCLUDES *abnormality of gait (781.2)*
AHA: 2Q, '04, 15; 4Q, '03, 66

§ ✓5th **719.8 Other specified disorders of joint**
[0-9]
Calcification of joint
Fistula of joint
EXCLUDES *temporomandibular joint-pain-dysfunction syndrome [Costen's syndrome] (524.60)*

§ ✓5th **719.9 Unspecified disorder of joint**
[0-9]

DORSOPATHIES (720-724)

EXCLUDES *curvature of spine (737.0-737.9)*
osteochondrosis of spine (juvenile) (732.0)
adult (732.8)

✓4th **720 Ankylosing spondylitis and other inflammatory spondylopathies**

720.0 Ankylosing spondylitis
Rheumatoid arthritis of spine NOS
Spondylitis:
Marie-Strümpell
rheumatoid
DEF: Rheumatoid arthritis of spine and sacroiliac joints; fusion and deformity in spine follows; affects mainly males; cause unknown.

720.1 Spinal enthesopathy
Disorder of peripheral ligamentous or muscular attachments of spine
Romanus lesion
DEF: Tendinous or muscular vertebral bone attachment abnormality.

720.2 Sacroiliitis, not elsewhere classified
Inflammation of sacroiliac joint NOS
DEF: Pain due to inflammation in joint, at juncture of sacrum and hip.

✓5th **720.8 Other inflammatory spondylopathies**

720.81 Inflammatory spondylopathies in diseases classified elsewhere
Code first underlying disease as:
tuberculosis (015.0)

720.89 Other

720.9 Unspecified inflammatory spondylopathy
Spondylitis NOS

✓4th **721 Spondylosis and allied disorders**
AHA: 2Q, '89, 14
DEF: Degenerative changes in spinal joint.

721.0 Cervical spondylosis without myelopathy
Cervical or cervicodorsal:
arthritis
osteoarthritis
spondylarthritis

721.1 Cervical spondylosis with myelopathy
Anterior spinal artery compression syndrome
Spondylogenic compression of cervical spinal cord
Vertebral artery compression syndrome

721.2 Thoracic spondylosis without myelopathy
Thoracic:
arthritis
osteoarthritis
spondylarthritis

721.3 Lumbosacral spondylosis without myelopathy
Lumbar or lumbosacral:
arthritis
osteoarthritis
spondylarthritis
AHA: 4Q, '02, 107

✓5th **721.4 Thoracic or lumbar spondylosis with myelopathy**

721.41 Thoracic region
Spondylogenic compression of thoracic spinal cord

721.42 Lumbar region
Spondylogenic compression of lumbar spinal cord

§ Requires fifth-digit. Valid digits are in [brackets] under each code. See beginning of section 710-739 for codes and defintions.

721.5 Kissing spine
Baastrup's syndrome
DEF: Compression of spinous processes of adjacent vertebrae; due to mutual contact.

721.6 Ankylosing vertebral hyperostosis

721.7 Traumatic spondylopathy
Kümmell's disease or spondylitis

721.8 Other allied disorders of spine

✓5th **721.9 Spondylosis of unspecified site**

721.90 Without mention of myelopathy
Spinal:
arthritis (deformans) (degenerative) (hypertrophic)
osteoarthritis NOS
Spondylarthrosis NOS

721.91 With myelopathy
Spondylogenic compression of spinal cord NOS

✓4th **722 Intervertebral disc disorders**
AHA: 1Q, '88, 10

722.0 Displacement of cervical intervertebral disc without myelopathy
Neuritis (brachial) or radiculitis due to displacement or rupture of cervical intervertebral disc
Any condition classifiable to 722.2 of the cervical or cervicothoracic intervertebral disc

✓5th **722.1 Displacement of thoracic or lumbar intervertebral disc without myelopathy**

722.10 Lumbar intervertebral disc without myelopathy
Lumbago or sciatica due to displacement of intervertebral disc
Neuritis or radiculitis due to displacement or rupture of lumbar intervertebral disc
Any condition classifiable to 722.2 of the lumbar or lumbosacral intervertebral disc
AHA: 1Q, '07, 9; 3Q, '03, 12; 1Q, '03, 7; 4Q, '02, 107

722.11 Thoracic intervertebral disc without myelopathy
Any condition classifiable to 722.2 of thoracic intervertebral disc

722.2 Displacement of intervertebral disc, site unspecified, without myelopathy
Discogenic syndrome NOS
Herniation of nucleus pulposus NOS
Intervertebral disc NOS:
extrusion
prolapse
protrusion
rupture
Neuritis or radiculitis due to displacement or rupture of intervertebral disc

Normal Anatomy of Vertebral Disc

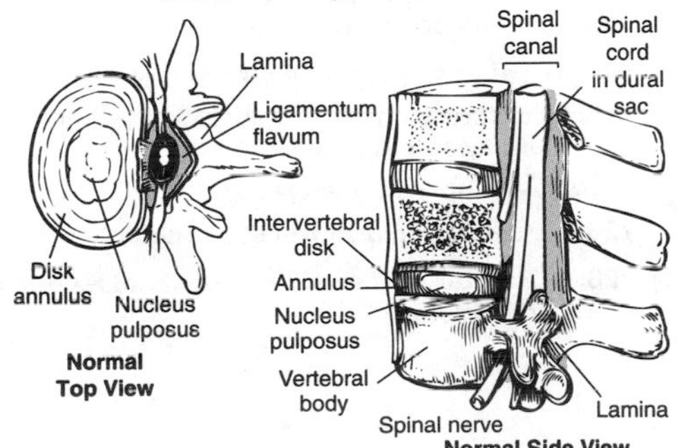

Derangement of Vertebral Disc

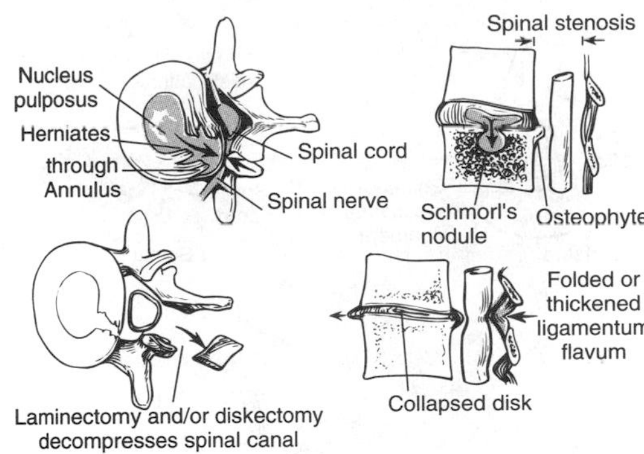

✓5th **722.3 Schmorl's nodes**
DEF: Irregular bone defect in the margin of the vertebral body; causes herniation into end plate of vertebral body.

722.30 Unspecified region

722.31 Thoracic region

722.32 Lumbar region

722.39 Other

722.4 Degeneration of cervical intervertebral disc
Degeneration of cervicothoracic intervertebral disc

✓5th **722.5 Degeneration of thoracic or lumbar intervertebral disc**

722.51 Thoracic or thoracolumbar intervertebral disc

722.52 Lumbar or lumbosacral intervertebral disc
AHA: 2Q, '06, 18; 4Q, '04, 133

722.6 Degeneration of intervertebral disc, site unspecified
Degenerative disc disease NOS
Narrowing of intervertebral disc or space NOS

✓5th **722.7 Intervertebral disc disorder with myelopathy**

722.70 Unspecified region

722.71 Cervical region

722.72 Thoracic region

722.73 Lumbar region

✓5th **722.8 Postlaminectomy syndrome**
AHA: J-F, '87, 7
DEF: Spinal disorder due to spinal laminectomy surgery.

722.80 Unspecified region

722.81 Cervical region

722.82 Thoracic region

722.83 Lumbar region
AHA: 2Q, '97, 15

✓5th **722.9 Other and unspecified disc disorder**
Calcification of intervertebral cartilage or disc
Discitis

722.90 Unspecified region
AHA: N-D, '84, 19

722.91 Cervical region

722.92 Thoracic region

722.93 Lumbar region

Stenosis in Cervical Region

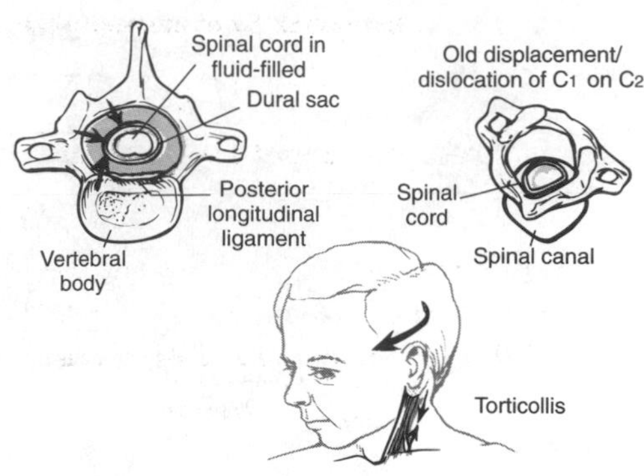

4th 723 Other disorders of cervical region

EXCLUDES *conditions due to:*
intervertebral disc disorders (722.0-722.9)
spondylosis (721.0-721.9)

AHA: 3Q, '94, 14; 2Q, '89, 14

723.0 Spinal stenosis in cervical region

AHA: 4Q, '03, 101

723.1 Cervicalgia

Pain in neck

DEF: Pain in cervical spine or neck region.

723.2 Cervicocranial syndrome

Barré-Liéou syndrome
Posterior cervical sympathetic syndrome

DEF: Neurologic disorder of upper cervical spine and nerve roots.

723.3 Cervicobrachial syndrome (diffuse)

AHA: N-D, '85, 12

DEF: Complex of symptoms due to scalenus anterior muscle compressing the brachial plexus; pain radiates from shoulder to arm or back of neck.

723.4 Brachial neuritis or radiculitis NOS

Cervical radiculitis
Radicular syndrome of upper limbs

723.5 Torticollis, unspecified

Contracture of neck

EXCLUDES *congenital (754.1)*
due to birth injury (767.8)
hysterical (300.11)
ocular torticollis (781.93)
psychogenic (306.0)
spasmodic (333.83)
traumatic, current (847.0)

AHA: 2Q, '01, 21; 1Q, '95, 7

DEF: Abnormally positioned neck relative to head; due to cervical muscle or fascia contractions; also called wryneck.

723.6 Panniculitis specified as affecting neck

DEF: Inflammation of the panniculus adiposus (subcutaneous fat) in the neck.

723.7 Ossification of posterior longitudinal ligament in cervical region

723.8 Other syndromes affecting cervical region

Cervical syndrome NEC
Klippel's disease
Occipital neuralgia

AHA: 1Q, '00, 7

723.9 Unspecified musculoskeletal disorders and symptoms referable to neck

Cervical (region) disorder NOS

4th 724 Other and unspecified disorders of back

EXCLUDES *collapsed vertebra (code to cause, e.g., osteoporosis, 733.00-733.09)*
conditions due to:
intervertebral disc disorders (722.0-722.9)
spondylosis (721.0-721.9)

AHA: 2Q, '89, 14

5th 724.0 Spinal stenosis, other than cervical

724.00 Spinal stenosis, unspecified region

724.01 Thoracic region

724.02 Lumbar region

AHA: ▶4Q, '07, 120;◀ 1Q, '07, 10, 20; 4Q, '99, 13

724.09 Other

724.1 Pain in thoracic spine

724.2 Lumbago

Low back pain
Low back syndrome
Lumbalgia

AHA: 2Q, '07, 11; N-D, '85, 12

724.3 Sciatica

Neuralgia or neuritis of sciatic nerve

EXCLUDES *specified lesion of sciatic nerve (355.0)*

AHA: 2Q, '89, 12

724.4 Thoracic or lumbosacral neuritis or radiculitis, unspecified

Radicular syndrome of lower limbs

AHA: 2Q, '99, 3

724.5 Backache, unspecified

Vertebrogenic (pain) syndrome NOS

724.6 Disorders of sacrum

Ankylosis } lumbosacral or sacroiliac (joint)
Instability }

5th 724.7 Disorders of coccyx

724.70 Unspecified disorder of coccyx

724.71 Hypermobility of coccyx

724.79 Other

Coccygodynia

724.8 Other symptoms referable to back

Ossification of posterior longitudinal ligament NOS
Panniculitis specified as sacral or affecting back

724.9 Other unspecified back disorders

Ankylosis of spine NOS
Compression of spinal nerve root NEC
Spinal disorder NOS

EXCLUDES *sacroiliitis (720.2)*

RHEUMATISM, EXCLUDING THE BACK (725-729)

INCLUDES disorders of muscles and tendons and their attachments, and of other soft tissues

725 Polymyalgia rheumatica

DEF: Joint and muscle pain, pelvis, and shoulder girdle stiffness, high sedimentation rate and temporal arteritis; occurs in elderly.

4th 726 Peripheral enthesopathies and allied syndromes

Note: Enthesopathies are disorders of peripheral ligamentous or muscular attachments.

EXCLUDES *spinal enthesopathy (720.1)*

726.0 Adhesive capsulitis of shoulder

5th 726.1 Rotator cuff syndrome of shoulder and allied disorders

726.10 Disorders of bursae and tendons in shoulder region, unspecified
Rotator cuff syndrome NOS
Supraspinatus syndrome NOS
AHA: 2Q, '01, 11

726.11 Calcifying tendinitis of shoulder

726.12 Bicipital tenosynovitis

726.19 Other specified disorders
EXCLUDES *complete rupture of rotator cuff, nontraumatic (727.61)*

726.2 Other affections of shoulder region, not elsewhere classified
Periarthritis of shoulder
Scapulohumeral fibrositis

✓5th 726.3 Enthesopathy of elbow region

726.30 Enthesopathy of elbow, unspecified

726.31 Medial epicondylitis

726.32 Lateral epicondylitis
Epicondylitis NOS
Golfers' elbow
Tennis elbow

726.33 Olecranon bursitis
Bursitis of elbow

726.39 Other

726.4 Enthesopathy of wrist and carpus
Bursitis of hand or wrist
Periarthritis of wrist

726.5 Enthesopathy of hip region
Bursitis of hip
Gluteal tendinitis
Iliac crest spur
Psoas tendinitis
Trochanteric tendinitis

✓5th 726.6 Enthesopathy of knee

726.60 Enthesopathy of knee, unspecified
Bursitis of knee NOS

726.61 Pes anserinus tendinitis or bursitis
DEF: Inflamed tendons of sartorius, gracilis and semitendinosus muscles of medial aspect of knee.

726.62 Tibial collateral ligament bursitis
Pellegrini-Stieda syndrome

726.63 Fibular collateral ligament bursitis

726.64 Patellar tendinitis

726.65 Prepatellar bursitis
AHA: 2Q, '06, 15

726.69 Other
Bursitis:
infrapatellar
subpatellar

✓5th 726.7 Enthesopathy of ankle and tarsus

726.70 Enthesopathy of ankle and tarsus, unspecified
Metatarsalgia NOS
EXCLUDES *Morton's metatarsalgia (355.6)*

726.71 Achilles bursitis or tendinitis

726.72 Tibialis tendinitis
Tibialis (anterior) (posterior) tendinitis

726.73 Calcaneal spur
DEF: Overgrowth of calcaneous bone; causes pain on walking; due to chronic avulsion injury of plantar fascia from calcaneus.

726.79 Other
Peroneal tendinitis

726.8 Other peripheral enthesopathies

✓5th 726.9 Unspecified enthesopathy

726.90 Enthesopathy of unspecified site
Capsulitis NOS
Periarthritis NOS
Tendinitis NOS

726.91 Exostosis of unspecified site
Bone spur NOS
AHA: 2Q, '01, 15

✓4th 727 Other disorders of synovium, tendon, and bursa

✓5th 727.0 Synovitis and tenosynovitis

727.00 Synovitis and tenosynovitis, unspecified
Synovitis NOS
Tenosynovitis NOS

727.01 *Synovitis and tenosynovitis in diseases classified elsewhere*
Code first underlying disease as:
tuberculosis (015.0-015.9)
EXCLUDES *crystal-induced (275.4)*
gonococcal (098.51)
gouty (274.0)
syphilitic (095.7)

727.02 Giant cell tumor of tendon sheath

727.03 Trigger finger (acquired)
DEF: Stenosing tenosynovitis or nodule in flexor tendon; cessation of flexion or extension movement in finger, followed by snapping into place.

727.04 Radial styloid tenosynovitis
de Quervain's disease

727.05 Other tenosynovitis of hand and wrist

727.06 Tenosynovitis of foot and ankle

727.09 Other

727.1 Bunion
DEF: Enlarged first metatarsal head due to inflamed bursa; results in laterally displaced great toe.

727.2 Specific bursitides often of occupational origin
Beat:
elbow
hand
knee
Chronic crepitant synovitis of wrist
Miners':
elbow
knee

727.3 Other bursitis
Bursitis NOS
EXCLUDES *bursitis:*
gonococcal (098.52)
subacromial (726.19)
subcoracoid (726.19)
subdeltoid (726.19)
syphilitic (095.7)
"frozen shoulder" (726.0)

Bunion

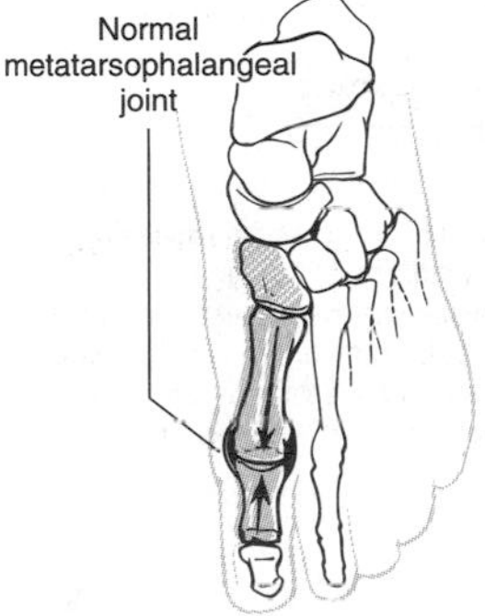

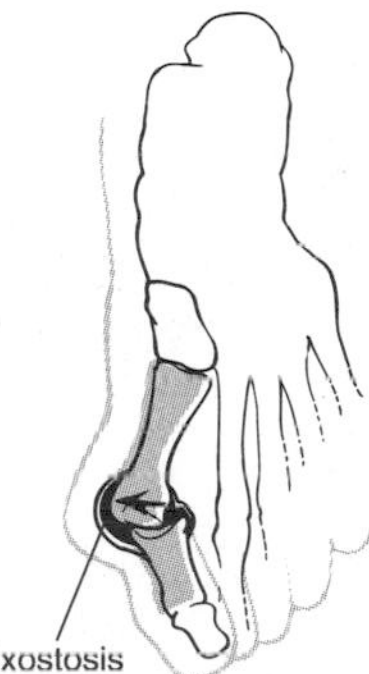

Ganglia

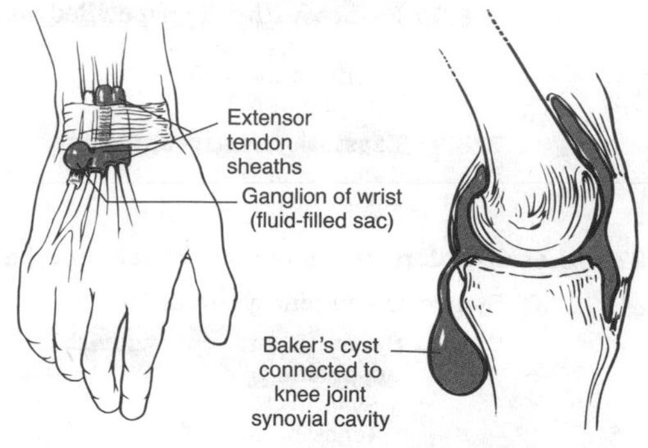

✓5th **727.4 Ganglion and cyst of synovium, tendon, and bursa**

727.40 Synovial cyst, unspecified

EXCLUDES *that of popliteal space (727.51)*

AHA: 2Q, '97, 6

727.41 Ganglion of joint

727.42 Ganglion of tendon sheath

727.43 Ganglion, unspecified

727.49 Other

Cyst of bursa

✓5th **727.5 Rupture of synovium**

727.50 Rupture of synovium, unspecified

727.51 Synovial cyst of popliteal space

Baker's cyst (knee)

727.59 Other

✓5th **727.6 Rupture of tendon, nontraumatic**

727.60 Nontraumatic rupture of unspecified tendon

727.61 Complete rupture of rotator cuff

727.62 Tendons of biceps (long head)

727.63 Extensor tendons of hand and wrist

727.64 Flexor tendons of hand and wrist

727.65 Quadriceps tendon

727.66 Patellar tendon

727.67 Achilles tendon

727.68 Other tendons of foot and ankle

727.69 Other

✓5th **727.8 Other disorders of synovium, tendon, and bursa**

727.81 Contracture of tendon (sheath)

Short Achilles tendon (acquired)

727.82 Calcium deposits in tendon and bursa

Calcification of tendon NOS
Calcific tendinitis NOS

EXCLUDES *peripheral ligamentous or muscular attachments (726.0-726.9)*

727.83 Plica syndrome

Plica knee

AHA: 4Q, '00, 44

DEF: A fold in the synovial tissue that begins to form before birth, creating a septum between two pockets of synovial tissue; two most common plicae are the medial patellar plica and the suprapatellar plica. Plica syndrome, or plica knee, refers to symptomatic plica. Experienced by females more commonly than males.

727.89 Other

Abscess of bursa or tendon

EXCLUDES *xanthomatosis localized to tendons (272.7)*

AHA: 2Q, '89, 15

727.9 Unspecified disorder of synovium, tendon, and bursa

✓4th **728 Disorders of muscle, ligament, and fascia**

EXCLUDES *enthesopathies (726.0-726.9)*
muscular dystrophies (359.0-359.1)
myoneural disorders (358.00-358.9)
myopathies (359.2-359.9)
▶*nontraumatic hematoma of muscle (729.92)*◀
old disruption of ligaments of knee (717.81-717.89)

728.0 Infective myositis

Myositis:
purulent
suppurative

EXCLUDES *myositis:*
epidemic (074.1)
interstitial (728.81)
syphilitic (095.6)
tropical (040.81)

DEF: Inflamed connective septal tissue of muscle.

✓5th **728.1 Muscular calcification and ossification**

728.10 Calcification and ossification, unspecified

Massive calcification (paraplegic)

728.11 Progressive myositis ossificans

DEF: Progressive myositic disease; marked by bony tissue formed by voluntary muscle; occurs among very young.

728.12 Traumatic myositis ossificans

Myositis ossificans (circumscripta)

728.13 Postoperative heterotopic calcification

DEF: Abnormal formation of calcium deposits in muscular tissue after surgery, marked by a corresponding loss of muscle tone and tension.

728.19 Other

Polymyositis ossificans

728.2 Muscular wasting and disuse atrophy, not elsewhere classified

Amyotrophia NOS
Myofibrosis

EXCLUDES *neuralgic amyotrophy (353.5)*
pelvic muscle wasting and disuse atrophy (618.83)
progressive muscular atrophy (335.0-335.9)

728.3 Other specific muscle disorders

Arthrogryposis
Immobility syndrome (paraplegic)

EXCLUDES *arthrogryposis multiplex congenita (754.89)*
stiff-man syndrome (333.91)

728.4 Laxity of ligament

728.5 Hypermobility syndrome

728.6 Contracture of palmar fascia A

Dupuytren's contracture

DEF: Dupuytren's contracture: flexion deformity of finger, due to shortened, thickened fibrosing of palmar fascia; cause unknown; associated with long-standing epilepsy; occurs more often in males.

✓5th **728.7 Other fibromatoses**

728.71 Plantar fascial fibromatosis
Contracture of plantar fascia
Plantar fasciitis (traumatic)

DEF: Plantar fascia fibromatosis; causes nodular swelling and pain; not associated with contractures.

728.79 Other
Garrod's or knuckle pads
Nodular fasciitis
Pseudosarcomatous fibromatosis (proliferative) (subcutaneous)

DEF: Knuckle pads: Pea-size nodules on dorsal surface of interphalangeal joints; new growth of fibrous tissue with thickened dermis and epidermis.

✓5th **728.8 Other disorders of muscle, ligament, and fascia**

728.81 Interstitial myositis

DEF: Inflammation of septal connective parts of muscle tissue.

728.82 Foreign body granuloma of muscle
Talc granuloma of muscle

728.83 Rupture of muscle, nontraumatic

728.84 Diastasis of muscle
Diastasis recti (abdomen)

EXCLUDES *diastasis recti complicating pregnancy, labor, and delivery (665.8)*

DEF: Muscle separation, such as recti abdominis after repeated pregnancies.

728.85 Spasm of muscle

728.86 Necrotizing fasciitis
Use additional code to identify:
infectious organism (041.00-041.89)
gangrene (785.4), if applicable

AHA: 4Q, '95, 54

DEF: Fulminating infection begins with extensive cellulitis, spreads to superficial and deep fascia; causes thrombosis of subcutaneous vessels, and gangrene of underlying tissue.

728.87 Muscle weakness (generalized)

EXCLUDES *generalized weakness (780.79)*

AHA: 1Q, '05, 13; 4Q, '03, 66

728.88 Rhabdomyolysis

AHA: 4Q, '03, 66

DEF: A disintegration or destruction of muscle; an acute disease characterized by the excretion of myoglobin into the urine.

728.89 Other
Eosinophilic fasciitis
Use additional E code to identify drug, if drug induced

AHA: 3Q, '06, 13; 3Q, '02, 28; 2Q, '01, 14, 15

DEF: Eosinophilic fasciitis: inflammation of fascia of extremities associated with eosinophilia, edema, and swelling; occurs alone or as part of myalgia syndrome.

728.9 Unspecified disorder of muscle, ligament, and fascia

AHA: 4Q, '88, 11

✓4th **729 Other disorders of soft tissues**

EXCLUDES *acroparesthesia (443.89)*
carpal tunnel syndrome (354.0)
disorders of the back (720.0-724.9)
entrapment syndromes (354.0-355.9)
palindromic rheumatism (719.3)
periarthritis (726.0-726.9)
psychogenic rheumatism (306.0)

729.0 Rheumatism, unspecified and fibrositis

DEF: General term describes diseases of muscle, tendon, nerve, joint, or bone; symptoms include pain and stiffness.

729.1 Myalgia and myositis, unspecified
Fibromyositis NOS

DEF: Myalgia: muscle pain.

DEF: Myositis: inflamed voluntary muscle.

DEF: Fibromyositis: inflamed fibromuscular tissue.

729.2 Neuralgia, neuritis, and radiculitis, unspecified

EXCLUDES *brachial radiculitis (723.4)*
cervical radiculitis (723.4)
lumbosacral radiculitis (724.4)
mononeuritis (354.0-355.9)
radiculitis due to intervertebral disc involvement (722.0-722.2, 722.7)
sciatica (724.3)

DEF: Neuralgia: paroxysmal pain along nerve; symptoms include brief pain and tenderness at point nerve exits.

DEF: Neuritis: inflamed nerve, symptoms include paresthesia, paralysis and loss of reflexes at nerve site.

DEF: Radiculitis: inflamed nerve root.

✓5th **729.3 Panniculitis, unspecified**

DEF: Inflammatory reaction of subcutaneous fat; causes nodules; often develops in abdominal region.

729.30 Panniculitis, unspecified site
Weber-Christian disease

DEF: Febrile, nodular, nonsuppurative, relapsing inflammation of subcutaneous fat.

729.31 Hypertrophy of fat pad, knee
Hypertrophy of infrapatellar fat pad

729.39 Other site

EXCLUDES *panniculitis specified as (affecting):*
back (724.8)
neck (723.6)
sacral (724.8)

729.4 Fasciitis, unspecified

EXCLUDES *necrotizing fasciitis (728.86)*
nodular fasciitis (728.79)

AHA: 2Q, '94, 13

729.5 Pain in limb

AHA: 2Q, '07, 11

729.6 Residual foreign body in soft tissue

EXCLUDES *foreign body granuloma:*
muscle (728.82)
skin and subcutaneous tissue (709.4)

✓5th **729.7 Nontraumatic compartment syndrome**

EXCLUDES *compartment syndrome NOS (958.90)*
traumatic compartment syndrome (958.90-958.99)

►Code first, if applicable, postprocedural complication (998.89)◄

DEF: Compression of nerves and blood vessels within an enclosed space, leading to impaired blood flow and muscle and nerve damage.

729.71 Nontraumatic compartment syndrome of upper extremity
Nontraumatic compartment syndrome of shoulder, arm, forearm, wrist, hand, and fingers

AHA: 4Q, '06, 100-102

729.72 Nontraumatic compartment syndrome of lower extremity
Nontraumatic compartment syndrome of hip, buttock, thigh, leg, foot, and toes

AHA: 4Q, '06, 100-102

729.73 Nontraumatic compartment syndrome of abdomen

AHA: 4Q, '06, 100-102

729.79 Nontraumatic compartment syndrome of other sites

AHA: 4Q, '06, 100-102

✓5th **729.8 Other musculoskeletal symptoms referable to limbs**

729.81 Swelling of limb

AHA: 4Q, '88, 6

729.82 Cramp

729.89 Other

EXCLUDES *abnormality of gait (781.2)*
tetany (781.7)
transient paralysis of limb (781.4)

AHA: 4Q, '88, 12

✓5th **729.9 Other and unspecified disorders of soft tissue**

● **729.90 Disorders of soft tissue, unspecified**

● **729.91 Post-traumatic seroma**

EXCLUDES *seroma complicating a procedure (998.13)*

● **729.92 Nontraumatic hematoma of soft tissue**

Nontraumatic hematoma of muscle

● **729.99 Other disorders of soft tissue**

Polyalgia

OSTEOPATHIES, CHONDROPATHIES, AND ACQUIRED MUSCULOSKELETAL DEFORMITIES (730-739)

✓4th **730 Osteomyelitis, periostitis, and other infections involving bone**

EXCLUDES *jaw (526.4-526.5)*
petrous bone (383.2)

Use additional code to identify organism, such as Staphylococcus (041.1)

The following fifth-digit subclassification is for use with codes 730; valid digits are in [brackets] under each code. See list at beginning of chapter for definitions.

- **0 site unspecified**
- **1 shoulder region**
- **2 upper arm**
- **3 forearm**
- **4 hand**
- **5 pelvic region and thigh**
- **6 lower leg**
- **7 ankle and foot**
- **8 other specified sites**
- **9 multiple sites**

AHA: 4Q, '97, 43

DEF: Osteomyelitis: bacterial inflammation of bone tissue and marrow.

DEF: Periostitis: inflammation of specialized connective tissue; causes swelling of bone and aching pain.

§ ✓5th **730.0 Acute osteomyelitis**
[0-9]

Abscess of any bone except accessory sinus, jaw, or mastoid

Acute or subacute osteomyelitis, with or without mention of periostitis

Use additional code to identify major osseous defect, if applicable (731.3)

AHA: 4Q, '06, 103; **For code 730.06:** 1Q, '02, 4; **For code 730.07:** 1Q, '04, 14

§ ✓5th **730.1 Chronic osteomyelitis**
[0-9]

Brodie's abscess

Chronic or old osteomyelitis, with or without mention of periostitis

Sequestrum of bone

Sclerosing osteomyelitis of Garré

Use additional code to identify major osseous defect, if applicable (731.3)

EXCLUDES *aseptic necrosis of bone (733.40-733.49)*

AHA: 4Q, '06, 103; **For code 730.17:** 3Q, '00, 4

§ ✓5th **730.2 Unspecified osteomyelitis**
[0-9]

Osteitis or osteomyelitis NOS, with or without mention of periostitis

Use additional code to identify major osseous defect, if applicable (731.3)

AHA: 4Q, '06, 103

§ ✓5th **730.3 Periostitis without mention of osteomyelitis**
[0-9]

Abscess of periosteum } without mention of osteomyelitis
Periostosis }

EXCLUDES *that in secondary syphilis (091.61)*

§ ✓5th ***730.7 Osteopathy resulting from poliomyelitis***
[0-9]

Code first underlying disease (045.0-045.9)

§ ✓5th ***730.8 Other infections involving bone in diseases classified elsewhere***
[0-9]

Code first underlying disease as:
tuberculosis (015.0-015.9)
typhoid fever (002.0)

EXCLUDES *syphilis of bone NOS (095.5)*

AHA: 2Q, '97, 16; 3Q, '91, 10

§ ✓5th **730.9 Unspecified infection of bone**
[0-9]

✓4th **731 Osteitis deformans and osteopathies associated with other disorders classified elsewhere**

DEF: Osteitis deformans: Bone disease marked by episodes of increased bone loss, excessive repair attempts follow; causes weakened, deformed bones with increased mass, bowed long bones, deformed flat bones, pain and pathological fractures; may be fatal if associated with congestive heart failure, giant cell tumors or bone sarcoma; also called Paget's disease.

731.0 Osteitis deformans without mention of bone tumor

Paget's disease of bone

731.1 Osteitis deformans in diseases classified elsewhere

Code first underlying disease as:
malignant neoplasm of bone (170.0-170.9)

731.2 Hypertrophic pulmonary osteoarthropathy

Bamberger-Marie disease

DEF: Clubbing, of fingers and toes; related to enlarged ends of long bones; due to chronic lung and heart disease.

731.3 Major osseous defects

Code first underlying disease, if known, such as:
aseptic necrosis (733.40-733.49)
malignant neoplasm of bone (170.0-170.9)
osteomyelitis (730.00-730.29)
osteoporosis (733.00-733.09)
peri-prosthetic osteolysis (996.45)

AHA: 4Q, '06, 103

731.8 Other bone involvement in diseases classified elsewhere

Code first underlying disease as:
diabetes mellitus ▶(249.8, 250.8)◀

Use additional code to specify bone condition, such as:
acute osteomyelitis (730.00-730.09)

AHA: 1Q, '04, 14; 4Q, '97, 43; 2Q, '97, 16

§ Requires fifth-digit. Valid digits are in [brackets] under each code. See beginning of section 710-739 for codes and defintions.

Slipped Femoral Epiphysis

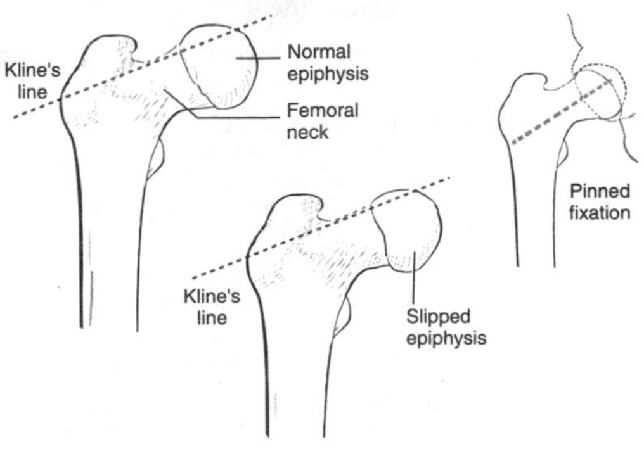

✓4th 732 Osteochondropathies

DEF: Conditions related to both bone and cartilage, or conditions in which cartilage is converted to bone (enchondral ossification).

732.0 Juvenile osteochondrosis of spine
Juvenile osteochondrosis (of):
marginal or vertebral epiphysis (of Scheuermann)
spine NOS
Vertebral epiphysitis
EXCLUDES *adolescent postural kyphosis (737.0)*

732.1 Juvenile osteochondrosis of hip and pelvis
Coxa plana
Ischiopubic synchondrosis (of van Neck)
Osteochondrosis (juvenile) of:
acetabulum
head of femur (of Legg-Calvé-Perthes)
iliac crest (of Buchanan)
symphysis pubis (of Pierson)
Pseudocoxalgia

732.2 Nontraumatic slipped upper femoral epiphysis
Slipped upper femoral epiphysis NOS

732.3 Juvenile osteochondrosis of upper extremity
Osteochondrosis (juvenile) of:
capitulum of humerus (of Panner)
carpal lunate (of Kienbock)
hand NOS
head of humerus (of Haas)
heads of metacarpals (of Mauclaire)
lower ulna (of Burns)
radial head (of Brailsford)
upper extremity NOS

732.4 Juvenile osteochondrosis of lower extremity, excluding foot
Osteochondrosis (juvenile) of:
lower extremity NOS
primary patellar center (of Köhler)
proximal tibia (of Blount)
secondary patellar center (of Sinding-Larsen)
tibial tubercle (of Osgood-Schlatter)
Tibia vara

732.5 Juvenile osteochondrosis of foot
Calcaneal apophysitis
Epiphysitis, os calcis
Osteochondrosis (juvenile) of:
astragalus (of Diaz)
calcaneum (of Sever)
foot NOS
metatarsal
second (of Freiberg)
fifth (of Iselin)
os tibiale externum (of Haglund)
tarsal navicular (of Köhler)

732.6 Other juvenile osteochondrosis
Apophysitis, Epiphysitis, Osteochondritis, Osteochondrosis } specified as juvenile, of other site, or site NOS

732.7 Osteochondritis dissecans

732.8 Other specified forms of osteochondropathy
Adult osteochondrosis of spine

732.9 Unspecified osteochondropathy
Apophysitis, Epiphysitis, Osteochondritis, Osteochondrosis } NOS; not specified as adult or juvenile, of unspecified site

✓4th 733 Other disorders of bone and cartilage

EXCLUDES *bone spur (726.91)*
cartilage of, or loose body in, joint (717.0-717.9, 718.0-718.9)
giant cell granuloma of jaw (526.3)
osteitis fibrosa cystica generalisata (252.01)
osteomalacia (268.2)
polyostotic fibrous dysplasia of bone (756.54)
prognathism, retrognathism (524.1)
xanthomatosis localized to bone (272.7)

✓5th 733.0 Osteoporosis
Use additional code to identify major osseous defect, if applicable (731.3)
▶Use additional code to identify personal history of pathologic (healed) fracture (V13.51)◀
AHA: 4Q, '06, 103
DEF: Bone mass reduction that ultimately results in fractures after minimal trauma; dorsal kyphosis or loss of height often occur.

733.00 Osteoporosis, unspecified
Wedging of vertebra NOS
AHA: 4Q, '07, 92;1Q, '07, 22; 3Q, '01, 19; 2Q, '98, 12

733.01 Senile osteoporosis
Postmenopausal osteoporosis
AHA: 1Q, '07, 5, 6

733.02 Idiopathic osteoporosis

733.03 Disuse osteoporosis

733.09 Other
Drug-induced osteoporosis
Use additional E code to identify drug
AHA: 4Q, '03, 108

✓5th 733.1 Pathologic fracture
Spontaneous fracture
EXCLUDES *stress fracture (733.93-733.95)*
traumatic fracture (800-829)
AHA: 1Q, '07, 3-4; 4Q, '93, 25; N-D, '86, 10; N-D, '85, 16
DEF: Fracture due to bone structure weakening by pathological processes (e.g., osteoporosis, neoplasms and osteomalacia).

733.10 Pathologic fracture, unspecified site

733.11 Pathologic fracture of humerus

733.12 Pathologic fracture of distal radius and ulna
Wrist NOS

733.13 Pathologic fracture of vertebrae
Collapse of vertebra NOS
AHA: 1Q, '07, 5, 6, 22; 3Q, '99, 5

733.14 Pathologic fracture of neck of femur
Femur NOS
Hip NOS
AHA: 1Q, '01, 1; 1Q, '96, 16

733.15 Pathologic fracture of other specified part of femur
AHA: 2Q, '98, 12

733.16 Pathologic fracture of tibia or fibula
Ankle NOS

733.19 Pathologic fracture of other specified site
AHA: 1Q, '07, 20

5th **733.2 Cyst of bone**

733.20 Cyst of bone (localized), unspecified

733.21 Solitary bone cyst
Unicameral bone cyst

733.22 Aneurysmal bone cyst
DEF: Solitary bone lesion, bulges into periosteum; marked by calcified rim.

733.29 Other
Fibrous dysplasia (monostotic)
EXCLUDES *cyst of jaw (526.0-526.2, 526.89)*
osteitis fibrosa cystica (252.01)
polyostotic fibrousdyplasia of bone (756.54)

733.3 Hyperostosis of skull
Hyperostosis interna frontalis Leontiasis ossium
DEF: Abnormal bone growth on inner aspect of cranial bones.

5th **733.4 Aseptic necrosis of bone**
Use additional code to identify major osseous defect, if applicable (731.3)
EXCLUDES *osteochondropathies (732.0-732.9)*
AHA: 4Q, '06, 103
DEF: Infarction of bone tissue due to a nonfectious etiology, such as a fracture, ischemic disorder or administration of immunosuppressive drugs; leads to degenerative joint disease or nonunion of fractures.

733.40 Aseptic necrosis of bone, site unspecified

733.41 Head of humerus

733.42 Head and neck of femur
Femur NOS
EXCLUDES *Legg-Calvé-Perthes disease (732.1)*

733.43 Medial femoral condyle

733.44 Talus

733.45 Jaw
Use additional E code to identify drug, if drug-induced
EXCLUDES *osteoradionecrosis of jaw (526.89)*
AHA: 4Q, '07, 91

733.49 Other

733.5 Osteitis condensans
Piriform sclerosis of ilium
DEF: Idiopathic condition marked by low back pain; associated with oval or triangular sclerotic, opaque bone next to sacroiliac joints in the ileum.

733.6 Tietze's disease
Costochondral junction syndrome
Costochondritis
DEF: Painful, idiopathic, nonsuppurative, swollen costal cartilage sometimes confused with cardiac symptoms because the anterior chest pain resembles that of coronary artery disease.

733.7 Algoneurodystrophy
Disuse atrophy of bone Sudeck's atrophy
DEF: Painful, idiopathic complex reflex sympathetic dystrophy, a chronic progressive disease characterized by severe pain, swelling, and changes in the skin..

5th **733.8 Malunion and nonunion of fracture**
AHA: 2Q, '94, 5

733.81 Malunion of fracture

733.82 Nonunion of fracture
Pseudoarthrosis (bone)

5th **733.9 Other unspecified disorders of bone and cartilage**

733.90 Disorder of bone and cartilage unspecified

733.91 Arrest of bone development or growth
Epiphyseal arrest

733.92 Chondromalacia
Chondromalacia:
NOS
localized, except patella
systemic
tibial plateau
EXCLUDES *chondromalacia of patella (717.7)*
DEF: Articular cartilage softening.

733.93 Stress fracture of tibia or fibula
Stress reaction of tibia or fibula
▶Use additional external cause code(s) to identify the cause of the stress fracture◀
AHA: 4Q, '01, 48

733.94 Stress fracture of the metatarsals
Stress reaction of metatarsals
▶Use additional external cause code(s) to identify the cause of the stress fracture◀
AHA: 4Q, '01, 48

733.95 Stress fracture of other bone
Stress reaction of other bone
▶Use additional external cause code(s) to identify the cause of the stress fracture◀
EXCLUDES ▶*stress fracture of:*
femoral neck (733.96)
fibula (733.93)
metatarsals (733.94)
pelvis (733.98)
shaft of femur (733.97)
tibia (733.93)◀

● **733.96 Stress fracture of femoral neck**
Stress reaction of femoral neck
Use additional external cause code(s) to identify the cause of the stress fracture

● **733.97 Stress fracture of shaft of femur**
Stress reaction of shaft of femur
Use additional external cause code(s) to identify the cause of the stress fracture

● **733.98 Stress fracture of pelvis**
Stress reaction of pelvis
Use additional external cause code(s) to identify the cause of the stress fracture

733.99 Other
Diaphysitis
Hypertrophy of bone
Relapsing polychondritis
AHA: J-F, '87, 14

734 Flat foot
Pes planus (acquired)
Talipes planus (acquired)
EXCLUDES *congenital (754.61)*
rigid flat foot (754.61)
spastic (everted) flat foot (754.61)

4th **735 Acquired deformities of toe**
EXCLUDES *congenital (754.60-754.69, 755.65-755.66)*

735.0 Hallux valgus (acquired)
DEF: Angled displacement of the great toe, causing it to ride over or under other toes.

735.1 Hallux varus (acquired)
DEF: Angled displacement of the great toe toward the body midline, away from the other toes.

735.2 Hallux rigidus
DEF: Limited flexion movement at metatarsophalangeal joint of great toe; due to degenerative joint disease.

735.3 Hallux malleus
DEF: Extended proximal phalanx, flexed distal phalanges, of great toe; foot resembles claw or hammer.

735.4 Other hammer toe (acquired)

735.5 Claw toe (acquired)
DEF: Hyperextended proximal phalanges, flexed middle and distal phalanges.

735.8 Other acquired deformities of toe
AHA: 4Q, '07, 123

735.9 Unspecified acquired deformity of toe

✓4th **736 Other acquired deformities of limbs**
EXCLUDES *congenital (754.3-755.9)*

✓5th **736.0 Acquired deformities of forearm, excluding fingers**

736.00 Unspecified deformity
Deformity of elbow, forearm, hand, or wrist (acquired) NOS

736.01 Cubitus valgus (acquired)
DEF: Deviation of the elbow away from the body midline upon extension; it occurs when the palm is turning outward.

736.02 Cubitus varus (acquired)
DEF: Elbow joint displacement angled laterally; when the forearm is extended, it is deviated toward the midline of the body; also called "gun stock" deformity.

736.03 Valgus deformity of wrist (acquired)
DEF: Abnormal angulation away from the body midline.

736.04 Varus deformity of wrist (acquired)
DEF: Abnormal angulation toward the body midline.

736.05 Wrist drop (acquired)
DEF: Inability to extend the hand at the wrist due to extensor muscle paralysis

Acquired Deformities of Toe

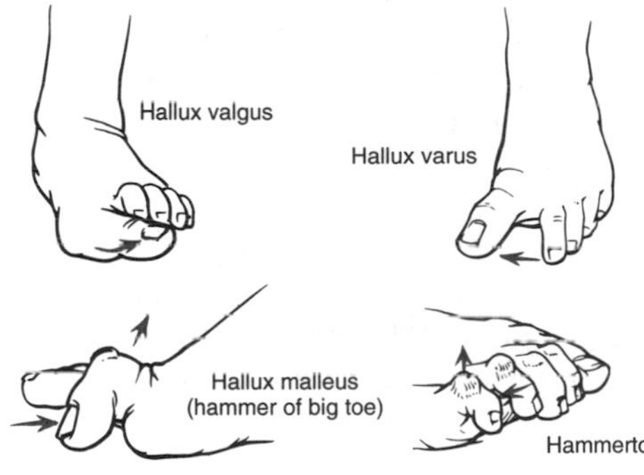

Acquired Deformities of Forearm

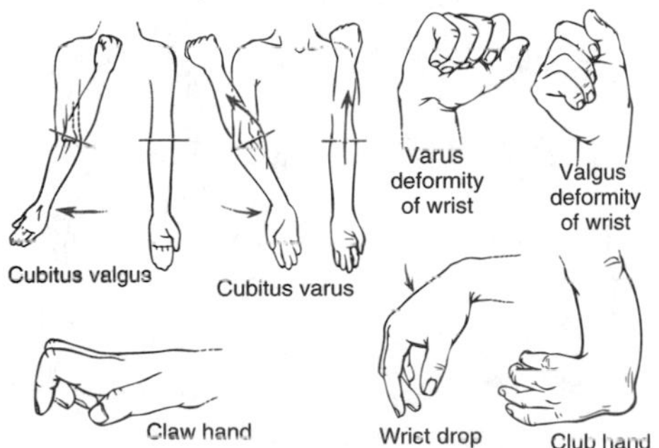

736.06 Claw hand (acquired)
DEF: Flexion and atrophy of the hand and fingers; found in ulnar nerve lesions, syringomyelia, and leprosy.

736.07 Club hand, acquired
DEF: Twisting of the hand out of shape or position; caused by the congenital absence of the ulna or radius.

736.09 Other

736.1 Mallet finger
DEF: Permanently flexed distal phalanx.

✓5th **736.2 Other acquired deformities of finger**

736.20 Unspecified deformity
Deformity of finger (acquired) NOS

736.21 Boutonniere deformity
DEF: A deformity of the finger caused by flexion of the proximal interphalangeal joint and hyperextension of the distal joint; also called buttonhole deformity.

736.22 Swan-neck deformity
DEF: Flexed distal and hyperextended proximal interphalangeal joint.

736.29 Other
EXCLUDES *trigger finger (727.03)*
AHA: 2Q, '05, 7; 2Q, '89, 13

✓5th **736.3 Acquired deformities of hip**

736.30 Unspecified deformity
Deformity of hip (acquired) NOS

736.31 Coxa valga (acquired)
DEF: Increase of at least 140 degrees in the angle formed by the axis of the head and the neck of the femur, and the axis of its shaft.

736.32 Coxa vara (acquired)
DEF: The bending downward of the neck of the femur: causing difficulty in movement; a right angle or less may be formed by the axis of the head and neck of the femur, and the axis of its shaft.

736.39 Other
AHA: ▶2Q, '08, 4;◀ 2Q, '91, 18

✓5th **736.4 Genu valgum or varum (acquired)**

736.41 Genu valgum (acquired)
DEF: Abnormally close together and an abnormally large space between the ankles; also called "knock-knees."

736.42 Genu varum (acquired)
DEF: Abnormally separated knees and the inward bowing of the legs; it is also called "bowlegs."

736.5 Genu recurvatum (acquired)
DEF: Hyperextended knees; also called "backknee."

736.6 Other acquired deformities of knee
Deformity of knee (acquired) NOS

Deformities of Lower Limb

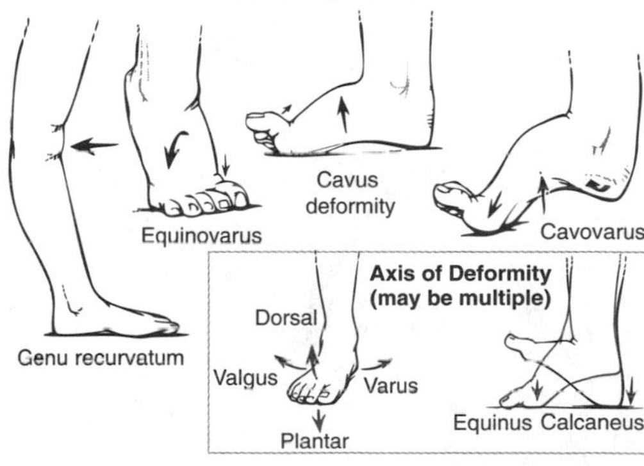

Acquired Deformities of Hip

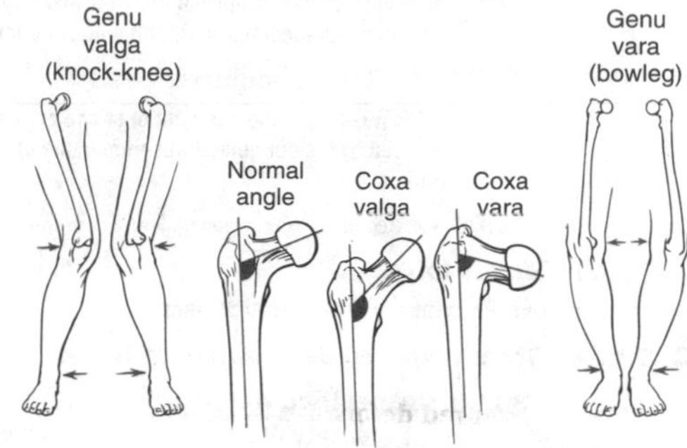

5th **736.7 Other acquired deformities of ankle and foot**

EXCLUDES *deformities of toe (acquired) (735.0-735.9)*
pes planus (acquired) (734)

736.70 Unspecified deformity of ankle and foot, acquired

736.71 Acquired equinovarus deformity

Clubfoot, acquired

EXCLUDES *clubfoot not specified as acquired (754.5-754.7)*

736.72 Equinus deformity of foot, acquired

DEF: A plantar flexion deformity that forces people to walk on their toes.

736.73 Cavus deformity of foot

EXCLUDES *that with claw foot (736.74)*

DEF: Abnormally high longitudinal arch of the foot.

736.74 Claw foot, acquired

DEF: High foot arch with hyperextended toes at metatarsophalangeal joint and flexed toes at distal joints; also called "main en griffe."

736.75 Cavovarus deformity of foot, acquired

DEF: Inward turning of the heel from the midline of the leg and an abnormally high longitudinal arch.

736.76 Other calcaneus deformity

736.79 Other

Acquired:
pes } not elsewhere classified
talipes }

5th **736.8 Acquired deformities of other parts of limbs**

736.81 Unequal leg length (acquired)

736.89 Other

Deformity (acquired):
arm or leg, not elsewhere classified
shoulder

AHA: ▶2Q, '08, 5◀

736.9 Acquired deformity of limb, site unspecified

Kyphosis and Lordosis

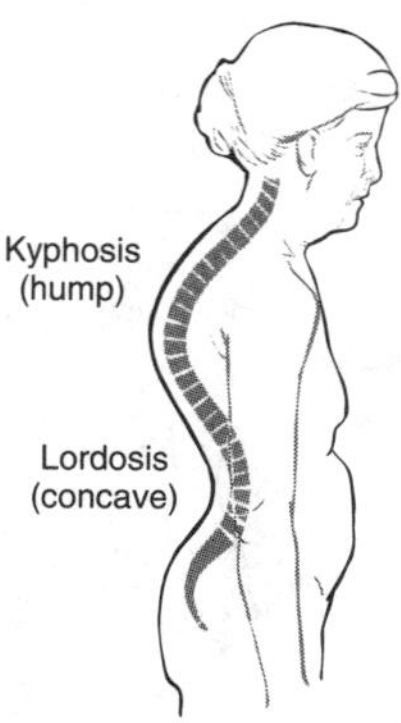

4th **737 Curvature of spine**

EXCLUDES *congenital (754.2)*

737.0 Adolescent postural kyphosis

EXCLUDES *osteochondrosis of spine (juvenile) (732.0)*
adult (732.8)

5th **737.1 Kyphosis (acquired)**

737.10 Kyphosis (acquired) (postural)

737.11 Kyphosis due to radiation

737.12 Kyphosis, postlaminectomy

AHA: J-F, '87, 7

737.19 Other

EXCLUDES *that associated with conditions classifiable elsewhere (737.41)*

AHA: 1Q, '07, 20

5th **737.2 Lordosis (acquired)**

DEF: Swayback appearance created by an abnormally increased spinal curvature; it is also referred to as "hollow back" or "saddle back."

737.20 Lordosis (acquired) (postural)

737.21 Lordosis, postlaminectomy

737.22 Other postsurgical lordosis

737.29 Other

EXCLUDES *that associated with conditions classifiable elsewhere (737.42)*

5th **737.3 Kyphoscoliosis and scoliosis**

DEF: Kyphoscoliosis: backward and lateral curvature of the spinal column; it is found in vertebral osteochondrosis.

DEF: Scoliosis: an abnormal deviation of the spine to the left or right of the midline

737.30 Scoliosis [and kyphoscoliosis], idiopathic

AHA: 3Q, '03, 19

737.31 Resolving infantile idiopathic scoliosis

737.32 Progressive infantile idiopathic scoliosis

AHA: 3Q, '02, 12

737.33 Scoliosis due to radiation

737.34 Thoracogenic scoliosis

737.39 Other

EXCLUDES *that associated with conditions classifiable elsewhere (737.43)*
that in kyphoscoliotic heart disease (416.1)

AHA: 2Q, '02, 16

Scoliosis and Kyphoscoliosis

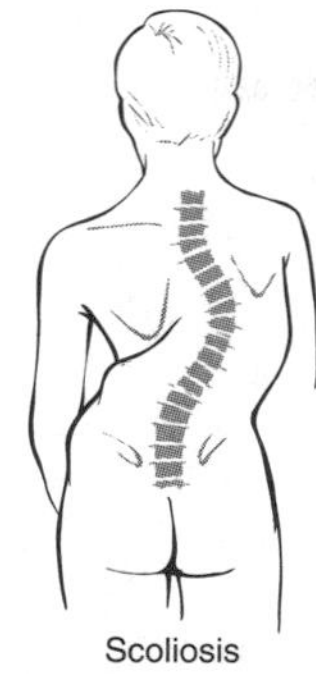
Scoliosis

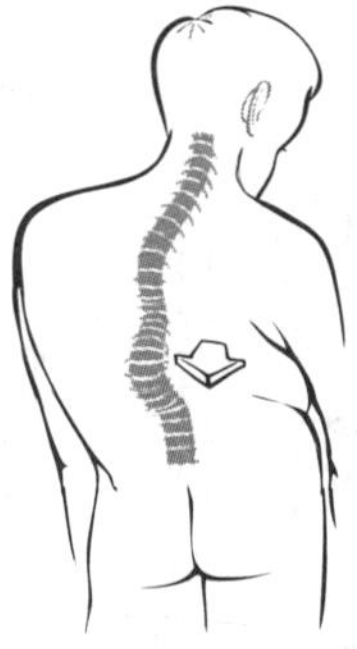
Kyphoscoliosis

✓5th **737.4 Curvature of spine associated with other conditions**

Code first associated condition as:
Charcôt-Marie-Tooth disease (356.1)
mucopolysaccharidosis (277.5)
neurofibromatosis (237.7)
osteitis deformans (731.0)
osteitis fibrosa cystica (252.01)
osteoporosis (733.00-733.09)
poliomyelitis (138)
tuberculosis [Pott's curvature] (015.0)

737.40 Curvature of spine, unspecified

737.41 Kyphosis

737.42 Lordosis

737.43 Scoliosis

737.8 Other curvatures of spine

737.9 Unspecified curvature of spine
Curvature of spine (acquired) (idiopathic) NOS
Hunchback, acquired
EXCLUDES *deformity of spine NOS (738.5)*

✓4th **738 Other acquired deformity**

EXCLUDES *congenital (754.0-756.9, 758.0-759.9)*
dentofacial anomalies (524.0-524.9)

738.0 Acquired deformity of nose
Deformity of nose (acquired)
Overdevelopment of nasal bones
EXCLUDES *deflected or deviated nasal septum (470)*

✓5th **738.1 Other acquired deformity of head**

738.10 Unspecified deformity

738.11 Zygomatic hyperplasia
DEF: Abnormal enlargement of the zygoma (processus zygomaticus temporalis).

738.12 Zygomatic hypoplasia
DEF: Underdevelopment of the zygoma (processus zygomaticus temporalis).

738.19 Other specified deformity
AHA: 1Q, '06, 8; 2Q, '03, 13

738.2 Acquired deformity of neck

738.3 Acquired deformity of chest and rib
Deformity:
chest (acquired)
rib (acquired)
Pectus:
carinatum, acquired
excavatum, acquired

738.4 Acquired spondylolisthesis
Degenerative spondylolisthesis
Spondylolysis, acquired
EXCLUDES *congenital (756.12)*
AHA: 4Q, '07, 120; 1Q, '07, 10
DEF: Vertebra displaced forward over another; due to bilateral defect in vertebral arch, eroded articular surface of posterior facts and elongated pedicle between fifth lumbar vertebra and sacrum.

738.5 Other acquired deformity of back or spine
Deformity of spine NOS
EXCLUDES *curvature of spine (737.0-737.9)*
AHA: ►1Q, '08, 11◄

738.6 Acquired deformity of pelvis
Pelvic obliquity
EXCLUDES *intrapelvic protrusion of acetabulum (718.6)*
that in relation to labor and delivery (653.0-653.4, 653.8-653.9)
DEF: Pelvic obliquity: slanting or inclination of the pelvis at an angle between 55 and 60 degrees between the plane of the pelvis and the horizontal plane.

738.7 Cauliflower ear
DEF: Abnormal external ear; due to injury, subsequent perichondritis.

738.8 Acquired deformity of other specified site
Deformity of clavicle
AHA: 2Q, '01, 15

738.9 Acquired deformity of unspecified site

✓4th **739 Nonallopathic lesions, not elsewhere classified**

INCLUDES segmental dysfunction
somatic dysfunction

DEF: Disability, loss of function or abnormality of a body part that is neither classifiable to a particular system nor brought about therapeutically to counteract another disease.

739.0 Head region
Occipitocervical region

739.1 Cervical region
Cervicothoracic region

739.2 Thoracic region
Thoracolumbar region

739.3 Lumbar region
Lumbosacral region

739.4 Sacral region
Sacrococcygeal region
Sacroiliac region

739.5 Pelvic region
Hip region
Pubic region

739.6 Lower extremities

739.7 Upper extremities
Acromioclavicular region
Sternoclavicular region

739.8 Rib cage
Costochondral region
Costovertebral region
Sternochondral region

739.9 Abdomen and other
AHA: 2Q, '89, 14

14. CONGENITAL ANOMALIES (740-759)

✓4th 740 Anencephalus and similar anomalies

740.0 Anencephalus
Acrania
Amyelencephalus
Hemicephaly
Hemianencephaly
DEF: Fetus without cerebrum, cerebellum and flat bones of skull.

740.1 Craniorachischisis
DEF: Congenital slit in cranium and vertebral column

740.2 Iniencephaly
DEF: Spinal cord passes through enlarged occipital bone (foramen magnum); absent vertebral bone layer and spinal processes; resulting in both reduction in number and proper fusion of the vertebrae.

✓4th 741 Spina bifida

EXCLUDES *spina bifida occulta (756.17)*

The following fifth-digit subclassification is for use with category 741:
0 unspecified region
1 cervical region
2 dorsal [thoracic] region
3 lumbar region

AHA: 3Q, '94, 7
DEF: Lack of closure of spinal cord's bony encasement; marked by cord protrusion into lumbosacral area; evident by elevated alpha-fetoprotein of amniotic fluid

§ ✓5th **741.0 With hydrocephalus**
[0-3]
Arnold-Chiari syndrome, type II
Chiari malformation, type II
Any condition classifiable to 741.9 with any condition classifiable to 742.3
AHA: 4Q, '97, 51; 4Q, '94, 37; S-O, '87, 10

§ ✓5th **741.9 Without mention of hydrocephalus**
[0-3]
Hydromeningocele (spinal)
Hydromyelocele
Meningocele (spinal)
Meningomyelocele
Myelocele
Myelocystocele
Rachischisis
Spina bifida (aperta)
Syringomyelocele

Spina Bifida

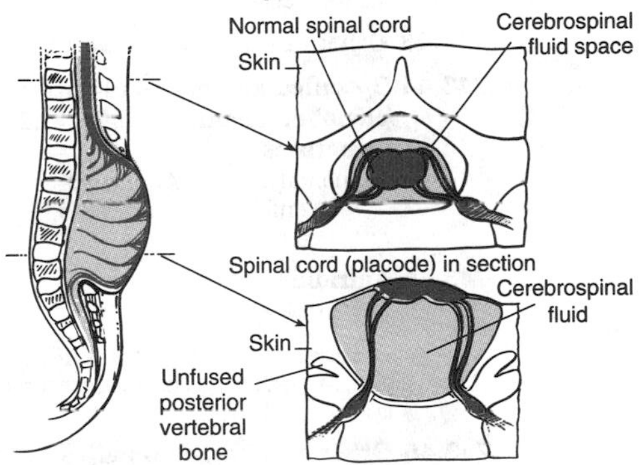

✓4th 742 Other congenital anomalies of nervous system

EXCLUDES *congenital central alveolar hypoventilation syndrome (327.25)*

742.0 Encephalocele
Encephalocystocele
Encephalomyelocele
Hydroencephalocele
Hydromeningocele, cranial
Meningocele, cerebral
Meningoencephalocele
AHA: 4Q, '94, 37
DEF: Brain tissue protrudes through skull defect.

742.1 Microcephalus
Hydromicrocephaly
Micrencephaly
DEF: Extremely small head or brain.

742.2 Reduction deformities of brain
Absence, Agenesis, Aplasia, Hypoplasia } of part of brain
Agyria
Arhinencephaly
Holoprosencephaly
Microgyria
AHA: 3Q, '03, 15; 4Q, '94, 37

742.3 Congenital hydrocephalus
Aqueduct of Sylvius:
  anomaly
  obstruction, congenital
  stenosis
Atresia of foramina of Magendie and Luschka
Hydrocephalus in newborn

EXCLUDES *hydrocephalus:*
  acquired (331.3-331.4)
  due to congenital toxoplasmosis (771.2)
  with any condition classifiable to 741.9 (741.0)

AHA: 4Q, '05, 83
DEF: Fluid accumulation within the skull; involves subarachnoid (external) or ventricular (internal) brain spaces.

Normal Ventricles and Hydrocephalus

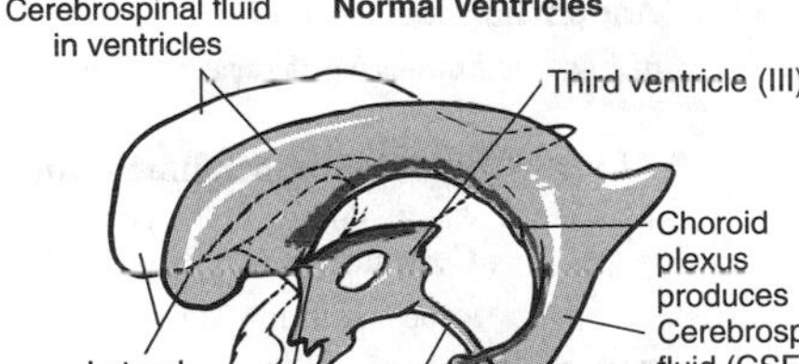
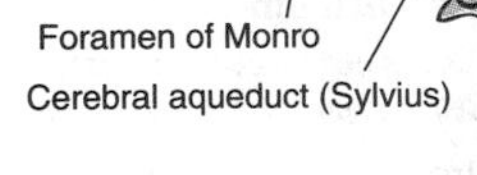

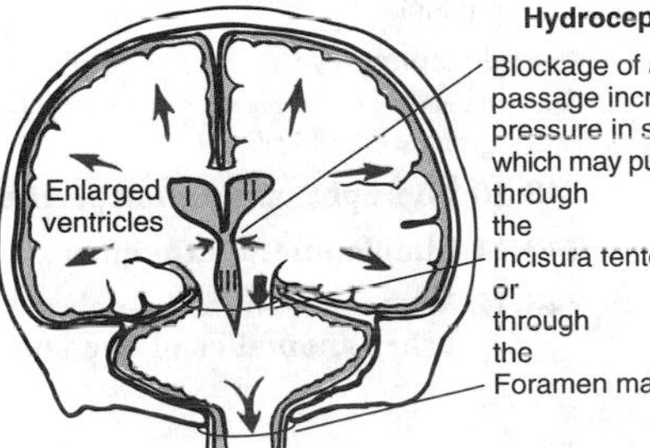

§ Requires fifth-digit. Valid digits are in [brackets] under each code. See category 741 for codes and defintions.

742.4 Other specified anomalies of brain
Congenital cerebral cyst
Macroencephaly
Macrogyria
Megalencephaly
Multiple anomalies of brain NOS
Porencephaly
Ulegyria
AHA: 1Q, '99, 9; 3Q, '92, 12

5th **742.5 Other specified anomalies of spinal cord**

742.51 Diastematomyelia
DEF: Congenital anomaly often associated with spina bifida; the spinal cord is separated into halves by a bony tissue resembling a "spike" (a spicule), each half surrounded by a dural sac.

742.53 Hydromyelia
Hydrorhachis
DEF: Dilated central spinal cord canal; characterized by increased fluid accumulation.

742.59 Other
Amyelia
Atelomyelia
Congenital anomaly of spinal meninges
Defective development of cauda equina
Hypoplasia of spinal cord
Myelatelia
Myelodysplasia
AHA: 2Q, '91, 14; 1Q, '89, 10

742.8 Other specified anomalies of nervous system
Agenesis of nerve
Displacement of brachial plexus
Familial dysautonomia
Jaw-winking syndrome
Marcus-Gunn syndrome
Riley-Day syndrome
EXCLUDES *neurofibromatosis (237.7)*

742.9 Unspecified anomaly of brain, spinal cord, and nervous system
Anomaly / Congenital: disease, lesion / Deformity } of: { brain, nervous system, spinal cord

4th **743 Congenital anomalies of eye**

5th **743.0 Anophthalmos**
DEF: Complete absence of the eyes or the presence of vestigial eyes.

743.00 Clinical anophthalmos, unspecified
Agenesis / Congenital absence } of eye
Anophthalmos NOS

743.03 Cystic eyeball, congenital

743.06 Cryptophthalmos
DEF: Skin is continuous over eyeball, results in apparent absence of eyelids.

5th **743.1 Microphthalmos**
Dysplasia / Hypoplasia } of eye
Rudimentary eye
DEF: Abnormally small eyeballs, may be opacities of cornea and lens, scarring of choroid and retina.

743.10 Microphthalmos, unspecified

743.11 Simple microphthalmos

743.12 Microphthalmos associated with other anomalies of eye and adnexa

5th **743.2 Buphthalmos**
Glaucoma:
congenital
newborn
Hydrophthalmos
EXCLUDES *glaucoma of childhood (365.14)*
traumatic glaucoma due to birth injury (767.8)
DEF: Distended, enlarged fibrous coats of eye; due to intraocular pressure of congenital glaucoma.

743.20 Buphthalmos, unspecified

743.21 Simple buphthalmos

743.22 Buphthalmos associated with other ocular anomalies
Keratoglobus, congenital / Megalocornea } associated with buphthalmos

5th **743.3 Congenital cataract and lens anomalies**
EXCLUDES *infantile cataract (366.00-366.09)*
DEF: Opaque eye lens.

743.30 Congenital cataract, unspecified

743.31 Capsular and subcapsular cataract

743.32 Cortical and zonular cataract

743.33 Nuclear cataract

743.34 Total and subtotal cataract, congenital

743.35 Congenital aphakia
Congenital absence of lens

743.36 Anomalies of lens shape
Microphakia
Spherophakia

743.37 Congenital ectopic lens

743.39 Other

5th **743.4 Coloboma and other anomalies of anterior segment**
DEF: Coloboma: ocular tissue defect associated with defect of ocular fetal intraocular fissure; may cause small pit on optic disk, major defects of iris, ciliary body, choroid, and retina.

743.41 Anomalies of corneal size and shape
Microcornea
EXCLUDES *that associated with buphthalmos (743.22)*

743.42 Corneal opacities, interfering with vision, congenital

743.43 Other corneal opacities, congenital

743.44 Specified anomalies of anterior chamber, chamber angle, and related structures
Anomaly:
Axenfeld's
Peters'
Anomaly:
Rieger's

743.45 Aniridia
AHA: 3Q, '02, 20
DEF: Incompletely formed or absent iris; affects both eyes; dominant trait; also called congenital hyperplasia of iris.

743.46 Other specified anomalies of iris and ciliary body
Anisocoria, congenital
Atresia of pupil
Coloboma of iris
Corectopia

743.47 Specified anomalies of sclera

743.48 Multiple and combined anomalies of anterior segment

743.49 Other

743.5 Congenital anomalies of posterior segment

743.51 Vitreous anomalies
Congenital vitreous opacity

743.52 Fundus coloboma
DEF: Absent retinal and choroidal tissue; occurs in lower fundus; a bright white ectatic zone of exposed sclera extends into and changes the optic disk.

743.53 Chorioretinal degeneration, congenital

743.54 Congenital folds and cysts of posterior segment

743.55 Congenital macular changes

743.56 Other retinal changes, congenital
AHA: 3Q, '99, 12

743.57 Specified anomalies of optic disc
Coloboma of optic disc (congenital)

743.58 Vascular anomalies
Congenital retinal aneurysm

743.59 Other

743.6 Congenital anomalies of eyelids, lacrimal system, and orbit

743.61 Congenital ptosis
DEF: Drooping of eyelid.

743.62 Congenital deformities of eyelids
Ablepharon
Absence of eyelid
Accessory eyelid
Congenital:
- ectropion
- entropion

AHA: 1Q, '00, 22

743.63 Other specified congenital anomalies of eyelid
Absence, agenesis, of cilia

743.64 Specified congenital anomalies of lacrimal gland

743.65 Specified congenital anomalies of lacrimal passages
Absence, agenesis of:
- lacrimal apparatus
- punctum lacrimale

Accessory lacrimal canal

743.66 Specified congenital anomalies of orbit

743.69 Other
Accessory eye muscles

743.8 Other specified anomalies of eye
EXCLUDES *congenital nystagmus (379.51)*
ocular albinism (270.2)
optic nerve hypoplasia (377.43)
retinitis pigmentosa (362.74)

743.9 Unspecified anomaly of eye
Congenital:
anomaly NOS, deformity NOS } of eye (any part)

744 Congenital anomalies of ear, face, and neck
EXCLUDES *anomaly of:*
- *cervical spine (754.2, 756.10-756.19)*
- *larynx (748.2-748.3)*
- *nose (748.0-748.1)*
- *parathyroid gland (759.2)*
- *thyroid gland (759.2)*

cleft lip (749.10-749.25)

744.0 Anomalies of ear causing impairment of hearing
EXCLUDES *congenital deafness without mention of cause (389.0-389.9)*

744.00 Unspecified anomaly of ear with impairment of hearing

744.01 Absence of external ear
Absence of:
- auditory canal (external)
- auricle (ear) (with stenosis or atresia of auditory canal)

744.02 Other anomalies of external ear with impairment of hearing
Atresia or stricture of auditory canal (external)

744.03 Anomaly of middle ear, except ossicles
Atresia or stricture of osseous meatus (ear)

744.04 Anomalies of ear ossicles
Fusion of ear ossicles

744.05 Anomalies of inner ear
Congenital anomaly of:
- membranous labyrinth
- organ of Corti

744.09 Other
Absence of ear, congenital

744.1 Accessory auricle
Accessory tragus
Polyotia
Preauricular appendage
Supernumerary:
- ear
- lobule

DEF: Redundant tissue or structures of ear.

744.2 Other specified anomalies of ear
EXCLUDES *that with impairment of hearing (744.00-744.09)*

744.21 Absence of ear lobe, congenital

744.22 Macrotia
DEF: Abnormally large pinna of ear.

744.23 Microtia
DEF: Hypoplasia of pinna; associated with absent or closed auditory canal.

744.24 Specified anomalies of Eustachian tube
Absence of Eustachian tube

744.29 Other
Bat ear
Darwin's tubercle
Pointed ear
Prominence of auricle
Ridge ear
EXCLUDES *preauricular sinus (744.46)*

744.3 Unspecified anomaly of ear
Congenital:
anomaly NOS, deformity NOS } of ear, not elsewhere classified

744.4 Branchial cleft cyst or fistula; preauricular sinus

744.41 Branchial cleft sinus or fistula
Branchial:
- sinus (external) (internal)
- vestige

DEF: Cyst due to failed closure of embryonic branchial cleft.

744.42 Branchial cleft cyst

744.43 Cervical auricle

744.46 Preauricular sinus or fistula

744.47 Preauricular cyst

744.49 Other
Fistula (of):
- auricle, congenital
- cervicoaural

744.5 Webbing of neck
Pterygium colli
DEF: Thick, triangular skinfold, stretches from lateral side of neck across shoulder; associated with Turner's and Noonan's syndromes.

✓5th **744.8 Other specified anomalies of face and neck**

744.81 Macrocheilia
Hypertrophy of lip, congenital
DEF: Abnormally large lips.

744.82 Microcheilia
DEF: Abnormally small lips.

744.83 Macrostomia
DEF: Bilateral or unilateral anomaly, of mouth due to malformed maxillary and mandibular processes; results in mouth extending toward ear.

744.84 Microstomia
DEF: Abnormally small mouth.

744.89 Other
EXCLUDES *congenital fistula of lip (750.25)*
musculoskeletal anomalies (754.0-754.1, 756.0)

744.9 Unspecified anomalies of face and neck
Congenital:
anomaly NOS } of face [any part] or neck [any part]
deformity NOS }

✓4th **745 Bulbus cordis anomalies and anomalies of cardiac septal closure**

745.0 Common truncus
Absent septum } between aorta and pulmonary artery
Communication (abnormal) }
Aortic septal defect
Common aortopulmonary trunk
Persistent truncus arteriosus

✓5th **745.1 Transposition of great vessels**

745.10 Complete transposition of great vessels
Transposition of great vessels:
NOS
classical

745.11 Double outlet right ventricle
Dextratransposition of aorta
Incomplete transposition of great vessels
Origin of both great vessels from right ventricle
Taussig-Bing syndrome or defect

745.12 Corrected transposition of great vessels

745.19 Other

Heart Defects

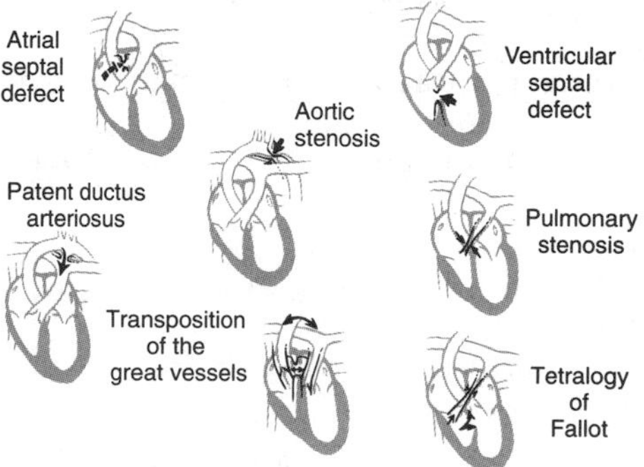

745.2 Tetralogy of Fallot
Fallot's pentalogy
Ventricular septal defect with pulmonary stenosis or atresia, dextraposition of aorta, and hypertrophy of right ventricle
EXCLUDES *Fallot's triad (746.09)*
DEF: Obstructed cardiac outflow causes pulmonary stenosis, interventricular septal defect and right ventricular hypertrophy.

745.3 Common ventricle
Cor triloculare biatriatum
Single ventricle

745.4 Ventricular septal defect
Eisenmenger's defect or complex
Gerbo dedefect
Interventricular septal defect
Left ventricular-right atrial communication
Roger's disease
EXCLUDES *common atrioventricular canal type (745.69)*
single ventricle (745.3)

745.5 Ostium secundum type atrial septal defect
Defect:
atrium secundum
fossa ovalis
Lutembacher's syndrome
Patent or persistent:
foramen ovale
ostium secundum
DEF: Opening in atrial septum due to failure of the septum secondum and the endocardial cushions to fuse; there is a rim of septum surrounding the defect.

✓5th **745.6 Endocardial cushion defects**
DEF: Atrial and/or ventricular septal defects causing abnormal fusion of cushions in atrioventricular canal.

745.60 Endocardial cushion defect,unspecified type
DEF: Septal defect due to imperfect fusion of endocardial cushions.

745.61 Ostium primum defect
Persistent ostium primum
DEF: Opening in low, posterior septum primum; causes cleft in basal portion of atrial septum; associated with cleft mitral valve.

745.69 Other
Absence of atrial septum
Atrioventricular canal type ventricular septal defect
Common atrioventricular canal
Common atrium

745.7 Cor biloculare
Absence of atrial and ventricular septa
DEF: Atrial and ventricular septal defect; marked by heart with two cardiac chambers (one atrium, one ventricle), and one atrioventricular valve.

745.8 Other

745.9 Unspecified defect of septal closure
Septal defect NOS

✓4th **746 Other congenital anomalies of heart**
EXCLUDES *endocardial fibroelastosis (425.3)*

✓5th **746.0 Anomalies of pulmonary valve**
EXCLUDES *infundibular or subvalvular pulmonic stenosis (746.83)*
tetralogy of Fallot (745.2)

746.00 Pulmonary valve anomaly, unspecified

746.01 Atresia, congenital
Congenital absence of pulmonary valve

746.02 Stenosis, congenital

DEF: Stenosis of opening between pulmonary artery and right ventricle; causes obstructed blood outflow from right ventricle.

746.09 Other

Congenital insufficiency of pulmonary valve
Fallot's triad or trilogy

746.1 Tricuspid atresia and stenosis, congenital

Absence of tricuspid valve

746.2 Ebstein's anomaly

DEF: Malformation of the tricuspid valve characterized by septal and posterior leaflets attaching to the wall of the right ventricle; causing the right ventricle to fuse with the atrium producing a large right atrium and a small ventricle; causes a malfunction of the right ventricle with accompanying complications such as heart failure and abnormal cardiac rhythm.

746.3 Congenital stenosis of aortic valve

Congenital aortic stenosis

EXCLUDES *congenital:*
subaortic stenosis (746.81)
supravalvular aortic stenosis (747.22)

AHA: 4Q, '88, 8

DEF: Stenosis of orifice of aortic valve; obstructs blood outflow from left ventricle.

746.4 Congenital insufficiency of aortic valve

Bicuspid aortic valve
Congenital aortic insufficiency

DEF: Impaired functioning of aortic valve due to incomplete closure; causes backflow (regurgitation) of blood from aorta to left ventricle.

746.5 Congenital mitral stenosis

Fused commissure } of mitral valve
Parachute deformity } of mitral valve
Supernumerary cusps } of mitral valve

AHA: 3Q, '07, 3

DEF: Stenosis of left atrioventricular orifice.

746.6 Congenital mitral insufficiency

DEF: Impaired functioning of mitral valve due to incomplete closure; causes backflow of blood from left ventricle to left atrium.

746.7 Hypoplastic left heart syndrome

Atresia, or marked hypoplasia, of aortic orifice or valve, with hypoplasia of ascending aorta and defective development of left ventricle (with mitral valve atresia)

✓5th **746.8 Other specified anomalies of heart**

746.81 Subaortic stenosis

AHA: 3Q, '07, 3

DEF: Stenosis, of left ventricular outflow tract due to fibrous tissue ring or septal hypertrophy below aortic valve.

746.82 Cor triatriatum

DEF: Transverse septum divides left atrium due to failed resorption of embryonic common pulmonary vein; results in three atrial chambers.

746.83 Infundibular pulmonic stenosis

Subvalvular pulmonic stenosis

DEF: Stenosis of right ventricle outflow tract within infundibulum due to fibrous diaphragm below valve or long, narrow fibromuscular channel.

746.84 Obstructive anomalies of heart, not elsewhere classified

►Shone's syndrome◄
Uhl's disease
►Use additional code for associated anomalies, such as:
coarctation of aorta (747.10)
congenital mitral stenosis (746.5)
subaortic stenosis (746.81)◄

746.85 Coronary artery anomaly

Anomalous origin or communication of coronary artery
Arteriovenous malformation of coronary artery
Coronary artery:
absence
arising from aorta or pulmonary trunk
single

AHA: N-D, '85, 3

746.86 Congenital heart block

Complete or incomplete atrioventricular [AV] block

DEF: Impaired conduction of electrical impulses; due to maldeveloped junctional tissue.

746.87 Malposition of heart and cardiac apex

Abdominal heart
Dextrocardia
Ectopia cordis
Levocardia (isolated)
Mesocardia

EXCLUDES *dextrocardia with complete transposition of viscera (759.3)*

746.89 Other

Atresia } of cardiac vein
Hypoplasia } of cardiac vein
Congenital:
cardiomegaly
diverticulum, left ventricle
pericardial defect

AHA: 3Q, '00, 3; 1Q, '99, 11; J-F, '85, 3

746.9 Unspecified anomaly of heart

Congenital:
anomaly of heart NOS
heart disease NOS

✓4th **747 Other congenital anomalies of circulatory system**

747.0 Patent ductus arteriosus

Patent ductus Botalli
Persistent ductus arteriosus

DEF: Open lumen in ductus arteriosus causes arterial blood recirculation in lungs; inhibits blood supply to aorta; symptoms such as shortness of breath more noticeable upon activity.

✓5th **747.1 Coarctation of aorta**

DEF: Localized deformity of aortic media seen as a severe constriction of the vessel lumen; major symptom is high blood pressure in the arms and low pressure in the legs; a CVA, rupture of the aorta, bacterial endocarditis or congestive heart failure can follow if left untreated.

747.10 Coarctation of aorta (preductal) (postductal)

Hypoplasia of aortic arch

AHA: 3Q, '07, 3; 1Q, '99, 11; 4Q, '88, 8

747.11 Interruption of aortic arch

✓5th **747.2 Other anomalies of aorta**

747.20 Anomaly of aorta, unspecified

747.21 Anomalies of aortic arch

Anomalous origin, right subclavian artery
Dextraposition of aorta
Double aortic arch
Kommerell's diverticulum
Overriding aorta
Persistent:
convolutions, aortic arch
right aortic arch
Vascular ring

EXCLUDES *hypoplasia of aortic arch (747.10)*

AHA: 1Q, '03, 15

747.22 Atresia and stenosis of aorta

Absence, Aplasia, Hypoplasia, Stricture } of aorta

Supra (valvular)-aortic stenosis

EXCLUDES *congenital aortic (valvular) stenosis or stricture, so stated (746.3)*
hypoplasia of aorta in hypoplastic left heart syndrome (746.7)

747.29 Other

Aneurysm of sinus of Valsalva
Congenital:
aneurysm, dilation } of aorta

747.3 Anomalies of pulmonary artery

Agenesis, Anomaly, Atresia, Coarctation, Hypoplasia, Stenosis } of pulmonary artery

Pulmonary arteriovenous aneurysm

AHA: 1Q, '04, 16; 1Q, '94, 15; 4Q, '88, 8

✓5th **747.4 Anomalies of great veins**

747.40 Anomaly of great veins, unspecified

Anomaly NOS of:
pulmonary veins
vena cava

747.41 Total anomalous pulmonary venous connection

Total anomalous pulmonary venous return [TAPVR]:
subdiaphragmatic
supradiaphragmatic

747.42 Partial anomalous pulmonary venous connection

Partial anomalous pulmonary venous return

747.49 Other anomalies of great veins

Absence, Congenital stenosis } of vena cava (inferior) (superior)

Persistent:
left posterior cardinal vein
left superior vena cava
Scimitar syndrome
Transposition of pulmonary veins NOS

747.5 Absence or hypoplasia of umbilical artery

Single umbilical artery

✓5th **747.6 Other anomalies of peripheral vascular system**

Absence, Anomaly, Atresia } of artery or vein, NEC

Arteriovenous aneurysm (peripheral)
Arteriovenous malformation of the peripheral vascular system
Congenital:
aneurysm (peripheral)
phlebectasia
stricture, artery
varix
Multiple renal arteries

EXCLUDES *anomalies of:*
cerebral vessels (747.81)
pulmonary artery (747.3)
congenital retinal aneurysm (743.58)
hemangioma (228.00-228.09)
lymphangioma (228.1)

747.60 Anomaly of the peripheral vascular system, unspecified site

747.61 Gastrointestinal vessel anomaly

AHA: 3Q, '96, 10

747.62 Renal vessel anomaly

747.63 Upper limb vessel anomaly

747.64 Lower limb vessel anomaly

747.69 Anomalies of other specified sites of peripheral vascular system

✓5th **747.8 Other specified anomalies of circulatory system**

747.81 Anomalies of cerebrovascular system

Arteriovenous malformation of brain
Cerebral arteriovenous aneurysm, congenital
Congenital anomalies of cerebral vessels

EXCLUDES *ruptured cerebral (arteriovenous) aneurysm (430)*

747.82 Spinal vessel anomaly

Arteriovenous malformation of spinal vessel

AHA: 3Q, '95, 5

747.83 Persistent fetal circulation N

Persistent pulmonary hypertension
Primary pulmonary hypertension of newborn

AHA: 4Q, '02, 62

DEF: A return to fetal-type circulation due to constriction of pulmonary arterioles and opening of the ductus arteriosus and foramen ovale, right-to-left shunting occurs, oxygenation of the blood does not occur, and the lungs remain constricted after birth; PFC is seen in term or post-term infants causes include asphyxiation, meconium aspiration syndrome, acidosis, sepsis, and developmental immaturity.

747.89 Other

Aneurysm, congenital, specified site not elsewhere classified

EXCLUDES *congenital aneurysm:*
coronary (746.85)
peripheral (747.6)
pulmonary (747.3)
retinal (743.58)

AHA: 4Q, '02, 63

747.9 Unspecified anomaly of circulatory system

Persistent Fetal Circulation

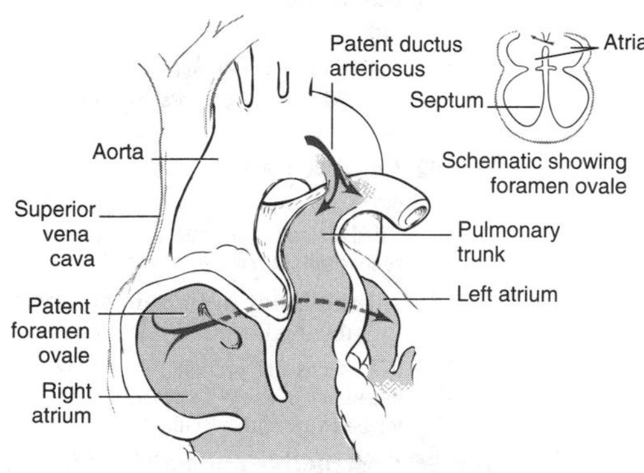

✓4th 748 Congenital anomalies of respiratory system

EXCLUDES *congenital central alveolar hypoventilation syndrome (327.25)*
congenital defect of diaphragm (756.6)

748.0 Choanal atresia

Atresia } of nares (anterior)
Congenital stenosis } (posterior)

DEF: Occluded posterior nares (choana), bony or membranous due to failure of embryonic bucconasal membrane to rupture.

748.1 Other anomalies of nose

Absent nose
Accessory nose
Cleft nose
Congenital:
deformity of nose
notching of tip of nose
perforation of wall of nasal sinus
Deformity of wall of nasal sinus

EXCLUDES *congenital deviation of nasal septum (754.0)*

748.2 Web of larynx

Web of larynx:
NOS
glottic
subglottic

DEF: Malformed larynx; marked by thin, translucent, or thick, fibrotic spread between vocal folds; affects speech.

748.3 Other anomalies of larynx, trachea, and bronchus

Absence or agenesis of:
bronchus
larynx
trachea
Anomaly (of):
cricoid cartilage
epiglottis
thyroid cartilage
tracheal cartilage
Atresia (of):
epiglottis
glottis
larynx
trachea
Cleft thyroid, cartilage, congenital
Congenital:
dilation, trachea
stenosis:
larynx
trachea
tracheocele
Diverticulum:
bronchus
trachea
Fissure of epiglottis
Laryngocele
Posterior cleft of cricoid cartilage (congenital)
Rudimentary tracheal bronchus
Stridor, laryngeal, congenital

AHA: 1Q, '99, 14

748.4 Congenital cystic lung

Disease, lung:
cystic, congenital
polycystic, congenital
Honeycomb lung, congenital

EXCLUDES *acquired or unspecified cystic lung (518.89)*

DEF: Enlarged air spaces of lung parenchyma.

748.5 Agenesis, hypoplasia, and dysplasia of lung

Absence of lung (fissures) (lobe) (lobe)
Aplasia of lung
Hypoplasia of lung
Sequestration of lung

✓5th **748.6 Other anomalies of lung**

748.60 Anomaly of lung, unspecified

748.61 Congenital bronchiectasis

748.69 Other

Accessory lung (lobe)
Azygos lobe (fissure), lung

748.8 Other specified anomalies of respiratory system

Abnormal communication between pericardial and pleural sacs
Anomaly, pleural folds
Atresia of nasopharynx
Congenital cyst of mediastinum

748.9 Unspecified anomaly of respiratory system

Anomaly of respiratory system NOS

✓4th 749 Cleft palate and cleft lip

✓5th **749.0 Cleft palate**

749.00 Cleft palate, unspecified

749.01 Unilateral, complete

749.02 Unilateral, incomplete

Cleft uvula

749.03 Bilateral, complete

749.04 Bilateral, incomplete

✓5th **749.1 Cleft lip**

Cheiloschisis
Congenital fissure of lip
Harelip
Labium leporinum

749.10 Cleft lip, unspecified

749.11 Unilateral, complete

749.12 Unilateral, incomplete

749.13 Bilateral, complete

749.14 Bilateral, incomplete

✓5th **749.2 Cleft palate with cleft lip**

Cheilopalatoschisis

749.20 Cleft palate with cleft lip, unspecified

749.21 Unilateral, complete

749.22 Unilateral, incomplete

749.23 Bilateral, complete

AHA: 1Q, '96, 14

749.24 Bilateral, incomplete

749.25 Other combinations

Cleft Lip and Palate

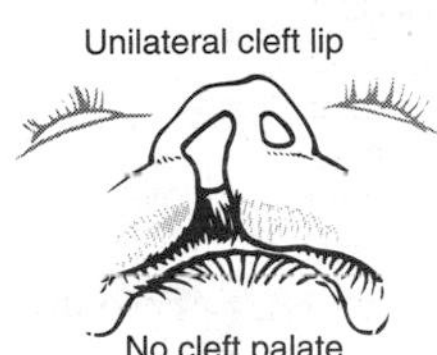

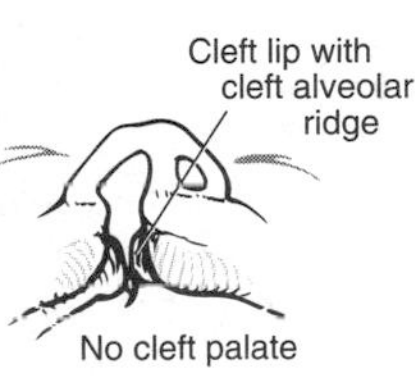

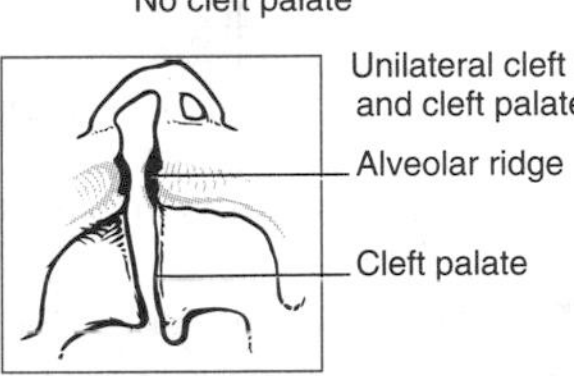

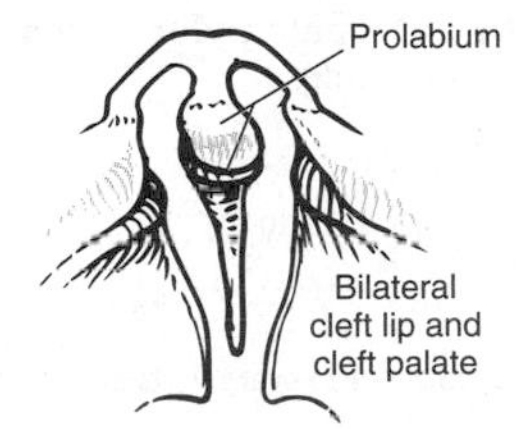

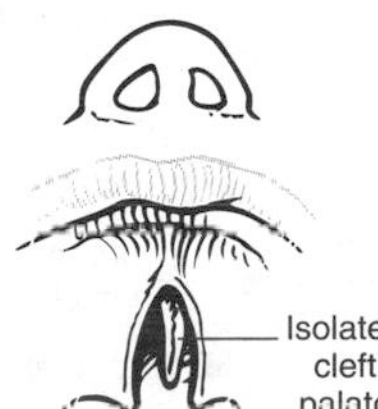

✓4th 750 Other congenital anomalies of upper alimentary tract

EXCLUDES *dentofacial anomalies (524.0-524.9)*

750.0 Tongue tie
Ankyloglossia
DEF: Restricted tongue movement due to lingual frenum extending toward tip of tongue. Tongue may be fused to mouth floor affecting speech.

✓5th 750.1 Other anomalies of tongue

750.10 Anomaly of tongue, unspecified

750.11 Aglossia
DEF: Absence of tongue.

750.12 Congenital adhesions of tongue

750.13 Fissure of tongue
Bifid tongue
Double tongue

750.15 Macroglossia
Congenital hypertrophy of tongue

750.16 Microglossia
Hypoplasia of tongue

750.19 Other

✓5th 750.2 Other specified anomalies of mouth and pharynx

750.21 Absence of salivary gland

750.22 Accessory salivary gland

750.23 Atresia, salivary duct
Imperforate salivary duct

750.24 Congenital fistula of salivary gland

750.25 Congenital fistula of lip
Congenital (mucus) lip pits

750.26 Other specified anomalies of mouth
Absence of uvula

750.27 Diverticulum of pharynx
Pharyngeal pouch

750.29 Other specified anomalies of pharynx
Imperforate pharynx

750.3 Tracheoesophageal fistula, esophageal atresia and stenosis
Absent esophagus
Atresia of esophagus
Congenital:
esophageal ring
stenosis of esophagus
stricture of esophagus
Congenital fistula:
esophagobronchial
esophagotracheal
Imperforate esophagus
Webbed esophagus

750.4 Other specified anomalies of esophagus
Dilatation, congenital } (of) esophagus
Displacement, congenital } (of) esophagus
Diverticulum } (of) esophagus
Duplication } (of) esophagus
Giant } (of) esophagus
Esophageal pouch
EXCLUDES *congenital hiatus hernia (750.6)*
AHA: J-F, '85, 3

750.5 Congenital hypertrophic pyloric stenosis
Congenital or infantile:
constriction } of pylorus
hypertrophy } of pylorus
spasm } of pylorus
stenosis } of pylorus
stricture } of pylorus
DEF: Obstructed pylorus due to overgrowth of pyloric muscle.

750.6 Congenital hiatus hernia
Displacement of cardia through esophageal hiatus
EXCLUDES *congenital diaphragmatic hernia (756.6)*

750.7 Other specified anomalies of stomach
Congenital:
cardiospasm
hourglass stomach
Displacement of stomach
Diverticulum of stomach, congenital
Duplication of stomach
Megalogastria
Microgastria
Transposition of stomach

750.8 Other specified anomalies of upper alimentary tract

750.9 Unspecified anomaly of upper alimentary tract
Congenital:
anomaly NOS } of upper alimentary tract [any part, except tongue]
deformity NOS } of upper alimentary tract [any part, except tongue]

✓4th 751 Other congenital anomalies of digestive system

751.0 Meckel's diverticulum
Meckel's diverticulum (displaced) (hypertrophic)
Persistent:
omphalomesenteric duct
vitelline duct
AHA: 1Q, '04, 10
DEF: Malformed sacs or appendages of ileum of small intestine; can cause strangulation, volvulus and intussusception.

751.1 Atresia and stenosis of small intestine P
Atresia of:
duodenum
ileum
intestine NOS
Congenital:
absence } of small intestine or intestine NOS
obstruction } of small intestine or intestine NOS
stenosis } of small intestine or intestine NOS
stricture } of small intestine or intestine NOS
Imperforate jejunum

751.2 Atresia and stenosis of large intestine rectum, and anal canal P
Absence:
anus (congenital)
appendix, congenital
large intestine, congenital
rectum
Atresia of:
anus
colon
rectum
Congenital or infantile:
obstruction of large intestine
occlusion of anus
stricture of anus
Imperforate:
anus
rectum
Stricture of rectum, congenital
AHA: 2Q, '98, 16

751.3 Hirschsprung's disease and other congenital functional disorders of colon
Aganglionosis
Congenital dilation of colon
Congenital megacolon
Macrocolon
DEF: Hirschsprung's disease: enlarged or dilated colon (megacolon), with absence of ganglion cells in the narrowed wall distally; causes inability to defecate.

751.4 Anomalies of intestinal fixation
Congenital adhesions:
omental, anomalous
peritoneal
Jackson's membrane
Malrotation of colon
Rotation of cecum or colon:
failure of
incomplete
insufficient
Universal mesentery

751.5 Other anomalies of intestine
Congenital diverticulum, colon
Dolichocolon
Duplication of:
anus
appendix
cecum
intestine
Ectopic anus
Megaloappendix
Megaloduodenum
Microcolon
Persistent cloaca
Transposition of:
appendix
colon
intestine
AHA: 3Q, '02, 11; 3Q, '01, 8

✓5th **751.6 Anomalies of gallbladder, bile ducts, and liver**

751.60 Unspecified anomaly of gallbladder, bile ducts, and liver

751.61 Biliary atresia P
Congenital:
absence, hypoplasia, obstruction, stricture } of bile duct (common) of passage
AHA: S-O, '87, 8

751.62 Congenital cystic disease of liver
Congenital polycystic disease of liver
Fibrocystic disease of liver

751.69 Other anomalies of gallbladder, bile ducts, and liver
Absence of:
gallbladder, congenital
liver (lobe)
Accessory:
hepatic ducts
liver
Congenital:
choledochal cyst
hepatomegaly
Duplication of:
biliary duct
cystic duct
gallbladder
liver
Floating:
gallbladder
liver
Intrahepatic gallbladder
AHA: S-O, '87, 8

751.7 Anomalies of pancreas
Absence, Accessory, Agenesis, Annular, Hypoplasia } (of) pancreas
Ectopic pancreatic tissue
Pancreatic heterotopia
EXCLUDES *diabetes mellitus ►(249.0-249.9, 250.0-250.9)◄*
fibrocystic disease of pancreas (277.00-277.09)
►neonatal diabetes mellitus (775.1)◄

751.8 Other specified anomalies of digestive system
Absence (complete) (partial) of alimentary tract NOS
Duplication, Malposition, congenital } of digestive organs NOS
EXCLUDES *congenital diaphragmatic hernia (756.6)*
congenital hiatus hernia (750.6)

751.9 Unspecified anomaly of digestive system
Congenital:
anomaly NOS, deformity NOS } of digestive system NOS

✓4th **752 Congenital anomalies of genital organs**
EXCLUDES *syndromes associated with anomalies in the number and form of chromosomes (758.0-758.9)*

752.0 Anomalies of ovaries ♀
Absence, congenital, Accessory, Ectopic, Streak } (of) ovary

✓5th **752.1 Anomalies of fallopian tubes and broad ligaments**

752.10 Unspecified anomaly of fallopian tubes and broad ligaments ♀

752.11 Embryonic cyst of fallopian tubes and broad ligaments ♀
Cyst:
epoophoron
fimbrial
parovarian
AHA: S-O, '85, 13

752.19 Other ♀
Absence, Accessory, Atresia } (of) fallopian tube or broad ligament

752.2 Doubling of uterus ♀
Didelphic uterus
Doubling of uterus [any degree] (associated with doubling of cervix and vagina)

752.3 Other anomalies of uterus ♀
Absence, congenital, Agenesis, Aplasia, Bicornuate } (of) uterus
Uterus unicornis
Uterus with only one functioning horn
AHA: 3Q, '06, 18

✓5th **752.4 Anomalies of cervix, vagina, and external female genitalia**

752.40 Unspecified anomaly of cervix, vagina, and external female genitalia ♀

752.41 Embryonic cyst of cervix, vagina, and external female genitalia ♀
Cyst of:
canal of Nuck, congenital
Gartner's duct
vagina, embryonal
vulva, congenital

DEF: Embryonic fluid-filled cysts, of cervix, vagina or external female genitalia.

752.42 Imperforate hymen ♀

DEF: Complete closure of membranous fold around external opening of vagina.

752.49 Other anomalies of cervix, vagina, and external female genitalia ♀
Absence } of cervix, clitoris, vagina, or vulva
Agenesis }
Congenital stenosis or stricture of:
cervical canal
vagina

EXCLUDES *double vagina associated with total duplication (752.2)*

AHA: 3Q, '06, 18

✓5th **752.5 Undescended and retractile testicle**
AHA: 4Q, '96, 33

752.51 Undescended testis ♂
Cryptorchism
Ectopic testis

752.52 Retractile testis ♂

✓5th **752.6 Hypospadias and epispadias and other penile anomalies**
AHA: 4Q, '96, 34, 35

752.61 Hypospadias ♂
AHA: 4Q, '03, 67-68; 3Q, '97, 6

DEF: Abnormal opening of urethra on the ventral surface of the penis or perineum; also a rare defect of vagina.

752.62 Epispadias ♂
Anaspadias

DEF: Urethra opening on dorsal surface of penis; in females appears as a slit in the upper wall of urethra.

752.63 Congenital chordee ♂

DEF: Ventral bowing of penis due to fibrous band along corpus spongiosum; occurs with hypospadias.

752.64 Micropenis ♂

752.65 Hidden penis ♂

752.69 Other penile anomalies ♂

Hypospadias and Epispadias

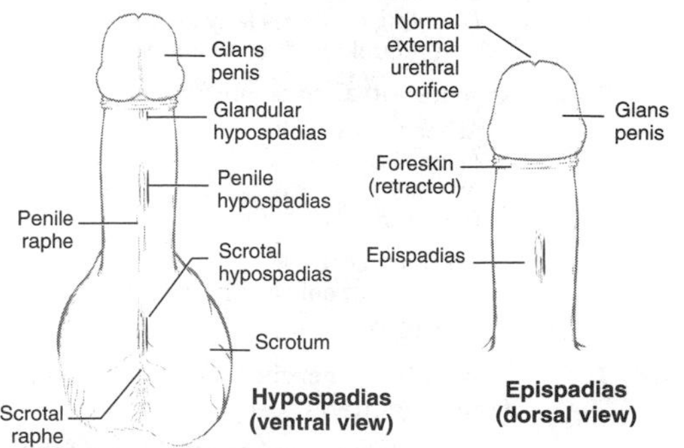

752.7 Indeterminate sex and pseudohermaphroditism
Gynandrism
Hermaphroditism
Ovotestis
Pseudohermaphroditism (male) (female)
Pure gonadal dysgenesis

EXCLUDES ►*androgen insensitivity (259.50-259.52)*◄
pseudohermaphroditism:
female, with adrenocortical disorder (255.2)
male, with gonadal disorder (257.8)
with specified chromosomal anomaly (758.0-758.9)
►*testicular feminization syndrome (259.50-259.52)*◄

DEF: Pseudohermaphroditism: presence of gonads of one sex and external genitalia of other sex.

✓5th **752.8 Other specified anomalies of genital organs**

EXCLUDES *congenital hydrocele (778.6)*
penile anomalies (752.61-752.69)
phimosis or paraphimosis (605)

752.81 Scrotal transposition ♂
AHA: 4Q, '03, 67-68

752.89 Other specified anomalies of genital organs
Absence of:
prostate
spermatic cord
vas deferens
Anorchism
Aplasia (congenital) of:
prostate
round ligament
testicle
Atresia of:
ejaculatory duct
vas deferens
Fusion of testes
Hypoplasia of testis
Monorchism
Polyorchism

752.9 Unspecified anomaly of genital organs
Congenital:
anomaly NOS } of genital organ, not elsewhere classified
deformity NOS }

✓4th **753 Congenital anomalies of urinary system**

753.0 Renal agenesis and dysgenesis
Atrophy of kidney:
congenital
infantile
Congenital absence of kidney(s)
Hypoplasia of kidney(s)

✓5th **753.1 Cystic kidney disease**

EXCLUDES *acquired cyst of kidney (593.2)*

AHA: 4Q, '90, 3

753.10 Cystic kidney disease, unspecified

753.11 Congenital single renal cyst

753.12 Polycystic kidney, unspecified type

753.13 Polycystic kidney, autosomal dominant

DEF: Slow progressive disease characterized by bilateral cysts causing increased kidney size and impaired function.

753.14 Polycystic kidney, autosomal recessive

DEF: Rare disease characterized by multiple cysts involving kidneys and liver, producing renal and hepatic failure in childhood or adolescence.

753.15 Renal dysplasia

753.16 Medullary cystic kidney
Nephronopthisis
DEF: Diffuse kidney disease results in uremia onset prior to age 20.

753.17 Medullary sponge kidney
DEF: Dilated collecting tubules; usually asymptomatic but calcinosis in tubules may cause renal insufficiency.

753.19 Other specified cystic kidney disease
Multicystic kidney

✓5th **753.2 Obstructive defects of renal pelvis and ureter**
AHA: 4Q, '96, 35

753.20 Unspecified obstructive defect of renal pelvis and ureter

753.21 Congenital obstruction of ureteropelvic junction
DEF: Stricture at junction of ureter and renal pelvis.

753.22 Congenital obstruction of ureterovesical junction
Adynamic ureter
Congenital hydroureter
DEF: Stricture at junction of ureter and bladder.

753.23 Congenital ureterocele

753.29 Other

753.3 Other specified anomalies of kidney
Accessory kidney
Congenital:
  calculus of kidney
  displaced kidney
Discoid kidney
Double kidney with double pelvis
Ectopic kidney
Fusion of kidneys
Giant kidney
Horseshoe kidney
Hyperplasia of kidney
Lobulation of kidney
Malrotation of kidney
Trifid kidney (pelvis)
AHA: 1Q, '07, 23

753.4 Other specified anomalies of ureter
Absent ureter
Accessory ureter
Deviation of ureter
Displaced ureteric orifice
Double ureter
Ectopic ureter
Implantation, anomalous of ureter

753.5 Exstrophy of urinary bladder
Ectopia vesicae
Extroversion of bladder
DEF: Absence of lower abdominal and anterior bladder walls with posterior bladder wall protrusion.

753.6 Atresia and stenosis of urethra and bladder neck
Congenital obstruction:
  bladder neck
  urethra
Congenital stricture of:
  urethra (valvular)
  urinary meatus
  vesicourethral orifice
Imperforate urinary meatus
Impervious urethra
Urethral valve formation

753.7 Anomalies of urachus
Cyst, Fistula, Patent } (of) urachussinus
Persistent umbilical sinus

753.8 Other specified anomalies of bladder and urethra
Absence, congenital of:
  bladder
  urethra
Accessory:
  bladder
  urethra
Congenital:
  diverticulum of bladder
  hernia of bladder
  prolapse of:
    bladder (mucosa)
    urethra
  urethrorectal fistula
Double:
  urethra
  urinary meatus

753.9 Unspecified anomaly of urinary system
Congenital:
  anomaly NOS, deformity NOS } of urinary system [any part, except urachus]

✓4th **754 Certain congenital musculoskeletal deformities**

INCLUDES nonteratogenic deformities which are considered to be due to intrauterine malposition and pressure

754.0 Of skull, face, and jaw
Asymmetry of face
Compression facies
Depressions in skull
Deviation of nasal septum, congenital
Dolichocephaly
Plagiocephaly
Potter's facies
Squashed or bent nose, congenital
EXCLUDES *dentofacial anomalies (524.0-524.9)*
syphilitic saddle nose (090.5)

754.1 Of sternocleidomastoid muscle
Congenital sternomastoid torticollis
Congenital wryneck
Contracture of sternocleidomastoid (muscle)
Sternomastoid tumor

754.2 Of spine
Congenital postural:
  lordosis
  scoliosis

✓5th **754.3 Congenital dislocation of hip**

754.30 Congenital dislocation of hip, unilateral
Congenital dislocation of hip NOS

754.31 Congenital dislocation of hip, bilateral

754.32 Congenital subluxation of hip, unilateral
Congenital flexion deformity, hip or thigh
Predislocation status of hip at birth
Preluxation of hip, congenital

754.33 Congenital subluxation of hip, bilateral

754.35 Congenital dislocation of one hip with subluxation of other hip

✓5th **754.4 Congenital genu recurvatum and bowing of long bones of leg**

754.40 Genu recurvatum
DEF: Backward curving of knee joint.

754.41 Congenital dislocation of knee (with genu recurvatum)

754.42 Congenital bowing of femur

754.43 Congenital bowing of tibia and fibula

754.44 Congenital bowing of unspecified long bones of leg

✓5th **754.5 Varus deformities of feet**

EXCLUDES *acquired (736.71, 736.75, 736.79)*

754.50 Talipes varus
Congenital varus deformity of foot, unspecified
Pes varus
DEF: Inverted foot marked by outer sole resting on ground.

754.51 Talipes equinovarus
Equinovarus (congenital)
DEF: Elevated, outward rotation of heel; also called clubfoot.

754.52 Metatarsus primus varus
DEF: Malformed first metatarsal bone, with bone angled toward body.

754.53 Metatarsus varus

754.59 Other
Talipes calcaneovarus

✓5th **754.6 Valgus deformities of feet**

EXCLUDES *valgus deformity of foot (acquired) (736.79)*

754.60 Talipes valgus
Congenital valgus deformity of foot, unspecified

754.61 Congenital pes planus
Congenital rocker bottom flat foot
Flat foot, congenital

EXCLUDES *pes planus (acquired) (734)*

754.62 Talipes calcaneovalgus

754.69 Other
Talipes:
equinovalgus
planovalgus

✓5th **754.7 Other deformities of feet**

EXCLUDES *acquired (736.70-736.79)*

754.70 Talipes, unspecified
Congenital deformity of foot NOS

754.71 Talipes cavus
Cavus foot (congenital)

754.79 Other
Asymmetric talipes
Talipes:
calcaneus
equinus

✓5th **754.8 Other specified nonteratogenic anomalies**

754.81 Pectus excavatum
Congenital funnel chest

754.82 Pectus carinatum
Congenital pigeon chest [breast]

754.89 Other
Club hand (congenital)
Congenital:
deformity of chest wall
dislocation of elbow
Generalized flexion contractures of lower limb joints, congenital
Spade-like hand (congenital)

✓4th **755 Other congenital anomalies of limbs**

EXCLUDES *those deformities classifiable to 754.0-754.8*

✓5th **755.0 Polydactyly**

755.00 Polydactyly, unspecified digits
Supernumerary digits

755.01 Of fingers
Accessory fingers

755.02 Of toes
Accessory toes

✓5th **755.1 Syndactyly**
Symphalangy
Webbing of digits

755.10 Of multiple and unspecified sites

755.11 Of fingers without fusion of bone

755.12 Of fingers with fusion of bone

755.13 Of toes without fusion of bone

755.14 Of toes with fusion of bone

✓5th **755.2 Reduction deformities of upper limb**

755.20 Unspecified reduction deformity of upper limb
Ectromelia NOS } of upper limb
Hemimelia NOS } of upper limb
Shortening of arm, congenital

755.21 Transverse deficiency of upper limb
Amelia of upper limb
Congenital absence of:
fingers, all (complete or partial)
forearm, including hand and fingers
upper limb, complete
Congenital amputation of upper limb
Transverse hemimelia of upper limb

755.22 Longitudinal deficiency of upper limb, not elsewhere classified
Phocomelia NOS of upper limb
Rudimentary arm

755.23 Longitudinal deficiency, combined, involving humerus, radius, and ulna (complete or incomplete)
Congenital absence of arm and forearm (complete or incomplete) with or without metacarpal deficiency and/or phalangeal deficiency, incomplete
Phocomelia, complete, of upper limb

755.24 Longitudinal deficiency, humeral, complete or partial (with or without distal deficiencies, incomplete)
Congenital absence of humerus (with or without absence of some [but not all] distal elements)
Proximal phocomelia of upper limb

755.25 Longitudinal deficiency, radioulnar, complete or partial (with or without distal deficiencies, incomplete)
Congenital absence of radius and ulna (with or without absence of some [but not all] distal elements)
Distal phocomelia of upper limb

755.26 Longitudinal deficiency, radial, complete or partial (with or without distal deficiencies, incomplete)
Agenesis of radius
Congenital absence of radius (with or without absence of some [but not all] distal elements)

755.27 Longitudinal deficiency, ulnar, complete or partial (with or without distal deficiencies, incomplete)
Agenesis of ulna
Congenital absence of ulna (with or without absence of some [but not all] distal elements)

755.28 Longitudinal deficiency, carpals or metacarpals, complete or partial (with or without incomplete phalangeal deficiency)

755.29 Longitudinal deficiency, phalanges, complete or partial
Absence of finger, congenital
Aphalangia of upper limb, terminal, complete or partial
EXCLUDES *terminal deficiency of all five digits (755.21)*
transverse deficiency of phalanges (755.21)

5th **755.3 Reduction deformities of lower limb**

755.30 Unspecified reduction deformity of lower limb
Ectromelia NOS } of lower limb
Hemimelia NOS } of lower limb
Shortening of leg, congenital

755.31 Transverse deficiency of lower limb
Amelia of lower limb
Congenital absence of:
foot
leg, including foot and toes
lower limb, complete
toes, all, complete
Transverse hemimelia of lower limb

755.32 Longitudinal deficiency of lower limb, not elsewhere classified
Phocomelia NOS of lower limb

755.33 Longitudinal deficiency, combined, involving femur, tibia, and fibula (complete or incomplete)
Congenital absence of thigh and (lower) leg (complete or incomplete) with or without metacarpal deficiency and/or phalangeal deficiency, incomplete
Phocomelia, complete, of lower limb

755.34 Longitudinal deficiency, femoral, complete or partial (with or without distal deficiencies, incomplete)
Congenital absence of femur (with or without absence of some [but not all] distal elements)
Proximal phocomelia of lower limb

755.35 Longitudinal deficiency, tibiofibular, complete or partial (with or without distal deficiencies, incomplete)
Congenital absence of tibia and fibula (with or without absence of some [but not all] distal elements)
Distal phocomelia of lower limb

755.36 Longitudinal deficiency, tibia, complete or partial (with or without distal deficiencies, incomplete)
Agenesis of tibia
Congenital absence of tibia (with or without absence of some [but not all] distal elements)

755.37 Longitudinal deficiency, fibular, complete or partial (with or without distal deficiencies, incomplete)
Agenesis of fibula
Congenital absence of fibula (with or without absence of some [but not all] distal elements)

755.38 Longitudinal deficiency, tarsals or metatarsals, complete or partial (with or without incomplete phalangeal deficiency)

755.39 Longitudinal deficiency, phalanges, complete or partial
Absence of toe, congenital
Aphalangia of lower limb, terminal, complete or partial
EXCLUDES *terminal deficiency of all five digits (755.31)*
transverse deficiency of phalanges (755.31)

755.4 Reduction deformities, unspecified limb
Absence, congenital (complete or partial) of limb NOS
Amelia, Ectromelia, Hemimelia, Phocomelia } of unspecified limb

5th **755.5 Other anomalies of upper limb, including shoulder girdle**

755.50 Unspecified anomaly of upper limb

755.51 Congenital deformity of clavicle

755.52 Congenital elevation of scapula
Sprengel's deformity

755.53 Radioulnar synostosis
DEF: Osseous adhesion of radius and ulna.

755.54 Madelung's deformity
DEF: Distal ulnar overgrowth or radial shortening; also called carpus curvus.

755.55 Acrocephalosyndactyly
Apert's syndrome
DEF: Premature cranial suture fusion (craniostenosis); marked by cone-shaped or pointed (acrocephaly) head and webbing of the fingers (syndactyly); similar to craniofacial dysostosis.

755.56 Accessory carpal bones

755.57 Macrodactylia (fingers)
DEF: Abnormally large fingers, toes.

755.58 Cleft hand, congenital
Lobster-claw hand
DEF: Extended separation between fingers into metacarpus; also may refer to large fingers and absent middle fingers of hand.

755.59 Other
Cleidocranial dysostosis
Cubitus:
valgus, congenital
varus, congenital
EXCLUDES *club hand (congenital) (754.89)*
congenital dislocation of elbow (754.89)

5th **755.6 Other anomalies of lower limb, including pelvic girdle**

755.60 Unspecified anomaly of lower limb

755.61 Coxa valga, congenital
DEF: Abnormally wide angle between the neck and shaft of the femur.

755.62 Coxa vara, congenital
DEF: Diminished angle between neck and shaft of femur.

755.63 Other congenital deformity of hip (joint)
Congenital anteversion of femur (neck)
EXCLUDES *congenital dislocation of hip (754.30-754.35)*
AHA: 1Q, '94, 15; S-O, '84, 15

755.64 Congenital deformity of knee (joint)
Congenital:
absence of patella
genu valgum [knock-knee]
genu varum [bowleg]
Rudimentary patella

755.65 Macrodactylia of toes
DEF: Abnormally large toes.

755.66 Other anomalies of toes
Congenital:
hallux valgus
hallux varus
hammer toe

755.67 Anomalies of foot, not elsewhere classified
Astragaloscaphoid synostosis
Calcaneonavicular bar
Coalition of calcaneus
Talonavicular synostosis
Tarsal coalitions

755.69 Other
Congenital:
angulation of tibia
deformity (of):
ankle (joint)
sacroiliac (joint)
fusion of sacroiliac joint

755.8 Other specified anomalies of unspecified limb

755.9 Unspecified anomaly of unspecified limb
Congenital:
anomaly NOS } of unspecified limb
deformity NOS } of unspecified limb
EXCLUDES *reduction deformity of unspecified limb (755.4)*

✓4th 756 Other congenital musculoskeletal anomalies
EXCLUDES ▶*congenital myotonic chondrodystrophy (359.23)*◀
those deformities classifiable to 754.0-754.8

756.0 Anomalies of skull and face bones
Absence of skull bones
Acrocephaly
Congenital deformity of forehead
Craniosynostosis
Crouzon's disease
Hypertelorism
Imperfect fusion of skull
Oxycephaly
Platybasia
Premature closure of cranial sutures
Tower skull
Trigonocephaly
EXCLUDES *acrocephalosyndactyly [Apert's syndrome] (755.55)*
dentofacial anomalies (524.0-524.9)
skull defects associated with brain anomalies, such as:
anencephalus (740.0)
encephalocele (742.0)
hydrocephalus (742.3)
microcephalus (742.1)
AHA: 3Q, '98, 9; 3Q, '96, 15

✓5th 756.1 Anomalies of spine

756.10 Anomaly of spine, unspecified

756.11 Spondylolysis, lumbosacral region
Prespondylolisthesis (lumbosacral)
DEF: Bilateral or unilateral defect through the pars interarticularis of a vertebra causes spondylolisthesis.

756.12 Spondylolisthesis
DEF: Downward slipping of lumbar vertebra over next vertebra; usually related to pelvic deformity.

756.13 Absence of vertebra, congenital

756.14 Hemivertebra
DEF: Incomplete development of one side of a vertebra.

756.15 Fusion of spine [vertebra], congenital

756.16 Klippel-Feil syndrome
DEF: Short, wide neck; limits range of motion due to ab-normal number of cervical vertebra or fused hemivertebrae.

756.17 Spina bifida occulta
EXCLUDES *spina bifida (aperta) (741.0-741.9)*
DEF: Spina bifida marked by a bony spinal canal defect without a protrusion of the cord or meninges; it is diagnosed by radiography and has no symptoms.

756.19 Other
Platyspondylia
Supernumerary vertebra

756.2 Cervical rib
Supernumerary rib in the cervical region
DEF: Costa cervicalis: extra rib attached to cervical vertebra.

756.3 Other anomalies of ribs and sternum
Congenital absence of:
rib
sternum
Congenital:
fissure of sternum
fusion of ribs
Sternum bifidum
EXCLUDES *nonteratogenic deformity of chest wall (754.81-754.89)*

756.4 Chondrodystrophy
Achondroplasia
Chondrodystrophia (fetalis)
Dyschondroplasia
Enchondromatosis
Ollier's disease
EXCLUDES *congenital myotonic chondrodystrophy (359.23)*
lipochondrodystrophy [Hurler's syndrome] (277.5)
Morquio's disease (277.5)
AHA: 2Q, '02, 16; S-O, '87, 10
DEF: Abnormal development of cartilage.

✓5th 756.5 Osteodystrophies

756.50 Osteodystrophy, unspecified

756.51 Osteogenesis imperfecta
Fragilitas ossium
Osteopsathyrosis
DEF: A collagen disorder commonly characterized by brittle, osteoporotic, easily fractured bones, hypermobility of joints, blue sclerae, and a tendency to hemorrhage.

756.52 Osteopetrosis
DEF: Abnormally dense bone, optic atrophy, hepatosplenomegaly, deafness; sclerosing depletes bone marrow and nerve foramina of skull; often fatal.

756.53 Osteopoikilosis
DEF: Multiple sclerotic foci on ends of long bones, stippling in round, flat bones; identified by x-ray.

756.54 Polyostotic fibrous dysplasia of bone
DEF: Fibrous tissue displaces bone results in segmented ragged-edge café-au-lait spots; occurs in girls of early puberty.

756.55 Chondroectodermal dysplasia
Ellis-van Creveld syndrome
DEF: Inadequate enchondral bone formation; impaired development of hair and teeth, polydactyly, and cardiac septum defects.

756.56 Multiple epiphyseal dysplasia

756.59 Other
Albright (-McCune)-Sternberg syndrome

756.6 Anomalies of diaphragm
Absence of diaphragm
Congenital hernia:
diaphragmatic
foramen of Morgagni
Eventration of diaphragm
EXCLUDES *congenital hiatus hernia (750.6)*

✓5th **756.7 Anomalies of abdominal wall**

756.70 Anomaly of abdominal wall, unspecified

756.71 Prune belly syndrome
Eagle-Barrett syndrome
Prolapse of bladder mucosa
AHA: 4Q, '97, 44
DEF: Prune belly syndrome: absence of lower rectus abdominis muscle and lower and medial oblique muscles; results in dilated bladder and ureters, dysplastic kidneys and hydronephrosis; more common in male infants with undescended testicles.

756.79 Other congenital anomalies of abdominal wall
Exomphalos
Gastroschisis
Omphalocele
EXCLUDES *umbilical hernia (551-553 with .1)*
DEF: Exomphalos: umbilical hernia prominent navel.
DEF: Gastroschisis: fissure of abdominal wall, results in protruding small or large intestine.
DEF: Omphalocele: hernia of umbilicus due to impaired abdominal wall; results in membrane-covered intestine protruding through peritoneum and amnion.

✓5th **756.8 Other specified anomalies of muscle, tendon, fascia, and connective tissue**

756.81 Absence of muscle and tendon
Absence of muscle (pectoral)

756.82 Accessory muscle

756.83 Ehlers-Danlos syndrome
DEF: Danlos syndrome: connective tissue disorder causes hyperextended skin and joints; results in fragile blood vessels with bleeding, poor wound healing and subcutaneous pseudotumors.

756.89 Other
Amyotrophia congenita
Congenital shortening of tendon
AHA: 3Q, '99, 16

756.9 Other and unspecified anomalies of musculoskeletal system
Congenital:
anomaly NOS } of musculoskeletal system, not
deformity NOS } elsewhere classified

✓4th **757 Congenital anomalies of the integument**
INCLUDES anomalies of skin, subcutaneous tissue, hair, nails, and breast
EXCLUDES *hemangioma (228.00-228.09)*
pigmented nevus (216.0-216.9)

757.0 Hereditary edema of legs
Congenital lymphedema
Hereditary trophedema
Milroy's disease

757.1 Ichthyosis congenita
Congenital ichthyosis
Harlequin fetus
Ichthyosiform erythroderma
DEF: Overproduction of skin cells causes scaling of skin; may result in stillborn fetus or death soon after birth.

757.2 Dermatoglyphic anomalies
Abnormal palmar creases
DEF: Abnormal skin-line patterns of fingers, palms, toes and soles; initial finding of possible chromosomal abnormalities.

✓5th **757.3 Other specified anomalies of skin**

757.31 Congenital ectodermal dysplasia
DEF: Tissues and structures originate in embryonic ectoderm; includes anhidrotic and hidrotic ectodermal dysplasia and EEC syndrome.

757.32 Vascular hamartomas
Birthmarks
Port-wine stain
Strawberry nevus
DEF: Benign tumor of blood vessels; due to malformed angioblastic tissues.

757.33 Congenital pigmentary anomalies of skin
Congenital poikiloderma
Urticaria pigmentosa
Xeroderma pigmentosum
EXCLUDES *albinism (270.2)*

757.39 Other
Accessory skin tags, congenital
Congenital scar
Epidermolysis bullosa
Keratoderma (congenital)
EXCLUDES *pilonidal cyst (685.0-685.1)*

757.4 Specified anomalies of hair
Congenital:
alopecia
atrichosis
beaded hair
hypertrichosis
monilethrix
Persistent lanugo

757.5 Specified anomalies of nails
Anonychia
Congenital:
clubnail
koilonychia
leukonychia
onychauxis
pachyonychia

757.6 Specified anomalies of breast
Absent } breast or nipple
Accessory }
Supernumerary }
EXCLUDES *absence of pectoral muscle (756.81)*
►*hypoplasia of breast (611.82)*◄

757.8 Other specified anomalies of the integument

757.9 Unspecified anomaly of the integument
Congenital:
anomaly NOS } of integument
deformity NOS }

✓4th **758 Chromosomal anomalies**
INCLUDES syndromes associated with anomalies in the number and form of chromosomes
Use additional codes for conditions associated with the chromosomal anomalies

758.0 Down's syndrome
Mongolism
Translocation Down's syndrome
Trisomy:
21 or 22
G

758.1 Patau's syndrome
Trisomy:
13
D_1
DEF: Trisomy of 13th chromosome; characteristic failure to thrive, severe mental impairment, seizures, abnormal eyes, low-set ears and sloped forehead.

758.2 Edwards' syndrome
Trisomy:
18
E_3
DEF: Trisomy of 18th chromosome; characteristic mental and physical impairments; mainly affects females.

✓5th **758.3 Autosomal deletion syndromes**

758.31 Cri-du-chat syndrome
Deletion 5p
DEF: Hereditary congenital syndrome caused by a microdeletion of short arm of chromosome 5; characterized by catlike cry in newborn, microenceph-aly, severe mental deficiency, and hypertelorism.

758.32 Velo-cardio-facial syndrome
Deletion 22q11.2
DEF: Microdeletion syndrome affecting multiple organs; characteristic cleft palate, heart defects, elongated face with almond-shaped eyes, wide nose, small ears, weak immune systems, weak musculature, hypothyroidism, short stature, and scoliosis; deletion at q11.2 on the long arm of the chromosome 22.

758.33 Other microdeletions
Miller-Dieker syndrome
Smith-Magenis syndrome
DEF: Miller-Dieker syndrome: deletion from the short arm of chromosome 17; characteristic mental retardation, speech and motor development delays, neurological complications, and multiple abnormalities affecting the kidneys, heart, gastrointestinal tract, and other organ; death in infancy or early childhood.
DEF: Smith-Magenis syndrome: deletion in a certain area of chromosome 17 that results in craniofacial changes, speech delay, hoarse voice, hearing loss in many, and behavioral problems, such as self-destructive head banging, wrist biting, and tearing at nails.

758.39 Other autosomal deletions

758.4 Balanced autosomal translocation in normal individual

758.5 Other conditions due to autosomal anomalies
Accessory autosomes NEC

758.6 Gonadal dysgenesis
Ovarian dysgenesis
XO syndrome
Turner's syndrome
EXCLUDES *pure gonadal dysgenesis (752.7)*

758.7 Klinefelter's syndrome ♂
XXY syndrome
DEF: Impaired embryonic development of seminiferous tubes; results in small testes, azoospermia, infertility and enlarged mammary glands.

✓5th **758.8 Other conditions due to chromosome anomalies**

758.81 Other conditions due to sex chromosome anomalies

758.89 Other

758.9 Conditions due to anomaly of unspecified chromosome

✓4th **759 Other and unspecified congenital anomalies**

759.0 Anomalies of spleen
Aberrant, Absent, Accessory } spleen
Congenital splenomegaly
Ectopic spleen
Lobulation of spleen

759.1 Anomalies of adrenal gland
Aberrant, Absent, Accessory } adrenal gland
EXCLUDES *adrenogenital disorders (255.2)*
congenital disorders of steroid metabolism (255.2)

759.2 Anomalies of other endocrine glands
Absent parathyroid gland
Accessory thyroid gland
Persistent thyroglossal or thyrolingual duct
Thyroglossal (duct) cyst
EXCLUDES *congenital:*
goiter (246.1)
hypothyroidism (243)

759.3 Situs inversus
Situs inversus or transversus:
abdominalis
thoracis
Transposition of viscera:
abdominal
thoracic
EXCLUDES *dextrocardia without mention of complete transposition (746.87)*
DEF: Laterally transposed thoracic and abdominal viscera.

759.4 Conjoined twins
Craniopagus
Dicephalus
Pygopagus
Thoracopagus
Xiphopagus

759.5 Tuberous sclerosis
Bourneville's disease
Epiloia
DEF: Hamartomas of brain, retina and viscera, impaired mental ability, seizures and adenoma sebaceum.

759.6 Other hamartoses, not elsewhere classified
Syndrome:
Peutz-Jeghers
Sturge-Weber (-Dimitri)
von Hippel-Lindau
EXCLUDES *neurofibromatosis (237.7)*
AHA: 3Q, '92, 12
DEF: Peutz-Jeghers: hereditary syndrome characterized by hamartomas of small intestine.
DEF: Sturge-Weber: congenital syndrome characterized by unilateral port-wine stain over trigeminal nerve, underlying meninges and cerebral cortex.
DEF: von Hipple-Lindau: hereditary syndrome of congenital angiomatosis of the retina and cerebellum.

759.7 Multiple congenital anomalies, so described
Congenital:
anomaly, multiple NOS
deformity, multiple NOS

✓5th **759.8 Other specified anomalies**
AHA: S-O, '87, 9; S-O, '85, 11

759.81 Prader-Willi syndrome

759.82 Marfan syndrome
AHA: 3Q, '93, 11

759.83 Fragile X syndrome
AHA: 4Q, '94, 41

759.89 Other

Congenital malformation syndromes affecting multiple systems, not elsewhere classified

Laurence-Moon-Biedl syndrome

AHA: 3Q, '06, 21; 2Q, '05, 17; 2Q, '04, 12; 1Q, '01, 3; 3Q, '99, 17, 18; 3Q, '98, 8

759.9 Congenital anomaly, unspecified

15. CERTAIN CONDITIONS ORIGINATING IN THE PERINATAL PERIOD (760-779)

INCLUDES conditions which have their origin in the perinatal period, before birth through the first 28 days after birth, even though death or morbidity occurs later

Use additional code(s) to further specify condition

MATERNAL CAUSES OF PERINATAL MORBIDITY AND MORTALITY (760-763)

AHA: 2Q, '89, 14; 3Q, '90, 5

✓4th **760 Fetus or newborn affected by maternal conditions which may be unrelated to present pregnancy**

INCLUDES the listed maternal conditions only when specified as a cause of mortality or morbidity of the fetus or newborn

EXCLUDES *maternal endocrine and metabolic disorders affecting fetus or newborn (775.0-775.9)*

AHA: 1Q, '94, 8; 2Q, '92, 12; N-D, '84, 11

760.0 Maternal hypertensive disorders

Fetus or newborn affected by maternal conditions classifiable to 642

760.1 Maternal renal and urinary tract diseases

Fetus or newborn affected by maternal conditions classifiable to 580-599

760.2 Maternal infections

Fetus or newborn affected by maternal infectious disease classifiable to 001-136 and 487, but fetus or newborn not manifesting that disease

EXCLUDES *congenital infectious diseases (771.0-771.8)*
maternal genital tract and other localized infections (760.8)

760.3 Other chronic maternal circulatory and respiratory diseases

Fetus or newborn affected by chronic maternal conditions classifiable to 390-459, 490-519, 745-748

760.4 Maternal nutritional disorders

Fetus or newborn affected by:
maternal disorders classifiable to 260-269
maternal malnutrition NOS

EXCLUDES *fetal malnutrition (764.10-764.29)*

760.5 Maternal injury

Fetus or newborn affected by maternal conditions classifiable to 800-995

▲ ✓5th **760.6 Surgical operation on mother and fetus**

EXCLUDES *cesarean section for present delivery (763.4)*
damage to placenta from amniocentesis, cesarean section, or surgical induction (762.1)

● **760.61 Newborn affected by amniocentesis**

EXCLUDES *fetal complications from amniocentesis (679.1)*

● **760.62 Newborn affected by other in utero procedure**

EXCLUDES *fetal complications of in utero procedure (679.1)*

● **760.63 Newborn affected by other surgical operations on mother during pregnancy**

EXCLUDES *newborn affected by previous surgical procedure on mother not associated with pregnancy (760.64)*

● **760.64 Newborn affected by previous surgical procedure on mother not associated with pregnancy**

✓5th **760.7 Noxious influences affecting fetus or newborn via placenta or breast milk**

Fetus or newborn affected by noxious substance transmitted via placenta or breast milk

EXCLUDES *anesthetic and analgesic drugs administered during labor and delivery (763.5)*
drug withdrawal syndrome in newborn (779.5)

AHA: 3Q, '91, 21

760.70 Unspecified noxious substance

Fetus or newborn affected by:
Drug NEC

760.71 Alcohol

Fetal alcohol syndrome

760.72 Narcotics

760.73 Hallucinogenic agents

760.74 Anti-infectives

Antibiotics
Antifungals

760.75 Cocaine

AHA: 3Q, '94, 6; 2Q, '92, 12; 4Q, '91, 26

760.76 Diethylstilbestrol [DES]

AHA: 4Q, '94, 45

760.77 Anticonvulsants N

Carbamazepine
Phenobarbital
Phenytoin
Valproic acid

AHA: 4Q, '05, 82

760.78 Antimetabolic agents N

Methotrexate
Retinoic acid
Statins

AHA: 4Q, '05, 82-83

760.79 Other

Fetus or newborn affected by:
immune sera } transmitted via placenta or breast
medicinal agents NEC } transmitted via placenta or breast
toxic substance NEC } transmitted via placenta or breast

760.8 Other specified maternal conditions affecting fetus or newborn

Maternal genital tract and other localized infection affecting fetus or newborn, but fetus or newborn not manifesting that disease

EXCLUDES *maternal urinary tract infection affecting fetus or newborn (760.1)*

760.9 Unspecified maternal condition affecting fetus or newborn

✓4th **761 Fetus or newborn affected by maternal complications of pregnancy**

INCLUDES the listed maternal conditions only when specified as a cause of mortality or morbidity of the fetus or newborn

761.0 Incompetent cervix

DEF: Inadequate functioning of uterine cervix.

761.1 Premature rupture of membranes

761.2 Oligohydramnios

EXCLUDES *that due to premature rupture of membranes (761.1)*

DEF: Deficient amniotic fluid.

761.3 Polyhydramnios

Hydramnios (acute) (chronic)

DEF: Excess amniotic fluid.

761.4 Ectopic pregnancy
Pregnancy:
abdominal
intraperitoneal
tubal

761.5 Multiple pregnancy
Triplet (pregnancy)
Twin (pregnancy)

761.6 Maternal death

761.7 Malpresentation before labor
Breech presentation, External version, Oblique lie, Transverse lie, Unstable lie } before labor

761.8 Other specified maternal complications of pregnancy affecting fetus or newborn
Spontaneous abortion, fetus

761.9 Unspecified maternal complication of pregnancy affecting fetus or newborn

4th 762 Fetus or newborn affected by complications of placenta, cord, and membranes

INCLUDES the listed maternal conditions only when specified as a cause of mortality or morbidity in the fetus or newborn

AHA: 1Q, '94, 8

762.0 Placenta previa N
DEF: Placenta developed in lower segment of uterus; causes hemorrhaging in last trimester.

762.1 Other forms of placental separation and hemorrhage N
Abruptio placentae
Antepartum hemorrhage
Damage to placenta from amniocentesis, cesarean section, or surgical induction
Maternal blood loss
Premature separation of placenta
Rupture of marginal sinus

762.2 Other and unspecified morphological and functional abnormalities of placenta N
Placental:
dysfunction
infarction
insufficiency

762.3 Placental transfusion syndromes N
Placental and cord abnormality resulting in twin-to-twin or other transplacental transfusion
Use additional code to indicate resultant condition in fetus or newborn:
fetal blood loss (772.0)
polycythemia neonatorum (776.4)

762.4 Prolapsed cord N
Cord presentation

762.5 Other compression of umbilical cord N
Cord around neck
Entanglement of cord
Knot in cord
Torsion of cord
AHA: 2Q, '03, 9

762.6 Other and unspecified conditions of umbilical cord N
Short cord
Thrombosis, Varices, Velamentous insertion } of umbilical cord
Vasa previa
EXCLUDES *infection of umbilical cord (771.4)*
single umbilical artery (747.5)

762.7 Chorioamnionitis N
Amnionitis
Membranitis
Placentitis
DEF: Inflamed fetal membrane.

762.8 Other specified abnormalities of chorion and amnion N

762.9 Unspecified abnormality of chorion and amnion N

4th 763 Fetus or newborn affected by other complications of labor and delivery

INCLUDES the listed conditions only when specified as a cause of mortality or morbidity in the fetus or newborn

EXCLUDES ▶*newborn affected by surgical procedures on mother (760.61-760.64)*◀

AHA: 1Q, '94, 8

763.0 Breech delivery and extraction N

763.1 Other malpresentation, malposition, and disproportion during labor and delivery N
Fetus or newborn affected by:
abnormality of bony pelvis
contracted pelvis
persistent occipitoposterior position
shoulder presentation
transverse lie
Fetus or newborn affected by conditions classifiable to 652, 653, and 660

763.2 Forceps delivery N
Fetus or newborn affected by forceps extraction

763.3 Delivery by vacuum extractor N

763.4 Cesarean delivery N
EXCLUDES *placental separation or hemorrhage from cesarean section (762.1)*

763.5 Maternal anesthesia and analgesia N
Reactions and intoxications from maternal opiates and tranquilizers during labor and delivery
EXCLUDES *drug withdrawal syndrome in newborn (779.5)*

763.6 Precipitate delivery N
Rapid second stage

763.7 Abnormal uterine contractions N
Fetus or newborn affected by:
contraction ring
hypertonic labor
hypotonic uterine dysfunction
uterine inertia or dysfunction
Fetus or newborn affected by conditions classifiable to 661, except 661.3

5th 763.8 Other specified complications of labor and delivery affecting fetus or newborn
AHA: 4Q, '98, 46

763.81 Abnormality in fetal heart rate or rhythm before the onset of labor N

763.82 Abnormality in fetal heart rate or rhythm during labor N
AHA: 4Q, '98, 46

763.83 Abnormality in fetal heart rate or rhythm, unspecified as to time of onset N

763.84 **Meconium passage during delivery** N

EXCLUDES *meconium aspiration (770.11, 770.12)*
meconium staining (779.84)

AHA: 4Q, '05, 83

DEF: Fetal intestinal activity that increases in response to a distressed state during delivery; anal sphincter relaxes, and meconium is passed into the amniotic fluid.

763.89 **Other specified complications of labor and delivery affecting fetus or newborn** N

Fetus or newborn affected by:
abnormality of maternal soft tissues
destructive operation on live fetus to facilitate delivery
induction of labor (medical)
other procedures used in labor and delivery
Fetus or newborn affected by other conditions classifiable to 650-669

763.9 **Unspecified complication of labor and delivery affecting fetus or newborn** N

OTHER CONDITIONS ORIGINATING IN THE PERINATAL PERIOD (764-779)

The following fifth-digit subclassification is for use with category 764 and codes 765.0-765.1 to denote birthweight:

0 **unspecified [weight]**
1 **less than 500 grams**
2 **500-749 grams**
3 **750-999 grams**
4 **1,000-1,249 grams**
5 **1,250-1,499 grams**
6 **1,500-1,749 grams**
7 **1,750-1,999 grams**
8 **2,000-2,499 grams**
9 **2,500 grams and over**

4th **764 Slow fetal growth and fetal malnutrition**

AHA: 3Q, '04, 4; 4Q, '02, 63; 1Q,'94, 8; 2Q, '91, 19; 2Q, '89, 15

§ 5th 764.0 **"Light-for-dates" without mention of fetal malnutrition** N
[0-9]
Infants underweight for gestational age
"Small-for-dates"

§ 5th 764.1 **"Light-for-dates" with signs of fetal malnutrition** N
[0-9]
Infants "light-for-dates" classifiable to 764.0, who in addition show signs of fetal malnutrition, such as dry peeling skin and loss of subcutaneous tissue

§ 5th 764.2 **Fetal malnutrition without mention of "light-for-dates"** N
[0-9]
Infants, not underweight for gestational age, showing signs of fetal malnutrition, such as dry peeling skin and loss of subcutaneous tissue
Intrauterine malnutrition

§ 5th 764.9 **Fetal growth retardation, unspecified** N
[0-9]
Intrauterine growth retardation

AHA: For code 764.97: 1Q, '97, 6

4th **765 Disorders relating to short gestation and low birthweight**

INCLUDES the listed conditions, without further specification, as causes of mortality, morbidity, or additional care, in fetus or newborn

AHA: 1Q, '97, 6; 1Q, '94, 8; 2Q, '91, 19; 2Q, '89, 15

§ 5th 765.0 **Extreme immaturity** N
[0-9]
Note: Usually implies a birthweight of less than 1000 grams.

Use additional code for weeks of gestation (765.20-765.29)

AHA: 3Q, '04, 4; 4Q, '02, 63; For code 765.03: 4Q, '01, 51

§ 5th 765.1 **Other preterm infants** N
[0-9]
Note: Usually implies a birthweight of 1000-2499 grams.

Prematurity NOS
Prematurity or small size, not classifiable to 765.0 or as "light-for-dates" in 764

Use additional code for weeks of gestation (765.20-765.29)

AHA: 3Q, '04, 4; 4Q, '02, 63; For code 765.10: 1Q, '94, 14; For code 765.17: 1Q, '97, 6; For code 765.18: 4Q, '02, 64

5th 765.2 **Weeks of gestation**

AHA: 3Q, '04, 4; 4Q, '02, 63

765.20 **Unspecified weeks of gestation** N

765.21 **Less than 24 completed weeks of gestation** N

765.22 **24 completed weeks of gestation** N

765.23 **25-26 completed weeks of gestation** N

765.24 **27-28 completed weeks of gestation** N

765.25 **29-30 completed weeks of gestation** N

765.26 **31-32 completed weeks of gestation** N

765.27 **33-34 completed weeks of gestation** N

765.28 **35-36 completed weeks of gestation** N

AHA: 4Q, '02, 64

765.29 **37 or more completed weeks of gestation** N

4th **766 Disorders relating to long gestation and high birthweight**

INCLUDES the listed conditions, without further specification, as causes of mortality, morbidity, or additional care, in fetus or newborn

766.0 **Exceptionally large baby** N

Note: Usually implies a birthweight of 4500 grams or more.

766.1 **Other "heavy-for-dates" infants** N

Other fetus or infant "heavy-" or "large-for-dates" regardless of period of gestation

5th 766.2 **Late infant, not "heavy-for-dates"**

AHA: 2Q, '06, 12; 4Q, '03, 69

766.21 **Post-term infant** N

Infant with gestation period over 40 completed weeks to 42 completed weeks

766.22 **Prolonged gestation of infant** N

Infant with gestation period over 42 completed weeks
Postmaturity NOS

4th **767 Birth trauma**

767.0 **Subdural and cerebral hemorrhage** N

Subdural and cerebral hemorrhage, whether described as due to birth trauma or to intrapartum anoxia or hypoxia
Subdural hematoma (localized)
Tentorial tear

Use additional code to identify cause

EXCLUDES *intraventricular hemorrhage (772.10-772.14)*
subarachnoid hemorrhage (772.2)

§ Requires fifth-digit. Valid digits are in [brackets] under each code. See beginning of section 764-779 for codes and definitions.

Epicranial Aponeurosis

Skin
Subcutaneous tissues
Areolar space
Frontalis muscle
Epicranial aponeurosis
Pericranium
Occipitalis muscle
Frontal sinus
Inion

✓5th **767.1 Injuries to scalp**

AHA: 4Q, '03, 69

767.11 Epicranial subaponeurotic hemorrhage (massive) N

Subgaleal hemorrhage

DEF: A hemorrhage that occurs within the space between the galea aponeurotica, or epicranial aponeurosis, a thin tendinous structure that is attached to the skull laterally and provides an insertion site for the occipitalis posteriorly and the frontalis muscle anteriorly, and the periosteum of the skull.

767.19 Other injuries to scalp N

Caput succedaneum
Cephalhematoma
Chignon (from vacuum extraction)

767.2 Fracture of clavicle N

767.3 Other injuries to skeleton N

Fracture of:
long bones
skull

EXCLUDES *congenital dislocation of hip (754.30-754.35)*
fracture of spine, congenital (767.4)

767.4 Injury to spine and spinal cord N

Dislocation / Fracture / Laceration / Rupture } of spine or spinal cord due to birth trauma

767.5 Facial nerve injury N

Facial palsy

767.6 Injury to brachial plexus N

Palsy or paralysis:
brachial
Erb (-Duchenne)
Klumpke (-Déjérine)

767.7 Other cranial and peripheral nerve injuries N

Phrenic nerve paralysis

767.8 Other specified birth trauma N

Eye damage
Hematoma of:
liver (subcapsular)
testes
vulva
Rupture of:
liver
spleen
Scalpel wound
Traumatic glaucoma

EXCLUDES *hemorrhage classifiable to 772.0-772.9*

767.9 Birth trauma, unspecified N

Birth injury NOS

✓4th **768 Intrauterine hypoxia and birth asphyxia**

Use only when associated with newborn morbidity classifiable elsewhere

EXCLUDES *acidemia NOS of newborn (775.81)*
acidosis NOS of newborn (775.81)
cerebral ischemia NOS (779.2)
hypoxia NOS of newborn (770.88)
mixed metabolic and respiratory acidosis of newborn (775.81)
respiratory arrest of newborn (770.87)

AHA: 4Q, '92, 20

DEF: Oxygen intake insufficiency due to interrupted placental circulation or premature separation of placenta.

768.0 Fetal death from asphyxia or anoxia before onset of labor or at unspecified time N

768.1 Fetal death from asphyxia or anoxia during labor N

768.2 Fetal distress before onset of labor, in liveborn infant N

Fetal metabolic acidemia before onset of labor, in liveborn infant

768.3 Fetal distress first noted during labor and delivery, in liveborn infant N

Fetal metabolic acidemia first noted during labor and delivery, in liveborn infant

768.4 Fetal distress, unspecified as to time of onset, in liveborn infant N

Fetal metabolic acidemia unspecified as to time of onset, in liveborn infant

AHA: N-D, '86, 10

768.5 Severe birth asphyxia N

Birth asphyxia with neurologic involvement

EXCLUDES *hypoxic-ischemic encephalopathy [HIE] (768.7)*

AHA: N-D, '86, 3

768.6 Mild or moderate birth asphyxia N

Other specified birth asphyxia (without mention of neurologic involvement)

EXCLUDES *hypoxic-ischemic encephalopathy [HIE] (768.7)*

AHA: N-D, '86, 3

768.7 Hypoxic-ischemic encephalopathy [HIE] N

AHA: 4Q, '06, 104

768.9 Unspecified birth asphyxia in liveborn infant N

Anoxia / Asphyxia } NOS, in liveborn infant

769 Respiratory distress syndrome N

Cardiorespiratory distress syndrome of newborn
Hyaline membrane disease (pulmonary)
Idiopathic respiratory distress syndrome [IRDS or RDS] of newborn
Pulmonary hypoperfusion syndrome

EXCLUDES *transient tachypnea of newborn (770.6)*

AHA: 1Q, '89, 10; N-D, '86, 6

DEF: Severe chest contractions upon air intake and expiratory grunting; infant appears blue due to oxygen deficiency and has rapid respiratory rate; formerly called hyaline membrane disease.

✓4th **770 Other respiratory conditions of fetus and newborn**

770.0 Congenital pneumonia N

Infective pneumonia acquired prenatally

EXCLUDES *pneumonia from infection acquired after birth (480.0-486)*

AHA: 1Q, '05, 10

5th **770.1 Fetal and newborn aspiration**

EXCLUDES *aspiration of postnatal stomach contents (770.85, 770.86)*
meconium passage during delivery (763.84)
meconium staining (779.84)

AHA: 4Q, '05, 83

770.10 Fetal and newborn aspiration, unspecified N

770.11 Meconium aspiration without respiratory symptoms N
Meconium aspiration NOS

770.12 Meconium aspiration with respiratory symptoms N
Meconium aspiration pneumonia
Meconium aspiration pneumonitis
Meconium aspiration syndrome NOS
Use additional code to identify any secondary pulmonary hypertension (416.8), if applicable

DEF: Meconium aspiration syndrome: aspiration of fetal intestinal material during or prior to delivery, usually a complication of placental insufficiency, causing pneumonitis and bronchial obstruction (inflammatory reaction of lungs).

770.13 Aspiration of clear amniotic fluid without respiratory symptoms N
Aspiration of clear amniotic fluid NOS

770.14 Aspiration of clear amniotic fluid with respiratory symptoms N
Aspiration of clear amniotic fluid with pneumonia
Aspiration of clear amniotic fluid with pneumonitis
Use additional code to identify any secondary pulmonary hypertension (416.8), if applicable

770.15 Aspiration of blood without respiratory symptoms N
Aspiration of blood NOS

770.16 Aspiration of blood with respiratory symptoms N
Aspiration of blood with pneumonia
Aspiration of blood with pneumonitis
Use additional code to identify any secondary pulmonary hypertension (416.8), if applicable

770.17 Other fetal and newborn aspiration without respiratory symptoms N

770.18 Other fetal and newborn aspiration with respiratory symptoms N
Other aspiration pneumonia
Other aspiration pneumonitis
Use additional code to identify any secondary pulmonary hypertension (416.8), if applicable

770.2 Interstitial emphysema and related conditions N
Pneumomediastinum, Pneumopericardium, Pneumothorax } originating in the perinatal period

770.3 Pulmonary hemorrhage N
Hemorrhage:
alveolar (lung), intra-alveolar (lung), massive pulmonary } originating in the perinatal period

770.4 Primary atelectasis N
Pulmonary immaturity NOS

DEF: Alveoli fail to expand causing insufficient air intake by newborn.

770.5 Other and unspecified atelectasis N
Atelectasis:
NOS, partial, secondary } originating in the perinatal period
Pulmonary collapse } originating in the perinatal period

770.6 Transitory tachypnea of newborn N
Idiopathic tachypnea of newborn
Wet lung syndrome

EXCLUDES *respiratory distress syndrome (769)*

AHA: 4Q, '95, 4; 1Q, '94, 12; 3Q, '93, 7; 1Q, '89, 10; N-D, '86, 6

DEF: Quick, shallow breathing of newborn; short-term problem.

770.7 Chronic respiratory disease arising in the perinatal period
Bronchopulmonary dysplasia
Interstitial pulmonary fibrosis of prematurity
Wilson-Mikity syndrome

AHA: 2Q, '91, 19; N-D, '86, 11

5th **770.8 Other respiratory problems after birth**

EXCLUDES *mixed metabolic and respiratory acidosis of newborn (775.81)*

AHA: 4Q, '02, 65; 2Q, '98, 10; 2Q, '96, 10

770.81 Primary apnea of newborn N
Apneic spells of newborn NOS
Essential apnea of newborn
Sleep apnea of newborn

DEF: Cessation of breathing when a neonate makes no respiratory effort for 15 seconds, resulting in cyanosis and bradycardia.

770.82 Other apnea of newborn N
Obstructive apnea of newborn

770.83 Cyanotic attacks of newborn N

770.84 Respiratory failure of newborn N

EXCLUDES *respiratory distress syndrome (769)*

770.85 Aspiration of postnatal stomach contents without respiratory symptoms N
Aspiration of postnatal stomach contents NOS

AHA: 4Q, '05, 83

770.86 Aspiration of postnatal stomach contents with respiratory symptoms N
Aspiration of postnatal stomach contents with pneumonia
Aspiration of postnatal stomach contents with pneumonitis
Use additional code to identify any secondary pulmonary hypertension (416.8), if applicable

AHA: 4Q, '05, 83

770.87 Respiratory arrest of newborn N

AHA: 4Q, '06, 104-106

770.88 Hypoxemia of newborn N
Hypoxia NOS of newborn

AHA: 4Q, '06, 104-106

770.89 Other respiratory problems after birth N

770.9 Unspecified respiratory condition of fetus and newborn N

✓4th 771 Infections specific to the perinatal period

INCLUDES infections acquired before or during birth or via the umbilicus or during the first 28 days after birth

EXCLUDES *congenital pneumonia (770.0)*
congenital syphilis (090.0-090.9)
infant botulism (040.41)
maternal infectious disease as a cause of mortality or morbidity in fetus or newborn, but fetus or newborn not manifesting the disease (760.2)
ophthalmia neonatorum due to gonococcus (098.40)
other infections not specifically classified to this category

AHA: N-D, '85, 4

771.0 Congenital rubella N
Congenital rubella pneumonitis

771.1 Congenital cytomegalovirus infection N
Congenital cytomegalic inclusion disease

771.2 Other congenital infections N

Congenital:	Congenital:
herpes simplex	toxoplasmosis
listeriosis	tuberculosis
malaria	

771.3 Tetanus neonatorum N
Tetanus omphalitis
EXCLUDES *hypocalcemic tetany (775.4)*
DEF: Severe infection of central nervous system; due to exotoxin of tetanus bacillus from navel infection prompted by nonsterile technique during umbilical ligation.

771.4 Omphalitis of the newborn N
Infection:
navel cord
umbilical stump
EXCLUDES *tetanus omphalitis (771.3)*
DEF: Inflamed umbilicus.

771.5 Neonatal infective mastitis N
EXCLUDES *noninfective neonatal mastitis (778.7)*

771.6 Neonatal conjunctivitis and dacryocystitis N
Ophthalmia neonatorum NOS
EXCLUDES *ophthalmia neonatorum due to gonococcus (098.40)*

771.7 Neonatal Candida infection N
Neonatal moniliasis
Thrush in newborn

✓5th **771.8 Other infection specific to the perinatal period**
Use additional code to identify organism (041.00-041.9)
AHA: 4Q, '02, 66

771.81 Septicemia [sepsis] of newborn N
▶Use additional codes to identify severe sepsis (995.92) and any associated acute organ dysfunction, if applicable◀

771.82 Urinary tract infection of newborn N

771.83 Bacteremia of newborn N

771.89 Other infections specific to the perinatal period N
Intra-amniotic infection of fetus NOS
Infection of newborn NOS

✓4th 772 Fetal and neonatal hemorrhage

EXCLUDES *hematological disorders of fetus and newborn (776.0-776.9)*

772.0 Fetal blood loss N
Fetal blood loss from:
cut end of co-twin's cord
placenta
ruptured cord
vasa previa
Fetal exsanguination
Fetal hemorrhage into:
co-twin
mother's circulation

✓5th **772.1 Intraventricular hemorrhage**
Intraventricular hemorrhage from any perinatal cause
AHA: 4Q, '01, 49; 3Q, '92, 8; 4Q, '88, 8

772.10 Unspecified grade N

772.11 Grade I N
Bleeding into germinal matrix

772.12 Grade II N
Bleeding into ventricle

772.13 Grade III N
Bleeding with enlargement of ventricle
AHA: 4Q, '01, 51

772.14 Grade IV N
Bleeding into cerebral cortex

772.2 Subarachnoid hemorrhage N
Subarachnoid hemorrhage from any perinatal cause
EXCLUDES *subdural and cerebral hemorrhage (767.0)*

772.3 Umbilical hemorrhage after birth N
Slipped umbilical ligature

772.4 Gastrointestinal hemorrhage N
EXCLUDES *swallowed maternal blood (777.3)*

772.5 Adrenal hemorrhage N

772.6 Cutaneous hemorrhage N
Bruising, Ecchymoses, Petechiae, Superficial hematoma } in fetus or newborn

772.8 Other specified hemorrhage of fetus or newborn N
EXCLUDES *hemorrhagic disease of newborn (776.0)*
pulmonary hemorrhage (770.3)

772.9 Unspecified hemorrhage of newborn N

✓4th 773 Hemolytic disease of fetus or newborn, due to isoimmunization

DEF: Hemolytic anemia of fetus or newborn due to maternal antibody formation against fetal erythrocytes; infant blood contains nonmaternal antigen.

773.0 Hemolytic disease due to Rh isoimmunization N
Anemia, Erythroblastosis (fetalis), Hemolytic disease (fetus) (newborn), Jaundice } due to RH: antibodies, isoimmunization, maternal/fetal incompatibility
Rh hemolytic disease
Rh isoimmunization

773.1 Hemolytic disease due to ABO isoimmunization N
ABO hemolytic disease
ABO isoimmunization
Anemia / Erythroblastosis (fetalis) / Hemolytic disease (fetus) (newborn) / Jaundice — due to ABO: antibodies, isoimmunization, maternal/fetal incompatibility

AHA: 3Q, '92, 8

DEF: Incompatible Rh fetal-maternal blood grouping; prematurely destroys red blood cells; detected by Coombs test.

773.2 Hemolytic disease due to other and unspecified isoimmunization N
Eythroblastosis (fetalis) (neonatorum) NOS
Hemolytic disease (fetus) (newborn) NOS
Jaundice or anemia due to other and unspecified blood-group incompatibility

AHA: 1Q, '94, 13

773.3 Hydrops fetalis due to isoimmunization N
Use additional code to identify type of isoimmunization (773.0-773.2)

DEF: Massive edema of entire body and severe anemia; may result in fetal death or stillbirth.

773.4 Kernicterus due to isoimmunization N
Use additional code to identify type of isoimmunization (773.0-773.2)

DEF: Complication of erythroblastosis fetalis associated with severe neural symptoms, high blood bilirubin levels and nerve cell destruction; results in bilirubin-pigmented gray matter of central nervous system.

773.5 Late anemia due to isoimmunization N

✓4th **774 Other perinatal jaundice**

774.0 *Perinatal jaundice from hereditary hemolytic anemias* N
Code first underlying disease (282.0-282.9)

774.1 Perinatal jaundice from other excessive hemolysis N
Fetal or neonatal jaundice from:
bruising
drugs or toxins transmitted from mother
infection
polycythemia
swallowed maternal blood
Use additional code to identify cause

EXCLUDES *jaundice due to isoimmunization (773.0-773.2)*

774.2 Neonatal jaundice associated with preterm delivery N
Hyperbilirubinemia of prematurity
Jaundice due to delayed conjugation associated with preterm delivery

AHA: 3Q, '91, 21

✓5th **774.3 Neonatal jaundice due to delayed conjugation from other causes**

774.30 Neonatal jaundice due to delayed conjugation, cause unspecified N

DEF: Jaundice of newborn with abnormal bilirubin metabolism; causes excess accumulated unconjugated bilirubin in blood.

774.31 *Neonatal jaundice due to delayed conjugation in diseases classified elsewhere* N
Code first underlying diseases as:
congenital hypothyroidism (243)
Crigler-Najjar syndrome (277.4)
Gilbert's syndrome (277.4)

774.39 Other N
Jaundice due to delayed conjugation from causes, such as:
breast milk inhibitors
delayed development of conjugating system

774.4 Perinatal jaundice due to hepatocellular damage N
Fetal or neonatal hepatitis
Giant cell hepatitis
Inspissated bile syndrome

774.5 *Perinatal jaundice from other causes* N
Code first underlying cause as:
congenital obstruction of bile duct (751.61)
galactosemia (271.1)
mucoviscidosis (277.00-277.09)

774.6 Unspecified fetal and neonatal jaundice N
Icterus neonatorum
Neonatal hyperbilirubinemia (transient)
Physiologic jaundice NOS in newborn

EXCLUDES *that in preterm infants (774.2)*

AHA: 1Q, '94, 13; 2Q, '89, 15

774.7 Kernicterus not due to isoimmunization N
Bilirubin encephalopathy
Kernicterus of newborn NOS

EXCLUDES *kernicterus due to isoimmunization (773.4)*

✓4th **775 Endocrine and metabolic disturbances specific to the fetus and newborn**

INCLUDES transitory endocrine and metabolic disturbances caused by the infant's response to maternal endocrine and metabolic factors, its removal from them, or its adjustment to extrauterine existence

775.0 Syndrome of "infant of a diabetic mother" N
Maternal diabetes mellitus affecting fetus or newborn (with hypoglycemia)

AHA: 1Q, '04, 7-8; 3Q, '91, 5

775.1 Neonatal diabetes mellitus N
Diabetes mellitus syndrome in newborn infant

AHA: 3Q, '91, 6

775.2 Neonatal myasthenia gravis N

775.3 Neonatal thyrotoxicosis N
Neonatal hyperthydroidism (transient)

775.4 Hypocalcemia and hypomagnesemia of newborn N
Cow's milk hypocalcemia
Hypocalcemic tetany, neonatal
Neonatal hypoparathyroidism
Phosphate-loading hypocalcemia

775.5 Other transitory neonatal electrolyte disturbances N
Dehydration, neonatal

AHA: 1Q, '05, 9

775.6 Neonatal hypoglycemia N

EXCLUDES *infant of mother with diabetes mellitus (775.0)*

AHA: 1Q '94, 8

775.7 Late metabolic acidosis of newborn N

✓5th **775.8 Other neonatal endocrine and metabolic disturbances**

775.81 Other acidosis of newborn N
Acidemia NOS of newborn
Acidosis of newborn NOS
Mixed metabolic and respiratory acidosis of newborn

AHA: 4Q, '06, 104-106

775.89 Other neonatal endocrine and metabolic disturbances N
Amino-acid metabolic disorders described as transitory
AHA: 4Q, '06, 104-106

775.9 Unspecified endocrine and metabolic disturbances specific to the fetus and newborn N

▲ ✓4th **776 Hematological disorders of newborn**
INCLUDES ▶disorders specific to the newborn though possibly originating in utero◀
EXCLUDES ▶*fetal hematologic conditions (678.0)*◀

776.0 Hemorrhagic disease of newborn N
Hemorrhagic diathesis of newborn
Vitamin K deficiency of newborn
EXCLUDES *fetal or neonatal hemorrhage (772.0-772.9)*

776.1 Transient neonatal thrombocytopenia N
Neonatal thrombocytopenia due to:
exchange transfusion
idiopathic maternal thrombocytopenia
isoimmunization
DEF: Temporary decrease in blood platelets of newborn.

776.2 Disseminated intravascular coagulation in newborn N
DEF: Disseminated intravascular coagulation of newborn: clotting disorder due to excess thromboplastic agents in blood as a result of disease or trauma; causes blood clotting within vessels and reduces available elements necessary for blood coagulation.

776.3 Other transient neonatal disorders of coagulation N
Transient coagulation defect, newborn

776.4 Polycythemia neonatorum N
Plethora of newborn
Polycythemia due to:
donor twin transfusion
maternal-fetal transfusion
DEF: Abnormal increase of total red blood cells of newborn.

776.5 Congenital anemia N
Anemia following fetal blood loss
EXCLUDES *anemia due to isoimmunization (773.0-773.2, 773.5)*
hereditary hemolytic anemias (282.0-282.9)

776.6 Anemia of prematurity N

776.7 Transient neonatal neutropenia N
Isoimmune neutropenia
Maternal transfer neutropenia
EXCLUDES *congenital neutropenia (nontransient) (288.01)*
DEF: Decreased neutrophilic leukocytes in blood of newborn.

776.8 Other specified transient hematological disorders N

776.9 Unspecified hematological disorder specific to fetus or newborn N

✓4th **777 Perinatal disorders of digestive system**
INCLUDES disorders specific to the fetus and newborn
EXCLUDES *intestinal obstruction classifiable to 560.0-560.9*

777.1 Meconium obstruction N
Congenital fecaliths
Delayed passage of meconium
Meconium ileus NOS
Meconium plug syndrome
EXCLUDES *meconium ileus in cystic fibrosis (277.01)*
DEF: Meconium blocked digestive tract of newborn.

777.2 Intestinal obstruction due to inspissated milk N

777.3 Hematemesis and melena due to swallowed maternal blood N
Swallowed blood syndrome in newborn
EXCLUDES *that not due to swallowed maternal blood (772.4)*

777.4 Transitory ileus of newborn N
EXCLUDES *Hirschsprung's disease (751.3)*

▲ ✓5th **777.5 Necrotizing enterocolitis in newborn**
Pseudomembranous enterocolitis in newborn
DEF: Acute inflammation of small intestine due to pseudomembranous plaque over ulceration; may be due to aggressive antibiotic therapy.

● **777.50 Necrotizing enterocolitis in newborn, unspecified** N
Necrotizing enterocolitis in newborn, NOS

● **777.51 Stage I necrotizing enterocolitis in newborn** N

● **777.52 Stage II necrotizing enterocolitis in newborn** N
Necrotizing enterocolitis with pneumatosis, without perforation

● **777.53 Stage III necrotizing enterocolitis in newborn** N
Necrotizing enterocolitis with perforation
Necrotizing enterocolitis with pneumatosis and perforation

777.6 Perinatal intestinal perforation N
Meconium peritonitis

777.8 Other specified perinatal disorders of digestive system N

777.9 Unspecified perinatal disorder of digestive system N

778 Conditions involving the integument and temperature regulation of fetus and newborn

778.0 Hydrops fetalis not due to isoimmunization N
Idiopathic hydrops
EXCLUDES *hydrops fetalis due to isoimmunization (773.3)*
DEF: Edema of entire body, unrelated to immune response.

778.1 Sclerema neonatorum N
Subcutaneous fat necrosis
DEF: Diffuse, rapidly progressing white, waxy, nonpitting hardening of tissue, usually of legs and feet, life-threatening; found in preterm or debilitated infants; unknown etiology.

778.2 Cold injury syndrome of newborn N

778.3 Other hypothermia of newborn N

778.4 Other disturbances of temperature regulation of newborn N
Dehydration fever in newborn
Environmentally-induced pyrexia
Hyperthermia in newborn
Transitory fever of newborn

778.5 Other and unspecified edema of newborn N
Edema neonatorum

778.6 Congenital hydrocele
Congenital hydrocele of tunica vaginalis

778.7 Breast engorgement in newborn N
Noninfective mastitis of newborn
EXCLUDES *infective mastitis of newborn (771.5)*

778.8 Other specified conditions involving the integument of fetus and newborn N
Urticaria neonatorum
EXCLUDES *impetigo neonatorum (684)*
pemphigus neonatorum (684)

778.9 Unspecified condition involving the integument and temperature regulation of fetus and newborn N

4th 779 Other and ill-defined conditions originating in the perinatal period

779.0 Convulsions in newborn N

Fits } in newborn
Seizures } in newborn

AHA: N-D, '94, 11

779.1 Other and unspecified cerebral irritability in newborn N

779.2 Cerebral depression, coma, and other abnormal cerebral signs N

Cerebral ischemia NOS of newborn
CNS dysfunction in newborn NOS

EXCLUDES *cerebral ischemia due to birth trauma (767.0)*
intrauterine cerebral ischemia (768.2-768.9)
intraventricular hemorrhage (772.10-772.14)

779.3 Feeding problems in newborn N

Regurgitation of food } in newborn
Slow feeding } in newborn
Vomiting } in newborn

AHA: 2Q, '89, 15

779.4 Drug reactions and intoxications specific to newborn N

Gray syndrome from chloramphenicol administration in newborn

EXCLUDES *fetal alcohol syndrome (760.71)*
reactions and intoxications from maternal opiates and tranquilizers (763.5)

779.5 Drug withdrawal syndrome in newborn N

Drug withdrawal syndrome in infant of dependent mother

EXCLUDES *fetal alcohol syndrome (760.71)*

AHA: 3Q, '94, 6

779.6 Termination of pregnancy (fetus) N

Fetal death due to:
induced abortion
termination of pregnancy

EXCLUDES *spontaneous abortion (fetus) (761.8)*

779.7 Periventricular leukomalacia

AHA: 4Q, '01, 50, 51

DEF: Necrosis of white matter adjacent to lateral ventricles with the formation of cysts; cause of PVL has not been firmly established, but thought to be related to inadequate blood flow in certain areas of the brain.

5th 779.8 Other specified conditions originating in the perinatal period

AHA: 4Q, '02, 67; 1Q, '94, 15

779.81 Neonatal bradycardia N

EXCLUDES *abnormality in fetal heart rate or rhythm complicating labor and delivery (763.81-763.83)*
bradycardia due to birth asphyxia (768.5-768.9)

779.82 Neonatal tachycardia N

EXCLUDES *abnormality in fetal heart rate or rhythm complicating labor and delivery (763.81-763.83)*

779.83 Delayed separation of umbilical cord N

AHA: 4Q, '03, 71

779.84 Meconium staining N

EXCLUDES *meconium aspiration (770.11, 770.12)*
meconium passage during delivery (763.84)

AHA: 4Q, '05, 83, 88

779.85 Cardiac arrest of newborn N

AHA: 4Q, '06, 104-106

779.89 Other specified conditions originating in the perinatal period N

Use additional code to specify condition

AHA: 1Q, '06, 18; 2Q, '05, 15; 1Q, '05, 9

779.9 Unspecified condition originating in the perinatal period N

Congenital debility NOS
Stillbirth NEC

16. SYMPTOMS, SIGNS, AND ILL-DEFINED CONDITIONS (780-799)

This section includes symptoms, signs, abnormal results of laboratory or other investigative procedures, and ill-defined conditions regarding which no diagnosis classifiable elsewhere is recorded.

Signs and symptoms that point rather definitely to a given diagnosis are assigned to some category in the preceding part of the classification. In general, categories 780-796 include the more ill-defined conditions and symptoms that point with perhaps equal suspicion to two or more diseases or to two or more systems of the body, and without the necessary study of the case to make a final diagnosis. Practically all categories in this group could be designated as "not otherwise specified," or as "unknown etiology," or as "transient." The Alphabetic Index should be consulted to determine which symptoms and signs are to be allocated here and which to more specific sections of the classification; the residual subcategories numbered .9 are provided for other relevant symptoms which cannot be allocated elsewhere in the classification.

The conditions and signs or symptoms included in categories 780-796 consist of: (a) cases for which no more specific diagnosis can be made even after all facts bearing on the case have been investigated; (b) signs or symptoms existing at the time of initial encounter that proved to be transient and whose causes could not be determined; (c) provisional diagnoses in a patient who failed to return for further investigation or care; (d) cases referred elsewhere for investigation or treatment before the diagnosis was made; (e) cases in which a more precise diagnosis was not available for any other reason; (f) certain symptoms which represent important problems in medical care and which it might be desired to classify in addition to a known cause.

SYMPTOMS (780-789)

AHA: 1Q, '91, 12; 2Q, '90, 3; 2Q, '90, 5; 2Q, '90, 15; M-A, '85, 3

✓4th **780 General symptoms**

✓5th **780.0 Alteration of consciousness**

EXCLUDES *coma:*
diabetic ►(249.2-249.3, 250.2-250.3)◄
hepatic (572.2)
originating in the perinatal period (779.2)

AHA: 4Q, '92, 20

780.01 Coma

AHA: 3Q, '96, 16

DEF: State of unconsciousness from which the patient cannot be awakened.

780.02 Transient alteration of awareness

DEF: Temporary, recurring spells of reduced consciousness.

780.03 Persistent vegetative state

DEF: Persistent wakefulness without consciousness due to nonfunctioning cerebral cortex.

780.09 Other

Drowsiness
Semicoma
Somnolence
Stupor
Unconsciousness

780.1 Hallucinations

Hallucinations:
NOS
auditory
gustatory
olfactory
tactile

EXCLUDES *those associated with mental disorders, as functional psychoses (295.0-298.9)*
organic brain syndromes (290.0-294.9, 310.0-310.9)
visual hallucinations (368.16)

DEF: Perception of external stimulus in absence of stimulus; inability to distinguish between real and imagined.

780.2 Syncope and collapse

Blackout
Fainting
(Near) (Pre) syncope
Vasovagal attack

EXCLUDES *carotid sinus syncope (337.0)*
heat syncope (992.1)
neurocirculatory asthenia (306.2)
orthostatic hypotension (458.0)
shock NOS (785.50)

AHA: 1Q, '02, 6; 3Q, '00, 12; 3Q, '95, 14; N-D, '85, 12

DEF: Sudden unconsciousness due to reduced blood flow to brain.

✓5th **780.3 Convulsions**

EXCLUDES *convulsions:*
epileptic (345.10-345.91)
in newborn (779.0)

AHA: 2Q, '97, 8; 1Q, '97, 12; 3Q, '94, 9; 1Q, '93, 24; 4Q, '92, 23; N-D, '87, 12

DEF: Sudden, involuntary contractions of the muscles.

780.31 Febrile convulsions (simple), unspecified

Febrile seizure NOS

AHA: 4Q, '97, 45

780.32 Complex febrile convulsions

Febrile seizure:
atypical
complex
complicated

EXCLUDES *status epilepticus (345.3)*

AHA: 4Q, '06, 106

780.39 Other convulsions

Convulsive disorder NOS
Fit NOS
Recurrent convulsions NOS
Seizure NOS

AHA: ►1Q, '08, 17;◄ 3Q, '06, 22; 4Q, '04, 51; 1Q, '03, 7; 2Q, '99, 17; 4Q, '98, 39

780.4 Dizziness and giddiness

Light-headedness
Vertigo NOS

EXCLUDES *Ménière's disease and other specified vertiginous syndromes (386.0-386.9)*

AHA: 2Q, '03, 11; 3Q, '00, 12; 2Q, '97, 9; 2Q, '91, 17

DEF: Whirling sensations in head with feeling of falling.

✓5th **780.5 Sleep disturbances**

EXCLUDES *circadian rhythm sleep disorders (327.30-327.39)*
organic hypersomnia (327.10-327.19)
organic insomnia (327.00-327.09)
organic sleep apnea (327.20-327.29)
organic sleep related movement disorders (327.51-327.59)
parasomnias (327.40-327.49)
that of nonorganic origin (307.40-307.49)

AHA: 4Q, '05, 59

780.50 Sleep disturbance, unspecified

780.51 Insomnia with sleep apnea, unspecified

DEF: Transient cessation of breathing disturbing sleep.

780.52 Insomnia, unspecified

DEF: Inability to maintain adequate sleep cycle.

780.53 Hypersomnia with sleep apnea, unspecified

AHA: 1Q, '93, 28; N-D, '85, 4

DEF: Autonomic response inhibited during sleep; causes insufficient oxygen intake, acidosis and pulmonary hypertension.

780.54 Hypersomnia, unspecified
DEF: Prolonged sleep cycle.

780.55 Disruptions of 24 hour sleep wake cycle, unspecified

780.56 Dysfunctions associated with sleep stages or arousal from sleep

780.57 Unspecified sleep apnea
AHA: 1Q, '01, 6; 1Q, '97, 5; 1Q, '93, 28

780.58 Sleep related movement disorder, unspecified
EXCLUDES *restless legs syndrome (333.94)*
AHA: 4Q, '04, 95

780.59 Other

▲ ✓5th **780.6 Fever and other physiologic disturbances of temperature regulation**
EXCLUDES ▶*effects of reduced environmental temperature (991.0-991.9)*
effects of heat and light (992.0-992.9)
fever, chills or hypothermia associated with confirmed infection – code to infection◀
AHA: 3Q, '05, 16; 3Q, '00,13; 4Q, '99, 26; 2Q, '91, 8

● **780.60 Fever, unspecified**
Chills with fever
Fever NOS
Fever of unknown origin (FUO)
Hyperpyrexia NOS
Pyrexia NOS
Pyrexia of unknown origin
EXCLUDES *chills without fever (780.64)*
neonatal fever (778.4)
pyrexia of unknown origin (during):
in newborn (778.4)
labor (659.2)
the puerperium (672)

● **780.61 Fever presenting with conditions classified elsewhere**
Code first underlying condition when associated fever is present, such as with:
leukemia (conditions classifiable to 204-208)
neutropenia (288.00-288.09)
sickle-cell disease (282.60-282.69)

● **780.62 Postprocedural fever**
EXCLUDES *postvaccination fever (780.63)*

● **780.63 Postvaccination fever**
Postimmunization fever

● **780.64 Chills (without fever)**
Chills NOS
EXCLUDES *chills with fever (780.60)*

● **780.65 Hypothermia not associated with low environmental temperature**
EXCLUDES *hypothermia:*
associated with low environmental temperature (991.6)
due to anesthesia (995.89)
of newborn (778.2, 778.3)

✓5th **780.7 Malaise and fatigue**
EXCLUDES *debility, unspecified (799.3)*
fatigue (during):
combat (308.0-308.9)
heat (992.6)
pregnancy (646.8)
neurasthenia (300.5)
senile asthenia (797)
AHA: 4Q, '88, 12; M-A, '87, 8

780.71 Chronic fatigue syndrome
AHA: 4Q, '98, 48
DEF: Persistent fatigue, symptoms include weak muscles, sore throat, lymphadenitis, headache, depression and mild fever; no known cause; also called chronic mononucleosis, benign myalgic encephalomyelitis, Iceland disease and neurosthenia.

● **780.72 Functional quadriplegia**
Complete immobility due to severe physical disability or frailty
EXCLUDES *hysterical paralysis (300.11)*
immobility syndrome (728.3)
neurologic quadriplegia (344.00-344.09)
quadriplegia NOS (344.00)

780.79 Other malaise and fatigue
Asthenia NOS
Lethargy
Postviral (asthenic) syndrome
Tiredness
AHA: 4Q, '04, 78; 1Q, '00, 6; 4Q, '99, 26
DEF: Asthenia: Any weakness, lack of strength or loss of energy, especially neuromuscular.
DEF: Lethargy: Listlessness, drowsiness, stupor and apathy.
DEF: Malaise: Vague feeling of debility or lack of good health.
DEF: Postviral (asthenic) syndrome: Listlessness, drowsiness, stupor and apathy; follows acute viral infection.
DEF: Tiredness: General exhaustion or fatigue.

780.8 Generalized hyperhidrosis
Diaphoresis
Excessive sweating
Secondary hyperhidrosis
EXCLUDES *focal (localized) (primary) (secondary) hyperhidrosis (705.21-705.22)*
Frey's syndrome (705.22)
DEF: Excessive sweating, appears as droplets on skin; general or localized.

✓5th **780.9 Other general symptoms**
EXCLUDES *hypothermia:*
NOS (accidental) (991.6)
due to anesthesia (995.89)
of newborn (778.2-778.3)
memory disturbance as part of a pattern of mental disorder
AHA: 4Q, '02, 67; 4Q, '99, 10; 3Q, '93, 11; N-D, '85, 12

780.91 Fussy infant (baby) P

780.92 Excessive crying of infant (baby) N
EXCLUDES *excessive crying of child, adolescent or adult (780.95)*

780.93 Memory loss
Amnesia (retrograde)
Memory loss NOS
EXCLUDES *mild memory disturbance due to organic brain damage (310.1)*
transient global amnesia (437.7)
AHA: 4Q, '03, 71

780.94 Early satiety
AHA: 4Q, '03, 72
DEF: The premature feeling of being full; mechanism of satiety is mutlifactorial.

780.95 Excessive crying of child, adolescent, or adult
EXCLUDES *excessive crying of infant (baby) (780.92)*
AHA: 4Q, '05, 89

780.96 Generalized pain
Pain NOS
AHA: 4Q, '06, 79-81

780.97 Altered mental status
Change in mental status
EXCLUDES *altered level of consciousness (780.01-780.09)*
altered mental status due to known condition–code to condition
delirium NOS (780.09)
AHA: 4Q, '06, 107

780.99 Other general symptoms
AHA: 4Q, '03, 103

✓4th **781 Symptoms involving nervous and musculoskeletal systems**
EXCLUDES *depression NOS (311)*
disorders specifically relating to:
back (724.0-724.9)
hearing (388.0-389.9)
joint (718.0-719.9)
limb (729.0-729.9)
neck (723.0-723.9)
vision (368.0-369.9)
pain in limb (729.5)

781.0 Abnormal involuntary movements
Abnormal head movements
Fasciculation
Spasms NOS
Tremor NOS
EXCLUDES *abnormal reflex (796.1)*
chorea NOS (333.5)
infantile spasms (345.60-345.61)
spastic paralysis (342.1, 343.0-344.9)
specified movement disorders classifiable to 333 (333.0-333.9)
that of nonorganic origin (307.2-307.3)

781.1 Disturbances of sensation of smell and taste
Anosmia
Parageusia
Parosmia
DEF: Anosmia: loss of sense of smell due to organic factors, including loss of olfactory nerve conductivity, cerebral disease, nasal fossae formation and peripheral olfactory nerve diseases; can also be psychological disorder.
DEF: Parageusia: distorted sense of taste, or bad taste in mouth.
DEF: Parosmia: distorted sense of smell.

781.2 Abnormality of gait
Gait:
ataxic
paralytic
spastic
staggering
EXCLUDES *ataxia:*
NOS (781.3)
locomotor (progressive) (094.0)
difficulty in walking (719.7)
AHA: 2Q, '05, 6; 2Q, '04, 15
DEF: Abnormal, asymmetric gait.

781.3 Lack of coordination
Ataxia NOS
Muscular incoordination
EXCLUDES *ataxic gait (781.2)*
cerebellar ataxia (334.0-334.9)
difficulty in walking (719.7)
vertigo NOS (780.4)
AHA: 4Q, '04, 51; 3Q, '97, 12

781.4 Transient paralysis of limb
Monoplegia, transient NOS
EXCLUDES *paralysis (342.0-344.9)*

781.5 Clubbing of fingers
DEF: Enlarged soft tissue of distal fingers.

781.6 Meningismus
Dupré's syndrome
Meningism
AHA: 3Q, '00,13; J-F, '87, 7
DEF: Condition with signs and symptoms that resemble meningeal irritation; it is associated with febrile illness and dehydration with no evidence of infection.

781.7 Tetany
Carpopedal spasm
EXCLUDES *tetanus neonatorum (771.3)*
tetany:
hysterical (300.11)
newborn (hypocalcemic) (775.4)
parathyroid (252.1)
psychogenic (306.0)
DEF: Nerve and muscle hyperexcitability; symptoms include muscle spasms, twitching, cramps, laryngospasm with inspiratory stridor, hyperreflexia and choreiform movements.

781.8 Neurologic neglect syndrome
Asomatognosia
Hemi-akinesia
Hemi-inattention
Hemispatial neglect
Left-sided neglect
Sensory extinction
Sensory neglect
Visuospatial neglect
AHA: 4Q, '94, 37

✓5th **781.9 Other symptoms involving nervous and musculoskeletal systems**
AHA: 4Q, '00, 45

781.91 Loss of height
EXCLUDES *osteoporosis (733.00-733.09)*

781.92 Abnormal posture

781.93 Ocular torticollis
AHA: 4Q, '02, 68
DEF: Abnormal head posture as a result of a contracted state of cervical muscles to correct a visual disturbance; either double vision or a visual field defect.

781.94 Facial weakness
Facial droop
EXCLUDES *facial weakness due to late effect of cerebrovascular accident (438.83)*
AHA: 4Q, '03, 72

781.99 Other symptoms involving nervous and musculoskeletal systems

✓4th **782 Symptoms involving skin and other integumentary tissue**
EXCLUDES *symptoms relating to breast (611.71-611.79)*

782.0 Disturbance of skin sensation
Anesthesia of skin
Burning or prickling sensation
Hyperesthesia
Hypoesthesia
Numbness
Paresthesia
Tingling

782.1 Rash and other nonspecific skin eruption
Exanthem
EXCLUDES *vesicular eruption (709.8)*

782.2 Localized superficial swelling, mass, or lump
Subcutaneous nodules
EXCLUDES *localized adiposity (278.1)*

782.3 Edema
Anasarca
Dropsy
Localized edema NOS
EXCLUDES *ascites (789.51-789.59)*
edema of:
newborn NOS (778.5)
pregnancy (642.0-642.9, 646.1)
fluid retention (276.6)
hydrops fetalis (773.3, 778.0)
hydrothorax ►(511.81-511.89)◄
nutritional edema (260, 262)

AHA: 2Q, '00, 18
DEF: Edema: excess fluid in intercellular body tissue.
DEF: Anasarca: massive edema in all body tissues.
DEF: Dropsy: serous fluid accumulated in body cavity or cellular tissue.
DEF: Localized edema: edema in specific body areas.

782.4 Jaundice, unspecified, not of newborn
Cholemia NOS
Icterus NOS
EXCLUDES *jaundice in newborn (774.0-774.7)*
due to isoimmunization (773.0-773.2, 773.4)

DEF: Bilirubin deposits of skin, causing yellow cast.

782.5 Cyanosis
EXCLUDES *newborn (770.83)*

DEF: Deficient oxygen of blood; causes blue cast to skin.

✓5th **782.6 Pallor and flushing**

782.61 Pallor

782.62 Flushing
Excessive blushing

782.7 Spontaneous ecchymoses
Petechiae
EXCLUDES *ecchymosis in fetus or newborn (772.6)*
purpura (287.0-287.9)

DEF: Hemorrhagic spots of skin; resemble freckles.

782.8 Changes in skin texture
Induration } of skin
Thickening } of skin

782.9 Other symptoms involving skin and integumentary tissues

✓4th **783 Symptoms concerning nutrition, metabolism, and development**

783.0 Anorexia
Loss of appetite
EXCLUDES *anorexia nervosa (307.1)*
loss of appetite of nonorganic origin (307.59)

783.1 Abnormal weight gain
EXCLUDES *excessive weight gain in pregnancy (646.1)*
obesity (278.00)
morbid (278.01)

✓5th **783.2 Abnormal loss of weight and underweight**
Use additional code to identify Body Mass Index (BMI), if known (V85.0-V85.54)

AHA: 4Q, '00, 45

783.21 Loss of weight
AHA: 4Q, '05, 96

783.22 Underweight
AHA: 4Q, '05, 96

783.3 Feeding difficulties and mismanagement
Feeding problem (elderly) (infant)
EXCLUDES *feeding disturbance or problems:*
in newborn (779.3)
of nonorganic origin (307.50-307.59)

AHA: 3Q, '97, 12

✓5th **783.4 Lack of expected normal physiological development in childhood**
EXCLUDES *delay in sexual development and puberty (259.0)*
gonadal dysgenesis (758.6)
pituitary dwarfism (253.3)
slow fetal growth and fetal malnutrition (764.00-764.99)
specific delays in mental development (315.0-315.9)

AHA: 4Q, '00, 45; 3Q, '97, 4

783.40 Lack of normal physiological development, unspecified
Inadequate development
Lack of development

783.41 Failure to thrive P
Failure to gain weight

AHA: 1Q, '03, 12
DEF: Organic failure to thrive: acute or chronic illness that interferes with nutritional intake, absorption, metabolism excretion and energy requirements. Nonorganic FTT is symptom of neglect or abuse.

783.42 Delayed milestones P
Late talker
Late walker

783.43 Short stature
Growth failure
Growth retardation
Lack of growth
Physical retardation

DEF: Constitutional short stature: stature inconsistent with chronological age. Genetic short stature is when skeletal maturation matches chronological age.

783.5 Polydipsia
Excessive thirst

783.6 Polyphagia
Excessive eating
Hyperalimentation NOS
EXCLUDES *disorders of eating of nonorganic origin (307.50-307.59)*

783.7 Adult failure to thrive A

783.9 Other symptoms concerning nutrition, metabolism, and development
Hypometabolism
EXCLUDES *abnormal basal metabolic rate (794.7)*
dehydration (276.51)
other disorders of fluid, electrolyte, and acid-base balance (276.0-276.9)

AHA: 2Q, '04, 3

✓4th **784 Symptoms involving head and neck**
EXCLUDES *encephalopathy NOS (348.30)*
specific symptoms involving neck classifiable to 723 (723.0-723.9)

784.0 Headache
Facial pain
Pain in head NOS
EXCLUDES *atypical face pain (350.2)*
migraine (346.0-346.9)
tension headache (307.81)

AHA: 3Q, '06, 22; 2Q, '06, 17; 3Q, '00, 13; 1Q, '90, 4; 3Q, '92, 14

784.1 Throat pain

EXCLUDES *dysphagia (787.20-787.29)*
neck pain (723.1)
sore throat (462)
chronic (472.1)

784.2 Swelling, mass, or lump in head and neck

Space-occupying lesion, intracranial NOS

AHA: 1Q, '03, 8

784.3 Aphasia

EXCLUDES *aphasia due to late effects of cerebrovascular disease (438.11)*
developmental aphasia (315.31)

AHA: 4Q, '04, 78; 4Q, '98, 87; 3Q, '97, 12

DEF: Inability to communicate through speech, written word, or sign language.

✓5th **784.4 Voice disturbance**

784.40 Voice disturbance, unspecified

784.41 Aphonia

Loss of voice

784.49 Other

Change in voice
Dysphonia
Hoarseness
Hypernasality
Hyponasality

784.5 Other speech disturbance

Dysarthria
Dysphasia
Slurred speech

EXCLUDES *stammering and stuttering (307.0)*
that of nonorganic origin (307.0, 307.9)

✓5th **784.6 Other symbolic dysfunction**

EXCLUDES *developmental learning delays (315.0-315.9)*

784.60 Symbolic dysfunction, unspecified

784.61 Alexia and dyslexia

Alexia (with agraphia)

DEF: Alexia: Inability to understand written word due to central brain lesion.

DEF: Dyslexia: Ability to recognize letters but inability to read, spell, and write words; genetic.

784.69 Other

Acalculia
Agnosia
Agraphia NOS
Apraxia

784.7 Epistaxis

Hemorrhage from nose   Nosebleed

AHA: 3Q, '04, 7

784.8 Hemorrhage from throat

EXCLUDES *hemoptysis (786.3)*

✓5th **784.9 Other symptoms involving head and neck**

784.91 Postnasal drip

AHA: 4Q, '06, 108

784.99 Other symptoms involving head and neck

Choking sensation
Feeling of foreign body in throat
Halitosis
Mouth breathing
Sneezing

EXCLUDES *foreign body in throat (933.0)*

AHA: 4Q, '06, 108

✓4th **785 Symptoms involving cardiovascular system**

EXCLUDES *heart failure NOS (428.9)*

785.0 Tachycardia, unspecified

Rapid heart beat

EXCLUDES *neonatal tachycardia (779.82)*
paroxysmal tachycardia (427.0-427.2)

AHA: 2Q, '03, 11

DEF: Excessively rapid heart rate.

785.1 Palpitations

Awareness of heart beat

EXCLUDES *specified dysrhythmias (427.0-427.9)*

785.2 Undiagnosed cardiac murmurs

Heart murmurs NOS

AHA: 4Q, '92, 16

785.3 Other abnormal heart sounds

Cardiac dullness, increased or decreased
Friction fremitus, cardiac
Precordial friction

785.4 Gangrene

Gangrene:
NOS
spreading cutaneous
Gangrenous cellulitis
Phagedena

Code first any associated underlying condition

EXCLUDES *gangrene of certain sites – see Alphabetic Index*
gangrene with atherosclerosis of the extremities (440.24)
gas gangrene (040.0

AHA: 1Q, '04, 14; 3Q, '91, 12; 3Q, '90, 15; M-A, '86, 12

DEF: Gangrene: necrosis of skin tissue due to bacterial infection, diabetes, embolus and vascular supply loss.

DEF: Gangrenous cellulitis: group A streptococcal infection; begins with severe cellulitis, spreads to superficial and deep fascia; produces gangrene of underlying tissues.

✓5th **785.5 Shock without mention of trauma**

785.50 Shock, unspecified

Failure of peripheral circulation

AHA: 2Q, '96, 10

DEF: Peripheral circulatory failure due to heart insufficiencies.

785.51 Cardiogenic shock

AHA: 3Q, '05, 14

DEF: Shock syndrome: associated with myocardial infarction, cardiac tamponade and massive pulmonary embolism; symptoms include mental confusion, reduced blood pressure, tachycardia, pallor and cold, clammy skin.

785.52 Septic shock

Shock:
endotoxic
gram-negative

Code first:
systemic inflammatory response syndrome due to infectious process with organ dysfunction (995.92)

AHA: 4Q, '06, 113; 2Q, '05, 18-19; 4Q, '03, 73, 79

785.59 Other
Shock:
hypovolemic
EXCLUDES *shock (due to):*
anesthetic (995.4)
anaphylactic (995.0)
due to serum (999.4)
electric (994.8)
following abortion (639.5)
lightning (994.0)
obstetrical (669.1)
postoperative (998.0)
traumatic (958.4)
AHA: 2Q, '00, 3

785.6 Enlargement of lymph nodes
Lymphadenopathy
"Swollen glands"
EXCLUDES *lymphadenitis (chronic) (289.1-289.3)*
acute (683)

785.9 Other symptoms involving cardiovascular system
Bruit (arterial)
Weak pulse

✓4th 786 Symptoms involving respiratory system and other chest symptoms

✓5th 786.0 Dyspnea and respiratory abnormalities

786.00 Respiratory abnormality, unspecified

786.01 Hyperventilation
EXCLUDES *hyperventilation, psychogenic (306.1)*
DEF: Rapid breathing causes carbon dioxide loss from blood.

786.02 Orthopnea
DEF: Difficulty breathing except in upright position.

786.03 Apnea
EXCLUDES *apnea of newborn (770.81, 770.82)*
sleep apnea (780.51, 780.53, 780.57)
AHA: 4Q, '98, 50
DEF: Cessation of breathing.

786.04 Cheyne-Stokes respiration
AHA: 4Q, '98, 50
DEF: Rhythmic increase of depth and frequency of breathing with apnea; occurs in frontal lobe and diencephalic dysfunction.

786.05 Shortness of breath
AHA: 4Q, '99, 25; 1Q, '99, 6; 4Q, '98, 50
DEF: Inability to take in sufficient oxygen.

786.06 Tachypnea
EXCLUDES *transitory tachypnea of newborn (770.6)*
AHA: 4Q, '98, 50
DEF: Abnormal rapid respiratory rate; called hyperventilation.

786.07 Wheezing
EXCLUDES *asthma (493.00-493.92)*
AHA: 4Q, '98, 50
DEF: Stenosis of respiratory passageway; causes whistling sound; due to asthma, coryza, croup, emphysema, hay fever, edema, and pleural effusion.

786.09 Other
Respiratory:
distress
insufficiency
EXCLUDES *respiratory distress:*
following trauma and surgery (518.5)
newborn (770.89)
syndrome (newborn) (769)
adult (518.5)
respiratory failure (518.81, 518.83-518.84)
newborn (770.84)
AHA: 4Q, '05, 90; 2Q, '98, 10; 1Q, '97, 7; 1Q, '90, 9

786.1 Stridor
EXCLUDES *congenital laryngeal stridor (748.3)*
DEF: Obstructed airway causes harsh sound.

786.2 Cough
EXCLUDES *cough:*
psychogenic (306.1)
smokers' (491.0)
with hemorrhage (786.3)
AHA: 4Q, '99, 26

786.3 Hemoptysis
Cough with hemorrhage
Pulmonary hemorrhage NOS
EXCLUDES *pulmonary hemorrhage of newborn (770.3)*
AHA: 2Q, '06, 17; 4Q, '90, 26
DEF: Coughing up blood or blood-stained sputum.

786.4 Abnormal sputum
Abnormal:
amount }
color } (of) sputum
odor }
Excessive }

✓5th 786.5 Chest pain

786.50 Chest pain, unspecified
AHA: 1Q, '07, 19; 2Q, '06, 7; 1Q, '03, 6; 1Q, '02, 4; 4Q, '99, 25

786.51 Precordial pain
DEF: Chest pain over heart and lower thorax.

786.52 Painful respiration
Pain:
anterior chest wall
pleuritic
Pleurodynia
EXCLUDES *epidemic pleurodynia (074.1)*
AHA: N-D, '84, 17

786.59 Other
Discomfort }
Pressure } in chest
Tightness }
EXCLUDES *pain in breast (611.71)*
AHA: 1Q, '02, 6

786.6 Swelling, mass, or lump in chest
EXCLUDES *lump in breast (611.72)*

786.7 Abnormal chest sounds
Abnormal percussion, chest
Friction sounds, chest
Rales
Tympany, chest
EXCLUDES *wheezing (786.07)*

786.8 Hiccough
EXCLUDES *psychogenic hiccough (306.1)*

786.9 Other symptoms involving respiratory system and chest
Breath-holding spell

4th 787 Symptoms involving digestive system

EXCLUDES *constipation (564.00-564.09)*
pylorospasm (537.81)
congenital (750.5)

5th 787.0 Nausea and vomiting
Emesis
EXCLUDES *hematemesis NOS (578.0)*
vomiting:
bilious, following gastrointestinal surgery (564.3)
cyclical (536.2)
▶associated with migraine (346.2)◀
psychogenic (306.4)
excessive, in pregnancy (643.0-643.9)
habit (536.2)
of newborn (779.3)
psychogenic NOS (307.54)

AHA: M-A, '85, 11

787.01 Nausea with vomiting
AHA: 1Q, '03, 5

787.02 Nausea alone
AHA: 3Q, '00, 12; 2Q, '97, 9

787.03 Vomiting alone

787.1 Heartburn
Pyrosis
Waterbrash
EXCLUDES *dyspepsia or indigestion (536.8)*
AHA: 2Q, '01, 6

5th 787.2 Dysphagia
Code first, if applicable, dysphagia due to late effect of cerebrovascular accident (438.82)
AHA: 4Q, '07, 92-94; 3Q, '07, 7; 4Q, '03, 103, 109; 2Q, '01, 4

787.20 Dysphagia, unspecified
Difficulty in swallowing NOS

787.21 Dysphagia, oral phase

787.22 Dysphagia, oropharyngeal phase
AHA: 4Q, '07, 94

787.23 Dysphagia, pharyngeal phase

787.24 Dysphagia, pharyngoesophageal phase

787.29 Other dysphagia
Cervical dysphagia
Neurogenic dysphagia

787.3 Flatulence, eructation, and gas pain
Abdominal distention (gaseous)
Bloating
Tympanites (abdominal) (intestinal)
EXCLUDES *aerophagy (306.4)*
DEF: Flatulence: excess air or gas in intestine or stomach.
DEF: Eructation: belching, expelling gas through mouth.
DEF: Gas pain: gaseous pressure affecting gastrointestinal system.

787.4 Visible peristalsis
Hyperperistalsis
DEF: Increase in involuntary movements of intestines.

787.5 Abnormal bowel sounds
Absent bowel sounds
Hyperactive bowel sounds

787.6 Incontinence of feces
Encopresis NOS
Incontinence of sphincter ani
EXCLUDES *that of nonorganic origin (307.7)*
AHA: 1Q, '97, 9

787.7 Abnormal feces
Bulky stools
EXCLUDES *abnormal stool content (792.1)*
melena:
NOS (578.1)
newborn (772.4, 777.3)

Phases of Swallowing

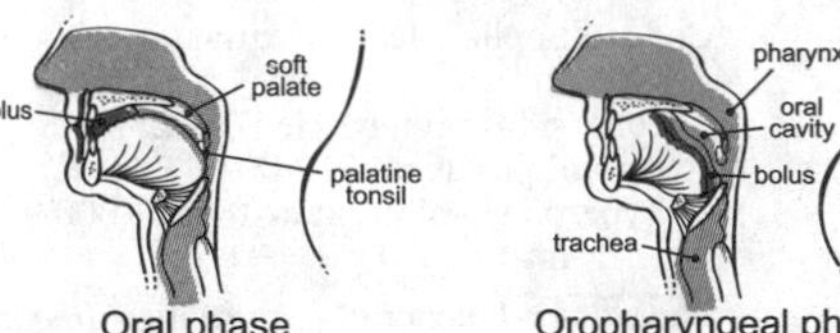

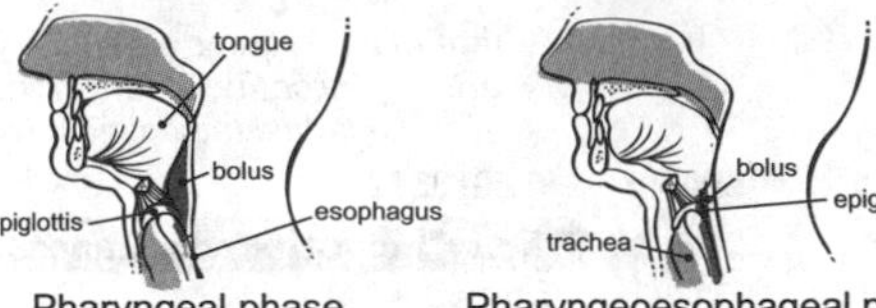

5th 787.9 Other symptoms involving digestive system
EXCLUDES *gastrointestinal hemorrhage (578.0-578.9)*
intestinal obstruction (560.0-560.9)
specific functional digestive disorders:
esophagus (530.0-530.9)
stomach and duodenum (536.0-536.9)
those not elsewhere classified (564.00-564.9)

787.91 Diarrhea
Diarrhea NOS
AHA: 4Q, '95, 54

787.99 Other
Change in bowel habits
Tenesmus (rectal)
DEF: Tenesmus: Painful, ineffective straining at the rectum with limited passage of fecal matter.

4th 788 Symptoms involving urinary system

EXCLUDES *hematuria ▶(599.70-599.72)◀*
nonspecific findings on examination of the urine (791.0-791.9)
small kidney of unknown cause (589.0-589.9)
uremia NOS (586)
urinary obstruction (599.60, 599.69)

788.0 Renal colic
Colic (recurrent) of:
kidney
ureter
AHA: 3Q, '04, 8
DEF: Kidney pain.

788.1 Dysuria
Painful urination
Strangury

5th 788.2 Retention of urine
Code, if applicable, any causal condition first, such as:
hyperplasia of prostate (600.0-600.9 with fifth-digit 1)
DEF: Accumulation of urine in the bladder due to inability to void

788.20 Retention of urine, unspecified
AHA: 4Q, '06, 93, 95; 2Q, '04, 18; 3Q, '03, 12-13; 1Q, '03, 6; 3Q, '96, 10

788.21 Incomplete bladder emptying
AHA: 4Q, '06, 93

788.29 Other specified retention of urine

✓5th **788.3 Urinary incontinence**

Code, if applicable, any causal condition first, such as:
congenital ureterocele (753.23)
genital prolapse (618.00-618.9)
hyperplasia of prostate (600.0-600.9 with fifth-digit 1)

EXCLUDES ►*functional urinary incontinence (788.91)*◄
that of nonorganic origin (307.6)
►*urinary incontinence associated with cognitive impairment (788.91)*◄

AHA: 4Q, '06, 93; 4Q, '92, 22

788.30 Urinary incontinence, unspecified
Enuresis NOS

788.31 Urge incontinence
AHA: 1Q, '00, 19
DEF: Inability to control urination, upon urge to urinate.

788.32 Stress incontinence, male ♂
EXCLUDES *stress incontinence, female (625.6)*
DEF: Inability to control urination associated with weak sphincter in males.

788.33 Mixed incontinence, (male) (female)
Urge and stress
DEF: Urge, stress incontinence: involuntary discharge of urine due to anatomic displacement.

788.34 Incontinence without sensory awareness
DEF: Involuntary discharge of urine without sensory warning.

788.35 Post-void dribbling
DEF: Involuntary discharge of residual urine after voiding.

788.36 Nocturnal enuresis
DEF: Involuntary discharge of urine during the night.

788.37 Continuous leakage
DEF: Continuous, involuntary urine seepage.

788.38 Overflow incontinence
DEF: Leakage caused by pressure of retained urine in the bladder after the bladder has fully contracted due to weakened bladder muscles or an obstruction of the urethra.

788.39 Other urinary incontinence

✓5th **788.4 Frequency of urination and polyuria**

Code, if applicable, any causal condition first, such as:
hyperplasia of prostate (600.0-600.9 with fifth-digit 1)

788.41 Urinary frequency
Frequency of micturition
AHA: 4Q, '06, 93

788.42 Polyuria
DEF: Excessive urination.

788.43 Nocturia
AHA: 4Q, '06, 93
DEF: Urination affecting sleep patterns.

788.5 Oliguria and anuria

Deficient secretion of urine
Suppression of urinary secretion

EXCLUDES *that complicating:*
abortion (634-638 with .3, 639.3)
ectopic or molar pregnancy (639.3)
pregnancy, childbirth, or the puerperium (642.0-642.9, 646.2)

DEF: Oliguria: diminished urinary secretion related to fluid intake.
DEF: Anuria: lack of urinary secretion due to renal failure or obstructed urinary tract.

✓5th **788.6 Other abnormality of urination**

Code, if applicable, any causal condition first, such as:
hyperplasia of prostate (600.0-600.9 with fifth-digit 1)

788.61 Splitting of urinary stream
Intermittent urinary stream

788.62 Slowing of urinary stream
Weak stream
AHA: 4Q, '06, 93

788.63 Urgency of urination
EXCLUDES *urge incontinence (788.31, 788.33)*
AHA: 4Q, '06, 93; 4Q, '03, 74
DEF: Feeling of intense need to urinate; abrupt sensation of imminent urination.

788.64 Urinary hesitancy
AHA: 4Q, '06, 93, 109

788.65 Straining on urination
AHA: 4Q, '06, 93, 109

788.69 Other

788.7 Urethral discharge

Penile discharge
Urethrorrhea

788.8 Extravasation of urine

DEF: Leaking or infiltration of urine into tissues.

✓5th **788.9 Other symptoms involving urinary system**

AHA: 1Q, '05, 12; 4Q, '88, 1

● **788.91 Functional urinary incontinence**
Urinary incontinence due to cognitive impairment, or severe physical disability or immobility
EXCLUDES *urinary incontinence due to physiologic condition (788.30-788.39)*

● **788.99 Other symptoms involving urinary system**
Extrarenal uremia
Vesical:
pain
tenesmus

✓4th 789 Other symptoms involving abdomen and pelvis

EXCLUDES *symptoms referable to genital organs:*
female (625.0-625.9)
male (607.0-608.9)
psychogenic (302.70-302.79))

The following fifth-digit subclassification is to be used for codes 789.0. 789.3, 789.4, 789.6:
0 unspecified site
1 right upper quadrant
2 left upper quadrant
3 right lower quadrant
4 left lower quadrant
5 periumbilic
6 epigastric
7 generalized
9 other specified site
Multiple sites

§ ✓5th **789.0 Abdominal pain**
[0-7, 9]
Colic:
NOS
infantile
Cramps, abdominal
EXCLUDES *renal colic (788.0)*
AHA: 1Q, '95, 3; For code 789.06: 1Q, '02, 5

789.1 Hepatomegaly
Enlargement of liver

789.2 Splenomegaly
Enlargement of spleen

§ ✓5th **789.3 Abdominal or pelvic swelling, mass, or lump**
[0-7, 9]
Diffuse or generalized swelling or mass:
abdominal NOS
umbilical
EXCLUDES *abdominal distention (gaseous) (787.3)*
ascites (789.51-789.59)

§ ✓5th **789.4 Abdominal rigidity**
[0-7, 9]

✓5th **789.5 Ascites**
Fluid in peritoneal cavity
AHA: 4Q, '07, 95; 2Q, '05, 8; 4Q, '89, 11
DEF: Serous fluid effusion and accumulation in abdominal cavity.

789.51 Malignant ascites
Code first malignancy, such as:
malignant neoplasm of ovary (183.0)
secondary malignant neoplasm of retroperitoneum and peritoneum (197.6)
AHA: 4Q, '07, 96

789.59 Other ascites

§ ✓5th **789.6 Abdominal tenderness**
[0-7, 9]
Rebound tenderness

789.9 Other symtoms involving abdomen and pelvis
Umbilical:
bleeding
discharge

NONSPECIFIC ABNORMAL FINDINGS (790-796)

AHA: 2Q, '90, 16

✓4th 790 Nonspecific findings on examination of blood

EXCLUDES *abnormality of:*
platelets (287.0-287.9)
thrombocytes (287.0-287.9)
white blood cells (288.00-288.9)

✓5th **790.0 Abnormality of red blood cells**
EXCLUDES *anemia:*
congenital (776.5)
newborn, due to isoimmunization (773.0-773.2, 773.5)
of premature infant (776.6)
other specified types (280.0-285.9)
hemoglobin disorders (282.5-282.7)
polycythemia:
familial (289.6)
neonatorum (776.4)
secondary (289.0)
vera (238.4)
AHA: 4Q, '00, 46

790.01 Precipitous drop in hematocrit
Drop in hematocrit

790.09 Other abnormality of red blood cells
Abnormal red cell morphology NOS
Abnormal red cell volume NOS
Anisocytosis
Poikilocytosis

790.1 Elevated sedimentation rate

✓5th **790.2 Abnormal glucose**
EXCLUDES *diabetes mellitus ►(249.00-249.91, 250.00-250.93)◄*
dysmetabolic syndrome X (277.7)
gestational diabetes (648.8)
glycosuria (791.5)
hypoglycemia (251.2)
that complicating pregnancy, childbirth, or puerperium (648.8)
AHA: 4Q, '03, 74; 3Q, '91, 5

790.21 Impaired fasting glucose
Elevated fasting glucose

790.22 Impaired glucose tolerance test (oral)
Elevated glucose tolerance test

790.29 Other abnormal glucose
Abnormal glucose NOS
Abnormal non-fasting glucose
Hyperglycemia NOS
Pre-diabetes NOS
AHA: 2Q, '05, 21

790.3 Excessive blood level of alcohol
Elevated blood-alcohol
AHA: S-O, '86, 3

790.4 Nonspecific elevation of levels of transaminase or lactic acid dehydrogenase [LDH]

790.5 Other nonspecific abnormal serum enzyme levels
Abnormal serum level of:
acid phosphatase
alkaline phosphatasc
amylase
lipase
EXCLUDES *deficiency of circulating enzymes (277.6)*

§ Requires fifth-digit. Valid digits are in [brackets] under each code. See category 789 for codes and definitions.

790.6 Other abnormal blood chemistry

Abnormal blood level of:
cobalt
copper
iron
lead
lithium
magnesium
mineral
zinc

EXCLUDES *abnormality of electrolyte or acid-base balance (276.0-276.9)*
hypoglycemia NOS (251.2)
lead poisoning (984.0-984.9)
specific finding indicating abnormality of:
amino-acid transport and metabolism (270.0-270.9)
carbohydrate transport and metabolism (271.0-271.9)
lipid metabolism (272.0-272.9)
uremia NOS (586)

AHA: 4Q, '88, 1

790.7 Bacteremia

EXCLUDES *bacteremia of newborn (771.83)*
septicemia (038)

Use additional code to identify organism (041)

AHA: 2Q, '03, 7; 4Q, '93, 29; 3Q, '88, 12

DEF: Laboratory finding of bacteria in the blood in the absence of two or more signs of sepsis; transient in nature, progresses to septicemia with severe infectious process.

790.8 Viremia, unspecified

AHA: 4Q, '88, 10

DEF: Presence of a virus in the blood stream.

✓5th **790.9 Other nonspecific findings on examination of blood**

AHA: 4Q, '93, 29

790.91 Abnormal arterial blood gases

790.92 Abnormal coagulation profile

Abnormal or prolonged:
bleeding time
coagulation time
partial thromboplastin time [PTT]
prothrombin time [PT]

EXCLUDES *coagulation (hemorrhagic) disorders (286.0-286.9)*

790.93 Elevated prostate specific antigen, [PSA] A ♂

790.94 Euthyroid sick syndrome

AHA: 4Q, '97, 45

DEF: Transient alteration of thyroid hormone metabolism due to nonthyroid illness or stress.

790.95 Elevated C-reactive protein [CRP]

DEF: Inflammation in an arterial wall results in elevated C-reactive protein (CRP) in the blood; CRP is a recognized risk factor in cardiovascular disease.

790.99 Other

AHA: 2Q, '03, 14

✓4th **791 Nonspecific findings on examination of urine**

EXCLUDES *hematuria NOS ►(599.70-599.72)◄*
specific findings indicating abnormality of:
amino-acid transport and metabolism (270.0-270.9)
carbohydrate transport and metabolism (271.0-271.9)

791.0 Proteinuria

Albuminuria
Bence-Jones proteinuria

EXCLUDES *postural proteinuria (593.6)*
that arising during pregnancy or the puerperium (642.0-642.9, 646.2)

AHA: 3Q, '91, 8

DEF: Excess protein in urine.

791.1 Chyluria

EXCLUDES *filarial (125.0-125.9)*

DEF: Excess chyle in urine.

791.2 Hemoglobinuria

DEF: Free hemoglobin in blood due to rapid hemolysis of red blood cells.

791.3 Myoglobinuria

DEF: Myoglobin (oxygen-transporting pigment) in urine.

791.4 Biliuria

DEF: Bile pigments in urine.

791.5 Glycosuria

EXCLUDES *renal glycosuria (271.4)*

DEF: Sugar in urine.

791.6 Acetonuria

Ketonuria

DEF: Excess acetone in urine.

791.7 Other cells and casts in urine

791.9 Other nonspecific findings on examination of urine

Crystalluria
Elevated urine levels of:
17-ketosteroids
catecholamines
indolacetic acid
vanillylmandelic acid [VMA]
Melanuria

AHA: 1Q, '05, 12

✓4th **792 Nonspecific abnormal findings in other body substances**

EXCLUDES *that in chromosomal analysis (795.2)*

792.0 Cerebrospinal fluid

792.1 Stool contents

Abnormal stool color
Fat in stool
Mucus in stool
Occult stool
Pus in stool

EXCLUDES *blood in stool [melena] (578.1)*
newborn (772.4, 777.3)

AHA: 2Q, '92, 9

792.2 Semen ♂

Abnormal spermatozoa

EXCLUDES *azoospermia (606.0)*
oligospermia (606.1)

792.3 Amniotic fluid M ♀

AHA: N-D, '86, 4

DEF: Nonspecific abnormal findings in amniotic fluid.

792.4 Saliva

EXCLUDES *that in chromosomal analysis (795.2)*

792.5 Cloudy (hemodialysis) (peritoneal) dialysis effluent

AHA: 4Q, '00, 46

792.9 Other nonspecific abnormal findings in body substances

Peritoneal fluid
Pleural fluid
Synovial fluid
Vaginal fluids

✓4th 793 Nonspecific abnormal findings on radiological and other examination of body structure

INCLUDES nonspecific abnormal findings of:
thermography
ultrasound examination [echogram]
x-ray examination

EXCLUDES *abnormal results of function studies and radioisotope scans (794.0-794.9)*

793.0 Skull and head

EXCLUDES *nonspecific abnormal echoencephalogram (794.01)*

AHA: 3Q, '06, 22

793.1 Lung field

Coin lesion } (of) lung
Shadow }

DEF: Coin lesion of lung: coin-shaped, solitary pulmonary nodule.

793.2 Other intrathoracic organ

Abnormal:
echocardiogram
heart shadow
ultrasound cardiogram
Mediastinal shift

793.3 Biliary tract

Nonvisualization of gallbladder

793.4 Gastrointestinal tract

793.5 Genitourinary organs

Filling defect:
bladder
kidney
ureter

793.6 Abdominal area, including retroperitoneum

793.7 Musculoskeletal system

✓5th 793.8 Breast

AHA: 4Q, '01, 51

793.80 Abnormal mammogram, unspecified

793.81 Mammographic microcalcification

EXCLUDES *mammographic calcification (793.89)*
mammographic calculus (793.89)

DEF: Calcium and cellular debris deposits in the breast that cannot be felt but can be detected on a mammogram; can be a sign of cancer, benign conditions, or changes in the breast tissue as a result of inflammation, injury, or obstructed duct.

793.89 Other abnormal findings on radiological examination of breast

Mammographic calcification
Mammographic calculus

✓5th 793.9 Other

EXCLUDES *abnormal finding by radioisotope localization of placenta (794.9)*

793.91 Image test inconclusive due to excess body fat

Use additional code to identify Body Mass Index (BMI), if known (V85.0-V85.54)

AHA: 4Q, '06, 109

793.99 Other nonspecific abnormal findings on radiological and other examinations of body structure

Abnormal:
placental finding by x-ray or ultrasound method
radiological findings in skin and subcutaneous tissue

AHA: 4Q, '06, 109

✓4th 794 Nonspecific abnormal results of function studies

INCLUDES radioisotope:
scans
uptake studies
scintiphotography

✓5th 794.0 Brain and central nervous system

794.00 Abnormal function study, unspecified

794.01 Abnormal echoencephalogram

794.02 Abnormal electroencephalogram [EEG]

794.09 Other

Abnormal brain scan

✓5th 794.1 Peripheral nervous system and special senses

794.10 Abnormal response to nerve stimulation, unspecified

794.11 Abnormal retinal function studies

Abnormal electroretinogram [ERG]

794.12 Abnormal electro-oculogram [EOG]

794.13 Abnormal visually evoked potential

794.14 Abnormal oculomotor studies

794.15 Abnormal auditory function studies

AHA: 1Q, '04, 15-16

794.16 Abnormal vestibular function studies

794.17 Abnormal electromyogram [EMG]

EXCLUDES that of eye (794.14)

794.19 Other

794.2 Pulmonary

Abnormal lung scan
Reduced:
ventilatory capacity
vital capacity

✓5th 794.3 Cardiovascular

794.30 Abnormal function study, unspecified

794.31 Abnormal electrocardiogram [ECG] [EKG]

EXCLUDES *long QT syndrome (426.82)*

794.39 Other

Abnormal:
ballistocardiogram
phonocardiogram
vectorcardiogram

794.4 Kidney

Abnormal renal function test

794.5 Thyroid

Abnormal thyroid:
scan
uptake

794.6 Other endocrine function study

794.7 Basal metabolism

Abnormal basal metabolic rate [BMR]

794.8 Liver

Abnormal liver scan

794.9 Other

Bladder
Pancreas
Placenta
Spleen

4th 795 Other and nonspecific abnormal cytological, histological, immunological and DNA test findings

EXCLUDES ▶*abnormal cytologic smear of anus and anal HPV (796.70-796.79)*◀
nonspecific abnormalities of red blood cells (790.01-790.09)

5th 795.0 Abnormal Papanicolaou smear of cervix and cervical HPV

Abnormal thin preparation smear of cervix
Abnormal cervical cytology

EXCLUDES ▶*abnormal cytologic smear of vagina and vaginal HPV (795.10-795.19)*
carcinoma in situ of cervix (233.1)◀
cervical intraepithelial neoplasia I (CIN I) (622.11)
cervical intraepithelial neoplasia II (CIN II) (622.12)
cervical intraepithelial neoplasia III (CIN III) (233.1)
dysplasia (histologically confirmed) of cervix (uteri) NOS (622.10)
mild ▶*cervical*◀ *dysplasia (histologically confirmed) (622.11)*
moderate ▶*cervical*◀ *dysplasia (histologically confirmed) (622.12)*
severe ▶*cervical*◀ *dysplasia (histologically confirmed) (233.1)*

AHA: 4Q, '02, 69

795.00 Abnormal glandular Papanicolaou smear of cervix ♀
Atypical endocervical cells NOS
Atypical endometrial cells NOS
Atypical ▶cervical◀ glandular cells NOS

795.01 Papanicolaou smear of cervix with atypical squamous cells of undetermined significance [ASC-US] ♀
AHA: 2Q, '06, 4

795.02 Papanicolaou smear of cervix with atypical squamous cells cannot exclude high grade squamous intraepithelial lesion [ASC-H] ♀

795.03 Papanicolaou smear of cervix with low grade squamous intraepithelial lesion [LGSIL] ♀

795.04 Papanicolaou smear of cervix with highgrade squamous intraepithelial lesion [HGSIL] ♀

795.05 Cervical high risk human papillomavirus [HPV] DNA test positive ♀

795.06 Papanicolaou smear of cervix with cytologic evidence of malignancy ♀
AHA: 4Q, '06, 110

● **795.07 Satisfactory cervical smear but lacking transformation zone** ♀

▲ **795.08 Unsatisfactory cervical cytology smear** ♀
Inadequate ▶cervical cytology◀ sample
AHA: 2Q, '06, 4

795.09 Other abnormal Papanicolaou smear of cervix and cervical HPV ♀
Cervical low risk human papillomavirus (HPV) DNA test positive
Use additional code for associated human papillomavirus (079.4)

EXCLUDES *encounter for Papanicolaou cervical smear to confirm findings of recent normal smear following initial abnormal smear (V72.32)*

▲ **5th 795.1 Abnormal Papanicolaou smear of vagina and vaginal HPV**

▶Abnormal thin preparation smear of vagina NOS
Abnormal vaginal cytology NOS◀

▶Use additional code to identify acquired absence of uterus and cervix, if applicable (V88.01-V88.03)◀

EXCLUDES ▶*abnormal cytologic smear of cervix and cervical HPV (795.00-795.09)*
carcinoma in situ of vagina (233.31)
carcinoma in situ of vulva (233.32)
dysplasia (histologically confirmed) of vagina NOS (623.0, 233.31)
dysplasia (histologically confirmed) of vulva NOS (624.01, 624.02, 233.32)
mild vaginal dysplasia (histologically confirmed) (623.0)
mild vulvar dysplasia (histologically confirmed) (624.01)
moderate vaginal dysplasia (histologically confirmed) (623.0)
moderate vulvar dysplasia (histologically confirmed) (624.02)
severe vaginal dysplasia (histologically confirmed) (233.31)
severe vulvar dysplasia (histologically confirmed) (233.32)
vaginal intraepithelial neoplasia I (VAIN I) (623.0)
vaginal intraepithelial neoplasia II (VAIN II) (623.0)
vaginal intraepithelial neoplasia III (VAIN III) (233.31)
vulvar intraepithelial neoplasia I (VIN I) (624.01)
vulvar intraepithelial neoplasia II (VIN II) (624.02)
vulvar intraepithelial neoplasia III (VIN III) (233.32)◀

● **795.10 Abnormal glandular Papanicolaou smear of vagina** ♀
Atypical vaginal glandular cells NOS

● **795.11 Papanicolaou smear of vagina with atypical squamous cells of undetermined significance [ASC-US]** ♀

● **795.12 Papanicolaou smear of vagina with atypical squamous cells cannot exclude high grade squamous intraepithelial lesion [ASC-H]** ♀

● **795.13 Papanicolaou smear of vagina with low grade squamous intraepithelial lesion [LGSIL]** ♀

● **795.14 Papanicolaou smear of vagina with high grade squamous intraepithelial lesion [HGSIL]** ♀

● **795.15 Vaginal high risk human papillomavirus [HPV] DNA test positive** ♀

EXCLUDES *condyloma acuminatum (078.11)*
genital warts (078.11)

● **795.16 Papanicolaou smear of vagina with cytologic evidence of malignancy** ♀

● **795.18 Unsatisfactory vaginal cytology smear** ♀
Inadequate vaginal cytology sample

● **795.19 Other abnormal Papanicolaou smear of vagina and vaginal HPV** ♀
Vaginal low risk human papillomavirus (HPV) DNA test positive
Use additional code for associated human papillomavirus (079.4)

795.2 Nonspecific abnormal findings on chromosomal analysis
Abnormal karyotype

✓5th **795.3 Nonspecific positive culture findings**
Positive culture findings in:
nose
throat
sputum
wound

EXCLUDES *that of:*
blood (790.7-790.8)
urine (791.9)

795.31 Nonspecific positive findings for anthrax
Positive findings by nasal swab
AHA: 4Q, '02, 70

795.39 Other nonspecific positive culture findings

795.4 Other nonspecific abnormal histological findings

795.5 Nonspecific reaction to tuberculin skin test without active tuberculosis
Abnormal result of Mantoux test
PPD positive
Tuberculin (skin test):
positive
reactor

795.6 False positive serological test for syphilis
False positive Wassermann reaction

✓5th **795.7 Other nonspecific immunological findings**

EXCLUDES *abnormal tumor markers (795.81-795.89)*
elevated prostate specific antigen [PSA] (790.93)
elevated tumor associated antigens (795.81-795.89)
isoimmunization, in pregnancy (656.1-656.2)
affecting fetus or newborn (773.0-773.2)

AHA: 2Q, '93, 6

795.71 Nonspecific serologic evidence of human immunodeficiency virus [HIV]
Inclusive human immunodeficiency [HIV] test (adult) (infant)
Note: This code is **only** to be used when a test finding is reported as nonspecific. Asymptomatic positive findings are coded to V08. If any HIV infection symptom or condition is present, see code 042. Negative findings are not coded.

EXCLUDES *acquired immunodeficiency syndrome [AIDS] (042)*
asymptomatic human immunodeficiency virus, [HIV] infection status (V08)
HIV infection, symptomatic (042)
human immunodeficiency virus [HIV] disease (042)
positive (status) NOS (V08)

AHA: 2Q, '04, 11; 1Q, '93, 21; 1Q, '93, 22; 2Q, '92, 11; J-A, '87, 24

795.79 Other and unspecified nonspecific immunologoical findings
Raised antibody titer
Raised level of immunoglobulins

✓5th **795.8 Abnormal tumor markers**
Elevated tumor associated antigens [TAA]
Elevated tumor specific antigens [TSA]

EXCLUDES *elevated prostate specific antigen [PSA] (790.93)*

795.81 Elevated carcinoembryonic antigen [CEA]
AHA: 4Q, '06, 111

795.82 Elevated cancer antigen 125 [CA 125] ♀
AHA: 4Q, '06, 111

795.89 Other abnormal tumor markers
AHA: 4Q, '06, 111

✓4th **796 Other nonspecific abnormal findings**

796.0 Nonspecific abnormal toxicological findings
Abnormal levels of heavy metals or drugs in blood, urine, or other tissue

EXCLUDES *excessive blood level of alcohol (790.3)*

AHA: 1Q, '97, 16

796.1 Abnormal reflex

796.2 Elevated blood pressure reading without diagnosis of hypertension
Note: This category is to be used to record an episode of elevated blood pressure in a patient in whom no formal diagnosis of hypertension has been made, or as an incidental finding.
AHA: 2Q, '03, 11; 3Q, '90, 4; J-A, '84, 12

796.3 Nonspecific low blood pressure reading

796.4 Other abnormal clinical findings
AHA: 1Q, '97, 16

796.5 Abnormal finding on antenatal screening ♀ M
AHA: 4Q, '97, 46

796.6 Abnormal findings on neonatal screening N

EXCLUDES *nonspecific serologic evidence of human immunodeficiency virus [HIV] (795.71)*

AHA: 4Q, '04, 99

● ✓5th **796.7 Abnormal cytologic smear of anus and anal HPV**

EXCLUDES *abnormal cytologic smear of cervix and cervical HPV (795.00-795.09)*
abnormal cytologic smear of vagina and vaginal HPV (795.10-795.19)
anal intraepithelial neoplasia I (AIN I) (569.44)
anal intraepithelial neoplasia II (AIN II) (569.44)
anal intraepithelial neoplasia III (AIN III) (230.5, 230.6)
carcinoma in situ of anus (230.5, 230.6)
dysplasia (histologically confirmed) of anus NOS (569.44)
mild anal dysplasia (histologically confirmed) (569.44)
moderate anal dysplasia (histologically confirmed) (569.44)
severe anal dysplasia (histologically confirmed) (569.44)

● **796.70 Abnormal glandular Papanicolaou smear of anus**
Atypical anal glandular cells NOS

● **796.71 Papanicolaou smear of anus with atypical squamous cells of undetermined significance [ASC-US]**

● **796.72 Papanicolaou smear of anus with atypical squamous cells cannot exclude high grade squamous intraepithelial lesion [ASC-H]**

• **796.73 Papanicolaou smear of anus with low grade squamous intraepithelial lesion [LGSIL]**

• **796.74 Papanicolaou smear of anus with high grade squamous intraepithelial lesion [HGSIL]**

• **796.75 Anal high risk human papillomavirus [HPV] DNA test positive**

• **796.76 Papanicolaou smear of anus with cytologic evidence of malignancy**

• **796.77 Satisfactory anal smear but lacking transformation zone**

• **796.78 Unsatisfactory anal cytology smear**
Inadequate anal cytology sample

• **796.79 Other abnormal Papanicolaou smear of anus and anal HPV**
Anal low risk human papillomavirus (HPV) DNA test positive
Use additional code for associated human papillomavirus (079.4)

796.9 Other

ILL-DEFINED AND UNKNOWN CAUSES OF MORBIDITY AND MORTALITY (797-799)

797 Senility without mention of psychosis
▶Frailty◀
Old age
Senescence
Senile asthenia
Senile:
debility
exhaustion
EXCLUDES *senile psychoses (290.0-290.9)*

✓4th **798 Sudden death, cause unknown**

798.0 Sudden infant death syndrome P
Cot death
Crib death
Sudden death of nonspecific cause in infancy
DEF: Death of infant under age one due to nonspecific cause.

798.1 Instantaneous death

798.2 Death occurring in less than 24 hours from onset of symptoms, not otherwise explained
Death known not to be violent or instantaneous, for which no cause could be discovered
Died without sign of disease

798.9 Unattended death
Death in circumstances where the body of the deceased was found and no cause could be discovered
Found dead

✓4th **799 Other ill-defined and unknown causes of morbidity and mortality**

✓5th **799.0 Asphyxia and hypoxemia**
EXCLUDES *asphyxia and hypoxemia (due to):*
carbon monoxide (986)
hypercapnia (786.09)
inhalation of food or foreign body (932-934.9)
newborn (768.0-768.9)
traumatic (994.7)

799.01 Asphyxia
AHA: 4Q, '05, 90
DEF: Lack of oxygen in inspired air, causing a deficiency of oxygen in tissues (hypoxia) and elevated levels of arterial carbon dioxide (hypercapnia).

799.02 Hypoxemia
AHA: 2Q, '06, 24, 25; 4Q, '05, 90
DEF: Deficient oxygenation of the blood.

799.1 Respiratory arrest
Cardiorespiratory failure
EXCLUDES *cardiac arrest (427.5)*
failure of peripheral circulation (785.50)
respiratory distress:
NOS (786.09)
acute (518.82)
following trauma and surgery (518.5)
newborn (770.89)
syndrome (newborn) (769)
adult (following trauma and surgery) (518.5)
other (518.82)
respiratory failure (518.81, 518.83-518.84)
newborn (770.84)
respiratory insufficiency (786.09)
acute (518.82)

799.2 Nervousness
"Nerves"

799.3 Debility, unspecified
EXCLUDES *asthenia (780.79)*
nervous debility (300.5)
neurasthenia (300.5)
senile asthenia (797)

799.4 Cachexia
Wasting disease
Code first underlying condition, if known
AHA: 3Q, '06, 14, 15; 3Q, '90, 17
DEF: General ill health and poor nutrition.

✓5th **799.8 Other ill-defined conditions**

799.81 Decreased libido A
Decreased sexual desire
EXCLUDES *psychosexual dysfunction with inhibited sexual desire (302.71)*
AHA: 4Q, '03, 75

799.89 Other ill-defined conditions

799.9 Other unknown and unspecified cause
Undiagnosed disease, not specified as to site or system involved
Unknown cause of morbidity or mortality
AHA: 1Q, '98,.4; 1Q, '90, 20

17. INJURY AND POISONING (800-999)

Use E code(s) to identify the cause and intent of the injury or poisoning (E800-E999)

Note:

1. The principle of multiple coding of injuries should be followed wherever possible. Combination categories for multiple injuries are provided for use when there is insufficient detail as to the nature of the individual conditions, or for primary tabulation purposes when it is more convenient to record a single code; otherwise, the component injuries should be coded separately.

   Where multiple sites of injury are specified in the titles, the word "with" indicates involvement of both sites, and the word "and" indicates involvement of either or both sites. The word "finger" includes thumb.
2. Categories for "late effect" of injuries are to be found at 905-909.

FRACTURES (800-829)

EXCLUDES *malunion (733.81)*
nonunion (733.82)
pathological or spontaneous fracture (733.10-733.19)
stress fractures (733.93-733.95)

The terms "condyle," "coronoid process," "ramus," and "symphysis" indicate the portion of the bone fractured, not the name of the bone involved.

The descriptions "closed" and "open" used in the fourth-digit subdivisions include the following terms:

closed (with or without delayed healing):
- comminuted
- depressed
- elevated
- fissured
- fracture NOS
- greenstick
- impacted
- linear
- simple
- slipped epiphysis
- spiral

open (with or without delayed healing):
- compound
- infected
- missile
- puncture
- with foreign body

Note: A fracture not indicated as closed or open should be classified as closed.

AHA: 1Q, '07, 3-4; 4Q, '90, 26; 3Q, '90, 5; 3Q, '90, 13; 2Q, '90, 7; 2Q, '89, 15, S-O, '85, 3

FRACTURE OF SKULL (800-804)

The following fifth-digit subclassification is for use with the appropriate codes in category 800, 801, 803, and 804:

0 unspecified state of consciousness
1 with no loss of consciousness
2 with brief [less than one hour] loss of consciousness
3 with moderate [1-24 hours] loss of consciousness
4 with prolonged [more than 24 hours] loss of consciousness and return to pre-existing conscious level
5 with prolonged [more than 24 hours] loss of consciousness, without return to pre-existing conscious level
Use fifth-digit 5 to designate when a patient is unconscious and dies before regaining consciousness, regardless of the duration of the loss of consciousness
6 with loss of consciousness of unspecified duration
9 with concussion, unspecified

4th **800 Fracture of vault of skull**

INCLUDES frontal bone
parietal bone

AHA: 4Q,'96, 36

DEF: Fracture of bone that forms skull dome and protects brain.

§ 5th **800.0 Closed without mention of intracranial injury** [0-6, 9]

§ 5th **800.1 Closed with cerebral laceration and contusion** [0-6, 9]

Fractures

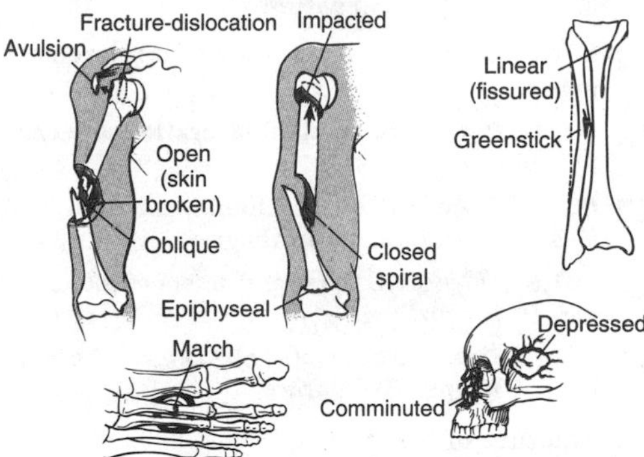

§ 5th **800.2 Closed with subarachnoid, subdural, and extradural hemorrhage** [0-6, 9]

§ 5th **800.3 Closed with other and unspecified intracranial hemorrhage** [0-6, 9]

§ 5th **800.4 Closed with intracranial injury of other and unspecified nature** [0-6, 9]

§ 5th **800.5 Open without mention of intracranial injury** [0-6, 9]

§ 5th **800.6 Open with cerebral laceration and contusion** [0-6, 9]

§ 5th **800.7 Open with subarachnoid, subdural, and extradural hemorrhage** [0-6, 9]

§ 5th **800.8 Open with other and unspecified intracranial hemorrhage** [0-6, 9]

§ 5th **800.9 Open with intracranial injury of other and unspecified nature** [0-6, 9]

4th **801 Fracture of base of skull**

INCLUDES fossa:
- anterior
- middle
- posterior

occiput bone
orbital roof
sinus:
- ethmoid
- frontal

sphenoid bone
temporal bone

AHA: 4Q, '96, 36

DEF: Fracture of bone that forms skull floor.

§ 5th **801.0 Closed without mention of intracranial injury** [0-6, 9]

§ 5th **801.1 Closed with cerebral laceration and contusion** [0-6, 9] **AHA:** For code 801.15: 4Q, '96, 36

§ 5th **801.2 Closed with subarachnoid, subdural, and extradural hemorrhage** [0-6, 9]

§ 5th **801.3 Closed with other and unspecified intracranial hemorrhage** [0-6, 9]

Skull

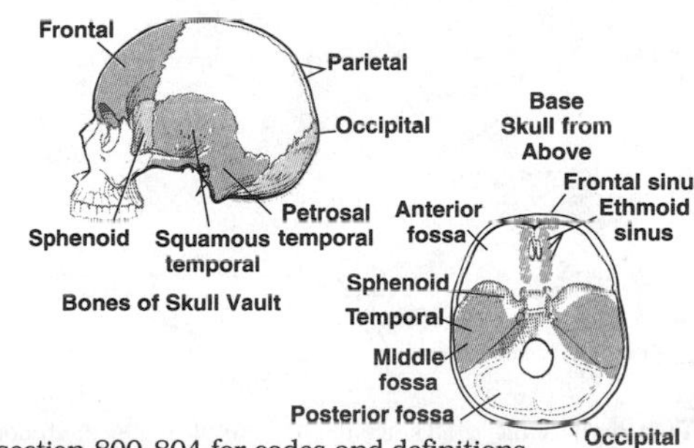

§ Requires fifth-digit. Valid digits are in [brackets] under each code. See beginning of section 800-804 for codes and definitions.

§ ✓5th **801.4 Closed with intracranial injury of other and unspecified nature**
[0-6, 9]

§ ✓5th **801.5 Open without mention of intracranial injury**
[0-6, 9]

§ ✓5th **801.6 Open with cerebral laceration and contusion**
[0-6, 9]

§ ✓5th **801.7 Open with subarachnoid, subdural, and extradural hemorrhage**
[0-6, 9]

§ ✓5th **801.8 Open with other and unspecified intracranial hemorrhage**
[0-6, 9]

§ ✓5th **801.9 Open with intracranial injury of other and unspecified nature**
[0-6, 9]

✓4th **802 Fracture of face bones**

AHA: 4Q, '96, 36

802.0 Nasal bones, closed

802.1 Nasal bones, open

✓5th **802.2 Mandible, closed**

Inferior maxilla
Lower jaw (bone)

802.20 Unspecified site

802.21 Condylar process

802.22 Subcondylar

802.23 Coronoid process

802.24 Ramus, unspecified

802.25 Angle of jaw

802.26 Symphysis of body

802.27 Alveolar border of body

802.28 Body, other and unspecified

802.29 Multiple sites

✓5th **802.3 Mandible, open**

802.30 Unspecified site

802.31 Condylar process

802.32 Subcondylar

802.33 Coronoid process

802.34 Ramus, unspecified

802.35 Angle of jaw

802.36 Symphysis of body

802.37 Alveolar border of body

802.38 Body, other and unspecified

802.39 Multiple sites

802.4 Malar and maxillary bones, closed

Superior maxilla
Upper jaw (bone)
Zygoma
Zygomatic arch

802.5 Malar and maxillary bones, open

Facial Fracture

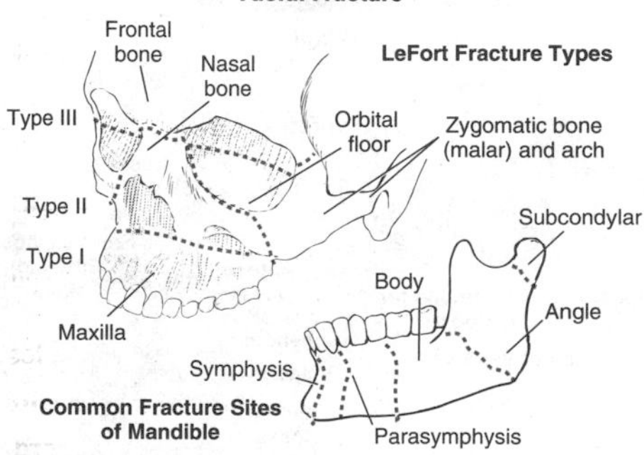

802.6 Orbital floor (blow-out), closed

802.7 Orbital floor (blow-out), open

802.8 Other facial bones, closed

Alveolus
Orbit:
NOS
part other than roof or floor
Palate

EXCLUDES *orbital:*
floor (802.6)
roof (801.0-801.9)

802.9 Other facial bones, open

✓4th **803 Other and unqualified skull fractures**

INCLUDES skull NOS
skull multiple NOS

AHA: 4Q, '96, 36

§ ✓5th **803.0 Closed without mention of intracranial injury**
[0-6, 9]

§ ✓5th **803.1 Closed with cerebral laceration and contusion**
[0-6, 9]

§ ✓5th **803.2 Closed with subarachnoid, subdural, and extradural hemorrhage**
[0-6, 9]

§ ✓5th **803.3 Closed with other and unspecified intracranial hemorrhage**
[0-6, 9]

§ ✓5th **803.4 Closed with intracranial injury of other and unspecified nature**
[0-6, 9]

§ ✓5th **803.5 Open without mention of intracranial injury**
[0-6, 9]

§ ✓5th **803.6 Open with cerebral laceration and contusion**
[0-6, 9]

§ ✓5th **803.7 Open with subarachnoid, subdural, and extradural hemorrhage**
[0-6, 9]

§ ✓5th **803.8 Open with other and unspecified intracranial hemorrhage**
[0-6, 9]

§ ✓5th **803.9 Open with intracranial injury of other and unspecified nature**
[0-6, 9]

✓4th **804 Multiple fractures involving skull or face with other bones**

AHA: 4Q, '96, 36

§ ✓5th **804.0 Closed without mention of intracranial injury**
[0-6, 9]

§ ✓5th **804.1Closed with cerebral laceration and contusion**
[0-6, 9] AHA: For code 804.10: 1Q, '06, 6

§ ✓5th **804.2 Closed with subarachnoid, subdural, and extradural hemorrhage**
[0-6, 9]

§ ✓5th **804.3 Closed with other and unspecified intracranial hemorrhage**
[0-6, 9]

§ ✓5th **804.4 Closed with intracranial injury of other and unspecified nature**
[0-6, 9]

§ ✓5th **804.5 Open without mention of intracranial injury**
[0-6, 9]

§ ✓5th **804.6 Open with cerebral laceration and contusion**
[0-6, 9]

§ ✓5th **804.7 Open with subarachnoid, subdural, and extradural hemorrage**
[0-6, 9]

§ ✓5th **804.8 Open with other and unspecified intracranial hemorrhage**
[0-6, 9]

§ ✓5th **804.9 Open with intracranial injury of other and unspecified nature**
[0-6, 9]

§ Requires fifth-digit. Valid digits are in [brackets] under each code. See beginning of section 800-804 for codes and definitions.

FRACTURE OF NECK AND TRUNK (805-809)

✓4th 805 Fracture of vertebral column without mention of spinal cord injury

INCLUDES neural arch
spine
spinous process
transverse process
vertebra

The following fifth-digit subclassification is for use with codes 805.0-805.1:

- **0 cervical vertebra, unspecified level**
- **1 first cervical vertebra**
- **2 second cervical vertebra**
- **3 third cervical vertebra**
- **4 fourth cervical vertebra**
- **5 fifth cervical vertebra**
- **6 sixth cervical vertebra**
- **7 seventh cervical vertebra**
- **8 multiple cervical vertebrae**

§ ✓5th **805.0 Cervical, closed**
[0-8] Atlas
Axis

§ ✓5th **805.1 Cervical, open**
[0-8]

805.2 Dorsal [thoracic], closed

805.3 Dorsal [thoracic], open

805.4 Lumbar, closed
AHA: 1Q, '07, 7; 4Q, '99, 12

805.5 Lumbar, open

805.6 Sacrum and coccyx, closed

805.7 Sacrum and coccyx, open

805.8 Unspecified, closed

805.9 Unspecified, open

Vertebral Column

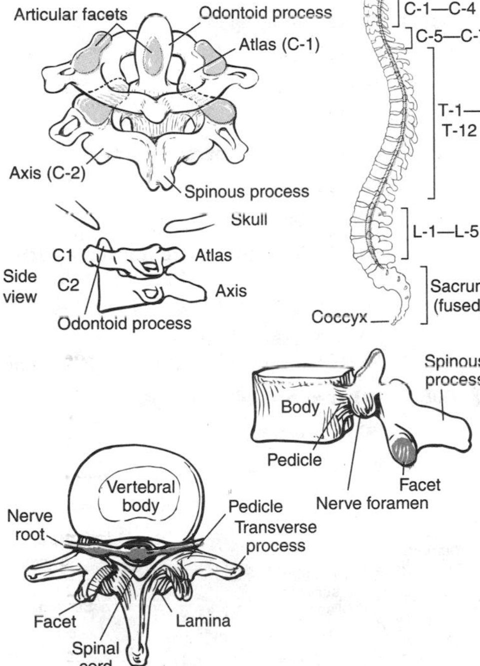

✓4th 806 Fracture of vertebral column with spinal cord injury

INCLUDES any condition classifiable to 805 with:
complete or incomplete transverse lesion (of cord)
hematomyelia
injury to:
cauda equina
nerve
paralysis
paraplegia
quadriplegia
spinal concussion

✓5th **806.0 Cervical, closed**

806.00 C_1-C_4 level with unspecified spinal cord injury
Cervical region NOS with spinal cord injury NOS

806.01 C_1-C_4 level with complete lesion of cord

806.02 C_1-C_4 level with anterior cord syndrome

806.03 C_1-C_4 level with central cord syndrome

806.04 C_1-C_4 level with other specified spinal cord injury
C_1-C_4 level with:
incomplete spinal cord lesion NOS
posterior cord syndrome

806.05 C_5-C_7 level with unspecified spinal cord injury

806.06 C_5-C_7 level with complete lesion of cord

806.07 C_5-C_7 level with anterior cord syndrome

806.08 C_5-C_7 level with central cord syndrome

806.09 C_5-C_7 level with other specified spinal cord injury
C_5-C_7 level with:
incomplete spinal cord lesion NOS
posterior cord syndrome

✓5th **806.1 Cervical, open**

806.10 C_1-C_4 level with unspecified spinal cord injury

806.11 C_1-C_4 level with complete lesion of cord

806.12 C_1-C_4 level with anterior cord syndrome

806.13 C_1-C_4 level with central cord syndrome

806.14 C_1-C_4 level with other specified spinal cord injury
C_1-C_4 level with:
incomplete spinal cord lesion NOS
posterior cord syndrome

806.15 C_5-C_7 level with unspecified spinal cord injury

806.16 C_5-C_7 level with complete lesion of cord

806.17 C_5-C_7 level with anterior cord syndrome

806.18 C_5-C_7 level with central cord syndrome

806.19 C_5-C_7 level with other specified spinal cord injury
C_5-C_7 level with:
incomplete spinal cord lesion NOS
posterior cord syndrome

✓5th **806.2 Dorsal [thoracic], closed**

806.20 T_1-T_6 level with unspecified spinal cord injury
Thoracic region NOS with spinal cord injury NOS

806.21 T_1-T_6 level with complete lesion of cord

806.22 T_1-T_6 level with anterior cord syndrome

806.23 T_1-T_6 level with central cord syndrome

§ Requires fifth-digit. Valid digits are in [brackets] under each code. See category 805 for codes and definitions.

806.24 T_1-T_6 level with other specified spinal cord injury
T_1-T_6 level with:
incomplete spinal cord lesion NOS
posterior cord syndrome

806.25 T_7-T_{12} level with unspecified spinal cord injury

806.26 T_7-T_{12} level with complete lesion of cord

806.27 T_7-T_{12} level with anterior cord syndrome

806.28 T_7-T_{12} level with central cord syndrome

806.29 T_7-T_{12} level with other specified spinal cord injury
T_7-T_{12} level with:
incomplete spinal cord lesion NOS
posterior cord syndrome

✓5th **806.3 Dorsal [thoracic], open**

806.30 T_1-T_6 level with unspecified spinal cord injury

806.31 T_1-T_6 level with complete lesion of cord

806.32 T_1-T_6 level with anterior cord syndrome

806.33 T_1-T_6 level with central cord syndrome

806.34 T_1-T_6 level with other specified spinal cord injury
T_1-T_6 level with:
incomplete spinal cord lesion NOS
posterior cord syndrome

806.35 T_7-T_{12} level with unspecified spinal cord injury

806.36 T_7-T_{12} level with complete lesion of cord

806.37 T_7-T_{12} level with anterior cord syndrome

806.38 T_7-T_{12} level with central cord syndrome

806.39 T_7-T_{12} level with other specified spinal cord injury
T_7-T_{12} level with:
incomplete spinal cord lesion NOS
posterior cord syndrome

806.4 Lumbar, closed
AHA: 4Q, '99, 11, 13

806.5 Lumbar, open

✓5th **806.6 Sacrum and coccyx, closed**

806.60 With unspecified spinal cord injury

806.61 With complete cauda equina lesion

806.62 With other cauda equina injury

806.69 With other spinal cord injury

✓5th **806.7 Sacrum and coccyx, open**

806.70 With unspecified spinal cord injury

Ribs, Sternum, Larynx, and Trachea

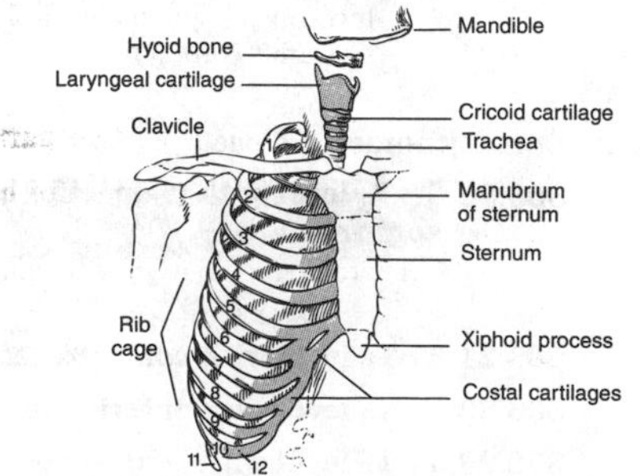

806.71 With complete cauda equina lesion

806.72 With other cauda equina injury

806.79 With other spinal cord injury

806.8 Unspecified, closed

806.9 Unspecified, open

✓4th **807 Fracture of rib(s), sternum, larynx, and trachea**

The following fifth-digit subclassification is for use with codes 807.0-807.1:
0 rib(s) unspecifed
1 one rib
2 two ribs
3 three ribs
4 four ribs
5 five ribs
6 six ribs
7 seven ribs
8 eight or more ribs
9 multiple ribs, unspecified

§ ✓5th **807.0 Rib(s), closed**
[0-9]

§ ✓5th **807.1 Rib(s), open**
[0-9]

807.2 Sternum, closed
DEF: Break in flat bone (breast bone) in anterior thorax.

807.3 Sternum, open
DEF: Break, with open wound, in flat bone in mid anterior thorax.

807.4 Flail chest

807.5 Larynx and trachea, closed
Hyoid bone
Thyroid cartilage
Trachea

807.6 Larynx and trachea, open

✓4th **808 Fracture of pelvis**

808.0 Acetabulum, closed

808.1 Acetabulum, open

808.2 Pubis, closed
AHA: ▶1Q, '08, 9◀

808.3 Pubis, open

✓5th **808.4 Other specified part, closed**

808.41 Ilium

808.42 Ischium

808.43 Multiple pelvic fractures with disruption of pelvic circle
AHA: ▶1Q, '08, 9◀

808.49 Other
Innominate bone
Pelvic rim

✓5th **808.5 Other specified part, open**

808.51 Ilium

808.52 Ischium

Pelvis and Pelvic Fractures

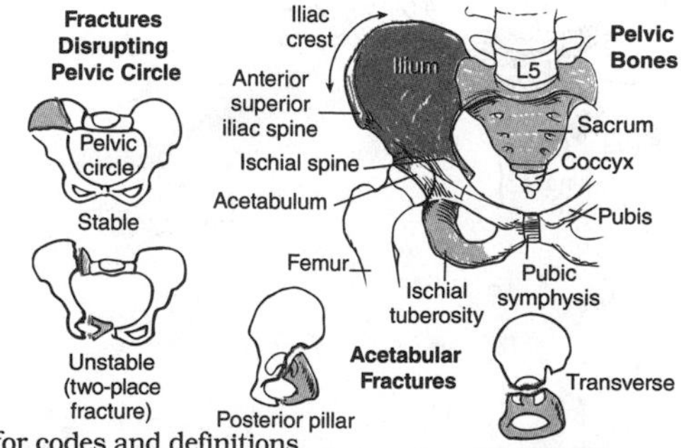

§ Requires fifth-digit. Valid digits are in [brackets] under each code. See category 807 for codes and definitions.

N Newborn Age: 0 P Pediatric Age: 0-17 M Maternity Age: 12-55 A Adult Age: 15-124

808.53 **Multiple pelvic fractures with disruption of pelvic circle**

808.59 **Other**

808.8 **Unspecified, closed**

808.9 **Unspecified, open**

4th 809 Ill-defined fractures of bones of trunk

INCLUDES bones of trunk with other bones except those of skull and face
multiple bones of trunk

EXCLUDES *multiple fractures of:*
pelvic bones alone (808.0-808.9)
ribs alone (807.0-807.1, 807.4)
ribs or sternum with limb bones (819.0-819.1, 828.0-828.1)
skull or face with other bones (804.0-804.9)

809.0 **Fracture of bones of trunk, closed**

809.1 **Fracture of bones of trunk, open**

FRACTURE OF UPPER LIMB (810-819)

4th 810 Fracture of clavicle

INCLUDES collar bone
interligamentous part of clavicle

The following fifth-digit subclassification is for use with category 810:
- **0 unspecified part**
  Clavicle NOS
- **1 sternal end of clavicle**
- **2 shaft of clavicle**
- **3 acromial end of clavicle**

§ 5th **810.0 Closed**
[0-3]

§ 5th **810.1 Open**
[0-3]

4th 811 Fracture of scapula

INCLUDES shoulder blade

The following fifth-digit subclassification is for use with category 811:
- **0 unspecified part**
- **1 acromial process**
  Acromion (process)
- **2 coracoid process**
- **3 glenoid cavity and neck of scapula**
- **9 other**

§ 5th **811.0 Closed**
[0-3, 9]

§ 5th **811.1 Open**
[0-3, 9]

4th 812 Fracture of humerus

5th **812.0 Upper end, closed**

812.00 **Upper end, unspecified part**
Proximal end
Shoulder

Right Clavicle and Scapula, Anterior View

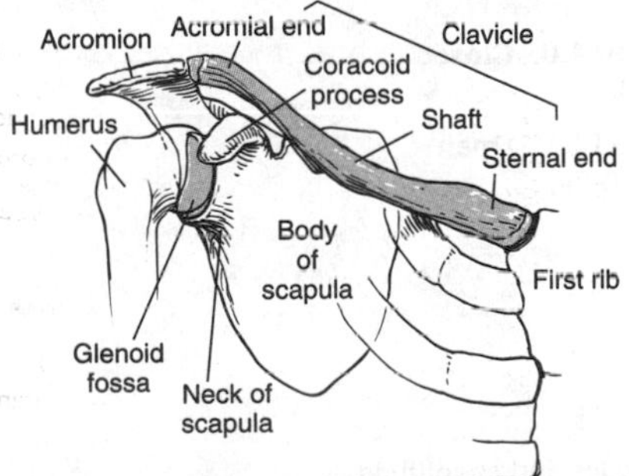

Right Humerus, Anterior View

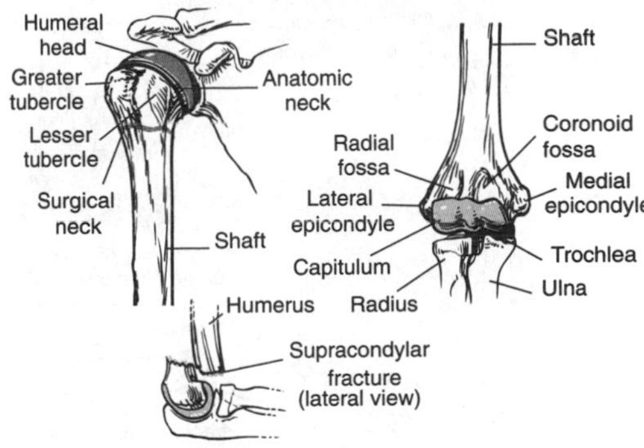

812.01 **Surgical neck**
Neck of humerus NOS

812.02 **Anatomical neck**

812.03 **Greater tuberosity**

812.09 **Other**
Head
Lesser tuberosity
Upper epiphysis

5th **812.1 Upper end, open**

812.10 **Upper end, unspecified part**

812.11 **Surgical neck**

812.12 **Anatomical neck**

812.13 **Greater tuberosity**

812.19 **Other**

5th **812.2 Shaft or unspecified part, closed**

812.20 **Unspecified part of humerus**
Humerus NOS
Upper arm NOS

812.21 **Shaft of humerus**
AHA: 4Q, '05, 129; 3Q, '99, 14

5th **812.3 Shaft or unspecified part, open**

812.30 **Unspecified part of humerus**

812.31 **Shaft of humerus**

5th **812.4 Lower end, closed**
Distal end of humerus
Elbow

812.40 **Lower end, unspecified part**

812.41 **Supracondylar fracture of humerus**

812.42 **Lateral condyle**
External condyle

812.43 **Medial condyle**
Internal epicondyle

812.44 **Lower end, unspecified part**
Articular process NOS
Lower epiphysis NOS

812.49 **Other**
Multiple fractures of lower end
Trochlea

5th **812.5 Lower end, open**

812.50 **Lower end, unspecified part**

812.51 **Supracondylar fracture of humerus**

812.52 **Lateral condyle**

812.53 **Medial condyle**

812.54 **Condyle(s), unspecified**

812.59 **Other**

§ Requires fifth-digit. Valid digits are in [brackets] under each code. See appropriate category for codes and definitions.

Right Radius and Ulna, Anterior View

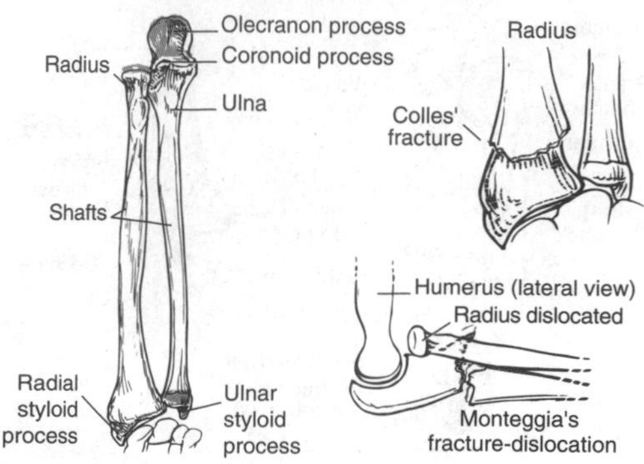

4th **813 Fracture of radius and ulna**

5th **813.0 Upper end, closed**
Proximal end

813.00 Upper end of forearm, unspecified

813.01 Olecranon process of ulna

813.02 Coronoid process of ulna

813.03 Monteggia's fracture
DEF: Fracture near the head of the ulnar shaft, causing dislocation of the radial head.

813.04 Other and unspecified fractures of proximal end of ulna (alone)
Multiple fractures of ulna, upper end

813.05 Head of radius

813.06 Neck of radius

813.07 Other and unspecified fractures of proximal end of radius (alone)
Multiple fractures of radius, upper end

813.08 Radius with ulna, upper end [any part]

5th **813.1 Upper end, open**

813.10 Upper end of forearm, unspecified

813.11 Olecranon process of ulna

813.12 Coronoid process of ulna

813.13 Monteggia's fracture

813.14 Other and unspecified fractures of proximal end of ulna (alone)

813.15 Head of radius

813.16 Neck of radius

813.17 Other and unspecified fractures of proximal end of radius (alone)

813.18 Radius with ulna, upper end [any part]

5th **813.2 Shaft, closed**

813.20 Shaft, unspecified

813.21 Radius (alone)

813.22 Ulna (alone)

813.23 Radius with ulna

5th **813.3 Shaft, open**

813.30 Shaft, unspecified

813.31 Radius (alone)

813.32 Ulna (alone)

813.33 Radius with ulna

5th **813.4 Lower end, closed**
Distal end

813.40 Lower end of forearm, unspecified

813.41 Colles' fracture
Smith's fracture
DEF: Break of lower end of radius; associated with backward movement of the radius lower section.

813.42 Other fractures of distal end of radius (alone)
Dupuytren's fracture, radius
Radius, lower end
DEF: Dupuytren's fracture: fracture and dislocation of the forearm; the fracture is of the radius above the wrist, and the dislocation is of the ulna at the lower end.

813.43 Distal end of ulna (alone)
Ulna:
head
lower end
lower epiphysis
styloid process

813.44 Radius with ulna, lower end
AHA: 1Q, '07, 7

813.45 Torus fracture of radius
AHA: 4Q, '02, 70

5th **813.5 Lower end, open**

813.50 Lower end of forearm, unspecified

813.51 Colles' fracture

813.52 Other fractures of distal end of radius (alone)

813.53 Distal end of ulna (alone)

813.54 Radius with ulna, lower end

5th **813.8 Unspecified part, closed**

813.80 Forearm, unspecified

813.81 Radius (alone)
AHA: 2Q, '98, 19

813.82 Ulna (alone)

813.83 Radius with ulna

5th **813.9 Unspecified part, open**

813.90 Forearm, unspecified

813.91 Radius (alone)

813.92 Ulna (alone)

813.93 Radius with ulna

4th **814 Fracture of carpal bone(s)**

The following fifth-digit subclassification is for use with category 814:
- **0 carpal bone, unspecified**
  Wrist NOS
- **1 navicular [scaphoid] of wrist**
- **2 lunate [semilunar] bone of wrist**
- **3 triquetral [cuneiform] bone of wrist**
- **4 pisiform**
- **5 trapezium bone [larger multangular]**
- **6 trapezoid bone [smaller multangular]**
- **7 capitate bone [os magnum]**
- **8 hamate [unciform] bone**
- **9 other**

§ 5th **814.0 Closed**
[0-9]

§ 5th **814.1 Open**
[0-9]

§ Requires fifth-digit. Valid digits are in [brackets] under each code. See category 814 for codes and definitions.

N Newborn Age: 0 P Pediatric Age: 0-17 M Maternity Age: 12-55 A Adult Age: 15-124

Hand Fractures

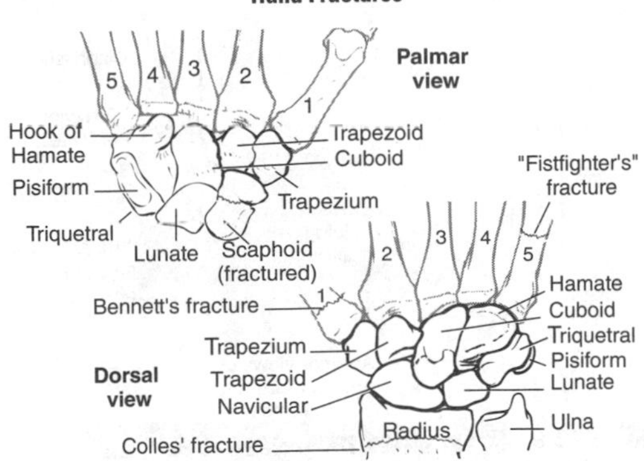

✓4th 815 Fracture of metacarpal bone(s)

INCLUDES hand [except finger]
metacarpus

The following fifth-digit subclassification is for use with category 815:

0 metacarpal bone(s), site unspecified
1 base of thumb [first] metacarpal
Bennett's fracture
2 base of other metacarpal bone(s)
3 shaft of metacarpal bone(s)
4 neck of metacarpal bone(s)
9 multiple sites of metacarpus

§ ✓5th **815.0 Closed**
[0-4, 9]

§ ✓5th **815.1 Open**
[0-4, 9]

✓4th 816 Fracture of one or more phalanges of hand

INCLUDES finger(s) thumb

The following fifth-digit subclassification is for use with category 816:

0 phalanx or phalanges, unspecified
1 middle or proximal phalanx or phalanges
2 distal phalanx or phalanges
3 multiple sites

§ ✓5th **816.0 Closed**
[0-3]

§ ✓5th **816.1 Open**
[0-3] AHA: For code 816.12: 4Q, '03, 77

✓4th 817 Multiple fractures of hand bones

INCLUDES metacarpal bone(s) with phalanx or phalanges of same hand

817.0 Closed

817.1 Open

✓4th 818 Ill-defined fractures of upper limb

INCLUDES arm NOS
multiple bones of same upper limb

EXCLUDES *multiple fractures of:*
metacarpal bone(s) with phalanx or phalanges (817.0-817.1)
phalanges of hand alone (816.0-816.1)
radius with ulna (813.0-813.9)

818.0 Closed

818.1 Open

✓4th 819 Multiple fractures involving both upper limbs, and upper limb with rib(s) and sternum

INCLUDES arm(s) with rib(s) or sternum
both arms [any bones]

819.0 Closed

819.1 Open

FRACTURE OF LOWER LIMB (820-829)

✓4th 820 Fracture of neck of femur

✓5th **820.0 Transcervical fracture, closed**

820.00 Intracapsular section, unspecified

820.01 Epiphysis (separation) (upper)
Transepiphyseal

820.02 Midcervical section
Transcervical NOS
AHA: 3Q, '03, 12

820.03 Base of neck
Cervicotrochanteric section

820.09 Other
Head of femur
Subcapital

✓5th **820.1 Transcervical fracture, open**

820.10 Intracapsular section, unspecified

820.11 Epiphysis (separation) (upper)

820.12 Midcervical section

820.13 Base of neck

820.19 Other

✓5th **820.2 Pertrochanteric fracture, closed**

820.20 Trochanteric section, unspecified
Trochanter:
NOS
greater
lesser

820.21 Intertrochanteric section

820.22 Subtrochanteric section

✓5th **820.3 Pertrochanteric fracture, open**

820.30 Trochanteric section, unspecified

820.31 Intertrochanteric section

820.32 Subtrochanteric section

820.8 Unspecified part of neck of femur, closed
Hip NOS
Neck of femur NOS

820.9 Unspecified part of neck of femur, open

✓4th 821 Fracture of other and unspecified parts of femur

✓5th **821.0 Shaft or unspecified part, closed**

821.00 Unspecified part of femur
Thigh
Upper leg
EXCLUDES *hip NOS (820.8)*

821.01 Shaft
AHA: 1Q, '07, 4; 1Q, '99, 5

✓5th **821.1 Shaft or unspecified part, open**

821.10 Unspecified part of femur

821.11 Shaft

Right Femur, Anterior View

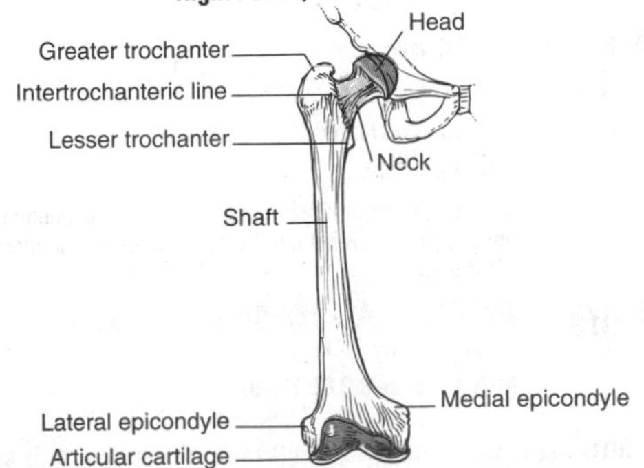

§ Requires fifth-digit. Valid digits are in [brackets] under each code. See appropriate category for codes and definitions.

Right Tibia and Fibula, Anterior View

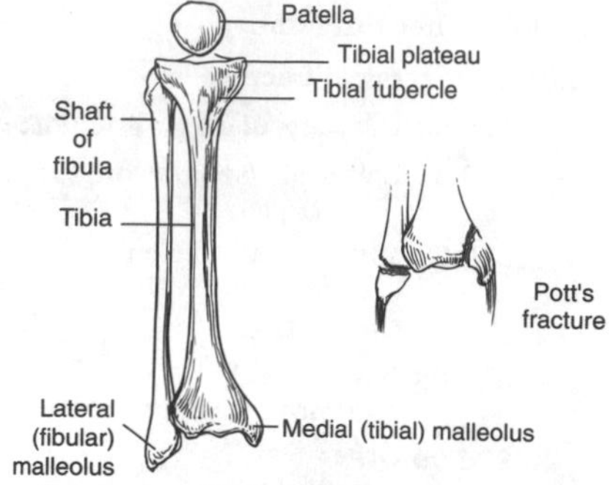

✓5th **821.2 Lower end, closed**
Distal end

821.20 Lower end, unspecified part

821.21 Condyle, femoral

821.22 Epiphysis, lower (separation)

821.23 Supracondylar fracture of femur

821.29 Other
Multiple fractures of lower end

✓5th **821.3 Lower end, open**

821.30 Lower end, unspecified part

821.31 Condyle, femoral

821.32 Epiphysis, lower (separation)

821.33 Supracondylar fracture of femur

821.39 Other

✓4th **822 Fracture of patella**

822.0 Closed

822.1 Open

✓4th **823 Fracture of tibia and fibula**

EXCLUDES *Dupuytren's fracture (824.4-824.5)*
ankle (824.4-824.5)
radius (813.42, 813.52)
Pott's fracture (824.4-824.5)
that involving ankle (824.0-824.9)

The following fifth-digit subclassification is for use with category 823:
0 tibia alone
1 fibula alone
2 fibula with tibia

§ ✓5th **823.0 Upper end, closed**
[0-2]
Head
Proximal end
Tibia:
condyles
tuberosity

§ ✓5th **823.1 Upper end, open**
[0-2]

§ ✓5th **823.2 Shaft, closed**
[0-2]

§ ✓5th **823.3 Shaft, open**
[0-2]

§ ✓5th **823.4 Torus fracture**
[0-2]
AHA: 4Q, '02, 70

DEF: A bone deformity in children, occurring commonly in the tibia and fibula, in which the bone bends and buckles but does not fracture.

§ ✓5th **823.8 Unspecified part, closed**
[0-2]
Lower leg NOS
AHA: For code 823.82: 1Q, '97, 8

Torus Fracture

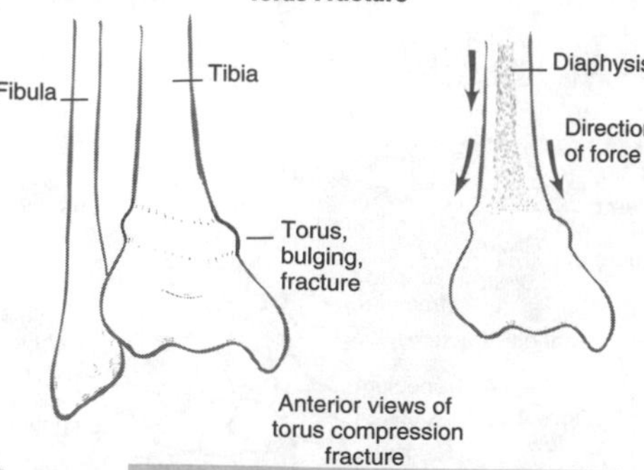

§ ✓5th **823.9 Unspecified part, open**
[0-2]

✓4th **824 Fracture of ankle**

824.0 Medial malleolus, closed
Tibia involving:
ankle
malleolus
AHA: 1Q, '04, 9

824.1 Medial malleolus, open

824.2 Lateral malleolus, closed
Fibula involving:
ankle
malleolus
AHA: 2Q, '02, 3

824.3 Lateral malleolus, open

824.4 Bimalleolar, closed
Dupuytren's fracture, fibula
Pott's fracture

DEF: Bimalleolar, closed: Breaking of both nodules (malleoli) on either side of ankle joint, without an open wound.

DEF: Dupuytren's fracture (Pott's fracture): The breaking of the farthest end of the lower leg bone (fibula), with injury to the farthest end joint of the other lower leg bone (tibia).

824.5 Bimalleolar, open

824.6 Trimalleolar, closed
Lateral and medial malleolus with anterior or posterior lip of tibia

824.7 Trimalleolar, open

824.8 Unspecified, closed
Ankle NOS
AHA: 3Q, '00, 12

824.9 Unspecified, open

✓4th **825 Fracture of one or more tarsal and metatarsal bones**

825.0 Fracture of calcaneus, closed
Heel bone
Os calcis

825.1 Fracture of calcaneus, open

Right Foot, Dorsal

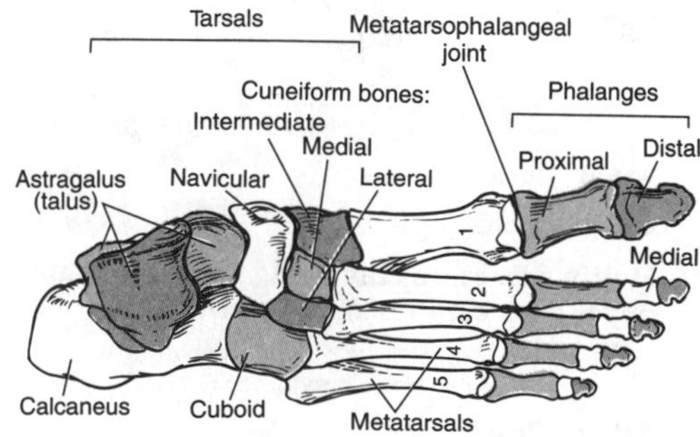

§ Requires fifth-digit. Valid digits are in [brackets] under each code. See category 823 for codes and definitions.

N Newborn Age: 0 P Pediatric Age: 0-17 M Maternity Age: 12-55 A Adult Age: 15-124

✓5th **825.2 Fracture of other tarsal and metatarsal bones, closed**

825.20 Unspecified bone(s) of foot [except toes]
Instep

825.21 Astragalus
Talus

825.22 Navicular [scaphoid], foot

825.23 Cuboid

825.24 Cuneiform, foot

825.25 Metatarsal bone(s)

825.29 Other
Tarsal with metatarsal bone(s) only
EXCLUDES *calcaneus (825.0)*

✓5th **825.3 Fracture of other tarsal and metatarsal bones, open**

825.30 Unspecified bone(s) of foot [except toes]

825.31 Astragalus

825.32 Navicular [scaphoid], foot

825.33 Cuboid

825.34 Cuneiform, foot

825.35 Metatarsal bone(s)

825.39 Other

✓4th **826 Fracture of one or more phalanges of foot**

INCLUDES toe(s)

826.0 Closed

826.1 Open

✓4th **827 Other, multiple, and ill-defined fractures of lower limb**

INCLUDES leg NOS
multiple bones of same lower limb

EXCLUDES *multiple fractures of:*
ankle bones alone (824.4-824.9)
phalanges of foot alone (826.0-826.1)
tarsal with metatarsal bones (825.29, 825.39)
tibia with fibula (823.0-823.9 with fifth-digit 2)

827.0 Closed

827.1 Open

✓4th **828 Multiple fractures involving both lower limbs, lower with upper limb, and lower limb(s) with rib(s) and sternum**

INCLUDES arm(s) with leg(s) [any bones]
both legs [any bones]
leg(s) with rib(s) or sternum

828.0 Closed

828.1 Open

✓4th **829 Fracture of unspecified bones**

829.0 Unspecified bone, closed

829.1 Unspecified bone, open

DISLOCATION (830-839)

INCLUDES displacement
subluxation

EXCLUDES *congenital dislocation (754.0-755.8)*
pathological dislocation (718.2)
recurrent dislocation (718.3)

The descriptions "closed" and "open," used in the fourth-digit subdivisions, include the following terms:

closed:	open:
complete	compound
dislocation NOS	infected
partial	with foreign body
simple	
uncomplicated	

A dislocation not indicated as closed or open should be classified as closed.

AHA: 3Q, '90, 12

✓4th **830 Dislocation of jaw**

INCLUDES jaw (cartilage) (meniscus)
mandible
maxilla (inferior)
temporomandibular (joint)

830.0 Closed dislocation

830.1 Open dislocation

✓4th **831 Dislocation of shoulder**

EXCLUDES *sternoclavicular joint (839.61, 839.71)*
sternum (839.61, 839.71)

The following fifth-digit subclassification is for use with category 831:
0 shoulder, unspecified
Humerus NOS
1 anterior dislocation of humerus
2 posterior dislocation of humerus
3 inferior dislocation of humerus
4 acromioclavicular (joint)
Clavicle
9 other
Scapula

§ ✓5th **831.0 Closed dislocation**
[0-4, 9]

§ ✓5th **831.1 Open dislocation**
[0-4, 9]

✓4th **832 Dislocation of elbow**

The following fifth-digit subclassification is for use with category 832:
0 elbow, unspecified
1 anterior dislocation of elbow
2 posterior dislocation of elbow
3 medial dislocation of elbow
4 lateral dislocation of elbow
9 other

§ ✓5th **832.0 Closed dislocation**
[0-4, 9]

§ ✓5th **832.1 Open dislocation**
[0-4, 9]

§ Requires fifth-digit. Valid digits are in [brackets] under each code. See appropriate category for codes and definitions.

✓4th 833 Dislocation of wrist

The following fifth-digit subclassification is for use with category 833:
- **0 wrist unspecified part**
  - Carpal (bone)
  - Radius, distal end
- **1 radioulnar (joint), distal**
- **2 radiocarpal (joint)**
- **3 midcarpal (joint)**
- **4 carpometacarpal (joint)**
- **5 metacarpal (bone), proximal end**
- **9 other**
  - Ulna, distal end

§ ✓5th **833.0 Closed dislocation**
[0-5, 9]

§ ✓5th **833.1 Open dislocation**
[0-5, 9]

✓4th 834 Dislocation of finger

INCLUDES finger(s)
phalanx of hand
thumb

The following fifth-digit subclassification is for use with category 834:
- **0 finger unspecified part**
- **1 metacarpophalangeal (joint)**
  - Metacarpal (bone), distal end
- **2 interphalangeal (joint), hand**

§ ✓5th **834.0 Closed dislocation**
[0-2]

§ ✓5th **834.1 Open dislocation**
[0-2]

✓4th 835 Dislocation of hip

The following fifth-digit subclassification is for use with category 835:
- **0 dislocation of hip, unspecified**
- **1 posterior dislocation**
- **2 obturator dislocation**
- **3 other anterior dislocation**

§ ✓5th **835.0 Closed dislocation**
[0-3]

§ ✓5th **835.1 Open dislocation**
[0-3]

✓4th 836 Dislocation of knee

EXCLUDES *dislocation of knee:*
old or pathological (718.2)
recurrent (718.3)
internal derangement of knee joint (717.0-717.5, 717.8-717.9)
old tear of cartilage or meniscus of knee (717.0-717.5, 717.8-717.9)

836.0 Tear of medial cartilage or meniscus of knee, current
Bucket handle tear:
NOS } current injury
medial meniscus } current injury

836.1 Tear of lateral cartilage or meniscus of knee, current

836.2 Other tear of cartilage or meniscus of knee, current
Tear of:
cartilage (semilunar) } current injury, not specified as medial or lateral
meniscus } current injury, not specified as medial or lateral

836.3 Dislocation of patella, closed

836.4 Dislocation of patella, open

✓5th **836.5 Other dislocation of knee, closed**

836.50 Dislocation of knee, unspecified

836.51 Anterior dislocation of tibia, proximal end
Posterior dislocation of femur, distal end

836.52 Posterior dislocation of tibia, proximal end
Anterior dislocation of femur, distal end

836.53 Medial dislocation of tibia, proximal end

836.54 Lateral dislocation of tibia, proximal end

836.59 Other

✓5th **836.6 Other dislocation of knee, open**

836.60 Dislocation of knee, unspecified

836.61 Anterior dislocation of tibia, proximal end

836.62 Posterior dislocation of tibia, proximal end

836.63 Medial dislocation of tibia, proximal end

836.64 Lateral dislocation of tibia, proximal end

836.69 Other

✓4th 837 Dislocation of ankle

INCLUDES astragalus
fibula, distal end
navicular, foot
scaphoid, foot
tibia, distal end

837.0 Closed dislocation

837.1 Open dislocation

✓4th 838 Dislocation of foot

The following fifth-digit subclassification is for use with category 838:
- **0 foot unspecified**
- **1 tarsal (bone), joint unspecified**
- **2 midtarsal (joint)**
- **3 tarsometatarsal (joint)**
- **4 metatarsal (bone), joint unspecified**
- **5 metatarsophalangeal (joint)**
- **6 interphalangeal (joint), foot**
- **9 other**
  - Phalanx of foot
  - Toe(s)

§ ✓5th **838.0 Closed dislocation**
[0-6, 9]

§ ✓5th **838.1 Open dislocation**
[0-6, 9]

✓4th 839 Other, multiple, and ill-defined dislocations

✓5th **839.0 Cervical vertebra, closed**
Cervical spine
Neck

839.00 Cervical vertebra, unspecified

839.01 First cervical vertebra

839.02 Second cervical vertebra

839.03 Third cervical vertebra

839.04 Fourth cervical vertebra

839.05 Fifth cervical vertebra

839.06 Sixth cervical vertebra

839.07 Seventh cervical vertebra

839.08 Multiple cervical vertebrae

✓5th **839.1 Cervical vertebra, open**

839.10 Cervical vertebra, unspecified

§ Requires fifth-digit. Valid digits are in [brackets] under each code. See appropriate category for codes and definitions.

N Newborn Age: 0 P Pediatric Age: 0-17 M Maternity Age: 12-55 A Adult Age: 15-124

839.11 **First cervical vertebra**

839.12 **Second cervical vertebra**

839.13 **Third cervical vertebra**

839.14 **Fourth cervical vertebra**

839.15 **Fifth cervical vertebra**

839.16 **Sixth cervical vertebra**

839.17 **Seventh cervical vertebra**

839.18 **Multiple cervical vertebrae**

5th 839.2 **Thoracic and lumbar vertebra, closed**

839.20 **Lumbar vertebra**

839.21 **Thoracic vertebra**
Dorsal [thoracic] vertebra

5th 839.3 **Thoracic and lumbar vertebra, open**

839.30 **Lumbar vertebra**

839.31 **Thoracic vertebra**

5th 839.4 **Other vertebra, closed**

839.40 **Vertebra, unspecified site**
Spine NOS

839.41 **Coccyx**

839.42 **Sacrum**
Sacroiliac (joint)

839.49 **Other**

5th 839.5 **Other vertebra, open**

839.50 **Vertebra, unspecified site**

839.51 **Coccyx**

839.52 **Sacrum**

839.59 **Other**

5th 839.6 **Other location, closed**

839.61 **Sternum**
Sternoclavicular joint

839.69 **Other**
Pelvis

5th 839.7 **Other location, open**

839.71 **Sternum**

839.79 **Other**

839.8 **Multiple and ill-defined, closed**
Arm
Back
Hand
Multiple locations, except fingers or toes alone
Other ill-defined locations
Unspecified location

839.9 **Multiple and ill-defined, open**

SPRAINS AND STRAINS OF JOINTS AND ADJACENT MUSCLES (840-848)

INCLUDES avulsion, hemarthrosis, laceration, rupture, sprain, strain, tear } of: joint capsule, ligament, muscle, tendon

EXCLUDES *laceration of tendon in open wounds (880-884 and 890-894 with .2)*

4th **840 Sprains and strains of shoulder and upper arm**

840.0 **Acromioclavicular (joint) (ligament)**

840.1 **Coracoclavicular (ligament)**

840.2 **Coracohumeral (ligament)**

840.3 **Infraspinatus (muscle) (tendon)**

840.4 **Rotator cuff (capsule)**
EXCLUDES *complete rupture of rotator cuff, nontraumatic (727.61)*

840.5 **Subscapularis (muscle)**

840.6 **Supraspinatus (muscle) (tendon)**

840.7 **Superior glenoid labrum lesion**
SLAP lesion
AHA: 4Q,'01, 52
DEF: Detachment injury of the superior aspect of the glenoid labrum which is the ring of fibrocartilage attached to the rim of the glenoid cavity of the scapula.

840.8 **Other specified sites of shoulder and upper arm**

840.9 **Unspecified site of shoulder and upper arm**
Arm NOS
Shoulder NOS

4th **841 Sprains and strains of elbow and forearm**

841.0 **Radial collateral ligament**

841.1 **Ulnar collateral ligament**

841.2 **Radiohumeral (joint)**

841.3 **Ulnohumeral (joint)**

841.8 **Other specified sites of elbow and forearm**

841.9 **Unspecified site of elbow and forearm**
Elbow NOS

4th **842 Sprains and strains of wrist and hand**

5th 842.0 **Wrist**

842.00 **Unspecified site**

842.01 **Carpal (joint)**

842.02 **Radiocarpal (joint) (ligament)**

842.09 **Other**
Radioulnar joint, distal

5th 842.1 **Hand**

842.10 **Unspecified site**

842.11 **Carpometacarpal (joint)**

842.12 **Metacarpophalangeal (joint)**

842.13 **Interphalangeal (joint)**

842.19 **Other**
Midcarpal (joint)

4th **843 Sprains and strains of hip and thigh**

843.0 **Iliofemoral (ligament)**

843.1 **Ischiocapsular (ligament)**

843.8 **Other specified sites of hip and thigh**

843.9 **Unspecified site of hip and thigh**
Hip NOS
Thigh NOS

4th **844 Sprains and strains of knee and leg**

844.0 **Lateral collateral ligament of knee**

844.1 **Medial collateral ligament of knee**

844.2 **Cruciate ligament of knee**

844.3 **Tibiofibular (joint) (ligament), superior**

844.8 **Other specified sites of knee and leg**

844.9 **Unspecified site of knee and leg**
Knee NOS
Leg NOS

4th **845 Sprains and strains of ankle and foot**

5th 845.0 **Ankle**

845.00 **Unspecified site**
AHA: 2Q, '02, 3

845.01 Deltoid (ligament), ankle
Internal collateral (ligament), ankle

845.02 Calcaneofibular (ligament)

845.03 Tibiofibular (ligament), distal
AHA: 1Q, '04, 9

845.09 Other
Achilles tendon

5th **845.1 Foot**

845.10 Unspecified site

845.11 Tarsometatarsal (joint) (ligament)

845.12 Metatarsophalangeal (joint)

845.13 Interphalangeal (joint), toe

845.19 Other

4th **846 Sprains and strains of sacroiliac region**

846.0 Lumbosacral (joint) (ligament)

846.1 Sacroiliac ligament

846.2 Sacrospinatus (ligament)

846.3 Sacrotuberous (ligament)

846.8 Other specified sites of sacroiliac region

846.9 Unspecified site of sacroiliac region

4th **847 Sprains and strains of other and unspecified parts of back**

EXCLUDES *lumbosacral (846.0)*

847.0 Neck
Anterior longitudinal (ligament), cervical
Atlanto-axial (joints)
Atlanto-occipital (joints)
Whiplash injury

EXCLUDES *neck injury NOS (959.0)*
thyroid region (848.2)

847.1 Thoracic

847.2 Lumbar

847.3 Sacrum
Sacrococcygeal (ligament)

847.4 Coccyx

847.9 Unspecified site of back
Back NOS

4th **848 Other and ill-defined sprains and strains**

848.0 Septal cartilage of nose

848.1 Jaw
Temporomandibular (joint) (ligament)

848.2 Thyroid region
Cricoarytenoid (joint) (ligament)
Cricothyroid (joint) (ligament)
Thyroid cartilage

848.3 Ribs
Chondrocostal (joint) } without mention of
Costal cartilage } injury to sternum

5th **848.4 Sternum**

848.40 Unspecified site

848.41 Sternoclavicular (joint) (ligament)

848.42 Chondrosternal (joint)

848.49 Other
Xiphoid cartilage

848.5 Pelvis
Symphysis pubis

EXCLUDES *that in childbirth (665.6)*

848.8 Other specified sites of sprains and strains

848.9 Unspecified site of sprain and strain

INTRACRANIAL INJURY, EXCLUDING THOSE WITH SKULL FRACTURE (850-854)

EXCLUDES *intracranial injury with skull fracture (800-801 and 803-804, except .0 and .5)*
open wound of head without intracranial injury (870.0-873.9)
skull fracture alone (800-801 and 803-804 with .0, .5)

Note: The description "with open intracranial wound," used in the fourth-digit subdivisions, includes those specified as open or with mention of infection or foreign body.

The following fifth-digit subclassification is for use with categories 851-854:

0 unspecified state of consciousness
1 with no loss of consciousness
2 with brief [less than one hour] loss of consciousness
3 with moderate [1-24 hours] loss of consciousness
4 with prolonged [more than 24 hours] loss of consciousness and returen to pre-existing conscious level
5 with prolonged [more than 24 hours] loss of consciousness without return to pre-existing conscious level
Use fifth-digit 5 to designate when a patient is unconscious and dies before regaining cosciousness, regardless of the duration of the loss of consciousness
6 with loss of consciousness of unspecified duration
9 with concussion, unspecified

AHA: 1Q, '93, 22

850 Concussion

INCLUDES commotio cerebri

EXCLUDES *concussion with:*
cerebral laceration or contusion (851.0-851.9)
cerebral hemorrhage (852-853)
head injury NOS (959.01)

AHA: 2Q, '96, 6; 4Q, '90, 24

850.0 With no loss of consciousness
Concussion with mental confusion or disorientation, without loss of consciousness

5th **850.1 With brief loss of consciousness**
Loss of consciousness for less than one hour
AHA: 4Q, '03, 76; 1Q, '99, 10; 2Q, '92, 5

850.11 With loss of consciousness of 30 minutes or less

850.12 With loss of consciousness from 31 to 59 minutes

850.2 With moderate loss of consciousness
Loss of consciousness for 1-24 hours

850.3 With prolonged loss of consciousness and return to pre-existing conscious level
Loss of consciousness for more than 24 hours with complete recovery

850.4 With prolonged loss of consciousness, without return to pre-existing conscious level

850.5 With loss of consciousness of unspecified duration

850.9 Concussion, unspecified

4th **851 Cerebral laceration and contusion**
AHA: 4Q, '96, 36; 1Q, '93, 22; 4Q, '90, 24

§ 5th **851.0 Cortex (cerebral) contusion without mention of open intracranial wound**
[0-6, 9]

§ 5th **851.1 Cortex (cerebral) contusion with open intracranial wound**
[0-6, 9]
AHA: 1Q, '92, 9

§ 5th **851.2 Cortex (cerebral) laceration without mention of open intracranial wound**
[0-6, 9]

§ Requires fifth-digit. Valid digits are in [brackets] under each code. See beginning of section 850-854 for codes and definitions.

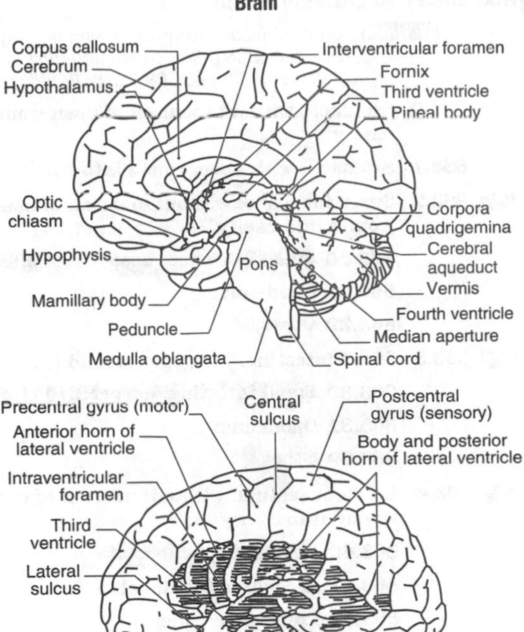

§ 5th **851.3 Cortex (cerebral) laceration with open intracranial wound**
[0-6, 9]

§ 5th **851.4 Cerebellar or brain stem contusion without mention of open intracranial wound**
[0-6, 9]

§ 5th **851.5 Cerebellar or brain stem contusion with open intracranial wound**
[0-6, 9]

§ 5th **851.6 Cerebellar or brain stem laceration without mention of open intracranial wound**
[0-6, 9]

§ 5th **851.7 Cerebellar or brain stem laceration with open intracranial wound**
[0-6, 9]

§ 5th **851.8 Other and unspecified cerebral laceration and contusion, without mention of open intracranial wound**
[0-6, 9]
Brain (membrane) NOS
AHA: 4Q, '96, 37

§ 5th **851.9 Other and unspecified cerebral laceration and contusion, with open intracranial wound**
[0-6, 9]

4th **852 Subarachnoid, subdural, and extradural hemorrhage, following injury**

EXCLUDES *Cerebral contusion or laceration (with hemorrhage) (851.0-851.9)*

DEF: Bleeding from lining of brain; due to injury.

§ 5th **852.0 Subarachnoid hemorrhage following injury without mention of open intracranial wound**
[0-6, 9]
Middle meningeal hemorrhage following injury

§ 5th **852.1 Subarachnoid hemorrhage following injury with open intracranial wound**
[0-6, 9]

§ 5th **852.2 Subdural hemorrhage following injury without mention of open intracranial wound**
[0-6, 9]
AHA: 4Q, '96, 43; For codes 852.21-852.29: 4Q, '07, 107

§ 5th **852.3 Subdural hemorrhage following injury with open intracranial wound**
[0-6, 9]

§ 5th **852.4 Extradural hemorrhage following injury without mention of open intracranial wound**
[0-6, 9]
Epidural hematoma following injury

§ 5th **852.5 Extradural hemorrhage following injury with open intracranial wound**
[0-6, 9]

4th **853 Other and unspecified intracranial hemorrhage following injury**

§ 5th **853.0 Without mention of open intracranial wound**
[0-6, 9]
Cerebral compression due to injury
Intracranial hematoma following injury
Traumatic cerebral hemorrhage
AHA: 3Q, '90, 14

§ 5th **853.1 With open intracranial wound**
[0-6, 9]

4th **854 Intracranial injury of other and unspecified nature**

INCLUDES brain injury NOS
cavernous sinus
intracranial injury

EXCLUDES *any condition classifiable to 850-853*
head injury NOS (959.01)

AHA: 1Q, '99, 10; 2Q, '92, 6

§ 5th **854.0 Without mention of open intracranial wound**
[0-6, 9] AHA: For code 854.00: 2Q, '05, 6

§ 5th **854.1 With open intracranial wound**
[0-6, 9]

INTERNAL INJURY OF THORAX, ABDOMEN, AND PELVIS (860-869)

INCLUDES blast injuries, blunt trauma, bruise, concussion injuries (except cerebral), crushing, hematoma, laceration, puncture, tear, traumatic rupture } of internal organs

EXCLUDES *concussion NOS (850.0-850.9)*
flail chest (807.4)
foreign body entering through orifice (930.0-939.9)
injury to blood vessels (901.0-902.9)

Note: The description "with open wound," used in the fourth-digit subdivisions, includes those with mention of infection or foreign body.

4th **860 Traumatic pneumothorax and hemothorax**

AHA: 2Q, '93, 4

DEF: Traumatic pneumothorax: air or gas leaking into pleural space of lung due to trauma.

DEF: Traumatic hemothorax: blood buildup in pleural space of lung due to trauma.

860.0 Pneumothorax without mention of open wound into thorax

860.1 Pneumothorax with open wound into thorax

860.2 Hemothorax without mention of open wound into thorax

860.3 Hemothorax with open wound into thorax

860.4 Pneumohemothorax without mention of open wound into thorax

860.5 Pneumohemothorax with open wound into thorax

§ Requires fifth-digit. Valid digits are in [brackets] under each code. See beginning of section 850-854 for codes and definitions.

4th 861 Injury to heart and lung

EXCLUDES *injury to blood vessels of thorax (901.0-901.9)*

5th 861.0 Heart, without mention of open wound into thorax

AHA: 1Q, '92, 9

861.00 Unspecified injury

861.01 Contusion

Cardiac contusion
Myocardial contusion

DEF: Bruising within the pericardium with no mention of open wound.

861.02 Laceration without penetration of heart chambers

DEF: Tearing injury of heart tissue, without penetration of chambers; no open wound.

861.03 Laceration with penetration of heart chambers

5th 861.1 Heart, with open wound into thorax

861.10 Unspecified injury

861.11 Contusion

861.12 Laceration without penetration of heart chambers

861.13 Laceration with penetration of heart chambers

5th 861.2 Lung, without mention of open wound into thorax

861.20 Unspecified injury

861.21 Contusion

DEF: Bruising of lung without mention of open wound.

861.22 Laceration

5th 861.3 Lung, with open wound into thorax

861.30 Unspecified injury

861.31 Contusion

861.32 Laceration

4th 862 Injury to other and unspecified intrathoracic organs

EXCLUDES *injury to blood vessels of thorax (901.0-901.9)*

862.0 Diaphragm, without mention of open wound into cavity

862.1 Diaphragm, with open wound into cavity

5th 862.2 Other specified intrathoracic organs, without mention of open wound into cavity

862.21 Bronchus

862.22 Esophagus

862.29 Other

Pleura
Thymus gland

5th 862.3 Other specified intrathoracic organs, with open wound into cavity

862.31 Bronchus

862.32 Esophagus

862.39 Other

862.8 Multiple and unspecified intrathoracic organs, without mention of open wound into cavity

Crushed chest
Multiple intrathoracic organs

862.9 Multiple and unspecified intrathoracic organs, with open wound into cavity

4th 863 Injury to gastrointestinal tract

EXCLUDES *anal sphincter laceration during delivery (664.2)*
bile duct (868.0-868.1 with fifth-digit 2)
gallbladder (868.0-868.1 with fifth-digit 2)

863.0 Stomach, without mention of open wound into cavity

863.1 Stomach, with open wound into cavity

5th 863.2 Small intestine, without mention of open wound into cavity

863.20 Small intestine, unspecified site

863.21 Duodenum

863.29 Other

5th 863.3 Small intestine, with open wound into cavity

863.30 Small intestine, unspecified site

863.31 Duodenum

863.39 Other

5th 863.4 Colon or rectum, without mention of open wound into cavity

863.40 Colon, unspecified site

863.41 Ascending [right] colon

863.42 Transverse colon

863.43 Descending [left] colon

863.44 Sigmoid colon

863.45 Rectum

863.46 Multiple sites in colon and rectum

863.49 Other

5th 863.5 Colon or rectum, with open wound into cavity

863.50 Colon, unspecified site

863.51 Ascending [right] colon

863.52 Transverse colon

863.53 Descending [left] colon

863.54 Sigmoid colon

863.55 Rectum

863.56 Multiple sites in colon and rectum

863.59 Other

5th 863.8 Other and unspecified gastrointestinal sites, without mention of open wound into cavity

863.80 Gastrointestinal tract, unspecified site

863.81 Pancreas, head

863.82 Pancreas, body

863.83 Pancreas, tail

863.84 Pancreas, multiple and unspecified sites

863.85 Appendix

863.89 Other

Intestine NOS

5th 863.9 Other and unspecified gastrointestinal sites, with open wound into cavity

863.90 Gastrointestinal tract, unspecified site

863.91 Pancreas, head

863.92 Pancreas, body

863.93 Pancreas, tail

863.94 Pancreas, multiple and unspecified sites

863.95 Appendix

863.99 Other

✓4th 864 Injury to liver

The following fifth-digit subclassification is for use with category 864:

- **0 unspecified injury**
- **1 hematoma and contusion**
- **2 laceration, minor**
  Laceration involving capsule only, or without significant involvement of hepatic parenchyma [i.e., less than 1 cm deep]
- **3 laceration, moderate**
  Laceration involving parenchyma but without major disruption of parenchyma [i.e., less than 10 cm long and less than 3 cm deep]
- **4 laceration, major**
  Laceration with significant disruption of hepatic parenchyma [i.e., 10 cm long and 3 cm deep]
  Multiple moderate lacerations, with or without hematoma
  Stellate lacerations of liver
- **5 laceration, unspecified**
- **9 other**

§ ✓5th **864.0 Without mention of open wound into cavity**
[0-5, 9]

§ ✓5th **864.1 With open wound into cavity**
[0-5, 9]

✓4th 865 Injury to spleen

The following fifth-digit subclassification is for use with category 865:

- **0 unspecified injury**
- **1 hematoma without rupture of capsule**
- **2 capsular tears, without major disruption of parenchyma**
- **3 laceration extending into parenchyma**
- **4 massive parenchymal disruption**
- **9 other**

§ ✓5th **865.0 Without mention of wound into cavity**
[0-4, 9]

§ ✓5th **865.1 With open wound into cavity**
[0-4, 9]

✓4th 866 Injury to kidney

EXCLUDES ▶*acute kidney injury (nontraumatic) (584.9)*◀

The following fifth-digit subclassification is for use with category 866:

- **0 unspecified injury**
- **1 hematoma without rupture of capsule**
- **2 laceration**
- **3 complete disruption of kidney parenchyma**

§ ✓5th **866.0 Without mention of open wound into cavity**
[0-3]

§ ✓5th **866.1 With open wound into cavity**
[0-3]

✓4th 867 Injury to pelvic organs

EXCLUDES *injury during delivery (664.0-665.9)*

867.0 Bladder and urethra, without mention of open wound into cavity
AHA: N-D, '85, 15

867.1 Bladder and urethra, with open wound into cavity

867.2 Ureter, without mention of open wound into cavity

867.3 Ureter, with open wound into cavity

867.4 Uterus, without mention of open wound into cavity ♀

867.5 Uterus, with open wound into cavity ♀

867.6 Other specified pelvic organs, without mention of open wound into cavity
Fallopian tube
Ovary
Prostate
Seminal vesicle
Vas deferens

867.7 Other specified pelvic organs, with open wound into cavity

867.8 Unspecified pelvic organ, without mention of open wound into cavity

867.9 Unspecified pelvic organ, with open wound into cavity

✓4th 868 Injury to other intra-abdominal organs

The following fifth-digit subclassification is for use with category 868:

- **0 unspecified intra-abdominal organ**
- **1 adrenal gland**
- **2 bile duct and gallbladder**
- **3 peritoneum**
- **4 retroperitoneum**
- **9 other and multiple intra-abdominal organs**

§ ✓5th **868.0 Without mention of open wound into cavity**
[0-4, 9]

§ ✓5th **868.1 With open wound into cavity**
[0-4, 9]

✓4th 869 Internal injury to unspecified or ill-defined organs

INCLUDES internal injury NOS
multiple internal injury NOS

869.0 Without mention of open wound into cavity

869.1 With open wound into cavity
AHA: 2Q, '89, 15

OPEN WOUND (870-897)

INCLUDES animal bite
avulsion
cut
laceration
puncture wound
traumatic amputation

Use additional code to identify infection

EXCLUDES *burn (940.0-949.5)*
crushing (925-929.9)
puncture of internal organs (860.0-869.1)
superficial injury (910.0-919.9)
that incidental to:
dislocation (830.0-839.9)
fracture (800.0-829.1)
internal injury (860.0-869.1)
intracranial injury (851.0-854.1)

Note: The description "complicated" used in the fourth-digit subdivisions includes those with mention of delayed healing, delayed treatment, foreign body, or infection.

AHA: 4Q, '01, 52

OPEN WOUND OF HEAD, NECK, AND TRUNK (870-879)

✓4th 870 Open wound of ocular adnexa

870.0 Laceration of skin of eyelid and periocular area

870.1 Laceration of eyelid, full-thickness, not involving lacrimal passages

870.2 Laceration of eyelid involving lacrimal passages

870.3 Penetrating wound of orbit, without mention of foreign body

870.4 Penetrating wound of orbit with foreign body

EXCLUDES *retained (old) foreign body in orbit (376.6)*

§ Requires fifth-digit. Valid digits are in [brackets] under each code. See appropriate category for codes and definitions.

870.8 Other specified open wounds of ocular adnexa

870.9 Unspecified open wound of ocular adnexa

✓4th **871 Open wound of eyeball**

EXCLUDES *2nd cranial nerve [optic] injury (950.0-950.9)*
3rd cranial nerve [oculomotor] injury (951.0)

871.0 Ocular laceration without prolapse of intraocular tissue
AHA: 3Q, '96, 7
DEF: Tear in ocular tissue without displacing structures.

871.1 Ocular laceration with prolapse or exposure of intraocular tissue

871.2 Rupture of eye with partial loss of intraocular tissue
DEF: Forcible tearing of eyeball, with tissue loss.

871.3 Avulsion of eye
Traumatic enucleation
DEF: Traumatic extraction of eyeball from socket.

871.4 Unspecified laceration of eye

871.5 Penetration of eyeball with magnetic foreign body
EXCLUDES *retained (old) magnetic foreign body in globe (360.50-360.59)*

871.6 Penetration of eyeball with (nonmagnetic) foreign body
EXCLUDES *retained (old) (nonmagnetic) foreign body in globe (360.60-360.69)*

871.7 Unspecified ocular penetration

871.9 Unspecified open wound of eyeball

✓4th **872 Open wound of ear**

✓5th **872.0 External ear, without mention of complication**

872.00 External ear, unspecified site

872.01 Auricle, ear
Pinna
DEF: Open wound of fleshy, outer ear.

872.02 Auditory canal
DEF: Open wound of passage from external ear to eardrum.

✓5th **872.1 External ear, complicated**

872.10 External ear, unspecified site

872.11 Auricle, ear

872.12 Auditory canal

✓5th **872.6 Other specified parts of ear, without mention of complication**

872.61 Ear drum
Drumhead
Tympanic membrane

872.62 Ossicles

872.63 Eustachian tube
DEF: Open wound of channel between nasopharynx and tympanic cavity.

872.64 Cochlea
DEF: Open wound of snail shell shaped tube of inner ear.

872.69 Other and multiple sites

✓5th **872.7 Other specified parts of ear, complicated**

872.71 Ear drum

872.72 Ossicles

872.73 Eustachian tube

872.74 Cochlea

872.79 Other and multiple sites

872.8 Ear, part unspecified, without mention of complication
Ear NOS

872.9 Ear, part unspecified, complicated

✓4th **873 Other open wound of head**

873.0 Scalp, without mention of complication

873.1 Scalp, complicated

✓5th **873.2 Nose, without mention of complication**

873.20 Nose, unspecified site

873.21 Nasal septum
DEF: Open wound between nasal passages.

873.22 Nasal cavity
DEF: Open wound of nostrils.

873.23 Nasal sinus
DEF: Open wound of mucous-lined respiratory cavities.

873.29 Multiple sites

✓5th **873.3 Nose, complicated**

873.30 Nose, unspecified site

873.31 Nasal septum

873.32 Nasal cavity

873.33 Nasal sinus

873.39 Multiple sites

✓5th **873.4 Face, without mention of complication**

873.40 Face, unspecified site

873.41 Cheek

873.42 Forehead
Eyebrow
AHA: 4Q, '96, 43

873.43 Lip

873.44 Jaw

873.49 Other and multiple sites

✓5th **873.5 Face, complicated**

873.50 Face, unspecified site

873.51 Cheek

873.52 Forehead

873.53 Lip

873.54 Jaw

873.59 Other and multiple sites

✓5th **873.6 Internal structures of mouth, without mention of complication**

873.60 Mouth, unspecified site

873.61 Buccal mucosa
DEF: Open wound of inside of cheek.

873.62 Gum (alveolar process)

873.63 Tooth (broken) (fractured) (due to trauma)
EXCLUDES *cracked tooth (521.81)*
AHA: 1Q, '04, 17

873.64 Tongue and floor of mouth

873.65 Palate
DEF: Open wound of roof of mouth.

873.69 Other and multiple sites

✓5th **873.7 Internal structures of mouth, complicated**

873.70 Mouth, unspecified site

873.71 **Buccal mucosa**

873.72 **Gum (alveolar process)**

873.73 **Tooth (broken) (fractured) (due to trauma)**

EXCLUDES *cracked tooth (521.81)*

AHA: 1Q, '04, 17

873.74 **Tongue and floor of mouth**

873.75 **Palate**

873.79 **Other and multiple sites**

873.8 **Other and unspecified open wound of head without mention of complication**
Head NOS

873.9 **Other and unspecified open wound of head complicated**

874 Open wound of neck

874.0 **Larynx and trachea, without mention of complication**

874.00 **Larynx with trachea**

874.01 **Larynx**

874.02 **Trachea**

874.1 **Larynx and trachea, complicated**

874.10 **Larynx with trachea**

874.11 **Larynx**

874.12 **Trachea**

874.2 **Thyroid gland, without mention of complication**

874.3 **Thyroid gland, complicated**

874.4 **Pharynx, without mention of complication**
Cervical esophagus

874.5 **Pharynx, complicated**

874.8 **Other and unspecified parts, without mention of complication**
Nape of neck
Supraclavicular region
Throat NOS

874.9 **Other and unspecified parts, complicated**

875 Open wound of chest (wall)

EXCLUDES *open wound into thoracic cavity (860.0-862.9)*
traumatic pneumothorax and hemothorax (860.1, 860.3, 860.5)

AHA: 3Q, '93, 17

875.0 **Without mention of complication**

875.1 **Complicated**

876 Open wound of back

INCLUDES loin
lumbar region

EXCLUDES *open wound into thoracic cavity (860.0-862.9)*
traumatic pneumothorax and hemothorax (860.1, 860.3, 860.5)

876.0 **Without mention of complication**

876.1 **Complicated**

877 Open wound of buttock

INCLUDES sacroiliac region

877.0 **Without mention of complication**

877.1 **Complicated**

878 Open wound of genital organs (external), including traumatic amputation

EXCLUDES *injury during delivery (664.0-665.9)*
internal genital organs (867.0-867.9)

878.0 **Penis, without mention of complication** ♂

878.1 **Penis, complicated** ♂

878.2 **Scrotum and testes, without mention of complication** ♂

878.3 **Scrotum and testes, complicated** ♂

878.4 **Vulva, without mention of complication** ♀
Labium (majus) (minus)

878.5 **Vulva, complicated** ♀

878.6 **Vagina, without mention of complication** ♀

878.7 **Vagina, complicated** ♀

878.8 **Other and unspecified parts, without mention of complication**

878.9 **Other and unspecified parts, complicated**

879 Open wound of other and unspecified sites, except limbs

879.0 **Breast, without mention of complication**

879.1 **Breast, complicated**

879.2 **Abdominal wall, anterior, without mention of complication**
Abdominal wall NOS
Epigastric region
Hypogastric region
Pubic region
Umbilical region

AHA: 2Q, '91, 22

879.3 **Abdominal wall, anterior, complicated**

879.4 **Abdominal wall, lateral, without mention of complication**
Flank
Groin
Hypochondrium
Iliac (region)
Inguinal region

879.5 **Abdominal wall, lateral, complicated**

879.6 **Other and unspecified parts of trunk, without mention of complication**
Pelvic region
Perineum
Trunk NOS

879.7 **Other and unspecified parts of trunk, complicated**

879.8 **Open wound(s) (multiple) of unspecified site(s) without mention of complication**
Multiple open wounds NOS
Open wound NOS

879.9 **Open wound(s) (multiple) of unspecified site(s), complicated**

OPEN WOUND OF UPPER LIMB (880-887)

AHA: N-D, '85, 5

880 Open wound of shoulder and upper arm

The following fifth-digit subclassification is for use with category 880:
0 shoulder region
1 scapular region
2 axillary region
3 upper arm
9 multiple sites

§ 880.0 **Without mention of complication**
[0-3, 9]

§ 880.1 **Complicated**
[0-3, 9] AHA: 2Q, '06, 7

§ 880.2 **With tendon involvement**
[0-3, 9]

§ Requires fifth-digit. Valid digits are in [brackets] under each code. See category 880 for codes and definitions.

4th 881 Open wound of elbow, forearm, and wrist

The following fifth-digit subclassification is for use with category 881:
- **0 forearm**
- **1 elbow**
- **2 wrist**

§ 5th **881.0 Without mention of complication**
[0-2]

§ 5th **881.1 Complicated**
[0-2]

§ 5th **881.2 With tendon involvement**
[0-2]

4th 882 Open wound of hand except finger(s) alone

882.0 Without mention of complication

882.1 Complicated

882.2 With tendon involvement

4th 883 Open wound of finger(s)

INCLUDES fingernail
thumb (nail)

883.0 Without mention of complication

883.1 Complicated

883.2 With tendon involvement

4th 884 Multiple and unspecified open wound of upper limb

INCLUDES arm NOS
multiple sites of one upper limb
upper limb NOS

884.0 Without mention of complication

884.1 Complicated

884.2 With tendon involvement

4th 885 Traumatic amputation of thumb (complete) (partial)

INCLUDES thumb(s) (with finger(s) of either hand)

885.0 Without mention of complication
AHA: 1Q, '03, 7

885.1 Complicated

4th 886 Traumatic amputation of other finger(s) (complete) (partial)

INCLUDES finger(s) of one or both hands, without mention of thumb(s)

886.0 Without mention of complication

886.1 Complicated

4th 887 Traumatic amputation of arm and hand (complete) (partial)

887.0 Unilateral, below elbow, without mention of complication

887.1 Unilateral, below elbow, complicated

887.2 Unilateral, at or above elbow, without mention of complication

887.3 Unilateral, at or above elbow, complicated

887.4 Unilateral, level not specified, without mention of complication

887.5 Unilateral, level not specified, complicated

887.6 Bilateral [any level], without mention of complication
One hand and other arm

887.7 Bilateral [any level], complicated

OPEN WOUND OF LOWER LIMB (890-897)

AHA: N-D, '85, 5

4th 890 Open wound of hip and thigh

890.0 Without mention of complication

890.1 Complicated

890.2 With tendon involvement

4th 891 Open wound of knee, leg [except thigh], and ankle

INCLUDES leg NOS
multiple sites of leg, except thigh

EXCLUDES *that of thigh (890.0-890.2)*
with multiple sites of lower limb (894.0-894.2)

891.0 Without mention of complication

891.1 Complicated

891.2 With tendon involvement

4th 892 Open wound of foot except toe(s) alone

INCLUDES heel

892.0 Without mention of complication

892.1 Complicated

892.2 With tendon involvement

4th 893 Open wound of toe(s)

INCLUDES toenail

893.0 Without mention of complication

893.1 Complicated

893.2 With tendon involvement

4th 894 Multiple and unspecified open wound of lower limb

INCLUDES lower limb NOS
multiple sites of one lower limb, with thigh

894.0 Without mention of complication

894.1 Complicated

894.2 With tendon involvement

4th 895 Traumatic amputation of toe(s) (complete) (partial)

INCLUDES toe(s) of one or both feet

895.0 Without mention of complication

895.1 Complicated

4th 896 Traumatic amputation of foot (complete) (partial)

896.0 Unilateral, without mention of complication

896.1 Unilateral, complicated

896.2 Bilateral, without mention of complication

EXCLUDES *one foot and other leg (897.6-897.7)*

896.3 Bilateral, complicated

4th 897 Traumatic amputation of leg(s) (complete) (partial)

897.0 Unilateral, below knee, without mention of complication

897.1 Unilateral, below knee, complicated

897.2 Unilateral, at or above knee, without mention of complication

897.3 Unilateral, at or above knee, complicated

897.4 Unilateral, level not specified, without mention of complication

897.5 Unilateral, level not specified, complicated

897.6 Bilateral [any level], without mention of complication
One foot and other leg

897.7 Bilateral [any level], complicated
AHA: 3Q, '90, 5

§ Requires fifth-digit. Valid digits are in [brackets] under each code. See category 881 for codes and definitions.

INJURY TO BLOOD VESSELS (900-904)

INCLUDES arterial hematoma, avulsion, cut, laceration, rupture, traumatic aneurysm or fistula (arteriovenous) } of blood vessel secondary to other injuries, e.g.; fracture or open wound

EXCLUDES *accidental puncture or laceration during medical procedure (998.2)*
intracranial hemorrhage following injury (851.0-854.1)

AHA: 3Q, '90, 5

✓4th 900 Injury to blood vessels of head and neck
- ✓5th **900.0 Carotid artery**
  - **900.00 Carotid artery, unspecified**
  - **900.01 Common carotid artery**
  - **900.02 External carotid artery**
  - **900.03 Internal carotid artery**
- **900.1 Internal jugular vein**
- ✓5th **900.8 Other specified blood vessels of head and neck**
  - **900.81 External jugular vein**
    Jugular vein NOS
  - **900.82 Multiple blood vessels of head and neck**
  - **900.89 Other**
- **900.9 Unspecified blood vessel of head and neck**

✓4th 901 Injury to blood vessels of thorax

EXCLUDES *traumatic hemothorax (860.2-860.5)*

- **901.0 Thoracic aorta**
- **901.1 Innominate and subclavian arteries**
- **901.2 Superior vena cava**
- **901.3 Innominate and subclavian veins**
- ✓5th **901.4 Pulmonary blood vessels**
  - **901.40 Pulmonary vessel(s), unspecified**
  - **901.41 Pulmonary artery**
  - **901.42 Pulmonary vein**
- ✓5th **901.8 Other specified blood vessels of thorax**
  - **901.81 Intercostal artery or vein**
  - **901.82 Internal mammary artery or vein**
  - **901.83 Multiple blood vessels of thorax**
  - **901.89 Other**
    Azygos vein
    Hemiazygos vein
- **901.9 Unspecified blood vessel of thorax**

✓4th 902 Injury to blood vessels of abdomen and pelvis
- **902.0 Abdominal aorta**
- ✓5th **902.1 Inferior vena cava**
  - **902.10 Inferior vena cava, unspecified**
  - **902.11 Hepatic veins**
  - **902.19 Other**
- ✓5th **902.2 Celiac and mesenteric arteries**
  - **902.20 Celiac and mesenteric arteries, unspecified**
  - **902.21 Gastric artery**
  - **902.22 Hepatic artery**
  - **902.23 Splenic artery**
  - **902.24 Other specified branches of celiac axis**
  - **902.25 Superior mesenteric artery (trunk)**
  - **902.26 Primary branches of superior mesenteric artery**
    Ileocolic artery
  - **902.27 Inferior mesenteric artery**
  - **902.29 Other**
- ✓5th **902.3 Portal and splenic veins**
  - **902.31 Superior mesenteric vein and primary subdivisions**
    Ileocolic vein
  - **902.32 Inferior mesenteric vein**
  - **902.33 Portal vein**
  - **902.34 Splenic vein**
  - **902.39 Other**
    Cystic vein
    Gastric vein
- ✓5th **902.4 Renal blood vessels**
  - **902.40 Renal vessel(s), unspecified**
  - **902.41 Renal artery**
  - **902.42 Renal vein**
  - **902.49 Other**
    Suprarenal arteries
- ✓5th **902.5 Iliac blood vessels**
  - **902.50 Iliac vessel(s), unspecified**
  - **902.51 Hypogastric artery**
  - **902.52 Hypogastric vein**
  - **902.53 Iliac artery**
  - **902.54 Iliac vein**
  - **902.55 Uterine artery** ♀
  - **902.56 Uterine vein** ♀
  - **902.59 Other**
- ✓5th **902.8 Other specified blood vessels of abdomen and pelvis**
  - **902.81 Ovarian artery** ♀
  - **902.82 Ovarian vein** ♀
  - **902.87 Multiple blood vessels of abdomen and pelvis**
  - **902.89 Other**
- **902.9 Unspecified blood vessel of abdomen and pelvis**

✓4th 903 Injury to blood vessels of upper extremity
- ✓5th **903.0 Axillary blood vessels**
  - **903.00 Axillary vessel(s), unspecified**
  - **903.01 Axillary artery**
  - **903.02 Axillary vein**
- **903.1 Brachial blood vessels**
- **903.2 Radial blood vessels**
- **903.3 Ulnar blood vessels**
- **903.4 Palmar artery**
- **903.5 Digital blood vessels**
- **903.8 Other specified blood vessels of upper extremity**
  Multiple blood vessels of upper extremity
- **903.9 Unspecified blood vessel of upper extremity**

✓4th 904 Injury to blood vessels of lower extremity and unspecified sites
- **904.0 Common femoral artery**
  Femoral artery above profunda origin
- **904.1 Superficial femoral artery**

904.2 Femoral veins

904.3 Saphenous veins
Saphenous vein (greater) (lesser)

5th **904.4 Popliteal blood vessels**

904.40 Popliteal vessel(s), unspecified

904.41 Popliteal artery

904.42 Popliteal vein

5th **904.5 Tibial blood vessels**

904.50 Tibial vessel(s), unspecified

904.51 Anterior tibial artery

904.52 Anterior tibial vein

904.53 Posterior tibial artery

904.54 Posterior tibial vein

904.6 Deep plantar blood vessels

904.7 Other specified blood vessels of lower extremity
Multiple blood vessels of lower extremity

904.8 Unspecified blood vessel of lower extremity

904.9 Unspecified site
Injury to blood vessel NOS

LATE EFFECTS OF INJURIES, POISONINGS, TOXIC EFFECTS, AND OTHER EXTERNAL CAUSES (905-909)

Note: These categories are to be used to indicate conditions classifiable to 800-999 as the cause of late effects, which are themselves classified elsewhere. The "late effects" include those specified as such, or as sequelae, which may occur at any time after the acute injury.

4th **905 Late effects of musculoskeletal and connective tissue injuries**
AHA: 1Q, '95, 10; 2Q, '94, 3

905.0 Late effect of fracture of skull and face bones
Late effect of injury classifiable to 800-804
AHA: 3Q, '97, 12

905.1 Late effect of fracture of spine and trunk without mention of spinal cord lesion
Late effect of injury classifiable to 805, 807-809
AHA: 1Q, '07, 20

905.2 Late effect of fracture of upper extremities
Late effect of injury classifiable to 810-819

905.3 Late effect of fracture of neck of femur
Late effect of injury classifiable to 820

905.4 Late effect of fracture of lower extremities
Late effect of injury classifiable to 821-827

905.5 Late effect of fracture of multiple and unspecified bones
Late effect of injury classifiable to 828-829

905.6 Late effect of dislocation
Late effect of injury classifiable to 830-839

905.7 Late effect of sprain and strain without mention of tendon injury
Late effect of injury classifiable to 840-848, except tendon injury

905.8 Late effect of tendon injury
Late effect of tendon injury due to:
open wound [injury classifiable to 880-884 with .2, 890-894 with .2]
sprain and strain [injury classifiable to 840-848]
AHA: 2Q, '89, 13; 2Q, '89, 15

905.9 Late effect of traumatic amputation
Late effect of injury classifiable to 885-887, 895-897
EXCLUDES *late amputation stump complication (997.60-997.69)*

4th **906 Late effects of injuries to skin and subcutaneous tissues**

906.0 Late effect of open wound of head, neck, and trunk
Late effect of injury classifiable to 870-879

906.1 Late effect of open wound of extremities without mention of tendon injury
Late effect of injury classifiable to 880-884, 890-894 except .2

906.2 Late effect of superficial injury
Late effect of injury classifiable to 910-919

906.3 Late effect of contusion
Late effect of injury classifiable to 920-924

906.4 Late effect of crushing
Late effect of injury classifiable to 925-929

906.5 Late effect of burn of eye, face, head, and neck
Late effect of injury classifiable to 940-941
AHA: 4Q, '04, 76

906.6 Late effect of burn of wrist and hand
Late effect of injury classifiable to 944
AHA: 4Q, '94, 22

906.7 Late effect of burn of other extremities
Late effect of injury classifiable to 943 or 945
AHA: 4Q, '94, 22

906.8 Late effect of burns of other specified sites
Late effect of injury classifiable to 942, 946-947
AHA: 4Q, '94, 22

906.9 Late effect of burn of unspecified site
Late effect of injury classifiable to 948-949
AHA: 4Q, '94, 22

4th **907 Late effects of injuries to the nervous system**

907.0 Late effect of intracranial injury without mention of skull fracture
Late effect of injury classifiable to 850-854
AHA: 4Q, '03, 103; 3Q, '90, 14

907.1 Late effect of injury to cranial nerve
Late effect of injury classifiable to 950-951

907.2 Late effect of spinal cord injury
Late effect of injury classifiable to 806, 952
AHA: 4Q, '03, 103; 4Q, '98, 38

907.3 Late effect of injury to nerve root(s), spinal plexus(es), and other nerves of trunk
Late effect of injury classifiable to 953-954
AHA: 2Q, '07, 11

907.4 Late effect of injury to peripheral nerve of shoulder girdle and upper limb
Late effect of injury classifiable to 955

907.5 Late effect of injury to peripheral nerve of pelvic girdle and lower limb
Late effect of injury classifiable to 956

907.9 Late effect of injury to other and unspecified nerve
Late effect of injury classifiable to 957

4th **908 Late effects of other and unspecified injuries**

908.0 Late effect of internal injury to chest
Late effect of injury classifiable to 860-862

908.1 Late effect of internal injury to intra-abdominal organs
Late effect of injury classifiable to 863-866, 868

908.2 Late effect of internal injury to other internal organs
Late effect of injury classifiable to 867 or 869

908.3 Late effect of injury to blood vessel of head, neck, and extremities
Late effect of injury classifiable to 900, 903-904

908.4 Late effect of injury to blood vessel of thorax, abdomen, and pelvis
Late effect of injury classifiable to 901-902

908.5 Late effect of foreign body in orifice
Late effect of injury classifiable to 930-939

908.6 Late effect of certain complications of trauma
Late effect of complications classifiable to 958

908.9 Late effect of unspecified injury
Late effect of injury classifiable to 959
AHA: 3Q, '00, 4

4th 909 Late effects of other and unspecified external causes

909.0 Late effect of poisoning due to drug, medicinal or biological substance
Late effect of conditions classifiable to 960-979
EXCLUDES *late effect of adverse effect of drug, medicinal or biological substance (909.5)*
AHA: 4Q, '03, 103

909.1 Late effect of toxic effects of nonmedical substances
Late effect of conditions classifiable to 980-989

909.2 Late effect of radiation
Late effect of conditions classifiable to 990

909.3 Late effect of complications of surgical and medical care
Late effect of conditions classifiable to 996-999
AHA: 1Q, '93, 29

909.4 Late effect of certain other external causes
Late effect of conditions classifiable to 991-994

909.5 Late effect of adverse effect of drug, medical or biological substance
EXCLUDES *late effect of poisoning due to drug, medicinal or biological substance (909.0)*
AHA: 4Q, '94, 48

909.9 Late effect of other and unspecified external causes

SUPERFICIAL INJURY (910-919)

EXCLUDES *burn (blisters) (940.0-949.5)*
contusion (920-924.9)
foreign body:
granuloma (728.82)
inadvertently left in operative wound (998.4)
residual in soft tissue (729.6)
insect bite, venomous (989.5)
open wound with incidental foreign body (870.0-897.7)

AHA: 2Q, '89, 15

4th 910 Superficial injury of face, neck, and scalp except eye

INCLUDES cheek
ear
gum
lip
nose
throat

EXCLUDES *eye and adnexa (918.0-918.9)*

910.0 Abrasion or friction burn without mention of infection

910.1 Abrasion or friction burn, infected

910.2 Blister without mention of infection

910.3 Blister, infected

910.4 Insect bite, nonvenomous, without mention of infection

910.5 Insect bite, nonvenomous, infected

910.6 Superficial foreign body (splinter) without major open wound and without mention of infection

910.7 Superficial foreign body (splinter) without major open wound, infected

910.8 Other and unspecified superficial injury of face, neck, and scalp without mention of infection

910.9 Other and unspecified superficial injury of face, neck, and scalp, infected

4th 911 Superficial injury of trunk

INCLUDES abdominal wall
anus
back
breast
buttock
chest wall
flank
groin
interscapular region
labium (majus) (minus)
penis
perineum
scrotum
testis
vagina
vulva

EXCLUDES *hip (916.0-916.9)*
scapular region (912.0-912.9)

911.0 Abrasion or friction burn without mention of infection
AHA: 3Q, '01, 10

911.1 Abrasion or friction burn, infected

911.2 Blister without mention of infection

911.3 Blister, infected

911.4 Insect bite, nonvenomous, without mention of infection

911.5 Insect bite, nonvenomous, infected

911.6 Superficial foreign body (splinter) without major open wound and without mention of infection

911.7 Superficial foreign body (splinter) without major open wound, infected

911.8 Other and unspecified superficial injury of trunk without mention of infection

911.9 Other and unspecified superficial injury of trunk, infected

4th 912 Superficial injury of shoulder and upper arm

INCLUDES axilla
scapular region

912.0 Abrasion or friction burn without mention of infection

912.1 Abrasion or friction burn, infected

912.2 Blister without mention of infection

912.3 Blister, infected

912.4 Insect bite, nonvenomous, without mention of infection

912.5 Insect bite, nonvenomous, infected

912.6 Superficial foreign body (splinter) without major open wound and without mention of infection

912.7 Superficial foreign body (splinter) without major open wound, infected

912.8 Other and unspecified superficial injury of shoulder and upper arm without mention of infection

912.9 Other and unspecified superficial injury of shoulder and upper arm, infected

913 Superficial injury of elbow, forearm, and wrist

913.0 Abrasion or friction burn without mention of infection

913.1 Abrasion or friction burn, infected

913.2 Blister without mention of infection

913.3 Blister, infected

913.4 Insect bite, nonvenomous, without mention of infection

913.5 Insect bite, nonvenomous, infected

913.6 Superficial foreign body (splinter) without major open wound and without mention of infection

913.7 Superficial foreign body (splinter) without major open wound, infected

913.8 Other and unspecified superficial injury of elbow, forearm, and wrist without mention of infection

913.9 Other and unspecified superficial injury of elbow, forearm, and wrist, infected

914 Superficial injury of hand(s) except finger(s) alone

914.0 Abrasion or friction burn without mention of infection

914.1 Abrasion or friction burn, infected

914.2 Blister without mention of infection

914.3 Blister, infected

914.4 Insect bite, nonvenomous, without mention of infection

914.5 Insect bite, nonvenomous, infected

914.6 Superficial foreign body (splinter) without major open wound and without mention of infection

914.7 Superficial foreign body (splinter) without major open wound, infected

914.8 Other and unspecified superficial injury of hand without mention of infection

914.9 Other and unspecified superficial injury of hand, infected

915 Superficial injury of finger(s)

INCLUDES fingernail
thumb (nail)

915.0 Abrasion or friction burn without mention of infection

915.1 Abrasion or friction burn, infected

915.2 Blister without mention of infection

915.3 Blister, infected

915.4 Insect bite, nonvenomous, without mention of infection

915.5 Insect bite, nonvenomous, infected

915.6 Superficial foreign body (splinter) without major open wound and without mention of infection

915.7 Superficial foreign body (splinter) without major open wound, infected

915.8 Other and unspecified superficial injury of fingers without mention of infection

AHA: 3Q, '01, 10

915.9 Other and unspecified superficial injury of fingers, infected

916 Superficial injury of hip, thigh, leg, and ankle

916.0 Abrasion or friction burn without mention of infection

916.1 Abrasion or friction burn, infected

916.2 Blister without mention of infection

916.3 Blister, infected

916.4 Insect bite, nonvenomous, without mention of infection

916.5 Insect bite, nonvenomous, infected

916.6 Superficial foreign body (splinter) without major open wound and without mention of infection

916.7 Superficial foreign body (splinter) without major open wound, infected

916.8 Other and unspecified superficial injury of hip, thigh, leg, and ankle without mention of infection

916.9 Other and unspecified superficial injury of hip, thigh, leg, and ankle, infected

917 Superficial injury of foot and toe(s)

INCLUDES heel
toenail

917.0 Abrasion or friction burn without mention of infection

917.1 Abrasion or friction burn, infected

917.2 Blister without mention of infection

917.3 Blister, infected

917.4 Insect bite, nonvenomous, without mention of infection

917.5 Insect bite, nonvenomous, infected

917.6 Superficial foreign body (splinter) without major open wound and without mention of infection

917.7 Superficial foreign body (splinter) without major open wound, infected

917.8 Other and unspecified superficial injury of foot and toes without mention of infection

AHA: 1Q, '03, 13

917.9 Other and unspecified superficial injury of foot and toes infected

AHA: 1Q, '03, 13

918 Superficial injury of eye and adnexa

EXCLUDES *burn (940.0-940.9)*
foreign body on external eye (930.0-930.9)

918.0 Eyelids and periocular area

Abrasion
Insect bite
Superficial foreign body (splinter)

918.1 Cornea

Corneal abrasion
Superficial laceration

EXCLUDES *corneal injury due to contact lens (371.82)*

918.2 Conjunctiva

918.9 Other and unspecified superficial injuries of eye

Eye (ball) NOS

919 Superficial injury of other, multiple, and unspecified sites

EXCLUDES *multiple sites classifiable to the same three-digit category (910.0-918.9)*

919.0 Abrasion or friction burn without mention of infection

919.1 Abrasion or friction burn, infected

919.2 Blister without mention of infection

919.3 Blister, infected

919.4 Insect bite, nonvenomous, without mention of infection

919.5 Insect bite, nonvenomous, infected

919.6 Superficial foreign body (splinter) without major open wound and without mention of infection

919.7 Superficial foreign body (splinter) without major open wound, infected

919.8 Other and unspecified superficial injuries without mention of infection

919.9 Other and unspecified superficial injury, infected

CONTUSION WITH INTACT SKIN SURFACE (920-924)

INCLUDES bruise } without fracture or open wound
hematoma } without fracture or open wound

EXCLUDES *concussion (850.0-850.9)*
hemarthrosis (840.0-848.9)
internal organs (860.0-869.1)
that incidental to:
crushing injury (925-929.9)
dislocation (830.0-839.9)
fracture (800.0-829.1)
internal injury (860.0-869.1)
intracranial injury (850.0-854.1)
nerve injury (950.0-957.9)
open wound (870.0-897.7)

920 Contusion of face, scalp, and neck except eye(s)
Cheek
Ear (auricle)
Gum
Lip
Mandibular joint area
Nose
Throat

4th **921 Contusion of eye and adnexa**

921.0 Black eye, not otherwise specified

921.1 Contusion of eyelids and periocular area

921.2 Contusion of orbital tissues

921.3 Contusion of eyeball

921.9 Unspecified contusion of eye
Injury of eye NOS

4th **922 Contusion of trunk**

922.0 Breast

922.1 Chest wall

922.2 Abdominal wall
Flank
Groin

5th **922.3 Back**
AHA: 4Q, '96, 39

922.31 Back
EXCLUDES *interscapular region (922.33)*
AHA: 3Q, '99, 14

922.32 Buttock

922.33 Interscapular region

922.4 Genital organs
Labium (majus) (minus)
Penis
Perineum
Scrotum
Testis
Vagina
Vulva

922.8 Multiple sites of trunk

922.9 Unspecified part
Trunk NOS

4th **923 Contusion of upper limb**

5th **923.0 Shoulder and upper arm**

923.00 Shoulder region

923.01 Scapular region

923.02 Axillary region

923.03 Upper arm

923.09 Multiple sites

5th **923.1 Elbow and forearm**

923.10 Forearm

923.11 Elbow

5th **923.2 Wrist and hand(s), except finger(s) alone**

923.20 Hand(s)

923.21 Wrist

923.3 Finger
Fingernail
Thumb (nail)

923.8 Multiple sites of upper limb

923.9 Unspecified part of upper limb
Arm NOS

4th **924 Contusion of lower limb and of other and unspecified sites**

5th **924.0 Hip and thigh**

924.00 Thigh

924.01 Hip

5th **924.1 Knee and lower leg**

924.10 Lower leg

924.11 Knee

5th **924.2 Ankle and foot, excluding toe(s)**

924.20 Foot
Heel

924.21 Ankle

924.3 Toe
Toenail

924.4 Multiple sites of lower limb

924.5 Unspecified part of lower limb
Leg NOS

924.8 Multiple sites, not elsewhere classified
AHA: 1Q, '03, 7

924.9 Unspecified site

CRUSHING INJURY (925-929)

Use additional code to identify any associated injuries, such as:
fractures (800-829)
internal injuries (860.0-869.1)
intracranial injuries (850.0-854.1)

AHA: 4Q, '03, 77; 2Q, '93, 7

4th **925 Crushing injury of face, scalp, and neck**
Cheek
Ear
Larynx
Pharynx
Throat

925.1 Crushing injury of face and scalp
Cheek
Ear

925.2 Crushing injury of neck
Larynx
Pharynx
Throat

✓4th **926 Crushing injury of trunk**

926.0 External genitalia
Labium (majus) (minus)
Penis
Scrotum
Testis
Vulva

✓5th **926.1 Other specified sites**

926.11 Back

926.12 Buttock

926.19 Other
Breast

926.8 Multiple sites of trunk

926.9 Unspecified site
Trunk NOS

✓4th **927 Crushing injury of upper limb**

✓5th **927.0 Shoulder and upper arm**

927.00 Shoulder region

927.01 Scapular region

927.02 Axillary region

927.03 Upper arm

927.09 Multiple sites

✓5th **927.1 Elbow and forearm**

927.10 Forearm

927.11 Elbow

✓5th **927.2 Wrist and hand(s), except finger(s) alone**

927.20 Hand(s)

927.21 Wrist

927.3 Finger(s)
AHA: 4Q, '03, 77

927.8 Multiple sites of upper limb

927.9 Unspecified site
Arm NOS

✓4th **928 Crushing injury of lower limb**

✓5th **928.0 Hip and thigh**

928.00 Thigh

928.01 Hip

✓5th **928.1 Knee and lower leg**

928.10 Lower leg

928.11 Knee

✓5th **928.2 Ankle and foot, excluding toe(s) alone**

928.20 Foot
Heel

928.21 Ankle

928.3 Toe(s)

928.8 Multiple sites of lower limb

928.9 Unspecified site
Leg NOS

✓4th **929 Crushing injury of multiple and unspecified sites**

929.0 Multiple sites, not elsewhere classified

929.9 Unspecified site

EFFECTS OF FOREIGN BODY ENTERING THROUGH ORIFICE (930-939)

EXCLUDES *foreign body:*
granuloma (728.82)
inadvertently left in operative wound (998.4, 998.7)
in open wound (800-839, 851-897)
residual in soft tissues (729.6)
superficial without major open wound (910-919 with .6 or .7)

✓4th **930 Foreign body on external eye**

EXCLUDES *foreign body in penetrating wound of:*
eyeball (871.5-871.6)
retained (old) (360.5-360.6)
ocular adnexa (870.4)
retained (old) (376.6)

930.0 Corneal foreign body

930.1 Foreign body in conjunctival sac

930.2 Foreign body in lacrimal punctum

930.8 Other and combined sites

930.9 Unspecified site
External eye NOS

931 Foreign body in ear
Auditory canal
Auricle

932 Foreign body in nose
Nasal sinus
Nostril

✓4th **933 Foreign body in pharynx and larynx**

933.0 Pharynx
Nasopharynx
Throat NOS

933.1 Larynx
Asphyxia due to foreign body
Choking due to:
food (regurgitated)
phlegm

✓4th **934 Foreign body in trachea, bronchus, and lung**

934.0 Trachea

934.1 Main bronchus
AHA: 3Q, '02, 18

934.8 Other specified parts
Bronchioles
Lung

934.9 Respiratory tree, unspecified
Inhalation of liquid or vomitus, lower respiratory tract NOS

✓4th **935 Foreign body in mouth, esophagus, and stomach**

935.0 Mouth

935.1 Esophagus
AHA: 1Q, '88, 13

935.2 Stomach

936 Foreign body in intestine and colon

937 Foreign body in anus and rectum
Rectosigmoid (junction)

938 Foreign body in digestive system, unspecified
Alimentary tract NOS
Swallowed foreign body

✓4th **939 Foreign body in genitourinary tract**

939.0 Bladder and urethra

939.1 Uterus, any part ♀

EXCLUDES *intrauterine contraceptive device:*
complications from (996.32, 996.65)
presence of (V45.51)

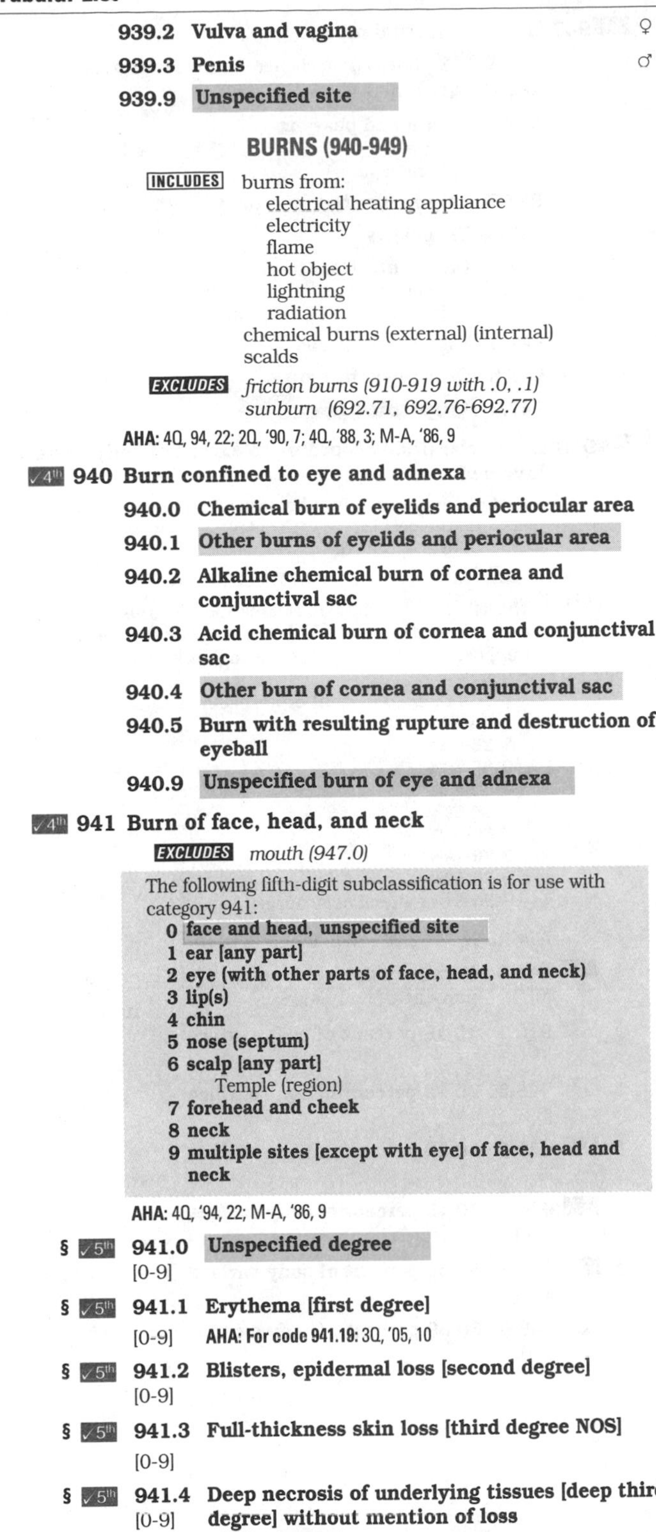

939.2 Vulva and vagina ♀

939.3 Penis ♂

939.9 Unspecified site

BURNS (940-949)

INCLUDES burns from:
- electrical heating appliance
- electricity
- flame
- hot object
- lightning
- radiation

chemical burns (external) (internal)
scalds

EXCLUDES *friction burns (910-919 with .0, .1)*
sunburn (692.71, 692.76-692.77)

AHA: 4Q, 94, 22; 2Q, '90, 7; 4Q, '88, 3; M-A, '86, 9

4th 940 Burn confined to eye and adnexa

940.0 Chemical burn of eyelids and periocular area

940.1 Other burns of eyelids and periocular area

940.2 Alkaline chemical burn of cornea and conjunctival sac

940.3 Acid chemical burn of cornea and conjunctival sac

940.4 Other burn of cornea and conjunctival sac

940.5 Burn with resulting rupture and destruction of eyeball

940.9 Unspecified burn of eye and adnexa

4th 941 Burn of face, head, and neck

EXCLUDES *mouth (947.0)*

The following fifth-digit subclassification is for use with category 941:
- **0 face and head, unspecified site**
- **1 ear [any part]**
- **2 eye (with other parts of face, head, and neck)**
- **3 lip(s)**
- **4 chin**
- **5 nose (septum)**
- **6 scalp [any part]**
  - Temple (region)
- **7 forehead and cheek**
- **8 neck**
- **9 multiple sites [except with eye] of face, head and neck**

AHA: 4Q, '94, 22; M-A, '86, 9

§ 5th **941.0 Unspecified degree**
[0-9]

§ 5th **941.1 Erythema [first degree]**
[0-9] **AHA: For code 941.19:** 3Q, '05, 10

§ 5th **941.2 Blisters, epidermal loss [second degree]**
[0-9]

§ 5th **941.3 Full-thickness skin loss [third degree NOS]**
[0-9]

§ 5th **941.4 Deep necrosis of underlying tissues [deep third degree] without mention of loss of a body part**
[0-9]

§ 5th **941.5 Deep necrosis of underlying tissues [deep third degree] with loss of a body part**
[0-9]

4th 942 Burn of trunk

EXCLUDES *scapular region (943.0-943.5 with fifth-digit 6)*

The following fifth-digit subclassificaiton is for use with category 942:
- **0 trunk, unspecified site**
- **1 breast**
- **2 chest wall, excluding breast and nipple**
- **3 abdominal wall**
  - Flank
  - Groin
- **4 back [any part]**
  - Buttock
  - Interscapular region
- **5 genitalia**
  - Labium (majus) (minus
  - Penis
  - Perineum
  - Scrotum
  - Testis
  - Vulva
- **9 other and multiple sites of trunk**

AHA: 4Q, '94, 22; M-A, '86, 9

§ 5th **942.0 Unspecified degree**
[0-5, 9]

§ 5th **942.1 Erythema [first degree]**
[0-5, 9]

§ 5th **942.2 Blisters, epidermal loss [second degree]**
[0-5, 9]

§ 5th **942.3 Full-thickness skin loss [third degree NOS]**
[0-5, 9]

§ 5th **942.4 Deep necrosis of underlying tissues[deep third degree] without mention of loss of a body part**
[0-5, 9]

§ 5th **942.5 Deep necrosis of underlying tissues[deep third degree] with loss of a body part**
[0-5, 9]

4th 943 Burn of upper limb, except wrist and hand

The following fifth-digit subclassificaiton is for use with category 943:
- **0 upper limb, unspecified site**
- **1 forearm**
- **2 elbow**
- **3 upper arm**
- **4 axilla**
- **5 shoulder**
- **6 scapular region**
- **9 multiple sites of upper limb, except wrist and hand**

AHA: 4Q, '94, 22; M-A, '06, 9

§ 5th **943.0 Unspecified degree**
[0-6, 9]

§ 5th **943.1 Erythema [first degree]**
[0-6, 9]

§ 5th **943.2 Blisters, epidermal loss [second degree]**
[0-6, 9]

§ 5th **943.3 Full-thickness skin loss [third degree NOS]**
[0-6, 9]

§ 5th **943.4 Deep necrosis of underlying tissues [deep third degree] without mention of loss of a body part**
[0-6, 9]

§ 5th **943.5 Deep necrosis of underlying tissues [deep third degree] with loss of a body part**
[0-6, 9]

§ Requires fifth-digit. Valid digits are in [brackets] under each code. See appropriate category for codes and definitions.

✓4th 944 Burn of wrist(s) and hand(s)

The following fifth-digit subclassification is for use with category 944:

0 hand, unspecified site
1 single digit [finger (nail)] other than thumb
2 thumb (nail)
3 two or more digits, not including thumb
4 two or more digits including thumb
5 palm
6 back of hand
7 wrist
8 multiple sites of wrist(s) and hand(s)

§ ✓5th **944.0 Unspecified degree**
[0-8]

§ ✓5th **944.1 Erythema [first degree]**
[0-8]

§ ✓5th **944.2 Blisters, epidermal loss [second degree]**
[0-8]

§ ✓5th **944.3 Full-thickness skin loss [third degree NOS]**
[0-8]

§ ✓5th **944.4 Deep necrosis of underlying tissues [deep third degree] without mention of loss of a body part**
[0-8]

§ ✓5th **944.5 Deep necrosis of underlying tissues [deep third degree] withloss of a body part**
[0-8]

✓4th 945 Burn of lower limb(s)

The following fifth-digit subclassification is for use with category 945:

0 lower limb [leg], unspecified site
1 toe(s) (nail)
2 foot
3 ankle
4 lower leg
5 knee
6 thigh [any part]
9 multiple sites of lower limb(s)

AHA: 4Q, '94, 22; M-A, '86, 9

§ ✓5th **945.0 Unspecified degree**
[0-6, 9]

§ ✓5th **945.1 Erythema [first degree]**
[0-6, 9]

§ ✓5th **945.2 Blisters, epidermal loss [second degree]**
[0-6, 9]

§ ✓5th **945.3 Full-thickness skin loss [third degree NOS]**
[0-6, 9]

§ ✓5th **945.4 Deep necrosis of underlying tissues [deep third degree] without mention of loss of a body part**
[0-6, 9]

§ ✓5th **945.5 Deep necrosis of underlying tissues [deep third degree] with loss of a body part**
[0-6, 9]

✓4th 946 Burns of multiple specified sites

INCLUDES burns of sites classifiable to more than one three-digit category in 940-945

EXCLUDES *multiple burns NOS (949.0-949.5)*

AHA: 4Q, '94, 22; M-A, '86, 9

946.0 Unspecified degree

946.1 Erythema [first degree]

946.2 Blisters, epidermal loss [second degree]

946.3 Full-thickness skin loss [third degree NOS]

946.4 Deep necrosis of underlying tissues [deep third degree] without mention of loss of a body part

946.5 Deep necrosis of underlying tissues [deep third degree] with loss of a body part

✓4th 947 Burn of internal organs

INCLUDES burns from chemical agents (ingested)

AHA: 4Q, '94, 22; M-A, '86, 9

947.0 Mouth and pharynx
Gum
Tongue

947.1 Larynx, trachea, and lung

947.2 Esophagus

947.3 Gastrointestinal tract
Colon
Rectum
Small intestine
Stomach

947.4 Vagina and uterus ♀

947.8 Other specified sites

947.9 Unspecified site

✓4th 948 Burns classified according to extent of body surface involved

Note: This category is to be used when the site of the burn is unspecified, or with categories 940-947 when the site is specified.

EXCLUDES *sunburn (692.71, 692.76-692.77)*

The following fifth-digit subclassification is for use with category 948 to indicate the percent of body surface with third degree burn; valid digits are in [brackets] under each code:

0 less than 10 percent or unspecified
1 10-19%
2 20-29%
3 30-39%
4 40-49%
5 50-59%
6 60-69%
7 70-79%
8 80-89%
9 90% or more of body surface

AHA: 4Q, '94, 22; 4Q, '88, 3; M-A, '86, 9; N-D, '84, 13

§ ✓5th **948.0 Burn [any degree] involving less than 10 percent of body surface**
[0]

§ ✓5th **948.1 10-19 percent of body surface**
[0-1]

§ ✓5th **948.2 20-29 percent of body surface**
[0-2]

§ ✓5th **948.3 30-39 percent of body surface**
[0-3]

§ ✓5th **948.4 40-49 percent of body surface**
[0-4]

§ ✓5th **948.5 50-59 percent of body surface**
[0-5]

§ ✓5th **948.6 60-69 percent of body surface**
[0-6]

§ Requires fifth-digit. Valid digits are in [brackets] under each code. See appropriate category for codes and definitions.

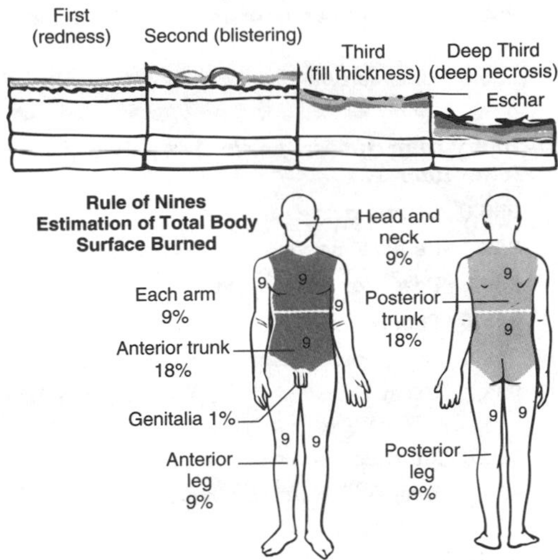

§ 5th **948.7 70-79 percent of body surface**
[0-7]

§ 5th **948.8 80-89 percent of body surface**
[0-8]

§ 5th **948.9 90 percent or more of body surface**
[0-9]

4th **949 Burn, unspecified**

INCLUDES burn NOS
multiple burns NOS

EXCLUDES *burn of unspecified site but with statement of the extent of body surface involved (948.0-948.9)*

AHA: 4Q, '94, 22; M-A, '86, 9

949.0 Unspecified degree

949.1 Erythema [first degree]

949.2 Blisters, epidermal loss [second degree]

949.3 Full-thickness skin loss [third degree NOS]

949.4 Deep necrosis of underlying tissues [deep third degree] without mention of loss of a body part

949.5 Deep necrosis of underlying tissues [deep third degree] with loss of a body part

INJURY TO NERVES AND SPINAL CORD (950-957)

INCLUDES division of nerve
lesion in continuity
traumatic neuroma
traumatic transient paralysis
(with open wound)

EXCLUDES *accidental puncture or laceration during medical procedure (998.2)*

4th **950 Injury to optic nerve and pathways**

950.0 Optic nerve injury
Second cranial nerve

950.1 Injury to optic chiasm

950.2 Injury to optic pathways

950.3 Injury to visual cortex

950.9 Unspecified
Traumatic blindness NOS

4th **951 Injury to other cranial nerve(s)**

951.0 Injury to oculomotor nerve
Third cranial nerve

951.1 Injury to trochlear nerve
Fourth cranial nerve

951.2 Injury to trigeminal nerve
Fifth cranial nerve

951.3 Injury to abducens nerve
Sixth cranial nerve

951.4 Injury to facial nerve
Seventh cranial nerve

951.5 Injury to acoustic nerve
Auditory nerve
Eighth cranial nerve
Traumatic deafness NOS

951.6 Injury to accessory nerve
Eleventh cranial nerve

951.7 Injury to hypoglossal nerve
Twelfth cranial nerve

951.8 Injury to other specified cranial nerves
Glossopharyngeal [9th cranial] nerve
Olfactory [1st cranial] nerve
Pneumogastric [10th cranial] nerve
Traumatic anosmia NOS
Vagus [10th cranial] nerve

951.9 Injury to unspecified cranial nerve

4th **952 Spinal cord injury without evidence of spinal bone injury**

5th **952.0 Cervical**

952.00 C_1-C_4 level with unspecified spinal cord injury
Spinal cord injury, cervical region NOS

952.01 C_1-C_4 level with complete lesion of spinal cord

952.02 C_1-C_4 level with anterior cord syndrome

952.03 C_1-C_4 level with central cord syndrome

952.04 C_1-C_4 level with other specified spinal cord injury
Incomplete spinal cord lesion at C_1 C_4 level:
NOS
with posterior cord syndrome

952.05 C_5-C_7 level with unspecified spinal cord injury

952.06 C_5-C_7 level with complete lesion of spinal cord

952.07 C_5-C_7 level with anterior cord syndrome

952.08 C_5-C_7 level with central cord syndrome

952.09 C_5-C_7 level with other specified spinal cord injury
Incomplete spinal cord lesion at C_5-C_7 level:
NOS
with posterior cord syndrome

Spinal Nerve Roots

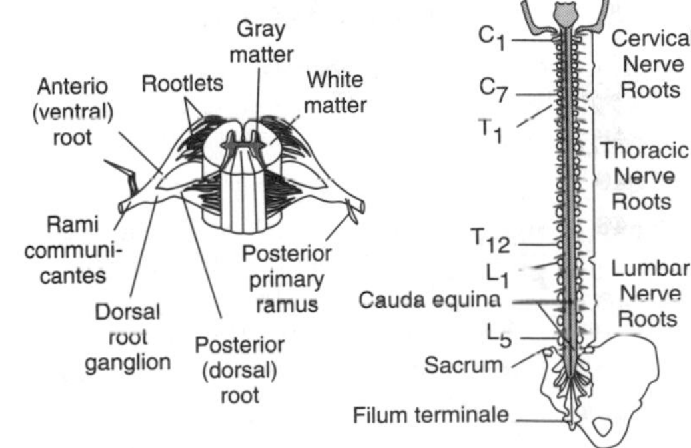

§ Requires fifth-digit. Valid digits are in [brackets] under each code. See category 948 for codes and definitions.

5th **952.1 Dorsal [thoracic]**

952.10 T_1-T_6 level with unspecified spinal cord injury
Spinal cord injury, thoracic region NOS

952.11 T_1-T_6 level with complete lesion of spinal cord

952.12 T_1-T_6 level with anterior cord syndrome

952.13 T_1-T_6 level with central cord syndrome

952.14 T_1-T_6 level with other specified spinal cord injury
Incomplete spinal cord lesion at T_1-T_6 level:
NOS
with posterior cord syndrome

952.15 T_7-T_{12} level with unspecified spinal cord injury

952.16 T_7-T_{12} level with complete lesion of spinal cord

952.17 T_7-T_{12} level with anterior cord syndrome

952.18 T_7-T_{12} level with central cord syndrome

952.19 T_7-T_{12} level with other specified spinal cord injury
Incomplete spinal cord lesion at T_7-T_{12} level:
NOS
with posterior cord syndrome

952.2 Lumbar

952.3 Sacral

952.4 Cauda equina

952.8 Multiple sites of spinal cord

952.9 Unspecified site of spinal cord

4th **953 Injury to nerve roots and spinal plexus**

953.0 Cervical root

953.1 Dorsal root

953.2 Lumbar root

953.3 Sacral root

953.4 Brachial plexus

953.5 Lumbosacral plexus

953.8 Multiple sites

953.9 Unspecified site

4th **954 Injury to other nerve(s) of trunk, excluding shoulder and pelvic girdles**

954.0 Cervical sympathetic

954.1 Other sympathetic
Celiac ganglion or plexus
Inferior mesenteric plexus
Splanchnic nerve(s)
Stellate ganglion

954.8 Other specified nerve(s) of trunk

954.9 Unspecified nerve of trunk

4th **955 Injury to peripheral nerve(s) of shoulder girdle and upper limb**

955.0 Axillary nerve

955.1 Median nerve

955.2 Ulnar nerve

955.3 Radial nerve

955.4 Musculocutaneous nerve

955.5 Cutaneous sensory nerve, upper limb

955.6 Digital nerve

955.7 Other specified nerve(s) of shoulder girdle and upper limb

955.8 Multiple nerves of shoulder girdle and upper limb

955.9 Unspecified nerve of shoulder girdle and upper limb

4th **956 Injury to peripheral nerve(s) of pelvic girdle and lower limb**

956.0 Sciatic nerve

956.1 Femoral nerve

956.2 Posterior tibial nerve

956.3 Peroneal nerve

956.4 Cutaneous sensory nerve, lower limb

956.5 Other specified nerve(s) of pelvic girdle and lower limb

956.8 Multiple nerves of pelvic girdle and lower limb

956.9 Unspecified nerve of pelvic girdle and lower limb

4th **957 Injury to other and unspecified nerves**

957.0 Superficial nerves of head and neck

957.1 Other specified nerve(s)

957.8 Multiple nerves in several parts
Multiple nerve injury NOS

957.9 Unspecified site
Nerve injury NOS

CERTAIN TRAUMATIC COMPLICATIONS AND UNSPECIFIED INJURIES (958-959)

4th **958 Certain early complications of trauma**

EXCLUDES *adult respiratory distress syndrome (518.5)*
flail chest (807.4)
▶*post-traumatic seroma (729.91)*◀
shock lung (518.5)
that occurring during or following medical procedures (996.0-999.9)

958.0 Air embolism
Pneumathemia

EXCLUDES *that complicating:*
abortion (634-638 with .6, 639.6)
ectopic or molar pregnancy (639.6)
pregnancy, childbirth, or the puerperium (673.0)

DEF: Arterial obstruction due to introduction of air bubbles into the veins following surgery or trauma.

958.1 Fat embolism

EXCLUDES *that complicating:*
abortion (634-638 with .6, 639.6)
pregnancy, childbirth, or the puerperium (673.8)

DEF: Arterial blockage due to the entrance of fat in circulatory system, after fracture of large bones or administration of corticosteroids.

958.2 Secondary and recurrent hemorrhage

958.3 Posttraumatic wound infection, not elsewhere classified

EXCLUDES *infected open wounds-code to complicated open wound of site*

AHA: 4Q, '01, 53; S-O, '85, 10

958.4 Traumatic shock
Shock (immediate) (delayed) following injury
EXCLUDES *shock:*
anaphylactic (995.0)
due to serum (999.4)
anesthetic (995.4)
electric (994.8)
following abortion (639.5)
lightning (994.0)
nontraumatic NOS (785.50)
obstetric (669.1)
postoperative (998.0)
DEF: Shock, immediate or delayed following injury.

958.5 Traumatic anuria
Crush syndrome
Renal failure following crushing
EXCLUDES *that due to a medical procedure (997.5)*
DEF: Complete suppression of urinary secretion by kidneys due to trauma.

958.6 Volkmann's ischemic contracture
Posttraumatic muscle contracture
DEF: Muscle deterioration due to loss of blood supply from injury or tourniquet; causes muscle contraction and results in inability to extend the muscles fully.

958.7 Traumatic subcutaneous emphysema
EXCLUDES *subcutaneous emphysema resulting from a procedure (998.81)*

958.8 Other early complications of trauma
AHA: 2Q, '92, 13

✓5th **958.9 Traumatic compartment syndrome**
EXCLUDES *nontraumatic compartment syndrome (729.71-729.79)*
DEF: Compression of nerves and blood vessels within an enclosed space due to previous trauma, which leads to impaired blood flow and muscle and nerve damage.

958.90 Compartment syndrome, unspecified
AHA: 4Q, '06, 100-102

958.91 Traumatic compartment syndrome of upper extremity
Traumatic compartment syndrome of shoulder, arm, forearm, wrist, hand, and fingers
AHA: 4Q, '06, 100-102

958.92 Traumatic compartment syndrome of lower extremity
Traumatic compartment syndrome of hip, buttock, thigh, leg, foot, and toes
AHA: 4Q, '06, 100-102

958.93 Traumatic compartment syndrome of abdomen
AHA: 4Q, '06, 100-102

958.99 Traumatic compartment syndrome of other sites
AHA: 4Q, '06, 100-102

✓4th **959 Injury, other and unspecified**
INCLUDES injury NOS
EXCLUDES *injury NOS of:*
blood vessels (900.0-904.9)
eye (921.0-921.9)
internal organs (860.0-869.1)
intracranial sites (854.0-854.1)
nerves (950.0-951.9, 953.0-957.9)
spinal cord (952.0-952.9)

✓5th **959.0 Head, face and neck**

959.01 Head injury, unspecified
EXCLUDES *concussion (850.1-850.9)*
with head injury NOS (850.1-850.9)
head injury NOS with loss of consciousness (850.1-850.5)
specified head injuries (850.0-854.1)
AHA: 4Q, '97, 46

959.09 Injury of face and neck
Cheek
Ear
Eyebrow
Lip
Mouth
Nose
Throat
AHA: 4Q, '97, 46

✓5th **959.1 Trunk**
EXCLUDES *scapular region (959.2)*
AHA: 4Q, '03, 78; 1Q, '99, 10

959.11 Other injury of chest wall

959.12 Other injury of abdomen

959.13 Fracture of corpus cavernosum penis ♂

959.14 Other injury of external genitals

959.19 Other injury of other sites of trunk
Injury of trunk NOS

959.2 Shoulder and upper arm
Axilla
Scapular region

959.3 Elbow, forearm, and wrist
AHA: 1Q, '97, 8

959.4 Hand, except finger

959.5 Finger
Fingernail
Thumb (nail)

959.6 Hip and thigh
Upper leg

959.7 Knee, leg, ankle, and foot

959.8 Other specified sites, including multiple
EXCLUDES *multiple sites classifiable to the same four-digit category (959.0-959.7)*

959.9 Unspecified site

POISONING BY DRUGS, MEDICINAL AND BIOLOGICAL SUBSTANCES (960-979)

INCLUDES overdose of these substances
wrong substance given or taken in error

Use additional code to specify the effects of the poisoning

EXCLUDES *adverse effects ["hypersensitivity," "reaction," etc.] of correct substance properly administered. Such cases are to be classified according to the nature of the adverse effect, such as:*
adverse effect NOS (995.20)
allergic lymphadenitis (289.3)
aspirin gastritis (535.4)
blood disorders (280.0-289.9)
dermatitis:
contact (692.0-692.9)
due to ingestion (693.0-693.9)
nephropathy (583.9)
[The drug giving rise to the adverse effect may be identified by use of categories E930-E949.]
drug dependence (304.0-304.9)
drug reaction and poisoning affecting the newborn (760.0-779.9)
nondependent abuse of drugs (305.0-305.9)
pathological drug intoxication (292.2)

AHA: 2Q, '90, 11

4th 960 Poisoning by antibiotics

EXCLUDES *antibiotics:*
ear, nose, and throat (976.6)
eye (976.5)
local (976.0)

960.0 Penicillins
Ampicillin
Carbenicillin
Cloxacillin
Penicillin G

960.1 Antifungal antibiotics
Amphotericin B
Griseofulvin
Nystatin
Trichomycin

EXCLUDES *preparations intended for topical use (976.0-976.9)*

960.2 Chloramphenicol group
Chloramphenicol
Thiamphenicol

960.3 Erythromycin and other macrolides
Oleandomycin
Spiramycin

960.4 Tetracycline group
Doxycycline
Minocycline
Oxytetracycline

960.5 Cephalosporin group
Cephalexin
Cephaloglycin
Cephaloridine
Cephalothin

960.6 Antimycobacterial antibiotics
Cycloserine
Kanamycin
Rifampin
Streptomycin

960.7 Antineoplastic antibiotics
Actinomycin such as:
Bleomycin
Cactinomycin
Dactinomycin
Daunorubicin
Mitomycin

960.8 Other specified antibiotics

960.9 Unspecified antibiotic

4th 961 Poisoning by other anti-infectives

EXCLUDES *anti-infectives:*
ear, nose, and throat (976.6)
eye (976.5)
local (976.0)

961.0 Sulfonamides
Sulfadiazine
Sulfafurazole
Sulfamethoxazole

961.1 Arsenical anti-infectives

961.2 Heavy metal anti-infectives
Compounds of:
antimony
bismuth
lead
mercury

EXCLUDES *mercurial diuretics (974.0)*

961.3 Quinoline and hydroxyquinoline derivatives
Chiniofon
Diiodohydroxyquin

EXCLUDES *antimalarial drugs (961.4)*

961.4 Antimalarials and drugs acting on other blood protozoa
Chloroquine
Cycloguanil
Primaquine
Proguanil [chloroguanide]
Pyrimethamine
Quinine

961.5 Other antiprotozoal drugs
Emetine

961.6 Anthelmintics
Hexylresorcinol
Piperazine
Thiabendazole

961.7 Antiviral drugs
Methisazone

EXCLUDES *amantadine (966.4)*
cytarabine (963.1)
idoxuridine (976.5)

961.8 Other antimycobacterial drugs
Ethambutol
Ethionamide
Isoniazid
Para-aminosalicylic acid derivatives
Sulfones

961.9 Other and unspecified anti-infectives
Flucytosine
Nitrofuran derivatives

4th 962 Poisoning by hormones and synthetic substitutes

EXCLUDES *oxytocic hormones (975.0)*

962.0 Adrenal cortical steroids
Cortisone derivatives
Desoxycorticosterone derivatives
Fluorinated corticosteroids

962.1 Androgens and anabolic congeners
Methandriol
Nandrolone
Oxymetholone
Testosterone

962.2 Ovarian hormones and synthetic substitutes
Contraceptives, oral
Estrogens
Estrogens and progestogens, combined
Progestogens

962.3 Insulins and antidiabetic agents
Acetohexamide
Biguanide derivatives, oral
Chlorpropamide
Glucagon
Insulin
Phenformin
Sulfonylurea derivatives, oral
Tolbutamide
AHA: M-A, '85, 8

962.4 Anterior pituitary hormones
Corticotropin
Gonadotropin
Somatotropin [growth hormone]

962.5 Posterior pituitary hormones
Vasopressin
EXCLUDES *oxytocic hormones (975.0)*

962.6 Parathyroid and parathyroid derivatives

962.7 Thyroid and thyroid derivatives
Dextrothyroxin
Levothyroxine sodium
Liothyronine
Thyroglobulin

962.8 Antithyroid agents
Iodides
Thiouracil
Thiourea

962.9 Other and unspecified hormones and synthetic substitutes

✓4th **963 Poisoning by primarily systemic agents**

963.0 Antiallergic and antiemetic drugs
Antihistamines
Chlorpheniramine
Diphenhydramine
Diphenylpyraline
Thonzylamine
Tripelennamine
EXCLUDES *phenothiazine-based tranquilizers (969.1)*

963.1 Antineoplastic and immunosuppressive drugs
Azathioprine
Busulfan
Chlorambucil
Cyclophosphamide
Cytarabine
Fluorouracil
Mercaptopurine
thio-TEPA
EXCLUDES *antineoplastic antibiotics (960.7)*

963.2 Acidifying agents

963.3 Alkalizing agents

963.4 Enzymes, not elsewhere classified
Penicillinase

963.5 Vitamins, not elsewhere classified
Vitamin A
Vitamin D
EXCLUDES *nicotinic acid (972.2)*
vitamin K (964.3)

963.8 Other specified systemic agents
Heavy metal antagonists

963.9 Unspecified systemic agent

✓4th **964 Poisoning by agents primarily affecting blood constituents**

964.0 Iron and its compounds
Ferric salts
Ferrous sulfate and other ferrous salts

964.1 Liver preparations and other antianemic agents
Folic acid

964.2 Anticoagulants
Coumarin
Heparin
Phenindione
Warfarin sodium
AHA: 1Q, '94, 22

964.3 Vitamin K [phytonadione]

964.4 Fibrinolysis-affecting drugs
Aminocaproic acid
Streptodornase
Streptokinase
Urokinase

964.5 Anticoagulant antagonists and other coagulants
Hexadimethrine
Protamine sulfate

964.6 Gamma globulin

964.7 Natural blood and blood products
Blood plasma
Human fibrinogen
Packed red cells
Whole blood
EXCLUDES *transfusion reactions (999.4-999.8)*

964.8 Other specified agents affecting blood constituents
Macromolecular blood substitutes
Plasma expanders

964.9 Unspecified agent affecting blood constituents

✓4th **965 Poisoning by analgesics, antipyretics, and antirheumatics**
EXCLUDES *drug dependence (304.0-304.9)*
nondependent abuse (305.0-305.9)

✓5th **965.0 Opiates and related narcotics**

965.00 Opium (alkaloids), unspecified
AHA: ▶3Q, '07, 6◀

965.01 Heroin
Diacetylmorphine

965.02 Methadone

965.09 Other
Codeine [methylmorphine]
Meperidine [pethidine]
Morphine
AHA: ▶3Q, '07, 6◀

965.1 Salicylates
Acetylsalicylic acid [aspirin]
Salicylic acid salts
AHA: N-D, '94, 15

965.4 Aromatic analgesics, not elsewhere classified
Acetanilid
Paracetamol [acetaminophen]
Phenacetin [acetophenetidin]

965.5 Pyrazole derivatives
Aminophenazone [aminopyrine]
Phenylbutazone

✓5th **965.6 Antirheumatics [antiphlogistics]**
EXCLUDES *salicylates (965.1)*
steroids (962.0-962.9)
AHA: 4Q, '98, 50

965.61 Propionic acid derivatives
Fenoprofen
Flurbiprofen
Ibuprofen
Ketoprofen
Naproxen
Oxaprozin
AHA: 4Q, '98, 50

965.69 **Other antirheumatics**
Gold salts
Indomethacin

965.7 **Other non-narcotic analgesics**
Pyrabital

965.8 **Other specified analgesics and antipyretics**
Pentazocine

965.9 **Unspecified analgesic and antipyretic**

✓4th **966 Poisoning by anticonvulsants and anti-Parkinsonism drugs**

966.0 **Oxazolidine derivatives**
Paramethadione
Trimethadione

966.1 **Hydantoin derivatives**
Phenytoin

966.2 **Succinimides**
Ethosuximide
Phensuximide

966.3 **Other and unspecified anticonvulsants**
Primidone
EXCLUDES *barbiturates (967.0)*
sulfonamides (961.0)

966.4 **Anti-Parkinsonism drugs**
Amantadine
Ethopropazine [profenamine]
Levodopa [L-dopa]

✓4th **967 Poisoning by sedatives and hypnotics**
EXCLUDES *drug dependence (304.0-304.9)*
nondependent abuse (305.0-305.9)

967.0 **Barbiturates**
Amobarbital [amylobarbitone]
Barbital [barbitone]
Butabarbital [butabarbitone]
Pentobarbital [pentobarbitone]
Phenobarbital [phenobarbitone]
Secobarbital [quinalbarbitone]
EXCLUDES *thiobarbiturate anesthetics (968.3)*

967.1 **Chloral hydrate group**

967.2 **Paraldehyde**

967.3 **Bromine compounds**
Bromide
Carbromal (derivatives)

967.4 **Methaqualone compounds**

967.5 **Glutethimide group**

967.6 **Mixed sedatives, not elsewhere classified**

967.8 **Other sedatives and hypnotics**

967.9 **Unspecified sedative or hypnotic**
Sleeping:
drug } NOS
pill } NOS
tablet } NOS

✓4th **968 Poisoning by other central nervous system depressants and anesthetics**
EXCLUDES *drug dependence (304.0-304.9)*
nondependent abuse (305.0-305.9)

968.0 **Central nervous system muscle-tone depressants**
Chlorphenesin (carbamate)
Mephenesin
Methocarbamol

968.1 **Halothane**

968.2 **Other gaseous anesthetics**
Ether
Halogenated hydrocarbon derivatives, except halothane
Nitrous oxide

968.3 **Intravenous anesthetics**
Ketamine
Methohexital [methohexitone]
Thiobarbiturates, such as thiopental sodium

968.4 **Other and unspecified general anesthetics**

968.5 **Surface [topical] and infiltration anesthetics**
Cocaine
Lidocaine [lignocaine]
Procaine
Tetracaine
AHA: 1Q, '93, 25

968.6 **Peripheral nerve- and plexus-blocking anesthetics**

968.7 **Spinal anesthetics**

968.9 **Other and unspecified local anesthetics**

✓4th **969 Poisoning by psychotropic agents**
EXCLUDES *drug dependence (304.0-304.9)*
nondependent abuse (305.0-305.9)

969.0 **Antidepressants**
Amitriptyline
Imipramine
Monoamine oxidase [MAO] inhibitors
AHA: ▶3Q, '07, 6◀

969.1 **Phenothiazine-based tranquilizers**
Chlorpromazine
Fluphenazine
Prochlorperazine
Promazine

969.2 **Butyrophenone-based tranquilizers**
Haloperidol
Spiperone
Trifluperidol

969.3 **Other antipsychotics, neuroleptics, and major tranquilizers**

969.4 **Benzodiazepine-based tranquilizers**
Chlordiazepoxide
Diazepam
Flurazepam
Lorazepam
Medazepam
Nitrazepam

969.5 **Other tranquilizers**
Hydroxyzine
Meprobamate

969.6 **Psychodysleptics [hallucinogens]**
Cannabis (derivatives)
Lysergide [LSD]
Marihuana (derivatives)
Mescaline
Psilocin
Psilocybin

969.7 **Psychostimulants**
Amphetamine
Caffeine
EXCLUDES *central appetite depressants (977.0)*
AHA: 2Q, '03, 11

969.8 **Other specified psychotropic agents**

969.9 **Unspecified psychotropic agent**

✓4th **970 Poisoning by central nervous system stimulants**

970.0 **Analeptics**
Lobeline
Nikethamide

970.1 **Opiate antagonists**
Levallorphan
Nalorphine
Naloxone

970.8 Other specified central nervous system stimulants

AHA: 1Q, '05, 6

970.9 Unspecified central nervous system stimulant

4th 971 Poisoning by drugs primarily affecting the autonomic nervous system

971.0 Parasympathomimetics [cholinergics]

Acetylcholine
Anticholinesterase:
organophosphorus
reversible
Pilocarpine

971.1 Parasympatholytics [anticholinergics and antimuscarinics] and spasmolytics

Atropine
Homatropine
Hyoscine [scopolamine]
Quaternary ammonium derivatives

EXCLUDES *papaverine (972.5)*

971.2 Sympathomimetics [adrenergics]

Epinephrine [adrenalin]
Levarterenol [noradrenalin]

971.3 Sympatholytics [antiadrenergics]

Phenoxybenzamine
Tolazolinehydrochloride

971.9 Unspecified drug primarily affecting autonomic nervous system

4th 972 Poisoning by agents primarily affecting the cardiovascular system

972.0 Cardiac rhythm regulators

Practolol
Procainamide
Propranolol
Quinidine

EXCLUDES *lidocaine (968.5)*

972.1 Cardiotonic glycosides and drugs of similar action

Digitalis glycosides
Digoxin
Strophanthins

972.2 Antilipemic and antiarteriosclerotic drugs

Clofibrate
Nicotinic acid derivatives

972.3 Ganglion-blocking agents

Pentamethonium bromide

972.4 Coronary vasodilators

Dipyridamole
Nitrates [nitroglycerin]
Nitrites

972.5 Other vasodilators

Cyclandelate
Diazoxide
Papaverine

EXCLUDES *nicotinic acid (972.2)*

972.6 Other antihypertensive agents

Clonidine
Guanethidine
Rauwolfia alkaloids
Reserpine

972.7 Antivaricose drugs, including sclerosing agents

Sodium morrhuate
Zinc salts

972.8 Capillary-active drugs

Adrenochrome derivatives
Metaraminol

972.9 Other and unspecified agents primarily affecting the cardiovascular system

4th 973 Poisoning by agents primarily affecting the gastrointestinal system

973.0 Antacids and antigastric secretion drugs

Aluminum hydroxide
Magnesium trisilicate

AHA: 1Q, '03, 19

973.1 Irritant cathartics

Bisacodyl
Castor oil
Phenolphthalein

973.2 Emollient cathartics

Dioctyl sulfosuccinates

973.3 Other cathartics, including intestinal atonia drugs

Magnesium sulfate

973.4 Digestants

Pancreatin
Papain
Pepsin

973.5 Antidiarrheal drugs

Kaolin
Pectin

EXCLUDES *anti-infectives (960.0-961.9)*

973.6 Emetics

973.8 Other specified agents primarily affecting the gastrointestinal system

973.9 Unspecified agent primarily affecting the gastrointestinal system

4th 974 Poisoning by water, mineral, and uric acid metabolism drugs

974.0 Mercurial diuretics

Chlormerodrin
Mercaptomerin
Mersalyl

974.1 Purine derivative diuretics

Theobromine
Theophylline

EXCLUDES *aminophylline [theophylline ethylenediamine] (975.7)*
caffeine (969.7)

974.2 Carbonic acid anhydrase inhibitors

Acetazolamide

974.3 Saluretics

Benzothiadiazides
Chlorothiazide group

974.4 Other diuretics

Ethacrynic acid
Furosemide

974.5 Electrolytic, caloric, and water-balance agents

974.6 Other mineral salts, not elsewhere classified

974.7 Uric acid metabolism drugs

Allopurinol
Colchicine
Probenecid

4th 975 Poisoning by agents primarily acting on the smooth and skeletal muscles and respiratory system

975.0 Oxytocic agents

Ergot alkaloids
Oxytocin
Prostaglandins

975.1 Smooth muscle relaxants

Adiphenine
Metaproterenol [orciprenaline]

EXCLUDES *papaverine (972.5)*

975.2 Skeletal muscle relaxants

975.3 Other and unspecified drugs acting on muscles

975.4 Antitussives
Dextromethorphan
Pipazethate

975.5 Expectorants
Acetylcysteine
Guaifenesin
Terpin hydrate

975.6 Anti-common cold drugs

975.7 Antiasthmatics
Aminophylline [theophylline ethylenediamine]

975.8 Other and unspecified respiratory drugs

✓4th **976 Poisoning by agents primarily affecting skin and mucous membrane, ophthalmological, otorhinolaryngological, and dental drugs**

976.0 Local anti-infectives and anti-inflammatory drugs

976.1 Antipruritics

976.2 Local astringents and local detergents

976.3 Emollients, demulcents, and protectants

976.4 Keratolytics, keratoplastics, other hair treatment drugs and preparations

976.5 Eye anti-infectives and other eye drugs
Idoxuridine

976.6 Anti-infectives and other drugs and preparations for ear, nose, and throat

976.7 Dental drugs topically applied
EXCLUDES *anti-infectives (976.0)*
local anesthetics (968.5)

976.8 Other agents primarily affecting skin and mucous membrane
Spermicides [vaginal contraceptives]

976.9 Unspecified agent primarily affecting skin and mucous membrane

✓4th **977 Poisoning by other and unspecified drugs and medicinal substances**

977.0 Dietetics
Central appetite depressants

977.1 Lipotropic drugs

977.2 Antidotes and chelating agents, not elsewhere classified

977.3 Alcohol deterrents

977.4 Pharmaceutical excipients
Pharmaceutical adjuncts

977.8 Other specified drugs and medicinal substances
Contrast media used for diagnostic x-ray procedures
Diagnostic agents and kits

977.9 Unspecified drug or medicinal substance

✓4th **978 Poisoning by bacterial vaccines**

978.0 BCG

978.1 Typhoid and paratyphoid

978.2 Cholera

978.3 Plague

978.4 Tetanus

978.5 Diphtheria

978.6 Pertussis vaccine, including combinations with a pertussis component

978.8 Other and unspecified bacterial vaccines

978.9 Mixed bacterial vaccines, except combinations with a pertussis component

✓4th **979 Poisoning by other vaccines and biological substances**
EXCLUDES *gamma globulin (964.6)*

979.0 Smallpox vaccine

979.1 Rabies vaccine

979.2 Typhus vaccine

979.3 Yellow fever vaccine

979.4 Measles vaccine

979.5 Poliomyelitis vaccine

979.6 Other and unspecified viral and rickettsial vaccines
Mumps vaccine

979.7 Mixed viral-rickettsial and bacterial vaccines, except combinations with a pertussis component
EXCLUDES *combinations with a pertussis component (978.6)*

979.9 Other and unspecified vaccines and biological substances

TOXIC EFFECTS OF SUBSTANCES CHIEFLY NONMEDICINAL AS TO SOURCE (980-989)

Use additional code to specify the nature of the toxic effect
EXCLUDES *burns from chemical agents (ingested) (947.0-947.9)*
localized toxic effects indexed elsewhere (001.0-799.9)
respiratory conditions due to external agents (506.0-508.9)

✓4th **980 Toxic effect of alcohol**

980.0 Ethyl alcohol
Denatured alcohol
Grain alcohol
Ethanol

Use additional code to identify any associated:
acute alcohol intoxication (305.0)
in alcoholism (303.0)
drunkenness (simple) (305.0)
pathological (291.4)

AHA: 3Q, '96, 16

980.1 Methyl alcohol
Methanol
Wood alcohol

980.2 Isopropyl alcohol
Dimethyl carbinol
Isopropanol
Rubbing alcohol

980.3 Fusel oil
Alcohol:
amyl
butyl
propyl

980.8 Other specified alcohols

980.9 Unspecified alcohol

981 Toxic effect of petroleum products
Benzine
Gasoline
Kerosene
Paraffin wax
Petroleum:
ether
naphtha
spirit

✓4th **982 Toxic effect of solvents other than petroleum-based**

982.0 Benzene and homologues

982.1 Carbon tetrachloride

982.2 Carbon disulfide
Carbon bisulfide

982.3 Other chlorinated hydrocarbon solvents
Tetrachloroethylene
Trichloroethylene
EXCLUDES *chlorinated hydrocarbon preparations other than solvents (989.2)*

982.4 Nitroglycol

982.8 Other nonpetroleum-based solvents
Acetone

4th 983 Toxic effect of corrosive aromatics, acids, and caustic alkalis

983.0 Corrosive aromatics
Carbolic acid or phenol
Cresol

983.1 Acids
Acid:
hydrochloric
nitric
sulfuric

983.2 Caustic alkalis
Lye
Potassium hydroxide
Sodium hydroxide

983.9 Caustic, unspecified

4th 984 Toxic effect of lead and its compounds (including fumes)

INCLUDES that from all sources except medicinal substances

984.0 Inorganic lead compounds
Lead dioxide
Lead salts

984.1 Organic lead compounds
Lead acetate
Tetraethyl lead

984.8 Other lead compounds

984.9 Unspecified lead compound

4th 985 Toxic effect of other metals

INCLUDES that from all sources except medicinal substances

985.0 Mercury and its compounds
Minamata disease

985.1 Arsenic and its compounds

985.2 Manganese and its compounds

985.3 Beryllium and its compounds

985.4 Antimony and its compounds

985.5 Cadmium and its compounds

985.6 Chromium

985.8 Other specified metals
Brass fumes
Copper salts
Iron compounds
Nickel compounds

AHA: 1Q, '88, 5

985.9 Unspecified metal

986 Toxic effect of carbon monoxide
Carbon monoxide from any source

4th 987 Toxic effect of other gases, fumes, or vapors

987.0 Liquefied petroleum gases
Butane
Propane

987.1 Other hydrocarbon gas

987.2 Nitrogen oxides
Nitrogen dioxide
Nitrous fumes

987.3 Sulfur dioxide

987.4 Freon
Dichloromonofluoromethane

987.5 Lacrimogenic gas
Bromobenzyl cyanide
Chloroacetophenone
Ethyliodoacetate

987.6 Chlorine gas

987.7 Hydrocyanic acid gas

987.8 Other specified gases, fumes, or vapors
Phosgene
Polyester fumes

987.9 Unspecified gas, fume, or vapor

AHA: 3Q, '05, 10

4th 988 Toxic effect of noxious substances eaten as food

EXCLUDES *allergic reaction to food, such as:*
gastroenteritis (558.3)
rash (692.5, 693.1)
food poisoning (bacterial) (005.0-005.9)
toxic effects of food contaminants, such as:
aflatoxin and other mycotoxin (989.7)
mercury (985.0)

988.0 Fish and shellfish

988.1 Mushrooms

988.2 Berries and other plants

988.8 Other specified noxious substances eaten as food

988.9 Unspecified noxious substance eaten as food

4th 989 Toxic effect of other substances, chiefly nonmedicinal as to source

989.0 Hydrocyanic acid and cyanides
Potassium cyanide
Sodium cyanide
EXCLUDES *gas and fumes (987.7)*

989.1 Strychnine and salts

989.2 Chlorinated hydrocarbons
Aldrin
Chlordane
DDT
Dieldrin
EXCLUDES *chlorinated hydrocarbon solvents (982.0-982.3)*

989.3 Organophosphate and carbamate
Carbaryl
Dichlorvos
Malathion
Parathion
Phorate
Phosdrin

989.4 Other pesticides, not elsewhere classified
Mixtures of insecticides

989.5 Venom
Bites of venomous snakes, lizards, and spiders
Tick paralysis

989.6 Soaps and detergents

989.7 Aflatoxin and other mycotoxin [food contaminants]

5th 989.8 Other substances, chiefly nonmedicinal as to source

AHA: 4Q, '95, 60

989.81 Asbestos
EXCLUDES *asbestosis (501)*
exposure to asbestos (V15.84)

989.82 **Latex**

989.83 **Silicone**

EXCLUDES *silicone used in medical devices, implants and grafts (996.00-996.79)*

989.84 **Tobacco**

989.89 **Other**

989.9 **Unspecified substance, chiefly nonmedicinal as to source**

OTHER AND UNSPECIFIED EFFECTS OF EXTERNAL CAUSES (990-995)

990 **Effects of radiation, unspecified**

Complication of:
- phototherapy
- radiation therapy

Radiation sickness

EXCLUDES *specified adverse effects of radiation. Such conditions are to be classified according to the nature of the adverse effect, as:*
burns (940.0-949.5)
dermatitis (692.7-692.8)
leukemia (204.0-208.9)
pneumonia (508.0)
sunburn (692.71, 692.76-692.77)
[The type of radiation giving rise to the adverse effect may be identified by use of the E codes.]

4th 991 **Effects of reduced temperature**

991.0 **Frostbite of face**

991.1 **Frostbite of hand**

991.2 **Frostbite of foot**

991.3 **Frostbite of other and unspecified sites**

991.4 **Immersion foot**

Trench foot

DEF: Paresthesia, edema, blotchy cyanosis of foot, the skin is soft (macerated), pale and wrinkled, and the sole is swollen with surface ridging and following sustained immersion in water.

991.5 **Chilblains**

Erythema pernio
Perniosis

DEF: Red, swollen, itchy skin; follows damp cold exposure; also associated with pruritus and a burning feeling, in hands, feet, ears, and face in children, legs and toes in women, and hands and fingers in men.

991.6 **Hypothermia**

Hypothermia (accidental)

EXCLUDES *hypothermia following anesthesia (995.89)*
hypothermia not associated with low environmental temperature ▶(780.65)◀

DEF: Reduced body temperature due to low environmental temperatures.

991.8 **Other specified effects of reduced temperature**

991.9 **Unspecified effect of reduced temperature**

Effects of freezing or excessive cold NOS

4th 992 **Effects of heat and light**

EXCLUDES *burns (940.0-949.5)*
diseases of sweat glands due to heat (705.0-705.9)
malignant hyperpyrexia following anesthesia (995.86)
sunburn (692.71, 692.76-692.77)

992.0 **Heat stroke and sunstroke**

Heat apoplexy
Heat pyrexia
Ictus solaris
Siriasis
Thermoplegia

DEF: Headache, vertigo, cramps and elevated body temperature due to high environmental temperatures.

992.1 **Heat syncope**

Heat collapse

992.2 **Heat cramps**

992.3 **Heat exhaustion, anhydrotic**

Heat prostration due to water depletion

EXCLUDES *that associated with salt depletion (992.4)*

992.4 **Heat exhaustion due to salt depletion**

Heat prostration due to salt (and water) depletion

992.5 **Heat exhaustion, unspecified**

Heat prostration NOS

992.6 **Heat fatigue, transient**

992.7 **Heat edema**

DEF: Fluid retention due to high environmental temperatures.

992.8 **Other specified heat effects**

992.9 **Unspecified**

4th 993 **Effects of air pressure**

993.0 **Barotrauma, otitic**

Aero-otitis media
Effects of high altitude on ears

DEF: Ringing ears, deafness, pain and vertigo due to air pressure changes.

993.1 **Barotrauma, sinus**

Aerosinusitis
Effects of high altitude on sinuses

993.2 **Other and unspecified effects of high altitude**

Alpine sickness
Andes disease
Anoxia due to high altitude
Hypobaropathy
Mountain sickness

AHA: 3Q, '88, 4

993.3 **Caisson disease**

Bends
Compressed-air disease
Decompression sickness
Divers' palsy or paralysis

DEF: Rapid reduction in air pressure while breathing compressed air; symptoms include skin lesions, joint pains, respiratory and neurological problems.

993.4 **Effects of air pressure caused by explosion**

993.8 **Other specified effects of air pressure**

993.9 **Unspecified effect of air pressure**

4th 994 **Effects of other external causes**

EXCLUDES *certain adverse effects not elsewhere classified (995.0-995.8)*

994.0 **Effects of lightning**

Shock from lightning
Struck by lightning NOS

EXCLUDES *burns (940.0-949.5)*

994.1 **Drowning and nonfatal submersion**

Bathing cramp
Immersion

AHA: 3Q, '88, 4

994.2 **Effects of hunger**

Deprivation of food
Starvation

994.3 **Effects of thirst**

Deprivation of water

994.4 Exhaustion due to exposure

994.5 Exhaustion due to excessive exertion
▶Exhaustion due to◀ overexertion

994.6 Motion sickness
Air sickness
Seasickness
Travel sickness

994.7 Asphyxiation and strangulation
Suffocation (by):
bedclothes
cave-in
constriction
mechanical
plastic bag
pressure
strangulation

EXCLUDES *asphyxia from:*
carbon monoxide (986)
inhalation of food or foreign body (932-934.9)
other gases, fumes, and vapors (987.0-987.9)

994.8 Electrocution and nonfatal effects of electric current
Shock from electric current
▶Shock from electroshock gun (taser)◀

EXCLUDES *electric burns (940.0-949.5)*

994.9 Other effects of external causes
Effects of:
abnormal gravitational [G] forces or states
weightlessness

✓4th **995 Certain adverse effects not elsewhere classified**

EXCLUDES *complications of surgical and medical care (996.0-999.9)*

995.0 Other anaphylactic shock
Allergic shock, Anaphylactic reaction, Anaphylaxis } NOS or due to adverse effect of correct medicinal substance properly administered

Use additional E code to identify external cause, such as:
adverse effects of correct medicinal substance properly administered [E930-E949]

EXCLUDES *anaphylactic reaction to serum (999.4)*
anaphylactic shock due to adverse food reaction (995.60-995.69)

AHA: 4Q, '93, 30

DEF: Immediate sensitivity response after exposure to specific antigen; results in life-threatening respiratory distress; usually followed by vascular collapse, shock, urticaria, angioedema and pruritus.

995.1 Angioneurotic edema
Giant urticaria

EXCLUDES *urticaria:*
due to serum (999.5)
other specified (698.2, 708.0-708.9, 757.33)

DEF: Circulatory response of deep dermis, subcutaneous or submucosal tissues; causes localized edema and wheals.

✓5th **995.2 Other and unspecified adverse effect of drug, medicinal and biological substance**
Adverse effect, Allergic reaction, Hypersensitivity, Idiosyncrasy } (due) to correct medicinal substance properly administered

Drug:
hypersensitivity NOS
reaction NOS

EXCLUDES *pathological drug intoxication (292.2)*

AHA: 2Q, '97, 12; 3Q, '95, 13; 3Q, '92, 16

995.20 Unspecified adverse effect of unspecified drug, medicinal and biological substance

AHA: 4Q, '06, 112

995.21 Arthus phenomenon
Arthus reaction

AHA: 4Q, '06, 112

995.22 Unspecified adverse effect of anesthesia

AHA: 4Q, '06, 112

995.23 Unspecified adverse effect of insulin

AHA: 4Q, '06, 112

995.27 Other drug allergy
Drug allergy NOS
Drug hypersensitivity NOS

AHA: 4Q, '06, 112

995.29 Unspecified adverse effect of other drug, medicinal and biological substance

AHA: 4Q, '06, 112

995.3 Allergy, unspecified
Allergic reaction NOS
Hypersensitivity NOS
Idiosyncrasy NOS

EXCLUDES *allergic reaction NOS to correct medicinal substance properly administered (995.27)*
allergy to existing dental restorative materials (525.66)
specific types of allergic reaction, such as:
allergic diarrhea (558.3)
dermatitis (691.0-693.9)
hayfever (477.0-477.9)

995.4 Shock due to anesthesia
Shock due to anesthesia in which the correct substance was properly administered

EXCLUDES *complications of anesthesia in labor or delivery (668.0-668.9)*
overdose or wrong substance given (968.0-969.9)
postoperative shock NOS (998.0)
specified adverse effects of anesthesia classified elsewhere, such as:
anoxic brain damage (348.1)
hepatitis (070.0-070.9), etc.
unspecified adverse effect of anesthesia (995.22)

✓5th **995.5 Child maltreatment syndrome**
Use additional code(s), if applicable, to identify any associated injuries

Use additional E code to identify:
nature of abuse (E960-E968)
perpetrator (E967.0-E967.9)

AHA: 1Q, '98, 11

995.50 Child abuse, unspecified P

995.51 Child emotional/psychological abuse P

AHA: 4Q, '96, 38, 40

995.52 Child neglect (nutritional) P

AHA: 4Q, '96, 38, 40

995.53 Child sexual abuse P

AHA: 4Q, '96, 39, 40

995.54 Child physical abuse P
Battered baby or child syndrome

EXCLUDES *shaken infant syndrome (995.55)*

AHA: 3Q, '99, 14; 4Q, '96, 39, 40

995.55 Shaken infant syndrome P

Use additional code(s) to identify any associated injuries

AHA: 4Q, '96, 40, 43

995.59 Other child abuse and neglect P

Multiple forms of abuse

✓5th **995.6 Anaphylactic shock due to adverse food reaction**

▶Anaphylactic reaction due to food◀

Anaphylactic shock due to nonpoisonous foods

AHA: 4Q, '93, 30

995.60 Due to unspecified food

995.61 Due to peanuts

995.62 Due to crustaceans

995.63 Due to fruits and vegetables

995.64 Due to tree nuts and seeds

AHA: ▶1Q, '08, 12◀

995.65 Due to fish

995.66 Due to food additives

995.67 Due to milk products

995.68 Due to eggs

995.69 Due to other specified food

995.7 Other adverse food reactions, not elsewhere classified

Use additional code to identify the type of reaction, such as:
- hives (708.0)
- wheezing (786.07)

EXCLUDES *anaphylactic shock due to adverse food reaction (995.60-995.69)*
asthma (493.0, 493.9)
dermatitis due to food (693.1)
in contact with skin (692.5)
gastroenteritis and colitis due to food (558.3)
rhinitis due to food (477.1)

✓5th **995.8 Other specified adverse effects, not elsewhere classified**

995.80 Adult maltreatment, unspecified A

Abused person NOS

Use additional code to identify:
- any associated injury
- perpetrator (E967.0-E967.9)

AHA: 4Q, '96, 41, 43

995.81 Adult physical abuse A

Battered:
- person syndrome NEC
- man
- spouse
- woman

Use additional code to identify:
- any association injury
- nature of abuse (E960-E968)
- perpetrator (E967.0-E967.9)

AHA: 4Q, '96, 42, 43

995.82 Adult emotional/psychological abuse A

Use additional E code to identify perpetrator (E967.0-E967.9)

995.83 Adult sexual abuse A

Use additional code(s) to identify:
- any associated injury
- perpetrator (E967.0-E967.9)

995.84 Adult neglect (nutritional) A

Use additional code(s) to identify:
- intent of neglect (E904.0, E968.4)
- perpetrator (E967.0-E967.9)

995.85 Other adult abuse and neglect A

Multiple forms of abuse and neglect

Use additional code(s) to identify
- any associated injury
- intent of neglect (E904.0, E968.4)
- nature of abuse (E960-E968)
- perpetrator (E967.0-E967.9)

995.86 Malignant hyperthermia

Malignant hyperpyrexia due to anesthesia

AHA: 4Q, '98, 51

995.89 Other

Hypothermia due to anesthesia

AHA: 2Q, '04, 18; 3Q, '03, 12

✓5th **995.9 Systemic inflammatory response syndrome (SIRS)**

AHA: 4Q, '06, 113-116; 2Q, '04, 16; 4Q, '02, 71

DEF: Clinical response to infection or trauma that can trigger an acute inflammatory reaction and progresses to coagulation, impaired fibrinolysis, and organ failure; manifested by two or more of the following symptoms: fever, tachycardia, tachypnea, leukocytosis or leukopenia.

995.90 Systemic inflammatory response syndrome, unspecified

SIRS NOS

995.91 Sepsis

Systemic inflammatory response syndrome due to infectious process without acute organ dysfunction

Code first underlying infection

EXCLUDES *sepsis with acute organ dysfunction (995.92)*
sepsis with multiple organ dysfunction (995.92)
severe sepsis (995.92)

AHA: 4Q, '07, 86; 4Q, '06, 113-116; 2Q, '04, 16; 4Q, '03, 79

995.92 Severe sepsis

Sepsis with acute organ dysfunction

Sepsis with multiple organ dysfunction (MOD)

Systemic inflammatory response syndrome due to infectious process with acute organ dysfunction

Code first underlying infection

Use additional code to specify acuteorgan dysfunction, such as:
- acute renal failure (584.5-584.9)
- acute respiratory failure (518.81)
- critical illness myopathy (359.81)
- critical illness polyneuropathy (357.82)
- disseminated intravascular coagulopathy [DIC] (286.6)
- encephalopathy (348.31)
- hepatic failure (570)
- septic shock (785.52)

AHA: 4Q, '07, 97; 4Q, '06, 113-116; 2Q, '05, 18-19; 1Q, '05, 7; 1Q, '05, 7; 2Q, '04, 16; 4Q, '03, 73, 79

Continuum of Illness Due to Infection

Bacteremia ➡ Septicemia ➡ Sepsis ➡ Severe Sepsis ➡ Severe Sepsis with Septic Shock ➡ MODS (Multiple Organ Dysfunction Syndrome) ➡ Death

995.93 Systemic inflammatory response syndrome due to noninfectious process without acute organ dysfunction

Code first underlying conditions, such as:
acute pancreatitis (577.0)
trauma

EXCLUDES *systemic inflammatory response syndrome due to noninfectious process with acute organ dysfunction (995.94)*

AHA: 4Q, '06, 113-116

995.94 Systemic inflammatory response syndrome due to noninfectious process with acute organ dysfunction

Code first underlying conditions, such as:
acute pancreatitis (577.0)
trauma

Use additional code to specify acute organ dysfunction, such as:
acute renal failure (584.5-584.9)
acute respiratory failure (518.81)
critical illness myopathy (359.81)
critical illness polyneuropathy (357.82)
disseminated intravascular coagulopathy [DIC] syndrome (286.6)
encephalopathy (348.31)
hepatic failure (570)

EXCLUDES *severe sepsis (995.92)*

AHA: 4Q, '06, 113-116; 4Q, '03, 79

COMPLICATIONS OF SURGICAL AND MEDICAL CARE, NOT ELSEWHERE CLASSIFIED (996-999)

EXCLUDES *adverse effects of medicinal agents (001.0-799.9, 995.0-995.8)*
burns from local applications and irradiation (940.0-949.5)
complications of:
conditions for which the procedure was performed
surgical procedures during abortion, labor, and delivery (630-676.9)
poisoning and toxic effects of drugs and chemicals (960.0-989.9)
postoperative conditions in which no complications are present, such as:
artificial opening status (V44.0-V44.9)
closure of external stoma (V55.0-V55.9)
fitting of prosthetic device (V52.0-V52.9)
specified complications classified elsewhere
anesthetic shock (995.4)
electrolyte imbalance (276.0-276.9)
postlaminectomy syndrome (722.80-722.83)
postmastectomy lymphedema syndrome (457.0)
postoperative psychosis (293.0-293.9)
any other condition classified elsewhere in the Alphabetic Index when described as due to a procedure

✓4th **996 Complications peculiar to certain specified procedures**

INCLUDES complications, not elsewhere classified, in the use of artificial substitutes [e.g., Dacron, metal, Silastic, Teflon] or natural sources [e.g., bone] involving:
anastomosis (internal)
graft (bypass) (patch)
implant
internal device:
catheter
electronic
fixation
prosthetic
reimplant
transplant

EXCLUDES *accidental puncture or laceration during procedure (998.2)*
▶*capsular contracture of breast implant (611.83)*◀
complications of internal anastomosis of:
gastrointestinal tract (997.4)
urinary tract (997.5)
endosseous dental implant failures (525.71-525.79)
intraoperative floppy iris syndrome [IFIS] (364.81)
mechanical complication of respirator (V46.14)
other specified complications classified elsewhere, such as:
hemolytic anemia (283.1)
functional cardiac disturbances (429.4)
serum hepatitis (070.2-070.3)

AHA: 1Q, '94, 3

✓5th **996.0 Mechanical complication of cardiac device, implant, and graft**

Breakdown (mechanical)
Displacement
Leakage
Obstruction, mechanical
Perforation
Protrusion

AHA: 2Q, '93, 9

996.00 Unspecified device, implant, and graft

996.01 Due to cardiac pacemaker (electrode)

AHA: 2Q, '06, 15; 2Q, '99, 11

996.02 Due to heart valve prosthesis

996.03 Due to coronary bypass graft

EXCLUDES *atherosclerosis of graft (414.02, 414.03)*
embolism [occlusion NOS] [thrombus] of graft (996.72)

AHA: 2Q, '95, 17; N-D, '86, 5

996.04 Due to automatic implantable cardiac defibrillator

AHA: 2Q, '05, 3

996.09 Other

AHA: 2Q, '93, 9

996.1 Mechanical complication of other vascular device, implant, and graft

Mechanical complications involving:
- aortic (bifurcation) graft (replacement)
- arteriovenous:
  - dialysis catheter, fistula, shunt } surgically created
- balloon (counterpulsation) device, intra-aortic
- carotid artery bypass graft
- femoral-popliteal bypass graft
- umbrella device, vena cava

EXCLUDES *atherosclerosis of biological graft (440.30-440.32)*
embolism [occlusion NOS] [thrombus] of (biological) (synthetic) graft (996.74)
peritoneal dialysis catheter (996.56)

AHA: 1Q, '06, 10; 2Q, '05, 8; 1Q, '02, 13; 1Q, '95, 3

996.2 Mechanical complication of nervous system device, implant, and graft

Mechanical complications involving:
- dorsal column stimulator
- electrodes implanted in brain [brain "pacemaker"]
- peripheral nerve graft
- ventricular (communicating) shunt

AHA: 2Q, '99, 4; S-O, '87, 10

✓5th **996.3 Mechanical complication of genitourinary device, implant, and graft**

AHA: 3Q, '01, 13; S-O, '85, 3

996.30 Unspecified device, implant, and graft

996.31 Due to urethral [indwelling] catheter

996.32 Due to intrauterine contraceptive device ♀

996.39 Other

Cystostomy catheter
Prosthetic reconstruction of vas deferens
Repair (graft) of ureter without mention of resection

EXCLUDES *complications due to:*
external stoma of urinary tract (997.5)
internal anastomosis of urinary tract (997.5)

✓5th **996.4 Mechanical complication of internal orthopedic device, implant, and graft**

Mechanical complications involving:
- external (fixation) device utilizing internal screw(s), pin(s) or other methods of fixation
- grafts of bone, cartilage, muscle, or tendon
- internal (fixation) device such as nail, plate, rod, etc.

Use additional code to identify prosthetic joint with mechanical complication (V43.60-V43.69)

EXCLUDES *complications of external orthopedic device, such as:*
pressure ulcer due to cast (707.00-707.09)

AHA: 4Q, '05, 91; 2Q, '99, 10; 2Q, '98, 19; 2Q, '96, 11; 3Q, '95, 16; N-D, '85, 11

996.40 Unspecified mechanical complication of internal orthopedic device, implant, and graft

996.41 Mechanical loosening of prosthetic joint

Aseptic loosening

AHA: 4Q, '05, 112

996.42 Dislocation of prosthetic joint

Instability of prosthetic joint
Subluxation of prosthetic joint

996.43 Prosthetic joint implant failure

Breakage (fracture) of prosthetic joint

996.44 Peri-prosthetic fracture around prosthetic joint

AHA: 4Q, '05, 93

996.45 Peri-prosthetic osteolysis

Use additional code to identify major osseous defect, if applicable (731.3)

AHA: 4Q, '06, 103

996.46 Articular bearing surface wear of prosthetic joint

996.47 Other mechanical complication of prosthetic joint implant

Mechanical complication of prosthetic joint NOS

996.49 Other mechanical complication of other internal orthopedic device, implant, and graft

►Breakage of internal fixation device in bone
Dislocation of internal fixation device in bone◄

EXCLUDES *mechanical complication of prosthetic joint implant (996.41-996.47)*

✓5th **996.5 Mechanical complication of other specified prosthetic device, implant, and graft**

Mechanical complications involving:
- prosthetic implant in:
  - bile duct
  - breast
  - chin
  - orbit of eye
- nonabsorbable surgical material NOS
- other graft, implant, and internal device, not elsewhere classified

AHA: 1Q, '98, 11

996.51 Due to corneal graft

996.52 Due to graft of other tissue, not elsewhere classified

EXCLUDES *failure of artificial skin graft (996.55)*
failure of decellularized allodermis (996.55)
sloughing of temporary skin allografts or xenografts (pigskin) — omit code

AHA: 1Q, '96, 10

996.53 Due to ocular lens prosthesis

EXCLUDES *contact lenses–code to condition*

AHA: 1Q, '00, 9

996.54 Due to breast prosthesis

Breast capsule (prosthesis)
Mammary implant

AHA: 2Q, '98, 14; 3Q, '92, 4

996.55 Due to artificial skin graft and decellularized allodermis

Dislodgement
Displacement
Failure
Non-adherence
Poor incorporation
Shearing

AHA: 4Q, '98, 52

996.56 Due to peritoneal dialysis catheter
EXCLUDES *mechanical complication of arteriovenous dialysis catheter (996.1)*
AHA: 4Q, '98, 54

996.57 Due to insulin pump
AHA: 4Q, '03, 81-82

996.59 Due to other implant and internal device, not elsewhere classified
Nonabsorbable surgical material NOS
Prosthetic implant in:
bile duct
chin
orbit of eye
AHA: 2Q, '99, 13; 3Q, '94, 7

✓5th **996.6 Infection and inflammatory reaction due to internal prosthetic device, implant, and graft**
Infection (causing obstruction) / Inflammation } due to (presence of) any device, implant, and graft classifiable to 996.0-996.5
Use additional code to identify specified infections
AHA: 2Q, '89, 16; J-F, '87, 14

996.60 Due to unspecified device, implant, and graft

996.61 Due to cardiac device, implant, and graft
Cardiac pacemaker or defibrillator:
electrode(s), lead(s)
pulse generator
subcutaneous pocket
Coronary artery bypass graft
Heart valve prosthesis

996.62 Due to other vascular device, implant, and graft
Arterial graft
Arteriovenous fistula or shunt
Infusion pump
Vascular catheter (arterial) (dialysis) (peripheral venous)
EXCLUDES *infection due to:*
central venous catheter (999.31)
Hickman catheter (999.31)
peripherally inserted central catheter [PICC] (999.31)
▶*portacath (port-a-cath) (999.31)*◀
triple lumen catheter (999.31)
▶*umbilical venous catheter (999.31)*◀
AHA: 4Q, '07, 88; 2Q, '04, 16, 1Q, '04, 5; 4Q, '03, 107, 111; 2Q, '03, 7; 2Q, '94, 13

996.63 Due to nervous system device, implant, and graft
Electrodes implanted in brain
Peripheral nerve graft
Spinal canal catheter
Ventricular (communicating) shunt (catheter)

996.64 Due to indwelling urinary catheter
Use additional code to identify specified infections, such as:
Cystitis (595.0-595.9)
Sepsis (038.0-038.9)
AHA: 3Q, '93, 6

996.65 Due to other genitourinary device implant, and graft
Intrauterine contraceptive device
AHA: 1Q, '00, 15

996.66 Due to internal joint prosthesis
Use additional code to identify infected prosthetic joint (V43.60-V43.69)
AHA: ▶2Q, '08, 3-5;◀ 2Q, '07, 7; 4Q, '05, 91, 113; 2Q, '91, 18

996.67 Due to other internal orthopedic device, implant, and graft
Bone growth stimulator (electrode)
Internal fixation device (pin) (rod) (screw)

996.68 Due to peritoneal dialysis catheter
Exit-site infection or inflammation
AHA: 4Q, '98, 54

996.69 Due to other internal prosthetic device, implant, and graft
Breast prosthesis
Ocular lens prosthesis
Prosthetic orbital implant
AHA: ▶2Q, '08, 11;◀ 4Q, '03, 108; 4Q, '98, 52

✓5th **996.7 Other complications of internal (biological) (synthetic) prosthetic device, implant, and graft**
Complication NOS / Occlusion NOS / Embolism / Fibrosis / Hemorrhage / Pain / Stenosis / Thrombus } due to (presence of) any device, implant, and graft classifiable to 996.0-996.5
Use additional code to identify complication, such as:
pain due to presence of device, implant or graft (338.18-338.19, 338.28-338.29)
EXCLUDES ▶*disruption (dehiscence) of internal suture material (998.31)*◀
transplant rejection (996.8)
AHA: 2Q, '07, 12; 4Q, '05, 94; 1Q, '89, 9; N-D, '86, 5

996.70 Due to unspecified device, implant, and graft

996.71 Due to heart valve prosthesis

996.72 Due to other cardiac device, implant, and graft
Cardiac pacemaker or defibrillator:
electrode(s), lead(s)
subcutaneous pocket
Coronary artery bypass (graft)
EXCLUDES *occlusion due to atherosclerosis (414.02-414.06)*
AHA: 3Q, '06, 8, 25; 3Q, '01, 20

996.73 Due to renal dialysis device, implant, and graft
AHA: 2Q, '91, 18

996.74 Due to other vascular device, implant, and graft
EXCLUDES *occlusion of biological graft due to atherosclerosis (440.30-440.32)*
AHA: 1Q, '03, 16, 17

996.75 Due to nervous system device, implant, and graft

996.76 Due to genitourinary device, implant, and graft
AHA: 1Q, '00, 15

996.77 Due to internal joint prosthesis
Use additional code to identify prosthetic joint (V43.60-V43.69)
AHA: 4Q, '05, 91

996.78 Due to other internal orthopedic device, implant, and graft
AHA: 2Q, '03, 14

996.79 **Due to other internal prosthetic device, implant, and graft**
AHA: 2Q, '04, 7; 1Q,'01, 8; 3Q, '95, 14; 3Q, '92, 4

5th 996.8 **Complications of transplanted organ**
Transplant failure or rejection
Use additional code to identify nature of complication, such as:
cytomegalovirus (CMV) infection (078.5)
▶graft-versus-host disease (279.50-279.53)
malignancy associated with organ transplant (199.2)
post-transplant lymphoproliferative disorder (PTLD) (238.77)◀
AHA: 3Q, '01, 12; 3Q, '93, 3, 4; 2Q, '93, 11; 1Q, '93, 24

996.80 **Transplanted organ, unspecified**

996.81 **Kidney**
AHA: 3Q, '03, 16; 3Q, '98, 6, 7; 3Q, '94, 8; 2Q, '94, 9; 1Q, '93, 24

996.82 **Liver**
AHA: 3Q, '03, 17; 3Q, '98, 3, 4

996.83 **Heart**
AHA: 3Q, '03, 16; 4Q, '02, 53; 3Q, '98, 5

996.84 **Lung**
AHA: 2Q, '03, 12; 3Q, '98, 5

996.85 **Bone marrow**
AHA: 4Q, '90, 4

996.86 **Pancreas**

996.87 **Intestine**

996.89 **Other specified transplanted organ**
AHA: 3Q, '94, 5

5th 996.9 **Complications of reattached extremity or body part**

996.90 **Unspecified extremity**

996.91 **Forearm**

996.92 **Hand**

996.93 **Finger(s)**

996.94 **Upper extremity, other and unspecified**

996.95 **Foot and toe(s)**

996.96 **Lower extremity, other and unspecified**

996.99 **Other specified body part**

4th 997 **Complications affecting specified body systems, not elsewhere classified**
Use additional code to identify complications
EXCLUDES *the listed conditions when specified as:*
causing shock (998.0)
complications of:
anesthesia:
adverse effect (001.0-799.9, 995.0-995.8)
in labor or delivery (668.0-668.9)
poisoning (968.0-969.9)
implanted device or graft (996.0-996.9)
obstetrical procedures (669.0-669.4)
reattached extremity (996.90-996.96)
transplanted organ (996.80-996.89)
AHA: 1Q, '94, 4; 1Q, '93, 26

5th 997.0 **Nervous system complications**

997.00 **Nervous system complication, unspecified**

997.01 **Central nervous system complication**
Anoxic brain damage
Cerebral hypoxia
EXCLUDES *cerebrovascular hemorrhage or infarction (997.02)*
AHA: 1Q, '07, 22; 1Q, '06, 15

997.02 **Iatrogenic cerebrovascular infarction or hemorrhage**
Postoperative stroke
AHA: 3Q, '06, 6; 2Q, '04, 8; 4Q, '95, 57

997.09 **Other nervous system complications**

997.1 **Cardiac complications**
Cardiac:
arrest
insufficiency
Cardiorespiratory failure
Heart failure
} during or resulting from a procedure
EXCLUDES *the listed conditions as long-term effects of cardiac surgery or due to the presence of cardiac prosthetic device (429.4)*
AHA: 2Q, '02, 12

997.2 **Peripheral vascular complications**
Phlebitis or thrombophlebitis during or resulting from a procedure
EXCLUDES *the listed conditions due to:*
implant or catheter device (996.62)
infusion, perfusion, or transfusion (999.2)
complications affecting blood vessels (997.71-997.79)
AHA: 1Q, '03, 6; 3Q, '02, 24-26

5th 997.3 **Respiratory complications**
EXCLUDES *iatrogenic [postoperative] pneumothorax (512.1)*
iatrogenic pulmonary embolism (415.11)
Mendelson's syndrome in labor and delivery (668.0)
specified complications classified elsewhere, such as:
adult respiratory distress syndrome (518.5)
pulmonary edema, postoperative (518.4)
respiratory insufficiency, acute, postoperative (518.5)
shock lung (518.5)
tracheostomy complications (519.00-519.09)
transfusion related acute lung injury [TRALI] (518.7)
AHA: 1Q, '97, 10; 2Q, '93, 3; 2Q, '93, 9; 4Q, '90, 25

● 997.31 **Ventilator associated pneumonia**
Use additional code to identify organism

● 997.39 **Other respiratory complications**
Mendelson's syndrome resulting from a procedure
Pneumonia (aspiration) resulting from a procedure
DEF: Mendelson's syndrome: acid pneumonitis due to aspiration of gastric acids, may occur after anesthesia or sedation.

997.4 Digestive system complications

Complications of:
intestinal (internal) anastomosis and bypass, not elsewhere classified, except that involving urinary tract

Hepatic failure, Hepatorenal syndrome, Intestinal obstruction NOS } specified as due to a procedure

EXCLUDES *gastrostomy complications (536.40-536.49)*
specified gastrointestinal complications classified elsewhere, such as:
blind loop syndrome (579.2)
colostomy and enterostomy complications (569.60-569.69)
gastrojejunal ulcer (534.0-534.9)
infection of esophagostomy (530.86)
infection of external stoma (569.61)
mechanical complication of esophagostomy (530.87)
pelvic peritoneal adhesions, female (614.6)
peritoneal adhesions (568.0)
peritoneal adhesions with obstruction (560.81)
postcholecystectomy syndrome (576.0)
postgastric surgery syndromes (564.2)
vomiting following gastrointestinal surgery (564.3)

AHA: 2Q, '01, 4-6; 3Q, '99, 4; 2Q, '99, 14; 3Q, '97, 7; 1Q, '97, 11; 2Q, '95, 7; 1Q, '93, 26; 3Q, '92, 15; 2Q, '89, 15; 1Q, '88, 14

997.5 Urinary complications

Complications of:
external stoma of urinary tract
internal anastomosis and bypass of urinary tract, including that involving intestinal tract

Oliguria or anuria, Renal: failure (acute), insufficiency (acute), Tubular necrosis (acute) } specified as due to procedure

EXCLUDES *specified complications classified elsewhere, such as:*
postoperative stricture of:
ureter (593.3)
urethra (598.2)

AHA: 3Q, '03, 13; 3Q, '96, 10, 15; 4Q, '95, 73; 1Q, '92, 13; 2Q, '89, 16; M-A, '87, 10; S-O, '85, 3

5th **997.6 Amputation stump complication**

EXCLUDES *admission for treatment for a current traumatic amputation – code to complicated traumatic amputation*
phantom limb (syndrome) (353.6)

AHA: 4Q, '95, 82

997.60 Unspecified complication

997.61 Neuroma of amputation stump

DEF: Hyperplasia generated nerve cell mass following amputation.

997.62 Infection (chronic)

Use additional code to identify the organism

AHA: 1Q, '05, 15 4Q, '96, 46

997.69 Other

AHA: 1Q, '05, 15

5th **997.7 Vascular complications of other vessels**

EXCLUDES *peripheral vascular complications (997.2)*

997.71 Vascular complications of mesenteric artery

AHA: 4Q, '01, 53

997.72 Vascular complications of renal artery

997.79 Vascular complications of other vessels

5th **997.9 Complications affecting other specified body systems, not elsewhere classified**

EXCLUDES *specified complications classified elsewhere, such as:*
broad ligament laceration syndrome (620.6)
postartificial menopause syndrome (627.4)
postoperative stricture of vagina (623.2)

997.91 Hypertension

EXCLUDES *essential hypertension (401.0-401.9)*

AHA: 4Q, '95, 57

997.99 Other

Vitreous touch syndrome

AHA: 2Q, '94, 12; 1Q, '94, 17

DEF: Vitreous touch syndrome: vitreous protruding through pupil and attaches to corneal epithelium; causes aqueous fluid in vitreous body; marked by corneal edema, loss of lucidity; complication of cataract surgery.

4th **998 Other complications of procedures, not elsewhere classified**

AHA: 1Q, '94, 4

998.0 Postoperative shock

Collapse NOS, Shock (endotoxic) (hypovolemic septic) } during or resulting from a surgical procedure

EXCLUDES *shock:*
anaphylactic due to serum (999.4)
anesthetic (995.4)
electric (994.8)
following abortion (639.5)
obstetric (669.1)
traumatic (958.4)

5th **998.1 Hemorrhage or hematoma or seroma complicating a procedure**

EXCLUDES *hemorrhage, hematoma, or seroma:*
complicating cesarean section or puerperal perineal wound (674.3)
due to implanted device or graft (996.70-996.79)

998.11 Hemorrhage complicating a procedure

AHA: 3Q, '03, 13; 1Q, '03, 4; 4Q, '97, 52; 1Q, '97, 10

998.12 Hematoma complicating a procedure

AHA: 3Q, '06, 12; 1Q, '03, 6; 3Q, '02, 24, 26

998.13 Seroma complicating a procedure

AHA: 4Q, '96, 46; 1Q, '93, 26; 2Q, '92, 15; S-O, '87, 8

998.2 Accidental puncture or laceration during a procedure

Accidental perforation by catheter or other instrument during a procedure on:
blood vessel
nerve
organ

EXCLUDES *iatrogenic [postoperative] pneumothorax (512.1)*
puncture or laceration caused by implanted device intentionally left in operation wound (996.0-996.5)
specified complications classified elsewhere, such as:
broad ligament laceration syndrome (620.6)
▶dural tear (349.31)
incidental durotomy (349.31)◀
trauma from instruments during delivery (664.0-665.9)

AHA: 2Q, '07, 9; 1Q, '06, 15; 3Q, '02, 24, 26; 3Q, '94, 6; 3Q, '90, 17; 3Q, '90, 18

▲ ✓5th **998.3 Disruption of wound**

Dehiscence } of operation wound
Rupture }

▶Disruption of any suture materials or other closure method◀

EXCLUDES *disruption of:*
cesarean wound (674.1)
perineal wound, puerperal (674.2)

AHA: 4Q, '02, 73; 1Q, '93, 19

● **998.30 Disruption of wound, unspecified**

Disruption of wound NOS

▲ **998.31 Disruption of internal operation (surgical) wound**

▶Disruption or dehiscence of closure of:
fascia, superficial or muscular
internal organ
muscle or muscle flap
ribs or rib cage
skull or craniotomy
sternum or sternotomy
tendon or ligament
Deep disruption or dehiscence of operation wound NOS◀

EXCLUDES *▶complications of internal anastomosis of:*
gastrointestinal tract (997.4)
urinary tract (997.5)◀

▲ **998.32 Disruption of external operation (surgical) wound**

Disruption of operation wound NOS
▶Disruption or dehiscence of closure of:
cornea
mucosa
skin
subcutaneous tissue
Full-thickness skin disruption or dehiscence
Superficial disruption or dehiscence of operation wound◀

AHA: 1Q, '06, 8; 1Q, '05, 11; 4Q, '03, 104, 106

● **998.33 Disruption of traumatic injury wound repair**

Disruption or dehiscence of closure of traumatic laceration (external) (internal)

998.4 Foreign body accidentally left during a procedure

Adhesions } due to foreign body accidentally left
Obstruction } in operative wound or body
Perforation } cavity during a procedure

EXCLUDES *obstruction or perforation caused by implanted device intentionally left in body (996.0-996.5)*

AHA: 1Q, '89, 9

✓5th **998.5 Postoperative infection**

EXCLUDES *bleb associated endophthalmitis (379.63)*
infection due to:
implanted device (996.60-996.69)
infusion, perfusion, or transfusion (999.31-999.39)
postoperative obstetrical wound infection (674.3)

998.51 Infected postoperative seroma

Use additional code to identify organism

AHA: 4Q, '96, 46

998.59 Other postoperative infection

Abscess: } postoperative
intra-abdominal
stitch
subphrenic
wound
Septicemia
Use additional code to identify infection

AHA: 2Q, '06, 23; 4Q, '04, 76; 4Q, '03, 104, 106-107; 3Q, '98, 3; 3Q, '95, 5; 2Q, '95, 7; 3Q, '94, 6; 1Q, '93, 19; J-F, '87, 14

998.6 Persistent postoperative fistula

AHA: J-F, '87, 14

998.7 Acute reaction to foreign substance accidentally left during a procedure

Peritonitis:
aseptic
chemical

✓5th **998.8 Other specified complications of procedures, not elsewhere classified**

AHA: 4Q, '94, 46; 1Q, '89, 9

998.81 Emphysema (subcutaneous) (surgical) resulting from a procedure

998.82 Cataract fragments in eye following cataract surgery

998.83 Non-healing surgical wound

AHA: 4Q, '96, 47

998.89 Other specified complications

AHA: 3Q, '06, 9; 3Q, '05, 16; 3Q, '99, 13; 2Q, '98, 16

998.9 Unspecified complication of procedure, not elsewhere classified

Postoperative complication NOS

EXCLUDES *complication NOS of obstetrical, surgery or procedure (669.4)*

AHA: 4Q, '93, 37

✓4th 999 Complications of medical care, not elsewhere classified

INCLUDES complications, not elsewhere classified, of:
dialysis (hemodialysis) (peritoneal) (renal)
extracorporeal circulation
hyperalimentation therapy
immunization
infusion
inhalation therapy
injection
inoculation
perfusion
transfusion
vaccination
ventilation therapy

Use additional code, where applicable, to identify specific complication

EXCLUDES *specified complications classified elsewhere such as:*
complications of implanted device (996.0-996.9)
contact dermatitis due to drugs (692.3)
dementia dialysis (294.8)
transient (293.9)
dialysis disequilibrium syndrome (276.0-276.9)
poisoning and toxic effects of drugs and chemicals (960.0-989.9)
postvaccinal encephalitis (323.51)
water and electrolyte imbalance (276.0-276.9)

999.0 Generalized vaccinia

EXCLUDES ▶*vaccinia not from vaccine (051.02)*◀

DEF: Skin eruption, self-limiting; follows vaccination; due to transient viremia with virus localized in skin.

999.1 Air embolism

Air embolism to any site following infusion, perfusion, or transfusion

EXCLUDES *embolism specified as:*
complicating:
abortion (634-638 with .6, 639.6)
ectopic or molar pregnancy (639.6)
pregnancy, childbirth, or the puerperium (673.0)
due to implanted device (996.7)
traumatic (958.0)

999.2 Other vascular complications

Phlebitis, Thromboembolism, Thrombophlebitis } following infusion, perfusion, or transfusion

EXCLUDES ▶*extravasation of vesicant drugs (999.81, 999.82)*◀
the listed conditions when specified as:
due to implanted device (996.61 996.62, 996.72-996.74)
postoperative NOS (997.2, 997.71 997.79)

AHA: 2Q, '97, 5

✓5th 999.3 Other infection

Infection, Sepsis, Septicemia } following infusion, injection, transfusion, or vaccination

Use additional code to identify the specified infection, such as:
septicemia (038.0-038.9)

EXCLUDES *the listed conditions when specified as:*
due to implanted device (996.60-996.69)
postoperative NOS (998.51-998.59)

AHA: 4Q, '07, 96; 2Q, '01, 11, 12; 2Q, '97, 5; J-F, '87, 14

999.31 Infection due to central venous catheter

Catheter-related bloodstream infection (CRBSI) ▶NOS◀
Infection due to:
Hickman catheter
peripherally inserted central catheter (PICC)
▶portacath (port-a-cath)◀
triple lumen catheter
▶umbilical venous catheter◀

EXCLUDES *infection due to:*
arterial catheter (996.62)
catheter NOS (996.69)
peripheral venous catheter (996.62)
urinary catheter (996.64)

AHA: 4Q, '07, 97

999.39 Infection following other infusion, injection, transfusion, or vaccination

999.4 Anaphylactic shock due to serum

▶Anaphylactic reaction due to serum◀

EXCLUDES *shock:*
allergic NOS (995.0)
anaphylactic:
NOS (995.0)
due to drugs and chemicals (995.0)

DEF: Life-threatening hypersensitivity to foreign serum; causes respiratory distress, vascular collapse, and shock.

999.5 Other serum reaction

Intoxication by serum
Protein sickness
Serum rash
Serum sickness
Urticaria due to serum

EXCLUDES *serum hepatitis (070.2-070.3)*

DEF: Serum sickness: Hypersensitivity to foreign serum; causes fever, hives, swelling, and lymphadenopathy.

999.6 ABO incompatibility reaction

Incompatible blood transfusion
Reaction to blood group incompatibility in infusion or transfusion

999.7 Rh incompatibility reaction

Elevation of Rh titer
Reactions due to Rh factor in infusion or transfusion

▲ **✓5th 999.8 Other infusion and transfusion reaction**

EXCLUDES *postoperative shock (998.0)*
transfusion related acute lung injury [TRALI] (518.7)

AHA: 3Q, '00, 9

● **999.81 Extravasation of vesicant chemotherapy**

Infiltration of vesicant chemotherapy

● **999.82 Extravasation of other vesicant agent**

Infiltration of other vesicant agent

● **999.88 Other infusion reaction**

● **999.89 Other transfusion reaction**

Transfusion reaction NOS
Use additional code to identify graft-versus-host reaction (279.5)

999.9 Other and unspecified complications of medical care, not elsewhere classified

Complications, not elsewhere classified, of:

electroshock, inhalation, ultrasound, ventilation } therapy

Unspecified misadventure of medical care

EXCLUDES *unspecified complication of:*
phototherapy (990)
radiation therapy (999)
▶*ventilator associated pneumonia (997.31)*◀

AHA: 3Q, '06, 25; 1Q, '03, 19; 2Q, '97, 5

SUPPLEMENTARY CLASSIFICATION OF FACTORS INFLUENCING HEALTH STATUS AND CONTACT WITH HEALTH SERVICES ▶(V01-V89)◀

This classification is provided to deal with occasions when circumstances other than a disease or injury classifiable to categories 001-999 (the main part of ICD) are recorded as "diagnoses" or "problems." This can arise mainly in three ways:

a) When a person who is not currently sick encounters the health services for some specific purpose, such as to act as a donor of an organ or tissue, to receive prophylactic vaccination, or to discuss a problem which is in itself not a disease or injury. This will be a fairly rare occurrence among hospital inpatients, but will be relatively more common among hospital outpatients and patients of family practitioners, health clinics, etc.

b) When a person with a known disease or injury, whether it is current or resolving, encounters the health care system for a specific treatment of that disease or injury (e.g., dialysis for renal disease; chemotherapy for malignancy; cast change).

c) When some circumstance or problem is present which influences the person's health status but is not in itself a current illness or injury. Such factors may be elicited during population surveys, when the person may or may not be currently sick, or be recorded as an additional factor to be borne in mind when the person is receiving care for some current illness or injury classifiable to categories 001-999.

In the latter circumstances the V code should be used only as a supplementary code and should not be the one selected for use in primary, single cause tabulations. Examples of these circumstances are a personal history of certain diseases, or a person with an artificial heart valve in situ.

AHA: J-F, '87, 8

PERSONS WITH POTENTIAL HEALTH HAZARDS RELATED TO COMMUNICABLE DISEASES (V01-V06)

EXCLUDES *family history of infectious and parasitic diseases (V18.8)*
personal history of infectious and parasitic diseases (V12.0)

✓4th **V01 Contact with or exposure to communicable diseases**

V01.0 Cholera
Conditions classifiable to 001

V01.1 Tuberculosis
Conditions classifiable to 010-018

V01.2 Poliomyelitis
Conditions classifiable to 045

V01.3 Smallpox
Conditions classifiable to 050

V01.4 Rubella
Conditions classifiable to 056

V01.5 Rabies
Conditions classifiable to 071

V01.6 Venereal diseases
Conditions classifiable to 090-099
AHA: 4Q, '07, 125

✓5th **V01.7 Other viral diseases**
Conditions classifiable to 042-078 and V08, except as above
AHA: 2Q, '92, 11

V01.71 Varicella

V01.79 Other viral diseases

✓5th **V01.8 Other communicable diseases**
Conditions classifiable to 001-136, except as above
AHA: J-A, '87, 24

V01.81 Anthrax
AHA: 4Q, '02, 70, 78

V01.82 Exposure to SARS-associated coronavirus
AHA: 4Q, '03, 46-47

V01.83 Escherichia coli (E. coli)

V01.84 Meningococcus

V01.89 Other communicable diseases

V01.9 Unspecified communicable diseases

✓4th **V02 Carrier or suspected carrier of infectious diseases**

INCLUDES ▶colonization status◀

AHA: 3Q, '95, 18; 3Q, '94, 4

V02.0 Cholera

V02.1 Typhoid

V02.2 Amebiasis

V02.3 Other gastrointestinal pathogens

V02.4 Diphtheria

✓5th **V02.5 Other specified bacterial diseases**

V02.51 Group B streptococcus
AHA: 3Q, '06, 14; 1Q, '02, 14; 4Q, '98, 56

V02.52 Other streptococcus

● **V02.53 Methicillin susceptible Staphylococcus aureus**
MSSA colonization

● **V02.54 Methicillin resistant Staphylococcus aureus**
MRSA colonization

V02.59 Other specified bacterial diseases
Meningococcal
Staphylococcal

✓5th **V02.6 Viral hepatitis**
Hepatitis Australian-antigen [HAA] [SH] carrier
Serum hepatitis carrier

V02.60 Viral hepatitis carrier, unspecfied
AHA: 4Q, '97, 47

V02.61 Hepatitis B carrier
AHA: 4Q, '97, 47

V02.62 Hepatitis C carrier
AHA: 4Q, '97, 47

V02.69 Other viral hepatitis carrier
AHA: 4Q, '97, 47

V02.7 Gonorrhea

V02.8 Other venereal diseases

V02.9 Other specified infectious organism
AHA: 3Q, '95, 18; 1Q, '93, 22; J-A, '87, 24

✓4th **V03 Need for prophylactic vaccination and inoculation against bacterial diseases**

EXCLUDES *vaccination not carried out (V64.00-V64.09)*
vaccines against combinations of diseases (V06.0-V06.9)

V03.0 Cholera alone

V03.1 Typhoid-paratyphoid alone [TAB]

V03.2 Tuberculosis [BCG]

V03.3 Plague

V03.4 Tularemia

V03.5 Diphtheria alone

V03.6 Pertussis alone

V03.7 Tetanus toxoid alone

✓5th **V03.8 Other specified vaccinations against single bacterial diseases**

V03.81 Hemophilus influenza, type B [Hib]

V03.82 Streptococcus pneumoniae [pneumococcus]

V03.89 Other specified vaccination
AHA: 2Q, '00, 9

V03.9 Unspecified single bacterial disease

✓4th V04 Need for prophylactic vaccination and inoculation against certain viral diseases
EXCLUDES *vaccines against combinations of diseases (V06.0-V06.9)*

V04.0 Poliomyelitis

V04.1 Smallpox

V04.2 Measles alone

V04.3 Rubella alone

V04.4 Yellow fever

V04.5 Rabies

V04.6 Mumps alone

V04.7 Common cold

✓5th V04.8 Other viral diseases
AHA: 4Q, '03, 83

V04.81 Influenza

V04.82 Respiratory syncytial virus (RSV)

V04.89 Other viral diseases
AHA: 2Q, '07, 9

✓4th V05 Need for other prophylactic vaccination and inoculation against single diseases
EXCLUDES *vaccines against combinations of diseases (V06.0-V06.9)*

V05.0 Athropod-borne viral encephalitis

V05.1 Other arthropod-borne viral diseases

V05.2 Leshmaniasis

V05.3 Viral hepatitis

V05.4 Varicella
Chickenpox

V05.8 Other specified disease
AHA: 1Q, '01, 4; 3Q, '91, 20

V05.9 Unspecified single disease

✓4th V06 Need for prophylactic vaccination and inoculation against combinations of diseases
Note: Use additional single vaccination codes from categories V03-V05 to identify any vaccinations not included in a combination code.

V06.0 Cholera with typhoid-paratyphoid [cholera+TAB]

V06.1 Diphtheria-tetanus-pertussis, combined [DTP] [DTaP]
AHA: 4Q, '03, 83; 3Q, '98, 13

V06.2 Diphtheria-tetanus-pertussis with typhoid-paratyphoid [DTP+TAB]

V06.3 Diphtheria-tetanus-pertussis with poliomyelitis [DTP+polio]

V06.4 Measles-mumps-rubella [MMR]

V06.5 Tetanus-diphtheria [Td] [DT]
AHA: 4Q, '03, 83

V06.6 Streptococcus pneumoniae [pneumococcus] and influenza

V06.8 Other combinations
EXCLUDES *multiple single vaccination codes (V03.0-V05.9)*
AHA: 1Q, '94, 19

V06.9 Unspecified combined vaccine

PERSONS WITH NEED FOR ISOLATION, OTHER POTENTIAL HEALTH HAZARDS AND PROPHYLACTIC MEASURES (V07-V09)

✓4th V07 Need for isolation and other prophylactic measures
EXCLUDES *prophylactic organ removal (V50.41-V50.49)*

V07.0 Isolation
Admission to protect the individual from his surroundings or for isolation of individual after contact with infectious diseases

V07.1 Desensitization to allergens

V07.2 Prophylactic immunotherapy
Administration of:
antivenin
immune sera [gamma globulin]
RhoGAM
tetanus antitoxin

✓5th V07.3 Other prophylactic chemotherapy

V07.31 Prophylactic fluoride administration

V07.39 Other prophylactic chemotherapy
EXCLUDES *maintenance chemotherapy following disease (V58.11)*

V07.4 Hormone replacement therapy (postmenopausal) ♀

● ✓5th V07.5 Prophylactic use of agents affecting estrogen receptors and estrogen levels
Code first, if applicable:
malignant neoplasm of breast (174.0-174.9, 175.0-175.9)
malignant neoplasm of prostate (185)
Use additional code, if applicable, to identify:
estrogen receptor positive status (V86.0)
family history of breast cancer (V16.3)
genetic susceptibility to cancer (V84.01-V84.09)
personal history of breast cancer (V10.3)
personal history of prostate cancer (V10.46)
postmenopausal status (V49.81)
EXCLUDES *hormone replacement therapy (postmenopausal) (V07.4)*

● V07.51 Prophylactic use of selective estrogen receptor modulators [SERMs]
Prophylactic use of:
raloxifene (Evista)
tamoxifen (Nolvadex)
toremifene (Fareston)

● V07.52 Prophylactic use of aromatase inhibitors
Prophylactic use of:
anastrozole (Arimidex)
exemestar (Aromasin)
letrozole (Femara)

● V07.59 Prophylactic use of other agents affecting estrogen receptors and estrogen levels
Prophylactic use of:
estrogen receptor downregulators
fulvestrant (Faslodex)
gonadotropin-releasing hormone (GnRH) agonist
goserelin acetate (Zoladex)
leuprolide acetate (leuprorelin) (Lupron)
megestrol acetate (Megace)

V07.8 Other specified prophylactic measure
AHA: 1Q, '92, 11

V07.9 Unspecified prophylactic measure

V08 Asymptomatic human immunodeficiency virus [HIV] infection status

HIV positive NOS

Note: This code is only to be used when no HIV infection symptoms or conditions are present. If any HIV infec-tion symptoms or conditions are present, see code 042.

EXCLUDES *AIDS (042)*
human immunodeficiency virus [HIV] disease (042)
exposure to HIV (V01.79)
nonspecific serologic evidence of HIV (795.71)
symptomatic human immunodeficiency virus [HIV] infection (042)

AHA: 2Q, '04, 11; 2Q, '99, 8; 3Q, '95, 18

4th **V09 Infection with drug-resistant microorganisms**

Note: This category is intended for use as an additional code for infectious conditions classified elsewhere to indicate the presence of drug-resistance of the infectious organism.

AHA: 3Q, '94, 4; 4Q, '93, 22

V09.0 Infection with microorganisms resistant to penicillins SDx

AHA: 2Q, '06, 16; 4Q, '03, 104, 106

V09.1 Infection with microorganisms resistant to cephalosporins and other B-lactam antibiotics SDx

V09.2 Infection with microorganisms resistant to macrolides SDx

V09.3 Infection with microorganisms resistant to tetracyclines SDx

V09.4 Infection with microorganisms resistant to aminoglycosides SDx

5th **V09.5 Infection with microorganisms resistant to quinolones and fluoroquinolones**

V09.50 Without mention of resistance to multiple quinolones and fluoroquinoles SDx

V09.51 With resistance to multiple quinolones and fluoroquinoles SDx

V09.6 Infection with microorganisms resistant to sulfonamides SDx

5th **V09.7 Infection with microorganisms resistant to other specified antimycobacterial agents**

EXCLUDES *Amikacin (V09.4)*
Kanamycin (V09.4)
Streptomycin [SM] (V09.4)

V09.70 Without mention of resistance to multiple antimycobacterial agents SDx

V09.71 With resistance to multiple antimycobacterial agents SDx

5th **V09.8 Infection with microorganisms resistant to other specified drugs**

Vancomycin (glycopeptide) intermediate staphylococcus aureus (VISA/GISA)
Vancomycin (glycopeptide) resistant enterococcus (VRE)
Vancomycin (glycopeptide) resistant staphylococcus aureus (VRSA/GRSA)

V09.80 Without mention of resistance to multiple drugs SDx

V09.81 With resistance to multiple drugs SDx

5th **V09.9 Infection with drug-resistant microorganisms, unspecified**

Drug resistance, NOS

V09.90 Without mention of multiple drug resistance SDx

V09.91 With multiple drug resistance SDx

Multiple drug resistance NOS

PERSONS WITH POTENTIAL HEALTH HAZARDS RELATED TO PERSONAL AND FAMILY HISTORY (V10-V19)

EXCLUDES *obstetric patients where the possibility that the fetus might be affected is the reason for observation or management during pregnancy (655.0-655.9)*

AHA: J-F, '87, 1

4th **V10 Personal history of malignant neoplasm**

►Code first any continuing functional activity, such as: carcinoid syndrome (259.2)◄

AHA: 4Q, '02, 80; 4Q, '98, 69; 1Q, '95, 4; 3Q, '92, 5; M-J, '85, 10; 2Q, '90, 9

5th **V10.0 Gastrointestinal tract**

History of conditions classifiable to 140-159

V10.00 Gastrointestinal tract, unspecified

V10.01 Tongue

V10.02 Other and unspecified oral cavity and pharynx

V10.03 Esophagus

V10.04 Stomach

V10.05 Large intestine

AHA: 3Q, '99, 7; 1Q, '95, 4

V10.06 Rectum, rectosigmoid junction, and anus

V10.07 Liver

V10.09 Other

AHA: 4Q, '03, 111

5th **V10.1 Trachea, bronchus, and lung**

History of conditions classifiable to 162

V10.11 Bronchus and lung

V10.12 Trachea

5th **V10.2 Other respiratory and intrathoracic organs**

History of conditions classifiable to 160, 161, 163-165

V10.20 Respiratory organ, unspecified

V10.21 Larynx

AHA: 4Q, '03, 108, 110

V10.22 Nasal cavities, middle ear, and accessory sinuses

V10.29 Other

V10.3 Breast

History of conditions classifiable to 174 and 175

AHA: 3Q, '07, 4; 1Q, '07, 6; 2Q, '03, 5; 4Q, '01, 66; 4Q, '98, 65; 4Q, '97, 50; 1Q, '91, 16; 1Q, '90, 21

5th **V10.4 Genital organs**

History of conditions classifiable to 179-187

V10.40 Female genital organ, unspecfied ♀

V10.41 Cervix uteri ♀

AHA: 4Q, '07, 99

V10.42 Other parts of uterus ♀

V10.43 Ovary ♀

V10.44 Other female genital organs ♀

V10.45 Male genital organ, unspecfied ♂

V10.46 Prostate ♂

V10.47 Testis ♂

V10.48 Epididymis ♂

V10.49 Other male genital organs ♂

5th **V10.5 Urinary organs**

History of conditions classifiable to 188 and 189

V10.50 Urinary organ, unspecified

V10.51 Bladder

V10.52 Kidney

EXCLUDES *renal pelvis (V10.53)*

AHA: 2Q, '04, 4

V10.53 Renal pelvis

AHA: 4Q, '01, 55

V10.59 Other

✓5th **V10.6 Leukemia**

Conditions classifiable to 204-208

EXCLUDES *leukemia in remission (204-208)*

AHA: 2Q, '92, 13; 4Q, '91, 26; 4Q, '90, 3

V10.60 Leukemia, unspecified

V10.61 Lymphoid leukemia

V10.62 Myeloid leukemia

V10.63 Monocytic leukemia

V10.69 Other

✓5th **V10.7 Other lymphatic and hematopoietic neoplasms**

Conditions classifiable to 200-203

EXCLUDES *listed conditions in 200-203 in remission*

AHA: M-J, '85, 18

V10.71 Lymphosarcoma and reticulosarcoma

V10.72 Hodgkin's disease

V10.79 Other

✓5th **V10.8 Personal history of malignant neoplasm of other sites**

History of conditions classifiable to 170-173, 190-195

V10.81 Bone

AHA: 2Q, '03, 13

V10.82 Malignant melanoma of skin

V10.83 Other malignant neoplasm of skin

V10.84 Eye

V10.85 Brain

AHA: 1Q, '01, 6

V10.86 Other parts of the nervous system

EXCLUDES *peripheral sympathetic, and parasympathetic nerves (V10.89)*

V10.87 Thyroid

V10.88 Other endocrine glands and related structures

V10.89 Other

V10.9 Unspecified personal history of malignant neoplasm

✓4th **V11 Personal history of mental disorder**

V11.0 Schizophrenia

EXCLUDES *that in remission (295.0-295.9 with fifth-digit 5)*

V11.1 Affective disorders

Personal history of manic-depressive psychosis

EXCLUDES *that in remission (296.0-296.6 with fifth-digit 5, 6)*

V11.2 Neurosis

V11.3 Alcoholism

V11.8 Other mental disorders

V11.9 Unspecified mental disorder

✓4th **V12 Personal history of certain other diseases**

AHA: 3Q, '92, 11

✓5th **V12.0 Infectious and parasitic diseases**

EXCLUDES *personal history of infectious diseases specific to a body system*

V12.00 Unspecified infectious and parasitic disease

V12.01 Tuberculosis

V12.02 Poliomyelitis

V12.03 Malaria

● **V12.04 Methicillin resistant Staphylococcus aureus**

MRSA

V12.09 Other

V12.1 Nutritional deficiency

V12.2 Endocrine, metabolic, and immunity disorders

EXCLUDES *history of allergy (V14.0-V14.9, V15.01-V15.09)*

AHA: 3Q, '07, 5

V12.3 Diseases of blood and blood-forming organs

✓5th **V12.4 Disorders of nervous system and sense organs**

V12.40 Unspecified disorder of nervous system and sense organs

V12.41 Benign neoplasm of the brain

AHA: 4Q, '97, 48

V12.42 Infections of the central nervous system

Encephalitis Meningitis

AHA: 4Q, '05, 95

V12.49 Other disorders of nervous system and sense organs

AHA: 4Q, '98, 59

✓5th **V12.5 Diseases of circulatory system**

EXCLUDES *old myocardial infarction (412)*
postmyocardial infarction syndrome (411.0)

AHA: 4Q, '95, 61

V12.50 Unspecified circulatory disease

V12.51 Venous thrombosis and embolism

Pulmonary embolism

AHA: 3Q, '06, 12; 4Q, '03, 108; 1Q, '02, 15

V12.52 Thrombophlebitis

V12.53 Sudden cardiac arrest

Sudden cardiac death successfully resuscitated

AHA: 4Q, '07, 98

V12.54 Transient ischemic attack [TIA], and cerebral infarction without residual deficits

Prolonged reversible ischemic neurological deficit [PRIND]
Reversible ischemic neurologic deficit [RIND]
Stroke NOS without residual deficits

EXCLUDES *late effects of cerebrovascular disease (438.0-438.9)*

AHA: 4Q, '07, 98

V12.59 Other

AHA: 2Q, '07, 3; 4Q, '99, 4; 4Q, '98, 88; 4Q, '97, 37

✓5th **V12.6 Diseases of respiratory system**

EXCLUDES *tuberculosis (V12.01)*

V12.60 Unspecified disease of respiratory system

V12.61 Pneumonia (recurrent)

AHA: 4Q, '05, 95

V12.69 Other diseases of respiratory system

✓5th V12.7 Diseases of digestive system
AHA: 1Q, '95, 3; 2Q, '89, 16

V12.70 Unspecified digestive disease

V12.71 Peptic ulcer disease

V12.72 Colonic polyps
AHA: 3Q, '02, 15

V12.79 Other

✓4th **V13 Personal history of other diseases**

✓5th V13.0 Disorders of urinary system

V13.00 Unspecified urinary disorder

V13.01 Urinary calculi

V13.02 Urinary (tract) infection
AHA: 4Q, '05, 95

V13.03 Nephrotic syndrome
AHA: 4Q, '05, 95

V13.09 Other

V13.1 Trophoblastic disease ♀
EXCLUDES *supervision during a current pregnancy (V23.1)*

✓5th V13.2 Other genital system and obstetric disorders
EXCLUDES *habitual aborter (646.3)*
without current pregnancy (629.81)
supervision during a current pregnancy of a woman with poor obstetric history (V23.0-V23.9)

V13.21 Personal history of pre-term labor ♀
EXCLUDES *current pregnancy with history of pre-term labor (V23.41)*
AHA: 4Q, '02, 78

V13.22 Personal history of cervical dysplasia ♀
Personal history of conditions classifiable to 622.10-622.12
EXCLUDES *personal history of malignant neoplasm of cervix uteri (V10.41)*
AHA: 4Q, '07, 98

V13.29 Other genital system and obstetric disorders ♀

V13.3 Diseases of skin and subcutaneous tissue

V13.4 Arthritis

✓5th V13.5 Other musculoskeletal disorders

● V13.51 Pathologic fracture
Healed pathologic fracture
EXCLUDES *personal history of traumatic fracture (V15.51)*

● V13.52 Stress fracture
Healed stress fracture
EXCLUDES *personal history of traumatic fracture (V15.51)*

● V13.59 Other musculoskeletal disorders

✓5th V13.6 Congenital malformations
AHA: 4Q, '98, 63

V13.61 Hypospadias SDx ♂

V13.69 Other congenital malformations
AHA: 1Q, '04, 16

V13.7 Perinatal problems
EXCLUDES *low birth weight status (V21.30-V21.35)*

V13.8 Other specified diseases

V13.9 Unspecified disease
AHA: 4Q, '06, 117

✓4th **V14 Personal history of allergy to medicinal agents**

V14.0 Penicillin SDx

V14.1 Other antibiotic agent SDx

V14.2 Sulfonamides SDx

V14.3 Other anti-infective agent SDx

V14.4 Anesthetic age SDx

V14.5 Narcotic agent SDx

V14.6 Analgesic agent SDx

V14.7 Serum or vaccine SDx

V14.8 Other specified medicinal agents SDx

V14.9 Unspecified medicinal agent SDx

✓4th **V15 Other personal history presenting hazards to health**
EXCLUDES ▶*personal history of drug therapy (V87.41-V87.49)*◀

✓5th V15.0 Allergy, other than to medicinal agents
EXCLUDES *allergy to food substance used as base for medicinal agent (V14.0-V14.9)*
AHA: 4Q, '00, 42, 49

V15.01 Allergy to peanuts SDx

V15.02 Allergy to milk products SDx
EXCLUDES *lactose intolerance (271.3)*
AHA: 1Q, '03, 12

V15.03 Allergy to eggs SDx

V15.04 Allergy to seafood SDx
Seafood (octopus) (squid) ink
Shellfish

V15.05 Allergy to other foods SDx
Food additives
Nuts other than peanuts

V15.06 Allergy to insects SDx
Bugs
Insect bites and stings
Spiders

V15.07 Allergy to latex SDx
Latex sensitivity

V15.08 Allergy to radiographic dye SDx
Contrast media used for diagnostic x-ray procedures

V15.09 Other allergy, other than to medicinal agents SDx

V15.1 Surgery to heart and great vessels SDx
EXCLUDES *replacement by transplant or other means (V42.1-V42.2, V43.2-V43.4)*
AHA: 1Q, '04, 16

▲ ✓5th V15.2 Surgery to other organs
EXCLUDES *replacement by transplant or other means (V42.0-V43.8)*

● V15.21 Personal history of undergoing in utero procedure during pregnancy SDx

● V15.22 Personal history of undergoing in utero procedure while a fetus SDx

● V15.29 Surgery to other organs SDx

V15.3 Irradiation SDx
Previous exposure to therapeutic or other ionizing radiation

✓5th V15.4 Psychological trauma
EXCLUDES *history of condition classifiable to 290-316 (V11.0-V11.9)*

V15.41 History of physical abuse SDx
Rape
AHA: 3Q, '99, 15

V15.42 **History of emotional abuse** SDx
Neglect
AHA: 3Q, '99, 15

V15.49 **Other** SDx
AHA: 3Q, '99, 15

✓5th **V15.5 Injury**

● V15.51 **Traumatic fracture** SDx
Healed traumatic fracture
EXCLUDES *personal history of pathologic and stress fracture (V13.51, V13.52)*

● V15.59 **Other injury** SDx

V15.6 Poisoning SDx

V15.7 Contraception
EXCLUDES *current contraceptive management (V25.0-V25.4)*
presence of intrauterine contraceptive device as incidental finding (V45.5)

✓5th **V15.8 Other specified personal history presenting hazards to health**
EXCLUDES ▶*contact with and (suspected) exposure to:*
aromatic compounds and dyes (V87.11-V87.19)
arsenic and other metals (V87.01-V87.09)
molds (V87.31)◀
AHA: 4Q, '95, 62

V15.81 **Noncompliance with medical treatment** SDx
EXCLUDES ▶*noncompliance with renal dialysis (V45.12)*◀
AHA: 3Q, '07, 9; 4Q, '06, 136; 2Q, '03, 7; 2Q, '01, 11, 12, 13; 2Q, '99, 17; 2Q, '97, 11; 1Q, '97, 12; 3Q, '96, 9

V15.82 **History of tobacco use** SDx
EXCLUDES *tobacco dependence (305.1)*

V15.84 **Exposure to asbestos** SDx

V15.85 **Exposure to potentially hazardous body fluids** SDx

V15.86 **Exposure to lead** SDx

V15.87 **History of extracorporeal membrane oxygenation [ECMO]** SDx
AHA: 4Q, '03, 84

V15.88 **History of fall**
At risk for falling
AHA: 4Q, '05, 95

V15.89 **Other** SDx
EXCLUDES ▶*contact with and (suspected) exposure to other potentially hazardous:*
chemicals (V87.2)
substances (V87.39)◀
AHA: 3Q, '07, 5; 1Q, '90, 21; N-D, '84, 12

V15.9 Unspecified personal history presenting hazards to health SDx

✓4th **V16 Family history of malignant neoplasm**

V16.0 Gastrointestinal tract
Family history of condition classifiable to 140-159
AHA: 1Q, '99, 4

V16.1 Trachea, bronchus, and lung
Family history of condition classifiable to 162

V16.2 Other respiratory and intrathoracic organs
Family history of condition classifiable to 160-161, 163-165

V16.3 Breast
Family history of condition classifiable to 174
AHA: 4Q, '04, 107; 2Q, '03, 4; 2Q, '00, 8; 1Q, '92, 11

✓5th **V16.4 Genital organs**
Family history of condition classifiable to 179-187
AHA: 4Q, '97, 48

V16.40 **Genital organ, unspecified**

V16.41 **Ovary**

V16.42 **Prostate**

V16.43 **Testis**

V16.49 **Other**
AHA: 2Q, '06, 2

✓5th **V16.5 Urinary organs**
Family history of condition classifiable to 188-189

V16.51 **Kidney**

V16.52 **Bladder**
AHA: 4Q, '07, 98

V16.59 **Other**

V16.6 Leukemia
Family history of condition classifiable to 204-208

V16.7 Other lymphatic and hematopoietic neoplasms
Family history of condition classifiable to 200-203

V16.8 Other specified malignant neoplasm
Family history of other condition classifiable to 140-199

V16.9 Unspecified malignant neoplasm

✓4th **V17 Family history of certain chronic disabling diseases**

V17.0 Psychiatric condition
EXCLUDES *family history of mental retardation (V18.4)*

V17.1 Stroke (cerebrovascular)

V17.2 Other neurological diseases
Epilepsy
Huntington's chorea

V17.3 Ischemic heart disease

✓5th **V17.4 Other cardiovascular diseases**
AHA: 1Q, '04, 6

V17.41 **Family history of sudden cardiac death [SCD]**
EXCLUDES *family history of ischemic heart disease (V17.3)*
family history of myocardial infarction (V17.3)
AHA: 4Q, '07, 98

V17.49 **Family history of other cardiovascular diseases**
Family history of cardiovascular disease NOS

V17.5 Asthma

V17.6 Other chronic respiratory conditions

V17.7 Arthritis

✓5th **V17.8 Other musculoskeletal diseases**

V17.81 **Osteoporosis**
AHA: 4Q, '05, 95

V17.89 **Other musculoskeletal diseases**

✓4th **V18 Family history of certain other specific conditions**

V18.0 Diabetes mellitus
AHA: 1Q, '04, 8

✓5th **V18.1 Other endocrine and metabolic diseases**

V18.11 **Multiple endocrine neoplasia [MEN] syndrome**
AHA: 4Q, '07, 98, 100

V18.19 **Other endocrine and metabolic diseases**

V18.2 **Anemia**

V18.3 **Other blood disorders**

V18.4 **Mental retardation**

✓5th V18.5 **Digestive disorders**

V18.51 **Colonic polyps**
EXCLUDES *family history of malignant neoplasm of gastrointestinal tract (V16.0)*
AHA: 4Q, '06, 117

V18.59 **Other digestive disorders**

✓5th V18.6 **Kidney diseases**

V18.61 **Polycystic kidney**

V18.69 **Other kidney diseases**

V18.7 **Other genitourinary diseases**

V18.8 **Infectious and parasitic diseases**

V18.9 **Genetic disease carrier**
AHA: 4Q, '05, 95

✓4th **V19 Family history of other conditions**

V19.0 **Blindness or visual loss**

V19.1 **Other eye disorders**

V19.2 **Deafness or hearing loss**

V19.3 **Other ear disorders**

V19.4 **Skin conditions**

V19.5 **Congenital anomalies**

V19.6 **Allergic disorders**

V19.7 **Consanguinity**

V19.8 **Other condition**

PERSONS ENCOUNTERING HEALTH SERVICES IN CIRCUMSTANCES RELATED TO REPRODUCTION AND DEVELOPMENT (V20-V29)

✓4th **V20 Health supervision of infant or child**

V20.0 **Foundling** PDx P

V20.1 **Other healthy infant or child receiving care** PDx P
Medical or nursing care supervision of healthy infant in cases of:
maternal illness, physical or psychiatric
socioeconomic adverse condition at home
too many children at home preventing or interfering with normal care
AHA: 1Q, '00, 25; 3Q, '89, 14

V20.2 **Routine infant or child health check** PDx P
Developmental testing of infant or child
Immunizations appropriate for age
Initial and subsequent routine newborn check
Routine vision and hearing testing
Use additional code(s) to identify:
special screening examination(s) performed (V73.0-V82.9)
EXCLUDES *special screening for developmental handicaps (V79.3)*
AHA: 1Q, '04, 15

✓4th **V21 Constitutional states in development**

V21.0 **Period of rapid growth in childhood** SDx

V21.1 **Puberty** SDx

V21.2 **Other adolecsence** SDx

✓5th V21.3 **Low birth weight status**
EXCLUDES *history of perinatal problems*
AHA: 4Q, '00, 51

V21.30 **Low birth weight status, unspecified** SDx

V21.31 **Low birth weight status, less than 500 grams** SDx

V21.32 **Low birth weight status, 500-999 grams** SDx

V21.33 **Low birth weight status, 1000-1499 grams** SDx

V21.34 **Low birth weight status, 1500-1999 grams** SDx

V21.35 **Low birth weight status, 2000-2500 grams** SDx

V21.8 **Other specified constitutional states in development** SDx

V21.9 **Unspecified constitutional state in development** SDx

✓4th **V22 Normal pregnancy**
EXCLUDES *pregnancy examination or test, pregnancy unconfirmed (V72.40)*
AHA: 4Q, '07, 125

V22.0 **Supervision of normal first pregnancy** PDx ♀
AHA: 3Q, '99, 16

V22.1 **Supervision of other normal pregnancy** PDx ♀
AHA: 3Q, '99, 16

V22.2 **Pregnant state, incidental** SDx ♀
Pregnant state NOS

✓4th **V23 Supervision of high-risk pregnancy**
AHA: 1Q, '90, 10

V23.0 **Pregnancy with history of infertility** M ♀

V23.1 **Pregnancy with history of trophoblastic disease** M ♀
Pregnancy with history of:
hydatidiform mole
vesicular mole
EXCLUDES *that without current pregnancy (V13.1)*

V23.2 **Pregnancy with history of abortion** M ♀
Pregnancy with history of conditions classifiable to 634-638
EXCLUDES *habitual aborter:*
care during pregnancy (646.3)
that without current pregnancy (629.81)

V23.3 **Grand multiparity** M ♀
EXCLUDES *care in relation to labor and delivery (659.4)*
that without current pregnancy (V61.5)

✓5th V23.4 **Pregnancy with other poor obstetric history**
Pregnancy with history of other conditions classifiable to 630-676

V23.41 **Pregnancy with history of labor pre-term** M ♀
AHA: 4Q, '02, 79

V23.49 **Pregnancy with other poor obstetric history** M ♀

V23.5 **Pregnancy with other poor reproductive history** M ♀
Pregnancy with history of stillbirth or neonatal death

V23.7 **Insufficient prenatal care** M ♀
History of little or no prenatal care

5th **V23.8 Other high-risk pregnancy**
AHA: 4Q, '98, 56, 63

V23.81 Elderly primigravida M♀
First pregnancy in a woman who will be 35 years of age or older at expected date of delivery
EXCLUDES *elderly primigravida complicating pregnancy (659.5)*

V23.82 Elderly multigravida M♀
Second or more pregnancy in a woman who will be 35 years of age or older at expected date of delivery
EXCLUDES *elderly multigravida complicating pregnancy (659.6)*

V23.83 Young primigravida M♀
First pregnancy in a female less than 16 years old at expected date of delivery
EXCLUDES *young primigravida complicating pregnancy (659.8)*

V23.84 Young multigravida M♀
Second or more pregnancy in a female less than 16 years old at expected date of delivery
EXCLUDES *young multigravida complicating pregnancy (659.8)*

● **V23.85 Pregnancy resulting from assisted reproductive technology** M♀
Pregnancy resulting from in vitro fertilization

● **V23.86 Pregnancy with history of in utero procedure during previous pregnancy** M♀
EXCLUDES *management of pregnancy affected by in utero procedure during current pregnancy (678.0-678.1)*

V23.89 Other high-risk pregnancy M♀
AHA: 3Q, '06, 14

V23.9 Unspecified high-risk pregnancy M♀

4th **V24 Postpartum care and examination**

V24.0 Immediately after delivery PDx M♀
Care and observation in uncomplicated cases
AHA: 3Q, '06, 11

V24.1 Lactating mother PDx♀
Supervision of lactation

V24.2 Routine postpartum follow-up PDx♀

4th **V25 Encounter for contraceptive management**
AHA: 4Q, '92, 24

5th **V25.0 General counseling and advice**

V25.01 Prescription of oral contraceptives ♀

V25.02 Initiation of other contraceptive measures
Fitting of diaphragm
Prescription of foams, creams, or other agents
AHA: 3Q, '97, 7

V25.03 Encounter for emergency contraceptive counseling and prescription
Encounter for postcoital contraceptive counseling and prescription
AHA: 4Q, '03, 84

V25.04 Counseling and instruction in natural family planning to avoid pregnancy
AHA: 4Q, '07, 99

V25.09 Other
Family planning advice

V25.1 Insertion of intrauterine contraceptive device♀

V25.2 Sterilization
Admission for interruption of fallopian tubes or vas deferens

V25.3 Menstrual extraction ♀
Menstrual regulation

5th **V25.4 Surveillance of previously prescribed contraceptive methods**
Checking, reinsertion, or removal of contraceptive device
Repeat prescription for contraceptive method
Routine examination in connection with contraceptive maintenance
EXCLUDES *presence of intrauterine contraceptive device as incidental finding (V45.5)*

V25.40 Contraceptive surveillance, unspecified

V25.41 Contraceptive pill ♀

V25.42 Intrauterine contraceptive device ♀
Checking, reinsertion, or removal of intrauterine device

V25.43 Implantable subdermal contraceptive ♀

V25.49 Other contraceptive method
AHA: 3Q, '97, 7

V25.5 Insertion of implantable subdermal contraceptive ♀
AHA: 3Q, '92, 9

V25.8 Other specified contraceptive management
Postvasectomy sperm count
EXCLUDES *sperm count following sterilization reversal (V26.22)*
sperm count for fertility testing (V26.21)
AHA: 3Q, '96, 9

V25.9 Unspecified contraceptive management

4th **V26 Procreative management**

V26.0 Tuboplasty or vasoplasty after previous sterilization
AHA: 2Q, '95, 10

V26.1 Artificial insemination ♀

5th **V26.2 Investigation and testing**
EXCLUDES *postvasectomy sperm count (V25.8)*
AHA: 4Q, '00, 56

V26.21 Fertility testing
Fallopian insufflation
Sperm count for fertility testing
EXCLUDES *genetic counseling and testing (V26.31-V26.39)*

V26.22 Aftercare following sterilization reversal
Fallopian insufflation following sterilization reversal
Sperm count following sterilization reversal

V26.29 Other investigation and testing
AHA: 2Q, '96, 9; N-D, '85, 15

5th **V26.3 Genetic counseling and testing**

EXCLUDES *fertility testing (V26.21)*
nonprocreative genetic screening (V82.71, V82.79)

AHA: 4Q, '05, 96

V26.31 Testing of female for genetic disease carrier status ♀

AHA: 4Q, '06, 117

V26.32 Other genetic testing of female ♀

Use additional code to identify habitual aborter (629.81, 646.3)

AHA: 4Q, '06, 117

V26.33 Genetic counseling

V26.34 Testing of male for genetic disease carrier status ♂

AHA: 4Q, '06, 117

V26.35 Encounter for testing of male partner of habitual aborter ♂

AHA: 4Q, '06, 117

V26.39 Other genetic testing of male ♂

AHA: 4Q, '06, 117

5th **V26.4 General counseling and advice**

V26.41 Procreative counseling and advice using natural family planning

AHA: 4Q, '07, 99

V26.49 Other procreative management, counseling and advice

5th **V26.5 Sterilization status**

V26.51 Tubal ligation status SDx ♀

EXCLUDES *infertility not due to previous tubal ligation (628.0-628.9)*

V26.52 Vasectomy status SDx ♂

5th **V26.8 Other specified procreative management**

V26.81 Encounter for assisted reproductive fertility procedure cycle PDx ♀

Patient undergoing in vitro fertilization cycle

Use additional code to identify the type of infertility

EXCLUDES *pre-cycle diagnosis and testing—code to reason for encounter*

AHA: 4Q, '07, 99

V26.89 Other specified procreative management

V26.9 Unspecified procreative management

4th **V27 Outcome of delivery**

Note: This category is intended for the coding of the outcome of delivery on the mother's record.

AHA: 2Q, '91, 16

V27.0 Single liveborn SDx M ♀

AHA: 4Q, '05, 81; 2Q, '03, 9; 2Q, '02, 10; 1Q, '01, 10; 3Q, '00, 5; 4Q, '98, 77; 4Q, '95, 59; 1Q, '92, 9

V27.1 Single stillborn SDx M ♀

V27.2 Twins, both liveborn SDx M ♀

V27.3 Twins, one liveborn and one stillborn SDx M ♀

V27.4 Twins, both stillborn SDx M ♀

V27.5 Other multiple birth, all liveborn SDx M ♀

V27.6 Other multiple birth, some liveborn SDx M ♀

V27.7 Other multiple birth, all stillborn SDx M ♀

V27.9 Unspecified outcome of delivery SDx M ♀

Single birth } outcome to infant unspecified
Multiple birth }

4th **V28 Encounter for antenatal screening of mother**

EXCLUDES *abnormal findings on screening — code to findings*
routine prenatal care (V22.0-V23.9)
▶*suspected fetal conditions affecting management of pregnancy (655.00-655.93, 656.00-656.93, 657.00-657.03, 658.00-658.93)*
suspected fetal conditions not found (V89.01-V89.09)◀

AHA: 4Q, '06, 117; 1Q, '04, 11

V28.0 Screening for chromosomal anomalies by amniocentesis M ♀

V28.1 Screening for raised alpha-fetoprotein levels in amniotic fluid M ♀

V28.2 Other screening based on amniocentesis M ♀

▲ **V28.3 Encounter for routine screening for malformation using ultrasonics** ♀

▶Encounter for routine fetal ultrasound NOS◀

EXCLUDES ▶*encounter for fetal anatomic survey (V28.81)*
genetic counseling and testing (V26.31-V26.39)◀

V28.4 Screening for fetal growth retardation using ultrasonics ♀

V28.5 Screening for isoimmunization ♀

V28.6 Screening for Streptococcus B M ♀

AHA: 4Q, '97, 46

5th **V28.8 Other specified antenatal screening**

AHA: 3Q, '99, 16

● **V28.81 Encounter for fetal anatomic survey** ♀

● **V28.82 Encounter for screening for risk of pre-term labor** ♀

● **V28.89 Other specified antenatal screening** ♀

Chorionic villus sampling
Genomic screening
Nuchal translucency testing
Proteomic screening

V28.9 Unspecified antenatal screening ♀

4th **V29 Observation and evaluation of newborns and infants for suspected condition not found**

Note: This category is to be used for newborns, within the neonatal period, (the first 28 days of life) who are suspected of having an abnormal condition resulting from exposure from the mother or the birth process, but without signs or symptoms, and, which after examination and observation, is found not to exist.

EXCLUDES ▶*suspected fetal conditions not found (V89.01-V89.09)*◀

AHA: 1Q, '00, 25; 4Q, '94, 47; 1Q, '94, 9; 4Q, '92, 21

[1] **V29.0 Observation for suspected infectious condition** N

AHA: 1Q, '01, 10

[1] **V29.1 Observation for suspected neurological condition** N

[1] **V29.2 Observation for suspected respiratory condition** N

[1] **V29.3 Observation for suspected genetic or metabolic condition** N

AHA: 2Q, '05, 21; 4Q, '98, 59, 68

[1] **V29.8 Observation for other specified suspected condition** N

AHA: 2Q, '03, 15

[1] A code from the V30–V39 series may be sequenced before the V29 on the newborn medical record

[1] **V29.9 Observation for unspecified suspected condition** N
AHA: 1Q, '02, 6

LIVEBORN INFANTS ACCORDING TO TYPE OF BIRTH (V30-V39)

Note: These categories are intended for the coding of liveborn infants who are consuming health care [e.g., crib or bassinet occupancy].

The following fouth-digit subdivisions are for use with categories V30-V39

✓5th **0 Born in hospital** N
1 Born before admission to hospital N
2 Born outside hospital and not hospitalized

The following two fifth-digits are for use with the fourth-digit .0, Born in hospital:
0 delivered without mention of cesarean delivery
1 delivered by cesarean delivery

AHA: 1Q, '01, 10

§ ✓4th **V30 Single liveborn** PDx
AHA: 2Q, '03, 9; 4Q, '98, 46, 59; 1Q, '94, 9; For code V30.00: 1Q, '04, 8, 16; 4Q, '03, 68; For code V30.01: 4Q, '05, 88; For code V30.10: 3Q, '06, 10

§ ✓4th **V31 Twin, mate liveborn** PDx
AHA: 3Q, '92, 10

§ ✓4th **V32 Twin, mate stillborn** PDx

§ ✓4th **V33 Twin, unspecified** PDx

§ ✓4th **V34 Other multiple, mates all liveborn** PDx

§ ✓4th **V35 Other multiple, mates all stillborn** PDx

§ ✓4th **V36 Other multiple, mates live and stillborn** PDx

§ ✓4th **V37 Other multiple, unspecified** PDx

§ ✓4th **V39 Unspecified** PDx

PERSONS WITH A CONDITION INFLUENCING THEIR HEALTH STATUS (V40-V49)

Note: These categories are intended for use when these conditions are recorded as "diagnoses" or "problems."

✓4th **V40 Mental and behavioral problems**

V40.0 Problems with learning
V40.1 Problems with communication [including speech]
V40.2 Other mental problems
V40.3 Other behavioral problems
V40.9 Unspecified mental or behavioral problem

✓4th **V41 Problems with special senses and other special functions**

V41.0 Problems with sight
V41.1 Other eye problems
V41.2 Problems with hearing
V41.3 Other ear problems
V41.4 Problems with voice production
V41.5 Problems with smell and taste
V41.6 Problems with swallowing and mastication
V41.7 Problems with sexual function

EXCLUDES *marital problems (V61.10)*
psychosexual disorders (302.0-302.9)

V41.8 Other problems with special functions
V41.9 Unspecified problem with special functions

✓4th **V42 Organ or tissue replaced by transplant**

INCLUDES *homologous or heterologous (animal) (human) transplant organ status*

AHA: 3Q, '98, 3, 4

V42.0 Kidney SDx
AHA: ▶1Q, '08, 10;◀ 1Q, '03, 10; 3Q, '01, 12
V42.1 Heart SDx
AHA: 3Q, '03, 16; 3Q, '01, 13
V42.2 Heart valve SDx
V42.3 Skin SDx
V42.4 Bone SDx
V42.5 Cornea SDx
V42.6 Lung SDx
V42.7 Liver SDx

✓5th **V42.8 Other specified organ or tissue**
AHA: 4Q, '98, 64; 4Q, '97, 49

V42.81 Bone marrow SDx
V42.82 Peripheral stem cells SDx
V42.83 Pancreas SDx
AHA: 1Q, '03, 10; 2Q, '01, 16
V42.84 Intestines SDx
AHA: 4Q, '00, 48, 50
V42.89 Other SDx

V42.9 Unspecified organ or tissue SDx

✓4th **V43 Organ or tissue replaced by other means**

INCLUDES organ or tissue assisted by other means
replacement of organ by:
artificial device
mechanical device
prosthesis

EXCLUDES *cardiac pacemaker in situ (V45.01)*
fitting and adjustment of prosthetic device (V52.0-V52.9)
renal dialysis status ▶(V45.11)◀

V43.0 Eye globe SDx
V43.1 Lens SDx
Pseudophakos
AHA: 4Q, '98, 65

✓5th **V43.2 Heart**
Fully implantable artificial heart
Heart assist device
AHA: 4Q, '03, 85

V43.21 Heart assist device SDx
V43.22 Fully implantable artificial heart

V43.3 Heart valve SDx
AHA: 3Q, '06, 7; 3Q, '02, 13, 14
V43.4 Blood vessel SDx
V43.5 Bladder SDx

✓5th **V43.6 Joint**
AHA: 4Q, '05, 91

V43.60 Unspecified joint SDx
V43.61 Shoulder SDx
V43.62 Elbow SDx
V43.63 Wrist SDx
V43.64 Hip SDx
AHA: ▶2Q, '08, 3-5;◀ 3Q, '06, 4, 5; 4Q, '05, 93, 112; 2Q, '04, 15

[1] A code from the V30–V39 series may be sequenced before the V29 on the newborn medical record.
§ Require fourth- and fifth-digits. See beginning of section V30-V39 for codes and definitions.

V43.65 Knee SDx
AHA: 3Q, '06, 5

V43.66 Ankle SDx

V43.69 Other SDx

V43.7 Limb SDx

5th V43.8 Other organ or tissue

V43.81 Larynx SDx
AHA: 4Q, '95, 55

V43.82 Breast SDx
AHA: 4Q, '95, 55

V43.83 Artificial skin SDx

V43.89 Other SDx

4th **V44 Artificial opening status**

EXCLUDES *artificial openings requiring attention or management (V55.0-V55.9)*

V44.0 Tracheostomy SDx
AHA: 4Q, '03, 103, 107, 111; 1Q, '01, 6

V44.1 Gastrostomy SDx
AHA: 4Q, '03, 103, 107-108, 110; 1Q, '01, 12; 3Q, '97, 12; 1Q, '93, 26

V44.2 Ileostomy SDx

V44.3 Colostomy SDx
AHA: 4Q, '03, 110

V44.4 Other artificial opening of gastrointestinal tract SDx

5th V44.5 Cystostomy

V44.50 Cystostomy, unspecified SDx

V44.51 Cutaneous-vesicostomy SDx

V44.52 Appendico-vesicostomy SDx

V44.59 Other cystostomy SDx

V44.6 Other artificial opening of urinary tract SDx
Nephrostomy
Urethrostomy
Ureterostomy

V44.7 Artificial vagina SDx

V44.8 Other artificial opening status SDx

V44.9 Unspecified artificial opening status SDx

4th **V45 Other postprocedural states**

EXCLUDES *aftercare management (V51-V58.9)*
malfunction or other complication — code to condition

AHA: 4Q, '03, 85

5th V45.0 Cardiac device in situ

EXCLUDES *artificial heart (V43.22)*
heart assist device (V43.21)

V45.00 Unspecified cardiac device SDx

V45.01 Cardiac pacemaker SDx

V45.02 Automatic implantable cardiac defibrillator SDx

V45.09 Other specified cardiac device SDx
Carotid sinus pacemaker in situ

5th V45.1 Renal dialysis status

EXCLUDES *admission for dialysis treatment or session (V56.0)*

AHA: ▶1Q, '08, 7;◀ 4Q, '07, 86; 3Q, '07, 9; 4Q, '06, 136; 4Q, '05, 96; 2Q, '03, 7; 2Q, '01, 12, 13

● V45.11 Renal dialysis status SDx
Hemodialysis status
Patient requiring intermittent renal dialysis
Peritoneal dialysis status
Presence of arterial-venous shunt (for dialysis)

● V45.12 Noncompliance with renal dialysis SDx

V45.2 Presence of cerebrospinal fluid drainage device SDx
Cerebral ventricle (communicating) shunt, valve, or device in situ

EXCLUDES *malfunction (996.2)*

AHA: 4Q, '03, 106

V45.3 Intestinal bypass or anastomosis status SDx

EXCLUDES *bariatric surgery status (V45.86)*
gastric bypass status (V45.86)
obesity surgery status (V45.86)

V45.4 Arthrodesis status SDx
AHA: N-D, '84, 18

5th V45.5 Presence of contraceptive device

EXCLUDES *checking, reinsertion, or removal of device (V25.42)*
complication from device (996.32)
insertion of device (V25.1)

V45.51 Intrauterine contraceptive device SDx ♀

V45.52 Subdermal contraceptive implant SDx

V45.59 Other SDx

5th V45.6 States following surgery of eye and adnexa

Cataract extraction, Filtering bleb, Surgical eyelid adhesion } state following eye surgery

EXCLUDES *aphakia (379.31)*
artificial eye globe (V43.0)

AHA: 4Q, '98, 65; 4Q, '97, 49

V45.61 Cataract extraction status SDx
Use additional code for associated artificial lens status (V43.1)

V45.69 Other states following surgery of eye and adnexa SDx
AHA: 2Q, '01, 16; 1Q, '98, 10; 4Q, '97, 19

5th V45.7 Acquired absence of organ
AHA: 4Q, '98, 65; 4Q, '97, 50

▲ V45.71 Acquired absence of breast and nipple

V45.72 Acquired absence of intestine (large)(small)

V45.73 Acquired absence of kidney

V45.74 Other parts of urinary tract
Bladder
AHA: 4Q, '00, 51

V45.75 Stomach
AHA: 4Q, '00, 51

V45.76 Lung
AHA: 4Q, '00, 51

V45.77 Genital organs

EXCLUDES *▶acquired absence of cervix and uterus (V88.01-V88.03)◀*
female genital mutilation status (629.20-629.29)

AHA: 1Q, '03, 13, 14; 4Q, '00, 51

V45.78 Eye
AHA: 4Q, '00, 51

V45.79 Other acquired absence of organ
AHA: 4Q, '00, 51

5th V45.8 Other postprocedural status

V45.81 Aortocoronary bypass status SDx
AHA: 4Q, '03, 105; 3Q, '01, 15; 3Q, '97, 16

V45.82 Percutaneous transluminal coronary angioplasty status SDx

V45.83 Breast implant removal status SDx
AHA: 4Q, '95, 55

V45.84 Dental restoration status SDx
Dental crowns status
Dental fillings status
AHA: 4Q, '01, 54

V45.85 Insulin pump status SDx

V45.86 Bariatric surgery status SDx
Gastric banding status
Gastric bypass status for obesity
Obesity surgery status
EXCLUDES *bariatric surgery status complicating pregnancy, childbirth or the puerperium (649.2)*
intestinal bypass or anastomosis status (V45.3)
AHA: 4Q, '06, 118

● **V45.87 Transplanted organ removal status** SDx
Transplanted organ previously removed due to complication, failure, rejection or infection
EXCLUDES *encounter for removal of transplanted organ — code to complication of transplanted organ (996.80-996.89)*

● **V45.88 Status post administration of tPA (rtPA) in a different facility within the last 24 hours prior to admission to current facility** SDx
Code first condition requiring tPA administration, such as:
acute cerebral infarction (433.0-433.9 with fifth-digit 1, 434.0-434.9 with fifth digit 1)
acute myocardial infarction (410.00-410.92)

V45.89 Other SDx
Presence of neuropacemaker or other electronic device
EXCLUDES *artificial heart valve in situ (V43.3)*
vascular prosthesis in situ (V43.4)
AHA: 1Q, '95, 11

▲ 4th **V46 Other dependence on machines and devices**

V46.0 Aspirator SDx

5th **V46.1 Respirator [Ventilator]**
Iron lung
AHA: 4Q, '05, 96; 4Q, '03, 103; 1Q, '01, 12; J-F, '87, 7 3

V46.11 Dependence on respirator, status SDx
AHA: 4Q, '04, 100

V46.12 Encounter for respirator dependence during power failure PDx
AHA: 4Q, '04, 100

V46.13 Encounter for weaning from respirator [ventilator] PDx

V46.14 Mechanical complication of respirator [ventilator]
Mechanical failure of respirator [ventilator]

V46.2 Supplemental oxygen SDx
Long-term oxygen therapy
AHA: 4Q, '03, 108; 4Q, '02, 79

● **V46.3 Wheelchair dependence** SDx
Wheelchair confinement status
Code first cause of dependence, such as:
muscular dystrophy (359.1)
obesity (278.00, 278.01)

V46.8 Other enabling machines SDx
Hyperbaric chamber
Possum [Patient-Operated-Selector-Mechanism]
EXCLUDES *cardiac pacemaker (V45.0)*
kidney dialysis machine ►(V45.11)◄

V46.9 Unspecified machine dependence
AHA: 4Q, '06, 117

4th **V47 Other problems with internal organs**

V47.0 Deficiencies of internal organs

V47.1 Mechanical and motor problems with internal organs

V47.2 Other cardiorespiratory problems
Cardiovascular exercise intolerance with pain (with):
at rest
less than ordinary activity
ordinary activity

V47.3 Other digestive problems

V47.4 Other urinary problems

V47.5 Other genital problems

V47.9 Unspecified

4th **V48 Problems with head, neck, and trunk**

V48.0 Deficiencies of head
EXCLUDES *deficiencies of ears, eyelids, and nose (V48.8)*

V48.1 Deficiencies of neck and trunk

V48.2 Mechanical and motor problems with head

V48.3 Mechanical and motor problems with neck and trunk

V48.4 Sensory problem with head

V48.5 Sensory problem with neck and trunk

V48.6 Disfigurements of head

V48.7 Disfigurements of neck and trunk

V48.8 Other problems with head, neck, and trunk

V48.9 Unspecified problem with head, neck, or trunk

4th **V49 Other conditions influencing health status**

V49.0 Deficiencies of limbs

V49.1 Mechanical problems with limbs

V49.2 Motor problems with limbs

V49.3 Sensory problems with limbs

V49.4 Disfigurements of limbs

V49.5 Other problems of limbs

5th **V49.6 Upper limb amputation status**
AHA: 4Q, '05, 94; 4Q, '98, 42; 4Q, '94, 39

V49.60 Unspecified level

V49.61 Thumb

V49.62 Other finger(s)
AHA: 2Q, '05, 7

V49.63 Hand

V49.64 Wrist
Disarticulation of wrist

V49.65 Below elbow

V49.66 Above elbow
Disarticulation of elbow

V49.67 Shoulder
Disarticulation of shoulder

✓5th **V49.7 Lower limb amputation status**
AHA: 3Q, '06, 5; 4Q, '05, 94; 4Q, '98, 42; 4Q, '94, 39

V49.70 Unspecified level

V49.71 Great toe

V49.72 Other toe(s)

V49.73 Foot

V49.74 Ankle
Disarticulation of ankle

V49.75 Below knee

V49.76 Above knee
Disarticulation of knee

V49.77 Hip
Disarticulation of hip

✓5th **V49.8 Other specified conditions influencing health status**
AHA: 4Q, '00, 51

V49.81 Asymptomatic postmenopausal status (age-related) (natural) A ♀
EXCLUDES *menopausal and premenopausal disorder (627.0-627.9)*
postsurgical menopause (256.2)
premature menopause (256.31)
symptomatic menopause (627.0-627.9)
AHA: 4Q, '02, 79; 4Q, '00, 54

V49.82 Dental sealant status SDx
AHA: 4Q, '01, 54

V49.83 Awaiting organ transplant status SDx

V49.84 Bed confinement status
AHA: 4Q, '05, 96

V49.85 Dual sensory impairment SDx
Blindness with deafness
Combined visual hearing impairment
Code first:
hearing impairment (389.00-389.9)
visual impairment (369.00-369.9)
AHA: 4Q, '07, 100

V49.89 Other specified conditions influencing health status
AHA: 4Q, '05, 94

V49.9 Unspecified

PERSONS ENCOUNTERING HEALTH SERVICES FOR SPECIFIC PROCEDURES AND AFTERCARE (V50-V59)

Note: Categories V51-V59 are intended for use to indicate a reason for care in patients who may have already been treated for some disease or injury not now present, or who are receiving care to consolidate the treatment, to deal with residual states, or to prevent recurrence.

EXCLUDES *follow-up examination for medical surveillance following treatment (V67.0-V67.9)*

✓4th **V50 Elective surgery for purposes other than remedying health states**

V50.0 Hair transplant

V50.1 Other plastic surgery for unacceptable cosmetic appearance
Breast augmentation or reduction
Face-lift
EXCLUDES ▶*encounter for breast reduction (611.1)*◀
plastic surgery following healed injury or operation ▶*(V51.0-V51.8)*◀

V50.2 Routine or ritual circumcision ♂
Circumcision in the absence of significant medical indication

V50.3 Ear piercing

✓5th **V50.4 Prophylactic organ removal**
EXCLUDES *organ donations (V59.0-V59.9)*
therapeutic organ removal — code to condition
AHA: 4Q, '94, 44

V50.41 Breast
AHA: 4Q, '04, 107

V50.42 Ovary ♀

V50.49 Other

V50.8 Other

V50.9 Unspecified

✓4th **V51 Aftercare involving the use of plastic surgery**
Plastic surgery following healed injury or operation
EXCLUDES *cosmetic plastic surgery (V50.2)*
▶*plastic surgery as treatment for current condition or injury — code to condition or injury*◀
repair of scarred tissue — code to scar

● **V51.0 Encounter for breast reconstruction following mastectomy**
EXCLUDES *deformity and disproportion of reconstructed breast (612.0-612.1)*

● **V51.8 Other aftercare involving the use of plastic surgery**

✓4th **V52 Fitting and adjustment of prosthetic device and implant**
INCLUDES removal of device
EXCLUDES *malfunction or complication of prosthetic device (996.0-996.7)*
status only, without need for care (V43.0-V43.8)
AHA: 4Q, '05, 94; 4Q, '95, 55 ; 1Q, '90, 7

V52.0 Artificial arm (complete) (partial)

V52.1 Artificial leg (complete) (partial)

V52.2 Artificial eye

V52.3 Dental prosthetic device

V52.4 Breast prosthesis and implant ♀
▶Elective implant exchange (different material) (different size)
Removal of tissue expander without synchronous insertion of permanent implant◀
EXCLUDES ▶*admission for initial breast implant insertion for breast augmentation (V50.1)*
complications of breast implant (996.54, 996.69, 996.79)
encounter for breast reconstruction following mastectomy (V51.0)◀
AHA: 4Q, '95, 80, 81

V52.8 Other specified prosthetic device
AHA: 2Q, '02, 12, 16

V52.9 Unspecified prosthetic device

✓4th **V53 Fitting and adjustment of other device**
INCLUDES removal of device
replacement of device
EXCLUDES *status only, without need for care (V45.0-V45.8)*

✓5th **V53.0 Devices related to nervous system and special senses**
AHA: 4Q, '98, 66; 4Q, '97, 51

V53.01 Fitting and adjustment of cerebral ventricular (communicating) shunt
AHA: 4Q, '97, 51

V53.02 Neuropacemaker (brain) (peripheral nerve) (spinal cord)

V53.09 Fitting and adjustment of other devices related to nervous system and special senses
Auditory substitution device
Visual substitution device
AHA: 2Q, '99, 4

V53.1 Spectacles and contact lenses

V53.2 Hearing aid

✓5th **V53.3 Cardiac device**
Reprogramming
AHA: 3Q, '92, 3; 1Q, '90, 7; M-J, '87, 8 ; N-D, '84, 18

V53.31 Cardiac pacemaker
EXCLUDES *mechanical complication of cardiac pacemaker (996.01)*
AHA: 1Q, '02, 3

V53.32 Automatic implantable cardiac defibrillator
AHA: 3Q, '05, 8

V53.39 Other cardiac device
AHA: ►2Q, '08, 9;◄ 1Q, '07, 20

V53.4 Orthodontic devices

V53.5 Other intestinal appliance
EXCLUDES *colostomy (V55.3)*
ileostomy (V55.2)
other artificial opening of digestive tract (V55.4)

V53.6 Urinary devices
Urinary catheter
EXCLUDES *cystostomy (V55.5)*
nephrostomy (V55.6)
ureterostomy (V55.6)
urethrostomy (V55.6)

V53.7 Orthopedic devices
Orthopedic:
brace
cast
corset
shoes
EXCLUDES *other orthopedic aftercare (V54)*

V53.8 Wheelchair

✓5th **V53.9 Other and unspecified device**
AHA: 2Q, '03, 6

V53.90 Unspecified device

V53.91 Fitting and adjustment of insulin pump
Insulin pump titration

V53.99 Other device

✓4th **V54 Other orthopedic aftercare**
EXCLUDES *fitting and adjustment of orthopedic devices (V53.7)*
malfunction of internal orthopedic device (996.40-996.49)
other complication of nonmechanical nature (996.60-996.79)
AHA: 1Q, '07, 3-4; 3Q, '95, 3

✓5th **V54.0 Aftercare involving internal fixation device**
EXCLUDES *malfunction of internal orthopedic device (996.40-996.49)*
other complication of nonmechanical nature (996.60-996.79)
removal of external fixation device (V54.89)
AHA: 4Q, '03, 87

V54.01 Encounter for removal of internal fixation device

V54.02 Encounter for lengthening/adjustment of growth rod

V54.09 Other aftercare involving internal fixation device

✓5th **V54.1 Aftercare for healing traumatic fracture**
EXCLUDES *aftercare for amputation stump (V54.89)*
AHA: 4Q, '02, 80

V54.10 Aftercare for healing traumatic fracture of arm, unspecified

V54.11 Aftercare for healing traumatic fracture of upper arm

V54.12 Aftercare for healing traumatic fracture of lower arm
AHA: 1Q, '07, 7

V54.13 Aftercare for healing traumatic fracture of hip
AHA: 4Q, '03, 103, 105; 2Q, '03, 16

V54.14 Aftercare for healing traumatic fracture of leg, unspecified

V54.15 Aftercare for healing traumatic fracture of upper leg
EXCLUDES *aftercare for healing traumatic fracture of hip (V54.13)*
AHA: 3Q, '06, 6

V54.16 Aftercare for healing traumatic fracture of lower leg

V54.17 Aftercare for healing traumatic fracture of vertebrae

V54.19 Aftercare for healing traumatic fracture of other bone
AHA: 1Q, '05, 13; 4Q, '02, 80

✓5th **V54.2 Aftercare for healing pathologic fracture**
AHA: 4Q, '02, 80

V54.20 Aftercare for healing pathologic fracture of arm, unspecified

V54.21 Aftercare for healing pathologic fracture of upper arm

V54.22 Aftercare for healing pathologic fracture of lower arm

V54.23 Aftercare for healing pathologic fracture of hip

V54.24 Aftercare for healing pathologic fracture of leg, unspecified

V54.25 Aftercare for healing pathologic fracture of upper leg
EXCLUDES *aftercare for healing pathologic fracture of hip (V54.23)*

V54.26 Aftercare for healing pathologic fracture of lower leg

V54.27 Aftercare for healing pathologic fracture of vertebrae
AHA: 1Q, '07, 6; 4Q, '03, 108

V54.29 Aftercare for healing pathologic fracture of other bone
AHA: 4Q, '02, 80

✓5th **V54.8 Other orthopedic aftercare**
AHA: 3Q, '01, 19; 4Q, '99, 5

V54.81 Aftercare following joint replacement
Use additional code to identify joint replacement site (V43.60-V43.69)
AHA: 3Q, '06, 4; 2Q, '04, 15; 4Q, '02, 80

V54.89 Other orthopedic aftercare
Aftercare for healing fracture NOS

V54.9 Unspecified orthopedic aftercare

✓4th V55 Attention to artificial openings

INCLUDES adjustment or repositioning of catheter
closure
passage of sounds or bougies
reforming
removal or replacement of catheter
toilet or cleansing

EXCLUDES *complications of external stoma (519.00-519.09, 569.60-569.69, 997.4, 997.5)*
status only, without need for care (V44.0-V44.9)

V55.0 Tracheostomy

V55.1 Gastrostomy
AHA: 4Q, '99, 9; 3Q, '97, 7, 8; 1Q, '96, 14; 3Q, '95, 13

V55.2 Ileostomy

V55.3 Colostomy
AHA: 2Q, '05, 4; 3Q, '97, 9

V55.4 Other artificial opening of digestive tract
AHA: 2Q, '05, 14; 1Q, '03, 10

V55.5 Cystostomy

V55.6 Other artificial opening of urinary tract
Nephrostomy
Ureterostomy
Urethrostomy

V55.7 Artificial vagina

V55.8 Other specified artificial opening

V55.9 Unspecified artificial opening

✓4th V56 Encounter for dialysis and dialysis catheter care
Use additional code to identify the associated condition

EXCLUDES *dialysis preparation — code to condition*

AHA: 4Q, '98, 66; 1Q, '93, 29

V56.0 Extracorporeal dialysis PDx
Dialysis (renal) NOS
EXCLUDES *dialysis status ▶(V45.11)◀*
AHA: 4Q, '05, 79; 1Q, '04, 23; 4Q, '00, 40; 3Q, '98, 6; 2Q, '98, 20

V56.1 Fitting and adjustment of extracorporeal dialysis catheter
Removal or replacement of catheter
Toilet or cleansing
Use additional code for any concurrent extracorporeal dialysis (V56.0)
AHA: 2Q, '98, 20

V56.2 Fitting and adjustment of peritoneal dialysis catheter
Use additional code for any concurrent peritoneal dialysis (V56.8)
AHA: 4Q, '98, 55

✓5th V56.3 Encounter for adequacy testing for dialysis
AHA: 4Q, '00, 55

V56.31 Encounter for adequacy testing for hemodialysis

V56.32 Encounter for adequacy testing for peritoneal dialysis
Peritoneal equilibration test

V56.8 Other dialysis
Peritoneal dialysis
AHA: 4Q, '98, 55

✓4th V57 Care involving use of rehabilitation procedures
Use additional code to identify underlying condition
AHA: 3Q, '06, 3; 1Q, '02, 19; 3Q, '97, 12; 1Q, '90, 6; S-O, '86, 3

V57.0 Breathing exercises PDx

V57.1 Other physical therapy PDx
Therapeutic and remedial exercises, except breathing
AHA: 3Q, '06, 4; 2Q, '04, 15; 4Q, '02, 56; 4Q, '99, 5

✓5th V57.2 Occupational therapy and vocational rehabilitation

V57.21 Encounter for occupational therapy PDx
AHA: 4Q, '99, 7

V57.22 Encounter for vocational therapy PDx

V57.3 Speech therapy PDx
AHA: 4Q, '97, 36

V57.4 Orthoptic training PDx

✓5th V57.8 Other specified rehabilitation procedure

V57.81 Orthotic training PDx
Gait training in the use of artificial limbs

V57.89 Other PDx
Multiple training or therapy
AHA: 4Q, '07, 94; 3Q, '06, 6; 4Q, '03, 105-106, 108; 2Q, '03, 16; 1Q '02, 16; 3Q, '01, 21; 3Q, '97, 11, 12; S-O, '86, 4

V57.9 Unspecified rehabilitation procedure PDx

✓4th V58 Encounter for other and unspecified procedures and aftercare

EXCLUDES *convalescence and palliative care (V66)*

V58.0 Radiotherapy PDx
Encounter or admission for radiotherapy
EXCLUDES *encounter for radioactive implant — code to condition*
radioactive iodine therapy — code to condition
AHA: 3Q, '92, 5; 2Q, '90, 7; J-F, '87, 13

✓5th V58.1 Encounter for antineoplastic chemotherapy and immunotherapy
Encounter or admission for chemotherapy
EXCLUDES *chemotherapy and immunotherapy for nonneoplastic conditions — code to condition*
AHA: 1Q, '04, 13; 2Q, '03, 16; 3Q, '93, 4; 2Q, '92, 6; 2Q, '91, 17; 2Q, '90, 7; S-O, '84, 5

V58.11 Encounter for antineoplastic chemotherapy PDx
AHA: 4Q, '07, 104; 2Q, '06, 20-21; 4Q, '05, 98

V58.12 Encounter for antineoplastic immunotherapy PDx
AHA: 4Q, '05, 98

V58.2 Blood transfusion, without reported diagnosis

✓5th V58.3 Attention to dressings and sutures
Change or removal of wound packing
EXCLUDES *attention to drains (V58.49)*
planned postoperative wound closure (V58.41)
AHA: 2Q, '05, 14

V58.30 Encounter for change or removal of nonsurgical wound dressing
Encounter for change or removal of wound dressing NOS
AHA: 4Q, '06, 117

V58.31 Encounter for change or removal of surgical wound dressing
AHA: 4Q, '06, 117

V58.32 Encounter for removal of sutures
Encounter for removal of staples
AHA: 4Q, '06, 117

✓5th **V58.4 Other aftercare following surgery**
Note: Codes from this subcategory should be used in conjunction with other aftercare codes to fully identify the reason for the aftercare encounter
EXCLUDES *aftercare following sterilization reversal surgery (V26.22)*
attention to artificial openings (V55.0-V55.9)
orthopedic aftercare (V54.0-V54.9)
AHA: 4Q, '99, 9; N-D, '87, 9

V58.41 Encounter for planned postoperative wound closure
EXCLUDES *disruption of operative wound ▶(998.31-998.32)◀*
encounter for dressings and suture aftercare (V58.30-V58.32)
AHA: 4Q, '99, 15

V58.42 Aftercare following surgery for neoplasm
Conditions classifiable to 140-239
AHA: 4Q, '02, 80

V58.43 Aftercare following surgery for injury and trauma
Conditions classifiable to 800-999
EXCLUDES *aftercare for healing traumatic fracture (V54.10-V54.19)*
AHA: 4Q, '02, 80

V58.44 Aftercare following organ transplant
Use additional code to identify the organ transplanted (V42.0-V42.9)
AHA: 4Q, '04, 101

V58.49 Other specified aftercare following surgery
Change or removal of drains
AHA: 1Q, '96, 8, 9

V58.5 Orthodontics
EXCLUDES *fitting and adjustment of orthodontic device (V53.4)*

✓5th **V58.6 Long-term (current) drug use**
EXCLUDES *▶drug abuse and dependence complicating pregnancy (648.3-648.4)◀*
drug abuse (305.00-305.93)
drug dependence (304.00-304.93)
hormone replacement therapy (postmenopausal) (V07.4)
▶prophylactic use of agents affecting estrogen receptors and estrogen levels (V07.51-V07.59)◀
AHA: 4Q, '03, 85; 4Q, '02, 84; 3Q, '02, 15; 4Q, '95, 61

V58.61 Long-term (current) use of anticoagulants SDx
EXCLUDES *long-term (current) use of aspirin (V58.66)*
AHA: 3Q, '06, 13; 3Q, '04, 7; 4Q, '03, 108; 3Q, '02, 13-16; 1Q, '02, 15, 16

V58.62 Long-term (current) use of antibiotics SDx
AHA: 4Q, '98, 59

V58.63 Long-term (current) use of antiplatelets/antithrombotics SDx
EXCLUDES *long-term (current) use of aspirin (V58.66)*

V58.64 Long-term (current) use of non-steroidal anti-inflammatories (NSAID) SDx
EXCLUDES *long-term (current) use of aspirin (V58.66)*

V58.65 Long-term (current) use of steroids SDx

V58.66 Long-term (current) use of aspirin SDx
AHA: 4Q, '04, 102

V58.67 Long-term (current) use of insulin SDx
AHA: 4Q, '04, 55-56, 103

V58.69 Long-term (current) use of other medications SDx
Other high-risk medications
▶Long term current use of methadone
Long term current use of opiate analgesic◀
AHA: 2Q, '04, 10; 1Q, '04, 13; 1Q, '03, 11; 2Q, '00, 8; 3Q, '99, 13; 2Q, '99, 17; 1Q, '97, 12; 2Q, '96, 7

✓5th **V58.7 Aftercare following surgery to specified body systems, not elsewhere classified**
Note: Codes from this subcategory should be used in conjunction with other aftercare codes to fully identify the reason for the aftercare encounter
EXCLUDES *aftercare following organ transplant (V58.44)*
aftercare following surgery for neoplasm (V58.42)
AHA: 4Q, '03, 104; 4Q, '02, 80

V58.71 Aftercare following surgery of the sense organs, NEC
Conditions classifiable to 360-379, 380-389

V58.72 Aftercare following surgery of the nervous system, NEC
Conditions classifiable to 320-359
EXCLUDES *aftercare following surgery of the sense organs, NEC (V58.71)*

V58.73 Aftercare following surgery of the circulatory system, NEC
Conditions classifiable to 390-459
AHA: 4Q, '03, 105

V58.74 Aftercare following surgery of the respiratory system, NEC
Conditions classifiable to 460-519

V58.75 Aftercare following surgery of the teeth, oral cavity and digestive system, NEC
Conditions classifiable to 520-579
AHA: 2Q, '05, 14

V58.76 Aftercare following surgery of the genitourinary system, NEC
Conditions classifiable to 580-629
EXCLUDES *aftercare following sterilization reversal (V26.22)*
AHA: 1Q, '05, 11-12

V58.77 Aftercare following surgery of the skin and subcutaneous tissue, NEC
Conditions classifiable to 680-709

V58.78 Aftercare following surgery of the musculoskeletal system, NEC
Conditions classifiable to 710-739
EXCLUDES *orthopedic aftercare (V54.01-V54.9)*

✓5th **V58.8 Other specified procedures and aftercare**
AHA: 4Q, '94, 45; 2Q, '94, 8

V58.81 **Fitting and adjustment of vascular catheter**
Removal or replacement of catheter
Toilet or cleansing
EXCLUDES *complication of renal dialysis (996.73)*
complication of vascular catheter (996.74)
dialysis preparation — code to condition
encounter for dialysis (V56.0-V56.8)
fitting and adjustment of dialysis catheter (V56.1)

V58.82 **Fitting and adjustment of nonvascular catheter, NEC**
Removal or replacement of catheter
Toilet or cleansing
EXCLUDES *fitting and adjustment of peritoneal dialysis catheter (V56.2)*
fitting and adjustment of urinary catheter (V53.6)

V58.83 **Encounter for therapeutic drug monitoring**
Use additional code for any associated long- term (current) drug use (V58.61-V58.69)
EXCLUDES *blood-drug testing for med-icolegal reasons (V70.4)*
AHA: 2Q, '04, 10; 1Q, '04, 13;4Q, '03, 85; 4Q, '02, 84; 3Q, '02, 13-16
DEF: Drug monitoring: Measurement of the level of a specific drug in the body or measurement of a specific function to assess effectiveness of a drug.

V58.89 **Other specified aftercare**
AHA: 4Q, '98, 59

V58.9 **Unspecified aftercare**

4th **V59 Donors**
EXCLUDES *examination of potential donor (V70.8)*
self-donation of organ or tissue — code to condition
AHA: 4Q, '95, 62; 1Q, '90, 10; N-D, '84, 8

5th V59.0 **Blood**
V59.01 **Whole blood** PDx
V59.02 **Stem cells** PDx
V59.09 **Other** PDx
V59.1 **Skin** PDx
V59.2 **Bone** PDx
V59.3 **Bone marrow** PDx
V59.4 **Kidney** PDx
V59.5 **Cornea** PDx
V59.6 **Liver** PDx

5th V59.7 **Egg (oocyte) (ovum)**
AHA: 4Q, '05, 99
V59.70 **Egg (oocyte) (ovum) donor, unspecified** PDx ♀
V59.71 **Egg (oocyte) (ovum) donor, under age 35, anonymous recipient** PDx ♀
Egg donor, under age 35 NOS
V59.72 **Egg (oocyte) (ovum) donor, under age 35, designated recipient** PDx ♀
V59.73 **Egg (oocyte) (ovum) donor, age 35 and over, anonymous recipient** PDx ♀
Egg donor, age 35 and over NOS
V59.74 **Egg (oocyte) (ovum) donor, age 35 and over, designated recipient** PDx ♀

V59.8 **Other specified organ or tissue** PDx
AHA: 3Q, '02, 20

V59.9 **Unspecified organ or tissue** PDx

PERSONS ENCOUNTERING HEALTH SERVICES IN OTHER CIRCUMSTANCES (V60-V69)

4th **V60 Housing, household, and economic circumstances**

V60.0 **Lack of housing** SDx
Hobos
Social migrants
Tramps
Transients
Vagabonds

V60.1 **Inadequate housing** SDx
Lack of heating
Restriction of space
Technical defects in home preventing adequate care

V60.2 **Inadequate material resources** SDx
Economic problem
Poverty NOS

V60.3 **Person living alone** SDx

V60.4 **No other household member able to render care** SDx
Person requiring care (has) (is):
family member too handicapped, ill, or otherwise unsuited to render care
partner temporarily away from home
temporarily away from usual place of abode
EXCLUDES *holiday relief care (V60.5)*

V60.5 **Holiday relief care** SDx
Provision of health carc facilities to a person normally cared for at home, to enable relatives to take a vacation

V60.6 **Person living in residential institution** SDx
Boarding school resident

V60.8 **Other specified housing or economic circumstances** SDx

V60.9 **Unspecified housing or economic circumstance** SDx

4th **V61 Other family circumstances**
INCLUDES when these circumstances or fear of them, affecting the person directly involved or others, are mentioned as the reason, justified or not, for seeking or receiving medical advice or care
AHA: 1Q, '90, 9

5th V61.0 **Family disruption**

● V61.01 **Family disruption due to family member on military deployment**
Individual or family affected by other family member being on deployment

● V61.02 **Family disruption due to return of family member from military deploymen**
Individual or family affected by other family member having returned from deployment (current or past conflict)

● V61.03 **Family disruption due to divorce or legal separation**

● V61.04 **Family disruption due to parent-child estrangement**
EXCLUDES *other family estrangement (V61.09)*

● V61.05 **Family disruption due to child in welfare custody**

● **V61.06 Family disruption due to child in foster care or in care of non-parental family member**

● **V61.09 Other family disruption**
Family estrangement NOS

✓5th **V61.1 Counseling for marital and partner problems**
EXCLUDES *problems related to:*
psychosexual disorders (302.0-302.9)
sexual function (V41.7)

V61.10 Counseling for marital and partner problems, unspecified
Marital conflict
Marital relationship problem
Partner conflict
Partner relationship problem

V61.11 Counseling for victim of spousal and partner abuse
EXCLUDES *encounter for treatment of current injuries due to abuse (995.80-995.85)*

V61.12 Counseling for perpetrator of spousal and partner abuse

✓5th **V61.2 Parent-child problems**

V61.20 Counseling for parent-child problem, unspecified
Concern about behavior of child
Parent-child conflict
Parent-child relationship problem

V61.21 Counseling for victim of child abuse
Child battering Child neglect
EXCLUDES *current injuries due to abuse (995.50-995.59)*

V61.22 Counseling for perpetrator of parental child abuse
EXCLUDES *counseling for non-parental abuser (V62.83)*

V61.29 Other
Problem concerning adopted or foster child
AHA: 3Q, '99, 16

V61.3 Problems with aged parents or in-laws

✓5th **V61.4 Health problems within family**

V61.41 Alcoholism in family

V61.49 Other
Care of } sick or handicapped
Presence of } person in family or household

V61.5 Multiparity

V61.6 Illegitimacy or illegitimate pregnancy M♀

V61.7 Other unwanted pregnancy M♀

V61.8 Other specified family circumstances
Problems with family members NEC
Sibling relationship problem

V61.9 Unspecified family circumstance

✓4th **V62 Other psychosocial circumstances**
INCLUDES those circumstances or fear of them, affecting the person directly involved or others, mentioned as the reason, justified or not, for seeking or receiving medical advice or care
EXCLUDES *previous psychological trauma (V15.41-V15.49)*

V62.0 Unemployment SDx
EXCLUDES *circumstances when main problem is economic inadequacy or poverty (V60.2)*

V62.1 Adverse effects of work environment SDx

✓5th **V62.2 Other occupational circumstances or maladjustment**

● **V62.21 Personal current military deployment status** SDx
Individual (civilian or military) currently deployed in theater or in support of military war, peacekeeping and humanitarian operations

● **V62.22 Personal history of return from military deployment** SDx
Individual (civilian or military) with past history of military war, peacekeeping and humanitarian deployment (current or past conflict)

● **V62.29 Other occupational circumstances or maladjustment** SDx
Career choice problem
Dissatisfaction with employment
Occupational problem

V62.3 Educational circumstances SDx
Academic problem
Dissatisfaction with school environment
Educational handicap

V62.4 Social maladjustment SDx
Acculturation problem
Cultural deprivation
Political, religious, or sex discrimination
Social:
isolation
persecution

V62.5 Legal circumstances SDx
Imprisonment Litigation
Legal investigation Prosecution

V62.6 Refusal of treatment for reasons of religion or conscience SDx

✓5th **V62.8 Other psychological or physical stress, not elsewhere classified**

V62.81 Interpersonal problems, not elsewhere classified SDx
Relational problem NOS

V62.82 Bereavement, uncomplicated SDx
EXCLUDES *bereavement as adjustment reaction (309.0)*

V62.83 Counseling for perpetrator of physical/sexual abuse SDx
EXCLUDES *counseling for perpetrator of parental child abuse (V61.22)*
counseling for perpetrator of spousal and partner abuse (V61.12)

V62.84 Suicidal ideation SDx
EXCLUDES *suicidal tendencies (300.9)*
AHA: 4Q, '05, 96
DEF: Thoughts of committing suicide; no actual attempt of suicide has been made.

V62.89 Other SDx
Borderline intellectual functioning
Life circumstance problems
Phase of life problems
Religious or spiritual problem

V62.9 Unspecified psychosocial circumstance SDx

✓4th **V63 Unavailability of other medical facilities for care**
AHA: 1Q, '91, 21

V63.0 Residence remote from hospital or other health care facility

V63.1 Medical services in home not available

EXCLUDES *no other household member able to render care (V60.4)*

AHA: 4Q, '01, 67; 1Q, '01, 12

V63.2 Person awaiting admission to adequate facility elsewhere

V63.8 Other specified reasons for unavailability of medical facilities

Person on waiting list undergoing social agency investigation

V63.9 Unspecified reason for unavailability of medical facilities

✓4th **V64 Persons encountering health services for specific procedures, not carried out**

✓5th **V64.0 Vaccination not carried out**

AHA: 4Q, '05, 99

V64.00 Vaccination not carried out, unspecified reason SDx

V64.01 Vaccination not carried out because of acute illness SDx

V64.02 Vaccination not carried out because of chronic illness or condition SDx

V64.03 Vaccination not carried out because of immune compromised state SDx

V64.04 Vaccination not carried out because of allergy to vaccine or component SDx

V64.05 Vaccination not carried out because of caregiver refusal SDx

Guardian refusal Parent refusal

EXCLUDES ►*vaccination not carried out because of caregiver refusal for religious reasons (V64.07)*◄

AHA: 1Q, '07, 12

V64.06 Vaccination not carried out because of patient refusal SDx

V64.07 Vaccination not carried out for religious reasons SDx

V64.08 Vaccination not carried out because patient had disease being vaccinated against SDx

V64.09 Vaccination not carried out for other reason SDx

V64.1 Surgical or other procedure not carried out because of contraindication SDx

V64.2 Surgical or other procedure not carried out because of patient's decision SDx

AHA: 2Q, '01, 8

V64.3 Procedure not carried out for other reasons SDx

✓5th **V64.4 Closed surgical procedure converted to open procedure**

AHA: 4Q, '03, 87; 4Q, '98, 68; 4Q, '97, 52

V64.41 Laparoscopic surgical procedure converted to open procedure SDx

V64.42 Thoracoscopic surgical procedure converted to open procedure SDx

V64.43 Arthroscopic surgical procedure converted to open procedure SDx

✓4th **V65 Other persons seeking consultation**

V65.0 Healthy person accompanying sick person

Boarder

✓5th **V65.1 Person consulting on behalf of another person**

Advice or treatment for nonattending third party

EXCLUDES *concern (normal) about sick person in family (V61.41-V61.49)*

AHA: 4Q, '03, 84

V65.11 Pediatric pre-birth visit for expectant mother M ♀

V65.19 Other person consulting on behalf of another person

V65.2 Person feigning illness

Malingerer Peregrinating patient

AHA: 3Q, '99, 20

V65.3 Dietary surveillance and counseling

Dietary surveillance and counseling (in):
- NOS
- colitis
- diabetes mellitus
- food allergies or intolerance
- gastritis
- hypercholesterolemia
- hypoglycemia
- obesity

Use additional code to identify Body Mass Index (BMI), if known (V85.0-V85.54)

AHA: 4Q, '05, 96

✓5th **V65.4 Other counseling, not elsewhere classified**

Health:
- advice
- education
- instruction

EXCLUDES *counseling (for):*
- *contraception (V25.40-V25.49)*
- *genetic (V26.31-V26.39)*
- *on behalf of third party (V65.11-V65.19)*
- *procreative management (V26.41-V26.49)*

V65.40 Counseling NOS

V65.41 Exercise counseling

V65.42 Counseling on substance use and abuse

V65.43 Counseling on injury prevention

V65.44 Human immunodeficiency virus [HIV] counseling

V65.45 Counseling on other sexually transmitted diseases

V65.46 Encounter for insulin pump training

V65.49 Other specified counseling

AHA: 2Q, '00, 8

V65.5 Person with feared complaint in whom no diagnosis was made

Feared condition not demonstrated
Problem was normal state
"Worried well"

V65.8 Other reasons for seeking consultation

EXCLUDES *specified symptoms*

AHA: 3Q, '92, 4

V65.9 Unspecified reason for consultation

✓4th **V66 Convalescence and palliative care**

V66.0 Following surgery PDx

V66.1 Following radiotherapy PDx

V66.2 Following chemotherapy PDx

V66.3 Following psychotherapy and other treatment for mental disorder PDx

V66.4 Following treatment of fracture PDx

V66.5 Following other treatment PDx

V66.6 Following combined treatment PDx

V66.7 Encounter for palliative care SDx

End of life care
Hospice care
Terminal care

Code first underlying disease

AHA: 2Q, '05, 9; 4Q, '03, 107; 1Q, '98, 11; 4Q, '96, 47, 48

V66.9 Unspecified convalescence PDx

AHA: 4Q, '99, 8

4th V67 Follow-up examination

INCLUDES surveillance only following completed treatment

EXCLUDES *surveillance of contraception (V25.40-V25.49)*

AHA: 2Q, '03, 5; 4Q, '94, 98

5th V67.0 Following surgery

AHA: 4Q, '00, 56; 4Q, '98, 69; 4Q, '97, 50; 2Q, '95, 8;1Q, '95, 4; 3Q, '92, 11

V67.00 Following surgery, unspecified

V67.01 Follow-up vaginal pap smear ♀

Vaginal pap-smear, status-post hysterectomy for malignant condition

Use additional code to identify:
acquired absence of uterus ▶(V88.01-V88.03)◀
personal history of malignant neoplasm (V10.40-V10.44)

EXCLUDES *vaginal pap smear status-post hysterectomy for non-malignant condition (V76.47)*

V67.09 Following other surgery

EXCLUDES *sperm count following sterilization reversal (V26.22)*
sperm count for fertility testing (V26.21)

AHA: 3Q, '03, 16; 3Q, '02, 15

V67.1 Following radiotherapy

V67.2 Following chemotherapy

Cancer chemotherapy follow-up

V67.3 Following psychotherapy and other treatment for mental disorder

V67.4 Following treatment of healed fracture

EXCLUDES *current (healing) fracture aftercare (V54.0-V54.9)*

AHA: 1Q, '90, 7

5th V67.5 Following other treatment

V67.51 Following completed treatment with high-risk medications, not elsewhere classified

EXCLUDES *long-term (current) drug use (V58.61-V58.69)*

AHA: 1Q, '99, 5, 6;4Q, '95, 61 ; 1Q, '90, 18

V67.59 Other

V67.6 Following combined treatment

V67.9 Unspecified follow-up examination

4th V68 Encounters for administrative purposes

5th V68.0 Issue of medical certificates

EXCLUDES *encounter for general medical examination (V70.0-V70.9)*

V68.01 Disability examination PDx

Use additional code(s) to identify specific examination(s), screening and testing performed (V72.0-V82.9)

AHA: 4Q, '07, 101

V68.09 Other issue of medical certificates PDx

V68.1 Issue of repeat prescriptions PDx

Issue of repeat prescription for:
appliance
glasses
medications

EXCLUDES *repeat prescription for contraceptives (V25.41-V25.49)*

V68.2 Request for expert evidence PDx

5th V68.8 Other specified administrative purpose

V68.81 Referral of patient without examination or treatment PDx

V68.89 Other PDx

V68.9 Unspecified administrative purpose PDx

4th V69 Problems related to lifestyle

AHA: 4Q, '94, 48

V69.0 Lack of physical exercise

V69.1 Inappropriate diet and eating habits

EXCLUDES *anorexia nervosa (307.1)*
bulimia (783.6)
malnutrition and other nutritional deficiencies (260-269.9)
other and unspecified eating disorders (307.50-307.59)

V69.2 High-risk sexual behavior

V69.3 Gambling and betting

EXCLUDES *pathological gambling (312.31)*

V69.4 Lack of adequate sleep

Sleep deprivation

EXCLUDES *insomnia (780.52)*

V69.5 Behavioral insomnia of childhood P

AHA: 4Q, '05, 99

DEF: Behaviors on the part of the child or caregivers that cause negative compliance with a child's sleep schedule; results in lack of adequate sleep.

V69.8 Other problems related to lifestyle

Self-damaging behavior

V69.9 Problem related to lifestyle, unspecified

PERSONS WITHOUT REPORTED DIAGNOSIS ENCOUNTERED DURING EXAMINATION AND INVESTIGATION OF INDIVIDUALS AND POPULATIONS (V70-V82)

Note: Nonspecific abnormal findings disclosed at the time of these examinations are classifiable to categories 790-796.

✓4th V70 General medical examination

Use additional code(s) to identify any special screening examination(s) performed (V73.0-V82.9)

V70.0 Routine general medical examination at a health care facility PDx

Health checkup

EXCLUDES *health checkup of infant or child (V20.2)*
pre-procedural general physical examination (V72.83)

V70.1 General psychiatric examination, requested by the authority PDx

V70.2 General psychiatric examination, other and unspecified PDx

V70.3 Other medical examination for administrative purposes PDx

General medical examination for:
- admission to old age home
- adoption
- camp
- driving license
- immigration and naturalization
- insurance certification
- marriage
- prison
- school admission
- sports competition

EXCLUDES *attendance for issue of medical certificates (V68.0)*
pre-employment screening (V70.5)

AHA: 1Q, '90, 6

V70.4 Examination for medicolegal reasons PDx

Blood-alcohol tests
Paternity testing
Blood-drug tests

EXCLUDES *examination and observation following:*
accidents (V71.3, V71.4)
assault (V71.6)
rape (V71.5)

V70.5 Health examination of defined subpopulations PDx

- Armed forces personnel
- Inhabitants of institutions
- Occupational healthexaminations
- Pre-employment screening
- Preschool children
- Prisoners
- Prostitutes
- Refugees
- School children
- Students

V70.6 Health examination in population surveys PDx

EXCLUDES *special screening (V73.0-V82.9)*

V70.7 Examination of participant in clinical trial

Examination of participant or control in clinical research

AHA: 2Q, '06, 5-6; 4Q, '01, 55

V70.8 Other specified general medical examinations PDx

Examination of potential donor of organ or tissue

V70.9 Unspecified general medical examination PDx

✓4th V71 Observation and evaluation for suspected conditions not found

INCLUDES This category is to be used when persons without a diagnosis are suspected of having an abnormal condition, without signs or symptoms, which requires study, but after examination and observation, is found not to exist. This category is also for use for administrative and legal observation status.

EXCLUDES ▶*suspected maternal and fetal conditions not found (V89.01-V89.09)*◀

AHA: 4Q, '94, 47; 2Q, '90, 5; M-A, '87, 1

✓5th V71.0 Observation for suspected mental condition

V71.01 Adult antisocial behavior A PDx

Dyssocial behavior or gang activity in adult without manifest psychiatric disorder

V71.02 Childhood or adolescent antisocial behavior PDx

Dyssocial behavior or gang activity in child or adolescent without manifest psychiatric disorder

V71.09 Other suspected mental condition PDx

V71.1 Observation for suspected malignant neoplasm PDx

V71.2 Observation for suspected tuberculosis PDx

V71.3 Observation following accident at work PDx

V71.4 Observation following other accident PDx

Examination of individual involved in motor vehicle traffic accident

AHA: 1Q, '06, 9

V71.5 Observation following alleged rape or seduction PDx

Examination of victim or culprit

V71.6 Observation following other inflicted injury PDx

Examination of victim or culprit

V71.7 Observation for suspected cardiovascular disease PDx

AHA: 1Q, '04, 6; 3Q, '90, 10; S-O, '87, 10

✓5th V71.8 Observation and evaluation for other specified suspected conditions

EXCLUDES ▶*contact with and (suspected) exposure to (potentially) hazardous substances (V15.84-V15.86, V87.0-V87.31)*◀

AHA: 4Q, '00, 54 ; 1Q, '90, 19

V71.81 Abuse and neglect PDx

EXCLUDES *adult abuse and neglect (995.80-995.85)*
child abuse and neglect (995.50-995.59)

AHA: 4Q, '00, 55

V71.82 Observation and evaluation for suspected exposure to anthrax PDx

AHA: 4Q, '02, 70, 85

V71.83 Observation and evaluation for suspected exposure to other biological agent PDx

AHA: 4Q, '03, 47

V71.89 Other specified suspected conditions PDx

AHA: 2Q, '03, 15

V71.9 Observation for unspecified suspected condition PDx

AHA: 1Q, '02, 6

4th V72 Special investigations and examinations

INCLUDES routine examination of specific system

Use additional code(s) to identify any special screening examination(s) performed (V73.0-V82.9)

EXCLUDES *general medical examination (V70.0-V70.4)*
general screening examination of defined population groups (V70.5, V70.6, V70.7)
routine examination of infant or child (V20.2)

V72.0 Examination of eyes and vision
AHA: 1Q, '04, 15

5th **V72.1 Examination of ears and hearing**
AHA: 1Q, '04, 15

V72.11 Encounter for hearing examination following failed hearing screening
AHA: 4Q, '06, 118

V72.12 Encounter for hearing conservation and treatment
AHA: 4Q, '07, 100

V72.19 Other examination of ears and hearing

V72.2 Dental examination

5th **V72.3 Gynecological examination**

EXCLUDES *cervical Papanicolaou smear without general gynecological examination (V76.2)*
routine examination in contraceptive management (V25.40-V25.49)

V72.31 Routine gynecological examination ♀
General gynecological examination with or without Papanicolaou cervical smear
Pelvic examination (annual) (periodic)
Use additional code to identify:
human papillomavirus (HPV) screening (V73.81)
routine vaginal Papanicolaou smear (V76.47)
AHA: 2Q, '06, 2-3; 4Q, '05, 98

V72.32 Encounter for Papanicolaou cervical smear to confirm findings of recent normal smear following initial abnormal smear ♀
AHA: 2Q, '06, 4

5th **V72.4 Pregnancy examination or test**
AHA: 4Q, '05, 98

V72.40 Pregnancy examination or test, pregnancy unconfirmed ♀
Possible pregnancy, not (yet) confirmed

V72.41 Pregnancy examination or test, negative result ♀

V72.42 Pregnancy examination or test, positive result ♀ M

V72.5 Radiological examination, not elsewhere classified
Routine chest x-ray
EXCLUDES *examination for suspected tuberculosis (V71.2)*
AHA: 1Q, '90, 19

V72.6 Laboratory examination
EXCLUDES *that for suspected disorder (V71.0-V71.9)*
AHA: 2Q, '06, 4; 1Q, '90, 22

V72.7 Diagnostic skin and sensitization tests
Allergy tests
Skin tests for hypersensitivity
EXCLUDES *diagnostic skin tests for bacterial diseases (V74.0-V74.9)*

5th **V72.8 Other specified examinations**

V72.81 Pre-operative cardiovascular examination
Pre-procedural cardiovascular examination

V72.82 Pre-operative respiratory examination
Pre-procedural respiratory examination
AHA: 3Q, '96, 14

V72.83 Other specified pre-operative examination
Other pre-procedural examination
Pre-procedural general physical examination
EXCLUDES *routine general medical examination (V70.0)*
AHA: 3Q, '96, 14

V72.84 Pre-operative examination, unspecified
Pre-procedural examination, unspecified

V72.85 Other specified examination
AHA: 4Q, '05, 96; 1Q, '04, 12

V72.86 Encounter for blood typing

V72.9 Unspecified examination
AHA: 4Q, '06, 117

4th V73 Special screening examination for viral and chlamydial diseases
AHA: 1Q, '04, 11

V73.0 Poliomyelitis

V73.1 Smallpox

V73.2 Measles

V73.3 Rubella

V73.4 Yellow fever

V73.5 Other arthropod-borne viral diseases
Dengue fever
Hemorrhagic fever
Viral encephalitis:
mosquito-borne
tick-borne

V73.6 Trachoma

5th **V73.8 Other specified viral and chlamydial diseases**

V73.81 Human papillomavirus [HPV]
AHA: 4Q, '07, 100

V73.88 Other specified chlamydial diseases
AHA: 4Q, '07, 124

V73.89 Other specified viral diseases

5th **V73.9 Unspecified viral and chlamydial disease**

V73.98 Unspecified chlamydial disease

V73.99 Unspecified viral disease

4th V74 Special screening examination for bacterial and spirochetal diseases

INCLUDES diagnostic skin tests for these diseases

AHA: 1Q, '04, 11

V74.0 Cholera

V74.1 Pulmonary tuberculosis

V74.2 Leprosy [Hansen's disease]

V74.3 Diphtheria

V74.4 Bacterial conjunctivitis

V74.5 Venereal disease
Screening for bacterial and spirochetal sexually transmitted diseases
Screening for sexually transmitted diseases NOS
EXCLUDES *special screening for nonbacterial sexually transmitted diseases (V73.81-V73.89, V75.4, V75.8)*
AHA: 4Q, '07, 124

V74.6 Yaws

V74.8 Other specified bacterial and spirochetal diseases
Brucellosis
Leptospirosis
Plague
Tetanus
Whooping cough

V74.9 Unspecified bacterial and spirochetal disease

✓4th **V75 Special screening examination for other infectious diseases**
AHA: 1Q, '04, 11

V75.0 Rickettsial diseases

V75.1 Malaria

V75.2 Leishmaniasis

V75.3 Trypanosomiasis
Chagas' disease
Sleeping sickness

V75.4 Mycotic infections

V75.5 Schistosomiasis

V75.6 Filariasis

V75.7 Intestinal helminthiasis

V75.8 Other specified parasitic infections

V75.9 Unspecified infectious disease

✓4th **V76 Special screening for malignant neoplasms**
AHA: 1Q, '04, 11

V76.0 Respiratory organs

✓5th **V76.1 Breast**
AHA: 4Q, '98, 67

V76.10 Breast screening, unspecified

V76.11 Screening mammogram for high-risk patient ♀
AHA: 2Q, '03, 4

V76.12 Other screening mammogram
AHA: 2Q, '06, 10; 2Q, '03, 3-4

V76.19 Other screening breast examination

V76.2 Cervix ♀
Routine cervical Papanicolaou smear
EXCLUDES *special screening for human papillomavirus (V73.81)*
that as part of a general gynecological examination (V72.31)

V76.3 Bladder

✓5th **V76.4 Other sites**

V76.41 Rectum

V76.42 Oral cavity

V76.43 Skin

V76.44 Prostate ♂

V76.45 Testis ♂

V76.46 Ovary ♀
AHA: 4Q, '00, 52

V76.47 Vagina ♀
Vaginal pap smear status-post hysterectomy for non-malignant condition
Use additional code to identify acquired absence of uterus ►(V88.01-V88.03)◄
EXCLUDES *vaginal pap smear status-post hysterectomy for malignant condition (V67.01)*
AHA: 4Q, '00, 52

V76.49 Other sites
AHA: 1Q, '99, 4

✓5th **V76.5 Intestine**
AHA: 4Q, '00, 52

V76.50 Intestine, unspecified

V76.51 Colon
EXCLUDES *rectum (V76.41)*
AHA: 4Q, '01, 56

V76.52 Small intestine

✓5th **V76.8 Other neoplasm**
AHA: 4Q, '00, 52

V76.81 Nervous system

V76.89 Other neoplasm

V76.9 Unspecified

✓4th **V77 Special screening for endocrine, nutritional, metabolic, and immunity disorders**
AHA: 1Q, '04, 11

V77.0 Thyroid disorders

V77.1 Diabetes mellitus

V77.2 Malnutrition

V77.3 Phenylketonuria [PKU]

V77.4 Galactosemia

V77.5 Gout

V77.6 Cystic fibrosis
Screening for mucoviscidosis

V77.7 Other inborn errors of metabolism

V77.8 Obesity

✓5th **V77.9 Other and unspecified endocrine, nutritional, metabolic, and immunity disorders**
AHA: 4Q, '00, 53

V77.91 Screening for lipoid disorders
Screening for cholesterol level
Screening for hypercholesterolemia
Screening for hyperlipidemia

V77.99 Other and unspecified endocrine nutritional metabolic and immunity disorders

✓4th **V78 Special screening for disorders of blood and blood-forming organs**
AHA: 1Q, '04, 11

V78.0 Iron deficiency anemia

V78.1 Other and unspecified deficiency anemia

V78.2 Sickle cell disease or trait

V78.3 Other hemoglobinopathies

V78.8 Other disorders of blood and blood-forming organs

V78.9 Unspecified disorder of blood and blood-forming organs

✓4th **V79 Special screening for mental disorders and developmental handicaps**

AHA: 1Q, '04, 11

V79.0 Depression

V79.1 Alcoholism

V79.2 Mental retardation

V79.3 Developmental handicaps in early childhood

V79.8 Other specified mental disorders and developmental handicaps

V79.9 Unspecified mental disorder and developmental handicap

✓4th **V80 Special screening for neurological, eye, and ear diseases**

AHA: 1Q, '04, 11

V80.0 Neurological conditions

V80.1 Glaucoma

V80.2 Other eye conditions

Screening for:
cataract
congenital anomaly of eye
senile macular lesions

EXCLUDES *general vision examination (V72.0)*

V80.3 Ear diseases

EXCLUDES *general hearing examination (V72.11-V72.19)*

✓4th **V81 Special screening for cardiovascular, respiratory, and genitourinary diseases**

AHA: 1Q, '04, 11

V81.0 Ischemic heart disease

V81.1 Hypertension

V81.2 Other and unspecified cardiovascular conditions

V81.3 Chronic bronchitis and emphysema

V81.4 Other and unspecified respiratory conditions

EXCLUDES *screening for:*
lung neoplasm (V76.0)
pulmonary tuberculosis (V74.1)

V81.5 Nephropathy

Screening for asymptomatic bacteriuria

V81.6 Other and unspecified genitourinary conditions

✓4th **V82 Special screening for other conditions**

AHA: 1Q, '04, 11

V82.0 Skin conditions

V82.1 Rheumatoid arthritis

V82.2 Other rheumatic disorders

V82.3 Congenital dislocation of hip

V82.4 Maternal postnatal screening for chromosomal anomalies ♀

EXCLUDES *antenatal screening by amniocentesis (V28.0)*

V82.5 Chemical poisoning and other contamination

Screening for:
heavy metal poisoning
ingestion of radioactive substance
poisoning from contaminated water supply
radiation exposure

V82.6 Multiphasic screening

✓5th **V82.7 Genetic screening**

EXCLUDES *genetic testing for procreative management (V26.31-V26.39)*

V82.71 Screening for genetic disease carrier status

AHA: 4Q, '06, 118

V82.79 Other genetic screening

AHA: 4Q, '06, 118

✓5th **V82.8 Other specified conditions**

AHA: 4Q, '00, 53

V82.81 Osteoporosis

Use additional code to identify:
hormone replacement therapy (postmenopausal) status (V07.4)
postmenopausal (age-related) (natural) status (V49.81)

AHA: 4Q, '00, 54

V82.89 Other specified conditions

V82.9 Unspecified condition

GENETICS (V83-V84)

✓4th **V83 Genetic carrier status**

AHA: 4Q, '02, 79; 4Q, '01, 54

✓5th **V83.0 Hemophilia A carrier**

V83.01 Asymptomatic hemophilia A carrier

V83.02 Symptomatic hemophilia A carrier

✓5th **V83.8 Other genetic carrier status**

V83.81 Cystic fibrosis gene carrier

V83.89 Other genetic carrier status

✓4th **V84 Genetic susceptibility to disease**

INCLUDES confirmed abnormal gene

Use additional code, if applicable, for any associated family history of the disease (V16-V19)

AHA: 4Q, '04, 106

✓5th **V84.0 Genetic susceptibility to malignant neoplasm**

Code first, if applicable, any current malignant neoplasms (140.0-195.8, 200.0-208.9, 230.0-234.9)

Use additional code, if applicable, for any personal history of malignant neoplasm (V10.0-V10.9)

V84.01 Genetic susceptibility to malignant neoplasm of breast SDx

AHA: 4Q, '04, 107

V84.02 Genetic susceptibility to malignant neoplasm of ovary SDx ♀

V84.03 Genetic susceptibility to malignant neoplasm of prostate SDx ♂

V84.04 Genetic susceptibility to malignant neoplasm of endometrium SDx ♀

V84.09 Genetic susceptibility to other malignant neoplasm SDx

✓5th **V84.8 Genetic susceptibility to other disease**

V84.81 Genetic susceptibility to multiple endocrine neoplasia [MEN] SDx

AHA: 4Q, '07, 100

V84.89 Genetic susceptibility to other disease SDx

BODY MASS INDEX (V85)

✓4th **V85 Body Mass Index [BMI]**

Kilograms per meters squared

Note: BMI adult codes are for use for persons over 20 years old

AHA: 4Q, '05, 97

V85.0 Body Mass Index less than 19, adult SDx A

V85.1 **Body Mass Index between 19-24, adult** SDx A

✓5th V85.2 **Body Mass Index between 25-29, adult**

V85.21 **Body Mass Index 25.0-25.9, adult** SDx A

V85.22 **Body Mass Index 26.0-26.9, adult** SDx A

V85.23 **Body Mass Index 27.0-27.9, adult** SDx A

V85.24 **Body Mass Index 28.0-28.9, adult** SDx A

V85.25 **Body Mass Index 29.0-29.9, adult** SDx A

✓5th V85.3 **Body Mass Index between 30-39, adult**

V85.30 **Body Mass Index 30.0-30.9, adult** SDx A

V85.31 **Body Mass Index 31.0-31.9, adult** SDx A

V85.32 **Body Mass Index 32.0-32.9, adult** SDx A

V85.33 **Body Mass Index 33.0-33.9, adult** SDx A

V85.34 **Body Mass Index 34.0-34.9, adult** SDx A

V85.35 **Body Mass Index 35.0-35.9, adult** SDx A

V85.36 **Body Mass Index 36.0-36.9, adult** SDx A

V85.37 **Body Mass Index 37.0-37.9, adult** SDx A

V85.38 **Body Mass Index 38.0-38.9, adult** SDx A

V85.39 **Body Mass Index 39.0-39.9, adult** SDx A

V85.4 **Body Mass Index 40 and over, adult** SDx A

✓5th V85.5 **Body Mass Index, pediatric**

Note: BMI pediatric codes are for use for persons age 2-20 years old. These percentiles are based on the growth charts published by the Centers for Disease Control and Prevention (CDC)

AHA: 4Q, '06, 118

V85.51 **Body Mass Index, pediatric, less than 5th percentile for age** SDx P

V85.52 **Body Mass Index, pediatric, 5th percentile to less than 85th percentile for age** SDx P

V85.53 **Body Mass Index, pediatric, 85th percentile to less than 95th percentile for age** SDx P

V85.54 **Body Mass Index, pediatric, greater than or equal to 95th percentile for age** SDx P

ESTROGEN RECEPTOR STATUS (V86)

✓4th **V86 Estrogen receptor status**

Code first malignant neoplasm of breast (174.0-174.9, 175.0-175.9)

AHA: 4Q, '06, 118

V86.0 **Estrogen receptor positive status [ER+]** SDx

V86.1 **Estrogen receptor negative status [ER-]** SDx

▶OTHER SPECIFIED PERSONAL EXPOSURES AND HISTORY PRESENTING HAZARDS TO HEALTH (V87)◀

● ✓4th **V87 Other specified personal exposures and history presenting hazards to health**

● ✓5th V87.0 **Contact with and (suspected) exposure to hazardous metals**

EXCLUDES *exposure to lead (V15.86)*
toxic effect of metals (984.0-985.9)

● V87.01 **Arsenic**

● V87.09 **Other hazardous metals**

Chromium compounds
Nickel dust

● ✓5th V87.1 **Contact with and (suspected) exposure to hazardous aromatic compounds**

EXCLUDES *toxic effects of aromatic compounds (982.0, 983.0)*

● V87.11 **Aromatic amines**

● V87.12 **Benzene**

● V87.19 **Other hazardous aromatic compounds**

Aromatic dyes NOS
Polycyclic aromatic hydrocarbons

● ✓5th V87.2 **Contact with and (suspected) exposure to other potentially hazardous chemicals**

Dyes NOS

EXCLUDES *exposure to asbestos (V15.84)*
toxic effect of chemicals (980-989)

● ✓5th V87.3 **Contact with and (suspected) exposure to other potentially hazardous substances**

EXCLUDES *contact with and (suspected) exposure to potentially hazardous body fluids (V15.85)*
toxic effect of substances (980-989)

● V87.31 **Exposure to mold**

● V87.39 **Contact with and (suspected) exposure to other potentially hazardous substances**

● ✓5th V87.4 **Personal history of drug therapy**

EXCLUDES *long-term (current) drug use (V58.61-V58.69)*

● V87.41 **Personal history of antineoplastic chemotherapy**

● V87.42 **Personal history of monoclonal drug therapy**

● V87.49 **Personal history of other drug therapy**

▶ACQUIRED ABSENCE OF OTHER ORGANS AND TISSUE (V88)◀

● ✓4th **V88 Acquired absence of other organs and tissue**

● ✓5th V88.0 **Acquired absence of cervix and uterus**

● V88.01 **Acquired absence of both cervix and uterus**

Acquired absence of uterus NOS
Status post total hysterectomy

● V88.02 **Acquired absence of uterus with remaining cervical stump**

Status post partial hysterectomy with remaining cervical stump

● V88.03 **Acquired absence of cervix with remaining uterus**

▶OTHER SUSPECTED CONDITIONS NOT FOUND (V89)◀

● ✓4th **V89 Other suspected conditions not found**

● ✓5th V89.0 **Suspected maternal and fetal conditions not found**

EXCLUDES *known or suspected fetal anomalies affecting management of mother, not ruled out (655.00, 655.93, 656.00-656.93, 657.00-657.03, 658.00-658.93)*
newborn and perinatal conditions — code to condition

● V89.01 **Suspected problem with amniotic cavity and membrane not found**

Suspected oligohydramnios not found
Suspected polyhydramnios not found

● V89.02 **Suspected placental problem not found**

● V89.03 **Suspected fetal anomaly not found**

● V89.04 **Suspected problem with fetal growth not found**

- V89.05 **Suspected cervical shortening not found**
- V89.09 **Other suspected maternal and fetal condition not found**

SUPPLEMENTARY CLASSIFICATION OF EXTERNAL CAUSES OF INJURY AND POISONING (E800-E999)

This section is provided to permit the classification of environmental events, circumstances, and conditions as the cause of injury, poisoning, and other adverse effects. Where a code from this section is applicable, it is intended that it shall be used in addition to a code from one of the main chapters of ICD-9-CM, indicating the nature of the condition. Certain other conditions which may be stated to be due to external causes are classified in Chapters 1 to 16 of ICD-9-CM. For these, the "E" code classification should be used as an additional code for more detailed analysis.

Machinery accidents [other than those connected with transport] are classifiable to category E919, in which the fourth-digit allows a broad classification of the type of machinery involved. If a more detailed classification of type of machinery is required, it is suggested that the "Classification of Industrial Accidents according to Agency," prepared by the International Labor Office, be used in addition. This is reproduced in Appendix D for optional use.

Categories for "late effects" of accidents and other external causes are to be found at E929, E959, E969, E977, E989, and E999.

DEFINITIONS AND EXAMPLES RELATED TO TRANSPORT ACCIDENTS

(a) A **transport accident** (E800-E848) is any accident involving a device designed primarily for, or being used at the time primarily for, conveying persons or goods from one place to another.

INCLUDES accidents involving:
- aircraft and spacecraft (E840-E845)
- watercraft (E830-E838)
- motor vehicle (E810-E825)
- railway (E800-E807)
- other road vehicles (E826-E829)

In classifying accidents which involve more than one kind of transport, the above order of precedence of transport accidents should be used.

Accidents involving agricultural and construction machines, such as tractors, cranes, and bulldozers, are regarded as transport accidents only when these vehicles are under their own power on a highway [otherwise the vehicles are regarded as machinery]. Vehicles which can travel on land or water, such as hovercraft and other amphibious vehicles, are regarded as watercraft when on the water, as motor vehicles when on the highway, and as off-road motor vehicles when on land, but off the highway.

EXCLUDES *accidents:*
- *in sports which involve the use of transport but where the transport vehicle itself was not involved in the accident*
- *involving vehicles which are part of industrial equipment used entirely on industrial premises*
- *occurring during transportation but unrelated to the hazards associated with the means of transportation [e.g., injuries received in a fight on board ship; transport vehicle involved in a cataclysm such as an earthquake]*
- *to persons engaged in the maintenance or repair of transport equipment or vehicle not in motion, unlesss injured by another vehicle in motion*

(b) A **railway accident** is a transport accident involving a railway train or other railway vehicle operated on rails, whether in motion or not.

EXCLUDES *accidents:*
- *in repair shops*
- *in roundhouse or on turntable*
- *on railway premises but not involving a train or other railway vehicle*

(c) A **railway train** or **railway vehicle** is any device with or without cars coupled to it, desiged for traffic on a railway.

INCLUDES interurban:
- electric car, street car (operated chiefly on its own right-of-way, not open to other traffic)
- railway train, any power [diesel] [electric] [steam]
  - funicular
  - monorail or two-rail
  - subterranean or elevated
- other vehicle designed to run on a railway track

EXCLUDES *interurban electric cars [streetcars] specified to be operating on a right-of-way that forms part of the public street or highway [definition (h)]*

(d) A **railway** or **railroad** is a right-of-way designed for traffic on rails, which is used by carriages or wagons transporting passengers or freight, and by other rolling stock, and which is not open to other public vehicular traffic.

(e) A **motor vehicle accident** is a transport accident involving a motor vehicle. It is defined as a motor vehicle traffic accident or as a motor vehicle nontraffic accident according to whether the accident occurs on a public highway or elsewhere.

EXCLUDES
- *injury or damage due to cataclysm*
- *injury or damage while a motor vehicle, not under its own power, is being loaded on, or unloaded from, another conveyance*

(f) A **motor vehicle traffic accident** is any motor vehicle accident occurring on a public highway [i.e., originating, terminating, or involving a vehicle partially on the highway]. A motor vehicle accident is assumed to have occurred on the highway unless another place is specified, except in the case of accidents involving only off-road motor vehicles which are classified as nontraffic accidents unless the contrary is stated.

(g) A **motor vehicle nontraffic accident** is any motor vehicle accident which occurs entirely in any place other than a public highway.

(h) A **public highway [trafficway]** or **street** is the entire width between property lines [or other boundary lines] of every way or place, of which any part is open to the use of the public for purposes of vehicular traffic as a matter of right or custom. A **roadway** is that part of the public highway designed, improved, and ordinarily used, for vehicular travel.

INCLUDES approaches (public) to:
- docks
- public building
- station

EXCLUDES
- *driveway (private)*
- *parking lot*
- *ramp*
- *roads in:*
  - *airfield*
  - *farm*
  - *industrial premises*
  - *mine*
  - *private grounds*
  - *quarry*

(i) A **motor vehicle** is any mechanically or electrically powered device, not operated on rails, upon which any person or property may be transported or drawn upon a highway. Any object such as a trailer, coaster, sled, or wagon being towed by a motor vehicle is considered a part of the motor vehicle.

INCLUDES automobile [any type]
bus
construction machinery, farm and industrial machinery, steam roller, tractor, army tank, highway grader, or similar vehicle on wheels or treads, while in transport under own power
fire engine (motorized)
motorcycle
motorized bicycle [moped] or scooter
trolley bus not operating on rails
truck
van

EXCLUDES *devices used solely to move persons or materials within the confines of a building and its premises, such as:*
building elevator
coal car in mine
electric baggage or mail truck used solely within a railroad station
electric truck used solely within an industrial plant
moving overhead crane

(j) A **motorcycle** is a two-wheeled motor vehicle having one or two riding saddles and sometimes having a third wheel for the support of a sidecar. The sidecar is considered part of the motorcycle.

INCLUDES motorized:
bicycle [moped]
scooter
tricycle

(k) An **off-road motor vehicle** is a motor vehicle of special design, to enable it to negotiate rough or soft terrain or snow. Examples of special design are high construction, special wheels and tires, driven by treads, or support on a cushion of air.

INCLUDES all terrain vehicle [ATV]
army tank
hovercraft, on land or swamp
snowmobile

(l) A **driver** of a motor vehicle is the occupant of the motor vehicle operating it or intending to operate it. A **motorcyclist** is the driver of a motorcycle. Other authorized occupants of a motor vehicle are **passengers**.

(m) An **other road vehicle** is any device, except a motor vehicle, in, on, or by which any person or property may be transported on a highway.

INCLUDES animal carrying a person or goods
animal-drawn vehicles
animal harnessed to conveyance
bicycle [pedal cycle]
streetcar
tricycle (pedal)

EXCLUDES *pedestrian conveyance [definition (q)]*

(n) A **streetcar** is a device designed and used primarily for transporting persons within a municipality, running on rails, usually subject to normal traffic control signals, and operated principally on a right-of-way that forms part of the traffic way. A trailer being towed by a streetcar is considered a part of the streetcar.

INCLUDES interurban or intraurban electric or streetcar, when specified to be operating on a street or public highway
tram (car)
trolley (car)

(o) A **pedal cycle** is any road transport vehicle operated solely by pedals.

INCLUDES bicycle
pedal cycle
tricycle

EXCLUDES *motorized bicycle [definition (j)]*

(p) A **pedal cyclist** is any person riding on a pedal cycle or in a sidecar attached to such a vehicle.

(q) A **pedestrian conveyance** is any human powered device by which a pedestrian may move other than by walking or by which a walking person may move another pedestrian.

INCLUDES baby carriage
coaster wagon
►heelies, wheelies◄
ice skates
perambulator
pushcart
pushchair
roller skates
scooter
skateboard
skis
sled
wheelchair

(r) A **pedestrian** is any person involved in an accident who was not at the time of the accident riding in or on a motor vehicle, railroad train, streetcar, animal-drawn or other vehicle, or on a bicycle or animal.

INCLUDES person:
changing tire of vehicle
in or operating a pedestrian conveyance
making adjustment to motor of vehicle
on foot

(s) A **watercraft** is any device for transporting passengers or goods on the water.

(t) A **small boat** is any watercraft propelled by paddle, oars, or small motor, with a passenger capacity of less than ten.

INCLUDES boat NOS
canoe
coble
dinghy
punt
raft
rowboat
rowing shell
scull
skiff
small motorboat

EXCLUDES *barge*
lifeboat (used after abandoning ship)
raft (anchored) being used as a diving platform
yacht

(u) An **aircraft** is any device for transporting passengers or goods in the air.

INCLUDES airplane [any type]
balloon
bomber
dirigible
glider (hang)
military aircraft
parachute

(v) A **commercial transport aircraft** is any device for collective passenger or freight transportation by air, whether run on commercial lines for profit or by government authorities, with the exception of military craft.

RAILWAY ACCIDENTS (E800-E807)

Note: For definitions of railway accident and related terms see definitions (a) to (d).

EXCLUDES *accidents involving railway train and:*
aircraft (E840.0-E845.9)
motor vehicle (E810.0-E825.9)
watercraft (E830.0-E838.9)

The following fourth-digit subdivisions are for use with categories E800-E807 to identify the injured person:

.0 Railway employee
Any person who by virtue of his employment in connection with a railway, whether by the railway company or not, is at increased risk of involvement in a railway accident, such as:
catering staff of train
driver
guard
porter
postal staff on train
railway fireman
shunter
sleeping car attendant

.1 Passenger on railway
Any authorized person traveling on a train, except a railway employee.
EXCLUDES *intending passenger waiting at station (.8)*
unauthorized rider on railway vehicle (.8)

.2 Pedestrian
See definition (r)

.3 Pedal cyclist
See definition (p)

.8 Other specified person
Intending passenger or bystander waiting at station
Unauthorized rider on railway vehicle

.9 Unspecified person

§ 4th **E800 Railway accident involving collision with rolling stock**
INCLUDES collision between railway trains or railway vehicles, any kind
collision NOS on railway
derailment with antecedent collision with rolling stock or NOS

§ 4th **E801 Railway accident involving collision with other object**
INCLUDES collision of railway train with:
buffers
fallen tree on railway
gates
platform
rock on railway
streetcar
other nonmotor vehicle
other object
EXCLUDES *collision with:*
aircraft (E840.0-E842.9)
motor vehicle (E810.0-E810.9, E820.0-E822.9)

§ 4th **E802 Railway accident involving derailment without antecedent collision**

§ 4th **E803 Railway accident involving explosion, fire, or burning**
EXCLUDES *explosion or fire, with antecedent derailment (E802.0-E802.9)*
explosion or fire, with mention of antecedent collision (E800.0-E801.9)

§ 4th **E804 Fall in, on, or from railway train**
INCLUDES fall while alighting from or boarding railway train
EXCLUDES *fall related to collision, derailment, or explosion of railway train (E800.0-E803.9)*

§ 4th **E805 Hit by rolling stock**
INCLUDES crushed, injured, killed, knocked down, run over } by railway train or part
EXCLUDES *pedestrian hit by object set in motion by railway train (E806.0-E806.9)*

§ 4th **E806 Other specified railway accident**
INCLUDES hit by object falling in railway train
injured by door or window on railway train
nonmotor road vehicle or pedestrian hit by object set in motion by railway train
railway train hit by falling:
earth NOS
rock
tree
other object
EXCLUDES *railway accident due to cataclysm (E908-E909)*

§ 4th **E807 Railway accident of unspecified nature**
INCLUDES found dead, injured } on railway right-of-way NOS
railway accident NOS

MOTOR VEHICLE TRAFFIC ACCIDENTS (E810-E819)

Note: For definitions of motor vehicle traffic accident, and related terms, see definitions (e) to (k).

EXCLUDES *accidents involving motor vehicle and aircraft (E840.0-E845.9)*

The following fourth-digit subdivisions are for use with categories E810-E819 to identify the injured person:

.0 Driver of motor vehicle other than motorcycle
See definition (l)

.1 Passenger in motor vehicle other than motorcycle
See definition (l)

.2 Motorcyclist
See definition (l)

.3 Passenger on motorcycle
See definition (l)

.4 Occupant of streetcar

.5 Rider of animal; occupant of animal-drawn vehicle

.6 Pedal cyclist
See definition (p)

.7 Pedestrian
See definition (r)

.8 Other specified person
Occupant of vehicle other than above
Person in railway train involved in accident
Unauthorized rider of motor vehicle

.9 Unspecified person

§ 4th **E810 Motor vehicle traffic accident involving collision with train**
EXCLUDES *motor vehicle collision with object set in motion by railway train (E815.0-E815.9)*
railway train hit by object set in motion by motor vehicle (E818.0-E818.9)

§ 4th **E811 Motor vehicle traffic accident involving re-entrant collision with another motor vehicle**
INCLUDES collision between motor vehicle which accidentally leaves the roadway then re-enters the same roadway, or the opposite roadway on a divided highway, and another motor vehicle
EXCLUDES *collision on the same roadway when none of the motor vehicles involved have left and re-entered the highway (E812.0-E812.9)*

§ Requires fourth-digit. See beginning of appropriate section for codes and definitions.

§ ✓4th **E812 Other motor vehicle traffic accident involving collision with motor vehicle**

INCLUDES collision with another motor vehicle parked, stopped, stalled, disabled, or abandoned on the highway
motor vehicle collision NOS

EXCLUDES *collision with object set in motion by another motor vehicle (E815.0-E815.9)*
re-entrant collision with another motor vehicle (E811.0-E811.9)

§ ✓4th **E813 Motor vehicle traffic accident involving collision with other vehicle**

INCLUDES collision between motor vehicle, any kind, and:
other road (nonmotor transport) vehicle, such as:
animal carrying a person
animal-drawn vehicle
pedal cycle
streetcar

EXCLUDES *collision with:*
object set in motion by nonmotor road vehicle (E815.0-E815.9)
pedestrian (E814.0-E814.9)
nonmotor road vehicle hit by object set in motion by motor vehicle (E818.0-E818.9)

§ ✓4th **E814 Motor vehicle traffic accident involving collision with pedestrian**

INCLUDES collision between motor vehicle, any kind, and pedestrian
pedestrian dragged, hit, or run over by motor vehicle, any kind

EXCLUDES *pedestrian hit by object set in motion by motor vehicle (E818.0-E818.9)*

§ ✓4th **E815 Other motor vehicle traffic accident involving collision on the highway**

INCLUDES collision (due to loss of control) (on highway) between motor vehicle, any kind, and:
abutment (bridge) (overpass)
animal (herded) (unattended)
fallen stone, traffic sign, tree, utility pole
guard rail or boundary fence
interhighway divider
landslide (not moving)
object set in motion by railway train or road vehicle (motor) (nonmotor)
object thrown in front of motor vehicle
other object, fixed, movable, or moving
safety island
temporary traffic sign or marker
wall of cut made for road

EXCLUDES *collision with:*
any object off the highway (resulting from loss of control) (E816.0-E816.9)
any object which normally would have been off the highway and is not stated to have been on it (E816.0-E816.9)
motor vehicle parked, stopped, stalled, disabled, or abandoned on highway (E812.0-E812.9)
moving landslide (E909)
motor vehicle hit by object:
set in motion by railway train or road vehicle (motor) (nonmotor) (E818.0-E818.9)
thrown into or on vehicle (E818.0-E818.9)

§ ✓4th **E816 Motor vehicle traffic accident due to loss of control, without collision on the highway**

INCLUDES motor vehicle:
failing to make curve
going out of control (due to):
blowout
burst tire
driver falling asleep
drive inattention
excessive speed
failure of mechanical part
} and:
coliding with object off the highway
overturning
stopping abruptly off the highway

EXCLUDES *collision on highway following loss of control (E810.0-E815.9)*
loss of control of motor vehicle following collision on the highway (E810.0-E815.9)

§ ✓4th **E817 Noncollision motor vehicle traffic accident while boarding or alighting**

INCLUDES fall down stairs of motor bus
fall from car in street
injured by moving part of the vehicle
trapped by door of motor bus
} while boarding or alighting

§ ✓4th **E818 Other noncollision motor vehicle traffic accident**

INCLUDES accidental poisoning from exhaust gas generated by
breakage of any part of
explosion of any part of
fall, jump, or being accidentally pushed from
fire starting in
hit by object thrown into or on
injured by being thrown against some part of, or object in
injury from moving part of
object falling in or on
object thrown on
} motor vehicle while in motion
collision of railway train or road vehicle except motor vehicle, with object set in motion by motor vehicle
motor vehicle hit by object set in motion by railway train or road vehicle (motor) (nonmotor)
pedestrian, railway train, or road vehicle (motor) (nonmotor) hit by object set in motion by motor vehicle

EXCLUDES *collision between motor vehicle and:*
object set in motion by railway train or road vehicle (motor) (nonmotor) (E815.0-E815.9)
object thrown towards the motor vehicle (E815.0-E815.9)
person overcome by carbon monoxide generated by stationary motor vehicle off the roadway with motor running (E868.2)

§ ✓4th **E819 Motor vehicle traffic accident of unspecified nature**

INCLUDES motor vehicle traffic accident NOS
traffic accident NOS

§ Requires fourth-digit. See beginning of appropriate section for codes and definitions.

MOTOR VEHICLE NONTRAFFIC ACCIDENTS (E820-E825)

Note: For definitions of motor vehicle nontraffic accident and related terms see definition (a) to (k).

INCLUDES accidents involving motor vehicles being used in recreational or sporting activities off the highway
collision and noncollision motor vehicle accidents occurring entirely off the highway

EXCLUDES *accidents involving motor vehicle and:*
aircraft (E840.0-E845.9)
watercraft (E830.0-E838.9)
accidents, not on the public highway, involving agricultural and construction machinery but not involving another motor vehicle (E919.0, E919.2, E919.7)

The following fourth-digit subdivisions are for use with categories E820-E825 to identify the injured person:

.0 Driver of motor vehicle other than motorcycle
See definition (l)
.1 Passenger in motor vehicle other than motorcycle
See definition (l)
.2 Motorcyclist
See definition (l)
.3 Passenger on motorcycle
See definition (l)
.4 Occupant of streetcar
.5 Rider of animal; occupant of animal-drawn vehicle
.6 Pedal cyclist
See definition (p)
.7 Pedestrian
See definition (r)
.8 Other specified person
Occupant of vehicle other than above
Person in railway train involved in accident
Unauthorized rider of motor vehicle
.9 Unspecified person

§ 4th **E820 Nontraffic accident involving motor-driven snow vehicle**

INCLUDES breakage of part of | fall from | hit by | overturning of | run over or dragged by } motor-driven snow vehicle (not on public highway)
collision of motor-driven snow vehicle with:
animal (being ridden) (-drawn vehicle)
another off-road motor vehicle
other motor vehicle, not on public highway
railway train
other object, fixed or movable
injury caused by rough landing of motor-driven snow vehicle (after leaving ground on rough terrain)

EXCLUDES *accident on the public highway involving motor driven snow vehicle (E810.0-E819.9)*

§ 4th **E821 Nontraffic accident involving other off-road motor vehicle**

INCLUDES breakage of part of | fall from | hit by | overturning of | run over or dragged by | thrown against some part of or object in } off-road motorvehicle except snow vehicle (not on public highway
collision with:
animal (being ridden) (-drawn vehicle)
another off-road motor vehicle, except snow vehicle
other motor vehicle, not on public highway
other object, fixed or movable

EXCLUDES *accident on public highway involving off-road motor vehicle (E810.0-E819.9)*
collision between motor driven snow vehicle and other off-road motor vehicle (E820.0-E820.9)
hovercraft accident on water (E830.0-E838.9)

§ 4th **E822 Other motor vehicle nontraffic accident involving collision with moving object**

INCLUDES collision, not on public highway, between motor vehicle, except off-road motor vehicle and:
animal
nonmotor vehicle
other motor vehicle, except off-road motor vehicle
pedestrian
railway train
other moving object

EXCLUDES *collision with:*
motor-driven snow vehicle (E820.0-E820.9)
other off-road motor vehicle (E821.0-E821.9)

§ 4th **E823 Other motor vehicle nontraffic accident involving collision with stationary object**

INCLUDES collision, not on public highway, between motor vehicle, except off-road motor vehicle, and any object, fixed or movable, but not in motion

§ 4th **E824 Other motor vehicle nontraffic accident while boarding and alighting**

INCLUDES fall | injury from oving part of motor vehicle | trapped by door of motor vehhicle } while boarding or alighting from motor vehicle, except off-road motor vehicle, not on public highway

§ 4th **E825 Other motor vehicle nontraffic accident of other and unspecified nature**

INCLUDES accidental poisoning from carbon monoxide generated by | breakage of any part of | explosion of any part of | fall, jump, or being accidentally pushed from | fire starting in | hit by object thrown into, towards, or on | injured by being thrown against some part of, or object in | injury from moving part of | object falling in or on } motor vehicle while in motion, not on public highway
motor vehicle nontraffic accident NOS

EXCLUDES *fall from or in stationary motor vehicle (E884.9, E885.9)*
overcome by carbon monoxide or exhaust gas generated by stationary motor vehicle off the roadway with motor running (E868.2)
struck by falling object from or in stationary motor vehicle (E916)

§ Requires fourth-digit. See beginning of appropriate section for codes and definitions.

OTHER ROAD VEHICLE ACCIDENTS (E826-E829)

Note: Other road vehicle accidents are transport accidents involving road vehicles other than motor vehicles. For definitions of other road vehicle and related terms see definitions (m) to (o).

INCLUDES accidents involving other road vehicles being used in recreational or sporting activities

EXCLUDES *collision of other road vehicle [any] with:*
aircraft (E840.0-E845.9)
motor vehicle (E813.0-E813.9, E820.0-E822.9)
railway train (E801.0-E801.9))

The following fourth-digit subdivisions are for use with categories E826-E829 to identify the injured person:

.0 Pedestrian
See definition (r)
.1 Pedal cyclist
See definition (p)
.2 Rider of animal
.3 Occupant of animal-drawn vehicle
.4 Occupant of streetcar
.8 Other specified person
.9 Unspecified person

§ 4th **E826 Pedal cycle accident**
[0-9]
INCLUDES breakage of any part of pedal cycle
collision between pedal cycle and:
animal (being ridden) (herded) (unattended)
another pedal cycle
any pedestrian
nonmotor road vehicle
other object, fixed, movable, or moving, not set in motion by motor vehicle, railway train, or aircraft
entanglement in wheel of pedal cycle
fall from pedal cycle
hit by object falling or thrown on the pedal cycle
pedal cycle accident NOS
pedal cycle overturned

§ 4th **E827 Animal-drawn vehicle accident**
[0,2,4,8,9]
INCLUDES breakage of any part of vehicle
collision between animal-drawn vehicle and:
animal (being ridden) (herded) (unattended)
nonmotor road vehicle, except pedal cycle
pedestrian, pedestrian conveyance, or pedestrian vehicle
other object, fixed, movable, or moving, not set in motion by motor vehicle, railway train, or aircraft
fall from / knocked down by / overturning of / running over by / thrown from } animal drawn vehicle

EXCLUDES *collision of animal-drawn vehicle with pedal cycle (E826.0-E826.9)*

§ 4th **E828 Accident involving animal being ridden**
[0,2,4,8,9]
INCLUDES collision between animal being ridden and:
another animal
nonmotor road vehicle, except pedal cycle, and animal-drawn vehicle
pedestrian, pedestrian conveyance, or pedestrian vehicle
other object, fixed, movable, or moving, not set in motion by motor vehicle, railway train, or aircraft
fall from / knocked down by / thrown from / trampled by } animal being ridden
ridden animal stumbled and fell

EXCLUDES *collision of animal being ridden with:*
animal-drawn vehicle (E827.0-E827.9)
pedal cycle (E826.0-E826.9)

§ 4th **E829 Other road vehicle accidents**
[0,4,8,9]
INCLUDES accident while boarding or alighting from / blow from object in / breakage of any part of / caught in door of / derailment of / fall in, on, or from / fire in } streetcar, nonmotor road vehicle not classifiable to E826-E828
collision between streetcar or nonmotor road vehicle, except as in E826-E828, and:
animal (not being ridden)
another nonmotor road vehicle not classifiable to E826-E828
pedestrian
other object, fixed, movable, or moving, not set in motion by motor vehicle, railway train, or aircraft
nonmotor road vehicle accident NOS
streetcar accident NOS

EXCLUDES *collision with:*
animal being ridden (E828.0-E828.9)
animal-drawn vehicle (E827.0-E827.9)
pedal cycle (E826.0-E826.9)

WATER TRANSPORT ACCIDENTS (E830-E838)

Note: For definitions of water transport accident and related terms see definitions (a), (s), and (t).

INCLUDES watercraft accidents in the course of recreational activities

EXCLUDES *accidents involving both aircraft, including objects set in motion by aircraft, and watercraft (E840.0-E845.9)*

The following fourth-digit subdivisions are for use with categories E830-E838 to identify the injured person:

.0 Occupant of small boat, unpowered
.1 Occupant of small boat, powered
See definition (t)
EXCLUDES *water skier (.4)*
.2 Occupant of other watercraft – crew
Persons:
engaged in operation of watercraft
providing passenger services [cabin attendants, ship's physician, catering personnel]
working on ship during voyage in other capacity [musician in band, operators of shops and beauty parlors
.3 Occupant of other watercraft – other than crew
Passenger
Occupant of lifeboat, other than crew, after abandoning ship
.4 Water skier
.5 Swimmer
.6 Dockers, stevedores
Longshoreman employed on the dock in loading and unloading ships
.8 Other specified person
Immigration and custom officials on board ship
Person:
accompanying passenger or member of crew visiting boat
Pilot (guiding ship into port)
.9 Unspecified person

§ 4th **E830 Accident to watercraft causing submersion**
INCLUDES submersion and drowning due to:
boat overturning
boat submerging
falling or jumping from burning ship
falling or jumping from crushed watercraft
ship sinking
other accident to watercraft

§ Requires fourth-digit. Valid digits are in [brackets] under each code. See beginning of appropriate section for codes and definitions.

§ 4th **E831 Accident to watercraft causing other injury**

INCLUDES any injury, except submersion and drowning, as a result of an accident to watercraft
burned while ship on fire
crushed between ships in collision
crushed by lifeboat after abandoning ship
fall due to collision or other accident to watercraft
hit by falling object due to accident to watercraft
injured in watercraft accident involving collision
struck by boat or part thereof after fall or jump from damaged boat

EXCLUDES *burns from localized fire or explosion on board ship (E837.0-E837.9)*

§ 4th **E832 Other accidental submersion or drowning in water transport accident**

INCLUDES submersion or drowning as a result of an accident other than accident to the watercraft, such as:
fall:
from gangplank
from ship
overboard
thrown overboard by motion of ship
washed overboard

EXCLUDES *submersion or drowning of swimmer or diver who voluntarily jumps from boat not involved in an accident (E910.0-E910.9)*

§ 4th **E833 Fall on stairs or ladders in water transport**

EXCLUDES *fall due to accident to watercraft (E831.0-E831.9)*

§ 4th **E834 Other fall from one level to another in water transport**

EXCLUDES *fall due to accident to watercraft (E831.0-E831.9)*

§ 4th **E835 Other and unspecified fall in water transport**

EXCLUDES *fall due to accident to watercraft (E831.0-E831.9)*

§ 4th **E836 Machinery accident in water transport**

INCLUDES injuries in water transport caused by:
deck, engine room, galley, laundry, loading } machinery

§ 4th **E837 Explosion, fire, or burning in watercraft**

INCLUDES explosion of boiler on steamship
localized fire on ship

EXCLUDES *burning ship (due to collision or explosion) resulting in:*
submersion or drowning (E830.0-E830.9)
other injury (E831.0-E831.9)

§ 4th **E838 Other and unspecified water transport accident**

INCLUDES accidental poisoning by gases or fumes on ship
atomic power plant malfunction in watercraft
crushed between ship and stationary object [wharf]
crushed between ships without accident to watercraft
crushed by falling object on ship or while loading or unloading
hit by boat while water skiing
struck by boat or part thereof (after fall from boat)
watercraft accident NOS

AIR AND SPACE TRANSPORT ACCIDENTS (E840-E845)

Note: For definition of aircraft and related terms see definitions (u) and (v).

The following fourth-digit subdivisions are for use with categories E840-E845 to identify the injured person. Valid fourth digits are in [brackets] under codes E842-E845:

.0 Occupant of spacecraft

.1 Occupant of military aircraft, any
Crew in military aircraft [air force] [army] [national guard] [navy]
Passenger (civilian) (military) in military aircraft [air force] [army] [national guard] [navy]
Troops in military aircraft [air force] [army] [national guard] [navy]

EXCLUDES *occupants of aircraft operated under jurisdiction of police departments (.5)*
parachutist (.7)

.2 Crew of commercial aircraft (powered) in surface to surface transport

.3 Other occupant of commercial aircraft (powered) in surface to surface transport
Flight personnel:
not part of crew
on familiarization flight
Passenger on aircraft (powered) NOS

.4 Occupant of commercial aircraft (powered) in surface to air transport
Occupant [crew] [passenger] of aircraft (powered) engaged in activities, such as:
aerial spraying (crops) (fire retardants)
air drops of emergency supplies
air drops of parachutists, except from military craft
crop dusting
lowering of construction material [bridge or telephone pole]
sky writing

.5 Occupant of other powered aircraft
Occupant [crew] [passenger] of aircraft (powered) engaged in activities, such as:
aerobatic flying
aircraft racing
rescue operation
storm surveillance
traffic surveillance
Occupant of private plane NOS

.6 Occupant of unpowered aircraft, except parachutist
Occupant of aircraft classifiable to E842

.7 Parachutist (military) (other)
Person making voluntary descent

EXCLUDES *person making descent after accident to aircraft (.1-.6)*

.8 Ground crew, airline employee
Persons employed at airfields (civil) (military) or launching pads, not occupants of aircraft

.9 Other person

§ 4th **E840 Accident to powered aircraft at takeoff or landing**

INCLUDES collision of aircraft with any object, fixed, movable, or moving; crash; explosion on aircraft; fire on aircraft; forced landing } while taking off or landing

§ 4th **E841 Accident to powered aircraft, other and unspecified**

INCLUDES aircraft accident NOS
aircraft crash or wreck NOS
any accident to powered aircraft while in transit or when not specified whether in transit, taking off, or landing
collision of aircraft with another aircraft, bird, or any object, while in transit
explosion on aircraft while in transit
fire on aircraft while in transit

§ Requires fourth-digit. See beginning of appropriate section for codes and definitions.

§ ✓4th **E842 Accident to unpowered aircraft**

[6-9] INCLUDES any accident, except collision with powered aircraft, to:
balloon
glider
hang glider
kite carrying a person
hit by object falling from unpowered aircraft

§ ✓4th **E843 Fall in, on, or from aircraft**

[0-9] INCLUDES accident in boarding or alighting from aircraft, any kind
fall in, on, or from aircraft [any kind], while in transit, taking off, or landing, except when as a result of an accident to aircraft

§ ✓4th **E844 Other specified air transport accidents**

[0-9] INCLUDES hit by:
aircraft
object falling from aircraft
injury by or from:
machinery of aircraft
rotating propellar
voluntary parachute descent
poisoning by carbon monoxide from aircraft while in transit
sucked into jet
} without accident to aircraft
any accident involving other transport vehicle (motor) (nonmotor) due to being hit by object set in motion by aircraft (powered)

EXCLUDES *air sickness (E903)*
effects of:
high altitude (E902.0-E902.1)
pressure change (E902.0-E902.1)
injury in parachute descent due to accident to aircraft (E840.0-E842-9)

§ ✓4th **E845 Accident involving spacecraft**

[0,8,9] INCLUDES launching pad accident
EXCLUDES *effects of weightlessness in spacecraft (E928.0)*

VEHICLE ACCIDENTS NOT ELSEWHERE CLASSIFIABLE (E846-E848)

E846 Accidents involving powered vehicles used solely within the buildings and premises of industrial or commercial establishment

Accident to, on, or involving:
battery powered airport passenger vehicle
battery powered trucks (baggage) (mail)
coal car in mine
logging car
self propelled truck, industrial
station baggage truck (powered)
tram, truck, or tub (powered) in mine or quarry
Collision with:
pedestrian
other vehicle or object within premises
Explosion of
Fall from
Overturning of
Struck by
} powered vehicle, industrial or commercial

EXCLUDES *accidental poisoning by exhaust gas from vehicle not elsewhere classifiable (E868.2)*
injury by crane, lift (fork), or elevator (E919.2)

E847 Accidents involving cable cars not running on rails

Accident to, on, or involving:
cable car, not on rails
ski chair-lift
ski-lift with gondola
téléférique
Breakage of cable
Caught or dragged by
Fall or jump from
Object thrown from or in
} cable car, not on rails

E848 Accidents involving other vehicles, not elsewhere classifiable

Accident to, on, or involving:
ice yacht
land yacht
nonmotor, nonroad vehicle NOS

✓4th ***E849 Place of occurrence***

The following category is for use to denote the place where the injury or poisoning occurred.

E849.0 Home

Apartment
Boarding house
Farm house
Home premises
House (residential)
Noninstitutional place of residence
Private:
driveway
garage
garden
home
walk
Swimming pool in private house or garden
Yard of home

EXCLUDES *home under construction but not yet occupied (E849.3)*
institutional place of residence (E849.7)

E849.1 Farm

Farm:
buildings
land under cultivation

EXCLUDES *farm house and home premises of farm (E849.0)*

E849.2 Mine and quarry

Gravel pit
Sand pit
Tunnel under construction

E849.3 Industrial place and premises

Building under construction
Dockyard
Dry dock
Factory
building
premises
Garage (place of work)
Industrial yard
Loading platform (factory) (store)
Plant, industrial
Railway yard
Shop (place of work)
Warehouse
Workhouse

E849.4 Place for recreation and sport

Amusement park
Baseball field
Basketball court
Beach resort
Cricket ground
Fives court
Football field
Golf course
Gymnasium
Hockey field
Holiday camp
Ice palace
Lake resort
Mountain resort
Playground, including school playground
Public park
Racecourse
Resort NOS
Riding school
Rifle range
Seashore resort
Skating rink
Sports palace
Stadium
Swimming pool, public
Tennis court
Vacation resort

EXCLUDES *that in private house or garden (E849.0)*

E849.5 Street and highway

§ Requires fourth-digit. Valid digits are in [brackets] under each code. See beginning of section E840–E845 for codes and definitions.

E849.6 Public building

Building (including adjacent grounds) used by the general public or by a particular group of the public, such as:

airport
bank
café
casino
church
cinema
clubhouse
courthouse
dance hall
garage building (for car storage)
hotel
market (grocery or other commodity)
movie house
music hall
nightclub
office
office building
opera house
post office
public hall
radio broadcasting station
restaurant
school (state) (public) (private)
shop, commercial
station (bus) (railway)
store
theater

EXCLUDES *home garage (E849.0)*
industrial building or workplace (E849.3)

E849.7 Residential institution

Children's home
Dormitory
Hospital
Jail
Old people's home
Orphanage
Prison
Reform school

E849.8 Other specified places

Beach NOS
Canal
Caravan site NOS
Derelict house
Desert
Dock
Forest
Harbor
Hill
Lake NOS
Mountain
Parking lot
Parking place
Pond or pool (natural)
Prairie
Public place NOS
Railway line
Reservoir
River
Sea
Seashore NOS
Stream
Swamp
Trailer court
Woods

E849.9 Unspecified place

ACCIDENTAL POISONING BY DRUGS, MEDICINAL SUBSTANCES, AND BIOLOGICALS (E850-E858)

INCLUDES accidental overdose of drug, wrong drug given or taken in error, and drug taken inadvertently
accidents in the use of drugs and biologicals in medical and surgical procedures

EXCLUDES *administration with suicidal or homicidal intent or intent to harm, or in circumstances classifiable to E980-E989 (E950.0-E950.5, E962.0, E980.0-E980.5)*
correct drug properly administered in therapeutic or prophylactic dosage, as the cause of adverse effect (E930.0-E949.9)

See Alphabetic Index for more complete list of specific drugs to be classified under the fourth-digit subdivisions. The American Hospital Formulary numbers can be used to classify new drugs listed by the American Hospital Formulary Service (AHFS). See Appendix C.

✓4th **E850 Accidental poisoning by analgesics, antipyretics, and antirheumatics**

E850.0 Heroin
Diacetylmorphine

E850.1 Methadone

E850.2 Other opiates and related narcotics
Codeine [methylmorphine]
Meperidine [pethidine]
Morphine
Opium (alkaloids)

E850.3 Salicylates
Acetylsalicylic acid [aspirin]
Amino derivatives of salicylic acid
Salicylic acid salts

E850.4 Aromatic analgesics, not elsewhere classified
Acetanilid
Paracetamol [acetaminophen]
Phenacetin [acetophenetidin]

E850.5 Pyrazole derivatives
Aminophenazone [amidopyrine]
Phenylbutazone

E850.6 Antirheumatics [antiphlogistics]
Gold salts
Indomethacin

EXCLUDES *salicylates (E850.3)*
steroids (E858.0)

E850.7 Other non-narcotic analgesics
Pyrabital

E850.8 Other specified analgesics and antipyretics
Pentazocine

E850.9 Unspecified analgesic or antipyretic

E851 Accidental poisoning by barbiturates
Amobarbital [amylobarbitone]
Barbital [barbitone]
Butabarbital [butabarbitone]
Pentobarbital [pentobarbitone]
Phenobarbital [phenobarbitone]
Secobarbital [quinalbarbitone]

EXCLUDES *thiobarbiturates (E855.1)*

✓4th **E852 Accidental poisoning by other sedatives and hypnotics**

E852.0 Chloral hydrate group

E852.1 Paraldehyde

E852.2 Bromine compounds
Bromides
Carbromal (derivatives)

E852.3 Methaqualone compounds

E852.4 Glutethimide group

E852.5 Mixed sedatives, not elsewhere classified

E852.8 Other specified sedatives and hypnotics

E852.9 Unspecified sedative or hypnotic
Sleeping:
drug | pill | tablet — NOS

✓4th E853 Accidental poisoning by tranquilizers

E853.0 Phenothiazine-based tranquilizers
Chlorpromazine
Fluphenazine
Prochlorperazine
Promazine

E853.1 Butyrophenone-based tranquilizers
Haloperidol
Spiperone
Trifluperidol

E853.2 Benzodiazepine-based tranquilizers
Chlordiazepoxide
Diazepam
Flurazepam
Lorazepam
Medazepam
Nitrazepam

E853.8 Other specified tranquilizers
Hydroxyzine
Meprobamate

E853.9 Unspecified tranquilizer

✓4th E854 Accidental poisoning by other psychotropic agents

E854.0 Antidepressants
Amitriptyline
Imipramine
Monoamine oxidase [MAO] inhibitors

E854.1 Psychodysleptics [hallucinogens]
Cannabis derivatives
Lysergide [LSD]
Marihuana (derivatives)
Mescaline
Psilocin
Psilocybin

E854.2 Psychostimulants
Amphetamine
Caffeine
EXCLUDES *central appetite depressants (E858.8)*

E854.3 Central nervous system stimulants
Analeptics
Opiate antagonists

E854.8 Other psychotropic agents

✓4th E855 Accidental poisoning by other drugs acting on central and autonomic nervous system

E855.0 Anticonvulsant and anti-Parkinsonism drugs
Amantadine
Hydantoin derivatives
Levodopa [L-dopa]
Oxazolidine derivatives [paramethadione] [trimethadione]
Succinimides

E855.1 Other central nervous system depressants
Ether
Gaseous anesthetics
Halogenated hydrocarbon derivatives
Intravenous anesthetics
Thiobarbiturates, such as thiopental sodium

E855.2 Local anesthetics
Cocaine
Lidocaine [lignocaine]
Procaine
Tetracaine

E855.3 Parasympathomimetics [cholinergics]
Acetylcholine
Anticholinesterase:
organophosphorus
reversible
Pilocarpine

E855.4 Parasympatholytics [anticholinergics and antimuscarinics] and spasmolytics
Atropine
Homatropine
Hyoscine [scopolamine]
Quaternary ammonium derivatives

E855.5 Sympathomimetics [adrenergics]
Epinephrine [adrenalin]
Levarterenol [noradrenalin]

E855.6 Sympatholytics [antiadrenergics]
Phenoxybenzamine
Tolazoline hydrochloride

E855.8 Other specified drugs acting on central and autonomic nervous systems

E855.9 Unspecified drug acting on central and autonomic nervous systems

E856 Accidental poisoning by antibiotics

E857 Accidental poisoning by other anti-infectives

✓4th E858 Accidental poisoning by other drugs

E858.0 Hormones and synthetic substitutes

E858.1 Primarily systemic agents

E858.2 Agents primarily affecting blood constituents

E858.3 Agents primarily affecting cardiovascular system

E858.4 Agents primarily affecting gastrointestinal system

E858.5 Water, mineral, and uric acid metabolism drugs

E858.6 Agents primarily acting on the smooth and skeletal muscles and respiratory system

E858.7 Agents primarily affecting skin and mucous membrane, ophthalmological, otorhinolaryngological, and dental drugs

E858.8 Other specified drugs
Central appetite depressants

E858.9 Unspecified drug

ACCIDENTAL POISONING BY OTHER SOLID AND LIQUID SUBSTANCES, GASES, AND VAPORS (E860-E869)

Note: Categories in this section are intended primarily to indicate the external cause of poisoning states classifiable to 980-989. They may also be used to indicate external causes of localized effects classifiable to 001-799.

✓4th E860 Accidental poisoning by alcohol, not elsewhere classified

E860.0 Alcoholic beverages
Alcohol in preparations intended for consumption

E860.1 Other and unspecified ethyl alcohol and its products
Denatured alcohol
Ethanol NOS
Grain alcohol NOS
Methylated spirit

E860.2 Methyl alcohol
Methanol
Wood alcohol

E860.3 Isopropyl alcohol
Dimethyl carbinol
Isopropanol
Rubbing alcohol subsitute
Secondary propyl alcohol

E860.4 Fusel oil
Alcohol:
amyl
butyl
propyl

E860.8 Other specified alcohols

E860.9 Unspecified alcohol

✓4th E861 Accidental poisoning by cleansing and polishing agents, disinfectants, paints, and varnishes

E861.0 Synthetic detergents and shampoos

E861.1 Soap products

E861.2 Polishes

E861.3 Other cleansing and polishing agents
Scouring powders

E861.4 Disinfectants
Household and other disinfectants not ordinarily used on the person
EXCLUDES *carbolic acid or phenol (E864.0)*

E861.5 Lead paints

E861.6 Other paints and varnishes

Lacquers
Oil colors
Paints, other than lead
White washes

E861.9 Unspecified

E862 Accidental poisoning by petroleum products, other solvents and their vapors, not elsewhere classified (4th)

E862.0 Petroleum solvents

Petroleum:
ether
benzine
Petroleum:
naphtha

E862.1 Petroleum fuels and cleaners

Antiknock additives to petroleum fuels
Gas oils
Gasoline or petrol
Kerosene

EXCLUDES *kerosene insecticides (E863.4)*

E862.2 Lubricating oils

E862.3 Petroleum solids

Paraffin wax

E862.4 Other specified solvents

Benzene

E862.9 Unspecified solvent

E863 Accidental poisoning by agricultural and horticultural chemical and pharmaceutical preparations other than plant foods and fertilizers (4th)

EXCLUDES *plant foods and fertilizers (E866.5)*

E863.0 Insecticides of organochlorine compounds

Benzene hexachloride
Chlordane
DDT
Dieldrin
Endrine
Toxaphene

E863.1 Insecticides of organophosphorus compounds

Demeton
Diazinon
Dichlorvos
Malathion
Methyl parathion
Parathion
Phenylsulphthion
Phorate
Phosdrin

E863.2 Carbamates

Aldicarb
Carbaryl
Propoxur

E863.3 Mixtures of insecticides

E863.4 Other and unspecified insecticides

Kerosene insecticides

E863.5 Herbicides

2, 4-Dichlorophenoxyacetic acid [2, 4-D]
2, 4, 5-Trichlorophenoxyacetic acid [2, 4, 5-T]
Chlorates
Diquat
Mixtures of plant foods and fertilizers with herbicides
Paraquat

E863.6 Fungicides

Organic mercurials (used in seed dressing)
Pentachlorophenols

E863.7 Rodenticides

Fluoroacetates
Squill and derivatives
Thallium
Warfarin
Zinc phosphide

E863.8 Fumigants

Cyanides
Methyl bromide
Phosphine

E863.9 Other and unspecified

E864 Accidental poisoning by corrosives and caustics, not elsewhere classified (4th)

EXCLUDES *those as components of disinfectants (E861.4)*

E864.0 Corrosive aromatics

Carbolic acid or phenol

E864.1 Acids

Acid:
hydrochloric
nitric
Acid:
sulfuric

E864.2 Caustic alkalis

Lye

E864.3 Other specified corrosives and caustics

E864.4 Unspecified corrosives and caustics

E865 Accidental poisoning from poisonous foodstuffs and poisonous plants (4th)

INCLUDES any meat, fish, or shellfish
plants, berries, and fungi eaten as, or in mistake for, food, or by a child

EXCLUDES *anaphylactic shock due to adverse food reaction (995.60-995.69)*
food poisoning (bacterial) (005.0-005.9)
poisoning and toxic reactions to venomous plants (E905.6-E905.7)

E865.0 Meat

E865.1 Shellfish

E865.2 Other fish

E865.3 Berries and seeds

E865.4 Other specified plants

E865.5 Mushrooms and other fungi

E865.8 Other specified foods

E865.9 Unspecified foodstuff or poisonous plant

E866 Accidental poisoning by other and unspecified solid and liquid substances (4th)

EXCLUDES *these substances as a component of:*
medicines (E850.0-E858.9)
paints (E861.5-E861.6)
pesticides (E863.0-E863.9)
petroleum fuels (E862.1)

E866.0 Lead and its compounds and fumes

E866.1 Mercury and its compounds and fumes

E866.2 Antimony and its compounds and fumes

E866.3 Arsenic and its compounds and fumes

E866.4 Other metals and their compounds and fumes

Beryllium (compounds)
Brass fumes
Cadmium (compounds)
Copper salts
Iron (compounds)
Manganese (compounds)
Nickel (compounds)
Thallium (compounds)

E866.5 Plant foods and fertilizers

EXCLUDES *mixtures with herbicides (E863.5)*

E866.6 Glues and adhesives

E866.7 Cosmetics

E866.8 Other specified solid or liquid substances

E866.9 Unspecified solid or liquid substance

E867 Accidental poisoning by gas distributed by pipeline

Carbon monoxide from incomplete combustion of piped gas
Coal gas NOS
Liquefied petroleum gas distributed through pipes (pure or mixed with air)
Piped gas (natural) (manufactured)

E868 Accidental poisoning by other utility gas and other carbon monoxide (4th)

E868.0 Liquefied petroleum gas distributed in mobile containers

Butane
Liquefied hydrocarbon gas NOS
Propane
} or carbon monoxide from incomplete conbustion of these gases

E868.1 Other and unspecified utility gas

Acetylene
Gas NOS used for lighting, heating, or cooking
Water gas
} or carbon monoxide from incomplete conbustion of these gases

E868.2 Motor vehicle exhaust gas

Exhaust gas from:
- any type of combustion engine not in watercraft
- farm tractor, not in transit
- gas engine
- motor pump
- motor vehicle, not in transit

EXCLUDES *poisoning by carbon monoxide from:*
aircraft while in transit (E844.0-E844.9)
motor vehicle while in transit (E818.0-E818.9)
watercraft whether or not in transit (E838.0-E838.9)

E868.3 Carbon monoxide from incomplete combustion of other domestic fuels

Carbon monoxide from incomplete combustion of:
coal
coke
kerosene
wood
} in domestic stove or fireplace

EXCLUDES *carbon monoxide from smoke and fumes due to conflagration (E890.0-E893.9)*

E868.8 Carbon monoxide from other sources

Carbon monoxide from:
- blast furnace gas
- incomplete combustion of fuels in industrial use
- kiln vapor

E868.9 Unspecified carbon monoxide

✓4th **E869 Accidental poisoning by other gases and vapors**

EXCLUDES *effects of gases used as anesthetics (E855.1, E938.2)*
fumes from heavy metals (E866.0-E866.4)
smoke and fumes due to conflagration or explosion (E890.0-E899)

E869.0 Nitrogen oxides

E869.1 Sulfur dioxide

E869.2 Freon

E869.3 Lacrimogenic gas [tear gas]

Bromobenzyl cyanide
Chloroacetophenone
Ethyliodoacetate

E869.4 Second-hand tobacco smoke

E869.8 Other specified gases and vapors

Chlorine
Hydrocyanic acid gas

E869.9 Unspecified gases and vapors

MISADVENTURES TO PATIENTS DURING SURGICAL AND MEDICAL CARE (E870-E876)

EXCLUDES *accidental overdose of drug and wrong drug given in error (E850.0-E858.9)*
surgical and medical procedures as the cause of abnormal reaction by the patient, without mention of misadventure at the time of procedure (E878.0-E879.9)

✓4th **E870 Accidental cut, puncture, perforation, or hemorrhage during medical care**

E870.0 Surgical operation

E870.1 Infusion or transfusion

E870.2 Kidney dialysis or other perfusion

E870.3 Injection or vaccination

E870.4 Endoscopic examination

E870.5 Aspiration of fluid or tissue, puncture, and catheterization

Abdominal paracentesis
Aspirating needle biopsy
Blood sampling
Lumbar puncture
Thoracentesis

EXCLUDES *heart catheterization (E870.6)*

E870.6 Heart catheterization

E870.7 Administration of enema

E870.8 Other specified medical care

E870.9 Unspecified medical care

✓4th **E871 Foreign object left in body during procedure**

E871.0 Surgical operation

E871.1 Infusion or transfusion

E871.2 Kidney dialysis or other perfusion

E871.3 Injection or vaccination

E871.4 Endoscopic examination

E871.5 Aspiration of fluid or tissue, puncture, and catheterization

Abdominal paracentesis
Aspiration needle biopsy
Blood sampling
Lumbar puncture
Thoracentesis

EXCLUDES *heart catheterization (E871.6)*

E871.6 Heart catheterization

E871.7 Removal of catheter or packing

E871.8 Other specified procedures

E871.9 Unspecified procedure

✓4th **E872 Failure of sterile precautions during procedure**

E872.0 Surgical operation

E872.1 Infusion or transfusion

E872.2 Kidney dialysis and other perfusion

E872.3 Injection or vaccination

E872.4 Endoscopic examination

E872.5 Aspiration of fluid or tissue, puncture, and catheterization

Abdominal paracentesis
Aspiration needle biopsy
Blood sampling
Lumbar puncture
Thoracentesis

EXCLUDES *heart catheterization (E872.6)*

E872.6 Heart catheterization

E872.8 Other specified procedures

E872.9 Unspecified procedure

✓4th **E873 Failure in dosage**

EXCLUDES *accidental overdose of drug, medicinal or biological substance (E850.0-E858.9)*

E873.0 Excessive amount of blood or other fluid during transfusion or infusion

E873.1 Incorrect dilution of fluid during infusion

E873.2 Overdose of radiation in therapy

E873.3 Inadvertent exposure of patient to radiation during medical care

E873.4 Failure in dosage in electroshock or insulin-shock therapy

E873.5 Inappropriate [too hot or too cold] temperature in local application and packing

E873.6 Nonadministration of necessary drug or medicinal substance

E873.8 Other specified failure in dosage

E873.9 Unspecified failure in dosage

4th **E874 Mechanical failure of instrument or apparatus during procedure**

E874.0 Surgical operation

E874.1 Infusion and transfusion
Air in system

E874.2 Kidney dialysis and other perfusion

E874.3 Endoscopic examination

E874.4 Aspiration of fluid or tissue, puncture, and catheterization
Abdominal paracentesis
Aspiration needle biopsy
Blood sampling
Lumbar puncture
Thoracentesis
EXCLUDES *heart catheterization (E874.5)*

E874.5 Heart catheterization

E874.8 Other specified procedures

E874.9 Unspecified procedure

4th **E875 Contaminated or infected blood, other fluid, drug, or biological substance**

INCLUDES presence of:
bacterial pyrogens
endotoxin-producing bacteria
serum hepatitis-producing agent

E875.0 Contaminated substance transfused or infused

E875.1 Contaminated substance injected or used for vaccination

E875.2 Contaminated drug or biological substance administered by other means

E875.8 Other

E875.9 Unspecified

4th **E876 Other and unspecified misadventures during medical care**

E876.0 Mismatched blood in transfusion

E876.1 Wrong fluid in infusion

E876.2 Failure in suture and ligature during surgical operation

E876.3 Endotracheal tube wrongly placed during anesthetic procedure

E876.4 Failure to introduce or to remove other tube or instrument
EXCLUDES *foreign object left in body during procedure (E871.0 E871.9)*

E876.5 Performance of inappropriate operation

E876.8 Other specified misadventures during medical care
Performance of inappropriate treatment NEC

E876.9 Unspecified misadventure during medical care

SURGICAL AND MEDICAL PROCEDURES AS THE CAUSE OF ABNORMAL REACTION OF PATIENT OR LATER COMPLICATION, WITHOUT MENTION OF MISADVENTURE AT THE TIME OF PROCEDURE (E878-E879)

INCLUDES procedures as the cause of abnormal reaction, such as:
displacement or malfunction of prosthetic device
hepatorenal failure, postoperative
malfunction of external stoma
postoperative intestinal obstruction
rejection of transplanted organ

EXCLUDES *anesthetic management properly carried out as the cause of adverse effect (E937.0-E938.9)*
infusion and transfusion, without mention of misadventure in the technique of procedure (E930.0-E949.9)

4th **E878 Surgical operation and other surgical procedures as the cause of abnormal reaction of patient, or of later complication, without mention of misadventure at the time of operation**

E878.0 Surgical operation with transplant of whole organ
Transplantation of:
heart
kidney
Transplantation of:
liver

E878.1 Surgical operation with implant of artificial internal device
Cardiac pacemaker
Electrodes implanted in brain
Heart valve prosthesis
Internal orthopedic device

E878.2 Surgical operation with anastomosis, bypass, or graft, with natural or artificial tissues used as implant
Anastomosis:
arteriovenous
gastrojejunal
Graft of blood vessel, tendon, or skin
EXCLUDES *external stoma (E878.3)*

E878.3 Surgical operation with formation of external stoma
Colostomy
Cystostomy
Duodenostomy
Gastrostomy
Ureterostomy

E878.4 Other restorative surgery

E878.5 Amputation of limb(s)

E878.6 Removal of other organ (partial) (total)

E878.8 Other specified surgical operations and procedures

E878.9 Unspecified surgical operations and procedures

4th **E879 Other procedures, without mention of misadventure at the time of procedure, as the cause of abnormal reaction of patient, or of later complication**

E879.0 Cardiac catheterization

E879.1 Kidney dialysis

E879.2 Radiological procedure and radiotherapy
EXCLUDES *radio-opaque dyes for diagnostic x-ray procedures (E947.8)*

E879.3 Shock therapy
Electroshock therapy
Insulin-shock therapy

E879.4 Aspiration of fluid
Lumbar puncture
Thoracentesis

E879.5 Insertion of gastric or duodenal sound

E879.6 Urinary catheterization

E879.7 Blood sampling

E879.8 Other specified procedures
Blood transfusion

E879.9 Unspecified procedure

ACCIDENTAL FALLS (E880-E888)

EXCLUDES *falls (in or from):*
burning building (E890.8, E891.8)
into fire (E890.0-E899)
into water (with submersion or drowning) (E910.0-E910.9)
machinery (in operation) (E919.0-E919.9)
on edged, pointed, or sharp object (E920.0-E920.9)
transport vehicle (E800.0-E845.9)
vehicle not elsewhere classifiable (E846-E848)

✓4th **E880 Fall on or from stairs or steps**

E880.0 Escalator

E880.1 Fall on or from sidewalk curb
EXCLUDES *fall from moving sidewalk (E885.9)*

E880.9 Other stairs or steps

✓4th **E881 Fall on or from ladders or scaffolding**

E881.0 Fall from ladder

E881.1 Fall from scaffolding

E882 Fall from or out of building or other structure
Fall from:
balcony
bridge
building
flagpole
tower
turret
viaduct
wall
window
Fall through roof

EXCLUDES *collapse of a building or structure (E916)*
fall or jump from burning building (E890.8, E891.8)

✓4th **E883 Fall into hole or other opening in surface**
INCLUDES fall into:
cavity
dock
hole
pit
quarry
shaft
swimming pool
tank
well

EXCLUDES *fall into water NOS (E910.9)*
that resulting in drowning or submersion without mention of injury (E910.0-E910.9)

E883.0 Accident from diving or jumping into water [swimming pool]
Strike or hit:
against bottom when jumping or diving into water
wall or board of swimming pool
water surface

EXCLUDES *diving with insufficient air supply (E913.2)*
effects of air pressure from diving (E902.2)

E883.1 Accidental fall into well

E883.2 Accidental fall into storm drain or manhole

E883.9 Fall into other hole or other opening in surface

✓4th **E884 Other fall from one level to another**

E884.0 Fall from playground equipment
EXCLUDES *recreational machinery (E919.8)*

E884.1 Fall from cliff

E884.2 Fall from chair

E884.3 Fall from wheelchair

E884.4 Fall from bed

E884.5 Fall from other furniture

E884.6 Fall from commode
Toilet

E884.9 Other fall from one level to another
Fall from:
embankment
haystack
stationary vehicle
tree

✓4th **E885 Fall on same level from slipping, tripping, or stumbling**

E885.0 Fall from (nonmotorized) scooter

E885.1 Fall from roller skates
▶Heelies◀
In-line skates
▶Wheelies◀

E885.2 Fall from skateboard

E885.3 Fall from skis

E885.4 Fall from snowboard

E885.9 Fall from other slipping, tripping, or stumbling
Fall on moving sidewalk

✓4th **E886 Fall on same level from collision, pushing, or shoving, by or with other person**
EXCLUDES *crushed or pushed by a crowd or human stampede (E917.1, E917.6)*

E886.0 In sports
Tackles in sports
EXCLUDES *kicked, stepped on, struck by object, in sports (E917.0, E917.5)*

E886.9 Other and unspecified
Fall from collision of pedestrian (conveyance) with another pedestrian (conveyance)

E887 Fracture, cause unspecified

✓4th **E888 Other and unspecified fall**
Accidental fall NOS
Fall on same level NOS

E888.0 Fall resulting in striking against sharp object
Use additional external cause code to identify object (E920)

E888.1 Fall resulting in striking against other object

E888.8 Other fall

E888.9 Unspecified fall
Fall NOS

ACCIDENTS CAUSED BY FIRE AND FLAMES (E890-E899)

INCLUDES asphyxia or poisoning due to conflagration or ignition
burning by fire
secondary fires resulting from explosion

EXCLUDES *arson (E968.0)*
fire in or on:
machinery (in operation) (E919.0-E919.9)
transport vehicle other than stationary vehicle (E800.0-E845.9)
vehicle not elsewhere classifiable (E846-E848)

✓4th **E890 Conflagration in private dwelling**
INCLUDES conflagration in:
apartment
boarding house
camping place
caravan
farmhouse
house
lodging house
mobile home
private garage
rooming house
tenement
conflagration originating from sources classifiable to E893-E898 in the above buildings

E890.0 Explosion caused by conflagration

E890.1 Fumes from combustion of polyvinylchloride [PVC] and similar material in conflagration

E890.2 Other smoke and fumes from conflagration

Carbon monoxide, Fumes NOS, Smoke NOS } from conflagration in private building

E890.3 Burning caused by conflagration

E890.8 Other accident resulting from conflagration

Collapse of, Fall from, Hit by object falling from, Jump from } burning private building

E890.9 Unspecified accident resulting from conflagration in private dwelling

✓4th **E891 Conflagration in other and unspecified building or structure**

Conflagration in:
- barn
- church
- convalescent and other residential home
- dormitory of educational institution
- factory
- farm outbuildings
- hospital
- hotel
- school
- store
- theater

Conflagration originating from sources classifiable to E893-E898, in the above buildings

E891.0 Explosion caused by conflagration

E891.1 Fumes from combustion of polyvinylchloride [PVC] and similar material in conflagration

E891.2 Other smoke and fumes from conflagration

Carbon monoxide, Fumes NOS, Smoke NOS } from conflagration in private building or structure

E891.3 Burning caused by conflagration

E891.8 Other accident resulting from conflagration

Collapse of, Fall from, Hit by object falling from, Jump from } burning private building or structure

E891.9 Unspecified accident resulting from conflagration of other and unspecified building or structure

E892 Conflagration not in building or structure

Fire (uncontrolled) (in) (of):
- forest
- grass
- hay
- lumber
- mine
- prairie
- transport vehicle [any], except while in transit
- tunnel

✓4th **E893 Accident caused by ignition of clothing**

EXCLUDES *ignition of clothing:*
- *from highly inflammable material (E894)*
- *with conflagration (E890.0-E892)*

E893.0 From controlled fire in private dwelling

Ignition of clothing from:
- normal fire (charcoal) (coal) (electric) (gas) (wood) in:
  - brazier
  - fireplace
  - furnace
  - stove

} in private dwelling (as listed in E890)

E893.1 From controlled fire in other building or structure

Ignition of clothing from:
- normal fire (charcoal) (coal) (electric) (gas) (wood) in:
  - brazier
  - fireplace
  - furnace
  - stove

} in other building or structure (as listed in E891)

E893.2 From controlled fire not in building or structure

Ignition of clothing from:
- bonfire (controlled)
- brazier fire (controlled), not in building or structure
- trash fire (controlled)

EXCLUDES *conflagration not in building (E892)*
trash fire out of control (E892)

E893.8 From other specified sources

Ignition of clothing from:
- blowlamp
- blowtorch
- burning bedspread
- candle
- cigar

Ignition of clothing from:
- cigarette
- lighter
- matches
- pipe
- welding torch

E893.9 Unspecified source

Ignition of clothing (from controlled fire NOS) (in building NOS) NOS

E894 Ignition of highly inflammable material

Ignition of:
- benzine
- gasoline
- fat
- kerosene
- paraffin
- petrol

} (with ignition of clothing)

EXCLUDES *ignition of highly inflammable material with:*
- *conflagration (E890.0-E892)*
- *explosion (E923.0-E923.9)*

E895 Accident caused by controlled fire in private dwelling

Burning by (flame of) normal fire (charcoal) (coal) (electric) (gas) (wood) in:
- brazier
- fireplace
- furnace
- stove

} in private dwelling (as listed in E890)

EXCLUDES *burning by hot objects not producing fire or flames (E924.0-E924.9)*
ignition of clothing from these sources (E893.0)
poisoning by carbon monoxide from incomplete combustion of fuel (E867-E868.9)
that with conflagration (E890.0-E890.9)

E896 Accident caused by controlled fire in other and unspecified building or structure

Burning by (flame of) normal fire (charcoal) (coal)(electric)(gas)(wood) in:
- brazier
- fireplace
- furnace
- stove

} in other building or structure (as listed in E891)

EXCLUDES *burning by hot objects not producing fire or flames (E924.0-E924.9)*
ignition of clothing from these sources (E893.1)
poisoning by carbon monoxide from incomplete combustion of fuel (E867-E868.9)
that with conflagration (E891.0-E891.9)

E897 Accident caused by controlled fire not in building or structure

Burns from flame of:
- bonfire } controlled
- brazier fire, not in building or structure } controlled
- trash fire } controlled

EXCLUDES *ignition of clothing from these sources (E893.2)*
trash fire out of control (E892)
that with conflagration (E892)

4th **E898 Accident caused by other specified fire and flames**

EXCLUDES *conflagration (E890.0-E892)*
that with ignition of:
clothing (E893.0-E893.9)
highly inflammable material (E894)

E898.0 Burning bedclothes

Bed set on fire NOS

E898.1 Other

Burning by:
- blowlamp
- blowtorch
- candle
- cigar
- cigarette
- fire in room NOS

Burning by:
- lamp
- lighter
- matches
- pipe
- welding torch

E899 Accident caused by unspecified fire

Burning NOS

ACCIDENTS DUE TO NATURAL AND ENVIRONMENTAL FACTORS (E900-E909)

4th **E900 Excessive heat**

E900.0 Due to weather conditions

Excessive heat as the external cause of:
- ictus solaris
- siriasis
- sunstroke

E900.1 Of man-made origin

Heat (in):
- boiler room
- drying room
- factory
- furnace room

Heat (in):
- generated in transport vehicle
- kitchen

E900.9 Of unspecified origin

4th **E901 Excessive cold**

E901.0 Due to weather conditions

Excessive cold as the cause of:
- chilblains NOS
- immersion foot

E901.1 Of man-made origin

Contact with or inhalation of:
- dry ice
- liquid air
- liquid hydrogen
- liquid nitrogen

Prolonged exposure in:
- deep freeze unit
- refrigerator

E901.8 Other specified origin

E901.9 Of unspecified origin

4th **E902 High and low air pressure and changes in air pressure**

E902.0 Residence or prolonged visit at high altitude

Residence or prolonged visit at high altitude as the cause of:
- Acosta syndrome
- Alpine sickness
- altitude sickness
- Andes disease
- anoxia, hypoxia
- barotitis, barodontalgia, barosinusitis, otitic barotrauma
- hypobarism, hypobaropathy
- mountain sickness
- range disease

E902.1 In aircraft

Sudden change in air pressure in aircraft during ascent or descent as the cause of:
- aeroneurosis
- aviators' disease

E902.2 Due to diving

High air pressure from rapid descent in water } as the cause of:
Reduction in atmospheric pressure while surfacing from deep water diving } as the cause of:
- caisson disease
- divers' disease
- divers' palsy or paralysis

E902.8 Due to other specified causes

Reduction in atmospheric pressure whilesurfacing from underground

E902.9 Unspecified cause

E903 Travel and motion

4th **E904 Hunger, thirst, exposure, and neglect**

EXCLUDES *any condition resulting from homicidal intent (E968.0-E968.9)*
hunger, thirst, and exposure resulting from accidents connected with transport (E800.0-E848)

E904.0 Abandonment or neglect of infants and helpless persons

Exposure to weather conditions } resulting from abandonment or neglect
Hunger or thirst } resulting from abandonment or neglect

Desertion of newborn
Inattention at or after birth
Lack of care (helpless person) (infant)

EXCLUDES *criminal [purposeful] neglect (E968.4)*

E904.1 Lack of food

Lack of food as the cause of:
- inanition
- insufficient nourishment
- starvation

EXCLUDES *hunger resulting from abandonment or neglect (E904.0)*

E904.2 Lack of water

Lack of water as the cause of:
- dehydration
- inanition

EXCLUDES *dehydration due to acute fluid loss (276.51)*

E904.3 Exposure (to weather conditions), not elsewhere classifiable

Exposure NOS
Humidity
Struck by hailstones

EXCLUDES *struck by lightning (E907)*

E904.9 Privation, unqualified

Destitution

4th **E905 Venomous animals and plants as the cause of poisoning and toxic reactions**

INCLUDES chemical released by animal
insects
release of venom through fangs, hairs, spines, tentacles, and other venom apparatus

EXCLUDES *eating of poisonous animals or plants (E865.0-E865.9)*

E905.0 Venomous snakes and lizards

- Cobra
- Copperhead snake
- Coral snake
- Fer de lance
- Gila monster
- Krait
- Mamba
- Rattlesnake
- Sea snake
- Snake (venomous)
- Viper
- Water moccasin

EXCLUDES *bites of snakes and lizards known to be nonvenomous (E906.2)*

E905.1 Venomous spiders
Black widow spider
Brown spider
Tarantula (venomous)

E905.2 Scorpion

E905.3 Hornets, wasps, and bees
Yellow jacket

E905.4 Centipede and venomous millipede (tropical)

E905.5 Other venomous arthropods
Sting of:
ant
caterpillar

E905.6 Venomous marine animals and plants
Puncture by sea urchin spine
Sting of:
coral
jelly fish
nematocysts
sea anemone
sea cucumber
other marine animal or plant

EXCLUDES *bites and other injuries caused by nonvenomous marine animal (E906.2-E906.8)*
bite of sea snake (venomous) (E905.0)

E905.7 Poisoning and toxic reactions caused by other plants
Injection of poisons or toxins into or through skin by plant thorns, spines, or other mechanisms

EXCLUDES *puncture wound NOS by plant thorns or spines (E920.8)*

E905.8 Other specified

E905.9 Unspecified
Sting NOS
Venomous bite NOS

✓4th **E906 Other injury caused by animals**

EXCLUDES *poisoning and toxic reactions caused by venomous animals and insects (E905.0-E905.9)*
road vehicle accident involving animals (E827.0-E828.9)
tripping or falling over an animal (E885.9)

E906.0 Dog bite

E906.1 Rat bite

E906.2 Bite of nonvenomous snakes and lizards

E906.3 Bite of other animal except arthropod

Cats	Rodents, except rats
Moray eel	Shark

E906.4 Bite of nonvenomous arthropod
Insect bite NOS

E906.5 Bite by unspecified animal
Animal bite NOS

E906.8 Other specified injury caused by animal
Butted by animal
Fallen on by horse or other animal, not being ridden
Gored by animal
Implantation of quills of porcupine
Pecked by bird
Run over by animal, not being ridden
Stepped on by animal, not being ridden

EXCLUDES *injury by animal being ridden (E828.0-E828.9)*

E906.9 Unspecified injury caused by animal

E907 Lightning

EXCLUDES *injury from:*
fall of tree or other object caused by lightning (E916)
fire caused by lightning (E890.0-E892)

✓4th **E908 Cataclysmic storms, and floods resulting from storms**

EXCLUDES *collapse of dam or man-made structure causing flood (E909.3)*

E908.0 Hurricane
Storm surge
"Tidal wave" caused by storm action
Typhoon

E908.1 Tornado
Cyclone
Twisters

E908.2 Floods
Torrential rainfall
Flash flood

EXCLUDES *collapse of dam or man-made structure causing flood (E909.3)*

E908.3 Blizzard (snow)(ice)

E908.4 Dust storm

E908.8 Other cataclysmic storms
Cloudburst

E908.9 Unspecified cataclysmic storms, and floods resulting from storms
Storm NOS

✓4th **E909 Cataclysmic earth surface movements and eruptions**

E909.0 Earthquakes

E909.1 Volcanic eruptions
Burns from lava
Ash inhalation

E909.2 Avalanche, landslide, or mudslide

E909.3 Collapse of dam or man-made structure

E909.4 Tidalwave caused by earthquake
Tidalwave NOS
Tsunami

EXCLUDES *tidalwave caused by tropical storm (E908.0)*

E909.8 Other cataclysmic earth surface movements and eruptions

E909.9 Unspecified cataclysmic earth surface movements and eruptions

ACCIDENTS CAUSED BY SUBMERSION, SUFFOCATION, AND FOREIGN BODIES (E910-E915)

✓4th **E910 Accidental drowning and submersion**

INCLUDES immersion
swimmers' cramp

EXCLUDES *diving accident (NOS) (resulting in injury except drowning) (E883.0)*
diving with insufficient air supply (E913.2)
drowning and submersion due to:
cataclysm (E908-E909)
machinery accident (E919.0-E919.9)
transport accident (E800.0-E845.9)
effect of high and low air pressure (E902.2)
injury from striking against objects while in running water (E917.2)

E910.0 While water-skiing
Fall from water skis with submersion or drowning

EXCLUDES *accident to water-skier involving a watercraft and resulting in submersion or other injury (E830.4, E831.4)*

E910.1 While engaged in other sport or recreational activity with diving equipment
Scuba diving NOS
Skin diving NOS
Underwater spear fishing NOS

E910.2 While engaged in other sport or recreational activity without diving equipment

Fishing or hunting, except from boat or with diving equipment
Ice skating
Playing in water
Surfboarding
Swimming NOS
Voluntarily jumping from boat, not involved in accident, for swim NOS
Wading in water

EXCLUDES *jumping into water to rescue another person (E910.3)*

E910.3 While swimming or diving for purposes other than recreation or sport

Marine salvage, Pearl diving, Placement of fishing nets, Rescue (attempt) of another person, Underwater construction or repairs } (with diving equipment)

E910.4 In bathtub

E910.8 Other accidental drowning or submersion

Drowning in:
quenching tank
swimming pool

E910.9 Unspecified accidental drowning or submersion

Accidental fall into water NOS
Drowning NOS

E911 Inhalation and ingestion of food causing obstruction of respiratory tract or suffocation

Aspiration and inhalation of food [any] (into respiratory tract) NOS
Asphyxia by, Choked on, Suffocation by } food [including bone, seed in food, regurgitated food]
Compression of trachea, Interruption of respiration, Obstruction of respiration } by food lodged in esophagus
Obstruction of pharynx by food (bolus)

EXCLUDES *injury, except asphyxia and obstruction of respiratory passage, caused by food (E915)*
obstruction of esophagus by food without mention of asphyxia or obstruction of respiratory passage (E915)

E912 Inhalation and ingestion of other object causing obstruction of respiratory tract or suffocation

Aspiration and inhalation of foreign body except food (into respiratory tract) NOS
Foreign object [bean] [marble] in nose
Obstruction of pharynx by foreign body
Compression, Interruption of respiration, Obstruction of respiration } by foreign body in esophagus

EXCLUDES *injury, except asphyxia and obstruction of respiratory passage, caused by foreign body (E915)*
obstruction of esophagus by foreign body without mention of asphyxia or obstruction in respiratory passage (E915)

✓4th **E913 Accidental mechanical suffocation**

EXCLUDES *mechanical suffocation from or by:*
accidental inhalation or ingestion of:
food (E911)
foreign object (E912)
cataclysm (E908-E909)
explosion (E921.0-E921.9, E923.0-E923.9)
machinery accident (E919.0-E919.9)

E913.0 In bed or cradle

EXCLUDES *suffocation by plastic bag (E913.1)*

E913.1 By plastic bag

E913.2 Due to lack of air (in closed place)

Accidentally closed up in refrigerator or other airtight enclosed space
Diving with insufficient air supply

EXCLUDES *suffocation by plastic bag (E913.1)*

E913.3 By falling earth or other substance

Cave-in NOS

EXCLUDES *cave-in caused by cataclysmic earth surface movements and eruptions (E909)*
struck by cave-in without asphyxiation or suffocation (E916)

E913.8 Other specified means

Accidental hanging, except in bed or cradle

E913.9 Unspecified means

Asphyxia, mechanical NOS
Strangulation NOS
Suffocation NOS

E914 Foreign body accidentally entering eye and adnexa

EXCLUDES *corrosive liquid (E924.1)*

E915 Foreign body accidentally entering other orifice

EXCLUDES *aspiration and inhalation of foreign body, any, (into respiratory tract) NOS (E911-E912)*

OTHER ACCIDENTS (E916-E928)

E916 Struck accidentally by falling object

Collapse of building, except on fire
Falling:
rock
snowslide NOS
stone
tree
Object falling from:
machine, not in operation
stationary vehicle
Code first:
collapse of building on fire (E890.0-E891.9)
falling object in:
cataclysm (E908-E909)
machinery accidents (E919.0-E919.9)
transport accidents (E800.0-E845.9)
vehicle accidents not elsewhere classifiable (E846-E848)
object set in motion by:
explosion (E921.0-E921.9, E923.0-E923.9)
firearm (E922.0-E922.9)
projected object (E917.0-E917.9)

✓4th **E917 Striking against or struck accidentally by objects or persons**

INCLUDES bumping into or against, colliding with, kicking against, stepping on, struck by } object (moving) (projected) (stationary), pedestrian conveyance, person

EXCLUDES *fall from:*
collision with another person, except when caused by a crowd (E886.0-E886.9)
stumbling over object (E885.9)
fall resulting in striking against object (E888.0, E888.1)
injury caused by:
assault (E960.0-E960.1, E967.0-E967.9)
cutting or piercing instrument (E920.0-E920.9)
explosion (E921.0-E921.9, E923.0-E923.9)
firearm (E922.0-E922.9)
machinery (E919.0-E919.9)
transport vehicle (E800.0-E845.9)
vehicle not elsewhere classifiable (E846-E848)

E917.0 In sports without subsequent fall
Kicked or stepped on during game (football) (rugby)
Struck by hit or thrown ball
Struck by hockey stick or puck

E917.1 Caused by a crowd, by collective fear or panic without subsequent fall
Crushed, Pushed, Stepped on } by crowd or human stampede

E917.2 In running water without subsequent fall
EXCLUDES *drowning or submersion (E910.0-E910.9)*
that in sports (E917.0, E917.5)

E917.3 Furniture without subsequent fall
EXCLUDES *fall from furniture (E884.2, E884.4-E884.5)*

E917.4 Other stationary object without subsequent fall
Bath tub
Fence
Lamp-post

E917.5 Object in sports with subsequent fall
Knocked down while boxing

E917.6 Caused by a crowd, by collective fear or panic with subsequent fall

E917.7 Furniture with subsequent fall
EXCLUDES *fall from furniture (E884.2, E884.4-E884.5)*

E917.8 Other stationary object with subsequent fall
Bath tub
Fence
Lamp-post

E917.9 Other striking against with or without subsequent fall

E918 Caught accidentally in or between objects
Caught, crushed, jammed, or pinched in or between moving or stationary objects, such as:
escalator
folding object
hand tools, appliances, or implements
sliding door and door frame
under packing crate
washing machine wringer

EXCLUDES *injury caused by:*
cutting or piercing instrument (E920.0-E920.9)
machinery (E919.0-E919.9)
transport vehicle (E800.0-E845.9)
vehicle not elsewhere classifiable (E846-E848)
struck accidentally by:
falling object (E916)
object (moving) (projected) (E917.0 E917.9)

4th **E919 Accidents caused by machinery**
INCLUDES burned by, caught in (moving parts of), collapse of, crushed by, cut or pierced by, drowning or submersion caused by, expolosion of, on, in, fall from or into moving part of, fire starting in or on, mechanical suffocation caused by, object falling from, on, in motion by, overturning of, pinned under, run over by, struck by, thrown from } machinery (accident)
caught between machinery and other object
machinery accident NOS

EXCLUDES *accidents involving machinery, not in operation (E884.9, E916-E918)*
injury caused by:
electric current in connection with machinery (E925.0-E925.9)
escalator (E880.0, E918)
explosion of pressure vessel in connection with machinery (E921.0-E921.9)
moving sidewalk (E885.9)
powered hand tools, appliances, and implements (E916-E918, E920.0-E921.9, E923.0-E926.9)
transport vehicle accidents involving machinery (E800.0-E848)
poisoning by carbon monoxide generated by machine (E868.8)

E919.0 Agricultural machines
Animal-powered agricultural machine
Combine
Derrick, hay
Farm machinery NOS
Farm tractor
Harvester
Hay mower or rake
Reaper
Thresher

EXCLUDES *that in transport under own power on the highway (E810.0-E819.9)*
that being towed by another vehicle on the highway (E810.0-E819.9, E827.0-E827.9, E829.0-E829.9)
that involved in accident classifiable to E820-E829 (E820.0-E829.9)

E919.1 Mining and earth-drilling machinery
Bore or drill (land) (seabed)
Shaft hoist
Shaft lift
Under-cutter
EXCLUDES *coal car, tram, truck, and tub in mine (E846)*

E919.2 Lifting machines and appliances
Chain hoist, Crane, Derrick, Elevator (building) (grain), Forklift truck, Lift, Pulley block, Winch } except in agricultural or mining operations

EXCLUDES *that being towed by another vehicle on the highway (E810.0-E819.9, E827.0-E827.9, E829.0-829.9)*
that in transport under own power on the highway (E810.0-E819.9)
that involved in accident classifiable to E820-E829 (E820.0-E829.9)

E919.3 Metalworking machines

Abrasive wheel
Forging machine
Lathe
Mechanical shears
Metal:
drilling machine
milling machine
power press
rolling-mill
sawing machine

E919.4 Woodworking and forming machines

Band saw
Bench saw
Circular saw
Molding machine
Overhead plane
Powered saw
Radial saw
Sander

EXCLUDES *hand saw (E920.1)*

E919.5 Prime movers, except electrical motors

Gas turbine
Internal combustion engine
Steam engine
Water driven turbine

EXCLUDES *that being towed by other vehicle on the highway (E810.0-E819.9, E827.0-E827.9, E829.0-E829.9)*
that in transport under own power on the highway (E810.0-E819.9)

E919.6 Transmission machinery

Transmission:
belt
cable
chain
gear
pinion
pulley
shaft

E919.7 Earth moving, scraping, and other excavating machines

Bulldozer
Road scraper
Steam shovel

EXCLUDES *that being towed by other vehicle on the highway (E810.0-E819.9, E827.0-E827.9, E829.0-E829.9)*
that in transport under own power on the highway (E810.0-E819.9)

E919.8 Other specified machinery

Machines for manufacture of:
clothing
foodstuffs and beverages
paper
Printing machine
Recreational machinery
Spinning, weaving, and textile machines

E919.9 Unspecified machinery

E920 Accidents caused by cutting and piercing instruments or objects (4th)

INCLUDES accidental injury (by) object } edged, pointed, sharp

E920.0 Powered lawn mower

E920.1 Other powered hand tools

Any powered hand tool [compressed air] [electric] [explosive cartridge] [hydraulic power], such as:
drill
hand saw
hedge clipper
rivet gun
snow blower
staple gun

EXCLUDES *band saw (E919.4)*
bench saw (E919.4)

E920.2 Powered household appliances and implements

Blender
Electric:
beater or mixer
can opener
fan
knife
sewing machine
Garbage disposal appliance

E920.3 Knives, swords, and daggers

E920.4 Other hand tools and implements

Axe
Can opener NOS
Chisel
Fork
Hand saw
Hoe
Ice pick
Needle (sewing)
Paper cutter
Pitchfork
Rake
Scissors
Screwdriver
Sewing machine, not powered
Shovel

E920.5 Hypodermic needle

Contaminated needle
Needle stick

E920.8 Other specified cutting and piercing instruments or objects

Arrow
Broken glass
Dart
Edge of stiff paper
Lathe turnings
Nail
Plant thorn
Splinter
Tin can lid

EXCLUDES *animal spines or quills (E906.8)*
flying glass due to explosion (E921.0-E923.9)

E920.9 Unspecified cutting and piercing instrument or object

E921 Accident caused by explosion of pressure vessel (4th)

INCLUDES accidental explosion of pressure vessels, whether or not part of machinery

EXCLUDES *explosion of pressure vessel on transport vehicle (E800.0-E845.9)*

E921.0 Boilers

E921.1 Gas cylinders

Air tank
Pressure gas tank

E921.8 Other specified pressure vessels

Aerosol can
Automobile tire
Tin can lid

E921.9 Unspecified pressure vessel

E922 Accident caused by firearm, and air gun missile (4th)

E922.0 Handgun

Pistol
Revolver

EXCLUDES *Verey pistol (E922.8)*

E922.1 Shotgun (automatic)

E922.2 Hunting rifle

E922.3 Military firearms

Army rifle
Machine gun

E922.4 Air gun

BB gun
Pellet gun

E922.5 Paintball gun

E922.8 Other specified firearm missile

Verey pistol [flare]

E922.9 Unspecified firearm missile

Gunshot wound NOS
Shot NOS

E923 Accident caused by explosive material (4th)

INCLUDES flash burns and other injuries resulting from explosion of explosive material
ignition of highly explosive material with explosion

EXCLUDES *explosion:*
in or on machinery (E919.0-E919.9)
on any transport vehicle, except stationary motor vehicle (E800.0-E848)
with conflagration (E890.0, E891.0,E892)
secondary fires resulting from explosion (E890.0-E899)

E923.0 Fireworks

E923.1 Blasting materials

Blasting cap
Detonator
Dynamite
Explosive [any] used in blasting operations

E923.2 Explosive gases

Acetylene
Butane
Coal gas
Explosion in mine NOS
Fire damp
Gasoline fumes
Methane
Propane

E923.8 Other explosive materials

Bomb
Explosive missile
Grenade
Mine
Shell
Torpedo
Explosion in munitions:
dump
factory

E923.9 Unspecified explosive material

Explosion NOS

✓4th E924 Accident caused by hot substance or object, caustic or corrosive material, and steam

EXCLUDES *burning NOS (E899)*
chemical burn resulting from swallowing a corrosive substance (E860.0-E864.4)
fire caused by these substances and objects (E890.0-E894)
radiation burns (E926.0-E926.9)
therapeutic misadventures (E870.0-E876.9)

E924.0 Hot liquids and vapors, including steam

Burning or scalding by:
boiling water
hot or boiling liquids not primarily caustic or corrosive
liquid metal
steam
other hot vapor

EXCLUDES *hot (boiling) tap water (E924.2)*

E924.1 Caustic and corrosive substances

Burning by:
acid [any kind]
ammonia
caustic oven cleaner or other substance
corrosive substance
lye
vitriol

E924.2 Hot (boiling) tap water

E924.8 Other

Burning by:
heat from electric heating appliance
hot object NOS
light bulb
steam pipe

E924.9 Unspecified

✓4th E925 Accident caused by electric current

INCLUDES electric current from exposed wire, faulty appliance, high voltage cable, live rail, or open electric socket as the cause of:
burn
cardiac fibrillation
convulsion
electric shock
electrocution
puncture wound
respiratory paralysis

EXCLUDES *burn by heat from electrical appliance (E924.8)*
lightning (E907)

E925.0 Domestic wiring and appliances

E925.1 Electric power generating plants, distribution stations, transmission lines

Broken power line

E925.2 Industrial wiring, appliances, and electrical machinery

Conductors
Control apparatus
Electrical equipment and machinery
Transformers

E925.8 Other electric current

Wiring and appliances in or on:
farm [not farmhouse]
outdoors
public building
residential institutions
schools

E925.9 Unspecified electric current

Burns or other injury from electric current NOS
Electric shock NOS
Electrocution NOS

✓4th E926 Exposure to radiation

EXCLUDES *abnormal reaction to or complication of treatment without mention of misadventure (E879.2)*
atomic power plant malfunction in water transport (E838.0-E838.9)
misadventure to patient in surgical and medical procedures (E873.2-E873.3)
use of radiation in war operations (E996-E997.9)

E926.0 Radiofrequency radiation

Overexposure to:	from:
microwave radiation radar radiation radiofrequency radiofrequency radiation [any]	high-powered radio and television transmitters industrial radiofrequency induction heaters radar installations

E926.1 Infrared heaters and lamps

Exposure to infrared radiation from heaters and lamps as the cause of:
blistering
burning
charring
inflammatory change

EXCLUDES *physical contact with heater or lamp (E924.8)*

E926.2 Visible and ultraviolet light sources

Arc lamps
Black light sources
Electrical welding arc
Oxygas welding torch
Sun rays
Tanning bed

EXCLUDES *excessive heat from these sources (E900.1-E900.9)*

E926.3 X-rays and other electromagnetic ionizing radiation

Gamma rays
X-rays (hard) (soft)

E926.4 Lasers

E926.5 Radioactive isotopes

Radiobiologicals
Radiopharmaceuticals

E926.8 Other specified radiation

Artificially accelerated beams of ionized particles generated by:
betatrons
synchrotrons

E926.9 Unspecified radiation

Radiation NOS

▲ **✓4th E927 Overexertion and strenuous and repetitive movements or loads**

● **E927.0 Overexertion from sudden strenuous movement**

Sudden trauma from strenuous movement

● **E927.1 Overexertion from prolonged static position**
Overexertion from maintaining prolonged positions, such as:
holding
sitting
standing

● **E927.2 Excessive physical exertion from prolonged activity**

● **E927.3 Cumulative trauma from repetitive motion**
Cumulative trauma from repetitive movements

● **E927.4 Cumulative trauma from repetitive impact**

● **E927.8 Other overexertion and strenuous and repetitive movements or loads**

● **E927.9 Unspecified overexertion and strenuous and repetitive movements or loads**

✓4th **E928 Other and unspecified environmental and accidental causes**

E928.0 Prolonged stay in weightless environment
Weightlessness in spacecraft (simulator)

E928.1 Exposure to noise
Noise (pollution)
Sound waves
Supersonic waves

E928.2 Vibration

E928.3 Human bite

E928.4 External constriction caused by hair

E928.5 External constriction caused by other object

E928.6 Environmental exposure to harmful algae and toxins

Algae bloom NOS	Florida red tide
Blue-green algae bloom	Harmful algae bloom
Brown tide	Pfiesteria piscicida
Cyanobacteria bloom	Red tide

E928.8 Other

E928.9 Unspecified accident

Accident NOS Blow NOS Casualty (not due to war) Decapitation	stated as accidentally inflicted
Knocked down Killed Injury [any part of body, or unspecified] Mangled Wound	stated as accidentally inflicted, but not otherwise specified

EXCLUDES *fracture, cause unspecified (E887)*
injuries undetermined whether accidentally or purposely inflicted (E980.0-E989)

LATE EFFECTS OF ACCIDENTAL INJURY (E929)

Note: This category is to be used to indicate accidental injury as the cause of death or disability from late effects, which are themselves classifiable elsewhere. The "late effects" include conditions reported as such, or as sequelae which may occur at any time after the attempted suicide or self-inflicted injury.

✓4th **E929 Late effects of accidental injury**

EXCLUDES *late effects of:*
surgical and medical procedures (E870.0-E879.9)
therapeutic use of drugs and medicines (E930.0-E949.9)

E929.0 Late effects of motor vehicle accident
Late effects of accidents classifiable to E810-E825

E929.1 Late effects of other transport accident
Late effects of accidents classifiable to E800-E807, E826-E838, E840-E848

E929.2 Late effects of accidental poisoning
Late effects of accidents classifiable to E850-E858, E860-E869

E929.3 Late effects of accidental fall
Late effects of accidents classifiable to E880-E888

E929.4 Late effects of accident caused by fire
Late effects of accidents classifiable to E890-E899

E929.5 Late effects of accident due to natural and environmental factors
Late effects of accidents classifiable to E900-E909

E929.8 Late effects of other accidents
Late effects of accidents classifiable to E910-E928.8

E929.9 Late effects of unspecified accident
Late effects of accidents classifiable to E928.9

DRUGS, MEDICINAL AND BIOLOGICAL SUBSTANCES CAUSING ADVERSE EFFECTS IN THERAPEUTIC USE (E930-E949)

INCLUDES correct drug properly administered in therapeutic or prophylactic dosage, as the cause of any adverse effect including allergic or hypersensitivity reactions

EXCLUDES *accidental overdose of drug and wrong drug given or taken in error (E850.0-E858.9)*
accidents in the technique of administration of drug or biological substance, such as accidental puncture during injection, or contamination of drug (E870.0-E876.9)
administration with suicidal or homicidal intent or intent to harm, or in circumstances classifiable to E980-E989 (E950.0-E950.5, E962.0, E980.0-E980.5)

See Alphabetic Index for more complete list of specific drugs to be classified under the fourth-digit subdivisions. The American Hospital Formulary numbers can be used to classify new drugs listed by the American Hospital Formulary Service (AHFS). See Appendix C.

✓4th **E930 Antibiotics**

EXCLUDES *that used as eye, ear, nose, and throat [ENT], and local anti-infectives (E946.0-E946.9)*

E930.0 Penicillins

Natural Synthetic Semisynthetic, such as: ampicillin	Semisynthetic, such as: cloxacillin nafcillin oxacillin

E930.1 Antifungal antibiotics

Amphotericin B	Hachimycin [trichomycin]
Griseofulvin	Nystatin

E930.2 Chloramphenicol group

Chloramphenicol	Thiamphenicol

E930.3 Erythromycin and other macrolides

Oleandomycin	Spiramycin

E930.4 Tetracycline group

Doxycycline	Oxytetracycline
Minocycline	

E930.5 Cephalosporin group

Cephalexin	Cephaloridine
Cephaloglycin	Cephalothin

E930.6 Antimycobacterial antibiotics

Cycloserine	Rifampin
Kanamycin	Streptomycin

E930.7 Antineoplastic antibiotics
Actinomycins, such as:
Bleomycin
Cactinomycin
Dactinomycin
Daunorubicin
Mitomycin

EXCLUDES *other antineoplastic drugs (E933.1)*

E930.8 Other specified antibiotics

E930.9 Unspecified antibiotic

E931 Other anti-infectives

EXCLUDES *ENT, and local anti-infectives (E946.0-E946.9)*

E931.0 Sulfonamides
Sulfadiazine
Sulfafurazole
Sulfamethoxazole

E931.1 Arsenical anti-infectives

E931.2 Heavy metal anti-infectives
Compounds of:
antimony
bismuth
lead
mercury

EXCLUDES *mercurial diuretics (E944.0)*

E931.3 Quinoline and hydroxyquinoline derivatives
Chiniofon
Diiodohydroxyquin

EXCLUDES *antimalarial drugs (E931.4)*

E931.4 Antimalarials and drugs acting on other blood protozoa
Chloroquine phosphate
Cycloguanil
Primaquine
Proguanil [chloroguanide]
Pyrimethamine
Quinine (sulphate)

E931.5 Other antiprotozoal drugs
Emetine

E931.6 Anthelmintics
Hexylresorcinol
Male fern oleoresin
Piperazine
Thiabendazole

E931.7 Antiviral drugs
Methisazone

EXCLUDES *amantadine (E936.4)*
cytarabine (E933.1)
idoxuridine (E946.5)

E931.8 Other antimycobacterial drugs
Ethambutol
Ethionamide
Isoniazid
Para-aminosalicylic acid derivatives
Sulfones

E931.9 Other and unspecified anti-infectives
Flucytosine
Nitrofuranderivatives

E932 Hormones and synthetic substitutes

E932.0 Adrenal cortical steroids
Cortisone derivatives
Desoxycorticosterone derivatives
Fluorinated corticosteroid

E932.1 Androgens and anabolic congeners
Nandrolone phenpropionate
Oxymetholone
Testosterone and preparations

E932.2 Ovarian hormones and synthetic substitutes
Contraceptives, oral
Estrogens
Estrogens and progestogens combined
Progestogens

E932.3 Insulins and antidiabetic agents
Acetohexamide
Biguanide derivatives, oral
Chlorpropamide
Glucagon
Insulin
Phenformin
Sulfonylurea derivatives, oral
Tolbutamide

EXCLUDES *adverse effect of insulin administered for shock therapy (E879.3)*

E932.4 Anterior pituitary hormones
Corticotropin
Gonadotropin
Somatotropin [growth hormone]

E932.5 Posterior pituitary hormones
Vasopressin

EXCLUDES *oxytocic agents (E945.0)*

E932.6 Parathyroid and parathyroid derivatives

E932.7 Thyroid and thyroid derivatives
Dextrothyroxine
Levothyroxine sodium
Liothyronine
Thyroglobulin

E932.8 Antithyroid agents
Iodides
Thiouracil
Thiourea

E932.9 Other and unspecified hormones and synthetic substitutes

E933 Primarily systemic agents

E933.0 Antiallergic and antiemetic drugs
Antihistamines
Chlorpheniramine
Diphenhydramine
Diphenylpyraline
Thonzylamine
Tripelennamine

EXCLUDES *phenothiazine-based tranquilizers (E939.1)*

E933.1 Antineoplastic and immunosuppressive drugs
Azathioprine
Busulfan
Chlorambucil
Cyclophosphamide
Cytarabine
Fluorouracil
Mechlorethamine hydrochloride
Mercaptopurine
Triethylenethiophosphoramide [thio-TEPA]

EXCLUDES *antineoplastic antibiotics (E930.7)*

E933.2 Acidifying agents

E933.3 Alkalizing agents

E933.4 Enzymes, not elsewhere classified
Penicillinase

E933.5 Vitamins, not elsewhere classified
Vitamin A
Vitamin D

EXCLUDES *nicotinic acid (E942.2)*
vitamin K (E934.3)

E933.6 Oral bisphosphonates

E933.7 Intravenous bisphosphonates

E933.8 Other systemic agents, not elsewhere classified
Heavy metal antagonists

E933.9 Unspecified systemic agent

E934 Agents primarily affecting blood constituents

E934.0 Iron and its compounds
Ferric salts
Ferrous sulphate and other ferrous salts

E934.1 Liver preparations and other antianemic agents
Folic acid

E934.2 Anticoagulants
Coumarin
Heparin
Phenindione
Prothrombin synthesis inhibitor
Warfarin sodium

E934.3 Vitamin K [phytonadione]

E934.4 Fibrinolysis-affecting drugs
Aminocaproic acid
Streptodornase
Streptokinase
Urokinase

E934.5 Anticoagulant antagonists and other coagulants
Hexadimethrine bromide
Protamine sulfate

E934.6 Gamma globulin

E934.7 Natural blood and blood products
Blood plasma
Human fibrinogen
Packed red cells
Whole blood

E934.8 Other agents affecting blood constituents
Macromolecular blood substitutes

E934.9 Unspecified agent affecting blood constituents

4th E935 Analgesics, antipyretics, and antirheumatics

E935.0 Heroin
Diacetylmorphine

E935.1 Methadone

E935.2 Other opiates and related narcotics
Codeine [methylmorphine]
Meperidine [pethidine]
Morphine
Opium (alkaloids)

E935.3 Salicylates
Acetylsalicylic acid [aspirin]
Amino derivatives of salicylic acid
Salicylic acid salts

E935.4 Aromatic analgesics, not elsewhere classified
Acetanilid
Paracetamol [acetaminophen]
Phenacetin [acetophenetidin]

E935.5 Pyrazole derivatives
Aminophenazone [aminopyrine]
Phenylbutazone

E935.6 Antirheumatics [antiphlogistics]
Gold salts
Indomethacin

EXCLUDES *salicylates (E935.3)*
steroids (E932.0)

E935.7 Other non-narcotic analgesics
Pyrabital

E935.8 Other specified analgesics and antipyretics
Pentazocine

E935.9 Unspecified analgesic and antipyretic

4th E936 Anticonvulsants and anti-Parkinsonism drugs

E936.0 Oxazolidine derivatives
Paramethadione
Trimethadione

E936.1 Hydantoin derivatives
Phenytoin

E936.2 Succinimides
Ethosuximide
Phensuximide

E936.3 Other and unspecified anticonvulsants
Beclamide
Primidone

E936.4 Anti-Parkinsonism drugs
Amantadine
Ethopropazine [profenamine]
Levodopa [L-dopa]

4th E937 Sedatives and hypnotics

E937.0 Barbiturates
Amobarbital [amylobarbitone]
Barbital [barbitone]
Butabarbital [butabarbitone]
Pentobarbital [pentobarbitone]
Phenobarbital [phenobarbitone]
Secobarbital [quinalbarbitone]

EXCLUDES *thiobarbiturates (E938.3)*

E937.1 Chloral hydrate group

E937.2 Paraldehyde

E937.3 Bromine compounds
Bromide
Carbromal (derivatives)

E937.4 Methaqualone compounds

E937.5 Glutethimide group

E937.6 Mixed sedatives, not elsewhere classified

E937.8 Other sedatives and hypnotics

E937.9 Unspecified
Sleeping:
drug } NOS
pill } NOS
tablet } NOS

4th E938 Other central nervous system depressants and anesthetics

E938.0 Central nervous system muscle-tone depressants
Chlorphenesin (carbamate)
Mephenesin
Methocarbamol

E938.1 Halothane

E938.2 Other gaseous anesthetics
Ether
Halogenated hydrocarbon derivatives, except halothane
Nitrous oxide

E938.3 Intravenous anesthetics
Ketamine
Methohexital [methohexitone]
Thiobarbiturates, such as thiopental sodium

E938.4 Other and unspecified general anesthetics

E938.5 Surface and infiltration anesthetics
Cocaine
Lidocaine [lignocaine]
Procaine
Tetracaine

E938.6 Peripheral nerve- and plexus-blocking anesthetics

E938.7 Spinal anesthetics

E938.9 Other and unspecified local anesthetics

4th E939 Psychotropic agents

E939.0 Antidepressants
Amitriptyline
Imipramine
Monoamine oxidase [MAO] inhibitors

E939.1 Phenothiazine-based tranquilizers
Chlorpromazine
Fluphenazine
Phenothiazine
Prochlorperazine
Promazine

E939.2 Butyrophenone-based tranquilizers
Haloperidol
Spiperone
Trifluperidol

E939.3 Other antipsychotics, neuroleptics, and major tranquilizers

E939.4 Benzodiazepine-based tranquilizers
Chlordiazepoxide
Diazepam
Flurazepam
Lorazepam
Medazepam
Nitrazepam

E939.5 Other tranquilizers
Hydroxyzine
Meprobamate

E939.6 Psychodysleptics [hallucinogens]
Cannabis (derivatives)
Lysergide [LSD]
Marihuana (derivatives)
Mescaline
Psilocin
Psilocybin

4th Fourth-digit Required ▶◀ Revised Text ● New Code ▲ Revised Code TitleDx

E939.7 Psychostimulants
Amphetamine
Caffeine
EXCLUDES *central appetite depressants (E947.0)*

E939.8 Other psychotropic agents

E939.9 Unspecified psychotropic agent

E940 Central nervous system stimulants

E940.0 Analeptics
Lobeline
Nikethamide

E940.1 Opiate antagonists
Levallorphan
Nalorphine
Naloxone

E940.8 Other specified central nervous system stimulants

E940.9 Unspecified central nervous system stimulant

E941 Drugs primarily affecting the autonomic nervous system

E941.0 Parasympathomimetics [cholinergics]
Acetylcholine
Anticholinesterase:
organophosphorus
reversible
Pilocarpine

E941.1 Parasympatholytics [anticholinergics and antimuscarinics] and spasmolytics
Atropine
Homatropine
Hyoscine [scopolamine]
Quaternary ammonium derivatives
EXCLUDES *papaverine (E942.5)*

E941.2 Sympathomimetics [adrenergics]
Epinephrine [adrenalin]
Levarterenol [noradrenalin]

E941.3 Sympatholytics [antiadrenergics]
Phenoxybenzamine
Tolazolinehydrochloride

E941.9 Unspecified drug primarily affecting the autonomic nervous system

E942 Agents primarily affecting the cardiovascular system

E942.0 Cardiac rhythm regulators
Practolol
Procainamide
Propranolol
Quinidine

E942.1 Cardiotonic glycosides and drugs of similar action
Digitalis glycosides
Digoxin
Strophanthins

E942.2 Antilipemic and antiarteriosclerotic drugs
Cholestyramine
Clofibrate
Nicotinic acid derivatives
Sitosterols
EXCLUDES *dextrothyroxine (E932.7)*

E942.3 Ganglion-blocking agents
Pentamethonium bromide

E942.4 Coronary vasodilators
Dipyridamole
Nitrates [nitroglycerin]
Nitrites
Prenylamine

E942.5 Other vasodilators
Cyclandelate
Diazoxide
Hydralazine
Papaverine

E942.6 Other antihypertensive agents
Clonidine
Guanethidine
Rauwolfia alkaloids
Reserpine

E942.7 Antivaricose drugs, including sclerosing agents
Monoethanolamine
Zinc salts

E942.8 Capillary-active drugs
Adrenochrome derivatives
Bioflavonoids
Metaraminol

E942.9 Other and unspecified agents primarily affecting the cardiovascular system

E943 Agents primarily affecting gastrointestinal system

E943.0 Antacids and antigastric secretion drugs
Aluminum hydroxide
Magnesium trisilicate

E943.1 Irritant cathartics
Bisacodyl
Castor oil
Phenolphthalein

E943.2 Emollient cathartics
Sodium dioctyl sulfosuccinate

E943.3 Other cathartics, including intestinal atonia drugs
Magnesium sulfate

E943.4 Digestants
Pancreatin
Papain
Pepsin

E943.5 Antidiarrheal drugs
Bismuth subcarbonate Pectin or Kaolin
EXCLUDES *anti-infectives (E930.0-E931.9)*

E943.6 Emetics

E943.8 Other specified agents primarily affecting the gastrointestinal system

E943.9 Unspecified agent primarily affecting the gastrointestinal system

E944 Water, mineral, and uric acid metabolism drugs

E944.0 Mercurial diuretics
Chlormerodrin
Mercaptomerin
Mercurophylline
Mersalyl

E944.1 Purine derivative diuretics
Theobromine
Theophylline
EXCLUDES *aminophylline [theophylline ethylenediamine] (E945.7)*

E944.2 Carbonic acid anhydrase inhibitors
Acetazolamide

E944.3 Saluretics
Benzothiadiazides
Chlorothiazide group

E944.4 Other diuretics
Ethacrynic acid
Furosemide

E944.5 Electrolytic, caloric, and water-balance agents

E944.6 Other mineral salts, not elsewhere classified

E944.7 Uric acid metabolism drugs
Cinchophen and congeners
Colchicine
Phenoquin
Probenecid

E945 Agents primarily acting on the smooth and skeletal muscles and respiratory system

E945.0 Oxytocic agents
Ergot alkaloids
Prostaglandins

E945.1 Smooth muscle relaxants
Adiphenine
Metaproterenol [orciprenaline]
EXCLUDES *papaverine (E942.5)*

E945.2 Skeletal muscle relaxants
Alcuronium chloride
Suxamethonium chloride

E945.3 Other and unspecified drugs acting on muscles

E945.4 Antitussives
Dextromethorphan
Pipazethate hydrochloride

E945.5 Expectorants
Acetylcysteine
Cocillana
Guaifenesin [glyceryl guaiacolate]
Ipecacuanha
Terpin hydrate

E945.6 Anti-common cold drugs

E945.7 Antiasthmatics
Aminophylline [theophylline ethylenediamine]

E945.8 Other and unspecified respiratory drugs

4th E946 Agents primarily affecting skin and mucous membrane, ophthalmological, otorhinolaryngological, and dental drugs

E946.0 Local anti-infectives and anti-inflammatory drugs

E946.1 Antipruritics

E946.2 Local astringents and local detergents

E946.3 Emollients, demulcents, and protectants

E946.4 Keratolytics, kerstoplastics, other hair treatment drugs and preparations

E946.5 Eye anti-infectives and other eye drugs
Idoxuridine

E946.6 Anti-infectives and other drugs and preparations for ear, nose, and throat

E946.7 Dental drugs topically applied

E946.8 Other agents primarily affecting skin and mucous membrane
Spermicides

E946.9 Unspecified agent primarily affecting skin and mucous membrane

4th E947 Other and unspecified drugs and medicinal substances

E947.0 Dietetics

E947.1 Lipotropic drugs

E947.2 Antidotes and chelating agents, not elsewhere classified

E947.3 Alcohol deterrents

E947.4 Pharmaceutical excipients

E947.8 Other drugs and medicinal substances
Contrast media used for diagnostic x-ray procedures
Diagnostic agents and kits

E947.9 Unspecified drug or medicinal substance

4th E948 Bacterial vaccines

E948.0 BCG vaccine

E948.1 Typhoid and paratyphoid

E948.2 Cholera

E948.3 Plague

E948.4 Tetanus

E948.5 Diphtheria

E948.6 Pertussis vaccine, including combinations with a pertussis component

E948.8 Other and unspecified bacterial vaccines

E948.9 Mixed bacterial vaccines, except combinations with a pertussis component

4th E949 Other vaccines and biological substances
EXCLUDES *gamma globulin (E934.6)*

E949.0 Smallpox vaccine

E949.1 Rabies vaccine

E949.2 Typhus vaccine

E949.3 Yellow fever vaccine

E949.4 Measles vaccine

E949.5 Poliomyelitis vaccine

E949.6 Other and unspecified viral and rickettsial vaccines
Mumps vaccine

E949.7 Mixed viral-rickettsial and bacterial vaccines, except combinations with a pertussis component
EXCLUDES *combinations with a pertussis component (E948.6)*

E949.9 Other and unspecified vaccines and biological substances

SUICIDE AND SELF-INFLICTED INJURY (E950-E959)

INCLUDES injuries in suicide and attempted suicide
self-inflicted injuries specified as intentional

4th E950 Suicide and self-inflicted poisoning by solid or liquid substances

E950.0 Analgesics, antipyretics, and antirheumatics

E950.1 Barbiturates

E950.2 Other sedatives and hypnotics

E950.3 Tranquilizers and other psychotropic agents

E950.4 Other specified drugs and medicinal substances

E950.5 Unspecified drug or medicinal substance

E950.6 Agricultural and horticultural chemical and pharmaceutical preparations other than plant foods and fertilizers

E950.7 Corrosive and caustic substances
Suicide and self-inflicted poisoning by substances classifiable to E864

E950.8 Arsenic and its compounds

E950.9 Other and unspecified solid and liquid substances

4th E951 Suicide and self-inflicted poisoning by gases in domestic use

E951.0 Gas distributed by pipeline

E951.1 Liquefied petroleum gas distributed in mobile containers

E951.8 Other utility gas

4th E952 Suicide and self-inflicted poisoning by other gases and vapors

E952.0 Motor vehicle exhaust gas

E952.1 Other carbon monoxide

E952.8 Other specified gases and vapors

E952.9 Unspecified gases and vapors

4th E953 Suicide and self-inflicted injury by hanging, strangulation, and suffocation

E953.0 Hanging

E953.1 Suffocation by plastic bag

E953.8 Other specified means

E953.9 Unspecified means

E954 Suicide and self-inflicted injury by submersion [drowning]

4th E955 Suicide and self-inflicted injury by firearms, air guns and explosives

E955.0 Handgun

E955.1 Shotgun

E955.2 Hunting rifle

E955.3 **Military firearms**

E955.4 **Other and unspecified firearm**
Gunshot NOS
Shot NOS

E955.5 **Explosives**

E955.6 **Air gun**
BB gun
Pellet gun

E955.7 **Paintball gun**

E955.9 **Unspecified**

E956 Suicide and self-inflicted injury by cutting and piercing instrument

4th **E957 Suicide and self-inflicted injuries by jumping from high place**

E957.0 **Residential premises**

E957.1 **Other man-made structures**

E957.2 **Natural sites**

E957.9 **Unspecified**

4th **E958 Suicide and self-inflicted injury by other and unspecified means**

E958.0 **Jumping or lying before moving object**

E958.1 **Burns, fire**

E958.2 **Scald**

E958.3 **Extremes of cold**

E958.4 **Electrocution**

E958.5 **Crashing of motor vehicle**

E958.6 **Crashing of aircraft**

E958.7 **Caustic substances, except poisoning**
EXCLUDES *poisoning by caustic substance (E950.7)*

E958.8 **Other specified means**

E958.9 **Unspecified means**

E959 Late effects of self-inflicted injury
Note:This category is to be used to indicate circumstances classifiable to E950-E958 as the cause of death or disability from late effects, which are themselves classifiable elsewhere. The "late effects" include conditions reported as such, or as sequelae which may occur at any time after the attempted suicide or self-inflicted injury.

HOMICIDE AND INJURY PURPOSELY INFLICTED BY OTHER PERSONS (E960-E969)

INCLUDES injuries inflicted by another person with intent to injure or kill, by any means

EXCLUDES *injuries due to:*
legal intervention (E970-E978)
operations of war (E990-E999)
terrorism (E979)

4th **E960 Fight, brawl, rape**

E960.0 **Unarmed fight or brawl**
Beatings NOS
Brawl or fight with hands, fists, feet
Injured or killed in fight NOS
EXCLUDES *homicidal:*
injury by weapons (E965.0-E966, E969)
strangulation (E963)
submersion (E964)

E960.1 **Rape**

E961 Assault by corrosive or caustic substance, except poisoning
Injury or death purposely caused by corrosive or caustic substance, such as:
acid [any]
corrosive substance
vitriol
EXCLUDES *burns from hot liquid (E968.3)*
chemical burns from swallowing a corrosive substance (E962.0-E962.9)

4th **E962 Assault by poisoning**

E962.0 **Drugs and medicinal substances**
Homicidal poisoning by any drug or medicinal substance

E962.1 **Other solid and liquid substances**

E962.2 **Other gases and vapors**

E962.9 **Unspecified poisoning**

E963 Assault by hanging and strangulation
Homicidal (attempt):
garrotting or ligature
hanging
strangulation
suffocation

E964 Assault by submersion [drowning]

4th **E965 Assault by firearms and explosives**

E965.0 **Handgun**
Pistol
Revolver

E965.1 **Shotgun**

E965.2 **Hunting rifle**

E965.3 **Military firearms**

E965.4 **Other and unspecified firearm**

E965.5 **Antipersonnel bomb**

E965.6 **Gasoline bomb**

E965.7 **Letter bomb**

E965.8 **Other specified explosive**
Bomb NOS (placed in):
car
house
Dynamite

E965.9 **Unspecified explosive**

E966 Assault by cutting and piercing instrument
Assassination (attempt), homicide (attempt) by any instrument classifiable under E920
Homicidal:
cut, puncture, stab } any part of the body
Stabbed any part of the body

4th **E967 Perpetrator of child and adult abuse**
Note: Selection of the correct perpetrator code is based on the relationship between the perpetrator and the victim

E967.0 **By father, stepfather, or boyfriend**
Male partner of child's parent or guardian

E967.1 **By other specified person**

E967.2 **By mother, stepmother, or girlfriend**
Female partner of child's parent or guardian

E967.3 **By spouse or partner**
Abuse of spouse or partner by ex-spouse or ex partner

E967.4 **By child**

E967.5 **By sibling**

E967.6 **By grandparent**

E967.7 **By other relative**

E967.8 By non-related caregiver

E967.9 By unspecified person

✓4th **E968 Assault by other and unspecified means**

E968.0 Fire

Arson
Homicidal burns NOS

EXCLUDES *burns from hot liquid (E968.3)*

E968.1 Pushing from a high place

E968.2 Striking by blunt or thrown object

E968.3 Hot liquid

Homicidal burns by scalding

E968.4 Criminal neglect

Abandonment of child, infant, or other helpless person with intent to injure or kill

E968.5 Transport vehicle

Being struck by other vehicle or run down with intent to injure
Pushed in front of, thrown from, or dragged by moving vehicle with intent to injure

E968.6 Air gun

BB gun
Pellet gun

E968.7 Human bite

E968.8 Other specified means

E968.9 Unspecified means

Assassination (attempt) NOS
Homicidal (attempt):
injury NOS
wound NOS
Manslaughter (nonaccidental)
Murder (attempt) NOS
Violence, non-accidental

E969 Late effects of injury purposely inflicted by other person

Note: This category is to be used to indicate circumstances classifiable to E960-E968 as the cause of death or disability from late effects, which are themselves classifiable elsewhere. The "late effects" include conditions reported as such, or as sequelae which may occur at any time after injury purposely inflicted by another person.

LEGAL INTERVENTION (E970-E978)

INCLUDES injuries inflicted by the police or other law-enforcing agents, including military on duty, in the course of arresting or attempting to arrest lawbreakers, suppressing disturbances, maintaining order, and other legal action
legal execution

EXCLUDES *injuries caused by civil insurrections (E990.0-E999)*

E970 Injury due to legal intervention by firearms

Gunshot wound
Injury by:
machine gun
revolver
rifle pellet or rubber bullet
shot NOS

E971 Injury due to legal intervention by explosives

Injury by:
dynamite
explosive shell
grenade
mortar bomb

E972 Injury due to legal intervention by gas

Asphyxiation by gas
Injury by tear gas
Poisoning by gas

E973 Injury due to legal intervention by blunt object

Hit, struck by:
baton (nightstick)
blunt object
stave

E974 Injury due to legal intervention by cutting and piercing instrument

Cut
Incised wound
Injured by bayonet
Stab wound

E975 Injury due to legal intervention by other specified means

Blow
Manhandling

E976 Injury due to legal intervention by unspecified means

E977 Late effects of injuries due to legal intervention

Note: This category is to be used to indicate circumstances classifiable to E970-E976 as the cause of death or disability from late effects, which are themselves classifiable elsewhere. The "late effects" include conditions reported as such, or as sequelae, which may occur at any time after the injury due to legal intervention.

E978 Legal execution

All executions performed at the behest of the judiciary or ruling authority [whether permanent or temporary] as:
asphyxiation by gas
beheading, decapitation (by guillotine)
capital punishment
electrocution
hanging
poisoning
shooting
other specified means

TERRORISM (E979)

✓4th **E979 Terrorism**

Injuries resulting from the unlawful use of force or violence against persons or property to intimidate or coerce a Government, the civilian population, or any segment thereof, in furtherance of political or social objective

E979.0 Terrorism involving explosion of marine weapons

Depth-charge
Marine mine
Mine NOS, at sea or in harbour
Sea-based artillery shell
Torpedo
Underwater blast

E979.1 Terrorism involving destruction of aircraft

Aircraft used as a weapon
Aircraft:
burned
exploded
shot down
Crushed by falling aircraft

E979.2 Terrorism involving other explosions and fragments
Antipersonnel bomb (fragments)
Blast NOS
Explosion (of):
artillery shell
breech-block
cannon block
mortar bomb
munitions being used in terrorism
NOS
Fragments from:
artillery shell
bomb
grenade
guided missile
land-mine
rocket
shell
shrapnel
Mine NOS

E979.3 Terrorism involving fires, conflagration and hot substances
Burning building or structure:
collapse of
fall from
hit by falling object in
jump from
Conflagration NOS
Fire (causing):
Asphyxia
Burns
NOS
Other injury
Melting of fittings and furniture in burning
Petrol bomb
Smouldering building or structure

E979.4 Terrorism involving firearms
Bullet:
carbine
machine gun
pistol
rifle
rubber (rifle)
Pellets (shotgun)

E979.5 Terrorism involving nuclear weapons
Blast effects
Exposure to ionizing radiation from nuclear weapon
Fireball effects
Heat from nuclear weapon
Other direct and secondary effects of nuclear weapons

E979.6 Terrorism involving biological weapons
Anthrax
Cholera
Smallpox

E979.7 Terrorism involving chemical weapons
Gases, fumes, chemicals
Hydrogen cyanide
Phosgene
Sarin

E979.8 Terrorism involving other means
Drowning and submersion
Lasers
Piercing or stabbing instruments
Terrorism NOS

E979.9 Terrorism, secondary effects
Note: This code is for use to identify conditions occurring subsequent to a terrorist attack not those that are due to the initial terrorist act

EXCLUDES *late effect of terrorist attack (E999.1)*

INJURY UNDETERMINED WHETHER ACCIDENTALLY OR PURPOSELY INFLICTED (E980-E989)

Note: Categories E980-E989 are for use when it is unspecified or it cannot be determined whether the injuries are accidental (unintentional), suicide (attempted), or assault.

✓4th **E980 Poisoning by solid or liquid substances, undetermined whether accidentally or purposely inflicted**

E980.0 Analgesics, antipyretics, and antirheumatics

E980.1 Barbiturates

E980.2 Other sedatives and hypnotics

E980.3 Tranquilizers and other psychotropic agents

E980.4 Other specified drugs and medicinal substances

E980.5 Unspecified drug or medicinal substance

E980.6 Corrosive and caustic substances
Poisoning, undetermined whether accidental or purposeful, by substances classifiable to E864

E980.7 Agricultural and horticultural chemical and pharmaceutical preparations other than plant foods and fertilizers

E980.8 Arsenic and its compounds

E980.9 Other and unspecified solid and liquid substances

✓4th **E981 Poisoning by gases in domestic use, undetermined whether accidentally or purposely inflicted**

E981.0 Gas distributed by pipeline

E981.1 Liquefied petroleum gas distributed in mobile containers

E981.8 Other utility gas

✓4th **E982 Poisoning by other gases, undetermined whether accidentally or purposely inflicted**

E982.0 Motor vehicle exhaust gas

E982.1 Other carbon monoxide

E982.8 Other specified gases and vapors

E982.9 Unspecified gases and vapors

✓4th **E983 Hanging, strangulation, or suffocation, undetermined whether accidentally or purposely inflicted**

E983.0 Hanging

E983.1 Suffocation by plastic bag

E983.8 Other specified means

E983.9 Unspecified means

E984 Submersion [drowning], undetermined whether accidentally or purposely inflicted

✓4th **E985 Injury by firearms, air guns and explosives, undetermined whether accidentally or purposely inflicted**

E985.0 Handgun

E985.1 Shotgun

E985.2 Hunting rifle

E985.3 Military firearms

E985.4 Other and unspecified firearm

E985.5 Explosives

E985.6 Air gun
BB gun
Pellet gun

E985.7 Paintball gun

E986 Injury by cutting and piercing instruments, undetermined whether accidentally or purposely inflicted

✓4th **E987 Falling from high place, undetermined whether accidentally or purposely inflicted**

E987.0 Residential premises

E987.1 Other man-made structures

E987.2 Natural sites

E987.9 Unspecified site

✓4th **E988 Injury by other and unspecified means, undetermined whether accidentally or purposely inflicted**

E988.0 Jumping or lying before moving object

E988.1 Burns, fire

E988.2 Scald

E988.3 Extremes of cold

E988.4 Electrocution

E988.5 Crashing of motor vehicle

E988.6 Crashing of aircraft

E988.7 Caustic substances, except poisoning

E988.8 Other specified means

E988.9 Unspecified means

E989 Late effects of injury, undetermined whether accidentally or purposely inflicted

Note: This category is to be used to indicate circumstances classifiable to E980-E988 as the cause of death or disability from late effects, which are themselves classifiable elsewhere. The "late effects" include conditions reported as such, or as sequelae, which may occur at any time after injury, undetermined whether accidentally or purposely inflicted.

INJURY RESULTING FROM OPERATIONS OF WAR (E990-E999)

INCLUDES injuries to military personnel and civilians caused by war and civil insurrections and occurring during the time of war and insurrection

EXCLUDES *accidents during training of military personnel manufacture of war material and transport, unless attributable to enemy action*

✓4th **E990 Injury due to war operations by fires and conflagrations**

INCLUDES asphyxia, burns, or other injury originating from fire caused by a fire-producing device or indirectly by any conventional weapon

E990.0 From gasoline bomb

E990.9 From other and unspecified source

✓4th **E991 Injury due to war operations by bullets and fragments**

E991.0 Rubber bullets (rifle)

E991.1 Pellets (rifle)

E991.2 Other bullets

Bullet [any, except rubber bullets and pellets]
- carbine
- machine gun
- pistol
- rifle
- shotgun

E991.3 Antipersonnel bomb (fragments)

E991.9 Other and unspecified fragments

Fragments from:
- artillery shell
- bombs, except anti-personnel
- grenade
- guided missile
- land mine
- rockets
- shell

Shrapnel

E992 Injury due to war operations by explosion of marine weapons

Depth charge
Marine mines
Mine NOS, at sea or in harbor
Sea-based artillery shell
Torpedo
Underwater blast

E993 Injury due to war operations by other explosion

Accidental explosion of munitions being used in war
Accidental explosion of own weapons
Air blast NOS
Blast NOS
Explosion NOS
Explosion of:
- artillery shell
- breech block
- cannon block
- mortar bomb

Injury by weapon burst

E994 Injury due to war operations by destruction of aircraft

Airplane:
- burned
- exploded

Airplane:
- shot down

Crushed by falling airplane

E995 Injury due to war operations by other and unspecified forms of conventional warfare

Battle wounds
Bayonet injury
Drowned in war operations

E996 Injury due to war operations by nuclear weapons

Blast effects
Exposure to ionizing radiation from nuclear weapons
Fireball effects
Heat
Other direct and secondary effects of nuclear weapons

✓4th **E997 Injury due to war operations by other forms of unconventional warfare**

E997.0 Lasers

E997.1 Biological warfare

E997.2 Gases, fumes, and chemicals

E997.8 Other specified forms of unconventional warfare

E997.9 Unspecified form of unconventional warfare

E998 Injury due to war operations but occurring after cessation of hostilities

Injuries due to operations of war but occurring after cessation of hostilities by any means classifiable under E990-E997

Injuries by explosion of bombs or mines placed in the course of operations of war, if the explosion occurred after cessation of hostilities

✓4th **E999 Late effect of injury due to war operations and terrorism**

Note: This category is to be used to indicate circumstances classifiable to E979, E990-E998 as the cause of death or disability from late effects, which are themselves classifiable elsewhere. The "late effects" include conditions reported as such, or as sequelae, which may occur at any time after the injury, resulting from operations of war or terrorism

E999.0 Late effect of injury due to war operations

E999.1 Late effect of injury due to terrorism

Official ICD-9-CM Government Appendixes

MORPHOLOGY OF NEOPLASMS

The World Health Organization has published an adaptation of the International Classification of Diseases for oncology (ICD-O). It contains a coded nomenclature for the morphology of neoplasms, which is reproduced here for those who wish to use it in conjunction with Chapter 2 of the International Classification of Diseases, 9th Revision, Clinical Modification.

The morphology code numbers consist of five digits; the first four identify the histological type of the neoplasm and the fifth indicates its behavior. The one-digit behavior code is as follows:

/0	Benign
/1	Uncertain whether benign or malignant Borderline malignancy
/2	Carcinoma in situ Intraepithelial Noninfiltrating Noninvasive
/3	Malignant, primary site
/6	Malignant, metastatic site Secondary site
/9	Malignant, uncertain whether primary or metastatic site

In the nomenclature below, the morphology code numbers include the behavior code appropriate to the histological type of neoplasm, but this behavior code should be changed if other reported information makes this necessary. For example, "chordoma (M9370/3)" is assumed to be malignant; the term "benign chordoma" should be coded M9370/0. Similarly, "superficial spreading adenocarcinoma (M8143/3)" described as "noninvasive" should be coded M8143/2 and "melanoma (M8720/3)" described as "secondary" should be coded M8720/6.

The following table shows the correspondence between the morphology code and the different sections of Chapter 2:

Morphology Code Histology/Behavior		ICD-9-CM Chapter 2	
Any	0	210-229	Benign neoplasms
M8000-M8004	1	239	Neoplasms of unspecified nature
M8010+	1	235-238	Neoplasms of uncertain behavior
Any	2	230-234	Carcinoma in situ
Any	3	140-195 200-208	Malignant neoplasms, stated or presumed to be primary
Any	6	196-198	Malignant neoplasms, stated or presumed to be secondary

The ICD-O behavior digit /9 is inapplicable in an ICD context, since all malignant neoplasms are presumed to be primary (/3) or secondary (/6) according to other information on the medical record.the first-listed term of the full ICD-O morphology nomenclature appears against each code number in the list below. The ICD-9-CM Alphabetical Index (Volume 2), however, includes all the ICD-O synonyms as well as a number of other morphological names still likely to be encountered on medical records but omitted from ICD-O as outdated or otherwise undesirable.

A coding difficulty sometimes arises where a morphological diagnosis contains two qualifying adjectives that have different code numbers. An example is "transitional cell epidermoid carcinoma." "Transitional cell carcinoma NOS" is M8120/3 and "epidermoid carcinoma NOS" is M8070/3. In such circumstances, the higher number (M8120/3 in this example) should be used, as it is usually more specific.

CODED NOMENCLATURE FOR MORPHOLOGY OF NEOPLASMS

M800	**Neoplasms NOS**
M8000/0	*Neoplasm, benign*
M8000/1	*Neoplasm, uncertain whether benign or malignant*
M8000/3	*Neoplasm, malignant*
M8000/6	*Neoplasm, metastatic*
M8000/9	*Neoplasm, malignant, uncertain whether primary or metastatic*
M8001/0	*Tumor cells, benign*
M8001/1	*Tumor cells, uncertain whether benign or malignant*
M8001/3	*Tumor cells, malignant*
M8002/3	*Malignant tumor, small cell type*
M8003/3	*Malignant tumor, giant cell type*
M8004/3	*Malignant tumor, fusiform cell type*
M801-M804	**Epithelial neoplasms NOS**
M8010/0	*Epithelial tumor, benign*
M8010/2	*Carcinoma in situ NOS*
M8010/3	*Carcinoma NOS*
M8010/6	*Carcinoma, metastatic NOS*
M8010/9	*Carcinomatosis*
M8011/0	*Epithelioma, benign*
M8011/3	*Epithelioma, malignant*
M8012/3	*Large cell carcinoma NOS*
M8020/3	*Carcinoma, undifferentiated type NOS*
M8021/3	*Carcinoma, anaplastic type NOS*
M8022/3	*Pleomorphic carcinoma*
M8030/3	*Giant cell and spindle cell carcinoma*
M8031/3	*Giant cell carcinoma*
M8032/3	*Spindle cell carcinoma*
M8033/3	*Pseudosarcomatous carcinoma*
M8034/3	*Polygonal cell carcinoma*
M8035/3	*Spheroidal cell carcinoma*
M8040/1	*Tumorlet*
M8041/3	*Small cell carcinoma NOS*
M8042/3	*Oat cell carcinoma*
M8043/3	*Small cell carcinoma, fusiform cell type*
M805-M808	**Papillary and squamous cell neoplasms**
M8050/0	*Papilloma NOS (except Papilloma of urinary bladder M8120/1)*
M8050/2	*Papillary carcinoma in situ*
M8050/3	*Papillary carcinoma NOS*
M8051/0	*Verrucous papilloma*
M8051/3	*Verrucous carcinoma NOS*
M8052/0	*Squamous cell papilloma*
M8052/3	*Papillary squamous cell carcinoma*
M8053/0	*Inverted papilloma*
M8060/0	*Papillomatosis NOS*
M8070/2	*Squamous cell carcinoma in situ NOS*
M8070/3	*Squamous cell carcinoma NOS*
M8070/6	*Squamous cell carcinoma, metastatic NOS*
M8071/3	*Squamous cell carcinoma, keratinizing type NOS*
M8072/3	*Squamous cell carcinoma, large cell, nonkeratinizing type*
M8073/3	*Squamous cell carcinoma, small cell, nonkeratinizing type*
M8074/3	*Squamous cell carcinoma, spindle cell type*
M8075/3	*Adenoid squamous cell carcinoma*
M8076/2	*Squamous cell carcinoma in situ with questionable stromal invasion*
M8076/3	*Squamous cell carcinoma, microinvasive*
M8080/2	*Queyrat's erythroplasia*
M8081/2	*Bowen's disease*
M8082/3	*Lymphoepithelial carcinoma*
M809-M811	**Basal cell neoplasms**
M8090/1	*Basal cell tumor*
M8090/3	*Basal cell carcinoma NOS*
M8091/3	*Multicentric basal cell carcinoma*
M8092/3	*Basal cell carcinoma, morphea type*
M8093/3	*Basal cell carcinoma, fibroepithelial type*
M8094/3	*Basosquamous carcinoma*
M8095/3	*Metatypical carcinoma*
M8096/0	*Intraepidermal epithelioma of Jadassohn*
M8100/0	*Trichoepithelioma*
M8101/0	*Trichofolliculoma*
M8102/0	*Tricholemmoma*
M8110/0	*Pilomatrixoma*
M812-M813	**Transitional cell papillomas and carcinomas**
M8120/0	*Transitional cell papilloma NOS*
M8120/1	*Urothelial papilloma*
M8120/2	*Transitional cell carcinoma in situ*
M8120/3	*Transitional cell carcinoma NOS*
M8121/0	*Schneiderian papilloma*
M8121/1	*Transitional cell papilloma, inverted type*
M8121/3	*Schneiderian carcinoma*
M8122/3	*Transitional cell carcinoma, spindle cell type*
M8123/3	*Basaloid carcinoma*
M8124/3	*Cloacogenic carcinoma*
M8130/3	*Papillary transitional cell carcinoma*
M814-M838	**Adenomas and adenocarcinomas**
M8140/0	*Adenoma NOS*
M8140/1	*Bronchial adenoma NOS*
M8140/2	*Adenocarcinoma in situ*
M8140/3	*Adenocarcinoma NOS*
M8140/6	*Adenocarcinoma, metastatic NOS*
M8141/3	*Scirrhous adenocarcinoma*
M8142/3	*Linitis plastica*
M8143/3	*Superficial spreading adenocarcinoma*
M8144/3	*Adenocarcinoma, intestinal type*
M8145/3	*Carcinoma, diffuse type*
M8146/0	*Monomorphic adenoma*
M8147/0	*Basal cell adenoma*
M8150/0	*Islet cell adenoma*
M8150/3	*Islet cell carcinoma*
M8151/0	*Insulinoma NOS*
M8151/3	*Insulinoma, malignant*
M8152/0	*Glucagonoma NOS*
M8152/3	*Glucagonoma, malignant*
M8153/1	*Gastrinoma NOS*
M8153/3	*Gastrinoma, malignant*
M8154/3	*Mixed islet cell and exocrine adenocarcinoma*
M8160/0	*Bile duct adenoma*
M8160/3	*Cholangiocarcinoma*
M8161/0	*Bile duct cystadenoma*
M8161/3	*Bile duct cystadenocarcinoma*
M8170/0	*Liver cell adenoma*
M8170/3	*Hepatocellular carcinoma NOS*
M8180/0	*Hepatocholangioma, benign*

M8180/3 *Combined hepatocellular carcinoma and cholangiocarcinoma*
M8190/0 *Trabecular adenoma*
M8190/3 *Trabecular adenocarcinoma*
M8191/0 *Embryonal adenoma*
M8200/0 *Eccrine dermal cylindroma*
M8200/3 *Adenoid cystic carcinoma*
M8201/3 *Cribriform carcinoma*
M8210/0 *Adenomatous polyp NOS*
M8210/3 *Adenocarcinoma in adenomatous polyp*
M8211/0 *Tubular adenoma NOS*
M8211/3 *Tubular adenocarcinoma*
M8220/0 *Adenomatous polyposis coli*
M8220/3 *Adenocarcinoma in adenomatous polyposis coli*
M8221/0 *Multiple adenomatous polyps*
M8230/3 *Solid carcinoma NOS*
M8231/3 *Carcinoma simplex*
M8240/1 *Carcinoid tumor NOS*
M8240/3 *Carcinoid tumor, malignant*
M8241/1 *Carcinoid tumor, argentaffin NOS*
M8241/3 *Carcinoid tumor, argentaffin, malignant*
M8242/1 *Carcinoid tumor, nonargentaffin NOS*
M8242/3 *Carcinoid tumor, nonargentaffin, malignant*
M8243/3 *Mucocarcinoid tumor, malignant*
M8244/3 *Composite carcinoid*
M8250/1 *Pulmonary adenomatosis*
M8250/3 *Bronchiolo-alveolar adenocarcinoma*
M8251/0 *Alveolar adenoma*
M8251/3 *Alveolar adenocarcinoma*
M8260/0 *Papillary adenoma NOS*
M8260/3 *Papillary adenocarcinoma NOS*
M8261/1 *Villous adenoma NOS*
M8261/3 *Adenocarcinoma in villous adenoma*
M8262/3 *Villous adenocarcinoma*
M8263/0 *Tubulovillous adenoma*
M8270/0 *Chromophobe adenoma*
M8270/3 *Chromophobe carcinoma*
M8280/0 *Acidophil adenoma*
M8280/3 *Acidophil carcinoma*
M8281/0 *Mixed acidophil-basophil adenoma*
M8281/3 *Mixed acidophil-basophil carcinoma*
M8290/0 *Oxyphilic adenoma*
M8290/3 *Oxyphilic adenocarcinoma*
M8300/0 *Basophil adenoma*
M8300/3 *Basophil carcinoma*
M8310/0 *Clear cell adenoma*
M8310/3 *Clear cell adenocarcinoma NOS*
M8311/1 *Hypernephroid tumor*
M8312/3 *Renal cell carcinoma*
M8313/0 *Clear cell adenofibroma*
M8320/3 *Granular cell carcinoma*
M8321/0 *Chief cell adenoma*
M8322/0 *Water-clear cell adenoma*
M8322/3 *Water-clear cell adenocarcinoma*
M8323/0 *Mixed cell adenoma*
M8323/3 *Mixed cell adenocarcinoma*
M8324/0 *Lipoadenoma*
M8330/0 *Follicular adenoma*
M8330/3 *Follicular adenocarcinoma NOS*
M8331/3 *Follicular adenocarcinoma, well differentiated type*
M8332/3 *Follicular adenocarcinoma, trabecular type*
M8333/0 *Microfollicular adenoma*
M8334/0 *Macrofollicular adenoma*
M8340/3 *Papillary and follicular adenocarcinoma*
M8350/3 *Nonencapsulated sclerosing carcinoma*
M8360/1 *Multiple endocrine adenomas*
M8361/1 *Juxtaglomerular tumor*
M8370/0 *Adrenal cortical adenoma NOS*
M8370/3 *Adrenal cortical carcinoma*
M8371/0 *Adrenal cortical adenoma, compact cell type*
M8372/0 *Adrenal cortical adenoma, heavily pigmented variant*
M8373/0 *Adrenal cortical adenoma, clear cell type*
M8374/0 *Adrenal cortical adenoma, glomerulosa cell type*
M8375/0 *Adrenal cortical adenoma, mixed cell type*
M8380/0 *Endometrioid adenoma NOS*
M8380/1 *Endometrioid adenoma, borderline malignancy*
M8380/3 *Endometrioid carcinoma*
M8381/0 *Endometrioid adenofibroma NOS*
M8381/1 *Endometrioid adenofibroma, borderline malignancy*
M8381/3 *Endometrioid adenofibroma, malignant*

M839-M842 Adnexal and skin appendage neoplasms

M8390/0 *Skin appendage adenoma*
M8390/3 *Skin appendage carcinoma*
M8400/0 *Sweat gland adenoma*
M8400/1 *Sweat gland tumor NOS*
M8400/3 *Sweat gland adenocarcinoma*
M8401/0 *Apocrine adenoma*
M8401/3 *Apocrine adenocarcinoma*
M8402/0 *Eccrine acrospiroma*
M8403/0 *Eccrine spiradenoma*
M8404/0 *Hidrocystoma*
M8405/0 *Papillary hydradenoma*
M8406/0 *Papillary syringadenoma*
M8407/0 *Syringoma NOS*
M8410/0 *Sebaceous adenoma*
M8410/3 *Sebaceous adenocarcinoma*
M8420/0 *Ceruminous adenoma*
M8420/3 *Ceruminous adenocarcinoma*

M843 Mucoepidermoid neoplasms

M8430/1 *Mucoepidermoid tumor*
M8430/3 *Mucoepidermoid carcinoma*

M844-M849 Cystic, mucinous, and serous neoplasms

M8440/0 *Cystadenoma NOS*
M8440/3 *Cystadenocarcinoma NOS*
M8441/0 *Serous cystadenoma NOS*
M8441/1 *Serous cystadenoma, borderline malignancy*
M8441/3 *Serous cystadenocarcinoma NOS*
M8450/0 *Papillary cystadenoma NOS*
M8450/1 *Papillary cystadenoma, borderline malignancy*
M8450/3 *Papillary cystadenocarcinoma NOS*
M8460/0 *Papillary serous cystadenoma NOS*
M8460/1 *Papillary serous cystadenoma, borderline malignancy*
M8460/3 *Papillary serous cystadenocarcinoma*
M8461/0 *Serous surface papilloma NOS*
M8461/1 *Serous surface papilloma, borderline malignancy*
M8461/3 *Serous surface papillary carcinoma*
M8470/0 *Mucinous cystadenoma NOS*
M8470/1 *Mucinous cystadenoma, borderline malignancy*
M8470/3 *Mucinous cystadenocarcinoma NOS*
M8471/0 *Papillary mucinous cystadenoma NOS*
M8471/1 *Papillary mucinous cystadenoma, borderline malignancy*
M8471/3 *Papillary mucinous cystadenocarcinoma*
M8480/0 *Mucinous adenoma*
M8480/3 *Mucinous adenocarcinoma*
M8480/6 *Pseudomyxoma peritonei*
M8481/3 *Mucin-producing adenocarcinoma*
M8490/3 *Signet ring cell carcinoma*
M8490/6 *Metastatic signet ring cell carcinoma*

M850-M854 Ductal, lobular, and medullary neoplasms

M8500/2 *Intraductal carcinoma, noninfiltrating NOS*
M8500/3 *Infiltrating duct carcinoma*
M8501/2 *Comedocarcinoma, noninfiltrating*
M8501/3 *Comedocarcinoma NOS*
M8502/3 *Juvenile carcinoma of the breast*
M8503/0 *Intraductal papilloma*
M8503/2 *Noninfiltrating intraductal papillary adenocarcinoma*
M8504/0 *Intracystic papillary adenoma*
M8504/2 *Noninfiltrating intracystic carcinoma*
M8505/0 *Intraductal papillomatosis NOS*
M8506/0 *Subareolar duct papillomatosis*
M8510/3 *Medullary carcinoma NOS*
M8511/3 *Medullary carcinoma with amyloid stroma*
M8512/3 *Medullary carcinoma with lymphoid stroma*
M8520/2 *Lobular carcinoma in situ*
M8520/3 *Lobular carcinoma NOS*
M8521/3 *Infiltrating ductular carcinoma*
M8530/3 *Inflammatory carcinoma*
M8540/3 *Paget's disease, mammary*
M8541/3 *Paget's disease and infiltrating duct carcinoma of breast*
M8542/3 *Paget's disease, extramammary (except Paget's disease of bone)*

M855 Acinar cell neoplasms

M8550/0 *Acinar cell adenoma*
M8550/1 *Acinar cell tumor*
M8550/3 *Acinar cell carcinoma*

M856-M858 Complex epithelial neoplasms

M8560/3 *Adenosquamous carcinoma*
M8561/0 *Adenolymphoma*
M8570/3 *Adenocarcinoma with squamous metaplasia*
M8571/3 *Adenocarcinoma with cartilaginous and osseous metaplasia*
M8572/3 *Adenocarcinoma with spindle cell metaplasia*
M8573/3 *Adenocarcinoma with apocrine metaplasia*
M8580/0 *Thymoma, benign*
M8580/3 *Thymoma, malignant*

M859-M867 Specialized gonadal neoplasms

M8590/1 *Sex cord-stromal tumor*
M8600/0 *Thecoma NOS*
M8600/3 *Theca cell carcinoma*
M8610/0 *Luteoma NOS*
M8620/1 *Granulosa cell tumor NOS*
M8620/3 *Granulosa cell tumor, malignant*
M8621/1 *Granulosa cell-theca cell tumor*
M8630/0 *Androblastoma, benign*
M8630/1 *Androblastoma NOS*
M8630/3 *Androblastoma, malignant*
M8631/0 *Sertoli-Leydig cell tumor*
M8632/1 *Gynandroblastoma*
M8640/0 *Tubular androblastoma NOS*
M8640/3 *Sertoli cell carcinoma*
M8641/0 *Tubular androblastoma with lipid storage*
M8650/0 *Leydig cell tumor, benign*
M8650/1 *Leydig cell tumor NOS*
M8650/3 *Leydig cell tumor, malignant*
M8660/0 *Hilar cell tumor*
M8670/0 *Lipid cell tumor of ovary*
M8671/0 *Adrenal rest tumor*

M868-M871 Paraganglionmas and glomus tumors

M8680/1 *Paraganglioma NOS*
M8680/3 *Paraganglioma, malignant*
M8681/1 *Sympathetic paraganglioma*
M8682/1 *Parasympathetic paraganglioma*
M8690/1 *Glomus jugulare tumor*
M8691/1 *Aortic body tumor*
M8692/1 *Carotid body tumor*
M8693/1 *Extra-adrenal paraganglioma NOS*
M8693/3 *Extra-adrenal paraganglioma, malignant*
M8700/0 *Pheochromocytoma NOS*
M8700/3 *Pheochromocytoma, malignant*
M8710/3 *Glomangiosarcoma*
M8711/0 *Glomus tumor*
M8712/0 *Glomangioma*

M872-M879 Nevi and melanomas

M8720/0 *Pigmented nevus NOS*
M8720/3 *Malignant melanoma NOS*
M8721/3 *Nodular melanoma*
M8722/0 *Balloon cell nevus*
M8722/3 *Balloon cell melanoma*
M8723/0 *Halo nevus*
M8724/0 *Fibrous papule of the nose*
M8725/0 *Neuronevus*
M8726/0 *Magnocellular nevus*
M8730/0 *Nonpigmented nevus*
M8730/3 *Amelanotic melanoma*
M8740/0 *Junctional nevus*
M8740/3 *Malignant melanoma in junctional nevus*
M8741/2 *Precancerous melanosis NOS*
M8741/3 *Malignant melanoma in precancerous melanosis*
M8742/2 *Hutchinson's melanotic freckle*
M8742/3 *Malignant melanoma in Hutchinson's melanotic freckle*
M8743/3 *Superficial spreading melanoma*
M8750/0 *Intradermal nevus*
M8760/0 *Compound nevus*
M8761/1 *Giant pigmented nevus*
M8761/3 *Malignant melanoma in giant pigmented nevus*
M8770/0 *Epithelioid and spindle cell nevus*
M8771/3 *Epithelioid cell melanoma*
M8772/3 *Spindle cell melanoma NOS*
M8773/3 *Spindle cell melanoma, type A*
M8774/3 *Spindle cell melanoma, type B*
M8775/3 *Mixed epithelioid and spindle cell melanoma*
M8780/0 *Blue nevus NOS*
M8780/3 *Blue nevus, malignant*
M8790/0 *Cellular blue nevus*

M880 Soft tissue tumors and sarcomas NOS

M8800/0 *Soft tissue tumor, benign*
M8800/3 *Sarcoma NOS*
M8800/9 *Sarcomatosis NOS*
M8801/3 *Spindle cell sarcoma*
M8802/3 *Giant cell sarcoma (except of bone M9250/3)*
M8803/3 *Small cell sarcoma*
M8804/3 *Epithelioid cell sarcoma*

M881-M883 Fibromatous neoplasms

M8810/0 *Fibroma NOS*
M8810/3 *Fibrosarcoma NOS*
M8811/0 *Fibromyxoma*
M8811/3 *Fibromyxosarcoma*
M8812/0 *Periosteal fibroma*
M8812/3 *Periosteal fibrosarcoma*
M8813/0 *Fascial fibroma*
M8813/3 *Fascial fibrosarcoma*
M8814/3 *Infantile fibrosarcoma*
M8820/0 *Elastofibroma*
M8821/1 *Aggressive fibromatosis*
M8822/1 *Abdominal fibromatosis*
M8823/1 *Desmoplastic fibroma*
M8830/0 *Fibrous histiocytoma NOS*
M8830/1 *Atypical fibrous histiocytoma*
M8830/3 *Fibrous histiocytoma, malignant*
M8831/0 *Fibroxanthoma NOS*
M8831/1 *Atypical fibroxanthoma*
M8831/3 *Fibroxanthoma, malignant*
M8832/0 *Dermatofibroma NOS*
M8832/1 *Dermatofibroma protuberans*
M8832/3 *Dermatofibrosarcoma NOS*

M884 Myxomatous neoplasms

M8840/0 *Myxoma NOS*
M8840/3 *Myxosarcoma*

M885-M888 Lipomatous neoplasms

M8850/0 *Lipoma NOS*
M8850/3 *Liposarcoma NOS*
M8851/0 *Fibrolipoma*
M8851/3 *Liposarcoma, well differentiated type*
M8852/0 *Fibromyxolipoma*
M8852/3 *Myxoid liposarcoma*
M8853/3 *Round cell liposarcoma*
M8854/3 *Pleomorphic liposarcoma*
M8855/3 *Mixed type liposarcoma*
M8856/0 *Intramuscular lipoma*
M8857/0 *Spindle cell lipoma*
M8860/0 *Angiomyolipoma*
M8860/3 *Angiomyoliposarcoma*
M8861/0 *Angiolipoma NOS*
M8861/1 *Angiolipoma, infiltrating*
M8870/0 *Myelolipoma*
M8880/0 *Hibernoma*
M8881/0 *Lipoblastomatosis*

M889-M892 Myomatous neoplasms

M8890/0 *Leiomyoma NOS*
M8890/1 *Intravascular leiomyomatosis*
M8890/3 *Leiomyosarcoma NOS*
M8891/1 *Epithelioid leiomyoma*
M8891/3 *Epithelioid leiomyosarcoma*
M8892/1 *Cellular leiomyoma*
M8893/0 *Bizarre leiomyoma*
M8894/0 *Angiomyoma*
M8894/3 *Angiomyosarcoma*
M8895/0 *Myoma*
M8895/3 *Myosarcoma*
M8900/0 *Rhabdomyoma NOS*
M8900/3 *Rhabdomyosarcoma NOS*
M8901/3 *Pleomorphic rhabdomyosarcoma*
M8902/3 *Mixed type rhabdomyosarcoma*
M8903/0 *Fetal rhabdomyoma*
M8904/0 *Adult rhabdomyoma*
M8910/3 *Embryonal rhabdomyosarcoma*
M8920/3 *Alveolar rhabdomyosarcoma*

M893-M899 Complex mixed and stromal neoplasms

M8930/3 *Endometrial stromal sarcoma*
M8931/1 *Endolymphatic stromal myosis*
M8932/0 *Adenomyoma*
M8940/0 *Pleomorphic adenoma*
M8940/3 *Mixed tumor, malignant NOS*
M8950/3 *Mullerian mixed tumor*
M8951/3 *Mesodermal mixed tumor*
M8960/1 *Mesoblastic nephroma*
M8960/3 *Nephroblastoma NOS*
M8961/3 *Epithelial nephroblastoma*
M8962/3 *Mesenchymal nephroblastoma*
M8970/3 *Hepatoblastoma*
M8980/3 *Carcinosarcoma NOS*
M8981/3 *Carcinosarcoma, embryonal type*
M8982/0 *Myoepithelioma*
M8990/0 *Mesenchymoma, benign*
M8990/1 *Mesenchymoma NOS*
M8990/3 *Mesenchymoma, malignant*
M8991/3 *Embryonal sarcoma*

M900-M903 Fibroepithelial neoplasms

M9000/0 *Brenner tumor NOS*
M9000/1 *Brenner tumor, borderline malignancy*
M9000/3 *Brenner tumor, malignant*
M9010/0 *Fibroadenoma NOS*
M9011/0 *Intracanalicular fibroadenoma NOS*
M9012/0 *Pericanalicular fibroadenoma*
M9013/0 *Adenofibroma NOS*
M9014/0 *Serous adenofibroma*
M9015/0 *Mucinous adenofibroma*
M9020/0 *Cellular intracanalicular fibroadenoma*
M9020/1 *Cystosarcoma phyllodes NOS*
M9020/3 *Cystosarcoma phyllodes, malignant*
M9030/0 *Juvenile fibroadenoma*

M904 Synovial neoplasms

M9040/0 *Synovioma, benign*
M9040/3 *Synovial sarcoma NOS*
M9041/3 *Synovial sarcoma, spindle cell type*
M9042/3 *Synovial sarcoma, epithelioid cell type*
M9043/3 *Synovial sarcoma, biphasic type*
M9044/3 *Clear cell sarcoma of tendons and aponeuroses*

M905 Mesothelial neoplasms

M9050/0 *Mesothelioma, benign*
M9050/3 *Mesothelioma, malignant*
M9051/0 *Fibrous mesothelioma, benign*
M9051/3 *Fibrous mesothelioma, malignant*
M9052/0 *Epithelioid mesothelioma, benign*
M9052/3 *Epithelioid mesothelioma, malignant*
M9053/0 *Mesothelioma, biphasic type, benign*
M9053/3 *Mesothelioma, biphasic type, malignant*
M9054/0 *Adenomatoid tumor NOS*

M906-M909 Germ cell neoplasms

M9060/3 *Dysgerminoma*
M9061/3 *Seminoma NOS*
M9062/3 *Seminoma, anaplastic type*
M9063/3 *Spermatocytic seminoma*
M9064/3 *Germinoma*
M9070/3 *Embryonal carcinoma NOS*
M9071/3 *Endodermal sinus tumor*
M9072/3 *Polyembryoma*
M9073/1 *Gonadoblastoma*
M9080/0 *Teratoma, benign*
M9080/1 *Teratoma NOS*
M9080/3 *Teratoma, malignant NOS*
M9081/3 *Teratocarcinoma*
M9082/3 *Malignant teratoma, undifferentiated type*
M9083/3 *Malignant teratoma, intermediate type*
M9084/0 *Dermoid cyst*
M9084/3 *Dermoid cyst with malignant transformation*
M9090/0 *Struma ovarii NOS*
M9090/3 *Struma ovarii, malignant*
M9091/1 *Strumal carcinoid*

M910 Trophoblastic neoplasms

M9100/0 *Hydatidiform mole NOS*
M9100/1 *Invasive hydatidiform mole*
M9100/3 *Choriocarcinoma*
M9101/3 *Choriocarcinoma combined with teratoma*
M9102/3 *Malignant teratoma, trophoblastic*

M911 Mesonephromas

M9110/0 *Mesonephroma, benign*
M9110/1 *Mesonephric tumor*
M9110/3 *Mesonephroma, malignant*
M9111/1 *Endosalpingioma*

M912-M916 Blood vessel tumors

M9120/0 *Hemangioma NOS*
M9120/3 *Hemangiosarcoma*
M9121/0 *Cavernous hemangioma*
M9122/0 *Venous hemangioma*
M9123/0 *Racemose hemangioma*

M9124/3 *Kupffer cell sarcoma*
M9130/0 *Hemangioendothelioma, benign*
M9130/1 *Hemangioendothelioma NOS*
M9130/3 *Hemangioendothelioma, malignant*
M9131/0 *Capillary hemangioma*
M9132/0 *Intramuscular hemangioma*
M9140/3 *Kaposi's sarcoma*
M9141/0 *Angiokeratoma*
M9142/0 *Verrucous keratotic hemangioma*
M9150/0 *Hemangiopericytoma, benign*
M9150/1 *Hemangiopericytoma NOS*
M9150/3 *Hemangiopericytoma, malignant*
M9160/0 *Angiofibroma NOS*
M9161/1 *Hemangioblastoma*

M917 Lymphatic vessel tumors
M9170/0 *Lymphangioma NOS*
M9170/3 *Lymphangiosarcoma*
M9171/0 *Capillary lymphangioma*
M9172/0 *Cavernous lymphangioma*
M9173/0 *Cystic lymphangioma*
M9174/0 *Lymphangiomyoma*
M9174/1 *Lymphangiomyomatosis*
M9175/0 *Hemolymphangioma*

M918-M920 Osteomas and osteosarcomas
M9180/0 *Osteoma NOS*
M9180/3 *Osteosarcoma NOS*
M9181/3 *Chondroblastic osteosarcoma*
M9182/3 *Fibroblastic osteosarcoma*
M9183/3 *Telangiectatic osteosarcoma*
M9184/3 *Osteosarcoma in Paget's disease of bone*
M9190/3 *Juxtacortical osteosarcoma*
M9191/0 *Osteoid osteoma NOS*
M9200/0 *Osteoblastoma*

M921-M924 Chondromatous neoplasms
M9210/0 *Osteochondroma*
M9210/1 *Osteochondromatosis NOS*
M9220/0 *Chondroma NOS*
M9220/1 *Chondromatosis NOS*
M9220/3 *Chondrosarcoma NOS*
M9221/0 *Juxtacortical chondroma*
M9221/3 *Juxtacortical chondrosarcoma*
M9230/0 *Chondroblastoma NOS*
M9230/3 *Chondroblastoma, malignant*
M9240/3 *Mesenchymal chondrosarcoma*
M9241/0 *Chondromyxoid fibroma*

M925 Giant cell tumors
M9250/1 *Giant cell tumor of bone NOS*
M9250/3 *Giant cell tumor of bone, malignant*
M9251/1 *Giant cell tumor of soft parts NOS*
M9251/3 *Malignant giant cell tumor of soft parts*

M926 Miscellaneous bone tumors
M9260/3 *Ewing's sarcoma*
M9261/3 *Adamantinoma of long bones*
M9262/0 *Ossifying fibroma*

M927-M934 Odontogenic tumors
M9270/0 *Odontogenic tumor, benign*
M9270/1 *Odontogenic tumor NOS*
M9270/3 *Odontogenic tumor, malignant*
M9271/0 *Dentinoma*
M9272/0 *Cementoma NOS*
M9273/0 *Cementoblastoma, benign*
M9274/0 *Cementifying fibroma*
M9275/0 *Gigantiform cementoma*
M9280/0 *Odontoma NOS*
M9281/0 *Compound odontoma*
M9282/0 *Complex odontoma*
M9290/0 *Ameloblastic fibro-odontoma*
M9290/3 *Ameloblastic odontosarcoma*
M9300/0 *Adenomatoid odontogenic tumor*
M9301/0 *Calcifying odontogenic cyst*
M9310/0 *Ameloblastoma NOS*
M9310/3 *Ameloblastoma, malignant*
M9311/0 *Odontoameloblastoma*
M9312/0 *Squamous odontogenic tumor*
M9320/0 *Odontogenic myxoma*
M9321/0 *Odontogenic fibroma NOS*
M9330/0 *Ameloblastic fibroma*
M9330/3 *Ameloblastic fibrosarcoma*
M9340/0 *Calcifying epithelial odontogenic tumor*

M935-M937 Miscellaneous tumors
M9350/1 *Craniopharyngioma*
M9360/1 *Pinealoma*
M9361/1 *Pineocytoma*
M9362/3 *Pineoblastoma*
M9363/0 *Melanotic neuroectodermal tumor*
M9370/3 *Chordoma*

M938-M948 Gliomas
M9380/3 *Glioma, malignant*
M9381/3 *Gliomatosis cerebri*
M9382/3 *Mixed glioma*
M9383/1 *Subependymal glioma*
M9384/1 *Subependymal giant cell astrocytoma*
M9390/0 *Choroid plexus papilloma NOS*
M9390/3 *Choroid plexus papilloma, malignant*
M9391/3 *Ependymoma NOS*
M9392/3 *Ependymoma, anaplastic type*
M9393/1 *Papillary ependymoma*
M9394/1 *Myxopapillary ependymoma*
M9400/3 *Astrocytoma NOS*
M9401/3 *Astrocytoma, anaplastic type*
M9410/3 *Protoplasmic astrocytoma*
M9411/3 *Gemistocytic astrocytoma*
M9420/3 *Fibrillary astrocytoma*
M9421/3 *Pilocytic astrocytoma*
M9422/3 *Spongioblastoma NOS*
M9423/3 *Spongioblastoma polare*
M9430/3 *Astroblastoma*
M9440/3 *Glioblastoma NOS*
M9441/3 *Giant cell glioblastoma*
M9442/3 *Glioblastoma with sarcomatous component*
M9443/3 *Primitive polar spongioblastoma*
M9450/3 *Oligodendroglioma NOS*
M9451/3 *Oligodendroglioma, anaplastic type*
M9460/3 *Oligodendroblastoma*
M9470/3 *Medulloblastoma NOS*
M9471/3 *Desmoplastic medulloblastoma*
M9472/3 *Medullomyoblastoma*
M9480/3 *Cerebellar sarcoma NOS*
M9481/3 *Monstrocellular sarcoma*

M949-M952 Neuroepitheliomatous neoplasms
M9490/0 *Ganglioneuroma*
M9490/3 *Ganglioneuroblastoma*
M9491/0 *Ganglioneuromatosis*
M9500/3 *Neuroblastoma NOS*
M9501/3 *Medulloepithelioma NOS*
M9502/3 *Teratoid medulloepithelioma*
M9503/3 *Neuroepithelioma NOS*
M9504/3 *Spongioneuroblastoma*
M9505/1 *Ganglioglioma*
M9506/0 *Neurocytoma*
M9507/0 *Pacinian tumor*
M9510/3 *Retinoblastoma NOS*
M9511/3 *Retinoblastoma, differentiated type*
M9512/3 *Retinoblastoma, undifferentiated type*
M9520/3 *Olfactory neurogenic tumor*
M9521/3 *Esthesioneurocytoma*
M9522/3 *Esthesioneuroblastoma*
M9523/3 *Esthesioneuroepithelioma*

M953 Meningiomas
M9530/0 *Meningioma NOS*
M9530/1 *Meningiomatosis NOS*
M9530/3 *Meningioma, malignant*
M9531/0 *Meningotheliomatous meningioma*
M9532/0 *Fibrous meningioma*
M9533/0 *Psammomatous meningioma*
M9534/0 *Angiomatous meningioma*
M9535/0 *Hemangioblastic meningioma*
M9536/0 *Hemangiopericytic meningioma*
M9537/0 *Transitional meningioma*
M9538/1 *Papillary meningioma*
M9539/3 *Meningeal sarcomatosis*

M954-M957 Nerve sheath tumor
M9540/0 *Neurofibroma NOS*
M9540/1 *Neurofibromatosis NOS*
M9540/3 *Neurofibrosarcoma*
M9541/0 *Melanotic neurofibroma*
M9550/0 *Plexiform neurofibroma*
M9560/0 *Neurilemmoma NOS*
M9560/1 *Neurinomatosis*
M9560/3 *Neurilemmoma, malignant*
M9570/0 *Neuroma NOS*

M958 Granular cell tumors and alveolar soft part sarcoma
M9580/0 *Granular cell tumor NOS*
M9580/3 *Granular cell tumor, malignant*
M9581/3 *Alveolar soft part sarcoma*

M959-M963 Lymphomas, NOS or diffuse
M9590/0 *Lymphomatous tumor, benign*
M9590/3 *Malignant lymphoma NOS*
M9591/3 *Malignant lymphoma, non Hodgkin's type*
M9600/3 *Malignant lymphoma, undifferentiated cell type NOS*
M9601/3 *Malignant lymphoma, stem cell type*
M9602/3 *Malignant lymphoma, convoluted cell type NOS*
M9610/3 *Lymphosarcoma NOS*
M9611/3 *Malignant lymphoma, lymphoplasmacytoid type*
M9612/3 *Malignant lymphoma, immunoblastic type*
M9613/3 *Malignant lymphoma, mixed lymphocytic-histiocytic NOS*
M9614/3 *Malignant lymphoma, centroblastic-centrocytic, diffuse*
M9615/3 *Malignant lymphoma, follicular center cell NOS*
M9620/3 *Malignant lymphoma, lymphocytic, well differentiated NOS*
M9621/3 *Malignant lymphoma, lymphocytic, intermediate differentiation NOS*
M9622/3 *Malignant lymphoma, centrocytic*
M9623/3 *Malignant lymphoma, follicular center cell, cleaved NOS*
M9630/3 *Malignant lymphoma, lymphocytic, poorly differentiated NOS*
M9631/3 *Prolymphocytic lymphosarcoma*
M9632/3 *Malignant lymphoma, centroblastic type NOS*
M9633/3 *Malignant lymphoma, follicular center cell, noncleaved NOS*

M964 *Reticulosarcomas*
M9640/3 *Reticulosarcoma NOS*
M9641/3 *Reticulosarcoma, pleomorphic cell type*
M9642/3 *Reticulosarcoma, nodular*

M965-M966 *Hodgkin's disease*
M9650/3 *Hodgkin's disease NOS*
M9651/3 *Hodgkin's disease, lymphocytic predominance*
M9652/3 *Hodgkin's disease, mixed cellularity*
M9653/3 *Hodgkin's disease, lymphocytic depletion NOS*
M9654/3 *Hodgkin's disease, lymphocytic depletion, diffuse fibrosis*

M9655/3 *Hodgkin's disease, lymphocytic depletion, reticular type*
M9656/3 *Hodgkin's disease, nodular sclerosis NOS*
M9657/3 *Hodgkin's disease, nodular sclerosis, cellular phase*
M9660/3 *Hodgkin's paragranuloma*
M9661/3 *Hodgkin's granuloma*
M9662/3 *Hodgkin's sarcoma*

M969 Lymphomas, nodular or follicular
M9690/3 *Malignant lymphoma, nodular NOS*
M9691/3 *Malignant lymphoma, mixed lymphocytic-histiocytic, nodular*
M9692/3 *Malignant lymphoma, centroblastic-centrocytic, follicular*
M9693/3 *Malignant lymphoma, lymphocytic, well differentiated, nodular*
M9694/3 *Malignant lymphoma, lymphocytic, intermediate differentiation, nodular*
M9695/3 *Malignant lymphoma, follicular center cell, cleaved, follicular*
M9696/3 *Malignant lymphoma, lymphocytic, poorly differentiated, nodular*
M9697/3 *Malignant lymphoma, centroblastic type, follicular*
M9698/3 *Malignant lymphoma, follicular center cell, noncleaved, follicular*

M970 Mycosis fungoides
M9700/3 *Mycosis fungoides*
M9701/3 *Sezary's disease*

M971-M972 Miscellaneous reticuloendothelial neoplasms
M9710/3 *Microglioma*
M9720/3 *Malignant histiocytosis*
M9721/3 *Histiocytic medullary reticulosis*
M9722/3 *Letterer-Siwe's disease*

M973 Plasma cell tumors
M9730/3 *Plasma cell myeloma*
M9731/0 *Plasma cell tumor, benign*
M9731/1 *Plasmacytoma NOS*
M9731/3 *Plasma cell tumor, malignant*

M974 Mast cell tumors
M9740/1 *Mastocytoma NOS*
M9740/3 *Mast cell sarcoma*
M9741/3 *Malignant mastocytosis*

M975 Burkitt's tumor
M9750/3 *Burkitt's tumor*

M980-M994 Leukemias NOS
M9800/3 Leukemias NOS
M9800/3 *Leukemia NOS*
M9801/3 *Acute leukemia NOS*
M9802/3 *Subacute leukemia NOS*
M9803/3 *Chronic leukemia NOS*
M9804/3 *Aleukemic leukemia NOS*

M981 Compound leukemias
M9810/3 *Compound leukemia*

M982 Lymphoid leukemias
M9820/3 *Lymphoid leukemia NOS*
M9821/3 *Acute lymphoid leukemia*
M9822/3 *Subacute lymphoid leukemia*
M9823/3 *Chronic lymphoid leukemia*
M9824/3 *Aleukemic lymphoid leukemia*
M9825/3 *Prolymphocytic leukemia*

M983 Plasma cell leukemias
M9830/3 *Plasma cell leukemia*

M984 Erythroleukemias
M9840/3 *Erythroleukemia*
M9841/3 *Acute erythremia*
M9842/3 *Chronic erythremia*

M985 Lymphosarcoma cell leukemias
M9850/3 *Lymphosarcoma cell leukemia*

M986 Myeloid leukemias
M9860/3 *Myeloid leukemia NOS*
M9861/3 *Acute myeloid leukemia*
M9862/3 *Subacute myeloid leukemia*
M9863/3 *Chronic myeloid leukemia*
M9864/3 *Aleukemic myeloid leukemia*
M9865/3 *Neutrophilic leukemia*
M9866/3 *Acute promyelocytic leukemia*

M987 Basophilic leukemias
M9870/3 *Basophilic leukemia*

M988 Eosinophilic leukemias
M9880/3 *Eosinophilic leukemia*

M989 Monocytic leukemias
M9890/3 *Monocytic leukemia NOS*
M9891/3 *Acute monocytic leukemia*
M9892/3 *Subacute monocytic leukemia*
M9893/3 *Chronic monocytic leukemia*
M9894/3 *Aleukemic monocytic leukemia*

M990-M994 Miscellaneous leukemias
M9900/3 *Mast cell leukemia*
M9910/3 *Megakaryocytic leukemia*
M9920/3 *Megakaryocytic myelosis*
M9930/3 *Myeloid sarcoma*
M9940/3 *Hairy cell leukemia*

M995-M997 Miscellaneous myeloproliferative and lymphoproliferative disorders
M9950/1 *Polycythemia vera*
M9951/1 *Acute panmyelosis*
M9960/1 *Chronic myeloproliferative disease*
M9961/1 *Myelosclerosis with myeloid metaplasia*
M9962/1 *Idiopathic thrombocythemia*
M9970/1 *Chronic lymphoproliferative disease*

APPENDIX B WAS OFFICIALLY DELETED OCTOBER 1, 2004

CLASSIFICATION OF DRUGS BY AMERICAN HOSPITAL FORMULARY SERVICE LIST NUMBER AND THEIR ICD-9-CM EQUIVALENTS

The coding of adverse effects of drugs is keyed to the continually revised Hospital Formulary of the American Hospital Formulary Service (AHFS) published under the direction of the American Society of Hospital Pharmacists.

The following section gives the ICD-9-CM diagnosis code for each AHFS list.

	AHFS* List	ICD-9-CM Diagnosis Code
4:00	ANTIHISTAMINE DRUGS	963.0
8:00	ANTI-INFECTIVE AGENTS	
8:04	Amebacides	961.5
	hydroxyquinoline derivatives	961.3
	arsenical anti-infectives	961.1
	quinoline derivatives	961.3
8:12.04	Antifungal Antibiotics	960.1
	nonantibiotics	961.9
8:12.06	Cephalosporins	960.5
8:12.08	Chloramphenicol	960.2
8:12.12	The Erythromycins	960.3
8:12.16	The Penicillins	960.0
8:12.20	The Streptomycins	960.6
8:12.24	The Tetracyclines	960.4
8:12.28	Other Antibiotics	960.8
	antimycobacterial antibiotics	960.6
	macrolides	960.3
8:16	Antituberculars	961.8
	antibiotics	960.6
8:18	Antivirals	961.7
8:20	Plasmodicides (antimalarials)	961.4
8:24	Sulfonamides	961.0
8:26	The Sulfones	961.8
8:28	Treponemicides	961.2
8:32	Trichomonacides	961.5
	hydroxyquinoline derivatives	961.3
	nitrofuran derivatives	961.9
8:36	Urinary Germicides	961.9
	quinoline derivatives	961.3
8:40	Other Anti-Infectives	961.9
10:00	ANTINEOPLASTIC AGENTS	963.1
	antibiotics	960.7
	progestogens	962.2
12:00	AUTONOMIC DRUGS	
12:04	Parasympathomimetic (Cholinergic) Agents	971.0
12:08	Parasympatholytic (Cholinergic Blocking) Agents	971.1
12:12	Sympathomimetic (Adrenergic) Agents	971.2
12:16	Sympatholytic (Adrenergic Blocking) Agents	971.3
12:20	Skeletal Muscle Relaxants	975.2
	central nervous system muscle-tone depressants	968.0
16:00	BLOOD DERIVATIVES	964.7
20:00	BLOOD FORMATION AND COAGULATION	
20:04	Antianemia Drugs	964.1
20:04.04	Iron Preparations	964.0
20:04.08	Liver and Stomach Preparations	964.1
20:12.04	Anticoagulants	964.2
20:12.08	Antiheparin Agents	964.5
20:12.12	Coagulants	964.5
20.12.16	Hemostatics	964.5
	capillary-active drugs	972.8
	fibrinolysis-affecting agents	964.4
	natural products	964.7
24:00	CARDIOVASCULAR DRUGS	
24:04	Cardiac Drugs	972.9
	cardiotonic agents	972.1
	rhythm regulators	972.0
24:06	Antilipemic Agents	972.2
	thyroid derivatives	962.7
24:08	Hypotensive Agents	972.6
	adrenergic blocking agents	971.3
	ganglion-blocking agents	972.3
	vasodilators	972.5
24:12	Vasodilating Agents	972.5
	coronary	972.4
	nicotinic acid derivatives	972.2
24:16	Sclerosing Agents	972.7
28:00	CENTRAL NERVOUS SYSTEM DRUGS	
28:04	General Anesthetics	968.4
	gaseous anesthetics	968.2
	halothane	968.1
	intravenous anesthetics	968.3
28:08	Analgesics and Antipyretics	965.9
	antirheumatics	965.61-965.69
	aromatic analgesics	965.4
	non-narcotics NEC	965.7
	opium alkaloids	965.00
	heroin	965.01
	methadone	965.02
	specified type NEC	965.09
	pyrazole derivatives	965.5
	salicylates	965.1
	specified type NEC	965.8
28:10	Narcotic Antagonists	970.1
28:12	Anticonvulsants	966.3
	barbiturates	967.0
	benzodiazepine-based tranquilizers	969.4
	bromides	967.3
	hydantoin derivatives	966.1
	oxazolidine derivative	966.0
	succinimides	966.2
28:16.04	Antidepressants	969.0
28:16.08	Tranquilizers	969.5
	benzodiazepine-based	969.4
	butyrophenone-based	969.2
	major NEC	969.3
	phenothiazine-based	969.1
28:16.12	Other Psychotherapeutic Agents	969.8
28:20	Respiratory and Cerebral Stimulants	970.9
	analeptics	970.0
	anorexigenic agents	977.0
	psychostimulants	969.7
	specified type NEC	970.8
28:24	Sedatives and Hypnotics	967.9
	barbiturates	967.0
	benzodiazepine-based tranquilizers	969.4
	chloral hydrate group	967.1
	glutethamide group	967.5
	intravenous anesthetics	968.3
	methaqualone	967.4
	paraldehyde	967.2
	phenothiazine-based tranquilizers	969.1
	specified type NEC	967.8
	thiobarbiturates	968.3
	tranquilizer NEC	969.5
36:00	DIAGNOSTIC AGENTS	977.8
40:00	ELECTROLYTE, CALORIC, AND WATER BALANCE AGENTS NEC	974.5
40:04	Acidifying Agents	963.2
40:08	Alkalinizing Agents	963.3
40:10	Ammonia Detoxicants	974.5
40:12	Replacement Solutions NEC	974.5
	plasma volume expanders	964.8
40:16	Sodium-Removing Resins	974.5
40:18	Potassium-Removing Resins	974.5
40:20	Caloric Agents	974.5
40:24	Salt and Sugar Substitutes	974.5
40:28	Diuretics NEC	974.4
	carbonic acid anhydrase inhibitors	974.2
	mercurials	974.0
	purine derivatives	974.1
	saluretics	974.3
40:36	Irrigating Solutions	974.5
40:40	Uricosuric Agents	974.7

	AHFS* List	ICD-9-CM Diagnosis Code
44:00	ENZYMES NEC	963.4
	fibrinolysis-affecting agents	964.4
	gastric agents	973.4
48:00	EXPECTORANTS AND COUGH PREPARATIONS	
	antihistamine agents	963.0
	antitussives	975.4
	codeine derivatives	965.09
	expectorants	975.5
	narcotic agents NEC	965.09
52:00	EYE, EAR, NOSE, AND THROAT PREPARATIONS	
52:04	Anti-Infectives	
	ENT	976.6
	ophthalmic	976.5
52:04.04	Antibiotics	
	ENT	976.6
	ophthalmic	976.5
52:04.06	Antivirals	
	ENT	976.6
	ophthalmic	976.5
52:04.08	Sulfonamides	
	ENT	976.6
	ophthalmic	976.5
52:04.12	Miscellaneous Anti-Infectives	
	ENT	976.6
	ophthalmic	976.5
52:08	Anti-Inflammatory Agents	
	ENT	976.6
	ophthalmic	976.5
52:10	Carbonic Anhydrase Inhibitors	974.2
52:12	Contact Lens Solutions	976.5
52:16	Local Anesthetics	968.5
52:20	Miotics	971.0
52:24	Mydriatics	
	adrenergics	971.2
	anticholinergics	971.1
	antimuscarinics	971.1
	parasympatholytics	971.1
	spasmolytics	971.1
	sympathomimetics	971.2
52:28	Mouth Washes and Gargles	976.6
52:32	Vasoconstrictors	971.2
52:36	Unclassified Agents	
	ENT	976.6
	ophthalmic	976.5
56:00	GASTROINTESTINAL DRUGS	
56:04	Antacids and Absorbents	973.0
56:08	Anti-Diarrhea Agents	973.5
56:10	Antiflatulents	973.8
56:12	Cathartics NEC	973.3
	emollients	973.2
	irritants	973.1
56:16	Digestants	973.4
56:20	Emetics and Antiemetics	
	antiemetics	963.0
	emetics	973.6
56:24	Lipotropic Agents	977.1
60:00	GOLD COMPOUNDS	965.69
64:00	HEAVY METAL ANTAGONISTS	963.8
68:00	HORMONES AND SYNTHETIC SUBSTITUTES	
68:04	Adrenals	962.0
68:08	Androgens	962.1
68:12	Contraceptives	962.2
68:16	Estrogens	962.2
68:18	Gonadotropins	962.4
68:20	Insulins and Antidiabetic Agents	962.3
68:20.08	Insulins	962.3
68:24	Parathyroid	962.6
68:28	Pituitary	
	anterior	962.4
	posterior	962.5
68:32	Progestogens	962.2
68:34	Other Corpus Luteum Hormones	962.2

	AHFS* List	ICD-9-CM Diagnosis Code
68:36	Thyroid and Antithyroid	
	antithyroid	962.8
	thyroid	962.7
72:00	LOCAL ANESTHETICS NEC	968.9
	topical (surface) agents	968.5
	infiltrating agents (intradermal) (subcutaneous) (submucosal)	968.5
	nerve blocking agents (peripheral) (plexus) (regional)	968.6
	spinal	968.7
76:00	OXYTOCICS	975.0
78:00	RADIOACTIVE AGENTS	990
80:00	SERUMS, TOXOIDS, AND VACCINES	
80:04	Serums	979.9
	immune globulin (gamma) (human)	964.6
80:08	Toxoids NEC	978.8
	diphtheria	978.5
	and tetanus	978.9
	with pertussis component	978.6
	tetanus	978.4
	and diphtheria	978.9
	with pertussis component	978.6
80:12	Vaccines NEC	979.9
	bacterial NEC	978.8
	with other bacterial component	978.9
	pertussis component	978.6
	viral and rickettsial component	979.7
	rickettsial NEC	979.6
	with bacterial component	979.7
	pertussis component	978.6
	viral component	979.7
	viral NEC	979.6
	with bacterial component	979.7
	pertussis component	978.6
	rickettsial component	979.7
84:00	SKIN AND MUCOUS MEMBRANE PREPARATIONS	
84:04	Anti-Infectives	976.0
84:04.04	Antibiotics	976.0
84:04.08	Fungicides	976.0
84:04.12	Scabicides and Pediculicides	976.0
84:04.16	Miscellaneous Local Anti-Infectives	976.0
84:06	Anti-Inflammatory Agents	976.0
84:08	Antipruritics and Local Anesthetics	
	antipruritics	976.1
	local anesthetics	968.5
84:12	Astringents	976.2
84:16	Cell Stimulants and Proliferants	976.8
84:20	Detergents	976.2
84:24	Emollients, Demulcents, and Protectants	976.3
84:28	Keratolytic Agents	976.4
84:32	Keratoplastic Agents	976.4
84:36	Miscellaneous Agents	976.8
86:00	SPASMOLYTIC AGENTS	975.1
	antiasthmatics	975.7
	papaverine	972.5
	theophyllin	974.1
88:00	VITAMINS	
88:04	Vitamin A	963.5
88:08	Vitamin B Complex	963.5
	hematopoietic vitamin	964.1
	nicotinic acid derivatives	972.2
88:12	Vitamin C	963.5
88:16	Vitamin D	963.5
88:20	Vitamin E	963.5
88:24	Vitamin K Activity	964.3
88:28	Multivitamin Preparations	963.5
92:00	UNCLASSIFIED THERAPEUTIC AGENTS	977.8

* American Hospital Formulary Service

CLASSIFICATION OF INDUSTRIAL ACCIDENTS ACCORDING TO AGENCY

Annex B to the Resolution concerning Statistics of Employment Injuries adopted by the Tenth International Conference of Labor Statisticians on 12 October 1962

1 MACHINES

11 Prime-Movers, except Electrical Motors
111 *Steam engines*
112 *Internal combustion engines*
119 *Others*
12 Transmission Machinery
121 *Transmission shafts*
122 *Transmission belts, cables, pulleys, pinions, chains, gears*
129 *Others*
13 Metalworking Machines
131 *Power presses*
132 *Lathes*
133 *Milling machines*
134 *Abrasive wheels*
135 *Mechanical shears*
136 *Forging machines*
137 *Rolling-mills*
139 *Others*
14 *Wood and Assimilated Machines*
141 *Circular saws*
142 *Other saws*
143 *Molding machines*
144 *Overhand planes*
149 *Others*
15 *Agricultural Machines*
151 *Reapers (including combine reapers)*
152 *Threshers*
159 *Others*
16 *Mining Machinery*
161 *Under-cutters*
169 *Others*
19 *Other Machines Not Elsewhere Classified*
191 *Earth-moving machines, excavating and scraping machines, except means of transport*
192 *Spinning, weaving and other textile machines*
193 *Machines for the manufacture of food- stuffs and beverages*
194 *Machines for the manufacture of paper*
195 *Printing machines*
199 *Others*

2 MEANS OF TRANSPORT AND LIFTING EQUIPMENT

21 *Lifting Machines and Appliances*
211 *Cranes*
212 *Lifts and elevators*
213 *Winches*
214 *Pulley blocks*
219 *Others*
22 *Means of Rail Transport*
221 *Inter-urban railways*
222 *Rail transport in mines, tunnels, quarries, industrial establishments, docks, etc.*
229 *Others*
23 *Other Wheeled Means of Transport, Excluding Rail Transport*
231 *Tractors*
232 *Lorries*
233 *Trucks*
234 *Motor vehicles, not elsewhere classified*
235 *Animal-drawn vehicles*
236 *Hand-drawn vehicles*
239 *Others*
24 *Means of Air Transport*
25 *Means of Water Transport*
251 *Motorized means of water transport*
252 *Non-motorized means of water transport*
26 *Other Means of Transport*
261 *Cable-cars*
262 *Mechanical conveyors, except cable-cars*
269 *Others*

3 OTHER EQUIPMENT

31 *Pressure Vessels*
311 *Boilers*
312 *Pressurized containers*
313 *Pressurized piping and accessories*
314 *Gas cylinders*
315 *Caissons, diving equipment*
319 *Others*
32 *Furnaces, Ovens, Kilns*
321 *Blast furnaces*
322 *Refining furnaces*
323 *Other furnaces*
324 *Kilns*
325 *Ovens*
33 *Refrigerating Plants*
34 *Electrical Installations, Including Electric Motors, but Excluding Electric Hand Tools*
341 *Rotating machines*
342 *Conductors*
343 *Transformers*
344 *Control apparatus*
349 *Others*
35 *Electric Hand Tools*
36 *Tools, Implements, and Appliances, Except Electric Hand Tools*
361 *Power-driven hand tools, except electrichand tools*
362 *Hand tools, not power-driven*
369 *Others*
37 *Ladders, Mobile Ramps*
38 *Scaffolding*
39 *Other Equipment, Not Elsewhere Classified*

4 MATERIALS, SUBSTANCES AND RADIATIONS

41 *Explosives*
42 *Dusts, Gases, Liquids and Chemicals, Excluding Explosives*
421 *Dusts*
422 *Gases, vapors, fumes*
423 *Liquids, not elsewhere classified*
424 *Chemicals, not elsewhere classified*
43 *Flying Fragments*
44 *Radiations*
441 *Ionizing radiations*
449 *Others*
49 *Other Materials and Substances Not Elsewhere Classified*

5 WORKING ENVIRONMENT

51 *Outdoor*
511 *Weather*
512 *Traffic and working surfaces*
513 *Water*
519 *Others*
52 *Indoor*
521 *Floors*
522 *Confined quarters*
523 *Stairs*
524 *Other traffic and working surfaces*
525 *Floor openings and wall openings*
526 *Environmental factors (lighting, ventilation, temperature, noise, etc.)*
529 *Others*
53 *Underground*
531 *Roofs and faces of mine roads and tunnels, etc.*
532 *Floors of mine roads and tunnels, etc.*
533 *Working-faces of mines, tunnels, etc.*
534 *Mine shafts*
535 *Fire*
536 *Water*
539 *Others*

6 OTHER AGENCIES, NOT ELSEWHERE CLASSIFIED

61 *Animals*
611 *Live animals*
612 *Animal products*
69 *Other Agencies, Not Elsewhere Classified*

7 AGENCIES NOT CLASSIFIED FOR LACK OF SUFFICIENT DATA

LIST OF THREE-DIGIT CATEGORIES

1. INFECTIOUS AND PARASITIC DISEASES

Intestinal infectious diseases (001-009)
001 Cholera
002 Typhoid and paratyphoid fevers
003 Other salmonella infections
004 Shigellosis
005 Other food poisoning (bacterial)
006 Amebiasis
007 Other protozoal intestinal diseases
008 Intestinal infections due to other organisms
009 Ill-defined intestinal infections

Tuberculosis (010-018)
010 Primary tuberculous infection
011 Pulmonary tuberculosis
012 Other respiratory tuberculosis
013 Tuberculosis of meninges and central nervous system
014 Tuberculosis of intestines, peritoneum, and mesenteric glands
015 Tuberculosis of bones and joints
016 Tuberculosis of genitourinary system
017 Tuberculosis of other organs
018 Miliary tuberculosis

Zoonotic bacterial diseases (020-027)
020 Plague
021 Tularemia
022 Anthrax
023 Brucellosis
024 Glanders
025 Melioidosis
026 Rat-bite fever
027 Other zoonotic bacterial diseases

Other bacterial diseases (030-042)
030 Leprosy
031 Diseases due to other mycobacteria
032 Diphtheria
033 Whooping cough
034 Streptococcal sore throat and scarlatina
035 Erysipelas
036 Meningococcal infection
037 Tetanus
038 Septicemia
039 Actinomycotic infections
040 Other bacterial diseases
041 Bacterial infection in conditions classified elsewhere and of unspecified site

Human immunodeficiency virus (042)
042 Human immunodeficiency virus [HIV] disease

Poliomyelitis and other non-arthropod-borne viral diseases and prion diseases of central nervous system (045-049)
045 Acute poliomyelitis
046 Slow virus infections and prion diseases of central nervous system
047 Meningitis due to enterovirus
048 Other enterovirus diseases of central nervous system
049 Other non-arthropod-borne viral diseases of central nervous system

Viral diseases accompanied by exanthem (050-058)
050 Smallpox
051 Cowpox and paravaccinia
052 Chickenpox
053 Herpes zoster
054 Herpes simplex
055 Measles
056 Rubella
057 Other viral exanthemata
058 Other human herpesvirus
059 Other poxvirus infections

Arthropod-borne viral diseases (060-066)
060 Yellow fever
061 Dengue
062 Mosquito-borne viral encephalitis
063 Tick-borne viral encephalitis
064 Viral encephalitis transmitted by other and unspecified arthropods
065 Arthropod-borne hemorrhagic fever
066 Other arthropod-borne viral diseases

Other diseases due to viruses and Chlamydiae (070-079)
070 Viral hepatitis
071 Rabies
072 Mumps
073 Ornithosis
074 Specific diseases due to Coxsackievirus
075 Infectious mononucleosis
076 Trachoma
077 Other diseases of conjunctiva due to viruses and Chlamydiae
078 Other diseases due to viruses and Chlamydiae
079 Viral infection in conditions classified elsewhere and of unspecified site

Rickettsioses and other arthropod-borne diseases (080-088)
080 Louse-borne [epidemic] typhus
081 Other typhus
082 Tick-borne rickettsioses
083 Other rickettsioses
084 Malaria
085 Leishmaniasis
086 Trypanosomiasis
087 Relapsing fever
088 Other arthropod-borne diseases

Syphilis and other venereal diseases (090-099)
090 Congenital syphilis
091 Early syphilis, symptomatic
092 Early syphilis, latent
093 Cardiovascular syphilis
094 Neurosyphilis
095 Other forms of late syphilis, with symptoms
096 Late syphilis, latent
097 Other and unspecified syphilis
098 Gonococcal infections
099 Other venereal diseases

Other spirochetal diseases (100-104)
100 Leptospirosis
101 Vincent's angina
102 Yaws
103 Pinta
104 Other spirochetal infection

Mycoses (110-118)
110 Dermatophytosis
111 Dermatomycosis, other and unspecified
112 Candidiasis
114 Coccidioidomycosis
115 Histoplasmosis
116 Blastomycotic infection
117 Other mycoses
118 Opportunistic mycoses

Helminthiases (120-129)
120 Schistosomiasis [bilharziasis]
121 Other trematode infections
122 Echinococcosis
123 Other cestode infection
124 Trichinosis
125 Filarial infection and dracontiasis
126 Ancylostomiasis and necatoriasis
127 Other intestinal helminthiases
128 Other and unspecified helminthiases
129 Intestinal parasitism, unspecified

Other infectious and parasitic diseases (130-136)
130 Toxoplasmosis
131 Trichomoniasis
132 Pediculosis and phthirus infestation
133 Acariasis
134 Other infestation
135 Sarcoidosis
136 Other and unspecified infectious and parasitic diseases

Late effects of infectious and parasitic diseases (137-139)
137 Late effects of tuberculosis
138 Late effects of acute poliomyelitis
139 Late effects of other infectious and parasitic diseases

2. NEOPLASMS

Malignant neoplasm of lip, oral cavity, and pharynx (140-149)
140 Malignant neoplasm of lip
141 Malignant neoplasm of tongue
142 Malignant neoplasm of major salivary glands
143 Malignant neoplasm of gum
144 Malignant neoplasm of floor of mouth
145 Malignant neoplasm of other and unspecified parts of mouth
146 Malignant neoplasm of oropharynx
147 Malignant neoplasm of nasopharynx
148 Malignant neoplasm of hypopharynx
149 Malignant neoplasm of other and ill-defined sites within the lip, oral cavity, and pharynx

Malignant neoplasm of digestive organs and peritoneum (150-159)
150 Malignant neoplasm of esophagus
151 Malignant neoplasm of stomach
152 Malignant neoplasm of small intestine, including duodenum
153 Malignant neoplasm of colon
154 Malignant neoplasm of rectum, rectosigmoid junction, and anus
155 Malignant neoplasm of liver and intrahepatic bile ducts
156 Malignant neoplasm of gallbladder and extrahepatic bile ducts
157 Malignant neoplasm of pancreas
158 Malignant neoplasm of retroperitoneum and peritoneum
159 Malignant neoplasm of other and ill-defined sites within the digestive organs and peritoneum

Malignant neoplasm of respiratory and intrathoracic organs (160-165)
160 Malignant neoplasm of nasal cavities, middle ear, and accessory sinuses
161 Malignant neoplasm of larynx
162 Malignant neoplasm of trachea, bronchus, and lung
163 Malignant neoplasm of pleura
164 Malignant neoplasm of thymus, heart, and mediastinum
165 Malignant neoplasm of other and ill-defined sites within the respiratory system and intrathoracic organs

Malignant neoplasm of bone, connective tissue, skin, and breast (170-176)
170 Malignant neoplasm of bone and articular cartilage
171 Malignant neoplasm of connective and other soft tissue
172 Malignant melanoma of skin
173 Other malignant neoplasm of skin
174 Malignant neoplasm of female breast
175 Malignant neoplasm of male breast
176 Kaposi's sarcoma

Malignant neoplasm of genitourinary organs (179-189)

179 Malignant neoplasm of uterus, part unspecified
180 Malignant neoplasm of cervix uteri
181 Malignant neoplasm of placenta
182 Malignant neoplasm of body of uterus
183 Malignant neoplasm of ovary and other uterine adnexa
184 Malignant neoplasm of other and unspecified female genital organs
185 Malignant neoplasm of prostate
186 Malignant neoplasm of testis
187 Malignant neoplasm of penis and other male genital organs
188 Malignant neoplasm of bladder
189 Malignant neoplasm of kidney and other unspecified urinary organs

Malignant neoplasm of other and unspecified sites (190-199)

190 Malignant neoplasm of eye
191 Malignant neoplasm of brain
192 Malignant neoplasm of other and unspecified parts of nervous system
193 Malignant neoplasm of thyroid gland
194 Malignant neoplasm of other endocrine glands and related structures
195 Malignant neoplasm of other and ill-defined sites
196 Secondary and unspecified malignant neoplasm of lymph nodes
197 Secondary malignant neoplasm of respiratory and digestive systems
198 Secondary malignant neoplasm of other specified sites
199 Malignant neoplasm without specification of site

Malignant neoplasm of lymphatic and hematopoietic tissue (200-208)

200 Lymphosarcoma and reticulosar-coma and other specified malignant tumors of lymphatic tissue
201 Hodgkin's disease
202 Other malignant neoplasm of lymphoid and histiocytic tissue
203 Multiple myeloma and immunoproliferative neoplasms
204 Lymphoid leukemia
205 Myeloid leukemia
206 Monocytic leukemia
207 Other specified leukemia
208 Leukemia of unspecified cell type

Neuroendocrine tumors (209)

209 Neuroendocrine tumors

Benign neoplasms (210-229)

210 Benign neoplasm of lip, oral cavity, and pharynx
211 Benign neoplasm of other parts of digestive system
212 Benign neoplasm of respiratory and intrathoracic organs
213 Benign neoplasm of bone and articular cartilage
214 Lipoma
215 Other benign neoplasm of connective and other soft tissue
216 Benign neoplasm of skin
217 Benign neoplasm of breast
218 Uterine leiomyoma
219 Other benign neoplasm of uterus
220 Benign neoplasm of ovary
221 Benign neoplasm of other female genital organs
222 Benign neoplasm of male genital organs
223 Benign neoplasm of kidney and other urinary organs
224 Benign neoplasm of eye
225 Benign neoplasm of brain and other parts of nervous system
226 Benign neoplasm of thyroid gland
227 Benign neoplasm of other endocrine glands and related structures
228 Hemangioma and lymphangioma, any site
229 Benign neoplasm of other and unspecified sites

Carcinoma in situ (230-234)

230 Carcinoma in situ of digestive organs
231 Carcinoma in situ of respiratory system
232 Carcinoma in situ of skin
233 Carcinoma in situ of breast and genitourinary system
234 Carcinoma in situ of other and unspecified sites

Neoplasms of uncertain behavior (235-238)

235 Neoplasm of uncertain behavior of digestive and respiratory systems
236 Neoplasm of uncertain behavior of genitourinary organs
237 Neoplasm of uncertain behavior of endocrine glands and nervous system
238 Neoplasm of uncertain behavior of other and unspecified sites and tissues

Neoplasms of unspecified nature (239)

239 Neoplasm of unspecified nature

3. ENDOCRINE, NUTRITIONAL AND METABOLIC DISEASES, AND IMMUNITY DISORDERS

Disorders of thyroid gland (240-246)

240 Simple and unspecified goiter
241 Nontoxic nodular goiter
242 Thyrotoxicosis with or without goiter
243 Congenital hypothyroidism
244 Acquired hypothyroidism
245 Thyroiditis
246 Other disorders of thyroid

Diseases of other endocrine glands (249-259)

249 Secondary diabetes mellitus
250 Diabetes mellitus
251 Other disorders of pancreatic internal secretion
252 Disorders of parathyroid gland
253 Disorders of the pituitary gland and its hypothalamic control
254 Diseases of thymus gland
255 Disorders of adrenal glands
256 Ovarian dysfunction
257 Testicular dysfunction
258 Polyglandular dysfunction and related disorders
259 Other endocrine disorders

Nutritional deficiencies (260-269)

260 Kwashiorkor
261 Nutritional marasmus
262 Other severe protein-calorie malnutrition
263 Other and unspecified protein-calorie malnutrition
264 Vitamin A deficiency
265 Thiamine and niacin deficiency states
266 Deficiency of B-complex components
267 Ascorbic acid deficiency
268 Vitamin D deficiency
269 Other nutritional deficiencies

Other metabolic disorders and immnity disorders (270-279)

270 Disorders of amino-acid transport and metabolism
271 Disorders of carbohydrate transport and metabolism
272 Disorders of lipoid metabolism
273 Disorders of plasma protein metabolism
274 Gout
275 Disorders of mineral metabolism
276 Disorders of fluid, electrolyte, and acid-base balance
277 Other and unspecified disorders of metabolism
278 Overweight, obesity and other hyperalimentation
279 Disorders involving the immune mechanism

4. DISEASES OF BLOOD AND BLOOD-FORMING ORGANS (280-289)

280 Iron deficiency anemias
281 Other deficiency anemias
282 Hereditary hemolytic anemias
283 Acquired hemolytic anemias
284 Aplastic anemia
285 Other and unspecified anemias
286 Coagulation defects
287 Purpura and other hemorrhagic conditions
288 Diseases of white blood cells
289 Other diseases of blood and blood-forming organs

5. MENTAL DISORDERS

Organic psychotic conditions (290-294)

290 Senile and presenile organic psychotic conditions
291 Alcoholic psychoses
292 Drug psychoses
293 Transient organic psychotic conditions
294 Other organic psychotic conditions (chronic)

Other psychoses (295-299)

295 Schizophrenic psychoses
296 Affective psychoses
297 Paranoid states
298 Other nonorganic psychoses
299 Psychoses with origin specific to childhood

Neurotic disorders, personality disorders, and other nonpsychotic mental disorders (300-316)

300 Neurotic disorders
301 Personality disorders
302 Sexual and gender identity disorders
303 Alcohol dependence syndrome
304 Drug dependence
305 Nondependent abuse of drugs
306 Physiological malfunction arising from mental factors
307 Special symptoms or syndromes, not elsewhere classified
308 Acute reaction to stress
309 Adjustment reaction
310 Specific nonpsychotic mental disorders following organic brain damage
311 Depressive disorder, not elsewhereclassified
312 Disturbance of conduct, not elsewhere classified
313 Disturbance of emotions specific tochildhood and adolescence
314 Hyperkinetic syndrome of childhood
315 Specific delays in development
316 Psychic factors associated with diseases classified elsewhere

Mental retardation (317-319)

317 Mild mental retardation
318 Other specified mental retardation
319 Unspecified mental retardation

6. DISEASES OF THE NERVOUS SYSTEM AND SENSE ORGANS

Inflammatory diseases of the central nervous system (320-326)

320 Bacterial meningitis

321 Meningitis due to other organisms
322 Meningitis of unspecified cause
323 Encephalitis, myelitis, and encephalomyelitis
324 Intracranial and intraspinal abscess
325 Phlebitis and thrombophlebitis of intracranial venous sinuses
326 Late effects of intracranial abscess or pyogenic infection

Organic Sleep Disorders (327)

327 Organic sleep disorders

Hereditary and degenerative diseases of the central nervous system (330-337)

330 Cerebral degenerations usually manifest in childhood
331 Other cerebral degenerations
332 Parkinson's disease
333 Other extrapyramidal diseases and abnormal movement disorders
334 Spinocerebellar disease
335 Anterior horn cell disease
336 Other diseases of spinal cord
337 Disorders of the autonomic nervous system

Pain (338)

338 Pain, not elsewhere classified

Other headache syndromes (339)

339 Other headache syndromes

Other disorders of the central nervous system (340-349)

340 Multiple sclerosis
341 Other demyelinating diseases of central nervous system
342 Hemiplegia and hemiparesis
343 Infantile cerebral palsy
344 Other paralytic syndromes
345 Epilepsy and recurrent seizures
346 Migraine
347 Cataplexy and narcolepsy
348 Other conditions of brain
349 Other and unspecified disorders of the nervous system

Disorders of the peripheral nervous system (350-359)

350 Trigeminal nerve disorders
351 Facial nerve disorders
352 Disorders of other cranial nerves
353 Nerve root and plexus disorders
354 Mononeuritis of upper limb and mononeuritis multiplex
355 Mononeuritis of lower limb
356 Hereditary and idiopathic peripheral neuropathy
357 Inflammatory and toxic neuropathy
358 Myoneural disorders
359 Muscular dystrophies and other myopathies

Disorders of the eye and adnexa (360-379)

360 Disorders of the globe
361 Retinal detachments and defects
362 Other retinal disorders
363 Chorioretinal inflammations and scars and other disorders of choroid
364 Disorders of iris and ciliary body
365 Glaucoma
366 Cataract
367 Disorders of refraction and accommodation
368 Visual disturbances
369 Blindness and low vision
370 Keratitis
371 Corneal opacity and other disorders of cornea
372 Disorders of conjunctiva
373 Inflammation of eyelids
374 Other disorders of eyelids
375 Disorders of lacrimal system
376 Disorders of the orbit
377 Disorders of optic nerve and visual pathways
378 Strabismus and other disorders of binocular eye movements
379 Other disorders of eye

Diseases of the ear and mastoid process (380-389)

380 Disorders of external ear
381 Nonsuppurative otitis media and Eustachian tube disorders
382 Suppurative and unspecified otitis media
383 Mastoiditis and related conditions
384 Other disorders of tympanic membrane
385 Other disorders of middle ear and mastoid
386 Vertiginous syndromes and other disorders of vestibular system
387 Otosclerosis
388 Other disorders of ear
389 Hearing loss

7. DISEASES OF THE CIRCULATORY SYSTEM

Acute rheumatic fever (390-392)

390 Rheumatic fever without mention of heart involvement
391 Rheumatic fever with heart involvement
392 Rheumatic chorea

Chronic rheumatic heart disease (393-398)

393 Chronic rheumatic pericarditis
394 Diseases of mitral valve
395 Diseases of aortic valve
396 Diseases of mitral and aortic valves
397 Diseases of other endocardial structures
398 Other rheumatic heart disease

Hypertensive disease (401-405)

401 Essential hypertension
402 Hypertensive heart disease
403 Hypertensive kidney disease
404 Hypertensive heart and kidney disease
405 Secondary hypertension

Ischemic heart disease (410-414)

410 Acute myocardial infarction
411 Other acute and subacute form of ischemic heart disease
412 Old myocardial infarction
413 Angina pectoris
414 Other forms of chronic ischemic heart disease

Diseases of pulmonary circulation (415-417)

415 Acute pulmonary heart disease
416 Chronic pulmonary heart disease
417 Other diseases of pulmonary circulation

Other forms of heart disease (420-429)

420 Acute pericarditis
421 Acute and subacute endocarditis
422 Acute myocarditis
423 Other diseases of pericardium
424 Other diseases of endocardium
425 Cardiomyopathy
426 Conduction disorders
427 Cardiac dysrhythmias
428 Heart failure
429 Ill-defined descriptions and complications of heart disease

Cerebrovascular disease (430-438)

430 Subarachnoid hemorrhage
431 Intracerebral hemorrhage
432 Other and unspecified intracranial hemorrhage
433 Occlusion and stenosis of precerebral arteries
434 Occlusion of cerebral arteries
435 Transient cerebral ischemia
436 Acute but ill-defined cerebrovascular disease
437 Other and ill-defined cerebrovascular disease
438 Late effects of cerebrovascular disease

Diseases of arteries, arterioles, and capillaries (440-449)

440 Atherosclerosis
441 Aortic aneurysm and dissection
442 Other aneurysm
443 Other peripheral vascular disease
444 Arterial embolism and thrombosis
445 Atheroembolism
446 Polyarteritis nodosa and allied conditions
447 Other disorders of arteries and arterioles
448 Diseases of capillaries
449 Septic arterial embolism

Diseases of veins and lymphatics, and other diseases of circulatory system (451-459)

451 Phlebitis and thrombophlebitis
452 Portal vein thrombosis
453 Other venous embolism and thrombosis
454 Varicose veins of lower extremities
455 Hemorrhoids
456 Varicose veins of other sites
457 Noninfective disorders of lymphatic channels
458 Hypotension
459 Other disorders of circulatory system

8. DISEASES OF THE RESPIRATORY SYSTEM

Acute respiratory infections (460-466)

460 Acute nasopharyngitis [common cold]
461 Acute sinusitis
462 Acute pharyngitis
463 Acute tonsillitis
464 Acute laryngitis and tracheitis
465 Acute upper respiratory infections of multiple or unspecified sites
466 Acute bronchitis and bronchiolitis

Other diseases of upper respiratory tract (470-478)

470 Deviated nasal septum
471 Nasal polyps
472 Chronic pharyngitis and nasopharyngitis
473 Chronic sinusitis
474 Chronic disease of tonsils and adenoids
475 Peritonsillar abscess
476 Chronic laryngitis and aryngotracheitis
477 Allergic rhinitis
478 Other diseases of upper respiratory tract

Pneumonia and influenza (480-488)

480 Viral pneumonia
481 Pneumococcal pneumonia [Streptococcus pneumoniae pneumonia]
482 Other bacterial pneumonia
483 Pneumonia due to other specified organism
484 Pneumonia in infectious diseases classified elsewhere
485 Bronchopneumonia, organism unspecified
486 Pneumonia, organism unspecified
487 Influenza
488 Influenza due to identified avian influenza virus

Chronic obstructive pulmonary disease and allied conditions (490-496)

490 Bronchitis, not specified as acute or chronic
491 Chronic bronchitis
492 Emphysema
493 Asthma
494 Bronchiectasis
495 Extrinsic allergic alveolitis

496 Chronic airways obstruction, not elsewhere classified

Pneumoconioses and other lung diseases due to external agents (500-508)

500 Coal workers' pneumoconiosis
501 Asbestosis
502 Pneumoconiosis due to other silica or silicates
503 Pneumoconiosis due to other inorganic dust
504 Pneumopathy due to inhalation of other dust
505 Pneumoconiosis, unspecified
506 Respiratory conditions due to chemical fumes and vapors
507 Pneumonitis due to solids and liquids
508 Respiratory conditions due to other and unspecified external agents

Other diseases of respiratory system (510-519)

510 Empyema
511 Pleurisy
512 Pneumothorax
513 Abscess of lung and mediastinum
514 Pulmonary congestion and hypostasis
515 Postinflammatory pulmonary fibrosis
516 Other alveolar and parietoalveolar pneumopathy
517 Lung involvement in conditions classified elsewhere
518 Other diseases of lung
519 Other diseases of respiratory system

9. DISEASES OF THE DIGESTIVE SYSTEM

Diseases of oral cavity, salivary glands, and jaws (520-529)

520 Disorders of tooth development and eruption
521 Diseases of hard tissues of teeth
522 Diseases of pulp and periapical tissues
523 Gingival and periodontal diseases
524 Dentofacial anomalies, including malocclusion
525 Other diseases and conditions of the teeth and supporting structures
526 Diseases of the jaws
527 Diseases of the salivary glands
528 Diseases of the oral soft tissues, excluding lesions specific for gingiva and tongue
529 Diseases and other conditions of the tongue

Diseases of esophagus, stomach, and duodenum (530-538)

530 Diseases of esophagus
531 Gastric ulcer
532 Duodenal ulcer
533 Peptic ulcer, site unspecified
534 Gastrojejunal ulcer
535 Gastritis and duodenitis
536 Disorders of function of stomach
537 Other disorders of stomach and duodenum
538 Gastrointestinal mucositis (ulcerative)

Appendicitis (540-543)

540 Acute appendicitis
541 Appendicitis, unqualified
542 Other appendicitis
543 Other diseases of appendix

Hernia of abdominal cavity (550-553)

550 Inguinal hernia
551 Other hernia of abdominal cavity, with gangrene
552 Other hernia of abdominal cavity, with ob-struction, but without mention of gangrene
553 Other hernia of abdominal cavity without mention of obstruction or gangrene

Noninfective enteritis and colitis (555-558)

555 Regional enteritis
556 Ulcerative colitis
557 Vascular insufficiency of intestine
558 Other noninfective gastroenteritis and colitis

Other diseases of intestines and peritoneum (560-569)

560 Intestinal obstruction without mention of hernia
562 Diverticula of intestine
564 Functional digestive disorders, not elsewhere classified
565 Anal fissure and fistula
566 Abscess of anal and rectal regions
567 Peritonitis and retroperitoneal infections
568 Other disorders of peritoneum
569 Other disorders of intestine

Other diseases of digestive system (570-579)

570 Acute and subacute necrosis of liver
571 Chronic liver disease and cirrhosis
572 Liver abscess and sequelae of chronic liver disease
573 Other disorders of liver
574 Cholelithiasis
575 Other disorders of gallbladder
576 Other disorders of biliary tract
577 Diseases of pancreas
578 Gastrointestinal hemorrhage
579 Intestinal malabsorption

10. DISEASES OF THE GENITOURINARY SYSTEM

Nephritis, nephrotic syndrome, and nephrosis (580-589)

580 Acute gloerulonephritis
581 Nephrotic syndrome
582 Chronic glomerulonephritis
583 Nephritis and nephropathy, not specified as acute or chronic
584 Acute renal failure
585 Chronic kidney disease (CKD)
586 Renal failure, unspecified
587 Renal sclerosis, unspecified
588 Disorders resulting from impaired renal function
589 Small kidney of unknown cause

Other diseases of urinary system (590-599)

590 Infections of kidney
591 Hydronephrosis
592 Calculus of kidney and ureter
593 Other disorders of kidney and ureter
594 Calculus of lower urinary tract
595 Cystitis
596 Other disorders of bladder
597 Urethritis, not sexually transmitted, and urethral syndrome
598 Urethral stricture
599 Other disorders of urethra and urinary tract

Diseases of male genital organs (600-608)

600 Hyperplasia of prostate
601 Inflammatory diseases of prostate
602 Other disorders of prostate
603 Hydrocele
604 Orchitis and epididymitis
605 Redundant prepuce and phimosis
606 Infertility, male
607 Disorders of penis
608 Other disorders of male genital organs

Disorders of breast (610-612)

610 Benign mammary dysplasias
611 Other disorders of breast
612 Deformity and disproportion of reconstructed breast

Inflammatory disease of female pelvic organs (614-616)

614 Inflammatory disease of ovary, fallopian tube, pelvic cellular tissue, and peritoneum
615 Inflammatory diseases of uterus, except cervix
616 Inflammatory disease of cervix, vagina, and vulva

Other disorders of female genital tract (617-629)

617 Endometriosis
618 Genital prolapse
619 Fistula involving female genital tract
620 Noninflammatory disorders of ovary, fallopian tube, and broad ligament
621 Disorders of uterus, not elsewhere classified
622 Noninflammatory disorders of cervix
623 Noninflammatory disorders of vagina
624 Noninflammatory disorders of vulva and perineum
625 Pain and other symptoms associated with female genital organs
626 Disorders of menstruation and other abnormal bleeding from female genital tract
627 Menopausal and postmenopausal disorders
628 Infertility, female
629 Other disorders of female genital organs

11. COMPLICATIONS OF PREGNANCY, CHILDBIRTH AND THE PUERPERIUM

Ectopic and molar pregnancy and other pregnancy with abortive outcome (630-639)

630 Hydatidiform mole
631 Other abnormal product of conception
632 Missed abortion
633 Ectopic pregnancy
634 Spontaneous abortion
635 Legally induced abortion
636 Illegally induced abortion
637 Unspecified abortion
638 Failed attempted abortion
639 Complications following abortion and ectopic and molar pregnancies

Complications mainly related to pregnancy (640-649)

640 Hemorrhage in early pregnancy
641 Antepartum hemorrhage, abruptio placentae, and placenta previa
642 Hypertension complicating pregnancy, childbirth, and the puerperium
643 Excessive vomiting in pregnancy
644 Early or threatened labor
645 Prolonged pregnancy
646 Other complications of pregnancy, not elsewhere classified
647 Infective and parasitic conditions in the mother classifiable elsewhere but complicating pregnancy, childbirth, and the puerperium
648 Other current conditions in the mother classifiable elsewhere but complicating pregnancy, childbirth, and the puerperium
649 Other conditions or status of the mother complicating pregnancy, childbirth, or puerperium

Normal delivery, and other indications for care in pregnancy, labor, and delivery (650-659)

650 Normal delivery
651 Multiple gestation
652 Malposition and malpresentation of fetus
653 Disproportion

654 Abnormality of organs and soft tissues of pelvis
655 Known or suspected fetal abnormality affecting management of mother
656 Other fetal and placental problems affecting management of mother
657 Polyhydramnios
658 Other problems associated with amniotic cavity and membranes
659 Other indications for care or intervention related to labor and delivery and not elsewhere classified

Complications occurring mainly in the course of labor and delivery (660-669)
660 Obstructed labor
661 Abnormality of forces of labor
662 Long labor
663 Umbilical cord complications
664 Trauma to perineum and vulva during delivery
665 Other obstetrical trauma
666 Postpartum hemorrhage
667 Retained placenta or membranes, without hemorrhage
668 Complications of the administration of anesthetic or other sedation in labor and delivery
669 Other complications of labor and delivery, not elsewhere classified

Complications of the puerperium (670-677)
670 Major puerperal infection
671 Venous complications in pregnancy and the puerperium
672 Pyrexia of unknown origin during the puerperium
673 Obstetrical pulmonary embolism
674 Other and unspecified complications of the puerperium, not elsewhere classified
675 Infections of the breast and nipple associated with childbirth
676 Other disorders of the breast associated with childbirth, and disorders of lactation
677 Late effect of complication of pregnancy, childbirth, and the puerperium

Other maternal and fetal complications (678-679)
678 Other fetal conditions
679 Complications of in utero procedures

12. DISEASES OF THE SKIN AND SUBCUTANEOUS TISSUE

Infections of skin and subcutaneous tissue (680-686)
680 Carbuncle and furuncle
681 Cellulitis and abscess of finger and toe
682 Other cellulitis and abscess
683 Acute lymphadenitis
684 Impetigo
685 Pilonidal cyst
686 Other local infections of skin and subcutaneous tissue

Inflammatory conditions of skin and subcutaneous tissue (690-698)
690 Erythematosquamous dermatosis
691 Atopic dermatitis and related conditions
692 Contact dermatitis and other eczema
693 Dermatitis due to substances taken internally
694 Bullous dermatoses
695 Erythematous conditions
696 Psoriasis and similar disorders
697 Lichen
698 Pruritus and related conditions

Other diseases of skin and subcutaneous tissue (700-709)
700 Corns and callosities
701 Other hypertrophic and atrophic conditions of skin
702 Other dermatoses
703 Diseases of nail
704 Diseases of hair and hair follicles
705 Disorders of sweat glands
706 Diseases of sebaceous glands
707 Chronic ulcer of skin
708 Urticaria
709 Other disorders of skin and subcutaneous tissue

13. DISEASES OF THE MUSCULOSKELETAL SYSTEM AND CONNECTIVE TISSUE

Arthropathies and related disorders (710-719)
710 Diffuse diseases of connective tissue
711 Arthropathy associated with infections
712 Crystal arthropathies
713 Arthropathy associated with other disorders classified elsewhere
714 Rheumatoid arthritis and other inflammatory polyarthropathies
715 Osteoarthrosis and allied disorders
716 Other and unspecified arthropathies
717 Internal derangement of knee
718 Other derangement of joint
719 Other and unspecified disorder of joint

Dorsopathies (720-724)
720 Ankylosing spondylitis and other inflammatory spondylopathies
721 Spondylosis and allied disorders
722 Intervertebral disc disorders
723 Other disorders of cervical region
724 Other and unspecified disorders of back

Rheumatism, excluding the back (725-729)
725 Polymyalgia rheumatica
726 Peripheral enthesopathies and allied syndromes
727 Other disorders of synovium, tendon, and bursa
728 Disorders of muscle, ligament, and fascia
729 Other disorders of soft tissues

Osteopathies, chondropathies, and acquired musculoskeletal deformities (730-739)
730 Osteomyelitis, periostitis, and other infections involving bone
731 Osteitis deformans and osteopathies associated with other disorders classified elsewhere
732 Osteochondropathies
733 Other disorders of bone and cartilage
734 Flat foot
735 Acquired deformities of toe
736 Other acquired deformities of limbs
737 Curvature of spine
738 Other acquired deformity
739 Nonallopathic lesions, not elsewhere classified

14. CONGENITAL ANOMALIES

740 Anencephalus and similar anomalies
741 Spina bifida
742 Other congenital anomalies of nervous system
743 Congenital anomalies of eye
744 Congenital anomalies of ear, face, and neck
745 Bulbus cordis anomalies and anomalies of cardiac septal closure
746 Other congenital anomalies of heart
747 Other congenital anomalies of circulatory system
748 Congenital anomalies of respiratory system
749 Cleft palate and cleft lip
750 Other congenital anomalies of upper alimentary tract
751 Other congenital anomalies of digestive system
752 Congenital anomalies of genital organs
753 Congenital anomalies of urinary system
754 Certain congenital musculoskeletal deformities
755 Other congenital anomalies of limbs
756 Other congenital musculoskeletal anomalies
757 Congenital anomalies of the integument
758 Chromosomal anomalies
759 Other and unspecified congenital anomalies

15. CERTAIN CONDITIONS ORIGINATING IN THE PERINATAL PERIOD

Maternal causes of perinatal morbidity and mortality (760-763)
760 Fetus or newborn affected by maternal conditions which may be unrelated to present pregnancy
761 Fetus or newborn affected by maternal complications of pregnancy
762 Fetus or newborn affected by complications of placenta, cord, and membranes
763 Fetus or newborn affected by other complications of labor and delivery

Other conditions originating in the perinatal period (764-779)
764 Slow fetal growth and fetal malnutrition
765 Disorders relating to short gestation and unspecified low birthweight
766 Disorders relating to long gestation and high birthweight
767 Birth trauma
768 Intrauterine hypoxia and birth asphyxia
769 Respiratory distress syndrome
770 Other respiratory conditions of fetus and newborn
771 Infections specific to the perinatal period
772 Fetal and neonatal hemorrhage
773 Hemolytic disease of fetus or newborn, due to isoimmunization
774 Other perinatal jaundice
775 Endocrine and metabolic disturbances specific to the fetus and newborn
776 Hematological disorders of newborn
777 Perinatal disorders of digestive system
778 Conditions involving the integument and temperature regulation of fetus and newborn
779 Other and ill-defined conditions originating in the perinatal period

16. SYMPTOMS, SIGNS, AND ILL-DEFINED CONDITIONS

Symptoms (780-789)
780 General symptoms
781 Symptoms involving nervous and musculoskeletal systems
782 Symptoms involving skin and other integumentary tissue
783 Symptoms concerning nutrition, metabolism, and development
784 Symptoms involving head and neck
785 Symptoms involving cardiovascular system
786 Symptoms involving respiratory system and other chest symptoms
787 Symptoms involving digestive system
788 Symptoms involving urinary system
789 Other symptoms involving abdomen and pelvis

Nonspecific abnormal findings (790-796)

790 Nonspecific findings on examination of blood
791 Nonspecific findings on examination of urine
792 Nonspecific abnormal findings in other body substances
793 Nonspecific abnormal findings on radiological and other examination of body structure
794 Nonspecific abnormal results of function studies
795 Nonspecific abnormal histological and immunological findings
796 Other nonspecific abnormal findings

Ill-defined and unknown causes of morbidity and mortality (797-799)

797 Senility without mention of psychosis
798 Sudden death, cause unknown
799 Other ill-defined and unknown causes of morbidity and mortality

17. INJURY AND POISONING

Fracture of skull (800-804)

800 Fracture of vault of skull
801 Fracture of base of skull
802 Fracture of face bones
803 Other and unqualified skull fractures
804 Multiple fractures involving skull or face with other bones

Fracture of spine and trunk (805-809)

805 Fracture of vertebral column without mention of spinal cord lesion
806 Fracture of vertebral column with spinal cord lesion
807 Fracture of rib(s), sternum, larynx, and trachea
808 Fracture of pelvis
809 Ill-defined fractures of bones of trunk

Fracture of upper limb (810-819)

810 Fracture of clavicle
811 Fracture of scapula
812 Fracture of humerus
813 Fracture of radius and ulna
814 Fracture of carpal bone(s)
815 Fracture of metacarpal bone(s)
816 Fracture of one or more phalanges of hand
817 Multiple fractures of hand bones
818 Ill-defined fractures of upper limb
819 Multiple fractures involving both upper limbs, and upper limb with rib(s) and sternum

Fracture of lower limb (820-829)

820 Fracture of neck of femur
821 Fracture of other and unspecified parts of femur
822 Fracture of patella
823 Fracture of tibia and fibula
824 Fracture of ankle
825 Fracture of one or more tarsal and metatarsal bones
826 Fracture of one or more phalanges of foot
827 Other, multiple, and ill-defined fractures of lower limb
828 Multiple fractures involving both lower limbs, lower with upper limb, and lower limb(s) with rib(s) and sternum
829 Fracture of unspecified bones

Dislocation (830-839)

830 Dislocation of jaw
831 Dislocation of shoulder
832 Dislocation of elbow
833 Dislocation of wrist
834 Dislocation of finger
835 Dislocation of hip
836 Dislocation of knee
837 Dislocation of ankle
838 Dislocation of foot
839 Other, multiple, and ill-defined dislocations

Sprains and strains of joints and adjacent muscles (840-848)

840 Sprains and strains of shoulder and upper arm
841 Sprains and strains of elbow and forearm
842 Sprains and strains of wrist and hand
843 Sprains and strains of hip and thigh
844 Sprains and strains of knee and leg
845 Sprains and strains of ankle and foot
846 Sprains and strains of sacroiliac region
847 Sprains and strains of other and unspecified parts of back
848 Other and ill-defined sprains and strains

Intracranial injury, excluding those with skull fracture (850-854)

850 Concussion
851 Cerebral laceration and contusion
852 Subarachnoid, subdural, and extradural hemorrhage, following injury
853 Other and unspecified intracranial hemorrhage following injury
854 Intracranial injury of other and unspecified nature

Internal injury of chest, abdomen, and pelvis (860-869)

860 Traumatic pneumothorax and hemothorax
861 Injury to heart and lung
862 Injury to other and unspecified intrathoracic organs
863 Injury to gastrointestinal tract
864 Injury to liver
865 Injury to spleen
866 Injury to kidney
867 Injury to pelvic organs
868 Injury to other intra-abdominal organs
869 Internal injury to unspecified or ill-defined organs

Open wound of head, neck, and trunk (870-879)

870 Open wound of ocular adnexa
871 Open wound of eyeball
872 Open wound of ear
873 Other open wound of head
874 Open wound of neck
875 Open wound of chest (wall)
876 Open wound of back
877 Open wound of buttock
878 Open wound of genital organs (external), including traumatic amputation
879 Open wound of other and unspecified sites, except limbs

Open wound of upper limb (880-887)

880 Open wound of shoulder and upper arm
881 Open wound of elbow, forearm, and wrist
882 Open wound of hand except finger(s) alone
883 Open wound of finger(s)
884 Multiple and unspecified open wound of upper limb
885 Traumatic amputation of thumb (complete) (partial)
886 Traumatic amputation of other finger(s) (complete) (partial)
887 Traumatic amputation of arm and hand (complete) (partial)

Open wound of lower limb (890-897)

890 Open wound of hip and thigh
891 Open wound of knee, leg [except thigh], and ankle
892 Open wound of foot except toe(s) alone
893 Open wound of toe(s)
894 Multiple and unspecified open wound of lower limb
895 Traumatic amputation of toe(s) (complete) (partial)
896 Traumatic amputation of foot (complete) (partial)
897 Traumatic amputation of leg(s) (complete) (partial)

Injury to blood vessels (900-904)

900 Injury to blood vessels of head and neck
901 Injury to blood vessels of thorax
902 Injury to blood vessels of abdomen and pelvis
903 Injury to blood vessels of upper extremity
904 Injury to blood vessels of lower extremity and unspecified sites

Late effects of injuries, poisonings, toxic effects, and other external causes (905-909)

905 Late effects of musculoskeletal and connective tissue injuries
906 Late effects of injuries to skin and subcutaneous tissues
907 Late effects of injuries to the nervous system
908 Late effects of other and unspecified injuries
909 Late effects of other and unspecified external causes

Superficial injury (910-919)

910 Superficial injury of face, neck, and scalp except eye
911 Superficial injury of trunk
912 Superficial injury of shoulder and upper arm
913 Superficial injury of elbow, forearm, and wrist
914 Superficial injury of hand(s) except finger(s) alone
915 Superficial injury of finger(s)
916 Superficial injury of hip, thigh, leg, and ankle
917 Superficial injury of foot and toe(s)
918 Superficial injury of eye and adnexa
919 Superficial injury of other, multiple, and unspecified sites

Contusion with intact skin surface (920-924)

920 Contusion of face, scalp, and neck except eye(s)
921 Contusion of eye and adnexa
922 Contusion of trunk
923 Contusion of upper limb
924 Contusion of lower limb and of other and unspecified sites

Crushing injury (925-929)

925 Crushing injury of face, scalp, and neck
926 Crushing injury of trunk
927 Crushing injury of upper limb
928 Crushing injury of lower limb
929 Crushing injury of multiple and unspecified sites

Effects of foreign body entering through orifice (930-939)

930 Foreign body on external eye
931 Foreign body in ear
932 Foreign body in nose
933 Foreign body in pharynx and larynx
934 Foreign body in trachea, bronchus, and lung
935 Foreign body in mouth, esophagus, and stomach
936 Foreign body in intestine and colon
937 Foreign body in anus and rectum
938 Foreign body in digestive system, unspecified

939 Foreign body in genitourinary tract

Burns (940-949)

940 Burn confined to eye and adnexa
941 Burn of face, head, and neck
942 Burn of trunk
943 Burn of upper limb, except wrist and hand
944 Burn of wrist(s) and hand(s)
945 Burn of lower limb(s)
946 Burns of multiple specified sites
947 Burn of internal organs
948 Burns classified according to extent of body surface involved
949 Burn, unspecified

Injury to nerves and spinal cord (950-957)

950 Injury to optic nerve and pathways
951 Injury to other cranial nerve(s)
952 Spinal cord injury without evidence of spinal bone injury
953 Injury to nerve roots and spinal plexus
954 Injury to other nerve(s) of trunk excluding shoulder and pelvic girdles
955 Injury to peripheral nerve(s) of shoulder girdle and upper limb
956 Injury to peripheral nerve(s) of pelvic girdle and lower limb
957 Injury to other and unspecified nerves

Certain traumatic complications and unspecified injuries (958-959)

958 Certain early complications of trauma
959 Injury, other and unspecified

Poisoning by drugs, medicinals and biological substances (960-979)

960 Poisoning by antibiotics
961 Poisoning by other anti-infectives
962 Poisoning by hormones and synthetic substitutes
963 Poisoning by primarily systemic agents
964 Poisoning by agents primarily affecting blood constituents
965 Poisoning by analgesics, antipyretics, and antirheumatics
966 Poisoning by anticonvulsants and anti-Parkinsonism drugs
967 Poisoning by sedatives and hypnotics
968 Poisoning by other central nervous system depressants and anesthetics
969 Poisoning by psychotropic agents
970 Poisoning by central nervous system stimulants
971 Poisoning by drugs primarily affecting the autonomic nervous system
972 Poisoning by agents primarily affecting the cardiovascular system
973 Poisoning by agents primarily affecting the gastrointestinal system
974 Poisoning by water, mineral, and uric acid metabolism drugs
975 Poisoning by agents primarily acting on the smooth and skeletal muscles and respiratory system
976 Poisoning by agents primarily affecting skin and mucous membrane, ophthalmological, otorhinolaryngological, and dental drugs
977 Poisoning by other and unspecified drugs and medicinals
978 Poisoning by bacterial vaccines
979 Poisoning by other vaccines and biological substances

Toxic effects of substances chiefly nonmedicinal as to source (980-989)

980 Toxic effect of alcohol
981 Toxic effect of petroleum products
982 Toxic effect of solvents other than petroleum-based
983 Toxic effect of corrosive aromatics, acids, and caustic alkalis
984 Toxic effect of lead and its compounds (including fumes)
985 Toxic effect of other metals
986 Toxic effect of carbon monoxide
987 Toxic effect of other gases, fumes, or vapors
988 Effect of noxious substances eaten as food
989 Toxic effect of other substances, chiefly nonmedicinal as to source

Other and unspecified effects of external causes (990-995)

990 Effects of radiation, unspecified
991 Effects of reduced temperature
992 Effects of heat and light
993 Effects of air pressure
994 Effects of other external causes
995 Certain adverse effects, not elsewhere classified

Complications of surgical and medical care, not elsewhere classified (996-999)

996 Complications peculiar to certain specified procedures
997 Complications affecting specified body systems, not elsewhere classified
998 Other complications of procedures, not elsewhere classified
999 Complications of medical care, not elsewhere classified

SUPPLEMENTARY CLASSIFICATION OF FACTORS INFLUENCING HEALTH STATUS AND CONTACT WITH HEALTH SERVICES

Persons with potential health hazards related to communicable diseases (V01-V09)

V01 Contact with or exposure to communicable diseases
V02 Carrier or suspected carrier of infectious diseases
V03 Need for prophylactic vaccination and inoculation against bacterial diseases
V04 Need for prophylactic vaccination and inoculation against certain viral diseases
V05 Need for other prophylactic vaccination and inoculation against single diseases
V06 Need for prophylactic vaccination and inoculation against combinations of diseases
V07 Need for isolation and other prophylactic measures
V08 Asymptomatic human immunodeficiency virus [HIV] infection status
V09 Infection with drug-resistant microorganisms

Persons with potential health hazards related to personal and family history (V10-V19)

V10 Personal history of malignant neoplasm
V11 Personal history of mental disorder
V12 Personal history of certain other diseases
V13 Personal history of other diseases
V14 Personal history of allergy to medicinal agents
V15 Other personal history presenting hazards to health
V16 Family history of malignant neoplasm
V17 Family history of certain chronic disabling diseases
V18 Family history of certain other specific conditions
V19 Family history of other conditions

Persons encountering health services in circumstances related to reproduction and development (V20-V29)

V20 Health supervision of infant or child
V21 Constitutional states in development
V22 Normal pregnancy
V23 Supervision of high-risk pregnancy
V24 Postpartum care and examination
V25 Encounter for contraceptive management
V26 Procreative management
V27 Outcome of delivery
V28 Antenatal screening
V29 Observation and evaluation of newborns and infants for suspected condition not found

Liveborn infants according to type of birth (V30-V39)

V30 Single liveborn
V31 mate liveborn
V32 Twin, mate stillborn
V33 Twin, unspecified
V34 Other multiple, mates all liveborn
V35 Other multiple, mates all stillborn
V36 Other multiple, mates live- and stillborn
V37 Other multiple, unspecified
V39 Unspecified

Persons with a condition influencing their health status (V40-V49)

V40 Mental and behavioral problems
V41 Problems with special senses and other special functions
V42 Organ or tissue replaced by transplant
V43 Organ or tissue replaced by other means
V44 Artificial opening status
V45 Other postprocedural states
V46 Other dependence on machines
V47 Other problems with internal organs
V48 Problems with head, neck, and trunk
V49 Other conditions influencing health status

Persons encountering health services for specific procedures and aftercare (V50-V59)

V50 Elective surgery for purposes other than remedying health states
V51 Aftercare involving the use of plastic surgery
V52 Fitting and adjustment of prosthetic device
V53 Fitting and adjustment of other device
V54 Other orthopedic aftercare
V55 Attention to artificial openings
V56 Encounter for dialysis and dialysis catheter care
V57 Care involving use of rehabilitation procedures
V58 Encounter for other and unspecified procedures and aftercare
V59 Donors

Persons encountering health services in other circumstances (V60-V69)

V60 Housing, household, and economic circumstances
V61 Other family circumstances
V62 Other psychosocial circumstances
V63 Unavailability of other medical facilities for care
V64 Persons encountering health services for specific procedures, not carried out
V65 Other persons seeking consultation
V66 Convalescence and palliative care
V67 Follow-up examination
V68 Encounters for administrative purposes
V69 Problems related to lifestyle

Persons without reported diagnosis encountered during examination and investigation of individuals and populations (V70-V82)

V70 General medical examination
V71 Observation and evaluation for suspected conditions not found
V72 Special investigations and examinations
V73 Special screening examination for viral and chlamydial diseases

V74 Special screening examination for bacterial and spirochetal diseases
V75 Special screening examination for other infectious diseases
V76 Special screening for malignant neoplasms
V77 Special screening for endocrine, nutritional, metabolic, and immunity disorders
V78 Special screening for disorders of blood and blood-forming organs
V79 Special screening for mental disorders and developmental handicaps
V80 Special screening for neurological, eye, and ear diseases
V81 Special screening for cardiovascular, respiratory, and genitourinary diseases
V82 Special screening for other conditions

Genetics (V83-V84)
V83 Genetic carrier status
V84 Genetic susceptibility to disease

Body mass index (V85)
V85 Body Mass Index

Estrogen receptor status (V86)
V86 Estrogen receptor status

Other specified personal exposures and history presenting hazards to health (V87)
V87 Other specified personal exposures and history presenting hazards to health

Acquired absence of other organs and tissue (V88)
V88 Acquired absence of other organs and tissue

Other suspected conditions not found (V89)
V89 Other suspected conditions not found

SUPPLEMENTARY CLASSIFICATION OF EXTERNAL CAUSES OF INJURY AND POISONING

Railway accidents (E800-E807)
E800 Railway accident involving collision with roling stock
E801 Railway accident involving collision with other object
E802 Railway accident involving derailment without antecedent collision
E803 Railway accident involving explosion, fire, or burning
E804 Fall in, on, or from railway train
E805 Hit by rolling stock
E806 Other specified railway accident
E807 Railway accident of unspecified nature

Motor vehicle traffic accidents (E810-E819)
E810 Motor vehicle traffic accident involving collision with train
E811 Motor vehicle traffic accident involving re-entrant collision with another motor vehicle
E812 Other motor vehicle traffic accident involving collision with another motor vehicle
E813 Motor vehicle traffic accident involving collision with other vehicle
E814 Motor vehicle traffic accident involving collision with pedestrian
E815 Other motor vehicle traffic accident involving collision on the highway
E816 Motor vehicle traffic accident due to loss of control, without collision on the highway
E817 Noncollision motor vehicle traffic accident while boarding or alighting
E818 Other noncollision motor vehicle traffic accident
E819 Motor vehicle traffic accident of unspecified nature

Motor vehicle nontraffic accidents (E820-E825)
E820 Nontraffic accident involving motor-driven snow vehicle
E821 Nontraffic accident involving other off-road motor vehicle
E822 Other motor vehicle nontraffic accident involving collision with moving object
E823 Other motor vehicle nontraffic accident involving collision with stationary object
E824 Other motor vehicle nontraffic accident while boarding and alighting
E825 Other motor vehicle nontraffic accident of other and unspecified nature

Other road vehicle accidents (E826-E829)
E826 Pedal cycle accident
E827 Animal-drawn vehicle accident
E828 Accident involving animal being ridden
E829 Other road vehicle accidents

Water transport accidents (E830-E838)
E830 Accident to watercraft causing submersion
E831 Accident to watercraft causing other injury
E832 Other accidental submersion or drowning in water transport accident
E833 Fall on stairs or ladders in water transport
E834 Other fall from one level to another in water transport
E835 Other and unspecified fall in water transport
E836 Machinery accident in water transport
E837 Explosion, fire, or burning in watercraft
E838 Other and unspecified water transport accident

Air and space transport accidents (E840-E845)
E840 Accident to powered aircraft at takeoff or landing
E841 Accident to powered aircraft, other and unspecified
E842 Accident to unpowered aircraft
E843 Fall in, on, or from aircraft
E844 Other specified air transport accidents
E845 Other involving spacecraft

Vehicle accidents, not elsewhere classfiable (E846-E849)
E846 Accidents involving powered vehicles used solely within the buildings and premises of an industrial or commercial establishment
E847 Accidents involving cable cars not running on rails
E848 Accidents involving other vehicles, not elsewhere classifiable
E849 Place of occurrence

Accidental poisoning by drugs, medicinal substances, and biologicals (E850-E858)
E850 Accidental poisoning by analgesics, antipyretics, and antirheumatics
E851 Accidental poisoning by barbiturates
E852 Accidental poisoning by other sedatives and hypnotics
E853 Accidental poisoning by tranquilizers
E854 Accidental poisoning by other psychotropic agents
E855 Accidental poisoning by other drugs acting on central and autonomic nervous systems
E856 Accidental poisoning by antibiotics
E857 Accidental poisoning by anti-infectives
E858 Accidental poisoning by other drugs

Accidental poisoning by other solid and liquid substances, gases, and vapors (E860-E869)
E860 Accidental poisoning by alcohol, not elsewhere classified
E861 Accidental poisoning by cleansing and polishing agents, disinfectants, paints, and varnishes
E862 Accidental poisoning by petroleum products, other solvents and their vapors, not elsewhere classified
E863 Accidental poisoning by agricultural and horticultural chemical and pharmaceutical preparations other than plant foods and fertilizers
E864 Accidental poisoning by corrosives and caustics, not elsewhere classified
E865 Accidental poisoning from poisonous foodstuffs and poisonous plants
E866 Accidental poisoning by other and unspecified solid and liquid substances
E867 Accidental poisoning by gas distributed by pipeline
E868 Accidental poisoning by other utility gas and other carbon monoxide
E869 Accidental poisoning by other gases and vapors

Misadventures to patients during surgical and medical care (E870-E876)
E870 Accidental cut, puncture, perforation, or hemorrhage during medical care
E871 Foreign object left in body during procedure
E872 Failure of sterile precautions during procedure
E873 Failure in dosage
E874 Mechanical failure of instrument or apparatus during procedure
E875 Contaminated or infected blood, other fluid, drug, or biological substance
E876 Other and unspecified misadventures during medical care

Surgical and medical procedures as the cause of abnormal reaction of patient or later complication, without mention of misadventure at the time of procedure (E878-E879)
E878 Surgical operation and other surgical procedures as the cause of abnormal reaction of patient, or of later complication, without mention of misadventure at the time of operation
E879 Other procedures, without mention of misadventure at the time of procedure, as the cause of abnormal reaction of patient, or of later complication

Accidental falls (E880-E888)
E880 Fall on or from stairs or steps
E881 Fall on or from ladders or scaffolding
E882 Fall from or out of building or other structure
E883 Fall into hole or other opening in surface
E884 Other fall from one level to another
E885 Fall on same level from slipping, tripping, or stumbling
E886 Fall on same level from collision, pushing or shoving, by or with other person
E887 Fracture, cause unspecified
E888 Other and unspecified fall

Accidents caused by fire and flames (E890-E899)
E890 Conflagration in private dwelling
E891 Conflagration in other and unspecified building or structure
E892 Conflagration not in building or structure
E893 Accident caused by ignition of clothing
E894 Ignition of highly inflammable material
E895 Accident caused by controlled fire in private dwelling

E896 Accident caused by controlled fire in other and unspecified building or structure
E897 Accident caused by controlled fire not in building or structure
E898 Accident caused by other specified fire and flames
E899 Accident caused by unspecified fire

Accidents due to natural and environmental factors (E900-E909)

E900 Excessive heat
E901 Excessive cold
E902 High and low air pressure and changes in air pressure
E903 Travel and motion
E904 Hunger, thirst, exposure, and neglect
E905 Venomous animals and plants as the cause of poisoning and toxic reactions
E906 Other injury caused by animals
E907 Lightning
E908 Cataclysmic storms, and floods resulting from storms
E909 Cataclysmic earth surface movements and eruptions

Accidents caused by submersion, suffocation, and foreign bodies (E910-E915)

E910 Accidental drowning and submersion
E911 Inhalation and ingestion of food causing obstruction of respiratory tract or suffocation
E912 Inhalation and ingestion of other object causing obstruction of respiratory tract or suffocation
E913 Accidental mechanical suffocation
E914 Foreign body accidentally entering eye and adnexa
E915 Foreign body accidentally entering other orifice

Other accidents (E916-E928)

E916 Struck accidentally by falling object
E917 Striking against or struck accidentally by objects or persons
E918 Caught accidentally in or between objects
E919 Accidents caused by machinery
E920 Accidents caused by cutting and piercing instruments or objects
E921 Accident caused by explosion of pressure vessel
E922 Accident caused by firearm missile
E923 Accident caused by explosive material
E924 Accident caused by hot substance or object, caustic or corrosive material, and steam
E925 Accident caused by electric current
E926 Exposure to radiation
E927 Overexertion and strenuous movements
E928 Other and unspecified environmental and accidental causes

Late effects of accidental injury (E929)

E929 Late effects of accidental injury

Drugs, medicinal and biological substances causing adverse effects in therapeutic use (E930-E949)

E930 Antibiotics
E931 Other anti-infectives
E932 Hormones and synthetic substitutes
E933 Primarily systemic agents
E934 Agents primarily affecting blood constituents
E935 Analgesics, antipyretics, and antirheumatics
E936 Anticonvulsants and anti-Parkinsonism drugs
E937 Sedatives and hypnotics
E938 Other central nervous system depressants and anesthetics
E939 Psychotropic agents
E940 Central nervous system stimulants
E941 Drugs primarily affecting the autonomic nervous system
E942 Agents primarily affecting the cardiovascular system
E943 Agents primarily affecting gastrointestinal system
E944 Water, mineral, and uric acid metabolism drugs
E945 Agents primarily acting on the smooth and skeletal muscles and respiratory system
E946 Agents primarily affecting skin and mucous membrane, ophthalmological, otorhinolaryngological, and dental drugs
E947 Other and unspecified drugs and medicinal substances
E948 Bacterial vaccines
E949 Other vaccines and biological substances

Suicide and self-inflicted injury (E950-E959)

E950 Suicide and self-inflicted poisoning by solid or liquid substances
E951 Suicide and self-inflicted poisoning by gases in domestic use
E952 Suicide and self-inflicted poisoning by other gases and vapors
E953 Suicide and self-inflicted injury by hanging, strangulation, and suffocation
E954 Suicide and self-inflicted injury by submersion [drowning]
E955 Suicide and self-inflicted injury by firearms and explosives
E956 Suicide and self-inflicted injury by cutting and piercing instruments
E957 Suicide and self-inflicted injuries by jumping from high place
E958 Suicide and self-inflicted injury by other and unspecified means
E959 Late effects of self-inflicted injury

Homicide and injury purposely inflicted by other persons (E960-E969)

E960 Fight, brawl, and rape
E961 Assault by corrosive or caustic substance, except poisoning
E962 Assault by poisoning
E963 Assault by hanging and strangulation
E964 Assault by submersion [drowning]
E965 Assault by firearms and explosives
E966 Assault by cutting and piercing instrument
E967 Child and adult battering and other maltreatment
E968 Assault by other and unspecified means
E969 Late effects of injury purposely inflicted by other person

Legal intervention (E970-E978)

E970 Injury due to legal intervention by firearms
E971 Injury due to legal intervention by explosives
E972 Injury due to legal intervention by gas
E973 Injury due to legal intervention by blunt object
E974 Injury due to legal intervention by cutting and piercing instruments
E975 Injury due to legal intervention by other specified means
E976 Injury due to legal intervention by unspecified means
E977 Late effects of injuries due to legal intervention
E978 Legal execution

Terrorism (E979)

E979 Terrorism

Injury undetermined whether accidentally or purposely inflicted (E980-E989)

E980 Poisoning by solid or liquid substances, undetermined whether accidentally or purposely inflicted
E981 Poisoning by gases in domestic use, undetermined whether accidentally or purposely inflicted
E982 Poisoning by other gases, undetermined whether accidentally or purposely inflicted
E983 Hanging, strangulation, or suffocation, undetermined whether accidentally or purposely inflicted
E984 Submersion [drowning], undetermined whether accidentally or purposely inflicted
E985 Injury by firearms and explosives, undetermined whether accidentally or purposely inflicted
E986 Injury by cutting and piercing instruments, undetermined whether accidentally or purposely inflicted
E987 Falling from high place, undetermined whether accidentally or purposely inflicted
E988 Injury by other and unspecified means, undetermined whether accidentally or purposely inflicted
E989 Late effects of injury, undetermined whether accidentally or purposely inflicted

Injury resulting from operations of war (E990-E999)

E990 Injury due to war operations by fires and conflagrations
E991 Injury due to war operations by bullets and fragments
E992 Injury due to war operations by explosion of marine weapons
E993 Injury due to war operations by other explosion
E994 Injury due to war operations by destruction of aircraft
E995 Injury due to war operations by other and unspecified forms of conventional warfare
E996 Injury due to war operations by nuclear weapons
E997 Injury due to war operations by other forms of unconventional warfare
E998 Injury due to war operations but occurring after cessation of hostilities
E999 Late effects of injury due to war operations